McGraw Hill connect™

# Student Instructions: Registration & Sign In Process

1. To begin go to http://www.mhconnectenglish.com and click on "*First-time Registration*" in the upper right-hand corner.

2. If you are a new user, you will see two options. Either click "*First-time using Connect English*" to enter your registration code and new user information.

   **OR**

   Click "*Already using Connect English*" to enter your registration code and proceed with your existing account information.

3. Next, enter the 20 character registration code that is listed below and click "*Submit*".

| REGISTRATION CODE | [redacted] |
|---|---|

4. Fill in your information, making note of your username (e-mail address) and password. Then click "*Create Account*".

5. Enter the "*Class Code*" given to you by your instructor, then click the "*Join Class*" button. Then, click the "*Proceed to Contents*" button. ***If your instructor did not provide you with a class/section code, click the "Skip Section Code" button.**

6. At your Connect homepage, you can access your assignments, study center, grades, and other resources provided by your instructor. Start by clicking any of the assignment titles displayed on the list, or go to the Table of Contents to access resources on your own.

If you need assistance contact Digital CARE:
1-800-331-5094 or for email support at http://mpss.mhhe.com/contact.php.

ISBN-13: 978-0-07-752713-6 / ISBN-10: 0-07-752713-5

McGraw Hill Learning Solutions

The McGraw·Hill Companies

# About the Authors

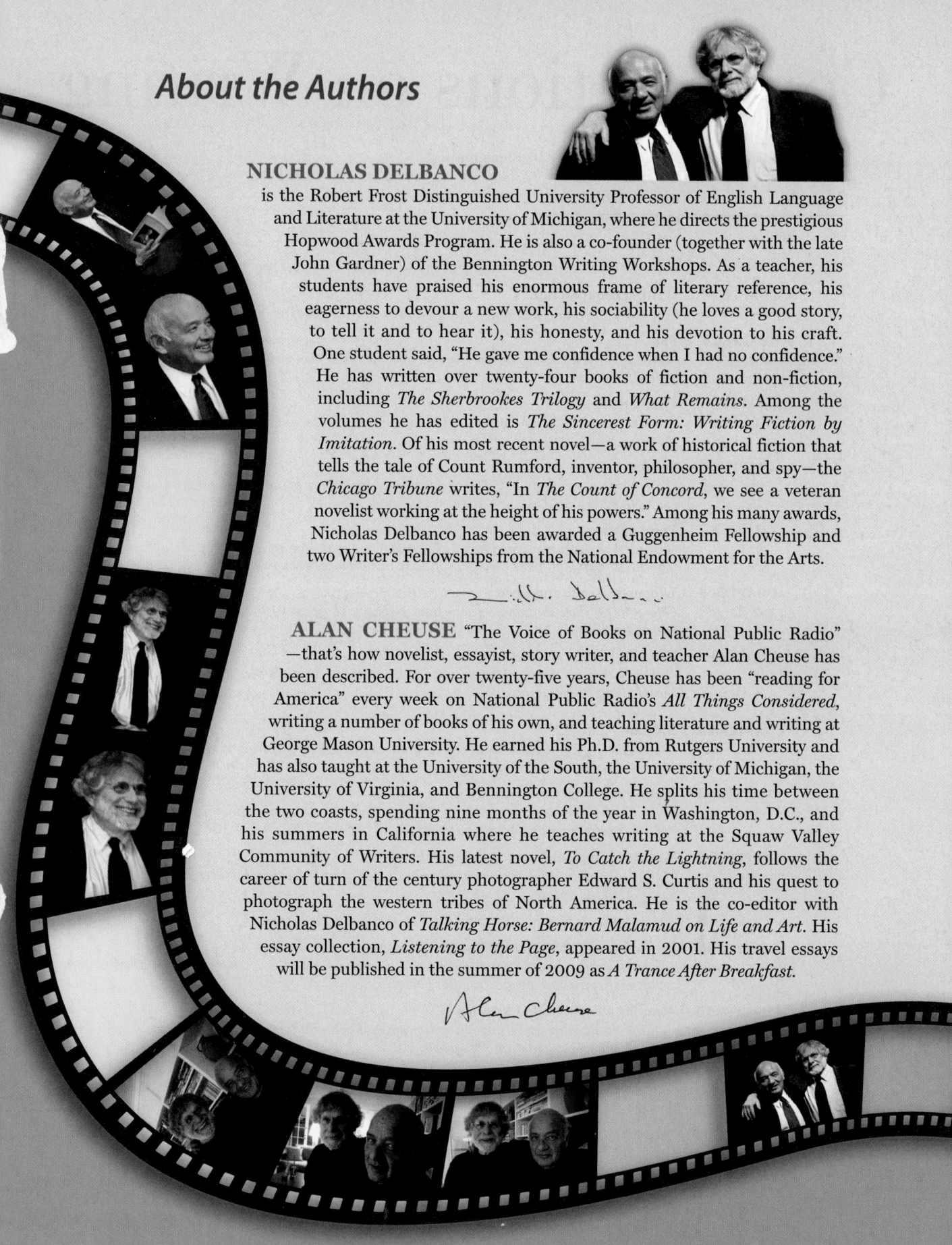

**NICHOLAS DELBANCO** is the Robert Frost Distinguished University Professor of English Language and Literature at the University of Michigan, where he directs the prestigious Hopwood Awards Program. He is also a co-founder (together with the late John Gardner) of the Bennington Writing Workshops. As a teacher, his students have praised his enormous frame of literary reference, his eagerness to devour a new work, his sociability (he loves a good story, to tell it and to hear it), his honesty, and his devotion to his craft. One student said, "He gave me confidence when I had no confidence." He has written over twenty-four books of fiction and non-fiction, including *The Sherbrookes Trilogy* and *What Remains*. Among the volumes he has edited is *The Sincerest Form: Writing Fiction by Imitation*. Of his most recent novel—a work of historical fiction that tells the tale of Count Rumford, inventor, philosopher, and spy—the *Chicago Tribune* writes, "In *The Count of Concord*, we see a veteran novelist working at the height of his powers." Among his many awards, Nicholas Delbanco has been awarded a Guggenheim Fellowship and two Writer's Fellowships from the National Endowment for the Arts.

**ALAN CHEUSE** "The Voice of Books on National Public Radio"—that's how novelist, essayist, story writer, and teacher Alan Cheuse has been described. For over twenty-five years, Cheuse has been "reading for America" every week on National Public Radio's *All Things Considered*, writing a number of books of his own, and teaching literature and writing at George Mason University. He earned his Ph.D. from Rutgers University and has also taught at the University of the South, the University of Michigan, the University of Virginia, and Bennington College. He splits his time between the two coasts, spending nine months of the year in Washington, D.C., and his summers in California where he teaches writing at the Squaw Valley Community of Writers. His latest novel, *To Catch the Lightning*, follows the career of turn of the century photographer Edward S. Curtis and his quest to photograph the western tribes of North America. He is the co-editor with Nicholas Delbanco of *Talking Horse: Bernard Malamud on Life and Art*. His essay collection, *Listening to the Page*, appeared in 2001. His travel essays will be published in the summer of 2009 as *A Trance After Breakfast*.

# Conversations on Writing

**CHAPTER 1** John Updike
**Reading a Story for Its Elements**
*"Your job as a writer of fiction is not to present an ideal world but to try to present the world that you see and hear around you."*

**CHAPTER 2** Richard Ford
**Going Further with Reading**
*"Writing stories is much more mosaical than it is linear."*

Amy Tan
*"I think of fiction as being subversive in a good way. It seduces you."*

**CHAPTER 3** Jamaica Kincaid
**Writing about Fiction**
*"The advice I would give anyone who wants to write is: Read a lot."*

**CHAPTER 4** T. Coraghessan Boyle
**Plot**
*"You don't really know what the story means until you have written it, and until you find out what the ending is."*

**CHAPTER 5** Gish Jen
**Character**
*"I think [character's] where the conflict comes from and I think it's where the plot comes from: that's where the story comes from."*

**CHAPTER 6** Barry Lopez
**Setting**
*"I think setting is often part of what determines the nature of the story, and the nature of the characters."*

**CHAPTER 7** ZZ Packer
**Point of View**
*"I think that in the end voice and craft together can make for an incredibly powerful story, because you end up using all your tools of craft to render a voice believable."*

**CHAPTER 8** Aimee Bender
**Language, Tone, and Style**
*"There isn't a story that doesn't have tone or theme. Those are just things that come from the language itself."*

**CHAPTER 9** Chimamanda Ngozi Adichie
**Theme**
*"If I must think in terms of theme, I would think about multiple themes, that a story can do so many things at the same time."*

**CHAPTER 10** Tim O'Brien
**Symbol**
*"Symbolism has to do with what objects of the world end up meaning to us. The object has meaning, has resonance and has echoes, and that's what symbolism for me really is."*

**CHAPTER 11** Joyce Carol Oates
**Fiction As Social Commentary**
*"I've always been very interested in holding a kind of mirror, sometimes a slightly distorting mirror, up to contemporary American society."*

**CHAPTER 12** William Kittredge
**American Regionalism and Sense of Place**
*"I think one of the ways to not somehow lose track of your dreams is to keep expanding what you see and find in the world."*

Dagoberto Gilb
*"I absolutely think place is everything. I think place is a character."*

**CHAPTER 14** Amy Hempel
**An Anthology of Stories for Further Reading**
*"One of the things that interests me most in story writing is that . . . there's a point where it stops being your story and becomes the story's story."*

**CHAPTER 15** Carolyn Forché
**Reading a Poem in Its Elements**
*"I think the more we know about how a poem makes its rhythms and musics and patternings, the more deeply we can enter into the poem."*

**CHAPTER 16** Stephen Mitchell
**Going Further: An Interactive Reading**
*"There's a whole world of beauty and profundity out there for people who don't know poetry—that's just waiting for you."*

## Videos available online at http://www.mhhe.com/delbanco1e

**CHAPTER 17** Li-Young Lee
**Writing about Poetry**
*"The minute I wake up I feel as if I'm in the presence of a poem: the whole cosmos, the whole world, seems to exist to me like a giant poem."*

**CHAPTER 18** Marie Howe
**Words**
*"It's the greatest feeling in the whole world, to be in the hands of something bigger than oneself."*

**CHAPTER 19** Stephen Dunn
**Voice**
*"So that good literature has a way of bringing us into the common fold, of making us part of the world."*

**CHAPTER 20** Jane Hirshfield
**Imagery and Symbol**
*"Image is one of the most powerful ways a poem both carries meaning and changes and enlarges it, which is the work that every good poem is trying to do."*

**CHAPTER 21** Robert Pinsky
**Figures of Speech**
*"I think one of the thrills of art is the sense that something may be going too far, or is about to go too far."*

**CHAPTER 22** Thomas Lynch
**Sound**
*"It does embolden you once you get a poem right. And there is a pleasure to it, I must say. And the pleasure is acoustic."*

**CHAPTER 23** Edward Hirsch
**Fixed Forms**
*"The only way you can write a good formal poem is if you can control the form, so that the form becomes the way in which you can express what you need to say."*

**CHAPTER 24** Robert Hass
**Open Forms**
*"Poetry is about catching the way we speak and the way things are said, and the rhythms of it, and making a shape from it."*

**CHAPTER 25** Al Young
**Spoken Word and Song**
*"Poetry is a wonderful opportunity to do two things at once. You can say something or not say something and you can sing through language."*

**CHAPTER 30** Marian Seldes
**Reading and Viewing a Play in Its Elements**
*"One of the wonderful things about reading a play is that you can go back and read the page again. You can take your time with it. Lovingly."*

**CHAPTER 31** Edward Albee
**Going Further: An Interactive Reading**
*"If art isn't engaging or troubling in some sense, it is a total waste of time."*

**CHAPTER 32** Edwin Wilson
**Writing about Drama**
*"In writing, whatever it is, you reread it and you'll be amazed at some of the changes you want to make to your own work."*

**CHAPTER 33** Gregory Nagy
**Ancient Greek Drama: Sophocles**
*"Imagine looking down at a sea of faces, twenty thousand pairs of eyes are weeping simultaneously, twenty thousand people have their hair stand on end in terror."*

**CHAPTER 34** Ralph Williams
**A Case Study on William Shakespeare**
*"One of the frightening and thrilling aspects of Shakespeare's plays is the constant reminder of how tentative it is that life turns out to be tragedy or comedy."*

**CHAPTER 35** Arthur Miller
**Modern Drama**
*"All we can hope for is to illuminate something so that people can make up their own minds based upon the reality of the situation."*

Ruben Santiago-Hudson
*"When you can sit down and open up a book and spend time in a whole different world—no matter whether it's five minutes or an hour—that's a privilege."*

**CHAPTER 36** Arthur Kopit
**A Case Study on Contemporary Theater**
*"To fully get a play, you need to imagine the impact on a crowd. The play is not complete until the audience completes it."*

# Literature

# Fiction: Craft and Voice

Nicholas Delbanco
*University of Michigan*

Alan Cheuse
*George Mason University*

# To Our Students

**Higher Education**

Published by McGraw-Hill, an imprint of The McGraw-Hill Companies, Inc., 1221 Avenue of the Americas, New York, NY 10020. 

This book is printed on acid-free paper.

8 9 0 DOW/DOW 0

ISBN: 978-0-07-310444-7
MHID: 0-07-310444-2

Editor in Chief: *Michael Ryan*
Publisher: *Lisa Moore*
Executive Marketing Manager: *Allison Jones*
Editorial Coordinator: *Stephen Sachs*
Production Editor: *Leslie LaDow*
Manuscript Editor: *Susan Norton*
Cover Designer: *Jeanne Schreiber*
Interior Designers: *Jeanne Schreiber and Linda Robertson*
Senior Photo Research Coordinator: *Nora Agbayani*
Lead Media Project Manager: *Ron Nelms*
Production Supervisor: *Louis Swaim*
Composition: *9.25/11.25 Miller Roman by Thompson Type*
Printing: *45# NewPage Orion Gloss, R. R. Donnelley & Sons/Willard, OH*

Cover: Frog: Photex/Jupiterimages. Dock: Gary John Norman/Getty Images.

Credits: The credits section for this book begins on page C-1 and is considered an extension of the copyright page.

**Library of Congress Cataloging-in-Publication Data**

Delbanco, Nicholas.
Literature : craft and voice / Nicholas Delbanco, Alan Cheuse.—1st ed.
p. cm.
Includes index.
3 vols. planned.
ISBN-13: 978-0-07-310444-7 (v. 1 : acid-free paper)
ISBN-10: 0-07-310444-2 (v. 1 : acid-free paper) 1. Literature. I. Cheuse, Alan. II. Title.
PN45.D457 2009
800—dc22
2008051003

The Internet addresses listed in the text were accurate at the time of publication. The inclusion of a Web site does not indicate an endorsement by the authors or McGraw-Hill, and McGraw-Hill does not guarantee the accuracy of the information presented at these sites.

# Contents

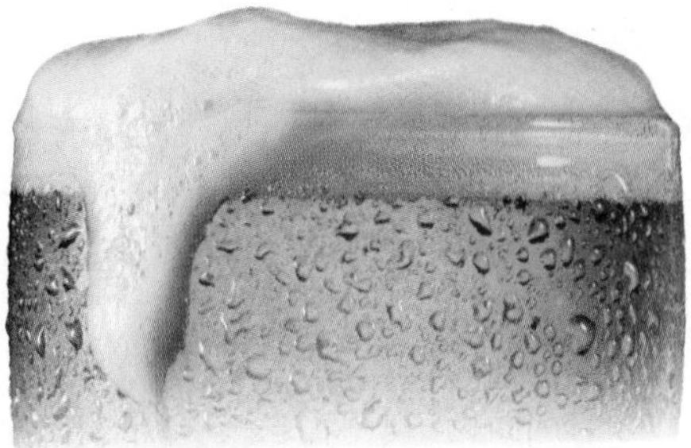

## FICTION

## 3 Writing about Fiction 50

## 4 Plot 74

GARY
VIETNAM
68-71
HOW YA
GONNA ACT?

# 11 Fiction as Social Commentary 362

# 12 American Regionalism and a Sense of Place 382

## 14 An Anthology of Stories for Further Reading 483

# A HANDBOOK FOR WRITING FROM READING H-1

## 1 Critical Approaches to Literature H-3



## 2 Writing from Reading H-25

# Preface for Instructors

"*Literature: Craft and Voice* speaks to students who have grown up in a media-blitzed world who do not really know how or why they should read."

—Shirley Nelson, Chattanooga State Community College

William James once called our first glimpse as infants of the paradoxical world we live in "one great blooming, buzzing confusion." Students today, at the outset of their college years, seem to live a much more supercharged technological life than ever before. We see it in our own lives as well. But especially for the students, the buzzing and confusion if unchecked keeps on blooming. Over the years, we have watched our own students struggle with the avalanche of unfiltered information as well as support one another in new families of virtual community, and McGraw-Hill researchers took this further by following thousands of students at hundreds of institutions from sunup to sundown (and well after) as they work, play, and study. We took to heart what we know and what we learned when creating this book. Students need to slow down. They need a private study spot. They need to feel connected, not only to one another but also to their reading. They need different ways of gaining entry to reading and different ways of slowing themselves down mentally so they can concentrate on analysis, synthesis, and interaction with a text.

William Blake urges us to see "a world in a grain of sand." The grains of sand in this book are fiction, poetry, and drama. We poured into this text our combined multiple decades of love for teaching students, our love of reading and discovering new writers, and our experience as writers in the service of what we believe is an extremely effective multimedia pedagogy that brings writers to readers and readers to writing. We have incorporated into that pedagogy various technologies, with an emphasis on video interviews with nearly three dozen writers, scholars, and theater people, which will, we hope, deepen and broaden even further the student's engagement with literature and the growth of his or her own ability to think and write critically.

"I think the video is very important for engaging students in discussion. A video is going to be more engaging than text for many people, so there is more opportunity to reach people who wouldn't otherwise participate."

—Kaitlyn Taylor, student, University of Delaware

## Reading in a Visual Age and Harnessing the Power of the Media

How do we read in a visual age? We came to this project with a desire to harness the power of media and use it to help students learn the art of sustained reading. This activity may be for pleasure or it may have a specific purpose such as the research paper, but it predates and is not a natural extension of the skim-and-grab reading that permeates our Internet culture. Like you, we believe that, in order to succeed in college, all students need to be able to apply critical thought to complex texts. To do this, they should engage their senses; they must listen as well as look. In this text, each chapter is accompanied by an ancillary video interview (sometimes two) of a featured writer discussing the topic of the chapter as well as what reading and writing have meant to him or her. In this way, we hope a visual and aural approach will enliven student interest in the act of reading.

"I appreciate the effort to appeal to a variety of learning styles. Having authors look students in the eye and talk about their writing has got to appeal and reinforce what teachers are saying in the classroom, whether it's a face-to-face classroom or a cyber classroom."

—April Childress, Greenville Technical College

## Bringing Writers to Readers Brings Readers to Writing

Who doesn't appreciate the human voice? In each video, the featured writer reads from a selection of his or her writing included in the chapter and provides a personal insight

A Conversation on Writing with Joyce Carol Oates, Chapter 11

A Conversation on Writing with Li-Young Lee, Chapter 17

A Conversation on Writing with Ruben Santiago-Hudson, Chapter 35

"I'm impressed by the thought that has gone into meeting younger 'generation internet students' on their own grounds. I think that "Literature Bibles' sometimes ignore who makes up their audience or marginalize how technology engages the same senses—see/hear/touch—that pen-and-ink fiction, poetry, and drama seek to capture."

—Jennifer Diamond, Bucks County Community College

"I was compelled into reading by the interviews. Once I read the interview, I wanted to continue reading the chapter and the selection for that chapter. It reminded me that I love poetry—I'm not a teacher of poetry but a lover of poetry. Quite a difference huh?"

—Tammy Mata, Tarrant County College

into its composition. Actually hearing the voice of the author is one way to experience a text. It is also one way to begin to think independently. With so many writers talking about how they experience writing, there are inevitably exciting differences, such as those who love revision (Joyce Carol Oates) and those who don't revise (Jamaica Kincaid). Discovering writers are real flesh-and-blood people not only makes students more inclined to read but also gives them ideas for writing. These interviews can be important creative energizers for classroom discussion and independent analytical thought for your students.

## Providing Media Designed Exclusively for Classroom Use with This Book

These interviews were created exclusively for their application to this project. As mentioned, each interview includes a writer's thoughts on how he or she came to reading; how the writer has worked with the element of craft that is under discussion in the chapter in his or her own work; a reading from the selection included in the chapter; and a personal assessment of what a new reader might find interesting about that work, as well as a discussion of the writing process. Quotations from these interviews and an extended boxed excerpt are included in each chapter. This creates a human connection to each subject and starts a conversation carried through with other quotations from these sessions that are included throughout the book. In this way, these writers' voices are sustained in the pages, along with our unifying discussion, making a complex text more personally inviting to students.

"The use of author interviews not only provides a sense of cohesion but also creates interest as students see and hear professional authors discussing their own writing processes and problems. I also like the emphasis and instruction on sustained reading skills needed for both analyzing and writing about literature."

—Linda Smith, Midlands Technical Community College

"The anthology's treatment of authors and the depth with which the anthology invites students to engage with authors as writers (not unlike themselves) make it a terrifically enabling experience for students."

—Elizabeth Rich, Saginaw Valley State University

*It's more important to read than to write.*

Q&A

*I'm really interested in breaking the form. . . .*

## *A Conversation on Writing*

### Jamaica Kincaid

#### On Reading and Writing

The advice I always give to people who are going to write is: It's more important to read than to write. I sometimes think I became a writer really to have the opportunity to read some more, because it's the only excuse. It's the only way you are really allowed to read and say, "Well I'm writing. You think I'm reading but really it's part of writing." . . . So, no, reading is the most important thing, and not your own work, reading other things.

#### On Form, the Voice in "Girl," and Her Mother

Whatever a novel is, I'm not it, and whatever a short story is, I'm not it. If I had to follow these forms, I couldn't write. I'm really interested in breaking the form. . . . With "Girl," I wanted to write something new. . . . Certainly at the time I wrote ["Girl"], I didn't know how to interpret my own experience. I had only the voice . . . of my mother . . . firmly embedded in and interwoven into the way I express myself. . . . I was taught all those instructions. Yes, everything was by her.

#### On the Writing Process

I generally only have one draft. The first draft is the last draft, but that's because I tend not to commit things to paper before I've fully worked them out in my head. I'm really writing all the time; it sometimes will take me a week to complete a sentence. But that's because it's not right, it doesn't sound right the way I see it in my head. And then when it's completed, and I can judge it, I can see how it works inside my head, I put it to paper and there it is.

To watch this entire interview and hear the author read from "Girl," go to **www.mhhe.com/delbanco1e.**

Jamaica Kincaid was born Elaine Potter Richardson in St. Johns, Antigua, a small Caribbean island in the British West Indies. Images of Kincaid's mother and the close bond they shared run through much of her writing. Kincaid was a precocious child educated in the government school system, which was largely shaped by British influence and which fostered in this particular student a growing disdain for England. Indeed, the British use the expression "don't tell stories" when they reprimand their children for lying—but Jamaica Kincaid has been telling stories ever since.

At the age of seventeen, Kincaid traveled to the United States to work as a nanny for the children of affluent families—an experience reported in her novel *Lucy.* Before long she found her way to New York City, changed her name, and began writing for magazines such as *Ms., Ingenue,* and the *Village Voice.* She became a regular writer for *The New Yorker,* which published her first short stories as well as brief prose pieces in its "Talk of the Town" page; these have been collected in *Talk Stories* (2001).

Kincaid is perhaps best known for turning the facts of her personal history into fictions that blend fantasy and reality, the imagined and the actual. Her first published collection of stories, *At the Bottom of the River* (1983), and novels such as *Annie John* (1985), *Lucy* (1991), *The Autobiography of My Mother* (1996), and *Mr. Potter* (2002) all explore the boundaries of actual and imagined life, or memoir and dream. Her books defy easy classification, falling into the gray area between autobiography and fiction: the incantatory rhythms of her first-person narrator have the quality of song.

**RESEARCH ASSIGNMENT** In her interview, Kincaid talks about her relationship with her mother. Listen to the interview and comment on how you think this influences the writing of "Girl."

The "Interactive Reading" sections are incredibly useful. . . . While these models are presented as reading tools, the active reading, deciphering, interpreting, and wordsmithing teach students not only to read but how to write. . . . They see firsthand how to break down and comment on various aspects of the work, obviously an integral part of research or explication."

—Kristin Le Veness, Nassau Community College

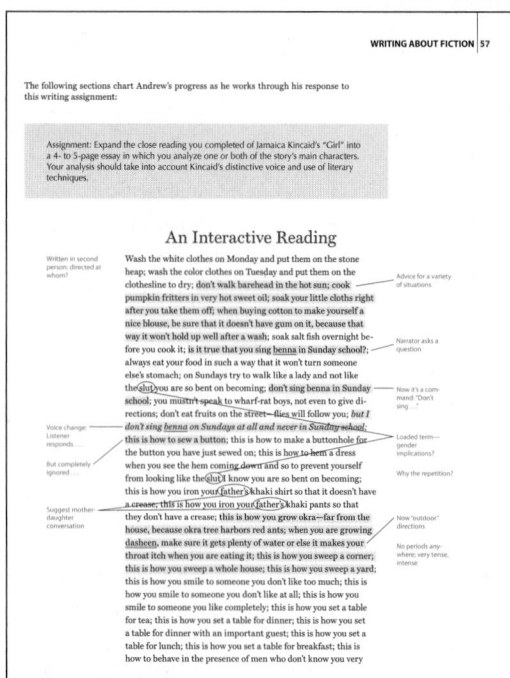

WRITING ABOUT FICTION | 57

The following sections chart Andrew's progress as he works through his response to this writing assignment:

Assignment: Expand the close reading you completed of Jamaica Kincaid's "Girl" into a 4- to 5-page essay in which you analyze one or both of the story's main characters. Your analysis should take into account Kincaid's distinctive voice and use of literary techniques.

### An Interactive Reading

Wash the white clothes on Monday and put them on the stone heap; wash the color clothes on Tuesday and put them on the clothesline to dry; don't walk barehead in the hot sun; cook pumpkin fritters in very hot sweet oil; soak your little cloths right after you take them off; when buying cotton to make yourself a nice blouse, be sure that it doesn't have gum on it, because that way it won't hold up well after a wash; soak salt fish overnight before you cook it; is it true that you sing benna in Sunday school?; always eat your food in such a way that it won't turn someone else's stomach; on Sundays try to walk like a lady and not like the slut you are so bent on becoming; don't sing benna in Sunday school; you mustn't speak to wharf-rat boys, not even to give directions; don't eat fruits on the street—flies will follow you; *but I don't sing benna on Sundays at all and never in Sunday school;* this is how to sew a button; this is how to make a buttonhole for the button you have just sewed on; this is how to hem a dress when you see the hem coming down and so to prevent yourself from looking like the slut I know you are so bent on becoming; this is how you iron your father's khaki shirt so that it doesn't have a crease; this is how you iron your father's khaki pants so that they don't have a crease; this is how you grow okra—far from the house, because okra tree harbors red ants; when you are growing dasheen, make sure it gets plenty of water or else it makes your throat itch when you are eating it; this is how you sweep a corner; this is how you sweep a whole house; this is how you sweep a yard; this is how you smile to someone you don't like too much; this is how you smile to someone you don't like at all; this is how you smile to someone you like completely; this is how you set a table for tea; this is how you set a table for dinner; this is how you set a table for dinner with an important guest; this is how you set a table for lunch; this is how you set a table for breakfast; this is how to behave in the presence of men who don't know you very

Written in second person: directed at whom?

Advice for a variety of situations

Narrator asks a question

Now it's a command: "Don't sing . . ."

Voice change: Listener responds . . .

But completely ignored . . .

Loaded term—gender implications?

Why the repetition?

Suggest mother-daughter conversation

Now "outdoor" directions

No periods anywhere; very tense, intense

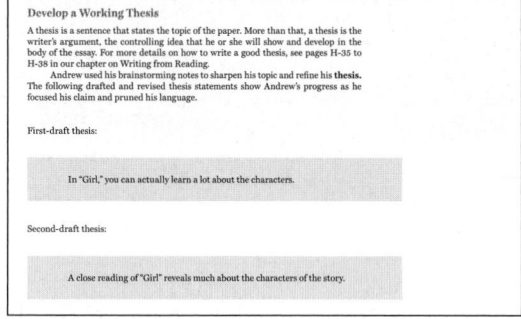

#### Develop a Working Thesis

A thesis is a sentence that states the topic of the paper. More than that, a thesis is the writer's argument, the controlling idea that he or she will show and develop in the body of the essay. For more details on how to write a good thesis, see pages H-35 to H-38 in our chapter on Writing from Reading.

Andrew used his brainstorming notes to sharpen his topic and refine his **thesis.** The following drafted and revised thesis statements show Andrew's progress as he focused his claim and pruned his language.

First-draft thesis:

In "Girl," you can actually learn a lot about the characters.

Second-draft thesis:

A close reading of "Girl" reveals much about the characters of the story.

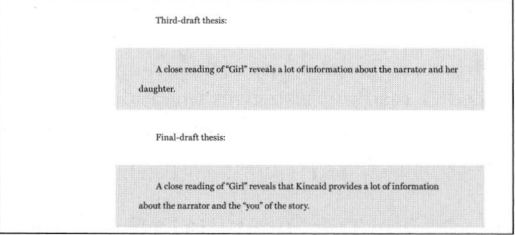

Third-draft thesis:

A close reading of "Girl" reveals a lot of information about the narrator and her daughter.

Final-draft thesis:

A close reading of "Girl" reveals that Kincaid provides a lot of information about the narrator and the "you" of the story.

"I was pleased to learn of the emphasis on sustained reading, as this skill will be called upon in every college course these students enter. . . . *Literature: Craft and Voice* addresses the needs of disengaged readers and writers. It is essential to their success."

—Carol Warren, Georgia Perimeter College

## Emphasizing the Kind of Sustained Reading Students Need for College Success

In addition to media enhancement, each section of the book pays significant attention to the skill of sustained reading, with two chapters per genre devoted to developing critical reading skills, one that provides an overview of the reading to analyze elements in a work, and the next that provides an interactive reading—an annotated work that shows an analysis of a work—and a discussion of context. We begin with the reading and writing process so that students are familiar with that set of skills as they approach reading for academic life. This additional guidance is intended to help students develop the tools they need to communicate their thoughts in *writing.*

Jack London A WICKED WOMAN | 135

## Jack London (1876–1916)

Born to an unmarried mother in California, John ("Jack") London sought employment from age ten in order to lessen his family's poverty. In jobs such as working at a cannery, shoveling coal at a power plant, and pirating oysters from commercial oyster operations, London experienced firsthand the life of an average worker and determined to better himself through education. He turned to writing after taking part in the Yukon gold rush, working with a self-imposed rule that he must write 1,000 publishable words every day. His first collection of short stories, *The Son of the Wolf,* appeared in 1900, and within the next several years, he published many of the novels that made him famous, including *The Call of the Wild* (1903), *The Sea Wolf* (1904), and *White Fang* (1906). These novels of survival in a harsh natural world made London famous all over the globe, and he is one of the few early twentieth century writers to have become rich from his fiction. Despite his rags-to-riches life story, London believed in socialism and used his celebrity status to speak and write in favor of it. London was a man of prodigious energy, and his hobbies ranged from sailing to agriculture to building his dream house. He died when just forty years old, of uremia, although some have speculated that his death may have been a suicide.

AS YOU READ As you read, notice your responses to the rather large cast of characters. Which do you get to know best? Do any of them seem familiar to you?

TIP FOR INTERACTIVE READING . . . As you read, mark the text in the places where about Loretta. How does she describe Loretta to her husband? How does she describ ford? What do the differences in the descriptions tell you about Mrs. Hemingway?

## A Wicked Woman

1 IT was because she had broken with Billy that Loretta had come visiting to Santa Clara. Billy could not understand. His sister had reported that he had walked the floor and cried all night. Loretta had not slept all night either, while she had wept most of the night. Daisy knew this, because it was in her arms that the weeping had been done. And Daisy's husband, Captain Kitt, knew, too. The tears of Loretta, and the comforting by Daisy, had lost him some sleep.

Now Captain Kitt did not like to ther did he want Loretta to marry Bil else. It was Captain Kitt's belief tha the help of her younger sister in the he did not say this aloud. Instead, he that Loretta was too young to think o was Captain Kitt's idea that Loretta s off on a visit to Mrs. Hemingway. Th any Billy there.

110 | CHARACTER

Taiwan, but most of the time I watch bloopers with Bess. Also, I watch the bird feeder—so many, many kinds of birds come. The Shea sons hang around all the time, asking when will I go home, but Bess tell them, Get lost.

She's a permanent resident, say Bess. She isn't going anywhere.

Then she wink at me, and switch the channel with the remote control.

Of course, I shouldn't say Irish this, Irish that, especially now I am become honorary Irish myself, according to Bess. Me! Who's Irish? I say, and she laugh. All the same, if I could mention one thing about some of the Irish, not all of them of course, I like to mention this: Their talk just stick. I don't know how Bess Shea learn to use her words, but sometimes I hear what she say a long time later. *Permanent resident. Not going anywhere.* Over and over I hear it, the voice of Bess. 150

ASSIMILATION in its widest sense has been a part of our national literature from the start. If you like Gish Jen's "Who's Irish?" you might also like other stories that take up the subject matter of the life of first-generation Americans, such as Sylvia Watanabe's "Talking to the Dead," (chapter 12), Junot Diaz's "How to Date a Browngirl, Blackgirl, Whitegirl, or Halfie" (chapter 8), Amy Tan's "Two Kinds" (chapter 2), Jhumpa Lahiri's "Interpreter of Maladies" (chapter 9), and Dagoberto Gilb's "Romero's Shirt" (chapter 12).

GOING FURTHER Timothy Mo's *Sour Sweet* and Fae Myenne Ng's *Bone* also explore Asian characters with one foot in one cultural world and the other foot in another.

## Writing from Reading

**Summarize**

1 Summarize the narrator's views of her Irish in-laws at the beginning of the story, then summarize her views at the end. Discuss how these views have changed, and how they've stayed the same.

**Analyze Craft**

2 Discuss how Jen uses the grandmother's dialect to create her character. What details about the grandmother does this dialect suggest that are never mentioned in the story? Explain how the story would change if it were written in Jen's standard English voice, with only the dialogue in dialect.

**Analyze Voice**

3 Consider the use of humor in "Who's Irish?" Find and list specific examples of misunderstandings and explore why these are (or are not) used for humorous purposes.

4 Discuss the narrator's view of the words *supportive* and *creative.* What does her view reveal about cultural differences?

**Synthesize Summary and Analysis**

5 Describe how Jen uses the topic of Sophie's skin color to reveal character.

6 Imagine "Who's Irish?" told by a neutral party. How would your impressions of the various characters change if viewed without the grandmother's direct opinions?

**Interpret the Story**

7 A central theme of "Who's Irish?" is the speaker's adjustment—as restaurant owner, wife, mother, and grandmother—to the values and systems of behavior in America. Based on her various reactions and interactions throughout the story, do you think she has adjusted?

*"Literature: Craft and Voice* walks students slowly and clearly through the steps of approaching works of literature. The word 'gentle' comes to mind; students daunted by reading or interpreting literature would not be intimidated."

—Shellie Michael, Volunteer State Community College

"My absolute favorite [feature] is the "If you liked the story, try. . . ." I'm always looking for good suggestions."

—Drew Henry, student, New York University

"I especially like the emphasis on the . . . connection between reading and writing. The discussion of these two concepts is superior to what I've found in most other anthologies."

—Joe Lostracco, Austin Community College

## Making Reading-Writing Connections

Our chapter on writing in each section walks students through how reading interactively with a text is the basis of writing your own interpretation of a text. This is reinforced in the question sets that follow the readings included in the discussion in each chapter, a building block approach to critical thinking from summarizing (for comprehension), to analyzing craft and voice, synthesizing summary and analysis, and using that synthesis to interpret a text. You'll also find tips for interactive reading and As You Read suggestions for most selections. Students responded very positively to this approach in our focus groups.

In addition, we wanted to maintain a wide range of works not only for the instructor to find something interesting to teach but also so that students might go from texts that are assigned to those they might find deeply meaningful personally—the gothic component of Southern literature, perhaps, or the discovery of the role of music in the literature of Langston Hughes. In our suggestions for further reading, we continue to encourage reading with the added enhancement of "If you like this, you might like this" suggestions to draw a student into another selection in the book.

"The tips for interactive reading are a very useful feature. These suggestions help students read poetry effectively, demystifying poems so that students aren't so afraid of the demand to know how to approach them."

—Jessica Rabin, Anne Arundel Community College

"I really like how your textbook organizes the questions about the stories—the categories of 'summarize,' 'analyze craft,' 'analyze voice,' 'synthesize summary and analysis,' and 'interpret the story' are excellent. This allows the student to build to a deeper understanding of the text."

—James Kirkpatrick, Central Piedmont Community College

310 | THEME

## Reading for Theme

When reading for **theme,** go beyond the plot and subject of the story and ask yourself what truths or insights about the human experience the story offers.

| | |
|---|---|
| **Does the title point to a major symbol, character, or subject from which themes develop?** | EXAMPLES: "The Jilting of Granny Weatherall," "The Death of Ivan Ilych," and "Why I Live at the P.O." |
| **Does the title point to a central irony that is thematic?** | EXAMPLES: "The Short Happy Life of Francis Macomber," "No One's a Mystery." |
| **Does the title point to thematic concerns of the story?** | EXAMPLES:<br>• "Who's Irish?" calls up the question of identity.<br>• "Araby" conjures an exotic dream.<br>• "The Rememberer" calls to mind the person left behind after a loss. |
| **Does the narrator or another character make general statements as observations that may offer insight into the writer's theme?** | EXAMPLE: *Moby-Dick's* narrator asserts that a subject must be larger than ordinary or everyday to accommodate a large theme. |
| **What changes in the main character? What does the main character come to realize?** | EXAMPLES:<br>• In Alice Munro's "An Ounce of Cure," the narrator says in the last line, "I am a grown-up woman now."<br>• In John Updike's "A&P," the young narrator realizes "how hard the world was going to be to me from here on in." |
| **Note powerful details and ask yourself why this is important. What does this make you feel? How do events or details thread together the meaning beyond a particular situation?** | EXAMPLES:<br>• The frail back of the old man on the wet floor (*What* do *I* feel when I think about that old man?).<br>• The uneaten rice (*How* did these events affect Nnamabia?).<br>• The tears in the brother's eyes (*Why* did the sister feel that tenderness?).<br>Continued |

"The conversational tone . . . puts the student at ease about analyzing literature. The editors acknowledge the student's fears . . . and offer encouragement, a you-can-do-it message . . . [that] allay[s] the fears of the nonreader. The editors' focus on connections . . . is also a strength."

—Ethel Bonds, Virginia Western Community College

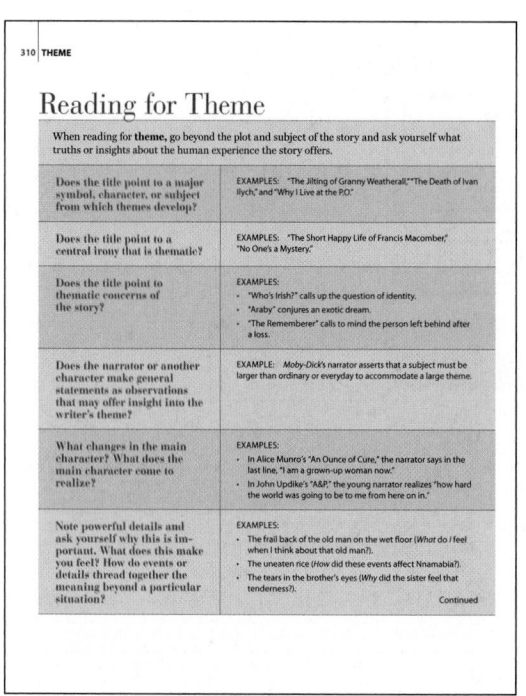

## Providing the Vocabulary of Craft for Analysis

As with all things, knowledge of the working pieces of a project will help the student understand it better. Reading is the starting point for most of what is written; therefore, we use our own experience as writers to delve into the craft of composition from the inside out. In every case, some attention to the context, purpose, and genre of a work is needed for sustained response. In fiction, poetry, and drama, we have the opportunity to examine language at its most powerful, to analyze how that power is created and how it affects an individual. The importance of technique in writing is self-evident. Each successful writer employs technique in ways specific to his or her experience of the world in which he or she writes. The effective use of artistic craft and voice creates an overall effect on individual readers living at the same time as the writer, and—if the work is of enduring quality—in readers born centuries later.

## Connecting Craft to the Variety of Composition Processes in Student Work

"I personally enjoy getting a glimpse into the writing and thought process of the people I'm reading. I think this really opens the texts up for both comprehension and analysis. . . . With so many author interviews students can begin to see how varied the writing process can be and how essential it is to rewrite. Also, the writing prompts are excellent."

—Heidi Johnsen, La Guardia Community College

As teachers who have brought our own students to reading and writing by demonstrating a personal connection to the work, we bring an intimate knowledge of the struggles all writers face and the composition process in all its variety. The various featured authors and scholars all have something to say about the composition process that should inspire as well as support a student's own writing process. The following statement by Richard Ford gives a taste of what students will hear in this text about writing, the kind of observation we hope will show them how they themselves can write not just creatively but for every course in the curriculum.

> *People see a story on the page and what they think is that the writer started and then wrote to the end and this is how it looked. And in fact the writer . . . started at the beginning and wrote to the end, and then he started at the end and wrote to the beginning, and then he plucked things out of the middle and closed up the places where he took something out.*

## Supporting Writing and Research with Enhanced Coverage of Avoiding Plagiarism

In addition to a chapter on writing that walks a student through three drafts of a student paper in each section, our case studies provide a springboard for research. We include a list of credible sources—both print and online—to get started, secondary sources online, and a research project involving the subject of the case study. Papers written on the subject of our case studies are found in our Handbook for Writing from Reading, which also provides additional support for students who will need to quote, paraphrase, summarize, and document their sources. The specific needs of today's students in writing, not only about literature but across the curriculum, encouraged us to provide pointed and direct guidance on avoiding plagiarism, whether using a single source or multiple sources. You'll find two chapters in our handbook that draw out issues on avoiding plagiarism, along with an MLA documentation style guide, and we believe these aids are crucial in helping students understand the requirements of the college experience.

"The bridge from reading to writing . . . provides important information . . . good information on critical approaches, suggestions for writing assignments, documentation, plagiarism, and MLA Guidelines."

—Kathleen A. Carlson, Brevard Community College

"Once students master critical reading skills, they still have great difficulty incorporating others' ideas about texts into their own interpretations."

—John Schaffer, Blinn College

## Selecting Works for Powerful Personal Resonance

Ultimately reading, research, and writing can't exist without a subject: The subject for practicing these skills in this text is, in the broadest sense, literature. It is *alpha* and *omega* here from first to final page. There are many advantages to making literature a jumping-off point for the college experience. First, literature provides a pleasurable and personal place to begin. It offers the kind of complex text that generates, in the best of circumstances, a visceral response. Most people don't read well at first. Most don't write well. But the process does grow simpler when works have been selected to provide a rich introduction to these critical components of college life.

So, a word about selection: We believe in meeting the students halfway, without either blindly adhering to the assumptions of the past or veering too much toward the attractive if fleeting fads of the immediate present. We believe that exercise enhances performance, but that solid performance without the foundation of sound literary taste can be an empty exercise in itself. We believe as most of you do in a practical approach to literary study and that the study of good writing leads to the making of good writers.

This book provides a range of stories, poems, and plays that are testaments to language at its best, examples both well known and new. The selection of contemporary works by writers from a variety of backgrounds should help us demonstrate that literature is alive and well today. And the living, breathing presence of authors on our videos should help dispel the notion that all art is deathly dull and was produced by the dead. But we also wanted to bring to the students' attention enduring works by writers from the past—texts they may only have heard of or studied only glancingly (such as "Beowulf" or Chekhov's fiction) or may read for the first time in this course (such as the poems of Thomas Hardy or the plays of Sophocles). As the table of contents will demonstrate, our examples are numerous and various; their common denominator is that we think them worth sustained attention on the student's part.

"Well chosen . . . I'm delighted with the inclusion of Ha Jin and a number of stories that could be used to introduce students to multicultural literature."

—Richard C. Taylor, East Carolina University

"The fiction section is outstanding. I like that . . . it has a section on regionalism with authors grouped in the American West and the American South . . . [and] that wonderful chapter 13, Visual Arts, Film, and Fiction, with selections from *Beowulf,* Gardner, and Crichton."

—Grace Haddox, El Paso Community College

## Designing a Text for Reading

Enormous thought and care and research has gone into this design, which students tell us makes them want to read further! By beginning with a compelling chapter opener and a quotation from literature itself, students find themselves reading before they've thought about whether they will or want to read this work. This text's design should be an invitation to explore further, think harder, and write. Our student responses have been unanimous and gratifying.

"I love the chapter openings! They're not just random pictures—they relate to the text. The spread also includes more than just a plot summary . . . it has a snippet of the text for every kind of reader and personality: a summary, a quote from the text, and a quote from the author."

—Alexandra V. Loizzo, student, Barnard College

"I really like the opening image. It fits the story really well. The image . . . make you think, what happened here? . . . which makes me want to read and find out more about what took place."

—Alvin Flete, student, Stony Brook University

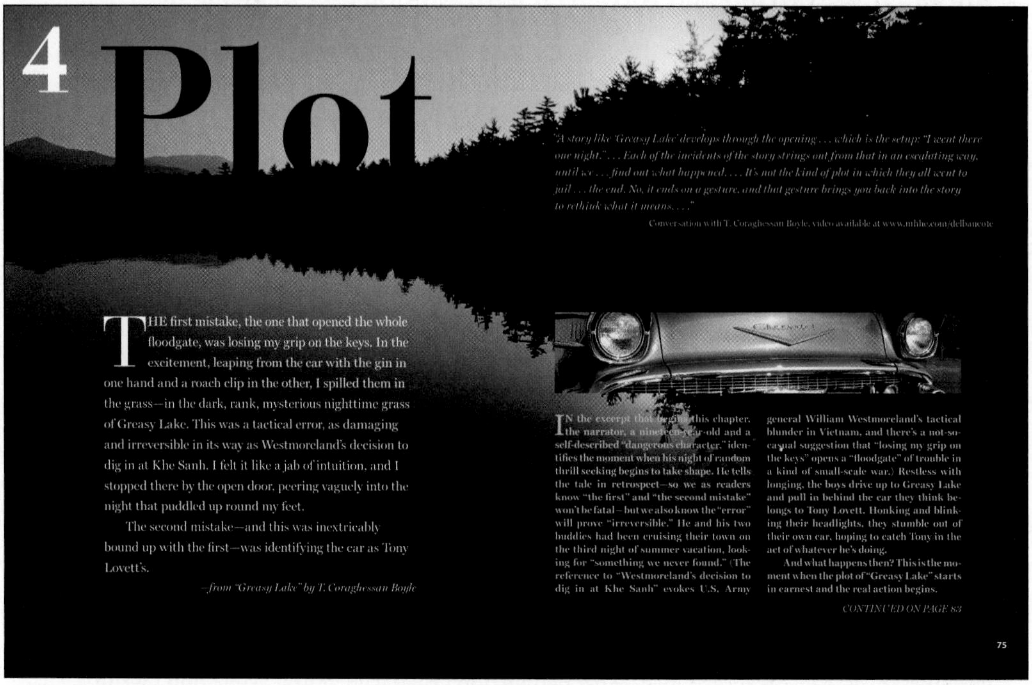

4 Plot

"A story like 'Greasy Lake' develops through the opening . . . which is the setup: "I went there one night." . . . Each of the incidents of the story strings out from that in an escalating way, until we . . . find out what happened. . . . It's not the kind of plot in which they all went to jail . . . the end. No, it ends on a gesture, and that gesture brings you back into the story to rethink what it means. . . ."

Conversation with T. Coraghessan Boyle, video available at www.mhhe.com/delbancote

THE first mistake, the one that opened the whole floodgate, was losing my grip on the keys. In the excitement, leaping from the car with the gin in one hand and a roach clip in the other, I spilled them in the grass—in the dark, rank, mysterious nighttime grass of Greasy Lake. This was a tactical error, as damaging and irreversible in its way as Westmoreland's decision to dig in at Khe Sanh. I felt it like a jab of intuition, and I stopped there by the open door, peering vaguely into the night that puddled up round my feet.

The second mistake—and this was inextricably bound up with the first—was identifying the car as Tony Lovett's.

—from "Greasy Lake" by T. Coraghessan Boyle

IN the excerpt that begins this chapter, the narrator, a nineteen-year-old and a self-described "dangerous character," identifies the moment when his night of random thrill seeking begins to take shape. He tells the tale in retrospect—so we as readers know "the first" and "the second mistake" won't be fatal—but we also know the "error" will prove "irreversible." He and his two buddies had been cruising their town on the third night of summer vacation, looking for "something we never found." (The reference to "Westmoreland's decision to dig in at Khe Sanh" evokes U.S. Army general William Westmoreland's tactical blunder in Vietnam, and there's a not-so-casual suggestion that "losing my grip on the keys" opens a "floodgate" of trouble in a kind of small-scale war.) Restless with longing, the boys drive up to Greasy Lake and pull in behind the car they think belongs to Tony Lovett. Honking and blinking their headlights, they stumble out of their own car, hoping to catch Tony in the act of whatever he's doing.

And what happens then? This is the moment when the plot of "Greasy Lake" starts in earnest and the real action begins.

CONTINUED ON PAGE 83

75

"I understand that we're dealing with a generation of students who are much more geared toward the visual. They are the post-MTV generation."

—Cleatta R. Morris, Lousiana State University, Shreveport

"I do appreciate the consideration of design that is going on in this text."

—Leigh Anne Duck, University of Memphis

"One of the strengths of *Literature: Craft and Voice* is how it's laid out. The organization is immediately clear."

—Danel Olson, North Harris College

All would prefer to read from this book when they compare it to the usual suspects. One student brought her sample home to show her sister, as she said, "My sister hates reading but she won't hate it when she sees this." We do hope we have created a twenty-first-century approach to our common task of education.

Our student research also tells us that students don't like a big book. But they don't like it small if all that has happened is that type size is shrunk and more words are crammed onto a page. However, research is clear that a student's ability to toss a book into a backpack makes it more likely he or she can find a quick moment here and there to read. Students in our focus group told us they read on the subway to the New York office because they couldn't wait to see what happened next. They googled authors themselves to find out more after they saw their interviews. This is the kind of engagement we hope this new format brings to the course.

Finally, a word about craft and voice and our names: The wonderful twentieth-century American novelist and poet Robert Penn Warren once described himself to students, when he was in his early eighties, as someone who woke up every day and sat down at his desk and was still trying to be a writer. That's how we both feel about the work of trying to become the best readers and best writers we can. Though we've come a long way from when we first tried "to be a writer," our own work as novelists, essayists, and reviewers brings us face-to-face every day with the hard labor of making sense with words.

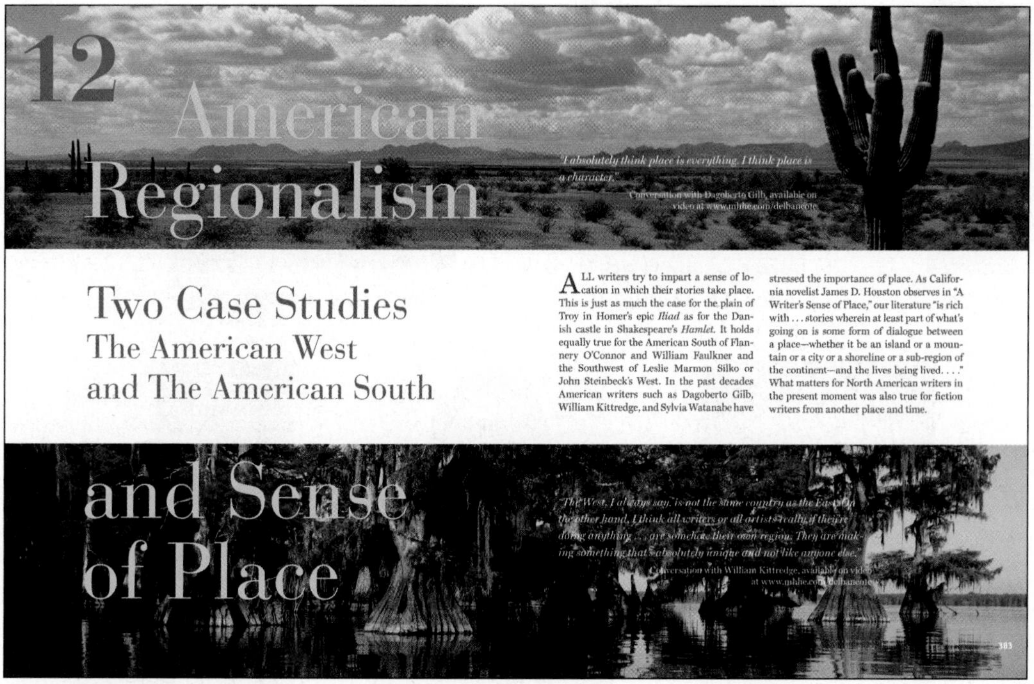
12

American Regionalism and Sense of Place

"I absolutely think place is everything. I think place is a character."

Conversation with Dagoberto Gilb, available on video at www.mhhe.com/delbancote

Two Case Studies
The American West
and The American South

ALL writers try to impart a sense of location in which their stories take place. This is just as much the case for the plain of Troy in Homer's epic *Iliad* as for the Danish castle in Shakespeare's *Hamlet*. It holds equally true for the American South of Flannery O'Connor and William Faulkner and the Southwest of Leslie Marmon Silko or John Steinbeck's West. In the past decades American writers such as Dagoberto Gilb, William Kittredge, and Sylvia Watanabe have stressed the importance of place. As California novelist James D. Houston observes in "A Writer's Sense of Place," our literature "is rich with . . . stories wherein at least part of what's going on is some form of dialogue between a place—whether it be an island or a mountain or a city or a shoreline or a sub-region of the continent—and the lives being lived. . . ." What matters for North American writers in the present moment was also true for fiction writers from another place and time.

"The West, I always say, is not the same country as the East. On the other hand, I think all writers or all artists really, if they're doing anything . . . are somehow their own region. They are making something that's absolutely unique and not like anyone else."

Conversation with William Kittredge, available on video at www.mhhe.com/delbancote

383

The discovery of *craft*—the techniques that taken together engender a work—and its relation to *voice*—the way a story or poem or play sounds to our ear—allows even the novice writer to begin to make his or her mark on the page. This forms the essence of our vision and the central tenet of our text. Remembering where we began has made us better teachers, too, because, as most of you know, nothing helps an instructor help a student so much as firsthand knowledge of the place that student starts from. As writer-teachers, we hope to create an instructive method by which students can help themselves to become better writers. To that end, we, Nicholas Delbanco (pronounced delb-ah-nco) and Alan Cheuse (pronounced *choose*), wish professors and students alike good reading and good writing!

*Nicholas Delbanco*

*Alan Cheuse*

"I believe your anthology will be a godsend to students hoping to write better essays and a blessing to professors who are . . . teaching rhetoric."

—William C. Myers, University of Colorado at Colorado Springs

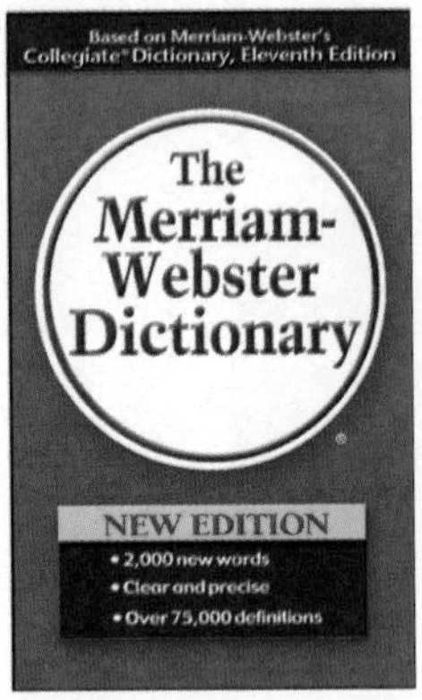

ISBN: 0-07-310057-9

ISBN: 0-07-310057-9

ISBN: 0-07-310057-9

# Ancillaries

**Instructor Resources for Teaching Literature: Craft and Voice** are available online and include an alternate thematic table of contents, sample syllabi, PowerPoints, quizzes (that students can take online), and support for teaching every selection and video associated with *Literature: Craft and Voice.* For students, we put our casebook sources online, to keep our book easy to carry and inviting (which both students and instructors asked for) and provide a reliable place for students to get started on their research. Additional student resources include an interactive tutorial for avoiding plagiarism and evaluating sources, plus resources for conducting research and formatting works cited pages. Blackboard cartridges are available for hybrid and online courses. Our online learning solutions support team can work with qualified adopters to adapt any of these materials to the learning management system at your institution.

**Select trade titles and reference sources** can be packaged at a discount with *Literature: Craft and Voice.* If you are interested in a dictionary, thesaurus, or any of the following titles, please contact your local McGraw-Hill representative or our Marketing Coordinator for English at English@McGraw-Hill.com.

# TRADE TITLES FROM RANDOM HOUSE

Any paperback novel or work of nonfiction published by Random House can be packaged at a discount with *Literature: Craft and Voice.* Below are just a few suggestions. If the work you are looking for is not listed, please contact your McGraw-Hill representative!

Edward Abbey, *The Monkey Wrench Gang*
ISBN: 0-07-243424-4

Chinua Achebe, *Things Fall Apart*
ISBN: 0-07-243518-6

Sherman Alexie, *The Lone Ranger and Tonto Fistfight in Heaven*
ISBN: 0-07-243418-X

Louisa May Alcott, *Little Women*
ISBN: 0-07-724088-X

Maya Angelou, *I Know Why the Caged Bird Sings*
ISBN: 0-07-313592-5

Margaret Atwood, *The Handmaid's Tale*
ISBN: 0-07-724089-8

Jane Austen, *Pride and Prejudice*
ISBN: 0-07-724090-1

H. G. Bissinger, *Friday Night Lights*
ISBN: 0-07-285654-8

Charlotte Brontë, *Jane Eyre*
ISBN: 0-07-724091-X

Sandra Cisneros, *The House on Mango Street*
ISBN: 0-07-243517-8

Joseph Conrad, *Heart of Darkness*
ISBN: 0-07-243513-5

Annie Dillard, *Pilgrim at Tinker Creek*
ISBN: 0-07-243417-1

Buchi Emecheta, *Second-Class Citizen*
ISBN: 0-07-724084-7

Louise Erdrich, *Love Medicine*
ISBN: 0-07-243419-8

Laura Esquivel, *Like Water for Chocolate*
ISBN: 0-07-313589-5

Zora Neale Hurston, *Their Eyes Were Watching God*
ISBN: 0-07-243422-8

Peter Jenkins, *A Walk across America*
ISBN: 0-07-285657-2

Ha Jin, *Waiting*
ISBN: 0-07-313588-7

Jamaica Kincaid, *Lucy*
ISBN: 0-07-724081-2

Maxine Hong Kingston, *Woman Warrior*
ISBN: 0-07-243519-4

Jhumpa Lahiri, *The Namesake*
ISBN: 0-07-724082-0

N. Scott Momaday, *House Made of Dawn*
ISBN: 0-07-243420-1

Toni Morrison, *Beloved*
ISBN: 0-07-313591-7

Azar Nafasi, *Reading Lolita in Tehran*
ISBN: 0-07-313587-9

Jean Rhys, *Wide Sargasso Sea*
ISBN: 0-07-724085-5

Bapsi Sidhwa, *Cracking India*
ISBN: 0-07-724083-9

Art Spiegelman, *Maus,* Vol. 1
ISBN: 0-07-313593-3

Amy Tan, *Joy Luck Club*
ISBN: 0-07-243509-7

Edith Wharton, *The House of Mirth*
ISBN: 0-07-724094-4

E. B. White, *Essays of E. B. White*
ISBN: 0-07-243427-9

Zoë Wicomb, *Playing in the Light*
ISBN: 0-07-724086-3

Virginia Woolf, *Mrs. Dalloway*
ISBN: 0-07-724087-1

## MODERN LIBRARY CLASSICS EDITIONS

William Blake, *Selected Poetry and Prose*
ISBN: 0-07-553661-7

James Boswell, *Life of Samuel Johnson*
ISBN: 0-07-553645-5

William Bradford, *Plymouth Plantation 1620–1647*
ISBN: 0-07-554281-1

Albert Camus, *The Plague*
ISBN: 0-07-553649-8

Kate Chopin, *The Awakening and Selected Stories*
ISBN: 0-07-554269-2

Stephen Crane, *The Red Badge of Courage*
ISBN: 0-07-555608-1

John Donne, *Poetry and Prose*
ISBN: 0-07-553663-3

Fyodor Dostoyevsky, *The Brothers Karamazov*
ISBN: 0-07-553575-0

Fyodor Dostoyevsky, *Crime and Punishment*
ISBN: 0-07-553574-2

Frederick Douglass, *Frederick Douglass: The Narrative and Selected Writings*
ISBN: 0-07-554375-3

John Dryden, *Selected Writings of Dryden*
ISBN: 0-07-553553-X

Ralph Waldo Emerson, *The Selected Writings*
ISBN: 0-07-554265-X

William Faulkner, *Absalom, Absalom!*
ISBN: 0-07-553657-9

William Faulkner, *Light in August*
ISBN: 0-07-553648-X

William Faulkner, *The Sound and the Fury*
ISBN: 0-07-553666-8

Gustav Flaubert, *Madame Bovary*
ISBN: 0-07-554378-8

Jacques Guicharnaud, *Seventeenth-Century French Drama*
ISBN: 0-07-553656-0

Allen G. Halline, *Six Modern American Plays*
ISBN: 0-07-553660-9

Alexander Hamilton, John Jay, and James Madison, *The Federalist*
ISBN: 0-07-553644-7

Nathaniel Hawthorne, *The Scarlet Letter and Selected Writings*
ISBN: 0-07-555475-5

Herodotus, *The Persian Wars*
ISBN: 0-07-553640-4

Washington Irving, *Selected Writings*
ISBN: 0-07-554394-X

Henry James, *The Portrait of a Lady*
ISBN: 0-07-553637-4

Roger Sherman Loomis, and Laura Hibbard Loomis, *Medieval Romances*
ISBN: 0-07-553650-1

John Milton, *Paradise Lost*
ISBN: 0-07-553668-4

Frederick Law Olmsted, *The Cotton Kingdom*
ISBN: 0-07-554413-X

Eugene O'Neill, *Later Plays of Eugene O'Neill*
ISBN: 0-07-553664-1

Edgar Allan Poe, *Selected Poetry and Prose*
ISBN: 0-07-553641-2

Marcel Proust, *Swann's Way*
ISBN: 0-07-553647-1

Ricardo Quintana, *Eighteenth-Century Plays*
ISBN: 0-07-553659-5

Jonathan Swift, *Gulliver's Travels*
ISBN: 0-07-553630-7

Henry David Thoreau, *Walden and Other Writings*
ISBN: 0-07-554267-6

Thucydides, *The Peloponnesian War*
ISBN: 0-07-554372-9

Alexis de Tocqueville, *Democracy in America*
ISBN: 0-07-554273-0

Leo Tolstoy, *Anna Karenina*
ISBN: 0-07-553632-3

Walt Whitman, *Leaves of Grass and Selected Prose*
ISBN: 0-07-554263-3

M. L. Wine, *Drama of the English Renaissance*
ISBN: 0-07-553569-6

William Wordsworth, *Selected Poetry*
ISBN: 0-07-553635-8

# Acknowledgments

This book is, truly, a collective effort: no single person or pair of authors could have produced it alone. From the first to the final chapter, we have relied upon the work of others; our Table of Contents represents the essence of shared enterprise. The individual voices here became a kind of chorus, and our first debt of gratitude goes to the splendid writers (some of them anonymous) who produced the fiction and poetry and plays that *Literature: Craft and Voice* contains.

We have dedicated this book to our students. In addition to our own students, there were more than 4,000 others at 132 institutions across the country who participated in ethnographic research by letting us into their daily lives and discussing how they live and learn. We thank them for allowing us to observe them at work, at leisure, and in their place of study. To the thousands of young people across the country who participated in this ethnographic research, we thank you, and we extend a special thanks to the several students who gave up their time to provide detailed information and in some cases meet with us personally:

Danielle Crochiere, Colby College; Brittany Davis, University of Southern Mississippi; Alvin Flete, SUNY Stony Brook; Rosellen Flete, SUNY New Paltz; Jane Fountain, Central Piedmont Community College; Drew Henry, New York University; Nancy Kurien, Hunter College; Alex Limanowski, Roosevelt University; Alexandra Loizzo, Barnard College; Selena Poznak, Tulane University; Emily Rejouis, Cornell University; Josie Sayegh, University of California, Santa Cruz; Kaitlyn Taylor, University of Delaware; Liz Wechter, University of Illinois; Brian Yu, University of Michigan.

We also wish to express our gratitude to the professors, colleagues, and students who have contributed to *Literature: Craft and Voice.* Many professors took the time to let some book people from McGraw-Hill into their offices to discuss their challenges with this course. The surveys that emerged from these interviews helped us create a new pedagogical program that we hope these friends recognize as emerging from their thoughtful comments about teaching today.

Heidi Ajrami, Victoria College
Norma Akins, Heart of Georgia Technical College
Frank Albert, Community College of Beaver County
Deborah Albritton, Jefferson Davis Community College–Brewton
Michael Alleman, Louisiana State University–Eunice
Michael Allen, North Central State College
Stephanie Almagno, Piedmont College
Maribeth Anderson, Ivy Tech Community College of Indiana
Helane Androne, Miami University–Middletown
Judith Angona, Ocean County College
Sonia Apgar Begert, Olympic College
Sue Apshaga, Community College of Rhode Island
Saye Atkinson, Georgia Military College
Les Bailey, Saint Martin's University
Ronda Bailey, Fort Scott Community College
Eileen Baland, East Texas Baptist University
John Balcer, Shenandoah University
Allison Bartlett, Wor-Wic Community College
Kathleen Bartlett, Florida Institute of Technology
Jonathan Barz, University of Dubuque
Janice Baskin, Azusa Pacific University
Lynne Belcher, Southern Arkansas University
John Bennett, Lake Land College
Bill Berry, Cape Cod Community College
Ken Bishop, Itawamba Community College
Mark Blaauw-hara, North Central Michigan College
Lawrence Blasco, Wor-Wic Community College
Laura Bloxham, Whitworth University
Paula Bolduc, Salve Regina University
Laurel Bollinger, University of Alabama–Huntsville
Ellen Boose, Bossier Parish Community College
Troy Boucher, Southwestern College
Michelle Bowie, Southern Nazarene University
David Breith, University of the Southwest
Jason Brown, Herkimer County Community College
Kristin Brunnemer, Pierce College
Mitzi Brunsdale, Mayville State University
Laurie Buchanan, Clark State Community College

Dawn Buckey, Charleston Southern University
Suzanne Bufamanti, Niagara County Community College
Dottie Burkhart, Davidson County Community College
Kelly Ann Butterbaugh, Lehigh Carbon Community College
Dona Cady, Middlesex Community College
Mechel Camp, Jackson State Community College
Sarah Canfield-Fuller, Shenandoah University
Robert Canipe, Catawba Valley Community College
Joan Canty, Columbia College
Judith Cavanaugh, Clinton Community College
Sean Cavanaugh, Assumption College
Marlys Cervantes, Cowley County Community College
Diane Chambers, Malone University
Windy Charles, Piedmont College
Maria Chiancola, Salve Regina University
Bill Church, Missouri Western State University
Lori Cinotte, Illinois Valley Community College
Stacy Clanton, Southern Arkansas University
Pam Clark, Frederick Community College
Jessica Cobbs, Bossier Parish Community College
Stanly Coberly, West Virginia University–Parkersburg
Michael Cocchiarale, Widener University
Rose Collins, Dallas Baptist University
Jim Compton, Muscatine Community College
Nancy Corbett, Maysville Community and Technical College
Jean Crockett, Cleveland State Community College
Sarah Dangelantonio, Franklin Pierce University
Judy Daniel, McMurry University
Cherie Dargan, Hawkeye Community College
Rebecca Dark, Dallas Baptist University
Bonita Dattner-Garza, St. Mary's University
Daniel de Roulet, Vanguard University
Laurie Delaney, Kent State University–Stark Campus
Mikee Delony, Abilene Christian University
Louise DeSantis Deutsch, Cape Cod Community College
Anna Crowe Dewart, College of Coastal Georgia
Betty Dobry, Redlands Community College
Scott Douglass, Chattanooga State Technical Community College
Lisa Dresdner, Norwalk Community College
Marilyn Durham, University of Wisconsin–Whitewater
Linda Eicken, Cape Fear Community College
Margaret Ellington, Georgia Southwestern State University
Scott Emmert, University of Wisconsin–Fox Valley
Joseph Ervin, Rend Lake College
Cassandra Falke, East Texas Baptist University
Tyler Farrell, University of Dubuque
William Feeler, Midland College
Sandy Feinstein, Penn State Berks
Maribeth Fell, College of Coastal Georgia
Robin Field, King's College
Jim Fisher, Peninsula College
Michael Flaherty, Triton College
Joey Flamm-Costello, Reading Area Community College
Juliene Forrestal, Olivet Nazarene University
Chriss Foster, San Francisco State University
Deborah Fox, Matanuska-Susitna College
Holly French, Bossier Parish Community College
Julie Fulbright, Cleveland State Community College
Robert Furstoss, Ocean County College
Joanne Gabel, Reading Area Community College
Naomi Gal, Moravian College
Xiongya Gao, Southern University at New Orleans
Maryanne Garbowsky, County College of Morris
Jennifer Garlen, University of Alabama in Huntsville
Vicki Garton, Crowder Community College–Nevada
Tony Giffone, Farmingdale State College
Wayne Gilbert, Community College of Aurora
Michelle Gompf, Concord University
Ron Goulet, Northland Pioneer College
Judith Griffith, Wartburg College
Brian Hale, Chattanooga State Technical Community College
Gary Hall, Victoria College
Carol Harding, Western Oregon University
Simon Hay, Connecticut College
Hunter Hayes, Texas A&M University–Commerce
Catherine Heath, Victoria College
Michael Helfin, Cape Cod University
Sue Henderson, East Central College
Marylou Horn, Middlesex Community College
Dianne Hunter, Trinity College
Deborah Hysell, North Central State College
Adriane Ivey, Oxford College of Emory University
Joanne Jacobs, Shenandoah University
John Jacobs, Shenandoah University
Kathleen Jacquette, Farmingdale State College
Kelli Johnson, Miami University–Hamilton
Dean Karpowicz, University of Wisconsin–Parkside
Robert Kellerman, University of Maine at Augusta
Tim Kelley, Northwest-Shoals Community College
Nora Kindley, Ulster Community College
Mark King, Gordon College
Bette Kirschstein, Pace University
Deborah Klein, Truman State University
John Krafft, Miami University–Hamilton
Theresa Kulbaga, Miami University–Hamilton
Celena Kusch, University of South Carolina Upstate
James Lake, Louisiana State University in Shreveport
Dana Lauro, Ocean County College
David Leigh, Seattle University
Bruce Litte, Northwest Missouri State University
Keming Liu, Medgar Evers College
Megan Lloyd, King's College
Deborah Luoma, Gavilan Community College
Brent Lynn, Wayland Baptist University
Robert Mahon, East Central University
Kathleen Maloney, St. Mary's University
Kelli Maloy, University of Pittsburgh at Greensburg

Beulah Manuel, Columbia Union College
Michael Martin, University of Wisconsin
Cindy McClenagan, Wayland Baptist University
Jeannine McDevitt, Pennsylvania Highlands Community College
Kathleen McDonald, Norwich University
Amy Minervini-Dodson, Arizona Western College
Brooke Mitchell, Wingate University
Kelly Moffett, Kentucky Wesleyan College
D'Juana Montgomery, Southwestern Assemblies of God University
Margaret Morlier, Reinhardt College
David Murdoch, Gadsden State Community College
Josephine Neill-Browning, Holmes Community College
Jeff Nelson, University of Alabama in Huntsville
Ode Ogede, North Carolina Central University
Michael Olendzenski, Cape Cod Community College
Salisa Olmstead, Lake Land College
Kim Overcash, Central Carolina Community College
Renelda Owen, Delta State University
Allison Palumbo, Elizabethtown Community and Technical College
Jeff Patridge, Capital Community College
Michelle Paulsen, Victoria College
Jared Pearce, William Penn University
Shannon Phillips, Lake Land College
Meenakshi Ponnoswami, Bucknell University
Nancy Popkin, Harris-Stowe State University
David Pulling, Louisiana State University–Eunice
Ken Raines, Eastern Arizona College
Wilbur Reames, Erskine College
Shirley Rehberg, Lake City Community College
Margaret Reimer, University of Southern Maine
Chauncey Ridley, Sacramento State University
Nancy Risch, Florence Darlington Technical College
Jason Roberts, Sierra College
Mary Rogerson, West Liberty State College
Patricia Roy, Mount Ida College
Jill Rubinson, University of Maine at Augusta
Wolfgang Runzi, Rogue Community College
Christine Ryan, Middlesex Community College
Elizabeth Sachs, Niagara County Community College
Joe Sarnowski, San Diego Christian College
Jane Schreck, Bismarck State College
Tracy Schrems, St. Bonaventure University
Jolly Sharp, University of the Cumberlands
Maggie Shear, South Suburban College
Deepa Sitaraman, Shawnee State University
Amy Smith, Hilbert College
Matt Smith, University of St. Francis
Amos St. Germain, Wentworth Institute of Technology
Gabriele Stauf, Georgia Southwestern State University
Michael Steven, Wayland Baptist University
Bill Stifler, Chattanooga State Technical Community College
Ron Stormer, Culver-Stockton College
Monnette Sturgill, Big Sandy Community and Technical College
Richard Swanson, University of Wisconsin–Stout
Nannette Tamer, Stevenson University
Richard Terdiman, University of California–Santa Cruz
Jennifer Thompson, Saint Xavier University
Alan Trusky, Florence-Darlington Technical College
Randal Urwiller, Texas College
Scott Vander Ploeg, Madisonville Community College
Leila Wells, Griffin Technical College
Eleanor Welsh, Chesapeake College
Cynthia Wesson, Cowley County Community College
Jeana West, Murray State College
Patricia White, Norwich University
Edward Whitelock, Gordon College
Brenda Williams, University of New Haven
Mary Williams, Midland College
Daniel Wolkow, Eastern New Mexico University–Roswell
Whitney Womack Smith, Miami University–Hamilton
Jane Wood, Park University
P. J. Yongbloed, Springfield Technical Community College
Adam Young, Middle Georgia College
Sarah Young, Baker University
J. B. Zwilling, Allen Community College

In addition, over 175 professors from 113 institutions provided their responses about design, selections, and content by way of WebEx, symposia, focus groups, phone interviews, design surveys, and detailed manuscript reviews. A special thanks to our students Margaret Dean and Valerie Laken, and especially Elizabeth Eshelman, Nicholas Harp, and Anne Stameshkin, who, with Professors Santi Buscemi (Middlesex County College) and Chris Thaiss (University of California, Davis), contributed importantly to the shape and sense of our handbook for writing from reading as well as to the other sections on fiction, poetry, and drama in this book. Tom Kitts (St. John's University) not only reviewed our text but deserves special recognition here for his herculean service to our resources for teaching. We can safely say that every page of this volume has been guided by at least a dozen people dedicated to education and to literature. And for that, to all of you, we offer our sincerest thanks.

Emory Reginald Abbott, Georgia Perimeter College
Kirk Adams, Tarrant Community College
Donna Allego, Gwynedd-Mercy College
Francesco Ancona, Sussex County Community College
Brian Anderson, Central Piedmont Community College
Peter Auski, University of Western Ontario
Beverly Bailey, Seminole Community College
Cynthia Baker-Schverak, Brevard Community College
Elizabeth Barnes, Daytona Beach Community College
Jim Baskin, Joliet Junior College
Amy Beaudry, Quinsigamond Community College
Valerie Belew, Nashville State Community College
Cole Bennett, Abilene Christian University
Randy Blankenship, Valencia Community College
Ethel Bonds, Virginia Western Community College
Debbie Borchers, Pueblo Community College
Patricia Bostian, Central Piedmont Community College
Linda Bow, Blinn College
Steve Brahlek, Palm Beach Community College–Lake Worth
Tamara Brattoli, Joliet Junior College
Joe Bryan, El Paso Community College
JoAnne Bryant, Troy University–Montgomery Campus
Donna Campbell, Washington State University
Patricia Campbell, Lake Sumter Community College
Carlos Campo, College of Southern Nevada
Kathy Carlson, Brevard Community College
Rosa Maria Chacon, California State University, Northridge
Lisbeth Chapin, Gwynedd-Mercy College
April Childress, Greenville Technical College
Kathleen Chrismon, Northeastern Oklahoma A&M University
John Cole, Community College of Rhode Island–Flanagan
Susan Constantine, Keystone College
Linda Cook, Sam Houston State University
Susan Dauer, Valencia Community College
Curtis Derrick, Midlands Technical College
Jason Dew, Georgia Perimeter College
Jennifer Diamond, Bucks County College
Joshua Dickinson, Jefferson Community College
Charles Dielman, Erie Community College
Regina Dilgen, Palm Beach Community College–Lake Worth
Scott Douglass, Chattanooga State Technical Community College
Caroline Dreyer, Pensacola Junior College
Leigh Anne Duck, University of Memphis
Jennifer Duncan, Chattanooga State Community College
Mildred Duprey-Smith, College of Southern Nevada
Heather Elko, Brevard Community College
John Esperian, College of Southern Nevada
Renee Field, Moberly Area Community College
John Freeman, El Paso Community College
Muriel Fuqua, Daytona Beach Community College
Fernando Ganivet, Florida International University
Stephen Gardner, University of South Carolina–Aiken
Richard Gaspar, Hillsboro Community College
Michael Gavin, Prince George's Community College
Joanna Gibson, Texas A&M University
Janine Gilbert, Brigham Young University–Idaho
Kimberly Greenfield, Lorain County Community College
Ross Gresham, U.S. Air Force Academy
Loren Gruber, Missouri Valley College
Frank Gunshanan, Daytona Beach Community College
Grace Haddox, El Paso Community College
Jill Hampton, University of South Carolina–Aiken
Holly Hassel, University of Wisconsin–Marathon County
Levia Hayes, College of Southern Nevada
Joel Henderson, Chattanooga State Community College
Deana Holifield, Pearl River Community College
Matthew Horton, Gainesville State College
Christine Hubbard, Tarrant County Community College
Mary Huffer, Lake Sumter Community College
Rob Hurd, Anne Arundel Community College
Heidi Johnsen, La Guardia Community College
Ken Johnson, Georgia Perimeter College
Theodore Johnston, El Paso Community College
Pamela Kannady, Tulsa Community College–Metro Campus

Barbara Kenney, Texas State Technical College
Nancy Kersell, Northern Kentucky University
Elizabeth Kessler, University of Houston
Rachel Key, East Central University
James Kirkpatrick, Central Piedmont Community College
Tom Kitts, St. John's University
Elaine Kromhout, Indian River Community College
Joseph Kronick, Louisiana State University
Kris Kurrus, Spokane Falls Community College
Angela Laflen, Marist College
James Lake, Louisiana State University
Ilona Law, University of South Carolina–Aiken
Kristin Le Veness, Nassau Community College
Sandy Longhorn, Pulaski Technical College
Joe Lostracco, Austin Community College
Cecilia Macheski, La Guardia Community College
Angela Macri, Pulaski Technical College
Al Maginnes, Wake Technical Community College
Tammy Mata, Tarrant County College
Virgin Mathes, University of New Mexico
Michael Matthews, Central Texas College
Beth Maxfield, Henderson State University
Laura McBride, College of Southern Nevada
Nicole McDaniel, Texas A&M University
Denise McNelly, Old Dominion University
Agnetta Mendoza, Nashville State Community College
Shellie Michael, Volunteer State Community College
Lawrence Milbourn, El Paso Community College
Dorothy Minor, Tulsa Community College–Metro Campus
David Mirchman, Moorpark College
Deborah Montuori, Shippensburg University
Cleatta Morris, Louisiana State University
Jake Morris, Louisiana State University, Shreveport
Kevin Morris, Greenville Technical College
Paul Munn, Saginaw Valley State University
William Myers, University of Colorado
Michelle Navarro, Dallas County Community College
Louise Nayer, City College of San Francisco
Jennifer Nelson, College of Southern Nevada
Shirley Nelson, Chattanooga State Community College
Andrea Neptune, Sierra College
Sally Nielsen, Florida Community College–Jacksonville
Cheryl Nixon, University of Massachusetts
Troy Nordman, Butler Community College
Claire O'Donoghue, St. John's University
Jay O'Leary, Santa Fe Community College
Ben Olguin, University of Texas at San Antonio
Danel Olsen, North Harris College
Thomas O'Neal, St. Johns River Community College
John Padgett, Brevard Community College
Neil Placky, Broward Community College
H. F. Poehlmann, Blinn College
Doranne Polcrack, Kutztown University
Tony Procell, El Paso Community College
Roberta Proctor, Palm Beach Community College–Lake Worth
Jessica Rabin, Anne Arundel Community College
Mary Anne Reiss, Elizabethtown Community and Technical College
Dana Resente, Montgomery County Community College
Elizabeth Rich, Saginaw Valley State University
Nandi Riley, Florida A&M University
Lou Ethel Roliston, Bergen Community College
Valerie Russell, Valencia Community College
Robert Saba, Florida International University
Mark Sanders, Lewis and Clark State College
John Schaffer, Blinn College
Ann Shillinglaw, Moraine Valley Community College
Ronald Shumaker, University of New Mexico
Gerald Siegel, York College
Mary Simpson, Dominican University
Donald Skinner, Indian River Community College
Patrick Slattery, University of Arkansas–Fayetteville
Beverly Slaughter, Brevard Community College
Derek Soles, Drexel University
Jean Sorensen, Grayson Community College
Anne Spurlock, Mississippi State University
Joyce Steelman, Catawba Valley Community College
Greg Stone, Tulsa Community College–Metro Campus
Victor Strandberg, Duke University
Beverly Stroud, Greenville Technical College
Richard Taylor, East Carolina University
Patricia Teel, Victor Valley College
Tracy Teel, California State University–Northridge
Matthew Teutsch, University of Louisiana, Monroe
Amber Flora Thomas, University of Alaska, Fairbanks
Anne-Marie Thomas, Austin Community College
Andrew Tomko, Bergen Community College
Pauline Uchmanowicz, SUNY–New Paltz
Carla Walker, St. Louis Community College
Brad Waltman, College of Southern Nevada
Carol Warren, Georgia Perimeter College
Linda Weeks, Dyersburg State Community College
Bridgette Weir, Nashville State Community College
Bart Welling, University of North Florida
Eleanor Welsh, Chesapeake College
Marian Wernicke, Pensacola Junior College
Sharon Wilson, University of Northern Colorado
Julie Wishart, Butler Community College
Jane Wood, Park University
Daphne Young, College of Southern Nevada
Robyn Younkin, Community College of Rhode Island
John Ziebell, College of Southern Nevada

The video interviews themselves were a labor of love for all those who participated—those interviewed were brought on board by their own deep love of students, writing, and literature. These conversations are as lively and varied and richly engaging as the work of the writers that we've included to represent them in *Literature: Craft and Voice*. Here we want to also add our sincerest thanks for the advice of our board of video advisors, many of whom provided their insight on other aspects of the project as well. These professors from across the country worked with our project for several months to guide the way for its use as part of an effective learning experience.

Paul Andrews, St. Johns River Community College

Christian Clark, College of Southern Nevada–Las Vegas

Chad Hammett, Texas State University

Ruth McAdams, Tarrant County College

Louise McKinney, Georgia Perimeter College–Dunwoody

Roxanne Munch, Joliet Junior College

Deborah Prickett, Jacksonville State University

Linda Smith, Midlands Technical College

Kathy Sanchez, Lone Star College–Tomball

Donna Thomsen, Johnson & Wales University

We are deeply grateful to McGraw-Hill for its many contributions to the development of this new learning program. In particular, we thank Paul Banks (our expert media maven), Betty Chen, David Chodoff, Josh Feldman, Susan Gouijnstook, Meredith Grant, Susan Messer, Andrea Pasquarelli (who took over for Paul Banks midstream and who made sure our videos were nipped and tucked into final shape), Lisa Pinto, and Karen Smith. This list is alphabetical, but Steev Sachs (arigatoo) deserves special mention and to be singled out; for the last weeks and months he seems to have been working twenty-five-hour days. Brian Jones was more than Executive Producer for our media project; he played cameraman, coach, and set designer on more than one occasion, and we were sorry to see him go, but we were also delighted to welcome Aoife Dempsey, Vice President of Digital. Jay Chakrapani, Vice President of Product Development, from the media group also brought information to the table for delivering media to students. The media program at McGraw-Hill has worked hand in hand with the editorial staff to bring out a new kind of program for teaching and learning in composition courses. Thanks also to Patrick Murphy of the University of Michigan for a pair of video interviews and to Laurence Goldstein of MQR and John Darnton of *The New York Times* for assistance with procuring the interviews of Arthur Miller and Edward Albee respectively. For tireless negotiation to make sure our book's permissions came in on budget and just in time to send our pages off to press, we thank the brilliantly efficient and professional Virginia Creeden.

We've had a special opportunity to spend time with many in the marketing and sales group, including the driving force of Suzanne Guinn, Director of Market Development; Allison Jones, Executive Marketing Manager; and Sharon Loeb, Director of Marketing. These muses brought in our sales champions Cristy Acosta, Hector Alvero, Colleen Balco, Jen Edwards, Carolyn Ghazi-Tehrani, Courtney Jones, Matt Parks, and Jack Powers: enthusiasts from the field who took their excitement back to their sales colleagues. With Simon Heathcote's excellent creative direction we looked without blinking at the camera when it came our turn to talk directly into its eye. Some of our field publishers have seen this project through from beginning to end. Byron Hopkins was there at our initial lunch, quoting poetry and wondering if this project would ever come to fruition. Our Senior Field Publisher, Ray Kelley, came to our speeches and sat in on several of our interviews. We met others along the way such as the super-reader Barbara Siry and the avid promoter Paula Radosevich; in California, Brian Gore brought his San Francisco style and love of all things literary and musical to support of our project. Jen Nelson, marketing coordinator, has been there on email, at our dress rehearsal, and throughout the marketing effort with good cheer and hard work to keep our marketing efforts running smoothly. Thank you, all.

We've saved for our penultimate note of thanks to McGraw-Hill a special thanks to those who've designed our book. Jeanne Schreiber, Creative Director, brought her tremendous design talent to the look of a new generation of textbooks—along with the midnight oil of many others in the editorial, design, and production group, especially Terri Schiesl, Vice President, Editing, Design, and Production; Leslie LaDow, Senior Production Editor; Nora Agbayani, Photo Research Coordinator; Preston Thomas, Design Manager; and Susan Norton, Copy Editor.

This book would not have come into existence had it not been for Steve Debow, President of Humanities and Social Sciences for McGraw-Hill Higher Education, and Michael Ryan, Editor-in-Chief for the Humanities and Social Sciences. Both lent their ears and time and drive to *Literature: Craft and Voice,* bringing McGraw-Hill's extensive resources to bear on innovation and learning in the twenty-first century.

And finally, our great gratitude to Lisa Moore, our editor and publisher, from whom we learned that writing a textbook is at least as difficult—and as rewarding—as writing novels. Lisa was the first to suggest this project, its tireless supervisor, enthusiastic sponsor, and pitch-perfect voice of experience; without her devotion to detail and eye for quality control we could neither be as proud of nor as pleased with the result.

The authors would like to register their gratitude to their respective agents, Gail Hochman, of Hochman and Brandt, and Timothy Seldes, of Russell & Volkening; they have been careful stewards from the first. Nicholas Delbanco would like to thank the Institute for the Humanities at the University of Michigan (and its director, Daniel Herwitz) for safe haven at this project's start, and Alan Cheuse is grateful to George Mason University for a leave of absence that helped bring it to completion. From the very beginning of this shared enterprise, through the many years of composition and labor, we have had the great good luck of being married to two close critics indeed. Elena Delbanco and Kristin O'Shee were indispensable to this endeavor, as they have long been to our lives; all thanks to each and both of them for everything they do and everything they are.

# Foreword to the Student

## LITERATURE REWARDS CLOSE READING

There's an important difference between life and art. You only live once. But you can turn and return to the best stories, poems, and plays; the great ones continue to live. So even if they were created in the sixth or the sixteenth century, you learn from the mistakes of characters you read about, revel in their pleasures, and grieve at their dismay. And as you spend time with them, you discover explanations for your own behavior as well.

There are other advantages to making literature a jumping-off point for the college experience. Any work of literature is a complex text. Reading it closely—carefully, analytically, within its own context and tradition—may seem strange at first. Yet it's like learning how to break down and rebuild an automobile engine or construct a defense in football or dance the tango or prepare a meal; you need to study the turns and twists of these various activities.

And there's a difference here too. Unlike taking the controls of an airplane, or performing surgery before you're fully trained, you can read a story and take control of it without doing damage to yourself or someone else in the process. There's reason to hope that you will understand great fiction or poetry or drama in a better and deeper way each time you read it again. By *understanding* we mean *learning* about how works are made up out of language that's carefully crafted and shaped. And learning about the way the characters think and feel. And learning about the world in which they find themselves. In other words, you can acquire all those things that lend depth and breadth to your own sense of life.

## READING PREPARES YOU FOR WRITING

So our first article of faith is that *literature rewards close reading.* And as professional writers of many years' experience, we can testify to this book's second article of faith: *reading prepares you for writing.* The ability to read closely and to write clearly about what you've read has practical value; these skills will help you in your other courses as well.

Repeated application—practice—is the key. In sports you know how important it is to practice. If you play a musical instrument, you know you have to practice. If you perform as a singer or actor or work as a salesman or auto mechanic, you know how critical it is to have been taught and, month after month, to rehearse what you do. All these activities have their techniques and depend upon instruction.

Reading literature will help you to think in new and different and powerful ways; writing about it will help you express what you think. It will help you to know yourself and make yourself known to others. Your success in college will depend on your ability to write well, and the better reader you train yourself to be the better you prepare yourself to become a better writer. (Notice, for example, how the previous sentence uses the same word three times; does the repeated "better" seem like a good idea?) It is not easy to read well. It is not easy to write well. But the process does grow simpler when works have been selected to provide a rich introduction to these critical components of your college life.

# A FEW FEATURES OF *LITERATURE: CRAFT AND VOICE*

## Our Selection of Fiction, Poetry, and Drama

We looked for works you'd enjoy reading as much as your teacher would enjoy teaching. Poetry about love (Pablo Neruda's "Do Not Love You Except Because I Love You") or happiness (Jane Kenyon's "The Suitor"), or grief (Marie Howe's "What the Living Do"). Plays about quick anger and tragic fate (from Sophocles' *Oedipus the King* to Arthur Miller's *Death of a Salesman*). A wide range of fiction from the novella nightmare of Franz Kafka's "The Metamorphosis" to young writers like Chimamanda Ngozi Adichie reporting on a prison cell in Africa, even fiction and film in a section on adaptations of the ancient Beowulf story. We wanted to show you literature at its best, both classic and new. A glance at our table of contents will show you how much we include. But the works here—no matter how numerous and various—have one thing in common: we believe them worth sustained attention on your part. You might not like everything you read, but we'd wager you'll find some that you won't be able to stop thinking about. The professional secret we'll whisper and shout is that reading and writing are fun.

## Media Brings Writers to Reading and Readers to Writing

The living, breathing presence of many of the authors we've included in this book is another way we wanted to bring you the full experience of reading literature. For one thing, our accompanying videos should help dispel the notion that all art is deathly dull and was produced by the honored dead. These writers were interviewed exclusively for this book. They prepared for their interviews by thinking about what they wanted to say directly to you. Our authors come in all sizes, ages, shapes, backgrounds. Pulitzer Prize winners, National Book Award winners, PEN/Faulkner Award winners, and Poet Laureates joined us in this endeavor. What they have in common is they wanted to tell you why they love to read, to talk about their trials in coming to love reading, and to reveal how their own writing process might be akin to yours. As has been famously said, every writer is a beginner; we all of us begin again each time we go to the desk.

## Designed for Reading

You'll see straightaway that this book doesn't look like other books. We know we live in a visual world. We know that unless you think you might one day be an English major, you're not likely to enjoy page after page of unbroken text, no matter how vivid the pictures the words make in your mind. Literature is not boring, so why should the design not be an invitation to enjoy reading?

We also could have made a thick book, a heavy one, one you would lift or open out of duty not desire. Your teacher tells you to turn to page 7 or 700 or 1700, and you groan and ask yourself why. Those books are doorstops and who knows what your chiropractor would say about your carrying them around. The easier it is to toss your book into your backpack, the more likely it is for you to find that spare moment to read. We wanted this exercise to be a little lighter; it is your intellectual muscles that should be the ones to grow strong.

## WHAT'S IN A NAME?

A last word about unusual names: If you have ever listened to National Public Radio, you may already know how to pronounce Alan Cheuse. If not, we invite you to listen to "the voice of books," and we also give you the correct pronunciation here: *Cheuse* sounds like *shoes* and rhymes with *booze* and *choose.* Nicholas Delbanco is quite used to hearing his last name mispronounced; it's *Delb-ah-nco,* as if you're preparing to sneeze. But both of us care less about the way you say our names than that you read these pages (sometimes out loud) and find the kind of pleasure in taking them apart that we ourselves took in putting them together. We wish you great fun and good luck.

*Nicholas Delbanco*

*Alan Cheuse*

# Literature Fiction

# 1 Reading a Story for its Elements

THE store's pretty empty, it being Thursday afternoon, so there was nothing much to do except lean on the register and wait for the girls to show up again. The whole store was like a pinball machine and I didn't know which tunnel they'd come out of. After a while they come around out of the far aisle, around the lightbulbs, records at discount of the Caribbean Six or Tony Martin Sings or some such gunk you wonder they waste the wax on, six-packs of candy bars, and plastic toys done up in cellophane that fall apart when a kid looks at them anyway. Around they come, Queenie still leading the way, and holding a little gray jar in her hand. Slots Three through Seven are unmanned and I could see her wondering between Stokes and me, but Stokesie with his usual luck draws an old party in baggy gray pants who stumbles up with four giant cans of pineapple juice (what do these bums do with all that pineapple juice? I've often asked myself) so the girls come to me. Queenie puts down the jar and I take it into my fingers icy cold.

*—from "A&P" by John Updike*

## A FIRST READING

Most of us read *casually* most of the time, not worrying too much about the way the piece—whether fiction or nonfiction—is put together. The first time we read something is one of the most fruitful times. When you first are exposed to a good story, you experience the pleasure of surprise, because the fiction writer has used a sophisticated grasp of technique to create a fresh impression—permitting you to see and feel and recognize something new. Sometimes that first experience will be a physical sensation like those "icy cold" fingers on the jar in the last sentence of the excerpt from "A&P." Sometimes that experience will be something more complex, like the jaded anticipation of the narrator at the cash register as he or she (we don't yet know which) follows the movements of customers at the A&P. You will probably have a gut feeling about the characters and what happens to them. You may feel sympathy with or confusion at the character's thoughts or actions. You may enjoy the tale's beautiful language or find the dialogue between characters amusing. But *why* do you have these responses?

*"The reading habit and the love of books physically, this particular package of words, the smell of the glue, the look of the print, was all that mattered to me to the point that I thought it would be wonderful to create such objects."*

Conversation with John Updike, available on video at www.mhhe.com/delbanco1e

## A CRITICAL READING

A writer creates a story out of material he or she has observed in the world and from incidents or feelings in his or her own life. But the result will not hold up well if the writer lacks a firm grasp of the **craft,** or conscious artistry, of fiction. As a noun, craft refers to the elements that comprise a story; as a verb, craft refers to the process of making or fashioning a story out of those elements. When authors write fiction, what they think they know—or believe or dream about or feel—needs to be made clear to others, and that process of transmission requires skill. Among the major elements of the craft of fiction are the following:

- **plot**—the sequence of events in a story (see chapter 4)
- **character**—the depiction of human beings (and nonhumans) within the story (see chapter 5)
- **setting**—when and where a story takes place (see chapter 6)
- **point of view**—who tells the story (see chapter 7)
- **language, tone, and style**—the elements that conjure a story's particular flavor and voice, as achieved because of the words the author chooses and the rhythm with which he or she puts the words together (see chapter 8)
- **theme**—the large meanings and connections explored in a piece of writing. Theme is what a story is "about" beyond the specific characters and events of the story (see chapter 9)
- **symbol**—an object or an event that transcends literal interpretation. A symbol works by using a particular object or event to represent something larger than the object or event itself (see chapter 10)

None of these elements operates in isolation, of course, but focusing on one in each chapter will allow us—as readers and writers—a particular "way in" or way of seeing how the story functions as a whole. By reading deeply and examining not just the obvious content of a story but also its context and form, its craft and voice, you can see beyond the story's surface, beyond merely "what" is happening.

This kind of critical reading begins when you actively engage with the story. As you read a story, mark it up with questions, ideas, and comments. Underline phrases and sentences you admire. Does the main character in a story seem to contradict himself? Does the author suddenly flash forward twenty years on page 2? Ask yourself why. If an author uses the word "idled" instead of "paused," circle the word and ask yourself why she made that choice. If an author titles a story "Would You Please Be Quiet, Please?" ask why he chooses to repeat the word "please." In other words, by formulating questions when you read, you can begin to grasp the techniques that make powerful expression possible.

*CONTINUED ON PAGE 9*

*. . . you . . . draw with words when you write.*

*I had to be firm against the forces of censorship.*

# Q&A
# A Conversation on Writing
## John Updike

Born in Reading, Pennsylvania, John Updike (1932–2009) began writing at a young age; his mother suggested it might cure him of a stammer. By the time of his death from lung cancer, at the age of seventy-six, he had become one of America's most celebrated authors, with abundant honors and a widespread readership. He published over fifty titles of fiction, nonfiction, and poetry—including two volumes of art criticism and several children's books. Updike began his career writing "Talk of the Town" pieces for *The New Yorker,* the magazine where his first published story appeared—and where his stories, essays, and book reviews are published to this day. Much (but not all) of Updike's fiction concerns the conflicts—internal and external—among middle-class Protestants in the American Northeast. He is most famous for his "Rabbit" quartet; these four novels follow an ex-basketball player named Harry "Rabbit" Angstrom, who struggles with the lack of fulfillment he feels in the presence of—and when deprived of—his family. (Those novels are, in order of publication, *Rabbit, Run; Rabbit Redux; Rabbit Is Rich;* and *Rabbit at Rest*—notice the pattern of repeated "R"s.) While some of Updike's characters do reprehensible or embarrassing things, the author manages to elicit our sympathy for them. He convinces us, even in the short space of a story, that his characters live and breathe in the American landscape—and that their problems are similar to ours. A number of Updike's short stories, including "A&P" (1961), are considered classic examples of the form.

### Writing and the Visual Arts

The pictorial and the verbal are similar in that they both take place in two dimensions on paper or canvas. . . . Drawing was a part of the gentleman's equipment, in fact, in the nineteenth century, just like operating a camera is for a twentieth-century person. . . . Handwriting is itself a kind of drawing and the letters are in a way visual objects. . . . I wanted to be a cartoonist but I fairly slowly saw that there were others more gifted than I at drawing [, so] I contented myself with being a writer in the theory that in a way you . . . draw with words when you write.

### Reading "A&P"

As I read those two paragraphs things come back to me that I'm tempted to share. One was the line "with a good tan and a sweet, soft, broad looking can." Some of the publishers who had to deal with this story in an anthology had great trouble with that *can*. . . . If they wanted to put it in there they should put it all in and let the kids get the shock of the word *can* in print. . . . The parenthetical thought, "Do you really think it's a mind in there or just a little buzz like a bee in a glass jar?" I think has served as the start of a lot of classroom discussions. But to me it seemed true of Sammy's worldview. Your job as a writer of fiction is not to present an ideal world but to try to present the world that you see and hear around you.

**To watch this entire interview and hear the author read from "A&P," go to www.mhhe.com/delbanco1e.**

**RESEARCH ASSIGNMENT:** In his interview, Updike talks about how he originally wrote several more scenes in this story—Sammy leaving the A&P, then going to the beach in order to look for the girls. But his editor at *The New Yorker,* William Maxwell, convinced him that the story should end where it does—thereby preserving the "unities" of time, place, and action. Which would you prefer—the ending as it is, suggesting a continuation of life lived off the page, or the kind of strong resolution the author originally planned? Explain your answer.

**AS YOU READ** As you read "A&P," consider who is telling the story and how you feel about this storyteller. Would you want this person for a friend? Why or why not? Does the outcome of this story surprise you? What outcome might you have predicted?

# A&P (1961)

1 IN walks these three girls in nothing but bathing suits. I'm in the second checkout slot, with my back to the door, so I don't see them until they're over by the bread. The one that caught my eye first was the one in the plaid green two-piece. She was a chunky kid, with a good tan and a sweet broad soft-looking can with those two crescents of white just under it, where the sun never seems to hit, at the top of the backs of her legs. I stood there with my hand on a box of Hi Ho crackers trying to remember if I rang it up or not. I ring it up again and the customer starts giving me hell. She's one of these cash-register-watchers, a witch about fifty with rouge on her cheekbones and no eyebrows, and I know it made her day to trip me up. She'd been watching cash registers for fifty years and probably never seen a mistake before.

2 By the time I got her feathers smoothed and her goodies into a bag—she gives me a little snort in passing, if she'd been born at the right time they would have burned her over in Salem—by the time I get her on her way the girls had circled around the bread and were coming back, without a pushcart, back my way along the counters, in the aisle between the checkouts and the Special bins. They didn't even have shoes on. There was this chunky one, with the two-piece—it was bright green and the seams on the bra were still sharp and her belly was still pretty pale so I guessed she just got it (the suit)—there was this one, with one of those chubby berry-faces, the lips all bunched together under her nose, this one, and a tall one, with black hair that hadn't quite frizzed right, and one of these sunburns right across under the eyes, and a chin that was too long—you know, the kind of girl other girls think is very "striking" and "attractive" but never quite makes it, as they very well know, which is why they like her so much—and then the third one, who wasn't quite so tall. She was the queen. She kind of led them, the other two peeking around and hunching over a little. She didn't look around, not this queen, she just walked straight on slowly, on these long white prima-donna legs. She came down a little hard on her heels, as if she didn't walk in her bare feet that much, putting down her heels and then letting the weight move along to her toes as if she was testing the floor with every step, putting a little deliberate extra action into it. You never know for sure how girls' minds work (do you really think it's a mind in there or just a little buzz like a bee in a glass jar?) but you got the idea she had talked the other two into coming in here with her, and now she was showing them how to do it, walk slow and hold yourself straight.

She had on a kind of dirty-pink—beige maybe, I don't know—bathing suit with a little nubble all over it and, what got me, the straps were down. They were off her shoulders looped loose around the cool tops of her arms, and I guess as a result the suit had slipped a little on her, so all around the top of the cloth there was this shining rim. If it hadn't been there you wouldn't have known there could have been anything whiter than those shoulders. With the straps pushed off, there was nothing between the top of the suit and the top of her head except just *her*, this clean bare plane of the top of her chest down from the shoulder bones like a dented sheet of metal tilted in the light. I mean, it was more than pretty. 3

She had sort of oaky hair that the sun and salt had bleached, done up in a bun that was unravelling, and 4 a kind of prim face. Walking into the A&P with your straps down, I suppose it's the only kind of face you *can* have. She held her head so high her neck, coming up out of those white shoulders, looked kind of stretched, but I didn't mind. The longer her neck was, the more of her there was.

5 She must have felt in the corner of her eye me and over my shoulder Stokesie in the first slot watching, but she didn't tip. Not this queen. She kept her eyes moving across the racks, and stopped, and turned so slow it made my stomach rub the inside of my apron, and buzzed to the other two, who kind of huddled against her for relief, and then they all three of them went up the cat-and-dog-food-breakfast-cereal-macaroni-rice-raisins-seasonings-spreads-spaghetti-soft-drinks-crackers-and-cookies aisle. From my slot I can look straight up this aisle to the meat counter, and I watched them all the way. The fat one with the tan sort of fumbled with the cookies, but on second thought she put the package back. The sheep pushing their carts down the aisle—the girls were walking against the usual traffic (not that we have one-way signs or anything)—were pretty hilarious. You could see them, when Queenie's white shoulders dawned on them, kind of jerk, or hop, or hiccup, but their eyes snapped back to their own baskets and on they pushed. I bet you could set off dynamite in an A&P and the people would by and large keep reaching and checking oatmeal off their lists and muttering "Let me see, there was a third thing, began with *A*, asparagus, no, ah, yes, applesauce!" or whatever it is they do mutter. But there was no doubt, this jiggled them. A few houseslaves in pin curlers even looked around after pushing their carts past to make sure what they had seen was correct.

The whole store was like a pinball machine . . .

6 You know, it's one thing to have a girl in a bathing suit down on the beach, where what with the glare nobody can look at each other much anyway, and another thing in the cool of the A&P, under the fluorescent lights, against all those stacked packages, with her feet paddling along naked over our checkerboard green-and-cream rubber-tile floor.

7 "Oh Daddy," Stokesie said beside me. "I feel so faint."

8 "Darling," I said. "Hold me tight." Stokesie's married, with two babies chalked up on his fuselage already, but as far as I can tell that's the only difference. He's twenty-two, and I was nineteen this April.

9 "Is it done?" he asks, the responsible married man finding his voice. I forgot to say he thinks he's going to be manager some sunny day, maybe in 1990 when it's called the Great Alexandrov and Petrooshki Tea Company or something.

10 What he meant was, our town is five miles from a beach, with a big summer colony out on the Point, but we're right in the middle of town, and the women generally put on a shirt or shorts or something before they get out of the car into the street. And anyway these are usually women with six children and varicose veins mapping their legs and nobody, including them, could care less. As I say, we're right in the middle of town, and if you stand at our front doors you can see two banks and the Congregational church and the newspaper store and three real-estate offices and about twenty-seven old freeloaders tearing up Central Street because the sewer broke again. It's not as if we're on the Cape; we're north of Boston and there's people in this town haven't seen the ocean for twenty years.

11 The girls had reached the meat counter and were asking McMahon something. He pointed, they pointed, and they shuffled out of sight behind a pyramid of Diet Delight peaches. All that was left for us to see was old McMahon patting his mouth and looking after them sizing up their joints. Poor kids, I began to feel sorry for them, they couldn't help it.

12 NOW here comes the sad part of the story, at least my family says it's sad, but I don't think it's so sad myself. The store's pretty empty, it being Thursday afternoon, so there was nothing much to do except lean on the register and wait for the girls to show up again. The whole store was like a pinball machine and I didn't know which tunnel they'd come out of. After a while they come around out of the far aisle, around the lightbulbs, records at discount of the Caribbean Six or Tony Martin Sings or some such gunk you wonder they waste the wax on, six-packs of candy bars, and plastic toys done up in cellophane that fall apart when a kid looks at them anyway. Around they come, Queenie still leading the way, and holding a little gray jar in her hand. Slots Three through Seven are unmanned and I could see her wondering between Stokes and me, but Stokesie with his usual luck draws an old party in baggy gray pants who stumbles up with four giant cans of pineapple juice (what do these bums *do* with all that pineapple juice? I've often asked myself) so the girls come to me. Queenie puts down the jar and I take it into my fingers icy cold. Kingfish Fancy Herring Snacks in Pure Sour Cream: 49¢. Now her hands are empty, not a ring or a bracelet, bare as God made

them, and I wonder where the money's coming from. Still with that prim look she lifts a folded dollar bill out of the hollow at the center of her nubbled pink top. The jar went heavy in my hand. Really, I thought that was so cute.

13 Then everybody's luck begins to run out. Lengel comes in from haggling with a truck full of cabbages on the lot and is about to scuttle into that door marked MANAGER behind which he hides all day when the girls touch his eye. Lengel's pretty dreary, teaches Sunday school and the rest, but he doesn't miss that much. He comes over and says,"Girls, this isn't the beach."

14 Queenie blushes, though maybe it's just a brush of sunburn I was noticing for the first time, now that she was so close. "My mother asked me to pick up a jar of herring snacks." Her voice kind of startled me, the way voices do when you see the people first, coming out so flat and dumb yet kind of tony, too, the way it ticked over "pick up" and "snacks." All of a sudden I slid right down her voice into her living room. Her father and the other men were standing around in ice-cream coats and bow ties and the women were in sandals picking up herring snacks on toothpicks off a big glass plate and they were all holding drinks the color of water with olives and sprigs of mint in them. When my parents have somebody over they get lemonade and if it's a real racy affair Schlitz in tall glasses with "They'll Do It Every Time" cartoons stencilled on.

15 "That's all right," Lengel said."But this isn't the beach." His repeating this struck me as funny, as if it had just occurred to him, and he had been thinking all these years the A&P was a great big dune and he was the head lifeguard. He didn't like my smiling—as I say, he doesn't miss much—but he concentrates on giving the girls that sad Sunday-school-superintendent stare.

16 Queenie's blush is no sunburn now, and the plump one in plaid, that I liked better from the back—a really sweet can—pipes up, "We weren't doing any shopping. We just came in for the one thing."

17 "That makes no difference," Lengel tells her, and I could see from the way his eyes went that he hadn't noticed she was wearing a two-piece before. "We want you decently dressed when you come in here."

18 "We *are* decent," Queenie says suddenly, her lower lip pushing, getting sore now that she remembers her place, a place from which the crowd that runs the A&P must look pretty crummy. Fancy Herring Snacks flashed in her very blue eyes.

19 "Girls, I don't want to argue with you. After this come in here with your shoulders covered. It's our policy." He turns his back. That's policy for you. Policy is what the kingpins want. What the others want is juvenile delinquency.

All this while, the customers had been showing up with their carts but, you know, sheep, seeing a scene, they had all bunched up on Stokesie, who shook open a paper bag as gently as peeling a peach, not wanting to miss a word. I could feel in the silence everybody getting nervous, most of all Lengel, who asks me, "Sammy, have you rung up their purchase?" 20

I thought and said "No" but it wasn't about that I was thinking. I go through the punches, 4, 9, GROC, TOT—it's more complicated than you think, and after you do it often enough, it begins to make a little song, that you hear words to, in my case "Hello (*bing*) there, you (*gung*) hap-py *pee*-pul (*splat*)!"—the *splat* being the drawer flying out. I uncrease the bill, tenderly as you may imagine, it just having come from between the two smoothest scoops of vanilla I had ever known were there, and pass a half and a penny into her narrow pink palm, and nestle the herrings in a bag and twist its neck and hand it over, all the time thinking. 21

The girls, and who'd blame them, are in a hurry to get out, so I say "I quit" to Lengel quick enough for them to hear, hoping they'll stop and watch me, their unsuspected hero. They keep right on going, into the electric eye; the door flies open and they flicker across the lot to their car, Queenie and Plaid and Big Tall Goony-Goony (not that as raw material she was so bad), leaving me with Lengel and a kink in his eyebrow. 22

"Did you say something, Sammy?" 23

"I said I quit." 24

"I thought you did." 25

"You didn't have to embarrass them." 26

"It was they who were embarrassing us." 27

I started to say something that came out "Fiddle-de-doo." It's a saying of my grandmother's, and I know she would have been pleased. 28

"I don't think you know what you're saying," Lengel said. 29

"I know you don't," I said. "But I do." I pull the bow at the back of my apron and start shrugging it off my shoulders. A couple customers that had been 30 heading for my slot begin to knock against each other, like scared pigs in a chute.

31 Lengel sighs and begins to look very patient and old and gray. He's been a friend of my parents for years. "Sammy, you don't want to do this to your mom and dad," he tells me. It's true, I don't. But it seems to me that once you begin a gesture it's fatal not to go through with it. I fold the apron, "Sammy" stitched in red on the pocket, and put it on the counter, and drop the bow tie on top of it. The bow tie is theirs, if you've ever wondered. "You'll feel this for the rest of your life," Lengel says, and I know that's true, too, but remembering how he made that pretty girl blush makes me so scrunchy inside I punch the No Sale tab and the machine whirs "*pee*-pul" and the drawer splats out. One advantage to this scene taking place in summer, I can follow it up with a clean exit, there's no fumbling around getting your coat and galoshes, I just saunter into the electric eye in my white shirt that my mother ironed the night before, and the door heaves itself open, and outside the sunshine is skating around on the asphalt.

32 I look around for my girls, but they're gone, of course. There wasn't anybody but some young married screaming with her children about some candy they didn't get by the door of a powder-blue Falcon station wagon. Looking back in the big windows, over the bags of peat moss and aluminum lawn furniture stacked on the pavement, I could see Lengel in my place in the slot, checking the sheep through. His face was dark gray and his back stiff, as if he'd just had an injection of iron, and my stomach kind of fell as I felt how hard the world was going to be to me from here on in.

*To hear Updike on the importance of making the reader see, go to* **www.mhhe.com/delbanco1e**.

IF you like this story, you may like other initiation stories—stories about growing up and acquiring increased awareness of our relation to the world—James Joyce's "Araby," for example, in chapter 4. You might also want to compare what the future holds for the narrator in "A&P" with the remembrances of the narrator in Alice Munro's "An Ounce of Cure" at the end of this chapter.

**GOING FURTHER** John Updike's novels, several of which are listed in the note about the author, may also interest you. In the eyes of many readers and critics, no one surpasses Updike when it comes to describing the manners and way of life of Americans during the last four decades.

# Writing from Reading

### Summarize

1 What are the literal events—the incidents—of this narrative? How do these events add up to Sammy's decision at the end of the story?

### Analyze Craft

2 "A&P" is confined to one setting (the inside of a supermarket) and a brief period of time. How would the *plot* change if it began with Sammy waking up at his house on the morning of the same day?

### Analyze Voice

3 Discuss the impact of Sammy's attitude on the narrative. Point to places in the text where Sammy interprets events rather than reports them objectively. What events might be reported differently (or left out altogether) if the story were told by Stokesie, or Queenie?

### Synthesize Summary and Analysis

4 In the interview, Updike talks about the importance of making the reader "see." Did he succeed in making you see the scene he was describing? Choose two images that you were able to see very clearly and analyze what Updike did to help you see them.

### Interpret the Story

5 Discuss why Sammy quits his job. What does he mean when he recognizes "how hard the world was going to be to me from here on in"?

6 Imagine an alternative ending to "A&P." What ideas in the story lead you to your version of the ending?

*CONTINUED FROM PAGE 3*

The word *fiction* derives from a Latin word, *fingere,* meaning "to fashion or form." Thus, fiction has to do with shaping, the way a sculptor fashions form. It has to do with making a narrative where nothing existed before. Each work of fiction, as the late Bernard Malamud once wrote, "predicates," or brings to life, an entire world.

Some of the earliest fiction consisted of **fables** and **parables,** short tales designed to impart a moral lesson. In one famous ancient Greek fable, for example, a shepherd boy, tending his family's flock, grows lonely and, to attract company, cries out the alarm signal "wolf!" Villagers come running to the boy's aid, but when they see

"I discovered a world that opened out to me in all kinds of directions. I began to understand things I hadn't understood before. And I began to find other things that I didn't understand yet that I wanted to understand. The world became more interesting to me. Fuller and richer. And I got all of that from reading." Conversation with William Kittredge

**STORY AND HISTORY**

The words *story* and *history* share a common root, the Latin word *historia,* which means a presumably true account of events and persons from a more or less remote past. In their earliest forms, stories were about purportedly real figures—sometimes gods and goddesses, sometimes human beings. The Latin words in turn go back to the Greek *historia,* meaning "narrative or history," from *histor* or "learned, wise man."

no wolves, they leave. Again the boy cries "wolf!" and once more the neighbors come running but can find no wolves. Eventually, the villagers ignore the boy's cries, and one day, when wolves really do appear, nobody comes to his aid. The moral? No one believes a liar, even when he's telling the truth. This story about seeking attention by deliberately raising a false alarm is the source of the expression "to cry wolf."

"I came to reading, in a way, by way of drawing. I certainly could appreciate cartooning before I could read it, and there was a kind of children's book called 'Big Little Books,' which had a panel of a comic strip opposite a little page of print. And I think it was those books that I first read." Conversation with John Updike

Today, much fiction is referred to according to its contemporary category: horror, spy, romance, etc. Categories such as these have stricter conventions of form than most of contemporary fiction. Horror stories, for example, evoke a world of supernatural or psychological terror:

> *From a private hospital for the insane near Providence, Rhode Island, there recently disappeared an exceedingly singular person. He bore the name of Charles Dexter Ward, and was placed under restraint most reluctantly by the grieving father who had watched his aberration grow from a mere eccentricity to a dark mania involving both a possibility of murderous tendencies and a profound and peculiar change in the apparent contents of his mind. Doctors confess themselves quite baffled by his case, since it presented oddities of a general physiological as well as psychological character.*
>
> *In the first place, the patient seemed oddly older than his twenty-six years would warrant. . . .*
>
> —from "The Case of Charles Dexter Ward," by H. P. Lovecraft

Spy thrillers create a sense of suspense, often involving an international crisis:

> *It took only two minutes from the time Willy's car arrived at the White House grounds to the time he was knocking on Nelson Cummin's door. Willy had done the trip many times. He reckoned that between security checks, registration, elevators, and a little wait in the outer office of the national security advisor, the average entry time to see Nelson—from entering the White House grounds to shaking his hand—was fifteen to twenty minutes. This time his car was waved through and a secretary waited for him at the side door of the building. . . .*
>
> —from *Point of Entry,* by Peter Schechter

Science fiction is set in an imagined future, often on other planets:

> *Got a job for you. Pays a billion.*
>
> *The message blinked at the top of the screen three times, then disappeared. Rod Morgan smiled. He had been hearing rumors about a quasi-multigovernment, quasi-commercial consortium that was raising capital to sponsor a risky trip to Saturn. He closed down his game of WARPWORLD, and switched to net-mail to read the rest of the message. He'd guessed right, it was from the consortium. The job must really be risky for them to be offering a billion dollars. Although the penny was no longer legal tender, a billion dollars was still a large fortune. . . .*
>
> —from *Saturn Rukh,* by Robert L. Forward

Genres like romance, crime, or fantasy help you know what to expect when you read particular texts. Suppose you picked up *Saturn Rukh,* the novel from which we took the preceding example, and you knew it was science fiction. It would not surprise you to see a reference to a trip to Saturn. But if you were unaware of the science fiction genre, you might have a hard time deciding how to approach the information about a trip to Saturn—whether to take it seriously or to laugh at it. Genre fiction is powerful because of the way in which it manipulates your response: What might seem utterly ridiculous or out of place in the real world becomes something we understand if we know to approach it based on the set of expectations created by genre.

Many works of fiction do not fall into a category like crime, horror, or romance; texts that defy this type of classification are generally referred to as mainstream or literary fiction. Most of the stories you will encounter in this book are examples of literary fiction. As with any fashioned form, the art of fiction comes in many sizes, from the briefest story (for an example, see Amy Hempel's couldn't-be-shorter "San Francisco" in our Stories for Further Reading) to novels of a thousand pages or more, such as Leo Tolstoy's *War and Peace.* Novels almost by definition need to tell more than one story, but short stories are dense and intense. Simply put, a **short story** is a brief fictional narrative. It attempts to dramatize or illustrate the effect or meaning of a single incident or small group of incidents in the life of a single character or small group of characters. Even in these compressed lengths, however, you'll find elements of horror (see Edgar Allan Poe's "The Fall of the House of Usher" in chapter 6), science fiction (see Ursula LeGuin's "Kerastion" in Stories for Further Reading), and detective romance (see William Faulkner's "A Rose for Emily" in the casebook on the American South).

> "There's a whole range of people writing, and somewhere in there is somebody who respects you, and when you read their stories, you're thinking, "I'm in here, and I can feel myself coming to life." Conversation with Barry Lopez

Whatever the category, reading can expand our emotional range, as Heather King suggests in her memoir, *Parched:*

> *I loved the way books looked, loved the way books smelled, loved that books made me forget. My favorites were* The Diary of Anne Frank, The Yearling, Uncle Tom's Cabin: *tales of grotesque cruelty and unbearable loss. That was precisely why I liked them. Even back then I understood the real purpose of literature. I didn't want to hear that people lived happily ever after. I wanted to know that other people suffered, too.*

You may prefer something with a lighter touch, but reading can give you a view into another world, and the analytical ability you develop from reading critically will stand you in good stead whether you're reading fiction or sociology or a political pamphlet.

## WHAT READING FICTION GIVES US

As the early-twentieth-century Austrian writer Robert Musil once put it, when troubled, we like to imagine that there is only one law of life, the law of narrative order. What he meant is that we tend to view our lives as meaningful, and endowed with the same kind of narrative coherence found in good fiction. Fiction allows us a close look

"Stories console me. If I'm lying in bed at night I'm a little less alone in a lonely universe. Stories connect me not to just other people, but to myself." Conversation with Tim O'Brien

at characters as it explicitly or implicitly tells the stories of their lives in an effort to make sense of them. Reading fiction gives us the opportunity to investigate our own lives by comparison, to notice how we put together the elements of our own stories—our family or friends, our emotions, our decisions, and our hopes—in order to try and understand who we are, where we have come from, and where we might be going. As we delve into good stories in order to understand them better, we come to better understand ourselves.

# Kate Chopin (1851–1904)

The daughter of an Irish father and a French Creole mother, Kate Chopin grew up in Saint Louis, where she studied French and English literature at a Catholic school. Her father died in a work-related accident when she was very young, an event that may have inspired this story. By the time she was married to the wealthy businessman Oscar Chopin and living in Louisiana, she was known as an unconventional woman. She drank, smoked, held her own opinions, and even ran her late husband's business for a year—all the while raising six children. Like many stories in this book, this story follows what some call the "unities" of time, place, and action that are found in classical drama and in a great deal of short fiction. The title suggests that this story will be brief. But when you read to write, remember that a short story, however brief, is not merely a joke or an anecdote—a funny thing that happened on the way to the parking lot or how your sister's cat got stuck in a tree. The fiction writer must take it further—selecting and arranging events in an artful way to show, for example, how a girl whose cat gets stuck in a tree comes to understand what really matters to her and why she calls for help.

**AS YOU READ** Notice the pace of the story. Where does it speed up and slow down? How are you feeling as the pace slows and quickens? Where are the surprises in the story? How do they make you feel?

**TIP** **FOR INTERACTIVE READING . . .** "The Story of an Hour" is not written in Louise's voice, but the narrator does seem to know Louise's thoughts. Annotate in the margins instances where the narrator offers insights into Louise's personal thoughts or past. Based on your notes, do you think the narrator tells the story objectively or with a bias?

# The Story of an Hour (1894)

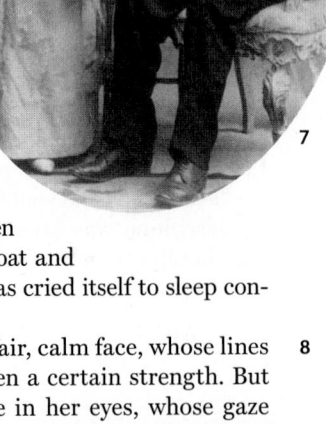

1 KNOWING that Mrs. Mallard was afflicted with a heart trouble, great care was taken to break to her as gently as possible the news of her husband's death.

2 It was her sister Josephine who told her, in broken sentences; veiled hints that revealed in half concealing. Her husband's friend Richards was there, too, near her. It was he who had been in the newspaper office when intelligence of the railroad disaster was received, with Brently Mallard's name leading the list of "killed." He had only taken the time to assure himself of its truth by a second telegram, and had hastened to forestall any less careful, less tender friend in bearing the sad message.

3 She did not hear the story as many women have heard the same, with a paralyzed inability to accept its significance. She wept at once, with sudden, wild abandonment, in her sister's arms. When the storm of grief had spent itself she went away to her room alone. She would have no one follow her.

4 There stood, facing the open window, a comfortable, roomy armchair. Into this she sank, pressed down by a physical exhaustion that haunted her body and seemed to reach into her soul.

5 She could see in the open square before her house the tops of trees that were all aquiver with the new spring life. The delicious breath of rain was in the air. In the street below a peddler was crying his wares. The notes of a distant song which some one was singing reached her faintly, and countless sparrows were twittering in the eaves.

6 There were patches of blue sky showing here and there through the clouds that had met and piled one above the other in the west facing her window.

7 She sat with her head thrown back upon the cushion of the chair, quite motionless, except when a sob came up into her throat and shook her, as a child who has cried itself to sleep continues to sob in its dreams.

8 She was young, with a fair, calm face, whose lines bespoke repression and even a certain strength. But now there was a dull stare in her eyes, whose gaze was fixed away off yonder on one of those patches of blue sky. It was not a glance of reflection, but rather indicated a suspension of intelligent thought.

9 There was something coming to her and she was waiting for it, fearfully. What was it? She did not know; it was too subtle and elusive to name. But she felt it, creeping out of the sky, reaching toward her through the sounds, the scents, the color that filled the air.

10 Now her bosom rose and fell tumultuously. She was beginning to recognize this thing that was approaching to possess her, and she was striving to beat it back with her will—as powerless as her two white slender hands would have been.

11 When she abandoned herself a little whispered word escaped her slightly parted lips. She said it over and over under her breath: "free, free, free!" The vacant stare and the look of terror that had followed it went from her eyes. They stayed keen and bright. Her pulses beat fast, and the coursing blood warmed and relaxed every inch of her body.

12 She did not stop to ask if it were or were not a monstrous joy that held her. A clear and exalted perception enabled her to dismiss the suggestion as trivial.

13 She knew that she would weep again when she saw the kind, tender hands folded in death; the face that had never looked save with love upon her, fixed and gray and dead. But she saw beyond that bitter moment a long procession of years to come that would belong to her absolutely. And she opened and spread her arms out to them in welcome.

She breathed a quick prayer that life might be long.

14 There would be no one to live for her during those coming years; she would live for herself. There would be no powerful will bending hers in that blind persistence with which men and women believe they have a right to impose a private will upon a fellow-creature. A kind intention or a cruel intention made the act seem no less a crime as she looked upon it in that brief moment of illumination.

15 And yet she had loved him—sometimes. Often she had not. What did it matter! What could love, the unsolved mystery, count for in face of this possession of self-assertion which she suddenly recognized as the strongest impulse of her being!

16 "Free! Body and soul free!" she kept whispering.

17 Josephine was kneeling before the closed door with her lips to the keyhold, imploring for admission. "Louise, open the door! I beg; open the door—you will make yourself ill. What are you doing, Louise? For heaven's sake open the door."

"Go away. I am not making myself ill." No; she 18
was drinking in a very elixir of life through that open window.

Her fancy was running riot 19
along those days ahead of her. Spring days, and summer days, and all sorts of days that would be her own. She breathed a quick prayer that life might be long. It was only yesterday she had thought with a shudder that life might be long.

She arose at length and opened the door to her 20
sister's importunities. There was a feverish triumph in her eyes, and she carried herself unwittingly like a goddess of Victory. She clasped her sister's waist, and together they descended the stairs. Richards stood waiting for them at the bottom.

Some one was opening the front door with a 21
latchkey. It was Brently Mallard who entered, a little travel-stained, composedly carrying his grip-sack and umbrella. He had been far from the scene of accident, and did not even know there had been one. He stood amazed at Josephine's piercing cry; at Richards' quick motion to screen him from the view of his wife.

But Richards was too late. 22

When the doctors came they said she had died of 23
heart disease—of joy that kills.

IF you like "The Story of an Hour," you may like other stories with strong heroines who desire more from life than being a wife or mother, such as "The Yellow Wallpaper" by Charlotte Perkins Gilman (in Stories for Further Reading), another classic feminist work.

**GOING FURTHER** Although the public responded well to Chopin's less controversial fiction about French Creole life, you may be interested in reading the book that lost her work its critical favor, *The Awakening* (1899), which critics called immoral. It is quite well-regarded today.

# Writing from Reading

### Summarize

1 Summarize the development of Louise's emotions over the course of the story. Is it ultimately joy or disappointment that causes her death?

### Analyze Craft

2 How well has Chopin succeeded in making you *see* the details of this story? Which images are particularly vivid, and how does Chopin make them so?

### Analyze Voice

3 How would you describe Chopin's attitude toward her character; does she admire or disdain the way Louise behaves? A "mallard" is a male duck; what does the name "Mrs. Mallard" suggest? What specific language from the story suggests how Chopin wanted the reader to respond to Louise?

### Synthesize Summary and Analysis

4 Though "The Story of an Hour" describes only one hour's time, its events are predicated upon the emotions Louise has developed over the course of her entire marriage. Summarize what we know about Louise's relationship with her husband, and discuss whether Chopin provides enough detail to justify Louise's death by the end.

### Interpret the Story

5 The first line of the story says that "Mrs. Mallard was afflicted with a heart trouble." Discuss whether Chopin undermines or reinforces the emotional significance of Louise's death by announcing her heart condition so early in the story.

# Alice Munro (b. 1931)

Alice Munro (née Laidlaw) was born on a farm in Wingham, Ontario, to a family of fox and potato farmers. She published her first short story at the age of nineteen while attending college and working as a waitress, library clerk, and tobacco picker. After leaving school to marry James Munro, she moved with her husband to British Columbia, where the couple ran a bookstore. In 1968, she published her first collection of stories, *Dance of the Happy Shades,* and in 1971 her first and only novel, *Lives of Girls and Women.* When her marriage ended in 1972, Munro returned to Ontario, remarried (to Gerald Fremlin, a geographer), and went on to publish eleven more collections of short stories (including *The Beggar Maid, The Moons of Jupiter, Friend of My Youth, Open Secrets, Runaway,* and, recently, *The View from Castle Rock,* in 2006). Her work has won many literary awards, including three of Canada's Governor General's Literary Awards and its Giller Prize; the Rea Award for Short Fiction; and the U.S. National Book Critics Circle Award. Her stories continue to appear in magazines such as *The New Yorker, The Atlantic Monthly,* and *The Paris Review.* Because of her ability to portray everyday human relationships—particularly, though not only, in Ontario—and her clean prose, Munro is widely considered to be one of the most accomplished short story writers alive today. She finds the extraordinary in the ordinary, the strange in the familiar; her influence is large.

**AS YOU READ** As you read, imagine yourself face-to-face with this narrator as she tells her story. What does she say that makes you laugh? What makes you gasp? What makes you shake your head in disbelief or amazement? Does she seem real to you?

TIP

**FOR INTERACTIVE READING . . .** Annotate the text using two systems of notation. Mark all the places in the text where the narrator says "I remember." Now mark the places where she says "I don't remember."

# An Ounce of Cure (1968)

1 MY parents didn't drink. They weren't rabid about it, and in fact I remember that when I signed the pledge in grade seven, with the rest of that superbly if impermanently indoctrinated class, my mother said, "It's just nonsense and fanaticism, children of that age." My father would drink a beer on a hot day, but my mother did not join him, and—whether accidentally or symbolically—this drink was always consumed *outside* the house. Most of the people we knew were the same way, in the small town where we lived. I ought not to say that it was this which got me into difficulties, because the difficulties I got into were a faithful expression of my own incommodious nature—the same nature that caused my mother to look at me, on any occasion which traditionally calls for feelings of pride and maternal accomplishment (my departure for my first formal dance, I mean, or my hellbent preparations for a descent on college) with an expression of brooding and fascinated despair, as if she could not possibly expect, did not ask, that it should go with me as it did with other girls; the dreamed-of spoils of daughters—orchids, nice boys, diamond rings—would be borne home in due course by the daughters of her friends, but not by me; all she could do was hope for a lesser rather than a greater disaster—an elopement, say, with a boy who could never earn his living, rather than an abduction into the White Slave trade.

But ignorance, my mother said, ignorance, or innocence if you like, is not always such a fine thing as people think and I am not sure it may not be dangerous for a girl like you; then she emphasized her point, as she had a habit of doing, with some quotation which had an innocent promposity and odour of mothballs. I didn't even wince at it, knowing full well how it must have worked wonders with Mr. Berryman. 2

The evening I baby-sat for the Berrymans must have been in April. I had been in love all year, or at least since the first week in September, when a boy named Martin Collingwood had given me a surprised, appreciative, and rather ominously complacent smile in the school assembly. I never knew what surprised him; I was not looking like anybody but me; I had an old blouse on and my home-permanent had turned out badly. A few weeks after that he took me out for the first time, and kissed me 3 on the dark side of the porch—also, I ought to say, on the mouth; I am sure it was the first time anybody had ever kissed me effectively, and I know that I did not wash my face that night or the next morning, in order to keep the imprint of those kisses intact. (I showed the most painful banality in the conduct of this whole affair, as you will see.) Two months, and a few amatory stages later, he dropped me. He had fallen for the girl who played opposite him in the Christmas production of *Pride and Prejudice.*

I am sure it was the first time anybody had ever kissed me effectively . . .

4 I said I was not going to have anything to do with that play, and I got another girl to work on Makeup in my place, but of course I went to it after all, and sat down in front with my girl friend Joyce, who pressed my hand when I was overcome with pain and delight at the sight of Mr. Darcy in white breeches, silk waistcoat, and sideburns. It was surely seeing Martin as Darcy that did it for me; every girl is in love with Darcy anyway, and the part gave Martin an arrogance and male splendour in my eyes which made it impossible to remember that he was simply a high-school senior, passably good-looking and of medium intelligence (and with a reputation slightly tainted, at that, by such preferences as the Drama Club and the Cadet *Band*) who happened to be the first boy, the first really presentable boy, to take an interest in me. In the last act they gave him a chance to embrace Elizabeth (Mary Bishop, with a sallow complexion and no figure, but big vivacious eyes) and during this realistic encounter I dug my nails bitterly into Joyce's sympathetic palm.

5 That night was the beginning of months of real, if more or less self-inflicted, misery for me. Why is it a temptation to refer to this sort of thing lightly, with irony, with amazement even, at finding oneself involved with such preposterous emotions in the unaccountable past? That is what we are apt to do, speaking of love; with adolescent love, of course, it's practically obligatory; you would think we sat around, dull afternoons, amusing ourselves with these tidbit recollections of pain. But it really doesn't make me feel very gay—worse still, it doesn't really surprise me—to remember all the stupid, sad, half-ashamed things I did, that people in love always do. I hung around the places where he might be seen, and then pretended not to see him; I made absurdly roundabout approaches, in conversation, to the bitter pleasure of casually mentioning his name. I daydreamed endlessly; in fact if you want to put it mathematically, I spent perhaps ten times as many hours thinking about Martin Collingwood—yes, pining and weeping for him—as I ever spent with him; the idea of him dominated my mind relentlessly and, after a while, against my will. For if at first I had dramatized my feelings, the time came when I would have been glad to escape them; my well-worn daydreams had become depressing and not even temporarily consoling. As I worked my math problems I would torture myself, quite mechanically and helplessly, with an exact recollection of Martin kissing my throat. I had an exact recollection of *everything.* One night I had an impulse to swallow all the aspirins in the bathroom cabinet, but stopped after I had taken six.

My mother noticed that something was wrong and got me some iron pills. She said, "Are you sure everything is going all right at school?" *School!* When I told her that Martin and I had broken up all she said was, "Well so much the better for that. I never saw a boy so stuck on himself." "Martin has enough conceit to sink a battleship," I said morosely and went upstairs and cried. 6

The night I went to the Berrymans was a Saturday night. I baby-sat for them quite often on Saturday nights because they liked to drive over to Baileyville, a much bigger, livelier town about twenty miles away, and perhaps have supper and go to a show. They had been living in our town only two or three years—Mr. Berryman had been brought in as plant manager of the new door-factory—and they remained, I suppose by choice, on the fringes of its society; most of their friends were youngish couples like themselves, born in other places, who lived in new ranch-style houses on a hill outside town where we used to go tobogganing. This Saturday night they had two other couples in for drinks before they all drove over to Baileyville for the opening of a new supper-club; they were all rather festive. I sat in the kitchen and pretended to do Latin. Last night had been the Spring Dance at the High School. I had not gone, since the 7

only boy who had asked me was Millerd Crompton, who asked so many girls that he was suspected of working his way through the whole class alphabetically. But the dance was held in the Armouries, which was only half a block away from our house; I had been able to see the boys in dark suits, the girls in long pale formals under their coats, passing gravely under the street-lights, stepping around the last patches of snow. I could even hear the music and I have not forgotten to this day that they played "Ballerina," and—oh, song of my aching heart—"Slow Boat to China." Joyce had phoned me up this morning and told me in her hushed way (we might have been discussing an incurable disease I had) that yes, M.C. *had* been there with M.B., and she had on a formal that must have been made out of somebody's old lace tablecloth, it just *hung*.

8 When the Berrymans and their friends had gone I went into the living room and read a magazine. I was mortally depressed. The big softly lit room, with its green and leaf-brown colours, made an uncluttered setting for the development of the emotions, such as you would get on a stage. At home the life of the emotions went on all right, but it always seemed to get buried under the piles of mending to be done, the ironing, the children's jigsaw puzzles and rock collections. It was the sort of house where people were always colliding with one another on the stairs and listening to hockey games and Superman on the radio.

9 I got up and found the Berrymans' "Danse Macabre" and put it on the record player and turned out the living-room lights. The curtains were only partly drawn. A street light shone obliquely on the windowpane, making a rectangle of thin dusty gold, in which the shadows of bare branches moved, caught in the huge sweet winds of spring. It was a mild black night when the last snow was melting. A year ago all this—the music, the wind and darkness, the shadows of the branches—would have given me tremendous happiness; when they did not do so now, but only called up tediously familiar, somehow humiliatingly personal thoughts, I gave up my soul for dead and walked into the kitchen and decided to get drunk.

10 No, it was not like that. I walked into the kitchen to look for a coke or something in the refrigerator, and there on the front of the counter were three tall beautiful bottles, all about half full of gold. But even after I had looked at them and lifted them to feel their weight I had not decided to get drunk; I had decided to have a drink.

Now here is where my ignorance, my disastrous innocence, comes in. It is true that I had seen the Berrymans and their friends drinking their highballs as casually as I would drink a coke, but I did not apply this attitude to myself. No; I thought of hard liquor as something as to be taken in extremities, and relied upon for extravagant results, one way or another. My approach could not have been less casual if I had been the Little Mermaid drinking the witch's crystal potion. Gravely, with a glance at my set face in the black window above the sink, I poured a little whisky from each of the bottles (I think now there were two brands of rye and an expensive Scotch) until I had my glass full. For I had never in my life seen anyone pour a drink and I had no idea that people frequently diluted their liquor with water, soda, et cetera, and I had seen that the glasses the Berrymans' guests were holding when I came through the living room were nearly full. 11

I drank it off as quickly as possible. I set the glass down and stood looking at my face in the window, half expecting to see it altered. My throat was burning, but I felt nothing else. It was very disappointing, when I had worked myself up to it. But I was not going to let it go at that. I poured another full glass, then filled each of the bottles with water to approximately the level I had seen when I came in. I drank the second glass only a little more slowly than the first. I put the empty glass down on the counter with care, perhaps feeling in my head a rustle of things to come, and went and sat down on a chair in the living room. I reached up and turned on a floor lamp beside the chair, and the room jumped on me. 12

WHEN I say that I was expecting extravagant results I do not mean that I was expecting this. I had thought of some sweeping emotional change, an upsurge of gaiety and irresponsibility, a feeling of lawlessness and escape, accompanied by a little dizziness and perhaps a tendency to giggle out loud. I did not have in mind the ceiling spinning like a great plate somebody had thrown at me, nor the pale green blobs 13 of the chairs swelling, converging, disintegrating, playing with me a game full of enormous senseless inanimate malice. My head sank back; I closed my eyes. And at once opened them, opened them wide, threw myself out of the chair and down the hall and reached—thank God, thank God!—the Berrymans' bathroom, where I was sick everywhere, everywhere, and dropped like a stone.

14 From this point on I have no continuous picture of what happened; my memories of the next hour or two are split into vivid and improbable segments, with nothing but murk and uncertainty between. I do remember lying on the bathroom floor looking sideways at the little six-sided white tiles, which lay together in such an admirable and logical pattern, seeing them with the brief broken gratitude and sanity of one who has just been torn to pieces with vomiting. Then I remember sitting on the stool in front of the hall phone, asking weakly for Joyce's number. Joyce was not home. I was told by her mother (a rather rattlebrained woman, who didn't seem to notice a thing the matter—for which I felt weakly, mechanically grateful) that she was at Kay Stringer's house. I didn't know Kay's number so I just asked the operator; I felt I couldn't risk looking down at the telephone book.

She loved a crisis, particularly one like this, which had a shady and scandalous aspect and which must be kept secret from the adult world.

15 Kay Stringer was not a friend of mine but a new friend of Joyce's. She had a vague reputation for wildness and a long switch of hair, very oddly, though naturally, coloured—from soap-yellow to caramel-brown. She knew a lot of boys more exciting than Martin Collingwood, boys who had quit school or been imported into town to play on the hockey team. She and Joyce rode around in these boys' cars, and sometimes went with them—having lied of course to their mothers—to the Gay-la dance hall on the highway north of town.

16 I got Joyce on the phone. She was very keyed-up, as she always was with boys around, and she hardly seemed to hear what I was saying.

17 "Oh, I can't tonight," she said. "Some kids are here. We're going to play cards. You know Bill Kline? He's here. Ross Armour—"

18 "I'm *sick*," I said trying to speak distinctly; it came out an inhuman croak. "I'm *drunk*. Joyce!" Then I fell off the stool and the receiver dropped out of my hand and banged for a while dismally against the wall.

I had not told Joyce where I was, so after think- 19
ing about it for a moment she phoned my mother, and using the elaborate and unnecessary subterfuge that young girls delight in, she found out. She and Kay and the boys—there were three of them—told some story about where they were going to Kay's mother, and got into the car and drove out. They found me still lying on the broadloom carpet in the hall; I had been sick again, and this time I had not made it to the bathroom.

It turned out that Kay Stringer, who arrived on 20
this scene only by accident, was exactly the person I needed. She loved a crisis, particularly one like this, which had a shady and scandalous aspect and which must be kept secret from the adult world. She became excited, aggressive, efficient; that energy which was termed wildness was simply the overflow of a great female instinct to manage, comfort and control. I could hear her voice coming at me from all directions, telling me not to worry, telling Joyce to find the biggest coffeepot they had and make it full of coffee (*strong* coffee, she said), telling the boys to pick me up and carry me to the sofa. Later, in the fog beyond my reach, she was calling for a scrub-brush.

Then I was lying on the sofa, covered with some 21
kind of crocheted throw they had found in the bedroom. I didn't want to lift my head. The house was full of the smell of coffee. Joyce came in, looking very pale; she said that the Berryman kids had wakened up but she had given them a cookie and told them to go back to bed, it was all right; she hadn't let them out of their room and she didn't believe they'd remember. She said that she and Kay had cleaned up the bathroom and the hall though she was afraid there was still a spot on the rug. The coffee was ready. I didn't understand anything very well. The boys had turned on the radio and were going through the Berrymans' record collection; they had it out on the floor. I felt there was something odd about this but I could not think what it was.

Kay brought me a huge breakfast mug full of coffee. 22

23 "I don't know if I can," I said. "Thanks."

24 "Sit up," she said briskly, as if dealing with drunks was an everyday business for her, I had no need to feel myself important. (I met, and recognized, that tone of voice years later, in the maternity ward.) "Now drink," she said. I drank, and at the same time realized that I was wearing only my slip. Joyce and Kay had taken off my blouse and skirt. They had brushed off the skirt and washed out the blouse, since it was nylon; it was hanging in the bathroom. I pulled the throw up under my arms and Kay laughed. She got everybody coffee. Joyce brought in the coffeepot and on Kay's instructions she kept filling my cup whenever I drank from it. Somebody said to me with interest. "You must have really wanted to tie one on."

25 "No," I said rather sulkily, obediently drinking my coffee. "I only had two drinks."

26 Kay laughed, "Well it certainly gets to you, I'll say that. What time do you expect *they'll* be back?" she said.

27 "Late, after one I think."

28 "You should be all right by that time. Have some more coffee."

29 Kay and one of the boys began dancing to the radio. Kay danced very sexily, but her face had the gently superior and indulgent, rather cold look it had when she was lifting me up to drink the coffee. The boy was whispering to her and she was smiling, shaking her head. Joyce said she was hungry, and she went out to the kitchen to see what there was—potato chips or crackers, or something like that, that you could eat without making too noticeable a dint. Bill Kline came over and sat on the sofa beside me and patted my legs through the crocheted throw. He didn't say anything to me, just patted my legs and looked at me with what seemed to me a very stupid, half-sick, absurd and alarming expression. I felt very uncomfortable; I wondered how it had ever got around that Bill Kline was so good looking, with an expression like that. I moved my legs nervously and he gave me a look of contempt, not ceasing to pat me. Then I scrambled off the sofa, pulling the throw around me, with the idea of going to the bathroom to see if my blouse was dry. I lurched a little when I started to walk, and for some reason—probably to show Bill Kline that he had not panicked me—I immediately exaggerated this, and calling out, "Watch me walk a straight line!" I lurched and stumbled, to the accompaniment of everyone's laughter, towards the hall. I was standing in the archway between the hall and the living room when the knob of the front door turned with a small matter-of-fact click and everything became silent behind me except the radio of course and the crocheted throw inspired by some delicate malice of its own slithered down around my feet and there—oh, delicious moment in a well-organized farce!—there stood the Berrymans, Mr. and Mrs., with expressions on their faces as appropriate to the occasion as any old-fashioned director of farces could wish. They must have been preparing those expressions, of course; they could not have produced them in the first moment of shock; with the noise we were making, they had no doubt heard us as soon as they got out of the car; for the same reason, we had not heard them. I don't think I ever knew what brought them home so early—a headache, an argument—and I was not really in a position to ask.

MR. Berryman drove me home. I don't remember how I got into that car, or how I found my clothes and put them on, or what kind of a good-night, if any, I said to Mrs. Berryman. I don't remember what happened to my friends, though I imagine they gathered up their coats and fled, covering up the ignominy of their departure with a mechanical roar of defiance. I remember Joyce with a box of crackers in her hand, saying that I had become terribly sick from eating—I think she said *sauerkraut*—for supper, and that I had called them for help. (When I asked her later what they made of this she said, "It wasn't any use. You *reeked*.") I remember also her saying, "Oh, no, Mr. Berryman I beg of you, my mother is a terribly nervous person I don't know what the shock might do to her. I will go down on my knees to you if you like but *you must not phone my mother*." I have no picture of her down on her knees—and she would have done it in a minute—so it seems this threat was not carried out. 30

Mr. Berryman said to me, "Well I guess you know your behaviour tonight is a pretty serious thing." He made it sound as if I might be charged with crimi- 31 nal negligence or something worse. “It would be very wrong of me to overlook it,” he said. I suppose that besides being angry and disgusted with *me,* he was worried about taking me home in this condition to my strait-laced parents, who could always say I got the liquor in his house. Plenty of Temperance people would think that enough to hold him responsible, and the town was full of Temperance people. Good relations with the town were very important to him from a business point of view.

32 “I have an idea it wasn’t the first time,” he said. “If it was the first time, would a girl be smart enough to fill three bottles up with water? No. Well in this case, she *was* smart enough, but not smart enough to know I could spot it. What do you say to that?” I opened my mouth to answer and although I was feeling quite sober the only sound that came out was a loud, desolate-sounding giggle. He stopped in front of our house. “Light’s on,” he said. “Now go in and tell your parents the straight truth. And if you don’t, remember I will.” He did not mention paying me for my baby-sitting services of the evening and the subject did not occur to me either.

33 I went into the house and tried to go straight upstairs but my mother called to me. She came into the front hall, where I had not turned on the light, and she must have smelled me at once for she ran forward with a cry of pure amazement, as if she had seen somebody falling, and caught me by the shoulders as I did indeed fall down against the bannister, overwhelmed by my fantastic lucklessness, and I told everything from the start, not omitting even the name of Martin Collingwood and my flirtation with the aspirin bottle, which was a mistake.

34 On Monday morning my mother took the bus over to Baileyville and found the liquor store and bought a bottle of Scotch whisky. Then she had to wait for a bus back, and she met some people she knew and she was not quite able to hide the bottle in her bag; she was furious with herself for not bringing a proper shopping-bag. As soon as she got back she walked out to the Berrymans’; she had not even had lunch. Mr. Berryman had not gone back to the factory. My mother went in and had a talk with both of them and made an excellent impression and then Mr. Berryman drove her home. She talked to them in the forthright and unemotional way she had, which was always agreeably surprising to people prepared to deal with a mother, and she told them that although I seemed to do well enough at school I was extremely backward—or perhaps eccentric—in my emotional development. I imagine that this analysis of my behaviour was especially effective with Mrs. Berryman, a great reader of Child Guidance books. Relations between them warmed to the point where my mother brought up a specific instance of my difficulties, and disarmingly related the whole story of Martin Collingwood.

> “. . . I will go down on my knees to you if you like but *you must not phone my mother.*”

Within a few days it was all 35
over town and the school that I had tried to commit suicide over Martin Collingwood. But it was already all over school and the town that the Berrymans had come home on Saturday night to find me drunk, staggering, wearing nothing but my slip, in a room with three boys, one of whom was Bill Kline. My mother had said that I was to pay for the bottle she had taken the Berrymans out of my baby-sitting earnings, but my clients melted away like the last April snow, and it would not be paid for yet if newcomers to town had not moved in across the street in July, and needed a baby sitter before they talked to any of their neighbours.

My mother also said that it had been a great mis- 36
take to let me go out with boys and that I would not be going out again until well after my sixteenth birthday, if then. This did not prove to be a concrete hardship at all, because it was at least that long before anybody asked me. If you think that news of the Berrymans’ adventure would put me in demand for whatever gambols and orgies were going on in and around that town, you could not be more mistaken. The extraordinary publicity which attended my first debauch may have made me seemed marked for a special kind of ill luck, like the girl whose illegitimate baby turns out to be triplets: nobody wants to have anything to do with her. At any rate I had at the same time one of the most silent telephones and positively the most sinful reputation in the whole High School. I had to put up with this until the next fall, when a fat blonde girl in Grade Ten ran away with a married man and was picked up two months later, living in sin—though not with the same man—in the city of Sault Ste. Marie. Then everybody forgot about me.

But there was a positive, a splendidly unexpected, 37
result of this affair: I got completely over Martin Collingwood. It was not only that he at once said, publicly, that he had always thought I was a nut; where

he was concerned I had no pride, and my tender fancy could have found a way around that, a month, a week, before. What was it that brought me back into the world again? It was the terrible and fascinating reality of my disaster; it was *the way things happened.* Not that I enjoyed it; I was a self-conscious girl and I suffered a good deal from all this exposure. But the development of events on that Saturday night—that fascinated me; I felt that I had had a glimpse of the shameless, marvellous, shattering absurdity with which the plots of life, though not of fiction, are improvised. I could not take my eyes off it.

38 And of course Martin Collingwood wrote his Senior Matric that June, and went away to the city to take a course at a school for Morticians, as I think it is called, and when he came back he went into his uncle's undertaking business. We lived in the same town and we would hear most things that happened to each other but I do not think we met face to face or saw one another, except at a distance, for years. I went to a shower for the girl he married, but then everybody went to everybody else's showers. No, I do not think I really saw him again until I came home after I had been married several years, to attend a relative's funeral. Then I saw him; not quite Mr. Darcy but still very nice-looking in those black clothes. And I saw him looking over at me with an expression as close to a reminiscent smile as the occasion would permit, and I knew that he had been surprised by a memory either of my devotion or my little buried catastrophe. I gave him a gentle uncomprehending look in return. I am a grown-up woman now; let him unbury his own catastrophes.

IF you liked "An Ounce of Cure," you might also like Richard Ford's "Optimists" in the next chapter, another narrator looking back on a youthful experience, with surprising conclusions.

**GOING FURTHER** Alice Munro is one of many in the group of contemporary Canadian writers with international acclaim. You may also want to look at her work in the context of books by her fellow Canadians, like Michael Ondaatje's *The English Patient* or Margaret Atwood's *The Handmaid's Tale.* Both of these authors are also poets, and samples of their poetry have been included in this book.

# Writing from Reading

## Summarize

1 The narrator and her mother have very defined views of each other. Summarize their respective opinions, and discuss how they shape (or are shaped by) the events of the story.

## Analyze Craft

2 Munro describes the narrator's drunken experience using the same language she uses throughout the story. What words and techniques does she use to convey "drunkenness"?

## Analyze Voice

3 Is the description of the narrator's drunken escapade meant to be humorous or tragic? Which aspects of Munro's language create this tone?

## Synthesize Summary and Analysis

4 The narrator tells the story as an adult, looking back on an awkward, confusing, and sometimes painful phase in her life. Discuss how the narrator's distance from the story affects the details she presents, and the plot overall.

## Interpret the Story

5 "An Ounce of Cure" opens with a description of the narrator's relationship with her parents, and closes with a description of her relationship with Martin Collingwood. Compare and contrast these two relationships, and discuss how both affect and are affected by the narrator's first drinking experience.

# Suggestions for Writing

1. The narrator of "A&P" is young and facing forward; the narrator of "An Ounce of Cure" is older, looking back. What might happen, do you think, if the authors had changed their narrative strategies and, for instance, told "A&P" from the vantage point of the store manager or "An Ounce of Cure" as a conversation between the Berrymans?
2. Nothing in "A&P" and "An Ounce of Cure" is *important* in the traditional sense; nobody falls in love eternally or fights to the finish or dies. Discuss what *does* seem to matter in each, and why the authors might have chosen to produce these modest-seeming tales.
3. In the case of "The Story of an Hour," although the situation is also domestic, matters of life and death are indeed under discussion and life itself is at stake. Notice that the narration here comes from "outside" the character and not as a first-person memory. Do you find you know more about the feelings of the first-person narrators in "A&P" and "An Ounce of Cure" than you do about Mrs. Mallard's feelings in "The Story of an Hour"? Or is the outside narrator in "The Story of an Hour" able to convey all that you need to know?

# 2 Going Further with Reading

YOU can best develop your reading skills by closely examining a piece of literature—whether short story, novel, poem, or any other form—and the craft behind it. In this kind of an examination you will use examples from the work itself as evidence to support your analysis. For example, you might argue that a story's theme is a comment on current day celebrity culture, using quotations from the work itself as evidence. You might argue that the ending of a story is particularly effective or ineffective. Examining the language, characters, and structure of a story helps you write meaningfully about a work. Reading a work critically allows you to make supportable associations that are personally important to you. It can also help you begin to develop your own writing powers and your own voice. Take a moment to look at one student's reading of Anton Chekhov's "Rapture."

## A STUDENT'S INITIAL REACTION TO "RAPTURE"

When I first read this, I thought it was amazing how short it is—and how funny it is! Mitya, the main character, doesn't have a clue. He sounds like some of the people I know on campus who like to tell stories about what happened when they were drunk. I had to look up what "Rapture" meant, and I'm still thinking about what it means. When I read this a second time, I plan to make some notes in the margin.

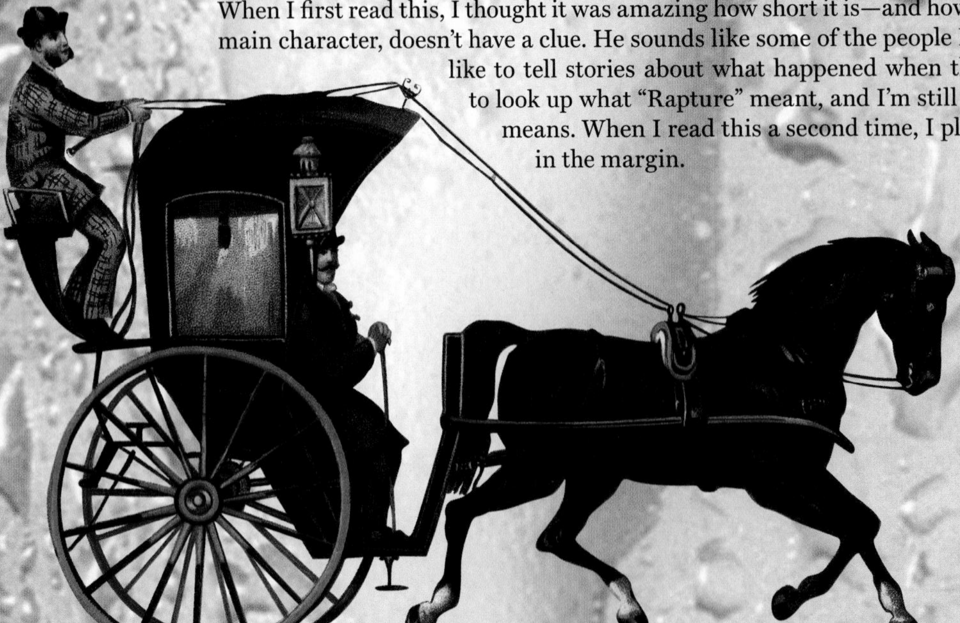

# An Interactive Reading of Anton Chekhov's "Rapture"

## Rapture

"Rapture" means "ecstasy," "transported to Heaven"—this title tells me the story is about this emotion.

Setting: The story takes place in the middle of the night in his parents' apartment. Looks like the stage is set for trouble.

Midnight.

Wild-eyed and disheveled, Mitya Kuldarov burst into his parents' flat and dashed into every room. His parents were about to go to bed. His sister was in bed already and had just got on to the last page of her novel. His schoolboy brothers were asleep.

"Where've you come from?" his parents exclaimed in astonishment. Is something wrong?"

Plot: As the parents see it, there's something "wrong," but the title suggests something else.

Character: Mitya and his parents are the main characters. Is this a story about their relationship?

"Oh, I don't know how to tell you! I'm staggered, absolutely staggered. It's . . . it's quite incredible!"

Mitya burst out laughing and collapsed into an armchair, overcome with happiness.

Mitya is "wild." Mitya's oblivious to everyone around him. Has he done this before? He is behaving so strangely.

"It's incredible! You'll never believe it! Take a look at this!"

Plot: Why is Mitya so happy (when nobody else is)? More uneasy suspense.

His sister jumped out of bed and came over to him, wrapping a blanket around her. The schoolboys woke up.

Plot: The whole house is in an uproar now.

"Is something wrong? You look awful."

Tone, Language, Style: "burst"—same word, twice.

"I'm so happy, Mum, that's why! Now everyone in Russia knows about me! Everyone! Till now only you knew of the existence of clerical officer of the fourteenth grade, Dimitry Kuldarov, but now everyone in Russia knows! O Lord, Mum!"

Tone, Language, Style: Second time Mitya has used word "incredible."

Theme: fame?

Mitya jumped up, ran round every room and sat down again.

Plot: Mitya's constant motion contributes to the tension.

"But tell us what's happened, for goodness sake."

"Oh, you lie here like savages, you don't read the papers, you've no ideas what's going on, and the papers are full of such remarkable things! As soon as anything happens, they make it all public, it's down there in black and white! O Lord, I'm so happy! Only famous people get their names in the paper, then all of a sudden—they go and print a story about me!"

Tone, Language, Style: Mitya keeps saying "happy."

Plot: Is this the turning point in the plot?

Theme: Mitya believes he is famous now. His name is in the paper. This is what has made him rapturous.

"What? Where?"

Dad turned pale. Mum looked up at the icon and crossed herself. The schoolboys jumped out of bed and ran over to their elder brother, wearing nothing but their short little nightshirts.

His parents are worried as if to say "nothing good can come of this." It feels like this isn't the first time they've had to worry about Mitya.

"They have! About me! Now I'm known all over Russia! You'd better keep this copy, Mum, and we can take it out now and then and read it. Look!"

Mitya pulled the newspaper out of this pocket and handed it to his father, jabbing his finger at a passage ringed with blue pencil. "Read it out!"

Father put on his glasses.

"Go on, read it!"

Mum looked up at the icon and crossed herself. Dad cleared his throat and began: "On December 29th at 11 p.m. clerical officer of the fourteenth grade, Dimitry Kuldarov—"

"See? See? Go on, Dad!"

". . . clerical officer of the fourteenth grade, Dimitry Kuldarov, emerging from the public ale-house situated on the ground floor of Kozikhin's Buildings in Little Bronnaya Street and being in a state of intoxication—"

"It was me and Semyon Petrovich . . . They've got all the details! Go on! Now listen, listen to this bit!"

". . . and being in a state of intoxication, slipped and fell in front of a cab-horse belonging to Ivan Knoutoff, peasant, from the village of Bumpkino in Pnoff district, which was standing at that spot. The frightened horse, stepping across Kuldarov, dragged over him the sledge in which was seated Ivan Lukov, merchant of the Second Guild in Moscow, bloted down the street and was arrested in its flight by some yard-porters. Kuldarov, being at first in a state of unconsciousness, was taken to the police-station and examined by a doctore. The blow which he had received on the back of the head—"

"I did it on the shaft, Dad. Go on and read the rest of the story."

". . . which he had received on the back of his head, was classified as superficial. A police report was drawn up concerning the incident. Medical assistance was rendered to the victim."

"They dabbed the back of my head with cold water. Finished? So what do you say to that, eh? It'll be all over Russia by now! Give it here!"

Mitya grabbed the newspaper, folded it and stuffed it into his pocket.

"Must run now and show the Makarovs . . . Then on to the Ivanitsky's, Nataliya Ivanova and Anisim Vasilich . . . Can't stop! Bye."

Mitya put on his official cap with the cockade and radiant, triumphant, ran out into the street.

Tone, Language, Style: Second time she has done this, as if to imply, My God, what has he gotten himself into this time?

Character: Mitya's impatient. If it's not about him, he doesn't care. He's already played superior to his parents by calling them "savages."

Theme: So he's famous for being intoxicated. Why isn't he embarrassed? Why is he so happy about this? What is the point here?

Plot: The story is now winding down.

Character: Mitya is a joke. His "rapture" about his fame shows how comical a character he is.

Point of View: The author really doesn't think much of Mitya.

Plot: His parents read the story instead of telling him off. They play along with his delusion. They let him go on thinking this is a great thing. Why? It looks like the parents didn't really expect much more from him.

Character: Mitya is impatient again. Why is it so important to him that he is now "known"? He might have been intoxicated throughout the whole story, accounting for his sloppy collapsing in a chair and wild outbursts.

Theme: Kind of a sad statement about people. Mitya is a fool. He is proud to be famous for being drunk. He's so deluded that he even wants his parents to know, and his parents do nothing to stop him. He seems ridiculous to me, but he's not acting all that different from how some celebrities act these days.

I don't know if I like this ending. Mitya never grows up. His parents just let him go on like this.

"Rapture" is one of Anton Chekhov's earliest pieces; it dramatizes the effects of alcohol on a young civil servant's ego, and it demonstrates the multiple ways in which people can perceive experience. If you liked this story, you may also enjoy Chekhov's masterwork "The Lady with the Pet Dog" (in Stories for Further Reading), composed when he had more fully discovered both his craft and his voice.

## READING IN CONTEXT

Sometimes while working closely with a story and its meanings, the reader loses sight of the bigger picture, the context. For example, "Rapture" is set in another country, in another century, and was written in another language. Nineteenth-century Russia—with its unpronounceable names and detailed newspaper stories and "official cap with the cockade"—may seem very distant. Yet no piece of writing exists in a vacuum. Each story has an author, a time and place in which it was written, and a tradition of stories

> "I remember reading books about people in Russia, people in India, and people in England, and understanding them—and how surprising this was. Because on the one hand, you realize they're so different from me. But on the other hand, what literature does [is] remind you of how there is that human bond that we all have in common."
>
> Conversation with Chimamanda Ngozi Adichie

and criticism it explicitly or implicitly responds to; taking these aspects into consideration is called **contextual reading.** Traditional research, research that includes multiple sources outside the work itself, can shed light on the context within which a story was written. The most complete analyses of craft and voice push us in the direction of contextual reading, just as the right kind of contextual reading pushes us, throughout the process of analysis, to turn back to the text itself. So reading from the "inside out" in this case means ignoring the fact that we're dealing with a "cab-horse," not a car, and that "Rapture" takes place in Moscow, not Chicago or Los Angeles or Atlanta. Despite the distance, Anton Chekhov's "Rapture" comes nonetheless alive today as an example of the way we may be dazzled by fame. Now, let's look at the critical response paper that is based on the previous reading of "Rapture." In the next chapter we will look more closely at *process* and a set of student drafts; here is the finished *result:*

Lau 1

Liane Lau

Professor Cheuse

Composition 120

23 April 2007

Mitya's False Finale: A Critical Response to Chekhov's "Rapture"

Although it is difficult to talk about language as such in Anton Chekhov's "Rapture," written in Russian in nineteenth-century Moscow, the structure of the story transcends language barriers. Chekhov's setting is domestic: an apartment serves as the location for the entire action, a stage of sorts. The young clerk runs in, stirs up his family and makes them read a newspaper article in which he has been named. Then, still raving about his new-found fame, he runs out again. He is "wild-eyed and disheveled" (25). He runs from room to room. He has laughing outbursts and collapses in a chair. Chekhov paints the portrait of a man out of control, one in an unvoiced conflict with his parents who are "pale" with worry, asking Mitya "Is something wrong? You look awful" (25). Mitya appears to want everyone, beginning with his family, to know his name—he wants to establish himself in the minds of others as someone *important.* However, the young "clerical officer of the fourteenth grade" does not come to any new realization or perception, and therefore, the resolution of the story is not ultimately satisfying (25).

The setting of the story looks like a scene from a play (and it's worth mentioning here that Anton Chekhov would also become a great Russian playwright). The story breaks into three distinct parts. First, the clerk runs in, announcing himself,

Introductory sentence focuses the reader immediately: Essay will center on story elements.

Introduction provides story elements: setting, characters, plot.

Quotes support statements, lend credibility, bring Chekhov's voice to the paper as an ally.

Thesis statement, presents paper's argument: Story elements (listed in paragraph's body) do not add up to a satisfying resolution.

"Three distinct parts": As stated in lead sentence, this argument is based on story structure.

Lau 2

disrupting the household, waking his brothers. Second, Mitya takes out the newspaper and urges his father to read it aloud. He adds his own enthusiastic comments to propel the action forward, and we discover that he was drunk the night before; quite plausibly he remains under the influence now. In the third sequence, a reader may expect something to happen as a result of Mitya's *rapture,* that he has become famous because his name is in the paper and on the police record. The use of the word *rapture* in itself ironically underscores how far it is between Mitya's experience of the truth and the actual truth of his situation. There is nothing elevated about his actions, and to some extent the whole story turns comically on this divide.

Paragraph two critically analyzes elements detailed in intro paragraph.

Critical evidence builds up to the initial debate: Does the story have a clear, satisfying ending.

However, as the ancient philosopher and critic Aristotle might put it, what is the dramatic purpose here? It looks like Mitya's parents are used to his antics as his mother crosses herself twice in anticipation of Mitya's supposedly "incredible" news (25). His parents and his siblings humor him instead of contradicting or berating him, thus making change less likely for Mitya. Mitya is completely happy with his newfound notoriety, even though it announces to the world that he is a drunkard. As we readers come to understand the nature of Mitya's delusion, we are entitled to wonder what Chekhov is after—what point is he attempting to make? Is "Rapture" a story about the folly of ambition? Is it, perhaps, a presage of our publicity-hungry world and the press agent's promise that any mention in the newspaper is more important than none? Or is it simply poking fun at a simple soul? The reader is left to wonder what the point is, and without that concluding action, the dramatic purpose is unclear, the story is incomplete, and ultimately unsatisfying.

Topic sentence states the question posed by preceding paragraphs: Do the story elements allow us to determine whether this is a tragedy or a comedy?

Conclusion restates the thesis, including logic established by body of the paper.

Questions reflect the argument that Chekhov has offered no clear resolution.

Quick, challenging question statements build tension that the conclusion sentence relieves.

Works Cited

Chekhov, Anton. "Rapture." Trans. Patrick Miles and Harvey Pitcher. *Literature: Craft & Voice.* Eds. Nicholas Delbanco and Alan Cheuse. New York: McGraw-Hill, 2009. Print.

For more discussion on how to form a text-based argument, refer to the student paper on Jamaica Kincaid (chapter 3).

Whether or not you care more for the factual than the fictional, or ever paid much attention to stories other people made up, or found your way to the library, you can take on the job of forming a text-based argument. You will need to understand what to make of twenty-six separate things (the English alphabet), crack the code of sentences and paragraphs, and solve the mysteries of punctuation. Are the words mostly long or short? Is the text dominated by descriptive prose or lots of dialogue? However you approach the text, you will of necessity go from outside in. Annotate what you read or keep a reading journal. As you grow more comfortable, what was strange becomes familiar, and what was a puzzle gets solved. Reading stories is like passing through a door and entering a world not precisely our own. We meet people in the throes of private trouble or private pleasure, and when our brief exposure to their lives has ended, we relate to them, however briefly, as if they were our family or loved ones or close friends—or ourselves.

"There's only so many people you're going to meet in the world, and so many people who are going to tell you their story, but you know you can multiply that amount of people by whatever degree or whatever number you want to when you're able to go and read a book." Conversation with ZZ Packer

## VOICE: LISTENING TO THE PAGE

In every work of fiction, a voice inhabits the page. Try to hear the writers' voices in this book. Each writer will have a special way of using language that sets his or her work apart. Some voices derive from a study of Latin, others from the street, some from the language of the Bible, others from the cadence of the blues. The language in a story may reflect the influence of tribal elders or a beloved teacher. Some writers may rely on the presentation of events, action, or dialogue in brief, condensed form to fill readers in on the story's background, a technique called **exposition.** You are likely to also see moment-by-moment passages, like **scenes** from a movie or play, with characters responding to each other as if onstage in real time. Fiction relies on genuine encounters between characters, usually fully conveyed by the words of a conversation itself. **Dialogue** can signal class, education, intelligence, ethnicity, and attitude—a whole host of characteristics—in the people represented on the page. At its best, it both expresses character and moves the action along.

"How different what a Northeasterner hears in his mind and what Faulkner heard in his mind is. We all have to learn to love these irregularities and these personal qualities that fiction has. Fiction's a fairly tough vehicle if it's done right, and it can survive, and engender life in a reader's mind." Conversation with John Updike

## DIALOGUE AND MONOLOGUE

*Dialogue* is a by-product of theatrical productions that began in ancient Greece. Even Plato's political treatise *The Republic* is written in dialogue to mimic the famous plays of the period (some critics suggest Plato wanted to be a playwright himself). A *monologue* is a long speech by a single speaker. Whether dialogue or monologue, in fiction as in drama, each line reveals something about the speaker's character as it moves the action forward.

In some ways, any story that is told by the main character is a kind of extended **monologue.** Characters in stories such as "A&P" and "An Ounce of Cure" from the previous chapter are, in effect, speaking to the reader, transmitting what they want the reader to know about what happened to them. (For more on "Point of View," see chapter 7.) Creating dialogue that sounds natural is important in such stories as a way of portraying the world as it exists. This is especially true of **dialect,** which attempts to reproduce the particular sound, accent, cadence, or emphasis of a character's speech. We require dialogue in order to *see* what we *hear*—that is, to visualize in our mind's eye what we have heard in our mind's ear. The *way* a thing is said, or asked, tells us more than the actual words themselves. If a character says, "Get outta my face," he is not likely to remark in another context, "Would you kindly depart our domicile?"

The next two stories, Richard Ford's "Optimists" and Amy Tan's "Two Kinds," examine questions of family. Tan employs dialect in "Two Kinds" in the mother's speech—"Not the best. Because you not trying." Ford discusses his use of dialogue in his interview. Both stories come to us from the perspective of a narrator who looks back. Compare and contrast how Ford and Tan dramatize a young character coming to terms with the adult world—and in particular the behavior of their parents—as you work with the texts and listen to the voices they create.

*I was dyslexic when I was a little boy . . .*

*. . . I spend as much time at my desk as I can.*

# Q&A
# A Conversation on Writing
## Richard Ford

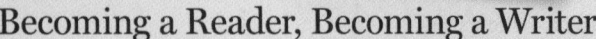

### Becoming a Reader, Becoming a Writer

I started reading fiction—other than reading *Freddie the Pig* novels when I was a kid—when I was nineteen. I was dyslexic when I was a little boy and am still at age sixty-two, but I've learned how to overcome that. . . . It's often the case with dyslexic kids that they are much better at . . . putting out language than they are given to taking language in. So, it was kind of natural to me . . . to try when I was seventeen. . . . long before I read a book through, to write a story.

### On the Writing Process

I go about writing as though it was a job that I liked. I get up in the morning, and I go to work about eight o'clock, and I work all day. And I spend as much time at my desk as I can. And in writing stories, I write with a pen, with a Bic pen, and then after I've written a whole story or whole novel with a Bic pen then I type it all up and work on those typed pages in editing and correcting and making things better.

### On Revision

People see a story on the page and what they think is that the writer started and then wrote to the end and this is how it looked. And in fact the writer started at the beginning and wrote to the end, and then he started at the end and wrote to the beginning, and then he plucked things out of the middle and closed up the places where he took something out. Writing stories is much more mosaical than it is linear.

**To watch this entire interview and hear the author read from "Optimists," go to www.mhhe.com/delbanco1e.**

Richard Ford was born in Jackson, Mississippi, and was raised in Mississippi and Arkansas. He has since lived in New Orleans, Maine, Montana, California, Michigan, New Jersey, and France. Although internationally acclaimed for his fiction, Ford has also committed, as he puts it, "random acts of journalism" and has taught at Harvard, Princeton, and the University of Michigan, among other places. *A Piece of My Heart,* his first book, was published in 1976 and has been followed to date by eight other works of fiction, including both novels and short story collections. His novel *Independence Day* (1995) is the only novel ever to have been accorded both the Pulitzer Prize and the PEN/Faulkner Award. Ford's protagonists are often restless men, adrift and alone; his characteristic first-person narrative mode links action with meditation. In "Optimists," note the span of years that separates the narrator—looking back upon a crucial event of his youth—and the event itself. From his present vantage, the narrator attempts to make sense of the past, seeing not so much an occasion for regret as a mapping of the road not taken, a consideration of what might have been.

**RESEARCH ASSIGNMENT** Richard Ford talks about how in "Optimists" parents and children are equals. Listen to the interview and discuss Ford's own upbringing and how this contributed to this view of family in "Optimists."

**AS YOU READ** Ask yourself about the title of this story—if the optimistic dreams of the characters are realized, and when not, why not. As the narrator observes, ". . . situations have possibilities in them, and we have only to be present to be involved." Keep track of your involvement in the situation here.

# Optimists (1986)

1 ALL of this that I am about to tell happened when I was only fifteen years old, in 1959, the year my parents were divorced, the year when my father killed a man and went to prison for it, the year I left home and school, told a lie about my age to fool the Army, and then did not come back. The year, in other words, when life changed for all of us and forever—ended, really, in a way none of us could ever have imagined in our most brilliant dreams of life.

2 My father was named Roy Brinson, and he worked on the Great Northern Railway, in Great Falls, Montana. He was a switch-engine fireman, and when he could not hold that job on the seniority list, he worked the extra-board as a hostler, or as a hostler's helper, shunting engines through the yard, onto and off the freight trains that went south and east. He was thirty-seven or thirty-eight years old in 1959, a small, young-appearing man, with dark blue eyes. The railroad was a job he liked, because it paid high wages and the work was not hard, and because you could take off days when you wanted to, or even months, and have no one to ask you questions. It was a union shop, and there were people who looked out for you when your back was turned. "It's a workingman's paradise," my father would say, and then laugh.

3 My mother did not work then, though she *had* worked—at waitressing and in the bars in town—and she had liked working. My father thought, though, that Great Falls was coming to be a rougher town than it had been when he grew up there, a town going downhill, like its name, and that my mother should be at home more, because I was at an age when trouble came easily. We lived in a rented two-story house on Edith Street, close to the freight yards and the Missouri River, a house where from my window at night I could hear the engines as they sat throbbing, could see their lights move along the dark rails. My mother was at home most of her time, reading or watching television or cooking meals, though sometimes she would go out to movies in the afternoon, or would go to the YWCA and swim in the indoor pool. Where she was from—in Havre, Montana, much farther north—there was never such a thing as a pool indoors, and she thought that to swim in the winter, with snow on the ground and the wind howling, was the greatest luxury. And she would come home late in the afternoon, with her brown hair wet and her face flushed, and in high spirits, saying she felt freer.

The night that I want to tell about happened in November. It was not then a good time for railroads—not in Montana especially—and for firemen not at all, anywhere. It was the featherbed time, and everyone knew, including my father, that they would—all of them—eventually lose their jobs, though no one knew exactly when, or who would go first, or, clearly, what the future would be. My father had been hired out ten years, and had worked on coal-burners and oil-burners out of Forsythe, Montana, on the 4

Sheridan spur. But he was still young in the job and low on the list, and he felt that when the cut came young heads would go first. "They'll do something for us, but it might not be enough," he said, and I had heard him say that other times—in the kitchen, with my mother, or out in front, working on his motorcycle, or with me, fishing the whitefish flats up the Missouri. But I do not know if he truly thought that or in fact had any reason to think it. He was an optimist. Both of them were optimists, I think.

5 I know that by the end of summer in that year he had stopped taking days off to fish, had stopped going out along the coulee rims to spot deer. He worked more then and was gone more, and he talked more about work when he was home: about what the union said on this subject and that, about court cases in Washington, D.C., a place I knew nothing of, and about injuries and illnesses to men he knew, that threatened their livelihoods, and by association with them, threatened his own—threatened, he must've felt, our whole life.

6 Because my mother swam at the YWCA she had met people there and made friends. One was a large woman named Esther, who came home with her once and drank coffee in the kitchen and talked about her boyfriend and laughed out loud for a long time, but who I never saw again. And another was a woman named Penny Mitchell whose husband, Boyd, worked for the Red Cross in Great Falls and had an office upstairs in the building with the YWCA, and who my mother would sometimes play canasta with on the nights my father worked late. They would set up a card table in the living room, the three of them, and drink and eat sandwiches until midnight. And I would lie in bed with my radio tuned low to the Calgary station, listening to a hockey match beamed out over the great empty prairie, and could hear the cards snap and laughter downstairs, and later I would hear footsteps leaving, hear the door shut, the dishes rattle in the sink, cabinets close. And in a while the door to my room would open and the light would fall inside, and my mother would set a chair back in. I could see her silhouette. She would always say, "Go back to sleep, Frank." And then the door would shut again, and I would almost always go to sleep in a minute.

IT was on a night that Penny and Boyd Mitchell were in our house that trouble came about. My father had been working his regular bid-in job on the switch engine, plus a helper's job off the extra-board—a practice that was illegal by the railroad's rules, but ignored by the union, who could see bad times coming and knew there would be nothing to help it when they came, and so would let men work if they wanted to. I was in the kitchen, eating a sandwich alone at the table, and my mother was in the living room playing cards with Penny and Boyd Mitchell. They were drinking vodka and eating the other sandwiches my mother had made, when I heard my father's motorcycle outside in the dark. It was eight o'clock at night, and I knew he was not expected home until midnight. 7

"Roy's home," I heard my mother say. "I hear Roy. That's wonderful." I heard chairs scrape and glasses tap. 8

"Maybe he'll want to play," Penny Mitchell said. "We can play four-hands." 9

I went to the kitchen door and stood looking through the dining room at the front. I don't think I knew something was wrong, but I think I knew something was unusual, something I would want to know about firsthand. 10

My mother was standing beside the card table when my father came inside. She was smiling. But I have never seen a look on a man's face that was like the look on my father's face at that moment. He looked wild. His eyes were wild. His whole face was. It was cold outside, and the wind was coming up, and he had ridden home from the train yard in only his flannel shirt. His face was red, and his hair was strewn around his bare head, and I remember his fists were clenched white, as if there was no blood in them at all. 11

"My God," my mother said. "What is it, Roy? You look crazy." She turned and looked for me, and I knew she was thinking that this was something I might not need to see. But she didn't say anything. She just looked back at my father, stepped toward him and touched his hand, where he must've been coldest. Penny and Boyd Mitchell sat at the card table, looking up. Boyd Mitchell was smiling for some reason. 12

"Something awful happened," my father said. He reached and took a corduroy jacket off the coat nail and put it on, right in the living room, then sat down on the couch and hugged his arms. His face seemed to get redder then. He was wearing black steel-toe boots, the boots he wore every day, and I stared at them and felt how cold he must be, even in his own house. I did not come any closer. 13

14 "Roy, what is it?" my mother said, and she sat down beside him on the couch and held his hand in both of hers.

15 My father looked at Boyd Mitchell and at his wife, as if he hadn't known they were in the room until then. He did not know them very well, and I thought he might tell them to get out, but he didn't.

16 "I saw a man be killed tonight," he said to my mother, then shook his head and looked down. He said, "We were pushing into that old hump yard on Ninth Avenue. A cut of coal cars. It wasn't even an hour ago. I was looking out my side, the way you do when you push out a curve. And I could see this one open boxcar in the cut, which isn't unusual. Only this guy was in it and was trying to get off, sitting in the door, scooting. I guess he was a hobo. Those cars had come in from Glasgow tonight. And just the second he started to go off, the whole cut buckled up. It's a thing that'll happen. But he lost his balance just when he hit the gravel, and he fell backwards underneath. I looked right at him. And one set of trucks rolled right over his foot." My father looked at my mother then. "It hit his foot," he said.

He didn't look scared, he just looked like a man doing something that was hard for him to do.

17 "My God," my mother said and looked down at her lap.

18 My father squinted. "But then he moved, he sort of bucked himself like he was trying to get away. He didn't yell, and I could see his face. I'll never forget that. He didn't look scared, he just looked like a man doing something that was hard for him to do. He looked like he was concentrating on something. But when he bucked he pushed back, and the other trucks caught his hand." My father looked at his own hands then, and made fists out of them and squeezed them.

19 "What did you do? my mother said. She looked terrified.

20 "I yelled out. And Sherman stopped pushing. But it wasn't that fast."

21 "Did you do anything then," Boyd Mitchell said.

22 "I got down," my father said, "and I went up there. But here's a man cut in three pieces in front of me. What can you do? You can't do very much. I squatted down and touched his good hand. And it was like ice. His eyes were open and roaming all up in the sky."

23 "Did he say anything?" my mother said.

24 "He said, 'Where am I today?' And I said to him, 'It's all right, bud, you're in Montana. You'll be all right.' Though, my God, he wasn't. I took my jacket off and put it over him. I didn't want him to see what had happened."

25 "You should've put tourniquets on," Boyd Mitchell said gruffly. "That could've helped. That could've saved his life."

26 My father looked at Boyd Mitchell then as if he had forgotten he was there and was surprised that he spoke. "I don't know about that," my father said. "I don't know anything about those things. He was already dead. A boxcar had run over him. He was breathing, but he was already dead to me."

27 "That's only for a licensed doctor to decide," Boyd Mitchell said. "You're morally obligated to do all you can." And I could tell from his tone of voice that he did not like my father. He hardly knew him, but he did not like him. I had no idea why. Boyd Mitchell was a big, husky, red-faced man with curly hair—handsome in a way, but with a big belly—and I knew only that he worked for the Red Cross, and that my mother was a friend of his wife's, and maybe of his, and that they played cards when my father was gone.

28 My father looked at my mother in a way I knew was angry. "Why have you got these people over here now, Dorothy? They don't have any business here."

29 "Maybe that's right," Penny Mitchell said, and she put down her hand of cards and stood up at the table. My mother looked around the room as though an odd noise had occurred inside of it and she couldn't find the source.

30 "Somebody definitely should've done something," Boyd Mitchell said, and he leaned forward on the table toward my father. "That's all there is to say." He was shaking his head *no*. "That man didn't have to die." Boyd Mitchell clasped his big hands on top of his playing cards and stared at my father. "The unions'll cover this up, too, I guess, won't they? That's what happens in these things."

31 My father stood up then, and his face looked wide, though it looked young, still. He looked like a young man who had been scolded and wasn't sure how he should act. "You get out of here," he said in a loud voice. "My God. What a thing to say. I don't even know you."

32 "I know you, though," Boyd Mitchell said angrily. "You're another featherbedder. You aren't good to do anything. You can't even help a dying man. You're bad for this country, and you won't last."

33 "Boyd, my goodness," Penny Mitchell said. "Don't say that. Don't say that to him."

34 Boyd Mitchell glared up at his wife. "I'll say anything I want to," he said. "And he'll listen, because he's helpless. He can't do anything."

35 "Stand up," my father said. "Just stand up on your feet." His fists were clinched again.

36 "All right, I will," Boyd Mitchell said. He glanced up at his wife. And I realized that Boyd Mitchell was drunk, and it was possible that he did not even know what he was saying, or what had happened, and that words just got loose from him this way, and anybody who knew him knew it. Only my father didn't. He only knew what had been said.

37 Boyd Mitchell stood up and put his hands in his pockets. He was much taller than my father. He had on a white Western shirt and whipcords and cowboy boots and was wearing a big silver wristwatch. "All right," he said. "Now I'm standing up. What's supposed to happen?" He weaved a little. I saw that.

38 And my father hit Boyd Mitchell then, hit him from across the card table—hit him with his right hand, square into the chest, not a lunging blow, just a hard, hitting blow that threw my father off balance and made him make a *chuffing* sound with his mouth. Boyd Mitchell groaned, "Oh," and fell down immediately, his big, thick, heavy body hitting the floor already doubled over. And the sound of him hitting the floor in our house was like no sound I had ever heard before. It was the sound of a man's body hitting a floor, and it was only that. In my life I have heard it other places, in hotel rooms and in bars, and it is one you do not want to hear.

Maybe she thought about the rest of her life then and what that might be like after tonight.

39 You can hit a man in a lot of ways, I know that, and I knew that then, because my father had told me. You can hit a man to insult him, or you can hit a man to bloody him, or to knock him down, or lay him out. Or you can hit a man to kill him. Hit him that hard. And that is how my father hit Boyd Mitchell—as hard as he could, in the chest and not in the face, the way someone might think who didn't know about it.

40 "Oh my God," Penny Mitchell said. Boyd Mitchell was lying on his side in front of the TV, and she had gotten down on her knees beside him. "Boyd," she said. "Are you hurt? Oh, look at this. Stay where you are, Boyd. Stay on the floor."

41 "Now then. All right," my father said. "Now. All right." He was standing against the wall, over to the side of where he had been when he hit Boyd Mitchell from across the card table. Light was bright in the room, and my father's eyes were wide and touring around. He seemed out of breath and both his fists were clenched, and I could feel his heart beating in my own chest. "All right, now, you son of a bitch," my father said, and loudly. I don't think he was even talking to Boyd Mitchell. He was just saying words that came out of him.

42 "Roy," my mother said calmly. "Boyd's hurt now. He's hurt." She was just looking down at Boyd Mitchell. I don't think she knew what to do.

43 "Oh, no," Penny Mitchell said in an excited voice. "Look up, Boyd. Look up at Penny. You've been hurt." She had her hands flat on Boyd Mitchell's chest, and her skinny shoulders close to him. She wasn't crying, but I think she was hysterical and couldn't cry.

44 All this had taken only five minutes, maybe even less time. I had never even left the kitchen door. And for that reason I walked out into the room where my father and mother were, and where Boyd and Penny Mitchell were both of them on the floor. I looked down at Boyd Mitchell, at his face. I wanted to see what had happened to him. His eyes had cast back up into their sockets. His mouth was open, and I could see his big pink tongue inside. He was breathing heavy breaths, and his fingers—the fingers on both his hands—were moving, moving in the way a man would move them if he was nervous or anxious about something. I think he was dead then, and I think even Penny Mitchell knew he was dead, because she was saying, "Oh please, please, please, Boyd."

45 That is when my mother called the police, and I think it is when my father opened the front door and stepped out into the night.

46 ALL that happened next is what you would expect to happen. Boyd Mitchell's chest quit breathing in a minute, and he turned pale and cold and began to look dead right on our living-room floor. He made a noise in his throat once, and Penny Mitchell cried out, and my mother got down on her knees and held Penny's shoulders while she cried. Then my mother made Penny get up and go into the bedroom—hers and my father's—and lie on the bed. Then she and I sat in the brightly lit living room, with Boyd Mitchell dead on the floor, and simply looked at each other—maybe for ten minutes, maybe for twenty. I don't know what my mother could've been thinking during that time, because she did not say. She did not ask about my father. She did not tell me to leave the room. Maybe she thought

about the rest of her life then and what that might be like after tonight. Or maybe she thought this: that people can do the worst things they are capable of doing and in the end the world comes back to normal. Possibly, she was just waiting for something normal to begin to happen again. That would make sense, given her particular character.

47 Though what I thought myself, sitting in that room with Boyd Mitchell dead, I remember very well, because I have thought it other times, and to a degree I began to date my real life from that moment and that thought. It is this: that situations have possibilities in them, and we have only to be present to be involved. Tonight was a very bad one. But how were we to know it would turn out this way until it was too late and we had all been changed forever? I realized though, that trouble, real trouble, was something to be avoided, inasmuch as once it has passed by, you have only yourself to answer to, even if, as I was, you are the cause of nothing.

48 In a little while the police arrived to our house. First one and then two more cars with their red lights turning in the street. Lights were on in the neighbors' houses—people came out and stood in the cold in their front yards watching, people I didn't know and who didn't know us. "It's a circus now," my mother said to me when we looked through the window. "We'll have to move somewhere else. They won't let us alone."

49 An ambulance came, and Boyd Mitchell was taken away on a stretcher, under a sheet. Penny Mitchell came out of the bedroom and went with them, though she did not say anything to my mother, or to anybody, just got in a police car and left into the dark.

50 Two policemen came inside, and one asked my mother some questions in the living room, while the other one asked me questions in the kitchen. He wanted to know what I had seen, and I told him. I said Boyd Mitchell had cursed at my father for some reason I didn't know, then had stood up and tried to hit him, and that my father had pushed Boyd, and that was all. He asked me if my father was a violent man, and I said no. He asked if my father had a girlfriend, and I said no. He asked if my mother and father had ever fought, and I said no. He asked me if I loved my mother and father, and I said I did. And then that was all.

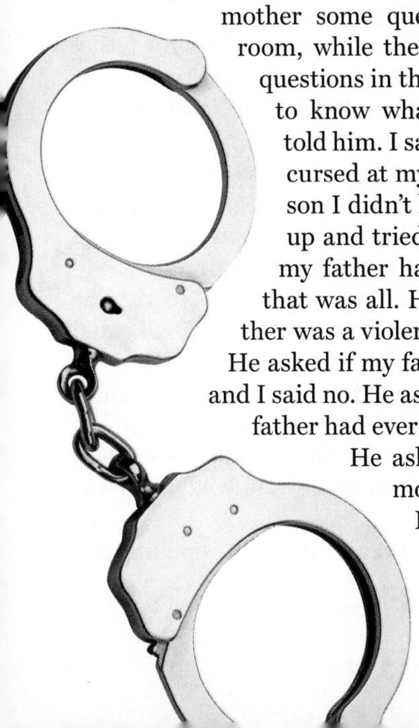

51 I went out into the living room then, and my mother was there, and when the police left we stood at the front door, and there was my father outside, standing by the open door of a police car. He had on handcuffs. And for some reason he wasn't wearing a shirt or his corduroy jacket but was bare-chested in the cold night, holding his shirt behind him. His hair looked wet to me. I heard a policeman say, "Roy, you're going to catch cold," and then my father say, "I wish I was a long way from here right now. China maybe." He smiled at the policeman. I don't think he ever saw us watching, or if he did he didn't want to admit it. And neither of us did anything, because the police had him, and when that is the case, there is nothing you can do to help.

52 ALL this happened by ten o'clock. At midnight my mother and I drove down to the city jail and got my father out. I stayed in the car while my mother went in—sat and watched the high windows of the jail, which were behind wire mesh and bars. Yellow lights were on there, and I could hear voices and see figures move past the lights, and twice someone called out, "Hello, hello. Marie, are you with me?" And then it was quiet, except for the cars that drove slowly past ours.

53 On the ride home, my mother drove and my father sat and stared out at the big electrical stacks by the river, and the lights of houses on the other side, in Black Eagle. He had on a checked shirt someone inside had given him, and his hair was neatly combed. No one said anything, but I did not understand why the police would put anyone in jail because he had killed a man and in two hours let him out again. It was a mystery to me, even though I wanted him to be out and for our life to resume, and even though I did not see any way it could and, in fact, knew it never would.

54 Inside our house, all the lights were burning when we got back. It was one o'clock and there were still lights in some neighbors' houses. I could see a man at the window across the street, both his hands to the glass, watching out, watching us.

55 My mother went into the kitchen, and I could hear her running water for coffee and taking down cups. My father stood in the middle of the living room and looked around, looking at the chairs, at the card table with cards still on it, at the open doorways to the other rooms. It was as if he had forgotten his own house and now saw it again and didn't like it.

56 "I don't feel I know what he had against me," my father said. He said this to me, but he said it to anyone,

too. "You'd think you'd know what a man had against you, wouldn't you, Frank?"

57 "Yes," I said, "I would." We were both just standing together, my father and I, in the lighted room there. We were not about to do anything.

58 "I want us to be happy here now," my father said. "I want us to enjoy life. I don't hold anything against anybody. Do you believe that?"

59 "I believe that," I said. My father looked at me with his dark blue eyes and frowned. And for the first time I wished my father had not done what he did but had gone about things differently. I saw him as a man who made mistakes, as a man who could hurt people, ruin lives, risk their happiness. A man who did not understand enough. He was like a gambler, though I did not even know what it meant to be a gambler then.

"'You don't belong in jail. You stand up too straight.'"

60 "It's such a quickly changing time now," my father said. My mother, who had come into the kitchen doorway, stood looking at us. She had on a flowered pink apron, and was standing where I had stood earlier that night. She was looking at my father and at me as if we were one person. "Don't you think it is, Dorothy?" he said. "All this turmoil. Everything just flying by. Look what's happened here."

61 My mother seemed very certain about things then, very precise. "You should've controlled yourself more," she said. "That's all."

62 "I know that," my father said. "I'm sorry. I lost control over my mind. I didn't expect to ruin things, but now I think I have. It was all wrong." My father picked up the vodka bottle, unscrewed the cap and took a big swallow, then put the bottle back down. He had seen two men killed tonight. Who could've blamed him?

63 "When I was in jail tonight," he said, staring at a picture on the wall, a picture by the door to the hallway. He was just talking again. "There was a man in the cell with me. And I've never been in jail before, not even when I was a kid. But this man said to me tonight, 'I can tell you've never been in jail before just by the way you stand up straight. Other people don't stand that way. They stoop. You don't belong in jail. You stand up too straight.'" My father looked back at the vodka bottle as if he wanted to drink more out of it, but he only looked at it. "Bad things happen," he said, and he let his open hands tap against his legs like clappers against a bell. "Maybe he was in love with you, Dorothy," he said. "Maybe that's what the trouble was."

64 And what I did then was stare at the picture on the wall, the picture my father had been staring at, a picture I had seen every day. Probably I had seen it a thousand times. It was two people with a baby on a beach. A man and a woman sitting in the sand with an ocean behind. They were smiling at the camera, wearing bathing suits. In all the times I had seen it I'd thought that it was a picture in which I was the baby, and the two people were my parents. But I realized as I stood there, that it was not me at all; it was my father who was the child in the picture, and the parents there were his parents—two people I'd never known, and who were dead—and the picture was so much older than I had thought it was. I wondered why I hadn't known that before, hadn't understood it for myself, hadn't always known it. Not even that it mattered. What mattered was, I felt, that my father had fallen down now, as much as the man he had watched fall beneath the train just hours before. And I was as helpless to do anything as he had been. I wanted to tell him that I loved him, but for some reason I did not.

LATER in the night I lay in my bed with the radio playing, listening to news that was far away, in Calgary and in Saskatoon, and even farther, in Regina and Winnipeg—cold, dark cities I knew I would never see in my life. My window was raised above the sill, and for a long time I had sat and looked out, hearing my parents talk softly down below, hearing their footsteps, hearing my father's steel-toed boots strike the floor, and then their bedsprings squeeze and then be quiet. From out across the sliding river I could hear trucks—stock trucks and grain trucks heading toward Idaho, or down toward Helena, or into the train yards where my father hostled engines. The neighborhood houses were dark again. My father's motorcycle sat in the yard, and out in the night air I felt I could hear even the falls themselves, could hear every sound of them, sounds that found me and whirled and filled my room—could even feel them, cold and wintry, so that warmth seemed like a possibility I would never know again. 65

After a time my mother came in my room. The light fell on my bed, and she set a chair inside. I could see that she was looking at me. She closed the door, came and turned off my radio, then took her chair to the window, closed it, and sat so that I could see her face silhouetted against the streetlight. She lit a cigarette and did not look at me, still cold under the covers of my bed. 66

"How do you feel, Frank," she said, smoking her cigarette. 67

68 "I feel all right," I said.

69 "Do you think your house is a terrible house now?"

70 "No," I said.

71 "I hope not," my mother said. "Don't feel it is. Don't hold anything against anyone. Poor Boyd. He's gone."

72 "Why do you think that happened?" I said, though I didn't think she would answer, and wondered if I even wanted to know.

73 My mother blew smoke against the window glass, then sat and breathed. "He must've seen something in your father he just hated. I don't know what it was. Who knows? Maybe your father felt the same way." She shook her head and looked out into the street-lamp light. "I remember once," she said. "I was still in Havre, in the thirties. We were living in a motel my father part-owned out Highway Two, and my mother was around then, but wasn't having any of us. My father had this big woman named Judy Belknap as his girlfriend. She was an Assiniboin. Just some squaw. But we used to go on nature tours when he couldn't put up with me anymore. She'd take me. Way up above the Milk River. All this stuff she knew about, animals and plants and ferns—she'd tell me all that. And once we were sitting watching some gadwall ducks on the ice where a creek had made a little turn-out. It was getting colder, just like now. And Judy just all at once stood up and clapped. Just clapped her hands. And all these ducks got up, all except for one that stayed on the ice, where its feet were frozen, I guess. It didn't even try to fly. It just sat. And Judy said to me, 'It's just a coincidence, Dottie. It's wildlife. Some always get left back.' And that seemed to leave her satisfied for some reason. We walked back to the car after that. So," my mother said. "Maybe that's what this is. Just a coincidence."

74 She raised the window again, dropped her cigarette out, blew the last smoke from her throat, and said, "Go to sleep, Frank. You'll be all right. We'll all survive this. Be an optimist."

75 When I was asleep that night, I dreamed. And what I dreamed was of a plane crashing, a bomber, dropping out of the frozen sky, bouncing as it hit the icy river, sliding and turning on the ice, its wings like knives, and coming into our house where we were sleeping, leveling everything. And when I sat up in bed I could hear a dog in the yard, its collar jingling, and I could hear my father crying, "Boo-hoo-hoo, boo-hoo-hoo,"—like that, quietly—though afterward I could never be sure if I had heard him crying in just that way, or if all of it was a dream, a dream I wished I had never had.

THE most important things of your life can change so suddenly, so unrecoverably, that you can forget even the most important of them and their connections, you are so taken up by the chanciness of all that's happened and by all that could and will happen next. I now no longer remember the exact year of my father's birth, or how old he was when I last saw him, or even when that last time took place. When you're young, these things seem unforgettable and at the heart of everything. But they slide away and are gone when you are not so young. 76

My father went to Deer Lodge Prison and stayed five months for killing Boyd Mitchell by accident, for using too much force to hit him. In Montana you cannot simply kill a man in your living room and walk off free from it, and what I remember is that my father pleaded no contest, the same as guilty. 77

My mother and I lived in our house for the months he was gone. But when he came out and went back on the railroad as a switchman the two of them argued about things, about her wanting us to go someplace else to live—California or Seattle were mentioned. And then they separated, and she moved out. And after that I moved out by joining the Army and adding years to my age, which was sixteen. 78

I know about my father only that after a time he began to live a life he himself would never have believed. He fell off the railroad, divorced my mother, who would now and then resurface in his life. Drinking was involved in that, and gambling, embezzling money, even carrying a pistol, is what I heard. I was apart from all of it. And when you are the age I was then, and loose on the world and alone, you can get along better than at almost any other time, because 79 it's a novelty, and you can act for what you want, and you can think that being alone will not last forever. All I know of my father, finally, is that he was once in Laramie, Wyoming, and not in good shape, and then he simply disappeared from view.

80 A month ago I saw my mother. I was buying groceries at a drive-in store by the interstate in Anaconda, Montana, not far from Deer Lodge itself, where my father had been. It had been fifteen years, I think, since I had seen her, though I am forty-three years old now, and possibly it was longer. But when I saw her I walked across the store to where she was and I said, "Hello, Dorothy. It's Frank."

81 She looked at me and smiled and said, "Oh, Frank. How are you? I haven't seen you in a long time. I'm glad to see you now, though." She was dressed in blue jeans and boots and a Western shirt, and she looked like a woman who could be sixty years old. Her hair was tied back and she looked pretty, though I think she had been drinking. It was ten o'clock in the morning.

82 There was a man standing near her, holding a basket of groceries, and she turned to him and said, "Dick, come here and meet my son, Frank. We haven't seen each other in a long time. This is Dick Spivey, Frank."

83 I shook hands with Dick Spivey, who was a man younger than my mother but older than me—a tall, thin-faced man with coarse blue-black hair—and who was wearing Western boots like hers. "Let me say a word to Frank, Dick," my mother said, and she put her hand on Dick's wrist and squeezed it and smiled at him. And he walked up toward the checkout to pay for his groceries.

84 "So. What are you doing now, Frank," my mother asked, and put her hand on my wrist the way she had on Dick Spivey's, but held it there. "These years," she said.

85 "I've been down in Rock Springs, on the coal boom," I said. "I'll probably go back down there."

86 "And I guess you're married, too."

87 "I was," I said. "But not right now."

88 "That's fine," she said. "You look fine." She smiled at me. "You'll never get anything fixed just right. That's your mother's word. Your father and I had a marriage made in Havre—that was our joke about us. We used to laugh about it. You didn't know that, of course. You were too young. A lot of it was just wrong."

89 "It's a long time ago." I said. "I don't know about that."

90 "I remember those times very well," my mother said. "They were happy enough times. I guess something *was* in the air, wasn't there? Your father was so jumpy. And Boyd got so mad, just all of a sudden. There was some hopelessness to it, I suppose. All that union business. We were the last to understand any of it, of course. We were trying to be decent people."

91 "That's right," I said. And I believed that was true of them.

92 "I still like to swim," my mother said. She ran her fingers back through her hair as if it were wet. She smiled at me again. "It still makes me feel freer."

93 "Good," I said. "I'm happy to hear that."

94 "Do you ever see your dad?"

95 "No," I said. "I never do."

96 "I don't either," my mother said. "You just reminded me of him." She looked at Dick Spivey, who was standing at the front window, holding a sack of groceries, looking out at the parking lot. It was March, and some small bits of snow were falling onto the cars in the lot. He didn't seem in any hurry. "Maybe I didn't appreciate your father enough," she said. "Who knows? Maybe we weren't even made for each other. Losing your love is the worst thing, and that's what we did." I didn't answer her, but I knew what she meant, and that it was true. "I wish we knew each other better, Frank," my mother said to me. She looked down, and I think she may have blushed. "We have our deep feelings, though, don't we? Both of us."

97 "Yes," I said. "We do."

98 "So. I'm going out now," my mother said. "Frank." She squeezed my wrist, and walked away through the checkout and into the parking lot, with Dick Spivey carrying their groceries beside her.

99 But when I had bought my own groceries and paid, and gone out to my car and started up, I saw Dick Spivey's green Chevrolet drive back into the lot and stop, and watched my mother get out and hurry across the snow to where I was, so that for a moment we faced each other through the open window.

100 "Did you ever think," my mother said, snow freezing in her hair. "Did you ever think back then that I was in love with Boyd Mitchell? Anything like that? Did you ever?"

101 "No," I said. "I didn't."

102 "No, well, I wasn't," she said. "Boyd was in love with Penny. I was in love with Roy. That's how things were. I want you to know it. You have to believe that. Do you?"

103 "Yes," I said. "I believe you."

104 And she bent down and kissed my cheek through the open window and touched my face with both her hands, held me for a moment that seemed like a long time before she turned away, finally, and left me there alone.

RICHARD Ford indicates in his interview that he grew up in the same neighborhood as Eudora Welty and cut his teeth on the novels of fellow Mississipian William Faulkner. Ford doesn't consider himself a Southern writer. His work ranges in location from Montana to New Jersey to Louisiana to New York, but if you like "Optimists," you may enjoy comparing Ford's story to Welty's thoroughly Southern "Why I Live at the P.O." (chapter 6) or the Faulkner stories in the casebook on the American South.

**GOING FURTHER** You may also want to read Ford's Pulitzer Prize–winning novel *Independence Day.*

# Writing from Reading

## Summarize

1 What details does Ford provide about Frank's mother's relationship to Boyd? Based on what you know, discuss whether his mother is telling the truth at the end when she says there was nothing between her and Boyd.

## Analyze Craft

2 Where in the story does Ford compress his characters' speech, and where does he let them talk? Where is the stress, the urgency, placed in what's said or left unexpressed? Consider the ways in which the dialogue in "Optimists" *instructs* the reader.

## Analyze Voice

3 "Optimists" is told retrospectively from Frank's perspective. All these years later, is it possible that Frank (now forty-three) recalls exactly what was said when he was a child? Are we supposed to believe that the words within the quotation marks are true to the letter? If not, what kind of dramatic license does Ford take with this story's dialogue?

## Synthesize Summary and Analysis

4 Consider why Ford has Dick Spivey present during Frank's final encounter with his mother. Why does he have Dick remain silent? Discuss how the final scene would change if Ford had left Dick Spivey out.

## Interpret the Story

5 The last words of this story are "and left me there alone." What do we know and what can we deduce about Frank's present life; is he an "optimist"?

# Q&A

# A Conversation on Writing

## Amy Tan

One of the first serious novelists of the post–Vietnam War era to make her mark on the imagination of a general readership, Amy Tan was born in Oakland, California, to Chinese immigrants. After college she became successful as a business writer and took up jazz piano as a hobby, a young Chinese American woman who had not yet clearly faced the matter of her cultural origins. It wasn't until after her marriage to a Bay Area tax attorney that she eventually began to try to write fiction based on her cultural heritage.

Like many first-generation Americans, Tan had not fully explored her relations to her parents' culture until she had established herself as a successful working adult. After her father and brother died within a year from brain tumors, she and her mother were left to work out their own difficulties. Her troubled relations with her mother eventually smoothed out, and after her mother recovered from a serious illness, the two of them traveled to China. There Tan got a firsthand look at the country of her parents' birth, beginning to explore her origins as possible material for fiction. This led to the composition of a series of stories, which Tan revised and made into the novel *The Joy Luck Club*. That book became a national best seller in 1989, and Tan has since published the novels *The Kitchen God's Wife, The Hundred Secret Senses, The Bonesetter's Daughter, Saving Fish from Drowning,* and two children's books, *The Moon Lady* and *Sagwa*.

### Becoming a Reader

I was a very lonely child much of my childhood. Books were a place where I could find someone who understood me. That someone could have lived 200 years ago. Jane Eyre had nothing to do with my life. And yet she did. She was that lonely girl nobody understood . . . and I imagined myself living that life. I realized as a young reader, I could really go anywhere. I could go to the prairie and the big woods, I could be living in a different time. I could wear all these different clothes. I could have romances with the most popular boy. . . . That made me not feel so lonely.

### On Voice and the Writing Process

When I started to write, I had this basic question that was posed to me by a woman named Molly Giles, a wonderful writer. She had read my work. And she said, "You know, what you've written here is not a story. It is the beginnings of a dozen stories." And she pointed out these sentences. She said, "This is the beginning of a story, this is the beginning of a story, this is the beginning. This is a voice, this is a voice, this is a voice." And I thought, Well, what is a voice? And what's a story? What are the things that make this up? But I feel now, now that I've been doing this for a while, that the questions are still there. And there's no absolute answer. And that you discover it each time you sit down and write. . . .

To watch this entire interview online and hear the author read from "Two Kinds," go to **www.mhhe.com/delbanco1e.**

**RESEARCH ASSIGNMENT** Amy Tan says in her interview that reading and writing fiction are subversive. Listen to the interview and explain what she means. Do you agree with her?

**AS YOU READ** As is the case with "Optimists," the narrator here describes her past from a present vantage point; she's a good deal older than the character described. Consider the perspective from which this tale is told.

# Two Kinds (1989)

1 MY mother believed you could be anything you wanted to be in America. You could open a restaurant. You could work for the government and get good retirement. You could buy a house with almost no money down. You could become rich. You could become instantly famous.

2 "Of course, you can be prodigy, too," my mother told me when I was nine. "You can be best anything. What does Auntie Lindo know? Her daughter, she is only best tricky."

3 America was where all my mother's hopes lay. She had come here in 1949 after losing everything in China: her mother and father, her family home, her first husband, and two daughters, twin baby girls. But she never looked back with regret. There were so many ways for things to get better

4 WE didn't immediately pick the right kind of prodigy. At first my mother thought I could be a Chinese Shirley Temple. We'd watch Shirley's old movies on TV as though they were training films. My mother would poke my arm and say, *"Ni kan"* —You watch. And I would see Shirley tapping her feet, or singing a sailor song, or pursing her lips into a very round O while saying "Oh, my goodness."

5 *"Ni kan,"* said my mother, as Shirley's eyes flooded with tears. "You already know how. Don't need talent for crying!"

6 Soon after my mother got this idea about Shirley Temple, she took me to a beauty training school in the Mission district and put me in the hands of a student who could barely hold the scissors without shaking. Instead of getting big fat curls, I emerged with an uneven mass of crinkly black fuzz. My mother dragged me off to the bathroom and tried to wet down my hair.

"You look like Negro Chinese," she lamented, as if I had done this on purpose. 7

The instructor of the beauty training school had to lop off these soggy clumps to make my hair even again. "Peter Pan is very popular these days," the instructor assured my mother. I now had hair the length of a boy's, with straight-across bangs that hung at a slant two inches above my eyebrows. I liked the haircut and it made me actually look forward to my future fame. 8

In fact, in the beginning, I was just as excited as my mother, maybe even more so. I pictured this prodigy part of me as many different images, trying each one on for size. I was a dainty ballerina girl standing by the curtains, waiting to hear the right music that would send me floating on my tiptoes. I was like the Christ child lifted out of the straw manger, crying with holy indignity. I was Cinderella stepping from her pumpkin carriage with sparkly cartoon music filling the air. 9

In all of my imaginings, I was filled with a sense that I would soon become *perfect*. My mother and father would adore me. I would be beyond reproach. I would never feel the need to sulk for anything. 10

But sometimes the prodigy in me became impatient. "If you don't hurry up and get me out of here, I'm disappearing for good," it warned. "And then you'll always be nothing." 11

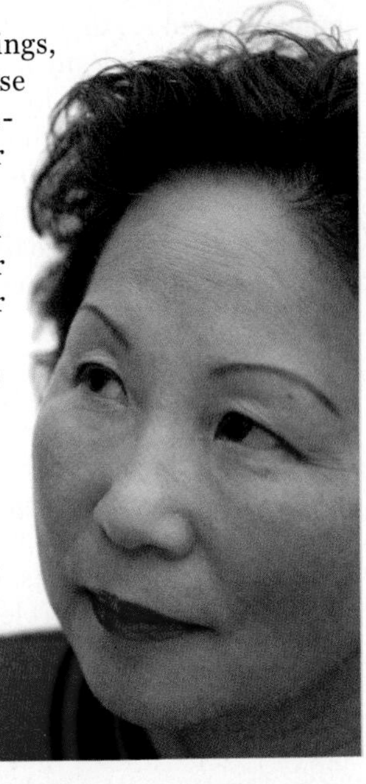

12 EVERY night after dinner, my mother and I would sit at the Formica kitchen table. She would present new tests, taking her examples from stories of amazing children she had read in *Ripley's Believe It or Not,* or *Good Housekeeping, Reader's Digest,* and a dozen other magazines she kept in a pile in our bathroom. My mother got these magazines from people whose houses she cleaned. And since she cleaned many houses each week, we had a great assortment. She would look through them all, searching for stories about remarkable children.

I won't let her change me, I promised myself.

13 The first night she brought out a story about a three-year-old boy who knew the capitals of all the states and even most of the European countries. A teacher was quoted as saying the little boy could also pronounce the names of the foreign cities correctly.

14 "What's the capital of Finland?" my mother asked me, looking at the magazine story.

15 All I knew was the capital of California, because Sacramento was the name of the street we lived on in Chinatown. "Nairobi!" I guessed, saying the most foreign word I could think of. She checked to see if that was possibly one way to pronounce "Helsinki" before showing me the answer.

16 The tests got harder—multiplying numbers in my head, finding the queen of hearts in a deck of cards, trying to stand on my head without using my hands, predicting the daily temperatures in Los Angeles, New York, and London.

17 One night I had to look at a page from the Bible for three minutes and then report everything I could remember. "Now Jehoshaphat had riches and honor in abundance and . . . that's all I remember, Ma," I said.

18 And after seeing my mother's disappointed face once again, something inside of me began to die. I hated the tests, the raised hopes and failed expectations. Before going to bed that night, I looked in the mirror above the bathroom sink and when I saw only my face staring back—and that it would always be this ordinary face—I began to cry. Such a sad, ugly girl! I made high-pitched noises like a crazed animal, trying to scratch out the face in the mirror.

19 And then I saw what seemed to be the prodigy side of me—because I had never seen that face before. I looked at my reflection, blinking so that I could see more clearly. The girl staring back at me was angry, powerful. This girl and I were the same. I had new thoughts, willful thoughts, or rather thoughts filled with lots of won'ts. I won't let her change me, I promised myself. I won't be what I'm not.

So now on nights when my mother presented her tests, I performed listlessly, my head propped on one arm. I pretended to be bored. And I was. I got so bored I started counting the bellows of the foghorns out on the bay while my mother drilled me in other areas. The sound was comforting and reminded me of the cow jumping over the moon. And the next day, I played a game with myself, seeing if my mother would give up on me before eight bellows. After a while I usually counted only one, maybe two bellows at most. At last she was beginning to give up hope. 20

TWO or three months had gone by without any mention of my being a prodigy again. And then one day my mother was watching *The Ed Sullivan Show* on TV. The TV was old and the sound kept shorting out. Every time my mother got halfway up from the sofa to adjust the set, the sound would go back on and Ed would be talking. As soon as she sat down, Ed would go silent again. She got up, the TV broke into loud piano music. She sat down. Silence. Up and down, back and forth, quiet and loud. It was like a stiff embraceless dance between her and the TV set. Finally she stood by the set with her hand on the sound dial. 21

She seemed entranced by the music, a little frenzied piano piece with this mesmerizing quality, sort of quick passages and then teasing lilting ones before it returned to the quick playful parts. 22

*"Ni kan,"* my mother said, calling me over with hurried hand gestures, "Look here." 23

I could see why my mother was fascinated by the music. It was being pounded out by a little Chinese girl, about nine years old, with a Peter Pan haircut. The girl had the sauciness of a Shirley Temple. She was proudly modest like a proper Chinese child. And she also did this fancy sweep of a curtsy, so that the fluffy skirt of her white dress cascaded slowly to the floor like the petals of a large carnation. 24

In spite of these warning signs, I wasn't worried. Our family had no piano and we couldn't afford to buy one, let alone reams of sheet music and piano lessons. So I could be generous in my comments when my mother bad-mouthed the little girl on TV. 25

"Play note right, but doesn't sound good! No singing sound," complained my mother. 26

"What are you picking on her for?" I said carelessly. "She's pretty good. Maybe she's not the best, but she's trying hard." I knew almost immediately I would be sorry I said that. 27

28 "Just like you," she said. "Not the best. Because you not trying." She gave a little huff as she let go of the sound dial and sat down on the sofa.

29 The little Chinese girl sat down also to play an encore of "Anitra's Dance" by Grieg. I remember the song, because later on I had to learn how to play it.

30 THREE days after watching *The Ed Sullivan Show,* my mother told me what my schedule would be for piano lessons and piano practice. She had talked to Mr. Chong, who lived on the first floor of our apartment building. Mr. Chong was a retired piano teacher and my mother had traded housecleaning services for weekly lessons and a piano for me to practice on every day, two hours a day, from four until six.

31 When my mother told me this, I felt as though I had been sent to hell. I whined and then kicked my foot a little when I couldn't stand it anymore.

32 "Why don't you like me the way I am? I'm *not* a genius! I can't play the piano. And even if I could, I wouldn't go on TV if you paid me a million dollars!" I cried.

33 My mother slapped me. "Who ask you to be genius?" she shouted. "Only ask you be your best. For you sake. You think I want you to be genius? Hnnh! What for! Who ask you!"

34 "So ungrateful," I heard her mutter in Chinese. "If she had as much talent as she has temper, she would be famous now."

35 Mr. Chong, whom I secretly nicknamed Old Chong, was very strange, always tapping his fingers to the silent music of an invisible orchestra. He looked ancient in my eyes. He had lost most of the hair on top of his head, and he wore thick glasses and had eyes that always looked tired and sleepy. But he must have been younger than I thought, since he lived with his mother and was not yet married.

36 I met Old Lady Chong once and that was enough. She had this peculiar smell like a baby that had done something in its pants. And her fingers felt like a dead person's, like an old peach I once found in the back of the refrigerator; the skin just slid off the meat when I picked it up.

37 I soon found out why Old Chong had retired from teaching piano. He was deaf. "Like Beethoven!" he shouted to me. "We're both listening only in our head!" And he would start to conduct his frantic silent sonatas.

38 Our lessons went like this. He would open the book and point to different things, explaining their purpose: "Key! Treble! Bass! No sharps or flats! So this is C major! Listen now and play after me!"

39 And then he would play the C scale a few times, a simple chord, and then, as if inspired by an old unreachable itch, he gradually added more notes and running trills and a pounding bass until the music was really something quite grand.

40 I would play after him, the simple scale, the simple chord, and then I just played some nonsense that sounded like a cat running up and down on top of garbage cans. Old Chong smiled and applauded and then said, "Very good! But now you must learn to keep time!"

41 So that's how I discovered that Old Chong's eyes were too slow to keep up with the wrong notes I was playing. He went through the motions in half-time. To help me keep rhythm, he stood behind me, pushing down on my right shoulder for every beat. He balanced pennies on top of my wrists so I would keep them still as I slowly played scales and arpeggios. He had me curve my hand around an apple and keep that shape when playing chords. He marched stiffly to show me how to make each finger dance up and down, staccato like an obedient little soldier.

42 He taught me all these things, and that was how I also learned I could be lazy and get away with mistakes, lots of mistakes. If I hit the wrong notes because I hadn't practiced enough, I never corrected myself. I just kept playing in rhythm. And Old Chong kept conducting his own private reverie.

43 So maybe I never really gave myself a fair chance. I did pick up the basics pretty quickly, and I might have become a good

pianist at that young age. But I was so determined not to try, not to be anybody different that I learned to play only the most ear-splitting preludes, the most discordant hymns.

44 Over the next year, I practiced like this, dutifully in my own way. And then one day I heard my mother and her friend Lindo Jong both talking in a loud bragging tone of voice so others could hear. It was after church, and I was leaning against the brick wall wearing a dress with stiff white petticoats. Auntie Lindo's daughter, Waverly, who was about my age, was standing farther down the wall about five feet away. We had grown up together and shared all the closeness of two sisters squabbling over crayons and dolls. In other words, for the most part, we hated each other. I thought she was snotty. Waverly Jong had gained a certain amount of fame as "Chinatown's Littlest Chinese Chess Champion."

45 "She bring home too many trophy," lamented Auntie Lindo that Sunday. "All day she play chess. All day I have no time do nothing but dust off her winnings." She threw a scolding look at Waverly, who pretended not to see her.

46 "You lucky you don't have this problem," said Auntie Lindo with a sigh to my mother.

47 And my mother squared her shoulders and bragged: "Our problem worser than yours. If we ask Jing-mei wash dish, she hear nothing but music. It's like you can't stop this natural talent."

48 And right then I was determined to put a stop to her foolish pride.

49 A FEW weeks later, Old Chong and my mother conspired to have me play in a talent show which would be held in the church hall. By then, my parents had saved up enough to buy me a secondhand piano, a black Wurlitzer spinet with a scarred bench. It was the showpiece of our living room.

50 For the talent show, I was to play a piece called "Pleading Child" from Schumann's *Scenes from Childhood*. It was a simple, moody piece that sounded more difficult than it was. I was supposed to memorize the whole thing, playing the repeat parts twice to make the piece sound longer. But I dawdled over it, playing a few bars and then cheating, looking up to see what notes followed. I never really listened to what I was playing. I daydreamed about being somewhere else, about being someone else.

51 The part I liked to practice best was the fancy curtsy: right foot out, touch the rose on the carpet with a pointed foot, sweep to the side, left leg bends, look up and smile.

My parents invited all the couples from the Joy Luck Club to witness my debut. Auntie Lindo and Uncle Tin were there. Waverly and her two older brothers had also come. The first two rows were filled with children both younger and older than I was. The littlest ones got to go first. They recited simple nursery rhymes, squawked out tunes on miniature violins, twirled Hula Hoops, pranced in pink ballet tutus, and when they bowed or curtsied, the audience would sigh in unison, "Awww," and then clap enthusiastically. 52

When my turn came, I was very confident. I remember my childish excitement. It was as if I knew, without a doubt, that the prodigy side of me really did exist. I had no fear whatsoever, no nervousness. I remember thinking to myself, This is it! This is it! I looked out over the audience, at my mother's blank face, my father's yawn, Auntie Lindo's stiff-lipped smile, Waverly's sulky expression. I had on a white dress layered with sheets of lace, and a pink bow in my Peter Pan haircut. As I sat down I envisioned people jumping to their feet and Ed Sullivan rushing up to introduce me to everyone on TV. 53

And I started to play. It was so beautiful. I was so caught up in how lovely I looked that at first I didn't worry how I would sound. So it was a surprise to me when I hit the first wrong note and I realized something didn't sound quite right. And then I hit another and another followed that. A chill started at the top of my head and began to trickle down. Yet I couldn't stop playing, as though my hands were bewitched. I kept thinking my fingers would adjust themselves back, like a train switching to the right track. I played this strange jumble through two repeats, the sour notes staying with me all the way to the end. 54

When I stood up, I discovered my legs were shaking. Maybe I had just been nervous and the audience, like Old Chong, had seen me go through the right motions and had not heard anything wrong at all. I swept my right foot out, went down on my knee, looked up and smiled. The room was quiet, except for Old Chong, who was beaming and shouting, "Bravo! Bravo! Well done!" But then I saw my mother's face, her stricken face. The audience clapped weakly, and as I walked back to my chair, with my whole face 55 quivering as I tried not to cry, I heard a little boy whisper loudly to his mother, "That was awful," and the mother whispered back, "Well, she certainly tried."

56 And now I realized how many people were in the audience, the whole world it seemed. I was aware of eyes burning into my back. I felt the shame of my mother and father as they sat stiffly throughout the rest of the show.

57 We could have escaped during intermission. Pride and some strange sense of honor must have anchored my parents to their chairs. And so we watched it all: the eighteen-year-old boy with a fake mustache who did a magic show and juggled flaming hoops while riding a unicycle. The breasted girl with white makeup who sang from *Madama Butterfly* and got honorable mention. And the eleven-year-old boy who won first prize playing a tricky violin song that sounded like a busy bee.

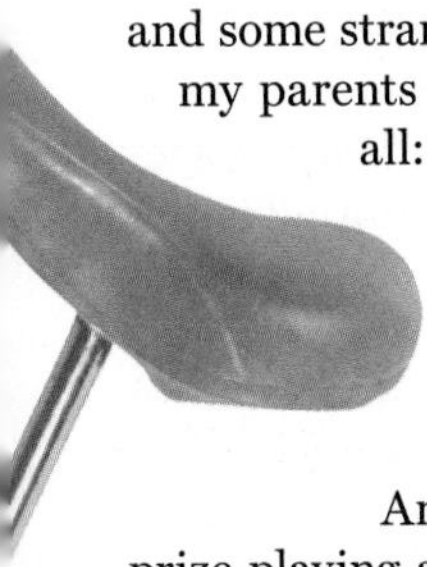

58 After the show, the Hsus, the Jongs, and the St. Clairs from the Joy Luck Club came up to my mother and father.

59 "Lots of talented kids," Auntie Lindo said vaguely, smiling broadly.

60 "That was somethin' else," said my father, and I wondered if he was referring to me in a humorous way, or whether he even remembered what I had done.

61 Waverly looked at me and shrugged her shoulders. "You aren't a genius like me," she said matter-of-factly. And if I hadn't felt so bad, I would have pulled her braids and punched her stomach.

62 But my mother's expression was what devastated me: a quiet, blank look that said she had lost everything. I felt the same way, and it seemed as if everybody were now coming up, like gawkers at the scene of an accident, to see what parts were actually missing. When we got on the bus to go home, my father was humming the busy-bee tune and my mother was silent. I kept thinking she wanted to wait until we got home before shouting at me. But when my father unlocked the door to our apartment, my mother walked in and then went to the back, into the bedroom. No accusations. No blame. And in a way, I felt disappointed. I had been waiting for her to start shouting, so I could shout back and cry and blame her for all my misery.

63 I ASSUMED my talent-show fiasco meant I never had to play the piano again. But two days later, after school, my mother came out of the kitchen and saw me watching TV.

"Four clock," she reminded me as if it were any other day. I was stunned, as though she were asking me to go through the talent-show torture again. I wedged myself more tightly in front of the TV. 64

"Turn off TV," she called from the kitchen five minutes later. 65

I didn't budge. And then I decided. I didn't have to do what my mother said anymore. I wasn't her slave: This wasn't China. I had listened to her before and look what happened. She was the stupid one. 66

She came out from the kitchen and stood in the arched entryway of the living room. "Four clock," she said once again, louder. 67

"I'm not going to play anymore," I said nonchalantly. "Why should I? I'm not a genius." 68

She walked over and stood in front of the TV. I saw her chest was heaving up and down in an angry way. 69

"No!" I said, and I now felt stronger, as if my true self had finally emerged. So this was what had been inside me all along. 70

"No! I won't!" I screamed. 71

She yanked me by the arm, pulled me off the floor, snapped off the TV. She was frighteningly strong, half pulling, half carrying me toward the piano as I kicked the throw rugs under my feet. She lifted me up and onto the hard bench. I was sobbing by now, looking at her bitterly. Her chest was heaving even more and her mouth was open, smiling crazily as if she were pleased I was crying. 72

"You want me to be someone that I'm not!" I sobbed. "I'll never be the kind of daughter you want me to be!" 73

"Only two kinds of daughters," she shouted in Chinese. "Those who are obedient and those who follow their own mind! Only one kind of daughter can live in this house. Obedient daughter!" 74

"Then I wish I wasn't your daughter. I wish you weren't my mother," I shouted. As I said these things I got scared. It felt like worms and toads and slimy things crawling out of my chest, but it also felt good, as if this awful side of me had surfaced, at last. 75

"Too late to change this," my mother said shrilly. 76

And I could sense her anger rising to its breaking point. I wanted to see it spill over. And that's when I remembered the babies she had lost in China, the ones we never talked about. "Then I wish I'd never been born!" I shouted. "I wish I were dead! Like them." 77

It was as if I had said the magic words. Alakazam!—and her face went blank, her mouth closed, her arms went slack, and she backed out of the room, stunned, as if she were blowing away like a small brown leaf, thin, brittle, lifeless. 78

79 IT was not the only disappointment my mother felt in me. In the years that followed, I failed her so many times, each time asserting my own will, my right to fall short of expectations. I didn't get straight As. I didn't become class president. I didn't get into Stanford. I dropped out of college.

80 For unlike my mother, I did not believe I could be anything I wanted to be. I could only be me.

81 And for all those years, we never talked about the disaster at the recital or my terrible accusations afterward at the piano bench. All that remained unchecked, like a betrayal that was now unspeakable. So I never found a way to ask her why she had hoped for something so large that failure was inevitable.

82 And even worse, I never asked her what frightened me the most: Why had she given up hope?

83 For after our struggle at the piano, she never mentioned my playing again. The lessons stopped. The lid to the piano was closed, shutting out the dust, my misery, and her dreams.

84 So she surprised me. A few years ago, she offered to give me the piano, for my thirtieth birthday. I had not played in all those years. I saw the offer as a sign of forgiveness, a tremendous burden removed.

85 "Are you sure?" I asked shyly. "I mean, won't you and Dad miss it?"

86 "No, this your piano," she said firmly. "Always your piano. You only one can play."

87 "Well, I probably can't play anymore," I said. "It's been years."

88 "You pick up fast," said my mother, as if she knew this was certain. "You have natural talent. You could been genius if you want to."

89 "No, I couldn't."

90 "You just not trying," said my mother. And she was neither angry nor sad. She said it as if to announce a fact that could never be disproved. "Take it," she said.

But I didn't at first. It was enough that she had offered it to me. And after that, every time I saw it in my parents' living room, standing in front of the bay windows, it made me feel proud, as if it were a shiny trophy I had won back. 91

LAST week I sent a tuner over to my parent's apartment and had the piano reconditioned, for purely sentimental reasons. My mother had died a few months before and I had been been getting things in order for my father, a little bit at a time. I put the jewelry in special silk pouches. The sweaters she had knitted in yellow, pink, bright orange—all the colors I hated—I put those in moth-proof boxes. I found some old Chinese silk dresses, the kind with little slits up the sides. I rubbed the old silk against my skin, then wrapped them in tissue and decided to take them home with me. 92

After I had the piano tuned, I opened the lid and touched the keys. It sounded even richer than I remembered. Really, it was a very good piano. Inside the bench were the same exercise notes with handwritten scales, the same secondhand music books with their covers held together with yellow tape. 93

I opened up the Schumann book to the dark little piece I had played at the recital. It was on the left-hand side of the page, "Pleading Child." It looked more difficult than I remembered. I played a few bars, surprised at how easily the notes came back to me. 94

I played a few bars, surprised at how easily the notes came back to me.

And for the first time, or so it seemed, I noticed the piece on the right-hand side. It was called "Perfectly Contented." I tried to play this one as well. It had a lighter melody but the same flowing rhythm and turned out to be quite easy. "Pleading Child" was shorter but slower; "Perfectly Contented" was longer, but faster. And after I played them both a few times, I realized they were two halves of the same song. 95

IF you like "Two Kinds," you may also like other stories with distinctive voices, such as that of Bernard Malamud's marriage broker in "The Magic Barrel" (chapter 6) or Gish Jen's irate speaker in "Who's Irish?" (chapter 5).

**GOING FURTHER** Amy Tan says in her interview that she is reading writers in translation to get a different point of view. You may be interested in some of these works as well, such as Dai Sijie's *Balzac and the Little Chinese Seamstress,* or *The Sand Child,* by Moroccan Tahar Ben Jelloun.

# Writing from Reading

### Summarize

1 Some of these memories are comic, some bitter, some loving, some aggrieved. Summarize the daughter's reactions to her mother's expectations and see how and where they change.

### Analyze Craft

2 All dialogue by the narrator's mother is written in broken English, even when she is speaking in her native Chinese. What effect does this dialect have on your impression of the mother?

### Analyze Voice

3 Tan writes as a first-generation American, a writer from the West Coast. Are there any details in the story that highlight her situation? Is there anything in the way the narrator speaks that calls these facts to mind?

### Synthesize Summary and Analysis

4 How does the dialect in the mother's speech reflected in the dialogue between the mother and child establish the narrator's identity as a second-generation Chinese American?

### Interpret the Story

5 The first line of "Two Kinds" reads, "My mother believed you could be anything you wanted to be in America." This line is repeated throughout the story. Find instances in the story that prove or refute this statement. Based on the story, do you think Tan believes this idea?

# Suggestions for Writing

1. Reread "Optimists." How does your understanding of it differ from the first reading? How did Ford's own comments about the story and his goals as a writer enhance or diminish your responses?
2. Which character do you feel you know better—Mitya or Frank? What elements of craft or voice has the author used to help you know this character? Give examples.
3. Chekhov, a great playwright, envisions "Rapture" almost as a one-act play and sets it up "in scene." How would it be altered if in fact this were a play and not short fiction? What role does dialogue play in "Optimists" and "Two Kinds"? Write an essay that explores the functions of dialogue in the chapter's three stories.
4. Reread the opening sentences of "Optimists," "Two Kinds," and "Rapture." What is the dramatic effect of these opening sentences? How do they work to launch the stories?

# 3 Writing about Fiction

WASH the white clothes on Monday and put them on the stone heap; wash the color clothes on Tuesday and put them on the clothesline to dry; don't walk barehead in the hot sun; cook pumpkin fritters in very hot sweet oil; soak your little cloths right after you take them off . . .

*—from "Girl" by Jamaica Kincaid*

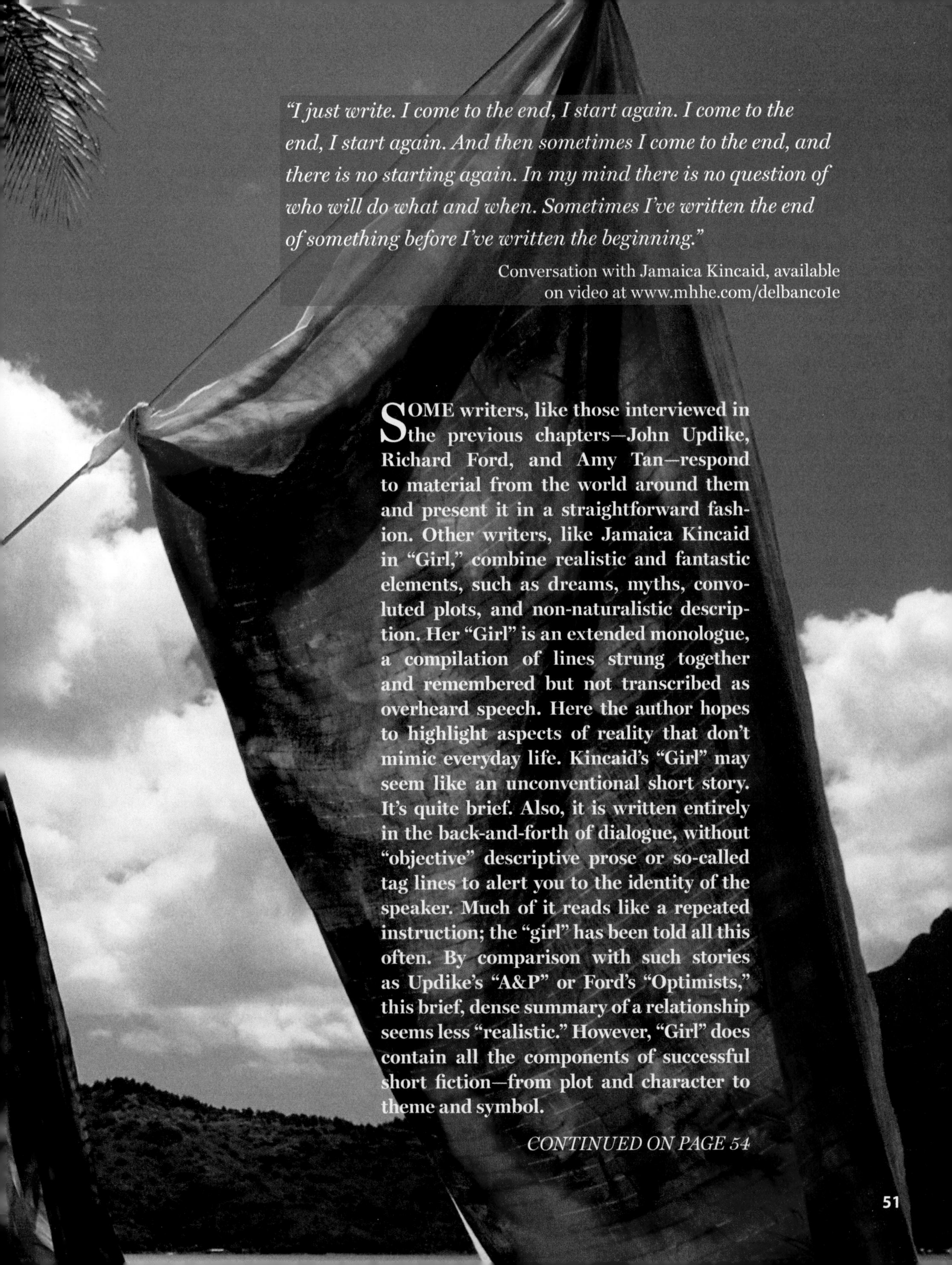

*"I just write. I come to the end, I start again. I come to the end, I start again. And then sometimes I come to the end, and there is no starting again. In my mind there is no question of who will do what and when. Sometimes I've written the end of something before I've written the beginning."*

Conversation with Jamaica Kincaid, available on video at www.mhhe.com/delbanco1e

**SOME writers, like those interviewed in the previous chapters—John Updike, Richard Ford, and Amy Tan—respond to material from the world around them and present it in a straightforward fashion. Other writers, like Jamaica Kincaid in "Girl," combine realistic and fantastic elements, such as dreams, myths, convoluted plots, and non-naturalistic description. Her "Girl" is an extended monologue, a compilation of lines strung together and remembered but not transcribed as overheard speech. Here the author hopes to highlight aspects of reality that don't mimic everyday life. Kincaid's "Girl" may seem like an unconventional short story. It's quite brief. Also, it is written entirely in the back-and-forth of dialogue, without "objective" descriptive prose or so-called tag lines to alert you to the identity of the speaker. Much of it reads like a repeated instruction; the "girl" has been told all this often. By comparison with such stories as Updike's "A&P" or Ford's "Optimists," this brief, dense summary of a relationship seems less "realistic." However, "Girl" does contain all the components of successful short fiction—from plot and character to theme and symbol.**

*CONTINUED ON PAGE 54*

*It's more important to read than to write.*

*I'm really interested in breaking the form. . . .*

# Q&A
# *A Conversation on Writing*

## Jamaica Kincaid

### On Reading and Writing

The advice I always give to people who are going to write is: It's more important to read than to write. I sometimes think I became a writer really to have the opportunity to read some more, because it's the only excuse. It's the only way you are really allowed to read and say, "Well I'm writing. You think I'm reading but really it's part of writing." . . . So, no, reading is the most important thing, and not your own work, reading other things.

### On Form, the Voice in "Girl," and Her Mother

Whatever a novel is, I'm not it, and whatever a short story is, I'm not it. If I had to follow these forms, I couldn't write. I'm really interested in breaking the form. . . . With "Girl," I wanted to write something new. . . . Certainly at the time I wrote ["Girl"], I didn't know how to interpret my own experience. I had only the voice . . . of my mother . . . firmly embedded in and interwoven into the way I express myself. . . . I was taught all those instructions. Yes, everything was by her.

### On the Writing Process

I generally only have one draft. The first draft is the last draft, but that's because I tend not to commit things to paper before I've fully worked them out in my head. I'm really writing all the time; it sometimes will take me a week to complete a sentence. But that's because it's not right, it doesn't sound right the way I see it in my head. And then when it's completed, and I can judge it, I can see how it works inside my head, I put it to paper and there it is.

To watch this entire interview and hear the author read from "Girl," go to **www.mhhe.com/delbanco1e**.

Jamaica Kincaid was born Elaine Potter Richardson in St. Johns, Antigua, a small Caribbean island in the British West Indies. Images of Kincaid's mother and the close bond they shared run through much of her writing. Kincaid was a precocious child educated in the government school system, which was largely shaped by British influence and which fostered in this particular student a growing disdain for England. Indeed, the British use the expression "don't tell stories" when they reprimand their children for lying—but Jamaica Kincaid has been telling stories ever since.

At the age of seventeen, Kincaid traveled to the United States to work as a nanny for the children of affluent families—an experience reported in her novel *Lucy.* Before long she found her way to New York City, changed her name, and began writing for magazines such as *Ms., Ingenue,* and the *Village Voice.* She became a regular writer for *The New Yorker,* which published her first short stories as well as brief prose pieces in its "Talk of the Town" page; these have been collected in *Talk Stories* (2001).

Kincaid is perhaps best known for turning the facts of her personal history into fictions that blend fantasy and reality, the imagined and the actual. Her first published collection of stories, *At the Bottom of the River* (1983), and novels such as *Annie John* (1985), *Lucy* (1991), *The Autobiography of My Mother* (1996), and *Mr. Potter* (2002) all explore the boundaries of actual and imagined life, or memoir and dream. Her books defy easy classification, falling into the gray area between autobiography and fiction: the incantatory rhythms of her first-person narrator have the quality of song.

**RESEARCH ASSIGNMENT** In her interview, Kincaid talks about her relationship with her mother. Listen to the interview and comment on how you think this influences the writing of "Girl."

**AS YOU READ** As you read "Girl," ask yourself who the main speaker is and how she reveals herself. If she were speaking to you, how would you feel? How do you feel as you listen to her? How does "Girl" achieve the inclusion of all the traditional elements of fiction, from plot to theme, in such limited space?

# Girl (1983)

1 WASH the white clothes on Monday and put them on the stone heap; wash the color clothes on Tuesday and put them on the clothesline to dry; don't walk barehead in the hot sun; cook pumpkin fritters in very hot sweet oil; soak your little cloths right after you take them off; when buying cotton to make yourself a nice blouse, be sure that it doesn't have gum on it, because that way it won't hold up well after a wash; soak salt fish overnight before you cook it; is it true that you sing *benna*[1] in Sunday school?; always eat your food in such a way that it won't turn someone else's stomach; on Sundays try to walk like a lady and not like the slut you are so bent on becoming; don't sing benna in Sunday school; you mustn't speak to wharf-rat boys, not even to give directions; don't eat fruits on the street—flies will follow you, *but I don't sing benna on Sundays at all and never in Sunday school;* this is how to sew a button; this is how to make a buttonhole for the button you have just sewed on; this is how to hem a dress when you see the hem coming down and so to prevent yourself from looking like the slut I know you are so bent on becoming; this is how you iron your father's khaki shirt so that it doesn't have a crease; this is how you iron your father's khaki pants so that they don't have a crease; this is how you grow okra—far from the house, because okra tree harbors red ants; when you are growing *dasheen,*[2] make sure it gets plenty of water or else it makes your throat itch when you are eating it; this is how you sweep a corner; this is how you sweep a whole house; this is how you sweep a yard; this is how you smile to someone you don't like too much; this is how you smile to someone you don't like at all; this is how you smile to someone you like completely; this is how you set a table for tea; this is how you set a table for dinner; this is how you set a table for dinner with an important guest; this is how you set a table for lunch; this is how you set a table for breakfast; this is how to behave in the presence of men who don't know you very well, and this way they won't recognize immediately the slut I have warned you against becoming; be sure to wash every day, even if it is with your own spit; don't squat down to play marbles—you are not a boy, you know; don't pick people's flowers—you might catch something; don't throw stones at blackbirds, because it might not be a blackbird at all; this is how to make a bread pudding; this is how to make *doukona;*[3] this is how to make *pepper pot;*[4] this is how to make a good medicine for a cold; this is how to make a good medicine to throw away a child before it even becomes a child; this is how to catch a fish; this is how to throw back a fish you don't like, and that way something bad won't fall on you; this is how to bully a man; this is how a man bullies you; this is how to love a man, and if this doesn't work there are other ways, and if they don't work don't feel too bad about giving up; this is how to spit up in the air if you feel like it, and this is how to move quick so that it doesn't fall on you; this is how to make ends meet; always squeeze bread to make sure it's fresh; *but what if the baker won't let me feel the bread?;* you mean to say that after all you are really going to be the kind of woman who the baker won't let near the bread?

. . . this is how you smile to someone you don't like too much . . .

[1]A form of folk music that originated in the Caribbean islands of Antigua and Barbuda and is usually about lewd or scandalous subjects.

[2]A tropical plant, similar in appearance to elephant ear plants, that grows up to seven feet tall and has edible roots.

[3]A spicy pudding.

[4]A Caribbean stew made of meat, vegetables, and spices.

IF you like "Girl," you might have a taste for magical realism—a style that emerged in the literature of the Caribbean region during the mid-twentieth century and gained practitioners throughout South America—and would enjoy reading the work of Gabriel García Márquez, whose story "The Handsomest Drowned Man in the World" appears in Stories for Further Reading.

**GOING FURTHER** In her interview, Kincaid says "Girl" is in a way a condensed version of her novel *Annie John,* which you might like to read in relation to this short work.

# Writing from Reading

### Summarize

1 Who are the story's characters, and what do you know about them?

### Analyze Craft

2 Consider the structure of the story, the order in which the author presents the pieces of advice. How important is the organization of information, and what does it mean?

3 What do you know about the setting of the story? Give examples that reveal and describe it.

4 Is there dialogue in the story? If so, what form does it take and what function does it serve?

### Analyze Voice

5 How does the way the girl receives and responds to advice serve to characterize her? Is she a passive character? Why or why not?

### Synthesize Summary and Analysis

6 What are the distinct characteristics of the two voices in the story? Discuss how these two voices help generate the implied setting and motion of the story. How would your mental image of the story change if Kincaid had not included the girl's responses?

### Interpret the Story

7 In her interview, Kincaid says that the voice in "Girl" is the voice of her mother, but she also says that there is no difference between her voice and the voice in which she writes. Discuss whether Kincaid has captured her mother's voice, or whether she has filtered that voice through her own.

*(CONTINUED FROM PAGE 51)*

## FROM READING TO WRITING

"I think that you really can't be a writer without being a reader."
Conversation with ZZ Packer

The first two chapters discussed how reading critically is the means to get your writing started. You look at the title of the work, find out about the author and the context within which a piece was written, and record your impressions by annotating a text or keeping a reading journal about how the elements of craft and the writer's voice work in a particular story. Whatever your assignment—a summary of the work, a short critical response, or a full-fledged research paper requiring multiple sources—one crucial component of writing effectively emerges when you discover something in the subject that is meaningful to *you*. Here is a quick checklist for writing a paper that may help you get started.

# Checklist for Writing

✓ EXPLORE YOUR IDEAS.

Journal, annotate, brainstorm, freewrite, surf the Web, browse the library, and recognize this: Finding meaning is a complex issue that involves multiple perspectives. Toward what aspect of a story do you find yourself turning in thought? What aspect of the story stirs your emotions the most? These turns of mind and feeling will often alert you to your special interest in a story.

✓ DEVELOP A WORKING THESIS.

Make a strong claim that is specific and significant. To maintain a thoughtful tone, you may want to frame your claim as a question you will explore throughout your paper.

✓ CREATE A PLAN.

Outlines (formal and informal) can help you support and develop your claim with evidence.

✓ GENERATE A FIRST DRAFT.

Avoid straight summary (unless this is the assignment), and, unless you revise in your head like Jamaica Kincaid, give yourself time to go back to revise, edit, and format your paper. At this point you may want to get comments from other readers; their comments may help you revise your paper.

✓ REVISE YOUR DRAFT.

Focus on the purpose of your writing and rethink to revise: test your thesis (an exploration of any topic might lead you somewhere you didn't originally set out to go); check that your introduction states your claim; make sure the organization of your paper is clear; note whether your paragraphs are unified and cohesive; check the effectiveness of your transitions; check and double-check your use of quotation and paraphrase; make sure your conclusion answers the question of why your topic (as expressed in your thesis) is important. Save your drafts, label revised drafts with different names, and print hard copies frequently.

✓ EDIT YOUR SENTENCES.

Grammar-checkers are unreliable, and editing is more than a spell-check. A spell-check can't tell you if your sentences are correct and clear.

✓ PROOFREAD AND FORMAT YOUR PAPER.

Spell-checkers don't always catch your typos. Read over your paper carefully and format it according to the instructions of your instructor, or follow the guidelines outlined by the Modern Language Association. Some tips: Use a 12-point typeface, ragged right margin, one-inch margins on all four sides of your paper, double-space, and assign page numbers. Usually a paper will need your name, the professor's name, and the course and section number at the top of the page.

## A SAMPLE STUDENT ESSAY IN PROGRESS

When Andrew Papadopoulis read "Girl," he annotated the story and took notes on his initial responses. Both his annotations and his notes, reproduced here, show him engaged with the text. He reads *actively* to scrutinize the story's language, asks questions about possible meanings, records thoughts and reactions, and notes important insights. By highlighting and annotating the story, this student interacts, or converses, with it, moving back and forth between the story's details and his developing understanding of those details. As he notes in his commentary, "Girl" condenses the elements of fiction into a single paragraph.

"My writing process, I don't really have one. I read. I find that both walk hand in hand, that when I'm writing, I have to read. Somehow I find that it feeds my own work, and not in a direct way." Conversation with Chimamanda Ngozi Adichie

Andrew focuses on the relationship between the story's two main characters—the second-person narrator, who uses *you* and commands ("Wash the white clothes on Monday"), and the listener, the girl of the story's title. He uncovers meaning from the details contained within this brief narrative to understand who the main characters are and where the story takes place. He notes those clues that point to the nature of the relationship between the speaker and the listener—the speaker's repeated use of the word *slut;* her admonitory, accusatory, and sometimes humorous tone; her reference to "your father"; and her advice on how to behave like a proper woman who tends to home and husband. Andrew interprets the story as an interaction between mother and daughter and isolates the details that reveal the story's domestic setting: okra, dasheen, doukona, and a host of household chores. He makes connections between the story's portrayal of domesticity and its broader implications of gender roles, identity, and society.

Next Andrew develops this initial exploration into a full-length essay that examines how Kincaid's distinctive use of literary techniques—especially the way her narrator addresses the readers directly with *you* (second-person point of view, see chapter 7)—allows the reader to feel like a participant in the story, an eavesdropper on a series of telling exchanges between mother and daughter. As this student demonstrates, fiction can be a lens through which we better visualize our relationship to literature and to the world. It can help us to see aspects of our own lives in new ways, or to catch a glimpse of imaginative worlds we find strange and interesting.

"There is a kind of magic to writing. . . . Anybody here who has written a term paper knows that there is a kind of magic to it. You don't know what it will be. You take notes, but the final product is utterly different from your initial conception of it. That's the joy of writing something." Conversation with T. Coraghessan Boyle

We emphasize throughout this text that literary works don't possess a *single* meaning, but rather *multiple* meanings; these are in turn revealed by reading and writing about a story with a close critical eye. We offer this not as a "finished" critique of "Girl" but as a way of demonstrating the process of responding to a text.

The following sections chart Andrew's progress as he works through his response to this writing assignment:

> Assignment: Expand the close reading you completed of Jamaica Kincaid's "Girl" into a 4- to 5-page essay in which you analyze one or both of the story's main characters. Your analysis should take into account Kincaid's distinctive voice and use of literary techniques.

# An Interactive Reading

Written in second person: directed at whom?

Wash the white clothes on Monday and put them on the stone heap; wash the color clothes on Tuesday and put them on the clothesline to dry; don't walk barehead in the hot sun; cook pumpkin fritters in very hot sweet oil; soak your little cloths right after you take them off; when buying cotton to make yourself a nice blouse, be sure that it doesn't have gum on it, because that way it won't hold up well after a wash; soak salt fish overnight before you cook it; is it true that you sing benna in Sunday school?; always eat your food in such a way that it won't turn someone else's stomach; on Sundays try to walk like a lady and not like the slut you are so bent on becoming; don't sing benna in Sunday school; you mustn't speak to wharf-rat boys, not even to give directions; don't eat fruits on the street—flies will follow you; *but I don't sing benna on Sundays at all and never in Sunday school;* this is how to sew a button; this is how to make a buttonhole for the button you have just sewed on; this is how to hem a dress when you see the hem coming down and so to prevent yourself from looking like the slut I know you are so bent on becoming; this is how you iron your father's khaki shirt so that it doesn't have a crease; this is how you iron your father's khaki pants so that they don't have a crease; this is how you grow okra—far from the house, because okra tree harbors red ants; when you are growing dasheen, make sure it gets plenty of water or else it makes your throat itch when you are eating it; this is how you sweep a corner; this is how you sweep a whole house; this is how you sweep a yard; this is how you smile to someone you don't like too much; this is how you smile to someone you don't like at all; this is how you smile to someone you like completely; this is how you set a table for tea; this is how you set a table for dinner; this is how you set a table for dinner with an important guest; this is how you set a table for lunch; this is how you set a table for breakfast; this is how to behave in the presence of men who don't know you very

Advice for a variety of situations

Narrator asks a question

Now it's a command: "Don't sing . . ."

Voice change: Listener responds . . .

But completely ignored . . .

Loaded term—gender implications?

Why the repetition?

Suggest mother-daughter conversation

Now "outdoor" directions

No periods anywhere; very tense, intense

well, and this way they won't recognize immediately the slut I have warned you against becoming; be sure to wash every day, even if it is with your own spit; don't squat down to play marbles—you are not a boy, you know, don't pick people's flowers—you might catch something; don't throw stones at blackbirds, because it might not be a blackbird at all; this is how to make a bread pudding; this is how to make doukona, this is how to make pepper pot; this is how to make a good medicine for a cold; this is how to make a good medicine to throw away a child before it becomes a child; this is how to catch a fish; this is how to throw back a fish you don't like, and that way something bad won't fall on you; this is how to bully a man; this is how a man bullies you; this is how to love a man, and if this doesn't work there are other ways, and if they don't work don't feel too bad about giving up; this is how to spit up in the air if you feel like it, and this is how to move quick so that it doesn't fall on you; this is how to make ends meet; always squeeze bread to make sure it's fresh; *but what if the baker won't let me feel the bread?;* you mean to say that after all you are really going to be the kind of woman who the baker won't let near the bread?

What else would a blackbird be? A soul?

Unwanted fish and child treated the same.

Attitude toward love is same as attitude toward work, etc.

Finally acknowledged at the end . . .

## Initial Response

Write an initial response to the text without concern for how formal it sounds or even how logically it flows. In other words, this response is simply your first impressions of the story. Did something stand out to you as important? Were there confusing elements? Don't worry at this point if you don't understand major parts of the story; the more you review the notes you've made and the text itself, the more you will begin to understand.

The first time I read "Girl," I thought it might be difficult to find a lot to say about such a short piece. But after a second and third reading, I realized the story is packed with layers of detail that make it a rich fictional work. I tried to highlight revealing words and phrases and draw connections among sections to show how Kincaid develops elements of craft—like character and setting—and how Kincaid's voice affected my understanding of the story. I found the relationship between the speaker and listener especially interesting; the mother's (I think she's her mother) warnings and advice, and the daughter's sparse, interspersed retorts, define what it means (and doesn't mean) to be a "girl." Being a good "girl," of course, has all sorts of implications about being a good woman, wife, and mother. I'd like to explore these ideas further.

## Explore Your Ideas

**Freewriting** is similar to the initial response—once again, do not worry about the flow of ideas or the language you are using. The difference is that freewriting comes after you have had some time to think about the story and reread it. In a sense, it's your "second response," rather than your initial one, and as such, you may find that you have more ideas and that your freewriting runs longer.

"There's nothing worse than a sheet of blank paper in front of you." Conversation with William Kittredge

After carefully considering his assignment, Andrew reread his close reading of "Girl" and the notes he took during his initial readings of the story. Andrew then moved on to freewrite about the story, writing continuously to get his ideas down on paper, without worrying about making mistakes or whether his initial ideas could be developed into a suitable paper topic. The following excerpt comes from Andrew's freewriting exercise.

This was a very strange but a very beautiful story. For the first few lines I was def. confused, but the more I read the more I got it. It's a mother talking to her daughter, telling her everything she needs to know. I wonder where this story is set? Need to do some research to find out—need to look up a lot of the terms in the dictionary. But even w/o knowing where the story is set, I liked it. My mother always gives me tons & tons of advice. My mother and this mother are actually pretty similar in a lot of ways, even though my mother doesn't like to cook or garden or anything. It's different, too, that I'm a son not a daughter; must keep the diff. in mind. That's prob. the mark of a good piece of writing, that you can get into it even if it doesn't directly relate to you.

**Journaling** is a writing exercise that helps you focus the ideas you generated in your notes and freewriting. This is the first step in which you should begin to feel your ideas coming together to form something that will eventually become a paper. The idea you found the most interesting from your reading and notes is a good starting place for a journal entry.

Andrew put aside his freewriting for several hours and returned to the story with a fresh perspective. In the following journal entry, he expands his initial freewriting into a more focused discussion of his growing understanding of the story. He considers how the story's characterizations and point of view create interesting effects.

My initial reaction to the first few lines of "Girl" was confusion. But the further I read, the more I warmed up to the character of the narrator. I realized that she is not totally different from my mother, even though it seems clear that this mother and my mother are from very different worlds. But my mother, like the narrator, is constantly emphasizing the right way (or maybe I should say her way) of doing things. And, like the narrator, although my mother can come across as harsh, I know she cares deeply about my success in life.

What's interesting to me, also, is how or why I assume I know that this story is about a mother talking to her daughter. Maybe it's because of the word "slut"—something my mother wd obviously never say to me! And Kincaid never states this directly. In fact, in "Girl," almost nothing about character is stated directly. And yet, after reading this story, I feel like I have a good idea of who the narrator is, and, just as importantly, who the person being talked to is. It would be interesting to go back and see just where and how Kincaid reveals personality and other character details in this story.

All in all, I really enjoyed "Girl." You don't read many stories written from this perspective (the "you" perspective), and it's an interesting way to experience a narrative. Once I pushed through some initial confusion, I found "Girl" was definitely an engaging piece of writing.

**Brainstorming** may take the form of a list or a web connecting your thoughts. Once you have used a journal entry to narrow down your interests, use your brainstorming session to generate ideas on how to turn the topics that interest you most into a paper.

Andrew's freewriting and journal entry sparked more and more ideas about how he might develop his character analysis. In the following **brainstorming** excerpt, Andrew lists possible topics for his paper, charts details about the story's characterizations, and works toward a **thesis statement.**

Most interesting topics:

—narrator's personality (funny)

—daughter's personality

—setting (Caribbean)

—WHY does the mother say all this . . .

WHO is the narrator and WHO is the daughter—

Learning WHO the characters are and WHY they do things.

| CHARACTERS' ACTION | MOTIVATION |
|---|---|
| Mother telling about cooking | Teaching girl how to run a household |
| Mother telling her not to talk to wharf-rat boys | Teaching girl how to behave like a girl. My sister Eleni? |
| Girl arguing with mother | Being independent, tough |

Reading "Girl" = much interesting info

Reading the story "Girl," you can learn a lot about who the characters are and why they do what they do.

## Develop a Working Thesis

A thesis is a sentence that states the topic of the paper. More than that, a thesis is the writer's argument, the controlling idea that he or she will show and develop in the body of the essay. For more details on how to write a good thesis, see pages H-35 to H-38 in our chapter on Writing from Reading.

Andrew used his brainstorming notes to sharpen his topic and refine his **thesis.** The following drafted and revised thesis statements show Andrew's progress as he focused his claim and pruned his language.

First-draft thesis:

In "Girl," you can actually learn a lot about the characters.

Second-draft thesis:

A close reading of "Girl" reveals much about the characters of the story.

Third-draft thesis:

A close reading of "Girl" reveals a lot of information about the narrator and her daughter.

Final-draft thesis:

A close reading of "Girl" reveals that Kincaid provides a lot of information about the narrator and the "you" of the story.

Revised final-draft thesis:

A careful, close reading of "Girl" reveals that Kincaid has painted a portrait of both the narrator and the "you" to whom the story is directed.

### Create a Plan

With his thesis in mind, Andrew next considered how he would organize his paper to best support his points. He drafted a **topic outline** to guide him through the writing and revising process.

I. Introduction
   a. "Girl" initially confusing
   b. Thesis: A careful, close reading of "Girl" reveals that Kincaid provides a great deal of information about the narrator and the "you" to whom the story is directed.

II. Identity of characters
   a. Discussion of tone
   b. Analysis of clues about gender and relationship of characters
      i. Specific lines directly related to gender
      ii. Nature of narrator's advice

III. Analysis of the narrator
   a. Tone can be humorous
   b. Demonstrates warmth
IV. Analysis of the listener
   a. Independent and uninterested in mother's advice
   b. Actually similar to her mother
V. Narrator's motives
   a. Discussion of story's final line
   b. Mother's advice meant to make daughter a respectable woman
VI. Conclusion
   a. Analysis of setting of "Girl"
   b. Story transcends specific setting

## Generate a First Draft

After completing his topic outline, Andrew was now ready to write his first draft. He tried to follow the organization of his outline, making each of the important points he planned to elaborate on and support with examples in subsequent drafts.

**FIRST DRAFT**

A Mother's Advice

Jamaica Kincaid's short-short story "Girl" can seem weird, if not totally bizarre. But careful, repeated reading reveals that Kincaid provides a great deal of information about the narrator and the person the narrator talks to. In other words, "Girl" hides much beneath its mysterious surface.

The first clues as to the identity of the narrator of "Girl" can be found in the story's tone. The narrator's speech is mean and tough. From the language, it is clear that the speaker is someone who is used to being in charge, believes they know the right way to do things, and believes that the person listening must obey. For these reasons, it is likely that the narrator is a parent, speaking to his or her child.

Further, the narrator is probably a woman talking to her daughter. The narrator even says, at one point, "You are not a boy." The narrator's identity as the girl's mother is suggested by the line: "This is how you iron your father's khaki pants so

Parenthetical citation of page number is not necessary for a story printed on one page. The page reference should appear in the Works Cited only.

that they don't have a crease." This instruction suggests a relationship among the narrator, the girl, and the girl's father. The most obvious characterization of this relationship is that the speaker is the girl's mother. The nature of the advice the narrator gives only reinforces this idea, that "Girl" consists of mother-to-daughter counsel.

Kincaid offers other insight into the characters of the story. As mentioned previously, the tone suggests that the narrator is strict and authoritarian. At times, though, she can be humorous. At other times, the narrator shows affection for her daughter.

What we learn about the listener is of course filtered through the view of the narrator. From the more direct statements her mother makes, one could conclude that the girl is in grave danger of becoming a slut. But beyond this, it is possible to learn something of her personality. The sheer amount of advice she is given suggests that she has a lot to learn, at least about cooking and all of that stuff. Thus, she could very well be independent, disinterested in the traditional activities about which her mother instructs her. Even more interestingly, she is probably very similar to her mother: stubborn and strong-willed.

Why is the narrator giving so much advice? We need to look at the final line to answer that question. After the daughter, in another moment of italicized response, questions whether the baker will let her squeeze the bread to see if it's fresh, the narrator says: "You mean to say that after all you are really going to be the kind of woman who the baker won't let near the bread?" This seems to get at what the mother is trying to teach her daughter: what *kind* of woman she should turn out to be.

All the counsel the mother gives the daughter in "Girl" is specific to the setting, the Caribbean. Nonetheless, in the mother's resolve to make her daughter into the kind of woman she envisions, there is something that transcends the specifics. Every parent wants his or her child to grow up to be a respectable adult, and whether the parent goes about it by saving money for college, exposing the child to different languages and cultures, or, as in the story, giving instructions on how to behave, this drive seems as innate as eating or sleeping. Hence, nearly any mother or father can identify with what the narrator is trying to accomplish.

### WRITER'S BLOCK

Sometimes called *the midnight disease,* writer's block can be avoided, especially with freewriting, brainstorming, and other exploratory techniques to get you started. Additional strategies to avoid writer's block include:

**Resist the temptation to be a perfectionist.** Save getting the right word, the stylish phrase, or even the correct spelling for your revising and editing stages.

**Take it "bird by bird."** Writer Anne Lamott passes along her father's advice to her brother, who had procrastinated on a report about birds—"Bird by bird, buddy, just take it bird by bird"—when she counsels students to break down writing assignments into manageable units.

**Start anywhere.** If you're stuck on the beginning, pick another section. Go back later and work out the introduction.

**Generate more ideas.** If you are drawing a blank, you may need to do some more reading or brainstorming. But don't let yourself use "reading some more" as a stalling tactic.

—from Maimon et al., *A Writer's Resource*, 3rd ed. (New York: McGraw-Hill, 2009).

## Revise Your Draft

Andrew's second draft includes his changes and annotations to remind himself to clarify and refine his language, provide more textual evidence to bolster his claims, and format his paper according to MLA guidelines (see chapter 40 in this text).

"You're asking [for] a reader's time, so to my way of thinking, you owe them. You owe them clarity." Conversation with Barry Lopez

### SECOND DRAFT

Andrew Papadopoulis

Professor Delbanco

Composition 102

A Mother's Advice

Jamaica Kincaid's short-short story "Girl" can seem weird, if not totally bizarre. A full appreciation of "Girl" requires careful, and even repeated, reading. Such an approach, though, reveals that Kincaid provides a great deal of information about the narrator and the "you" to whom the story is directed. In other words, "Girl" hides much beneath its initially mysterious surface.

Why? Explain what's so weird, why you need to be careful.

Be more specific. More formal language?

Much what? Characterization? Details?

The first clues as to the identity of the narrator of "Girl" can be found in the story's tone. The narrator's speech is admonitory, domineering, and tough. From

Quote example from the story.

this blunt language, it is clear that the speaker is someone who is used to being in charge, believes he or she knows the right way to do things, and believes that the person listening must obey. For these reasons, it is likely that the narrator is a parent, speaking to his or her child.

Further, it is not difficult to conclude that the narrator is a woman, talking to her daughter. The narrator even says, at one point, "You are not a boy." The narrator's identity as the girl's mother is suggested by a different line. The narrator says: "This is how you iron your father's khaki pants so that they don't have a crease." This instruction, with its casual reference to "your father," suggests a relationship among the narrator, the girl, and the girl's father. The most obvious characterization of this relationship is that the speaker is the girl's mother, and she is telling her daughter how to iron her father's pants. The nature of the advice the narrator gives only reinforces the idea that "Girl" consists of mother-to-daughter counsel.

Explain "so what"?

Other ways this shows up?

More specific.

Kincaid offers other insight into the characters of the story. As mentioned previously, the tone suggests that the narrator is strict and authoritarian. At times, though, she can be humorous. At other times, the narrator shows affection for her daughter.

Paragraph's too short. Fill out with text examples.

What we learn about the listener is of course mainly filtered through the view of the narrator. From the more direct statements her mother makes, one could conclude that the girl is in grave danger of becoming a "slut." But beyond this, it is possible to learn something of her personality. The sheer amount of advice she is given suggests that she has a lot to learn, at least about cooking and all of that stuff. Thus, she could very well be independent, disinterested in the traditional activities about which her mother instructs her. This idea is supported by the brief moments of interaction in the story (the daughter's responses to her mother's words are set off in italics). These show her questioning her mother and arguing with her assertions. For instance, she insists, *"But I don't sing benna on Sundays at all and never in Sunday school."* From this sort of headstrong defense one can conclude that this girl is very much her mother's daughter, strong-willed and determined.

Too informal—clean up.

Need to show how mom's strong willed?

The larger motives of the narrator can be detected in the story's final line. After her daughter, in another moment of italicized response, questions whether the baker will let her squeeze the bread to see if it's fresh, the narrator says: "You mean to say that after all you are really going to be the kind of woman who the baker won't let near the bread?" This seems to get at what the mother is trying to teach her daughter. Ultimately, it is not important *what* the girl knows, but the "kind of woman" the girl becomes.

Too deep. Need to relate to the thesis—what's hidden?

Need text proof?

All the counsel the mother gives the daughter in "Girl" is specific to the setting, the Caribbean. Nonetheless, in the mother's resolve to make her daughter into the kind of woman she envisions, there is something that transcends the specifics. Every parent wants his or her child to grow up to be a respectable adult, and whether the parent goes about it by saving money for college, exposing them to different languages and cultures, or, as in the story, giving instructions on how to behave, this drive seems as innate as eating or sleeping. Hence, nearly any mother or father can identify with what the narrator is trying to accomplish.

Sentence too long—break up or rewrite.

## Edit Your Sentences, Proofread and Format Your Paper

Andrew uses these notes to develop his final draft, in which he fleshes out his character analysis and discusses the significance of the story's point of view, tone, and setting. For the final draft, he also checks his spelling, word choice, transitions, and sentences for clarity and grammatical correctness. He also makes sure he has provided ample evidence from the story itself with quotations, and he checks to make sure these quotations are correctly formatted in-text references, which correspond to a Work Cited page at the end of his paper (see the handbook for writing from reading for MLA formatting guidelines). He also incorporates paraphrase and summary where context is needed but quotations are not necessary. Andrew's progress shows his easeful back and forth with the story as he continually revises his interpretation of it.

"I was not a good student. I was not particularly good in English. Yet I am a writer. And this, I think, points to something relevant which is that it's not about talent, necessarily. You [just need to] do whatever is required, because you want it more. That was my experience."

Conversation with Amy Hempel

**FINAL DRAFT**

Papadopoulis 1

Student name, instructor name, course number, and date

Andrew Papadopoulis

Professor Delbanco

Composition 102

15 April 2008

A Mother's Advice

Essay title

On first encounter, Jamaica Kincaid's short-short story "Girl" can seem enigmatic, if not simply baffling. While most works of fiction are written in either the first or the third person, "Girl" is written in the second person: the "you" voice. This makes the beginning of the story fairly disorienting, as the reader is likely unaccustomed to this narrative perspective. Additionally, because the story is so short, the reader may reach the end before the feeling of disorientation ever goes away. A full appreciation of "Girl" requires careful, and even repeated, reading. Such an approach, though, reveals that Kincaid provides a great deal of information about the narrator and the "you" to whom the story is directed. In other words, "Girl" hides much beneath its initially mysterious surface, mainly, details about the characters.

Introduction leading toward thesis

Thesis

The first clues as to the identity of the narrator of "Girl" can be found in the story's tone. From the first lines, the narrator's speech is admonitory, domineering, and tough. The story begins with "Wash the white clothes on Monday and put them on the stone heap; wash the color clothes on Tuesday and put them on the clothesline to dry; don't walk barehead in the hot sun." From this direct, blunt language, it

Discussion of tone illustrated with example

Papadopoulis 2

is clear that the speaker is someone who is used to being in charge, believes he or she knows the right way to do things, and, importantly, believes that the person listening must obey. For these reasons, it is likely that the narrator is a parent, speaking to his or her child. This interpretation certainly fits the relationship suggested by the story's commanding language.

Further, it is not difficult to conclude that the narrator is a woman, talking to her daughter. The narrator even says, at one point, "You are not a boy." This fairly well clears up any mystery as to the listener's gender! The narrator's identity as the girl's mother is suggested by a line earlier in the story. The narrator says, "This is how you iron your father's khaki pants so that they don't have a crease." This instruction, with its casual reference to "your father," suggests a relationship among the narrator, the girl, and the girl's father. The most obvious characterization of this relationship is that the speaker is the girl's mother, and she is telling her daughter how to iron her father's pants.

Textual analysis as part of a discussion of the characters' genders.

The nature of the advice the narrator gives only reinforces the idea that "Girl" consists of mother-to-daughter counsel. The narrator has recommendations for cleaning, cooking, gardening, and washing—all domestic chores, traditionally considered women's work. Further, the narrator has plenty of ideas on how to behave like a "lady" and not a "slut." Obviously, this is the sort of gender etiquette one woman would pass on to another, particularly a mother to a daughter.

Further textual analysis of characters' relationship

Papadopoulis 3

In addition to the familial relationship between the narrator and the listener, Kincaid offers other insight into the characters of the story. As mentioned previously, the tone suggests that the narrator is strict and authoritarian. At times, though, she can be humorous, as when she says, "Always eat your food in such a way that it won't turn someone else's stomach." Although the statement implies criticism (specifically, that the girl eats in a way that *does* turn people's stomachs), the advice cannot be taken as wholly serious. At other times, the narrator demonstrates affection for her daughter. For example, about men, she says, "This is how to love a man, and if this doesn't work there are other ways, and if they don't work don't feel too bad about giving up." There is a warmth to these lines that shows the narrator truly cares that her daughter avoids the deeper pitfalls of love.

Character analysis of the narrator

What we learn about the listener, the "girl" of the story's title, is of course mainly filtered through the view of the narrator. From the more direct statements her mother makes, one could conclude that the girl is in grave danger of becoming a "slut." But beyond this, it is possible to learn something of her personality. The sheer amount of advice she is given suggests that she has a lot to learn, at least about cooking and such. Thus, she could very well be independent, disinterested in the traditional activities about which her mother instructs her. This idea is supported by the brief moments of interaction in the story (the daughter's responses to her mother's words are set off in italics). These show her questioning her mother and arguing with her assertions. For instance, she insists, "*But I don't sing benna on*

Character analysis of the listener

Papadopoulis 4

*Sundays at all and never in Sunday school."* From this sort of headstrong defense one can conclude that this girl is very much her mother's daughter, strong willed and determined.

Given what can be learned about the two characters in the story—mother and daughter—it is interesting to consider *why* the narrator feels compelled to give the girl so much advice. It almost seems as if she wants to tell her daughter every single thing she will need to know, but this of course is impossible. Her larger motives can be detected in the story's final line. After her daughter, in another moment of italicized response, questions whether the baker will let her squeeze the bread to see if it's fresh, the narrator says, "You mean to say that after all you are really going to be the kind of woman who the baker won't let near the bread?" This seems to get at the heart of what the mother is trying to teach her daughter. Ultimately, it is not important *what* the girl knows, but the "kind of woman" the girl becomes. The many lessons of the story represent the accumulated knowledge of a particular type of woman—dignified, competent, capable, wise. These are the qualities the mother hopes to pass on, more than tips about planting okra.

Larger discussion of the narrator's motives

All the counsel the mother gives the daughter in "Girl" is specific to a particular setting. From the details of food (okra, dasheen) and music (*benna*), one can conjecture that this setting is in the Caribbean, where Jamaica Kincaid grew up. Further, all the counsel deals with the rural, domestic realm the mother inhabits and controls. Nonetheless, in the mother's resolve to make her daughter into the kind of

Papadopoulis 5

woman she envisions, there is certainly an element that transcends these specifics. Every parent wants his or her child to grow up to be a respectable adult. Whether the parent goes about it by saving money for the child's college, exposing him or her to different languages and cultures, or, as in "Girl," giving instructions on how to behave like a lady, this drive seems as innate as any fundamental parental instinct. Hence, nearly any mother or father, or even anyone who has mentored another in any capacity, can identify with what the narrator is trying to accomplish.

Conclusion broadening the essay's argument to a more general point

Work Cited

Kincaid, Jamaica. "Girl." *Literature: Craft and Voice.* Eds. Nicholas Delbanco and Alan Cheuse. New York: McGraw-Hill, 2009. 53. Print.

Work Cited page and entry in MLA format

# Compiling a Writing Portfolio

If you are compiling a portfolio or just several drafts of a single paper for your instructor, here's some advice:

- Gather your writing.
- Review what you have gathered and make selections.
- Arrange selections in a deliberate order.
- Write a reflective essay or letter to explain what is in your portfolio.
- Suggest who you are as a writer—that is, highlight your strengths and tell how you envision your writing taking shape in future written work.

Your instructor may prefer you to submit your work as an e-portfolio.

- Use the opening screen to establish your purpose and appeal to your audience.
- Provide links to help readers navigate your portfolio.
- Consider using links to connect with related files external to the portfolio like audio or video clips.
- Navigate through it all the way to make sure it's conceptually and structurally right before releasing it.

# 4 Plot

THE first mistake, the one that opened the whole floodgate, was losing my grip on the keys. In the excitement, leaping from the car with the gin in one hand and a roach clip in the other, I spilled them in the grass—in the dark, rank, mysterious nighttime grass of Greasy Lake. This was a tactical error, as damaging and irreversible in its way as Westmoreland's decision to dig in at Khe Sanh. I felt it like a jab of intuition, and I stopped there by the open door, peering vaguely into the night that puddled up round my feet.

The second mistake—and this was inextricably bound up with the first—was identifying the car as Tony Lovett's.

*—from "Greasy Lake" by T. Coraghessan Boyle*

*"A story like 'Greasy Lake' develops through the opening . . . which is the setup: "I went there one night." . . . Each of the incidents of the story strings out from that in an escalating way, until we . . . find out what happened. . . . It's not the kind of plot in which they all went to jail . . . the end. No, it ends on a gesture, and that gesture brings you back into the story to rethink what it means. . . ."*

Conversation with T. Coraghessan Boyle, video available at www.mhhe.com/delbanco1e

IN the excerpt that begins this chapter, the narrator, a nineteen-year-old and a self-described "dangerous character," identifies the moment when his night of random thrill seeking begins to take shape. He tells the tale in retrospect—so we as readers know "the first" and "the second mistake" won't be fatal—but we also know the "error" will prove "irreversible." He and his two buddies had been cruising their town on the third night of summer vacation, looking for "something we never found." (The reference to "Westmoreland's decision to dig in at Khe Sanh" evokes U.S. Army general William Westmoreland's tactical blunder in Vietnam, and there's a not-so-casual suggestion that "losing my grip on the keys" opens a "floodgate" of trouble in a kind of small-scale war.) Restless with longing, the boys drive up to Greasy Lake and pull in behind the car they think belongs to Tony Lovett. Honking and blinking their headlights, they stumble out of their own car, hoping to catch Tony in the act of whatever he's doing.

And what happens then? This is the moment when the plot of "Greasy Lake" starts in earnest and the real action begins.

*CONTINUED ON PAGE 83*

*I don't consciously make a plot beforehand . . .*

Q&A

*For me it just happens, and it happens slowly . . .*

# A Conversation on Writing

## T. Coraghessan Boyle

### From Music to Writing

As a teenager . . . I wanted to be a serious musician, and I went to music college. I played a saxophone and clarinet. . . . As soon as I got there . . . I realized that I couldn't hack it. The others were so much more advanced and better than I at their instruments. . . . In the first English course I took, which was on the contemporary short story, I discovered Flannery O'Connor, her story "A Good Man Is Hard to Find" [in chapter 12]. And it was a revelation for me, because here was a very funny story about a family going on vacation, and it's hilarious. You've got the brat kids, the old grandmother—she sneaks her cat into the car. The father of the family, Bailey, is overwrought and harassed like any guy on TV. And then the story turns on you and becomes utterly tragic and heartbreaking. And it just woke me up, and I thought, "This is an amazing thing."

### On Plot and His Writing Process

I don't consciously make a plot beforehand, nor do I make a plot in revision. . . . I revise as I go along, so that the story that you see is exactly what it was. I don't ever write scenes and change them around or anything like that. . . . For me it just happens, and it happens slowly . . . , and I perfect each line. I couldn't go on if I didn't feel that what is behind me is good. And at some point the end arrives. There's no major revision after that, and there's no detailing for plot, or theme, or symbols, or anything else. They are organic, it all just happens as one whole. So I don't do any revision whatsoever, beyond daily revision of each line till I think it's right.

To watch this entire interview and hear the author read from "Greasy Lake," go to **www.mhhe.com/delbanco1e.**

**RESEARCH ASSIGNMENT:** In the interview, Boyle says, "Plot is essential to all fiction." After watching the interview, explain why Boyle feels that way. Do you agree with him? What stories can you think of that either support or refute his claim?

T. Coraghessan Boyle (also known as T. C. Boyle), born Thomas John Boyle in Peekskill, New York (1948), is a novelist and short story writer. Boyle earned a B.A. in English and history from the State University of New York at Potsdam in 1968, after which he taught for four years at the high school in his hometown where his mother worked as head secretary and his father as a janitor. After being accepted to the Iowa Writers' Workshop in 1972, Boyle served as fiction editor for the *Iowa Review* and, in 1977, received a Creative Writing Fellowship from the National Endowment for the Arts. In 1988, he received a Guggenheim. Boyle has since received many literary awards, including the PEN/Faulkner Award, the PEN/Malamud Prize, the PEN/West Literary Prize, the Commonwealth Gold Medal for Literature, and the National Academy of Arts and Letters Award for Prose Excellence. His novels include *World's End* (1987, winner of the PEN/Faulkner Award for Fiction); *The Road to Wellville* (1993); and *The Tortilla Curtain* (1995, winner of France's Prix Médicis Étranger). Boyle is also one of America's most accomplished short story writers; his story collections include *Descent of Man* (1979), *Greasy Lake* (1985), *If the River Was Whiskey* (1989), and *Without a Hero* (1994). His short stories regularly appear in major American magazines, including *The New Yorker, Harper's, Esquire, The Atlantic Monthly,* and *Playboy.*

Now the author of nineteen books of fiction, Boyle is known for his imagination and humor as he writes on such subjects as hippies, the environment, illegal immigration, the nineteenth-century health food movement, and identity theft. He describes writing as an addiction and explains that in his own fiction "the themes and obsessions—the search for the father, racism, class and community, predetermination versus free will, cultural imperialism, sexual war and sexual truce—keep repeating. I can see this, but only in retrospect. That's the beauty of this addiction—you have to move on, no retirement here, look out ahead, though you can't see where you're going." Boyle has taught at the University of Southern California since 1978.

**AS YOU READ** As you read "Greasy Lake," consider these questions: Where does the tension mount? Why? As the plot unfolds, what does the main character worry about? What do you worry about?

# Greasy Lake (1985)

*It's about a mile down on the dark side of Route 88.*

—Bruce Springsteen

1 THERE was a time when courtesy and winning ways went out of style, when it was good to be bad, when you cultivated decadence like a taste. We were all dangerous characters then. We wore torn-up leather jackets, slouched around with toothpicks in our months, sniffed glue and ether and what somebody claimed was cocaine. When we wheeled our parents' whining station wagons out onto the street we left a patch of rubber half a block long. We drank gin and grape juice, Tango, Thunderbird, and Bali Hai. We were nineteen. We were bad. We read André Gide and struck elaborate poses to show that we didn't give a shit about anything. At night, we went up to Greasy Lake.

2 Through the center of town, up the strip, past the housing developments and shopping malls, street lights giving way to the thin streaming illumination of the headlights, trees crowding the asphalt in a black unbroken wall: that was the way out to Greasy Lake. The Indians had called it Wakan, a reference to the clarity of its waters. Now it was fetid and murky, the mud banks glittering with broken glass and strewn with beer cans and the charred remains of bonfires. There was a single ravaged island a hundred yards from shore, so stripped of vegetation it looked as if the air force had strafed it. We went up to the lake because everyone went there, because we wanted to snuff the rich scent of possibility on the breeze, watch a girl take off her clothes and plunge into the festering murk, drink beer, smoke pot, howl at the stars, savor the incongruous full-throated roar of rock and roll against the primeval susurrus of frogs and crickets. This was nature.

3 I was there one night, late, in the company of two dangerous characters. Digby wore a gold star in his right ear and allowed his father to pay his tuition at Cornell; Jeff was thinking of quitting school to become a painter/musician/head-shop proprietor. They were both expert in the social graces, quick with a sneer, able to manage a Ford with lousy shocks over a rutted and gutted blacktop road at eighty-five while rolling a joint as compact as a Tootsie Roll Pop stick. They could lounge against a bank of booming speakers and trade "man"s with the best of them or roll out across the dance floor as if their joints worked on bearings. They were slick and quick and they wore their mirror shades at breakfast and dinner, in the shower, in closets and caves. In short, they were bad.

I drove. Digby pounded the dashboard and shouted 4
along with Toots & the Maytals while Jeff hung his head out the window and streaked the side of my mother's Bel Air with vomit. It was early June, the air soft as a hand on your cheek, the third night of summer vacation. The first two nights we'd been out till dawn, looking for something we never found. On this, the third night, we'd cruised the strip sixty-seven times, been in and out of every bar and club we could think of in a twenty-mile radius, stopped twice for bucket chicken and forty-cent hamburgers, debated going to a party at the house of a girl Jeff's sister knew, and chucked two dozen raw eggs at mailboxes and hitchhikers. It was 2:00 A.M.; the bars were closing. There was nothing to do but take a bottle of lemon-flavored gin up to Greasy Lake.

The taillights of a 5
single car winked at us as we swung into the dirt lot with its tufts

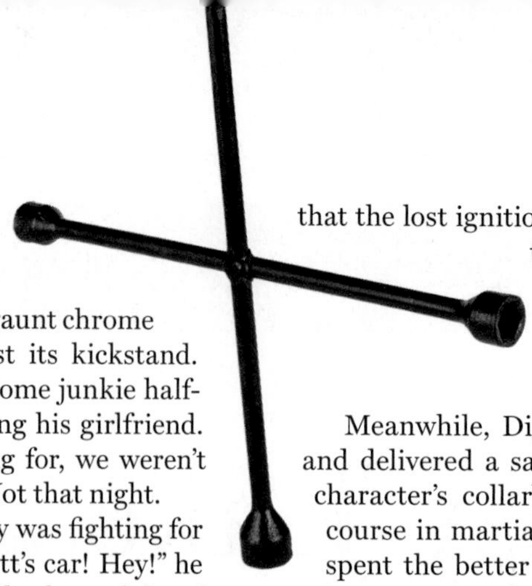

of weed and washboard corrugations; '57 Chevy, mint, metallic blue. On the far side of the lot, like the exoskeleton of some gaunt chrome insect, a chopper leaned against its kickstand. And that was it for excitement: some junkie halfwit biker and a car freak pumping his girlfriend. Whatever it was we were looking for, we weren't about to find it at Greasy Lake. Not that night.

6 But then all of a sudden Digby was fighting for the wheel. "Hey, that's Tony Lovett's car! Hey!" he shouted, while I stabbed at the brake pedal and the Bel Air nosed up to the gleaming bumper of the parked Chevy. Digby leaned on the horn, laughing, and instructed me to put my brights on. I flicked on the brights. This was hilarious. A joke. Tony would experience premature withdrawal and expect to be confronted by grim-looking state troopers with flashlights. We hit the horn, strobed the lights, and then jumped out of the car to press our witty faces to Tony's windows; for all we knew we might even catch a glimpse of some little fox's tit, and then we could slap backs with red-faced Tony, roughhouse a little, and go on to new heights of adventure and daring.

7 The first mistake, the one that opened the whole floodgate, was losing my grip on the keys. In the excitement, leaping from the car with the gin in one hand and a roach clip in the other, I spilled them in the grass—in the dark, rank, mysterious nighttime grass of Greasy Lake. This was a tactical error, as damaging and irreversible in its way as Westmoreland's decision to dig in at Khe Sanh. I felt it like a jab of intuition, and I stopped there by the open door, peering vaguely into the night that puddled up round my feet.

8 The second mistake—and this was inextricably bound up with the first—was identifying the car as Tony Lovett's. Even before the very bad character in greasy jeans and engineer boots ripped out of the driver's door, I began to realize that this chrome blue was much lighter than the robin's-egg of Tony's car, and that Tony's car didn't have rear-mounted speakers. Judging from their expressions, Digby and Jeff were privately groping toward the same inevitable and unsettling conclusion as I was.

9 In any case, there was no reasoning with this bad greasy character—clearly he was a man of action. The first lusty Rockette kick of his steel-toed boot caught me under the chin, chipped my favorite tooth, and left me sprawled in the dirt. Like a fool, I'd gone down on one knee to comb the stiff hacked grass for the keys, my mind making connections in the most dragged-out, testudineous way, knowing that things had gone wrong, that I was in a lot of trouble, and that the lost ignition key was my grail and my salvation. The three or four succeeding blows were mainly absorbed by my right buttock and the tough piece of bone at the base of my spine.

Meanwhile, Digby vaulted the kissing bumpers and delivered a savage kung-fu blow to the greasy character's collarbone. Digby had just finished a course in martial arts for phys-ed credit and had spent the better part of the past two nights telling us apocryphal tales of Bruce Lee types and of the raw power invested in lightning blows shot from coiled wrists, ankles, and elbows. The greasy character was unimpressed. He merely backed off a step, his face like a Toltec mask, and laid Digby out with a single whistling roundhouse blow . . . but by now Jeff had got into the act, and I was beginning to extricate myself from the dirt, a tinny compound of shock, rage, and impotence wadded in my throat. 10

Jeff was on the guy's back, biting at his ear. Digby was on the ground, cursing. I went for the tire iron I kept under the driver's seat. I kept it there because bad characters always keep tire irons under the driver's seat, for just such an occasion as this. Never mind that I hadn't been involved in a fight since sixth grade, when a kid with a sleepy eye and two streams of mucus depending from his nostrils hit me in the knee with a Louisville slugger, never mind that I'd touched the tire iron exactly twice before, to change tires: it was there. And I went for it. 11

I was terrified. Blood was beating in my ears, my hands were shaking, my heart turning over like a dirtbike in the wrong gear. My antagonist was shirtless, and a single cord of muscle flashed across his chest as he bent forward to peel Jeff from his back like a wet overcoat. "Motherfucker," he spat, over and over, and I was aware in that instant that all four of us—Digby, Jeff, and myself included—were chanting "motherfucker, motherfucker," as if it were a battle cry. (What happened next? The detective asks the murderer from beneath the turned-down brim of his porkpie hat. I don't know, the murderer says, something came over me. Exactly.) 12

13 Digby poked the flat of his hand in the bad character's face and I came at him like a kamikaze, mindless, raging, stung with humiliation—the whole thing, from the initial boot in the chin to this murderous primal instant involving no more than sixty hyperventilating, gland-flooding seconds—I came at him and brought the tire iron down across his ear. The effect was instantaneous, astonishing. He was a stunt man and this was Hollywood, he was a big grimacing toothy balloon and I was a man with a straight pin. He collapsed. Wet his pants. Went loose in his boots.

14 A single second, big as a zeppelin, floated by. We were standing over him in a circle, gritting our teeth, jerking our necks, our limbs and hands and feet twitching with glandular discharges. No one said anything. We just stared down at the guy, the car freak, the lover, the bad greasy character laid low. Digby looked at me; so did Jeff. I was still holding the tire iron, a tuft of hair clinging to the crook like dandelion fluff, like down. Rattled, I dropped it in the dirt, already envisioning the headlines, the pitted faces of the police inquisitors, the gleam of handcuffs, clank of bars, the big black shadows rising from the back of the cell . . . when suddenly a raw torn shriek cut through me like all the juice in all the electric chairs in the country.

We were bad characters, and we were scared and hot and three steps over the line . . .

15 It was the fox. She was short, barefoot, dressed in panties and a man's shirt. "Animals!" she screamed, running at us with her fists clenched and wisps of blow-dried hair in her face. There was a silver chain round her ankle, and her toenails flashed in the glare of the headlights. I think it was the toenails that did it. Sure, the gin and the cannabis and even the Kentucky Fried may have had a hand in it, but it was the sight of those flaming toes that set us off—the toad emerging from the loaf in *Virgin Spring*, lipstick smeared on a child; she was already tainted. We were on her like Bergman's deranged brothers—see no evil, hear none, speak none—panting, wheezing, tearing at her clothes, grabbing for flesh. We were bad characters, and we were scared and hot and three steps over the line—anything could have happened.

16 It didn't.

17 Before we could pin her to the hood of the car, our eyes masked with lust and greed and the purest primal badness, a pair of headlights swung into the lot. There we were, dirty, bloody, guilty, dissociated from humanity and civilization, the first of the Ur-crimes behind us, the second in progress, shreds of nylon panty and spandex brassiere dangling from our fingers, our flies open, lips licked—there we were, caught in the spotlight. Nailed.

We bolted. First for the car, and then, realizing we had no way of starting it, for the woods. I thought nothing. I thought escape. The headlights came at me like accusing fingers. I was gone. 18

Ram-bam-bam, across the parking lot, past the chopper and into the feculent undergrowth at the lake's edge, insects flying up in my face, weeds whipping, frogs and snakes and red-eyed turtles splashing off into the night: I was already ankle-deep in muck and tepid water and still going strong. Behind me, the girl's screams rose in intensity, disconsolate, incriminating, the screams of the Sabine women, the Christian martyrs, Anne Frank dragged from the garret. I kept going, pursued by those cries, imagining cops and bloodhounds. The water was up to my knees when I realized what I was doing: I was going to swim for it. Swim the breadth of Greasy Lake and hide myself in the thick clot of woods on the far side. They'd never find me there. 19

I was breathing in sobs, in gasps. The water lapped at my waist as I looked out over the moon-burnished ripples, the mats of algae that clung to the surface like scabs. Digby and Jeff had vanished. I paused. Listened. The girl was quieter now, screams tapering to sobs, but there were male voices, angry, excited, and the high-pitched ticking of the second car's engine. I waded deeper, stealthy, hunted, the ooze sucking at my sneakers. As I was about to take the plunge—at the very instant I dropped my shoulder for the first slashing stroke—I blundered into something. Something unspeakable, obscene, something soft, wet, moss-grown. A patch of weed? A log? When I reached out to touch it, it gave like a rubber duck, it gave like flesh. 20

In one of those nasty little epiphanies for which we are prepared by films and TV and childhood visits to the funeral home to ponder the shrunken painted forms of dead grandparents, I understood what it was that bobbed there so inadmissibly in the dark. Understood, and stumbled back in horror and revulsion, my mind yanked in six different directions (I was nineteen, a mere child, an infant, and here in the space of five minutes I'd struck down one greasy character and blundered into the waterlogged carcass of a second), thinking, The keys, the keys, why did I have to go and 21

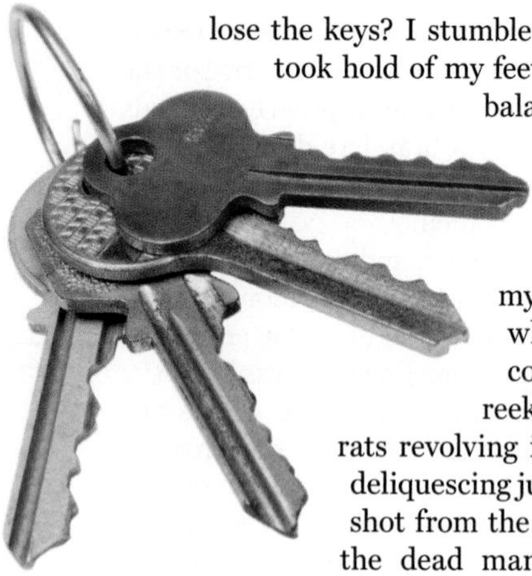

lose the keys? I stumbled back, but the muck took hold of my feet—a sneaker snagged, balance lost—and suddenly I was pitching face forward into the buoyant black mass, throwing out my hands in desperation while simultaneously conjuring the image of reeking frogs and muskrats revolving in slicks of their own deliquescing juices. AAAAArrrgh! I shot from the water like a torpedo, the dead man rotating to expose a mossy beard and eyes cold as the moon. I must have shouted out, thrashing around in the weeds, because the voices behind me suddenly became animated.

22 "What was that?"

23 "It's them, it's them: they tried to, tried to . . . *rape* me!" Sobs.

24 A man's voice, flat Midwestern accent. "You sons a bitches, we'll kill you!"

25 Frogs, crickets.

26 Then another voice, harsh, *r*-less, Lower East Side: "Motherfucker!" I recognized the verbal virtuosity of the bad greasy character in the engineer boots. Tooth chipped, sneakers gone, coated in mud and slime and worse, crouching breathless in the weeds waiting to have my ass thoroughly and definitively kicked and fresh from the hideous stinking embrace of a three-days-dead-corpse, I suddenly felt a rush of joy and vindication: the son of a bitch was alive! Just as quickly, my bowels turned to ice. "Come on out of there, you pansy mothers!" the bad greasy character was screaming. He shouted curses till he was out of breath.

27 The crickets started up again, then the frogs. I held my breath. All at once was a sound in the reeds, a swishing, a splash: thunk-a-thunk. They were throwing rocks. The frogs fell silent. I cradled my head. Swish, swish, thunk-a-thunk. A wedge of feldspar the size of a cue ball glanced off my knee. I bit my finger.

28 It was then that they turned to the car. I heard a door slam, a curse, and then the sound of the headlights shattering—almost a good-natured sound, celebratory, like corks popping from the necks of bottles. This was succeeded by the dull booming of the fenders, metal on metal, and then the icy crash of the windshield. I inched forward, elbows and knees, my belly pressed to the muck; thinking of guerrillas and commandos and *The Naked and the Dead*. I parted the weeds and squinted the length of the parking lot.

The second car—it was a Trans-Am—was still running, its high beams washing the scene in a lurid stagy light. Tire iron flailing, the greasy bad character was laying into the side of my mother's Bel Air like an avenging demon, his shadow riding up the trunks of the trees. Whomp. Whomp. Whomp-whomp. The other two guys—blond types, in fraternity jackets—were helping out with tree branches and skull-sized boulders. One of them was gathering up bottles, rocks, muck, candy wrappers, used condoms, poptops, and other refuse and pitching it through the window on the driver's side. I could see the fox, a white bulb behind the windshield of the '57 Chevy. "Bobbie," she whined over the thumping, "come on." The greasy character paused a moment, took one good swipe at the left taillight, and then heaved the tire iron halfway across the lake. Then he fired up the '57 and was gone. 29

Blond head nodded at blond head. One said something to the other, two low for me to catch. They were no doubt thinking that in helping to annihilate my mother's car they'd committed a fairly rash act, and thinking too that there were three bad characters connected with that very car watching them from the woods. Perhaps other possibilities occurred to them as well—police, jail cells, justices of the peace, reparations, lawyers, irate parents, fraternal censure. Whatever they were thinking, they suddenly dropped branches, bottles, and rocks and sprang for their car in unison, as if they'd choreographed it. Five seconds. That's all it took. The engine shrieked, the tires squealed, a cloud of dust rose from the rutted lot and then settled back on darkness. 30

I don't know how long I lay there, the bad breath of decay all around me, my jacket heavy as a bear, the primordial ooze subtly reconstituting itself to accommodate my upper thighs and testicles. My jaws ached, my knee throbbed, my coccyx was on fire. I contemplated suicide, wondered if I'd need bridgework, scraped the recesses of my brain for some sort of excuse to give my parents—a tree had fallen on the car, I was blinded by a bread truck, hit and run, vandals had got to it while we were playing chess at Digby's. Then I thought of the dead man. He was probably the only person on the planet worse off than I was. I thought about him, fog on the lake, insects chirring eerily, and felt the tug of fear, felt the darkness opening up inside me like a set of jaws. Who was he, I wondered, this victim of time and circumstance bobbing sorrowfully in the lake at my back. The owner of the chopper, no doubt, a bad older character come to this. Shot during a murky drug deal, drowned while drunkenly frolicking in the lake. Another headline. My car was wrecked; he was dead. 31

32 When the eastern half of the sky went from black to cobalt and the trees began to separate themselves from the shadows, I pushed myself up from the mud and stepped out into the open. By now the birds had begun to take over for the crickets, and dew lay slick on the leaves. There was a smell in the air, raw and sweet at the same time, the smell of the sun firing buds and opening blossoms. I contemplated the car. It lay there like a wreck along the highway, like a steel sculpture left over from a vanished civilization. Everything was still. This was nature.

**Then I thought of the dead man.**

**He was probably the only person on the planet worse off than I was.**

33 I was circling the car, as dazed and bedraggled as the sole survivor of an air blitz, when Digby and Jeff emerged from the trees behind me. Digby's face was crosshatched with smears of dirt; Jeff's jacket was gone and his shirt was torn across the shoulder. They slouched across the lot, looking sheepish, and silently came up beside me to gape at the ravaged automobile. No one said a word. After a while Jeff swung open the driver's door and began to scoop the broken glass and garbage off the seat. I looked at Digby. He shrugged. "At least they didn't slash the tires," he said.

34 It was true: the tires were intact. There was no windshield, the headlights were staved in, and the body looked as if it had been sledge-hammered for a quarter a shot at the county fair, but the tires were inflated to regulation pressure. The car was drivable. In silence, all three of us bent to scrape the mud and shattered glass from the interior. I said nothing about the biker. When we were finished, I reached in my pocket for the keys, experienced a nasty stab of recollection, cursed myself, and turned to search the grass. I spotted them almost immediately, no more than five feet from the open door, glinting like jewels in the first tapering shaft of sunlight. There was no reason to get philosophical about it: I eased into the seat and turned the engine over.

35 It was at that precise moment that the silver Mustang with the flame decals rumbled into the lot. All three of us froze; then Digby and Jeff slid into the car and slammed the door. We watched as the Mustang rocked and bobbed across the ruts and finally jerked to a halt beside the forlorn chopper at the far end of the lot. "Let's go," Digby said. I hesitated, the Bel Air wheezing beneath me.

36 Two girls emerged from the Mustang. Tight jeans, stiletto heels, hair like frozen fur. They bent over the motorcycle, paced back and forth aimlessly, glanced once or twice at us, and then ambled over to where the reeds sprang up in a green fence round the perimeter of the lake. One of them cupped her hands to her mouth. "Al," she called. "Hey, Al!"

37 "Come on," Digby hissed. "Let's get out of here."

38 But it was too late. The second girl was picking her way across the lot, unsteady on her heels, looking up at us and then away. She was older—twenty-five or -six—and as she came closer we could see there was something wrong with her: she was stoned or drunk, lurching now and waving her arms for balance. I gripped the steering wheel as if it were the ejection lever of a flaming jet, and Digby spat out my name, twice, terse and impatient.

39 "Hi," the girl said.

40 We looked at her like zombies, like war veterans, like deaf-and-dumb pencil peddlers.

41 She smiled, her lips cracked and dry. "Listen," she said, bending from the waist to look in the window, "you guys seen Al?" Her pupils were pinpoints, her eyes glass. She jerked her neck. "That's his bike over there—Al's. You seen him?"

42 Al. I didn't know what to say. I wanted to get out of the car and retch, I wanted to go home to my parents' house and crawl into bed. Digby poked me in the ribs. "We haven't seen anybody," I said.

43 The girl seemed to consider this, reaching out a slim veiny arm to brace herself against the car. "No matter," she said, slurring the *t*'s, "he'll turn up." And then, as if she'd just taken stock of the whole scene—the ravaged car and our battered faces, the desolation of the place—she said: "Hey, you guys look like some pretty bad characters—been fightin', huh?" We stared straight ahead, rigid as catatonics. She was fumbling in her pocket and muttering something. Finally she held out a handful of tablets in glassine wrappers: "Hey, you want to party, you want to do some of these with me and Sarah?"

44 I just looked at her. I thought I was going to cry. Digby broke the silence. "No, thanks," he said, leaning over me. "Some other time."

45 I put the car in gear and it inched forward with a groan, shaking off pellets of glass like an old dog shedding water after a bath, heaving over the ruts on its worn springs, creeping toward the highway. There was a sheen of sun on the lake. I looked back. The girl was still standing there, watching us, her shoulders slumped, hand outstretched.

EACH of the stories in the plot chapter deals with the coming of age, or initiation into adult life, of a young character, somewhat innocent as the story begins and more knowledgeable by the story's end. If you like the way T.C. Boyle treats this subject matter, you might want to compare it with John Updike's disaffected hero in "A&P" in chapter 1.

**GOING FURTHER** You can find another comic antihero, like Boyle's, in *Garden State* by Rick Moody, and you may enjoy the comic sensibility in the essays of Steve Almond *(Not That You Asked) Rants, Exploits, and Obsessions.*

"And everybody has been to Greasy Lake" Conversation with T. Coraghessan Boyle

# Writing from Reading

### Summarize

1 Consider all the plot complications the author introduces to keep the tension in the story mounting. At what point does the story reach its climax (point of greatest tension)? Discuss whether or not the events following the climax decline to a resolution for the story.

2 When the narrator wades into the lake, he "blundered into something. Something unspeakable, obscene." What does he blunder into and what impact does it have on him? How does this plot complication differ from the others?

### Analyze Craft

3 Describe how Boyle reveals the characters' context. What is the socioeconomic status of the three main characters in "Greasy Lake"? What clues does Boyle give to reveal this? How is economic status a factor in the plot of this story?

### Analyze Voice

4 In the first paragraph of the story, the narrator describes what it means to be "bad." Does his voice throughout the story suggest he thinks of himself as a "bad guy"? How does the narrator's description of events support or refute his idea of himself as a "bad guy"?

### Synthesize Summary and Analysis

5 "Greasy Lake" is written in past tense, presumably some time after the events of the story. How does this distance affect the tone of the story? Discuss how the plot and the description of events might change if the story were told in present tense by the narrator at age nineteen.

### Interpret the Story

6 Discuss the relationship between plot and character. When the girls arrive at the end of the story, the boys turn down the chance to party with them because, as Boyle says in his interview, "these boys have their tails between their legs." Why do they now have their "tails between their legs"? Use examples from the text to support your answer.

*CONTINUED FROM PAGE 75*

# AN ARTFUL ARRANGEMENT OF INCIDENTS

When we lose ourselves in fiction, are we caught up in the story or its plot? Do *plot* and *story* mean the same thing? In *Aspects of the Novel,* E. M. Forster distinguishes between story and plot with this illustration:

> *"The king died, and then the queen died" is a story. "The king died, and then the queen died of grief" is a plot.*

If an event takes place in a story, we say, "and then?" If it is in a plot we ask, "why?" A **plot** is the artful arrangement of incidents in a story, with each incident building on the next in a series of causes and effects. If the three restless teens in "Greasy Lake" had simply spent the night driving and drinking, stopping at friends' houses, and throwing eggs at mailboxes, the story would be a mere arrangement of chronological events. Once the narrator loses his car keys and taunts the wrong guy, however, the "plot thickens." Event piles on event, succeeding each other in causal but unpredictable ways. The reader becomes engaged, wondering "What next?"

This creates **suspense**—a sense of anticipation or excitement about what will happen and how the characters will deal with their newfound predicament. It's worth remembering that a secondary meaning of the word *plot* is *conspiracy.* In this sense, the word has negative connotations and suggests something faintly illegal, as in: *there was a plot against the king.* What keeps readers enthralled is most often not the root sequence of story, the *and then and then and then* of events; it's the surprise, the *then and therefore* that introduces the idea of motive and permits us to question behavior. Since unexplained behavior lies at the root of mystery, *plot* in its sophisticated manifestations offers the promise of surprise and the excitement of suspense.

As T. C. Boyle says in his interview, "The rest of the story—that's where the plot evolves: what happened that night. Each of the incidents of the story strings out from that in an escalating way, until we try to wrap it up and find out what happened." Authors arrange the incidents of their stories in a variety of ways to show us as readers "what happened."

## Crafting Plot

One way writers set up a story and try to draw a reader into the plot is by means of **exposition,** the presentation of necessary information about the character, setting, or characters' history provided to make the reader care what happens to the characters

> "Plot is the essential element of all stories."
>
> Conversation with T. Coraghessan Boyle

in the story. In Anton Chekhov's "The Lady with the Pet Dog" (chapter 14), the story starts off with this technique. The opening paragraphs set up the situation: A man alone, on vacation, perhaps restless after two weeks, notices a woman alone and considers approaching her.

> *It was said that a new person had appeared on the sea-front: a lady with a little dog. Dmitri Dmitritch Gurov, who had by then been a fortnight at Yalta, and so was fairly at home there, had begun to take an interest in new arrivals. Sitting in Verney's pavilion, he saw, walking on the sea-front, a fair-haired young lady of medium height, wearing a* béret; *a white Pomeranian dog was running behind her.*

*And afterwards he met her in the public gardens and in the square several times a day. She was walking alone, always wearing the same* béret, *and always with the same white dog; no one knew who she was, and every one called her simply "the lady with the dog."*

*"If she is here alone without a husband or friends, it wouldn't be amiss to make her acquaintance," Gurov reflected.*

Some stories begin ***in medias res,*** or in the middle of things. In "The Story of an Hour" (chapter 1), for example, we immediately learn what's at stake: Mr. Mallard has died, and someone has to inform the fragile Mrs. Mallard. This is a common technique in dramatic presentations—an almost standard strategy in plays and movies and on TV. The first episode of the popular television show "Lost" began with a plane crash, leaving dozens of survivors stranded on a strange island. The story line was built on a series of **flashbacks,** the device of moving back in time to a point before the primary action of the story, to reveal how and why this particular group of people crashed in this particular place—but the "backstory" is only slowly revealed.

"Characters may not want to do what you want them to do in the story. They may want to do something that's just going to ruin the story. Guess what, they get to do it." Conversation with William Kittredge

Authors also use **foreshadowing,** a hint about plot elements to come, to both advance the plot and build suspense. For example, in "Greasy Lake," Boyle "flashes forward" with this line, about his narrator's "mistakes": "This was a tactical error, as damaging and irreversible in its way as Westmoreland's decision to dig in at Khe Sanh." He's letting the reader know that trouble surely lies ahead, trouble as bad as a bad decision made by a military officer during the Vietnam War.

All stories have a **protagonist,** the main figure (or principal actor) in a work of literature. Like any human being, a protagonist will have desires or objectives. A story's plot hinges equally on the protagonist's efforts to realize his or her desires and to cope with failure if and when plans are thwarted and desires left unfulfilled. Thus, the characters in a story often drive plot development.

The moment of greatest tension in a story is its **climax,** the narrative's turning point in a struggle between opposing forces.

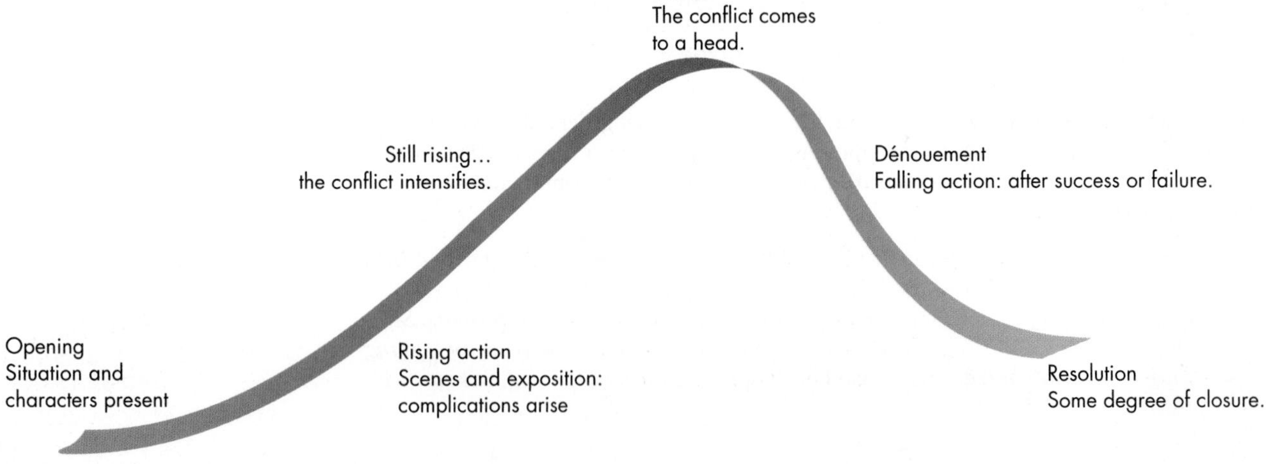

Conflict in a narrative can consist of struggles within the mind and soul of the protagonist, and it can also involve physical struggles. Complications that deepen the protagonist's predicament create the **rising action** of the story. Characters' emotional and psychological conflicts intensify their **conflict** with one or more **antagonists.** The internal and external worlds stand at odds; desires oppose each other; opposition mounts.

In J. R. R. Tolkien's classic story *The Lord of the Rings,* the main character, Frodo, faces a powerful inner struggle: He must resist the corrupting spell of the magic ring so that he can pursue his mission to destroy it and save Middle Earth. He also faces numerous external struggles on his journey, as a series of enemies seeks to kill him and steal the ring. These confrontations with his enemies intensify his internal conflict—the desire to use the ring for his own benefit. The climax in *The Lord of the Rings* occurs when Frodo stands before the Lake of Fire in his mission to destroy the ring forever. Frequently, the climax causes the protagonist to change or at least to gain new understanding.

At this moment of internal conflict, Gollum attacks Frodo, and the climax resolves with both the ring and Gollum plunging into the fire toward everlasting destruction.

The conclusion of the story, or the resolution that follows the climactic moment, is referred to as the **dénouement,** the **falling action** and **resolution.** Here conflicts are resolved and the story comes—at least provisionally—to an end. In the dénouement of *The Lord of the Rings,* peace is restored to Middle Earth, the new king marries his queen, and Frodo and his companions return home to the Shire.

Gollum (Andy Serkis) plummets into the Lake of Fire holding the magic ring, resolving the overarching conflict of the story and advancing the plot toward the dénouement.

"Faulkner said, 'Fiction is the human heart in conflict with itself.' And it does seem to me that the human heart is always in conflict with itself, and that it is the fiction writer's job to understand the nature of that conflict and to make fiction out of it." Conversation with Gish Jen

Often, the internal transformation of the protagonist is the focal point of the story. The majority of modern and contemporary short fictions hinge on such moments, in which a significant truth or the essence of something is revealed to a character—and, by extension, the reader. Conflict, in other words, need not consist of a kick in the chin or a battle by a Lake of Fire; its resolution can be as simple as a character saying "Yes" or "No" or "Please stay" or "Go."

It is important to remember that no writer sitting at the work desk (except perhaps a screen-writer) says, "Well, I've had my anticlimax, now I need a falling action and a dénouement," or "I've had my turning point and must write a resolution." The terminology we use to describe the craft of fiction is used to understand how the story makes its impact on us—long after the fact of it being written. The language is useful primarily as a tool for analytic discussion as we share our thoughts about how stories are put together, how they work, and which ones work best.

# James Joyce (1882–1941)

Born in Ireland in 1882, James Joyce chose to live much of his life as an expatriate in Paris, Zurich, and Trieste. The country of his birth, however, is the subject of almost all his fiction.

The publication of Joyce's short story collection *Dubliners* (1914) was held up for years for fear of libel; the characters and places of his stories were based on real people and locations in Dublin, and publishers feared readers would recognize them as such. Joyce rendered the Dublin of his novel *Ulysses* so accurately that he once joked the city could be reconstructed solely by consulting the "map" of his book. Ezra Pound wrote of Joyce: "He presents his people swiftly and vividly, he does not sentimentalize over them, he does not weave convulsions. He is a realist. . . . He gives the thing as it is. He is not bound by the tiresome convention that any part of life, to be interesting, must be shaped into the conventional form of a 'story.'"

The story "Araby," like the others in *Dubliners,* reflects the influence of nineteenth-century realism, an artistic movement that advocated portraying the world as it is, without idealizing it. His later works—*A Portrait of the Artist As a Young Man, Ulysses,* and *Finnegans Wake*—become progressively more experimental in terms of language and form. Although it is longer than some nineteenth-century epic novels that span generations, the real-time action of *Ulysses* takes place entirely within the span of a single day.

**AS YOU READ** As you read "Araby," consider these questions: Who is telling the story? What does he want? What complications does he face in getting what he wants? How do these desires and confusions drive the story's plot?

# Araby (1914)

1 NORTH Richmond Street, being blind, was a quiet street except at the hour when the Christian Brothers' School set the boys free. An uninhabited house of two storeys stood at the blind end, detached from its neighbours in a square ground. The other houses of the street, conscious of decent lives within them, gazed at one another with brown imperturbable faces.

2 The former tenant of our house, a priest, had died in the back drawing-room. Air, musty from having been long enclosed, hung in all the rooms, and the waste room behind the kitchen was littered with old useless papers. Among these I found a few paper-covered books, the pages of which were curled and damp: *The Abbot,* by Walter Scott, *The Devout Communicant* and *The Memoirs of Vidocq.* I liked the last best because its leaves were yellow. The wild garden behind the house contained a central apple-tree and a few straggling bushes under one of which I found the late tenant's rusty bicycle-pump. He had been a very charitable priest; in his will he had left all his money to institutions and the furniture of his house to his sister.

When the short days of winter came dusk fell before we had well eaten our dinners. When we met in the street the houses had grown sombre. The space of sky above us was the colour of ever-changing violet and towards it the lamps of the street lifted their 3 feeble lanterns. The cold air stung us and we played till our bodies glowed. Our shouts echoed in the silent street. The career of our play brought us through the dark muddy lanes behind the houses where we ran the gantlet of the rough tribes from the cottages, to the back doors of the dark dripping gardens where odours arose from the ashpits, to the dark odorous stables where a coachman smoothed and combed the horse or shook music from the buckled harness. When we returned to the street light from the kitchen windows had filled the areas. If my uncle was seen turning the corner we hid in the shadow until we had seen him safely housed. Or if Mangan's sister came out on the doorstep to call her brother in to his tea we watched her from our shadow peer up and down the street. We waited to see whether she would remain or go in and, if she remained, we left our shadow and walked up to Mangan's steps resignedly. She was waiting for us, her figure defined by the light from the half-opened door. Her brother always teased her before he obeyed and I stood by the railings looking at her. Her dress swung as she moved her body and the soft rope of her hair tossed from side to side.

I had never spoken to her, except for a few casual words, and yet her name was like a summons to all my foolish blood.

4 Every morning I lay on the floor in the front parlour watching her door. The blind was pulled down to within an inch of the sash so that I could not be seen. When she came out on the doorstep my heart leaped. I ran to the hall, seized my books and followed her. I kept her brown figure always in my eye and, when we came near the point at which our ways diverged, I quickened my pace and passed her. This happened morning after morning. I had never spoken to her, except for a few casual words, and yet her name was like a summons to all my foolish blood.

5 Her image accompanied me even in places the most hostile to romance. On Saturday evenings when my aunt went marketing I had to go to carry some of the parcels. We walked through the flaring streets, jostled by drunken men and bargaining women, amid the curses of labourers, the shrill litanies of shop-boys who stood on guard by the barrels of pigs' cheeks, the nasal chanting of street-singers, who sang a *come-all-you* about O'Donovan Rossa, or a ballad about the troubles in our native land. These noises converged in a single sensation of life for me: I imagined that I bore my chalice safely through a throng of foes. Her name sprang to my lips at moments in strange prayers and praises which I myself did not understand. My eyes were often full of tears (I could not tell why) and at times a flood from my heart seemed to pour itself out into my bosom. I thought little of the future. I did not know whether I would ever speak to her or not or, if I spoke to her, how I could tell her of my confused adoration. But my body was like a harp and her words and gestures were like fingers running upon the wires.

6 One evening I went into the back drawing-room in which the priest had died. It was a dark rainy evening and there was no sound in the house. Through one of the broken panes I heard the rain impinge upon the earth, the fine incessant needles of water playing in the sodden beds. Some distant lamp or lighted window gleamed below me. I was thankful that I could see so little. All my senses seemed to desire to veil themselves and, feeling that I was about to slip from them, I pressed the palms of my hands together until they trembled, murmuring: *O love! O love!* many times.

7 At last she spoke to me. When she addressed the first words to me I was so confused that I did not know what to answer. She asked me was I going to *Araby*. I forget whether I answered yes or no. It would be a splendid bazaar, she said; she would love to go.

8 —And why can't you? I asked.

9 While she spoke she turned a silver bracelet round and round her wrist. She could not go, she said, because there would be a retreat that week in her convent. Her brother and two other boys were fighting for their caps and I was alone at the railings. She held one of the spikes, bowing her head towards me. The light from the lamp opposite our door caught the white curve of her neck, lit up her hair that rested there and, falling, lit up the hand upon the railing. It fell over one side of her dress and caught the white border of a petticoat, just visible as she stood at ease.

10 —It's well for you, she said.

11 —If I go, I said, I will bring you something.

12 What innumerable follies laid waste my waking and sleeping thoughts after that evening! I wished to annihilate the tedious intervening days. I chafed against the work of school. At night in my bedroom and by day in the classroom her image came between me and the page I strove to read. The syllables of the word *Araby* were called to me through the silence in which my soul luxuriated and cast an Eastern enchantment over me. I asked for leave to go to the bazaar Saturday night. My aunt was surprised and

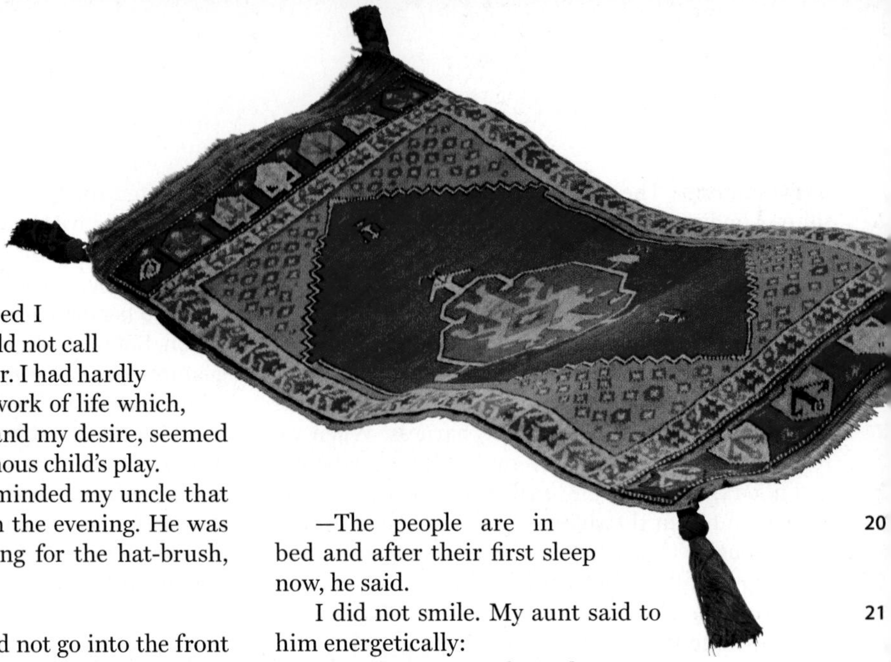

hoped it was not some Freemason affair. I answered few questions in class. I watched my master's face pass from amiability to sternness; he hoped I was not beginning to idle. I could not call my wandering thoughts together. I had hardly any patience with the serious work of life which, now that it stood between me and my desire, seemed to me child's play, ugly monotonous child's play.

13 On Saturday morning I reminded my uncle that I wished to go to the bazaar in the evening. He was fussing at the hallstand, looking for the hat-brush, and answered me curtly:

14 —Yes, boy, I know.

15 As he was in the hall I could not go into the front parlour and lie at the window. I left the house in bad humour and walked slowly towards the school. The air was pitilessly raw and already my heart misgave me.

16 When I came home to dinner my uncle had not yet been home. Still it was early. I sat staring at the clock for some time and, when its ticking began to irritate me, I left the room. I mounted the staircase and gained the upper part of the house. The high cold empty gloomy rooms liberated me and I went from room to room singing. From the front window I saw my companions playing below in the street. Their cries reached me weakened and indistinct and, leaning my forehead against the cool glass, I looked over at the dark house where she lived. I may have stood there for an hour, seeing nothing but the brown-clad figure cast by my imagination, touched discreetly by the lamplight at the curved neck, at the hand upon the railings and at the border below the dress.

17 When I came downstairs again I found Mrs. Mercer sitting at the fire. She was an old garrulous woman, a pawnbroker's widow, who collected used stamps for some pious purpose. I had to endure the gossip of the tea-table. The meal was prolonged beyond an hour and still my uncle did not come. Mrs. Mercer stood up to go: she was sorry she couldn't wait any longer, but it was after eight o'clock and she did not like to be out late, as the night air was bad for her. When she had gone I began to walk up and down the room, clenching my fists. My aunt said:

18 —I'm afraid you may put off your bazaar for this night of Our Lord.

19 At nine o'clock I heard my uncle's latchkey in the halldoor. I heard him talking to himself and heard the hallstand rocking when it had received the weight of his overcoat. I could interpret these signs. When he was midway through his dinner I asked him to give me the money to go to the bazaar. He had forgotten.

—The people are in bed and after their first sleep now, he said. 20

I did not smile. My aunt said to him energetically: 21

—Can't you give him the money and let him go? You've kept him late enough as it is. 22

My uncle said he was very sorry he had forgotten. He said he believed in the old saying: *All work and no play makes Jack a dull boy.* He asked me where I was going and, when I had told him a second time he asked me did I know *The Arab's Farewell to his Steed.* When I left the kitchen he was about to recite the opening lines of the piece to my aunt. 23

I held a florin tightly in my hand as I strode down Buckingham Street towards the station. The sight of the streets thronged with buyers and glaring with gas recalled to me the purpose of my journey. I took my seat in a third-class carriage of a deserted train. After an intolerable delay the train moved out of the station slowly. It crept onward among ruinous houses and over the twinkling river. At Westland Row Station a crowd of people pressed to the carriage doors; but the porters moved them back, saying that it was a special train for the bazaar. I remained alone in the bare carriage. In a few minutes the train drew up beside an improvised wooden platform. I passed out on to the road and saw by the lighted dial of a clock that it was ten minutes to ten. In front of me was a large building which displayed the magical name. 24

I could not find any sixpenny entrance and, fearing that the bazaar would be closed, I passed in quickly through a turnstile, handing a shilling to a weary-looking man. I found myself in a big hall girdled at half its height by a gallery. Nearly all the stalls were closed and the greater part of the hall was in darkness. I recognised a silence like that which pervades a church after a service. I walked into the centre of the bazaar timidly. A few people were gathered about the stalls which were still open. Before a curtain, over which the words *Café Chantant* were written in 25 coloured lamps, two men were counting money on a salver. I listened to the fall of the coins.

26 Remembering with difficulty why I had come I went over to one of the stalls and examined porcelain vases and flowered tea-sets. At the door of the stall a young lady was talking and laughing with two young gentlemen. I remarked their English accents and listened vaguely to their conversation.

27 —O, I never said such a thing!

28 —O, but you did!

29 —O, but I didn't!

30 —Didn't she say that?

31 —Yes. I heard her.

32 —O, there's a . . . fib!

33 Observing me the young lady came over and asked me did I wish to buy anything. The tone of her voice was not encouraging; she seemed to have spoken to me out of a sense of duty. I looked humbly at the great jars that stood like eastern guards at either side of the dark entrance to the stall and murmured:

—No, thank you. 34

The young lady changed the position of one of the vases and went back to the two young men. They began to talk of the same subject. Once or twice the young lady glanced at me over her shoulder. 35

I lingered before her stall, though I knew my stay was useless, to make my interest in her wares seem the more real. Then I turned away slowly and walked down the middle of the bazaar. I allowed the two pennies to fall against the sixpence in my pocket. I heard a voice call from one end of the gallery that the light was out. The upper part of the hall was now completely dark. 36

Gazing up into the darkness I saw myself as a creature driven and derided by vanity; and my eyes burned with anguish and anger. 37

IF you liked "Araby," you might like "The Odour of Chrysanthemums" (chapter 9) by D. H. Lawrence, a working-class writer from neighboring England who created a scandal with the publication of his novel *Lady Chatterley's Lover.*

**GOING FURTHER** Joyce's stories can be found in his collection *Dubliners.* His novel *A Portrait of the Artist As a Young Man* takes the theme of growing up and enlarges it to include the main character's initiation into matters of family, love, religion, art, and politics.

# Writing from Reading

### Summarize

1 The story begins with a long expository section in which the narrator describes the setting and his state of mind. Mark the place in the story where it shifts into a scene and the plot is launched.

2 List all the causes and effects you can find in the plot. What role does cause/effect have in the development of the plot?

### Analyze Craft

3 Does the terse, isolated dialogue serve to advance the plot of *Araby*? Describe how more detailed interactions would affect the pace of the story.

### Analyze Voice

4 The narrator reports this story as he looks back on it from a future time. Based on the language and voice, how distant in time is the narrator from the events he recounts? Using textual evidence, can you piece together the age and social status of the narrator as the story unfolds?

(continued)

### Synthesize Summary and Analysis

5 Consider the role of the priest who died in the drawing room in relation to the events of the story. Note the two instances in which the narrator visits the room where the priest died, and discuss these scenes in relation to the rising tension of the story.

### Interpret the Story

6 At the end of the story, the narrator recognizes himself as a "creature driven and derided by vanity." Consider whether he is becoming such a person at that moment—whether the events of the story have brought about a change in him—or whether he is having an epiphany about the person he has always been. Which of the narrator's actions in the story support your conclusion?

# Naguib Mahfouz (1911–2006)

The first Arab to win the Nobel Prize in Literature, Naguib Mahfouz lived in Cairo, Egypt, his entire life. Mahfouz wrote historical fiction inspired by Sir Walter Scott before turning to social realism to depict everyday life in his native city. *The Cairo Trilogy,* his trilogy about a middle-class family in Cairo, published in the late 1950s and won him widespread fame in the Arab-speaking world. Although many of his works were made into popular Arab films and he was a major influence on Arab literature, Mahfouz never made his living from writing. Instead, he worked as a civil servant for thirty-five years, writing and reading in the evenings after a full day of work. As Mahfouz's work progressed, it increasingly made political statements hidden in allegory and symbolism, combined with elements of realism. Some of his writing was controversial, notably *Children of Gebelawi,* which was banned in Egypt because of its alleged representation of God and the prophets. An outward sign of this controversy came in 1994 when an Islamist extremist stabbed Mahfouz in the neck because he found Mahfouz's portrayal of religion offensive. Although Mahfouz never fully recovered his health, he continued writing and published his last book, *The Seventh Heaven,* in the year preceding his death.

**AS YOU READ** **As you read, notice the way Mahfouz's plot twists transform a simple errand into something far more complex. Why is it so difficult for the narrator to do his mother's bidding? Do you identify with him and his troubles?**

TIP **FOR INTERACTIVE READING . . .** The action of this story is advanced by a series of conflicts and temporary resolutions. As you read, note each new complication and resolution. Based on your notes, draw the plot curve of the story, identifying rising action, the climax, falling action, and the resolution.

# The Conjurer Made Off with the Dish (1969)

"THE time has come for you to be useful," said my mother to me, and she slipped her hand into her pocket, saying:

"Take this piastre and go off and buy some beans. Don't play on the way, and keep away from the cars."

I took the dish, put on my clogs and went out, humming a tune. Finding a crowd in front of the bean-seller, I waited until I discovered a way through to the marble table.

"A piastre's worth of beans, mister," I called out in my shrill voice.

He asked me impatiently:

"Beans alone? With oil? With cooking butter?"

I didn't answer and he said to me roughly:

"Make way for someone else."

I withdrew, overcome by embarrassment, and returned home defeated.

"Returning with an empty dish?" my mother shouted at me. "What did you do—spill the beans or lose the piastre, you naughty boy?"

"Beans alone? With oil? With cooking butter?—you didn't tell me," I protested.

"You stupid, what do you eat every morning?"

"I don't know."

"You good-for-nothing, ask him for beans with oil."

I went off to the man and said:

"A piastre's worth of beans with oil, mister."

With a frown of impatience he asked:

"Linseed oil? Nut oil? Olive oil?"

I was taken aback and again made no answer:

"Make way for someone else," he shouted at me.

I returned in a rage to my mother, who called out in astonishment:

"You've come back empty-handed—no beans and no oil."

"Linseed oil? Nut oil? Olive oil?—you didn't tell me," I said angrily.

"Beans with oil means beans with linseed oil."

"How should I know?"

"You're a good-for-nothing and he's a tiresome man—tell him beans with linseed oil."

"How should I know?"

I went off quickly and called out to the man while still some yards from his shop:

"Beans with linseed oil, mister."

"Put the piastre on the counter," he said, plunging the ladle into the pot.

I put my hand into my pocket but didn't find the piastre. I searched round for it anxiously. I turned my pocket inside out but found no trace of it. The man withdrew the ladle empty, saying with disgust:

"You've lost the piastre—you're not a boy to be depended on."

"I haven't lost it," I said, looking under my feet and round about me. "It's been in my pocket all the time."

"Make way for someone else and don't make trouble."

I returned to my mother with an empty dish.

"Good grief, you idiot boy!"

"The piastre . . ."

"What of it?"

"It wasn't in my pocket."

"Did you buy sweets with it?"

"I swear I didn't."

"How did you lose it?"

"I don't know."

"Do you swear by the Koran you didn't buy anything with it?"

"I swear."

"There's a hole in your pocket."

"No there isn't."

"Maybe you gave it to the man the first time or the second."

"Maybe."

"Are you sure of nothing?"

"I'm hungry."

She clapped her hands together in a gesture of resignation.

"Never mind," she said. "I'll give you another piastre but I'll take it out of your money-box, and if you come back with an empty dish I'll break your head."

I went off at a run, dreaming of a delicious breakfast. At the turning leading to the alleyway where the bean-seller was I saw a crowd of children and heard merry, festive sounds. My feet dragged as my heart was pulled towards them. At least let me have a fleeting glance. I slipped in amongst them and found the conjurer looking straight at me. A stupefying joy overwhelmed me; I was completely taken out of myself. With the whole of my being I became involved in the tricks of the rabbits and the eggs, and the snakes and the ropes. When the man came up to collect money, I drew back mumbling, "I haven't got any money."

A stupefying joy overwhelmed me;

I was completely taken out of myself.

He rushed at me savagely and I escaped only with difficulty. I ran off, my back almost broken by his blow, and yet I was utterly happy as I made my way to the seller of beans.

"Beans with linseed oil for a piastre, mister," I said.

He went on looking at me without moving, so I repeated my request.

"Give me the dish," he demanded angrily.

The dish! Where was the dish? Had I dropped it while running? Had the conjurer made off with it?

"Boy, you're out of your mind."

I turned back, searching along the way for the lost dish. The place where the conjurer had been I found empty, but the voices of children led me to him in a nearby lane. I moved round the circle; when the conjurer spotted me he shouted out threateningly:

"Pay up or you'd better scram."

"The dish!" I called out despairingly.

"What dish, you little devil?"

"Give me back the dish."

"Scram or I'll make you into food for snakes."

He had stolen the dish, yet fearfully I moved away out of sight and wept. Whenever a passer-by asked me why I was crying I would reply:

"The conjurer made off with the dish."

Through my misery I became aware of a voice saying:

"Come along and watch."

I looked behind me and saw a peep-show had been set up. I saw dozens of children hurrying towards it and taking it in turns to stand in front of the peepholes, while the man began making his commentary on the pictures:

"There you've got the gallant knight and the most beautiful of all ladies, Zainat al-Banat."

Drying my tears, I gazed up in fascination at the box, completely forgetting the conjurer and the dish. Unable to overcome the temptation, I paid over the piastre and stood in front of the peephole next to a girl who was standing in front of the other one, and there flowed across our vision enchanting picture stories. When I came back to my own world I realized I had lost both the piastre and the dish, and there was no sign of the conjurer. However, I gave no thought to the loss, so taken up was I with the pictures of chivalry, love and deeds of daring. I forgot my hunger; I forgot the fear of what threatened me back home. I took a few paces back so as to lean against an ancient wall of what had once been a Treasury and the seat of office of the Cadi, and gave myself up wholly to my reveries. For a long while I dreamt of chivalry, of Zainat al-Banat and the ghoul. In my dream I spoke aloud, giving meaning to my words with gestures. Thrusting home the imaginary lance, I said:

"Take that, O ghoul, right in the heart!"

"And he raised Zainat al-Banat up behind him on his horse," came back a gentle voice.

I looked to my right and saw the young girl who had been beside me at the performance. She was wearing a dirty dress and coloured clogs and was playing with her long plait of hair; in her other hand were the red and white sweets called "Lady's fleas," which she was leisurely sucking. We exchanged glances and I lost my heart to her.

"Let's sit down and rest," I said to her.

She appeared to be agreeable to my suggestion, so I took her by the arm and we went through the gateway of the ancient wall and sat down on the step of a stairway that went nowhere, a stairway that rose up until it ended in a platform behind which there could be seen a blue sky and minarets. We sat in silence, side by side. I pressed her hand and we sat on in silence, not knowing what to say. I experienced feelings that were new, strange and obscure. Putting my face close to hers, I breathed in the natural smell of her hair, mingled with an odour of earth, and the fragrance of breath mixed with the aroma of sweets. I kissed her lips. I swallowed my saliva which had taken on a sweetness from the dissolved "Lady's fleas." I put my arm round her, without her uttering a word, kissing her cheek and lips. Her lips grew still as they received the kiss, then went back to sucking at the sweets. At last she decided we should get up. I seized her arm anxiously.

"Sit down," I said.

80 "I'm going," she said simply.

"Where to?" I asked irritably.

"To the midwife Umm Ali," and she pointed to a house at the bottom of which was a small ironing shop.

"Why?"

"To tell her to come quickly."

85 "Why?"

"My mother's crying in pain at home. She told me to go to the midwife Umm Ali and to take her along quickly."

"And you'll come back after that?"

She nodded her head in assent. Her mentioning her mother reminded me of my own and my heart missed a beat. Getting up from the ancient stairway, I made my way back home. I wept out loud, a tried method by which I would defend myself. I expected she would come to me but she did not. I wandered from the kitchen to the bedroom but found no trace of her. Where had my mother gone? When would she return? I was bored with being in the empty house. An idea occurred to me: I took a dish from the kitchen and a piastre from my savings and went off immediately to the seller of beans. I found him asleep on a bench outside the shop, his face covered over by his arm. The pots of beans had vanished and the long-necked bottles of oil had been put back on the shelf and the marble top washed down.

"Mister," I whispered, approaching.

90 Hearing nothing but his snoring, I touched his shoulder. He raised his arm in alarm and looked at me through reddened eyes.

"Mister."

"What do you want?" he asked roughly, becoming aware of my presence and recognizing me.

"A piastre's worth of beans with linseed oil."

"Eh?"

"I've got the piastre and I've got the dish." 95

"You're crazy, boy," he shouted at me. "Get out or I'll bash your brains in."

When I didn't move he pushed me so violently I went sprawling onto my back. I got up painfully, struggling to hold back the crying that was twisting my lips. My hands were clenched, one on the dish and the other on the piastre. I threw him an angry look. I thought about returning with my hopes dashed, but dreams of heroism and valour altered my plan of action. Resolutely, I made a quick decision and with all my strength threw the dish at him. It flew through the air and struck him on the head, while I took to my heels, heedless of everything. I was convinced I'd killed him, just as the knight had killed the ghoul. I didn't stop running till I was near the ancient wall. Panting, I looked behind me but saw no signs of any pursuit. I stopped to get my breath back, then asked myself what I should do now that the second dish was lost. Something warned me not to return home directly, and soon I had given myself over to a wave of indifference that bore me off where it willed. It meant a beating, neither more nor less, on my return, so let me put it off for a time. Here was the piastre in my hand and I could have some sort of enjoyment with it before being punished. I decided to pretend I had forgotten my having done wrong—but where was the conjurer, where was the peep-show? I looked everywhere for them but to no avail.

Worn out by this fruitless searching, I went off to the ancient stairway to keep my appointment. I sat down to wait, imagining to myself the meeting. I yearned for another kiss redolent with the fragrance of sweets. I admitted to myself that the little girl had given me sensations I had never experienced before. As I waited and dreamed, a whispering sound came to me from far away behind me. I climbed the stairs

cautiously and at the final landing I lay down flat on my face in order to see what was behind it, without anyone being able to spot me. I saw some ruins surrounded by a high wall, the last of what remained of the Treasury and the Chief Cadi's house. Directly under the stairs sat a man and a woman, and it was from them that the whispering came. The man looked like a tramp; the woman like one of those gypsies that tend sheep. An inner voice told me that their meeting was similar to the one I had had. Their lips and eyes revealed this, but they showed astonishing expertise in the extraordinary things they did. My gaze became rooted upon them with curiosity, surprise, pleasure, and a certain amount of disquiet. At last they sat down side by side, neither of them taking any notice of the other. After quite a while the man said:

"The money!"

"You're never satisfied," she said irritably.

Spitting on the ground, he said: "You're crazy."

"You're a thief."

He slapped her hard with the back of his hand, and she gathered up a handful of earth and threw it in his face. Then he sprang at her, fastening his fingers on her windpipe. In vain she gathered all her strength to escape from his grip. Her voice failed her, her eyes bulged out of their sockets, while her feet struck out at the air. In dumb terror I stared at the scene till I saw a thread of blood trickling down from her nose. A scream escaped from my mouth. Before the man raised his head, I had crawled backwards; descending the stairs at a jump, I raced off like mad to wherever my legs might carry me. I didn't stop running till I was out of breath. Gasping for breath, I was quite unaware of my whereabouts, but when I came to myself I found I was under a raised vault at the middle of a crossroads. I had never set foot there before and had no idea of where I was in relation to our quarter. On both sides sat sightless beggars, and crossing it from all directions were people who paid attention to no one. In terror I realized I had lost my way and that countless difficulties lay in wait for me before I would find my way home. Should I resort to asking one of the passers-by to direct me? What, though, would happen if chance should lead me to a man like the vendor of beans or the tramp of the waste plot? Would a miracle come about whereby I'd see my mother approaching so that I could eagerly hurry towards her? Should I try to make my own way, wandering about till I came across some familiar landmark that would indicate the direction I should take? I told myself that I should be resolute and take a quick decision: the day was passing and soon mysterious darkness would descend.

*Translated by Denys Johnson-Davies*

IF you liked Mahfouz's "The Conjurer Made Off with the Dish," you might also like a story by a writer whose work, among that of many modernists, including James Joyce in this chapter, influenced Mahfouz: Franz Kafka's "The Metamorphosis" (chapter 10).

**GOING FURTHER** Salman Rushdie, like Mahfouz, experienced death threats when he published *The Satanic Verses,* a novel that Mahfouz defended.

# Writing from Reading

## Summarize

1 What is the boy's level of responsibility for the various complications in the story? At which points is he relatively innocent? At which points does he make decisions that get him into further trouble?

2 Describe the role of the young girl in the story. How does her presence drive the plot?

## Analyze Craft

3 Examine the instances of dialogue in the story, and discuss how Mahfouz uses dialogue differently at different points through the story.

4 "The Conjurer Made Off with the Dish" is written in first person. Analyze how the story would change if it were written in third person, and discuss what is gained or lost by hearing events described by the boy narrator.

5 Although the story is named after the conjurer, the boy's complications involve many different characters. Identify one of these characters as the antagonist, citing proof from the story to make your argument.

### Analyze Voice

6 Naguib Mahfouz was born in Cairo, and his story takes place in Egypt. How does setting affect the plot and the complications that the narrator encounters? Discuss which elements of the story would differ and which would remain the same if it were told by a boy in a modern American city.

### Synthesize Summary and Analysis

7 Consider all the complications and momentary resolutions throughout the story. At what point, if ever, does the narrator undergo a change? Discuss the events of the story that drive the boy toward, or keep him from, changing by the end of the story.

### Interpret the Story

8 In the last line of the story, the boy resolves to make a quick decision. Discuss the irony of this conclusion in light of the events of the story. Consider what, if anything, the boy has learned from the day's events, and argue whether his adventure is finished or just beginning.

# Pramoedya Ananta Toer (1925–2006)

Called Indonesia's greatest writer, Pramoedya (Prah-MOO-dia) Ananta Toer spent more than fourteen years in prison because of his political views. A supporter of Indonesian independence at a time when the country was ruled first by the Dutch, then by the Japanese, Pramoedya was beaten so badly upon his arrest that he lost much of his hearing. He suffered other abuses, including no communication with his wife and children while in prison and the destruction of his manuscripts and notes. Nevertheless, Pramoedya produced novels, short stories, and essays that have been translated into more than thirty languages. His best-known work, the *Buru Quartet,* is a series of four novels about the Indonesian nationalist movement—*This Earth of Mankind* (1980), *Child of All Nations* (1980), *Footsteps* (1985), and *House of Glass* (1988). He began working on the quartet while imprisoned on the island of Buru, originally telling stories to his fellow prisoners, who enjoyed them so much that they took on Pramoedya's prison labor to allow him to write; he composed on scraps of paper that had to be smuggled from the prison. Although the books were banned in Indonesia, they were well-received internationally, securing Pramoedya's place as the leading literary voice of the Indonesian struggle for independence.

**AS YOU READ** As you read, notice how straightforward the basic plot is. Notice also how the tension in the story rises and falls as the plot advances. How does the narrator manage his feelings of anxiety? How do the narrator's feelings about events influence your feelings?

# Circumcision (1969)

1 LIKE other village children, I spent my evenings at the local prayer house learning to recite the Quran. Nothing could have pleased us more than to be there. For recitation lessons we paid two and a half cents per week, which was used to buy oil for the lamps. Lessons began at five thirty in the evening and continued until nine; they were the one and only excuse we had for getting out of doing our homework.

2 What I'm calling recitation lessons was actually nothing more than telling jokes, talking in fevered whispers about sex, and annoying other devotees who came to say their sunset or evening prayers while we waited for our own turn to be called. This was my world at the age of nine.

3 Like my friends, I wanted to be a good Muslim, though few of us, at our age, had been circumcised. But then, one day, one of my friends did get circumcised and a large celebration was held for him. This is when I began to think, if I hadn't been circumcised was I really a Muslim? I mulled over this question but didn't let anyone know what I was thinking.

4 In my small hometown of Blora, boys were usually circumcised somewhere between the ages of eight and thirteen, generally in as grand a style as family circumstances permitted. Girls underwent symbolic circumcision at the age of fifteen days, without any kind of celebration.

5 One night, my father came home and talked to me about circumcision. I had no idea where he had been, but he was in a very buoyant mood. The house was dark; all the lamps had been extinguished except for one in the central hall, where I was sitting with my mother, listening to her tell me a story about an old man—a pious one, presumably, since he had been to Mecca and was called *haji*[1] to indicate that he had made the pilgrimage to Islam's most holy seat—who kept on getting married. The story was a good one, but because of my father's sudden return it died then and there.

6 "Do you think you're brave enough to be circumcised?" he asked me, a hopeful smile on his lips.

7 I didn't know what to say. I wanted to be a good Muslim, but my father's surprise offer terrified me. Then again, my father always terrified me. But, for some reason, his smile that night made all my fears disappear.

"Yes, I am!" I told him. 8

His smile broadened and he laughed congenially. 9
"What would you like to wear to your circumcision, a wraparound *kain*,[2] or a sarong?"

"A *kain*," I answered. 10

He then turned to my seven-year-old brother, who 11
was also in the room. "And what about you, Tato? Are you brave enough, too?"

Tato laughed happily: "Sure I am!" 12

Father, too, laughed contentedly and the light 13
from the lamp illuminated his even white teeth and pink gums.

Mother rose from the mat she had rolled out on 14
the floor earlier, before starting her bedtime story.

"When do you want to have them circumcised?" 15
she asked.

"As soon as possible," my father replied. 16

He then rose from his chair and walked away, into 17
the darkness of the house and his bedroom.

Mother stretched out on the mat again but did not 18
continue her story about the marriage-happy *haji*. Instead, she looked at us: "You boys must give thanks to God that your father is going to have you both circumcised."

"We will, Mother," we answered in unison. 19

"Your dear departed grandmother and all your 20
other ancestors in heaven will be very pleased to know that you have been circumcised."

"Yes, Mother," we said again. 21

THAT night I could scarcely sleep as I thought 22
of how much the circumcision would hurt. But then I also began to think of the new *kain* and new pair of sandals I would likely receive—along with all the other new clothes, and a headcloth and prayer mat as well. On top of that, I wouldn't have to go to school and there would be numerous guests. I was almost sure to receive lots of gifts.

I imagined the happiness I would feel from own- 23
ing my own *kain* and headcloth, for these items were not only a sign of being a good Muslim; they were a

[1]A Muslim honorific indicating one has made the pilgrimage to Mecca.

[2]A cloth skirt similar to a sarong, but with the ends sewn together.

sign of being a good Javanese as well, something I also wanted to be.

24 I was sure to be given at least one sarong, maybe two or even three. My uncircumcised friends would be jealous; that thought, too, gave me a thrill.

25 The next morning I rose from my bed full of excitement. Tato and I set off for school with plenty of time to spare. Usually, our legs balked at walking to school, but that day they flew. All of our classmates soon heard the news, and the boys who weren't circumcised, especially the older ones, looked on us with newfound respect. Even the teachers cast a kindly gaze on us, for soon we were going to be true Muslims, bona fide circumcised Muslims. And when that happened—and this was the most important thing of all—we would have the right to a place in heaven. We'd no longer have to wish for the many beautiful things that we'd always hoped for but had never been able to obtain, for they would be ours.

I suddenly felt taller, more important than my friends.

26 At the prayer house, the news also created a sensation among my friends, and our religious teacher gave me the same kindly look that my teachers at school had displayed. I suddenly felt taller, more important than my friends. I could see it very clearly: heaven's gates standing wide open for me. And sure enough, just as our religious teacher had also promised, there they were—the beautiful *houri,* young maidens waiting to tend to my needs. Each one was as beautiful as a certain girl at my school that all the boys talked about.

27 "After I'm circumcised, I'll be a true Muslim," I told the *kiai.*[3] "I'll have the right to go to heaven!"

28 The man laughed cheerfully. "And you'll have forty-four *houri* to wait on you!"

29 "But I don't want any who has six or eight breasts, like a dog," I told him. "I want them to look like Sriati, my classmate at school. She's beautiful."

30 The *kiai* laughed again.

31 "And I'll go fishing in rivers of milk every day," Tato chimed in.

32 Our teacher's mouth opened wider with laughter, baring a disgusting set of teeth that looked like they'd never been brushed.

33 Our older and uncircumcised friends listened to this conversation silently. I could see fear in their eyes: the fear of missing out on their share of *houri* and the fear of going not to heaven but to hell.

34 Starting that evening, we followed our recitation lessons diligently and we made sure to finish our homework in short order too. We also fasted, every week, from Monday to Thursday, until the end of the school year. As a result of this extra labor, I easily passed to the next grade.

Two weeks before the end of the school year, my father, the principal of our school, decided to stage a play with the children as actors. Our circumcision ceremony would be held the following day. Father had decided, then and there, to make this an annual event. That way, the poorer boys in school whose parents could not afford to hold a separate celebration would have the chance to get circumcised as well. 35

For this, my father's first attempt at starting a new tradition, the response of the townspeople was not what Father had expected it to be. Many parents with sons of circumcision age were apparently embarrassed to have someone else pay for their sons' circumcision ceremony. In the end, there were only six boys to be circumcised: my brother Tato and I, a ten-year-old cousin of ours, a sixteen-year-old foster brother, and two boys from poor families who lived outside of town. Another foster brother, who was eighteen and had already had a child with our servant, refused to participate. He insisted that his own father would arrange a ceremony for him. 36

Five days before the celebration, the boys who were to be circumcised were made to memorize a *panembrama,* a Javanese welcome song. On the night of the play, we were to appear onstage and announce to the audience in song that we were to be circumcised the next day; we were also to request that they offer their prayers for a successful event. 37

One of our teachers wrote a play about a lost goat in which all the roles were played by the male students. 38

Finally, the day that we had long awaited approached. The evening before, our grandmother gave Tato and me green silk sarongs. Our mother gave us lacquered wooden sandals and blue shirts. The girls in school gave us switches for keeping flies away during the ceremony, and our father gave us eight Dutch-language children's books. All these gifts made us forget about the pain we were to feel the following day. 39

ON the night of the play, the school was jam-packed with spectators. Food was served: sweet potatoes and boiled peanuts, fermented cassava, *gemblong*[4] made of sweetened sticky 40

[3]An authority on Islamic religious affairs.

[4]An Indonesian dessert.

rice, and other snacks. Before the performance was to begin, the six of us who were to be circumcised were made to line up on stage. I was outfitted in a *kain* and headcloth, as was my brother, Tato. The other boys were bareheaded. When the curtain opened, the *gamelan*[5] orchestra began to play, and we bowed in respect to the audience. I felt so incredibly proud of myself at that moment. All eyes were focused on us as we sang out that tomorrow we were to be circumcised. The girls looked on us with awe; there would soon be six more eligible men in town.

41 After our song the audience clapped loudly and we took another bow. The curtain was then closed and we were relieved from further responsibility.

42 In my hometown, there was very little public entertainment, which is why, I suppose, people came from all parts of the city to watch our performance of *The Lost Goat.* The school's large central classroom, which was usually subdivided into four sections during the regular school day, had been transformed into one large hall that was now filled with people.

When my foster brother was led out of the hut, he could scarcely walk.

43 The musical entertainment that night varied greatly; besides *gamelan* orchestral works, there were new popular songs such as "Peanut Flower" and "Rose Mary," cowboy songs, theatrical tunes, and older popular songs with a Western influence.

44 After the performance, many people from the audience patted our shoulders or pounded our backs, giving all six of us greater encouragement and making us feel very special. Later that night, after we had returned home, Tato continued to sing in his bed until he could stay awake no longer; his voice grew softer and softer until it finally died and he drifted to sleep.

45 In my hometown, the day of a boy's circumcision was a day of great significance, as important as one's birthday or wedding day, the anniversary of a person's death, or even a public holiday. Although my mother had sent out no formal invitations, news of the ceremony had spread far and wide, and she received contributions for the event from all parts of town.

46 As was usually the case with major life rituals, even though we had stayed up late the night before, on the day of our circumcision we woke up extra early; by four thirty in the morning the house was already very busy. The candidates for circumcision bathed and were then each dressed in his new *kain* and a prayer cap or headcloth. My sisters wore new clothes and my mother dressed in a new *kain* with a *parang rusak*[6] motif. For a top, she wore a long blouse with embroidered lapels and edging, a gift from an aunt who taught at the girls' school in Rembang. A green rainbow-motif shoulder sash completed her outfit.

47 My father had on his school uniform: a wraparound *kain* with a broken dagger motif that matched my mother's and a long-sleeved button-up jacket. As usual he was barefooted. (My father never wore shoes; only at home might he sometimes wear wooden cloppers or sandals.)

48 As if infected by my family's state of readiness, our neighbors rose early too. All dressed in new clothing as well, they then gathered at our house to escort us to the school, where the ceremony was to be held, about a half kilometer away.

49 Inside the school a small tentlike shelter with sides made of mosquito netting had been erected for the circumcision ceremony. The six of us who were to be circumcised occupied a row of chairs nearby. As the time for the ceremony approached, the number of visitors around the shelter grew larger, both adults and children too. The girls remained at a slight distance.

50 Finally, a circumcision specialist, the *calak*, arrived, and proceeded to unwrap three straight-edge blades from their handkerchief covers. As he was doing this, an older man offered us words of advice: "Don't be afraid. It won't hurt. It's a bit like being bitten by a red ant. I laughed when I was circumcised."

51 His was only one of many comforting voices, but no matter how reassuring the tone, we couldn't completely expunge our anxiety and fear.

52 Then came the time for the ceremony to begin. My father and mother, who were seated in a pair of large chairs among the crowd of visitors, rose and approached the netted shelter. Pride and elation showed on their faces.

53 The first boy to enter the hut was my parents' foster son, the sixteen-year-old, because he was the oldest one among us. The other foster son, the one who had refused to be circumcised, was nowhere to be seen in the crowd. The children who had come to witness the ceremony crowded so close to the shelter that the adults were forced to shoo them away.

54 I was incredibly scared. I wanted to be a good Muslim, but that wasn't enough to still my terror. And when the *calak* suddenly began to bawl out an incom-

---

[5]An Indonesian musical ensemble composed mostly of percussion instruments.

[6]"Broken knife"; a traditional Javanese pattern.

prehensible prayer, the pounding of my heart in my chest grew all the more strong. When my foster brother was led out of the hut, he could scarcely walk. His face was drained of blood and his lips looked almost white. He had no strength. The ushers seated him in his chair and placed a large earthenware saucer that was filled with fine ash from the kitchen hearth between his legs to catch and sop up the blood that was dripping from his penis.

55 One by one, the older boys entered the shelter. As with my foster brother, when they reemerged they looked pale-faced and walked with an unsteady gait. As I stood up to enter the tent, I felt several people take hold of my shoulders, as if they were afraid I would try to run away. I was then ushered inside the hut, where the *calak* was waiting impatiently, with a ferocious gleam in his eye—at least that's how he looked to me.

56 I was placed in a chair and my head pulled backward so that I was now facing up, toward the roof of the tent. While one of the ushers, an older man, held my shoulders tightly to steady me, another pair of old hands attached themselves to my temples so that I could not look down. Below me, on the floor, was an earthenware bowl filled with ash. I felt a hand grope my penis, and then my foreskin being twisted tightly until it began to sting and feel very hot. Just at that moment, a razor severed that knot of my skin. It was over; I was circumcised. The old man who had been holding my temples back released his hands. I looked down to see blood dripping from the end of my penis.

57 "Don't move," one of the men said.

58 "You have to wait until the first flow of blood has stopped," another added.

59 I stared at the stream of blood—a blackened cord as it began to coagulate—and watched it as it slowly fell and disappeared into the fine ash in the saucer directly below.

60 Because Tato was the youngest, he was the last to be circumcised; and when his operation was over, he too was led out from the shelter and put back on the seat beside me. Blood continued to drip into the earthenware dishes below our legs. All eyes were upon us. Mother came to me and kissed my cheeks; her display of affection caused tears to well in my eyes. She kissed Tato on the cheek too. Then Father came over to congratulate us: "Well done, well done."

61 The visitors began to leave, first the children and then the adults, who took their leave one by one. After that, the six of us who had just been circumcised made our way home on foot as well.

62 We were treated like kings that day. Our wishes were commands. The families of the two poor boys who had also been circumcised came to our home bearing gifts of chicken and rice.

63 "Now that you've been circumcised, do you feel that something's changed?" my mother asked me.

64 "I feel really happy," I told her.

65 "And do you feel like a true Muslim?" she then inquired.

66 Her question gave me pause; the fact was, I didn't feel any different.

67 "I feel like I did yesterday," I tried to explain, "... and the day before. I still don't feel like a true Muslim."

68 "Could it be because you don't perform the daily prayers?" Mother then asked.

69 "No, I always do all five," I told her.

70 "Your grandfather's been to Mecca. Maybe if you made the pilgrimage, you'd feel the change, and know that you were a true Muslim."

71 "Would we go by ship?" Tato chirped.

72 "Yes, you'd sail to Arabia," Mother answered.

73 "Wouldn't we have to be really rich to do that?" I then posed.

74 "Yes, you would," Mother said.

75 And with that all my hopes of becoming a true Muslim vanished. I knew that my parents weren't well off and that we could never afford to make the pilgrimage.

76 "Why hasn't Father ever been to Mecca?" I asked.

77 "Because your father doesn't have the money."

78 Although I suddenly wanted to be rich, I also knew that this would never be the case. And after I had healed, the thought of becoming a true Muslim never again entered my mind.

IF you liked this story, "Circumcision," you might also like Chimamanda Ngozi Adichie's "Cell One," about political repression in Nigeria (chapter 9).

**GOING FURTHER** The nationalist movement that led to Pramoedya's arrest spawned many Indonesian writers, among them the pioneer in modernizing the Indonesian language, Sutan Takdir Alisjahbana, whose best-known novel is *Open Sail*.

# Writing from Reading

### Summarize

1 Break down the story into individual events. Does this story follow the traditional pattern described in the chapter? That is, can you identify a conflict or conflicts, rising action, climax, and dénouement or resolution? What are they?

### Analyze Craft

2 Does the story have a protagonist and antagonist? Explain.

3 Describe the relationship between the narrator and his father. How does this relationship affect the plot?

### Analyze Voice

4 The narrator is relating a deeply personal story, which in some cultures might make for great embarrassment. How would you describe the tone he uses to tell about these events? Does he take a longer view than just focusing on the ritual practice of the title?

### Synthesize Summary and Analysis

5 Analyze the relationship between plot and character. How does this story's plot hinge on the protagonist's efforts to realize his desire and his abilities to cope with failure?

6 How do the themes of wealth and poverty affect the characters and the plot of this story? In the narrator's mind, how do economic factors affect his ability to be a "good Muslim"?

7 Reread the paragraphs in which the circumcision occurs. Describe a ceremony or ritual from your own culture, using details and suspense the way this author does.

### Interpret the Story

8 What pain does the narrator feel that may be greater than the physical pain? How do you explain the narrator's falling off of devotion at the end?

# Reading for Plot

When reading for plot, ask yourself how the author has arranged the incidents in the story for cause and effect leading to the climax and the resolution of the story. We'll use a familiar fairy-tale as an example.

| | | |
|---|---|---|
| **How does the story begin?** | • Is exposition included in the story? | EXAMPLE In those days, it wasn't so unusual for a little girl to walk in the forest by herself—especially since her grandmother's house was close by. |
| | • Does it begin ***in medias res***? | EXAMPLE The forest felt especially dark and creepy, she thought, as she set off in her red cloak with a basket of goodies for her grandmother. |

| | | |
|---|---|---|
| **How does the plot unfold?** | • Does it include **flashbacks**? | EXAMPLE There had been another time—last spring, when the animals were hungrier than usual, after the long deprivation of winter—that she had felt afraid. She'd seen a wolf, at the bend of the path, and then again, by the pond, drinking. Both times, she passed quickly, not making eye contact, telling herself that so close to grandmother's, nothing could harm her. |
| | • Does the story include **foreshadowing**? | EXAMPLE Little Red Riding Hood shivered as she walked, drawing her cloak around her, listening for cries of wild animals, wondering whether she really should have come alone, whether that quick movement was the wind . . . or something else. |
| **Which elements of plot can you identify?** | • Who is the **protagonist**? | EXAMPLE Little Red Riding Hood |
| | • Who/what is the **antagonist**? | EXAMPLE the wolf |
| | • What is the **conflict**? | EXAMPLE The big bad wolf is leading the poor, defenseless Little Red Riding Hood into a trap. |
| | • What is the **climax**? | EXAMPLE The wolf tore off its cap and leapt from the bed, teeth and claws bared. |
| | • What is the **dénouement, resolution,** or **conclusion**? | EXAMPLE The woodcutter dusted off the little girl, found the grandmother, and they all had a lovely little snack together. |

# Suggestions for Writing about Plot

1. Consider the order of incidents in "The Conjurer Made Off with the Dish." Why do you think Mahfouz placed the scenes in this particular order?
2. Compare the setting of "Araby" with that of "Greasy Lake." How do the grim settings of these stories propel the plot?
3. Compare the way each story in this chapter employs plot to achieve its dramatic purpose. What similarities do you see in the writers' techniques? Choose two stories and discuss the elements of plot that are common to both.
4. Make a case for how the young narrators of the stories in this chapter respond to new situations or opportunities. Who takes action and who does not? Which characters reach new levels of perception? Does anyone fulfill his or her desire?

# 5

IN China, daughter take care of mother. Here it is the other way around. Mother help daughter, mother ask, Anything else I can do? Otherwise daughter complain mother is not supportive. I tell daughter, We do not have this word in Chinese, *supportive*. But my daughter too busy to listen, she has to go to meeting, she has to write memo while her husband go to the gym to be a man. My daughter say otherwise he will be depressed. Seems like all his life he has this trouble, depression.

*—from "Who's Irish?" by Gish Jen*

# Chara

*"All characters are individual, first and foremost. I don't think that any successful piece of fiction can start from any premise, such as 'I am trying to represent an American, an Asian-American, or an Irish-American,' or any kind of anything. I think that I have certain pre-occupations and those things arise naturally; but, first and foremost, I am concerned with character, individuals as individuals, but also in their place in the world."*

Conversation with Gish Jen, available on video at www.mhhe.com/delbanco1e

WHOSE voice is this, and what can you tell about her from this short excerpt? You can tell quite a bit, actually. It's likely that the first thing you notice is the way the person speaks—with the inaccurate spelling and grammar of a person not native to English. It's also clear from the context that the speaker is female, the mother of a married daughter whose husband is depressed. "Here"—the first word of the second sentence—suggests that the speaker's no longer at home but is instead an immigrant, a stranger in what seems to her a strange land. The character/narrator doesn't use articles or pronouns, and she fails to use appropriate verb forms; her nouns and verbs disagree. The grammatically correct first sentence would have been "In China, *a* daughter *takes* care of *her* mother."

Next, because she knows the ways of China and the Chinese, we can safely guess where the mother comes from and what her native language is. Even the single word "supportive" provides us with much evidence; the speaker tells her daughter that there's no such word in Chinese, and she's evidently repeating a term the daughter—a better English speaker—has previously used. So there's a family disagreement going on; the daughter has complained her mother's not being supportive while she, the younger woman, is earning a living—going to meetings, writing memos "while her husband go to the gym." Jen replicates the sound, accent, and cadence of inflected speech, bringing the character vividly to life.

Even in this brief excerpt, we get a sense of the mother's nature. Her flood of words has an edge. This narrator is not just reporting facts about her life and family; she's *complaining*, even *ranting*. Her daughter's entire way of life is, to the speaker, a puzzle. The mother doesn't approve of a husband who has to "go to the gym to be a man." That phrase, more than any other in the passage, underlines her disapproval and confusion; the behavior of the younger generation is hard for her to swallow, and roles have been reversed. Her child fails to provide her with the respectful attention an elder in China expects. We know that we will read a story about the clash of values, about generations in conflict and cultures at odds with each other.

*CONTINUED ON PAGE 111*

cter

*. . . the character is absolutely the font of all fiction.*

# Q&A

*. . . I am interested in so many questions of ethnicity and identity . . .*

# A Conversation on Writing

## Gish Jen

### Using Character to Drive Fiction

I think the character is absolutely the font of all fiction. I think that's where the conflict comes from and I think it's where the plot comes from: that's where the story comes from. And so when I feel that something is not going well, that it doesn't have its own drive, I don't look at the incidents to try to understand what's going wrong. I look at the character, and in particular I look at the character's ambivalence.

### Using Humor to Confront Loaded Topics

[Humor] does seem to have a particular use in my writing, because I am interested in so many questions of ethnicity and identity, which are pretty loaded. With humor, it's like everything is just floating on a sea where they can all move around. And things, which perhaps would be crashing into each other in a very unpleasant way, are suddenly able to float.

### On the Pleasure of Reading

I at least feel much more alive reading than I do living sometimes. I mean, there is a way in which life itself can be kind of a disappointment, which literature never is.

### On the Writing Process

You know, when I was a younger writer, I used to have a system where I kept a little notebook of index cards. These were 4-by-6 index cards that were spiral bound. That was a very useful way of keeping notes because after you write things down you can tear them out and file them. So, all of your thoughts about character, for instance, can be put in one place. . . . Now that I'm an older person and more in need of such devices I actually . . . rely more heavily on my imagination.

"I *am* the kind of person who would make a joke on someone's deathbed, tacky as it may seem," Gish Jen once said in an interview. And while she may have been speaking lightheartedly, she captured one of the essential elements of her craft—her ability to blend tragedy and humor. Born (1955) as Lillian Jen to Chinese immigrant parents in Scarsdale, New York, she changed her first name to "Gish" in honor of the silent film actress Lillian Gish. After graduating from Harvard, Jen taught English to engineers in China, later returning to the United States and earning her M.F.A. from the Iowa Writers' Workshop. She is the author of three novels—*Typical American* (1991), its sequel, *Mona in the Promised Land* (1996), and *The Love Wife* (2004)—as well as a collection of short stories, *Who's Irish?* (2000). In her fiction, Jen explores ideas of ethnic and cultural identity, assimilation, and integration, and how these ideas change for her characters as they adapt to new surroundings or situations. She now lives in Cambridge, Massachusetts, with her husband and two children.

**To watch this entire interview and hear the author read from "Who's Irish?" go to www.mhhe.com/delbanco1e.**

**RESEARCH ASSIGNMENT** In Jen's interview, she reflects on this quotation about story writing: "If you don't surprise yourself, you will not surprise the reader." What does this mean to Jen?

**AS YOU READ** As you read, imagine that you are sitting across the table from the narrator of this story. Imagine that she is speaking directly to you. How do you feel about what she is telling you? What would you like to say to her? Would you say everything you are thinking?

# Who's Irish? (1999)

1 IN China, people say mixed children are supposed to be smart, and definitely my granddaughter Sophie is smart. But Sophie is wild, Sophie is not like my daughter Natalie, or like me. I am work hard my whole life, and fierce besides. My husband always used to say he is afraid of me, and in our restaurant, busboys and cooks all afraid of me too. Even the gang members come for protection money, they try to talk to my husband. When I am there, they stay away. If they come by mistake, they pretend they are come to eat. They hide behind the menu, they order a lot of food. They talk about their mothers. Oh, my mother have some arthritis, need to take herbal medicine, they say. Oh, my mother getting old, her hair all white now.

I say, Your mother's hair used to be white, but since she dye it, it become black again. Why don't you go home once in a while and take a look? I tell them, Confucius say a filial son knows what color his mother's hair is.

My daughter is fierce too, she is vice president in the bank now. Her new house is big enough for everybody to have their own room, including me. But Sophie take after Natalie's husband's family, their name is Shea. Irish. I always thought Irish people are like Chinese people, work so hard on the railroad, but now I know why the Chinese beat the Irish. Of course, not all Irish are like the Shea family, of course not. My daughter tell me I should not say Irish this, Irish that.

How do you like it when people say the Chinese this, the Chinese that, she say.

5 You know, the British call the Irish heathen, just like they call the Chinese, she say.

You think the Opium War was bad, how would you like to live right next door to the British, she say.

And that is that. My daughter have a funny habit when she win an argument, she take a sip of something and look away, so the other person is not embarrassed. So I am not embarrassed. I do not call anybody anything either. I just happen to mention about the Shea family, an interesting fact: four brothers in the family, and not one of them work. The mother, Bess, have a job before she got sick, she was executive secretary in a big company. She is handle everything for a big shot, you would be surprised how complicated her job is, not just type this, type that. Now she is a nice woman with a clean house. But her boys, every one of them is on welfare, or so-called severance pay, or so-called disability pay. Something. They say they cannot find work, this is not the economy of the fifties, but I say, Even the black people doing better these days, some of them live so fancy, you'd be surprised. Why the Shea family have so much trouble? They are white people, they speak English. When I come to this country, I have no money and do not speak English. But my husband and I own our restaurant before he die. Free and clear, no mortgage. Of course, I understand I am just lucky; come from a country where the food is popular all over the world. I understand it is not the Shea family's fault they come from a country where everything is boiled. Still, I say.

She's right, we should broaden our horizons, say one brother Jim, at Thanksgiving. Forget about the car business. Think about egg rolls.

Pad thai, say another brother, Mike. I'm going to make my fortune in pad thai. It's going to be the new pizza.

10 I say, You people too picky about what you sell. Selling egg rolls not good enough for you, but at least my husband and I can say, We made it. What can you say? Tell me. What can you say?

Everybody chew their tough turkey.

I especially cannot understand my daughter's husband John, who has no job but cannot take care of Sophie either. Because he is a man, he say, and that's the end of the sentence.

Plain boiled food, plain boiled thinking. Even his name is plain boiled: John. Maybe because I grew up with black bean sauce and hoisin sauce and garlic sauce, I always feel something is missing when my son-in-law talk.

But, okay: so my son-in-law can be man, I am baby-sitter. Six hours a day, same as the old sitter, crazy Amy, who quit. This is not so easy, now that I am sixty-eight, Chinese age almost seventy. Still, I try. In China, daughter take care of mother. Here it is the other way around. Mother help daughter, mother ask, Anything else I can do? Otherwise daughter complain mother is not supportive. I tell daughter, We do not have this word in Chinese, *supportive.* But my daughter too busy to listen, she has to go to meeting, she has to write memo while her husband go to the gym to be a man. My daughter say otherwise he will be depressed. Seems like all his life he has this trouble, depression.

No one wants to hire someone who is depressed, she say. It is important for him to keep his spirits up.

Beautiful wife, beautiful daughter, beautiful house, oven can clean itself automatically. No money left over, because only one income, but lucky enough, got the baby-sitter for free. If John lived in China, he would be very happy. But he is not happy. Even at the gym things go wrong. One day, he pull a muscle. Another day, weight room too crowded. Always something.

Until finally, hooray, he has a job. Then he feel pressure.

I need to concentrate, he say. I need to focus.

He is going to work for insurance company. Salesman job. A paycheck, he say, and at least he will wear clothes instead of gym shorts. My daughter buy him some special candy bars from the health-food store. They say THINK! on them, and are supposed to help John think.

John is a good-looking boy, you have to say that, especially now that he shave so you can see his face.

I am an old man in a young man's game, say John.

I will need a new suit, say John.

This time I am not going to shoot myself in the foot, say John.

Good, I say.

She means to be supportive, my daughter say. Don't start the send her back to China thing, because we can't.

SOPHIE is three years old American age, but already I see her nice Chinese side swallowed up by her wild Shea side. She looks like mostly Chinese. Beautiful black hair, beautiful black eyes. Nose perfect size, not so flat looks like something fell down, not so large looks like some big deal got stuck in wrong face. Everything just right, only her skin is a brown surprise to John's family. So brown, they say. Even John say it. She never goes in the sun, still she is that color, he say. Brown. They say, Nothing the matter with brown. They are just surprised. So brown. Nattie is not that brown, they say. They say, It seems like Sophie should be a color in between Nattie and John. Seems funny, a girl named Sophie Shea be brown. But she is brown, maybe her name should be Sophie Brown. She never go in the sun, still she is that color, they say. Nothing the matter with brown. They are just surprised.

The Shea family talk is like this sometimes, going around and around like a Christmas-tree train.

Maybe John is not her father, I say one day, to stop the train. And sure enough, train wreck. None of the brothers ever say the word *brown* to me again.

Instead, John's mother, Bess, say, I hope you are not offended.

She say, I did my best on those boys. But raising four boys with no father is no picnic.

You have a beautiful family, I say.

I'm getting old, she say.

You deserve a rest, I say. Too many boys make you old.

I never had a daughter, she say. You have a daughter.

I have a daughter, I say. Chinese people don't think a daughter is so great, but you're right. I have a daughter.

I was never against the marriage, you know, she say. I never thought John was marrying down. I always thought Nattie was just as good as white.

I was never against the marriage either, I say. I just wonder if they look at the whole problem.

Of course you pointed out the problem, you are a mother, she say. And now we both have a granddaughter. A little brown granddaughter, she is so precious to me.

I laugh. A little brown granddaughter, I say. To tell you the truth, I don't know how she came out so brown.

40 We laugh some more. These days Bess need a walker to walk. She take so many pills, she need two glasses of water to get them all down. Her favorite TV show is about bloopers, and she love her bird feeder. All day long, she can watch that bird feeder, like a cat.

I can't wait for her to grow up, Bess say. I could use some female company.

Too many boys, I say.

Boys are fine, she say. But they do surround you after a while.

You should take a break, come live with us, I say. Lots of girls at our house.

45 Be careful what you offer, say Bess with a wink. Where I come from, people mean for you to move in when they say a thing like that.

NOTHING the matter with Sophie's outside, that's the truth. It is inside that she is like not any Chinese girl I ever see. We go to the park, and this is what she does. She stand up in the stroller. She take off all her clothes and throw them in the fountain.

Sophie! I say. Stop!

But she just laugh like a crazy person. Before I take over as baby-sitter, Sophie has that crazy-person sitter, Amy the guitar player. My daughter thought this Amy very creative—another word we do not talk about in China. In China, we talk about whether we have difficulty or no difficulty. We talk about whether life is bitter or not bitter. In America, all day long, people talk about creative. Never mind that I cannot even look at this Amy, with her shirt so short that her belly button showing. This Amy think Sophie should love her body. So when Sophie take off her diaper, Amy laugh. When Sophie run around naked, Amy say she wouldn't want to wear a diaper either. When Sophie go *shu-shu* in her lap, Amy laugh and say there are no germs in pee. When Sophie take off her shoes, Amy say bare feet is best, even the pediatrician say so. That is why Sophie now walk around with no shoes like a beggar child. Also why Sophie love to take off her clothes.

Turn around! say the boys in the park. Let's see that ass!

50 Of course, Sophie does not understand. Sophie clap her hands, I am the only one to say, No! This is not a game.

It has nothing to do with John's family, my daughter say. Amy was too permissive, that's all.

But I think if Sophie was not wild inside, she would not take off her shoes and clothes to begin with.

You never take off your clothes when you were little, I say. All my Chinese friends had babies, I never saw one of them act wild like that.

Look, my daughter say. I have a big presentation tomorrow.

55 John and my daughter agree Sophie is a problem, but they don't know what to do.

You spank her, she'll stop, I say another day.

But they say, Oh no.

In America, parents not supposed to spank the child.

It gives them low self-esteem, my daughter say. And that leads to problems later, as I happen to know.

60 My daughter never have big presentation the next day when the subject of spanking come up.

I don't want you to touch Sophie, she say. No spanking, period.

Don't tell me what to do, I say.

I'm not telling you what to do, say my daughter. I'm telling you how I feel.

I am not your servant, I say. Don't you dare talk to me like that.

65 My daughter have another funny habit when she lose an argument. She spread out all her fingers and look at them, as if she like to make sure they are still there.

My daughter is fierce like me, but she and John think it is better to explain to Sophie that clothes are a good idea. This is not so hard in the cold weather. In the warm weather, it is very hard.

Use your words, my daughter say. That's what we tell Sophie. How about if you set a good example.

As if good example mean anything to Sophie. I am so fierce, the gang members who used to come to the restaurant all afraid of me, but Sophie is not afraid.

I say, Sophie, if you take off your clothes, no snack.

70 I say, Sophie, if you take off your clothes, no lunch.

I say, Sophie, if you take off your clothes, no park.

Pretty soon we are stay home all day, and by the end of six hours she still did not have one thing to eat. You never saw a child stubborn like that.

I'm hungry! she cry when my daughter come home.

What's the matter, doesn't your grandmother feed you? My daughter laugh.

75 No! Sophie say. She doesn't feed me anything!

My daughter laugh again. Here you go, she say.

She say to John, Sophie must be growing.

Growing like a weed, I say.

Still Sophie take off her clothes, until one day I spank her. Not too hard, but she cry and cry, and when I tell her if she doesn't put her clothes back on I'll spank her again, she put her clothes back on. Then I tell her she is good girl, and give her some food to eat. The next

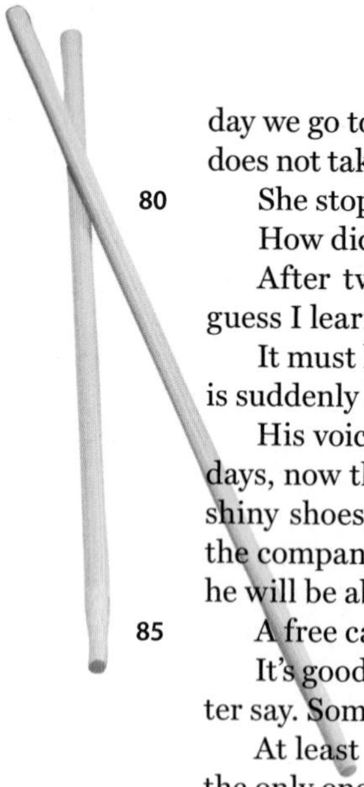

day we go to the park and, like a nice Chinese girl, she does not take off her clothes.

She stop taking off her clothes, I report. Finally!

How did you do it? my daughter ask.

After twenty-eight years experience with you, I guess I learned something, I say.

It must have been a phase, John say, and his voice is suddenly like an expert.

His voice is like an expert about everything these days, now that he carry a leather briefcase, and wear shiny shoes, and can go shopping for a new car. On the company, he say. The company will pay for it, but he will be able to drive it whenever he want.

A free car, he say. How do you like that.

It's good to see you in the saddle again, my daughter say. Some of your family patterns are scary.

At least I don't drink, he say. He say, And I'm not the only one with scary family patterns.

That's for sure, say my daughter.

EVERYONE is happy. Even I am happy, because there is more trouble with Sophie, but now I think I can help her Chinese side fight against her wild side. I teach her to eat food with fork or spoon or chopsticks, she cannot just grab into the middle of a bowl of noodles. I teach her not to play with garbage cans. Sometimes I spank her, but not too often, and not too hard.

Still, there are problems. Sophie like to climb everything. If there is a railing, she is never next to it. Always she is on top of it. Also, Sophie like to hit the mommies of her friends. She learn this from her playground best friend, Sinbad, who is four. Sinbad wear army clothes every day and like to ambush his mommy. He is the one who dug a big hole under the play structure, a foxhole he call it, all by himself. Very hardworking. Now he wait in the foxhole with a shovel full of wet sand. When his mommy come, he throw it right at her.

Oh, it's all right, his mommy say. You can't get rid of war games, it's part of their imaginative play. All the boys go through it.

Also, he like to kick his mommy, and one day he tell Sophie to kick his mommy too.

I wish this story is not true.

Kick her, kick her! Sinbad say.

Sophie kick her. A little kick, as if she just so happened was swinging her little leg and didn't realize that big mommy leg was in the way. Still I spank Sophie and make Sophie say sorry, and what does the mommy say?

Really, it's all right, she say. It didn't hurt.

After that, Sophie learn she can attack mommies in the playground, and some will say, Stop, but others will say, Oh, she didn't mean it, especially if they realize Sophie will be punished.

THIS is how, one day, bigger trouble come. The bigger trouble start when Sophie hide in the foxhole with that shovel full of sand. She wait, and when I come look for her, she throw it at me. All over my nice clean clothes.

Did you ever see a Chinese girl act this way?

Sophie! I say. Come out of there, say you're sorry.

But she does not come out. Instead, she laugh. Naaah, naah-na, naaa-naaa, she say.

I am not exaggerate: millions of children in China, not one act like this.

Sophie! I say. Now! Come out now!

But she know she is in big trouble. She know if she come out, what will happen next. So she does not come out. I am sixty-eight, Chinese age almost seventy, how can I crawl under there to catch her? Impossible. So I yell, yell, yell, and what happen? Nothing. A Chinese mother would help, but American mothers, they look at you, they shake their head, they go home. And, of course, a Chinese child would give up, but not Sophie.

I hate you! she yell. I hate you, Meanie!

Meanie is my new name these days.

Long time this goes on, long long time. The foxhole is deep, you cannot see too much, you don't know where is the bottom. You cannot hear too much either. If she does not yell, you cannot even know she is still there or not. After a while, getting cold out, getting dark out. No one left in the playground, only us.

Sophie, I say. How did you become stubborn like this? I am go home without you now.

I try to use a stick, chase her out of there, and once or twice I hit her, but still she does not come out. So finally I leave. I go outside the gate.

Bye-bye! I say. I'm go home now.

But still she does not come out and does not come out. Now it is dinnertime, the sky is black. I think I should maybe go get help, but how can I leave a little girl by herself in the playground? A bad man could come. A rat could come. I go back in to see what is happen to Sophie. What if she have a shovel and is making a tunnel to escape?

Sophie! I say.

No answer.

Sophie!

I don't know if she is alive. I don't know if she is fall asleep down there. If she is crying, I cannot hear her.

So I take the stick and poke.

Sophie! I say. I promise I no hit you. If you come out, I give you a lollipop.

No answer. By now I worried. What to do, what to do, what to do? I poke some more, even harder, so that I am poking and poking when my daughter and John suddenly appear.

What are you doing? What is going on? say my daughter.

Put down that stick! say my daughter.

You are crazy! say my daughter.

John wiggle under the structure, into the foxhole, to rescue Sophie.

She fell asleep, say John the expert. She's okay. That is one big hole.

Now Sophie is crying and crying.

Sophia, my daughter say, hugging her. Are you okay, peanut? Are you okay?

She's just scared, say John.

Are you okay? I say too. I don't know what happen, I say.

She's okay, say John. He is not like my daughter, full of questions. He is full of answers until we get home and can see by the lamplight.

Will you look at her? he yell then. What the hell happened?

Bruises all over her brown skin, and a swollen-up eye.

You are crazy! say my daughter. Look at what you did! You are crazy!

I try very hard, I say.

How could you use a stick? I told you to use your words!

She is hard to handle, I say.

She's three years old! You cannot use a stick! say my daughter.

She is not like any Chinese girl I ever saw, I say.

I brush some sand off my clothes. Sophie's clothes are dirty too, but at least she has her clothes on.

Has she done this before? ask my daughter. Has she hit you before?

She hits me all the time, Sophie say, eating ice cream.

Your family, say John.

Believe me, say my daughter.

A DAUGHTER I have, a beautiful daughter. I took care of her when she could not hold her head up. I took care of her before she could argue with me, when she was a little girl with two pigtails, one of them always crooked. I took care of her when we have to escape from China, I took care of her when suddenly we live in a country with cars everywhere, if you are not careful your little girl get run over. When my husband die, I promise him I will keep the family together, even though it was just two of us, hardly a family at all.

But now my daughter take me around to look at apartments. After all, I can cook, I can clean, there's no reason I cannot live by myself, all I need is a telephone. Of course, she is sorry. Sometimes she cry, I am the one to say everything will be okay. She say she have no choice, she doesn't want to end up divorced. I say divorce is terrible, I don't know who invented this terrible idea. Instead of live with a telephone, though, surprise, I come to live with Bess. Imagine that. Bess make an offer and, sure enough, where she come from, people mean for you to move in when they say things like that. A crazy idea, go to live with someone else's family, but she like to have some female company, not like my daughter, who does not believe in company. These days when my daughter visit, she does not bring Sophie. Bess say we should give Nattie time, we will see Sophie again soon. But seems like my daughter have more presentation than ever before, every time she come she have to leave.

I have a family to support, she say, and her voice is heavy, as if soaking wet. I have a young daughter and a depressed husband and no one to turn to.

When she say no one to turn to, she mean me.

These days my beautiful daughter is so tired she can just sit there in a chair and fall asleep. John lost his job again, already, but still they rather hire a baby-sitter than ask me to help, even they can't afford it. Of course, the new baby-sitter is much younger, can run around. I don't know if Sophie these days is wild or not wild. She call me Meanie, but she like to kiss me too, sometimes. I remember that every time I see a child on TV. Sophie like to grab my hair, a fistful in each hand, and then kiss me smack on the nose. I never see any other child kiss that way.

The satellite TV has so many channels, more channels than I can count, including a Chinese channel from the Mainland and a Chinese channel from

Taiwan, but most of the time I watch bloopers with Bess. Also, I watch the bird feeder—so many, many kinds of birds come. The Shea sons hang around all the time, asking when will I go home, but Bess tell them, Get lost.

She's a permanent resident, say Bess. She isn't going anywhere.

Then she wink at me, and switch the channel with the remote control.

Of course, I shouldn't say Irish this, Irish that, es- 15
pecially now I am become honorary Irish myself, according to Bess. Me! Who's Irish? I say, and she laugh. All the same, if I could mention one thing about some of the Irish, not all of them of course, I like to mention this: Their talk just stick. I don't know how Bess Shea learn to use her words, but sometimes I hear what she say a long time later. *Permanent resident. Not going anywhere.* Over and over I hear it, the voice of Bess.

ASSIMILATION in its widest sense has been a part of our national literature from the start. If you like Gish Jen's "Who's Irish?" you might also like other stories that take up the subject matter of the life of first-generation Americans, such as Sylvia Watanabe's "Talking to the Dead," (chapter 12), Junot Diaz's "How to Date a Browngirl, Blackgirl, Whitegirl, or Halfie" (chapter 8), Amy Tan's "Two Kinds" (chapter 2), Jhumpa Lahiri's "Interpreter of Maladies" (chapter 9), and Dagoberto Gilb's "Romero's Shirt" (chapter 12).

**GOING FURTHER** Timothy Mo's *Sour Sweet* and Fae Myenne Ng's *Bone* also explore Asian characters with one foot in one cultural world and the other foot in another.

# Writing from Reading

## Summarize

1 Summarize the narrator's views of her Irish in-laws at the beginning of the story, then summarize her views at the end. Discuss how these views have changed, and how they've stayed the same.

## Analyze Craft

2 Discuss how Jen uses the grandmother's dialect to create her character. What details about the grandmother does this dialect suggest that are never mentioned in the story? Explain how the story would change if it were written in Jen's standard English voice, with only the dialogue in dialect.

## Analyze Voice

3 Consider the use of humor in "Who's Irish?" Find and list specific examples of misunderstandings and explore why these are (or are not) used for humorous purposes.

4 Discuss the narrator's view of the words *supportive* and *creative.* What does her view reveal about cultural differences?

## Synthesize Summary and Analysis

5 Describe how Jen uses the topic of Sophie's skin color to reveal character.

6 Imagine "Who's Irish?" told by a neutral party. How would your impressions of the various characters change if viewed without the grandmother's direct opinions?

## Interpret the Story

7 A central theme of "Who's Irish?" is the speaker's adjustment—as restaurant owner, wife, mother, and grandmother—to the values and systems of behavior in America. Based on her various reactions and interactions throughout the story, do you think she has adjusted?

*CONTINUED FROM PAGE 103*

## THE CRAFT OF CHARACTERIZATION

**Characters**—the people who inhabit literary works—should capture and hold our attention as they suffer, rejoice, rebel, and sometimes perish within the world of the story. It's the sleeping passenger who makes us care whether her train runs off the tracks and plunges into a ravine; it's the child in the upstairs bedroom who makes us hope the firefighters reach his burning house in time. Theirs are the faces we see, the voices we hear, the decisions we sympathize with or marvel at, and the fates we come to share and care about while we read.

"I don't sit down in the morning and say, 'Well how am I going to enter this character?' For me it's something which comes naturally, so all I have to do is be quiet. I sit and I listen and the voices come." Conversation with Gish Jen

**Characterization,** or the way a writer crafts and defines personality, gives us an insight into thoughts and actions that real life rarely permits. We may seek out a story for its plot, admire its setting, and delight in the beauty of its language—but most of us keep turning the page to find out what happens to the characters an author has conjured into life. A character's name, appearance, behavior, words, manner of speech, and inner thoughts all reveal who he or she is. As Gish Jen demonstrates in "Who's Irish?" this process can begin with a tale's opening line. We continue to read to remain in a character's company and understand his or her behavior better, page by page.

"Fiction really starts with this: I have to understand the people."
Conversation with William Kittredge

One of the many benefits of fiction is that it allows us to get *inside the minds* of invented characters—something we cannot do, in most cases, even with our closest friends, whose actions may seem mysterious. In "The Jilting of Granny Weatherall," in this chapter, Katherine Anne Porter allows readers to share Granny's thoughts as she lies on her deathbed, listening to her daughter Cornelia and the doctor discuss her condition:

> *Well, and what if she was? She still had ears. It was like Cornelia to whisper around doors. She always kept things secret in such a public way. She was always being tactful and kind. Cornelia was dutiful; that was the trouble with her. Dutiful and good: "So good and dutiful," said Granny, "that I'd like to spank her."*

Together, the few sentences of that paragraph, combined with Granny's one line of dialogue ("So good and dutiful . . . that I'd like to spank her") bring the character to life. She's cantankerous and quarrelsome, impatient with Cornelia, and surprising us as readers with that desire to spank her daughter for being, of all things, "good and dutiful."

In fiction, because we have access to unspoken thoughts, we can understand **motivation,** or what causes people to behave as they do. In Alice Munro's "An Ounce of Cure" (chapter 1), a heartbroken, melancholy teenage girl tells readers one version of what motivated her to act as she did the night she babysat for the Berryman family:

*I got up and found the Berrymans' "Danse Macabre" and put it on the record player and turned out the living-room lights. The curtains were only partly drawn. A street light shone obliquely on the windowpane, making a rectangle of thin dusty gold, in which the shadows of bare branches moved, caught in the huge sweet winds of spring. It was a mild black night when the last snow was melting. A year ago all this—the music, the wind and the darkness, the shadows of the branches—would have given me tremendous happiness; when they did not do so now, but only called up tediously familiar, somehow humiliatingly personal thoughts, I gave up my soul for dead and walked into the kitchen and decided to get drunk.*

"[Characters] aren't invented for the purposes of function and a plot. . . . They appear as I write." Conversation with Tim O'Brien

In the next paragraph, she changes her story somewhat, leaving readers to assemble their own explanation of her motives:

*No, it was not like that. I walked into the kitchen to look for a coke or something in the refrigerator, and there on the front of the counter were three tall beautiful bottles, all about half full of gold. But even after I had looked at them and lifted them to feel their weight I had not decided to get drunk; I had decided to have a drink.*

Motivation, she seems to say in these two paragraphs, is a complex matter but something people want and need to understand. It becomes more complex, she might have added, when one is trying to remember one's own motivation many years later—as does the speaker here.

### What You See Is What You Get

Because we usually judge people first on their appearance, the writers of prose fiction give great thought to sketching in and filling out a character's looks—the curve of a nose, the crease between brows, the shape of a hulking or a slender frame. However, in literature, physical appearance has meaning beyond a simple list of features. For example, one would make a character seven feet tall and 350 pounds only if the size and heft of the person have some significance signaling the impact he has on those around him, how he views himself, and what frustrations or powers he carries with him as a result. The following portrait of Captain Ahab from *Moby-Dick* uses physical traits to establish character and portend aspects of the plot.

*His whole high, broad form, seemed made of solid bronze, and shaped in an unalterable mould. . . . Threading its way out from among his grey hairs, and continuing right down one side of his tawny scorched face and neck, till it disappeared in his clothing, you saw a slender rod-like mark, lividly whitish. It resembled that perpendicular seam sometimes made in the straight, lofty trunk of a great tree, when the upper lightning tearingly darts down it, and without wrenching a single twig, peels and grooves out the bark from top to bottom, ere running off into the soil, leaving the tree still greenly alive, but branded. Whether that mark was born with him, or whether it was the scar left by some desperate wound, no one could certainly say. . . .*

Everything about Ahab is striking and distinctive: his statue-like form, his gray hair, his tanned face and neck, and especially the scar that seems to run the length of his body, a scar that Melville compares to a lightning strike. But this passage goes beyond describing his bodily attributes. It also suggests, in the concluding lines about the mark, that his fate may be a product either of his inner nature or of some encounter at sea, which raises the question about the essence of his character.

> "Somebody said to me once, 'You know, you'll never write a novel. . . . You care too much about people. You got to use people; you got to put a person in a book and use them for what you need and then get rid of them. But you won't do that, so you're never going to write a novel.'" Conversation with Barry Lopez

## What's in a Name?

Authors may reveal aspects of character by their choice of names, though the meaning of those names may often turn ironic. A character named Swift may be slow. A character named Rough may be gentle. A writer may choose a name to suggest a certain nature, as does Nathaniel Hawthorne in the case of Goodman Brown (chapter 10), who enters into a profound struggle between good and evil, thereby earning the "good" part of his name. Katherine Anne Porter's Granny Weatherall is a person who has thus far "weathered all"—meaning she has overcome multiple hardships in her life. Since "clothes make the man," characters can also be known by what they wear. Does a woman wear designer ball gowns or denim overalls? Does she shop at K-Mart or Saks Fifth Avenue or at a showroom for haute couture in Paris? These details allow readers to learn about a character's social class, lifestyle, and in some cases, aspirations.

## The Clothes Make the Man

In "Paul's Case," Willa Cather focuses closely on the clothing of her protagonist. She does so because clothing is important to Paul, who envisions himself in a life different and grander than the one he leads. The following description comes near the beginning of the story:

> *His clothes were a trifle outgrown, and the tan velvet on the collar of his open overcoat was frayed and worn; but for all that there was something of the dandy about him, and he wore an opal pin in his neatly knotted black four-in-hand, and a red carnation in his buttonhole. The latter adornment the faculty somehow felt was not properly significant of the contrite spirit befitting a boy under the ban of suspension.*

Paul, with his outgrown and frayed clothing, is not a wealthy boy. Still, the velvet of the collar suggests an eye for luxury, and he has a certain attitude despite his limitations. He has added the opal pin, the neatly knotted tie, and the red carnation. Notice how Cather gives extra meaning to the carnation by letting us see it through the offended eyes of the teachers.

## We Are What We (Repeatedly) Do

What characters do can include a wide array of possibilities that represent who they are: what they eat (brown rice and tofu versus fast-food burgers), what attracts their attention (the bud or the thorns on a rosebush), and how they respond to others—for example, with puzzlement and exasperation, as the narrator does in "Who's Irish?"

They also interact with others, being arrogant or meek or devious, spurring responses that help us as readers know them. For example, we learn about Paul from the way his teachers respond.

### Can You Hear Me Now?

Another significant means of understanding characters comes to us through dialogue, or conversation between two or more participants in a scene. We've talked a bit about dialogue in chapter 2, and we will discuss it further in chapter 8 (Language, Tone, and Style). As a way to define a character's behavior, dialogue reveals personality in addition to motivation. When the principal confronts Paul for insulting a teacher, Paul responds by saying, "I don't know. . . . I didn't mean to be polite or impolite, either. I guess it's a sort of way I have of saying things regardless." This is one of the few lines of

"Dialogue in stories is when characters seem the most like real people." Conversation with Richard Ford

dialogue in "Paul's Case," one of the only times we get to hear Paul *in his own words,* and they reinforce the impression that he is a difficult person to understand. His words at least suggest the possibility that he is neither intentionally impertinent nor rude. He is simply being himself and doesn't expect to change or apologize for it.

Dialogue, then, can add dimension to a character. In the bittersweet, teasing voice of Mangan's sister in James Joyce's "Araby" (chapter 4), you can hear the lilt of turn-of-the-century Dublin's middle-class English. The distinctive voice Bernard Malamud achieves with Pinye Salzman in "The Magic Barrel" (chapter 6) emerges from the music of the character's language. At its best—as with dialogue in a stage play—speech both reveals character and advances a story's action. In this exchange in the story "No One's a Mystery" by Elizabeth Tallent (chapter 10), the uninterrupted conversation tells us a lot about what's at stake and what's at risk. Here, Jack, a married man, has just given his teenage girlfriend a diary.

> *"Tonight you'll write, 'I love Jack. This is my birthday present from him. I can't imagine anybody loving anybody more than I love Jack.'"*
>
> *"I can't."*
>
> *"In a year you'll write, 'I wonder what I ever really saw in Jack. I wonder why I spent so many days just riding around in his pickup. It's true he taught me something about sex. It's true there wasn't ever much else to do in Cheyenne.'"*
>
> *"I won't write that."*
>
> *"In two years you'll write, 'I wonder what that old guy's name was, the one with the curly hair and the filthy dirty pickup truck and time on his hands.'"*
>
> *"I won't write that."*

The relationship has a certain playfulness. The characters are at ease with each other, comfortable in their shared space. We're getting to know him: he's being clever, flirtatious, playful, as he puts himself in her shoes, imagining what she'll write in the diary. At the same time, he's a realist—projecting into the future, considering how she'll see him as the years pass, revealing somewhat how he may see himself (too old for her, directionless, a diversion). And there's a whiff of self-pity, too, in his prediction that he'll be forgotten, that his girlfriend will remember his "filthy dirty pickup truck" but not his own actual name. So far, she hasn't declared what she *will* write—only what she won't. The exchange moves the plot along because it piques the reader's curiosity—well, what *would* she have to say?

## ROUND AND FLAT CHARACTERS

Reading fiction is a bit like eavesdropping or spying; it allows an intimate sense of how people think and live. What gives us that sense of life lived off (as well as on) the page? What makes a character real?

We usually talk about characters in literature in terms of their psychological makeup, the way we speak of family members and friends. *He is a talker. She's a brain. He worries a lot about money. She smokes incessantly and doesn't seem capable of standing up to her mother.* In a story, we come to know characters by way of the sum of their physical and mental attributes or **characteristics.** *He has dark hair, gestures while he speaks, and chews on his lower lip. She wears a silver comb in her hair, taps her right foot while she smokes, and her voice rises into the high upper register when she gets upset.*

If this sum of characteristics is complex and multifaceted, the characters seem real, or, in the terminology of twentieth-century British writer E. M. Forster (in his book *Aspects of the Novel),* they grow **round.** By contrast, in Forster's view, a **flat** character possesses a very narrow range of speech and action; these figures are predictable and do not develop over the course of the plot. In other words, they are **static,** meaning that they are unchanging. Roundness and flatness can be a matter of degree, with characters in a story falling along a spectrum.

This distinction between round and flat characters is a crucial one. Forster suggests, in effect, that no one is either entirely good or entirely bad, completely brave or cowardly, wholly smart or stupid. Instead, we're all a compound or mixture of opposite qualities, and the combination or proportion of these qualities can change. A story's

> "I like characters who have agency, who make the choice to change—who act, rather than having life or having the world act on them." Conversation with Chimamanda Ngozi Adichie

protagonist, or central actor, is almost always round. Such characters are **dynamic,** meaning that their personality and behavior alter over the course of the action in response to challenges and changing circumstances. A protagonist who initially behaves as a coward, for instance, may well become valiant at a crucial moment.

### A HISTORY OF CHARACTER

The word *character* comes from *kharakter,* the Greek word for a stamping tool. Thus, the ancient Greeks believed that an individual's character—those defining traits that inform behavior and action—was static. Character made up one's fate or destiny. Whether a person was generous, loving, calm, excitable, level-headed, jittery, easily embarrassed, fearful, or brave, human personalities were seen as stable.

More recent notions of character have grown less absolute. In the nineteenth century, the age of psychology revolutionized and complicated our understanding of the human mind and, consequently, of character. Most people no longer regard personality and behavior as fixed. Instead, a person's behavior could be mutable, contradictory, unpredictable.

Far from a fixed stamp or *kharakter,* characterization and the study of character are, at least in part, ways of exploring an individual's capacity for change within the pages of a story *and* in our own lives.

In most fiction, the developing (or disintegrating) relationship between the protagonist and the antagonist (see chapter 4) has a significant effect on both people. A particular kind of protagonist who often appears in contemporary fiction is referred to as an **antihero**—a main character who acts outside the usual lines of heroic behavior (brave, honest, true). In "Paul's Case" (this chapter) the teachers and principal

"I think that most of the people that turn up in my stories are somewhat lost. . . . If you have a character who finds herself less than adequate in any situation, that makes that character appealing. You would think that we would see this person as sort of pathetic, but often it doesn't work that way at all."
Conversation with Amy Hempel

meet with Paul to voice their complaints about his insolence and misbehavior in their classes. If they were only punitive, we might be able to dismiss them, give them less thought. But Cather allows readers access to the teachers' minds and hearts, and in this way shows that they can't help feeling that Paul is sad and damaged, and that they, as adults, bear some blame:

> *His teachers left the building dissatisfied and unhappy; humiliated to have felt so vindictive toward a mere boy, to have uttered this feeling in cutting terms, and to have set each other on, as it were, in the gruesome game of intemperate reproach. Some of them remembered having seen a miserable street cat set at bay by a ring of tormentors.*

In contrast to round characters, flat or **stock characters** represent a concept or type of behavior, such as *mean teacher* or *mischievous student,* and offer readers the comforts of repetition and reliability. Often, such characters are comic and provide us with comic relief—overeating, taking pratfalls, losing their glasses, and bumping into doors. The difference here, as we suggested, is the distinction between characters who are dynamic and those who are static. And it's not always the case that round is desirable and flat is less so; most fictions require both kinds of portrayals to fully establish a plot. Flat characters often play a limited role in a story's plot. As such, they may serve as **foils,** or contrasts, to a central player. A devious friend, for example, might bring out a protagonist's trusting nature, or a happy-go-lucky uncle might make his niece's sadness all the more noticeable.

"If I have a character walking down the street and all the buildings fall down, it may be reflecting something about a feeling, as opposed to the actual reality of all the buildings falling down."
Conversation with Aimee Bender

## *Character* in Context

The four stories in this chapter use details to create characters who come to life, emerging from the page—and who do so by being (to some extent) unpredictable. In turn, each story has a distinctive voice that flows from the worlds these figures inhabit. Gish Jen's "Who's Irish?" Katherine Anne Porter's "The Jilting of Granny Weatherall," Willa Cather's "Paul's Case," and Jack London's "A Wicked Woman" focus closely on a single protagonist, but the writers make various choices as to vocabulary, rhythm, and phrasing. Characterization, like personality, does not exist in a vacuum; in each story, consider how other characters influence the protagonist's development. What we learn from these insights into fictional characters helps satisfy our hunger for knowledge about real people in the real world—and, perhaps, may offer insight into our own behavior.

# Katherine Anne Porter (1890–1980)

Callie Porter, a girl who grew up motherless and in extreme poverty, was destined to become Katherine Anne Porter, a writer, traveler, and woman of expensive tastes who changed her name after divorcing her first of four husbands. An independent woman with an active interest in life and politics, Porter worked on and off as a journalist, essayist, and book reviewer in a range of places, including Colorado, New York, Washington, D.C., and Mexico. Her work, while not voluminous, is known for its intensity of emotion and its refined and meticulously crafted prose. In her fiction, the personal becomes universal, as her stories are based on her own experiences. Although she lived to age ninety, her zest for life and her perfectionist approach to completing a story hindered her output. She published four collections of short stories—including *Flowering Judas* (1935) and *Pale Horse, Pale Rider* (1939)—and one novel, *Ship of Fools* (1962). Her work was much celebrated in her lifetime, and she won the Pulitzer Prize and the National Book Award in 1966 for her collected stories.

**AS YOU READ** **As you read, notice the way you're drawn into the thoughts of the main character. Notice how her thoughts move back and forth through time, in and out of the present. How well do you get to know her as a result of being allowed to enter the privacy of her mind?**

**TIP**

**FOR INTERACTIVE READING . . .** Note when Granny Weatherall is experiencing events from the past. Based on your notation, describe Granny as a young woman. Do the events you've noted explain how she's become the woman in the story's present?

# The Jilting of Granny Weatherall (1930)

1 SHE flicked her wrist neatly out of Doctor Harry's pudgy careful fingers and pulled the sheet up to her chin. The brat ought to be in knee breeches. Doctoring around the country with spectacles on his nose! "Get along now, take your schoolbooks and go. There's nothing wrong with me."

2 Doctor Harry spread a warm paw like a cushion on her forehead where the forked green vein danced and made her eyelids twitch. "Now, now, be a good girl, and we'll have you up in no time."

3 "That's no way to speak to a woman nearly eighty years old just because she's down. I'd have you respect your elders, young man."

4 "Well, Missy, excuse me." Doctor Harry patted her cheek. "But I've got to warn you, haven't I? You're a marvel, but you must be careful or you're going to be good and sorry."

5 "Don't tell me what I'm going to be. I'm on my feet now, morally speaking. It's Cornelia. I had to go to bed to get rid of her."

6 Her bones felt loose, and floated around in her skin, and Doctor Harry floated like a balloon around the foot of the bed. He floated and pulled down his waistcoat and swung his glasses on a cord. "Well, stay where you are, it certainly can't hurt you."

7 "Get along and doctor your sick," said Granny Weatherall. "Leave a well woman alone. I'll call for you when I want you. . . . Where were you forty years ago when I pulled through milk-leg and double pneumonia? You weren't even born. Don't let Cornelia lead you on," she shouted, because Doctor Harry appeared to float up to the ceiling and out. "I pay my own bills, and I don't throw my money away on nonsense!"

8 She meant to wave good-by, but it was too much trouble. Her eyes closed of themselves, it was like a dark curtain drawn around the bed. The pillow rose and floated under her, pleasant as a hammock in a light wind. She listened to the leaves rustling outside the window. No, somebody was swishing newspapers: no, Cornelia and Doctor Harry were whispering together. She leaped broad awake, thinking they whispered in her ear.

"She was never like this, *never* like this!" "Well, 9
what can we expect?" "Yes, eighty years old. . . ."

Well, and what if she was? She still had ears. It 10
was like Cornelia to whisper around doors. She always kept things secret in such a public way. She was always being tactful and kind. Cornelia was dutiful; that was the trouble with her. Dutiful and good: "So good and dutiful," said Granny, "that I'd like to spank her." She saw herself spanking Cornelia and making a fine job of it.

"What'd you say, Mother?" 11

Granny felt her face tying up in hard knots. 12

"Can't a body think, I'd like to know?" 13

"I thought you might want something." 14

"I do. I want a lot of things. First off, go away and 15
don't whisper."

She lay and drowsed, hoping in her sleep that the 16
children would keep out and let her rest a minute. It had been a long day. Not that she was tired. It was always pleasant to snatch a minute now and then. There was always so much to be done, let me see: tomorrow.

Tomorrow was far away and there was nothing to 17
trouble about. Things were finished somehow when the time came; thank God there was always a little margin over for peace: then a person could spread out the plan of life and tuck in the edges orderly. It was good to have everything clean and folded away, with the hair brushes and tonic bottles sitting straight on the white, embroidered linen: the day started without fuss and the pantry shelves laid out with rows of jelly glasses and brown jugs and white stone-china jars with blue whirligigs and words painted on them: coffee, tea, sugar, ginger, cinnamon, allspice: and the bronze clock with the lion on top nicely dusted off. The dust that lion could collect in twenty-four hours! The box in the attic with all those letters tied up, well, she'd have to go through that tomorrow. All those letters—George's letters and John's letters and her letters to them both—

lying around for the children to find afterwards made her uneasy. Yes, that would be tomorrow's business. No use to let them know how silly she had been once.

18 While she was rummaging around she found death in her mind and it felt clammy and unfamiliar. She had spent so much time preparing for death there was no need for bringing it up again. Let it take care of itself now. When she was sixty she had felt very old, finished, and went around making farewell trips to see her children and grandchildren, with a secret in her mind: This is the very last of your mother, children! Then she made her will and came down with a long fever. That was all just a notion like a lot of other things, but it was lucky too, for she had once for all got over the idea of dying for a long time. Now she couldn't be worried. She hoped she had better sense now. Her father had lived to be one hundred and two years old and had drunk a noggin of strong hot toddy on his last birthday. He told the reporters it was his daily habit, and he owed his long life to that. He had made quite a scandal and was very pleased about it. She believed she'd just plague Cornelia a little.

19 "Cornelia! Cornelia!" No footsteps, but a sudden hand on her cheek. "Bless you, where have you been?"

20 "Here, Mother."

21 "Well, Cornelia, I want a noggin of hot toddy."

22 "Are you cold, darling?"

23 "I'm chilly, Cornelia. Lying in bed stops the circulation. I must have told you that a thousand times."

24 Well, she could just hear Cornelia telling her husband that Mother was getting a little childish and they'd have to humor her. The thing that most annoyed her was that Cornelia thought she was deaf, dumb, and blind. Little hasty glances and tiny gestures tossed around her and over her head saying, "Don't cross her, let her have her way, she's eighty years old," and she sitting there as if she lived in a thin glass cage. Sometimes Granny almost made up her mind to pack up and move back to her own house where nobody could remind her every minute that she was old. Wait, wait, Cornelia, till your own children whisper behind your back!

25 In her day she had kept a better house and had got more work done. She wasn't too old yet for Lydia to be driving eighty miles for advice when one of the children jumped the track, and Jimmy still dropped in and talked things over: "Now, Mammy, you've a good business head, I want to know what you think of this? . . ." Old. Cornelia couldn't change the furniture around without asking. Little things, little things! They had been so sweet when they were little. Granny wished the old days were back again with the children young and everything to be done over. It had been a hard pull, but not too much for her. When she thought of all the food she had cooked, and all the clothes she had cut and sewed, and all the gardens she had made—well, the children showed it. There they were, made out of her, and they couldn't get away from that. Sometimes she wanted to see John again and point to them and say, Well, I didn't do so badly, did I? But that would have to wait. That was for tomorrow. She used to think of him as a man, but now all the children were older than their father, and he would be a child beside her if she saw him now. It seemed strange and there was something wrong in the idea. Why, he couldn't possibly recognize her. She had fenced in a hundred acres once, digging the post holes herself and clamping the wires with just a negro boy to help. That changed a woman. John would be looking for a young woman with the peaked Spanish comb in her hair and the painted fan. Digging post holes changed a woman. Riding country roads in the winter when women had their babies was another thing: sitting up nights with sick horses and sick negroes and sick children and hardly ever losing one. John, I hardly ever lost one of them! John would see that in a minute, that would be something he could understand, she wouldn't have to explain anything!

It made her feel like rolling up her sleeves and put- 26
ting the whole place to rights again. No matter if Cornelia was determined to be everywhere at once, there were a great many things left undone on this place. She would start tomorrow and do them. It was good to be strong enough for everything, even if all you made melted and changed and slipped under your hands, so that by the time you finished you almost forgot what you were working for. What was it I set out to do? she asked herself intently, but she could not remember. A fog rose over the valley, she saw it marching across the creek swallowing the trees and moving up the hill

like an army of ghosts. Soon it would be at the near edge of the orchard, and then it was time to go in and light the lamps. Come in, children, don't stay out in the night air.

27 Lighting the lamps had been beautiful. The children huddled up to her and breathed like little calves waiting at the bars in the twilight. Their eyes followed the match and watched the flame rise and settle in a blue curve, then they moved away from her. The lamp was lit, they didn't have to be scared and hang on to mother any more. Never, never, never more. God, for all my life, I thank Thee. Without Thee, my God, I could never have done it. Hail, Mary, full of grace.

Plenty of girls get jilted.

28 I want you to pick all the fruit this year and see that nothing is wasted. There's always someone who can use it. Don't let good things rot for want of using. You waste life when you waste good food. Don't let things get lost. It's bitter to lose things. Now, don't let me get to thinking, not when I'm tired and taking a little nap before supper. . . .

29 The pillow rose about her shoulders and pressed against her heart and the memory was being squeezed out of it: oh, push down the pillow, somebody: it would smother her if she tried to hold it. Such a fresh breeze blowing and such a green day with no threats in it. But he had not come, just the same. What does a woman do when she has put on the white veil and set out the white cake for a man and he doesn't come? She tried to remember. No, I swear he never harmed me but in that. He never harmed me but in that . . . and what if he did? There was the day, the day, but a whirl of dark smoke rose and covered it, crept up and over into the bright field where everything was planted so carefully in orderly rows. That was hell, she knew hell when she saw it. For sixty years she had prayed against remembering him and against losing her soul in the deep pit of hell, and now the two things were mingled in one and the thought of him was a smoky cloud from hell that moved and crept in her head when she had just got rid of Doctor Harry and was trying to rest a minute. Wounded vanity, Ellen, said a sharp voice in the top of her mind. Don't let your wounded vanity get the upper hand of you. Plenty of girls get jilted. You were jilted, weren't you? Then stand up to it. Her eyelids wavered and let in streamers of blue-gray light like tissue paper over her eyes. She must get up and pull the shades down or she'd never sleep. She was in bed again and the shades were not down. How could that happen? Better turn over, hide from the light, sleeping in the light gave you nightmares. "Mother, how do you feel now?" and a stinging wetness on her forehead. But I don't like having my face washed in cold water!

Hapsy? George? Lydia? Jimmy? No, Cornelia, and 30
her features were swollen and full of little puddles. "They're coming, darling, they'll all be here soon." Go wash your face, child, you look funny.

Instead of obeying, Cornelia knelt down and put her 31
head on the pillow. She seemed to be talking but there was no sound. "Well, are you tongue-tied? Whose birthday is it? Are you going to give a party?"

Cornelia's mouth moved urgently in strange shapes. 32
"Don't do that, you bother me, daughter."

"Oh, no, Mother. Oh, no . . ." 33

Nonsense. It was strange about children. They 34
disputed your every word. "No what, Cornelia?"

"Here's Doctor Harry." 35

"I won't see that boy again. He just left five min- 36
utes ago."

"That was this morning, Mother. It's night now. 37
Here's the nurse."

"This is Doctor Harry, Mrs. Weatherall. I never 38
saw you look so young and happy!"

"Ah, I'll never be young again—but I'd be happy if 39
they'd let me lie in peace and get rested."

She thought she spoke up loudly, but no one an- 40
swered. A warm weight on her forehead, a warm bracelet on her wrist, and a breeze went on whispering, trying to tell her something. A shuffle of leaves in the everlasting hand of God, He blew on them and they danced and rattled. "Mother, don't mind, we're going to give you a little hypodermic." "Look here, daughter, how do ants get in this bed? I saw sugar ants yesterday." Did you send for Hapsy too?

It was Hapsy she really wanted. She had to go a 41
long way back through a great many rooms to find Hapsy standing with a baby on her arm. She seemed to herself to be Hapsy also, and the baby on Hapsy's arm was Hapsy and himself and herself, all at once, and there was no surprise in the meeting. Then Hapsy melted from within and turned flimsy as gray gauze and the baby was a gauzy shadow, and Hapsy came up close and said, "I thought you'd never come," and looked at her very searchingly and said, "You haven't changed a bit!" They leaned forward to kiss, when Cornelia began whispering from a long way off, "Oh,

is there anything you want to tell me? Is there anything I can do for you?"

42 Yes, she had changed her mind after sixty years and she would like to see George. I want you to find George. Find him and be sure to tell him I forgot him. I want him to know I had my husband just the same and my children and my house like any other woman. A good house too and a good husband that I loved and fine children out of him. Better than I had hoped for even. Tell him I was given back everything he took away and more. Oh, no, oh, God, no, there was something else besides the house and the man and the children. Oh, surely they were not all? What was it? Something not given back. . . . Her breath crowded down under her ribs and grew into a monstrous frightening shape with cutting edges; it bored up into her head, and the agony was unbelievable: Yes, John, get the Doctor now, no more talk, my time has come.

43 When this one was born it should be the last. The last. It should have been born first, for it was the one she had truly wanted. Everything came in good time. Nothing left out, left over. She was strong, in three days she would be as well as ever. Better. A woman needed milk in her to have her full health.

44 "Mother, do you hear me?"

45 "I've been telling you—"

46 "Mother, Father Connolly's here."

47 "I went to Holy Communion only last week. Tell him I'm not so sinful as all that."

48 "Father just wants to speak to you."

49 He could speak as much as he pleased. It was like him to drop in and inquire about her soul as if it were a teething baby, and then stay on for a cup of tea and a round of cards and gossip. He always had a funny story of some sort, usually about an Irishman who made his little mistakes and confessed them, and the point lay in some absurd thing he would blurt out in the confessional showing his struggles between native piety and original sin. Granny felt easy about her soul. Cornelia, where are your manners? Give Father Connolly a chair. She had her secret comfortable understanding with a few favorite saints who cleared a straight road to God for her. All as surely signed and sealed as the papers for the new Forty Acres. Forever . . . heirs and assigns forever. Since the day the wedding cake was not cut, but thrown out and wasted. The whole bottom dropped out of the world, and there she was blind and sweating with nothing under her feet and the walls falling away. His hand had caught her under the breast, she had not fallen, there was the freshly polished floor with the green rug on it, just as before. He had cursed like a sailor's parrot and said, "I'll kill him for you." Don't lay a hand on him, for my sake leave something to God. "Now, Ellen, you must believe what I tell you. . . ."

So there was nothing, nothing to worry about any more, except sometimes in the night one of the children screamed in a nightmare, and they both hustled out shaking and hunting for the matches and calling, "There, wait a minute, here we are!" John, get the doctor now, Hapsy's time has come. But there was Hapsy standing by the bed in a white cap. "Cornelia, tell Hapsy to take off her cap. I can't see her plain." 50

Her eyes opened very wide and the room stood out like a picture she had seen somewhere. Dark colors with the shadows rising toward the ceiling in long angles. The tall black dresser gleamed with nothing on it but John's picture, enlarged from a little one, with John's eyes very black when they should have been blue. You never saw him, so how do you know how he looked? But the man insisted the copy was perfect, it was very rich and handsome. For a picture, yes, but it's not my husband. The table by the bed had a linen cover and a candle and a crucifix. The light was blue from Cornelia's silk lampshades. No sort of light at all, just frippery. You had to live forty years with kerosene lamps to appreciate honest electricity. She felt very strong and she saw Doctor Harry with a rosy nimbus around him. 51

"You look like a saint, Doctor Harry, and I vow that's as near as you'll ever come to it." 52

"She's saying something." 53

"I heard you Cornelia. What's all this carrying on?" 54

"Father Connolly's saying—" 55

Cornelia's voice staggered and bumped like a cart in a bad road. It rounded corners and turned back again and arrived nowhere. Granny stepped up in the cart very lightly and reached for the reins, but a man sat beside her and she knew him by his hands, driving the cart. She did not look in his face, for she knew without seeing, but looked instead down the road where the trees leaned over and bowed to each 56 other and a thousand birds were singing a Mass. She felt like singing too, but she put her hand in the bosom of her dress and pulled out a rosary, and Father Connolly murmured Latin in a very solemn voice and tickled her feet. My God, will you stop that nonsense? I'm a married woman. What if he did run away and leave me to face the priest by myself? I found another a whole world better. I wouldn't have exchanged my husband for anybody except St. Michael himself, and you may tell him that for me with a thank you in the bargain.

So, my dear Lord, this is my death and I wasn't even thinking about it.

57 Light flashed on her closed eyelids, and a deep roaring shook her. Cornelia, is that lightning? I hear thunder. There's going to be a storm. Close all the windows. Call the children in. . . . "Mother, here we are, all of us." "Is that you, Hapsy?" "Oh, no, I'm Lydia. We drove as fast as we could." Their faces drifted above her, drifted away. The rosary fell out of her hands and Lydia put it back. Jimmy tried to help, their hands fumbled together, and Granny closed two fingers around Jimmy's thumb. Beads wouldn't do, it must be something alive. She was so amazed her thoughts ran round and round. So, my dear Lord, this is my death and I wasn't even thinking about it. My children have come to see me die. But I can't, it's not time. Oh, I always hated surprises. I wanted to give Cornelia the amethyst set—Cornelia, you're to have the amethyst set, but Hapsy's to wear it when she wants, and, Doctor Harry, do shut up. Nobody sent for you. Oh, my dear Lord, do wait a minute. I meant to do something about the Forty Acres, Jimmy doesn't need it and Lydia will later on, with that worthless husband of hers. I meant to finish the altar cloth and send six bottles of wine to Sister Borgia for her dyspepsia. I want to send six bottles of wine to Sister Borgia, Father Connolly, now don't let me forget.

Cornelia's voice made short turns and tilted over and crashed. "Oh, Mother, oh, Mother, oh, Mother . . ." 58

"I'm not going, Cornelia. I'm taken by surprise. I can't go." 59

You'll see Hapsy again. What about her? "I thought you'd never come." Granny made a long journey outward, looking for Hapsy. What if I don't find her? What then? Her heart sank down and down, there was no bottom to death, she couldn't come to the end of it. The blue light from Cornelia's lampshade drew into a tiny point in the center of her brain, it flickered and winked like an eye, quietly it fluttered and dwindled. Granny lay curled down within herself, amazed and watchful, staring at the point of light that was herself; her body was now only a deeper mass of shadow in an endless darkness and this darkness would curl around the light and swallow it up. God, give a sign! 60

For the second time there was no sign. Again no bridegroom and the priest in the house. She could not remember any other sorrow because this grief wiped them all away. Oh, no, there's nothing more cruel than this—I'll never forgive it. She stretched herself with a deep breath and blew out the light. 61

DEATH—the darkest theme. If you like Katherine Anne Porter's "The Jilting of Granny Weatherall," you can read another great writer, perhaps the greatest novelist of them all, on the same subject in Leo Tolstoy's "Death of Ivan Ilych" (in the For Further Reading section of this anthology).

**GOING FURTHER** Porter concentrates a single life into the briefest of times in the Granny Weatherall story, but she has produced a number of variations on the question of characters living, and dying, over the long years of a life. In her quasi-allegorical novel *Ship of Fools,* she attempts to tell the story of an entire generation of Americans adrift.

# Writing from Reading

### Summarize

1 How many children did Granny have, and what are their names? Which of them are present in the room with her as she lies on her deathbed?

2 Although the author does not reveal a specific era or place for this story, she provides many details related to setting. Go through the text and find all the details you can that give you a feel for where and when these events occur. Write a paragraph summarizing your findings.

### Analyze Craft

3 In revealing Granny's mental/emotional state, Porter sometimes layers past with present or mixes emotional pain with physical pain. Find two examples of this layering and mixing and discuss the effect.

4 How do the minor characters in this story—such as Doctor Harry and Cornelia—add dimension to Granny Weatherall's character? Are these minor characters flat? Support your reasoning with examples from the story.

### Analyze Voice

5 How do Porter's use of dialogue and her description of the characters' gestures (particularly Granny's) make them seem real?

### Synthesize Summary and Analysis

6 "The Jilting of Granny Weatherall" is written from Granny's limited point of view. How does this limited scope affect your understanding of the major and minor characters?

7 Because of Granny's increasing disorientation, you are able to get a snapshot of all the major moments in her life. Put these events in order and consider them as a story of their own. Is Granny a round or a flat character in this underlying plot? Discuss how her character in the past compares to her character in the present.

### Interpret the Story

8 At the end of the story, Granny appears finally to become aware of her impending death. Do you believe she's been ignorant of her situation throughout the whole story? Search the story for evidence of Granny's recognition or ignorance, and discuss how her state of awareness affects your understanding of the story's conclusion.

# Willa Cather (1873–1947)

Although any citizen of the United States who publishes fiction could be called an "American writer," some writers, because of a particular mix of subject matter and its presentation, stand out as quintessentially American. Early-twentieth-century writer Willa Cather was one of those—or, as the title of one of her novels puts it, *One of Ours*. Her biography includes some interesting geography, including several locations that affect her work. Born in Virginia, she moved with her family to the Nebraska plains when still a child and lived in the region long enough to attend high school and the University of Nebraska; that state claims her as a "favorite daughter" today. Although she moved to Pittsburgh after graduation and worked as a journalist there and in New York City, she focused in much of her best-known work on life in the small towns and farms of the Great Plains. An independent woman at a time when many were not, Cather never married, preferring instead female friendship. She struggled, however, with the increasingly material society that surrounded her, and some of her later work emphasizes nonmaterialistic values. Her best-known novels—*My Ántonia, O Pioneers,* and *Death Comes for the Archbishop*—put forward serious themes about identity and life in a masterly prose style, crossing state and regional borders in their subjects. In the story that follows, "Paul's Case," she dramatizes the opposition between disparate locales, dealing with a character who moves from city to city in an attempt to "belong" or feel at home.

**AS YOU READ** As you read, mark the sections that portray Paul in a negative light—lying, devious, impertinent, ungrateful, or angry—and use a different notation to mark the sections where Paul is portrayed in a positive light—happy, satisfied, gracious, or charming. What do the occasions for these various portrayals say about Paul's temperament?

# Paul's Case (1905)

1 IT was Paul's afternoon to appear before the faculty of the Pittsburgh High School to account for his various misdemeanours. He had been suspended a week ago, and his father had called at the Principal's office and confessed his perplexity about his son. Paul entered the faculty room suave and smiling. His clothes were a trifle outgrown, and the tan velvet on the collar of his open overcoat was frayed and worn; but for all that there was something of the dandy about him, and he wore an opal pin in his neatly knotted black four-in-hand, and a red carnation in his buttonhole. This latter adornment the faculty somehow felt was not properly significant of the contrite spirit befitting a boy under the ban of suspension.

2 Paul was tall for his age and very thin, with high, cramped shoulders and a narrow chest. His eyes were remarkable for a certain hysterical brilliancy, and he continually used them in a conscious, theatrical sort of way, peculiarly offensive in a boy. The pupils were abnormally large, as though he were addicted to belladonna, but there was a glassy glitter about them which that drug does not produce.

3 When questioned by the Principal as to why he was there, Paul stated, politely enough, that he wanted to come back to school. This was a lie, but Paul was quite accustomed to lying; found it, indeed, indispensable for overcoming friction. His teachers were asked to state their respective charges against him, which they did with such a rancour and aggrievedness as evinced that this was not a usual case. Disorder and impertinence were among the offences named, yet each of his instructors felt that it was scarcely possible to put into words the real cause of the trouble, which lay in a sort of hysterically defiant manner of the boy's; in the contempt which they all knew he felt for them, and which he seemingly made not the least effort to conceal. Once, when he had been making a synopsis of a paragraph at the blackboard, his English teacher had stepped to his side and attempted to guide his hand. Paul had started back with a shudder and thrust his hands violently behind him. The astonished woman could scarcely have been more hurt and embarrassed had he struck at her. The insult was so involuntary and definitely personal as to be unforgettable. In one way and another, he had made all his teachers, men and women alike, conscious of the same feeling of physical aversion. In one class he habitually sat with his hand shading his eyes; in another he always looked out of the window during the recitation; in another he made a running commentary on the lecture, with humorous intent.

4 His teachers felt this afternoon that his whole attitude was symbolized by his shrug and his flippantly red carnation flower, and they fell upon him without mercy, his English teacher leading the pack. He stood through it smiling, his pale lips parted over his white teeth. (His lips were continually twitching, and he had a habit of raising his eyebrows that was contemptuous and irritating to the last degree.) Older boys than Paul had broken down and shed tears under that ordeal, but his set smile did not once desert him, and his only sign of discomfort was the nervous trembling of the fingers that toyed with the buttons of his overcoat, and an occasional jerking of the other hand which held his hat. Paul was always smiling, always glancing about him, seeming to feel that people might be watching him and trying to detect some-

thing. This conscious expression, since it was as far as possible from boyish mirthfulness, was usually attributed to insolence or "smartness."

5 As the inquisition proceeded, one of his instructors repeated an impertinent remark of the boy's, and the Principal asked him whether he thought that a courteous speech to make to a woman. Paul shrugged his shoulders slightly and his eyebrows twitched.

6 "I don't know," he replied. "I didn't mean to be polite or impolite, either. I guess it's a sort of way I have, of saying things regardless."

7 The Principal asked him whether he didn't think that a way it would be well to get rid of. Paul grinned and said he guessed so. When he was told that he could go, he bowed gracefully and went out. His bow was like a repetition of the scandalous red carnation.

8 His teachers were in despair, and his drawing master voiced the feeling of them all when he declared there was something about the boy which none of them understood. He added: "I don't really believe that smile of his comes altogether from insolence; there's something sort of haunted about it. The boy is not strong, for one thing. There is something wrong about the fellow."

9 The drawing master had come to realize that, in looking at Paul, one saw only his white teeth and the forced animation of his eyes. One warm afternoon the boy had gone to sleep at his drawing-board, and his master had noted with amazement what a white, blue-veined face it was; drawn and wrinkled like an old man's about the eyes, the lips twitching even in his sleep.

10 His teachers left the building dissatisfied and unhappy; humiliated to have felt so vindictive toward a mere boy, to have uttered this feeling in cutting terms, and to have set each other on, as it were, in the grewsome game of intemperate reproach. Some of them remembered having seen a miserable street cat set at bay by a ring of tormentors.

11 As for Paul, he ran down the hill whistling the Soldiers' Chorus from *Faust,* looking wildly behind him now and then to see whether some of his teachers were not there to witness his light-heartedness. As it was now late in the afternoon and Paul was on duty that evening as usher at Carnegie Hall, he decided that he would not go home to supper.

12 When he reached the concert hall the doors were not yet open. It was chilly outside, and he decided to go up into the picture gallery—always deserted at this hour—where there were some of Raffelli's gay studies of Paris streets and an airy blue Venetian scene or two that always exhilarated him. He was delighted to find no one in the gallery but the old guard, who sat in the corner, a newspaper on his knee, a black patch over one eye and the other closed. Paul possessed himself of the place and walked confidently up and down, whistling under his breath. After a while he sat down before a blue Rico and lost himself. When he bethought him to look at his watch, it was after seven o'clock, and he rose with a start and ran downstairs, making a face at Augustus Cæsar, peering out from the cast-room, and an evil gesture at the Venus of Milo as he passed her on the stairway.

13 When Paul reached the ushers' dressing-room half-a-dozen boys were there already, and he began excitedly to tumble into his uniform. It was one of the few that at all approached fitting, and Paul thought it very becoming—though he knew the tight, straight coat accentuated his narrow chest, about which he was exceedingly sensitive. He was always excited while he dressed, twanging all over to the tuning of the strings and the preliminary flourishes of the horns in the music-room; but tonight he seemed quite beside himself, and he teased and plagued the boys until, telling him that he was crazy, they put him down on the floor and sat on him.

14 Somewhat calmed by his suppression, Paul dashed out to the front of the house to seat the early comers. He was a model usher. Gracious and smiling he ran up and down the aisles. Nothing was too much trouble for him; he carried messages and brought programs as though it were his greatest pleasure in life, and all the people in his section thought him a charming boy, feeling that he remembered and admired

them. As the house filled, he grew more and more vivacious and animated, and the colour came to his cheeks and lips. It was very much as though this were a great reception and Paul were the host. Just as the musicians came out to take their places, his English teacher arrived with checks for the seats which a prominent manufacturer had taken for the season. She betrayed some embarrassment when she handed Paul the tickets, and a *hauteur* which subsequently made her feel very foolish. Paul was startled for a moment, and had the feeling of wanting to put her out; what business had she here among all these fine people and gay colours? He looked her over and decided that she was not appropriately dressed and must be a fool to sit downstairs in such togs. The tickets had probably been sent her out of kindness, he reflected, as he put down a seat for her, and she had about as much right to sit there as he had.

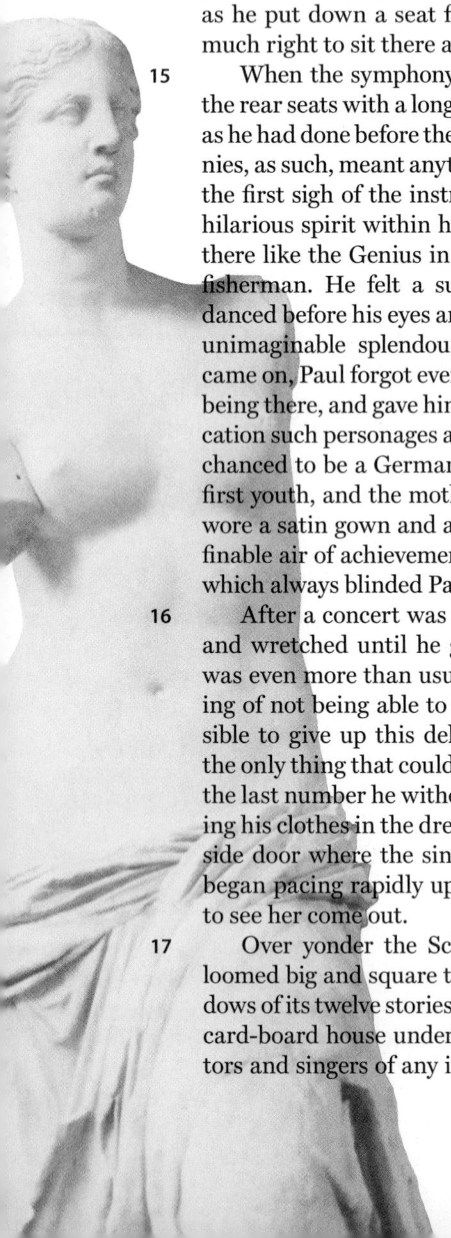

15 When the symphony began Paul sank into one of the rear seats with a long sigh of relief, and lost himself as he had done before the Rico. It was not that symphonies, as such, meant anything in particular to Paul, but the first sigh of the instruments seemed to free some hilarious spirit within him; something that struggled there like the Genius in the bottle found by the Arab fisherman. He felt a sudden zest of life; the lights danced before his eyes and the concert hall blazed into unimaginable splendour. When the soprano soloist came on, Paul forgot even the nastiness of his teacher's being there, and gave himself up to the peculiar intoxication such personages always had for him. The soloist chanced to be a German woman, by no means in her first youth, and the mother of many children; but she wore a satin gown and a tiara, and she had that indefinable air of achievement, that world-shine upon her, which always blinded Paul to any possible defects.

16 After a concert was over, Paul was often irritable and wretched until he got to sleep,—and tonight he was even more than usually restless. He had the feeling of not being able to let down; of its being impossible to give up this delicious excitement which was the only thing that could be called living at all. During the last number he withdrew and, after hastily changing his clothes in the dressing-room, slipped out to the side door where the singer's carriage stood. Here he began pacing rapidly up and down the walk, waiting to see her come out.

17 Over yonder the Schenley, in its vacant stretch, loomed big and square through the fine rain, the windows of its twelve stories glowing like those of a lighted card-board house under a Christmas tree. All the actors and singers of any importance stayed there when they were in the city, and a number of the big manufacturers of the place lived there in the winter. Paul had often hung about the hotel, watching the people go in and out, longing to enter and leave school-masters and dull care behind him for ever.

At last the singer came out, accompanied by the 18
conductor, who helped her into her carriage and closed the door with a cordial *auf wiedersehen,*—which set Paul to wondering whether she were not an old sweetheart of his. Paul followed the carriage over to the hotel, walking so rapidly as not to be far from the entrance when the singer alighted and disappeared behind the swinging glass doors which were opened by a negro in a tall hat and a long coat. In the moment that the door was ajar, it seemed to Paul that he, too, entered. He seemed to feel himself go after her up the steps, into the warm, lighted building, into an exotic, a tropical world of shiny, glistening surfaces and basking ease. He reflected upon the mysterious dishes that were brought into the dining-room, the green bottles in buckets of ice, as he had seen them in the supper party pictures of the Sunday supplement. A quick gust of wind brought the rain down with sudden vehemence, and Paul was startled to find that he was still outside in the slush of the gravel driveway; that his boots were letting in the water and his scanty overcoat was clinging wet about him; that the lights in front of the concert hall were out, and that the rain was driving in sheets between him and the orange glow of the windows above him. There it was, what he wanted—tangibly before him, like the fairy world of a Christmas pantomime; as the rain beat in his face, Paul wondered whether he were destined always to shiver in the black night outside, looking up at it.

He turned and walked reluctantly toward the car 19
tracks. The end had to come sometime; his father in his nightclothes at the top of the stairs, explanations that did not explain, hastily improvised fictions that were forever tripping him up, his upstairs room and its horrible yellow wallpaper, the creaking bureau with the greasy plush collar-box, and over his painted wooden bed the pictures of George Washington and John Calvin, and the framed motto, "Feed my Lambs," which had been worked in red worsted by his mother, whom Paul could not remember.

Half an hour later, Paul alighted from the Neg- 20
ley Avenue car and went slowly down one of the side streets off the main thoroughfare. It was a highly respectable street, where all the houses were exactly alike, and where business men of moderate means begot and reared large families of children, all of whom went to Sabbath-school and learned the

shorter catechism, and were interested in arithmetic; all of whom were as exactly alike as their homes, and of a piece with the monotony in which they lived. Paul never went up Cordelia Street without a shudder of loathing. His home was next the house of the Cumberland minister. He approached it tonight with the nerveless sense of defeat, the hopeless feeling of sinking back forever into ugliness and commonness that he had always had when he came home. The moment he turned into Cordelia Street he felt the waters close above his head. After each of these orgies of living, he experienced all the physical depression which follows a debauch; the loathing of respectable beds, of common food, of a house permeated by kitchen odours; a shuddering repulsion for the flavourless, colourless mass of every-day existence; a morbid desire for cool things and soft lights and fresh flowers.

21 The nearer he approached the house, the more absolutely unequal Paul felt to the sight of it all; his ugly sleeping chamber; the cold bath-room with the grimy zinc tub, the cracked mirror, the dripping spiggots; his father, at the top of the stairs, his hairy legs sticking out from his nightshirt, his feet thrust into carpet slippers. He was so much later than usual that there would certainly be inquiries and reproaches. Paul stopped short before the door. He felt that he could not be accosted by his father tonight; that he could not toss again on that miserable bed. He would not go in. He would tell his father that he had no car fare, and it was raining so hard he had gone home with one of the boys and stayed all night.

22 Meanwhile, he was wet and cold. He went around to the back of the house and tried one of the basement windows, found it open, raised it cautiously, and scrambled down the cellar wall to the floor. There he stood, holding his breath, terrified by the noise he had made; but the floor above him was silent, and there was no creak on the stairs. He found a soapbox, and carried it over to the soft ring of light that streamed from the furnace door, and sat down. He was horribly afraid of rats, so he did not try to sleep, but sat looking distrustfully at the dark, still terrified lest he might have awakened his father. In such reactions, after one of the experiences which made days and nights out of the dreary blanks of the calendar, when his senses were deadened, Paul's head was always singularly clear. Suppose his father had heard him getting in at the window and had come down and shot him for a burglar? Then, again, suppose his father had come down, pistol in hand, and he had cried out in time to save himself, and his father had been horrified to think how nearly he had killed him? Then, again, suppose a day should come when his father would remember that night, and wish there had been no warning cry to stay his hand? With this last supposition Paul entertained himself until daybreak.

The following Sunday was fine; the sodden November chill was broken by the last flash of autumnal summer. In the morning Paul had to go to church and Sabbath-school, as always. On seasonable Sunday afternoons the burghers of Cordelia Street usually sat out on their front "stoops," and talked to their neighbours on the next stoop, or called to those across the street in neighbourly fashion. The men sat placidly on gay cushions placed upon the steps that led down to the sidewalk, while the women, in their Sunday "waists," sat in rockers on the cramped porches, pretending to be greatly at their ease. The children played in the streets; there were so many of them that the place resembled the recreation grounds of a kindergarten. The men on the steps—all in their shirt sleeves, their vests unbuttoned—sat with their legs well apart, their stomachs comfortably protruding, and talked of the prices of things, or told anecdotes of the sagacity of their various chiefs and overlords. They occasionally looked over the multitude of squabbling children, listened affectionately to their high-pitched, nasal voices, smiling to see their own proclivities reproduced in their offspring, and interspersed their legends of the iron kings with remarks about their sons' progress at school, their grades in arithmetic, and the amounts they had saved in their toy banks. 23

On this last Sunday of November, Paul sat all the afternoon on the lowest step of his "stoop," staring into the street, while his sisters, in their rockers, were talking to the minister's daughters next door about how many shirt-waists they had made in the last week, and how many waffles some one had eaten at the last church supper. When the weather was warm, and his father was in a particularly jovial frame of mind, the girls made lemonade, which was always brought out in a red-glass pitcher, ornamented with forget-me-nots in blue enamel. This the girls thought very fine, and the neighbours always joked about the suspicious colour of the pitcher. 24

Today Paul's father, on the top step, was talking to a young man who shifted a restless baby from knee to knee. He happened to be the young man who was daily held up to Paul as a model, and after whom it 25 was his father's dearest hope that he would pattern. This young man was of a ruddy complexion, with a compressed, red mouth, and faded, near-sighted eyes, over which he wore thick spectacles, with gold bows that curved about his ears. He was clerk to one of the magnates of a great steel corporation, and was looked upon in Cordelia Street as a young man with a future. There was a story that, some five years ago—he was now barely twenty-six—he had been a trifle "dissipated," but in order to curb his appetites and save the loss of time and strength that a sowing of wild oats might have entailed, he had taken his chief's advice, oft reiterated to his employés, and at twenty-one had married the first woman whom he could persuade to share his fortunes. She happened to be an angular school-mistress, much older than he, who also wore thick glasses, and who had now borne him four children, all near-sighted, like herself.

This was Paul's fairy tale, and it had for him all the allurement of a secret love.

26 The young man was relating how his chief, now cruising in the Mediterranean, kept in touch with all the details of the business, arranging his office hours on his yacht just as though he were at home, and "knocking off work enough to keep two stenographers busy." His father told, in turn, the plan his corporation was considering, of putting in an electric railway plant in Cairo. Paul snapped his teeth; he had an awful apprehension that they might spoil it all before he got there. Yet he rather liked to hear these legends of the iron kings, that were told and retold on Sundays and holidays; these stories of palaces in Venice, yachts on the Mediterranean, and high play at Monte Carlo appealed to his fancy, and he was interested in the triumphs of cash boys who had become famous, though he had no mind for the cash-boy stage.

27 After supper was over, and he had helped to dry the dishes, Paul nervously asked his father whether he could go to George's to get some help in his geometry, and still more nervously asked for car-fare. This latter request he had to repeat, as his father, on principle, did not like to hear requests for money, whether much or little. He asked Paul whether he could not go to some boy who lived nearer, and told him that he ought not to leave his school work until Sunday; but he gave him the dime. He was not a poor man, but he had a worthy ambition to come up in the world. His only reason for allowing Paul to usher was that he thought a boy ought to be earning a little.

28 Paul bounded upstairs, scrubbed the greasy odour of the dish-water from his hands with the ill-smelling soap he hated, and then shook over his fingers a few drops of violet water from the bottle he kept hidden in his drawer. He left the house with his geometry conspicuously under his arm, and the moment he got out of Cordelia Street and boarded a downtown car, he shook off the lethargy of two deadening days, and began to live again.

The leading juvenile of the permanent stock company which played at one of the downtown theatres was an acquaintance of Paul's, and the boy had been invited to drop in at the Sunday-night rehearsals whenever he could. For more than a year Paul had spent every available moment loitering about Charley Edwards's dressing-room. He had won a place among Edwards's following not only because the young actor, who could not afford to employ a dresser, often found him useful, but because he recognized in Paul something akin to what churchmen term "vocation." 29

It was at the theatre and at Carnegie Hall that Paul really lived; the rest was but a sleep and a forgetting. This was Paul's fairy tale, and it had for him all the allurement of a secret love. The moment he inhaled the gassy, painty, dusty odour behind the scenes, he breathed like a prisoner set free, and felt within him the possibility of doing or saying splendid, brilliant things. The moment the cracked orchestra beat out the overture from *Martha,* or jerked at the serenade from *Rigoletto,* all stupid and ugly things slid from him, and his senses were deliciously, yet delicately fired. 30

Perhaps it was because, in Paul's world, the natural nearly always wore the guise of ugliness, that a certain element of artificiality seemed to him necessary in beauty. Perhaps it was because his experience of life elsewhere was so full of Sabbath-school picnics, petty economies, wholesome advice as to how to succeed in life, and the unescapable odours of cooking, that he found this existence so alluring, these smartly-clad men and women so attractive, that he was so moved by these starry apple orchards that bloomed perennially under the lime-light. 31

It would be difficult to put it strongly enough how convincingly the stage entrance of that theatre was for Paul the actual portal of Romance. Certainly none of the company ever suspected it, least of all Charley Edwards. It was very like the old stories that used to float about London of fabulously rich Jews, who had subterranean halls, with palms, and fountains, and soft lamps and richly apparelled women 32

who never saw the disenchanting light of London day. So, in the midst of that smoke-palled city, enamoured of figures and grimy toil, Paul had his secret temple, his wishing-carpet, his bit of blue-and-white Mediterranean shore bathed in perpetual sunshine.

33 Several of Paul's teachers had a theory that his imagination had been perverted by garish fiction; but the truth was, he scarcely ever read at all. The books at home were not such as would either tempt or corrupt a youthful mind, and as for reading the novels that some of his friends urged upon him—well, he got what he wanted much more quickly from music; any sort of music, from an orchestra to a barrel organ. He needed only the spark, the indescribable thrill that made his imagination master of his senses, and he could make plots and pictures enough of his own. It was equally true that he was not stage-struck—not, at any rate, in the usual acceptation of that expression. He had no desire to become an actor, any more than he had to become a musician. He felt no necessity to do any of these things; what he wanted was to see, to be in the atmosphere, float on the wave of it, to be carried out, blue league after blue league, away from everything.

34 After a night behind the scenes, Paul found the schoolroom more than ever repulsive; the bare floors and naked walls; the prosy men who never wore frock coats, or violets in their buttonholes; the women with their dull gowns, shrill voices, and pitiful seriousness about prepositions that govern the dative. He could not bear to have the other pupils think, for a moment, that he took these people seriously; he must convey to them that he considered it all trivial, and was there only by way of a joke, anyway. He had autograph pictures of all the members of the stock company which he showed his classmates, telling them the most incredible stories of his familiarity with these people, of his acquaintance with the soloists who came to Carnegie Hall, his suppers with them and the flowers he sent them. When these stories lost their effect, and his audience grew listless, he would bid all the boys good-bye, announcing that he was going to travel for awhile; going to Naples, to California, to Egypt. Then, next Monday, he would slip back, conscious and nervously smiling; his sister was ill, and he would have to defer his voyage until spring.

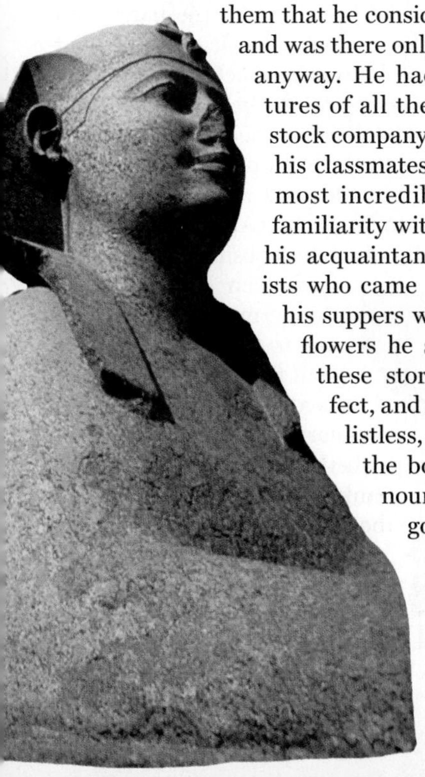

Matters went steadily worse with Paul at school. 35
In the itch to let his instructors know how heartily he despised them, and how thoroughly he was appreciated elsewhere, he mentioned once or twice that he had no time to fool with theorems; adding—with a twitch of the eyebrows and a touch of that nervous bravado which so perplexed them—that he was helping the people down at the stock company; they were old friends of his.

The upshot of the matter was, that the Principal 36
went to Paul's father, and Paul was taken out of school and put to work. The manager at Carnegie Hall was told to get another usher in his stead; the doorkeeper at the theatre was warned not to admit him to the house; and Charley Edwards remorsefully promised the boy's father not to see him again.

The members of the stock company were vastly 37
amused when some of Paul's stories reached them—especially the women. They were hard-working women, most of them supporting indolent husbands or brothers, and they laughed rather bitterly at having stirred the boy to such fervid and florid inventions. They agreed with the faculty and with his father, that Paul's was a bad case.

THE east-bound train was ploughing through 38
a January snow-storm; the dull dawn was beginning to show grey when the engine whistled a mile out of Newark. Paul started up from the seat where he had lain curled in uneasy slumber, rubbed the breath-misted window glass with his hand, and peered out. The snow was whirling in curling eddies above the white bottom lands, and the drifts lay already deep in the fields and along the fences, while here and there the long dead grass and dried weed stalks protruded black above it. Lights shone from the scattered houses, and a gang of labourers who stood beside the track waved their lanterns.

Paul had slept very little, and he felt grimy and 39
uncomfortable. He had made the all-night journey in a day coach because he was afraid if he took a Pullman he might be seen by some Pittsburgh business man who had noticed him in Denny & Carson's office. When the whistle woke him, he clutched quickly at his breast pocket, glancing about him with an uncertain smile. But the little, clay-bespattered Italians were still sleeping, the slatternly women across the aisle were in open-mouthed oblivion, and even the crumby, crying babies were for the nonce stilled. Paul settled back to struggle with his impatience as best he could.

40 When he arrived at the Jersey City station, he hurried through his breakfast, manifestly ill at ease and keeping a sharp eye about him. After he reached the Twenty-third Street station, he consulted a cabman, and had himself driven to a men's furnishing establishment which was just opening for the day. He spent upward of two hours there, buying with endless reconsidering and great care. His new street suit he put on in the fitting-room; the frock coat and dress clothes he had bundled into the cab with his new shirts. Then he drove to a hatter's and a shoe house. His next errand was at Tiffany's, where he selected silver mounted brushes and a scarf-pin. He would not wait to have his silver marked, he said. Lastly, he stopped at a trunk shop on Broadway, and had his purchases packed into various travelling bags.

41 It was a little after one o'clock when he drove up to the Waldorf, and, after settling with the cabman, went into the office. He registered from Washington; said his mother and father had been abroad, and that he had come down to await the arrival of their steamer. He told his story plausibly and had no trouble, since he offered to pay for them in advance, in engaging his rooms; a sleeping-room, sitting-room, and bath.

42 Not once, but a hundred times Paul had planned this entry into New York. He had gone over every detail of it with Charley Edwards, and in his scrap book at home there were pages of description about New York hotels, cut from the Sunday papers.

43 When he was shown to his sitting-room on the eighth floor, he saw at a glance that everything was as it should be; there was but one detail in his mental picture that the place did not realize, so he rang for the bell boy and sent him down for flowers. He moved about nervously until the boy returned, putting away his new linen and fingering it delightedly as he did so. When the flowers came, he put them hastily into water, and then tumbled into a hot bath. Presently he came out of his white bath-room, resplendent in his new silk underwear, and playing with the tassels of his red robe. The snow was whirling so fiercely outside his windows that he could scarcely see across the street; but within, the air was deliciously soft and fragrant. He put the violets and jonquils on the tabouret beside the couch, and threw himself down with a long sigh, covering himself with a Roman blanket. He was thoroughly tired; he had been in such haste, he had stood up to such a strain, covered so much ground in the last twenty-four hours, that he wanted to think how it had all come about. Lulled by the sound of the wind, the warm air, and the cool fragrance of the flowers, he sank into deep, drowsy retrospection.

It had been wonderfully simple; when they had shut him out of the theatre and concert hall, when they had taken away his bone, the whole thing was virtually determined. The rest was a mere matter of opportunity. The only thing that at all surprised him was his own courage—for he realized well enough that he had always been tormented by fear, a sort of apprehensive dread that, of late years, as the meshes of the lies he had told closed about him, had been pulling the muscles of his body tighter and tighter. Until now, he could not remember a time when he had not been dreading something. Even when he was a little boy, it was always there—behind him, or before, or on either side. There had always been the shadowed corner, the dark place into which he dared not look, but from which something seemed always to be watching him—and Paul had done things that were not pretty to watch, he knew. 44

But now he had a curious sense of relief, as though he had at last thrown down the gauntlet to the thing in the corner. 45

Yet it was but a day since he had been sulking in the traces; but yesterday afternoon that he had been sent to the bank with Denny & Carson's deposit, as usual—but this time he was instructed to leave the book to be balanced. There was above two thousand dollars in checks, and nearly a thousand in the bank notes which he had taken from the book and quietly transferred to his pocket. At the bank he had made out a new deposit slip. His nerves had been steady enough to permit of his returning to the office, where he had finished his work and asked for a full day's holiday tomorrow, Saturday, giving a perfectly reasonable pretext. The bank book, he knew, would not be returned before Monday or Tuesday, and his father would be out of town for the next week. From the time he slipped the bank notes into his pocket 46

until he boarded the night train for New York, he had not known a moment's hesitation.

47 How astonishingly easy it had all been; here he was, the thing done; and this time there would be no awakening, no figure at the top of the stairs. He watched the snow flakes whirling by his window until he fell asleep.

48 WHEN he awoke, it was four o'clock in the afternoon. He bounded up with a start; one of his precious days gone already! He spent nearly an hour in dressing, watching every stage of his toilet carefully in the mirror. Everything was quite perfect; he was exactly the kind of boy he had always wanted to be.

49 When he went downstairs, Paul took a carriage and drove up Fifth avenue toward the Park. The snow had somewhat abated; carriages and tradesmen's wagons were hurrying soundlessly to and fro in the winter twilight; boys in woollen mufflers were shovelling off the doorsteps; the avenue stages made fine spots of colour against the white street. Here and there on the corners whole flower gardens blooming behind glass windows, against which the snow flakes stuck and melted; violets, roses, carnations, lilies of the valley—somehow vastly more lovely and alluring that they blossomed thus unnaturally in the snow. The Park itself was a wonderful stage winterpiece.

50 When he returned, the pause of the twilight had ceased, and the tune of the streets had changed. The snow was falling faster, lights streamed from the hotels that reared their many stories fearlessly up into the storm, defying the raging Atlantic winds. A long, black stream of carriages poured down the avenue, intersected here and there by other streams, tending horizontally. There were a score of cabs about the entrance of his hotel, and his driver had to wait. Boys in livery were running in and out of the awning stretched across the sidewalk, up and down the red velvet carpet laid from the door to the street. Above, about, within it all, was the rumble and roar, the hurry and toss of thousands of human beings as hot for pleasure as himself, and on every side of him towered the glaring affirmation of the omnipotence of wealth.

51 The boy set his teeth and drew his shoulders together in a spasm of realization; the plot of all dramas, the text of all romances, the nerve-stuff of all sensations was whirling about him like the snow flakes. He burnt like a faggot in a tempest.

52 When Paul came down to dinner, the music of the orchestra floated up the elevator shaft to greet him. As he stepped into the thronged corridor, he sank back into one of the chairs against the wall to get his breath. The lights, the chatter, the perfumes, the bewildering medley of colour—he had, for a moment, the feeling of not being able to stand it. But only for a moment; these were his own people, he told himself. He went slowly about the corridors, through the writing-rooms, smoking-rooms, reception-rooms, as though he were exploring the chambers of an enchanted palace, built and peopled for him alone.

When he reached the dining-room he sat down at a table near a window. The flowers, the white linen, the many-coloured wine glasses, the gay toilettes of the women, the low popping of corks, the undulating repetitions of the *Blue Danube* from the orchestra, all flooded Paul's dream with bewildering radiance. When the roseate tinge of his champagne was added—that cold, precious, bubbling stuff that creamed and foamed in his glass—Paul wondered that there were honest men in the world at all. This was what all the world was fighting for, he reflected; this was what all the struggle was about. He doubted the reality of his past. Had he ever known a place called Cordelia Street, a place where fagged looking business men boarded the early car? Mere rivets in a machine they seemed to Paul,—sickening men, with combings of children's hair always hanging to their coats, and the smell of cooking in their clothes. Cordelia Street—Ah, that belonged to another time and country! Had he not always been thus, had he not sat here night after night, from as far back as he could remember, looking pensively over just such shimmering textures, and slowly twirling the stem of a glass like this one between his thumb and middle finger? He rather thought he had. 53

He was not in the least abashed or lonely. He had no especial desire to meet or to know any of these people; all he demanded was the right to look on and conjecture, to watch the pageant. The mere stage properties were all he contended for. Nor was he lonely later in the evening, in his loge at the Opera. He was entirely rid of his nervous misgivings, of his forced aggressiveness, of the imperative desire to show himself different from his surroundings. He felt now that his surroundings explained him. Nobody questioned the purple; he had only to wear it passively. He had only to glance down at his dress coat to reassure himself that here it would be impossible for anyone to humiliate him. 54

55 He found it hard to leave his beautiful sitting-room to go to bed that night, and sat long watching the raging storm from his turret window. When he went to sleep, it was with the lights turned on in his bedroom; partly because of his old timidity, and partly so that, if he should wake in the night, there would be no wretched moment of doubt, no horrible suspicion of yellow wall-paper, or of Washington and Calvin above his bed.

The mere release from the necessity of petty lying, lying every day and every day, restored his self-respect.

56 On Sunday morning the city was practically snowbound. Paul breakfasted late, and in the afternoon he fell in with a wild San Francisco boy, a freshman at Yale, who said he had run down for a "little flyer" over Sunday. The young man offered to show Paul the night side of the town, and the two boys went off together after dinner, not returning to the hotel until seven o'clock the next morning. They had started out in the confiding warmth of a champagne friendship, but their parting in the elevator was singularly cool. The freshman pulled himself together to make his train, and Paul went to bed. He awoke at two o'clock in the afternoon, very thirsty and dizzy, and rang for ice-water, coffee, and the Pittsburgh papers.

57 On the part of the hotel management, Paul excited no suspicion. There was this to be said for him, that he wore his spoils with dignity and in no way made himself conspicuous. His chief greediness lay in his ears and eyes, and his excesses were not offensive ones. His dearest pleasures were the grey winter twilights in his sitting-room; his quiet enjoyment of his flowers, his clothes, his wide divan, his cigarette and his sense of power. He could not remember a time when he had felt so at peace with himself. The mere release from the necessity of petty lying, lying every day and every day, restored his self-respect. He had never lied for pleasure, even at school; but to make himself noticed and admired, to assert his difference from other Cordelia Street boys; and he felt a good deal more manly, more honest, even, now that he had no need for boastful pretensions, now that he could, as his actor friends used to say, "dress the part." It was characteristic that remorse did not occur to him. His golden days went by without a shadow, and he made each as perfect as he could.

58 On the eighth day after his arrival in New York, he found the whole affair exploited in the Pittsburgh papers, exploited with a wealth of detail which indicated that local news of a sensational nature was at a low ebb. The firm of Denny & Carson announced that the boy's father had refunded the full amount of his theft, and that they had no intention of prosecuting. The Cumberland minister had been interviewed, and expressed his hope of yet reclaiming the motherless lad, and Paul's Sabbath-school teacher declared that she would spare no effort to that end. The rumour had reached Pittsburgh that the boy had been seen in a New York hotel, and his father had gone East to find him and bring him home.

Paul had just come in to 59
dress for dinner; he sank into a chair, weak in the knees, and clasped his head in his hands. It was to be worse than jail, even; the tepid waters of Cordelia Street were to close over him finally and forever. The grey monotony stretched before him in hopeless, unrelieved years; Sabbath-school, Young People's Meeting, the yellow-papered room, the damp dish-towels; it all rushed back upon him with sickening vividness. He had the old feeling that the orchestra had suddenly stopped, the sinking sensation that the play was over. The sweat broke out on his face, and he sprang to his feet, looked about him with his white, conscious smile, and winked at himself in the mirror, With something of the childish belief in miracles with which he had so often gone to class, all his lessons unlearned, Paul dressed and dashed whistling down the corridor to the elevator.

He had no sooner entered the dining-room and 60
caught the measure of the music, than his remembrance was lightened by his old elastic power of claiming the moment, mounting with it, and finding it all sufficient. The glare and glitter about him, the mere scenic accessories had again, and for the last time, their old potency. He would show himself that he was game, he would finish the thing splendidly. He doubted, more than ever, the existence of Cordelia Street, and for the first time he drank his wine recklessly. Was he not, after all, one of these fortunate beings? Was he not still himself, and in his own place? He drummed a nervous accompaniment to the music and looked about him, telling himself over and over that it had paid.

He reflected drowsily, to the swell of the violin 61
and the chill sweetness of his wine, that he might have done it more wisely. He might have caught an outbound steamer and been well out of their clutches before now. But the other side of the world had seemed too far away and too uncertain then; he could not have

waited for it; his need had been too sharp. If he had to choose over again, he would do the same thing tomorrow. He looked affectionately about the dining-room, now gilded with a soft mist. Ah, it had paid indeed!

62 Paul was awakened next morning by a painful throbbing in his head and feet. He had thrown himself across the bed without undressing, and had slept with his shoes on. His limbs and hands were lead heavy, and his tongue and throat were parched. There came upon him one of those fateful attacks of clear-headedness that never occurred except when he was physically exhausted and his nerves hung loose. He lay still and closed his eyes and let the tide of realities wash over him.

63 His father was in New York; "stopping at some joint or other," he told himself. The memory of successive summers on the front stoop fell upon him like a weight of black water. He had not a hundred dollars left; and he knew now, more than ever, that money was everything, the wall that stood between all he loathed and all he wanted. The thing was winding itself up; he had thought of that on his first glorious day in New York, and had even provided a way to snap the thread. It lay on his dressing-table now; he had got it out last night when he came blindly up from dinner,—but the shiny metal hurt his eyes, and he disliked the look of it, anyway.

64 He rose and moved about with a painful effort, succumbing now and again to attacks of nausea. It was the old depression exaggerated; all the world had become Cordelia Street. Yet somehow he was not afraid of anything, was absolutely calm; perhaps because he had looked into the dark corner at last, and knew. It was bad enough, what he saw there; but somehow not so bad as his long fear of it had been. He saw everything clearly now. He had a feeling that he had made the best of it, that he had lived the sort of life he was meant to live, and for half an hour he sat staring at the revolver. But he told himself that was not the way, so he went downstairs and took a cab to the ferry.

65 When Paul arrived at Newark, he got off the train and took another cab, directing the driver to follow the Pennsylvania tracks out of the town. The snow lay heavy on the roadways and had drifted deep in the open fields. Only here and there the dead grass or dried weed stalks projected, singularly black, above it. Once well into the country, Paul dismissed the carriage and walked, floundering along the tracks, his mind a medley of irrelevant things. He seemed to hold in his brain an actual picture of everything he had seen that morning. He remembered every feature of both his drivers, the toothless old woman from whom he had bought the red flowers in his coat, the agent from whom he had got his ticket, and all of his fellow-passengers on the ferry. His mind, unable to cope with vital matters near at hand, worked feverishly and deftly at sorting and grouping these images. They made for him a part of the ugliness of the world, of the ache in his head, and the bitter burning on his tongue. He stooped and put a handful of snow into his mouth as he walked, but that, too, seemed hot. When he reached a little hillside, where the tracks ran through a cut some twenty feet below him, he stopped and sat down.

66 The carnations in his coat were drooping with the cold, he noticed; all their red glory over. It occurred to him that all the flowers he had seen in the show windows that first night must have gone the same way, long before this. It was only one splendid breath they had, in spite of their brave mockery at the winter outside the glass. It was a losing game in the end, it seemed, this revolt against the homilies by which the world is run. Paul took one of the blossoms carefully from his coat and scooped a little hole in the snow, where he covered it up. Then he dozed a while, from his weak condition, seeming insensible to the cold.

67 The sound of an approaching train woke him, and he started to his feet, remembering only his resolution, and afraid lest he should be too late. He stood watching the approaching locomotive, his teeth chattering, his lips drawn away from them in a frightened smile; once or twice he glanced nervously sidewise, as though he were being watched. When the right moment came, he jumped. As he fell, the folly of his haste occurred to him with merciless clearness, the vastness of what he had left undone. There flashed through his brain, clearer than ever before, the blue of Adriatic water, the yellow of Algerian sands.

68 He felt something strike his chest,—his body was being thrown swiftly through the air, on and on, immeasurably far and fast, while his limbs gently relaxed. Then, because the picture making mechanism was crushed, the disturbing visions flashed into black, and Paul dropped back into the immense design of things.

IF you liked this story of a troubled young man in Willa Cather's "Paul's Case," you might look again at "Greasy Lake" by T. Coraghessan Boyle in chapter 4 or at the soldiers of Tim O'Brien's "The Things They Carried" in chapter 10, or the family members in Alice Walker's "Everyday Use" in Stories for Further Reading.

**GOING FURTHER** Paul, an ordinary young person moving in a downward spiral, is an interesting variation on the nature of human character, which Willa Cather has explored at length in her many novels. Most of her characters strive upward, such as the immigrant girl Ántonia in *My Ántonia,* the gifted Midwestern opera singer in *The Song of the Lark,* and Father Latour, the nineteenth-century priest, based on an actual historical figure, in the novel *Death Comes for the Archbishop.*

# Writing from Reading

## Summarize

1 The story's subtitle, "A Study in Temperament," suggests dispassionate analysis—as if we were about to read a clinician's case study or a police report. What are the facts that make up this "case"? Summarize the events.

## Analyze Craft

2 Cather first presents Paul from the perspective of his teachers, who see him as smug, flippant, difficult, and beyond their ability to understand. Why does Cather open the story this way, and does this approach affect your response to him as a character?

3 Describe what Paul experiences when he watches the symphony. What, specifically, does he hear, see, and feel? How does his response to the music, especially the soprano soloist, help to characterize him?

4 Compare and contrast the two locations of the story—Pittsburgh and New York—and explore how, in rendering them, Cather also characterizes Paul and the changes in his life. Consider other aspects of setting—times of day, the weather, the season—in your analysis.

## Analyze Voice

5 This story raises a series of psychological questions: What motivates Paul to make the choices he does? What does he seek? What is his desire? Discuss how the story's narrator answers these questions.

6 In what ways does Cather's language make this seem more like a "case," a presentation of facts and details, than it does a story?

## Synthesize Summary and Analysis

7 Paul is an antihero, a protagonist whose actions do not meet our expectations of courage and honesty. Discuss how Cather makes the reader relate to Paul despite his unacceptable behavior.

## Interpret the Story

8 Make a case for Paul as round or flat, and static or dynamic. Consider how Paul has or hasn't changed over the course of the story, citing the events that altered or maintained his character.

# Jack London (1876–1916)

Born to an unmarried mother in California, John ("Jack") London sought employment from age ten in order to lessen his family's poverty. In jobs such as working at a cannery, shoveling coal at a power plant, and pirating oysters from commercial oyster operations, London experienced firsthand the life of an average worker and determined to better himself through education. He turned to writing after taking part in the Yukon gold rush, working with a self-imposed rule that he must write 1,000 publishable words every day. His first collection of short stories, *The Son of the Wolf,* appeared in 1900, and within the next several years, he published many of the novels that made him famous, including *The Call of the Wild* (1903), *The Sea Wolf* (1904), and *White Fang* (1906). These novels of survival in a harsh natural world made London famous all over the globe, and he is one of the few early twentieth century writers to have become rich from his fiction. Despite his rags-to-riches life story, London believed in socialism and used his celebrity status to speak and write in favor of it. London was a man of prodigious energy, and his hobbies ranged from sailing to agriculture to building his dream house. He died when just forty years old, of uremia, although some have speculated that his death may have been a suicide.

**AS YOU READ** **As you read, notice your responses to the rather large cast of characters. Which do you get to know best? Do any of them seem familiar to you?**

**TIP** **FOR INTERACTIVE READING . . .** As you read, mark the text in the places where Mrs. Hemingway talks about Loretta. How does she describe Loretta to her husband? How does she describe Loretta to Ned Bashford? What do the differences in the descriptions tell you about Mrs. Hemingway?

# A Wicked Woman (1906)

1 IT was because she had broken with Billy that Loretta had come visiting to Santa Clara. Billy could not understand. His sister had reported that he had walked the floor and cried all night. Loretta had not slept all night either, while she had wept most of the night. Daisy knew this, because it was in her arms that the weeping had been done. And Daisy's husband, Captain Kitt, knew, too. The tears of Loretta, and the comforting by Daisy, had lost him some sleep.

Now Captain Kitt did not like to lose sleep. Neither did he want Loretta to marry Billy—nor anybody else. It was Captain Kitt's belief that Daisy needed the help of her younger sister in the household. But he did not say this aloud. Instead, he always insisted that Loretta was too young to think of marriage. So it was Captain Kitt's idea that Loretta should be packed off on a visit to Mrs. Hemingway. There wouldn't be any Billy there. 2

3 Before Loretta had been at Santa Clara a week, she was convinced that Captain Kitt's idea was a good one. In the first place, though Billy wouldn't believe it, she did not want to marry Billy. And in the second place, though Captain Kitt wouldn't believe it, she did not want to leave Daisy. By the time Loretta had been at Santa Clara two weeks, she was absolutely certain that she did not want to marry Billy. But she was not so sure about not wanting to leave Daisy. Not that she loved Daisy less, but that she—had doubts.

> He did not believe in the truth of women . . .

4 The day of Loretta's arrival, a nebulous plan began shaping itself in Mrs. Hemingway's brain. The second day she remarked to Jack Hemingway, her husband, that Loretta was so innocent a young thing that were it not for her sweet guilelessness she would be positively stupid. In proof of which, Mrs. Hemingway told her husband several things that made him chuckle. By the third day Mrs. Hemingway's plan had taken recognizable form. Then it was that she composed a letter. On the envelope she wrote: "Mr. Edward Bashford, Athenian Club, San Francisco."

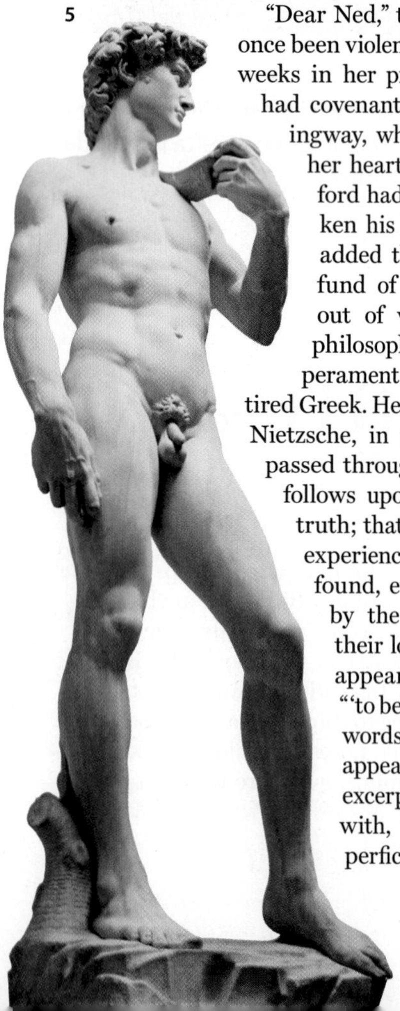

5 "Dear Ned," the letter began. She had once been violently loved by him for three weeks in her pre-marital days. But she had covenanted herself to Jack Hemingway, who had prior claims, and her heart as well; and Ned Bashford had philosophically not broken his heart over it. He merely added the experience to a large fund of similarly collected data out of which he manufactured philosophy. Artistically and temperamentally he was a Greek—a tired Greek. He was fond of quoting from Nietzsche, in token that he, too, had passed through the long sickness that follows upon the ardent search for truth; that he too had emerged, too experienced, too shrewd, too profound, ever again to be afflicted by the madness of youths in their love of truth. "To worship appearance," he often quoted; "'to believe in forms, in tones, in words, in the whole Olympus of appearance!'" This particular excerpt he always concluded with, "Those Greeks were superficial—*out of profundity*!"

He was a fairly young Greek, jaded and worn. Women were faithless and unveracious, he held—at such times that he had relapses and descended to pessimism from his wonted high philosophical calm. He did not believe in the truth of women; but, faithful to his German master, he did not strip from them the airy gauzes that veiled their untruth. He was content to accept them as appearances and to make the best of it. He was superficial—*out of profundity*. 6

"Jack says to be sure to say to you, 'good swimming,'" Mrs. Hemingway wrote in her letter; "and also 'to bring your fishing duds along.'" Mrs. Hemingway wrote other things in the letter. She told him that at last she was prepared to exhibit to him an absolutely true, unsullied, and innocent woman. "A more guileless, immaculate bud of womanhood never blushed on the planet," was one of the several ways in which she phrased the inducement. And to her husband she said triumphantly, "If I don't marry Ned off this time—" leaving unstated the terrible alternative that she lacked either vocabulary to express or imagination to conceive. 7

Contrary to all her forebodings, Loretta found that she was not unhappy at Santa Clara. True, Billy wrote to her every day, but his letters were less distressing than his presence. Also, the ordeal of being away from Daisy was not so severe as she had expected. For the first time in her life she was not lost in eclipse in the blaze of Daisy's brilliant and mature personality. Under such favorable circumstances Loretta came rapidly to the front, while Mrs. Hemingway modestly and shamelessly retreated into the background. 8

Loretta began to discover that she was not a pale orb shining by reflection. Quite unconsciously she became a small centre of things. When she was at the piano, there was some one to turn the pages for her and to express preferences for certain songs. When she dropped her handkerchief, there was some one to pick it up. And there was some one to accompany her in ramblings and flower gatherings. Also, she learned to cast flies in still pools and below savage riffles, and how not to entangle silk lines and gut-leaders with the shrubbery. 9

Jack Hemingway did not care to teach beginners, and fished much by himself, or not at all, thus giving Ned Bashford ample time in which to consider Loretta as an appearance. As such, she was all that his philosophy demanded. Her blue eyes had the direct gaze of a boy, and out of his profundity he delighted in them and forbore to shudder at the duplic- 10 ity his philosophy bade him to believe lurked in their depths. She had the grace of a slender flower, the fragility of color and line of fine china, in all of which he pleasured greatly, without thought of the Life Force palpitating beneath and in spite of Bernard Shaw—in whom he believed.

11 Loretta bourgeoned. She swiftly developed personality. She discovered a will of her own and wishes of her own that were not everlastingly entwined with the will and the wishes of Daisy. She was petted by Jack Hemingway, spoiled by Alice Hemingway, and devotedly attended by Ned Bashford. They encouraged her whims and laughed at her follies, while she developed the pretty little tyrannies that are latent in all pretty and delicate women. Her environment acted as a soporific upon her ancient desire always to live with Daisy. This desire no longer prodded her as in the days of her companionship with Billy. The more she saw of Billy, the more certain she had been that she could not live away from Daisy. The more she saw of Ned Bashford, the more she forgot her pressing need of Daisy.

12 Ned Bashford likewise did some forgetting. He confused superficiality with profundity, and entangled appearance with reality until he accounted them one. Loretta was different from other women. There was no masquerade about her. She was real. He said as much to Mrs. Hemingway, and more, who agreed with him and at the same time caught her husband's eyelid drooping down for the moment in an unmistakable wink.

There seemed to emanate from her the perfect sweetness of a child—"the aura of a white soul."

13 It was at this time that Loretta received a letter from Billy that was somewhat different from his others. In the main, like all his letters, it was pathological. It was a long recital of symptoms and sufferings, his nervousness, his sleeplessness, and the state of his heart. Then followed reproaches, such as he had never made before. They were sharp enough to make her weep, and true enough to put tragedy into her face. This tragedy she carried down to the breakfast table. It made Jack and Mrs. Hemingway speculative, and it worried Ned. They glanced to him for explanation, but he shook his head.

14 "I'll find out to-night," Mrs. Hemingway said to her husband.

15 But Ned caught Loretta in the afternoon in the big living-room. She tried to turn away. He caught her hands, and she faced him with wet lashes and trembling lips. He looked at her, silently and kindly. The lashes grew wetter.

"There, there, don't cry, little one," he said soothingly. 16

He put his arm protectingly around her shoulder. And to his shoulder, like a tired child, she turned her face. He thrilled in ways unusual for a Greek who has recovered from the long sickness. 17

"Oh, Ned," she sobbed on his shoulder, "if you only knew how wicked I am!" 18

He smiled indulgently, and breathed in a great breath freighted with the fragrance of her hair. He thought of his world-experience of women, and drew another long breath. There seemed to emanate from her the perfect sweetness of a child—"the aura of a white soul," was the way he phrased it to himself. 19

Then he noticed that her sobs were increasing. 20

"What's the matter, little one?" he asked pettingly and almost paternally. "Has Jack been bullying you? Or has your dearly beloved sister failed to write?" 21

She did not answer, and he felt that he really must kiss her hair, that he could not be responsible if the situation continued much longer. 22

"Tell me, "he said gently, "and we'll see what I can do." 23

"I can't. You will despise me.—Oh, Ned, I am so ashamed!" 24

He laughed incredulously, and lightly touched her hair with his lips—so lightly that she did not know. 25

"Dear little one, let us forget all about it, whatever it is. I want to tell you how I love—" 26

She uttered a sharp cry that was all delight, and then moaned— 27

"Too late!" 28

"Too late?" he echoed in surprise. 29

"Oh, why did I? Why did I?" she was moaning. 30

He was aware of a swift chill at his heart. 31

"What?" he asked. 32

"Oh, I . . . he . . . Billy. 33

"I am such a wicked woman, Ned. I know you will never speak to me again." 34

"This—er—this Billy," he began haltingly. "He is your brother?" 35

"No . . . he . . . I didn't know. I was so young. I could not help it. Oh, I shall go mad! I shall go mad!" 36

It was then that Loretta felt his shoulder and the encircling arm become limp. He drew away from her gently, and gently he deposited her in a big chair, where she buried her face and sobbed afresh. He twisted his mustache fiercely, then drew up another chair and sat down. 37

"I—I do not understand," he said. 38

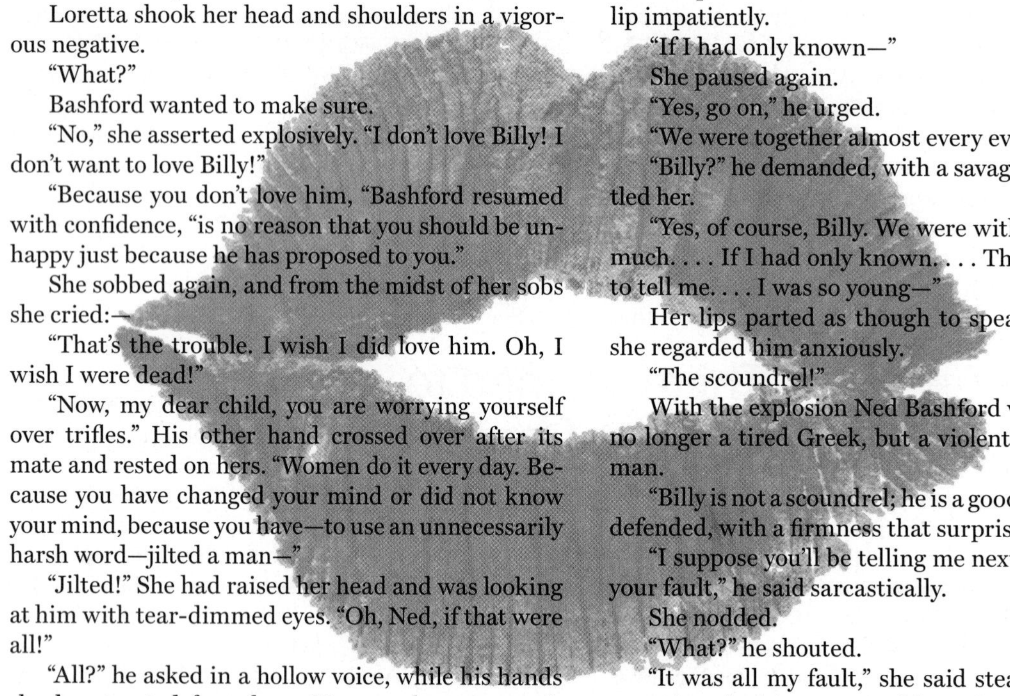

39 "I am so unhappy," she wailed.

40 "Why unhappy?"

41 "Because . . . he . . . he wants me to marry him."

42 His face cleared on the instant, and he placed a hand soothingly on hers.

43 "That should not make any girl unhappy," he remarked sagely. "Because you don't love him is no reason—of course, you don't love him?"

44 Loretta shook her head and shoulders in a vigorous negative.

45 "What?"

46 Bashford wanted to make sure.

47 "No," she asserted explosively. "I don't love Billy! I don't want to love Billy!"

48 "Because you don't love him, "Bashford resumed with confidence, "is no reason that you should be unhappy just because he has proposed to you."

49 She sobbed again, and from the midst of her sobs she cried:—

50 "That's the trouble. I wish I did love him. Oh, I wish I were dead!"

51 "Now, my dear child, you are worrying yourself over trifles." His other hand crossed over after its mate and rested on hers. "Women do it every day. Because you have changed your mind or did not know your mind, because you have—to use an unnecessarily harsh word—jilted a man—"

52 "Jilted!" She had raised her head and was looking at him with tear-dimmed eyes. "Oh, Ned, if that were all!"

53 "All?" he asked in a hollow voice, while his hands slowly retreated from hers. He was about to speak further, then remained silent.

54 "But I don't want to marry him," Loretta broke forth protestingly.

55 "Then I shouldn't," he counselled.

56 "But I ought to marry him."

57 "*Ought* to marry him?"

58 She nodded.

59 "That is a strong word."

60 "I know it is," she acquiesced, while she strove to control her trembling lips. Then she spoke more calmly. "I am a wicked woman, a terribly wicked woman. No one knows how wicked I am—except Billy."

61 There was a pause. Ned Bashford's face was grave, and he looked queerly at Loretta.

62 "He—Billy knows?" he asked finally.

63 A reluctant nod and flaming cheeks was the reply.

64 He debated with himself for a while, seeming, like a diver, to be preparing himself for the plunge.

65 "Tell me about it." He spoke very firmly. "You must tell me all of it."

66 "And will you—ever—forgive me?" she asked in a faint, small voice.

67 He hesitated, drew a long breath, and made the plunge.

68 "Yes," he said desperately. "I'll forgive you. Go ahead."

69 "There was no one to tell me," she began. "We were with each other so much. I did not know anything of the world—then."

70 She paused to meditate. Bashford was biting his lip impatiently.

71 "If I had only known—"

72 She paused again.

73 "Yes, go on," he urged.

74 "We were together almost every evening."

75 "Billy?" he demanded, with a savageness that startled her.

76 "Yes, of course, Billy. We were with each other so much. . . . If I had only known. . . . There was no one to tell me. . . . I was so young—"

77 Her lips parted as though to speak further, and she regarded him anxiously.

78 "The scoundrel!"

79 With the explosion Ned Bashford was on his feet, no longer a tired Greek, but a violently angry young man.

80 "Billy is not a scoundrel; he is a good man," Loretta defended, with a firmness that surprised Bashford.

81 "I suppose you'll be telling me next that it was all your fault," he said sarcastically.

82 She nodded.

83 "What?" he shouted.

84 "It was all my fault," she said steadily. "I should never have let him. I was to blame."

85 Bashford ceased from his pacing up and down, and when he spoke, his voice was resigned.

86 "All right," he said. "I don't blame you in the least, Loretta. And you have been very honest. But Billy is right, and you are wrong. You must get married."

87 "To Billy?" she asked, in a dim, far-away voice.

88 "Yes, to Billy. I'll see to it. Where does he live? I'll make him."

89 "But I don't want to marry Billy!" she cried out in alarm. "Oh, Ned, you won't do that?"

90 "I shall," he answered sternly. "You must. And Billy must. Do you understand?"

91 Loretta buried her face in the cushioned chair back, and broke into a passionate storm of sobs.

92 All that Bashford could make out at first, as he listened, was: "But I don't want to leave Daisy! I don't want to leave Daisy!"

93 He paced grimly back and forth, then stopped curiously to listen.

94 "How was I to know?—Boo-hoo," Loretta was crying. "He didn't tell me. Nobody else ever kissed me. I never dreamed a kiss could be so terrible . . . until,

boo-hoo . . . until he wrote to me. I only got the letter this morning."

95 His face brightened. It seemed as though light was dawning on him.

96 "Is that what you're crying about?"

97 "N-no."

98 His heart sank.

99 "Then what are you crying about?" he asked in a hopeless voice.

100 "Because you said I had to marry Billy. And I don't want to marry Billy. I don't want to leave Daisy. I don't know what I want. I wish I were dead."

101 He nerved himself for another effort.

102 "Now look here, Loretta, be sensible. What is this about kisses? You haven't told me everything."

103 "I—I don't want to tell you everything."

104 She looked at him beseechingly in the silence that fell.

105 "Must I?" she quavered finally.

106 "You must," he said imperatively. 'You must tell me everything."

107 "Well, then . . . must I?"

108 "You must."

109 "He . . . I . . . we . . ." she began flounderingly. Then blurted out, "I let him, and he kissed me."

110 "Go on," Bashford commanded desperately.

111 "That's all," she answered.

112 "All?" There was a vast incredulity in his voice.

113 "All?" In her voice was an interrogation no less vast.

114 "I mean—er—nothing worse?" He was overwhelmingly aware of his own awkwardness.

115 "Worse?" She was frankly puzzled. "As though there could be! Billy said—"

116 "When did he say it?" Bashford demanded abruptly.

117 "In his letter I got this morning. Billy said that my . . . our . . . our kisses were terrible if we didn't get married."

Bashford's head was swimming. 118

"What else did Billy say?" he asked. 119

"He said that when a woman allowed a man to kiss her, she always married him—that it was terrible if she didn't. It was the custom, he said; and I say it is a bad, wicked custom, and I don't like it. I know I'm terrible," she added defiantly, "but I can't help it." 110

Bashford absent-mindedly brought out a cigarette. 111

"Do you mind if I smoke?" he asked, as he struck a match. 1112

Then he came to himself. 113

"I beg your pardon," he cried, flinging away match and cigarette. "I don't want to smoke. I didn't mean that at all. What I mean is—" 114

He bent over Loretta, caught her hands in his, then sat on the arm of the chair and softly put one arm around her. 115

"Loretta, I am a fool. I mean it. And I mean something more. I want you to be my wife." 116

He waited anxiously in the pause that followed. 117

"You might answer me," he urged. 118

"I will . . . if—" 119

"Yes, go on. If what?" 120

"If I don't have to marry Billy." 121

"You can't marry both of us," he almost shouted. 122

"And it isn't the custom . . . what . . . what Billy said?" 123

"No, it isn't the custom. Now, Loretta, will you marry me?" 124

"Don't be angry with me," she pouted demurely. 125

He gathered her into his arms and kissed her. 126

"I wish it were the custom," she said in a faint voice, from the midst of the embrace, "because then I'd have to marry you, Ned . . . dear . . . wouldn't I?" 127

SUCCESSFUL comedy in fiction is a rare quality. If you like "A Wicked Woman," look at Eudora Welty's "Why I Live at the P.O." (chapter 6), Lorrie Moore's slyly narrated "How to Become a Writer or, Have You Earned This Cliché?" (chapter 7), and the bitter wit in Amy Hempel's "San Francisco" (chapter 14).

**GOING FURTHER** Although much of London's material came from personal experience, some scholars have claimed he purchased plots and ideas from fellow writer Sinclair Lewis. In his first commercially successful novel, *Main Street,* Lewis provides a realistic picture of small-town America, featuring a strong female protagonist.

# Writing from Reading

## Summarize

**1** List all the characters in this story (including Loretta herself) and summarize their impressions of Loretta.

**2** Summarize what Loretta actually wishes for herself, based first on the narrator's exposition in the story, then on Loretta's own spoken confessions. Compare and contrast these two conclusions.

## Analyze Craft

**3** Do you consider the characters in this story to be round or flat? Why? Place them along a spectrum from roundest to flattest, and explain why you have arranged them in that way.

**4** Discuss the character of Loretta. Does she change in the course of the story, and in what ways? Who are her antagonists, and what sort of impact do they have on her development?

## Analyze Voice

**5** This story was published in 1908. How current does it seem a century later, and how does its date affect the credibility of events in the story?

## Synthesize Summary and Analysis

**6** Consider the dialogue between Ned and Loretta at the end of the story. What characteristics differentiate the two characters' voices? What aspects of their characters lend to the confusion of their argument? Explain how the same confusion the characters feel is extended to the reader.

## Interpret the Story

**7** Considering the disparity between the narrator's exposition and Loretta's own assertions, and in light of Loretta's agreement to marry Ned and her final statement, do you think Loretta's behavior with Ned is genuine or preconceived? In other words, has she fooled Ned into a proposal? Provide evidence from the story that supports or denies Loretta's own profession that she is "a wicked woman."

# Reading for Character

When reading for character, ask yourself how the author characterizes the personality and motivation that make a character behave in a certain way.

| | |
|---|---|
| **Which elements of characterization can you identify?** | • What does the physical appearance of the character tell you?<br>• Does the name of the character reveal anything?<br>• How is the character dressed, and what does this reveal?<br>• What actions has a character taken that tell you about his or her motivation?<br>• How does the character's voice, by means of either internal thoughts or dialogue, emerge on the page, how does that voice "sound," and what does this tell you about the character? |

| | |
|---|---|
| **Is the character complex—exhibiting both good and bad traits—and able to change?** | • That character is a ***round, dynamic*** character. |
| **Does the main character exhibit traits that are sympathetic but not heroic in the traditional sense?** | • That character is likely an ***antihero.*** |
| **Does the character represent primarily one characteristic, such as greed or vanity?** | • That character is a ***flat, stock*** character. |
| **What function do the flat characters play in the story?** | • A flat character may be used to reveal the hero more clearly, functioning as the hero's ***foil.*** |

# Suggestions for Writing about Character

1. Write an argument for or against the usefulness of flat secondary characters in fiction; back up your main point with examples from at least two stories in this chapter.
2. "Who's Irish?" is told in first person, whereas "The Jilting of Granny Weatherall" is told in third person. (See chapter 7 for a discussion of point of view.) How do the two narrators' biases and personalities affect your responses to the other characters and events in the stories?
3. Consider the role of motivation in a story's protagonist as well as in its antagonist. Choose two stories in this chapter and discuss the thoughts, feelings, beliefs, needs, and wants that drive the main characters.
4. Of the characters in the four stories from this chapter, which seems the most real and the roundest to you? Which seems the least real and the flattest? Compare and contrast these two characters, using examples to show what makes your round character round and your flat one flat.

IN late June 1844, after Foster had begun to despair of ever understanding either the fact or the meaning of the disappearance of the river, after a time of ritual cleansing and dreaming, perhaps agoraphobic or maddened by the interweaving of literalisms and metaphors and forms of proof, Foster began throwing his manuscripts into the river. According to a Pawnee called Wolf Finger, who spoke with the historian Henry Lake, Foster would go down naked in the afternoon, wade out into the Niobrara and hurl a fistful of pages into the water, or from the shore he would skip a journal across the surface like a stone. Eventually he threw everything he'd ever written down into the Niobrara River, turned the pack mules out with the Pawnee horses, and left. He went away to the north, "like a surprised grouse whirring off across the prairie."

—*from "The Location of the River" by Barry Lopez*

# 6 Setting

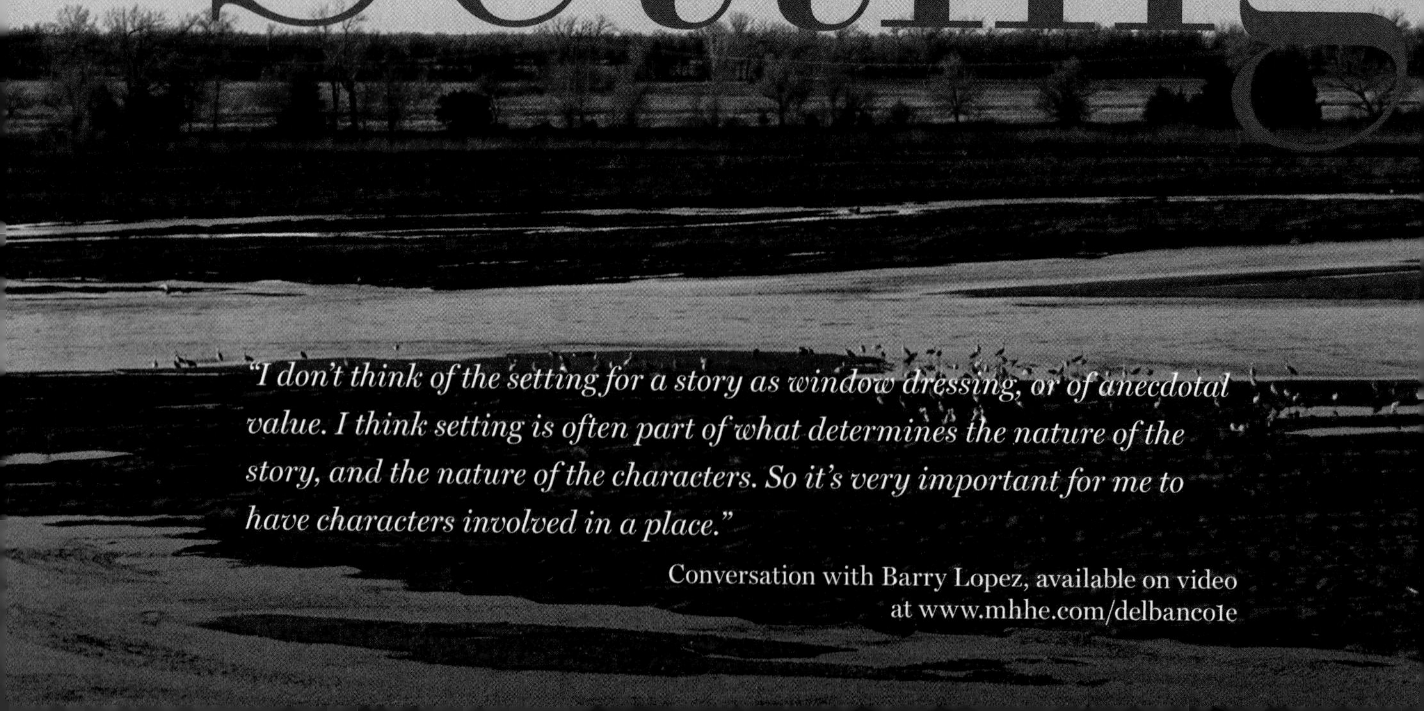

*"I don't think of the setting for a story as window dressing, or of anecdotal value. I think setting is often part of what determines the nature of the story, and the nature of the characters. So it's very important for me to have characters involved in a place."*

Conversation with Barry Lopez, available on video at www.mhhe.com/delbanco1e

THIS passage sets us down in a specific place on the earth: western Nebraska, on the banks of the Niobrara River. The year is 1844. In this story, wandering historian Benjamin Foster has set out to solve a mystery. Had, as the Pawnee told him, the upper Niobrara truly disappeared the previous summer? As Foster attempts to understand how or whether such an occurrence was possible, he engages more and more deeply with the surrounding landscape and the people who inhabit it—the Pawnee, the Sioux, the Arapaho, the Arikara, and others. Increasingly preoccupied by what he does and does not know, what he can and cannot prove, he abandons the quest, perhaps half-mad, as portrayed in the excerpt at the beginning of the chapter.

## SETTING AS PHYSICAL ENVIRONMENT

Consider the variety of settings you have encountered in the stories in this book: a grim view of Dublin in the early twentieth century in Joyce's "Araby," the crowded streets of Cairo in Mahfouz's "The Conjurer Made Off with the Dish," the 1800s in America in a well-appointed home in Chopin's "The Story of an Hour," the checkout counter of a grocery store in Updike's "A&P," and many more. Each **setting**—each particular time and place—comes with its own sights, sounds, and smells. Each creates a set of expectations among readers for the cast of characters they're likely to encounter and the range of events likely to occur in such a setting; little by little we understand the "local" customs described, as well as the rules of appropriate behavior.

In its most basic sense, the term *setting* refers to the time and place in which a story unfolds. The conceptual meanings of time and place can be various in a work of fiction. Time, of course, can refer to the particular time of day and time of year. It can also refer to the era in which a story occurs—in Lopez's story, the mid-nineteenth century. Setting also includes weather. For example, the season dictates what characters will wear, what they will eat, see, smell, touch, and hear—what challenges of comfort or survival they will face. All these elements make up the physical environment of the story, and each decision the author makes in this regard shapes the story.

In his essay "A Writer's Sense of Place," novelist James D. Houston describes the power of setting when "the place is profoundly felt, as a feature of the narrative that is working on the characters or through the characters or is somehow bearing upon their lives." "Our literature," he continues, "is rich with such works, stories wherein at least part of what's going on is some form of dialogue between a place—whether it be an island or a mountain or a city or a shoreline or a subregion of the continent—and the lives being lived. I look upon this as one more version of the endless dialogue we're all involved in, between the human imagination and the world we find ourselves inhabiting. . . ."

*. . . I love the idea of making that place come alive like another person.*

Q&A

*I can feel it in my mind, and I can pull it out, . . .*

# A Conversation on Writing

## Barry Lopez

### The Role of Setting in a Story

I'm very comfortable writing a story in which a character just moves through a place, because I love the idea of making that place come alive like another person. . . . It's the thing that's outside the self. . . . And it's not until you get outside the self that you can come alive.

### Setting in "The Location of the River"

In a story like "The Location of the River," I can go back and remember a time driving cross-country where I just pulled my truck off the road on the Niobrara River, and slept the night there. . . . So somewhere in my tissues is the sound of that river . . . I can feel it in my mind, and I can pull it out, and it's attached to other things, and then it just unfolds in front of me. It's like the story is inside a little thing that happened when I was young and camping. . . . Years go by, and . . . it pulls all of the things out of my history of observation, and it's turned itself into a world. And then that world is where the story unfolds.

### An Intimate Conversation

I feel that push in me all the time, when I'm in a place I've never been before, to have a conversation with it. "Who are you? Talk to me." If I can make myself vulnerable to a place, it senses that, and then it starts to talk to you. You have to trust, because trust is the only way to get to vulnerability, and vulnerability is the only way to get to intimacy. And that's what I want when I'm in a place, that intimate conversation with a place.

To watch this entire interview and hear the author read from "The Location of the River," go to **www.mhhe.com/delbanco1e**.

Among his many achievements, Barry Lopez counts creating a university major—the B.A. in Natural Sciences and the Humanities at Texas Tech University. The major blends the very elements around which Lopez has built his career as he writes about the relationship between human beings and the physical environments they inhabit: how people are shaped, changed, or haunted by a landscape—and how they, in turn, shape the land. Lopez was born in New York (1945) and grew up both there and in California. After earning his bachelor's and graduate degrees from Notre Dame University, Lopez moved to Oregon, where he has lived ever since, devoting himself full-time to writing. His writing, which includes essay, memoir, and fiction, has earned awards such as the Pushcart Prize for both fiction and nonfiction, and his meditation on life in the northern latitudes, *Arctic Dreams,* received the National Book Award for nonfiction in 1986. Lopez also frequently collaborates with people engaged in other arts, such as the composers John Luther Adams and Arvo Pärt, and the illustrator Tom Pohrt. Above all else, Lopez loves the written word; as one of his characters in *Crow and Weasel* (1998), a children's story, says, "Sometimes a person needs a story more than food to stay alive. That is why we put these stories in each other's memory."

**RESEARCH ASSIGNMENT** Listen to the interview with Barry Lopez and explain what he means when he talks about a story "fighting" you off. Do you relate to this? Why or why not?

**AS YOU READ** As you read this story, picture the setting. In what ways is it hospitable and in what ways inhospitable? Does it seem like an inviting place, one you would like to see for yourself? Why or why not?

**TIP** **FOR INTERACTIVE READING . . .** Go through the story and mark all the details of physical setting, including names of towns or other landmarks, plant and animal life, and geographical features. Consult a map to get a feel for the region where the events in the story took place.

# The Location of the River (1986)

1 ACCORDING to a journal kept by Benjamin Foster, a historian returning along the Platte River from the deserts of the Great Basin at the time, the spring of 1844 came early to western Nebraska. He recorded the first notes of a horned lark on the sixteenth of February. This unseasonable good weather induced him to stay a few weeks with a band of Pawnee camped just south of the Niobrara River. One morning he volunteered to go out with two men to look for stray horses. They found the horses grazing near an island of oak and ash trees on the prairie, along the edge of the river. When he saw the current and quicksand Foster was glad the horses had not crossed over.

2 On the way back, writes Foster—little of his last journal survives, but some fragments relevant to this incident are preserved—the Pawnee told him that the previous summer the upper Niobrara had disappeared.

3 At first Foster took this for a figurative statement about a severe drought, but the other Pawnee told him, no, the Niobrara had not run dry—in fact, the spring of 1843 had been very wet. It disappeared. That Foster took this information seriously, that he did not treat it with skepticism or derision, was characteristic of him.

The Pawnee, he goes to say, did not associate the disappearance of the river with any one particular phenomenon (Foster, I should say, was a confidant; he spoke fluent Pawnee and I'm sure they felt he was both knowledgeable and trustworthy); they attributed its disappearance to a sort of willful irritation, which they found amusing. They told Foster that the earth, the rivers, did not belong to men but were only to be used by them, and that the earth, though it was pleased with the Pawnee, was very disappointed in the white man. It suited the earth's purpose, they said, to suddenly abandon a river for a while, to confound men who were too dependent on such things always being there. 4

Foster thought this explanation narrow and self-serving and told the Pawnee so. But they were adamant. Foster writes that he himself was increasingly at a loss to understand what had happened, but he had been among Indians long enough to appreciate their sense of humor and to know their strength for allegory. He pointed out to them that if the river had shifted course or disappeared, the Pawnee would be as 5

affected by it as the white men; but the Pawnee said, no, this was not so, because they saw things like this all the time and were not bothered by them.

6 It is difficult to fathom what happened to the river or to Foster either, once he concluded, as he apparently did, that the Pawnee were literally correct, that sometime during the summer of 1843 the upper reaches of the Niobrara River, above the present town of Marshland and westward into Wyoming, did vanish for four or five months.

7 An initial thought, he wrote, was that the people he was camped with were not Pawnee. He thought they might be a little too far north—in Sioux or possibly Arapaho country. Even though they spoke, ate, dressed, and even played at sleight-of-hand like Pawnee, they could be somebody else, with a cavalier regard for local truth. In others of his papers Foster writes about a rite of imitation in which a band of people from one tribe, Arikara, for example, would imitate a band from some other tribe for long periods of time, fifteen years or more. They began doing this on the northern plains in the 1820s, imitating each other in exacting detail, as a form of amusement. There was no way Foster could be certain he was not among Oglala Sioux pretending to be Pawnee and playing the Long Joke, fooling a white man and making at the same time a joke about their star-gazing neighbors the Pawnee who might not know what was going on at their very feet. But he had been intimate with the Pawnee; after extensive inquiry he believed he was among them, not someone else.

8 It appears Foster tried systematically to establish a basis for belief in the river's disappearance, and pursued this course with increasing determination, as though he intuited the truth of the thing but didn't know how to demonstrate it. I don't know why, but I feel that, by that point, the man had begun to wonder at all he had seen in his life, and what of any of it would be believed.

9 The possibility that the river had simply changed its channel seemed plausible to him, but after reconnoitering extensively through the hills he discounted it. And the river had not switched channels or run dry, it was repeatedly emphasized to him, it had vanished. There were no willows on the islands. There were no islands. There were no mud flats, no smooth places even in the sand, no abandoned channels, nothing. With the aid of survey maps made in 1840, and a theodolite, compass, artificial mercury horizon, and other instruments he borrowed from Fort Laramie some hundred miles to the southwest, Foster tried to compare the present location of the river with its location in November 1840, when the maps were made. The disagreements were too insignificant to have meaning, however, what one would have to expect given the crudeness of tools and methods in those days.

10 Foster subsequently was unable to find any permanent resident to question, or to learn anything from men garrisoned at Fort Laramie or Fort Platte to the south. He rode as far north as the Sioux Agency in South Dakota looking for people to talk to. Exhausting all these traditional methods, he turned finally to something less conventional. It had long been his personal belief (and he was bolstered in this by some of those with whom he lived) that the history of the earth was revealed anew each spring in the shapes of the towering cumulus clouds that moved over the country from the north and west. If a man were blessed, were *wakan,* and had the patience and watched from the time of the first thunderstorm until the first prairie grass fire, he would see it. There was no sequence; the events unfurled in an order of their own, so Foster prepared himself for a long vigil. One April afternoon, seventeen days after he had begun, he saw on the horizon with the aid of an interpreter, as clear as the blades of blue grama grass and his moccasined feet before him, the fading and disappearance of the upper Niobrara River in the clouds. He judged the time of year to be late June.

11 This must have been slightly disquieting for Foster, living in two worlds as he did, lying there on his back under the inexorable movement of clouds, feeling the earth turn under him, thinking what he did and did not know, could and could not prove. On the basis of what is a man to be believed?

12 There is something else here, too. In a letter to Foster dated July 7, 1831, the American explorer and painter George Catlin remarks on his terror of open space in Nebraska. While on foot in the tallgrass prairie, he and his party used a sextant and chronometer, as though at sea. I don't know whether having underlined this passage in Catlin's letter (it survives) means Foster's own perception of the prairie was oceanic—people later spoke of the "coasts of Nebraska"—or whether on his own he had always felt unsettled by the unbounded space, as he might particularly have been that spring.

13 THE disappearance of the upper Niobrara might never have come to light at all had it not been for Foster's breakdown at that point and, much later, the interest of a graduate student at Idaho State University called Anton Breverton. Breverton tried to document Foster's career in the west in his history thesis and he tried especially to clarify this one episode on the Niobrara. I lost touch with Breverton some years ago. He is either living today in obscurity, possibly in Europe, or he has passed on. His thesis, I am sorry to say, is also unavailable. The archival librarian at Pocatello believes his was among some twenty theses lost when the library transferred its collections to a new building in 1948. I read Breverton's thesis at his request when it came out, made a few notes, and returned it. Reconstructing Foster's life had been a preoccupation of mine, too, since coming into possession of the notes and journals he failed to destroy that spring.

I imagine Foster, a brilliant man much troubled by the destruction of native cultures, simply fell prey to a final madness.

14 Breverton read extensively in the literature of western Nebraska, in science and history, from both native and white sources, trying to find some hint of explanation for the disappearance of the river or what was meant by the Pawnee who told Foster this. He combed emigrants' journals, reports from Smithsonian, the Carnegie Institution—all fruitless. He even read regional novels, including those of Mari Sandoz, going so far as to go to New York and interview Miss Sandoz. An unusually sensitive woman who grew up in that country at the turn of the century, Sandoz had been particularly attentive to the stories of the region. But Breverton was unable to corroborate any part of it. He finally left it out of his thesis.

15 I understand a colleague of Breverton, irritated by the entire issue, nearly enraged in fact, secured some military funding to conduct a soil analysis throughout Dawes, Sioux, and Box Butte counties in Nebraska where the river flows, but I do not know what became of this information. I myself have communicated with the Pawnee Tribal Council, with friends among the Arapaho, and with faculty at the University of Nebraska who could be expected to add something, but to no avail.

16 FOR my part, I do not think the river ever disappeared. I imagine Foster, a brilliant man much troubled by the destruction of native cultures, simply fell prey to a final madness.

A catalytic event occurred in Foster's life in 1808 when he was living in a large Chippewa village near the present town of Bayfield, Wisconsin. Representatives of the Shawnee Prophet had come among them and instructed the people to extinguish all their fires, to rekindle fire in the old way with sticks, and to never let it go out. They said the old lifeways would return, that the prophet himself would bring back the dead. The psychologically depressed Chippewa enthusiastically adopted the beliefs of these impassioned young men. A demonstration of allegiance they required was that of throwing away one's personal possessions. As an eleven-year-old boy, Foster saw the shore of Lake Superior lined with the medicine bundles of a thousand men, all washed up by the waves. These small bundles, decorated with trade beads, strips of bright cloth, feathers, and quill work, must have been gathered up by someone (perhaps even Foster) and taken somewhere, for one morning the beaches were empty. 17

From this time forward, I am sure Foster was possessed of the idea of recording the beliefs of native tribes before they fell victim to whites or to the panic of their own spiritual leaders. This much is clearly implied by a boyhood friend of Foster who wrote about the incident on the lake in *A Narrative of the Captivity and Adventures of John Tanner.* (It is further substantiated in the private papers of W. W. Warren in the manuscript collection of the Minnesota Historical Society. You can appreciate perhaps the difficulty of piecing together Foster's career, in the wake of the destruction of all his notes.) 18

Foster spent the next thirty years with six or seven different tribes. He is occasionally mentioned in the correspondence of Ogden, Sublette, and others as a translator and Indian expert of exceptional skill. He would apparently live for years with a tribe before moving on. Though loath to do it, he deposited this steady accumulation of field notes periodically at various American and British trading posts for safekeeping, intending one day to collect them all. This is what he was doing in 1844 when he was waylaid by the Pawnee and good weather. He had eleven pack mules with him at the time, all of them burdened with manuscripts. His writings were more detailed, complete, inclusive of fantastic incident, rigorous, and perceptive (to judge from the scraps) than anything Fontenelle, Maximilian, Ruxton, Stewart, or any of the rest ever wrote down. He was en route to 19

Kansas City, where the great trading family of Chouteau had offered him money for publication. The collection would have equalled in scope and importance the collected volumes on the west edited by Reuben Thwaites some sixty years later. It is one of the great tragedies of American history that he did not arrive and that his manuscripts were ruined.

20 In late June 1844, after Foster had begun to despair of ever understanding either the fact or the meaning of the disappearance of the river, after a time of ritual cleansing and dreaming, perhaps agoraphobic or maddened by the interweaving of literalisms and metaphors and forms of proof, Foster began throwing his manuscripts into the river. According to a Pawnee called Wolf Finger, who spoke with the historian Henry Lake, Foster would go down naked in the afternoon, wade out into the Niobrara and hurl a fistful of pages into the water, or from the shore he would skip a journal across the surface like a stone. Eventually he threw everything he'd ever written down into the Niobrara River, turned the pack mules out with the Pawnee horses, and left. He went away to the north, "like a surprised grouse whirring off across the prairie."

Eventually he threw everything he'd ever written down into the Niobrara River . . .

21 WHAT was left of these documents came into my hands though my father, a tax assessor. He found them in a barn near Lusk, Wyoming, in 1901. Among them—there was about enough to fill one cardboard box—was the first page of an essay entitled "Studying the Indian." I have no idea of the date. In the first paragraph Foster says, "I have been among the Absarokee when they left the battlefield like sparrows. I have watched Navajo men run down antelope on foot and smother their last breath in a handful of corn pollen. One bad summer in the Desert of the Black Rocks I saw Shoshoni women go out at sunset and because they were starving call in the quail. I have heard the soft syllables of the Arapaho tongue and the choking sound of the Kiowa and the hissing Cheyenne sounds. A woman called Reaches Deep taught me how to dance, and once I danced until I entered the sun. But already in the fall of 1826, in Judith Basin, a Piegan called Coyote in the Camp had told me I was learning everything wrong. . . ." Foster goes on, a few words, the rest is washed out and sun bleached.

22 In an attempt to understand what little Foster had written down about the disappearance of the Niobrara (and with a sense of compassion for him), I visited that part of the state in 1963. I stayed in a small hotel, the Plainview, in the town of Box Butte. I had with me all of Foster's water-stained notes, which I had spread around the room and was examining again for perhaps the hundredth time. During the night a tremendous rainstorm broke over the prairie. The Niobrara threatened to flood and I was awakened by the motel operator. I drove across the river—in the cone of my headlights I could see the fast brown water surging against the bridge supports—and spent the rest of the night in my car on high ground, at some distance from the town, in some hills the name of which I do not remember. In the morning I became confused on farm roads and was unable to find my way back to the river. In desperation I stopped at a place I recognized having been at the day before and proceeded from there on foot toward the river, until I became lost in the fields themselves. I met a man on a tractor who told me the river had never come over in that direction. Ever. And to get away.

23 I have not been back in that country since.

THERE are many stories in this book in which landscape plays a significant role in the meaning of the story. If you enjoyed Barry Lopez's "The Location of the River," you may also enjoy Leslie Marmon Silko's "The Man to Send Rain Clouds" (chapter 12).

**GOING FURTHER** Barry Lopez has spent a large part of his career writing about the relationship between landscape—setting—and narrative or story making. His award-winning nonfiction work *Arctic Dreams* was a major step in this direction. *Home Ground,* an anthology he edited with his wife, Debra Gwartney, offers descriptive definitions by dozens of American writers on the various elements of landscape, such as arroyo, swale, muskeg, and so forth.

# Writing from Reading

## Summarize

1 Compare and contrast the various theories of the river's disappearance—the Native American views and the views of the white researchers: Foster, Breverton, and the narrator.

## Analyze Craft

2 Most of this story is related almost as a report. How does this affect the information we receive about the setting? Do we see the place as a scientist would, or as an artist or sightseeing traveler might view it?

## Analyze Voice

3 Who is the narrator of this story? When and how does the narrator become an active participant? What is the role of this narrator?

4 Consider the narrator's descriptions of setting compared to Foster's. Discuss the fundamental differences and similarities between the narrator and Foster based on what they see.

## Synthesize Summary and Analysis

5 Consider the comparison between open space in Nebraska and the open sea. How does George Catlin's use of a sextant and chronometer in the tallgrass prairie—and Foster's interest in this story—contribute to the story's setting, characterizations, and theme? What effect does this extended metaphor have on you as a reader?

6 List all the things in the story that are lost. Also note the people who get lost or lose their way. Based on your findings, discuss how "loss" operates as a theme in "The Location of the River."

## Interpret the Story

7 Consider the passage from the first page of Foster's essay "Studying the Indian," where he is told by an Indian that he has learned everything wrong. Compare this passage to the narrator's study of Foster in the preceding pages. By including the passage, what is Lopez suggesting about the narrator's conclusions?

*CONTINUED FROM PAGE 143*

## SETTING AS SOCIAL ENVIRONMENT

Growing out of the physical environment of a story is something more various called the **social environment.** Elements such as the era and location combined with a character's living and working conditions make up the social environment. To understand social environment, consider the challenges and community being portrayed in any work of fiction. For example, in Lopez's story, Foster is a white man and an historian who is performing research among native peoples on the Great Plains of Wyoming and Nebraska in 1844. His physical environment consists of the great, uncharted outdoors, where he is often alone. When he is not alone, the Pawnee and Sioux, Arapaho and Arikara are his companions. Cultural differences, however, make it unclear how much trust exists in these relationships. Thus, Foster inhabits a social environment characterized by a particular kind of isolation.

"I think one of the things that people read for is gossip, curiosity. They want to find out how things work. They want to understand what it's like to be somewhere." Conversation with William Kittredge

## SETTING AND MOOD

Writers approach setting the way designers use sets for plays or films. Each object is placed deliberately in order to create a particular effect. Consider the following excerpt from the 1957 short story "Wine" by British author Doris Lessing.

> *A man and woman walked toward the boulevard from a little hotel in a side street.*
>
> *The trees were still leafless, black, cold; but the fine twigs were swelling toward spring, so that looking upward it was with an expectation of the first glimmering greenness. Yet everything was calm, and the sky was a calm, classic blue.*
>
> *The couple drifted slowly along. Effort, after days of laziness, seemed impossible; and almost at once they turned into a café and sank down, as if exhausted, in the glass-walled space that was thrust forward into the street.*
>
> *The place was empty. People were seeking the midday meal in the restaurants. Not all: that morning crowds had been demonstrating, a procession had just passed, and its straggling end could still be seen. The sounds of violence, shouted slogans and singing, no longer absorbed the din of Paris traffic; but it was these sounds that had roused the couple from sleep.*

Lessing places the couple in Paris, conjuring up images of romance. They are there in the spring, so we have the promise of new life and the possibility of a new beginning. It is midday, so they are people of leisure, at least at the moment. These details lend a flavor, and the setting sets a mood. These details also hint at plot developments—the demonstrators in the background, the possibility that something is about to change.

## SETTING AND CHARACTER

A setting, however, can play a bigger role than simply serving as backdrop and mood. A character's location often shapes his or her identity. A character who lives on a fifty-five-acre farm, for instance, will develop quite differently from a character who takes a crowded subway to work. In James Joyce's novel *A Portrait of the Artist As a Young Man* (1916), the protagonist Stephen Dedalus defines himself as a student, an Irish citizen, and a citizen of the world as he places himself at the top of the list he jots down in his geography book:

*Stephen Dedalus*
*Class of Elements*
*Clongowes Wood College*
*Sallins*
*County Kildare*
*Ireland*
*Europe*
*The World*
*The Universe*

The setting can also explicitly reflect and symbolize the inner lives of characters, as in the opening passage of Edgar Allan Poe's "The Fall of the House of Usher."

> *During the whole of a dull, dark, and soundless day in the autumn of the year, when the clouds hung oppressively low in the heavens, I had been passing alone, on horseback, through a singularly dreary tract of country; and at length found myself, as the shades of the evening drew on, within view of the melancholy House of Usher. . . . I looked upon the scene before me—upon the mere house, and the simple landscape features of the domain—upon the bleak walls—upon the vacant eye-like windows—upon a few rank sedges—and upon a few white trunks of decayed trees—with an utter depression of soul which I can compare to no earthly sensation more properly than to the after-dream of the reveller upon opium—the bitter lapse into everyday life—the hideous dropping off of the veil.*

In this passage, Poe's scene includes lowering clouds and festering vegetation around a "melancholy" mansion, establishing a mood of intense gloom and foreboding. The images shape the reader's experience of the story—showing us not only where it takes place but also how it feels for characters to occupy that space. Just imagine for a moment how the story would change if it opened by saying, "During the whole of a bright, light, and bird-song-filled day in the spring of the year, when no single cloud appeared in the sky, I had been passing . . ." Poe's word choices—"dull, dark," "oppressively low," "dreary tract of country," "melancholy," "bleak," "vacant," and so on—create a sense of dread, foreshadowing terrors to come. More than this, the images reflect the distraught interior life and psyche of his characters, making their flaws and fallibilities

### REGIONAL WRITERS

Critics sometimes refer to authors whose work tends to focus on a particular setting and its characters, customs, dialect, and topography as *regional writers,* a term historically used in a negative fashion. Texas writer Larry McMurtry, one of the most popular American writers of his generation, once joked in protest about the way in which Southern writers especially were defined as "regional" and thus put in a pigeonhole by reviewers. He had T-shirts made that said "Regional Writer" and passed them out to his friends. Today, we no longer object to writers merely because of their ties to a particular region. In fact, it's almost impossible *not* to have such ties or a sense of preferred location.

external. Thus, the physical structure of the mansion and the surrounding landscape become a symbol of the disintegration of the family within—the "ancient," "time-honored" Ushers. Even the name Usher stands as a sign pointing to the transitional nature of life and the house stands as a gateway to another world (for more on symbols and symbolism, see chapter 10).

Finally, the setting can itself be a character. Landscape can entwine with personality so that it expresses the soul of the narrator, as it does in Lopez's story. The Great Plains are a vast, unknowable presence baffling Foster and the others who follow him in trying to understand it. Together, the setting, characters, and plot express the writer's feeling about the impossibility of knowing anything with certainty in this vast world.

## *SETTING* IN CONTEXT

Writers locate their stories by selecting particular details that transport us to new places as well as to new ways of seeing familiar ones. As you read, notice how the quite dissimilar stories in this chapter develop from the details of the various landscapes described. The best way to understand the role setting plays with regard to mood, character, or theme is to ask yourself, "Why has the author chosen this particular setting? What would change if the story were set elsewhere?"

The four stories in this chapter explore the ways in which settings shape and reflect mood, character, or theme. Each was composed in America; one in the nineteenth century, the others in the twentieth. There the similarities end. As we've discussed, Barry Lopez's story takes place in the vast, uninhabited lands of the Great Plains. Edgar Allan Poe's story, by contrast, is *interior;* we enter an isolated and decaying mansion. Eudora Welty also confines us to an interior landscape: the conflict-ridden house of a family in the rural South. Bernard Malamud conjures the world of a rabbinical student and a matchmaker in the Yiddish culture of uptown Manhattan and the Bronx.

Together, these stories demonstrate just how much the experience of living can differ from region to region. We should notice also the paradox that despite the differences in time and place and social environment, the problems these characters wrestle with are familiar. These stories, then, help us understand that life anywhere is, simply, life lived everywhere.

# Edgar Allan Poe (1809–1849)

Edgar Allan Poe was born Edgar Arnold Poe in Boston. His parents were actors, and both died by 1811, leaving him orphaned. He spent much of his youth in Virginia under the care of John Allan, a tobacco merchant. Allan sent Poe to college at the University of Virginia, but when Poe turned to gambling, Allan withdrew his support, forcing Poe to drop out in 1826. That same year, Poe published his first book of poetry, *Tamerlane and Other Poems.* In the years that followed, Poe wore many hats. He briefly attended West Point Military Academy and served briefly in the U.S. Army. In 1836 he married his thirteen-year-old cousin, Virginia Clem. Editing and contributing to the *Southern Literary Messenger, Graham's Magazine,* and other publications, Poe also wrote book reviews for various periodicals. He published his own writing in popular magazines such as *The Broadway Journal,* and he dreamed of founding his own literary journal. Poe started out as a poet (his most famous poem is "The Raven"), and he did publish one short novel, *The Narrative of Arthur Gordon Pym* (1838), but he mostly devoted himself to short fiction. Today, he is best known for his horror stories (including "The Fall of the House of Usher," "The Masque of the

Red Death," "The Black Cat," "The Tell-Tale Heart," and many others). Critics consider Poe to have invented the genre of the detective mystery with such stories as "The Purloined Letter" and "The Murders in the Rue Morgue."

In his horror stories, Poe uses lush language to render setting in great detail, creating an atmosphere of terror and, often, despair. His unsettling plots rely on suspense and the revelation of terrible secrets, but the settings, as perceived by troubled narrators who are drawn into the horror as actors or observers, are what give these stories their dark and bizarre flavor. In the tale that follows, "The Fall of the House of Usher," a house takes on the literal and symbolic importance of a main character; in such fiction, setting both drives and embodies the plot.

Poe died in Baltimore in1849 when he was forty years old. The circumstances of his death were mysterious and have been the source of much speculation. His official obituary reported only "a congestion of the brain."

**AS YOU READ** As you read, notice the way you enter the world of the story and the interior of the house with the narrator, relying on him for description and interpretation. Does the setting overshadow the characters and/or the plot? How does it make you feel?

# The Fall of the House of Usher (1839)

*Son cœur est un luth suspendu;*
*Sitôt qu'on le touche il résonne.*[1]

De Béranger

1 DURING the whole of a dull, dark, and soundless day in the autumn of the year, when the clouds hung oppressively low in the heavens, I had been passing alone, on horseback, through a singularly dreary tract of country; and at length found myself, as the shades of evening drew on, within view of the melancholy House of Usher. I know not how it was—but, with the first glimpse of the building, a sense of insufferable gloom pervaded my spirit. I say insufferable; for the feeling was unrelieved by any of that half-pleasurable, because poetic, sentiment, with which the mind usually receives even the sternest natural images of the desolate or terrible. I looked upon the scene before me—upon the mere house, and the simple landscape features of the domain—upon the bleak walls—upon the vacant eye-like windows—upon a few rank sedges—and upon a few white trunks of decayed trees—with an utter depression of soul which I can compare to no earthly sensation more properly than to the after-dream of the reveller upon opium—the bitter lapse into everyday life—the hideous dropping off of the veil. There was iciness, a sinking, a sickening of the heart—an unredeemed

[1] "His heart is a lute hanging (in air) / when touched it resonates."

dreariness of thought which no goading of the imagination could torture into aught of the sublime. What was it—I paused to think—what was it that so unnerved me in the contemplation of the House of Usher? It was a mystery all insoluble; nor could I grapple with the shadowy fancies that crowded upon me as I pondered. I was forced to fall back upon the unsatisfactory conclusion, that while, beyond doubt, there *are* combinations of very simple natural objects which have the power of thus affecting us, still the analysis of this power lies among considerations beyond our depth. It was possible, I reflected, that a mere different arrangement of the particulars of the scene, of the details of the picture, would be sufficient to modify, or perhaps to annihilate its capacity for sorrowful impression; and, acting upon this idea, I reined my horse to the precipitous brink of a black and lurid tarn that lay in unruffled luster by the dwelling, and gazed down—but with a shudder even more thrilling than before—upon the remodelled and inverted images of the gray sedge, and the ghastly tree-stems, and the vacant and eye-like windows.

> . . . with the first glimpse of the building, a sense of insufferable gloom pervaded my spirit.

2 Nevertheless, in this mansion of gloom I now proposed to myself a sojourn of some weeks. Its proprietor, Roderick Usher, had been one of my boon companions in boyhood; but many years had elapsed since our last meeting. A letter, however, had lately reached me in a distant part of the country—a letter from him—which, in its wildly importunate nature, had admitted of no other than a personal reply. The MS. gave evidence of nervous agitation. The writer spoke of acute bodily illness—of a mental disorder which oppressed him—and of an earnest desire to see me, as his best, and indeed his only personal friend, with a view of attempting, by the cheerfulness of my society, some alleviation of his malady. It was the manner in which all this, and much more, was said—it was the apparent *heart* that went with his request—which allowed me no room for hesitation; and I accordingly obeyed forthwith what I still considered a very singular summons.

3 Although, as boys, we had been even intimate associates, yet I really knew little of my friend. His reserve had been always excessive and habitual. I was aware, however, that his very ancient family had been noted, time out of mind, for a peculiar sensibility of temperament, displaying itself, through long ages, in many works of exalted art, and manifested, of late, in repeated deeds of munificent yet unobtrusive charity, as well as in a passionate devotion to the intricacies, perhaps even more than to the orthodox and easily recognizable beauties, of musical science. I had learned, too, the very remarkable fact, that the stem of the Usher race, all time-honored as it was, had put forth, at no period, any enduring branch; in other words, that the entire family lay in the direct line of descent, and had always, with very trifling and very temporary variation, so lain. It was this deficiency, I considered, while running over in thought the perfect keeping of the character of the premises with the accredited character of the people, and while speculating upon the possible influence which the one, in the long lapse of centuries, might have exercised upon the other—it was this deficiency, perhaps, of collateral issue, and the consequent undeviating transmission, from sire to son, of the patrimony with the name, which had, at length, so identified the two as to merge the original title of the estate in the quaint and equivocal appellation of the "House of Usher"—an appellation which seemed to include, in the minds of the peasantry who used it, both the family and the family mansion.

I have said that the sole effect of my somewhat childish experiment—that of looking down within the tarn—had been to deepen the first singular impression. There can be no doubt that the consciousness of the rapid increase of my superstition—for why should I not so term it?—served mainly to accelerate the increase itself. Such, I have long known, is the paradoxical law of all sentiments having terror as a basis. And it might have been for this reason only, that, when I again uplifted my eyes to the house itself, from its image in the pool, there grew in my mind a strange fancy—a fancy so ridiculous, indeed, that I but mention it to show the vivid force of the sensations which oppressed me. I had so worked upon my imagination as really to believe that about the whole mansion and domain there hung an atmosphere peculiar to themselves and their immediate vicinity—an atmosphere which had no affinity with the air of heaven, but which had reeked up from the decayed trees, and the gray wall, and the silent tarn—a pestilent and mystic vapor, dull, sluggish, faintly discernible, and leaden-hued. 4

Shaking off from my spirit what *must* have been a dream, I scanned more narrowly the real aspect of the building. Its principal feature seemed to be that of an excessive antiquity. The discoloration of ages had been great. Minute fungi overspread the whole exte- 5

rior, hanging in a fine tangled web-work from the eaves. Yet all this was apart from any extraordinary dilapidation. No portion of the masonry had fallen; and there appeared to be a wild inconsistency between its still perfect adaptation of parts, and the crumbling condition of the individual stones. In this there was much that reminded me of the specious totality of old wood-work which has rotted for long years in some neglected vault, with no disturbance from the breath of the external air. Beyond this indication of extensive decay, however, the fabric gave little token of instability. Perhaps the eye of a scrutinizing observer might have discovered a barely perceptible fissure, which, extending from the roof of the building in front, made its way down the wall in a zigzag direction, until it became lost in the sullen waters of the tarn.

6 Noticing these things, I rode over a short causeway to the house. A servant in waiting took my horse, and I entered the Gothic archway of the hall. A valet, of stealthy step, thence conducted me, in silence, through many dark and intricate passages in my progress to the *studio* of his master. Much that I encountered on the way contributed, I know not how, to heighten the vague sentiments of which I have already spoken. While the objects around me—while the carvings of the ceilings, the somber tapestries of the walls, the ebon blackness of the floors, and the phantasmagoric armorial trophies which rattled as I strode, were but matters to which, or to such as which, I had been accustomed from my infancy—while I hesitated not to acknowledge how familiar was all this—I still wondered to find how unfamiliar were the fancies which ordinary images were stirring up. On one of the staircases, I met the physician of the family. His countenance, I thought, wore a mingled expression of low cunning and perplexity. He accosted me with trepidation and passed on. The valet now threw open a door and ushered me into the presence of his master.

7 The room in which I found myself was very large and lofty. The windows were long, narrow, and pointed, and at so vast a distance from the black oaken floor as to be altogether inaccessible from within. Feeble gleams of encrimsoned light made their way through the trellised panes, and served to render sufficiently distinct the more prominent objects around; the eye, however, struggled in vain to reach the remoter angles of the chamber, or the recesses of the vaulted and fretted ceiling. Dark draperies hung upon the walls. The general furniture was profuse, comfortless, antique, and tattered. Many books and musical instruments lay scattered about, but failed to give any vitality to the scene. I felt that I breathed an atmosphere of sorrow. An air of stern, deep, and irredeemable gloom hung over and pervaded all.

Upon my entrance, Usher arose 8
from a sofa on which he had been lying at full length, and greeted me with a vivacious warmth which had much in it, I at first thought, of an overdone cordiality—of the constrained effort of the *ennuyé* man of the world. A glance, however, at his countenance, convinced me of his perfect sincerity. We sat down; and for some moments, while he spoke not, I gazed upon him with a feeling half of pity, half of awe. Surely, a man had never before so terribly altered, in so brief a period, as had Roderick Usher! It was with difficulty that I could bring myself to admit the identity of the wan being before me with the companion of my early boyhood. Yet the character of his face had been at all times remarkable. A cadaverousness of complexion; an eye large, liquid, and luminous beyond comparison; lips somewhat thin and very pallid, but of a surpassingly beautiful curve; a nose of a delicate Hebrew model, but with a breadth of nostril unusual in similar formations; a finely moulded chin, speaking, in its want of prominence, of a want of moral energy; hair of a more than web-like softness and tenuity; these features, with an inordinate expansion above the regions of the temple, made up altogether a countenance not easily to be forgotten. And now in the mere exaggeration of the prevailing character of these features, and of the expression they were wont to convey, lay so much of change that I doubted to whom I spoke. The now ghastly pallor of the skin, and the now miraculous luster of the eye, above all things startled and even awed me. The silken hair, too, had been suffered to grow all unheeded, and as, in its wild gossamer texture, it floated rather than fell about the face, I could not, even with effort, connect its arabesque expression with any idea of simple humanity.

In the manner of my friend I was at once struck 9
with an incoherence—an inconsistency; and I soon found this to arise from a series of feeble and futile struggles to overcome an habitual trepidancy—an excessive nervous agitation. For something of this nature I had indeed been prepared, no less by his letter, than by reminiscences of certain boyish traits, and by

conclusions deduced from his peculiar physical conformation and temperament. His action was alternatively vivacious and sullen. His voice varied rapidly from a tremulous indecision (when the animal spirits seemed utterly in abeyance) to that of energetic concision—that abrupt, weighty, unhurried, and hollow-sounding enunciation—that leaden, self-balanced and perfectly modulated guttural utterance, which may be observed in the lost drunkard, or the irreclaimable eater of opium, during the periods of his most intense excitement.

10 It was thus that he spoke of the object of my visit, of his earnest desire to see me, and of the solace he expected me to afford him. He entered, at some length, into what he conceived to be the nature of his malady. It was, he said, a constitutional and a family evil, and one for which he despaired to find a remedy—a mere nervous affection, he immediately added, which would undoubtedly soon pass off. It displayed itself in a host of unnatural sensations. Some of these, as he detailed them, interested and bewildered me; although, perhaps, the terms, and the general manner of the narration had their weight. He suffered much from a morbid acuteness of the senses; the most insipid food was alone endurable; he could wear only garments of certain texture; the odors of all flowers were oppressive; his eyes were tortured by even a faint light; and there were but peculiar sounds, and these from stringed instruments, which did not inspire him with horror.

11 To an anomalous species of terror I found him a bounded slave. "I shall perish," said he, "I *must* perish in this deplorable folly. Thus, thus, and not otherwise, shall I be lost. I dread the events of the future, not in themselves but in their results. I shudder at the thought of any, even the most trivial, incident, which may operate upon this intolerable agitation of soul. I have, indeed, no abhorrence of danger, except in its absolute effect—in terror. In this unnerved—in this pitiable condition—I feel that the period will sooner or later arrive when I must abandon life and reason together, in some struggle with the grim phantasm, FEAR."

12 I learned, moreover, at intervals, and through broken and equivocal hints, another singular feature of his mental condition. He was enchained by certain superstitious impressions in regard to the dwelling which he tenanted, and whence, for many years, he had never ventured forth—in regard to an influence whose suppositious force was conveyed in terms too shadowy here to be re-stated—an influence which some peculiarities in the mere form and substance of his family mansion, had, by dint of long sufferance, he said, obtained over his spirit—an effect which the *physique* of the gray walls and turrets, and of the dim tarn into which they all looked down, had, at length, brought about upon the *morale* of his existence.

13 He admitted, however, although with hesitation, that much of the peculiar gloom which thus afflicted him could be traced to a more natural and far more palpable origin—to the severe and long-continued illness—indeed to the evidently approaching dissolution—of a tenderly beloved sister—his sole companion for long years—his last and only relative on earth. "Her decease," he said, with a bitterness which I can never forget, "would leave him (him the hopeless and the frail) the last of the ancient race of the Ushers." While he spoke, the lady Madeline (for so was she called) passed slowly through a remote portion of the apartment, and, without having noticed my presence, disappeared. I regarded her with an utter astonishment not unmingled with dread—and yet I found it impossible to account for such feelings. A sensation of stupor oppressed me, as my eyes followed her retreating steps. When a door, at length, closed upon her, my glance sought instinctively and eagerly the countenance of the brother—but he had buried his face in his hands, and I could only perceive that a far more than ordinary wanness had overspread the emaciated fingers through which trickled many passionate tears.

14 The disease of the lady Madeline had long baffled the skill of her physicians. A settled apathy, a gradual wasting away of the person, and frequent although transient affections of a partially cataleptical character, were the unusual diagnosis. Hitherto she had steadily borne up against the pressure of her malady, and had not betaken herself finally to bed; but, on the closing in of the evening of my arrival at the house, she succumbed (as her brother told me at night with inexpressible agitation) to the prostrating power of the destroyer; and I learned that the glimpse I had obtained of her person would thus probably be the last I should obtain—that the lady, at least while living, would be seen by me no more.

The disease of the lady Madeline had long baffled the skill of her physicians.

15 For several days ensuing, her name was unmentioned by either Usher or myself: and during this period I was busied in earnest endeavors to alleviate the melancholy of my friend. We painted and read together;

or I listened, as if in a dream, to the wild improvisations of his speaking guitar. And thus, as a closer and still closer intimacy admitted me more unreservedly into the recesses of his spirit, the more bitterly did I perceive the futility of all attempt at cheering a mind from which darkness, as if an inherent positive quality, poured forth upon all objects of the moral and physical universe, in one unceasing radiation of gloom.

16 I shall ever bear about me a memory of the many solemn hours I thus spent alone with the master of the House of Usher. Yet I should fail in any attempt to convey an idea of the exact character of the studies, or of the occupations, in which he involved me, or led me the way. An excited and highly distempered ideality threw a sulphureous luster over all. His long improvised dirges will ring forever in my ears. Among other things, I hold painfully in mind a certain singular perversion and amplification of the wild air of the last waltz of Von Weber. From the paintings over which his elaborate fancy brooded, and which grew, touch by touch, into vaguenesses at which I shuddered the more thrillingly, because I shuddered knowing not why;—from these paintings (vivid as their images now are before me) I would in vain endeavor to educe more than a small portion which should lie within the compass of merely written words. By the utter simplicity, by the nakedness of his designs, he arrested and over-awed attention. If ever mortal painted an idea, that mortal was Roderick Usher. For me at least—in the circumstances then surrounding me—there arose out of the pure abstractions which the hypochondriac contrived to throw upon his canvas, an intensity of intolerable awe, no shadow of which felt I ever yet in the contemplation of the certainly glowing yet too concrete reveries of Fuseli.

17 One of the phantasmagoric conceptions of my friend, partaking not so rigidly of the spirit of abstraction, may be shadowed forth, although feebly, in words. A small picture presented the interior of an immensely long and rectangular vault or tunnel, with low walls, smooth, white, and without interruption or device. Certain accessory points of the design served well to convey the idea that this excavation lay at an exceeding depth below the surface of the earth. No outlet was observed in any portion of its vast extent, and no torch, or other artificial source of light was discernible; yet a flood of intense rays rolled throughout, and bathed the whole in a ghastly and inappropriate splendor.

18 I have just spoken of that morbid condition of the auditory nerve which rendered all music intolerable to the sufferer, with the exception of certain effects of stringed instruments. It was, perhaps, the narrow limits to which he thus confined himself upon the guitar, which gave birth, in great measure, to the fantastic character of his performances. But the fervid *facility* of his *impromptus* could not be so accounted for. They must have been, and were, in the notes, as well as in the words of his wild fantasias (for he not unfrequently accompanied himself with rhymed verbal improvisations), the result of that intense mental collectedness and concentration to which I have previously alluded as observable only in particular moments of the highest artificial excitement. The words of one of these rhapsodies I have easily remembered. I was, perhaps, the more forcibly impressed with it, as he gave it, because, in the under or mystic current of its meaning, I fancied that I perceived, and for the first time, a full consciousness on the part of Usher, of the tottering of his lofty reason upon her throne. The verses, which were entitled "The Haunted Palace," ran very nearly, if not accurately, thus:

I

In the greenest of our valleys,
  By good angels tenanted,
Once a fair and stately palace—
  Radiant palace—reared its head.
In the monarch Thought's dominion—
  It stood there!
Never seraph spread a pinion
  Over fabric half so fair.

II

Banners yellow, glorious, golden,
  On its roof did float and flow;
(This—all this—was in the olden
  Time long ago)
And every gentle air that dallied,
  In that sweet day,
Along the ramparts plumed and pallid,
  A winged odor went away.

III

Wanderers in that happy valley
  Through two luminous windows saw
Spirits moving musically
  To a lute's well-tunèd law,
Round about a throne, where sitting
  (Porphyrogene!)
In state his glory well befitting,
  The ruler of the realm was seen.

IV

And all with pearl and ruby glowing
 Was the fair palace door,
Through which came flowing, flowing, flowing
 And sparkling evermore,
A troop of Echoes whose sweet duty
 Was but to sing,
In voices of surpassing beauty,
 The wit and wisdom of their king.

V

But evil things, in robes of sorrow,
 Assailed the monarch's high estate;
(Ah, let us mourn, for never morrow
 Shall dawn upon him, desolate!)
And, round about his home, the glory
 That blushed and bloomed
Is but a dim-remembered story
 Of the oldtime entombed.

VI

And travellers now within that valley,
 Through the red-litten windows, see
Vast forms that move fantastically
 To a discordant melody;
While, like a rapid ghastly river,
 Through the pale door,
A hideous throng rush out forever,
 And laugh—but smile no more.

I well remember that suggestions arising from this ballad, led us into a train of thought wherein there became manifest an opinion of Usher's which I mention not so much on account of its novelty (for other men that have thought thus), as on account of the pertinacity with which he maintained it. This opinion, in its general form, was that of the sentience of all vegetable things. But, in his disordered fancy, the idea had assumed a more daring character, and trespassed, under certain conditions, upon the kingdom of inorganization. I lack words to express the full extent, of the earnest *abandon* of his persuasion. The belief, however, was connected (as I have previously hinted) with the gray stones of the home of his forefathers. The conditions of the sentience had been here, he imagined, fulfilled in the method of collocation of these stones—in the order of their arrangement, as well as in that of the many *fungi* which overspread them, and of the decayed trees which stood around—above all, in the long undisturbed endurance of this arrangement, and in its reduplication in the still waters of the tarn. Its evidence—the evidence of the sentience—was to be seen, he said (and I here started as he spoke), in the gradual yet certain condensation of an atmosphere of their own about the waters and the walls. The result was discoverable, he added, in that silent, yet importunate and terrible influence which for centuries had moulded the destinies of his family, and which made *him* what I now saw him—what he was. Such opinions need no comment, and I will make none.

Our books—the books which, for years, had 19
formed no small portion of the mental existence of the invalid—were, as might be supposed, in strict keeping with this character of phantasm. We pored together over such works as the Vervet et Chartreuse of Gresset; the Belphegor of Machiavelli; the Heaven and Hell of Swedenborg; the Subterranean Voyage of Nicholas Klimm by Holberg; the Chiromancy of Robert Flud, of Jean D'Indaginé, and of De la Chambre; the Journey into the Blue Distance of Tieck; and the City of the Sun of Campanella. One favorite volume was a small octavo edition of the *Directorium Inquisitorum*, by the Dominican Eymeric de Gironne; and there were passages in Pomponius Mela, about the old African Satyrs and Ægipans, over which Usher would sit dreaming for hours. His chief delight, however, was found in the perusal of an exceedingly rare and curious book in quarto Gothic—the manual of a forgotten church—the *Vigilæ Mortuorum secundum Chorum Ecclesiæ Maguntinæ.*

I could not help thinking of the wild ritual of this 20
work, and of its probable influence upon the hypochondriac, when, one evening, having informed me abruptly that the lady Madeline was no more, he stated his intention of preserving her corpse for a fortnight (previously to its final interment), in one of the numerous vaults within the main walls of the building. The worldly reason, however, assigned for this singular proceeding, was one which I did not feel at liberty to dispute. The brother had been led to his resolution (so he told me) by consideration of the unusual character of the malady of the deceased, of certain obstrusive and eager inquiries on the part of her medical men, and of the remote and exposed situation of the burial-ground of the family. I will not deny that when I called to mind the sinister countenance of the person whom I met upon the staircase, on the day of my arrival at the house, I had no desire to oppose what I regarded as at best but a harmless, and by no means an unnatural, precaution.

21 At the request of Usher, I personally aided him in the arrangements for the temporary entombment. The body having been encoffined, we two alone bore it to its rest. The vault in which we placed it (and which had been so long unopened that our torches, half smothered in its oppressive atmosphere, gave us little opportunity for investigation) was small, damp, and entirely without means of admission for light; lying, at great depth, immediately beneath that portion of the building in which was my own sleeping apartment. It had been used, apparently, in remote feudal times, for the worst purposes of a donjon-keep, and, in later days, as a place of deposit for powder, or some other highly combustible substance, as a portion of its floor, and the whole interior of a long archway through which we reached it, were carefully sheathed with copper. The door, of massive iron, had been, also, similarly protected. Its immense weight caused an unusually sharp grating sound, as it moved upon its hinges.

The body having been encoffined, we two alone bore it to its rest.

22 Having deposited our mournful burden upon tressels within this region of horror, we partially turned aside the yet unscrewed lid of the coffin, and looked upon the face of the tenant. A striking similitude between the brother and sister now first arrested my attention; and Usher, divining, perhaps, my thoughts, murmured out some few words from which I learned that the deceased and himself had been twins, and that sympathies of a scarcely intelligible nature had always existed between them. Our glances, however, rested not long upon the dead—for we could not regard her unawed. The disease which had thus entombed the lady in the maturity of youth, had left, as usual in all maladies of a strictly cataleptical character, the mockery of a faint blush upon the bosom and the face, and that suspiciously lingering smile upon the lip which is so terrible in death. We replaced and screwed down the lid, and, having secured the door of iron, made our way, with toil, into the scarcely less gloomy apartments of the upper portion of the house.

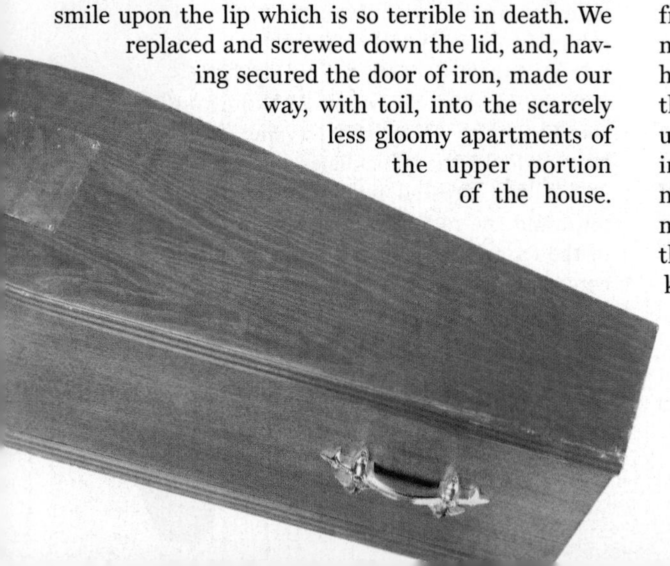

23 And now, some days of bitter grief having elapsed, an observable change came over the features of the mental disorder of my friend. His ordinary manner had vanished. His ordinary occupations were neglected or forgotten. He roamed from chamber to chamber with hurried, unequal, and objectless step. The pallor of his countenance had assumed, if possible, a more ghastly hue—but the luminousness of his eye had utterly gone out. The once occasional huskiness of his tone was heard no more; and a tremulous quaver, as if of extreme terror, habitually characterized his utterance. There were times, indeed, when I thought his unceasingly agitated mind was laboring with some oppressive secret, to divulge which he struggled for the necessary courage. At times, again, I was obliged to resolve all into the mere inexplicable vagaries of madness, for I beheld him gazing upon vacancy for long hours, in an attitude of the profoundest attention, as if listening to some imaginary sound. It was no wonder that his condition terrified—that it infected me. I felt creeping upon me, by slow yet certain degrees, the wild influences of his own fantastic yet impressive superstitions.

24 It was, especially, upon retiring to bed late in the night of the seventh or eighth day after the placing of the lady Madeline within the donjon, that I experienced the full power of such feelings. Sleep came not near my couch—while the hours waned and waned away. I struggled to reason off the nervousness which had dominion over me. I endeavored to believe that much, if not all of what I felt, was due to the bewildering influence of the gloomy furniture of the room—of the dark and tattered draperies, which, tortured into motion by the breath of a rising tempest, swayed fitfully to and fro upon the walls, and rustled uneasily about the decorations of the bed. But my efforts were fruitless. An irrepressible tremor gradually pervaded my frame; and, at length, there sat upon my very heart an incubus of utterly causeless alarm. Shaking this off with a gasp and a struggle, I uplifted myself upon the pillows, and, peering earnestly within the intense darkness of the chamber, hearkened—I know not why, except that an instinctive spirit prompted me—to certain low and indefinite sounds which came, through the pauses of the storm, at long intervals, I knew not whence. Overpowered by an intense sentiment of horror, unaccountable yet unendurable, I threw my clothes on with haste (for I felt that I should sleep no more during the night), and endeavored to arouse myself from the pitiable condition

into which I had fallen, by pacing rapidly to and fro through the apartment.

25 I had taken but few turns in this manner, when a light step on an adjoining staircase arrested my attention. I presently recognized it as that of Usher. In an instant afterward he rapped, with a gentle touch, at my door, and entered, bearing a lamp. His countenance was, as usual, cadaverously wan—but, moreover, there was a species of mad hilarity in his eyes—an evidently restrained *hysteria* in his whole demeanor. His air appalled me—but anything was preferable to the solitude which I had so long endured, and I even welcomed his presence as a relief.

26 "And you have not seen it?" he said abruptly, after having stared about him for some moments in silence—"you have not then seen it?—but, stay! you shall." Thus speaking, and having carefully shaded his lamp, he hurried to one of the casements, and threw it freely open to the storm.

27 The impetuous fury of the entering gust nearly lifted us from our feet. It was, indeed, a tempestuous yet sternly beautiful night, and one wildly singular in its terror and its beauty. A whirlwind had apparently collected its force in our vicinity; for there were frequent and violent alterations in the direction of the wind; and the exceeding density of the clouds (which hung so low as to press upon the turrets of the house) did not prevent our perceiving the lifelike velocity with which they flew careering from all points against each other, without passing away into the distance. I say that even their exceeding density did not prevent our perceiving this—yet we had no glimpse of the moon or stars—nor was there any flashing forth of the lightening. But the under surfaces of the huge masses of agitated vapor, as well as all terrestrial objects immediately around us, were glowing in the unnatural light of a faintly luminous and distinctly visible gaseous exhalation which hung about and enshrouded the mansion.

28 "You must not—you shall not behold this!" said I, shudderingly, to Usher, as I led him, with a gentle violence, from the window to a seat. "These appearances, which bewilder you, are merely electrical phenomena not uncommon—or it may be that they have their ghastly origin in the rank miasma of the tarn. Let us close this casement; —the air is chilling and dangerous to your frame. Here is one of your favorite romances. I will read, and you shall listen; —and so we will pass away this terrible night together."

29 The antique volume which I had taken up was the "Mad Trist" of Sir Launcelot Canning; but I had called it a favorite of Usher's more in sad jest than in earnest; for, in truth, there is little in its uncouth and unimaginative prolixity which could have had interest for the lofty and spiritual ideality of my friend. It was, however, the only book immediately at hand; and I indulged a vague hope that the excitement which now agitated the hypochondriac, might find relief (for the history of mental disorder is full of similar anomalies) even in the extremeness of the folly which I should read. Could I have judged, indeed, by the wild overstrained air of vivacity with which he hearkened, or apparently hearkened, to the words of the tale, I might well have congratulated myself upon the success of my design.

I had arrived at that well-known portion of the 30
story where Ethelred, the hero of the Trist, having sought in vain for peaceable admission into the dwelling of the hermit, proceeds to make good an entrance by force. Here, it will be remembered, the words of the narrative run thus:

"And Ethelred, who was by nature of a doughty 31
heart, and who was now mighty withal, on account of the powerfulness of the wine which he had drunken, waited no longer to hold parley with the hermit, who, in sooth, was of an obstinate and maliceful turn, but, feeling the rain upon his shoulders, and fearing the rising of the tempest, uplifted his mace outright, and, with blows, made quickly room in the plankings of the door for his gauntleted hand; and now pulling therewith sturdily, he so cracked, and ripped, and tore all asunder, that the noise of the dry and hollow-sounding wood alarumed and reverberated throughout the forest."

At the termination of this sentence I 32
started, and for a moment, paused; for it appeared to me (although I at once concluded that my excited fancy had deceived me)—it appeared to me that, from some very remote portion of the mansion, there came indistinctly, to my ears, what might have been, in its exact similarity of character, the echo (but a stifled and dull one certainly) of the very cracking and ripping sound which Sir Launcelot had so particularly described. It was, beyond doubt, the coincidence alone which had arrested my attention; for, amid the rattling of the sashes of the casements, and the ordinary commingled noises of the still increasing storm, the sound, in itself, had nothing, surely, which should have interested or disturbed me. I continued the story:

33 "But the good champion Ethelred, now entering within the door, was sore enraged and amazed to perceive no signal of the maliceful hermit; but, in the stead thereof, a dragon of a scaly and prodigious demeanor, and of a fiery tongue, which sate in guard before a palace of gold, with a floor of silver; and upon the wall there hung a shield of shining brass with this legend enwritten—

Who entereth herein, a conqueror hath bin;
Who slayeth the dragon, the shield he shall win;

And Ethelred uplifted his mace, and struck upon the head of the dragon, which fell before him, and gave up his pesty breath, with a shriek so horrid and harsh, and withal so piercing, that Ethelred had fain to close his ears with his hands against the dreadful noise of it, the like whereof was never before heard."

*We have put her living in the tomb!*

34 Here again, I paused abruptly, and now with a feeling of wild amazement—for there could be no doubt whatever that, in this instance, I did actually hear (although from what direction it proceeded I found it impossible to say) a low and apparently distant, but harsh, protracted, and most unusual screaming or grating sound—the exact counterpart of what my fancy had already conjured up for the dragon's unnatural shriek as described by the romancer.

35 Oppressed, as I certainly was, upon the occurrence of the second and most extraordinary coincidence, by a thousand conflicting sensations, in which wonder and extreme terror were predominant, I still retained sufficient presence of mind to avoid exciting, by any observation, the sensitive nervousness of my companion. I was by no means certain that he had noticed the sounds in question; although, assuredly, a strange alteration had, during the last few minutes, taken place in his demeanor. From a position fronting my own, he had gradually brought round his chair, so as to sit with his face to the door of the chamber; and thus I could but partially perceive his features, although I saw that his lips trembled as if he were murmuring inaudibly. His head had dropped upon his breast—yet I knew that he was not asleep, from the wide and rigid opening of the eye as I caught a glance of it in profile. The motion of his body, too, was at variance with this idea—for he rocked from side to side with a gentle yet constant and uniform sway. Having rapidly taken notice of all this, I resumed the narrative of Sir Launcelot, which thus proceeded:

"And now, the champion, having escaped from the terrible fury of the dragon, bethinking himself of the brazen shield, and of the breaking up of the enchantment which was upon it, removed the carcass from out of the way before him, and approached valorously over the silver pavement of the castle to where the shield was upon the wall; which in sooth tarried not for his full coming, but fell down at his feet upon the silver floor, with a mighty great and terrible ringing sound." 36

No sooner had these syllables passed my lips, than—as if a shield of brass had indeed, at the moment, fallen heavily upon a floor of silver—I became aware of a distinct, hollow, metallic, and clangorous, yet apparently muffled reverberation. Completely unnerved, I leaped to my feet; but the measured rocking movement of Usher was undisturbed. I rushed to the chair in which he sat. His eyes were bent fixedly before him, and throughout his whole countenance there reigned a stony rigidity. But, as I placed my hand upon his shoulder, there came a strong shudder over his whole person; a sickly smile quivered about his lips; and I saw that he spoke in a low, hurried, and gibbering murmur, as if unconscious of my presence. Bending closely over him, I at length drank in the hideous import of his words. 37

"Not hear it? —yes, I hear it, and *have* heard it. Long—long—long—many minutes, many hours, many days, have I heard it—yet I dared not—oh, pity me, miserable wretch that I am!—I dared not—I *dared* not speak! *We have put her living in the tomb!* Said I not that my senses were acute? I *now* tell you that I heard her first feeble movements in the hollow coffin. I heard them—many, many days ago—yet I dared not—*I dared not speak!* And now—to-night—Ethelred—ha! ha! —the breaking of the hermit's door, and the death-cry of the dragon, and the clangor of the shield! —say, rather, the rending of her coffin, and the grating of the iron hinges of her prison, and her struggles within the coppered archway of the vault! Oh whither shall I fly? Will she not be here anon? Is she not hurrying to upbraid me for my haste? Have I not heard her footstep on the stair? Do I not distinguish that heavy and horrible beating of her heart? MADMAN!" here he sprang 38

furiously to his feet, and shrieked out his syllables, as if in the effort he were giving up his soul—"MADMAN! I TELL YOU THAT SHE NOW STANDS WITHOUT THE DOOR!"

39 As if in the superhuman energy of his utterance there had been found the potency of a spell—the huge antique panels to which the speaker pointed, threw slowly back, upon the instant, their ponderous and ebony jaws. It was the work of the rushing gust—but then without those doors there *did* stand the lofty and enshrouded figure of the lady Madeline of Usher. There was blood upon her white robes, and the evidence of some bitter struggle upon every portion of her emaciated frame. For a moment she remained trembling and reeling to and fro upon the threshold, then, with a low moaning cry, fell heavily inward upon the person of her brother, and in her violent and now final death-agonies, bore him to the floor a corpse, and a victim to the terrors he had anticipated.

40 From that chamber, and from that mansion, I fled aghast. The storm was still abroad in all its wrath as I found myself crossing the old causeway. Suddenly there shot along the path a wild light, and I turned to see whence a gleam so unusual could have issued; for the vast house and its shadows were alone behind me. The radiance was that of the full, setting, and blood-red moon which now shone vividly through that once barely-discernible fissure of which I have before spoken as extending from the roof of the building, in a zigzag direction, to the base. While I gazed, this fissure rapidly widened—there came a fierce breath of the whirlwind—the entire orb of the satellite burst at once upon my sight—my brain reeled as I saw the mighty walls rushing asunder—there was a long tumultuous shouting sound like the voice of a thousand waters—and the deep and dark tarn at my feet closed sullenly and silently over the fragments of the "HOUSE OF USHER."

IF you liked reading Poe's description of the physical setting of the Usher mansion, you may enjoy encountering the dramatic settings in a number of other stories, such as the New York City streets in Bernard Malamud's "The Magic Barrel" in this chapter or in Herman Melville's New York story "Bartleby, the Scrivener" in chapter 14.

**GOING FURTHER** In many of his other stories Poe conjures up settings and landscapes somewhere between actual geography and dreamworld. In his novella *The Narrative of Arthur Gordon Pym* he creates a distinctive polar setting without ever having traveled anywhere near the regions he describes.

# Writing from Reading

## Summarize

1 How would you characterize the relationship between Roderick Usher and his sister Madeline? Use details from the story to back up your claim.

2 Why has the narrator come to visit Roderick Usher? What is his history with the Usher family? How does he feel about entering the house? How has his relationship with the "House of Usher" changed by the time he leaves the house?

## Analyze Craft

3 Find the words the narrator uses to describe the valet who guides him through the house and the physician he meets on the stairs. How do these words contribute to your impressions

of the narrator and/or the situation in the house?

4 Describe how the house and its surroundings serve as a character in this story.

### Analyze Voice

5 Poe invokes three different voices in this story: the narrator's voice, Roderick's voice in the ballad "The Haunted Palace," and Sir Launcelot's voice in "Mad Trist." Compare and contrast these three different styles and intonations. How is each still uniquely Poe's own voice?

### Synthesize Summary and Analysis

6 Discuss the setting of "The Fall of the House of Usher" in relation to the settings within the story of "The Haunted Palace" and the cave where Ethelred confronts his dragon. What is the effect of these three parallel settings?

### Interpret the Story

7 Discuss the effect of the storm on your experience at the end of the story. Consider the contrast between the chaotic storm and the stillness that dominates the rest of the story. How would the ending experience be different if there were no storm to accompany Madeline's appearance and the collapse of the house?

8 How does the overall effect of the story depend on the mood created by the narrator?

9 How might the story, with its emphasis on mood and European-like setting, change your impression of what constitutes "American" literature?

# Eudora Welty (1909–2001)

Eudora Welty was born in Jackson, Mississippi, where she lived and worked for most of her life. In the 1930s, she wrote articles for the newspaper *Commercial Appeal,* worked at a Jackson radio station, and became a publicity agent for the Works Progress Administration. Welty began publishing short stories in the mid-1930s. During her long writing career, she received many literary awards, including a Pulitzer Prize. Despite ample opportunities to live abroad or in major cities, Welty always returned to Jackson; arguably, the setting she lived and wrote in was a powerful influence on the timbre of her writing. Many consider her to be one of the most important stylists of the twentieth century; it is hard to talk about a "southern" voice without mentioning Eudora Welty. (For more on southern writers, see chapter 12, the casebook on the American South.) Always willing to experiment with the voice, tone, and form of her stories, she evoked powerful, often hilarious relationships among eccentric (but recognizable) southern families. In addition to four short story collections, she wrote several books of nonfiction—*One Writer's Beginnings* is about the art of writing—one children's book, and five novels. Welty was also a photographer and published two books of photographs.

Of her work, and certainly relevant to "Why I Live at the P.O," she once wrote, "I was trying to write about the way people who live away off from nowhere have to amuse themselves by dramatizing every situation that comes along by exaggerating it—'telling it.' I used the exaggerations and ways of talking I have heard all my life. It's just the way they keep life interesting—they make an experience out of the ordinary. I wasn't trying to do anything but show that. I thought it was cheerful, on the whole."

**AS YOU READ** As you read this story, notice the manner in which the characters speak to each other—both the tone and the phrasing. Notice other details that relate to the particular place and time in which the story is set.

# Why I Live at the P.O. (1941)

1 I was getting along fine with Mama, Papa-Daddy and Uncle Rondo until my sister Stella-Rondo just separated from her husband and came back home again. Mr. Whitaker! Of course I went with Mr. Whitaker first, when he first appeared here in China Grove, taking "Pose Yourself" photos, and Stella-Rondo broke us up. Told him I was one-sided. Bigger on one side than the other, which is a deliberate, calculated falsehood: I'm the same. Stella-Rondo is exactly twelve months to the day younger than I am and for that reason she's spoiled.

2 She's always had anything in the world she wanted and then she'd throw it away. Papa-Daddy gave her this gorgeous Add-a-Pearl necklace when she was eight years old and she threw it away playing baseball when she was nine, with only two pearls.

3 So as soon as she got married and moved away from home the first thing she did was separate! From Mr. Whitaker! This photographer with the popeyes she said she trusted. Came home from one of those towns up in Illinois and to our complete surprise brought this child of two.

4 Mama said she like to made her drop dead for a second. "Here you had this marvelous blonde child and never so much as wrote your mother a word about it," says Mama. "I'm thoroughly ashamed of you." But of course she wasn't.

5 Stella-Rondo just calmly takes off this *hat*, I wish you could see it. She says, "Why, Mama, Shirley-T.'s adopted, I can prove it."

6 "How?" says Mama, but all I says was, "H'm!" There I was over the hot stove, trying to stretch two chickens over five people and a completely unexpected child into the bargain, without one moment's notice.

7 "What do you mean—'H'm!'?" says Stella-Rondo, and Mama says, "I heard that, Sister."

8 I said that oh, I didn't mean a thing, only that whoever Shirley-T. was, she was the spit-image of Papa-Daddy if he'd cut off his beard, which of course he'd never do in the world. Papa-Daddy's Mama's papa and sulks.

9 Stella-Rondo got furious! She said, "Sister, I don't need to tell you you got a lot of nerve and always did have and I'll thank you to make no future reference to my adopted child whatsoever."

10 "Very well," I said. "Very well, very well. Of course I noticed at once she looks like Mr. Whitaker's side too. That frown. She looks like a cross between Mr. Whitaker and Papa-Daddy."

11 "Well, all I can say is she isn't."

12 "She looks exactly like Shirley Temple to me," says Mama, but Shirley-T. just ran away from her. So the first thing Stella-Rondo did at the table was turn Papa-Daddy against me.

13 "Papa-Daddy," she says. He was trying to cut up his meat. "Papa-Daddy!" I was taken completely by surprise. Papa-Daddy is about a million years old and's got this long-long beard. "Papa-Daddy, Sister says she fails to understand why you don't cut off your beard."

14 So Papa-Daddy l-a-y-s down his knife and fork! He's real rich. Mama says he is, he says he isn't. So he says, "Have I heard correctly? You don't understand why I don't cut off my beard?"

15 "Why," I says, "Papa-Daddy, of course I understand, I did not say any such of a thing, the idea!"

16 He says, "Hussy!"

17 I says, "Papa-Daddy, you know I wouldn't any more want you to cut off your beard than the man in the moon. It was the farthest thing from my mind! Stella-Rondo sat there and made that up while she was eating breast of chicken."

18 But he says, "So the postmistress fails to understand why I don't cut off my beard. Which job I got you through my influence with the government. 'Bird's nest'—is that what you call it?"

19 Not that it isn't the next to smallest P.O. in the entire state of Mississippi.

While she was married she got this peculiar idea that it's cooler with the windows shut and locked.

20 I says, "Oh, Papa-Daddy," I says, "I didn't say any such of a thing, I never dreamed it was a bird's nest, I have always been grateful though this is the next to smallest P.O. in the state of Mississippi, and I do not enjoy being referred to as a hussy by my own grandfather."

21 But Stella-Rondo says, "Yes, you did say it too. Anybody in the world could of heard you, that had ears."

22 "Stop right there," says Mama, looking at *me*.

23 So I pulled my napkin straight back through the napkin ring and left the table.

24 As soon as I was out of the room Mama says, "Call her back, or she'll starve to death," but Papa-Daddy says, "This is the beard I started growing on the Coast when I was fifteen years old." He would of gone on till nightfall if Shirley-T. hadn't lost the Milky Way she ate in Cairo.

25 So Papa-Daddy says, "I am going out and lie in the hammock, and you can all sit here and remember my words: I'll never cut off my beard as long as I live, even one inch, and I don't appreciate it in you at all." Passed right by me in the hall and went straight out and got in the hammock.

26 It would be a holiday. It wasn't five minutes before Uncle Rondo suddenly appeared in the hall in one of Stella-Rondo's flesh-colored kimonos, all cut on the bias, like something Mr. Whitaker probably thought was gorgeous.

27 "Uncle Rondo!" I says. "I didn't know who that was! Where are you going?"

28 "Sister," he says, "get out of my way, I'm poisoned."

"If you're poisoned stay away from Papa-Daddy," 29
I says. "Keep out of the hammock. Papa-Daddy will certainly beat you on the head if you come within forty miles of him. He thinks I deliberately said he ought to cut off his beard after he got me the P.O., and I've told him and told him and told him, and he acts like he just don't hear me. Papa-Daddy must of gone stone deaf."

"He picked a fine day to do it then," says Uncle 30
Rondo, and before you could say "Jack Robinson" flew out in the yard.

What he'd really done, he'd drunk another bottle 31
of that prescription. He does it every single Fourth of July as sure as shooting, and it's horribly expensive. Then he falls over in the hammock and snores. So he insisted on zigzagging right on out to the hammock, looking like a half-wit.

Papa-Daddy woke up with 32
this horrible yell and right there without moving an inch he tried to turn Uncle Rondo against me. I heard every word he said. Oh, he told Uncle Rondo I didn't learn to read till I was eight years old and he didn't see how in the world I ever got the mail put up at the P.O., much less read it all, and he said if Uncle Rondo could only fathom the lengths he had gone to to get me that job! And he said on the other hand he thought Stella-Rondo had a brilliant mind and deserved credit for getting out of town. All the time he was just lying there swinging as pretty as you please and looping out his beard, and poor Uncle Rondo was *pleading* with him to slow down the hammock, it was making him as dizzy as a witch to watch it. But that's what Papa-Daddy likes about a hammock. So Uncle Rondo was too dizzy to get turned against me for the time being. He's Mama's only brother and is a good case of a one-track mind. Ask anybody. A certified pharmacist.

Just then I heard Stella-Rondo raising the up- 33
stairs window. While she was married she got this peculiar idea that it's cooler with the windows shut and locked. So she has to raise the window before she can make a soul hear her outdoors.

So she raises the window and says, *"Oh!"* You 34
would have thought she was mortally wounded.

Uncle Rondo and Papa-Daddy didn't even look 35
up, but kept right on with what they were doing. I had to laugh.

I flew up the stairs and threw the door open! I says, 36
"What in the wide world's the matter, Stella-Rondo? You mortally wounded?"

37 "No," she says, "I am not mortally wounded but I wish you would do me the favor of looking out that window there and telling me what you see.

38 So I shade my eyes and look out the window.

39 "I see the front yard," I says.

40 "Don't you see any human beings?" she says.

41 "I see Uncle Rondo trying to run Papa-Daddy out of the hammock," I says. "Nothing more. Naturally, it's so suffocating-hot in the house, with all the windows shut and locked, everybody who cares to stay in their right mind will have to go out and get in the hammock before the Fourth of July is over."

42 "Don't you notice anything different about Uncle Rondo?" asks Stella-Rondo.

43 "Why, no, except he's got on some terrible-looking flesh-colored contraption I wouldn't be found dead in, is all I can see," I says.

44 "Never mind, you won't be found dead in it, because it happens to be part of my trousseau, and Mr. Whitaker took several dozen photographs of me in it," says Stella-Rondo. "What on earth could Uncle Rondo *mean* by wearing part of my trousseau out in the broad open daylight without saying so much as 'Kiss my foot,' *knowing* I only got home this morning after my separation and hung my negligee up on the bathroom door, just as nervous as I could be?"

45 "I'm sure I don't know, and what do you expect me to do about it?" I says. "Jump out the window?"

46 "No, I expect nothing of the kind. I simply declare that Uncle Rondo looks like a fool in it, that's all," she says. "It makes me sick to my stomach."

47 "Well, he looks as good as he can," I says. "As good as anybody in reason could." I stood up for Uncle Rondo, please remember. And I said to Stella-Rondo, "I think I would do well not to criticize so freely if I were you and came home with a two-year-old child I had never said a word about, and no explanation whatever about my separation."

48 "I asked you the instant I entered this house not to refer one more time to my adopted child, and you gave me your word of honor you would not," was all Stella-Rondo would say, and started pulling out every one of her eyebrows with some cheap Kress tweezers.

49 So I merely slammed the door behind me and went down and made some green-tomato pickle. Somebody had to do it. Of course Mama had turned both the niggers loose; she always said no earthly power could hold one anyway on the Fourth of July, so she wouldn't even try. It turned out that Jaypan fell in the lake and came within a very narrow limit of drowning.

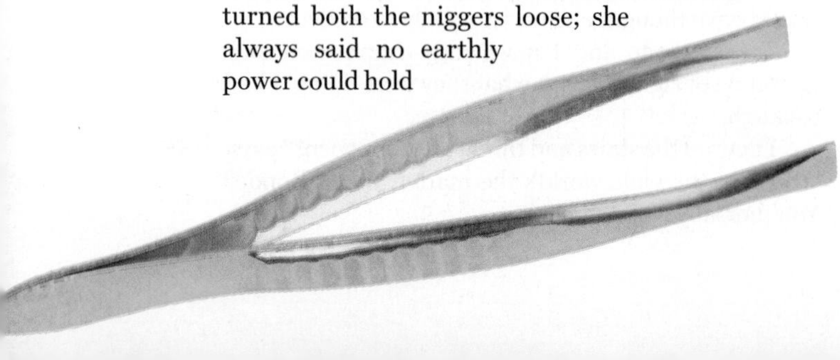

So Mama trots in. Lifts up the lid and says, "H'm! 50
Not very good for your Uncle Rondo in his precarious condition, I must say. Or poor little adopted Shirley-T. Shame on you!"

That made me tired. I says, "Well, Stella-Rondo 51
had better thank her lucky stars it was her instead of me came trotting in with that very peculiar-looking child. Now if it had been me that trotted in from Illinois and brought a peculiar-looking child of two, I shudder to think of the reception I'd of got, much less controlled the diet of an entire family."

"But you must remember, Sister, that you were 52
never married to Mr. Whitaker in the first place and didn't go up to Illinois to live," says Mama, shaking a spoon in my face. "If you had I would of been just as overjoyed to see you and your little adopted girl as I was to see Stella-Rondo, when you wound up with your separation and came on back home."

"You would not," I says. 53

"Don't contradict me, I would," says Mama. 54

But I said she couldn't convince me though she 55
talked till she was blue in the face. Then I said, "Besides, you know as well as I do that that child is not adopted."

"She most certainly is adopted," says Mama, stiff 56
as a poker.

I says, "Why, Mama, Stella-Rondo had her just as 57
sure as anything in this world, and just too stuck up to admit it."

"Why, Sister," said Mama. "Here I thought we were 58
going to have a pleasant Fourth of July, and you start right out not believing a word your own baby sister tells you!"

"Just like Cousin Annie Flo. Went to her grave de- 59
nying the facts of life," I remind Mama.

"I told you if you ever mentioned Annie Flo's name 60
I'd slap your face," says Mama, and slaps my face.

"All right, you wait and see," I says. 61

"I," says Mama, "*I* prefer to take my children's word 62
for anything when it's humanly possible." You ought to see Mama, she weighs two hundred pounds and has real tiny feet.

Just then something perfectly horrible occurred 63
to me.

"Mama," I says, "can that child talk?" I simply had 64
to whisper! "Mama, I wonder if that child can be—you know—in any way? Do you realize," I says, "that she hasn't spoken one single, solitary word to a human being up to this minute? This is the way she looks," I says, and I looked like this.

65 Well, Mama and I just stood there and stared at each other. It was horrible!

66 "I remember well that Joe Whitaker frequently drank like a fish," says Mama. "I believed to my soul he drank *chemicals.*" And without another word she marches to the foot of the stairs and calls Stella-Rondo.

67 "Stella-Rondo? O-o-o-o-o! Stella-Rondo!"

68 "What?" says Stella-Rondo from upstairs. Not even the grace to get up off the bed.

69 "Can that child of yours talk?" asks Mama.

70 Stella-Rondo says, "Can she what?"

71 "Talk! Talk!" says Mama. "Burdyburdyburdyburdy!"

72 So Stella-Rondo yells back, "Who says she can't talk?"

73 "Sister says so," says Mama.

74 "You didn't have to tell me, I know whose word of honor don't mean a thing in this house," says Stella-Rondo.

". . . 'Uncle Rondo certainly does look like a fool in that pink kimono!'"

75 And in a minute the loudest Yankee voice I ever heard in my life yells out, "OE'm Pop-OE the Sailor-r-r-r Ma-a-an!" and then somebody jumps up and down in the upstairs hall. In another second the house would of fallen down.

76 "Not only talks, she can tap-dance!" calls Stella-Rondo. "Which is more than some people I won't name can do."

77 "Why, the little precious darling thing!" Mama says, so surprised. "Just as smart as she can be!" Starts talking baby talk right there. Then she turns on me. "Sister, you ought to be thoroughly ashamed! Run upstairs this instant and apologize to Stella-Rondo and Shirley-T."

78 "Apologize for what?" I says. "I merely wondered if the child was normal, that's all. Now that she's proved she is, why, I have nothing further to say."

79 But Mama just turned on her heel and flew out, furious. She ran right upstairs and hugged the baby. She believed it was adopted. Stella-Rondo hadn't done a thing but turn her against me from upstairs while I stood there helpless over the hot stove. So that made Mama, Papa-Daddy and the baby all on Stella-Rondo's side.

80 Next, Uncle Rondo.

81 I must say that Uncle Rondo has been marvelous to me at various times in the past and I was completely unprepared to be made to jump out of my skin, the way it turned out. Once Stella-Rondo did something perfectly horrible to him—broke a chain letter from Flanders Field—and he took the radio back he had given her and gave it to me. Stella Rondo was furious! For six months we all had to call her Stella instead of Stella-Rondo, or she wouldn't answer. I always thought Uncle Rondo had all the brains of the entire family. Another time he sent me to Mammoth Cave, with all expenses paid.

82 But this would be the day he was drinking that prescription, the Fourth of July.

83 So at supper Stella-Rondo speaks up and says she thinks Uncle Rondo ought to try to eat a little something. So finally Uncle Rondo said he would try a little cold biscuits and ketchup, but that was all. So *she* brought it to him.

84 "Do you think it wise to disport with ketchup in Stella-Rondo's flesh-colored kimono?" I says. Trying to be considerate! If Stella-Rondo couldn't watch out for her trousseau, somebody had to.

85 "Any objections?" asks Uncle Rondo, just about to pour out all the ketchup.

86 "Don't mind what she says, Uncle Rondo," says Stella-Rondo. "Sister has been devoting this solid afternoon to sneering out my bedroom window at the way you look."

87 "What's that?" says Uncle Rondo. Uncle Rondo has got the most terrible temper in the world. Anything is liable to make him tear the house down if it comes at the wrong time.

88 So Stella-Rondo says, "Sister says, 'Uncle Rondo certainly does look like a fool in that pink kimono!'"

89 Do you remember who it was really said that?

90 Uncle Rondo spills out all the ketchup and jumps out of his chair and tears off the kimono and throws it down on the dirty floor and puts his foot on it. It had to be sent all the way to Jackson to the cleaners and repleated.

91 "So that's your opinion of your Uncle Rondo, is it?" he says. "I look like a fool, do I? Well, that's the last straw. A whole day in this house with nothing to do, and then to hear you come out with a remark like that behind my back!"

92 "I didn't say any such of a thing, Uncle Rondo," I says, "and I'm not saying who did, either. Why, I think you look all right. Just try to take care of yourself and not talk and eat at the same time," I says. "I think you better go lie down."

93 "Lie down my foot," says Uncle Rondo. I ought to of known by that he was fixing to do something perfectly horrible.

94 So he didn't do anything that night in the precarious state he was in—just played Casino with Mama and Stella-Rondo and Shirley-T. and gave Shirley-T. a

nickel with a head on both sides. It tickled her nearly to death, and she called him "Papa." But at 6:30 A.M. the next morning, he threw a whole five-cent package of some unsold one-inch firecrackers from the store as hard as he could into my bedroom and they every one went off. Not one bad one in the string. Anybody else, there'd be one that wouldn't go off.

95 Well, I'm just terribly susceptible to noise of any kind, the doctor has always told me I was the most sensitive person he had ever seen in his whole life, and I was simply prostrated. I couldn't eat! People tell me they heard it as far as the cemetery, and old Aunt Jep Patterson, that had been holding her own so good, thought it was Judgment Day and she was going to meet her whole family. It's usually so quiet here.

96 And I'll tell you it didn't take me any longer than a minute to make up my mind what to do. There I was with the whole entire house on Stella-Rondo's side and turned against me. If I have anything at all I have pride.

97 So I just decided I'd go straight down to the P.O. There's plenty of room there in the back, I says to myself.

98 Well! I made no bones about letting the family catch on to what I was up to. I didn't try to conceal it.

The first thing they knew, I marched in where they were all playing Old Maid and pulled the electric oscillating fan out by the plug, and everything got real hot. Next I snatched the pillow I'd done the needlepoint on right off the davenport from behind Papa-Daddy. He went "Ugh!" I beat Stella-Rondo up the stairs and finally found my charm bracelet in her bureau drawer under a picture of Nelson Eddy.

99 "So that's the way the land lies," says Uncle Rondo. There he was, piecing on the ham. "Well, Sister, I'll be glad to donate my army cot if you got any place to set it up, providing you'll leave right this minute and let me get some peace." Uncle Rondo was in France.

100 "Thank you kindly for the cot and 'peace' is hardly the word I would select if I had to resort to firecrackers at 6:30 A.M. in a young girl's bedroom," I says back to him. "And as to where I intend to go, you seem to forget my position as postmistress of China Grove, Mississippi," I says. "I've always got the P.O."

Well, that made them all sit up and take notice. 101

I went out front and started digging up some four-o'clocks to plant around the P.O. 102

"Ah-ah-ah!" says Mama, raising the window. "Those happen to be my four-o'clocks. Everything planted in that star is mine. I've never known you to make anything grow in your life." 103

"You can just let my mail lie there and *rot,* for all I care . . ."

"Very well," I says. "But I take the fern. Even you, Mama, can't stand there and deny that I'm the one watered that fern. And I happen to know where I can send in a box top and get a packet of one thousand mixed seeds, no two the same kind, free." 104

"Oh, where?" Mama wants to know. 105

But I says, "Too late. You 'tend to your house, and I'll 'tend to mine. You hear things like that all the time if you know how to listen to the radio. Perfectly marvelous offers. Get anything you want free." 106

So I hope to tell you I marched in and got that radio, and they could of all bit a nail in two, especially Stella-Rondo, that it used to belong to, and she well knew she couldn't get it back, I'd sue for it like a shot. And I very politely took the sewing-machine motor I helped pay the most on to give Mama for Christmas back in 1929, and a good big calendar, with the first-aid remedies on it. The thermometer and the Hawaiian ukulele certainly were rightfully mine, and I stood on the step-ladder and got all my watermelon-rind preserves and every fruit and vegetable I'd put up, every jar. Then I began to pull the tacks out of the bluebird wall vases on the archway to the dining room. 107

"Who told you you could have those, Miss Priss?" says Mama, fanning as hard as she could. 108

"I bought 'em and I'll keep track of 'em," I says. "I'll tack 'em up one on each side the post-office window, and you can see 'em when you come to ask me for your mail, if you're so dead to see 'em." 109

"Not I! I'll never darken the door to that post office again if I live to be a hundred," Mama says. "Ungrateful child! After all the money we spent on you at the Normal." 110

"Me either," says Stella-Rondo. "You can just let my mail lie there and *rot,* for all I care. I'll never come and relieve you of a single, solitary piece." 111

"I should worry," I says. "And who you think's going to sit down and write you all those big fat letters and 112 postcards, by the way? Mr. Whitaker? Just because he was the only man ever dropped down in China Grove and you got him—unfairly—is he going to sit down and write you a lengthy correspondence after you come home giving no rhyme nor reason whatsoever for your separation and no explanation for the presence of that child? I may not have your brilliant mind, but I fail to see it."

13 So Mama says, "Sister, I've told you a thousand times that Stella-Rondo simply got homesick, and this child is far too big to be hers," and she says, "Now, why don't you all just sit down and play Casino?"

14 Then Shirley-T. sticks out her tongue at me in this perfectly horrible way. She has no more manners than the man in the moon. I told her she was going to cross her eyes like that some day and they'd stick.

15 "It's too late to stop me now," I says. "You should have tried that yesterday. I'm going to the P.O. and the only way you can possibly see me is to visit me there."

16 So Papa-Daddy says, "You'll never catch me setting foot in that post office, even if I should take a notion into my head to write a letter some place." He says, "I won't have you reachin' out of that little old window with a pair of shears and cuttin' off any beard of mine. I'm too smart for you!"

17 "We all are," says Stella-Rondo.

18 But I said, "If you're so smart, where's Mr. Whitaker?"

19 So then Uncle Rondo says, "I'll thank you from now on to stop reading all the orders I get on postcards and telling everybody in China Grove what you think is the matter with them," but I says, "I draw my own conclusions and will continue in the future to draw them." I says, "If people want to write their inmost secrets on penny postcards, there's nothing in the wide world you can do about it, Uncle Rondo."

20 "And if you think we'll ever *write* another postcard you're sadly mistaken," says Mama.

21 "Cutting off your nose to spite your face then," I says. "But if you're all determined to have no more to do with the U. S. mail, think of this: What will Stella-Rondo do now, if she wants to tell Mr. Whitaker to come after her?"

22 "Wah!" says Stella-Rondo. I knew she'd cry. She had a conniption fit right there in the kitchen.

23 "It will be interesting to see how long she holds out," I says. "And now—I am leaving."

24 "Good-bye," says Uncle Rondo.

25 "Oh, I declare," says Mama, "to think that a family of mine should quarrel on the Fourth of July, or the day after, over Stella-Rondo leaving old Mr. Whitaker and having the sweetest little adopted child! It looks like we'd all be glad!"

"Wah!" says Stella-Rondo, and has a fresh conniption fit. 126

"*He* left *her*—you mark my words," I says. "That's Mr. Whitaker. I know Mr. Whitaker. After all, I knew him first. I said from the beginning he'd up and leave her. I foretold every single thing that's happened." 127

"Where did he go?" asks Mama. 128

"Probably to the North Pole, if he knows what's good for him," I says. 129

But Stella-Rondo just bawled and wouldn't say another word. She flew to her room and slammed the door. 130

"Now look what you've gone and done, Sister," says Mama. "You go apologize." 131

"I haven't got time, I'm leaving," I says. 132

"Well, what are you waiting around for?" asks Uncle Rondo. 133

So I just picked up the kitchen clock and marched off, without saying "Kiss my foot" or anything, and never did tell Stella-Rondo good-bye. 134

There was a nigger girl going along on a little wagon right in front. 135

"Nigger girl," I says, "come help me haul these things down the hill, I'm going to live in the post office." 136

Took her nine trips in her express wagon. Uncle Rondo came out on the porch and threw her a nickel. 137

AND that's the last I've laid eyes on my family or my family laid eyes on me for five solid days and nights. Stella-Rondo may be telling the most horrible tales in the world about Mr. Whitaker, but I haven't heard them. As I tell everybody, I draw my own conclusions. 138

But oh, I like it here. It's ideal, as I've been saying. You see, I've got everything cater-cornered, the way I like it. Hear the radio? All the war news. Radio, sewing machine, book ends, ironing board and 139

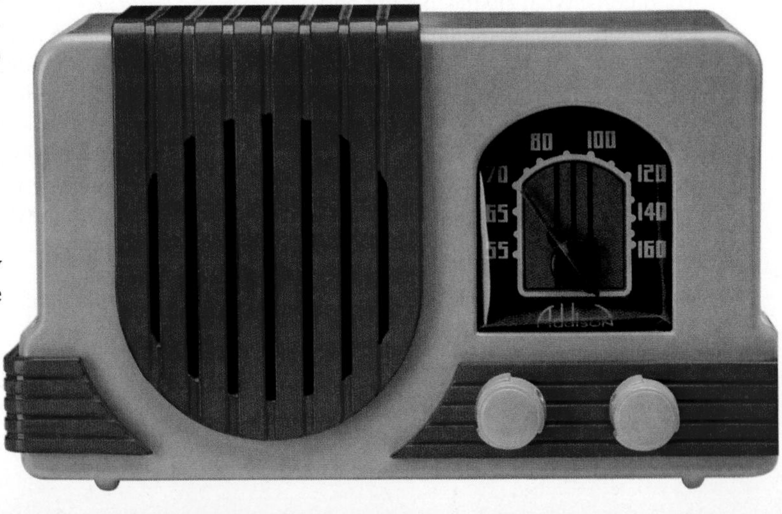

that great big piano lamp—peace, that's what I like. Butter-bean vines planted all along the front where the strings are.

Of course, there's not much mail. My family are naturally the main people in China Grove, and if they prefer to vanish from the face of the earth, for all the mail they get or the mail they write, why, I'm not going to open my mouth. Some of the folks here in town are taking up for me and some turned against me. I know which is which. There are always people who will quit buying stamps just to get on the right side of Papa-Daddy.

But here I am, and here I'll stay. I want the world to know I'm happy.

And if Stella-Rondo should come to me this minute, on bended knees, and *attempt* to explain the incidents of her life with Mr. Whitaker, I'd simply put my fingers in both my ears and refuse to listen.

IF you like how the physicality of the setting for "Why I Live at the P.O." might be imagined as the setting for a stage play, you may like the way this same treatment could work for the subway platform in Thomas Wolfe's story "Only the Dead Know Brooklyn" in chapter 8.

**GOING FURTHER** The American South, with its farms and woods, rural roads and rivers, and, as in "No Place for You, My Love," Welty's passionate celebration of New Orleans and the lower Mississippi Delta provides a distinctive setting for her lifework. In novel after novel she makes the post-Faulknerian landscape come alive.

# Writing from Reading

## Summarize

1 List details Welty gives about the setting: the house, the town, the season, and the time period.

2 Describe the social environment of these characters. What are these characters' living and working conditions? What are the rhythms and challenges of the community being portrayed?

## Analyze Craft

3 Sister's relationship to Mr. Whitaker is mentioned only twice in the story, once at the beginning and once toward the end, but it makes for a conflict central to the story. Explore why Welty chooses in the context to hide this conflict, and discuss how the quarrel between sisters might differ if they were more open.

## Analyze Voice

4 How does the narrator's informal voice affect your impression of her? Do you trust her side of the story more or less because she is speaking naturally? How do you think your impression is affected by your familiarity or unfamiliarity with the dialect and the setting of the story?

## Synthesize Summary and Analysis

5 Why is it significant that Sister works at (and eventually moves into) a post office? Analyze Welty's choice of this setting and the profession of postmaster.

## Interpret the Story

6 Stella-Rondo, unlike Sister, escaped to another place and another life, if only for a short time. What impact might this change of setting have had on Stella-Rondo and her view of her home and family? What impact might

this change have had on her relationship with Sister? Demonstrate this impact with examples.

7 At the end of the story, Sister describes her home at the P.O., telling the reader to experience the setting firsthand. Discuss the narrator's (and Welty's) purpose in involving the reader so directly at the end of the story.

# Bernard Malamud (1914–1986)

Bernard Malamud was born in New York City in 1914 and died there in 1986. However, he spent much of his professional life away from the city, teaching writing first at Oregon State College, then at Bennington College in Vermont. In *The Natural* (1952), he wrote about baseball, in *The Fixer* (1966), of Anti-Semitism in Russia. Despite his range of residencies and the variety of fictional locations in his work, Malamud remains best known as a chronicler of urban poverty and the immigrant experience; his characters are city dwellers, often, though not exclusively, Jewish and adrift. In many of his short stories and several of his novels, the world of the New York City tenement frames, as he put it, "my sad and comic tales." Much celebrated in the United States and abroad, Malamud received numerous honors for his work, including the Pulitzer Prize in 1967. *The Magic Barrel,* a collection of stories of which this chapter's selection is the title piece, won the National Book Award for fiction in 1958; he captured this award again in 1967 for *The Fixer.* In 1983 he published *The Stories of Bernard Malamud* and received the American Academy and Institute's Gold Medal for Fiction.

If Richard Ford's characters speak in "standard" English (chapter 2), the spoken utterance of Malamud's characters everywhere betrays its origin and their recent arrival on America's shores. In "The Magic Barrel," the marriage broker Salzman and his wife appear almost to be speaking in translation; their English is recently acquired and poor. In contrast, the seminarian Finkle and the prospective bride Lily Hirschorn are better assimilated, more fluent in the language and therefore "Americanized."

Critics saw Malamud as a Jewish-American writer, but he resisted this label, preferring to be known as a Jew who lived and wrote in America. His fiction reflects his interest in fable and allegory—the way a figure can be both particular and representative, both specific and abstract.

Of this story, he said, "["The Magic Barrel"] has been interpreted in two ways, as realism and as fantasy. I had meant it to be realistic, but two things conditioned some people's reading of it. In the original version Salzman says somewhere, referring to his daughter, 'For her to be poor was a sin. That is why she is dead now.' And the Chagallean imagery of the ending convinces some that it was meant to be fantasy. Either interpretation suits me, I thought, but then in the manuscript I sent to the publisher I altered Salzman's speech so that it now reads, 'This is why to me she is dead now.'"

**AS YOU READ** As you read, notice the details of setting that Malamud provides. What kind of a world is he leading readers into? Is it a world that seems foreign or familiar to you?

# The Magic Barrel (1958)

1 NOT long ago there lived in uptown New York, in a small, almost meager room, though crowded with books, Leo Finkle, a rabbinical student at the Yeshiva University. Finkle, after six years of study, was to be ordained in June and had been advised by an acquaintance that he might find it easier to win himself a congregation if he were married. Since he had no present prospects of marriage, after two tormented days of turning it over in his mind, he called in Pinye Salzman, a marriage broker whose two-line advertisement he had read in the *Forward.*

He remarked in passing that the function of the marriage broker was ancient and honorable . . .

2 The matchmaker appeared one night out of the dark fourth-floor hallway of the graystone rooming house where Finkle lived, grasping a black, strapped portfolio that had been worn thin with use. Salzman, who had been long in the business, was of slight but dignified build, wearing an old hat, and an overcoat too short and tight for him. He smelled frankly of fish, which he loved to eat, and although he was missing a few teeth, his presence was not displeasing, because of an amiable manner curiously contrasted with mournful eyes. His voice, his lips, his wisp of beard, his bony fingers were animated, but give him a moment of repose and his mild blue eyes revealed a depth of sadness, a characteristic that put Leo a little at ease although the situation, for him, was inherently tense.

3 He at once informed Salzman why he had asked him to come, explaining that but for his parents, who had married comparatively late in life, he was alone in the world. He had for six years devoted himself almost entirely to his studies, as a result of which, understandably, he had found himself without time for a social life and the company of young women. Therefore he thought it the better part of trial and error—of embarrassing fumbling—to call in an experienced person to advise him on these matters. He remarked in passing that the function of the marriage broker was ancient and honorable, highly approved in the Jewish community, because it made practical the necessary without hindering joy. Moreover, his own parents had been brought together by a matchmaker. They had made, if not a financially profitable marriage—since neither had possessed any worldly goods to speak of—at least a successful one in the sense of their everlasting devotion to each other. Salzman listened in embarrassed surprise, sensing a sort of apology. Later, however, he experienced a glow of pride in his work, an emotion that had left him years ago, and he heartily approved of Finkle.

The two went to their business. Leo had led Salzman to 4
the only clear place in the room, a table near a window that overlooked the lamp-lit city. He seated himself at the matchmaker's side but facing him, attempting by an act of will to suppress the unpleasant tickle in his throat. Salzman eagerly unstrapped his portfolio and removed a loose rubber band from a thin packet of much-handled cards. As he flipped through them, a gesture and sound that physically hurt Leo, the student pretended not to see and gazed steadfastly out the window. Although it was still February, winter was on its last legs, signs of which he had for the first time in years begun to notice. He now observed the round white moon, moving high in the sky through a cloud menagerie, and watched with half-open mouth as it penetrated a huge hen, and dropped out of her like an egg laying itself. Salzman, though pretending through eyeglasses he had just slipped on to be engaged in scanning the writing on the cards, stole occasional glances at the young man's distinguished face, noting with pleasure the long, severe scholar's nose, brown eyes heavy with learning, sensitive yet ascetic lips, and a certain almost hollow quality of the dark cheeks. He gazed around

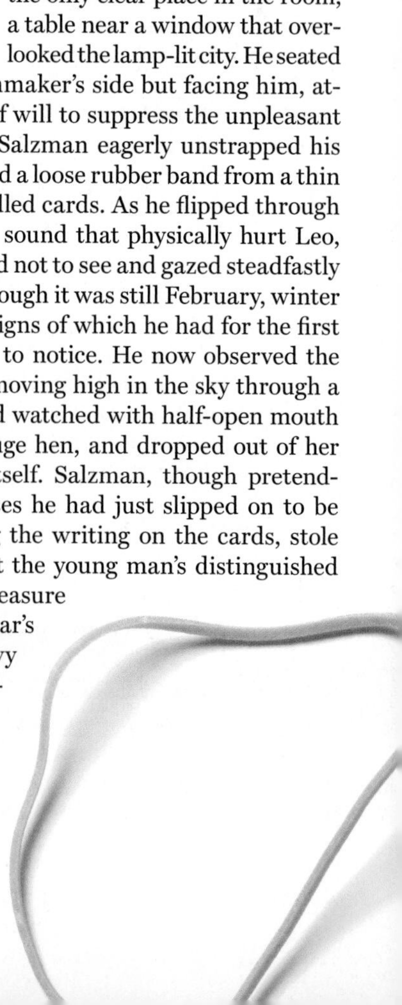

at shelves upon shelves of books and let out a soft, contented sigh.

5 When Leo's eyes fell upon the cards, he counted six spread out in Salzman's hand.

6 "So few?" he asked in disappointment.

7 "You wouldn't believe me how much cards I got in my office," Salzman replied. "The drawers are already filled to the top, so I keep them now in a barrel, but is every girl good for a new rabbi?"

8 Leo blushed at this, regretting all he had revealed of himself in a curriculum vitae he had sent to Salzman. He had thought it best to acquaint him with his strict standards and specifications but, in having done so, felt he had told the marriage broker more than was absolutely necessary.

9 He hesitantly inquired, "Do you keep photographs of your clients on file?"

10 "First comes family, amount of dowry, also what kind promises," Salzman replied, unbuttoning his tight coat and settling himself in the chair. "After comes pictures, rabbi."

11 "Call me Mr. Finkle. I'm not yet a rabbi."

12 Salzman said he would, but instead called him doctor, which he changed to rabbi when Leo was not listening too attentively.

13 Salzman adjusted his horn-rimmed spectacles, gently cleared his throat and read in an eager voice the contents of the top card:

14 "Sophie P. Twenty four years. Widow one year. No children. Educated high school and two years college. Father promises eight thousand dollars. Has wonderful wholesale business. Also real estate. On the mother's side comes teachers, also one actor. Well known on Second Avenue."

15 Leo gazed up in surprise. "Did you say a widow?"

16 "A widow don't mean spoiled, rabbi. She lived with her husband maybe four months. He was a sick boy she made a mistake to marry him."

17 "Marrying a widow has never entered my mind."

18 "This is because you have no experience. A widow, especially if she is young and healthy like this girl, is a wonderful person to marry. She will be thankful to you the rest of her life. Believe me, if I was looking now for a bride, I would marry a widow.

19 Leo reflected, then shook his head.

20 Salzman hunched his shoulders in an almost imperceptible gesture of disappointment. He placed the card down on the wooden table and began to read another:

21 "Lily H. High school teacher. Regular. Not a substitute. Has savings and new Dodge car. Lived in Paris one year. Father is successful dentist thirty-five years. Interested in professional man. Well-Americanized family. Wonderful opportunity."

22 "I know her personally," said Salzman. "I wish you could see this girl. She is a doll. Also very intelligent. All day you could talk to her about books and theayter and whatnot. She also knows current events."

23 "I don't believe you mentioned her age?"

24 "Her age?" Salzman said, raising his brows. "Her age is thirty-two years."

25 Leo said after a while, "I'm afraid that seems a little too old."

26 Salzman let out a laugh. "So how old are you, rabbi?"

27 "Twenty-seven."

28 "So what is the difference, tell me, between twenty-seven and thirty-two? My own wife is seven years older than me. So what did I suffer?— Nothing. If Rothschild's daughter wants to marry you, would you say on account her age, no?"

29 "Yes," Leo said dryly.

30 Salzman shook off the no in the yes. "Five years don't mean a thing. I give you my word that when you will live with her for one week you will forget her age. What does it mean five years—that she lived more and knows more than somebody who is younger? On this girl, God bless her, years are not wasted. Each one that it comes makes better the bargain."

31 "What subject does she teach in high school?"

32 "Languages. If you heard the way she speaks French, you will think it is music. I am in the business twenty-five years, and I recommend her with my whole heart. Believe me, I know what I'm talking, rabbi."

33 "What's on the next card?" Leo said abruptly.

34 Salzman reluctantly turned up the third card:

35 "Ruth K. Nineteen years. Honor student. Father offers thirteen thousand cash to the right bridegroom. He is a medical doctor. Stomach specialist with marvelous practice. Brother-in-law owns own garment business. Particular people."

36 Salzman looked as if he had read his trump card.

37 "Did you say nineteen?" Leo asked with interest.

38 "On the dot."

39 "Is she attractive?" He blushed. "Pretty?"

40 Salzman kissed his fingertips. "A little doll. On this I give you my word. Let me call the father tonight and you will see what means pretty."

41 But Leo was troubled. "You're sure she's that young?"

42 "This I am positive. The father will show you the birth certificate."

43 "Are you positive there isn't something wrong with her?" Leo insisted.

44 "Who says there is wrong?"

45 "I don't understand why an American girl her age should go to a marriage broker."

46 A smile spread over Salzman's face.

47 "So for the same reason you went, she comes."

48 Leo flushed. "I am pressed for time."

49 Salzman, realizing he had been tactless, quickly explained. "The father came, not her. He wants she should have the best, so he looks around himself. When we will locate the right boy he will introduce him and encourage. This makes a better marriage than if a young girl without experience takes for herself. I don't have to tell you this."

"Love comes with the right person, not before."

50 "But don't you think this young girl believes in love?" Leo spoke uneasily.

51 Salzman was about to guffaw but caught himself and said soberly, "Love comes with the right person, not before."

52 Leo parted dry lips but did not speak. Noticing that Salzman had snatched a glance at the next card, he cleverly asked, "How is her health?"

53 "Perfect," Salzman said, breathing with difficulty. "Of course, she is a little lame on her right foot from an auto accident that it happened to her when she was twelve years, but nobody notices on account she is so brilliant and also beautiful."

54 Leo got up heavily and went to the window. He felt curiously bitter and upbraided himself for having called in the marriage broker. Finally, he shook his head.

55 "Why not?" Salzman persisted, the pitch of his voice rising.

56 "Because I detest stomach specialists."

57 "So what do you care what is his business? After you marry her do you need him? Who says he must come every Friday night in your house?"

58 Ashamed of the way the talk was going, Leo dismissed Salzman, who went home with heavy, melancholy eyes.

59 Though he had felt only relief at the marriage broker's departure, Leo was in low spirits the next day. He explained it as arising from Salzman's failure to produce a suitable bride for him. He did not care for his type of clientele. But when Leo found himself hesitating whether to seek out another matchmaker, one more polished than Pinye, he wondered if it could be—his protestations to the contrary, and although he honored his father and mother—that he did not, in essence, care for the matchmaking institution? This thought he quickly put out of mind yet found himself still upset. All day he ran around in the woods—missed an important appointment, forgot to give out his laundry, walked out of a Broadway cafeteria without paying and had to run back with the ticket in his hand; had even not recognized his landlady in the street when she passed with a friend and courteously called out, "A good evening to you, Dr. Finkle." By nightfall, however, he had regained sufficient calm to sink his nose into a book and there found peace from his thoughts.

60 Almost at once there came a knock on the door. Before Leo could say enter, Salzman, commercial Cupid, was standing in the room. His face was gray and meager, his expression hungry, and he looked as if he would expire on his feet. Yet the marriage broker managed, by some trick of the muscles, to display a broad smile.

61 "So good evening. I am invited?"

62 Leo nodded, disturbed to see him again, yet unwilling to ask the man to leave.

63 Beaming still, Salzman laid his portfolio on the table, "Rabbi, I got for you tonight good news."

64 "I've asked you not to call me rabbi. I'm still a student."

65 "Your worries are finished. I have for you a first-class bride."

66 "Leave me in peace concerning this subject." Leo pretended lack of interest.

67 "The world will dance at your wedding."

68 "Please, Mr. Salzman, no more."

69 "But first must come back my strength," Salzman said weakly. He fumbled with the portfolio straps and took out of the leather case an oily paper bag, from which he extracted a hard, seeded roll and a small, smoked whitefish. With a quick motion of his hand he stripped the fish out of its skin and began ravenously to chew. "All day in a rush," he muttered.

70 Leo watched him eat.

71 "A sliced tomato you have maybe?" Salzman hesitantly inquired.

72 "No."

73 The marriage broker shut his eyes and ate. When he had finished he carefully cleaned up the crumbs and rolled up the remains of the fish, in the paper bag. His spectacled eyes roamed the room until he discovered, amid some piles of books, a one-burner gas stove. Lifting his hat he humbly asked, "A glass tea you got, rabbi?"

74 Conscience-stricken, Leo rose and brewed the tea. He served it with a chunk of lemon and two cubes of lump sugar, delighting Salzman.

75 After he had drunk his tea, Salzman's strength and good spirits were restored.

76 "So tell me, rabbi," he said amiably, "you considered some more the three clients I mentioned yesterday?"

77 "There was no need to consider."

78 "Why not?"

79 "None of them suits me."

80 "What then suits you?"

81 Leo let it pass because he could give only a confused answer.

82 Without waiting for a reply, Salzman asked, "You remember this girl I talked to you—the high school teacher?"

83 "Age thirty-two?"

84 But, surprisingly, Salzman's face lit in a smile. "Age twenty-nine."

85 Leo shot him a look. "Reduced from thirty-two?"

86 "A mistake," Salzman avowed. "I talked today with the dentist. He took me to his safety deposit box and showed me the birth certificate. She was twenty-nine years last August. They made her a party in the mountains where she went for her vacation. When her father spoke to me the first time I forgot to write the age and I told you thirty-two, but now I remember this was a different client, a widow."

87 "The same one you told me about, I thought she was twenty-four?"

88 "A different. Am I responsible that the world is filled with widows?"

89 "No, but I'm not interested in them, nor for that matter, in schoolteachers."

90 Salzman pulled his clasped hands to his breast. Looking at the ceiling he devoutly exclaimed, "Yidishe kinder, what can I say to somebody that he is not interested in high school teachers? So what then you are interested?"

91 Leo flushed but controlled himself.

92 "In what else will you be interested," Salzman went on, "if you not interested in this fine girl that she speaks four languages and has personally in the bank ten thousand dollars? Also her father guarantees further twelve thousand. Also she has a new car, wonderful clothes, talks on all subjects, and she will give you a first-class home and children. How near do we come in our life to paradise?"

"If she's so wonderful, why wasn't she married ten years ago?" 93

"Why?" said Salzman with a heavy laugh. "—Why? Because she is *partikiler*. This is why. She wants the *best*." 94

Leo was silent, amused at how he had entangled himself. But Salzman had aroused his interest in Lily H., and he began seriously to consider calling on her. When the marriage broker observed how intently Leo's mind was at work on the facts he had supplied, he felt certain they would soon come to an agreement. 95

LATE Saturday afternoon, conscious of Salzman, Leo Finkle walked with Lily Hirschorn along Riverside Drive. He walked briskly and erectly, wearing with distinction the black fedora he had that morning taken with trepidation out of the dusty hat box on his closet shelf, and the heavy black Saturday coat he had thoroughly whisked clean. Leo also owned a walking stick, a present from a distant relative, but quickly put temptation aside and did not use it. Lily, petite and not unpretty, had on something signifying the approach of spring. She was au courant, animatedly, with all sorts of subjects, and he weighed her words and found her surprisingly sound—score another for Salzman, whom he uneasily sensed to be somewhere around, hiding perhaps high in a tree along the street, flashing the lady signals with a pocket mirror; or perhaps a cloven-hoofed Pan, piping nuptial ditties as he danced his invisible way before them, strewing wild buds on the walk and purple grapes in their path, symbolizing fruit of a union, though there was of course still none. 96

Lily startled Leo by remarking, "I was thinking of Mr. Salzman, a curious figure wouldn't you say?" 97

Not certain what to answer, he nodded. 98

She bravely went on, blushing, "I for one am grateful for his introducing us. Aren't you?" 99

He courteously replied, "I am." 100

"I mean," she said with a little laugh—and it was all in good taste, or at least gave the effect of being not in bad—"do you mind that we came together so?" 101

He was not displeased with her honesty, recognizing that she meant to set the relationship aright, and understanding that it took a certain amount of experience in life, and courage, to want to do it quite that way. One had to have some sort of past to make that kind of beginning. 102

He said that he did not mind. Salzman's function was traditional and honorable—valuable for what it might achieve, which, he pointed out, was frequently nothing. 103

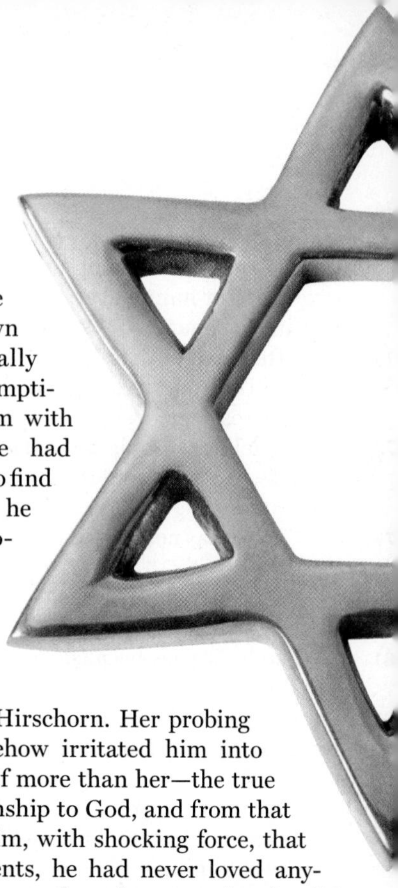

104 Lily agreed with a sigh. They walked on for a while and she said after a long silence, again with a nervous laugh, "Would you mind if I asked you something a little bit personal? Frankly, I find the subject fascinating." Although Leo shrugged, she went on half-embarrassedly, "How was it that you came to your calling? I mean, was it a sudden passionate inspiration?"

105 Leo, after a time, slowly replied, "I was always interested in the Law."

106 "You saw revealed in it the presence of the Highest?"

107 He nodded and changed the subject. "I understand that you spent a little time in Paris, Miss Hirschorn?"

108 "Oh, did Mr. Salzman tell you, Rabbi Finkle?" Leo winced but she went on, "It was ages ago and almost forgotten. I remember I had to return for my sister's wedding."

109 And Lily would not be put off. "When," she asked in a slightly trembly voice, "did you become enamored of God?"

110 He stared at her. Then it came to him that she was talking about not Leo Finkle but a total stranger, some mystical figure, perhaps even passionate prophet that Salzman had dreamed up for her—no relation to the living or dead. Leo trembled with rage and weakness. The trickster had obviously sold her a bill of goods, just as he had him, who'd expected to become acquainted with a young lady of twenty-nine, only to behold, the moment he had laid eyes upon her strained and anxious face, a woman past thirty-five and aging rapidly. Only his self-control had kept him this long in her presence.

111 "I am not," he said gravely, "a talented religious person," and, in seeking words to go on, found himself possessed by shame and fear. "I think," he said in a strained manner, "that I came to God not because I loved Him but because I did not."

112 This confession he spoke harshly because its unexpectedness shook him.

113 Lily wilted. Leo saw a profusion of loaves of bread go flying like ducks high over his head, not unlike the winged loaves by which he had counted himself to sleep last night. Mercifully, then, it snowed, which he would not put past Salzman's machinations.

114 HE was infuriated with the marriage broker and swore he would throw him out of the room the minute he reappeared. But Salzman did not come that night, and when Leo's anger had subsided, an unaccountable despair grew in its place. At first he thought this was caused by his disappointment in Lily, but before long it became evident that he had involved himself with Salzman without a true knowledge of his own intent. He gradually realized—with an emptiness that seized him with six hands—that he had called in the broker to find him a bride because he was incapable of doing it himself. This terrifying insight he had derived as a result of his meeting and conversation with Lily Hirschorn. Her probing questions had somehow irritated him into revealing—to himself more than her—the true nature of his relationship to God, and from that it had come upon him, with shocking force, that apart from his parents, he had never loved anyone. Or perhaps it went the other way, that he did not love God so well as he might, because he had not loved man. It seemed to Leo that his whole life stood starkly revealed and he saw himself for the first time as he truly was—unloved and loveless. This bitter but somehow not fully unexpected revelation brought him to a point of panic, controlled only by extraordinary effort. He covered his face with his hands and cried.

The week that followed was the worst of his life. 11
He did not eat and lost weight. His beard darkened and grew ragged. He stopped attending seminars and almost never opened a book. He seriously considered leaving the Yeshiva, although he was deeply troubled at the thought of the loss of all his years of study—saw them like pages torn from a book, strewn over the city—and at the devastating effect of this decision upon his parents. But he had lived without knowledge of himself, and never in the Five Books and all the Commentaries—mea culpa—had the truth been revealed to him. He did not know where to turn, and in all this desolating loneliness there was no *to whom,* although he often thought of Lily but not once could bring himself to go downstairs and make the call. He became touchy and irritable, especially with his landlady, who asked him all manner of personal questions; on the other hand, sensing his own disagreeableness, he waylaid her on the stairs and apologized abjectly, until, mortified, she ran from him. Out of this, how-

ever, he drew the consolation that he was a Jew and that a Jew suffered. But gradually, as the long and terrible week drew to a close, he regained his composure and some idea of purpose in life: to go on as planned. Although he was imperfect, the ideal was not. As for his quest of a bride, the thought of continuing afflicted him with anxiety and heartburn, yet perhaps with this new knowledge of himself he would be more successful than in the past. Perhaps love would now come to him and a bride to that love. And for this sanctified seeking who needed a Salzman?

16 The marriage broker, a skeleton with haunted eyes, returned that very night. He looked, withal, the picture of frustrated expectancy—as if he had steadfastly waited the week at Miss Lily Hirschorn's side for a telephone call that never came.

17 Casually coughing, Salzman came immediately to the point: "So how did you like her?"

18 Leo's anger rose and he could not refrain from chiding the matchmaker: "Why did you lie to me, Salzman?"

19 Salzman's pale face went dead white, the world had snowed on him.

20 "Did you not state that she was twenty-nine?" Leo insisted.

21 "I give you my word—"

22 "She was thirty-five, if a day. *At least* thirty-five."

23 "Of this don't be too sure. Her father told me—"

24 "Never mind. The worst of it is that you lied to her."

25 "How did I lie to her, tell me?"

26 "You told her things about me that weren't true. You made me out to be more, consequently less than I am. She had in mind a totally different person, a sort of semi-mystical Wonder Rabbi.

27 "All I said, you was a religious man."

28 "I can imagine."

29 Salzman sighed. "This is my weakness that I have," he confessed. "My wife says to me I shouldn't be a salesman, but when I have two fine people that they would be wonderful to be married, I am so happy that I talk too much." He smiled wanly. "This is why Salzman is a poor man."

30 Leo's anger left him. "Well, Salzman, I'm afraid that's all."

31 The marriage broker fastened hungry eyes on him.

32 "You don't want anymore a bride?"

"I do," said Leo, "but I have decided to seek her 133
in another way. I am no longer interested in an arranged marriage. To be frank, I now admit the necessity of premarital love. That is, I want to be in love with the one I marry."

"Love?" said Salzman, astounded. After a mo- 134
ment he remarked, "For us, our love is our life, not for the ladies. In the ghetto they—"

"I know, I know," said Leo. "I've thought of it of- 135
ten. Love, I have said to myself, should be a product of living and worship rather than its own end. Yet for myself I find it necessary to establish the level of my need and fulfill it."

Salzman shrugged but answered, "Listen, rabbi, if 136
you want love, this I can find for you also. I have such beautiful clients that you will love them the minute your eyes will see them."

Leo smiled unhappily. "I'm afraid you don't 137
understand."

But Salzman hastily unstrapped his portfolio and 138
withdrew a manila packet from it.

"Pictures," he said, quickly laying the envelope on 139
the table.

Leo called after him to take the pictures away, but as 140
if on the wings of the wind, Salzman had disappeared.

March came. Leo had returned to his regular rou- 141
tine. Although he felt not quite himself yet—lacked energy—he was making plans for a more active social life. Of course it would cost something, but he was an expert in cutting corners; and when there were no corners left he would make circles rounder. All the while Salzman's pictures had lain on the table, gathering dust. Occasionally as Leo sat studying, or enjoying a cup of tea, his eyes fell on the manila envelope, but he never opened it.

The days went by and no social life to speak of 142
developed with a member of the opposite sex—it was difficult, given the circumstances of his situation. One morning Leo toiled up the stairs to his room and stared out the window at the city. Although the day was bright his view of it was dark. For some time he watched the people in the street below hurrying along and then turned with a heavy heart to his little room. On the table was the packet. With a sudden relentless gesture he tore it open. For a half hour he stood by the table in a state of excitement, examining the photographs of the ladies Salzman had included. Finally, with a deep sigh he put them down. There were six, of varying degrees of attractiveness, but look at them long enough and they all became Lily Hirschorn: all past their prime, all starved behind bright smiles, not a true personality in the lot. Life, despite their frantic

yoohooings, had passed them by; they were pictures in a briefcase that stank of fish. After a while, however, as Leo attempted to return the photographs into the envelope, he found in it another, a snapshot of the type taken by a machine for a quarter. He gazed at it a moment and let out a low cry.

143 Her face deeply moved him. Why, he could at first not say. It gave him the impression of youth—spring flowers, yet age—a sense of having been used to the bone, wasted; this came from the eyes, which were hauntingly familiar, yet absolutely strange. He had a vivid impression that he had met her before, but try as he might he could not place her although he could almost recall her name, as if he had read it in her own handwriting. No, this couldn't be; he would have remembered her. It was not, he affirmed, that she had an extraordinary beauty—no, though her face was attractive enough; it was that *something* about her moved him. Feature for feature, even some of the ladies of the photographs could do better; but she leaped forth to his heart—had *lived,* or wanted to—more than just wanted, perhaps regretted how she had lived—had somehow deeply suffered: it could be seen in the depths of those reluctant eyes, and from the way the light enclosed and shone from her, and within her, opening realms of possibility: this was her own. Her he desired. His head ached and eyes narrowed with the intensity of his gazing, then as if an obscure fog had blown up in the mind, he experienced fear of her and was aware that he had received an impression, somehow, of evil. He shuddered, saying softly, It is thus with us all. Leo brewed some tea in a small pot and sat sipping it without sugar, to calm himself. But before he had finished drinking, again with excitement he examined the face and found it good: good for Leo Finkle. Only such a one could understand him and help him seek whatever he was seeking. She might, perhaps, love him. How she had happened to be among the discards in Salzman's barrel he could never guess, but he knew he must urgently go find her.

He had a vivid impression that he had met her before . . .

144 Leo rushed downstairs, grabbed up the Bronx telephone book, and searched for Salzman's home address. He was not listed, nor was his office. Neither was he in the Manhattan book. But Leo remembered having written down the address on a slip of paper after he had read Salzman's advertisement in the "personals" column of the *Forward.* He ran up to his room and tore through his papers, without luck. It was exasperating. Just when he needed the matchmaker he was nowhere to be found. Fortunately Leo remembered to look in his wallet. There on a card he found his name written and a Bronx address. No phone number was listed, the reason—Leo now recalled—he had originally communicated with Salzman by letter. He got on his coat, put a hat on over his skullcap, and hurried to the subway station. All the way to the far end of the Bronx he sat on the edge of his seat. He was more than once tempted to take out the picture and see if the girl's face was as he remembered, but he refrained, allowing the snapshot to remain in his inside coat pocket, content to have her so close. When the train pulled into the station he was waiting at the door and bolted out. He quickly located the street Salzman had advertised.

The building he sought was less than a block from the subway, but it was not an office building, nor even a loft, nor a store in which one could rent office space. It was a very old tenement house. Leo found Salzman's name in pencil on a soiled tag under the bell and climbed three dark flights to his apartment. When he knocked, the door was opened by a thin, asthmatic, gray-haired woman, in felt slippers. 145

"Yes?" she said, expecting nothing. She listened without listening. He could have sworn he had seen her, too, before but knew it was an illusion. 146

"Salzman—does he live here? Pinye Salzman," he said, "the matchmaker?" 147

She stared at him a long minute. "Of course." 148

He felt embarrassed. "Is he in?" 149

"No." Her mouth, though left open, offered nothing more. 150

"The matter is urgent. Can you tell me where his office is?" 151

"In the air." She pointed upward. 152

"You mean he has no office?" Leo asked. 153

"In his socks." 154

He peered into the apartment. It was sunless and dingy, one large room divided by a half-open curtain, beyond which he could see a sagging metal bed. The near side of the room was crowded with rickety chairs, old bureaus, a three-legged table, racks of cooking utensils, and all the apparatus of a kitchen. But there was no sign of Salzman or his magic barrel, probably also a figment of the imagination. An odor of frying fish made Leo weak to the knees. 155

"Where is he?" he insisted. "I've got to see your husband." 156

At length she answered, "So who knows where he is? Every time he thinks a new thought he runs to a different place. Go home, he will find you." 157

"Tell him Leo Finkle." 158

159 She gave no sign she had heard.

160 He walked downstairs, depressed.

161 But Salzman, breathless, stood waiting at his door.

162 Leo was astounded and overjoyed. "How did you get here before me?"

163 "I rushed."

164 "Come inside."

165 They entered. Leo fixed tea, and a sardine sandwich for Salzman. As they were drinking he reached behind him for the packet of pictures and handed them to the marriage broker.

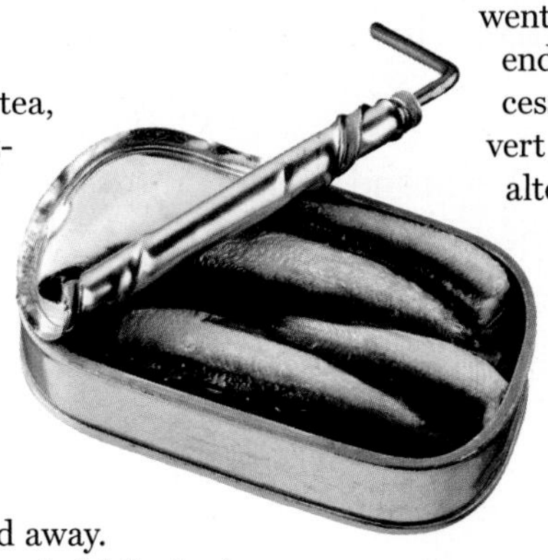

166 Salzman put down his glass and said expectantly, "You found somebody you like?"

167 "Not among these."

168 The marriage broker turned away.

169 "Here is the one I want." Leo held forth the snapshot.

170 Salzman slipped on his glasses and took the picture into his trembling hand. He turned ghastly and let out a groan.

171 "What's the matter?" cried Leo.

172 "Excuse me. Was an accident this picture. She isn't for you."

173 Salzman frantically shoved the manila packet into his portfolio. He thrust the snapshot into his pocket and fled down the stairs.

174 Leo, after momentary paralysis, gave chase and cornered the marriage broker in the vestibule. The landlady made hysterical outcries but neither of them listened.

175 "Give me back the picture, Salzman."

176 "No." The pain in his eyes was terrible.

177 "Tell me who she is then."

178 "This I can't tell you. Excuse me."

179 He made to depart, but Leo, forgetting himself, seized the matchmaker by his tight coat and shook him frenziedly.

180 "Please," sighed Salzman. "*Please.*"

181 Leo ashamedly let him go. "Tell me who she is," he begged. "It's very important for me to know."

182 "She is not for you. She is a wild one—wild, without shame. This is not a bride for a rabbi."

183 "What do you mean wild?"

184 "Like an animal. Like a dog. For her to be poor was a sin. This is why to me she is dead now."

185 "In God's name, what do you mean?"

186 "Her I can't introduce to you," Salzman cried.

187 "Why are you so excited?"

188 "Why, he asks," Salzman said, bursting into tears. "This is my baby, my Stella, she should burn in hell."

LEO hurried up to bed and hid under the covers. Under the covers he thought his life through. Although he soon fell asleep he could not sleep her out of his mind. He woke, beating his breast. Though he prayed to be rid of her, his prayers went unanswered. Through days of torment he endlessly struggled not to love her; fearing success, he escaped it. He then concluded to convert her to goodness, himself to God. The idea alternately nauseated and exalted him. 189

He perhaps did not know that he had come to a final decision until he encountered Salzman in a Broadway caferia. He was sitting alone at a rear table, sucking the bony remains of a fish. The marriage broker appeared haggard, and transparent to the point of vanishing. 190

Salzman looked up at first without recognizing him. Leo had grown a pointed beard and his eyes were weighted with wisdom. 191

"Salzman," he said, "love has at last come to my heart." 192

"Who can love from a picture?" mocked the marriage broker. 193

"It is not impossible." 194

"If you can love her, then you can love anybody. Let me show you some new clients that they just sent me their photographs. One is a little doll." 195

"Just her I want," Leo murmured. 196

"Don't be a fool, doctor. Don't bother with her." 197

"Put me in touch with her, Salzman," Leo said humbly. "Perhaps I can be of service." 198

Salzman had stopped eating and Leo understood with emotion that it was now arranged. 199

Leaving the cafeteria, he was, however, afflicted by a tormenting suspicion that Salzman had planned it all to happen this way. 200

LEO was informed by letter that she would meet him on a certain corner, and she was there one spring night, waiting under a street lamp. He appeared, carrying a small bouquet of violets and rosebuds. Stella stood by the lamppost, smoking. She wore white with red shoes, which fitted his expectations, although in a troubled moment he had imagined the dress red, and only the shoes white. She waited uneasily and shyly. From afar he saw that her eyes—clearly her father's—were filled with desperate innocence. He pictured, in her, his own redemption. Violins and lit candles revolved in the sky. Leo ran forward with flowers outthrust. 201

Around the corner, Salzman, leaning against a wall, chanted prayers for the dead. 202

FROM reading this story closely you will have noticed that you can consider the interior of a room or apartment a setting in itself. If you like this variety of setting in "The Magic Barrel," you may want to look at the interiors of "Cell One" by Chimamanda Ngozi Adichie in chapter 9 and the interior of the pickup truck in "No One's a Mystery" by Elizabeth Tallent in chapter 10.

**GOING FURTHER** Malamud is a master of detail and, in the context of our discussion in this chapter, of the creation of settings. From the inside of the small grocery store in his novel *The Assistant* to the Italy of his story-sequence *Pictures of Fidelman* to the Vermont countryside in *Dubin's Lives* and the Pacific island in *God's Grace,* his settings seem absolutely suited to the action of the novels.

# Writing from Reading

## Summarize

1 Examine Leo's reasoning for rejecting all the various women Salzman presents, then read the description of Stella at the end. Compare and contrast Stella with the ideal Salzman seems to seek at the beginning of the story.

## Analyze Craft

2 In many ways, with his "magic" barrel, Pinye Salzman seems more magician than marriage broker. Consider how Malamud constructs the setting and atmosphere of scenes in which Salzman appears to make himself seem larger than life.

## Analyze Voice

3 Consider the setting, plot, and characters of the story. How might things differ if Malamud himself weren't a Jew living in America? What details might be omitted or changed?

## Synthesize Summary and Analysis

4 Consider the various settings in the story: Leo's and Salzman's apartments, the park, the cafeteria, beneath the streetlamp. Compare and contrast Malamud's description of each. In what ways are Leo's reactions determined by his environment?

## Interpret the Story

5 At the end of the story, Leo has the suspicion he has been tricked by Salzman. Use evidence from the story to build a case for Salzman's honesty (or dishonesty). According to your conclusion, who is "the dead" that Salzman prays for at the end?

# Reading for Setting

When reading for setting, ask yourself how *time* and *place* create a series of expectations among readers for the cast of characters they're likely to encounter and the range of events likely to occur, and play a role in the overall *effect* of the story.

| | |
|---|---|
| **What *elements* of setting can you identify?** | • What is the story's location?<br>• What mood does the setting create?<br>• How is setting a window into character?<br>• How does setting shape character?<br>• Is setting a character itself?<br>• Is setting an expression of the story's theme?<br>• How is setting a window into a particular region? |
| **What is the *physical or social environment* of the setting?** | • When does the story occur (day, year, era)?<br>• Is weather a part of the setting?<br>• Is the setting a comfortable one, or is it unpleasant, even brutalizing?<br>• What are the living and working conditions?<br>• What are the social conditions in the era in which the story occurs? |

# Suggestions for Writing about Setting

1. After reading the introduction to this chapter and the stories within it, what would you add to our definition of "setting"? Use evidence from the stories to illustrate your new definition.
2. "Why I Live at the P.O." and "The Fall of the House of Usher" both feature narrators with distinctive voices. How do Welty and Poe use these voices to establish a sense of place? Give examples.
3. The main events of Lopez's story occur in the first half of the 1800s. What were the conditions for native people in Nebraska at that time? How might those conditions have influenced the relationship between Foster and the Pawnee and other tribes?
4. In Poe's "The Fall of the House of Usher" and Lopez's "The Location of the River," bodies of water take on literal and metaphoric significance. Analyze the role the Niobrara River plays in Lopez's story and the role of the tarn in Poe's.
5. All four stories challenge readers as to what they can or should believe. Write an essay in which you discuss the role of uncertainty and mystery in each story, how they affect the reading experience, and how, possibly, the setting influenced your understanding of these questions.

# 7

# Point of View

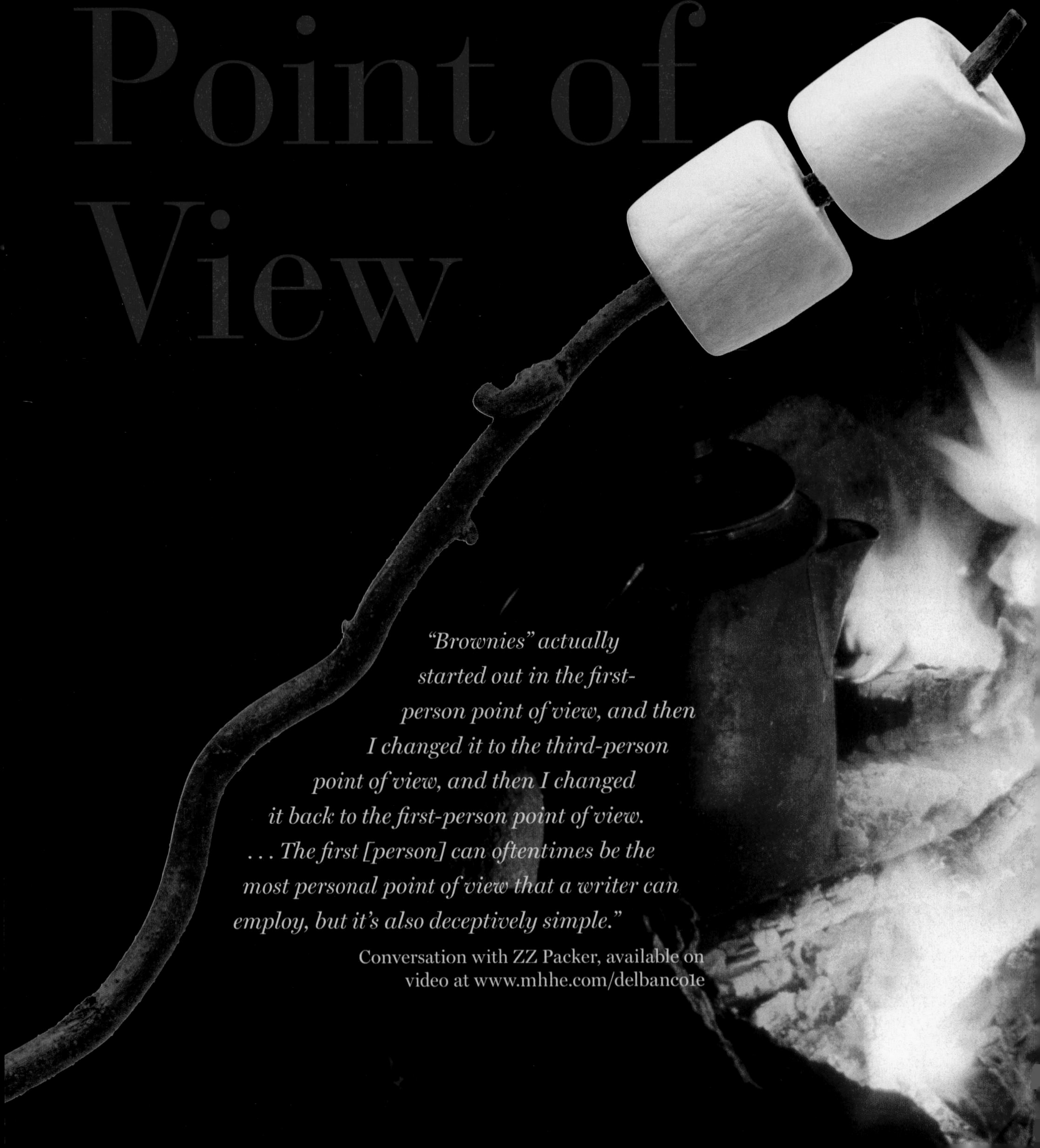

*"Brownies" actually started out in the first-person point of view, and then I changed it to the third-person point of view, and then I changed it back to the first-person point of view. . . . The first [person] can oftentimes be the most personal point of view that a writer can employ, but it's also deceptively simple."*

Conversation with ZZ Packer, available on video at www.mhhe.com/delbanco1e

"DAPHNE!" Arnetta asked. "Are you coming?"

We all looked back at the bending girl, the thin of her back hunch like the back of a custodian sweeping a stage, caught in limelight. strands of her hair were lit near-transparent, thin fiber-optic threads. She not nod yes to the question, nor did she shake her head no. She abided, be Then she began again, picking up leaves, wads of paper, the cotton fluff in from a torn stuffed toy. She did it so methodically, so exquisitely, so humb must have been trained. I thought of those dresses she wore, faded and ol so pressed and clean. I then saw the poverty in them; I then could imagin mother, cleaning the houses of others, returning home, weary.

*—from "Brownies" by ZZ*

**THE character whose thoughts are revealed in this passage is Laurel, nicknamed Snot. Laurel is the narrator, or the person who tells the story. The narrator relates events through the filter of her experiences, and it is from her point of view, or perspective, that the reader views the action. As Laurel reflects on Daphne, "the bending girl," she comes to a new understanding of the nature of Daphne's life. As the Brownie troop waits for a response to Arnetta's query—"Are you coming?"—Laurel looks closely at Daphne's movements and clothing and slowly recognizes that the "bending girl" is poor.**

## NARRATOR AND POINT OF VIEW

When the writer of an autobiography or memoir uses the first-person pronoun *I*, we're entitled to believe that *I* means the person writing the memoir. However, in fiction the narrator of a story is not the same as the writer. Writers create narrators to bring a story to life, and they provide a **point of view** by which to tell the tale. The writer's choice of narrator and point of view determines a great deal about what readers learn and when and how they learn it. Sometimes, as in the case of "Brownies," the story is told by means of a **first-person narrator,** a character in the story identified by use of the pronoun *I* or the plural first-person *we.* In contrast, many stories and novels use a **third-person narrator,** as in Hemingway's story in this chapter, "The Short Happy Life of Francis Macomber," in which the narrator refers to all the characters in the story with the pronouns *he, she,* or *they.* A third option, used less commonly, is for a story to be told via a **second-person narrator,** who addresses the reader directly (you), as is done in the story by Lorrie Moore in this chapter.

*CONTINUED ON PAGE 195*

*. . . I put it in third person so that I could see some of my blind spots.*

# Q&A

*. . . there's almost . . . no better way to be a part of the world than to read.*

# *A Conversation on Writing*

## ZZ Packer

### Using Point of View to Craft "Brownies"

I found it very good to begin with that [first-person] voice because I felt as though I could just tell the story the way I thought that Laurel/Snot would. . . . And then I put it in third person so that I could see some of my blind spots. . . . This particular third person could see some things about the rest of the world but might not have access to everything that Laurel had access to. So then that allowed me to see beyond Laurel's point of view. So switching the point of view for me enabled me to get the voice, which I wanted, which was the first-person voice, but also to get the knowledge and range of information that sometimes authors can only get when they travel into the third-person point of view.

### The Power of the First-Person Point of View

I like to think of first person [as] here's the "I" that's telling the story. . . . A lot of writers tend to believe that, Oh, it's really me telling the story and so sometimes they just pour everything in . . . [but] they don't realize that the voice, which can be confessional . . . is a storytelling voice, [a storytelling voice that] can easily get out of the writer's grasp because it's so powerful.

### Reading to Be a Citizen of the World

I encounter people who don't like to read. I mean to me it doesn't seem to be taking away from your time in the world, but just enriching it. When you read *War and Peace,* it's almost like having lived an extra ten years or something like that. So to me . . . there's almost . . . no better way to be a part of the world than to read. It almost seems the opposite of the way people think of it as a very solitary and even sort of solipsistic kind of activity. But I can't think of any other that would make me more of a citizen of the world.

ZZ Packer was born (1973) Zuwena Packer in Chicago. As she grew up in Atlanta and Louisville, her friends and family shortened Zuwena—Swahili for "good"—to ZZ, the name that she uses today. While attending Yale, Packer considered a career in engineering but ultimately turned to writing. Her debut short story collection, *Drinking Coffee Elsewhere* (2003), received great critical and popular acclaim; named a *New York Times* Notable Book, it was also picked for the *Today Show* Book Club by John Updike. In addition to appearing in *The New Yorker, Harper's,* and *Ploughshares,* her work has been anthologized in collections featuring young writers, southern writers, and black women writers, among others. Her stories present a range of characters, most of whom struggle to fit into their community, and she often captures aspects of the African-American experience. Like her varied characters, Packer herself has a résumé that includes stints as a barmaid, a high school teacher, and a coffee shop barista as well as a Stegner Fellow at Stanford University's prestigious writing program. Packer currently lives and writes in San Francisco.

**To watch this entire interview and hear the author read from "Brownies," go to www. mhhe .com/delbanco1e.**

**RESEARCH ASSIGNMENT** In her interview, what does ZZ Packer say she is trying to tell a story about? Do you agree this is the subject of the story? How does she get her point across?

**AS YOU READ** As you read this story, notice the shifting levels of happiness and unhappiness among the characters. Notice also the shifting alliances among the characters at the center of the story.

**TIP** **FOR INTERACTIVE READING . . .** As you read, take note every time the story refers to a father. What is the significance of the various fathers mentioned? How does this tie in with the lesson the girls experience at camp?

# Brownies (1999)

1 BY our second day at Camp Crescendo, the girls in my Brownie troop had decided to kick the asses of each and every girl in Brownie Troop 909. Troop 909 was doomed from the first day of camp; they were white girls, their complexions a blend of ice cream: strawberry, vanilla. They turtled out from their bus in pairs, their rolled-up sleeping bags chromatized with Disney characters: Sleeping Beauty, Snow White, Mickey Mouse; or the generic ones cheap parents bought: washed-out rainbows, unicorns, curly-eyelashed frogs. Some clutched Igloo coolers and still others held on to stuffed toys like pacifiers, looking all around them like tourists determined to be dazzled.

2 Our troop was wending its way past their bus, past the ranger station, past the colorful trail guide drawn like a treasure map, locked behind glass.

3 "Man, did you smell them?" Arnetta said, giving the girls a slow once-over, "They smell like Chihuahuas. *Wet* Chihuahuas." Their troop was still at the entrance, and though we had passed them by yards, Arnetta raised her nose in the air and grimaced.

4 Arnetta said this from the very rear of the line, far away from Mrs. Margolin, who always strung our troop behind her like a brood of obedient ducklings. Mrs. Margolin even looked like a mother duck—she had hair cropped close to a small ball of a head, almost no neck, and huge, miraculous breasts. She wore enormous belts that looked like the kind that weightlifters wear, except hers would be cheap metallic gold or rabbit fur or covered with gigantic fake sunflowers, and often these belts would become nature lessons in and of themselves. "See," Mrs. Margolin once said to us, pointing to her belt, "this one's made entirely from the feathers of baby pigeons."

The belt layered with feathers 5
was uncanny enough, but I was more disturbed by the realization that I had never actually *seen* a baby pigeon. I searched weeks for one, in vain—scampering after pigeons whenever I was downtown with my father.

But nature lessons were not Mrs. Margolin's top 6
priority. She saw the position of troop leader as an evangelical post. Back at the A.M.E. church where our Brownie meetings were held, Mrs. Margolin was especially fond of imparting religious aphorisms by means of acrostics—"Satan" was the "Serpent Always Tempting and Noisome"; she'd refer to the "Bible" as "Basic Instructions Before Leaving Earth." Whenever she quizzed us on these, expecting to hear the acrostics parroted back to her, only Arnetta's correct replies soared over our vague mumblings. "Jesus?" Mrs. Margolin might ask expectantly, and Arnetta alone would dutifully answer, "Jehovah's Example, Saving Us Sinners."

Arnetta always made a point of listening to Mrs. 7
Margolin's religious talk and giving her what she wanted to hear. Because of this, Arnetta could have blared through a megaphone that the white girls of

Troop 909 were "wet Chihuahuas" without so much as a blink from Mrs. Margolin. Once, Arnetta killed the troop goldfish by feeding it a french fry covered in ketchup, and when Mrs. Margolin demanded that she explain what had happened, claimed the goldfish had been eyeing her meal for *hours,* then the fish—giving in to temptation—had leapt up and snatched a whole golden fry from her fingertips.

8 "*Serious* Chihuahua," Octavia added, and though neither Arnetta nor Octavia could *spell* "Chihuahua," had ever *seen* a Chihuahua, trisyllabic words had gained a sort of exoticism within our fourth-grade set at Woodrow Wilson Elementary. Arnetta and Octavia would flip through the dictionary, determined to work the vulgar-sounding ones like "Djibouti" and "asinine" into conversation.

9 "*Caucasian* Chihuahuas," Arnetta said.

10 That did it. The girls in my troop turned elastic: Drema and Elise doubled up on one another like inextricably entwined kites; Octavia slapped her belly; Janice jumped straight up in the air, then did it again, as if to slam-dunk her own head. They could not stop laughing. No one had laughed so hard since a boy named Martez had stuck a pencil in the electric socket and spent the whole day with a strange grin on his face.

The word took off from there, and soon everything was Caucasian.

11 "Girls, girls," said our parent helper, Mrs. Hedy. Mrs. Hedy was Octavia's mother, and she wagged her index finger perfunctorily, like a windshield wiper. "Stop it, now. Be good." She said this loud enough to be heard, but lazily, bereft of any feeling or indication that she meant to be obeyed, as though she could say these words again at the exact same pitch if a button somewhere on her were pressed.

12 But the rest of the girls didn't stop; they only laughed louder. It was the word "Caucasian" that got them all going. One day at school, about a month before the Brownie camping trip, Arnetta turned to a boy wearing impossibly high-ankled floodwater jeans and said, "What are you? *Caucasian?*" The word took off from there, and soon everything was Caucasian. If you ate too fast you ate like a Caucasian, if you ate too slow you ate like a Caucasian. The biggest feat anyone at Woodrow Wilson could do was to jump off the swing in midair, at the highest point in its arc, and if you fell (as I had, more than once) instead of landing on your feet, knees bent Olympic gymnast–style, Arnetta and Octavia were prepared to comment. They'd look at each other with the silence of passengers who'd narrowly escaped an accident, then nod their heads, whispering with solemn horror, "*Caucasian.*"

Even the only white kid in our school, Dennis, got in on the Caucasian act. That time when Martez stuck a pencil in the socket, Dennis had pointed and yelled, "That was *so* Caucasian!" 13

WHEN you lived in the south suburbs of Atlanta, it was easy to forget about whites. Whites were like those baby pigeons: real and existing, but rarely seen or thought about. Everyone had been to Rich's to go clothes shopping, everyone had seen white girls and their mothers coo-cooing over dresses; everyone had gone to the downtown library and seen white businessmen swish by importantly, wrists flexed in front of them to check the time as though they would change from Clark Kent into Superman at any second. But those images were as fleeting as cards shuffled in a deck, whereas the ten white girls behind us—*invaders,* Arnetta would later call them—were instantly real and memorable, with their long, shampoo-commercial hair, straight as spaghetti from the box. This alone was reason for envy and hatred. The only black girl most of us had ever seen with hair that long was Octavia, whose hair hung past her butt like a Hawaiian hula dancer's. The sight of Octavia's mane prompted other girls to listen to her reverentially, as though whatever she had to say would somehow activate their own follicles. For example, when, on the first day of camp, Octavia made as if to speak, and everyone fell silent. "Nobody," Octavia said, "calls us niggers." 14

At the end of that first day, when half of our troop made their way back to the cabin after tag-team restroom visits, Arnetta said she'd heard one of the Troop 909 girls call Daphne a nigger. The other half of the girls and I were helping Mrs. Margolin clean up the pots and pans from the campfire ravioli dinner. When we made our way to the restrooms to wash up and brush our teeth, we met up with Arnetta midway. 15

"Man, I completely heard the girl," Arnetta reported. "Right, Daphne?" 16

Daphne hardly ever spoke, but when she did, her voice was petite and tinkly, the voice one might expect from a shiny new earring. She'd written a poem once, for Langston Hughes Day, a poem brimming with all the teacher-winning ingredients—trees and oceans, sunsets and moons—but what cinched the poem for 17 the grown-ups, snatching the win from Octavia's musical ode to Grandmaster Flash and the Furious Five, were Daphne's last lines:

> You are my father, the veteran
> When you cry in the dark
> It rains and rains and rains in my heart

18 She'd always worn clean, though faded, jumpers and dresses when Chic jeans were the fashion, but when she went up to the dais to receive her prize journal, pages trimmed in gold, she wore a new dress with a velveteen bodice and a taffeta skirt as wide as an umbrella. All the kids clapped, though none of them understood the poem. I'd read encyclopedias the way others read comics, and I didn't get it. But those last lines pricked me, they were so eerie, and as my father and I ate cereal, I'd whisper over my Froot Loops, like a mantra, "*You are my father, the veteran. You are my father, the veteran, the veteran, the veteran,*" until my father, who acted in plays as Caliban and Othello and was not a veteran, marched me up to my teacher one morning and said, "Can you tell me what's wrong with this kid?"

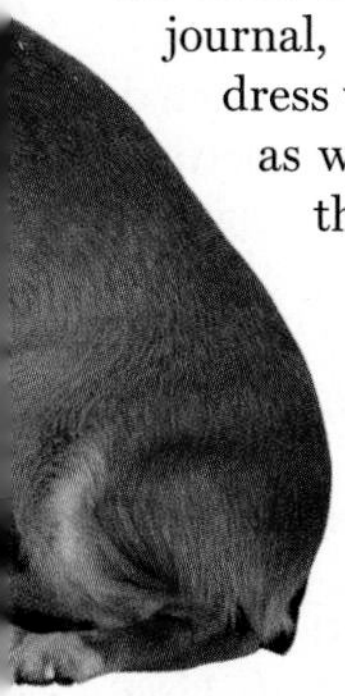

19 I thought Daphne and I might become friends, but I think she grew spooked by me whispering those lines to her, begging her to tell me what they meant, and I soon understood that two quiet people like us were better off quiet alone.

20 "Daphne? Didn't you hear them call you a nigger?" Arnetta asked, giving Daphne a nudge.

21 The sun was setting behind the trees, and their leafy tops formed a canopy of black lace for the flame of the sun to pass through. Daphne shrugged her shoulders at first, then slowly nodded her head when Arnetta gave her a hard look.

22 Twenty minutes later, when my restroom group returned to the cabin, Arnetta was still talking about Troop 909. My restroom group had passed by some of the 909 girls. For the most part, they deferred to us, waving us into the restrooms, letting us go even though they'd gotten there first.

23 We'd seen them, but from afar, never within their orbit enough to see whether their faces were the way all white girls appeared on TV—ponytailed and full of energy, bubbling over with love and money. All I could see was that some of them rapidly fanned their faces with their hands, though the heat of the day had long passed. A few seemed to be lolling their heads in slow circles, half purposefully, as if exercising the muscles of their necks, half ecstatically, like Stevie Wonder.

"We can't let them get away with that," Arnetta said, dropping her voice to a laryngitic whisper. "We can't let them get away with calling us niggers. I say we teach them a lesson." She sat down cross-legged on a sleeping bag, an embittered Buddha, eyes glimmering acrylic-black. "We can't go telling Mrs. Margolin, either. Mrs. Margolin'll say something about doing unto others and the path of righteousness and all. Forget that shit." She let her eyes flutter irreverently till they half closed, as though ignoring an insult not worth returning. We could all hear Mrs. Margolin outside, gathering the last of the metal campware. 24

Nobody said anything for a while. Usually people were quiet after Arnetta spoke. Her tone had an upholstered confidence that was somehow both regal and vulgar at once. It demanded a few moments of silence in its wake, like the ringing of a church bell or the playing of taps. Sometimes Octavia would ditto or dissent to whatever Arnetta had said, and this was the signal that others could speak. But this time Octavia just swirled a long cord of hair into pretzel shapes. 25

"*Well?*" Arnetta said. She looked as if she had discerned the hidden severity of the situation and was waiting for the rest of us to catch up. Everyone looked from Arnetta to Daphne. It was, after all, Daphne who had supposedly been called the name, but Daphne sat on the bare cabin floor, flipping through the pages of the Girl Scout handbook, eyebrows arched in mock wonder, as if the handbook were a catalogue full of bright and startling foreign costumes. Janice broke the silence. She clapped her hands to broach her idea of a plan. 26

"They gone be sleeping," she whispered conspiratorially, "then we gone sneak into they cabin, then we'll put daddy longlegs in they sleeping bags. Then they'll wake up. Then we gone beat 'em up till they're as flat as frying pans!" She jammed her fist into the palm of her hand, then made a sizzling sound. 27

Janice's country accent was laughable, her looks homely, her jumpy acrobatics embarrassing to behold. Arnetta and Octavia volleyed amused, arrogant smiles whenever Janice opened her mouth, but Janice never caught the hint, spoke whenever she wanted, fluttered around Arnetta and Octavia futilely offering her opinions to their departing backs. Whenever Arnetta and Octavia shooed her away, Janice loitered until the two would finally sigh and ask, "What *is* it, Miss Caucausoid? What do you *want*?" 28

"Shut up, Janice," Octavia said, letting a fingered loop of hair fall to her waist as though just the sound of Janice's voice had ruined the fun of her hair twisting. 29

Janice obeyed, her mouth hung open in a loose grin, unflappable, unhurt. 30

31 "All right," Arnetta said, standing up. "We're going to have a secret meeting and talk about what we're going to do."

32 Everyone gravely nodded her head. The word "secret" had a built-in importance, the modifier form of the word carried more clout than the noun. A secret meant nothing; it was like gossip: just a bit of unpleasant knowledge about someone who happened to be someone other than yourself. A secret *meeting*, or a secret *club* was entirely different.

A secret meant nothing; it was like gossip . . .

33 That was when Arnetta turned to me as though she knew that doing so was both a compliment and a charity.

34 "Snot, you're not going to be a bitch and tell Mrs. Margolin, are you?"

35 I had been called "Snot" ever since first grade, when I'd sneezed in class and two long ropes of mucus had splattered a nearby girl.

36 "Hey," I said. "Maybe you didn't hear them right—I mean—"

37 "Are you gonna tell on us or not?" was all Arnetta wanted to know, and by the time the question was asked, the rest of our Brownie troop looked at me as though they'd already decided their course of action, me being the only impediment.

38 CAMP Crescendo used to double as a high-school-band and field hockey camp until an arcing field hockey ball landed on the clasp of a girl's metal barrette, knifing a skull nerve and paralyzing the right side of her body. The camp closed down for a few years and the girl's teammates built a memorial, filling the spot on which the girl fell with hockey balls, on which they had painted—all in nail polish—get-well tidings, flowers, and hearts. The balls were still stacked there, like a shrine of ostrich eggs embedded in the ground.

39 On the second day of camp, Troop 909 was dancing around the mound of hockey balls, their limbs jangling awkwardly, their cries like the constant summer squeal of an amusement park. There was a stream that bordered the field hockey lawn, and the girls from my troop settled next to it, scarfing down the last of lunch: sandwiches made from salami and slices of tomato that had gotten waterlogged from the melting ice in the cooler. From the stream bank, Arnetta eyed the Troop 909 girls, scrutinizing their movements to glean inspiration for battle.

40 "Man," Arnetta said, "we could bumrush them right now if that damn lady would *leave*."

41 The 909 troop leader was a white woman with the severe pageboy hairdo of an ancient Egyptian. She lay on a picnic blanket, sphinx-like, eating a banana, sometimes holding it out in front of her like a microphone. Beside her sat a girl slowly flapping one hand like a bird with a broken wing. Occasionally, the leader would call out the names of girls who'd attempted leapfrogs and flips, or of girls who yelled too loudly or strayed far from the circle.

"I'm just glad Big Fat Mama's not following us here," Octavia said. "At least we don't have to worry about her." Mrs. Margolin, Octavia assured us, was having her Afternoon Devotional, shrouded in mosquito netting, in a clearing she'd found. Mrs. Hedy was cleaning mud from her espadrilles in the cabin. 42

"I handled them." Arnetta sucked on her teeth and proudly grinned. "I told her we was going to gather leaves." 43

"Gather leaves," Octavia said, nodding respectfully. "That's a good one. Especially since they're so mad-crazy about this camping thing." She looked from ground to sky, sky to ground. Her hair hung down her back in two braids like a squaw's. "I mean, I really don't know why it's called *camping*—all we ever do with Nature is find some twigs and say something like, 'Wow, this fell from a tree.'" She then studied her sandwich. With two disdainful fingers, she picked out a slice of dripping tomato, the sections congealed with red slime. She pitched it into the stream embrowned with dead leaves and the murky effigies of other dead things, but in the opaque water, a group of small silver-brown fish appeared. They surrounded the tomato and nibbled. 44

"Look!" Janice cried. "Fishes! Fishes!" As she scrambled to the edge of the stream to watch, a covey of insects threw up tantrums from the wheatgrass and nettle, a throng of tiny electric machines, all going at once. Octavia sneaked up behind Janice as if to push her in. Daphne and I exchanged terrified looks. It seemed as though only we knew that Octavia was close enough—and bold enough—to actually push Janice into the stream. Janice turned around quickly, but Octavia was already staring serenely into the still water as though she was gathering some sort of courage from it. "What's so funny?" Janice said, eyeing them all suspiciously. 45

Elise began humming the tune to "Karma Chameleon," all the girls joining in, their hums light and facile. Janice also began to hum, against everyone else, the high-octane opening chords of "Beat It." 46

"I love me some Michael Jackson," Janice said when she'd finished humming, smacking her lips as though Michael Jackson were a favorite meal. "I *will* marry Michael Jackson." 47

8 Before anyone had a chance to impress upon Janice the impossibility of this, Arnetta suddenly rose, made a sun visor of her hand, and watched Troop 909 leave the field hockey lawn.

9 "Dammit!" she said. "We've got to get them *alone.*"

0 "They won't ever be alone," I said. All the rest of the girls looked at me, for I usually kept quiet. If I spoke even a word, I could count on someone calling me Snot. Everyone seemed to think that we could beat up these girls; no one entertained the thought that they might fight *back*. "The only time they'll be unsupervised is in the bathroom."

1 "Oh shut up, Snot," Octavia said.

2 But Arnetta slowly nodded her head. "The bathroom," she said. "The bathroom," she said, again and again. "The bathroom! The bathroom!"

3 ACCORDING to Octavia's watch, it took us five minutes to hike to the restrooms, which were midway between our cabin and Troop 909's. Inside, the mirrors above the sinks returned only the vaguest of reflections, as though someone had taken a scouring pad to their surfaces to obscure the shine. Pine needles, leaves, and dirty, flattened wads of chewing gum covered the floor like a mosaic. Webs of hair matted the drain in the middle of the floor. Above the sinks and below the mirrors, stacks of folded white paper towels lay on a long metal counter. Shaggy white balls of paper towels sat on the sinktops in a line like corsages on display. A thread of floss snaked from a wad of tissues dotted with the faint red-pink of blood. One of those white girls, I thought, had just lost a tooth.

Pine needles, leaves, and dirty, flattened wads of chewing gum covered the floor like a mosaic.

4 Though the restroom looked almost the same as it had the night before, it somehow seemed stranger now. We hadn't noticed the wooden rafters coming together in great V's. We were, it seemed, inside a whale, viewing the ribs of the roof of its mouth.

5 "Wow. It's a mess," Elise said.

6 "You can say that again."

7 Arnetta leaned against the doorjamb of a restroom stall. "This is where they'll be again," she said. Just seeing the place, just having a plan seemed to satisfy her. "We'll go in and talk to them. You know, 'How you doing? How long'll you be here?' That sort of thing. Then Octavia and I are gonna tell them what happens when they call any one of us a nigger."

8 "I'm going to say something, too," Janice said.

9 Arnetta considered this. "Sure," she said. "Of course. Whatever you want."

Janice pointed her finger like a gun at Octavia and rehearsed the line she'd thought up, "'We're gonna teach you a *lesson*!' That's what I'm going to say." She narrowed her eyes like a TV mobster. "'We're gonna teach you little girls a lesson!'" 60

With the back of her hand, Octavia brushed Janice's finger away. "You couldn't teach me to shit in a toilet." 61

"But," I said, "what if they say, 'We didn't say that. We didn't call anyone an N-I-G-G-E-R.'" 62

"Snot," Arnetta said, and then sighed. "Don't think. Just fight. If you even know how." 63

Everyone laughed except Daphne. Arnetta gently laid her hand on Daphne's shoulder. "Daphne. You don't have to fight. We're doing this for you." 64

Daphne walked to the counter, took a clean paper towel, and carefully unfolded it like a map. With it, she began to pick up the trash all around. Everyone watched. 65

"C'mon," Arnetta said to everyone. "Let's beat it." We all ambled toward the doorway, where the sunshine made one large white rectangle of light. We were immediately blinded, and we shielded our eyes with our hands and our forearms. 66

"Daphne?" Arnetta asked. "Are you coming?" 67

We all looked back at the bending girl, the thin of her back hunched like the back of a custodian sweeping a stage, caught in limelight. Stray strands of her hair were lit near-transparent, thin fiber-optic threads. She did not nod yes to the question, nor did she shake her head no. She abided, bent. Then she began again, picking up leaves, wads of paper, the cotton fluff innards from a torn stuffed toy. She did it so methodically, so exquisitely, so humbly, she must have been trained. I thought of those dresses she wore, faded and old, yet so pressed and clean. I then saw the poverty in them; I then could imagine her mother, cleaning the houses of others, returning home, weary. 68

"I guess she's not coming." 69

We left her and headed back to our cabin, over pine needles and leaves, taking the path full of shade. 70

"What about our secret meeting?" Elise asked. 71

Arnetta enunciated her words in a way that defied contradiction: "We just had it." 72

IT was nearing our bedtime, but the sun had not yet set. 73

"Hey, your mama's coming," Arnetta said to Octavia when she saw Mrs. Hedy walk toward the 74 cabin, sniffling. When Octavia's mother wasn't giving bored, parochial orders, she sniffled continuously, mourning an imminent divorce from her husband. She might begin a sentence, "I don't know what Robert will do when Octavia and I are gone. Who'll buy him cigarettes?" and Octavia would hotly whisper, "*Mama,*" in a way that meant: Please don't talk about our problems in front of everyone. Please shut up.

75 But when Mrs. Hedy began talking about her husband, thinking about her husband, seeing clouds shaped like the head of her husband, she couldn't be quiet, and no one could dislodge her from the comfort of her own woe. Only one thing could perk her up—Brownie songs. If the girls were quiet, and Mrs. Hedy was in her dopey, sorrowful mood, she would say, "Y'all know I like those songs, girls. Why don't you sing one?" Everyone would groan, except me and Daphne. I, for one, liked some of the songs.

76 "C'mon, everybody," Octavia said drearily. "She likes the Brownie song best."

77 We sang, loud enough to reach Mrs. Hedy:

> "I've got something in my pocket;
> It belongs across my face.
> And I keep it very close at hand
>   in a most convenient place.
> I'm sure you couldn't guess it
> If you guessed a long, long while.
> So I'll take it out and put it on—
> It's a great big Brownie smile!"

78 The Brownie song was supposed to be sung cheerfully, as though we were elves in a workshop, singing as we merrily cobbled shoes, but everyone except me hated the song so much that they sang it like a maudlin record, played on the most sluggish of rpms.

79 "That was good," Mrs. Hedy said, closing the cabin door behind her. "Wasn't that nice, Linda?"

80 "Praise God," Mrs. Margolin answered without raising her head from the chore of counting out Popsicle sticks for the next day's craft session.

81 "Sing another one," Mrs. Hedy said. She said it with a sort of joyful aggression, like a drunk I'd once seen who'd refused to leave a Korean grocery.

82 "God, Mama, get over it," Octavia whispered in a voice meant only for Arnetta, but Mrs. Hedy heard it and started to leave the cabin.

83 "Don't go," Arnetta said. She ran after Mrs. Hedy and held her by the arm. "We haven't finished singing." She nudged us with a single look. "Let's sing the 'Friends Song.' For Mrs. Hedy."

84 Although I liked some of the songs, I hated this one:

> Make new friends
> But keep the o-old,
> One is silver
> And the other gold.

If most of the girls in the troop could be any type of metal, they'd be bunched-up wads of tinfoil, maybe, or rusty iron nails you had to get tetanus shots for. 85

"No, no, no," Mrs. Margolin said before anyone could start in on the "Friends Song." "An uplifting song. Something to lift her up and take her mind off all these earthly burdens." 86

Arnetta and Octavia rolled their eyes. Everyone knew what song Mrs. Margolin was talking about, and no one, no one, wanted to sing it. 87

"Please, no," a voice called out. "Not 'The Doughnut Song.'" 88

"Please not 'The Doughnut Song,'" Octavia pleaded. 89

"I'll brush my teeth two times if I don't have to sing 'The Doughnut—'" 90

"Sing!" Mrs. Margolin demanded. 91

We sang: 92

> "Life without Jesus is like a do-ough-nut!
> Like a do-ooough-nut!
> Like a do-ooough-nut!
> Life without Jesus is like a do-ough-nut!
> There's a hole in the middle of my soul!"

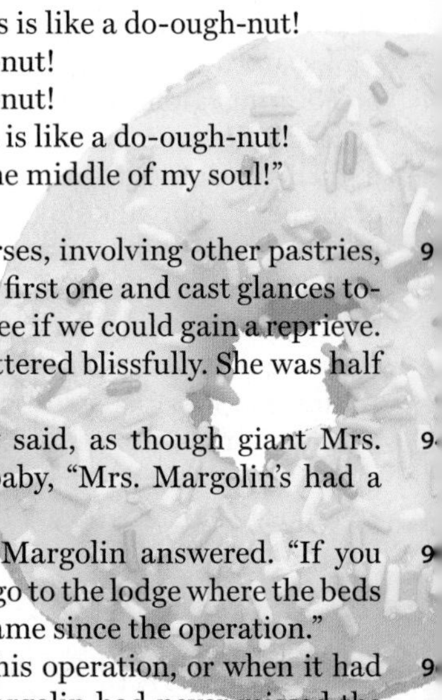

There were other verses, involving other pastries, but we stopped after the first one and cast glances toward Mrs. Margolin to see if we could gain a reprieve. Mrs. Margolin's eyes fluttered blissfully. She was half asleep. 93

"Awww," Mrs. Hedy said, as though giant Mrs. Margolin were a cute baby, "Mrs. Margolin's had a long day." 94

"Yes, indeed," Mrs. Margolin answered. "If you don't mind, I might just go to the lodge where the beds are. I haven't been the same since the operation." 95

I had not heard of this operation, or when it had occurred, since Mrs. Margolin had never missed the once-a-week Brownie meetings, but I could see from Daphne's face that she was concerned, and I could see that the other girls had decided that Mrs. Margolin's operation must have happened long ago in some remote time unconnected to our own. Nevertheless, they put on sad faces. We had all been taught that adulthood was full of sorrow and pain, taxes and bills, dreaded work and dealings with whites, sickness and death. I tried to do what the others did. I tried to look silent. 96

97 "Go right ahead, Linda," Mrs. Hedy said. "I'll watch the girls." Mrs. Hedy seemed to forget about divorce for a moment; she looked at us with dewy eyes, as if we were mysterious, furry creatures. Meanwhile, Mrs. Margolin walked through the maze of sleeping bags until she found her own. She gathered a neat stack of clothes and pajamas slowly, as though doing so was almost painful. She took her toothbrush, her toothpaste, her pillow. "All right!" Mrs. Margolin said, addressing us all from the threshold of the cabin. "Be in bed by nine." She said it with a twinkle in her voice, letting us know she was allowing us to be naughty and stay up till nine-fifteen.

98 "C'mon everybody," Arnetta said after Mrs. Margolin left. "Time for us to wash up."

99 Everyone watched Mrs. Hedy closely, wondering whether she would insist on coming with us since it was night, making a fight with Troop 909 nearly impossible. Troop 909 would soon be in the bathroom, washing their faces, brushing their teeth—completely unsuspecting of our ambush.

00 "We won't be long," Arnetta said. "We're old enough to go to the restrooms by ourselves."

01 Mrs. Hedy pursed her lips at this dilemma. "Well, I guess you Brownies are almost Girl Scouts, right?"

02 "Right!"

03 "Just one more badge," Drema said.

04 "And about," Octavia droned, "a million more cookies to sell." Octavia looked at all of us, *Now's our chance,* her face seemed to say, but our chance to do *what,* I didn't exactly know.

05 Finally, Mrs. Hedy walked to the doorway where Octavia stood dutifully waiting to say goodbye but looking bored doing it. Mrs. Hedy held Octavia's chin. "You'll be good?"

06 "Yes, Mama."

07 "And remember to pray for me and your father? If I'm asleep when you get back?"

08 "Yes, Mama."

09 WHEN the other girls had finished getting their toothbrushes and washcloths and flashlights for the group restroom trip, I was drawing pictures of tiny birds with too many feathers. Daphne was sitting on her sleeping bag, reading.

10 "You're not going to come?" Octavia asked.

11 Daphne shook her head.

12 "I'm gonna stay, too," I said. "I'll go to the restroom when Daphne and Mrs. Hedy go."

13 Arnetta leaned down toward me and whispered so that Mrs. Hedy, who'd taken over Mrs. Margolin's task of counting Popsicle sticks, couldn't hear. "No, Snot. If we get in trouble, you're going to get in trouble with the rest of us."

WE made our way through the darkness by flashlight. The tree branches that had shaded us just hours earlier, along the same path, now looked like arms sprouting menacing hands. The stars sprinkled the sky like spilled salt. They seemed fastened to the darkness, high up and holy, their places fixed and definite as we stirred beneath them. 114

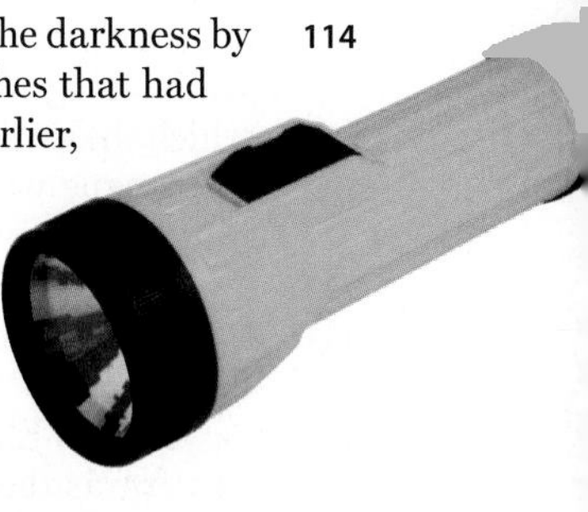

Some, like me, were quiet because we were afraid of the dark; others were talking like crazy for the same reason. 115

"Wow!" Drema said, looking up. "Why are all the stars out here? I never see stars back on Oneida Street." 116

"It' a camping trip, that's why," Octavia said. "You're supposed to see stars on camping trips." 117

Janice said, "This place smells like my mother's air freshener." 118

"These woods are *pine,*" Elise said. "Your mother probably uses *pine* air freshener." 119

Janice mouthed an exaggerated "Oh," nodding her head as though she just then understood one of the world's great secrets. 120

No one talked about fighting. Everyone was afraid enough just walking through the infinite deep of the woods. Even though I didn't fight to fight, was afraid of fighting, I felt I was part of the rest of the troop; like I was defending something. We trudged against the slight incline of the path, Arnetta leading the way. 121

"You know," I said, "their leader will be there. Or they won't even be there. It's dark already. Last night the sun was still in the sky. I'm sure they're already finished." 122

Arnetta acted as if she hadn't heard me. I followed her gaze with my flashlight, and that's when I saw the squares of light in the darkness. The bathroom was just ahead. 123

BUT the girls were there. We could hear them before we could see them. 124

"Octavia and I will go in first so they'll think there's just two of us, then wait till I say, 'We're gonna teach you a lesson,'" Arnetta said. "Then, bust in. That'll surprise them." 125

"That's what I was supposed to say," Janice said. 126

Arnetta went inside, Octavia next to her. Janice followed, and the rest of us waited outside. 127

They were in there for what seemed like whole minutes, but something was wrong. Arnetta hadn't 128 given the signal yet. I was with the girls outside when I heard one of the Troop 909 girls say, "NO. That did NOT happen!"

129 That was to be expected, that they'd deny the whole thing. What I hadn't expected was *the voice* in which the denial was said. The girl sounded as though her tongue was caught in her mouth. "That's a BAD word!" the girl continued. "We don't say BAD words!"

130 "Let's go in," Elise said.

131 "No," Drema said, "I don't want to. What if we get beat up?"

132 "Snot?" Elise turned to me, her flashlight blinding. It was the first time anyone had asked my opinion, though I knew they were just asking because they were afraid.

133 "I say we go inside, just to see what's going on."

134 "But Arnetta didn't give us the signal," Drema said. "She's supposed to say, 'We're gonna teach you a lesson,' and I didn't hear her say it."

135 "C'mon," I said. "Let's just go in."

136 We went inside. There we found the white girls—about five girls huddled up next to one big girl. I instantly knew she was the owner of the voice we'd heard. Arnetta and Octavia inched toward us as soon as we entered.

137 "Where's Janice?" Elise asked, then we heard a flush. "Oh."

138 "I think," Octavia said, whispering to Elise, "they're retarded."

139 "We ARE NOT retarded!" the big girl said, though it was obvious that she was. That they all were. The girls around her began to whimper.

140 "They're just pretending," Arnetta said, trying to convince herself. "I know they are."

141 Octavia turned to Arnetta. "Arnetta. Let's just leave."

142 Janice came out of a stall, happy and relieved, then she suddenly remembered her line, pointed to the big girl, and said, "We're gonna teach you a lesson."

143 "Shut up, Janice," Octavia said, but her heart was not in it. Arnetta's face was set in a lost, deep scowl. Octavia turned to the big girl and said loudly, slowly, as if they were all deaf, "We're going to leave. It was nice meeting you, O.K.? You don't have to tell anyone that we were here. O.K.?"

144 "Why not?" said the big girl, like a taunt. When she spoke, her lips did not meet, her mouth did not close. Her tongue grazed the roof of her mouth, like a little pink fish. "You'll get in trouble. I know. *I* know."

145 Arnetta got back her old cunning. "If you said anything, then you'd be a tattletale."

146 The girl looked sad for a moment, then perked up quickly. A flash of genius crossed her face. "I *like* tattletale."

IT'S all right, girls. It's gonna be all right!" the 909 troop leader said. All of Troop 909 burst into tears. It was as though someone had instructed them all to cry at once. The troop leader had girls under her arm, and all the rest of the girls crowded about her. It reminded me of a hog I'd seen on a field trip, where all the little hogs gathered about the mother at feeding time, latching onto her teats. The 909 troop leader had come into the bathroom, shortly after the big girl had threatened to tell. Then the ranger came, then, once the ranger had radioed the station, Mrs. Margolin arrived with Daphne in tow. 147

The ranger had left the restroom area, but everyone else was huddled just outside, swatting mosquitoes. 148

"Oh. They *will* apologize," Mrs. Margolin said to the 909 troop leader, but she said this so angrily, I knew she was speaking more to us than to the other troop leader. "When their parents find out, every one a them will be on punishment." 149

"It's all right, it's all right," the 909 troop leader reassured Mrs. Margolin. Her voice lilted in the same way it had when addressing the girls. She smiled the whole time she talked. She was like one of those TV-cooking-show women who talk and dice onions and smile all at the same time. 150

"See. It could have happened. I'm not calling your girls fibbers or anything." She shook her head ferociously from side to side, her Egyptian-style pageboy flapping against her cheeks like heavy drapes. "It *could* have happened. See. Our girls are *not* retarded. They are *delayed* learners." She said this in a syrupy instructional voice, as though our troop might be delayed learners as well. "We're from the Decatur Children's Academy. Many of them just have special needs." 151

"Now we won't be able to walk to the bathroom by ourselves!" the big girl said. 152

"Yes you will," the troop leader said, "but maybe we'll wait till we get back to Decatur—" 153

"I don't want to wait!" the girl said. "I want my Independence badge!" 154

The girls in my troop were entirely speechless. Arnetta looked stoic, as though she were soon to be tortured but was determined not to appear weak. Mrs. Margolin pursed her lips solemnly and said, "Bless them, Lord. Bless them." 155

In contrast, the Troop 909 leader was full of words and energy. "Some of our girls are echolalic—" She smiled and happily presented one of the girls hanging onto her, but the girl widened her eyes in horror, and violently withdrew herself from the center of attention, sensing she was being sacrificed for the village sins. "Echolalic," the troop leader continued. "That means they will say whatever they hear, like an echo—that's where the word comes from. It comes from 'echo.'" 156

She ducked her head apologetically, "I mean, not all of them have the most *progressive* of parents, so if they heard a bad word, they might have repeated it. But I guarantee it would not have been *intentional.*"

157 Arnetta spoke. "I saw her say the word. I heard her." She pointed to a small girl, smaller than any of us, wearing an oversized T-shirt that read: "Eat Bertha's Mussels."

158 The troop leader shook her head and smiled, "That's impossible. She doesn't speak. She can, but she doesn't."

159 Arnetta furrowed her brow. "No. It wasn't her. That's right. It was *her.*"

160 The girl Arnetta pointed to grinned as though she'd been paid a compliment. She was the only one from either troop actually wearing a full uniform: the mocha-colored A-line shift, the orange ascot, the sash covered with badges, though all the same one—the Try-It patch. She took a few steps toward Arnetta and made a grand sweeping gesture toward the sash. "See," she said, full of self-importance, "I'm a Brownie." I had a hard time imagining this girl calling anyone a "nigger"; the girl looked perpetually delighted, as though she would have cuddled up with a grizzly if someone had let her.

161 ON the fourth morning, we boarded the bus to go home.

162 The previous day had been spent building miniature churches from Popsicle sticks. We hardly left the cabin. Mrs. Margolin and Mrs. Hedy guarded us so closely, almost no one talked for the entire day.

163 Even on the day of departure from Camp Crescendo, all was serious and silent. The bus ride began quietly enough. Arnetta had to sit beside Mrs. Margolin; Octavia had to sit beside her mother. I sat beside Daphne, who gave me her prize journal without a word of explanation.

164 "You don't want it?"

165 She shook her head no. It was empty.

166 Then Mrs. Hedy began to weep. "Octavia," Mrs. Hedy said to her daughter without looking at her, "I'm going to sit with Mrs. Margolin. All right?"

167 Arnetta exchanged seats with Mrs. Hedy. With the two women up front, Elise felt it safe to speak. "Hey," she said, then she set her face into a placid, vacant stare, trying to imitate that of a Troop 909 girl. Emboldened, Arnetta made a gesture of mock pride toward an imaginary sash, the way the girl in full uniform had done. Then they all made a game of it, trying to do the most exaggerated imitations of the Troop 909 girls, all without speaking, all without laughing loud enough to catch the women's attention.

Daphne looked down at her shoes, white with sneaker polish. I opened the journal she'd given me. I looked out the window, trying to decide what to write, searching for lines, but nothing could compare with what Daphne had written, *"My father, the veteran,"* my favorite line of all time. It replayed itself in my head, and I gave up trying to write. 168

By then, it seemed that the rest of the troop had given up making fun of the girls in Troop 909. They were now quietly gossiping about who had passed notes to whom in school. For a moment the gossiping fell off, and all I heard was the hum of the bus as we sped down the road and the muffled sounds of Mrs. Hedy and Mrs. Margolin talking about serious things. 169

"You know," Octavia whispered, "why did *we* have to be stuck at a camp with retarded girls? You know?" 170

"*You* know why," Arnetta answered. She narrowed her eyes like a cat. "My mama and I were in the mall in Buckhead, and this white lady just kept looking at us. I mean, like we were foreign or something. Like we were from China." 171

"What did the woman say?" Elise asked. 172

"Nothing," Arnetta said. "She didn't say nothing." 173

A few girls quietly nodded their heads. 174

"There was this time," I said, "when my father and I were in the mall and—" 175

"Oh shut up, Snot," Octavia said. 176

I stared at Octavia, then rolled my eyes from her to the window. As I watched the trees blur, I wanted nothing more than to be through with it all: the bus ride, the troop, school—all of it. But we were going home. I'd see the same girls in school the next day. We were on a bus, and there was nowhere else to go. 177

"Go on, Laurel," Daphne said to me. It seemed like the first time she'd spoken the whole trip, and she'd said my name. I turned to her and smiled weakly so as not to cry, hoping she'd remember when I'd tried to be her friend, thinking maybe that her gift of the journal was an invitation of friendship. But she didn't smile back. All she said was, "What happened?" 178

I studied the girls, waiting for Octavia to tell me to shut up again before I even had a chance to utter another word, but everyone was amazed that Daphne had 179

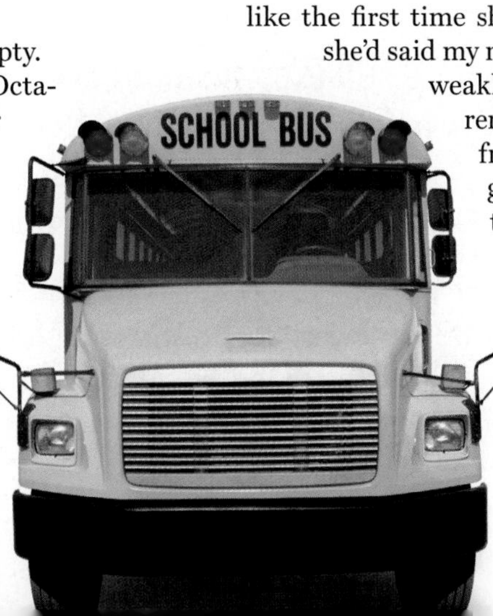

spoken. The bus was silent. I gathered my voice. "Well," I said. "My father and I were in this mall, but *I* was the one doing the staring." I stopped and glanced from face to face. I continued. "There were these white people dressed like Puritans or something, but they weren't Puritans. They were Mennonites. They're these people who, if you ask them to do a favor, like paint your porch or something, they have to do it. It's in their rules."

180 "That sucks," someone said.

181 "C'mon," Arnetta said. "You're lying."

182 "I am not."

183 "How do you know that's not just some story someone made up?" Elise asked, her head cocked full of daring. "I mean, who's gonna do whatever you ask?"

184 "It's not made up. I know because when I was looking at them, my father said, 'See those people? If you ask them to do something, they'll do it. Anything you want.'"

185 No one would call anyone's father a liar—then they'd have to fight the person. But Drema parsed her words carefully. "How does your *father* know that's not just some story? Huh?"

186 "Because," I said, "he went up to the man and asked him would he paint our porch, and the man said yes. It's their religion."

187 "Man, I'm glad I'm a Baptist," Elise said, shaking her head in sympathy for the Mennonites.

188 "So did the guy do it?" Drema asked, scooting closer to hear if the story got juicy.

189 "Yeah," I said. "His whole family was with him. My dad drove them to our house. They all painted our porch. The woman and girl were in bonnets and long, long skirts with buttons up to their necks. The guy wore this weird hat and these huge suspenders."

When you've been made to feel bad for so long, you jump at the chance to do it to others.

"Why," Arnetta asked archly, as though she didn't believe a word, "would someone pick a *porch*? If they'll do anything, why not make them paint the whole *house*? Why not ask for a hundred bucks?" 19

I thought about it, and then remembered the words my father had said about them painting our porch, though I had never seemed to think about his words after he'd said them. 19

"He said," I began, only then understanding the words as they uncoiled from my mouth, "it was the only time he'd have a white man on his knees doing something for a black man for free." 19

I now understood what he meant, and why he did it, though I didn't like it. When you've been made to feel bad for so long, you jump at the chance to do it to others. I remembered the Mennonites bending the way Daphne had bent when she was cleaning the restroom. I remembered the dark blue of their bonnets, the black of their shoes. They painted the porch as though scrubbing a floor. I was already trembling before Daphne asked quietly, "Did he thank them?" 19

I looked out the window. I could not tell which were the thoughts and which were the trees. "No," I said, and suddenly knew there was something mean in the world that I could not stop. 1

Arnetta laughed. "If I asked them to take off their long skirts and bonnets and put on some jeans, would they do it?" 1

And Daphne's voice, quiet, steady: "Maybe they would. Just to be nice." 1

ZZ Packer is a young writer who is still experimenting with the use of point of view in her work, and, as with most literary matters, it seems difficult to predict where she will go next. If you like "Brownies," you might also like "Traveling Madness," by another young writer, Ana Menendez (in Stories for Further Reading), who stands at a similar point in her writing career.

**GOING FURTHER** As of this writing Packer is at work on her first novel, a story about the "Buffalo Soldiers," black Union Army veterans who went west during and after the Civil War. With her contemporary Danzy Senna (*Caucasia* and *Symptomatic*) and the slightly younger Tayari Jones (*Leaving Atlanta*) and Asali Solomon (*Get Down*), she is carving out space for new black American women writers.

# Writing from Reading

### Summarize

1 What are Snot/Laurel's feelings about her father? What does she tell the reader directly? What can you infer from what she says and when she says it?

2 Locate all the scenes where Laurel's troop actually encounters Troop 909. What details does Laurel include that foreshadow their later discovery about the white girls? What details are omitted because we get only Laurel's view?

### Analyze Craft

3 Packer includes several sets of lyrics in "Brownies," including Daphne's poem, and the songs the girls are asked to sing. What is the effect of including the full text of these lyrics? Why does Packer choose to leave out the lyrics of the Michael Jackson song?

### Analyze Voice

4 Analyze the difference between Laurel's voice as narrator of the story and her voice when she speaks in the story. Based on this comparison, do you think Packer was trying to use the voice of a young girl narrator or of a grown-up looking back?

### Synthesize Summary and Analysis

5 Compare the descriptions of Laurel's troop members to the descriptions of the girls in Troop 909. Does Packer draw a comparison between the two troops? Examine why Packer chose to distance Troop 909 both racially and mentally.

### Interpret the Story

6 Think about the protagonists, antagonists, and foils of this story. Can they be divided evenly into groups by race, age, or troop? What is the overarching conflict the protagonists are up against, and how does the story of the Mennonites help bring resolution to this conflict?

*CONTINUED FROM PAGE 183*

## A PARTICIPANT, OR FIRST-PERSON, NARRATOR

The first-person narrator is always a participant in the story and can be either a major or a minor character. This type of tale telling relies on the perspective of a single character through whose eyes, and by means of whose voice, we come to understand the action in the story. Readers enter the narrator's mind, gaining access to his or her thoughts and emotions. In the opening passage, with Laurel as the first-person narrator, our entry to the narrative comes through her eyes and words.

First person is by its nature limited because we have only one set of eyes. As participants in a story, first-person narrators have their own interests and motivations—

> "You have to create a little distance from yourself to make . . . a story; otherwise it's just you talking. . . . As a story . . . you want to be able to walk around in some way. However closely it relates to your own autobiography, it has to be a little different. There has to be some space between you and it and the voice is one way to establish a little space." Conversation with John Updike

and, like the rest of us, cannot be entirely objective. They can give only their version of the tale. Often, readers see more than the narrator can, and sometimes this broader vantage point allows us to recognize an **unreliable narrator,** or one who cannot be trusted to present an undistorted account of the action. Not all narrators are unreliable, but those who are have many reasons for their unreliability, ranging from inexperience, ignorance, and personal bias to intentional deceptiveness and even insanity. The narrator of Eudora Welty's story "Why I Live at the P.O." in the previous chapter is so intent on feeling like a victim that she fails to acknowledge any part in or responsibility for the trouble in her family. The reader realizes quickly that her self-pity and jealousy of her younger sister prevent her from understanding anyone else's point of view.

A specific type of unreliable narrator is the **naïve narrator,** who remains unaware of the full complexity of events in the story being told. A narrator may be naïve because of youth, innocence, or lack of cultural alertness. Writers intentionally use naïve narrators to reveal a truth, raise questions in the reader's mind, or otherwise emphasize a point. In Harper Lee's classic novel *To Kill a Mockingbird,* young Scout is the naïve narrator who describes the members of her family and the characters and events in her town. Tom Robinson, a black man, has been falsely accused of raping a white woman. Scout takes us into the courtroom where her father, the town's highly respected lawyer, defends Tom. Scout, an avid observer, still cannot understand how Tom can be convicted when the evidence overwhelmingly supports his innocence. The critical reader, having some knowledge of the social conventions of life in the American South in the 1930s, understands that Tom is the victim of the town's deep-rooted racism. By the use of Scout's perspective, therefore, Harper Lee effectively reveals the injustice of the town's racist attitudes.

## A NONPARTICIPANT, OR THIRD-PERSON, NARRATOR

Third-person narrators are never characters in the story. These narrators relate the events of a story as unseen observers, referring to all the characters as *he, she,* or *they.* This particular narrative vantage remains the most common strategy for tale telling, though there are gradations within it, and it's worth spelling them out. Third-person narrators come in three basic varieties:

- **Omniscient narrator.** Omniscient, or all-knowing, third-person narrators observe the thoughts and describe the actions of multiple characters in the story, as does the narrator in Ernest Hemingway's "The Short Happy Life of Francis Macomber" in this chapter.
- **Limited omniscient narrator.** Limited third-person narrators typically enter into the thoughts and emotions of one character, as does the narrator in Kate Chopin's "The Story of an Hour" (chapter 1).
- **Objective point-of-view narrator.** Objective third-person narrators report only what can be seen and heard.

The **omniscient narrator** can see beyond the physical actions and dialogue of characters and is able to reveal the inner thoughts and emotions of anyone in the story. This narrator moves freely between the thoughts of characters and across time and space. The term comes from the Latin *omni scientia, "all-knowing,"* and it suggests a kind of godlike or infallible witness—often one who offers his or her opinion on the action as it unfolds. The omniscient narrator chooses which thoughts are important to the story, and when to tell them.

### A BRIEF HISTORY OF POINT OF VIEW

In the earliest narratives of Western culture, news about the world comes down to the poets from a literally omniscient source—the gods or God. Both *The Iliad* and *The Odyssey,* for example, begin by asking a goddess—called the Muse—to relate the events of the story. So, too, the first five books of the Bible are held to be the word of God as revealed to Moses. However, over time, more varied perspectives on life and history emerged; the fourteenth-century English poet Geoffrey Chaucer (in *The Canterbury Tales*) and the Italian Renaissance story writer Boccaccio (in *The Decameron*) told tales about men and women of differing backgrounds and social positions as if the characters were speaking in their own words. The stories became as varied as their narrators, and the point of view changed as each new narrator told a tale. Once numerous and partial points of view began to replace omniscience, or all-knowingness, skill in this aspect of the writer's craft grew crucial.

Using this perspective, for example, Hemingway's narrator at a certain point gives us a glimpse into Mrs. Macomber's thoughts as she sits with Wilson, the safari leader, and her husband, Mr. Macomber: "She looked at both these men as though she had never seen them before. One, Wilson, the white hunter, she knew she had never truly seen before."

At other times, the narrator reveals Wilson's thoughts about Mrs. Macomber: "When she left, Wilson was thinking, when she went off to cry, she seemed a hell of a fine woman. She seemed to understand, to realize, to be hurt for him and for herself and to know how things really stood."

The reader also has access to Mr. Macomber's thoughts, as in the following instance when he lies in bed, unable to fall asleep: "But more than shame he felt cold, hollow fear in him. The fear was still there like a cold slimy hollow in all the emptiness where once his confidence had been and it made him feel sick." The omniscient narrator chooses what should be revealed, and when, providing a deep insight into the nature of each character.

> "Once you break with the first person, then you do discover the wonderful world of multiple view points, and you can fly through space, and go from head to head, and you get out and you become a character in your own right, you become the omniscient author presiding." Conversation with John Updike

Omniscient narrators are not always objective. Sometimes a narrator shows **editorial omniscience,** inserting his or her own commentary about the characters or the events. By contrast, a narrator who shows **impartial omniscience** remains neutral, relating events and characters' thoughts without passing judgment or offering an opinion. Many novels employ the all-knowing third-person (impartial omniscient) approach to their material, as in, for example, the opening of World War II writer James Jones's *The Pistol.* The novel begins on the morning when the Japanese attack Pearl Harbor, and the passage is straightforward enough that you might easily find it in a work of history or general nonfiction:

> *When the first bombs hit at Wheeler Field on December 7, 1941, Pfc Richard Mast was eating breakfast. He was also wearing a pistol. From where Mast sat,*

> *amidst the bent heads, quiet murmur, and soft, cutlery-against-china sounds of breakfast, in a small company mess in one of the infantry quadrangles of Schofield Barracks, it was perhaps a mile to Wheeler Field, and it took several seconds for the sound of the explosions, followed soon after by the shockwave through the earth, to reach his ears.*

Few omniscient narrators are purely editorial or purely impartial, however; in most works of fiction, you will find both kinds of storytelling.

A **limited omniscient narrator** describes the vision and insights of one character only, as if telling the story "over the shoulder" of that character. Unlike a first-person narrator, the limited omniscient narrator is separate from the main character and serves as the interpreter—not the source—of his or her thoughts. The reader can trust that the narrator's observations are more or less objective. Kate Chopin's "The Story of an Hour" uses limited omniscient narration, with the focus on Mrs. Mallard, the only character whose consciousness we enter. In other words, the narrator can relate only what Mrs. Mallard can see and hear, and what she herself feels and thinks.

> *There were patches of blue sky showing here and there through the clouds that had met and piled one above the other in the west facing her window. . . . There was something coming to her and she was waiting for it, fearfully. What was it? She did not know; it was too subtle and elusive to name. But she felt it, creeping out of the sky, reaching toward her through the sounds, the scents, the color that filled the air.*
>
> *Now her bosom rose and fell tumultuously. She was beginning to recognize this thing that was approaching to possess her, and she was striving to beat it back with her will—as powerless as her two white slender hands would have been. When she abandoned herself a little whispered word escaped her slightly parted lips. She said it over and over under the breath: "free, free, free!"*

In this passage, Mrs. Mallard has left her guests downstairs to go to her room. The narrator describes Mrs. Mallard's movements and feelings in great detail, following her gaze outside the window, as her mind begins to understand what her body has already grasped. She feels as free as the blue sky showing through the clouds.

An omniscient narrator who goes very deeply into the mind of a character may use the technique of interior monologue, in which a character's conscious or unconscious thought processes are narrated as they occur, with only minimal guidance from the narrator. These thoughts can be disconnected, moving rapidly and randomly from one idea to the next. Kate Chopin briefly uses the interior monologue technique in the passage about Mrs. Mallard. A similar but more random-seeming approach is **stream of consciousness,** in which thoughts flow by in free association and the literary convention suggests that there is no writer mediating the consciousness of the subject. The following example comes from James Joyce's novel *Ulysses;* here, the thoughts of a character named Molly Bloom pour onto the page:

> *. . . and Ronda with the old windows of the posadas glancing eyes a lattice hid for her lover to kiss the iron and the wineshops half open at night and the castanets and the night we missed the boat at Algeciras the watchman going about serene with his lamp and O that awful deepdown torrent O and the sea the sea crimson sometimes like fire and the glorious sunsets and the fig trees in the Alameda gardens yes . . .*

In contrast to the narrator with limited omniscience, who delves into the consciousness of a particular character, an **objective point-of-view** narrator seems almost disinterested, relating only what all characters in the story see or hear. This type of narrator is often compared to the "fly on the wall" who sees and hears all. Similarly, the objective narrator provides no insight into the thoughts, emotions, or motivations of any single character. "I am a camera," as the narrator declares in Christopher Isherwood's *Berlin Stories,* suggesting a kind of objective assessment—one that's neither naïve nor editorialized. Reading a story with an objective narrator is much like watching a play, because the reader comes to understand what the characters think and feel based only on what they do and say. An objective narrator never lets the reader enter the consciousness of a particular character, the way Chopin did with Mrs. Mallard. The reader must use the clues of dialogue and behavior to infer what people truly think and feel.

## THE SECOND-PERSON NARRATOR

The least commonly used point of view is that of the second-person narrator, who addresses readers directly with the pronoun *you* or with imperatives (*do this and that*). Second-person narration can make a reader feel like a participant in the story. It also creates a sense of closeness to the protagonist—as if the character is talking to himself or herself. In the following selection from Lorrie Moore's "How to Become a Writer," notice how the familiar, conversational use of "you" draws the reader in.

> *You spend too much time slouched and demoralized. Your boyfriend suggests bicycling. Your roommate suggests a new boyfriend. You are said to be self-mutilating and losing weight, but you continue writing. The only happiness you have is writing something new, in the middle of the night, armpits damp, heart pounding, something no one has yet seen. You have only those brief, fragile untested moments of exhilaration when you know: you are a genius. Understand what you must do. Switch majors. The kids in your nursery project will be disappointed but you have a calling, an urge, a delusion, an unfortunate habit. You have, as your mother would say, fallen in with a bad crowd.*

Drawing the reader directly into the story can prove challenging when creating a work of fiction. For example, not all readers will identify with the "you" being portrayed, thinking, "I don't have a boyfriend," or "My mother would never say something like that." Nevertheless, Lorrie Moore and others have created innovative and compelling fiction by the use of second-person narrators; there's an intimacy (as if we overhear internal monologue) involved.

## *POINT OF VIEW* IN CONTEXT

The stories in this chapter represent points of view from first person in ZZ Packer's "Brownies" to omniscient third person in Hemingway's "The Short Happy Life of Francis Macomber." Each point of view lets you into a different frame of mind and has different powers and limitations. Third person can't feel as intimate as first person. First person can't see as many sides of an issue as third. It's interesting in this regard to notice the role that *fashion* plays in point of view. The omniscient narrator was more common in the eighteenth and nineteenth centuries, for example, than is the case today. In the contemporary moment, we tend to deploy the first-person narrator, either as a reliable or unreliable witness—and the proportion of novels and short stories using the first person, as opposed to the third, has enlarged. Perhaps in the next fifty years the second-person narrator will take center stage.

# Lorrie Moore (b. 1957)

Growing up in Glens Falls, New York, Lorrie Moore was so skinny, she feared falling through sidewalk grates. Her fiction, however, has not been lost on critics and readers, who have responded enthusiastically to Moore's ability to blend comedy, pathos, and poignancy. After winning *Seventeen*'s writing contest at age nineteen, Moore's next literary success came when she published *Self-Help* (1985), a collection of stories pulled largely from the graduate thesis she completed at Cornell University. Moore's use of the second-person point of view and witty application of self-help-manual rhetoric in this first collection earned her immediate critical praise. Her stories have since continued to appear in the most prestigious literary venues, including *The New Yorker* and *The Best American Short Stories* series, as she experiments with reverse chronology, sequential accounts, and fragmented narration. A professor of English at the University of Wisconsin since 1984, Moore now boasts two novels, three collections of short stories, and awards including the Rea Award for the Short Story and the O. Henry Prize. Her work treats serious themes such as loneliness and the difficulties of love, both familial and romantic, but in such a way that the darker thematic undertones are highlighted by humor and wit.

**AS YOU READ** As you read this story, consider how you feel about being addressed directly by the narrator. What do you think of this narrator? Can you see yourself living the life she is describing?

# How to Become a Writer Or, Have You Earned This Cliché? (1985)

1 FIRST, try to be something, anything, else. A movie star/astronaut. A movie star/missionary. A movie star/kindergarten teacher. President of the World. Fail miserably. It is best if you fail at an early age—say, fourteen. Early, critical disillusionment is necessary so that at fifteen you can write long haiku sequences about thwarted desire. It is a pond, a cherry blossom, a wind brushing against spar-

row wing leaving for mountain. Count the syllables. Show it to your mom. She is tough and practical. She has a son in Vietnam and a husband who may be having an affair. She believes in wearing brown because it hides spots. She'll look briefly at your writing, then back up at you with a face blank as a donut. She'll say: "How about emptying the dishwasher?" Look away. Shove the forks in the fork drawer. Accidentally break one of the freebie gas station glasses. This is the required pain and suffering. This is only for starters.

2 In your high school English class look at Mr. Killian's face. Decide faces are important. Write a villanelle about pores. Struggle. Write a sonnet. Count the syllables: nine, ten, eleven, thirteen. Decide to experiment with fiction. Here you don't have to count syllables. Write a short story about an elderly man and woman who accidentally shoot each other in the head, the result of an inexplicable malfunction of a shotgun which appears mysteriously in their living room one night. Give it to Mr. Killian as your final project. When you get it back, he has written on it: "Some of your images are quite nice, but you have no sense of plot." When you are home, in the privacy of your own room, faintly scrawl in pencil beneath his black-inked comments: "Plots are for dead people, pore-face."

3 Take all the babysitting jobs you can get. You are great with kids. They love you. You tell them stories about old people who die idiot deaths. You sing them songs like "Blue Bells of Scotland," which is their favorite. And when they are in their pajamas and have finally stopped pinching each other, when they are fast asleep, you read every sex manual in the house, and wonder how on earth anyone could ever do those things with someone they truly loved. Fall asleep in a chair reading Mr. McMurphy's *Playboy*. When the McMurphys come home, they will tap you on the shoulder, look at the magazine in your lap, and grin. You will want to die. They will ask you if Tracey took her medicine all right. Explain, yes, she did, that you promised her a story if she would take it like a big girl and that seemed to work out just fine. "Oh, marvelous," they will exclaim.

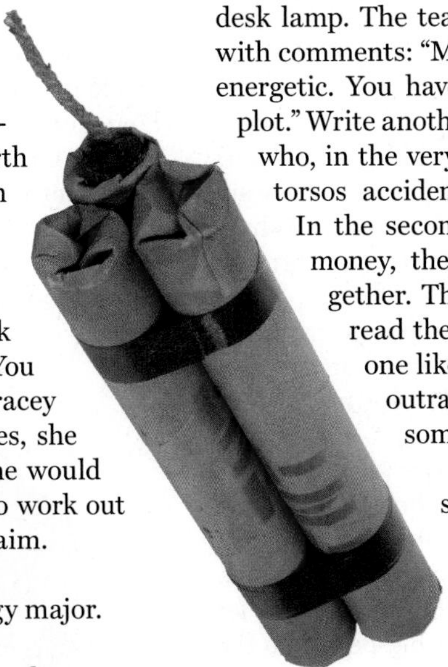

4 Try to smile proudly.

5 Apply to college as a child psychology major.

6 AS a child psychology major, you have some electives. You've always liked kids. Sign up for something called "The Ornithological Field Trip." It meets Tuesdays and Thursdays at two. When you arrive at Room 134 on the first day of class, everyone is sitting around a seminar table talking about metaphors. You've heard of these. After a short, excruciating while, raise your hand and say diffidently, "Excuse me, isn't this Birdwatching One-oh-one?" The class stops and turns to look at you. They seem to all have one face—giant and blank as a vandalized clock. Someone with a beard booms out, "No, this is Creative Writing." Say: "Oh—right," as if perhaps you knew all along. Look down at your schedule. Wonder how the hell you ended up here. The computer, apparently, has made an error. You start to get up to leave and then don't. The lines at the registrar this week are huge. Perhaps you should stick with this mistake. Perhaps your creative writing isn't all that bad. Perhaps it is fate. Perhaps this is what your dad meant when he said, "It's the age of computers, Francie, it's the age of computers."

DECIDE that you like college life. In your dorm you meet many nice people. Some are smarter than you. And some, you notice, are dumber than you. You will continue, unfortunately, to view the world in exactly these terms for the rest of your life. 7

THE assignment this week in creative writing is to narrate a violent happening. Turn in a story about driving with your Uncle Gordon and another one about two old people who are accidentally electrocuted when they go to turn on a badly wired desk lamp. The teacher will hand them back to you with comments: "Much of your writing is smooth and energetic. You have, however, a ludicrous notion of plot." Write another story about a man and a woman who, in the very first paragraph, have their lower torsos accidentally blitzed away by dynamite. In the second paragraph, with the insurance money, they buy a frozen yogurt stand together. There are six more paragraphs. You read the whole thing out loud in class. No one likes it. They say your sense of plot is outrageous and incompetent. After class someone asks you if you are crazy. 8

Decide that perhaps you should stick to comedies. Start dating someone who is funny, someone who has what in high school you called a "really great sense of humor" and what now your creative writing class calls "self-contempt giving rise to comic form." Write down all of his jokes, but don't tell him you are doing this. Make up anagrams of his old girlfriend's name and name all of your socially handicapped characters with 9 them. Tell him his old girlfriend is in all of your stories and then watch how funny he can be, see what a really great sense of humor he can have.

10 Your child psychology advisor tells you you are neglecting courses in your major. What you spend the most time on should be what you're majoring in. Say yes, you understand.

11 IN creative writing seminars over the next two years, everyone continues to smoke cigarettes and ask the same things: "But does it work?" "Why should we care about this character?" "Have you earned this cliché?" These seem like important questions.

12 On days when it is your turn, you look at the class hopefully as they scour your mimeographs for a plot. They look back up at you, drag deeply, and then smile in a sweet sort of way.

13 YOU spend too much time slouched and demoralized. Your boyfriend suggests bicycling. Your roommate suggests a new boyfriend. You are said to be self-mutilating and losing weight, but you continue writing. The only happiness you have is writing something new, in the middle of the night, armpits damp, heart pounding, something no one has yet seen. You have only those brief, fragile, untested moments of exhilaration when you know: you are a genius. Understand what you must do. Switch majors. The kids in your nursery project will be disappointed, but you have a calling, an urge, a delusion, an unfortunate habit. You have, as your mother would say, fallen in with a bad crowd.

14 WHY write? Where does writing come from? These are questions to ask yourself. They are like: Where does dust come from? Or: Why is there war? Or: If there's a God, then why is my brother now a cripple?

15 These are questions that you keep in your wallet, like calling cards. These are questions, your creative writing teacher says, that are good to address in your journals but rarely in your fiction.

16 The writing professor this fall is stressing the Power of the Imagination. Which means he doesn't want long descriptive stories about your camping trip last July. He wants you to start in a realistic context but then to alter it. Like recombinant DNA. He wants you to let your imagination sail, to let it grow big-bellied in the wind. This is a quote from Shakespeare.

17 TELL your roommate your great idea, your great exercise of imaginative power: a transformation of Melville to contemporary life. It will be about monomania and the fish-eat-fish world of life insurance in Rochester, New York. The first line will be "Call me Fishmeal," and it will feature a menopausal suburban husband named Richard, who because he is so depressed all the time is called "Mopey Dick" by his witty wife Elaine. Say to your roommate: "Mopey Dick, get it?" Your roommate looks at you, her face blank as a large Kleenex. She comes up to you, like a buddy, and puts an arm around your burdened shoulders. "Listen, Francie," she says, slow as speech therapy. "Let's go out and get a big beer."

THE seminar doesn't like this one either. You suspect they are beginning to feel sorry for you. They say: "You have to think about what is happening. Where is the story here?" 18

THE next semester the writing professor is obsessed with writing from personal experience. You must write from what you know, from what has happened to you. He wants deaths, he wants camping trips. Think about what has happened to you. In three years there have been three things: you lost your virginity; your parents got divorced; and your brother came home from a forest ten miles from the Cambodian border with only half a thigh, a permanent smirk nestled into one corner of his mouth. 19

About the first you write: "It created a new space, which hurt and cried in a voice that wasn't mine, 'I'm not the same anymore, but I'll be okay.'" 20

About the second you write an elaborate story of an old married couple who stumble upon an unknown land mine in their kitchen and accidentally blow themselves up. You call it: "For Better or for Liverwurst." 21

About the last you write nothing. 22
There are no words for this. Your typewriter hums. You can find no words.

23 AT undergraduate cocktail parties, people say, "Oh, you write? What do you write about?" Your roommate, who has consumed too much wine, too little cheese, and no crackers at all, blurts: "Oh, my god, she always writes about her dumb boyfriend."

24 Later on in life you will learn that writers are merely open, helpless texts with no real understanding of what they have written and therefore must half-believe anything and everything that is said of them. You, however, have not yet reached this stage of literary criticism. You stiffen and say, "I do not," the same way you said it when someone in the fourth grade accused you of really liking oboe lessons and your parents really weren't just making you take them.

25 Insist you are not very interested in any one subject at all, that you are interested in the music of language, that you are interested in—in—syllables, because they are the atoms of poetry, the cells of the mind, the breath of the soul. Begin to feel woozy. Stare into your plastic wine cup.

26 "Syllables?" you will hear someone ask, voice trailing off, as they glide slowly toward the reassuring white of the dip.

27 BEGIN to wonder what you do write about. Or if you have anything to say. Or if there even is such a thing as a thing to say. Limit these thoughts to no more than ten minutes a day; like sit-ups, they can make you thin.

28 You will read somewhere that all writing has to do with one's genitals. Don't dwell on this. It will make you nervous.

29 YOUR mother will come visit you. She will look at the circles under your eyes and hand you a brown book with a brown briefcase on the cover. It is entitled: *How to Become a Business Executive.* She has also brought the *Names for Baby* encyclopedia you asked for; one of your characters, the aging clown-school teacher, needs a new name. Your mother will shake her head and say: "Francie, Francie, remember when you were going to be a child psychology major?"

30 Say: "Mom, I like to write."

31 She'll say: "Sure you like to write. Of course. Sure you like to write."

32 WRITE a story about a confused music student and title it: "Schubert Was the One with the Glasses, Right?" It's not a big hit, although your roommate likes the part where the two violinists accidentally blow themselves up in a recital room. "I went out with a violinist once," she says, snapping her gum.

Thank god you are taking other courses. You can find sanctuary in nineteenth-century ontological snags and invertebrate courting rituals. Certain globular mollusks have what is called "Sex by the Arm." The male octopus, for instance, loses the end of one arm when placing it inside the female body during intercourse. Marine biologists call it "Seven Heaven." Be glad you know these things. Be glad you are not just a writer. Apply to law school. 33

FROM here on in, many things can happen. But the main one will be this: you decide not to go to law school after all, and, instead, you spend a good, big chunk of your adult life telling people how you decided not to go to law school after all. Somehow you end up writing again. Perhaps you go to graduate school. Perhaps you work odd jobs and take writing courses at night. Perhaps you are working on a novel and writing down all the clever remarks and intimate personal confessions you hear during the day. Perhaps you are losing your pals, your acquaintances, your balance. 34

You have broken up with your boyfriend. You now go out with men who, instead of whispering "I love you," shout: "Do it to me baby." This is good for your writing. 35

Sooner or later you have a finished manuscript more or less. People look at it in a vaguely troubled sort of way and say, "I'll bet becoming a writer was always a fantasy of yours, wasn't it?" Your lips dry to salt. Say that of all the fantasies possible in the world, you can't imagine being a writer even making the top twenty. Tell them you were going to be a child psychology major. "I bet," they always sigh, "you'd be great with kids." Scowl fiercely. Tell them you're a walking blade. 36

QUIT classes. Quit jobs. Cash in old savings bonds. Now you have time like warts on your hands. Slowly copy all of your friends' addresses into a new address book. 37

Vacuum. Chew cough drops. Keep a folder full of fragments. 38

*An eyelid darkening sideways.* 39

*World as conspiracy.* 40

*Possible plot? A woman gets on a bus.* 41

*Suppose you threw a love affair and nobody came.* 42

AT home drink a lot of coffee. At Howard Johnson's order the cole slaw. Consider how it looks like the soggy confetti of a map: where you've been, where you're going—"You Are Here," says the red star on the back of the menu. 43

44 Occasionally a date with a face blank as a sheet of paper asks you whether writers often become discouraged. Say that sometimes they do and sometimes they do. Say it's a lot like having polio.

"Interesting," smiles your date, and then he looks 45
down at his arm hairs and starts to smooth them, all, always, in the same direction.

A STORY about story writing is not to everyone's taste. If you like this one, you should try the Jorge Luis Borges story "The Circular Ruins" in Stories for Further Reading in this anthology.

**GOING FURTHER** Moore's comic meta-fiction was influenced early on by the work of Donald Barthelme, a father to many postmodernists, and Gilbert Sorrentino, whose hilarious examination of the literary imagination is captured in his classic novel *Mulligan Stew*.

# Writing from Reading

### Summarize

1 Make a list of the events and changes that occur in the life of the "you" of this story. Does the narrator reveal how the "you" feels about these events and changes? Give examples.

### Analyze Craft

2 Examine the instances of dialogue in the story. Analyze how Moore uses dialogue differently from other authors you have read.

3 What is the plot of this story? Discuss how using the second-person point of view tells a different story than one the same events would describe in third or first person.

### Analyze Voice

4 Who is the "you" of this story? Who is the narrator? Who is Francie? Are they all the same person? Does Lorrie Moore provide a clear answer? Explain.

### Synthesize Summary and Analysis

5 Which events does the narrator portray in a scene-like way, and which events does she merely refer to in exposition? What effect does dramatizing one event rather than another have on the story?

### Interpret the Story

6 Lorrie Moore uses humor in her writing, but she confronts some very serious topics, like self-mutilation, loneliness, and the Vietnam War. Do you think Moore intends this story to be a satire—a joke—or an actual caution to potential writers? Provide examples of instances of Moore being humorous and instances of her being serious, and contrast the two.

# Ernest Hemingway (1899–1961)

Born in Oak Park, Illinois, Ernest Hemingway became one of the most influential American authors of the twentieth century. In novels, short stories, and nonfiction alike, Hemingway celebrated the ideal of "grace under pressure" as a way to live and a way to write. He distrusted fancy phrasing and abstract utterance, making a case in much of his work for concrete speech. Under the influence of Gertrude Stein and Sherwood Anderson, he went about the business of renovating the American literary sentence. Writing stories made him into an artist. Novel writing made him famous. His first novel, *The Sun Also Rises* (1926), deals with American expatriates in France and Spain; his novel *A Farewell to Arms* (1929) is set in Italy and Switzerland during World War I. A prolific writer, Hemingway is also the author of *For Whom the Bell Tolls, The Old Man and the Sea, A Moveable Feast,* and numerous other works of fiction and nonfiction. He spent many years abroad and married four times. He was known—and self-described—as writing's "heavyweight champ"; both he and his characters are known for their unapologetic bravado. The men in his fiction are matadors, soldiers, and big-game hunters, a tight-lipped and cool-headed lot in the face of danger. A Nobel laureate and a world-famous public figure, Hemingway was nonetheless prone to suicidal depression; he took his own life in 1961 in Ketchum, Idaho.

**AS YOU READ** As you read this story, notice the shifting levels of happiness and unhappiness among the characters. Notice also the shifting alliances in the triangle of characters at the center of the story. Which of them do you most sympathize with and feel compassion for? Why?

**TIP**

**FOR INTERACTIVE READING . . .** As you move through the story, mark sections and paragraphs according to whose perspective is represented. What do these glimpses into each character's thoughts reveal about their motivations and weaknesses?

# The Short Happy Life of Francis Macomber (1936)

1 IT was now lunch time and they were all sitting under the double green fly of the dining tent pretending that nothing had happened.

2 "Will you have lime juice or lemon squash?" Macomber asked.

3 "I'll have a gimlet," Robert Wilson told him.

4 "I'll have a gimlet too. I need something," Macomber's wife said.

5 "I suppose it's the thing to do," Macomber agreed. "Tell him to make three gimlets."

6 The mess boy had started them already, lifting the bottles out of the canvas cooling bags that sweated wet

in the wind that blew through the trees that shaded the tents.

7 "What had I ought to give them?" Macomber asked.

8 "A quid would be plenty," Wilson told him. "You don't want to spoil them."

9 "Will the headman distribute it?"

10 "Absolutely."

11 Francis Macomber had, half an hour before, been carried to his tent from the edge of the camp in triumph on the arms and shoulders of the cook, the personal boys, the skinner and the porters. The gun-bearers had taken no part in the demonstration. When the native boys put him down at the door of his tent, he had shaken all their hands, received their congratulations, and then gone into the tent and sat on the bed until his wife came in. She did not speak to him when she came in and he left the tent at once to wash his face and hands in the portable wash basin outside and go over to the dining tent to sit in a comfortable canvas chair in the breeze and the shade.

12 "You've got your lion," Robert Wilson said to him, "and a damned fine one too."

13 Mrs. Macomber looked at Wilson quickly. She was an extremely handsome and well kept woman of the beauty and social position which had, five years before, commanded five thousand dollars as the price of endorsing, with photographs, a beauty product which she had never used. She had been married to Francis Macomber for eleven years.

14 "He is a good lion, isn't he?" Macomber said. His wife looked at him now. She looked at both these men as though she had never seen them before.

15 One, Wilson, the white hunter, she knew she had never truly seen before. He was about middle height with sandy hair, a stubby mustache, a very red face and extremely cold blue eyes with faint white wrinkles at the corners that grooved merrily when he smiled. He smiled at her now and she looked away from his face at the way his shoulders sloped in the loose tunic he wore with the four big cartridges held in loops where the left breast pocket should have been, at his big brown hands, his old slacks, his very dirty boots and back to his red face again. She noticed where the baked red of his face stopped in a white line that marked the circle left by his Stetson hat that hung now from one of the pegs of the tent pole.

"Well, here's to the lion," Robert Wilson said. He 16
smiled at her again and, not smiling, she looked curiously at her husband.

Francis Macomber was very tall, very well built if 17
you did not mind that length of bone, dark, his hair cropped like an oarsman, rather thin-lipped, and was considered handsome. He was dressed in the same sort of safari clothes that Wilson wore except that his were new, he was thirty-five years old, kept himself very fit, was good at court games, had a number of big-game fishing records, and had just shown himself, very publicly, to be a coward.

"Here's to the lion," he said. "I can't ever thank you 18
for what you did."

Margaret, his wife, looked away from him and 19
back to Wilson.

"Let's not talk about the lion," she said. 20

Wilson looked over at her without smiling and 21
now she smiled at him.

"It's been a very strange day," she said. "Hadn't 22
you ought to put your hat on even under the canvas at noon? You told me that, you know."

"Might put it on," said Wilson. 23

"You know you have a very red face, Mr. Wilson," 24
she told him and smiled again.

"Drink," said Wilson. 25

"I don't think so," she said. "Francis drinks a great 26
deal, but his face is never red."

"It's red today," Macomber tried a joke. 27

"No," said Margaret. "It's mine that's red today. 28
But Mr. Wilson's is always red."

"Must be racial," said Wilson. "I say, you wouldn't 29
like to drop my beauty as a topic, would you?"

"I've just started on it." 30

"Let's chuck it," said Wilson.

"Conversation is going to be so difficult," Marga- 31
ret said.

"Don't be silly, Margot," her husband said. 32

"No difficulty," Wilson said. "Got a damn fine lion." 33

Margot looked at them both and they both saw 34
that she was going to cry. Wilson had seen it coming for a long time and he dreaded it. Macomber was past dreading it.

"I wish it hadn't happened. Oh, I wish it hadn't 35
happened," she said and started for her tent. She made no noise of crying but they could see that her shoul-

ders were shaking under the rose-colored, sun-proofed shirt she wore.

36 "Women upset," said Wilson to the tall man. "Amounts to nothing. Strain on the nerves and one thing'n another."

37 "No," said Macomber. "I suppose that I rate that for the rest of my life now."

38 "Nonsense. Let's have a spot of the giant killer," said Wilson. "Forget the whole thing. Nothing to it anyway."

You most certainly could not tell a damned thing about an American.

39 "We might try," said Macomber. "I won't forget what you did for me though."

40 "Nothing," said Wilson. "All nonsense."

41 So they sat there in the shade where the camp was pitched under some wide-topped acacia trees with a boulder-strewn cliff behind them, and a stretch of grass that ran to the bank of a boulder-filled stream in front with forest beyond it, and drank their just-cool lime drinks and avoided one another's eyes while the boys set the table for lunch. Wilson could tell that the boys all knew about it now and when he saw Macomber's personal boy looking curiously at his master while he was putting dishes on the table he snapped at him in Swahili. The boy turned away with his face blank.

42 "What were you telling him?" Macomber asked.

43 "Nothing. Told him to look alive or I'd see he got about fifteen of the best."

44 "What's that? Lashes?"

45 "It's quite illegal," Wilson said. "You're supposed to fine them."

46 "Do you still have them whipped?"

47 "Oh, yes. They could raise a row if they chose to complain. But they don't. They prefer it to the fines."

48 "How strange!" said Macomber.

49 "Not strange, really," Wilson said. "Which would you rather do? Take a good birching or lose your pay?"

50 Then he felt embarrassed at asking it and before Macomber could answer he went on, "We all take a beating every day, you know, one way or another."

51 This was no better. "Good God," he thought. "I am a diplomat, aren't I?"

52 "Yes, we take a beating," said Macomber, still not looking at him. "I'm awfully sorry about that lion business. It doesn't have to go any further, does it? I mean no one will hear about it, will they?"

53 "You mean will I tell it at the Mathaiga Club?" Wilson looked at him now coldly. He had not expected this. So he's a bloody four-letter man as well as a bloody coward, he thought. I rather liked him too until today. But how is one to know about an American?

54 "No," said Wilson. "I'm a professional hunter. We never talk about our clients. You can be quite easy on that. It's supposed to be bad form to ask us not to talk though."

He had decided now that to break would be much 55
easier. He would eat, then, by himself and could read a book with his meals. They would eat by themselves. He would see them through the safari on a very formal basis—what was it the French called it? Distinguished consideration—and it would be a damn sight easier than having to go through this emotional trash. He'd insult him and make a good clean break. Then he could read a book with his meals and he'd still be drinking their whisky. That was the phrase for it when a safari went bad. You ran into another white hunter and you asked, "How is everything going?" and he answered, "Oh, I'm still drinking their whisky," and you knew everything had gone to pot.

"I'm sorry," Macomber said and looked at him with 56
his American face that would stay adolescent until it became middle-aged, and Wilson noted his crew-cropped hair, fine eyes only faintly shifty, good nose, thin lips and handsome jaw. "I'm sorry I didn't realize that. There are lots of things I don't know."

So what could he do, Wilson thought. He was all 57
ready to break it off quickly and neatly and here the beggar was apologizing after he had just insulted him. He made one more attempt. "Don't worry about me talking," he said. "I have a living to make. You know in Africa no woman ever misses her lion and no white man ever bolts."

"I bolted like a rabbit," Macomber said. 58

Now what in hell were you going to do about a 59
man who talked like that, Wilson wondered.

Wilson looked at Macomber with his flat, blue, 60
machine-gunner's eyes and the other smiled back at him. He had a pleasant smile if you did not notice how his eyes showed when he was hurt.

"Maybe I can fix it up on buffalo," he said. "We're 61
after them next, aren't we?"

"In the morning if you like," Wilson told him. Per- 62
haps he had been wrong. This was certainly the way to take it. You most certainly could not tell a damned thing about an American. He was all for Macomber again. If you could forget the morning. But, of course, you couldn't. The morning had been about as bad as they come.

"Here comes the Memsahib," he said. She was 63
walking over from her tent looking refreshed and cheerful and quite lovely. She had a very perfect oval face, so perfect that you expected her to be stupid. But she wasn't stupid, Wilson thought, no, not stupid.

64 "How is the beautiful red-faced Mr. Wilson? Are you feeling better, Francis, my pearl?"

65 "Oh, much," said Macomber.

66 "I've dropped the whole thing," she said, sitting down at the table. "What importance is there to whether Francis is any good at killing lions? That's not his trade. That's Mr. Wilson's trade. Mr. Wilson is really very impressive killing anything. You do kill anything, don't you?"

67 "Oh, anything," said Wilson. "Simply anything." They are, he thought, the hardest in the world; the hardest, the cruelest, the most predatory and the most attractive and their men have softened or gone to pieces nervously as they have hardened. Or is it that they pick men they can handle? They can't know that much at the age they marry, he thought. He was grateful that he had gone through his education on American women before now because this was a very attractive one.

How should a woman act when she discovers her husband is a bloody coward?

68 "We're going after buff in the morning," he told her.

69 "I'm coming," she said.

70 "No, you're not."

71 "Oh, yes, I am. Mayn't I, Francis?"

72 "Why not stay in camp?"

73 "Not for anything," she said. "I wouldn't miss something like today for anything."

74 When she left, Wilson was thinking, when she went off to cry, she seemed a hell of a fine woman. She seemed to understand, to realize, to be hurt for him and for herself and to know how things really stood. She is away for twenty minutes and now she is back, simply enamelled in that American female cruelty. They are the damnedest women. Really the damnedest.

75 "We'll put on another show for you tomorrow," Francis Macomber said.

76 "You're not coming," Wilson said.

77 "You're very mistaken," she told him. "And I want *so* to see you perform again. You were lovely this morning. That is if blowing things' heads off is lovely."

78 "Here's the lunch," said Wilson. "You're very merry, aren't you?"

79 "Why not? I didn't come out here to be dull."

80 "Well, it hasn't been dull," Wilson said. He could see the boulders in the river and the high bank beyond with the trees and he remembered the morning.

81 "Oh, no," she said. "It's been charming. And tomorrow. You don't know how I look forward to tomorrow."

82 "That's eland he's offering you," Wilson said.

83 "They're the big cowy things that jump like hares, aren't they?"

84 "I suppose that describes them," Wilson said.

"It's very good meat," Macomber said. 85

"Did you shoot it, Francis?" she asked. 86

"Yes." 87

"They're not dangerous, are they?" 88

"Only if they fall on you," Wilson told her. 89

"I'm so glad." 90

"Why not let up on the bitchery just a little, Margot," Macomber said, cutting the eland steak and putting some mashed potato, gravy and carrot on the downturned fork that tined through the piece of meat. 91

"I suppose I could," she said, "since you put it so prettily." 92

"Tonight we'll have champagne for the lion," Wilson said. "It's a bit too hot at noon." 93

"Oh, the lion," Margot said. "I'd forgotten the lion!" 94

So, Robert Wilson thought to himself, she *is* giving him a ride, isn't she? Or do you suppose that's her idea of putting up a good show? How should a woman act when she discovers her husband is a bloody coward? She's damn cruel but they're all cruel. They govern, of course, and to govern one has to be cruel sometimes. Still, I've seen enough of their damn terrorism. 95

"Have some more eland," he said to her politely. 96

That afternoon, late, Wilson and Macomber went out in the motor car with the native driver and the two gun-bearers. Mrs. Macomber stayed in the camp. It was too hot to go out, she said, and she was going with them in the early morning. As they drove off Wilson saw her standing under the big tree, looking pretty rather than beautiful in her faintly rosy khaki, her dark hair drawn back off her forehead and gathered in a knot low on her neck, her face as fresh, he thought, as though she were in England. She waved to them as the car went off through the swale of high grass and curved around through the trees into the small hills of orchard bush. 97

In the orchard bush they found a herd of impala, and leaving the car they stalked one old ram with long, wide-spread horns and Macomber killed it with a very creditable shot that knocked the buck down at a good two hundred yards and sent the herd off bounding wildly and leaping over one another's backs in long, leg-drawn-up leaps as unbelievable and as floating as those one makes sometimes in dreams. 98

"That was a good shot," Wilson said. "They're a small target." 99

"Is it a worth-while head?" Macomber asked. 100

"It's excellent," Wilson told him. "You shoot like that and you'll have no trouble." 101

"Do you think we'll find buffalo tomorrow?" 102

03 "There's a good chance of it. They feed out early in the morning and with luck we may catch them in the open."

04 "I'd like to clear away that lion business," Macomber said. "It's not very pleasant to have your wife see you do something like that."

05 I should think it would be even more unpleasant to do it, Wilson thought, wife or no wife, or to talk about having done it. But he said, "I wouldn't think about that any more. Any one could be upset by his first lion. That's all over."

06 But that night after dinner and a whisky and soda by the fire before going to bed, as Francis Macomber lay on his cot with the mosquito bar over him and listened to the night noises it was not all over. It was neither all over nor was it beginning. It was there exactly as it happened with some parts of it indelibly emphasized and he was miserably ashamed at it. But more than shame he felt cold, hollow fear in him. The fear was still there like a cold slimy hollow in all the emptiness where once his confidence had been and it made him feel sick. It was still there with him now.

07 It had started the night before when he had wakened and heard the lion roaring somewhere up along the river. It was a deep sound and at the end there were sort of coughing grunts that made him seem just outside the tent, and when Francis Macomber woke in the night to hear it he was afraid. He could hear his wife breathing quietly, asleep. There was no one to tell he was afraid, nor to be afraid with him, and, lying alone, he did not know the Somali proverb that says a brave man is always frightened three times by a lion; when he first sees his track, when he first hears him roar and when he first confronts him. Then while they were eating breakfast by lantern light out in the dining tent, before the sun was up, the lion roared again and Francis thought he was just at the edge of camp.

108 "Sounds like an old-timer," Robert Wilson said, looking up from his kippers and coffee. "Listen to him cough."

109 "Is he very close?"

110 "A mile or so up the stream."

111 "Will we see him?"

112 "We'll have a look."

113 "Does his roaring carry that far? It sounds as though he were right in camp."

114 "Carries a hell of a long way," said Robert Wilson. "It's strange the way it carries. Hope he's a shootable cat. The boys said there was a very big one about here."

115 "If I get a shot, where should I hit him," Macomber asked, "to stop him?"

116 "In the shoulders," Wilson said. "In the neck if you can make it. Shoot for bone. Break him down."

117 "I hope I can place it properly," Macomber said.

118 "You shoot very well," Wilson told him. "Take your time. Make sure of him. The first one in is the one that counts."

119 "What range will it be?"

120 "Can't tell. Lion has something to say about that. Don't shoot unless it's close enough so you can make sure."

121 "At under a hundred yards?" Macomber asked.

122 Wilson looked at him quickly.

123 "Hundred's about right. Might have to take him a bit under. Shouldn't chance a shot at much over that. A hundred's a decent range. You can hit him wherever you want at that. Here comes the Memsahib."

124 "Good morning," she said. "Are we going after that lion?"

125 "As soon as you deal with your breakfast," Wilson said. "How are you feeling?"

126 "Marvellous," she said. "I'm very excited."

127 "I'll just go and see that everything is ready." Wilson went off. As he left the lion roared again.

128 "Noisy beggar," Wilson said. "We'll put a stop to that."

129 "What's the matter, Francis?" his wife asked him.

130 "Nothing," Macomber said.

131 "Yes, there is," she said. "What are you upset about?"

132 "Nothing," he said.

133 "Tell me," she looked at him. "Don't you feel well?"

134 "It's that damned roaring," he said. "It's been going on all night, you know."

135 "Why didn't you wake me," she said. "I'd love to have heard it."

136 "I've got to kill the damned thing," Macomber said, miserably.

137 "Well, that's what you're out here for, isn't it?"

138 "Yes. But I'm nervous. Hearing the thing roar gets on my nerves."

139 "Well then, as Wilson said, kill him and stop his roaring."

140 "Yes, darling," said Francis Macomber. "It sounds easy, doesn't it?"

141 "You're not afraid, are you?"

142 "Of course not. But I'm nervous from hearing him roar all night."

143 "You'll kill him marvellously," she said. "I know you will. I'm awfully anxious to see it."

144 "Finish your breakfast and we'll be starting."

145 "It's not light yet," she said. "This is a ridiculous hour."

146 Just then the lion roared in a deep-chested moaning, suddenly guttural, ascending vibration that seemed to shake the air and ended in a sigh and a heavy, deep-chested grunt.

147 "He sounds almost here," Macomber's wife said.

148 "My God," said Macomber. "I hate that damned noise."

149 "It's very impressive."

150 "Impressive. It's frightful."

151 Robert Wilson came up then carrying his short, ugly, shockingly big-bored .505 Gibbs and grinning.

152 "Come on," he said. "Your gun-bearer has your Springfield and the big gun. Everything's in the car. Have you solids?"

153 "Yes."

154 "I'm ready," Mrs. Macomber said.

155 "Must make him stop that racket," Wilson said. "You get in front. The Memsahib can sit back here with me."

156 They climbed into the motor car and, in the gray first daylight, moved off up the river through the trees. Macomber opened the breech of his rifle and saw he had metal-cased bullets, shut the bolt and put the rifle on safety. He saw his hand was trembling. He felt in his pocket for more cartridges and moved his fingers over the cartridges in the loops of his tunic front. He turned back to where Wilson sat in the rear seat of the doorless, box-bodied motor car beside his wife, them both grinning with excitement, and Wilson leaned forward and whispered,

157 "See the birds dropping. Means the old boy has left his kill."

158 On the far bank of the stream Macomber could see, above the trees, vultures circling and plummeting down.

159 "Chances are he'll come to drink along here," Wilson whispered. "Before he goes to lay up. Keep an eye out."

160 They were driving slowly along the high bank of the stream which here cut deeply to its boulder-filled bed, and they wound in and out through big trees as they drove. Macomber was watching the opposite bank when he felt Wilson take hold of his arm. The car stopped.

161 "There he is," he heard the whisper. "Ahead and to the right. Get out and take him. He's a marvellous lion."

162 Macomber saw the lion now. He was standing almost broadside, his great head up and turned toward them. The early morning breeze that blew toward them was just stirring his dark mane, and the lion looked huge, silhouetted on the rise of bank in the gray morning light, his shoulders heavy, his barrel of a body bulking smoothly.

"How far is he?" asked Macomber, raising his rifle. 16

"About seventy-five. Get out and take him." 16

"Why not shoot from where I am?" 16

"You don't shoot them from cars," he heard Wilson saying in his ear. "Get out. He's not going to stay there all day." 16

Macomber stepped out of the curved opening at the side of the front seat, onto the step and down onto the ground. The lion still stood looking majestically and coolly toward this object that his eyes only showed in silhouette, bulking like some super-rhino. There was no man smell carried toward him and he watched the object, moving his great head a little from side to side. Then watching the object, not afraid, but hesitating before going down the bank to drink with such a thing opposite him, he saw a man figure detach itself from it and he turned his heavy head and swung away toward the cover of the trees as he heard a cracking crash and felt the slam of a .30-06 220-grain solid bullet that bit his flank and ripped in sudden hot scalding nausea through his stomach. He trotted, heavy, big-footed, swinging wounded full-bellied, through the trees toward the tall grass and cover, and the crash came again to go past him ripping the air apart. Then it crashed again and he felt the blow as it hit his lower ribs and ripped on through, blood sudden hot and frothy in his mouth, and he galloped toward the high grass where he could crouch and not be seen and make them bring the crashing thing close enough so he could make a rush and get the man that held it. 16

Macomber had not thought how the lion felt as he got out of the car. He only knew his hands were shaking and as he walked away from the car it was almost impossible for him to make his legs move. They were stiff in the thighs, but he could feel the muscles fluttering. He raised the rifle, sighted on the junction of the lion's head and shoulders and pulled the 16

trigger. Nothing happened though he pulled until he thought his finger would break. Then he knew he had the safety on and as he lowered the rifle to move the safety over he moved another frozen pace forward, and the lion seeing his silhouette flow clear of the silhouette of the car, turned and started off at a trot, and, as Macomber fired, he heard a whunk that meant that the bullet was home; but the lion kept on going. Macomber shot again and every one saw the bullet throw a spout of dirt beyond the trotting lion. He shot again, remembering to lower his aim, and they all heard the bullet hit, and the lion went into a gallop and was in the tall grass before he had the bolt pushed forward.

> . . . a wounded lion's going to charge.

69 Macomber stood there feeling sick at his stomach, his hands that held the Springfield still cocked, shaking, and his wife and Robert Wilson were standing by him. Beside him too were the two gun-bearers chattering in Wakamba.

70 "I hit him," Macomber said. "I hit him twice."

71 "You gut-shot him and you hit him somewhere forward," Wilson said without enthusiasm. The gun-bearers looked very grave. They were silent now.

72 "You may have killed him," Wilson went on. "We'll have to wait a while before we go in to find out."

73 "What do you mean?"

74 "Let him get sick before we follow him up."

75 "Oh," said Macomber.

76 "He's a hell of a fine lion," Wilson said cheerfully. "He's gotten into a bad place though."

77 "Why is it bad?"

78 "Can't see him until you're on him."

79 "Oh," said Macomber.

80 "Come on," said Wilson. "The Memsahib can stay here in the car. We'll go to have a look at the blood spoor."

81 "Stay here, Margot," Macomber said to his wife. His mouth was very dry and it was hard for him to talk.

82 "Why?" she asked.

83 "Wilson says to."

84 "We're going to have a look," Wilson said. "You stay here. You can see even better from here."

85 "All right."

86 Wilson spoke in Swahili to the driver. He nodded and said, "Yes, Bwana."

87 Then they went down the steep bank and across the stream, climbing over and around the boulders and up the other bank, pulling up by some projecting roots, and along it until they found where the lion had been trotting when Macomber first shot. There was dark blood on the short grass that the gun-bearers pointed out with grass stems, and that ran away behind the river bank trees.

"What do we do?" asked Macomber. 188

"Not much choice," said Wilson. "We can't bring the car over. Bank's too steep. We'll let him stiffen up a bit and then you and I'll go in and have a look for him." 189

"Can't we set the grass on fire?" Macomber asked. 190

"Too green." 191

"Can't we send beaters?" 192

Wilson looked at him appraisingly. "Of course we can," he said. "But it's just a touch murderous. You see, we know the lion's wounded. You can drive an unwounded lion—he'll move on ahead of a noise—but a wounded lion's going to charge. You can't see him until you're right on him. He'll make himself perfectly flat in cover you wouldn't think would hide a hare. You can't very well send boys in there to that sort of a show. Somebody bound to get mauled." 193

"What about the gun-bearers?" 194

"Oh, they'll go with us. It's their *shauri*. You see, they signed on for it. They don't look too happy though, do they?" 195

"I don't want to go in there," said Macomber. It was out before he knew he'd said it. 196

"Neither do I," said Wilson very cheerily. "Really no choice though." Then, as an afterthought, he glanced at Macomber and saw suddenly how he was trembling and the pitiful look on his face. 197

"You don't have to go in, of course," he said. "That's what I'm hired for, you know. That's why I'm so expensive." 198

"You mean you'd go in by yourself? Why not leave him there?" 199

Robert Wilson, whose entire occupation had been with the lion and the problem he presented, and who had not been thinking about Macomber except to note that he was rather windy, suddenly felt as though he had opened the wrong door in a hotel and seen something shameful. 200

"What do you mean?" 201

"Why not just leave him?" 202

"You mean pretend to ourselves he hasn't been hit?" 203

"No. Just drop it." 204

"It isn't done." 205

"Why not?" 206

"For one thing, he's certain to be suffering. For another, some one else might run onto him." 207

"I see." 208

"But you don't have to have anything to do with it." 209

"I'd like to," Macomber said. "I'm just scared, you know." 210

"I'll go ahead when we go in," Wilson said, "with Kongoni tracking. You keep behind me and a little to one side. Chances are we'll hear him growl. If we see 211 him we'll both shoot. Don't worry about anything. I'll keep you backed up. As a matter of fact, you know, perhaps you'd better not go. It might be much better. Why don't you go over and join the Memsahib while I just get it over with?"

212 "No, I want to go."

213 "All right," said Wilson. "But don't go in if you don't want to. This is my *shauri* now, you know."

214 "I want to go," said Macomber.

215 They sat under a tree and smoked.

216 "Want to go back and speak to the Memsahib while we're waiting?" Wilson asked.

217 "No."

218 "I'll just step back and tell her to be patient."

219 "Good," said Macomber. He sat there, sweating under his arms, his mouth dry, his stomach hollow feeling, wanting to find courage to tell Wilson to go on and finish off the lion without him. He could not know that Wilson was furious because he had not noticed the state he was in earlier and sent him back to his wife. While he sat there Wilson came up. "I have your big gun," he said. "Take it. We've given him time, I think. Come on."

220 Macomber took the big gun and Wilson said:

221 "Keep behind me and about five yards to the right and do exactly as I tell you." Then he spoke in Swahili to the two gun-bearers who looked the picture of gloom.

222 "Let's go," he said.

223 "Could I have a drink of water?" Macomber asked. Wilson spoke to the older gun-bearer, who wore a canteen on his belt, and the man unbuckled it, unscrewed the top and handed it to Macomber, who took it noticing how heavy it seemed and how hairy and shoddy the felt covering was in his hand. He raised it to drink and looked ahead at the high grass with the flat-topped trees behind it. A breeze was blowing toward them and the grass rippled gently in the wind. He looked at the gun-bearer and he could see the gun-bearer was suffering too with fear.

224 Thirty-five yards into the grass the big lion lay flattened out along the ground. His ears were back and his only movement was a slight twitching up and down of his long, black-tufted tail. He had turned at bay as soon as he had reached this cover and he was sick with the wound through his full belly, and weakening with the wound through his lungs that brought a thin foamy red to his mouth each time he breathed. His flanks were wet and hot and flies were on the little openings the solid bullets had made in his tawny hide, and his big yellow eyes, narrowed with hate, looked straight ahead, only blinking when the pain came as he breathed, and his claws dug in the soft baked earth. All of him, pain, sickness, hatred and all of his remaining strength, was tightening into an absolute concentration for a rush. He could hear the men talking and he waited, gathering all of himself into this preparation for a charge as soon as the men would come into the grass. As he heard their voices his tail stiffened to twitch up and down, and, as they came into the edge of the grass, he made a coughing grunt and charged.

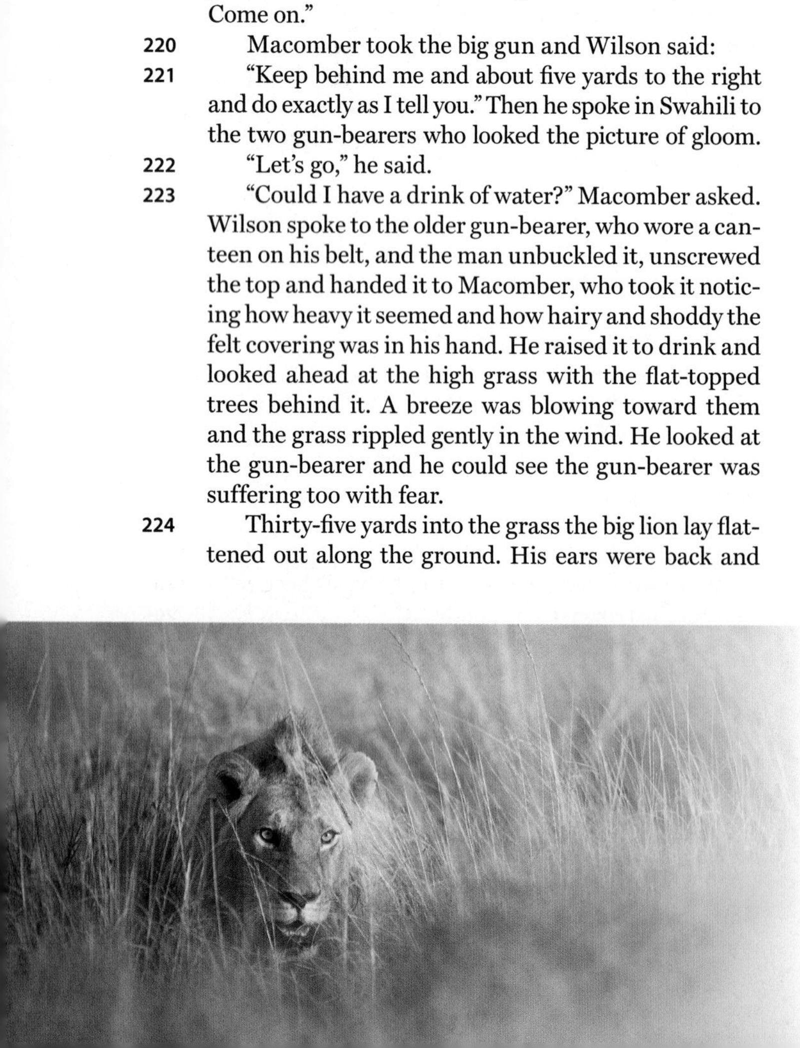

Kongoni, the old gun-bearer, in the lead watch- 22
ing the blood spoor, Wilson watching the grass for any movement, his big gun ready, the second gun-bearer looking ahead and listening, Macomber close to Wilson, his rifle cocked, they had just moved into the grass when Macomber heard the blood-choked coughing grunt, and saw the swishing rush in the grass. The next thing he knew he was running; running wildly, in panic in the open, running toward the stream.

He heard the *ca-ra-wong!* of Wilson's big rifle, and 22
again in a second crashing *carawong!* and turning saw the lion, horrible-looking now, with half his head seeming to be gone, crawling toward Wilson in the edge of the tall grass while the red-faced man worked the bolt on the short ugly rifle and aimed carefully as another blasting *carawong!* came from the muzzle, and the crawling, heavy, yellow bulk of the lion stiffened and the huge, mutilated head slid forward and Macomber, standing by himself in the clearing where he had run, holding a loaded rifle, while two black men and a white man looked back at him in contempt, knew the lion was dead. He came toward Wilson, his tallness all seeming a naked reproach, and Wilson looked at him and said:

"Want to take pictures?" 22

"No," he said. 22

That was all any one had said until they reached 22
the motor car. Then Wilson had said:

"Hell of a fine lion. Boys will skin him out. We 23
might as well stay here in the shade."

Macomber's wife had not looked at him nor he at 23
her and he had sat by her in the back seat with Wilson sitting in the front seat. Once he had reached over and taken his wife's hand without looking at her and

she had removed her hand from his. Looking across the stream to where the gun-bearers were skinning out the lion he could see that she had been able to see the whole thing. While they sat there his wife had reached forward and put her hand on Wilson's shoulder. He turned and she had leaned forward over the low seat and kissed him on the mouth.

2 "Oh, I say," said Wilson, going redder than his natural baked color.

3 "Mr. Robert Wilson," she said. "The beautiful red-faced Mr. Robert Wilson."

4 Then she sat down beside Macomber again and looked away across the stream to where the lion lay, with uplifted, white-muscled, tendon-marked naked forearms, and white bloating belly, as the black men fleshed away the skin. Finally the gun-bearers brought the skin over, wet and heavy, and climbed in behind with it, rolling it up before they got in, and the motor car started. No one had said anything more until they were back in camp.

5 That was the story of the lion. Macomber did not know how the lion had felt before he started his rush, nor during it when the unbelievable smash of the .505 with a muzzle velocity of two tons had hit him in the mouth, nor what kept him coming after that, when the second ripping crash had smashed his hind quarters and he had come crawling on toward the crashing, blasting thing that had destroyed him. Wilson knew something about it and only expressed it by saying, "Damned fine lion," but Macomber did not know how Wilson felt abut things either. He did not know how his wife felt except that she was through with him.

6 His wife had been through with him before but it never lasted. He was very wealthy, and would be much wealthier, and he knew she would not leave him ever now. That was one of the few things that he really knew. He knew about that, about motor cycles—that was earliest—about motor cars, about duck-shooting, about fishing, trout, salmon and big-sea, about sex in books, many books, too many books, about all court games, about dogs, not much about horses, about hanging on to his money, about most of the other things his world dealt in, and about his wife not leaving him. His wife had been a great beauty and she was still a great beauty in Africa, but she was not a great enough beauty any more at home to be able to leave him and better herself and she knew it and he knew it. She had missed the chance to leave him and he knew it. If he had been better with women she would probably have started to worry about him getting another new, beautiful wife; but she knew too much about him to worry about him either. Also, he had always had a great tolerance which seemed the nicest thing about him if it were not the most sinister.

Margot was too beautiful for Macomber to divorce her and Macomber had too much money for Margot ever to leave him.

All in all they were known as a comparatively happily married couple, one of those whose disruption is often rumored but never occurs, and as the society columnist put it, they were adding more than a spice of *adventure* to their much envied and ever-enduring *Romance* by a *Safari* in what was known as *Darkest Africa* until the Martin Johnsons lighted it on so many silver screens where they were pursuing *Old Simba* the lion, the buffalo, *Tembo* the elephant and as well collecting specimens for the Museum of Natural History. This same columnist had reported them *on the verge* at least three times in the past and they had been. But they always made it up. They had a sound basis of union. Margot was too beautiful for Macomber to divorce her and Macomber had too much money for Margot ever to leave him. 237

It was now about three o'clock in the morning and Francis Macomber, who had been asleep a little while after he had stopped thinking about the lion, wakened and then slept again, woke suddenly, frightened in a dream of the bloody-headed lion standing over him, and listening while his heart pounded, he realized that his wife was not in the other cot in the tent. He lay awake with that knowledge for two hours. 238

At the end of that time his wife came into the tent, lifted her mosquito bar and crawled cozily into bed. 239

"Where have you been?" Macomber asked in the darkness. 240

"Hello," she said. "Are you awake?" 241

"Where have you been?" 242

"I just went out to get a breath of air." 243

"You did, like hell." 244

"What do you want me to say, darling?" 245

"Where have you been?" 246

"Out to get a breath of air." 247

"That's a new name for it. You *are* a bitch." 248

"Well, you're a coward." 249

"All right," he said. "What of it?" 250

"Nothing as far as I'm concerned. But please let's not talk, darling, because I'm very sleepy." 251

"You think that I'll take anything." 252

253 "I know you will, sweet."

254 "Well, I won't."

255 "Please, darling, let's not talk. I'm so very sleepy."

256 "There wasn't going to be any of that. You promised there wouldn't be."

257 "Well, there is now," she said sweetly.

258 "You said if we made this trip that there would be none of that. You promised."

259 "Yes, darling. That's the way I meant it to be. But the trip was spoiled yesterday. We don't have to talk about it, do we?"

260 "You don't wait long when you have an advantage, do you?"

261 "Please let's not talk. I'm so sleepy, darling."

262 "I'm going to talk."

263 "Don't mind me then, because I'm going to sleep." And she did.

264 At breakfast they were all three at the table before daylight and Francis Macomber found that, of all the many men that he had hated, he hated Robert Wilson the most.

265 "Sleep well?" Wilson asked in his throaty voice, filling a pipe.

266 "Did you?"

267 "Topping," the white hunter told him.

268 You bastard, thought Macomber, you insolent bastard.

269 So she woke him when she came in, Wilson thought, looking at them both with his flat, cold eyes. Well, why doesn't he keep his wife where she belongs? What does he think I am, a bloody plaster saint? Let him keep her where she belongs. It's his own fault.

270 "Do you think we'll find buffalo?" Margot asked, pushing away a dish of apricots.

271 "Chance of it," Wilson said and smiled at her. "Why don't you stay in camp?"

272 "Not for anything," she told him.

273 "Why not order her to stay in camp?" Wilson said to Macomber.

274 "You order her," said Macomber coldly.

275 "Let's not have any ordering, nor," turning to Macomber, "any silliness, Francis," Margot said quite pleasantly.

276 "Are you ready to start?" Macomber asked.

277 "Any time," Wilson told him. "Do you want the Memsahib to go?"

278 "Does it make any difference whether I do or not?"

279 The hell with it, thought Robert Wilson. The utter complete hell with it. So this is what it's going to be like. Well, this is what it's going to be like, then.

"Makes no difference," he said.

"You're sure you wouldn't like to stay in camp with her yourself and let me go out and hunt the buffalo?" Macomber asked.

"Can't do that," said Wilson. "Wouldn't talk rot if I were you."

"I'm not talking rot. I'm disgusted."

"Bad word, disgusted."

"Francis, will you please try to speak sensibly," his wife said.

"I speak too damned sensibly," Macomber said. "Did you ever eat such filthy food?"

"Something wrong with the food?" asked Wilson quietly.

"No more than with everything else."

"I'd pull yourself together, laddybuck," Wilson said very quietly. "There's a boy waits at table that understands a little English."

"The hell with him."

Wilson stood up and puffing on his pipe strolled away, speaking a few words in Swahili to one of the gun-bearers who was standing waiting for him. Macomber and his wife sat on at the table. He was staring at his coffee cup.

"If you make a scene I'll leave you, darling," Margot said quietly.

"No, you won't."

"You can try it and see."

"You won't leave me."

"No," she said. "I won't leave you and you'll behave yourself."

"Behave myself? That's a way to talk. Behave myself."

"Yes. Behave yourself."

"Why don't *you* try behaving?"

"I've tried it so long. So very long."

"I hate that red-faced swine," Macomber said. "I loathe the sight of him."

"He's really *very* nice."

"Oh, *shut up,*" Macomber almost shouted. Just then the car came up and stopped in front of the dining tent and the driver and the two gun-bearers got out. Wilson walked over and looked at the husband and wife sitting there at the table.

"Going, shooting?" he asked.

"Yes," said Macomber, standing up. "Yes."

"Better bring a woolly. It will be cool in the car," Wilson said.

"I'll get my leather jacket," Margot said.

"The boy has it," Wilson told her. He climbed into the front with the driver and Francis Macomber and his wife sat, not speaking, in the back seat.

309 Hope the silly beggar doesn't take a notion to blow the back of my head off, Wilson thought to himself. Women *are* a nuisance on safari.

310 The car was grinding down to cross the river at a pebbly ford in the gray daylight and then climbed, angling up the steep bank, where Wilson had ordered a way shovelled out the day before so they could reach the parklike wooded rolling country on the far side.

311 It was a good morning, Wilson thought. There was a heavy dew and as the wheels went through the grass and low bushes he could smell the odor of the crushed fronds. It was an odor like verbena and he liked this early morning smell of the dew, the crushed bracken and the look of the tree trunks showing black through the early morning mist, as the car made its way through the untracked, parklike country. He had put the two in the back seat out of his mind now and was thinking about buffalo. The buffalo that he was after stayed in the daytime in a thick swamp where it was impossible to get a shot, but in the night they fed out into an open stretch of country and if he could come between them and their swamp with the car, Macomber would have a good chance at them in the open. He did not want to hunt buff with Macomber in thick cover. He did not want to hunt buff or anything else with Macomber at all, but he was a professional hunter and he had hunted with some rare ones in his time. If they got buff today there would only be rhino to come and the poor man would have gone through his dangerous game and things might pick up. He'd have nothing more to do with the woman and Macomber would get over that too. He must have gone through plenty of that before by the look of things. Poor beggar. He must have a way of getting over it. Well, it was the poor sod's own bloody fault.

They were his standards in all except the shooting.

312 He, Robert Wilson, carried a double size cot on safari to accommodate any windfalls he might receive. He had hunted for a certain clientele, the international, fast, sporting set, where the women did not feel they were getting their money's worth unless they had shared that cot with the white hunter. He despised them when he was away from them although he liked some of them well enough at the time, but he made his living by them; and their standards were his standards as long as they were hiring him.

313 They were his standards in all except the shooting. He had his own standards about the killing and they could live up to them or get some one else to hunt them. He knew, too, that they all respected him for this. This Macomber was an odd one though. Damned if he wasn't. Now the wife. Well, the wife. Yes, the wife. Hm, the wife. Well he'd dropped all that. He looked around at them. Macomber sat grim and furious. Margot smiled at him. She looked younger today, more innocent and fresher and not so professionally beautiful. What's in her heart God knows, Wilson thought. She hadn't talked much last night. At that it was a pleasure to see her.

The motor car climbed up a slight rise and went on through the trees and then out into a grassy prairie-like opening and kept in the shelter of the trees along the edge, the driver going slowly and Wilson looking carefully out across the prairie and all along its far side. He stopped the car and studied the opening with his field glasses. Then he motioned to the driver to go on and the car moved slowly along, the driver avoiding warthog holes and driving around the mud castles ants had built. Then, looking across the opening, Wilson suddenly turned and said, 314

"By God, there they are!" 315

And looking where he pointed, while the car jumped forward and Wilson spoke in rapid Swahili to the driver, Macomber saw three huge, black animals looking almost cylindrical in their long heaviness, like big black tank cars, moving at a gallop across the far edge of the open prairie. They moved at a stiff-necked, stiff bodied gallop and he could see the upswept wide black horns on their heads as they galloped heads out; the heads not moving. 316

"They're three old bulls," Wilson said. "We'll cut them off before they get to the swamp." 317

The car was going a wild forty-five miles an hour across the open and as Macomber watched, the buffalo got bigger and bigger until he could see the gray, hairless, scabby look of one huge bull and how his neck was a part of his shoulders and the shiny black of his horns as he galloped a little behind the others that were strung out in that steady plunging gait; and then, the car swaying as though it had just jumped a road, they drew up close and he could see the plunging hugeness of the bull, and the dust in his sparsely haired hide, the wide boss of horn and his outstretched, wide-nostrilled muzzle, and he was raising his rifle when Wilson shouted, "Not from the car, you fool!" and he had no fear, only hatred of Wilson, while the brakes clamped on and the car skidded, plowing sideways to an almost stop and Wilson was out on one side and he on the other, stumbling as his feet hit the still speeding-by of the earth, and then he was shooting at the bull as he moved away, hearing the bullets whunk into him, emptying his rifle at him as he moved steadily away, finally remembering to get his shots forward into the 318 shoulder, and as he fumbled to re-load, he saw the bull was down. Down on his knees, his big head tossing, and seeing the other two still galloping he shot at the leader and hit him. He shot again and missed and he heard the *carawonging* roar as Wilson shot and saw the leading bull slide forward onto his nose.

319 "Get that other," Wilson said. "Now you're shooting!"

320 But the other bull was moving steadily at the same gallop and he missed, throwing a spout of dirt, and Wilson missed and the dust rose in a cloud and Wilson shouted, "Come on. He's too far!" and grabbed his arm and they were in the car again, Macomber and Wilson hanging on the sides and rocketing swayingly over the uneven ground, drawing up on the steady, plunging, heavy-necked, straight-moving gallop of the bull.

321 They were behind him and Macomber was filling his rifle, dropping shells onto the ground, jamming it, clearing the jam, then they were almost up with the bull when Wilson yelled "Stop," and the car skidded so that it almost swung over and Macomber fell forward onto his feet, slammed his bolt forward and fired as far forward as he could aim into the galloping, rounded black back, aimed and shot again, then again, then again, and the bullets, all of them hitting, had no effect on the buffalo that he could see. Then Wilson shot, the roar deafening him, and he could see the bull stagger. Macomber shot again, aiming carefully, and down he came, onto his knees.

322 "All right," Wilson said. "Nice work. That's the three."

323 Macomber felt a drunken elation.

324 "How many times did you shoot?" he asked.

325 "Just three," Wilson said. "You killed the first bull. The biggest one. I helped you finish the other two. Afraid they might have got into cover. You had them killed. I was just mopping up a little. You shot damn well."

326 "Let's go to the car," said Macomber. "I want a drink."

327 "Got to finish off that buff first," Wilson told him. The buffalo was on his knees and he jerked his head furiously and bellowed in pig-eyed, roaring rage as they came toward him.

328 "Watch he doesn't get up," Wilson said. Then, "Get a little broadside and take him in the neck just behind the ear."

329 Macomber aimed carefully at the center of the huge, jerking, rage-driven neck and shot. At the shot the head dropped forward.

"That does it," said Wilson. "Got the spine. They're 33
a hell of a looking thing, aren't they?"

"Let's get the drink," said Macomber. In his life he 33
had never felt so good.

"In the car Macomber's wife sat very white-faced. 33
"You were marvellous, darling," she said to Macomber. "What a ride."

"Was it rough?" Wilson asked. 33

"It was frightful. I've never been more frightened 33
in my life."

"Let's all have a drink," Macomber said. 33

"By all means," said Wilson. "Give it to the Mem- 33
sahib." She drank the neat whisky from the flask and shuddered a little when she swallowed. She handed the flask to Macomber who handed it to Wilson.

She drank the neat whisky from the flask and shuddered a little when she swallowed.

"It was frightfully exciting," 33
she said. "It's given me a dreadful headache. I didn't know you were allowed to shoot them from cars though."

"No one shot from cars," said Wilson coldly. 33

"I mean chase them from cars." 33

"Wouldn't ordinarily," Wilson said. "Seemed sport- 34
ing enough to me though while we were doing it. Taking more chance driving that way across the plain full of holes and one thing and another than hunting on foot. Buffalo could have charged us each time we shot if he liked. Gave him every chance. Wouldn't mention it to anyone though. It's illegal if that's what you mean."

"It seemed very unfair to me," Margot said, "chas- 34
ing those big helpless things in a motor car."

"Did it?" said Wilson. 34

"What would happen if they heard about it in 34
Nairobi?"

"I'd lose my licence for one thing. Other unpleas- 34
antnesses," Wilson said, taking a drink from the flask. "I'd be out of business."

"Really?" 34

"Yes, really." 34

"Well," said Macomber, and he smiled for the first 34
time all day. "Now she has something on you."

"You have such a pretty way of putting things, Fran- 34
cis," Margot Macomber said. Wilson looked at them both. If a four-letter man marries a five-letter woman, he was thinking, what number of letters would their children be? What he said was, "We lost a gun-bearer. Did you notice it?"

"My God, no," Macomber said. 34

"Here he comes," Wilson said. "He's all right. He 35
must have fallen off when we left the first bull."

Approaching them was the middle-aged gun-bearer, 35
limping along in his knitted cap, khaki tunic, shorts

and rubber sandals, gloomy-faced and disgusted looking. As he came up he called out to Wilson in Swahili and they all saw the change in the white hunter's face.

2 "What does he say?" asked Margot

3 "He says the first bull got up and went into the bush," Wilson said with no expression in his voice.

4 "Oh," said Macomber blankly.

5 "Then it's going to be just like the lion," said Margot, full of anticipation.

6 "It's not going to be a damned bit like the lion," Wilson told her. "Did you want another drink, Macomber?"

7 "Thanks, yes," Macomber said. He expected the feeling he had had about the lion to come back but it did not. For the first time in his life he really felt wholly without fear. Instead of fear he had a feeling of definite elation.

8 "We'll go and have a look at the second bull," Wilson said. "I'll tell the driver to put the car in the shade."

9 "What are you going to do?" asked Margaret Macomber.

0 "Take a look at the buff," Wilson said.

1 "I'll come."

2 "Come along."

3 The three of them walked over to where the second buffalo bulked blackly in the open, head forward on the grass, the massive horns swung wide.

4 "He's a very good head," Wilson said. "That's close to a fifty-inch spread."

5 Macomber was looking at him with delight.

6 "He's hateful looking," said Margot. "Can't we go into the shade?"

7 "Of course," Wilson said. "Look," he said to Macomber, and pointed. "See that patch of bush?"

8 "Yes."

9 "That's where the first bull went in. The gun-bearer said when he fell off the bull was down. He was watching us helling along and the other two buff galloping. When he looked up there was the bull up and looking at him. Gun-bearer ran like hell and the bull went off slowly into that bush."

0 "Can we go in after him now?" asked Macomber eagerly.

1 Wilson looked at him appraisingly. Damned if this isn't a strange one, he thought. Yesterday he's scared sick and today he's a ruddy fire eater.

2 "No, we'll give him a while."

3 "Let's please go into the shade," Margot said. Her face was white and she looked ill.

4 They made their way to the car where it stood under a single, wide-spreading tree and all climbed in.

5 "Chances are he's dead in there," Wilson remarked. "After a little we'll have a look."

6 Macomber felt a wild unreasonable happiness that he had never known before.

"By God, that was a chase," he said. "I've never felt any such feeling. Wasn't it marvellous, Margot?" 377

"I hated it." 378

"Why?" 379

"I hated it," she said bitterly. "I loathed it." 380

"You know I don't think I'd ever be afraid of anything again," Macomber said to Wilson. "Something happened in me after we first saw the buff and started after him. Like a dam bursting. It was pure excitement." 381

"Cleans out your liver," said Wilson. "Damn funny things happen to people." 382

Macomber's face was shining. "You know something did happen to me," he said. "I feel absolutely different." 383

His wife said nothing and eyed him strangely. She was sitting far back in the seat and Macomber was sitting forward talking to Wilson who turned sideways talking over the back of the front seat. 384

"You know, I'd like to try another lion," Macomber said. "I'm really not afraid of them now. After all, what can they do to you?" 385

"That's it," said Wilson. "Worst one can do is kill you. How does it go? Shakespeare. Damned good. See if I can remember. Oh, damned good. Used to quote it to myself at one time. Let's see. 'By my troth, I care not; a man can die but once; we owe God a death and let it go which way it will, he that dies this year is quit for the next.' Damned fine, eh?" 386

He was very embarrassed, having brought out this thing he had lived by, but he had seen men come of age before and it always moved him. It was not a matter of their twenty-first birthday. 387

It had taken a strange chance of hunting, a sudden precipitation into action without opportunity for worrying beforehand, to bring this about with Macomber, but regardless of how it had happened it had most certainly happened. Look at the beggar now, Wilson thought. It's that some of them stay little boys so long, Wilson thought. Sometimes all their lives. Their figures stay boyish when they're fifty. The great Ameri- 388

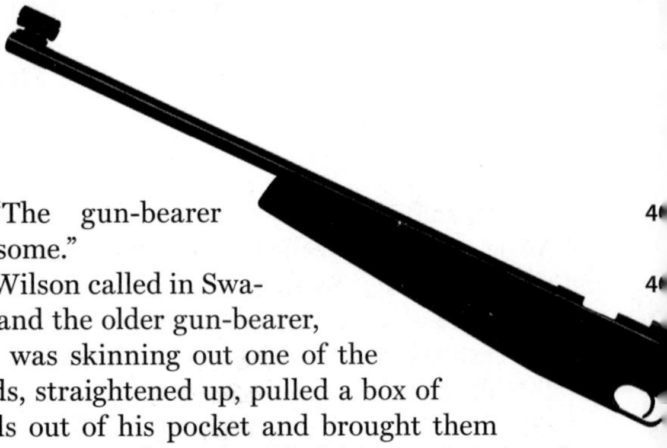

can boy-men. Damned strange people. But he liked this Macomber now. Damned strange fellow. Probably meant the end of cuckoldry too. Well, that would be a damned good thing. Damned good thing. Beggar had probably been afraid all his life. Don't know what started it. But over now. Hadn't had time to be afraid with the buff. That and being angry too. Motor car too. Motor cars made it familiar. Be a damn fire eater now. He'd seen it in the war work the same way. More of a change than any loss of virginity. Fear gone like an operation. Something else grew in its place. Main thing a man had. Made him into a man. Women knew it too. No bloody fear.

389 From the far corner of the seat Margaret Macomber looked at the two of them. There was no change in Wilson. She saw Wilson as she had seen him the day before when she had first realized what his great talent was. But she saw the change in Francis Macomber now.

390 "Do you have that feeling of happiness about what's going to happen?" Macomber asked, still exploring his new wealth.

391 "You're not supposed to mention it," Wilson said, looking in the other's face. "Much more fashionable to say you're scared. Mind you, you'll be scared too, plenty of times."

392 But you *have* a feeling of happiness about action to come?"

393 "Yes," said Wilson. "There's that. Doesn't do to talk too much about all this. Talk the whole thing away. No pleasure in anything if you mouth it up too much.

394 "You're both talking rot," said Margot. "Just because you've chased some helpless animals in a motor car you talk like heroes."

395 "Sorry," said Wilson. "I have been gassing too much." She's worried about it already, he thought.

396 "If you don't know what we're talking about why not keep out of it?" Macomber asked his wife.

397 "You've gotten awfully brave, awfully suddenly," his wife said contemptuously, but her contempt was not secure. She was very afraid of something.

398 Macomber laughed, a very natural hearty laugh. "You know I *have*," he said. "I really have."

399 "Isn't it sort of late?" Margot said bitterly. Because she had done the best she could for many years back and the way they were together now was no one person's fault.

400 "Not for me," said Macomber.

401 Margot said nothing but sat back in the corner of the seat.

402 "Do you think we've given him time enough?" Macomber asked Wilson cheerfully.

403 "We might have a look," Wilson said. "Have you any solids left?"

"The gun-bearer has some." 404

Wilson called in Swahili and the older gun-bearer, who was skinning out one of the heads, straightened up, pulled a box of solids out of his pocket and brought them over to Macomber, who filled his magazine and put the remaining shells in his pocket. 405

"You might as well shoot the Springfield," Wilson said. "You're used to it. We'll leave the Mannlicher in the car with the Memsahib. Your gun-bearer can carry your heavy gun. I've this damned cannon. Now let me tell you about them." He had saved this until the last because he did not want to worry Macomber. "When a buff comes he comes with his head high and thrust straight out. The boss of the horns covers any sort of a brain shot. The only shot is straight into the nose. The only other shot is into his chest or, if you're to one side, into the neck or the shoulders. After they've been hit once they take a hell of a lot of killing. Don't try anything fancy. Take the easiest shot there is. They've finished skinning out that head now. Should we get started?" 406

He called to the gun-bearers, who came up wiping their hands, and the older one got into the back. 407

"I'll only take Kongoni," Wilson said. "The other can watch to keep the birds away." 408

As the car moved slowly across the open space toward the island of brushy trees that ran in a tongue of foliage along a dry water course that cut the open swale, Macomber felt his heart pounding and his mouth was dry again, but it was excitement, not fear. 409

"Here's where he went in," Wilson said. Then to the gun-bearer in Swahili, "Take the blood spoor." 410

The car was parallel to the patch of bush. Macomber, Wilson and the gun-bearer got down. Macomber, looking back, saw his wife, with the rifle by her side, looking at him. He waved to her and she did not wave back. 411

The brush was very thick ahead and the ground was dry. The middle-aged gun-bearer was sweating heavily and Wilson had his hat down over his eyes and his red neck showed just ahead of Macomber. Suddenly the gun-bearer said something in Swahili to Wilson and ran forward. 412

"He's dead in there," Wilson said. "Good work," and he turned to grip Macomber's hand and as they shook hands, grinning at each other, the gun-bearer shouted wildly and they saw him coming out of the bush sideways, fast as a crab, and the bull coming, nose out, mouth tight closed, blood dripping, massive head straight out, coming in a charge, his little pig eyes bloodshot as he looked at them. Wilson, who 413 was ahead, was kneeling shooting, and Macomber, as he fired, unhearing his shot in the roaring of Wilson's gun, saw fragments like slate burst from the huge boss of the horns, and the head jerked, he shot again at the wide nostrils and saw the horns jolt again and fragments fly, and he did not see Wilson now and, aiming carefully, shot again with the buffalo's huge bulk almost on him and his rifle almost level with the on-coming head, nose out, and he could see the little wicked eyes and the head started to lower and he felt a sudden white-hot, blinding flash explode inside his head and that was all he ever felt.

14 Wilson had ducked to one side to get in a shoulder shot. Macomber had stood solid and shot for the nose, shooting a touch high each time and hitting the heavy horns, splintering and chipping them like hitting a slate roof, and Mrs. Macomber, in the car, had shot at the buffalo with the 6.5 Mannlicher as it seemed about to gore Macomber and had hit her husband about two inches up and a little to one side of the base of his skull.

"... Why didn't you poison him? That's what they do in England."

15 Francis Macomber lay now, face down, not two yards from where the buffalo lay on his side and his wife knelt over him with Wilson beside her.

16 "I wouldn't turn him over," Wilson said.

17 The woman was crying hysterically.

18 "I'd get back in the car," Wilson said. "Where's the rifle?"

19 She shook her head, her face contorted. The gun-bearer picked up the rifle.

20 "Leave it as it is," said Wilson. Then, "Go get Abdulla so that he may witness the manner of the accident."

He knelt down, took a handkerchief from his pocket, and spread it over Francis Macomber's crew-cropped head where it lay. The blood sank into the dry, loose earth. 421

Wilson stood up and saw the buffalo on his side, his legs out, his thinly-haired belly crawling with ticks. "Hell of a good bull," his brain registered automatically. "A good fifty inches, or better. Better." He called to the driver and told him to spread a blanket over the body and stay by it. Then he walked over to the motor car where the woman sat crying in the corner. 422

"That was a pretty thing to do," he said in a toneless voice. "He *would* have left you too." 423

"Stop it," she said. 424

"Of course it's an accident," he said. "I know that." 425

"Stop it," she said. 426

"Don't worry," he said. "There will be a certain amount of unpleasantness but I will have some photographs taken that will be very useful at the inquest. There's the testimony of the gun-bearers and the driver too. You're perfectly all right." 427

"Stop it," she said. 428

"There's a hell of a lot to be done," he said. "And I'll have to send a truck off to the lake to wireless for a plane to take the three of us into Nairobi. Why didn't you poison him? That's what they do in England." 429

"Stop it. Stop it. Stop it," the woman cried. 430

Wilson looked at her with his flat blue eyes. 431

"I'm through now," he said. "I was a little angry. I'd begun to like your husband." 432

"Oh, please stop it," she said. "Please stop it." 433

"That's better," Wilson said. "Please is much better. Now I'll stop." 434

If you like "The Short Happy Life of Francis Macomber," you may enjoy looking at some of the other third-person stories and seeing how they dip in and out of the perspective of one or another of the characters besides the main character. Take a look again at Willa Cather's story "Paul's Case" and see if the author herself makes a judgment or two about the situation as the story unfolds.

**GOING FURTHER** If you like the Hemingway story, you can dive into any one of a number of his novels and story collections. His nonfiction book *The Green Hills of Africa* takes you back to the setting of this story. To read about Africa from the point of view of an African writer, you can find novels that cover the great continent from the work of Tahar Ben Jelloun in the north all the way down to Nadine Gordimer and Zakes Mda in the south.

# Writing from Reading

## Summarize

1 Summarize the events of the two hunts described in the story, noting their similarities. Discuss the points of view from which Hemingway chooses to describe these parallel events. Do the point-of-view shifts match, or do we see similar events from different points of view?

## Analyze Craft

2 The point of view in the story shifts many times. Discuss the ways in which Hemingway signifies this shift to the reader.

3 This story begins *in medias res,* the first hunt of the lion and Macomber's first show of cowardice already having happened. Why does Hemingway choose to begin after the first hunt, rather than before? Explain how the story would change if your introduction to Francis was as a wealthy, attractive American embarking on his first safari.

4 Why does Hemingway choose to show us the lion's point of view? Some readers think of this passage as a triumphant demonstration of Hemingway's narrative style and imaginative reach; others think of it as overreaching or too showy. Criticize or defend the use of the lion's point of view, considering its context in the larger story.

## Analyze Voice

5 The story is told by a third-person omniscient narrator who jumps from one character's thoughts to the next. Consider whether the narrator identifies with one character more than the others, and explain your conclusion using clues from the text.

6 Note the parts of the story in which the narrator becomes most objective, acting as an observer who remains outside all the characters. What do these more distant perspectives contribute?

## Synthesize Summary and Analysis

7 Thanks to the narrator's omniscient point of view, we are able to see characters in their own minds as well as through the eyes of others. Discuss how Hemingway characterizes Francis Macomber using Francis's thoughts as well as Wilson's impressions of Francis. How does the dual impression affect you as a reader? Are you inclined to believe one source more than the other? Consider how you would view Francis if you never saw him from Wilson's point of view.

## Interpret the Story

8 At the end of the story, Wilson accuses Margot of killing her husband on purpose. Do you agree or disagree with Wilson? What evidence from the text supports or denies Wilson's accusations? Consider in your analysis why Hemingway rarely writes from Margot's point of view.

# Charlotte Perkins Gilman (1860–1935)

Born in Connecticut, Charlotte Perkins Gilman became a reluctant wife when she was twenty-four—reluctant because she feared the duties of a housewife would interfere with her desire to be active and productive in her own work. When the birth of her first child sent Gilman into depression, her doctor prescribed a rest cure consisting of an entirely domestic life free of physical and intellectual activity. As Gilman explained, "I went home and obeyed those directions for some three months, and came so near the border line of utter mental ruin that I could see over." She recovered by ignoring her doctor's orders and resuming her work as a writer and dedicated feminist. Gilman's most famous short story, "The Yellow Wallpaper," tells the story of a woman secluded from any activity and her consequent descent into madness—the author's way of speaking out against harmful patterns of preventing women's participation in society. In addition to creating stories that promoted feminist ideals, she also wrote nonfiction treatises on behalf of women's rights—most notably, *Women and Economics* (1898)—and lectured widely. Suffering from breast cancer and the loss of her second husband, Gilman ended her own life with chloroform at seventy-five.

**AS YOU READ** Notice the images that are repeated—for example, the house, the grounds surrounding it, the journal, the husband, the room where most of the story takes place, and of course, the wallpaper. How does the narrator's view of these crucial images change over the course of the story? How does the narrator herself change over the course of the story?

# The Yellow Wallpaper (1892)

1 IT is very seldom that mere ordinary people like John and myself secure ancestral halls for the summer.

2 A colonial mansion, a hereditary estate, I would say a haunted house and reach the height of romantic felicity—but that would be asking too much of fate!

3 Still I will proudly declare that there is something queer about it.

4 Else, why should it be let so cheaply? And why have stood so long untenanted?

5 John laughs at me, of course, but one expects that.

6 John is practical in the extreme. He has no patience with faith, an intense horror of superstition, and he scoffs openly at any talk of things not to be felt and seen and put down in figures.

7 John is a physician, and *perhaps*—(I would not say it to a living soul, of course, but this is dead paper and a great relief to my mind)—*perhaps* that is one reason I do not get well faster.

8 You see, he does not believe I am sick! And what can one do?

9 If a physician of high standing, and one's own husband, assures friends and relatives that there is really nothing the matter with one but temporary nervous depression—a slight hysterical tendency—what is one to do?

10 My brother is also a physician, and also of high standing, and he says the same thing.

11 So I take phosphates or phosphites—whichever it is—and tonics, and air and exercise, and journeys, and am absolutely forbidden to "work" until I am well again.

12 Personally, I disagree with their ideas.

13 Personally, I believe that congenial work, with excitement and change, would do me good.

14 But what is one to do?

15 I did write for a while in spite of them; but it *does* exhaust me a good deal—having to be so sly about it, or else meet with heavy opposition.

16 I sometimes fancy that in my condition, if I had less opposition and more society and stimulus—but John says the very worst thing I can do is to think about my condition, and I confess it always makes me feel bad.

17 So I will let it alone and talk about the house.

18 The most beautiful place! It is quite alone, standing well back from the road, quite three miles from the village. It makes me think of English places that you read about, for there are hedges and walls and

gates that lock, and lots of separate little houses for the gardeners and people.

19 There is a *delicious* garden! I never saw such a garden—large and shady, full of box-bordered paths, and lined with long grape-covered arbors with seats under them.

20 There were greenhouses, but they are all broken now.

21 There was some legal trouble, I believe, something about the heirs and coheirs; anyhow, the place has been empty for years.

22 That spoils my ghostliness, I am afraid, but I don't care—there is something strange about the house—I can feel it.

. . . there is something strange about the house— I can feel it.

23 I even said so to John one moonlight evening, but he said what I felt was a *draught,* and shut the window.

24 I get unreasonably angry with John sometimes. I'm sure I never used to be so sensitive. I think it is due to this nervous condition.

25 But John says if I feel so I shall neglect proper self-control; so I take pains to control myself—before him, at least, and that makes me very tired.

26 I don't like our room a bit. I wanted one downstairs that opened onto the piazza and had roses all over the window, and such pretty old-fashioned chintz hangings! But John would not hear of it.

27 He said there was only one window and not room for two beds, and no near room for him if he took another.

28 He is very careful and loving, and hardly lets me stir without special direction.

29 I have a schedule prescription for each hour in the day; he takes all care from me, and so I feel basely ungrateful not to value it more.

30 He said he came here solely on my account, that I was to have perfect rest and all the air I could get. "Your exercise depends on your strength, my dear," said he, "and your food somewhat on your appetite; but air you can absorb all the time." So we took the nursery at the top of the house.

31 It is a big, airy room, the whole floor nearly, with windows that look all ways, and air and sunshine galore. It was a nursery first, and then playroom and gymnasium, I should judge, for the windows are barred for little children, and there are rings and things in the walls.

32 The paint and paper look as if a boys' school had used it. It is stripped off—the paper—in great patches all around the head of my bed, about as far as I can reach, and in a great place on the other side of the room low down. I never saw a worse paper in my life. One of those sprawling, flamboyant patterns committing every artistic sin.

33 It is dull enough to confuse the eye in following, pronounced enough constantly to irritate and provoke study, and when you follow the lame uncertain curves for a little distance they suddenly commit suicide—plunge off at outrageous angles, destroy themselves in unheard-of contradictions.

34 The color is repellent, almost revolting: a smouldering unclean yellow, strangely faded by the slow-turning sunlight. It is a dull yet lurid orange in some places, a sickly sulphur tint in others.

35 No wonder the children hated it! I should hate it myself if I had to live in this room long.

36 There comes John, and I must put this away—he hates to have me write a word.

37 WE have been here two weeks, and I haven't felt like writing before, since that first day.

38 I am sitting by the window now, up in this atrocious nursery, and there is nothing to hinder my writing as much as I please, save lack of strength.

39 John is away all day, and even some nights when his cases are serious.

40 I am glad my case is not serious!

41 But these nervous troubles are dreadfully depressing.

42 John does not know how much I really suffer. He knows there is no *reason* to suffer, and that satisfies him.

43 Of course it is only nervousness. It does weigh on me so not to do my duty in any way!

44 I meant to be such a help to John, such a real rest and comfort, and here I am a comparative burden already!

45 Nobody would believe what an effort it is to do what little I am able—to dress and entertain, and order things.

46 It is fortunate Mary is so good with the baby. Such a dear baby!

47 And yet I *cannot* be with him, it makes me so nervous.

48 I suppose John never was nervous in his life. He laughs at me so about this wallpaper!

49 At first he meant to repaper the room, but afterward he said that I was letting it get the better of me, and that nothing was worse for a nervous patient than to give way to such fancies.

50 He said that after the wallpaper was changed it would be the heavy bedstead, and then the barred windows, and then that gate at the head of the stairs, and so on.

51 "You know the place is doing you good," he said, "and really, dear, I don't care to renovate the house just for a three months' rental."

52 "Then do let us go downstairs," I said. "There are such pretty rooms there."

53 Then he took me in his arms and called me a blessed little goose, and said he would go down to the cellar, if I wished, and have it whitewashed into the bargain.

54 But he is right enough about the beds and windows and things.

55 It is as airy and comfortable a room as anyone need wish, and, of course, I would not be so silly as to make him uncomfortable just for a whim.

56 I'm really getting quite fond of the big room, all but that horrid paper.

57 Out of one window I can see the garden—those mysterious deep-shaded arbors, the riotous old-fashioned flowers, and bushes and gnarly trees.

58 Out of another I get a lovely view of the bay and a little private wharf belonging to the estate. There is a beautiful shaded lane that runs down there from the house. I always fancy I see people walking in these numerous paths and arbors, but John has cautioned me not to give way to fancy in the least. He says that with my imaginative power and habit of storymaking, a nervous weakness like mine is sure to lead to all manner of excited fancies, and that I ought to use my will and good sense to check the tendency. So I try.

59 I think sometimes that if I were only well enough to write a little it would relieve the press of ideas and rest me.

60 But I find I get pretty tired when I try.

61 It is so discouraging not to have any advice and companionship about my work. When I get really well, John says we will ask Cousin Henry and Julia down for a long visit; but he says he would as soon put fireworks in my pillow-case as to let me have those stimulating people about now.

62 I wish I could get well faster.

63 But I must not think about that. This paper looks to me as if it *knew* what a vicious influence it had!

64 There is a recurrent spot where the pattern lolls like a broken neck and two bulbous eyes stare at you upside down.

65 I get positively angry with the impertinence of it and the everlastingness. Up and down and sideways they crawl, and those absurd unblinking eyes are everywhere. There is one place where two breadths didn't match, and the eyes go all up and down the line, one a little higher than the other.

66 I never saw so much expression in an inanimate thing before, and we all know how much expression they have! I used to lie awake as a child and get more entertainment and terror out of blank walls and plain furniture than most children could find in a toy-store.

67 I remember what a kindly wink the knobs of our big old bureau used to have, and there was one chair that always seemed like a strong friend.

68 I used to feel that if any of the other things looked too fierce I could always hop into that chair and be safe.

69 The furniture in this room is no worse than inharmonious, however, for we had to bring it all from downstairs. I suppose when this was used as a playroom they had to take the nursery things out, and no wonder! I never saw such ravages as the children have made here.

70 The wallpaper, as I said before, is torn off in spots, and it sticketh closer than a brother—they must have had perseverance as well as hatred.

71 Then the floor is scratched and gouged and splintered, the plaster itself is dug out here and there, and this great heavy bed, which is all we found in the room, looks as if it had been through the wars.

72 But I don't mind it a bit—only the paper.

73 There comes John's sister. Such a dear girl as she is, and so careful of me! I must not let her find me writing.

74 She is a perfect and enthusiastic housekeeper, and hopes for no better profession. I verily believe she thinks it is the writing which made me sick!

75 But I can write when she is out, and see her a long way off from these windows.

76 There is one that commands the road, a lovely shaded winding road, and one that just looks off over the country. A lovely country, too, full of great elms and velvet meadows.

77 This wallpaper has a kind of subpattern in a different shade, a particularly irritating one, for you can only see it in certain lights, and not clearly then.

78 But in the places where it isn't faded and where the sun is just so—I can see a strange, provoking, formless sort of figure that seems to skulk about behind that silly and conspicuous front design.

79 THERE'S sister on the stairs!

80 Well, the Fourth of July is over! The people are all gone, and I am tired out. John thought it might do me good to see a little company, so we just had Mother and Nellie and the children down for a week.

81 Of course I didn't do a thing. Jennie sees to everything now.

82 But it tired me all the same.

83 John says if I don't pick up faster he shall send me to Weir Mitchell in the fall.

84 But I don't want to go there at all. I had a friend who was in his hands once, and she says he is just like John and my brother, only more so!

85 Besides, it is such an undertaking to go so far.

86 I don't feel as if it was worthwhile to turn my hand over for anything, and I'm getting dreadfully fretful and querulous.

87 I cry at nothing, and cry most of the time.

88 Of course I don't when John is here, or anybody else, but when I am alone.

89 And I am alone a good deal just now. John is kept in town very often by serious cases, and Jennie is good and lets me alone when I want her to.

90 So I walk a little in the garden or down that lovely lane, sit on the porch under the roses, and lie down up here a good deal.

91 I'm getting really fond of the room in spite of the wallpaper. Perhaps *because* of the wallpaper.

92 It dwells in my mind so!

93 I lie here on this great immovable bed—it is nailed down, I believe—and follow that pattern about by the hour. It is as good as gymnastics, I assure you. I start, we'll say, at the bottom, down in the corner over there where it has not been touched, and I determine for the thousandth time that I *will* follow that pointless pattern to some sort of a conclusion.

94 I know a little of the principle of design, and I know this thing was not arranged on any laws of radiation, or alternation, or repetition, or symmetry, or anything else that I ever heard of.

95 It is repeated, of course, by the breadths, but not otherwise.

96 Looked at in one way, each breadth stands alone; the bloated curves and flourishes—a kind of "debased Romanesque" with *delirium tremens*—go waddling up and down in isolated columns of fatuity.

97 But, on the other hand, they connect diagonally, and the sprawling outlines run off in great slanting waves of optic horror, like a lot of wallowing seaweeds in full chase.

98 The whole thing goes horizontally, too, at least it seems so, and I exhaust myself trying to distinguish the order of its going in that direction.

99 They have used a horizontal breadth for a frieze, and that adds wonderfully to the confusion.

I'm getting really fond of the room in spite of the wallpaper.

100 There is one end of the room where it is almost intact, and there, when the crosslights fade and the low sun shines directly upon it, I can almost fancy radiation after all—the interminable grotesque seems to form around a common center and rush off in headlong plunges of equal distraction.

101 It makes me tired to follow it. I will take a nap, I guess.

102 I don't know why I should write this.

103 I don't want to.

104 I don't feel able.

105 And I know John would think it absurd. But I *must* say what I feel and think in some way—it is such a relief!

106 BUT the effort is getting to be greater than the relief.

107 Half the time now I am awfully lazy, and lie down ever so much. John says I mustn't lose my strength, and has me take cod liver oil and lots of tonics and things, to say nothing of ale and wines and rare meat.

108 Dear John! He loves me very dearly, and hates to have me sick. I tried to have a real earnest reasonable talk with him the other day, and tell him how I wish he would let me go and make a visit to Cousin Henry and Julia.

109 But he said I wasn't able to go, nor able to stand it after I got there; and I did not make out a very good case for myself, for I was crying before I had finished.

110 It is getting to be a great effort for me to think straight. Just this nervous weakness, I suppose.

111 And dear John gathered me up in his arms, and just carried me upstairs and laid me on the bed, and sat by me and read to me till it tired my head.

112 He said I was his darling and his comfort and all he had, and that I must take care of myself for his sake, and keep well.

113 He says no one but myself can help me out of it, that I must use my will and self-control and not let any silly fancies run away with me.

114 There's one comfort—the baby is well and happy, and does not have to occupy this nursery with the horrid wallpaper.

115 If we had not used it, that blessed child would have! What a fortunate escape! Why, I wouldn't have a child of mine, an impressionable little thing, live in such a room for worlds.

116 I never thought of it before, but it is lucky that John kept me here after all; I can stand it so much easier than a baby, you see.

117 Of course I never mention it to them any more—I am too wise—but I keep watch for it all the same.

118 There are things in the wallpaper that nobody knows about but me, or ever will.

119 Behind that outside pattern the dim shapes get clearer every day.

120 It is always the same shape, only very numerous.

121 And it is like a woman stooping down and creeping about behind that pattern. I don't like it a bit. I wonder—I begin to think—I wish John would take me away from here!

122 It is so hard to talk with John about my case, because he is so wise, and because he loves me so.

123 But I tried it last night.

124 It was moonlight. The moon shines in all around just as the sun does.

125 I hate to see it sometimes, it creeps so slowly, and always comes in by one window or another.

126 John was asleep and I hated to waken him, so I kept still and watched the moonlight on that undulating wallpaper till I felt creepy.

127 The faint figure behind seemed to shake the pattern, just as if she wanted to get out.

128 I got up softly and went to feel and see if the paper *did* move, and when I came back John was awake.

129 "What is it, little girl?" he said. "Don't go walking about like that—you'll get cold."

130 I thought it was a good time to talk, so I told him that I really was not gaining here, and that I wished he would take me away.

131 "Why, darling!" said he, "Our lease will be up in three weeks, and I can't see how to leave before.

132 "The repairs are not done at home, and I cannot possibly leave town just now. Of course, if you were in any danger, I could and would, but you really are better, dear, whether you can see it or not. I am a doctor, dear, and I know. You are gaining flesh and color, your appetite is better, I feel really much easier about you."

133 "I don't weigh a bit more," said I, "nor as much; and my appetite may be better in the evening when you are here but it is worse in the morning when you are away!"

"Bless her little heart!" said he with a big hug. "She shall be as sick as she pleases! But now let's improve the shining hours by going to sleep, and talk about it in the morning!" 134

"And you won't go away?" I asked gloomily. 135

"Why, how can I, dear? It is only three weeks more and then we will take a nice little trip for a few days while Jennie is getting the house ready. Really, dear, you are better!" 136

"Better in body perhaps—" I began, and stopped short, for he sat up straight and looked at me with such a stern, reproachful look that I could not say another word. 137

"My darling," said he, "I beg you, for my sake and for our child's sake, as well as for your own, that you will never for one instant let that idea enter your mind! There is nothing so dangerous, so fascinating, to a temperament like yours. It is a false and foolish fancy. Can you not trust me as a physician when I tell you so?" 138

So of course I said no more on that score, and we went to sleep before long. He thought I was asleep first, but I wasn't, and lay there for hours trying to decide whether that front pattern and the back pattern really did move together or separately. 139

On a pattern like this, by daylight, there is a lack of sequence, a defiance of law, that is a constant irritant to a normal mind. 140

The color is hideous enough, and unreliable enough, and infuriating enough, but the pattern is torturing. 141

You think you have mastered it, but just as you get well under way in following, it turns a back-somersault and there you are. It slaps you in the face, knocks you down, and tramples upon you. It is like a bad dream. 142

The outside pattern is a florid arabesque, reminding one of a fungus. If you can imagine a toadstool in joints, an interminable string of toadstools, budding and sprouting in endless convolutions—why, that is something like it. 143

That is, sometimes! 144

There is one marked peculiarity about this paper, a thing nobody seems to notice but myself, and that is that it changes as the light changes. 145

When the sun shoots in through the east window—I always watch for that first long, straight ray—it changes so quickly that I never can quite believe it. 146

That is why I watch it always. 147

148 By moonlight—the moon shines in all night when there is a moon—I wouldn't know it was the same paper.

149 At night in any kind of light, in twilight, candlelight, lamplight, and worst of all by moonlight, it becomes bars! The outside pattern, I mean, and the woman behind it is as plain as can be.

150 I didn't realize for a long time what the thing was that showed behind, that dim subpattern, but now I am quite sure it is a woman.

151 By daylight she is subdued, quiet. I fancy it is the pattern that keeps her so still. It is so puzzling. It keeps me quiet by the hour.

The fact is I am getting a little afraid of John.

152 I lie down ever so much now. John says it is good for me, and to sleep all I can.

153 Indeed he started the habit by making me lie down for an hour after each meal.

154 It is a very bad habit, I am convinced, for you see, I don't sleep.

155 And that cultivates deceit, for I don't tell them I'm awake—oh, no!

156 The fact is I am getting a little afraid of John.

157 He seems very queer sometimes, and even Jennie has an inexplicable look.

158 It strikes me occasionally, just as a scientific hypothesis, that perhaps it is the paper!

159 I have watched John when he did not know I was looking, and come into the room suddenly on the most innocent excuses, and I've caught him several times *looking at the paper!* And Jennie too. I caught Jennie with her hand on it once.

160 She didn't know I was in the room, and when I asked her in a quiet, a very quiet voice, with the most restrained manner possible, what she was doing with the paper, she turned around as if she had been caught stealing, and looked quite angry—asked me why I should frighten her so!

161 Then she said that the paper stained everything it touched, that she had found yellow smooches on all my clothes and John's and she wished we would be more careful!

162 Did not that sound innocent? But I know she was studying that pattern, and I am determined that nobody shall find it out but myself!

163 LIFE is very much more exciting now than it used to be. You see, I have something more to expect, to look forward to, to watch. I really do eat better, and am more quiet than I was.

John is so pleased to see me improve! He laughed a little the other day, and said I seemed to be flourishing in spite of my wallpaper. 164

I turned it off with a laugh. I had no intention of telling him it was *because* of the wallpaper—he would make fun of me. He might even want to take me away. 165

I don't want to leave now until I have found it out. There is a week more, and I think that will be enough. 166

I'm feeling so much better! 167

I don't sleep much at night, for it is so interesting to watch developments; but I sleep a good deal during the daytime. 168

In the daytime it is tiresome and perplexing. 169

There are always new shoots on the fungus, and new shades of yellow all over it. I cannot keep count of them, though I have tried conscientiously. 170

It is the strangest yellow, that wallpaper! It makes me think of all the yellow things I ever saw—not beautiful ones like buttercups, but old foul, bad yellow things. 171

But there is something else about that paper—the smell! I noticed it the moment we came into the room, but with so much air and sun it was not bad. Now we have had a week of fog and rain, and whether the windows are open or not, the smell is here. 172

It creeps all over the house. 173

I find it hovering in the dining-room, skulking in the parlor, hiding in the hall, lying in wait for me on the stairs. 174

It gets into my hair. 175

Even when I go to ride, if I turn my head suddenly and surprise it—there is that smell! 176

Such a peculiar odor, too! I have spent hours in trying to analyze it, to find what it smelled like. 177

It is not bad—at first—and very gentle, but quite the subtlest, most enduring odor I ever met. 178

In this damp weather it is awful. I wake up in the night and find it hanging over me. 179

It used to disturb me at first. I thought seriously of burning the house—to reach the smell. 180

But now I am used to it. The only thing I can think of that it is like is the *color* of the paper! A yellow smell. 181

There is a very funny mark on this wall, low down, near the mopboard. A streak that runs round the room. It goes behind every piece of furniture, except the bed, a long, straight, even *smooch,* as if it had been rubbed over and over. 182

I wonder how it was done and who did it, and what they did it for. Round and round and round—round and round and round—it makes me dizzy! 183

184 I really have discovered something at last.

185 Through watching so much at night, when it changes so, I have finally found out.

186 The front pattern *does* move—and no wonder! The woman behind shakes it!

187 Sometimes I think there are a great many women behind, and sometimes only one, and she crawls around fast, and her crawling shakes it all over.

188 Then in the very bright spots she keeps still, and in the very shady spots she just takes hold of the bars and shakes them hard.

189 And she is all the time trying to climb through. But nobody could climb through that pattern—it strangles so; I think that is why it has so many heads.

190 They get through and then the pattern strangles them off and turns them upside down, and makes their eyes white!

191 If those heads were covered or taken off it would not be half so bad.

192 I think that woman gets out in the daytime!

193 And I'll tell you why—privately—I've seen her!

194 I can see her out of every one of my windows!

195 It is the same woman, I know, for she is always creeping, and most women do not creep by daylight.

196 I see her in that long shaded lane, creeping up and down. I see her in those dark grape arbors, creeping all round the garden.

197 I see her on that long road under the trees, creeping along, and when a carriage comes she hides under the blackberry vines.

198 I don't blame her a bit. It must be very humiliating to be caught creeping by daylight!

199 I always lock the door when I creep by daylight. I can't do it at night, for I know John would suspect something at once.

200 And John is so queer now that I don't want to irritate him. I wish he would take another room! Besides, I don't want anybody to get that woman out at night but myself.

201 I often wonder if I could see her out of all the windows at once.

202 But, turn as fast as I can, I can only see out of one at one time.

203 And though I always see her, she *may* be able to creep faster than I can turn! I have watched her sometimes away off in the open country, creeping as fast as a cloud shadow in a wind.

204 If only that top pattern could be gotten off from the under one! I mean to try it, little by little.

205 I have found out another funny thing, but I shan't tell it this time! It does not do to trust people too much.

There are only two more days to get this paper off, 206
and I believe John is beginning to notice. I don't like the look in his eyes.

And I heard him ask Jennie a lot of professional 207
questions about me. She had a very good report to give.

She said I slept a good deal in the daytime. 208

John knows I don't sleep very well at night, for all 209
I'm so quiet!

He asked me all sorts of questions too, and pre- 210
tended to be very loving and kind.

As if I couldn't see through him! 211

Still, I don't wonder he acts so, sleeping under this 212
paper for three months.

It only interests me, but I feel sure John and Jen- 213
nie are affected by it.

HURRAH! This is the last day, but it is 214
enough. John is to stay in town over night, and won't be out until this evening.

Jennie wanted to sleep with me—the 215
sly thing; but I told her I should undoubtedly rest better for a night all alone.

That was clever, for really I wasn't alone a bit! As 216
soon as it was moonlight and that poor thing began to crawl and shake the pattern, I got up and ran to help her.

I pulled and she shook, I shook and she pulled, and 217
before morning we had peeled off yards of that paper.

A strip about as high as my head and half around 218
the room.

And then when the sun came and that awful pat- 219
tern began to laugh at me, I declared I would finish it today!

We go away tomorrow, and they are moving all 220
my furniture down again to leave things as they were before.

Jennie looked at the wall in amazement, but I told 221
her merrily that I did it out of pure spite at the vicious thing.

She laughed and said she wouldn't mind doing it 222
herself, but I must not get tired.

How she betrayed herself that time! 223

But I am here, and no person touches this paper 224
but Me—not *alive!*

She tried to get me out of the room—it was too 225
patent! But I said it was so quiet and empty and clean now that I believed I would lie down again and sleep all I could, and not to wake me even for dinner—I would call when I woke.

So now she is gone, and the servants are gone, and 226
the things are gone, and there is nothing left but that

great bedstead nailed down, with the canvas mattress we found on it.

227 We shall sleep downstairs tonight, and take the boat home tomorrow.

228 I quite enjoy the room, now it is bare again.

229 How those children did tear about here!

230 This bedstead is fairly gnawed!

231 But I must get to work.

232 I have locked the door and thrown the key down into the front path.

233 I don't want to go out, and I don't want to have anybody come in, till John comes.

234 I want to astonish him.

235 I've got a rope up here that even Jennie did not find. If that woman does get out, and tries to get away, I can tie her!

236 But I forgot I could not reach far without anything to stand on!

237 This bed will *not* move!

238 I tried to lift and push it until I was lame, and then I got so angry I bit off a little piece at one corner—but it hurt my teeth.

239 Then I peeled off all the paper I could reach standing on the floor. It sticks horribly and the pattern just enjoys it! All those strangled heads and bulbous eyes and waddling fungus growths just shriek with derision!

240 I am getting angry enough to do something desperate. To jump out of the window would be admirable exercise, but the bars are too strong even to try.

241 Besides I wouldn't do it. Of course not. I know well enough that a step like that is improper and might be misconstrued.

242 I don't like to *look* out of the windows even—there are so many of those creeping women, and they creep so fast.

243 I wonder if they all come out of that wallpaper as I did!

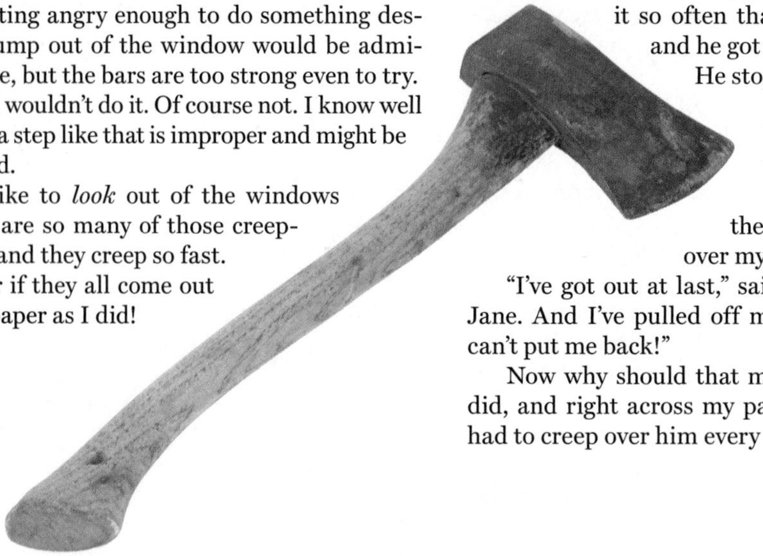

But I am securely fastened now by my well-hidden 244
rope—you don't get *me* out in the road there!

I suppose I shall have to get back behind the pat- 245
tern when it comes night, and that is hard!

It is so pleasant to be out in this great room and 246
creep around as I please!

I don't want to go outside. I won't, even if Jennie 247
asks me to.

For outside you have to creep on the ground, and 248
everything is green instead of yellow.

But here I can creep smoothly on the floor, and 249
my shoulder just fits in that long smooch around the wall, so I cannot lose my way.

Why, there's John at the door! 250

It is no use, young man, you can't open it! 251

How he does call and pound! 252

Now he's crying to Jennie for an axe. 253

It would be a shame to break down that beautiful 254
door!

"John, dear!" said I in the gentlest voice. "The key 255
is down by the front steps, under a plantain leaf!"

That silenced him for a few moments. 256

Then he said, very quietly indeed, "Open the door, 257
my darling!"

"I can't," said I. "The key is down by the front door 258
under a plantain leaf!" And then I said it again, several times, very gently and slowly, and said it so often that he had to go and see, and he got it of course, and came in. He stopped short by the door.

"What is the matter?" 259
he cried. "For God's sake, what are you doing!"

I kept on creeping just 260
the same, but I looked at him over my shoulder.

"I've got out at last," said I, "in spite of you and 261
Jane. And I've pulled off most of the paper, so you can't put me back!"

Now why should that man have fainted? But he 262
did, and right across my path by the wall, so that I had to creep over him every time!

YOU can find themes pertaining to the lives of modern women in a number of other stories in the book, including Kate Chopin's "The Story of an Hour" and Amy Tan's "Two Kinds," in chapter 2, and Jamaica Kincaid's "Girl" in chapter 3, among others.

**GOING FURTHER** One of the classic texts of the modern feminist movement, "The Yellow Wallpaper" points toward a long line of future fiction on similar themes, such as Joan Didion's novels *Run River* and *Play It As It Lays* and Margaret Atwood's *The Handmaid's Tale.*

# Writing from Reading

### Summarize

1 Describe the wallpaper's pattern in literal terms. What does it look like?

2 The narrator's relationship with the wallpaper goes through various stages. Identify and describe those stages.

### Analyze Craft

3 Analyze John's character and his role in the story. How does he help and/or harm his wife?

4 Discuss the themes of censorship, silencing, and imprisonment in this story.

### Analyze Voice

5 Consider the use of a first-person narrator in this story. Could the same story be told from a different point of view, or would the effect change entirely? What does your answer to this question say about the narrator's reliability?

### Synthesize Summary and Analysis

6 Scan the story for each mention of the narrator's journal, underlining these references when you find them. Form a conclusion about the role of the journal in the story. Why does the narrator have to keep it a secret from John and his sister?

### Interpret the Story

7 Identify a conflict central to the story. Discuss how that conflict affects the various characters. Is the conflict resolved by the end?

# Reading for Point of View

| | | |
|---|---|---|
| **When reading for point of view, ask yourself, *who is telling the story?*** | • A participant, or first-person narrator? (I/we) | EXAMPLE: I'm still not sure why I agreed to go with him in the first place. |
| | • Is s/he **naïve** because of age, experience, or cultural difference? Is s/he **unreliable** because of bias, character, or mental condition? | EXAMPLE: I was running on only three hours of sleep. Plus, he paid for my coffee, and he had a nice enough smile. |
| | • A nonparticipant, or third-person narrator? (he/she/they) | EXAMPLE: As the lights in the theater dimmed, he reached over and took her hand. |
| | • Is the narrator **omniscient,** or aware of the thoughts of multiple characters? | EXAMPLE: Her heart leaped, and her mind buzzed, so that she missed the entire introduction to the film and had to ask him what was going on. "They're robbing this bank," he replied nonchalantly, silently thrilled she hadn't pulled away. |
| | • Is the narrator **editorial,** inserting judgments about the character? | EXAMPLE: Later she might reflect on the cruelty of excusing herself to go to the bathroom and abandoning him there at the theater, but at the time all she could think about was freedom. |
| | • Is the narrator **impartial,** relating events without judging them? | EXAMPLE: So she left him there, alone, waiting patiently for her return. She went and bought herself a frozen yogurt. |
| | • Is the omniscience limited to one character? | EXAMPLE: There were two cute guys sitting in the bed of the truck next to her car when she exited the ice cream parlor. She tripped as she approached them and experienced a moment of utter terror. The looks on the guys' faces were blank, and she convinced herself they hadn't noticed. |
| | • Does the narrator allow readers into a character's **interior monologue,** following the natural path of the person's thought processes? | EXAMPLE: Don't stare, she told herself. Let them speak to you first. Then a voice in her head reminded her that she'd already blown off one guy tonight, and all she currently had to look forward to was a night of reruns. |

CONTINUED

| | | |
|---|---|---|
| | • Is the narrator **objective**? | EXAMPLE: She said hello, and they said hello back. |
| | • A second-person narrator, or a narrator who addresses you directly? (you) | EXAMPLE: You taste your frozen yogurt to distract yourself from the race of your heartbeat. You try to look just above and to the right of the nearest guy's eyes—Don't stare into them, you tell yourself, don't show so much interest. You struggle for something to say. They're waiting for you to say something. |

# Suggestions for Writing about Point of View

1. In her interview, ZZ Packer talks about reading as a way to "live an extra ten years" and become "a citizen of the world." How could reading "The Short Happy Life of Francis Macomber" help you achieve these goals? What did the story teach you about the world? What did it teach you about Africa? What did it teach you about power relationships, including those involving the Africans who work for Wilson?
2. Of the characters you encountered in this chapter's stories, which is the roundest (see chapter 5, Character)? Explain what makes that character particularly round by citing examples from the story you chose. How did the author's use of point of view contribute to your sense of that character's roundness?
3. Write a short profile of the "you" character in "How to Become a Writer" and of the first-person narrator in "The Yellow Wallpaper." Does one type of narration allow you to know more about a character than another type of narration, or are they equally effective in conveying character?
4. Compare the first-person narrator of "Brownies" to the first-person narrator of "The Yellow Wallpaper." Find an example of each narrator's naïveté. By the end of each story, how would you describe their levels of self-awareness?

# 8 Language, Tone, and Style

*"I remember in high school I would play a game with my friends, If you were a color, you would be a light blue . . . if Jenny were an animal, she would be a giraffe. Then we would figure out these reasons why. . . . There's something about tone in that. . . . Every word is going to convey a color, a feeling, a tone like a musical instrument, a mood. . . . If you start to look at the words . . . those are just things that come from the language itself."*

Conversation with Aimee Bender, available on video at www.mhhe.com/delbanco1e

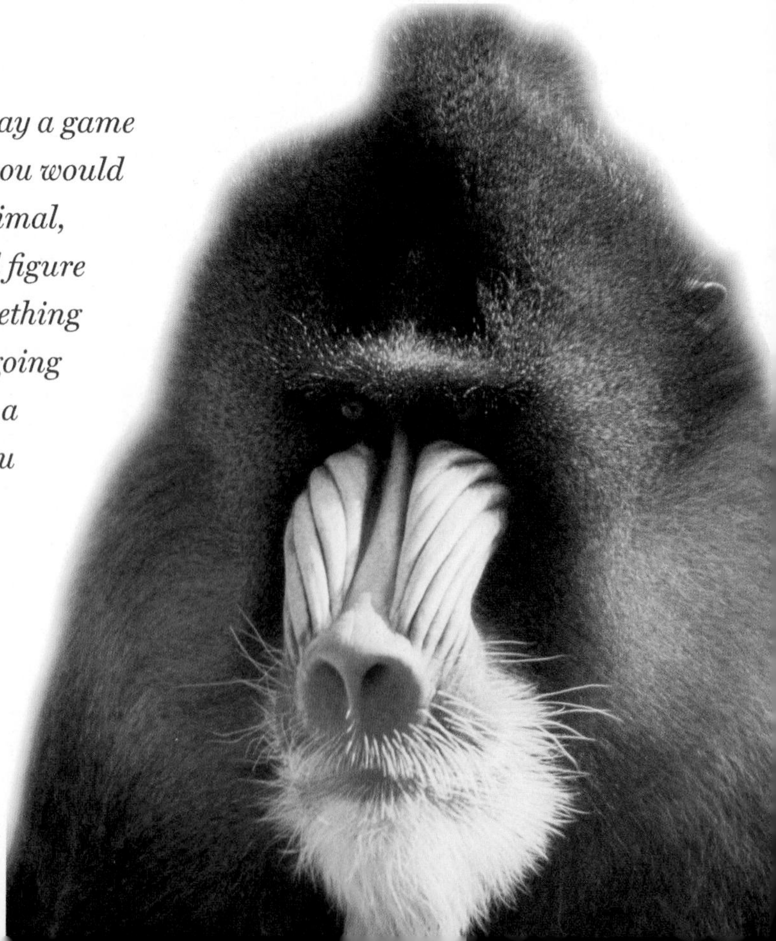

MY lover is experiencing reverse evolution. I tell no one. I don't know how it happened, only that one day he was my lover and the next he was some kind of ape. It's been a month and now he's a sea turtle.

I keep him on the counter, in a glass baking pan filled with salt water.

"Ben," I say to his small protruding head, "can you understand me?" and he stares with eyes like little droplets of tar and I drip tears into the pan, a sea of me.

He is shedding a million years a day.

—*from "The Rememberer," by Aimee Bender*

IN this opening passage, Aimee Bender uses simple, straightforward language. The **language** she has chosen has the narrator sound confessional, a little befuddled, and sad. Of her lover's bizarre transformation, she simply says, "I don't know how it happened." She unblinkingly reports the facts, thereby bringing the reader step by step, word by word, into this odd reality in which a man can devolve into a turtle. In this story, and others that Bender has written, she creates fantastical worlds. This mix of the realistic with the fantastic is a central element of her **style**—meaning the characteristic way in which she, or any writer, uses language and story.

Style is closely related to **tone**—the author's attitude toward his or her characters or subject matter. Think of tone in writing in the same way you think of tone of voice in speech. Depending on the tone of voice your friend uses when she says *Dude,* she may be signaling affection, awe, disdain, pleasure, or disgust. In turn, the tone shapes how you respond to her message. Authors convey tone by word choice and style as well as with their selection of details and images. How do Aimee Bender's style and tone shape our response to her narrator? Readers are likely to feel an odd mix of compassion for her loss and a startled "*What* did she just say about her lover!?"

*CONTINUED ON PAGE 238*

*We need more magic in our imaginative lives . . .*

*There is something . . . about the intimacy of reader and writer . . .*

Q&A

# A Conversation on Writing

## Aimee Bender

In 1998, a *San Francisco Chronicle* review said of Aimee Bender (b. 1969): "Once in a while, a writer comes along who makes you grateful for the very existence of language." Bender's first collection of stories, *The Girl in the Flammable Skirt* (1998), received enthusiastic praise from critics and readers alike. In this book—as in her novel *An Invisible Sign of My Own* (2000) and her second story collection, *Willful Creatures* (2005)—Bender's works push the limits of realism, relaying what seems impossible (a man comes back from the war without lips; a woman gives birth to her own recently deceased mother; a man suffers from an accelerated form of reverse evolution) with a straightforwardness that acknowledges but also fully accepts the fantastic. The surreal subjects of her stories are aided by the lyrical quality of her prose, which combines a straightforward tone with playful diction. Bender holds an M.F.A. from the University of California, Irvine, and she now teaches creative writing at the University of Southern California. She is currently at work on a new novel.

**To watch this entire interview and hear Aimee Bender read from "The Rememberer," go to www.mhhe.com/delbanco1e.**

**RESEARCH ASSIGNMENT** In her interview, Aimee Bender talks about realism in fiction. She also talks about fairy tales, magic, and poetry. What is the author's attitude toward realism and fantasy in fiction? Can you relate to what Aimee Bender describes? How did her attitude affect her decision to become a writer? When she did become a writer, and why did she choose to write fiction over other forms, like plays?

### About "The Rememberer"

This story came from a dream. . . . I had had a dream . . . where I was going through reverse evolution with a friend, and we became dolphins, and swam around in a tank. . . . About five years later I was thinking about loss a lot, and I was thinking about it in terms of a relationship that was ending, and somehow that dream came back. And I sat down, and that first line popped into my head, "My lover's going through reverse evolution," and then I followed it to the end.

### Fiction and Magic

As a kid I loved books that had magic in them. . . . There was something about that leap into metaphor and into imagination that just thrilled me. I really assumed that part of puberty, and part of growing up, meant a move to realism—that in order to become an adult, you had to give away those trappings of magic. . . . It was only later when I [discovered writers who] were taking on adult issues . . . but were doing it through metaphor, and imaginative leaps, and magical realism. I could start writing things . . . that . . . responded to so much [that I loved] as a kid but now [could write about] with hopefully more depth and perspective. . . . We need more magic in our imaginative lives, because . . . it's freeing, and . . . can be a way to get to feelings that are hard to look at straight on.

### The Intimacy of Reading and Writing

There is something . . . about the intimacy of reader and writer, the action of sitting and reading something as one writer, one reader.

In writing . . . I was trying to put something out there for a future reader, and then it was so satisfying when people read things and responded to them.

**AS YOU READ** As you read this story, notice the narrator's tone. Does anything that happens seem to surprise her? Do events in the story surprise you? How do you account for the differences, if any, between her responses and yours?

# The Rememberer (1997)

1 MY lover is experiencing reverse evolution. I tell no one. I don't know how it happened, only that one day he was my lover and the next he was some kind of ape. It's been a month and now he's a sea turtle.

2 I keep him on the counter, in a glass baking pan filled with salt water.

3 "Ben," I say to his small protruding head, "can you understand me?" and he stares with eyes like little droplets of tar and I drip tears into the pan, a sea of me.

4 He is shedding a million years a day. I am no scientist, but this is roughly what I figured out. I went to the old biology teacher at the community college and asked him for an approximate time line of our evolution. He was irritated at first—he wanted money. I told him I'd be happy to pay and then he cheered up quite a bit. I can hardly read his time line—he should've typed it—and it turns out to be wrong. According to him, the whole process should take about a year, but from the way things are going, I think we have less than a month left.

5 At first, people called on the phone and asked me where was Ben. Why wasn't he at work? Why did he miss his lunch date with those clients? His out-of-print special-ordered book on civilization had arrived at the bookstore, would he please pick it up? I told them he was sick, a strange sickness, and to please stop calling. The stranger thing was, they did. They stopped calling. After a week, the phone was silent and Ben, the baboon, sat in a corner by the window, wrapped up in drapery, chattering to himself.

6 Last day I saw him human, he was sad about the world.

7 This was not unusual. He was always sad about the world. It was a large reason why I loved him. We'd sit together and be sad and think about being sad and sometimes discuss sadness.

8 On his last human day, he said, "Annie, don't you see? We're all getting too smart. Our brains are just getting bigger and bigger, and the world dries up and dies when there's too much thought and not enough heart."

9 He looked at me pointedly, blue eyes unwavering. "Like us, Annie," he said. "We think far too much."

10 I sat down. I remembered how the first time we had sex, I left the lights on, kept my eyes wide open, and concentrated really hard on letting go; then I noticed that his eyes were open too and in the middle of everything we sat down on the floor and had an hour-long conversation about poetry. It was all very peculiar. It was all very familiar.

11 Another time he woke me up in the middle of the night, lifted me off the pale blue sheets, led me outside to the stars and whispered: *Look, Annie, look—there is no space for anything but dreaming.* I listened, sleepily, wandered back to bed and found myself wide awake, staring at the ceiling, unable to dream at all. Ben fell asleep right away, but I crept back outside. I tried to dream up to the stars, but I didn't know how to do that. I tried to find a star no one in all of history had ever wished on before, and wondered what would happen if I did.

12 On his last human day, he put his head in his hands and sighed and I

stood up and kissed the entire back of his neck, covered that flesh, made wishes there because I knew no woman had ever been so thorough, had ever kissed his every inch of skin. I coated him. What did I wish for? I wished for good. That's all. Just good. My wishes became generalized long ago, in childhood; I learned quick the consequence of wishing specific.

13 I took him in my arms and made love to him, my sad man. "See, we're not thinking," I whispered into his ear while he kissed my neck, "we're not thinking at all" and he pressed his head into my shoulder and held me tighter. Afterward, we went outside again; there was no moon and the night was dark. He said he hated talking and just wanted to look into my eyes and tell me things that way. I let him and it made my skin lift, the things in his look. Then he told me he wanted to sleep outside for some reason and in the morning when I woke up in bed, I looked out to the patio and there was an ape sprawled on the cement, great furry arms covering his head to block out the glare of the sun.

I walk around the block at night in case he doesn't quite remember which house it is.

14 Even before I saw the eyes, I knew it was him. And once we were face to face, he gave me his same sad look and I hugged those enormous shoulders. I didn't even really care, then, not at first, I didn't panic and call 911. I sat with him outside and smoothed the fur on the back of his hand. When he reached for me, I said No, loudly, and he seemed to understand and pulled back. I have limits here.

15 We sat on the lawn together and ripped up the grass. I didn't miss human Ben right away; I wanted to meet the ape too, to take care of my lover like a son, a pet; I wanted to know him every possible way but I didn't realize he wasn't coming back.

16 Now I come home from work and look for his regular-size shape walking and worrying and realize, over and over, that he's gone. I pace the halls. I chew whole packs of gum in mere minutes. I review my memories and make sure they're still intact because if he's not here, then it is my job to remember. I think of the way he wrapped his arms around my back and held me so tight it made me nervous and the way his breath felt in my ear: right.

When I go to the kitchen, I peer in the glass and see he's some kind of salamander now. He's small. 17

"Ben," I whisper, "do you remember me? Do you remember?" 18

His eyes roll up in his head and I dribble honey into the water. He used to love honey. He licks at it and then swims to the other end of the pan. 19

This is the limit of my limits: here it is. You don't ever know for sure where it is and then you bump against it and bam, you're there. Because I cannot bear to look down into the water and not be able to find him at all, to search the tiny clear waves with a microscope lens and to locate my lover, the one-celled wonder, bloated and bordered, brainless, benign, heading clear and small like an eye-floater into nothingness. 20

I put him in the passenger seat of the car, and drive him to the beach. Walking down the sand, I nod at people on towels, laying their bodies out to the sun and wishing. At the water's edge, I stoop down and place the whole pan on the tip of a baby wave. It floats well, a cooking boat, for someone to find washed up on shore and to make cookies in, a lucky catch for a poor soul with all the ingredients but no container. 21

Ben the salamander swims out. I wave to the water with both arms, big enough for him to see if he looks back. 22

I turn around and walk back to the car. 23

Sometimes I think he'll wash up on shore. A naked man with a startled look. Who has been to history and back. I keep my eyes on the newspaper. I make sure my phone number is listed. I walk around the block at night in case he doesn't quite remember which house it is. I feed the birds outside and sometimes before I put my one self to bed, I place my hands around my skull to see if it's growing, and wonder what, of any use, would fill it if it did. 24

IF you like Aimee Bender's "The Rememberer," you may also enjoy other stories in the book that step over the line from realism into the fantastic, such as Jorge Luis Borges's "The Circular Ruins" (chapter 14).

**GOING FURTHER** In Bender's interview, she mentions that Anne Sexton's *Transformations,* the retelling of fairy tales from a contemporary perspective, was a personal favorite of hers growing up; another version of fairy tales comes in the funny and fantastic *Italian Folktales* by Italo Calvino, whose work influenced Bender. She marches in a line of writers who incorporate the supernatural and the metaphysical into fiction, such as Gabriel García Márquez (*One Hundred Years of Solitude*), Alejo Carpentier (*The Kingdom of This World*), Miguel Angel Asturias (*Men of Maize*), and the American Bernard Malamud (*God's Grace*).

# Writing from Reading

### Summarize

1 List the different animals we glimpse Ben as throughout the story. Discuss why Bender has chosen these snapshots of de-evolution out of the entire array of animals.

### Analyze Craft

2 Briefly describe the narrator's level of vocabulary (i.e., does she use difficult words that you need a dictionary to decode, or simpler words that you might hear in everyday conversation?). Discuss why Bender would write at this level of vocabulary, considering what effect it has on the tone (the emotional effect) of the story.

### Analyze Voice

3 "The Rememberer" provides very little background on the characters Annie and Ben. What can you glean about them, their backgrounds, and their style of life from the narrator's voice and the details she provides (or doesn't provide)?

### Synthesize Summary and Analysis

4 Discuss Annie's use of the word *limits* throughout the story. What are the different contexts in which she mentions limits? What are her limits, and why?

### Interpret the Story

5 The scientist forecasts a year for Ben's de-evolution, but it happens much faster. Why does Bender make a point of mentioning the scientist and his discrepancy? Explore the commentary she might be making about human history, citing the text.

6 Discuss the roles of science, realism, and fantasy in this story. How does Bender use the three to make the world portrayed in this story a convincing place?

*CONTINUED FROM PAGE 233*

You may have noticed that most chapters in this book focus on a single topic—plot, character, setting, point of view—whereas this chapter groups three topics together. This is because language, tone, and style are difficult to separate from one another. The type of language an author uses establishes his or her tone. In "The Fall of the House of Usher" (chapter 6), for example, Poe uses language that connotes darkness and decay. This, in turn, establishes a melancholy tone, one that suggests the attitude that both narrator and reader take toward the house of Usher is one of sadness at the decline of a once-great family. At the same time, the language of darkness and decay creates a sense of foreboding, even if we don't know at the beginning what causes that feeling. Poe's language, then, gives rise to a tone that we can describe as both melancholy and chilling.

Putting those elements together—the darkness and decay evoked by the language, the melancholy and foreboding tone—you arrive at Poe's style. As you most likely know if you have encountered Poe before, he is famous for his horror stories and mysteries. This reputation is based on a tonal choice, the mood which his work consists of and evokes. Consider his well-known poem "The Raven," which begins with the line "Once upon a midnight dreary." Characteristic of Poe's style, the language here, as in "The Fall of the House of Usher," is dark and immediately sets a melancholy ("dreary"), foreboding ("midnight") tone.

In this chapter, we focus on three stories that we think demonstrate a particularly clear use of language, tone, and style. But remember, all stories contain these three elements—after all, stories are made of language, which in turn creates a tone that combines with the language to form an author's distinctive style.

## CRAFTING STYLE AND TONE

Everyone knows what style looks like or feels the effect of it. We see it in the distinctive way a base runner moves, a basketball player goes for a layup, or a kid does turns on a skateboard. We see a person's style in the way she does (or doesn't do) her nails, the choice and placement of a tattoo or a piercing, a particular combination of shirt, jeans, vest, and scarf—with high-top sneakers, cowboy boots, high heels, flip-flops, or anything else in the vast array of potential footwear.

> "I know that there are many things that can open a story, that can start a person working. For me it's language. It's not an idea."
>
> Conversation with Amy Hempel

The distinctive style combined with the writer's tone molds the reader's impressions. Tone establishes how the narrator regards the story and the people in it—for example, with contempt, longing, passionate curiosity, sympathy, or ambivalence. The writer's tone influences how the reader will relate and respond to the characters and the course of events. Reading a literary work critically comes down to an intense scrutiny of the work's style and tone with these questions in mind:

- *What* is being said, and *how* and *why*?
- What effect does the author wish to create?
- What effect does the writing have on you?

Each of the stories in this chapter evokes a setting or scene and does so with a unique style and tone. As you read them, ask yourself why the authors chose the particular words and images they did. What tone (of voice) do you hear? Where does the style fall on a spectrum of formal to informal, direct to roundabout, concrete to abstract, serious to wry to comedic? Are the sentences long and complex, or short and simple? Does the author use the language of the street or that of academia? Taken together, these are qualities that make up an author's style and tone.

The tone of "The Rememberer" is intimate and informal when the first-person narrator stands weeping over her boyfriend-turned-sea-turtle. Her tone and style arise from her **diction,** an author's or character's distinctive choice of words and style of expression. Now consider a passage written by Ernest Hemingway.

> *You know how it is there early in the morning in Havana with the bums still asleep against the walls of the buildings; before even the ice wagons come by with the ice for the bars? Well, we came across the square from the dock to the Pearl of San Francisco Café to get coffee and there was only one beggar awake in the square and he was getting a drink out of the fountain. But when we got inside the café and sat down, there were the three of them waiting for us. . . .*
>
> —from "One Trip Across" (1934)

In this story, which became the opening lines of his novel *To Have and Have Not* (1937), Hemingway uses the everyday language of his American character, a smuggler living in Cuba. The tone is casual, conversational, and hard-boiled. With that "You know how it is," the narrator speaks to us directly, drawing us in as confederates who are just as street savvy as he is, who have been up that early in the morning. The style is realistic, concrete, and economical, and the details reveal that the place is exotic (Havana), and just a little bit seedy, with its bums and beggars.

> "I thought, well what is a voice? And what's a story? What are the things that make this up? And if I know, you know, ABCD, these components, I can sit down and write these things. But I feel now, now that I've been doing this for a while, that the questions are still there. And there's no absolute answer. And that you discover it each time you sit down and write."
>
> Conversation with Amy Tan

Notice what the narrator reveals—in an offhand way. He's been around, the kind of man who has seen enough "bums still asleep against the walls of the buildings" that they barely have an impact on him. There's plenty we don't yet know: why this narrator has come from the dock, who's with him, who's waiting for him at the bar and why. With style, tone, and careful selection of words and details, Hemingway creates an effect: a narrator in motion, leading the reader to a rendezvous with something that seems like trouble. "Follow him," Hemingway seems to say of his narrator. "So he's a little shady. He's still the one to watch."

## STYLE AND DICTION

A number of elements contribute to a work's overall style and to the effect it creates on the reader. As we noted, diction, whether formal or informal, is important in writing because of what it reveals about character. Diction, for example, is a central concern of

Thomas Wolfe's "Only the Dead Know Brooklyn." In this story, Wolfe shows how vast the possibilities are for the English language. He wants us to "know Brooklyn" in its own language, in its own words, to know what it's really like to walk those streets and live in that world.

> *Now is the winter of our discontent made glorious by dis mont' of May, and all the long-drowned desolation of our souls in the green fire and radiance of the Springtime buried.*
>
> *We are the dead—ah! We were drowned so long ago—and now we thrust our feelers in distressful ooze upon the sea-floors of the buried world. We are the drowned—blind crawls and eyeless gropes and mindless sucks that swirl and scuttle in the jungle depths, immense and humid skies bend desolately upon us, and our flesh is gray.*
>
> *We are lost, the eyeless atoms of the jungle depth, we grope and crawl and scuttle with blind feelers, and we have no way but this.*
>
> *Dere's no guy livin' dat knows Brooklyn t'roo an' t'roo, (only the dead know Brooklyn t'roo and t'roo), because it'd take a lifetime just to find his way aroun' duh goddam town (—only the dead know Brooklyn t'roo and t'roo, even the dead will quarrel an' bicker over the sprawl and web of jungle desolation that is Brooklyn t'roo and t'roo).*

Part of the first sentence comes from Shakespeare's *Richard III,* which begins with the phrase "Now is the winter of our discontent made glorious summer by this sun of York." But instead of "glorious summer," Wolfe substitutes "dis mont'" (or "this month") of May. The next two paragraphs continue in this Shakespearian-poetic style, but the fourth drops into the exaggeratedly coarse Brooklynese. The contrast between the two

"At some point the sound of the language becomes the story: the sounds of characters talking, what comes out of their mouths, the sound of your own prose as you write a bit of narrative, a bit of description, or whatever. You're discovering meaning as you're doing it through the sound of the prose." Conversation with Tim O'Brien

kinds of language and diction is startling. The opening implies his hope that we would admire the speaker of Brooklynese English as much as we do Shakespeare's speaker, and that the lives of ordinary Brooklynites will have as much resonance and drama as do the lives of kings. Once you've read the story, try to imagine what it would be like if Wolfe had used standard English—how the color and spirit of the story would change. Consider how much flavor you gain because of the work he did to capture the authentic diction of the place.

## TONE AND IRONY

Before his transformation, Ben, the narrator's lover in the Bender story, was a melancholy type, always bemoaning the human condition—that people had become too smart, that they thought too much, that they talked too much. So his fate—changing from man, to ape, to sea turtle so that he no longer needs to suffer the human condition—makes "sense," but with a twist. Expecting, as we all do, to live forward in time and evolve as a human being, Ben instead evolves backward, thus experiencing

> "Tone is the attitude that the writer lays over the story itself . . . whereas voice is to me the music of the story's intelligence, which is to say it's how the story sounds in your ear—when you're reading it aloud or you're reading it silently—how the story sounds when it's being most itself, when it's being as smart as it is, when it's being as characteristic as it is."
>
> Conversation with Richard Ford

a striking example of ironic reversal. Once you know what it looks and sounds like, **irony** may be the most distinctive and easily recognizable tone to identify. Irony, a difference between what occurs and what you expect to occur or between what is said and what is meant, often involves some sort of reversal in circumstances or fate.

Irony has other manifestations that grow out of the technique of radical reversal. For example, a football player intercepts a pass but becomes confused and runs the ball in the wrong direction, toward his own goal line. A president wants to bring glory to his country but takes actions that lead to disgrace and defeat. A nerdy young man courts a girl by taking acting lessons, buying a new suit, and getting a fresh haircut only to be rejected by the girl who wanted a natural sort of guy. The idea of reversal is central to the fate of Ben in "The Rememberer."

The term *irony* also refers to an incongruity between what someone says and what someone means. For example, your neighbor catches you taking out the garbage in your old wrinkled pajamas, with your hair wildly askew, and says, "You're looking fabulous today." This is an example of **verbal irony**—a person saying one thing and meaning another. When someone speaks in a mean-spirited, critical, or malicious way, we call it **sarcasm.** Sarcasm is not common in literature, but verbal irony is, as in this passage about war by Kurt Vonnegut from his novel *Slaughterhouse Five:*

> *Wherever you went there were women who would do anything for food or protection for themselves and their children and the old people . . . the whole point of war is to put women everywhere in that condition. It's always the men against the women, with the men only pretending to fight among themselves . . . the ones who pretend the hardest get their pictures in the paper and medals afterwards.*

### A BRIEF HISTORY OF IRONY

Irony is a concept that comes down to us from the time of Greek tragedy. In that era, it was a philosophical, if not theological, lens through which the Greeks viewed all of life, and it has proved useful to writers throughout the history of literature in the West. While irony was a complex process in the Greek tragedies, the essence of irony is reversal, and reversal is a simple concept: A beggar discovers treasure, or a man at the height of his powers loses everything. In the European Middle Ages, the sign of fortune was a great wheel; irony defined that circling course. The hero's fortune could reside at the top of the wheel, but it could just as easily fall to the bottom. During the thousand years and more when Europe was united in the belief that Christianity was the answer to all questions about life and death, irony became less useful as a general idea. Those who accepted Christ found life after death, so the human outcome was clear.

No one would seriously claim that "the whole point of war" is to turn women's lives into a desperate struggle to protect themselves and others, and Vonnegut does not expect the reader to buy this. He says one thing but means another in order to get at a truth about the *effects* of war and to convey an attitude about war—that it is a horrific and senseless human activity. At the same time, he feigns innocence, as if he is describing a set of simple facts, as if he truly believes that jeopardizing women is "the whole point of war."

"... you draw with words when you write. . . . Conrad talked about the need to make the reader see. [Although you also hope to make him or her hear, and smell even, and appeal to all the senses,] nevertheless the seeing seems to be what it's ultimately all about."
Conversation with John Updike

How does a reader know when an author is being ironic? In Vonnegut's case, you know because Vonnegut pushes his point to extremes. When he says "the whole point," and when he talks about "men only pretending to fight," you know that he is up to something other than a straight-faced discussion of war. He also uses an ironic tone—which borders here on sarcasm—because of the extreme points he makes, as if he were saying, "You idiots, can't you see?"

The fable "Appointment in Samarra," retold below by British novelist W. Somerset Maugham, illustrates an aspect of irony that we introduced before—a discrepancy between acts and results, or between what occurs and what the character expected to occur. In this story, the narrator is Death.

> *There was a merchant in Bagdad who sent his servant to market to buy provisions and in a little while the servant came back, white and trembling, and said, Master, just now when I was in the marketplace I was jostled by a woman in the crowd and when I turned I saw it was Death that jostled me. She looked at me and made a threatening gesture. Now, lend me your horse, and I will ride away from this city and avoid my fate. I will go to Samarra and there Death will not find me. The merchant lent him his horse, and the servant mounted it, and he dug his spurs in its flanks and as fast as the horse could gallop he went. Then the merchant went down to the marketplace and he saw me standing in the crowd and he came to me and said, Why did you make a threatening gesture to my servant when you saw him this morning? That was not a threatening gesture, I said, it was only a start of surprise. I was astonished to see him in Bagdad, for I had an appointment with him tonight in Samarra.*

The outcome for the poor servant is ironic because he hopes to avoid death by leaving his home and going to hide in Samarra. In doing so, however, he unknowingly guarantees that he will be precisely at the place where Death intends to seek him. The reader can see what the outcome will be, but the servant cannot, which gives the reader an advantage but also a feeling of apprehension or, in some cases, sorrow. This literary device is referred to as **dramatic irony,** a situation in which an author or narrator lets the reader know more about a situation than a character does.

## *LANGUAGE, TONE, AND STYLE* IN CONTEXT

For the most part, a prose style, including its tone, is as complex and unique as a fingerprint, as is its genesis. In this chapter, we have looked closely at the topic of style—where it comes from, how to recognize and describe it—and also the faces of irony in literature, and the intricate relationship both style and irony have with tone.

> "There are writers that I just deeply admire for the sentences that they write. And they're the ones I go back to read when writing isn't going well." Conversation with Chimamanda Ngozi Adichie

The styles of today's fiction are varied. Its language can be lush or lean, and the language of fiction is *creative;* it provides a window through which we as readers see new worlds, or come to see our own world differently. This chapter offers four short stories, each written in a distinctive literary style. As you read, consider how each writer's voice emerges from the story's tone, style, and language.

# Thomas Wolfe (1900–1938)

Thomas Wolfe was born in Asheville, North Carolina, and he attended Harvard, where he read voraciously in the classics. Migrating to New York City, he made a striking figure at literary parties—he was well over six feet tall and broad in girth—and wrote in the kitchen of his Brooklyn apartment by standing in front of his refrigerator and using the top as his writing desk. His work has been lauded primarily for its opulent language and wide range of voices; he was always trying new styles, experimenting with new ways to tell stories that were largely autobiographical. In addition to numerous short stories, Wolfe published two novels, *Look Homeward, Angel* (1929) and *Of Time and the River* (1935); a short-story collection, *From Death to Morning* (1935); and a long essay, *The Story of a Novel* (1936). In 1938, at the age of thirty-eight, after a long, tiring journey through the American West, he succumbed to tuberculosis; it's worth noting that he wrote his entire, relatively small body of work in the span of seven years. After his death, however, dedicated scholars of his work compiled material from his unfinished manuscripts and published four posthumous books: *The Web and the Rock, You Can't Go Home Again, The Hills Beyond,* and—most recently—*The Party at Jack's.*

**AS YOU READ** As you read this story, let yourself hear the sound of the speaker's voice and the way he pronounces his words. Imagine the sounds of the city and of the train as the two characters travel along together. Imagine or remember how it feels to ask directions in a new place, and all the ways a newcomer stands out from the "natives."

# Only the Dead Know Brooklyn (1935)

1 NOW is the winter of our discontent made glorious by dis mont' of May, and all the long-drowned desolation of our souls in the green fire and radiance of Springtime buried.

2 We are the dead—ah! We were drowned so long ago—and now we thrust our feelers in distressful ooze upon the sea-floors of the buried world. We are the drowned—blind crawls and eyeless gropes and mindless sucks that swirl and scuttle in the jungle depths, immense and humid skies bend desolately upon us, and our flesh is gray.

3 We are lost, the eyeless atoms of the jungle depth, we grope and crawl and scuttle with blind feelers, and we have no way but this.

4 DERE'S no guy livin' dat knows Brooklyn t'roo an' t'roo, because it'd take a guy a lifetime just to find his way aroun' duh f——— town.

5 So like I say, I'm waitin' for my train t' come when I sees dis big guy standin' deh—dis is duh foist I eveh see of him. Well, he's lookin' wild, y'know, an' I can see dat he's had plenty, but still he's holdin' it; he talks good an' is walkin' straight enough. So den, dis big guy steps up to a little guy dat's standin' deh, an' says, "How d'yuh get t' Eighteent' Avenoo an' Sixty-sevent' Street?" he says.

"Jesus! Yuh got me, chief," duh little guy says to him. 6
"I ain't been heah long myself. Where is duh place?" he says. "Out in duh Flatbush section somewhere?"

"Nah," duh big guy says. "It's out in Bensonhoist. 7
But I was neveh deh befoeh. How d'yuh get deh?"

"Jesus," duh little guy says, scratchin' his head, 8
y'know—yuh could see duh litle guy didn't know his way about—"yuh got me, chief. I neveh hoid of it. Do any of youse guys know where it is?" he says to me.

"Sure," I says. "It's out in Bensonhoist. Yuh take duh 9
Fourt' Avenoo express, get off at Fifty-nint' Street, change to a Sea Beach local deh, get off at Eighteent' Avenoo an' Sixty-toid, an' den walk down foeh blocks. Dat's all yuh got to do," I says.

"G'wan!" some wise guy dat I neveh seen befoeh 1
pipes up. "Whatcha talkin' about?" he says—oh, he was wise, y'know. "Duh guy is crazy! I tell yuh what yuh do," he says to duh big guy. "Yuh change to duh West End line at Toity-sixt'," he tells him. "Get off at Noo Utrecht an' Sixteent' Avenoo," he says. "Walk two blocks oveh, foeh blocks up," he says, "an' you'll be right deh." Oh, a *wise* guy, y'know.

"Oh, yeah?" I says. "Who told *you* so much?" He 1
got me sore because he was so wise about it. "How long you been livin' heah?" I says.

"All my life," he says. "I was bawn in Williamsboig," 1
he says. "An' I can tell you t'ings about dis town you neveh hoid of," he says.

"Yeah?" I says. 1

"Yeah," he says. 1

"Well, den, you can tell me t'ings about dis town dat nobody else has eveh hoid of, either. Maybe you make it all up yoehself at night," I says, "befoeh you go to sleep—like cuttin' out papeh dolls, or somp'n."

"Oh, yeah?" he says. "You're pretty wise, ain't yuh?"

"Oh, I don't know," I says. "Duh boids ain't usin' my head for Lincoln's statue yet," I says. "But I'm wise enough to know a phony when I see one."

"Yeah?" he says. "A wise guy, huh? Well, you're so wise dat some one's goin' t'bust yuh one right on duh snoot some day," he says. "Dat's how wise *you* are."

Whatcha gonna do wit a guy as dumb as dat?

WELL, my train was comin', or I'da smacked him den and dere, but when I seen duh train was comin', all I said was, "All right, mugg! I'm sorry I can't stay to take keh of you, but I'll be seein' yuh sometime, I hope, out in duh cemetery." So den I says to duh big guy, who'd been standin' deh all duh time, "You come wit me," I says. So when we gets onto duh train I says to him, "Where yuh goin' out in Bensonhoist?" I says. "What numbeh are yuh lookin' for?" I says. *You* know—I t'ought if he told me duh address I might be able to help him out.

20 "Oh," he says, "I'm not lookin' for no one. I don't know no one out deh."

21 "Then whatcha goin' out deh for?" I says.

22 "Oh," duh guy says, "I'm just goin' out to see duh place," he says. "I like duh sound of duh name—Bensonhoist, y'know—so I t'ought I'd go out an' have a look at it."

23 "Whatcha tryin' t'hand me?" I says. "Whatcha tryin' t'do—kid me?" *You* know, I t'ought duh guy was bein' wise wit me.

24 "No," he says. "I'm tellin' yuh duh troot. I like to go out an' take a look at places wit nice names like dat. I like to go out an' look at all kinds of places," he says.

25 "How'd yuh know deh was such a place," I says, "if yuh neveh been deh befoeh?"

26 "Oh," he says, "I got a map."

27 "A *map?*" I says.

28 "Sure," he says, "I got a map dat tells me about all dese places. I take it wit me every time I come out heah," he says.

29 And Jesus! Wit dat, he pulls it out of his pocket, an' so help me, but he's *got* it—he's tellin' duh troot—a big map of duh whole f——— place with all duh different pahts mahked out. You know—Canarsie an' East Noo Yawk an' Flatbush, Bensonhoist, Sout' Brooklyn, duh Heights, Bay Ridge, Greenpernt—duh whole goddam layout, he's got it right deh on duh map.

"You been to any of dose places?" I says. 30

"Sure," he says, "I been to most of 'em. I was down in Red Hook just last night," he says. 31

"Jesus! Red Hook!" I says. "Whatcha do down deh?" 32

"Oh," he says, "nuttin' much. I just walked aroun'. I went into a coupla places an' had a drink," he says, "but most of the time I just walked aroun'." 33

"Just walked aroun'?" I says. 34

"Sure," he says, "just lookin' at t'ings, y'know." 35

"Where'd yuh go?" I asts him. 36

"Oh," he says, "I don't know duh name of duh place, but I could find it on my map," he says. "One time I was walkin' across some big fields where deh ain't no houses," he says, "but I could see ships oveh deh all lighted up. Dey was loadin'. So I walks across duh fields," he says, "to where duh ships are." 37

"Sure," I says, "I know where you was. You was down to duh Erie Basin." 38

"Yeah," he says. "I guess dat was it. Dey had some of dose big elevators an' cranes an' dey was loadin' ships, an' I could see some ships in drydock all lighted up, so I walks across duh fields to where dey are," he says. 39

"Den what did yuh do?" I says. 40

"Oh," he says, "nuttin' much. I came on back across duh fields after a while an' went into a coupla places an' had a drink." 41

"Didn't nuttin' happen while yuh was in dere?" I says. 42

"No," he says. "Nuttin' much. A coupla guys was drunk in one of duh places an' started a fight, but dey bounced 'em out," he says, "an' den one of duh guys stahted to come back again, but duh bartender gets his baseball bat out from under duh counteh, so duh guy goes on." 43

"Jesus!" I said. "Red Hook!" 44

"Sure," he says. "Dat's where it was, all right." 45

"Well, you keep outa deh," I says. "You stay away from deh." 46

"Why?" he says. "What's wrong wit it?" 47

"Oh," I says, "it's a good place to stay away from, dat's all. It's a good place to keep out of." 48

"Why?" he says. "Why is it?" 49

Jesus! Whatcha gonna do wit a guy as dumb as dat? I saw it wasn't no use to try to tell him nuttin', he wouldn't know what I was talkin' about, so I just says to him, "Oh, nuttin'. Yuh might get lost down deh, dat's all." 50

51 "Lost?" he says. "No, I wouldn't get lost. I got a map," he says.

52 A map! Red Hook! Jesus!

53 SO den duh guy begins to ast me all kinds of nutty questions: how big was Brooklyn an' could I find my way aroun' in it, an' how long would it take a guy to know duh place.

54 "Listen!" I says. "You get dat idea outa yoeh head right now," I says. "You ain't neveh gonna get to know Brooklyn," I says. "Not in a hundred yeahs. I been livin' heah all my life," I says, "an' I don't even know all deh is to know about it, so how do you expect to know duh town," I says, "when you don't even live heah?"

55 "Yes," he says, "but I got a map to help me find my way about."

56 "Map or no map," I says, "yuh ain't gonna get to know Brooklyn wit no map," I says.

57 "Can you swim?" he says, just like dat. Jesus! By dat time, y'know, I begun to see dat duh guy was some kind of nut. He'd had plenty to drink, of course, but he had dat crazy look in his eye I didn't like. "Can you swim?" he says.

58 "Sure," I says. "Can't you?"

59 "No," he says. "Not more'n a stroke or two. I neveh loined good."

60 "Well, it's easy," I says. "All yuh need is a little confidence. Duh way I loined, me older bruddeh pitched me off duh dock one day when I was eight yeahs old, cloes an' all. 'You'll swim,' he says. 'You'll swim all right—or drown.' An', believe me, I *swam*! When yuh know yuh got to, you'll do it. Duh only t'ing yuh need is confidence. An' once you've loined," I says, "you've got nuttin' else to worry about. You'll neveh forget it. It's somp'n dat stays wit yuh as long as yuh live."

61 "Can yuh swim good?" he says.

62 "Like a fish," I tells him. "I'm a regulah fish in duh wateh," I says. "I loined to swim right off duh docks wit all duh oddeh kids," I says.

63 "What would you do if yuh saw a man drownin'?" duh guy says.

64 "Do? Why, I'd jump in an' pull him out," I says. "Dat's what I'd do."

65 "Did yuh eveh see a man drown?" he says.

66 "Sure, " I says. "I see two guys—bot' times at Coney Island. Dey got out too far, an' neider one could swim. Dey drowned befoeh any one could get to 'em."

67 "What becomes of people after dey've drowned out heah?" he says.

68 "Drowned out where?" I says.

69 "Out heah in Brooklyn."

70 "I don't know whatcha mean," I says. "Neveh hoid of no one drownin' heah in Brooklyn, unless you mean a swimmin' pool. Yuh can't drown in Brooklyn," I says. "Yuh gotta drown somewhere else—in duh ocean, where dere's wateh."

"Drownin'," duh guy says, lookin' at his map. "Drownin'." Jesus! I could see by den he was some kind of nut, he had dat crazy expression in his eyes when he looked at you, an' I didn't know what he might do. So we was comin' to a station, an' it wasn't my stop, but I got off anyway, an' waited for duh next train.

"Well, so long, chief," I says. "Take it easy, now."

"Drownin'," duh guy says, lookin' at his map. "Drownin'."

Jesus! I've t'ought about dat guy a t'ousand times since den an' wondered what eveh happened to 'm goin' out to look at Bensonhoist because he liked duh name! Walkin' aroun' t'roo Red Hook by himself at night an' lookin' at his map! How many people did I see get drowned out heah in Brooklyn! How long would it take a guy wit a good map to know all deh was to know about Brooklyn!

Jesus! What a nut *he* was! I wondeh what eveh happened to 'im, anyway! I wondeh if some one knocked him on duh head, or if he's still wanderin' aroun' in duh subway in duh middle of duh night wit his little map! Duh poor guy! Say, I've got to laugh, at dat, when I t'ink about him! Maybe he's found out by now dat he'll neveh live long enough to know duh whole of Brooklyn. It'd take a guy a lifetime to know Brooklyn t'roo an' t'roo. An' even den, yuh wouldn't know it all.

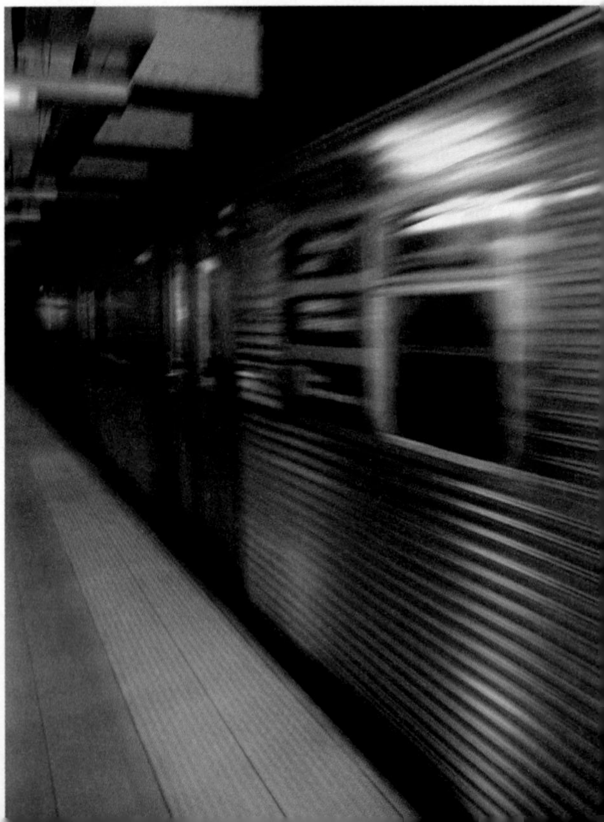

ONCE the story shifts from the high literary tone in its opening to the low speech of the ordinary Brooklyn subway passenger, you hear a celebration of life and death in the exuberant dialect. You may want to compare this dialect with those you find in the stories by Gish Jen (chapter 5), or Amy Tan (chapter 2), or William Faulkner or Flannery O'Connor (chapter 12).

**GOING FURTHER** All this infusion of linguistic energy as a component of American character goes back to Herman Melville's *Moby-Dick* and Mark Twain's *The True Adventures of Huckleberry Finn,* but you may want to read some of Wolfe's contemporaries to see how they handle American speech. "I am an American, Chicago born—Chicago, that somber city . . .": the opening lines of Saul Bellow's 1953 novel *The Adventures of Augie March* explode with much the same exuberance as the Wolfe story does.

# Writing from Reading

### Summarize

1 Who are the main characters of this story? Describe their personalities and individual traits. Discuss how the narrator's tone changes when he talks about different characters.

2 Who is the "I" of this story? What do you know about him based on the way he speaks and the words he chooses? Use some of his distinctive phrases and expressions as examples to support your view.

### Analyze Craft

3 Choose a section of the story and read it aloud. What effect does *hearing* the narrator's voice have? How is it different from imagining how it would sound while reading silently?

### Analyze Voice

4 Tone is defined as the author's attitude toward his or her characters or subject matter. Analyze Thomas Wolfe's attitude toward the characters in this story—especially the narrator. How do you think Wolfe would want readers to feel about these people?

### Synthesizing Summary and Analysis

5 Describe the tone of the story when the narrator and the big man are discussing Red Hook. Now describe the tone when they discuss swimming and drowning. How are the tones different? Discuss what Wolfe might be showing us through this tone shift that the narrator might be blind to.

### Interpret the Story

6 What do you think the man with the map is up to? Why does he ask what happens to men who drown in Brooklyn? What is he looking for—beyond the places on the map? Support your answer by citing instances of tone shifts or uses of irony.

7 What does the story say about the difference between outsiders and insiders? Although all dialogue is delivered in the narrator's native Brooklynese, identify other ways Wolfe makes distinctions between outsiders and insiders.

# Ha Jin (b. 1956)

If it hadn't been for the Tiananmen Square Massacre in 1989, Ha Jin—born Jin Xuefei in northern China—most likely would never have written the award-winning short stories, novels, and poetry that he is known for today. In fact, Jin had no plans to be a writer; he had served in the Chinese army for five years before pursuing his education, first in China, then in the United States. But when the massacre occurred, he and his wife decided to remain in the United States to raise their son. Upon Jin's completion of his Ph.D. at Brandeis University, and after several odd jobs, he eventually earned a professorship at Emory University as a result of his success in writing. He kept writing, he says, to keep his job. After publishing two books of poetry, *Between Silences* (1990) and *Facing Shadows* (1996), he published two collections of short stories, *Ocean of Words* (1996) and *Under the Red Flag* (1997), before turning to longer works. His novels *Waiting* (1999) and *War Trash* (2004) were each given the PEN/Faulkner award, making him one of only three writers to win the prestigious award more than once. Although Jin sets much of his work in China and has an interest in immigrant literature, he writes in English, a language he didn't begin learning until he was twenty years old. His precise use of language and detail allows him to fully realize the intersection between characters and society, though he pays attention to the inner lives of his characters above all else. His first work of nonfiction, *The Writer As Migrant* (2008), takes up the question of modern literary exiles and immigrants such as himself. He currently teaches writing and literature at Boston University.

**AS YOU READ** **As you read, pay attention to the details the narrator focuses on—the sights, the sounds, the tastes. Notice your feelings about these details. How does the author's choice of words and details affect your feelings about the events and characters?**

# Saboteur (2000)

1 MR. CHIU and his bride were having lunch in the square before Muji Train Station. On the table between them were two bottles of soda spewing out brown foam and two paper boxes of rice and sautéed cucumber and pork. "Let's eat," he said to her, and broke the connected ends of the chopsticks. He picked up a slice of streaky pork and put it into his mouth. As he was chewing, a few crinkles appeared on his thin jaw.

2 To his right, at another table, two railroad policemen were drinking tea and laughing; it seemed that the stout, middle-aged man was telling a joke to his young comrade, who was tall and of athletic build. Now and again they would steal a glance at Mr. Chiu's table.

3 The air smelled of rotten melon. A few flies kept buzzing above the couple's lunch. Hundreds of people were rushing around to get on the platform or to catch buses to downtown. Food and fruit vendors were crying for customers in lazy voices. About a dozen young women, representing the local hotels, held up placards which displayed the daily prices and words as large as a palm, like FREE MEALS, AIR-CONDITIONING, and ON THE RIVER. In the center of the square stood

a concrete statue of Chairman Mao, at whose feet peasants were napping, their backs on the warm granite and their faces toward the sunny sky. A flock of pigeons perched on the Chairman's raised hand and forearm.

4 The rice and cucumber tasted good, and Mr. Chiu was eating unhurriedly. His sallow face showed exhaustion. He was glad that the honeymoon was finally over and that he and his bride were heading back for Harbin. During the two weeks' vacation, he had been worried about his liver, because three months ago he had suffered from acute hepatitis; he was afraid he might have a relapse. But he had had no severe symptoms, despite his liver being still big and tender. On the whole he was pleased with his health, which could endure even the strain of a honeymoon; indeed, he was on the course of recovery. He looked at his bride, who took off her wire glasses, kneading the root of her nose with her fingertips. Beads of sweat coated her pale cheeks.

5 "Are you all right, sweetheart?" he asked.

6 "I have a headache. I didn't sleep well last night."

7 "Take an aspirin, will you?"

8 "It's not that serious. Tomorrow is Sunday and I can sleep in. Don't worry."

9 As they were talking, the stout policeman at the next table stood up and threw a bowl of tea in their direction. Both Mr. Chiu's and his bride's sandals were wet instantly.

10 "Hooligan!" she said in a low voice.

11 Mr. Chiu got to his feet and said out loud, "Comrade Policeman, why did you do this?" He stretched out his right foot to show the wet sandal.

12 "Do what?" the stout man asked huskily, glaring at Mr. Chiu while the young fellow was whistling.

13 "See, you dumped tea on our feet."

14 "You're lying. You wet your shoes yourself."

15 "Comrade Policeman, your duty is to keep order, but you purposely tortured us common citizens. Why violate the law you are supposed to enforce?" As Mr. Chiu was speaking, dozens of people began gathering around.

16 With a wave of his hand, the man said to the young fellow, "Let's get hold of him!"

17 They grabbed Mr. Chiu and clamped handcuffs around his wrists. He cried, "You can't do this to me. This is utterly unreasonable."

"Shut up!" The man pulled out his pistol. "You can use your tongue at our headquarters." 18

The young fellow added, "You're a saboteur, you know that? You're disrupting public order." 19

The bride was too petrified to say anything coherent. She was a recent college graduate, had majored in fine arts, and had never seen the police make an arrest. All she could say was, "Oh, please, please!" 20

The policemen were pulling Mr. Chiu, but he refused to go with them, holding the corner of the table and shouting, "We have a train to catch. We already bought the tickets." 21

The stout man punched him in the chest. "Shut up. Let your ticket expire." With the pistol butt he chopped Mr. Chiu's hands, which at once released the table. Together the two men were dragging him away to the police station. 22

Realizing he had to go with them, Mr. Chiu turned his head and shouted to his bride, "Don't wait for me here. Take the train. If I'm not back by tomorrow morning, send someone over to get me out." 23

She nodded, covering her sobbing mouth with her palm. 24

AFTER removing his belt, they locked Mr. Chiu into a cell in the back of the Railroad Police Station. The single window in the room was blocked by six steel bars; it faced a spacious yard, in which stood a few pines. Beyond the trees, two swings hung from an iron frame, swaying gently in the breeze. Somewhere in the building a cleaver was chopping rhythmically. There must be a kitchen upstairs, Mr. Chiu thought. 25

He was too exhausted to worry about what they would do to him, so he lay down on the narrow bed and shut his eyes. He wasn't afraid. The Cultural Revolution was over already, and recently the Party had been propagating the idea that all citizens were equal before the law. The police ought to be a law-abiding model for common people. As long as he remained coolheaded and reasoned with them, they probably wouldn't harm him. 26

Late in the afternoon he was taken to the Interrogation Bureau on the second floor. On his way there, in the stairwell, he ran into the middle-aged policeman who had manhandled him. The man grinned, rolling his bulgy eyes and pointing his fingers at him 27 as if firing a pistol. Egg of a tortoise! Mr. Chiu cursed mentally.

28 The moment he sat down in the office, he burped, his palm shielding his mouth. In front of him, across a long desk, sat the chief of the bureau and a donkey-faced man. On the glass desktop was a folder containing information on his case. He felt it bizarre that in just a matter of hours they had accumulated a small pile of writing about him. On second thought he began to wonder whether they had kept a file on him all the time. How could this have happened? He lived and worked in Harbin, more than three hundred miles away, and this was his first time in Muji City.

> We can easily prove you are guilty.

29 The chief of the bureau was a thin, bald man who looked serene and intelligent. His slim hands handled the written pages in the folder in the manner of a lecturing scholar. To Mr. Chiu's left sat a young scribe, with a clipboard on his knee and a black fountain pen in his hand.

30 "Your name?" the chief asked, apparently reading out the question from a form.

31 "Chiu, Maguang."

32 "Age?"

33 "Thirty-four."

34 "Profession?"

35 "Lecturer."

36 "Work unit?"

37 "Harbin University."

38 "Political status?"

39 "Communist Party member."

40 The chief put down the paper and began to speak. "Your crime is sabotage, although it hasn't induced serious consequences yet. Because you are a Party member, you should be punished more. You have failed to be a model for the masses and you—"

41 "Excuse me, sir," Mr. Chiu cut him off.

42 "What?"

43 "I didn't do anything. Your men are the saboteurs of our social order. They threw hot tea on my feet and on my wife's feet. Logically speaking, you should criticize them, if not punish them."

44 "That statement is groundless. You have no witness. Why should I believe you?" the chief said matter-of-factly.

45 "This is my evidence." He raised his right hand. "Your man hit my fingers with a pistol."

46 "That doesn't prove how your feet got wet. Besides, you could have hurt your fingers yourself."

47 "But I am telling the truth!" Anger flared up in Mr. Chiu. "Your police station owes me an apology. My train ticket has expired, my new leather sandals are ruined, and I am late for a conference in the provincial capital. You must compensate me for the damage and losses. Don't mistake me for a common citizen who would tremble when you sneeze. I'm a scholar, a philosopher, and an expert in dialectical materialism. If necessary, we will argue about this in *The Northeastern Daily,* or we will go to the highest People's Court in Beijing. Tell me, what's your name?" He got carried away with his harangue, which was by no means trivial and had worked to his advantage on numerous occasions.

"Stop bluffing us," the donkey-faced man broke in. "We have seen a lot of your kind. We can easily prove you are guilty. Here are some of the statements given by eyewitnesses." He pushed a few sheets of paper toward Mr. Chiu. 4

Mr. Chiu was dazed to see the different handwritings, which all stated that he had shouted in the square to attract attention and refused to obey the police. One of the witnesses had identified herself as a purchasing agent from a shipyard in Shanghai. Something stirred in Mr. Chiu's stomach, a pain rising to his rib. He gave out a faint moan. 4

"Now you have to admit you are guilty," the chief said. "Although it's a serious crime, we won't punish you severely, provided you write out a self-criticism and promise that you won't disrupt the public order again. In other words, your release will depend on your attitude toward this crime." 5

"You're daydreaming," Mr. Chiu cried. "I won't write a word, because I'm innocent. I demand that you provide me with a letter of apology so I can explain to my university why I'm late." 5

Both the interrogators smiled contemptuously. "Well, we've never done that," said the chief, taking a puff at his cigarette. 5

"Then make this a precedent." 5

"That's unnecessary. We are pretty certain that you will comply with our wishes." The chief blew a column of smoke toward Mr. Chiu's face. 5

At the tilt of the chief's head, two guards stepped forward and grabbed the criminal by the arms. Mr. Chiu meanwhile went on saying, "I shall report you to the Provincial Administration. You'll have to pay for this! You are worse than the Japanese military police." 5

They dragged him out of the room. 5

AFTER dinner, which consisted of a bowl of millet porridge, a corn bun, and a piece of pickled turnip, Mr. Chiu began to have a fever, shaking with a chill and sweating pro- 5 fusely. He knew that the fire of anger had gotten into his liver and that he was probably having a relapse. No medicine was available, because his briefcase had been left with his bride. At home it would have been time for him to sit in front of their color TV, drinking jasmine tea and watching the evening news. It was so lonesome in here. The orange bulb above the single bed was the only source of light, which enabled the guards to keep him under surveillance at night. A moment ago he had asked them for a newspaper or a magazine to read, but they turned him down.

8 Through the small opening on the door noises came in. It seemed that the police on duty were playing cards or chess in a nearby office; shouts and laughter could be heard now and then. Meanwhile, an accordion kept coughing from a remote corner in the building. Looking at the ballpoint and the letter paper left for him by the guards when they took him back from the Interrogation Bureau, Mr. Chiu remembered the old saying, "When a scholar runs into soldiers, the more he argues, the muddier his point becomes." How ridiculous this whole thing was. He ruffled his thick hair with his fingers.

9 He felt miserable, massaging his stomach continually. To tell the truth, he was more upset than frightened, because he would have to catch up with his work once he was back home—a paper that was due at the printers next week, and two dozen books he ought to read for the courses he was going to teach in the fall.

0 A human shadow flitted across the opening. Mr. Chiu rushed to the door and shouted through the hole, "Comrade Guard, Comrade Guard!"

1 What do you want?" a voice rasped.

2 "I want you to inform your leaders that I'm very sick. I have heart disease and hepatitis. I may die here if you keep me like this without medication."

3 "No leader is on duty on the weekend. You have to wait till Monday."

4 "What? You mean I'll stay in here tomorrow?"

5 "Yes."

6 "Your station will be held responsible if anything happens to me."

7 "We know that. Take it easy, you won't die."

8 It seemed illogical that Mr. Chiu slept quite well that night, though the light above his head had been on all the time and the straw mattress was hard and infested with fleas. He was afraid of ticks, mosquitoes, cockroaches—any kind of insect but fleas and bedbugs. Once, in the countryside, where his school's faculty and staff had helped the peasants harvest crops for a week, his colleagues had joked about his flesh, which they said must have tasted nonhuman to fleas. Except for him, they were all afflicted with hundreds of bites.

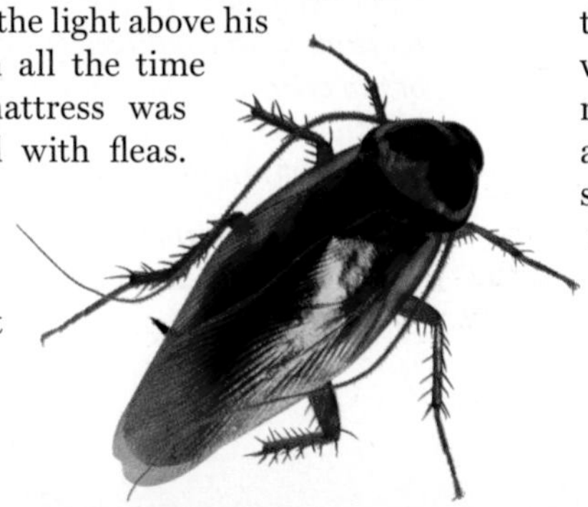

More amazing now, he didn't miss his bride a lot. He even enjoyed sleeping alone, perhaps because the honeymoon had tired him out and he needed more rest. 69

The backyard was quiet on Sunday morning. Pale sunlight streamed through the pine branches. A few sparrows were jumping on the ground, catching caterpillars and ladybugs. Holding the steel bars, Mr. Chiu inhaled the morning air, which smelled meaty. There must have been an eatery or a cooked-meat stand nearby. He reminded himself that he should take this detention with ease. A sentence that Chairman Mao had written to a hospitalized friend rose in his mind: "Since you are already in here, you may as well stay and make the best of it." 70

His desire for peace of mind originated in his fear that his hepatitis might get worse. He tried to remain unperturbed. However, he was sure that his liver was swelling up, since the fever still persisted. For a whole day he lay in bed, thinking about his paper on the nature of contradictions. Time and again he was overwhelmed by anger, cursing aloud, "A bunch of thugs!" He swore that once he was out, he would write an article about this experience. He had better find out some of the policemen's names. 71

It turned out to be a restful day for the most part; he was certain that his university would send somebody to his rescue. All he should do now was remain calm and wait patiently. Sooner or later the police would have to release him, although they had no idea that he might refuse to leave unless they wrote him an apology. Damn those hoodlums, they had ordered more than they could eat! 72

WHEN he woke up on Monday morning, it was already light. Somewhere a man was moaning; the sound came from the backyard. After a long yawn, and kicking off the tattered blanket, Mr. Chiu climbed out of bed and went to the window. In the middle of the yard, a young man was fastened to a pine, his wrists handcuffed around the trunk from behind. He was wriggling and swearing loudly, but there was no sight of anyone else in the yard. He looked familiar to Mr. Chiu. 73

Mr. Chiu squinted his eyes to see who it was. To his astonishment, he recognized the man, who was 74

Fenjin, a recent graduate from the Law Department at Harbin University. Two years ago Mr. Chiu had taught a course in Marxist materialism, in which Fenjin had enrolled. Now, how on earth had this young devil landed here?

75 Then it dawned on him that Fenjin must have been sent over by his bride. What a stupid woman! A bookworm, who only knew how to read foreign novels! He had expected that she would contact the school's Security Section, which would for sure send a cadre here. Fenjin held no official position; he merely worked in a private law firm that had just two lawyers; in fact, they had little business except for some detective work for men and women who suspected their spouses of having extramarital affairs. Mr. Chiu was overcome with a wave of nausea.

76 Should he call out to let his student know he was nearby? He decided not to, because he didn't know what had happened. Fenjin must have quarreled with the police to incur such a punishment. Yet this could never have occurred if Fenjin hadn't come to his rescue. So no matter what, Mr. Chiu had to do something. But what could he do?

77 It was going to be a scorcher. He could see purple steam shimmering and rising from the ground among the pines. Poor devil, he thought, as he raised a bowl of corn glue to his mouth, sipped, and took a bite of a piece of salted celery.

78 When a guard came to collect the bowl and the chopsticks, Mr. Chiu asked him what had happened to the man in the backyard. "He called our boss 'bandit,'" the guard said. "He claimed he was a lawyer or something. An arrogant son of a rabbit."

79 Now it was obvious to Mr. Chiu that he had to do something to help his rescuer. Before he could figure out a way, a scream broke out in the backyard. He rushed to the window and saw a tall policeman standing before Fenjin, an iron bucket on the ground. It was the same young fellow who had arrested Mr. Chiu in the square two days before. The man pinched Fenjin's nose, then raised his hand, which stayed in the air for a few seconds, then slapped the lawyer across the face. As Fenjin was groaning, the man lifted up the bucket and poured water on his head.

80 "This will keep you from getting sunstroke, boy. I'll give you some more every hour," the man said loudly.

81 Fenjin kept his eyes shut, yet his wry face showed that he was struggling to hold back from cursing the policeman, or, more likely, that he was sobbing in silence. He sneezed, then raised his face and shouted, "Let me go take a piss."

82 "Oh yeah?" the man bawled. "Pee in your pants."

Still Mr. Chiu didn't make any noise, gripping 83
the steel bars with both hands, his fingers white. The policeman turned and glanced at the cell's window; his pistol, partly holstered, glittered in the sun. With a snort he spat his cigarette butt to the ground and stamped it into the dust.

Then the door opened and the guards motioned 84
Mr. Chiu to come out. Again they took him upstairs to the Interrogation Bureau.

The same men were in the office, though this time 85
the scribe was sitting there empty-handed. At the sight of Mr. Chiu the chief said, "Ah, here you are. Please be seated."

After Mr. Chiu sat down, the chief waved a white 86
silk fan and said to him, "You may have seen your lawyer. He's a young man without manners, so our director had him taught a crash course in the backyard."

"It's illegal to do that. Aren't you afraid to appear 87
in a newspaper?"

"No, we are not, not even on TV. What else can you 88
do? We are not afraid of any story you make up. We call it fiction. What we do care about is that you cooperate with us. That is to say, you must admit your crime."

"What if I refuse to cooperate?" 89

"Then your lawyer will continue his education in 90
the sunshine."

A swoon swayed Mr. Chiu, and he held the arms 91
of the chair to steady himself. A numb pain stung him in the upper stomach and nauseated him, and his head was throbbing. He was sure that the hepatitis was finally attacking him. Anger was flaming up in his chest; his throat was tight and clogged.

The chief resumed, "As a matter of fact, you don't 92
even have to write out your self-criticism. We have your crime described clearly here. All we need is your signature."

Holding back his rage, Mr. Chiu said, "Let me look 93
at that."

With a smirk the donkey-faced man handed him 94
a sheet, which carried these words:

> *I hereby admit that on July 13 I disrupted public order at Muji Train Station, and that I refused to listen to reason when the railroad police issued their warning. Thus I myself am responsible for my arrest. After two days' detention, I have realized the reactionary nature of my crime. From now on, I shall continue to educate myself with all my effort and shall never commit this kind of crime again.*

A voice started screaming in Mr. Chiu's ears, "Lie, 95
lie!" But he shook his head and forced the voice away.

He asked the chief, "If I sign this, will you release both my lawyer and me?"

6 "Of course, we'll do that." The chief was drumming his fingers on the blue folder—their file on him.

7 Mr. Chiu signed his name and put his thumbprint under his signature.

8 "Now you are free to go," the chief said with a smile, and handed him a piece of paper to wipe his thumb with.

9 Mr. Chiu was so sick that he couldn't stand up from the chair at first try. Then he doubled his effort and rose to his feet. He staggered out of the building to meet his lawyer in the backyard, having forgotten to ask for his belt back. In his chest he felt as though there were a bomb. If he were able to, he would have razed the entire police station and eliminated all their families. Though he knew he could do nothing like that, he made up his mind to do something.

0 "I'M sorry about this torture, Fenjin," Mr. Chiu said when they met.

1 "It doesn't matter. They are savages." The lawyer brushed a patch of dirt off his jacket with trembling fingers. Water was still dribbling from the bottoms of his trouser legs.

2 "Let's go now," the teacher said.

3 The moment they came out of the police station, Mr. Chiu caught sight of a tea stand. He grabbed Fenjin's arm and walked over to the old woman at the table. "Two bowls of black tea," he said and handed her a one-yuan note.

After the first bowl, they each had another one. Then they set out for the train station. But before they walked fifty yards, Mr. Chiu insisted on eating a bowl of tree-ear soup at a food stand. Fenjin agreed. He told his teacher, "You mustn't treat me like a guest." 104

"No, I want to eat something myself." 105

As if dying of hunger, Mr. Chiu dragged his lawyer from restaurant to restaurant near the police station, but at each place he ordered no more than two bowls of food. Fenjin wondered why his teacher wouldn't stay at one place and eat his fill. 106

Mr. Chiu bought noodles, wonton, eight-grain porridge, and chicken soup, respectively, at four restaurants. While eating, he kept saying through his teeth, "If only I could kill all the bastards!" At the last place he merely took a few sips of the soup without tasting the chicken cubes and mushrooms. 107

Fenjin was baffled by his teacher, who looked ferocious and muttered to himself mysteriously, and whose jaundiced face was covered with dark puckers. For the first time Fenjin thought of Mr. Chiu as an ugly man. 108

WITHIN a month over eight hundred people contracted acute hepatitis in Muji. Six died of the disease, including two children. Nobody knew how the epidemic had started. 109

THE direct declarative telling of the story makes this piece by Pulitzer Prize–winner Ha Jin all the more powerful, and you may want to read Ralph Ellison's two stories in the casebook on the American South (chapter 12) in the same light, as fiction dealing with a difficult time in a difficult place.

**GOING FURTHER** Modern Chinese life, including that of the army, politics, the professions, and the university, has served as the major focus of Ha Jin's work. However, in *A Free Life,* his 2007 novel, he turned his attention to immigrant life in America, shifting away from his usual material.

# Writing from Reading

### Summarize

1 Examine the various acts of sabotage in this story and write a description of "saboteur." Now identify the various "saboteurs" (not just those indicated specifically by the story) and name their crimes. Which characters in the story don't commit some act of sabotage?

### Analyze Craft

2 What is the narrator's attitude toward Mr. Chiu's plight? How do you know this? What clues does the author provide by use of details and tone?

### Analyze Voice

3 Whom does Ha Jin agree with, the narrator or the law system? Cite examples of Jin's use of specific language and tone when describing certain characters and events.

### Synthesize Summary and Analysis

4 What is the narrator's attitude toward the police? How do you know this? What clues does the author provide through details and tone? Discuss the ironic aspects of the story.

5 How does the author portray power relations in China? Consider the various roles mentioned—policemen, scholar, lawyer, chief of the bureau.

### Interpret the Story

6 Does the story end as you might have expected? Who has won the struggle for power?

7 Does your attitude toward Mr. Chiu change over the course of the story? Discuss how and when, and whether you think Ha Jin has purposely influenced this attitude change.

# Junot Diaz (b. 1968)

Today, Junot Diaz's success as both a writer and a professor at MIT may lull others into forgetting the difficulties he faced as a boy who immigrated to the United States from the Dominican Republic when he was six. However, the poverty he experienced in Santo Domingo and the unpleasantness of growing up next door to a landfill in New Jersey left an indelible mark on Diaz and his fiction, which seeks to give voice to the difficulties of the immigrant life. A blend of sharp, slang-filled prose and narrators that include drug dealers and young boys struggling to make their way in an adopted country, Diaz's first book, a collection of stories titled *Drown* (1996), met with such acclaim that Diaz found himself a celebrity overnight; he was named one of *Newsweek*'s "New Faces of 1996." Although Diaz tends to write at a slow pace—ten years elapsed between *Drown* and his first novel, *The Brief Wondrous Life of Oscar Wao*—he has published stories in the most prestigious venues including *The New Yorker, The Paris Review,* and the *Best American Short Stories* series. His subject is the immigrant experience in the United States, which he portrays with great detail, right down to the feeling of constant uncertainty and the desire to fit in—a subject that allows his work to be semiautobiographical. And while he writes to set a precedent for future Latino writers, he also helps foster future writers through both his college teaching job and his volunteer work with urban high school students.

**AS YOU READ** Consider the narrator's tone. What voice do you hear as you're reading? How do you feel about his message? When do you feel comfortable with what he's saying, and when do you feel uncomfortable? What does he hide and what does he reveal?

# How to Date a Browngirl, Blackgirl, Whitegirl, or Halfie (1995)

1 WAIT for your brother and your mother to leave the apartment. You've already told them that you're feeling too sick to go to Union City to visit that tía who likes to squeeze your nuts. (He's gotten big, she'll say.) And even though your moms knows you ain't sick you stuck to your story until finally she said, Go ahead and stay, malcriado.

2 Clear the government cheese from the refrigerator. If the girl's from the Terrace stack the boxes behind the milk. If she's from the Park or Society Hill hide the cheese in the cabinet above the oven, way up where she'll never see. Leave yourself a reminder to get it out before morning or your moms will kick your ass. Take down any embarrassing photos of your family in the campo, especially the one with the half-naked kids dragging a goat on a rope leash. The kids are your cousins and by now they're old enough to understand why you're doing what you're doing. Hide the pictures of yourself with an Afro. Make sure the bathroom is presentable. Put the basket with all the crapped-on toilet paper under the sink. Spray the bucket with Lysol, then close the cabinet.

Shower, comb, dress. Sit on the couch and watch TV. If she's an outsider her father will be bringing her, maybe her mother. Neither of them want her seeing any boys from the Terrace—people get stabbed in the Terrace—but she's strong-headed and this time will get her way. If she's a white girl you know you'll at least get a hand job. 3

The directions were in your best handwriting, so her parents won't think you're an idiot. Get up from the couch and check the parking lot. Nothing. If the girl's local, don't sweat it. She'll flow over when she's good and ready. Sometimes she'll run into her other friends and a whole crowd will show up at your apartment and even though that means you ain't getting shit it will be fun anyway and you'll wish these people would come over more often. Sometimes the girl won't flow over at all and the next day in school she'll say sorry, smile and you'll be stupid enough to believe her and ask her out again. 4

Wait and after an hour go out to your corner. The neighborhood is full of traffic. Give one of your boys a shout and when he says, Are you still waiting on that bitch? Say, Hell yeah. 5

Get back inside. Call her house and when her father picks up ask if she's there. He'll ask, Who is this? Hang up. 6

He sounds like a principal or a police chief, the sort of dude with a big neck, who never has to watch his back. Sit and wait. By the time your stomach's ready to give out on you, a Honda or maybe a Jeep pulls in and out she comes.

7 Hey, you'll say.

8 Look, she'll say. My mom wants to meet you. She's got herself all worried about nothing.

9 Don't panic. Say, Hey, no problem. Run a hand through your hair like the whiteboys do even though the only thing that runs easily through your hair is Africa. She will look good. The white ones are the ones you want the most, aren't they, but usually the out-of-towners are black, blackgirls who grew up with ballet and Girl Scouts, who have three cars in their driveways. If she's a halfie don't be surprised that her mother is white. Say, Hi. Her moms will say hi and you'll see that you don't scare her, not really. She will say that she needs easier directions to get out and even though she has the best directions in her lap give her new ones. Make her happy.

As you walk to the restaurant talk about school.

10 You have choices. If the girl's from around the way, take her to El Cibao for dinner. Order everything in your busted-up Spanish. Let her correct you if she's Latina and amaze her if she's black. If she's not from around the way, Wendy's will do. As you walk to the restaurant talk about school. A local girl won't need stories about the neighborhood but the other ones might. Supply the story about the loco who'd been storing canisters of tear gas in his basement for years, how one day the canisters cracked and the whole neighborhood got a dose of the military-strength stuff. Don't tell her that your moms knew right away what it was, that she recognized its smell from the year the United States invaded your island.

11 Hope that you don't run into your nemesis, Howie, the Puerto Rican kid with the two killer mutts. He walks them all over the neighborhood and every now and then the mutts corner themselves a cat and tear it to shreds, Howie laughing as the cat flips up in the air, its neck twisted around like an owl, red meat showing through the soft fur. If his dogs haven't cornered a cat, he will walk behind you and ask, Hey, Yunior, is that your new fuckbuddy?

12 Let him talk. Howie weighs about two hundred pounds and could eat you if he wanted. At the field he will turn away. He has new sneakers, and doesn't want them muddy. If the girl's an outsider she will hiss now and say, What a fucking asshole. A homegirl would have been yelling back at him the whole time, unless she was shy. Either way don't feel bad that you didn't do anything. Never lose a fight on a first date or that will be the end of it.

Dinner will be tense. You are not good at talking 13
to people you don't know. A halfie will tell you that her parents met in the Movement, will say, Back then people thought it a radical thing to do. It will sound like something her parents made her memorize. Your brother once heard that one and said, Man, that sounds like a whole lot of Uncle Tomming to me. Don't repeat this.

Put down your hamburger 14
and say, It must have been hard.

She will appreciate your in- 15
terest. She will tell you more. Black people, she will say, treat me real bad. That's why I don't like them. You'll wonder how she feels about Dominicans. Don't ask. Let her speak on it and when you're both finished eating walk back into the neighborhood. The skies will be magnificent. Pollutants have made Jersey sunsets one of the wonders of the world. Point it out. Touch her shoulder and say, That's nice, right?

Get serious. Watch TV but stay alert. Sip some of 16
the Bermúdez your father left in the cabinet, which nobody touches. A local girl may have hips and a thick ass but she won't be quick about letting you touch. She has to live in the same neighborhood you do, has to deal with you being all up in her business. She might just chill with you and then go home. She might kiss you and then go, or she might, if she's reckless, give it up, but that's rare. Kissing will suffice. A whitegirl might just give it up right then. Don't stop her.

She'll take her gum out of her mouth, stick it to the plastic sofa covers and then will move close to you. You have nice eyes, she might say.

17 Tell her that you love her hair, that you love her skin, her lips, because, in truth, you love them more than you love your own.

18 She'll say, I like Spanish guys, and even though you've never been to Spain, say, I like you. You'll sound smooth.

19 You'll be with her until about eight-thirty and then she will want to wash up. In the bathroom she will hum a song from the radio and her waist will keep the beat against the lip of the sink. Imagine her old lady coming to get her, what she would say if she knew her daughter had just lain under you and blown your name, pronounced with her eighth-grade Spanish, into your ear. While she's in the bathroom call one of your boys and say, Lo hice, loco. Or just sit back on the couch and smile.

20 But usually it won't work this way. Be prepared. She will not want to kiss you. Just cool it, she'll say. The halfie might lean back, breaking away from you. She will cross her arms, say, I hate my tits. Stroke her hair but she will pull away. I don't like anybody touching my hair, she will say. She will act like somebody you don't know. In school she is known for her attention-grabbing laugh, as high and far-ranging as a gull, but here she will worry you. You will not know what to say.

You're the only kind of guy who asks me out, she 21
will say. Your neighbors will start their hyena calls, now that the alcohol is in them. You and the blackboys.

Say nothing. Let her button her 22
shirt, let her comb her hair, the sound of it stretching like a sheet of fire between you. When her father pulls in and beeps, let her go without too much of a good-bye. She won't want it. During the next hour the phone will ring. You will be tempted to pick it up. Don't. Watch the shows you want to watch, without a family around to debate you. Don't go downstairs. Don't fall asleep. It won't help. Put the government cheese back in its place before your moms kills you.

In many ways this is the most playful story in the book, and if you like the tone of it you may notice it has some affinities to Lorrie Moore's story "How to Become a Writer" (chapter 7)—they both use the second-person point of view—or the story by Sherman Alexie in the Anthology of Stories for Further Reading.

**GOING FURTHER** Playfulness, even when treating some of the most serious subjects, goes all the way back to Laurence Sterne's *Tristram Shandy* in the eighteenth century and to *Don Quixote,* the classic Spanish novel composed by Miguel de Cervantes and first published in 1605. Today you might find similarities between Diaz's tone and the tone in *Extremely Loud & Incredibly Close* by Jonathan Safran Foer.

# Writing from Reading

### Summarize

1 Describe the narrator's attitudes toward each kind of girl mentioned in the title. What attracts him about each? What complaints does he have about each?

2 Consider whether this story is meant to be a recipe for *successful* dating. Does the narrator end up where he means to be in each scenario? What is his goal for the date?

### Analyze Craft

3 Discuss the use of irony in the story. Are there incongruities (1) between acts and results, (2) between what occurs and what the character expected to occur, or (3) between what is said and what is meant?

### Analyze Voice

4 What does the narrator hide and what does he reveal? Discuss how his secrets and confessions affect your attitudes toward him.

### Synthesize Summary and Analysis

5 Discuss the attitudes that this narrator reveals about race, class, and ethnicity. Cite examples to demonstrate how Diaz uses tone to affect your response to the narrator's suggestions.

### Interpret the Story

6 Consider the form the story would take if written in first person, as a straight-forward dramatic scene. Discuss how the tone and language of the story might change, and what the effect would be on your impression of the boy on the date.

# Reading for Language, Tone, and Style

When reading for language, tone, and style, make notes about how the author uses language to express a particular attitude toward the characters and events.

- *What* is being said, and *how* and *why*?
- What effect does the author wish to create?
- What effect does the writing have on you?

| | |
|---|---|
| ***What kind of language or diction* did the author choose to shape the style and tone of the story?** | • Are there particular words that are important to the style and tone of the story?<br>• Are there key images that have an impact on the style and tone?<br>• How would you describe the language chosen by the writer? |

| | |
|---|---|
| **What tone (of voice) do you hear?** | • **Serious or comedic?**<br>• **Distant or intimate?**<br>• **Direct or roundabout?**<br>• **Restrained or emotional?**<br>• **Ominous or lighthearted?**<br>• **Straightforward or ironic?** |
| **Is the author being ironic?** | • Is the irony **verbal?**<br>• Is the irony **dramatic?** |
| **How do the language and tone work together to define the writer's style?** | • Is the language lush or lean?<br>• Are the sentences long and complex, or short and simple?<br>• What kind of tone is created in the story?<br>• How would you describe the style: elegant? hard-boiled? lyrical? unadorned? ornate? self-conscious? |

# Suggestions for Writing about Language, Tone, and Style

1. In her interview, Aimee Bender says that she uses her imagination in writing as "a way to get to feelings that are hard to look at straight on." Discuss this aspect of her style as represented by "The Rememberer." How effective is this style for exploring the subject of loss?
2. "The Rememberer" and "How to Date a Browngirl, Blackgirl, Whitegirl, or Halfie" both explore intimate relationships—the limitations and possibilities between members of a couple. Using specific examples, argue how each of the narrators might define love. What words would they use? What kind of language?
3. Briefly describe the style of each story in this chapter, and then compare and contrast the authors' approaches. Why is each style fitting for its particular story?
4. The titles "Only the Dead Know Brooklyn" and "How to Date a Browngirl, Blackgirl, Whitegirl, or Halfie" are both bold declarations. What do these titles suggest about the way language will be used in the stories that follow? How do other lines of dialogue or description reinforce or refute the sense of certainty in the titles?

"THE next day, Nnamabia barely touched his rice. He said that the policemen had splashed soapy water on the floor and walls of the cell, as they usually did, and that the old man, who had not bathed in a week, had yanked his shirt off and rubbed his frail back against the wet floor. The policemen started to laugh when they saw him do this, and then they asked him to take all his clothes off and parade in the corridor outside the cell; as he did, they laughed louder and asked whether his son the thief knew that Papa's buttocks were so shrivelled. Nnamabia was staring at his yellow-orange rice as he spoke, and when he looked up his eyes were filled with tears, my worldly brother, and I felt a tenderness for him that I would not have been able to describe if I had been asked to."

*—from "Cell One" by Chimamanda Ngozi Adichie*

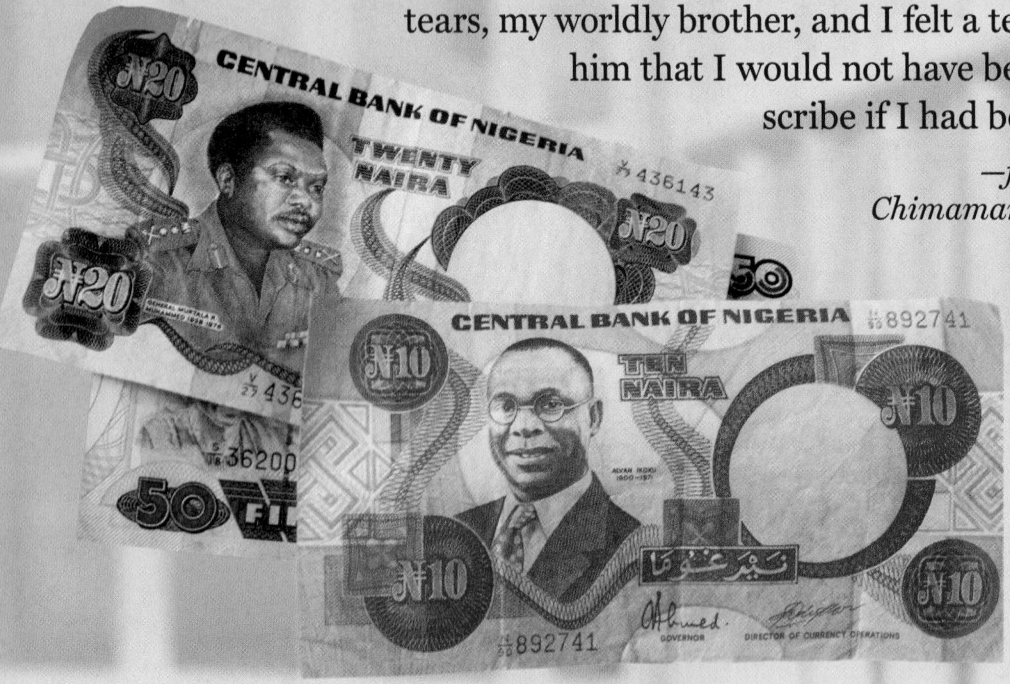


*"The germ of the story came from a small story that my brother Okey had told me . . . about an old man in a cell. . . . I was haunted . . . and heartbroken . . . but I knew I wanted to use it . . . and wanted it also to be about my brother. I wanted to write about how my brother was redeemed in the most unlikely way. . . . I think that the story's about redemption—my brother's redemption—but in some ways it also redeemed me."*

Conversation with Chimamanda Ngozi Adichie, available on video at www.mhhe.com/delbanco1e

# 9 THEME

NNAMABIA, the young man who is the focus of this passage, is Nigerian. He is handsome, popular, well-educated, from a good family, attractive to women, and he has enjoyed every minute of his privileged life. Now, however, he is in prison because he has been linked, perhaps unjustly, to gang activity and the murder of three students on a college campus. While he is in prison, his mother, father, and sister—who is the narrator of the story—visit him almost daily. During one visit, he tells this story of the old man.

This passage is central to "cell one" because it reveals a change in Nnamabia. The imprisonment has stirred a social consciousness in him, an awareness that life is a serious matter. The passage also reveals the impact this change has on his sister. Nnamabia doesn't say, "I am beginning to understand justice and injustice and human cruelty." His sister certainly doesn't explain why she felt that rush of tenderness. She says that she cannot. Still, as readers, we sense the significance of the old man's mistreatment and its impact on these characters. As we move toward understanding this new situation, we move toward understanding the **theme**—that is, the central or underlying meanings of a literary work.

When we talk about theme, we're talking about broad ideas. Theme is what a story is "about" beyond the specific characters and events of the story. So, we can say that in the passage from Adichie's story, the development of social conscience, the horror of human brutality, and the significance of human connection emerge as thematic concerns. To put these concerns together in a complete thought, we might say that "Cell One" explores the brutal lessons that are sometimes needed to awaken social consciousness and a sense of justice.

*CONTINUED ON PAGE 270*

*I like to think about multiple themes . . .*

Q&A

*I grew up fortunate enough to be surrounded by books . . .*

# *A Conversation on Writing*

## Chimamanda Ngozi Adichie

### On Multiple Themes in "Cell One"

The notion of just one theme in a story sometimes just reduces a work of fiction. I like to think about multiple themes, that a story can do so many things at the same time. I do think ["Cell One"] is about redemption. . . . but it's also about gender. . . . and also [about] how, in my opinion, unreasonable family love can be. . . . And I wanted to explore middle-class comfort versus wartime deprivation and how it changes how people feel about each other.

### Bagels, Longing, and Literature

I grew up in a small university town in western Nigeria. I grew up fortunate enough to be surrounded by books, and I was fascinated by this word *bagel*. . . . because these characters in the books had these things for breakfast. . . . I had never seen one. . . . I think what that showed me was how you don't need to know what it is to long for it. . . . What underlies it all is that human thing that I think is common—that we all long to be loved, and want to love. . . . For me I hope that's really what comes out of my work, and that the other things, the Nigerian food and the language, all of which I love and want to celebrate . . . will be secondary.

### On Reading

You don't have to love everything, first of all, and you won't love everything, but . . . you will find something to love. . . . Very often we see literature as something difficult. . . . Sometimes we forget that literature should be something that we enjoy and have fun doing.

When readers think of Nigerian authors, Chinua Achebe is the major name that has come to mind for the past few decades. Today, however, Nigerian writer Chimamanda Ngozi Adichie is following in his footsteps—almost literally, as she grew up in the house where Achebe once lived. Adichie came to the United States when she was nineteen to complete her undergraduate degree; she also earned a master's in creative writing from Johns Hopkins University. Her first novel, *Purple Hibiscus* (2003), met with great success; it was shortlisted for the Orange Fiction Prize and won the Commonwealth Writers' Prize for Best First Book. Like *Purple Hibiscus,* her second novel, *Half of a Yellow Sun,* is set in Nigeria, but whereas her first novel portrayed a Nigerian family and their struggle with religion and authority, this novel takes for its subject the Nigerian Civil War. Adichie's short stories have also met with success; she won an O. Henry Prize in 2003, and her stories have appeared in *Granta, The Iowa Review,* and *The New Yorker.* She was awarded the MacArthur "genius grant" in 2008. She currently divides her time between Nigeria and the United States.

**RESEARCH ASSIGNMENT** In her interview, Adichie talks about authenticity in her writing. How does she achieve this authenticity? Do you agree with her about the "ideal of authenticity" in fiction? Why or why not?

To watch this entire interview and hear the author read from "Cell One," go to **www.mhhe.com/delbanco1e.**

**AS YOU READ** As you read, notice how these characters change in the course of the story. Which events lead to these changes? How do these changes rise to the level of thematic importance?

**TIP** **FOR INTERACTIVE READING . . .** What is Cell One? Find and mark all references to it in the story. When you are finished reading, describe everything you know about it, including the characters' attitudes about it.

# Cell One (2007)

1 THE first time our house was robbed, it was our neighbor Osita who climbed in through the dining-room window and stole our TV and VCR, and the "Purple Rain" and "Thriller" videotapes that my father had brought back from America. The second time our house was robbed, it was my brother Nnamabia, who faked a break-in and stole my mother's jewelry. It happened on a Sunday. My parents had travelled to their home town to visit our grandparents, so Nnamabia and I went to church alone. He drove my mother's green Peugeot 504. We sat together in church as we usually did, but we did not have time to nudge each other and stifle giggles about somebody's ugly hat or threadbare caftan, because Nnamabia left without a word after ten minutes. He came back just before the priest said, "The Mass is ended, go in peace." I was a little piqued. I imagined that he had gone off to smoke or to see some girl, since he had the car to himself for once; but he could at least have told me. We drove home in silence, and when he parked in our long driveway I stayed back to pick some ixora flowers while Nnamabia unlocked the front door. I went inside to find him standing in the middle of the parlor.

2 "We've been robbed!" he said.

3 It took me a moment to take in the room. Even then, I felt that there was a theatrical quality to the way the drawers had been flung open. Or perhaps it was simply that I knew my brother too well. Later, when my parents had come home and neighbors began to troop in to say *ndo*—sorry—and to snap their fingers and heave their shoulders up and down, I sat alone in my room upstairs and realized what the queasiness in my gut was: Nnamabia had done it, I knew. My father knew, too. He pointed out that the window louvres had been slipped out from the inside, rather than from the outside (Nnamabia was usually smarter than that—perhaps he had been in a hurry to get back to church before Mass ended), and that the robber knew exactly where my mother's jewelry was: in the back left corner of her metal trunk. Nnamabia stared at my father with wounded eyes and said that he may have done horrible things in the past, things that had caused my parents pain, but that he had done nothing in this case. He walked out the back door and did not come home that night. Or the next night. Or the night after. Two weeks later, he came home gaunt, smelling of beer, crying, saying he was sorry, that he had pawned the jewelry to the Hausa traders in Enugu, and that all the money was gone.

"How much did they give you for my gold?" our mother asked him. And when he told her she placed both hands on her head and cried, "Oh! Oh! *Chi m egbuo m!* My God has killed me!" I wanted to slap her. My father asked Nnamabia to write a report: how he had pawned the jewelry, what he had spent the money on, with whom he had spent it. I didn't think that Nnamabia would tell the truth, and I don't think that my father thought he would, but he liked reports, my professor father, he liked to have things written down and nicely documented. Besides, Nnamabia was seventeen, with 4

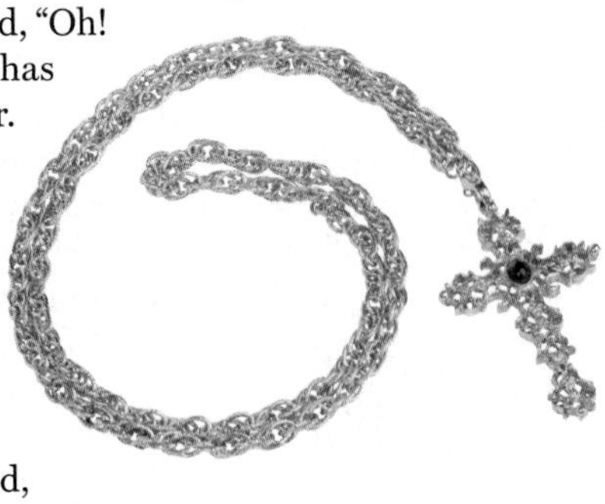

a carefully tended beard. He was already between secondary school and university, and was too old for caning. What else could my father have done? After Nnamabia had written the report, my father filed it in the steel cabinet in his study where he kept our school papers.

5 "That he could hurt his mother like that!" was the last thing my father said on the subject.

6 But Nnamabia hadn't set out to hurt her. He had done it because my mother's jewelry was the only thing of any value in the house: a lifetime's accumulation of solid-gold pieces. He had done it, too, because other sons of professors were doing it. This was the season of thefts on our serene campus. Boys who had grown up watching "Sesame Street," reading Enid Blyton, eating cornflakes for breakfast, and attending the university staff primary school in polished brown sandals were now cutting through the mosquito netting of their neighbors' windows, sliding out glass louvres, and climbing in to steal TVs and VCRs. We knew the thieves. Still, when the professors saw one another at the staff club or at church or at a faculty meeting, they were careful to moan about the riffraff from town coming onto their sacred campus to steal.

7 The thieving boys were the popular ones. They drove their parents' cars in the evening, their seats pushed back and their arms stretched out to reach the steering wheel. Osita, our neighbor who had stolen our TV only weeks before Nnamabia's theft, was lithe and handsome in a brooding sort of way, and walked with the grace of a cat. His shirts were always crisply ironed, and I used to watch him across the hedge, then close my eyes and imagine that he was walking toward me, coming to claim me as his. He never noticed me. When he stole from us, my parents did not go over to Professor Ebube's house to ask for our things back. But they knew it was Osita. Osita was two years older than Nnamabia; most of the thieving boys were a little older than Nnamabia, and maybe that was why Nnamabia had not stolen from another person's house. Perhaps he did not feel old enough, qualified enough, for anything more serious than my mother's jewelry.

8 Nnamabia looked just like my mother—he had her fair complexion and large eyes, and a generous mouth that curved perfectly. When my mother took us to the market, traders would call out, "Hey! Madam, why did you waste your fair skin on a boy and leave the girl so dark? What is a boy doing with all this beauty?" And my mother would chuckle, as though she took a mischievous and joyful responsibility for Nnamabia's looks. When, at eleven, Nnamabia broke the window of his classroom with a stone, my mother gave him the money to replace it and didn't tell my father. When, a few years later, he took the key to my father's car and pressed it into a bar of soap that my father found before Nnamabia could take it to a locksmith, she made vague sounds about how he was just experimenting and it didn't mean anything. When he stole the exam questions from the study and sold them to my father's students, she yelled at him, but then told my father that Nnamabia was sixteen, after all, and really should be given more pocket money.

9 I don't know whether Nnamabia felt remorse for stealing her jewelry. I could not always tell from my brother's gracious, smiling face what he really felt. He and I did not talk about it, and neither did my parents. Even though my mother's sisters sent her their gold earrings, even though she bought a new gold chain from Mrs. Mozie—the glamorous woman who imported gold from Italy—and began to drive to Mrs. Mozie's house once a month to pay in installments, we never talked about what had happened to her jewelry. It was as if by pretending that Nnamabia had not done the things he had done we could give him the opportunity to start afresh. The robbery might never have been mentioned again if Nnamabia had not been arrested two years later, in his second year of university.

10 BY then, it was the season of cults on the Nsukka campus, when signs all over the university read in bold letters, "SAY NO TO CULTS." The Black Axe, the Buccaneers, and the Pirates were the best known. They had once been benign fraternities, but they had evolved, and now eighteen-year-olds who had mastered the swagger of American rap videos were undergoing secret initiations that sometimes left one or two of them dead on Odim Hill. Guns and tortured loyalties became common. A boy would leer at a girl who turned out to be the girlfriend of the Capone of the Black Axe, and that boy, as he walked to a kiosk later to buy a cigarette, would be stabbed in the thigh. He would turn out to be a Buccaneer, and so one of his fellow-Buccaneers would go

to a beer parlor and shoot the nearest Black Axe in the leg, and then the next day another Buccaneer would be shot dead in the refectory, his body falling onto aluminum plates of *garri,* and that evening a Black Axe—a professor's son—would be hacked to death in his room, his CD player splattered with blood. It was inane. It was so abnormal that it quickly became normal. Girls stayed in their rooms after classes, and lecturers quivered, and when a fly buzzed too loudly people jumped. So the police were called in. They sped across campus in their rickety blue Peugeot 505 and glowered at the students, their rusty guns poking out of the car windows. Nnamabia came home from his lectures laughing. He thought that the police would have to do better than that; everyone knew the cult boys had newer guns.

11 My parents watched Nnamabia with silent concern, and I knew that they, too, were wondering if he was in a cult. Cult boys were popular, and Nnamabia was very popular. Boys yelled out his nickname—"The Funk!"—and shook his hand whenever he passed by, and girls, especially the popular ones, hugged him for too long when they said hello. He went to all the parties, the tame ones on campus and the wilder ones in town, and he was the kind of ladies' man who was also a guy's guy, the kind who smoked a packet of Rothmans a day and was reputed to be able to finish a case of Star beer in a single sitting. But it seemed more his style to befriend all the cult boys and yet not be one himself. And I was not entirely sure, either, that my brother had whatever it took—guts or diffidence—to join a cult.

Outside, the bodies lay on the lawn.

12 The only time I asked him if he was in a cult, he looked at me with surprise, as if I should have known better than to ask, before replying, "Of course not." I believed him. My dad believed him, too, when he asked. But our believing him made little difference, because he had already been arrested for belonging to a cult.

13 THIS is how it happened. On a humid Monday, four cult members waited at the campus gate and waylaid a professor driving a red Mercedes. They pressed a gun to her head, shoved her out of the car, and drove it to the Faculty of Engineering, where they shot three boys who were coming out of the building. It was noon. I was in a class nearby, and when we heard the shots our lecturer was the first to run out the door. There was loud screaming, and suddenly the stairwells were packed with scrambling students unsure where to run. Outside, the bodies lay on the lawn. The Mercedes had already screeched away. Many students hastily packed their bags, and *okada* drivers charged twice the usual fare to take them to the motor park to get on a bus. The vice-chancellor announced that all evening classes would be cancelled and everyone had to stay indoors after 9 P.M. This did not make much sense to me, since the shooting had happened in sparkling daylight, and perhaps it did not make sense to Nnamabia, either, because the first night of the curfew he didn't come home. I assumed that he had spent the night at a friend's; he did not always come home anyway. But the next morning a security man came to tell my parents that Nnamabia had been arrested at a bar with some cult boys and was at the police station.

My mother screamed, "*Ekwuzikwana!* Don't say that!" My father calmly thanked the security man. We drove to the police station in town, and there a constable chewing on the tip of a dirty pen said, "You mean those cult boys arrested last night? They have been taken to Enugu. Very serious case! We must stop this cult business once and for all!"

We got back into the car, and a new fear gripped us all. Nsukka, which was made up of our slow, insular campus and the slower, more insular town, was manageable; my father knew the police superintendent. But Enugu was anonymous. There the police could do what they were famous for doing when under pressure to produce results: kill people. 14

THE Enugu police station was in a sprawling, sandy compound. My mother bribed the policemen at the desk with money, and with jollof rice and meat, and they allowed Nnamabia to come out of his cell and sit on a bench under a mango tree with us. Nobody asked why he had stayed out the night before. Nobody said that the police were wrong to walk into a bar and arrest all the boys drinking there, including the barman. Instead, we listened to Nnamabia talk. 15

"If we ran Nigeria like this cell," he said, "we would have no problems. Things are so organized. Our cell has a chief and he has a second-in-command, and when you come in you are expected to give them some money. If you don't, you're in trouble." 16

"And did you have any money?" my mother asked. 17

Nnamabia smiled, his face more beautiful than ever, despite the new pimple-like insect bite on his forehead, and said that he had slipped his money into his anus shortly after the arrest. He knew the policemen would take it if he didn't hide it, and he knew 18 that he would need it to buy his peace in the cell. My parents said nothing for a while. I imagined Nnamabia rolling hundred-naira notes into a thin cigarette shape and then reaching into the back of his trousers to slip them into himself. Later, as we drove back to Nsukka, my father said, "This is what I should have done when he stole your jewelry. I should have had him locked up in a cell."

19 My mother stared out the window.

20 "Why?" I asked.

21 "Because this has shaken him. Couldn't you see?" my father asked with a smile. I couldn't see it. Nnamabia had seemed fine to me, slipping his money into his anus and all.

22 Nnamabia's first shock was seeing a Buccaneer sobbing. The boy was tall and tough, rumored to have carried out one of the killings and likely to become Capone next semester, and yet there he was in the cell, cowering and sobbing after the chief gave him a light slap on the back of the head. Nnamabia told me this in a voice lined with both disgust and disappointment; it was as if he had suddenly been made to see that the Incredible Hulk was really just painted green. His second shock was learning about the cell farthest away from his, Cell One. He had never seen it, but every day two policemen carried a dead man out of Cell One, stopping by Nnamabia's cell to make sure that the corpse was seen by all.

23 Those in the cell who could afford to buy old plastic paint cans of water bathed every other morning. When they were let out into the yard, the policemen watched them and often shouted, "Stop that or you are going to Cell One now!" Nnamabia could not imagine a place worse than his cell, which was so crowded that he often stood pressed against the wall. The wall had cracks where tiny *kwalikwata* lived; their bites were fierce and sharp, and when he yelped his cellmates mocked him. The biting was worse during the night, when they all slept on their sides, head to foot, to make room for one another, except the chief, who slept with his whole back lavishly on the floor. It was also the chief who divided up the two plates of rice that were pushed into the cell every day. Each person got two mouthfuls.

24 Nnamabia told us this during the first week. As he spoke, I wondered if the bugs in the wall had bitten his face or if the bumps spreading across his forehead were due to an infection. Some of them were tipped with cream-colored pus. Once in a while, he scratched at them. I wanted him to stop talking. He seemed to enjoy his new role as the sufferer of indignities, and he did not understand how lucky he was that the policemen allowed him to come out and eat our food, or how stupid he'd been to stay out drinking that night, and how uncertain his chances were of being released.

25 WE visited him every day for the first week. We took my father's old Volvo, because my mother's Peugeot was unsafe for trips outside Nsukka. By the end of the week, I noticed that my parents were acting differently—subtly so, but differently. My father no longer gave a monologue, as soon as we were waved through the police checkpoints, on how illiterate and corrupt the police were. He did not bring up the day when they had delayed us for an hour because he'd refused to bribe them, or how they had stopped a bus in which my beautiful cousin Ogechi was travelling and singled her out and called her a whore because she had two cell phones, and asked her for so much money that she had knelt on the ground in the rain begging them to let her go. My mother did not mumble that the policemen were symptoms of a larger malaise. Instead, my parents remained silent. It was as if by refusing to criticize the police they would somehow make Nnamabia's freedom more likely. "Delicate" was the word the superintendent at Nsukka had used. To get Nnamabia out anytime soon would be delicate, especially with the police commissioner in Enugu giving gloating, preening interviews about the arrest of the cultists. The cult problem was serious. Big Men in Abuja were following events. Everybody wanted to seem as if he were doing something.

26 The second week, I told my parents that we were not going to visit Nnamabia. We did not know how long this would last, and petrol was too expensive for us to drive three hours every day. Besides, it would not hurt Nnamabia to fend for himself for one day.

27 My mother said that nobody was begging me to come—I could sit there and do nothing while my innocent brother suffered. She started walking toward the car, and I ran after her. When I got outside, I was not sure what to do, so I picked up a stone near the ixora bush and hurled it at the windshield of the Volvo. I heard the brittle sound and saw the tiny lines spreading like rays on the glass before I turned and dashed upstairs and locked myself in my room. I heard my mother shouting. I heard my father's voice. Finally, there was silence. Nobody went to see Nnamabia that day. It surprised me, this little victory.

28 WE visited him the next day. We said nothing about the windshield, although the cracks had spread out like ripples on a frozen stream. The policeman at the

desk, the pleasant dark-skinned one, asked why we had not come the day before—he had missed my mother's jollof rice. I expected Nnamabia to ask, too, even to be upset, but he looked oddly sober. He did not eat all of his rice.

29 "What is wrong?" my mother said, and Nnamabia began to speak almost immediately, as if he had been waiting to be asked. An old man had been pushed into his cell the day before—a man perhaps in his mid-seventies, white-haired, skin finely wrinkled, with an old-fashioned dignity about him. His son was wanted for armed robbery, and when the police had not been able to find his son they had decided to lock up the father.

30 "The man did nothing," Nnamabia said.

31 "But you did nothing, either," my mother said.

32 Nnamabia shook his head as if our mother did not understand. The following days, he was more subdued. He spoke less, and mostly about the old man: how he could not afford bathing water, how the others made fun of him or accused him of hiding his son, how the chief ignored him, how he looked frightened and so terribly small.

33 "Does he know where his son is?" my mother asked.

34 "He has not seen his son in four months," Nnamabia said.

35 "Of course it is wrong," my mother said. "But this is what the police do all the time. If they do not find the person they are looking for, they lock up his relative."

36 "The man is ill," Nnamabia said. "His hands shake, even when he's asleep."

37 He closed the container of rice and turned to my father. "I want to give him some of this, but if I bring it into the cell the chief will take it."

38 My father went over and asked the policeman at the desk if we could be allowed to see the old man in Nnamabia's cell for a few minutes. The policeman was the light-skinned acerbic one who never said thank you when my mother handed over the rice-and-money bribe, and now he sneered in my father's face and said that he could well lose his job for letting even Nnamabia out and yet now we were asking for another person? Did we think this was visiting day at a boarding school? My father came back and sat down with a sigh, and Nnamabia silently scratched at his bumpy face.

The next day, Nnamabia barely 39
touched his rice. He said that the policemen had splashed soapy water on the floor and walls of the cell, as they usually did, and that the old man, who had not bathed in a week, had yanked his shirt off and rubbed his frail back against the wet floor. The policemen started to laugh when they saw him do this, and then they asked him to take all his clothes off and parade in the corridor outside the cell; as he did, they laughed louder and asked whether his son the thief knew that Papa's buttocks were so shrivelled. Nnamabia was staring at his yellow-orange rice as he spoke, and when he looked up his eyes were filled with tears, my worldly brother, and I felt a tenderness for him that I would not have been able to describe if I had been asked to.

THERE was another attack on campus—a boy 40
hacked another boy with an axe—two days later.

"This is good," my mother said. "Now they 41
cannot say that they have arrested all the cult boys." We did not go to Enugu that day; instead my parents went to see the local police superintendent, and they came back with good news. Nnamabia and the barman were to be released immediately. One of the cult boys, under questioning, had insisted that Nnamabia was not a member. The next day, we left earlier than usual, without jollof rice. My mother was always nervous when we drove, saying to my father, "*Nekwa ya!* Watch out!," as if he could not see the cars making dangerous turns in the other lane, but this time she did it so often that my father pulled over before we got to Ninth Mile and snapped, "Just who is driving this car?"

Two policemen were flogging a man with *koboko* 42
as we drove into the police station. At first, I thought it was Nnamabia, and then I thought it was the old man from his cell. It was neither. I knew the boy on the ground, who was writhing and shouting with each lash. He was called Aboy and had the grave ugly face of a hound; he drove a Lexus around campus and was said to be a Buccaneer. I tried not to look at him as we walked inside. The policeman on duty, the one with tribal marks on his cheeks who always said "God bless you" when he took his bribe, looked away when he saw us, and I knew that something was wrong. My parents

gave him the note from the superintendent. The policeman did not even glance at it. He knew about the release order, he told my father; the barman had already been released, but there was a complication with the boy. My mother began to shout, "What do you mean? Where is my son?"

43 The policeman got up. "I will call my senior to explain to you."

My father did not stop at any of the police checkpoints on the road . . .

44 My mother rushed at him and pulled on his shirt. "Where is my son? Where is my son?" My father pried her away, and the policeman brushed at his chest, as if she had left some dirt there, before he turned to walk away.

45 "Where is our son?" my father asked in a voice so quiet, so steely, that the policeman stopped.

46 "They took him away, sir," he said.

47 "They took him away? What are you saying?" my mother was yelling. "Have you killed my son? Have you killed my son?"

48 "Where is our son?" my father asked again.

49 "My senior said I should call him when you came," the policeman said, and this time he hurried through a door.

50 It was after he left that I felt suddenly chilled by fear; I wanted to run after him and, like my mother, pull at his shirt until he produced Nnamabia. The senior policeman came out, and I searched his blank face for clues.

51 "Good day, sir," he said to my father.

52 "Where is our son?" my father asked. My mother breathed noisily.

53 "No problem, sir. It is just that we transferred him. I will take you there right away." There was something nervous about the policeman; his face remained blank, but he did not meet my father's eyes.

54 "Transferred him?"

55 "We got the order this morning. I would have sent somebody for him, but we don't have petrol, so I was waiting for you to come so that we could go together."

56 "Why was he transferred?"

57 "I was not here, sir. They said that he misbehaved yesterday and they took him to Cell One, and then yesterday evening there was a transfer of all the people in Cell One to another site."

58 "He misbehaved? What do you mean?"

59 "I was not here, sir."

60 My mother spoke in a broken voice: "Take me to my son! Take me to my son right now!"

61 I sat in the back with the policeman, who smelled of the kind of old camphor that seemed to last forever in my mother's trunk. No one spoke except for the policeman when he gave my father directions. We arrived about fifteen minutes later, my father driving inordinately fast. The small, walled compound looked neglected, with patches of overgrown grass strewn with old bottles and plastic bags. The policeman hardly waited for my father to stop the car before he opened the door and hurried out, and again I felt chilled. We were in a godforsaken part of town, and there was no sign that said "Police Station." There was a strange deserted feeling in the air. But the policeman soon emerged with Nnamabia. There he was, my handsome brother, walking toward us, seemingly unchanged, until he came close enough for my mother to hug him, and I saw him wince and back away—his arm was covered in soft-looking welts. There was dried blood around his nose.

"Why did they beat you like this?" my mother 62
asked him. She turned to the policeman. "Why did you people do this to my son? Why?"

The man shrugged. There was a new insolence 63
to his demeanor; it was as if he had been uncertain about Nnamabia's well-being but now, reassured, could let himself talk. "You cannot raise your children properly—all of you people who feel important because you work at the university—and when your children misbehave you think they should not be punished. You are lucky they released him."

My father said, "Let's go." 64

He opened the door and Nnamabia climbed in, 65
and we drove home. My father did not stop at any of the police checkpoints on the road, and, once, a policeman gestured threateningly with his gun as we sped past. The only time my mother opened her mouth on the drive home was to ask Nnamabia if he wanted us to stop and buy some *okpa*. Nnamabia said no. We had arrived in Nsukka before he finally spoke.

"Yesterday, the policemen asked the old man if he 66
wanted a free half bucket of water. He said yes. So they told him to take his clothes off and parade the corridor. Most of my cellmates were laughing. Some of them said it was wrong to treat an old man like that." Nnamabia paused. "I shouted at the policeman. I told him the old man was innocent and ill, and if they kept him here it wouldn't help them find his son, because the man did not even know where his son was. They said that I should shut up immediately, that they would take me to Cell One. I didn't care. I didn't shut up. So they pulled me out and slapped me and took me to Cell One."

67 Nnamabia stopped there, and we asked him nothing else. Instead, I imagined him calling the policeman a stupid idiot, a spineless coward, a sadist, a bastard, and I imagined the shock of the policemen—the chief staring openmouthed, the other cellmates stunned at the audacity of the boy from the university. And I imagined the old man himself looking on with surprised pride and quietly refusing to undress. Nnamabia did not say what had happened to him in Cell One, or what happened at the new site. It would have been so easy for him, my charming brother, to make a sleek drama of his story, but he did not.

If you like Adichie's "Cell One," you will find similarities in "Saboteur," Ha Jin's story of political turmoil in China.

**GOING FURTHER** In her interview, Adichie praises the traditional oral storytelling in the work of African writer Ama Ata Aidoo, whose novels include *Our Sister Killjoy; Or, Reflections from a Black-Eyed Squint* and *Changes*. Other novels set on the continent of Africa include Amos Tutuola's *The Palm-Wine Drunkard* and Nigeria's own Chinua Achebe's *Things Fall Apart*. Notable among contemporary Nigerian writers currently living in the United States are Helon Habila and Chris Abani.

# Writing from Reading

## Summarize

1 Describe Nnamabia. Explain everything you know about him. What does he learn in the course of the story? Do you think he is treated differently from other prisoners because of his social class and level of education?

2 Explain the role of the sister. Why does she break the car windshield? Why is this act important?

## Analyze Craft

3 Adichie begins "Cell One" by describing Nnamabia's various trespasses and potential gang involvement. How does her treatment of Nnamabia change once he is imprisoned? Analyze her purpose in including Nnamabia's criminal past.

## Analyze Voice

4 Adichie herself grew up in Nigeria. What evidence is there of her own voice coming through in the narrator's description of events? Identify specific phrases or scenes, and describe what sets them apart as more personal to the author.

## Synthesize Summary and Analysis

5 Over the course of the story, the narrator seldom takes any action—that is, she mostly remains a detached observer. What single incident turns on the narrator's own actions? Discuss the effect of this scene on the story.

6 Note all the times the narrator expresses her impression of her brother and then says that her father saw the same thing. At what point does the narrator's father think something different from her? Explore what this sudden discrepancy suggests about the theme of the story.

## Interpret the Story

7 Adichie named her story after Cell One, a place never glimpsed in the actual story. What is Cell One, literally in the story as well as figuratively? How does the existence of Cell One, and Nnamabia's stay there, influence the theme of the story? Consider how the theme would change if Nnamabia was just beaten up by the guards for his outcry.

*CONTINUED FROM PAGE 261*

"I figured part of what fiction was, or writing creatively, was to write your view of life." Conversation with Amy Tan

## CRAFT AND THEME

Each element of craft—including plot, characterization, setting, and point of view—contributes to the thematic meaning of the tale. Theme connects fiction to the human experience, giving a single story relevance and reach. When we say that we read fiction for the truths or insights it offers—for its ideas—we are reading for theme.

"Fiction's a fairly tough vehicle if it's done right, and it can survive, and engender life in a reader's mind out of a fairly unpromising or difficult base." Conversation with John Updike

## WHAT THEME IS NOT

Readers sometimes confuse theme with subject or situation. Take Hemingway's "The Short Happy Life of Francis Macomber" (chapter 7) as an example. We can say that its subject is big-game hunting, but that is not its theme. Similarly, if we say that Hemingway's story is about a man struggling with notions of manhood and cowardice and courage, we are accurately summarizing the situation, but we are still not stating a theme. This statement is too specific to the story to be thematic.

Readers also often confuse theme and plot. Plot tells us in a literal, specific sense *what happens* in a story. To summarize the plot of Hemingway's story, then, you might say that a husband and wife go big-game hunting. The husband struggles with his own cowardice when he faces a lion, but in the end, driven by the complex triangle of relationships among himself, his wife, and their hunting guide, he becomes shockingly bold. In contrast, a theme goes beyond the particulars of the story, revealing something general and universal.

"I'm sort of aware of themes emerging. Sometimes it's helpful for me not to know so much about what themes are coming up, because I think it can get in the way of my investigation." Conversation with Aimee Bender

You can further see the difference between plot and theme by considering other stories in this book. On the level of plot, Alice Munro's "An Ounce of Cure" (chapter 1) is about a high school girl, melancholy over an unrequited love, who gets drunk one night while babysitting. In terms of theme, however, the story raises important questions about adolescents and how they learn the ways of the world. Thematically, the story emphasizes the timeless issue of entry into the world of womanhood. These ideas are organic or intrinsic to the narrative; they don't declare themselves immediately or in a topic sentence.

Finally, a theme, especially in contemporary literature, rarely boils down to a life lesson. Because Hemingway's story encompasses such a complex mix of feelings and events, it would be difficult to reduce it to a simple message or "teaching moment," such as "Don't go big-game hunting if you don't know what you're doing." However, if you dig toward the ideas that link all its elements as well as their meanings, you could articulate a theme such as: "The Short Happy Life of Francis Macomber" is a story about marriage and manhood and the testing of courage in both.

## WHAT THEME IS

Some stories do, of course, communicate lessons. "There's no place like home," Dorothy says at the end of *The Wizard of Oz*. This statement is indeed a theme of L. Frank Baum's tale of wonder and danger—because it goes beyond the specific details of the story to a general statement about human life. It is also thematic because it ties elements of the story together, including its beginning, when we see that Dorothy doesn't appreciate her home. Instead, she is frustrated and restless in the confines of that Kansas farm.

> "So [it] was very important for me to understand that people could write about rage and political action, whether it was metaphorical or literal." Conversation with Dagoberto Gilb

A literary work can, of course, put forward multiple themes. Consider Shakespeare's *Hamlet* (chapter 33). Depending on the lens through which we read the work, *Hamlet*'s themes can be seen as the anguish and consequences of indecision, the roots of suicidal melancholy, the repercussions of the Oedipal conflict, the perennial intermingling of power and corruption, or any combination of those ideas. By contrast, on the level of subject or plot, *Hamlet* could be summarized as a play about a man who loves his mother or a melancholic prince who can't make up his mind. The greatness of Shakespeare's play, of course, is that it is all this, and more: Shakespeare gives us a constantly shifting and surprising creation that cannot be reduced to any single reading or meaning.

**THEMES THROUGH TIME**

Some themes, or thematic questions, persist in literature through the ages. Do we determine the course of our own lives, or do the gods make our fates? From the epics of Homer onward, the Greeks put forward that great question, and fiction writers, poets, and playwrights have taken it up as a theme ever since. Some writers recast this theme as how to live a good life in a world full of turmoil and trouble. Cervantes did so in a semi-comical tone in his seventeenth-century novel *Don Quixote*.

Shakespeare presents a great variety of themes about love and power and the yearning for a meaningful life and asks the audience to draw its own conclusions. Similarly, contemporary story writers and novelists tend to dramatize the quandaries and troubles of their characters—but without drawing any conclusions or suggesting any moralistic answers.

In modern literature, many writers disdain the notion of theme. The pleasure the work offers to the reader becomes everything. Hemingway famously suggested that "if you want a message, go to Western Union." Nevertheless, as we've shown, themes emerge, even in the work of writers, such as Hemingway, who downplay their importance.

## IDENTIFYING THEMES

An understanding of theme can come from a work's title. Titles may point to a major symbol, character, or subject from which themes develop, as do "The Jilting of Granny Weatherall," "The Death of Ivan Ilych," and "Why I Live at the P.O." They may also point to a central irony that is thematic, as do "The Short Happy Life of Francis Macomber" and "No One's a Mystery." The title "Who's Irish?" calls up the question of identity, while "Araby" conjures an exotic dream, and "The Rememberer" calls to mind the person left behind after a loss—all thematic concerns of those stories.

"I'm trying to create a world in which some of the strange stuff of our life comes to the surface, and we say, "I know that. The circumstances of my life are different from this person's story, but I know that feeling." Conversation with Barry Lopez

As you question the text, notice general statements the narrator or another character makes, because such observations may well offer insight into the writer's theme. In Herman Melville's classic novel *Moby-Dick,* the narrator asserts that a great book needs a great theme—and that a subject must be large to accommodate a large theme. A flea will not do. This novel describes the voyage of Captain Ahab and his crew on a hunt for the great whale. The novel has numerous and wide-ranging subjects and themes: whaling, society, nature, defiance, comradeship, and the human struggle for meaning. The narrator is Ishmael, the sole survivor of that voyage.

Tolstoy's novel *War and Peace,* a surpassing work of fiction that came out of the European realist tradition, demonstrates beyond dispute the truth of Melville's assertion about theme. In its very title, as well as its meticulous execution, it embraces everything there is for us in life and sets it down on the page.

All stories include insights from narrators or characters, and these insights often relate to theme. In Alice Munro's "An Ounce of Cure" (chapter 1), at tale's end, the first-person narrator who got drunk while babysitting says, "I was a self-conscious girl and I suffered a good deal from all the exposure. But the development of events on that Saturday night—that fascinated me." In John Updike's "A&P" (chapter 1), the young narrator realizes "how hard the world was going to be to me from here on in." In both cases, the characters acknowledge a new level of awareness and responsibility; it's not entirely welcome or pleasurable, but it seems to be inevitable, a rite of passage to adulthood.

In music a theme is a recurring motif. In these two stories the theme that recurs calls to our minds the troubles, turmoil, and sometime pleasures of coming of age. At the thematic level, these stories belong to a certain variety of fiction. Theme? Think of a horse as a theme among the general category of land mammals or a whale as a theme among the general category of sea mammals.

## *THEME* IN CONTEXT

Works of serious fiction do not generally give up their meanings easily, and this is why we often feel intimidated or tentative when it comes to articulating a theme. So why, despite the risks and difficulties, should we strive to understand theme? Why not sim-

"To write a true war story, to write a true story about anything, is difficult—on all kinds of levels. On the most simple level, truth evaporates." Conversation with Tim O'Brien

ply enjoy the plot and the characters and leave it at that? First of all, reading closely enough to gather the threads of theme reveals the greatest potential of a story. Second, delving into the world of a story for its theme can point up truths about the way the world works. Finally, reading with an eye for theme in fiction can teach a great deal about how to get at the essence of other kinds of texts that are required reading in college, and it helps create the skill of linkage and expressiveness in writing for college.

To understand theme, then, readers can ask questions that go beyond the surface and the events. In this chapter you will find four quite different short stories about quite different subjects. Each is rooted in a version of the author's experience. In each, the theme grows seamlessly from plot, setting, style, characterization, and all the other elements of the writer's craft. In each, theme emerges from our reading and questioning of the story in all its twists and permutations. As you saw with the excerpt from "Cell One" at the beginning of the chapter, the theme is not the frail back of the old man on the wet floor or the uneaten rice or even the tears in the brother's eyes. It is embedded in those details and emerges from them. It is the *why* of those details, the thread that ties them together and gives them meaning beyond this particular story and situation. It emerges from asking and answering questions such as, "*How* did these events affect Nnamabia?" and "*Why* did the sister feel that tenderness?" and "*What* do *I* feel when I think about that old man?" and "Why is this important?"

"So it started off sort of as a memory, and it became, I guess, a story when I began thinking about just the ways in which victims can so easily become victimizers . . ."

Conversation with ZZ Packer

Common themes in literature include the struggle of justice against injustice, as in Adichie's "Cell One"; comradeship and cooperation, as in "The Open Boat"; the ever-present cycles of life and death, as in "The Odour of Chrysanthemums"; and youth and age, as in "Interpreter of Maladies." But this is stating theme very broadly. Remember that truly identifying theme means paying attention to how that theme is addressed in a specific story. So, for example, you might amend the preceding sentence to say that "Cell One" is about how justice requires a person to think beyond his or her own selfish preoccupations. Or you might refine youth and age in "Interpreter of Maladies" to the theme that age does not necessarily bring wisdom, while youth is capable of being stained by worldly experience. You can probably think of many other broad themes—love and loss, power and powerlessness, freedom and responsibility, death and faith, and love and family. Leaving home, going on a journey, falling in love, proving one's heroism or goodness, making a new start in a new place, or joining with a new family group: these are just a few of the major themes that emerge from the stories in this book, and once you identify them, you can see their variations as you encounter these themes in other courses and in the world after college. In other words, all the most important ideas in life arise as themes in literature.

# Stephen Crane (1871–1900)

Stephen Crane was born in Newark, New Jersey. By the time he was sixteen, he was already contributing articles to *The New York Tribune*. Crane moved to New York City, where he conducted extensive research for both fiction and nonfiction projects. To render an accurate account of life in poverty, for example, he lived in the slums while writing his first novel, *Maggie: A Girl of the Streets* (1893). This and Crane's other works—most famously *The Red Badge of Courage* (1895)—are examples of the literary style of *naturalism,* a technique that features characters carried along by fate in realistic, bleak circumstances. The indifference of nature is a popular theme in naturalistic fiction. The story that follows, "The Open Boat," was inspired by Crane's own experience on an 1896 expedition to Cuba. When the ship he was traveling on, the S.S. *Commodore,* was wrecked, Crane and other survivors drifted at sea for two weeks. During this time, he developed what would turn out to be a fatal strain of tuberculosis; he died in 1900. Crane wrote many stories about his experiences in Cuba, among them "Flanagan and His Short Filibustering Adventure" (1897) and "This Majestic Lie" (1900). A poet as well as a prose writer, Crane composed poetry that was experimental in its use of free verse and which put forward a dark view of the human condition. His career was unhappily brief, cut short by his death at age twenty-eight.

**AS YOU READ** As you read, notice the changes in the relationships among the four characters. Notice their peaks and valleys of hope and despair, of determination and exhaustion. What ideas do you perceive about the struggle for survival and the impact it has on these men?

**TIP**

**FOR INTERACTIVE READING . . .** Keep track of repeated lines as you read. Consider what effect these repetitions have on the tone of the story, and on your own memory of certain events or characters. Are there any similarities between the repeated phrases?

# The Open Boat:

## *A Tale Intended to Be after the Fact: Being the Experience of Four Men from the Sunk Steamer Commodore* (1897)

### I

1 None of them knew the color of the sky. Their eyes glanced level, and were fastened upon the waves that swept toward them. These waves were of the hue of slate, save for the tops, which were of foaming white, and all of the men knew the colors of the sea. The horizon narrowed and widened, and dipped and rose, and at all times its edge was jagged with waves that seemed thrust up in points like rocks.

2 Many a man ought to have a bath-tub larger than the boat which here rode upon the sea. These waves were most wrongfully and barbarously abrupt and tall, and each froth-top was a problem in small boat navigation.

3 The cook squatted in the bottom and looked with both eyes at the six inches of gunwale which separated him from the ocean. His sleeves were rolled over his fat forearms, and the two flaps of his unbuttoned vest dangled as he bent to bail out the boat. Often he said: "Gawd! That was a narrow clip." As he remarked it he invariably gazed eastward over the broken sea.

The oiler, steering with one of the two oars in the boat, sometimes raised himself suddenly to keep clear of water that swirled in over the stern. It was a thin little oar and it seemed often ready to snap. 4

The correspondent, pulling at the other oar, watched the waves and wondered why he was there. 5

The injured captain, lying in the bow, was at this time buried in that profound dejection and indifference which comes, temporarily at least, to even the bravest and most enduring when, willy nilly, the firm fails, the army loses, the ship goes down. The mind of the master of a vessel is rooted deep in the timbers of her, though he command for a day or a decade, and this captain had on him the stern impression of a scene in the grays of dawn of seven turned faces, and later a stump of a top-mast with a white ball on it that slashed to and fro at the waves, went low and lower, and down. Thereafter there was something strange in his voice. Although steady, it was deep with mourning, and of a quality beyond oration or tears. 6

"Keep'er a little more south, Billie," said he. 7

"'A little more south,' sir," said the oiler in the stern. 8

9 A seat in this boat was not unlike a seat upon a bucking broncho, and, by the same token, a broncho is not much smaller. The craft pranced and reared, and plunged like an animal. As each wave came, and she rose for it, she seemed like a horse making at a fence outrageously high. The manner of her scramble over these walls of water is a mystic thing, and, moreover, at the top of them were ordinarily these problems in white water, the foam racing down from the summit of each wave, requiring a new leap, and a leap from the air. Then, after scornfully bumping a crest, she would slide, and race, and splash down a long incline and arrive bobbing and nodding in front of the next menace.

The craft pranced and reared, and plunged like an animal.

10 A singular disadvantage of the sea lies in the fact that after successfully surmounting one wave you discover that there is another behind it just as important and just as nervously anxious to do something effective in the way of swamping boats. In a ten-foot dingey one can get an idea of the resources of the sea in the line of waves that is not probable to the average experience, which is never at sea in a dingey. As each slaty wall of water approached, it shut all else from the view of the men in the boat, and it was not difficult to imagine that this particular wave was the final outburst of the ocean, the last effort of the grim water. There was a terrible grace in the move of the waves, and they came in silence, save for the snarling of the crests.

11 In the wan light, the faces of the men must have been gray. Their eyes must have glinted in strange ways as they gazed steadily astern. Viewed from a balcony, the whole thing would doubtlessly have been weirdly picturesque. But the men in the boat had no time to see it, and if they had had leisure there were other things to occupy their minds. The sun swung steadily up the sky, and they knew it was broad day because the color of the sea changed from slate to emerald-green, streaked with amber lights, and the foam was like tumbling snow. The process of the breaking day was unknown to them. They were aware only of this effect upon the color of the waves that rolled toward them.

12 In disjointed sentences the cook and the correspondent argued as to the difference between a life-saving station and a house of refuge. The cook had said: "There's a house of refuge just north of the Mosquito Inlet Light, and as soon as they see us, they'll come off in their boat and pick us up."

13 "As soon as who see us?" said the correspondent.

14 "The crew," said the cook.

15 "Houses of refuge don't have crews," said the correspondent. "As I understand them, they are only places where clothes and grub are stored for the benefit of shipwrecked people. They don't carry crews."

16 "Oh, yes, they do," said the cook.

17 "No, they don't," said the correspondent.

18 "Well, we're not there yet, anyhow," said the oiler, in the stern.

19 "Well," said the cook, "perhaps it's not a house of refuge that I'm thinking of as being near Mosquito Inlet Light. Perhaps it's a life-saving station."

20 "We're not there yet," said the oiler, in the stern.

## II

21 As the boat bounced from the top of each wave, the wind tore through the hair of the hatless men, and as the craft plopped her stern down again the spray slashed past them. The crest of each of these waves was a hill, from the top of which the men surveyed, for a moment, a broad tumultuous expanse, shining and wind-riven. It was probably splendid. It was probably glorious, this play of the free sea, wild with lights of emerald and white and amber.

22 "Bully good thing it's an on-shore wind," said the cook. "If not, where would we be? Wouldn't have a show."

23 "That's right," said the correspondent.

24 The busy oiler nodded his assent.

25 Then the captain, in the bow, chuckled in a way that expressed humor, contempt, tragedy, all in one. "Do you think we've got much of a show, now, boys?" said he.

26 Whereupon the three were silent, save for a trifle of hemming and hawing. To express any particular optimism at this time they felt to be childish and stupid, but they all doubtless possessed this sense of the situation in their mind. A young man thinks doggedly at such times. On the other hand, the ethics of their condition was decidedly against any open suggestion of hopelessness. So they were silent.

27 "Oh, well," said the captain, soothing his children, "we'll get ashore all right."

28 But there was that in his tone which made them think, so the oiler quoth: "Yes! If this wind holds!"

29 The cook was bailing: "Yes! If we don't catch hell in the surf."

30 Canton flannel gulls flew near and far. Sometimes they sat down on the sea, near patches of brown sea-weed that rolled over the waves with a movement like carpets on a line in a gale. The birds sat comfortably in groups, and they were envied by some in the dingey, for the wrath of the sea was no more to them than it was to a covey of prairie chickens a thousand miles inland. Often they came very close and stared at the men with black bead-like eyes. At these times they were uncanny and sinister in their unblinking scrutiny, and the men hooted angrily at them, telling them to be gone. One came, and evidently decided to alight on the top of the captain's head. The bird flew parallel to the boat and did not circle, but made short sidelong jumps in the air in chicken-fashion. His black eyes were wistfully fixed upon the captain's head. "Ugly brute," said the oiler to the bird. "You look as if you were made with a jack-knife." The cook and the correspondent swore darkly at the creature. The captain naturally wished to knock it away with the end of the heavy painter, but he did not dare do it, because anything resembling an emphatic gesture would have capsized this freighted boat, and so with his open hand, the captain gently and carefully waved the gull away. After it had been discouraged from the pursuit the captain breathed easier on account of his hair, and others breathed easier because the bird struck their minds at this time as being somehow grewsome and ominous.

31 In the meantime the oiler and the correspondent rowed. And also they rowed.

32 They sat together in the same seat, and each rowed an oar. Then the oiler took both oars; then the correspondent took both oars; then the oiler; then the correspondent. They rowed and they rowed. The very ticklish part of the business was when the time came for the reclining one in the stern to take his turn at the oars. By the very last star of truth, it is easier to steal eggs from under a hen than it was to change seats in the dingey. First the man in the stern slid his hand along the thwart and moved with care, as if he were of Sèvres. Then the man in the rowing seat slid his hand along the other thwart. It was all done with the most extraordinary care. As the two sidled past each other, the whole party kept watchful eyes on the coming wave, and the captain cried: "Look out now! Steady there!"

33 The brown mats of sea-weed that appeared from time to time were like islands, bits of earth. They were travelling, apparently, neither one way nor the other. They were, to all intents, stationary. They informed the men in the boat that it was making progress slowly toward the land.

34 The captain, rearing cautiously in the bow, after the dingey soared on a great swell, said that he had seen the light-house at Mosquito Inlet. Presently the cook remarked that he had seen it. The correspondent was at the oars, then, and for some reason he too wished to look at the light-house, but his back was toward the far shore and the waves were important, and for some time he could not seize an opportunity to turn his head. But at last there came a wave more gentle than the others, and when at the crest of it he swiftly scoured the western horizon.

35 "See it?" said the captain.

36 "No," said the correspondent, slowly, "I didn't see anything."

37 "Look again," said the captain. He pointed. "It's exactly in that direction."

38 At the top of another wave, the correspondent did as he was bid, and this time his eyes chanced on a small still thing on the edge of the swaying horizon. It was precisely like the point of a pin. It took an anxious eye to find a light-house so tiny.

39 "Think we'll make it, Captain?"

40 "If this wind holds and the boat don't swamp, we can't do much else," said the captain.

41 The little boat, lifted by each towering sea, and splashed viciously by the crests, made progress that in the absence of sea-weed was not apparent to those in her. She seemed just a wee thing wallowing, miraculously, top-up, at the mercy of five oceans. Occasionally, a great spread of water, like white flames, swarmed into her.

42 "Bail her, cook," said the captain, serenely.

43 "All right, captain," said the cheerful cook.

## III

44 It would be difficult to describe the subtle brotherhood of men that was here established on the seas. No one said that it was so. No one mentioned it. But it dwelt in the boat, and each man felt it warm him. They were a captain, an oiler, a cook, and a correspondent, and they were friends, friends in a more curiously iron-bound degree than may be common. The hurt captain, lying against the water-jar in the bow, spoke always in a low voice and calmly, but he could never command a more ready and swiftly obedient crew than the motley three of the dingey. It was more than a mere recognition of what was best for the

common safety. There was surely in it a quality that was personal and heartfelt. And after this devotion to the commander of the boat there was this comradeship that the correspondent, for instance, who had been taught to be cynical of men, knew even at the time was the best experience of his life. But no one said that it was so. No one mentioned it.

45 "I wish we had a sail," remarked the captain. "We might try my overcoat on the end of an oar and give you two boys a chance to rest." So the cook and the correspondent held the mast and spread wide the overcoat. The oiler steered, and the little boat made good way with her new rig. Sometimes the oiler had to scull sharply to keep a sea from breaking into the boat, but otherwise sailing was a success.

Slowly and beautifully the land loomed out of the sea.

46 Meanwhile the light-house had been growing slowly larger. It had now almost assumed color, and appeared like a little gray shadow on the sky. The man at the oars could not be prevented from turning his head rather often to try for a glimpse of this little gray shadow.

47 At last, from the top of each wave the men in the tossing boat could see land. Even as the light-house was an upright shadow on the sky, this land seemed but a long black shadow on the sea. It certainly was thinner than paper. "We must be about opposite New Smyrna," said the cook, who had coasted this shore often in schooners. "Captain, by the way, I believe they abandoned that life-saving station there about a year ago."

48 "Did they?" said the captain.

49 The wind slowly died away. The cook and the correspondent were not now obliged to slave in order to hold high the oar. But the waves continued their old impetuous swooping at the dingey, and the little craft, no longer under way, struggled woundily over them. The oiler or the correspondent took the oars again.

50 Shipwrecks are *apropos* of nothing. If men could only train for them and have them occur when the men had reached pink condition, there would be less drowning at sea. Of the four in the dingey none had slept any time worth mentioning for two days and two nights previous to embarking in the dingey, and in the excitement of clambering about the deck of a foundering ship they had also forgotten to eat heartily.

51 For these reasons, and for others, neither the oiler nor the correspondent was fond of rowing at this time. The correspondent wondered ingenuously how in the name of all that was sane could there be people who thought it amusing to row a boat. It was not an amusement; it was a diabolical punishment, and even a genius of mental aberrations could never conclude that it was anything but a horror to the muscles and a crime against the back. He mentioned to the boat in general how the amusement of rowing struck him, and the weary-faced oiler smiled in full sympathy. Previously to the foundering, by the way, the oiler had worked double-watch in the engine-room of the ship.

52 "Take her easy, now, boys," said the captain. "Don't spend yourselves. If we have to run a surf you'll need all your strength, because we'll sure have to swim for it. Take your time."

53 Slowly the land arose from the sea. From a black line it became a line of black and a line of white—trees and sand. Finally, the captain said that he could make out a house on the shore. "That's the house of refuge, sure," said the cook. "They'll see us before long, and come out after us."

54 The distant light-house reared high. "The keeper ought to be able to make us out now, if he's looking through a glass," said the captain. "He'll notify the life-saving people."

55 "None of those other boats could have got ashore to give word of the wreck," said the oiler, in a low voice. "Else the life-boat would be out hunting us."

56 Slowly and beautifully the land loomed out of the sea. The wind came again. It had veered from the northeast to the southeast. Finally, a new sound struck the ears of the men in the boat. It was the low thunder of the surf on the shore. "We'll never be able to make the light-house now," said the captain. "Swing her head a little more north, Billie."

57 "'A little more north,' sir," said the oiler.

58 Whereupon the little boat turned her nose once more down the wind, and all but the oarsman watched the shore grow. Under the influence of this expansion doubt and direful apprehension was leaving the minds of the men. The management of the boat was still most absorbing, but it could not prevent a quiet cheerfulness. In an hour, perhaps, they would be ashore.

59 Their back-bones had become thoroughly used to balancing in the boat and they now rode this wild colt of a dingey like circus men. The correspondent thought that he had been drenched to the skin, but happening to feel in the top pocket of his coat, he found therein eight cigars. Four of them were soaked with sea-water; four were perfectly scatheless. After a search, somebody produced three dry matches, and thereupon the four waifs rode impudently in their little boat, and with an assurance of an impending rescue shining in their eyes, puffed at the big cigars

and judged well and ill of all men. Everybody took a drink of water.

## IV

60 "Cook," remarked the captain, "there don't seem to be any signs of life about your house of refuge."

61 "No," replied the cook. "Funny they don't see us!"

62 A broad stretch of lowly coast lay before the eyes of the men. It was of dunes topped with dark vegetation. The roar of the surf was plain, and sometimes they could see the white lip of a wave as it spun up the

beach. A tiny house was blocked out black upon the sky. Southward, the slim light-house lifted its little gray length.

63 Tide, wind, and waves were swinging the dingey northward. "Funny they don't see us," said the men.

64 The surf's roar was here dulled, but its tone was, nevertheless, thunderous and mighty. As the boat swam over the great rollers, the men sat listening to this roar. "We'll swamp sure," said everybody.

65 It is fair to say here that there was not a life-saving station within twenty miles in either direction, but the men did not know this fact and in consequence they made dark and opprobrious remarks concerning the eyesight of the nation's life-savers. Four scowling men sat in the dingey and surpassed records in the invention of epithets.

66 "Funny they don't see us."

67 The light-heartedness of a former time had completely faded. To their sharpened minds it was easy to conjure pictures of all kinds of incompetency and blindness and, indeed, cowardice. There was the shore of the populous land, and it was bitter and bitter to them that from it came no sign.

68 "Well," said the captain, ultimately, "I suppose we'll have to make a try for ourselves. If we stay out here too long, we'll none of us have strength left to swim after the boat swamps."

69 And so the oiler, who was at the oars, turned the boat straight for the shore. There was a sudden tightening of muscles. There was some thinking.

70 "If we don't all get ashore—" said the captain. "If we don't all get ashore, I suppose you fellows know where to send news of my finish?"

They then briefly exchanged some addresses and admonitions. As for the reflections of the men, there was a great deal of rage in them. Perchance they might be formulated thus: "If I am going to be drowned—if I am going to be drowned—if I am going to be drowned, why, in the name of the seven mad gods who rule the sea, was I allowed to come thus far and contemplate sand and trees? Was I brought here merely to have my nose dragged away as I was about to nibble the sacred cheese of life? It is preposterous. If this old ninny-woman, Fate, cannot do better than this, she should be deprived of the management of men's fortunes. She is an old hen who knows not her intention. If she has decided to drown me, why did she not do it in the beginning and save me all this trouble. The whole affair is absurd. . . . But, no, she cannot mean to drown me. She dare not drown me. She cannot drown me. Not after all this work." Afterward the man might have had an impulse to shake his fist at the clouds: "Just you drown me, now, and then hear what I call you!" 71

The billows that came at this time were more formidable. They seemed always just about to break and roll over the little boat in a turmoil of foam. There was a preparatory and long growl in the speech of them. No mind unused to the sea would have concluded that the dingey could ascend these sheer heights in time. The shore was still afar. The oiler was a wily surfman. "Boys," he said, swiftly, "she won't live three minutes more and we're too far out to swim. Shall I take her to sea again, Captain?" 72

"Yes! Go ahead!" said the captain. 73

This oiler, by a series of quick miracles, and fast and steady oarsmanship, turned the boat in the middle of the surf and took her safely to sea again. 74

There was a considerable silence as the boat bumped over the furrowed sea to deeper water. Then somebody in gloom spoke. "Well, anyhow, they must have seen us from the shore by now." 75

The gulls went in slanting flight up the wind toward the gray desolate east. A squall, marked by dingy clouds, and clouds brick-red, like smoke from a burning building, appeared from the southeast. 76

"What do you think of those life-saving people? Ain't they peaches?" 77

"Funny they haven't seen us." 78

"Maybe they think we're out here for sport! Maybe they think we're fishin'. Maybe they think we're damned fools." 79

It was a long afternoon. A changed tide tried to force them southward, but wind and wave said northward. Far ahead, where coast-line, sea, and sky formed their mighty angle, there were little dots which seemed to indicate a city on the shore. 80

81 "St. Augustine?"

82 The captain shook his head. "Too near Mosquito Inlet."

83 And the oiler rowed, and then the correspondent rowed. Then the oiler rowed. It was a weary business. The human back can become the seat of more aches and pains than are registered in books for the composite anatomy of a regiment. It is a limited area, but it can become the theatre of innumerable muscular conflicts, tangles, wrenches, knots, and other comforts.

84 "Did you ever like to row, Billie?" asked the correspondent.

85 "No," said the oiler. "Hang it."

86 When one exchanged the rowing-seat for a place in the bottom of the boat, he suffered a bodily depression that caused him to be careless of everything save an obligation to wiggle one finger. There was cold seawater swashing to and fro in the boat, and he lay in it. His head, pillowed on a thwart, was within an inch of the swirl of a wave crest, and sometimes a particularly obstreperous sea came in-board and drenched him once more. But these matters did not annoy him. It is almost certain that if the boat had capsized he would have tumbled comfortably out upon the ocean as if he felt sure it was a great soft mattress.

87 "Look! There's a man on the shore!"

88 "Where?"

89 "There! See 'im? See 'im?"

90 "Yes, sure! He's walking along."

91 "Now he's stopped. Look! He's facing us!"

92 "He's waving at us!"

93 "So he is! By thunder!"

94 "Ah, now, we're all right! Now we're all right! There'll be a boat out here for us in half an hour."

95 "He's going on. He's running. He's going up to that house there."

96 The remote beach seemed lower than the sea, and it required a searching glance to discern the little black figure. The captain saw a floating stick and they rowed to it. A bath-towel was by some weird chance in the boat, and, tying this on the stick, the captain waved it. The oarsman did not dare turn his head, so he was obliged to ask questions.

97 "What's he doing now?"

98 "He's standing still again. He's looking, I think. . . . There he goes again. Toward the house. . . . Now he's stopped again."

99 "Is he waving at us?"

100 "No, not now! he was, though."

101 "Look! There comes another man!"

102 "He's running."

103 "Look at him go, would you."

"Why, he's on a bicycle. Now he's met the other man. They're both waving at us. Look!" 104

"There comes something up the beach." 105

"What the devil is that thing?" 106

"Why, it looks like a boat." 107

"Why, certainly it's a boat." 108

"No, it's on wheels." 109

"Yes, so it is. Well, that must be the life-boat. They drag them along shore on a wagon." 110

"That's the life-boat, sure." 111

"No, by—, it's—it's an omnibus." 112

"I tell you it's a life-boat." 113

"It is not! It's an omnibus. I can see it plain. See? One of these big hotel omnibuses." 114

"By thunder, you're right. It's an omnibus, sure as fate. What do you suppose they are doing with an omnibus? Maybe they are going around collecting the life-crew, hey?" 115

"That's it, likely. Look! There's a fellow waving a little black flag. He's standing on the steps of the omnibus. There come those other two fellows. Now they're all talking together. Look at the fellow with the flag. Maybe he ain't waving it!" 116

"That ain't a flag, is it? That's his coat. Why, certainly, that's his coat." 117

"So it is. It's his coat. He's taken it off and is waving it around his head. But would you look at him swing it!" 118

"Oh, say, there isn't any life-saving station there. That's just a winter resort hotel omnibus that has brought over some of the boarders to see us drown." 119

"What's that idiot with the coat mean? What's he signaling, anyhow?" 120

"It looks as if he were trying to tell us to go north. There must be a life-saving station up there." 121

"No! He thinks we're fishing. Just giving us a merry hand. See? Ah, there, Willie." 122

"Well, I wish I could make something out of those signals. What do you suppose he means?" 123

"He don't mean anything. He's just playing." 124

"Well, if he'd just signal us to try the surf again, or to go to sea and wait, or go north, or go south, or go to hell—there would be some reason in it. But look at him. He just stands there and keeps his coat revolving like a wheel. The ass!" 125

"There come more people." 126

"Now there's quite a mob. Look! Isn't that a boat?" 127

"Where? Oh, I see where you mean. No, that's no boat." 128

"That fellow is still waving his coat." 129

"He must think we like to see him do that. Why don't he quit it. It don't mean anything." 130

31 "I don't know. I think he is trying to make us go north. It must be that there's a life-saving station there somewhere."

32 "Say, he ain't tired yet. Look at 'im wave."

33 "Wonder how long he can keep that up. He's been revolving his coat ever since he caught sight of us. He's an idiot. Why aren't they getting men to bring a boat out? A fishing boat—one of those big yawls—could come out here all right. Why don't he do something?"

34 "Oh, it's all right, now."

35 "They'll have a boat out here for us in less than no time, now that they've seen us."

36 A faint yellow tone came into the sky over the low land. The shadows on the sea slowly deepened. The wind bore coldness with it, and the men began to shiver.

37 "Holy smoke!" said one, allowing his voice to express his impious mood, "if we keep on monkeying out here! If we've got to flounder out here all night!"

38 "Oh, we'll never have to stay here all night! Don't you worry. They've seen us now, and it won't be long before they'll come chasing out after us."

39 The shore grew dusky. The man waving a coat blended gradually into this gloom, and it swallowed in the same manner the omnibus and the group of people. The spray, when it dashed uproariously over the side, made the voyagers shrink and swear like men who were being branded.

40 "I'd like to catch the chump who waved the coat. I feel like soaking him one, just for luck."

41 "Why? What did he do?"

42 "Oh, nothing, but then he seemed so damned cheerful."

43 In the meantime the oiler rowed, and then the correspondent rowed, and then the oiler rowed. Grayfaced and bowed forward, they mechanically, turn by turn, plied the leaden oars. The form of the lighthouse had vanished from the southern horizon, but finally a pale star appeared, just lifting from the sea. The streaked saffron in the west passed before the all-merging darkness, and the sea to the east was black. The land had vanished, and was expressed only by the low and drear thunder of the surf.

44 "If I am going to be drowned—if I am going to be drowned—if I am going to be drowned, why, in the name of the seven mad gods who rule the sea, was I allowed to come thus far and contemplate sand and trees? Was I brought here merely to have my nose dragged away as I was about to nibble the sacred cheese of life?"

45 The patient captain, drooped over the water-jar, was sometimes obliged to speak to the oarsman.

"Keep her head up! Keep her head up!" 146

"'Keep her head up,' sir." The voices were weary and low. 147

This was surely a quiet evening. All save the oarsman lay heavily and listlessly in the boat's bottom. As for him, his eyes were just capable of noting the tall black waves that swept forward in a most sinister silence, save for an occasional subdued growl of a crest. 148

The cook's head was on a thwart, and he looked without interest at the water under his nose. He was deep in other scenes. Finally he spoke. "Billie," he murmured, dreamfully, "what kind of pie do you like best?" 149

## V

"Pie," said the oiler and the correspondent, agitatedly. "Don't talk about those things, blast you!" 150

"Well," said the cook, "I was just thinking about ham sandwiches, and—" 151

A night on the sea in an open boat is a long night. As darkness settled finally, the shine of the light, lifting from the sea in the south, changed to full gold. On the northern horizon a new light appeared, a small bluish gleam on the edge of the waters. These two lights were the furniture of the world. Otherwise there was nothing but waves. 152

A night on the sea in an open boat is a long night.

Two men huddled in the stern, and distances were so magnificent in the dingey that the rower was enabled to keep his feet partly warmed by thrusting them under his companions. Their legs indeed extended far under the rowing-seat until they touched the feet of the captain forward. Sometimes, despite the efforts of the tired oarsman, a wave came piling into the boat, an icy wave of the night, and the chilling water soaked them anew. They would twist their bodies for a moment and groan, and sleep the dead sleep once more, while the water in the boat gurgled about them as the craft rocked. 153

The plan of the oiler and the correspondent was for one to row until he lost the ability, and then arouse the other from his sea-water couch in the bottom of the boat. 154

The oiler plied the oars until his head drooped forward, and the overpowering sleep blinded him. And he rowed yet afterward. Then he touched a man in the bottom of the boat, and called his name. "Will you spell me for a little while?" he said, meekly. 155

"Sure, Billie," said the correspondent, awakening and dragging himself to a sitting position. They exchanged places carefully, and the oiler, cuddling 156 down in the sea-water at the cook's side, seemed to go to sleep instantly.

157 The particular violence of the sea had ceased. The waves came without snarling. The obligation of the man at the oars was to keep the boat headed so that the tilt of the rollers would not capsize her, and to preserve her from filling when the crests rushed past. The black waves were silent and hard to be seen in the darkness. Often one was almost upon the boat before the oarsman was aware.

158 In a low voice the correspondent addressed the captain. He was not sure that the captain was awake, although this iron man seemed to be always awake. "Captain, shall I keep her making for that light north, sir?"

159 The same steady voice answered him. "Yes. Keep it about two points off the port bow."

160 The cook had tied a life-belt around himself in order to get even the warmth which this clumsy cork contrivance could donate, and he seemed almost stove-like when a rower, whose teeth invariably chattered wildly as soon as he ceased his labor, dropped down to sleep.

161 The correspondent, as he rowed, looked down at the two men sleeping under foot. The cook's arm was around the oiler's shoulders, and, with their fragmentary clothing and haggard faces, they were the babes of the sea, a grotesque rendering of the old babes in the wood.

162 Later he must have grown stupid at his work, for suddenly there was a growling of water, and a crest came with a roar and a swash into the boat, and it was a wonder that it did not set the cook afloat in his life-belt. The cook continued to sleep, but the oiler sat up, blinking his eyes and shaking with the new cold.

163 "Oh, I'm awful sorry, Billie," said the correspondent, contritely.

164 "That's all right, old boy," said the oiler, and lay down again and was asleep.

165 Presently it seemed that even the captain dozed, and the correspondent thought that he was the one man afloat on all the oceans. The wind had a voice as it came over the waves, and it was sadder than the end.

166 There was a long, loud swishing astern of the boat, and a gleaming trail of phosphorescence, like blue flame, was furrowed on the black waters. It might have been made by a monstrous knife.

167 Then there came a stillness, while the correspondent breathed with the open mouth and looked at the sea.

168 Suddenly there was another swish and another long flash of bluish light, and this time it was alongside the boat, and might almost have been reached with an oar. The correspondent saw an enormous fin speed like a shadow through the water, hurling the crystalline spray and leaving the long glowing trail.

The correspondent looked over his shoulder at the captain. His face was hidden, and he seemed to be asleep. He looked at the babes of the sea. They certainly were asleep. So, being bereft of sympathy, he leaned a little way to one side and swore softly into the sea. 16

But the thing did not then leave the vicinity of the boat. Ahead or astern, on one side or the other, at intervals long or short, fled the long sparkling streak, and there was to be heard the whiroo of the dark fin. The speed and power of the thing was greatly to be admired. It cut the water like a gigantic and keen projectile. 17

The presence of this biding thing did not affect the man with the same horror that it would if he had been a picnicker. He simply looked at the sea dully and swore in an undertone. 17

Nevertheless, it is true that he did not wish to be alone with the thing. He wished one of his companions to awaken by chance and keep him company with it. But the captain hung motionless over the water-jar and the oiler and the cook in the bottom of the boat were plunged in slumber. 17

## VI

"If I am going to be drowned—if I am going to be drowned—if I am going to be drowned, why, in the name of the seven mad gods who rule the sea, was I allowed to come thus far and contemplate sand and trees?" 17

During this dismal night, it may be remarked that a man would conclude that it was really the intention of the seven mad gods to drown him, despite the abominable injustice of it. For it was certainly an abominable injustice to drown a man who had worked so hard, so hard. The man felt it would be a crime most unnatural. Other people had drowned at sea since galleys swarmed with painted sails, but still— 17

When it occurs to a man that nature does not regard him as important, and that she feels she would not maim the universe by disposing of him, he at first wishes to throw bricks at the temple, and he hates deeply the fact that there are no bricks and no temples. Any visible expression of nature would surely be pelleted with his jeers. 1

Then, if there be no tangible thing to hoot he feels, perhaps, the desire to confront a personification and indulge in pleas, bowed to one knee, and with hands supplicant, saying: "Yes, but I love myself." 1

77 A high cold star on a winter's night is the word he feels that she says to him. Thereafter he knows the pathos of his situation.

78 The men in the dingey had not discussed these matters, but each had, no doubt, reflected upon them in silence and according to his mind. There was seldom any expression upon their faces save the general one of complete weariness. Speech was devoted to the business of the boat.

79 To chime the notes of his emotion, a verse mysteriously entered the correspondent's head. He had even forgotten that he had forgotten this verse, but it suddenly was in his mind.

> A soldier of the Legion lay dying in Algiers,
> There was lack of woman's nursing, there was
> dearth of woman's tears;
> But a comrade stood beside him, and he took
> that comrade's hand,
> And he said: "I never more shall see my own,
> my native land."

80 In his childhood, the correspondent had been made acquainted with the fact that a soldier of the Legion lay dying in Algiers, but he had never regarded it as important. Myriads of his school-fellows had informed him of the soldier's plight, but the dinning had naturally ended by making him perfectly indifferent. He had never considered it his affair that a soldier of the Legion lay dying in Algiers, nor had it appeared to him as a matter for sorrow. It was less to him than the breaking of a pencil's point.

81 Now, however, it quaintly came to him as a human, living thing. It was no longer merely a picture of a few throes in the breast of a poet, meanwhile drinking tea and warming his feet at the grate; it was an actuality—stern, mournful, and fine.

82 The correspondent plainly saw the soldier. He lay on the sand with his feet out straight and still. While his pale left hand was upon his chest in an attempt to thwart the going of his life, the blood came between his fingers. In the far Algerian distance, a city of low square forms was set against a sky that was faint with the last sunset hues. The correspondent, plying the oars and dreaming of the slow and slower movements of the lips of the soldier, was moved by a profound and perfectly impersonal comprehension. He was sorry for the soldier of the Legion who lay dying in Algiers.

83 The thing which had followed the boat and waited had evidently grown bored at the delay. There was no longer to be heard the slash of the cut-water, and there was no longer the flame of the long trail. The light in the north still glimmered, but it was apparently no nearer to the boat. Sometimes the boom of the surf rang in the correspondent's ears, and he turned the craft seaward then and rowed harder. Southward, some one had evidently built a watch-fire on the beach. It was too low and too far to be seen, but it made a shimmering, roseate reflection upon the bluff back of it, and this could be discerned from the boat. The wind came stronger, and sometimes a wave suddenly raged out like a mountain-cat and there was to be seen the sheen and sparkle of a broken crest.

The captain, in the bow, moved on his water-jar and sat erect. "Pretty long night," he observed to the correspondent. He looked at the shore. "Those life-saving people take their time." 184

"Did you see that shark playing around?" 185

"Yes, I saw him. He was a big fellow, all right." 186

"Wish I had known you were awake." 187

Later the correspondent spoke into the bottom of the boat. 188

"Billie!" There was a slow and gradual disentanglement. "Billie, will you spell me?" 189

"Sure," said the oiler. 190

As soon as the correspondent touched the cold comfortable sea-water in the bottom of the boat, and had huddled close to the cook's life-belt he was deep in sleep, despite the fact that his teeth played all the popular airs. This sleep was so good to him that it was but a moment before he heard a voice call his name in a tone that demonstrated the last stages of exhaustion. "Will you spell me?" 191

"Sure, Billie." 192

The light in the north had mysteriously vanished, but the correspondent took his course from the wide-awake captain. 193

Later in the night they took the boat farther out to sea, and the captain directed the cook to take one oar at the stern and keep the boat facing the seas. He was to call out if he should hear the thunder of the surf. This plan enabled the oiler and the correspondent to get respite together. "We'll give those boys a chance to get into shape again," said the captain. They curled down and, after a few preliminary chatterings and trembles, slept once more the dead sleep. Neither knew they had bequeathed to the cook the company of another shark, or perhaps the same shark. 194

As the boat caroused on the waves, spray occasionally bumped over the side and gave them a fresh 195 soaking, but this had no power to break their repose. The ominous slash of the wind and the water affected them as it would have affected mummies.

196 "Boys," said the cook, with the notes of every reluctance in his voice, "she's drifted in pretty close. I guess one of you had better take her to sea again." The correspondent, aroused, heard the crash of the toppled crests.

197 As he was rowing, the captain gave him some whiskey and water, and this steadied the chills out of him. "If I ever get ashore and anybody shows me even a photograph of an oar—"

It merely occurred to him that if he should drown it would be a shame.

198 At last there was a short conversation.

199 "Billie. . . . Billie, will you spell me?"

200 "Sure," said the oiler.

## VII

201 When the correspondent again opened his eyes, the sea and the sky were each of the gray hue of the dawning. Later, carmine and gold was painted upon the waters. The morning appeared finally, in its splendor, with a sky of pure blue, and the sunlight flamed on the tips of the waves.

202 On the distant dunes were set many little black cottages, and a tall white wind-mill reared above them. No man, nor dog, nor bicycle appeared on the beach. The cottages might have formed a deserted village.

203 The voyagers scanned the shore. A conference was held in the boat. "Well," said the captain, "if no help is coming, we might better try a run through the surf right away. If we stay out here much longer we will be too weak to do anything for ourselves at all." The others silently acquiesced in this reasoning. The boat was headed for the beach. The correspondent wondered if none ever ascended the tall wind-tower, and if then they never looked seaward. This tower was a giant, standing with its back to the plight of the ants. It represented in a degree, to the correspondent, the serenity of nature amid the struggles of the individual—nature in the wind, and nature in the vision of men. She did not seem cruel to him then, nor beneficent, nor treacherous, nor wise. But she was indifferent, flatly indifferent. It is, perhaps, plausible that a man in this situation, impressed with the unconcern of the universe, should see the innumerable flaws of his life and have them taste wickedly in his mind and wish for another chance. A distinction between right and wrong seems absurdly clear to him, then, in this new ignorance of the grave-edge, and he understands that if he were given another opportunity he would mend his conduct and his words, and be better and brighter during an introduction, or at a tea.

"Now, boys," said the captain, "she is going to swamp sure. All we can do is to work her in as far as possible, and then when she swamps, pile out and scramble for the beach. Keep cool now, and don't jump until she swamps sure." 20

The oiler took the oars. Over his shoulders he scanned the surf. "Captain," he said, "I think I'd better bring her about, and keep her head-on to the seas and back her in." 20

"All right, Billie," said the captain. "Back her in." The oiler swung the boat then and, seated in the stern, the cook and the correspondent were obliged to look over their shoulders to contemplate the lonely and indifferent shore. 20

The monstrous inshore rollers heaved the boat high until the men were again enabled to see the white sheets of water scudding up the slanted beach. "We won't get in very close," said the captain. Each time a man could wrest his attention from the rollers, he turned his glance toward the shore, and in the expression of the eyes during this contemplation there was a singular quality. The correspondent, observing the others, knew that they were not afraid, but the full meaning of their glances was shrouded. 20

As for himself, he was too tired to grapple fundamentally with the fact. He tried to coerce his mind into thinking of it, but the mind was dominated at this time by the muscles, and the muscles said they did not care. It merely occurred to him that if he should drown it would be a shame. 20

There were no hurried words, no pallor, no plain agitation. The men simply looked at the shore. "Now, remember to get well clear of the boat when you jump," said the captain. 20

Seaward the crest of a roller suddenly fell with a thunderous crash, and the long white comber came roaring down upon the boat. 21

"Steady now," said the captain. The men were silent. They turned their eyes from the shore to the comber and waited. The boat slid up the incline, leaped at the furious top, bounced over it, and swung down the long back of the wave. Some water had been shipped and the cook bailed it out. 21

But the next crest crashed also. The tumbling boiling flood of white water caught the boat and whirled it almost perpendicular. Water swarmed in from all sides. The correspondent had his hands on the gunwale at this time, and when the water entered at that 21 place he swiftly withdrew his fingers, as if he objected to wetting them.

13 The little boat, drunken with this weight of water, reeled and snuggled deeper into the sea.

14 "Bail her out, cook! Bail her out," said the captain.

15 "All right, Captain," said the cook.

16 "Now, boys, the next one will do for us, sure," said the oiler. "Mind to jump clear of the boat."

17 The third wave moved forward, huge, furious, implacable. It fairly swallowed the dingey, and almost simultaneously the men tumbled into the sea. A piece of life-belt had lain in the bottom of the boat, and as the correspondent went overboard he held this to his chest with his left hand.

18 The January water was icy, and he reflected immediately that it was colder than he had expected to find it off the coast of Florida. This appeared to his dazed mind as a fact important enough to be noted at the time. The coldness of the water was sad; it was tragic. This fact was somehow so mixed and confused with his opinion of his own situation that it seemed almost a proper reason for tears. The water was cold.

19 When he came to the surface he was conscious of little but the noisy water. Afterward he saw his companions in the sea. The oiler was ahead in the race. He was swimming strongly and rapidly. Off to the correspondent's left, the cook's great white and corked back bulged out of the water, and in the rear the captain was hanging with his one good hand to the keel of the overturned dingey.

20 There is a certain immovable quality to a shore, and the correspondent wondered at it amid the confusion of the sea.

21 It seemed also very attractive, but the correspondent knew that it was a long journey, and he paddled leisurely. The piece of life-preserver lay under him, and sometimes he whirled down the incline of a wave as if he were on a hand-sled.

22 But finally he arrived at a place in the sea where travel was beset with difficulty. He did not pause swimming to inquire what manner of current had caught him, but there his progress ceased. The shore was set before him like a bit of scenery on a stage, and he looked at it and understood with his eyes each detail of it.

23 As the cook passed, much farther to the left, the captain was calling to him, "Turn over on your back, cook! Turn over on your back and use the oar."

24 "All right, sir." The cook turned on his back, and, paddling with an oar, went ahead as if he were a canoe.

25 Presently the boat also passed to the left of the correspondent with the captain clinging with one hand to the keel. He would have appeared like a man raising himself to look over a board fence, if it were not for the extraordinary gymnastics of the boat. The correspondent marvelled that the captain could still hold to it.

They passed on, nearer to shore—the oiler, the cook, 226
the captain—and following them went the water-jar, bouncing gayly over the seas.

The correspondent remained in the grip of this 227
strange new enemy—a current. The shore, with its white slope of sand and its green bluff, topped with little silent cottages, was spread like a picture before him. It was very near to him then, but he was impressed as one who in a gallery looks at a scene from Brittany or Holland.

He thought: "I am going to drown? Can it be pos- 228
sible? Can it be possible? Can it be possible?" Perhaps an individual must consider his own death to be the final phenomenon of nature.

But later a wave perhaps whirled him out of this 229
small deadly current, for he found suddenly that he could again make progress toward the shore. Later still, he was aware that the captain, clinging with one hand to the keel of the dingey, had his face turned away from the shore and toward him, and was calling his name. "Come to the boat! Come to the boat!"

In his struggle to reach the captain and the boat, 230
he reflected that when one gets properly wearied, drowning must really be a comfortable arrangement, a cessation of hostilities accompanied by a large degree of relief, and he was glad of it, for the main thing in his mind for some moments had been horror of the temporary agony. He did not wish to be hurt.

Presently he saw a man running along the shore. 231
He was undressing with most remarkable speed. Coat, trousers, shirt, everything flew magically off him.

"Come to the boat," called the captain. 232

"All right, Captain." As the correspondent paddled, 233
he saw the captain let himself down to bottom and leave the boat. Then the correspondent performed his one little marvel of the voyage. A large wave caught him and flung him with ease and supreme speed completely over the boat and far beyond it. It struck him even then as an event in gymnastics, and a true miracle of the sea. An overturned boat in the surf is not a plaything to a swimming man.

The correspondent arrived in water that reached 234
only to his waist, but his condition did not enable him to stand for more than a moment. Each wave knocked him into a heap, and the under-tow pulled at him.

Then he saw the man who had been running 235
and undressing, and undressing and running, come bounding into the water. He dragged ashore the cook, and then waded toward the captain, but the captain

waved him away, and sent him to the correspondent. He was naked, naked as a tree in winter, but a halo was about his head, and he shone like a saint. He gave a strong pull, and a long drag, and a bully heave at the correspondent's hand. The correspondent, schooled in the minor formulae, said: "Thanks, old man." But suddenly the man cried: "What's that?" He pointed a swift finger. The correspondent said: "Go."

In the shallows, face downward, lay the oiler.

236 In the shallows, face downward, lay the oiler. His forehead touched sand that was periodically, between each wave, clear of the sea.

237 The correspondent did not know all that transpired afterward. When he achieved safe ground he fell, striking the sand with each particular part of his body. It was as if he had dropped from a roof, but the thud was grateful to him.

It seems that instantly the beach was populated 23
with men with blankets, clothes, and flasks, and women with coffee-pots and all the remedies sacred to their minds. The welcome of the land to the men from the sea was warm and generous, but a still and dripping shape was carried slowly up the beach, and the land's welcome for it could only be the different and sinister hospitality of the grave.

When it came night, the white waves paced to and 23
fro in the moonlight, and the wind brought the sound of the great sea's voice to the men on shore, and they felt that they could then be interpreters.

IF you liked the struggle between human beings and indifferent nature in "The Open Boat," you will also find it in a subtle form in Barry Lopez's "The Location of the River" in chapter 6.

**GOING FURTHER** Similar struggles are also found in the short stories and novels of Joseph Conrad, which offer excellent examples of men adrift or with particular goals at sea and in strange lands. The novels of Ernest Hemingway offer similar themes.

# Writing from Reading

## Summarize

1 The story begins in the middle of things, with the crew already stranded at sea. What details does Crane provide about the shipwreck? Which does he leave out?

2 The swim for shore is described only from the correspondent's point of view. What details are there of the other passengers' swims? Use what information you have to piece together an explanation for the oiler's death.

## Analyze Craft

3 Explain what Crane achieves by repeating certain passages of dialogue, reflection, and description within the story. What are some of these repeated lines and how many times do they recur? Do their meanings change with repetition or with the changing contexts in which they occur?

4 Only the oiler is ever called by his name in the story, and then never by the narrator. What is the significance of naming just the one character? Discuss this significance in light of Billie's death.

## Analyze Voice

5 This story was written in 1897. Consider how the era in which it was written affected its language. What words appear that you don't know without the aid of a dictionary? Are there any that sound old-fashioned to you?

### Synthesize Summary and Analysis

6 What is the narrator's role in this story? How would you describe the narrative distance? In other words, how close is the tale teller to the story and to its characters? Does the distance change over the course of the story? How?

### Interpret the Story

7 There are several themes in "The Open Boat," including comradeship, the struggle to survive, and nature's indifference. Choose one of these, or identify another theme in the story, and discuss incidents in the story where the theme becomes most clear. Explain how Crane emphasizes the theme, citing passages from the text.

# D. H. Lawrence (1855–1930)

David Herbert Lawrence was born in the coal mining district of Eastwood, Nottinghamshire, in the center of England, his father a hard-drinking coal miner and his mother a schoolteacher. He attended high school there and went on to Nottingham University, from which he graduated in his early twenties with a teaching certificate. A few years later, after he had moved to London and taken up a teaching position, he came under the tutelage of writer and magazine editor Ford Madox Ford, who published Lawrence in the *English Review.* By 1910 Lawrence had published his first novel, *The White Peacock,* and was entirely committed to the writing life. After the death of his mother from cancer, he published his autobiographical masterpiece *Sons and Lovers* (1913), and this was followed by other major titles such as *The Rainbow* (1915), *Women in Love* (1920), *Aaron's Rod* (1922), *The Plumed Serpent* (1926), and, perhaps most notoriously, *Lady Chatterley's Lover,* in 1928.

This last book created a scandal, because of its frank sexuality as well as its discussion of class; the "lady's" lover is a gardener, a man beneath her standing in society. In his personal life, as well, Lawrence broke social taboos; he ran off with Frieda von Richthofen Weekley, the wife of his university language professor. Thus began a period of extended travel with only occasional trips back to England; after the end of World War I, he and Frieda embraced a life of self-imposed exile. Mediterranean Europe, Australia, North America, and Mexico became Lawrence's shifting home grounds.

While he was living outside of England, a torrent of language poured forth from his pen; story after story, poem after poem, novel after novel appeared in rapid succession. He wrote travel books and articles and social tracts and plays. Lawrence used Aztec mythology, British social class distinctions, modern history—just about everything in modern life seemed useful to him in the composition of his work. Above all else—and this is truly why he matters to readers and writers of modern fiction—he found a forceful, direct, and appropriate diction by which to dramatize in physical form the volatile nature of interior states of mind and feeling. Upon his death from tuberculosis at the age of forty-four, he left behind one of the great modern bodies of work.

**AS YOU READ** Notice the sights and sounds, both of machines and in the natural world, that come to you line by line. Do you get the sense that all of this information points toward some important event? Do you feel this as a premonition of something good or something bad about to occur?

# The Odour of Chrysanthemums (1911)

## I

1 The small locomotive engine, Number 4, came clanking, stumbling down from Selston with seven full waggons. It appeared round the corner with loud threats of speed, but the colt that it startled from among the gorse, which still flickered indistinctly in the raw afternoon, outdistanced it at a canter. A woman, walking up the railway line to Underwood, drew back into the hedge, held her basket aside, and watched the footplate of the engine advancing. The trucks thumped heavily past, one by one, with slow inevitable movement, as she stood insignificantly trapped between the jolting black waggons and the hedge; then they curved away towards the coppice where the withered oak leaves dropped noiselessly, while the birds, pulling at the scarlet hips beside the track, made off into the dusk that had already crept into the spinney. In the open, the smoke from the engine sank and cleaved to the rough grass. The fields were dreary and forsaken, and in the marshy strip that led to the whimsey, a reedy pit-pond, the fowls had already abandoned their run among the alders, to roost in the tarred fowl-house. The pit-bank loomed up beyond the pond, flames like red sores licking its ashy sides, in the afternoon's stagnant light. Just beyond rose the tapering chimneys and the clumsy black headstocks of Brinsley Colliery. The two wheels were spinning fast up against the sky, and the winding-engine rapped out its little spasms. The miners were being turned up.

2 The engine whistled as it came into the wide bay of railway lines beside the colliery, where rows of trucks stood in harbour.

3 Miners, single, trailing and in groups, passed like shadows diverging home. At the edge of the ribbed level of sidings squat a low cottage, three steps down from the cinder track. A large bony vine clutched at the house, as if to claw down the tiled roof. Round the bricked yard grew a few wintry primroses. Beyond, the long garden sloped down to a bush-covered brook course. There were some twiggy apple trees, winter-crack trees, and ragged cabbages. Beside the path hung dishevelled pink chrysanthemums, like pink cloths hung on bushes. A woman came stooping out of the felt-covered fowl-house, half-way down the garden. She closed and padlocked the door, then drew herself erect, having brushed some bits from her white apron.

4 She was a tall woman of imperious mien, handsome, with definite black eyebrows. Her smooth black hair was parted exactly. For a few moments she stood steadily watching the miners as they passed along the railway: then she turned towards the brook course. Her face was calm and set, her mouth was closed with disillusionment. After a moment she called:

5 "John!" There was no answer. She waited, and then said distinctly:

6 "Where are you?"

7 "Here!" replied a child's sulky voice from among the bushes. The woman looked piercingly through the dusk.

8 "Are you at that brook?" she asked sternly.

9 For answer the child showed himself before the raspberry-canes that rose like whips. He was a small, sturdy boy of five. He stood quite still, defiantly.

10 "Oh!" said the mother, conciliated. "I thought you were down at that wet brook—and you remember what I told you—"

11 The boy did not move or answer.

12 "Come, come on in," she said more gently, "it's getting dark. There's your grandfather's engine coming down the line!"

13 The lad advanced slowly, with resentful, taciturn movement. He was dressed in trousers and waistcoat of cloth that was too thick and hard for the size of the garments. They were evidently cut down from a man's clothes.

14 As they went slowly towards the house he tore at the ragged wisps of chrysanthemums and dropped the petals in handfuls along the path.

15 "Don't do that—it does look nasty," said his mother. He refrained, and she, suddenly pitiful, broke off a twig with three or four wan flowers and held them against her face. When mother and son reached the yard her hand hesitated, and instead of laying the flower aside, she pushed it in her apron-band. The mother and son stood at the foot of the three steps looking across the bay of lines at the passing home of the miners. The trundle of the small train was imminent. Suddenly the engine loomed past the house and came to a stop opposite the gate.

16 The engine-driver, a short man with round grey beard, leaned out of the cab high above the woman.

17 "Have you got a cup of tea?" he said in a cheery, hearty fashion.

18 It was her father. She went in, saying she would mash. Directly, she returned.

19 "I didn't come to see you on Sunday," began the little grey-bearded man.

20 "I didn't expect you," said his daughter.

21 The engine-driver winced; then, reassuming his cheery, airy manner, he said:

22 "Oh, have you heard then? Well, and what do you think—?"

23 "I think it is soon enough," she replied.

24 At her brief censure the little man made an impatient gesture, and said coaxingly, yet with dangerous coldness:

25 "Well, what's a man to do? It's no sort of life for a man of my years, to sit at my own hearth like a stranger. And if I'm going to marry again it may as well be soon as late—what does it matter to anybody?"

26 The woman did not reply, but turned and went into the house. The man in the engine-cab stood assertive, till she returned with a cup of tea and a piece of bread and butter on a plate. She went up the steps and stood near the footplate of the hissing engine.

27 "You needn't 'a' brought me bread an' butter," said her father. "But a cup of tea"—he sipped appreciatively—"it's very nice." He sipped for a moment or two, then: "I hear as Walter's got another bout on," he said.

28 "When hasn't he?" said the woman bitterly.

29 "I heered tell of him in the 'Lord Nelson' braggin' as he was going to spend that b—— afore he went: half a sovereign that was."

30 "When?" asked the woman.

31 "A' Sat'day night—I know that's true."

32 "Very likely," she laughed bitterly. "He gives me twenty-three shillings."

33 "Aye, it's a nice thing, when a man can do nothing with his money but make a beast of himself!" said the grey-whiskered man. The woman turned her head away. Her father swallowed the last of his tea and handed her the cup.

34 "Aye," he sighed, wiping his mouth. "It's a settler, it is—"

35 He put his hand on the lever. The little engine strained and groaned, and the train rumbled towards the crossing. The woman again looked across the metals. Darkness was settling over the spaces of the railway and trucks: the miners, in grey sombre groups, were still passing home. The winding-engine pulsed hurriedly, with brief pauses. Elizabeth Bates looked at the dreary flow of men, then she went indoors. Her husband did not come.

36 The kitchen was small and full of firelight; red coals piled glowing up the chimney mouth. All the life of the room seemed in the white, warm hearth and the steel fender reflecting the red fire. The cloth was laid for tea; cups glinted in the shadows. At the back, where the lowest stairs protruded into the room, the boy sat struggling with a knife and a piece of whitewood. He was almost hidden in the shadow. It was half-past four. They had but to await the father's coming to begin tea. As the mother watched her son's sullen little struggle with the wood, she saw herself in his silence and pertinacity; she saw the father in her child's indifference to all but himself. She seemed to be occupied by her husband. He had probably gone past his home, slung past his own door, to drink before he came in, while his dinner spoiled and wasted in waiting. She glanced at the clock, then took the potatoes to strain them in the yard. The garden and fields beyond the brook were closed in uncertain darkness. When she rose with the saucepan, leaving the drain steaming into the night behind her, she saw the yellow lamps were lit along the high road that went up the hill away beyond the space of the railway lines and the field.

37 Then again she watched the men trooping home, fewer now and fewer.

38 Indoors the fire was sinking and the room was dark red. The woman put her saucepan on the hob, and set a batter pudding near the mouth of the oven. Then she stood unmoving. Directly, gratefully, came quick young steps to the door. Someone hung on the latch a moment, then a little girl entered and began pulling off her outdoor things, dragging a mass of

curls, just ripening from gold to brown, over her eyes with her hat.

39 Her mother chid her for coming late from school, and said she would have to keep her at home the dark winter days.

40 "Why, mother, it's hardly a bit dark yet. The lamp's not lighted, and my father's not home."

41 "No, he isn't. But it's a quarter to five! Did you see anything of him?"

42 The child became serious. She looked at her mother with large, wistful blue eyes.

As she reached up, her figure displayed itself just rounding with maternity.

43 "No, mother, I've never seen him. Why? Has he come up an' gone past, to Old Brinsley? He hasn't, mother, 'cos I never saw him."

44 "He'd watch that," said the mother bitterly, "he'd take care as you didn't see him. But you may depend upon it, he's seated in the 'Prince o' Wales.' He wouldn't be this late."

45 The girl looked at her mother piteously.

46 "Let's have our teas, mother, should we?" said she.

47 The mother called John to table. She opened the door once more and looked out across the darkness of the lines. All was deserted: she could not hear the winding-engines.

48 "Perhaps," she said to herself, "he's stopped to get some ripping done."

49 They sat down to tea. John, at the end of the table near the door, was almost lost in the darkness. Their faces were hidden from each other. The girl crouched against the fender slowly moving a thick piece of bread before the fire. The lad, his face a dusky mark on the shadow, sat watching her who was transfigured in the red glow.

50 "I do think it's beautiful to look in the fire," said the child.

51 "Do you?" said her mother. "Why?"

52 "It's so red, and full of little caves—and it feels so nice, and you can fair smell it."

53 "It'll want mending directly," replied her mother, "and then if your father comes he'll carry on and say there never is a fire when a man comes home sweating from the pit. A public-house is always warm enough."

54 There was silence till the boy said complainingly: "Make haste, our Annie."

55 "Well, I am doing! I can't make the fire do it no faster, can I?"

56 "She keeps wafflin' it about so's to make 'er slow," grumbled the boy.

57 "Don't have such an evil imagination, child," replied the mother.

Soon the room was busy in the darkness with the crisp sound of crunching. The mother ate very little. She drank her tea determinedly, and sat thinking. When she rose her anger was evident in the stern unbending of her head. She looked at the pudding in the fender, and broke out: 58

"It is a scandalous thing as a man can't even come home to his dinner! If it's crozzled up to a cinder I don't see why I should care. Past his very door he goes to get to a public-house, and here I sit with his dinner waiting for him—" 59

She went out. As she dropped piece after piece of coal on the red fire, the shadows fell on the walls, till the room was almost in total darkness. 60

"I canna see," grumbled the invisible John. In spite of herself, the mother laughed. 61

"You know the way to your mouth," she said. She set the dustpan outside the door. When she came again like a shadow on the hearth, the lad repeated, complaining sulkily: 62

"I canna see." 63

"Good gracious!" cried the mother irritably, "you're as bad as your father if it's a bit dusk!" 64

Nevertheless she took a paper spill from a sheaf on the mantelpiece and proceeded to light the lamp that hung from the ceiling in the middle of the room. As she reached up, her figure displayed itself just rounding with maternity. 65

"Oh, mother—!" exclaimed the girl. 66

"What?" said the woman, suspended in the act of putting the lamp glass over the flame. The copper reflector shone handsomely on her, as she stood with uplifted arm, turning to face her daughter. 67

"You've got a flower in your apron!" said the child, in a little rapture at this unusual event. 68

"Goodness me!" exclaimed the woman, relieved. "One would think the house was afire." She replaced the glass and waited a moment before turning up the wick. A pale shadow was seen floating vaguely on the floor. 69

"Let me smell!" said the child, still rapturously, coming forward and putting her face to her mother's waist. 70

"Go along, silly!" said the mother, turning up the lamp. The light revealed their suspense so that the woman felt it almost unbearable. Annie was still bending at her waist. Irritably, the mother took the flowers out from her apron-band. 71

"Oh, mother—don't take them out!" Annie cried, catching her hand and trying to replace the sprig. 72

3 "Such nonsense!" said the mother, turning away. The child put the pale chrysanthemums to her lips, murmuring:

4 "Don't they smell beautiful!"

5 Her mother gave a short laugh.

6 "No," she said, "not to me. It was chrysanthemums when I married him, and chrysanthemums when you were born, and the first time they ever brought him home drunk, he'd got brown chrysanthemums in his button-hole."

7 She looked at the children. Their eyes and their parted lips were wondering. The mother sat rocking in silence for some time. Then she looked at the clock.

8 "Twenty minutes to six!" In a tone of fine bitter carelessness she continued: "Eh, he'll not come now till they bring him. There he'll stick! But he needn't come rolling in here in his pit-dirt, for *I* won't wash him. He can lie on the floor—Eh, what a fool I've been, what a fool! And this is what I came here for, to this dirty hole, rats and all, for him to slink past his very door. Twice last week—he's begun now—"

9 She silenced herself, and rose to clear the table.

0 While for an hour or more the children played, subduedly intent, fertile of imagination, united in fear of the mother's wrath, and in dread of their father's home-coming, Mrs. Bates sat in her rocking-chair making a "singlet" of thick cream-coloured flannel, which gave a dull wounded sound as she tore off the grey edge. She worked at her sewing with energy, listening to the children, and her anger wearied itself, lay down to rest, opening its eyes from time to time and steadily watching, its ears raised to listen. Sometimes even her anger quailed and shrank, and the mother suspended her sewing, tracing the footsteps that thudded along the sleepers outside; she would lift her head sharply to bid the children "hush," but she recovered herself in time, and the footsteps went past the gate, and the children were not flung out of their play-world.

1 But at last Annie sighed, and gave in. She glanced at her waggon of slippers, and loathed the game. She turned plaintively to her mother.

2 "Mother!"—but she was inarticulate.

3 John crept out like a frog from under the sofa. His mother glanced up.

4 "Yes," she said, "just look at those shirt-sleeves!"

5 The boy held them out to survey them, saying nothing. Then somebody called in a hoarse voice away down the line, and suspense bristled in the room, till two people had gone by outside, talking.

36 "It is time for bed," said the mother.

37 "My father hasn't come," wailed Annie plaintively. But her mother was primed with courage.

"Never mind. They'll bring him when he does come—like a log." She meant there would be no scene. "And he may sleep on the floor till he wakes himself. I know he'll not go to work to-morrow after this!" 88

The children had their hands and faces wiped with a flannel. They were very quiet. When they had put on their nightdresses, they said their prayers, the boy mumbling. The mother looked down at them, at the brown silken bush of intertwining curls in the nape of the girl's neck, at the little black head of the lad, and her heart burst with anger at their father who caused all three such distress. The children hid their faces in her skirts for comfort. 89

When Mrs. Bates came down, the room was strangely empty, with a tension of expectancy. She took up her sewing and stitched for some time without raising her head. Meantime her anger was tinged with fear. 90

## II

The clock struck eight and she rose suddenly, dropping her sewing on her chair. She went to the stairfoot door, opened it, listening. Then she went out, locking the door behind her. 91

Something scuffled in the yard, and she started, though she knew it was only the rats with which the place was overrun. The night was very dark. In the great bay of railway lines, bulked with trucks, there was no trace of light, only away back she could see a few yellow lamps at the pit-top, and the red smear of the burning pit-bank on the night. She hurried along the edge of the track, then, crossing the converging lines, came to the stile by the white gates, whence she emerged on the road. Then the fear which had led her shrank. People were walking up to New Brinsley; she saw the lights in the houses; twenty yards further on were the broad windows of the "Prince of Wales," very warm and bright, and the loud voices of men could be heard distinctly. What a fool she had been to imagine that anything had happened to him! He was merely drinking over there at the "Prince of Wales." She faltered. She had never yet been to fetch him, and she never would go. So she continued her walk towards the long straggling line of houses, standing blank on the highway. She entered a passage between the dwellings. 92

93 "Mr. Rigley?—Yes! Did you want him? No, he's not in at this minute."

94 The raw-boned woman leaned forward from her dark scullery and peered at the other, upon whom fell a dim light through the blind of the kitchen window.

95 "Is it Mrs. Bates?" she asked in a tone tinged with respect.

96 "Yes. I wondered if your Master was at home. Mine hasn't come yet."

97 "'Asn't 'e! Oh, Jack's been 'ome an' 'ad 'is dinner an' gone out. 'E's just gone for 'alf an hour afore bed-time. Did you call at the 'Prince of Wales'?"

98 "No—"

99 "No, you didn't like—! It's not very nice." The other woman was indulgent. There was an awkward pause. "Jack never said nothink about—about your Mester," she said.

100 "No!—I expect he's stuck in there!"

101 Elizabeth Bates said this bitterly, and with recklessness. She knew that the woman across the yard was standing at her door listening, but she did not care. As she turned:

102 "Stop a minute! I'll just go an' ask Jack if 'e knows anythink," said Mrs. Rigley.

103 "Oh, no—I wouldn't like to put—!"

104 "Yes, I will, if you'll just step inside an' see as th' childer doesn't come downstairs and set theirselves afire."

105 Elizabeth Bates, murmuring a remonstrance, stepped inside. The other woman apologized for the state of the room.

106 The kitchen needed apology. There were little frocks and trousers and childish undergarments on the squab and on the floor, and a litter of playthings everywhere. On the black American cloth of the table were pieces of bread and cake, crusts, slops, and a teapot with cold tea.

107 "Eh, ours is just as bad," said Elizabeth Bates, looking at the woman, not at the house. Mrs. Rigley put a shawl over her head and hurried out, saying:

108 "I shanna be a minute."

109 The other sat, noting with faint disapproval the general untidiness of the room. Then she fell to counting the shoes of various sizes scattered over the floor. There were twelve. She sighed and said to herself, "No wonder!"—glancing at the litter. There came the scratching of two pairs of feet on the yard, and the Rigleys entered. Elizabeth Bates rose. Rigley was a big man, with very large bones. His head looked particularly bony. Across his temple was a blue scar, caused by a wound got in the pit, a wound in which the coal-dust remained blue like tattooing.

"'Asna 'e come whoam yit?" asked the man, without any form of greeting, but with deference and sympathy. "I couldna say wheer he is—'e's non ower theer!"—he jerked his head to signify the "Prince of Wales." 1

"'E's 'appen gone up to th' 'Yew,'" said Mrs. Rigley. 1

There was another pause. Rigley had evidently something to get off his mind: 1

"Ah left 'im finishin' a stint," he began. "Loose-all 'ad bin gone about ten minutes when we com'n away, an' I shouted, 'Are ter comin', Walt?' an' 'e said, 'Go on, Ah shanna be but a'ef a minnit,' so we com'n ter th' bottom, me an' Bowers, thinkin' as 'e wor just behint, an' 'ud come up i' th' next bantle—" 1

He stood perplexed, as if answering a charge of deserting his mate. Elizabeth Bates, now again certain of disaster, hastened to reassure him: 1

"I expect 'e's gone up to th' 'Yew Tree,' as you say. It's not the first time. I've fretted myself into a fever before now. He'll come home when they carry him." 11

"Ay, isn't it too bad!" deplored the other woman. 11

"I'll just step up to Dick's an' see if 'e *is* theer," offered the man, afraid of appearing alarmed, afraid of taking liberties. 11

"Oh, I wouldn't think of bothering you that far," said Elizabeth Bates, with emphasis, but he knew she was glad of his offer. 11

As they stumbled up the entry, Elizabeth Bates heard Rigley's wife run across the yard and open her neighbour's door. At this, suddenly all the blood in her body seemed to switch away from her heart. 11

"Mind!" warned Rigley. "Ah've said many a time as Ah'd fill up them ruts in this entry, sumb'dy 'll be breakin' their legs yit." 12

She recovered herself and walked quickly along with the miner. 12

"I don't like leaving the children in bed, and nobody in the house," she said. 12

"No, you dunna!" he replied courteously. They were soon at the gate of the cottage. 12

"Well, I shanna be many minnits. Dunna you be frettin' now, 'e'll be all right," said the butty. 12

"Thank you very much, Mr. Rigley," she replied. 12

"You're welcome!" he stammered, moving away. "I shanna be many minnits." 12

The house was quiet. Elizabeth Bates took off her hat and shawl, and rolled back the rug. When she had finished, she sat down. It was a few minutes past nine. She was startled by the rapid chuff of the winding-engine at the pit, and the sharp whirr of the brakes on the rope as it descended. Again she felt the painful sweep of her blood, and she put her hand to her 12 side, saying aloud, "Good gracious!—it's only the nine o'clock deputy going down," rebuking herself.

28 She sat still, listening. Half an hour of this, and she was wearied out.

29 "What am I working myself up like this for?" she said pitiably to herself, "I s'll only be doing myself some damage."

30 She took out her sewing again.

31 At a quarter to ten there were footsteps. One person! She watched for the door to open. It was an elderly woman, in a black bonnet and a black woollen shawl—his mother. She was about sixty years old, pale, with blue eyes, and her face all wrinkled and lamentable. She shut the door and turned to her daughter-in-law peevishly.

32 "Eh, Lizzie, whatever shall we do, whatever shall we do!" she cried.

33 Elizabeth drew back a little, sharply.

34 "What is it, mother?" she said.

35 The elder woman seated herself on the sofa.

36 "I don't know, child, I can't tell you!"—she shook her head slowly. Elizabeth sat watching her, anxious and vexed.

37 "I don't know," replied the grandmother, sighing very deeply. "There's no end to my troubles, there isn't. The things I've gone through, I'm sure it's enough—!" She wept without wiping her eyes, the tears running.

38 "But, mother," interrupted Elizabeth, "what do you mean? What is it?"

39 The grandmother slowly wiped her eyes. The fountains of her tears were stopped by Elizabeth's directness. She wiped her eyes slowly.

40 "Poor child! Eh, you poor thing!" she moaned. "I don't know what we're going to do, I don't—and you as you are—it's a thing, it is indeed!"

41 Elizabeth waited.

42 "Is he dead?" she asked, and at the words her heart swung violently, though she felt a slight flush of shame at the ultimate extravagance of the question. Her words sufficiently frightened the old lady, almost brought her to herself.

43 "Don't say so, Elizabeth! We'll hope it's not as bad as that; no, may the Lord spare us that, Elizabeth. Jack Rigley came just as I was sittin' down to a glass afore going to bed, an' 'e said, ''Appen you'll go down th' line, Mrs. Bates. Walt's had an accident. 'Appen you'll go an' sit wi' 'er till we can get him home.' I hadn't time to ask him a word afore he was gone. An' I put my bonnet on an' come straight down, Lizzie. I thought to myself, 'Eh, that poor blessed child, if anybody should come an' tell her of a sudden, there's no knowin' what'll 'appen to 'er.' You mustn't let it upset you, Lizzie—or you know what to expect. How long is it, six months—or is it five, Lizzie? Ay!"—the old woman shook her head—"time slips on, it slips on! Ay!"

Elizabeth's thoughts were busy elsewhere. If he 144
was killed—would she be able to manage on the little pension and what she could earn?—she counted up rapidly. If he was hurt—they wouldn't take him to the hospital—how tiresome he would be to nurse!—but perhaps she'd be able to get him away from the drink and his hateful ways. She would—while he was ill. The tears offered to come to her eyes at the picture. But what sentimental luxury was this she was beginning? She turned to consider the children. At any rate she was absolutely necessary for them. They were her business.

"Ay!" repeated the old woman, "it seems but a week 145
or two since he brought me his first wages. Ay—he was a good lad, Elizabeth, he was, in his way. I don't know why he got to be such a trouble, I don't. He was a happy lad at home, only full of spirits. But there's no mistake he's been a handful of trouble, he has! I hope the Lord'll spare him to mend his ways. I hope so, I hope so. You've had a sight o' trouble with him, Elizabeth, you have indeed. But he was a jolly enough lad wi' me, he was, I can assure you. I don't know how it is. . . ."

The old woman continued to muse aloud, a mo- 146
notonous irritating sound, while Elizabeth thought concentratedly, startled once, when she heard the winding-engine chuff quickly, and the brakes skirr with a shriek. Then she heard the engine more slowly, and the brakes made no sound. The old woman did not notice. Elizabeth waited in suspense. The mother-in-law talked, with lapses into silence.

"But he wasn't your son, Lizzie, an' it makes a 147
difference. Whatever he was, I remember him when he was little, an' I learned to understand him and to make allowances. You've got to make allowances for them—"

It was half-past ten, and the old woman was say- 148
ing: "But it's trouble from beginning to end; you're never too old for trouble, never too old for that—" when the gate banged back, and there were heavy feet on the steps.

"I'll go, Lizzie, let me go," cried the old woman, 149
rising. But Elizabeth was at the door. It was a man in pit-clothes.

"They're bringin' 'im, Missis," he said. Elizabeth's 150
heart halted a moment. Then it surged on again, almost suffocating her.

"Is he—is it bad?" she asked. 151

The man turned away, looking at the darkness: 152

153 "The doctor says 'e'd been dead hours. 'E saw 'im i' th' lamp-cabin."

154 The old woman, who stood just behind Elizabeth, dropped into a chair, and folded her hands, crying: "Oh, my boy, my boy!"

155 "Hush!" said Elizabeth, with a sharp twitch of a frown. "Be still, mother, don't waken th' children: I wouldn't have them down for anything!"

156 The old woman moaned softly, rocking herself. The man was drawing away. Elizabeth took a step forward.

157 "How was it?" she asked.

158 "Well, I couldn't say for sure," the man replied, very ill at ease. "'E wor finishin' a stint an' th' butties 'ad gone, an' a lot o' stuff come down atop 'n 'im."

159 "And crushed him?" cried the widow, with a shudder.

160 "No," said the man, "it fell at th' back of 'im. 'E wor under th' face, an' it niver touched 'im. It shut 'im in. It seems 'e wor smothered."

161 Elizabeth shrank back. She heard the old woman behind her cry:

162 "What?—what did 'e say it was?"

163 The man replied, more loudly: "'E wor smothered!"

164 Then the old woman wailed aloud, and this relieved Elizabeth.

165 "Oh, mother," she said, putting her hand on the old woman, "don't waken th' children, don't waken th' children."

166 She wept a little, unknowing, while the old mother rocked herself and moaned. Elizabeth remembered that they were bringing him home, and she must be ready. "They'll lay him in the parlour," she said to herself, standing a moment pale and perplexed.

167 Then she lighted a candle and went into the tiny room. The air was cold and damp, but she could not make a fire, there was no fireplace. She set down the candle and looked round. The candlelight glittered on the lustre-glasses, on the two vases that held some of the pink chrysanthemums, and on the dark mahogany. There was a cold, deathly smell of chrysanthemums in the room. Elizabeth stood looking at the flowers. She turned away, and calculated whether there would be room to lay him on the floor, between the couch and the chiffonier. She pushed the chairs aside. There would be room to lay him down and to step round him. Then she fetched the old red tablecloth, and another old cloth, spreading them down to save her bit of carpet. She shivered on leaving the parlour; so, from the dresser-drawer she took a clean shirt and put it at the fire to air. All the time her mother-in-law was rocking herself in the chair and moaning.

"You'll have to move from there, mother," said 168
Elizabeth. "They'll be bringing him in. Come in the rocker."

The old mother rose mechanically, and seated her- 169
self by the fire, continuing to lament. Elizabeth went into the pantry for another candle, and there, in the little penthouse under the naked tiles, she heard them coming. She stood still in the pantry doorway, listening. She heard them pass the end of the house, and come awkwardly down the three steps, a jumble of shuffling footsteps and muttering voices. The old woman was silent. The men were in the yard.

Then Elizabeth heard Mat- 170
thews, the manager of the pit, say: "You go in first, Jim. Mind!"

The door came open, and the 171
two women saw a collier backing into the room, holding one end of a stretcher, on which they could see the nailed pit-boots of the dead man. The two carriers halted, the man at the head stooping to the lintel of the door.

"Wheer will you have him?" asked the manager, a 172
short, white-bearded man.

Elizabeth roused herself and came from the pan- 173
try carrying the unlighted candle.

"In the parlour," she said. 174

"In there, Jim!" pointed the manager, and the carri- 175
ers backed round into the tiny room. The coat with which they had covered the body fell off as they awkwardly turned through the two doorways, and the women saw their man, naked to the waist, lying stripped for work. The old woman began to moan in a low voice of horror.

"Lay th' stretcher at th' side," snapped the man- 176
ager, "an' put 'im on th' cloths. Mind now, mind! Look you now—!"

One of the men had knocked off a vase of chrysan- 177
themums. He stared awkwardly, then they set down the stretcher. Elizabeth did not look at her husband. As soon as she could get in the room, she went and picked up the broken vase and the flowers.

"Wait a minute!" she said. 178

The three men waited in silence while she mopped 179
up the water with a duster.

"Eh, what a job, what a job, to be sure!" the man- 180
ager was saying, rubbing his brow with trouble and perplexity. "Never knew such a thing in my life, never! He'd no business to ha' been left. I never knew such a thing in my life! Fell over him clean as a whistle, an' shut him in. Not four foot of space, there wasn't—yet it scarce bruised him."

He looked down at the dead man, lying prone, half 181
naked, all grimed with coal-dust.

There was a cold, deathly smell of chrysanthemums in the room.

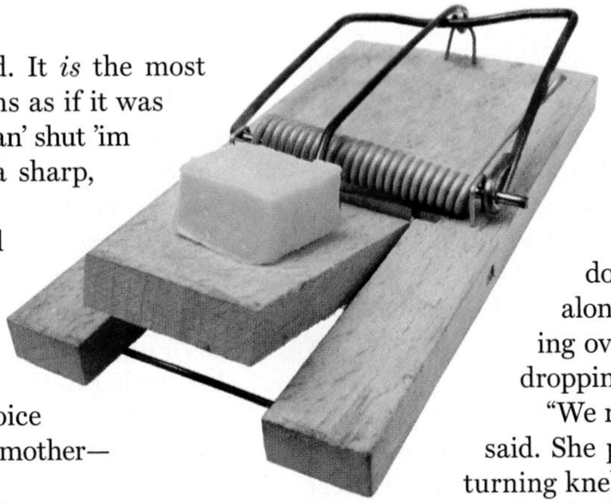

182 "'Sphyxiated,' the doctor said. It *is* the most terrible job I've ever known. Seems as if it was done o' purpose. Clean over him, an' shut 'im in, like a mouse-trap"—he made a sharp, descending gesture with his hand.

183 The colliers standing by jerked aside their heads in hopeless comment.

184 The horror of the thing bristled upon them all.

185 Then they heard the girl's voice upstairs calling shrilly: "Mother, mother—who is it? Mother, who is it?"

186 Elizabeth hurried to the foot of the stairs and opened the door:

187 "Go to sleep!" she commanded sharply. "What are you shouting about? Go to sleep at once—there's nothing—"

188 Then she began to mount the stairs. They could hear her on the boards, and on the plaster floor of the little bedroom. They could hear her distinctly:

189 "What's the matter now?—what's the matter with you, silly thing?"—her voice was much agitated, with an unreal gentleness.

190 "I thought it was some men come," said the plaintive voice of the child. "Has he come?"

191 "Yes, they've brought him. There's nothing to make a fuss about. Go to sleep now, like a good child."

192 They could hear her voice in the bedroom, they waited whilst she covered the children under the bedclothes.

193 "Is he drunk?" asked the girl, timidly, faintly.

194 "No! No—he's not! He—he's asleep."

195 "Is he asleep downstairs?"

196 "Yes—and don't make a noise."

197 There was silence for a moment, then the men heard the frightened child again:

198 "What's that noise?"

199 "It's nothing, I tell you, what are you bothering for?"

200 The noise was the grandmother moaning. She was oblivious of everything, sitting on her chair rocking and moaning. The manager put his hand on her arm and bade her "Sh—sh!!"

201 The old woman opened her eyes and looked at him. She was shocked by this interruption, and seemed to wonder.

202 "What time is it?"—the plaintive thin voice of the child, sinking back unhappily into sleep, asked this last question.

203 "Ten o'clock," answered the mother more softly. Then she must have bent down and kissed the children.

204 Matthews beckoned to the men to come away. They put on their caps and took up the stretcher. Stepping over the body, they tiptoed out of the house. None of them spoke till they were far from the wakeful children.

205 When Elizabeth came down she found her mother alone on the parlour floor, leaning over the dead man, the tears dropping on him.

206 "We must lay him out," the wife said. She put on the kettle, then returning knelt at the feet, and began to unfasten the knotted leather laces. The room was clammy and dim with only one candle, so that she had to bend her face almost to the floor. At last she got off the heavy boots and put them away.

207 "You must help me now," she whispered to the old woman. Together they stripped the man.

208 When they arose, saw him lying in the naïve dignity of death, the women stood arrested in fear and respect. For a few moments they remained still, looking down, the old mother whimpering. Elizabeth felt countermanded. She saw him, how utterly inviolable he lay in himself. She had nothing to do with him. She could not accept it. Stooping, she laid her hand on him, in claim. He was still warm, for the mine was hot where he had died. His mother had his face between her hands, and was murmuring incoherently. The old tears fell in succession as drops from wet leaves; the mother was not weeping, merely her tears flowed. Elizabeth embraced the body of her husband, with cheek and lips. She seemed to be listening, inquiring, trying to get some connection. But she could not. She was driven away. He was impregnable.

209 She rose, went into the kitchen, where she poured warm water into a bowl, brought soap and flannel and a soft towel.

210 "I must wash him," she said.

211 Then the old mother rose stiffly, and watched Elizabeth as she carefully washed his face, carefully brushing the big blond moustache from his mouth with the flannel. She was afraid with a bottomless fear, so she ministered to him. The old woman, jealous, said:

212 "Let me wipe him!"—and she kneeled on the other side drying slowly as Elizabeth washed, her big black bonnet sometimes brushing the dark head of her daughter-in-law. They worked thus in silence for a long time. They never forgot it was death, and the touch of the man's dead body gave them strange emotions, different in each of the women; a great dread possessed them both, the mother felt the lie was given

to her womb, she was denied; the wife felt the utter isolation of the human soul, the child within her was a weight apart from her.

213 At last it was finished. He was a man of handsome body, and his face showed no traces of drink. He was blond, full-fleshed, with fine limbs. But he was dead.

214 "Bless him," whispered his mother, looking always at his face, and speaking out of sheer terror. "Dear lad—bless him!" She spoke in a faint, sibilant ecstasy of fear and mother love.

215 Elizabeth sank down again to the floor, and put her face against his neck, and trembled and shuddered. But she had to draw away again. He was dead, and her living flesh had no place against his. A great dread and weariness held her: she was so unavailing. Her life was gone like this.

216 "White as milk he is, clear as a twelve-month baby, bless him, the darling!" the old mother murmured to herself. "Not a mark on him, clear and clean and white, beautiful as ever a child was made," she murmured with pride. Elizabeth kept her face hidden.

217 "He went peaceful, Lizzie—peaceful as sleep. Isn't he beautiful, the lamb? Ay—he must ha' made his peace, Lizzie. 'Appen he made it all right, Lizzie, shut in there. He'd have time. He wouldn't look like this if he hadn't made his peace. The lamb, the dear lamb. Eh, but he had a hearty laugh. I loved to hear it. He had the heartiest laugh, Lizzie, as a lad—"

218 Elizabeth looked up. The man's mouth was fallen back, slightly open under the cover of the moustache. The eyes, half shut, did not show glazed in the obscurity. Life with its smoky burning gone from him, had left him apart and utterly alien to her. And she knew what a stranger he was to her. In her womb was ice of fear, because of this separate stranger with whom she had been living as one flesh. Was this what it all meant—utter, intact separateness, obscured by heat of living? In dread she turned her face away. The fact was too deadly. There had been nothing between them, and yet they had come together, exchanging their nakedness repeatedly. Each time he had taken her, they had been two isolated beings, far apart as now. He was no more responsible than she. The child was like ice in her womb. For as she looked at the dead man, her mind, cold and detached, said clearly: "Who am I? What have I been doing? I have been fighting a husband who did not exist. *He* existed all the time. What wrong have I done? What was that I have been living with? There lies the reality, this man." And her soul died in her for fear: she knew she had never seen him, he had never seen her, they had met in the dark and had fought in the dark, not knowing whom they met nor whom they fought. And now she saw, and turned silent in seeing. For she had been wrong. She had said he was something he was not; she had felt familiar with him. Whereas he was apart all the while, living as she never lived, feeling as she never felt.

In fear and shame she looked at his naked body, 219
that she had known falsely. And he was the father of her children. Her soul was torn from her body and stood apart. She looked at his naked body and was ashamed, as if she had denied it. After all, it was itself. It seemed awful to her. She looked at his face, and she turned her own face to the wall. For his look was other than hers, his way was not her way. She had denied him what he was—she saw it now. She had refused him as himself. And this had been her life, and his life. She was grateful to death, which restored the truth. And she knew she was not dead.

She felt that in the next world he would be a stranger to her.

And all the while her heart was bursting with 220
grief and pity for him. What had he suffered? What stretch of horror for this helpless man! She was rigid with agony. She had not been able to help him. He had been cruelly injured, this naked man, this other being, and she could make no reparation. There were the children—but the children belonged to life. This dead man had nothing to do with them. He and she were only channels through which life had flowed to issue in the children. She was a mother—but how awful she knew it now to have been a wife. And he, dead now, how awful he must have felt it to be a husband. She felt that in the next world he would be a stranger to her. If they met there, in the beyond, they would only be ashamed of what had been before. The children had come, for some mysterious reason, out of both of them. But the children did not unite them. Now he was dead, she knew how eternally he was apart from her, how eternally he had nothing more to do with her. She saw this episode of her life closed. They had denied each other in life. Now he had withdrawn. An anguish came over her. It was finished then: it had become hopeless between them long before he died. Yet he had been her husband. But how little!

"Have you got his shirt, 'Lizabeth?" 221

Elizabeth turned without answering, though she 222
strove to weep and behave as her mother-in-law expected. But she could not, she was silenced. She went into the kitchen and returned with the garment.

23 "It is aired," she said, grasping the cotton shirt here and there to try. She was almost ashamed to handle him; what right had she or any one to lay hands on him; but her touch was humble on his body. It was hard work to clothe him. He was so heavy and inert. A terrible dread gripped her all the while: that he could be so heavy and utterly inert, unresponsive, apart. The horror of the distance between them was almost too much for her—it was so infinite a gap she must look across.

At last it was finished. They covered him with a sheet and left him lying, with his face bound. And she fastened the door of the little parlour, lest the children should see what was lying there. Then, with peace sunk heavy on her heart, she went about making tidy the kitchen. She knew she submitted to life, which was her immediate master. But from death, her ultimate master, she winced with fear and shame. 224

IF you like the Lawrence story, you might enjoy comparing it with John Steinbeck's "The Chrysanthemums" (chapter 12) and noting any similarities and differences in the use of the flower in evoking theme.

**GOING FURTHER** You can find the renewal of life in the cycle of death and birth at work in D. H. Lawrence's many books, from the early *Sons and Lovers* to later work such as *The Plumed Serpent,* his mystically tinged novel set in rural Mexico.

# Writing from Reading

## Summarize

1 Explore why Lawrence has Elizabeth's father visit at the beginning of the story. What information do we learn, and what is the effect of our learning it from this specific interaction?

2 Trace Elizabeth's emotions while she awaits her husband's homecoming. Based on this progression, discuss whether or not she truly cares about him.

## Analyze Craft

3 What is the setting (place, time period) of the story? Explain how you know, indicating examples from the text.

4 Discuss the techniques Lawrence uses to mount tension as the story progresses. Why is it almost a relief when you finally discover Walter's fate?

## Analyze Voice

5 Write a couple of sentences describing the voice of the narrator in terms of diction, tone, and syntax. Discuss why this particular voice complements the theme of longing for beauty in "The Odour of Chrysanthemums."

## Synthesize Summary and Analysis

6 Discuss why the setting of a coal mining town seems particularly appropriate for this story. Would the tone and themes of the story remain unchanged if Walt were caught in a factory machine or trampled in a stampede instead of being smothered by coal?

## Interpret the Story

7 Consider what the chrysanthemums represent in this story—to Elizabeth and to the children. What does it signify when the men carrying Walter's dead body knock over the vase of chrysanthemums? In light of this image, propose an overarching theme for the story, and try to imagine the future in store for the widow and her children.

# Jhumpa Lahiri (b. 1967)

Growing up in Rhode Island as the daughter of South Asian parents, Jhumpa Lahiri struggled with her identity, later reflecting that "my conflicting selves always cancel[ed] each other out." Although she was born in London, her parents moved to the United States when she was two, so Lahiri's two conflicting selves became Indian and American. These identities form the touchstone of her fiction, as she explores issues faced by Indian immigrants (especially Bengalis) as they adapt to new surroundings and cultural expectations. After earning three master's degrees—in English, creative writing, and comparative studies in literature and the arts—and a Ph.D in Renaissance studies from Boston University, Lahiri taught creative writing at Boston University and the Rhode Island School of Art and Design. Her life, however, was disrupted by celebrity when she published *Interpreter of Maladies,* a collection of short stories that won a Pulitzer Prize and the PEN/Hemingway Award, among others, and became an international best seller translated into twenty-nine languages. She became so famous, in fact, that the media had to be held at bay at her wedding to Alberto Vourvoulias, a Guatemalan-Greek journalist. Lahiri published her first novel, *The Namesake,* in 2003. Like her short stories, *The Namesake* focuses on themes such as marital and family difficulties, on the attempts of first- and second-generation immigrants to understand one another, and particularly on what it means to be Indian and to be assimilated. The novel was made into a major motion picture in 2006. Her most recent collection of stories, *Unaccustomed Earth,* was published in 2008.

As she said in an interview, the "question of identity is always a difficult one, but especially so for those who are culturally displaced, as immigrants are, or those who grow up in two worlds simultaneously, as is the case for their children. The older I get, the more I am aware that I have somehow inherited a sense of exile from my parents, even though in many ways I am so much more American than they are. In fact, it is still very hard to think of myself as an American."

**AS YOU READ** As you read, notice how the personalities and situations of the characters are revealed. How do your feelings about them change as you get to know them better? How do you interpret their maladies?

TIP

**FOR INTERACTIVE READING . . .** Trace the theme of interpretation and translation over the course of the story. Mark places in the text where any of the characters offers an interpretation.

# Interpreter of Maladies (1999)

1 AT the tea stall Mr. and Mrs. Das bickered about who should take Tina to the toilet. Eventually Mrs. Das relented when Mr. Das pointed out that he had given the girl her bath the night before. In the rearview mirror Mr. Kapasi watched as Mrs. Das emerged slowly from his bulky white Ambassador, dragging her shaved, largely bare legs across the back seat. She did not hold the little girl's hand as they walked to the rest room.

2 They were on their way to see the Sun Temple at Konarak. It was a dry, bright Saturday, the mid-July heat tempered by a steady ocean breeze, ideal weather for sightseeing. Ordinarily Mr. Kapasi would not have stopped so soon along the way, but less than five minutes after he'd picked up the family that morning in front of Hotel Sandy Villa, the little girl had complained. The first thing Mr. Kapasi had noticed when he saw Mr. and Mrs. Das, standing with their children under the portico of the hotel, was that they were very young, perhaps not even thirty. In addition to Tina they had two boys, Ronny and Bobby, who appeared very close in age and had teeth covered in a network of flashing silver wires. The family looked Indian but dressed as foreigners did, the children in stiff, brightly colored clothing and caps with translucent visors. Mr. Kapasi was accustomed to foreign tourists; he was assigned to them regularly because he could speak English. Yesterday he had driven an elderly couple from Scotland, both with spotted faces and fluffy white hair so thin it exposed their sunburnt scalps. In comparison, the tanned youthful faces of Mr. and Mrs. Das were all the more striking. When he'd introduced himself, Mr. Kapasi had pressed his palms together in greeting, but Mr. Das squeezed hands like an American so that Mr. Kapasi felt it in his elbow. Mrs. Das, for her part, had flexed one side of her mouth, smiling dutifully at Mr. Kapasi, without displaying any interest in him.

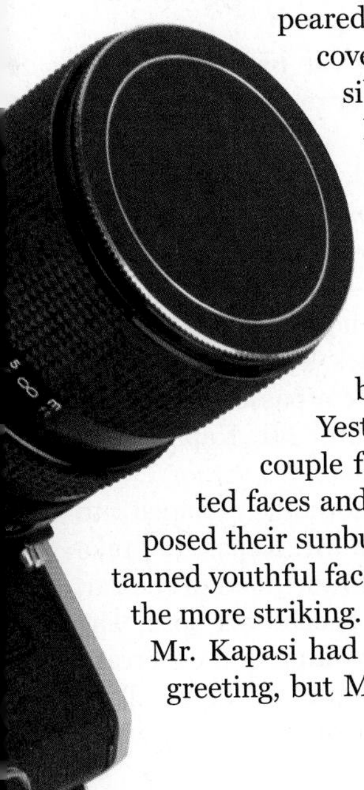

3 As they waited at the tea stall, Ronny, who looked like the older of the two boys, clambered suddenly out of the back seat, intrigued by a goat tied to a stake in the ground.

4 "Don't touch it," Mr. Das said. He glanced up from his paperback tour book, which said "INDIA" in yellow letters and looked as if it had been published abroad. His voice, somehow tentative and a little shrill, sounded as though it had not yet settled into maturity.

5 "I want to give it a piece of gum," the boy called back as he trotted ahead.

6 Mr. Das stepped out of the car and stretched his legs by squatting briefly to the ground. A clean-shaven man, he looked exactly like a magnified version of Ronny. He had a sapphire blue visor, and was dressed in shorts, sneakers, and a T-shirt. The camera slung around his neck, with an impressive telephoto lens and numerous buttons and markings, was the only complicated thing he wore. He frowned, watching as Ronny rushed toward the goat, but appeared to have no intention of intervening. "Bobby, make sure that your brother doesn't do anything stupid."

7 "I don't feel like it," Bobby said, not moving. He was sitting in the front seat beside Mr. Kapasi, studying a picture of the elephant god taped to the glove compartment.

8 "No need to worry," Mr. Kapasi said. "They are quite tame." Mr. Kapasi was forty-six years old, with receding hair that had gone completely silver, but his butterscotch complexion and his unlined brow, which he treated in spare moments to dabs of lotus-oil balm, made it easy to imagine what he must have looked like at an earlier age. He wore gray trousers and a matching jacket-style shirt, tapered at the waist, with short sleeves and a large pointed collar, made of a thin but durable synthetic material. He had specified both the

cut and the fabric to his tailor—it was his preferred uniform for giving tours because it did not get crushed during his long hours behind the wheel. Through the windshield he watched as Ronny circled around the goat, touched it quickly on its side, then trotted back to the car.

9 "You left India as a child?" Mr. Kapasi asked when Mr. Das had settled once again into the passenger seat.

10 "Oh, Mina and I were both born in America," Mr. Das announced with an air of sudden confidence. "Born and raised. Our parents live here now, in Assansol. They retired. We visit them every couple years." He turned to watch as the little girl ran toward the car, the wide purple bows of her sundress flopping on her narrow brown shoulders. She was holding to her chest a doll with yellow hair that looked as if it had been chopped, as a punitive measure, with a pair of dull scissors. "This is Tina's first trip to India, isn't it, Tina?"

11 "I don't have to go to the bathroom anymore," Tina announced.

12 "Where's Mina?" Mr. Das asked.

13 Mr. Kapasi found it strange that Mr. Das should refer to his wife by her first name when speaking to the little girl. Tina pointed to where Mrs. Das was purchasing something from one of the shirtless men who worked at the tea stall. Mr. Kapasi heard one of the shirtless men sing a phrase from a popular Hindi love song as Mrs. Das walked back to the car, but she did not appear to understand the words of the song, for she did not express irritation, or embarrassment, or react in any other way to the man's declarations.

14 He observed her. She wore a red-and-white-checkered skirt that stopped above her knees, slip-on shoes with a square wooden heel, and a close-fitting blouse styled like a man's undershirt. The blouse was decorated at chest-level with a calico appliqué in the shape of a strawberry. She was a short woman, with small hands like paws, her frosty pink fingernails painted to match her lips, and was slightly plump in her figure. Her hair, shorn only a little longer than her husband's, was parted far to one side. She was wearing large dark brown sunglasses with a pinkish tint to them, and carried a big straw bag, almost as big as her torso, shaped like a bowl, with a water bottle poking out of it. She walked slowly, carrying some puffed rice tossed with peanuts and chili peppers in a large packet made from newspapers. Mr. Kapasi turned to Mr. Das.

15 "Where in America do you live?"

16 "New Brunswick, New Jersey."

17 "Next to New York?"

18 "Exactly. I teach middle school there."

19 "What subject?"

20 "Science. In fact, every year I take my students on a trip to the Museum of Natural History in New York City. In a way we have a lot in common, you could say, you and I. How long have you been a tour guide, Mr. Kapasi?"

21 "Five years."

22 Mrs. Das reached the car. "How long's the trip?" she asked, shutting the door.

23 "About two and a half hours," Mr. Kapasi replied.

24 At this Mrs. Das gave an impatient sigh, as if she had been traveling her whole life without pause. She fanned herself with a folded Bombay film magazine written in English.

25 "I thought that the Sun Temple is only eighteen miles north of Puri," Mr. Das said, tapping on the tour book.

26 "The roads to Konarak are poor. Actually it is a distance of fifty-two miles," Mr. Kapasi explained.

27 Mr. Das nodded, readjusting the camera strap where it had begun to chafe the back of his neck.

28 Before starting the ignition, Mr. Kapasi reached back to make sure the cranklike locks on the inside of each of the back doors were secured. As soon as the car began to move the little girl began to play with the lock on her side, clicking it with some effort forward and backward, but Mrs. Das said nothing to stop her. She sat a bit slouched at one end of the back seat, not offering her puffed rice to anyone. Ronny and Tina sat on either side of her, both snapping bright green gum.

29 "Look," Bobby said as the car began to gather speed. He pointed with his finger to the tall trees that lined the road. "Look."

30 "Monkeys!" Ronny shrieked. "Wow!"

31 They were seated in groups along the branches, with shining black faces, silver bodies, horizontal eyebrows, and crested heads. Their long gray tails dangled like a series of ropes among the leaves. A few scratched themselves with black leathery hands, or swung their feet, staring as the car passed.

32 "We call them the hanuman," Mr. Kapasi said. "They are quite common in the area."

33 As soon as he spoke, one of the monkeys leaped into the middle of the road, causing Mr. Kapasi to brake suddenly. Another bounced onto the hood of the car, then sprang away. Mr. Kapasi beeped his horn. The children began to get excited, sucking in their breath and covering their faces partly with their hands. They had never seen monkeys outside of a zoo, Mr. Das ex-

plained. He asked Mr. Kapasi to stop the car so that he could take a picture.

34 While Mr. Das adjusted his telephoto lens, Mrs. Das reached into her straw bag and pulled out a bottle of colorless nail polish, which she proceeded to stroke on the tip of her index finger.

35 The little girl stuck out a hand. "Mine too. Mommy, do mine too."

36 "Leave me alone," Mrs. Das said, blowing on her nail and turning her body slightly. "You're making me mess up."

37 The little girl occupied herself by buttoning and unbuttoning a pinafore on the doll's plastic body.

38 "All set," Mr. Das said, replacing the lens cap.

39 The car rattled considerably as it raced along the dusty road, causing them all to pop up from their seats every now and then, but Mrs. Das continued to polish her nails. Mr. Kapasi eased up on the accelerator, hoping to produce a smoother ride. When he reached for the gearshift the boy in front accommodated him by swinging his hairless knees out of the way. Mr. Kapasi noted that this boy was slightly paler than the other children. "Daddy, why is the driver sitting on the wrong side in this car, too?" the boy asked.

40 "They all do that here, dummy," Ronny said.

41 "Don't call your brother a dummy," Mr. Das said. He turned to Mr. Kapasi. "In America, you know . . . it confuses them."

42 "Oh yes, I am well aware," Mr. Kapasi said. As delicately as he could, he shifted gears again, accelerating as they approached a hill in the road. "I see it on *Dallas*, the steering wheels are on the left-hand side."

43 "What's *Dallas?*" Tina asked, banging her now naked doll on the seat behind Mr. Kapasi.

44 "It went off the air," Mr. Das explained. "It's a television show."

45 They were all like siblings, Mr. Kapasi thought as they passed a row of date trees. Mr. and Mrs. Das behaved like an older brother and sister, not parents. It seemed that they were in charge of the children only for the day; it was hard to believe they were regularly responsible for anything other than themselves. Mr. Das tapped on his lens cap, and his tour book, dragging his thumbnail occasionally across the pages so that they made a scraping sound. Mrs. Das continued to polish her nails. She had still not removed her sunglasses. Every now and then Tina renewed her plea that she wanted her nails done, too, and so at one point Mrs. Das flicked a drop of polish on the little girl's finger before depositing the bottle back inside her straw bag.

"Isn't this an air-conditioned car?" she asked, still blowing on her hand. The window on Tina's side was broken and could not be rolled down. 46

"Quit complaining," Mr. Das said. "It isn't so hot." 47

"I told you to get a car with air-conditioning," Mrs. Das continued. "Why do you do this, Raj, just to save a few stupid rupees. What are you saving us, fifty cents?" 48

Their accents sounded just like the ones Mr. Kapasi heard on American television programs, though not like the ones on *Dallas*. 49

"Doesn't it get tiresome, Mr. Kapasi, showing people the same thing every day?" Mr. Das asked, rolling down his own window all the way. "Hey, do you mind stopping the car. I just want to get a shot of this guy." 50

Mr. Kapasi pulled over to the side of the road as Mr. Das took a picture of a barefoot man, his head wrapped in a dirty turban, seated on top of a cart of grain sacks pulled by a pair of bullocks. Both the man and the bullocks were emaciated. In the back seat Mrs. Das gazed out another window, at the sky, where nearly transparent clouds passed quickly in front of one another. 51

"I look forward to it, actually," Mr. Kapasi said as they continued on their way. "The Sun Temple is one of my favorite places. In that way it is a reward for me. I give tours on Fridays and Saturdays only. I have another job during the week." 52

"Oh? Where?" Mr. Das asked. 53

"I work in a doctor's office." 54

"You're a doctor?" 55

"I am not a doctor. I work with one. As an interpreter." 56

"What does a doctor need an interpreter for?" 57

"He has a number of Gujarati patients. My father was Gujarati, but many people do not speak Gujarati in this area, including the doctor. And so the doctor asked me to work in his office, interpreting what the patients say." 58

"Interesting. I've never heard of anything like that," Mr. Das said. 59

60 Mr. Kapasi shrugged. “It is a job like any other.”

61 “But so romantic,” Mrs. Das said dreamily, breaking her extended silence. She lifted her pinkish brown sunglasses and arranged them on top of her head like a tiara. For the first time, her eyes met Mr. Kapasi’s in the rearview mirror: pale, a bit small, their gaze fixed but drowsy.

62 Mr. Das craned to look at her. “What’s so romantic about it?”

63 “I don’t know. Something.” She shrugged, knitting her brows together for an instant. “Would you like a piece of gum, Mr. Kapasi?” she asked brightly. She reached into her straw bag and handed him a small square wrapped in green-and-white-striped paper. As soon as Mr. Kapasi put the gum in his mouth a thick sweet liquid burst onto his tongue.

64 “Tell us more about your job, Mr. Kapasi,” Mrs. Das said.

65 “What would you like to know, madame?”

66 “I don’t know,” she shrugged, munching on some puffed rice and licking the mustard oil from the corners of her mouth. “Tell us a typical situation.” She settled back in her seat, her head tilted in a patch of sun, and closed her eyes. “I want to picture what happens.”

67 “Very well. The other day a man came in with a pain in his throat.”

68 “Did he smoke cigarettes?”

69 “No. It was very curious. He complained that he felt as if there were long pieces of straw stuck in his throat. When I told the doctor he was able to prescribe the proper medication.”

70 “That’s so neat.”

71 “Yes,” Mr. Kapasi agreed after some hesitation.

72 “So these patients are totally dependent on you,” Mrs. Das said. She spoke slowly, as if she were thinking aloud. “In a way, more dependent on you than the doctor.”

73 “How do you mean? How could it be?”

74 “Well, for example, you could tell the doctor that the pain felt like a burning, not straw. The patient would never know what you had told the doctor, and the doctor wouldn’t know that you had told the wrong thing. It’s a big responsibility.”

75 “Yes, a big responsibility you have there, Mr. Kapasi,” Mr. Das agreed.

76 Mr. Kapasi had never thought of his job in such complimentary terms. To him it was a thankless occupation. He found nothing noble in interpreting people’s maladies, assiduously translating the symptoms of so many swollen bones, countless cramps of bellies and bowels, spots on people’s palms that changed color, shape, or size. The doctor, nearly half his age, had an affinity for bell-bottom trousers and made humorless jokes about the Congress party. Together they worked in a stale little infirmary where Mr. Kapasi’s smartly tailored clothes clung to him in the heat, in spite of the blackened blades of a ceiling fan churning over their heads.

**Mr. Kapasi had never thought of his job in such complimentary terms.**

77 The job was a sign of his failings. In his youth he’d been a devoted scholar of foreign languages, the owner of an impressive collection of dictionaries. He had dreamed of being an interpreter for diplomats and dignitaries, resolving conflicts between people and nations, settling disputes of which he alone could understand both sides. He was a self-educated man. In a series of notebooks, in the evenings before his parents settled his marriage, he had listed the common etymologies of words, and at one point in his life he was confident that he could converse, if given the opportunity, in English, French, Russian, Portuguese, and Italian, not to mention Hindi, Bengali, Orissi, and Gujarati. Now only a handful of European phrases remained in his memory, scattered words for things like saucers and chairs. English was the only non-Indian language he spoke fluently anymore. Mr. Kapasi knew it was not a remarkable talent. Sometimes he feared that his children knew better English than he did, just from watching television. Still, it came in handy for the tours.

78 He had taken the job as an interpreter after his first son, at the age of seven, contracted typhoid—that was how he had first made the acquaintance of the doctor. At the time Mr. Kapasi had been teaching English in a grammar school, and he bartered his skills as an interpreter to pay the increasingly exorbitant medical bills. In the end the boy had died one evening in his mother’s arms, his limbs burning with fever, but then there was the funeral to pay for, and the other children who were born soon enough, and the newer, bigger house, and the good schools and tutors, and the fine shoes and the television, and the countless other ways he tried to console his wife and to keep her from crying in her sleep, and so when the doctor offered to pay him twice as much as he earned at the grammar school, he accepted. Mr. Kapasi knew that his wife had little regard for his career as an interpreter. He knew it reminded her of the son she’d lost, and that she resented the other lives he helped, in his own small way, to save. If ever she referred to his position, she used the phrase “doctor’s assistant,” as if the

process of interpretation were equal to taking someone's temperature, or changing a bedpan. She never asked him about the patients who came to the doctor's office, or said that his job was a big responsibility.

79 For this reason it flattered Mr. Kapasi that Mrs. Das was so intrigued by his job. Unlike his wife, she had reminded him of its intellectual challenges. She had also used the word "romantic." She did not behave in a romantic way toward her husband, and yet she had used the word to describe him. He wondered if Mr. and Mrs. Das were a bad match, just as he and his wife were. Perhaps they, too, had little in common apart from three children and a decade of their lives. The signs he recognized from his own marriage were there—the bickering, the indifference, the protracted silences. Her sudden interest in him, an interest she did not express in either her husband or her children, was mildly intoxicating. When Mr. Kapasi thought once again about how she had said "romantic," the feeling of intoxication grew.

80 He began to check his reflection in the rearview mirror as he drove, feeling grateful that he had chosen the gray suit that morning and not the brown one, which tended to sag a little in the knees. From time to time he glanced through the mirror at Mrs. Das. In addition to glancing at her face he glanced at the strawberry between her breasts, and the golden brown hollow in her throat. He decided to tell Mrs. Das about another patient, and another: the young woman who had complained of a sensation of raindrops in her spine, the gentleman whose birthmark had begun to sprout hairs. Mrs. Das listened attentively, stroking her hair with a small plastic brush that resembled an oval bed of nails, asking more questions, for yet another example. The children were quiet, intent on spotting more monkeys in the trees, and Mr. Das was absorbed by his tour book, so it seemed like a private conversation between Mr. Kapasi and Mrs. Das. In this manner the next half hour passed, and when they stopped for lunch at a roadside restaurant that sold fritters and omelette sandwiches, usually something Mr. Kapasi looked forward to on his tours so that he could sit in peace and enjoy some hot tea, he was disappointed. As the Das family settled together under a magenta umbrella fringed with white and orange tassels, and placed their orders with one of the waiters who marched about in tricornered caps, Mr. Kapasi reluctantly headed toward a neighboring table.

81 "Mr. Kapasi, wait. There's room here," Mrs. Das called out. She gathered Tina onto her lap, insisting that he accompany them. And so, together, they had bottled mango juice and sandwiches and plates of onions and potatoes deep-fried in graham-flour batter. After finishing two omelette sandwiches Mr. Das took more pictures of the group as they ate.

"How much longer?" he asked Mr. Kapasi as he 82
paused to load a new roll of film in the camera.

"About half an hour more." 83

By now the children had gotten 84
up from the table to look at more monkeys perched in a nearby tree, so there was a considerable space between Mrs. Das and Mr. Kapasi. Mr. Das placed the camera to his face and squeezed one eye shut, his tongue exposed at one corner of his mouth. "This looks funny. Mina, you need to lean in closer to Mr. Kapasi."

She did. He could smell a scent on her skin, like a 85
mixture of whiskey and rosewater. He worried suddenly that she could smell his perspiration, which he knew had collected beneath the synthetic material of his shirt. He polished off his mango juice in one gulp and smoothed his silver hair with his hands. A bit of the juice dripped onto his chin. He wondered if Mrs. Das had noticed.

She had not. "What's your address, Mr. Kapasi?" 86
she inquired, fishing for something inside her straw bag.

"You would like my address?" 87

"So we can send you copies," she said. "Of the pic- 88
tures." She handed him a scrap of paper which she had hastily ripped from a page of her film magazine. The blank portion was limited, for the narrow strip was crowded by lines of text and a tiny picture of a hero and heroine embracing under a eucalyptus tree.

The paper curled as Mr. Kapasi wrote his address 89
in clear, careful letters. She would write to him, asking about his days interpreting at the doctor's office, and he would respond eloquently, choosing only the most entertaining anecdotes, ones that would make her laugh out loud as the read them in her house in New Jersey. In time she would reveal the disappointment of her marriage, and he his. In this way their friendship would grow, and flourish. He would possess a picture of the two of them, eating fried onions under a magenta umbrella, which he would keep, he decided, safely tucked between the pages of his Russian grammar. As his mind raced, Mr. Kapasi experienced a mild and pleasant shock. It was similar to a feeling he used to experience long ago when, after months of translating with the aid of a dictionary, he would finally read a passage from a French novel, or an Italian sonnet, and understand the words, one after another, unencumbered by his own efforts. In those moments Mr. Kapasi used to believe that all

was right with the world, that all struggles were rewarded, that all of life's mistakes made sense in the end. The promise that he would hear from Mrs. Das now filled him with the same belief.

90 When he finished writing his address Mr. Kapasi handed her the paper, but as soon as he did so he worried that he had either misspelled his name, or accidentally reversed the numbers of his postal code. He dreaded the possibility of a lost letter, the photograph never reaching him, hovering somewhere in Orissa, close but ultimately unattainable. He thought of asking for the slip of paper again, just to make sure he had written his address accurately, but Mrs. Das had already dropped it into the jumble of her bag.

91 THEY reached Konarak at two-thirty. The temple, made of sandstone, was a massive pyramid-like structure in the shape of a chariot. It was dedicated to the great master of life, the sun, which struck three sides of the edifice as it made its journey each day across the sky. Twenty-four giant wheels were carved on the north and south sides of the plinth. The whole thing was drawn by a team of seven horses, speeding as if through the heavens. As they approached, Mr. Kapasi explained that the temple had been built between A.D. 1243 and 1255, with the efforts of twelve hundred artisans, by the great ruler of the Ganga dynasty, King Narasimhadeva the First, to commemorate his victory against the Muslim army.

92 "It says the temple occupies about a hundred and seventy acres of land," Mr. Das said, reading from his book.

93 "It's like a desert," Ronny said, his eyes wandering across the sand that stretched on all sides beyond the temple.

94 "The Chandrabhaga River once flowed one mile north of here. It is dry now," Mr. Kapasi said, turning off the engine.

95 They got out and walked toward the temple, posing first for pictures by the pair of lions that flanked the steps. Mr. Kapasi led them next to one of the wheels of the chariot, higher than any human being, nine feet in diameter.

96 "'The wheels are supposed to symbolize the wheel of life,'" Mr. Das read. "'They depict the cycle of creation, preservation, and achievement of realization.' Cool." He turned the page of his book. "'Each wheel is divided into eight thick and thin spokes, dividing the day into eight equal parts. The rims are carved with designs of birds and animals, whereas the medallions in the spokes are carved with women in luxurious poses, largely erotic in nature.'"

What he referred to were the countless friezes of 97
entwined naked bodies, making love in various positions, women clinging to the necks of men, their knees wrapped eternally around their lovers' thighs. In addition to these were assorted scenes from daily life, of hunting and trading, of deer being killed with bows and arrows and marching warriors holding swords in their hands.

It was no longer possible to enter the temple, for 98
it had filled with rubble years ago, but they admired the exterior, as did all the tourists Mr. Kapasi brought there, slowly strolling along each of its sides. Mr. Das trailed behind, taking pictures. The children ran ahead, pointing to figures of naked people, intrigued in particular by the Nagamithunas, the half-human, half-serpentine couples who were said, Mr. Kapasi told them, to live in the deepest waters of the sea. Mr. Kapasi was pleased that they liked the temple, pleased especially that it appealed to Mrs. Das. She stopped every three or four paces, staring silently at the carved lovers, and the processions of elephants, and the topless female musicians beating on two-sided drums.

Though Mr. Kapasi had been to the temple count- 99
less times, it occurred to him, as he, too, gazed at the topless women, that he had never seen his own wife fully naked. Even when they had made love she kept the panels of her blouse hooked together, the string of her petticoat knotted around her waist. He had never admired the backs of his wife's legs the way he now admired those of Mrs. Das, walking as if for his benefit alone. He had, of course, seen plenty of bare limbs before, belonging to the American and European ladies who took his tours. But Mrs. Das was different. Unlike the other women, who had an interest only in the temple, and kept their noses buried in a guidebook, or their eyes behind the lens of a camera, Mrs. Das had taken an interest in him.

Mr. Kapasi was anxious to be alone with her, to 100
continue their private conversation, yet he felt nervous to walk at her side. She was lost behind her sunglasses, ignoring her husband's requests that she pose for another picture, walking past her children as if they were strangers. Worried that he might disturb her, Mr. Kapasi walked ahead, to admire, as he always did, the three life-sized bronze avatars of Surya, the sun god, each emerging from its own niche on the temple facade to greet the sun at dawn, noon, and evening. They wore elaborate headdresses, their languid, elongated eyes closed, their bare chests draped with carved chains and amulets. Hibiscus petals, offerings from previous visitors, were strewn at their gray-green feet. The last statue, on the northern wall of the tem-

ple, was Mr. Kapasi's favorite. This Surya had a tired expression, weary after a hard day of work, sitting astride a horse with folded legs. Even his horse's eyes were drowsy. Around his body were smaller sculptures of women in pairs, their hips thrust to one side.

1 "Who's that? Mrs. Das asked. He was startled to see that she was standing beside him.

2 "He is the Astachala-Surya," Mr. Kapasi said. "The setting sun."

3 "So in a couple of hours the sun will set right here?" She slipped a foot out of one of her square-heeled shoes, rubbed her toes on the back of her other leg.

4 "That is correct."

5 She raised her sunglasses for a moment, then put them back on again. "Neat."

6 Mr. Kapasi was not certain exactly what the word suggested, but he had a feeling it was a favorable response. He hoped that Mrs. Das had understood Surya's beauty, his power. Perhaps they would discuss it further in their letters. He would explain things to her, things about India, and she would explain things to him about America. In its own way this correspondence would fulfill his dream, of serving as an interpreter between nations. He looked at her straw bag, delighted that his address lay nestled among its contents. When he pictured her so many thousands of miles away he plummeted, so much so that he had an overwhelming urge to wrap his arms around her, to freeze with her, even for an instant, in an embrace witnessed by his favorite Surya. But Mrs. Das had already started walking.

7 "When do you return to America?" he asked, trying to sound placid.

8 "In ten days."

9 He calculated: A week to settle in, a week to develop the pictures, a few days to compose her letter, two weeks to get to India by air. According to his schedule, allowing room for delays, he would hear from Mrs. Das in approximately six weeks' time.

0 THE family was silent as Mr. Kapasi drove them back, a little past four-thirty, to Hotel Sandy Villa. The children had bought miniature granite versions of the chariot's wheels at a souvenir stand, and they turned them round in their hands. Mr. Das continued to read his book. Mrs. Das untangled Tina's hair with her brush and divided it into two little ponytails.

Mr. Kapasi was beginning to dread the thought of dropping them off. He was not prepared to begin his six-week wait to hear from Mrs. Das. As he stole glances at her in the rearview mirror, wrapping elastic bands around Tina's hair, he wondered how he might make the tour last a little longer. Ordinarily he sped back to Puri using a shortcut, eager to return home, scrub his feet and hands with sandalwood soap, and enjoy the evening newspaper and a cup of tea that his wife would serve him in silence. The thought of that silence, something to which he'd long been resigned, now oppressed him. It was then that he suggested visiting the hills at Udayagiri and Khandagiri, where a number of monastic dwellings were hewn out of the ground, facing one another across a defile. It was some miles away, but well worth seeing, Mr. Kapasi told them. 111

The thought of that silence, something to which he'd long been resigned, now oppressed him.

Oh yeah, there's something mentioned about it in this book," Mr. Das said. "Built by a Jain king or something." 112

"Shall we go then?" Mr. Kapasi asked. He paused at a turn in the road. "It's to the left." 113

Mr. Das turned to look at Mrs. Das. Both of them shrugged. 114

"Left, left," the children chanted. 115

Mr. Kapasi turned the wheel, almost delirious with relief. He did not know what he would do or say to Mrs. Das once they arrived at the hills. Perhaps he would tell her what a pleasing smile she had. Perhaps he would compliment her strawberry shirt, which he found irresistibly becoming. Perhaps, when Mr. Das was busy taking a picture, he would take her hand. 116

He did not have to worry. When they got to the hills, divided by a steep path thick with trees, Mrs. Das refused to get out of the car. All along the path, dozens of monkeys were seated on stones, as well as on the branches of the trees. Their hind legs were stretched out in front and raised to shoulder level, their arms resting on their knees. 117

"My legs are tired," she said, sinking low in her seat. "I'll stay here." 118

"Why did you have to wear those stupid shoes?" Mr. Das said. "You won't be in the pictures." 119

"Pretend I'm there." 120

"But we could use one of these pictures for our Christmas card this year. We didn't get one of all five of us at the Sun Temple. Mr. Kapasi could take it." 121

122 "I'm not coming. Anyway, those monkeys give me the creeps."

123 "But they're harmless," Mr. Das said. He turned to Mr. Kapasi. "Aren't they?"

124 "They are more hungry than dangerous," Mr. Kapasi said. "Do not provoke them with food, and they will not bother you."

125 Mr. Das headed up the defile with the children, the boys at his side, the little girl on his shoulders. Mr. Kapasi watched as they crossed paths with a Japanese man and woman, the only other tourists there, who paused for a final photograph, then stepped into a nearby car and drove away. As the car disappeared out of view some of the monkeys called out, emitting soft whooping sounds, and then walked on their flat black hands and feet up the path. At one point a group of them formed a little ring around Mr. Das and the children. Tina screamed in delight. Ronny ran in circles around his father. Bobby bent down and picked up a fat stick on the ground. When he extended it, one of the monkey's approached him and snatched it, then briefly beat the ground.

126 "I'll join them," Mr. Kapasi said, unlocking the door on his side. "There is much to explain about the caves."

127 "No. Stay a minute," Mrs. Das said. She got out of the back seat and slipped in beside Mr. Kapasi. "Raj has his dumb book anyway." Together, through the windshield, Mrs. Das and Mr. Kapasi watched as Bobby and the monkey passed the stick back and forth between them.

128 "A brave little boy," Mr. Kapasi commented.

129 "It's not so surprising," Mrs. Das said.

130 "No?"

131 "He's not his."

"I beg your pardon?" 132

"Raj's. He's not Raj's son." 133

Mr. Kapasi felt a prickle on his skin. He reached into his shirt pocket for the small tin of lotus-oil balm he carried with him at all times, and applied it to three spots on his forehead. He knew that Mrs. Das was watching him, but he did not turn to face her. Instead he watched as the figures of Mr. Das and the children grew smaller, climbing up the steep path, pausing every now and then for a picture, surrounded by a growing number of monkeys. 134

"Are you surprised?" The way she put it made him choose his words with care. 135

"It's not the type of thing one assumes," Mr. Kapasi replied slowly. He put the tin of lotus-oil balm back in his pocket. 136

"No, of course not. And no one knows, of course. No one at all. I've kept it a secret for eight whole years." She looked at Mr. Kapasi, tilting her chin as if to gain a fresh perspective. "But now I've told you." 137

Mr. Kapasi nodded. He felt suddenly parched, and his forehead was warm and slightly numb from the balm. He considered asking Mrs. Das for a sip of water, then decided against it. 138

"We met when we were very young," she said. She reached into her straw bag in search of something, then pulled out a packet of puffed rice. "Want some?" 139

"No, thank you." 140

She put a fistful in her mouth, sank into the seat a little, and looked away from Mr. Kapasi, out the window on her side of the car. "We married when we were still in college. We were in high school when he proposed. We went to the same college, of course. Back then we couldn't stand the thought of being separated, not for a day, not for a minute. Our parents were best friends who lived in the same town. My entire life I saw him every weekend, either at our house or theirs. We were sent upstairs to play together while our parents joked about our marriage. Imagine! They never caught us at anything, though in a way I think it was all more or less a setup. The things we did those Friday and Saturday nights, while our parents sat downstairs drinking tea . . . I could tell you stories, Mr. Kapasi." 141

As a result of spending all her time in college with Raj, she continued, she did not make many close friends. There was no one to confide in about him at the end of a difficult day, or to share a passing thought or a worry. Her parents now lived on the other side of the world, but she had never been very close to them, anyway. After marrying so young she was overwhelmed by it all, having a child so quickly, and nursing, and warming up bottles of milk and testing their temperature against her wrist while Raj was at work, 142 dressed in sweaters and corduroy pants, teaching his students about rocks and dinosaurs. Raj never looked cross or harried, or plump as she had become after the first baby.

143 Always tired, she declined invitations from her one or two college girlfriends, to have lunch or shop in Manhattan. Eventually the friends stopped calling her, so that she was left at home all day with the baby, surrounded by toys that made her trip when she walked or wince when she sat, always cross and tired. Only occasionally did they go out after Ronny was born, and even more rarely did they entertain. Raj didn't mind; he looked forward to coming home from teaching and watching television and bouncing Ronny on his knee. She had been outraged when Raj told her that a Punjabi friend, someone whom she had once met but did not remember, would be staying with them for a week for some job interviews in the New Brunswick area.

144 Bobby was conceived in the afternoon, on a sofa littered with rubber teething toys, after the friend learned that a London pharmaceutical company had hired him, while Ronny cried to be freed from his playpen. She made no protest when the friend touched the small of her back as she was about to make a pot of coffee, then pulled her against his crisp navy suit. He made love to her swiftly, in silence, with an expertise she had never known, without the meaningful expressions and smiles Raj always insisted on afterward. The next day Raj drove the friend to JFK. He was married now, to a Punjabi girl, and they lived in London still, and every year they exchanged Christmas cards with Raj and Mina, each couple tucking photos of their families into the envelopes. He did not know that he was Bobby's father. He never would.

145 "I beg your pardon, Mrs. Das, but why have you told me this information?" Mr. Kapasi asked when she had finally finished speaking, and had turned to face him once again.

146 "For God's sake, stop calling me Mrs. Das. I'm twenty-eight. You probably have children my age."

147 "Not quite." It disturbed Mr. Kapasi to learn that she thought of him as a parent. The feeling he had had toward her, that had made him check his reflection in the rearview mirror as they drove, evaporated a little.

148 "I told you because of your talents." She put the packet of puffed rice back into her bag without folding over the top.

149 "I don't understand," Mr. Kapasi said.

150 "Don't you see? For eight years I haven't been able to express this to anybody, not to friends, certainly not to Raj. He doesn't even suspect it. He thinks I'm still in love with him. Well, don't you have anything to say?"

He thinks I'm still in love with him.

"About what?" 151

"About what I've just told you. About my secret, 152
and about how terrible it makes me feel. I feel terrible looking at my children, and at Raj, always terrible. I have terrible urges, Mr. Kapasi, to throw things away. One day I had the urge to throw everything I own out the window, the television, the children, everything. Don't you think it's unhealthy?"

He was silent. 153

"Mr. Kapasi, don't you have anything to say? I 154
thought that was your job."

"My job is to give tours, Mrs. Das." 155

"Not that. Your other job. As an interpreter." 156

"But we do not face a language barrier. What need 157
is there for an interpreter?"

"That's not what I mean. I would never have told 158
you otherwise. Don't you realize what it means for me to tell you?"

"What does it mean?" 159

"It means that I'm tired of feeling so terrible all the 160
time. Eight years, Mr. Kapasi, I've been in pain eight years. I was hoping you could help me feel better, say the right thing. Suggest some kind of remedy."

He looked at her, in her red plaid skirt and straw- 161
berry T-shirt, a woman not yet thirty, who loved neither her husband nor her children, who had already fallen out of love with life. Her confession depressed him, depressed him all the more when he thought of Mr. Das at the top of the path, Tina clinging to his shoulders, taking pictures of ancient monastic cells cut into the hills to show his students in America, unsuspecting and unaware that one of his sons was not his own. Mr. Kapasi felt insulted that Mrs. Das should ask him to interpret her common, trivial little secret. She did not resemble the patients in the doctor's office, those who came glassy-eyed and desperate, unable to sleep or breathe or urinate with ease, unable, above all, to give words to their pains. Still, Mr. Kapasi believed it was his duty to assist Mrs. Das. Perhaps he ought to tell her to confess the truth to Mr. Das. He would explain that honesty was the best policy. Honesty, surely, would help her feel better, as she'd put it. Perhaps he would offer to preside over the discussion, as a mediator. He decided to begin with the most obvious question, to get to the heart of the matter, and so he asked, "Is it really pain you feel, Mrs. Das, or is it guilt?"

She turned to him and glared, mustard oil thick 162
on her frosty pink lips. She opened her mouth to say something, but as she glared at Mr. Kapasi some

certain knowledge seemed to pass before her eyes, and she stopped. It crushed him; he knew at that moment that he was not even important enough to be properly insulted. She opened the car door and began walking up the path, wobbling a little on her square wooden heels, reaching into her straw bag to eat handfuls of puffed rice. It fell through her fingers, leaving a zigzagging trail, causing a monkey to leap down from a tree and devour the little white grains. In search of more, the monkey began to follow Mrs. Das. Others joined him, so that she was soon being followed by about half a dozen of them, their velvety tails dragging behind.

163 Mr. Kapasi stepped out of the car. He wanted to holler, to alert her in some way, but he worried that if she knew they were behind her, she would grow nervous. Perhaps she would lose her balance. Perhaps they would pull at her bag or her hair. He began to jog up the path, taking a fallen branch in his hand to scare away the monkeys. Mrs. Das continued walking, oblivious, trailing grains of puffed rice. Near the top of the incline, before a group of cells fronted by a row of squat stone pillars, Mr. Das was kneeling on the ground, focusing the lens of his camera. The children stood under the arcade, now hiding, now emerging from view.

164 "Wait for me," Mrs. Das called out. "I'm coming."

165 Tina jumped up and down. "Here comes Mommy!"

166 "Great," Mr. Das said without looking up. "Just in time. We'll get Mr. Kapasi to take a picture of the five of us."

167 Mr. Kapasi quickened his pace, waving his branch so that the monkeys scampered away, distracted, in another direction.

168 "Where's Bobby?" Mrs. Das asked when she stopped.

169 Mr. Das looked up from the camera. "I don't know. Ronny, where's Bobby?"

170 Ronny shrugged. "I thought he was right here."

171 "Where is he?" Mrs. Das repeated sharply. "What's wrong with all of you?"

172 They began calling his name, wandering up and down the path a bit. Because they were calling, they did not initially hear the boy's screams. When they found him, a little farther down the path under a tree, he was surrounded by a group of monkeys, over a dozen of them, pulling at his T-shirt with their long black fingers. The puffed rice Mrs. Das had spilled was scattered at his feet, raked over by the monkeys' hands. The boy was silent, his body frozen, swift tears running down his startled face. His bare legs were dusty and red with welts from where one of the monkeys struck him repeatedly with the stick he had given it earlier.

"Daddy, the monkey's hurting Bobby," Tina said. 1

Mr. Das wiped his palms on the front of his shorts. 1
In his nervousness he accidentally pressed the shutter on his camera; the whirring noise of the advancing film excited the moneys, and the one with the stick began to beat Bobby more intently. "What are we supposed to do? What if they start attacking?"

"Mr. Kapasi," Mrs. Das shrieked, noticing him 1
standing to one side. "Do something, for God's sake, do something!"

The animals retreated slowly, with a measured gait, obedient but unintimidated.

Mr. Kapasi took his branch 1
and shooed them away, hissing at the ones that remained, stomping his feet to scare them. The animals retreated slowly, with a measured gait, obedient but unintimidated. Mr. Kapasi gathered Bobby in his arms and brought him back to where his parents and siblings were standing. As he carried him he was tempted to whisper a secret into the boy's ear. But Bobby was stunned, and shivering with fright, his legs bleeding slightly where the stick had broken the skin. When Mr. Kapasi delivered him to his parents, Mr. Das brushed some dirt off the boy's T-shirt and put the visor on him the right way. Mrs. Das reached into her straw bag to find a bandage which she taped over the cut on his knee. Ronny offered his brother a fresh piece of gum. "He's fine. Just a little scared, right, Bobby?" Mr. Das said, patting the top of his head.

"God, let's get out of here," Mrs. Das said. She 1
folded her arms across the strawberry on her chest. "This place gives me the creeps."

"Yeah. Back to the hotel, definitely," Mr. Das 1
agreed.

"Poor Bobby," Mrs. Das said. "Come here a second. 1
Let Mommy fix your hair." Again she reached into her straw bag, this time for her hairbrush, and began to run it around the edges of the translucent visor. When she whipped out the hairbrush, the slip of paper with Mr. Kapasi's address on it fluttered away in the wind. No one but Mr. Kapasi noticed. He watched as it rose, carried higher and higher by the breeze, into the trees where the monkeys now sat, solemnly observing the scene below. Mr. Kapasi observed it too, knowing that this was the picture of the Das family he would preserve forever in his mind.

IF you enjoyed "Interpreter of Maladies," you will probably admire "An Astrologer's Day" (in Stories for Further Reading), by R. K. Narayan, an Indian writer to whom Lahiri herself looks for inspiration.

**GOING FURTHER** Lahiri's more recent fiction, such as *The Namesake* and *Unaccustomed Earth,* belongs to a long line of books that dramatize in universal ways the themes that grow out of immigration to the United States. Examples include Henry Roth's 1934 classic *Call It Sleep,* about immigrant Jews living in New York City's slums, Edwidge Danticat's *The Dew Breaker,* and Junot Diaz's Pulitzer Prize–winning novel of 2007, *The Brief Wondrous Life of Oscar Wao.*

# Writing from Reading

### Summarize

1 Examine Mr. Kapasi's daydreams of his future with Mrs. Das. What does he expect from their interactions? What is it that he is looking for that he doesn't currently have with his wife?

### Analyze Craft

2 Discuss why the story begins with Mr. Kapasi's observations of Mrs. Das, and how they help set up what the story is *about.*

3 Analyze the thematic importance of the story's title. What are the maladies in this story? What does it mean to be an interpreter of maladies?

### Analyze Voice

4 Jhumpa Lahiri has referred to her conflicting selves—the Indian and the American. How does this dual cultural background come through in her narration of "Interpreter of Maladies"? What details and themes strike you as more American or more Indian? Explain why.

### Synthesize Summary and Analysis

5 Discuss what role the monkeys play in the story. Consider when and where they appear and how various characters respond to them.

### Interpret the Story

6 While they wait for Tina and Mrs. Das to emerge from the bathroom, Mr. Das says to Mr. Kapasi: "We have a lot in common, you could say, you and I." Is this true? What do these two men have in common? Explain how the rest of the story serves to prove, disprove, or change the meaning of this statement.

# Reading for Theme

When reading for **theme**, go beyond the plot and subject of the story and ask yourself what truths or insights about the human experience the story offers.

| | |
|---|---|
| **Does the title point to a major symbol, character, or subject from which themes develop?** | EXAMPLES: "The Jilting of Granny Weatherall," "The Death of Ivan Ilych," and "Why I Live at the P.O." |
| **Does the title point to a central irony that is thematic?** | EXAMPLES: "The Short Happy Life of Francis Macomber," "No One's a Mystery." |
| **Does the title point to thematic concerns of the story?** | EXAMPLES:<br>• "Who's Irish?" calls up the question of identity.<br>• "Araby" conjures an exotic dream.<br>• "The Rememberer" calls to mind the person left behind after a loss. |
| **Does the narrator or another character make general statements as observations that may offer insight into the writer's theme?** | EXAMPLE: *Moby-Dick*'s narrator asserts that a subject must be larger than ordinary or everyday to accommodate a large theme. |
| **What changes in the main character? What does the main character come to realize?** | EXAMPLES:<br>• In Alice Munro's "An Ounce of Cure," the narrator says in the last line, "I am a grown-up woman now."<br>• In John Updike's "A&P," the young narrator realizes "how hard the world was going to be to me from here on in." |
| **Note powerful details and ask yourself why this is important. What does this make you feel? How do events or details thread together the meaning beyond a particular situation?** | EXAMPLES:<br>• The frail back of the old man on the wet floor (*What* do *I* feel when I think about that old man?).<br>• The uneaten rice (*How* did these events affect Nnamabia?).<br>• The tears in the brother's eyes (*Why* did the sister feel that tenderness?).<br>Continued |

| | | |
|---|---|---|
| A literary work can have multiple themes. Does the proposed theme tie the elements of the story together? Ask questions that go beyond the surface and the events. Theme grows seamlessly from plot, setting, style, characterization, and all the other elements of the writer's craft. In each, theme emerges from our reading and questioning of the story in all its twists and permutations. | | |
| **How do you state a theme?** | • Formulate a general idea that is not tied to specific details in the story or to a particular character in the story but to all human beings. | **Too limited:** "The Short Happy Life of Francis Macomber" is about a man who struggles with questions of courage during a big-game hunt.<br>**More precise:** "The Short Happy Life of Francis Macomber" is a story about marriage and manhood and the testing of courage in both. |
| | • Write a complete sentence that goes beyond the subject and includes some conclusion or attitude about the subject. | **Too broad:** Adulthood<br>**More precise:** Adulthood can be a burden but also a highly prized period of life. |

# Suggestions for Writing about Theme

1. How do Stephen Crane and Jhumpa Lahiri raise thematic issues by use of descriptions of setting? Compare the authors' techniques in "The Open Boat" and "Interpreter of Maladies."
2. Select two stories in this chapter and show how, although their plots differ, they explore a similar theme. Throughout, back up your claims with specific lines or passages from the story.
3. Compare and contrast the role of monkeys in "Interpreter of Maladies" with that of the seagulls in "The Open Boat."
4. Compare and contrast the theme of change in Adichie's "Cell One" and Crane's "The Open Boat." In each, how do the characters change and what are the factors that prompt the change?

# 10

# SYM

"BRIEFLY, in the rain, Lieutenant Cross saw Martha's gray eyes gazing back at him.

He understood.

It was very sad, he thought. The things men carried inside. The things men did or felt they had to do.

He almost nodded at her, but didn't.

Instead he went back to his maps. He was now determined to perform his duties firmly and without negligence. It wouldn't help Lavender, he knew that, but from this point on he would comport himself as an officer. He would dispose of his good-luck pebble. Swallow it, maybe, or use Lee Strunk's slingshot, or just drop it along the trail."

*—from "The Things They Carried" by Tim O'Brien*

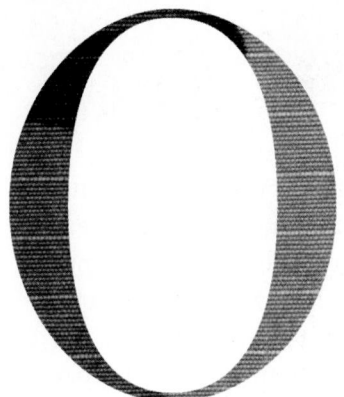

*"A symbol, although it's a literary-sounding word . . . has a meaning that goes beyond textbooks. It has to do with what objects of the world, things of the world, end up meaning to us. . . . In ["The Things They Carried"] the book starts with a list of physical objects . . . The pebble that Jimmy Cross carried and the pantyhose carried by Henry Dobbins and all the military paraphernalia all the men carry. . . . The object has meaning, has resonance and has echoes . . . [ in] the spiritual burdens that not only the soldiers carry through a war—but the burden[s] that all of us carry through our lives: fear, piety, loss, grief, love, nostalgia."*

Conversation with Tim O'Brien, available on video at www.mhhe.com/delbanco1e

# BOL

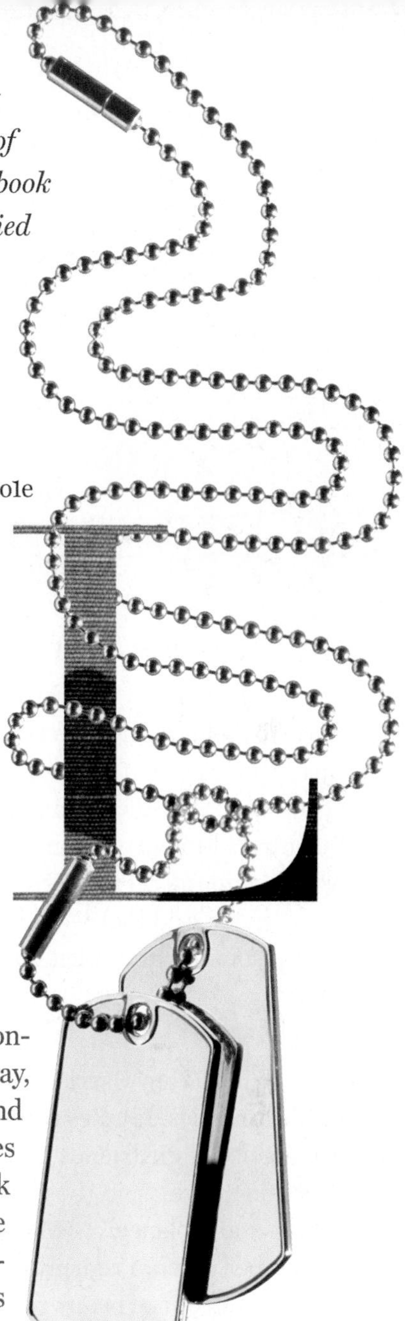

A YOUNG American lieutenant in Vietnam during the war imagines the eyes of Martha, a girl back home who has become the center of his fantasies. During much of the action, he dreams of her love; now he understands that she has been a distraction and he must focus on duty instead. We've caught him in a sad, contemplative moment—coming to an understanding about the burdens of leadership and how he must "perform his duties firmly and without negligence." The boy at the beginning of the story has "understood" and grown into a man.

This narrative introduces the members of Lieutenant Cross's platoon—describing in an inventory-like manner what each carries on his back as well as in his heart. They trek through jungles and villages; they deal with weather, boredom, and enemy attack. By telling us what the soldiers carry, O'Brien shows us who they are—each with his special burden, each terrified and confused and, in his own way, heroic. If you think beyond the surface of the images in the story—the good-luck pebble, the maps, even the names Cross and Lavender—you enter it in terms of its symbolic resonance. A **symbol,** in the literary sense, is any object, image, character, or action that suggests meaning beyond the everyday literal level. In contemporary literature, symbols don't work in a simple equation of *A = B* or *This means that.* They acquire meaning from a rich matrix of associations. All elements—plot, character, point of view, setting, tone, and theme—contribute to the effect.

*CONTINUED ON PAGE 324*

*Art can be born out of playful intent, having fun.*

*. . . I began to recognize something that mattered . . .*

# Q&A
# *A Conversation on Writing*
## Tim O'Brien

### On Becoming a Writer in Vietnam

I think that somewhere during those months in Vietnam, as I sat in those foxholes at night, was when writing became serious for me. It was serious not in the sense of "I'm going to publish" or "I'm going to be a writer," but the writing itself was serious. It was written partly, I think, as kind of a testament that, if I were to be killed, these words would be found on my person, would be sent to my mom or my dad or my sister, and they would have some sense of their son and brother's personality and spirit during those life-and-death days of war.

### On Memory and Writing about War

"The Things They Carried" is organized around, just in terms of locale, foxholes. It takes place largely around men talking and reminiscing about girlfriends and hometowns and religion and the world they don't have . . . in those hours a soldier has that aren't full of horror and violence. . . . Moments in Vietnam were horrible. I don't remember much. I remember saying, "Dear Jesus, dear Jesus," as I was wounded, but I can't remember much before that or much afterwards, for that matter. What I do remember vividly are those quiet moments when you'd reflect back on what happened.

### On the Writing Process

I had originally started writing *The Things They Carried* playfully as a game. . . . . Art can be born out of playful intent, having fun. And my idea was to have fun with the word "carry." I wanted to find how many ways can I use the word: *carry* himself with poise; *carry* yourself with dignity; *carried* in the usual sense; "*carry* on, men."

**To watch this entire interview and hear the author read from "The Things They Carried," go to www.mhhe.com/delbanco1e.**

Tim O'Brien's biography begins like many American biographies, and a summary might include: He grew up in Minnesota and had a successful college career. However, the summer after graduation, O'Brien was drafted into the Vietnam War and embarked upon an experience that shaped the rest of his life and much of his fiction. He fought for a little over a year, earning both a Purple Heart and a Bronze Star. His first book was a memoir, *If I Die in a Combat Zone: Box Me Up and Ship Me Home* (1973), and two years thereafter he published his first novel, *Northern Lights*.

Like many of the characters in his fiction, O'Brien seems haunted by the experience of combat, unable to relegate it comfortably to the past. Although he has written on other topics, the majority of his books deal in some way with Vietnam and the transforming effects of battle—a battle from which (though the deserter in *Going after Cacciato* literally walks out of Southeast Asia) there's no true escape. Continually, even obsessively, O'Brien describes the condition of life as a soldier and war's aftermath. It is his great subject and recurrent theme.

Such books as *Going after Cacciato* (1978), *The Things They Carried* (1990), and *The Nuclear Age* (1985) masterfully blend short story and memoir, fiction and nonfiction, while exploring themes of courage, morality, love, truth, and ambiguity. In *The Things They Carried,* for example, O'Brien highlights "story truth" as the truth that the reader's stomach believes and "happening truth" as the mere facts of what occurred.

**RESEARCH ASSIGNMENT** In his interview, O'Brien says he could have set "The Things They Carried" in a different locale. How would this have changed the story, and what do you think the foxholes add to the setting of the story?

**AS YOU READ** As you read, notice the differences between "the things" the characters carry on their backs and "the things" they carry in their minds and hearts. How do the two kinds of burdens weigh on these men? What do they carry that inspires or soothes them?

**TIPS**

**FOR INTERACTIVE READING . . .**

- Choose three characters and circle all the things they carried. How do these objects characterize them? What do the objects reveal about them? Do these objects complete our understanding of the men or limit it?
- O'Brien introduces a vocabulary of war. Find and circle the special terms the men have for what they do and what they experience.

# The Things They Carried (1986)

1 FIRST Lieutenant Jimmy Cross carried letters from a girl named Martha, a junior at Mount Sebastian College in New Jersey. They were not love letters, but Lieutenant Cross was hoping, so he kept them folded in plastic at the bottom of his rucksack. In the late afternoon, after a day's march, he would dig his foxhole, wash his hands under a canteen, unwrap the letters, hold them with the tips of his fingers, and spend the last hour of light pretending. He would imagine romantic camping trips into the White Mountains in New Hampshire. He would sometimes taste the envelope flaps, knowing her tongue had been there. More than anything, he wanted Martha to love him as he loved her, but the letters were mostly chatty, elusive on the matter of love. She was a virgin, he was almost sure. She was an English major at Mount Sebastian, and she wrote beautifully about her professors and roommates and midterm exams, about her respect for Chaucer and her great affection for Virginia Woolf. She often quoted lines of poetry; she never mentioned the war, except to say, Jimmy, take care of yourself. The letters weighed ten ounces. They were signed "Love, Martha," but Lieutenant Cross understood that "Love" was only a way of signing and did not mean what he sometimes pretended it meant. At dusk, he would carefully return the letters to his rucksack. Slowly, a bit distracted, he would get up and move among his men, checking the perimeter, then at full dark he would return to his hole and watch the night and wonder if Martha was a virgin.

The things they carried were largely determined 2
by necessity. Among the necessities or near necessities were P-38 can openers, pocket knives, heat tabs, wrist watches, dog tags, mosquito repellant, chewing gum, candy, cigarettes, salt tablets, packets of Kool-Aid, lighters, matches, sewing kits, Military Payment Certificates, C rations, and two or three canteens of water. Together, these items weighed between fifteen and twenty pounds, depending upon a man's habits or rate of metabolism. Henry Dobbins, who was a big man, carried extra rations; he was especially fond of canned peaches in heavy syrup over pound cake. Dave Jensen, who practiced field hygiene, carried a toothbrush, dental floss, and several hotel-size bars of soap he'd stolen on R&R in Sydney, Australia. Ted Lavender, who was scared, carried tranquilizers until he was shot in the head outside the village of Than Khe in mid-April. By necessity, and because it was SOP, they all carried steel helmets that weighed five pounds including the liner and camouflage cover. They carried the standard fatigue jackets and trousers. Very few

carried underwear. On their feet they carried jungle boots—2.1 pounds—and Dave Jensen carried three pairs of socks and a can of Dr. Scholl's foot powder as a precaution against trench foot. Until he was shot, Ted Lavender carried six or seven ounces of premium dope, which for him was a necessity. Mitchell Sanders, the RTO, carried condoms. Norman Bowker carried a diary. Rat Kiley carried comic books. Kiowa, a devout Baptist, carried an illustrated New Testament that had been presented to him by his father, who taught Sunday school in Oklahoma City, Oklahoma. As a hedge against bad times, however, Kiowa also carried his grandmother's distrust of the white man, his grandfather's old hunting hatchet. Necessity dictated. Because the land was mined and booby-trapped, it was SOP for each man to carry a steel-centered, nylon-covered flak jacket, which weighed 6.7 pounds, but which on hot days seemed much heavier. Because you could die so quickly, each man carried at least one large compress bandage, usually in the helmet band for easy access. Because the nights were cold, and because the monsoons were wet, each carried a green plastic poncho that could be used as a raincoat or groundsheet or makeshift tent. With its quilted liner, the poncho weighed almost two pounds, but it was worth every ounce. In April, for instance, when Ted Lavender was shot, they used his poncho to wrap him up, then to carry him across the paddy, then to lift him into the chopper that took him away.

He carried a strobe light and the responsibility for the lives of his men.

3 THEY were called legs or grunts.

4 To carry something was to "hump" it, as when Lieutenant Jimmy Cross humped his love for Martha up the hills and through the swamps. In its intransitive form, "to hump," meant "to walk," or "to march," but it implied burdens far beyond the intransitive.

5 Almost everyone humped photographs. In his wallet, Lieutenant Cross carried two photographs of Martha. The first was a Kodachrome snapshot signed "Love," though he knew better. She stood against a brick wall. Her eyes were gray and neutral, her lips slightly open as she stared straight-on at the camera. At night, sometimes, Lieutenant Cross wondered who had taken the picture, because he knew she had boyfriends, because he loved her so much, and because he could see the shadow of the picture taker spreading out against the brick wall. The second photograph had been clipped from the 1968 Mount Sebastian yearbook. It was an action shot—women's volleyball—and Martha was bent horizontal to the floor, reaching, the palms of her hands in sharp focus, the tongue taut, the expression frank and competitive. There was no visible sweat. She wore white gym shorts. Her legs, he thought, were almost certainly the legs of a virgin, dry and without hair, the left knee cocked and carrying her entire weight, which was just over one hundred pounds. Lieutenant Cross remembered touching that left knee. A dark theater, he remembered, and the movie was *Bonnie and Clyde,* and Martha wore a tweed skirt, and during the final scene, when he touched her knee, she turned and looked at him in a sad, sober way that made him pull his hand back, but he would always remember the feel of the tweed skirt and the knee beneath it and the sound of the gunfire that killed Bonnie and Clyde, how embarrassing it was, how slow and oppressive. He remembered kissing her good night at the dorm door. Right then, he thought, he should've done something brave. He should've carried her up the stairs to her room and tied her to the bed and touched that left knee all night long. He should've risked it. Whenever he looked at the photographs, he thought of new things he should've done.

WHAT they carried was partly a function of rank, partly of field specialty. 6

As a first lieutenant and platoon leader, Jimmy Cross carried a compass, maps, code books, binoculars, and a .45-caliber pistol that weighed 2.9 pounds fully loaded. He carried a strobe light and the responsibility for the lives of his men. 7

As an RTO, Mitchell Sanders carried the PRC-25 radio, a killer, twenty-six pounds with its battery. 8

As a medic, Rat Kiley carried a canvas satchel filled with morphine and plasma and malaria tablets and surgical tape and comic books and all the things a medic must carry, including M&M's for especially bad wounds, for a total weight of nearly twenty pounds. 9

As a big man, therefore a machine gunner, Henry Dobbins carried the M-60, which weighed twenty-three pounds unloaded, but which was almost always loaded. In addition, Dobbins carried between ten and fifteen pounds of ammunition draped in belts across his chest and shoulders. 10

As PFCs or Spec 4s, most of them were common grunts and carried the standard M-16 gas-operated assault rifle. The weapon weighed 7.5 pounds unloaded, 8.2 pounds with its full twenty-round magazine. Depending on numerous factors, such as topography 11 and psychology, the riflemen carried anywhere from twelve to twenty magazines, usually in cloth bandoliers, adding on another 8.4 pounds at minimum, fourteen pounds at maximum. When it was available, they also carried M-16 maintenance gear—rods and steel brushes and swabs and tubes of LSA oil—all of which weighed about a pound. Among the grunts, some carried the M-79 grenade launcher, 5.9 pounds unloaded, a reasonably light weapon except for the ammunition, which was heavy. A single round weighed ten ounces. The typical load was twenty-five rounds. But Ted Lavender, who was scared, carried thirty-four rounds when he was shot and killed outside Than Khe, and he went down under an exceptional burden, more than twenty pounds of ammunition, plus the flak jacket and helmet and rations and water and toilet paper and tranquilizers and all the rest, plus the unweighed fear. He was dead weight. There was no twitching or flopping. Kiowa, who saw it happen, said it was like watching a rock fall, or a big sandbag or something—just boom, then down—not like the movies where the dead guy rolls around and does fancy spins and goes ass over teakettle—not like that, Kiowa said, the poor bastard just flat-fuck fell. Boom. Down. Nothing else. It was a bright morning in mid-April. Lieutenant Cross felt the pain. He blamed himself. They stripped off Lavender's canteens and ammo, all the heavy things, and Rat Kiley said the obvious, the guy's dead, and Mitchell Sanders used his radio to report one U.S. KIA and to request a chopper. Then they wrapped Lavender in his poncho. They carried him out to a dry paddy, established security, and sat smoking the dead man's dope until the chopper came. Lieutenant Cross kept to himself. He pictured Martha's smooth young face, thinking he loved her more than anything, more than his men, and now Ted Lavender was dead because he loved her so much and could not stop thinking about her. When the dust-off arrived, they carried Lavender aboard. Afterward they burned Than Khe. They marched until dusk, then dug their holes, and that night Kiowa kept explaining how you had to be there, how fast it was, how the poor guy just dropped like so much concrete, Boom-down, he said. Like cement.

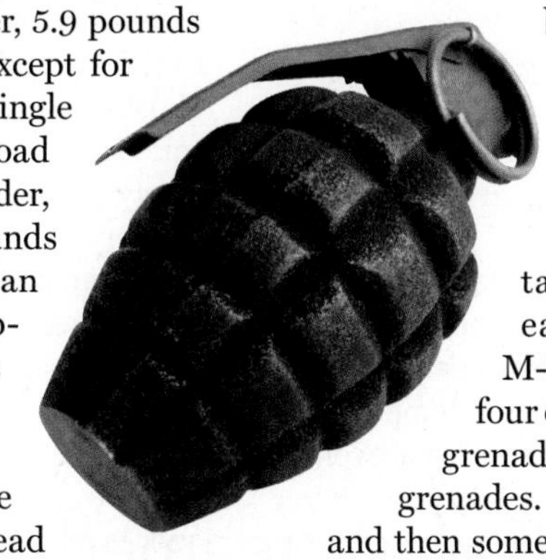

2 IN addition to the three standard weapons—the M-60, M-16, and M-79—they carried whatever presented itself, or whatever seemed appropriate as a means of killing or staying alive. They carried catch-as-catch-can. At various times, in various situations, they carried M-14s and CAR-15s and Swedish Ks and grease guns and captured AK-47s and ChiCom's and RPGs and Simonov carbines and black-market Uzis and .38-caliber Smith & Wesson handguns and 66 mm LAW's and shotguns and silencers and blackjacks and bayonets and C-4 plastic explosives. Lee Strunk carried a slingshot; a weapon of last resort, he called it. Mitchell Sanders carried brass knuckles. Kiowa carried his grandfather's feathered hatchet. Every third or fourth man carried a Claymore antipersonnel mine—3.5 pounds with its firing device. They all carried fragmentation grenades—fourteen ounces each. They all carried at least one M-18 colored smoke grenade—twenty-four ounces. Some carried CS or tear-gas grenades. Some carried white-phosphorus grenades. They carried all they could bear, and then some, including a silent awe for the terrible power of the things they carried.

In the first week of April, before Lavender died, 13
Lieutenant Jimmy Cross received a good-luck charm from Martha. It was a simple pebble, an ounce at most. Smooth to the touch, it was a milky-white color with flecks of orange and violet, oval-shaped, like a miniature egg. In the accompanying letter, Martha wrote that she had found the pebble on the Jersey shoreline, precisely where the land touched water at high tide, where things came together but also separated. It was this separate-but-together quality, she wrote, that had inspired her to pick up the pebble and to carry it in her breast pocket for several days, where it seemed weightless, and then to send it through the mail, by air, as a token of her truest feelings for him. Lieutenant Cross found this romantic. But he wondered what her truest feelings were, exactly, and what she meant by separate-but-together. He wondered how the tides and waves had come into play on that afternoon along the Jersey shoreline when Martha saw the pebble and bent down to rescue it from geology. He imagined bare feet. Martha was a poet, with the poet's sensibilities, and her feet would be brown and bare, the toenails unpainted, the eyes chilly and somber like the ocean in March, and though it was painful, he wondered who had been with her that afternoon. He imagined a pair of shadows moving along the strip of sand where things came together but also separated. It was phantom jealousy, he knew, but he couldn't help himself. He loved her so much. On the march, through the hot days of early April, he carried the pebble in his mouth, turning it with his tongue, tasting sea salts and moisture. His mind wandered. He had difficulty keeping

his attention on the war. On occasion he would yell at his men to spread out the column, to keep their eyes open, but then he would slip away into daydreams, just pretending, walking barefoot along the Jersey shore, with Martha, carrying nothing. He would feel himself rising. Sun and waves and gentle winds, all love and lightness.

14 WHAT they carried varied by mission.

15 When a mission took them to the mountains, they carried mosquito netting, machetes, canvas tarps, and extra bug juice.

16 If a mission seemed especially hazardous, or if it involved a place they knew to be bad, they carried everything they could. In certain heavily mined AOs, where the land was dense with Toe Poppers and Bouncing Betties, they took turns humping a twenty-eight-pound mine detector. With its headphones and big sensing plate, the equipment was a stress on the lower back and shoulders, awkward to handle, often useless because of the shrapnel in the earth, but they carried it anyway, partly for safety, partly for the illusion of safety.

**If you screamed, how far would the sound carry?**

17 On ambush, or other night missions, they carried peculiar little odds and ends. Kiowa always took along his New Testament and a pair of moccasins for silence. Dave Jensen carried night-sight vitamins high in carotene. Lee Strunk carried his slingshot; ammo, he claimed, would never be a problem. Rat Kiley carried brandy and M&M's. Until he was shot, Ted Lavender carried the starlight scope, which weighed 6.3 pounds with its aluminum carrying case. Henry Dobbins carried his girlfriend's pantyhose wrapped around his neck as a comforter. They all carried ghosts. When dark came, they would move out single file across the meadows and paddies to their ambush coordinates, where they would quietly set up the Claymores and lie down and spend the night waiting.

18 Other missions were more complicated and required special equipment. In mid-April, it was their mission to search out and destroy the elaborate tunnel complexes in the Than Khe area south of Chu Lai. To blow the tunnels, they carried one-pound blocks of pentrite high explosives; four blocks to a man, sixty-eight pounds in all. They carried wiring, detonators, and battery-powered clackers. Dave Jensen carried earplugs. Most often, before blowing the tunnels, they were ordered by higher command to search them, which was considered bad news, but by and large they just shrugged and carried out orders. Because he was a big man, Henry Dobbins was excused from tunnel duty. The others would draw numbers. Before Lavender died there were seventeen men in the platoon, and whoever drew the number seventeen would strip off his gear and crawl in head first with a flashlight and Lieutenant Cross's .45-caliber pistol. The rest of them would fan out as security. They would sit down or kneel, not facing the hole, listening to the ground beneath them, imagining cobwebs and ghosts, whatever was down there—the tunnel walls squeezing in—how the flashlight seemed impossibly heavy in the hand and how it was tunnel vision in the very strictest sense, compression in all ways, even time, and how you had to wiggle in—ass and elbows—a swallowed-up feeling—and how you found yourself worrying about odd things—will your flashlight go dead? Do rats carry rabies? If you screamed, how far would the sound carry? Would your buddies hear it? Would they have the courage to drag you out? In some respects, though not many, the waiting was worse than the tunnel itself. Imagination was a killer.

On April 16, when Lee Strunk drew the number seventeen, he laughed and muttered something and went down quickly. The morning was hot and very still. Not good, Kiowa said. He looked at the tunnel opening, then out across a dry paddy toward the village of Than Khe. Nothing moved. No clouds or birds or people. As they waited, the men smoked and drank Kool-Aid, not talking much, feeling sympathy for Lee Strunk but also feeling the luck of the draw, You win some, you lose some, said Mitchell Sanders, and sometimes you settle for a rain check. It was a tired line and no one laughed. 19

Henry Dobbins ate a tropical chocolate bar. Ted Lavender popped a tranquilizer and went off to pee. 20

After five minutes, Lieutenant Jimmy Cross moved to the tunnel, leaned down, and examined the darkness. Trouble, he thought—a cave-in maybe. And then suddenly, without willing it, he was thinking about Martha. The stresses and fractures, the quick collapse, the two of them buried alive under all that weight. Dense, crushing love. Kneeling, watching the hole, he tried to concentrate on Lee Strunk and the war, all the dangers, but his love was too much for him, he felt paralyzed, he wanted to sleep inside her lungs and breathe her blood and be smothered. He wanted her to be a virgin and not a virgin, all at once. He wanted to know her. Intimate secrets—why poetry? Why so sad? Why the grayness in her eyes? Why so alone? Not lonely, just alone—riding her bike across campus or sitting off by herself in the cafeteria. Even dancing, she danced 21 alone—and it was the aloneness that filled him with love. He remembered telling her that one evening. How she nodded and looked away. And how, later, when he kissed her, she received the kiss without returning it, her eyes wide open, not afraid, not a virgin's eyes, just flat and uninvolved.

2 Lieutenant Cross gazed at the tunnel. But he was not there. He was buried with Martha under the white sand at the Jersey shore. They were pressed together, and the pebble in his mouth was her tongue. He was smiling. Vaguely, he was aware of how quiet the day was, the sullen paddies, yet he could not bring himself to worry about matters of security. He was beyond that. He was just a kid at war, in love. He was twenty-two years old. He couldn't help it.

3 A few moments later Lee Strunk crawled out of the tunnel. He came up grinning, filthy but alive. Lieutenant Cross nodded and closed his eyes while the others clapped Strunk on the back and made jokes about rising from the dead.

4 Worms, Rat Kiley said. Right out of the grave. Fuckin' zombie.

5 The men laughed. They all felt great relief.

6 Spook City, said Mitchell Sanders.

7 Lee Strunk made a funny ghost sound, a kind of moaning, yet very happy, and right then, when Strunk made that high happy moaning sound, when he went *Ahhooooo,* right then Ted Lavender was shot in the head on his way back from peeing. He lay with his mouth open. The teeth were broken. There was a swollen black bruise under his left eye. The cheekbone was gone. Oh shit, Rat Kiley said, the guy's dead. The guy's dead, he kept saying, which seemed profound—the guy's dead. I mean really.

8 THE things they carried were determined to some extent by superstition. Lieutenant Cross carried his good-luck pebble. Dave Jensen carried a rabbit's foot. Norman Bowker, otherwise a very gentle person, carried a thumb that had been presented to him as a gift by Mitchell Sanders. The thumb was dark brown, rubbery to the touch, and weighed four ounces at most. It had been cut from a VC corpse, a boy of fifteen or sixteen. They'd found him at the bottom of an irrigation ditch, badly burned, flies in his mouth and eyes. The boy wore black shorts and sandals. At the time of his death he had been carrying a pouch of rice, a rifle, and three magazines of ammunition.

You want my opinion, Mitchell Sanders said, there's a definite moral here. 29

He put his hand on the dead boy's wrist. He was quiet for a time, as if counting a pulse, then he patted the stomach, almost affectionately, and used Kiowa's hunting hatchet to remove the thumb. 30

Henry Dobbins asked what the moral was. 31

Moral? 32

You know. *Moral.* 33

Sanders wrapped the thumb in toilet paper and handed it across to Norman Bowker. There was no blood. Smiling, he kicked the boy's head, watched the files scatter, and said, It's like with that old TV show—Paladin. Have gun, will travel. 34

Henry Dobbins thought about it. 35

Yeah, well, he finally said. I don't see no moral. 36

There it *is,* man. 37

Fuck off. 38

THEY carried USO stationery and pencils and pens. They carried Sterno, safety pins, trip flares, signal flares, spools of wire, razor blades, chewing tobacco, liberated joss sticks and statuettes of the smiling Buddha, candles, grease pencils, *The Stars and Stripes,* fingernail clippers, Psy Ops leaflets, bush hats, bolos, and much more. Twice a week, when the resupply choppers came in, they carried hot chow in green Mermite cans and large canvas bags filled with iced beer and soda pop. They carried plastic water containers, each with a two-gallon capacity. Mitchell Sanders carried a set of starched tiger fatigues for special occasions. Henry Dobbins carried Black Flag insecticide. Dave Jensen carried empty sandbags that could be filled at night for added protection. Lee Strunk carried tanning lotion. Some things they carried in common. Taking turns, they carried the big PRC-77 scrambler radio, which weighed thirty pounds with its battery. They shared the weight of memory. They took up what others could no longer bear. Often, they carried each other, the wounded or weak. They carried infections. They carried chess sets, basketballs, Vietnamese-English dictionaries, insignia of rank, Bronze Stars and Purple Hearts, plastic cards imprinted with the Code of Conduct. They carried diseases, among them malaria and dysentery. They carried lice and ringworm and leeches and paddy algae and various rots and molds. They carried the land itself—Vietnam, the place, the soil—a powdery orange-red dust 39 that covered their boots and fatigues and faces. They carried the sky. The whole atmosphere, they carried it, the humidity, the monsoons, the stink of fungus and decay, all of it, they carried gravity. They moved like mules. By daylight they took sniper fire, at night they were mortared, but it was not battle, it was just the endless march, village to village, without purpose, nothing won or lost. They marched for the sake of the march. They plodded along slowly, dumbly, leaning forward against the heat, unthinking, all blood and bone, simple grunts, soldiering with their legs, toiling up the hills and down into the paddies and across the rivers and up again and down, just humping, one step and then the next and then another, but no volition, no will, because it was automatic, it was anatomy, and the war was entirely a matter of posture and carriage, the hump was everything, a kind of inertia, a kind of emptiness, a dullness of desire and intellect and conscience and hope and human sensibility. Their principles were in their feet. Their calculations were biological. They had no sense of strategy or mission. They searched the villages without knowing what to look for, not caring, kicking over jars of rice, frisking children and old men, blowing tunnels, sometimes setting fires and sometimes not, then forming up and moving on to the next village, then other villages, where it would always be the same. They carried their own lives. The pressures were enormous. In the heat of early afternoon, they would remove their helmets and flak jackets, walking bare, which was dangerous but which helped ease the strain. They would often discard things along the route of march. Purely for comfort, they would throw away rations, blow their Claymores and grenades, no matter, because by nightfall the resupply choppers would arrive with more of the same, then a day or two later still more, fresh watermelons and crates of ammunition and sunglasses and woolen sweaters—the resources were stunning—sparklers for the Fourth of July, colored eggs for Easter. It was the great American war chest—the fruits of science, the smokestacks, the canneries, the arsenals at Hartford, the Minnesota forests, the machine shops, the vast fields of corn and wheat—they carried like freight trains; they carried it on their backs and shoulders—and for all the ambiguities of Vietnam, all the mysteries and unknowns, there was at least the single abiding certainty that they would never be at a loss for things to carry.

AFTER the chopper took Lavender away, Lieutenant Jimmy Cross led his men into the village of Than Khe. They burned everything. They shot chickens and dogs, they trashed the village well, they called in artillery and watched the wreckage, then they marched for several hours through the hot afternoon, and then at dusk, while Kiowa explained how Lavender died, Lieutenant Cross found himself trembling. 40

He tried not to cry. With his entrenching tool, which weighed five pounds, he began digging a hole in the earth. 41

He felt shame. He hated himself. He had loved Martha more than his men, and as a consequence Lavender was now dead, and this was something he would have to carry like a stone in his stomach for the rest of the war. 42

All he could do was dig. He used his entrenching tool like an ax, slashing, feeling both love and hate, and then later, when it was full dark, he sat at the bottom of his foxhole and wept. It went on for a long while. In part, he was grieving for Ted Lavender, but mostly it was for Martha, and for himself, because she belonged to another world, which was not quite real, and because she was a junior at Mount Sebastian College in New Jersey, a poet and a virgin and uninvolved, and because he realized she did not love him and never would. 43

LIKE cement, Kiowa whispered in the dark. I swear to God—boom-down. Not a word. 44

I've heard this, said Norman Bowker. 45

A pisser, you know? Still zipping himself up. Zapped while zipping. 46

All right, fine. That's enough. 47

Yeah, but you had to see it, the guy just— 48

I *heard,* man. Cement. So why not shut the fuck *up?* 49

Kiowa shook his head sadly and glanced over at the hole where Lieutenant Jimmy Cross sat watching the night. The air was thick and wet. A warm, dense fog had settled over the paddies and there was the stillness that precedes rain. 50

After a time Kiowa sighed. 51

One thing for sure, he said. The Lieutenant's in some deep hurt. I mean that crying jag—the way he was carrying on—it wasn't fake or anything, it was real heavy-duty hurt. The man cares. 52

Sure, Norman Bowker said. 53

Say what you want, the man does care. 54

5 We all got problems.

6 Not Lavender.

7 No, I guess not, Bowker said. Do me a favor, though.

8 Shut up?

9 That's a smart Indian. Shut up.

0 Shrugging, Kiowa pulled off his boots. He wanted to say more, just to lighten up his sleep, but instead he opened his New Testament and arranged it beneath his head as a pillow. The fog made things seem hollow and unattached. He tried not to think about Ted Lavender, but then he was thinking how fast it was, no drama, down and dead, and how it was hard to feel anything except surprise. It seemed un-Christian. He wished he could find some great sadness, or even anger, but the emotion wasn't there and he couldn't make it happen. Mostly he felt pleased to be alive. He liked the smell of the New Testament under his cheek, the leather and ink and paper and glue, whatever the chemicals were. He liked hearing the sounds of night. Even his fatigue, it felt fine, the stiff muscles and the prickly awareness of his own body, a floating feeling. He enjoyed not being dead. Lying there, Kiowa admired Lieutenant Jimmy Cross's capacity for grief. He wanted to share the man's pain, he wanted to care as Jimmy Cross cared. And yet when he closed his eyes, all he could think was Boom-down, and all he could feel was the pleasure of having his boots off and the fog curling in around him and the damp soil and the Bible smells and the plush comfort of night.

1 After a moment Norman Bowker sat up in the dark.

2 What the hell, he said. You want to talk, *talk*. Tell it to me.

3 Forget it.

4 No, man, go on. One thing I hate, it's a silent Indian.

5 FOR the most part they carried themselves with poise, a kind of dignity. Now and then, however, there were times of panic, when they squealed or wanted to squeal but couldn't, when they twitched and made moaning sounds and covered their heads and said Dear Jesus and flopped around on the earth and fired their weapons blindly and cringed and sobbed and begged for the noise to stop and went wild and made stupid promises to themselves and to God and to their mothers and fathers, hoping not to die. In different ways, it happened to all of them. Afterward, when the firing ended, they would blink and peek up. They would touch their bodies, feeling shame, then quickly hiding it. They would force themselves to stand. As if in slow motion, frame by frame, the world would take on the old logic—absolute silence, then the wind, then sunlight, then voices. It was the burden of being alive. Awkwardly, the men would reassemble themselves, first in private, then in groups, becoming soldiers again. They would repair the leaks in their eyes. They would check for casualties, call in dust-offs, light cigarettes, try to smile, clear their throats and spit and begin cleaning their weapons. After a time someone would shake his head and say, No lie, I almost shit my pants, and someone else would laugh, which meant it was bad, yes, but the guy had obviously not shit his pants, it wasn't that bad, and in any case nobody would ever do such a thing and then go ahead and talk about it. They would squint into the dense, oppressive sunlight. For a few moments, perhaps, they would fall silent, lighting a joint and tracking its passage from man to man, inhaling, holding in the humiliation. Scary stuff, one of them might say. But then someone else would grin or flick his eyebrows and say, Roger-dodger, almost cut me a new asshole, *almost*.

There were numerous such poses. Some carried themselves with a sort of wistful resignation, others with pride or stiff soldierly discipline or good humor or macho zeal. They were afraid of dying but they were even more afraid to show it. 66

They were afraid of dying but they were even more afraid to show it.

They found jokes to tell. 67

They used a hard vocabulary to contain the terrible softness. *Greased,* they'd say. *Offed, lit up, zapped while zipping.* It wasn't cruelty, just stage presence. They were actors and the war came at them in 3-D. When someone died, it wasn't quite dying, because in a curious way it seemed scripted, and because they had their lines mostly memorized, irony mixed with tragedy, and because they called it by other names, as if to encyst and destroy the reality of death itself. They kicked corpses. They cut off thumbs. They talked grunt lingo. They told stories about Ted Lavender's supply of tranquilizers, how the poor guy didn't feel a thing, how incredibly tranquil he was. 68

There's a moral here, said Mitchell Sanders. 69

They were waiting for Lavender's chopper, smoking the dead man's dope. 70

The moral's pretty obvious, Sanders said, and winked. Stay away from drugs. No joke, they'll ruin your day every time. 71

Cute, said Henry Dobbins. 72

Mind-blower, get it? Talk about wiggy—nothing left, just blood and brains. 73

They made themselves laugh. 74

75 There it is, they'd say, over and over, as if the repetition itself were an act of poise, a balance between crazy and almost crazy, knowing without going. There it is, which meant be cool, let it ride, because oh yeah, man, you can't change what can't be changed, there it is, there it absolutely and positively and fucking well *is*.

76 They were tough.

77 They carried all the emotional baggage of men who might die. Grief, terror, love, longing—these were intangibles, but the intangibles had their own mass and specific gravity, they had tangible weight. They carried shameful memories. They carried the common secret of cowardice barely restrained, the instinct to run or freeze or hide, and in many respects this was the heaviest burden of all, for it could never be put down, it required perfect balance and perfect posture. They carried their reputations. They carried the soldier's greatest fear, which was the fear of blushing. Men killed, and died, because they were embarrassed not to. It was what had brought them to the war in the first place, nothing positive, no dreams of glory or honor, just to avoid the blush of dishonor. They died so as not to die of embarrassment. They crawled into tunnels and walked point and advanced under fire. Each morning, despite the unknowns, they made their legs move. They endured. They kept humping. They did not submit to the obvious alternative, which was simply to close the eyes and fall. So easy, really. Go limp and tumble to the ground and let the muscles unwind and not speak and not budge until your buddies picked you up and lifted you into the chopper that would roar and dip its nose and carry you off to the world. A mere matter of falling, yet no one ever fell. It was not courage, exactly; the object was not valor. Rather, they were too frightened to be cowards.

Men killed, and died, because they were embarrassed not to.

78 By and large they carried these things inside, maintaining the masks of composure. They sneered at sick call. They spoke bitterly about guys who had found release by shooting off their own toes or fingers. Pussies, they'd say. Candyasses. It was fierce, mocking talk, with only a trace of envy or awe, but even so, the image played itself out behind their eyes.

They imagined the muzzle against flesh. They imagined the quick, sweet pain, then the evacuation to Japan, then a hospital with warm beds and cute geisha nurses.

79 They dreamed of freedom birds.

80 At night, on guard, staring into the dark, they were carried away by jumbo jets. They felt the rush of takeoff. *Gone!* they yelled. And then velocity, wings and engines, a smiling stewardess—but it was more than a plane, it was a real bird, a big sleek silver bird with feathers and talons and high screeching. They were flying. The weights fell off, there was nothing to bear. They laughed and held on tight, feeling the cold slap of wind and altitude, soaring, thinking *It's over, I'm gone!*—they were naked, they were light and free—it was all lightness, bright and fast and buoyant, light as light, a helium buzz in the brain, a giddy bubbling in the lungs as they were taken up over the clouds and the war, beyond duty, beyond gravity and mortification and global entanglements—*Sin loi!* they yelled, *I'm sorry, motherfuckers, but I'm out of it, I'm goofed, I'm on a space cruise, I'm gone!*—and it was a restful, disencumbered sensation, just riding the light waves, sailing that big silver freedom bird over the mountains and oceans, over America, over the farms and great sleeping cities and cemeteries and highways and the golden arches of McDonald's. It was flight, a kind of fleeing, a kind of falling, falling higher and higher, spinning off the edge of the earth and beyond the sun and through the vast, silent vacuum where there were no burdens and where everything weighed exactly nothing. *Gone!* they screamed, *I'm sorry but I'm gone!* And so at night, not quite dreaming, they gave themselves over to lightness, they were carried, they were purely borne.

ON the morning after Ted Lavender died, 81
First Lieutenant Jimmy Cross crouched at the bottom of his foxhole and burned Martha's letters. Then he burned the two photographs. There was a steady rain falling, which made it difficult, but he used heat tabs and Sterno to build a small fire, screening it with his body, holding the photographs over the tight blue flame with the tips of his fingers.

He realized it was only a gesture. Stupid, he 82
thought. Sentimental, too, but mostly just stupid.

Lavender was dead. You couldn't burn the blame. 83

Besides, the letters were in his head. And even 84
now, without photographs, Lieutenant Cross could see Martha playing volleyball in her white gym shorts and yellow T-shirt. He could see her moving in the rain.

When the fire died out, Lieutenant Cross pulled 85
his poncho over his shoulders and ate breakfast from a can.

There was no great mystery, he decided. 86

In those burned letters Martha had never men- 87
tioned the war, except to say, Jimmy take care of yourself. She wasn't involved. She signed the letters "Love,"

but it wasn't love, and all the fine lines and technicalities did not matter.

88 The morning came up wet and blurry. Everything seemed part of everything else, the fog and Martha and the deepening rain.

89 It was a war, after all.

90 Half smiling, Lieutenant Jimmy Cross took out his maps. He shook his head hard, as if to clear it, then bent forward and began planning the day's march. In ten minutes, or maybe twenty, he would rouse the men and they would pack up and head west, where the maps showed the country to be green and inviting. They would do what they had always done. The rain might add some weight, but otherwise it would be one more day layered upon all the other days.

91 He was realistic about it. There was that new hardness in his stomach.

92 No more fantasies, he told himself.

93 Henceforth, when he thought about Martha, it would be only to think that she belonged elsewhere. He would shut down the daydreams. This was not Mount Sebastian, it was another world, where there were no pretty poems or midterm exams, a place where men died because of carelessness and gross stupidity. Kiowa was right. Boom-down, and you were dead, never partly dead.

94 Briefly, in the rain, Lieutenant Cross saw Martha's gray eyes gazing back at him.

95 He understood.

96 It was very sad, he thought. The things men carried inside. The things men did or felt they had to do.

97 He almost nodded at her, but didn't.

98 Instead he went back to his maps. He was now determined to perform his duties firmly and without negligence. It wouldn't help Lavender, he knew that, but from this point on he would comport himself as a soldier. He would dispose of his good-luck pebble. Swallow it, maybe, or use Lee Strunk's slingshot, or just drop it along the trail. On the march he would impose strict field discipline. He would be careful to send out flank security, to prevent straggling or bunching up, to keep his troops moving at the proper pace and at the proper interval. He would insist on clean weapons. He would confiscate the remainder of Lavender's dope. Later in the day, perhaps, he would call the men together and speak to them plainly. He would accept the blame for what had happened to Ted Lavender. He would be a man about it. He would look them in the eyes, keeping his chin level, and he would issue the new SOPs in a calm, impersonal tone of voice, an officer's voice, leaving no room for argument or discussion. Commencing immediately, he'd tell them, they would no longer abandon equipment along the route of march. They would police up their acts. They would get their shit together, and keep it together, and maintain it neatly and in good working order.

He would not tolerate laxity. He would show 99
strength, distancing himself.

Among the men there would be grumbling, of 100
course, and maybe worse, because their days would seem longer and their loads heavier, but Lieutenant Cross reminded himself that his obligation was not to be loved but to lead. He would dispense with love; it was not now a factor. And if anyone quarreled or complained, he would simply tighten his lips and arrange his shoulders in the correct command posture. He might give a curt little nod. Or he might not. He might just shrug and say Carry on, then they would saddle up and form into a column and move out toward the villages of Than Khe.

IF you enjoyed mulling over the meaning, ultimately mysterious, of the stone in "The Things They Carried," you might also enjoy considering possible interpretations of the grandmother's dance regalia in Sherman Alexie's "What You Pawn I Will Redeem" (in chapter 11) or the car keys in T. Coraghessan Boyle's "Greasy Lake" (chapter 4).

**GOING FURTHER** War is what Herman Melville (see chapter 14) would call a "great" theme, and in our tumultuous modern age it often serves as literary material, as in, for example, the novels of Joseph Heller (*Catch-22*), Norman Mailer (*The Naked and the Dead*), and James Jones (*The Thin Red Line*). As we suggested, war has emerged in the work of Tim O'Brien as his great subject, sometimes overshadowing the domestic aspects of life in his fiction.

# Writing from Reading

## Summarize

1 Explain why Cross burns Martha's letters after Lavender's death.

2 O'Brien mentions various reasons why the men carried things. For example, they carried a number of things "by necessity." What are the other reasons given? How does the reason given affect the story that follows?

## Analyze Craft

3 Discuss how O'Brien uses lists in this story. How do the lists affect the tone and themes of the story?

4 Consider the names Cross and Lavender. What symbolic meanings do these names suggest?

## Analyze Voice

5 Identify passages and details in the story that seem to come from O'Brien's personal experience. What makes them seem this way?

6 The men in this story are soldiers in the Vietnam War. Which of their experiences and the things they carry are specific to that war? Consider reasons of era, culture, climate, and terrain. Which would apply to any war?

## Synthesize Summary and Analysis

7 What symbolic meaning does Ted Lavender's death take on? Find each reference to Lavender and to his death and explore the effect the repetition has on you as a reader.

## Interpret the Story

8 Consider why O'Brien includes so many detailed passages about Lieutenant Jimmy Cross. How might his thoughts, fears, and fantasies about Martha represent the feelings of all soldiers who served in Vietnam?

*CONTINUED FROM PAGE 313*

## SYMBOLS IN EVERYDAY LIFE AND LITERATURE

We use symbols whenever we speak or write, draw or gesture. Those little icons on your computer screen—the picture of a trash can, the picture of a disk—are symbols. An image represents an idea; a picture stands for a thing. Symbols in literature, however, rarely have single, unambiguous meanings. Symbolism takes us deep into the tangled web of words and characters, incidents and objects in a story. Because symbols are compact and efficient, they can communicate a broad array of feelings and impressions. Moreover, a symbol doesn't boil down to a single "correct" meaning. When a symbolic object or act is successfully embedded in a story, it imbues the story with multiple meanings—and therefore the possibility of multiple interpretations.

In "The Things They Carried," for example, the pebble is a gift from Martha; it's something she has touched, so for Cross it embodies her essence. It comes from a beach back home, so it also carries the essence of "beach"—a place of serenity as well as carefree pleasures. It seems a kind of rabbit's foot, a good-luck charm. Yet it is also a mere piece of stone. Although Martha herself sees symbolic meaning in the stone—she points out the "separate-but-together quality" of the tide line where she found it—anybody else strolling the beach would likely have passed it by as just another ordinary pebble. Now, layered with associations and memories, it becomes symbolic of Cross's longing for romantic love and also with the promise and possibility of escape from brutal war. Lieutenant Cross carries the pebble in his mouth, guarding it, tasting it, absorbing all it carries. Shown in these various lights, the pebble acquires so much significance by the time Cross vows to discard it that we know he's giving a great deal away by doing so.

> "So in this story I take on death—a huge subject. But in this story the way into that huge subject is through the watch that is left behind by a woman who has died, which her daughters are now fighting over." Conversation with Amy Hempel

Just as an object or character can hold many shades of meaning, so can a **symbolic act,** a gesture or action beyond the everyday practical definition. When Lieutenant Cross discards Martha's pebble, he discards an entire dream. In the symbolic act of *carrying,* the weary soldiers not only shoulder a host of physical objects—letters, can openers, pocket knives, salt tablets, ammunition, dental floss—they also bear a host of emotional burdens: the fear of death, the horrors of what they've seen, the fatigue of war.

## SYMBOL AND ALLEGORY

Authors have not always used or thought of symbols in this way. Most literature was once allegorical. An **allegory** is a story in which major elements such as characters and settings represent universal truths or moral lessons in a one-to-one correspondence, as they do in the fable of the grasshopper and the ant. In this fable the grasshopper is careless all the way through, frittering away its time, while the ant labors diligently to put away food for the winter. When winter comes, you can guess which one will be secure and which one will suffer. In this allegorical narrative, the lesson to be learned is that it is best to prepare for future necessity. Each character represents a single form of behavior—"irresponsibility" for the grasshopper versus "conscientiousness" for the ant. Allegorical figures are one-dimensional and constant; "what they carry" does not change.

Allegory is a cardboard cutout kind of symbolism; in allegory, a value such as "virtue" or "vice" remains constant from beginning to end. In our discussion of "Character" (chapter 5), we drew the distinction between "flat" and "round" characters; in this regard an allegorical figure would be *flat,* whereas a symbolic figure or object—

### THE HISTORY OF SYMBOLISM

The use of allegory stems from the old pagan religions, in which the gods were understood to have created certain constant values—good, evil, heroism, fidelity—in human beings, who were seen as incapable of change. These values gradually adapted to Christian symbols of salvation and redemption. Toward the end of the eighteenth century, poetry and fiction moved largely away from allegory and toward a more multidimensional symbolism. By the mid-nineteenth century, most serious writers produced work that was decidedly symbolic rather than allegorical. Readers, too, took on the new task of interpreting literature in multiple ways, contributing new perspectives and initiating new discussions about the growing literary cannon. What once was myth—an age-old and collective story—became, in time, an individual's tale. If you want to look at these developments in political terms, you might say that allegory is the mode of kings and religious uniformity, while symbolism is the mode of democracy and governments made up of a multiplicity of views.

what O'Brien identifies as "the pebble or the shooting of a baby water buffalo"—would be understood as *round.* In contrast to allegory, symbols convey multiple meanings, and the meaning may expand and become more complex over the course of the story.

## RECOGNIZING AND APPRECIATING SYMBOLS

Symbolic meanings are not "hidden," as many readers have come to believe. Their context suggests them, as does the way characters view them. The red carnation the protagonist wears in Willa Cather's "Paul's Case" (chapter 5) becomes far more than a flower in a lapel. The decoration, in one sense, seems a symbol of Paul's aspiration, of his belief that he belongs elsewhere, above the dreary situation he was born into. Yet, from his teachers' perspective, his lapel carnations are a sign of his insubordination and pretentiousness—precisely what they dislike about him. It's also important to notice that a carnation is scarcely *original* as a flower to wear; it's not as if he puts a sunflower in his buttonhole, or an elaborate orchid; his is a conventional choice. Late in the story, after Paul has escaped into a new life, the carnations embody the futility of his dream.

> "We know from Greek myth and from many mythic structures, the three witches, the three sisters, Cinderella and her two sisters, and on and on. It's just a very organic form, and the triangle is, in general, a very important figure for a fiction writer to have in mind."
>
> Conversation with John Updike

It's possible to go deeper still. For example, we can ask, "Why, of all flowers, a carnation?" With a little digging, we learn that it is one of the oldest cultivated flowers—dating back to ancient Greece and Rome—and that its botanical name *dianthus* means divine flower. From this comes a feeling that Paul's dreams are ancient, enduring, perhaps even cosmic. Furthermore, in the dictionary, we see that one root of the word is *carne,* or flesh. These images add to and deepen the sense we have of Paul as one who aspires to something grand, something divine, while bound to the earth and the realities of his own flesh. We cannot know whether Cather intended these additional meanings, but we do know that writers choose images carefully, for their resonance.

How can you tell when an image, character, or act is significant in a symbolic sense? First, look at the title of a work. O'Brien sets us up to know what is going to be laden with symbolic importance in his title, "The Things They Carried." Notice also images that you see repeated throughout the story, like the carnations in "Paul's Case." Recurrence, especially, gives an image importance, drawing attention to it, suggesting it has significance beyond the ordinary. Sometimes the author focuses on a precise detail in a way that seems to be saying, "Notice this; it says something important," as in the story in this chapter, "No One's a Mystery," when the narrator describes the manure clinging to Jack's boots. Reflect on how an image is used in a story and how it connects to the characters, especially the protagonist, as in Gregor Samsa in Franz Kafka's "The Metamorphosis" in this chapter.

## *SYMBOLISM* IN CONTEXT

When we read fiction, we are invited—in fact, called upon—to interpret objects, characters, and behavior beyond their literal meanings, and to look for multiple, not simply single, truths or meanings. The four stories in this chapter are filled with richly layered images. As you read, consider how the predominant symbols might be interpreted in multiple ways. How might each symbol be read both literally and figuratively, both as it actually is (a pebble) and as what it represents (longing)? What we learn from reading with symbolic potential in mind not only deepens our reading experience but also prepares us to understand the significance of events in our own lives.

# Nathaniel Hawthorne (1804–1864)

Shortly after graduating from Bowdoin College, Nathaniel Hawthorne published his first novel, *Fanshawe* (1828), at his own expense, only to reclaim and destroy nearly every copy. Hawthorne also struggled with holding ordinary jobs—in his case, those of bookkeeper and customs-house employee—while trying to be a writer. Despite these difficulties, Hawthorne became famous with his publication of *The Scarlet Letter* (1850) and has remained in the American canon ever since. A native of Massachusetts and a descendant of prosecutors in the Salem witch trials, Hawthorne was fascinated with the Puritanical influence in New England, and his work is known for its exploration of sin, punishment, and atonement. Even during his most productive period—when he and his wife lived in Concord, Massachusetts, and maintained friendships with writers Ralph Waldo Emerson and Henry David Thoreau, who were part of a movement called *transcendentalism* and focused on how humans were basically good and connected to the natural world—Hawthorne explored the dark side of human nature in his fiction. To do this, he often turned to a modified form of allegory, making his characters less like real individuals and more like representations of a theme or concept. His writing is a blend of realism and romanticism, and he is known as a Romantic in the sense that he fused unreal occurrences or situations with his often all-too-human characters. "Young Goodman Brown," a story from his collection *Mosses from an Old Manse* (1846), is quintessential Hawthorne; he uses Goodman Brown's slightly fantastical encounter in the woods to expose the sin present in even the most pious people.

**AS YOU READ** **As you read, watch for repeated images—concrete details the author wishes to bring to your attention. How do these particular objects or images alter over the course of the story? What kinds of feelings do they stir in you?**

**TIP**

**FOR INTERACTIVE READING . . .** Circle the repeated images. Make brief notes in the margin regarding their portrayal. Based on the context, what feeling or value do you associate with each?

# Young Goodman Brown (1835)

1 YOUNG Goodman Brown came forth at sunset into the street of Salem village; but put his head back, after crossing the threshold, to exchange a parting kiss with his young wife. And Faith, as the wife was aptly named, thrust her own pretty head into the street, letting the wind play with the pink ribbons of her cap while she called to Goodman Brown.

2 "Dearest heart," whispered she, softly and rather sadly, when her lips were close to his ear, "prithee put off your journey until sunrise and sleep in your own bed to-night. A lone woman is troubled with such dreams and such thoughts that she's afeard of herself sometimes. Pray tarry with me this night, dear husband, of all nights in the year."

3 "My love and my Faith," replied young Goodman Brown, "of all nights in the year, this one night must I tarry away from thee. My journey, as thou callest it, forth and back again, must needs be done 'twixt now and sunrise. What, my sweet, pretty wife, dost thou doubt me already, and we but three months married?"

4 "Then God bless you!" said Faith, with the pink ribbons; "and may you find all well when you come back."

5 "Amen!" cried Goodman Brown. "Say thy prayers, dear Faith, and go to bed at dusk, and no harm will come to thee."

6 So they parted; and the young man pursued his way until, being about to turn the corner by the meeting house, he looked back and saw the head of Faith still peeping after him with a melancholy air, in spite of her pink ribbons.

7 "Poor little Faith!" thought he, for his heart smote him. "What a wretch am I to leave her on such an errand! She talks of dreams, too. Methought as she spoke there was trouble in her face, as if a dream had warned her what work is to be done to-night. But no, no; 'twould kill her to think it. Well, she's a blessed angel on earth; and after this one night I'll cling to her skirts and follow her to heaven."

With this excellent resolve for the future, Goodman Brown felt himself justified in making more haste on his present evil purpose. He had taken a dreary road, darkened by all the gloomiest trees of the forest, which barely stood aside to let the narrow path creep through, and closed immediately behind. It was all as lonely as could be; and there is this peculiarity in such a solitude, that the traveller knows not who may be concealed by the innumerable trunks and thick boughs overhead; so that with lonely footsteps he may yet be passing through an unseen multitude. 8

"There may be a devilish Indian behind every tree," said Goodman Brown to himself; and he glanced fearfully behind him as he added, "What if the devil himself should be at my very elbow!" 9

His head being turned back, he passed a crook of the road, and, looking forward again, beheld the figure of a man, in grave and decent attire, seated at the foot of an old tree. He arose at Goodman Brown's approach and walked onward side by side with him. 10

"You are late, Goodman Brown," said he. "The clock of the Old South was striking as I came through Boston; and that is full fifteen minutes agone." 11

"Faith kept me back a while," replied the young man, with a tremor in his voice, caused by the sudden appearance of his companion, though not wholly unexpected. 12

It was now deep dusk in the forest, and deepest in that part of it where these two were journeying. As nearly as could be discerned, the second traveller was about fifty years old, apparently in the same rank of life as Goodman Brown, and bearing a considerable resemblance to him, though perhaps more in expression than features. Still they might have been taken for father and son. And yet, though the elder person was as simply clad as the younger, and as simple in manner too, he had an indescribable air of one who knew the world, and who would not have felt abashed at the gov- 13 ernor's dinner table or in King William's court, were it possible that his affairs should call him thither. But the only thing about him that could be fixed upon as remarkable was his staff, which bore the likeness of a great black snake, so curiously wrought that it might almost be seen to twist and wriggle itself like a living serpent. This, of course, must have been an ocular deception, assisted by the uncertain light.

14 "Come, Goodman Brown," cried his fellow-traveller, "this is a dull pace for the beginning of a journey. Take my staff, if you are so soon weary."

15 "Friend," said the other, exchanging his slow pace for a full stop, "having kept covenant by meeting thee here, it is my purpose now to return whence I came. I have scruples touching the matter thou wot'st of."

16 "Sayest thou so?" replied he of the serpent, smiling apart. "Let us walk on, nevertheless, reasoning as we go; and if I convince thee not thou shalt turn back. We are but a little way in the forest yet."

17 "Too far! too far!" exclaimed the goodman, unconsciously resuming his walk. "My father never went into the woods on such an errand, nor his father before him. We have been a race of honest men and good Christians since the days of the martyrs; and shall I be the first of the name of Brown that ever took this path and kept——"

18 "Such company, thou wouldst say," observed the elder person, interpreting his pause. "Well said, Goodman Brown! I have been as well acquainted with your family as with ever a one among the Puritans; and that's no trifle to say. I helped your grandfather, the constable, when he lashed the Quaker woman so smartly through the streets of Salem; and it was I that brought your father a pitch-pine knot, kindled at my own hearth, to set fire to an Indian village, in King Philip's war. They were my good friends, both; and many a pleasant walk have we had along this path, and returned merrily after midnight. I would fain be friends with you for their sake."

19 "If it be as thou sayest," replied Goodman Brown, "I marvel they never spoke of these matters; or, verily, I marvel not, seeing that the least rumor of the sort would have driven them from New England. We are a people of prayer, and good works to boot, and abide no such wickedness."

20 "Wickedness or not," said the traveller with the twisted staff, "I have a very general acquaintance here in New England. The deacons of many a church have drunk the communion wine with me; the selectmen of divers towns make me their chairman; and a majority of the Great and General Court are firm supporters of my interest. The governor and I, too—But these are state secrets."

"Can this be so?" cried Goodman Brown, with a stare of amazement at his undisturbed companion. "Howbeit, I have nothing to do with the governor and council; they have their own ways, and are no rule for a simple husbandman like me. But, were I to go on with thee, how should I meet the eye of that good old man, our minister, at Salem village? O, his voice would make me tremble both Sabbath day and lecture day." 21

Thus far the elder traveller had listened with due gravity; but now burst into a fit of irrepressible mirth, shaking himself so violently that his snakelike staff actually seemed to wriggle in sympathy. 22

"Ha! ha! ha!" shouted he again and again; then composing himself. "Well, go on, Goodman Brown, go on; but, prithee, don't kill me with laughing." 23

"Well, then, to end the matter at once," said Goodman Brown, considerably nettled, "there is my wife, Faith. It would break her dear little heart; and I'd rather break my own." 24

"Nay, if that be the case," answered the other, "e'en go thy ways, Goodman Brown. I would not for twenty old women like the one hobbling before us that Faith should come to any harm." 25

As he spoke, he pointed his staff at a female figure on the path, in whom Goodman Brown recognized a very pious and exemplary dame, who had taught him his catechism in youth, and was still his moral and spiritual adviser, jointly with the minister and Deacon Gookin. 26

"A marvel, truly, that Goody Cloyse should be so far in the wilderness at nightfall," said he. "But, with your leave, friend, I shall take a cut through the woods until we have left this Christian woman behind. Being a stranger to you, she might ask whom I was consorting with and whither I was going." 27

"Be it so," said his fellow-traveller. "Betake you to the woods, and let me keep the path." 28

Accordingly the young man turned aside, but took care to watch his companion, who advanced softly along the road until he had come within a staff's length of the old dame. She, meanwhile, was making the best of her way, with singular speed for so aged a woman, and mumbling some indistinct words—a 29 prayer, doubtless—as she went. The traveller put forth his staff and touched her withered neck with what seemed the serpent's tail.

30 "The devil!" screamed the pious old lady.

31 "Then Goody Cloyse knows her old friend?" observed the traveller, confronting her and leaning on his writhing stick.

32 "Ah, forsooth, and is it your worship indeed?" cried the good dame. "Yea, truly is it, and in the very image of my old gossip, Goodman Brown, the grandfather of the silly fellow that now is. But—would your worship believe it?—my broomstick hath strangely disappeared, stolen, as I suspect, by that unhanged witch, Goody Cory, and that, too, when I was all anointed with the juice of smallage, and cinquefoil, and wolf's bane—"

33 "Mingled with fine wheat and the fat of a new-born babe," said the shape of old Goodman Brown.

34 "Ah, your worship knows the recipe," cried the old lady, cackling aloud. "So, as I was saying, being all ready for the meeting, and no horse to ride on, I made up my mind to foot it; for they tell me there is a nice young man to be taken into communion to-night. But now your good worship will lend me your arm, and we shall be there in a twinkling."

35 "That can hardly be," answered her friend. "I may not spare you my arm, Goody Cloyse; but here is my staff, if you will."

36 So saying, he threw it down at her feet, where, perhaps, it assumed life, being one of the rods which its owner had formerly lent to the Egyptian magi. Of this fact, however, Goodman Brown could not take cognizance. He had cast up his eyes in astonishment, and, looking down again, beheld neither Goody Cloyse nor the serpentine staff, but his fellow-traveller alone, who waited for him as calmly as if nothing had happened.

37 "That old woman taught me my catechism," said the young man; and there was a world of meaning in this simple comment.

38 They continued to walk onward, while the elder traveller exhorted his companion to make good speed and persevere in the path, discoursing so aptly that his arguments seemed rather to spring up in the bosom of his auditor than to be suggested by himself. As they went, he plucked a branch of maple to serve for a walking stick, and began to strip it of the twigs and little boughs, which were wet with evening dew. The moment his fingers touched them they became strangely withered and dried up as with a week's sunshine. Thus the pair proceeded, at a good free pace, until suddenly, in a gloomy hollow of the road, Goodman Brown sat himself down on the stump of a tree and refused to go any farther.

39 "Friend," said he, stubbornly, "my mind is made up. Not another step will I budge on this errand. What if a wretched old woman do choose to go to the devil when I thought she was going to heaven: is that any reason why I should quit my dear Faith and go after her?"

40 "You will think better of this by and by," said his acquaintance, composedly. "Sit here and rest yourself a while; and when you feel like moving again, there is my staff to help you along."

41 Without more words, he threw his companion the maple stick, and was as speedily out of sight as if he had vanished into the deepening gloom. The young man sat a few moments by the roadside, applauding himself greatly, and thinking with how clear a conscience he should meet the minister in his morning walk, nor shrink from the eye of good old Deacon Gookin. And what calm sleep would be his that very night, which was to have been spent so wickedly, but so purely and sweetly now, in the arms of Faith! Amidst these pleasant and praiseworthy meditations, Goodman Brown heard the tramp of horses along the road, and deemed it advisable to conceal himself within the verge of the forest, conscious of the guilty purpose that had brought him thither, though now so happily turned from it.

42 On came the hoof tramps and the voices of the riders, two grave old voices, conversing soberly as they drew near. These mingled sounds appeared to pass along the road, within a few yards of the young man's hidingplace; but, owing doubtless to the depth of the gloom at that particular spot, neither the travellers nor their steeds were visible. Though their figures brushed the small boughs by the wayside, it could not be seen that they intercepted, even for a moment, the faint gleam from the strip of bright sky athwart which they must have passed. Goodman Brown alternately crouched and stood on tiptoe, pulling aside the branches and thrusting forth his head as far as he durst without discerning so much as a shadow. It vexed him the more, because he could have sworn, were such a thing possible, that he recognized the voices of the minister and Deacon Gookin, jogging along quietly, as they were wont to do, when bound to

The moment his fingers touched them they became strangely withered and dried up as with a week's sunshine.

some ordination or ecclesiastical council. While yet within hearing, one of the riders stopped to pluck a switch.

43 "Of the two, reverend sir," said the voice like the deacon's, "I had rather miss an ordination dinner than to-night's meeting. They tell me that some of our community are to be here from Falmouth and beyond, and others from Connecticut and Rhode Island, besides several of the Indian powwows, who, after their fashion, know almost as much deviltry as the best of us. Moreover, there is a goodly young woman to be taken into communion."

44 "Mighty well, Deacon Gookin!" replied the solemn old tones of the minister. "Spur up, or we shall be late. Nothing can be done, you know, until I get on the ground."

45 The hoofs clattered again; and the voices, talking so strangely in the empty air, passed on through the forest, where no church had ever been gathered or solitary Christian prayed. Whither, then, could these holy men be journeying so deep into the heathen wilderness? Young Goodman Brown caught hold of a tree for support, being ready to sink down on the ground, faint and overburdened with the heavy sickness of his heart. He looked up to the sky, doubting whether there really was a heaven above him. Yet there was the blue arch, and the stars brightening in it.

He looked up to the sky, doubting whether there really was a heaven above him.

46 "With heaven above and Faith below, I will yet stand firm against the devil!" cried Goodman Brown.

47 While he still gazed upward into the deep arch of the firmament and had lifted his hands to pray, a cloud, though no wind was stirring, hurried across the zenith and hid the brightening stars. The blue sky was still visible except directly overhead, where this black mass of cloud was sweeping swiftly northward. Aloft in the air, as if from the depths of the cloud, came a confused and doubtful sound of voices. Once the listener fancied that he could distinguish the accents of townspeople of his own, men and women, both pious and ungodly, many of whom he had met at the communion table, and had seen others rioting at the tavern. The next moment, so indistinct were the sounds, he doubted whether he had heard aught but the murmur of the old forest, whispering without a wind. Then came a stronger swell of those familiar tones, heard daily in the sunshine at Salem village, but never until now from a cloud of night There was one voice, of a young woman, uttering lamentations, yet with an uncertain sorrow, and entreating for some favor, which, perhaps, it would grieve her to obtain; and all the unseen multitude, both saints and sinners, seemed to encourage her onward.

"Faith!" shouted Goodman Brown, in a voice of agony and desperation; and the echoes of the forest mocked him, crying, "Faith! Faith!" as if bewildered wretches were seeking her all through the wilderness. 48

The cry of grief, rage, and terror was yet piercing the night, when the unhappy husband held his breath for a response. There was a scream, drowned immediately in a louder murmur of voices, fading into far-off laughter, as the dark cloud swept away, leaving the clear and silent sky above Goodman Brown. But something fluttered lightly down through the air and caught on the branch of a tree. The young man seized it, and beheld a pink ribbon. 49

"My Faith is gone!" cried he, after one stupefied moment. "There is no good on earth; and sin is but a name. Come, devil; for to thee is this world given." 50

And, maddened with despair, so that he laughed loud and long, did Goodman Brown grasp his staff and set forth again, at such a rate that he seemed to fly along the forest path rather than to walk or run. The road grew wilder and drearier and more faintly traced, and vanished at length, leaving him in the heart of the dark wilderness, still rushing onward with the instinct that guides mortal man to evil. The whole forest was peopled with frightful sounds—the creaking of the trees, the howling of wild beasts, and the yell of Indians; while sometimes the wind tolled like a distant church bell, and sometimes gave a broad roar around the traveller, as if all Nature were laughing him to scorn. But he was himself the chief horror of the scene, and shrank not from its other horrors. 51

"Ha! ha! ha!" roared Goodman Brown when the wind laughed at him. "Let us hear which will laugh loudest. Think not to frighten me with your deviltry. Come witch, come wizard, come Indian powwow, come devil himself, and here comes Goodman Brown. You may as well fear him as he fear you." 52

In truth, all through the haunted forest there could be nothing more frightful than the figure of Goodman Brown. On he flew among the black pines, brandishing his staff with frenzied gestures, now giving vent to an inspiration of horrid blasphemy, and now shouting forth such laughter as set all the echoes of the forest laughing like demons around him. The fiend in his own shape is less hideous than when he rages in the breast of man. Thus sped the demoniac 53 on his course, until, quivering among the trees, he saw a red light before him, as when the felled trunks and branches of a clearing have been set on fire, and throw up their lurid blaze against the sky, at the hour of midnight. He paused, in a lull of the tempest that had driven him onward, and heard the swell of what seemed a hymn, rolling solemnly from a distance with the weight of many voices. He knew the tune; it was a familiar one in the choir of the village meeting house. The verse died heavily away, and was lengthened by a chorus, not of human voices, but of all the sounds of the benighted wilderness pealing in awful harmony together. Goodman Brown cried out; and his cry was lost to his own ear by its unison with the cry of the desert.

"But where is Faith?" thought Goodman Brown, and, as hope came into his heart, he trembled.

54 In the interval of silence he stole forward until the light glared full upon his eyes. At one extremity of an open space, hemmed in by the dark wall of the forest, arose a rock, bearing some rude, natural resemblance either to an altar or a pulpit, and surrounded by four blazing pines, their tops aflame, their stems untouched, like candles at an evening meeting. The mass of foliage that had overgrown the summit of the rock was all on fire, blazing high into the night and fitfully illuminating the whole field. Each pendent twig and leafy festoon was in a blaze. As the red light arose and fell, a numerous congregation alternately shone forth, then disappeared in shadow, and again grew, as it were, out of the darkness, peopling the heart of the solitary woods at once.

55 "A grave and dark-clad company," quoth Goodman Brown.

56 In truth they were such. Among them, quivering to and fro between gloom and splendor, appeared faces that would be seen next day at the council board of the province, and others which, Sabbath after Sabbath, looked devoutly heavenward, and benignantly over the crowded pews, from the holiest pulpits in the land. Some affirm that the lady of the governor was there. At least there were high dames well known to her, and wives of honored husbands, and widows, a great multitude, and ancient maidens, all of excellent repute, and fair young girls, who trembled lest their mothers should espy them. Either the sudden gleams of light flashing over the obscure field bedazzled Goodman Brown, or he recognized a score of the church members of Salem village famous for their especial sanctity. Good old Deacon Gookin had arrived, and waited at the skirts of that venerable saint, his revered pastor. But, irreverently consorting with these grave, reputable, and pious people, these elders of the church, these chaste dames and dewy virgins, there were men of dissolute lives and women of spotted fame, wretches given over to all mean and filthy vice, and suspected even of horrid crimes. It was strange to see that the good shrank not from the wicked, nor were the sinners abashed by the saints. Scattered also among their pale-faced enemies were the Indian priests, or powwows, who had often scared their native forest with more hideous incantations than any known to English witchcraft.

"But where is Faith?" thought Goodman Brown, 57
and, as hope came into his heart, he trembled.

Another verse of the hymn arose, a slow and 58
mournful strain, such as the pious love, but joined to words which expressed all that our nature can conceive of sin, and darkly hinted at far more. Unfathomable to mere mortals is the lore of fiends. Verse after verse was sung; and still the chorus of the desert swelled between the deepest tone of a mighty organ; and with the final peal of that dreadful anthem there came a sound, as if the roaring wind, the rushing streams, the howling beasts, and every other voice of the unconverted wilderness were mingling and according with the voice of guilty man in homage to the prince of all. The four blazing pines threw up a loftier flame, and obscurely discovered shapes and visages of horror on the smoke wreaths above the impious assembly. At the same moment the fire on the rock shot redly forth and formed a glowing arch above its base, where now appeared a figure. With reverence be it spoken, the figure bore no slight similitude, both in garb and manner, to some grave divine of the New England churches.

"Bring forth the converts!" cried a voice that 59
echoed through the field and rolled into the forest.

At the word, Goodman Brown stepped forth from 60
the shadow of the trees and approached the congregation, with whom he felt a loathful brotherhood by the sympathy of all that was wicked in his heart. He could have well nigh sworn that the shape of his own dead father beckoned him to advance, looking downward from a smoke wreath, while a woman, with dim features of despair, threw out her hand to warn him back. Was it his mother? But he had no power to retreat one step, nor to resist, even in thought, when the minister and good old Deacon Gookin seized his arms and led him to the blazing rock. Thither came also the slender form of a veiled female, led between Goody Cloyse, that pious teacher of the catechism, and Mar-

tha Carrier, who had received the devil's promise to be queen of hell. A rampant hag was she. And there stood the proselytes beneath the canopy of fire.

61 "Welcome, my children," said the dark figure, "to the communion of your race. Ye have found thus young your nature and your destiny. My children, look behind you!"

62 They turned; and flashing forth, as it were, in a sheet of flame, the fiend worshippers were seen; the smile of welcome gleamed darkly on every visage.

63 "There," resumed the sable form, "are all whom ye have reverenced from youth. Ye deemed them holier than yourselves, and shrank from your own sin, contrasting it with their lives of righteousness and prayerful aspirations heavenward. Yet here are they all in my worshipping assembly. This night it shall be granted you to know their secret deeds; how hoary-bearded elders of the church have whispered wanton words to the young maids of their households; how many a woman, eager for widows' weeds, has given her husband a drink at bedtime and let him sleep his last sleep in her bosom; how beardless youths have made haste to inherit their fathers' wealth; and how fair damsels—blush not, sweet ones—have dug little graves in the garden, and bidden me, the sole guest, to an infant's funeral. By the sympathy of your human hearts for sin ye shall scent out all the places—whether in church, bed chamber, street, field, or forest—where crime has been committed, and shall exult to behold the whole earth one stain of guilt, one mighty blood spot. Far more than this. It shall be yours to penetrate, in every bosom, the deep mystery of sin, the fountain of all wicked arts, and which inexhaustibly supplies more evil impulses than human power—than my power at its utmost—can make manifest in deeds. And now, my children, look upon each other."

Evil must be your only happiness.

64 They did so; and, by the blaze of the hell-kindled torches, the wretched man beheld his Faith, and the wife her husband, trembling before that unhallowed altar.

65 "Lo, there ye stand, my children," said the figure, in a deep and solemn tone, almost sad with its despairing awfulness, as if his once angelic nature could yet mourn for our miserable race. "Depending upon one another's hearts, ye had still hoped that virtue were not all a dream. Now are ye undeceived. Evil is the nature of mankind. Evil must be your only happiness. Welcome again, my children, to the communion of your race."

66 "Welcome," repeated the fiend worshippers, in one cry of despair and triumph.

And there they stood, the only pair, as it seemed, 67
who were yet hesitating on the verge of wickedness in this dark world. A basin was hollowed, naturally, in the rock. Did it contain water, reddened by the lurid light? or was it blood? or, perchance, a liquid flame? Herein did the shape of evil dip his hand and prepare to lay the mark of baptism upon their foreheads, that they might be partakers of the mystery of sin, more conscious of the secret guilt of others, both in deed and thought, than they could now be of their own. The husband cast one look at his pale wife, and Faith at him. What polluted wretches would the next glance show them to each other, shuddering alike at what they disclosed and what they saw!

"Faith! Faith!" cried the hus- 68
band, "look up to heaven, and resist the wicked one."

Whether Faith obeyed, he knew not. Hardly had 69
he spoken when he found himself amid calm night and solitude, listening to a roar of the wind which died heavily away through the forest. He staggered against the rock, and felt it chill and damp; while a hanging twig, that had been all on fire, besprinkled his cheek with the coldest dew.

The next morning young Goodman Brown came 70
slowly into the street of Salem village, staring around him like a bewildered man. The good old minister was taking a walk along the graveyard to get an appetite for breakfast and meditate his sermon, and bestowed a blessing, as he passed, on Goodman Brown. He shrank from the venerable saint as if to avoid an anathema. Old Deacon Gookin was at domestic worship, and the holy words of his prayer were heard through the open window. "What God doth the wizard pray to?" quoth Goodman Brown. Goody Cloyse, that excellent old Christian, stood in the early sunshine at her own lattice, catechizing a little girl who had brought her a pint of morning's milk. Goodman Brown snatched away the child as from the grasp of the fiend himself. Turning the corner by the meeting house, he spied the head of Faith, with the pink ribbons, gazing anxiously forth, and bursting into such joy at sight of him that she skipped along the street and almost kissed her husband before the whole village. But Goodman Brown looked sternly and sadly into her face, and passed on without a greeting.

Had Goodman Brown fallen asleep in the forest 71
and only dreamed a wild dream of a witch meeting?

Be it so, if you will; but, alas; it was a dream of 72
evil omen for young Goodman Brown. A stern, a sad, a darkly meditative, a distrustful, if not a desperate, man did he become from the night of that fearful

dream. On the Sabbath day, when the congregation were singing a holy psalm, he could not listen, because an anthem of sin rushed loudly upon his ear and drowned all the blessed strain. When the minister spoke from the pulpit, with power and fervid eloquence and with his hand on the open Bible, of the sacred truths of our religion, and of saintlike lives and triumphant deaths, and of future bliss or misery unutterable, then did Goodman Brown turn pale, dreading lest the roof should thunder down upon the gray blasphemer and his hearers. Often, awaking suddenly at midnight, he shrank from the bosom of Faith; and at morning or eventide, when the family knelt down at prayer, he scowled, and muttered to himself, and gazed sternly at his wife, and turned away. And when he had lived long, and was borne to his grave, a hoary corpse, followed by Faith, an aged woman, and children and grandchildren, a goodly procession, besides neighbors not a few, they carved no hopeful verse upon his tombstone; for his dying hour was gloom.

IF you enjoyed "Young Goodman Brown," you might also look at the dark woods and listen to the voices at one's shoulder in the work of Barry Lopez and William Kittredge, though their landscape is very different from that of New Englander Nathaniel Hawthorne.

**GOING FURTHER** The world's literature abounds in spiritual quest stories, from the Gilgamesh epic to J. R. R. Tolkien's *Lord of the Rings* novels. You might be interested in the works of C. S. Lewis, another Christian quester given to playing with allegory in the modern world.

# Writing from Reading

## Summarize

1 What does the story tell you about Goodman Brown's ancestors? What kind of people are they? Does he follow in their footsteps? Explain your answer.

2 What exactly is the wickedness that Goodman Brown witnesses? How does he participate in it? How does Faith?

## Analyze Craft

3 Discuss Hawthorne's use of the forest as a symbol. What does the forest represent to Goodman Brown? What does it represent to you as a reader? How and why might those images be different?

4 Discuss the ways in which the scenes that play out for Goodman Brown in the forest reflect his wavering faith. Does Goodman Brown's role as observer of these scenes make the incidents more or less personal, and why?

## Analyze Voice

5 Consider the time period in which Hawthorne wrote this story. Identify words and symbols that seem dated or have changed over time. Propose modern equivalents.

## Synthesize Summary and Analysis

6 "Faith kept me back a while," says young Goodman Brown, and by "Faith" he means more than his wife. Is her name merely allegorical? Or does she waver in her "faith" and thus become a more complex character? Explore how each character's name makes him or her symbolic—and how he or she lives up to (or defies) this promise.

## Interpret the Story

7 When he finally reaches Salem, Goodman Brown finds business as usual. The narrator wonders "Had Goodman Brown fallen asleep . . . and only dreamed a wild dream of a witch meeting?" Does Goodman Brown share this suspicion? Argue yes or no, using evidence from the story. Consider the implications of your argument—that is, how does the story's statement on human nature change when you view Goodman Brown's experience as a dream instead of reality, or vice versa?

# Franz Kafka (1883–1924)

Born in Prague to a German-speaking Jewish family, Kafka was relatively unknown during his lifetime but has since come to be recognized internationally as one of the first major modern writers. Kafka, who wrote in German, published a small amount of short fiction in his lifetime and requested that all his unpublished manuscripts be destroyed upon his death. However, his friend and biographer Max Brod disobeyed Kafka's wish, and from the manuscripts he rescued, we have three of Kafka's best-known novels: *The Castle* (1930), *The Trial* (1937), and *Amerika* (1938). An insecure man who never severed his emotional dependency on his parents, Kafka created fiction that uniquely captures the helpless feeling of the individual in a modern, uncaring world. His works are often fantastical or surreal—for example, a man awaking to find he has become a giant insect as in "The Metamorphosis," or a man caught in an inescapable court trial for no clear reason as in *The Trial*—so that the events in his works are symbolic rather than realistic. His clear, direct tone and unreal plots give his fiction the feeling of an unending nightmare, and like a dream, his work can be interpreted in so many ways that a complete understanding eludes even an advanced reader. Kafka never married and spent his life working as a civil servant by day and a writer by night. He contracted tuberculosis in 1917 and died seven years later.

**AS YOU READ** As you read, picture Gregor Samsa's appearance. He, of course, undergoes a profound metamorphosis, but other things and characters also change in the course of the story. Notice these many changes.

**TIP** **FOR INTERACTIVE READING . . .** Scan the text for references to doors. Mark these references. Why do the doors play such an important part in the story? Describe the symbolic ways they are used.

# The Metamorphosis (1915)

## I

1 When Gregor Samsa awoke in his bed one morning from unquiet dreams, he found himself transformed into an enormous insect. He lay on a back as hard as armor and saw, when he raised his head slightly, a jutting brown underbelly divided into arching segments. The bedcovers could barely cover it; they threatened to slide off altogether. His many legs, pitifully thin in comparison with the rest of his bulk, fluttered helplessly before his eyes.

2 "What has happened to me?" he thought. It wasn't a dream. His room—a decent enough room for a person, if slightly too small—lay quietly between the four familiar walls. Over the table on which was spread his unpacked collections of fabric samples—Samsa was a traveling salesman—hung the picture that he had recently cut out of an illustrated magazine and fit into an attractive gilt frame. The picture was of a woman clad in a fur hat and a fur stole; she sat upright and held out to the viewer a thick fur muff into which her entire forearm disappeared.

3 Gregor's gaze then directed itself to the window. The dreary weather—one could hear raindrops hit the metal awning over the window—made him quite melancholy. "What if I slept a bit longer and forgot all this foolishness," he thought. But that was altogether impossible, because he was used to sleeping on his right side, and his current condition made working himself into this position impossible. No matter how vigorously he swung himself over to the right, he immediately rolled again onto his back. He tried what seemed hundreds of times, closing his eyes in order to avoid having to see his wriggling legs. He finally gave up only when he began to feel in his side a small dull ache that he had never felt before.

4 "Oh, God," he thought, "what a strenuous profession I've chosen—traveling day in, day out! The demands of business are far greater on the road than they are at the home office, and I'm burdened with the annoyances of travel besides: the worry about train connections; the irregular, bad meals; a social life limited to passing acquaintances who never become real friends. To hell with it!" He felt an itch on his belly, and he shoved himself back against the bedpost so he could lift his head more easily. He found the spot that itched: it was covered with small white dots that he couldn't identify. He went to touch the spot with one of his legs but drew it back immediately, because the touch made him shudder.

5 He slid back into his former position. "This early rising," he thought, "can make you into a complete idiot. A man needs his sleep. Other travelers live like women in a harem. When, for example, I go back to my hotel during the course of the morning to write up orders, these gentlemen are just sitting down to breakfast. I should try that with the Director: I'd be fired on the spot. Who knows, though—that might be good for me. If it weren't for my parents, I would have given notice long ago: I would have confronted the Director and given him a piece of my mind. He would have fallen off his chair! It's incredible the way he has of sitting perched at his reading desk and speaking from on high to employees who, on top of everything, have to draw very near owing to his slight deafness. Oh well, I shouldn't give up hope altogether: once I have the money to pay off my parents' debt—it should only be another five or six years—I'll definitely do it. Then I'll make my big break. In the meantime, I have to get up—my train leaves at five."

6 And he looked over at the alarm clock that ticked on the bureau. "God in heaven!" he thought. It was six-thirty, and the hands of the clock went quietly on; it was even later than six-thirty—it was closer to six-forty-five. Shouldn't the alarm have gone off? He could see from the bed that it was correctly set for four o'clock; it must have gone off. But was it possible to sleep peacefully through that furniture-rattling noise? Of course, he hadn't actually slept peacefully, but he had no doubt for that reason slept more deeply. But what should he do now? The next train left at seven o'clock. In order to catch that one, he'd have to rush like a madman, and his samples weren't packed up yet. He hardly felt alert or energetic enough. And even if he caught the train, he wouldn't avoid the Director's wrath, because the office porter had been waiting at the five-o'clock train and would long since have reported his failure to appear. The porter was completely under the Director's thumb—he had neither a backbone nor brains. What if Gregor were to report himself sick? But that would be highly awkward and suspicious, because he had not been sick once in five years of service. The Director would certainly come with the insurance doctor. He would reproach his parents for their lazy son and dismiss all rejoinders by referring them to the doctor, who considered all people completely healthy, but work-averse. And would he be so wrong in this case? Gregor actually felt completely fine, despite a fatigue completely unwarranted after such a long sleep. He even had a powerful appetite.

7 As he thought all this over hurriedly, without being able to decide whether to leave his bed—the clock had just struck six-forty-five—there was a knock on the door near the head of his bed. "Gregor," he heard—it was his mother—"it's a quarter to seven. Weren't you going on a trip?" What a gentle voice! Gregor was terrified when he heard his answer. It was unmistakably in his old voice, but had mixed in, as if from down deep, an irrepressible, painful, squeaking noise, which allowed words to be heard clearly when first uttered, but as they resonated, distorted them to such an extent that they were difficult to understand. Gregor had wanted to answer in detail and explain everything, but in light of the circumstances he limited himself to saying: "Yes, yes, thanks, Mother, I'm getting up." The wooden door seemed to make the change in Gregor's voice imperceptible outside the room, because his mother was satisfied with his explanation and shuffled away. But through this brief exchange the other family members had become aware that Gregor was unexpectedly still at home, and his father was already knocking on one side door—lightly, but with his fist. "Gregor, Gregor," he called, "What's going on?" And after a short pause he urged again, with a deeper voice: "Gregor! Gregor!" At the other side door, his sister fretted softly: "Gregor? Are you ill? Do you need something?" To both sides, Gregor answered,

"I'm just about ready to go," and he made an effort to ban anything conspicuous from his voice by the most painstaking enunciation and by inserting long pauses between individual words. His father returned to his breakfast, but his sister whispered: "Gregor, open up, I beg you." Gregor had no intention of opening the door, however—instead he gave thanks for his habitual precaution, born of much travel, of locking all doors during the night, even at home.

8 First he wanted to get up, quietly and undisturbed, get dressed, and above all eat breakfast—only then did he want to think over what came next, because he could see that he would come to no reasonable conclusions as along as he lay in bed. In the past he had often felt one mild pain or another while lying in bed, possibly from lying in an awkward position, that proved to be sheer imagination once he got up. He was eager to see how today's fantasies would gradually resolve themselves. He didn't doubt in the least that the change in his voice was nothing more than the harbinger of a hearty cold, one of the occupational hazards of traveling salesmen.

He was eager to see how today's fantasies would gradually resolve themselves.

9 Throwing off the covers was perfectly simple: he only needed to puff himself up a bit and they fell off on their own. But doing more than that was difficult, especially because he was so strangely broad. He would normally have used his arms and hands to get up: now, he had only the many little legs which were continuously moving in every direction and which he could not seem to control. If he meant to bend one, it would be the first one to stretch itself out; if he finally succeeded in enforcing his will with one leg, all the rest of them worked furiously, as if liberated, in extreme, painful agitation. "You can't just lie here in bed doing nothing," Gregor said to himself.

10 At first he intended to get out of the bed with the lower part of his body foremost, but this lower part, which he had moreover not yet seen and of which he could not form a proper mental image, proved too difficult to move. It went extremely slowly. When, nearly frantic, he finally gathered his strength and recklessly shoved himself forward, he misjudged the direction and violently struck the lower bed post. The burning pain he felt convinced him that the lower part of his body was at least at the moment the most sensitive part.

11 He afterwards attempted to get his upper body out of bed and carefully turned his head towards the edge of the bed. This he could do easily, and in spite of its bulk and weight, the mass of his body finally slowly followed the direction of his head. But when he held his head at last free of the bed, he became afraid to shift further in this direction, because if he ultimately let himself fall like that, it would be a miracle if his head were not injured. And now, of all times, he could not afford to lose consciousness; he would rather remain in bed.

12 After continued effort, however, he found himself lying exactly as before, and heaved a sigh. He saw his little legs struggling against one another even more furiously, if that were possible, and he saw no way of introducing calm and order to this anarchy. At this point he repeated to himself that he could not possibly lie in bed any longer and that it would be most sensible to risk everything, even if there were only the smallest hope of thereby freeing himself from bed. At the same time, however, he kept reminding himself that calm deliberation was always better than rash decision-making. All the while he tried hard to focus on the view from the window, but unfortunately there was little encouragement or cheer to gain from the sight of the morning fog, which shrouded even the opposite side of the narrow street. "Already seven o'clock," he said to himself with the latest striking of the alarm clock, "already seven o'clock and still such fog." And he lay quiet a short while, breathing shallowly, as if he thought complete stillness might restore things to their true and natural state.

13 After a bit, however, he said to himself, "Before it strikes seven-fifteen, I must without fail be completely out of bed. For one thing, someone from the company will have come by then to inquire after me, because the office opens before seven." And he concentrated his efforts toward swinging his entire body out of the bed all at the same time. If he let himself fall out of bed in this manner, his head, which he would raise sharply during the fall, would presumably remain uninjured. His back seemed to be hard; nothing would happen to it in the fall onto the carpet. His greatest source of misgiving was anticipation of the loud crash that would follow, which would probably arouse anxiety, if not terror, beyond the doors. That would have to be risked, however.

14 When, by rocking back and forth, Gregor moved halfway off of the bed—the new method was more a game than an exertion—it occurred to him how simple everything would be if someone would come help him. Two strong people—he thought of his father and the servant girl—would be more than adequate. They would only have to shove their arms under his domed back, pry him up out of bed, prop up his bulk by crouching low, and then help him complete the turn over onto the floor, where hopefully his little legs would gain some sense of purpose. Quite apart from the fact that the doors were locked, though, should he really call for help? In spite of his predicament he couldn't suppress a smile at the thought.

15 He was already so far along that he could hardly maintain his balance when he rocked forcefully. Very soon he would have to make a final decision, because in five minutes it would be seven-fifteen. Just then the front doorbell rang. "That's someone from the company," he said to himself and virtually froze, though his little legs only danced more hurriedly. Everything remained quiet for a moment. "They're not opening the door," Gregor said to himself, momentarily carried away by some absurd hope. But then, naturally, as always, the servant girl directed her firm step to the door and opened it. Gregor needed to hear only the first word of greeting from the visitor and he already knew who it was—the Deputy Director himself. Why was Gregor condemned to work at a company where the least infraction immediately attracted the greatest suspicion? Were all employees then without exception scoundrels; were there among them no loyal, devoted individuals who, when they had merely missed a few morning hours of service, would become so tormented by pangs of conscience that they would be frankly unable to leave their beds? Wouldn't it really have been enough to send an apprentice to inquire—if indeed this inquiry were necessary at all? Did the Deputy Director himself have to come, thereby showing the entire innocent family that the investigation of this suspicious situation could only be entrusted to the Deputy Director himself? And more as a result of the agitation into which this line of thought transported Gregor, than as a result of a proper decision, he swung himself with all his might out of the bed. There was a loud thump, but no actual crash. The fall was muffled a bit by the carpet, and his back was more elastic than Gregor had thought—these things accounted for the fairly inconspicuous dull thump. He had failed only to raise his head carefully enough and had struck it. He twisted it back and forth and rubbed it into the carpet out of anger and pain.

16 "Something happened inside there," said the Deputy Director in the room to the left. Gregor tried to imagine something similar to what had happened to him today happening to the Deputy Director; it really was possible, after all. But as if in cruel response to this question the Deputy Director took a few decisive steps in the next room, making his patent leather boots creak. From the room to the right Gregor's sister whispered to inform him: "Gregor, the Deputy Director is here." "I know," said Gregor to himself; but he did not dare to raise his voice loud enough for his sister to hear.

17 "Gregor," his father now said from the room to the left, "the Deputy Director has come and inquires as to why you did not leave with the early morning train. We don't know what we should say to him. Furthermore, he wants to speak to you directly. So please open the door. He will surely have the goodness to excuse the disorder of your room." "Good morning, Mr. Samsa," the Deputy Director called out at the same time in a friendly manner. "He is not well," his mother said to the Deputy Director, while his father still spoke at the door, "he is not well, believe me, sir. Why would Gregor otherwise miss a train? The boy has nothing in his head but the company. I almost worry that he never goes out at night; he has been in the city eight days now, but he was at home every night. He sits with us at the table and quietly reads the newspaper or studies train schedules. Busying himself with woodworking is as far as he goes in the way of amusement. In the course of two, three evenings, for example, he cut himself a small frame; you would be astounded at how pretty it is. It's hanging in his room; you will see it right away, when Gregor opens up. I am happy, in any case, that you're here, Deputy Director. We could not have persuaded Gregor to open the door alone; he is so stubborn; and there's certainly something wrong with him, although he denied it this morning." "I'm coming right away," said Gregor slowly and carefully, while not moving at all, in order not to miss a word of the conversation. "Otherwise, dear woman, I can't explain it myself, either," said the Deputy Director. "Hopefully, it's nothing serious. Though I must say, that we businessmen—either fortunately or unfortunately, as you will—must often ignore a trivial indisposition in the interest of business." "So can the Deputy Director come in to see you?" asked his impatient father, knocking again at the door. "No," said Gregor. In the room to the left there arose an awkward silence; in the room to the right, his sister began sobbing.

18 Why didn't his sister join the others? She had most likely just now arisen from bed and had not yet begun to get dressed. And why was she crying? Because he did not stand up and let the Deputy Director in; because he was in danger of losing his position and because the Director would then persecute his parents

with the old demands? Those were unnecessary worries, for the time being. Gregor was still here and did not in the least contemplate leaving his family. At the moment he was lying on the carpet, and no one who was aware of his condition would seriously request that he let the Deputy Director in. Gregor could not possibly be dismissed just for this minor breach of politeness; he could easily find a suitable excuse later. And it seemed to Gregor far more reasonable to leave him in peace now, instead of disturbing him with tears and entreaties. But it was the uncertainty of it all that distressed the others and so excused their behavior.

19 "Mr. Samsa," the Deputy Director now called in a raised voice, "what's the matter? You barricade yourself there in your room, answer merely with yes and no, burden your parents with profound, unnecessary worries and—this only mentioned incidentally—neglect your business responsibilities in an unheard-of way. I speak here in the name of your parents and your Director and earnestly request of you an immediate, clear explanation. I am amazed; I am amazed. I thought I knew you as a quiet, reasonable person, and now you suddenly begin to exhibit extraordinary capriciousness. The Director told me early this morning of a possible explanation for your dereliction—it related to the cash account recently entrusted to you—but I actually almost gave him my word of honor that this explanation could not be accurate. Now, however, I see your incomprehensible stubbornness here, and I lose any desire to vouch for you in the least. And your position is not the most secure. I originally had the intention of saying all of this just between the two of us, but since you force me to waste my time here needlessly, I don't know why your parents should not also hear it. Your performance recently has been very unsatisfying. It is not the time of the year, of course, to do extraordinary business, we recognize that; but there is no time of year in which to do *no* business, Mr. Samsa—there cannot be."

He ignored the pain in his lower body, despite the fact that it burned.

20 "But sir," called out Gregor, beside himself, forgetting everything else in his agitation, "I'll open up immediately, this instant. A mild indisposition—an attack of dizziness—has kept me from getting up. I'm still lying in bed. I'm completely recovered now, though. I'm climbing out of bed right now. Just one moment of patience! I thought things were not quite back to normal yet. But I'm already well again. How it can suddenly come over a person! I was fine yesterday evening, my parents know that, or perhaps I should say that yesterday evening I had a slight premonition of it. It must have been easy to see in me. Why didn't I report it to the office yesterday! But one always thinks that one can ride out illness without having to stay home. Sir! Spare my parents! There is no basis for all the reproaches you've made against me; no one said anything about them to me before now. Perhaps you haven't seen the latest orders that I sent in. In any case, I will be starting my trip on the eight o'clock train. These few hours of rest have strengthened me. Don't let me hold you up, though, sir; I'll soon be in the office myself, and please have the goodness to say so, and to send my greetings to the Director."

And while Gregor hurriedly blurted all this out, 21
hardly knowing what he said, he moved effortlessly closer to the chest, thanks to the practice he had had in bed, and attempted to raise himself against it to an upright position. He actually wanted to open the door, actually wanted to let them see him and to speak with the Deputy Director. He was eager to know what they all would say to him when they finally saw him, after so much urging. Would they be afraid? If so, Gregor would be absolved of responsibility and could relax. If they took it all in stride, however, then, too, he would have no cause for worry, and he really could be at the train station at eight, if he hurried. At first he simply slid a few times down the side of the slippery chest; finally, however, he gave himself one last swing and stood upright. He ignored the pain in his lower body, despite the fact that it burned. Now he let himself fall against the back of a nearby chair and held tight to its sides with his legs. This helped him regain his self-control, and he stayed quiet, so that he could hear the Deputy Director speak.

"Did you understand one word?" the Deputy Di- 22
rector asked his parents. "Surely he's making fun of us?" "For God's sake," cried his mother in the midst of tears, "he might be seriously ill, and we're all plaguing him. Grete! Grete!" she then screamed. "Mother?" called his sister from the other side. They were communicating through Gregor's room. "You must go fetch the doctor this minute. Gregor is ill. Quickly, to the doctor. Did you hear Gregor speak just now?" "That was the voice of an animal," said the Deputy Director, noticeably quiet, by contrast with the screaming of his mother. "Anna! Anna!" called his father towards the kitchen, clapping his hands, "Get a locksmith immediately!" And the two girls ran, their skirts rustling, through the foyer—how had his sister gotten dressed so quickly?—and flung the apartment door open. There was no noise of the door slamming; they had probably left it open, as was usual in apartments where some great misfortune had occurred.

23 Gregor had become much calmer, however. It was true that they didn't understand his speech, but it sounded clear enough to him, clearer than previously, perhaps because his ear had adjusted to it. But they did still believe that something was wrong with him, and they were prepared to help him. He was pleased by the confidence and certainty with which the first arrangements had been made. He felt drawn once again into the circle of humanity and expected great things from both the doctor and the locksmith, without really making a distinction between them. In order to develop the clearest possible voice for the decisive discussions to come, he coughed a bit, although he tried to do this in a muted fashion, because this, too, might sound very different from a human cough—he no longer trusted himself to judge. It had now fallen completely silent in the next room. His parents might have been sitting at the table, whispering with the Deputy Director, or perhaps they were all pressed against the door, listening.

24 Using the chair, Gregor slowly shoved himself forward, and then let go, throwing himself against the door, and holding himself upright against it. The balls of his feet had some sticky substance on them. He took a moment to recover from the exertion. Then he applied himself to turning the key in the lock. Unfortunately, it seemed as if he had no real teeth—what then could he grip the key with?—but his jaws, on the other hand, were powerful. With their help he started to turn the key. He paid no attention to the fact that he obviously did some harm to himself in the process—a brown discharge came out from his mouth, flowing over the key and dripping on the floor. "Listen now," said the Deputy Director in the next room, "he's turning the key." That encouraged Gregor greatly, but all of them should have cheered him on, his father and mother, too: "Come on, Gregor," they should have called, "keep at it, keep working the lock!" And imagining that all his efforts were being watched with rapt attention, he recklessly bit down on the key with all his might. He danced around the lock, following the key as it turned; holding himself upright entirely with his mouth, he either pulled up on the key or forced it down with the full weight of his body, as necessary. The crisp click of the lock finally snapping back elated him. Breathing a sigh of relief he said to himself, "I didn't even need the locksmith," and he laid his head on the door handle, in order to open the door.

25 Because he had to open the door in this way, he was not yet visible even when it was opened wide. If he didn't want to fall flat on his back just before his entrance into the next room, he would first have to slowly make his way around the open panel of the double door. He was still busy with this difficult maneuver and had not yet had a moment to think of the others, when he heard the Deputy Director force out a loud "Oh!" It sounded like a gust of wind. Now he could also see the Deputy, who was nearest the door—he pressed his hand to his open mouth and slowly shrank back, as if an invisible, irresistible force drove him. His mother—who stood, despite the presence of the Deputy Director, with her hair still loose, and sticking up in parts from her night's sleep—first looked at his father with her hands clasped; then she walked two steps towards Gregor and sank to the ground in the midst of her billowing skirts, her face completely hidden, sunk upon her breast. His father balled his fist with a fierce expression, as if he wanted to knock Gregor back into his room; then he looked uncertainly around the living room, covered his eyes with his hands, and sobbed so that his powerful chest shook.

Gregor had not yet entered the outer room; instead, he leaned from within against the door panel 26
that was still fastened, so that only half of his body and his head, craned to one side in order to see them, were visible. It had become much brighter outside in the meantime: one could clearly see a section of the endless, gray-black building—it was a hospital—that stood across the street, its severe, uniform windows breaking up its facade. The rain still fell, but only in large, singly visible and singly plummeting drops. The table teemed with breakfast dishes; his father considered breakfast the most important meal of the day, and he protracted it for hours reading various periodicals. On the wall just opposite hung a photograph of Gregor from his military days, which showed him dressed as a lieutenant, with a carefree smile, his hand on his dagger, his bearing and his uniform commanding respect. The door to the foyer was open, and because the door to the apartment was open as well, one could see the outer hall and the top of the staircase leading downwards.

"Now," said Gregor—and he was well aware that 27
he was the only one remaining calm—"I will just get dressed, pack my samples up, and be off. Will you all allow me to go? Deputy Director, you see that I'm not obstinate and that I want to work. Traveling is demanding, but I couldn't live without it. Where do you intend to go now, Deputy Director? To the office? Yes? Will you report everything accurately? A person might be unable to work for a time, but it is precisely then that one must consider his past accomplishments and keep in mind that once the hindrance is past, he will certainly work even harder and more efficiently. I owe a great deal to the Director—you know that only too well. On the other hand, I have the care of my par-

ents and sister. I'm in a fix, but I'll work my way out again. But please don't make it more difficult for me than it already is. Take my part in the office! I know the traveling salesmen aren't popular. People think we earn a huge amount of money and lead grand lives. People just don't have any particular reason to think this prejudice through carefully. You, however, Deputy Director, you have a better perspective on how things work than most of the staff—I might say, confidentially, a better perspective than even the Director himself, who, in his capacity as owner, as easily be misled in his judgment about an employee. You know very well that the traveling salesman, because he is away from the office the better part of the year, easily falls victim to gossip, to chance misfortune, and groundless complaints. It's impossible for him to defend himself against these complaints, as he ordinarily learns nothing of them; it's only when he comes home at the end of a trip completely exhausted that he feels the terrible consequences, whose origins he can't divine, in his very body. Deputy Director, don't leave without saying one word that shows me that you agree with me at least in part!"

I'm in a fix, but I'll work my way out again.

28 But the Deputy Director had turned away at Gregor's first words, and was staring back at Gregor over one twitching shoulder, his mouth agape. During Gregor's speech he had not stood still for a moment, but, never taking his eyes off of Gregor, moved steadily but surreptitiously towards the door, as if there were some secret prohibition against leaving the room. He had already reached the foyer, and judging by the sudden movement with which he pulled his foot out of the room at his last step, one would have thought his sole was on fire. Once in the foyer, he stretched his hand out towards the staircase as if divine deliverance awaited him there.

29 Gregor realized that the Deputy Director could under no circumstances be allowed to leave this way, if his position at the company were not to be endangered. His parents didn't understand this as well as he did. They had over the years persuaded themselves that he was guaranteed permanent employment in the company, and besides, they had so much to do in dealing with their own distress at the moment, that their foresight had vanished. But Gregor had this foresight. The Deputy Director must be detained, calmed, persuaded, and finally won over—the future of Gregor and his family depended on it. If only his sister were here! She was clever: she was already crying when Gregor was still calmly lying on his back. And the Deputy Director, that ladies' man, would surely have let her sway him: she would have closed the apartment door and talked him out of his fear in the foyer. But his sister was not there, so Gregor would have to handle it himself. And without thinking about the fact that he had no idea yet how well he could move, without thinking that his speech was possibly—well, very probably—incomprehensible, he let go of the door panel, forcing himself through the opening, and headed for the Deputy Director, who was already at the landing in the hall and hugging himself in a comical manner. With a small cry, scrambling in vain for something to hold on to, Gregor immediately fell down onto his many little legs. This had hardly happened, when for the first time that morning he felt a sense of physical well-being. His little legs had solid ground beneath them; they obeyed him completely, as he noted to his delight. They even strove to carry him where he wanted to go. Suddenly, he believed that the ultimate relief of all his suffering was at hand. But at that moment, as he lay on the floor trembling with suppressed energy, close to his mother and directly opposite her, she sprang up—she who had seemed so lost in thought—with her arms outstretched, her fingers splayed, and cried out: "Help, for God's sake, help!" She kept her head turned towards him, as if she wanted to be able to see him better, but, following a contradictory impulse, she ran heedlessly backwards, forgetting that the table full of dishes lay behind her. She quickly sat down when she reached it, as if absent-mindedly, seeming not to notice that next to her the coffeepot had been knocked over and coffee was streaming freely out onto the carpet.

"Mother, Mother," Gregor said softly, and looked 30
up at her. The Deputy Director vanished from his mind momentarily, and he couldn't stop himself from snapping his jaws at the empty air several times at the sight of the flowing coffee. His mother began screaming again over this, fled from the table, and fell into the arms of his father, who was hurrying towards her. But Gregor had no time then for his parents. The Deputy Director was already on the stairs. His chin on the railing, he looked back one last time. Gregor took a running start, in order to have the best chance of catching up to him. The Deputy Director must have sensed something, as he sprang down several steps and then disappeared. "Ahh!" he screamed; it echoed throughout the entire stairwell.

Unfortunately, the flight of the Deputy Director 31
seemed to have completely unhinged his father, who up until then had been relatively self-controlled. Instead of running after the Deputy Director or at least not restraining Gregor from pursuing him, with his right hand he grabbed the walking stick that the Deputy Director had left behind on an armchair together

with his hat and coat; with his left hand he picked up a large newspaper from the table; then, stamping his feet, he began to drive Gregor back into his room by swatting at him with the stick and the newspaper. None of Gregor's pleas helped—none of his pleas were understood. The more submissively he bowed his head, the more vigorously his father stamped his feet. Across the room, despite the cool weather, his mother had thrown open a window and, leaning far out of the window, pressed her face into her hands. Between the street and the stairwell there arose a strong cross-draft: the window curtains flew up; the newspapers on the table rustled, and a few pages fluttered to the floor. His father drove him back mercilessly, spitting out hissing noises like a wild beast. Gregor, however, still was unpracticed in moving backwards, so he went very slowly. If he had only been allowed time to turn around, he would have gone immediately back into his room, but he was afraid of making his father impatient. At every moment the stick in his father's hand threatened to deal him a fatal blow to his back or head. Finally, however, Gregor found he had no choice, as he noted with terror that he seemed unable to keep going in the right direction when he moved backwards. He therefore began, with frequent side-glances at his father, to turn around as quickly as he could, which was actually very slowly. His father might have understood his good intentions, because he did not disturb him while he was doing this; in fact, he actually directed him here and there from a distance with the point of his stick. If only there weren't this unbearable hissing from his father! It unnerved Gregor completely. He was already almost completely turned around when, listening to this hissing, he made a mistake and turned a bit in the wrong direction. When he was finally, fortunately, headfirst at the opening of the door, it appeared that his body was too wide to go through without further ado. In his present state of mind it was naturally far from occurring to his father to open the other door panel in order to make a wide enough passageway for Gregor. He was obsessed merely with getting Gregor into his room as quickly as possible. He would never have allowed the preparations necessary for Gregor to raise himself up and possibly go through the door that way. Instead, making a great deal of noise, he drove Gregor forward as if there were no obstacle before him. The noise coming from behind Gregor didn't sound any longer like the voice of his father. It was clearly no laughing matter, so Gregor forced himself—happen what would—through the door. One side of his body was hoisted upwards. He lay crookedly in the doorway. One of his flanks was rubbed raw, and on the white door ugly smears remained behind. He was soon stuck fast, and couldn't move at all anymore. His little legs hung twitching on one side, and those on the other side were pressed painfully against the floor. Then his father liberated him with a powerful shove from behind, and he flew, bleeding heavily, a long way into his room. The door was slammed shut with the stick, and then it was finally quiet.

He immediately dunked his head in the milk nearly up to his eyes.

## II

32 It was already twilight when Gregor awoke from a deep, dreamless sleep. He would not have arisen much later even without having been disturbed, for he felt well rested and no longer sleepy, but it seemed to him that he had been awakened by the sounds of a fleeting footstep and of the door to the foyer carefully being shut. The glare from the electric street lamp outside lay palely here and there on the ceiling of his room and on the upper surfaces of the furniture, but down by Gregor it was dark. He shoved himself slowly towards the door, awkwardly groping with the feelers he had just then come to appreciate, in order to see what had happened there. His left side seemed to be a single, long, unpleasantly taut scar, and he had to positively limp on his row of legs. One leg had been seriously injured during the events of the morning: it dragged limply behind him.

33 It was only when he was at the door that he realized what had actually lured him there: it was the smell of something edible. Standing there was a basin filled with fresh milk, swimming with small pieces of white bread. He could almost have laughed for joy, for he was even hungrier than he had been that morning. He immediately dunked his head in the milk nearly up to his eyes. But he soon pulled back, disappointed. It wasn't only that his tender left side made it hard for him to eat—for it seemed he was able to eat only if his entire panting body cooperated—it was rather that the milk, which had always been his favorite drink, and which his sister certainly placed here for that reason, didn't taste good to him at all. He turned away from the basin with something like revulsion and crept back into the middle of the room.

34 The gas lamps had been turned on in the living room, as Gregor saw through the crack in the door. Whereas ordinarily at this hour his father would read the afternoon paper out loud to his mother and some-

times to his sister, now there wasn't a sound. Perhaps the reading, which his sister had frequently told him and wrote him about, had lately dropped out of their routine. It was completely quiet, though the apartment was certainly not empty. "What a quiet life the family leads," Gregor said to himself and felt great pride, as he stared into the darkness before him, that he had been able to provide his parents and his sister with such a life, in such a nice apartment. But what if terror now drove away all quiet, all prosperity, all contentment? Rather than surrender to such thoughts, Gregor preferred to move about, so he crawled back and forth in the room.

35 Once during the long evening one of the side doors and later the other was opened a crack and then hastily shut again. Someone had probably needed to come in, but had then thought better of it. Gregor now stopped directly in front of the door to the living room, determined somehow to get the hesitant visitor to come in, or at least to find out who it was, but the doors were not opened again and Gregor waited in vain. Early on, when the doors were locked, everyone had wanted to come in; now, when he had unlocked one door and the others had clearly been unlocked during the day, no one came, and the keys had been moved to the outside.

36 It was late at night before the light in the living room was turned out, and it was now clear that his parents and sister had been awake until then, for all three could clearly be heard departing on tiptoes. Now surely no one would come to see Gregor until morning; he therefore had quite a while in which to consider undisturbed how he should newly arrange his life. But he was uneasy lying flat on the ground in the high-ceilinged open room. He did not know why this should be, for he had lived in the room for five years already. Half unconsciously, and not without some shame, he scurried under the sofa where, despite the fact that his back was a bit crushed and he could no longer lift his head, he immediately felt more comfortable, regretting only that his body was too broad to fit completely underneath.

37 He remained there the entire night. He spent part of it in a light sleep, out of which hunger kept jolting him awake, and part of it awake, consumed by worries and by vague hopes that all led to the same conclusion: that for the time being he should keep calm and, by exercising patience and the greatest consideration for his family, try to make bearable the unpleasantness that he would in his present condition inevitably cause them.

Early the next morning—it was nearly still night—Gregor had a chance to test the firmness of his resolve, for his sister, already half-dressed, opened the door leading from the foyer and looked tensely inside. She couldn't find him right away, but when she noticed him under the sofa—God, he had to be someplace, he couldn't have just flown away—she was so shocked that without being able to stop herself, she slammed the door shut again. But as if she regretted her behavior, she opened the door again immediately, and came inside on tiptoe, as if she were in the presence of someone severely ill, or even a complete stranger. Gregor shoved his head forward just to the edge of the sofa and watched her. He wondered whether she would notice that he had left the milk standing, though not from lack of hunger, and whether she would bring him some other food that suited him better. If she didn't do it on her own, he would rather starve than make her aware of it, although he felt a strong urge to shoot out from beneath the sofa, throw himself at her feet, and beg her for something good to eat. But his sister, with some amazement, right away noticed the still full basin: only a bit of milk had been spilled around its edges. She picked it up immediately, though with a rag, not with her bare hands, and took it away. Gregor was extremely curious to see what she would bring as a replacement and thought a great deal about it. He could never have guessed, however, what his sister in her goodness actually did. In order to test his preferences, she brought him an entire assortment of foods spread out on an old newspaper. There were old, half-rotten vegetables; bones from last night's meal, covered with congealed white sauce; a few raisins and almonds; a cheese that Gregor had declared inedible two days before; a piece of dry bread, a piece of bread smeared with butter, and a piece with butter and salt. Beside this she placed the basin that seemed now to be designated permanently for Gregor, which she had filled with water. And out of tact, because she knew Gregor would not eat in front of her, she departed hastily, even going so far as to turn the key in the lock, just so that Gregor would know that he could make himself as comfortable as he wanted. Gregor's legs quivered, now that the meal lay waiting. His wounds must moreover have completely healed. He felt no impairment now, and was astonished at this, thinking of how he had cut himself very slightly with a knife more than a month ago, and how the wound had still hurt him considerably the day before yesterday. "Am I less sensitive than before?" he wondered, and sucked greedily at the cheese, to which he had found himself urgently drawn, before everything else. In rapid succession, amidst tears of joy, he devoured the cheese, the vegetables, and the sauce. He didn't like the taste
38 of the fresh foods, however—he couldn't even bear their smell, and dragged the foods that he wanted to eat a bit farther away. He had long since finished

everything and lay lazily in the same spot when his sister slowly turned the key in the lock, as a sign that he should withdraw. That jolted him awake immediately, though he was almost dozing, and he hurried back under the sofa. But it took great self-control for him to remain under the sofa even for the brief time that his sister was in the room, for his body had swelled a bit with the ample meal, and he could hardly breathe in the narrow space. Half-suffocating, he looked out with slightly bulging eyes as his sister, who noticed nothing, swept up with a broom not just the remainder of the food Gregor had eaten, but also the food that he had not even touched, as if this were no longer useable. She put it all in a container that she closed with a wooden lid, and then carried everything out. She had hardly turned around when Gregor pulled himself out from under the sofa and exhaled.

39 In this way Gregor now received his daily meals: the first in the morning, while his parents and the servant girl still slept, and the second after the common midday meal, for his parents slept a bit afterwards, and his sister sent the serving girl away on one errand or another. It was not that the others wanted him to starve, but experiencing his meals at secondhand might have been all they could bear; or perhaps his sister simply wanted to spare them even this minor source of sorrow, since they were already suffering enough.

40 With what kinds of excuses they had managed to get the doctor and the locksmith out of the apartment the first morning, Gregor didn't manage to find out. Because no one could understand him, it didn't occur to anyone—not even to his sister—that he could understand them, so he had to content himself, when his sister was in his room, with listening to her occasional sighs and appeals to the saints. It was only later, when she had gotten used to things a bit—getting used to them completely was out of the question, of course—that Gregor sometimes seized on a remark that was meant in a friendly way or that could be taken that way. "Today he liked it," she said, if he had made a real dent in the meal, while in the contrary case, which occurred ever more frequently of late, she used to say almost sadly: "Everything untouched again."

41 Though Gregor could not learn any news directly, he overheard some from the rooms next door. The moment he heard voices, he immediately ran to the door and pressed his entire body up against it. Especially in the early days, there was no conversation that did not somehow, if only indirectly, relate to him. For two days there were consultations at every meal about what they should do; between meals, too, they discussed the same thing. There were always at least two family members at home, because no one wanted to remain home alone, and they couldn't under any circumstances all leave the apartment at the same time. On the very first day the girl who cooked for them had begged his mother on bended knee—it wasn't exactly clear what and how much she knew of what had happened—to dismiss her. As she departed fifteen minutes later, she tearfully thanked them for her dismissal, as if for the greatest favor that had ever been done her, and swore a terrible oath, without anyone having asked her to do so, not to betray the least of what she knew to anyone.

Now his sister had to do the cooking, together with 42
his mother. This didn't take much effort, however, because they ate practically nothing. Gregor heard them again and again urge each other to eat and receive no other answer than "Thanks, I've had enough," or something similar. It seemed they didn't drink anything, either. His sister often asked his father if he would like a beer, cheerfully offering to get it herself. When his father said nothing, she offered to send the porter for it, in case he didn't want to trouble her. When his father finally uttered a firm "No," the subject was dropped.

In the course of the first few days his father ex- 43
plained their entire financial situation and their prospects to his mother and to his sister. Now and then he stood up from the table and took various documents and notebooks out of the small safe that he had rescued from the bankruptcy of his business five years before. He could be heard opening the complicated lock and closing it again after removing what he sought. His father's explanations contained the first heartening news that Gregor had heard since his imprisonment. He had been under the impression that his father had absolutely nothing left over from his business. At least, he had said nothing to the contrary, and Gregor had certainly never asked him about it. Gregor's concern at the time of the bankruptcy had been to arrange everything so that the family could forget as soon as possible the financial misfortune that had brought them to a state of complete despair. And so he had begun to work with pronounced fervor. Practically overnight he was elevated from a minor clerk into a traveling salesman, which naturally gave him completely different financial prospects. His successes at work translated directly into cash that he could lay on the table at home before his astonished and pleased

family. Those had been fine times, but they had never recurred, at least not with the same warm feelings, although Gregor later earned so much money that he was in a position to support the entire family, and he did so. They simply got used to it—the family, as well as Gregor. They gratefully accepted his money, and he gladly offered it, but that special warmth did not reappear. Only his sister remained close to Gregor. Because she loved music very much, unlike Gregor, and could play the violin movingly, he secretly planned to send her to the conservatory next year, despite the great cost, which would have to be made up somehow. The conservatory came up often in conversations with his sister during Gregor's brief stays in the city, but only as a beautiful dream whose realization was unthinkable. His parents didn't even like to hear them utter those innocent musings. But Gregor had given it a good deal of thought and intended to announce his decision with due ceremony on Christmas Eve.

44 These thoughts, completely futile in his present situation, went through his head while he clung to the door and listened. Sometimes, from sheer exhaustion, he could listen no more and would let his head fall against the door, but then immediately catch himself, for even the faint noise that he made in doing so was heard next door and caused them all to fall silent. "What's he doing now?" said his father after a pause, obviously turned towards the door. Only then was the interrupted conversation gradually taken up again.

45 Gregor now learned—for his father tended to repeat himself often in his explanations, partly because he had not concerned himself with these matters for a long while, and partly, too, because his mother didn't immediately understand everything the first time—that despite all their misfortunes, a certain sum, though a very small one, was left over from the old days. The untouched interest on the sum had moreover in the meantime allowed it to grow a bit. Besides this, the money that Gregor had brought home every month—he had only kept a few florins for himself—had not been completely exhausted and had accumulated into a small amount of capital. Gregor, behind the door, nodded eagerly, overjoyed at this unexpected foresight and thriftiness. It occurred to him that he might have used that extra money to further pay down the debt his father owed the Director, bringing closer the day that he could quit his job, but the way his father had arranged things was no doubt better.

46 The sum that had been saved was not, however, large enough to allow his family to live off of the interest. It would have been enough to support them for a year, or at most two years, but no longer. The sum really shouldn't be touched; it should be set aside for emergencies. To live, money would have to be earned. His father was a healthy but old man, who had not worked now for five years and couldn't in any case take on too much. During these five years, which had been the first free time of his hardworking but unsuccessful life, he had put on a great deal of weight and had become downright sluggish. But was his elderly mother supposed to earn money now—his mother, who suffered from asthma, for whom even a stroll through the apartment was considerable exertion, and who spent every other day on the sofa by the open window, gasping for breath? Or his sister, who at seventeen was still a child, and whose lifestyle up to that point had consisted of dressing herself neatly, sleeping late, helping out in the household, taking part in a few modest pleasures, and above all playing the violin? Whenever the conversation turned towards the necessity of earning money, Gregor left the door and threw himself on the leather sofa that stood nearby, for he burned with shame and sorrow.

Often he lay there the long night through, though he was unable to sleep for a moment and just scratched for hours at the leather. Or he would go to great pains to shove an armchair to the window, then crawl up to the windowsill and, bolstered by the armchair, lean against the window. He did so only in some kind of nostalgia for the feeling of freedom he had previously found in looking out the window, for the fact was that every day he saw things that were even a short distance away less and less clearly. He could no longer see the hospital that lay across the way, whose all too massive prospect he had earlier cursed. If he had not known very well that he lived in the quiet, but distinctly urban Charlotte Street, he could have believed that he looked out of his window into a desert in which the gray sky and the gray earth merged indistinguishably. His alert sister only had to see the armchair standing by the window twice before she began to shove the chair precisely back to the spot by the window after she straightened up the room. She even left the inner casement open from then on. 47

If Gregor had been able to speak to his sister and thank her for everything she had to do for him, he would have been able to bear her assistance more easily; as it was, however, it caused him some pain. His sister tried to hide the awkwardness of the whole thing as much as possible, and the longer it went on, the better she succeeded, but Gregor felt everything more acutely as time went on. Even her entrance was terrible for him. She had hardly entered, when, without even taking the time to shut the doors, though she otherwise took such pains to spare everyone the sight of Gregor's room, she ran to the window and hastily flung it open, as if she were suffocating. Then she remained for a time by the window, cold as it still was, 48 and breathed deeply. With this running and commotion she alarmed Gregor twice daily. He trembled under the sofa the entire time and yet he knew very well that she would gladly have spared him, if only it had been possible to stay in a room where Gregor was with the windows closed.

He especially liked hanging upside down from the ceiling.

49 Once—one month had already passed since Gregor's transformation, and there was no longer any reason for his sister to be astonished by his appearance—she came a bit earlier than usual and encountered Gregor as he was staring out the window, motionless and perfectly positioned to frighten someone. Gregor would not have been surprised if she had not come in, since his position hindered her from immediately opening the window, but she not only refrained from coming in, she actually turned around and locked the door. A stranger would have thought that Gregor had lain in wait for her and tried to bite her. Gregor naturally hid himself immediately under the sofa, but he had to wait until midday for her return, and she seemed then more agitated than usual. He realized from this that his appearance was still unbearable to her and that it would remain so—that she had to steel herself to keep from running at the sight of even the small portion of his body that jutted out from beneath the sofa. In order to spare her the sight, one day he dragged a sheet onto the sofa—it took him four hours to do so—and arranged it in such a way that he was completely covered. His sister could not have seen him even if she bent down. If the sheet had not been necessary, in her opinion, she could have removed it, for it obviously couldn't be pleasant for Gregor to block himself off so completely. But she left the sheet where it was, and Gregor thought he even noticed a grateful glance when he once carefully lifted the sheet with his head in order to see how his sister liked the new arrangement.

50 In the first two weeks his parents could not bring themselves to come in to see him, and he often heard them praise his sister's current industry, whereas they had previously complained a great deal about her, as she had then seemed to them a rather idle girl. In those early days, both his father and his mother often waited in front of Gregor's room while his sister straightened up, and as soon as she came out, she had to tell them precisely what it looked like in the room, what Gregor had eaten, how he had behaved, and whether there were perhaps any slight improvement in his condition. His mother also wanted to visit Gregor early on, but his father and sister dissuaded her with sound reasons to which Gregor listened very attentively, and which he completely supported. Later, however, she had to be restrained with force. When she cried out, "Let me in to see Gregor; he's my poor son! Don't you understand that I must go to him?" Gregor thought that it might be good if his mother did come in—not every day, of course, but perhaps once a week. After all, she knew how to do things much better than his sister, who, despite her courage, was still only a child, and who likely took on such a heavy burden only out of childish thoughtlessness.

Gregor's wish to see his mother was soon fulfilled. 51
During the day, for his parents' sake, Gregor did not want to show himself at the window, but he did not have much room to crawl in the few square meters of floor space. It was hard enough for him to bear lying quietly during the night, and eating soon gave him not the least bit of pleasure, so in order to distract himself, he had adopted the habit of crawling across the walls and ceiling. He especially liked hanging upside down from the ceiling. It was completely different from lying on the floor: he could breathe more freely; his entire body swayed gently; and in the nearly happy distraction in which he found himself above, it sometimes happened that he unexpectedly let himself fall and crashed to the ground. But these days he had better control of his body, so he did not hurt himself even in a great fall. His sister immediately noticed the new amusement that Gregor had found for himself—he left a trace of stickiness behind him here and there while crawling—and so she got it in her head to allow him to crawl to his utmost by removing the furniture that hindered it, especially the chest of drawers and desk. She was not capable of doing this herself, however. She didn't dare ask her father for help. The servant girl would certainly not help her: this roughly sixteen-year-old girl had stuck it out quite bravely since the dismissal of the former cook, but she had asked for the privilege of keeping the kitchen door always locked and only having to open it when specifically asked. So his sister had no choice but to enlist her mother one time when her father was absent. With cries of great joy his mother approached, but fell silent at the door of Gregor's room. His sister checked first, of course, to see that the room was in order; only then did she let her mother enter. In great haste Gregor pulled the sheet lower and gathered more material around him. It looked like a sheet had merely been carelessly thrown over the sofa. Gregor also refrained from spying out from under the sheet. He deprived himself of the sight of his mother and took his pleasure entirely from the fact that she had come. "Come on, you can't see him," said his sister, and she apparently led

her mother in by the hand. Gregor then heard the two frail women shove the heavy old chest of drawers from its place. His sister reserved the greatest part of the labor for herself, ignoring the warnings of her mother, who feared that she would overexert herself. It took a very long time. After fifteen minutes of work, his mother said that they should just leave the chest where it was, first, because it was too heavy—they wouldn't be finished before his father returned, and so would end up leaving the chest in the middle of the room, where it would block Gregor at every turn—and second, because it was not at all certain that they were doing Gregor a favor by removing the furniture. It seemed to her rather the opposite: the sight of the empty wall oppressed her heart. Why should Gregor not feel the same way? He had been used to the room's furniture for so long, that he would surely feel lost in an empty room. "And isn't it so," concluded his mother very softly—almost whispering, as if she wanted to keep Gregor, of whose precise whereabouts she wasn't certain, from hearing even the sound of her voice, for she was convinced that he could not understand the words—"isn't it so, that by removing the furniture we seem to be saying that we give up all hope of his recovery, and abandon him absolutely? I think it would be best if we left the room in exactly the same condition it was in before, so that when Gregor returns to us, he'll find everything unchanged, and so more easily forget what's happened in the meantime."

52 In listening to his mother's words, Gregor realized that the lack of any direct human communication over the course of the past two months, together with the monotonous life he led in the midst of the family, must have deranged his mind; otherwise he couldn't explain why he had earnestly desired that his room be emptied. Did he really want to let them transform the warm room, comfortably outfitted with inherited furnishings, into a cave? Granted, he would be able to crawl undisturbed in all directions, but he would at the same time forget, quickly and completely, his human past. He was already close to forgetting it, but his mother's voice, so long unheard, had roused him. Nothing should be removed; everything had to stay. He could not afford to lose the good influence the furniture had on his condition. If the furniture hindered him from carrying on his mindless crawling about, that was no drawback, it was rather a great advantage.

53 But his sister was unfortunately of a different opinion. She had become accustomed, not completely without justification, to playing the expert when it came to discussing anything that concerned Gregor with her parents. And so her mother's advice now led her to insist on the removal not only of the chest and the desk, which was all she had first intended, but of all of the furniture, with the exception of the indispensable sofa. Of course, it was not just childish stubbornness and the hard-won self-confidence she had recently and unexpectedly acquired that determined her on the this course: she had actually observed that Gregor needed a great deal of room to crawl around in, and that he did not use the furniture at all, as far as she could see. It might also have been the romantic nature of girls of her age, which sought some outlet at every opportunity, and made her want Gregor's situation to be even more terrifying, so that she could do even more than before to help him. For in a space in which Gregor, completely alone, ruled the empty walls, no person but Grete would dare to enter.

And so she did not allow herself to be swayed by 54
her mother, who faltered from sheer uneasiness at being in the room, soon fell silent, and finally helped his sister as much as she was able in shoving the chest out of the room. Gregor could spare the chest if he must, but the desk had to stay. The women had hardly left the room with the chest, pushing at it and gasping for air, when Gregor stuck his head out from under the sofa, in order to see where he could intervene, as carefully and as considerately as possible. But unfortunately it was his mother who returned first, while Grete in the next room gripped the chest and rocked it back and forth alone, without, naturally, being able to move it from its spot. His mother was not, however, used to the sight of Gregor—he might have made her sick—so Gregor, alarmed, rushed back to the opposite end of the sofa. He could not, however, prevent the sheet from moving a bit at the front. That was enough to put his mother on the alert. She froze, stood still a moment, and then returned to Grete.

Though Gregor kept telling himself that nothing 55
extraordinary was happening—a few pieces of furniture were merely being moved around—he soon realized that this continual back and forth on the part of the women, their soft calls to one another, and the scraping of the furniture on the floor affected him like the greatest of commotions closing in on him from all sides. However closely he drew in his head and legs and however firmly he pressed his body to the floor, he realized he couldn't stand it much longer. They were emptying out his room; they were taking from him everything that he held dear. They had carried out the chest which held his fret saw and other tools; they were already working free the desk from the grooves it had worn into the floor—the desk at which he had written his exercises as a student at trade school, at secondary school, and even at primary school. At this point he did not have the patience to contemplate the women's good intentions, the existence of which he had at any rate almost forgotten. Exhausted, they

worked now in complete silence, and only the heavy tread of their feet could be heard.

56 And so he burst forth from under the sofa—the women were just leaning against the desk in the next room, in order to catch their breath—though he changed the direction of his charge four times, for he really did not know what to save first. On one otherwise empty wall he distinctly saw the picture of the woman dressed entirely in furs. He crept hurriedly up to it and pressed himself against the glass, which held him fast and soothed his hot belly. At least no one could take away this picture, which Gregor now completely covered with his body. He turned his head towards the door of the living room in order to observe the women on their return.

57 They weren't allowing themselves much rest and so came back directly. Grete had put her arm around her mother and seemed practically to carry her. "Well, what should we take now?" said Grete and looked around. Then her glance met Gregor's as he clung to the wall. She maintained her composure—surely only due to her mother's presence—bent her face to her mother, in order to keep her from looking around, and said hastily, a tremor in her voice, "Come, let's go back in the living room for a moment." Grete's intention was clear to Gregor: she wanted to bring her mother to safety and then chase him down off of the wall. Well, she could try! He would sit on the picture and not give it up. He would rather spring in Grete's face.

58 But Grete's words had for the first time really unsettled his mother. She moved to the side, spotted the giant brown fleck on the flowered wallpaper, and cried out in a screeching, raw voice, before she was really fully conscious that it was Gregor that she saw, "Oh my God; oh my God!" She then fell onto the sofa with widespread arms, as if she were altogether giving up, and didn't move. "Gregor, you—!" cried his sister with a raised fist and piercing gaze. They were the first words she had directly addressed to Gregor since his transformation. She ran into the next room in order to get some scent with which she could wake her mother out of her faint. Gregor wanted to help, too—there was still time to save the picture—but he was stuck to the glass and had to tear himself free. He, too, ran into the next room, as if he could give his sister some advice, as in earlier days, but then he had to stand helplessly behind her while she rummaged through various bottles. She was startled when she turned around; a bottle fell to the floor and broke. A sliver of glass cut Gregor's face, and some burning medicine spilled over him. Grete took as many bottles as she could carry and ran with them in to her mother. She then slammed the door shut with her foot. Gregor was now shut off from his mother, who was through his fault possibly near death. He couldn't open the door, if he did not want to chase away his sister, who had to remain with his mother. He had nothing left to do but wait. Oppressed by self-reproaches and worry, he began to crawl. He crawled over everything—walls, furniture, and ceiling—and finally, in his despair, he fell, the entire room spinning around him, onto the center of the large table.

A short time passed, and Gregor lay limply there. 59
All around was quiet. Perhaps that was a good sign. Then the bell rang. The servant girl was naturally locked into her kitchen, and so Grete had to go open the door. His father had returned. "What happened?" were his first words. The look on Grete's face betrayed everything to him. Grete answered with a muffled voice—she was obviously pressing her face against her father's chest: "Mother fainted, but she's already better. Gregor broke out." "I was waiting for this," said his father, "I always said it would happen, but you women didn't want to hear it." It was clear to Gregor that his father had interpreted Grete's all-too-brief announcement in the worst possible way, and assumed that Gregor had been guilty of some act of violence. Therefore Gregor had to try to mollify his father, for he had neither the time nor the ability to enlighten him. And so he fled to the door of his room and pressed against it, so that his father could see immediately on leaving the hallway that Gregor had every intention of returning right away to his room. It would not be necessary to drive him back, just to open the door, and he would disappear instantly.

But his father was not in the mood to notice such 60
subtleties: "Ah!" he cried out on entering, in a tone that made him seem at once furious and glad. Gregor drew his head back from the door and turned it toward his father. His father's appearance was different from the way he remembered it. Lately, due to his new habit of crawling about, Gregor had concerned himself less with the goings-on in the rest of the apartment; he should therefore really have been prepared to encounter new developments. But still, still, was this really his father? The same man who lay, tired out, buried deep in his bed, when Gregor was all set to go on a business trip? The man who, dressed in a nightshirt, had greeted him when he returned in the evenings from an easy chair, and, unable to stand up, only raised his arms to show his joy at his return? The man who, on the rare walks he took together with Gregor and his mother on a few Sundays and the most important holidays of the year, walked packed into his old coat even more slowly than they did, though they walked slowly enough, laboring forward with a deliberately placed cane, and who nearly always stopped when he wanted to say something, gathering his

companions around him? Now, he was quite well put together. He was dressed in the kind of close-fitting blue uniform with gold buttons that doormen at the banking houses wore; over the high stiff collar of the coat his pronounced double chin protruded; under his bushy eyebrows the glance of his dark eyes sprang forth fresh and alert; the formerly disheveled white hair was combed flat into a painfully exact, shining part. He threw his hat, which bore a gold monogram—probably that of a bank—in an arc across the room and onto the sofa. He moved towards Gregor, the ends of his long coat pushed back, his hands in his pants pockets, his face grim. He probably did not know himself what he planned to do. In any case he lifted his feet unusually high, and Gregor was astonished at the gigantic size of the soles of his boots. But he didn't let his astonishment distract him. He had known from the first day of his new life that his father considered the greatest severity appropriate in dealing with him. And so he ran away from his father. He froze when his father stood still and hurried forward again when his father moved a muscle. In this way they circled the room several times, without anything decisive happening; the whole thing moved at such a slow tempo that it didn't even look like a pursuit. For the time being, Gregor stayed on the floor. He was afraid that his father might consider flight toward the walls or the ceiling as particular wickedness. But Gregor realized that he couldn't keep up even this pace for long, for when his father took a single step, he had to carry out myriad movements. He soon felt short of breath; his lungs had not been reliable even in the old days. As he staggered forward, he could barely keep his eyes open, so hard did he try to concentrate his energy for running. In his dullness he was simply unable to think of any other means of deliverance. He had almost forgotten already that the walls were open to him, though they were obstructed here by painstakingly carved furniture full of points and sharp edges. Suddenly something lightly thrown flew just past him and rolled ahead. It was an apple. Another immediately followed. Gregor froze in fear. Running further was pointless, for his father had decided to bombard him. He had filled his pockets from the fruit bowl on the credenza and now threw apple after apple, without for the time being aiming very carefully. These small red apples rolled around on the ground, knocking into each other as if charged with electricity. A weakly thrown apple strafed Gregor's back, but glanced off without doing any harm. One that flew immediately in its wake actually embedded itself in his back, however. Gregor tried to drag himself forward, as if he could outrun the unbelievable pain by changing position, but he felt as if he were nailed to the spot and lay sprawled upon the ground, in complete distraction of all of his senses. With his last conscious glance he watched as the door to his room was ripped open and, ahead of his screaming sister, his mother ran out of the room in her slip—for his sister had undressed her to let her breathe freely while in her faint—and raced towards his father, her untied skirts slipping down to the floor one after another; he watched as, stumbling on the skirts, she embraced his father, fully at one with him—but Gregor's vision now failed him utterly—and, with her hands clasped around the back of his head, begged him to spare Gregor's life.

Gregor was a member of the family who should not be treated as an enemy.

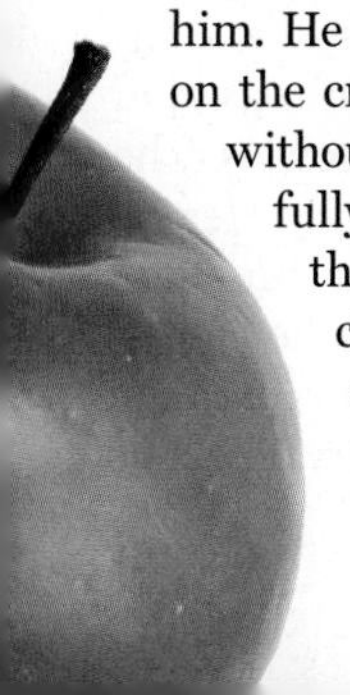

## III

61 The deep injury from which Gregor had suffered for over a month—the apple remained embedded in his flesh as a visible memento, as no one had dared to remove it—seemed to have reminded even his father that despite his present sad and repulsive state, Gregor was a member of the family who should not be treated as an enemy. The law of familial obligation dictated, rather, that one had to swallow one's revulsion and be tolerant, simply be tolerant.

62 And though Gregor had probably permanently lost some mobility through his injury, and now, like an invalid, took many, many minutes to cross his room—crawling on high was out of the question—this degeneration in his condition brought with it a compensation that was to his mind completely satisfactory. Toward evening they now opened the living room door so that, lying in the darkness of his room and invisible from the living room, he could watch the entire family at the lighted table and listen to their conversation by general consent, as it were—a complete change from the early days when he used to watch the door like a hawk an hour or two before they gathered.

63 Of course, the conversations were not as lively as in earlier days. Gregor used to recall them longingly in the small hotel rooms where he had had to throw himself, exhausted, into the damp bedclothes. These days everything was mostly very quiet. His father fell asleep in his armchair soon after the evening meal; his mother and sister urged one another to silence. His mother now sewed fine lingerie for a boutique, bend-

ing close to her work under the light. His sister, who had taken a job as a salesclerk, studied stenography and French at night, in order to find a better position one day. Sometimes his father awoke and, as if he didn't realize that he had been sleeping, would say to his mother: "How long you're sewing again today!" Then he would fall asleep again immediately, while his mother and sister exchanged tired smiles.

64 With a kind of stubbornness his father refused to take off his work uniform when he returned home, and while his nightshirt hung, useless, on a clothes hook, he dozed at his place fully clothed, as if he were always on duty and awaited the call of his superiors. As a result, the uniform, which hadn't been new in the first place, became less than pristine, despite the care his mother and sister took with it. Gregor often spent whole evenings looking at the badly stained coat, its oft-polished gold buttons shining, in which the old man slept highly uncomfortably, but quietly.

What really kept the family from changing apartments was despair . . .

65 As soon as the clock struck ten, his mother tried to wake his father by speaking softly to him, and tried to persuade him to go to bed, for he couldn't sleep well there, and a good sleep was absolutely essential, since he had to be at work by six. But in the stubbornness that had come over him since he became a bank employee, he always insisted on remaining longer where he was, although he regularly fell asleep again, and required much effort to persuade in exchanging the armchair for his bed. His mother and sister could press him with gentle remonstrances as much as they liked—for a quarter of an hour at a time he slowly shook his head, his eyes closed, and refused to stand up. His mother plucked at his sleeve, and whispered endearments in his ear; his sister left her work in order to help her mother, but got nowhere with him. He only sank deeper into his armchair. Only when the women grasped him under the arms would he open his eyes, look in turn at Gregor's mother and sister, and say, "What a life. This is the peace and quiet of my old age." And bracing himself against the women, he hoisted himself up laboriously, as if he were his own greatest burden, and allowed himself to be led to the door. He waved them off then and went on under his own power, but Gregor's mother would hastily throw down her sewing and his sister her quill in order to run after him and be of further help to him.

66 Who in this overworked and overtired family had time to worry about Gregor more than was absolutely necessary? The household was ever more reduced in circumstances. The servant girl had been dismissed, and a gigantic, bony servant with white hair that fluttered about her head came in the mornings and the evenings to do the hardest labor. Everything else his mother took care of, in addition to her abundant sewing work. It even came to pass that various pieces of family jewelry, which his mother and sister had previously worn with pleasure at parties and celebrations, were sold, as Gregor learned one evening from a general conversation about the prices obtained. Their greatest source of complaint, however, was that the apartment, far too large for them under the circumstances, could not be left, because it was unthinkable that Gregor be relocated. But Gregor realized that it was not consideration for him that hindered a relocation, for they could have transported him easily in a suitable carton with a few air holes. What really kept the family from changing apartments was despair, and the thought that they had been afflicted by misfortune such as had struck no one in their circle of relatives and acquaintances. They did everything that the world demanded of poor people—his father fetched breakfast for the junior bank clerks; his mother dedicated herself to making underwear for strangers; his sister ran back and forth behind the counter at the beck and call of customers—but they could do no more than that. And the wound in his back began to hurt Gregor anew when his mother and sister would return from putting his father to bed, let their work lie, and huddle close together, cheek to cheek. His mother, gesturing towards Gregor's room, said, "Close the door, Grete," and Gregor was in the dark again, while next door the women mingled tears or stared, dry-eyed and numb, down at the table.

Gregor passed the days and nights nearly without 67
sleep. Sometimes he considered taking the affairs of the family in hand again, the next time the door was opened. After some time, he thought again about the Director and the Deputy Director, the clerks and the apprentices, the slow-witted porter, two or three friends from other companies, a chambermaid from a hotel in the provinces—a dear, fleeting memory—and a cashier from a hat store whom he had courted seriously, though too slowly. They reappeared in his thoughts together with strangers or people he had already forgotten, but instead of helping him and his family, they all remained detached, and he was glad when they disappeared. At other times, however, he was not in the mood to worry about his family. He was filled with rage at the poor care they took of him, and though he could think of nothing for which he had an appetite, he made plans to reach the pantry and take what was due him, even if he were not hungry. Without

considering any longer what might especially please Gregor, mornings and afternoons before returning to the store his sister hurriedly shoved any old kind of food into his room with her foot, only in order to sweep it out with a whisk of the broom in the evenings, indifferent as to whether it might have been merely tasted or—as was usually the case—it remained completely untouched. Her cleaning of the room, which she now always did in the evening, could not have been done any more hastily. Smears of dirt ran along the walls, and here and there lay balls of dust and filth. In the early days Gregor used to position himself upon the arrival of his sister in a particularly grubby corner, in order to reproach her. But he could have remained there for weeks, and his sister would still not have changed her ways. She saw the dirt as well as he did, but she had simply decided to leave it there. At the same time, with a touchiness entirely new to her that had now possessed the entire family, she was vigilant in making sure that the straightening of Gregor's room was left to her. His mother once undertook a thorough cleaning of Gregor's room, which had required several buckets of water—the moisture bothered Gregor, and he lay broad, embittered, and unmoving on top of the sofa—but his mother did not go unpunished. That evening his sister had hardly registered the change in Gregor's room when, highly insulted, she ran into the living room, and despite her mother's beseechingly raised hands, broke into a spasm of tears that his parents—his father had naturally been frightened out of his seat—at first simply watched, helpless with astonishment. Then they, too, were affected: on one side, his father reproached his mother for not leaving the cleaning of Gregor's room to his sister; on the other side, he shouted at his sister that she would never be allowed to clean Gregor's room again. In the meantime, his mother tried to drag his father, who was beside himself with agitation, into the bedroom; his sister, racked by sobs, hammered the table with her small fists; and Gregor hissed loudly with fury that no one thought to close the door and so spare him the scene and the noise.

68 But even if his sister, exhausted from her work, could no longer manage to care for Gregor as she had earlier, his mother would still not have had to intervene in order to keep Gregor from being neglected. For there was still the servant. This old widow, who had weathered the worst in her long life with the help of a powerful frame, felt no especial revulsion towards Gregor. Without exactly being curious, she had once by chance opened the door to Gregor's room and stood staring at the sight of him, her hands folded across her chest. Gregor was completely taken by surprise, and despite the fact that no one was chasing him, he began to run back and forth. Since that time, she hadn't missed a chance to open the door quickly in the morning and the evening to look in at Gregor. At first she called him over to her with words that she probably considered friendly, like "Come on over here, you old dung beetle!" or "Look at the old dung beetle!" Gregor did not respond to such overtures, but remained motionless in his place, as if the door had not even been opened. If only they would order this servant to clean his room daily, instead of letting her needlessly disturb him at will! Once in the early morning—a hard rain, perhaps already a sign of the coming spring, beat on the windowpanes—Gregor became so embittered when the servant began to speak that he turned towards her, as if to attack, though slowly and feebly. Instead of being afraid, however, the servant simply lifted high into the air a chair that stood in reach of the door. As she stood there with her mouth opened wide, it was clear that she intended to shut her mouth only after the chair in her hands had come down on Gregor's back. "That's it, then?" she asked, as Gregor turned around again, and she put the chair quietly back in its corner.

Gregor now ate almost nothing. When he hap- 69
pened to pass by the food prepared for him, he sometimes idly took a bite and held it in his mouth for an hour or so, only to spit most of it out again. At first he thought that his sorrow over the state of his room kept him from eating, but he had actually reconciled himself very soon to the changes. The family had gotten into the habit of putting into his room things that wouldn't fit anywhere else: there were now many such things, as they had rented one room in the apartment to three lodgers. These three serious gentlemen—all three had full beards, as Gregor discovered once by looking through the crack in the door—were painfully focused on order, not only in their room, but, simply because they had taken lodgings there, in the entire household, especially in the kitchen. They would not put up with useless or dirty things. And in any case, they had brought with them most of their own furnishings. For this reason, many things that were not saleable, but that the family did not want to throw away, had become superfluous. All of this made its way into Gregor's room—even, eventually, the ash bin and the rubbish bin from the kitchen. The servant, who was

always in a rush, simply slung anything that was at the moment unuseable into Gregor's room. Fortunately Gregor usually saw only the relevant object and the hand that held it. The servant might once have intended to take the things out again when time and opportunity permitted, or perhaps to throw them all out together once and for all, but in practice they lay wherever they were tossed, unless Gregor wound his way through the clutter and stirred it up—first because he had no other place to crawl, and later with growing pleasure, although after such forays, tired to death and full of sorrow, he could not stir for hours.

70 Because the lodgers sometimes took their evening meal in the common living room, the living room door remained closed on some evenings. Gregor managed without it very well. On some evenings when it was open he did not even take advantage of it, but without the family's knowing it, lay in the darkest corner of his room. Once, however, the servant left the door to his room open a bit, and it remained open, even as the lodgers came in that evening and the light was turned on. They sat at the head of the table, where in former days his father, mother, and Gregor had eaten, unfolded their napkins, and took their knives and forks in hand. His mother immediately appeared in the doorway with a dish of meat and his sister directly behind her with a dish piled high with potatoes. The steaming food gave off a rich smell. The lodgers bent over the dishes placed before them as if they wanted to check them before eating, and the one in the middle, whom the other two appeared to consider an authority, actually cut off a piece of meat still in the serving dish, obviously to test whether it were tender enough, or whether it might perhaps need to be sent back to the kitchen. He was satisfied, and mother and sister, who had watched the proceedings tensely, breathed again and smiled.

71 The family themselves ate in the kitchen. Nevertheless, his father, before he went into the kitchen, came into the room and made a single long bow while circling the table, cap in hand. The lodgers all rose together and murmured something into their beards. When they were alone again, they ate in near total silence. It seemed strange to Gregor that, among all the various sounds of eating, he could pick out the sound of their chewing teeth—it was as if Gregor were thereby reminded that one needed teeth in order to eat, and that one could do nothing with even the most beautiful toothless jaws. "I do have an appetite," said Gregor sorrowfully to himself, "but not for these things. How these lodgers feed themselves, while I'm dying of hunger!"

72 On this very evening, though Gregor did not remember having heard it once before during that whole time, the violin sounded from the kitchen. The lodgers had already finished their meal. The middle one had pulled out a newspaper and given each of the others one page. They now read, leaning back, and smoked. As the violin began to play, they became alert, arose and went on tiptoes to the hall door, where they stood pressed up against one another. They must have heard them in the kitchen, for his father called out: "Do you gentlemen perhaps dislike the playing? It can be stopped immediately." "On the contrary," said the lodger in the middle, "wouldn't the young lady like to come out and play here in this room, where it's much more comfortable and convenient?" "Oh, please!" called his father, as if he were the violin player. The lodgers moved back into the room and waited. His father soon came in with the music stand, his mother with the music, and his sister with the violin. His sister quietly prepared to play. His parents, who had never rented a room out before and so exaggerated the courtesy due the lodgers, did not dare to sit on their own chairs. His father leaned against the door, his right hand stuck between two buttons of his fastened livery coat. His mother, however, accepted a chair offered by one of the lodgers, and sat off in the corner where he had happened to place the chair.

His sister began to play. His father and mother, 73
on either side of her, followed every note, attentive to the movements of her hands. Gregor, drawn by the music, had ventured a bit further forward. His head was already in the living room. He hardly wondered at himself for being so inconsiderate towards the others of late; earlier, this consideration had been a great source of pride. And just now he had more reason than before to hide himself. Because of the dust everywhere in his room that flew up at the least movement, he was himself covered in dust. Threads, hairs, and bits of leftover food stuck to his back and sides. His general apathy was much too great for him now to lie on his back and scrub himself on the carpet, as he used to do several times a day. Despite his condition, however, he had no qualms about advancing a bit onto the immaculate living room floor.

But no one paid any attention to him. His fam- 74
ily was entirely absorbed in the playing of the violin. The lodgers, on the other hand, who had at first, their hands in their pants pockets, taken up positions inconveniently close to his sister's music stand, in order to see all the notes, soon withdrew to the window, their heads bowed amidst whispered conversation, and remained there with Gregor's father worriedly observing them. It was now painfully obvious that they were disappointed in what they had assumed would be a beautiful or entertaining performance, and that they were sick of the entire production and now al-

lowed their quiet to be disturbed only out of politeness. They way they all blew their cigar smoke out of their mouths and noses indicated great irritation. But his sister played so beautifully! Her face was turned to the side; her gaze followed the lines of notes, searching and sorrowful. Gregor crept further forward and held his head close to the floor, in order to meet her gaze if possible. The music gripped him—was he then an animal? He felt as if he were being guided to the sustenance he had unknowingly desired. He was determined to press on all the way to his sister, to pull on her skirt and let her know that she could come into his room with her violin. No one here knew how to appreciate her playing the way he did. He wanted never to let her out of his room again, at least not as long as he lived. His terrifying shape would finally be of some use to him: he would be at all doors of his room at once, hissing at all intruders. His sister, though, would not be forced, but would rather stay with him willingly. She would sit next to him on the sofa, her ear inclined towards him, and he would confide in her that he had intended to send her to the conservatory, and that, were it not for the misfortune that had occurred, he had intended to announce it to everyone last Christmas—Christmas had surely passed already?—ignoring any possible objections. After this declaration, his sister would surely burst into tears of emotion, and Gregor would lift himself up to her shoulder and kiss her neck, which she now left uncovered, without ribbon or collar, since she had begun working at the store.

> The music gripped him—was he then an animal?

75 "Mr. Samsa!" called the middle lodger and without wasting another word, pointed at Gregor, who was slowly inching his way forward. The violin fell silent. The middle lodger smiled at first, shaking his head at his friends, and then looked down again at Gregor. His father seemed to consider it more urgent to reassure the lodgers than to drive Gregor back, despite the fact that they seemed calm and more entertained by Gregor than by the violin. He hurried over to them and tried with outspread arms to urge them into their room; at the same time, he wanted to block their view of Gregor with his body. They actually became a bit angry now, though it was unclear whether this was over his father's behavior or over the dawning recognition that, unbeknownst to them, they had all the while had a neighbor like Gregor. They asked his father for an explanation, raised their arms, pulled agitatedly at their beards and only reluctantly retreated into their room. In the meantime his sister had come out of the trance into which she had fallen after her playing had been so suddenly broken off. For a time she had held her violin and bow in her limply hanging hands and continued to stare at the music, as if she were still playing. Now, all at once, she pulled herself together, laid the instrument in the lap of her mother, who, short of breath and gasping for air, was still seated, and ran into the next room, which the lodgers were now approaching more quickly at the urging of her father. Under her practiced hands, the covers and pillows flew high in the air and arranged themselves. Before the lodgers had reached the room, she was finished readying the beds and had slipped out. His father's stubbornness seemed to have returned to the extent that he forgot all respect that he owed his lodgers. He kept urging them and urging them, until finally at the threshold the gentleman in the middle resoundingly stamped his foot and so brought his father to a standstill. "I hereby declare," he said, and, raising his hand, sought the gaze of Gregor's mother and sister, as well, "that, in consideration of the revolting conditions existing in this apartment and this family"—and here, without a moment's hesitation, he spat on the ground—"I give notice this instant. I will naturally pay absolutely nothing for the days I have lived here; on the contrary, I will consider bringing charges against you, which will—believe me—be very easy to prove." He fell silent and stared straight ahead, as if he were waiting for something. His two friends then obliged him by chiming in with the words: "We, too, give notice this instant." At that, he seized the door handle and shut the door with a crash.

His father staggered to his chair, his hands 76
stretched out before him, and fell into it. It looked as if he were stretching himself out for his usual evening nap, but his head, sharply, ceaselessly nodding, showed that he was not sleeping at all. Gregor had lain all this time in the same spot where the lodgers had discovered him. His disappointment at the failure of his plans—perhaps, though, too, the weakness caused by his long hunger—made it impossible for him to move. He was distinctly afraid that in the next moment everything was going to come crashing down on top of him. He waited. Not even the violin roused him, which slipped from his mother's trembling fingers and fell from her lap, emitting a ringing tone.

"My dear parents," said his sister and struck her 77
hand on the table by way of preamble, "we can't go on like this. If you can't see it, I can. I don't want to use the name of my brother in front of this monster, so let me just say this: we have to try to get rid of it. We have tried as much as humanly possible to care for it and to put up with it. I don't think it could reproach us in the least."

78 "She is absolutely right," said his father under his breath. His mother, who seemed not to have caught her breath yet, began to emit a muffled cough into the hand she held before her, a crazed expression in her eyes.

79 His sister hurried to his mother and put her hand to her forehead. His sister's words seemed to have put his father's thoughts in a surer course. He sat up straight, fiddling with his uniform cap amongst the plates that still sat on the table from the lodgers' evening meal, and looked for a time down at the quiet Gregor.

80 "We must try to get rid of it," his sister finally said to his father, for his mother heard nothing in the midst of her coughing. "It's going to kill you both; I can see it coming. When people have to work as hard as we do, they can't bear this kind of constant torture at home. I can't bear it any more." And she began crying so hard that her tears flowed down her mother's face, where she began mechanically wiping them away with her hand.

81 "But my child," said his father, sympathetically and with striking compassion, "what should we do?"

82 His sister only shrugged her shoulders as a sign of the helplessness that had during her crying spell taken the place of her former certainty. "But if he understood us—" his father said, questioningly. His sister, in the midst of her tears, waved her hand violently as a sign that that was out of the question.

83 "If he understood us," his father repeated, and by closing his eyes, tried to absorb her certainty that it was impossible, "then we might able be to arrive at some arrangement with him. But as things stand—"

84 "It has to go," cried his sister. "That is the only way, father. You must simply try to rid yourself of the thought that it's Gregor. Our real misfortune is that we believed it for so long. But how can it be Gregor? If it were Gregor, he would have seen long ago that such an animal cannot live with people and he would have left voluntarily. We would then have had no brother, but we could have lived on and honored his memory. But this beast persecutes us, drives off the lodgers, and obviously wants to take over the apartment and force us to sleep out in the alley. Just look, Father," she suddenly screamed, "he's starting again!" And in a state of terror totally incomprehensible to Gregor, his sister abandoned his mother and practically vaulted off her chair, as if she would rather sacrifice her than remain in Gregor's vicinity. She hurried behind her father who, agitated entirely through her behavior, stood up as well and half raised his arms as if to protect her.

85 But it wasn't at all Gregor's intent to upset anyone, especially not his sister. He had just begun to turn himself around in order to make his way back into his room. Of course, that procedure looked peculiar enough, because his ailing condition meant that in order to turn even with difficulty he had to help with his head, which he lifted repeatedly and braced against the ground. He paused and looked around. His good intentions seemed to be recognized: it had only been a momentary fright. They all looked at him, silent and sorrowful. His mother lay in her chair, her legs stretched before her and pressed together; her eyes were nearly falling shut from exhaustion. His father and sister sat next to one another, his sister with her hand laid around her father's neck.

"Maybe they'll allow me to turn around now," 86
thought Gregor, and started to work on it again. He could not suppress the wheezing caused by his exertion, and he had to stop and rest now and then. No one rushed him: he was left to his own devices. When he had completed the turn, he immediately headed straight back. He was astonished by the vast distance that divided him from his room, and he could not grasp how in his weakened condition he had put the entire distance behind him, almost without noticing it. Focused solely on crawling as quickly as possible, he hardly noticed that no word and no outcry from his family disturbed him. He turned his head only when he was already at the door—not all the way, for he felt his neck getting stiff, but enough to see that nothing had changed behind him, except for the fact that his sister had stood up. His last glance fell on his mother, who was now fast asleep.

He was hardly in his room when the door was 87
hastily pushed to, bolted fast and locked. The sudden noise behind him frightened Gregor so much that his legs buckled beneath him. It was his sister who had rushed to do it. She had stood, waiting, and had suddenly sprung forward, light-footed—Gregor had not even heard her coming—crying out to her parents "Finally!" as she turned the key in the lock.

"And now?" Gregor asked himself, and looked 88
around in the dark. He soon discovered that he could no longer move at all. He didn't wonder at this; on the contrary, it had seemed unnatural to him that he had actually been able to move before on such thin legs. Besides that, however, he felt relatively comfortable. He did have pains all over his body, but it seemed to him that they were becoming weaker and weaker and would finally die away altogether. He could hardly feel the rotten apple in his back or the inflamed surrounding area, which was now completely covered in moist dust. He thought of his family with compassion and love. His conviction that he had to disappear was even more definite than his sister's. He remained in this state of empty and peaceful contemplation until the clock tower struck three. He experienced once more

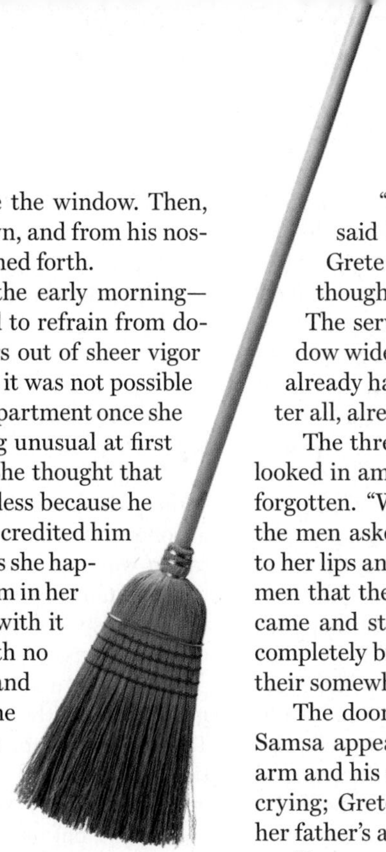

the approach of daylight outside the window. Then, unwilled, his head sank fully down, and from his nostrils his last breath weakly streamed forth.

89 When the servant came in the early morning—though she had often been asked to refrain from doing so, she slammed all the doors out of sheer vigor and haste, to such an extent that it was not possible to sleep quietly anywhere in the apartment once she had arrived—she noticed nothing unusual at first in her morning visit to Gregor. She thought that he intentionally lay there motionless because he found her behavior insulting; she credited him with all manner of intelligence. As she happened to be holding her long broom in her hand, she tried to tickle Gregor with it from the door. When she met with no response, she became irritated and poked him a bit. Only when she had shoved him from his spot without meeting any resistance did she become alert. She soon understood the situation. Her eyes widened, and she whistled out loud. It wasn't long before she had flung the door of the master bedroom open and called loudly into the darkness: "Look, everyone, it's kicked the bucket; it's lying there, dead as a doornail!"

90 The Samsas sat bolt upright in bed and had first to overcome their alarm at the servant's behavior before they could understand her report. Then, however, they climbed hurriedly out of bed, one on each side. Mr. Samsa threw the blanket over his shoulders; Mrs. Samsa emerged in her nightgown. In this manner they entered Gregor's room. In the meantime Grete had opened the door to the living room, where she had been sleeping since the arrival of the lodgers. She was completely dressed, as if she had not slept; her pale face confirmed the impression. "Dead?" said Mrs. Samsa, and looked questioningly up at the servant, although she could have made her own investigation or even have recognized the fact without making any investigation. "I'd say so," said the servant, and as proof, she pushed Gregor's corpse further to one side with the broom. Mrs. Samsa moved as if she wanted to hold her back, but she didn't. "Well," said Mr. Samsa, "now we can thank God." He crossed himself, and the three women followed his example. Grete, who did not take her eyes from the corpse, said: "Just look at how thin he was. He hadn't eaten anything for so long. The food came out just the way it went in." Gregor's body was indeed completely flat and dry; it was really only possible to see it now that he was off his legs and nothing else distracted the eye.

"Come, Grete, come sit with us for a bit," 91
said Mrs. Samsa with a wistful smile, and Grete followed her parents into their bedroom, though not without looking back at the corpse. The servant shut the door and opened the window wide. Despite the early morning the fresh air already had something mild mixed in it. It was, after all, already the end of March.

The three lodgers emerged from their room and 92
looked in amazement for their breakfast. It had been forgotten. "Where is breakfast?" the middlemost of the men asked the servant sullenly. She laid a finger to her lips and then silently and hastily signaled to the men that they might come into Gregor's room. They came and stood around Gregor's corpse in the now completely bright room, their hands in the pockets of their somewhat shabby coats.

The door to the bedroom opened then, and Mr. 93
Samsa appeared in his livery with his wife on one arm and his daughter on the other. They had all been crying; Grete pressed her face from time to time to her father's arm.

"Leave my apartment immediately!" said Mr. 94
Samsa and pointed to the door, without letting the women leave his side. "What do you mean?" said the middle lodger, somewhat dismayed, and smiled mawkishly. The two others held their hands behind their backs and rubbed them together continuously, as if in joyful expectation of a great fight, which would, they were sure, end favorably for them. "I mean exactly what I say," answered Mr. Samsa, and advanced in a line with his companions toward the lodger. He stood quietly, at first, and looked at the ground, as if the things in his head were arranging themselves in a new order. "Then we'll go," he said and looked up at Mr. Samsa, as if a sudden access of humility required him to seek renewed approval even for this decision. Mr. Samsa merely nodded shortly several times, his eyes wide and staring. At this, the man immediately walked with long strides into the foyer. His two friends had listened at first, their hands completely still, and they now skipped after him directly, as if in fear that Mr. Samsa could step in front of them in the foyer and disrupt their connection to their leader. In the hall all three of them took their hats from the rack, drew their walking sticks from the stand, bowed mutely, and left the apartment. In what proved to be a completely unnecessary precaution, Mr. Samsa walked out with the two women onto the landing. Leaning on the railing, they watched as the three men slowly but steadily descended the stairs, disappearing on every floor at the turning of the stairwell, and emerging again after a few moments. The lower they went, the more the

Samsa family lost interest in them, and as a butcher's boy carrying his burden on his head with dignity passed them and then climbed high above them, Mr. Samsa left the landing with the women and they all returned, as if freed from a burden, to their apartment.

95 They decided to spend the day resting and taking a stroll. They had not only earned this rest from work, they absolutely needed it. And so they sat at the table and wrote three letters of excuse, Mr. Samsa to the bank directors, Mrs. Samsa to her employer, and Grete to her supervisor. While they were writing the servant entered in order to say that she was leaving, as her morning work was finished. Writing, the three of them merely nodded at first, without looking up; only when the servant failed to depart did they look up angrily. "Well?" asked Mr. Samsa. The servant stood in the door, smiling, as if she had some great piece of good news to report to the family, but would only do so if she were thoroughly interrogated. The nearly upright little ostrich feather on her hat, which had annoyed Mr. Samsa the entire time she had been employed there, waved freely in all directions. "Well, what do you want?" asked Mrs. Samsa, for whom the servant had the most respect. "Well," the servant answered, and could not say more right away, fairly bursting with friendly laughter, "well, you needn't worry about getting rid of that thing next door. It's all been taken care of." Mrs. Samsa and Grete bent to their letters again, as if they wanted to continue writing. Mr. Samsa, who saw that the servant was about to begin describing everything in great detail, decisively headed this off with an outstretched hand. Since she was not going to be allowed to tell her story, she suddenly remembered her great haste, and, obviously deeply insulted, called out, "'Bye, everyone," then spun around wildly and left the apartment amidst a terrific slamming of doors.

96 "Tonight we're firing her," said Mr. Samsa, but received no answer either from his wife or from his daughter, for the servant seemed to have disturbed their but newly restored calm. They rose, went to the window, and remained there, their arms around each other. Mr. Samsa turned in his chair as they went and quietly observed them for a while. Then he called out, "Well, come over here. Let what's past be past. And take some care of me, for once." The women obeyed immediately, hurrying over to him and caressing him, and then quickly finished their letters.

97 Then all three of them left the apartment together, which they had not done for months, and took a trolley to the open air beyond the city. The car they sat in was drenched with warm sunlight. Leaning back comfortably in their seats, they discussed their future prospects, and it emerged that these were not at all bad on closer inspection, for all three of their positions, were altogether favorable at present and, most importantly, had great potential for the future. The greatest improvement of their present situation would have to come, naturally, from a change of apartments. They would want a smaller and cheaper apartment, but one that was better located and generally more convenient than their current apartment, which Gregor had originally found for them. While they conversed in this way, it occurred to both Mr. and Mrs. Samsa in the same moment in looking at their ever more lively daughter that despite the recent ordeals that had made her cheeks so pale, she had blossomed into a pretty and well-developed young woman. Becoming quieter and almost unconsciously communicating through glances, they realized that it would soon be time to look for a good husband for her. And it seemed to them a confirmation of their new dreams and good intentions, when, at the end of their journey, their daughter rose first and stretched her young body.

*translated by Alexis Walker*

IF you like the way that Kafka employs the older form of allegory to new ends, leading the reader away from fixed meanings into the world of ambiguity, you may enjoy rereading Thomas Wolfe's "Only the Dead Know Brooklyn" and Stephen Crane's "The Open Boat." "The Gilded Six Bits," by Zora Neale Hurston (see chapter 14) also gives multiple meanings to its titular "six bits."

**GOING FURTHER** A few great modern novels waver between—or perhaps encompass both—allegory and symbolism. Among these are Albert Camus's *The Stranger* and Thomas Pynchon's *V.*

# Writing from Reading

## Summarize

1 Describe how the family viewed Gregor before the metamorphosis. What was his role in the family?

2 Describe each family member's reaction when he or she first discovers Gregor's transformation. What do their responses reveal about them as characters and about their relationship with Gregor?

## Analyze Craft

3 Discuss the symbolic aspect of the desk in Gregor's room. What role does it play in his life before and after his metamorphosis?

4 Discuss the three boarders as a symbol. What role do they play in the life of the family? What effect do they have on the family's peculiar situation?

## Analyze Voice

5 Gregor's condition is extraordinary, but nobody ever seems to question it. Discuss how Kafka handles this fantastical aspect in his otherwise very practical story. Is he successful in making the surreal believable?

## Synthesize Summary and Analysis

6 What happens to the father in the course of the story? Contrast his life before Gregor's metamorphosis with his life afterward.

## Interpret the Story

7 Discuss the removal of the furniture in Gregor's room as a symbolic act. In your discussion, contrast the mother's view of the removal with that of Gregor and of his sister.

8 In the original German, Gregor is transformed into an *Ungeziefer,* which does not translate directly to "insect." There are other possible translations, but each fails in some way to capture the same connotations of uncleanness and unpleasantness. Discuss how the use of the word "insect" (as opposed to other possible translations like "pest" or "vermin") affects your reading of the story.

# Elizabeth Tallent (b. 1954)

Born in Washington, D.C., Elizabeth Tallent has an impressive teaching record that includes the creative writing programs at the University of California, Irvine, the University of California, Davis, the Iowa Writer's Workshop, and—currently—Stanford University. Although she has published a novel, *Museum Pieces* (1985), and a volume of criticism on John Updike's writing, *Married Men and Magic Tricks* (1982), Tallent is best known for her short stories. She has published three collections—*In Constant Flight* (1983), *Time with Children* (1987), and *Honey* (1993)—each of which chronicles contemporary familial relationships, marriage, and adultery. Tallent's fiction has been featured in a wide variety of literary magazines and journals, including *The New Yorker, Grand Street,* and *The Paris Review,* as well as in *The Best American Short Stories.*

**AS YOU READ** As you read, note the easy way the two characters talk with each other. Notice what the narrator notices. Where does her eye take you and why?

TIPS

**FOR INTERACTIVE READING . . .**

- Create a marking system and use it to note what's inside the truck, what's outside the truck, and what's in the imaginations of the two characters. How do these three worlds of the story interact with one another?
- Circle the objects in the story that you feel have symbolic resonance. Make brief notes in the margin about associations you have with the circled objects.

# No One's a Mystery (1985)

1 FOR my eighteenth birthday Jack gave me a five-year diary with a latch and a little key, light as a dime. I was sitting beside him scratching at the lock, which didn't seem to want to work, when he thought he saw his wife's Cadillac in the distance, coming toward us. He pushed me down onto the dirty floor of the pickup and kept one hand on my head while I inhaled the musk of his cigarettes in the dashboard ashtray and sang along with Rosanne Cash on the tape deck. We'd been drinking tequila and the bottle was between his legs, resting up against his crotch, where the seam of his Levi's was bleached linen-white, though the Levi's were nearly new. I don't know why his Levi's always bleached like that, along the seams and at the knees. In a curve of cloth his zipper glinted, gold.

2 "It's her," he said. "She keeps the lights on in the daytime. I can't think of a single habit in a woman that irritates me more than that." When he saw that I was going to stay still he took his hand from my head and ran it through his own dark hair.

3 "Why does she?" I said.

4 "She thinks it's safer. Why does she need to be safer? She's driving exactly fifty-five miles an hour. She believes in those signs: 'Speed Monitored by Aircraft.' It doesn't matter that you can look up and see that the sky is empty."

5 "She'll see your lips move, Jack. She'll know you're talking to someone."

6 "She'll think I'm singing along with the radio."

7 He didn't lift his head, just raised the fingers in salute while the pressure of his palm steadied the wheel, and I heard the Cadillac honk twice, musically; he was driving easily eighty miles an hour. I studied his boots. The elk heads stitched into the leather were bearded with frayed thread, the toes were scuffed, and there was a compact wedge of muddy manure between the heel and the sole—the same boots he'd been wearing for the two years I'd known him. On the tape deck Rosanne Cash sang, "Nobody's into me, no one's a mystery."

8 "Do you think she's getting famous because of who her daddy is or for herself?" Jack said.

9 "There are about a hundred pop tops on the floor, did you know that? Some little kid could cut a bare foot on one of these, Jack."

10 "No little kids get into this truck except for you."

11 "How come you let it get so dirty?"

12 "'How come,'" he mocked. "You even sound like a kid. You can get back into the seat now, if you want. She's not going to look over her shoulder and see you."

13 "How do you know?"

14 "I just know," he said. "Like I know I'm going to get meat loaf for supper. It's in the air. Like I know what you'll be writing in that diary."

15 "What will I be writing?" I knelt on my side of the seat and craned around to look at the butterfly of dust printed on my jeans. Outside the window Wyoming

was dazzling in the heat. The wheat was fawn and yellow and parted smoothly by the thin dirt road. I could smell the water in the irrigation ditches hidden in the wheat.

16 "Tonight you'll write, 'I love Jack. This is my birthday present from him. I can't imagine anybody loving anybody more than I love Jack.'"

17 "I can't."

18 "In a year you'll write, 'I wonder what I ever really saw in Jack. I wonder why I spent so many days just riding around in his pickup. It's true he taught me something about sex. It's true there wasn't ever much else to do in Cheyenne.'"

19 "I won't write that."

20 "In two years you'll write, 'I wonder what that old guy's name was, the one with the curly hair and the filthy dirty pickup truck and time on his hands.'"

21 "I won't write that."

22 "No?"

23 "Tonight I'll write, 'I love Jack. This is my birthday present from him. I can't imagine anybody loving anybody more than I love Jack.'"

24 "No, you can't," he said. "You can't imagine it."

25 "In a year I'll write, 'Jack should be home any minute now. The table's set—my grandmother's linen and her old silver and the yellow candles left over from the wedding—but I don't know if I can wait until after the trout à la Navarra to make love to him.'"

26 "It must have been a fast divorce."

27 "In two years I'll write, 'Jack should be home by now. Little Jack is hungry for his supper. He said his first word today besides "Mama" and "Papa." He said "kaka."'"

28 Jack laughed. "He was probably trying to fingerpaint with kaka on the bathroom wall when you heard him say it."

"In three years I'll write, 'My nipples are a little sore from nursing Eliza Rosamund.'" 29

"Rosamund. Every little girl should have a middle name she hates." 30

"'Her breath smells like vanilla and her eyes are just Jack's color of blue.'" 31

"That's nice," Jack said. 32

"So, which one do you like?" 33

"I like yours," he said. "But I believe mine." 34

"It doesn't matter. I believe mine." 35

"Not in your heart of hearts, you don't." 36

"You're wrong." 37

"I'm not wrong," he said. "And her breath would smell like your milk, and it's kind of a bittersweet smell, if you want to know the truth." 38

IF you like "No One's a Mystery," about the education of a young girl bordering on the scandalous, you might also enjoy the casebook on Joyce Carol Oates that includes the cautionary tale "Where Are You Going, Where Have You Been?"

**GOING FURTHER** Tallent and Oates rank high among a large number of contemporary women who work on material once reserved only for male writers, as in Oates's depiction of a sexually obsessed real-estate salesman in her novel *What I Lived For,* Susanna Moore's focus on violent crime in her novel *In the Cut,* and Alice Walker's depiction of black sexuality in *The Color Purple.*

# Writing from Reading

### Summarize

1 Describe Jack's life situation as it's suggested by the text. Cite specific details from the text that support your conclusions. Do some details seem incongruous with the Jack portrayed by the narrator?

2 Jack accuses the narrator of acting childish. In what ways does she act childish, and in what ways, if any, does she demonstrate the maturity of the adult she's just become?

### Analyze Craft

3 Tallent provides very little physical description of her characters. Consider the things Tallent does choose to describe: How do these descriptions reflect on the characters and their situation?

### Analyze Voice

4 Discuss how having a young woman as a narrator lends extra weight to symbols like the diary and the pop song and breast milk. Would these symbols have the same effect if the story were told from Jack's point of view?

### Synthesize Summary and Analysis

5 Compare and contrast the diary entries that the two characters imagine. What do their fantasies reveal about them and the differences between them?

### Interpret the Story

6 Discuss the significance of the diary as a central image in this story. Why does Tallent choose to have the diary locked? Does this portend anything for the narrator's future with Jack? Analyze the locked diary by considering other symbols in the story.

# Reading for Symbols

When reading for **symbols**—objects, images, characters, or actions that suggest meaning beyond the literal level—notice the images that receive special emphasis. Ask yourself these questions:

| | | |
|---|---|---|
| **Is this an *allegory*—a story in which key elements such as characters and settings represent universal truths or moral lessons in a one-to-one correspondence?** | | EXAMPLE: the ant and the grasshopper |
| **Is this a *symbolic object* or *symbolic character*—one that appears to have meaning beyond the literal level?** | | EXAMPLES: the pebble that Martha sent; Paul's red carnation |

| | | |
|---|---|---|
| **Is this a *symbolic act*—a gesture or action that conveys something beyond the literal level?** | | EXAMPLE: Lieutenant Cross discarding the pebble |
| **How do you identify an image with symbolic potential?** | • Consider whether it is repeated, portrayed in detail or given emotional weight in the lives of the characters or narrator. | |
| **How do you understand the meanings of a symbol?** | • Consider the characters' attitudes about it, the effect it has on the characters, especially the protagonist, or how it changes over the course of the story, and how attitudes toward it change. | |

# Suggestions for Writing about Symbolism

1. In "The Metamorphosis" and "Young Goodman Brown," what, if any, qualities of an allegory can you identify? Compare the two stories. On the whole, would you label either story as an allegory?
2. Choose any two of the stories in this chapter and articulate their major themes. How do symbols in these stories support and establish the themes? What do these stories suggest about the relationship between theme and symbol in fiction?
3. Exploring the relationship between setting and symbol, "The Things They Carried" and "Young Goodman Brown" both feature characters who find themselves away from home in strange and dangerous places. How does each author establish a sense of place, as in Hawthorne's deep forest in New England and O'Brien's jungle battlefield in Vietnam? Use examples from each story to illustrate how the symbolic resonance of particular details enhances these settings.

# 11

# Fiction As Social Commentary

## A Case Study

### *Joyce Carol Oates*

AS a witness to society, Joyce Carol Oates (b. 1938) has few if any equals; for more than forty years she has reported on America, its brightly lit arenas as well as its dark corners. Joyce Carol Oates calls attention to many facets of society, including the dark and violent side, as in "Where Are You Going, Where Have You Been?" A story like "Three Girls" gives a new perspective on celebrity and what our society does to an individual with fame. Her tales are often fringed with menace and their resolutions violent; a storyteller's energy infuses every page. She's—there's no other word for it—prodigious, and though the quality of her written work may vary, the quantity is nearly nonpareil. She produces learned assessments of little-known or long-forgotten authors but is never far away from popular culture in her book reviews, essays, and fiction about figures such as Muhammad Ali, Edward Kennedy, and Marilyn Monroe.

*"I like to write about my own time, and I always tell my students that we write for our own time. . . . We can't be writing for people far in the future because we don't know who they are. So, we write for our own time. . . . I address myself to these issues of the present time."*

—from a conversation with Joyce Carol Oates, available on video at www.mhhe.com/delbanco1e

**Although Oates experiments with different voices in her fiction, she does speak in her own voice in her nonfiction. Deeply intellectual yet not afraid to add a casual personal remark, Oates in her nonfiction voice has commented on a host of topics related to writing in general (as in *The Faith of a Writer*), on her own writing (in *The New York Times*), on other authors' work (as in her collection *Uncensored: Views and (Re)views,* a compilation of Oates's discussions of authors from Emily Brontë to Don DeLillo), and on the sport of boxing, a love of which she acquired as a young girl in the company of her father.**

"I've always been very interested in holding a kind of mirror, sometimes a slightly distorting mirror, up to contemporary American society." Conversation with Joyce Carol Oates

**The stories reprinted here are among her most famous, and they also exemplify the major themes of much of Oates's work. Here are ordinary people in extraordinary moments; there are questions of identity, the female experience, and the threat of violence. "All my life," Oates says, "I've been fascinated with the mystery of human personality."**

*CONTINUED ON PAGE 366*

*I hope readers read without thinking it's a work of fiction.*

*I always felt reading was my freedom.*

# Q&A
# A Conversation on Writing
## Joyce Carol Oates

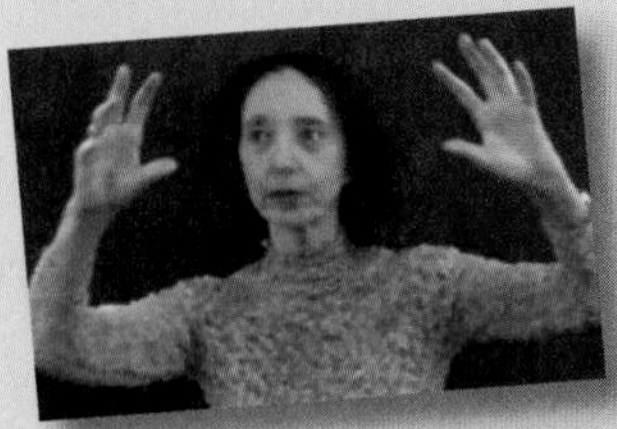

### Falling in Love with Your Subject

You may see something happen and it lodges very deeply in you for a reason that you can't understand. I think it's almost like falling in love. . . . You might see something on television. It makes almost no impression. It just sort of glimmers and goes past you. But once in a while something will enter into you and it imprints itself very deeply into you because it struck a resonance with your own unconscious and your own personal life. I don't think that one can write or create any kind of art that doesn't have a deep resonance in the artist or writer's unconscious.

### Daydreaming, Integrity, and the Writing Process

I become really haunted by something. Sometimes I see a photograph; sometimes I'm just drawn by a story. Sometimes it's a dream image. Sometimes it's something that has happened to me. . . . It becomes something of a meditation. . . . I have this meditation, as I say, it can be very haunting. . . . I'm a runner. I just run, and I allow my mind to be very open and kind of loose and sort of in a daydreaming mode. . . . Then when I come back from this experience I . . . write down what I remember from what I had worked out. . . . So the act of remembering to me is very thrilling . . . but then the act of writing . . . becomes a very different sort of experience . . . choosing the right language, the right sentences, using maybe compound sentences or complex sentences, long sentences, short sentences—that's the most challenging part of it. The daydreaming part is enjoyable and interesting and has its own integrity. But then the writing part is much more challenging.

### The Sport of Revision

Well, the process of revision I find so thrilling. And I encourage my students to deal with revision in a way that's competitive. They take a work of theirs that they've done several weeks ago, and you look through it quickly. And you say to yourself, "I can do better. I can do better than this." And it's true. You can always do better. Every sentence could be rewritten, paragraphs could be rewritten, the whole thing could be kind of restructured. You could have a different opening—more interesting—you could have a different ending, a different title. The whole thing belongs to you, and you say to yourself, "I can make this better." And the fact is that nobody else can touch that except you. You are the sole proprietor and owner of that material.

To watch this entire interview and hear the author read from her work, go to **www.mhhe.com/delbanco1e.**

**RESEARCH ASSIGNMENT** In her interview, Oates talks about the original title of "Where Are You Going, Where Have You Been?" and how she originally thought about that story. What made her change her title and with it her story? Do you agree with her decision?

# Joyce Carol Oates (b. 1938)

"I'm very struck by how ordinary people can rise to levels of extraordinary behavior. That people, maybe all of us, could be capable of heroic actions." Conversation with Joyce Carol Oates

First educated in a one-room schoolhouse in rural western New York, Joyce Carol Oates is now a professor of creative writing at Princeton University. For her fourteenth birthday, Oates received a typewriter, began writing, and went on to become one of America's most prominent contemporary authors. At age nineteen, Oates won *Mademoiselle* magazine's prestigious short story contest, continued to write steadily as an undergraduate at Syracuse University, published her first book at the age of twenty-eight, and established a rate of production of at least two books per year. She and her late husband, Raymond Smith, settled at the University of Windsor, near Detroit, after she earned her master's degree from the University of Wisconsin. Together they founded the *Ontario Review,* which they continued to edit after the couple moved to Princeton.

"Genuine artists create their own modes of art and nothing interests them except the free play of the imagination," Oates once said in an interview. From the very beginning, Oates engaged in the "free play" of the imagination—painting and drawing stories before she knew how to read. As she reached her teenage years and began reading great American novelists, she wrote stories in which she mimicked their styles, from Hemingway's spartan prose to Faulkner's lush language. Today, however, her own fiction is it's "own mode of art," and Oates is often offended when critics call attention to her sex and to the violence that her female protagonists often face. Oates's fiction is concerned with more than female suffering.

While it is often the violence, or suggestion of violence, that draws attention to Oates's writing, this is a single aspect of her fascination with human behavior and the way—even in the face of destructive outside forces—people create identity. "To write," she says in her interview, "you have to have an emotional thread."—an emotional connection between a writer and her work. Oates explains the connection in her interview: "I sometimes write about people who are ordinary people in extraordinary moments because I think that people are much stronger and more interesting than they appear to be. Literature and art take people to places of conflict, where what is buried in them and perhaps even asleep in them is awakened suddenly. . . . And so with all of us I think we awaken from a kind of a sleep of ordinary life by some stressful thing that happens to us."

As a testament to the quality of her prose, twenty-eight of her stories have won O. Henry Prizes for Short Fiction and eleven Pushcart Prizes, and for her work in the form she was awarded the PEN/Malamud Award for Excellence in Short Fiction. Thirty-nine of her books have been *New York Times* Notable Books of the Year. Oates's literary achievement is both broad—in terms of the number of books, collections, stories, and articles she has published—and deep. Among her better-known novels are *them* (1969), winner of the National Book Award, *Black Water* (1992), a finalist for the Pulitzer Prize, and *We Were the Mulvaneys* (2001), selected for Oprah's Book Club.

Her prizes are as numerous, it sometimes seems, as her titles. Best known as a writer of contemporary gothic fiction that incorporates feminism, violence, the normal and the paranormal, Oates explores the outer limits of human personality and the depths of American society. Her subjects range from the anonymous citizen to the iconic American celebrity; she writes of family life and loneliness, of conviction and delusion, the mall and the family farm.

Additionally, Oates has written in several genres of fiction, including gothic, romance, and mystery. Her celebrity as a writer seems at odds with the humble way she describes her daily writing process: "I have always lived a very conventional life of moderation, absolutely regular hours, nothing exotic, no need, even, to organize my time." The result is an author whose varied awards point to how we might best read her—while some were given to a specific novel or story, others were bestowed for overall influence and ongoing achievement.

"I saw a snapshot of Norma Jean Baker that had been taken when she was sixteen or seventeen years old . . . when you saw her as a high school student, you would not have thought she was anyone that special. . . . I thought it was so interesting how an ordinary girl could be made into a starlet, could become world famous, one day would be called by *Playboy* magazine 'the sexiest female of the twentieth century' . . . how an ordinary person becomes extraordinary." Conversation with Joyce Carol Oates

# Three Girls (2002)

1 IN Strand Used Books on Broadway and Twelfth one snowy March early evening in 1956 when the streetlights on Broadway glimmered with a strange sepia glow, we were two NYU girl-poets drifting through the warehouse of treasures as through an enchanted forest. Just past 6:00 P.M. Above the light-riddled Manhattan, opaque night. Snowing, and sidewalks encrusted with ice so there were fewer customers in the Strand than usual at this hour but *there we were.* Among other cranky brooding regulars. In our army-surplus jackets, baggy khaki pants, and zip-up rubber boots. In our matching wool caps (knitted by your restless fingers) pulled down low over our pale-girl foreheads. Enchanted by books. Enchanted by the Strand.

2 No bookstore of merely "new" books with elegant show window displays drew us like the drafty Strand, bins of books untidy and thumbed through as merchants' sidewalk bins on Fourteenth Street, NEW THIS WEEK, BEST BARGAINS, WORLD CLASSICS, ART BOOKS

50% OFF, REVIEWERS' COPIES, HIGHEST PRICE $1.98, REMAINDERS 25¢—$1.00. Hard-cover/paperback. Spotless/battered. Beautiful books/cheaply printed pulp paper. And at the rear and sides in that vast echoing space massive shelves of books books books rising to a ceiling of hammered tin fifteen feet above! Stacked shelves so high they required ladders to negotiate a monkey nimbleness (like yours) to climb.

3 We were enchanted with the Strand and with each other in the Strand. Overseen by surly young clerks who were poets like us, or playwrights/actors/artists. In an agony of unspoken young love I watched you. As always on these romantic evenings at the Strand, prowling the aisles sneering at those luckless books, so many of them, unworthy of your attention. Bestsellers, how-tos, arts and crafts, too-simple *histories of.* Women's romances, sentimental love poems. Patriotic books, middlebrow books, books lacking esoteric covers. We were girl-poets passionately enamored of T. S. Eliot but scornful of Robert Frost whom we'd been made to memorize in high school—slyly we communicated in code phrases from Eliot in the presence of obtuse others in our dining hall and residence. We were admiring of though confused by the poetry of Yeats, we were yet more confused by the lauded worth of Pound, enthusiastically drawn to the bold metaphors of Kafka (that cockroach!) and Dostoevsky (sexy murderer Raskolnikov and the Underground Man were our rebel heroes) and Sartre ("Hell is other people"—we knew this), and had reason to believe that we were their lineage though admittedly we were American middle class, and Caucasian, and female. (Yet we were not "conventional" females. In fact, we shared male contempt for the merely "conventional" female.)

4 Brooding above a tumble of books that quickened the pulse, almost shyly touching Freud's *Civilization and Its Discontents,* Crane Brinton's *The Age of*

*Reason,* Margaret Mead's *Coming of Age in Samoa,* D. H. Lawrence's *The Rainbow,* Kierkegaard's *Fear and Trembling,* Mann's *Death in Venice*—there suddenly you glided up behind me to touch my wrist (as never you'd done before, had you?) and whispered, "Come here," in a way that thrilled me for its meaning *I have something wonderful/unexpected/startling to show you.* Like poems these discoveries in the Strand were, to us, found poems to be cherished. And eagerly I turned to follow you though disguising my eagerness, "Yes, what?" as if you'd interrupted me, for possibly we'd had a quarrel earlier that day, a flaring up of tense girl-tempers. Yes, you were childish and self-absorbed and given to sulky silences and mercurial moods in the presence of showy superficial people, and I adored and feared you knowing you'd break my heart, my heart that had never before been broken because never before so exposed.

. . . I saw that she was Marilyn Monroe.

5 So eagerly yet with my customary guardedness I followed you through a maze of book bins and shelves and stacks to the ceiling ANTHROPOLOGY, ART/ANCIENT, ART/RENAISSANCE, ART/MODERN, ART/ASIAN, ART/WESTERN, TRAVEL, PHILOSOPHY, COOKERY, POETRY/MODERN where the way was treacherously lighted only by bare sixty-watt bulbs, and where customers as cranky as we two stood in the aisles reading books, or sat hunched on footstools glancing up annoyed at our passage, and unquestioning I followed you until at POETRY/MODERN you halted, and pushed me ahead and around a corner, and I stood puzzled staring, not knowing what I was supposed to be seeing until impatiently you poked me in the ribs and pointed, and now I perceived an individual in the aisle pulling down books from shelves, peering at them, clearly absorbed by what she read, a woman nearly my height (I was tall for a girl, in 1956) in a man's navy coat to her ankles and with sleeves past her wrists, a man's beige fedora hat on her head, scrunched low as we wore our knitted caps, and most of her hair hidden by the hat except for a six-inch blond plait at the nape of her neck; and she wore black trousers tucked into what appeared to be salt-stained cowboy boots. Someone we knew? An older, good-looking student from one of our classes? *A girl-poet like ourselves?* I was about to nudge you in the ribs in bafflement when the blond woman turned, taking down another book from the shelf (e. e. cummings' *Tulips and Chimneys*—always I would remember that title!), and I saw that she was Marilyn Monroe.

6 Marilyn Monroe. In the Strand. Just like us. And she seemed to be alone.

*Marilyn Monroe, alone!* 7

Wholly absorbed in browsing amid books, oblivious of her surroundings and of us. No one seemed to have recognized her (yet) except you. 8

Here was the surprise: this woman was/was not Marilyn Monroe. For this woman was an individual wholly absorbed in selecting, leafing through, pausing to read books. You could see that this individual was a *reader.* One of those who *reads.* With concentration, with passion. With her very soul. And it was poetry she was reading, her lips pursed, silently shaping words. Absent-mindedly she wiped her nose on the edge of her hand, so intent was she on what she was reading. For when you truly read poetry, poetry reads *you.* 9

Still, this woman was—Marilyn Monroe. And despite our common sense, our scorn for the silly clichés of Hollywood romance, still we halfway expected a Leading Man to join her: Clark Gable, Robert Taylor, Marlon Brando. 10

Halfway we expected the syrupy surge of movie music, to glide us into the scene. 11

But no man joined Marilyn Monroe in her disguise as one of us in the Strand. No Leading Man, no dark prince. 12

Like us (we began to see) this Marilyn Monroe required no man. 13

For what seemed like a long time but was probably no more than half an hour, Marilyn Monroe browsed in the POETRY/MODERN shelves, as from a distance of approximately ten feet two girl-poets watched covertly, clutching each other's hands. We were stunned to see that this woman looked very little like the glamorous "Marilyn Monroe." That figure was a garish blond showgirl, a Hollywood "sexpot" of no interest to intellectuals (*we* thought, we who knew nothing of the secret romance between Marilyn Monroe and Arthur Miller); this figure more resembled us (almost) than she resembled her Hollywood image. We were dying of curiosity to see whose poetry books Marilyn Monroe was examining: Elizabeth Bishop, H. D., Robert Lowell, Muriel Rukeyser, Harry Crosby, Denise Levertov . . . Five or six of these Marilyn Monroe decided to purchase, then moved on, leather bag slung over her shoulder and fedora tilted down on her head. 14

We couldn't resist, we had to follow! Cautious not to whisper together like excited schoolgirls, still less to giggle wildly as we were tempted; 15

you nudged me in the ribs to sober me, gave me a glare signaling *Don't be rude, don't ruin this for all of us.* I conceded: I was the more pushy of the two of us, a tall gawky Rima the Bird Girl with springy carroty-red hair like an exotic bird's crest, while you were petite and dark haired and attractive with long-lashed Semitic sloe eyes, you the wily gymnast and I the aggressive basketball player, you the "experimental" poet and I drawn to "forms," our contrary talents bred in our bones. Which of us would marry, have babies, disappear into "real" life, and which of us would persevere into her thirties before starting to be published and becoming, in time, a "real" poet—could anyone have predicted, this snowy March evening in 1956?

16 Marilyn Monroe drifted through the maze of books and we followed in her wake as through a maze of dreams, past SPORTS, past MILITARY, past WAR, past HISTORY/ANCIENT, past the familiar figures of Strand regulars frowning into books, past surly yawning bearded clerks who took no more heed of the blond actress than they ever did of us, and so to NATURAL HISTORY where she paused, and there again for unhurried minutes (the Strand was open until 9:00 P.M.) Marilyn Monroe in her mannish disguise browsed and brooded, pulling down books, seeking what? at last crouched leafing through an oversized illustrated book (curiosity overcame me! I shoved away your restraining hand; politely I eased past Marilyn Monroe murmuring "excuse me" without so much as brushing against her and without being noticed), Charles Darwin's *Origin of Species* in a deluxe edition. Darwin! *Origin of Species!* We were poet-despisers-of-science, or believed we were, or must be, to be true poets in the exalted mode of T. S. Eliot and William Butler Yeats; such a choice, for Marilyn Monroe, seemed perverse to us. But this book was one Marilyn quickly decided to purchase, hoisting it into her arms and moving on.

17 That rakish fedora we'd come to covet, and that single chunky blonde braid. (Afterward we would wonder: Marilyn Monroe's hair in a braid? Never had we seen Marilyn Monroe with her hair braided in any movie or photo. What did this mean? Did it mean anything? *Had she quit films, and embarked on a new, anonymous life in our midst?*)

18 Suddenly Marilyn Monroe glanced back at us, frowning as a child might frown (had we spoken aloud? had she heard our thoughts?), and there came into her face a look of puzzlement, not alarm or annoyance but a childlike puzzlement: *Who are you? You two? Are you watching me?* Quickly we looked away. We were engaged in a whispering dispute over a book one of us had fumbled from a shelf, *A History of Botanical Gardens in England.* So we were undetected. We hoped!

But wary now, and sobered. For what if Marilyn 19
Monroe had caught us, and knew that we knew?

She might have abandoned her books and fled the 20
Strand. What a loss for her, and for the books! For us, too.

Oh, we worried at Marilyn Monroe's recklessness! 21
We dreaded her being recognized by a (male) customer or (male) clerk. A girl or woman would have kept her secret (so we thought) but no man could resist staring openly at her, following her, and at last speaking to her. Of course, the blond actress in Strand Used Books wasn't herself, not at all glamorous, or "sexy," or especially blond, in her inconspicuous man's clothing and those salt-stained boots; she might have been anyone, female or male, hardly a Hollywood celebrity, a movie goddess. Yet if you stared, you'd recognize her. If you tried, with any imagination you'd see "Marilyn Monroe." It was like a child's game in which you stare at foliage, grass, clouds in the sky, and suddenly you see a face or a figure, and after that recognition you can't not see the hidden shape, it's staring you in the face. So too with Marilyn Monroe. Once we saw her, it seemed to us she must be seen—and recognized—by anyone who happened to glance at her. If any man saw! We were fearful her privacy would be destroyed. Quickly the blond actress would become surrounded, mobbed. It was risky and reckless of her to have come to Strand Used Books by herself, we thought. Sure, she could shop at Tiffany's, maybe; she could stroll through the lobby of the Plaza, or the Waldorf-Astoria; she'd be safe from fans and unwanted admirers in privileged settings on the Upper East Side, but—here? In the egalitarian Strand, on Broadway and Twelfth?

We were perplexed. Almost, I was annoyed with 22
her. Taking such chances! But you, gripping my wrist, had another, more subtle thought.

"She thinks she's like *us.*" 23

You meant: a human being, anonymous. Female, 24
like us. Amid the ordinary unspectacular customers (predominantly male) of the Strand.

And that was the sadness in it, Marilyn Monroe's 25
wish. To be *like us.* For it was impossible, of course. For anyone could have told Marilyn Monroe, even two young girl-poets, that it was too late for her in history. Already, at age thirty (we could calculate afterward

that this was her age) "Marilyn Monroe" had entered history, and there was no escape from it. Her films, her photos. Her face, her figure, her name. To enter history is to be abducted spiritually, with no way back. As if lightning were to strike the building that housed the Strand, as if an actual current of electricity were to touch and transform only one individual in the great cavernous space and that lone individual, by pure chance it might seem, the caprice of fate, would be the young woman with the blond braid and the fedora slanted across her face. Why? Why her, and not another? You could argue that such a destiny is absurd, and underserved, for one individual among many, and logically you would be correct. And yet: "Marilyn Monroe" has entered history, and you have not. She will endure, though the young woman with the blond braid will die. *And even should she wish to die, "Marilyn Monroe" cannot.*

26 By this time she—the young woman with the blond braid—was carrying an armload of books. We were hoping she'd almost finished and would be leaving soon, before strangers' rude eyes lighted upon her and exposed her, but no: she surprised us by heading for a section called JUDAICA. In that forbidding aisle, which we'd never before entered, there were books in numerous languages: Hebrew, Yiddish, German, Russian, French. Some of these books looked ancient! Complete sets of the Talmud. Cryptically printed tomes on the cabala. Luckily for us, the titles Marilyn Monroe pulled out were all in English: *Jews of Eastern Europe; The Chosen People: A Complete History of the Jews: Jews of the New World.* Quickly Marilyn Monroe placed her bag and books on the floor, sat on a footstool, and leafed through pages with the frowning intensity of a young girl, as if searching for something urgent, something she knew—knew!—must be there; in this comfortable posture she remained for at least fifteen minutes, wetting her fingers to turn pages that stuck together, pages that had not been turned, still less read, for decades. She was frowning, yet smiling too; fain vertical lines appeared between her eyebrows, in the intensity of her concentration; her eyes moved rapidly along lines of print, then returned, and moved more slowly. By this time we were close enough to observe the blond actress's feverish cheeks and slightly parted moist lips that seemed to move silently. *What is she reading in that ancient book, what can possibly mean so much to her? A secret, revealed? A secret, to save her life?*

> But this young woman was beautiful without makeup, without even lipstick . . .

27 "Hey you!" a clerk called out in a nasal, insinuating voice.

The three of us looked up, startled. 28

But the clerk wasn't speaking to us. Not to the blond actress frowning over *The Chosen People,* and not to us who were hovering close by. The clerk had caught someone slipping a book into an overcoat pocket, not an unusual sight at the Strand. 29

After this mild upset, Marilyn Monroe became uneasy. She turned to look frankly at us, and though we tried clumsily to retreat, her eyes met ours. *She knows!* But after a moment, she simply turned back to her book, stubborn and determined to finish what she was reading, while we continued to hover close by, exposed now, and blushing, yet feeling protective of her. *She has seen us, she knows. She trusts us.* We saw that Marilyn Monroe was beautiful in her anonymity as she had never seemed, to us, to be beautiful as "Marilyn Monroe." All that was makeup, fakery, cartoon sexiness subtle as a kick in the groin. All that was vulgar and infantile. But this young woman was beautiful without makeup, without even lipstick; in her mannish clothes, her hair in a stubby braid. Beautiful: her skin luminous and pale and her eyes a startling clear blue. Almost shyly she glanced back at us, to note that we were still there, and she smiled. *Yes, I see you two. Thank you for not speaking my name.* 30

Always you and I would remember: that smile of gratitude, and sweetness. 31

Always you and I would remember: that she trusted us, as perhaps we would not have trusted ourselves. 32

So many years later, I'm proud of us. We were so young. 33

Young, headstrong, arrogant, insecure though "brilliant"—or so we'd been let to believe. Not that we thought of ourselves as young: you were nineteen, I was twenty. We were mature for our ages, and we were immature. We were intellectually sophisticated, and emotionally unpredictable. We revered something we called *art,* we were disdainful of something we called *life.* We were overly conscious of ourselves. And yet: how patient, how protective, watching over Marilyn Monroe squatting on a footstool in the JUDAICA stacks as stray customers pushed past muttering "excuse me!" or not even seeming to notice her, or the two of us standing guard. And at last—a relief—Marilyn Monroe shut the unwieldy book, having decided to buy it, and rose from the footstool gathering up her many things. And—this was a temptation!—we held back, not offering to help her carry her things as we so badly wanted to, but only just following at 34

a discreet distance as Marilyn Monroe made her way through the labyrinth of the bookstore to the front counter. (Did she glance back at us? Did she understand you and I were her protectors?) If anyone dared to approach her, we intended to intervene. We would push between Marilyn Monroe and whomever it was. Yet how strange the scene was: none of the other Strand customers, lost in books, took any special notice of her, any more than they took notice of us. Book lovers, especially used-book lovers, are not ones to stare curiously at others, but only at books. At the front of the store—it was a long hike—the cashiers would be more alert, we thought. One of them seemed to be watching Marilyn Monroe approach. Did he know? Could he guess? Was he waiting for her?

35 Nearing the front counter and the bright fluorescent lights overhead, Marilyn Monroe seemed for the first time to falter. She fumbled to extract out of her shoulder bag a pair of dark glasses and managed to put them on. She turned up the collar of her navy coat. She lowered her hat brim.

36 Still she was hesitant, and it was then that I stepped forward and said quietly, "Excuse me. Why don't I buy your books for you? That way you won't have to talk to anyone."

37 The blond actress stared at me through her oversized dark glasses. Her eyes were only just visible behind the lenses. A shy-girl's eyes, startled and grateful.

38 And so I did. With you helping me. Two girl-poets, side by side, all brisk and businesslike, making Marilyn Monroe's purchases for her: a total of sixteen books!—hardcover and paperback, relatively new books, old battered thumbed-through books—at a cost of $55.85. A staggering sum! Never in my two years of coming into the Strand had I handed over more than a few dollars to the cashier, and this time my hand might have trembled as I pushed twenty-dollar bills at him, half expecting the bristly bearded man to interrogate me: "Where'd you get so much money?" But as usual the cashier hardly gave me a second glance. And Marilyn Monroe, burdened with no books, had already slipped through the turnstile and was awaiting us at the front door.

There, when we handed over her purchases in two sturdy bags, she leaned forward. For a breathless moment we thought she might kiss our cheeks. Instead she pressed into our surprised hands a slender volume she lifted from one of the bags: *Selected Poems of Marianne Moore*. We stammered thanks, but already the blond actress had pulled the fedora down more tightly over her head and had stepped out into the lightly falling snow, headed south on Broadway. We trailed behind her, unable to resist, waiting for her to hail a taxi, but she did not. We knew we must not follow her. By this time we were giddy with the strain of the past hour, gripping each other's hands in childlike elation. So happy! 39

"Oh. Oh God. Marilyn Monroe. She gave us a book. Was any of it real?" 40

It was real: we had *Selected Poems of Marianne Moore* to prove it. 41

That snowy early evening in March at Strand Used Books. That magical evening of Marilyn Monroe, when I kissed you for the first time. 42

# Questions for Critical Thinking

1 Describe the basic plot of the girls spotting Marilyn Monroe. Then consider the last line, "when I kissed you for the first time." How would you describe this second plot line?

2 Are there conflicts beyond the central conflict of keeping Marilyn Monroe a secret from the outside world? Describe them.

3 Although this is a one-scene story, it contains the elements of a traditional story—conflict, rising action, climax, dénouement. Identify where each of these elements takes place.

4 This story has a specific, carefully described setting. What elements of this setting build toward the sense that something "magical" occurs that evening?

5 The narrator says "we were not 'conventional' females." What does she mean by this? How does her voice as she tells the story prove or refute the statement that she is "unconventional"?

6 As the title suggests, gender plays a large role in this story. The girls clearly have expectations of gender, such as when they expect the Leading Man to join Marilyn Monroe in the bookstore. Considering the three female characters, how are men portrayed in this story?

7 *Three Girls* is as much about creating identity as it is about erasing it. Using examples from the text, create an argument for or against this statement.

"What was so interesting about the original event was not so much that a serial killer had been preying on young people, which is unfortunately all too common, but that the young people had known about it. They had known that some girls had been killed and buried in the desert, but they kept the secret because their allegiance was to this man. And I wanted to write a story about that phenomenon." Conversation with Joyce Carol Oates

# Where Are You Going, Where Have You Been? (1970)

*For Bob Dylan*

1 HER name was Connie. She was fifteen and she had a quick nervous giggling habit of craning her neck to glance into mirrors, or checking other people's faces to make sure her own was all right. Her mother, who noticed everything and knew everything and who hadn't much reason any longer to look at her own face, always scolded Connie about it. "Stop gawking at yourself, who are you? You think you're so pretty?" she would say. Connie would raise her eyebrows at these familiar complaints and look right through her mother, into a shadowy vision of herself as she was right at that moment: she knew she was pretty and that was everything. Her mother had been pretty once too, if

you could believe those old snapshots in the album, but now her looks were gone and that was why she was always after Connie.

2 "Why don't you keep your room clean like your sister? How've you got your hair fixed—what the hell stinks? Hair spray? You don't see your sister using that junk."

3 Her sister June was twenty-four and still lived at home. She was a secretary in the high school Connie attended, and if that wasn't bad enough—with her in the same building—she was so plain and chunky and steady that Connie had to hear her praised all the time by her mother and her mother's sisters. June did this, June did that, she saved money and helped clean the house and cooked and Connie couldn't do a thing, her mind was all filled with trashy daydreams. Their father was away at work most of the time and when he came home he wanted supper and he read the newspaper at supper and after supper he went to bed. He didn't bother talking much to them, but around his bent head Connie's mother kept picking at her until Connie wished her mother was dead and she herself was dead and it was all over. "She makes me want to throw up sometimes," she complained to her friends. She had a high, breathless, amused voice which made everything she said sound a little forced, whether it was sincere or not.

He wagged a finger and laughed and said, "Gonna get you, baby."

4 There was one good thing: June went places with girl friends of hers, girls who were just as plain and steady as she, and so when Connie wanted to do that her mother had no objections. The father of Connie's best girl friend drove the girls the three miles to town and left them off at a shopping plaza, so that they could walk through the stores or go to a movie, and when he came to pick them up again at eleven he never bothered to ask what they had done.

5 They must have been familiar sights, walking around that shopping plaza in their shorts and flat ballerina slippers that always scuffed the sidewalk, with charm bracelets jingling on their thin wrists; they would lean together to whisper and laugh secretly if someone passed by who amused or interested them. Connie had long dark blond hair that drew anyone's eye to it, and she wore part of it pulled up on her head and puffed out and the rest of it she let fall down her back. She wore a pullover jersey blouse that looked one way when she was at home and another way when she was away from home. Everything about her had two sides to it, one for home and one for anywhere that was not home: her walk that could be childlike and bobbing, or languid enough to make anyone think she was hearing music in her head, her mouth which was pale and smirking most of the time, but bright and pink on these evenings out, her laugh which was cynical and drawling at home—"Ha, ha, very funny"—but high-pitched and nervous anywhere else, like the jingling of the charms on her bracelet.

6 Sometimes they did go shopping or to a movie, but sometimes they went across the highway, ducking fast across the busy road, to a drive-in restaurant where older kids hung out. The restaurant was shaped like a big bottle, though squatter than a real bottle, and on its cap was a revolving figure of a grinning boy who held a hamburger aloft. One night in mid-summer they ran across, breathless with daring, and right away someone leaned out a car window and invited them over, but it was just a boy from high school they didn't like. It made them feel good to be able to ignore him. They went up through the maze of parked and cruising cars to the bright-lit, fly-infested restaurant, their faces pleased and expectant as if they were entering a sacred building that loomed out of the night to give them what haven and what blessing they yearned for. They sat at the counter and crossed their legs at the ankles, their thin shoulders rigid with excitement, and listened to the music that made everything so good: the music was always in the background like music at a church service, it was something to depend upon.

7 A boy named Eddie came in to talk with them. He sat backwards on his stool, turning himself jerkily around in semi-circles and then stopping and turning again, and after a while he asked Connie if she would like something to eat. She said she did and so she tapped her friend's arm on her way out—her friend pulled her face up into a brave droll look—and Connie said she would meet her at eleven, across the way. "I just hate to leave her like that," Connie said earnestly, but the boy said that she wouldn't be alone for long. So they went out to his car and on the way Connie couldn't help but let her eyes wander over the windshields and faces all around her, her face gleaming with a joy that had nothing to do with Eddie or even this place; it might have been the music. She drew her shoulders up and sucked in her breath with the pure pleasure of being alive, and just at that moment she happened to glance at a face just a few feet from hers. It was a boy with shaggy black hair, in a convertible jalopy painted gold. He stared at her and then his lips widened into a grin. Connie slit her eyes at him and turned away, but she couldn't help glancing back and there he was still watching her. He wagged a finger and laughed and

said, "Gonna get you, baby," and Connie turned away again without Eddie noticing anything.

8 She spent three hours with him, at the restaurant where they ate hamburgers and drank Cokes in wax cups that were always sweating, and then down an alley a mile or so away, and when he left her off at five to eleven only the movie house was still open at the plaza. Her girl friend was there, talking with a boy. When Connie came up the two girls smiled at each other and Connie said, "How was the movie?" and the girl said, "*You* should know." They rode off with the girl's father, sleepy and pleased, and Connie couldn't help but look at the darkened shopping plaza with its big empty parking lot and its signs that were faded and ghostly now, and over at the drive-in restaurant where cars were still circling tirelessly. She couldn't hear the music at this distance.

9 Next morning June asked her how the movie was and Connie said, "So-so."

10 She and that girl and occasionally another girl went out several times a week that way, and the rest of the time Connie spent around the house—it was summer vacation—getting in her mother's way and thinking, dreaming, about the boys she met. But all the boys fell back and dissolved into a single face that was not even a face, but an idea, a feeling, mixed up with the urgent insistent pounding of the music and the humid night air of July. Connie's mother kept dragging her back to the daylight by finding things for her to do or saying, suddenly, "What's this about the Pettinger girl?"

11 And Connie would say nervously, "Oh, her. That dope." She always drew thick clear lines between herself and such girls, and her mother was simple and kindly enough to believe her. Her mother was so simple, Connie thought, that it was maybe cruel to fool her so much. Her mother went scuffling around the house in old bedroom slippers and complained over the telephone to one sister about the other, then the other called up and the two of them complained about the third one. If June's name was mentioned her mother's tone was approving, and if Connie's name was mentioned it was disapproving. This did not really mean she disliked Connie and actually Connie thought that her mother preferred her to June because she was prettier, but the two of them kept up a pretense of exasperation, a sense that they were tugging and struggling over something of little value to either of them. Sometimes, over coffee, they were almost friends, but something would come up—some vexation that was like a fly buzzing suddenly around their heads—and their faces went hard with contempt.

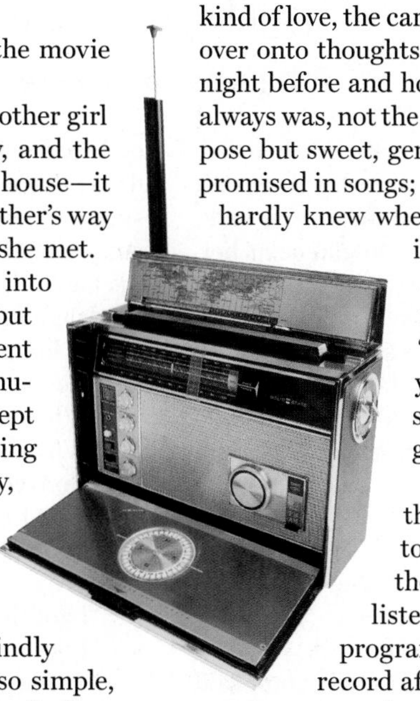

One Sunday Connie got up at eleven—none of them bothered with church—and washed her hair so that it could dry all day long, in the sun. Her parents and sister were going to a barbecue at an aunt's house and Connie said no, she wasn't interested, rolling her eyes to let her mother know just what she thought of it. "Stay home alone then," her mother said sharply. Connie sat out back in a lawn chair and watched them drive away, her father quiet and bald, hunched around so that he could back the car out, her mother with a look that was still angry and not at all softened through the windshield, and in the back seat poor old June all dressed up as if she didn't know what a barbecue was, with all the running yelling kids and the flies. Connie sat with her eyes closed in the sun, dreaming and dazed with the warmth about her as if this were a kind of love, the caresses of love, and her mind slipped over onto thoughts of the boy she had been with the night before and how nice he had been, how sweet it always was, not the way someone like June would suppose but sweet, gentle, the way it was in movies and promised in songs; and when she opened her eyes she hardly knew where she was, the back yard ran off into weeds and a fence-line of trees and behind it the sky was perfectly blue and still. The asbestos "ranch house" that was now three years old startled her—it looked small. She shook her head as if to get awake. 12

It was too hot. She went inside the house and turned on the radio to drown out the quiet. She sat on the edge of her bed, barefoot, and listened for an hour and a half to a program called XYZ Sunday Jamboree, record after record of hard, fast, shrieking songs she sang along with, interspersed by exclamations from "Bobby King": "An' look here you girls at Napoleon's—Son and Charley want you to pay real close attention to this song coming up!" 13

And Connie paid close attention herself, bathed in a glow of slow-pulsed joy that seemed to rise mysteriously out of the music itself and lay languidly about the airless little room, breathed in and breathed out with each gentle rise and fall of her chest. 14

After a while she heard a car coming up the drive. She sat up at once, startled, because it couldn't be her father so soon. The gravel kept crunching all the way in from the road—the driveway was long—and Connie ran to the window. It was a car she didn't know. It was an open jalopy, painted a bright gold that caught the sunlight opaquely. Her heart began to pound and her fingers snatched at her hair, checking it, and she 15 whispered "Christ, Christ," wondering how bad she looked. The car came to a stop at the side door and the horn sounded four short taps as if this were a signal Connie knew.

16 She went into the kitchen and approached the door slowly, then hung out the screen door, her bare toes curling down off the step. There were two boys in the car and now she recognized the driver: he had shaggy, shabby black hair that looked crazy as a wig and he was grinning at her.

17 "I ain't late, am I?" he said.

18 "Who the hell do you think you are?" Connie said.

19 "Toldja I'd be out, didn't I?"

20 "I don't even know who you are."

21 She spoke sullenly, careful to show no interest or pleasure, and he spoke in a fast bright monotone. Connie looked past him to the other boy, taking her time. He had fair brown hair, with a lock that fell onto his forehead. His sideburns gave him a fierce, embarrassed look, but so far he hadn't even bothered to glance at her. Both boys wore sunglasses. The driver's glasses were metallic and mirrored everything in miniature.

> The way he straightened and recovered from his fit of laughing showed that it had been all fake.

22 "You wanta come for a ride?" he said.

23 Connie smirked and let her hair fall loose over one shoulder.

24 "Don'tcha like my car? New paint job," he said. "Hey."

25 "What?"

26 "You're cute."

27 She pretended to fidget, chasing flies away from the door.

28 "Don'tcha believe me, or what?" he said.

29 "Look, I don't even know who you are," Connie said in disgust.

30 "Hey, Ellie's got a radio, see. Mine's broke down." He lifted his friend's arm and showed her the little transistor the boy was holding, and now Connie began to hear the music. It was the same program that was playing inside the house.

31 "Bobby King?" she said.

32 "I listen to him all the time. I think he's great."

33 "He's kind of great," Connie said reluctantly.

34 "Listen, that guy's *great*. He knows where the action is."

35 Connie blushed a little, because the glasses made it impossible for her to see just what this boy was looking at. She couldn't decide if she liked him or if he was just a jerk, and so she dawdled in the doorway and wouldn't come down or go back inside. She said, "What's all that stuff painted on your car?"

"Can'tcha read it?" He opened the door very carefully, as if he was afraid it might fall off. He slid out just as carefully, planting his feet firmly on the ground, the tiny metallic world in his glasses slowing down like gelatine hardening and in the midst of it Connie's bright green blouse. "This here is my name, to begin with," he said. ARNOLD FRIEND was written in tarlike black letters on the side, with a drawing of a round grinning face that reminded Connie of a pumpkin, except it wore sunglasses. "I wanta introduce myself, I'm Arnold Friend and that's my real name and I'm gonna be your friend, honey, and inside the car's Ellie Oscar, he's kinda shy." Ellie brought his transistor radio up to his shoulder and balanced it there. "Now these numbers are a secret code, honey," Arnold Friend explained. He read off the numbers 33, 19, 17 and raised his eyebrows at her to see what she thought of that, but she didn't think much of it. The left rear fender had been smashed and around it was written, on the gleaming gold background: DONE BY CRAZY WOMAN DRIVER. Connie had to laugh at that. Arnold Friend was pleased at her laughter and looked up at her. "Around the other side's a lot more—you wanta come and see them?" 36

"No." 37

"Why not?" 38

"Why should I?" 39

"Don'tcha wanta see what's on the car? Don'tcha wanta go for a ride?" 40

"I don't know." 41

"Why not?" 42

"I got things to do." 43

"Like what?" 44

"Things." 45

He laughed as if she had said something funny. He slapped his thighs. He was standing in a strange way, leaning back against the car as if he were balancing himself. He wasn't tall, only an inch or so taller than she would be if she came down to him. Connie liked the way he was dressed, which was the way all of them dressed: tight faded jeans stuffed into black, scuffed boots, a belt that pulled his waist in and showed how lean he was, and a white pull-over shirt that was a little soiled and showed the hard small muscles of his arms and shoulders. He looked as if he probably did hard work, lifting and carrying things. Even his neck looked muscular. And his face was a familiar face, somehow: the jaw and chin and cheeks slightly darkened, because he hadn't shaved for a day or two, and the nose long and hawk-like, sniffing as if she were a treat he was going to gobble up and it was all a joke. 46

7 "Connie, you ain't telling the truth. This is your day set aside for a ride with me and you know it," he said, still laughing. The way he straightened and recovered from his fit of laughing showed that it had been all fake.

8 "How do you know what my name is?" she said suspiciously.

9 "It's Connie."

0 "Maybe and maybe not."

1 "I know my Connie," he said, wagging his finger. Now she remembered him even better, back at the restaurant, and her cheeks warmed at the thought of how she sucked in her breath just at the moment she passed him—how she must have looked to him. And he had remembered her. "Ellie and I come out here especially for you," he said. "Ellie can sit in back. How about it?"

2 "Where?"

3 "Where what?"

4 "Where're we going?"

5 He looked at her. He took off the sunglasses and she saw how pale the skin around his eyes was, like holes that were not in shadow but instead in light. His eyes were chips of broken glass that catch the light in an amiable way. He smiled. It was as if the idea of going for a ride somewhere, to some place, was a new idea to him.

6 "Just for a ride, Connie sweetheart."

7 "I never said my name was Connie," she said.

8 "But I know what it is. I know your name and all about you, lots of things," Arnold Friend said. He had not moved yet but stood still leaning back against the side of his jalopy. "I took a special interest in you, such a pretty girl, and found out all about you like I know your parents and sister are gone somewheres and I know where and how long they're going to be gone, and I know who you were with last night, and your best girl friend's name is Betty. Right?"

9 He spoke in a simple lilting voice, exactly as if he were reciting the words to a song. His smile assured her that everything was fine. In the car Ellie turned up the volume on his radio and did not bother to look around at them.

0 "Ellie can sit in the back seat," Arnold Friend said. He indicated his friend with a casual jerk of his chin, as if Ellie did not count and she should not bother with him.

1 "How'd you find out all that stuff?" Connie said.

2 "Listen: Betty Schultz and Tony Fitch and Jimmy Pettinger and Nancy Pettinger," he said, in a chant. "Raymond Stanley and Bob Hutter—"

3 "Do you know all those kids?"

4 "I know everybody."

5 "Look, you're kidding. You're not from around here."

"Sure." 66

"But—how come we never saw you before?" 67

"Sure you saw me before," he said. He looked down at his boots, as if he were a little offended. "You just don't remember." 68

"I guess I'd remember you," Connie said. 69

"Yeah?" He looked up at this, beaming. He was pleased. He began to mark time with the music from Ellie's radio, tapping his fists lightly together. Connie looked away from his smile to the car, which was painted so bright it almost hurt her eyes to look at it. She looked at that name, ARNOLD FRIEND. And up at the front fender was an expression that was familiar—MAN THE FLYING SAUCERS. It was an expression kids had used the year before, but didn't use this year. She looked at it for a while as if the words meant something to her that she did not yet know. 70

"What're you thinking about? Huh?" Arnold Friend demanded. "Not worried about your hair blowing around in the car, are you?" 71

"No." 72

"Think I maybe can't drive good?" 73

"How do I know?" 74

"You're a hard girl to handle. How come?" he said. "Don't you know I'm your friend? Didn't you see me put my sign in the air when you walked by?" 75

"What sign?" 76

"My sign." And he drew an X in the air, leaning out toward her. They were maybe ten feet apart. After his hand fell back to his side the X was still in the air, almost visible. Connie let the screen door close and stood perfectly still inside it, listening to the music from her radio and the boy's blend together. She stared at Arnold Friend. He stood there so stiffly relaxed, pretending to be relaxed, with one hand idly on the door handle as if he were keeping himself up that way and had no intention of ever moving again. She recognized most things about him, the tight jeans that showed his thighs and buttocks and the greasy leather boots and the tight shirt, and even that slippery friendly smile of his, that sleepy dreamy smile that all the boys used to get across ideas they didn't want to put into words. She recognized all this and also the singsong way he talked, slightly mocking, kidding, but serious and a little melancholy, and she recognized the way he tapped one fist against the other in homage to the perpetual music behind him. But all these things did not come together. 77

She said suddenly, "Hey, how old are you?" 78

His smile faded. She could see then that he wasn't a kid, he was much older—thirty, maybe more. At this knowledge her heart began to pound faster. 79

"That's a crazy thing to ask. Can'tcha see I'm your own age?" 80

81 "Like hell you are."

82 "Or maybe a coupla years older, I'm eighteen."

83 "Eighteen?" she said doubtfully.

84 He grinned to reassure her and lines appeared at the corners of his mouth. His teeth were big and white. He grinned so broadly his eyes became slits and she saw how thick the lashes were, thick and black as if painted with a black tar-like material. Then he seemed to become embarrassed, abruptly, and looked over his shoulder at Ellie. "*Him,* he's crazy," he said. "Ain't he a riot, he's a nut, a real character." Ellie was still listening to the music. His sunglasses told nothing about what he was thinking. He wore a bright orange shirt unbuttoned halfway to show his chest, which was a pale, bluish chest and not muscular like Arnold Friend's. His shirt collar was turned up all around and the very tips of the collar pointed out past his chin as if they were protecting him. He was pressing the transistor radio up against his ear and sat there in a kind of daze, right in the sun.

85 "He's kinda strange," Connie said.

86 "Hey, she says you're kinda strange! Kinda strange!" Arnold Friend cried. He pounded on the car to get Ellie's attention. Ellie turned for the first time and Connie saw with shock that he wasn't kid either—he had a fair, hairless face, cheeks reddened slightly as if the veins grew too close to the surface of his skin, the face of a forty-year-old baby. Connie felt a wave of dizziness rise in her at this sight and she stared at him as if waiting for something to change the shock of the moment, make it all right again. Ellie's lips kept shaping words, mumbling along, with the words blasting in his ear.

87 "Maybe you two better go away," Connie said faintly.

88 "What? How come?" Arnold Friend cried. "We come out here to take you for a ride. It's Sunday." He had the voice of the man on the radio now. It was the same voice, Connie thought. "Don'tcha know it's Sunday all day and honey, no matter who you were with last night today you're with Arnold Friend and don't you forget it!—Maybe you better step out here," he said, and this last was in a different voice. It was a little flatter, as if the heat was finally getting to him.

89 "No. I got things to do."

90 "Hey."

91 "You two better leave."

92 "We ain't leaving until you come with us."

93 "Like hell I am—"

94 "Connie, don't fool around with me. I mean, I mean, don't fool *around,*" he said, shaking his head. He laughed incredulously. He placed his sunglasses on top of his head, carefully, as if he were indeed wearing a wig, and brought the stems down behind his ears. Connie stared at him, another wave of dizziness and fear rising in her so that for a moment he wasn't even in focus but was just a blur, standing there against his gold car, and she had the idea that he had driven up the driveway all right but had come from nowhere before that and belonged nowhere and that everything about him and even about the music that was so familiar to her was only half real.

Connie stared at him, another wave of dizziness and fear rising in her . . .

"If my father comes and sees you—" 9

"He ain't coming. He's at the barbecue." 9

"How do you know that?" 9

"Aunt Tillie's. Right now they're—uh—they're drinking. Sitting around," he said vaguely, squinting as if he were staring all the way to town and over to Aunt Tillie's backyard. Then the vision seemed to get clear and he nodded energetically. "Yeah. Sitting around. There's your sister in a blue dress, huh? And high heels, the poor sad bitch—nothing like you, sweetheart! And your mother's helping some fat woman with the corn, they're cleaning the corn—husking the corn—" 9

"What fat woman?" Connie cried. 9

"How do I know what fat woman. I don't know every goddam fat woman in the world!" Arnold Friend laughed. 1

"Oh, that's Mrs. Hornby. . . . Who invited her?" Connie said. She felt a little light-headed. Her breath was coming quickly. 1

"She's too fat. I don't like them fat. I like them the way you are, honey," he said, smiling sleepily at her. They stared at each other for a while, through the screen door. He said softly, "Now what you're going to do is this: you're going to come out that door. You're going to sit up front with me and Ellie's going to sit in the back, the hell with Ellie, right? This isn't Ellie's date. You're my date. I'm your lover, honey." 1

"What? You're crazy—" 1

"Yes, I'm your lover. You don't know what that is but you will," he said. "I know that too. I know all about you. But look: it's real nice and you couldn't ask for nobody better than me, or more polite. I always keep my word. I'll tell you how it is, I'm always nice at first, the first time. I'll hold you so tight you won't think you have to try to get away or pretend anything because you'll know you can't. And I'll come inside you where it's all secret and you'll give in to me and you'll love me—" 1

"Shut up! You're crazy!" Connie said. She backed away from the door. She put her hands against her 1 ears as if she'd heard something terrible, something not meant for her. "People don't talk like that, you're crazy," she muttered. Her heart was almost too big now for her chest and its pumping made sweat break out all over her. She looked out to see Arnold Friend pause and then take a step toward the porch lurching. He almost fell. But, like a clever drunken man, he managed to catch his balance. He wobbled in his high boots and grabbed hold of one of the porch posts.

6 "Honey?" he said. "You still listening?"

7 "Get the hell out of here!"

8 "Be nice, honey. Listen."

9 "I'm going to call the police—"

0 He wobbled again and out of the side of his mouth came a fast spat curse, an aside not meant for her to hear. But even this "Christ!" sounded forced. Then he began to smile again. She watched this smile come, awkward as if he were smiling from inside a mask. His whole face was a mask, she thought wildly, tanned down onto his throat but then running out as if he had plastered makeup on his face but had forgotten about his throat.

1 "Honey—? Listen, here's how it is. I always tell the truth and I promise you this: I ain't coming in that house after you."

2 "You better not! I'm going to call the police if you—if you don't—"

3 "Honey," he said, talking right through her voice, "honey, I'm not coming in there but you are coming out here. You know why?"

4 She was panting. The kitchen looked like a place she had never seen before, some room she had run inside but which wasn't good enough, wasn't going to help her. The kitchen window had never had a curtain, after three years, and there were dishes in the sink for her to do—probably—and if you ran your hand across the table you'd probably feel something sticky there.

5 "You listening, honey? Hey?"

6 "—going to call the police—"

7 "Soon as you touch the phone I don't need to keep my promise and can come inside. You won't want that."

8 She rushed forward and tried to lock the door. Her fingers were shaking. "But why lock it," Arnold Friend said gently, talking right into her face. "It's just a screen door. It's just nothing." One of his boots was at a strange angle, as if his foot wasn't in it. It pointed out to the left, bent at the ankle. "I mean, anybody can break through a screen door and glass and wood and iron or anything else if he needs to, anybody at all and specially Arnold Friend. If the place got lit up with a fire honey you'd come running out into my arms, right into my arms and safe at home—like you knew I was your lover and'd stopped fooling around. I don't mind a nice shy girl but I don't like no fooling around." Part of those words were spoken with a slight rhythmic lilt, and Connie somehow recognized them—the echo of a song from last year, about a girl rushing into her boyfriend's arms and coming home again—

Connie stood barefoot on the linoleum floor, staring at him. "What do you want?" she whispered. 119

"I want you," he said. 120

"What?" 121

"Seen you that night and thought, that's the one, yes sir. I never needed to look any more." 122

"But my father's coming back. He's coming to get me. I had to wash my hair first—" She spoke in a dry, rapid voice, hardly raising it for him to hear. 123

"No, your daddy is not coming and yes, you had to wash your hair and you washed it for me. It's nice and shining and all for me, I thank you, sweetheart," he said, with a mock bow, but again he almost lost his balance. He had to bend and adjust his boots. Evidently his feet did not go all the way down; the boots must have been stuffed with something so that he would seem taller. Connie stared out at him and behind him Ellie in the car, who seemed to be looking off toward Connie's right, into nothing. This Ellie said, pulling the words out of the air one after another as if he were just discovering them, "You want me to pull out the phone?" 124

"Shut your mouth and keep it shut," Arnold Friend said, his face red from bending over or maybe from embarrassment because Connie had seen his boots. "This ain't none of your business." 125

"What—what are you doing? What do you want?" Connie said. "If I call the police they'll get you, they'll arrest you—" 126

"Promise was not to come in unless you touch that phone, and I'll keep that promise," he said. He resumed his erect position and tried to force his shoulders back. He sounded like a hero in a movie, declaring something important. He spoke too loudly and it was as if he were speaking to someone behind Connie. "I ain't made plans for coming in that house where I don't belong but just for you to come out to me, the way you should. Don't you know who I am?" 127

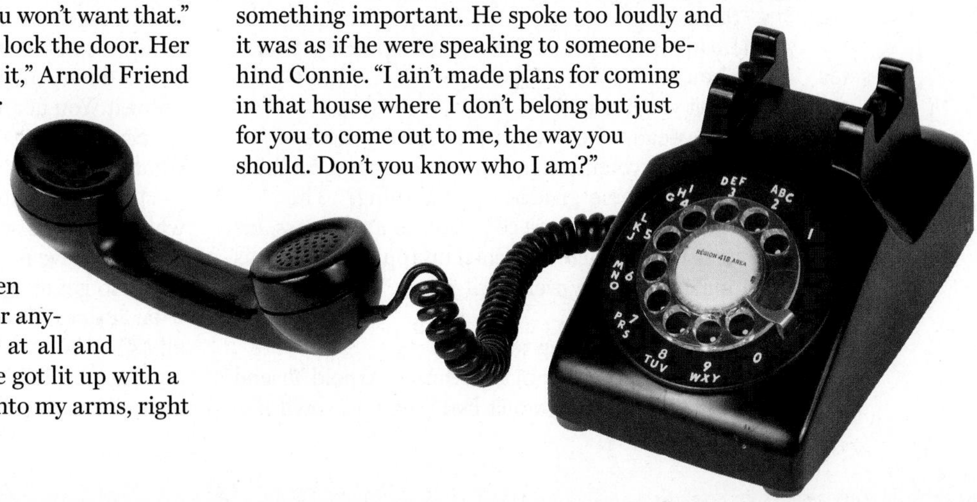

128 "You're crazy," she whispered. She backed away from the door but did not want to go into another part of the house, as if this would give him permission to come through the door. "What do you . . . You're crazy, you . . ."

129 "Huh? What're you saying, honey?"

130 Her eyes darted everywhere in the kitchen. She could not remember what it was, this room.

She thought, I'm not going to see my mother again.

131 "This is how it is, honey: you come out and we'll drive away, have a nice ride. But if you don't come out we're gonna wait till your people come home and then they're all going to get it."

132 "You want that telephone pulled out?" Ellie said. He held the radio away from his ear and grimaced, as if without the radio the air was too much for him.

133 "I toldja shut up, Ellie," Arnold Friend said, "you're deaf, get a hearing aid, right? Fix yourself up. This little girl's no trouble and's gonna be nice to me, so Ellie keep to yourself, this ain't your date—right? Don't hem in on me. Don't hog. Don't crush. Don't bird dog. Don't trail me," he said in a rapid meaningless voice, as if he were running through all the expressions he'd learned but was no longer sure which one of them was in style, then rushing on to new ones, making them up with his eyes closed, "Don't crawl under my fence, don't squeeze in my chipmunk hole, don't sniff my glue, suck my popsicle, keep your own greasy fingers on yourself!" He shaded his eyes and peered in at Connie, who was backed against the kitchen table. "Don't mind him honey he's just a creep. He's a dope. Right? I'm the boy for you and like I said you come out here nice like a lady and give me your hand, and nobody else gets hurt, I mean, your nice old bald-headed daddy and your mummy and your sister in her high heels. Because listen: why bring them in this?"

134 "Leave me alone," Connie whispered.

135 "Hey, you know that old woman down the road, the one with the chickens and stuff—you know her?"

136 "She's dead!"

137 "Dead? What? You know her?" Arnold Friend said.

138 "She's dead—"

139 'Don't you like her?"

140 "She's dead—she's—she isn't here any more—"

141 "But don't you like her, I mean, you got something against her? Some grudge or something?" Then his voice dipped as if he were conscious of a rudeness. He touched the sunglasses perched on top of his head as if to make sure they were still there. "Now you be a good girl."

142 "What are you going to do?"

143 "Just two things, or maybe three," Arnold Friend said. "But I promise it won't last long and you'll like me that way you get to like people you're close to. You will. It's all over for you here, so come on out. You don't want your people in any trouble, do you?"

She turned and bumped against a chair or something, hurting her leg, but she ran into the back room and picked up the telephone. Something roared in her ear, a tiny roaring, and she was so sick with fear that she could do nothing but listen to it—the telephone was clammy and very heavy and her fingers groped down to the dial but were too weak to touch it. She began to scream into the phone, into the roaring. She cried out, she cried for her mother, she felt her breath start jerking back and forth in her lungs as if it were something Arnold Friend were stabbing her with again and again with no tenderness. A noisy sorrowful wailing rose all about her and she was locked inside it the way she was locked inside the house. 1

After a while she could hear again. She was sitting on the floor with her wet back against the wall. 1

Arnold Friend was saying from the door, "That's a good girl. Put the phone back." She kicked the phone away from her. 1

"No, honey. Pick it up. Put it back right."

She picked it up and put it back. The dial tone stopped.

"That's a good girl. Now come outside."

She was hollow with what had been fear, but what was now just an emptiness. All that screaming had blasted it out of her. She sat, one leg cramped under her, and deep inside her brain was something like a pinpoint of light that kept going and would not let her relax. She thought, I'm not going to see my mother again. She thought, I'm not going to sleep in my bed again. Her bright green blouse was all wet. 1

Arnold Friend said, in a gentle-loud voice that was like a stage voice, "The place where you came from ain't there any more, and where you had in mind to go is cancelled out. This place you are now—inside your daddy's house—is nothing but a cardboard box I can knock down any time. You know that and always did know it. You hear me?" 1

She thought, I have got to think. I have to know what to do. 1

"We'll go out to a nice field, out in the country here where it smells so nice and it's sunny," Arnold Friend said. "I'll have my arms around you so you won't need to try to get away and I'll show you what love is like, what it does. The hell with this house! It looks solid all right," he said. He ran a fingernail down the screen and the noise did not make Connie shiver, as it would have the day before. "Now put your hand on your 1

heart, honey. Feel that? That feels solid too but we know better, be nice to me, be sweet like you can because what else is there for a girl like you but to be sweet and pretty and give in?—and get away before her people come back?"

154 She felt her pounding heart. Her hand seemed to enclose it. She thought for the first time in her life that it was nothing that was hers, that belonged to her, but just a pounding, living thing inside this body that wasn't really hers either.

155 "You don't want them to get hurt," Arnold Friend went on. "Now get up, honey. Get up all by yourself."

156 She stood up.

157 "Now turn this way. That's right. Come over here to me—Ellie, put that away, didn't I tell you? You dope. You miserable creepy dope," Arnold Friend said. His words were not angry but only part of an incantation. The incantation was kindly. "Now come out through the kitchen to me honey and let's see a smile, try it, you're a brave sweet little girl and now they're eating corn and hotdogs cooked to bursting over an outdoor fire, and they don't know one thing about you and never did and honey you're better than them because not a one of them would have done this for you."

Connie felt the linoleum under her feet; it was cool. She brushed her hair back out of her eyes. Arnold Friend let go of the post tentatively and opened his arms for her, his elbows pointing in toward each other and his wrists limp, to show that this was an embarrassed embrace and a little mocking, he didn't want to make her self-conscious. 158

She put out her hand against the screen. She watched herself push the door slowly open as if she were safe back somewhere in the other doorway, watching this body and this head of long hair moving out into the sunlight where Arnold Friend waited. 159

"My sweet little blue-eyed girl," he said, in a half-sung sigh that had nothing to do with her brown eyes but was taken up just the same by the vast sunlit reaches of the land behind him and on all sides of him, so much land that Connie had never seen before and did not recognize except to know that she was going to it. 160

"What was so interesting about the original event was not so much that a serial killer had been preying on young people, which is unfortunately all too common, but that the young people had known about it. They had known that some girls had been killed and buried in the desert, but they kept the secret because their allegiance was to this man. And I wanted to write a story about that phenomenon."

Conversation with Joyce Carol Oates

# Questions for Critical Thinking

1 Describe what we know of Arnold Friend when he first appears at Connie's house. Then describe what we know of him by the end of the story. What effect does this change have on us as readers? In other words, how does Oates's pacing build suspense?

2 List the characters besides Connie and Arnold. How are they important to our understanding of Connie?

3 Consider Oates's use of dialogue, particularly the exchange between Arnold and Connie when he comes to her house. What in Arnold's speech suggests who he is and what he is doing? What in Connie's speech contributes to our understanding of her as a teenage girl?

4 Describe the setting—both time and place—of the story. Is it a place where we might expect to find someone like Arnold Friend? Why or why not?

5 The story opens with a bit of background exposition by the narrator. Discuss how this exposition is distinguished from the description of the story's main events. What relationship, if any, does the narrator seem to have or have had with Connie? Cite evidence from the text.

6 Oates builds Connie's character by means of a series of details about her age, her appearance, her habits, her clothes. Which details make Connie believable or familiar to you? Which details represent larger personality traits in Connie?

7 In her interview, Oates suggests Connie's act may be considered heroic in that she sacrifices herself to save her family. What details about Connie suggest her motivation for complying with Arnold Friend? In light of these details, make a case for whether Connie's act is or is not heroic.

8 Much of Oates's fiction deals with violence and the aftermath of such violence. Develop an argument about whether or not this is a violent story; consider the difference between including actual violence and simply suggesting it.

# Getting Started: A Research Project

Research is a skill that will carry you through your college career. You can find the research materials you need for this project on our website (**www.mhhe.com/delbanco1e**). Other ideas for research projects and sources appear at the end of this chapter.

A book's initial critical reception, the way reviewers and literary critics first respond to it, can offer some interesting material about the book and the time in which it is published. For example, when *Moby-Dick* was first published in 1851, it was not highly regarded, but today it is recognized as one of the greatest American novels. The best way of studying a critical reception—past or present—is by reading book reviews. Unlike a literary analysis, which builds a complex argument about a particular aspect of a work of literature, a book review gives an overview of what readers will find in the book, as well as the critic's opinion of its strengths and weaknesses. Intended more for a general than an academic audience, today's most influential book reviews are often found in newspapers such as *The Los Angeles Times* or *The New York Times* and on National Public Radio.

Oates's critical reception has been positive overall, as three reviews of *I Am No One You Know,* the short story collection in which "Three Girls" appears, illustrate (reviews available online at **www.mhhe.com/delbanco1e**). While these reviews yield three different views of the book, each compliments Oates's ability. Chanel Lee, writing for the *Village Voice,* draws attention to how Oates "artfully and uncomfortably examines the power of one's inner voice—the one no one can, or is supposed to, hear." An early review in *Publisher's Weekly* similarly points to Oates's intimacy with characters but emphasizes the two major categories those characters comprise: "In Oates's precise psychological renderings, victims are as complex as villains and almost always more interesting." Kevin Bicknell's review in the *Atlanta Journal-Constitution* describes her collection as "post-gothic. That is, Oates is less interested in the grotesque and the doomed than in ordinary people dealing with what Philip Roth called the 'American Berserk,' the sense that anybody's normal, well-ordered life can be thrown into chaos."

Book reviews provide concise summaries of the work so that, for example, after reading the reviews just mentioned here you would know to expect stories with sensational material, stories "populated by serial killers and their victims, murderers, stalkers, pedophiliac teachers, child abusers, the orphaned and the insane" on subjects including "murder, rape, arson and terrorism."

**Go to www.mhhe.com/delbanco1e and respond to several book reviews of Oates's work.**

1. Explain the ways in which "Three Girls" "artfully and uncomfortably examines the power of one's inner voice—the one no one can, or is supposed to, hear."
2. In what ways is Marilyn Monroe a victim in "Three Girls"? Is there a villain in the story?
3. Explain the notion of the "American Berserk" in relation to Oates's "Three Girls." In what ways are the protagonists' lives "thrown into chaos" with their sighting of Marilyn Monroe?

# Further Suggestions for Writing and Research

1. Review the two stories included in this chapter. Write a paragraph or two describing Oates's style—are her sentences short or long, full of metaphors or minimalist? Does she use elevated diction, or everyday expressions? Then research what another critic has to say about Oates's style. How is the critic's view similar to or different from your own?
2. One of Oates's major themes is shaping personal identity. Review the two stories included in this chapter and list details about the main characters' search for identity in each. Then consult other sources to see what critics have said about characters and identity in Oates's work. Do the two stories offer a different insight about identity? If so, explain how those stories show what the critic fails to examine. If not, use specific examples from your choices to support what the critic observes about identity in Oates's other work.
3. Find and read at least three of the dozens of articles on Joyce Carol Oates' website about "Where Are You Going, Where Have You Been?" Incorporating the critical views you found, give and develop your own interpretation of this story.
4. How does the interview with the writer aid your understanding of her work? Read one of the interviews she has given elsewhere about her work. Combining the information from these two sources, consider one of the following new perspectives you gained from hearing about her personal life, her view of her writing, or characteristics of contemporary American life.

**Some Sources for Research**


5. Johnson, Greg. *Invisible Writer.* New York: Dutton, 1998. The authoritative biography of Joyce Carol Oates.
6. *Celestial Timepiece,* a Joyce Carol Oates homepage, http://jco.usfca.edu/index.html. A website with comprehensive information on Oates's life, work, awards, and schedule of live appearances maintained by a reference librarian at the University of San Francisco.
7. Milazzo, Lee, ed. *Conversations with Joyce Carol Oates.* Jackson, MS: University Press of Mississippi, 1989. Contains interviews with Joyce Carol Oates.


**For examples of student papers, see chapter 3, Common Writing Assignments, and chapter 5, Writing the Research Paper, in the Handbook for Writing from Reading.**

# 12 American Regionalism and Sense of Place

## Two Case Studies
## The American West and The American South

ALL writers try to impart a sense of location in which their stories take place. This is just as much the case for the plain of Troy in Homer's epic *Iliad* as for the Danish castle in Shakespeare's *Hamlet*. It holds equally true for the American South of Flannery O'Connor and William Faulkner and the Southwest of Leslie Marmon Silko or John Steinbeck's West. In the past decades American writers such as Dagoberto Gilb, William Kittredge, and Sylvia Watanabe have stressed the importance of place. As California novelist James D. Houston observes in "A Writer's Sense of Place," our literature "is rich with . . . stories wherein at least part of what's going on is some form of dialogue between a place—whether it be an island or a mountain or a city or a shoreline or a sub-region of the continent—and the lives being lived. . . ." What matters for North American writers in the present moment was also true for fiction writers from another place and time.

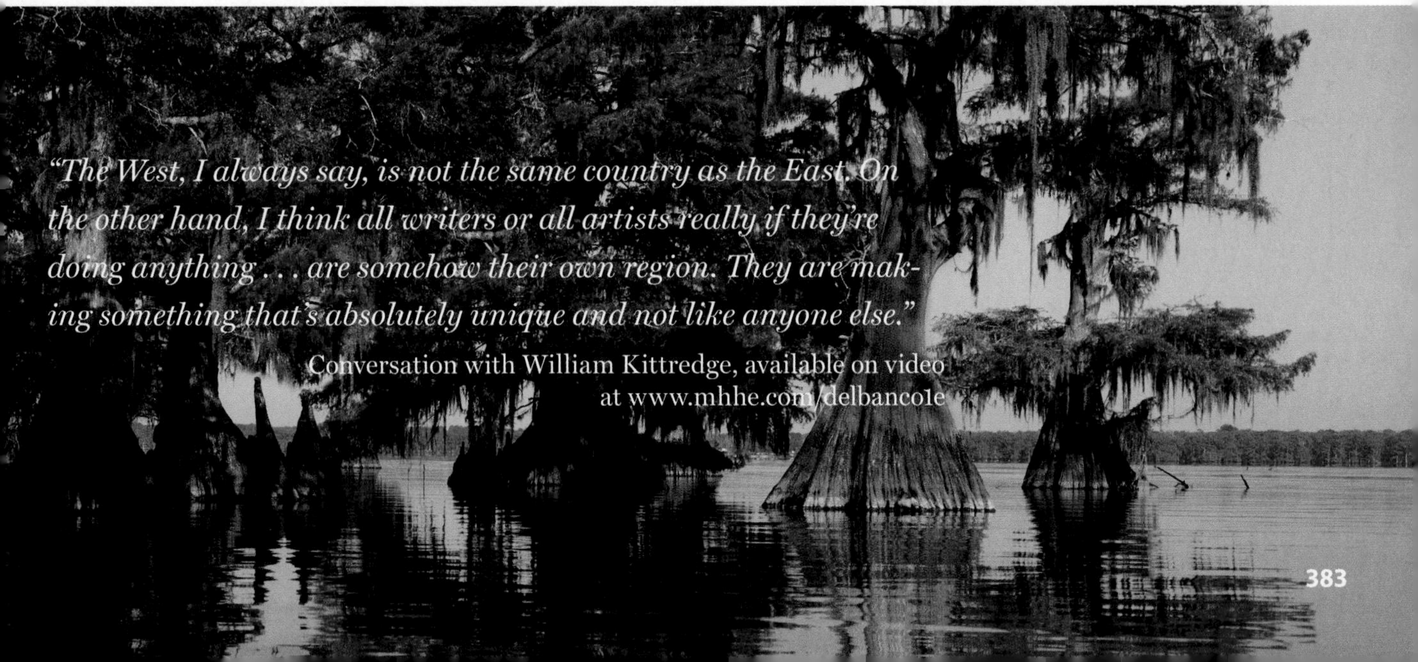

# The American West

William Kittredge
"Thirty-Four Seasons of Winter"

Dagoberto Gilb
"Romero's Shirt"

John Steinbeck
"The Chrysanthemums"

Leslie Marmon Silko
"The Man to Send Rain Clouds"

Sylvia Watanabe
"Talking to the Dead"

THE last major region of the continental United States to be settled, the West has played a special role in the American imagination. Its vast spaces and wide variety of landscapes—deserts, grazing lands, lush farming valleys, and mountains—have inspired Americans since the Lewis and Clark expedition (1804–1806) to explore the land. With the close of the frontier in the 1890s, the region changed. Cities began to compete with farms and ranches as centers of commercial and cultural experience. New immigrant populations mingled with native inhabitants. Although the romantic image of rugged cowboys and starkly individualistic settlers lives on in twentieth-century Western movies, serious Western literature of the twentieth century has become much more ambiguous—less certain of the good, morally upright settler taming the landscape and more aware of a growing society's willingness to exploit natural resources. With the emergence of Native American writers such as Leslie Marmon Silko, a sense of loss colors the literature; the traditional Native American way of life has long been at risk. Other writers, such as William Kittredge, are deeply attuned to the beauty of surrounding nature, displaying an awareness of the disjunction between the demands of modern life and the environment they so love. From the central plains to southern Texas to the California coast and, beyond, to the islands of Hawaii, the Old West has clearly become a New West, a region to rediscover.

*. . . my mother was a woman who valued the arts . . .*

# Q&A

*They're not autobiographical stories at all . . .*

# *A Conversation on Writing*

## William Kittredge

### Books and Cattle

I grew up on a great big cattle ranch in Southeastern Oregon. It was very isolated. The idea of literary culture was pretty nonexistent. We were 300 miles from probably the nearest really functional bookstore. But my mother was a woman who valued the arts, and she was one of those women who . . . belonged to the Book of the Month Club. And I remember when I was about fifteen years old working on the ranch in the summertime and sitting out on the screened-in porch in the evening reading a copy of *Big Sky,* Bud Guthrie's novel. And as I got farther and farther into it, I . . . marveled: How can anybody know this much about the world and their particular piece of the world? I didn't know anything. I didn't know that much about what was within five miles of me and much less all up and down the river and on and on and on. That stayed with me.

### Writing "Thirty-Four Seasons of Winter"

Worrying that story through and other stories too. By worrying I mean two things. I was writing about people and places and situations that I cared about deeply, that really were to some degree very close to home to me. They're not autobiographical stories at all, but nevertheless, I know that world and I know people; I had people in my mind's eye when I first started writing about it. And then those people coalesced and came together and became whatever they became in the story.

To watch this entire interview and hear the author read from "Thirty-Four Seasons of Winter," go to **www.mhhe.com/delbanco1e**.

William Kittredge has lived in the West for nearly his entire life; he grew up on a ranch in southeastern Oregon where he farmed into his thirties, after which he taught at the University of Montana for almost thirty years. In between, he studied writing at the Iowa Writers' Workshop and received Stanford University's prestigious Stegner Fellowship. Kittredge's subject is the West—but not the West of tough-grained cowboy heroes or seemingly unlimited resources.

In 2007, at the age of seventy-five, Kittredge published his first novel, *The Willow Trees.* This book deals with the education of a young cowboy whose adventures carry him from the early days of modern ranching to the politics of contemporary Western statehood. In his story collections *We Are Not in This Together* (1984) and *The Van Gogh Field* (1978), Kittredge portrays vulnerable men and complicated love relationships, even as he depicts the Western traditions of farming and ranching as in "Thirty-Four Seasons of Winter."

**RESEARCH ASSIGNMENT** In his interview, Kittredge says the West is a "museum culture." What does he mean by that? Do you agree? How does that affect how you read "Thirty-Four Seasons of Winter"?

# Thirty-Four Seasons of Winter (1984)

1 BEN Alton remembered years in terms of winter. Summers all ran together, each like the last, heat and baled hay and dust. "That was '59," he'd say. "The year I wintered in California." He'd be remembering manure-slick alleys of a feedlot outside Manteca, a flat horizon and constant rain.

2 Or flood years. "March of '64, when the levees went." Or open winters. "We fed cattle the whole of February in our shirtsleeves. For Old Man Swarthout." And then he'd be sad. "One week Art helped. We was done every day by noon and drunk by three." Sad because Art was his stepbrother and dead, and because there'd been nothing but hate between them when Art was killed.

3 Ben and Art fought only once, when they were thirteen. Ben's father, Corrie Alton, moved in with Art's old lady on her dryland place in the hills north of Davanero, and the boys bunked together in a back room. The house was surrounded by a fenced dirt yard where turkeys picked, shaded by three withering peach trees; and the room they shared was furnished with two steel-frame cots and a row of nails where they hung what extra clothing they owned. The first night, while the old people were drinking in town, the boys fought. Ben took a flattened nose and chipped tooth against one of the cot frames and was satisfied and didn't try again.

4 The next year Art's mother sold the place for money to drink on, and when that was gone Ben's old man pulled out, heading for Shafter, down out of Bakersfield, going to see friends and work a season in the spuds. Corrie never came back or sent word, so the next spring the boys took a job setting siphons for an onion farmer, doing the muddy and exhausting work of one man, supporting themselves and Art's mother. She died the spring they were seventeen; and Art began to talk about getting out of town, fighting in the ring, being somebody.

5 So he ran every night, and during the day he and Ben stacked alfalfa bales, always making their thousand a day, twenty bucks apiece, and then in the fall Art went to Portland and worked out in a gym each afternoon, learning to fight, and spent his evenings swimming at the YMCA or watching movies. Early in the winter he began to get some fights; and for at least the first year he didn't lose. People began to know his name in places like Salem and Yakima and Klamath Falls.

6 HE fought at home only once, a January night in the Peterson barn on the edge of town, snow falling steadily. The barn warmed slowly, losing its odor of harness leather and rotting hay; and under a circle of lights that illuminated the fighters in a blue glare, country people smoked and bet and drank. Circling a sweating and tiring Mexican boy, Art tapped his gloves and brushed back his thin blond hair with a quick forearm, sure and quiet. Then he moved under an overhand right, ducking in a quick new way he must have learned in Portland; and then he was inside, forcing, and flat on his feet, grunting as he followed each short chop with his body. The Mexican backed against one of the rough juniper posts supporting the ring, covered his face, gloves fumbling together as he began sink-

ing and twisting, knees folding; and it ended with the Mexican sprawled and cut beneath one eye, bleeding from the nose, and Art in his corner, breathing easily while he flexed and shook his arms as if he weren't loose yet. Art spit the white mouthpiece onto the wet, gray canvas and ducked away under the ropes.

7 That night, Ben sat in the top row of the little grandstand and watched two men drag the other fighter out of the ring and attempt to revive him by pouring water over his head. Ben hugged his knees and watched the crowd settle and heard the silence while everybody watched. Finally the Mexican boy shook his head and stood up, and the crowd moved in a great sigh.

Even tired she looked good.

8 THE next summer Art showed up with Clara, brought her back with him from a string of fights in California. It was an August afternoon, dead hot in the valley hayfields, and dust rose in long spirals from the field ahead where five balers were circling slowly, eating windrows of loose hay and leaving endless and uniform strings of bales. Ben was working the stack, unloading trucks, sweating through his pants every day before noon, shirtless and peeling.

9 The lemon-colored Buick convertible came across the stubble, bouncing and wheeling hard, just ahead of its own dust, and stopped twenty or thirty yards from the stack. Art jumped out holding a can of beer over his head. The girl stood beside the convertible in the dusty alfalfa stubble and squinted into the glaring light, moist and sleepy looking. She was maybe twenty, and her sleeveless white blouse was wrinkled from sleeping in the car and sweat-gray beneath the arms. But she was blond and tan and direct in the 100-degree heat of the afternoon. "Ain't she something?" Art said. "She's a kind of prize I brought home." He laughed and slapped her on the butt.

10 "Hello, Ben," she said. "Art told me about you." They drank a can of beer, iced and metallic tasting, and Art talked about the fighting in California, Fresno, and Tracy, and while he talked he ran his fingers slowly up and down Clara's bare arm. Ben crouched in the shade of the convertible with his beer and tried not to watch the girl. That night he lay awake and thought about her, and everything about that meeting seemed too large and real, like some memory of childhood.

11 Anyway, she was living and traveling with Art. Then the fall he was twenty-five, fighting in Seattle, Art broke his right hand in a way that couldn't be fixed and married Clara and came home to live, driving a logging truck in the summer and drinking in the bars and drawing his unemployment through the winters, letting Clara work as a barmaid when they were broke. The years got away until one afternoon in a tavern called The Tarpaper Shack, when Ben and Art were thirty-one. Art was sitting with a girl named Marie, and when Ben came in and wandered over to the booth she surprised him by being quiet and nice, with brown eyes and dark hair, not the kind Art ran with on his drunks; and by the end of the summer Marie and Ben were engaged.

WHICH caused no trouble until Christmas. 12
The stores were open late, but the streets with their decorations were deserted, looking like a carnival at four in the morning, lighted and ready to tear down and move.

"You gonna marry that pig?" Art said. Art was 13
drunk. The barkeeper, a woman called Virgie, was leaning on the counter.

"I guess I am," Ben said. "But don't sweat it." Then 14
he noticed Virgie looking past them to the far corner of the vaulted room. A worn row of booths ran there, beyond the lighted shuffleboard table and bowling machine. Above the last booth he saw the shadowed back of Clara's head. Just the yellow hair and yet certainly her. Art was grinning.

"You see her," he said talking to Ben. "She's got a 15
problem. She ain't getting any."

Ben finished the beer and eased the glass back to 16
the wooden counter, wishing he could leave, wanting no more of their trouble. Clara was leaning back, eyes closed and the table in front of her empty except for her clasped hands. She didn't move or look as he approached.

"Hello, Clara," he said. And when she opened 17
her eyes it was the same, like herons over the valley swamps, white against green. Even tired she looked good. "All right if I sit?" he asked. "You want a beer?"

She sipped from his, taking the glass without 18
speaking, touching his hand with her hand, then smiling and licking the froth from her lips. "Okay," she said, and he ordered another glass and sat down beside her.

"How you been?" he said. "All right?" 19

"You know," she said, looking sideways at him, 20
never glancing toward Art. "You got a pretty good idea how I been." Then she smiled. "I hear you're getting married."

"Just because you're tied up," he said, and she 21
grinned again, more like her old self now. "I mean it," he said. "Guess I ought to tell you once."

22 "Don't, she said. "For Christ sake. Not with that bastard over there laughing." She drank a little more of the beer. "I mean it," she said, after a moment. "Leave me alone."

23 Ben picked up his empty glass and walked toward the bar, turning the glass in his hand and feeling how it fit his grasp. He stood looking at the back of Art's head, the thin hair, fine and blond; and then he wrapped the glass in his fist and smashed it into the hollow of Art's neck, shattering the glass and driving Art's face into the counter. Then he ran, crashing out the door and onto the sidewalk.

24 His hand was cut and bleeding. He picked glass from his palm and wrapped his hand in his handkerchief as he walked, looking in the store windows, bright and lighted for Christmas.

25 Clara left for Sacramento that night, lived there with her father, worked in a factory southeast of town, making airplane parts and taking care of the old man, not coming back until he died. Sometimes Ben wondered if she would have come back anyway, even if the old man hadn't died. Maybe she's just been waiting for Art to come after her. And then one day on the street he asked, "You and Art going back together?" just hoping he could get her to talk awhile.

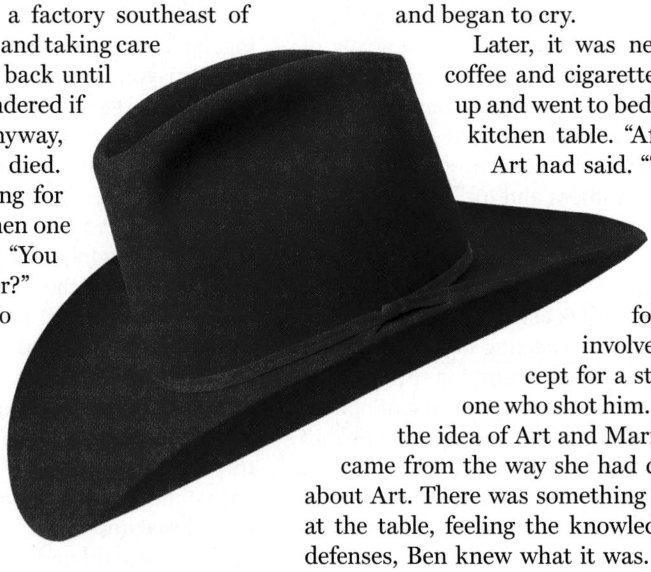

26 "I guess not," she said. "That's what he told me."

27 "I'm sorry," Ben said. And he was.

28 "I came back because I wanted," she said. "Guess I lived here too long."

29 THAT spring Ben and Marie were married and began living out of town, on a place her father owned; and the next fall his father was killed, crushed under a hillside combine in Washington, just north of Walla Walla, drunk and asleep at the leveling wheel, dead when they dug him out. And then the summer Art and Ben turned thirty-four Marie got pregnant and that winter Art was killed, shot in the back of the head by a girl named Stephanie Rudd, a thin red-haired girl just out of high school and, so people said, knocked up a little. Art was on the end stool in the The Tarpaper Shack, his usual place, when the girl entered quietly and shot before anyone noticed. He was dead when he hit the floor, face destroyed, blood spattered over the mirror and glasses behind the bar. And all the time music he'd punched was playing on the jukebox. *Trailer for sale or rent;* and *I can't stop loving you;* and *Time to bum again;* and, *That's what you get for loving me:* Roger Miller, Ray Charles, Waylon Jennings.

BEN awakened the night of the shooting and heard Marie on the phone, felt her shake him awake in the dim light of the bedroom. She seemed enormously frightened and continued to shake him, as if to awaken herself. She was eight months pregnant. 30

"He's dead." She spoke softly, seeming terrified, as if some idea she feared had been at last confirmed. "He never had a chance," she said. 31

"He had plenty." Ben sat up and put his arm around her, forced from his shock. 32

"They never gave him anything." She bent over and began to cry. 33

Later, it was nearly morning, after coffee and cigarettes, when Marie gave up and went to bed; Ben sat alone at the kitchen table. "Afraid of everything," Art had said. "That's how they are. Every stinking one." 34

Ben saw Art drunk and talking like he was ready for anything, actually involved with nothing except for a string of girls like the one who shot him. And then, somehow, the idea of Art and Marie got hold of Ben. It came from the way she had cried and carried on about Art. There was something wrong. Sitting there at the table, feeling the knowledge seep around his defenses, Ben knew what it was. He got up from the chair. 35

She was in the bedroom, curled under the blankets, crying softly. "What is it?" he asked. "There's something going on." She didn't open her eyes, but the crying seemed to slow a little. Ben waited, standing beside the bed, looking down, all the time wondering, as he became more sure, if it had happened in this bed, and all the time knowing it made no difference where it happened. And it was her fault. Not any fault of Art's. Art was what he was. She could have stopped him. Ben's hands felt strange, as if there was something to be done he couldn't recognize. He asked again, hearing his voice harsh and strained. "What is it, Marie?" 36

She didn't answer. He forced her onto her back and held her there, waiting for her to open her eyes while she struggled silently, twisting her upper body against his grip. His fingers sank into her shoulder 37 and his wrist trembled. They remained like that, forcing against each other. Then she relaxed and opened her eyes. "What is it?" he asked again. "It was something between you and Art, wasn't it?"

38 Her eyes were changed, shielded. She shook her head. "No," she said. "No."

39 "He was screwing you, wasn't he? Is it his kid?"

40 "It was a long time ago," she said.

41 "My ass." He let go of her shoulder. "That's why you're so tore up. Because you ain't getting any more from him." He walked around the bed, unable for some reason, because of what he was left with, to ask her if it happened here, in this bed. "Isn't that right?" he said. "How come you married me? He turn you down?"

"How come you married me? He turn you down?"

42 "Because I was afraid of him. I didn't want him. He was just fooling. I wanted you, not him."

43 Ben slapped her, and she curled quickly again, her hands pressed to her mouth, crying, shoulders hunching. He made her face him. "You ain't getting away," he said. "So I was a nice tame dog, and you took me."

44 "You'll hurt the baby."

45 "His goddamned baby!"

46 "It all broke off when I met you," she said. "He told me to go ahead, that you'd be good to me." It had surprised him when they met that she was with Art, but somehow he'd never until now gotten the idea they had anything going on. "It was only a few times after I knew you," she said. "He begged me."

47 "So I got stuck with the leavings." He cursed her again, at the same time listening to at least a little of what she said. "He begged me." That was sad. Remembering Art those last years, after he came home to stay, Ben believed her.

48 "So he dumped you off onto me," Ben said. "I wish I could thank him."

49 "It wasn't like that. He loved you. He said for me to marry you and be happy."

50 "So you did. And I was stupid enough to go for it."

51 "He was a little boy. It was fun, but he was a little boy."

52 "I'm happy," Ben said, "things worked out so nice for you." She shook her head and didn't answer. Ben wondered what he should do. It was as if he had never been married, had been right in always imagining his life as single. He'd watched his friends settle, seen their kids start to grow up, and it had seemed those were things he was not entitled to, that he was going to grow old in a habit of taverns, rented rooms, separate from the married world. And now he was still there, outside. And she'd kept it all a secret. "You stinking pig," he said slowly.

"Ben, it was a long time ago. Ben." 53

He was tired and his work was waiting. Maybe it was a long time ago and maybe it wasn't. He left her there crying while he dressed to go out and feed her father's cattle. 54

In the afternoon she had the house picked up and a meal waiting. She watched while he ate, but they didn't talk. He asked if she wanted to go to the funeral, and she said no and that was all. When he was drinking his coffee, calm now, and so tired his chest ached, he started thinking about Clara. He wondered if she'd known. Wouldn't have made any difference, he thought. Not after everything else. 55

THREE days later, heading for the burial, he was alone and hunched against the wheel, driving through new snow that softly drifted across the highway. His fingers were numb, the broken cracks in the rough calluses ingrained with black. A tire chain ticked a fender, but he kept going. He'd gone out at daylight to feed, a mandatory job that had to be done every day of winter, regardless of other 56

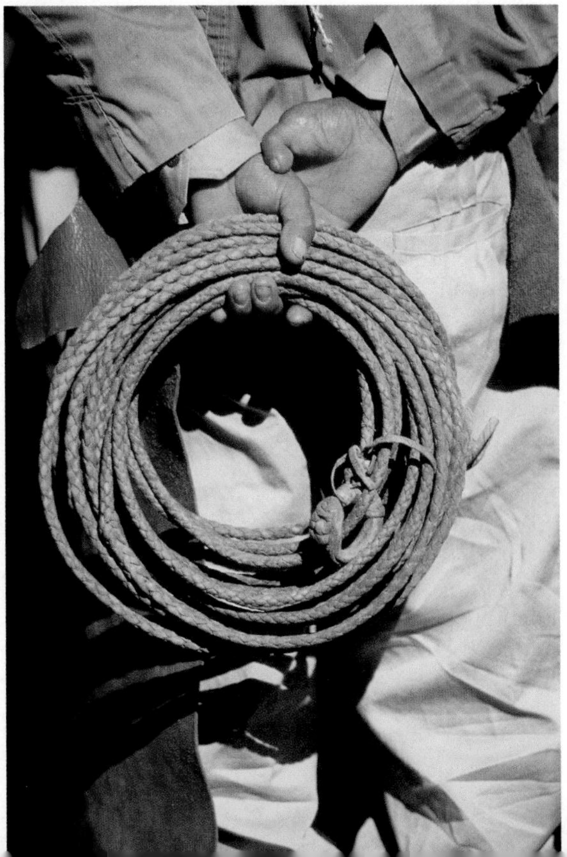

obligations. The rust-streaked Chevrolet swayed on the rutted ice beneath the snow. The steady and lumbering gait of the team he fed with, two massive frost-coated Belgian geldings, the creaking oceanic motion of the hay wagon, was still with him, more real than this.

57 The Derrick County cemetery was just below the road, almost five miles short of town. They were going to bury Art in the area reserved for charity burials, away from the lanes of Lombardy poplars and old-time lilacs. By dark the grave would be covered with snow. Ben parked and got out, and went over to look down in the hole. Far away in town, the bells of the Catholic church were faintly tolling. Ben stood a moment, then started back toward the car. He sat in the front seat with his hands cupped in his crotch, warming them. After a time, he backed slowly out of the graveyard.

58 Davanero was on the east side of the valley, scattered houses hung with ice, windows sealed against wind by tacked-on plastic sheeting. The still smoke of house fires rose straight up. Ben drove between lots heaped with snow-covered junk, past shacks with open, hanging doors where drifters lived in summer, into the center of town. The stores were open and a few people moved toward the coffee shops. He felt cut away from everything, as if this were an island in the center of winter.

59 The OPEN sign hung in the front window of The Tarpaper Shack. Ben wondered if Clara was tending bar and if she intended to go to the funeral. He parked and walked slowly through the snow to the door. The church bells were louder, close and direct now. Inside, the tavern was dark and barn-like, empty except for Clara, who was washing glasses in a metal sink. Ben went to the far end, where Art always sat, and eased onto a stool. "I'd take a shot," he said. "A double. Take one yourself."

60 "I'm closing up," she said. "So there's no use hanging around." She stayed at the sink and continued to wash glasses.

61 "You going to the funeral?" Ben said.

62 "I'm closing up." Her hands were still in the water. "I guess you need a drink," she said. "Go lock the door."

63 She was sitting in one of the booths when he got back. "You ain't going to the funeral?" he asked again.

64 "What good is that?"

65 "I guess you feel pretty bad."

66 "I guess." She drank quietly. "I would have took anything off him. Any damned thing. And that stupid bitch kills him. I would have given anything for his kid."

Ben finished his whiskey, and Clara took his glass and went for some more. "To hell with their goddamned funeral," he said. 6

Clara played some music on the jukebox, slow country stuff; and they danced staggering against the stools and the shuffleboard table, holding each other. She pushed him away after a few songs. "If you ain't one hell of a dancer," she said. "Art was a pretty dancer." She sat down in the booth and put an arm on the table and then lay her head alongside it, facing the wall. "Goddamn," she said. "I could cry. I ain't cried since I was a little girl," she said. "Not since then. Not since I was a little girl." 6

Ben wandered around the barroom, carrying his drink. He called his wife on the telephone. "You bet your sweet ass I'm drunk," he shouted when she answered, then hung up. 6

"Ain't you some hero," Clara said. She drank what whiskey was left in her glass. "You're nothing," she said. "Absolutely nothing." 7

Outside, the bells had stopped. Nothing. That was what he felt like. Nothing. Like his hands were without strength to steer the car. He sat awhile in the front seat, then drove to the jail, a gray brick building with heavy wire mesh over the windows. The deputy, a small bald man in a gray uniform, sat behind the desk in the center of the main room, coffee cup beside him. He smiled when he saw Ben, but he didn't say anything. 7

"How's chances of seeing that girl?" Ben asked. He didn't know why he'd come. It was just some idea that because she'd hated Art enough to kill him, because of that, maybe she understood and could tell him, Ben, why he wasn't nothing. He knew, even while he spoke, that it was a stupid, drunk idea. 7

73 "Okay," the deputy said, after a minute. "Come on. I guess you got a right."

74 THEY went through two locked doors, back into a large cinder-block room without any windows. Light came from a long fluorescent tube overhead. Two cells were separated by steel bars six inches apart. The room was warm. The girl was sitting on a cot in the left-hand cell, legs crossed, with red hair straight down over her shoulders and wearing a wrinkled blue smock without any pockets. She was looking at her hands, which were folded in her lap. "What now?" she said when she looked up. Her voice was surprisingly loud.

75 "Ben wanted to see you," the deputy said.

76 "Like a zoo, ain't it." The girl grinned and raised and lowered her shoulders.

77 "And you're not one bit sorry?" Ben said. "Just a little bit sorry for what you did?"

78 "Not one bit," the girl said. "I've had plenty of time to think about that. I'm not. I'm happy. I feel good."

79 "He wasn't no bad man," Ben said. "Not really. He never really was."

80 "He sure as hell wasn't Winston Churchill. He never even *tried* to make me happy." She put her hands in her lap.

81 "I don't see it," Ben said. "No way I can see you're right. He wasn't that bad."

82 "The thing I liked about him," she said, "was that he was old enough. He was like you. He was old enough to do anything. He could have been nice if he'd wanted."

83 The deputy laughed.

"I felt so bad before," the girl said, "killing him was easy. The only thing I feel bad about is that I never got down into him and made him crawl around. That's the only thing. I'm sorry about that, but that's all." 84

"He didn't owe you nothing," Ben said. 85

The girl looked at the deputy. "Make him leave," she said. 86

BEN drove slowly home in the falling snow. He could only see blurred outlines of the trees on either side of the lane that led to his house. He parked the car, kicked the snow from his boots, and went inside the house. Marie was in the bedroom, sleeping. The dim room was gray and cold, the bed a rumpled island. Marie was on her back, her stomach a mound beneath the blankets. Her mouth gaped a little. 87

After he got out of his clothes, Ben sat on the edge of the bed. Marie sighed in her sleep and moved a little, but she didn't waken. Ben reached to touch her shoulder and then stopped. Her eyelids flickered open. 88

"Come on," she said. "Get under the covers."

"In a minute," Ben said. He went back out to the kitchen and smoked a cigarette. Then he went back into the bedroom and crawled in beside her and put his hand on her belly, hoping to feel the baby move. He remembered a warm, shirtsleeve day in February, working with Art, hurrying while they fed a final load of bales to the cattle that trailed behind, eager to get to town, noon sun glaring off wind-glazed fields of snow. 89

"I felt so bad before," the girl said, "killing him was easy. . . ."

# Questions for Critical Thinking

1 Think about what you know of the West. Are there details in the story that fit your view of the West? If so, what are they? Are there any that surprised you? Could this story take place in another state or region and still evolve in the same way?

2 Consider the relationships among the four main characters. Which relationship seems to mean the most to Ben? Support your answer with details about the character that suggest his/her importance to Ben.

3 How does the writer portray nature in this story? You might want to consider how the characters are feeling when they are outdoors and what actions they perform while outdoors as opposed to in indoor scenes.

*. . . I had no idea that books existed, really.*

# Q&A

*I loved that you could be angry on the page . . .*

# A Conversation on Writing

## Dagoberto Gilb

### Growing Up Without Books

I did not grow up with books. . . . I had no idea that books existed, really. And it wasn't part of my own community or culture. I grew up with a mother that was a single mother, a Mexican-American and also as a person from the working class. . . . My friends whether they're black or white basically didn't read; we didn't have any concept of books. So I just came into it late as one of these odd things that seemed to have happened to me.

### Discovering Literature

To get through [school], you had to take that freshman comp class. I wasn't really dumb. What do you call that when you're not dumb but you can sort of survive? And you look dumb to all the teachers that are giving you dumb grades. I very wisely took a night class where I looked good because everybody was older and tired. I got a "B". . . . I did have to take one more [course]. I remember reading *Billy Budd* . . . but I had to look up a word every other line. . . . I couldn't believe an American writer wrote so oddly. And I just gave up literature . . . until I started reading others. . . . Luis Valdez . . . Jack Kerouac. . . . I learned, and very gratefully learned, that storytelling was about voice.

### Reading As Exercise for Writing

The brain is a muscle. And the muscle that makes the brain the strongest is reading . . . Anybody that sits down to read one book (I don't care if you read it twenty times, it doesn't have to be twenty books, it can be one book twenty times) . . . will get stronger and . . . see better. You'll breathe deeper. . . . And writing is the same thing. Actually writing doesn't exist without loving books and loving reading.

Born in Los Angeles to a Mexican mother and an American father, Dagoberto Gilb has become an increasingly recognized voice of the Mexican-American, and working-class, experience. Although he graduated with a double major and a master's degree from the University of California, Santa Barbara, Gilb turned to construction for his living and traveled between Los Angeles and El Paso for his work. He began to write during this period, joining a labor union as a class-A journeyman carpenter and working primarily on high-rise buildings. Thus, his writing captures a contemporary working-class perspective, beginning with his first full collection of short stories, *The Magic of Blood* (1993). Gilb has published a novel, *The Last Known Residence of Mickey Acuna* (1994); another collection of short stories, *Woodcuts of Women* (2001); a collection of essays, *Gritos* (1993); and, most recently, a novel, *The Flowers* (2008). His anthology *Hecho En Tejas, An Anthology of Texas-Mexican Literature* appeared in 2007.

**To watch this entire interview with Dagoberto Gilb, go to www.mhhe.com/delbanco1e.**

**RESEARCH ASSIGNMENT** In his interview, Gilb says, "I don't think an American white guy can write from a black point of view." What does he mean by this? Do you agree?

"A lot of times the world of books doesn't reflect your own neighborhood. I think in the Rio Grande Valley or in El Paso, Texas, or places like that where the majority of the population, I'd say seventy-five percent of the population, is Mexican-American, first generation to third. . . . They sit there and read about mutton and teapots, and go, ugh, and think, I don't know what I'm going to do in college. . . . There's never gorditas, there's no enchiladas, there's nothing about the neighborhood." Conversation with Dagoberto Gilb

# Romero's Shirt (1992)

1 JUAN Romero, a man not unlike many in this country, has had jobs in factories, shops, and stores. He has painted houses, dug ditches, planted trees, hammered, sawed, bolted, snaked pipes, picked cotton and chile and pecans, each and all for wages. Along the way he has married and raised his children and several years ago he finally arranged it so that his money might pay for the house he and his family live in. He is still more than twenty years away from being the owner. It is a modest house even by El Paso standards. The building, in an adobe style, is made of stone which is painted white, though the paint is gradually chipping off or being absorbed by the rock. It has two bedrooms, a den which is used as another, a small dining area, a living room, a kitchen, one bathroom, and a garage which, someday, he plans to turn into another place to live. Although in a development facing a paved street and in a neighborhood, it has the appearance of being on almost half an acre. At the front is a garden of cactus—nopal, ocotillo, and agave—and there are weeds that grow tall with yellow flowers which seed into thorn-hard burrs. The rest is dirt and rocks of various sizes, some of which have been lined up to form a narrow path out of the graded dirt, a walkway to the front porch—where, under a tile and one-by tongue and groove overhang, are a wooden chair and a love seat, covered by an old bedspread, its legless frame on the red cement slab. Once the porch looked onto oak trees. Two of them are dried-out stumps; the remaining one has a limb or two which still can produce leaves, but with so many amputations, its future is irreversible. Romero seldom runs water through a garden hose, though in the back yard some patchy grass can almost seem suburban, at least to him, when he does. Near the corner of his land, in the front, next to the sidewalk, is a juniper shrub, his only bright green plant, and Romero does not want it to yellow and die, so he makes special efforts on its behalf, washing off dust, keeping its leaves neatly pruned and shaped.

These days Romero calls himself a handyman. He 2
does odd jobs, which is exactly how he advertises—"no job too small"—in the throwaway paper. He hangs wallpaper and doors, he paints, lays carpet, does just about anything someone will call and ask him to do. It doesn't earn him much, and sometimes it's barely enough, but he's his own boss, and he's had so many bad jobs over those other years, ones no more dependable, he's learned that this suits him. At one time Romero did want more, and he'd believed that he could have it simply through work, but no matter what he did his children still had to be born at the county hospital. Even years later it was there that his oldest son went for serious medical treatment

because Romero couldn't afford the private hospitals. He tried not to worry about how he earned his money. In Mexico, where his parents were born and he spent much of his youth, so many things weren't available, and any work which allowed for food, clothes, and housing was to be honored—by the standards there, Romero lived well. Except this wasn't Mexico, and even though there were those who did worse even here, there were many who did better and had more, and a young Romero too often felt ashamed by what he saw as his failure. But time passed, and he got older. As he saw it, he didn't live in poverty, and *here,* he finally came to realize, was where he was, where he and his family were going to stay. Life in El Paso was much like the land—hard, but one could make do with what was offered. Just as his parents had, Romero always thought it was a beautiful place for a home.

**He denied his wife nothing,** but she was a woman who asked for little.

3 Yet people he knew left—to Houston, Dallas, Los Angeles, San Diego, Denver, Chicago—and came back for holidays with stories of high wages and acquisition. And more and more people crossed the river, in rags, taking work, his work, at any price. Romero constantly had to discipline himself by remembering the past, how his parents lived; he had to teach himself to appreciate what he did have. His car, for example, he'd kept up since his early twenties. He'd had it painted three times in that period and he worked on it so devotedly that even now it was in as good a condition as almost any car could be. For his children he tried to offer more—an assortment of clothes for his daughter, lots of toys for his sons. He denied his wife nothing, but she was a woman who asked for little. For himself, it was much less. He owned some work clothes and T-shirts necessary for his jobs as well as a set of good enough, he thought, shirts he'd had since before the car. He kept up a nice pair of custom boots, and in a closet hung a pair of slacks for a wedding or baptism or important mass. He owned two jackets, a leather one from Mexico and a warm nylon one for cold work days. And he owned a wool plaid Pendleton shirt, his favorite piece of clothing, which he'd bought right after the car and before his marriage because it really was good-looking besides being functional. He wore it anywhere and everywhere with confidence that its quality would always be both in style and appropriate.

4 THE border was less than two miles below Romero's home, and he could see, down the dirt street which ran alongside his property, the desert and mountains of Mexico. The street was one of the few in the city which hadn't yet been paved. Romero liked it that way, despite the runoff problems when heavy rains passed by, as they had the day before this day. A night wind had blown hard behind the rains, and the air was so clean he could easily see buildings in Juárez. It was sunny, but a breeze told him to put on his favorite shirt before he pulled the car up alongside the house and dragged over the garden hose to wash it, which was something he still enjoyed doing as much as anything else. He was organized, had a special bucket, a special sponge, and he used warm water from the kitchen sink. When he started soaping the car he worried about getting his shirt sleeves wet, and once he was moving around he decided a T-shirt would keep him warm enough. So he took off the wool shirt and draped it, conspicuously, over the juniper near him, at the corner of his property. He thought that if he couldn't help but see it, he couldn't forget it, and forgetting something outside was losing it. He lived near a school, and teenagers passed by all the time, and also there was regular foot-traffic—many people walked the sidewalk in front of his house, many who had no work.

After the car was washed, Romero went inside and brought out the car wax. Waxing his car was another thing he still liked to do, especially on a weekday like this one when he was by himself, when no one in his family was home. He could work faster, but he took his time, spreading with a damp cloth, waiting, then wiping off the crust with a dry cloth. The exterior done, he went inside the car and waxed the dash, picked up some trash on the floorboard, cleaned out the glove compartment. Then he went for some pliers he kept in 5

a toolbox in the garage, returned and began to wire up the rear license plate which had lost a nut and bolt and was hanging awkwardly. As he did this, he thought of other things he might do when he finished, like prune the juniper. Except his old shears had broken, and he hadn't found another used pair, because he wouldn't buy them new.

When he woke up he immediately remembered his shirt . . .

6 An old man walked up to him carrying a garden rake, a hoe, and some shears. He asked Romero if there was some yard work needing to be done. After spring, tall weeds grew in many yards, but it seemed a dumb question this time of year, particularly since there was obviously so little ever to be done in Romero's yard. But Romero listened to the old man. There were still a few weeds over there, and he could rake the dirt so it'd be even and level, he could clip that shrub, and probably there was something in the back if he were to look. Romero was usually brusque with requests such as these, but he found the old man unique and likeable and he listened and finally asked how much he would want for all those tasks. The old man thought as quickly as he spoke and threw out a number. Ten. Romero repeated the number, questioningly, and the old man backed up, saying well, eight, seven. Romero asked if that was for everything. Yes sir, the old man said, excited that he'd seemed to catch a customer. Romero asked if he would cut the juniper for three dollars. The old man kept his eyes on the evergreen, disappointed for a second, then thought better of it. Okay, okay, he said, but, I've been walking all day, you'll give me lunch? The old man rubbed his striped cotton shirt at his stomach.

7 Romero liked the old man and agreed to it. He told him how he should follow the shape which was already there, to cut it evenly, to take a few inches off all of it just like a haircut. Then Romero went inside, scrambled enough eggs and chile and cheese for both of them and rolled it all in some tortillas. He brought out a beer.

8 The old man was clearly grateful, but since his gratitude was keeping the work from getting done—he might talk an hour about his little ranch in Mexico, about his little turkeys and his pig—Romero excused himself and went inside. The old man thanked Romero for the food, and, as soon as he was finished with the beer, went after the work sincerely. With dull shears—he sharpened them, so to speak, against a rock wall—the old man snipped garishly, hopping and jumping around the bush, around and around. It gave Romero such great pleasure to watch that this was all he did from his front window.

The work didn't take long, so, as the old man was raking up the clippings, Romero brought out a five-dollar bill. He felt that the old man's dancing around that bush, in those baggy old checkered pants, was more inspiring than religion, and a couple of extra dollars was a cheap price to see old eyes whiten like a boy's. 9

The old man was so pleased that he invited Romero to that little ranch of his in Mexico where he was sure they could share some aguardiente, or maybe Romero could buy a turkey from him—they were skinny but they could by fattened—but in any case they could enjoy a bottle of tequila together, with some sweet lemons. The happy old man swore he would come back no matter what, for he could do many things for Romero at his beautiful home. He swore he would return, maybe in a week or two, for surely there was work that needed to be done in the back yard. 10

Romero wasn't used to feeling so virtuous. He so often was disappointed, so often dwelled on the difficulties of life, that he had become hard, guarding against compassion and generosity. So much so that he'd even become spare with his words, even with his family. His wife whispered to the children that this was because he was tired, and, since it wasn't untrue, he accepted it as the explanation too. It spared him that worry, and from having to discuss why he liked working weekends and taking a day off during the week, like this one. But now an old man had made Romero wish his family were there with him so he could give as much, *more,* to them too, so he could watch their spin around dances—he'd missed so many—and Romero swore he would take them all into Juárez that night for dinner. He might even convince them to take a day, maybe two, for a drive to his uncle's house in Chihuahua instead, because he'd promised that so many years ago—so long ago they probably thought about somewhere else by now, like San Diego, or Los Angeles. Then he'd take them there! They'd go for a week, spend whatever it took. No expense could be so great, and if happiness was as easy as some tacos and a five-dollar bill, then how stupid it had been of him not to have offered it all this time. 11

Romero felt so good, felt such relief, he napped on the couch. When he woke up he immediately remembered his shirt, that it was already gone before the old man had even arrived—he remembered they'd walked around the juniper before it was cut. Nevertheless, the possibility that the old man took it wouldn't leave Romero's mind. Since he'd never believed in letting 12 down, giving into someone like that old man, the whole experience became suspect. Maybe it was part of some ruse which ended with the old man taking his shirt, some food, money. This was how Romero thought. Though he held a hope that he'd left it somewhere else, that it was a lapse of memory on his part—he went outside, inside, looked everywhere twice, then one more time after that—his cynicism had flowered, colorful and bitter.

13 UNDERSTAND that it was his favorite shirt, that he'd never thought of replacing it and that its loss was all Romero could keep his mind on, though he knew very well it wasn't a son, or a daughter, or a wife, or a mother or father, not a disaster of any kind. It was a simple shirt, in the true value of things not very much to lose. But understand also that Romero was a good man who tried to do what was right and who would harm no one willfully. Understand that Romero was a man who had taught himself to not care, to not want, to not desire for so long that he'd lost many words, avoided many people, kept to himself, alone, almost always, even when his wife gave him his meals. Understand that it was his favorite shirt and though no more than that, for him it was no less. Then understand how he felt like a fool paying that old man who, he considered, might even have taken it, like a fool for feeling so friendly and generous, happy, when the shirt was already gone, like a fool for having all those and these thoughts for the love of a wool shirt, like a fool for not being able to stop thinking them all, but especially the one reminding him that this was what he had always believed in, that loss was what he was most prepared for. And so then you might understand why he began to stare out the window of his home, waiting for someone to walk by absently with it on, for the thief to pass by, careless. He kept a watch out the window as each of his children came in, then his wife. He told them only what had happened and, as always, they left him alone. He stared out that window onto the dirt street, past the ocotillos and nopales and agaves, the junipers and oaks and mulberries in front of other homes of brick or stone, painted or not, past them to the buildings in Juárez, and he watched the horizon darken and the sky light up with the moon and stars, and the land spread with shimmering lights, so bright in the dark blot of night. He heard dogs barking until another might bark farther away, and then another, back and forth like that, the small rectangles and squares of their fences plotted out distinctly in his mind's eye as his lids closed. Then he heard a gust of wind bend around his house, and then came the train, the metal rhythm getting closer until it was as close as it could be, the steel pounding the earth like a beating heart, until it diminished and then faded away and then left the air to silence, to its quiet and dark, so still it was like death, or rest, sleep, until he could hear a grackle, and then another gust of wind, and then finally a car.

He looked in on his daughter still so young, so beautiful, becoming a woman who would leave that bed for another, his sons still boys when they were asleep, who dreamed like men when they were awake, and his wife, still young in his eyes in the morning shadows of their bed. 14

Romero went outside. The juniper had been cut just as he'd wanted it. He got cold and came back in and went to the bed and blankets his wife kept so clean, so neatly arranged as she slept under them without him, and he lay down beside her. 15

# Questions for Critical Thinking

1 Notice how character and place interact: If you were called on to testify in court as a character witness for Romero, what might you say? If you were a city official in El Paso and asked to describe Romero's neighborhood, how might you depict it?

2 How much of a part does physical labor play in the story? Does it play a role in other stories you have found in this volume?

3 Where do you see links between geography—location—and symbolic implications about the meaning of Romero's life?

4 "Character and geography—location—are closely bound up together. Where we live says something about who we are." Do you agree or disagree with this statement? Support your answer with examples from the text. Consider how much of Romero's daily life might be the same, and how much might be different, if he were living in Atlanta or New York or Seattle.

# John Steinbeck (1902–1968)

The Salinas Valley area of central California, carries the nickname "Steinbeck Country," named, of course, for John Steinbeck, the Nobel Prize–winning author who was born and raised there. Steinbeck's summer job as a ranch hand and his mother's anecdotes about local people rooted him in his home county early on. Although he attended Stanford as an English major, Steinbeck dropped out to pursue his dream of success as a writer, a dream that did not pay off until several novels into his career. Today, his place in the American literary canon is secure with books like *The Grapes of Wrath* (1939), his Pulitzer Prize–winning epic about a family of Oklahomans who migrate to California; *East of Eden* (1952), an account of two families in the Salinas Valley; and *Of Mice and Men* (1937), the tragic tale of a farm laborer and his mentally handicapped friend.

Consider, for a moment, D. H. Lawrence's "The Odour of Chrysanthemums" (chapter 9), another story about the way people Ford Madox Ford called "the other half" live. But the landscape of the north of England is importantly different from the landscape of the American West, and a comparison of these two stories suggests the pervasive effect of a region. A writer conscious of the economic and social problems of his day, Steinbeck portrayed characters who struggle, whether internally with their own psyches or externally with a society permeated by intolerance. Most of the large body of his work—novels, stories, plays, essays, travel books, reportage—has remained in print since his death, a tribute by both publishers and readers to the enduring nature of his vision.

"Men do change, and change comes like a little wind that ruffles the curtains at dawn, and it comes like the stealthy perfume of wildflowers hidden in the grass." —John Steinbeck

# The Chrysanthemums (1938)

1 THE high grey-flannel fog of winter closed off the Salinas Valley from the sky and from all the rest of the world. On every side it sat like a lid on the mountains and made of the great valley a closed pot. On the broad, level land floor the gang plows bit deep and left the black earth shining like metal where the shares had cut. On the foothill ranches across the Salinas River, the yellow stubble fields seemed to be bathed in pale cold sunshine, but there was no sunshine in the valley now in December. The thick willow scrub along the river flamed with sharp and positive yellow leaves.

2 It was a time of quiet and of waiting. The air was cold and tender. A light wind blew up from the southwest

so that the farmers were mildly hopeful of a good rain before long; but fog and rain do not go together.

3 Across the river, on Henry Allen's foothill ranch there was little work to be done, for the hay was cut and stored and the orchards were plowed up to receive the rain deeply when it should come. The cattle on the higher slopes were becoming shaggy and rough-coated.

4 Elisa Allen, working in her flower garden, looked down across the yard and saw Henry, her husband, talking to two men in business suits. The three of them stood by the tractor shed, each man with one foot on the side of the little Fordson. They smoked cigarettes and studied the machine as they talked.

5 Elisa watched them for a moment and then went back to her work. She was thirty-five. Her face was lean and strong and her eyes were as clear as water. Her figure looked blocked and heavy in her gardening costume, a man's black hat pulled low down over her eyes, clodhopper shoes, a figured print dress almost completely covered by a big corduroy apron with four big pockets to hold the snips, the trowel and scratcher, the seeds and the knife she worked with. She wore heavy leather gloves to protect her hands while she worked.

She could stick anything in the ground and make it grow.

6 She was cutting down the old year's chrysanthemum stalks with a pair of short and powerful scissors. She looked down toward the men by the tractor shed now and then. Her face was eager and mature and handsome; even her work with the scissors was over-eager, over-powerful. The chrysanthemum stems seemed too small and easy for her energy.

7 She brushed a cloud of hair out of her eyes with the back of her glove, and left a smudge of earth on her cheek in doing it. Behind her stood the neat white farm house with red geraniums close-banked around it as high as the windows. It was a hard-swept looking little house with hard-polished windows, and a clean mud-mat on the front steps.

8 Elisa cast another glance toward the tractor shed. The strangers were getting into their Ford coupe. She took off a glove and put her strong fingers down into the forest of new green chrysanthemum sprouts that were growing around the old roots. She spread the leaves and looked down among the close-growing stems. No aphids were there, no sowbugs or snails or cutworms. Her terrier fingers destroyed such pests before they could get started.

9 Elisa started at the sound of her husband's voice. He had come near quietly, and he leaned over the wire fence that protected her flower garden from cattle and dogs and chickens.

"At it again," he said. "You've got a strong new crop 10
coming."

Elisa straightened her back and pulled on the gardening glove again. "Yes. They'll be strong this coming year." In her tone and on her face there was a little smugness. 11

"You've got a gift with things," Henry observed. 12
"Some of those yellow chrysanthemums you had this year were ten inches across. I wish you'd work out in the orchard and raise some apples that big."

Her eyes sharpened. "Maybe 13
I could do it, too. I've a gift with things, all right. My mother had it. She could stick anything in the ground and make it grow. She said it was having planters' hands that knew how to do it."

"Well, it sure works with flowers," he said. 14

"Henry, who were those men you were talking to?" 15

"Why, sure, that's what I came to tell you. They 16
were from the Western Meat Company. I sold those thirty head of three-year-old steers. Got nearly my own price, too."

"Good," she said. "Good for you." 17

"And I thought," he continued, "I thought how it's 18
Saturday afternoon, and we might go into Salinas for dinner at a restaurant, and then to a picture show—to celebrate, you see."

"Good," she repeated. "Oh, yes. That will be good." 19

Henry put on his joking tone. "There's fights to- 20
night. How'd you like to go to the fights?"

"Oh, no," she said breathlessly. "No, I wouldn't like 21
fights."

"Just fooling, Elisa. We'll go to a movie. Let's see. 22
It's two now. I'm going to take Scotty and bring down those steers from the hill. It'll take us maybe two hours. We'll go in town about five and have dinner at the Cominos Hotel. Like that?"

"Of course I'll like it. It's good to eat away from 23
home."

"All right, then. I'll go get up a couple of horses." 24

She said, "I'll have plenty of time to transplant 25
some of these sets, I guess."

She heard her husband calling Scotty down by the 26
barn. And a little later she saw the two men ride up the pale yellow hillside in search of the steers.

There was a little square sandy bed kept for root- 27
ing the chrysanthemums. With her trowel she turned the soil over and over, and smoothed it and patted it

firm. Then she dug ten parallel trenches to receive the sets. Back at the chrysanthemum bed she pulled out the little crisp shoots, trimmed off the leaves of each one with her scissors and laid it on a small orderly pile.

28 A squeak of wheels and plod of hoofs came from the road. Elisa looked up. The country road ran along the dense bank of willows and cottonwoods that bordered the river, and up this road came a curious vehicle, curiously drawn. It was an old spring-wagon, with a round canvas top on it like the cover of a prairie schooner. It was drawn by an old bay horse and a little grey-and-white burro. A big stubble-bearded man sat between the cover flaps and drove the crawling team. Underneath the wagon, between the hind wheels, a lean and rangy mongrel dog walked sedately. Words were painted on the canvas, in clumsy, crooked letters. "Pots, pans, knives, sisors, lawn mores, Fixed." Two rows of articles, and the triumphantly definitive "Fixed" below. The black paint had run down in little sharp points beneath each letter.

29 Elisa, squatting on the ground, watched to see the crazy, loose-jointed wagon pass by. But it didn't pass. It turned into the farm road in front of her house, crooked old wheels skirling and squeaking. The rangy dog darted from between the wheels and ran ahead. Instantly the two ranch shepherds flew out at him. Then all three stopped, and with stiff and quivering tails, with taut straight legs, with ambassadorial dignity, they slowly circled, sniffing daintily. The caravan pulled up to Elisa's wire fence and stopped. Now the newcomer dog, feeling out-numbered, lowered his tail and retired under the wagon with raised hackles and bared teeth.

30 The man on the wagon seat called out, "That's a bad dog in a fight when he gets started."

31 Elisa laughed. "I see he is. How soon does he generally get started?"

32 The man caught up her laughter and echoed it heartily. "Sometimes not for weeks and weeks," he said. He climbed stiffly down, over the wheel. The horse and the donkey drooped like unwatered flowers.

33 Elisa saw that he was a very big man. Although his hair and beard were greying, he did not look old. His worn black suit was wrinkled and spotted with grease. The laughter had disappeared from his face and eyes the moment his laughing voice ceased. His eyes were dark, and they were full of the brooding that gets in the eyes of teamsters and of sailors. The calloused hands he rested on the wire fence were cracked, and every crack was a black line. He took off his battered hat.

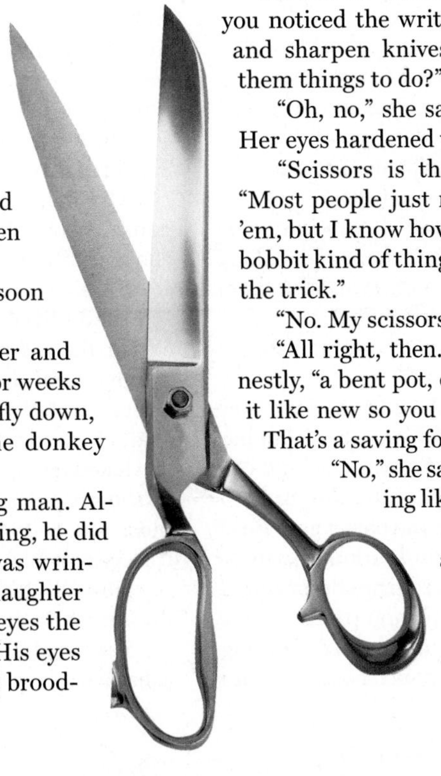

"I'm off my general road, ma'am," he said. "Does this dirt road cut over across the river to the Los Angeles highway?" 34

Elisa stood up and shoved the thick scissors in her apron pocket. "Well, yes, it does, but it winds around and then fords the river. I don't think your team could pull through the sand." 35

He replied with some asperity. "It might surprise you what them beasts can pull through." 36

"When they get started?" she asked. 37

He smiled for a second. "Yes. When they get started." 38

"Well," said Elisa, "I think you'll save time if you go back to the Salinas road and pick up the highway there." 39

He drew a big finger down the chicken wire and made it sing. "I ain't in any hurry, ma'am. I go from Seattle to San Diego and back every year. Takes all my time. About six months each way. I aim to follow nice weather." 40

Elisa took off her gloves and stuffed them in the apron pocket with the scissors. She touched the under edge of her man's hat, searching for fugitive hairs. "That sounds like a nice kind of a way to live," she said. 41

He leaned confidentially over the fence. "Maybe you noticed the writing on my wagon. I mend pots and sharpen knives and scissors. You got any of them things to do?" 42

"Oh, no," she said quickly. "Nothing like that." Her eyes hardened with resistance. 43

"Scissors is the worst thing," he explained. "Most people just ruin scissors trying to sharpen 'em, but I know how. I got a special tool. It's a little bobbit kind of thing, and patented. But it sure does the trick." 44

"No. My scissors are all sharp." 45

"All right, then. Take a pot," he continued earnestly, "a bent pot, or a pot with a hole. I can make it like new so you don't have to buy no new ones. That's a saving for you." 46

"No," she said shortly. "I tell you I have nothing like that for you to do." 47

His face fell to an exaggerated sadness. His voice took on a whining undertone. "I ain't had a thing to do today. Maybe I won't have no supper tonight. You see I'm off my regular road. 48

I know folks on the highway clear from Seattle to San Diego. They save their things for me to sharpen up because they know I do it so good and save them money."

49 "I'm sorry," Elisa said irritably. "I haven't anything for you to do."

50 His eyes left her face and fell to searching the ground. They roamed about until they came to the chrysanthemum bed where she had been working. "What's them plants, ma'am?"

51 The irritation and resistance melted from Elisa's face. "Oh, those are chrysanthemums, giant whites and yellows. I raise them every year, bigger than anybody around here."

52 "Kind of a long-stemmed flower? Looks like a quick puff of colored smoke?" he asked.

53 "That's it. What a nice way to describe them."

54 "They smell kind of nasty till you get used to them," he said.

55 "It's a good bitter smell," she retorted, "not nasty at all.

56 He changed his tone quickly. "I like the smell myself."

57 "I had ten-inch blooms this year," she said.

58 The man leaned farther over the fence. "Look. I know a lady down the road a piece, has got the nicest garden you ever seen. Got nearly every kind of flower but no chrysanthemums. Last time I was mending a copper-bottom washtub for her (that's a hard job but I do it good), she said to me, 'If you ever run acrost some nice chrysanthemums I wish you'd try to get me a few seeds.' That's what she told me."

59 Elisa's eyes grew alert and eager. "She couldn't have known much about chrysanthemums. You *can* raise them from seed, but it's much easier to root the little sprouts you see there."

60 "Oh," he said. "I s'pose I can't take none to her, then."

61 "Why yes you can," Elisa cried. "I can put some in damp sand, and you can carry them right along with you. They'll take root in the pot if you keep them damp. And then she can transplant them."

62 "She'd sure like to have some, ma'am. You say they're nice ones?"

63 "Beautiful," she said. "Oh, beautiful." Her eyes shone. She tore off the battered hat and shook out her dark pretty hair. "I'll put them in a flower pot, and you can take them right with you. Come into the yard."

64 While the man came through the picket gate Elisa ran excitedly along the geranium-bordered path to the back of the house. And she returned carrying a big red flower pot. The gloves were forgotten now. She kneeled on the ground by the starting bed and dug up the sandy soil with her fingers and scooped it into the bright new flower pot. Then she picked up the little pile of shoots she had prepared. With her strong fingers she pressed them in the sand and tamped around them with her knuckles. The man stood over her. "I'll tell you what to do," she said. "You remember so you can tell the lady."

"Yes, I'll try to remember." 65

"Well, look. These will take root in about a month. 66
Then she must set them out, about a foot apart in good rich earth like this, see?" She lifted a handful of dark soil for him to look at. "They'll grow fast and tall. Now remember this: In July tell her to cut them down, about eight inches from the ground."

"Before they bloom?" he asked. 67

"Yes, before they bloom." Her face was tight with 68
eagerness. "They'll grow right up again. About the last of September the buds will start."

She stopped and seemed perplexed. "It's the bud- 69
ding that takes the most care," she said hesitantly. "I don't know how to tell you." She looked deep into his eyes, searchingly. Her mouth opened a little, and she seemed to be listening. "I'll try to tell you," she said. "Did you ever hear of planting hands?"

"Can't say I have, ma'am." 70

"Well, I can only tell you what it feels like. It's when 71
you're picking off the buds you don't want. Everything goes right down into your fingertips. You watch your fingers work. They do it themselves. You can feel how it is. They pick and pick the buds. They never make a mistake. They're with the plant. Do you see? Your fingers and the plant. You can feel that, right up your arm. They know. They never make a mistake. You can feel it. When you're like that you can't do anything wrong. Do you see that? Can you understand that?"

She was kneeling on the ground looking up at him. 72
Her breast swelled passionately.

The man's eyes narrowed. He looked away self- 73
consciously. "Maybe I know," he said. "Sometimes in the night in the wagon there—"

Elisa's voice grew husky. She broke in on him, 74
"I've never lived as you do, but I know what you mean. When the night is dark—why, the stars are sharp-pointed, and there's quiet. Why, you rise up and up! Every pointed star gets driven into your body. It's like that. Hot and sharp and—lovely."

Kneeling there, her hand went out toward his legs 75
in the greasy black trousers. Her hesitant fingers almost touched the cloth. Then her hand dropped to the ground. She crouched low like a fawning dog.

He said, "It's nice, just like you say. Only when you 76
don't have no dinner, it ain't."

She stood up then, very straight, and her face was 77
ashamed. She held the flower pot out to him and placed

it gently in his arms. "Here. Put it in your wagon, on the seat, where you can watch it. Maybe I can find something for you to do."

78 At the back of the house she dug in the can pile and found two old and battered aluminum saucepans. She carried them back and gave them to him. "Here, maybe you can fix these."

79 His manner changed. He became professional. "Good as new I can fix them." At the back of his wagon he set a little anvil, and out of an oily tool box dug a small machine hammer. Elisa came through the gate to watch him while he pounded out the dents in the kettles. His mouth grew sure and knowing. At a difficult part of the work he sucked his under-lip.

80 "You sleep right in the wagon?" Elisa asked.

81 "Right in the wagon, ma'am. Rain or shine I'm dry as a cow in there."

82 "It must be nice," she said. "It must be very nice. I wish women could do such things."

83 "It ain't the right kind of a life for a woman."

". . . I wish women could do such things."

84 Her upper lip raised a little, showing her teeth. "How do you know? How can you tell?" she said.

85 "I don't know, ma'am," he protested. "Of course I don't know. Now here's your kettles, done. You don't have to buy no new ones."

86 "How much?"

87 "Oh, fifty cents'll do. I keep my prices down and my work good. That's why I have all them satisfied customers up and down the highway."

88 Elisa brought him a fifty-cent piece from the house and dropped it in his hand. "You might be surprised to have a rival some time. I can sharpen scissors, too. And I can beat the dents out of little pots. I could show you what a woman might do."

89 He put his hammer back in the oily box and shoved the little anvil out of sight. "It would be a lonely life for a woman, ma'am, and a scarey life, too, with animals creeping under the wagon all night." He climbed over the singletree, steadying himself with a hand on the burro's white rump. He settled himself in the seat, picked up the lines. "Thank you kindly, ma'am," he said. "I'll do like you told me; I'll go back and catch the Salinas road."

90 "Mind," she called, "if you're long in getting there, keep the sand damp."

91 "Sand, ma'am? . . . Sand? Oh, sure. You mean around the chrysanthemums. Sure I will." He clucked his tongue. The beasts leaned luxuriously into their collars. The mongrel dog took his place between the back wheels. The wagon turned and crawled out the entrance road and back the way it had come, along the river.

Elisa stood in front of her wire fence watching 92
the slow progress of the caravan. Her shoulders were straight, her head thrown back, her eyes half-closed, so that the scene came vaguely into them. Her lips moved silently, forming the words "Good-bye—good-bye." Then she whispered. "That's a bright direction. There's a glowing there." The sound of her whisper startled her. She shook herself free and looked about to see whether anyone had been listening. Only the dogs had heard. They lifted their heads toward her from their sleeping in the dust, and then stretched out their chins and settled asleep again. Elisa turned and ran hurriedly into the house.

In the kitchen she reached behind the stove and felt 93
the water tank. It was full of hot water from the noonday cooking. In the bathroom she tore off her soiled clothes and flung them into the corner. And then she scrubbed herself with a little block of pumice, legs and thighs, loins and chest and arms, until her skin was scratched and red. When she had dried herself she stood in front of a mirror in her bedroom and looked at her body. She tightened her stomach and threw out her chest. She turned and looked over her shoulder at her back.

After a while she began to dress, slowly. She put 94
on her newest underclothing and her nicest stockings and the dress which was the symbol of her prettiness. She worked carefully on her hair, penciled her eyebrows and rouged her lips.

Before she was finished she heard the little thun- 95
der of hoofs and the shouts of Henry and his helper as they drove the red steers into the corral. She heard the gate bang shut and set herself for Henry's arrival.

His step sounded on the porch. He entered the 96
house calling, "Elisa, where are you?"

"In my room, dressing. I'm not ready. There's hot 97
water for your bath. Hurry up. It's getting late."

When she heard him splashing in the tub, Elisa 98
laid his dark suit on the bed, and shirt and socks and tie beside it. She stood his polished shoes on the floor beside the bed. Then she went to the porch and sat primly and stiffly down. She looked toward the river road where the willow-line was still yellow with frosted leaves so that under the high grey fog they seemed a thin band of sunshine. This was the only color in the grey afternoon. She sat unmoving for a long time. Her eyes blinked rarely.

Henry came banging out of the door, shoving his 99
tie inside his vest as he came. Elisa stiffened and her

face grew tight. Henry stopped short and looked at her. "Why—why, Elisa. You look so nice!"

100 "Nice? You think I look nice? What do you mean by 'nice'?"

101 Henry blundered on. "I don't know. I mean you look different, strong and happy."

102 "I am strong? Yes, strong. What do you mean 'strong'?"

103 He looked bewildered. "You're playing some kind of a game," he said helplessly. "It's a kind of a play. You look strong enough to break a calf over your knee, happy enough to eat it like a watermelon."

104 For a second she lost her rigidity. "Henry! Don't talk like that. You didn't know what you said." She grew complete again. "I'm strong," she boasted. "I never knew before how strong."

105 Henry looked down toward the tractor shed, and when he brought his eyes back to her, they were his own again. "I'll get out the car. You can put on your coat while I'm starting."

106 Elisa went into the house. She heard him drive to the gate and idle down his motor, and then she took a long time to put on her hat. She pulled it here and pressed it there. When Henry turned the motor off she slipped into her coat and went out.

107 The little roadster bounced along on the dirt road by the river, raising the birds and driving the rabbits into the brush. Two cranes flapped heavily over the willow-line and dropped into the river-bed.

108 Far ahead on the road Elisa saw a dark speck. She knew.

109 She tried not to look as they passed it, but her eyes would not obey. She whispered to herself sadly, "He might have thrown them off the road. That wouldn't have been much trouble, not very much. But he kept the pot," she explained. "He had to keep the pot. That's why he couldn't get them off the road."

The roadster turned a bend and she saw the caravan ahead. She swung full around toward her husband so she could not see the little covered wagon and the mismatched team as the car passed them. 11

In a moment it was over. The thing was done. She did not look back.

She said loudly, to be heard above the motor, "It will be good, tonight, a good dinner." 11

"Now you're changed again," Henry complained. He took one hand from the wheel and patted her knee. "I ought to take you in to dinner oftener. It would be good for both of us. We get so heavy out on the ranch." 11

"Henry," she asked, "could we have wine at dinner?" 11

"Sure we could. Say! That will be fine." 11

She was silent for a while; then she said, "Henry, at those prize fights, do the men hurt each other very much?" 11

"Sometimes a little, not often. Why?" 11

"Well, I've read how they break noses, and blood runs down their chests. I've read how the fighting gloves get heavy and soggy with blood." 11

He looked around at her. "What's the matter, Elisa? I didn't know you read things like that." He brought the car to a stop, then turned to the right over the Salinas River bridge. 11

"Do any women ever go to the fights?" she asked. 11

"Oh, sure, some. What's the matter, Elisa? Do you want to go? I don't think you'd like it, but I'll take you if you really want to go." 12

She relaxed limply in the seat. "Oh, no. No. I don't want to go. I'm sure I don't." Her face was turned away from him. "It will be enough if we can have wine. It will be plenty." She turned up her coat collar so he could not see that she was crying weakly—like an old woman. 12

# Questions for Critical Thinking

1 Pay attention to Steinbeck's description of the Salinas Valley at the beginning of the story. What pattern of imagery do you notice? How does this contribute to your understanding of Elisa's conflict?

2 What is the conflict in this story? Is it an inner conflict or an external one?

3 Elisa, like Steinbeck, is clearly attuned to the world surrounding her. What does this suggest about her character? In other words, why do you think Steinbeck chose her to be adept at growing plants rather than focusing on other occupations such as sewing or cooking?

# Leslie Marmon Silko (b. 1948)

Leslie Marmon Silko grew up in Laguna, New Mexico, a town with a history of conflict between missionaries and the native inhabitants. Her own heritage is a mix of Native American, Hispanic, and Caucasian ancestry. As a young girl, Silko roamed the landscape, traversing it with her horse and her rifle. While an undergraduate at the University of New Mexico, Silko wrote and published "The Man to Send Rain Clouds," which she based on a story she had heard about a priest upset because he had not been asked to take over a Native American's funeral. Silko has been successful in a number of genres, with story collections such as *Storyteller* (1981); poetry like *Laguna Women* (1974); novels including *Ceremony* (1977) and *Almanac of the Dead* (1991); and essays as in *Yellow Woman and a Beauty of the Spirit* (1996). While Silko's subject varies, the heart of her fiction has to do with her mixed identity, her fascination with storytelling, and her reverence for the southwestern landscape and people.

# The Man to Send Rain Clouds (1969)

## ONE

1 They found him under a big cottonwood tree. His Levi jacket and pants were faded light-blue so that he had been easy to find. The big cottonwood tree stood apart from a small grove of winterbare cottonwoods which grew in the wide, sandy arroyo. He had been dead for a day or more, and the sheep had wandered and scattered up and down the arroyo. Leon and his brother-in-law, Ken, gathered the sheep and left them in the pen at the sheep camp before they returned to the cottonwood tree. Leon waited under the tree while Ken drove the truck through the deep sand to the edge of the arroyo. He squinted up at the sun and unzipped his jacket—it sure was hot for this time of year. But high and northwest the blue mountains were still deep in snow. Ken came sliding down the low, crumbling bank about fifty yards down, and he was bringing the red blanket.

Before they wrapped the old man, Leon took a piece of string out of his pocket and tied a small gray feather in the old man's long white hair. Ken gave him the paint. Across the brown wrinkled forehead he drew a streak of white and along the high cheekbones he drew a strip of blue paint. He paused and watched Ken throw pinches of corn meal and pollen into the wind that fluttered the small gray feather. Then Leon painted with yellow under the old man's broad nose, and finally, when he had painted green across the chin, he smiled. 2

"Send us rain clouds, Grandfather." They laid the bundle in the back of the pickup and covered it with with a heavy tarp before they started back to the pueblo. 3

They turned off the highway onto the sandy pueblo road. Not long after they passed the store and post office they saw Father Paul's car coming toward them. When he recognized their faces he slowed his car and 4

> "The oral tradition stays in the human brain and then it is a collective effort in the recollection. So when he is telling a story and she is telling a story and you are telling a story and one of us is listening and there is a slightly different version or a detail, then it is participatory when somebody politely says I remember it this way. It is a collective memory and depends upon the whole community. There is no single entity that controls information or dictates but this oral tradition is a constantly self-correcting process."
>
> —Leslie Marmon Silko (from "An Interview with Leslie Marmon Silko" by Thomas Irmer)

waved for them to stop. The young priest rolled down the car window.

5 "Did you find old Teofilo?" he asked loudly.

6 Leon stopped the truck. "Good morning, Father. We were just out to the sheep camp. Everything is O.K. now."

7 "Thank God for that. Teofilo is a very old man. You really shouldn't allow him to stay at the sheep camp alone."

8 "No, he won't do that any more now."

9 "Well, I'm glad you understand. I hope I'll be seeing you at Mass this week—we missed you last Sunday. See if you can get old Teofilo to come with you." The priest smiled and waved at them as they drove away.

## TWO

10 Louise and Teresa were waiting. The table was set for lunch, and the coffee was boiling on the black iron stove. Leon looked at Louise and then at Teresa.

11 "We found him under a cottonwood tree in the big arroyo near sheep camp. I guess he sat down to rest in the shade and never got up again." Leon walked toward the old man's bed. The red plaid shawl had been shaken and spread carefully over the bed, and a new brown flannel shirt and pair of stiff new Levis were arranged neatly beside the pillow. Louise held the screen door open while Leon and Ken carried in the red blanket. He looked small and shriveled, and after they dressed him in the new shirt and pants he seemed more shrunken.

It was noontime now because the church bells rang the Angelus. They ate the beans with hot bread, and nobody said anything until after Teresa poured the coffee. 12

Ken stood up and put on his jacket. "I'll see about the gravediggers. Only the top layer of soil is frozen. I think it can be ready before dark." 13

Leon nodded his head and finished his coffee. After Ken had been gone for a while, the neighbors and clanspeople came quietly to embrace Teofilo's family and to leave food on the table because the gravediggers would come to eat when they were finished. 14

## THREE

The sky in the west was full of pale-yellow light. Louise stood outside with her hands in the pockets of Leon's green army jacket that was too big for her. The funeral was over, and the old men had taken their candles and medicine bags and were gone. She waited until the body was laid into the pickup before she said anything to Leon. She touched his arm, and he noticed that her hands were still dusty from the corn meal that she had sprinkled around the old man. When she spoke, Leon could not hear her. 15

"What did you say? I didn't hear you." 16

"I said that I had been thinking about something." 17

18 "About what?"

19 "About the priest sprinkling holy water for Grandpa. So he won't be thirsty."

20 Leon stared at the new moccasins that Teofilo had made for the ceremonial dances in the summer. They were nearly hidden by the red blanket. It was getting colder, and the wind pushed gray dust down the narrow pueblo road. The sun was approaching the long mesa where it disappeared during the winter. Louise stood there shivering and watching his face. Then he zipped up his jacket and opened the truck door. "I'll see if he's there."

## FOUR

21 Ken stopped the pickup at the church, and Leon got out; and then Ken drove down the hill to the graveyard where people were waiting. Leon knocked at the old carved door with its symbols of the Lamb. While he waited he looked up at the twin bells from the king of Spain with the last sunlight pouring around them in their tower.

22 The priest opened the door and smiled when he saw who it was. "Come in! What brings you here this evening?"

23 The priest walked toward the kitchen, and Leon stood with his cap in his hand, playing with the earflaps and examining the living room—the brown sofa, the green armchair, and the brass lamp that hung down from the ceiling by links of chain. The priest dragged a chair out of the kitchen and offered it to Leon.

24 "No thank you, Father. I only came to ask you if you would bring your holy water to the graveyard."

The priest turned away from Leon and looked out the window at the patio full of shadows and the dining-room windows of the nuns' cloister across the patio. The curtains were heavy, and the light from within faintly penetrated; it was impossible to see the nuns inside eating supper. "Why didn't you tell me he was dead? I could have brought the Last Rites anyway." 25

Leon smiled. "It wasn't necessary, Father." 26

The priest stared down at his scuffed brown loafers and the worn hem of his cassock. "For a Christian burial it was necessary." 27

His voice was distant, and Leon thought that his blue eyes looked tired. 28

"It's O.K. Father, we just want him to have plenty of water." 29

The priest sank down into the green chair and picked up a glossy missionary magazine. He turned the colored pages full of lepers and pagans without looking at them. 30

"You know I can't do that, Leon. There should have been the Last Rites and a funeral Mass at the very least." 31

Leon put on his green cap and pulled the flaps down over his ears. "It's getting late, Father. I've got to go." 32

When Leon opened the door Father Paul stood up and said, "Wait." He left the room and came back wearing a long brown overcoat. He followed Leon out the door and across the dim churchyard to the adobe steps in front of the church. They both stooped to fit through the low adobe entrance. And when they started down the hill to the graveyard only half of the sun was visible above the mesa. 33

The priest approached the grave slowly, wondering how they had managed to dig into the frozen ground; and then he remembered that this was New Mexico, and saw the pile of cold loose sand beside the hole. The people stood close to each other with little clouds of steam puffing from their faces. The priest looked at them and saw a pile of jackets, gloves, and scarves in the yellow, dry tumbleweeds that grew in the graveyard. He looked at the red blanket, not sure that Teofilo was so small, wondering if it wasn't some perverse Indian trick—something they did in March to ensure a good harvest—wondering if maybe old Teofilo was actually at sheep camp corraling the sheep for the night. But there he was, facing into a cold dry wind and squinting at the last sunlight, ready to bury a red wool blanket while the faces of his parishioners were in shadow with the last warmth of the sun on their backs. 34

His fingers were stiff, and it took him a long time to twist the the lid off the holy water. Drops of water 35 fell on the red blanket and soaked into dark icy spots. He sprinkled the grave and the water disappeared almost before it touched the dim, cold sand; it reminded him of something—he tried to remember what it was, because he thought if he could remember he might understand this. He sprinkled more water; he shook the container until it was empty, and the water fell through the light from sundown like August rain that fell while the sun was still shining, almost evaporating before it touched the wilted squash flowers.

He sprinkled the grave and the water disappeared almost before it touched the dim, cold sand . . .

36 The wind pulled at the priest's brown Franciscan robe and swirled away the corn meal and pollen that had been sprinkled on the blanket. They lowered the bundle into the ground, and they didn't bother to untie the stiff pieces of new rope that were tied around the ends of the blanket. The sun was gone, and over on the highway the eastbound lane was full of headlights. The priest walked away slowly. Leon watched him climb the hill, and when he had disappeared within the tall, thick walls, Leon turned to look up at the high blue mountains in the deep snow that reflected a faint red light from the west. He felt good because it was finished, and he was happy about the sprinkling of the holy water; now the old man could send them big thunderclouds for sure.

# Questions for Critical Thinking

1. How would you describe the tone of this story? Pay particular attention to the ending. Do you read it as humorous or sad?

2. How large a part does religion play in the story? How much of the priest's actions grow from his official duties, how much from his common humanity?

3. Compare this selection with Sherman Alexie's story ("What You Pawn I Will Redeem") in chapter 14, keeping in mind that both he and Silko are prominent Native American writers. Then make a list of the main similarities and differences between the two.

4. In many places, this story makes history feel as if it bears closely on the present. Where do you see these intersections of time? You might want to begin by listing the details that make it clear the story takes place in the present.

# Sylvia Watanabe (b. 1953)

One of the best of a new generation of Hawaiian writers, Sylvia Watanabe was born on the island of Maui and raised on the island of Oahu, a third-generation Japanese-American. After completing her undergraduate degree at the University of Hawaii, she began a long self-imposed exile on the American mainland—doing graduate work at the University of Michigan, marrying a literature scholar, and teaching at various colleges and universities around the country, including Oberlin College in Ohio. In her work she focuses on the region of her birth, examining matters Hawaiian and thus extending the borders of our national literature to include the islands she calls home. Her stories reflect the vital setting of her native grounds and the struggle between traditional beliefs and contemporary necessities as her characters wrestle with personal needs often opposed to the customs of the modern world.

"I first began writing because I wanted to record a way of life which I loved and which seemed in danger of dying away—as the value of island real estate rose, tourism prospered, and the prospect of unlimited development loomed in our future. I wanted to tell how the Lahaina coast looked before it was covered with resorts, how the old-time fishermen went torching at night out on the reefs, and how the iron-rich earth of the canefields smelled in the afternoon sun. I wanted to save my parents' and grandparents' stories."

—from the "Afterword" of "Talking to the Dead"

# Talking to the Dead (1992)

1 WE spoke of her in whispers as Aunty Talking to the Dead, the half-Hawaiian kahuna lady. But whenever there was a death in the village, she was the first to be sent for; the priest came second. For it was she who understood the wholeness of things—the significance of directions and colors. Prayers to appease the hungry ghosts. Elixirs for grief. Most times, she'd be out on her front porch, already waiting—her boy, Clinton, standing behind with her basket of spells—when the messenger arrived. People said she could smell a death from clear on the other side of the island, even as the dying person breathed his last. And if she fixed her eyes on you and named a day, you were already as good as six feet under.

2 I went to work as her apprentice when I was eighteen. That was in '48, the year Clinton graduated from mortician school on the GI bill. It was the talk for weeks—how he'd returned to open the Paradise Mortuary in the heart of the village and had bought the scientific spirit of free enterprise to the doorstep of the hereafter. I remember the advertisements for the Grand Opening, promising to modernize the funeral trade with Lifelike Artistic Techniques and Stringent Standards of Sanitation. The old woman, who had waited out the war for her son's return, stoically took his defection in stride and began looking for someone else to help out with her business.

At the time, I didn't have many prospects—more schooling didn't interest me, and my mother's attempts at marrying me off inevitably failed when I stood to shake hands with a prospective bridegroom and ended up towering a foot above him. "It would be bad enough if she just looked like a horse," I heard one of them complain, "but she's as big as one, too." 3

My mother dressed me in navy blue, on the theory that dark colors make things look less conspicuous. "Yuri, sit down," she'd hiss, tugging at my skirt as the decisive moment approached. I'd nod, sip my tea, smile through the introductions and small talk, till the time came for sealing the bargain with handshakes. Then, nothing on earth could keep me from 4 getting to my feet. The go-between finally suggested that I consider taking up a trade. "After all, marriage isn't for everyone," she said. My mother said that that was a fact which remained to be proven, but meanwhile it wouldn't hurt if I took in sewing or learned to cut hair. I made up my mind to apprentice myself to Aunty Talking to the Dead.

5 The old woman's house was on the hill behind the village, just off the road to Chicken Fight Camp. She lived in an old plantation worker's bungalow with peeling green and white paint and a large, well-tended garden—mostly of flowering bushes and strong-smelling herbs.

6 "Aren't you a big one," a voice behind me said.

7 I started, then turned. It was the first time I had ever seen her up close.

8 "Hello, uh, Mrs. Dead," I stammered.

9 She was little, way under five feet, and wrinkled. Everything about her seemed the same color—her skin, her lips, her dress. Everything was just a slightly different shade of the same brown-gray, except her hair, which was absolutely white, and her tiny eyes, which glinted like metal. For a minute those eyes looked me up and down.

10 "Here," she said finally, thrusting an empty rice sack into my hands. "For collecting salt." Then she started down the road to the beach.

11 IN the next few months we walked every inch of the hills and beaches around the village, and then some. I struggled behind, laden with strips of bark and leafy twigs, while Aunty marched three steps ahead, chanting. "This is *a'ali'i* to bring sleep—it must be dried in the shade on a hot day. This is *noni* for the heart, and *awa* for every kind of grief. This is *uhaloa* with the deep roots. If you are like that, death cannot easily take you."

12 "This is where you gather salt to preserve a corpse," I hear her still. "This is where you cut to insert the salt." Her words marked the places on my body, one by one.

13 That whole first year, not a day passed when I didn't think of quitting. I tried to figure out a way of moving back home without making it seem like I was admitting anything.

"You know what people are saying, don't you?" my 14
mother said, lifting the lid of the bamboo steamer and setting a tray of freshly steamed meat buns on the already crowded table before me. It was one of my few visits since my apprenticeship, though I'd never been more than a couple of miles away, and she had stayed up the whole night before, cooking. She'd prepared a canned ham with yellow sweet potatoes, wing beans with pork, sweet and sour mustard cabbage, fresh raw yellowfin, pickled eggplant, and rice with red beans. I had not seen so much food since the night she tried to persuade Uncle Mongoose not to volunteer for the army. He went anyway, and on the last day of training, just before he was to be shipped to Italy, he shot himself in the head while cleaning his gun. "I always knew that boy would come to no good," was all Mama said when she heard the news.

"What do you mean you can't eat another bite?" 15
she fussed now. "Look at you, nothing but a bag of bones."

The truth was, there didn't seem to be much of a fu- 16
ture in my apprenticeship. In eleven and a half months I had memorized most of the minor rituals of mourning and learned to identify a couple of dozen herbs and all their medicinal uses, but I had not seen, much less gotten to practice on, a single honest-to-goodness corpse. "People live longer these days," Aunty claimed.

But I knew it was because everyone, even from vil- 17
lages across the bay, had begun taking their business to the Paradise Mortuary. The single event that had established Clinton's monopoly was the untimely death of old Mrs. Parmeter, the plantation owner's mother-in-law, who'd choked on a fishbone in the salmon mousse during a fund-raising luncheon for Famine Relief. Clinton had been chosen to be in charge of the funeral. After that, he'd taken to wearing three-piece suits, as a symbol of his new respectability, and was nominated as a Republican candidate for the village council.

"So, what are people saying?" I asked, finally push- 18
ing my plate away.

9 This was the cue that Mama had been waiting for. "They're saying That Woman has gotten herself a pet donkey, though that's not the word they're using, of course." She paused dramatically; the implication was clear.

0 I began remembering things about living in my mother's house. The navy-blue dresses. The humiliating weekly tea ceremony lessons at the Buddhist temple.

1 "Give up this foolishness," she wheedled. "Mrs. Koyama tells me the Barber Shop Lady is looking for help."

2 "I think I'll stay right where I am," I said.

3 My mother fell silent. Then she jabbed a meat bun with her serving fork and lifted it onto my plate. "Here, have another helping," she said.

4 A FEW weeks later Aunty and I were called outside the village to perform a laying-out. It was early afternoon when Sheriff Kanoi came by to tell us that the body of Mustard Hayashi, the eldest of the Hayashi boys, had just been pulled from an irrigation ditch by a team of field workers. He had apparently fallen in the night before, stone drunk, on his way home from the La Hula Rumba Bar and Grill.

5 I began hurrying around, assembling Aunty's tools and potions, and checking that everything was in working order, but the old woman didn't turn a hair; she just sat calmly rocking back and forth and puffing on her skinny, long-stemmed pipe.

6 "Yuri, you stop that rattling around back there," she snapped, then turned to the sheriff. "My son Clinton could probably handle this. Why don't you ask him?"

7 Sheriff Kanoi hesitated before replying, "This looks like a tough case that's going to need some real expertise."

8 Aunty stopped rocking. "That's true, it was a bad death," she mused.

9 "Very bad," the sheriff agreed.

0 "The spirit is going to require some talking to," she continued. "You know, so it doesn't linger."

1 "And the family asked especially for you," he added.

2 No doubt because they didn't have any other choice, I thought. That morning, I'd run into Chinky Malloy, the assistant mortician at the Paradise, so I happened to know that Clinton was at a morticians' conference in Los Angeles and wouldn't be back for several days. But I didn't say a word.

When we arrived at the Hayashis', Mustard's body was lying on the green Formica table in the kitchen. It was the only room in the house with a door that faced north. Aunty claimed that a proper laying-out required a room with a north-facing door, so the spirit could find its way home to the land of the dead without getting lost. 33

Mustard's mother was leaning over his corpse, wailing, and her husband stood behind her, looking white-faced, and absently patting her on the back. The tiny kitchen was jammed with sobbing, nose-blowing mourners, and the air was thick with the smells of grief—perspiration, ladies' cologne, the previous night's cooking, and the faintest whiff of putrefying flesh. Aunty gripped me by the wrist and pushed her way to the front. The air pressed close, like someone's hot, wet breath on my face. My head reeled, and the room broke apart into dots of color. From far away I heard somebody say, "It's Aunty Talking to the Dead." 34

"Make room, make room," another voice called. 35

I looked down at Mustard, lying on the table in front of me, his eyes half open in that swollen, purple face. The smell was much stronger close up, and there were flies everywhere. 36

"We'll have to get rid of some of this bloat," Aunty said, thrusting a metal object into my hand. 37

People were leaving the room. 38

She went around to the other side of the table. "I'll start here," she said. "You work over there. Do just like I told you." 39

I nodded. This was the long-awaited moment. My moment. But it was already the beginning of the end. My knees buckled, and everything went dark. 40

Aunty performed the laying-out alone and never mentioned the episode again. But it was talk of the village for weeks—how Yuri Shimabukuro, assistant to Aunty Talking to the Dead, passed out under the Hayashis' kitchen table and had to be tended by the grief-stricken mother of the dead boy. 41

My mother took to catching the bus to the plantation store three villages away whenever she needed to stock up on necessaries. "You're my daughter—how could I *not* be on your side?" was the way she put it, but the air buzzed with her unspoken recriminations. And whenever I went into the village, I was aware of the sly laughter behind my back, and Chinky Malloy smirking at me from behind the shutters of the Paradise Mortuary. 42

43 "SHE'S giving the business a bad name," Clinton said, carefully removing his jacket and draping it across the back of the rickety wooden chair. He dusted the seat, looked at his hand with distaste before wiping it off on his handkerchief, then drew up the legs of his trousers, and sat.

44 Aunty retrieved her pipe from the smoking tray next to her rocker and filled the tiny brass bowl from a pouch of Bull Durham. "I'm glad you found time to drop by," she said. "You still going out with that skinny white girl?"

45 "You mean Marsha?" Clinton sounded defensive. "Sure, I see her sometimes. But I didn't come here to talk about that." He glanced over at where I was sitting on the sofa. "You think we could have some privacy?"

46 Aunty lit her pipe and puffed. "Yuri's my right-hand girl. Couldn't do without her."

47 "The Hayashis probably have their own opinion about that."

48 Aunty dismissed his insinuation with a wave of her hand. "There's no pleasing some people," she said. "Yuri's just young; she'll learn." She reached over and patted me on the knee, then looked him straight in the face. "Like we all did."

> "You can talk to the dead till you're blue in the face, but *ain't no one listening. . . .*"

49 Clinton turned red. "Damn it, Mama," he sputtered, "this is no time to bring up the past. What counts is now, and right now your right-hand girl is turning you into a laughingstock!" His voice became soft, persuasive. "Look, you've worked hard all your life, and you deserve to retire. Now that my business is taking off, I can help you out. You know I'm only thinking about you."

50 "About the election to village council, you mean." I couldn't help it; the words just burst out of my mouth.

51 Aunty said, "You considering going into politics, son?"

52 "Mama, wake up!" Clinton hollered, like he'd wanted to all along. "You can talk to the dead till you're blue in the face, but *ain't no one listening.* The old ghosts have had it. You either get on the wheel of progress or you get run over."

53 For a long time after he left, Aunty sat in her rocking chair next to the window, rocking and smoking, without saying a word, just rocking and smoking, as the afternoon shadows spread beneath the trees and turned to night.

54 Then she began to sing—quietly, at first, but very sure. She sang the naming chants and the healing chants. She sang the stones, and trees, and stars back into their rightful places. Louder and louder she sang, making whole what had been broken.

EVERYTHING changed for me after Clinton's visit. I stopped going into the village and began spending all my time with Aunty Talking to the Dead. I followed her everywhere, carried her loads without complaint, memorized remedies, and mixed potions till my head spun and I went near blind. I wanted to know what *she* knew; I wanted to make what had happened at the Hayashis' go away. Not just in other people's minds. Not just because I'd become a laughingstock, like Clinton said. But because I knew that I had to redeem myself for that one thing, or my moment—the single instant of glory for which I had lived my entire life—would be snatched beyond my reach forever. 55

Meanwhile, there were other layings-out. The kitemaker who hanged himself. The crippled boy from Chicken Fight Camp. The Vagrant. The Blindman. The Blindman's dog. 56

"Do like I told you," Aunty would say before each one. Then, "Give it time," when it was done. 57

But it was like living the same nightmare over and over—just one look at a body and I was done for. For twenty-five years, people in the village joked about my "indisposition." Last fall, my mother's funeral was held at the Paradise Mortuary. While the service was going on, I stood outside on the cement walk for a long time, but I never made it through the door. Little by little, I'd begun to give up hope that my moment would ever arrive. 58

Then, a week ago, Aunty caught a chill, gathering *awa* in the rain. The chill developed into a fever, and for the first time since I'd known her, she took to her bed. I nursed her with the remedies she'd taught me—sweat baths; eucalyptus steam; tea made from *ko'oko'olau*—but the fever worsened. Her breathing became labored, and she grew weaker. My few hours of sleep were filled with bad dreams. Finally, aware of my betrayal, I walked to a house up the road and telephoned for an ambulance. 59

"I'm sorry, Aunty," I kept saying, as the flashing red light swept across the porch. The attendants had her on a stretcher and were carrying her out the front door. 60

She reached up and grasped my arm, her grip still strong. "You'll do okay, Yuri," the old woman whispered hoarsely. "Clinton used to get so scared, he messed his pants." She chuckled, then began to cough. One of the 61 attendants put an oxygen mask over her face. “Hush,” he said. “There’ll be plenty of time for talking later.”

62 ON the day of Aunty’s wake, the entrance to the Paradise Mortuary was blocked. Workmen had dug up the front walk and carted the old concrete tiles away. They’d left a mound of gravel on the grass, stacked some bags of concrete next to it, and covered the bags with black tarps. There was an empty wheelbarrow parked to one side of the gravel mound. The entire front lawn had been roped off and a sign had been put up that said, “Please follow the arrows around to the back. We are making improvements in Paradise. The Management.”

63 My stomach was beginning to play tricks, and I was feeling shaky. The old panic was mingled with an uneasiness which had not left me ever since I’d decided to call the ambulance. I kept thinking that it had been useless to call it since she’d gone and died anyway. Or maybe I had waited too long. I almost turned back, but I thought of what Aunty had told me about Clinton and pressed ahead. Numbly, I followed the two women in front of me.

64 “So, old Aunty Talking to the Dead has finally passed on,” one of them, whom I recognized as Emi McAllister, said. She was with Pearlie Woo. Both were old classmates of mine.

65 I was having difficulty seeing—it was getting dark, and my head was spinning so.

66 “How old do you suppose she was?” Pearlie asked.

67 “Gosh, even when we were kids it seemed like she was at least a hundred,” Emi said.

68 Pearlie laughed. “‘The Undead,’ my brother used to call her.”

69 “When we misbehaved,” Emi said, “our mother always threatened to abandon us on the hill where Aunty lived. Mama would be beating us with a wooden spoon and hollering, ‘This is gonna seem like nothing then.’”

70 Aunty had been laid out in a room near the center of the mortuary. The heavy, wine-colored drapes had been drawn across the windows and all the wall lamps turned very low, so it was darker indoors than it had been outside. Pearlie and Emi moved off into the front row. I headed for the back.

There were about thirty of us at the viewing, mostly from the old days—those who had grown up on stories about Aunty, or who remembered her from before the Paradise Mortuary. People got up and began filing past the casket. For a moment I felt dizzy again, but I glanced over at Clinton, looking prosperous and self-assured, accepting condolences, and I got into line. 71

The room was air conditioned and smelled of floor disinfectant and roses. Soft music came from speakers mounted on the walls. I drew nearer and nearer to the casket. Now there were four people ahead. Now three. I looked down at my feet, and I thought I would faint. 72

Then Pearlie Woo shrieked, “Her eyes!” People behind me began to murmur. “What—whose eyes?” Emi demanded. Pearlie pointed to the body in the casket. Emi cried, “My God, they’re open!” 73

My heart turned to ice. 74

“What?” voices behind me were asking. “What about her eyes?” 75

“She said they’re open,” someone said. 76

“Aunty Talking to the Dead’s eyes are open,” someone else said. 77

Now Clinton was hurrying over. 78

“That’s because she’s not dead,” still another voice added. 79

Clinton looked into the coffin, and his face went white. He turned quickly around and waved to his assistants across the room. 80

“I’ve heard about cases like this,” someone was saying. “It’s because she’s looking for someone.” 81

“I’ve heard that too! The old woman is trying to tell us something.” 82

I was the only one there who knew. Aunty was talking to *me*. I clasped my hands together, hard, but they wouldn’t stop shaking. 83

People began leaving the line. Others pressed in, trying to get a better look at the body, but a couple of Clinton’s assistants had stationed themselves in front 84

of the coffin, preventing anyone from getting too close. They had shut the lid, and Chinky Malloy was directing people out of the room.

85 "I'd like to take this opportunity to thank you all for coming here this evening," Clinton was saying. "I hope you will join us at the reception down the hall."

Then I knew. This was *it:* my moment had arrived.

86 WHILE everyone was eating, I stole back into the parlor and quietly—ever so quietly—went up to the casket, lifted the lid, and looked in.

87 At first I thought they had switched bodies on me and exchanged Aunty for some powdered and painted old grandmother, all pink and white, in a pink dress, and clutching a white rose to her chest. But there they were. Open. Aunty's eyes staring up at me.

88 Then I knew. This was *it:* my moment had arrived. Aunty Talking to the Dead had come awake to bear me witness.

89 I walked through the deserted front rooms of the mortuary and out the front door. It was night. I got the wheelbarrow, loaded it with one of the tarps covering the bags of cement, and wheeled it back to the room where Aunty was. It squeaked terribly, and I stopped often to make sure no one had heard. From the back of the building came the clink of glassware and the buzz of voices. I had to work quickly—people would be leaving soon.

But this was the hardest part. Small as she was, it 90
was very hard to lift her out of the coffin. She was horribly heavy, and unyielding as a bag of cement. I finally got her out and wrapped her in the tarp. I loaded her in the tray of the wheelbarrow—most of her, anyway; there was nothing I could do about her feet sticking out the front end. Then I wheeled her out of the mortuary, across the village square, and up the road, home.

NOW, in the dark, the old woman is singing. 91

I have washed her with my own hands 92
and worked the salt into the hollows of her body. I have dressed her in white and laid her in flowers.

Aunty, here are the beads you like to wear. Your 93
favorite cakes. A quilt to keep away the chill. Here is *noni* for the heart and *awa* for every kind of grief.

Down the road a dog howls, and the sound of ham- 94
mering echoes through the still air. "Looks like a burying tomorrow," the sleepers murmur, turning in their warm beds.

I bind the sandals to her feet and put the torch to 95
the pyre.

The sky turns to light. The smoke climbs. Her ashes 96
scatter, filling the wind.

And she sings, she sings, she sings. 97

# Questions for Critical Thinking

1 How does the location affect the characters in "Talking to the Dead"? Can you imagine this story taking place in the village, town, or city where you grew up? If so, how would it remain the same and how would it differ?

2 Note references in the story to a belief in the supernatural. Does the author appear to endorse these views or merely to describe them?

3 Do you agree with the statement "Island cultures are slow to change in comparison with a mainland culture"? Support your answer with examples from the text.

# The American South

William Faulkner

"A Rose for Emily"

"Barn Burning"

Flannery O'Connor

"A Good Man Is Hard to Find"

"Revelation"

Ralph Ellison

"Battle Royal"

"A Party Down at the Square"

THOUGH many of our major Southern writers lived in the twentieth century—as do those represented in this case study—the roots of Southern literature extend back to colonization and the slave culture of cotton and tobacco farming. The legacy of slavery forms the backdrop for what Flannery O'Connor describes as a region "rich in contradiction, rich in irony, rich in contrast, and particularly rich in its speech." Southern literature in the twentieth century continues to be haunted by its past; one critic has jokingly commented that every southern story has grandparents in it and very few northern stories go back a generation.

Perhaps no other region in America is so steeped in the oral tradition; the habit of tale telling and yarn spinning seems somehow to come with the territory below the Mason-Dixon line. Writers such as O'Connor and Eudora Welty capture the strangeness of rural life alongside often-satirical portraits of proud, white Southerners. William Faulkner lived much of his life in the small town of Oxford, Mississippi; Oklahoma-born Ralph Ellison—perhaps doubly displaced because of his skin color—attended school in the South and then moved to and stayed in the North. Modern Southern writers continue to treat issues such as troubled race relations, yet in an altered context and with a new sensibility.

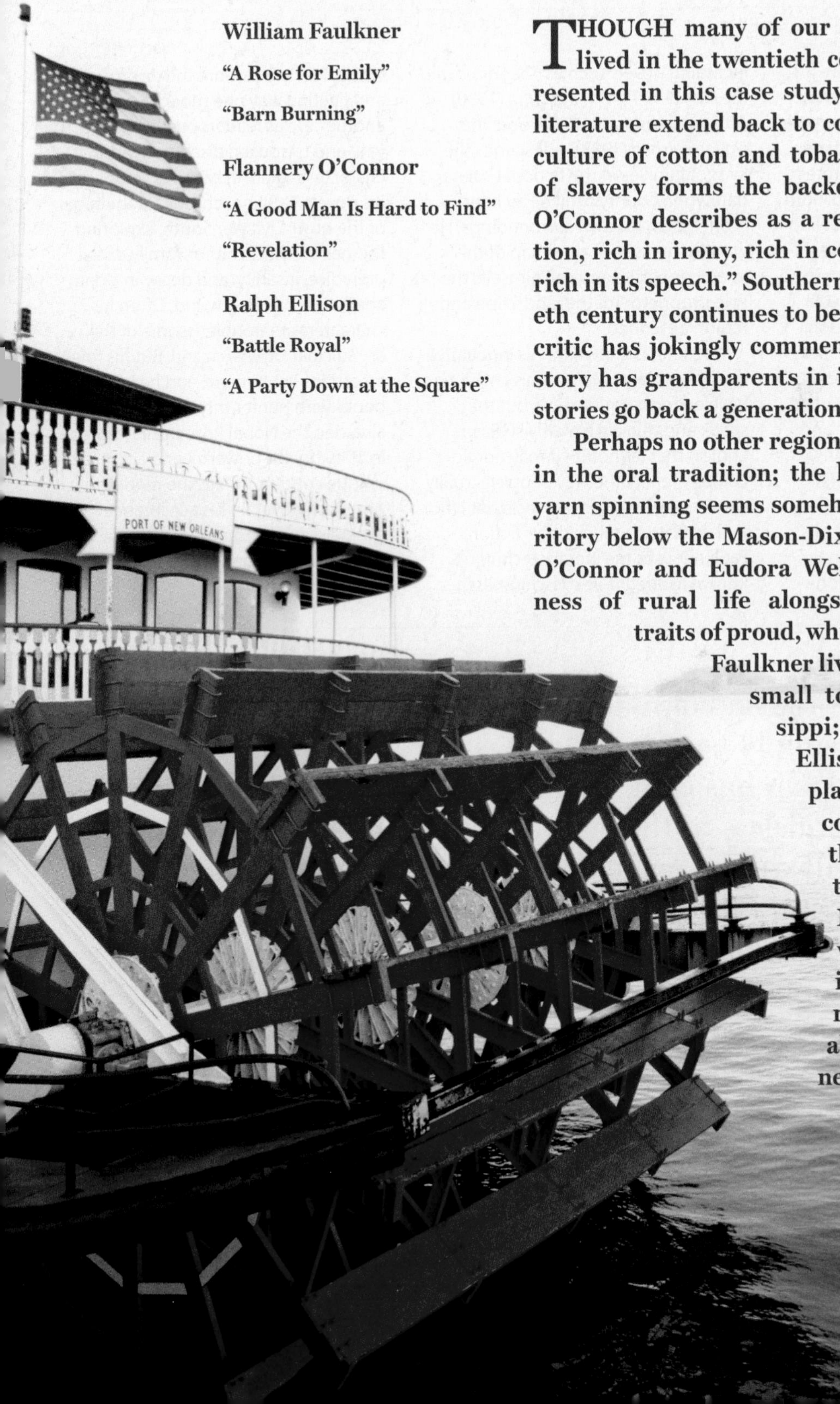

# William Faulkner (1897–1962)

Many of his best-known American contemporaries chose to travel abroad and live as, at least briefly, "expatriates." But William Faulkner lived and wrote in the region in which he was raised. Born in New Albany, Mississippi, he grew up in Oxford, Mississippi, and ultimately settled there. Ten years after dropping out of high school, Faulkner forged a friendship with Sherwood Anderson, who not only helped find a publisher for Faulkner's first novel but also encouraged the young Mississippi writer to take for his subject the people and places of his own life. Consequently, Faulkner wrote about the American South as someone deeply invested in its history and future as well as in its particular language and regional tradition. Much of Faulkner's fiction—including novels such as *The Sound and the Fury* (1929), *As I Lay Dying* (1930), *Absalom, Absalom!* (1936), and *The Unvanquished* (1938)—describes the lives of families in the fictional Yoknapatawpha County, which Faulkner modeled on his own surroundings. He went so far as to draw a map of this imaginary place and call himself "the sole proprietor" of the landscape and region described.

Faulkner is known for his innovative use of language. Many of his characters have no formal education, but they speak and think in a highly stylized English that (although it may not accurately reflect the way people actually converse) gives them a consistent lyric authenticity. In much of his fiction, Faulkner uses the literary technique known as *stream-of-consciousness,* which seeks to capture the disorganized and fleeting way one thought leads to another; we as readers *overhear* the private and unspoken discourse within a character's mind. In both his stories and his novels, Faulkner chronicles the saga of the post–Civil War South, exploring themes of justice, honor, family, racial prejudice, insanity, and decay in a damaged and changing world. Often his characters are troubled; some of them are suicidal, others, crazed. But his final assertions are hopeful, and he laces his books with humor throughout. He was awarded the Nobel Prize in Literature in 1949 "for his powerful and artistically unique contribution to the modern American novel." In his acceptance speech, Faulkner famously declared, "I believe that man will not merely endure: he will prevail."

"I decline to accept the end of man. It is easy enough to say that man is immortal simply because he will endure: that when the last dingdong of doom has clanged and faded from the last worthless rock hanging tideless in the last red and dying evening, that even then there will still be one more sound: that of his puny inexhaustible voice, still talking. I refuse to accept this. I believe that man will not merely endure: he will prevail. He is immortal, not because he alone among creatures has an inexhaustible voice, but because he has a soul, a spirit capable of compassion and sacrifice and endurance. The poet's, the writer's, duty is to write about these things. It is his privilege to help man endure by lifting his heart, by reminding him of the courage and honor and hope and pride and compassion and pity and sacrifice which have been the glory of his past. The poet's voice need not merely be the record of man, it can be one of the props, the pillars to help him endure and prevail." —William Faulkner, speech at the Nobel Banquet at the City Hall in Stockholm, 1949

# A Rose for Emily (1932)

## I

1 When Miss Emily Grierson died, our whole town went to her funeral: the men through a sort of respectful affection for a fallen monument, the women mostly out of curiosity to see the inside of her house, which no one save an old manservant—a combined gardener and cook—had seen in at least ten years.

2 It was a big, squarish frame house that had once been white, decorated with cupolas and spires and scrolled balconies in the heavily lightsome style of the seventies, set on what had once been our most select street. But garages and cotton gins had encroached and obliterated even the august names of that neighborhood; only Miss Emily's house was left, lifting its stubborn and coquettish decay above the cotton wagons and the gasoline pumps—an eyesore among eyesores. And now Miss Emily had gone to join the representatives of those august names where they lay in the cedar-bemused cemetery among the ranked and anonymous graves of Union and Confederate soldiers who fell at the battle of Jefferson.

3 Alive, Miss Emily had been a tradition, a duty, and a care; a sort of hereditary obligation upon the town, dating from that day in 1894 when Colonel Sartoris, the mayor—he who fathered the edict that no Negro woman should appear on the streets without an apron—remitted her taxes, the dispensation dating from the death of her father on into perpetuity. Not that Miss Emily would have accepted charity. Colonel Sartoris invented an involved tale to the effect that Miss Emily's father had loaned money to the town, which the town, as a matter of business, preferred this way of repaying. Only a man of Colonel Sartoris' generation and thought could have invented it, and only a woman could have believed it.

4 When the next generation, with its more modern ideas, became mayors and aldermen, this arrangement created some little dissatisfaction. On the first of the year they mailed her a tax notice. February came, and there was no reply. They wrote her a formal letter, asking her to call at the sheriff's office at her convenience. A week later the mayor wrote her himself, offering to call or to send his car for her, and received in reply a note on paper of an archaic shape, in a thin, flowing calligraphy in faded ink, to the effect that she no longer went out at all. The tax notice was also enclosed, without comment.

They called a special meeting of the Board of Al- 5
dermen. A deputation waited upon her, knocked at the door through which no visitor had passed since she ceased giving china-painting lessons eight or ten years earlier. They were admitted by the old Negro into a dim hall from which a stairway mounted into still more shadow. It smelled of dust and disuse—a close, dank smell. The Negro led them into the parlor. It was furnished in heavy, leather-covered furniture. When the Negro opened the blinds of one window, they could see that the leather was cracked; and when they sat down, a faint dust rose sluggishly about their thighs, spinning with slow motes in the single sun-ray. On a tarnished gilt easel before the fireplace stood a crayon portrait of Miss Emily's father.

They rose when she entered—a small, fat woman 6
in black, with a thin gold chain descending to her waist and vanishing into her belt, leaning on an ebony cane with a tarnished gold head. Her skeleton was small and spare; perhaps that was why what would have been merely plumpness in another was obesity in her. She looked bloated, like a body long submerged in motionless water, and of that pallid hue. Her eyes, lost in the fatty ridges of her face, looked like two small pieces of coal pressed into a lump of dough as they moved from one face to another while the visitors stated their errand.

She did not ask them to sit. She 7
just stood in the door and listened quietly until the spokesman came to a stumbling halt. Then they could hear the invisible watch ticking at the end of the gold chain.

Her voice was dry and 8
cold. "I have no taxes in Jefferson. Colonel Sartoris explained

it to me. Perhaps one of you can gain access to the city records and satisfy yourselves."

9 "But we have. We are the city authorities, Miss Emily. Didn't you get a notice from the sheriff, signed by him?"

10 "I received a paper, yes," Miss Emily said. "Perhaps he considers himself the sheriff . . . I have no taxes in Jefferson."

11 "But there is nothing on the books to show that, you see. We must go by the—"

12 "See Colonel Sartoris. I have no taxes in Jefferson."

13 "But, Miss Emily—"

14 "See Colonel Sartoris." (Colonel Sartoris had been dead almost ten years.) "I have no taxes in Jefferson. Tobe!" The Negro appeared. "Show these gentlemen out."

None of the young men were quite good enough for Miss Emily and such.

## II

15 So she vanquished them, horse and foot, just as she had vanquished their fathers thirty years before about the smell. That was two years after her father's death and a short time after her sweetheart—the one we believed would marry her—had deserted her. After her father's death she went out very little; after her sweetheart went away, people hardly saw her at all. A few of the ladies had the temerity to call, but were not received, and the only sign of life about the place was the Negro man—a young man then—going in and out with a market basket.

16 "Just as if a man—any man—could keep a kitchen properly," the ladies said; so they were not surprised when the smell developed. It was another link between the gross, teeming world and the high and mighty Griersons.

17 A neighbor, a woman, complained to the mayor, Judge Stevens, eighty years old.

18 "But what will you have me do about it, madam?" he said.

19 "Why, send her word to stop it," the woman said. "Isn't there a law?"

20 "I'm sure that won't be necessary," Judge Stevens said. "It's probably just a snake or a rat that nigger of hers killed in the yard. I'll speak to him about it."

21 The next day he received two more complaints, one from a man who came in diffident deprecation. "We really must do something about it, Judge. I'd be the last one in the world to bother Miss Emily, but we've got to do something." That night the Board of Aldermen met—three graybeards and one younger man, a member of the rising generation.

"It's simple enough," he said. "Send her word to 22
have her place cleaned up. Give her a certain time to do it in, and if she don't . . ."

"Dammit, sir," Judge Stevens said, "will you ac- 23
cuse a lady to her face of smelling bad?"

So the next night, after midnight, four men crossed 24
Miss Emily's lawn and slunk about the house like burglars, sniffing along the base of the brickwork and at the cellar openings while one of them performed a regular sowing motion with his hand out of a sack slung from his shoulder. They broke open the cellar door and sprinkled lime there, and in all the outbuildings. As they recrossed the lawn, a window that had been dark was lighted and Miss Emily sat in it, the light behind her, and her upright torso motionless as that of an idol. They crept quietly across the lawn and into the shadow of the locusts that lined the street. After a week or two the smell went away.

That was when people had begun to feel really 25
sorry for her. People in our town, remembering how old lady Wyatt, her great-aunt, had gone completely crazy at last, believed that the Griersons held themselves a little too high for what they really were. None of the young men were quite good enough for Miss Emily and such. We had long thought of them as a tableau, Miss Emily a slender figure in white in the background, her father a spraddled silhouette in the foreground, his back to her and clutching a horsewhip, the two of them framed by the back-flung front door. So when she got to be thirty and was still single, we were not pleased exactly, but vindicated; even with insanity in the family she wouldn't have turned down all of her chances if they had really materialized.

When her father died, it got about that the house 26
was all that was left to her; and in a way, people were glad. At last they could pity Miss Emily. Being left alone, and a pauper, she had become humanized. Now she too would know the old thrill and the old despair of a penny more or less.

The day after his death all the ladies prepared to 27
call at the house and offer condolence and aid, as is our custom. Miss Emily met them at the door, dressed as usual and with no trace of grief on her face. She told them that her father was not dead. She did that for three days, with the ministers calling on her, and the doctors, trying to persuade her to let them dispose of the body. Just as they were about to resort to law and force, she broke down, and they buried her father quickly.

28 We did not say she was crazy then. We believed she had to do that. We remembered all the young men her father had driven away, and we knew that with nothing left, she would have to cling to that which had robbed her, as people will.

## III

29 She was sick for a long time. When we saw her again, her hair was cut short, making her look like a girl, with a vague resemblance to those angels in colored church windows—sort of tragic and serene.

30 The town had just let the contracts for paving the sidewalks, and in the summer after her father's death they began the work. The construction company came with niggers and mules and machinery, and a foreman named Homer Barron, a Yankee—a big, dark, ready man, with a big voice and eyes lighter than his face. The little boys would follow in groups to hear him cuss the niggers, and the niggers singing in time to the rise and fall of picks. Pretty soon he knew everybody in town. Whenever you heard a lot of laughing anywhere about the square, Homer Barron would be in the center of the group. Presently, we began to see him and Miss Emily on Sunday afternoons driving in the yellow-wheeled buggy and the matched team of bays from the livery stable.

31 At first we were glad that Miss Emily would have an interest, because the ladies all said, "Of course a Grierson would not think seriously of a Northerner, a day laborer." But there were still others, older people, who said that even grief could not cause a real lady to forget *noblesse oblige*[1]—without calling it *noblesse oblige*. They just said, "Poor Emily. Her kinsfolk should come to her." She had some kin in Alabama; but years ago her father had fallen out with them over the estate of old lady Wyatt, the crazy woman, and there was no communication between the two families. They had not even been represented at the funeral.

32 And as soon as the old people said, "Poor Emily," the whispering began. "Do you suppose it's really so?" they said to one another. "Of course it is. What else could. . . ." This behind their hands; rustling of craned silk and satin behind jalousies closed upon the sun of Sunday afternoon as the thin, swift clop-clop-clop of the matched team passed: "Poor Emily."

33 She carried her head high enough—even when we believed that she was fallen. It was as if she demanded more than ever the recognition of her dignity as the last Grierson; as if it had wanted that touch of earthiness to reaffirm her imperviousness. Like when she bought the rat poison, the arsenic. That was over a year after they had begun to say "Poor Emily," and while the two female cousins were visiting her.

"I want some poison," she said to the druggist. 34
She was over thirty then, still a slight woman, though thinner than usual, with cold, haughty black eyes in a face the flesh of which was strained across the temples and about the eye-sockets as you imagine a lighthouse-keeper's face ought to look. "I want some poison," she said.

"Yes, Miss Emily. What kind? For rats and such? 35
I'd recom—"

"I want the best you have. I don't care what kind." 36

The druggist named several. "They'll kill any- 37
thing up to an elephant. But what you want is—"

"Arsenic," Miss Emily said. "Is that a good one?" 38

"Is . . . arsenic? Yes, ma'am. But what you want—" 39

"I want arsenic." 40

The druggist looked down at her. She looked back 41
at him, erect, her face like a strained flag. "Why, of course," the druggist said. "If that's what you want. But the law requires you to tell what you are going to use it for."

Miss Emily just stared at him, her head tilted back 42
in order to look him eye for eye, until he looked away and went and got the arsenic and wrapped it up. The Negro delivery boy brought her the package; the druggist didn't come back. When she opened the package at home there was written on the box, under the skull and bones: "For rats."

## IV

So the next day we all said, "She will kill herself"; and 43
we said it would be the best thing. When she had first begun to be seen with Homer Barron, we had said, "She will marry him." Then we said, "She will persuade him yet," because Homer himself had remarked—he liked men, and it was known that he drank with the younger men in the Elks' Club—that he was not a marrying man. Later we said, "Poor Emily," behind the jalousies as they passed on Sunday afternoon in the glittering buggy, Miss Emily with her head high and Homer Barron with his hat cocked and a cigar in his teeth, reins and whip in a yellow glove.

Then some of the ladies began to say that it was a 44
disgrace to the town and a bad example to the young people. The men did not want to interfere, but at last the ladies forced the Baptist minister—Miss Emily's people were Episcopal—to call upon her. He would never divulge what happened during that interview,

[1]French: a term used to describe the obligations and responsibilities of a member of the upper class.

but he refused to go back again. The next Sunday they again drove about the streets, and the following day the minister's wife wrote to Miss Emily's relations in Alabama.

45 So she had blood-kin under her roof again and we sat back to watch developments. At first nothing happened. Then we were sure that they were to be married. We learned that Miss Emily had been to the jeweler's and ordered a man's toilet set in silver, with the letters H.B. on each piece. Two days later we learned that she had bought a complete outfit of men's clothing, including a nightshirt, and we said, "They are married." We were really glad. We were glad because the two female cousins were even more Grierson than Miss Emily had ever been.

> A thin, acrid pall as of the tomb seemed to lie everywhere upon this room decked and furnished as for a bridal . . .

46 So we were not surprised when Homer Barron—the streets had been finished some time since—was gone. We were a little disappointed that there was not a public blowing-off, but we believed that he had gone on to prepare for Miss Emily's coming, or to give her a chance to get rid of the cousins. (By that time it was a cabal, and we were all Miss Emily's allies to help circumvent the cousins.) Sure enough, after another week they departed. And, as we had expected all along, within three days Homer Barron was back in town. A neighbor saw the Negro man admit him at the kitchen door at dusk one evening.

47 And that was the last we saw of Homer Barron. And of Miss Emily for some time. The Negro man went in and out with the market basket, but the front door remained closed. Now and then we would see her at a window for a moment, as the men did that night when they sprinkled the lime, but for almost six months she did not appear on the streets. Then we knew that this was to be expected too; as if that quality of her father which had thwarted her woman's life so many times had been too virulent and too furious to die.

48 When we next saw Miss Emily, she had grown fat and her hair was turning gray. During the next few years it grew grayer and grayer until it attained an even pepper-and-salt iron-gray, when it ceased turning. Up to the day of her death at seventy-four it was still that vigorous iron-gray, like the hair of an active man.

49 From that time on her front door remained closed, save for a period of six or seven years, when she was about forty, during which she gave lessons in china-painting. She fitted up a studio in one of the downstairs rooms, where the daughters and granddaughters of Colonel Sartoris' contemporaries were sent to her with the same regularity and in the same spirit that they were sent to church on Sundays with a twenty-five-cent piece for the collection plate. Meanwhile her taxes had been remitted.

Then the newer generation became the backbone and the spirit of the town, and the painting pupils grew up and fell away and did not send their children to her with boxes of color and tedious brushes and pictures cut from the ladies' magazines. The front door closed upon the last one and remained closed for good. When the town got free postal delivery, Miss Emily alone refused to let them fasten the metal numbers above her door and attach a mailbox to it. She would not listen to them. 50

Daily, monthly, yearly we watched the Negro grow grayer and more stooped, going in and out with the market basket. Each December we sent her a tax notice, which would be returned by the post office a week later, unclaimed. Now and then we would see her in one of the downstairs windows—she had evidently shut up the top floor of the house—like the carven torso of an idol in a niche, looking or not looking at us, we could never tell which. Thus she passed from generation to generation—dear, inescapable, impervious, tranquil, and perverse. 51

And so she died. Fell ill in the house filled with dust and shadows, with only a doddering Negro man to wait on her. We did not even know she was sick; we had long since given up trying to get any information from the Negro. He talked to no one, probably not even to her, for his voice had grown harsh and rusty, as if from disuse. 52

She died in one of the downstairs rooms, in a heavy walnut bed with a curtain, her gray head propped on a pillow yellow and moldy with age and lack of sunlight. 53

## V

The Negro met the first of the ladies at the front door and let them in, with their hushed, sibilant voices and their quick, curious glances, and then he disappeared. He walked right through the house and out the back and was not seen again. 54

The two female cousins came at once. They held the funeral on the second day, with the town coming to look at Miss Emily beneath a mass of bought flowers, with the crayon face of her father musing profoundly above the bier and the ladies sibilant and macabre; 55

and the very old men—some in their brushed Confederate uniforms—on the porch and the lawn, talking of Miss Emily as if she had been a contemporary of theirs, believing that they had danced with her and courted her perhaps, confusing time with its mathematical progression, as the old do, to whom all the past is not a diminishing road but, instead, a huge meadow which no winter ever quite touches, divided from them now by the narrow bottleneck of the most recent decade of years.

56 Already we knew that there was one room in that region above stairs which no one had seen in forty years, and which would have to be forced. They waited until Miss Emily was decently in the ground before they opened it.

57 The violence of breaking down the door seemed to fill this room with pervading dust. A thin, acrid pall as of the tomb seemed to lie everywhere upon this room decked and furnished as for a bridal: upon the valance curtains of faded rose color, upon the rose-shaded lights, upon the dressing table, upon the delicate array of crystal and the man's toilet things backed with tarnished silver, silver so tarnished that the monogram was obscured. Among them lay collar and tie, as if they had just been removed, which, lifted, left upon the surface a pale crescent in the dust. Upon a chair hung the suit, carefully folded; beneath it the two mute shoes and the discarded socks.

The man himself lay in the bed. 58

For a long while we just stood there, looking down 59
at the profound and fleshless grin. The body had apparently once lain in the attitude of an embrace, but now the long sleep that outlasts love, that conquers even the grimace of love, had cuckolded him. What was left of him, rotted beneath what was left of the nightshirt, had become inextricable from the bed in which he lay; and upon him and upon the pillow beside him lay that even coating of the patient and biding dust.

Then we noticed that in the second 60
pillow was the indentation of a head. One of us lifted something from it, and leaning forward, that faint and invisible dust dry and acrid in the nostrils, we saw a long strand of iron-gray hair.

# Questions for Critical Thinking

1 Faulkner is famous for his lush language and imagery. Choose a sentence that you like and which includes a detail unique to the South—whether a description of nature, a chore the characters perform, or a house. What is it about that sentence that speaks to you?

2 There is an element of mystery in this story. How does it affect the plot? What overall effect does it create for you as you read?

3 Imagine adapting the plot to a different time and place. What elements would you have to change in order to make these alterations work?

# Barn Burning (1939)

1 THE store in which the Justice of the Peace's court was sitting smelled of cheese. The boy, crouched on his nail keg at the back of the crowded room, knew he smelled cheese, and more: from where he sat he could see the ranked shelves close-packed with the solid, squat, dynamic shapes of tin cans whose labels his stomach read, not from the lettering which meant nothing to his mind but from the scarlet devils and the silver curve of fish—this, the cheese which he knew he smelled and the hermetic meat which his intestines believed he smelled coming in intermittent gusts momentary and brief between the other constant one, the smell and sense just a little of fear because mostly of despair and grief, the old fierce pull of blood. He could not see the table where the Justice sat and before which his father and his father's enemy (*our enemy* he thought in that despair: *ourn! Mine and hisn both! He's my father!*) stood, but he could hear them, the two of them that is, because his father had said no word yet:

"Do you want me to question this boy?"

2 "But what proof have you, Mr. Harris?"

3 "I told you. The hog got into my corn. I caught it up and sent it back to him. He had no fence that would hold it. I told him so, warned him. The next time I put the hog in my pen. When he came to get it I gave him enough wire to patch up his pen. The next time I put the hog up and kept it. I rode down to his house and saw the wire I gave him still rolled on to the spool in his yard. I told him he could have the hog when he paid me a dollar pound fee. That evening a nigger came with the dollar and got the hog. He was a strange nigger. He said, 'He say to tell you wood and hay kin burn.' I said, 'What?' 'That whut he say to tell you,' the nigger said. 'Wood and hay kin burn.' That night my barn burned. I got the stock out but I lost the barn."

4 "Where's the nigger? Have you got him?"

5 "He was a strange nigger, I tell you. I don't know what became of him."

6 "But that's not proof. Don't you see that's not proof?"

7 "Get that boy up here. He knows." For a moment the boy thought too that the man meant his older brother until Harris said, "Not him. The little one. The boy," and, crouching, small for his age, small and wiry like his father, in patched and faded jeans even too small for him, with straight, uncombed, brown hair and eyes gray and wild as storm scud, he saw the men between himself and the table part and become a lane of grim faces, at the end of which he saw the Justice, a shabby, collarless, graying man in spectacles, beckoning him. He felt no floor under his bare feet; he seemed to walk beneath the palpable weight of the grim turning faces. His father, still in his black Sunday coat donned not for the trial but for the moving, did not even look at him. *He aims for me to lie,* he thought, again with that frantic grief and despair. *And I will have to do hit.*

"What's your name, boy?" the Justice said. 8

"Colonel Sartoris Snopes," the boy whispered. 9

"Hey?" the Justice said. "Talk louder. Colonel Sar- 10
toris? I reckon anybody named for Colonel Sartoris in this country can't help but tell the truth, can they?" The boy said nothing. *Enemy! Enemy!* he thought; for a moment he could not even see, could not see that the Justice's face was kindly nor discern that his voice was troubled when he spoke to the man named Harris: "Do you want me to question this boy?" But he could hear, and during those subsequent long seconds while there was absolutely no sound in the crowded little room save that of quiet and intent breathing it was as if he had swung outward at the end of a grape vine, over a ravine, and at the top of the swing had been caught in a prolonged instant of mesmerized gravity, weightless in time.

"No!" Harris said violently, explosively. "Dam- 11
nation! Send him out of here!" Now time, the fluid world, rushed beneath him again, the voices coming to him again through the smell of cheese and sealed meat, the fear and despair and the old grief of blood:

"This case is closed. I can't find against you, Snopes, 12
but I can give you advice. Leave this country and don't come back to it."

His father spoke for the first time, his voice cold and 13
harsh, level, without emphasis: "I aim to. I don't figure to stay in a country among people who . . ." he said something unprintable and vile, addressed to no one.

14 "That'll do," the Justice said. "Take your wagon and get out of this country before dark. Case dismissed."

15 His father turned, and he followed the stiff black coat, the wiry figure walking a little stiffly from where a Confederate provost's man's musket ball had taken him in the heel on a stolen horse thirty years ago, followed the two backs now, since his older brother had appeared from somewhere in the crowd, no taller than the father but thicker, chewing tobacco steadily, between the two lines of grim-faced men and out of the store and across the worn gallery and down the sagging steps and among the dogs and half-grown boys in the mild May dust, where as he passed a voice hissed:

> ... the element of fire spoke to some deep mainspring of his father's being ...

16 "Barn burner!"

17 Again he could not see, whirling; there was a face in a red haze, moonlike, bigger than the full moon, the owner of it half again his size, he leaping in the red haze toward the face, feeling no blow, feeling no shock when his head struck the earth, scrabbling up and leaping again, feeling no blow this time either and tasting no blood, scrabbling up to see the other boy in full flight and himself already leaping into pursuit as his father's hand jerked him back, the harsh, cold voice speaking above him: "Go get in the wagon."

18 It stood in a grove of locusts and mulberries across the road. His two hulking sisters in their Sunday dresses and his mother and her sister in calico and sunbonnets were already in it, sitting on and among the sorry residue of the dozen and more movings which even the boy could remember—the battered stove, the broken beds and chairs, the clock inlaid with mother-of-pearl, which would not run, stopped at some fourteen minutes past two o'clock of a dead and forgotten day and time, which had been his mother's dowry. She was crying, though when she saw him she drew her sleeve across her face and began to descend from the wagon. "Get back," the father said.

19 "He's hurt. I got to get some water and wash his . . ."

20 "Get back in the wagon," his father said. He got in too, over the tail-gate. His father mounted to the seat where the older brother already sat and struck the gaunt mules two savage blows with the peeled willow, but without heat. It was not even sadistic; it was exactly that same quality which in later years would cause his descendants to over-run the engine before putting a motor car into motion, striking and reining back in the same movement. The wagon went on, the store with its quiet crowd of grimly watching men dropped behind; a curve in the road hid it. *Forever* he thought. *Maybe he's done satisfied now, now that he has* . . . stopping himself, not to say it aloud even to himself. His mother's hand touched his shoulder.

21 "Does hit hurt?" she said.

22 "Naw," he said. "Hit don't hurt. Lemme be."

23 "Can't you wipe some of the blood off before hit dries?"

24 "I'll wash to-night," he said. "Lemme be, I tell you."

25 The wagon went on. He did not know where they were going. None of them ever did or ever asked, because it was always somewhere, always a house of sorts waiting for them a day or two days or even three days away. Likely his father had already arranged to make a crop on another farm before he . . . Again he had to stop himself. He (the father) always did. There was something about his wolflike independence and even courage when the advantage was at least neutral which impressed strangers, as if they got from his latent ravening ferocity not so much a sense of dependability as a feeling that his ferocious conviction in the rightness of his own actions would be of advantage to all whose interest lay with his.

26 That night they camped, in a grove of oaks and beeches where a spring ran. The nights were still cool and they had a fire against it, of a rail lifted from a nearby fence and cut into lengths—a small fire, neat, niggard almost, a shrewd fire; such fires were his father's habit and custom always, even in freezing weather. Older, the boy might have remarked this and wondered why not a big one; why should not a man who had not only seen the waste and extravagance of war, but who had in his blood an inherent voracious prodigality with material not his own, have burned everything in sight? Then he might have gone a step farther and thought that that was the reason: that niggard blaze was the living fruit of nights passed during those four years in the woods hiding from all men, blue and gray, with his strings of horses (captured horses, he called them). And older still, he might have divined the true reason: that the element of fire spoke to some deep mainspring of his father's being, as the element of steel or of powder spoke to other men, as the one weapon for the preservation of integrity, else breath were not worth the breathing, and hence to be regarded with respect and used with discretion.

27 But he did not think this now and he had seen those same niggard blazes all his life. He merely ate his supper beside it and was already half asleep over his iron plate when his father called him, and once more he followed the stiff back, the stiff and ruthless limp,

up the slope and on to the starlit road where, turning, he could see his father against the stars but without face or depth—a shape black, flat, and bloodless as though cut from tin in the iron folds of the frockcoat which had not been made for him, the voice harsh like tin and without heat like tin:

28 "You were fixing to tell them. You would have told him."

29 He didn't answer. His father struck him with the flat of his hand on the side of the head, hard but without heat, exactly as he had struck the two mules at the store, exactly as he would strike either of them with any stick in order to kill a horse fly, his voice without heat or anger: "You're getting to be a man. You got to learn. You got to learn to stick to your own blood or you ain't going to have any blood to stick to you. Do you think either of them, any man there this morning, would? Don't you know all they wanted was a chance to get at me because they knew I had them beat? Eh?" Later, twenty years later, he was to tell himself, "If I had said they wanted only truth, justice, he would have hit me again." But now he said nothing. He was not crying. He just stood there. "Answer me," his father said.

30 "Yes," he whispered. His father turned.

31 "Get on to bed. We'll be there tomorrow."

32 Tomorrow they were there. In the early afternoon the wagon stopped before a paintless two-room house identical almost with the dozen others it had stopped before even in the boy's ten years, and again, as on the other dozen occasions, his mother and aunt got down and began to unload the wagon, although his two sisters and his father and brother had not moved.

33 "Likely hit ain't fitten for hawgs," one of the sisters said.

34 "Nevertheless, fit it will and you'll hog it and like it," his father said. "Get out of them chairs and help your Ma unload."

35 The two sisters got down, big, bovine, in a flutter of cheap ribbons; one of them drew from the jumbled wagon bed a battered lantern, the other a worn broom. His father handed the reins to the older son and began to climb stiffly over the wheel. "When they get unloaded, take the team to the barn and feed them." Then he said, and at first the boy thought he was still speaking to his brother: "Come with me."

36 "Me?" he said.

37 "Yes," his father said. "You."

38 "Abner," his mother said. His father paused and looked back—the harsh level stare beneath the shaggy, graying, irascible brows.

39 "I reckon I'll have a word with the man that aims to begin tomorrow owning me body and soul for the next eight months."

40 They went back up the road. A week ago—or before last night, that is—he would have asked where they were going, but not now. His father had struck him before last night but never before had he paused afterward to explain why; it was as if the blow and the following calm, outrageous voice still rang, repercussed, divulging nothing to him save the terrible handicap of being young, the light weight of his few years, just heavy enough to prevent his soaring free of the world as it seemed to be ordered but not heavy enough to keep him footed solid in it, to resist it and try to change the course of its events.

41 Presently he could see the grove of oaks and cedars and the other flowering trees and shrubs where the house would be, though not the house yet. They walked beside a fence massed with honeysuckle and Cherokee roses and came to a gate swinging open between two brick pillars, and now, beyond a sweep of drive, he saw the house for the first time and at that instant he forgot his father and the terror and despair both, and even when he remembered his father again (who had not stopped) the terror and despair did not return. Because, for all the twelve movings, they had sojourned until now in a poor country, a land of small farms and fields and houses, and he had never seen a house like this before. *Hit's big as a courthouse* he thought quietly, with a surge of peace and joy whose reason he could not have thought into words, being too young for that: *They are safe from him. People whose lives are a part of this peace and dignity are beyond his touch, he no more to them than a buzzing wasp: capable of stinging for a little moment but that's all; the spell of this peace and dignity rendering even the barns and stable and cribs which belong to it impervious to the puny flames he might contrive . . .* this, the peace and joy, ebbing for an instant as he looked again at the still black back, the stiff and implacable limp of the figure which was not dwarfed by the house, for the reason that it had never looked big anywhere and which now, against the serene columned backdrop, had more than ever that impervious quality of something cut ruthlessly from tin, depthless, as though, sidewise to the sun, it would cast no shadow. Watching him, the boy remarked the absolutely undeviating course which his father held and saw the stiff foot come squarely down in a pile of fresh droppings where a horse had stood in the drive and which his father could have avoided by a simple change of stride. But it ebbed only a moment, though he could not have thought this into words either, walking on in the spell of the house, which he could even want but without envy, without sorrow, certainly never with that raving and jealous rage which unknown to him walked in the ironlike black coat before him: *Maybe he will feel*

*it too. Maybe it will even change him now from what maybe he couldn't help but be.*

42 They crossed the portico. Now he could hear his father's stiff foot as it came down on the boards with clocklike finality, a sound out of all proportion to the displacement of the body it bore and which was not dwarfed either by the white door before it, as though it had attained to a sort of vicious and ravening minimum not to be dwarfed by anything—the flat, wide, black hat, the formal coat of broadcloth which had once been black but which had now that friction-glazed greenish cast of the bodies of old house flies, the lifted sleeve which was too large, the lifted hand like a curled claw. The door opened so promptly that the boy knew the Negro must have been watching them all the time, an old man with neat grizzled hair, in a linen jacket, who stood barring the door with his body, saying, "Wipe yo foots, white man, fo you come in here. Major ain't home nohow."

. . . the boy watched him pivot on the good leg and saw the stiff foot drag . . .

43 "Get out of my way, nigger," his father said, without heat too, flinging the door back and the Negro also and entering, his hat still on his head. And now the boy saw the prints of the stiff foot on the doorjamb and saw them appear on the pale rug behind the machinelike deliberation of the foot which seemed to bear (or transmit) twice the weight which the body compassed. The Negro was shouting "Miss Lula! Miss Lula!" somewhere behind them, then the boy, deluged as though by a warm wave by a suave turn of the carpeted stair and a pendant glitter of chandeliers and a mute gleam of gold frames, heard the swift feet and saw her too, a lady—perhaps he had never seen her like before either—in a gray, smooth gown with lace at the throat and an apron tied at the waist and the sleeves turned back, wiping cake or biscuit dough from her hands with a towel as she came up the hall, looking not at his father at all but at the tracks on the blond rug with an expression of incredulous amazement.

44 "I tried," the Negro cried. "I tole him to . . ."

45 "Will you please go away?" she said in a shaking voice. "Major de Spain is not at home. Will you please go away?"

46 His father had not spoken again. He did not speak again. He did not even look at her. He just stood stiff in the center of the rug, in his hat, the shaggy iron-gray brows twitching slightly above the pebble-colored eyes as he appeared to examine the house with brief deliberation. Then with the same deliberation he turned; the boy watched him pivot on the good leg and saw the stiff foot drag around the arc of the turning, leaving a final long and fading smear. His father never looked at it, he never once looked down at the rug. The Negro held the door. It closed behind them, upon the hysteric and indistinguishable woman-wail. His father stopped at the top of the steps and scraped his boot clean on the edge of it. At the gate he stopped again. He stood for a moment, planted stiffly on the stiff foot, looking back at the house. "Pretty and white, ain't it?" he said. "That's sweat. Nigger sweat. Maybe it ain't white enough yet to suit him. Maybe he wants to mix some white sweat with it."

Two hours later the boy was chopping wood behind the house within which his mother and aunt and the two sisters (the mother and aunt, not the two girls, he knew that; even at this distance and muffled by walls the flat loud voices of the two girls emanated an incorrigible idle inertia) were setting up the stove to prepare a meal, when he heard the hooves and saw the linen-clad man on a fine sorrel mare, whom he recognized even before he saw the rolled rug in front of the Negro youth following on a fat bay carriage horse—a suffused, angry face vanishing, still at full gallop, beyond the corner of the house where his father and brother were sitting in the two tilted chairs; and a moment later, almost before he could have put the axe down, he heard the hooves again and watched the sorrel mare go back out of the yard, already galloping again. Then his father began to shout one of the sisters' names, who presently emerged backward from the kitchen door dragging the rolled rug along the ground by one end while the other sister walked behind it. 47

"If you ain't going to tote, go on and set up the wash pot," the first said. 48

"You, Sarty!" the second shouted. "Set up the wash pot!" His father appeared at the door, framed against that shabbiness, as he had been against that other bland perfection, impervious to either, the mother's anxious face at his shoulder. 49

"Go on," the father said. "Pick it up." The two sisters stooped, broad, lethargic; stooping, they presented an incredible expanse of pale cloth and a flutter of tawdry ribbons. 50

"If I thought enough of a rug to have to git hit all the way from France I wouldn't keep hit where folks coming in would have to tromp on hit," the first said. They raised the rug. 51

"Abner," the mother said. "Let me do it." 52

"You go back and git dinner," his father said. "I'll tend to this." 53

54 From the woodpile through the rest of the afternoon the boy watched them, the rug spread flat in the dust beside the bubbling wash pot, the two sisters stooping over it with that profound and lethargic reluctance, while the father stood over them in turn, implacable and grim, driving them though never raising his voice again. He could smell the harsh homemade lye they were using; he saw his mother come to the door once and look toward them with an expression not anxious now but very like despair; he saw his father turn, and he fell to with the axe and saw from the corner of his eye his father raise from the ground a flattish fragment of field stone and examine it and return to the pot, and this time his mother actually spoke: "Abner. Abner. Please don't. Please, Abner."

"It cost a hundred dollars. But you never had a hundred dollars. You never will. . . ."

55 Then he was done too. It was dusk; the whippoorwills had already begun. He could smell coffee from the room where they would presently eat the cold food remaining from the mid-afternoon meal, though when he entered the house he realized they were having coffee again probably because there was a fire on the hearth, before which the rug now lay spread over the backs of the two chairs. The tracks of his father's foot were gone. Where they had been were now long, water-cloudy scoriations resembling the sporadic course of a lilliputian mowing machine.

56 It still hung there while they ate the cold food and then went to bed, scattered without order or claim up and down the two rooms, his mother in one bed, where his father would later lie, the older brother in the other, himself, the aunt, and the two sisters on pallets on the floor. But his father was not in bed yet. The last thing the boy remembered was the depthless, harsh silhouette of the hat and coat bending over the rug and it seemed to him that he had not even closed his eyes when the silhouette was standing over him, the fire almost dead behind it, the stiff foot prodding him awake. "Catch up the mule," his father said.

57 When he returned with the mule his father was standing in the back door, the rolled rug over his shoulder. "Ain't you going to ride?" he said.

58 "No. Give me your foot."

59 He bent his knee into his father's hand, the wiry, surprising power flowed smoothly, rising, he rising with it, on to the mule's bare back (they had owned a saddle once; the boy could remember it though not when or where) and with the same effortlessness his father swung the rug up in front of him. Now in the starlight they retraced the afternoon's path, up the dusty road rife with honeysuckle, through the gate and up the black tunnel of the drive to the lightless house, where he sat on the mule and felt the rough warp of the rug drag across his thighs and vanish.

60 "Don't you want me to help?" he whispered. His father did not answer and now he heard again that stiff foot striking the hollow portico with that wooden and clocklike deliberation, that outrageous overstatement of the weight it carried. The rug, hunched, not flung (the boy could tell that even in the darkness) from his father's shoulder struck the angle of wall and floor with a sound unbelievably loud, thunderous, then the foot again, unhurried and enormous; a light came on in the house and the boy sat, tense, breathing steadily and quietly and just a little fast, though the foot itself did not increase its beat at all, descending the steps now; now the boy could see him.

61 "Don't you want to ride now?" he whispered. "We kin both ride now," the light within the house altering now, flaring up and sinking. *He's coming down the stairs now,* he thought. He had already ridden the mule up beside the horse block; presently his father was up behind him and he doubled the reins over and slashed the mule across the neck, but before the animal could begin to trot the hard, thin arm came around him, the hard, knotted hand jerking the mule back to a walk.

62 In the first red rays of the sun they were in the lot, putting plow gear on the mules. This time the sorrel mare was in the lot before he heard it at all, the rider collarless and even bareheaded, trembling, speaking in a shaking voice as the woman in the house had done, his father merely looking up once before stooping again to the hame he was buckling, so that the man on the mare spoke to his stooping back:

63 "You must realize you have ruined that rug. Wasn't there anybody here, any of your women . . ." he ceased, shaking, the boy watching him, the older brother leaning now in the stable door, chewing, blinking slowly and steadily at nothing apparently. "It cost a hundred dollars. But you never had a hundred dollars. You never will. So I'm going to charge you twenty bushels of corn against your crop. I'll add it in your contract and when you come to the commissary you can sign it. That won't keep Mrs. de Spain quiet but maybe it will teach you to wipe your feet off before you enter her house again."

64 Then he was gone. The boy looked at his father, who still had not spoken or even looked up again, who was now adjusting the logger-head in the hame.

65 "Pap," he said. His father looked at him—the inscrutable face, the shaggy brows beneath where the gray eyes glinted coldly. Suddenly the boy went toward him, fast, stopping as suddenly. "You done the best you could!" he cried. "If he wanted hit done different why didn't he wait and tell you how? He won't git no twenty bushels! He won't git none! We'll gather hit and hide hit! I kin watch . . ."

66 "Did you put the cutter back in that straight stock like I told you?"

67 "No, sir," he said.

68 "Then go do it."

69 That was Wednesday. During the rest of that week he worked steadily, at what was within his scope and some which was beyond it, with an industry that did not need to be driven nor even commanded twice; he had this from his mother, with the difference that some at least of what he did he liked to do, such as splitting wood with the half-size axe which his mother and aunt had earned, or saved money somehow, to present him with at Christmas. In company with the two older women (and on one afternoon, even one of the sisters), he built pens for the shoat and the cow which were a part of his father's contract with the landlord, and one afternoon, his father being absent, gone somewhere on one of the mules, he went to the field.

70 They were running a middle buster now, his brother holding the plow straight while he handled the reins, and walking beside the straining mule, the rich black soil shearing cool and damp against his bare ankles, he thought *Maybe this is the end of it. Maybe even that twenty bushels that seems hard to have to pay for just a rug will be a cheap price for him to stop forever and always from being what he used to be;* thinking, dreaming now, so that his brother had to speak sharply to him to mind the mule: *Maybe he even won't collect the twenty bushels. Maybe it will all add up and balance and vanish—corn, rug, fire; the terror and grief; the being pulled two ways like between two teams of horses—gone, done with for ever and ever.*

71 Then it was Saturday; he looked up from beneath the mule he was harnessing and saw his father in the black coat and hat. "Not that," his father said. "The wagon gear." And then, two hours later, sitting in the wagon bed behind his father and brother on the seat, the wagon accomplished a final curve, and he saw the weathered paintless store with its tattered tobacco- and patent-medicine posters and the tethered wagons and saddle animals below the gallery. He mounted the gnawed steps behind his father and brother, and there again was the lane of quiet, watching faces for the three of them to walk through. He saw the man in spectacles sitting at the plank table and he did not need to be told this was a Justice of the Peace; he sent one glare of fierce, exultant, partisan defiance at the man in collar and cravat now, whom he had seen but twice before in his life, and that on a galloping horse, who now wore on his face an expression not of rage but of amazed unbelief which the boy could not have known was at the incredible circumstance of being sued by one of his own tenants, and came and stood against his father and cried at the Justice: "He ain't done it! He ain't burnt . . ."

"Go back to the wagon," his father said. 72

"Burnt?" the Justice said. "Do I understand this 73 rug was burned too?"

"Does anybody here claim it was?" his father said. 74 "Go back to the wagon." But he did not, he merely retreated to the rear of the room, crowded as that other had been, but not to sit down this time, instead, to stand pressing among the motionless bodies, listening to the voices:

"And you claim twenty bushels of corn is too high 75 for the damage you did to the rug?"

"He brought the rug to me and said he wanted the 76 tracks washed out of it. I washed the tracks out and took the rug back to him."

"But you didn't carry the rug back to him in the 77 same condition it was in before you made the tracks on it."

His father did not answer, and now for perhaps 78 half a minute there was no sound at all save that of breathing, the faint, steady suspiration of complete and intent listening.

"You decline to answer that, Mr. Snopes?" Again his 79 father did not answer. "I'm going to find against you, Mr. Snopes. I'm going to find that you were responsible for the injury to Major de Spain's rug and hold you liable for it. But twenty bushels of corn seems a little high for a man in your circumstances to have to pay. Major de Spain claims it cost a hundred dollars. October corn will be worth about fifty cents. I figure that if Major de Spain can stand a ninety-five dollar loss on something he paid cash for, you can stand a five-dollar loss you haven't earned yet. I hold you in damages to Major de Spain to the amount of ten bushels of corn over and above your contract with him, to be paid to him out of your crop at gathering time. Court adjourned."

It had taken no time hardly, the morning was but 80 half begun. He thought they would return home and perhaps back to the field, since they were late, far behind all other farmers. But instead his father passed on behind the wagon, merely indicating with his hand for the older brother to follow with it, and crossed the road toward the blacksmith shop opposite, pressing on after his father, overtaking him, speaking, whispering up at the harsh, calm face beneath the weathered hat: "He won't git no ten bushels either. He won't git one. We'll . . ." until his father glanced for an instant down at him, the face absolutely calm, the grizzled eyebrows tangled above the cold eyes, the voice almost pleasant, almost gentle:

81 "You think so? Well, we'll wait till October anyway."

82 The matter of the wagon—the setting of a spoke or two and the tightening of the tires—did not take long either, the business of the tires accomplished by driving the wagon into the spring branch behind the shop and letting it stand there, the mules nuzzling into the water from time to time, and the boy on the seat with the idle reins, looking up the slope and through the sooty tunnel of the shed where the slow hammer rang and where his father sat on an upended cypress bolt, easily, either talking or listening, still sitting there when the boy brought the dripping wagon up out of the branch and halted it before the door.

83 "Take them on to the shade and hitch," his father said. He did so and returned. His father and the smith and a third man squatting on his heels inside the door were talking, about crops and animals; the boy, squatting too in the ammoniac dust and hoof-parings and scales of rust, heard his father tell a long and unhurried story out of the time before the birth of the older brother even when he had been a professional horsetrader. And then his father came up beside him where he stood before a tattered last year's circus poster on the other side of the store, gazing rapt and quiet at the scarlet horses, the incredible poisings and convulsions of tulle and tights and the painted leers of comedians, and said, "It's time to eat."

84 But not at home. Squatting beside his brother against the front wall, he watched his father emerge from the store and produce from a paper sack a segment of cheese and divide it carefully and deliberately into three with his pocket knife and produce crackers from the same sack. They all three squatted on the gallery and ate, slowly, without talking; then in the store again, they drank from a tin dipper tepid water smelling of the cedar bucket and of living beech trees. And still they did not go home. It was a horse lot this time, a tall rail fence upon and along which men stood and sat and out of which one by one horses were led, to be walked and trotted and then cantered back and forth along the road while the slow swapping and buying went on and the sun began to slant westward, they—the three of them—watching and listening, the older brother with his muddy eyes and his steady, inevitable tobacco, the father commenting now and then on certain of the animals, to no one in particular.

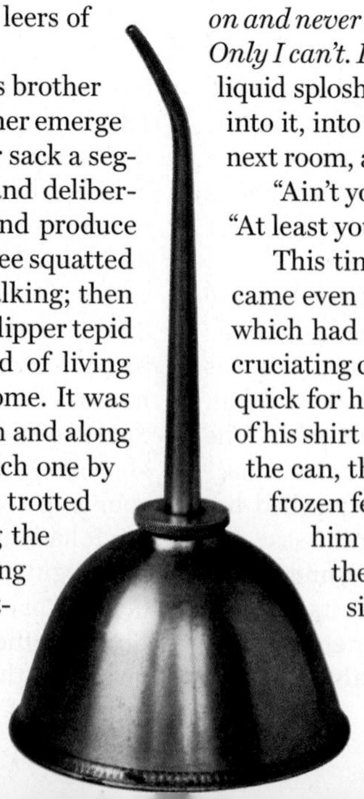

It was after sundown when they reached home. 85
They ate supper by lamplight, then, sitting on the doorstep, the boy watched the night fully accomplish, listening to the whippoorwills and the frogs, when he heard his mother's voice: "Abner! No! No! Oh, God. Oh, God. Abner!" and he rose, whirled, and saw the altered light through the door where a candle stub now burned in a bottle neck on the table and his father, still in the hat and coat, at once formal and burlesque as though dressed carefully for some shabby and ceremonial violence, emptying the reservoir of the lamp back into the five-gallon kerosene can from which it had been filled, while the mother tugged at his arm until he shifted the lamp to the other hand and flung her back, not savagely or viciously, just hard, into the wall, her hands flung out against the wall for balance, her mouth open and in her face the same quality of hopeless despair as had been in her voice. Then his father saw him standing in the door.

"Go to the barn and get that can of oil we were 86
oiling the wagon with," he said. The boy did not move. Then he could speak.

"What . . ." he cried. "What are you . . ." 87

"Go get that oil," his father said. "Go." 88

Then he was moving, running, outside the house, 89
toward the stable: this the old habit, the old blood which he had not been permitted to choose for himself, which had been bequeathed him willy nilly and which had run for so long (and who knew where, battening on what of outrage and savagery and lust) before it came to him. *I could keep on,* he thought. *I could run on and on and never look back, never need to see his face again. Only I can't. I can't,* the rusted can in his hand now, the liquid sploshing in it as he ran back to the house and into it, into the sound of his mother's weeping in the next room, and handed the can to his father.

"Ain't you going to even send a nigger?" he cried. 90
"At least you sent a nigger before!"

This time his father didn't strike him. The hand 91
came even faster than the blow had, the same hand which had set the can on the table with almost excruciating care flashing from the can toward him too quick for him to follow it, gripping him by the back of his shirt and on to tiptoe before he had seen it quit the can, the face stooping at him in breathless and frozen ferocity, the cold, dead voice speaking over him to the older brother who leaned against the table, chewing with that steady, curious, sidewise motion of cows:

"Empty the can into the big one and 92
go on. I'll catch up with you."

93 "Better tie him up to the bedpost," the brother said.

94 "Do like I told you," the father said. Then the boy was moving, his bunched shirt and the hard, bony hand between his shoulder-blades, his toes just touching the floor, across the room and into the other one, past the sisters sitting with spread heavy thighs in the two chairs over the cold hearth, and to where his mother and aunt sat side by side on the bed, the aunt's arm about his mother's shoulders.

95 "Hold him," the father said: The aunt made a startled movement. "Not you," the father said. "Lennie. Take hold of him. I want to see you do it." His mother took him by the wrist. "You'll hold him better than that. If he gets loose don't you know what he is going to do? He will go up yonder." He jerked his head toward the road. "Maybe I'd better tie him."

96 "I'll hold him," his mother whispered.

He did not know it was midnight and he did not know how far he had come.

97 "See you do then." Then his father was gone, the stiff foot heavy and measured upon the boards, ceasing at last.

98 Then he began to struggle. His mother caught him in both arms, he jerking and wrenching at them. He would be stronger in the end, he knew that. But he had no time to wait for it. "Lemme go!" he cried. "I don't want to have to hit you!"

99 "Let him go!" the aunt said. "If he don't go, before God, I am going up there myself!"

100 "Don't you see I can't?" his mother cried. "Sarty! Sarty! No! No! Help me, Lizzie!"

101 Then he was free. His aunt grasped at him but it was too late. He whirled, running, his mother stumbled forward on to her knees behind him, crying to the nearer sister: "Catch him, Net! Catch him!" But that was too late too, the sister (the sisters were twins, born at the same time, yet either of them now gave the impression of being, encompassing as much living meat and volume and weight as any other two of the family) not yet having begun to rise from the chair, her head, face, alone merely turned, presenting to him in the flying instant an astonishing expanse of young female features untroubled by any surprise even, wearing only an expression of bovine interest. Then he was out of the room, out of the house, in the mild dust of the starlit road and the heavy rifeness of honeysuckle, the pale ribbon unspooling with terrific slowness under his running feet, reaching the gate at last and turning in, running, his heart and lungs drumming, on up the drive toward the lighted house, the lighted door. He did not knock, he burst in, sobbing for breath, incapable for the moment of speech; he saw the astonished face of the Negro in the linen jacket without knowing when the Negro had appeared.

102 "De Spain!" he cried, panted. "Where's . . ." then he saw the white man too emerging from a white door down the hall. "Barn!" he cried. "Barn!"

103 "What?" the white man said. "Barn?"

104 "Yes!" the boy cried. "Barn!"

105 "Catch him!" the white man shouted.

106 But it was too late this time too. The Negro grasped his shirt, but the entire sleeve, rotten with washing, carried away, and he was out that door too and in the drive again, and had actually never ceased to run even while he was screaming into the white man's face.

107 Behind him the white man was shouting, "My horse! Fetch my horse!" and he thought for an instant of cutting across the park and climbing the fence into the road, but he did not know the park nor how the vine-massed fence might be and he dared not risk it. So he ran on down the drive, blood and breath roaring; presently he was in the road again though he could not see it. He could not hear either: the galloping mare was almost upon him before he heard her, and even then he held his course, as if the very urgency of his wild grief and need must in a moment more find him wings, waiting until the ultimate instant to hurl himself aside and into the weed-choked roadside ditch as the horse thundered past and on, for an instant in furious silhouette against the stars, the tranquil early summer night sky which, even before the shape of the horse and rider vanished, stained abruptly and violently upward: a long, swirling roar incredible and soundless, blotting the stars, and he springing up and into the road again, running again, knowing it was too late yet still running even after he heard the shot and an instant later, two shots, pausing now without knowing he had ceased to run, crying, "Pap! Pap!", running again before he knew he had begun to run, stumbling, tripping over something and scrabbling up again without ceasing to run, looking backward over his shoulder at the glare as he got up, running on among the invisible trees, panting, sobbing, "Father! Father!"

108 At midnight he was sitting on the crest of a hill. He did not know it was midnight and he did not know how far he had come. But there was no glare behind him now and he sat now, his back toward what he had called home for four days anyhow, his face toward the dark woods which he would enter when breath was strong again, small, shaking steadily in the chill darkness, hugging himself into the remainder of his thin, rotten shirt, the grief and despair now no longer

terror and fear but just grief and despair. *Father. My father,* he thought. "He was brave!" he cried suddenly, aloud but not loud, no more than a whisper. "He was! He was in the war! He was in Colonel Sartoris' cav'ry!" not knowing that his father had gone to that war a private in the fine old European sense, wearing no uniform, admitting the authority of and giving fidelity to no man or army or flag, going to war as Marlbrouck himself did: for booty—it meant nothing and less than nothing to him if it were enemy booty or his own.

109 The slow constellations wheeled on. It would be dawn and then sun-up after a while and he would be hungry. But that would be tomorrow and now he was only cold, and walking would cure that. His breathing was easier now and he decided to get up and go on, and then he found that he had been asleep because he knew it was almost dawn, the night almost over. He could tell that from the whippoorwills. They were everywhere now among the dark trees below him, constant and inflectioned and ceaseless, so that, as the instant for giving over to the day birds drew nearer and nearer, there was no interval at all between them. He got up. He was a little stiff, but walking would cure that too as it would the cold, and soon there would be the sun. He went on down the hill, toward the dark woods within which the liquid silver voices of the birds called unceasing—the rapid and urgent beating of the urgent and quiring heart of the late spring night. He did not look back.

# Questions for Critical Thinking

1 The smells and sounds of country life contribute largely to the effects of this story. Can you catalog these on a second reading of the story? Which senses—smell, touch, etc.—seem the most important?

2 Faulkner's phrases and sentences seem quite distinctive (as in "He went on down the hill, toward the dark woods within which the liquid silver voices of the birds called unceasing—the rapid and urgent beating of the urgent and quiring heart of the late spring night."). Do these seem "Southern" to you? What other terms might you use to describe Faulkner's style?

3 Note the references Faulkner makes to the Civil War. Based on what we learn about the father in the penultimate paragraph of "Barn Burning," how would you describe this author's view of Southern history?

4 Imagine the setting of "Barn Burning" in a northern city. Is it possible? How would it change the story?

"The first and most obvious characteristic of fiction is that it deals with reality through what can be seen, heard, smelt, tasted, and touched. Now this is something that can't be learrned only in the head; it has to be learned in the habits. It has to become a way that you habitually look at things. The fiction writer has to realize that he can't create compassion with compassion, or emotion with emotion, or thought with thought. He has to provide all these things with a body; he has to create a world with weight and extension. . . . The meaning of a story has to be embodied in it, has to be made concrete in it. A story is a way to say something that can't be said any other way, and it takes every word in the story to say what the meaning is." —Flannery O'Connor, 1969 (from "Writing Short Stories")

# Flannery O'Connor (1925–1964)

A Southern writer unlike any other, Flannery O'Connor is known for her satire on poor and middle-class Southern whites, her Catholic perspective, and her portrayal of the grotesque. Beyond these signature characteristics, O'Connor's prose jumps off the page with precision, wit, and sharpness—all calculated, as she put it, to show readers moments of God's grace. Born and raised in Savannah, Georgia, O'Connor moved with her parents to the small town of Milledgeville when her father became ill with lupus. She went to college in Georgia and then attended the Iowa Writers' Workshop, where she earned her M.F.A. Her teacher there, Paul Engle, described O'Connor's Georgia accent as so strong when they first met that, after several attempts to comprehend her speech, he finally had to ask her to write down what she wanted to say.

O'Connor became a shy, silent fixture in the back of the classroom, working hard at stories rooted in Southern culture and Catholic sensibility. The cadences of regional speech course through her fiction, and she urged other writers, too, to "[take] advantage of what's yours." There are traces of the influence of other Southern writers in her work—notably the gothic strain of her great predecessor William Faulkner—but much of her work defies comparison as well as easy imitation; it is, to use a much-overused word, *original.*

Her health—she, too, contracted lupus—forced her to return to the farm in Milledgeville and move in with her mother. She left home only occasionally to lecture or to accept an award; the rest of her time she spent writing and raising her beloved peacocks. O'Connor is most famous for her short stories, collected in *A Good Man Is Hard to Find* (1955) and *Everything That Rises Must Converge* (1965), but she also wrote two novels before her early death from lupus at age thirty-nine. In 1969 her occasional prose, speeches, and essays were collected in *Mystery and Manners,* and her complete stories were collected in a 1971 edition, which earned her a posthumous National Book Award. O'Connor is remembered not just as a modern master of the short story form but also—from interviews, letters, and speeches—for her wise and witty voice. When asked whether writing programs stifle writers, O'Connor famously replied, "My opinion is that they don't stifle enough of them."

# A Good Man Is Hard to Find (1955)

1 THE grandmother didn't want to go to Florida. She wanted to visit some of her connections in east Tennessee and she was seizing at every chance to change Bailey's mind. Bailey was the son she lived with, her only boy. He was sitting on the edge of his chair at the table, bent over the orange sports section of the *Journal*. "Now look here, Bailey," she said, "see here, read this," and she stood with one hand on her thin hip and the other rattling the newspaper at his bald head. "Here this fellow that calls himself The Misfit is aloose from the Federal Pen and headed toward Florida and you read here what it says he did to these people. Just you read it. I wouldn't take my children in any direction with a criminal like that aloose in it. I couldn't answer to my conscience if I did."

Bailey didn't look up from his reading so she wheeled around then and faced the children's mother, a young woman in slacks, whose face was as broad and innocent as a cabbage and was tied around with 2 a green head-kerchief that had two points on the top like a rabbit's ears. She was sitting on the sofa, feeding the baby his apricots out of a jar. "The children have been to Florida before," the old lady said. "You all ought to take them somewhere else for a change so they would see different parts of the world and be broad. They never have been to east Tennessee."

3 The children's mother didn't seem to hear her but the eight-year-old boy, John Wesley, a stocky child with glasses, said, "If you don't want to go to Florida, why dontcha stay at home?" He and the little girl, June Star, were reading the funny papers on the floor.

In case of an accident, anyone seeing her dead on the highway would know at once that she was a lady.

4 "She wouldn't stay at home to be queen for a day," June Star said without raising her yellow head.

5 "Yes and what would you do if this fellow, The Misfit, caught you?" the grandmother asked.

6 "I'd smack his face," John Wesley said.

7 "She wouldn't stay at home for a million bucks," June Star said. "Afraid she'd miss something. She has to go everywhere we go."

8 "All right, Miss," the grandmother said. "Just remember that the next time you want me to curl your hair."

9 June Star said her hair was naturally curly.

10 The next morning the grandmother was the first one in the car, ready to go. She had her big black valise that looked like the head of a hippopotamus in one corner, and underneath it she was hiding a basket with Pitty Sing, the cat, in it. She didn't intend for the cat to be left alone in the house for three days because he would miss her too much and she was afraid he might brush against one of the gas burners and accidentally asphyxiate himself. Her son, Bailey, didn't like to arrive at a motel with a cat.

11 She sat in the middle of the back seat with John Wesley and June Star on either side of her. Bailey and the children's mother and the baby sat in front and they left Atlanta at eight forty-five with the mileage on the car at 55890. The grandmother wrote this down because she thought it would be interesting to say how many miles they had been when they got back. It took them twenty minutes to reach the outskirts of the city.

12 The old lady settled herself comfortably, removing her white cotton gloves and putting them up with her purse on the shelf in front of the back window. The children's mother still had on slacks and still had her head tied up in a green kerchief, but the grandmother had on a navy blue straw sailor hat with a bunch of white violets on the brim and a navy blue dress with a small white dot in the print. Her collars and cuffs were white organdy trimmed with lace and at her neckline she had pinned a purple spray of cloth violets containing a sachet. In case of an accident, anyone seeing her dead on the highway would know at once that she was a lady.

She said she thought it was going to be a good 13
day for driving, neither too hot nor too cold, and she cautioned Bailey that the speed limit was fifty-five miles an hour and that the patrolmen hid themselves behind billboards and small clumps of trees and sped out after you before you had a chance to slow down. She pointed out interesting details of the scenery: Stone Mountain; the blue granite that in some places came up to both sides of the highway; the brilliant red clay banks slightly streaked with purple; and the various crops that made rows of green lace-work on the ground. The trees were full of silver-white sunlight and the meanest of them sparkled. The children were reading comic magazines and their mother had gone back to sleep.

"Let's go through Georgia fast so we won't have to 14
look at it much," John Wesley said.

"If I were a little boy," said the grandmother, "I 15
wouldn't talk about my native state that way. Tennessee has the mountains and Georgia has the hills."

"Tennessee is just a hillbilly dumping ground," 16
John Wesley said, "and Georgia is a lousy state too."

"You said it," June Star said. 17

"In my time," said the grandmother, folding her 18
thin veined fingers, "children were more respectful of their native states and their parents and everything else. People did right then. Oh look at the cute little pickaninny!" she said and pointed to a Negro child standing in the door of a shack. "Wouldn't that make a picture, now?" she asked and they all turned and looked at the little Negro out of the back window. He waved.

"He didn't have any britches on," June Star said. 19

"He probably didn't have any," the grandmother 20
explained. "Little niggers in the country don't have things like we do. If I could paint, I'd paint that picture," she said.

The children exchanged comic books. 21

The grandmother offered to hold the baby and the 22
children's mother passed him over the front seat to her.

She set him on her knee and bounced him and told him about the things they were passing. She rolled her eyes and screwed up her mouth and stuck her leathery thin face into his smooth bland one. Occasionally he gave her a faraway smile. They passed a large cotton field with five or six graves fenced in the middle of it, like a small island. "Look at the graveyard!" the grandmother said, pointing it out. "That was the old family burying ground. That belonged to the plantation."

23 "Where's the plantation?" John Wesley asked.

24 "Gone With the Wind," said the grandmother. "Ha. Ha."

25 When the children finished all the comic books they had brought, they opened the lunch and ate it. The grandmother ate a peanut butter sandwich and an olive and would not let the children throw the box and the paper napkins out the window. When there was nothing else to do they played a game by choosing a cloud and making the other two guess what shape it suggested. John Wesley took one of the shape of a cow and June Star guessed a cow and John Wesley said, no, an automobile, and June Star said he didn't play fair, and they began to slap each other over the grandmother.

26 The grandmother said she would tell them a story if they would keep quiet. When she told a story, she rolled her eyes and waved her head and was very dramatic. She said once when she was a maiden lady she had been courted by a Mr. Edgar Atkins Teagarden from Jasper, Georgia. She said he was a very good-looking man and a gentleman and that he brought her a watermelon every Saturday afternoon with his initials cut in it, E. A. T. Well, one Saturday, she said, Mr. Teagarden brought the watermelon and there was nobody at home and he left it on the front porch and returned in his buggy to Jasper, but she never got the watermelon, she said, because a nigger boy ate it when he saw the initials, E. A. T.! This story tickled John Wesley's funny bone and he giggled and giggled but June Star didn't think it was any good. She said she wouldn't marry a man that just brought her a watermelon on Saturday. The grandmother said she would have done well to marry Mr. Teagarden because he was a gentleman and had bought Coca-Cola stock when it first came out and that he had died only a few years ago, a very wealthy man.

They stopped at The Tower for barbecued sandwiches. The Tower was a part stucco and part wood filling station and dance hall set in a clearing outside of Timothy. A fat man named Red Sammy Butts ran it and there were signs stuck here and there on the building and for miles up and down the highway saying, TRY RED SAMMY'S FAMOUS BARBECUE. NONE LIKE FAMOUS RED SAMMY'S! RED SAM! THE FAT BOY WITH THE HAPPY LAUGH! A VETERAN! RED SAMMY'S YOUR MAN! 27

Red Sammy was lying on the bare ground outside The Tower with his head under a truck while a gray monkey about a foot high, chained to a small chinaberry tree, chattered nearby. The monkey sprang back into the tree and got on the highest limb as soon as he saw the children jump out of the car and run toward him. 28

Inside, The Tower was a long dark room with a counter at one end and tables at the other and dancing space in the middle. They sat down at a board table next to the nickelodeon and Red Sam's wife, a tall burnt-brown woman with hair and eyes lighter than her skin, came and took their order. The children's mother put a dime in the machine and played "The Tennessee Waltz," and the grandmother said that tune always made her want to dance. She asked Bailey if he would like to dance but he only glared at her. He didn't have a naturally sunny disposition like she did and trips made him nervous. The grandmother's brown eyes were very bright. She swayed her head from side to side and pretended she was dancing in her chair. June Star said play something she could tap to so the children's mother put in another dime and played a fast number and June Star stepped out onto the dance floor and did her tap routine. 29

"Ain't she cute?" Red Sam's wife said, leaning over the counter. "Would you like to come be my little girl?" 30

"No I certainly wouldn't," June Star said. "I wouldn't live in a broken-down place like this for a million bucks!" and she ran back to the table. 31

"Ain't she cute?" the woman repeated, stretching her mouth politely. 32

"Aren't you ashamed?" hissed the grandmother. 33

Red Sam came in and told his wife to quit lounging on the counter and hurry up with these people's order. His khaki trousers reached just to his hip bones and his stomach hung over them like a sack of meal swaying under his shirt. He came over and sat down at a table nearby and let out a combination sigh and yodel. "You can't win," he said. "You can't win," and he wiped his sweating red face off with a gray handkerchief. 34

"These days you don't know who to trust," he said. "Ain't that the truth?"

35 "People are certainly not nice like they used to be," said the grandmother.

36 "Two fellers come in here last week," Red Sammy said, "driving a Chrysler. It was a old beat-up car but it was a good one and these boys looked all right to me. Said they worked at the mill and you know I let them fellers charge the gas they bought? Now why did I do that?"

37 "Because you're a good man!" the grandmother said at once.

38 "Yes'm, I suppose so," Red Sam said as if he were stuck with this answer.

39 His wife brought the orders, carrying the five plates all at once without a tray, two in each hand and one balanced on her arm. "It isn't a soul in this green world of God's that you can trust," she said. "And I don't count nobody out of that, not nobody," she repeated, looking at Red Sammy.

The old lady said that in her opinion Europe was entirely to blame for the way things were now.

40 "Did you read about that criminal, The Misfit, that's escaped?" asked the grandmother.

41 "I wouldn't be a bit surprised if he didn't attact this place right here," said the woman. "If he hears about it being here, I wouldn't be none surprised to see him. If he hears it's two cent in the cash register, I wouldn't be a tall surprised if he . . ."

42 "That'll do," Red Sam said. "Go bring these people their Co'-Colas," and the woman went off to get the rest of the order.

43 "A good man is hard to find," Red Sammy said. "Everything is getting terrible. I remember the day you could go off and leave your screen door unlatched. Not no more."

44 He and the grandmother discussed better times. The old lady said that in her opinion Europe was entirely to blame for the way things were now. She said the way Europe acted you would think we were made of money and Red Sam said it was no use talking about it, she was exactly right. The children ran outside into the white sunlight and looked at the monkey in the lacy chinaberry tree. He was busy catching fleas on himself and biting each one carefully between his teeth as if it were a delicacy.

45 They drove off again into the hot afternoon. The grandmother took cat naps and woke up every few minutes with her own snoring. Outside of Toombsboro she woke up and recalled an old plantation that she had visited in this neighborhood once when she was a young lady. She said the house had six white columns across the front and that there was an avenue of oaks leading up to it and two little wooden trellis arbors on either side in front where you sat down with your suitor after a stroll in the garden. She recalled exactly which road to turn off to get to it. She knew that Bailey would not be willing to lose any time looking at an old house, but the more she talked about it, the more she wanted to see it once again and find out if the little twin arbors were still standing. "There was a secret panel in this house," she said craftily, not telling the truth but wishing that she were, "and the story went that all the family silver was hidden in it when Sherman came through but it was never found . . ."

"Hey!" John Wesley said. "Let's go see it! We'll find it! We'll poke all the woodwork and find it! Who lives there? Where do you turn off at? Hey Pop, can't we turn off there?" 46

"We never have seen a house with a secret panel!" June Star shrieked. "Let's go to the house with the secret panel! Hey Pop, can't we go see the house with the secret panel!" 47

"It's not far from here, I know," the grandmother said. "It wouldn't take over twenty minutes." 48

Bailey was looking straight ahead. His jaw was as rigid as a horseshoe. "No," he said. 49

The children began to yell and scream that they wanted to see the house with the secret panel. John Wesley kicked the back of the front seat and June Star hung over her mother's shoulder and whined desperately into her ear that they never had any fun even on their vacation, that they could never do what THEY wanted to do. The baby began to scream and John Wesley kicked the back of the seat so hard that his father could feel the blows in his kidney. 50

"All right!" he shouted and drew the car to a stop at the side of the road. "Will you all shut up? Will you all just shut up for one second? If you don't shut up, we won't go anywhere." 51

"It would be very educational for them," the grandmother murmured. 52

"All right," Bailey said, "but get this: this is the only time we're going to stop for anything like this. This is the one and only time." 53

"The dirt road that you have to turn down is about a mile back," the grandmother directed. "I marked it when we passed." 54

"A dirt road," Bailey groaned. 55

After they had turned around and were headed toward the dirt road, the grandmother recalled other 56 points about the house, the beautiful glass over the front doorway and the candle-lamp in the hall. John Wesley said that the secret panel was probably in the fireplace.

7 "You can't go inside this house," Bailey said. "You don't know who lives there."

8 "While you all talk to the people in front, I'll run around behind and get in a window," John Wesley suggested.

9 "We'll all stay in the car," his mother said.

0 They turned onto the dirt road and the car raced roughly along in a swirl of pink dust. The grandmother recalled the times when there were no paved roads and thirty miles was a day's journey. The dirt road was hilly and there were sudden washes in it and sharp curves on dangerous embankments. All at once they would be on a hill, looking down over the blue tops of trees for miles around, then the next minute, they would be in a red depression with the dust-coated trees looking down on them.

1 "This place had better turn up in a minute," Bailey said, "or I'm going to turn around."

2 The road looked as if no one had traveled on it in months.

3 "It's not much farther," the grandmother said and just as she said it, a horrible thought came to her. The thought was so embarrassing that she turned red in the face and her eyes dilated and her feet jumped up, upsetting her valise in the corner. The instant the valise moved, the newspaper top she had over the basket under it rose with a snarl and Pitty Sing, the cat, sprang onto Bailey's shoulder.

4 The children were thrown to the floor and their mother, clutching the baby, was thrown out the door onto the ground; the old lady was thrown into the front seat. The car turned over once and landed right-side-up in a gulch off the side of the road. Bailey remained in the driver's seat with the cat—gray-striped with a broad white face and an orange nose—clinging to his neck like a caterpillar.

5 As soon as the children saw they could move their arms and legs, they scrambled out of the car, shouting, "We've had an ACCIDENT!" The grandmother was curled up under the dashboard, hoping she was injured so that Bailey's wrath would not come down on her all at once. The horrible thought she had had before the accident was that the house she had remembered so vividly was not in Georgia but in Tennessee.

6 Bailey removed the cat from his neck with both hands and flung it out the window against the side of a pine tree. Then he got out of the car and started looking for the children's mother. She was sitting against the side of the red gutted ditch, holding the screaming baby, but she only had a cut down her face and a broken shoulder. "We've had an ACCIDENT!" the children screamed in a frenzy of delight.

67 "But nobody's killed," June Star said with disappointment as the grandmother limped out of the car, her hat still pinned to her head but the broken front brim standing up at a jaunty angle and the violet spray hanging off the side. They all sat down in the ditch, except the children, to recover from the shock. They were all shaking.

68 "Maybe a car will come along," said the children's mother hoarsely.

69 "I believe I have injured an organ," said the grandmother, pressing her side, but no one answered her. Bailey's teeth were clattering. He had on a yellow sport shirt with bright blue parrots designed in it and his face was as yellow as the shirt. The grandmother decided that she would not mention that the house was in Tennessee.

70 The road was about ten feet above and they could see only the tops of the trees on the other side of it. Behind the ditch they were sitting in there were more woods, tall and dark and deep. In a few minutes they saw a car some distance away on top of a hill, coming slowly as if the occupants were watching them. The grandmother stood up and waved both arms dramatically to attract their attention. The car continued to come on slowly, disappeared around a bend and appeared again, moving even slower, on top of the hill they had gone over. It was a big black battered hearse-like automobile. There were three men in it.

71 It came to a stop just over them and for some minutes, the driver looked down with a steady expressionless gaze to where they were sitting, and didn't speak. Then he turned his head and muttered something to the other two and they got out. One was a fat boy in black trousers and a red sweat shirt with a silver stallion embossed on the front of it. He moved around on the right side of them and stood staring, his mouth

partly open in a kind of loose grin. The other had on khaki pants and a blue striped coat and a gray hat pulled down very low, hiding most of his face. He came around slowly on the left side. Neither spoke.

72 The driver got out of the car and stood by the side of it, looking down at them. He was an older man than the other two. His hair was just beginning to gray and he wore silver-rimmed spectacles that gave him a scholarly look. He had a long creased face and didn't have on any shirt or undershirt. He had on blue jeans that were too tight for him and was holding a black hat and a gun. The two boys also had guns.

73 "We've had an ACCIDENT!" the children screamed.

74 The grandmother had the peculiar feeling that the bespectacled man was someone she knew. His face was as familiar to her as if she had known him all her life but she could not recall who he was. He moved away from the car and began to come down the embankment, placing his feet carefully so that he wouldn't slip. He had on tan and white shoes and no socks, and his ankles were red and thin. "Good afternoon," he said. "I see you all had you a little spill."

75 "We turned over twice!" said the grandmother.

76 "Oncet," he corrected. "We seen it happen. Try their car and see will it run, Hiram," he said quietly to the boy with the gray hat.

77 "What you got that gun for?" John Wesley asked. "Whatcha gonna do with that gun?"

78 "Lady," the man said to the children's mother, "would you mind calling them children to sit down by you? Children make me nervous. I want all you to sit down right together there where you're at."

79 "What are you telling US what to do for?" June Star asked.

80 Behind them the line of woods gaped like a dark open mouth. "Come here," said their mother.

Behind them the line of woods gaped like a dark open mouth.

81 "Look here now," Bailey began suddenly, "we're in a predicament! We're in . . ."

82 The grandmother shrieked. She scrambled to her feet and stood staring. "You're The Misfit!" she said. "I recognized you at once!"

83 "Yes'm," the man said, smiling slightly as if he were pleased in spite of himself to be known, "but it would have been better for all of you, lady, if you hadn't of reckernized me."

84 Bailey turned his head sharply and said something to his mother that shocked even the children. The old lady began to cry and The Misfit reddened.

"Lady," he said, "don't you get upset. Sometimes a man says things he don't mean. I don't reckon he meant to talk to you thataway."

"You wouldn't shoot a lady, would you?" the grandmother said and removed a clean handkerchief from her cuff and began to slap at her eyes with it.

The Misfit pointed the toe of his shoe into the ground and made a little hole and then covered it up again. "I would hate to have to," he said.

"Listen," the grandmother almost screamed, "I know you're a good man. You don't look a bit like you have common blood. I know you must come from nice people!"

"Yes mam," he said, "finest people in the world." When he smiled he showed a row of strong white teeth. "God never made a finer woman than my mother and my daddy's heart was pure gold," he said. The boy with the red sweat shirt had come around behind them and was standing with his gun at his hip. The Misfit squatted down on the ground. "Watch them children, Bobby Lee," he said. "You know they make me nervous." He looked at the six of them huddled together in front of him and he seemed to be embarrassed as if he couldn't think of anything to say. "Ain't a cloud in the sky," he remarked, looking up at it. "Don't see no sun but don't see no cloud neither."

"Yes, it's a beautiful day," said the grandmother. "Listen," she said, "you shouldn't call yourself The Misfit because I know you're a good man at heart. I can just look at you and tell."

"Hush!" Bailey yelled. "Hush! Everybody shut up and let me handle this!" He was squatting in the position of a runner about to sprint forward but he didn't move.

"I pre-chate that, lady," The Misfit said and drew a little circle in the ground with the butt of his gun.

"It'll take a half a hour to fix this here car," Hiram called, looking over the raised hood of it.

"Well, first you and Bobby Lee get him and that little boy to step over yonder with you," The Misfit said, pointing to Bailey and John Wesley. "The boys want to ast you something," he said to Bailey. "Would you mind stepping back in them woods there with them?"

"Listen," Bailey began, "we're in a terrible predicament! Nobody realizes what this is," his voice cracked. His eyes were as blue and intense as the parrots in his shirt and he remained perfectly still.

The grandmother reached up to adjust her hat brim as if she were going to the woods with him but it came

off in her hand. She stood staring at it and after a second she let it fall on the ground. Hiram pulled Bailey up by the arm as if he were assisting an old man. John Wesley caught hold of his father's hand and Bobby Lee followed. They went off toward the woods and just as they reached the dark edge, Bailey turned and supporting himself against a gray naked pine trunk, he shouted, "I'll be back in a minute, Mamma, wait on me!"

"Come back this instant!" his mother shrilled but they all disappeared into the woods.

"Bailey Boy!" the grandmother called in a tragic voice but she found she was looking at The Misfit squatting on the ground in front of her. "I just know you're a good man," she said desperately. "You're not a bit common!"

"Nome, I ain't a good man," The Misfit said after a second as if he had considered her statement carefully, "but I ain't the worst in the world neither. My daddy said I was a different breed of dog from my brothers and sisters. 'You know,' Daddy said, 'it's some that can live their whole life out without asking about it and it's others has to know why it is, and this boy is one of the latters. He's going to be into everything!'" He put on his black hat and looked up suddenly and then away deep into the woods as if he were embarrassed again. "I'm sorry I don't have on a shirt before you ladies," he said, hunching his shoulders slightly. "We buried our clothes that we had on when we escaped and we're just making do until we can get better. We borrowed these from some folks we met," he explained.

"That's perfectly all right," the grandmother said. "Maybe Bailey has an extra shirt in his suitcase."

"I'll look and see terrectly," The Misfit said.

"Where are they taking him?" the children's mother screamed.

"Daddy was a card himself," The Misfit said. "You 103
couldn't put anything over on him. He never got in trouble with the Authorities though. Just had the knack of handling them."

"You could be honest too if you'd only try," said the 104
grandmother. "Think how wonderful it would be to settle down and live a comfortable life and not have to think about somebody chasing you all the time."

The Misfit kept scratching in the ground with the 105
butt of his gun as if he were thinking about it. "Yes'm, somebody is always after you," he murmured.

The grandmother noticed how thin his shoulder 106
blades were just behind his hat because she was standing up looking down on him. "Do you ever pray?" she asked.

He shook his head. All she saw was the black hat 107
wiggle between his shoulder blades. "Nome," he said.

There was a pistol shot from the woods, followed 108
closely by another. Then silence. The old lady's head jerked around. She could hear the wind move through the tree tops like a long satisfied insuck of breath. "Bailey Boy!" she called.

"I was a gospel singer for a while," The Misfit said. 109
"I been most everything. Been in the arm service, both land and sea, at home and abroad, been twice married, been an undertaker, been with the railroads, plowed Mother Earth, been in a tornado, seen a man burnt alive oncet," and looked up at the children's mother and the little girl who were sitting close together, their faces white and their eyes glassy; "I even seen a woman flogged," he said.

"Pray, pray," the grandmother began, "pray, 110
pray . . ."

"I never was a bad boy that I remember of," The 111
Misfit said in an almost dreamy voice, "but somewheres along the line I done something wrong and got sent to the penitentiary. I was buried alive," and he looked up and held her attention to him by a steady stare.

""That's when you should have started to pray," 112
she said. "What did you do to get sent to the penitentiary that first time?"

"Turn to the right, it was a wall," The Misfit said, 113
looking up again at the cloudless sky. "Turn to the left, it was a wall. Look up it was a ceiling, look down it was a floor. I forget what I done, lady. I set there and set there, trying to remember what it was I done and I ain't recalled it to this day. Oncet in a while, I would think it was coming to me, but it never come."

"Maybe they put you in by mistake," the old lady 114
said vaguely.

"Nome," he said. "It wasn't no mistake. They had 115
the papers on me."

116 "You must have stolen something," she said.

117 The Misfit sneered slightly. "Nobody had nothing I wanted," he said. "It was a head-doctor at the penitentiary said what I had done was kill my daddy but I know that for a lie. My daddy died in nineteen ought nineteen of the epidemic flu and I never had a thing to do with it. He was buried in the Mount Hopewell Baptist churchyard and you can go there and see for yourself."

118 "If you would pray," the old lady said, "Jesus would help you."

119 "That's right," The Misfit said.

120 "Well then, why don't you pray?" she asked trembling with delight suddenly.

121 "I don't want no hep," he said. "I'm doing all right by myself."

122 Bobby Lee and Hiram came ambling back from the woods. Bobby Lee was dragging a yellow shirt with bright blue parrots in it.

123 "Throw me that shirt, Bobby Lee," The Misfit said. The shirt came flying at him and landed on his shoulder and he put it on. The grandmother couldn't name what the shirt reminded her of. "No, lady," The Misfit said while he was buttoning it up, "I found out the crime don't matter. You can do one thing or you can do another, kill a man or take a tire off his car, because sooner or later you're going to forget what it was you done and just be punished for it."

124 The children's mother had begun to make heaving noises as if she couldn't get her breath. "Lady," he asked, "would you and that little girl like to step off yonder with Bobby Lee and Hiram and join your husband?"

125 "Yes, thank you," the mother said faintly. Her left arm dangled helplessly and she was holding the baby, who had gone to sleep, in the other. "Hep that lady up, Hiram," The Misfit said as she struggled to climb out of the ditch, "and Bobby Lee, you hold onto that little girl's hand."

126 "I don't want to hold hands with him," June Star said. "He reminds me of a pig."

127 The fat boy blushed and laughed and caught her by the arm and pulled her off into the woods after Hiram and her mother.

128 Alone with The Misfit, the grandmother found that she had lost her voice. There was not a cloud in the sky nor any sun. There was nothing around her but woods. She wanted to tell him that he must pray. She opened and closed her mouth several times before anything came out. Finally she found herself saying, "Jesus, Jesus," meaning, Jesus will help you, but the way she was saying it, it sounded as if she might be cursing.

"Yes'm," The Misfit said as if he agreed. "Jesus thrown everything off balance. It was the same case with Him as with me except He hadn't committed any crime and they could prove I had committed one because they had the papers on me. Of course," he said, "they never shown me my papers. That's why I sign myself now. I said long ago, you get you a signature and sign everything you do and keep a copy of it. Then you'll know what you done and you can hold up the crime to the punishment and see do they match and in the end you'll have something to prove you ain't been treated right. I call myself The Misfit," he said, "because I can't make what all I done wrong fit what all I gone through in punishment."

There was a piercing scream from the woods, followed closely by a pistol report.

There was a piercing scream from the woods, followed closely by a pistol report. "Does it seem right to you, lady, that one is punished a heap and another ain't punished at all?"

"Jesus!" the old lady cried. "You've got good blood! I know you wouldn't shoot a lady! I know you come from nice people! Pray! Jesus, you ought not to shoot a lady. I'll give you all the money I've got!"

"Lady," The Misfit said, looking beyond her far into the woods, "there never was a body that give the undertaker a tip."

There were two more pistol reports and the grandmother raised her head like a parched old turkey hen crying for water and called, "Bailey Boy, Bailey Boy!" as if her heart would break.

"Jesus was the only One that ever raised the dead." The Misfit continued, "and He shouldn't have done it. He thrown everything off balance. If He did what He said, then it's nothing for you to do but throw away everything and follow Him, and if He didn't, then it's nothing for you to do but enjoy the few minutes you got left the best way you can—by killing somebody or burning down his house or doing some other meanness to him. No pleasure but meanness," he said and his voice had become almost a snarl.

"Maybe He didn't raise the dead," the old lady mumbled, not knowing what she was saying and feeling so dizzy that she sank down in the ditch with her legs twisted under her.

"I wasn't there so I can't say He didn't," The Misfit said. "I wisht I had of been there," he said, hitting the ground with his fist. "It ain't right I wasn't there because if I had of been there I would of known. Listen lady," he said in a high voice, "if I had of been there I would of known and I wouldn't be like I am now." His voice seemed about to crack and the grandmother's head cleared for an instant. She saw the man's face twisted close to her own as if he were going to cry and she murmured, "Why you're one of my babies. You're one of my own children!" She reached out and touched him on the shoulder. The Misfit sprang back as if a snake had bitten him and shot her three times through the chest. Then he put his gun down on the ground and took off his glasses and began to clean them.

37 Hiram and Bobby Lee returned from the woods and stood over the ditch, looking down at the grandmother who half sat and half lay in a puddle of blood with her legs crossed under her like a child's and her face smiling up at the cloudless sky.

138 Without his glasses, The Misfit's eyes were red-rimmed and pale and defenseless looking. "Take her off and throw her where you thrown the others," he said, picking up the cat that was rubbing itself against his leg.

139 "She was a talker, wasn't she?" Bobby Lee said, sliding down the ditch with a yodel.

140 "She would have been a good woman," The Misfit said, "if it had been somebody there to shoot her every minute of her life."

141 "Some fun!" Bobby Lee said.

142 "Shut up, Bobby Lee," The Misfit said. "It's no real pleasure in life."

# Questions for Critical Thinking

1 What is the grandmother's attitude toward the South as opposed to the rest of her family's attitude, particularly her grandson's? How do you account for the difference?

2 "It is the grandmother's 'Southern Pride' that leads to the family's downfall." In a short essay, explain whether you agree or disagree with this statement. Support your answer with examples from the text.

3 Review the story and mark the margins whenever you find an example of humor. How would you describe O'Connor's humor? What role does humor play in the story?

4 How much of a role does irony play in the story? How should we take The Misfit's final statement about the grandmother?

# Revelation (1965)

1 THE doctor's waiting room, which was very small, was almost full when the Turpins entered and Mrs. Turpin, who was very large, made it look even smaller by her presence. She stood looming at the head of the magazine table set in the center of it, a living demonstration that the room was inadequate and ridiculous. Her little bright black eyes took in all the patients as she sized up the seating situation. There was one vacant chair and a place on a sofa occupied by a blond child in a dirty blue romper who should have been told to move over and make room for the lady. He was five or six, but Mrs. Turpin saw at once that no one was going to tell him to move over. He was slumped down in the seat, his arms idle at his sides and his eyes idle in his head; his nose ran unchecked.

2 Mrs. Turpin put a firm hand on Claud's shoulder and said in a voice that included anyone who wanted

to listen, "Claud, you sit in that chair there," and gave him a push down into the vacant one. Claud was florid and bald and sturdy, somewhat shorter than Mrs. Turpin, but he sat down as if he were accustomed to doing what she told him to.

3 Mrs. Turpin remained standing. The only man in the room besides Claud was a lean stringy old fellow with a rusty hand spread out on each knee, whose eyes were closed as if he were asleep or dead or pretending to be so as not to get up and offer her his seat. Her gaze settled agreeably on a well-dressed grey-haired lady whose eyes met hers and whose expression said: if that child belonged to me, he would have some manners and move over—there's plenty of room there for you and him too.

4 Claud looked up with a sigh and made as if to rise.

5 "Sit down," Mrs. Turpin said. "You know you're not supposed to stand on that leg. He has an ulcer on his leg," she explained.

6 Claud lifted his foot onto the magazine table and rolled his trouser leg up to reveal a purple swelling on a plump marble-white calf.

7 "My!" the pleasant lady said. "How did you do that?"

8 "A cow kicked him," Mrs. Turpin said.

9 "Goodness!" said the lady.

10 Claud rolled his trouser leg down.

11 "Maybe the little boy would move over," the lady suggested, but the child did not stir.

12 "Somebody will be leaving in a minute," Mrs. Turpin said. She could not understand why a doctor—with as much money as they made charging five dollars a day to just stick their head in the hospital door and look at you—couldn't afford a decent-sized waiting room. This one was hardly bigger than a garage. The table was cluttered with limp-looking magazines and at one end of it there was a big green glass ash tray full of cigaret butts and cotton wads with little blood spots on them. If she had had anything to do with the running of the place, that would have been emptied every so often. There were no chairs against the wall at the head of the room. It had a rectangular-shaped panel in it that permitted a view of the office where the nurse came and went and the secretary listened to the radio. A plastic fern in a gold pot sat in the opening and trailed its fronds down almost to the floor. The radio was softly playing gospel music.

13 Just then the inner door opened and a nurse with the highest stack of yellow hair Mrs. Turpin had ever seen put her face in the crack and called for the next patient. The woman sitting beside Claud grasped the two arms of her chair and hoisted herself up; she pulled her dress free from her legs and lumbered through the door where the nurse had disappeared.

Mrs. Turpin eased into the vacant chair, which 14
held her tight as a corset. "I wish I could reduce," she said, and rolled her eyes and gave a comic sigh.

"Oh, *you* aren't fat," the stylish lady said. 15

"Ooooo I am too," Mrs. Turpin said. "Claud he eats 16
all he wants to and never weighs over one hundred and seventy-five pounds, but me I just look at something good to eat and I gain some weight," and her stomach and shoulders shook with laughter. "You can eat all you want to, can't you, Claud?" she asked, turning to him.

Claud only grinned. 17

"Well, as long as you have such a good disposi- 18
tion," the stylish lady said, "I don't think it makes a bit of difference what size you are. You just can't beat a good disposition."

Next to her was a fat girl of eighteen or nineteen, 19
scowling into a thick blue book which Mrs. Turpin saw was entitled *Human Development*. The girl raised her head and directed her scowl at Mrs. Turpin as if she did not like her looks. She appeared annoyed that anyone should speak while she tried to read. The poor girl's face was blue with acne and Mrs. Turpin thought how pitiful it was to have a face like that at that age. She gave the girl a friendly smile but the girl only scowled the harder. Mrs. Turpin herself was fat but she had always had good skin, and, though she was forty-seven years old, there was not a wrinkle in her face except around her eyes from laughing too much.

Next to the ugly girl was the child, still in exactly 20
the same position, and next to him was a thin leathery old woman in a cotton print dress. She and Claud had three sacks of chicken feed in their pump house that was in the same print. She had seen from the first that the child belonged with the old woman. She could tell by the way they sat—kind of vacant and white-trashy, as if they would sit there until Doomsday if nobody called and told them to get up. And at right angles but next to the well-dressed pleasant lady was a lank-faced woman who was certainly the child's mother. She had on a yellow sweat shirt and wine-colored slacks, both gritty-looking, and the rims of her lips were stained with snuff. Her dirty yellow hair was tied behind with a little piece of red paper ribbon. Worse than niggers any day, Mrs. Turpin thought.

The gospel hymn playing was, "When I looked up 21
and He looked down," and Mrs. Turpin, who knew it, supplied the last line mentally, "And wona these days I know I'll we-eara crown."

Without appearing to, Mrs. Turpin always no- 22
ticed people's feet. The well-dressed lady had on red and grey suede shoes to match her dress. Mrs. Turpin had on her good black patent leather pumps. The ugly

girl had on Girl Scout shoes and heavy socks. The old woman had on tennis shoes and the white-trashy mother had on what appeared to be bedroom slippers, black straw with gold braid threaded through them—exactly what you would have expected her to have on.

23 Sometimes at night when she couldn't go to sleep, Mrs. Turpin would occupy herself with the question of who she would have chosen to be if she couldn't have been herself. If Jesus had said to her before he made her, "There's only two places available for you. You can either be a nigger or white-trash," what would she have said? "Please, Jesus, please," she would have said, "just let me wait until there's another place available," and he would have said, "No, you have to go right now and I have only those two places so make up your mind." She would have wiggled and squirmed and begged and pleaded but it would have been no use and finally she would have said, "All right, make me a nigger then—but that don't mean a trashy one." And he would have made her a neat clean respectable Negro woman, herself but black.

Sometimes Mrs. Turpin occupied herself at night naming the classes of people.

24 Next to the child's mother was a red-headed youngish woman, reading one of the magazines and working a piece of chewing gum, hell for leather, as Claud would say. Mrs. Turpin could not see the woman's feet. She was not white-trash, just common. Sometimes Mrs. Turpin occupied herself at night naming the classes of people. On the bottom of the heap were most colored people, not the kind she would have been if she had been one, but most of them; then next to them—not above, just away from—were the white-trash; then above them were the home-owners, and above them the home-and-land owners, to which she and Claud belonged. Above she and Claud were people with a lot of money and much bigger houses and much more land. But here the complexity of it would begin to bear in on her, for some of the people with a lot of money were common and ought to be below she and Claud and some of the people who had good blood had lost their money and had to rent and then there were colored people who owned their homes and land as well. There was a colored dentist in town who had two red Lincolns and a swimming pool and a farm with registered white-face cattle on it. Usually by the time she had fallen asleep all the classes of people were moiling and roiling around in her head, and she would dream they were all crammed in together in a box car, being ridden off to be put in a gas oven.

25 "That's a beautiful clock," she said and nodded to her right. It was a big wall clock, the face encased in a brass sunburst.

26 "Yes, it's very pretty," the stylish lady said agreeably. "And right on the dot too," she added, glancing at her watch.

27 The ugly girl beside her cast an eye upward at the clock, smirked, then looked directly at Mrs. Turpin and smirked again. Then she returned her eyes to her book. She was obviously the lady's daughter because, although they didn't look anything alike as to disposition, they both had the same shape of face and the same blue eyes. On the lady they sparkled pleasantly but in the girl's seared face they appeared alternately to smolder and to blaze.

28 What if Jesus had said, "All right, you can be white-trash or a nigger or ugly"!

29 Mrs. Turpin felt an awful pity for the girl, though she thought it was one thing to be ugly and another to act ugly.

30 The woman with the snuff-stained lips turned around in her chair and looked up at the clock. Then she turned back and appeared to look a little to the side of Mrs. Turpin. There was a cast in one of her eyes. "You want to know wher you can get you one of them ther clocks?" she asked in a loud voice.

31 "No, I already have a nice clock," Mrs. Turpin said. Once somebody like her got a leg in the conversation, she would be all over it.

32 "You can get you one with green stamps," the woman said. "That's most likely wher he got hisn. Save you up enough, you can get you most anythang. I got me some joo'ry."

33 Ought to have got you a wash rag and some soap, Mrs. Turpin thought.

34 "I get contour sheets with mine," the pleasant lady said.

35 The daughter slammed her book shut. She looked straight in front of her, directly through Mrs. Turpin and on through the yellow curtain and the plate glass window which made the wall behind her. The girl's eyes seemed lit all of a sudden with a peculiar light, an unnatural light like night road signs give. Mrs. Turpin turned her head to see if there was anything going on outside that she should see, but she could not see anything. Figures passing cast only a pale shadow through the curtain. There was no reason the girl should single her out for her ugly looks.

36 "Miss Finley," the nurse said, cracking the door. The gum-chewing woman got up and passed in front

of her and Claud and went into the office. She had on red high-heeled shoes.

37 Directly across the table, the ugly girl's eyes were fixed on Mrs. Turpin as if she had some very special reason for disliking her.

38 "This is wonderful weather, isn't it?" the girl's mother said.

39 "It's good weather for cotton if you can get the niggers to pick it," Mrs. Turpin said, "but niggers don't want to pick cotton any more. You can't get the white folks to pick it and now you can't get the niggers—because they got to be right up there with the white folks."

40 "They gonna *try* anyways," the white-trash woman said, leaning forward.

41 "Do you have one of those cotton-picking machines?" the pleasant lady asked.

42 "No," Mrs. Turpin said, "they leave half the cotton in the field. We don't have much cotton anyway. If you want to make it farming now, you have to have a little of everything. We got a couple of acres of cotton and a few hogs and chickens and just enough white-face that Claud can look after them himself."

43 "One thang I don't want," the white-trash woman said, wiping her mouth with the back of her hands. "Hogs. Nasty stinking things, a-gruntin and a-rootin all over the place."

44 Mrs. Turpin gave her the merest edge of her attention. "Our hogs are not dirty and they don't stink," she said. "They're cleaner than some children I've seen. Their feet never touch the ground. We have a pig-parlor—that's where you raise them on concrete," she explained to the pleasant lady, "and Claud scoots them down with the hose every afternoon and washes off the floor." Cleaner by far than that child right there, she thought. Poor nasty little thing. He had not moved except to put the thumb of his dirty hand into his mouth.

45 The woman turned her face away from Mrs. Turpin. "I know I wouldn't scoot down no hog with no hose," she said to the wall.

46 You wouldn't have no hog to scoot down, Mrs. Turpin said to herself.

47 "A-gruntin and a-rootin and a-groanin," the woman muttered.

48 "We got a little of everything," Mrs. Turpin said to the pleasant lady. "It's no use in having more than you can handle yourself with help like it is. We found enough niggers to pick our cotton this year but Claud he has to go after them and take them home again in the evening. They can't walk that half a mile. No they can't. I tell you," she said and laughed merrily. "I sure am tired of buttering up niggers, but you got to love em if you want em to work for you. When they come in the morning, I run out and I say, 'Hi yawl this morning?' and when Claud drives them off to the field I just wave to beat the band and they just wave back." And she waved her hand rapidly to illustrate.

49 "Like you read out of the same book," the lady said, showing she understood perfectly.

50 "Child, yes," Mrs. Turpin said. "And when they come in from the field, I run out with a bucket of icewater. That's the way it's going to be from now on," she said. "You may as well face it."

51 "One thang I know," the white-trash woman said. "Two thangs I ain't going to do: love no niggers or scoot down no hog with no hose." And she let out a bark of contempt.

52 The look that Mrs. Turpin and the pleasant lady exchanged indicated they both understood that you had to *have* certain things before you could *know* certain things. But every time Mrs. Turpin exchanged a look with the lady, she was aware that the ugly girl's peculiar eyes were still on her, and she had trouble bringing her attention back to the conversation.

. . . they both understood that you had to *have* certain things before you could *know* certain things.

53 "When you got something," she said, "you got to look after it." And when you ain't got a thing but breath and britches, she added to herself, you can afford to come to town every morning and just sit on the Court House coping and spit.

54 A grotesque revolving shadow passed across the curtain behind her and was thrown palely on the opposite wall. Then a bicycle clattered down against the outside of the building. The door opened and a colored boy glided in with a tray from the drug store. It had two large red and white paper cups on it with tops on them. He was a tall, very black boy in discolored white pants and a green nylon shirt. He was chewing gum slowly, as if to music. He set the tray down in the office opening next to the fern and stuck his head through to look for the secretary. She was not in there. He rested his arms on the ledge and waited, his narrow bottom stuck out, swaying slowly to the left and right. He raised a hand over his head and scratched the base of his skull.

55 "You see that button there, boy?" Mrs. Turpin said. "You can punch that and she'll come. She's probably in the back somewhere."

56 "Is thas right?" the boy said agreeably, as if he had never seen the button before. He leaned to the right

and put his finger on it. "She sometime out," he said and twisted around to face his audience, his elbows behind him on the counter. The nurse appeared and he twisted back again. She handed him a dollar and he rooted in his pocket and made the change and counted it out to her. She gave him fifteen cents for a tip and he went out with the empty tray. The heavy door swung to slowly and closed at length with the sound of suction. For a moment no one spoke.

7 "They ought to send all them niggers back to Africa," the white-trash woman said. "That's wher they come from in the first place."

8 "Oh, I couldn't do without my good colored friends," the pleasant lady said.

9 "There's a heap of things worse than a nigger," Mrs. Turpin agreed. "It's all kinds of them just like it's all kinds of us."

0 "Yes, and it takes all kinds to make the world go round," the lady said in her musical voice.

1 As she said it, the raw-complexioned girl snapped her teeth together. Her lower lip turned downwards and inside out, revealing the pale pink inside of her mouth. After a second it rolled back up. It was the ugliest face Mrs. Turpin had ever seen anyone make and for a moment she was certain that the girl had made it at her. She was looking at her as if she had known and disliked her all her life—all of Mrs. Turpin's life, it seemed too, not just all the girl's life. Why, girl, I don't even know you, Mrs. Turpin said silently.

2 She forced her attention back to the discussion. "It wouldn't be practical to send them back to Africa," she said. "They wouldn't want to go. They got it too good here."

3 "Wouldn't be what they wanted—if I had anything to do with it," the woman said.

4 "It wouldn't be a way in the world you could get all the niggers back over there," Mrs. Turpin said. "They'd be hiding out and lying down and turning sick on you and wailing and hollering and raring and pitching. It wouldn't be a way in the world to get them over there."

5 "They got over here," the trashy woman said. "Get back like they got over."

6 "It wasn't so many of them then," Mrs. Turpin explained.

7 The woman looked at Mrs. Turpin as if here was an idiot indeed but Mrs. Turpin was not bothered by the look, considering where it came from.

8 "Nooo," she said, "they're going to stay here where they can go to New York and marry white folks and improve their color. That's what they all want to do, every one of them, improve their color."

"You know what comes of that, don't you?" Claud asked. 69

"No, Claud, what?" Mrs. Turpin said. 70

Claud's eyes twinkled. "White-faced niggers," he said with never a smile. 71

Everybody in the office laughed except the white-trash and the ugly girl. The girl gripped the book in her lap with white fingers. The trashy woman looked around her from face to face as if she thought they were all idiots. The old woman in the feed sack dress continued to gaze expressionless across the floor at the hightop shoes of the man opposite her, the one who had been pretending to be asleep when the Turpins came in. He was laughing heartily, his hands still spread out on his knees. The child had fallen to the side and was lying now almost face down in the old woman's lap. 72

While they recovered from their laughter, the nasal chorus on the radio kept the room from silence. 73

*"You go to blank blank*
*And I'll go to mine*
*But we'll all blank along*
*To-geth-ther,*
*And all along the blank*
*We'll hep each other out*
*Smile-ling in any kind of*
*Weath-ther!"*

Mrs. Turpin didn't catch every word but she caught enough to agree with the spirit of the song and it turned her thoughts sober. To help anybody out that needed it was her philosophy of life. She never spared herself when she found somebody in need, whether they were white or black, trash or decent. And of all she had to be thankful for, she was most thankful that this was so. If Jesus had said, "You can be high society and have all the money you want and be thin and svelte-like, but you can't be a good woman with it," she would have had to say, "Well don't make me that then. Make me a good woman and it don't matter what else, how fat or how ugly or how poor!" Her heart rose. He had not made her a nigger or white-trash or ugly! He had made her herself and given her a little of everything. Jesus, thank you! she said. Thank you thank you thank you! Whenever she counted her blessings she felt as buoyant as if she weighed one hundred and twenty-five pounds instead of one hundred and eighty. 74

75 "What's wrong with your little boy?" the pleasant lady asked the white-trashy woman.

76 "He has a ulcer," the woman said proudly. "He ain't give me a minute's peace since he was born. Him and her are just alike," she said, nodding at the old woman, who was running her leathery fingers through the child's pale hair. "Look like I can't get nothing down them two but Co' Cola and candy."

77 That's all you try to get down em, Mrs. Turpin said to herself. Too lazy to light the fire. There was nothing you could tell her about people like them that she didn't know already. And it was not just that they didn't have anything. Because if you gave them everything, in two weeks it would all be broken or filthy or they would have chopped it up for lightwood. She knew all this from her own experience. Help them you must, but help them you couldn't.

There was nothing you could tell her about people like them that she didn't know already.

78 All at once the ugly girl turned her lips inside out again. Her eyes were fixed like two drills on Mrs. Turpin. This time there was no mistaking that there was something urgent behind them.

79 Girl, Mrs. Turpin exclaimed silently, I haven't done a thing to you! The girl might be confusing her with somebody else. There was no need to sit by and let herself be intimidated. "You must be in college," she said boldly, looking directly at the girl. "I see you reading a book there."

80 The girl continued to stare and pointedly did not answer.

81 Her mother blushed at this rudeness. "The lady asked you a question, Mary Grace," she said under her breath.

82 "I have ears," Mary Grace said.

83 The poor mother blushed again. "Mary Grace goes to Wellesley College," she explained. She twisted one of the buttons on her dress. "In Massachusetts," she added with a grimace. "And in the summer she just keeps right on studying. Just reads all the time, a real book worm, She's done real well at Wellesley; she's taking English and Math and History and Psychology and Social Studies," she rattled on, "and I think it's too much. I think she ought to get out and have fun."

84 The girl looked as if she would like to hurl them all through the plate glass window.

85 "Way up north," Mrs. Turpin murmured and thought, well, it hasn't done much for her manners.

86 "I'd almost rather to have him sick," the white-trash woman said, wrenching the attention back to herself. "He's so mean when he ain't. Look like some children just take natural to meanness. It's some gets bad when they get sick but he was the opposite. Took sick and turned good. He don't give me no trouble now. It's me waitin to see the doctor," she said.

87 If I was going to send anybody back to Africa, Mrs. Turpin thought, it would be your kind, woman. "Yes, indeed," she said aloud, but looking up at the ceiling, "it's a heap of things worse than a nigger." And dirtier than a hog, she added to herself.

88 "I think people with bad dispositions are more to be pitied than anyone on earth," the pleasant lady said in a voice that was decidedly thin.

89 "I thank the Lord he has blessed me with a good one," Mrs. Turpin said. "The day has never dawned that I couldn't find something to laugh at."

90 "Not since she married me anyways," Claud said with a comical straight face.

91 Everybody laughed except the girl and the white-trash.

92 Mrs. Turpin's stomach shook. "He's such a caution," she said, "that I can't help but laugh at him."

93 The girl made a loud ugly noise through her teeth.

94 Her mother's mouth grew thin and straight. "I think the worst thing in the world," she said, "is an ungrateful person. To have everything and not appreciate it. I know a girl," she said, "who has parents who would give her anything, a little brother who loves her dearly, who is getting a good education, who wears the best clothes, but who can never say a kind word to anyone, who never smiles, who just criticizes and complains all day long."

95 "Is she too old to paddle?" Claud asked.

96 The girl's face was almost purple.

97 "Yes," the lady said, "I'm afraid there's nothing to do but leave her to her folly. Some day she'll wake up and it'll be too late."

98 "It never hurt anyone to smile," Mrs. Turpin said. "It just makes you feel better all over."

99 "Of course," the lady said sadly, "but there are just some people you can't tell anything to. They can't take criticism."

100 "If it's one thing I am," Mrs. Turpin said with feeling, "it's grateful. When I think who all I could have been besides myself and what all I got, a little of everything, and a good disposition besides, I just feel like shouting, 'Thank you, Jesus, for making everything the way it is!' It could have been different!" For one thing, somebody else could have got Claud. At the thought of this, she was flooded with gratitude and a terrible pang of joy ran through her. "Oh thank you, Jesus, Jesus, thank you!" she cried aloud.

01 The book struck her directly over her left eye. It struck almost at the same instant that she realized the girl was about to hurl it. Before she could utter a sound, the raw face came crashing across the table toward her, howling. The girl's fingers sank like clamps into the soft flesh of her neck. She heard the mother cry out and Claud shout, "Whoa!" There was an instant when she was certain that she was about to be in an earthquake.

02 All at once her vision narrowed and she saw everything as if it were happening in a small room far away, or as if she were looking at it through the wrong end of a telescope. Claud's face crumpled and fell out of sight. The nurse ran in, then out, then in again. Then the gangling figure of the doctor rushed out of the inner door. Magazines flew this way and that as the table turned over. The girl fell with a thud and Mrs. Turpin's vision suddenly reversed itself and she saw everything large instead of small. The eyes of the white-trashy woman were staring hugely at the floor. There the girl, held down on one side by the nurse and on the other by her mother, was wrenching and turning in their grasp. The doctor was kneeling astride her, trying to hold her arm down. He managed after a second to sink a long needle into it.

03 Mrs. Turpin felt entirely hollow except for her heart which swung from side to side as if it were agitated in a great empty drum of flesh.

04 "Somebody that's not busy call for the ambulance," the doctor said in the offhand voice young doctors adopt for terrible occasions.

5 Mrs. Turpin could not have moved a finger. The old man who had been sitting next to her skipped nimbly into the office and made the call, for the secretary still seemed to be gone.

6 "Claud!" Mrs. Turpin called.

7 He was not in his chair. She knew she must jump up and find him but she felt like some one trying to catch a train in a dream, when everything moves in slow motion and the faster you try to run the slower you go.

8 "Here I am," a suffocated voice, very unlike Claud's, said.

9 He was doubled up in the corner on the floor, pale as paper, holding his leg. She wanted to get up and go to him but she could not move. Instead, her gaze was drawn slowly downward to the churning face on the floor, which she could see over the doctor's shoulder.

The girl's eyes stopped rolling and focused on her. 110
They seemed a much lighter blue than before, as if a door that had been tightly closed behind them was now open to admit light and air.

Mrs. Turpin's head cleared and her power of mo- 111
tion returned. She leaned forward until she was looking directly into the fierce brilliant eyes. There was no doubt in her mind that the girl did know her, knew her in some intense and personal way, beyond time and place and condition. "What you got to say to me?" she asked hoarsely and held her breath, waiting, as for a revelation.

The girl raised her head. Her gaze locked with 112
Mrs. Turpin's. "Go back to hell where you came from, you old wart hog," she whispered. Her voice was low but clear. Her eyes burned for a moment as if she saw with pleasure that her message had struck its target.

Mrs. Turpin sank back in her chair. 113

After a moment the girl's eyes closed and she 114
turned her head wearily to the side.

The doctor rose and handed the nurse the 115
empty syringe. He leaned over and put both hands for a moment on the mother's shoulders, which were shaking. She was sitting on the floor, her lips pressed together, holding Mary Grace's hand in her lap. The girl's fingers were gripped like a baby's around her thumb. "Go on to the hospital," he said. "I'll call and make the arrangements."

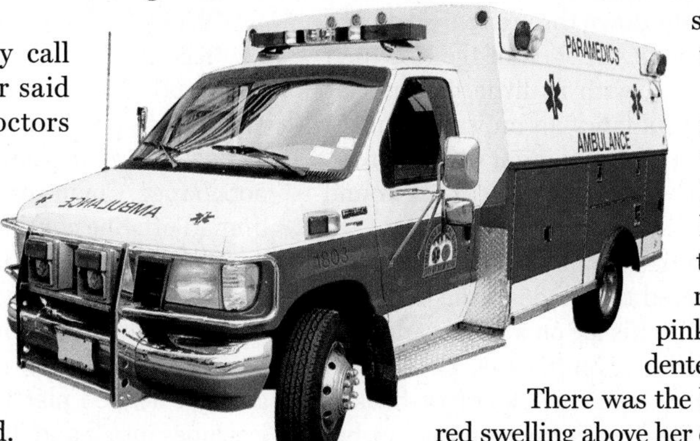


"Now let's see that 116
neck," he said in a jovial voice to Mrs. Turpin. He began to inspect her neck with his first two fingers. Two little moon-shaped lines like pink fish bones were indented over her windpipe. There was the beginning of an angry red swelling above her eye. His fingers passed over this also.

"Lea'me be," she said thickly and shook him off. 117
"See about Claud. She kicked him."

"I'll see about him in a minute," he said and felt her 118
pulse. He was a thin gray-haired man, given to pleasantries. "Go home and have yourself a vacation the rest of the day," he said and patted her on the shoulder.

Quit your pattin me, Mrs. Turpin growled to 119
herself.

"And put an ice pack over that eye," he said. Then 120
he went and squatted down beside Claud and looked at his leg. After a moment he pulled him up and Claud limped after him into the office.

121 Until the ambulance came, the only sounds in the room were the tremulous moans of the girl's mother, who continued to sit on the floor. The white-trash woman did not take her eyes off the girl. Mrs. Turpin looked straight ahead at nothing. Presently the ambulance drew up, a long dark shadow, behind the curtain. The attendants came in and set the stretcher down beside the girl and lifted her expertly onto it and carried her out. The nurse helped the mother gather up her things. The shadow of the ambulance moved silently away and the nurse came back in the office.

122 "That ther girl is going to be a lunatic, ain't she?" the white-trash woman asked the nurse, but the nurse kept on to the back and never answered her.

123 "Yes, she's going to be a lunatic," the white-trash woman said to the rest of them.

124 "Po' critter," the old woman murmured. The child's face was still in her lap. His eyes looked idly out over her knees. He had not moved during the disturbance except to draw one leg up under him.

125 "I thank Gawd," the white-trash woman said fervently, "I ain' a lunatic."

126 Claud came limping out and the Turpins went home.

127 As their pick-up truck turned into their own dirt road and made the crest of the hill, Mrs. Turpin gripped the window ledge and looked out suspiciously. The land sloped gracefully down through a field dotted with lavender weeds and at the start of the rise their small yellow frame house, with its little flower beds spread out around it like a fancy apron, sat primly in its accustomed place between two giant hickory trees. She would not have been startled to see a burnt wound between two blackened chimneys.

128 Neither of them felt like eating so they put on their house clothes and lowered the shade in the bedroom and lay down, Claud with his leg on a pillow and herself with a damp washcloth over her eye. The instant she was flat on her back, the image of a razor-backed hog with warts on its face and horns coming out behind its ears snorted into her head. She moaned, a low quiet moan.

129 "I am not," she said tearfully, "a wart hog. From hell." But the denial had no force. The girl's eyes and her words, even the tone of her voice, low but clear, directed only to her, brooked no repudiation. She had been singled out for the message, though there was trash in the room to whom it might justly have been applied. The full force of this fact struck her only now. There was a woman there who was neglecting her own child but she had been overlooked. The message had been given to Ruby Turpin, a respectable, hardworking, church-going woman. The tears dried. Her eyes began to burn instead with wrath.

130 She rose on her elbow and the washcloth fell into her hand. Claud was lying on his back, snoring. She wanted to tell him what the girl had said. At the same time, she did not wish to put the image of herself as a wart hog from hell into his mind.

131 "Hey, Claud," she muttered and pushed his shoulder.

132 Claud opened one pale baby blue eye.

133 She looked into it warily. He did not think about anything. He just went his way.

134 "Wha, whasit?" he said and closed the eye again.

135 "Nothing," she said. Does your leg pain you?"

136 "Hurts like hell," Claud said.

137 "It'll quit terreckly," she said and lay back down. In a moment Claud was snoring again. For the rest of the afternoon they lay there. Claud slept. She scowled at the ceiling. Occasionally she raised her fist and made a small stabbing motion over her chest as if she was defending her innocence to invisible guests who were like the comforters of Job, reasonable-seeming but wrong.

138 About five-thirty Claud stirred. "Got to go after those niggers," he sighed, not moving.

139 She was looking straight up as if there were unintelligible handwriting on the ceiling. The protuberance over her eye had turned a greenish-blue. "Listen here," she said.

140 "What?"

141 "Kiss me."

142 Claud leaned over and kissed her loudly on the mouth. He pinched her side and their hands interlocked. Her expression of ferocious concentration did not change. Claud got up, groaning and growling, and limped off. She continued to study the ceiling.

143 She did not get up until she heard the pick-up truck coming back with the Negroes. Then she rose and thrust her feet in her brown oxfords, which she did not bother to lace, and stumped out onto the back porch and got her red plastic bucket. She emptied a tray of ice cubes into it and filled it half full of water and went out into the back yard. Every afternoon after Claud brought the hands in, one of the boys helped him put out hay and the rest waited in the back of the truck until he was ready to take them home. The truck was parked in the shade under one of the hickory trees.

144 "Hi yawl this evening?" Mrs. Turpin asked grimly, appearing with the bucket and the dipper. There were three women and a boy in the truck.

145 "Us doin nicely," the oldest woman said. "Hi you doin?" and her gaze stuck immediately on the dark lump on Mrs. Turpin's forehead. "You done fell down, ain't you?" she asked in a solicitous voice. The old woman was dark and almost toothless. She had on an old felt hat of Claud's set back on her head. The other

two women were younger and lighter and they both had new bright green sun hats. One of them had hers on her head; the other had taken hers off and the boy was grinning beneath it.

6 Mrs. Turpin set the bucket down on the floor of the truck. "Yawl hep yourselves," she said. She looked around to make sure Claud had gone. "No. I didn't fall down," she said, folding her arms. "It was something worse than that."

7 "Ain't nothing bad happen to you!" the old woman said. She said it as if they all knew Mrs. Turpin was protected in some special way by Divine Providence. "You just had you a little fall."

8 "We were in town at the doctor's office for where the cow kicked Mr. Turpin," Mrs. Turpin said in a flat tone that indicated they could leave off their foolishness. "And there was this girl there. A big fat girl with her face all broke out. I could look at that girl and tell she was peculiar but I couldn't tell how. And me and her mama were just talking and going along and all of a sudden WHAM! She throws this big book she was reading at me and . . ."

9 "Naw!" the old woman cried out.

0 "And then she jumps over the table and commences to choke me."

1 "Naw!" they all exclaimed, "naw!"

2 "Hi come she do that?" the old woman asked. "What ail her?"

3 Mrs. Turpin only glared in front of her.

4 "Somethin ail her," the old woman said.

5 "They carried her off in an ambulance," Mrs. Turpin continued, "but before she went she was rolling on the floor and they were trying to hold her down to give her a shot and she said something to me." She paused. "You know what she said to me?"

6 "What she say?" they asked.

7 "She said," Mrs. Turpin began, and stopped, her face very dark and heavy. The sun was getting whiter and whiter, blanching the sky overhead so that the leaves of the hickory tree were black in the face of it. She could not bring forth the words. "Something real ugly," she muttered.

"She sho shouldn' said nothing ugly to you," the old woman said. "You so sweet. You the sweetest lady I know." 158

"She pretty too," the one with the hat on said. 159

"And stout," the other one said. "I never knowed no sweeter white lady." 160

"That's the truth befo' Jesus," the old woman said. "Amen! You des as sweet and pretty as you can be." 161

Mrs. Turpin knew just exactly how much Negro flattery was worth and it added to her rage: "She said," she began again and finished this time with a fierce rush of breath, "that I was an old wart hog from hell." 162

There was an astounded silence. 163

"Where she at?" the youngest woman cried in a piercing voice. 164

"Lemme see her. I'll kill her!" 165

"I'll kill her with you!" the other one cried. 166

"She b'long in the sylum," the old woman said emphatically. "You the sweetest white lady I know." 167

"She pretty too," the other two said. "Stout as she can be and sweet. Jesus satisfied with her!" 168

"Deed he is," the old woman declared. 169

Idiots! Mrs. Turpin growled to herself. You could never say anything intelligent to a nigger. You could talk at them but not with them. "Yawl ain't drunk your water," she said shortly. "Leave the bucket in the truck when you're finished with it. I got more to do than just stand around and pass the time of day," and she moved off and into the house. 170

She stood for a moment in the middle of the kitchen. The dark protuberance over her eye looked like a miniature tornado cloud which might any moment sweep across the horizon of her brow. Her lower lip protruded dangerously. She squared her massive shoulders. Then she marched into the front of the house and out the side door and started down the road to the pig parlor. She had the look of a woman going single-handed, weaponless, into battle. 171

The sun was a deep yellow now like a harvest moon and was riding westward very fast over the far tree line as if it meant to reach the hogs before she did. The road was rutted and she kicked several good-sized stones out of her path as she strode along. The pig parlor was on a little knoll at the end of a lane that ran off from the side of the barn. It was a square of concrete as large as a small room, with a board fence about four feet high around it. The concrete floor sloped slightly so that the hog wash could drain off into a trench where it was carried to the field for fertilizer. Claud was standing on the outside, on the edge of the concrete, hanging onto the top board, hosing 172 down the floor inside. The hose was connected to the faucet of a water trough nearby.

173 Mrs. Turpin climbed up beside him and glowered down at the hogs inside. There were seven long-snouted bristly shoats in it—tan with liver-colored spots—and an old sow a few weeks off from farrowing. She was lying on her side grunting. The shoats were running about shaking themselves like idiot children, their little slit pig eyes searching the floor for anything left. She had read that pigs were the most intelligent animal. She doubted it. They were supposed to be smarter than dogs. There had even been a pig astronaut. He had performed his assignment perfectly but died of a heart attack afterwards because they left him in his electric suit, sitting upright throughout his examination when naturally a hog should be on all fours.

174 A-gruntin and a-rootin and a-groanin.

175 "Gimme that hose," she said, yanking it away from Claud. "Go on and carry them niggers home and then get off that leg."

176 "You look like you might have swallowed a mad dog," Claud observed, but he got down and limped off. He paid no attention to her humors.

177 Until he was out of earshot, Mrs. Turpin stood on the side of the pen, holding the hose and pointing the stream of water at the hind quarters of any shoat that looked as if it might try to lie down. When he had had time to get over the hill, she turned her head slightly and her wrathful eyes scanned the path. He was nowhere in sight. She turned back again and seemed to gather herself up. Her shoulder rose and she drew in her breath.

"What do you send me a message like that for?" 1
she said in a low fierce voice, barely above a whisper but with the force of a shout in its concentrated fury. "How am I hog and me both? How am I saved from hell too?" Her free fist was knotted and with the other she gripped the hose, blindly pointing the stream of water in and out of the eye of the old sow whose outraged squeal she did not hear.

The pig parlor commanded a view of the back 1
pasture where their twenty beef cows were gathered around the hay-bales Claud and the boy had put out. The freshly cut pasture sloped down to the highway. Across it was their cotton field and beyond that a dark green dusty wood which they owned as well. The sun was behind the wood, very red, looking over the paling of trees like a farmer inspecting his own hogs.

"Why me?" she rumbled. "It's no trash around here, 1
black or white, that I haven't given to. And break my back to the bone every day working. And do for the church."

She appeared to be the right size woman to com- 1
mand the arena before her. "How am I a hog?" she demanded. "Exactly how am I like them?" and she jabbed the stream of water at the shoats. "There was plenty of trash there. It didn't have to be me.

"If you like trash better, go get yourself some trash 1
then," she railed. "You could have made me trash. Or a nigger. If trash is what you wanted why didn't you make me trash?" She shook her fist with the hose in it and a watery snake appeared momentarily in the air. "I could quit working and take it easy and be filthy,"

she growled. "Lounge about the sidewalks all day drinking root beer. Dip snuff and spit in every puddle and have it all over my face. I could be nasty.

3 "Or you could have made me a nigger. It's too late for me to be a nigger," she said with deep sarcasm, "but I could act like one. Lay down in the middle of the road and stop traffic. Roll on the ground."

4 In the deepening light everything was taking on a mysterious hue. The pasture was growing a peculiar glassy green and the streak of highway had turned lavender. She braced herself for a final assault and this time her voice rolled out over the pasture. "Go on," she yelled, "call me a hog! Call me a hog again. From hell. Call me a wart hog from hell. Put that bottom rail on top. There'll still be a top and bottom!"

5 A garbled echo returned to her.

6 A final surge of fury shook her and she roared, "Who do you think you are?"

7 The color of everything, field and crimson sky, burned for a moment with a transparent intensity. The question carried over the pasture and across the highway and the cotton field and returned to her clearly like an answer from beyond the wood.

8 She opened her mouth but no sound came out of it.

9 A tiny truck, Claud's, appeared on the highway, heading rapidly out of sight. Its gears scraped thinly. It looked like a child's toy. At any moment a bigger truck might smash into it and scatter Claud's and the niggers' brains all over the road.

0 Mrs. Turpin stood there, her gaze fixed on the highway, all her muscles rigid, until in five or six minutes the truck reappeared, returning. She waited until it had had time to turn into their own road. Then like a monumental statue coming to life, she bent her head slowly and gazed, as if through the very heart of mystery, down into the pig parlor at the hogs. They had settled all in one corner around the old sow who was grunting softly. A red glow suffused them. They appeared to pant with a secret life.

Until the sun slipped finally behind the tree line, 191 Mrs. Turpin remained there with her gaze bent to them as if she were absorbing some abysmal life-giving knowledge. At last she lifted her head. There was only a purple streak in the sky, cutting through a field of crimson and leading, like an extension of the highway, into the descending dusk. She raised her hands from the side of the pen in a gesture hieratic and profound. A visionary light settled in her eyes. She saw the streak as a vast swinging bridge extending upward from the earth through a field of living fire. Upon it a vast horde of souls were rumbling toward heaven. There were whole companies of white-trash, clean for the first time in their lives, and bands of black niggers in white robes, and battalions of freaks and lunatics shouting and clapping and leaping like frogs. And bringing up the end of the procession was a tribe of people whom she recognized at once as those who, like herself and Claud, had always had a little of everything and the God-given wit to use it right. She leaned forward to observe them closer. They were marching behind the others with great dignity, accountable as they had always been for good order and common sense and respectable behavior. They alone were on key. Yet she could see by their shocked and altered faces that even their virtues were being burned away. She lowered her hands and gripped the rail of the hog pen, her eyes small but fixed unblinkingly on what lay ahead. In a moment the vision faded but she remained where she was, immobile.

At length she got down and turned off the faucet 192 and made her slow way on the darkening path to the house. In the woods around her the invisible cricket choruses had struck up, but what she heard were the voices of the souls climbing upward into the starry field and shouting hallelujah.

# Questions for Critical Thinking

1 What does the title tell you about the theme of the story? How would you distinguish between Mrs. Turpin's final revelation in the story and the revelation of the overall story itself? Flannery O'Connor was a devout Catholic. How does that color her view of her characters, if at all?

2 What is the significance of the names chosen for the characters in this story?

3 What is the central conflict of the story and how does race play a role in defining that conflict?

# Ralph Ellison (1914–1994)

"If I'm going to be remembered as a novelist, I'd better produce a few more books," Ralph Ellison said in a 1981 interview. Indeed, Ellison failed to complete a second novel in his lifetime, but the quality and importance of his first novel, *Invisible Man,* was so great that his literary reputation remains intact long after his death. *Invisible Man* follows the life of an unnamed black man in New York City who is "invisible" because white 1940s society refuses to see him. Although Ellison was insistent that the book was first and foremost a piece of literature, it is difficult to read it without paying attention to its comment on race.

*Invisible Man* responds to life in the Jim Crow era, the time period from 1877 to the mid-1960s in which blacks were the victims of widespread racism. A phenomenon primarily of the Southern states, Jim Crow laws (the name comes from a black, servile character in a popular minstrel show) kept blacks legally segregated from whites with the idea of "separate but equal." In effect, facilities for blacks were rarely equal in quality to those for whites. Segregation was only one manifestation of the prevailing mentality that blacks were inferior to whites. At its worst, racist behavior took the form of lynching, a term that refers to the execution of an individual carried out by a mob, rather than by legal authorities. Blacks were often lynched without any reason and in brutal ways. Ellison's fiction captures both this overtly cruel form of racism, as in his story that appears in this chapter, "A Party Down at the Square," and the subtler, once-commonplace discrimination that leads the black protagonist of *Invisible Man* to believe his path ought to be humility.

Unlike his protagonist, who was born in the Deep South, Ellison was raised in Oklahoma City, then educated at Tuskegee Institute, where he studied music and became friends with important jazz musicians of the day. He went to New York City to earn money before his senior year at Tuskegee but never returned. Ellison wrote essays and reviews, edited publications such as *The Negro Quarterly,* and taught creative writing later in his life. In addition to *Invisible Man,* which won the National Book Award in 1953, Ellison published two books of essays, *Shadow and Act* (1964) and *Going to the Territory* (1986), and a number of short stories. His collection *Flying Home* appeared posthumously in 1996. Three years thereafter, literary scholar John Callahan published a highly edited version of Ellison's second novel as *Juneteenth.*

A kindly and gracious man, intense with his friends and patient with his students, Ellison suffered some harsh criticism from later generations of African-American writers, who wanted him to be more overtly political in his prose. He never faltered, however, in his belief that literature was one of the highest callings a human being might follow. And, although he died at eighty with just one published novel, he remained devoted to the craft. Music—jazz in particular—was a clear influence on this writer; he once described *Invisible Man* as having the structure of a jazz composition—a beginning theme and bass line with variations and improvised solos.

"The act of writing requires a constant plunging back into the shadow of the past where time hovers ghostlike." —Ralph Ellison

# Battle Royal (1952)

1 IT goes a long way back, some twenty years. All my life I had been looking for something, and everywhere I turned someone tried to tell me what it was. I accepted their answers too, though they were often in contradiction and even self-contradictory. I was naïve. I was looking for myself and asking everyone except myself questions which I, and only I, could answer. It took me a long time and much painful boomeranging of my expectations to achieve a realization everyone else appears to have been born with: That I am nobody but myself. But first I had to discover that I am an invisible man!

2 And yet I am no freak of nature, nor of history. I was in the cards, other things having been equal (or unequal) eighty-five years ago. I am not ashamed of my grandparents for having been slaves. I am only ashamed of myself for having at one time been ashamed. About eighty-five years ago they were told they were free, united with others of our country in everything pertaining to the common good, and, in everything social, separate like the fingers of the hand. And they believed it. They exulted in it. They stayed in their place, worked hard, and brought up my father to do the same. But my grandfather is the one. He was an odd old guy, my grandfather, and I am told I take after him. It was he who caused the trouble. On his deathbed he called my father to him and said, "Son, after I'm gone I want you to keep up the good fight. I never told you, but our life is a war and I have been a traitor all my born days, a spy in the enemy's country ever since I give up my gun back in the Reconstruction. Live with your head in the lion's mouth. I want you to overcome 'em with yeses, undermine 'em with grins, agree 'em to death and destruction, let 'em swoller you till they vomit or bust wide open." They thought the old man had gone out of his mind. He had been the meekest of men. The younger children were rushed from the room, the shades drawn and the flame of the lamp turned so low that it sputtered on the wick like the old man's breathing. "Learn it to the younguns," he whispered fiercely; then he died.

3 But my folks were more alarmed over his last words than over his dying. It was as though he had not died at all, his words caused so much anxiety. I was warned emphatically to forget what he had said and, indeed, this is the first time it has been mentioned outside the family circle. It had a tremendous effect upon me, however. I could never be sure of what he meant. Grandfather had been a quiet old man who never made any trouble, yet on his deathbed he had called himself a traitor and a spy, and he had spoken of his meekness as a dangerous activity. It became a constant puzzle which lay unanswered in the back of my mind. And whenever things went well for me I remembered my grandfather and felt guilty and uncomfortable. It was as though I was carrying out his advice in spite of myself. And to make it worse, everyone loved me for it. I was praised by the most lily-white men in town. I was considered an example of desirable conduct—just as my grandfather had been. And what puzzled me was that the old man had defined it as *treachery.* When I was praised for my conduct I felt a guilt that in some way I was doing something that was really against the wishes of the white folks, that if they had understood they would have desired me to act just the opposite, that I should have been sulky and mean, and that that really would have been what they wanted, even though they were fooled and thought they wanted me to act as I did. It made me afraid that some day they would look upon me as a traitor and I would be lost. Still I was more afraid to act any other way because they didn't like that at all. The old man's words were like a curse. On my graduation day I delivered an oration in which I showed that humility was the secret, indeed, the very essence of progress. (Not that I believed this—how could I, remembering my grandfather?—I only believed that it worked.) It was a great success. Everyone praised me and I was invited to give the speech at a gathering of the town's leading white citizens. It was a triumph for the whole community.

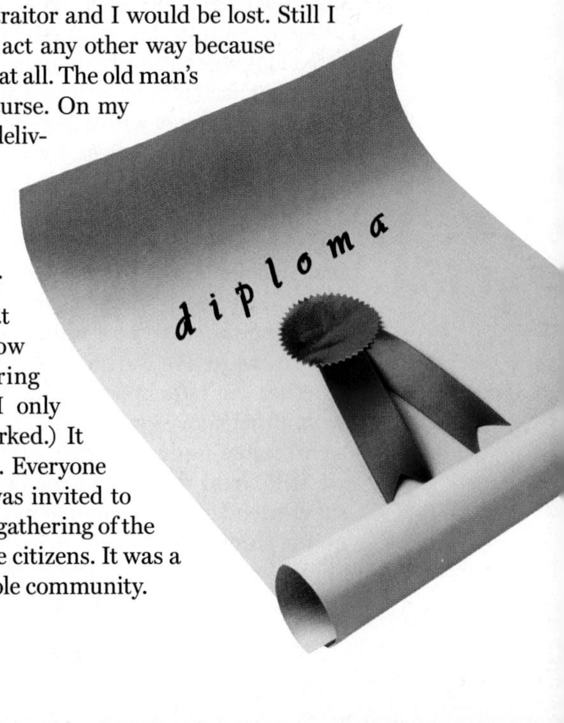

4 It was in the main ballroom of the leading hotel. When I got there I discovered that it was on the occasion of a smoker, and I was told that since I was to be there anyway I might as well take part in the battle royal to be fought by some of my schoolmates as part of the entertainment. The battle royal came first.

5 All of the town's big shots were there in their tuxedoes, wolfing down the buffet foods, drinking beer and whiskey and smoking black cigars. It was a large room with a high ceiling. Chairs were arranged in neat rows around three sides of a portable boxing ring. The fourth side was clear, revealing a gleaming space of polished floor. I had some misgivings over the battle royal, by the way. Not from a distaste for fighting but because I didn't care too much for the other fellows who were to take part. They were tough guys who seemed to have no grandfather's curse worrying their minds. No one could mistake their toughness. And besides, I suspected that fighting a battle royal might detract from the dignity of my speech. In those pre-invisible days I visualized myself as a potential Booker T. Washington. But the other fellows didn't care too much for me either, and there were nine of them. I felt superior to them in my way, and I didn't like the manner in which we were all crowded together in the servants' elevator. Nor did they like my being there. In fact, as the warmly lighted floors flashed past the elevator we had words over the fact that I, by taking part in the fight, had knocked one of their friends out of a night's work.

6 We were led out of the elevator through a rococo hall into an anteroom and told to get into our fighting togs. Each of us was issued a pair of boxing gloves and ushered out into the big mirrored hall, which we entered looking cautiously about us and whispering, lest we might accidentally be heard above the noise of the room. It was foggy with cigar smoke. And already the whiskey was taking effect. I was shocked to see some of the most important men of the town quite tipsy. They were all there—bankers, lawyers, judges, doctors, fire chiefs, teachers, merchants. Even one of the more fashionable pastors. Something we could not see was going on up front. A clarinet was vibrating sensuously and the men were standing up and moving eagerly forward. We were a small tight group, clustered together, our bare upper bodies touching and shining with anticipatory sweat: while up front the big shots were becoming increasingly excited over something we still could not see. Suddenly I heard the school superintendent, who had told me to come, yell, "Bring up the shines, gentlemen! Bring up the little shines!"

7 We were rushed up to the front of the ballroom, where it smelled even more strongly of tobacco and whiskey. Then we were pushed into place. I almost wet my pants. A sea of faces, some hostile, some amused, ringed around us, and in the center, facing us, stood a magnificent blonde—stark naked. There was dead silence. I felt a black of cold air chill me. I tried to back away, but they were behind me and around me. Some of the boys stood with lowered heads, trembling. I felt a wave of irrational guilt and fear. My teeth chattered, my skin turned to goose flesh, my knees knocked. Yet I was strongly attracted and looked in spite of myself. Had the price of looking been blindness, I would have looked. The hair was yellow like that of a circus kewpie doll, the face heavily powdered and rouged, as though to form an abstract mask, the eyes hollow and smeared a cool blue, the color of a baboon's butt. I felt a desire to spit upon her as my eyes brushed slowly over her body. Her breasts were firm and round as the domes of East Indian temples, and I stood so close as to see the fine skin texture and beads of pearly perspiration glistening like dew around the pink and erected buds of her nipples. I wanted at one and the same time to run from the room, to sink through the floor, or go to her and cover her from my eyes and the eyes of the others with my body; to feel the soft thighs, to caress her and destroy her, to love her and to murder her, to hide from her and yet to stroke where below the small American flag tattooed upon her belly her thighs formed a capital V. I had a notion that of all in the room she saw only me with her impersonal eyes.

And then she began to dance, a slow sensuous 8
movement; the smoke of a hundred cigars clinging to her like the thinnest of veils. She seemed like a fair bird-girl girdled in veils calling to me from the angry surface of some gray and threatening sea. I was transported. Then I became aware of the clarinet playing and the big shots yelling at us. Some threatened us if we looked and others if we did not. On my right I saw one boy faint. And now a man grabbed a silver pitcher from a table and stepped close as he dashed ice water upon him and stood him up and forced two of us to support him as his head hung and moans issued from his thick bluish lips. Another boy began to plead to go home. He was the largest of the group, wearing dark red fighting trunks much too small to conceal the erection which projected from him as though in answer to the insinuating low-registered moaning of the clarinet. He tried to hide himself with his boxing gloves.

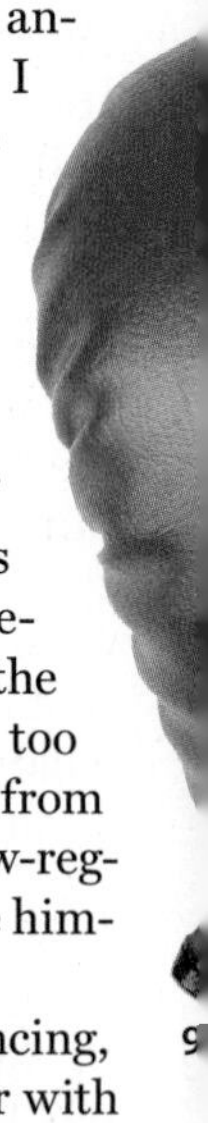

And all the while the blonde continued dancing, 9
smiling faintly at the big shots who watched her with fascination, and faintly smiling at our fear. I noticed a certain merchant who followed her hungrily, his

lips loose and drooling. He was a large man who wore diamond studs in a shirtfront which swelled with the ample paunch underneath, and each time the blonde swayed her undulating hips he ran his hand through the thin hair of his bald head and, with his arms upheld, his posture clumsy like that of an intoxicated panda, wound his belly in a slow and obscene grind. This creature was completely hypnotized. The music had quickened. As the dancer flung herself about with a detached expression on her face, the men began reaching out to touch her. I could see their beefy fingers sink into her soft flesh. Some of the others tried to stop them and she began to move around the floor in graceful circles, as they gave chase, slipping and sliding over the polished floor. It was mad. Chairs went crashing, drinks were spilt, as they ran laughing and howling after her. They caught her just as she reached a door, raised her from the floor, and tossed her as college boys are tossed at a hazing, and above her red, fixed-smiling lips I saw the terror and disgust in her eyes, almost like my own terror and that which I saw in some of the other boys. As I watched, they tossed her twice and her soft breasts seemed to flatten against the air and her legs flung wildly as she spun. Some of the more sober ones helped her to escape. And I started off the floor, heading for the anteroom with the rest of the boys.

10 Some were still crying and in hysteria. But as we tried to leave we were stopped and ordered to get into the ring. There was nothing to do but what we were told. All ten of us climbed under the ropes and allowed ourselves to be blindfolded with broad bands of white cloth. One of the men seemed to feel a bit sympathetic and tried to cheer us up as we stood with our backs against the ropes. Some of us tried to grin. "See that boy over there?" one of the men said. "I want you to run across at the bell and give it to him right in the belly. If you don't get him, I'm going to get you. I don't like his looks." Each of us was told the same. The blindfolds were put on. Yet even then I had been going over my speech. In my mind each word was as bright as a flame. I felt the cloth pressed into place, and frowned so that it would be loosened when I relaxed.

11 But now I felt a sudden fit of blind terror. I was unused to darkness, it was as though I had suddenly found myself in a dark room filled with poisonous cottonmouths. I could hear the bleary voices yelling insistently for the battle royal to begin.

12 "Get going in there!"

13 "Let me at that big nigger!"

14 I strained to pick up the school superintendent's voice, as though to squeeze some security out of that slightly more familiar sound.

15 "Let me at those black sonsabitches!" someone yelled.

16 "No, Jackson, no!" another voice yelled. "Here, somebody, help me hold Jack."

17 "I want to get at that ginger-colored nigger. Tear him limb from limb," the first voice yelled.

18 I stood against the ropes trembling. For in those days I was what they called ginger-colored, and he sounded as though he might crunch me between his teeth like a crisp ginger cookie.

19 Quite a struggle was going on. Chairs were being kicked about and I could hear voices grunting as with terrific effort. I wanted to see, to see more desperately than ever before. But the blindfold was as tight as a thick skin-puckering scab and when I raised my gloved hands to push the layers of white aside a voice yelled, "Oh, no you don't, black bastard! Leave that alone!"

20 "Ring the bell before Jackson kills him a coon!" someone boomed in the sudden silence. And I heard the bell clang and the sound of the feet scuffling forward.

21 A glove smacked against my head. I pivoted, striking out stiffly as someone went past, and felt the jar ripple along the length of my arm to my shoulder. Then it seemed as though all nine of the boys had turned upon me at once. Blows pounded me from all sides while I struck out as best I could. So many blows landed upon me that I wondered if I were not the only blindfolded fighter in the ring, or if the man called Jackson hadn't succeeded in getting me after all.

22 Blindfolded, I could no longer control my motions. I had no dignity. I stumbled about like a baby or a drunken man. The smoke had become thicker and with each new blow it seemed to sear and further restrict my lungs. My saliva became like hot bitter glue. A glove connected with my head, filling my mouth with warm blood. It was everywhere. I could not tell if the moisture I felt upon my body was sweat or blood. A blow landed hard against the nape of my neck. I felt myself going over, my head hitting the floor. Streaks of blue light filled the black world behind the blindfold. I lay prone, pretending that I was knocked out, but felt myself seized by hands and yanked to my feet. "Get going, black boy! Mix it up!" My arms were like

lead, my head smarting from blows. I managed to feel my way to the ropes and held on, trying to catch my breath. A glove landed in my midsection and I went over again, feeling as though the smoke had become a knife jabbed into my guts. Pushed this way and that by the legs milling around me, I finally pulled erect and discovered that I could see the black, sweat-washed forms weaving in the smoky-blue atmosphere like drunken dancers weaving to the rapid drum-like thuds of blows.

23 Everyone fought hysterically. It was complete anarchy. Everybody fought everybody else. No group fought together for long. Two, three, four, fought one, then turned to fight each other, were themselves attacked. Blows landed below the belt and in the kidney, with the gloves open as well as closed, and with my eye partly opened now there was not so much terror. I moved carefully, avoiding blows, although not too many to attract attention, fighting group to group. The boys groped about like blind, cautious crabs crouching to protect their midsections, their heads pulled in short against their shoulders, their arms stretched nervously before them, with their fists testing the smoke-filled air like the knobbed feelers of hypersensitive snails. In one corner I glimpsed a boy violently punching the air and heard him scream in pain as he smashed his hand against a ring post. For a second I saw him bent over holding his hand, then going down as a blow caught his unprotected head. I played one group against the other, slipping in and throwing a punch then stepping out of range while pushing the others into the melee to take the blows blindly aimed at me. The smoke was agonizing and there were no rounds, no bells at three minute intervals to relieve our exhaustion. The room spun round me, a swirl of lights, smoke, sweating bodies surrounded by tense white faces. I bled from both nose and mouth, the blood spattering upon my chest.

24 The men kept yelling, "Slug him, black boy! Knock his guts out!"

25 "Uppercut him! Kill him! Kill that big boy!"

26 Taking a fake fall, I saw a boy going down heavily beside me as though we were felled by a single blow, saw a sneaker-clad foot shoot into his groin as the two who had knocked him down stumbled upon him. I rolled out of range, feeling a twinge of nausea.

27 The harder we fought the more threatening the men became. And yet, I had begun to worry about my speech again. How would it go? Would they recognize my ability? What would they give me?

I was fighting automatically when suddenly I noticed that one after another of the boys was leaving the ring. I was surprised, filled with panic, as though I had been left alone with an unknown danger. Then I understood. The boys had arranged it among themselves. It was the custom for the two men left in the ring to slug it out for the winner's prize. I discovered this too late. When the bell sounded two men in tuxedoes leaped into the ring and removed the blindfold. I found myself facing Tatlock, the biggest of the gang. I felt sick at my stomach. Hardly had the bell stopped ringing in my ears than it clanged again and I saw him moving swiftly toward me. Thinking of nothing else to do I hit him smash on the nose. He kept coming, bringing the rank sharp violence of stale sweat. His face was a black blank of a face, only eyes alive—with hate of me and aglow with a feverish terror from what had happened to us all. I became anxious. I wanted to deliver my speech and he came at me as though he meant to beat it out of me. I smashed him again and again, taking his blows as they came. Then on a sudden impulse I struck him lightly and we clinched. I whispered, "Fake like I knocked you out, you can have the prize." 2

"I'll break your behind," he whispered hoarsely. 2

"For *them*?" 3

"For *me*, sonofabitch!" 3

They were yelling for us to break it up and Tatlock spun me half around with a blow, and as a joggled camera sweeps in a reeling scene, I saw the howling red faces crouching tense beneath the cloud of blue-gray smoke. For a moment the world wavered, unraveled, flowed, then my head cleared and Tatlock bounced before me. That fluttering shadow before my eyes was his jabbing left hand. Then falling forward, my head against his damp shoulder, I whispered. 3

"I'll make it five dollars more." 3

"Go to hell!" 3

But his muscles relaxed a trifle beneath my pressure and I breathed, "Seven?" 3

"Give it to your ma," he said, ripping me beneath the heart. 3

And while I still held him I butted him and moved away. I felt myself bombarded with punches. I fought back with hopeless desperation. I wanted to deliver my speech more than anything else in the world, because I felt that only these men could judge truly my ability, and now this stupid clown was ruining my chances. I began fighting carefully now, moving in to punch him and out again with my greater speed. A lucky blow to 3

I wanted to deliver my speech more than anything else in the world . . .

his chin and I had him going too—until I heard a loud voice yell, "I got my money on the big boy."

38 Hearing this, I almost dropped my guard. I was confused: Should I try to win against the voice out there? Would not this go against my speech, and was not this a moment for humility, for nonresistance? A blow to my head as I danced about sent my right eye popping like a jack-in-the-box and settled my dilemma. The room went red as I fell. It was a dream fall, my body languid and fastidious as to where to land, until the floor became impatient and smashed up to meet me. A moment later I came to. An hypnotic voice and said FIVE emphatically. And I lay there, hazily watching a dark red spot of my own blood shaping itself into a butterfly, glistening and soaking into the soiled gray world of the canvas.

39 When the voice drawled TEN I was lifted up and dragged to a chair. I sat dazed. My eye pained and swelled with each throb of my pounding heart and I wondered if now I would be allowed to speak. I was wringing wet, my mouth still bleeding. We were grouped along the wall now. The other boys ignored me as they congratulated Tatlock and speculated as to how much they would be paid. One boy whimpered over his smashed hand. Looking up front, I saw attendants in white jackets rolling the portable ring away and placing a small square rug in the vacant space surrounded by chairs. Perhaps, I thought, I will stand on the rug to deliver my speech.

40 Then the M.C. called to us. "Come on up here boys and get your money."

41 We ran forward to where the men laughed and talked in their chairs, waiting. Everyone seemed friendly now.

42 "There it is on the rug," the man said. I saw the rug covered with coins of all dimensions and a few crumpled bills. But what excited me, scattered here and there, were the gold pieces.

43 "Boys, it's all yours," the man said. "You get all you grab."

44 "That's right, Sambo," a blond man said, winking at me confidentially.

45 I trembled with excitement, forgetting my pain. I would get the gold and the bills. I thought. I would use both hands. I would throw my body against the boys nearest me to block them from the gold.

46 "Get down around the rug now," the man commanded, "and don't anyone touch it until I give the signal."

47 "This ought to be good," I heard.

48 As told, we got around the square rug on our knees. Slowly the man raised his freckled hand as we followed it upward with our eyes.

I heard, "These niggers look like they're about to pray!" 49

Then, "Ready," the man said. "Go!" 50

I lunged for a yellow coin lying on the blue design of the carpet, touching it and sending a surprised shriek to join those around me. I tried frantically to remove my hand but could not let go. A hot, violent force tore through my body, shaking me like a wet rat. The rug was electrified. The hair bristled up on my head as I shook myself free. My muscles jumped, my nerves jangled, writhed. But I saw that this was not stopping the other boys. Laughing in fear and embarrassment, some were holding back and scooping up the coins knocked off by the painful contortions of others. The men roared above us as we struggled. 51

"Pick it up, goddamnit, pick it up!" someone called like a bass-voiced parrot. "Go on, get it!" 52

I crawled rapidly around the floor, picking up the coins, trying to avoid the coppers and to get greenbacks and the gold. Ignoring the shock by laughing, as I brushed the coins off quickly, I discovered that I could contain the electricity—a contradiction but it works. Then the men began to push us onto the rug. Laughing embarrassedly, we struggled out of their hands and kept after the coins. We were all wet and slippery and hard to hold. Suddenly I saw a boy lifted into the air, glistening with sweat like a circus seal, and dropped, his wet back landing flush upon the charged rug, heard him yell and saw him literally dance upon his back, his elbows beating a frenzied tattoo upon the floor, his muscles twitching like the flesh of a horse stung by many flies. When he finally rolled off, his face was gray and no one stopped him when he ran from the floor amid booming laughter. 53

"Get the money," the M.C. called. "That's good hard American cash!" 54

And we snatched and grabbed, snatched and grabbed. I was careful not to come too close to the rug now, and when I felt the hot whiskey breath descend upon me like a cloud of foul air I reached out and grabbed the leg of a chair. It was occupied and I held on desperately. 55

"Leggo, nigger! Leggo!" 56

The huge face wavered down to mine as he tried to push me free. But my body was slippery and he was too drunk. It was Mr. Colcord, who owned a chain of movie houses and "entertainment palaces." Each time he grabbed me I slipped out of his hands. It became a real struggle. I feared the rug more than I did the drunk, so I held on, surprising myself for a moment by trying to topple *him* upon the rug. It was such an enormous idea that I found myself actually carrying it out. I tried not to be obvious, yet when I 57 grabbed his leg, trying to tumble him out of the chair, he raised up, roaring with laughter, and, looking at me with soberness dead in the eye, kicked me viciously in the chest. The chair leg flew out of my hand and I felt myself going and rolled. It was as though I had rolled through a bed of hot coals. It seemed a whole century would pass before I would roll free, a century in which I was seared through the deepest levels of my body to the fearful breath within me and the breath seared and heated to the point of explosion. It'll all be over in a flash, I thought as I rolled clear. It'll all be over in a flash.

58 But not yet, the men on the other side were waiting, red faces swollen as though from apoplexy as they bent forward in their chairs. Seeing their fingers coming toward me I rolled away as a fumbled football rolls off the receiver's fingertips, back into the coals. That time I luckily sent the rug sliding out of place and heard the coins ringing against the floor and the boys scuffling to pick them up and the M.C. calling, "All right, boys, that's all. Go get dressed and get your money."

59 I was limp as a dish rag. My back felt as though it had been beaten with wires.

60 When we had dressed the M.C. came in and gave us each five dollars, except Tatlock, who got ten for being the last in the ring. Then he told us to leave. I was not to get a chance to deliver my speech, I thought. I was going out into the dim alley in despair when I was stopped and told to go back. I returned to the ballroom, where the men were pushing back their chairs and gathering in small groups to talk.

61 The M.C. knocked on a table for quiet. "Gentlemen," he said, "we almost forgot an important part of the program. A most serious part, gentlemen. This boy was brought here to deliver a speech which he made at his graduation yesterday . . ."

62 "Bravo!"

63 "I'm told that he is the smartest boy we've got out there in Greenwood. I'm told that he knows more big words than a pocket-sized dictionary."

64 Much applause and laughter.

65 "So now, gentlemen, I want you to give him your attention."

66 There was still laughter as I faced them, my mouth dry, my eyes throbbing. I began slowly, but evidently my throat was tense, because they began shouting. "Louder! Louder!"

"We of the younger generation extol the wisdom of that great leader and educator," I shouted, "who first spoke these flaming words of wisdom: 'A ship lost at sea for many days suddenly sighted a friendly vessel. From the mast of the unfortunate vessel was seen a signal: "Water, water, we die of thirst!" The answer from the friendly vessel came back: "Cast down your bucket where you are." The captain of the distressed vessel, at last heeding the injunction, cast down his bucket, and it came up full of fresh sparkling water from the mouth of the Amazon River.' And like him I say, and in his words, 'To those of my race who depend upon bettering their condition in a foreign land, or who underestimate the importance of cultivating friendly relations with the Southern white man, who is his next-door neighbor, I would say: "Cast down your bucket where you are"—cast it down in making friends in every manly way of the people of all races by whom we are surrounded . . .'" 67

I spoke automatically and with such fervor that I did not realize that the men were still talking and laughing until my dry mouth, filling up with blood from the cut, almost strangled me. I coughed, wanting to stop and go to one of the tall brass, sand-filled spittoons to relieve myself, but a few of the men, especially the superintendent, were listening and I was afraid. So I gulped it down, blood, saliva and all, and continued. (What powers of endurance I had during those days! What enthusiasm! What a belief in the rightness of things!) I spoke even louder in spite of the pain. But still they talked and still they laughed, as though deaf with cotton in dirty ears. So I spoke with greater emotional emphasis. I closed my ears and swallowed blood until I was nauseated. The speech seemed a hundred times as long as before, but I could not leave out a single word. All had to be said, each memorized nuance considered, rendered. Nor was that all. Whenever I uttered a word of three or more syllables a group of voices would yell for me to repeat it. I used the phrase "social responsibility" and they yelled: 68

"What's that word you say, boy?" 69

"Social responsibility," I said. 70

"What?" 71

"Social . . ." 72

"Louder." 73

". . . responsibility." 74

"More!" 75

76 "Respon—"

77 "Repeat!"

78 "—sibility."

79 The room filled with the uproar of laughter until, no doubt, distracted by having to gulp down my blood, I made a mistake and yelled a phrase I had often seen denounced in newspaper editorials, heard debated in private.

80 "Social . . ."

81 "What?" they yelled.

82 ". . . equality—"

83 The laughter hung smokelike in the sudden stillness. I opened my eyes, puzzled. Sounds of displeasure filled the room. The M.C. rushed forward. They shouted hostile phrases at me. But I did not understand.

84 A small dry mustached man in the front row blared out, "Say that slowly, son!"

85 "What, sir?"

86 "What you just said!"

87 "Social responsibility, sir," I said.

88 "You weren't being smart, were you, boy?" he said, not unkindly.

89 "No, sir!"

90 "You sure that about 'equality' was a mistake?"

91 "Oh, yes, sir," I said. "I was swallowing blood."

92 "Well, you had better speak more slowly so we can understand. We mean to do right by you, but you've got to know your place at all times. All right, now, go on with your speech."

93 I was afraid. I wanted to leave but I wanted also to speak and I was afraid they'd snatch me down.

94 "Thank you, sir," I said, beginning where I had left off, and having them ignore me as before.

95 Yet when I finished there was a thunderous applause. I was surprised to see the superintendent come forth with a package wrapped in white tissue paper, and, gesturing for quiet, address the men.

96 "Gentlemen, you see that I did not overpraise the boy. He makes a good speech and some day he'll lead his people in the proper paths. And I don't have to tell you that this is important in these days and times. This is a good, smart boy, and so to encourage him in the right direction, in the name of the Board of Education I wish to present him a prize in the form of this . . ."

97 He paused, removing the tissue paper and revealing a gleaming calfskin briefcase.

". . . We mean to do right by you, but you've got to know your place at all times. . . ."

". . . in the form of this first-class article from Shad Whitmore's shop." 98

"Boy," he said, addressing me, "take this prize and keep it well. Consider it a badge of office. Prize it. Keep developing as you are and some day it will be filled with important papers that will help shape the destiny of your people." 99

I was so moved that I could hardly express my thanks. A rope of bloody saliva forming a shape like an undiscovered continent drooled upon the leather and I wiped it quickly away. I felt an importance that I had never dreamed. 100

"Open it and see what's inside," I was told. 101

My fingers a-tremble, I complied, smelling fresh leather and finding an official-looking document inside. It was a scholarship to the state college for Negroes. My eyes filled with tears and I ran awkwardly off the floor. 102

I was overjoyed; I did not even mind when I discovered the gold pieces I had scrambled for were brass pocket tokens advertising a certain make of automobile. 103

When I reached home everyone was excited. Next day the neighbors came to congratulate me. I even felt safe from grandfather, whose deathbed curse usually spoiled my triumphs. I stood beneath his photograph with my briefcase in hand and smiled triumphantly into his stolid black peasant's face. It was a face that fascinated me. The eyes seemed to follow everywhere I went. 104

That night I dreamed I was at a circus with him and that he refused to laugh at the clowns no matter what they did. Then later he told me to open my briefcase and read what was inside and I did, finding an official envelope stamped with the state seal: and inside the envelope I found another and another, endlessly, and I thought I would fall of weariness. "Them's years," he said. "Now open that one." And I did and in it I found an engraved stamp containing a short message in letters of gold. "Read it," my grandfather said. "Out loud." 105

"To Whom It May Concern," I intoned. "Keep This Nigger-Boy Running." 106

I awoke with the old man's laughter ringing in my ears. 107

# Questions for Critical Thinking

1 Unlike most writers who lived in the South (such as Faulkner and O'Connor), Ralph Ellison was not born there. What about "Battle Royal" makes it a Southern story? You might want to consider which, if any, themes it shares with the Faulkner and O'Connor selections.

2 Reread the protagonist's dream recounted at the end of the story. Given the time and place in which this story's action occurs, what do you think the boy's dream stands for or means?

3 The narrator tells his story from a future point in time, looking back on the occurrence of this battle royal. Identify the ironies you see in the story that are created from this disjuncture of point of view. How does the point of view of the non-Southern narrator of the second story affect its meaning?

# A Party Down at the Square (1966)

1 I DON'T know what started it. A bunch of men came by my Uncle Eds place and said there was going to be a party down at the Square, and my uncle hollered for me to come on and I ran with them through the dark and rain and there we were at the Square. When we got there everybody was mad and quiet and standing around looking at the nigger. Some of the men had guns, and one man kept goosing the nigger in his pants with the barrel of a shotgun, saying he ought to pull the trigger, but he never did. It was right in front of the courthouse, and the old clock in the tower was striking twelve. The rain was falling cold and freezing as it fell. Everybody was cold, and the nigger kept wrapping his arms around himself trying to stop the shivers.

2 Then one of the boys pushed through the circle and snatched off the nigger's shirt, and there he stood, with his black skin all shivering in the light from the fire, and looking at us with a scaired look on his face and putting his hands in his pants pockets. Folks started yelling to hurry up and kill the nigger. Somebody yelled: "Take your hands out of your pockets, nigger; we gonna have plenty heat in a minnit." But the nigger didn't hear him and kept his hands where they were.

I tell you the rain was cold. I had to stick my hands in my pockets they got so cold. The fire was pretty small, and they put some logs around the platform they had the nigger on and then threw on some gasoline, and you could see the flames light up the whole Square. It was late and the streetlights had been off for a long time. It was so bright that the bronze statue of the general standing there in the Square was like something alive. The shadows playing on his moldy green face made him seem to be smiling down at the nigger. 3

They threw on more gas, and it made the Square bright like it gets when the lights are turned on or when the sun is setting red. All the wagons and cars were standing around the curbs. Not like Saturday though—the niggers weren't there. Not a single nigger was there except this Bacote nigger and they dragged him there tied to the back of Jed Wilson's truck. On Saturday there's as many niggers as white folks. 4

5 Everybody was yelling crazy 'cause they were about to set fire to the nigger, and I got to the rear of the circle and looked around the Square to try to count the cars. The shadows of the folks was flickering on the trees in the middle of the Square. I saw some birds that the noise had woke up flying through the trees. I guess maybe they thought it was morning. The ice had started the cobblestones in the street to shine where the rain was falling and freezing. I counted forty cars before I lost count. I knew folks must have been there from Phenix City by all the cars mixed in with the wagons.

6 God, it was a hell of a night. It was some night all right. When the noise died down I heard the nigger's voice from where I stood in the back, so I pushed my way up front. The nigger was bleeding from his nose and ears, and I could see him all red where the dark blood was running down his black skin. He kept lifting first one foot and then the other, like a chicken on a hot stove. I looked down to the platform they had him on, and they had pushed a ring of fire up close to his feet. It must have been hot to him with the flames almost touching his big black toes. Somebody yelled for the nigger to say his prayers, but the nigger wasn't saying anything now. He just kinda moaned with his eyes shut and kept moving up and down on his feet, first one foot and then the other.

I wanted to run, and I wanted to stay and see what was going to happen.

7 I watched the flames burning the logs up closer and closer to the nigger's feet. They were burning good now, and the rain had stopped and the wind was rising, making the flames flare higher. I looked, and there must have been thirty-five women in the crowd, and I could hear their voices clear and shrill mixed in with those of the men. Then it happened. I heard the noise about the same time everyone else did. It was like the roar of a cyclone blowing up from the gulf, and everyone was looking up into the air to see what it was. Some of the faces looked surprised and scaired, all but the nigger. He didn't even hear the noise. He didn't even look up. Then the roar came closer, right above our heads and the wind was blowing higher and higher and the sound seemed to be going in circles.

8 Then I saw her. Through the clouds and fog I could see a red and green light on her wings. I could see them just for a second: then she rose up into the low clouds. I looked out for the beacon over the tops of the buildings in the direction of the airfield that's forty miles away, and it wasn't circling around. You usually could see it sweeping around the sky at night, but it wasn't there. Then, there she was again, like a big bird lost in the fog. I looked for the red and green lights, and they weren't there anymore. She was flying even closer to the tops of the buildings than before. The wind was blowing harder, and leaves started flying about, making funny shadows on the ground, and tree limbs were cracking and falling.

It was a storm all right. The pilot must have thought he was over the landing field. Maybe he thought the fire in the Square was put there for him to land by. Gosh, but it scaired the folks. I was scaired too. They started yelling: "He's going to land. He's going to land." And: "He's going to fall." A few started for their cars and wagons. I could hear the wagons creaking and chains jangling and cars spitting and missing as they started the engines up. Off to my right, a horse started pitching and striking his hooves against a car. 9

I didn't know what to do. I wanted to run, and I wanted to stay and see what was going to happen. The plane was close as hell. The pilot must have been trying to see where he was at, and her motors were drowning out all the sounds. I could even feel the vibration, and my hair felt like it was standing up under my hat. I happened to look over at the statue of the general standing with one leg before the other and leaning back on a sword, and I was fixing to run over and climb between his legs and sit there and watch when the roar stopped some, and I looked up and she was gliding just over the top of the trees in the middle of the Square. 10

Her motors stopped altogether and I could hear the sound of branches cracking and snapping off below her landing gear. I could see her plain now, all silver and shining in the light of the fire with T.W.A. in black letters under her wings. She was sailing smoothly out of the Square when she hit the high power lines that follow the Birmingham highway through the town. It made a loud crash. It sounded like the wind blowing the door of a tin barn shut. She only hit with her landing gear, but I could see the sparks flying, and the wires knocked loose from the poles were spitting blue sparks and whipping around like a bunch of snakes and leaving circles of blue sparks in the darkness. 11

The plane had knocked five or six wires loose, and they were dangling and swinging, and every time they touched they threw off more sparks. The wind was making them swing, and when I got over there, there was a crackling and spitting screen of blue haze across the highway. I lost my hat running over, but I didn't stop to look for it. I was among the first and I could hear the others pounding behind me across the grass 12 of the Square. They were yelling to beat all hell, and they came up fast, pushing and shoving, and someone got pushed against a swinging wire. It made a sound like when a blacksmith drops a red hot horseshoe into a barrel of water, and the steam comes up. I could smell the flesh burning. The first time I'd ever smelled it. I got up close and it was a woman. It must have killed her right off. She was lying in a puddle stiff as a board, with pieces of glass insulators that the plane had knocked off the poles lying all around her. Her white dress was torn, and I saw one of her tits hanging out in the water and her thighs. Some woman screamed and fainted and almost fell on a wire, but a man caught her. The sheriff and his men were yelling and driving folks back with guns shining in their hands, and everything was lit up blue by the sparks. The shock had turned the woman almost as black as the nigger. I was trying to see if she wasn't blue too, or if it was just the sparks, and the sheriff drove me away. As I backed off trying to see, I heard the motors of the plane start up again somewhere off to the right in the clouds.

13 The clouds were moving fast in the wind and the wind was blowing the smell of something burning over to me. I turned around, and the crowd was headed back to the nigger. I could see him standing there in the middle of the flames. The wind was making the flames brighter every minute. The crowd was running. I ran too. I ran back across the grass with the crowd. It wasn't so large now that so many had gone when the plane came. I tripped and fell over the limb of a tree lying in the grass and bit my lip. It ain't well yet I bit it so bad. I could taste the blood in my mouth as I ran over. I guess that's what made me sick. When I got there, the fire had caught the nigger's pants, and the folks were standing around watching, but not too close on account of the wind blowing the flames. Somebody hollered, "Well, nigger, it ain't so cold now, is it? You don't need to put your hands in your pockets now." And the nigger looked up with his great white eyes looking like they was 'bout to pop out of his head, and I had enough. I didn't want to see anymore. I wanted to run somewhere and puke, but I stayed. I stayed right there in the front of the crowd and looked.

14 The nigger tried to say something I couldn't hear for the roar of the wind in the fire, and I strained my ears. Jed Wilson hollered, "What you say there, nigger?" And it came back through the flames in his nigger voice: "Will one a you gentlemen please cut my throat?" he said. "Will somebody please cut my throat like a Christian?" And Jed hollered back, "Sorry, but ain't no Christians around tonight. Ain't no Jew-boys neither. We're just one hundred percent Americans."

Then the nigger was silent. Folks started laughing 15
at Jed. Jed's right popular with the folks, and the next year, my uncle says, they plan to run him for sheriff. The heat was too much for me, and the smoke was making my eyes to smart. I was trying to back away when Jed reached down and brought up a can of gasoline and threw it in the fire on the nigger. I could see the flames catching the gas in a puff as it went in in a silver sheet and some of it reached the nigger, making spurts of blue fire all over his chest.

Well, that nigger was tough. I have to give it to that 16
nigger; he was really tough. He had started to burn like a house afire and was making the smoke smell like burning hides. The fire was up around his head, and the smoke was so thick and black we couldn't see him. And him not moving—we thought he was dead. Then he started out. The fire had burned the ropes they had tied him with, and he started jumping and kicking about like he was blind, and you could smell his skin burning. He kicked so hard that the platform, which was burning too, fell in, and he rolled out of the fire at my feet. I jumped back so he wouldn't get on me. I'll never forget it. Every time I eat barbeque I'll remember that nigger. His back was just like a barbecued hog. I could see the prints of his ribs where they start around from his backbone and curve down and around. It was a sight to see, that nigger's back. He was right at my feet, and somebody behind pushed me and almost made me step on him, and he was still burning.

I didn't step on him though, and Jed and some- 17
body else pushed him back in the burning planks and logs and poured on more gas. I wanted to leave, but the folks were yelling and I couldn't move except to look around and see the statue. A branch the wind had broken was resting on his hat. I tried to push out and get away because my guts were gone, and all I got was spit and hot breath in my face from the woman and two men standing directly behind me. So I had to turn back around. The nigger rolled out of the fire again. He wouldn't stay put. It was on the other side this time. I couldn't see him very well through the flames and smoke. They got some tree limbs and held him there this time and he stayed there till he was ashes. I guess he stayed there. I know he burned to ashes because I saw Jed a week later, and he laughed and showed me some white finger bones still held together with little pieces of the nigger's skin. Anyway, I left when somebody moved around to see the nigger. I pushed my way through the crowd, and a woman in

the rear scratched my face as she yelled and fought to get up close.

18 I ran across the Square to the other side, where the sheriff and his deputies were guarding the wires that were still spitting and making a blue fog. My heart was pounding like I had been running a long ways, and I bent over and let my insides go. Everything came up and spilled in a big gush over the ground. I was sick, and tired, and weak, and cold. The wind was still high, and large drops of rain were beginning to fall. I headed down the street to my uncle's place past a store where the wind had broken a window, and glass lay over the sidewalk. I kicked it as I went by. I remember somebody's fool rooster crowing like it was morning in all that wind.

He said you get used to it in time.

19 The next day I was too weak to go out, and my uncle kidded me and called me "the gutless wonder from Cincinnati." I didn't mind. He said you get used to it in time. He couldn't go out hisself. There was too much wind and rain. I got up and looked out of the window, and the rain was pouring down and dead sparrows and limbs of trees were scattered all over the yard. There had been a cyclone all right. It swept a path right through the county, and we were lucky we didn't get the full force of it.

20 It blew for three days steady, and put the town in a hell of a shape. The wind blew sparks and set fire to the white-and-green-rimmed house on Jackson Avenue that had the big concrete lions in the yard and burned it down to the ground. They had to kill another nigger who tried to run out of the county after they burned this Bacote nigger. My Uncle Ed said they always have to kill niggers in pairs to keep the other niggers in place. I don't know though, the folks seem a little skittish of the niggers. They all came back, but they act pretty sullen. They look mean as hell when you pass them down at the store. The other day I was down to Brinkley's store, and a white cropper said it didn't do no good to kill the niggers 'cause things don't get no better. He looked hungry as hell. Most of the croppers look hungry. You'd be surprised how hungry white folks can look. Somebody said that he'd better shut his damn mouth, and he shut up. But from the look on his face he won't stay shut long. He went out of the store muttering to himself and spit a big chew of tobacco right down on Brinkley's floor. Brinkley said he was sore 'cause he wouldn't let him have credit. Anyway, it didn't seem to help things. First it was the nigger and the storm, then the plane, then the woman and the wires, and now I hear the airplane line is investigating to find who set the fire that almost wrecked their plane. All that in one night, and all of it but the storm over one nigger. It was some night all right. It was some party too. I was right there, see. I was right there watching it all. It was my first party and my last. God, but that nigger was tough. That Bacote nigger was some nigger!

# Questions for Critical Thinking

1. What role does setting play in this story?

2. Why does Ellison use the first-person narrator of a young boy? What does this accomplish?

3. Ellison asks readers to bear witness to this event. What does the title of the story reveal?

4. What is the point of the airplane in the story? What is Ellison trying to suggest to us by including this incident?

# Getting Started: A Research Project

Research is a skill that will carry you through your college career. You can find the research materials you need for this project on our website (**www.mhhe.com/delbanco1e**). Other ideas for research projects and sources appear at the end of this chapter.

Between the South and the West, decide which region's literature you liked the most in this chapter. Then, use one of the sources found at **www.mhhe.com/delbanco1e** to read more selections from that region. Formulate a thesis in which you identify what you believe to be the defining feature of literature from that region. But as you do this, take note of your own understanding or personally held myths about the region before you began and after you completed the reading. Consider how much of the region's identity comes from within, from its own inhabitants, and how much outside observers impose on it. For example, race relations in the South as depicted in fiction emerge as complex and painful on all sides; the heritage and memory of the Civil War—popularly known in the South as the War Between the States—holds different meanings for different races, and different meanings within social classes as well. In our national literature the war was a mostly subterranean subject, or as critic Daniel Aaron referred to it, an "unwritten war." The West has its own myths, some coming from within—as we noticed about the South—and some imposed on it from outside the region. The fairy-tale-large notion of "cowboys and Indians," for example, is something we grow up with. How realistic a view of the West does that image convey once you've read even a few selections about the country between the western bank of the Mississippi River and the Pacific Ocean?

**Go to www.mhhe.com/delbanco1e and respond to story selections from the South and the West.**

1. Choose a figure particular to one of the regions—the white farmer, say, in the South or the black fieldworker or the small-town shop-owner, or the western ranch owner or a Native American schoolteacher or reservation policeman—and, working with your instructor, draw up a reading list that will help you to flesh out a portrait of a person rooted in the region who seems recognizable to people living outside the region. Try to establish how much of that person's habits and views comes from local and regional influences and what aspect pertains to the national way of seeing the world.
2. Work from the outside in, beginning with a stereotype out of American popular or commercial culture, the Marlboro Man, for example, or the Southern Rebel soldier, and see how much the actual literature of the time, the stories and novels, lends support to these stereotypes.

# Further Suggestions for Writing and Research

1. Consider the three Southern authors you read in this chapter. Based on their fiction, how would you describe their attitudes toward the South? What characteristics of the region or its people do you see recur in more than one of the authors' works? Which aspects differ from author to author?
2. Are there such things as "regional" writers, or do all writers, even those from major cities, belong to a particular place, with habits and speech patterns and ways of seeing all their own?
3. Apply Thomas Wolfe's notion that "only the dead know Brooklyn" (from his story of the same name in chapter 8) to the South. Apply it to the West. Is there a particular place where you might imagine setting a Southern story equivalent to Wolfe's Brooklyn subway station? A Western story?

**Some Sources for Research**

Ayers, Edward L., and Bradley Mittendorf, eds. *The Oxford Book of the American South: Testimony, Memory, and Fiction.* New York: Oxford University Press, 1997.

Bercovitch, Sacvan. *Rites of Assent: Transformations in the Symbolic Construction of America.* New York: Routledge, 1993.

Fetterley, Judith, and Marjorie Pryse. *Regionalism, Women, and American Literary Culture.* Champaign, IL: University of Illinois Press, 2003. Especially chapters 1 and 2 and the Works Cited section.

Kittredge, William, ed. *The Portable Western Reader.* New York: Penguin, 1997.

Stegner, Wallace. "Western Record and Romance." *Literary History of the United States.* Ed. William Kittredge. New York: Penguin, 1997.

Work, James C., ed. *Prose and Poetry of the American West.* Lincoln: University of Nebraska Press, 1990.

**For examples of student papers, see chapter 3, Common Writing Assignments, and chapter 5, Writing the Research Paper, in the Handbook for Writing from Reading.**

# 13 Visual Arts,

AS you have seen throughout this textbook, writers use all aspects of technique—tone, point of view, character, symbols—to create a text. However, at the heart of their craft is the desire to tell a tale. Human beings have always delighted in telling and listening to stories, and that basic urge has lasted from the Greek epics to Biblical accounts to Elizabethan drama to the present day of TV, movies, email, text messages, and the Internet. The modes of delivery may have changed, but the hunger for story—both to tell it and hear it—remains.

As a result of these technologies, our culture has become increasingly based on visual media. Accordingly, we have found more visual ways to tell stories—including comics, television, movies, and—one of the newest and fastest growing formats—graphic novels. This chapter asks you to

# Film, & Fiction

think about the intersection between visual storytelling and the textual storytelling we have presented up to this point, with the hope of both learning about new ways to tell stories and illuminating what is unique to the written word. We will begin with comics, a hybrid of images and text, and their recent descendent, graphic novels. Then we'll explore adaptation—that is, how an old story is retold and reshaped into contemporary formats—as we chart *Beowulf* from its original epic poem format to current novel versions, to a major motion picture. In so doing, we hope you'll see how narratives, both old and new, really live all around us.

## COMICS

In his seminal book *Understanding Comics,* Scott McCloud traces comics all the way back to 1300 B.C. in Egyptian art. Although he admits that he cannot be sure where or when comics actually started, the point is that using a series of pictures to depict an action or a story is an age-old form. In the late 1930s and through the 1940s, however, comic books were marketed specifically for children, with superheroes like Superman and Wonder Woman high in popularity in the World War II era. Later, in the 1950s, comics became far more controversial as they began to take on adult themes with content closer to the hard-boiled edge of film noir and crime fiction than to stories suitable for children. As time passed, comics for adults continued to grow, even though adult comics today still fight the stereotype that they are a children's format.

Narrative prose requires time over which the story unfolds; in comics, however, space becomes an important element. Comics have their own set of techniques that the cartoonist can manipulate to create effects. One of the most important features of comics is the panel. Panels can be differently sized to create emphasis on certain images or moments. The gutter (the space between the panels) usually signals a time change from one panel to the next, and since not all minutiae of action are drawn, readers must fill in the gap between two panels as they read across the strip. Where a panel is positioned on the page generally determines where that panel occurs in time.

## GRAPHIC NOVELS

The term "graphic novel" is problematic in the eyes of many who create them. "Graphic" is all too easily and errantly associated with pornography, while many graphic novels are actually graphic memoirs or other genres like biography. Yet it is the term most widely used to describe a book-length comic that develops serious subject matter in roughly the length and depth of a novel. More than that, "graphic novel" signifies one of the fastest growing formats in terms of popularity and book sales; *Publisher's Weekly* estimated that graphic novels generated $330 million in sales in 2006, up from $75 million just five years earlier.

The first graphic novels were published in the late 1970s. In 1986, the first volume of Art Spiegelman's landmark graphic novel *Maus* was published, followed by the second volume in 1991. In 1992, the complete *Maus* won the Pulitzer Prize Special Award. *Maus* is at the heart of the graphic novel canon; a memoir more than a novel, it recounts Spiegelman's parents' survival of concentration camps during the Holocaust and the lasting effect the experience had on both them and on Spiegelman himself. Other widely known graphic novels include *The Sandman* (serialized 1989 to 1996) by Neil Gaiman, *Jimmy Corrigan* (2000) by Chris Ware, *Sin City* (serialized 1991–1992)

### GRAPHIC POETRY

Putting images with text is not, of course, a new invention. One of many artists to have done so is the early Romantic poet William Blake (1757-1827). In addition to a highly ornate style created by a unique printing process he invented, Blake's work is notable for the way that text and image work together to create meaning. For more on this topic, and to see samples of Blake's mix of graphics and poetry, see the William Blake casebook (chapter 26). For step-by-step help in "reading" graphics, refer to the "Learning to Read Images" exercise in that chapter.

by Frank Miller, *V for Vendetta* (originally serialized 1982–1985) by Alan Moore and David Lloyd, and *Persepolis* by Marjane Satrapi. *Sin City, V for Vendetta,* and *Persepolis* were adapted into major motion pictures. In the tradition of *Maus, Persepolis* is really a graphic memoir rather than a graphic novel. Like *Maus, Persepolis* also deals with political oppression and its effect on the people who live through it. Satrapi tells the story of her own childhood in Iran during the tumultuous times of the Shah's downfall and the installation of Islamic rule. Other graphic novels are themselves adaptations of previously told stories; a notable example is *Gemma Bovary (1999),* Posy Simmond's modern recasting of Flaubert's classic novel *Madame Bovary.*

Stills from the movie *Persepolis* (2007) by Marjane Satrapi and Vincent Paronnaud; based on the graphic novel by Marjane Satrapi

Graphic novels are as diverse in craft as are literary novels. Much has to do with the artist's individual style: Chris Ware's meticulous detail and his use of straight lines make for a clean, precise look that seems to reflect the isolation his characters feel, while Marjane Satrapi's stark black-and-white illustrations confront the reader in the same bold manner that her characters negotiate life in Iran. Compare the graphics from *Persepolis* to those by Gareth Hinds, who created *Beowulf: A Graphic Novel* in 2007, featuring full-color illustrations of the classic epic.

# Gareth Hinds (b. 1971)

# *Beowulf: A Graphic Novel*

## *[Grendel's Attack]* (2007)

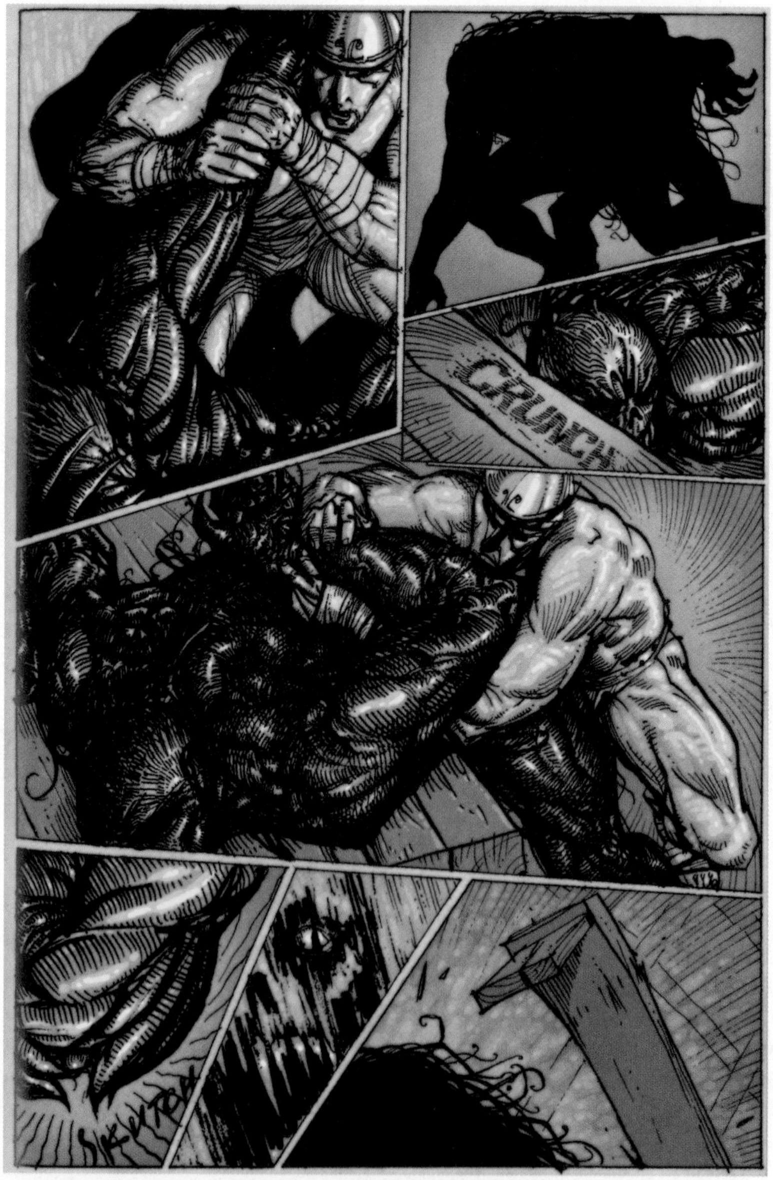

# Questions for Critical Thinking

1 A graphic novel usually brings text and pictures together. Describe the balance between text and images in Hinds's *Beowulf.* How effective do you find his visual rendition? What, if anything, would you change if you were the artist?

2 What details of Beowulf's depiction allow you to read him as a hero figure? What details of Grendel make it clear he is a villain?

3 Note the physical features of Beowulf and Grendel that are emphasized in the drawings. Are certain unique features emphasized for each character? Are certain features hidden? How do the two characters' portrayals influence your impressions of them?

## FILM ADAPTATIONS

When you hear the titles *Field of Dreams, Gone with the Wind,* and *Jaws,* you most likely think of Kevin Costner in a whispering cornfield, Clark Gable as Rhett Butler taking Vivien Leigh as Scarlett O'Hara into his arms, and the threatening bass music of the shark's approach. What you may not as readily think of are the novels these movies are based on—*Shoeless Joe* by Canadian novelist William P. Kinsella, *Gone with the Wind* by Margaret Mitchell, and *Jaws* by Peter Benchley—but each of these classic movies were novels first. Although estimates vary, it is safe to say that more than half of all movies made are drawn from literary sources. Screenwriters and filmmakers have adapted narratives and novels, and sometimes short stories, from Homer through Shakespeare, Tolstoy, and Hemingway into film. The transition from prose to the movie screen has advantages and disadvantages. Novels are frequently trimmed down, while filmmakers often plump up a short story, usually by presenting additional material about major characters. Certain aspects of a writer's voice or a narrator's presence can be difficult, if not impossible, to translate into film; often the closest approximation of a narrator is a voice-over in film. Almost by definition, the visual aspects of a work of literature come to life on the screen.

People who study film adaptation get frustrated with the oft-heard audience criticism that "it wasn't like that in the book." They would point out that there are several types of adaptation. Some do seek to be absolutely faithful to the original source. A frequently cited example is the BBC's production of Jane Austen's *Pride and Prejudice,* which takes approximately five hours to watch. Many adaptations incorporate differences to offer a reinterpretation of the original. A popular example you might be familiar with is *10 Things I Hate about You,* which is a contemporary interpretation of Shakespeare's *The Taming of the Shrew.* Reinterpretation doesn't have to be as dramatically different as placing a sixteenth-century drama in a modern-day high school; it can be as subtle as emphasizing a particular character more than the original does, or creating a mood or atmosphere that is augmented from the literary version.

A third type of adaptation is one in which the film uses a literary work as the germ of an idea, but takes it in such a different direction that the adaptation becomes its own work. A famous example is the 1979 film *Apocalypse Now,* which stands alone as a comment on the Vietnam War, yet clearly has at its heart Joseph Conrad's 1899 novella *Heart of Darkness.*

Those who study film adaptation lament that the criticism "It wasn't like the book" shows how thoughtlessly prejudiced many viewers are toward the original reading experience. The truth is that reading a book and watching a movie are completely different experiences, and comparing the two is most useful for understanding the story from various angles, rather than trying to precisely replicate one experience in another medium.

## CHARTING *BEOWULF*: FROM REINTERPRETATION TO FILM ADAPTATION

Stories are so important to a culture that writers and poets and playwrights tell them and retell them, over and over again. In the English and American literary tradition, one such story is *Beowulf,* an epic poem written around 1000 A.D. (although it likely existed in oral form as early as 700 A.D.). *Beowulf,* an epic poem in Old English by an anonymous author, tells the story of the Danes and the Geats, early Germanic tribes who lived in Denmark and southern Sweden. The poem was recorded by a Christian scribe, and so references to Christianity are inserted in an otherwise pagan society.

## BEOWULF STORY

King Hrothgar has built a magnificent hall named Heorot. But the hall is soon attacked by Grendel, a monster who is described as a descendant of Cain. Beowulf and his group of warriors arrive at Heorot from their homeland, and Beowulf offers to rid Hrothgar of his cursed monster. Beowulf fights Grendel hand-to-hand, and mortally wounds Grendel by tearing off his arm. Hrothgar's people are celebrating Beowulf's victory when another attack occurs, this time by Grendel's mother. Beowulf follows her to her lair and kills her as well. Victorious, Beowulf takes leave of Hrothgar and returns to his homeland. Years pass, and Beowulf eventually becomes king of the Geats. When Beowulf is old, a thief disturbs a nearby treasure trove that is guarded by a fierce dragon. The dragon threatens Beowulf's kingdom, and Beowulf sets out for one last fight. He is successful at slaying the dragon, but at the cost of his own life. Beowulf is mourned and honored as a hero by his people.

# Beowulf

## *[Grendel's attack and the fight with Beowulf]* **(circa 1000 A.D.)**

1 THE king's men lived, blissful and happy, until a certain one, a fiend of hell, began to plot mischief. This wrathful spirit was called Grendel, a mighty stalker of the marches, who haunted the moors, the fens and fastnesses. The wretched being had long inhabited the abode of the monster kind, e'er since the Creator had condemned him. The Lord eternal wreaked vengeance upon the kindred of Cain, because of the murder—the slaying of Abel. He got no pleasure in the feud, but the Lord banished him for that wicked deed far from mankind. From him there woke to life all the evil broods, monsters and elves and sea-beasts, and giants too, who long time strove with God. He gave them their reward! [. . .]

2 A thane of Hygelac,[1] great among the Geats, heard of these deeds of Grendel in his native land. In his strength he was the best of men in the day of this life, noble and mighty. He bade make ready for him a goodly ship, he said that he would go over the ocean-road unto that war-king, the great prince, since he had need of men. Little did his prudent thanes blame him for that journey, though he was dear to them; they encouraged him in his high purpose, and looked for good omens. The hero had warriors, chosen from among the Geats, the keenest he could find. Fifteen in all went down unto the ship. [. . .]

In his strength he was the best of men in the day of this life, noble and mighty.

[Beowulf arrives at Hrothgar's Kingdom.]

3 Then the mighty one arose with many a warrior round him,—it was a noble group of thanes! Some remained and guarded the armor as the chief bade them. The heroes hastened on, as the guide led them under the roof of Heorot. The great-hearted man, bold under his helmet, went on until he stood within the hall. Beowulf spoke,—on him gleamed his byrnie, his coat of mail linked by the smith's craft—: "Hail to thee, Hrothgar! I am Hygelac's kinsman and thane. Many an exploit have I undertaken in the days of my youth. In my native land I learned of Grendel's deeds; for seafarers say that this hall, this best of houses, stands empty and useless for all men, as soon as evening light is hidden under the vault of heaven. And my people, e'en the best and wisest men among them, urged me, king Hrothgar, to come unto thee, for they knew the strength of my might. They had themselves looked on when I came from the fight, stained with the blood of my foes. There I bound five of my enemies, destroyed a giant race, and slew by night the sea-beasts on the wave. I endured great distress, avenged the affliction of the Weder people,—they who had suffered woes! I ground the angry foe in pieces. And now I alone will decide the fight with Grendel, the giant monster. [. . .]

[Night falls.]

4 Then from the moorland, 'neath the misty hillsides, came Grendel drawing near; and God's anger was on him. The deadly foe was thinking to ensnare some man in that high hall. On he strode beneath the clouds, until he could see full well the wine-hall, the gilded house of men, all bright with gold. [. . .] The door, though fast in fire-hardened bands, sprang open straightway, soon as he touched it with his hands. Thus, plotting evil, he burst open the entrance to the hall, for he was swollen with rage. Quickly thereafter the fiend was treading upon the bright-paved floor, moving on in wrathful mood. Out of his eyes started a loathsome light, most like to flame. He saw in the hall many warriors, a kindred band together, a group of clansmen all asleep. And he laughed in his heart. The cursèd monster thought to take the life from each body, ere the day broke; for the hope of a plenteous feast was come to him. But it was not fated that he should devour any more of the race of men after that night.

The mighty kinsman of Hygelac was watching 5
to see how the deadly foe would go about his swift attacks. The monster thought not of tarrying, but sudden, for his first move, he seized upon a sleeping thane, rent him in pieces unawares, bit into the flesh, drank the blood from the veins, and swallowed him in huge pieces. In a moment he had devoured the whole corpse, even the hands and feet. He stepped on nearer and seized with his hands the great-hearted warrior on his bed. The fiend clutched at him with his claw, but Beowulf quickly grasped it with deadly purpose, fastening upon the arm. Straightway that master of evils discovered that never in this world in all the corners of the earth, had he met in any man a mightier hand-grip. But he could get away never the faster for that. He was eager to be gone; he wished to flee away into the darkness, to rejoin the horde of devils. He was not faring there as in the former days. Then the good kinsman of Hygelac bethought him of his speech at even; he stood upright and grappled him fast; his fingers cracked. The giant was making off. The hero followed him close. The monster was minded to fling loose, if he could, and flee away thence to the fen-hollows; but he knew that the strength of his arm was in the grasp of an angry foe. It was a dire journey that the destroyer had made to Heorot.

[. . .] Upon his shoulder a gaping wound appeared; 6
the sinews sprang asunder, the flesh was rent apart. The glory of the fight was given unto Beowulf. Grendel, sick to death, was doomed to flee thence and find out his joyless abode 'neath the fen-banks. Full well he knew that the end of his life was come, the appointed number of his days. By that deadly fight the desire of all the Danes was satisfied.

[1] "A thane of Hygelac" refers to Beowulf. A thane is a general term for a warrior; Hygelac is the name of Beowulf's kinsman.

# Questions for Critical Thinking

1 Grendel's physical appearance is one of the great mysteries of the Beowulf epic because very few direct details are provided in the text. How did you envision Grendel while reading the text?

2 Examine how Beowulf fits the traditional role of the hero. In what ways does he conform to typical conceptions of the hero? In what ways, if any, does he differ? Before you write, you may want to brainstorm qualities of heroes; in your introduction, offer a definition of the hero as you understand that archetype.

3 In what ways is Grendel a villain? Are there any ways in which he is sympathetic?

## TWO NOVEL ADAPTATIONS OF BEOWULF

The ancient epic has been reinterpreted in two contemporary novels, *Grendel* by John Gardner (1971) and *Eaters of the Dead* by Michael Crichton (1976). Popular novelist Crichton takes *Beowulf* and tells it from an outsider's perspective—Ibn Fadlan, an Arab who is conscripted into Beowulf's group of warriors. Crichton searches for the rational explanation of the events recounted in *Beowulf* and puts forth a story in which Grendel is not a single monster, but a group of Neanderthals who are ransacking the nearby village of the evolved Norsemen. He makes the novel read like the tenth-century eyewitness account of Ibn Fadlan; it includes many observations of Viking habits and way of life. Gardner provides another "outsider" perspective, telling the Beowulf tale through the eyes of the monster Grendel—whose tale is more a tragic coming-of-age story than an heroic epic. As you read, pay careful attention to the ways in which these modern interpretations adhere to the original epic, and to the ways in which they differ. Could these be, as Michael Crichton suggests, merely different accounts of the same actual event?

# John Gardner (1933–1982)

# *Grendel* (1971)

## GRENDEL'S ISOLATION

1 The sky ignores me, forever unimpressed. Him too I hate, the same as I hate these brainless budding trees, these brattling birds.

2 Not, of course, that I fool myself with thoughts that I'm more noble. Pointless, ridiculous monster crouched in the shadows, stinking of dead men, murdered children, martyred cows. (I am neither proud nor ashamed, understand. One more dull victim,

leering at seasons that never were meant to be observed.) "Ah, sad one, poor old freak!" I cry, and hug myself, and laugh, letting out salt tears, he he! till I fall down gasping and sobbing. (It's mostly fake.) The sun spins mindlessly overhead, the shadows lengthen and shorten as if by plan. Small birds, with a high-pitched yelp, lay eggs. The tender grasses peek up, innocent yellow, through the ground: the children of the dead. (It was just here, this shocking green, that once when the moon was tombed in clouds, I tore off sly old Athelgard's head. Here, where the startling tiny jaws of crocuses snap at the late-winter sun like the heads of baby water-snakes, here I killed the old woman with the iron-gray hair. She tasted of urine and spleen, which made me spit. Sweet mulch for yellow blooms. Such are the tiresome memories of a shadow-shooter, earth-rim-roamer, walker of the world's weird wall.) "Waaah!" I cry, with another quick, nasty face at the sky, mournfully observing the way it is, bitterly remembering the way it was, and idiotically casting tomorrow's nets. "Aargh! Yaww!" I reel, smash trees. Disfigured son of lunatics. The big-boled oaks gaze down at me yellow with morning, beneath complexity. "No offense," I say, with a terrible, sycophantish smile, and tip an imaginary hat.

3 It was not always like this, of course. On occasion, it's been worse.

## BEOWULF'S ARRIVAL

4 I am mad with joy.—At least I think it's joy. Strangers have come, and it's a whole new game. I kiss the ice on the frozen creeks, I press my ear to it, honoring the water that rattles below, for by water they came: the icebergs parted as if gently pushed back by enormous hands, and the ship sailed through, sea-eager, foamy-necked, white sails riding the swan-road, flying like a bird! O happy Grendel! Fifteen glorious heroes, proud in their battle dress, fat as cows! [. . .]

[Grendel watches as Hrothgar's coast guard questions Beowulf as to who he is.]

5 At last the coastguard's voice gave out—he bent over the pommel, coughing into his fist—and the leader answered. His voice, though powerful, was mild. Voice of a dead thing, calm as dry sticks and ice when the wind blows over them. He had a strange face that, little by little, grew unsettling to me: it was a face, or so it seemed for an instant, from a dream I had almost forgotten. The eyes slanted downward, never blinking, unfeeling as a snake's. He had no more beard than a fish. He smiled as he spoke, but it was as if the gentle voice, the child-like yet faintly ironic smile were holding something back, some magician-power that could blast stone cliffs to ashes as lightning blasts trees.

The eyes slanted downward, never blinking, unfeeling as a snake's.

6 "We're Geats," he said, "the hearth-companions of King Hygilac. You've heard of my father. A famous old man named Ecgtheow." His mind, as he spoke, seemed far away, as if, though polite, he were indifferent to all this—an outsider not only among the Danes but everywhere.

## FIGHT WITH BEOWULF

7 I touch the door with my fingertips and it bursts, for all its fire-forged bands—it jumps away like a terrified deer—and I plunge into the silent, hearth-lit hall with a laugh that I wouldn't much care to wake up to myself. I trample the planks that a moment before protected the hall like a hand raised in horror to a terrified mouth (sheer poetry, ah!) and the broken hinges rattle like swords down the timbered walls. The Geats are like stones, and whether it's because they're numb with terror or stiff from too much mead, I cannot tell. I am swollen with excitement, bloodlust and joy and a strange fear that mingle in my chest like the twisting rage of a bone-fire. I step onto the brightly shining floor and angrily advance on them. They're all asleep, the whole company! I can hardly believe my luck, and my wild heart laughs, but I let out no sound. Swiftly, softly, I will move from bed to bed and destroy them all, swallow every last man. I am blazing, half-crazy with joy. For pure, mad prank, I snatch a cloth from the nearest table and tie it around my neck to make a napkin. I delay no longer. I seize up a sleeping man, tear at him hungrily, bite through his bone-locks and suck hot, slippery blood. He goes down in huge morsels, head, chest, hips, legs, even the hands and feet. My face and arms are wet, matted. The napkin is sopping. The dark floor steams. I move on at once and I reach for another one (whispering, whispering, chewing the universe down to words), and I seize a wrist. A shock goes through me. Mistake!

8 It's a trick! His eyes are open, were open all the time, cold-bloodedly watching to see how I work. The eyes nail me now as his hand nails down my arm. I

jump back without thinking (whispering wildly: *jump back without thinking*). Now he's out of his bed, his hand still closed like a dragon's jaw on mine. Nowhere on middle-earth, I realize, have I encountered a grip like his. My whole arm's on fire, incredible, searing pain—it's as if his crushing fingers are charged like fangs with poison. I scream, facing him, grotesquely shaking hands—dear long-lost brother, kinsman-thane—and the timbered hall screams back at me. I feel the bones go, ground from their sockets, and I scream again. [. . .]

9 The room goes suddenly white, as if struck by lightning. I stare down, amazed. He has torn off my arm at the shoulder! Blood pours down where the limb was. I cry, I bawl like a baby. He stretched his blinding white wings and breathes out fire. I run for the door and through it. I move like wind. I stumble and fall, get up again. I'll die! I howl. The night is aflame with winged men. *No, no! Think!* I come suddenly awake once more from the nightmare. Darkness. I really will die! Every rock, every tree, every crystal of snow cries out cold-blooded objectness. Cold, sharp outlines, everything around me: distinct, detached as dead men. I understand. "Mama!" I bellow. "Mama, Mama! I'm dying!" But her love is history. His whispering follows me into the woods, though I've outrun him. "It was an accident," I bellow back. I will cling to what is true. "Blind, mindless, mechanical. Mere logic of chance." I am weak from loss of blood. No one follows me now. I stumble again and with my one weak arm I cling to the huge twisted roots of an oak. I look down past stars to a terrifying darkness. I seem to recognize the place, but it's impossible. "Accident," I whisper. I will fall. I seem to desire the fall, and though I fight it with all my will I know in advance that I can't win. Standing baffled, quaking with fear, three feet from the edge of a nightmare cliff, I find myself, incredibly, moving toward it. I look down, down, into bottomless blackness, feeling the dark power moving in me like an ocean current, some monster inside me, deep sea wonder, dread night monarch astir in his cave, moving me slowly to my voluble tumble into death.

# Questions for Critical Thinking

1 Write a description of Grendel as he appears in Gardner's novel. What can you say about his personality and attitude? Support your description with quotes from the excerpt.

2 How does being in Grendel's point of view affect the way you see Beowulf in Gardner's version? How similar or different do you find Beowulf from the original epic in which he was the main character?

3 Compare Gardner's Grendel to the monster in the original epic. Is he a more sympathetic character in Gardner's rendering? If so, formulate a thesis explaining what makes him more sympathetic in your view. If not, create a thesis in which you argue why he is not.

4 Read the excerpts from Michael Crichton's *Eaters of the Dead* below. Compare and contrast the Grendel monster from the original epic, Gardner's interpretation, and Crichton's depiction of the wendol. Are the various authors describing different characters altogether, or are they emphasizing different traits of the same creature?

# A FACTUAL NOTE ON ADAPTING *BEOWULF* FOR

## *Eaters of the Dead* by Michael Crichton

I started from the scholarly tradition that examined epic poetry and mythology as if it might have some underlying basis in fact. Heinrich Schliemann assumed the *Iliad* was true, and found what he claimed was Troy and Mycenae; Arthur Evans believed there was something to the myth of the Minotaur, and uncovered the Palace of Knossos on Crete; M. I. Finley and others had traced the route of Ulysses in the *Odyssey;* Lionel Casson had written about the real journeys that might underlie the myth of Jason and the Argonauts. Thus it seemed reasonable, within this tradition, to imagine that *Beowulf,* too, had originally been based on an actual event.

That event had been embellished over centuries of oral retelling, producing the fantastic narrative we read today. But I thought it might be possible to reverse the process, peeling away the poetic invention, and returning to a kernel of genuine human experience—something that had actually happened. . . .

Clearly, I wanted an eyewitness account. I could not extract it from the existing *Beowulf* narrative, and I did not want to invent it. That was my impasse. But at some point, I realized I did not have to invent it—I could *discover* it instead.

Suppose, I thought, a contemporary observer had been present at these battles, and had written an account of the events that were later transformed into a poem. Suppose, too, that this account *already existed,* but had never been recognized for what it was. If this were so, then no invention on my part would be necessary. I could merely reproduce the eyewitness narrative, and annotate it for the reader. . . .

What sort of narrative would be most desirable? I concluded the most useful account would be written by an outsider—someone not part of the culture, who could report objectively on the events as they occurred. But who would this outside observer have been? Where would he have come from?

On reflection, I realized I already knew of such a person. In the tenth century, an Arab named Ibn Fadlan had traveled north from Baghdad into what is now Russia, where he came in contact with the Vikings. His manuscript, well-known to scholars, provides one of the earliest eyewitness accounts of Viking life and culture. As a college undergraduate, I had read portions of the manuscript. Ibn Fadlan had a distinct voice and style. He was imitable. He was believable. He was unexpected. And after a thousand years, I felt that Ibn Fadlan would not mind being revived in a new role, as a witness to the events that led to the epic poem of *Beowulf.* . . .

I obtained the existing manuscript fragments and combined them, with only slight modifications, into the first three chapters of *Eaters of the Dead.* I then wrote the rest of the novel in the style of the manuscript to carry Ibn Fadlan on the rest of his now-fictional journey. . . .

# Michael Crichton (1942–2008)

# *Eaters of the Dead* (1976)

## FIRST GLIMPSE OF BULIWYF

1 Now, one of their number, a young noble called Buliwyf, was chosen to be their new leader, but he was not accepted while the sick chieftan still lived. This was the cause of uneasiness, at the time of our arrival. Yet also there was no aspect of sorrow or weeping among the people encamped on the Volga.

2 The Northmen place great importance on the duty of the host. They greet every visitor with warmth and hospitality, much food and clothing, and the earls and nobles compete for the honor of the greatest hospitality. The party of our caravan was brought before Buliwyf and a great feast was given us. Over this Buliwyf himself presided, and I saw him to be a tall man, and strong, with skin and hair and beard of pure white. He had the bearing of a leader.

## BATTLE WITH THE WENDOL

3 Now I noticed that Buliwyf and all his company did not drink that night, or only sparingly, and Rothgar took this as no insult, but rather acknowledged it as the natural course of things. There was no wind that night; the candles and flames of Hurot Hall did not flicker, and yet it was damp, and chill. I saw with my own eyes that out of doors the mist was rolling in from the hills, blocking the silvered light of the moon, cloaking all in blackness.

4 As the night continued, King Rothgar and his Queen departed for sleep, and the massive doors of Hurot Hall were locked and barred, and the nobles and earls remaining there fell into a drunken stupor and snored loudly.

5 Then Buliwyf and his men, still wearing their armor, went about the room, dousing the candles and seeing to the fires, that they should burn low and weak. I asked Herger the meaning of this, and he told me to pray for my life, and to feign sleep. I was given a weapon, a short sword, but it was little comfort to me; I was not a warrior and knew it full well.

Verily, all the men feigned sleep. Buliwyf and his 6
men joined the slumbering bodies of the King Rothgar's earls, who were truly snoring. How long we waited I do not know, for I think I slept awhile myself. Then all at once I was awake, in a manner of unnatural sharp alertness; I was not drowsy but instantly tense and alert, still lying on a bearskin cloth on the floor of the great hall. It was dark night; the candles in the hall burned low, and a faint breeze whispered through the hall and fluttered the yellow flames.

And then I heard a low grunting sound, like the 7
rooting of a pig, carried to me by the breeze, and I smelled a rank odor like the rot of a carcass after a month, and I feared greatly. This rooting sound, for I can call it none else, this grumbling, grunting, snorting sound, grew louder and more excited. It came from outdoors, at one side of the hall. Then I heard it from another side, and then another, and another. Verily the hall was surrounded.

I sat up on one elbow, my heart pounding, and I 8
looked about the hall. No man among the sleeping warriors moved, and yet there was Herger, lying with his eyes wide open. And there, too, Buliwyf, breathing in a snore, with his eyes also wide open. From this I gathered that all the warriors of Buliwyf were waiting to do battle with the wendol, whose sounds now filled the air. [. . .]

Then came the most fearsome moment. All sounds 9
ceased. There was utter silence, except for the snoring of the men and the low crackle of the fire. Still none of the warriors of Buliwyf stirred.

And then there was a mighty crash upon the solid 10
doors of the hall of Hurot, and these doors burst open, and a rush of reeking air gutted all the lights, and the black mist entered the room. I did not count their

number: verily it seemed thousands of black grunting shapes, and yet it might have been no more than five or six, huge black shapes hardly in the manner of men, and yet also manlike. The air stank of blood and death; I was cold beyond reason, and shivered. Yet still no warrior moved.

11 Then, with a curdling scream to wake the dead, Buliwyf leapt up, and in his arms he swung the giant sword Runding, which sang like a sizzling flame as it cut the air. And his warriors leapt up with him, and all joined in battle. The shouts of the men mingled with the pig-grunts and the odors of the black mist, and there was terror and confusion and great wracking and rending of the Hurot Hall. [. . .]

The air stank of blood and death;

12 I remember, most distinctly, the touch of these monsters upon me, especially the furry aspect of the bodies, for these mist monsters have hair as long as a hairy dog, and as thick, on all parts of their bodies. And then the black mist was gone, slunk away, grunting and panting and stinking, leaving behind destruction and death that we could not know until we had lighted fresh tapers. [. . .]

13 Herger said thus: "I saw two of their number carrying a third, who was dead." Perhaps this was so, for all generally agreed upon it. I learned that the mist monsters never leave one of their kind to the society of men, but rather will risk great dangers to retrieve him from human purview. So also will they go to extreme lengths to keep a victim's head, and we could not find the head of Edgtho in any place; the monsters had carried it off with them.

Then Buliwyf spoke, and Herger told me his words thus: "Look, I have retained a trophy of the night's bloody deeds. See, here is an arm of one of the fiends." 14

And, true to his word, Buliwyf held the arm of one of the mist monsters, cut off at the shoulder by the great sword Runding. All the warriors crowded around to examine it. I perceived it thusly: it appeared to be small, with a hand of abnormally large size. But the forearm and upper arm were not large to match it, although the muscles were powerful. There was long black matted hair on all parts of the arm except the palm of the hand. Finally it is to say that the arm stank as the whole beast stank, with the fetid smell of the black mist. 15

Now all the warriors cheered Buliwyf, and his sword Runding. The fiend's arm was hung from the rafters of the great hall of Hurot, and marveled at by all the people of the kingdom of Rothgar. Thus ended the first battle with the wendol. 16

# Questions for Critical Thinking

1 Compare Grendel in the original version to the wendol of *Eaters of the Dead.* In it, examine what is gained, as well as what is lost, by making these changes.

2 Crichton shifts the point of view of the story by making it a first-person account from an Arab—an outsider to the Northman tribe. Note the places in which you see the outsider status of the narrator giving Crichton the opportunity to expand on the details of Buliwyf's tribe. How do these details change your view of Beowulf and his brave warriors?

3 Take a small portion of Grendel's fight with Beowulf from the original epic and underline all the descriptions the author includes. Do the same for the wendol attack in *Eaters of the Dead.* In your opinion, which version more clearly brings the battle to life on the page?

4 Both Crichton and Gardner offer an "outsider's" view of Beowulf. Compare Crichton's Arab narrator's impression of Buliwyf to Grendel's first impression of Beowulf. What feelings do they share about him? What do the differences between their impressions say about their characters?

# TWO FILM ADAPTATIONS OF *BEOWULF*

Buliwyf, his sword bloody from battling his way into the subterranean wendol lair, prepares to do battle with the wendol queen. Contrast his weary expression and dirty clothes with the naked, glistening bravura of Beowulf from *Beowulf: The Movie.*

The wendol queen, adorned in snakes and human bones, casts a baleful look at Buliwyf. How does her warped humanity compare to the twisted, gigantic form of Grendel from *Beowulf: The Movie*?

Beowulf, naked and unarmed, steps forward to challenge Grendel in combat. In what ways is he "larger than life" compared to Buliwyf from *The 13th Warrior*? What effect does computer rendering of a real actor have on your perception of the Beowulf character?

The hulking, twisted Grendel bursts into Hrothgar's mead hall, intent on a feast of human flesh. Compare his bent posture to the coiled crouch of the wendol queen. Which "monster" seems more threatening?

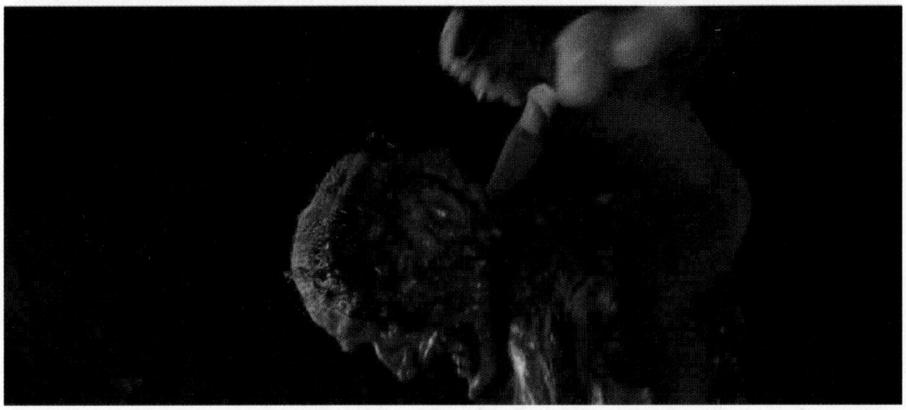

Beowulf gains the advantage over the giant Grendel and pummels him with his bare fists. Which version of the epic presented in this chapter does this representation remind you most of? Is this how you imagined the fight when you read the original epic?

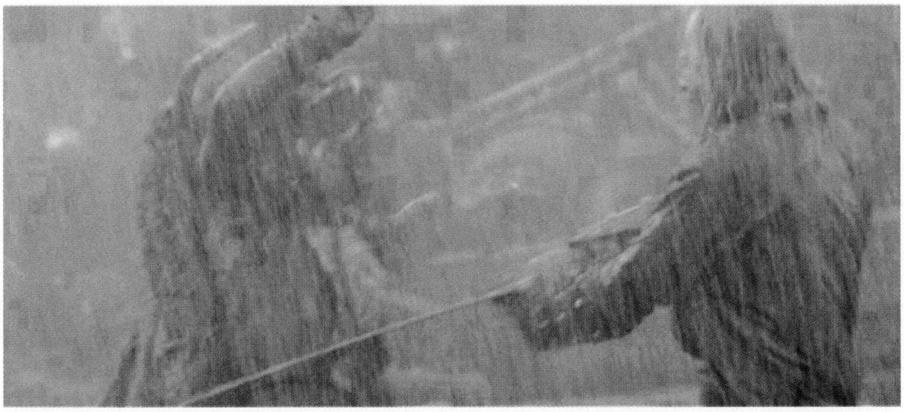

Buliwyf wields the mighty sword Huring in a fatal blow to the wendol leader. By using weapons and fighting foes his own size, does Buliwyf appear to be more or less heroic? Does he or the Beowulf of *Beowulf: The Movie* seem more believable?

# The 13th Warrior (1999)

*Adapted from the novel* Eaters of the Dead *by Michael Crichton*
*Screenplay by: William Wisher Jr. and Warren Lewis*
*Director: John McTiernan*
*Starring: Antonio Banderas (Ibn Fadlan), Vladimir Kulich (Buliwyf)*

1 AHMED Ibn Fadlan, an Arab charged to be an ambassador to the north, comes across a band of Vikings. They have been asked to help a far-off kingdom, and they cast lots to see which thirteen men will be sent. Since the thirteenth man must be a foreigner, Ahmed is conscripted to go along with the group, led by Buliwyf.

2 Disgusted by the Vikings' habits and hygiene, Ahmed is at first on the outskirts of the group. He begins to prove himself by picking up their language, showing off his horsemanship and maintaining his dignity as an Arab devoted to Allah.

3 When the warriors arrive in Hrothgar's land, they come upon a house in which all the inhabitants have been killed and their bodies gnawed on. They speak with Hrothgar and understand that it is the wendol, a group that comes with the mist, who have attacked his kingdom repeatedly. That night, Buliwyf's group feigns sleep and are alert and ready when the wendol come. Ahmed takes part in the fight, even though he does not want to. Bulywif takes the arm of one of the wendol, which are portrayed as hairy men with bear skins that cover their heads.

It is Ahmed who pieces together that they must 4
fight the source of the wendol in order to get rid of them, and so Buliwyf's men find the wendol's cave. In the cave, they see the remains of human victims who have been eaten by the wendol. Bulywif sneaks into the innermost room where the wendol's queen is kept. He kills her, but in so doing is himself wounded. Pursued by wendol, he escapes with his men by swimming under the cave and out into the sea (another of Ahmed's ideas).

Back at Hrothgar's hall, they prepare for a final 5
attack from the wendol. With his waning strength, Buliwyf fights in the battle and kills the leader of the wendol before dying himself. Ahmed fights, too, as he has become a brave warrior.

The movie ends with Ahmed, now a friend of the 6
Vikings, setting sail for home.

# Questions for Critical Thinking

1 In *Eaters of the Dead,* Ibn Fadlan and Buliwyf have a growing friendship over the course of the novel. In *The 13th Warrior,* Buliwyf remains far more distant. How does this alter the reader's/viewer's perception of Buliwyf? Why might the moviemakers have changed this aspect of Crichton's book?

2 *The 13th Warrior* is, in a way, twice removed from the original *Beowulf*—that is, it is a movie adaptation of a reinterpretation of the original. Can you trace similarities between the original epic and this reinterpreted movie adaptation? List any similarities you see, from the overall plot to the smallest detail. Does the number of similarities, whether small or large, surprise you?

3 After reading Michael Crichton's process in "A Factual Note on *Eaters of the Dead,*" evaluate whether the movie represents what Crichton was trying to do or takes the book in a new direction. What, if anything, does the film add to further Crichton's idea?

# Beowulf: The Movie (2007)

*Written by: Roger Avary and Neil Gaiman*
*Director: Robert Zemeckis*
*Starring: Anthony Hopkins (Hrothgar), Ray Winstone (Beowulf), Crispin Glover (Grendel), Angelina Jolie (Grendel's mother)*

1 RELEASED in 2007, the movie uses motion capture animation—that is, a technique in which infrared light captures the movements of real actors, which are then put into computer animation to create the look and color desired by the animators—and was originally released as a 3D movie. The major change to the plot of the original epic is that Beowulf is seduced by Grendel's mother, and their offspring is the dragon that Beowulf later fights. Other changes include that Hrothgar was also seduced by Grendel's mother, and—tormented by the fact that Grendel is his offspring—Hrothgar commits suicide, making Beowulf king of the Danes, not the Geats.

2 *Note:* This movie adaptation is not to be confused with the 2005 movie *Beowulf & Grendel. Beowulf: The Movie* begins with Grendel's attack on the mead hall, showing the destruction and death he causes, even though Grendel clearly avoids harming Hrothgar. Next, Beowulf arrives with his men and is taken to meet with Hrothgar, where he pledges to rid the king of his monster. After feasting, Beowulf strips off his armor to go to bed, reasoning that he will fight Grendel hand to hand. When Grendel bursts in, Beowulf fights him and breaks off Grendel's arm.

Grendel, who speaks Old English, returns to his mother's cave where he laments his missing arm and assures her he did not kill Hrothgar. All the movie shows of his mother at this point is a soft, seductive voice with flashes of a snake's tail. When Beowulf comes to the cave to slay Grendel's mother, he finds that she is a beautiful seductress. 3

After Beowulf returns and refuses to directly tell Hrothgar whether or not he killed Grendel's mother, Hrothgar—tormented by his concealment of the fact that he was himself seduced by Grendel's mother years ago and that Grendel is their love child—commits suicide, making Beowulf king. 4

The movie jumps ahead many years to show that Beowulf, though an adored king, is bothered by a former guilt. Only the queen seems to understand that guilt, and she is cold to Beowulf because of what she knows about his relation with Grendel's mother. It becomes clear that Beowulf, like Hrothgar before him, was seduced by Grendel's mother, and that their love child is a dragon. In the end, Beowulf slays the dragon—his own offspring—but is mortally wounded in the fight and dies. As Beowulf tells the queen before he dies, "Keep a memory of me, not as a king or a hero, but as a man, fallible and flawed." 5

# An Interview on Adapting *Beowulf* for the movie with Roger Avary & Neil Gaiman

*(from http://www.moviesonline.ca/movienews_13367.html)*

**Roger Avary:** The original genesis of the project began with questioning. You know when I read the eulogy itself, who is Grendel's father? Why has no one in academia ever addressed that? Why does Beowulf emerge from the cave with the head of Grendel and not the head of the mother and why was he in there for eight days? You know, these were questions that I didn't see anybody answering. . . .

And then I had heard much theorizing about the themes of the last half but no one had ever united it properly into a single story and so I was talking with Neil ten years ago in May and telling him my theories on Beowulf and the problem I was having with the second half, and Neil said, "But don't you see? If this and this and this that you say are true about Beowulf, if Hrothgar is Grendel's father and if Beowulf did indeed give in to the mother, don't you see the dragon is Beowulf's son come back to haunt him for his sins?" And it was like, had it been a snake it would have bit me. I stood up and I immediately told Neil, "When are you available? Let's go work on this."

**Neil Gaiman:** [. . .] [T]he problem with Beowulf is that we only have one manuscript and that manuscript, the Cotton Vitellius document, has frankly come to us through luck more than anything else. It was written over a thousand years ago. The manuscript has scorch marks on it from where it was rescued from a fire and thrown out of a window. Is it incomplete? Well no, it's not like we're missing pages of that version of Beowulf. Is that the only version of Beowulf that has that story that ever existed or was ever told? Obviously not. This was part of the oral tradition that was at the end of it. . . .

You know so it's like do we think that? When you tell a story in the oral tradition, you tend to adapt it to your audience. If your audience wants blood, you give them blood. If they want sex, you give them sex. If you are a Christian monk writing something down, if there were sexual elements, you're not going to put them in and they didn't. . . .

**Roger Avary:** So you can imagine that many changes could have occurred over it. And for us it was a matter of investigating why . . . were we not privy to the actual battles with Grendel's mother? Why was it told by Beowulf afterwards?

**Neil Gaiman:** Taking concepts like just the idea of an unreliable narrator and saying we think that the story of Beowulf is told by an unreliable narrator. And one of the things that our Beowulf is about is the idea of okay, at the end of it, we are told his song is going to be sung and this is the song of Beowulf but it's very obvious by the end of our film that the song of Beowulf that is being sung even then is not actually what happened. It's already changing and shifting. It's about the relationship between a man and his story in some ways.

# Questions for Critical Thinking

1 After watching Grendel's attack in *Beowulf* and the battle scenes in *The 13th Warrior,* compare the strengths of the movies. Which effects are particularly stimulating visually? How realistic or fantastic is each version? How do the effects build that sense of reality or fantasy?

2 Contrast the duels between Beowulf and Grendel from *Beowulf* the movie and from Gareth Hinds's graphic novel. How are the two battles different? Discuss how the differing dynamics of the battles impact your impressions of the Beowulf and Grendel characters.

3 Observe the Grendel character in the *Beowulf* movie. Is he sympathetic or a villain? Compare him to the Grendel characters from Crichton's and Gardner's versions, as well as from the original epic. Which "Grendel" does he have most in common with? Explain your answer with examples from the movie.

# Getting Started: A Research Project

Research is a skill that will carry you through your college career. You can find the research materials you need for this project on our website (www.mhhe.com/delbanco1e). Other ideas for research projects and sources appear at the end of this chapter.

As you've witnessed, when it comes to the classics, adaptation is a major way of honoring the original. We see this in the thousands-of-years-old tradition of staging and restaging Greek tragedy (see chapter 32) and Shakespeare's plays (see chapter 33) and in the adaptation of the Beowulf epic. Another long heroic poem that has gone through a number of changes and permutations is Homer's *Odyssey*. Its ancient original oral form—which was chanted by a group of rhetors or reciters at Greek religious festivals four times a year in the centuries leading up to the birth of writing—became a literary form. The story of Odysseus and the Trojan War was copied down on papyrus and read by Greek scholars up until the present moment. There have been a number of translations over the centuries (from say, that of Alexander Pope to Chapman's and Murray's), and some striking and powerful contemporary versions of the poem (Lattimore, Fitzgerald, Fagles); there was also a Classics Illustrated comic book version, and, with the advent of film technology, a number of cinematic versions.

An adventurous student may want to take on the task of reading the *Odyssey* in a few different translations and plotting the course of this epic's evolution from English version of the classical Greek poem to comic book to the movies. Focusing on a particular incident or scene in the original poem, such as Odysseus's trick of employing the so-called Trojan Horse to gain entry into the heavily fortified city of Troy, you can observe and comment upon the various changes and transformations. Add to this the various cinematic versions of the epic. From Italian costume epics to the 1997 TV movie made here in the United States and such variations on the story as we find in "O Brother, Where Art Thou?" the possibilities are rich for studying how a timeless story became adapted over time. A similarly rich trail of versions of Jane Austen's novels is something you can follow as well, or Shakespeare's *Othello* or *Hamlet*.

# Further Suggestions for Writing and Research

The Research in the World box at the end of each casebook directs you toward secondary sources available at www.mhhe.com/delbanco1e that enhance your understanding of the work or author by giving you another perspective. This casebook also offers another kind of research: working in depth with the literature itself. While the excerpts in this chapter have given you an idea of each work and its major similarities with and differences from the original epic, the topics below will ask you to read or watch a couple of works from this casebook in their entirety. Studying the entire work will give you the chance to make your own connections and form your own ideas.

1. The poet who recorded *Beowulf* was Christian, even if those who recited the epic in earlier centuries were not. There is an interesting mix, then, of Christian references and pagan norms. *Eaters of the Dead, The Thirteenth Warrior, Beowulf* the movie, and *Grendel* all involve the presence of religion in different ways. Along with the original epic, choose one of

continued

these adaptations to read or watch in its entirety. Then write a five-page paper in which you examine the portrayal of religion in each work. A good starting place for a thesis would be to state where you see the conflict between 1) religious belief and action, or 2) different religions within one work.

2. The hero is an important character to literature. After brainstorming your ideas about hero characters—and you may want to consider heroes from Odysseus all the way up to current heroes like Superman—write a paragraph that defines the hero and lists his qualities. Keep this paragraph handy as you read the original *Beowulf* and one other work or movie of your choice from this chapter. Then write a five-page paper in which you discuss who the hero is and how he is portrayed in the adaptation you chose. How do these versions of the hero complicate and expand your original definition? In other words, formulate a thesis that states how the concept of the hero is used in *Beowulf* and in an adaptation.
3. In addition to the original *Beowulf*, read one book and watch one movie presented in this chapter. Then write a five-page essay in which you place the three versions on a continuum of adaptation from the most to the least like the original epic. Make a decision about which of the adaptations you feel is most stimulating to a modern audience. What are the major differences? What is the effect of these differences? Do these differences enhance readers' experience of the epic or diminish it?
4. After reading the original *Beowulf* and viewing one of its reinterpretations, imagine what your own reinterpretation of *Beowulf* might look like. In five pages, outline your ideas, including decisions such as the medium you would use (i.e., book or movie or something else), the point of view or main character, the setting and time period, etc.

**Some Sources for Research**

5. A contemporary version of graphic poetry has recently developed around Billy Collins, U.S. poet laureate from 2001–2003. Independent animators have created short animation to accompany Collins's own reading of his poems. To sample some of this animated poetry, this poetry can be found at *www.bcactionpoet.org*. (Poems we particularly recommend: "Budapest" and "Forgetfulness")
6. "Why They Changed the Beowulf Story" http://www.moviesonline.ca/movienews_13367.html
7. The field is quite new and still truly wide open, so you can perform raw field research on your own by taking a character from your reading and seeing what adaptations you can find on the Web, reading the new versions, viewing the films, and writing down your own findings.

**For examples of student papers, see chapter 3, Common Writing Assignments, and chapter 5, Writing the Research Paper, in the Handbook for Writing from Reading.**

# 14

# An Anthology of Stories for Further Reading

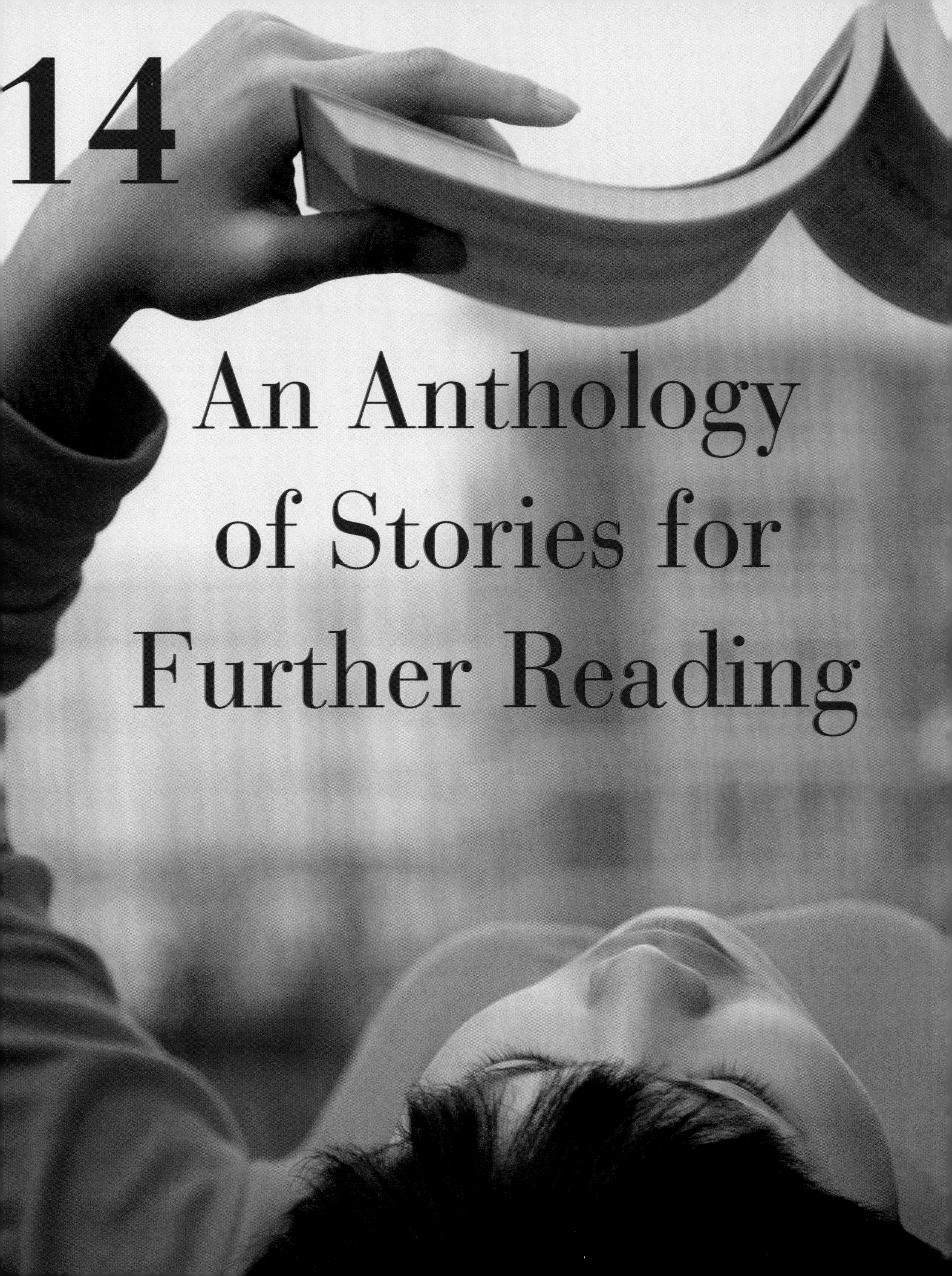

*I'll read stories where the stakes are high . . .*

Q&A

*I don't like to see a bad sentence on the page.*

# *A Conversation on Writing*

## Amy Hempel

### The Allure of Reading

I will read any story about somebody getting through a hard thing. Anybody who comes out the other side of a difficult experience—I want to know how that person did it. I'll read stories where the stakes are high, where it matters if things turn out right or not. I read people who are incredibly inventive with language, people who say things I've never heard before. People who have sentences with kind of a rhythm like music. I like the sounds of a sentence, the acoustics of a sentence, not just what it's saying or the information in it. In fact, information for me is often the least important part of the story. I'm interested in who it happened to and what he or she is making of it.

### Writing from Experience

One of the things that interests me most in story writing is that, even though you start maybe with things that really happened to you, people that you know, if you're paying attention there's a point where it stops being your story and becomes the story's story. It will veer off. And if you're paying attention and open to invention, that's when story really comes into being, I think. We mythologize ourselves, so even when you try to tell a true story, you tell a friend about a close call, you find yourself embellishing it, because it could have been a closer call. And I think everybody's alert to that without even trying. So I usually start with something that did happen with people I know. But almost without trying, it changes. They change. And they become somebody else or anybody else.

### Reading As a Refuge

My earliest memory of reading fiction is taking *The Secret Garden* into a fort that I had built in a family's home in Denver. It was a basement fort next to a crawl space. . . . I remember taking couch cushions off the couch and using sheets and building a fort. And I could just stay there for hours and hours.

Born in Chicago (1951), Amy Hempel lived in several different places throughout her childhood, among them California. Known as a minimalist in her writing—although she prefers Raymond Carver's term, "precisionist"—Hempel has made her reputation solely on short fiction. She has published four collections of short stories—*Reasons to Live* (1985), *At the Gates of the Animal Kingdom* (1990), *Tumble Home* (1997), and *The Dog of the Marriage* (2005). As this last title suggests, Hempel has an interest in dogs; she even co-edited an anthology of poems written in dogs' voices titled *Unleashed: Poems by Writers' Dogs* (1995). A well-respected and much anthologized writer (see the interview with Amy Tan), Hempel has taught at such institutions as Bennington College, Duke University, Princeton University, New York University, and Sarah Lawrence College.

Hempel's writing has been published in venues including *Harper's, Vanity Fair, The Quarterly,* and *Playboy.* She has received many honors, including a Guggenheim Fellowship and, in 2008, the REA Award for the Short Story. *The Collected Stories,* published in 2006 won the Ambassador Book Award for best fiction of the year, and was a finalist for the PEN/Faulkner Award. It was one of the *New York Times'* Ten Best Books of the Year. She is currently the director of the graduate fiction program at Brooklyn College, and makes her home in Manhattan.

**To watch this entire interview and hear the author read from "San Francisco," go to www.mhhe.com/delbanco1e.**

**RESEARCH ASSIGNMENT** In her interview, Amy Hempel discusses how her surroundings affect the subject matter and themes of her writing. How do you see these influences reflected in her story "San Francisco"?

# San Francisco (1985)

1 Do you know what I think?

I think it was the tremors. That's what must have done it. The way the floor rolled like bongo boards under our feet? Remember it was you and Daddy and me having lunch? "I guess that's not an earthquake," you said. "I guess you're shaking the table?"

That's when it must have happened. A watch on a dresser, a small thing like that—it must have been shaken right off, onto the floor.

And how would Maidy know? Maidy at the doctor's office? All those years on a psychiatrist's couch and suddenly the couch is *moving*.

5 Good God, she is on that couch when the big one hits.

Maidy didn't tell you, but you know what her doctor said? When she sprang from the couch and said, "My God, was that an earthquake?"

The doctor said this: "Did it *feel* like an earthquake to you?"

I think we are agreed, you have to look on the light side.

So that's when I think it must have happened. Not that it matters to me. Maidy is the one who wants to know. She thinks she has it coming, being the older daughter. Although where was the older daughter when it happened? Which daughter was it that found you?

10 When Maidy started asking about your watch, I felt I had to say it. I said, "With the body barely cold?"

Maidy said the body is not the person, that the *essence* is the person, and that the essence leaves the body behind it, along with the body's possessions—for example, its watch?

"Time flies," I said. "Like an arrow.

"*Fruit flies,*" I said, and Maidy said, "What?"

"Fruit flies," I said again. "Fruit flies like a banana."

15 That's how easy it is to play a joke on Maidy.

Remember how easy?

Now Maidy thinks I took your watch. She thinks because I got there first, my first thought was to take it. Maidy keeps asking, "Who took Mama's watch?" She says, "Did *you* take Mama's watch?"

If you like the exquisitely crafted "San Francisco," you may also like another spare, trim story, thought of as "minimalist" by some contemporary critics—"Cathedral" by Raymond Carver (in this section).

**GOING FURTHER** You might also enjoy the novelist Mary Robison's *Why Did I Ever,* also of the "less is more" school of writing, and the elegantly spare novels, particularly *Play It As It Lays,* of Joan Didion.

# Sherman Alexie (b. 1966)

SHERMAN ALEXIE GREW UP on the Spokane Indian Reservation in Washington (he is of Spokane/Coeur d'Alene Indian descent). He attended college with the goal of becoming a doctor. His career as a poet took off shortly after graduation; by 1993, he had received two major fellowships and published two books of poetry. Next, he returned to short stories with *The Lone Ranger and Tonto Fistfight In Heaven* (1993) and then produced a novel, *Reservation Blues* (1995). He also wrote the screenplay for the award-winning, independently produced film *Smoke Signals* (1998). His signature blend of irony, humor, cynicism, and critique of modern Native American life has won him many honors including the PEN/Hemingway award, the PEN/Malamud award, and the Pushcart Prize. In 2007 he received the National Book Award for Young People's Literature with *The Absolutely True Diary of a Part-Time Indian.* He calls Seattle home.

# What You Pawn I Will Redeem (2003)

## NOON

1 One day you have a home and the next you don't, but I'm not going to tell you my particular reasons for being homeless, because it's my secret story, and Indians have to work hard to keep secrets from hungry white folks.

I'm a Spokane Indian boy, an Interior Salish, and my people have lived within a hundred-mile radius of Spokane, Washington, for at least ten thousand years. I grew up in Spokane, moved to Seattle twenty-three years ago for college, flunked out after two semesters, worked various blue- and bluer-collar jobs, married two or three times, fathered two or three kids, and then went crazy. Of course, crazy is not the official definition of my mental problem, but I don't think asocial disorder fits it, either, because that makes me sound like I'm a serial killer or something. I've never hurt another human being, or, at least, not physically. I've broken a few hearts in my time, but we've all done that, so I'm nothing special in that regard. I'm a boring heartbreaker, too. I never dated or married more than one woman at a time. I didn't break hearts into pieces overnight. I broke them slowly and carefully. And I didn't set any land-speed records running out the door. Piece by piece, I disappeared. I've been disappearing ever since.

I've been homeless for six years now. If there's such a thing as an effective homeless man, then I suppose I'm effective. Being homeless is probably the only thing I've ever been good at. I know where to get the best free food. I've made friends with restaurant and convenience-store managers who let me use their bathrooms. And I don't mean the public bathrooms, either. I mean the employees' bathrooms, the clean ones hidden behind the kitchen or the pantry or the cooler. I know it sounds strange to be proud of this, but it means a lot to me, being trustworthy enough to piss in somebody else's clean bathroom. Maybe you don't understand the value of a clean bathroom, but I do.

Probably none of this interests you. Homeless Indians are everywhere in Seattle. We're common and boring, and you walk right on by us, with maybe a look of anger or disgust or even sadness at the terrible fate of the noble savage. But we have dreams and families. I'm friends with a homeless Plains Indian man whose son is the editor of a big-time newspaper back East. Of course, that's his story, but we Indians are great storytellers and liars and mythmakers, so maybe that Plains Indian hobo is just a plain old everyday Indian. I'm kind of suspicious of him, because he identifies himself only as Plains Indian, a generic term, and not by a specific tribe. When I asked him why he wouldn't tell me exactly what he is, he said, "Do any of us know exactly what we are?" Yeah, great, a philosophizing Indian. "Hey," I said, "you got to have a home to be that homely." He just laughed and flipped me the eagle and walked away.

5 I wander the streets with a regular crew—my teammates, my defenders, my posse. It's Rose of Sharon, Junior, and me. We matter to each other if we don't matter to anybody else. Rose of Sharon is a big woman, about seven feet tall if you're measuring over-all effect and about five feet tall if you're only talking about the physical. She's a Yakama Indian of the Wishram variety. Junior is a Colville, but there are about a hundred and ninety-nine tribes that make up the Colville, so he could be anything. He's good-looking, though, like he just stepped out of some "Don't Litter the Earth" public-service advertisement. He's got those great big cheekbones that are like planets, you know, with little moons orbiting them. He gets me jealous, jealous, and jealous. If you put Junior and me next to each other, he's the Before Columbus Arrived Indian and I'm the After Columbus

Arrived Indian. I am living proof of the horrible damage that colonialism has done to us Skins. But I'm not going to let you know how scared I sometimes get of history and its ways. I'm a strong man, and I know that silence is the best method of dealing with white folks.

This whole story really started at lunchtime, when Rose of Sharon, Junior, and I were panning the handle down at Pike Place Market. After about two hours of negotiating, we earned five dollars—good enough for a bottle of fortified courage from the most beautiful 7-Eleven in the world. So we headed over that way, feeling like warrior drunks, and we walked past this pawnshop I'd never noticed before. And that was strange, because we Indians have built-in pawnshop radar. But the strangest thing of all was the old powwow-dance regalia I saw hanging in the window.

"That's my grandmother's regalia," I said to Rose of Sharon and Junior.

"How you know for sure?" Junior asked.

I didn't know for sure, because I hadn't seen that regalia in person ever. I'd only seen photographs of my grandmother dancing in it. And those were taken before somebody stole it from her, fifty years ago. But it sure looked like my memory of it, and it had all the same color feathers and beads that my family sewed into our powwow regalia.

10 "There's only one way to know for sure," I said.

So Rose of Sharon, Junior, and I walked into the pawnshop and greeted the old white man working behind the counter.

"How can I help you?" he asked.

"That's my grandmother's powwow regalia in your window," I said. "Somebody stole it from her fifty years ago, and my family has been searching for it ever since."

The pawnbroker looked at me like I was a liar. I understood. Pawnshops are filled with liars.

15 "I'm not lying," I said. "Ask my friends here. They'll tell you."

"He's the most honest Indian I know," Rose of Sharon said.

"All right, honest Indian," the pawnbroker said. "I'll give you the benefit of the doubt. Can you prove it's your grandmother's regalia?"

Because they don't want to be perfect, because only God is perfect, Indian people sew flaws into their powwow regalia. My family always sewed one yellow bead somewhere on our regalia. But we always hid it so that you had to search really hard to find it.

"If it really is my grandmother's," I said, "there will be one yellow bead hidden somewhere on it."

20 "All right, then," the pawnbroker said. "Let's take a look."

He pulled the regalia out of the window, laid it down on the glass counter, and we searched for that yellow bead and found it hidden beneath the armpit.

"There it is," the pawnbroker said. He didn't sound surprised. "You were right. This is your grandmother's regalia."

"It's been missing for fifty years," Junior said.

"Hey, Junior," I said. "It's my family's story. Let me tell it."

25 "All right," he said. "I apologize. You go ahead."

"It's been missing for fifty years," I said.

"That's his family's sad story," Rose of Sharon said. "Are you going to give it back to him?"

"That would be the right thing to do," the pawnbroker said. "But I can't afford to do the right thing. I paid a thousand dollars for this. I can't just give away a thousand dollars."

"We could go to the cops and tell them it was stolen," Rose of Sharon said.

30 "Hey," I said to her. "Don't go threatening people."

The pawnbroker sighed. He was thinking about the possibilities.

"Well, I suppose you could go to the cops," he said. "But I don't think they'd believe a word you said."

He sounded sad about that. As if he was sorry for taking advantage of our disadvantages.

"What's your name?" the pawnbroker asked me.

35 "Jackson," I said.

"Is that first or last?"

"Both," I said.

"Are you serious?"

"Yes, it's true. My mother and father named me Jackson Jackson. My family nickname is Jackson Squared. My family is funny."

"All right, Jackson Jackson," the pawnbroker said. "You wouldn't happen to have a thousand dollars, would you?"

"We've got five dollars total," I said.

"That's too bad," he said, and thought hard about the possibilities. "I'd sell it to you for a thousand dollars if you had it. Heck, to make it fair, I'd sell it to you for nine hundred and ninety-nine dollars. I'd lose a dollar. That would be the moral thing to do in this case. To lose a dollar would be the right thing."

"We've got five dollars total," I said again.

"That's too bad," he said once more, and thought harder about the possibilities. "How about this? I'll give you twenty-four hours to come up with nine hundred and ninety-nine dollars. You come back here at lunchtime tomorrow with the money and I'll sell it back to you. How does that sound?"

"It sounds all right," I said.

"All right, then," he said. "We have a deal. And I'll get you started. Here's twenty bucks."

He opened up his wallet and pulled out a crisp twenty-dollar bill and gave it to me. And Rose of Sharon, Junior, and I walked out into the daylight to search for nine hundred and seventy-four more dollars.

## 1 P.M.

Rose of Sharon, Junior, and I carried our twenty-dollar bill and our five dollars in loose change over to the 7-Eleven and bought three bottles of imagination. We needed to figure out how to raise all that money in only one day. Thinking hard, we huddled in an alley beneath the Alaska Way Viaduct and finished off those bottles—one, two, and three.

## 2 P.M.

Rose of Sharon was gone when I woke up. I heard later that she had hitchhiked back to Toppenish and was living with her sister on the reservation.

Junior had passed out beside me and was covered in his own vomit, or maybe somebody else's vomit, and my head hurt from thinking, so I left him alone and walked down to the water. I love the smell of ocean water. Salt always smells like memory.

When I got to the wharf, I ran into three Aleut cousins, who sat on a wooden bench and stared out at the bay and cried. Most of the homeless Indians in Seattle come from Alaska. One by one, each of them hopped a big working boat in Anchorage or Barrow or Juneau, fished his way south to Seattle, jumped off the boat with a pocketful of cash to party hard at one of the highly sacred and traditional Indian bars, went broke and broker, and has been trying to find his way back to the boat and the frozen North ever since.

These Aleuts smelled like salmon, I thought, and they told me they were going to sit on that wooden bench until their boat came back.

"How long has your boat been gone?" I asked.

"Eleven years," the elder Aleut said.

I cried with them for a while.

"Hey," I said. "Do you guys have any money I can borrow?"

They didn't.

## 3 P.M.

I walked back to Junior. He was still out cold. I put my face down near his mouth to make sure he was breathing. He was alive, so I dug around in his bluejeans pockets and found half a cigarette. I smoked it all the way down and thought about my grandmother.

Her name was Agnes, and she died of breast cancer when I was fourteen. My father always thought Agnes caught her tumors from the uranium mine on the reservation. But my mother said the disease started when Agnes was walking back from a powwow one night and got run over by a motorcycle. She broke three ribs, and my mother always said those ribs never healed right, and tumors take over when you don't heal right.

Sitting beside Junior, smelling the smoke and the salt and the vomit, I wondered if my grandmother's cancer started when somebody stole her powwow regalia. Maybe the cancer started in her broken heart and then leaked out into her breasts. I know it's crazy, but I wondered whether I could bring my grandmother back to life if I bought back her regalia.

I needed money, big money, so I left Junior and walked over to the Real Change office.

## 4 P.M.

Real Change is a multifaceted organization that publishes a newspaper, supports cultural projects that empower the poor and the homeless, and mobilizes the public around poverty issues. Real Change's mission is to organize, educate, and build alliances to create solutions to homelessness and poverty. It exists to provide a voice for poor people in our community.

I memorized Real Change's mission statement because I sometimes sell the newspaper on the streets. But you have to stay sober to sell it, and I'm not always good at staying sober. Anybody can sell the paper. You buy each copy for thirty cents and sell it for a dollar, and you keep the profit.

"I need one thousand four hundred and thirty papers," I said to the Big Boss.

"That's a strange number," he said. "And that's a lot of papers."

"I need them."

The Big Boss pulled out his calculator and did the math.

"It will cost you four hundred and twenty-nine dollars for that many," he said.

"If I had that kind of money, I wouldn't need to sell the papers."

"What's going on, Jackson-to-the-Second-Power?" he asked. He is the only person who calls me that. He's a funny and kind man.

I told him about my grandmother's powwow regalia and how much money I needed in order to buy it back.

"We should call the police," he said.

"I don't want to do that," I said. "It's a quest now. I need to win it back by myself."

"I understand," he said. "And, to be honest, I'd give you the papers to sell if I thought it would work. But the record for the most papers sold in one day by one vender is only three hundred and two."

"That would net me about two hundred bucks," I said.

The Big Boss used his calculator. "Two hundred and eleven dollars and forty cents," he said.

"That's not enough," I said.

"And the most money anybody has made in one day is five hundred and twenty-five. And that's because somebody gave Old Blue five hundred-dollar bills for some dang reason. The average daily net is about thirty dollars."

"This isn't going to work."

"No."

"Can you lend me some money?"

"I can't do that," he said. "If I lend you money, I have to lend money to everybody."

"What can you do?"

"I'll give you fifty papers for free. But don't tell anybody I did it."

"O.K.," I said.

He gathered up the newspapers and handed them to me. I held them to my chest. He hugged me. I carried the newspapers back toward the water.

## 5 P.M.

Back on the wharf, I stood near the Bainbridge Island Terminal and tried to sell papers to business commuters boarding the ferry.

I sold five in one hour, dumped the other forty-five in a garbage can, and walked into McDonald's, ordered four cheeseburgers for a dollar each, and slowly ate them.

After eating, I walked outside and vomited on the sidewalk. I hated to lose my food so soon after eating it. As an alcoholic Indian with a busted stomach, I always hope I can keep enough food in me to stay alive.

## 6 P.M.

With one dollar in my pocket, I walked back to Junior. He was still passed out, and I put my ear to his chest and listened for his heartbeat. He was alive, so I took off his shoes and socks and found one dollar in his left sock and fifty cents in his right sock.

With two dollars and fifty cents in my hand, I sat beside Junior and thought about my grandmother and her stories.

When I was thirteen, my grandmother told me a story about the Second World War. She was a nurse at a military hospital in Sydney, Australia. For two years, she healed and comforted American and Australian soldiers.

One day, she tended to a wounded Maori soldier, who had lost his legs to an artillery attack. He was very dark-skinned. His hair was black and curly and his eyes were black and warm. His face was covered with bright tattoos.

"Are you Maori?" he asked my grandmother.

"No," she said. "I'm Spokane Indian. From the United States."

"Ah, yes," he said. "I have heard of your tribes. But you are the first American Indian I have ever met."

"There's a lot of Indian soldiers fighting for the United States," she said. "I have a brother fighting in Germany, and I lost another brother on Okinawa."

"I am sorry," he said. "I was on Okinawa as well. It was terrible."

"I am sorry about your legs," my grandmother said.

"It's funny, isn't it?" he said.

"What's funny?"

"How we brown people are killing other brown people so white people will remain free."

"I hadn't thought of it that way."

"Well, sometimes I think of it that way. And other times I think of it the way they want me to think of it. I get confused."

She fed him morphine.

"Do you believe in Heaven?" he asked.

"Which Heaven?" she asked.

"I'm talking about the Heaven where my legs are waiting for me."

They laughed.

"Of course," he said, "my legs will probably run away from me when I get to Heaven. And how will I ever catch them?"

"You have to get your arms strong," my grandmother said. "So you can run on your hands."

They laughed again.

Sitting beside Junior, I laughed at the memory of my grandmother's story. I put my hand close to Junior's mouth to make sure he was still breathing. Yes, Junior was alive, so I took my two dollars and fifty cents and walked to the Korean grocery store in Pioneer Square.

## 7 P.M.

At the Korean grocery store, I bought a fifty-cent cigar and two scratch lottery tickets for a dollar each. The maximum cash prize was five hundred dollars a ticket. If I won both, I would have enough money to buy back the regalia.

I loved Mary, the young Korean woman who worked the register. She was the daughter of the owners, and she sang all day.

"I love you," I said when I handed her the money.

"You always say you love me," she said.

"That's because I will always love you."

"You are a sentimental fool."

"I'm a romantic old man."

"Too old for me."

"I know I'm too old for you, but I can dream."

"O.K.," she said. "I agree to be a part of your dreams, but I will only hold your hand in your dreams. No kissing and no sex. Not even in your dreams."

"O.K.," I said. "No sex. Just romance."

"Goodbye, Jackson Jackson, my love. I will see you soon."

I left the store, walked over to Occidental Park, sat on a bench, and smoked my cigar all the way down.

Ten minutes after I finished the cigar, I scratched my first lottery ticket and won nothing. I could only win five hundred dollars now, and that would only be half of what I needed.

Ten minutes after I lost, I scratched the other ticket and won a free ticket—a small consolation and one more chance to win some money.

I walked back to Mary.

"Jackson Jackson," she said. "Have you come back to claim my heart?"

"I won a free ticket," I said.

"Just like a man," she said. "You love money and power more than you love me."

"It's true," I said. "And I'm sorry it's true."

She gave me another scratch ticket, and I took it outside. I like to scratch my tickets in private. Hopeful and sad, I scratched that third ticket and won real money. I carried it back inside to Mary.

"I won a hundred dollars," I said.

She examined the ticket and laughed.

"That's a fortune," she said, and counted out five twenties. Our fingertips touched as she handed me the money. I felt electric and constant.

"Thank you," I said, and gave her one of the bills.

"I can't take that," she said. "It's your money."

"No, it's tribal. It's an Indian thing. When you win, you're supposed to share with your family."

"I'm not your family."

"Yes, you are."

She smiled. She kept the money. With eighty dollars in my pocket, I said goodbye to my dear Mary and walked out into the cold night air.

## 8 P.M.

I wanted to share the good news with Junior. I walked back to him, but he was gone. I heard later that he had hitchhiked down to Portland, Oregon, and died of exposure in an alley behind the Hilton Hotel.

## 9 P.M.

Lonesome for Indians, I carried my eighty dollars over to Big Heart's in South Downtown. Big Heart's is an all-Indian bar. Nobody knows how or why Indians migrate to one bar and turn it into an official Indian bar. But Big Heart's has been an Indian bar for twenty-three years. It used to be way up on Aurora Avenue, but a crazy Lummi Indian burned that one down, and the owners moved to the new location, a few blocks south of Safeco Field.

I walked into Big Heart's and counted fifteen Indians—eight men and seven women. I didn't know any of them, but Indians like to belong, so we all pretended to be cousins.

"How much for whiskey shots?" I asked the bartender, a fat white guy.

"You want the bad stuff or the badder stuff?"

"As bad as you got."

"One dollar a shot."

I laid my eighty dollars on the bar top.

"All right," I said. "Me and all my cousins here are going to be drinking eighty shots. How many is that apiece?"

"Counting you," a woman shouted from behind me, "that's five shots for everybody."

I turned to look at her. She was a chubby and pale Indian woman, sitting with a tall and skinny Indian man.

"All right, math genius," I said to her, and then shouted for the whole bar to hear. "Five drinks for everybody!"

All the other Indians rushed the bar, but I sat with the mathematician and her skinny friend. We took our time with our whiskey shots.

"What's your tribe?" I asked.

"I'm Duwamish," she said. "And he's Crow."

"You're a long way from Montana," I said to him.

"I'm Crow," he said. "I flew here."

"What's your name?" I asked them.

"I'm Irene Muse," she said. "And this is Honey Boy."

She shook my hand hard, but he offered his hand as if I was supposed to kiss it. So I did. He giggled and blushed, as much as a dark-skinned Crow can blush.

"You're one of them two-spirits, aren't you?" I asked him.

"I love women," he said. "And I love men."

"Sometimes both at the same time," Irene said.

We laughed.

"Man," I said to Honey Boy. "So you must have about eight or nine spirits going on inside you, enit?"

"Sweetie," he said. "I'll be whatever you want me to be."

"Oh, no," Irene said. "Honey Boy is falling in love."

"It has nothing to do with love," he said.

We laughed.

"Wow," I said. "I'm flattered, Honey Boy, but I don't play on your team."

"Never say never," he said.

"You better be careful," Irene said. "Honey Boy knows all sorts of magic."

"Honey Boy," I said, "you can try to seduce me, but my heart belongs to a woman named Mary."

"Is your Mary a virgin?" Honey Boy asked.

We laughed.

And we drank our whiskey shots until they were gone. But the other Indians bought me more whiskey shots, because I'd been so generous with my money. And Honey Boy pulled out his credit card, and I drank and sailed on that plastic boat.

After a dozen shots, I asked Irene to dance. She refused. But Honey Boy shuffled over to the jukebox, dropped in a quarter, and selected Willie Nelson's "Help Me Make It Through the Night." As Irene and I sat at the table and laughed and drank more whiskey, Honey Boy danced a slow circle around us and sang along with Willie.

"Are you serenading me?" I asked him.

He kept singing and dancing.

"Are you serenading me?" I asked him again.

"He's going to put a spell on you," Irene said.

I leaned over the table, spilling a few drinks, and kissed Irene hard. She kissed me back.

## 10 P.M.

Irene pushed me into the women's bathroom, into a stall, shut the door behind us, and shoved her hand down my pants. She was short, so I had to lean over to kiss her. I grabbed and squeezed her everywhere I could reach, and she was wonderfully fat, and every part of her body felt like a large, warm, soft breast.

## MIDNIGHT

Nearly blind with alcohol, I stood alone at the bar and swore I had been standing in the bathroom with Irene only a minute ago.

"One more shot!" I yelled at the bartender.

"You've got no more money!" he yelled back.

"Somebody buy me a drink!" I shouted.

"They've got no more money!"

"Where are Irene and Honey Boy?"

"Long gone!"

## 2 A.M.

"Closing time!" the bartender shouted at the three or four Indians who were still drinking hard after a long, hard day of drinking. Indian alcoholics are either sprinters or marathoners.

"Where are Irene and Honey Boy?" I asked.

"They've been gone for hours," the bartender said.

"Where'd they go?"

"I told you a hundred times, I don't know."

"What am I supposed to do?"

"It's closing time. I don't care where you go, but you're not staying here."

"You are an ungrateful bastard. I've been good to you."

"You don't leave right now, I'm going to kick your ass."

"Come on, I know how to fight."

He came at me. I don't remember what happened after that.

## 4 A.M.

I emerged from the blackness and discovered myself walking behind a big warehouse. I didn't know where I was. My face hurt. I felt my nose and decided that it might be broken. Exhausted and cold, I pulled a plastic tarp from a truck bed, wrapped it around me like a faithful lover, and fell asleep in the dirt.

## 6 A.M.

Somebody kicked me in the ribs. I opened my eyes and looked up at a white cop.

"Jackson," the cop said. "Is that you?"

"Officer Williams," I said. He was a good cop with a sweet tooth. He'd given me hundreds of candy bars over the years. I wonder if he knew I was diabetic.

"What the hell are you doing here?" he asked.

"I was cold and sleepy," I said. "So I lay down."

"You dumb-ass, you passed out on the railroad tracks."

I sat up and looked around. I was lying on the railroad tracks. Dockworkers stared at me. I should have been a railroad-track pizza, a double Indian pepperoni with extra cheese. Sick and scared, I leaned over and puked whiskey.

"What the hell's wrong with you?" Officer Williams asked. "You've never been this stupid."

"It's my grandmother," I said. "She died."

"I'm sorry, man. When did she die?"

"Nineteen seventy-two."

"And you're killing yourself now?"

"I've been killing myself ever since she died."

He shook his head. He was sad for me. Like I said, he was a good cop.

"And somebody beat the hell out of you," he said. "You remember who?"

"Mr. Grief and I went a few rounds."

"It looks like Mr. Grief knocked you out."

"Mr. Grief always wins."

"Come on," he said. "Let's get you out of here."

He helped me up and led me over to his squad car. He put me in the back. "You throw up in there and you're cleaning it up," he said.

"That's fair."

He walked around the car and sat in the driver's seat. "I'm taking you over to detox," he said.

"No, man, that place is awful," I said. "It's full of drunk Indians."

We laughed. He drove away from the docks.

"I don't know how you guys do it," he said.

"What guys?" I asked.

"You Indians. How the hell do you laugh so much? I just picked your ass off the railroad tracks, and you're making jokes. Why the hell do you do that?"

"The two funniest tribes I've ever been around are Indians and Jews, so I guess that says something about the inherent humor of genocide."

We laughed.

"Listen to you, Jackson. You're so smart. Why the hell are you on the street?"

"Give me a thousand dollars and I'll tell you."

"You bet I'd give you a thousand dollars if I knew you'd straighten up your life."

He meant it. He was the second-best cop I'd ever known.

"You're a good cop," I said.

"Come on, Jackson," he said. "Don't blow smoke up my ass."

"No, really, you remind me of my grandfather."

"Yeah, that's what you Indians always tell me."

"No, man, my grandfather was a tribal cop. He was a good cop. He never arrested people. He took care of them. Just like you."

"I've arrested hundreds of scumbags, Jackson. And I've shot a couple in the ass."

"It don't matter. You're not a killer."

"I didn't kill them. I killed their asses. I'm an ass-killer."

We drove through downtown. The missions and shelters had already released their overnighters. Sleepy homeless men and women stood on street corners and stared up at a gray sky. It was the morning after the night of the living dead.

"Do you ever get scared?" I asked Officer Williams.

"What do you mean?"

"I mean, being a cop, is it scary?"

He thought about that for a while. He contemplated it. I liked that about him.

"I guess I try not to think too much about being afraid," he said. "If you think about fear, then you'll be afraid. The job is boring most of the time. Just driving and looking into dark corners, you know, and seeing nothing. But then things get heavy. You're chasing somebody, or fighting them or walking around a dark house, and you just know some crazy guy is hiding around a corner, and hell, yes, it's scary."

"My grandfather was killed in the line of duty," I said.

"I'm sorry. How'd it happen?"

I knew he'd listen closely to my story.

"He worked on the reservation. Everybody knew everybody. It was safe. We aren't like those crazy Sioux or Apache or any of those other warrior tribes. There've only been three murders on my reservation in the last hundred years."

"That is safe."

"Yeah, we Spokane, we're passive, you know. We're mean with words. And we'll cuss out anybody. But we don't shoot people. Or stab them. Not much, anyway."

"So what happened to your grandfather?"

"This man and his girlfriend were fighting down by Little Falls."

"Domestic dispute. Those are the worst."

"Yeah, but this guy was my grandfather's brother. My great-uncle."

"Oh, no."

"Yeah, it was awful. My grandfather just strolled into the house. He'd been there a thousand times. And his brother and his girlfriend were drunk and beating on each other. And my grandfather stepped between them, just as he'd done a hundred times before. And the girlfriend tripped or something. She fell down and hit her head and started crying. And my grandfather kneeled down beside her to make sure she was all right. And for some reason my great-uncle reached down, pulled my grandfather's pistol out of the holster, and shot him in the head."

"That's terrible. I'm sorry."

"Yeah, my great-uncle could never figure out why he did it. He went to prison forever, you know, and he always wrote these long letters. Like fifty pages of tiny little handwriting. And he was always trying to figure out why he did it. He'd write and write and write and try to figure it out. He never did. It's a great big mystery."

"Do you remember your grandfather?"

"A little bit. I remember the funeral. My grandmother wouldn't let them bury him. My father had to drag her away from the grave."

"I don't know what to say."

"I don't, either."

We stopped in front of the detox center.

"We're here," Officer Williams said.

"I can't go in there," I said.

"You have to."

"Please, no. They'll keep me for twenty-four hours. And then it will be too late."

"Too late for what?"

I told him about my grandmother's regalia and the deadline for buying it back.

"If it was stolen, you need to file a report," he said. "I'll investigate it myself. If that thing is really your grandmother's, I'll get it back for you. Legally."

"No," I said. "That's not fair. The pawnbroker didn't know it was stolen. And, besides, I'm on a mission here. I want to be a hero, you know? I want to win it back, like a knight."

"That's romantic crap."

"That may be. But I care about it. It's been a long time since I really cared about something."

Officer Williams turned around in his seat and stared at me. He studied me.

"I'll give you some money," he said. "I don't have much. Only thirty bucks. I'm short until payday. And it's not enough to get back the regalia. But it's something."

"I'll take it," I said.

"I'm giving it to you because I believe in what you believe. I'm hoping, and I don't know why I'm hoping it, but I hope you can turn thirty bucks into a thousand somehow."

"I believe in magic."

"I believe you'll take my money and get drunk on it."

"Then why are you giving it to me?"

"There ain't no such thing as an atheist cop."

"Sure, there is."

"Yeah, well, I'm not an atheist cop."

He let me out of the car, handed me two fivers and a twenty, and shook my hand.

"Take care of yourself, Jackson," he said. "Stay off the railroad tracks."

"I'll try," I said.

He drove away. Carrying my money, I headed back toward the water.

## 8 A.M.

On the wharf, those three Aleuts still waited on the wooden bench.

"Have you seen your ship?" I asked.

"Seen a lot of ships," the elder Aleut said. "But not our ship."

I sat on the bench with them. We sat in silence for a long time. I wondered if we would fossilize if we sat there long enough.

I thought about my grandmother. I'd never seen her dance in her regalia. And, more than anything, I wished I'd seen her dance at a powwow.

"Do you guys know any songs?" I asked the Aleuts.

"I know all of Hank Williams," the elder Aleut said.

"How about Indian songs?"

"Hank Williams is Indian."

"How about sacred songs?"

"Hank Williams is sacred."

"I'm talking about ceremonial songs. You know, religious ones. The songs you sing back home when you're wishing and hoping."

"What are you wishing and hoping for?"

"I'm wishing my grandmother was still alive."

"Every song I know is about that."

"Well, sing me as many as you can."

The Aleuts sang their strange and beautiful songs. I listened. They sang about my grandmother and about their grandmothers. They were lonesome for the cold and the snow. I was lonesome for everything.

## 10 A.M.

After the Aleuts finished their last song, we sat in silence for a while. Indians are good at silence.

"Was that the last song?" I asked.

"We sang all the ones we could," the elder Aleut said. "The others are just for our people."

I understood. We Indians have to keep our secrets. And these Aleuts were so secretive they didn't refer to themselves as Indians.

"Are you guys hungry?" I asked.

They looked at one another and communicated without talking.

"We could eat," the elder Aleut said.

## 11 A.M.

The Aleuts and I walked over to the Big Kitchen, a greasy diner in the International District. I knew they served homeless Indians who'd lucked into money.

"Four for breakfast?" the waitress asked when we stepped inside.

"Yes, we're very hungry," the elder Aleut said.

She took us to a booth near the kitchen. I could smell the food cooking. My stomach growled.

"You guys want separate checks?" the waitress asked.

"No, I'm paying," I said.

"Aren't you the generous one," she said.

"Don't do that," I said.

"Do what?" she asked.

"Don't ask me rhetorical questions. They scare me."

She looked puzzled, and then she laughed.

"O.K., Professor," she said. "I'll only ask you real questions from now on."

"Thank you."

"What do you guys want to eat?"

"That's the best question anybody can ask anybody," I said. "What have you got?"

"How much money you got?" she asked.

"Another good question," I said. "I've got twenty-five dollars I can spend. Bring us all the breakfast you can, plus your tip."

She knew the math.

"All right, that's four specials and four coffees and fifteen per cent for me."

The Aleuts and I waited in silence. Soon enough, the waitress returned and poured us four coffees, and we sipped at them until she returned again, with four plates of food. Eggs, bacon, toast, hash-brown potatoes. It's amazing how much food you can buy for so little money.

Grateful, we feasted.

## NOON

I said farewell to the Aleuts and walked toward the pawnshop. I heard later that the Aleuts had waded into the salt water near Dock 47 and disappeared. Some Indians swore they had walked on the water and headed north. Other Indians saw the Aleuts drown. I don't know what happened to them.

I looked for the pawnshop and couldn't find it. I swear it wasn't in the place where it had been before. I walked twenty or thirty blocks looking for the pawnshop, turned corners and bisected intersections, and looked up its name in the phone books and asked people walking past me if they'd ever heard of it. But that pawnshop seemed to have sailed away like a ghost ship. I wanted to cry. And just when I'd given up, when I turned one last corner and thought I might die if I didn't find that pawnshop, there it was, in a space I swear it hadn't occupied a few minutes ago.

I walked inside and greeted the pawnbroker, who looked a little younger than he had before.

"It's you," he said.

"Yes, it's me," I said.

"Jackson Jackson."

"That is my name."

"Where are your friends?"

"They went travelling. But it's O.K. Indians are everywhere."

"Do you have the money?"

"How much do you need again?" I asked, and hoped the price had changed.

"Nine hundred and ninety-nine dollars."

It was still the same price. Of course, it was the same price. Why would it change?

"I don't have that," I said.

"What do you have?"

"Five dollars."

I set the crumpled Lincoln on the countertop. The pawnbroker studied it.

"Is that the same five dollars from yesterday?"

"No, it's different."

He thought about the possibilities.

"Did you work hard for this money?" he asked.

"Yes," I said.

He closed his eyes and thought harder about the possibilities. Then he stepped into the back room and returned with my grandmother's regalia.

"Take it," he said, and held it out to me.

"I don't have the money."

"I don't want your money."

"But I wanted to win it."

"You did win it. Now take it before I change my mind."

Do you know how many good men live in this world? Too many to count!

I took my grandmother's regalia and walked outside. I knew that solitary yellow bead was part of me. I knew I was that yellow bead in part. Outside, I wrapped myself in my grandmother's regalia and breathed her in. I stepped off the sidewalk and into the intersection. Pedestrians stopped. Cars stopped. The city stopped. They all watched me dance with my grandmother. I was my grandmother, dancing.

If you enjoyed "What You Pawn I Will Redeem," you may enjoy "The Man to Send Rainclouds" by Leslie Marmon Silko in chapter 12, The Casebook on the American West.

**GOING FURTHER** Alexie and Silko come from a long line of American Indian fiction writers that includes Pulitzer Prize winner N. Scott Momaday and his lyrical work of fiction *The Way to Rainy Mountain*. You also might enjoy Louise Erdrich's novels *Tracks* or *The Beet Queen*.

## Margaret Atwood (b. 1939)

BORN IN TORONTO, Margaret Atwood has been, along with short story writer Alice Munro, one of the few Canadian writers with a major impact on the contemporary American reading public. A driving force in the literature scene to our north, she works in a wide range of genres and styles—seeming equally at home in the mode of historical fiction as that of science fiction. Her novels such as *Surfacing* (1972), *The Handmaid's Tale* (1985), and the Booker Prize–winning *The Blind Assassin* (2000) have won her great acclaim. Atwood is also a poet (see Poetry, chapter 21), essayist, and short story writer. In each of these genres and forms, she demonstrates keen attention to craft as well as theme.

# Happy Endings (1983)

1 John and Mary meet.

What happens next?

If you want a happy ending, try A.

### A

John and Mary fall in love and get married. They both have worthwhile and remunerative jobs which they find stimulating and challenging. They buy a charming house. Real estate values go up. Eventually, when they can afford live-in help, they have two children, to whom they are devoted. The children turn out well. John and Mary have a stimulating and challenging sex life and worthwhile friends. They go on fun vacations together. They retire. They both have hobbies which they find stimulating and challenging. Eventually they die. This is the end of the story.

### B

5 Mary falls in love with John but John doesn't fall in love with Mary. He merely uses her body for selfish pleasure and ego gratification of a tepid kind. He comes to her apartment twice a week and she cooks him dinner, you'll notice that he doesn't even consider her worth the price of a dinner out, and after he's eaten the dinner he fucks her and after that he falls asleep, while she does the dishes so he won't think she's untidy, having all those dirty dishes lying around, and puts on fresh lipstick so she'll look good when he wakes up, but when he wakes up he doesn't even notice, he puts on his socks and his shorts and his pants and his shirt and his tie and his shoes, the reverse order from the one in which he took them off. He doesn't take off Mary's clothes, she takes them off herself, she acts as if she's dying for it every time, not because she likes sex exactly, she doesn't, but she wants John to think she does because if they do it often enough surely he'll get used to her, he'll come to depend on her and they will get married, but John goes out the door with hardly so much as a good-night and three days later he turns up at six o'clock and they do the whole thing over again.

Mary gets run-down. Crying is bad for your face, everyone knows that and so does Mary but she can't stop. People at work notice. Her friends tell her John is a rat, a pig, a dog, he isn't good enough for her, but she can't believe it. Inside John, she thinks, is another John, who is much nicer. This other John will emerge like a butterfly from a cocoon, a Jack from a box, a pit from a prune, if the first John is only squeezed enough.

One evening John complains about the food. He has never complained about the food before. Mary is hurt.

Her friends tell her they've seen him in a restaurant with another woman, whose name is Madge. It's not even Madge that finally gets to Mary; it's the restaurant. John has never taken Mary to a restaurant. Mary collects all the sleeping pills and aspirins she can find, and takes them and a half a bottle of sherry. You can see what kind of a woman she is by the fact that it's not even whiskey. She leaves a note for John. She hopes he'll discover her and get her to the hospital in time and repent and then they can get married, but this fails to happen and she dies.

John marries Madge and everything continues as in A.

## C

10 John, who is an older man, falls in love with Mary, and Mary, who is only twenty-two, feels sorry for him because he's worried about his hair falling out. She sleeps with him even though she's not in love with him. She met him at work. She's in love with someone called James, who is twenty-two also and not yet ready to settle down.

John on the contrary settled down long ago: this is what is bothering him. John has a steady, respectable job and is getting ahead in his field, but Mary isn't impressed by him, she's impressed by James, who has a motorcycle and a fabulous record collection. But James is often away on his motorcycle, being free. Freedom isn't the same for girls, so in the meantime Mary spends Thursday evenings with John. Thursdays are the only days John can get away.

John is married to a woman called Madge and they have two children, a charming house which they bought just before the real estate values went up, and hobbies which they find stimulating and challenging, when they have the time. John tells Mary how important she is to him, but of course, he can't leave his wife because a commitment is a commitment. He goes on about this more than is necessary and Mary finds it boring, but older men can keep it up longer so on the whole she has a fairly good time.

One day James breezes in on his motorcycle with some top-grade California hybrid and James and Mary get higher than you'd believe possible and they climb into bed. Everything becomes very underwater, but along comes John, who has a key to Mary's apartment. He finds them stoned and entwined. He's hardly in any position to be jealous, considering Madge, but nevertheless he's overcome with despair. Finally he's middle-aged, in two years he'll be bald as an egg and he can't stand it. He purchases a handgun, saying he needs it for target practice—this is the thin part of the plot, but it can be dealt with later—and shoots the two of them and himself.

Madge, after a suitable period of mourning, marries an understanding man called Fred and everything continues as in A, but under different names.

## D

15 Fred and Madge have no problems. They get along exceptionally well and are good at working out any little difficulties that may arise. But their charming house is by the seashore and one day a giant tidal wave approaches. Real estate values go down. The rest of the story is about what caused the tidal wave and how they escape from it. They do, though thousands drown, but Fred and Madge are virtuous and lucky. Finally on high ground they clasp each other, wet and dripping and grateful, and continue as in A.

## E

Yes, but Fred has a bad heart. The rest of the story is about how kind and understanding they both are until Fred dies. Then Madge devotes herself to charity work until the end of A. If you like, it can be "Madge," "cancer," "guilty and confused," and "bird watching."

## F

If you think this is all too bourgeois, make John a revolutionary and Mary a counterespionage agent and see how far that gets you. Remember, this is Canada. You'll still end up with A, though in between you may get a lustful brawling saga of passionate involvement, a chronicle of our times, sort of.

You'll have to face it, the endings are the same however you slice it. Don't be deluded by any other endings, they're all fake, either deliberately fake, with malicious intent to deceive, or just motivated by excessive optimism if not by downright sentimentality.

The only authentic ending is the one provided here:

*John and Mary die. John and Mary die. John and Mary die.*

So much for endings. Beginnings are almost more fun. True connoisseurs, however, are known to favor the stretch in between, since it's the hardest to do anything with.

That's about all that can be said for plots, which anyway are just one thing after another, a what and a what and a what.

Now try How and Why.

If you like this story, you may also like "An Ounce of Cure" (chapter 1) by Atwood's fellow Canadian writer Alice Munro.

**GOING FURTHER** Atwood's literary mentor was a novelist and story writer named Margaret Laurence. Laurence's novel *The Diviners* is one of the finest examples you'll find of a female coming-of-age story, a powerful and important novel set mainly in western Canada.

# James Baldwin (1924–1987)

BORN IN NEW York City, James Baldwin grew up in Harlem, the mostly black section at the north end of Manhattan. Though his formal education ended in high school, he asserted his place in contemporary letters before the age of thirty with a powerful debut novel about childhood in a Pentecostal Harlem church, *Go Tell It on the Mountain* (1953). For the next three decades Baldwin made a place for himself in American letters as both a fiction writer and an essayist, gaining a place as well in the unfolding saga of the American Civil Rights movement. His novels *Giovanni's Room* (1956) and *Another Country* (1962) drew solid readerships, but his polemical essay *The Fire Next Time* (1955)—which first appeared in the pages of *The New Yorker* magazine and then as a book—brought him national attention.

He never relinquished it. Like his sometime mentor Richard Wright, Baldwin exiled himself in France—living first in Paris, then in the village of St. Paul de Vence—for a large part of his adult life. His focus was always on America, however, and while living abroad he continued to write about politics and race at home. The Civil War and the Civil Rights Movement were, to this writer, two chapters of the one story. Such nonfiction texts as *No Name in the Street* (1972) and *Evidence of Things Not Seen* (1985) focus both on race and politics; his final fiction and essays about black-and-white life in America attested equally to his sharp eye and a troubled dream of harmony.

A lifelong adept of jazz, Baldwin wrote that when he first moved to Paris he took along a phonograph record of the jazz singer Bessie Smith in order to remind himself of what he'd left behind. "Sonny's Blues" attests to this fascination with music, its sorrows and delights.

# Sonny's Blues (1957)

I read about it in the paper, in the subway, on my way to work. I read it, and I couldn't believe it, and I read it again. Then perhaps I just stared at it, at the newsprint spelling out his name, spelling out the story. I stared at it in the swinging lights of the subway car, and in the faces and bodies of the people, and in my own face, trapped in the darkness which roared outside.

It was not to be believed and I kept telling myself that, as I walked from the subway station to the high school. And at the same time I couldn't doubt it. I was scared, scared for Sonny. He became real to me again. A great block of ice got settled in my belly and kept melting there slowly all day long, while I taught my classes algebra. It was a special kind of ice. It kept melting, sending trickles of ice water all up and down my veins, but it never got less. Sometimes it hardened and seemed to expand until I felt my guts were going to come spilling out or that I was going to choke or scream. This would always be at a moment when I was remembering some specific thing Sonny had once said or done.

When he was about as old as the boys in my classes his face had been bright and open, there was a lot of copper in it; and he'd had wonderfully direct brown eyes, and great gentleness and privacy. I wondered what he looked like now. He had been picked up, the evening before, in a raid on an apartment downtown, for peddling and using heroin.

I couldn't believe it: but what I mean by that is that I couldn't find any room for it anywhere inside me. I had kept it outside me for a long time. I hadn't wanted to know. I had had suspicions, but I didn't name them, I kept putting them away. I told myself that Sonny was wild, but he wasn't crazy. And he'd always been a good boy, he hadn't ever turned hard or evil or disrespectful, the way kids can, so quick, so quick, especially in Harlem. I didn't want to believe that I'd ever see my brother going down, coming to nothing, all that light in his face gone out, in the condition I'd already seen so many others. Yet it had happened and here I was, talking about algebra to a lot of boys who might, every one of them for all I knew, be popping off needles every time they went to the head. Maybe it did more for them than algebra could.

I was sure that the first time Sonny had ever had horse, he couldn't have been much older than these boys were now. These boys, now, were living as we'd been living then, they were growing up with a rush and their heads bumped abruptly against the low ceiling of their actual possibilities. They were filled with rage. All they really knew were two darknesses, the darkness of their lives, which was now closing in on them, and the darkness of the movies, which had blinded them to that other darkness, and in which they now, vindictively, dreamed, at once more together than they were at any other time, and more alone.

When the last bell rang, the last class ended, I let out my breath. It seemed I'd been holding it for all that time. My clothes were wet—I may have looked as though I'd been sitting in a steam bath, all dressed up, all afternoon. I sat alone in the classroom a long time. I listened to the boys outside, downstairs, shouting and cursing and laughing. Their laughter struck me for perhaps the first time. It was not the joyous laughter which—God knows why—one associates with children. It was mocking and insular, its intent was to denigrate. It was disenchanted, and in this, also, lay the authority of their curses. Perhaps I was listening to them because I was thinking about my brother. And myself.

One boy was whistling a tune, at once very complicated and very simple, it seemed to be pouring out of him as though he were a bird, and it sounded very cool and moving through all that harsh, bright air, only just holding its own through all those other sounds.

I stood up and walked over to the window and looked down into the courtyard. It was the beginning of the spring and the sap was rising in the boys. A teacher passed through them every now and again, quickly, as though he or she couldn't wait to get out of that courtyard, to get those boys out of their sight and off their minds. I started collecting my stuff. I thought I'd better get home and talk to Isabel.

The courtyard was almost deserted by the time I got downstairs. I saw this boy standing in the shadow of a doorway, looking just like Sonny. I almost called his name. Then I saw that it wasn't

Sonny, but somebody we used to know, a boy from around our block. He'd been Sonny's friend. He'd never been mine, having been too young for me, and, anyway, I'd never liked him. And now, even though he was a grown-up man, he still hung around that block, still spent hours on the street corners, was always high and raggy. I used to run into him from time to time and he'd often work around to asking me for a quarter or fifty cents. He always had some real good excuse, too, and I always gave it to him, I don't know why.

10 But now, abruptly, I hated him. I couldn't stand the way he looked at me, partly like a dog, partly like a cunning child. I wanted to ask him what the hell he was doing in the school courtyard.

He sort of shuffled over to me, and he said, "I see you got the papers. So you already know about it."

"You mean about Sonny? Yes, I already know about it. How come they didn't get you?"

He grinned. It made him repulsive and it also brought to mind what he'd looked like as a kid. "I wasn't there. I stay away from them people."

"Good for you." I offered him a cigarette and I watched him through the smoke. "You come all the way down here just to tell me about Sonny?"

15 "That's right." He was sort of shaking his head and his eyes looked strange, as though they were about to cross. The bright sun deadened his damp dark brown skin and it made his eyes look yellow and showed up the dirt in his kinked hair. He smelled funky. I moved a little away from him and I said, "Well, thanks. But I already know about it and I got to get home."

"I'll walk you a little ways," he said. We started walking. There were a couple of kids still loitering in the courtyard and one of them said goodnight to me and looked strangely at the boy beside me.

"What're you going to do?" he asked me. "I mean, about Sonny?"

"Look. I haven't seen Sonny for over a year, I'm not sure I'm going to do anything. Anyway, what the hell *can* I do?"

"That's right," he said quickly, "ain't nothing you can do. Can't much help old Sonny no more, I guess."

20 It was what I was thinking and so it seemed to me he had no right to say it.

"I'm surprised at Sonny, though," he went on—he had a funny way of talking, he looked straight ahead as though he were talking to himself—"I thought Sonny was a smart boy, I thought he was too smart to get hung."

"I guess he thought so too," I said sharply, "and that's how he got hung. And how about you? You're pretty goddamn smart, I bet."

Then he looked directly at me, just for a minute. "I ain't smart," he said. "If I was smart, I'd have reached for a pistol a long time ago."

"Look. Don't tell *me* your sad story, if it was up to me, I'd give you one." Then I felt guilty—guilty, probably, for never having supposed that the poor bastard *had* a story of his own, much less a sad one, and I asked, quickly, "What's going to happen to him now?"

25 He didn't answer this. He was off by himself some place. "Funny thing," he said, and from his tone we might have been discussing the quickest way to get to Brooklyn, "when I saw the papers this morning, the first thing I asked myself was if I had anything to do with it. I felt sort of responsible."

I began to listen more carefully. The subway station was on the corner, just before us, and I stopped. He stopped, too. We were in front of a bar and he ducked slightly, peering in, but whoever he was looking for didn't seem to be there. The juke box was blasting away with something black and bouncy and I half watched the barmaid as she danced her way from the juke box to her place behind the bar. And I watched her face as she laughingly responded to something someone said to her, still keeping time to the music. When she smiled one saw the little girl, one sensed the doomed, still-struggling woman beneath the battered face of the semi-whore.

"I never *give* Sonny nothing," the boy said finally, "but a long time ago I come to school high and Sonny asked me how it felt." He paused, I couldn't bear to watch him, I watched the barmaid, and I listened to the music which seemed to be causing the pavement to shake. "I told him it felt great." The music stopped, the barmaid paused and watched the juke box until the music began again. "It did."

All this was carrying me some place I didn't want to go. I certainly didn't want to know how it felt. It filled everything, the people, the houses, the music, the dark, quicksilver barmaid, with menace; and this menace was their reality.

"What's going to happen to him now?" I asked again.

"They'll send him away some place and they'll try to cure him." He shook his head. "Maybe he'll even think he's kicked the habit. Then they'll let him loose"—he gestured, throwing his cigarette into the gutter. "That's all."

"What do you mean, that's *all*?"

But I knew what he meant.

"I *mean,* that's *all.*" He turned his head and looked at me, pulling down the corners of his mouth. "Don't you know what I mean?" he asked, softly.

"How the hell *would* I know what you mean?" I almost whispered it, I don't know why.

"That's right," he said to the air, "how would *he* know what I mean?" He turned toward me again, patient and calm, and yet I somehow felt him shaking, shaking as though he were going to fall apart. I felt that ice in my guts again, the dread I'd felt all afternoon; and again I watched the barmaid, moving about the bar, washing glasses, and singing. "Listen. They'll let him out and then it'll just start all over again. That's what I mean."

"You mean—they'll let him out. And then he'll just start working his way back in again. You mean he'll never kick the habit. Is that what you mean?"

"That's right," he said, cheerfully. "*You* see what I mean."

"Tell me," I said at last, "why does he want to die? He must want to die, he's killing himself, why does he want to die?"

He looked at me in surprise. He licked his lips. "He don't want to die. He wants to live. Don't nobody want to die, ever."

Then I wanted to ask him—too many things. He could not have answered, or if he had, I could not have borne the answers. I started walking. "Well, I guess it's none of my business."

"It's going to be rough on old Sonny," he said. We reached the subway station. "This is your station?" he asked. I nodded. I took one step down. "Damn!" he said, suddenly. I looked up at him. He grinned again. "Damn it if I didn't leave all my money home. You ain't got a dollar on you, have you? Just for a couple of days, is all."

All at once something inside gave and threatened to come pouring out of me. I didn't hate him any more. I felt that in another moment I'd start crying like a child.

"Sure," I said. "Don't sweat." I looked in my wallet and didn't have a dollar, I only had a five. "Here," I said. "That hold you?"

He didn't look at it—he didn't want to look at it. A terrible, closed look came over his face, as though he were keeping the number on the bill a secret from him and me. "Thanks," he said, and now he was dying to see me go. "Don't worry about Sonny. Maybe I'll write him or something."

"Sure," I said. "You do that. So long."

"Be seeing you," he said. I went on down the steps.

And I didn't write Sonny or send him anything for a long time. When I finally did, it was just after my little girl died, he wrote me back a letter which made me feel like a bastard.

Here's what he said:

> *Dear brother,*
>
> *You don't know how much I needed to hear from you. I wanted to write you many a time but I dug how much I must have hurt you and so I didn't write. But now I feel like a man who's been trying to climb up out of some deep, real deep and funky hole and just saw the sun up there, outside. I got to get outside.*
>
> *I can't tell you much about how I got here. I mean I don't know how to tell you. I guess I was afraid of something or I was trying to escape from something and you know I have never been very strong in the head (smile). I'm glad Mama and Daddy are dead and can't see what's happened to their son and I swear if I'd known what I was doing I would never have hurt you so, you and a lot of other fine people who were nice to me and who believed in me.*

*I don't want you to think it had anything to do with me being a musician. It's more than that. Or maybe less than that. I can't get anything straight in my head down here and I try not to think about what's going to happen to me when I get outside again. Sometime I think I'm going to flip and never get outside and sometime I think I'll come straight back. I tell you one thing, though, I'd rather blow my brains out than go through this again. But that's what they all say, so they tell me. If I tell you when I'm coming to New York and if you could meet me, I sure would appreciate it. Give my love to Isabel and the kids and I was sure sorry to hear about little Gracie. I wish I could be like Mama and say the Lord's will be done, but I don't know it seems to me that trouble is the one thing that never does get stopped and I don't know what good it does to blame it on the Lord. But maybe it does some good if you believe it.*

*Your brother,*
*Sonny*

55 Then I kept in constant touch with him and I sent him whatever I could and I went to meet him when he came back to New York. When I saw him many things I thought I had forgotten came flooding back to me. This was because I had begun, finally, to wonder about Sonny, about the life that Sonny lived inside. This life, whatever it was, had made him older and thinner and it had deepened the distant stillness in which he had always moved. He looked very unlike my baby brother. Yet, when he smiled, when we shook hands, the baby brother I'd never known looked out from the depths of his private life, like an animal waiting to be coaxed into the light.

"How you been keeping?" he asked me.

"All right. And you?"

"Just fine." He was smiling all over his face. "It's good to see you again."

"It's good to see you."

60 The seven years' difference in our ages lay between us like a chasm: I wondered if these years would ever operate between us as a bridge. I was remembering, and it made it hard to catch my breath, that I had been there when he was born; and I had heard the first words he had ever spoken. When he started to walk, he walked from our mother straight to me. I caught him just before he fell when he took the first steps he ever took in this world.

"How's Isabel?"

"Just fine. She's dying to see you."

"And the boys?"

"They're fine, too. They're anxious to see their uncle."

65 "Oh, come on. You know they don't remember me."

"Are you kidding? Of course they remember you."

He grinned again. We got into a taxi. We had a lot to say to each other, far too much to know how to begin.

As the taxi began to move, I asked, "You still want to go to India?"

He laughed. "You still remember that. Hell, no. This place is Indian enough for me."

70 "It used to belong to them," I said.

And he laughed again. "They damn sure knew what they were doing when they got rid of it."

Years ago, when he was around fourteen, he'd been all hipped on the idea of going to India. He read books about people sitting on rocks, naked, in all kinds of weather, but mostly bad, naturally, and walking barefoot through hot coals and arriving at wisdom. I used to say that it sounded to me as though they were getting away from wisdom as fast as they could. I think he sort of looked down on me for that.

"Do you mind," he asked, "if we have the driver drive alongside the park? On the west side—I haven't seen the city in so long."

"Of course not," I said. I was afraid that I might sound as though I were humoring him, but I hoped he wouldn't take it that way.

75 So we drove along, between the green of the park and the stony, lifeless elegance of hotels and apartment buildings, toward the vivid, killing streets of our childhood. These streets hadn't changed, though housing projects jutted up out of them now like rocks in the middle of a boiling sea. Most of the houses in which we had grown up had vanished, as had the stores from which we

had stolen, the basements in which we had first tried sex, the rooftops from which we had hurled tin cans and bricks. But houses exactly like the houses of our past yet dominated the landscape, boys exactly like the boys we once had been found themselves smothering in these houses, came down into the streets for light and air and found themselves encircled by disaster. Some escaped the trap, most didn't. Those who got out always left something of themselves behind, as some animals amputate a leg and leave it in the trap. It might be said, perhaps, that I had escaped, after all, I was a school teacher; or that Sonny had, he hadn't lived in Harlem for years. Yet, as the cab moved uptown through streets which seemed, with a rush, to darken with dark people, and as I covertly studied Sonny's face, it came to me that what we both were seeking through our separate cab windows was that part of ourselves which had been left behind. It's always at the hour of trouble and confrontation that the missing member aches.

We hit 110th Street and started rolling up Lenox Avenue. And I'd known this avenue all my life, but it seemed to me again, as it had seemed on the day I'd first heard about Sonny's trouble, filled with a hidden menace which was its very breath of life.

"We almost there," said Sonny.

"Almost." We were both too nervous to say anything more.

We live in a housing project. It hasn't been up long. A few days after it was up it seemed uninhabitably new, now, of course, it's already rundown. It looks like a parody of the good, clean, faceless life—God knows the people who live in it do their best to make it a parody. The beat-looking grass lying around isn't enough to make their lives green, the hedges will never hold out the streets, and they know it. The big windows fool no one, they aren't big enough to make space out of no space. They don't bother with the windows, they watch the TV screen instead. The playground is most popular with the children who don't play at jacks, or skip rope, or roller skate, or swing, and they can be found in it after dark. We moved in partly because it's not too far from where I teach, and partly for the kids; but it's really just like the houses in which Sonny and I grew up. The same things happen, they'll have the same things to remember. The moment Sonny and I started into the house I had the feeling that I was simply bringing him back into the danger he had almost died trying to escape.

Sonny has never been talkative. So I don't know why I was sure he'd be dying to talk to me when supper was over the first night. Everything went fine, the oldest boy remembered him, and the youngest boy liked him, and Sonny had remembered to bring something for each of them; and Isabel, who is really much nicer than I am, more open and giving, had gone to a lot of trouble about dinner and was genuinely glad to see him. And she's always been able to tease Sonny in a way that I haven't. It was nice to see her face so vivid again and to hear her laugh and watch her make Sonny laugh. She wasn't, or, anyway, she didn't seem to be, at all uneasy or embarrassed. She chatted as though there were no subject which had to be avoided and she got Sonny past his first, faint stiffness. And thank God she was there, for I was filled with that icy dread again. Everything I did seemed awkward to me, and everything I said sounded freighted with hidden meaning. I was trying to remember everything I'd heard about dope addiction and I couldn't help watching Sonny for signs. I wasn't doing it out of malice. I was trying to find out something about my brother. I was dying to hear him tell me he was safe.

"Safe!" my father grunted, whenever Mama suggested trying to move to a neighborhood which might be safer for children. "Safe, hell! Ain't no place safe for kids, nor nobody."

He always went on like this, but he wasn't, ever, really as bad as he sounded, not even on weekends, when he got drunk. As a matter of fact, he was always on the lookout for "something a little better," but he died before he found it. He died suddenly, during a drunken weekend in the middle of the war, when Sonny was fifteen. He and Sonny hadn't ever got on too well. And this was partly because Sonny was the apple of his father's eye. It was because he loved Sonny so much and was frightened for him, that he was always fighting with him. It doesn't do any good to fight with Sonny. Sonny just moves back, inside himself, where he can't be reached. But the principal reason that they never hit it off is that they were so much alike. Daddy was big and rough and loud-talking, just the opposite of Sonny, but they both had—that same privacy.

Mama tried to tell me something about this, just after Daddy died. I was home on leave from the army.

This was the last time I ever saw my mother alive. Just the same, this picture gets all mixed up in my mind with pictures I had of her when she was younger. The way I always see her is the way she used to be on a Sunday afternoon, say, when the old folks were talking after the big Sunday dinner. I always see her wearing pale blue. She'd be sitting on the sofa. And my father would be sitting in the easy chair, not far from her. And the living room would be full of church folks and relatives. There they sit, in chairs all around the living room, and the night is creeping up outside, but nobody knows it yet. You can see the darkness growing against the windowpanes and you hear the street noises every now and again, or maybe the jangling beat of a tambourine from one of the churches close by, but it's real quiet in the room. For a moment nobody's talking, but every face looks darkening, like the sky outside. And my mother rocks a little from the waist, and my father's eyes are closed. Everyone is looking at something a child can't see. For a minute they've forgotten the children. Maybe a kid is lying on the rug, half asleep. Maybe somebody's got a kid in his lap and is absent-mindedly stroking the kid's head. Maybe there's a kid, quiet and big-eyed, curled up in a big chair in the corner. The silence, the darkness coming, and the darkness in the faces frightens the child obscurely. He hopes that the hand which strokes his forehead will never stop—will never die. He hopes that there will never come a time when the old folks won't be sitting around the living room, talking about where they've come from, and what they've seen, and what's happened to them and their kinfolk.

But something deep and watchful in the child knows that this is bound to end, is already ending. In a moment someone will get up and turn on the light. Then the old folks will remember the children and they won't talk any more that day. And when light fills the room, the child is filled with darkness. He knows that every time this happens he's moved just a little closer to that darkness outside. The darkness outside is what the old folks have been talking about. It's what they've come from. It's what they endure. The child knows that they won't talk any more because if he knows too much about what's happened to *them,* he'll know too much too soon, about what's going to happen to *him.*

The last time I talked to my mother, I remember I was restless. I wanted to get out and see Isabel. We weren't married then and we had a lot to straighten out between us.

There Mama sat, in black, by the window. She was humming an old church song, *Lord, you brought me from a long ways off.* Sonny was out somewhere. Mama kept watching the streets.

"I don't know," she said, "if I'll ever see you again, after you go off from here. But I hope you'll remember the things I tried to teach you."

"Don't talk like that," I said, and smiled. "You'll be here a long time yet."

She smiled, too, but she said nothing. She was quiet for a long time. And I said, "Mama, don't you worry about nothing. I'll be writing all the time, and you be getting the checks. . . ."

"I want to talk to you about your brother," she said, suddenly. "If anything happens to me he ain't going to have nobody to look out for him."

"Mama," I said, "ain't nothing going to happen to you *or* Sonny. Sonny's all right. He's a good boy and he's got good sense."

"It ain't a question of his being a good boy," Mama said, "nor of his having good sense. It ain't only the bad ones, nor yet the dumb ones that gets sucked under." She stopped, looking at me. "Your Daddy once had a brother," she said, and she smiled in a way that made me feel she was in pain. "You didn't never know that, did you?"

"No," I said, "I never knew that," and I watched her face.

"Oh, yes," she said, "your Daddy had a brother." She looked out of the window again. "I know you never saw your Daddy cry. But *I* did—many a time, through all these years."

I asked her, "What happened to his brother? How come nobody's ever talked about him?"

This was the first time I ever saw my mother look old.

"His brother got killed," she said, "when he was just a little younger than you are now. I knew him. He was a fine boy. He was maybe a little full of the devil, but he didn't mean nobody no harm."

Then she stopped and the room was silent, exactly as it had sometimes been on those Sunday afternoons. Mama kept looking out into the streets.

"He used to have a job in the mill," she said, "and, like all young folks, he just liked to perform on Saturday nights. Saturday nights, him and your father would drift around to different places, go to dances and things like that, or just sit around with people they knew, and your father's brother would sing, he had a fine voice, and play along with himself on his guitar. Well, this particular Saturday night, him and your father was coming home from some place, and they were both a little drunk and there was a moon that night, it was bright like day. Your father's brother was feeling kind of good, and he was whistling to himself, and he had his guitar slung over his shoulder. They was coming down a hill and beneath them was a road that turned off from the highway. Well, your father's brother, being always kind of frisky, decided to run down this hill, and he did, with that guitar banging and clanging behind him, and he ran across the road, and he was making water behind a tree. And your father was sort of amused at him and he was still coming down the hill, kind of slow. Then he heard a car motor and that same minute his brother stepped from behind the tree, into the road, in the moonlight. And he started to cross the road. And your father started to run down the hill, he says he don't know why. This car was full of white men. They was all drunk, and when they seen your father's brother they let out a great whoop and holler and they aimed the car straight at him. They was having fun, they just wanted to scare him, the way they do sometimes, you know. But they was drunk. And I guess the boy, being drunk, too, and scared, kind of lost his head. By the time he jumped it was too late. Your father says he heard his brother scream when the car rolled over him, and he heard the wood of that guitar when it give, and he heard them strings go flying, and he heard them white men shouting, and the car kept on a-going and it ain't stopped till this day. And, time your father got down the hill, his brother weren't nothing but blood and pulp."

Tears were gleaming on my mother's face. There wasn't anything I could say.

"He never mentioned it," she said, "because I never let him mention it before you children. Your Daddy was like a crazy man that night and for many a night thereafter. He says he never in his life seen anything as dark as that road after the lights of that car had gone away. Weren't nothing, weren't nobody on that road, just your Daddy and his brother and that busted guitar. Oh, yes. Your Daddy never did really get right again. Till the day he died he weren't sure but that every white man he saw was the man that killed his brother."

She stopped and took out her handkerchief and dried her eyes and looked at me.

"I ain't telling you all this," she said, "to make you scared or bitter or to make you hate nobody. I'm telling you this because you got a brother. And the world ain't changed."

I guess I didn't want to believe this. I guess she saw this in my face. She turned away from me, toward the window again, searching those streets.

"But I praise my Redeemer," she said at last, "that He called your Daddy home before me. I ain't saying it to throw no flowers at myself, but, I declare, it keeps me from feeling too cast down to know I helped your father get safely through this world. Your father always acted like he was the roughest, strongest man on earth. And everybody took him to be like that. But if he hadn't had *me* there—to see his tears!"

She was crying again. Still, I couldn't move. I said, "Lord, Lord, Mama, I didn't know it was like that."

"Oh, honey," she said, "there's a lot that you don't know. But you are going to find it out." She stood up from the window and came over to me. "You got to hold on to your brother," she said, "and don't let him fall, no matter what it looks like is happening to him and no matter how evil you gets with him. You going to be evil with him many a time. But don't you forget what I told you, you hear?"

"I won't forget," I said. "Don't you worry, I won't forget. I won't let nothing happen to Sonny."

My mother smiled as though she were amused at something she saw in my face. Then, "You may not be able to stop nothing from happening. But you got to let him know you's *there*."

Two days later I was married, and then I was gone. And I had a lot of things on my mind and I pretty well forgot my promise to Mama until I got shipped home on a special furlough for her funeral.

And, after the funeral, with just Sonny and me alone in the empty kitchen, I tried to find out something about him.

"What do you want to do?" I asked him.

"I'm going to be a musician," he said.

115 For he had graduated, in the time I had been away, from dancing to the juke box to finding out who was playing what, and what they were doing with it, and he had bought himself a set of drums.

"You mean, you want to be a drummer?" I somehow had the feeling that being a drummer might be all right for other people but not for my brother Sonny.

"I don't think," he said, looking at me very gravely, "that I'll ever be a good drummer. But I think I can play a piano."

I frowned. I'd never played the role of the older brother quite so seriously before, had scarcely ever, in fact, *asked* Sonny a damn thing. I sensed myself in the presence of something I didn't really know how to handle, didn't understand. So I made my frown a little deeper as I asked: "What kind of musician do you want to be?"

He grinned. "How many kinds do you think there are?"

120 "Be *serious,*" I said.

He laughed, throwing his head back, and then looked at me. "I *am* serious."

"Well, then, for Christ's sake, stop kidding around and answer a serious question. I mean, do you want to be a concert pianist, you want to play classical music and all that, or—or what?" Long before I finished he was laughing again. "For Christ's *sake,* Sonny!"

He sobered, but with difficulty. "I'm sorry. But you sound so—*scared!*" and he was off again.

"Well, you may think it's funny now, baby, but it's not going to be so funny when you have to make your living at it, let me tell you *that.*" I was furious because I knew he was laughing at me and I didn't know why.

125 "No," he said, very sober now, and afraid, perhaps, that he'd hurt me, "I don't want to be a classical pianist. That isn't what interests me. I mean"—he paused, looking hard at me, as though his eyes would help me to understand, and then gestured helplessly, as though perhaps his hand would help—"I mean, I'll have a lot of studying to do, and I'll have to study *everything,* but, I mean, I want to play *with*—jazz musicians." He stopped. "I want to play jazz," he said.

Well, the word had never before sounded as heavy, as real, as it sounded that afternoon in Sonny's mouth. I just looked at him and I was probably frowning a real frown by this time. I simply couldn't see why on earth he'd want to spend his time hanging around nightclubs, clowning around on bandstands, while people pushed each other around a dance floor. It seemed—beneath him, somehow. I had never thought about it before, had never been forced to, but I suppose I had always put jazz musicians in a class with what Daddy called "good-time people."

"Are you *serious?*"

"Hell, *yes,* I'm serious."

He looked more helpless than ever, and annoyed, and deeply hurt.

130 I suggested, helpfully: "You mean—like Louis Armstrong?"

His face closed as though I'd struck him. "No. I'm not talking about none of that old-time, down home crap."

"Well, look, Sonny, I'm sorry, don't get mad. I just don't altogether get it, that's all. Name somebody—you know, a jazz musician you admire."

"Bird."

"Who?"

135 "Bird! Charlie Parker! Don't they teach you nothing in the goddamn army?"

I lit a cigarette. I was surprised and then a little amused to discover that I was trembling. "I've been out of touch," I said. "You'll have to be patient with me. Now. Who's this Parker character?"

"He's just one of the greatest jazz musicians alive," said Sonny, sullenly, his hands in his pockets, his back to me. "Maybe *the* greatest," he added, bitterly, "that's probably why *you* never heard of him."

"All right," I said, "I'm ignorant. I'm sorry. I'll go out and buy all the cat's records right away, all right?"

"It don't," said Sonny, with dignity, "make any difference to me. I don't care what you listen to. Don't do me no favors."

40 I was beginning to realize that I'd never seen him so upset before. With another part of my mind I was thinking that this would probably turn out to be one of those things kids go through and that I shouldn't make it seem important by pushing it too hard. Still, I didn't think it would do any harm to ask: "Doesn't all this take a lot of time? Can you make a living at it?"

He turned back to me and half leaned, half sat, on the kitchen table. "Everything takes time," he said, "and—well, yes, sure, I can make a living at it. But what I don't seem to be able to make you understand is that it's the only thing I want to do."

"Well, Sonny," I said, gently, "you know people can't always do exactly what they *want* to do—"

"*No,* I don't know that," said Sonny, surprising me. "I think people *ought* to do what they want to do, what else are they alive for?"

"You getting to be a big boy," I said desperately, "it's time you started thinking about your future."

45 "I'm thinking about my future," said Sonny, grimly. "I think about it all the time."

I gave up. I decided, if he didn't change his mind, that we could always talk about it later. "In the meantime," I said, "you got to finish school." We had already decided that he'd have to move in with Isabel and her folks. I knew this wasn't the ideal arrangement because Isabel's folks are inclined to be dicty and they hadn't especially wanted Isabel to marry me. But I didn't know what else to do. "And we have to get you fixed up at Isabel's."

There was a long silence. He moved from the kitchen table to the window. "That's a terrible idea. You know it yourself."

"Do you have a *better* idea?"

He just walked up and down the kitchen for a minute. He was as tall as I was. He had started to shave. I suddenly had the feeling that I didn't know him at all.

50 He stopped at the kitchen table and picked up my cigarettes. Looking at me with a kind of mocking, amused defiance, he put one between his lips. "You mind?"

"You smoking already?"

He lit the cigarette and nodded, watching me through the smoke. "I just wanted to see if I'd have the courage to smoke in front of you." He grinned and blew a great cloud of smoke to the ceiling. "It was easy." He looked at my face. "Come on, now. I bet you was smoking at my age, tell the truth."

I didn't say anything but the truth was on my face, and he laughed. But now there was something very strained in his laugh. "Sure. And I bet that ain't all you was doing."

He was frightening me a little. "Cut the crap," I said. "We already decided that you was going to go and live at Isabel's. Now what's got into you all of a sudden?"

55 "*You* decided it," he pointed out. "*I* didn't decide nothing." He stopped in front of me, leaning against the stove, arms loosely folded. "Look, brother. I don't want to stay in Harlem no more, I really don't." He was very earnest. He looked at me, then over toward the kitchen window. There was something in his eyes I'd never seen before, some thoughtfulness, some worry all his own. He rubbed the muscle of one arm. "It's time I was getting out of here."

"Where do you want to *go,* Sonny?"

"I want to join the army. Or the navy, I don't care. If I say I'm old enough, they'll believe me."

Then I got mad. It was because I was so scared. "You must be crazy. You goddamn fool, what the hell do you want to go and join the *army* for?"

"I just told you. To get out of Harlem."

60 "Sonny, you haven't even finished *school.* And if you really want to be a musician, how do you expect to study if you're in the *army?*"

He looked at me, trapped, and in anguish. "There's ways. I might be able to work out some kind of deal. Anyway, I'll have the G.I. Bill when I come out."

"*If* you come out." We stared at each other. "Sonny, please. Be reasonable. I know the setup is far from perfect. But we got to do the best we can."

"I ain't learning nothing in school," he said. "Even when I go." He turned away from me and opened the window and threw his cigarette out into the narrow alley. I watched his back. "At least, I ain't learning nothing you'd want me to learn." He slammed the window so hard I thought the glass would fly out, and turned back to me. "And I'm sick of the stink of these garbage cans!"

"Sonny," I said, "I know how you feel. But if you don't finish school now, you're going to be sorry later that you didn't." I grabbed him by the shoulders. "And you only got another year. It ain't so bad. And I'll come back and I swear I'll help you do *whatever* you want to do. Just try to put up with it till I come back. Will you please do that? For me?"

165 He didn't answer and he wouldn't look at me.

"Sonny. You hear me?"

He pulled away. "I hear you. But you never hear anything *I* say."

I didn't know what to say to that. He looked out of the window and then back at me. "OK," he said, and sighed. "I'll try."

Then I said, trying to cheer him up a little, "They got a piano at Isabel's. You can practice on it."

170 And as a matter of fact, it did cheer him up for a minute. "That's right," he said to himself. "I forgot that." His face relaxed a little. But the worry, the thoughtfulness, played on it still, the way shadows play on a face which is staring into the fire.

But I thought I'd never hear the end of that piano. At first, Isabel would write me, saying how nice it was that Sonny was so serious about his music and how, as soon as he came in from school, or wherever he had been when he was supposed to be at school, he went straight to that piano and stayed there until suppertime. And, after supper, he went back to that piano and stayed there until everybody went to bed. He was at the piano all day Saturday and all day Sunday. Then he bought a record player and started playing records. He'd play one record over and over again, all day long sometimes, and he'd improvise along with it on the piano. Or he'd play one section of the record, one chord, one change, one progression, then he'd do it on the piano. Then back to the record. Then back to the piano.

Well, I really don't know how they stood it. Isabel finally confessed that it wasn't like living with a person at all, it was like living with sound. And the sound didn't make any sense to her, didn't make any sense to any of them—naturally. They began, in a way, to be afflicted by this presence that was living in their home. It was as though Sonny were some sort of god, or monster. He moved in an atmosphere which wasn't like theirs at all. They fed him and he ate, he washed himself, he walked in and out of their door; he certainly wasn't nasty or unpleasant or rude, Sonny isn't any of those things; but it was as though he were all wrapped up in some cloud, some fire, some vision all his own; and there wasn't any way to reach him.

At the same time, he wasn't really a man yet, he was still a child, and they had to watch out for him in all kinds of ways. They certainly couldn't throw him out. Neither did they dare to make a great scene about that piano because even they dimly sensed, as I sensed, from so many thousands of miles away, that Sonny was at that piano playing for his life.

But he hadn't been going to school. One day a letter came from the school board and Isabel's mother got it—there had, apparently, been other letters but Sonny had torn them up. This day, when Sonny came in, Isabel's mother showed him the letter and asked where he'd been spending his time. And she finally got it out of him that he'd been down in Greenwich Village, with musicians and other characters, in a white girl's apartment. And this scared her and she started to scream at him and what came up, once she began—though she denies it to this day—was what sacrifices they were making to give Sonny a decent home and how little he appreciated it.

175 Sonny didn't play the piano that day. By evening, Isabel's mother had calmed down but then there was the old man to deal with, and Isabel herself. Isabel says she did her best to be calm but she broke down and started crying. She says she just watched Sonny's face. She could tell, by watching him, what was happening with him. And what was happening was that they penetrated his cloud, they had reached him. Even if their fingers had been a thousand times more gentle than human fingers ever are, he could hardly help feeling that they had stripped him naked and were spitting on that nakedness. For he also had to see that his presence, that music, which was life or death to him, had been torture for them and that they had endured it, not at all for his sake, but only for mine. And Sonny couldn't take that. He can take it a little better today than he could then but he's still not very good at it and, frankly, I don't know anybody who is.

The silence of the next few days must have been louder than the sound of all the music ever played since time began. One morning, before she went to work, Isabel was in his room for something and she suddenly realized that all of his records were gone. And she knew for certain that he was gone. And he was. He went as far as the navy would carry him. He finally sent me a postcard from some place in Greece and that was the first I knew that Sonny was still alive. I didn't see him any more until we were both back in New York and the war had long been over.

He was a man by then, of course, but I wasn't willing to see it. He came by the house from time to time, but we fought almost every time we met. I didn't like the way he carried himself, loose and dreamlike all the time, and I didn't like his friends, and his music seemed to be merely an excuse for the life he led. It sounded just that weird and disordered.

Then we had a fight, a pretty awful fight, and I didn't see him for months. By and by I looked him up, where he was living, in a furnished room in the Village, and I tried to make it up. But there were lots of other people in the room and Sonny just lay on his bed, and he wouldn't come downstairs with me, and he treated these other people as though they were his family and I weren't. So I got mad and then he got mad, and then I told him that he might just as well be dead as live the way he was living. Then he stood up and he told me not to worry about him any more in life, that he *was* dead as far as I was concerned. Then he pushed me to the door and the other people looked on as though nothing were happening, and he slammed the door behind me. I stood in the hallway, staring at the door. I heard somebody laugh in the room and then the tears came to my eyes. I started down the steps, whistling to keep from crying, I kept whistling to myself, *You going to need me, baby, one of these cold, rainy days.*

I read about Sonny's trouble in the spring. Little Grace died in the fall. She was a beautiful little girl. But she only lived a little over two years. She died of polio and she suffered. She had a slight fever for a couple of days, but it didn't seem like anything and we just kept her in bed. And we would certainly have called the doctor, but the fever dropped, she seemed to be all right. So we thought it had just been a cold. Then, one day, she was up, playing, Isabel was in the kitchen fixing lunch for the two boys when they'd come in from school, and she heard Grace fall down in the living room. When you have a lot of children you don't always start running when one of them falls, unless they start screaming or something. And, this time, Grace was quiet. Yet, Isabel says that when she heard that *thump* and then that silence, something happened in her to make her afraid. And she ran to the living room and there was little Grace on the floor, all twisted up, and the reason she hadn't screamed was that she couldn't get her breath. And when she did scream, it was the worst sound, Isabel says, that she'd ever heard in all her life, and she still hears it sometimes in her dreams. Isabel will sometimes wake me up with a low, moaning, strangled sound and I have to be quick to awaken her and hold her to me and where Isabel is weeping against me seems a mortal wound.

0 I think I may have written Sonny the very day that little Grace was buried. I was sitting in the living room in the dark, by myself, and I suddenly thought of Sonny. My trouble made his real.

One Saturday afternoon, when Sonny had been living with us, or, anyway, been in our house, for nearly two weeks, I found myself wandering aimlessly about the living room, drinking from a can of beer, and trying to work up the courage to search Sonny's room. He was out, he was usually out whenever I was home, and Isabel had taken the children to see their grandparents. Suddenly I was standing still in front of the living room window, watching Seventh Avenue. The idea of searching Sonny's room made me still. I scarcely dared to admit to myself what I'd be searching for. I didn't know what I'd do if I found it. Or if I didn't.

On the sidewalk across from me, near the entrance to a barbecue joint, some people were holding an old-fashioned revival meeting. The barbecue cook, wearing a dirty white apron, his conked hair reddish and metallic in the pale sun, and a cigarette between his lips, stood in the doorway, watching them. Kids and older people paused in their errands and stood there, along with some older men and a couple of very tough-looking women who watched everything that happened on the avenue, as though they owned it, or were maybe owned by it. Well, they were watching this, too. The revival was being carried on by three sisters in black, and a brother. All they had were their voices and their Bibles and a tambourine. The brother was testifying and while he testified two of the sisters stood together, seeming to say, amen, and the third sister walked around with the tambourine outstretched and a couple of people dropped coins into it. Then the brother's testimony ended and the sister who had been taking up the collection dumped the coins into her palm and transferred them to the pocket of her long black robe. Then she raised both hands, striking the tambourine against the air, and then against one hand, and she started to sing. And the two other sisters and the brother joined in.

It was strange, suddenly, to watch, though I had been seeing these street meetings all my life. So, of course, had everybody else down there. Yet, they paused and watched and listened and I stood still at the window. "*Tis the old ship of Zion,*" they sang, and the sister with the tambourine kept a steady, jangling beat, "*it has rescued many a thousand!*" Not a soul under the sound of their voices was hearing this song for the first time, not one of them had been rescued. Nor had they seen much in the way of rescue work being done around them. Neither did they especially believe in the holiness of the three sisters and the brother, they knew too much about them, knew where they lived, and how. The woman with the tambourine, whose voice dominated the air, whose face was bright with joy, was divided by very little from the woman who stood watching her, a cigarette between her heavy, chapped lips, her hair a cuckoo's nest, her face scarred and swollen from many beatings, and her black eyes glittering like coal. Perhaps they both knew this, which was why, when, as rarely, they addressed each other, they addressed each other as Sister. As the singing filled the air the watching, listening faces underwent a change, the eyes focusing on something within; the music seemed to soothe a poison out of them; and time seemed, nearly, to fall away from the sullen, belligerent, battered faces, as though they were fleeing back to their first condition, while dreaming of their last. The barbecue cook half shook his head and smiled, and dropped his cigarette and disappeared into his joint. A man fumbled in his pockets for change and stood holding it in his hand impatiently, as though he had just remembered a pressing appointment further up the avenue. He looked furious. Then I saw Sonny, standing on the edge of the crowd. He was carrying a wide, flat notebook with a green cover, and it made him look, from where I was standing, almost like a schoolboy. The coppery sun brought out the copper in his skin, he was very faintly smiling, standing very still. Then the singing stopped, the tambourine turned into a collection plate again. The furious man dropped in his coins and vanished, so did a couple of the women, and Sonny dropped some change in the plate, looking directly at the woman with a little smile. He started across the avenue, toward the house. He has a slow, loping walk, something like the way Harlem hipsters walk, only he's imposed on this his own half-beat. I had never really noticed it before.

I stayed at the window, both relieved and apprehensive. As Sonny disappeared from my sight, they began singing again. And they were still singing when his key turned in the lock.

185 "Hey," he said.

"Hey, yourself. You want some beer?"

"No. Well, maybe." But he came up to the window and stood beside me, looking out. "What a warm voice," he said.

They were singing *If I could only hear my mother pray again!*

"Yes," I said, "and she can sure beat that tambourine."

190 "But what a terrible song," he said, and laughed. He dropped his notebook on the sofa and disappeared into the kitchen. "Where's Isabel and the kids?"

"I think they went to see their grandparents. You hungry?"

"No." He came back into the living room with his can of beer. "You want to come some place with me tonight?"

I sensed, I don't know how, that I couldn't possibly say no. "Sure. Where?"

He sat down on the sofa and picked up his notebook and started leafing through it. "I'm going to sit in with some fellows in a joint in the Village."

195 "You mean, you're going to play, tonight?"

"That's right." He took a swallow of his beer and moved back to the window. He gave me a sidelong look. "If you can stand it."

"I'll try," I said.

He smiled to himself and we both watched as the meeting across the way broke up. The three sisters and the brother, heads bowed, were singing *God be with you till we meet again.* The faces around them were very quiet. Then the song ended. The small crowd dispersed. We watched the three women and the lone man walk slowly up the avenue.

"When she was singing before," said Sonny, abruptly, "her voice reminded me for a minute of what heroin feels like sometimes—when it's in your veins. It makes you feel sort of warm and cool at the same time. And distant. And—and sure." He sipped his beer, very deliberately not looking at me. I watched his face. "It makes you feel—in control. Sometimes you've got to have that feeling."

00 "Do you?" I sat down slowly in the easy chair.

"Sometimes." He went to the sofa and picked up his notebook again. "Some people do."

"In order," I asked, "to play?" And my voice was very ugly, full of contempt and anger.

"Well"—he looked at me with great, troubled eyes, as though, in fact, he hoped his eyes would tell me things he could never otherwise say—"they *think* so. And *if* they think so—!"

"And what do *you* think?" I asked.

05 He sat on the sofa and put his can of beer on the floor. "I don't know," he said, and I couldn't be sure if he were answering my question or pursuing his thoughts. His face didn't tell me. "It's not so much to *play*. It's to *stand* it, to be able to make it at all. On any level." He frowned and smiled: "In order to keep from shaking to pieces."

"But these friends of yours," I said, "they seem to shake themselves to pieces pretty goddamn fast."

"Maybe." He played with the notebook. And something told me that I should curb my tongue, that Sonny was doing his best to talk, that I should listen. "But of course you only know the ones that've gone to pieces. Some don't—or at least they haven't *yet* and that's just about all *any* of us can say." He paused. "And then there are some who just live, really, in hell, and they know it and they see what's happening and they go right on. I don't know." He sighed, dropped the notebook, folded his arms. "Some guys, you can tell from the way they play, they on something *all* the time. And you can see that, well, it makes something real for them. But of course," he picked up his beer from the floor and sipped it and put the can down again, "they *want* to, too, you've got to see that. Even some of them that say they don't—*some,* not all."

"And what about you?" I asked—I couldn't help it. "What about you? Do *you* want to?"

He stood up and walked to the window and remained silent for a long time. Then he sighed. "Me," he said. Then: "While I was downstairs before, on my way here, listening to that woman sing, it struck me all of a sudden how much suffering she must have had to go through—to sing like that. It's *repulsive* to think you have to suffer that much."

10 I said: "But there's no way not to suffer—is there, Sonny?"

"I believe not," he said and smiled, "but that's never stopped anyone from trying." He looked at me. "Has it?" I realized, with this mocking look, that there stood between us, forever, beyond the power of time or forgiveness, the fact that I had held silence—so long!—when he had needed human speech to help him. He turned back to the window. "No, there's no way not to suffer. But you try all kinds of ways to keep from drowning in it, to keep on top of it, and to make it seem—well, like *you*. Like you did something, all right, and now you're suffering for it. You know?" I said nothing. "Well you know," he said, impatiently, "why *do* people suffer? Maybe it's better to do something to give it a reason, *any* reason."

"But we just agreed," I said, "that there's no way not to suffer. Isn't it better, then, just to—take it?"

"But nobody just takes it," Sonny cried, "that's what I'm telling you! *Everybody* tries not to. You're just hung up on the *way* some people try—it's not *your* way!"

The hair on my face began to itch, my face felt wet. "That's not true," I said, "that's not true. I don't give a damn what other people do, I don't even care how they suffer. I just care how *you* suffer." And he looked at me. "Please believe me," I said, "I don't want to see you—die—trying not to suffer."

15 "I won't," he said, flatly, "die trying not to suffer. At least, not any faster than anybody else."

"But there's no need," I said, trying to laugh, "is there? in killing yourself."

I wanted to say more, but I couldn't. I wanted to talk about will power and how life could be—well, beautiful. I wanted to say that it was all within; but was it? or, rather, wasn't that exactly the trouble? And I wanted to promise that I would never fail him again. But it would all have sounded—empty words and lies.

So I made the promise to myself and prayed that I would keep it.

"It's terrible sometimes, inside," he said, "that's what's the trouble. You walk these streets, black and funky and cold, and there's not really a living ass to talk to, and there's nothing shaking, and there's no way of getting it out—that storm inside. You can't talk it and you can't make love with it, and when you finally try to get with it and play it, you realize *nobody's* listening. So *you've* got to listen. You got to find a way to listen."

220 And then he walked away from the window and sat on the sofa again, as though all the wind had suddenly been knocked out of him. "Sometimes you'll do *anything* to play, even cut your mother's throat." He laughed and looked at me. "Or your brother's." Then he sobered. "Or your own." Then: "Don't worry. I'm all right now and I think I'll *be* all right. But I can't forget—where I've been. I don't mean just the physical place I've been, I mean where I've *been*. And *what* I've been."

"What have you been, Sonny?" I asked.

He smiled—but sat sideways on the sofa, his elbow resting on the back, his fingers playing with his mouth and chin, not looking at me. "I've been something I didn't recognize, didn't know I could be. Didn't know anybody could be." He stopped, looking inward, looking helplessly young, looking old. "I'm not talking about it now because I feel *guilty* or anything like that—maybe it would be better if I did, I don't know. Anyway, I can't really talk about it. Not to you, not to anybody," and now he turned and faced me. "Sometimes, you know, and it was actually when I was most *out* of the world, I felt that I was in it, that I was *with* it, really, and I could play or I didn't really have to *play*, it just came out of me, it was there. And I don't know how I played, thinking about it now, but I know I did awful things, those times, sometimes, to people. Or it wasn't that I *did* anything to them—it was that they weren't real." He picked up the beer can; it was empty; he rolled it between his palms: "And other times—well, I needed a fix, I needed to find a place to lean, I needed to clear a space to *listen*—and I couldn't find it, and I—went crazy, I did terrible things to *me*, I was terrible *for* me." He began pressing the beer can between his hands, I watched the metal begin to give. It glittered, as he played with it, like a knife, and I was afraid he would cut himself, but I said nothing. "Oh well. I can never tell you. I was all by myself at the bottom of something, stinking and sweating and crying and shaking, and I smelled it, you know? *my* stink, and I thought I'd die if I couldn't get away from it and yet, all the same, I knew that everything I was doing was just locking me in with it. And I didn't know," he paused, still flattening the beer can, "I didn't know, I still *don't* know, something kept telling me that maybe it was good to smell your own stink, but I didn't think that *that* was what I'd been trying to do—and—who can stand it?" and he abruptly dropped the ruined beer can, looking at me with a small, still smile, and then rose, walking to the window as though it were the lodestone rock. I watched his face, he watched the avenue. "I couldn't tell you when Mama died—but the reason I wanted to leave Harlem so bad was to get away from drugs. And then, when I ran away, that's what I was running from—really. When I came back, nothing had changed, *I* hadn't changed, I was just—older." And he stopped, drumming with his fingers on the windowpane. The sun had vanished, soon darkness would fall. I watched his face. "It can come again," he said, almost as though speaking to himself. Then he turned to me. "It can come again," he repeated. "I just want you to know that."

"All right," I said, at last. "So it can come again. All right."

He smiled, but the smile was sorrowful. "I had to try to tell you," he said.

225 "Yes," I said. "I understand that."

"You're my brother," he said, looking straight at me, and not smiling at all.

"Yes," I repeated, "yes. I understand that."

He turned back to the window, looking out. "All that hatred down there," he said, "all that hatred and misery and love. It's a wonder it doesn't blow the avenue apart."

We went to the only nightclub on a short, dark street, downtown. We squeezed through the narrow, chattering, jam-packed bar to the entrance of the big room, where the bandstand was. And we stood there for a moment, for the lights were very dim in this room and we couldn't see. Then, "Hello, boy," said a voice and an enormous black man, much older than Sonny or myself, erupted out of all that atmospheric lighting and put an arm around Sonny's shoulder. "I been sitting right here," he said, "waiting for you."

30 He had a big voice, too, and heads in the darkness turned toward us.

Sonny grinned and pulled a little away, and said, "Creole, this is my brother. I told you about him."

Creole shook my hand. "I'm glad to meet you, son," he said, and it was clear that he was glad to meet me *there,* for Sonny's sake. And he smiled, "You got a real musician in *your* family," and he took his arm from Sonny's shoulder and slapped him, lightly, affectionately, with the back of his hand.

"Well. Now I've heard it all," said a voice behind us. This was another musician, and a friend of Sonny's, a coal-black, cheerful-looking man, built close to the ground. He immediately began confiding to me, at the top of his lungs, the most terrible things about Sonny, his teeth gleaming like a lighthouse and his laugh coming up out of him like the beginning of an earthquake. And it turned out that everyone at the bar knew Sonny, or almost everyone; some were musicians, working there, or nearby, or not working, some were simply hangers-on, and some were there to hear Sonny play. I was introduced to all of them and they were all very polite to me. Yet, it was clear that, for them, I was only Sonny's brother. Here, I was in Sonny's world. Or, rather: his kingdom. Here, it was not even a question that his veins bore royal blood.

They were going to play soon and Creole installed me, by myself, at a table in a dark corner. Then I watched them, Creole, and the little black man, and Sonny, and the others, while they horsed around, standing just below the bandstand. The light from the bandstand spilled just a little short of them and, watching them laughing and gesturing and moving about, I had the feeling that they, nevertheless, were being most careful not to step into that circle of light too suddenly: that if they moved into the light too suddenly, without thinking, they would perish in flame. Then, while I watched, one of them, the small, black man, moved into the light and crossed the bandstand and started fooling around with his drums. Then—being funny and being, also, extremely ceremonious—Creole took Sonny by the arm and led him to the piano. A woman's voice called Sonny's name and a few hands started clapping. And Sonny, also being funny and being ceremonious, and so touched, I think, that he could have cried, but neither hiding it nor showing it, riding it like a man, grinned, and put both hands to his heart and bowed from the waist.

35 Creole then went to the bass fiddle and a lean, very bright-skinned brown man jumped up on the bandstand and picked up his horn. So there they were, and the atmosphere on the bandstand and in the room began to change and tighten. Someone stepped up to the microphone and announced them. Then there were all kinds of murmurs. Some people at the bar shushed others. The waitress ran around, frantically getting in the last orders, guys and chicks got closer to each other, and the lights on the bandstand, on the quartet, turned to a kind of indigo. Then they all looked different there. Creole looked about him for the last time, as though he were making certain that all his chickens were in the coop, and then he—jumped and struck the fiddle. And there they were.

All I know about music is that not many people ever really hear it. And even then, on the rare occasions when something opens within, and the music enters, what we mainly hear, or hear corroborated, are personal, private, vanishing evocations. But the man who creates the music is hearing something else, is dealing with the roar rising from the void and imposing order on it as it hits the air. What is evoked in him, then, is of another order, more terrible because it has no words, and triumphant, too, for that same reason. And his triumph, when he triumphs, is ours. I just watched Sonny's face. His face was troubled, he was working hard, but he wasn't with it. And I had the feeling that, in a way, everyone on the bandstand was waiting for him, both waiting for him and pushing him along. But as I began to watch Creole, I realized that it was Creole who held them all back. He had them on a short rein. Up there, keeping the beat with his whole body, wailing on the fiddle, with his eyes half closed, he was listening to everything, but he was listening to Sonny. He was having a dialogue with Sonny. He wanted Sonny to leave the shoreline and strike out for the deep water. He was Sonny's witness that deep water and drowning were not the same thing—he had been there, and he knew. And he wanted Sonny to know. He was waiting for Sonny to do the things on the keys which would let Creole know that Sonny was in the water.

And, while Creole listened, Sonny moved, deep within, exactly like someone in torment. I had never before thought of how awful the relationship must be between the musician and his instrument. He has to fill it, this instrument, with the breath of life, his own. He has to make it do what he wants it to do. And a piano is just a piano. It's made out of so much wood and wires and little hammers and big ones, and ivory. While there's only so much you can do with it, the only way to find this out is to try; to try and make it do everything.

And Sonny hadn't been near a piano for over a year. And he wasn't on much better terms with his life, not the life that stretched before him now. He and the piano stammered, started one way, got scared, stopped; started another way, panicked, marked time, started again; then seemed to have found a direction, panicked again, got stuck. And the face I saw on Sonny I'd never seen before. Everything had been burned out of it, and, at the same time, things usually hidden were being burned in, by the fire and fury of the battle which was occurring in him up there.

Yet, watching Creole's face as they neared the end of the first set, I had the feeling that something had happened, something I hadn't heard. Then they finished, there was scattered applause, and then, without an instant's warning, Creole started into something else, it was almost sardonic, it was *Am I Blue*. And, as though he commanded, Sonny began to play. Something began to happen. And Creole let out the reins. The dry, low, black man said something awful on the drums, Creole answered, and the drums talked back. Then the horn insisted, sweet and high, slightly detached perhaps, and Creole listened, commenting now and then, dry, and driving, beautiful and calm and old. Then they all came together again, and Sonny was part of the family again. I could tell this from his face. He seemed to have found, right there beneath his fingers, a damn brand-new piano. It seemed that he couldn't get over it. Then, for awhile, just being happy with Sonny, they seemed to be agreeing with him that brand-new pianos certainly were a gas.

Then Creole stepped forward to remind them that what they were playing was the blues. He hit something in all of them, he hit something in me, myself, and the music tightened and deepened, apprehension began to beat the air. Creole began to tell us what the blues were all about. They were not about anything very new. He and his boys up there were keeping it new, at the risk of ruin, destruction, madness, and death, in order to find new ways to make us listen. For, while the tale of how we suffer, and how we are delighted, and how we may triumph is never new, it always must be heard. There isn't any other tale to tell, it's the only light we've got in all this darkness.

And this tale, according to that face, that body, those strong hands on those strings, has another aspect in every country, and a new depth in every generation. Listen, Creole seemed to be saying, listen. Now these are Sonny's blues. He made the little black man on the drums know it, and the bright, brown man on the horn. Creole wasn't trying any longer to get Sonny in the water. He was wishing him Godspeed. Then he stepped back, very slowly, filling the air with the immense suggestion that Sonny speak for himself.

Then they all gathered around Sonny and Sonny played. Every now and again one of them seemed to say, amen. Sonny's fingers filled the air with life, his life. But that life contained so many others. And Sonny went all the way back, he really began with the spare, flat statement of the opening phrase of the song. Then he began to make it his. It was very beautiful because it wasn't hurried and it was no longer a lament. I seemed to hear with what burning he had made it his, with what burning we had yet to make it ours, how we could cease lamenting. Freedom lurked around us and I understood, at last, that he could help us to be free if we would listen, that he would never be free until we did. Yet, there was no battle in his face now. I heard what he had gone through, and would continue to go through until he came to rest in earth. He had made it his: that long line, of which we knew only Mama and Daddy. And he was giving it back, as everything must be given back, so that, passing through death, it can live forever. I saw my mother's face again, and felt, for the first time, how the stones of the road she had walked on must have bruised her feet. I saw the moonlit road where my father's brother died. And it brought something else back to me, and carried me past it. I saw my little girl again and felt Isabel's tears again, and I felt my own tears begin to rise. And I was yet aware that this was only a moment, that the world waited outside, as hungry as a tiger, and that trouble stretched above us, longer than the sky.

Then it was over. Creole and Sonny let out their breath, both soaking wet, and grinning. There was a lot of applause and some of it was real. In the dark, the girl came by and I asked her to take drinks to the bandstand. There was a long pause, while they talked up there in the indigo light and after awhile I saw the girl put a Scotch and milk on top of the piano for Sonny. He didn't seem to notice it, but just before they started playing again, he sipped from it and looked toward me, and nodded. Then he put it back on top of the piano. For me, then, as they began to play again, it glowed and shook above my brother's head like the very cup of trembling.

If you like this story you may also like Ralph Ellison's "Battle Royal" and "A Party Down at the Square" (chapter 12) as well as "Everyday Use," by black fiction writer and essayist Alice Walker (at the end of this section), and ZZ Packer's "Brownies" (chapter 7).

**GOING FURTHER** Baldwin's predecessor Richard Wright, the author of *Native Son, Uncle Tom's Children,* and *Eight Men,* is one of the most important writers of the twentieth century. Both Wright and Baldwin fled America and settled in France. Wright nurtured Ralph Ellison and his work, and Ellison's "Battle Royal" is one of the opening scenes in his award-winning novel *Invisible Man.* Another major black novelist and story writer worth considering in relation to James Baldwin is John Edgar Wideman, particularly his novel *Sent for You Yesterday.*

## Jorge Luis Borges (1899–1986)

JORGE LUIS BORGES was born in Buenos Aires and spent most of his childhood there. When his family moved to Geneva he enrolled in the equivalent of a high school, returning only in the early 1920s to Argentina, where he began a career as a poet and then took to writing short fiction as well. Over the decades his reputation as a poet, story writer, and essayist continued to grow; his work made an enormous impact not only in Latin America but also around the world. As Mexican novelist Carlos Fuentes has noted, Borges renovated twentieth-century Latin American literary language and cleared the way for the new narrative styles of prose in New World Spanish.

By the end of his life he was clinically blind, but he never lost the inner vision that marked his learned imagination; as one of his titles—*The Book of Imaginary Beings*—suggests, he loved libraries and delighted in textual complexity. Questions about the nature of reality, time, personal identity, and history stand at the center of his concentrated "ficciones" or "fictions," his way of describing his version of the short story form.

# The Circular Ruins (1949)

And if he left off dreaming about you . . .
—*Through the Looking Glass, VI.*

No one saw him disembark in the unanimous night, no one saw the bamboo canoe sink into the sacred mud, but in a few days there was no one who did not know that the taciturn man came from the South and that his home had been one of those numberless villages upstream in the deeply cleft side of the mountain, where the Zend language has not been contaminated by Greek and where leprosy is infrequent. What is certain is that the gray man kissed the mud, climbed up the bank without pushing aside (probably, without feeling) the blades which were lacerating his flesh, and crawled, nauseated and bloodstained, up to the circular enclosure crowned with a stone tiger or horse, which sometimes was the color of flame and now was that of ashes. This circle was a temple which had been devoured by ancient fires, profaned by the miasmal jungle, and whose god no longer received the homage of men. The stranger stretched himself out beneath the pedestal. He was awakened by the sun high overhead. He was not astonished to find that his wounds had healed; he closed his pallid eyes and slept, not through weakness of flesh but through determination of will. He knew that this temple was the place required for his invincible intent; he knew that the incessant trees had not succeeded in strangling the ruins of another propitious temple downstream which had once belonged to gods now burned and dead; he knew that his immediate obligation was to dream. Toward midnight he was awakened by the inconsolable shriek of a bird. Tracks of bare feet, some figs and a jug warned him that the men of the region had been spying respectfully on his sleep, soliciting his protection or afraid of his magic. He felt a chill of fear, and sought out a sepulchral niche in the dilapidated wall where he concealed himself among unfamiliar leaves.

The purpose which guided him was not impossible, though supernatural. He wanted to dream a man; he wanted to dream him in minute entirety and impose him on reality. This magic project had exhausted the entire expanse of his mind; if some one had asked him his name or to relate some event of his former life, he would not have been able to give an answer. This uninhabited, ruined temple suited him, for it contained a minimum of visible world; the proximity of the workmen also suited him, for they took it upon themselves to provide for his frugal needs. The rice and fruit they brought him were nourishment enough for his body, which was consecrated to the sole task of sleeping and dreaming.

At first his dreams were chaotic; then in a short while they became dialectic in nature. The stranger dreamed that he was in the center of a circular amphitheater which was more or less the burnt temple; clouds of taciturn students filled the tiers of seats; the faces of the farthest ones hung at a distance of many centuries and as high as the stars, but their features were completely precise. The man lectured his pupils on anatomy, cosmography, and magic: the faces listened anxiously and tried to answer understandingly, as if they guessed the importance of that examination which would redeem one of them from his condition of empty illusion and interpolate him into the real world. Asleep or awake, the man thought over the answers of his phantoms, did not allow himself to be deceived by impostors, and in certain perplexities he sensed a growing intelligence. He was seeking a soul worthy of participating in the universe.

After nine or ten nights he understood with a certain bitterness that he could expect nothing from those pupils who accepted his doctrine passively, but that he could expect something from those who occasionally dared to oppose him. The former group, although worthy of love and affection, could not ascend to the level of individuals; the latter pre-existed to a slightly greater degree. One afternoon (now afternoons were also given over to sleep, now he was only awake for a couple of hours at daybreak) he dismissed the vast illusory student body for good and kept only one pupil. He was a taciturn, sallow boy, at times intractable, and whose sharp features resembled those of his dreamer. The brusque elimination of his fellow students did not disconcert him for long; after a few private lessons, his progress was enough to astound the teacher. Nevertheless, a catastrophe took place. One day, the man emerged from his sleep as if from a viscous desert, looked at the useless afternoon light which he immediately confused with the dawn, and understood that he had not dreamed. All that night and all day long, the intolerable lucidity of insomnia fell upon him. He tried exploring the forest, to lose his strength; among the hemlock he barely succeeded in experiencing several short snatchs of sleep, veined with fleeting, rudimentary visions that were useless. He tried to assemble the student body but scarcely had he articulated a few brief words of exhortation when it became deformed and was then erased. In his almost perpetual vigil, tears of anger burned his old eyes.

5 He understood that modeling the incoherent and vertiginous matter of which dreams are composed was the most difficult task that a man could undertake, even though he should penetrate all the enigmas of a superior and inferior order; much more difficult than weaving a rope out of sand or coining the faceless wind. He swore he would forget the enormous hallucination which had thrown him off at first, and he sought another method of work. Before putting it into execution, he spent a month recovering his strength, which had been squandered by his delirium. He abandoned all premeditation of dreaming and almost immediately succeeded in sleeping a reasonable part of each day. The few times that he had dreams during this period, he paid no attention to them. Before resuming his task, he waited until the moon's disk was perfect. Then, in the afternoon, he purified himself in the waters of the river, worshiped the planetary gods, pronounced the prescribed syllables of a mighty name, and went to sleep. He dreamed almost immediately, with his heart throbbing.

He dreamed that it was warm, secret, about the size of a clenched fist, and of a garnet color within the penumbra of a human body as yet without face or sex; during fourteen lucid nights he dreamt of it with meticulous love. Every night he perceived it more clearly. He did not touch it; he only permitted himself to witness it, to observe it, and occasionally to rectify it with a glance. He perceived it and lived it from all angles and distances. On the fourteenth night he lightly touched the pulmonary artery with his index finger, then the whole heart, outside and inside. He was satisfied with the examination. He deliberately did not dream for a night; he then took up the heart again, invoked the name of a planet, and undertook the vision of another of the principal organs. Within a year he had come to the skeleton and the eyelids. The innumerable hair was perhaps the most difficult task. He dreamed an entire man—a young man, but who did not sit up or talk, who was unable to open his eyes. Night after night, the man dreamt him asleep.

In the Gnostic cosmogonies, demiurges fashion a red Adam who cannot stand; as clumsy, crude and elemental as this Adam of dust was the Adam of dreams forged by the wizard's nights. One afternoon, the man almost destroyed his entire work, but then changed his mind. (It would have been better had he destroyed it.) When he had exhausted all supplications to the deities of the earth, he threw himself at the feet of the effigy which was perhaps a tiger or perhaps a colt and implored its unknown help. That evening, at twilight, he dreamt of the statue. He dreamt it was alive, tremulous: it was not an atrocious bastard of a tiger and a colt, but at the same time these two fiery creatures and also a bull, a rose, and a storm. This multiple god revealed to him that his earthly name was Fire, and that in this circular temple (and in others like it) people had once made sacrifices to him and worshiped him, and that he would magically animate the dreamed phantom, in such a way that all creatures, except Fire itself and the dreamer, would believe it to be a man of flesh and blood. He commanded that once this man had been instructed in all the rites, he should be sent to the other ruined temple whose pyramids were still standing downstream, so that some voice would glorify him in that deserted edifice. In the dream of the man that dreamed, the dreamed one awoke.

The wizard carried out the orders he had been given. He devoted a certain length of time (which finally proved to be two years) to instructing him in the mysteries of the universe and the cult of fire. Secretly, he was pained at the idea of being separated from him. On the pretext of pedagogical necessity, each day he increased the number of hours dedicated to dreaming. He also remade the right shoulder, which was somewhat defective. At times, he was disturbed by the impression that all this had already happened. . . . In general, his days were happy; when he closed his eyes, he thought: *Now I will be with my son.* Or, more rarely: *The son I have engendered is waiting for me and will not exist if I do not go to him.*

Gradually, he began accustoming him to reality. Once he ordered him to place a flag on a faraway peak. The next day the flag was fluttering on the peak. He tried other analogous experiments, each time more audacious. With a certain bitterness, he understood that his son was ready to be born—and perhaps impatient. That night he kissed him for the first time and sent him off to the other temple whose remains were turning white downstream, across many miles of inextricable jungle and marshes. Before doing this (and so that his son should never know that he was a phantom, so that he should think himself a man like any other) he destroyed in him all memory of his years of apprenticeship.

10 His victory and peace became blurred with boredom. In the twilight times of dusk and dawn, he would prostrate himself before the stone figure, perhaps imagining his unreal son carrying out identical rites in other circular ruins downstream; at night he no longer dreamed, or dreamed as any man does. His perceptions of the sounds and forms of the universe became somewhat pallid: his absent son was being nourished by these diminutions of his soul. The purpose of his life had been fulfilled; the man remained in a kind of ecstasy. After a certain time, which some chroniclers prefer to compute in years and others in decades, two oarsmen awoke him at midnight; he could not see their faces, but they spoke to him of a charmed man in a temple of the North, capable of walking on fire without burning himself. The wizard suddenly remembered the words of the god. He remembered that of all the creatures that people the earth, Fire was the only one who knew his son to be a phantom. This memory, which at first calmed him, ended by tormenting him. He feared lest his son should meditate on this abnormal privilege and by some means find out he was a mere simulacrum. Not to be a man, to be a projection of another man's dreams—what an incomparable humiliation, what madness! Any father is interested in the sons he has procreated (or permitted) out of the mere confusion of happiness; it was natural that the wizard should fear

for the future of that son whom he had thought out entrail by entrail, feature by feature, in a thousand and one secret nights.

His misgivings ended abruptly, but not without certain forewarnings. First (after a long drought) a remote cloud, as light as a bird, appeared on a hill; then, toward the South, the sky took on the rose color of leopard's gums; then came clouds of smoke which rusted the metal of the nights; afterwards came the panic-stricken flight of wild animals. For what had happened many centuries before was repeating itself. The ruins of the sanctuary of the god of Fire was destroyed by fire. In a dawn without birds, the wizard saw the concentric fire licking the walls. For a moment, he thought of taking refuge in the water, but then he understood that death was coming to crown his old age and absolve him from his labors. He walked toward the sheets of flame. They did not bite his flesh, they caressed him and flooded him without heat or combustion. With relief, with humiliation, with terror, he understood that he also was an illusion, that someone else was dreaming him.

—Translated by Anthony Bonner

If you like this story, you may also like "The Handsomest Drowned Man in the World" (in this section) by another Latin American writer, Gabriel García Márquez. The work of Borges and García Márquez has had a large impact on North American readers.

**GOING FURTHER** If you discover you have a taste for the Borgesian style you may also want to read works such as *Hopscotch* by the late Argentinian writer Julio Cortázar.

## Raymond Carver (1938–1988)

RAYMOND CARVER WAS born into a working-class family in the Pacific Northwest and spent most of his childhood in Yakima, Washington, before moving to California in his early twenties and attending classes at California State College, Chico. There he studied fiction writing with John Gardner and began the apprenticeship that would lead to his creation of some of the most celebrated short fiction of his time. Critics pointed to his stories about working-class and lower-middle-class people in desperate straits as evidence of the so-called minimalist style. Carver himself often pointed out that he saw his work in the tradition of Sherwood Anderson, Ernest Hemingway, and Anton Chekhov.

Carver was also a practicing poet and essayist; perhaps in keeping with the aesthetic of minimalism, however, he never wrote a novel. He possessed a keen sense of dialogue, and the director Robert Altman joined several of his short stories together for the 1993 film *Short Cuts*.

# Cathedral (1984)

1 This blind man, an old friend of my wife's, he was on his way to spend the night. His wife had died. So he was visiting the dead wife's relatives in Connecticut. He called my wife from his in-laws'. Arrangements were made. He would come by train, a five-hour trip, and my wife would meet him at the station. She hadn't seen him since she worked for him one summer in Seattle ten years ago. But she and the blind man had kept in touch. They made tapes and mailed them back and forth. I wasn't enthusiastic about his visit. He was no one I knew. And his being blind

bothered me. My idea of blindness came from the movies. In the movies, the blind moved slowly and never laughed. Sometimes they were led by seeing-eye dogs. A blind man in my house was not something I looked forward to.

That summer in Seattle she had needed a job. She didn't have any money. The man she was going to marry at the end of the summer was in officers' training school. He didn't have any money, either. But she was in love with the guy, and he was in love with her, etc. She'd seen something in the paper: HELP WANTED—*Reading to Blind Man,* and a telephone number. She phoned and went over, was hired on the spot. She'd worked with this blind man all summer. She read stuff to him, case studies, reports, that sort of thing. She helped him organize his little office in the county social-service department. They'd become good friends, my wife and the blind man. How do I know these things? She told me. And she told me something else. On her last day in the office, the blind man asked if he could touch her face. She agreed to this. She told me he touched his fingers to every part of her face, her nose—even her neck! She never forgot it. She even tried to write a poem about it. She was always trying to write a poem. She wrote a poem or two every year, usually after something really important had happened to her.

When we first started going out together, she showed me the poem. In the poem, she recalled his fingers and the way they had moved around over her face. In the poem, she talked about what she had felt at the time, about what went through her mind when the blind man touched her nose and lips. I can remember I didn't think much of the poem. Of course, I didn't tell her that. Maybe I just don't understand poetry. I admit it's not the first thing I reach for when I pick up something to read.

Anyway, this man who'd first enjoyed her favors, the officer-to-be, he'd been her childhood sweetheart. So okay. I'm saying that at the end of the summer she let the blind man run his hands over her face, said goodbye to him, married her childhood etc., who was now a commissioned officer, and she moved away from Seattle. But they'd kept in touch, she and the blind man. She made the first contact after a year or so. She called him up one night from an Air Force base in Alabama. She wanted to talk. They talked. He asked her to send him a tape and tell him about her life. She did this. She sent the tape. On the tape, she told the blind man about her husband and about their life together in the military. She told the blind man she loved her husband but she didn't like it where they lived and she didn't like it that he was a part of the military-industrial thing. She told the blind man she'd written a poem about what it was like to be an Air Force officer's wife. The poem wasn't finished yet. She was still writing it. The blind man made a tape. He sent her the tape. She made a tape. This went on for years. My wife's officer was posted to one base and then another. She sent tapes from Moody AFB, McGuire, McConnell, and finally Travis, near Sacramento, where one night she got to feeling lonely and cut off from people she kept losing in that moving-around life. She got to feeling she couldn't go it another step. She went in and swallowed all the pills and capsules in the medicine chest and washed them down with a bottle of gin. Then she got into a hot bath and passed out.

5 But instead of dying, she got sick. She threw up. Her officer—why should he have a name? he was the childhood sweetheart, and what more does he want?—came home from somewhere, found her, and called the ambulance. In time, she put it all on a tape and sent the tape to the blind man. Over the years, she put all kinds of stuff on tapes and sent the tapes off lickety-split. Next to writing a poem every year, I think it was her chief means of recreation. On one tape, she told the blind man she'd decided to live away from her officer for a time. On another tape, she told him about her divorce. She and I began going out, and of course she told her blind man about it. She told him everything, or so it seemed to me. Once she asked me if I'd like to hear the latest tape from the blind man. This was a year ago. I was on the tape, she said. So I said okay, I'd listen to it. I got us drinks and we settled down in the living room. We made ready to listen. First she inserted the tape into the player and adjusted a couple of dials. Then she pushed a lever. The tape squeaked and someone began to talk in this loud voice. She lowered the volume. After a few minutes of harmless chitchat, I heard my own name in the mouth of this stranger, this blind man I didn't even know! And then this: "From all you've said about him, I can only conclude—" But we were interrupted, a knock at the door, something, and we didn't ever get back to the tape. Maybe it was just as well. I'd heard all I wanted to.

Now this same blind man was coming to sleep in my house.

"Maybe I could take him bowling," I said to my wife. She was at the draining board doing scalloped potatoes. She put down the knife she was using and turned around.

"If you love me," she said, "you can do this for me. If you don't love me, okay. But if you had a friend, any friend, and the friend came to visit, I'd make him feel comfortable." She wiped her hands with the dish towel.

"I don't have any blind friends," I said.

10 "You don't have *any* friends," she said. "Period. Besides," she said, "goddamn it, his wife's just died! Don't you understand that? The man's lost his wife!"

I didn't answer. She'd told me a little about the blind man's wife. Her name was Beulah. Beulah! That's a name for a colored woman.

"Was his wife a Negro?" I asked.

"Are you crazy?" my wife said. "Have you just flipped or something?" She picked up a potato. I saw it hit the floor, then roll under the stove. "What's wrong with you?" she said. "Are you drunk?"

"I'm just asking," I said.

15 Right then my wife filled me in with more detail than I cared to know. I made a drink and sat at the kitchen table to listen. Pieces of the story began to fall into place.

Beulah had gone to work for the blind man the summer after my wife had stopped working for him. Pretty soon Beulah and the blind man had themselves a church wedding. It was a little wedding—who'd want to go to such a wedding in the first place?—just the two of them, plus the minister and the minister's wife. But it was a church wedding just the same. It was what Beulah had wanted, he'd said. But even then Beulah must have been carrying the cancer in her glands. After they had been inseparable for eight years—my wife's word, *inseparable*—Beulah's health went into a rapid decline. She died in a Seattle hospital room, the blind man sitting beside the bed and holding on to her hand. They'd married, lived and worked together, slept together—had sex, sure—and then the blind man had to bury her. All this without his having ever seen what the goddamned woman looked like. It was beyond my understanding. Hearing this, I felt sorry for the blind man for a little bit. And then I found myself thinking what a pitiful life this woman must have led. Imagine a woman who could never see herself as she was seen in the eyes of her loved one. A woman who could go on day after day and never receive the smallest compliment from her beloved. A woman whose husband could never read the expression on her face, be it misery or something better. Someone who could wear makeup or not—what difference to him? She could, if she wanted, wear green eye-shadow around one eye, a straight pin in her nostril, yellow slacks and purple shoes, no matter. And then to slip off into death, the blind man's hand on her hand, his blind eyes streaming tears—I'm imagining now—her last thought maybe this: that he never even knew what she looked like, and she on an express to the grave. Robert was left with a small insurance policy and half of a twenty-peso Mexican coin. The other half of the coin went into the box with her. Pathetic.

So when the time rolled around, my wife went to the depot to pick him up. With nothing to do but wait—sure, I blamed him for that—I was having a drink and watching the TV when I heard the car pull into the drive. I got up from the sofa with my drink and went to the window to have a look.

I saw my wife laughing as she parked the car. I saw her get out of the car and shut the door. She was still wearing a smile. Just amazing. She went around to the other side of the car to where the blind man was already starting to get out. This blind man, feature this, he was wearing a full beard! A beard on a blind man! Too much, I say. The blind man reached into the back seat and dragged out a suitcase. My wife took his arm, shut the car door, and, talking all the way, moved him down the drive and then up the steps to the front porch. I turned off the TV. I finished my drink, rinsed the glass, dried my hands. Then I went to the door.

My wife said, "I want you to meet Robert. Robert, this is my husband. I've told you all about him." She was beaming. She had this blind man by his coat sleeve.

20 The blind man let go of his suitcase and up came his hand.

I took it. He squeezed hard, held my hand, and then he let it go.

"I feel like we've already met," he boomed.

"Likewise," I said. I didn't know what else to say. Then I said, "Welcome. I've heard a lot about you." We began to move then, a little group, from the porch into the living room, my wife guiding him by the arm. The blind man was carrying his suitcase in his other hand. My wife said things like, "To your left here, Robert. That's right. Now watch it, there's a chair. That's it. Sit down right here. This is the sofa. We just bought this sofa two weeks ago."

I started to say something about the old sofa. I'd liked that old sofa. But I didn't say anything. Then I wanted to say something else, small-talk, about the scenic ride along the Hudson. How going *to* New York, you should sit on the right-hand side of the train, and coming *from* New York, the left-hand side.

"Did you have a good train ride?" I said. "Which side of the train did you sit on, by the way?"

"What a question, which side!" my wife said. "What's it matter which side?" she said.

"I just asked," I said.

"Right side," the blind man said. "I hadn't been on a train in nearly forty years. Not since I was a kid. With my folks. That's been a long time. I'd nearly forgotten the sensation. I have winter in my beard now," he said. "So I've been told, anyway. Do I look distinguished, my dear?" the blind man said to my wife.

"You look distinguished, Robert," she said. "Robert," she said. "Robert, it's just so good to see you."

My wife finally took her eyes off the blind man and looked at me. I had the feeling she didn't like what she saw. I shrugged.

I've never met, or personally known, anyone who was blind. This blind man was late forties, a heavy-set, balding man with stooped shoulders, as if he carried a great weight there. He wore brown slacks, brown shoes, a light-brown shirt, a tie, a sports coat. Spiffy. He also had this full beard. But he didn't use a cane and he didn't wear dark glasses. I'd always thought dark glasses were a must for the blind. Fact was, I wished he had a pair. At first glance, his eyes looked like anyone else's eyes. But if you looked close, there was something different about them. Too much white in the iris, for one thing, and the pupils seemed to move around in the sockets without his knowing it or being able to stop it. Creepy. As I stared at his face, I saw the left pupil turn in toward his nose while the other made an effort to keep in one place. But it was only an effort, for that eye was on the roam without his knowing it or wanting it to be.

I said, "Let me get you a drink. What's your pleasure? We have a little of everything. It's one of our pastimes."

"Bub, I'm a Scotch man myself," he said fast enough in this big voice.

"Right," I said. Bub! "Sure you are. I knew it."

He let his fingers touch his suitcase, which was sitting alongside the sofa. He was taking his bearings. I didn't blame him for that.

"I'll move that up to your room," my wife said.

"No, that's fine," the blind man said loudly. "It can go up when I go up."

"A little water with the Scotch?" I said.

"Very little," he said.

"I knew it," I said.

He said, "Just a tad. The Irish actor, Barry Fitzgerald? I'm like that fellow. When I drink water, Fitzgerald said, I drink water. When I drink whiskey, I drink whiskey." My wife laughed. The blind man brought his hand up under his beard. He lifted his beard slowly and let it drop.

I did the drinks, three big glasses of Scotch with a splash of water in each. Then we made ourselves comfortable and talked about Robert's travels. First the long flight from the West Coast to Connecticut, we covered that. Then from Connecticut up here by train. We had another drink concerning that leg of the trip.

I remembered having read somewhere that the blind didn't smoke because, as speculation had it, they couldn't see the smoke they exhaled. I thought I knew that much and that much only about blind people. But this blind man smoked his cigarette down to the nubbin and then lit another one. This blind man filled his ashtray and my wife emptied it.

When we sat down at the table for dinner, we had another drink. My wife heaped Robert's plate with cube steak, scalloped potatoes, green beans. I buttered him up two slices of bread. I said, "Here's bread and butter for you." I swallowed some of my drink. "Now let us pray," I said, and the blind man lowered his head. My wife looked at me, her mouth agape. "Pray the phone won't ring and the food doesn't get cold," I said.

45 We dug in. We ate everything there was to eat on the table. We ate like there was no tomorrow. We didn't talk. We ate. We scarfed. We grazed that table. We were into serious eating. The blind man had right away located his foods, he knew just where everything was on his plate. I watched with admiration as he used his knife and fork on the meat. He'd cut two pieces of meat, fork the meat into his mouth, and then go all out for the scalloped potatoes, the beans next, and then he'd tear off a hunk of buttered bread and eat that. He'd follow this up with a big drink of milk. It didn't seem to bother him to use his fingers once in a while, either.

We finished everything, including half a strawberry pie. For a few moments, we sat as if stunned. Sweat beaded on our faces. Finally, we got up from the table and left the dirty plates. We didn't look back. We took ourselves into the living room and sank into our places again. Robert and my wife sat on the sofa. I took the big chair. We had us two or three more drinks while they talked about the major things that had come to pass for them in the past ten years. For the most part, I just listened. Now and then I joined in. I didn't want him to think I'd left the room, and I didn't want her to think I was feeling left out. They talked of things that had happened to them— to them!—these past ten years. I waited in vain to hear my name on my wife's sweet lips: "And then my dear husband came into my life"—something like that. But I heard nothing of the sort. More talk of Robert. Robert had done a little of everything, it seemed, a regular blind jack-of-all-trades. But most recently he and his wife had had an Amway distributorship, from which, I gathered, they'd earned their living, such as it was. The blind man was also a ham radio operator. He talked in his loud voice about conversations he'd had with fellow operators in Guam, in the Philippines, in Alaska, and even in Tahiti. He said he'd have a lot of friends there if he ever wanted to go visit those places. From time to time, he'd turn his blind face toward me, put his hand under his beard, ask me something. How long had I been in my present position? (Three years.) Did I like my work? (I didn't.) Was I going to stay with it? (What were the options?) Finally, when I thought he was beginning to run down, I got up and turned on the TV.

My wife looked at me with irritation. She was heading toward a boil. Then she looked at the blind man and said, "Robert, do you have a TV?"

The blind man said, "My dear, I have two TVs. I have a color set and a black-and-white thing, an old relic. It's funny, but if I turn the TV on, and I'm always turning it on, I turn on the color set. It's funny, don't you think?"

I didn't know what to say to that. I had absolutely nothing to say to that. No opinion. So I watched the news program and tried to listen to what the announcer was saying.

50 "This is a color TV," the blind man said. "Don't ask me how, but I can tell."

"We traded up a while ago," I said.

The blind man had another taste of his drink. He lifted his beard, sniffed it, and let it fall. He leaned forward on the sofa. He positioned his ashtray on the coffee table, then put the lighter to his cigarette. He leaned back on the sofa and crossed his legs at the ankles.

My wife covered her mouth, and then she yawned. She stretched. She said, "I think I'll go upstairs and put on my robe. I think I'll change into something else. Robert, you make yourself comfortable," she said.

"I'm comfortable," the blind man said.

55 "I want you to feel comfortable in this house," she said.

"I am comfortable," the blind man said.

After she'd left the room, he and I listened to the weather report and then to the sports roundup. By that time, she'd been gone so long I didn't know if she was going to come back. I thought she might have gone to bed. I wished she'd come back downstairs. I didn't want to be left alone with a blind man. I asked if he wanted to smoke some dope with me. I said I'd just rolled a number. I hadn't, but I planned to do so in about two shakes.

"I'll try some with you," he said.

"Damn right," I said. "That's the stuff."

I got our drinks and sat down on the sofa with him. Then I rolled us two fat numbers. I lit one and passed it. I brought it to his fingers. He took it and inhaled.

"Hold it as long as you can," I said. I could tell he didn't know the first thing.

My wife came back downstairs wearing her pink robe and her pink slippers.

"What do I smell?" she said.

"We thought we'd have us some cannabis," I said.

My wife gave me a savage look. Then she looked at the blind man and said, "Robert, I didn't know you smoked."

He said, "I do now, my dear. There's a first time for everything. But I don't feel anything yet."

"This stuff is pretty mellow," I said. "This stuff is mild. It's dope you can reason with," I said. "It doesn't mess you up."

"Not much it doesn't, bub," he said, and laughed.

My wife sat on the sofa between the blind man and me. I passed her the number. She took it and toked and then passed it back to me. "Which way is this going?" she said. Then she said, "I shouldn't be smoking this. I can hardly keep my eyes open as it is. That dinner did me in. I shouldn't have eaten so much."

"It was the strawberry pie," the blind man said. "That's what did it," he said, and he laughed his big laugh. Then he shook his head.

"There's more strawberry pie," I said.

"Do you want some more, Robert?" my wife said.

"Maybe in a little while," he said.

We gave our attention to the TV. My wife yawned again. She said, "Your bed is made up when you feel like going to bed, Robert. I know you must have had a long day. When you're ready to go to bed, say so." She pulled his arm. "Robert?"

He came to and said, "I've had a real nice time. This beats tapes, doesn't it?"

I said, "Coming at you," and I put the number between his fingers. He inhaled, held the smoke, and then let it go. It was like he'd been doing it since he was nine years old.

"Thanks, bub," he said. "But I think this is all for me. I think I'm beginning to feel it," he said. He held the burning roach out for my wife.

"Same here," she said. "Ditto. Me, too." She took the roach and passed it to me. "I may just sit here for a while between you two guys with my eyes closed. But don't let me bother you, okay? Either one of you. If it bothers you, say so. Otherwise, I may just sit here with my eyes closed until you're ready to go to bed," she said. "Your bed's made up, Robert, when you're ready. It's right next to our room at the top of the stairs. We'll show you up when you're ready. You wake me up now, you guys, if I fall asleep." She said that and then she closed her eyes and went to sleep.

The news program ended. I got up and changed the channel. I sat back down on the sofa. I wished my wife hadn't pooped out. Her head lay across the back of the sofa, her mouth open. She'd turned so that her robe had slipped away from her legs, exposing a juicy thigh. I reached to draw her robe back over her, and it was then that I glanced at the blind man. What the hell! I flipped the robe open again.

"You say when you want some strawberry pie," I said.

"I will," he said.

I said, "Are you tired? Do you want me to take you up to your bed? Are you ready to hit the hay?"

"Not yet," he said. "No, I'll stay up with you, bub. If that's all right. I'll stay up until you're ready to turn in. We haven't had a chance to talk. Know what I mean? I feel like me and her monopolized the evening." He lifted his beard and he let it fall. He picked up his cigarettes and his lighter.

"That's all right," I said. Then I said, "I'm glad for the company."

85 And I guess I was. Every night I smoked dope and stayed up as long as I could before I fell asleep. My wife and I hardly ever went to bed at the same time. When I did go to sleep, I had these dreams. Sometimes I'd wake up from one of them, my heart going crazy.

Something about the church and the Middle Ages was on the TV. Not your run-of-the-mill TV fare. I wanted to watch something else. I turned to the other channels. But there was nothing on them, either. So I turned back to the first channel and apologized.

"Bub, it's all right," the blind man said. "It's fine with me. Whatever you want to watch is okay. I'm always learning something. Learning never ends. It won't hurt me to learn something tonight. I got ears," he said.

We didn't say anything for a time. He was leaning forward with his head turned at me, his right ear aimed in the direction of the set. Very disconcerting. Now and then his eyelids dropped and then they snapped open again. Now and then he put his fingers into his beard and tugged, like he was thinking about something he was hearing on the television.

On the screen, a group of men wearing cowls was being set upon and tormented by men dressed in skeleton costumes and men dressed as devils. The men dressed as devils wore devil masks, horns, and long tails. This pageant was part of a procession. The Englishman who was narrating the thing said it took place in Spain once a year. I tried to explain to the blind man what was happening.

90 "Skeletons," he said. "I know about skeletons," he said, and he nodded.

The TV showed this one cathedral. Then there was a long, slow look at another one. Finally, the picture switched to the famous one in Paris, with its flying buttresses and its spires reaching up to the clouds. The camera pulled away to show the whole of the cathedral rising above the skyline.

There were times when the Englishman who was telling the thing would shut up, would simply let the camera move around over the cathedrals. Or else the camera would tour the countryside, men in fields walking behind oxen. I waited as long as I could. Then I felt I had to say something. I said, "They're showing the outside of this cathedral now. Gargoyles. Little statues carved to look like monsters. Now I guess they're in Italy. Yeah, they're in Italy. There's paintings on the walls of this one church."

"Are those fresco paintings, bub?" he asked, and he sipped from his drink.

I reached for my glass. But it was empty. I tried to remember what I could remember. "You're asking me are those frescoes?" I said. "That's a good question. I don't know."

95 The camera moved to a cathedral outside Lisbon. The differences in the Portuguese cathedral compared with the French and Italian were not that great. But they were there. Mostly the interior stuff. Then something occurred to me, and I said, "Something has occurred to me. Do you have any idea what a cathedral is? What they look like, that is? Do you follow me? If somebody says cathedral to you, do you have any notion what they're talking about? Do you know the difference between that and a Baptist church, say?"

He let the smoke dribble from his mouth. "I know they took hundreds of workers fifty or a hundred years to build," he said. "I just heard the man say that, of course. I know generations of the same families worked on a cathedral. I heard him say that, too. The men who began their life's work on them, they never lived to see the completion of their work. In that wise, bub, they're no different from the rest of us, right?" He laughed. Then his eyelids drooped again. His head nodded. He seemed to be snoozing. Maybe he was imagining himself in Portugal. The TV was showing another cathedral now. This one was in Germany. The Englishman's voice droned on. "Cathedrals," the blind man said. He sat up and rolled his head back and forth. "If you want the truth, bub, that's about all I know. What I just said. What I heard him say. But maybe you could describe one to me? I wish you'd do it. I'd like that. If you want to know, I really don't have a good idea."

I stared hard at the shot of the cathedral on the TV. How could I even begin to describe it? But say my life depended on it. Say my life was being threatened by an insane guy who said I had to do it or else.

I stared some more at the cathedral before the picture flipped off into the countryside. There was no use. I turned to the blind man and said, "To begin with, they're very tall." I was looking around the room for clues. "They reach way up. Up and up. Toward the sky. They're so big, some of them, they have to have these supports. To help hold them up, so to speak. These supports are called buttresses. They remind me of viaducts, for some reason. But maybe you don't know viaducts, either? Sometimes the cathedrals have devils and such carved into the front. Sometimes lords and ladies. Don't ask me why this is," I said.

He was nodding. The whole upper part of his body seemed to be moving back and forth.

100 "I'm not doing so good, am I?" I said.

He stopped nodding and leaned forward on the edge of the sofa. As he listened to me, he was running his fingers through his beard. I wasn't getting through to him, I could see that. But he waited for me to go on just the same. He nodded, like he was trying to encourage me. I tried to think what else to say. "They're really big," I said. "They're massive. They're built of stone. Marble, too, sometimes. In those olden days, when they built cathedrals, men wanted to be close to God. In those olden days, God was an important part of everyone's life. You could tell this from their cathedral-building. I'm sorry," I said, "but it looks like that's the best I can do for you. I'm just no good at it."

"That's all right, bub," the blind man said. "Hey, listen. I hope you don't mind my asking you. Can I ask you something? Let me ask you a simple question, yes or no. I'm just curious and there's no offense. You're my host. But let me ask if you are in any way religious? You don't mind my asking?"

I shook my head. He couldn't see that, though. A wink is the same as a nod to a blind man. "I guess I don't believe in it. In anything. Sometimes it's hard. You know what I'm saying?"

"Sure, I do," he said.

105 "Right," I said.

The Englishman was still holding forth. My wife sighed in her sleep. She drew a long breath and went on with her sleeping.

"You'll have to forgive me," I said. "But I can't tell you what a cathedral looks like. It just isn't in me to do it. I can't do any more than I've done."

The blind man sat very still, his head down, as he listened to me.

I said, "The truth is, cathedrals don't mean anything special to me. Nothing. Cathedrals. They're something to look at on late-night TV. That's all they are."

110 It was then that the blind man cleared his throat. He brought something up. He took a handkerchief from his back pocket. Then he said, "I get it, bub. It's okay. It happens. Don't worry about it," he said. "Hey, listen to me. Will you do me a favor? I got an idea. Why don't you find us some heavy paper? And a pen. We'll do something. We'll draw one together. Get us a pen and some heavy paper. Go on, bub, get the stuff," he said.

So I went upstairs. My legs felt like they didn't have any strength in them. They felt like they did after I'd done some running. In my wife's room, I looked around. I found some ballpoints in a little basket on her table. And then I tried to think where to look for the kind of paper he was talking about.

Downstairs, in the kitchen, I found a shopping bag with onion skins in the bottom of the bag. I emptied the bag and shook it. I brought it into the living room and sat down with it near his legs. I moved some things, smoothed the wrinkles from the bag, spread it out on the coffee table.

The blind man got down from the sofa and sat next to me on the carpet.

He ran his fingers over the paper. He went up and down the sides of the paper. The edges, even the edges. He fingered the corners.

115 "All right," he said. "All right, let's do her."

He found my hand, the hand with the pen. He closed his hand over my hand. "Go ahead, bub, draw," he said. "Draw. You'll see. I'll follow along with you. It'll be okay. Just begin now like I'm telling you. You'll see. Draw," the blind man said.

So I began. First I drew a box that looked like a house. It could have been the house I lived in. Then I put a roof on it. At either end of the roof, I drew spires. Crazy.

"Swell," he said. "Terrific. You're doing fine," he said. "Never thought anything like this could happen in your lifetime, did you, bub? Well, it's a strange life, we all know that. Go on now. Keep it up."

I put in windows with arches. I drew flying buttresses. I hung great doors. I couldn't stop. The TV station went off the air. I put down the pen and closed and opened my fingers. The blind man felt around over the paper. He moved the tips of his fingers over the paper, all over what I had drawn, and he nodded.

120 "Doing fine," the blind man said.

I took up the pen again, and he found my hand. I kept at it. I'm no artist. But I kept drawing just the same.

My wife opened up her eyes and gazed at us. She sat up on the sofa, her robe hanging open. She said, "What are you doing? Tell me, I want to know."

I didn't answer her.

The blind man said, "We're drawing a cathedral. Me and him are working on it. Press hard," he said to me. "That's right. That's good," he said. "Sure. You got it, bub. I can tell. You didn't think you could. But you can, can't you? You're cooking with gas now. You know what I'm saying? We're going to really have us something here in a minute. How's the old arm?" he said. "Put some people in there now. What's a cathedral without people?"

125 My wife said, "What's going on? Robert, what are you doing? What's going on?"

"It's all right," he said to her. "Close your eyes now," the blind man said to me.

I did it. I closed them just like he said.

"Are they closed?" he said. "Don't fudge."

"They're closed," I said.

130 "Keep them that way," he said. He said, "Don't stop now. Draw."

So we kept on with it. His fingers rode my fingers as my hand went over the paper. It was like nothing else in my life up to now.

Then he said, "I think that's it. I think you got it," he said. "Take a look. What do you think?"

But I had my eyes closed. I thought I'd keep them that way for a little longer. I thought it was something I ought to do.

"Well?" he said. "Are you looking?"

135 My eyes were still closed. I was in my house. I knew that. But I didn't feel like I was inside anything.

"It's really something," I said.

Critics coined the term "minimalism" to describe a pared down type of realistic story. Carver didn't like the term. Nor did some of the other writers associated with this group, such as Amy Hempel. If you like "Cathedral," you may also want to read Hempel's "San Francisco" (in this chapter).

**GOING FURTHER** Jayne Anne Phillips writes stories made up of brief lyrical bursts of events. *Black Tickets* is a collection of her stories that may be of interest to those who like Carver.

# Anton Chekhov (1860–1904)

RUSSIAN WRITER ANTON Chekhov was born into poverty but trained to become a physician. Even at the start of his medical practice, he was trying out short fictional sketches on magazine editors in Moscow, discovering that he had a talent for creating characters with a few brief lines of prose. Around 1888 Chekhov began writing more extended pieces of fiction, such as "The Kiss" and "Gusev," that were acclaimed for their artistic merit, not just their entertainment value. Well known to his contemporaries as a writer of numerous stories, Chekhov counted Leo Tolstoy among his early admirers. Later in life, Chekhov wrote plays, including *The Seagull* (1896) and *The Cherry*

*Orchard* (1904); his stage works have become nearly as influential as his short stories, affecting playwrights such as George Bernard Shaw and Tennessee Williams. Today, Chekhov's work is even more widely read than during his lifetime, and many consider him to be the "father" of the modern short story (see his "Rapture" in chapter 2).

# The Lady with the Pet Dog (1899)

## I

A new person, it was said, had appeared on the esplanade: a lady with a pet dog. Dmitry Dmitrich Gurov, who had spent a fortnight at Yalta and had got used to the place, had also begun to take an interest in new arrivals. As he sat in Vernet's confectionery shop, he saw, walking on the esplanade, a fair-haired young woman of medium height, wearing a beret; a white Pomeranian was trotting behind her.

And afterwards he met her in the public garden and in the square several times a day. She walked alone, always wearing the same beret and always with the white dog; no one knew who she was and everyone called her simply "the lady with the pet dog."

"If she is here alone without husband or friends," Gurov reflected, "it wouldn't be a bad thing to make her acquaintance."

He was under forty, but he already had a daughter twelve years old, and two sons at school. They had found a wife for him when he was very young, a student in his second year, and by now she seemed half as old again as he. She was a tall, erect woman with dark eyebrows, stately and dignified and, as she said of herself, intellectual. She read a great deal, used simplified spelling in her letters, called her husband, not Dmitry, but Dimitry, while he privately considered her of limited intelligence, narrow-minded, dowdy, was afraid of her, and did not like to be at home. He had begun being unfaithful to her long ago—had been unfaithful to her often and, probably for that reason, almost always spoke ill of women, and when they were talked of in his presence used to call them "the inferior race."

5 It seemed to him that he had been sufficiently tutored by bitter experience to call them what he pleased, and yet he could not have lived without "the inferior race" for two days together. In the company of men he was bored and ill at ease, he was chilly and uncommunicative with them; but when he was among women he felt free, and knew what to speak to them about and how to comport himself; and even to be silent with them was no strain on him. In his appearance, in his character, in his whole makeup there was something attractive and elusive that disposed women in his favor and allured them. He knew that, and some force seemed to draw him to them, too.

Oft-repeated and really bitter experience had taught him long ago that with decent people—particularly Moscow people—who are irresolute and slow to move, every affair which at first seems a light and charming adventure inevitably grows into a whole problem of extreme complexity, and in the end a painful situation is created. But at every new meeting with an interesting woman this lesson of experience seemed to slip from his memory, and he was eager for life, and everything seemed so simple and diverting.

One evening while he was dining in the public garden the lady in the beret walked up without haste to take the next table. Her expression, her gait, her dress, and the way she did her hair told him that she belonged to the upper class, that she was married, that she was in Yalta for the first time and alone, and that she was bored there. The stories told of the immorality in Yalta are to a great extent untrue; he despised them, and knew that such stories were made up for the most part by persons who would have been glad to sin themselves if they had had the chance; but when the lady sat down at the next table three paces from him, he recalled these stories of easy conquests, of trips to the mountains, and the tempting thought of swift, fleeting liaison, a romance with an unknown woman of whose very name he was ignorant suddenly took hold him.

He beckoned invitingly to the Pomeranian, and when the dog approached him, shook his finger at it. The Pomeranian growled; Gurov threatened it again.

The lady glanced at him and at once dropped her eyes.

10 "He doesn't bite," she said and blushed.

"May I give him a bone?" he asked; and when she nodded he inquired affably, "Have you been in Yalta long?"

"About five days."

"And I am dragging out the second week here."

There was a short silence.

15 "Time passes quickly, and yet it is so dull here!" she said, not looking at him.

"It's only the fashion to say it's dull here. A provincial will live in Belyov or Zhizdra and not be bored, but when he comes here it's 'Oh, the dullness! Oh, the dust!' One would think he came from Granada."

She laughed. Then both continued eating in silence, like strangers, but after dinner they walked together and there sprang up between them the light banter of people who are free and contented, to whom it does not matter where they go or what they talk about. They walked and talked of the strange light on the sea; the water was a soft, warm, lilac color, and there was a golden band of moonlight upon it. They talked of how sultry it was after a hot day. Gurov told her that he was a native of Moscow, that he had studied languages and literature at the university, but had a post in a bank; that at one time he had trained to become an opera singer but had given it up, that he owned two houses in Moscow. And he learned from her that she had grown up in Petersburg, but had lived in S——— since her marriage two years previously, that she was going to stay in Yalta for about another month, and that her husband, who needed a rest, too, might perhaps come to fetch her. She was not certain whether her husband was a member of a Government Board or served on a Zemstvo Council, and this amused her. And Gurov learned too that her name was Anna Sergeyevna.

Afterwards in his room at the hotel he thought about her—and was certain that he would meet her the next day. It was bound to happen. Getting into bed he recalled that she had been a schoolgirl only recently, doing lessons like his own daughter; he thought how much timidity and angularity there was still in her laugh and her manner of talking with a stranger. It must have been the first time in her life that she was alone in a setting in which she was followed, looked at, and spoken to for one secret purpose alone, which she could hardly fail to guess. He thought of her slim, delicate throat, her lovely gray eyes.

"There's something pathetic about her, though," he thought, and dropped off.

## II

20 A week had passed since they had struck up an acquaintance. It was a holiday. It was close indoors, while in the street the wind whirled the dust about and blew people's hats off. One was thirsty all day, and Gurov often went into the restaurant and offered Anna Sergeyevna a soft drink or ice cream. One did not know what to do with oneself.

In the evening when the wind had abated they went out on the pier to watch the steamer come in. There were a great many people walking about the dock; they had come to welcome someone and they were carrying bunches of flowers. And two peculiarities of a festive Yalta crowd stood out: the elderly ladies were dressed like young ones and there were many generals.

Owing to the choppy sea, the steamer arrived late, after sunset, and it was a long time tacking about before it put in at the pier. Anna Sergeyevna peered at the steamer and the passengers through her lorgnette as though looking for acquaintances, and whenever she turned to Gurov her eyes were shining. She talked a great deal and asked questions jerkily, forgetting the next moment what she had asked; then she lost her lorgnette in the crush.

The festive crowd began to disperse; it was now too dark to see people's faces; there was no wind any more, but Gurov and Anna Sergeyevna still stood as though waiting to see someone else come off the steamer. Anna Sergeyevna was silent now, and sniffed her flowers without looking at Gurov.

"The weather has improved this evening," he said. "Where shall we go now? Shall we drive somewhere?"

She did not reply.

Then he looked at her intently, and suddenly embraced her and kissed her on the lips, and the moist fragrance of her flowers enveloped him; and at once he looked round him anxiously, wondering if anyone had seen them.

"Let us go to your place," he said softly. And they walked off together rapidly.

The air in her room was close and there was the smell of the perfume she had bought at the Japanese shop. Looking at her, Gurov thought: "What encounters life offers!" From the past he preserved the memory of carefree, good-natured women whom love made gay and who were grateful to him for the happiness he gave them, however brief it might be; and of women like his wife who loved without sincerity, with too many words, affectedly, hysterically, with an expression that it was not love or passion that engaged them but something more significant; and of two or three others, very beautiful, frigid women, across whose faces would suddenly flit a rapacious expression—an obstinate desire to take from life more than it could give, and these were women no longer young, capricious, unreflecting, domineering, unintelligent, and when Gurov grew cold to them their beauty aroused his hatred, and the lace on their lingerie seemed to him to resemble scales.

But here there was the timidity, the angularity of inexperienced youth, a feeling of awkwardness; and there was a sense of embarrassment, as though someone had suddenly knocked at the door. Anna Sergeyevna, "the lady with the pet dog," treated what had happened in a peculiar way, very seriously, as though it were her fall—so it seemed, and this was odd and inappropriate. Her features drooped and faded, and her long hair hung down sadly on either side of her face; she grew pensive and her dejected pose was that of a Magdalene in a picture by an old master.

"It's not right," she said. "You don't respect me now, you first of all."

There was a watermelon on the table. Gurov cut himself a slice and began eating it without haste. They were silent for at least half an hour.

There was something touching about Anna Sergeyevna; she had the purity of a well-bred, naive woman who has seen little of life. The single candle burning on the table barely illumined her face, yet it was clear that she was unhappy.

"Why should I stop respecting you, darling?" asked Gurov. "You don't know what you're saying."

"God forgive me," she said, and her eyes filled with tears. "It's terrible."

"It's as though you were trying to exonerate yourself."

"How can I exonerate myself? No. I am a bad, low woman; I despise myself and I have no thought of exonerating myself. It's not my husband but myself I have deceived. And not only just now; I have been deceiving myself for a long time. My husband may be a good, honest man, but he is a flunkey! I don't know what he does, what his work is, but I know he is a flunkey! I was twenty when I married him. I was tormented by curiosity; I wanted something better. 'There must be a different sort of life,' I said to myself. I wanted to live! To live, to live! Curiosity kept eating at me—you don't understand it, but I swear to God I could no longer control myself; something was going on in me: I could not be held back. I told my husband I was ill, and came here. And here I have been walking about as though in a daze, as though I were mad; and now I have become a vulgar, vile woman whom anyone may despise."

Gurov was already bored with her; he was irritated by her naive tone, by her repentance, so unexpected and so out of place; but for the tears in her eyes he might have thought she was joking or play-acting.

"I don't understand, my dear," he said softly. "What do you want?"

She hid her face on his breast and pressed close to him.

"Believe me, believe me, I beg you," she said, "I love honesty and purity, and sin is loathsome to me; I don't know what I'm doing. Simple people say, 'The Evil One has led me astray.' And I may say of myself now that the Evil One has led me astray."

"Quiet, quiet," he murmured.

He looked into her fixed, frightened eyes, kissed her, spoke to her softly and affectionately, and by degrees she calmed down, and her gaiety returned; both began laughing.

Afterwards when they went out there was not a soul on the esplanade. The town with its cypresses looked quite dead, but the sea was still sounding as it broke upon the beach; a single launch was rocking on the waves and on it a lantern was blinking sleepily.

They found a cab and drove to Oreanda.

45 "I found out your surname in the hall just now: it was written on the board—von Dideritz," said Gurov. "Is your husband German?"

"No; I believe his grandfather was German, but he is Greek Orthodox himself."

At Oreanda they sat on a bench not far from the church, looked down at the sea, and were silent. Yalta was barely visible through the morning mist; white clouds rested motionlessly on the mountaintops. The leaves did not stir on the trees, cicadas twanged, and the monotonous muffled sound of the sea that rose from below spoke of the peace, the eternal sleep awaiting us. So it rumbled below when there was no Yalta, no Oreanda here; so it rumbles now, and it will rumble as indifferently and as hollowly when we are no more. And in this constancy, in this complete indifference to the life and death of each of us, there lies, perhaps, a pledge of our eternal salvation, of the unceasing advance of life upon earth, of unceasing movement towards perfection. Sitting beside a young woman who in the dawn seemed so lovely, Gurov, soothed and spellbound by these magical surroundings—the sea, the mountains, the clouds, the wide sky—thought how everything is really beautiful in this world when one reflects: everything except what we think or do ourselves when we forget the higher aims of life and our own human dignity.

A man strolled up to them—probably a guard—looked at them and walked away. And this detail, too, seemed so mysterious and beautiful. They saw a steamer arrive from Feodosia, its lights extinguished in the glow of dawn.

"There is dew on the grass," said Anna Sergeyevna, after a silence.

50 "Yes, it's time to go home."

They returned to the city.

Then they met every day at twelve o'clock on the esplanade, lunched and dined together, took walks, admired the sea. She complained that she slept badly, that she had palpitations, asked the same questions, troubled now by jealousy and now by the fear that he did not respect her sufficiently. And often in the square or the public garden, when there was no one near them, he suddenly drew her to him and kissed her passionately. Complete idleness, these kisses in broad daylight exchanged furtively in dread of someone's seeing them, the heat, the smell of the sea, and the continual flitting before his eyes of idle, well-dressed, well-fed people, worked a complete change in him; he kept telling Anna Sergeyevna how beautiful she was, how seductive, was urgently passionate; he would not move a step away from her, while she was often pensive and continually pressed him to confess that he did not respect her, did not love her in the least, and saw in her nothing but a common woman. Almost every evening rather late they drove somewhere out of town, to Oreanda or to the waterfall; and the excursion was always a success, the scenery invariably impressed them as beautiful and magnificent.

They were expecting her husband, but a letter came from him saying that he had eye-trouble, and begging his wife to return home as soon as possible. Anna Sergeyevna made haste to go.

"It's a good thing I am leaving," she said to Gurov. "It's the hand of Fate!"

55 She took a carriage to the railway station, and he went with her. They were driving the whole day. When she had taken her place in the express, and when the second bell had rung, she said, "Let me look at you once more—let me look at you again. Like this."

She was not crying but was so sad that she seemed ill, and her face was quivering.

"I shall be thinking of you—remembering you," she said. "God bless you; be happy. Don't remember evil against me. We are parting forever—it has to be, for we ought never to have met. Well, God bless you."

The train moved off rapidly, its lights soon vanished, and a minute later there was no sound of it, as though everything had conspired to end as quickly as possible that sweet trance, that madness. Left alone on the platform, and gazing into the dark distance, Gurov listened to the twang of the grasshoppers and the hum of the telegraph wires, feeling as though he had just waked up. And he reflected, musing, that there had now been another episode or adventure in his life, and it, too, was at an end, and nothing was left of it but a memory. He was moved, sad, and slightly remorseful: this young woman whom he would never meet again had not been happy with him; he had been warm and affectionate with her, but yet in his manner, his tone, and his caresses there had been a shade of light irony, the slightly coarse arrogance of a happy male who was, besides, almost twice her age. She had constantly called him kind, exceptional, high-minded; obviously he had seemed to her different from what he really was, so he had involuntarily deceived her.

Here at the station there was already a scent of autumn in the air; it was a chilly evening.

60 "It is time for me to go north, too," thought Gurov as he left the platform. "High time!"

## III

At home in Moscow the winter routine was already established: the stoves were heated, and in the morning it was still dark when the children were having breakfast and getting ready for school, and the nurse would light the lamp for a short time. There were frosts already. When the first snow falls, on the first day the sleighs are out, it is pleasant to see the white earth, the white roofs; one draws easy, delicious breaths, and the season brings back the days of one's youth. The old limes and birches, white with hoar-frost, have a good-natured look; they are closer to one's heart than cypresses and palms, and near them one no longer wants to think of mountains and the sea.

Gurov, a native of Moscow, arrived there on a fine frosty day, and when he put on his fur coat and warm gloves and took a walk along Petrovka, and when on Saturday night he heard the bells ringing, his recent trip and the places he had visited lost all charm for him. Little by little he became immersed in Moscow life, greedily read three newspapers a day, and declared that he did not read the Moscow papers on principle. He already felt a longing for restaurants, clubs, formal dinners, anniversary celebrations, and it flattered him to entertain distinguished lawyers and actors, and to play cards with a professor at the physicians' club. He could eat a whole portion of meat stewed with pickled cabbage and served in a pan, Moscow style.

A month or so would pass and the image of Anna Sergeyevna, it seemed to him, would become misty in his memory, and only from time to time he would dream of her with her touching smile as he dreamed of others. But more than a month went by, winter came into its own, and everything was still clear in his memory as though he had parted from Anna Sergeyevna only yesterday. And his memories glowed more and more vividly. When in the evening stillness the voices of his children preparing their lessons reached his study, or when he listened to a song or to an organ playing in a restaurant, or when the storm howled in the chimney, suddenly everything would rise up in his memory: what had happened on the pier and the early morning with the mist on the mountains, and the steamer coming from Feodosia, and the kisses. He would pace about his room a long time, remembering and smiling; then his memories passed into reveries, and in his imagination the past would mingle with what was to come. He did not dream of Anna Sergeyevna, but she followed him about everywhere and watched him. When he shut his eyes he saw her before him as though she were there in the flesh; and she seemed to him lovelier, younger, tenderer than she had been, and he imagined himself a finer man than he had been in Yalta. Of evenings she peered out at him from the bookcase, from the fireplace, from the corner—he heard her breathing, the caressing rustle of her clothes. In the street he followed the women with his eyes, looking for someone who resembled her.

Already he was tormented by a strong desire to share his memories with someone. But in his home it was impossible to talk of his love, and he had no one to talk to outside; certainly he could not confide in his tenants or in anyone at the bank. And what was there to talk to about? He hadn't loved her then, had he? Had there been anything beautiful, poetical, edifying, or simply interesting in his relations with Anna Sergeyevna? And he was forced to talk vaguely of love, of women, and no one guessed what he meant; only his wife would twitch her black eyebrows and say, "The part of a philanderer does not suit you at all, Dimitry."

65 One evening, coming out of the physician's club with an official with whom he had been playing cards, he could not resist saying:

"If you only knew what a fascinating woman I became acquainted with at Yalta!"

The official got into his sledge and was driving away, but turned suddenly and shouted: "Dmitry Dmitrich!"

"What is it?"

"You were right this evening: the sturgeon was a bit high."

70 These words, so commonplace, for some reason moved Gurov to indignation, and struck him as degrading and unclean. What savage manners, what mugs! What stupid nights, what dull, humdrum days! Frenzied gambling, gluttony, drunkenness, continual talk always about the same things! Futile pursuits and conversations always about the same topics take up the better part of one's time, the better part of one's strength, and in the end there is left a life clipped and wingless, an absurd mess, and there is no escaping or getting away from it—just as though one were in a madhouse or a prison.

Gurov, boiling with indignation, did not sleep all night. And he had a headache all the next day. And the following nights too he slept badly; he sat up in bed, thinking, or paced up and down his room. He was fed up with his children, fed up with the bank; he had no desire to go anywhere or to talk of anything.

In December during the holidays he prepared to take a trip and told his wife he was going to Petersburg to do what he could for a young friend—and he set off for S———. What for? He did not know, himself. He wanted to see Anna Sergeyevna and talk with her, to arrange a rendezvous if possible.

He arrived at S——— in the morning, and at the hotel took the best room, in which the floor was covered with gray army cloth, and on the table there was an inkstand, gray with dust and topped by a figure on horseback, its hat in its raised hand and its head broken off. The porter gave him the necessary information: von Dideritz lived in a house of his own on Staro-Goncharnaya Street, not far from the hotel: he was rich and lived well and kept his own horses; everyone in the town knew him. The porter pronounced the name: "Dridiritz."

Without haste Gurov made his way to Staro-Goncharnaya Street and found the house. Directly opposite the house stretched a long gray fence studded with nails.

75 "A fence like that would make one run away," thought Gurov, looking now at the fence, now at the windows of the house.

He reflected: this was a holiday, and the husband was apt to be at home. And in any case, it would be tactless to go into the house and disturb her. If he were to send her a note, it might fall into her husband's hands, and that might spoil everything. The best thing was to rely on chance. And he kept walking up and down the street and along the fence, waiting for the chance. He saw a beggar go in at the gate and heard the dogs attack him; then an hour later he heard a piano, and the sound came to him faintly and indistinctly. Probably it was Anna Sergeyevna playing. The front door opened suddenly, and an old woman came out, followed by the familiar white Pomeranian. Gurov was on the point of calling to the dog, but his heart began beating violently, and in his excitement he could not remember the Pomeranian's name.

He kept walking up and down, and hated the gray fence more and more, and by now he thought irritably that Anna Sergeyevna had forgotten him, and was perhaps already diverting herself with another man, and that that was very natural in a young woman who from morning till night had to look at that damn fence. He went back to his hotel room and sat on the couch for a long while, not knowing what to do, then he had dinner and a long nap.

"How stupid and annoying all this is!" he thought when he woke and looked at the dark windows: it was already evening. "Here I've had a good sleep for some reason. What am I going to do at night?"

He sat on the bed, which was covered with a cheap gray blanket of the kind seen in hospitals, and he twitted himself in his vexation:

80 "So there's your lady with the pet dog. There's your adventure. A nice place to cool your heels in."

That morning at the station a playbill in large letters had caught his eye. *The Geisha* was to be given for the first time. He thought of this and drove to the theater.

"It's quite possible that she goes to first nights," he thought.

The theater was full. As in all provincial theaters, there was a haze above the chandelier, the gallery was noisy and restless; in the front row, before the beginning of the performance the local dandies were standing with their hands clasped behind their backs; in the Governor's box the Governor's daughter, wearing a boa, occupied the front seat, while the Governor himself hid modestly behind the portiere and only his hands were visible; the curtain swayed; the orchestra was a long time tuning up. While the audience were coming in and taking their seats, Gurov scanned the faces eagerly.

Anna Sergeyevna, too, came in. She sat down in the third row, and when Gurov looked at her his heart contracted, and he understood clearly that in the whole world there was no human being so near, so precious, and so important to him; she, this little, undistinguished woman, lost in a provincial crowd, with a vulgar lorgnette in her hand, filled his whole life now, was his sorrow and his joy, the only happiness that he now desired for himself, and to the sounds of the bad orchestra, of the miserable local violins, he thought how lovely she was. He thought and dreamed.

A young man with small side-whiskers, very tall and stooped, came in with Anna Sergeyevna and sat down beside her; he nodded his head at every step and seemed to be bowing continually. Probably this was the husband whom at Yalta, in an excess of bitter feeling, she had called a flunkey. And there really was in his lanky figure, his side-whiskers, his small bald patch, something of a flunkey's retiring manner; his smile was mawkish, and in his buttonhole there was an academic badge like a waiter's number.

During the first intermission the husband went out to have a smoke; she remained in her seat. Gurov, who was also sitting in the orchestra, went up to her and said in a shaky voice, with a forced smile:

"Good evening!"

She glanced at him and turned pale, then looked at him again in horror, unable to believe her eyes, and gripped the fan and the lorgnette tightly together in her hands, evidently trying to keep herself from fainting. Both were silent. She was sitting, he was standing, frightened by her distress and not daring to take a seat beside her. The violins and the flute that were being tuned up sang out. He suddenly felt frightened: it seemed as if all the people in the boxes were looking at them. She got up and went hurriedly to the exit; he followed her, and both of them walked blindly along the corridors and up and down stairs, and figures in the uniforms prescribed for magistrates, teachers, and officials of the Department of Crown Lands, all wearing badges, flitted before their eyes, as did also ladies, and fur coats on hangers; they were conscious of drafts and the smell of stale tobacco. And Gurov, whose heart was beating violently, thought:

"Oh, Lord! Why are these people here and this orchestra!"

And at that instant he suddenly recalled how when he had seen Anna Sergeyevna off at the station he had said to himself that all was over between them and that they would never meet again. But how distant the end still was!

On the narrow, gloomy staircase over which it said "To the Amphitheatre," she stopped.

"How you frightened me!" she said, breathing hard, still pale and stunned. "Oh, how you frightened me! I am barely alive. Why did you come? Why?"

"But do understand, Anna, do understand—" he said hurriedly, under his breath. "I implore you, do understand—"

She looked at him with fear, with entreaty, with love; she looked at him intently, to keep his features more distinctly in her memory.

"I suffer so," she went on, not listening to him. "All this time I have been thinking of nothing but you; I live only by the thought of you. And I wanted to forget, to forget; but why, oh, why have you come?"

On the landing above them two high school boys were looking down and smoking, but it was all the same to Gurov; he drew Anna Sergeyevna to him and began kissing her face and her hands.

"What are you doing, what are you doing!" she was saying in horror, pushing him away. "We have lost our senses. Go away today; go away at once—I conjure you by all that is sacred, I implore you—People are coming this way!"

Someone was walking up the stairs.

"You must leave," Anna Sergeyevna went on in a whisper. "Do you hear, Dmitry Dmitrich? I will come and see you in Moscow. I have never been happy; I am unhappy now, and I never, never shall be happy, never! So don't make me suffer still more! I swear I'll come to Moscow. But now let us part. My dear, good, precious one, let us part!"

100 She pressed his hand and walked rapidly downstairs, turning to look round at him, and from her eyes he could see that she really was unhappy. Gurov stood for a while, listening, then when all grew quiet, he found his coat and left the theater.

## IV

And Anna Sergeyevna began coming to see him in Moscow. Once every two or three months she left S———, telling her husband that she was going to consult a doctor about a woman's ailment from which she was suffering—and her husband did and did not believe her. When she arrived in Moscow she would stop at the Slavyansky Bazar Hotel, and at once send a man in a red cap to Gurov. Gurov came to see her, and no one in Moscow knew of it.

Once he was going to see her in this way on a winter morning (the messenger had come the evening before and not found him in). With him walked his daughter, whom he wanted to take to school: it was on the way. Snow was coming down in big wet flakes.

"It's three degrees above zero,[1] and yet it's snowing," Gurov was saying to his daughter. "But this temperature prevails only on the surface of the earth; in the upper layers of the atmosphere there is quite a different temperature."

"And why doesn't it thunder in winter, papa?"

105 He explained that, too. He talked, thinking all the while that he was on his way to a rendezvous, and no living soul knew of it, and probably no one would ever know. He had two lives: an open one, seen and known by all who needed to know it, full of conventional truth and conventional falsehood, exactly like the lives of his friends and acquaintances; and another life that went on in secret. And through some strange, perhaps accidental, combination of circumstances, everything that was of interest and importance to him, everything that was essential to him, everything about which he felt sincerely and did not deceive himself, everything that constituted the core of his life, was going on concealed from others; while all that was false, the shell in which he hid to cover the truth—his work at the bank, for instance, his discussions at the club, his references to the "inferior race," his appearances at anniversary celebrations with his wife—all that went on in the open. Judging others by himself, he did not believe what he saw, and always fancied that every man led his real, most interesting life under cover of secrecy as under cover of night. The personal life of every individual is based on secrecy, and perhaps it is partly for that reason that civilized man is so nervously anxious that personal privacy should be respected.

Having taken his daughter to school, Gurov went on to the Slavyansky Bazar Hotel. He took off his fur coat in the lobby, went upstairs, and knocked gently at the door. Anna Sergeyevna, wearing his favorite gray dress, exhausted by the journey and by waiting, had been expecting him since the previous evening. She was pale, and looked at him without a smile, and he had hardly entered when she flung herself on his breast. Their kiss was a long, lingering one, as though they had not seen one another for two years.

"Well, darling, how are you getting on there?" he asked. "What news?"

"Wait; I'll tell you in a moment—I can't speak."

She could not speak; she was crying. She turned away from him, and pressed her handkerchief to her eyes.

110 "Let her have her cry; meanwhile I'll sit down," he thought, and he seated himself in an armchair.

Then he rang and ordered tea, and while he was having his tea she remained standing at the window with her back to him. She was crying out of sheer agitation, in the sorrowful consciousness that their life was so sad; that they could only see each other in secret and had to hide from people like thieves! Was it not a broken life?

"Come, stop now, dear!" he said.

It was plain to him that this love of theirs would not be over soon, that the end of it was not in sight. Anna Sergeyevna was growing more and more attached to him. She adored him, and it

[1]Equal to approximately thirty-seven degrees Fahrenheit (Russia uses the Celsius scale).

was unthinkable to tell her that their love was bound to come to an end some day; besides, she would not have believed it!

He went up to her and took her by the shoulders, to fondle her and say something diverting, and at that moment he caught sight of himself in the mirror.

His hair was already beginning to turn gray. And it seemed odd to him that he had grown so much older in the last few years, and lost his looks. The shoulders on which his hands rested were warm and heaving. He felt compassion for this life, still so warm and lovely, but probably already about to begin to fade and wither like his own. Why did she love him so much? He always seemed to women different from what he was, and they loved in him not himself, but the man whom their imagination created and whom they had been eagerly seeking all their lives; and afterwards, when they saw their mistake, they loved him nevertheless. And not one of them had been happy with him. In the past he had met women, come together with them, parted from them, but he had never once loved; it was anything you please, but not love. And only now when his head was gray he had fallen in love, really, truly—for the first time in his life.

Anna Sergeyevna and he loved each other as people do who are very close and intimate, like man and wife, like tender friends; it seemed to them that Fate itself had meant them for one another, and they could not understand why he had a wife and she had a husband; and it was as though they were a pair of migratory birds, male and female, caught and forced to live in different cages. They forgave each other what they were ashamed of in their past, they forgave everything in the present, and felt that this love of theirs had altered them both.

Formerly in moments of sadness he had soothed himself with whatever logical arguments came into his head, but now he no longer cared for logic; he felt profound compassion, he wanted to be sincere and tender.

"Give it up now, my darling," he said. "You've had your cry; that's enough. Let us have a talk now, we'll think up something."

Then they spent a long time taking counsel together, they talked of how to avoid the necessity for secrecy, for deception, for living in different cities, and not seeing one another for long stretches of time. How could they free themselves from these intolerable fetters?

"How" How?" he asked, clutching his head. "How?"

And it seemed as though in a little while the solution would be found, and then a new and glorious life would begin; and it was clear to both of them that the end was still far off, and that what was to be most complicated and difficult for them was only just beginning.

—Translated by Avrahm Yarmolinsky

Most contemporary short story writers would agree that Chekhov's work is the source and inspiration of a large part of their own work. If you like this story you may want to read "Optimists" by Richard Ford (chapter 2), who served as editor for a recent collection of Chekhov's prose.

**GOING FURTHER** Works by the French Guy de Maupassant and the Russian Isaac Babel contribute, like Chekhov's stories, to the European legacy of the modern short story. Working in this tradition are also some Irish writers such as Frank O'Connor and William Trevor. The latter's *Collected Stories* offers a feast of modern short fiction.

# Gabriel García Márquez (b. 1928)

THE WINNER OF the 1982 Nobel Prize for Literature, Gabriel García Márquez was born in the small northern Colombian town of Aracataca. Originally a student of law, he ended his studies and went to work as a journalist, a profession that took him to Europe and eventually to the United States. There he made a pilgrimage to Oxford,

Mississippi, the hometown of his literary idol William Faulkner, whom he referred to in his Nobel Prize acceptance speech in laudatory terms. Márquez declared that the writer's goal was to create a "new and sweeping utopia of life, where no one will be able to decide for others how they die, where love will prove true and happiness be possible, and where the races condemned to one hundred years of solitude will have, at last and forever, a second opportunity on earth."

His style is that of "magical realism," in which supernatural events occur in otherwise natural contexts and settings. Marquez is famous for his ability to span decades in a sentence, to bring the dead to life, and to make even the cruelest fates a matter of course—all with utmost fluidity and believability. Along with his many other works of fiction and nonfiction, his masterwork, the novel *One Hundred Years of Solitude,* has illuminated life in the Americas for millions of readers.

# The Handsomest Drowned Man in the World (1972)

## A TALE FOR CHILDREN

1 The first children who saw the dark and slinky bulge approaching through the sea let themselves think it was an enemy ship. Then they saw it had no flags or masts and they thought it was a whale. But when it washed up on the beach, they removed the clumps of seaweed, the jellyfish tentacles, and the remains of fish and flotsam, and only then did they see that it was a drowned man.

They had been playing with him all afternoon, burying him in the sand and digging him up again, when someone chanced to see them and spread the alarm in the village. The men who carried him to the nearest house noticed that he weighed more than any dead man they had ever known, almost as much as a horse, and they said to each other that maybe he'd been floating too long and the water had got into his bones. When they laid him on the floor they said he'd been taller than all other men because there was barely enough room for him in the house, but they thought that maybe the ability to keep on growing after death was part of the nature of certain drowned men. He had the smell of the sea about him and only his shape gave one to suppose that it was the corpse of a human being, because the skin was covered with a crust of mud and scales.

They did not even have to clean off his face to know that the dead man was a stranger. The village was made up of only twenty-odd wooden houses that had stone courtyards with no flowers and which were spread about on the end of a desertlike cape. There was so little land that mothers always went about with the fear that the wind would carry off their children and the few dead that the years had caused among them had to be thrown off the cliffs. But the sea was calm and bountiful and all the men fit into seven boats. So when they found the drowned man they simply had to look at one another to see that they were all there.

That night they did not go out to work at sea. While the men went to find out if anyone was missing in neighboring villages, the women stayed behind to care for the drowned man. They took the mud off with grass swabs, they removed the underwater stones entangled in his hair, and they scraped the crust off with tools used for scaling fish. As they were doing that they noticed that the vegetation on him came from faraway oceans and deep water and that his clothes were in tatters, as if he had sailed through labyrinths of coral. They noticed too that he bore his death with pride, for he did not have the lonely look of other drowned men who came out of the sea or that haggard, needy look of men who drowned in rivers. But only when they finished cleaning him off did they become aware of the kind of man he was and it left them breathless. Not only was he the tallest, strongest, most virile, and best built man they had ever seen, but even though they were looking at him there was no room for him in their imagination.

5 They could not find a bed in the village large enough to lay him on nor was there a table solid enough to use for his wake. The tallest men's holiday pants would not fit him, nor the fattest ones' Sunday shirts, nor the shoes of the one with the biggest feet. Fascinated by his huge size and his beauty, the women then decided to make him some pants from a large piece of sail and a shirt from some bridal brabant linen so that he could continue through his death with dignity. As they sewed, sitting in a circle and gazing at the corpse between stitches, it seemed to them that the wind had never been so steady nor the sea so restless as on that night and they supposed that the change had something to do with the dead man. They thought that if that magnificent man had lived in the village, his house would have had the widest doors, the highest ceiling, and the strongest floor, his bedstead would have been made from a midship frame held together by iron bolts, and his wife would have been the happiest woman. They thought that he would have had so much authority that he could have drawn fish out of the sea simply by calling their names and that he would have put so much work into his land that springs would have burst forth from among the rocks so that he would have been able to plant flowers on the cliffs. They secretly compared him to their own men, thinking that for all their lives theirs were incapable of doing what he could do in one night, and they ended up dismissing them deep in their hearts as the weakest, meanest, and most useless creatures on earth. They were wandering through that maze of fantasy when the oldest woman, who as the oldest had looked upon the drowned man with more compassion than passion, sighed:

"He has the face of someone called Esteban."

It was true. Most of them had only to take another look at him to see that he could not have any other name. The more stubborn among them, who were the youngest, still lived for a few hours with the illusion that when they put his clothes on and he lay among the flowers in patent leather shoes his name might be Lautaro. But it was a vain illusion. There had not been enough canvas, the poorly cut and worse sewn pants were too tight, and the hidden strength of his heart popped the buttons on his shirt. After midnight the whistling of the wind died down and the sea fell into its Wednesday drowsiness. The silence put an end to any last doubts: he was Esteban. The women who had dressed him, who had combed his hair, had cut his nails and shaved him were unable to hold back a shudder of pity when they had to resign themselves to his being dragged along the ground. It was then that they understood how unhappy he must have been with that huge body since it bothered him even after death. They could see him in life, condemned to going through doors sideways, cracking his head on crossbeams, remaining on his feet during visits, not knowing what to do with his soft, pink, sea lion hands while the lady of the house looked for her most resistant chair and begged him, frightened to death, sit here, Esteban, please, and he, leaning against the wall, smiling, don't bother, ma'am, I'm fine where I am, his heels raw and his back roasted from having done the same thing so many times whenever he paid a visit, don't bother, ma'am, I'm fine where I am, just to avoid the embarrassment of breaking up the chair, and never knowing perhaps that the ones who said don't go, Esteban, at least wait till the coffee's ready, were the ones who later on would whisper the big boob finally left, how nice, the handsome fool has gone. That was what the women were thinking beside the body a little before dawn. Later, when they covered his face with a handkerchief so that the light would not bother him, he looked so forever dead, so defenseless, so much like their men that the first furrows of tears opened in their hearts. It was one of the younger ones who began the weeping. The others, coming to, went from sighs to wails, and the more they sobbed the more they felt like weeping, because the drowned man was becoming all the more Esteban for them, and so they wept so much, for he was the most destitute, most peaceful, and most obliging man on earth, poor Esteban. So when the men returned with the news that the drowned man was not from the neighboring villages either, the women felt an opening of jubilation in the midst of their tears.

"Praise the Lord," they sighed, "he's ours!"

The men thought the fuss was only womanish frivolity. Fatigued because of the difficult nighttime inquiries, all they wanted was to get rid of the bother of the newcomer once and for all before the sun grew strong on that arid, windless day. They improvised a litter with the remains of foremasts and gaffs, tying it together with rigging so that it would bear the weight of the body until they reached the cliffs. They wanted to tie the anchor from a cargo ship to him so that he would sink easily into the deepest waves, where fish are blind and divers die of nostalgia, and bad currents would not bring him back to shore, as had happened with other bodies. But the more they hurried, the more the women thought of ways to waste time. They walked about like startled hens, pecking with the sea charms on their breasts, some interfering on one side to put a scapular of the good wind on the drowned man, some on the other side to put a wrist compass on him, and after a great deal of *get away from there, woman, stay out of the way, look, you almost made me fall on top of the dead man,* the men began to feel mistrust in their livers and started grumbling about why so many main-altar decorations for a stranger, because no matter how many nails and holy-water jars he had on him, the sharks would chew him all the same, but the women kept piling on their junk relics, running back and forth, stumbling, while they released in sighs what they did not in tears, so that the men finally exploded with *since when has there ever been such a fuss over a drifting corpse, a drowned nobody, a piece of cold Wednesday meat.* One of the women, mortified by so much lack of care, then removed the handkerchief from the dead man's face and the men were left breathless too.

10 He was Esteban. It was not necessary to repeat it for them to recognize him. If they had been told Sir Walter Raleigh, even they might have been impressed with his gringo accent, the macaw on his shoulder, his cannibal-killing blunderbuss, but there could be only one Esteban in the world and there he was, stretched out like a sperm whale, shoeless, wearing the pants of an undersized child, and with those stony nails that had to be cut with a knife. They only had to take the handkerchief off his face to see that he was ashamed, that it was not his fault that he was so big or so heavy or so handsome, and if he had known that this was going to happen, he would have looked for a more discreet place to drown in, seriously, I even would have tied the anchor off a galleon around my neck and staggered off a cliff like someone who doesn't like things in order not to be upsetting people now with this Wednesday dead body, as you people say, in order not to be bothering anyone with this filthy piece of cold meat that doesn't have anything to do with me. There was so much truth in his manner that even the most mistrustful men, the ones who felt the bitterness of endless nights at sea fearing that their women would tire of dreaming about them and begin to dream of drowned men, even they and others who were harder still shuddered in the marrow of their bones at Esteban's sincerity.

That was how they came to hold the most splendid funeral they could ever conceive of for an abandoned drowned man. Some women who had gone to get flowers in the neighboring villages returned with other women who could not believe what they had been told, and those women went back for more flowers when they saw the dead man, and they brought more and more until there were so many flowers and so many people that it was hard to walk about. At the final moment it pained them to return him to the waters as an orphan and they chose a father and mother from among the best people, and aunts and uncles and cousins, so that through him all the inhabitants of the village became kinsmen. Some sailors who heard the weeping from a distance went off course and people heard of one who had himself tied to the mainmast, remembering ancient fables about sirens. While they fought for the privilege of carrying him on their shoulders along the steep escarpment by the cliffs, men and women became aware for the first time of the desolation of their streets, the dryness of their courtyards, the narrowness of their dreams as they faced the splendor and beauty of their drowned man. They let him go without an anchor so that he could come back if he wished and whenever he wished, and they all held their breath for the fraction of centuries the body took to fall into the abyss. They did not need to look at one another to realize that they were no longer all present, that they would never be. But they also knew that everything would be different from then on, that their houses would have wider doors, higher ceilings, and stronger floors so that Esteban's memory could go everywhere without bumping into beams and so that no one in the future would dare whisper the big boob finally died, too bad, the handsome fool has finally died, because they were going to paint their house fronts gay colors to make Esteban's memory eternal and they were going to break their backs digging for springs among the stones and planting flowers on the cliffs so that in future years at dawn the passengers on great liners would awaken, suffocated by the smell of gardens on the high seas, and the captain would have to come down from the bridge in his dress uniform, with his astrolabe, his pole star, and his row of war medals and, pointing to the promontory of roses on the horizon, he would say in fourteen languages, look there, where the wind is so peaceful now that it's gone to sleep beneath the beds, over there, where the sun's so bright that the sunflowers don't know which way to turn, yes, over there, that's Esteban's village.

If you like this story, you can find affinities with the style in the work of Franz Kafka, whose long story "The Metamorphosis" you can find in chapter 10, and in "The Rememberer" by Aimee Bender (chapter 8).

**GOING FURTHER** A number of U.S. writers have found themselves influenced by García Márquez's so-called magical realist style, among them Toni Morrison in her novel *Song of Solomon* and younger writers such as Mark Helprin in the stories collected in *A Dove of the East* and Jonathan Safran Foer in his 2005 novel *Extremely Loud and Incredibly Close.*

## Zora Neale Hurston (1891–1960)

GROWING UP IN Eatonville, Florida—an all-black town—Zora Neale Hurston did not experience racial prejudice. Instead, she saw examples of black role models, such as her father, who served as the town mayor. She began her education at Howard University in Washington, D.C., and finished her B.A. in anthropology at Barnard College in New York City. Her love of folk culture and literature led her to write novels, short stories, and collections of folklore that captured the common black person; unlike her contemporaries, including Langston Hughes, Hurston cared more about authenticity than about how her depictions made blacks appear to white audiences. An important figure of the Harlem Renaissance, Hurston is famous for her charming, vibrant personality that made her the center of parties and social life in Harlem. Some of her early fiction was published in *Opportunity,* a black magazine of the Harlem Renaissance. Her best work appeared in the 1930s and '40s with books such as *Mules and Men* (1935), which was the fruit of her ethnographic studies of blacks in Florida, and *Their Eyes Were Watching God* (1937), Hurston's classic novel about an African-American woman who forges her identity in relation to three different husbands. Although these works found an audience, Hurston sank into obscurity toward the end of her life. However, interest in her writing revived in the 1970s, thanks to Alice Walker's article "In Search of Zora Neale Hurston," which appeared in *Ms.* magazine. Today, Hurston is recognized as the most important African-American woman in early-twentieth-century literature.

# The Gilded Six-Bits (1933)

1 It was a Negro yard around a Negro house in a Negro settlement that looked to the payroll of the G and G Fertilizer works for its support.

But there was something happy about the place. The front yard was parted in the middle by a sidewalk from gate to door-step, a sidewalk edged on either side by quart bottles driven neck down into the ground on a slant. A mess of homey flowers planted without a plan but blooming cheerily from their helter-skelter places. The fence and house were whitewashed. The porch and steps scrubbed white.

The front door stood open to the sunshine so that the floor of the front room could finish drying after its weekly scouring. It was Saturday. Everything clean from the front gate to the privy house. Yard raked so that the strokes of the rake would make a pattern. Fresh newspaper cut in fancy edge on the kitchen shelves.

Missie May was bathing herself in the galvanized washtub in the bedroom. Her dark-brown skin glistened under the soapsuds that skittered down from her wash rag. Her stiff young breasts thrust forward aggressively, like broad-based cones with the tips lacquered in black.

She heard men's voices in the distance and glanced at the dollar clock on the dresser.

"Humph! Ah'm way behind time t'day! Joe gointer be heah 'fore Ah git mah clothes on if Ah don't make haste."

She grabbed the clean meal sack at hand and dried herself hurriedly and began to dress. But before she could tie her slippers, there came the ring of singing metal on wood. Nine times.

Missie May grinned with delight. She had not seen the big tall man come stealing in the gate and creep up the walk grinning happily at the joyful mischief he was about to commit. But she knew that it was her husband throwing silver dollars in the door for her to pick up and pile beside her plate at dinner. It was this way every Saturday afternoon. The nine dollars hurled into the open door, he scurried to a hiding place behind the cape jasmine bush and waited.

Missie May promptly appeared at the door in mock alarm.

"Who dat chunkin' money in mah do'way?" she demanded. No answer from the yard. She leaped off the porch and began to search the shrubbery. She peeped under the porch and hung over the gate to look up and down the road. While she did this, the man behind the jasmine darted to the chinaberry tree. She spied him and gave chase.

"Nobody ain't gointer be chunkin' money at me and Ah not do 'em nothin'," she shouted in mock anger. He ran around the house with Missie May at his heels. She overtook him at the kitchen door. He ran inside but could not close it after him before she crowded in and locked with him in a rough and tumble. For several minutes the two were a furious mass of male and female energy. Shouting, laughing, twisting, turning, tussling, tickling each other in the ribs; Missie May clutching onto Joe and Joe trying, but not too hard, to get away.

"Missie May, take yo' hand out mah pocket!" Joe shouted out between laughs.

"Ah ain't, Joe, not lessen you gwine gimme whateve' it is good you got in yo' pocket. Turn it go, Joe, do Ah'll tear yo' clothes."

"Go on tear 'em. You de one dat pushes de needles round heah. Move yo' hand Missie May."

"Lemme git dat paper sack out yo' pocket. Ah bet it's candy kisses."

"Tain't. Move yo' hand. Woman ain't got no business in a man's clothes no how. Go way."

Missie May gouged way down and gave an upward jerk and triumphed.

"Unhhunh! Ah got it! It 'tis so candy kisses. Ah knowed you had somethin' for me in yo' clothes. Now Ah got to see whut's in every pocket you got."

Joe smiled indulgently and let his wife go through all of his pockets and take out the things that he had hidden there for her to find. She bore off the chewing gum, the cake of sweet soap, the pocket handkerchief as if she had wrested them from him, as if they had not been bought for the sake of this friendly battle.

"Whew! dat play-fight done got me all warmed up," Joe exclaimed. "Got me some water in de kittle?"

"Yo' water is on de fire and yo' clean things is cross de bed. Hurry up and wash yo'self and git changed so we kin eat. Ah'm hongry." As Missie said this, she bore the steaming kettle into the bedroom.

"You ain't hongry, sugar," Joe contradicted her. "Youse jes' a little empty. Ah'm de one whut's hongry. Ah could eat up camp meetin', back off 'ssociation, and drink Jurdan dry. Have it on de table when Ah git out de tub."

"Don't you mess wid mah business, man. You git in yo' clothes. Ah'm a real wife, not no dress and breath. Ah might not look lak one, but if you burn me, you won't git a thing but wife ashes."

Joe splashed in the bedroom and Missie May fanned around in the kitchen. A fresh red and white checked cloth on the table. Big pitcher of buttermilk beaded with pale drops of butter from the churn. Hot fried mullet, crackling bread, ham hock atop a mound of string beans and new potatoes, and perched on the window-sill a pone of spicy potato pudding.

Very little talk during the meal but that little consisted of banter that pretended to deny affection but in reality flaunted it. Like when Missie May reached for a second helping of the tater pone. Joe snatched it out of her reach.

After Missie May had made two or three unsuccessful grabs at the pan, she begged, "Aw, Joe gimme some mo' dat tater pone."

"Nope, sweetenin' is for us men-folks. Y'all pritty lil frail eels don't need nothin' lak dis. You too sweet already."

"Please, Joe."

"Naw, naw. Ah don't want you to git no sweeter than whut you is already. We goin' down de road a lil piece t'night so you go put on yo' Sunday-go-to-meetin' things."

Missie May looked at her husband to see if he was playing some prank. "Sho nuff, Joe?"

"Yeah. We goin' to de ice cream parlor."

"Where de ice cream parlor at, Joe?"

"A new man done come heah from Chicago and he done got a place and took and opened it up for a ice cream parlor, and bein' as it's real swell, Ah wants you to be one de first ladies to walk in dere and have some set down."

"Do Jesus, Ah ain't knowed nothin' 'bout it. Who de man done it?"

"Mister Otis D. Slemmons, of spots and places—Memphis, Chicago, Jacksonville, Philadelphia and so on."

"Dat heavy-set man wid his mouth full of gold teethes?"

"Yeah. Where did you see 'im at?"

"Ah went down to de sto' tuh git a box of lye and Ah seen 'im standin' on de corner talkin' to some of de mens, and Ah come on back and went to scrubbin' de floor, and he passed and tipped his hat whilst Ah was scourin' de steps. Ah thought Ah never seen *him* befo'."

Joe smiled pleasantly. "Yeah, he's up to date. He got de finest clothes Ah ever seen on a colored man's back."

"Aw, he don't look no better in his clothes than you do in yourn. He got a puzzlegut on 'im and he so chuckle-headed, he got a pone behind his neck."

Joe looked down at his own abdomen and said wistfully: "Wisht Ah had a build on me lak he got. He ain't puzzlegutted, honey. He jes' got a corperation. Dat make 'm look lak a rich white man. All rich mens is got some belly on 'em."

"Ah seen de pitchers of Henry Ford and he's a spare-built man and Rockefeller look lak he ain't got but one gut. But Ford and Rockefeller and dis Slemmons and all de rest kin be as many-gutted as dey please, Ah'm satisfied wid you jes' lak you is, baby. God took pattern after a pine tree and built you noble. Youse a pritty man, and if Ah knowed any way to make you mo' pritty still Ah'd take and do it."

Joe reached over gently and toyed with Missie May's ear. "You jes' say dat cause you love me, but Ah know Ah can't hold no light to Otis D. Slemmons. Ah ain't never been nowhere and Ah ain't got nothin' but you."

Missie May got on his lap and kissed him and he kissed back in kind. Then he went on. "All de womens is crazy 'bout 'im everywhere he go."

"How you know dat, Joe?"

"He tole us so hisself."

"Dat don't make it so. His mouf is cut cross-ways, ain't it? Well, he kin lie jes' lak anybody else."

"Good Lawd, Missie! You womens sho is hard to sense into things. He's got a five-dollar gold piece for a stick-pin and he got a ten-dollar gold piece on his watch chain and his mouf is jes' crammed full of gold teethes. Sho wisht it wuz mine. And whut make it so cool, he got money 'cumulated. And womens give it all to 'im."

"Ah don't see whut de womens see on 'im. Ah wouldn't give 'im a wink if de sheriff wuz after 'im."

"Well, he tole us how de white womens in Chicago give 'im all dat gold money. So he don't 'low nobody to touch it at all. Not even put dey finger on it. Dey tole 'im not to. You kin make 'miration at it, but don't tetch it."

"Whyn't he stay up dere where dey so crazy 'bout 'im?"

"Ah reckon dey done made 'im vast-rich and he wants to travel some. He says dey wouldn't leave 'im hit a lick of work. He got mo' lady people crazy 'bout him than he kin shake a stick at."

"Joe, Ah hates to see you so dumb. Dat stray nigger jes' tell y'all anything and y'all b'lieve it."

"Go 'head on now, honey and put on yo' clothes. He talkin' 'bout his pritty womens—Ah want 'im to see *mine.*"

Missie May went off to dress and Joe spent the time trying to make his stomach punch out like Slemmons' middle. He tried the rolling swagger of the stranger, but found that his tall bone-and-muscle stride fitted ill with it. He just had time to drop back into his seat before Missie May came in dressed to go.

On the way home that night Joe was exultant. "Didn't Ah say ole Otis was swell? Can't he talk Chicago talk? Wuzn't dat funny whut he said when great big fat ole Ida Armstrong come in? He asted me, 'Who is dat broad wid de forte shake?' Dat's a new word. Us always thought forty was a set of figgers but he showed us where it means a whole heap of things. Sometimes he don't say forty, he jes' say thirty-eight and two and dat mean de same thing. Know whut he tole me when Ah wuz payin' for our ice cream? He say, 'Ah have to hand it to you, Joe. Dat wife of yours is jes' thirty-eight and two. Yessuh, she's forte!' Ain't he killin'?"

"He'll do in case of a rush. But he sho is got uh heap uh gold on 'im. Dat's de first time Ah ever seed gold money. It lookted good on him sho nuff, but it'd look a whole heap better on you."

"Who, me? Missie May, youse crazy! Where would a po' man lak me git gold money from?"

Missie May was silent for a minute, then she said, "Us might find some goin' long de road some time. Us could."

"Who would be losin' gold money round heah? We ain't even seen none dese white folks wearin' no gold money on dey watch chain. You must be figgerin' Mister Packard or Mister Cadillac goin' pass through heah."

"You don't know whut been lost 'round heah. Maybe somebody way back in memorial times lost they gold money and went on off and it ain't never been found. And then if we wuz to find it, you could wear some 'thout havin' no gang of womens lak dat Slemmons say he got."

Joe laughed and hugged her. "Don't be so wishful 'bout me. Ah'm satisfied de way Ah is. So long as Ah be yo' husband, Ah don't keer 'bout nothin' else. Ah'd ruther all de other womens in de world to be dead than for you to have de toothache. Less we go to bed and git our night rest."

It was Saturday night once more before Joe could parade his wife in Slemmons' ice cream parlor again. He worked the night shift and Saturday was his only night off. Every other evening around six o'clock he left home, and dying dawn saw him hustling home around the lake where the challenging sun flung a flaming sword from east to west across the trembling water.

That was the best part of life—going home to Missie May. Their whitewashed house, the mock battle on Saturday, the dinner and ice cream parlor afterwards, church on Sunday nights when Missie outdressed any woman in town—all, everything was right.

One night around eleven the acid ran out at the G and G. The foreman knocked off the crew and let the steam die down. As Joe rounded the lake on his way home, a lean moon rode the lake in a silver boat. If anybody had asked Joe about the moon on the lake, he would have said he hadn't paid it any attention. But he saw it with his feelings. It made him yearn painfully for Missie. Creation obsessed him. He thought about children. They had been married more than a year now. They had money put away. They ought to be making little feet for shoes. A little boy child would be about right.

He saw a dim light in the bedroom and decided to come in through the kitchen door. He could wash the fertilizer dust off himself before presenting himself to Missie May. It would be nice for her not to know that he was there until he slipped into his place in bed and hugged her back. She always liked that.

He eased the kitchen door open slowly and silently, but when he went to set his dinner bucket on the table he bumped it into a pile of dishes, and something crashed to the floor. He heard his wife gasp in fright and hurried to reassure her.

"Iss me, honey. Don't git skeered."

There was a quick, large movement in the bedroom. A rustle, a thud, and a stealthy silence. The light went out.

What? Robbers? Murderers? Some varmint attacking his helpless wife, perhaps. He struck a match, threw himself on guard and stepped over the door-sill into the bedroom

The great belt on the wheel of Time slipped and eternity stood still. By the match light he could see the man's legs fighting with his breeches in his frantic desire to get them on. He had both chance and time to kill the intruder in his helpless condition—half in and half out of his pants—but he was too weak to take action. The shapeless enemies of humanity that live in the hours of Time had waylaid Joe. He was assaulted in his weakness. Like Samson awakening after his haircut. So he just opened his mouth and laughed.

The match went out and he struck another and lit the lamp. A howling wind raced across his heart, but underneath its fury he heard his wife sobbing and Slemmons pleading for his life. Offering to buy it with all that he had. "Please, suh, don't kill me. Sixty-two dollars at de sto'. Gold money."

Joe just stood. Slemmons looked at the window, but it was screened. Joe stood out like a rough-backed mountain between him and the door. Barring him from escape, from sunrise, from life.

He considered a surprise attack upon the big clown that stood there laughing like a chessy cat. But before his fist could travel an inch, Joe's own rushed out to crush him like a battering ram. Then Joe stood over him.

75 "Git into yo' damn rags, Slemmons, and dat quick."

Slemmons scrambled to his feet and into his vest and coat. As he grabbed his hat, Joe's fury overrode his intentions and he grabbed at Slemmons with his left hand and struck at him with his right. The right landed. The left grazed the front of his vest. Slemmons was knocked a somersault into the kitchen and fled through the open door. Joe found himself alone with Missie May, with the golden watch charm clutched in his left fist. A short bit of broken chain dangled between his fingers.

Missie May was sobbing. Wails of weeping without words. Joe stood, and after awhile he found out that he had something in his hand. And then he stood and felt without thinking and without seeing with his natural eyes. Missie May kept on crying and Joe kept on feeling so much and not knowing what to do with all his feelings, he put Slemmons' watch charm in his pants pocket and took a good laugh and went to bed.

"Missie May, whut you cryin' for?"

"Cause Ah love you so hard and Ah know you don't love *me* no mo'."

80 Joe sank his face into the pillow for a spell then he said huskily, "You don't know de feelings of dat yet, Missie May."

"Oh Joe, honey, he said he wuz gointer give me dat gold money and he jes' kept on after me—"

Joe was very still and silent for a long time. Then he said, "Well, don't cry no mo', Missie May. Ah got yo' gold piece for you."

The hours went past on their rusty ankles. Joe still and quiet on one bed-rail and Missie May wrung dry of sobs on the other. Finally the sun's tide crept upon the shore of night and drowned all its hours. Missie May with her face stiff and streaked towards the window saw the dawn come into her yard. It was day. Nothing more. Joe wouldn't be coming home as usual. No need to fling open the front door and sweep off the porch, making it nice for Joe. Never no more breakfast to cook; no more washing and starching of Joe's jumper-jackets and pants. No more nothing. So why get up?

With this strange man in her bed, she felt embarrassed to get up and dress. She decided to wait till he had dressed and gone. Then she would get up, dress quickly and be gone forever beyond reach of Joe's looks and laughs. But he never moved. Red light turned to yellow, then white.

85 From beyond the no-man's land between them came a voice. A strange voice that yesterday had been Joe's.

"Missie May, ain't you gonna fix me no breakfus'?"

She sprang out of bed. "Yeah, Joe. Ah didn't reckon you wuz hongry."

No need to die today. Joe needed her for a few more minutes anyhow.

Soon there was a roaring fire in the cook stove. Water bucket full and two chickens killed. Joe loved fried chicken and rice. She didn't deserve a thing and good Joe was letting her cook him some breakfast. She rushed hot biscuits to the table as Joe took his seat.

90 He ate with his eyes in his plate. No laughter, no banter.

"Missie May, you ain't eatin' yo' breakfus'."

"Ah don't choose none, Ah thank yuh."

His coffee cup was empty. She sprang to refill it. When she turned from the stove and bent to set the cup beside Joe's plate, she saw the yellow coin on the table between them.

She slumped into her seat and wept into her arms.

95 Presently Joe said calmly, "Missie May, you cry too much. Don't look back lak Lot's wife and turn to salt."

The sun, the hero of every day, the impersonal old man that beams as brightly on death as on birth, came up every morning and raced across the blue dome and dipped into the sea of fire every evening. Water ran down hill and birds nested.

Missie knew why she didn't leave Joe. She couldn't. She loved him too much, but she could not understand why Joe didn't leave her. He was polite, even kind at times, but aloof.

There were no more Saturday romps. No ringing silver dollars to stack beside her plate. No pockets to rifle. In fact the yellow coin in his trousers was like a monster hiding in the cave of his pockets to destroy her.

She often wondered if he still had it, but nothing could have induced her to ask nor yet to explore his pockets to see for herself. Its shadow was in the house whether or no.

100 One night Joe came home around midnight and complained of pains in the back. He asked Missie to rub him down with liniment. It had been three months since Missie had touched his body and it all seemed strange. But she rubbed him. Grateful for the chance. Before morning, youth triumphed and Missie exulted. But the next day, as she joyfully made up their bed, beneath her pillow she found the piece of money with the bit of chain attached.

Alone to herself, she looked at the thing with loathing, but look she must. She took it into her hands with trembling and saw first thing that it was no gold piece. It was a gilded half dollar. Then she knew why Slemmons had forbidden anyone to touch his gold. He trusted village eyes at a distance not to recognize his stick-pin as a gilded quarter, and his watch charm as a four-bit piece.

She was glad at first that Joe had left it there. Perhaps he was through with her punishment. They were man and wife again. Then another thought came clawing at her. He had come home to buy from her as if she were any woman in the long house. Fifty cents for her love. As if to say that he could pay as well as Slemmons. She slid the coin into his Sunday pants pocket and dressed herself and left his house.

Halfway between her house and the quarters she met her husband's mother, and after a short talk she turned and went back home. Never would she admit defeat to that woman who prayed for it nightly. If she had not the substance of marriage she had the outside show. Joe must leave *her*. She let him see she didn't want his gold four-bits too.

She saw no more of the coin for some time though she knew that Joe could not help finding it in his pocket. But his health kept poor, and he came home at least every ten days to be rubbed.

105 The sun swept around the horizon, trailing its robes of weeks and days. One morning as Joe came in from work, he found Missie May chopping wood. Without a word he took the ax and chopped a huge pile before he stopped.

"You ain't got no business choppin' wood, and you know it."

"How come? Ah been choppin' it for de last longest."

"Ah ain't blind. You makin' feet for shoes."

"Won't you be glad to have a lil baby chile, Joe?"

110 "You know dat 'thout astin' me."

"Iss gointer be a boy chile and de very spit of you."

"You reckon, Missie May?"

"Who else could it look lak?"

Joe said nothing, but he thrust his hand deep into his pocket and fingered something there.

115 It was almost six months later Missie May took to bed and Joe went and got his mother to come wait on the house.

Missie May was delivered of a fine boy. Her travail was over when Joe came in from work one morning. His mother and the old women were drinking great bowls of coffee around the fire in the kitchen.

The minute Joe came into the room his mother called him aside.

"How did Missie May make out?" he asked quickly.

"Who, dat gal? She strong as a ox. She gointer have plenty mo'. We done fixed her wid de sugar and lard to sweeten her for de nex' one."

Joe stood silent awhile.

"You ain't ast 'bout de baby, Joe. You oughter be mighty proud cause he sho is de spittin' image of yuh, son. Dat's yourn all right, if you never git another one, dat un is yourn. And you know Ah'm mighty proud too, son, cause Ah never thought well of you marryin' Missie May cause her ma used tuh fan her foot round right smart and Ah been mighty skeered dat Missie May wuz gointer git misput on her road."

Joe said nothing. He fooled around the house till late in the day then just before he went to work, he went and stood at the foot of the bed and asked his wife how she felt. He did this every day during the week.

On Saturday he went to Orlando to make his market. It had been a long time since he had done that.

Meat and lard, meal and flour, soap and starch. Cans of corn and tomatoes. All the staples. He fooled around town for awhile and bought bananas and apples. Way after while he went around to the candy store.

"Hello, Joe," the clerk greeted him. "Ain't seen you in a long time."

"Nope, Ah ain't been heah. Been round in spots and places."

"Want some of them molasses kisses you always buy?"

"Yessuh." He threw the gilded half dollar on the counter. "Will dat spend?"

"What is it, Joe? Well, I'll be doggone! A gold-plated four-bit piece. Where'd you git it, Joe?"

"Offen a stray nigger dat come through Eatonville. He had it on his watch chain for a charm—goin' round making out iss gold money. Ha ha! He had a quarter on his tie pin and it wuz all golded up too. Tryin' to fool people. Makin' out he so rich and everything. Ha! Ha! Tryin' to tole off folkses wives from home."

"How did you git it, Joe? Did he fool you, too?"

"Who, me? Naw suh! He ain't fooled me none. Know whut Ah done? He come round me wid his smart talk. Ah hauled off and knocked 'im down and took his old four-bits way from 'im. Gointer buy my wife some good ole lasses kisses wid it. Gimme fifty cents worth of dem candy kisses."

"Fifty cents buys a mighty lot of candy kisses, Joe. Why don't you split it up and take some chocolate bars, too? They eat good, too."

"Yessuh, dey do, but Ah wants all dat in kisses. Ah got a lil boy chile home now. Tain't a week old yet, but he kin suck a sugar tit and maybe eat one them kisses hisself."

Joe got his candy and left the store. The clerk turned to the next customer. "Wisht I could be like these darkies. Laughin' all the time. Nothin' worries 'em."

Back in Eatonville, Joe reached his own front door. There was the ring of singing metal on wood. Fifteen times. Missie May couldn't run to the door, but she crept there as quickly as she could.

"Joe Banks, Ah hear you chunkin' money in mah do'way. You wait till Ah got mah strength back and Ah'm gointer fix you for dat."

Hurston is a Southern writer whose work you might consider in context with that of William Faulkner, Flannery O'Connor, and Ralph Ellison, all in the case study on the American South in chapter 12.

**GOING FURTHER** Hurston, a native of Alabama, did primary anthropological research among black populations in Florida and hobnobbed with the New York intellectual crowd in Manhattan during the period known as the Harlem Renaissance. Contemporary black American women writers such as Alice Walker and Toni Morrison point to her as an ancestor; the former's *The Color Purple* and the latter's *Song of Solomon* and *Beloved* owe much to the example of *Their Eyes Were Watching God.*

# Ursula K. Le Guin (b. 1929)

ONE OF THE foremost writers of imaginative fiction in our time, Ursula K. Le Guin was born Ursula Kroeber in Berkeley, California. Her parents were the anthropologist Alfred Kroeber and the writer Theodora Kroeber, author of *Ishi.* Although Le Guin is widely known as a science-fiction writer, her most successful and best-known books—novels such as *The Left Hand of Darkness* (1969) and *The Dispossessed* (1974), and her short fiction in collections such as *The Wind's Twelve Quarters* (1975) and *The Compass Rose* (1982)—have always expressed a certain anthropological cast of mind reminiscent of her parents' scientific study of human habits and customs.

Few writers working in a particular genre—in Le Guin's case, science fiction—have had such success as a "cross-over" writer, publishing stories in both popular and genre magazines, from *Galaxy* and *Fantasy & Science Fiction* to *The New Yorker,* and winning Hugo and Nebula awards for outstanding science fiction while garnering such prestigious literary prizes as the PEN/Malamud Award for Excellence in the Short Story. Le Guin has also written many volumes of fantasy fiction, childrens' books, and essays.

## The Kerastion (1994)

FOR ROUSSEL SARGENT, WHO INVENTED IT

1 The small caste of the Tanners was a sacred one. To eat food prepared by a Tanner would entail a year's purification to a Tinker or a Sculptor, and even low-power castes such as the Traders had to be cleansed by a night's ablutions after dealing for leather goods. Chumo had been a Tanner since she was five years old and had heard the willows whisper all night long at the Singing Sands. She had had her proving day, and since then had worn a Tanner's madder-red and blue shirt and doublet, woven of linen on a willow-wood loom. She had made her masterpiece, and since then had worn the Master Tanner's neckband of dried vauti-tuber incised with the double line and double circles. So clothed and ornamented she stood among the willows by the burying ground, waiting for the funeral procession of her brother, who had broken the law and betrayed his caste. She stood erect and silent, gazing towards the village by the river and listening for the drum.

She did not think; she did not want to think. But she saw her brother Kwatewa in the reeds down by the river, running ahead of her, a little boy too young to have caste, too young to be polluted by the sacred, a crazy little boy pouncing on her out of the tall reeds shouting, "I'm a mountain lion!"

A serious little boy watching the river run, asking, "Does it ever stop? Why can't it stop running, Chumo?"

A five-year-old coming back from the Singing Sands, coming straight to her, bringing her the joy, the crazy, serious joy that shone in his round face—"Chumo! I heard the sand singing! I heard it! I have to be a Sculptor, Chumo!"

5 She had stood still. She had not held out her arms. And he had checked his run towards her and stood still, the light going out of his face. She was only his wombsister. He would have truesibs, now. He and she were of different castes. They would not touch again.

Ten years after that day she had come with most of the townsfolk to Kwatewa's proving day, to see the sand-sculpture he had made in the Great Plain Place where the Sculptors performed their art. Not a breath of wind had yet rounded off the keen edges or leveled the lovely curves of the classic form he had executed with such verve and sureness, the Body of Amakumo. She saw admiration and envy in the faces of his truebrothers and truesisters. Standing aside among the sacred castes, she heard the speaker of the Sculptors dedicate Kwatewa's proving piece to Amakumo. As his voice ceased a wind came out of the desert north, Amakumo's wind, the maker hungry for the made—Amakumo the Mother eating her body, eating herself. Even while they watched, the wind destroyed Kwatewa's sculpture. Soon there was only a shapeless lump and a feathering of white sand blown across the proving ground. Beauty had gone back to the Mother. That the sculpture had been destroyed so soon and so utterly was a great honor to the maker.

The funeral procession was approaching. She heard or imagined she heard the drumbeat, soft, no more than a heartbeat.

Her own proving piece had been the traditional one for Tanner women, a drumhead. Not a funeral drum but a dancing drum, loud, gaudy with red paint and tassels. "Your drumhead, your maidenhead!" her truebrothers called it, and made fierce teasing jokes, but they couldn't make her blush. Tanners had no business blushing. They were outside shame. It had been an excellent drum, chosen at once from the proving ground by an old Musician, who had played it so much she soon wore off the bright paint and lost the red tassels; but the drumhead lasted through the winter and till the Roppi Ceremony, when it finally split wide open during the drumming for the all-night dancing under the moons, when Chumo and Karwa first twined their wristplaits. Chumo had been proud all winter when she heard the voice of her drum loud and clear across the dancing ground, she had been proud when it split and gave itself to the Mother; but that had been nothing to the pride she had felt in Kwatewa's sculptures. For if the work be well done and the thing made be powerful, it belongs to the Mother. She will desire it; she will not wait for it to give itself, but will take it. So the child dying young is called the Mother's Child. Beauty, the most sacred of all things, is hers; the body of the Mother is the most beautiful of all things. So all that is made in the likeness of the Mother is made in sand.

To keep your work, to try to keep it for yourself, to take her body from her. Kwatewa! How could you, how could you, my brother? her heart said. But she put the question back into the silence and stood silent among the willows, the trees sacred to her caste, watching the funeral procession come between the flaxfields. It was his shame, not hers. What was shame to a Tanner? It was pride she felt, pride. For that was her masterpiece that Dastuye the Musician held now and raised to his lips as he walked before the procession, guiding the new ghost to its body's grave.

10 She had made that instrument, the kerastion, the flute that is played only at a funeral. The kerastion is made of leather, and the leather is tanned human skin, and the skin is that of the wombmother or the foremother of the dead.

When Wekuri, wombmother of Chumo and Kwatewa, had died two winters ago, Chumo the Tanner had claimed her privilege. There had been an old, old kerastion to play at Wekuri's funeral, handed down from her grandmothers; but the Musician, when he had finished playing it, laid it on the mats that wrapped Wekuri in the open grave. For the night before, Chumo had flayed the left arm of the body, singing the songs of power of her caste as she worked, the songs that ask the dead mother to put her voice, her song into the instrument. She had kept and cured the piece of rawhide, rubbing it with the secret cures, wrapping it round a clay cylinder to harden, wetting it, oiling it, forming it and refining its form, till the clay went to powder and was knocked from the tube, which she then cleaned and rubbed and oiled and finished. It was a privilege which only the most powerful, the most truly shameless of the Tanners took, to make a kerastion of the mother's skin. Chumo had claimed it without fear or doubt. As she worked she had many times pictured the Musician leading the procession, playing the flute, guiding her own spirit to its grave. She had wondered which of the Musicians it might be, and who would follow her, walking in her funeral procession. Never once had she thought that it would be played for Kwatewa before it was played for her. How was she to think of him, so much younger, dying first?

He had killed himself out of shame. He had cut his wrist veins with one of the tools he had made to cut stone.

His death itself was no shame, since there had been nothing for him to do but die. There was no fine, no ablution, no purification, for what he had done.

Shepherds had found the cave where he had kept the stones, great marble pieces from the cave walls, carved into copies of his own sandsculptures, his own sacred work for the Solstice and the Hariba: sculptures of stone, abominable, durable, desecrations of the body of the Mother.

15 People of his caste had destroyed the things with hammers, beaten them to dust and sand, swept the sand down into the river. She had thought Kwatewa would follow them, but he had gone to the cave at night and taken the sharp tool and cut his wrists and let his blood run. Why can't it stop running, Chumo?

The Musician had come abreast of her now as she stood among the willows by the burying ground. Dastuye was old and skillful; his slow dancewalk seemed to float him above the ground in rhythm with the soft heartbeat of the drum that followed. Guiding the spirit and the body on its litter borne by four casteless men, he played the kerastion. His lips lay light on the leather mouthpiece, his fingers moved lightly as he played, and there was no sound at all. The kerastion flute has no stops and both its ends are plugged with disks of bronze. Tunes played on it are not heard by living ears. Chumo, listening, heard the drum and the whisper of the north wind in the willow leaves. Only Kwatewa in his woven grass shroud on the litter heard what song the Musician played for him, and knew whether it was a song of shame, or of grief, or of welcome.

If you like this story, you may also enjoy the use of the fantastic in Franz Kafka's "The Metamorphosis" and in Nathaniel Hawthorne's "Young Goodman Brown" (both in chapter 10).

**GOING FURTHER** The ranks of interesting American science-fiction writers are broad and deep. A British novelist who, like Le Guin, employs science-fiction motifs for other purposes is the prize-winning writer Jeanette Winterson, whose novel *The Stone Gods* (2008) crosses over into mainstream fiction.

## Katherine Mansfield (1888–1923)

KATHERINE MANSFIELD, ONE of the finest practitioners of the modern short story in English, was born Kathleen Mansfield Beauchamp in Wellington, New Zealand. As an adolescent she traveled to England to study and eventually left New Zealand permanently to make a life in bohemian literary circles in London and Europe.

Her short stories, influenced by Chekhov but glowing with a mastery all their own, won her both the praise and the envy of such modernist writers as Virginia Woolf. She died too young to leave behind a major body of work, but her eye for detail and sense of nuanced emotion have assured her a place in the circle of important writers of the twentieth century.

# Miss Brill (1920)

1 Although it was so brilliantly fine—the blue sky powdered with gold and great spots of light like white wine splashed over the Jardins Publiques—Miss Brill was glad that she had decided on her fur. The air was motionless, but when you opened your mouth there was just a faint chill, like a chill from a glass of iced water before you sip, and now and again a leaf came drifting—from nowhere, from the sky. Miss Brill put up her hand and touched her fur. Dear little thing! It was nice to feel it again. She had taken it out of its box that afternoon, shaken out the moth powder, given it a good brush, and rubbed the life back into the dim little eyes. "What has been happening to me?" said the sad little eyes. Oh, how sweet it was to see them snap at her again from the red eiderdown! . . . But the nose, which was of some black composition, wasn't at all firm. It must have had a knock, somehow. Never mind—a little dab of black sealing-wax when the time came—when it was absolutely necessary . . . Little rogue! Yes, she really felt like that

about it. Little rogue biting its tail just by her left ear. She could have taken it off and laid it on her lap and stroked it. She felt a tingling in her hands and arms, but that came from walking, she supposed. And when she breathed, something light and sad—no, not sad, exactly—something gentle seemed to move in her bosom.

There were a number of people out this afternoon, far more than last Sunday. And the band sounded louder and gayer. That was because the Season had begun. For although the band played all the year round on Sundays, out of season it was never the same. It was like some one playing with only the family to listen; it didn't care how it played if there weren't any strangers present. Wasn't the conductor wearing a new coat, too? She was sure it was new. He scraped with his foot and flapped his arms like a rooster about to crow, and the bandsmen sitting in the green rotunda blew out their cheeks and glared at the music. Now there came a little "flutey" bit—very pretty!—a little chain of bright drops. She was sure it would be repeated. It was; she lifted her head and smiled.

Only two people shared her "special" seat: a fine old man in a velvet coat, his hands clasped over a huge carved walking-stick, and a big old woman, sitting upright, with a roll of knitting on her embroidered apron. They did not speak. This was disappointing, for Miss Brill always looked forward to the conversation. She had become really quite expert, she thought, at listening as though she didn't listen, at sitting in other people's lives just for a minute while they talked round her.

She glanced, sideways, at the old couple. Perhaps they would go soon. Last Sunday, too, hadn't been as interesting as usual. An Englishman and his wife, he wearing a dreadful Panama hat and she button boots. And she'd gone on the whole time about how she ought to wear spectacles; she knew she needed them; but that it was no good getting any; they'd be sure to break and they'd never keep on. And he'd been so patient. He'd suggested everything—gold rims, the kind that curve round your ears, little pads inside the bridge. No, nothing would please her. "They'll always be sliding down my nose!" Miss Brill had wanted to shake her.

5 The old people sat on the bench, still as statues. Never mind, there was always the crowd to watch. To and fro, in front of the flower beds and the band rotunda, the couples and groups paraded, stopped to talk, to greet, to buy a handful of flowers from the old beggar who had his tray fixed to the railings. Little children ran among them, swooping and laughing; little boys with big white silk bows under their chins, little girls, little French dolls, dressed up in velvet and lace. And sometimes a tiny staggerer came suddenly rocking into the open from under the trees, stopped, stared, as suddenly sat down "flop," until its small high-stepping mother, like a young hen, rushed scolding to its rescue. Other people sat on the benches and green chairs, but they were nearly always the same, Sunday after Sunday, and—Miss Brill had often noticed—there was something funny about nearly all of them. They were odd, silent, nearly all old, and from the way they stared they looked as though they'd just come from dark little rooms or even—even cupboards!

Behind the rotunda the slender trees with yellow leaves down drooping, and through them just a line of sea, and beyond the blue sky with gold-veined clouds.

Tum-tum-tum tiddle-um! tiddle-um! tum tiddley-um tum ta! blew the band.

Two young girls in red came by and two young soldiers in blue met them, and they laughed and paired and went off arm-in-arm. Two peasant women with funny straw hats passed, gravely, leading beautiful smoke-colored donkeys. A cold, pale nun hurried by. A beautiful woman came along and dropped her bunch of violets, and a little boy ran after to hand them to her, and she took them and threw them away as if they'd been poisoned. Dear me! Miss Brill didn't know whether to admire that or not! And now an ermine toque and a gentleman in gray met just in front of her. He was tall, stiff, dignified, and she was wearing the ermine toque she'd bought when her hair was yellow. Now everything, her hair, her face, even her eyes, was the same color as the shabby ermine, and her hand, in its cleaned glove, lifted to dab her lips, was a tiny yellowish paw. Oh, she was so pleased to see him—delighted! She rather thought they were going to meet that afternoon. She described where she'd been—everywhere, here, there, along by the sea. The day was so charming—didn't he agree? And wouldn't he, perhaps? . . . But he shook his head, lighted a cigarette, slowly breathed a great deep puff into her face, and, even while she was still talking and laughing, flicked the match away and walked on. The ermine toque was alone; she smiled more brightly than ever. But even the band seemed to know what she was feeling and played more softly, played tenderly, and the drum beat, "The Brute! The Brute!" over and over. What would she do? What was going to happen now? But as Miss Brill wondered, the ermine toque turned, raised her hand as though she'd seen some one else, much nicer, just over there, and pattered away. And the band changed again and played more quickly, more gayly than ever, and the old couple on Miss Brill's seat got up and marched away, and such a funny old man with long whiskers hobbled along in time to the music and was nearly knocked over by four girls walking abreast.

Oh, how fascinating it was! How she enjoyed it! How she loved sitting here, watching it all! It was like a play. It was exactly like a play. Who could believe the sky at the back wasn't painted? But it wasn't till a little brown dog trotted on solemn and then slowly trotted off, like a little "theater" dog, a little dog that had been drugged, that Miss Brill discovered what it was that made it so exciting. They were all on stage. They weren't only the audience, not only looking on; they were acting. Even she had a part and came every Sunday. No doubt somebody would have noticed if she hadn't been there; she was part of the performance after all. How strange she'd never thought of it like that before! And yet it explained why she made such a point of starting from home at just the same time each week—so as not to be late for the performance—and it also explained why she had quite a queer, shy feeling at telling her English pupils how she spent her Sunday afternoons. No wonder! Miss Brill nearly laughed out loud. She was on the stage. She thought of the old invalid gentleman to whom she read the newspaper four afternoons a week while he slept in the garden. She had got quite used to the frail head on the cotton pillow, the hollowed eyes, the open mouth and the high pinched nose. If he'd been dead she mightn't have noticed for weeks; she wouldn't have minded. But suddenly he knew he was having the paper read to him by an actress! "An actress!" The old head lifted; two points of light quivered in the old eyes. "An actress—are ye?" And Miss Brill smoothed the newspaper as though it were the manuscript of her part and said gently: "Yes, I have been an actress for a long time."

10 The band had been having a rest. Now they started again. And what they played was warm, sunny, yet there was just a faint chill—a something, what was it?—not sadness—no, not sadness—a something that made you want to sing. The tune lifted, lifted, the light shone; and it seemed to Miss Brill that in another moment all of them, all the whole company, would begin singing. The young ones, the laughing ones who were moving together, they would begin, and the men's voices, very resolute and brave, would join them. And then she too, she too, and the others on the benches—they would come in with a kind of accompaniment—something low, that scarcely rose or fell, something so beautiful—moving . . . And Miss Brill's eyes filled with tears and she looked smiling at all the other members of the company. Yes, we understand, we understand, she thought—though what they understood she didn't know.

Just at that moment a boy and girl came and sat down where the old couple had been. They were beautifully dressed; they were in love. The hero and heroine, of course, just arrived from his father's yacht. And still soundlessly singing, still with that trembling smile, Miss Brill prepared to listen.

"No, not now," said the girl. "Not here, I can't."

"But why? Because of that stupid old thing at the end there?" asked the boy. "Why does she come here at all—who wants her? Why doesn't she keep her silly old mug at home?"

"It's her fu-fur which is so funny," giggled the girl. "It's exactly like a fried whiting."

15 "Ah, be off with you!" said the boy in an angry whisper. Then: "Tell me, ma petite chère—"

"No, not here," said the girl. "Not *yet*."

On her way home she usually bought a slice of honeycake at the baker's. It was her Sunday treat. Sometimes there was an almond in her slice, sometimes not. It made a great difference. If there was an almond it was like carrying home a tiny present—a surprise—something that might very well not have been there. She hurried on the almond Sundays and struck the match for the kettle in quite a dashing way.

But today she passed the baker's by, climbed the stairs, went into the little dark room—her room like a cupboard—and sat down on the red eiderdown. She sat there for a long time. The box that the fur came out of was on the bed. She unclasped the necklet quickly; quickly, without looking, laid it inside. But when she put the lid on she thought she heard something crying.

If you like this story, you may also like Katherine Anne Porter's "The Jilting of Granny Weatherall" and other character studies in chapter 5. You might ask yourself how Mansfield's drawing of character compares with those found in that chapter.

**GOING FURTHER** You may want to read her work alongside the dark psychological portraits, in *Mrs. Dalloway* or *To the Lighthouse,* by her contemporary Virginia Woolf.

# Herman Melville (1819–1891)

WHEN HERMAN MELVILLE died of a heart attack in 1891, his name was virtually unknown. His obituary in *Harper's* magazine consisted of only one line—and they got his age wrong: *September 27—In New York City, Herman Melville, aged seventy-three years* (he was actually seventy-two). Today he is considered one of our greatest writers, known for having produced what many critics consider America's most important novel, *Moby-Dick; or The Whale.* When he was a young man his desire for independence (financial and personal) led him to find work as a sailor. The sea and the ships that travel upon it were major subjects for many of Melville's fictions—including the novels *Typee* and *Omoo,* which report on his adventures in the South Seas, and his last brief masterpiece, the novella *Billy Budd.*

Melville spent much of the middle of his life in New England, where he forged a strong friendship with Nathaniel Hawthorne. As Melville's writing matured, his interest in metaphysics (the philosophy of being and reality) increasingly influenced his work. However, the complexity of his fiction was unappreciated if not unnoticed, and after the publication of several commercially unsuccessful novels, among them *Moby-Dick,* Melville stopped writing prose and took a job as a customs inspector in New York City. His description, here, of city life reads almost like a clinical analysis of both depression and the impersonal, corporate world; the famous phrase "I prefer not to" has become an emblem of passive resistance. It is the oppressiveness of this conventional, urban existence that Melville captures so poignantly in "Bartleby, the Scrivener."

# Bartleby, the Scrivener (1853)

## A STORY OF WALL STREET

1 I am a rather elderly man. The nature of my avocations, for the last thirty years, has brought me into more than ordinary contact with what would seem an interesting and somewhat singular set of men, of whom, as yet, nothing, that I know of, has ever been written—I mean, the law-copyists, or scriveners. I have known very many of them, professionally and privately, and, if I pleased, could relate divers histories, at which good-natured gentlemen might smile, and sentimental souls might weep. But I waive the biographies of all other scriveners, for a few passages in the life of Bartleby, who was a scrivener, the strangest I ever saw, or heard of. While, of other law-copyists, I might write the complete life, of Bartleby nothing of that sort can be done. I believe that no materials exist, for a full and satisfactory biography of this man. It is an irreparable loss to literature. Bartleby was one of those beings of whom nothing is ascertainable, except from the original sources, and in

his case, those are very small. What my own astonished eyes saw of Bartleby, *that* is all I know of him, except, indeed, one vague report, which will appear in the sequel.

Ere introducing the scrivener, as he first appeared to me, it is fit I make some mention of myself, my *employés,* my business, my chambers, and general surroundings, because some such description is indispensable to an adequate understanding of the chief character about to be presented. Imprimis: I am a man who, from his youth upwards, has been filled with a profound conviction that the easiest way of life is the best. Hence, though I belong to a profession proverbially energetic and nervous, even to turbulence, at times, yet nothing of that sort have I ever suffered to invade my peace. I am one of those unambitious lawyers who never address a jury, or in any way draw down public applause; but, in the cool tranquillity of a snug retreat, do a snug business among rich men's bonds and mortgages and title-deeds. All who know me consider me an eminently *safe* man. The late John Jacob Astor, a personage little given to poetic enthusiasm, had no hesitation in pronouncing my first grand point to be prudence; my next, method. I do not speak it in vanity, but simply record the fact, that I was not unemployed in my profession by the late John Jacob Astor; a name which, I admit, I love to repeat; for it hath a rounded and orbicular sound to it, and rings like unto bullion. I will freely add, that I was not insensible to the late John Jacob Astor's good opinion.

Some time prior to the period at which this little history begins, my avocations had been largely increased. The good old office, now extinct in the State of New York, of a Master in Chancery, had been conferred upon me. It was not a very arduous office, but very pleasantly remunerative. I seldom lose my temper; much more seldom indulge in dangerous indignation at wrongs and outrages; but I must be permitted to be rash here and declare, that I consider the sudden and violent abrogation of the office of Master of Chancery, by the new Constitution, as a —— premature act; inasmuch as I had counted upon a life-lease of the profits, whereas I only received those of a few short years. But this is by the way.

My chambers were up stairs at No. — Wall Street. At one end, they looked upon the white wall of the interior of a spacious skylight shaft, penetrating the building from top to bottom.

5 This view might have been considered rather tame than otherwise, deficient in what landscape painters call "life." But, if so, the view from the other end of my chambers offered, at least, a contrast, if nothing more. In that direction, my windows commanded an unobstructed view of a lofty brick wall, black by age and everlasting shade; which wall required no spyglass to bring out its lurking beauties, but, for the benefit of all near-sighted spectators, was pushed up to within ten feet of my window-panes. Owing to the great height of the surrounding buildings, and my chambers being on the second floor, the interval between this wall and mine not a little resembled a huge square cistern.

At the period just preceding the advent of Bartleby, I had two persons as copyists in my employment, and a promising lad as an office-boy. First, Turkey; second, Nippers; third, Ginger Nut. These may seem names, the like of which are not usually found in the Directory. In truth, they were nicknames, mutually conferred upon each other by my three clerks, and were deemed expressive of their respective persons or characters. Turkey was a short, pursy Englishman, of about my own age—that is, somewhere not far from sixty. In the morning, one might say, his face was of a fine florid hue, but after twelve o'clock, meridian—his dinner hour—it blazed like a grate full of Christmas coals; and continued blazing—but, as it were, with a gradual wane—till six o'clock, P.M., or thereabouts; after which, I saw no more of the proprietor of the face, which, gaining its meridian with the sun, seemed to set with it, to rise, culminate, and decline the following day, with the like regularity and undiminished glory. There are many singular coincidences I have known in the course of my life, not the least among which was the fact, that, exactly when Turkey displayed his fullest beams from his red and radiant countenance, just then, too, at that critical moment, began the daily period when I considered his business capacities as seriously disturbed for the remainder of the twenty-four hours. Not that he was absolutely idle, or averse to business then; far from it. The difficulty was, he was apt to be altogether too energetic. There was a strange, inflamed, flurried, flighty recklessness of activity about him. He would be incautious in dipping his pen into his inkstand. All his blots upon my documents were dropped there after twelve o'clock, meridian. Indeed, not only would he be reckless, and sadly given to making blots in the afternoon, but, some days, he went further, and was rather noisy. At such times, too, his face flamed with augmented blazonry, as if cannel coal had been heaped on anthracite. He made an unpleasant racket with his chair; spilled his sand-box; in mending his pens, impatiently split them all to pieces, and threw them on the floor in a sudden passion; stood up, and leaned over his table, boxing his papers about in a most indecorous manner, very sad to behold in an elderly man like him. Nevertheless, as he was in many ways a most valuable person to me, and all the time before twelve o'clock, meridian, was the quickest, steadiest creature, too, accomplishing a great deal of work in a style not easily to be matched—for these reasons, I was willing to overlook his eccentricities, though, indeed, occasionally, I remonstrated with him. I did this very gently, however, because, though the civilest, nay, the blandest and most reverential of men in the morning, yet, in the afternoon, he was disposed, upon provocation, to be slightly rash with his tongue—in fact, insolent. Now, valuing his morning services as I did, and resolved not to lose them—yet, at the same time, made uncomfortable by his inflamed ways after twelve o'clock—and being a man of peace, unwilling by my admonitions to call forth unseemly retorts from him, I took upon me, one Saturday noon (he was always worse on Saturdays) to hint to him, very kindly, that, perhaps, now that he was growing old, it might be well to abridge his labors; in short, he need not come to my chambers after twelve o'clock, but, dinner over, had best go home to his lodgings, and rest himself till tea-time. But no; he insisted upon his afternoon devotions. His countenance became intolerably fervid, as he oratorically assured me—gesticulating with a long ruler at the other end of the room—that if his services in the morning were useful, how indispensable, then, in the afternoon?

"With submission, sir," said Turkey, on this occasion, "I consider myself your right-hand man. In the morning I but marshal and deploy my columns; but in the afternoon I put myself at their head, and gallantly charge the foe, thus"—and he made a violent thrust with the ruler.

"But the blots, Turkey," intimated I.

"True; but, with submission, sir, behold these hairs! I am getting old. Surely, sir, a blot or two of a warm afternoon is not to be severely urged against gray hairs. Old age—even if it blot the page—is honorable. With submission, sir, we *both* are getting old."

10 This appeal to my fellow-feeling was hardly to be resisted. At all events, I saw that go he would not. So, I made up my mind to let him stay, resolving, nevertheless, to see to it that, during the afternoon, he had to do with my less important papers.

Nippers, the second on my list, was a whiskered, sallow, and, upon the whole, rather piratical-looking young man of about five-and-twenty. I always deemed him the victim of two evil powers—ambition and indigestion. The ambition was evinced by a certain impatience of the duties of a mere copyist, an unwarrantable usurpation of strictly professional affairs such as the original drawing up of legal documents. The indigestion seemed betokened in an occasional nervous testiness and grinning irritability, causing the teeth to audibly grind together over mistakes committed in copying; unnecessary maledictions, hissed, rather than spoken, in the heat of business; and especially by a continual discontent with the height of the table where he worked. Though of a very ingenious mechanical turn, Nippers could never get this table to suit him. He put chips under it, blocks of various sorts, bits of pasteboard, and at last went so far as to attempt an exquisite adjustment, by final pieces of folded blotting-paper. But no invention would answer. If, for the sake of easing his back, he brought the table-lid at a sharp angle well up towards his chin, and wrote there like a man using the steep roof of a Dutch house for his desk, then he declared that it stopped the circulation in his arms. If now he lowered the table to his waistbands, and stooped over it in writing, then there was a sore aching in his back. In short, the truth of the matter was, Nippers knew not what he wanted. Or, if he wanted anything, it was to be rid of a scrivener's table altogether. Among the manifestations of his diseased ambition was a fondness he had for receiving visits from certain ambiguous-looking fellows in seedy coats, whom he called his clients. Indeed, I was aware that not only was he, at times, considerable of a ward-politician, but he occasionally did a little business at the justices' courts, and was not unknown on the steps of the Tombs. I have good reason to believe, however, that one individual who called upon him at my chambers, and who, with a grand air, he insisted was his client, was no other than a dun, and the alleged title-deed, a bill. But, with all his failings, and the annoyances he caused me, Nippers, like his compatriot Turkey, was a very useful man to me; wrote a neat, swift hand; and, when he chose, was not deficient in a gentlemanly sort of deportment. Added to this, he always dressed in a gentlemanly sort of way; and so, incidentally, reflected credit upon my chambers. Whereas, with respect to Turkey, I had much ado to keep him from being a reproach to me. His clothes were apt to look oily, a smell of eating-houses. He wore his pantaloons very loose and baggy in summer. His coats were execrable, his hat not to be handled. But while the hat was a thing of indifference to me, inasmuch as his natural civility and deference, as a dependent Englishman, always led him to doff it the moment he entered the room, yet his coat was another matter. Concerning his coats, I reasoned with him; but with no effect. The truth was, I suppose, that a man with so small an income, could not afford to sport such a lustrous face and a lustrous coat at one and the same time. As Nippers once observed, Turkey's money went chiefly for red ink. One winter day, I presented Turkey with a highly respectable-looking coat of my own—a padded gray coat, of a most comfortable warmth, and which buttoned straight up from the knee to the neck. I thought Turkey would appreciate the favor, and abate his rashness and obstreperousness of afternoons. But no; I verily believe that buttoning himself up in so downy and blanket-like a coat had a pernicious effect upon him—upon the same principle that too much oats are bad for horses. In fact, precisely as a rash, restive horse is said to feel his oats, so Turkey felt his coat. It made him insolent. He was a man whom prosperity harmed.

Though, concerning the self-indulgent habits of Turkey, I had my own private surmises, yet, touching Nippers, I was well persuaded that, whatever might be his faults in other respects, he was, at least, a temperate young man. But indeed, nature herself seemed to have been his vintner, and, at his birth, charged him so thoroughly with an irritable, brandy-like disposition, that all subsequent potations were needless. When I consider how, amid the stillness of my chambers, Nippers would sometimes impatiently rise from his seat, and stooping over his table, spread his arms wide apart, seize the whole desk, and move it, and jerk it, with a grim, grinding motion on the floor, as if the table were a perverse voluntary agent, intent on thwarting and vexing him, I plainly perceive that, for Nippers, brandy-and-water were altogether superfluous.

It was fortunate for me that, owing to its peculiar cause—indigestion—the irritability and consequent nervousness of Nippers were mainly observable in the morning, while in the afternoon he was comparatively mild. So that, Turkey's paroxysms only coming on about twelve o'clock, I never had to do with their eccentricities at one time. Their fits relieved each other, like guards. When Nippers' was on, Turkey's was off; and *vice versa*. This was a good natural arrangement under the circumstances.

Ginger Nut, the third on my list, was a lad, some twelve years old. His father was a carman, ambitious of seeing his son on the bench instead of a cart, before he died. So he sent him to my office, as student at law, errand-boy, cleaner, and sweeper, at the rate of one dollar a week. He had a little desk to himself, but he did not use it much. Upon inspection, the drawer exhibited a great array of the shells of various sorts of nuts. Indeed, to this quick-witted youth, the whole noble science of the law was contained in a nutshell. Not the least among the employments of Ginger Nut, as well as one which he discharged with the most alacrity, was his duty as cake and apple purveyor for Turkey and Nippers. Copying lawpapers being proverbially a dry, husky sort of business, my two scriveners were fain to moisten their mouths very often with Spitzenbergs, to be had at the numerous stalls nigh the Custom House and Post Office. Also, they sent Ginger Nut very frequently for that peculiar cake—small, flat, round, and very spicy—after which he had been named by them. Of a cold morning, when business was but dull, Turkey would gobble up scores of these cakes, as if they were mere wafers—indeed, they sell them at the rate of six or eight for a penny—the scrape of his pen blending with the crunching of the crisp particles in his mouth. Of all the fiery afternoon blunders and flurried rashness of Turkey, was his once moistening a ginger-cake between his lips, and clapping it on to a mortgage, for a seal. I came within an ace of dismissing him then. But he mollified me by making an oriental bow, and saying—

15 "With submission, sir, it was generous of me to find you in stationery on my own account."

Now my original business—that of a conveyancer and title hunter, and drawer-up of recondite documents of all sorts—was considerably increased by receiving the master's office. There was now great work for scriveners. Not only must I push the clerks already with me, but I must have additional help.

In answer to my advertisement, a motionless young man one morning stood upon my office threshold, the door being open, for it was summer. I can see that figure now—pallidly neat, pitiably respectable, incurably forlorn! It was Bartleby.

After a few words touching his qualifications, I engaged him, glad to have among my corps of copyists a man of so singularly sedate an aspect, which I thought might operate beneficially upon the flighty temper of Turkey, and the fiery one of Nippers.

I should have stated before that ground-glass folding-doors divided my premises into two parts, one of which was occupied by my scriveners, the other by myself. According to my humor, I threw open these doors, or closed them. I resolved to assign Bartleby a corner by the folding-doors, but on my side of them, so as to have this quiet man within easy call, in case any trifling thing was to be done. I placed his desk close up to a small side-window in that part of the room, a window which originally had afforded a lateral view of certain grimy brickyards and bricks, but which, owing to subsequent erections, commanded at present no view at all, though it gave some light. Within three feet of the panes was a wall, and the light came down from far above, between two lofty buildings, as from a very small opening in a dome. Still further to a satisfactory arrangement, I procured a high green folding screen, which might entirely isolate Bartleby from my sight, though not remove him from my voice. And thus, in a manner, privacy and society were conjoined.

20 At first, Bartleby did an extraordinary quantity of writing. As if long famishing for something to copy, he seemed to gorge himself on my documents. There was no pause for digestion. He ran a day and night line, copying by sunlight and by candle-light. I should have been quite delighted with his application, had be been cheerfully industrious. But he wrote on silently, palely, mechanically.

It is, of course, an indispensable part of a scrivener's business to verify the accuracy of his copy, word by word. Where there are two or more scriveners in an office, they assist each other in this examination, one reading from the copy, the other holding the original. It is a very dull, wearisome, and lethargic affair. I can readily imagine that, to some sanguine temperaments, it would be altogether intolerable. For example, I cannot credit that the mettlesome poet, Byron, would have contentedly sat down with Bartleby to examine a law document of, say five hundred pages, closely written in a crimpy hand.

Now and then, in the haste of business, it had been my habit to assist in comparing some brief document myself, calling Turkey or Nippers for this purpose. One object I had, in placing Bartleby so handy to me behind the screen, was, to avail myself of his services on such trivial occasions. It was on the third day, I think, of his being with me, and before any necessity had arisen for having his own writing examined, that, being much hurried to complete a small affair I had in hand, I abruptly called to Bartleby. In my haste and natural expectancy of instant compliance, I sat with my head bent over the original on my desk, and my right hand sideways, and somewhat nervously extended with the copy, so that, immediately upon emerging from his retreat, Bartleby might snatch it and proceed to business without the least delay.

In this very attitude did I sit when I called to him, rapidly stating what it was I wanted him to do—namely, to examine a small paper with me. Imagine my surprise, nay, my consternation, when, without moving from his privacy, Bartleby, in a singularly mild, firm voice, replied, "I would prefer not to."

I sat awhile in perfect silence, rallying my stunned faculties. Immediately it occurred to me that my ears had deceived me, or Bartleby had entirely misunderstood my meaning. I repeated my request in the clearest tone I could assume; but in quite as clear a one came the previous reply, "I would prefer not to."

25 "Prefer not to," echoed I, rising in high excitement, and crossing the room with a stride. "What do you mean? Are you moonstruck? I want you to help me compare this sheet here—take it," and I thrust it towards him.

"I would prefer not to," said he.

I looked at him steadfastly. His face was leanly composed; his gray eye dimly calm. Not a wrinkle of agitation rippled him. Had there been the least uneasiness, anger, impatience, or impertinence in his manner; in other words, had there been anything ordinarily human about him, doubtless I should have violently dismissed him from the premises. But as it was, I should have as soon thought of turning my pale plaster-of-paris bust of Cicero out of doors. I stood gazing at him awhile, as he went on with his own writing, and then reseated myself at my desk. This is very strange, thought I. What had one best do? But my business hurried me. I concluded to forget the matter for the present, reserving it for my future leisure. So, calling Nippers from the other room, the paper was speedily examined.

A few days after this, Bartleby concluded four lengthy documents, being quadruplicates of a week's testimony taken before me in my High Court of Chancery. It became necessary to examine them. It was an important suit, and great accuracy was imperative. Having all things arranged, I called Turkey, Nippers, and Ginger Nut, from the next room, meaning to place the four copies in the hands of my four clerks, while I should read from the original. Accordingly, Turkey, Nippers, and Ginger Nut had taken their seats in a row, each with his document in his hand, when I called to Bartleby to join this interesting group.

"Bartleby! quick, I am waiting."

30 I heard a slow scrape of his chair legs on the uncarpeted floor, and soon he appeared standing at the entrance of his hermitage.

"What is wanted?" said he, mildly.

"The copies, the copies," said I, hurriedly. "We are going to examine them. There"—and I held towards him the fourth quadruplicate.

"I would prefer not to," he said, and gently disappeared behind the screen.

For a few moments I was turned into a pillar of salt, standing at the head of my seated column of clerks. Recovering myself, I advanced towards the screen, and demanded the reason for such extraordinary conduct.

35 "*Why* do you refuse?"

"I would prefer not to."

With any other man I should have flown outright into a dreadful passion, scorned all further words, and thrust him ignominiously from my presence. But there was something about Bartleby that not only strangely disarmed me, but, in a wonderful manner, touched and disconcerted me. I began to reason with him.

"These are your own copies we are about to examine. It is labor saving to you, because one examination will answer for your four papers. It is common usage. Every copyist is bound to help examine his copy. Is it not so? Will you not speak? Answer!"

"I prefer not to," he replied in a flute-like tone. It seemed to me that, while I had been addressing him, he carefully revolved every statement that I made; fully comprehended the meaning; could not gainsay the irresistible conclusion; but, at the same time, some paramount consideration prevailed with him to reply as he did.

40 "You are decided, then, not to comply with my request—a request made according to common usage and common sense?"

He briefly gave me to understand that on that point my judgment was sound. Yes: his decision was irreversible.

It is not seldom the case that, when a man is browbeaten in some unprecedented and violently unreasonable way, he begins to stagger in his own plainest faith. He begins, as it were, vaguely to surmise that, wonderful as it may be, all the justice and all the reason is on the other side. Accordingly, if any disinterested persons are present, he turns to them for some reinforcement for his own faltering mind.

"Turkey," said I, "what do you think of this? Am I not right?"

"With submission, sir," said Turkey, in his blandest tone, "I think that you are."

45 "Nippers," said I, "what do *you* think of it?"

"I think I should kick him out of the office."

(The reader of nice perceptions will have perceived that, it being morning, Turkey's answer is couched in polite and tranquil terms, but Nippers replies in ill-tempered ones. Or, to repeat a previous sentence, Nippers' ugly mood was on duty, and Turkey's off.)

"Ginger Nut," said I, willing to enlist the smallest suffrage in my behalf, "what do *you* think of it?"

"I think, sir, he's a little *luny,*" replied Ginger Nut, with a grin.

"You hear what they say," said I, turning towards the screen, "come forth and do your duty."

But he vouchsafed no reply. I pondered a moment in sore perplexity. But once more business hurried me. I determined again to postpone the consideration of this dilemma to my future leisure. With a little trouble we made out to examine the papers without Bartleby, though at every page or two Turkey deferentially dropped his opinion, that this proceeding was quite out of the common; while Nippers, twitching in his chair with a dyspeptic nervousness, ground out, between his set teeth, occasional hissing maledictions against the stubborn oaf behind the screen. And for his (Nippers') part, this was the first and the last time he would do another man's business without pay.

Meanwhile Bartleby sat in his hermitage, oblivious to every thing but his own peculiar business there.

Some days passed, the scrivener being employed upon another lengthy work. His late remarkable conduct led me to regard his ways narrowly. I observed that he never went to dinner; indeed, that he never went anywhere. As yet I had never, of my personal knowledge, known him to be outside of my office. He was a perpetual sentry in the corner. At about eleven o'clock though, in the morning, I noticed that Ginger Nut would advance toward the opening in Bartleby's screen, as if silently beckoned thither by a gesture invisible to me where I sat. The boy would then leave the office, jingling a few pence, and reappear with a handful of ginger-nuts, which he delivered in the hermitage, receiving two of the cakes for his trouble.

He lives, then, on ginger-nuts, thought I; never eats a dinner, properly speaking; he must be a vegetarian, then, but no; he never eats even vegetables, he eats nothing but ginger-nuts. My mind then ran on in reveries concerning the probable effects upon the human constitution of living entirely on ginger-nuts. Ginger-nuts are so called, because they contain ginger as one of their peculiar constituents, and the final flavoring one. Now, what was ginger? A hot, spicy thing. Was Bartleby hot and spicy? Not at all. Ginger, then, had no effect upon Bartleby. Probably he preferred it should have none.

Nothing so aggravates an earnest person as a passive resistance. If the individual so resisted be of a not inhumane temper, and the resisting one perfectly harmless in his passivity, then, in the better moods of the former, he will endeavor charitably to construe to his imagination what proves impossible to be solved by his judgment. Even so, for the most part, I regarded Bartleby and his ways. Poor fellow! thought I, he means no mischief; it is plain he intends no insolence; his aspect sufficiently evinces that his eccentricities are involuntary. He is useful to me. I can get along with him. If I turn him away, the chances are he will fall in with some less indulgent employer, and then he will be rudely treated, and perhaps driven forth miserably to starve. Yes. Here I can cheaply purchase a delicious self-approval. To befriend Bartleby; to humor him in his strange wilfulness, will cost me little or nothing, while I lay up in my soul what will eventually prove a sweet morsel for my conscience. But this mood was not invariable with me. The passiveness of Bartleby sometimes irritated me. I felt strangely goaded on to encounter him in new opposition—to elicit some angry spark from him answerable to my own. But, indeed, I might as well have essayed to strike fire with my knuckles against a bit of Windsor soap. But one afternoon the evil impulse in me mastered me, and the following little scene ensued:

"Bartleby," said I, "when those papers are all copied, I will compare them with you."

"I would prefer not to."

"How? Surely you do not mean to persist in that mulish vagary?"

No answer.

I threw open the folding-doors nearby, and turning upon Turkey and Nippers, exclaimed:

"Bartleby a second time says, he won't examine his papers. What do you think of it, Turkey?"

It was afternoon, be it remembered. Turkey sat glowing like a brass boiler; his bald head steaming; his hands reeling among his blotted papers.

"Think of it?" roared Turkey. "I think I'll just step behind his screen, and black his eyes for him!"

So saying, Turkey rose to his feet and threw his arms into a pugilistic position. He was hurrying away to make good his promise, when I detained him, alarmed at the effect of incautiously rousing Turkey's combativeness after dinner.

65 "Sit down, Turkey," said I, "and hear what Nippers has to say. What do you think of it, Nippers? Would I not be justified in immediately dismissing Bartleby?"

"Excuse me, that is for you to decide, sir. I think his conduct quite unusual, and, indeed, unjust, as regards Turkey and myself. But it may only be a passing whim."

"Ah," exclaimed I, "you have strangely changed your mind, then—you speak very gently of him now."

"All beer," cried Turkey; "gentleness is effects of beer—Nippers and I dined together to-day. You see how gentle *I* am, sir. Shall I go and black his eyes?"

"You refer to Bartleby, I suppose. No, not to-day, Turkey," I replied; "pray, put up your fists."

70 I closed the doors, and again advanced towards Bartleby. I felt additional incentives tempting me to my fate. I burned to be rebelled against again. I remembered that Bartleby never left the office.

"Bartleby," said I, "Ginger Nut is away; just step around to the Post Office, won't you?" (it was but a three minutes' walk) "and see if there is anything for me."

"I would prefer not to."

"You *will* not?"

"I *prefer* not."

75 I staggered to my desk, and sat there in a deep study. My blind inveteracy returned. Was there any other thing in which I could procure myself to be ignominiously repulsed by this lean, penniless wight?—my hired clerk? What added thing is there, perfectly reasonable, that he will be sure to refuse to do?

"Bartleby!"

No answer.

"Bartleby," in a louder tone.

No answer.

80 "Bartleby," I roared.

Like a very ghost, agreeably to the laws of magical invocation, at the third summons, he appeared at the entrance of his hermitage.

"Go to the next room, and tell Nippers to come to me."

"I prefer not to," he respectfully and slowly said, and mildly disappeared.

"Very good, Bartleby," said I, in a quiet sort of serenely-severe self-possessed tone, intimating the unalterable purpose of some terrible retribution very close at hand. At the moment I half intended something of the kind. But upon the whole, as it was drawing towards my dinner-hour, I thought it best to put on my hat and walk home for the day, suffering much from perplexity and distress of mind.

85 Shall I acknowledge it? The conclusion of this whole business was, that it soon became a fixed fact of my chambers, that a pale young scrivener, by the name of Bartleby, had a desk there; that he copied for me at the usual rate of four cents a folio (one hundred words); but he was permanently exempt from examining the work done by him, that duty being transferred to Turkey and Nippers, out of compliment, doubtless, to their superior acuteness; moreover, said Bartleby was never, on any account, to be dispatched on the most trivial errand of any sort; and that even if entreated to take upon him such a matter, it was generally understood that he would "prefer not to"—in other words, that he would refuse point-blank.

As days passed on, I became considerably reconciled to Bartleby. His steadiness, his freedom from all dissipation, his incessant industry (except when he chose to throw himself into a standing revery behind his screen), his great stillness, his unalterableness of demeanor under all circumstances, made him a valuable acquisition. One prime thing was this—*he was always there*—first in the morning, continually through the day, and the last at night. I had a singular confidence in his honesty. I felt my most precious papers perfectly safe in his hands. Sometimes, to be sure, I could not, for the very soul of me, avoid falling into sudden spasmodic passions with him. For it was exceeding difficult to bear in mind all the time those strange peculiarities, privileges, and unheard-of exemptions, forming the tacit stipulations on Bartleby's part under which he remained in my office. Now and then, in the eagerness of dispatching pressing business, I would inadvertently summon Bartleby, in a short, rapid tone, to put his finger, say, on the incipient tie of a bit of red tape with which I was about compressing some papers. Of course, from behind the screen the usual answer, "I prefer not to," was sure to come; and then, how could a human creature, with the common infirmities of our nature, refrain from bitterly exclaiming upon such perverseness—such unreasonableness? However, every added repulse of this sort which I received only tended to lessen the probability of my repeating the inadvertence.

Here is must be said, that, according to the custom of most legal gentlemen occupying chambers in densely populated law buildings, there were several keys to my door. One was kept by a woman residing in the attic, which person weekly scrubbed and daily swept and dusted my apartments. Another was kept by Turkey for convenience sake. The third I sometimes carried in my own pocket. The fourth I knew not who had.

Now, one Sunday morning I happened to go to Trinity Church, to hear a celebrated preacher, and finding myself rather early on the ground I thought I would walk round to my chambers for a while. Luckily I had my key with me; but upon applying it to the lock, I found it resisted by something inserted from the inside. Quite surprised, I called out; when to my consternation a key was turned from within; and thrusting his lean visage at me, and holding the door ajar, the apparition of Bartleby appeared, in his shirt-sleeves, and otherwise in a strangely tattered *deshabille,* saying quietly that he was sorry, but he was deeply engaged just then, and—preferred not admitting me at present. In a brief word or two, he moreover added, that perhaps I had better walk round the block two or three times, and by that time he would probably have concluded his affairs.

Now, the utterly unsurmised appearance of Bartleby, tenanting my law-chambers of a Sunday morning, with his cadaverously gentlemanly *nonchalance,* yet withal firm and self-possessed, had such a strange effect upon me, that incontinently I slunk away from my own door, and did as desired. But not without sundry twinges of impotent rebellion against the mild effrontery of this unaccountable scrivener. Indeed, it was his wonderful mildness chiefly, which not only disarmed me, but unmanned me, as it were. For I consider that one, for the time, is sort of unmanned when he tranquilly permits his hired clerk to dictate to him, and order him away from his own premises. Furthermore, I was full of uneasiness as to what Bartleby could possibly be doing in my office in his shirt-sleeves, and in an otherwise dismantled condition of a Sunday morning. Was anything amiss going on? Nay, that was out of the question. It was not to be thought of for a moment that Bartleby was an immoral person. But what could he be doing there?—copying? Nay again, whatever might be his eccentricities, Bartleby was an eminently decorous person. He would be the last man to sit down to his desk in any state approaching to nudity. Besides, it was Sunday; and there was something about Bartleby that forbade the supposition that he would by any secular occupation violate the proprieties of the day.

Nevertheless, my mind was not pacified; and full of a restless curiosity, at last I returned to the door. Without hindrance I inserted my key, opened it, and entered. Bartleby was not to be seen. I looked round anxiously, peeped behind his screen; but it was very plain that he was gone. Upon more closely examining the place, I surmised that for an indefinite period Bartleby must have ate, dressed, and slept in my office, and that too without plate, mirror, or bed. The cushioned seat of a rickety old sofa in one corner bore the faint impress of a lean, reclining form. Rolled away under his desk, I found a blanket; under the empty grate, a blacking box and brush; on a chair, a tin basin, with soap and a ragged towel; in a newspaper a few crumbs of ginger-nuts and a morsel of cheese. Yes, thought I, it is evident enough that Bartleby has been making his home here, keeping bachelor's hall all by himself. Immediately then the thought came sweeping across me, what miserable friendlessness and loneliness are here revealed! His poverty is great; but his solitude, how horrible! Think of it. Of a Sunday, Wall Street is deserted as Petra; and every night of every day it is an emptiness. This building, too, which of week-days hums with industry and life, at nightfall echoes with sheer vacancy, and all through Sunday is forlorn. And here Bartleby makes his home; sole spectator of a solitude which he has seen all populous—a sort of innocent and transformed Marius brooding among the ruins of Carthage?

For the first time in my life a feeling of overpowering stinging melancholy seized me. Before, I had never experienced aught but a not unpleasing sadness. The bond of a common humanity now drew me irresistibly to gloom. A fraternal melancholy! For both I and Bartleby were sons of Adam. I remembered the bright silks and sparkling faces I had seen that day, in gala trim, swan-like sailing down the Mississippi of Broadway; and I contrasted them with the pallid copyist, and thought to myself, Ah, happiness courts the light, so we deem the world is gay; but misery hides aloof, so we deem that misery there is none. These sad fancyings—chimeras, doubtless, of a sick and silly brain—led on to other and more special thoughts, concerning the eccentricities of Bartleby. Presentiments of strange discoveries hovered round me. The scrivener's pale form appeared to me laid out, among uncaring strangers, in its shivering winding-sheet.

Suddenly I was attracted by Bartleby's closed desk, the key in open sight left in the lock.

I mean no mischief, seek the gratification of no heartless curiosity, thought I; besides, the desk is mine, and its contents, too, so I will make bold to look within. Everything was methodically arranged, the papers smoothly placed. The pigeon-holes were deep, and removing the files of documents, I groped into their recesses. Presently I felt something there, and dragged it out. It was an old bandanna handkerchief, heavy and knotted. I opened it, and saw it was a saving's bank.

I now recalled all the quiet mysteries which I had noted in the man. I remembered that he never spoke but to answer; that, though at intervals he had considerable time to himself, yet I had never seen him reading—no, not even a newspaper; that for long periods he would stand looking out, at his pale window behind the screen, upon the dead brick wall; I was quite sure he never visited any refectory or eating-house; while his pale face clearly indicated that he never drank beer like Turkey, or tea and coffee even, like other men; that he never went anywhere in particular that I could learn; never went out for a walk, unless, indeed, that was the case at present; that he had declined telling who he was, or whence he came, or whether he had any relatives in the world; that though so thin and pale, he never complained of ill-health. And more than all, I remembered a certain unconscious air of pallid—how shall I call it?—of pallid haughtiness, say, or rather an austere reserve about him, which had positively awed me into my tame compliance with his eccentricities, when I had feared to ask him to do the slightest incidental thing for me, even though I might know, from his long-continued motionlessness, that behind his screen he must be standing in one of those dead-wall reveries of his.

95 Revolving all these things, and coupling them with the recently discovered fact, that he made my office his constant abiding place and home, and not forgetful of his morbid moodiness; revolving all these things, a prudential feeling began to steal over me. My first emotions had been those of pure melancholy and sincerest pity; but just in proportion as the forlornness of Bartleby grew and grew to my imagination, did that same melancholy merge into fear, that pity into repulsion. So true it is, and so terrible, too, that up to a certain point the thought or sight of misery enlists our best affections; but, in certain special cases, beyond that point it does not. They err who would assert that invariably this is owing to the inherent selfishness of the human heart. It rather proceeds from a certain hopelessness of remedying excessive and organic ill. To a sensitive being, pity is not seldom pain. And when at last it is perceived that such pity cannot lead to effectual succor, common sense bids the soul be rid of it. What I saw that morning persuaded me that the scrivener was the victim of innate and incurable disorder. I might give alms to his body; but his body did not pain him; it was his soul that suffered, and his soul I could not reach.

I did not accomplish the purpose of going to Trinity Church that morning. Somehow, the things I had seen disqualified me for the time from church-going. I walked homeward, thinking what I would do with Bartleby. Finally, I resolved upon this—I would put certain calm questions to him the next morning, touching his history, etc., and if he declined to answer then openly and unreservedly (and I supposed he would prefer not), then to give him a twenty dollar bill over and above whatever I might owe him, and tell him his services were no longer required; but that if in any other way I could assist him, I would be happy to do so, especially if he desired to return to his native place, wherever that might be, I would willingly help to defray the expenses. Moreover, if, after reaching home, he found himself at any time in want of aid, a letter from him would be sure of a reply.

The next morning came.

"Bartleby," said I, gently calling to him behind his screen.

No reply.

"Bartleby," said I, in a still gentler tone, "come here; I am not going to ask you to do anything you would prefer not to do—I simply wish to speak to you."

Upon this he noiselessly slid into view.

"Will you tell me, Bartleby, where you were born?"

"I would prefer not to."

"Will you tell me *anything* about yourself?"

"I would prefer not to."

"But what reasonable objection can you have to speak to me? I feel friendly towards you."

He did not look at me while I spoke, but kept his glance fixed upon my bust of Cicero, which, as I then sat, was directly behind me, some six inches above my head.

"What is your answer, Bartleby?" said I, after waiting a considerable time for a reply, during which his countenance remained immovable, only there was the faintest conceivable tremor of the white attenuated mouth.

"At present I prefer to give no answer," he said, and retired into his hermitage.

It was rather weak in me I confess, but his manner, on this occasion, nettled me. Not only did there seem to lurk in it a certain calm disdain, but his perverseness seemed ungrateful, considering the undeniable good usage and indulgence he had received from me.

Again I sat ruminating what I should do. Mortified as I was at his behavior, and resolved as I had been to dismiss him when I entered my office, nevertheless I strangely felt something superstitious knocking at my heart, and forbidding me to carry out my purpose, and denouncing me for a villain if I dared to breathe one bitter word against this forlornest of mankind. At last, familiarly drawing my chair behind his screen, I sat down and said: "Bartleby, never mind, then, about revealing your history; but let me entreat you, as a friend, to comply as far as may be with the usages of this office. Say now, you will help to examine papers tomorrow or next day: in short, say now, that in a day or two you will begin to be a little reasonable:—say so, Bartleby."

"At present I would prefer not to be a little reasonable," was his mildly cadaverous reply.

Just then the folding-doors opened, and Nippers approached. He seemed suffering from an unusually bad night's rest, induced by severer indigestion than common. He overheard those final words of Bartleby.

"*Prefer not,* eh?" gritted Nippers—"I'd *prefer* him, if I were you, sir," addressing me—"I'd *prefer* him; I'd give him preferences, the stubborn mule! What is it, sir, pray, that he *prefers* not to do now?"

Bartleby moved not a limb.

"Mr. Nippers," said I, "I'd prefer that you would withdraw for the present."

Somehow, of late, I had got into the way of involuntarily using this word "prefer" upon all sorts of not exactly suitable occasions. And I trembled to think that my contact with the scrivener had already and seriously affected me in a mental way. And what further and deeper aberration might it not yet produce? This apprehension had not been without efficacy in determining me to summary measures.

As Nippers, looking very sour and sulky, was departing, Turkey blandly and deferentially approached.

"With submission, sir," said he, "yesterday I was thinking about Bartleby here, and I think that if he would but prefer to take a quart of good ale every day, it would do much towards mending him, and enabling him to assist in examining his papers."

"So you have got the word, too," said I, slightly excited.

"With submission, what word, sir?" asked Turkey, respectfully crowding himself into the contracted space behind the screen, and by so doing, making me jostle the scrivener. "What word, sir?"

"I would prefer to be left alone here," said Bartleby, as if offended at being mobbed in his privacy.

"*That's* the word, Turkey," said I—"*that's* it."

"Oh, *prefer?* oh yes—queer word. I never use it myself. But, sir, as I was saying, if he would but prefer—"

125 "Turkey," interrupted I, "you will please withdraw."

"Oh certainly, sir, if you prefer that I should."

As he opened the folding-door to retire, Nippers at his desk caught a glimpse of me, and asked whether I would prefer to have a certain paper copied on blue paper or white. He did not in the least roguishly accent the word "prefer." It was plain that it involuntarily rolled from his tongue. I thought to myself, surely I must get rid of a demented man, who already has in some degree turned the tongues, if not the heads of myself and clerks. But I thought it prudent not to break the dismission at once.

The next day I noticed that Bartleby did nothing but stand at his window in his dead-wall revery. Upon asking him why he did not write, he said that he had decided upon doing no more writing.

"Why, how now? what next?" exclaimed I, "do no more writing?"

130 "No more."

"And what is the reason?"

"Do you not see the reason for yourself?" he indifferently replied.

I looked steadfastly at him, and perceived that his eyes looked dull and glazed. Instantly it occurred to me, that his unexampled diligence in copying by his dim window for the first few weeks of his stay with me might have temporarily impaired his vision.

I was touched. I said something in condolence with him. I hinted that of course he did wisely in abstaining from writing for a while; and urged him to embrace that opportunity of taking wholesome exercise in the open air. This, however, he did not do. A few days after this, my other clerks being absent, and being in a great hurry to dispatch certain letters by the mail, I thought that, having nothing else earthly to do, Bartleby would surely be less inflexible than usual, and carry these letters to the Post Office. But he blankly declined. So, much to my inconvenience, I went myself.

135 Still added days went by. Whether Bartleby's eyes improved or not, I could not say. To all appearance, I thought they did. But when I asked him if they did, he vouchsafed no answer. At all events, he would do no copying. At last, in replying to my urgings, he informed me that he had permanently given up copying.

"What!" exclaimed I; "suppose your eyes should get entirely well—better than ever before—would you not copy then?"

"I have given up copying," he answered, and slid aside.

He remained as ever, a fixture in my chamber. Nay—if that were possible—he became still more of a fixture than before. What was to be done? He would do nothing in the office; why should he stay there? In plain fact, he had now become a millstone to me, not only useless as a necklace, but afflictive to bear. Yet I was sorry for him. I speak less than truth when I say that, on his own account, he occasioned me uneasiness. If he would but have named a single relative or friend, I would instantly have written, and urged their taking the poor fellow away to some convenient retreat. But he seemed alone, absolutely alone in the universe. A bit of wreck in the mid-Atlantic. At length, necessities connected with my business tyrannized over all other considerations. Decently as I could, I told Bartleby that in six days' time he must unconditionally leave the office. I warned him to take measures, in the interval, for procuring some other abode. I offered to assist him in this endeavor, if he himself would but take the first step towards a removal. "And when you finally quit me, Bartleby," added I, "I shall see that you go not away entirely unprovided. Six days from this hour, remember."

At the expiration of that period, I peeped behind the screen, and lo! Bartleby was there.

140 I buttoned up my coat, balanced myself; advanced slowly towards him, touched his shoulder, and said, "The time has come; you must quit this place; I am sorry for you; here is money; but you must go."

"I would prefer not," he replied, with his back still towards me.

"You *must.*"

He remained silent.

Now I had an unbounded confidence in this man's common honesty. He had frequently restored to me sixpences and shillings carelessly dropped upon the floor, for I am apt to be very reckless in such shirt-button affairs. The proceeding, then, which followed will not be deemed extraordinary.

"Bartleby," said I, "I owe you twelve dollars on account; here are thirty-two, the odd twenty are yours—Will you take it?" and I handed the bills towards him.

But he made no motion.

"I will leave them here, then," putting them under a weight on the table. Then taking my hat and cane and going to the door, I tranquilly turned and added—"After you have removed your things from these offices, Bartleby, you will of course lock the door—since every one is now gone for the day but you—and if you please, slip your key underneath the mat, so that I may have it in the morning. I shall not see you again; so good-bye to you. If, hereafter, in your new place of abode, I can be of any service to you, do not fail to advise me by letter. Good-bye, Bartleby, and fare you well."

But he answered not a word; like the last column of some ruined temple, he remained standing mute and solitary in the middle of the otherwise deserted room.

As I walked home in a pensive mood, my vanity got the better of my pity. I could not but highly plume myself on my masterly management in getting rid of Bartleby. Masterly I call it, and such it must appear to any dispassionate thinker. The beauty of my procedure seemed to consist in its perfect quietness. There was no vulgar bullying, no bravado of any sort, no choleric hectoring, and striding to and fro across the apartment, jerking out vehement commands for Bartleby to bundle himself off with his beggarly traps. Nothing of the kind. Without loudly bidding Bartleby depart—as an inferior genius might have done—I *assumed* the ground that depart he must; and upon that assumption built all I had to say. The more I thought over my procedure, the more I was charmed with it. Nevertheless, next morning, upon awakening, I had my doubts—I had somehow slept off the fumes of vanity. One of the coolest and wisest hours a man has, is just after he awakes in the morning. My procedure seemed as sagacious as ever—but only in theory. How it would prove in practice—there was the rub. It was truly a beautiful thought to have assumed Bartleby's departure; but, after all, that assumption was simply my own, and none of Bartleby's. The great point was, not whether I had assumed that he would quit me, but whether he would prefer to do so. He was more a man of preferences than assumptions.

After breakfast, I walked down town, arguing the probabilities *pro* and *con.* One moment I thought it would prove a miserable failure, and Bartleby would be found all alive at my office as usual; the next moment it seemed certain that I should find his chair empty. And so I kept veering about. At the corner of Broadway and Canal Street, I saw quite an excited group of people standing in earnest conversation.

"I'll take odds he doesn't," said a voice as I passed.

"Doesn't go?—done!" said I, "put up your money."

I was instinctively putting my hand in my pocket to produce my own, when I remembered that this was an election day. The words I had overheard bore no reference to Bartleby, but to the success or non-success of some candidate for the mayoralty. In my intent frame of mind, I had, as it were, imagined that all Broadway shared in my excitement, and were debating the same question with me. I passed on, very thankful that the uproar of the street screened my momentary absent-mindedness.

As I had intended, I was earlier than usual at my office door. I stood listening for a moment. All was still. He must be gone. I tried the knob. The door was locked. Yes, my procedure had worked to a charm; he indeed must be vanished. Yet a certain melancholy mixed with this: I was almost sorry for my brilliant success. I was fumbling under the door mat for the key, which Bartleby was to have left there for me, when accidentally my knee knocked against a panel, producing a summoning sound, and in response a voice came to me from within—"Not yet; I am occupied."

It was Bartleby.

I was thunderstruck. For an instant I stood like the man who, pipe in mouth, was killed one cloudless afternoon long ago in Virginia, by summer lightning; at his own warm open window he was killed, and remained leaning out there upon the dreamy afternoon, till some one touched him, when he fell.

"Not gone!" I murmured at last. But again obeying that wondrous ascendancy which the inscrutable scrivener had over me, and from which ascendancy, for all my chafing, I could not completely escape, I slowly went down stairs and out into the street, and while walking round the block, considered what I should next do in this unheard-of perplexity. Turn the man out by an actual thrusting I could not; to drive him away by calling him hard names would not do; calling in the police was an unpleasant idea; and yet, permit him to enjoy his cadaverous triumph over me—this, too, I could not think of. What was to be done? or, if nothing could be done, was there anything further that I could *assume* in the matter? Yes, as before I had prospectively assumed that Bartleby would depart, so now I might retrospectively assume that departed he was. In the legitimate carrying out of this assumption, I might enter my office in a great hurry, and pretending not to see Bartleby at all, walk straight against him as if he were air. Such a proceeding would in a singular degree have the appearance of a home-thrust. It was hardly possible that Bartleby could withstand such an application of the doctrine of assumption. But upon second thoughts the success of the plan seemed rather dubious. I resolved to argue the matter over with him again.

"Bartleby," said I, entering the office, with a quietly severe expression, "I am seriously displeased. I am pained, Bartleby. I had thought better of you. I had imagined you of such a gentlemanly organization, that in any delicate dilemma a slight hint would suffice—in short, an assumption. But it appears I am deceived. Why," I added, unaffectedly starting, "you have not even touched that money yet," pointing to it, just where I had left it the evening previous.

He answered nothing.

"Will you, or will you not, quit me?" I now demanded in a sudden passion, advancing close to him.

"I would prefer *not* to quit you," he replied, gently emphasizing the *not*.

"What earthly right have you to stay here? Do you pay any rent? Do you pay my taxes? Or is this property yours?"

He answered nothing.

"Are you ready to go on and write now? Are your eyes recovered? Could you copy a small paper for me this morning? or help examine a few lines? or step round to the Post Office? In a word, will you do anything at all, to give a coloring to your refusal to depart the premises?"

He silently retired into his hermitage.

I was now in such a state of nervous resentment that I thought it but prudent to check myself at present from further demonstrations. Bartleby and I were alone. I remembered the tragedy of the unfortunate Adams and the still more unfortunate Colt in the solitary office of the latter; and how poor Colt, being dreadfully incensed by Adams, and imprudently permitting himself to get wildly excited, was at unawares hurried into his fatal act—an act which certainly no man could possibly deplore more than the actor himself. Often it had occurred to me in my ponderings upon the subject that had that altercation taken place in the public street, or at a private residence, it would not have terminated as it did. It was the circumstance of being alone in a solitary office, up stairs, of a building entirely unhallowed by humanizing domestic associations—an uncarpeted office, doubtless, of a dusty, haggard sort of appearance—this it must have been, which greatly helped to enhance the irritable desperation of the hapless Colt.

But when this old Adam of resentment rose in me and tempted me concerning Bartleby, I grappled him and threw him. How? Why, simply by recalling the divine injunction: "A new commandment give I unto you, that ye love one another." Yes, this it was that saved me. Aside from higher considerations, charity often operates as a vastly wise and prudent principle—a great safeguard to its possessor. Men have committed murder for jealousy's sake, and anger's sake, and hatred's sake, and selfishness' sake, and spiritual pride's sake; but no man, that ever I heard of, ever committed a diabolical murder for sweet charity's sake. Mere self-interest, then, if no better motive can be enlisted, should, especially with high-tempered men, prompt all beings to charity and philanthropy. At any rate, upon the occasion in question, I strove to drown my exasperated feelings towards the scrivener by benevolently construing his conduct. Poor fellow, poor fellow! thought I, he don't mean anything; and besides, he has seen hard times, and ought to be indulged.

I endeavored, also, immediately to occupy myself, and at the same time to comfort my despondency. I tried to fancy, that in the course of the morning, at such time as might prove agreeable to him, Bartleby, of his own free accord, would emerge from his hermitage and take up some decided line of march in the direction of the door. But no. Half-past twelve o'clock came; Turkey began to glow in the face, overturn his inkstand, and become generally obstreperous; Nippers abated down into quietude and courtesy; Ginger Nut munched his noon apple; and Bartleby remained standing at his window in one of his profoundest dead-wall reveries. Will it be credited? Ought I to acknowledge it? That afternoon I left the office without saying one further word to him.

Some days now passed, during which, at leisure intervals I looked a little into "Edwards on the Will," and "Priestley on Necessity." Under the circumstances, those books induced a salutary feeling. Gradually I slid into the persuasion that these troubles of mine, touching the scrivener, had been all predestined from eternity, and Bartleby was billeted upon me for some mysterious purpose of an all-wise Providence, which it was not for a mere mortal like me to fathom. Yes, Bartleby, stay there behind your screen, thought I; I shall persecute you no more; you are harmless and noiseless as any of these old chairs; in short, I never feel so private as when I know you are here. At least I see it, I feel it; I penetrate to the predestined purpose of my life. I am content. Others may have loftier parts to enact; but my mission in this world, Bartleby, is to furnish you with office-room for such period as you may see fit to remain.

I believe that this wise and blessed frame of mind would have continued with me, had it not been for the unsolicited and uncharitable remarks obtruded upon me by my professional friends who visited the rooms. But thus it often is, that the constant friction of illiberal minds wears out at last the best resolves of the more generous. Though to be sure, when I reflected upon it, it was not strange that people entering my office should be struck by the peculiar aspect of the unaccountable Bartleby, and so be tempted to throw out some sinister observations concerning him. Sometimes an attorney, having business with me, and calling at my office, and finding no one but the scrivener there, would undertake to obtain some sort of precise information from him touching my whereabouts; but without heeding his idle talk, Bartleby would remain standing immovable in the middle of the room. So after contemplating him in that position for a time, the attorney would depart, no wiser than he came.

Also, when a reference was going on, and the room full of lawyers and witnesses, and business driving fast, some deeply-occupied legal gentleman present, seeing Bartleby wholly unemployed, would request him to run round to his (the legal gentleman's) office and fetch some papers for him. Thereupon, Bartleby would tranquilly decline, and yet remain idle as before. Then the lawyer would give a great stare, and turn to me. And what could I say? At last I was made aware that all through the circle of my professional acquaintance, a whisper of wonder was running round, having reference to the strange creature I kept at my office. This worried me very much. And as the idea came upon me of his possibly turning out a long-lived man, and keeping occupying my chambers, and denying my authority; and perplexing my visitors; and scandalizing my professional reputation; and casting a general gloom over the premises; keeping soul and body together to the last upon his savings (for doubtless he spent but half a dime a day), and in the end perhaps outlive me, and claim possession of my office by right of his perpetual occupancy: as all these dark anticipations crowded upon me more and more, and my friends continually intruded their relentless remarks upon the apparition in my room; a great change was wrought in me. I resolved to gather all my faculties together, and forever rid me of this intolerable incubus.

Ere revolving any complicated project, however, adapted to this end, I first simply suggested to Bartleby the propriety of his permanent departure. In a calm and serious tone, I commended the idea to his careful and mature consideration. But, having taken three days to meditate upon it, he apprised me, that his original determination remained the same; in short, that he still preferred to abide with me.

What shall I do? I now said to myself, buttoning up my coat to the last button. What shall I do? what ought I to do? what does conscience say I *should* do with this man, or, rather, ghost. Rid myself of him, I must; go, he shall. But how? You will not thrust him, the poor, pale, passive mortal—you will not thrust such a helpless creature out of your door? you will not dishonor yourself by such cruelty? No, I will not, I cannot do that. Rather would I let him live and die here, and then mason up his remains in the wall. What, then, will you do? For all your coaxing, he will not budge. Bribes he leaves under your own paperweight on your table; in short, it is quite plain that he prefers to cling to you.

Then something severe, something unusual must be done. What! surely you will not have him collared by a constable, and commit his innocent pallor to the common jail? And upon what ground could you procure such a thing to be done?—a vagrant, is he? What! he a vagrant, a wanderer, who refuses to budge? It is because he will *not* be a vagrant, then, that you seek to count him *as* a vagrant. That is too absurd. No visible means of support: there I have him. Wrong again: for indubitably he *does* support himself, and that is the only unanswerable proof that any man can show of his possessing the means so to do. No more, then. Since he will not quit me, I must quit him. I will change my offices; I will move elsewhere, and give him fair notice, that if I find him on my new premises I will then proceed against him as a common trespasser.

175 Acting accordingly, next day I thus addressed him: "I find these chambers too far from the City Hall; the air is unwholesome. In a word, I propose to remove my offices next week, and shall no longer require your services. I tell you this now, in order that you may seek another place."

He made no reply, and nothing more was said.

On the appointed day I engaged carts and men, proceeded to my chambers, and having but little furniture, everything was removed in a few hours. Throughout, the scrivener remained standing behind the screen, which I directed to be removed the last thing. It was withdrawn; and, being folded up like a huge folio, left him the motionless occupant of a naked room. I stood in the entry watching him a moment, while something from within me upbraided me.

I re-entered, with my hand in my pocket—and—and my heart in my mouth.

"Good-bye, Bartleby; I am going—good-bye, and God some way bless you; and take that," slipping something in his hand. But it dropped upon the floor, and then—strange to say—I tore myself from him whom I had so longed to be rid of.

180 Established in my new quarters, for a day or two I kept the door locked, and started at every footfall in the passages. When I returned to my rooms, after any little absence, I would pause at the threshold for an instant, and attentively listen, ere applying my key. But these fears were needless. Bartleby never came nigh me.

I thought all was going well, when a perturbed-looking stranger visited me, inquiring whether I was the person who had recently occupied rooms at No. — Wall Street.

Full of forebodings, I replied that I was.

"Then, sir," said the stranger, who proved a lawyer, "you are responsible for the man you left there. He refuses to do any copying; he refuses to do anything; he says he prefers not to; and he refuses to quit the premises."

"I am very sorry, sir," said I, with assumed tranquillity, but an inward tremor, "but, really, the man you allude to is nothing to me—he is no relation or apprentice of mine, that you should hold me responsible for him."

185 "In mercy's name, who is he?"

"I certainly cannot inform you. I know nothing about him. Formerly I employed him as a copyist; but he has done nothing for me now for some time past."

"I shall settle him, then—good morning, sir."

Several days passed, and I heard nothing more; and though I often felt a charitable prompting to call at the place and see poor Bartleby, yet a certain squeamishness, of I know not what, withheld me.

All is over with him, by this time, thought I, at last, when, through another week, no further intelligence reached me. But, coming to my room the day after, I found several persons waiting at my door in a high state of nervous excitement.

"That's the man—here he comes," cried the foremost one, whom I recognized as the lawyer who had previously called upon me alone.

"You must take him away, sir, at once," cried a portly person among them, advancing upon me, and whom I knew to be the landlord of No. — Wall Street. "These gentlemen, my tenants, cannot stand it any longer; Mr. B———," pointing to the lawyer, "has turned him out of his room, and he now persists in haunting the building generally, sitting upon the banisters of the stairs by day, and sleeping in the entry by night. Everybody is concerned; clients are leaving the offices; some fears are entertained of a mob; something you must do, and that without delay."

Aghast at this torrent, I fell back before it, and would fain have locked myself in my new quarters. In vain I persisted that Bartleby was nothing to me—no more than to any one else. In vain—I was the last person known to have anything to do with him, and they held me to the terrible account. Fearful, then, of being exposed in the papers (as one person present obscurely threatened), I considered the matter, and, at length, said, that if the lawyer would give me a confidential interview with the scrivener, in his (the lawyer's) own room, I would, that afternoon, strive my best to rid them of the nuisance they complained of.

Going up stairs to my old haunt, there was Bartleby silently sitting upon the banister at the landing.

"What are you doing here, Bartleby?" said I.

"Sitting upon the banister," he mildly replied.

I motioned him into the lawyer's room, who then left us.

"Bartleby," said I, "are you aware that you are the cause of great tribulation to me, by persisting in occupying the entry after being dismissed from the office?"

No answer.

"Now one of two things must take place. Either you must do something, or something must be done to you. Now what sort of business would you like to engage in? Would you like to re-engage in copying for some one?"

"No; I would prefer not to make any change."

"Would you like a clerkship in a dry-goods store?"

"There is too much confinement about that. No, I would not like a clerkship; but I am not particular."

"Too much confinement," I cried, "why, you keep yourself confined all the time!"

"I would prefer not to take a clerkship," he rejoined, as if to settle that little item at once.

"How would a bar-tender's business suit you? There is no trying of the eye-sight in that."

"I would not like it at all; though, as I said before, I am not particular."

His unwonted wordiness inspirited me. I returned to the charge.

"Well, then, would you like to travel through the country collecting bills for the merchants? That would improve your health."

"No, I would prefer to be doing something else."

"How, then, would going as a companion to Europe, to entertain some young gentleman with your conversation—how would that suit you?"

"Not at all. It does not strike me that there is anything definite about that. I like to be stationary. But I am not particular."

"Stationary you shall be, then," I cried, now losing all patience, and, for the first time in all my exasperating connection with him, fairly flying into a passion. "If you do not go away from these premises before night, I shall feel bound—indeed I *am* bound—to—to quit the premises myself!" I rather absurdly concluded, knowing not with what possible threat to try to frighten his immobility into compliance. Despairing of all further efforts, I was precipitately leaving him, when a final thought occurred to me—one which had not been wholly unindulged before.

"Bartleby," said I, in the kindest tone I could assume under such exciting circumstances, "will you go home with me now—not to my office, but my dwelling—and remain there till we can conclude upon some convenient arrangement for you at our leisure? Come, let us start now, right away."

"No: at present I would prefer not to make any change at all."

215 I answered nothing; but, effectually dodging every one by the suddenness and rapidity of my flight, rushed from the building, ran up Wall Street towards Broadway, and, jumping into the first omnibus, was soon removed from pursuit. As soon as tranquillity returned, I distinctly perceived that I had now done all that I possibly could, both in respect to the demands of the landlord and his tenants, and with regard to my own desire and sense of duty, to benefit Bartleby, and shield him from rude persecution. I now strove to be entirely care-free and quiescent; and my conscience justified me in the attempt; though, indeed, it was not so successful as I could have wished. So fearful was I of being again hunted out by the incensed landlord and his exasperated tenants, that, surrendering my business to Nippers, for a few days, I drove about the upper part of the town and through the suburbs, in my rockaway; crossed over to Jersey City and Hoboken, and paid fugitive visits to Manhattanville and Astoria. In fact, I almost lived in my rockaway for the time.

When again I entered my office, lo, a note from the landlord lay upon the desk. I opened it with trembling hands. It informed me that the writer had sent to the police, and had Bartleby removed to the Tombs as a vagrant. Moreover, since I knew more about him than any one else, he wished me to appear at that place, and make a suitable statement of the facts. These tidings had a conflicting effect upon me. At first I was indignant; but, at last, almost approved. The landlord's energetic, summary disposition, had led him to adopt a procedure which I do not think I would have decided upon myself; and yet, as a last resort, under such peculiar circumstances, it seemed the only plan.

As I afterwards learned, the poor scrivener, when told that he must be conducted to the Tombs, offered not the slightest obstacle, but, in his pale, unmoving way, silently acquiesced.

Some of the compassionate and curious by-standers joined the party; and headed by one of the constables arm-in-arm with Bartleby, the silent procession filed its way through all the noise, and heat, and joy of the roaring thoroughfares at noon.

The same day I received the note, I went to the Tombs, or, to speak more properly, the Halls of Justice. Seeking the right officer, I stated the purpose of my call, and was informed that the individual I described was, indeed, within. I then assured the functionary that Bartleby was a perfectly honest man, and greatly to be compassionated, however unaccountably eccentric. I narrated all I knew, and closed by suggesting the idea of letting him remain in as indulgent confinement as possible, till something less harsh might be done—though, indeed, I hardly knew what. At all events, if nothing else could be decided upon, the almshouse must receive him. I then begged to have an interview.

220 Being under no disgraceful charge, and quite serene and harmless in all his ways, they had permitted him freely to wander about the prison, and, especially, in the inclosed grass-platted yards thereof. And so I found him there, standing all alone in the quietest of the yards, his face towards a high wall, while all around, from the narrow slits of the jail windows, I thought I saw peering out upon him the eyes of murderers and thieves.

"Bartleby!"

"I know you," he said, without looking round—"and I want nothing to say to you."

"It was not I that brought you here, Bartleby," said I, keenly pained at his implied suspicion. "And to you, this should not be so vile a place. Nothing reproachful attaches to you by being here. And see, it is not so sad a place as one might think. Look, there is the sky, and here is the grass."

"I know where I am," he replied, but would say nothing more, and so I left him.

225 As I entered the corridor again, a broad meat-like man, in an apron, accosted me, and jerking his thumb over his shoulder, said—"Is that your friend?"

"Yes."

"Does he want to starve? If he does, let him live on the prison fare, that's all."

"Who are you?" asked I, not knowing what to make of such an unofficially speaking person in such a place.

"I am the grub-man. Such gentlemen as have friends here, hire me to provide them with something good to eat."

230 "Is this so?" said I, turning to the turnkey.

He said it was.

"Well, then," said I, slipping some silver into the grub-man's hands (for so they called him), "I want you to give particular attention to my friend there; let him have the best dinner you can get. And you must be as polite to him as possible."

"Introduce me, will you?" said the grub-man, looking at me with an expression which seemed to say he was all impatience for an opportunity to give a specimen of his breeding.

Thinking it would prove of benefit to the scrivener, I acquiesced; and, asking the grub-man his name, went up with him to Bartleby.

"Bartleby, this is a friend; you will find him very useful to you."

"Your servant, sir, your servant," said the grub-man, making a low salutation behind his apron. "Hope you find it pleasant here, sir; nice grounds—cool apartments—hope you'll stay with us some time—try to make it agreeable. What will you have for dinner to-day?"

"I prefer not to dine to-day," said Bartleby, turning away. "It would disagree with me; I am unused to dinners." So saying, he slowly moved to the other side of the inclosure, and took up a position fronting the deadwall.

"How's this?" said the grub-man, addressing me with a stare of astonishment. "He's odd, aint he?"

"I think he is a little deranged," said I, sadly.

"Deranged? deranged is it? Well, now, upon my word, I thought that friend of yourn was a gentleman forger; they are always pale and genteel-like, them forgers. I can't help pity 'em—can't help it, sir. Did you know Monroe Edwards?" he added, touchingly, and paused. Then, laying his hand piteously on my shoulder, sighed, "He died of consumption at Sing-Sing. So you weren't acquainted with Monroe?"

"No, I was never socially acquainted with any forgers. But I cannot stop longer. Look to my friend yonder. You will not lose by it. I will see you again."

Some few days after this, I again obtained admission to the Tombs, and went through the corridors in quest of Bartleby; but without finding him.

"I saw him coming from his cell not long ago," said a turnkey, "may be he's gone to loiter in the yards."

So I went in that direction.

"Are you looking for the silent man?" said another turnkey, passing me. "Yonder he lies—sleeping in the yard there. 'Tis not twenty minutes since I saw him lie down."

The yard was entirely quiet. It was not accessible to the common prisoners. The surrounding walls, of amazing thickness, kept off all sounds behind them. The Egyptian character of the masonry weighed upon me with its gloom. But a soft imprisoned turf grew under foot. The heart of the eternal pyramids, it seemed, wherein, by some strange magic, through the clefts, grass-seed, dropped by birds, had sprung.

Strangely huddled at the base of the wall, his knees drawn up, and lying on his side, his head touching the cold stones, I saw the wasted Bartleby. But nothing stirred. I paused; then went close up to him; stooped over, and saw that his dim eyes were open; otherwise he seemed profoundly sleeping. Something prompted me to touch him. I felt his hand, when a tingling shiver ran up my arm and down my spine to my feet.

The round face of the grub-man peered upon me now. "His dinner is ready. Won't he dine to-day, either? Or does he live without dining?"

"Lives without dining," said I, and closed the eyes.

"Eh!—He's asleep, aint he?"

"With kings and counselors," murmured I.

There would seem little need for proceeding further in this history. Imagination will readily supply the meagre recital of poor Bartleby's interment. But, ere parting with the reader, let me say, that if this little narrative has sufficiently interested him, to awaken curiosity as to who Bartleby was, and what manner of life he led prior to the present narrator's making his acquaintance, I can only reply, that in such curiosity I fully share, but am wholly unable to gratify it. Yet here I hardly know whether I should divulge one little item of rumor, which came to my ear a few months after the scrivener's decease. Upon what basis it rested, I could never ascertain; and hence, how true it is I cannot now tell. But, inasmuch as this vague report has not been without a certain suggestive interest to me, however sad, it may prove the same with some others; and so I will briefly mention it. The report was this: that Bartleby had been a subordinate clerk in the Dead Letter Office at Washington, from which he had been suddenly removed by a change in the administration. When I think over this rumor, hardly can I express the emotions which seize me. Dead letters! does it not sound like dead men? Conceive a man by nature and misfortune prone to a pallid hopelessness, can any business seem more fitted to heighten it than that of continually handling these dead letters, and assorting them for the flames? For by the cart-load they are annually burned. Sometimes from out the folded paper the pale clerk takes a ring—the finger it was meant for, perhaps, moulders in the grave; a bank-note sent in swiftest charity—he whom it would relieve, nor eats nor hungers any more; pardon for those who died despairing; hope for those who died unhoping; good tidings for those who died stifled by unrelieved calamities. On errands of life, these letters speed to death.

Ah, Bartleby! Ah, humanity!

Bartleby's gradual descent into gloom—and ultimately death—because of his occupation is characterized by the same Gothic theme of entrapment in Edgar Allan Poe's "Fall of the House of Usher" (chapter 6). There's a similarity, too, between Bartleby's hopelessness and Gregor Samsa's transformation into an insect in Franz Kafka's *The Metamorphosis* (chapter 10).

**GOING FURTHER** The themes of failed intentions and mortality explored by Melville in "Bartleby, the Scrivener" can also be found in the fiction of a number of modern American writers, such as the novels *The Moviegoer* (1961) and *Lancelot* (1977) by Walker Percy.

## Ana Menendez (b. 1970)

ANA MENENDEZ WAS born in Los Angeles, the daughter of Cuban exiles. She is the author of two books of fiction: *In Cuba I Was a German Shepherd,* which was a 2001 *New York Times* Notable Book of the Year and whose title story won a Pushcart Prize, and the novel *Loving Che.* Her second novel, *The Last War,* was published in 2009 by HarperCollins. Since 1991, Menendez has worked as a journalist in the United States and abroad, including three years as a prize-winning columnist for *The Miami Herald.* She has a B.A. in English from Florida International University and an M.F.A from New York University. She was a 2008–2009 Fulbright Scholar in Cairo.

# Traveling Madness (2009)

1 All the men on my father's side of the family have been mad in one way or another.

There was my great-uncle Panchito, who joined the communist party in 1934 when it was a nothing party of dreamers only to quit in 1965 when the party officially denied him permission to fly to the moon. He could have turned all those years of underground meetings and patriotic songs into something, he could have cashed in and finally helped his family. Instead, he spent the last years of his life writing angry letters to the Ministry for Travel and Culture, arguing that if the Russians could send a flea-bitten dog into space, certainly the Cubans ought to be able to fly a loyal party monkey to the moon. His latter letters were scrupulously ignored. And he ended up dying in a rented room in his niece's apartment, fighting her until the last for the right to his homemade rum. In the end, the party would not even allow him to be buried in the Patriot's cemetery.

There was a cousin named Severino who hanged himself from a banyan one spring morning after a passing traveler told him there was buried treasure on the other side of the mountain. Severino, who had never even traveled beyond the swamp. As a boy he had been happy to sit out by a stream for hours and launch paper boats, waiting until one disappeared downstream before sending out the next one. The passing traveler was never seen or spoken of again until many years later when miners discovered a silver vein hard against the mountain. The townspeople, in an act of remembering common to those times, named the mine after Severino.

And, most recently, there was my grandfather Solomon, who, as an exile in Miami, one cool winter morning began digging a tunnel beneath the azaleas with the intention of surfacing some day in Havana.

5 The first two stories have been passed down through the family and I can't vouch for the truth in them. The last one I saw with my own eyes and can tell you that nothing can match the image of a shirtless old man with a dream. He had it all planned out, my grandfather did, for he was a man who took great pride in logic and the scientific method. Before he even began to dig, he filled a great many notebooks with figures that explained precisely how many shovels of dirt it would take, how wide the hole should be, and how many years would have to pass before he finally broke through the sand on the other side. I was only eight years old then, but sometimes after school I helped him dig. My grandfather had barely made it under the property line when his project ended abruptly. It seems the neighbors had called the police to say the old man next door was digging what appeared to be a mass grave. It took some days to sort out the complications that followed. But my grandfather never recovered from his disappointment. He sank into a deep sadness that didn't lift even after my father, also prone to making mathematical calculations, pointed out a mistake in his figures and said that it actually would have taken 16,742 years to dig to Havana.

But perhaps the most tragically brilliant of this mad lineage was Matias Padron, a third great-cousin of my father's though marriage by way of his mother. The family connection is tenuous, I know. But I feel a certain pride in claiming Matias, for his story has passed into the island lore of Cuba; his story is all our story.

Matias, so it is told, was not a very big man. This is also true of most of the men on my father's side of the family. But unlike most of the men, who tend to make up in width for what they lack in height, Matias was slightly built all around. He was, it is well known, even smaller and thinner than his wife, who scandalously abused her advantage to keep Matias timid and soft-spoken at home. Matias didn't seem to mind this and often played along good naturedly, now and then repeating a favorite phrase he had heard about the greatness of a man being measured not from the ground to his head, but from the distance of his head to God. The literal-minded took this to be an even greater disadvantage. But Matias knew what he was talking about.

Since he had turned 18, Matias had been running the post office in Santiago de Cuba. By the time he was 40 years old, he had browsed 22 Christmas catalogs from El Encanto, leafed through dozens of Bohemias, and read several hundred letters of love, the great majority of which were not between husbands and wives. But the task that took up most of his time and the one, that by all accounts, he adored above all the others, was predicting the weather. In those years, the postmaster also ran the local telegraph service. This meant that the postmaster, in addition to being the telegrapher, was also a sort of informal meteorologist as the telegraph, for the first time in the Caribbean, was being used to give advanced warnings of storms developing off shore. It was a duty that all the previous postmasters had taken very seriously. But none had thrown themselves into it with anything approaching the passion that Matias brought.

Matias and his wife lived above the post office in a house that, according to tradition, was paid and kept up by the municipality for the use of the postmaster and his family. It was a large house, two stories, with a wide balcony that wrapped around all four sides. But as Matias and his wife had never had children, vast areas of the house remained dark and unused. It was in one such sealed room that Matias established a small office. When he wasn't below in the post office reading other people's mail or receiving telegraphs about the latest events around the world, Matias was in his little office trying to predict the weather. He had all matter of instruments, barometers, thermometers. Probably, it wasn't too different from the type of things amateurs keep the world over. But Matias's secrecy about his room, even from his wife, soon led to talk in the town that Matias was an alchemist dealing in nefarious activities. It was the first chatter about Matias's supposed eccentricity. And just because it prefigured the extraordinary act he was about to embark on, it doesn't mean that it was necessarily a fair assessment. At that moment, I believe that Matias had truly developed a scientific interest in the weather. After all, not too many years had passed since a hurricane had devastated Varadero, cutting the narrow peninsula in half until both oceans met over the sand. Matias, I think, was trying to save Santiago from the next cataclysm.

10 He ordered all manner of new equipment from New York and tore at the packages when they arrived weeks later. Soon he built an observation deck on the roof and in clear weather began sending up weather balloons. At first, the balloons didn't carry anything—Matias merely used them to calculate wind speeds and air pressure. But as technology improved and radio transmitters began to gain wider currency, Matias arranged for bigger and bigger balloons that could carry more and more equipment. Soon he was launching balloons as big as oil drums carrying thermometers, barometers, humidity detectors all wired to a radio that could send the information back to Matias in his little room.

Every Friday, he posted the results on the front door of the post office as well as a small assessment of what the coming week's weather was likely to be. He was right more often than he was wrong and except for a few lapses when, for example, he announced that yesterday "rain had been very heavy" (something the townspeople could know well enough without consulting any instruments other than their memories) the people grew to respect his forecasts.

Cuba had prospered in those years and along with it, Santiago, and along with Santiago, Matias. The memory of hunger was fading. Children grew healthy. And Matias entered middle age in the prime of health. Even the hurricanes that had assaulted Cuba the previous decade seemed to ease and everyone everywhere seemed relaxed and content as if the more malevolent workings of the world had finally passed them by.

Matias continued to go into his office every afternoon and every Friday he emerged with the forecast for the following week. And of course he also continued to send up his balloons, each more elaborate than the last. The weather was not always perfect, but it was predictable. Soon everyone knew the rains would come in August and the heaviest thunder would be reserved for the late afternoon, when the sun began to dip low in the sky. By October, the skies would clear and the blue days return. Winters, whether Matias said so or not, were generally dry and pleasant.

Some nights, couples out for a walk noticed a dark figure above the post office—Matias with his hands on the railing looking up into the sky. But otherwise, few people paid much attention to Matias or his forecasts, anymore. They met him once a week, sometimes touched their fingers lightly to his when he handed them their mail and that was that. It seemed there was nothing left to fear.

15 There are eddies that develop in time, places where histories converge, and individuals caught inside the current find themselves suddenly unable to act for themselves. Perhaps this is what happened to Matias. Maybe everything that followed was as inevitable as history. I have to say things like this because there is really no other explanation for what came to pass. Outside of a family connection, there was nothing in Matias's character to suggest madness. The reports that came out later pointed out that there was no history of despondency. And nothing in the days preceding the event gave anyone any reason to believe that Matias had suffered a sudden depression. The weather, moreover, had been pleasantly uneventful, with, as Matias himself had noted, an abundance of bright days somewhat unusual for springtime.

And yet, the truth is this: One morning Matias was handing a stack of letters to Consuelo Perez and the next he was floating high above Santiago, his office chair dangling beneath four giant weather balloons with him in it.

Santiago had been the first city in Cuba to be linked by telegraph to the rest of the Caribbean. Santiago had been the first city to pioneer the use of observation balloons during war time. The telegraph had connected Cuba to the world, but in the end, the country learned it could not stand alone. Its prosperity and health were forever tethered to history and geography. Did Matias sense this? In those last years he had developed a habit of linking ideas one to the next until he'd convinced himself that there was an inherent logic running through the universe, governing even the impossible. When his own mind finally became untethered, where did it fly to?

His wife was the first to notice Matias had gone. She ran up to the observation deck and when she saw him just clearing the tops of the palms she began to shout at him, You insolent madman, you flying fool! Her shouting brought out a handful of people whose shouting brought out still more people. And soon the whole town was pointing at the sky where Matias floated, sometimes rising suddenly and sometimes hanging in the air, swaying from side to side just over the tree line, every second becoming a little bit smaller in the distance. A few of the men started off after him and when they were directly under his path began shouting instructions at him, in the venerable Cuban tradition: Cut one of the balloons! Jump now, the fronds will break your fall! When you make it over the swamp let the helium out very slowly! They continued to run and shout even after it became clear that Matias was not coming back. One of the men said that just when he was becoming so small that one could hardly make out his person, Matias glanced down at the others and there was a wide, white smile on his face. He was like a saint or a martyr, the man said. And for days, the man could talk of nothing else but Matias's calm happy gaze as he floated away from Santiago forever.

Matias seemed to know right where he was going. All those years of tracing wind patterns had given him a pilot's confidence. It was April, when the winds blow east to west. Before an hour was out he was a tiny speck out over the sea and then he was impossible to make out in the haze. After a while most of the people stopped searching the sky for Matias and began walking back to their homes. A few gathered in silence outside the post office. Matilde locked herself in the house and didn't emerge until the governor arrived two weeks later to take a report. Some days later, the police came for his papers. They carted off hundreds and hundreds of notebooks filled with strange drawings and algebraic calculations. But among the more curious of his possessions was a stuffed owl and a rare Cuban tern preserved in a bottle of formaldehyde.

Today, people in Cuba still say of an elusive fellow, He vanished like Matias Padron.

I think of Matias now and then. I am also a traveler. And nowadays after I have taken off my shoes and put them back on, after I have retrieved my naked laptop from the conveyor and had my purse rifled through, after I have emerged safely on the other side of the security cabal, I like to take a seat up close to the windows and watch the planes come and go. How generous of airport architects to design such large windows. And how good of the staff to keep them so clean and shiny. Coming upon these portals is like stumbling onto a new and intricate explanation of the possible.

I sit in one of the soft functional chairs and watch the planes land and I watch them lift off from the earth. And each time it seems like a miracle. There are so many planes flying in so many different directions that it is difficult to follow a single one. Too often, the flight path takes them beyond my line of vision. But now and then a plane will take off just so and fly straight out in view of all the airport, fly off to that point that everyone calls infinity but is really just the limits of our perception.

I'll follow the plane until it is nothing and know that soon I will be on one just like it. And I wonder, do we still know what it's like to dream about the other side of the mountain? At what point does one cross the crest of forgetting? And this is when I think of Matias, who breached the space of the known for nothing more than a glimpse of the white-blind city on the other side.

If you like this story, you may like the fiction from Latin America by Borges and García Márquez (both in this section), along with the work of Kafka ("The Metamorphosis," chapter 10). You may also like other writers who take up the subject matter of first-generation Americans, such as Chinese-American writer Gish Jen ("Who's Irish?" chapter 5) and Sylvia Watanabe ("Talking to the Dead," chapter 12). You can read Junot Diaz's story "How to Date a Browngirl, Blackgirl, Whitegirl, or Halfie" (chapter 8) in a similar light.

**GOING FURTHER** You may want to read Menendez in the company of her fellow Cuban-American writer Cristina Garcia (*Dreaming in Cuban*) or Haitian-American Edwidge Danticat, who, like Menendez, lives in Miami.

## R. K. Narayan (1906–2001)

R. K. NARAYAN, born in Madras (the southern Indian city now known as Chennai) and educated in English-language schools, was one of the most prolific novelists and story writers of his generation. For a number of decades his work stood as the main source from which many thousands of readers in the West learned about life in India from a native perspective—as opposed, say, to that of a fascinated visitor such as E. M. Forster, in his *Passage to India.* Narayan's close attention to the lives of ordinary people, with all of their foibles and failings, lends his tales about India a universal appeal—and in some ways he is the first of a series of authors to make the subcontinent's culture vividly available in prose.

His creation of a town called "Malgudi" as the setting for a number of his works of fiction shows his affinity with the work of William Faulkner, whose imaginary southern U.S. Yoknapatawpha County served the same purpose of establishing a fictional location that had the air of real geography about it.

# An Astrologer's Day (1947)

1 Punctually at midday he opened his bag and spread out his professional equipment, which consisted of a dozen cowrie shells, a square piece of cloth with obscure mystic charts on it, a notebook and a bundle of palmyra writing. His forehead was resplendent with sacred ash and vermilion, and his eyes sparkled with a sharp abnormal gleam which was really an outcome of a continual searching look for customers, but which his simple clients took to be a prophetic light and felt comforted. The power of his eyes was considerably enhanced by their position—placed as they were between the painted forehead and the dark whiskers which streamed down his cheeks: even a half-wit's eyes would sparkle in such a setting. To crown the effect he wound a saffron-coloured turban around his head. This colour scheme never failed. People were attracted to him as bees are attracted to cosmos or dahlia stalks. He sat under the boughs of a spreading tamarind tree which flanked a path running through the Town Hall Park. It was a remarkable place in many ways: a surging crowd was always moving up and down this narrow road morning till night. A variety of trades and occupations was represented all along its way: medicine-sellers,

sellers of stolen hardware and junk, magicians and, above all, an auctioneer of cheap cloth, who created enough din all day to attract the whole town. Next to him in vociferousness came a vendor of fried groundnuts, who gave his ware a fancy name each day, calling it Bombay Ice-Cream one day, and on the next Delhi Almond, and on the third Raja's Delicacy, and so on and so forth, and people flocked to him. A considerable portion of this crowd dallied before the astrologer too. The astrologer transacted his business by the light of a flare which crackled and smoked up above the groundnut heap nearby. Half the enchantment of the place was due to the fact that it did not have the benefit of municipal lighting. The place was lit up by shop lights. One or two had hissing gaslights, some had naked flares stuck on poles, some were lit up by old cycle lamps and one or two, like the astrologer's, managed without lights of their own. It was a bewildering crisscross of light rays and moving shadows. This suited the astrologer very well, for the simple reason that he had not in the least intended to be an astrologer when he began life; and he knew no more of what was going to happen to others than he knew what was going to happen to himself next minute. He was as much a stranger to the stars as were his innocent customers. Yet he said things which pleased and astonished everyone: that was more a matter of study, practice and shrewd guesswork. All the same, it was as much an honest man's labour as any other, and he deserved the wages he carried home at the end of a day.

He had left his village without any previous thought or plan. If he had continued there he would have carried on the work of his forefathers—namely, tilling the land, living, marrying and ripening in his cornfield and ancestral home. But that was not to be. He had to leave home without telling anyone, and he could not rest till he left it behind a couple of hundred miles. To a villager it is a great deal, as if an ocean flowed between.

He had a working analysis of mankind's troubles: marriage, money and the tangles of human ties. Long practice had sharpened his perception. Within five minutes he understood what was wrong. He charged three pies per question and never opened his mouth till the other had spoken for at least ten minutes, which provided him enough stuff for a dozen answers and advices. When he told the person before him, gazing at his palm, "In many ways you are not getting the fullest results for your efforts," nine out of ten were disposed to agree with him. Or he questioned: "Is there any woman in your family, maybe even a distant relative, who is not well disposed towards you?" Or he gave an analysis of character: "Most of your troubles are due to your nature. How can you be otherwise with Saturn where he is? You have an impetuous nature and a rough exterior." This endeared him to their hearts immediately, for even the mildest of us loves to think that he has a forbidding exterior.

The nuts-vendor blew out his flare and rose to go home. This was a signal for the astrologer to bundle up too, since it left him in darkness except for a little shaft of green light which strayed in from somewhere and touched the ground before him. He picked up his cowrie shells and paraphernalia and was putting them back into his bag when the green shaft of light was blotted out; he looked up and saw a man standing before him. He sensed a possible client and said: "You look so careworn. It will do you good to sit down for a while and chat with me." The other grumbled some vague reply. The astrologer pressed his invitation; whereupon the other thrust his palm under his nose, saying: "You call yourself an astrologer?" The astrologer felt challenged and said, tilting the other's palm towards the green shaft of light: "Yours is a nature . . ." "Oh, stop that," the other said. "Tell me something worthwhile . . ."

5 Our friend felt piqued. "I charge only three pies per question, and what you get ought to be good enough for your money . . ." At this the other withdrew his arm, took out an anna and flung it out to him, saying, "I have some questions to ask. If I prove you are bluffing, you must return that anna to me with interest."

"If you find my answers satisfactory, will you give me five rupees?"

"No."

"Or will you give me eight annas?"

"All right, provided you give me twice as much if you are wrong," said the stranger. This pact was accepted after a little further argument. The astrologer sent up a prayer to heaven as the other lit a cheroot. The astrologer caught a glimpse of his face by the match-light. There was a pause as cars hooted on the road, *jutka*-drivers swore at their horses and the babble of the crowd agitated the semi-darkness of the park. The other sat down, sucking his cheroot, puffing out, sat there ruthlessly. The astrologer felt very uncomfortable. "Here, take your anna back. I am not used to such challenges. It is late for me today . . ." He made preparations to bundle up. The other held his wrist and said, "You can't get out of it now. You dragged me in while I was passing." The astrologer shivered in his grip; and his voice shook and became faint. "Leave me today. I will speak to you tomorrow." The other thrust his palm in his face and said, "Challenge is challenge. Go on." The astrologer proceeded with his throat drying up. "There is a woman . . ."

"Stop," said the other. "I don't want all that. Shall I succeed in my present search or not? Answer this and go. Otherwise I will not let you go till you disgorge all your coins." The astrologer muttered a few incantations and replied, "All right. I will speak. But will you give me a rupee if what I say is convincing? Otherwise I will not open my mouth, and you may do what you like." After a good deal of haggling the other agreed. The astrologer said, "You were left for dead. Am I right?"

"Ah, tell me more."

"A knife has passed through you once?" said the astrologer.

"Good fellow!" He bared his chest to show the scar. "What else?"

"And then you were pushed into a well nearby in the field. You were left for dead."

"I should have been dead if some passer-by had not chanced to peep into the well," exclaimed the other, overwhelmed by enthusiasm. "When shall I get at him?" he asked, clenching his fist.

"In the next world," answered the astrologer. "He died four months ago in a far-off town. You will never see any more of him." The other groaned on hearing it. The astrologer proceeded.

"Guru Nayak—"

"You know my name!" the other said, taken aback.

"As I know all other things. Guru Nayak, listen carefully to what I have to say. Your village is two days' journey due north of this town. Take the next train and be gone. I see once again great danger to your life if you go from home." He took out a pinch of sacred ash and held it out to him. "Rub it on your forehead and go home. Never travel southward again, and you will live to be a hundred."

"Why should I leave home again?" the other said reflectively. "I was only going away now and then to look for him and to choke out his life if I met him." He shook his head regretfully. "He has escaped my hands. I hope at least he died as he deserved." "Yes," said the astrologer. "He was crushed under a lorry." The other looked gratified to hear it.

The place was deserted by the time the astrologer picked up his articles and put them into his bag. The green shaft was also gone, leaving the place in darkness and silence. The stranger had gone off into the night, after giving the astrologer a handful of coins.

It was nearly midnight when the astrologer reached home. His wife was waiting for him at the door and demanded an explanation. He flung the coins at her and said, "Count them. One man gave all that."

"Twelve and a half annas," she said, counting. She was overjoyed. "I can buy some *jaggery* and coconut tomorrow. The child has been asking for sweets for so many days now. I will prepare some nice stuff for her."

"The swine has cheated me! He promised me a rupee," said the astrologer. She looked up at him. "You look worried. What is wrong?"

"Nothing."

After dinner, sitting on the *pyol,* he told her, "Do you know a great load is gone from me today? I thought I had the blood of a man on my hands all these years. That was the reason why I ran away from home, settled here and married you. He is alive."

She gasped. "You tried to kill!"

"Yes, in our village, when I was a silly youngster. We drank, gambled and quarrelled badly one day—why think of it now? Time to sleep," he said, yawning, and stretched himself on the *pyol.*

If you like "An Astrologer's Day," you may also like "Interpreter of Maladies" by Jhumpa Lahiri (chapter 9).

**GOING FURTHER** Stories and novels by South Asian writers are plentiful these days, and such writers as Salman Rushdie and Amitav Ghosh sometimes reach the bestseller lists. Chitra Banerjee Divakaruni's *The Mistress of Spices* was, like Lahiri's *The Namesake,* made into a film.

## Leo Tolstoy (1828–1910)

ONE OF RUSSIA'S most famous authors—both today and in his lifetime—Leo Tolstoy began life in the upper-class gentry and ended in self-elected poverty. As a young man he joined the army and fought in the Crimean War. During this period, he published his first works, which were largely about growing up or army life. Always introspective, Tolstoy grew frustrated with his youthful propensities for gambling and women; his struggle against these temptations led him to proclaim a fervent faith in God. The next period of his life was the happiest, the time in which he married, began a family of nine children, and wrote his two major masterpieces, *War and Peace* (1869) and *Anna Karenina* (1877).

While finishing *Anna Karenina,* however, Tolstoy became depressed to the point that he considered suicide, viewing his career and literary accomplishments as vanities. He renounced ostentation, simplified his life by dividing his property among his children, and became a vegetarian who wore peasant clothing. Although these actions estranged him from his family, many people, including Mohandas Gandhi, were inspired by "Tolstoyism"—Tolstoy's belief that goodness is achieved through passive resistance to evil, a dogma based on Christian teachings. His fiction is noted for its psychological realism in exploring both male and female characters in the face of great historical moments, moral crises, and death.

# The Death of Ivan Ilych (1886)

### I

1 During an interval in the Melvinski trial in the large building of the Law Courts, the members and public prosecutor met in Ivan Egorovich Shebek's private room, where the conversation turned on the celebrated Krasovski case. Fëdor Vasilievich warmly maintained that it was not subject to their jurisdiction, Ivan Egorovich maintained the contrary, while Peter Ivanovich, not having entered into the discussion at the start, took no part in it but looked through the *Gazette* which had just been handed in.

"Gentlemen," he said, "Ivan Ilych has died!"

"You don't say so!"

"Here, read it yourself," replied Peter Ivanovich, handing Fëdor Vasilievich the paper still damp from the press. Surrounded by a black border were the words: "Praskovya Fëdorovna Goloviná, with profound sorrow, informs relatives and friends of the demise of her beloved husband Ivan Ilych Golovin, Member of the Court of Justice, which occurred on February the 4th of this year 1882. The funeral will take place on Friday at one o'clock in the afternoon."

Ivan Ilych had been a colleague of the gentlemen present and was liked by them all. He had been ill for some weeks with an illness said to be incurable. His post had been kept open for him, but there had been conjectures that in case of his death Alexeev might receive his appointment, and that either Vinnikov or Shtabel would succeed Alexeev. So on receiving the news of Ivan Ilych's death the first thought of each of the gentlemen in that private room was of the changes and promotions it might occasion among themselves or their acquaintances.

"I shall be sure to get Shtabel's place or Vinnikov's," thought Fëdor Vasilievich. "I was promised that long ago, and the promotion means an extra eight hundred rubles a year for me besides the allowance."

"Now I must apply for my brother-in-law's transfer from Kaluga," thought Peter Ivanovich. "My wife will be very glad, and then she won't be able to say that I never do anything for her relations."

"I thought he would never leave his bed again," said Peter Ivanovich aloud. "It's very sad."

"But what really was the matter with him?"

"The doctors couldn't say—at least they could, but each of them said something different. When last I saw him I thought he was getting better."

"And I haven't been to see him since the holidays. I always meant to go."

"Had he any property?"

"I think his wife had a little—but something quite trifling."

"We shall have to go to see her, but they live so terribly far away."

"Far away from you, you mean. Everything's far away from your place."

"You see, he never can forgive my living on the other side of the river," said Peter Ivanovich, smiling at Shebek. Then, still talking of the distances between different parts of the city, they returned to the Court.

Besides considerations as to the possible transfers and promotions likely to result from Ivan Ilych's death, the mere fact of the death of a near acquaintance aroused, as usual, in all who heard of it the complacent feeling that, "it is he who is dead and not I."

Each one thought or felt, "Well, he's dead but I'm alive!" But the more intimate of Ivan Ilych's acquaintances, his so-called friends, could not help thinking also that they would now have to fulfill the very tiresome demands of propriety by attending the funeral service and paying a visit of condolence to the widow.

Fëdor Vasilievich and Peter Ivanovich had been his nearest acquaintances. Peter Ivanovich had studied law with Ivan Ilych and had considered himself to be under obligations to him.

Having told his wife at dinner-time of Ivan Ilych's death and of his conjecture that it might be possible to get her brother transferred to their circuit, Peter Ivanovich sacrificed his usual nap, put on his evening clothes, and drove to Ivan Ilych's house.

At the entrance stood a carriage and two cabs. Leaning against the wall in the hall downstairs near the cloak-stand was a coffin-lid covered with cloth of gold, ornamented with gold cord and tassels, that had been polished up with metal powder. Two ladies in black were taking off their fur cloaks. Peter Ivanovich recognized one of them as Ivan Ilych's sister, but the other was a stranger to him. His colleague Schwartz was just coming downstairs, but on seeing Peter Ivanovich enter he stopped and winked at him, as if to say: "Ivan Ilych has made a mess of things—not like you and me."

Schwartz's face with his Piccadilly whiskers and his slim figure in evening dress had as usual an air of elegant solemnity which contrasted with the playfulness of his character and had a special piquancy here, or so it seemed to Peter Ivanovich.

Peter Ivanovich allowed the ladies to precede him and slowly followed them upstairs. Schwartz did not come down but remained where he was, and Peter Ivanovich understood that he wanted to arrange where they should play bridge that evening. The ladies went upstairs to the widow's room, and Schwartz with seriously compressed lips but a playful look in his eyes, indicated by a twist of his eyebrows the room to the right where the body lay.

Peter Ivanovich, like everyone else on such occasions, entered feeling uncertain what he would have to do. All he knew was that at such times it is always safe to cross oneself. But he was not quite sure whether one should make obeisances while doing so. He therefore adopted a middle course. On entering the room he began crossing himself and made a slight movement resembling a bow. At the same time, as far as the motion of his head and arm allowed, he surveyed the room. Two young men—apparently nephews, one of whom was a high-school pupil—were leaving the room, crossing themselves as they did so. An old woman was standing motionless, and a lady with strangely arched eyebrows was saying something to her in a whisper. A vigorous, resolute Church Reader, in a frock-coat, was reading something in a loud voice with an expression that precluded any contradiction. The butler's assistant, Gerasim, stepping lightly in front of Peter Ivanovich, was strewing something on the floor. Noticing this, Peter Ivanovich was immediately aware of a faint odor of a decomposing body.

The last time he had called on Ivan Ilych, Peter Ivanovich had seen Gerasim in the study. Ivan Ilych had been particularly fond of him and he was performing the duty of a sick nurse.

Peter Ivanovich continued to make the sign of the cross, slightly inclining his head in an intermediate direction between the coffin, the Reader, and the icons on the table in a corner of the room. Afterwards, when it seemed to him that this movement of his arm in crossing himself had gone on too long, he stopped and began to look at the corpse.

The dead man lay, as dead men always lie, in a specially heavy way, his rigid limbs sunk in the soft cushions of the coffin, with the head forever bowed on the pillow. His yellow waxen brow with bald patches over his sunken temples was thrust up in the way peculiar to the dead, the protruding nose seeming to press on the upper lip. He was much changed and had grown even thinner since Peter Ivanovich had last seen him, but, as is always the case with the dead, his face was handsomer and above all more dignified than when he was alive. The expression on the face said that what was necessary had been accomplished, and accomplished rightly. Besides this there was in that expression a reproach and a warning to the living. This warning seemed to Peter Ivanovich out of place, or at least not applicable to him. He felt a certain discomfort and so he hurriedly crossed himself once more and turned and went out the door—too hurriedly and too regardless of propriety, as he himself was aware.

Schwartz was waiting for him in the adjoining room with legs spread wide apart and both hands toying with his top-hat behind his back. The mere sight of that playful, well-groomed, and elegant figure refreshed Peter Ivanovich. He felt that Schwartz was above all these happenings and would not surrender to any depressing influences. His very look said that this incident of a church service for Ivan Ilych could not be a sufficient reason for infringing the order of the session—in other words, that it would certainly not prevent his unwrapping a new pack of cards and shuffling them that evening while a footman placed four fresh candles on the table: in fact, that there was no reason for supposing that this incident would hinder their spending the evening agreeably. Indeed he said this in a whisper as Peter Ivanovich passed him, proposing that they should meet for a game at Fēdor Vasilievich's. But apparently Peter Ivanovich was not destined to play bridge that evening. Praskovya Fēdorovna (a short, fat woman who despite all efforts to the contrary had continued to broaden steadily from her shoulders downwards and who had the same extraordinarily arched eyebrows as the lady who had been standing by the coffin), dressed all in black, her head covered with lace, came out of her own room with some other ladies, conducted them to the room where the dead body lay, and said: "The service will begin immediately. Please go in."

Schwartz, making an indefinite bow, stood still, evidently neither accepting nor declining this invitation. Praskovya Fēdorovna recognizing Peter Ivanovich, sighed, went close up to him, took his hand, and said: "I know you were a true friend to Ivan Ilych . . ." and looked at him awaiting some suitable response. And Peter Ivanovich knew that, just as it had been the right thing to cross himself in that room, so what he had to do here was to press her hand, sigh, and say, "Believe me. . . ." So he did all this and as he did it felt that the desired result had been achieved: that both he and she were touched.

"Come with me. I want to speak to you before it begins," said the widow. "Give me your arm."

Peter Ivanovich gave her his arm and they went to the inner rooms, passing Schwartz, who winked at Peter Ivanovich compassionately.

"That does for our bridge! Don't object if we find another player. Perhaps you can cut in when you do escape," said his playful look.

Peter Ivanovich sighed still more deeply and despondently, and Praskovya Fëdorovna pressed his arm gratefully. When they reached the drawing-room, upholstered in pink cretonne and lighted by a dim lamp, they sat down at the table—she on a sofa and Peter Ivanovich on a low pouffe, the springs of which yielded spasmodically under his weight. Praskovya Fëdorovna had been on the point of warning him to take another seat, but felt that such a warning was out of keeping with her present condition and so changed her mind. As he sat down on the pouffe Peter Ivanovich recalled how Ivan Ilych had arranged this room and had consulted him regarding this pink cretonne with green leaves. The whole room was full of furniture and knick-knacks, and on her way to the sofa the lace of the widow's black shawl caught on the carved edge of the table. Peter Ivanovich rose to detach it, and the springs of the pouffe, relieved of his weight, rose also and gave him a push. The widow began detaching her shawl herself, and Peter Ivanovich again sat down, suppressing the rebellious springs of the pouffe under him. But the widow had not quite freed herself and Peter Ivanovich got up again, and again the pouffe rebelled and even creaked. When this was all over she took out a clean cambric handkerchief and began to weep. The episode with the shawl and the struggle with the pouffe had cooled Peter Ivanovich's emotions and he sat there with a sullen look on his face. This awkward situation was interrupted by Sokolov, Ivan Ilych's butler, who came to report that the plot in the cemetery that Praskovya Fëdorovna had chosen would cost two hundred rubles. She stopped weeping and, looking at Peter Ivanovich with the air of a victim, remarked in French that it was very hard for her. Peter Ivanovich made a silent gesture signifying his full conviction that it must indeed be so.

"Please smoke," she said in a magnanimous yet crushed voice, and turned to discuss with Sokolov the price of the plot for the grave.

35 Peter Ivanovich while lighting his cigarette heard her inquiring very circumstantially into the prices of different plots in the cemetery and finally decide which she would take. When that was done she gave instructions about engaging the choir. Sokolov then left the room.

"I look after everything myself," she told Peter Ivanovich, shifting the albums that lay on the table; and noticing that the table was endangered by his cigarette-ash, she immediately passed him an ashtray, saying as she did so: "I consider it an affectation to say that my grief prevents my attending to practical affairs. On the contrary, if anything can—I won't say console me, but—distract me, it is seeing to everything concerning him." She again took out her handkerchief as if preparing to cry, but suddenly, as if mastering her feeling, she shook herself and began to speak calmly. "But there is something I want to talk to you about."

Peter Ivanovich bowed, keeping control of the springs of the pouffe, which immediately began quivering under him.

"He suffered terribly the last few days."

"Did he?" said Peter Ivanovich.

40 "Oh, terribly! He screamed unceasingly, not for minutes but for hours. For the last three days he screamed incessantly. It was unendurable. I cannot understand how I bore it; you could hear him three rooms off. Oh, what I have suffered!"

"Is it possible that he was conscious all that time?" asked Peter Ivanovich.

"Yes," she whispered. "To the last moment. He took leave of us a quarter of an hour before he died, and asked us to take Vasya away."

The thought of the sufferings of this man he had known so intimately, first as a merry little boy, then as a school-mate, and later as a grown-up colleague, suddenly struck Peter Ivanovich with horror, despite an unpleasant consciousness of his own and this woman's dissimulation. He again saw that brow, and that nose pressing down on the lip, and felt afraid for himself.

"Three days of frightful suffering and then death! Why, that might suddenly, at any time, happen to me," he thought, and for a moment felt terrified. But—he did not himself know how—the customary reflection at once occurred to him that this had happened to Ivan Ilych and not to him, and that it should not and could not happen to him, and that to think that it could would be yielding to depression which he ought not to do, as Schwartz's expression plainly showed. After which reflection Peter Ivanovich felt reassured, and began to ask with interest about the details of Ivan Ilych's death, as though death was an accident natural to Ivan Ilych but certainly not to himself.

After many details of the really dreadful physical sufferings Ivan Ilych had endured (which details he learnt only from the effect those sufferings had produced on Praskovya Fëdorovna's nerves) the widow apparently found it necessary to get to business.

"Oh, Peter Ivanovich, how hard it is! How terribly, terribly hard!" and she again began to weep.

Peter Ivanovich sighed and waited for her to finish blowing her nose. When she had done so he said, "Believe me . . ." and she again began talking and brought out what was evidently her chief concern with him—namely, to question him as to how she could obtain a grant of money from the government on the occasion of her husband's death. She made it appear that she was asking Peter Ivanovich's advice about her pension, but he soon saw that she already knew about that to the minutest detail, more even than he did himself. She knew how much could be got out of the government in consequence of her husband's death, but wanted to find out whether she could not possibly extract something more. Peter Ivanovich tried to think of some means of doing so, but after reflecting for a while and, out of propriety, condemning the government for its niggardliness, he said he thought that nothing more could be got. Then she sighed and evidently began to devise means of getting rid of her visitor. Noticing this, he put out his cigarette, rose, pressed her hand, and went out into the anteroom.

In the dining-room where the clock stood that Ivan Ilych had liked so much and had bought at an antique shop, Peter Ivanovich met a priest and a few acquaintances who had come to attend the service, and he recognized Ivan Ilych's daughter, a handsome young woman. She was in black and her slim figure appeared slimmer than ever. She had a gloomy, determined, almost angry expression, and bowed to Peter Ivanovich as though he were in some way to blame. Behind her, with the same offended look, stood a wealthy young man, an examining magistrate, whom Peter Ivanovich also knew and who was her fiancé, as he had heard. He bowed mournfully to them and was about to pass into the death-chamber, when from under the stairs appeared the figure of Ivan Ilych's schoolboy son, who was extremely like his father. He seemed a little Ivan Ilych, such as Peter Ivanovich remembered when they studied law together. His tear-stained eyes had in them the look that is seen in the eyes of boys of thirteen or fourteen who are not pureminded. When he saw Peter Ivanovich he scowled morosely and shamefacedly. Peter Ivanovich nodded to him and entered the death-chamber. The service began: candles, groans, incense, tears, and sobs. Peter Ivanovich stood looking gloomily down at his feet. He did not look once at the dead man, did not yield to any depressing influence, and was one of the first to leave the room. There was no one in the anteroom, but Gerasim darted out of the dead man's room, rummaged with his strong hands among the fur coats to find Peter Ivanovich's and helped him on with it.

"Well, friend Gerasim," said Peter Ivanovich, so as to say something. "It's a sad affair, isn't it?"

"It's God will. We shall all come to it some day," said Gerasim, displaying his teeth—the even white teeth of a healthy peasant—and, like a man in the thick of urgent work, he briskly opened the front door, called the coachman, helped Peter Ivanovich into the sledge, and sprang back to the porch as if in readiness for what he had to do next.

Peter Ivanovich found the fresh air particularly pleasant after the smell of incense, the dead body, and carbolic acid.

"Where to sir?" asked the coachman.

"It's not too late even now . . . I'll call round on Fëdor Vasilievich."

He accordingly drove there and found them just finishing the first rubber, so that it was quite convenient for him to cut in.

## II

Ivan Ilych's life had been most simple and most ordinary and therefore most terrible.

He had been a member of the Court of Justice, and died at the age of forty-five. His father had been an official who after serving in various ministries and departments in Petersburg had made the sort of career which brings men to positions from which by reason of their long service they cannot be dismissed, though they are obviously unfit to hold any responsible position, and for whom therefore posts are specially created, which though fictitious carry salaries of from six to ten thousand rubles that are not fictitious, and in receipt of which they live on to a great age.

Such was the Privy Councillor and superfluous member of various superfluous institutions, Ilya Epimovich Golovin.

He had three sons, of whom Ivan Ilych was the second. The eldest son was following in his father's footsteps only in another department, and was already approaching that stage in the service at which a similar sinecure would be reached. The third son was a failure. He had ruined his prospects in a number of positions and was now serving in the railway department. His father and brothers, and still more their wives, not merely disliked meeting him, but avoided remembering his existence unless compelled to do so. His sister had married Baron Greff, a Petersburg official of her father's type. Ivan Ilych was *le phénix de la famille*[1] as people said. He was neither as cold and formal as his elder brother nor as wild as the younger, but was a happy mean between them—an intelligent, polished, lively, and agreeable man. He had studied with his younger brother at the School of Law, but the latter had failed to complete the course and was expelled when he was in the fifth class. Ivan Ilych finished the course well. Even when he was at the School of Law he was just what he remained for the rest of his life: a capable, cheerful, good-natured, and sociable man, though strict in the fulfillment of what he considered to be his duty: and he considered his duty to be what was so considered by those in authority. Neither as a boy nor as a man was he a toady, but from early youth was by nature attracted to people of high station as a fly is drawn to the light, assimilating their ways and views of life and establishing friendly relations with them. All the enthusiasms of childhood and youth passed without leaving much trace on him; he succumbed to sensuality, to vanity, and latterly among the highest classes to liberalism, but always within limits which his instinct unfailingly indicated to him as correct.

At school he had done things which had formerly seemed to him very horrid and made him feel disgusted with himself when he did them; but when later on he saw that such actions were done by people of good position and that they did not regard them as wrong, he was able not exactly to regard them as right, but to forget about them entirely or not be at all troubled at remembering them.

60 Having graduated from the School of Law and qualified for the tenth rank of the civil service, and having received money from his father for his equipment, Ivan Ilych ordered himself clothes at Scharmer's, the fashionable tailor, hung a medallion inscribed *respice finem*[2] on his watch-chain, took leave of his professor and the prince who was patron of the school, had a farewell dinner with his comrades at Donon's first-class restaurant, and with his new and fashionable portmanteau, linen, clothes, shaving and other toilet appliances, and a traveling rug all purchased at the best shops, he set off for one of the provinces where through his father's influence, he had been attached to the Governor as an official for special service.

In the province Ivan Ilych soon arranged as easy and agreeable a position for himself as he had had at the School of Law. He performed his official tasks, made his career, and at the same time amused himself pleasantly and decorously. Occasionally he paid official visits to country districts, where he behaved with dignity both to his superiors and inferiors, and performed the duties entrusted to him, which related chiefly to the sectarians, with an exactness and incorruptible honesty of which he could not but feel proud.

In official matters, despite his youth and taste for frivolous gaiety, he was exceedingly reserved, punctilious, and even severe; but in society he was often amusing and witty, and always good-natured, correct in his manner, and *bon enfant*,[3] as the Governor and his wife—with whom he was like one of the family—used to say of him.

In the province he had an affair with a lady who made advances to the elegant young lawyer, and there was also a milliner; and there were carousals with aides-de-camp who visited the district, and after-supper visits to a certain outlying street of doubtful reputation; and there was too some obsequiousness to his chief and even to his chief's wife, but all this was done with such a tone of good breeding that no hard names could be applied to it. It all came under the heading

---

[1]French: "Paragon of the family"—the child most likely to succeed.

[2]Latin phrase meaning "Consider the end" (of one's life).

[3]French: "Good Child"—a phrase used to describe an amiable disposition.

of the French saying: "*Il faut que jeunesse se passe.*"[4] It was all done with clean hands, in clean linen, with French phrases, and above all among people of the best society and consequently with the approval of people of rank.

So Ivan Ilych served for five years and then came a change in his official life. The new and reformed judicial institutions were introduced, and new men were needed. Ivan Ilych became such a new man. He was offered the post of examining magistrate, and he accepted it though the post was in another province and obliged him to give up the connections he had formed and to make new ones. His friends met to give him a send-off; they had a group photograph taken and presented him with a silver cigarette-case, and he set off to his new post.

As examining magistrate Ivan Ilych was just as *comme il faut*[5] and decorous a man, inspiring general respect and capable of separating his official duties from his private life, as he had been when acting as an official on special service. His duties now as examining magistrate were far more interesting and attractive than before. In his former position it had been pleasant to wear an undress uniform made by Scharmer, and to pass through the crowd of petitioners and officials who were timorously awaiting an audience with the Governor, and who envied him as with free and easy gait he went straight into his chief's private room to have a cup of tea and a cigarette with him. But not many people had then been directly dependent on him—only police officials and the sectarians when he went on special missions—and he liked to treat them politely, almost as comrades, as if he were letting them feel that he who had the power to crush them was treating them in this simple, friendly way. There were then but few such people. But now, as an examining magistrate, Ivan Ilych felt that everyone without exception, even the most important and self-satisfied, was in his power, and that he need only write a few words on a sheet of paper with a certain heading, and this or that important, self-satisfied person would be brought before him in the role of an accused person or a witness, and if he did not choose to allow him to sit down, would have to stand before him and answer his questions. Ivan Ilych never abused his power; he tried on the contrary to soften its expression, but the consciousness of it and of the possibility of softening its effect, supplied the chief interest and attraction of his office. In his work itself, especially in his examinations, he very soon acquired a method of eliminating all considerations irrelevant to the legal aspect of the case, and reducing even the most complicated case to a form in which it would be presented on paper only in its externals, completely excluding his personal opinion of the matter, while above all observing every prescribed formality. The work was new and Ivan Ilych was one of the first men to apply the new Code of 1864.

On taking up the post of examining magistrate in a new town, he made new acquaintances and connections, placed himself on a new footing and assumed a somewhat different tone. He took up an attitude of rather dignified aloofness towards the provincial authorities, but picked out the best circle of legal gentlemen and wealthy gentry living in the town and assumed a tone of slight dissatisfaction with the government, of moderate liberalism, and of enlightened citizenship. At the same time, without at all altering the elegance of his toilet, he ceased shaving his chin and allowed his beard to grow as it pleased.

Ivan Ilych settled down very pleasantly in this new town. The society there, which inclined towards opposition to the Governor, was friendly, his salary was larger, and he began to play *vint*, which he found added not a little to the pleasure of life, for he had a capacity for cards, played good-humoredly, and calculated rapidly and astutely, so that he usually won.

After living there for two years he met his future wife, Praskovya Fëdorovna Mikhel, who was the most attractive, clever, and brilliant girl of the set in which he moved, and among other amusements and relaxations from his labors as examining magistrate, Ivan Ilych established light and playful relations with her.

While he had been an official on special service he had been accustomed to dance, but now as an examining magistrate it was exceptional for him to do so. If he danced now, he did it as if to show that though he served under the reformed order of things, and had reached the fifth official rank,

[4]French: "Youth must pass"—a phrase similar to "boys will be boys."

[5]French: "As it should be."

yet when it came to dancing he could do it better than most people. So at the end of an evening he sometimes danced with Praskovya Fëdorovna, and it was chiefly during these dances that he captivated her. She fell in love with him. Ivan Ilych had at first no definite intention of marrying, but when the girl fell in love with him he said to himself: "Really, why shouldn't I marry?"

70 Praskovya Fëdorovna came of a good family, was not bad-looking, and had some little property. Ivan Ilych might have aspired to a more brilliant match, but even this was good. He had his salary, and she, he hoped, would have an equal income. She was well connected, and was a sweet, pretty, and thoroughly correct young woman. To say that Ivan Ilych married because he fell in love with Praskovya Fëdorovna and found that she sympathized with his views of life would be as incorrect as to say that he married because his social circle approved of the match. He was swayed by both these considerations: the marriage gave him personal satisfaction, and at the same time it was considered the right thing by the most highly placed of his associates.

So Ivan Ilych got married.

The preparations for marriage and the beginning of married life, with its conjugal caresses, the new furniture, new crockery, and new linen, were very pleasant until his wife became pregnant—so that Ivan Ilych had begun to think that marriage would not impair the easy, agreeable, gay, and always decorous character of his life, approved of by society and regarded by himself as natural, but would even improve it. But from the first months of his wife's pregnancy, something new, unpleasant, depressing, and unseemly, and from which there was no way of escape, unexpectedly showed itself.

His wife, without any reason—*de gaieté de coeur*[6] as Ivan Ilych expressed it to himself—began to disturb the pleasure and propriety of their life. She began to be jealous without any cause, expected him to devote his whole attention to her, found fault with everything, and made coarse and ill-mannered scenes.

At first Ivan Ilych hoped to escape from the unpleasantness of this state of affairs by the same easy and decorous relation to life that had served him heretofore: he tried to ignore his wife's disagreeable moods, continued to live in his usual easy and pleasant way, invited friends to his house for a game of cards, and also tried going out to his club or spending his evenings with friends. But one day his wife began upbraiding him so vigorously, using such coarse words, and continued to abuse him every time he did not fulfill her demands, so resolutely and with such evident determination not to give way till he submitted—that is, till he stayed at home and was bored just as she was—that he became alarmed. He now realized that matrimony—at any rate with Praskovya Fëdorovna—was not always conducive to the pleasures and amenities of life, but on the contrary often infringed both comfort and propriety, and that he must therefore entrench himself against such infringement. And Ivan Ilych began to seek for means of doing so. His official duties were the one thing that imposed upon Praskovya Fëdorovna, and by means of his official work and the duties attached to it he began struggling with his wife to secure his own independence.

75 With the birth of their child, the attempts to feed it and the various failures in doing so, and with the real and imaginary illnesses of mother and child, in which Ivan Ilych's sympathy was demanded but about which he understood nothing, the need of securing for himself an existence outside his family life became still more imperative.

As his wife grew more irritable and exacting and Ivan Ilych transferred the center of gravity of his life more and more to his official work, so did he grow to like his work better and became more ambitious than before.

Very soon, within a year of his wedding, Ivan Ilych had realized that marriage, though it may add some comforts to life, is in fact a very intricate and difficult affair towards which in order to perform one's duty, that is, to lead a decorous life approved of by society, one must adopt a definite attitude just as towards one's official duties.

And Ivan Ilych evolved such an attitude towards married life. He only required of it those conveniences—dinner at home, housewife, and bed—which it could give him, and above all that propriety of external forms required by public opinion. For the rest he looked for light-

---

[6]French: "To the heart's delight."

hearted pleasure and propriety, and was very thankful when he found them, but if he met with antagonism and querulousness he at once retired into his separate fenced-off world of official duties, where he found satisfaction.

Ivan Ilych was esteemed a good official, and after three years was made Assistant Public Prosecutor. His new duties, their importance, the possibility of indicting and imprisoning anyone he chose, the publicity his speeches received, and the success he had in all these things, made his work still more attractive.

30 More children came. His wife became more and more querulous and ill-tempered, but the attitude Ivan Ilych had adopted towards his home life rendered him almost impervious to her grumbling.

After seven years' service in that town he was transferred to another province as Public Prosecutor. They moved, but were short of money and his wife did not like the place they moved to. Though the salary was higher the cost of living was greater, besides which two of their children died and family life became still more unpleasant for him.

Praskovya Fëdorovna blamed her husband for every inconvenience they encountered in their new home. Most of the conversations between husband and wife, especially as to the children's education, led to topics which recalled former disputes, and these disputes were apt to flare up again at any moment. There remained only those rare periods of amorousness which still came to them at times but did not last long. These were islets at which they anchored for a while and then again set out upon that ocean of veiled hostility which showed itself in their aloofness from one another. This aloofness might have grieved Ivan Ilych had he considered that it ought not to exist, but he now regarded the position as normal, and even made it the goal at which he aimed in family life. His aim was to free himself more and more from those unpleasantnesses and to give them a semblance of harmlessness and propriety. He attained this by spending less and less time with his family, and when obliged to be at home he tried to safeguard his position by the presence of outsiders. The chief thing, however, was that he had his official duties. The whole interest of his life now centered in the official world and that interest absorbed him. The consciousness of his power, being able to ruin anybody he wished to ruin, the importance, even the external dignity of his entry into court, or meetings with his subordinates, his success with superiors and inferiors, and above all his masterly handling of cases, of which he was conscious—all this gave him pleasure and filled his life, together with chats with his colleagues, dinners, and bridge. So that on the whole Ivan Ilych's life continued to flow as he considered it should do—pleasantly and properly.

So things continued for another seven years. His eldest daughter was already sixteen, another child had died, and only one son was left, a schoolboy and a subject of dissension. Ivan Ilych wanted to put him in the School of Law, but to spite him Praskovya Fëdorovna entered him at the High School. The daughter had been educated at home and had turned out well: the boy did not learn badly either.

## III

So Ivan Ilych lived for seventeen years after his marriage. He was already a Public Prosecutor of long standing, and had declined several proposed transfers while awaiting a more desirable post, when an unanticipated and unpleasant occurrence quite upset the peaceful course of his life. He was expecting to be offered the post of presiding judge in a University town, but Happe somehow came to the front and obtained the appointment instead. Ivan Ilych became irritable, reproached Happe, and quarreled both with him and with his immediate superiors—who became colder to him and again passed him over when other appointments were made.

35 This was in 1880, the hardest year of Ivan Ilych's life. It was then that it became evident on the one hand that his salary was insufficient for them to live on, and on the other that he had been forgotten, and not only this, but that what was for him the greatest and most cruel injustice appeared to others a quite ordinary occurrence. Even his father did not consider it his duty to help him. Ivan Ilych felt himself abandoned by everyone, and that they regarded his position with a salary of 3,500 rubles as quite normal and even fortunate. He alone knew that with the consciousness of the injustices done him, with his wife's incessant nagging, and with the debts he had contracted by living beyond his means, his position was far from normal.

In order to save money that summer he obtained a leave of absence and went with his wife to live in the country at her brother's place.

In the country, without his work, he experienced *ennui* for the first time in his life, and not only *ennui* but intolerable depression, and he decided that it was impossible to go on living like that, and that it was necessary to take energetic measures.

Having passed a sleepless night pacing up and down the veranda, he decided to go to Petersburg and bestir himself, in order to punish those who had failed to appreciate him and to get transferred to another ministry.

Next day, despite many protests from his wife and her brother, he started for Petersburg with the sole object of obtaining a post with a salary of five thousand rubles a year. He was no longer bent on any particular department, or tendency, or kind of activity. All he now wanted was an appointment to another post with a salary of five thousand rubles, either in the administration, in the banks, with the railways, in one of the Empress Marya's Institutions, or even in the customs—but it had to carry with it a salary of five thousand rubles and be in a ministry other than that in which they had failed to appreciate him.

90 And this quest of Ivan Ilych's was crowned with remarkable and unexpected success. At Kursk an acquaintance of his, F. I. Ilyin, got into the first-class carriage, sat down beside Ivan Ilych, and told him of a telegram just received by the Governor of Kursk announcing that a change was about to take place in the ministry: Peter Ivanovich was to be superseded by Ivan Semënovich.

The proposed change, apart from its significance for Russia, had a special significance for Ivan Ilych, because by bringing forward a new man, Peter Petrovich, and consequently his friend Zachar Ivanovich, it was highly favorable for Ivan Ilych, since Zachar Ivanovich was a friend and colleague of his.

In Moscow this news was confirmed, and on reaching Petersburg Ivan Ilych found Zachar Ivanovich and received a definite promise of an appointment in his former department of Justice.

A week later he telegraphed to his wife: "Zachar in Miller's place. I shall receive appointment on presentation of report."

Thanks to this change of personnel, Ivan Ilych had unexpectedly obtained an appointment in his former ministry which placed him two stages above his former colleagues besides giving him five thousand rubles salary and three thousand five hundred rubles for expenses connected with his removal. All his ill humor towards his former enemies and the whole department vanished, and Ivan Ilych was completely happy.

95 He returned to the country more cheerful and contented than he had been for a long time. Praskovya Fëdorovna also cheered up and a truce was arranged between them. Ivan Ilych told of how he had been fêted by everybody in Petersburg, how all those who had been his enemies were put to shame and now fawned on him, how envious they were of his appointment, and how much everybody in Petersburg had liked him.

Praskovya Fëdorovna listened to all this and appeared to believe it. She did not contradict anything, but only made plans for their life in the town to which they were going. Ivan Ilych saw with delight that these plans were his plans, that he and his wife agreed, and that, after a stumble, his life was regaining its due and natural character of pleasant lightheartedness and decorum.

Ivan Ilych had come back for a short time only, for he had to take up his new duties on the 10th of September. Moreover, he needed time to settle into the new place, to move all his belongings from the province, and to buy and order many additional things: in a word, to make such arrangements as he had resolved on, which were almost exactly what Praskovya Fëdorovna too had decided on.

Now that everything had happened so fortunately, and that he and his wife were at one in their aims and moreover saw so little of one another, they got on together better than they had done since the first years of marriage. Ivan Ilych had thought of taking his family away with him at once, but the insistence of his wife's brother and her sister-in-law, who had suddenly become particularly amiable and friendly to him and his family, induced him to depart alone.

So he departed, and the cheerful state of mind induced by his success and by the harmony between his wife and himself, the one intensifying the other, did not leave him. He found a delightful house, just the thing both he and his wife had dreamt of. Spacious, lofty reception rooms in the old style, a convenient and dignified study, rooms for his wife and daughter, a study for his son—it might have been specially built for them. Ivan Ilych himself superintended the arrangements, chose the wallpapers, supplemented the furniture (preferably with antiques which he considered particularly *comme il faut*), and supervised the upholstering. Everything progressed and progressed and approached the ideal he had set himself: even when things were only half completed they exceeded his expectations. He saw what a refined and elegant character, free from vulgarity, it would all have when it was ready. On falling asleep he pictured to himself how the reception-room would look. Looking at the yet unfinished drawing-room he could see the fireplace, the screen, the what-not, the little chairs dotted here and there, the dishes and plates on the walls, and the bronzes, as they would be when everything was in place. He was pleased by the thought of how his wife and daughter, who shared his taste in this matter, would be impressed by it. They were certainly not expecting as much. He had been particularly successful in finding, and buying cheaply, antiques which gave a particularly aristocratic character to the whole place. But in his letters he intentionally understated everything in order to be able to surprise them. All this so absorbed him that his new duties—though he liked his official work—interested him less than he had expected. Sometimes he even had moments of absentmindedness during the Court Sessions, and would consider whether he should have straight or curved cornices for his curtains. He was so interested in it all that he often did things himself, rearranging the furniture, or rehanging the curtains. Once when mounting a stepladder to show the upholsterer, who did not understand, how he wanted the hangings draped, he made a false step and slipped, but being a strong and agile man he clung on and only knocked his side against the knob of the window frame. The bruised place was painful but the pain soon passed, and he felt particularly bright and well just then. He wrote: "I feel fifteen years younger." He thought he would have everything ready by September, but it dragged on till mid-October. But the result was charming not only in his eyes but to everyone who saw it.

0 In reality it was just what is usually seen in the houses of people of moderate means who want to appear rich, and therefore succeed only in resembling others like themselves: there were damasks, dark wood, plants, rugs, and dull and polished bronzes—all the things people of a certain class have in order to resemble other people of that class. His house was so like the others that it would never have been noticed, but to him it all seemed to be quite exceptional. He was very happy when he met his family at the station and brought them to the newly furnished house all lit up, where a footman in a white tie opened the door into the hall decorated with plants, and when they went on into the drawing-room and the study uttering exclamations of delight. He conducted them everywhere, drank in their praises eagerly, and beamed with pleasure. At tea that evening, when Praskovya Fëdorovna among other things asked him about his fall, he laughed and showed them how he had gone flying and had frightened the upholsterer.

"It's a good thing I'm a bit of an athlete. Another man might have been killed, but I merely knocked myself, just there; it hurts when it's touched, but it's passing off already—it's only a bruise."

So they began living in their new home—in which, as always happens, when they got thoroughly settled in they found they were just one room short—and with the increased income, which as always was just a little (some five hundred rubles) too little, but it was all very nice.

Things went particularly well at first, before everything was finally arranged and while something had still to be done: this thing bought, that thing ordered, another thing moved, and something else adjusted. Though there were some disputes between husband and wife, they were both so well satisfied and had so much to do that it all passed off without any serious quarrels. When nothing was left to arrange it became rather dull and something seemed to be lacking, but they were then making acquaintances, forming habits, and life was growing fuller.

Ivan Ilych spent his mornings at the law courts and came home to dinner, and at first he was generally in a good humor, though he occasionally became irritable just on account of his house. (Every spot on the tablecloth or the upholstery, and every broken window-blind string, irritated him. He had devoted so much trouble to arranging it all that every disturbance of it distressed him.) But on the whole his life ran its course as he believed life should do: easily, pleasantly, and decorously.

5 He got up at nine, drank his coffee, read the paper, and then put on his undress uniform and went to the law courts. There the harness in which he worked had already been stretched to fit

him and he donned it without a hitch: petitioners, inquiries at the chancery, the chancery itself, and the sittings public and administrative. In all this the thing was to exclude everything fresh and vital, which always disturbs the regular course of official business, and to admit only official relations with people, and then only on official grounds. A man would come, for instance, wanting some information. Ivan Ilych, as one in whose sphere the matter did not lie, would have nothing to do with him: but if the man had some business with him in his official capacity, something that could be expressed on officially stamped paper, he would do everything, positively everything he could within the limits of such relations, and in doing so would maintain the semblance of friendly human relations, that is, would observe the courtesies of life. As soon as the official relations ended, so did everything else. Ivan Ilych possessed this capacity to separate his real life from the official side of affairs and not mix the two, in the highest degree, and by long practice and natural aptitude had brought it to such a pitch that sometimes, in the manner of a virtuoso, he would even allow himself to let the human and official relations mingle. He let himself do this just because he felt that he could at any time he chose resume the strictly official attitude again and drop the human relation. And he did it all easily, pleasantly, correctly, and even artistically. In the intervals between the sessions he smoked, drank tea, chatted a little about politics, a little about general topics, a little about cards, but most of all about official appointments. Tired, but with the feelings of a virtuoso—one of the first violins who has played his part in an orchestra with precision—he would return home to find that his wife and daughter had been out paying calls, or had a visitor, and that his son had been to school, had done his homework with his tutor, and was duly learning what is taught at High Schools. Everything was as it should be. After dinner, if they had no visitors, Ivan Ilych sometimes read a book that was being much discussed at the time, and in the evening settled down to work, that is, read official papers, compared the depositions of witnesses, and noted paragraphs of the Code applying to them. This was neither dull nor amusing. It was dull when he might have been playing bridge, but if no bridge was available it was at any rate better than doing nothing or sitting with his wife. Ivan Ilych's chief pleasure was giving little dinners to which he invited men and women of good social position, and just as his drawing-room resembled all other drawing-rooms so did his enjoyable little parties resemble all other such parties.

Once they even gave a dance. Ivan Ilych enjoyed it and everything went off well, except that it led to a violent quarrel with his wife about the cakes and sweets. Praskovya Fëdorovna had made her own plans, but Ivan Ilych insisted on getting everything from an expensive confectioner and ordered too many cakes, and the quarrel occurred because some of those cakes were left over and the confectioner's bill came to forty-five rubles. It was a great and disagreeable quarrel. Praskovya Fëdorovna called him "a fool and an imbecile," and he clutched at his head and made angry allusions to divorce.

But the dance itself had been enjoyable. The best people were there, and Ivan Ilych had danced with Princess Trufonova, a sister of the distinguished founder of the Society "Bear My Burden."

The pleasures connected with his work were pleasures of ambition; his social pleasures were those of vanity; but Ivan Ilych's greatest pleasure was playing bridge. He acknowledged that whatever disagreeable incident happened in his life, the pleasure that beamed like a ray of light above everything else was to sit down to bridge with good players, not noisy partners, and of course to four-handed bridge (with five players it was annoying to have to stand out, though one pretended not to mind), to play a clever and serious game (when the cards allowed it), and then to have supper and drink a glass of wine. After a game of bridge, especially if he had won a little (to win a large sum was unpleasant), Ivan Ilych went to bed in a specially good humor.

So they lived. They formed a circle of acquaintances among the best people and were visited by people of importance and by young folk. In their views as to their acquaintances, husband, wife, and daughter were entirely agreed, and tacitly and unanimously kept at arm's length and shook off the various shabby friends and relations who, with much show of affection, gushed into the drawing-room with its Japanese plates on the walls. Soon these shabby friends ceased to obtrude themselves and only the best people remained in the Golovins' set.

Young men made up to Lisa, and Petrishchev, an examining magistrate and Dmitri Ivanovich Petrishchev's son and sole heir, began to be so attentive to her that Ivan Ilych had already spoken to Praskovya Fëdorovna about it, and considered whether they should not arrange a party for them, or get up some private theatricals.

So they lived, and all went well, without change, and life flowed pleasantly.

## IV

They were all in good health. It could not be called ill health if Ivan Ilych sometimes said that he had a queer taste in his mouth and felt some discomfort in his left side.

But this discomfort increased and, though not exactly painful, grew into a sense of pressure in his side accompanied by ill humor. And his irritability became worse and worse and began to mar the agreeable, easy, and correct life that had established itself in the Golovin family. Quarrels between husband and wife became more and more frequent, and soon the ease and amenity disappeared and even the decorum was barely maintained. Scenes again became frequent, and very few of those islets remained on which husband and wife could meet without an explosion. Praskovya Fëdorovna now had good reason to say that her husband's temper was trying. With characteristic exaggeration she said he had always had a dreadful temper, and that it had needed all her good nature to put up with it for twenty years. It was true that now the quarrels were started by him. His bursts of temper always came just before dinner, often just as he began to eat his soup. Sometimes he noticed that a plate or dish was chipped, or the food was not right, or his son put his elbow on the table, or his daughter's hair was not done as he liked it, and for all this he blamed Praskovya Fëdorovna. At first she retorted and said disagreeable things to him, but once or twice he fell into such a rage at the beginning of dinner that she realized it was due to some physical derangement brought on by taking food, and so she restrained herself and did not answer, but only hurried to get the dinner over. She regarded this self-restraint as highly praiseworthy. Having come to the conclusion that her husband had a dreadful temper and made her life miserable, she began to feel sorry for herself, and the more she pitied herself the more she hated her husband. She began to wish he would die; yet she did not want him to die because then his salary would cease. And this irritated her against him still more. She considered herself dreadfully unhappy just because not even his death could save her, and though she concealed her exasperation, that hidden exasperation of hers increased his irritation also.

After one scene in which Ivan Ilych had been particularly unfair and after which he had said in explanation that he certainly was irritable but that it was due to his not being well, she said that if he was ill it should be attended to, and insisted on his going to see a celebrated doctor.

15 He went. Everything took place as he had expected and as it always does. There was the usual waiting and the important air assumed by the doctor, with which he was so familiar (resembling that which he himself assumed in court), and the sounding and listening, and the questions which called for answers that were foregone conclusions and were evidently unnecessary, and the look of importance which implied that "if only you put yourself in our hands we will arrange everything—we know indubitably how it has to be done, always in the same way for everybody alike." It was all just as it was in the law courts. The doctor put on just the same air towards him as he himself put on towards an accused person.

The doctor said that so-and-so indicated that there was so-and-so inside the patient, but if the investigation of so-and-so did not confirm this, then he must assume that and that. If he assumed that and that, then . . . and so on. To Ivan Ilych only one question was important: was his case serious or not? But the doctor ignored that inappropriate question. From his point of view it was not the one under consideration, the real question was to decide between a floating kidney, chronic catarrh, or appendicitis. It was not a question of Ivan Ilych's life or death, but one between a floating kidney and appendicitis. And that question the doctor solved brilliantly, as it seemed to Ivan Ilych, in favor of the appendix, with the reservation that should an examination of the urine give fresh indications the matter would be reconsidered. All this was just what Ivan Ilych had himself brilliantly accomplished a thousand times in dealing with men on trial. The doctor summed up just as brilliantly, looking over his spectacles triumphantly and even gaily at the accused. From the doctor's summing up Ivan Ilych concluded that things were bad, but that for the doctor, and perhaps for everybody else, it was a matter of indifference, though for him it was bad. And this conclusion struck him painfully, arousing in him a great feeling of pity for himself and of bitterness towards the doctor's indifference to a matter of such importance.

He said nothing of this, but rose, placed the doctor's fee on the table, and remarked with a sigh: "We sick people probably often put inappropriate questions. But tell me, in general, is this complaint dangerous, or not? . . ."

The doctor looked at him sternly over his spectacles with one eye, as if to say: "Prisoner, if you will not keep to the questions put to you, I shall be obliged to have you removed from the court."

"I have already told you what I consider necessary and proper. The analysis may show something more." And the doctor bowed.

120 Ivan Ilych went out slowly, seated himself disconsolately in his sledge, and drove home. All the way home he was going over what the doctor had said, trying to translate those complicated, obscure, scientific phrases into plain language and find in them an answer to the question: "Is my condition bad? Is it very bad? Or is there as yet nothing much wrong?" And it seemed to him that the meaning of what the doctor had said was that it was very bad. Everything in the streets seemed depressing. The cabmen, the houses, the passers-by, and the shops, were dismal. His ache, this dull gnawing ache that never ceased for a moment, seemed to have acquired a new and more serious significance from the doctor's dubious remarks. Ivan Ilych now watched it with a new and oppressive feeling.

He reached home and began to tell his wife about it. She listened, but in the middle of his account his daughter came in with her hat on, ready to go out with her mother. She sat down reluctantly to listen to this tedious story, but could not stand it long, and her mother too did not hear him to the end.

"Well, I am very glad," she said. "Mind now to take your medicine regularly. Give me the prescription and I'll send Gerasim to the chemist's." And she went to get ready to go out.

While she was in the room Ivan Ilych had hardly taken time to breathe, but he sighed deeply when she left it.

"Well," he thought, "perhaps it isn't so bad after all."

125 He began taking his medicine and following the doctor's directions, which had been altered after the examination of the urine. But then it happened that there was a contradiction between the indications drawn from the examination of the urine and the symptoms that showed themselves. It turned out that what was happening differed from what the doctor had told him, and that he had either forgotten, or blundered, or hidden something from him. He could not, however, be blamed for that, and Ivan Ilych still obeyed his orders implicitly and at first derived some comfort from doing so.

From the time of his visit to the doctor, Ivan Ilych's chief occupation was the exact fulfillment of the doctor's instructions regarding hygiene and the taking of medicine, and the observation of his pain and his excretions. His chief interests came to be people's ailments and people's health. When sickness, deaths, or recoveries were mentioned in his presence, especially when the illness resembled his own, he listened with agitation which he tried to hide, asked questions, and applied what he heard to his own case.

The pain did not grow less, but Ivan Ilych made efforts to force himself to think that he was better. And he could do this so long as nothing agitated him. But as soon as he had any unpleasantness with his wife, any lack of success in his official work, or held bad cards at bridge, he was at once acutely sensible of his disease. He had formerly borne such mischances, hoping soon to adjust what was wrong, to master it and attain success, or make a grand slam. But now every mischance upset him and plunged him into despair. He would say to himself: "There now, just as I was beginning to get better and the medicine had begun to take effect, comes this accursed misfortune, or unpleasantness. . . ." And he was furious with the mishap, or with the people who were causing the unpleasantness and killing him, for he felt that this fury was killing him but could not restrain it. One would have thought that it should have been clear to him that this exasperation with circumstances and people aggravated his illness, and that he ought therefore to ignore unpleasant occurrences. But he drew the very opposite conclusion: he said that he needed peace, and he watched for everything that might disturb it and became irritable at the slightest infringement of it. His condition was rendered worse by the fact that he read medical books and consulted doctors. The progress of his disease was so gradual that he could deceive himself when comparing one day with another—the difference was so slight. But when he consulted the doctors it seemed to him that he was getting worse, and even very rapidly. Yet despite this he was continually consulting them.

That month he went to see another celebrity, who told him almost the same as the first had done but put his questions rather differently, and the interview with this celebrity only increased Ivan Ilych's doubts and fears. A friend of a friend of his, a very good doctor, diagnosed his illness again quite differently from the others, and though he predicted recovery, his questions and suppositions bewildered Ivan Ilych still more and increased his doubts. A homeopathist diagnosed the disease in yet another way, and prescribed medicine which Ivan Ilych took secretly for a week. But after a week, not feeling any improvement and having lost confidence both in the former doctor's treatment and in this one's, he became still more despondent. One day a lady acquaintance mentioned a cure effected by a wonder-working icon. Ivan Ilych caught himself listening attentively and beginning to believe that it had occurred. This incident alarmed him. "Has my mind really weakened to such an extent?" he asked himself. "Nonsense! It's all rubbish. I mustn't give way to nervous fears but having chosen a doctor must keep strictly to his treatment. That is what I will do. Now it's all settled. I won't think about it, but will follow the treatment seriously till summer, and then we shall see. From now there must be no more of this wavering!" This was easy to say but impossible to carry out. The pain in his side oppressed him and seemed to grow worse and more incessant, while the taste in his mouth grew stranger and stranger. It seemed to him that his breath had a disgusting smell, and he was conscious of a loss of appetite and strength. There was no deceiving himself: something terrible, new, and more important than anything before in his life, was taking place within him of which he alone was aware. Those about him did not understand or would not understand it, but thought everything in the world was going on as usual. That tormented Ivan Ilych more than anything. He saw that his household, especially his wife and daughter who were in a perfect whirl of visiting, did not understand anything of it and were annoyed that he was so depressed and so exacting, as if he were to blame for it. Though they tried to disguise it he saw that he was an obstacle in their path, and that his wife had adopted a definite line in regard to his illness and kept to it regardless of anything he said or did. Her attitude was this: "You know," she would say to her friends, "Ivan Ilych can't do as other people do, and keep to the treatment prescribed for him. One day he'll take his drops and keep strictly to his diet and go to bed in good time, but the next day unless I watch him he'll suddenly forget his medicine, eat sturgeon—which is forbidden—and sit up playing cards till one o'clock in the morning."

"Oh, come, when was that?" Ivan Ilych would ask in vexation. "Only once at Peter Ivanovich's."

"And yesterday with Shebek."

"Well, even if I hadn't stayed up, this pain would have kept me awake."

"Be that as it may you'll never get well like that, but will always make us wretched."

Praskovya Fëdorovna's attitude to Ivan Ilych's illness, as she expressed it both to others and to him, was that it was his own fault and was another of the annoyances he caused her. Ivan ilych felt that this opinion escaped her involuntarily—but that did not make it easier for him.

At the law courts too, Ivan Ilych noticed, or thought he noticed, a strange attitude towards himself. It sometimes seemed to him that people were watching him inquisitively as a man whose place might soon be vacant. Then again, his friends would suddenly begin to chaff him in a friendly way about his low spirits, as if the awful, horrible, and unheard-of thing that was going on within him, incessantly gnawing at him and irresistibly drawing him away, was a very agreeable subject for jests. Schwartz in particular irritated him by his jocularity, vivacity, and *savoir-faire,* which reminded him of what he himself had been ten years ago.

Friends came to make up a set and they sat down to cards. They dealt, bending the new cards to soften them, and he sorted the diamonds in his hand and found he had seven. His partner said "No trumps" and supported him with two diamonds. What more could be wished for? It ought to be jolly and lively. They would make a grand slam. But suddenly Ivan Ilych was conscious of that gnawing pain, that taste in his mouth, and it seemed ridiculous that in such circumstances he should be pleased to make a grand slam.

He looked at his partner Mikhail Mikhaylovich, who rapped the table with his strong hand and instead of snatching up the tricks pushed the cards courteously and indulgently towards Ivan Ilych that he might have the pleasure of gathering them up without the trouble of stretching out his hand for them. "Does he think I am too weak to stretch out my arm?" thought Ivan Ilych, and forgetting what he was doing he over-trumped his partner, missing the grand slam by three tricks. And what was most awful of all was that he saw how upset Mikhail Mikhaylovich was about it but did not himself care. And it was dreadful to realize why he did not care.

They all saw that he was suffering, and said: "We can stop if you are tired. Take a rest." Lie down? No, he was not at all tired, and he finished the rubber. All were gloomy and silent. Ivan Ilych felt that he had diffused this gloom over them and could not dispel it. They had supper and went away, and Ivan Ilych was left alone with the consciousness that his life was poisoned and was poisoning the lives of others, and that this poison did not weaken but penetrated more and more deeply into his whole being.

With this consciousness, and with physical pain besides the terror, he must go to bed, often to lie awake the greater part of the night. Next morning he had to get up again, dress, go to the law courts, speak, and write; or if he did not go out, spend at home those twenty-four hours a day each of which was a torture. And he had to live thus all alone on the brink of an abyss, with no one who understood or pitied him.

## V

So one month passed and then another. Just before the New Year his brother-in-law came to town and stayed at their house. Ivan Ilych was at the law courts and Praskovya Fëdorovna had gone shopping. When Ivan Ilych came home and entered his study he found his brother-in-law there—a healthy, florid man—unpacking his portmanteau himself. He raised his head on hearing Ivan Ilych's footsteps and looked up at him for a moment without a word. That stare told Ivan Ilych everything. His brother-in-law opened his mouth to utter an exclamation of surprise but checked himself, and that action confirmed it all.

"I have changed, eh?"

"Yes, there is a change."

And after that, try as he would to get his brother-in-law to return to the subject of his looks, the latter would say nothing about it. Praskovya Fëdorovna came home and her brother went out to her. Ivan Ilych locked the door and began to examine himself in the glass, first full face, then in profile. He took up a portrait of himself taken with his wife, and compared it with what he saw in the glass. The change in him was immense. Then he bared his arms to the elbow, looked at them, drew the sleeves down again, sat down on an ottoman, and grew blacker than night.

"No, no, this won't do!" he said to himself, and jumped up, went to the table, took up some law papers, and began to read them, but could not continue. He unlocked the door and went into the reception-room. The door leading to the drawing-room was shut. He approached it on tiptoe and listened.

"No, you are exaggerating!" Praskovya Fëdorovna was saying.

"Exaggerating! Don't you see it? Why, he's a dead man! Look at his eyes—there's no light in them. But what is it that is wrong with him?"

"No one knows. Nikolaevich said something, but I don't know what. And Leshchetitsky said quite the contrary . . ."

Ivan Ilych walked away, went to his own room, lay down, and began musing; "The kidney, a floating kidney." He recalled all the doctors had told him of how it detached itself and swayed about. And by an effort of imagination he tried to catch that kidney and arrest it and support it. So little was needed for this, it seemed to him. "No, I'll go to see Peter Ivanovich again." He rang, ordered the carriage, and got ready to go.

"Where are you going, Jean?" asked his wife, with a specially sad and exceptionally kind look.

This exceptionally kind look irritated him. He looked morosely at her.

"I must go to see Peter Ivanovich."

He went to see Peter Ivanovich, and together they went to see his friend, the doctor. He was in, and Ivan Ilych had a long talk with him.

Reviewing the anatomical and physiological details of what in the doctor's opinion was going on inside him, he understood it all.

There was something, a small thing, in the vermiform appendix. It might all come right. Only stimulate the energy of one organ and check the activity of another, then absorption would take place and everything would come right. He got home rather late for dinner, ate his dinner, and conversed cheerfully, but could not for a long time bring himself to go back to work in his room. At last, however, he went to his study and did what was necessary, but the consciousness that he had put something aside—an important, intimate matter which he would revert to when his work was done—never left him. When he had finished his work he remembered that this intimate matter was the thought of his vermiform appendix. But he did not give himself up to it, and went to the drawing-room for tea. There were callers there, including the examining magistrate who was a desirable match for his daughter, and they were conversing, playing the piano, and singing. Ivan Ilych, as Praskovya Fëdorovna remarked, spent that evening more cheerfully than usual, but he never for a moment forgot that he had postponed the important matter of the appendix. At eleven o'clock he said good-night and went to his bedroom. Since his illness he had slept alone in a small room next to his study. He undressed and took up a novel by Zola, but instead of reading it he fell into thought, and in his imagination that desired improvement in the vermiform appendix occurred. There was the absorption and evacuation and the re-establishment of normal activity. "Yes, that's it!" he said to himself. "One need only assist nature, that's all." He remembered his medicine, rose, took it, and lay down on his back watching for the beneficent action of the medicine and for it to lessen the pain. "I need only take it regularly and avoid all injurious influences. I am already feeling better, much better." He began touching his side: it was not painful to the touch. "There, I really don't feel it. It's much better already." He put out the light and turned on his side . . . "The appendix is getting better, absorption is occurring." Suddenly he felt the old, familiar, dull, gnawing pain, stubborn and serious. There was the same familiar loathsome taste in his mouth. His heart sank and he felt dazed. "My God! My God!" he muttered. "Again, again! And it will never cease." And suddenly the matter presented itself in a quite different aspect. "Vermiform appendix! Kidney!" he said to himself. "It's not a question of appendix or kidney, but of life and . . . death. Yes, life was there and now it is going, going and I cannot stop it. Yes. Why deceive myself? Isn't it obvious to everyone but me that I'm dying, and that it's only a question of weeks, days . . . it may happen this moment. There was light and now there is darkness. I was here and now I'm going there! Where?" A chill came over him, his breathing ceased, and he felt only the throbbing of his heart.

"When I am not, what will there be? There will be nothing. Then where shall I be when I am no more? Can this be dying? No, I don't want to!" He jumped up and tried to light the candle, felt for it with trembling hands, dropped candle and candlestick on the floor, and fell back on his pillow.

55 "What's the use? It makes no difference," he said to himself, staring with wide-open eyes into the darkness. "Death. Yes, death. And none of them know or wish to know it, and they have no pity for me. Now they are playing." (He heard through the door the distant sound of a song and its accompaniment.) "It's all the same to them, but they will die too! Fools! I first, and they later, but it will be the same for them. And now they are merry . . . the beasts!"

Anger choked him and he was agonizingly, unbearably miserable. "It is impossible that all men have been doomed to suffer this awful horror!" He raised himself.

"Something must be wrong. I must calm myself—must think it all over from the beginning." And he again began thinking. "Yes, the beginning of my illness: I knocked my side, but I was still quite well that day and the next. It hurt a little, then rather more. I saw the doctors, then followed despondency and anguish, more doctors, and I drew nearer to the abyss. My strength grew less and I kept coming nearer and nearer, and now I have wasted away and there is no light in my eyes. I think of the appendix—but this is death! I think of mending the appendix, and all the while here is death! Can it really be death?" Again terror seized him and he gasped for breath. He leant down and began feeling for the matches, pressing with his elbow on the stand beside the bed. It was in his way and hurt him, he grew furious with it, pressed on it still harder, and upset it. Breathless and in despair he fell on his back, expecting death to come immediately.

Meanwhile the visitors were leaving. Praskovya Fëdorovna was seeing them off. She heard something fall and came in.

"What has happened?"

"Nothing. I knocked it over accidentally."

She went out and returned with a candle. He lay there panting heavily, like a man who has run a thousand yards, and stared upwards at her with a fixed look.

"What is it, Jean?"

"No . . . o . . . thing. I upset it." ("Why speak of it? She won't understand," he thought.)

And in truth she did not understand. She picked up the stand, lit his candle, and hurried away to see another visitor off. When she came back he still lay on his back, looking upwards.

"What is it? Do you feel worse?"

"Yes."

She shook her head and sat down.

"Do you know, Jean, I think we must ask Leshchetitsky to come and see you here."

This meant calling in the famous specialist, regardless of expense. He smiled malignantly and said "No." She remained a little longer and then went up to him and kissed his forehead.

While she was kissing him he hated her from the bottom of his soul and with difficulty refrained from pushing her away.

"Good-night. Please God you'll sleep."

"Yes."

## VI

Ivan Ilych saw that he was dying, and he was in continual despair.

In the depth of his heart he knew he was dying, but not only was he not accustomed to the thought, he simply did not and could not grasp it.

The syllogism he had learnt from Kiesewetter's Logic: "Caius is a man, men are mortal, therefore Caius is mortal," had always seemed to him correct as applied to Caius, but certainly not as applied to himself. That Caius—man in the abstract—was mortal, was perfectly correct, but he was not Caius, not an abstract man, but a creature quite, quite separate from all others. He had been little Vanya, with a mamma and a papa, with Mitya and Volodya, with the toys, a coachman and a nurse, afterwards with Katenka and with all the joys, griefs, and delights of childhood, boyhood, and youth. What did Caius know of the smell of that striped leather ball Vanya had been so fond of? Had Caius kissed his mother's hand like that, and did the silk of her dress rustle so for Caius? Had he rioted like that at school when the pastry was bad? Had Caius been in love like that? Could Caius preside at a session as he did? "Caius really was mortal, and it was right for him to die; but for me, little Vanya, Ivan Ilych, with all my thoughts and emotions, it's altogether a different matter. It cannot be that I ought to die. That would be too terrible."

Such was his feeling.

"If I had to die like Caius I would have known it was so. An inner voice would have told me so, but there was nothing of the sort in me and I and all my friends felt that our case was quite different from that of Caius. And now here it is!" he said to himself. "It can't be. It's impossible! But here it is. How is this? How is one to understand it?"

He could not understand it, and tried to drive this false, incorrect, morbid thought away and to replace it by other proper and healthy thoughts. But that thought, and not the thought only but the reality itself, seemed to come and confront him.

And to replace that thought he called up a succession of others, hoping to find in them some support. He tried to get back into the former current of thoughts that had once screened the thought of death from him. But strange to say, all that had formerly shut off, hidden, and destroyed his consciousness of death, no longer had that effect. Ivan Ilych now spent most of his time in attempting to re-establish that old current. He would say to himself: "I will take up my duties again—after all I used to live by them." And banishing all doubts he would go to the law courts, enter into conversation with his colleagues, and sit carelessly as was his wont, scanning the crowd with a thoughtful look and leaning both his emaciated arms on the arms of his oak chair; bending over as usual to a colleague and drawing his papers nearer he would interchange whispers with him, and then suddenly raising his eyes and sitting erect would pronounce certain words and open the proceedings. But suddenly in the midst of those proceedings the pain in his side, regardless of the stage the proceedings had reached, would begin its own gnawing work. Ivan Ilych would turn his attention to it and try to drive the thought of it away, but without success. *It* would come and stand before him and look at him, and he would be petrified and the light would die out of his eyes, and he would again begin asking himself whether *It* alone was true. And his colleagues and subordinates would see with surprise and distress that he, the brilliant and subtle judge, was becoming confused and making mistakes. He would shake himself, try to pull himself together, manage somehow to bring the sitting to a close, and return home with the sorrowful consciousness that his judicial labors could not as formerly hide from him what he wanted them to hide, and could not deliver him from *It*. And what was worst of all was that *It* drew his attention to itself not in order to make him take some action but only that he should look at *It*, look it straight in the face: look at it and, without doing anything, suffer inexpressibly.

80 And to save himself from this condition Ivan Ilych looked for consolation—new screens—and new screens were found and for a while seemed to save him, but then they immediately fell to pieces or rather became transparent, as if *It* penetrated them and nothing could veil *It*.

In these latter days he would go into the drawing-room he had arranged—that drawing-room where he had fallen and for the sake of which (how bitterly ridiculous it seemed) he had sacrificed his life—for he knew that his illness originated with that knock. He would enter and see that something had scratched the polished table. He would look for the cause of this and find that it was the bronze ornamentation of an album, that had got bent. He would take up the expensive album which he had lovingly arranged, and feel vexed with his daughter and her friends for their untidiness—for the album was torn here and there and some of the photographs turned upside down. He would put it carefully in order and bend the ornamentation back into position. Then it would occur to him to place all those things in another corner of the room, near the plants. He could call the footman, but his daughter or wife would come to help him. They would not agree, and his wife would contradict him, and he would dispute and grow angry. But that was all right, for then he did not think about *It*. *It* was invisible.

But then, when he was moving something himself, his wife would say: "Let the servants do it. You will hurt yourself again." And suddenly *It* would flash through the screen and he would see it. It was just a flash, and he hoped it would disappear, but he would involuntarily pay attention to his side. "It sits there as before, gnawing just the same!" And he could no longer forget *It*, but could distinctly see it looking at him from behind the flowers. "What is it all for?"

"It really is so! I lost my life over that curtain as I might have done when storming a fort. Is that possible? How terrible and how stupid. It can't be true! It can't, but it is."

He would go to his study, lie down, and again be alone with *It:* face to face with *It*. And nothing could be done with *It* except to look at it and shudder.

## VII

85 How it happened it is impossible to say because it came about step by step, unnoticed, but in the third month of Ivan Ilych's illness, his wife, his daughter, his son, his acquaintances, the doctors, the servants, and above all he himself, were aware that the whole interest he had for other people was whether he would soon vacate his place, and at last release the living from the discomfort caused by his presence and be himself released from his sufferings.

He slept less and less. He was given opium and hypodermic injections of morphine, but this did not relieve him. The dull depression he experienced in a somnolent condition at first gave him a little relief, but only as something new, afterwards it became as distressing as the pain itself or even more so.

Special foods were prepared for him by the doctors' orders, but all those foods became increasingly distasteful and disgusting to him.

For his excretions also special arrangements had to be made, and this was a torment to him every time—a torment from the uncleanliness, the unseemliness, and the smell, and from knowing that another person had to take part in it.

But just through his most unpleasant matter, Ivan Ilych obtained comfort. Gerasim, the butler's young assistant, always came in to carry the things out. Gerasim was a clean, fresh peasant lad, grown stout on town food and always cheerful and bright. At first the sight of him, in his clean Russian peasant costume, engaged on that disgusting task embarrassed Ivan Ilych.

Once when he got up from the commode too weak to draw up his trousers, he dropped into a soft armchair and looked with horror at his bare, enfeebled thighs with the muscles so sharply marked on them.

Gerasim with a firm light tread, his heavy boots emitting a pleasant smell of tar and fresh winter air, came in wearing a clean Hessian apron, the sleeves of his print shirt tucked up over his strong, bare young arms; and refraining from looking at his sick master out of consideration for his feelings, and restraining the joy of life that beamed from his face, he went up to the commode.

"Gerasim!" said Ivan Ilych in a weak voice.

Gerasim started, evidently afraid he might have committed some blunder, and with a rapid movement turned his fresh, kind, simple young face which just showed the first downy signs of a beard.

"Yes, sir?"

"That must be very unpleasant for you. You must forgive me. I am helpless."

"Oh, why, sir," and Gerasim's eyes beamed and he showed his glistening white teeth, "what's a little trouble? It's a case of illness with you, sir."

And his deft strong hands did their accustomed task, and he went out of the room stepping lightly. Five minutes later he as lightly returned.

Ivan Ilych was still sitting in the same position in the armchair.

"Gerasim," he said when the latter had replaced the freshly washed utensil. "Please come here and help me." Gerasim went up to him. "Lift me up. It is hard for me to get up, and I have sent Dmitri away."

Gerasim went up to him, grasped his master with his strong arms deftly but gently, in the same way that he stepped—lifted him, supported him with one hand, and with the other drew up his trousers and would have set him down again, but Ivan Ilych asked to be led to the sofa. Gerasim, without an effort and without apparent pressure, led him, almost lifting him, to the sofa, and placed him on it.

"Thank you. How easily and well you do it all!"

Gerasim smiled again and turned to leave the room. But Ivan Ilych felt his presence such a comfort that he did not want to let him go.

"One thing more, please move up that chair. No, the other one—under my feet. It is easier for me when my feet are raised."

Gerasim brought the chair, set it down gently in place, and raised Ivan Ilych's legs on to it. It seemed to Ivan Ilych that he felt better while Gerasim was holding up his legs.

"It's better when my legs are higher," he said. "Place that cushion under them."

Gerasim did so. He again lifted the legs and placed them, and again Ivan Ilych felt better while Gerasim held his legs. When he set them down Ivan Ilych fancied he felt worse.

"Gerasim," he said. "Are you busy now?"

"Not at all, sir," said Gerasim, who had learnt from the townsfolk how to speak to gentlefolk.

"What have you still to do?"

"What have I to do? I've done everything except chopping the logs for tomorrow."

"Then hold my legs up a bit higher, can you?"

"Of course I can. Why not?" and Gerasim raised his master's legs higher and Ivan Ilych thought that in that position he did not feel any pain at all.

"And how about the logs?"

"Don't trouble about that, sir. There's plenty of time."

15 Ivan Ilych told Gerasim to sit down and hold his legs, and began to talk to him. And strange to say it seemed to him that he felt better while Gerasim held his legs up.

After that Ivan Ilych would sometimes call Gerasim and get him to hold his legs on his shoulders, and he liked talking to him. Gerasim did it all easily, willingly, simply, and with a good nature that touched Ivan Ilych. Health, strength, and vitality in other people were offensive to him, but Gerasim's strength and vitality did not mortify but soothed him.

What tormented Ivan Ilych most was the deception, the lie, which for some reason they all accepted, that he was not dying but was simply ill, and that he only need keep quiet and undergo a treatment and then something very good would result. He, however, knew that do what they would nothing would come of it, only still more agonizing suffering and death. This deception tortured him—their not wishing to admit what they all knew and what he knew, but wanting to lie to him concerning his terrible condition, and wishing and forcing him to participate in that lie. Those lies—lies enacted over him on the eve of his death and destined to degrade this awful, solemn act to the level of their visitings, their curtains, their sturgeon for dinner—were a terrible agony for Ivan Ilych. And strangely enough, many times when they were going through their antics over him he had been within a hairbreadth of calling out to them: "Stop lying! You know and I know that I am dying. Then at least stop lying about it!" But he had never had the spirit to do it. The awful, terrible act of his dying was, he could see, reduced by those about him to the level of a casual, unpleasant, and almost indecorous incident (as if someone entered a drawing-room diffusing an unpleasant odor) and this was done by that very decorum which he had served all his life long. He saw that no one felt for him, because no one even wished to grasp his position. Only Gerasim recognized it and pitied him. And so Ivan Ilych felt at ease only with him. He felt comforted when Gerasim supported his legs (sometimes all night long) and refused to go to bed, saying: "Don't you worry, Ivan Ilych. I'll get sleep enough later on," or when he suddenly became familiar and exclaimed: "If you weren't sick it would be another matter, but as it is, why should I grudge a little trouble?" Gerasim alone did not lie; everything showed that he alone understood the facts of the case and did not consider it necessary to disguise them, but simply felt sorry for his emaciated and enfeebled master. Once when Ivan Ilych was sending him away he even said straight out: "We shall all of us die, so why should I grudge a little trouble?"—expressing the fact that he did not think his work burdensome, because he was doing it for a dying man and hoped someone would do the same for him when his time came.

Apart from this lying, or because of it, what most tormented Ivan Ilych was that no one pitied him as he wished to be pitied. At certain moments after prolonged suffering he wished most of all (though he would have been ashamed to confess it) for someone to pity him as a sick child is pitied. He longed to be petted and comforted. He knew he was an important functionary, that he had a beard turning grey, and that therefore what he longed for was impossible, but still he longed for it. And in Gerasim's attitude towards him there was something akin to what he wished for, and so that attitude comforted him. Ivan Ilych wanted to weep, wanted to be petted and cried over, and then his colleague Shebek would come, and instead of weeping and being petted, Ivan Ilych would assume a serious, severe, and profound air, and by force of habit would express his opinion on a decision of the Court of Cassation and would stubbornly insist on that view. This falsity around him and within him did more than anything else to poison his last days.

## VIII

It was morning. He knew it was morning because Gerasim had gone, and Peter the footman had come and put out the candles, drawn back one of the curtains, and begun quietly to tidy up. Whether it was morning or evening, Friday or Sunday, made no difference, it was all just the same: the gnawing, unmitigated, agonizing pain, never ceasing for an instant, the consciousness of life inexorably waning but not yet extinguished, the approach of that ever dreaded and hateful Death which was the only reality, and always the same falsity. What were days, weeks, hours, in such a case?

20 "Will you have some tea, sir?"

"He wants things to be regular, and wishes the gentlefolk to drink tea in the morning," thought Ivan Ilych, and only said "No."

"Wouldn't you like to move onto the sofa, sir?"

"He wants to tidy up the room, and I'm in the way. I am uncleanliness and disorder," he thought, and said only:

"No, leave me alone."

225 The man went on bustling about. Ivan Ilych stretched out his hand. Peter came up, ready to help.

"What is it, sir?"

"My watch."

Peter took the watch which was close at hand and gave it to his master.

"Half-past eight. Are they up?"

230 "No, sir, except Vasily Ivanovich" (the son) "who has gone to school. Praskovya Fëdorovna ordered me to wake her if you asked for her. Shall I do so?"

"No, there's no need to." "Perhaps I'd better have some tea," he thought, and added aloud: "Yes, bring me some tea."

Peter went to the door, but Ivan Ilych dreaded being left alone. "How can I keep him here? Oh yes, my medicine." "Peter, give me my medicine." "Why not? Perhaps it may still do some good." He took a spoonful and swallowed it. "No, it won't help. It's all tomfoolery, all deception," he decided as soon as he became aware of the familiar, sickly, hopeless taste. "No, I can't believe in it any longer. But the pain, why this pain? If it would only cease just for a moment!" And he moaned. Peter turned towards him. "It's all right. Go and fetch me some tea."

Peter went out. Left alone Ivan Ilych groaned not so much with pain, terrible though that was, as from mental anguish. Always and forever the same, always these endless days and nights. If only it would come quicker! If only *what* would come quicker? Death, darkness?. . . No, no! anything rather than death!

When Peter returned with the tea on a tray, Ivan Ilych stared at him for a time in perplexity, not realizing who and what he was. Peter was disconcerted by that look and his embarrassment brought Ivan Ilych to himself.

235 "Oh, tea! All right, put it down. Only help me to wash and put on a clean shirt."

And Ivan Ilych began to wash. With pauses for rest, he washed his hands and then his face, cleaned his teeth, brushed his hair, and looked in the glass. He was terrified by what he saw, especially by the limp way in which his hair clung to his pallid forehead.

While his shirt was being changed he knew that he would be still more frightened at the sight of his body, so he avoided looking at it. Finally he was ready. He drew on a dressing-gown, wrapped himself in a plaid, and sat down in the armchair to take his tea. For a moment he felt refreshed, but as soon as he began to drink the tea he was again aware of the same taste, and the pain also returned. He finished it with an effort, and then lay down stretching out his legs, and dismissed Peter.

Always the same. Now a spark of hope flashes up, then a sea of despair rages, and always pain; always pain, always despair, and always the same. When alone he had a dreadful and distressing desire to call someone, but he knew beforehand that with others present it would be still worse. "Another dose of morphine—to lose consciousness. I will tell him, the doctor, that he must think of something else. It's impossible, impossible, to go on like this."

An hour and another pass like that. But now there is a ring at the door bell. Perhaps it's the doctor? It is. He comes in fresh, hearty, plump, and cheerful, with that look on his face that seems to say: "There now, you're in a panic about something, but we'll arrange it all for you directly!" The doctor knows this expression is out of place here, but he has put it on once for all and can't take it off—like a man who has put on a frock-coat in the morning to pay a round of calls.

240 The doctor rubs his hands vigorously and reassuringly.

"Brr! How cold it is! There's such a sharp frost; just let me warm myself!" he says, as if it were only a matter of waiting till he was warm, and then he would put everything right.

"Well now, how are you?"

Ivan Ilych feels that the doctor would like to say: "Well, how are our affairs?" but that even he feels that this would not do, and says instead: "What sort of a night have you had?"

Ivan Ilych looks at him as much as to say: "Are you really never ashamed of lying?" But the doctor does not wish to understand this question, and Ivan Ilych says: "Just as terrible as ever. The pain never leaves me and never subsides. If only something . . ."

"Yes, you sick people are always like that. . . . There, now I think I am warm enough. Even Praskovya Fëdorovna, who is so particular, could find no fault with my temperature. Well, now I can say good-morning," and the doctor presses his patient's hand.

Then, dropping his former playfulness, he begins with a most serious face to examine the patient, feeling his pulse and taking his temperature, and then begins the sounding and auscultation.

Ivan Ilych knows quite well and definitely that all this is nonsense and pure deception, but when the doctor, getting down on his knee, leans over him, putting his ear first higher then lower, and performs various gymnastic movements over him with a significant expression on his face, Ivan Ilych submits to it all as he used to submit to the speeches of the lawyers, though he knew very well that they were all lying and why they were lying.

The doctor, kneeling on the sofa, is still sounding him when Praskovya Fëdorovna's silk dress rustles at the door and she is heard scolding Peter for not having let her know of the doctor's arrival.

She comes in, kisses her husband, and at once proceeds to prove that she has been up a long time already, and only owing to a misunderstanding failed to be there when the doctor arrived.

Ivan Ilych looks at her, scans her all over, sets against her the whiteness and plumpness and cleanness of her hands and neck, the gloss of her hair, and the sparkle of her vivacious eyes. He hates her with his whole soul. And the thrill of hatred he feels for her makes him suffer from her touch.

Her attitude towards him and his disease is still the same. Just as the doctor had adopted a certain relation to his patient which he could not abandon, so had she formed one towards him—that he was not doing something he ought to do and was himself to blame, and that she reproached him lovingly for this—and she could not now change that attitude.

"You see he doesn't listen to me and doesn't take his medicine at the proper time. And above all he lies in a position that is no doubt bad for him—with his legs up."

She described how he made Gerasim hold his legs up.

The doctor smiled with a contemptuous affability that said: "What's to be done? These sick people do have foolish fancies of that kind, but we must forgive them."

When the examination was over the doctor looked at his watch, and then Praskovya Fëdorovna announced to Ivan Ilych that it was of course as he pleased, but she had sent today for a celebrated specialist who would examine him and have a consultation with Michael Danilovich (their regular doctor).

"Please don't raise any objections. I am doing this for my own sake," she said ironically, letting it be felt that she was doing it all for his sake and only said this to leave him no right to refuse. He remained silent, knitting his brows. He felt that he was so surrounded and involved in a mesh of falsity that it was hard to unravel anything.

Everything she did for him was entirely for her own sake, and she told him she was doing for herself what she actually was doing for herself, as if that was so incredible that he must understand the opposite.

At half-past eleven the celebrated specialist arrived. Again the sounding began and the significant conversations in his presence and in another room, about the kidneys and the appendix, and the questions and answers, with such an air of importance that again, instead of the real question of life and death which now alone confronted him, the question arose of the kidney and appendix which were not behaving as they ought to and would now be attacked by Michael Danilovich and the specialist and forced to amend their ways.

The celebrated specialist took leave of him with a serious though not hopeless look, and in reply to the timid question Ivan Ilych, with eyes glistening with fear and hope, put to him as to whether there was a chance of recovery, said that he could not vouch for it but there was a possibility. The look of hope with which Ivan Ilych watched the doctor out was so pathetic that Praskovya Fëdorovna, seeing it, even wept as she left the room to hand the doctor his fee.

The gleam of hope kindled by the doctor's encouragement did not last long. The same room, the same pictures, curtains, wallpaper, medicine bottles, were all there, and the same aching suffering body, and Ivan Ilych began to moan. They gave him a subcutaneous injection and he sank into oblivion.

It was twilight when he came to. They brought him his dinner and he swallowed some beef tea with difficulty, and then everything was the same again and night was coming on.

After dinner, at seven o'clock, Praskovya Fëdorovna came into the room in evening dress, her full bosom pushed up by her corset, and with traces of powder on her face. She had reminded him in the morning that they were going to the theater. Sarah Bernhardt was visiting the town and they had a box, which he had insisted on their taking. Now he had forgotten about it and her toilet offended him, but he concealed his vexation when he remembered that he had himself insisted on their securing a box and going because it would be an instructive and aesthetic pleasure for the children.

Praskovya Fëdorovna came in, self-satisfied but yet with a rather guilty air. She sat down and asked how he was, but, as he saw, only for the sake of asking and not in order to learn about it, knowing that there was nothing to learn—and then went on to what she really wanted to say: that she would not on any account have gone but that the box had been taken and Helen and their daughter were going, as well as Petrishchev (the examining magistrate, their daughter's fiancé) and that it was out of the question to let them go alone; but that she would have much preferred to sit with him for a while; and he must be sure to follow the doctor's orders while she was away.

"Oh, and Fëdor Petrovich" (the fiancé) "would like to come in. May he? And Lisa?"

"All right."

Their daughter came in in full evening dress, her fresh young flesh exposed (making a show of that very flesh which in his own case caused so much suffering), strong, healthy, evidently in love, and impatient with illness, suffering, and death, because they interfered with her happiness.

Fëdor Petrovich came in too, in evening dress, his hair curled *à la Capoul,* a tight stiff collar round his long sinewy neck, an enormous white shirtfront, and narrow black trousers tightly stretched over his strong thighs. He had one white glove tightly drawn on, and was holding his opera hat in his hand.

Following him the schoolboy crept in unnoticed, in a new uniform, poor little fellow, and wearing gloves. Terribly dark shadows showed under his eyes, the meaning of which Ivan Ilych knew well.

His son had always seemed pathetic to him, and now it was dreadful to see the boy's frightened look of pity. It seemed to Ivan Ilych that Vasya was the only one besides Gerasim who understood and pitied him.

They all sat down and again asked how he was. A silence followed. Lisa asked her mother about the opera-glasses, and there was an altercation between mother and daughter as to who had taken them and where they had been put. This occasioned some unpleasantness.

Fëdor Petrovich inquired of Ivan Ilych whether he had ever seen Sarah Bernhardt. Ivan Ilych did not at first catch the question, but then replied: "No, have you seen her before?"

"Yes, in *Adrienne Lecouvreur.*"

Praskovya Fëdorovna mentioned some rôles in which Sarah Bernhardt was particularly good. Her daughter disagreed. Conversation sprang up as to the elegance and realism of her acting—the sort of conversation that is always repeated and is always the same.

In the midst of the conversation Fëdor Petrovich glanced at Ivan Ilych and became silent. The others also looked at him and grew silent. Ivan Ilych was staring with glittering eyes straight before him, evidently indignant with them. This had to be rectified, but it was impossible to do so. The silence had to be broken, but for a time no one dared to break it and they all became afraid that the conventional deception would suddenly become obvious and the truth become plain to all. Lisa was the first to pluck up courage and break that silence, but by trying to hide what everybody was feeling, she betrayed it.

"Well, if we are going it's time to start," she said, looking at her watch, a present from her father, and with a faint and significant smile at Fëdor Petrovich relating to something known only to them. She got up with a rustle of her dress.

They all rose, said good-night, and went away.

When they had gone it seemed to Ivan Ilych that he felt better; the falsity had gone with them. But the pain remained—that same pain and that same fear that made everything monotonously alike, nothing harder and nothing easier. Everything was worse.

Again minute followed minute and hour followed hour. Everything remained the same and there was no cessation. And the inevitable end of it all became more and more terrible.

"Yes, send Gerasim here," he replied to a question Peter asked.

## IX

His wife returned late at night. She came in on tiptoe, but he heard her, opened his eyes, and made haste to close them again. She wished to send Gerasim away and to sit with him herself, but he opened his eyes and said: "No, go away."

"Are you in great pain?"

"Always the same."

"Take some opium."

He agreed and took some. She went away.

Till about three in the morning he was in a state of stupefied misery. It seemed to him that he and his pain were being thrust into a narrow, deep black sack, but though they were pushed further and further in they could not be pushed to the bottom. And this, terrible enough in itself, was accompanied by suffering. He was frightened yet wanted to fall through the sack, he struggled but yet cooperated. And suddenly he broke through, fell, and regained consciousness. Gerasim was sitting at the foot of the bed dozing quietly and patiently, while he himself lay with his emaciated stockinged legs resting on Gerasim's shoulders; the same shaded candle was there and the same unceasing pain.

"Go away, Gerasim," he whispered.

"It's all right, sir. I'll stay a while."

"No. Go away."

He removed his legs from Gerasim's shoulders, turned sideways onto his arm, and felt sorry for himself. He only waited till Gerasim had gone into the next room and then restrained himself no longer but wept like a child. He wept on account of his helplessness, his terrible loneliness, the cruelty of man, the cruelty of God, and the absence of God.

"Why hast Thou done all this? Why hast Thou brought me here? Why, why dost Thou torment me so terribly?"

He did not expect an answer and yet wept because there was no answer and could be none. The pain grew more acute, but he did not stir and did not call. He said to himself: "Go on! Strike me! But what is it for? What have I done to Thee? What is it for?"

Then he grew quiet and not only ceased weeping but even held his breath and became all attention. It was as though he was listening not to an audible voice but to the voice of his soul, to the current of thoughts arising within him.

"What is it you want?" was the first clear conception capable of expression in words, that he heard.

"What do you want? What do you want?" he repeated to himself.

"What do I want? To live and not to suffer," he answered.

And again he listened with such concentrated attention that even his pain did not distract him.

"To live? How?" asked his inner voice.

"Why, to live as I used to—well and pleasantly."

"As you lived before, well and pleasantly?" the voice repeated.

And in imagination he began to recall the best moments of his pleasant life. But strange to say none of those best moments of his pleasant life now seemed at all what they had then seemed—none of them except the first recollections of childhood. There, in childhood, there had been something really pleasant with which it would be possible to live if it could return. But the child who had experienced that happiness existed no longer, it was like a reminiscence of somebody else.

As soon as the period began which had produced the present Ivan Ilych, all that had then seemed joys now melted before his sight and turned into something trivial and often nasty.

And the further he departed from childhood and the nearer he came to the present the more worthless and doubtful were the joys. This began with the School of Law. A little that was really good was still found there—there was lightheartedness, friendship, and hope. But in the upper classes there had already been fewer of such good moments. Then during the first years of his official career, when he was in the service of the Governor, some pleasant moments again occurred: they were the memories of love for a woman. Then all became confused and there was still less of what was good; later on again there was still less that was good, and the further he went the less there was. His marriage, a mere accident, then the disenchantment that followed it, his wife's bad breath and the sensuality and hypocrisy; then that deadly official life and those preoccupations about money, a year of it, and two, and ten, and twenty, and always the same thing. And the longer it lasted the more deadly it became. "It is as if I had been going downhill while I imagined I was going up. And that is really what it was. I was going up in public opinion, but to the same extent life was ebbing away from me. And now it is all done and there is only death."

"Then what does it mean? Why? It can't be that life is so senseless and horrible. But if it really has been so horrible and senseless, why must I die and die in agony? There is something wrong!"

"Maybe I did not live as I ought to have done," it suddenly occurred to him. "But how could that be, when I did everything properly?" he replied, and immediately dismissed from his mind this, the sole solution of all the riddles of life and death, as something quite impossible.

305 "Then what do you want now? To live? Live how? Live as you lived in the law courts when the usher proclaimed 'The judge is coming!' The judge is coming, the judge!" he repeated to himself. "Here he is, the judge. But I am not guilty!" he exclaimed angrily. "What is it for?" And he ceased crying, but turning his face to the wall continued to ponder on the same question: Why, and for what purpose, is there all this horror? But however much he pondered he found no answer. And whenever the thought occurred to him, as it often did, that it all resulted from his not having lived as he ought to have done, he at once recalled the correctness of his whole life and dismissed so strange an idea.

## X

Another fortnight passed. Ivan Ilych now no longer left his sofa. He would not lie in bed but lay on the sofa, facing the wall nearly all the time. He suffered ever the same unceasing agonies and in his loneliness pondered always on the same insoluble question: "What is this? Can it be that it is Death?" And the inner voice answered: "Yes, it is Death."

"Why these sufferings?" And the voice answered, "For no reason—they just are so." Beyond and besides this there was nothing.

From the very beginning of his illness, ever since he had first been to see the doctor, Ivan Ilych's life had been divided between two contrary and alternating moods: now it was despair and the expectation of this uncomprehended and terrible death, and now hope and an intently interested observation of the functioning of his organs. Now before his eyes there was only a kidney or an intestine that temporarily evaded its duty, and now only that incomprehensible and dreadful death from which it was impossible to escape.

These two states of mind had alternated from the very beginning of his illness, but the further it progressed the more doubtful and fantastic became the conception of the kidney, and the more real the sense of impending death.

310 He had but to call to mind what he had been three months before and what he was now, to call to mind with what regularity he had been going downhill, for every possibility of hope to be shattered.

Latterly during that loneliness in which he found himself as he lay facing the back of the sofa, a loneliness in the midst of a populous town and surrounded by numerous acquaintances and relations but that yet could not have been more complete anywhere—either at the bottom of the sea or under the earth—during that terrible loneliness Ivan Ilych had lived only in memories of the past. Pictures of his past rose before him one after another. They always began with what was nearest in time and then went back to what was most remote—to his childhood—and rested there. If he thought of the stewed prunes that had been offered him that day, his mind went back to the raw shrivelled French plums of his childhood, their peculiar flavor and the flow of saliva when he sucked their stones, and along with the memory of that taste came a whole series of memories of those days: his nurse, his brother, and their toys. "No, I mustn't think of that. . . . It is too painful," Ivan Ilych said to himself, and brought himself back to the present—to the button on the back of the sofa and the creases in its morocco. "Morocco is expensive, but it does not wear well: there had been a quarrel about it. It was a different kind of quarrel and a different kind of morocco that time when we tore father's portfolio and were punished, and mamma brought us some tarts. . . ." And again his thoughts dwelt on his childhood, and again it was painful and he tried to banish them and fix his mind on something else.

Then again together with that chain of memories another series passed through his mind—of how his illness had progressed and grown worse. There also the further back he looked the more life there had been. There had been more of what was good in life and more of life itself. The two merged together. "Just as the pain went on getting worse and worse, so my life grew worse and worse," he thought. "There is one bright spot there at the back, at the beginning of life, and afterwards all becomes blacker and blacker and proceeds more and more rapidly—in inverse ratio to the square of the distance from death," thought Ivan Ilych. And the example of a stone falling downwards with increasing velocity entered his mind. Life, a series of increasing sufferings, flies further and further towards its end—the most terrible suffering. "I am flying. . . ." He shuddered, shifted himself, and tried to resist, but was already aware that resistance was impossible, and again, with eyes weary of gazing but unable to cease seeing what was before them, he stared at the back of the sofa and waited—awaiting that dreadful fall and shock and destruction.

"Resistance is impossible!" he said to himself. "If I could only understand what it is all for! But that too is impossible. An explanation would be possible if it could be said that I have not lived as I ought to. But it is impossible to say that," and he remembered all the legality, correctitude, and propriety of his life. "That at any rate can certainly not be admitted," he thought, and his lips smiled ironically as if someone could see that smile and be taken in by it. "There is no explanation! Agony, death. . . . What for?"

## XI

Another two weeks went by in this way and during that fortnight an event occurred that Ivan Ilych and his wife had desired. Petrishchev formally proposed. It happened in the evening. The next day Praskovya Fëdorovna came into her husband's room considering how best to inform him of it, but that very night there had been a fresh change for the worse in his condition. She found him still lying on the sofa but in a different position. He lay on his back, groaning and staring fixedly straight in front of him.

15 She began to remind him of his medicines, but he turned his eyes towards her with such a look that she did not finish what she was saying; so great an animosity, to her in particular, did that look express.

"For Christ's sake let me die in peace!" he said.

She would have gone away, but just then their daughter came in and went up to say good morning. He looked at her as he had done at his wife, and in reply to her inquiry about his health said dryly that he would soon free them all of himself. They were both silent and after sitting with him for a while went away.

"Is it our fault?" Lisa said to her mother. "It's as if we were to blame! I am sorry for papa, but why should we be tortured?"

The doctor came at his usual time. Ivan Ilych answered "Yes" and "No," never taking his angry eyes from him, and at last said: "You know you can do nothing for me, so leave me alone."

20 "We can ease your sufferings."

"You can't even do that. Let me be."

The doctor went into the drawing-room and told Praskovya Fëdorovna that the case was very serious and that the only resource left was opium to allay her husband's sufferings, which must be terrible.

It was true, as the doctor said, that Ivan Ilych's physical sufferings were terrible, but worse than the physical sufferings were his mental sufferings, which were his chief torture.

His mental sufferings were due to the fact that one night, as he looked at Gerasim's sleepy, good-natured face with its prominent cheekbones, the question suddenly occurred to him: "What if my whole life has really been wrong?"

325 It occurred to him that what had appeared perfectly impossible before, namely that he had not spent his life as he should have done, might after all be true. It occurred to him that his scarcely perceptible attempts to struggle against what was considered good by the most highly placed people, those scarcely noticeable impulses which he had immediately suppressed, might have been the real thing, and all the rest false. And his professional duties and the whole arrangement of his life and of his family, and all his social and official interests, might all have been false. He tried to defend all those things to himself and suddenly felt the weakness of what he was defending. There was nothing to defend.

"But if that is so," he said to himself, "and I am leaving this life with the consciousness that I have lost all that was given me and it is impossible to rectify it—what then?"

He lay on his back and began to pass his life in review in quite a new way. In the morning when he saw first his footman, then his wife, then his daughter, and then the doctor, their every word and movement confirmed to him the awful truth that had been revealed to him during the night. In them he saw himself—all that for which he had lived—and saw clearly that it was not real at all, but a terrible and huge deception which had hidden both life and death. This consciousness intensified his physical suffering tenfold. He groaned and tossed about, and pulled at his clothing which choked and stifled him. And he hated them on that account.

He was given a large dose of opium and became unconscious, but at noon his sufferings began again. He drove everybody away and tossed from side to side.

His wife came to him and said:

330 "Jean, my dear, do this for me. It can't do any harm and often helps. Healthy people often do it."

He opened his eyes wide.

"What? Take communion? Why? It's unnecessary! However . . ."

She began to cry.

"Yes, do, my dear. I'll send for our priest. He is such a nice man."

335 "All right. Very well," he muttered.

When the priest came and heard his confession, Ivan Ilych was softened and seemed to feel a relief from his doubts and consequently from his sufferings, and for a moment there came a ray of hope. He again began to think of the vermiform appendix and the possibility of correcting it. He received the sacrament with tears in his eyes.

When they laid him down again afterwards he felt a moment's ease, and the hope that he might live awoke in him again. He began to think of the operation that had been suggested to him. "To live! I want to live!" he said to himself.

His wife came in to congratulate him after his communion, and when uttering the usual conventional words she added:

"You feel better, don't you?"

340 Without looking at her he said "Yes."

Her dress, her figure, the expression of her face, the tone of her voice, all revealed the same thing. "This is wrong, it is not as it should be. All you have lived for and still live for is falsehood and deception, hiding life and death from you." And as soon as he admitted that thought, his hatred and his agonizing physical suffering again sprang up, and with that suffering a consciousness of the unavoidable, approaching end. And to this was added a new sensation of grinding shooting pain and a feeling of suffocation.

The expression of his face when he uttered that "yes" was dreadful. Having uttered it, he looked her straight in the eyes, turned on his face with a rapidity extraordinary in his weak state and shouted:

"Go away! Go away and leave me alone!"

## XII

From that moment the screaming began that continued for three days, and was so terrible that one could not hear it through two closed doors without horror. At the moment he answered his wife he realized that he was lost, that there was no return, that the end had come, the very end, and his doubts were still unsolved and remained doubts.

"Oh! Oh! Oh!" he cried in various intonations. He had begun by screaming "I won't!" and continued screaming on the letter *O*.

For three whole days, during which time did not exist for him, he struggled in that black sack into which he was being thrust by an invisible, resistless force. He struggled as a man condemned to death struggles in the hands of the executioner, knowing that he cannot save himself. And every moment he felt that despite all his efforts he was drawing nearer and nearer to what terrified him. He felt that his agony was due to his being thrust into that black hole and still more to his not being able to get right into it. He was hindered from getting into it by his conviction that his life had been a good one. That very justification of his life held him fast and prevented his moving forward, and it caused him most torment of all.

Suddenly some force struck him in the chest and side, making it still harder to breathe, and he fell through the hole and there at the bottom was a light. What had happened to him was like the sensation one sometimes experiences in a railway carriage when one thinks one is going backwards while one is really going forwards and suddenly becomes aware of the real direction.

"Yes, it was all not the right thing," he said to himself, "but that's no matter. It can be done. But what *is* the right thing? he asked himself, and suddenly grew quiet.

This occurred at the end of the third day, two hours before his death. Just then his schoolboy son had crept softly in and gone up to the bedside. The dying man was still screaming desperately and waving his arms. His hand fell on the boy's head, and the boy caught it, pressed it to his lips, and began to cry.

At that very moment Ivan Ilych fell through and caught sight of the light, and it was revealed to him that though his life had not been what it should have been, this could still be rectified. He asked himself, "What *is* the right thing?" and grew still, listening. Then he felt that someone was kissing his hand. He opened his eyes, looked at his son, and felt sorry for him. His wife came up to him and he glanced at her. She was gazing at him open-mouthed, with undried tears on her nose and cheek and a despairing look on her face. He felt sorry for her too.

"Yes, I am making them wretched," he thought. "They are sorry, but it will be better for them when I die." He wished to say this but had not the strength to utter it. "Besides, why speak? I must act," he thought. With a look at his wife he indicated his son and said: "Take him away . . . sorry for him . . . sorry for you too. . . ." He tried to add, "Forgive me," but said "forgo" and waved his hand, knowing that He whose understanding mattered would understand.

And suddenly it grew clear to him that what had been oppressing him and would not leave him was all dropping away at once from two sides, from ten sides, and from all sides. He was sorry for them, he must act so as not to hurt them: release them and free himself from these sufferings. "How good and how simple!" he thought. "And the pain?" he asked himself. "What has become of it? Where are you, pain?"

He turned his attention to it.

"Yes, here it is. Well, what of it? Let the pain be."

"And death . . . where is it?"

He sought his former accustomed fear of death and did not find it. "Where is it? What death?" There was no fear because there was no death.

In place of death there was light.

"So that's what it is!" he suddenly exclaimed aloud. "What joy!"

To him all this happened in a single instant, and the meaning of that instant did not change. For those present his agony continued for another two hours. Something rattled in his throat, his emaciated body twitched, then the gasping and rattle became less and less frequent.

"It is finished!" said someone near him.

He heard these words and repeated them in his soul.
"Death is finished," he said to himself. "It is no more!"
He drew in a breath, stopped in the midst of a sigh, stretched out, and died.

If you like this story, you may be interested in reading short fiction by other major foreign writers, such as Egyptian writer Naguib Mahfouz's "The Conjurer Made Off with the Dish" and the Indonesian writer Pramoedya Ananta Toer's "Circumcision" (both in chapter 4).

**GOING FURTHER** Tolstoy's novels *War and Peace* and *Anna Karenina* stand at the summit of the greatest fiction in the Western world. The great tradition in Russia has been carried on by writers such as Aleksandr Solzhenitsyn (*Cancer Ward*), Vasily Aksyonov (*Generations of Winter*) and Victor Pelevin (*The Werewolf Problem in Central Russia*).

## Alice Walker (b. 1944)

ALICE WALKER WAS born in rural Georgia, attended Spelman College in Atlanta and Sarah Lawrence College in New York, and worked in New York City as a welfare worker before returning to the South in the midst of the turmoil of the Civil Rights movement. In the late 1960s and early '70s she began to publish fiction and poetry. In 1982 her novel *The Color Purple,* became a great critical as well as commercial success. Not only was it awarded the Pulitzer Prize for fiction, but it also became a movie directed by Stephen Spielberg. *The Color Purple* has become a central document in the literature of diversity—a book that celebrates black women in particular and the human spirit in general.

Alice Walker has lived for the past several decades in northern California.

# Everyday Use

### FOR YOUR GRANDMAMA

1 I will wait for her in the yard that Maggie and I made so clean and wavy yesterday afternoon. A yard like this is more comfortable than most people know. It is not just a yard. It is like an extended living room. When the hard clay is swept clean as a floor and the fine sand around the edges lined with tiny, irregular grooves anyone can come and sit and look up into the elm tree and wait for the breezes that never come inside the house.

Maggie will be nervous until after her sister goes: she will stand hopelessly in corners, homely and ashamed of the burn scars down her arms and legs, eyeing her sister with a mixture of envy and awe. She thinks her sister has held life always in the palm of one hand, that "no" is a word the world never learned to say to her.

You've no doubt seen those TV shows where the child who has "made it" is confronted, as a surprise, by her own mother and father, tottering in weakly from backstage. (A pleasant surprise, of course: What would they do if parent and child came on the show only to curse out and insult each other?) On TV mother and child embrace and smile into each other's faces. Sometimes the mother and father weep, the child wraps them in her arms and leans across the table to tell how she would not have made it without their help. I have seen these programs.

Sometimes I dream a dream in which Dee and I are suddenly brought together on a TV program of this sort. Out of a dark and soft-seated limousine I am ushered into a bright room filled with many people. There I meet a smiling, gray, sporty man like Johnny Carson who shakes my hand and tells me what a fine girl I have. Then we are on the stage and Dee is embracing me with tears in her eyes. She pins on my dress a large orchid, even though she has told me once that she thinks orchids are tacky flowers.

5 In real life I am a large, big-boned woman with rough, man-working hands. In the winter I wear flannel nightgowns to bed and overalls during the day. I can kill and clean a hog as mercilessly as a man. My fat keeps me hot in zero weather. I can work outside all day, breaking ice to get water for washing; I can eat pork liver cooked over the open fire minutes after it comes steaming from the hog. One winter I knocked a bull calf straight in the brain between the eyes with a sledge hammer and had the meat hung up to chill before nightfall. But of course all this does not show on television. I am the way my daughter would want me to be: a hundred pounds lighter, my skin like an uncooked barley pancake. My hair glistens in the hot bright lights. Johnny Carson has much to do to keep up with my quick and witty tongue.

But that is a mistake. I know even before I wake up. Who ever knew a Johnson with a quick tongue? Who can even imagine me looking a strange white man in the eye? It seems to me I have talked to them always with one foot raised in flight, with my head turned in whichever way is farthest from them. Dee, though. She would always look anyone in the eye. Hesitation was no part of her nature.

"How do I look, Mama?" Maggie says, showing just enough of her thin body enveloped in pink skirt and red blouse for me to know she's there, almost hidden by the door.

"Come out into the yard," I say.

Have you ever seen a lame animal, perhaps a dog run over by some careless person rich enough to own a car, sidle up to someone who is ignorant enough to be kind to him? That is the way my Maggie walks. She has been like this, chin on chest, eyes on ground, feet in shuffle, ever since the fire that burned the other house to the ground.

10 Dee is lighter than Maggie, with nicer hair and a fuller figure. She's a woman now, though sometimes I forget. How long ago was it that the other house burned? Ten, twelve years? Sometimes I can still hear the flames and feel Maggie's arms sticking to me, her hair smoking and her dress falling off her in little black papery flakes. Her eyes seemed stretched open, blazed open by the flames reflected in them. And Dee. I see her standing off under the sweet gum tree she used to dig gum out of; a look of concentration on her face as she watched the last dingy gray board of the house fall in toward the red-hot brick chimney. Why don't you do a dance around the ashes? I'd wanted to ask her. She had hated the house that much.

I used to think she hated Maggie, too. But that was before we raised the money, the church and me, to send her to Augusta to school. She used to read to us without pity; forcing words, lies, other folks' habits, whole lives upon us two, sitting trapped and ignorant underneath her voice. She washed us in a river of make-believe, burned us with a lot of knowledge we didn't necessarily need to know. Pressed us to her with the serious way she read, to shove us away at just the moment, like dimwits, we seemed about to understand.

Dee wanted nice things. A yellow organdy dress to wear to her graduation from high school; black pumps to match a green suit she'd made from an old suit somebody gave me. She was determined to stare down any disaster in her efforts. Her eyelids would not flicker for minutes at a time. Often I fought off the temptation to shake her. At sixteen she had a style of her own: and knew what style was.

I never had an education myself. After second grade the school was closed down. Don't ask me why: in 1927 colored asked fewer questions than they do now. Sometimes Maggie reads to me. She stumbles along good-naturedly but can't see well. She knows she is not bright. Like good looks and money, quickness passes her by. She will marry John Thomas (who has mossy teeth in an earnest face) and then I'll be free to sit here and I guess just sing church songs to myself. Although I never was a good singer. Never could carry a tune. I was always better at a man's job. I used to love to milk till I was hoofed in the side in '49. Cows are soothing and slow and don't bother you, unless you try to milk them the wrong way.

I have deliberately turned my back on the house. It is three rooms, just like the one that burned, except the roof is tin; they don't make shingle roofs any more. There are no real windows, just some holes cut in the sides, like the portholes in a ship, but not round and not square, with rawhide holding the shutters up on the outside. This house is in a pasture, too, like the other one. No doubt when Dee sees it she will want to tear it down. She wrote me once that no matter where we "choose" to live, she will manage to come see us. But she will never bring her friends. Maggie and I thought about this and Maggie asked me, "Mama, when did Dee ever *have* any friends?"

15 She had a few. Furtive boys in pink shirts hanging about on washday after school. Nervous girls who never laughed. Impressed with her they worshiped the well-turned phrase, the cute shape, the scalding humor that erupted like bubbles in lye. She read to them.

When she was courting Jimmy T she didn't have much time to pay to us, but turned all her faultfinding power on him. He *flew* to marry a cheap city girl from a family of ignorant flashy people. She hardly had time to recompose herself.

When she comes I will meet—but there they are!

Maggie attempts to make a dash for the house, in her shuffling way, but I stay her with my hand. "Come back here," I say. And she stops and tries to dig a well in the sand with her toe.

It is hard to see them clearly through the strong sun. But even the first glimpse of leg out of the car tells me it is Dee. Her feet were always neat-looking, as if God himself had shaped them with a certain style. From the other side of the car comes a short, stocky man. Hair is all over his head a foot long and hanging from his chin like a kinky mule tail. I hear Maggie suck in her breath. "Uhnnnh," is what it sounds like. Like when you see the wriggling end of a snake just in front of your foot on the road. "Uhnnnh."

20 Dee next. A dress down to the ground, in this hot weather. A dress so loud it hurts my eyes. There are yellows and oranges enough to throw back the light of the sun. I feel my whole face warming from the heat waves it throws out. Earrings, too, gold and hanging down to her shoulders. Bracelets dangling and making noises when she moves her arm up to shake the folds of the dress out of her armpits. The dress is loose and flows, and as she walks closer, I like it. I hear Maggie go "Uhnnnh" again. It is her sister's hair. It stands straight up like the wool on a sheep. It is black as night and around the edges are two long pigtails that rope about like small lizards disappearing behind her ears.

"Wa-su-zo-Tean-o!" she says, coming on in that gliding way the dress makes her move. The short stocky fellow with the hair to his navel is all grinning and he follows up with "Asalamalakim, my mother and sister!" He moves to hug Maggie but she falls back, right up against the back of my chair. I feel her trembling there and when I look up I see the perspiration falling off her chin.

"Don't get up," says Dee. Since I am stout it takes something of a push. You can see me trying to move a second or two before I make it. She turns, showing white heels through her sandals, and goes back to the car. Out she peeks next with a Polaroid. She stoops down quickly and lines up picture after picture of me sitting there in front of the house with Maggie cowering behind me. She never takes a shot without making sure the house is included. When a cow comes nibbling around the edge of the yard she snaps it and me and Maggie *and* the house. Then she puts the Polaroid in the back seat of the car, and comes up and kisses me on the forehead.

Meanwhile Asalamalakim is going through the motions with Maggie's hand. Maggie's hand is as limp as a fish, and probably as cold, despite the sweat, and she keeps trying to pull it back. It looks like Asalamalakim wants to shake hands but wants to do it fancy. Or maybe he don't know how people shake hands. Anyhow, he soon gives up on Maggie.

"Well," I say. "Dee."

"No, Mama," she says. "Not 'Dee,' Wangero Leewanika Kemanjo!"

"What happened to 'Dee'?" I wanted to know.

"She's dead," Wangero said. "I couldn't bear it any longer, being named after the people who oppress me."

"You know as well as me you was named after your aunt Dicie," I said. Dicie is my sister. She named Dee. We called her "Big Dee" after Dee was born.

"But who was *she* named after?" asked Wangero.

"I guess after Grandma Dee," I said.

"And who was she named after?" asked Wangero.

"Her mother," I said, and saw Wangero was getting tired. "That's about as far back as I can trace it," I said. Though, in fact, I probably could have carried it back beyond the Civil War through the branches.

"Well," said Asalamalakim, "there you are."

"Uhnnnh," I heard Maggie say.

"There I was not," I said, "before 'Dicie' cropped up in our family, so why should I try to trace it that far back?"

He just stood there grinning, looking down on me like somebody inspecting a Model A car. Every once in a while he and Wangero sent eye signals over my head.

"How do you pronounce this name?" I asked.

"You don't have to call me by it if you don't want to," said Wangero.

"Why shouldn't I?" I asked. "If that's what you want us to call you, we'll call you."

"I know it might sound awkward at first," said Wangero.

"I'll get used to it," I said. "Ream it out again."

Well, soon we got the name out of the way. Asalamalakim had a name twice as long and three times as hard. After I tripped over it two or three times he told me to just call him Hakim-a-barber. I wanted to ask him was he a barber, but I didn't really think he was, so I didn't ask.

"You must belong to those beef-cattle peoples down the road," I said. They said "Asalamalakim" when they met you, too, but they didn't shake hands. Always too busy: feeding the cattle, fixing the fences, putting up salt-lick shelters, throwing down hay. When the white folks poisoned some of the herd the men stayed up all night with rifles in their hands. I walked a mile and a half just to see the sight.

Hakim-a-barber said, "I accept some of their doctrines, but farming and raising cattle is not my style." (They didn't tell me, and I didn't ask, whether Wangero (Dee) had really gone and married him.)

We sat down to eat and right away he said he didn't eat collards and pork was unclean. Wangero, though, went on through the chitlins and corn bread, the greens and everything else. She talked a blue streak over the sweet potatoes. Everything delighted her. Even the fact that we still used the benches her daddy made for the table when we couldn't effort to buy chairs.

"Oh, Mama!" she cried. Then turned to Hakim-a-barber. "I never knew how lovely these benches are. You can feel the rump prints," she said, running her hands underneath her and along the bench. Then she gave a sigh and her hand closed over Grandma Dee's butter dish. "That's it!" she said. "I knew there was something I wanted to ask you if I could have." She jumped up from the table and went over in the corner where the churn stood, the milk in it clabber by now. She looked at the churn and looked at it.

"This churn top is what I need," she said. "Didn't Uncle Buddy whittle it out of a tree you all used to have?"

"Yes," I said.

"Uh huh," she said happily. "And I want the dasher, too."

"Uncle Buddy whittle that, too?" asked the barber.

Dee (Wangero) looked up at me.

"Aunt Dee's first husband whittled the dash," said Maggie so low you almost couldn't hear her. "His name was Henry, but they called him Stash."

"Maggie's brain is like an elephant's," Wangero said, laughing. "I can use the churn top as a centerpiece for the alcove table," she said, sliding a plate over the churn, "and I'll think of something artistic to do with the dasher."

When she finished wrapping the dasher the handle stuck out. I took it for a moment in my hands. You didn't even have to look close to see where hands pushing the dasher up and down to make butter had left a kind of sink in the wood. In fact, there were a lot of small sinks; you could see where thumbs and fingers had sunk into the wood. It was beautiful light yellow wood, from a tree that grew in the yard where Big Dee and Stash had lived.

After dinner Dee (Wangero) went to the trunk at the foot of my bed and started rifling through it. Maggie hung back in the kitchen over the dishpan. Out came Wangero with two quilts. They had been pieced by Grandma Dee and then Big Dee and me had hung them on the quilt frames on the front porch and quilted them. One was in the Lone Star pattern. The other was Walk Around the Mountain. In both of them were scraps of dresses Grandma Dee had won fifty and more years ago. Bits and pieces of Grandpa Jarrell's paisley shirts. And one teeny faded blue piece, about the piece of a penny matchbox, that was from Great Grandpa Ezra's uniform that he wore in the Civil War.

"Mama," Wangero said sweet as a bird. "Can I have these old quilts?"

I heard something fall in the kitchen, and a minute later the kitchen door slammed.

"Why don't you take one or two of the others?" I asked. "These old things was just done by me and Big Dee from some tops your grandma pieced before she died."

"No," said Wangero. "I don't want those. They are stitched around the borders by machine."

"That'll make them last better," I said.

"That's not the point," said Wangero. "These are all pieces of dresses Grandma used to wear. She did all this stitching by hand. Imagine!" She held the quilts securely in her arms, stroking them.

"Some of the pieces, like those lavender ones, come from old clothes her mother handed down to her," I said, moving up to touch the quilts. Dee (Wangero) moved back just enough so that I couldn't reach the quilts. They already belonged to her.

"Imagine!" she breathed again, clutching them closely to her bosom.

"The truth is," I said, "I promised to give them quilts to Maggie, for when she marries John Thomas."

She gasped like a bee had stung her.

"Maggie can't appreciate these quilts!" she said. "She'd probably be backward enough to put them to everyday use."

"I reckon she would," I said. "God knows I been saving 'em for long enough with nobody using 'em. I hope she will!" I didn't want to bring up how I had offered Dee (Wangero) a quilt when she went away to college. Then she had told me they were old-fashioned, out of style.

"But they're *priceless!*" she was saying now, furiously; for she has a temper. "Maggie would put them on the bed and in five years they'd be in rags. Less than that!"

"She can always make some more," I said. "Maggie knows how to quilt."

Dee (Wangero) looked at me with hatred. "You just will not understand. The point is these quilts, *these* quilts!"

"Well," I said, stumped. "What would *you* do with them?"

"Hang them," she said. As if that was the only thing you *could* do with quilts.

Maggie by now was standing in the door. I could almost hear the sound her feet made as they scraped over each other.

"She can have them, Mama," she said, like somebody used to never winning anything, or having anything reserved for her. "I can 'member Grandma Dee without the quilts."

I looked at her hard. She had filled her bottom lip with checkerberry snuff and it gave her face a kind of dopey, hangdog look. It was Grandma Dee and Big Dee who taught her how to quilt herself. She stood there with her scarred hands hidden in the folds of her skirt. She looked at her sister with something like fear but she wasn't mad at her. This was Maggie's portion. This was the way she knew God to work.

When I looked at her like that something hit me in the top of my head and ran down to the soles of my feet. Just like when I'm in church and the spirit of God touches me and I get happy and shout. I did something I never had done before: hugged Maggie to me, then dragged her on into the room, snatched the quilts out of Miss Wangero's hands and dumped them into Maggie's lap. Maggie just sat there on my bed with her mouth open.

"Take one or two of the others," I said to Dee.

But she turned without a word and went out to Hakim-a-barber.

"You just don't understand," she said, as Maggie and I came out to the car.

"What don't I understand?" I wanted to know.

"Your heritage," she said. And then she turned to Maggie, kissed her, and said, "You ought to try to make something of yourself, too, Maggie. It's really a new day for us. But from the way you and Mama still live you'd never know it."

She put on some sunglasses that hid everything above the tip of her nose and chin.

Maggie smiled; maybe at the sunglasses. But a real smile, not scared. After we watched the car dust settle I asked Maggie to bring me a dip of snuff. And then the two of us sat there just enjoying, until it was time to go in the house and go to bed.

If you like this story, you may be interested in reading Georgia-born Alice Walker in the context of the case study on the American South in chapter 12, with works by Flannery O'Connor, William Faulkner, and Ralph Ellison.

**GOING FURTHER** Succeeding generations of young, black short-story writers have made their mark on American literature, many of them looking to Walker as their mentor. One of the foremost of these is the Pulitzer–Prize winner Edward P. Jones, author of *Lost in the City* (1992) and *All Aunt Hagar's Children* (2006).

# NOTES

# NOTES

# NOTES

# NOTES

# Glossary of Literary Terms

**Abstract** A short **summary** at the beginning of a scholarly article that states the **thesis,** the major points of **evidence,** and the **conclusion** of the article.

**Abstract Diction** Language referring to a general or conceptual thing or quality, such as *progress,* or *justice.*

**Accent** The vocal emphasis on a syllable in a word. Often used interchangeably with **stress,** which sometimes refers to emphasis within a line of poetry, rather than a single word.

**Accentual Meter** A kind of **meter** or verse measure that uses a fixed number of stressed syllables in each line, although based on a number of unstressed syllables may vary. Accentual meters often can be heard in rap music and children's rhymes.

**Accentual-Syllabic Verse** A verse form that uses a fixed number of **stresses** and syllables per line. This is the most common verse form in English poetry, and includes, for example, **iambic pentameter,** where each line has five **stressed** syllables and five unstressed syllables.

**Act** A subdivision of the action of a play, similar to a chapter in a book. Acts generally occur during a change in **scenery,** cast of **characters,** or mood, and the end of an act usually suggests the advancement of time in the play. Acts are often divided into subunits called **scenes.**

**Allegory** A story in which major elements such as **characters** and settings represent universal truths or moral lessons in a one-to-one correspondence.

**Alliteration** The repetition of the initial consonant sounds of a sequence of words.

**Allusion** A reference to another work of art or literature, or to a person, place, or event outside the text.

**Amphibrach** A syllable pattern characterized by three syllables in the order *unstressed, stressed, unstressed.*

**Amphitheater** A stage surrounded on all sides by the audience, who watch the action from above.

***Anagnorisis*** In **tragedy,** a change from ignorance to knowledge, producing love or hate between the persons destined by the poet for good or bad fortune.

**Anagram** A word or phrase created using the letters that spell a different word or phrase. For example, *dirty room* is an anagram for *dormitory.*

**Analyze** To take a text apart and examine its elements: the different written devices the author uses (such as **point of view, plot,** and imagery) and the **voice** the author brings to the piece (**tone,** word choice).

**Anapestic Meter** A **meter** using feet with two unstressed syllables followed by a **stressed** syllable.

**Anecdote** A personal remembrance or brief story.

**Antagonist** A **character** in **conflict** with the **protagonist.** A story's **plot** often hinges on a protagonist's conflict with an antagonist.

**Anticlimax** The opposite of a **climax;** a point in a narrative that is striking for its *lack* of excitement, intensity, or emphasis. An anticlimax generally occurs at a point of high action where a true climax is expected to occur.

**Antihero** A main **character** who acts outside the usual lines of heroic behavior (brave, honest, true).

**Apostrophe** A **figure of speech** in which a writer directly addresses an unseen person, force, or personified idea. The term *apostrophe* derives from the Greek term meaning *turning away* and often marks a digression.

**Approximate Rhyme** *See* **Slant Rhyme.**

**Archetypal Criticism** *See* **Mythological Criticism.**

**Archetype** An **image** or **symbol** with a universal meaning that evokes a common emotional reaction in readers.

**Arena Theater** Also called *Theater in the Round,* an arena stage is surrounded on all sides by the audience, with all the action taking place on a stage in the center.

**Argument** A position or perspective based on a **claim** that can be supported with **evidence.**

**Aside** In drama, a remark made by an actor to the audience, which the other **characters** do not hear. This convention is sometimes discernable in fiction writing, when a self-conscious **narrator** breaks the flow of the narrative to make a remark directly to the reader.

**Assonance** A repetition of vowel sounds or patterns in neighboring words.

**Auditory Imagery** **Images** that appeal to a reader's sense of hearing.

**Augustan Age** A distinct period in early-eighteenth-century neoclassical English literature characterized by formal structure and diction. This Augustan Age is named after the great period of Roman literature during Emperor Augustus's reign, when Ovid, Horace, and Virgil were writing. Famous writers of the English Augustan Age were Alexander Pope, Thomas Gray, and Jonathan Swift.

**Authorial Intrusion** *See* **Editorial Omniscience.**

**Ballad Stanza** A **quatrain** in which the first and third lines possess four stresses, while the second and fourth have three stresses. The **rhyme scheme** is often *abcb.*

**Ballad** A song or poem that tells a lively or tragic story in simple language using rhyming four-line **stanzas** and a set **meter.**

***Bathos*** An error that occurs when a writer attempts elevated language but is accidentally trite or ridiculous; a sort of **anticlimax.**

**Beat Generation** A group of writers in the 1950s and '60s who represented the counterculture to 1950s American prosperity. The word "beat" comes from the slang for being down and worn out, suggesting their weariness with mainstream culture and their adoption of a freespirited attitude. Jack Kerouac's *On the Road* and Allen Ginsberg's poem "Howl" are major works of the Beat Generation.

**Bibliography** A list of the works consulted in the preparation of a paper, containing adequate information for readers to locate the source materials themselves.

***Bildungsroman*** A **coming of age story** that details the growth or maturity of a youth, usually an adolescent. The term is German, meaning "**novel** of formation."

**Biographical Criticism** **Literary criticism** that emphasizes the belief that literature is created by authors whose unique experiences shape their writing and therefore can inform our reading of their work. Biographical critics research and use an author's biography to interpret the text as well as the author's stated intentions or comments on the process of composition itself. These critics often consult the author's memoirs to uncover connections between the author's life and the author's work. They may also study the author's rough drafts to trace the evolution of a given text or examine the author's library to discern potential influences on the author's work.

**Biography** The factual account of a person's life.

**Blank Verse** Unrhymed **iambic pentameter,** often used in Shakespeare's plays or for epic subject matter, as in Milton's *Paradise Lost.*

**Blues** A form of music that originated in the Deep South. Descended from African-American spirituals and work songs, the blues reflects the hardships of life and love in its lyrics. Most blues songs follow a form made of three phrases equal in length: a first phrase, a second that repeats the first phrase, and a third phrase different from the first two that concludes the verse.

**Box Set** *See* **Proscenium Stage.**

**Brainstorming** A process of generating and collecting ideas on a topic.

**Burlesque** A work of drama or literature that ridicules its subject matter through exaggerated mockery and broad **comedy.**

**Cacophony** Harsh-sounding, grating, or even hard-to-pronounce language.

**Caesura** A pause, usually in the middle of a line, that marks a kind of rhythmic division.

**Canon** In a literary context, the group of works considered by academics and scholars to be essential to and representative of the body of respected literature.

***Carpe diem*** Latin for *seize the day.* A phrase used commonly in poetry that emphasizes the brevity of life and the importance of living in the moment.

**Catharsis** The purging of emotions which the audience experiences as a result of the powerful **climax** of a classical **tragedy**; the sense of relief and renewal experienced through art.

**Central Intelligence** Henry James's term for the **narrator** of a story—distinct from the author—whose impressions and ideas shape the telling of the story and determine the details revealed.

**Character** The depiction of human beings (and nonhumans) within a story.

**Characters** The actors (human and nonhuman) in a story.

**Characteristics** The physical and mental attributes of a **character,** established through **characterization.**

**Characterization** The way a writer crafts and defines a **character**'s personality to give an insight into that character's thoughts and actions.

**Charting** A technique for generating ideas that involves placing related concepts and themes in a chart to view their relationships.

**Chorus** A group of amateurs and trained actors who participated in traditional Greek plays. The chorus represents a group of citizens with worries and questions, expressed in poetry and music and dance movement.

**Claim** An idea or stance on a particular subject; a defendable claim is necessary for a strong **thesis.**

**Classifications of Drama** These four categories are generally assigned to Shakespeare's theater, but are commonly used in reference to the works of other **playwrights.** **Histories** focus on the reign of kings from the past, from Julius

Caesar to Henry V. Because histories naturally contain very astute and sometimes troubling political commentaries, playwrights had to limit their subjects to rulers of the distant past. **Comedies** are plays for entertainment, and as a convention end in the marriage of two main **characters.** A comedic **plot** generally begins with a complication or misunderstanding between two lovers, which is complicated by further scheming and misunderstandings until finally a **resolution** is attained and the two are wed. **Tragedies** are darker plays, with more complex **characters** and more dire consequences, usually dramatizing the fall from a high state of life of a royal or special **character. Romances** (from the French *roman,* which means an "extended narrative") involve lovers whose potential happiness is complicated by misunderstandings, mistaken identities, and any number of other difficulties. Although similar in plot to a **comedy,** a romance play does not guarantee a happy ending.

**Cliché** A **figure of speech** that has been used so commonly that it has become trite. The use of cliché may suggest an ironic tone.

**Climax** The narrative's turning point in a struggle between opposing forces. The point of highest **conflict** in a story.

**Close Reading** The **explication** of a text in order to **analyze** the ways in which distinct formal elements interact to create a unified artistic experience for the reader.

**Closed Couplet** A pair of rhymed lines that capture one complete idea. If the couplet is **end-stopped** and in **iambic pentameter,** it is called a **heroic couplet.**

**Closed Denouement** A **resolution** to a story that leaves no loose ends.

**Closed Form** *See* **Fixed Form.**

**Closet Drama** A piece of literature written as though for the stage, but intended only to be read.

**Collective Unconscious** A set of **characters, plots, symbols,** and **images** that each evoke a universal response.

**Colloquial Speech** Familiar and conversational speech.

**Comedy** A type of drama that deals with light or humorous subject matter and usually includes a happy ending. The opposite of **tragedy.** *See* **Classifications of Drama.**

**Comedy of Manners** A work of **satire** that pokes fun at human behavior in particular social circles. Since a comedy of manners concerns itself with social interactions, it tends to reveal the **characters'** foibles or follies as they try to appear or act in a certain way.

**Comic Relief** A **character** or situation that provides humor in the midst of a work that is predominantly serious. A classic example is the bumbling Falstaff, a character in Shakesepeare's *Henry IV* who makes the audience laugh, even as England's fate hangs in the balance.

**Coming of Age Story** A story that follows a **character's** physical, emotional, or spiritual maturation, often from youth into adulthood. *See* ***Bildungsroman.***

**Common Measure** A variation on **ballad** meter that uses **iambic quatrains** with the first and third lines containing four feet (**tetrameter**) and the second and fourth containing three feet (**trimeter**). The rhyme scheme is often *abab* rhyme. Common measure, also called *common meter,* is the **meter** most associated with hymns.

**Comparison** Looking at two or more texts, **characters,** authors, or other items side by side to draw similarities between them.

**Conceit** A complex comparison or **metaphor** that extends throughout a poem

**Conclusion** The final idea and **resolution** of a text. In a good essay, the conclusion not only reiterates the **thesis** but offers a reason for its significance or a reflection that pushes it toward a broader meaning beyond the essay itself. In a story or play, the conclusion refers to the resolution or **dénouement.**

**Concrete Diction** Language referring to a specific, definite thing or quality, such as *lawn mower* or *street light.*

**Concrete Poetry** Also called *visual poetry.* Poetry written in the shape of something it describes.

**Confessional Poetry** Poetry that includes pieces of a poet's autobiography or personal experience. This mode of poetry was prevalent in the mid-twentieth century with poets like Sylvia Plath, Anne Sexton, and Robert Lowell.

**Conflict** The central problem in a story. The source of tension between the **protagonist** and **antagonist.**

**Connotation** The associations a word carries beyond its literal meaning. Connotations are formed by the context of the word's popular usage; for example, *green,* aside from being a color, connotes money. The opposite of **denotation.**

**Consonance** A repetition of consonant sounds or similar patterns in neighboring words.

**Context** The literary, historical, biographical, or poetical situation that influences the writing of a work of literature.

**Contextual Reading** Reading and interpreting a story while mindful of its author, the time and place it was written, the traditions of its form, and the criticism it explicitly or implicitly responds to.

**Contrast** Looking at two or more texts, **characters,** authors, or other items side by side to highlight the differences between them.

**Convention** In literature, a feature or element of a **genre** that is commonly used and therefore widely accepted—and expected—

by readers and writers alike. For example, it is a convention of Shakespearean **comedy** to end with a marriage.

**Conventional Symbols** **Symbols** that have accrued a widely accepted **interpretation** through their repeated use in literature and the broader culture. For example, spring and winter are conventional symbols of birth and death, as they appear with that meaning in Shakespeare's works through Frost's poetry. Colors, too, can be used as conventional symbols; in contemporary society, a pink ribbon is a conventional symbol of breast cancer awareness.

**Cosmic Irony** A literary convention where forces beyond the control of **characters**—such as God or fate or the supernatural—foil plans or expectations.

**Couplet** Two lines of poetry forming one unit of meaning. Couplets are often **rhymed,** strung together without a break, and share the same **meter.**

***Cothurni*** Tall boots, worn by actors in the Ancient Greek theater, which served both to elevate an actor and make him more visible to the massive crowds, and also to make the **character**s seem larger than life.

**Craft** As a noun, craft refers to the elements that comprise a story; as a verb, craft refers to the process of making or fashioning a story out of those elements.

**Cretic** Also called *Amphimacer.* A syllable pattern characterized by three syllables in the order *stressed, unstressed, stressed.*

**Crisis** *See* **Climax.**

**Critical Reading** A process of digesting and understanding a text so you can appreciate not just the ideas it presents or the story it tells, but how it presents those ideas, why it presents them, and how those ideas exist in a certain context. Critical reading involves **summary, analysis, synthesis,** and **interpretation.**

**Critique** A **summary** accompanied by one's own personal opinion and perspectives.

**Cultural Studies** This critical perspective was developed mainly in England in the sixties by New Left writers, social philosophers, and sociologists. Cultural studies incorporates the techniques of literary analysis to **analyze** social life and social movements as though they were written texts.

**Dactylic Meter** A **meter** in which the foot contains a stressed syllable followed by two unstressed syllables.

**Deconstruction** A critical approach to analyzing literature based on the idea that texts do not have a single, stable meaning or **interpretation.** Deconstructionists seek to break down literature to reveal the inevitable inconsistency or lack of unity in even the most successful and revered texts, believing that the author's intentions have no bearing on the meaning of the text to the reader.

**Decorum** A certain level of propriety appropriate to a given text. As well as demanding a certain level of **diction,** decorum can also have bearing on the **characters, setting,** and **plot** events of a piece of literature.

**Denotation** The literal meaning of a word. The opposite of **connotation.**

**Denouement** The period after the story's **climax** when **conflicts** are addressed and/or resolved. Includes the **falling action** and **resolution** of a story.

***Deus ex machina*** Latin for *God from the machine;* a literary device, often seen in drama, where a **conflict** is resolved by unforeseen and often far-fetched means.

**Dialect** **Dialogue** written to phonetically or grammatically replicate a particular **sound,** cadence, **rhythm,** or emphasis in a **character's** speech.

**Dialogue** Spoken interaction between two or more **characters.** A **characterization** technique that can signal class, education, intelligence, ethnicity, and attitude in the characters involved.

**Diction** An author's or **character's** distinctive choice of words and style of expression.

**Didactic Literature** Literature, such as a fable or **allegory,** written to instruct or teach a moral.

**Dimeter** A poetic **meter** comprised of two poetic feet.

**Dirge** A funeral song.

**Doggerel** An obviously patterned piece of **rhyme,** often lunging or twisting word order in order to get a rhyme. Doggerel can sometimes seem almost childish and, when extensive, boring.

**Drama** A term that comes from the Greek word for doing or acting and refers to a literary work that is represented through performance.

**Dramatic Irony** A situation in which an author or **narrator** lets the reader know more about a situation than a **character** does.

**Dramatic Monologue** A poem in which a **character** addresses another character or the reader. Dramatic monologues are offshoots of the epic form.

**Dramatic Poetry** Poetry in which the speaker of the poem is not the poet. Dramatic poetry often tells a story.

**Dramatic Point of View** A **third-person point of view** in which the **narrator** presents only bare details and the **dialogue** of other **character**s.

**Dramatic Question** The overarching challenge or issue in a piece of drama—the complication which the events of a play work to resolve.

**Dynamic Character** A **character** whose personality and behavior alter over the course of the action in response to challenges and changing circumstances.

**Dramatis Personae** "People of the play"; a list of the **characters** in a play, usually one of the first elements of a script.

**Echo Verse** Poetry in which words at the ends of lines or **stanzas** are repeated, mimicking an echo.

**Economic Determinist Criticism** *See* **Marxist Criticism.**

**Editorial Omniscience** A **narrator** inserts his or her own commentary about **character**s or events into the narrative.

**Electra Complex** The female version of the **Oedipus Complex,** the Electra Complex suggests that female children are hostile toward their mothers because of subconscious sexual attraction to their fathers.

**Elegy** A poem of lamentation memorializing the dead or contemplating some nuance of life's melancholy. Early Greek elegies employed a fixed form of **dactylic hexameter** and **iambic pentameter couplets.**

**Elision** The omission of a vowel or consonant sound within or between words, such as "ne'er" for "never" and "o'er" for "over." Elision dramatizes language and allows for flexibility within a poem's **meter.**

**Ellipses** Three periods placed in succession (. . .) to illustrate that something has been omitted.

**End Rhyme** **Rhyme** that occurs at the end of two or more lines of poetry. An example of end rhyme can be found in "The Love Song of J. Alfred Prufrock": "Let us go through certain half-deserted streets, / The muttering retreats."

**End-stopped Line** A line that ends with a full stop or period.

**Endnote** Information placed at the end of a text in an explanatory note. In a research paper, endnotes are used to comment on sources or provide additional analysis that is slightly tangential to the focus of your paper. An endnote is indicated by a superscript number ( $^{1}$ ) in the text itself, which corresponds to a numbered explanatory note at the end.

**English Sonnet** *See* **Shakespearean Sonnet.**

**Enjambment** The running over of a phrase from one line into another so that closely related words belong to different lines.

**Envoi** The final **stanza** of a **sestina,** which summarizes the entire poem. Envoi is French for *farewell.*

**Epic** A long **narrative poem,** traditionally recited publicly, whose subject matter reflects the values of the culture from which it came by portraying important legends or heroes. Classical epics include the *Odyssey* and the *Aeneid,* while English epics include *Beowulf* and *Paradise Lost.*

**Epigram** A short, often satirical observation on a single subject.

**Epigraph** A quotation or brief passage from another source, included at the beginning of a piece of literature. Writers use epigraphs to suggest a major theme or idea in their work.

**Epiphany** A sudden realization or new understanding achieved by a **character** or speaker. In many short stories, the character's epiphany is the **climax** of the story.

**Episode** A unified event or incident within a longer narrative.

***Episodia*** The scenes of a Greek tragedy, divided by ***stasimon*** from the **Chorus.**

**Epistolary Novel** A novel written in the form of letters between two or more **characters,** or in the form of diary entries. Epistolary novels were particularly popular in the eighteenth century.

**Ethnic Studies** A critical approach to literature that seeks to give voice to literature that has previously been overlooked in the traditionally Euro-centric worldview—not simply by including ethnically diverse literature in the **canon,** but by attention to historically underrepresented groups, like African Americans and Native Americans.

**Euphony** Musically pleasing poetic language.

**Evidence** Reliable information, such as statistics, expert opinions, and anecdotes, used to support a **claim** in an **argument.**

**Exact Rhyme** A rhyme in which the final vowel and consonant sounds are identical, regardless of spelling. Also called *pure rhyme, perfect rhyme,* and *true rhyme.*

***Exodos*** The concluding scene of a Greek **tragedy.**

**Explication** a **close reading** of any text where the goal is to logically **analyze** details within the text itself to uncover deeper meanings or contradictions.

**Exposition:** The narrative presentation of necessary information about the **character, setting,** or character's history provided to make the reader care what happens to the characters in the story.

**Expressionism** A mode of theater in which the playwright attempts to portray his or her subjective emotions in a symbolic way on stage.

**Extended Metaphor** A figurative analogy that is woven through a poem.

**Eye Rhyme** Words that share similar spellings but—when spoken—have different sounds. For example, *lint* and *pint.* Also called *Sight Rhyme.*

**Fables** A short narrative in which the **characters** (often animals or inanimate things) illustrate a lesson. The characters in fables are *actors* rather than **symbols.**

**Fairy Tale** A story, usually for children, that involves magical creatures or circumstances and usually has a happy ending.

**Falling Action** The events following the **climax** and leading up to the **resolution.** These events reveal how the **protagonist** has been impacted by and dealt with the preceding **conflicts** of the story.

**Falling Meter** A **meter** comprised of feet that begin with a stressed syllable, followed by an unstressed syllable or syllables. **Trochaic** and **dactylic** feet both create falling meter, which is named for the effect of *falling* from the initial stressed syllable to the unstressed.

**Fantasy** A literary **genre** that uses magical **character**s or circumstances.

**Farce** A work of drama or literature that uses broad, often physical **comedy,** exaggerated **characters,** absurd situations, and improbable **plot** twists to evoke laughter without intending social criticism.

**Feminine Rhyme** Rhymes between multisyllable words in which the final syllable is unstressed, such as *bother* and *father.* Also called *falling rhyme.*

**Feminist Criticism** An approach to literary criticism that highlights literature written by women and the exploration of the experience of female **characters**; also a critical examination of the ways in which female characters are viewed with prejudice, are subjugated to male interests, or are simply overlooked in literature.

**Fiction** A genre of literature that describes events and **characters** invented by the author.

**Figurative Language** Language that describes one thing by relating it to something else.

**Figure of Speech** A technique of using language to describe one thing in terms of another, often comparing two unlike objects, such as *the sun* and *the face of the beloved,* to condense and heighten the effect of language, particularly the effect of **imagery** or **symbolism** in a poem.

**First-Person Narrator** The story is narrated by a **character** in the story, identified by use of the pronoun *I* or the plural first-person, *we.*

**Fixed Form** An arrangement of text that requires a poet to obey set written combinations, including line length, **meter, stanza** structure, and **rhyme scheme.** Also called ***closed form.***

**Flashback** The device of moving back in time to a point before the primary action of the story.

**Flat Character** A **character** with a narrow range of speech or action. Flat characters are predictable and do not develop over the course of the **plot.**

**Foil** A **character** who contrasts with the central character, often with the purpose of emphasizing some trait in the central character. For example, a cruel sister emphasizes the other sister's kindness.

**Folklore** A traditional **canon** of stories, sayings, and **characters.**

**Folktale** A short, often fantastic tale passed down over time.

**Foot** The smallest unit of measure in poetic **meter.** A foot usually contains a stressed syllable and one or two unstressed syllables. **Meter** is formed when the same foot repeats more than once. For example, in **iambic pentameter,** *iambic* refers to the type of foot (an unstressed syllable followed by a stressed syllable), while *pentameter* tells us that there are five (pent) iambic feet in each line.

**Footnote** Like an **endnote,** a way to include commentary on sources or other information tangential to the focus of a text. A footnote occurs at the bottom of the page on which the subject is most closely addressed. To create a footnote, a superscript number ($^1$) is placed in the text itself and corresponds to the number of the explanatory note at the bottom of the page.

**Foreshadowing** A hint about **plot** elements to come, both to advance the plot and build **suspense.**

**Form** The shape, structure, and style of a poem, as distinguishable from, but integral to, the content or substance of the poem.

**Formal Diction** Complex, grammatically proper, and often polysyllabic language in writing. It sounds grandiloquent—a *formal* word—and tends not to resemble the sort of talk heard in daily life.

**Formalist Criticism** An approach to literary criticism that considers a successful text to be a complete, independent, unified artifact whose meaning and value can be understood purely by analyzing the interaction of its formal and technical components, such as **plot, imagery,** structure, style, **symbol,** and **tone.** Rather than drawing their textual interpretations from *extrinsic* factors such as the historical, political, or biographical context of the work, formalist critics focus on the text's *intrinsic* formal elements.

**Found Poem** A poem created from already existing text that the poet reshapes and presents in poetic form. Text may come from advertisements, labels on household items, newspapers, magazines, or any other printed source not intended originally as poetry. A poet may piece together several sources like a collage, or he/she might take a short text exactly as it is and insert line breaks.

**Fourth Wall** The *invisible wall* of the stage, through which the audience views the action.

**Free Verse** Poetry in which the poet does not adhere to a preset metrical or **rhyme scheme.** Free verse has become increasingly prevalent since the nineteenth century, when it was first used. *See* **Open Form.**

**Freewrite** Writing continuously to generate ideas, without worrying about mistakes.

**Gay and Lesbian Criticism** A critical approach that is similar to **feminist criticism** in its quest to uncover previously overlooked undertones and themes in literature. Gay and lesbian criticism seeks to identify underlying homosexual themes in literature.

**Gender Criticism** A critical approach to literature that seeks to understand how gender and sexual identity reflect upon the interpretation of literary works. Feminist criticism and gay and lesbian criticism are derivatives of gender criticism.

**Genre** A literary category or form, such as the short story or novel, or a specific type of fiction, such as science fiction or mystery.

**Groundlings** "Standing room only" spectators in the Elizabethan theater who paid a penny to stand on the ground surrounding the stage.

**Haiku** A poetic form containing seventeen syllables in three lines of five, seven, and five syllables each. Haiku traditionally contain a natural-world reference or central **image.**

***Hamartia*** A tragic flaw or weakness in a tragic **character** that leads to his or her downfall. **Hubris** is a type of *hamartia.*

**Heptameter** A poetic **meter** that consists of seven feet in each line.

**Hero/Heroine** The **protagonist** of a story, often possessing positive traits such as courage or honesty.

**Heroic Couplet** Two successive rhyming lines in **iambic pentameter.**

**Hexameter** A poetic **meter** that consists of six feet in each line. If the six feet are **iambic,** the line is known as an alexandrine, which was the preferred line of French epic poetry.

**High Comedy** **Comedy,** often a satire of upper-class society, that relies on sophisticated wit and **irony.**

**Hip Hop** An intensely rhythmical form of popular music developed by African-Americans and Latinos in the 1970s in which vocalists deploy rhyme—known as rap—over the rhythm.

**Historical Criticism** An approach to **literary criticism** that emphasizes the relationship between a text and its historical context. When interpreting a text, historical critics highlight the cultural, philosophical, and political movements and ideologies prevalent during the text's creation and reception.

**Historical Fiction** A type of fiction writing wherein the author bases his or her **characters, plot,** or **setting** on actual people, events, or places.

**Histories** *See* **Classifications of Drama.**

**Hubris** Excessive arrogance or pride. In classical literature, the hero's tragic flaw was often hubris, which caused his downfall in the tragedy.

**Hyperbole** A type of figurative speech that uses verbal exaggeration to make a point. Hyperbole is sometimes called ***overstatement.***

**Iamb** A poetic **foot** consisting of an unstressed syllable followed by a stressed syllable.

**Iambic Meter** A poetic **meter** created when each line contains more than one **iamb** (a unit with an unstressed syllable followed by a stressed syllable).

**Iambic Pentameter** A poetic **meter** in which each line contains five feet, predominantly iambs. Iambic pentameter is the most commonly used meter in English poetry, comprising **sonnets,** much of Shakespeare's plays, Milton's *Paradise Lost,* Wordsworth's *The Prelude* and Wallace Stevens' "Sunday Morning."

**Iconography** **Symbols** that commonly engender a certain meaning. For example, a skull equals *death,* and a dove equals *peace.*

**Image** A sensory impression created by language. Not all images are visual pictures; an image can appeal to any of the five senses, emotions, or the intellect.

**Imagism** A poetic practice wherein the *thing itself*—the object seen and not discussed or **analyzed**—becomes the poet's focus and the poem's primary concern. Imagism is associated with poets like Ezra Pound and William Carlos Williams.

**Impartial Omniscience** A **narrator** who remains neutral, relating events and **characters'** thoughts without passing judgment or offering an opinion.

**Implied Metaphor** A suggested comparison that is never stated plainly.

**Impressionism** In literature, a style of writing that focuses on a **protagonist**'s reactions to external events rather than the events themselves.

**Indirect Discourse** A **narrator**'s description of an action or event as experienced by a **character** in the story.

**Informal Diction** An author's use of words that are conversational or easily understood, as opposed to elevated or formal language. For example, using *you* instead of *thou.*

**Initial Alliteration** The repetition of consonant or vowel sounds in the middle of a line of poetry.

**Initiation Story** *See* **Coming of Age Story** and ***Bildungsroman.***

***In medias res*** Latin for *in the middle of things.* A term applied when a story begins with relevant story events already having occurred.

**Innocent Narrator** *See* **Naïve Narrator.**

**Intentional Fallacy** The practice by **formalist** critics of discerning or trusting an author's own stated purpose for the meaning of a text.

**Interior Monologue** A **character's** conscious or unconscious thought processes, narrated as they occur, with only minimal-seeming guidance from the **narrator.**

**Internal Alliteration** The repetition of consonant or vowel sounds in the middle of a line of poetry.

**Internal Refrain** The repetition of words or phrases within the lines of a poem.

**Internal Rhyme** **Rhyme** that occurs within a line. The placement of internal rhyme can vary; for example, a word in the middle of the line might rhyme with the word at the end of that same line, or both rhyming words might occur in the middle of two consecutive lines.

**Interpret** The act of **interpretation.**

**Interpretation** The process of contributing to the overall understanding of some aspect of a work in order to illuminate its meaning.

**In-Text Parenthetical Citation** A reference within the body of a paper that links a **quotation, paraphrase,** or **summary** from another source to its full citation in the list of **works cited.**

**In the Round** *See* **Arena Theater.**

**Inverted Syntax** A reversal of expected or traditional word order, often used to aid a poem's sounds, **rhyme,** and/or **meter.**

**Ironic Point of View** Describes a **narrator** who does not understand the significance of the events of a story.

**Irony** A **tone** characterized by a distance between what occurs and what is expected to occur, or between what is said and what is meant.

**Italian Sonnet** *See* **Petrarchan Sonnet.**

**Jargon** Words used with specific meaning for a particular group of people. For example, *starboard* in nautical jargon refers to the right side of a ship.

**Journal Entry** A writing exercise that expands **freewriting** into a more focused discussion that reflects a growing understanding of a topic.

**Language, Tone, and Style** The elements that conjure a story's particular flavor and **voice,** as achieved by means of the words the author chooses and the **rhythm** with which he or she puts the words together

**Language** The words of a story, including **syntax** (how words or other elements of the sentence are arranged) and **diction** (what words the author chooses).

**Levels of Diction** Refers to the three major categories of diction: high, middle, and low diction. The level of diction a writer uses determines whether the words in the work will be formal or informal, poetic or conversational, etc.

**Limerick** A light, often humorous verse form consisting of five **anapestic** (two short syllables followed by one long one) lines, with a rhyme scheme of *aabba.* The first, second, and fifth lines consist of three feet, while lines three and four consist of two feet.

**Limited Omniscient Narrator** A **third-person narrator** who enters into the mind of only one **character** at a time. This narrator serves more as an interpreter than a source of the main **character's** thoughts.

**Line** A row of words containing phrases and/or sentences. The line is a defining feature of poetry, in which there are often set amounts of syllables or poetic feet in each line.

**Literary Ballad** A story told in **ballad** form.

**Literary Criticism** The acts of analyzing, interpreting, and commenting on literature.

**Literary Epic** *See* **Epic.**

**Literary Theory** The body of criticism and schools of thought (such as **Feminist, Deconstructionist,** or **Biographical** Criticism) that govern how we study literature.

**Low Comedy** An informal brand of **comedy** that uses crude humor and **slapstick.**

**Lyric** A short poem with a central pictorial **image** written in an uninflected (direct and personal) **voice.**

**Madrigal** A variety of contrapuntal song that originated in 16th-century Italy. Madrigal features secular verse sung by two or more voices without instrumental accompaniment.

**Magic Realism** A type of fiction in which something "magical" happens in an otherwise realistic world. The form is particularly associated with Latin American writers like Gabriel García Márquez. Unlike **fantasy** or science fiction, magic realism generally has only one fantastical element and the rest relies on realistic **characters** and settings. Notable examples in this book are Franz Kafka's *The Metamorphosis* and Aimee Bender's "The Rememberer."

**Marxist Criticism** Marxist or Economic Determinist Criticism is based on the writings of Karl Marx, who argued that economic concerns shape lives more than anything else, and that society is essentially a struggle between the working classes and the dominant capitalist classes. Rather than assuming that culture evolves naturally or autonomously out of individual human experience, Marxist critics maintain that culture—including literature—is shaped by the interests of the dominant or most powerful social class.

**Masculine Rhyme** The **end rhymes** of multisyllable words with a stressed final syllable, such as *remove* and *approve.* Also called rising rhyme.

**Melodrama** A literary work, mainly a stage play, movie, or television play or show in which **characters** display exaggerated emotions and the **plot** takes sensational turns, sometimes accompanied by music intended to lead the audience's feelings.

**Melody** The linear succession of various musical pitches recognized as a unit.

**Metafiction** A work of fiction that self-consciously draws attention to itself as a work of fiction. Rather than upholding the standard pretense, prevalent in realist fiction, that a story creates or refers to a "real world" beyond the text, metafiction self-consciously reveals the fact and sometimes the manner of its own construction. Metafiction is often associated with **postmodernism,** but examples of metafiction also occur in many other literary movements.

**Metaphor** A close comparison of two dissimilar things that creates a fusion of identity between the things that are compared. A metaphor joins two dissimilar things *without* using words such as *like* or *as.* While a **simile** suggests that X is *like* Y a metaphor states that X *is* Y.

**Meter** A measure of verse, based on regular patterns of sound.

**Metonymy** A **figure of speech** that uses an identifying emblem or closely associated object to represent another object. For example, the phrase *the power of the purse* makes little sense literally (there is no purse that has power), but in the metonymical sense, *purse* stands for money.

**Middle Diction** Poetic language characterized by sophisticated word usage and grammatical accuracy. Middle diction reads as educated, cultured language but is not extravagant like **poetic diction.**

**Mime** The act of performing a play without words.

**Miracle Plays** During the tenth century, when drama was suppressed by the church, these anonymous plays were acted out as religious instruction for the benefit of spectators who could not read the Bible.

**Mixed Metaphor** A failed comparison that results when a writer uses at least two separate, mismatched comparisons in one statement—to confusing, and sometimes comical effect. For example, *The early bird strikes when the iron's hot!*

**Monologue** A single **character's** discourse, without interaction or interruption by other **characters.**

**Monometer** A poetic **meter** comprised of one poetic foot.

**Monosyllabic** A word with one syllable.

**Moral** The lesson taught by a piece of **didactic literature** such as a fable. A moral is often phrased simply and memorably.

**Morality Play** A form of drama in which the figures on stage taught right and proper behavior—morality—to those who watched.

**Motif** A pattern of **imagery** or a concept that recurs throughout a work of literature.

**Motivation** A **character's** reason for doing something.

**Mystery Play** A play that enacted stories of the Bible, such as the Creation or the Crucifixion. These plays appeared during the tenth century, when drama was suppressed in England.

**Myth** The pre-Classical Greek word for sacred story or religious narrative, which by the Classical period had come to mean **plot,** as used in Aristotle's *Poetics.*

**Mythological Criticism** Also called the *archetypal approach,* mythological criticism stems from the work of Carl Jung, a Swiss psychoanalyst (and contemporary of Freud) who argued that humans share in a **collective unconscious,** or a set of **characters,** plots, symbols, and **images** that each evoke a universal response. Jung calls these recurring elements **archetypes,** and likens them to *instincts*—knowledge or associations with which humans are born. Mythological critics **analyze** the ways in which such archetypes function in literature and attempt to explain the power that literature has over us or the reasons why certain texts continue to hold power over audiences many centuries after their creation.

**Naïve Narrator** An unreliable **narrator** who remains unaware of the full complexity of events in the story being told, often due to youth, innocence, or lack of cultural awareness.

**Narrative Poem** A poem that tells a story. Examples include Tennyson's "The Charge of the Light Brigade," Longfellow's "The Midnight Ride of Paul Revere," and most ballads.

**Narrator** The **character** or consciousness that tells a story. For specific types of narrators, see **First-Person Narrator, Second-Person Narrator, Third-Person narrator, Omniscient Narrator, Limited Omniscient Narrator, Impartial Omniscience, Editorial Omniscience, Naïve Narrator,** and **Unreliable Narrator.**

**Naturalistic Theater** Drama that shines a light on the painful realities and problems of everyday life.

**Near Rhyme** *See* **Slant Rhyme.**

**New Criticism** *See* **Formalist Criticism.**

**New Historicism** A critical approach that emerged as a reaction to **new criticism**'s disregard of historical context, but also in response to the perceived shortcomings of older methods of **historical criticism.** Rather than focusing on texts in the **canon** as representations of the most powerful or dominant historical movements, new historicists give equal or greater attention to less dominant texts and non-literary texts (newspapers, pamphlets, legal documents, medical documents, etc.). New historicists attempt to highlight overlooked or suppressed texts, particularly those that express deviation from the dominant culture of the time. In this way, new historicists study not just the historical context of a major literary text, but the complex relationship between texts and culture, or the ways in which literature can challenge as well as support a given culture.

**Nonfiction Novel** A presentation of real events using the craft and technique of a fiction novel.

**Novel** A long fictional work. Because of their greater length, novels are typically complex and may follow more than one **character** or **plot.**

**Novella** A short novel, which generally means it has more complexity than a short story but without the usual length of a novel.

**Objective Point of View** The story is told by an observer who relates only facts, providing neither commentary nor insight into the **character's** thoughts or actions.

**Observer** A **first-person narrator** who does not participate in the action of the story.

**Octameter** A poetic **meter** that consists of eight feet in each line.

**Octave** Eight lines of poetry grouped together in a **stanza** or a unit of thought, as in the **Petrarchan sonnet** where the octave sets up a thought or feeling that the following **sestet** resolves.

**Ode** An elevated, formal **lyric** poem often written in ceremony to someone or to an abstract subject. In Greek **tragedy,** a song and dance performed by the **Chorus** between ***episodia.***

**Oedipus Complex:** Sigmund Freud's theory of behavior (derived from the **plot** of Sophocles's *Oedipus the King*) which holds that male children are jealous of the father because of their sexual attraction to the mother. In *Oedipus the King,* Oedipus kills his father and sleeps with his mother.

**Off Rhyme** *See* **Slant Rhyme.**

**O. Henry Ending** A short story ending that consists of a sudden surprise, often ironic or coincidental in nature, named for the short story writer O. Henry, who frequently ended his stories in this way. A classic example is O. Henry's "The Gift of the Magi" in which a husband and wife each give something precious of theirs to purchase a gift for the other; the ending reveals that each has sacrificed the very thing that would have allowed him or her to enjoy the gift received from their spouse.

**Omniscient Narrator** A **third-person narrator** who observes the thoughts and describes the actions of multiple **characters** in the story. The omniscient narrator can see beyond the physical actions and **dialogue** of **characters** and is able to reveal the inner thoughts and emotions of anyone in the story.

**One-Act Play** A play that consists of a single act that contains the entire action of the play. One-act plays usually portray a single **scene** with an exchange among a smaller number of **characters**; for example, Edward Albee's *The Zoo Story.*

**Onomatopoeia** The use of words that imitate the sounds they refer to, such as *buzz* or *pop.*

**Open Denoument** A **resolution** to a story that leaves loose ends and does not completely resolve the overarching **conflict.**

**Open Form** Poetry ungoverned by metrical or rhyme schemes. Also called free verse.

**Orchestra** The open area in front of the stage (or ***skene***) in the Greek **amphitheater.**

**Overstatement** *See* **Hyperbole.**

**Oxymoron** A version of **paradox** that combines contradictory words into a compact, often two-word term, such as *jumbo shrimp* or *definitely maybe.*

***Paean*** The final choral **ode** of a Greek **tragedy.**

**Pantoum** A variation on the **villanelle,** consisting of an unspecified number of **quatrains** with the rhyme scheme *abab.* The first line of each quatrain repeats the second line of the preceding quatrain, and the third line repeats the final line of the preceding quatrain. In the final quatrain, the second line repeats the third line of the first quatrain, and the last line of the poem repeats the first line of the poem.

**Parable** A short narrative that illustrates a lesson using comparison to familiar **characters** and events. The characters and events in parables often have obvious significance as **symbols** and **allegories.**

***Parados*** The **Chorus**' first **ode** in a Greek **tragedy.**

**Paradox** Seemingly contradictory statements that, when closely examined, have a deeper, sometimes complicated, meaning.

**Parallelism** The arrangement of words or phrases in a grammatically similar way.

**Paraphrase** Condensing a passage or idea from an existing text into your own words. Paraphrase does not mean simply changing the words from the original; rather, it should re-present the original in a way that demonstrates your understanding of it.

**Parody** Mimicking another author or work of literature in such a way as to make fun of the original, often by exaggerating its characteristic aspects.

**Participant narrator** A **first-person narrator** who takes part in the action of the story.

**Pastoral Poetry** A variety of poem in which life in the countryside, mainly among shepherds, is glorified and idealized.

**Pentameter** A poetic **meter** that consists of five feet in each line.

***Peripeteia*** An element of Greek **tragedy,** *peripeteia* occurs when an action has the opposite result of what was intended. In a **tragedy,** this generally occurs at a turning point for the **hero** and signals his downfall.

**Persona** A poem's speaker, which may or may not use the **voice** of the poet.

***Personae*** Masks, often representative of certain **iconography** and familiar **characters,** worn by actors in the Ancient Greek theater to enable one actor to perform as many **characters.** *Personae* often were designed to project an actor's voice to the far rows of the **amphitheater.**

**Personification** A **figure of speech** in which a writer ascribes human traits or behavior to something inhuman.

**Persuasion** The process of using **analysis** and logical **argument** to prove the validity of a certain **interpretation** or **point of view.**

**Petrarchan (Italian) Sonnet** A sonnet consisting of an **octave** and a **sestet,** all in **iambic pentameter,** with the rhyme scheme *abbaabba cdecde* or *abbaabba cdcdcd.* The **volta,** or turn, typically occurs between the octave and sestet, around line nine of the poem.

**Plagiarism** The act of taking credit for another's work or ideas.

**Play** A work of drama, usually performed before an audience.

**Players** Traveling actors, men and boys, who spoke their lines for pay.

**Play Review** The critique of a play.

**Playwright** The author of a dramatic work.

**Plot** The artful arrangement of incidents in a story, with each incident building on the next in a series of causes and effects.

**Poetic Diction** Lofty and elevated language, used traditionally in poetry written before the nineteenth century to separate poetic speech from common speech.

**Point of View** The perspective from which the story is told to the reader.

**Polysyllabic** A word that has many syllables.

**Portmanteau Word** A word invented by combining two other words to achieve the effect of both. Lewis Carroll's poem "Jabberwocky" is comprised largely of portmanteau words such as *slithy,* which means *slimy* and *lithe.*

**Postcolonialism** A critical approach to **literary criticism** that seeks to offer views of relations between the colonizing West and colonized nations and regions that differed sharply from the conventional Western perspectives.

**Poststructuralist Criticism** Criticism based on the belief that texts do not have a single, stable meaning or **interpretation,** in part because language itself is filled with ambiguity, multiple meanings, and meanings that can change with time or context.

**Precís** *See* **Summary Paper.**

**Preview** The process of gathering information about a piece of literature before you read it.

**Problem Play** A play about a social problem, written with an aim to create awareness of the problem.

**Prologue** The introduction to a literary work.

**Proscenium Stage** A realistic **setting** with three flat walls (two flat sides, and a ceiling) that simulates a room; the audience views the action through the missing **fourth wall.**

**Prose Poem** A poem that uses the devices and **imagery** characteristic of traditionally lined poetry, but in compact units without clearly defined line breaks.

**Prosody** The analysis of a poem's rhythm and metrical structures.

**Protagonist** The main figure (or principal actor) in a work of literature. A story's **plot** hinges equally on the protagonist's efforts to realize his or her desires and to cope with failure if and when plans are thwarted and desires left unfulfilled.

**Psalm** A sacred song, usually written to or in honor of a deity.

**Psychoanalytic Criticism** Also called *psychological criticism,* this approach in a sense studies **characters** and authors as one would patients, looking in the text for evidence of childhood trauma, repressed sexual impulses, preoccupation with death, and so on. Through the lens of psychology critics attempt to explain the motivations and meanings behind characters' actions. Psychological critics also use textual and biographical evidence as a means to better understand the author's psychology, as well as examine the process and nature of literary creation, studying the ways in which texts create an emotional and intellectual effect for their readers and authors.

**Pun** A play on words that reveals different meanings in words that are similar or even identical.

**Pyrrhic** A poetic foot characterized by two unstressed syllables.

**Quantitative Meter** A type of poetry that counts the length of syllables, rather than the emphasis they receive (as in **accentual meter** and syllabic verse). Quantitative meter primarily appears in Greek and Latin poetry and is rarely used in English since English vowel lengths are not clearly quantified.

**Quatrain** A four-line **stanza.** Quatrains are the most popular stanzaic form in English poetry because they are easily varied in **meter,** line length, and **rhyme scheme.**

**Queer Theory** The idea that power is reflected in language and that discourse itself shapes our sense of who we are and how we define ourselves sexually.

**Rap** An oral form of poetry that is akin to spoken word, but distinguished by musical qualities and choral repetitions. *See* **Hip Hop.**

**Reader-Response Criticism** The reader-response approach emphasizes that the reader is central to the writer-text-reader interaction. Reader-response critics believe a literary work is not complete until someone reads and **interprets** it.

Such critics acknowledge that because each reader has a different set of experiences and views, each reader's response to a text may be different.

**Realism** A mode of literature in which the author depicts **characters** and scenarios that could occur in real life. Unlike **fantasy** or **surrealism,** realism seeks to represent the world as it is.

**Recognition** The moment in a **tragedy** when the **hero** comes to recognize the actuality of events and is no longer under illusion.

**Refrain** A line or **stanza** that is repeated at regular intervals in a poem or song.

**Resolution** The end of the story, where the **conflict** is ultimately resolved and the effects of the story's events on the **protagonist** become evident.

**Restoration Comedy** A bawdy play about fallen virtue and infidelity that became popular after the Puritans were displaced in England in the mid-seventeenth century.

**Retrospect** *See* **Flashback.**

**Reversal** *See* ***Peripeteia.***

**Rhyme** The echoing repetition of sounds in the end syllables of words, often (though not always) at the end of a line of poetry.

**Rhyme Scheme** The pattern of **rhyme** throughout a particular poem.

**Rhythm** The sequence of stressed and unstressed sounds in a poem.

**Rising Action** Story events that increase tension and move the plot toward the climax.

**Rising Meter** A **meter** comprised of feet that begin with an unstressed syllable, followed by a stressed syllable or syllables. **Iambic** and **anapestic** feet both create rising meter, which is named for the effect of *rising* from the initial unstressed syllable to the stressed.

**Romance** *See* **Classifications of Drama.**

**Romantic Comedy** A type of **comedy** in which two would-be/should-be lovers find each other after a series of misunderstandings and false starts.

**Round Character** A **character** with complex, multifaceted characteristics. Round characters behave as real people. For example, a round **hero** may suffer temptation, and a round **villain** may show compassion.

**Run-On Line** A line of poetry that, when read, does not come to a natural conclusion where the line breaks. *See* **Enjambment.**

**Sarcasm** Verbal irony that is intended in a mean-spirited, malicious, or critical way.

**Satire** An artistic critique, sometimes heated, on some aspect of human immorality or absurdity.

**Satiric Comedy** A derisive and dark **comedy** in which there is no promise that good will prevail.

**Satyr Play** An often obscene satirical fourth play, provided after a trilogy of tragedies, meant to provide **comic relief.**

**Scansion** The process of determining the metrical pattern of a line of poetry by marking its stresses and feet.

**Scene** A defined moment of action or interaction in a story usually confined to a single **setting.** Scenes are the building blocks of a story's **plot.**

**Scenery** The set pieces and stage decorations onstage during the performance of a play.

**Scratch Outline** A multi-tiered, ordered list of topics that should be covered in a paper. A scratch outline goes into deeper detail than a topic outline.

**Screenplay** A script that is specifically tailored and structured for television or film rather than the stage.

**Script** The written text of a play, which may include set descriptions and actor cues.

**Second-Person Narrator** A **narrator** who addresses the character as *you,* often involving the reader by association.

**Semiotics** The study of how meaning is attached to and communicated by symbols.

**Sentence Outline** An outline that uses complete sentences instead of brief words or phrases.

**Sestet** Six lines of poetry grouped together in a stanza or a unit of thought, as in the **Petrarchan sonnet** where the last six lines of the poem resolve the idea or question set up by the initial **octave.**

**Sestina** A poem of six six-line **stanzas** and a three-line **envoi,** usually unrhymed, in which each stanza repeats the end words of the lines of the first stanza, but in different order, the envoi using the six words again, three in the middle of the lines and three at the end.

**Setting** The time and place where the story occurs. Setting creates expectations for the types of **characters** and situations encountered in the story.

**Shakespearean (English) Sonnet** A **sonnet** form composed of three quatrains and a final couplet, all in **iambic pentameter** and rhymed *abab cdcd efef gg.* The **volta,** or turn, occurs in the final **couplet** of the poem.

**Short Story** A brief fictional narrative that attempts to dramatize or illustrate the effect or meaning of a single incident or small group of incidents in the life of a single **character** or small group of characters.

**Simile** A direct comparison of two dissimilar things using the words *like* or *as.*

**Situational Irony** A situation portrayed in a poem when what occurs is the opposite or very different from what's expected to occur.

***Skene*** The stage in the Greek **amphitheater.**

**Slam** Poetry in a variety of styles, performed competitively in clubs and halls.

**Slant Rhyme** A case in which vowel or consonant sounds are similar but not exactly the same, such as *heap* and *rap* and *tape*. Also called *near rhyme, imperfect rhyme* and *off rhyme*.

**Slapstick** A type of low **comedy** characterized by unexpected, often physical humor. A classic example of slapstick is the man walking along who accidentally slips on a banana peel.

**Social Environment** A study of **setting** that considers era and location as well as a **character's** living and working conditions.

**Sociological Criticism** The study of literary texts as products of the cultural, political, and economic context of the author's time and place.

**Soliloquy** A **monologue** delivered by a **character** in a play who is alone onstage. Soliloquies generally have a **character** revealing his or her thoughts to the audience.

**Sonnet** A poem of fourteen lines of **iambic pentameter** in a recognizable pattern of **rhyme.** Sonnets contain a **volta,** or turn, in which the last lines resolve or change direction from the controlling idea of the preceding lines.

**Sound** The rhythmic structure of the lines of a poem, which draws the reader in, often utilizing **rhyme** and created through word choice and word order.

**Spoken Word Poetry** Poetry that derives from the **Beat** poets, characterized by emphasis of the *performance* of a poem over the written form. Spoken word often employs improvisation.

**Spondee** A poetic foot characterized by two stressed syllables.

**Stage Directions** Cues, included by the playwright in the script of a play, which inform the actions of the actors during the play.

**Stanza** A unit of two or more lines, set off by a space, often sharing the same **rhythm** and **meter.**

***Stasimon*** In Greek **tragedy,** an ode performed by the **Chorus** which interprets and responds to the preceding scene.

**Static Character** A **character,** often flat, who does not change over the course of the story.

**Stock Character** A **character** who represents a concept or type of behavior, such as a "mean teacher" or "mischievous student," and offers readers the comfort of repetition and reliability.

**Stream of Consciousness:** A **character's** thoughts are presented flowing by in free association, and the literary convention that rules is that there is no writer mediating the consciousness of the subject.

**Stress** The vocal emphasis on a syllable in a line of verse, largely a matter of pitch.

**Structuralism** Structuralist literary critics work from the belief that a given work of literature can be fully understood only when a reader considers the system of conventions, or the *genre* to which it belongs or responds.

**Style** The characteristic way in which any writer uses language.

**Subplot** A **plot** that is not the central plot of the work, but nonetheless appears in the same work. Longer works, like **novels** and plays, tend to have subplots that might follow side **characters** or somehow affect the action of the main plot.

**Summary** Restating concisely the main ideas of a text without adding opinion or commentary. The best approach to summary is to divide the text into its major sections and then write a sentence for each section stating its main idea.

**Summary Paper** A short paper that represents the main ideas of the text as the author has presented them, excluding any subjective ideas or interpretations.

**Surrealism** A technique of the modern theater in which the realms of conscious and unconscious experience are fused together to create a total reality. In this way the fiction writer, poet, and **playwright,** tap into the resources of the unconscious mind and the imagination and portray in story on the page or on the modern stage the stuff of human desire, hope, and dreams.

**Suspense** A sense of anticipation or excitement about what will happen and how the **characters** will deal with their newfound predicament.

**Syllabic verse** A verse form that uses a fixed number of syllables per line or stanza, regardless of the number of stressed or unstressed syllables.

**Symbol** Any object, **image, character,** or action that suggests meaning beyond the everyday literal level.

**Symbolic Act** A gesture or action beyond the everyday practical definition.

**Synecdoche** A **figure of speech** that uses a piece or part of a thing to represent the thing in its entirety. For example, in the Biblical saying that man does not live by bread alone, *bread* stands for the larger concept of food or physical sustenance.

**Synopsis** A **summary** or **précis** of a work.

**Syntax** The meaningful arrangement of words and phrases. Syntax can refer to word placement and order, as well as the overall length and shape of a sentence.

**Synthesis** The act of bringing together the ideas and observations generated by reading and analysis in order to make a concrete statement about a work.

**Tactile Imagery** Imagery that appeals to a reader's sense of touch.

**Tercet** A group of three lines of poetry, sometimes called a **triplet** when all three lines rhyme.

**Terminal Refrain** Repeated lines which appear at the end of each **stanza** in a poem.

**Terza Rima** A **tercet** fixed form featuring the interlocking rhyme scheme *aba, bcb, cdc, ded,* etc.

**Tetrameter** A poetic **meter** that contains four feet in each line.

**Theme** The central or underlying meanings of a literary work.

**Thesis Statement** A sentence, usually but not always included in a paper's introductory paragraph, that defines a paper's purpose and argument.

**Thesis** A paper's purpose and **argument,** defined by the **thesis statement** and proved by the paper's **conclusion.**

**Third-Person Narrator** A **narrator** who is outside the story. The narrator refers to all the **characters** in the story with the pronouns *he, she,* or *they.*

**Tiring House** In the Elizabethan theater, a room, adjoined to the stage, in which actors changed their costumes.

**Tone** The author's attitude toward his or her **characters** or subject matter.

**Topic Outline** A multi-tiered organization of a paper's topics and **arguments,** used to structure a paper.

**Tragedy** A dramatic form in which **characters** face serious and important challenges that end in disastrous failure or defeat for the **protagonist.** *See* **Classifications of Drama.**

**Tragic Flaw** In classical literature, the hero's weakness that causes his downfall.

**Tragic Hero** A heroic **protagonist** who from the beginning, due to some innate flaw in his **character** or some unforeseeable mistake (*see* **Tragic Flaw**), is doomed. The inevitability of a tragic hero's demise inspires sympathy in the audience.

**Tragic Irony** The situation in a **tragedy** where the audience is aware of the **tragic hero's** fate although the **character** has not yet become aware.

**Tragicomedy** A play with the elements of **tragedy** that ends happily.

**Transferred Epithet** A description that pairs an adjective with a noun that does not logically follow, such as *silver sounds.*

**Trimeter** A poetic **meter** that contains three feet in each line.

**Triplet** A **tercet** of three rhymed lines.

**Trochaic Meter:** A poetic **meter** created when each line contains more than one **trochee** (a unit with a stressed syllable followed by an unstressed syllable). Trochaic meter is a type of **falling meter.**

**Trochee** A poetic **foot** consisting of a stressed syllable followed by an unstressed syllable. The opposite of an **iamb,** and so sometimes called an "inverted foot," often beginning a line of **iambic pentameter.**

**Understatement** A purposeful underestimation of something, used to emphasize its actual magnitude.

**Unreliable Narrator** A **narrator** who cannot be trusted to present an undistorted account of the action because of inexperience, ignorance, personal bias, intentional deceptiveness, or even insanity.

**Verbal Irony** A statement in which the stated meaning is very different (sometimes opposite) from the implied meaning.

**Verisimilitude** How alike an imitation is to its original. The goal of literature, especially when written in the mode of realism, is to provide a likeness, or a verisimilitude, of real life.

**Verse** A broad term to describe poetic lines.

***Vers libre*** *See* **Free Verse.**

**Villanelle** A poem consisting of five **tercets** and a concluding **quatrain.** Each tercet rhymes *aba* and the final quatrain rhymes *abaa.* The poem's opening line repeats as the final line of the second and fourth stanzas, and in the second-to-last line of the poem. The last line of the first **stanza** repeats as the final line of the third and fifth stanzas and is also the final line of the poem overall.

**Visual imagery** **Imagery** and descriptions that appeal to a reader's sense of sight.

**Voice** The unique sound of an author's writing, created by elements such as **diction, tone,** and sentence construction.

**Volta** In a sonnet, the turn where a shift in thought or emotion occurs. In the **Petrarchan sonnet,** the **volta** occurs between the **octave** and the **sestet;** in the **Shakespearean sonnet,** the ending couplet provides the volta.

**Vulgate** A term to describe the common people, often used in reference to a level of speech or **diction.**

**Well-made Play** A type of theater popularized in France. Well-made plays feature a three-act sequence that *poses* a problem, *complicates* and then *resolves* it; usually that **resolution** comes when a **character's** past is revealed. The first act offers *exposition,* the second a *situation,* the third an unraveling or *completion.* Meticulous plotting and **suspense** are components of this mode of theater.

**Working Bibliography** A list of all the sources consulted in preparing a paper, as well as all the information necessary to cite them in the final list of works cited.

**Works Cited** A list of all the primary and secondary sources consulted in the creation of a paper.

# Credits

Adichi, Chimamanda Ngozi. "Cell One" first published in *The New Yorker,* January 29, 2007. Copyright © 2007 by Chimamanda Ngozi Adichie, reprinted with permission of The Wylie Agency, Inc.

Alexie, Sherman. "What You Pawn I Will Redeem" from *Ten Little Indians* by Sherman Alexie. Copyright © 2003 by Sherman Alexie. Used by permission of Grove/Atlantic.

Atwood, Margaret. "Happy Endings" from *Good Bones and Simple Murders* by Margaret Atwood, copyright © 1983, 1992, 1994, by O.W. Toad Ltd. A Nan A. Talese Book. Used by permission of Doubleday, a division of Random House, Inc. and McClelland & Stewart.

Baldwin, James. "Sonny's Blues" © 1957 by James Baldwin was originally published in *Partisan Review.* Copyright renewed. Collected in *Going to Meet the Man,* published by Vintage Books. Used by arrangement with the James Baldwin Estate.

Barthes, Roland. Excerpt from "The Death of the Author" from *Image/Music/Text* by Roland Barthes, translated by Stephen Heath. English translation copyright © 1977 by Stephen Heath. Reprinted by permission of Hill and Wang, a division of Farrar, Straus & Giroux, LLC.

Bender, Aimee. "The Rememberer" from *The Girl in the Flammable Skirt* by Aimee Bender, copyright © 1998 by Aimee Bender. Used by permission of Doubleday, a division of Random House, Inc.

Borges, Jorge Luis. "The Circular Ruins" from *Collected Fictions by Jorge Luis Borges,* translated by Andrew Hurley, copyright © 1998 by Maria Kodama; translation copyright © 1998 by Penguin Putnam Inc. Used by permission of Viking Penguin, a division of Penguin Group (USA) Inc.

Boyle, T. Coraghessan. "Greasy Lake" from *Greasy Lake and Other Stories* by T. Coraghessan Boyle, copyright © 1979, 1981, 1982, 1983, 1984, 1985 by T. Coraghessan Boyle. Used by permission of Viking Penguin, a division of Penguin Group (USA) Inc.

Burke, Kenneth. Excerpt from "The Poetic Process" from *Counter-Statement* by Kenneth Burke, second edition, University of California Press. Reprinted by permission of the Kenneth Burke Literary Trust.

Carver, Raymond. "Cathedral" from *Cathedral* by Raymond Carver. Copyright © 1981, 1982, 1983 by Raymond Carver. Used by permission of Alfred A. Knopf, a division of Random House, Inc.

Chekhov, Anton. "The Lady with the Pet Dog" translated by Avrahm Yarmolinsky, from *The Portable Chekhov by Anton Chekhov,* edited by Avrahm Yarmolinsky, copyright 1947, © 1968 by Viking Penguin, Inc., renewed © 1975 by Avrahm Yarmolinsky. Used by permission of Viking Penguin, a division of Penguin Group (USA) Inc.

Chekhov, Anton. "Rapture" translated by Patrick Miles and Harvey Pitcher. Reprinted from *Chekhov: The Comic Stories,* published by Andre Deutsch by permission of Carlton Publishing Group.

Crichton, Michael. Excerpt from *Eaters of the Dead* by Michael Crichton, copyright © 1976 and renewed 2004 by Michael Crichton. Used by permission of Alfred A. Knopf, a division of Random House, Inc.

Diaz, Junot. "How to Date a Browngirl, Blackgirl, Whitegirl, or Halfie" from *Drown* by Junot Diaz. Copyright © 1996 by Junot Diaz. Used by permission of Riverhead Books, an imprint of Penguin Group (USA) Inc.

Eikhenbaum, Boris. Excerpt from "The Theory of the Formal Method" by Boris Eikhenbaum collected in *Readings in Russian Poetics: Formalist and Structuralist Views,* edited by Ladislav Matejka and Krystyna Pomorska (Michigan Slavic Publications, 1998). Reprinted by permission.

Ellison, Ralph. "Battle Royal" copyright 1948 by Ralph Ellison, from *Invisible Man* by Ralph Ellison. Used by permission of Random House, Inc.

Ellison, Ralph. "A Party Down at the Square" copyright © 1996 by Fanny Ellison, from *Flying Home and Other Stories* by Ralph Ellison. Used by permission of Random House, Inc.

Faulkner, William. "Barn Burning" copyright 1950 by Random House, Inc. Copyright renewed 1977 by Jill Faulkner Summers. "A Rose for Emily" copyright 1930 and renewed 1958 by William Faulkner, from *Collected Stories of William Faulkner* by William Faulkner. Used by permission of Random House, Inc.

Fetterley, Judith: Excerpt from the Introduction to *The Resisting Reader: A Feminist Approach to American Fiction* by Judith Fetterley. Indiana University Press.

Ford, Richard. "Optimists" from *Rock Springs* by Richard Ford. Copyright © 1987 by Richard Ford. Used by permission of Grove/Atlantic, Inc.

Frye, Northrup. Excerpt from *Anatomy of Criticism* by Northrup Frye. Copyright © 1957 Princeton University Press, 1985 renewed Princeton University Press, 2000 paperback edition. Reprinted by permission of Princeton University Press.

García Márquez, Gabriel. "The Handsomest Drowned Man in the World" from *Leaf Storm and Other Stories* by Gabriel García Márquez. Copyright © 1971 by Gabriel García Márquez. Reprinted by permission of HarperCollins Publishers.

Gardner, John. Excerpt from *Grendel* by John Gardner, copyright © 1971 by John Gardner. Used by permission of Alfred A. Knopf, a division of Random House, Inc.

Gilb, Dagoberto. "Romero's Shirt" from *The Magic of Blood.* Copyright © 1993 by the University of New Mexico Press. Reprinted by permission.

Greenblatt, Stephen. Excerpt from Introduction to *The Power of Forms in the English Renaissance* edited by Stephen Greenblatt. Copyright © 1982. Published by Pilgrim Books.

Hemingway, Ernest. "The Short Happy Life of Francis Macomber" reprinted with permission of Scribner, a division of Simon & Schuster, Inc. from *The Short Stories of Ernest Hemingway.* Copyright 1936 by Ernest Hemingway. Copyright renewed © 1964 by Mary Hemingway. All rights reserved.

Hempel, Amy. "San Francisco" reprinted with the permission of Scribner, a division of Simon & Schuster, Inc., from *The Collected Stories of Amy Hempel* by Amy Hempel. Copyright © 1985 by Amy Hempel. All rights reserved.

Iser, Wolfgang. Excerpt from *The Act of Reading: A Theory of Aesthetic Response.* Copyright © 1978 The Johns Hopkins University Press. Reprinted by permission of The Johns Hopkins University Press.

Jen, Gish. "Who's Irish" copyright © 1998 by Gish Jen. First published in *The New Yorker.* From the collection *Who's Irish?* by Gish Jen published in 1999 by Alfred A. Knopf. Reprinted by permission of the author.

Jin, Ha. "Saboteur" from *The Bridegroom* by Ha Jin. Copyright © 2000 by Ha Jin. Used by permission of Pantheon Books, a division of Random House, Inc.

Kincaid, Jamaica. "Girl" from *At the Bottom of the River* by Jamaica Kincaid. Copyright © 1983 by Jamaica Kincaid. Reprinted by permission of Farrar, Straus and Giroux, LLC.

Kittredge, William. "Thirty-Four Seasons of Winter" copyright 2003 by William Kittredge. Reprinted from *The Best Short Stories of William Kittredge* with the permission of Graywolf Press, Saint Paul, Minnesota.

Lahiri, Jhumpa. "Interpreter of Maladies" from *Interpreter of Maladies* by Jhumpa Lahiri. Copyright © 1999 by Jhumpa Lahiri. Reprinted by permission of Houghton Mifflin Company. All rights reserved.

Le Guin, Ursula K. "The Kerastion" copyright © 1990 by Ursula K. Le Guin; first appeared in *Westercon 1990 Program Book*; from the author's collection *A Fisherman of the Island Sea*; reprinted by permission of the author and the author's agents, the Virginia Kidd Agency, Inc.

Leitch, Vincent B. Excerpt from *Cultural Criticism, Literary Theory, Postculturalism* by Vincent B. Leitch. Copyright © 1992. Reprinted by permission of Columbia University Press.

Lopez, Barry. "The Location of the River" from *Winter Count* by Barry Lopez. Reprinted by permission of SLL/Sterling Lord Literistic, Inc. Copyright by Barry Holstun Lopez.

Mahfouz, Naguib. "The Conjurer Made Off with the Dish" from *The Anchor Book of Modern Arabic Fiction,* edtied by Denys Johnson-Davies, copyright © 2006 by Denys Johnson-Davies. Used by permission of Anchor Books, a division of Random House, Inc.

Malamud, Bernard: "The Magic Barrel" from *The Stories of Bernard Malamud.* Copyright © 1983 by Bernard Malamud. Reprinted by permission of Farrar, Straus and Giroux, LLC.

Menendez, Ana. "Traveling Madness" © Ana Menendez. Used by permission of the author.

Moore, Lorrie. "How to Become a Writer" from *Self-Help* by Lorrie Moore, copyright © 1985 by M. L. Moore. Used by permission of Alfred A. Knopf, a division of Random House, Inc.

Munro, Alice. "An Ounce of Cure" from *Dance of the Happy Shades.* Copyright © 1968 by Alice Munro. Reprinted by permission of William Morris Agency, LLC on behalf of the author and McGraw-Hill Ryerson.

Narayan, R. K. "An Astrologer's Day" from *Malgudi Days* by R. K. Narayan, copyright © 1972, 1975, 1978, 1980, 1981, 1982 by R. K. Narayan. Used by permission of Viking Penguin, a division of Penguin Group (USA) Inc.

Oates, Joyce Carol. "Three Girls" from *I Am No One You Know* Copyright © 2004/2006 Ontario Review. "Where Are You Going, Where Have You Been?" published 1970 by Vanguard Press. Reprinted by permission of John Hawkins & Associates, Inc.

O'Brien, Tim. "The Things They Carried" from *The Things They Carried* by Tim O'Brien. Copyright © 1990 by Tim O'Brien. Reprinted by permission of Houghton Mifflin Harcourt Company. All rights reserved.

O'Connor, Flannery. "A Good Man Is Hard to Find" from *A Good Man Is Hard to Find and Other Stories,* copyright 1953 by Flannery O'Connor and renewed 1981 by Regina O'Connor. Reprinted by permission of Harcourt, Inc. "Revelation" from *The Complete Stories* by Flannery O'Connor. Copyright © 1971 by the Estate of Mary Flannery O'Connor. Reprinted by permission of Farrar, Straus and Giroux, LLC.

Packer, ZZ. "Brownies" from *Drinking Coffee Elsewhere* by ZZ Packer, copyright © 2003 by ZZ Packer. Used by permission of Riverhead Books, an imprint of Penguin Group (USA) Inc.

Porter, Katherine Anne. "The Jilting of Granny Weatherall" from *Flowering Judas and Other Stories.* Copyright 1930 and renewed 1958 by Katherine Anne Porter. Reprinted by permission of Harcourt, Inc.

Propp, Vladimir. Excerpt from "Fairy Tale Transformations," originally published as "Transformacii volšebnyx skazok," Poetika, 4 (Leningrad, 1928), pp. 70-89. Translated by C. H. Severens. Reprinted in *Readings in Russian Poetics: Formalist and Structuralist Views,* Ed. Ladislav Matejka and Krystyna Pomorska, (Michigan Slavic Publications, 1978) pp. 94-5. Reprinted by permission.

Silko, Leslie Marmon. "The Man to Send Rain Clouds" copyright © 1981 by Leslie Marmon Silko. Reprinted from *Storyteller* by Leslie Marmon Silko, published by Seaver Books, New York, New York.

Steinbeck, John. "The Chrysanthemums" copyright 1937, renewed © 1965 by John Steinbeck from *The Long Valley* by John Steinbeck. Used by permission of Viking Penguin, a division of Penguin Group (USA) Inc.

Stonum, Gary Lee. Excerpt from "Dickinson's Literary Background" from *The Emily Dickinson Handbook,* edited by Gudrun Gragher, Roland Hagenbüchle, Cristanne Miller. Copyright © 1998 by University of Massachusetts Press and published by the University of Massachusetts Press.

Tallent, Elizabeth. "No One's a Mystery" is reprinted by permission of the author.

Tan, Amy. "Two Kinds" from *The Joy Luck Club* by Amy Tan, copyright © 1989 by Amy Tan. Used by permission of G.P. Putnam's Sons, a division of Penguin Group (USA) Inc.

Toer, Pramoedya Ananta. "Circumcision" from *All That Is Gone* by Pramoedya Ananta Toer. Copyright © Pramoedya Ananta Toer. English translation copyright © 1994 Willem Samuels. Reprinted by permission of Hyperion. All rights reserved.

Updike, John. "A&P" from *The Early Stories, 1953-1975* by John Updike, copyright © 2003 by John Updike. Used by permission of Alfred A. Knopf, a division of Random House, Inc.

Walker, Alice. "Everyday Use" from *In Love & Trouble: Stories of Black Women,* copyright © 1973 by Alice Walker. Reprinted by permission of Harcourt, Inc.

Watanabe, Sylvia. "Talking to the Dead" from *Talking to the Dead* by Sylvia Watanabe, copyright © 1992 by Sylvia Watanabe. Used by permission of Doubleday, a division of Random House, Inc.

Welty, Eudora. "Why I Live at the P.O." from *A Curtain of Green and Other Stories,* copyright 1941 and renewed 1969 by Eudora Welty, reprinted by permission of Harcourt, Inc.

Wolfe, Thomas. "Only the Dead Know Brooklyn" from *From Death to Morning* by Thomas Wolfe. Copyright © 1935 by F-R Pub. Corp. Copyright renewed 1962 by Paul Gitlin, Administrator C.T.A., Estate of Thomas Wolfe. Reprinted with the permission of McIntosh and Otis, Inc.

# Photo Credits

**Page iv–v:** picturegarden/Getty Images; **xxxix:** ZenShui/Frederic Cirou/Getty Images; **2:** Comstock Images/Alamy; **2-3:** Chris Whitehead/Digital Vision/Getty Images; **5:** Brand X Pictures/PunchStock; **7 L:** Photodisc/Getty Images; **7R:** D. Hurst/Alamy; **8:** Royalty-Free/Corbis; **12:** Courtesy of Northwestern State University of Louisiana, Watson Memorial Library, Cammie G. Henry Research Center, Gladys Breazeale Collection, Folder 2; **13:** Library of Congress, Prints & Photographs Division [LC-USZ62-65696]; **15:** Paul Hawthorne/AP Images; **16:** Royalty Free/Corbis; **17:** Comstock/PunchStock; **18:** John A. Rizzo/Getty Images; **19:** Photodisc/PunchStock; **20:** BananaStock/PunchStock; **22:** D. Hurst/Alamy; **24:** Visual Language Illustration/Veer; **24–25:** Bruce Peebles/Corbis; **33:** Ryan McVay/Getty Images; **34:** Stockbyte ; **37:** Photodisc Collection/Getty Images; **39:** 2005 image100 Ltd. All Rights Reserved.; **43:** Amos Morgan/Getty Images; **45:** Photo Spin/Getty Images; **46:** Ingram Publishing/Fotosearch; **50–51:** Randy Faris/Corbis; **74–75:** David H. Wells/Photonica/Getty Images; **75:** Tom Brakefield/Corbis; **77:** Masterfile Royalty Free; **78 T:** Comstock/JupiterImages; **78 B–79 B:** Burke/Triolo/Brand X Pictures; **80:** Stockbyte/PunchStock; **88:** Photodisc/Getty Images; **90:** Amr Nabil/AP Images; **93:** Royalty-Free/Corbis; **95:** Suzanne Plunkett/AP Images; **102 L:** Daniel Hurst/Images.com; **102 R:** Mike Kemp/Punchstock; **106:** C Squared Studios/Getty Images; **108:** Brand X Pictures/PunchStock; **109:** Comstock Images; **117:** Hulton Archive/Getty Images; **118:** Anthony Saint James/Getty Images; **119:** Digital Vision/Getty Images; **120:** Cre8tive Studios/Alamy; **121:** Image Club; **123:** Library of Congress, Prints & Photographs Division, Carl Van Vechten Collection, [LC-USZ62-116087]; **125:** Photodisc/Getty Images; **126:** DAJ/Getty Images; **127:** Photodisc Collection/Getty Images; **129:** Ingram Publishing/Alamy; **130:** Ingram Publishing/Alamy; **131:** Comstock/PunchStock; **133:** Stockbyte/PunchStock; **136:** Philip Coblentz/Brand X Pictures/PictureQuest; **138:** Comstock Images/Alamy; **139:** Image Club; **142–143:** Joe Sartore/National Geographic/Getty Images; **143:** Alan & Sandy Carey/zefa/Corbis; **145:** Ingram Publishing/Alamy; **146 T:** Photodisc/Getty Images; **146 B:** Creatas Images; **148:** Joel Sartore/National Geographic/Getty Images; **152:** Library of Congress; **155:** Photodisc/Getty Images; **158–159:** Ingram Publishing/Fototsearch; **160–161:** Ingram Publishing/AGE Fotostock; **162:** Brand X Pictures/PunchStock; **163:** Tannen Maury/AP Images; **164 T:** Radlund & Associates/Getty Images; **164 B:** Radlund & Associates/Getty Images; **166:** Ingram Publishing/Fotosearch; **168:** Reven T.C. Wurman/Alamy; **169:** Classic PIO/Fotosearch; **171:** AP Images; **172:** The McGraw-Hill Companies Inc./Ken Cavanagh Photographer; **175:** The McGraw-Hill Companies, Inc./Jacques Cornell photographer; **176–177:** Steve Cole/Getty Images; **179:** Burke/Triolo Productions/Getty Images; **182:** C Squared Studios/Getty Images; **182–183:** Michael S. Quinton/National Geographic/Getty Images; **185:** Photodisc/PunchStock; **186–187:** Photodisc/Getty Images; **190:** Jules Frazier/Getty Images; **191:** Ingram Publishing/Alamy; **193:** Royalty-Free/Corbis; **194:** ImageState/Alamy; **200 T:** Andy Manis/AP Images; **200 B:** Comstock Images/Alamy; **201:** Ingram Publishing/Fotosearch; **202:** Getty Images; **206:** Digital Vision/PunchStock; **209:** Pixtal/SuperStock; **210:** Royalty-Free/Corbis; **212:** Digital Vision/PunchStock; **214:** Brand X Pictures; **217:** Brand X Pictures/PunchStock; **218:** Photodisc/Getty Images; **220:** Library of Congress [LC-USZ62-106490]; **221:** Library of Congress [LC-DIG-ppmsca-09485]; **223:** C Squared Studios/Getty Images; **225:** Ingram Publishing/Alamy; **228:** Ingram Publishing/Fotosearch; **232 L:** fotototo/Alamy; **232 R:** Brand X Pictures/Jupiterimages; **233:** Frank Greenaway/Dorling Kindersley/Getty Images; **235:** 1996 PhotoDisc, Inc./Getty Images; **236:** Ingram Publishing/Alamy; **243:** Library of Congress, Carl Van Vechten Collection,[LC-USZ62-42508]; **244:** Library of Congress; **246:** Royalty-Free/Corbis; **248:** Steven Senne/AP Images; **249:** moodboard/Punchstock; **251 B:** Creatas/PunchStock; **253:** Comstock Images/Alamy; **254:** Jim McKnight/AP Images; **255:** Photodisc/Getty Images; **256:** Stockbyte; **257:** Ingram Publishing/Alamy; **260:** Comstock Images/Jupiter Images; **260–261:** Hans Neleman/The Image Bank/Getty Images; **263:** Ingram Publishing/Fototsearch; **264:** Burke/Triolo Productions/Getty

Images; **267:** Ingram Publishing/Alamy; **268:** Ingram Publishing/Alamy; **274 B–275 B:** Stockdisc/Getty Images; **277:** Royalty-Free/Corbis; **279:** Comstock Images/Alamy; **283:** Ingram Publishing/Alamy; **285:** C Squared Studios/Getty Images; **287:** AP Images; **288:** C Squared Studios/Getty Images; **289:** Ingram Publishing/Alamy; **291:** Getty Images/Digital Vision; **295:** Stockbyte/PunchStock; **298:** Jennifer Graylock/AP Images; **299:** C Squared Studios/Getty Images; **300:** Ingram Publishing/Alamy; **301:** C Squared Studios/Getty Images; **303:** C Squared Studios/Getty Images; **304:** ephotocorp/Alamy; **306:** 2006 Glowimages, Inc.; **312 C:** Tom Schierlitz/Stone/Getty Images; **312 T:** Maciej Szubert/iStockphoto; **312 B:** Nathan Benn/Corbis; **313:** Davies and Starr/Stone/Getty Images; **315:** CMCD/Getty Images; **317:** Photodisc Collection/Getty Images; **319:** Photodisc/Getty Images; **320:** Steve Cole/Getty Images; **327:** Library of Congress, Prints & Photographs Division, [LC-DIG-cwpbh-03440]; **328:** Photodisc; **329:** Ingram Publishing/Fotosearch; **335 T:** Stockbyte; **337:** Image Source/Alamy; **338:** Janis Christie/Getty Images; **343:** Photodisc/PunchStock; **344:** Glenn Mitsui/Getty Images; **348–349:** D. Hurst/Alamy; **350–351:** Jules Frazier/Getty Images; **353:** Brand X Pictures/PunchStock; **355:** C Squared Studios/Getty Images; **357:** Courtesy of Elizabeth Tallent. Photo © Deirdre Lamb.; **358:** Comstock Images; **359:** Kent Knudson/PhotoLink/Getty Images; **362–363:** Marco Cristofori/Robert Harding World Imagery/Getty Images; **363:** Bettmann/Corbis; **363:** Silver Screen Collection/Hulton Archive/Getty Images; **366:** Dynamicgraphics/Jupiterimages; **367:** Image Club; **368:** Lawrence Manning/Corbis; **370:** The McGraw-Hill Companies Inc./Ken Cavanagh Photographer; **372:** Burke/Triolo Productions/Getty Images; **373:** Comstock/PunchStock; **375:** TRBfoto/Getty Images; **377:** Ingram Publishing/Fotosearch; **379:** Burke/Triolo Productions/Getty Images; **382 T:** Rich Reid/National Geographic/Getty Image; **382 B:** VisionsofAmerica/Joe Sohm/Getty Images; **384:** Grant Faint/Getty Images; **386:** Jules Frazier/Getty Images; **388:** Image Club; **389:** H. Fougere/Iconotec.com; **390:** Purestock/SuperStock; **394:** The McGraw-Hill Companies, Inc./John Flournoy, photographer; **399:** Comstock/JupiterImages; **400:** Brand X Pictures/PunchStock; **401:** Brand X Pictures/PunchStock; **402:** C Squared Studios/Getty Images; **403:** Christopher Felver/Corbis; **404:** Jeremy Woodhouse/Getty Images; **405:** Royalty-Free/Corbis; **406:** W.P. Osborn; **408:** PhotoLink/Getty Images; **409:** Comstock Images/Alamy; **411:** Michael T. Sedam/Corbis; **412:** Comstock Images/Alamy; **413:** Raymond Patrick/The Image Bank/Getty Images; **414:** Library of Congress, Prints & Photographs Division, Carl Van Vechten Collection, [LC-USZ62-42485]; **415:** BananaStock/PunchStock; **419:** C Squared Studios/Getty Images; **422:** Comstock/PunchStock; **425:** Photodisc/Getty Images; **426:** Royalty-Free/Corbis; **429:** AP Images; **430:** C Squared Studios/Getty Images; **433:** Anthony Ise/Getty Images; **435:** Pixtal/SuperStock; **438:** Comstock/JupiterImages; **441:** S. Solum/PhotoLink/Getty Images; **443:** Comstock Images; **445:** Royalty-Free/Corbis; **446:** Royalty-Free/Corbis; **448:** C Squared Studios/Getty Images; **450:** Image Club; **451:** Creatas Images/Jupiter Images; **453:** Don Farrall/Getty Images; **458:** Royalty-Free/Corbis; **462–463:** Lisa Zador/Getty Images; **487:** Shannon Fagan/Getty Images; **H-1:** Andre Jenny/Alamy; **H-86:** (**Google screenshot**) Reprinted by permission of Google Brand Features; **H-87:** (**NYU library catalog screenshot, JSTOR**) Reprinted courtesy of JSTOR. Copyright © 2008 JSTOR. All rights reserved; **H-90** (**PoemHunter.com screenshot and "Dream Deferred" by Langston Hughes, embedded within PoemHunter screenshot**) Reprinted by permission of Poemhunter.com.; From *The Collected Poems of Langston Hughes* by Langston Hughes, edited by Arnold Rampersad with David Roessel, Associate Editor. Copyright © 1994 by The Estate of Langston Hughes. Reprinted by permission of Harold Ober Associates Incorporated; **H-91:** (**Poetry Foundation screenshot; "Harlem" by Langston Hughes, embedded within Poetry Foundation screenshot**) Webpage reprinted by permission of the Poetry Foundation. Copyright © 2008 http://www.poetryfoundation.org; From *The Collected Poems of Langston Hughes* by Langston Hughes, edited by Arnold Rampersad with David Roessel, Associate Editor. Copyright © 1994 by The Estate of Langston Hughes. Reprinted by permission of Harold Ober Associates Incorporated; **H-97:** Michael Ochs Archives/Getty Images; **H-98:** Frank Driggs Collection/Getty Images; **H-107:** "Book Cover," copyright © 2000, from FROM SLAVERY TO FREEDOM by John H. Franklin and Evelyn Higginbotham. Used by permission of The McGraw Hill Companies; **H-114:** (**NYU library site for catalog page, SpringerLink**) Reprinted by permission of Springer.

# Index

Note: Page references in **boldface** refer to literary works included in their entirety.

# List of Authors and Selections for Fiction, Poetry, Drama, and Critical Approaches

## FICTION

CHIMAMANDA NGOZI ADICHIE, *Cell One*
SHERMAN ALEXIE, *What You Pawn I Will Redeem*
MARGARET ATWOOD, *Happy Endings*
ROGER AVERY AND NEIL GAIMON, *Interview on Adapting the Beowulf Story for Film*
JAMES BALDWIN, *Sonny's Blues*
AIMEE BENDER, *The Rememberer*
BEOWULF [GRENDEL'S ATTACK AND THE FIGHT WITH BEOWULF], *translated by CB Tinker*
BEOWULF: THE MOVIE (FILM STILLS OF BEOWULF AND GRENDEL)
J.L. BORGES, *The Circular Ruins, translated by Anthony Bonner*
T. CORAGHESSAN BOYLE, *Greasy Lake*
RAYMOND CARVER, *Cathedral*
WILLA CATHER, *Paul's Case*
ANTON CHEKHOV, *The Lady with the Pet Dog, translated by Avrahm Yarmolinsky*
——, *Rapture, translated by Patrick Miles and Harvey Pitcher*
KATE CHOPIN, *The Story of an Hour*
STEPHEN CRANE, *The Open Boat*
MICHAEL CRICHTON, *Eaters of the Dead [First Glimpse of Buliwyf; Battle with the Wendol]*
——, *A Factual Note on Adapting Beowulf for Eaters of the Dead*
JUNOT DIAZ, *How to Date a Browngirl, Blackgirl, Whitegirl, or Halfie*
RALPH ELLISON, *Battle Royal*
——, *A Party Down at the Square*
WILLIAM FAULKNER, *A Rose for Emily*
——, *Barn Burning*
RICHARD FORD, *Optimists*
JOHN GARDNER, *Grendel [Grendel's Isolation; Beowulf's Arrival; Fight with Beowulf]*
DAGOBERTO GILB, *Romero's Shirt*
CHARLOTTE PERKINS GILMAN, *The Yellow Wallpaper*
NATHANIEL HAWTHORNE, *Young Goodman Brown*
ERNEST HEMINGWAY, *The Short Happy Life of Francis Macomber*
AMY HEMPEL, *San Francisco*
GARETH HINDS, *Beowulf: The Graphic Novel [Grendel's Attack]*
ZORA NEALE HURSTON, *The Gilded Six-Bits*
GISH JEN, *Who's Irish?*
HA JIN, *Saboteur*
JAMES JOYCE, *Araby*
FRANZ KAFKA, *The Metamorphosis*
JAMAICA KINCAID, *Girl*
WILLIAM KITTREDGE, *Thirty-Four Seasons of Winter*
JHUMPA LAHIRI, *The Interpreter of Maladies*
D. H. LAWRENCE, *The Odour of Chrysanthemums*
URSULA K. LE GUIN, *The Kerastion*
JACK LONDON, *A Wicked Woman*
BARRY LOPEZ, *The Location of the River*
NAGUIB MAHFOUZ, *The Conjurer Made Off with the Dish, translated by Denys Johnson-Davies*
BERNARD MALAMUD, *The Magic Barrel*
KATHERINE MANSFIELD, *Miss Brill*
GABRIEL GARCÍA MÁRQUEZ, *The Handsomest Drowned Man in the World, translated by Gregory Rabassa*
HERMAN MELVILLE, *Bartleby, the Scrivener: A Story of Wall Street*
ANA MENENDEZ, *Traveling Madness*
LORRIE MOORE, *How to Become a Writer or, Have You Earned This Cliché?*

ALICE MUNRO, *An Ounce of Cure*
R. K. NARAYAN, *An Astrologer's Day*
JOYCE CAROL OATES, *Three Girls*
——, *Where Are You Going, Where Have You Been?*
TIM O'BRIEN, *The Things They Carried*
FLANNERY O'CONNOR, *A Good Man Is Hard to Find*
——, *Revelation*
Z Z PACKER, *Brownies*
EDGAR ALLAN POE, *The Fall of the House of Usher*
KATHERINE ANNE PORTER, *The Jilting of Granny Weatherall*
MARJANE SATRAPI, *Persepolis* (FILM STILLS BASED ON THE GRAPHIC NOVEL)
LESLIE MARMON SILKO, *The Man to Send Rain Clouds*
JOHN STEINBECK, *The Chrysanthemums*
ELIZABETH TALLENT, *No One's a Mystery*
AMY TAN, *Two Kinds*
THE 13TH WARRIOR (FILM STILLS OF BULIWYF AND THE WENDOL)
PRAMOEDYA ANANTA TOER, *Circumcision*
LEO TOLSTOY, *The Death of Ivan Ilych, translated by Louise and Aylmer Maude*
JOHN UPDIKE, *A&P*
ALICE WALKER, *Everyday Use*
SYLVIA WATANABE, *Talking to the Dead*
EUDORA WELTY, *Why I Live at the P.O.*
THOMAS WOLFE, *Only the Dead Know Brooklyn*

## POETRY

KIM ADDONIZIO, *First Poem for You*
AI, *Riot Act, April 29, 1992*
SHERMAN ALEXIE, *Defending Walt Whitman*
MIGUEL ALGARIN, *HIV*
JULIA ALVAREZ, *Woman's Work*
A. R. AMMONS, *Small Song*
——, *Their Sex Life*
ANONYMOUS, *Bonnie Barbara Allen*
ANONYMOUS, *Sir Patrick Spence*
ANONYMOUS, *Western Wind*
GLORIA ANZALDUA, *To live in the Borderlands means you*
MATTHEW ARNOLD, *Dover Beach*
MARGARET ATWOOD, *you fit into me*
W. H. AUDEN, *Funeral Blues*
——, *In Memory of W. B. Yeats*
——, *Musée des Beaux Arts* with Breughel's *Fall of Icarus*
——, *The Unknown Citizen*
JIMMY SANTIAGO BACA, *Choices*
MATSUO BASHŌ, *A caterpillar, translated by Robert Hass*
——, *Deep autumn—, translated by Robert Hass*
——, *Kyoto, translated by Robert Hass*
BHAGAVAD GITA, *[The Secret of Life], translated by Stephen Mitchell*
FRANK BIDART, *Herbert White*
ELIZABETH BISHOP, *The Fish*
——, *One Art*
——, *Sestina*
WILLIAM BLAKE, *Ah! Sun-flower*
——, *The Chimney Sweeper (Songs of Experience)*
——, *The Chimney Sweeper (Songs of Innocence)*
——, *The Clod & the Pebble*
——, *The Divine Image with Illustration*
——, *Earth's Answer*
——, *The Ecchoing Green with Illustrations*
——, *The Fly with Illustration*
——, *Frontispiece for Songs of Experience*
——, *Frontispiece for Songs of Innocence*
——, *The Garden of Love with Illustration*
——, *Holy Thursday (Songs of Experience) with Illustration*
——, *Holy Thursday (Songs of Innocence)*
——, *The Human Abstract*
——, *Introduction to Songs of Experience*
——, *Introduction to Songs of Innocence*
——, *The Little Black Boy*
——, *A Little Boy Lost*
——, *The Little Boy Lost*
——, *The Little Boy Found*
——, *A Little Girl Lost*
——, *The Lamb*
——, *London*
——, *Nurse's Song (Songs of Experience)*
——, *Nurse's Song (Songs of Innocence)*
——, *The Sick Rose*
——, *Title Page Illustration for Songs of Experience*
——, *Title Page Illustration for Songs of Innocence*
——, *The Tyger*
——, *The Voice of the Bard*
ROBERT BLY, *Driving to Town Late to Mail a Letter*
LOUISE BOGAN, *Changed Woman*
ANNE BRADSTREET, *The Author to Her Book*
——, *To My Dear and Loving Husband*
EMILY BRONTË, *Come Walk with Me*
GWENDOLYN BROOKS, *Sadie and Maud*
——, *We Real Cool*
ELIZABETH BARRETT BROWNING, *Go From Me*
——, *How Do I Love Thee? Let Me Count the Ways*
ROBERT BROWNING, *Love Among the Ruins*
——, *Meeting at Night*

GERDA MAYER, *Narcissus*
CLAUDE MCKAY, *The White City*
JAMES MERRILL, *The Victor Dog*
W. S. MERWIN, *For the Anniversary of My Death*
CHARLOTTE MEW, *I So Liked Spring*
EDNA ST. VINCENT MILLAY, *Not in a silver casket cool with pearls*
——, *Only until this cigarette is ended*
CZESLAW MILOSZ, *Encounter, translated by Czeslaw Milosz and Lillian Vallee*
JOHN MILTON, *Paradise Lost [Of Man's first disobedience . . .]*
——, *When I consider how my light is spent*
GABRIELLA MISTRAL, *Fugitive Woman, translated by Randall Couch*
MARIANNE MOORE, *The Fish*
PAUL MULDOON, *Symposium*
OGDEN NASH, *Gervaise*
MARILYN NELSON, *Chopin*
HOWARD NEMEROV, *The Blue Swallows*
PABLO NERUDA, *Do Not Love You Except Because I Love You, translated by Gustavo Escobedo*
——, *The Stolen Branch, translated by Donald D. Walsh*
NAOMI SHIHAB NYE, *The World In Translation*
SHARON OLDS, *Sex without Love*
MARY OLIVER, *At Blackwater Pond*
MICHAEL ONDAATJE, *Sweet Like a Crow*
JACQUELINE OSHEROW, *Song for the Music in the Warsaw Ghetto*
WILFRED OWEN, *Anthem for Doomed Youth*
——, *Dulce et Decorum Est*
GRACE PALEY, *Here*
DOROTHY PARKER, *Sonnet for the End of a Sequence*
LINDA PASTAN, *Ethics*
——, *Jump Cabling*
OCTAVIO PAZ, *Motion*
MOLLY PEACOCK, *Desire*
WILLIE PERDOMO, *Postcards of El Barrio*
LAURENCE PERRINE, *The limerick's never averse*
MARGE PIERCY, *The Secretary Chant*
ROBERT PINSKY, *Shirt*
——, *Sonnet*
——, *To Television*
SYLVIA PLATH, *Daddy*
——, *Metaphors*
——, *Mirror*
EDGAR ALLAN POE, *Annabel Lee*
ALEXANDER POPE, *True ease in Writing Comes from Art, Not Chance*
EZRA POUND, *In a Station of the Metro*
——, *The River-Merchant's Wife: A Letter*
SIR WALTER RALEIGH, *The Nymph's Reply to the Shepherd*
DUDLEY RANDALL, *The Ballad of Birmingham*
HENRY REED, *Naming of Parts*
ISHMAEL REED, *Beware: Do Not Read This Poem*
ADRIENNE RICH, *Aunt Jennifer's Tigers*
——, *Diving into the Wreck*
——, *Living In Sin*
RAINER MARIA RILKE, *Archaic Torso of Apollo, translated by Stephen Mitchell*
ALBERTO ALVARO RÍOS, *Naní*
EDWIN ARLINGTON ROBINSON, *Richard Cory*
THEODORE ROETHKE, *Elegy for Jane*
——, *My Papa's Waltz*
——, *Root Cellar*
WENDY ROSE, *Leaving Port Authority for the St. Regis Rezz*
CHRISTINA ROSSETTI, *A Birthday*
——, *Echo*
RUMI, *Some Kiss We Want, translated by Coleman Parks*
MARY JO SALTER, *Video Blues*
SONIA SANCHEZ, *Poem at Thirty*
CARL SANDBURG, *Fog*
SAPPHO, *A Fragment ["The moon has set"]*
CAROLE SATYAMARTI, *I Shall Paint My Nails Red*
GJERTRUD SCHNACKENBERG, *Snow Melting*
GIL SCOTT-HERON, *The Revolution Will Not Be Televised*
ANNE SEXTON, *Letter Written on a Ferry while Crossing Long Island Sound*
WILLIAM SHAKESPEARE, *Fear no more the heat o' the sun*
——, *Let me not to the marriage of true minds*
——, *My mistress' eyes are nothing like the sun*
——, *Not marble nor the gilded monuments*
——, *Shall I compare thee to a summer's day?*
——, *That time of the year thou mayest in me behold*
——, *When, in disgrace with Fortune and men's eyes*
JULIE SHEEHAN, *Hate Poem*
PERCY BYSSHE SHELLEY, *Ode to the West Wind*
——, *Ozymandias*
JANE SHORE, *My Mother's Chair*
SIR PHILLIP SIDNEY, *To the Sad Moon*
MARC SMITH, *Dusty Blues*
CATHY SONG, *Girl Powdering Her Neck* with Kitagawa Utamaro's Ukiyo-e print of *Girl Powdering Her Neck*
SONG OF SOLOMON 4:1-7 ["BEHOLD THOU ART FAIR, MY LOVE"], *King James Version*
GARY SOTO, *Mexicans Begin Jogging*

## DRAMA



## CRITICAL APPROACHES TO LITERATURE

# NOTES

# NOTES

# NOTES

# NOTES

## About the Authors

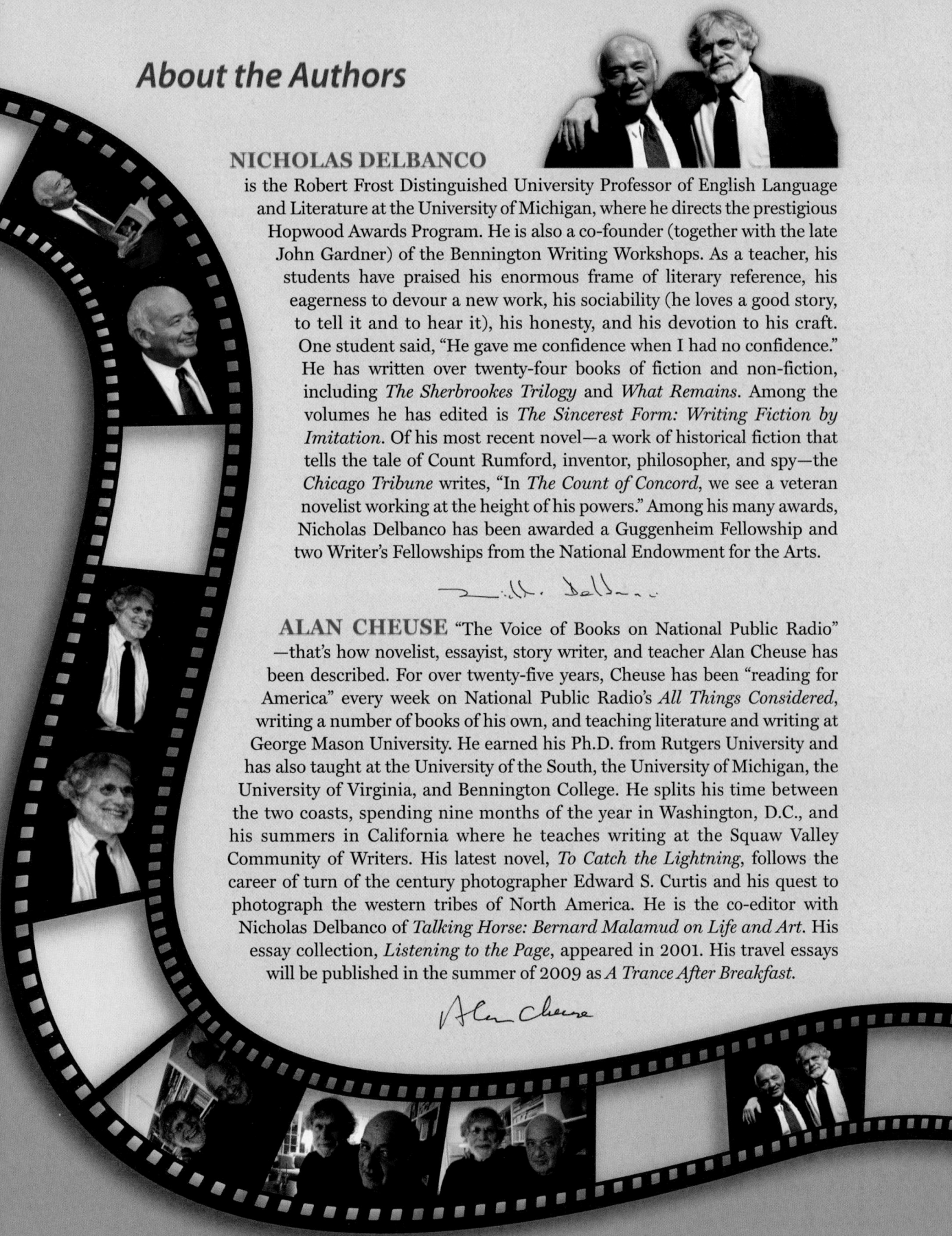

**NICHOLAS DELBANCO** is the Robert Frost Distinguished University Professor of English Language and Literature at the University of Michigan, where he directs the prestigious Hopwood Awards Program. He is also a co-founder (together with the late John Gardner) of the Bennington Writing Workshops. As a teacher, his students have praised his enormous frame of literary reference, his eagerness to devour a new work, his sociability (he loves a good story, to tell it and to hear it), his honesty, and his devotion to his craft. One student said, "He gave me confidence when I had no confidence." He has written over twenty-four books of fiction and non-fiction, including *The Sherbrookes Trilogy* and *What Remains*. Among the volumes he has edited is *The Sincerest Form: Writing Fiction by Imitation*. Of his most recent novel—a work of historical fiction that tells the tale of Count Rumford, inventor, philosopher, and spy—the *Chicago Tribune* writes, "In *The Count of Concord*, we see a veteran novelist working at the height of his powers." Among his many awards, Nicholas Delbanco has been awarded a Guggenheim Fellowship and two Writer's Fellowships from the National Endowment for the Arts.

**ALAN CHEUSE** "The Voice of Books on National Public Radio"—that's how novelist, essayist, story writer, and teacher Alan Cheuse has been described. For over twenty-five years, Cheuse has been "reading for America" every week on National Public Radio's *All Things Considered*, writing a number of books of his own, and teaching literature and writing at George Mason University. He earned his Ph.D. from Rutgers University and has also taught at the University of the South, the University of Michigan, the University of Virginia, and Bennington College. He splits his time between the two coasts, spending nine months of the year in Washington, D.C., and his summers in California where he teaches writing at the Squaw Valley Community of Writers. His latest novel, *To Catch the Lightning*, follows the career of turn of the century photographer Edward S. Curtis and his quest to photograph the western tribes of North America. He is the co-editor with Nicholas Delbanco of *Talking Horse: Bernard Malamud on Life and Art*. His essay collection, *Listening to the Page*, appeared in 2001. His travel essays will be published in the summer of 2009 as *A Trance After Breakfast*.

# Literature

## Poetry: Craft and Voice

**Nicholas Delbanco**
*University of Michigan*

**Alan Cheuse**
*George Mason University*

# To Our Students

Mc Graw Hill **Higher Education**

Published by McGraw-Hill, an imprint of The McGraw-Hill Companies, Inc., 1221 Avenue of the Americas, New York, NY 10020. 

This book is printed on acid-free paper.

5 6 7 8 9 0 DOW/DOW 0

ISBN: 978-0-07-721424-1
MHID: 0-07-721424-2

Editor in Chief: *Michael Ryan*
Publisher: *Lisa Moore*
Executive Marketing Manager: *Allison Jones*
Editorial Coordinator: *Stephen Sachs*
Production Editor: *Jasmin Tokatlian*
Manuscript Editor: *Susan Norton*
Cover Designer: *Jeanne Schreiber*
Interior Designers: *Jeanne Schreiber and Linda Robertson*
Senior Photo Research Coordinator: *Nora Agbayani*
Lead Media Project Manager: *Ron Nelms*
Production Supervisor: *Louis Swaim*
Composition: *9.25/11.25 Miller Roman by Thompson Type*
Printing: *45# NewPage Orion Gloss, R. R. Donnelley & Sons/Willard, OH*

Cover: © picturegarden/The Image Bank/Getty Images.

Credits: The credits section for this book begins on page C-1 and is considered an extension of the copyright page.

**Library of Congress Cataloging-in-Publication Data**

Delbanco, Nicholas.
Literature : craft and voice / Nicholas Delbanco, Alan Cheuse.—1st ed.
p. cm.
Includes index.
3 vols. planned.
ISBN-13: 978-0-07-721424-1 (v. 1 : acid-free paper)
ISBN-10: 0-07-721424-2 (v. 1 : acid-free paper) 1. Literature. I. Cheuse, Alan. II. Title.
PN45.D457 2009
800—dc22

2008051003



**www.mhhe.com**

# Contents

## POETRY

*Video interview with the authors available online at www.mhhe.com/delbancopreview*

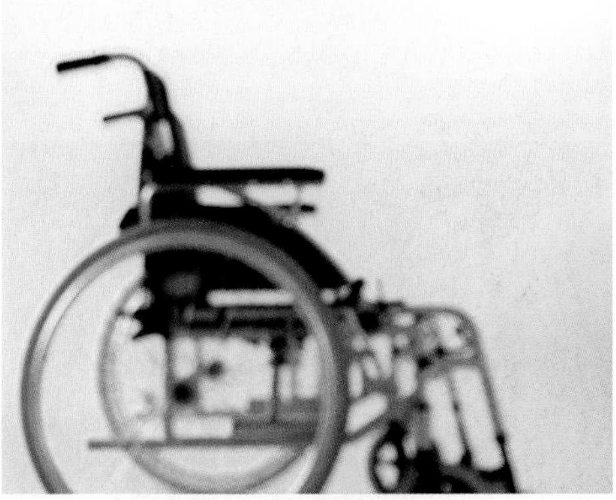

# 19 Voice: Tone, Persona, and Irony 102

## 20 Imagery and Symbol 144

## 21 Figures of Speech 176

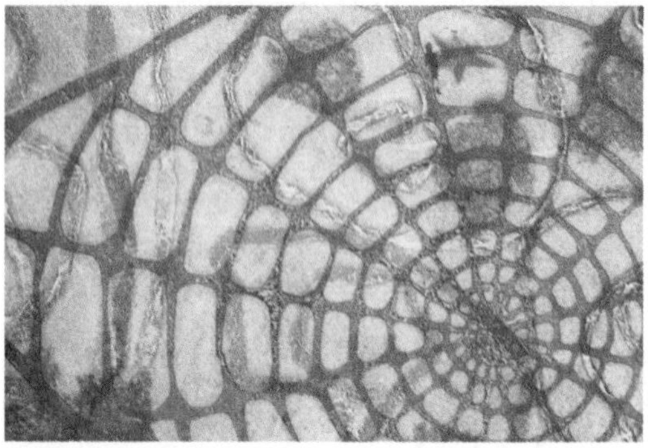

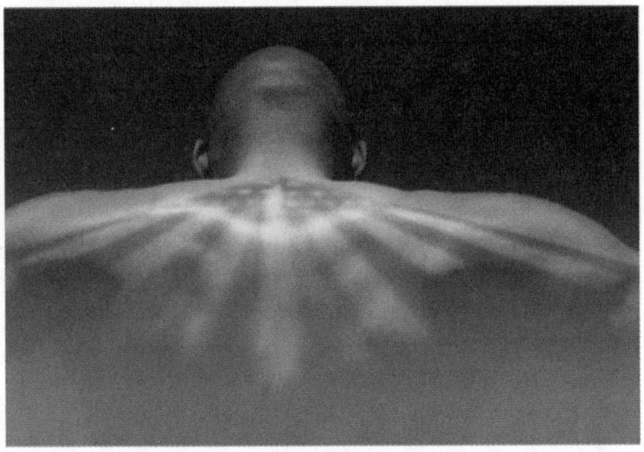

## 26 Langston Hughes 356



## 27 Art and Poetry 380

# A HANDBOOK FOR WRITING FROM READING H-1

## 1 Critical Approaches to Literature H-3



## 2 Writing from Reading H-25

# 15 Reading a Poem in Its Elements

THIS is your museum of stones, assembled in matchbox and tin,
collected from roadside, culvert, and viaduct,
battlefield, threshing floor, basilica, abattoir,
stones loosened by tanks in the streets
of a city whose earliest map was drawn in ink on linen,
schoolyard stones in the hand of a corpse,
pebble from Apollinaire's *oui*,
stone of the mind within us
carried from one silence to another . . .

*—from "The Museum of Stones," by Carolyn Forché*

NOWADAYS more people read fiction or go to the movies (our contemporary version of the theater) than read poetry. However, most writers think of poetry as the purest example of verbal expression; all of us acknowledge it as the mother form. Short stories and novels are relatively recent genres, but poetry has been a hallmark of civilization since civilization began. The earliest singers and bards expressed themselves in rhythm and rhyme long before prose was composed. When the first drum sounded or the first string was plucked, its verbal companion or accompaniment was what we have come to call verse.

While we may be more familiar with the techniques of prose fiction, the language of poetry is often where we turn to better express the emotion of a great occasion or a deeply personal one. At weddings and funerals everywhere, poems are being recited; they remain the "touchstones" of experience relived. Carolyn Forché tells us that "The Museum of Stones" is a memorial tribute to a dead friend—a man who kept a collection of

*"The more we know about how a poem makes its rhythms and musics and patternings, the more deeply we can enter into the poem. It doesn't mean that we can't read the poem with great pleasure knowing very little about those matters, it means that we'll have much more pleasure if we know more."*

Conversation with Carolyn Forché, available on video at www.mhhe.com/delbanco1e

stones to remind him of his travels. The long list of places where the stones in the poem were found provides a kind of encyclopedia of buildings seen and countries visited. This general human history is made vivid for the poet through personal loss. If we can open ourselves to the experience of reading poetry, its special language—its lists and repetitions—can touch our lives more deeply than ordinary speech.

## A FIRST READING: "DUFFING INTO IT"

When reading a poem for the first time, remember: We may start anywhere. As the great American poet Robert Frost expresses it, "We *duff* into our first reading of a poem. We read that poem imperfectly (thoroughness with it would be fatal), but the better to read the second. We read the second the better to read the third . . . ." A "duffer" is a beginner, and everyone who reads a poem for the first time duffs his or her way into it.

All children are alive to rhyme, the pleasures of repeated sound, and it's one of the ways we learn language: *pretty* rhymes with *witty, hiss* with *kiss* or *miss.* (Think of those nursery rhymes that have remained intact across the ages.) When you read a poem for the first time, it's that childhood pleasure you're after. Notice the way words edge up against each other, the way they match and shift. Let your mind drift, enjoy the words, and listen to the sound of the lines. What do the sounds make you think of? What words stand out for you? What associations does the poem have?

In her interview, Carolyn Forché says "as the reader" you should read the first time "without a preconception." As you begin to read poems in this chapter you will notice that some of them are easier to understand than others; some seem transparent with respect to their meaning while others may appear flat-out incomprehensible. Some will please you; some will not. Upon first reading, don't make finding the poem's meaning your sole aim. The sound and the shape of a poem will be as important as the final interpretation.

*CONTINUED ON PAGE 6*

*The poet is imagining you . . .*

Q&A

*You are as much this poem's important reader as the very first person who read it.*

# *A Conversation on Writing*

## Carolyn Forché

### Reading Poetry

A poet will tell you this if you ask. They go where the poem takes them, and they don't know in advance where the poem is going when they are writing it the first time. They don't know what the poem is going to be about, often. They certainly don't know what its destination is. So, your experience as the reader is also to go without a preconception, and to enter the poem and to read freshly. You are as much this poem's important reader as the very first person who read it. Writing does not recur. The poem is written and finished and goes into the world. But reading recurs, and you are a fresh reader.

### Interpreting Poetry

The poet is imagining you . . . and is attempting to become present to you and to celebrate your presence. . . . You are making a reading of the poem. If you are sitting in a circle of students, you will find that there might be six or seven different readings of this poem. Often the way to really solve the puzzle is to talk about all the different readings. Some of them might contradict each other and some of them might complement each other, but eventually you'll arrive at a full appreciation of what's before you on the page, and it's delightful.

### The Story of "The Museum of Stones"

I had a friend who, when he was traveling around the world, decided that instead of going to souvenir shops . . . would choose a little stone . . . from each place he visited. . . . He would put it on a little prong or block and he would label it. "Stone from beneath the Eiffel Tower, 1993, spring" . . . "Stone from the Banks of the Nile," "Stone from Hector's Garage in Illinois." You know, he had all kinds of different stones, and he called it his museum. I wrote this poem for him . . . after he died.

Known as a "poet of witness," Carolyn Forché (b. 1950)—a native of Detroit, Michigan—became a spokesperson for human rights through her poetry after traveling to El Salvador. Forché had a consciousness of atrocities from the time she was a young girl—she discovered a copy of *Look* magazine with pictures of the Holocaust, which her mother promptly hid—but it wasn't until her second book of poetry, *The Country Between Us* (1981), that she stirred controversy by dealing with political violence overtly. Her first collection, *Gathering the Tribes* (1976), won the Yale Series of Younger Poets Prize, and she has continued to receive prestigious awards and fellowships, including the Guggenheim and National Endowment of the Arts Creative Writing Fellowship. She has taught at George Mason University and Skidmore College; she now is a member of the faculty at Georgetown University.

**To watch this entire interview and hear the author read from her work, go to www.mhhe.com/delbanco1e.**

**RESEARCH ASSIGNMENT** Watch the interview and explain what Forché means when she says "form and content are intertwined." How does this relate to the word *stone* in the poem "The Museum of Stones"?

**AS YOU READ** Duff your way into the poem in a first reading. Notice the different stones mentioned in this poem.

# The Museum of Stones

**(2007)**

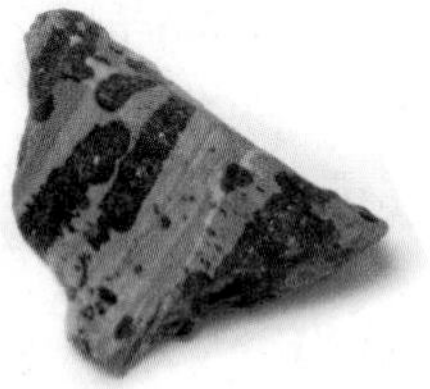

This is your museum of stones, assembled in matchbox and tin,
collected from roadside, culvert, and viaduct,
battlefield, threshing floor, basilica, abattoir,
stones loosened by tanks in the streets
of a city whose earliest map was drawn in ink on linen,
schoolyard stones in the hand of a corpse,
pebble from Apollinaire's *oui,*
stone of the mind within us
carried from one silence to another,
stone of cromlech and cairn, schist and shale, hornblende,
agate, marble, millstones, and ruins of choirs and shipyards,
chalk, marl, and mudstone from temples and tombs,
stone from the silvery grass near the scaffold,
stone from the tunnel lined with bones,
lava of the city's entombment,
chipped from lighthouse, cell wall, scriptorium,
paving stones from the hands of those who rose against the army,
stones where the bells had fallen, where the bridges were blown,
those that had flown through windows and weighted petitions,
feldspar, rose quartz, slate, blueschist, gneiss, and chert,
fragments of an abbey at dusk, sandstone toe
of a Buddha mortared at Bamiyan,
stone from the hill of three crosses and a crypt,
from a chimney where storks cried like human children,
stones newly fallen from stars, a stillness of stones, a heart,
altar and boundary stone, marker and vessel, first cast, lode, and hail,
bridge stones and others to pave and shut up with,
stone apple, stone basil, beech, berry, stone brake,
stone bramble, stone fern, lichen, liverwort, pippin, and root,
concretion of the body, as blind as cold as deaf,
all earth a quarry, all life a labor, stone-faced, stone-drunk
with hope that this assemblage, taken together, would become
a shrine or holy place, an ossuary, immovable and sacred,
like the stone that marked the path of the sun as it entered the human dawn.

"When we read a poem maybe the mind of the reader is a kind of solvent, like you drop the DNA, which is the poem, in the mind of the reader, and the poem begins to blossom, to bloom with all these meanings. Of course the information I'm talking about in a poem isn't just data, and it's not necessarily biographical information. It's emotional information, spiritual information, soulful information, erotic information, intellectual information, all of that stuff packed into a poem." Conversation with Li-Young Lee

# Writing from Reading

### Summarize

1 List the stones included here and describe how "this assemblage, taken together" can help us to understand the world.

### Analyze Craft

2 In her interview, Forché says, "In our culture it becomes more and more difficult for us to enter into, imaginatively at least, the consciousness of others. Literature is a way of doing that." How do you share in the speaker's experience of mourning by reading this poem? What in the poem makes that sadness clear?

3 Why do you think the speaker plays with the different *stone* words? What effect does the wordplay have on your reading of the poem?

4 Do the references to Apollinaire and Bamiyan require research on your part, or do they seem like private allusions?

### Analyze Voice

5 In her interview, Forché also indicates that "The first level of [a poem's] meaning is simply to be moved and to hear a speaker, to hear a voice giving voice to what is within the poet." In this poem, does "your museum of stones" mean the poet is talking to herself, or is she addressing someone else, or both?

### Synthesize Summary and Analysis

6 There is a great deal of information in this poem. Compare it to the listing technique of O'Brien's "The Things They Carried" (*Fiction*, chapter 10). In both instances, what is the effect of the writers' doing this?

### Interpret the Poem

7 Why do you think the poet uses the image of a "museum" in this poem; what about a museum lends additional meaning to the poem?

*(CONTINUED FROM PAGE 3)*

## A CRITICAL READING

In ways we'll come to understand, poetry often manages to use everyday language in uncommon ways—to rise above the commonplace and avoid cliché. A thing that's said too frequently can feel unimportant, and if we repeat the same phrase again and again its meaning empties out. Certain expressions—or words like *like*—come to us on automatic pilot, and we barely notice what we're saying or reading. When people say "No problem" now, they tend to mean "You're welcome," but neither of those phrases means precisely what the words say, and both of them get used with something less than conscious attention to word choice. "Good-bye," for example, is a contraction of "God be with ye," but which of us who shouts "Good-bye!" is conscious of its original meaning? "Farewell"—a slightly more formal expression at parting—has also been stripped of its resonance until we stop and think about what "fare well" might mean. To the poet—and poetry's careful reader—each word has its own history and every syllable counts.

> "You have to read the way a cook eats. How is it done? How is that put together?" Conversation with Robert Pinsky

"Be completely open—innocent, if you will, of the poem. Walk in, just like it's water, and say, "What is this?" And read it over and over again. . . . [Read] with that kind of ignorant joy, and [let] yourself be bewildered when you're bewildered."

Conversation with Marie Howe

Although such an assertion—that every syllable counts—seems simple and even self-evident, it involves a host of elements the following chapters will discuss in detail. No one element works in isolation from the others. Rather, rhythm depends on word choices, and word choices conjure up a speaker's voice; that voice will be inflected by the use of images, symbols, or figures of speech. These will be made shapely and arranged into a form, either a formal prescribed structure or one that emerges from the content and cadence of the words themselves. All these elements work together to create the effect the poem makes.

- **Words** are the language of poetry; a poet chooses "the best words" and puts them in "the best order" to describe an experience or feeling. Choices may be playful, lofty, direct, or unusual, and they lead directly to voice.
- **Voice** refers to every poem's speaker. The words and the order of the words that the poet chooses determine that speaker's tone of voice (stately, mournful, tender, angry). The speaker may or may not be the poet.
- **Images** in poetry transform the everyday thing that is experienced for itself into a vivid sensory impression.
- **Symbols** transcend the thing itself (a tree) and suggest a larger meaning (nature). Imagery and symbolism work in the service of word choice and tone of voice to generate emotion and establish the mood of the poem. Like language itself, they are a sign for something not present on the page.
- **Figures of speech** most commonly compare two unlike objects, such as "the sun" and "the face of the beloved," to condense and heighten the effect of language, particularly the effect of the imagery or symbolism used in a poem.
- **Sound,** the rhythmic structure of the lines that draws the reader in, often utilizes rhyme and is created through word choice and word order.
- **Form,** either formal or open, distinguishes poetry from prose through its arrangement in rhythmic lines of words.

As Carolyn Forché says in her interview, every reader gets to have a fresh reading. Forché also indicates that as her work on "The Museum of Stones" progressed, she went to the dictionary, to the thesaurus, to various sources of information on the sound and shape and look of these particular objects (she's not a geologist and had no previous expertise with rocks). The words became a kind of game for her, and she began to link

"Everybody plays with language, with the rhythms of language as part of what they do, you know, it's sort of our fundamental act of learning." Conversation with Robert Hass

three categories—animal, vegetable, and mineral—from the game "Twenty Questions." You do not need to know these things to read her poem critically, but do be mindful of the pleasure in the playfulness in the poet's language. Here is a sample reading of "The Museum of Stones" in which the reader looks at how the poet's choices helped create the experience of the first reading.

# An Interactive Reading of "The Museum of Stones"

This is your museum of stones, assembled in matchbox and tin,
collected from roadside, culvert, and viaduct,
battlefield, threshing floor, basilica, abattoir,
stones loosened by tanks in the streets
of a city whose earliest map was drawn in ink on linen,
schoolyard stones in the hand of a corpse,
pebble from Apollinaire's *oui*,
stone of the mind within us
carried from one silence to another,
stone of cromlech and cairn, schist and shale, hornblende,
agate, marble, millstones, and ruins of choirs and shipyards,
chalk, marl, and mudstone from temples and tombs,
stone from the silvery grass near the scaffold,
stone from the tunnel lined with bones,
lava of the city's entombment,
chipped from lighthouse, cell wall, scriptorium,
paving stones from the hands of those who rose against the army,
stones where the bells had fallen, where the bridges were blown,
those that had flown through windows and weighted petitions,
feldspar, rose quartz, slate, blueschist, gneiss, and chert,
fragments of an abbey at dusk, sandstone toe
of a Buddha mortared at Bamiyan,
stone from the hill of three crosses and a crypt,
from a chimney where storks cried like human children,
stones newly fallen from stars, a stillness of stones, a heart,
altar and boundary stone, marker and vessel, first cast, lode, and
  hail,
bridge stones and others to pave and shut up with,
stone apple, stone basil, beech, berry, stone brake,
stone bramble, stone fern, lichen, liverwort, pippin, and root,
concretion of the body, as blind as cold as deaf,
all earth a quarry, all life a labor, stone-faced, stone-drunk
with hope that this assemblage, taken together, would become
a shrine or holy place, an ossuary, immovable and sacred,
like the stone that marked the path of the sun as it entered the
  human dawn.

*Interpret:* great image!—a stone catching the sunlight in the morning. But here, it's not just any morning—it's the beginning of the whole human race. So maybe even though there is so much death and war earlier, it shows these stones and the human race still go on? I never quite figured out who the poet was addressing—"this is *your* museum of stones." The textbook says it's a dead friend of the poet, but I didn't get many clues about the "you." Still, the poem seems less personal and more universal to me.

*Image:* very violent—war; I'm picturing a dusty landscape.

*Interpret:* References to something outside the poem? What?

*Image:* Suddenly really abstract, in the middle of all this physical imagery . . .

*Interpret:* a long list of rock types. Can picture a ruined shipyard, but a ruined choir?

*Interpret:* Is this a story or a progression of related images? What's tying it all together?

*Words:* Look up "scriptorium"—what do these three words have in common?

*Words:* Another list of rock types . . . a break? or a type of momentum?

*Sound:* Repetition of "s" sounds . . . slows the line down—emphasis?

*Interpret:* She is clearly not talking just about stones—"all earth, all life" means this is about everything.

*Image:* Unexpected words . . . words for a person, not nature.

*Interpret:* Does "museum" equal "rock collection"?

*Words:* look up "culvert" and "abbatoir." Why such complicated words?

*Image:* shift in image . . . tanks on rock to ink on cloth. Change to softer tone?

*Words:* Types of rocks, I think—but why these? Sound of the words, maybe, more than the rocks themselves.

*Words:* "tomb" repeated, and lots of "grave" imagery. Is the collection a "museum" because something/someone has died?

*Rhyme:* "sandstone toe"—the sounds of the words are the same—almost a relief after the list of weird rock names.

*Interpret:* Significance of two different religious references in a row?

*Words:* repetition of "stone"—gives the impression of hardness over and over, even though basil, beech, and berry are nice images. But then, liverwort, lichen, and bramble aren't so pretty.

## THE CRAFT OF POETRY

Robert Burns is perhaps best known for his work with Scottish folk songs, and what we first notice in the seemingly simple work that follows is the rhythm and rhyme in the four-line stanzas of "O my luve's like a red, red rose." The poem is more a description of an emotion than an emotion itself. The only three-syllable word in the sixteen lines is "melodie"—a somewhat formal way of saying *song*. Burns wrote in Scottish dialect; the poem can be (and has been) set to music.

# Robert Burns (1759–1796)

One of Scotland's greatest poets, Robert Burns was born to a struggling tenant farm family. At age fifteen, Burns fell in love and consequently wrote his first poem. He became notorious for his love affairs, which shocked the Calvinist society surrounding him, and he cultivated his poetry based on his own broad reading. He published *Poems* in 1786 and became immensely popular in Edinburgh. But perhaps his greatest achievement was his preservation and creation of folk songs, which he did formally for two anthologies, *The Scots Musical Museum* and *Select Collection of Original Scottish Airs.* Burns is known for writing in Scots, an English dialect spoken by commoners and by eighteenth-century nobility. Burns's songs are still widely known today, especially "Auld Lang Syne."

**AS YOU READ** Note that the speaker addresses both his lover and an audience over her shoulder; the first stanza is a kind of general declaration, and the next three are specific to "my bonnie lass" herself.

# O my luve's like a red, red rose (1794)

O my luve's like a red, red rose,
  That's newly sprung in June.
O my luve's like the melodie
  That's sweetly play'd in tune.

As fair art thou, my bonnie lass,
  So deep in luve am I;
And I will luve thee still, my dear,
  Till a' the seas gang dry.

Till a' the seas gang dry, my dear,
  And the rocks melt wi' the sun;
And I will luve thee still, my dear,
  While the sands o' life shall run.

And fare thee weel, my only luve!
  And fare thee weel awhile!
And I will come again, my luve,
  Tho' it were ten thousand mile.

# Writing from Reading

### Summarize

**1** If this poem is a declaration, what is the speaker declaring? How long does he indicate his love will last?

**2** How far would he be willing to travel to see his love again?

### Analyze Craft

**3** Burns compiled and created Scottish folk songs in the Scots dialect. What about this poem seems musical to you?

**4** What two things does the poet compare to his "luve" in the first stanza? What do those comparisons help him accomplish in this poem? How does it set the stage for the rest of the poem?

**5** When is the rose that he compares his love to "sprung"? Why would the month be significant?

### Analyze Voice

**6** What words does the speaker use that show how "deep in luve am I"?

### Synthesize Summary and Analysis

**7** Burns has chosen the form of a song to declare his love. How does this choice make his declaration convincing?

### Interpret the Poem

**8** Although the poem is clearly a love poem, how would you characterize the love here? Do we know why the speaker is leaving his lover? Do we need to?

Here's a very different kind of love poem—one written by a son to the memory of his father. For Robert Burns, the problem with his "luve" is one of distance, and he promises he will return; for Robert Hayden, in the twentieth century, the distance is unbridgeable because his parent is dead. This is never made *explicit* in the fourteen lines that follow, but the sense of loss is *implicit* throughout, a muted if not mute regret that the poet failed to tell his father, "Thanks."

## Robert Hayden (1913–1980)

Though uneducated themselves, Robert Hayden's parents encouraged their son's intellectual efforts in his childhood spent in Detroit, Michigan. Of African-American descent, Hayden resisted a narrow view of his work as that of a "black" poet, even though it frequently engages with African-American history and experience. Hayden earned a bachelor's degree from Wayne State University in Detroit. He then worked for the Federal Writers' Project, published his first collection of poems in 1940, and married before earning his master's degree at the University of Michigan, where he studied with W. H. Auden. Known for his formal poetry on a range of subjects—including historical figures like Phillis Wheatley and Malcolm X—Hayden earned the position of Poet Laureate from 1976 to 1978. Aside from poetry, Hayden made his career as a professor of English at Fisk University and the University of Michigan.

**AS YOU READ** Try to hear the speaker's tone of voice, the sorrow here expressed.

# Those Winter Sundays (1962)

Sundays too my father got up early
and put his clothes on in the blueblack cold,
then with cracked hands that ached
from labor in the weekday weather made
banked fires blaze. No one ever thanked him.

I'd wake and hear the cold splintering, breaking.
When the rooms were warm, he'd call,
and slowly I would rise and dress,
fearing the chronic angers of that house,

Speaking indifferently to him,
who had driven out the cold
and polished my good shoes as well.
What did I know, what did I know
of love's austere and lonely offices?

# Writing from Reading

## Summarize

1 The poem's first two words are "Sundays too." This suggests that what he does on Sunday morning he does the other six days of the week. What evidence do we have of the socio-economic circumstance of this family? Is there a furnace, for instance?

2 What might be some of "the chronic angers of that house"?

## Analyze Craft

3 Imagine for a moment that the poem has been written in the present tense. Its title would be "These Winter Sundays," and the first line would report "my father gets up early." How does the use of the past tense instead suggest that these are memories, and that "No one ever thanked him" means they cannot do so now?

## Analyze Voice

4 Notice the way the poet repeats his regretful, "What did I know, what did I know . . ." Does this provide a kind of emphasis, and, if you were to read it aloud, where would the emphasis change?

## Synthesize Summary and Analysis

5 We know that this is a Sunday and that the father polishes his son's "good shoes." Does this suggest the family will soon go to church?

## Interpret the Poem

6 What does the poet mean by, and what do we learn about, "love's austere and lonely offices"? And why did Hayden choose to use that final word?

Ezra Pound writes in his eccentric but illuminating study *ABC of Reading*, "That poetry is best which is closest to music. . . ." Most people think of "lyric" as the words to a song, yet it is, in fact, a form of poetry, playing the same music from the ancient time of Sappho to the present moment: a song of love and loss. The speaker

"I just was entranced by [the poetry] I read, and I read it with a kind of fury. I felt kind of saved by it. Then I began to read poems that made a tremendous difference to me; I felt almost as if I had written them." Conversation with Edward Hirsch

of the following fragment finds herself in darkness, in the middle of the night. She yearns for company (with the presence in the visible sky of the constellation known as the Pleiades, or the Seven Sisters, suggesting it might be female company she desires). Here too the subject is isolation, some twenty-five hundred years before "Those Winter Sundays," and here too the context is different—but the tone of the two poems is in many ways the same.

## Sappho (c. 630–570 B.C.E.)

Although much of her biography is speculation rather than fact, we know Sappho lived on the island of Lesbos in ancient Greece. She was exiled to Sicily for a time before returning to Lesbos, where she had a husband and daughter. She also ran a school for girls. Sappho has been recognized throughout the centuries as the greatest ancient female poet, one whom Plato referred to as the "tenth muse" (in Greek mythology, there are nine). Her verse, which would have been sung to the accompaniment of the lyre, is direct and simple but overflows with emotion. Today, only fragments of Sappho's work survive, although in her lifetime, she likely produced nine collections of poetry. Sappho died either of old age or, according to legend, from jumping off a cliff for love of Phaon, a young boatman.

**AS YOU READ** **Notice the way the last line rises up and sweeps back against the first few lines, qualifying what went before.**

# A Fragment (c. 600 B.C.E.)

The moon has set,
The Pleiades have gone,
Midnight, and the hours pass,
I lie in my bed alone . . .

*—adapted by Alan Cheuse*

# Writing from Reading

### Summarize

1 Where is the speaker, and what time is it?

### Analyze Craft

2 What significance does the time have?

### Analyze Voice

3 Who is the speaker? What is her lament?

### Synthesize Summary and Analysis

4 What are the Pleiades? How do the night sky, the moon, and the Pleiades support the mood of the poem?

5 How would you describe the tone of the poem?

6 How does the setting of the poem reflect the loneliness of the speaker?

### Interpret the Poem

7 This is only a fragment, which has been recovered, of a longer work by Sappho. Many of her fragments, on similar themes, are all that we have of Sappho's work. Judging from this brief work, is her loneliness temporary, or will it be relieved?

There is more than mere sentiment or sentimentality in this poem. Everyone feels this variety of loneliness at some point in a lifetime. The poet finds a way to give that shared feeling or emotion a particular expression. If Sappho had written "with you" as opposed to "alone," the whole feel of the poem would change, and the mood of melancholy would likely be supplanted by one of celebration. If the last line read "with my dog Spot" or "with my daughter" or "with a man I met an hour ago," the tone would also shift; each word *matters,* and the word *alone* gives the fragment its negative force.

> "Reading good poetry helps a person feel less lonely. It's the evidence that someone else has felt what we feel, knowing what we know." Conversation with Jane Hirshfield

William Wordsworth, the nineteenth-century British poet, defined the essence of a poem as "the spontaneous overflow of powerful feelings . . . recollected in tranquility." Traditionally, the **lyric** poem speaks of the poet's misery over the loss of love or the loss of his or her affections toward the object of his or her love. Wordsworth dramatizes in the poem that follows the process by which a past event becomes transformed. The poet can nonetheless remember from his "couch" what it felt like to be out on a hillside, surrounded by flowers. (This poem is also known by the alternative title "The Daffodils.") The twentieth-century American poet John Ciardi spoke about the movement at the end of a poem as the "wave" that doubles back and breaks against all the lines that come before it. By reconstructing what he felt, the poet helps us as readers feel it anew: an experience described is an experience shared.

# William Wordsworth (1770–1850)

One of the major British Romantic poets, Wordsworth was born—and lived most of his life—in the Lake District of England. He and Samuel Taylor Coleridge developed a close friendship built on mutual admiration of each other's poetry. Together, they published *Lyrical Ballads* (1798), which contained one of Wordsworth's major poems, "Tintern Abbey." A poet with a deep reverence for nature and an interest in the individual, Wordsworth's touchstone work is "The Prelude" (1850), a long autobiographical poem full of reflections on past emotions. Although Wordsworth grew in stature and was named Poet Laureate in 1848, the quality of his poetry declined after 1810, perhaps because he relied on remembered emotions of his youth—an exhaustible resource—to fuel his poetry. Still, he shaped the course of British poetry with his famous "Preface" to *Lyrical Ballads* in which he argued that poetry should be about emotions and everyday experience, rather than the intellect and classical forms—a dictum Wordsworth followed in his own work.

**AS YOU READ** **Notice how perfect yet casual the rhyme appears to be. No one without conscious intention and considerable effort could shape past emotion into such a work of art.**

## I Wandered Lonely As a Cloud (1804)

I wandered lonely as a cloud
That floats on high o'er vales and hills,
When all at once I saw a crowd,
A host, of golden daffodils;
Beside the lake, beneath the trees,
Fluttering and dancing in the breeze.

Continuous as the stars that shine
And twinkle on the milky way,
They stretched in never-ending line
Along the margin of a bay:
Ten thousand saw I at a glance,
Tossing their heads in sprightly dance.

The waves beside them danced, but they
Out-did the sparkling leaves in glee;
A poet could not be but gay,
In such a jocund company;
I gazed—and gazed—but little thought
What wealth the show to me had brought:

For oft, when on my couch I lie
In vacant or in pensive mood,
They flash upon that inward eye
Which is the bliss of solitude;
And then my heart with pleasure fills,
And dances with the daffodils.

# Writing from Reading

### Summarize

1 What does the speaker mean by "that inward eye/ Which is the bliss of solitude"?

### Analyze Craft

2 Which words are formal here ("sprightly," "jocund," "pensive," etc.) and which ones less so ("lonely," "twinkle," "pleasure," etc.)?

3 How do the words chosen in the rhymes convey a casualness that supports the idea of "wandering" on a hill?

### Analyze Voice

4 Why does the speaker begin by mentioning he is lonely? Where does the tone change? What is the overall tone of this poem?

### Synthesize Summary and Analysis

5 Where does the poet locate himself in the first three stanzas; where is he in the fourth?

6 How does Wordsworth's loneliness compare with that of Sappho?

### Interpret the Poem

7 Why are daffodils a consolation?

Next come two examples of the art of "shaping" personal expression to suggest more than what the words say. In each case the poet addresses both the self and the reader, describing an encounter—with a body of water as well as a journey—in language that might seem casual but is carefully arranged. As Mary Oliver writes in her *Rules for the Dance: A Handbook for Writing and Reading Metrical Verse:* "Every poem is music—a determined, persuasive, reliable, enthusiastic, and crafted music. Without an understanding of this music, Shakespeare is only the sense we can make of him; he is the wisdom without the shapeliness, which is one half of the poem."

> "I've been looking for a safe place all my life, a refuge. . . . It might have something to do with the possibility that my own identity was nearly erased when I was born. Many Chinese lost their lives in Indonesia. . . . Maybe that's what . . . poetry is about ultimately . . . discovering who we are, being friends with who we are, getting friendly with your own mind."
>
> Conversation with Li-Young Lee

The music of "At Blackwater Pond" is easily "one half of the poem"; read it to yourself aloud and notice where your breath starts, stops. When the poet asks "what is that beautiful thing that just happened?" is she describing a cold drink of water or perhaps the effect of poetry itself? The "tossed waters" that "have settled after a night of rain" are similar to Wordsworth's "powerful feelings . . . recollected in tranquility"; here the natural world is, again, full of mystery for the poet who observes it, and one poem responds to the other.

# Mary Oliver (b. 1935)

Mary Oliver was born in Maple Heights, Ohio, and spent part of her teenage years living in the home of Edna St. Vincent Millay, where she helped organize the poet's remaining papers. She attended Ohio State University and Vassar College but received a degree from neither. Oliver's first collection of poetry, *No Voyage, and Other Poems,* was published in 1963. Since then she has published more than a dozen books of poetry, winning such prestigious honors as the Pulitzer Prize for Poetry for *American Primitive* (1983), the L. L. Winship/PEN New England Award for *House of Light* (1990), and the National Book Award for *New and Selected Poems* (1992). Oliver has taught at several institutions, including Case Western Reserve University, Bucknell University, and Bennington College in Vermont; she currently lives in Massachusetts.

**AS YOU READ** What "voice" are you hearing in the poem—who speaks to whom, and why? As in the case of Wordsworth, this poet also addresses both the self and the reader, describing an encounter—with a lake as well as a poem.

# At Blackwater Pond (1993)

At Blackwater Pond the tossed waters have settled
after a night of rain.
I dip my cupped hands. I drink
a long time. It tastes
like stone, leaves, fire. It falls cold
into my body, waking the bones. I hear them
deep inside me, whispering
oh what is that beautiful thing
that just happened?

# Writing from Reading

### Summarize

1 What did the speaker literally do at the pond?

2 What did the water taste like?

3 Drinking from the lake awakened "the bones . . . deep inside me." What kind of experience is the poet having as she drinks from the pond?

### Analyze Craft

4 In six lines, this poem includes six sentences. Given the experience the poet recalls, should the poem have been longer?

5 Discuss the tenses in this poem—what happens when.

### Analyze Voice

6 The poem is, in some ways, like a prayer. How does the poet establish a spiritual or meditative tone?

### Synthesize Summary and Analysis

7 What do you think "stone, leaves, fire" taste like, and how do bones wake and whisper? Describe what's "normal" in this poem and what seems most strange.

### Interpret the Poem

8 What is transformed in the speaker?

# William Butler Yeats (1865–1939)

An Irish poet of unparalleled importance to twentieth-century British literature, William Butler Yeats spent his childhood in Dublin, Sligo, and London. Of a religious nature but not devoted to one religion, Yeats explored folklore, mysticism, and neoplatonism, which enabled him to create a set of unique symbols and imagery in his poems. Yeats managed to combine a sense of Romantic dreaminess with colloquialism, clarity, and Celtic influence, making his poetry unlike any other. Also unlike most other poets, Yeats perfected his style in his later years, bringing his talent to full fruition in collections such as *The Tower* (1928) and *The Winding Stair* (1933). Yeats led an active life, taking part in the movement for Irish nationalism and co-founding the Irish National Theatre, in addition to writing plays. He was awarded the Nobel Prize in Literature in 1923.

**AS YOU READ** **Consider the poem in terms of time, not space. What refers to the past, the present, and what will happen in the future?**

TIP

**FOR INTERACTIVE READING . . .** Note each time the word *song* or *singing* is used. Track the changes in the way the word *song* is used in the poem.

# Sailing to Byzantium (1927)

I

That is no country for old men. The young
In one another's arms, birds in the trees
—Those dying generations—at their song,
The salmon-falls, the mackerel-crowded seas,
Fish, flesh, or fowl, commend all summer long
Whatever is begotten, born, and dies.
Caught in that sensual music all neglect
Monuments of unaging intellect.

II

An aged man is but a paltry thing,
A tattered coat upon a stick, unless
Soul clap its hands and sing, and louder sing
For every tatter in its mortal dress,
Nor is there singing school but studying
Monuments of its own magnificence;
And therefore I have sailed the seas and come
To the holy city of Byzantium.

III

O sages standing in God's holy fire
As in the gold mosaic of a wall,
Come from the holy fire, perne in a gyre,
And be the singing-masters of my soul.
Consume my heart away; sick with desire
And fastened to a dying animal
It knows not what it is; and gather me
Into the artifice of eternity.

IV

Once out of nature I shall never take
My bodily form from any natural thing,
But such a form as Grecian goldsmiths make
Of hammered gold and gold enameling
To keep a drowsy Emperor awake;
Or set upon a golden bough to sing
To lords and ladies of Byzantium
Of what is past, or passing, or to come.

# Writing from Reading

## Summarize

1 As a "voyage" poem, what journey does it describe the poet taking? Where does he arrive?

## Analyze Craft

2 How does the use of the triad (three terms in a row)—"what is past, or passing, or to come," "fish, flesh, or fowl"—affect the music of the poem? Can you point to other triads in the poem, where phrases repeat each other or vary only slightly?

3 How is the idea of a song used in this poem? In stanza I, for example, there's a "song" of "sensual music"; in stanza II this modulates to "sing, and louder sing" and "singing school." The "singing-masters" of line 20 instruct the poet how "to sing" and "keep a drowsy Emperor awake."

## Analyze Voice

4 What does Yeats feel about the journey to Byzantium?

## Synthesize Summary and Analysis

5 What does Yeats mean by "*That* is no country for old men"? Does he mean his native Ireland or also life in the world at his age?

## Interpret the Poem

6 What is meant by "the artifice of eternity"? How is eternity artificial instead of natural?

This is one of the most important and complex poems in Yeats's career; we can only scratch its surface here. Look at the way Yeats modulates from "old men" in the first stanza to "a tattered coat upon a stick" in the second, in which the "aged man" has become a scarecrow. In the third stanza, the scarecrow is burned up and melted down; the poet asks the "sages" (wise men) to "consume my heart away." By the last stanza, however, far from frightening the birds away, the poet has joined up with them and been "set upon a golden bough to sing." So the transformation of the "dying animal" into "such a form as Grecian goldsmiths make" is a journey *out* of nature and "into the artifice of eternity." The poem's subject is, appropriately enough, the very life cycle he will leave behind: "whatever is begotten, born, and dies."

In "Sailing to Byzantium," Yeats refers to the absence in Ireland of a "singing school." By the time of his death, he had gone a good distance to remedying that absence and was recognized worldwide as a major representative—perhaps the twentieth century's foremost practitioner—of the art of poetry. So one way to read his poems, as was the case with Mary Oliver, is to think about the way he built them word by word, and what the artifact itself reveals about its making. Poets often write about the art of poetry, addressing or revising or invoking their great predecessors, and in the chapters that follow there are several examples of this variety of conversation. The first comes from a poet featured in chapter 19.

# Stephen Dunn (b. 1939)

For a brief biography and A Conversation on Writing with Stephen Dunn, see chapter 19.

**AS YOU READ** Notice the use of humor and then the "awful" shift in the last lines of the poem.

# Poem for People That Are Understandably Too Busy to Read Poetry (1966)

Relax. This won't last long.
Or if it does, or if the lines
make you sleepy or bored,
give in to sleep, turn on
the T.V., deal the cards.
This poem is built to withstand
such things. Its feelings
cannot be hurt. They exist
somewhere in the poet,
and I am far away.
Pick it up anytime. Start it
in the middle if you wish.
It is as approachable as melodrama,
and can offer you violence
if it is violence you like. Look,
*there's a man on a sidewalk;*
*the way his leg is quivering*
*he'll never be the same again.*
This is your poem
and I know you're busy at the office
or the kids are into your last good nerve.
Maybe it's sex you've always wanted.
Well, *they lie together*
*like the party's unbuttoned coats,*
*slumped on the bed,*
*waiting for drunken arms to move them.*
I don't think you want me to go on;
everyone has his expectations, but this
is a poem for the entire family.
Right now, Budweiser
is dripping from a waterfall,
deodorants are hissing into armpits
of people you resemble,
and *the two lovers are dressing now,*
*saying farewell.*
I don't know what music this poem
can come up with, but clearly
it's needed. For it's apparent
*they will never see each other again*

and we need music for this
because there never was music when he or she
left *you* standing on that corner.
You see, I want this poem to be nicer
than life. I want you to look at it
when anxiety zigzags your stomach
and the last tranquilizer is gone
and you need someone to tell you
*I'll be here when you want me*
*like the sound inside a shell.*
The poem is saying that to you now.
But don't give up anything for this poem.
It doesn't expect much. It will never say more
than listening can explain.
Just keep it in your attache case
or in your house. And if you're not asleep
by now, or bored beyond sense,
the poem wants you to laugh. Laugh at
yourself, laugh at this poem, at all poetry.
Come on:

Good. Now here's what poetry can do.
Imagine you're a caterpillar:
*There's an awful shrug and, suddenly,*
*you're beautiful for as long as you live.*

# Writing from Reading

### Summarize

1 The poet says of his work that "It doesn't expect much. It will never say more / than listening can explain." What does that mean about poetry in general and "this poem" in particular?

### Analyze Craft

2 Discuss the language of this poem—sophisticated or familiar?—and how it achieves its effects.

### Analyze Voice

3 Who is the speaker addressing?

4 Is the speaker serious? Point to places in the poem that indicate the speaker is serious or, conversely, playful.

### Synthesize Summary and Analysis

5 You might want to look at the poem "Leda and the Swan" by William Butler Yeats, in the next chapter, and contrast and compare the two poets' uses of tone and imagery.

### Interpret the Poem

6 "This is your poem," says the speaker, and then compares his reader to a caterpillar. What does he mean by "awful shrug," and what will happen next?

# 16 Going Further with Reading

## *Reading in Context*

"THE way to read a poem," Robert Frost wrote, "is in the light of all the other poems ever written." Though none of us will ever know all the other poems ever written, it helps to have some sense of what went before. Understanding its tradition and **context**—the situation of, or reason for, the writing—also makes poetry richer. A first reading can bring you close to the music of speech. A second critical reading can help you see how the work has been constructed to achieve that music. A contextual reading will situate the poem for you; as is the case with fiction or drama, poems hold clues to their meaning embedded in each line.

Some of our most beautiful poetry was written in a different context from our own. William Shakespeare, the "Bard of Avon," was at work four hundred years ago, and much of our language has changed. He was writing for *his* audience, and the Elizabethan diction (or choice of words) that he and they found natural no longer sounds natural to us. The Elizabethan language in the following poem goes against the grain of the modern ear, and its diction may present a barrier to understanding. The strategy behind the poem—especially the way Shakespeare praises his lady love's qualities by playing them down—may seem confusing as well. This interactive reading can provide some tips for understanding the words artists used in other centuries and seeing the craft at work in poetry outside our own day.

*CONTINUED ON PAGE 24*

*"I read it over and over . . . at the end it seemed to me that the poet had written something that was not [just] literature, that this man had really seen something . . . and if I could understand what he had seen, I would have a way of dealing with this pain in my heart. . . . It felt like listening to the most profound, gorgeous music. I could hear it and know that it was crucial to my life."*

Conversation with Stephen Mitchell, available on video at www.mhhe.com/delbanco1e

## An Interactive Reading of William Shakespeare's "My mistress' eyes are nothing like the sun"

My mistress' eyes are nothing like the sun;  
Coral is far more red than her lips' red;  
If snow be white, why then her breasts are dun;  
If hairs be wires, black wires grow on her head.  
I have seen roses damasked, red and white,  
But no such roses see I in her cheeks;  
And in some perfumes is there more delight  
Than in the breath that from my mistress reeks.  
I love to hear her speak, yet well I know  
That music hath a far more pleasing sound;  
I grant I never saw a goddess go;  
My mistress when she walks treads on the ground.  
  And yet, by heaven, I think my love as rare  
  As any she belied with false compare.

*Paraphrase:* My lover's eyes are different from the sun. *Different how?*

*Words:* Coral is bright . . . he's saying her lips are less bright than coral?

*Voice:* "be white" and "be wires" . . . this is how Elizabethans spoke naturally, ok.

*Interpret:* Black wires grow on her head? No roses in her cheeks? Not the romantic comparisons I expected from Shakespeare.

*Words:* ???—look this up. I think it's a patterned kind of linen.

*Rhyme:* same sounds as "cheeks" and "reeks"—ties all of it together.

*Context:* means "has." Sounds old-fashioned, but was it back then?

*Interpret:* This last line is hard. What does "any" refer to? Maybe any of his other loves: "my love is as rare as any other lover . . ."?

*Words:* Look up "belied." "False compare" is maybe short for comparison? So, a false comparison?

*Figures of Speech:* Poem seems to mostly be a list of comparisons.

*Words:* I don't know this word, but it must describe her body.

*Rhyme:* "dun" rhymes with "sun" here . . . and "red" rhymes with "head." I can hear the rhythm.

*Rhyme:* "white" and "delight"; "cheeks" and "reeks" . . . more rhyming words.

*Voice:* inverted words here . . . common back then, or done on purpose?

*Context:* "reeks"—does that mean the same thing in Shakespeare's time as now?!

*Interpret:* all these negative comparisons are funny—a poem making fun of love poems: an anti-love Poem.

*Interpret:* not sure I get this line—a goddess go? go where?

*Words:* means walking, I guess. Elizabethan word.

*Interpret:* Last lines set apart—probably tie up the whole poem.

"I think my love as rare"—if something is rare, it's usually treasured because it's one of a kind. So . . . he's saying, 'I think my mistress, whom I love, is one of a kind in a way that makes me value her.'

"And yet" means "despite all that preceded." So, she's *different* from all the other poets' lovers . . . but he loves her because of that.

*CONTINUED FROM PAGE 22*

What Shakespeare suggests here is that too many poets indulge in "false compare." You don't need to belie the facts by comparing your mistress's eyes to the sun, her lips to coral, her body to snow—and so on and so forth. Her cheeks contain no actual roses; her breath is not actual perfume. She is *human,* not a goddess, and real love consists of recognizing and admitting this; the genuine commitment to truth telling is one of the hallmarks of art. It's not an accident that the two uses of the crucial word and the two phrases in which it's embedded—"I *love* to hear her speak" and "I think my *love* as rare . . ."—are reality based and straightforward in the choice of words.

A world away from Shakespeare's formal approach to the question of love is singer-songwriter-novelist-poet Leonard Cohen's brief contemporary poem that plays off against the Shakespearean sonnet. It's possible the language here will sound obscure to some English speaker four hundred years in the future—but to our ears the diction is natural and plain. Maybe the word *compare*—used three times in the poem's six lines—will confuse a future reader, but the idea of comparison is likely to endure. Poets often write this sort of echoing response to previous poems; it's a kind of conversation with what went before.

# Leonard Cohen (b. 1934)

Poet, novelist, and singer-songwriter, Leonard Cohen was born in Montreal, Canada, to Jewish parents. He attended McGill University in Montreal and published his first book of poetry, *Let Us Compare Mythologies* (1956), while still an undergraduate. His next collection, *The Spice-Box of Earth* (1961), earned him wide recognition throughout Canada. Cohen spent much of the sixties living on Hydra, a Greek island, where he enjoyed semi-isolation and published one more collection of poetry, *Flowers for Hitler* (1964), and two novels. In 1967, he relocated to New York City to pursue a music career. He has since produced eleven albums, and at age seventy-four continues to write, record, and perform music.

**AS YOU READ** Note the reference to Shakespeare's poem "My mistress' eyes are nothing like the sun"—as well, no doubt, as the sonnet "Shall I compare thee to a summer's day?"(chapter 18)—and the twist in the last lines.

## For Anne (1961)

With Annie gone,
Whose eyes to compare
With the morning sun?

Not that I did compare,
But I do compare
Now that she's gone.

# Writing from Reading

### Summarize

1 What does the speaker think about now that his love has left? And what does the shift in naming—the title uses the formal "Anne," the poem itself calls her "Annie"—suggest?

### Analyze Craft

2 Cohen is using Shakespeare's famous comparison as a starting point. How does the comparison change over the course of "For Anne"?

### Analyze Voice

3 Cohen is a songwriter. The music suggests a rhythm and you move to it, sometimes silently, internally, sometimes by snapping your fingers and stamping your feet to the beat. Can you imagine this poem sung?

### Synthesize Summary and Analysis

4 Would you be able to understand this poem without knowledge of what went before—Shakespeare's poems, for example?

### Interpret the Poem

5 Would it affect your hearing of the voice of the speaker if the poem were set to music? Does the speaker want his lost love to come back to him? How do we know?

## FORMS OF POETRY

We are much the richer for literature's variety and range. In James Joyce's novel *A Portrait of the Artist As a Young Man,* the main character—an intense young writer in the making named Stephen Dedalus—lectures his schoolmates about the three modes of creative expression. These are, according to him, lyric, epic, and dramatic. Of the epic and dramatic modes we'll have more to say later on; lyric—according to Joyce

> "The way to study a poem is to read the poem as you would anything else. There's not necessarily a code or a puzzle. You take in the lines and often read it aloud and pause at the end of the lines just a little so that you get a sense of . . . the music that the lines establish in the poem. Then read it again, and think about it, and let your mind drift and be open. A reading will become available to you." Conversation with Carolyn Forché

and Dedalus—comes first. It is "the simplest verbal vesture of an instant of emotion, a rhythmical cry such as ages ago cheered on the man who pulled at the oar or dragged stones up a slope. He who utters it is more conscious of the instant of emotion than of himself as feeling emotion."

### Lyric

A **lyric** is a short poem with a central pictorial image written in an *uninflected* voice—by which we mean a voice that's both direct and personal (usually using the first-person pronoun to create an intimate point of view). As the name implies, a lyric was originally sung to the accompaniment of a lyre; this was surely the case with the following work, from the Song of Solomon. A lyric poem relies on music, but it also conjures up a series of visual emblems—images to which our emotions adhere. In this way, whatever feelings the words of the poem create for you become crystallized in pictorial terms: we *see* as well as *hear* what the poet tries to say. The great love poem that follows was translated by a committee of scholars, under the sponsorship of King James I and for the King James Version of the Bible.

"I didn't start learning to read poetry in English—although I was reading the Bible, I guess. I was reading the Psalms and the Gospels and Genesis and Exodus, and those books just knocked me out. I thought they were weird and mysterious and otherworldly." Conversation with Li-Young Lee

In addition to considering the audience for whom a work was written, we have the added consideration that this is a sacred work, a poem written in celebration of God. (Indeed, the love of God and the secular devotion to "my love" become somehow *conflated*, or made one and the same; the singer celebrates both. There's no separation of body and soul or sacred and profane; this lyric conjoins them in praise.) How does such knowledge deepen our reading of this work? Does it feel modern? If so, what makes it feel modern? The answers to these questions help us place a poem in the context of its own tradition, in this case the tradition of lyric poetry, and help us read other lyric poems in the light of at least this one poem, if not "in the light of all the other poems ever written."

**AS YOU READ** Imagine that you hold a lyre—or, in the contemporary moment, a guitar—and sing these lines. What kind of melody would be most fitting here?

# Song of Solomon 4:1–7

## *—from the King James Bible [Behold, thou art fair, my love]* (1611)

Behold, thou art fair, my love; behold, thou art fair; thou hast doves' eyes within thy
locks: thy hair is as a flock of goats, that appear from mount Gilead.
Thy teeth are like a flock of sheep that are even shorn, which came up from the
washing; whereof every one bear twins, and none is barren among them.
Thy lips are like a thread of scarlet, and thy speech is comely: thy temples are like a
piece of a pomegranate within thy locks.
Thy neck is like the tower of David builded for an armoury, whereon there hang a
thousand bucklers, all shields of mighty men.

5 Thy two breasts are like two young roes that are twins, which feed among the lilies.
Until the day break, and the shadows flee away, I will get me to the mountain of myrrh, and to the hill of frankincense.
Thou art all fair, my love; there is no spot in thee.

# Writing from Reading

### Summarize

1 What kinds of comparisons does the poet-singer use to address his God?

### Analyze Craft

2 The poet compares parts of his beloved's body to various animals. List these. What is the effect of comparing his love this way?

### Analyze Voice

3 How does the poet's deep love affect the way he sings? Can the poem be read the way such poems as William Shakespeare's and Leonard Cohen's can be read—as the specific discussion of an individual "she"?

### Synthesize Summary and Analysis

4 Singing to his God, the poet dramatizes his emotion by a series of striking images. What does this technique accomplish?

### Interpret the Poem

5 What is the context for this poem? Why do you imagine the singer-poet chooses to express his love in this way?

We looked at D. H. Lawrence's short story "Odour of Chrysanthemums" (chapter 9); now consider a poem by the same author. (Many other authors in this volume—Margaret Atwood, Joyce Carol Oates, and John Updike, for example—write both prose fiction and verse.) "Piano" attests to the power of music and how it takes a listener back to "the old Sunday evenings at home."

## D. H. Lawrence (1885–1930)

David Herbert Lawrence was born in the coal mining district of Eastwood, Nottinghamshire, in the center of England, his father a hard-drinking coal miner and his mother a schoolteacher. He attended high school there and went on to Nottingham University, from which he graduated in his early twenties with a teaching certificate. A few years later, after he had moved to London and taken up a teaching position, he came under the tutelage of writer and magazine editor Ford Madox Ford, who published Lawrence in the English Review (see below). By 1910 Lawrence had published his first novel, The White Peacock, and was entirely committed to the writing life. After the death of his mother from cancer, he published his autobiographical masterpiece *Sons and Lovers* (1913), and this was followed by other major titles such as *The Rainbow* (1915), *Women in Love* (1920), *Aaron's Rod* (1922), *The Plumed Serpent* (1926) and, perhaps most notoriously, *Lady Chatterly's Lover*, in 1928. This last book created a scandal, because of its frank sexuality as well as its discussion of class; the "lady's" lover is a gardener, a man beneath her standing in society. In his personal life, as well, Lawrence broke social taboos; he ran off with

Frieda von Richthofen Weekley, the wife of his university language professor. Thus began a period of extended travel with only occasional trips back to England; after the end of World War I, he and Frieda embraced a life of self-imposed exile. Mediterranean Europe, Australia, North America and Mexico became Lawrence's shifting home grounds. While living outside of England a torrent of language poured forth from his pen; story after story, poem after poem, novel after novel appeared in rapid succession. He wrote travel books and articles and social tracts and plays. Lawrence used Aztec mythology, British social class distinctions, modern history—just about everything in modern life seemed useful to him in the composition of his work. Above all else—and this is truly why he matters to readers and writers of modern fiction—he found a forceful, direct, and appropriate diction by which to dramatize in physical form the volatile nature of interior states of mind and feeling. Upon his death from tuberculosis at the age of only forty-four he left behind one of the great modern bodies of work.

**AS YOU READ** **Notice that the title of the poem gets repeated in each of the three stanzas; notice how a musical instrument organizes the dozen lines that constitute the poem.**

# Piano (1918)

Softly, in the dusk, a woman is singing to me;
Taking me back down the vista of years, till I see
A child sitting under the piano, in the boom of the tingling strings
And pressing the small, poised feet of a mother who smiles as she sings.

In spite of myself, the insidious mastery of song
Betrays me back, till the heart of me weeps to belong
To the old Sunday evenings at home, with winter outside
And hymns in the cozy parlor, the tinkling piano our guide.

So now it is vain for the singer to burst into clamour
With the great black piano appassionato. The glamour
Of childish days is upon me, my manhood is cast
Down in the flood of remembrance, I weep like a child for the past.

# Writing from Reading

### Summarize

1 Do these three stanzas tell a story? Summarize the action in each.

### Analyze Craft

2 How is the present linked to the past?

### Analyze Voice

3 What does the speaker feel toward his remembrance? What words give you clues as to his feeling?

4 Who is speaking in the poem?

### Synthesize Summary and Analysis

5 Compare the two experiences of music here, the two pianos, the two musicians.

### Interpret the Poem

6 What does the speaker mean by "my manhood is cast down"? What in his childhood does he long for?

The speaker connects the occasion of the woman singing to him in the twilight hour and the set of emotions it calls up: his adult attention to the singer, his child's love for his mother, his deeply felt memories of long-ago evenings—all of this comes together in the image of the "Piano." The musical instrument he looks at and the one the poet remembers are both different and the same. When the speaker weeps "like a child for the past," it's clear that memory takes precedence; "the flood of remembrance" carries him away. So "the glamour" that would seem to attach to a woman "singing to me" in "the great black piano appassionato" in fact belongs to the recollection of past childhood, and the singer who begins "Softly, in the dusk," bursts merely into "clamour" in the present scene.

An image such as "the piano" is central to any lyric poem, and one of the first things to consider is the image pattern you discover as you read. An indelible part of the following poem by William Butler Yeats is the image of a swan, its "feathered glory." Were the poem about Leda to involve the kind of bird Yeats wrote of in "Sailing to Byzantium" (in chapter 15), or if that poem had involved a flock of swans, the poems would be less distinctive. This swan is thoroughly physical, not something "out of nature," and it's useful to contrast the two varieties of birds.

> "I can't imagine any writer or any artist doing anything of any good without knowing some or a lot of what preceded him." Conversation with Stephen Dunn

According to Greek myth, the swan is actually the god Zeus who has descended to earth, and this narrative focuses on a violent act, the disguised god's rape of a human woman. There's a complicated history here, as is often the case in Yeats's work. According to the Greeks, Leda gave birth to two sets of children after having been raped. One egg produced the twins Castor and Pollux, rendered immortal and "heavenly" in the night sky; out of the other came her daughters, Helen and Clytemnaestra—the wives of Menelaeus and Agamemnon respectively. The Trojan War resulted from Helen's abduction by Paris, and "the broken wall, the burning roof and tower, and Agamemnon dead" is how Yeats refers to the nine-year-long siege of the Greeks. This poem talks about "A sudden blow" and "a white rush"; the moment "engenders" consequences that will last long after this particular action is done.

## William Butler Yeats (1865–1939)

For a biography of William Butler Yeats, see chapter 15.

**AS YOU READ** Think about the differences between this bird and the birds described in "Sailing to Byzantium."

# Leda and the Swan (1924)

A sudden blow: the great wings beating still
Above the staggering girl, her thighs caressed
By the dark webs, her nape caught in his bill,
He holds her helpless breast upon his breast.

How can those terrified vague fingers push
The feathered glory from her loosening thighs?
And how can body, laid in that white rush,
But feel the strange heart beating where it lies?

A shudder in the loins engenders there
The broken wall, the burning roof and tower
And Agamemnon dead.
Being so caught up,
So mastered by the brute blood of the air,
Did she put on his knowledge with his power
Before the indifferent beak could let her drop?

# Writing from Reading

## Summarize

1 The poet takes a story from Greek mythology and describes it in close detail. What kind of picture does he paint, and what is going on?

## Analyze Craft

2 Parts of this poem are "descriptive" and parts ask questions. What kind of questions get asked?

## Analyze Voice

3 The voice has a kind of overview of history—looking back on what would happen as a result of the act described. In terms of point of view, is the speaker omniscient or merely informed? How does this affect the speaker's tone?

## Synthesize Summary and Analysis

4 "Knowledge" and "power" would seem to be opposing qualities. Is there a moment when they become one and the same?

## Interpret the Poem

5 The "strange heart" and "brute blood" and "indifferent beak" all belong to the animal kingdom. What is the poet saying about the part that animal behavior plays in human behavior?

Because the poet helps us visualize the event, the reader *sees* the questions the poem raises about the relation of wisdom and power, of frailty and strength. Notice also the frank—and frankly daring—sexuality of words like "laid in that white rush" or "the indifferent beak" and how the rhythms of the poem manage to suggest the physical encounter in and of itself. When it's over it's over for Zeus; he simply "let her drop." Yeats creates an image that stays in our mind of this unequal meeting between heaven and earth, this fusion of power and knowledge. If that pictorial image had been presented as an abstraction only, it would not stay with us long.

## Epic

Although the image is central to most modern verse, it's important to remember that this was not always the case. Poetry was originally very different. The first widespread use of poetry in Western culture comes in the form of the **epic,** a long narrative poem recited publicly. The earliest audiences took in these poems with their ears, not their eyes. Poetry was an oral and aural (spoken and heard) art form rather than a visual entity or a series of lines transcribed. The audience listened to but could not read them because until the late fourth century B.C. these epics were not written down.

> "Before television and before radio, and really, before typewriters and computers and all of that . . . the ability to stand up in public and speak was very important. . . . The teaching of poetry . . . had to do with learning to recite it, to say it in public." Conversation with Robert Hass

One function of the epic narrative derives from or is connected to the notion of community and a collective hearing. This sort of poem is more *public* rather than *private;* its intended audience is less the individual than the group. Bards called upon the goddess Memory to send down the words of the poem. The values of a culture—its sense of tradition, its very existence—were incorporated and communicated in the medium of poetry. "Voice" is crucial to the form—but less as individual intonation than as a communal voice, a kind of chanted chorus in which everybody learns to "sing along."

In Greece, *rhapsodes,* or reciters of poetry, performed by reciting the thousands and thousands of lines of the Homeric epics of the *Iliad* and the *Odyssey,* the earliest stories to arise in our civilization—with their heroes at the center, their large groups of secondary characters, their multiple sequences of events in war and peace. Great narrative poems such as these may contain powerful images—such as the intricately described shield of Achilles in the *Iliad* and the monstrous Cyclops in the *Odyssey*—but these poems usually derive their power from the strength of the language and the story's sound and flow.

After the two major Greek epic poems, the *Iliad* and the *Odyssey,* comes the *Aeneid,* the epic of the founding of Rome. Each of these three long narratives deals with the relationship between the gods and human beings, the past and present, the values, rules, laws, and customs of civilizations and empires, and the variety of heroes who keep them vital. Several long poems in old English also attempt this fusion of nature and culture. *Beowulf, Sir Gawain and the Green Knight,* and *Le Morte d'Arthur,* the story of Sir King Arthur and the knights of the fabled Round Table, all instruct their audience in the "proper" way to behave.

"Li-Young Lee says . . . memorizing poems . . . is a kind of yoga where you assume the same position, if you will, as the poet. When you memorize a poem . . . you actually inhabit the mind and heart of the poet, and every turn that poet has taken, and it's a remarkably great thing to do. It doesn't seem like it's going to help your writing, but of course it does. It provides syntactical moves and ways of thinking and feeling . . . that would never occur to you on your own. That's what all reading does." Conversation with Marie Howe

The extended poems that come later (such as Geoffrey Chaucer's *Canterbury Tales* and the early Italian Renaissance poet Dante Alighieri's *Divine Comedy*) build on the same principles as those of the ancient epic poets. In *Paradise Lost,* John Milton, the last great poet to create a Christian epic, describes it as justifying God's ways to man, an attempt to clarify the nature of religious and social relations. After Milton this variety of poem more or less disappears, although there do continue to be narratives in verse.

Ironically enough, the epic is the form least natural to modern culture. (Although some contemporary movies have been described as "epic," and may require years to produce and cost hundreds of millions of dollars, they take barely two hours of screen time and are not the kind of art form we mean here.) George Gordon, Lord Byron, takes a sardonic and comical approach to the genre, working with the epic but with a lighter touch. The Greeks traditionally invoked a goddess when they began to sing—and Milton, too, provided a Christian version of "the Goddess of Memory," calling her "Heavenly Muse." Byron, however, starts his long narrative poem "Don Juan" with an insulting address to one of his contemporaries.

# George Gordon, Lord Byron (1788–1824)

One of the great English Romantic poets, Lord Byron enjoyed a larger-than-life celebrity status after the publication of the first cantos of "Childe Harold's Pilgrimage" in 1811. His fame came largely from the public conflation of Byron himself with his character creation, the Byronic hero. The Byronic hero is one who stands apart from society, brooding and hating the rest of humankind, whom he considers unable to equal his capacity for passion. Byron's poetry ranges from lyrics that mimic older styles of complimenting women in verse to satires in the style of Pope, to extended poems like his capstone "Don Juan." Byron led a turbulent life up to his death at age thirty-six, while helping Greece gain its independence.

**AS YOU READ** **Enjoy the way the poet in the dedication calls out one of his contemporaries and then calls for a real hero as the poem proper begins.**

# [Bob Southey! You're a poet]

## —*from the Dedication to Don Juan* (1819)

Bob Southey! You're a poet—Poet-laureate,
And representative of all the race;
Although 'tis true that you turn'd out a Tory at
Last,—yours has lately been a common case;
And now, my Epic Renegade! what are ye at?
With all the Lakers, in and out of place?
A nest of tuneful persons, to my eye
Like "four and twenty Blackbirds in a pye;

"Which pye being open'd they began to sing"
(This old song and new simile holds good),
"A dainty dish to set before the King,"
Or Regent, who admires such kind of food;
And Coleridge, too, has lately taken wing,
But like a hawk encumber'd with his hood,
Explaining Metaphysics to the nation—
I wish he would explain his Explanation.

Writing in a time when, as he sees it, poets lack inspiration from the Goddess and in which great heroes no longer can be found, Bryon relies on humor to create a personal epic for his age. Notice how he plays with the nursery rhyme about blackbirds in a pie—saying that "This old song and new simile holds good"—turning the blackbirds into poets. Robert Southey and Samuel Taylor Coleridge, two of Byron's contemporaries, need to have their politics and metaphysics explained, and though he dedicates his lines to them, he does so tongue in cheek.

Here again, context helps. When Byron refers to "the Lakers," he's reporting not on a basketball team but on poets such as William Wordsworth, who liked to walk in England's Lake District. It may also help to know that the name *Southey* would have been pronounced *Suhthee* and that the Poet-laureate holds a position of honor—one that Byron with his scandalous private life could never expect to attain.

# [I want a hero]

## —*from Don Juan, Canto the First* (1819)

I want a hero: an uncommon want,
When every year and month sends forth a new one,
Till, after cloying the gazettes with cant,
The age discovers he is not the true one;
Of such as these I should not care to vaunt,
I'll therefore take our ancient friend Don Juan—
We all have seen him, in the pantomime,
Sent to the devil somewhat ere his time.

# Writing from Reading

### Summarize

1 The poet opens a long poem with a dedication and the first stanza. Who and what is he making fun of?

### Analyze Craft

2 The Greek epics narrate the deeds of heroes. How does Byron twist the form of an ancient Greek epic?

### Analyze Voice

3 What kind of tone does the mix of satire and elevated language create?

### Synthesize Summary and Analysis

4 Why does Byron use the epic form in a time when epic has fallen out of fashion?

### Interpret the Poem

5 What does the poet have in mind when he speaks of a "hero"? Why does he choose this particular figure—Don Juan—as his subject? Research this figure in the library or on the Internet.

### Dramatic

The dramatic poem, also called the **dramatic monologue,** in which a character addresses another character, or the reader, is an offshoot of the epic form and the third of James Joyce's three categories. The notion of "voice" in this case has more to do with impersonation than the personal or lyric "cry" of an individual; the poet assumes the "mask" or "persona" of a character not his or her own (for more on persona, see chapter 19, Voice). In the case of "My Last Duchess," Robert Browning becomes someone altogether other than the poet Robert Browning, creating a character engaged in soliloquy much as might a playwright. What we learn of the Duke here is more than the Duke might wish to confess—his pride and temper, his murderous distrust of his young wife, his chilly desire (stated almost unconsciously in the first line, with the possessive pronoun "my") to treat people as possessions. The "scene" (in Ferrara, Italy) is swiftly set; the speaker walks a silent witness—a kind of stand-in for the reader—through a picture gallery. By the second line, we learn what the title already suggests, that his "last duchess" is dead; near the poem's end, we learn that he's planning to marry again. The man who listens is a negotiator from "the Count your master," a rich man whose daughter the speaker intends to acquire as his next wife.

"In our culture it becomes more and more difficult for us to enter into, imaginatively at least, the consciousness of others. Literature is a way of doing that." Conversation with Carolyn Forché

# Robert Browning (1812–1889)

Robert Browning was one of the great Victorian poets, but his fame was eclipsed by that of Elizabeth Barrett (his wife) in his own time; today, however, he is recognized for his innovative use of the dramatic monologue. Browning's poems explore faith, doubt, crime, and madness using speakers who lived in past times, frequently from the Renaissance era. Browning was educated mostly at home and traveled little until he and Barrett eloped to Italy, where they lived for sixteen years (until Barrett's death). Among Browning's more famous poems are "Porphyria's Lover," "My Last Duchess," and "Fra Lippo Lippi," but his masterpiece is a four-volume dramatic monologue, *The Ring and the Book* (1868), that tells the story of a murder trial in seventeenth-century Italy.

**AS YOU READ** Listen in your mind's ear to the way in which the statements overlap the ends of lines and continue on to complete their meanings.

## My Last Duchess (1842)

### *Ferrara*

That's my last Duchess painted on the wall,
Looking as if she were alive. I call
That piece a wonder, now: Frà Pandolf's hands
Worked busily a day, and there she stands.
Will't please you sit and look at her? I said
"Frà Pandolf" by design, for never read
Strangers like you that pictured countenance,
The depth and passion of its earnest glance,
But to myself they turned (since none puts by
The curtain I have drawn for you, but I)
And seemed as they would ask me, if they durst,
How such a glance came there; so, not the first
Are you to turn and ask thus. Sir, 'twas not
Her husband's presence only, called that spot
Of joy into the Duchess' cheek: perhaps
Frà Pandolf chanced to say "Her mantle laps
Over my lady's wrist too much," or "Paint
Must never hope to reproduce the faint
Half-flush that dies along her throat." Such stuff
Was courtesy, she thought, and cause enough
For calling up that spot of joy. She had
A heart—how shall I say?—too soon made glad,
Too easily impressed; she liked whate'er
She looked on, and her looks went everywhere.
Sir, 'twas all one! My favour at her breast,
The dropping of the daylight in the West,
The bough of cherries some officious fool
Broke in the orchard for her, the white mule
She rode with round the terrace—all and each
Would draw from her alike the approving speech,

Or blush, at least. She thanked men—good! but thanked
Somehow—I know not how—as if she ranked
My gift of a nine-hundred-years-old name
With anybody's gift. Who'd stoop to blame
This sort of trifling? Even had you skill
In speech—(which I have not)—to make your will
Quite clear to such an one, and say, "Just this
Or that in you disgusts me; here you miss,
Or there exceed the mark"—and if she let
Herself be lessoned so, nor plainly set
Her wits to yours, forsooth, and make excuse,
—E'en then would be some stooping; and I choose
Never to stoop. Oh sir, she smiled, no doubt,
Whene'er I passed her; but who passed without
Much the same smile? This grew; I gave commands;
Then all smiles stopped together. There she stands
As if alive. Will't please you rise? We'll meet
The company below, then. I repeat,
The Count your master's known munificence
Is ample warrant that no just pretense
Of mine for dowry will be disallowed;
Though his fair daughter's self, as I avowed
At starting, is my object. Nay we'll go
Together down, sir. Notice Neptune, though,
Taming a sea-horse, thought a rarity,
Which Claus of Innsbruck cast in bronze for me!

# Writing from Reading

### Summarize

1 Who is the speaker of the poem? To whom does he give the tour? What brings the visitor to the viewing?

### Analyze Craft

2 The speaker is not the poet—the poet creates a character here, and a story. Can you describe the two characters in the poem and the woman in the painting whom the speaker describes?

### Analyze Voice

3 What are your first impressions of the speaker, and what are your final ones? How and where do they begin to change?

### Synthesize Summary and Analysis

4 What do you learn about his "last Duchess," and how do you imagine she felt about her husband?

### Interpret the Poem

5 When "all smiles stopped together," what do you think happened? Did he have her killed? Was she perhaps a suicide? Or did she simply—as old stories have it—"die of grief"?

The more we "listen" to this speaker, the more we come to mistrust him. Even such a simple word as "now" in the third line suggests its opposite, "then"; quite probably he wasn't as pleased by the smile of his living wife as he is by the portrait behind the curtain, which he alone is permitted to "draw." He keeps her beauty hidden, in effect, and for his private pleasure; soon enough we learn he was unable to do so while she was alive. She smiled at the painter, at other men, at common folk, and the proud duke did not approve of this. The lines "I gave commands; / Then all smiles stopped together" is bone chilling in its suggestiveness. At the very least he commanded his wife to stop smiling at and thanking other people; possibly he ordered her death. There's a long short story embedded in this narrative, and the dramatic monologue reveals an attitude and a situation the speaker tries to hide.

## AROUND THE WORLD

It's important early on to stress how many different languages enable creative expression, and how many of the world's masterworks were composed in other tongues. As we suggested at this chapter's start, the English of Shakespeare or the King James Version of the Bible (and, to a lesser degree, the English of Lord Byron and Robert Browning) can seem foreign to a modern reader; their language is not quite the one we use in daily speech. When we deal with foreign languages, that's literally the case. The poet Li-Young Lee (in chapter 17) describes his first experience of hearing and then speaking English; born in Indonesia, of Chinese ancestry, he came to this country when young. Having been exposed from infancy to his parents' love of ancient Chinese poetry, he grew up to write poetry himself, but he does so in his non-native English. We are more and more citizens of the world, and poetry and its global traditions are part of the context of reading.

The three poems that follow are translations, which means the translators did research in the language, the culture, the traditions—the context—that brought these works into being. Stephen Mitchell, in his interview, describes his experience of translating sacred texts almost as a spiritual journey. While translations have issues that

> "Translation makes the world accessible to us."
>
> Conversation with Robert Hass

are special to any work that links languages, all poetry is enhanced by an understanding of its context and history. In the previous chapter, you examined the language of poetry from your first experience to reading for word choices, patterns of images and sounds, and considerations of the way the structure of a poem supports your interpretation. In this chapter, we've examined very briefly the context of major traditions of poetry—the lyric, epic, and dramatic modes. While we might not all be multilingual, reading a poem is a little like doing a translation of your own, going on your own journey into language.

*There's a whole world of beauty . . . out there for people who don't know poetry . . .*

# Q&A

*. . . I needed to know what that God was all about.*

# A Conversation on Translation

## Stephen Mitchell

Born in Brooklyn, New York, in 1943, Stephen Mitchell went to Amherst College as a pre-med student. However, while studying in Paris, he was introduced to Rainer Maria Rilke's poetry. Mitchell learned German simply to read Rilke in his original language, and it was his translation of Rilke's poems that would launch his publishing career in 1982 with *The Selected Poems of Rainer Maria Rilke.* Although he has published original poetry in the collection *Parables and Portraits* (1990), he is best known for the poetry of his translations of ancient and modern texts. Mitchell is concerned with spirituality and religious wisdom, as is seen in his acclaimed translations *Bhagavad Gita* (2002), *The Book of Job* (1992), and *Tao Te Ching* (1988). He has also published a number of children's books, among them *Jesus: What He Really Said and Did* (2002), which presents his collection of sayings that he believes are authentic to the historical Jesus. Mitchell, who holds a degree in comparative literature from Yale, has an interest in Zen Buddhism, and he has collaborated with his wife, Byron Katie, on her books devoted to helping people achieve inner peace.

### Falling in Love, Learning Languages, and Reading Poetry

I've always learned a language because I've fallen in love with a consciousness. So I learned German because of Rilke, I learned Hebrew because of Job. And that was my focus. It wasn't to learn a language. It was so I could become intimate with a consciousness that I love very deeply. The value is indescribable. It's like if you ask the question, Why should I read poetry? Why should I learn Latin and other languages? It's like asking, Why should I listen to music? I mean, what would your life be without music? What an impoverishment. There's a whole world of beauty and profundity out there for people who don't know poetry, that's just waiting for you.

### A Love Song to God

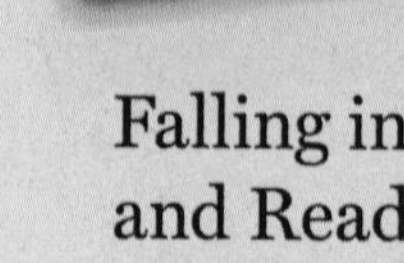

The Bhagavad Gita is . . . a love song to God, and that's actually a possible translation of the title. It is the central text of Hinduism . . . a very wise text, and also a very beautiful text. It's a book that I again fell in love with . . . and it astonished me to read a book with such a vast conception of God . . . It is really a hair-raising verse and the God who appears in the Bhagavad Gita says . . . in his most dreadful compassionate form . . . "I am death, I am what lies beyond all your small concepts of what should be and what is right and good." Anyway, this was a great riddle for me at first. . . . I needed to know what that God was all about.

**To watch the entire video and hear the author read from his work, go to www.mhhe.com/delbanco1e.**

**RESEARCH ASSIGNMENT** For Mitchell, translating texts has been a spiritual journey. Watch the interview and describe his writing and research process. What spiritual truths draw him to the texts he chooses to translate? What has Zen meant to his ability to translate texts effectively?

**AS YOU READ** Compare the approach to deity in these lines to the approach in the Song of Solomon.

# [The Secret of Life]

## *—from the Bhagavad Gita ("Love Song to God")* (c. 500–200 B.C.E.)

THE BLESSED LORD SAID:

Because you trust me, Arjuna,
I will tell you what wisdom is,
the secret of life: know it
and be free of suffering, forever.

This is the supreme wisdom,
the knowing beyond all knowing,
experienced directly, in a flash,
eternal, and a joy to practice.

Those who are without faith
in my teaching, cannot attain me;
they endlessly return to this world,
shuttling from death to death.

I permeate all the universe
in my unmanifest form.
All beings exist within me,
yet I am so inconceivably

vast, so beyond existence,
that though they are brought forth
and sustained by my limitless power,
I am not confined within them.

Just as the all-moving wind,
wherever it goes, always
remains in the vastness of space,
all beings remain within me.

They are gathered back into my womb
at the end of the cosmic cycle—
a hundred fifty thousand
billion of your earthly years—
and as a new cycle begins
I send them forth once again,
pouring from my abundance
the myriad forms of life.

These actions do not bind me, Arjuna.
I stand apart from them all,
indifferent to their outcome,
unattached, serene.

Under my guidance, Nature
brings forth all beings, all things
animate or inanimate,
and sets the whole universe in motion.

Foolish people despise me
in the human form that I take,
blind to my true nature
as the Lord of all life and death.

Their hopes and actions are vain,
their knowledge is sheer delusion;
turning from the light, they fall
into cruelty, selfishness, greed.

But the truly wise, Arjuna,
who dive deep into themselves,
fearless, one-pointed, know me
as the inexhaustible source.

Always chanting my praise,
steadfast in their devotion,
they make their lives an unending
hymn to my endless love.

*—translated by Stephen Mitchell*

# Writing from Reading

### Summarize

1 The Hindu God speaks, recounting his nature and his accomplishments. What does he say about the nature of those who worship him?

### Analyze Craft

2 Does this scripture resemble a drama in any way?

### Analyze Voice

3 Can you characterize the voice of the deity?

### Synthesize Summary and Analysis

4 The God speaks. What makes it possible for us to listen in?

### Interpret the Poem

5 In what ways are ideas in this poem similar to or different from those in the writings of your religion?

# Rumi (c. 1207–1273)

A Persian mystic and poet, Jalal al-Din Rumi was born in what is now Afghanistan and lived most of his life in present-day Turkey. Rumi was a well-respected teacher and theologian until 1244, when he met Shams of Tabriz, a wandering dervish (an Islamic mystic). Shams inspired Rumi to devote his life to Sufism (Islamic mysticism), and Rumi began to write mystical verse, much of it in praise of Shams. When Shams was murdered, Rumi continued to write in his praise. He also wrote the *Mathnawi,* an epic poem important to the Islamic world. Beyond his verse, Rumi is known as the founder of the whirling dervishes sect of Islam, a group that uses song, dance, and spinning as a means of reaching God. His verse remains widely known, particularly in Iran, and it has enjoyed a resurgence of popularity in the United States since the 1990s.

**AS YOU READ** Ask yourself if this is another hymn, in the form of a love poem, or a love poem in the form of a hymn.

# Some Kiss We Want (c. mid-thirteenth century)

There is some kiss we want
with our whole lives, the touch

of spirit on the body. Seawater
begs the pearl to break its shell.

And the lily, how passionately
it needs some wild darling!

At night, I open the window and ask
the moon to come and press its
face against mine.

Breathe into me. Close
the language-door and open the love-window.
The moon won't use the door,
only the window.

*—translated by Coleman Barks*

# Writing from Reading

### Summarize

1 To whom does the poet admit a desire? Who does he ask to come to him?

### Analyze Craft

2 How does the poet turn love of his God into a poem that seems to be about human love?

### Analyze Voice

3 How would you describe this voice? How is this similar to, or distinct from, the voice in the Song of Solomon?

### Synthesize Summary and Analysis

4 The poet seeks union with his beloved, expressing this need in language beyond the literal. What does he mean by "the moon won't use the door"?

### Interpret the Poem

5 What does the speaker want as expressed in such lines as "... Sea-water / begs the pearl to break its shell" or "the lily, how passionately ... it needs some wild darling!"?

## Pablo Neruda (1904–1973)

Ricardo Eliecer Neftalí Reyes Basoalto was born in southern Chile. He adopted the pen name Pablo Neruda to avoid conflict with his family, who disapproved of his poetic activity. Abandoning his studies at age twenty in order to devote himself to poetry, Neruda embarked on a diplomatic career that took him to Argentina, Spain, Mexico, and France. He became politically controversial when he supported the republican side of the Spanish Civil War, publishing the collection *España en el corazón* (1937), which forced him to end his period in Spain and return to Chile. He supported communism in Chile and was exiled as a result; during this time he wrote his keystone work *Canto General* (1950), an epic poem cataloguing the South American continent. A celebrated poet, Neruda won the Nobel Prize in Literature in 1971.

**AS YOU READ** Ask yourself what life must be like for a poet as passionate as Neruda describes himself here. Compare the passion in this poem to that of, say, Shakespeare or Leonard Cohen.

# I Do Not Love You Except Because I Love You (1959)

I do not love you—except because I love you;
and from loving you to not loving you,
from waiting to not waiting for you
my heart moves from the cold into
the fire. I love you only because it's you
I love; I hate you no end, and hating you
bend to you, and the measure of my changing love for you
is that I do not see you but love you

blindly. Maybe the January light will consume
my heart with its cruel
ray, stealing my key to true

calm. In this part of the story I am the one who
dies, the only one, and I will die of love because I love you
because I love you, Love, in fire and in blood.

*—translated by Gustavo Escobedo*

# Writing from Reading

### Summarize

1 To whom is this passionate poem about love and its power addressed?

### Analyze Craft

2 The poem seems to be so plain in its attitude: "I love you because I love you." How does the poet create the intensity of the poem? What emotionally charged words does he use?

### Analyze Voice

3 What is the emotional state of the speaker? How do you know?

### Synthesize Summary and Analysis

4 Why is it only the speaker who dies in this poem?

### Interpret the Poem

5 What is it that the speaker longs for?

# For Review and Further Study

## Elizabeth Barrett Browning (1806–1861)

*For a brief biography of Elizabeth Barrett Browning, see chapter 24.*

### Go From Me (1850)

Go from me. Yet I feel that I shall stand
Henceforth in thy shadow. Nevermore
Alone upon the threshold of my door
Of individual life, I shall command
The uses of my soul, nor lift my hand
Serenely in the sunshine as before,
Without the sense of that which I forbore—
Thy touch upon the palm. The widest land
Doom takes to part us, leaves thy heart in mine
With pulses that beat double. What I do
And what I dream include thee, as the wine
Must taste of its own grapes. And when I sue
God for myself, He hears that name of thine,
And sees within my eyes the tears of two.

### Questions for Interactive Reading and Writing

1. Try to reconstruct the context, the situation, in which the poet might feel this sense of being deeply bound to the beloved but also wanting to separate. Recall out of your own experience the deep sense of being bound to someone you love even after you part.

2. Read the poem aloud without pausing at the end of each line. Which do you believe controls the poem, the thoughts the poet expresses or the rhymes?
3. Can you paraphrase this sensual image: ". . . as the wine / Must taste of its own grapes . . ."?
4. List the series of orders the speaker issues to the beloved. What does the poet mean by saying, "I sue" God?
5. Does the beloved, whom the poet addresses, have any choice about whether to leave or stay in the poet's memory?

# Robert Browning (1812–1889)

*For a brief biography of Robert Browning, see the discussion of dramatic monologue earlier in this chapter.*

## Love Among the Ruins (1855)

I

Where the quiet-coloured end of evening smiles
  Miles and miles
On the solitary pastures where our sheep
  Half-asleep
Tinkle homeward thro' the twilight, stray or stop
  As they crop—
Was the site once of a city great and gay,
  (So they say)
Of our country's very capital, its prince
  Ages since
Held his court in, gathered councils, wielding far
  Peace or war.

II

Now—the country does not even boast a tree,
  As you see,
To distinguish slopes of verdure, certain rills
  From the hills
Intersect and give a name to, (else they run
  Into one)
Where the domed and daring palace shot its spires
  Up like fires
O'er the hundred-gated circuit of a wall
  Bounding all,
Made of marble, men might march on nor be pressed,
  Twelve abreast.

III

And such plenty and perfection, see, of grass
  Never was!
Such a carpet as, this summer-time, o'erspreads
  And embeds
Every vestige of the city, guessed alone,
  Stock or stone—
Where a multitude of men breathed joy and woe
  Long ago;
Lust of glory pricked their hearts up, dread of shame
  Struck them tame;
And that glory and that shame alike, the gold
  Bought and sold.

IV

Now,—the single little turret that remains
  On the plains,
By the caper overrooted, by the gourd
  Overscored,
While the patching houseleek's head of blossom winks
  Through the chinks—
Marks the basement whence a tower in ancient time
  Sprang sublime,
And a burning ring, all round, the chariots traced
  As they raced,
And the monarch and his minions and his dames
  Viewed the games.

V

And I know, while thus the quiet-coloured eve
  Smiles to leave
To their folding, all our many-tinkling fleece
  In such peace,
And the slopes and rills in undistinguished grey
  Melt away—
That a girl with eager eyes and yellow hair
  Waits me there
In the turret whence the charioteers caught soul
  For the goal,
When the king looked, where she looks now, breathless,
    dumb
  Till I come.

VI

But he looked upon the city, every side,
  Far and wide,
All the mountains topped with temples, all the glades'
  Colonnades,
All the causeys, bridges, aqueducts,—and then,
  All the men!
When I do come, she will speak not, she will stand,
  Either hand,
On my shoulder, give her eyes the first embrace
  Of my face,
Ere we rush, ere we extinguish sight and speech
  Each on each.

VII

In one year they sent a million fighters forth
  South and north,
And they built their gods a brazen pillar high
  As the sky,
Yet reserved a thousand chariots in full force—
  Gold, of course.
Oh, heart! oh, blood that freezes, blood that burns!
  Earth's returns
For whole centuries of folly, noise and sin!
  Shut them in,
With their triumphs and their glories and the rest!
  Love is best!

### Questions for Interactive Reading and Writing

1. What are the two story lines that coincide in this poem? Is the poem primarily about war and empire or about love?
2. How does the story about war and empire affect the love story?
3. To whom is the poet speaking? How does that affect the way he tells the poem?
4. What does the poem suggest about the relation of individuals, their lives and loves, in the context of the social situation of the state, of the country?
5. Does the way the poem sounds—its particular music as you read it aloud—contribute anything to the meaning?

# William Dickey (1928–1994)

## Therefore (1994)

Nothing exists that is not marred; therefore
we are obliged to imagine how things might be:
the sea
at its green uttermost, the shore
white to exaggeration, white before
it was checked and clouded by its spent debris.

Nothing exists that does not end, and so
to knowledge we must deliberately be untrue:
you
murmuring that you will not go, when you will go,
promising to do always what you cannot do:
hold the sun steady, and the sky new.

No one exists who can be loved the same
by day as by dark; it is that sleeping place,
lame,
we attempt to follow into, and cannot trace,
that makes us lie, saying we know his face,
as if we knew even half of his true name.

### Questions for Interactive Reading and Writing

1. Does the poet have an "argument" he is trying to put forward?
2. What is the relation, in the last two lines, of the words "lie" and "true"?
3. Who is the "we" in the poem?
4. How does the poet seem to marry his personal quest for happiness and a philosophical quest to understand human feelings? Try to imagine the personal situation that gave rise to these lines.

# Edna St. Vincent Millay (1892–1950)

## Not in a silver casket cool with pearls (1931)

Not in a silver casket cool with pearls
Or rich with red corundum or with blue,
Locked, and the key withheld, as other girls
Have given their loves, I give my love to you;
Not in a lovers'-knot, not in a ring
Worked in such fashion, and the legend plain—
*Semper fidelis,* where a secret spring
Kennels a drop of mischief for the brain:
Love in the open hand, no thing but that,
Ungemmed, unhidden, wishing not to hurt,
As one should bring you cowslips in a hat
Swung from the hand, or apples in her skirt,
I bring you, calling out as children do:
"Look what I have!—And these are all for you."

### Questions for Interactive Reading and Writing

1. Why does the poet choose to begin with a series of negative statements?
2. The Latin words *semper fidelis*—also the motto of the Marine Corps—mean "forever faithful." How does that connect to this poem's theme?
3. Do you like the phrase "love in the open hand"? Why does it please?

4. What does the image "apples in her skirt" conjure up? How does it compare with the opening image of "a silver casket cool with pearls"?
5. How would you feel if you were the recipient of this poem?

# Adrienne Rich (b. 1929)

## Living in Sin (1955)

She had thought the studio would keep itself;
no dust upon the furniture of love.
Half heresy, to wish the taps less vocal,
the panes relieved of grime. A plate of pears,
a piano with a Persian shawl, a cat
stalking the picturesque amusing mouse
had risen at his urging.
Not that at five each separate stair would writhe
under the milkman's tramp; that morning light
so coldly would delineate the scraps
of last night's cheese and three sepulchral bottles;
that on the kitchen shelf among the saucers
a pair of beetle-eyes would fix her own—
envoy from some village in the moldings . . .
Meanwhile, he, with a yawn,
sounded a dozen notes upon the keyboard,
declared it out of tune, shrugged at the mirror,
rubbed at his beard, went out for cigarettes;
while she, jeered by the minor demons,
pulled back the sheets and made the bed and found
a towel to dust the table-top,
and let the coffee-pot boil over on the stove.
By evening she was back in love again,
though not so wholly but throughout the night
she woke sometimes to feel the daylight coming
like a relentless milkman up the stairs.

### Questions for Interactive Reading and Writing

1. What makes the poet feel particularly uncomfortable in her current living arrangement?
2. How does the reference to the vermin—"a pair of beetle-eyes"—add to her feeling of being ill at ease?
3. Does the reference to the out-of-tune piano increase the discomfort?
4. Does the man feel as the poet-speaker does? What makes us able to move from a description of the piano to a description of the poet's feelings?
5. What supposedly new state does she find herself in at the end of the day?
6. Can you call this a love poem, or is it a poem of another sort?

# Rainer Maria Rilke (1875–1926)

## Archaic Torso of Apollo (1908)

We cannot know his legendary head
with eyes like ripening fruit. And yet his torso
is still suffused with brilliance from inside,
like a lamp, in which his gaze, now turned to low,

gleams in all its power. Otherwise
the curved breast could not dazzle you so, nor could
a smile run through the placid hips and thighs
to that dark center where procreation flared.

Otherwise this stone would seem defaced
beneath the translucent cascade of the shoulders
and would not glisten like a wild beast's fur:

would not, from all the borders of itself,
burst like a star: for here there is no place
that does not see you. You must change your life.

*—translated by Stephen Mitchell*

### Questions for Interactive Reading and Writing

1. While living in Paris, Rilke worked as a kind of private secretary to the sculptor Auguste Rodin. What does the poet look at when he sees "this stone"?
2. Look up the Greek god Apollo and make a list of his qualities. Relate them to what the poet sees here.
3. Who is the "you" in this poem, and does it also mean "I"?
4. Which images are "surface" images, and which relate to depths?
5. The poet lives in the present moment, but what he's looking at is "archaic" and comes from a civilization that flourished thousands of years before. Discuss this as an example of both "tradition" and "translation."
6. What does the last sentence of this poem mean, and who gives the order that "You must change your life"?

# 17 Writing about Poetry

I'VE pulled the last of the year's young onions.
The garden is bare now. The ground is cold,
brown and old. What is left of the day flames
in the maples at the corner of my
eye. I turn, a cardinal vanishes.
By the cellar door, I wash the onions,
then drink from the icy metal spigot.

—*from "Eating Alone" by Li-Young Lee*

*"'Eating Together' or 'Eating Alone'—those are about eating and all those other things—but . . . [when we write about poetry] we should be interrogating the quality of the imagination in the poem, the quality of the mind, the heart, the soul in the poem."*

Conversation with Li-Young Lee, available on video at www.mhhe.com/delbanco1e

HOW do we write about poetry? We do it in ways similar to writing about fiction, by analyzing the writer's craft and voice in terms of its technical aspects, in order to get closer to the meaning.

As suggested in the preceding chapters, there are many ways to **think about** and read poetry, based on your own thoughts and your eventual understanding of traditional techniques. First you read the poem to yourself, let the language flow over you and find general associations that the images and words bring up. This is your **first reading,** and it's not meant to be final or thorough, more a general impression that's a springboard to the work. In your first reading of "Eating Alone," you may notice how forlorn the speaker seems and how important onions are in the first and final stanzas. It's useful if you try your **second reading** out loud, the better to catch the sounds clearly and see what kind of rhythm has enforced its structure on the poem.

A **critical reading,** one in which you begin to apply various ways of looking at a poem, helps you fully understand a poem and may require a line-by-line **explication,** an examination of how the elements of craft work in each line. This kind of reading prepares you to write a **text-based argument.** Writing a text-based argument is a skill you will need for many of your college courses, and it's quite likely you will need such skill for your work and career outside of college. Lawyers, journalists, police detectives, managers of many varieties—all those who have to examine what is said between the lines—need to be able to look closely at how language works and find evidence in the text itself that supports an argument about the meaning of the work.

This chapter follows the development of a sample student essay from the earliest stages to the final draft. Emma Baldwin, a student, uses several of the prewriting and writing strategies that we discuss in depth in the Handbook for Writing from Reading at the end of this volume (see chapter 3 in the handbook on "Common Writing Assignments"). As was the case with fiction, we emphasize that most literary works don't possess a single meaning but rather offer multiple meanings and interpretations of the work.

*. . . I do think that writing poems is dealing with language on a quantum level . . .*

# Q&A

*I don't blame . . . people for being intimidated by poetry . . .*

# A Conversation on Writing

## Li-Young Lee

### The Strangeness of Poetry

I don't blame . . . people for being intimidated by poetry—especially lyric poetry. I'm not sure that poems belong in the same category as novels and essays and short stories. Poems are strange; they belong in a whole category of synchronicity or coincidence.

### Coincidence and Poetic Order

I think [the] experience of coincidence is the closest thing we have to [the] experience of poetry. . . . Things emerge simultaneously and we can't quite account for that particular emergence of simultaneous things at the same time. So I think [that] the most radical thing about poetry is that it proposes this other order. You know, I think other kinds of writing, ultimately they participate in and examine causal orderedness: cause and effect. And maybe poetry proposes that cause and effect aren't the only lord and lady ruling the universe. . . . I think that's ultimately what lyric poetry attempts to manifest.

### Language on a Quantum Level

What's so fascinating is this: I think one has to inhabit a particular state of consciousness in order to notice coincidence or synchronicity in the world. And it could be in fact that the more open we are to it, the more we realize, the more we maybe begin to notice that that's the deepest thing going on at any particular time, that cause and effect is a type of surface condition. Maybe down deep, at a deeper level, a quantum level of reality (and I do think that writing poems is dealing with language on a quantum level) . . . the synchronicities and coincidences begin to emerge, begin to yield themselves, begin to reveal themselves in language.

Li-Young Lee was born in 1957 to Chinese parents in Indonesia and came to this country when young. As he reports in his interview, the refugee experience—his family was persecuted, forced into exile—has deeply influenced his way of looking at the world; if the poet is always, to some degree, an "outsider," this one is literally so. Much of his writing has to do with tradition, the presence of the past—and what is lost, what remains. The growing and cooking and eating of food, for example, has a resonance beyond the merely literal, and for Lee such everyday procedures all partake of pilgrimage and even of the sacred. His language—direct and straightforward diction—celebrates the ordinary and sanctifies everyday life. For this, his work has received many honors, including three Puschart Prizes, the Lannan Literary Award, and the American Book Award. Lee's collection *Book of My Nights* was the winner of the Poetry Society of America's William Carlos Williams Award. His other books include *The City in Which I Love You, Rose, The Winged Seed: A Remembrance,* and, in 2008, *Behind My Eyes.*

**To view this entire interview and hear the author read from his work, go to www.mhhe.com/delbanco1e.**

**RESEARCH ASSIGNMENT** In his interview, Li-Young Lee talks about being a refugee. What happened to Li-Young Lee, and what does he think this meant for his poetry?

**AS YOU READ** Observe the way in which the poet focuses on two important aspects of life: first solitude and then companionship.

## *Two Poems by Li-Young Lee*

# Eating Alone (1986)

I've pulled the last of the year's young onions.
The garden is bare now. The ground is cold,
brown and old. What is left of the day flames
in the maples at the corner of my
eye. I turn, a cardinal vanishes.
By the cellar door, I wash the onions,
then drink from the icy metal spigot.

Once, years back, I walked beside my father
among the windfall pears. I can't recall
our words. We may have strolled in silence. But
I still see him bend that way—left hand braced
on knee, creaky—to lift and hold to my
eye a rotten pear. In it, a hornet
spun crazily, glazed in slow, glistening juice.

It was my father I saw this morning
waving to me from the trees. I almost
called to him, until I came close enough
to see the shovel, leaning where I had
left it, in the flickering, deep green shade.

White rice steaming, almost done. Sweet green peas
fried in onions. Shrimp braised in sesame
oil and garlic. And my own loneliness.
What more could I, a young man, want.

# Eating Together (1986)

In the steamer is the trout
seasoned with slivers of ginger,
two sprigs of green onion, and sesame oil.
We shall eat it with rice for lunch,
brothers, sister, my mother who will
taste the sweetest meat of the head,
holding it between her fingers
deftly, the way my father did
weeks ago. Then he lay down
to sleep like a snow-covered road
winding through pines older than him,
without any travelers, and lonely for no one.

# A Guide to Writing from Reading

Here are some guidelines for reading that will support your writing.

| | |
|---|---|
| **Summarize the poem.** | Some poems are more transparent than others, but poetic language is nevertheless different from everyday speech. Make sure you understand what is going on in the poem. A poem may have dramatic action, a plot almost, but it's just as likely to be a description. After you have gotten your first impressions, depending on the difficulty of the language, you may need to write in your own prose (**paraphrase**) what each line or stanza means. |
| **Analyze its craft.** | A poem works differently from prose, so how language pushes and pulls the prose meaning of the poem is critical to an analysis. Look for patterns of images or sounds, such as the images of stones in Carolyn Forché's "The Museum of Stones" or the rhymes in Shakespeare's "My mistress' eyes are nothing like the sun." Look for other kinds of patterns (like the clustering into threes—*begotten, born, and dies*—of Yeats's "Sailing to Byzantium") and for interesting or unusual word choices, word order, or rhythms. You may want to organize your paper as a walk-through of the lines of the poem. |
| **Analyze its voice.** | Each poem has a speaker; in your writing you shouldn't assume the speaker is the poet, even though the speaker in the poem uses an "I." Don't write "In Li-Young Lee's 'Eating Together' he finds fulfillment in the family meal." Instead write "In Li-Young Lee's 'Eating Together,' he creates *a speaker* who finds fulfillment in the family meal." In Li-Young Lee's interview, he tells us that the real subject of any poem is the speaker. Ask yourself who the speaker is, what motivated the speaker to tell the "story" in the poem, and why the speaker uses the kind of rhythm, sound, and imagery in a poem the way he or she (or it) does. |
| **Synthesize the summary and analysis.** | What are the larger issues in the poem? What themes are present, what conflicts or issues are dramatized? Describe the situation of the speaker. Think about how craft is used to tell the story of the poem, where sounds, for example, reflect happiness, mourning, or wonder. How do these sounds work together? Are the image patterns most important? Is it an intimate tone that gives the poem its power? You can use your synthesis to organize your thoughts, and this may become the way you organize your paper. |
| **Interpret the poem.** | Here is your argument. Two crucial components of writing effectively are discovering something meaningful to you and maintaining a questioning, thoughtful attitude in your exploration of the poem. You will need to make a claim about the poem, and the lines from the poem will be the evidence that supports your claim. If you're using outside sources, other critics' voices should be included only as a jumping-off point for your own interpretation. Do not end your paper with a quotation from an outside critic. Learning to support your own interpretation, based on your synthesis and analysis, is the point of writing about poetry. |

"Well, the writerly impulse—at least for me—proceeds from a readerly impulse." Conversation with Thomas Lynch

*(CONTINUED FROM PAGE 47)*

# A SAMPLE STUDENT ESSAY IN PROGRESS

Everyone has his or her own way of writing. Some think it all the way through before putting pen to paper; others create numerous notes and organize those notes into an outline before they begin. Whatever your process is, there is a sequence that can help break down the writing tasks into digestible chunks and keep the dreaded "blank screen" from causing writer's block. Here you can follow Emma Baldwin through the steps of her writing process to see how her understanding of the poem evolves as she responds to this assignment: *In 2–3 pages, do a close reading of Li-Young Lee's poem "Eating Alone" in which you analyze one or more elements of the poem.*

- Interact with the Reading
- Explore Your Ideas
- Develop a Thesis
- Create a Plan for Your Paper
- Generate a First Draft
- Revise Your Draft
- Edit and Format Your Paper

"I almost . . . never have the lines that I think are the good lines in the poem prior to the act of writing. They occur in the act of. And when you're good that day, you can be a little bit better than yourself." Conversation with Stephen Dunn

## Interact with the Reading

When Emma Baldwin read "Eating Alone," she annotated the poem and took notes on her initial responses. Both her annotations and notes, reproduced here, show how she engaged with the text.

### Initial Response

Overall, this poem seems very sad to me. I know that the young man is gardening and cooking, which are both fun hobbies, so it seems like the poem should be happier than it is. But I think he misses his father, since that is the only other person mentioned in the poem. I don't understand the significance of the hornet spinning in the rotten pear, but I can picture it exactly. I also don't understand the last lines—why would anyone want to be lonely? I did notice that the poem jumps around in time. Those jumps seem to occur with each stanza, so it seems like that is significant too. I think the thing I understood best in the poem was the imagery—I could relate to the smell of onions, icy cold water, the cardinal and maple trees. It was easy to picture everything in the poem, even the flickering shade and the shovel in the ground, and so I'd like to understand what it all means.

After a first reading of "Eating Alone," Emma reread the poem, scanned the first few lines to determine the meter, and made annotations. Her annotations are a combination of personal reaction and notation of formal elements, like rhyme and rhythm. At this stage in our discussion of the **craft** of poetry, you won't yet be familiar in detail with the formal elements of rhythm, rhyme, and structure—we simply allude to them here—but they are discussed in the chapters that follow. "A sonnet," for example, is a poetic "fixed form" examined at length in chapter 22. It's early innings yet, and we won't go into elaborate discussions of technique.

TIPS

**FOR INTERACTIVE READING . . .**

**Number the lines**—This will help you refer to specific details as you begin your writing process. It will also help you discover whether the poem follows a particular format; for example, if you find there are fourteen lines, chances are the poem is a sonnet.

**Scan the first several lines**—This allows you to determine if there is a set rhythm or if the poem is written in free verse (see chapter 22). The first three lines of the following poem have been annotated for scansion of the rhythm, marking ´ for stressed and ˘ for unstressed syllables.

**Identify rhyme**—This is another tactic that will enable you to know the form of the poem. If you find no consistent rhyme scheme, noting internal rhyme, assonance, and consonance will help you understand the emphasis on certain words.

# An Interactive Reading of "Eating Alone"

Ĭ've púlled thĕ *lást* ŏf thĕ yeár's yóung óniŏns.
Thĕ gárdĕn ĭs *báre nŏw*. Thĕ groúnd ĭs *cóld,*
*brówn* ănd *óld*. *Whăt ĭs léft* ŏf thĕ dáy flámes
in the maples at the corner of my
eye. I turn, a cardinal vanishes.
By the cellar door, I wash the onions,
then drink from the icy metal spigot.

Once, years back, I walked beside my father
among the windfall pears. I can't recall
our words. We may have strolled in silence. But
I still see him bend that way—left hand braced
on knee, creaky—to lift and hold to my
eye a rotten pear. In it, a hornet
spun crazily, glazed in slow, glistening juice.

It was my father I saw this morning
waving to me from the trees. I almost
called to him, until I came close enough
to see the shovel, leaning where I had
left it, in the flickering, deep green shade.

White rice steaming, almost done. Sweet green peas
fried in onions. Shrimp braised in sesame
oil and garlic. And my own loneliness.
What more could I, a young man, want.

*Image:* Imagery is barren, desolate

*Setting:* Present; pulling onions from garden

*Image:* Imagery brightens with "flames" and "cardinal"

*Rhyme:* Internal rhyme, wind*fall* and re*call*. kn*ee* and cr*eaky*. crazily and glazed

*Setting:* Past; "once, years back . . ."; walking with father, who is old

*Setting:* Earlier in the present day; "this morning"; mistakes a shovel for his father

*Setting:* Present; cooking the onions he has pulled from the garden in a meal

*Interpret:* Explicit statement of who narrator is (although I felt like I already knew—not sure why)

*Rhyme:*—cold/old

*Words:* Assonance: *day flames*

*Rhyme:* No formal rhyme scheme or set meter

*Image:* "Icy metal spigot"—striking; I can taste it and feel it

*Interpret:* Father must be old—creaky, difficulty moving

*Image:* Striking image—metaphor for something?

*Intepret:* A very sad moment—father is not there; dead, perhaps? shovel makes me think of burial

*Image:* Words engage sense of smell, taste, visual: very crisp and *present*

*Interpret:* Confusing last line . . . seems like a contradiction

"This notion of discovery is really important. It's something that's very difficult to remember. I've been writing now for twenty-five years; it's still hard for me to remember that I have to constantly go into the new. Stanley [Kunitz] used to say, he was about ninety, 'I go to write a poem, it's not where the last one was.'" Conversation with Marie Howe

## Explore Your Ideas

Although Emma did a great job annotating the poem, her confusion over the last lines suggests that she still does not have a full grasp on its meaning. There are several ways you might be able to refine your own ideas for your paper. Here are some examples of freewriting, journaling, and brainstorming. Choose what works best for you.

### Freewriting

The saddest moment in the poem is when he mistakes the shovel for his father. I think it means his father is dead, right? Because the poem is so sad, and also the idea of being alone is there from the very beginning, and when someone dies, you feel left alone. I also think he's dead because he seems very old in the flashback where he bends to pick up a pear; my grandpa moved like that towards the end of his life, so it definitely means the father is old. So then the situation is a son doing his normal routine of cooking and eating but without his father there because he is dead. I still don't get the hornet in the pear, but since the father showed it to him, maybe it has to do with the father? Or maybe it's just a vivid image and that's why Lee went with it. It's strange that this poem is hard to understand because the language is pretty simple. I didn't have to look anything up. Spigot is definitely the coolest word in here. Those last lines are still really confusing, too, because they seem to contradict each other. In the one, he talks about "loneliness," but then the next second, he's saying what more could he want? No one wants to be lonely, right? So how does that make sense? It seems like what he really wants is to have his father with him again.

### Journaling

In Li-Young Lee's poem, a son misses his father, who is apparently dead. The situation is pretty straightforward, but it does jump around a lot in time. At first the son is in the garden; then he remembers something about his father from a long time ago; then he talks about that morning; then he's cooking at the end.

One appealing aspect of the poem is the imagery. You can practically see, taste, and smell the very things the son sees, tastes, and smells. Some of the imagery is very pleasant, like the cooking smells and tastes at the end, but other imagery is not very attractive. Especially in the first stanza, there's a lot of detail about the garden being cold, brown, and old. And empty, since the son has pulled the "last" of the onions. I don't know if the hornet in the pear is an attractive image or not—the juice is cool, but a hornet and a rotten pear are not things you like to encounter. In any case, some of the images seem to be full of life—like the cooking at the end—but others seem to be dead—like the garden.

In a poem that's easy to understand in terms of the words themselves, the last lines are really hard to figure out. The last lines contradict each other, but I realize now that he's not asking a question. The last line says, "What more could I, a young man, want." So he's telling us he is satisfied somehow, even though his father is not with him. If it had been an actual question, I would have answered that he wants his father back—so maybe his statement means he has learned to be content despite his grief over his father's death.

**Brainstorming**

| LIFE | DEATH |
|---|---|
| son/speaker | father |
| young onions | bare garden—cold, brown, old |
| hornet | rotten pear |
| father waving | shovel |
| eating | eating alone |

"[Write] about something that really moves you and engages you; you must be there on the page." Conversation with Carolyn Forché

## Develop a Thesis

In your responses, annotations, and explorations, you have concentrated on the parts of the poem that make up the whole. At this point, you have an idea of the larger conflicts or issues the poem dramatizes. In developing a thesis, it helps if you choose something personally meaningful. Your thesis is your claim that the poem works a certain way or means a certain thing. It isn't a general statement with which no one can disagree, such as information on what you personally like or feel about a poem. Your thesis is a thoughtful and specific assertion that will organize your paper and for which you can provide support and evidence from the poem itself.

*First draft:* The imagery and the contrast in the last lines suggest contradictory feelings, although it is mostly sad.

*Second draft:* In a poem about a son missing his dead father, there are many contrasting elements.

*Third draft:* This poem, which is an expression of grief over a dead father, relies on contrasting elements like imagery, tone, and time in order to make us feel the narrator's loss.

*Final draft:* A close reading shows the entire poem is created out of contradictory elements. Through contrasts of imagery, tone, and the literal events of the poem, Lee uses paradox to give full expression to the grief his speaker feels about his father's death.

## Create a Plan for Your Paper

In any paper, your first paragraph sets up the issues that you will explore. There are as many ways to organize your paper as there are lines in the poem, but some general guidelines might help. You can examine the poem line by line, focus on the conflicts that are dramatized in the poem, or look at patterns, types of images, themes, or repeated words. When you are organizing your paper, advance your argument with evidence from the poem to avoid creating a laundry list that leads nowhere. Your paper will focus on the text itself, but your conclusion can make connections and raise questions and emphasize crucial issues. You do not need to repeat your thesis in your concluding paragraph. Sometimes an outline will help you plan your paper.

### Outlining

I. Introduction
  A. confusing because last lines contradict
  B. thesis: A close reading shows the entire poem is created out of contradictory elements. Through contrasts of imagery, tone, and the literal events of the poem, Lee uses paradox to give full expression to the grief his speaker feels about his father's death.

II. Imagery
  A. imagery that suggests life
  B. imagery that suggests death

III. Tone
  A. plain language
  B. syntax is not complicated . . .
  C. . . . but subject matter is. This = understatement

IV. Time/Literal Events
  A. present, past "years back," past "this morning"
  B. talk about contrast in time

VI. Conclusion
   A. address contrast in last lines
   B. we can understand them in context of poem

## Generate a First Draft

A first draft is just that: the *first*. Often you find clearer ways to express your thoughts as you go along. Sometimes you change your mind. With poetry, as with all literature, write in the present tense (He *misses* his father; not he *missed* his father). The event that the poem describes never changes, so it is the convention to use present tense when writing about literature.

**First Draft**

Baldwin 1

Emma Baldwin

Professor Stoller

English 102

September 22, 2008

Paradox in "Eating Alone"

On first reading Li-Young Lee's poem "Eating Alone," it doesn't make much sense. The speaker's conclusion that he is lonely *and* has everything he wants isn't logical. But on a closer reading, the entire poem is created out of contradictory elements. Through contrasts of imagery, tone, and the literal events of the poem, Lee uses paradox to give full expression to the grief his speaker feels about his father's death.

There is lots of imagery throughout the poem. A lot of it has to do with being alive, like the smell and taste of "sesame oil / and garlic" (lines 21–22). But a lot of it also has to do with death. The poem begins with the speaker picking "the last" (1) produce so that, "The garden is bare now" (2), and Lee further describes the ground as "cold, / brown and old" (2–3). These things remind the reader of death. The images seem to contradict themselves; on the one hand, they make the reader feel connected to the physical world, but on the other hand, they are cold, fleeting images that are related to death.

The father is dead, even though the poem doesn't state that. But it's obvious from the creaky way he bends that he is old. Since that is in a memory from years ago, chances are he has since passed away if he was so old to begin with.

Baldwin 2

In a poem about death, you might expect the words to be flowery, or even like passages from the Bible. You might also expect that the narrator is outwardly sad, or might even cry. But that doesn't happen. Instead, statements like "Once, years back, I walked beside my father / among the windfall pears" (8–9) sound as though they are said in casual conversation. By understating the situation of death, there is a contrast between the level of subject matter and the way that subject matter is expressed. This contrast highlights that even though death is a major and mystical event, it has become a fact of daily life for this speaker. The understated tone of the poem shows that grief is part of everyday life.

Several other contrasts are embedded in the poem. First is the matter of time. The young man in the present talks about a memory in the past. But beyond a simple past/present contrast, there's an immediate past in addition to a farther away past. The present action is the young man picking the onions, cleaning them, then using them to cook. The distant past is the memory that takes place in the second stanza, "years back," (8) while the immediate past is the occurrence recounted in the third stanza that occurred "this morning" (15). The purpose of the immediate past is that it links the past and present. In that stanza, he sees his father waving at him in the current moment; then he recognizes it is only a shovel in the shade, making the speaker painfully aware in the present of all he has lost from the past. In this way, that painful moment of father and shovel confusion highlights how the father was once alive but is now dead.

In summation, there are contradictory elements in almost every aspect of his poem. Because of this, I can come to understand the last stanza: "Shrimp braised in sesame / oil and garlic. And my own loneliness. / What more could I, a young man, want" (21–23). As noted previously, the fact that loneliness is part of what the young man wants is confusing. But since the whole poem is built on contrasts, the last contrast somehow seems to make sense.

Work Cited

Lee, Li-Young. "Eating Alone." *Literature: Craft & Voice.* Eds. Nicholas Delbanco and Alan Cheuse. New York: McGraw-Hill, 2009. 49. Print.

### Revise Your Draft

Before beginning her second draft, Emma looked back at her notes and annotations and compared those to her draft. She found that her notes frequently mentioned the image of the hornet in the pear, but that her final paper left out that image. She also found that the paper did not explicitly highlight the life-and-death contrast she had found so important to furthering her understanding of the poem. While you certainly do not need to incorporate every idea into the final version, Emma thought it would help her argument to include these elements in her paper.

"Here I have a tremendous kind of furious argument, and here I've got to try and tame it. I've got to enact it. I've got to find a way to formalize it so that someone else can experience what I experienced." Conversation with Edward Hirsch

In the second draft, look for how Emma (1) clarifies her argument by pointing out the life in death imagery; (2) adds textual support to her discussion of imagery; (3) works towards making her conclusion more related to her thesis; (4) adds citations.

**Second Draft**

Baldwin 1

Emma Baldwin

Professor Stoller

English 102

September 27, 2008

Paradox in Li-Young Lee's "Eating Alone"

On first reading Li-Young Lee's poem "Eating Alone," it doesn't make much sense. The speaker's conclusion that he is lonely *and* has everything he wants is not logical because loneliness means something is missing. In this case, it's the father, who is dead. The entire poem is created out of contradictory elements. Through contrasts of imagery, tone, and the literal events of the poem, Lee uses paradox to give full expression to the grief his speaker feels about his father's death.

Clarifies why the conclusion is not logical, which is an important facet of the thesis.

There is lots of imagery throughout the poem. A lot of it has to do with the different parts of being alive. There is sight when Lee describes "the shovel, leaning where I had / left it, in the flickering, deep green shade" (lines 18–19). There is sound from "the icy metal spigot" (7). There is touch when Lee talks about the cold ground and the cold water (2, 7). There is both taste and smell with the cooking, like with "sesame / oil and garlic" (21–22). But a lot of it also

Added textual support gives a solid basis for the argument. Emma has fleshed out the idea from the first draft with added examples.

Baldwin 2

has to do with death. The poem begins with the speaker picking "the last" produce so that, "The garden is bare now" (1, 2), and Lee further describes the ground as "cold, / brown and old" (2–3). Such images suggest that all has been harvested and that winter is coming, and this is linked to death. Even the image in line 5, "I turn, a cardinal vanishes," suggests the fleeting, changeable nature of all that surrounds the speaker, who himself is shown in the act of turning. The images seem to contradict themselves; on the one hand, they make the reader feel connected to the physical world, but on the other hand, they are cold, fleeting images that are related to death.

The father is dead, even though the poem doesn't state that. But it's obvious from the creaky way he bends that he is old. Since that is a memory from years ago, chances are he has since passed away if he was so old to begin with. In a poem about death, you might expect the words to be flowery, or even like passages from the Bible. You might also expect that the narrator is outwardly sad, or might even cry. But that doesn't happen. Instead, the syntax is straightforward, so that statements like "Once, years back, I walked beside my father / among the windfall pears" (8–9) sound as though they are said in casual conversation. By understating the situation of death, there is a contrast between the level of subject matter and the way that subject matter is expressed. This contrast highlights that even though death is a major and mystical event, it has become a fact of daily life for this speaker. The understated tone of the poem shows that grief is part of everyday life.

This paragraph was already well expressed, so Emma opted for no changes.

Several other contrasts are embedded in the poem. First is the matter of time. The young man in the present talks about a memory in the past. But beyond a simple past/present contrast, Lee adds an immediate past in addition to a farther away past. The present action is the young man picking the onions, cleaning them, then using them to cook. The distant past is the memory that takes place in the second stanza, "years back" (8), while the immediate past is the occurrence recounted in the third stanza that occurred "this morning." The purpose of the immediate past is that it links the past and present. In that stanza, he sees his father waving at him in the current moment; then he recognizes it is only a shovel in the shade, making the speaker painfully aware

More formal language added—tenses clarified.

Refined language more clearly articulates the importance of the moment described.

Added paragraph to highlight additional contrasts in the poem. Since the thesis statement is about contrast, this new paragraph lends further support to the argument.

Further refinement of the thesis. The previous draft asked the reader to make too many leaps in figuring out what Emma was trying to say; here she has made her argument clear.

Baldwin 2

in the present of all he has lost from the past. In this way, that painful moment of father and shovel confusion encapsulates two realities—the past reality that his father was once alive, and the present reality that the father is dead.

Life and death is another contrast placed in the poem. The title, "Eating Alone," and the fact that the poem ends with the speaker preparing his food, emphasizes the act of eating. Eating sustains life; therefore, the speaker engages in an action that highlights his state as a living being, even as he thinks of his father, who is dead. The hornet in the rotten pear is another expression of life and death in the same space. A rotten pear connotes decay, which equates with death, while the spinning hornet is clearly alive.

In summation, there are contradictory elements in almost every aspect of his poem. Because of this, I can come to understand the last stanza: "Shrimp braised in sesame / oil and garlic. And my own loneliness. / What more could I, a young man, want" (21–23). As noted previously, the fact that loneliness is part of what the young man wants is confusing. But in the context of a poem where Lee has shown death alongside life, past and present brushing shoulders in the same instant, and everyday speech coupled with as great an event as death, we instinctively understand that it is in the intersection of contradictory elements that fullness is achieved—whether that be a full life, or a full expression of grief.

Work Cited

Lee, Li-Young. "Eating Alone." *Literature: Craft & Voice.* Eds. Nicholas Delbanco and Alan Cheuse. New York: McGraw-Hill, 2009. 49. Print.

## Edit and Format Your Paper

When you're ready to create your final draft, carefully go back and edit your sentences. Make sure your punctuation is correct, your spellings are accurate, and your grammar is in order. These formal considerations are not as much about the meaning of your thesis, but they are the clothes you put on it. After inserting additional content in the second draft, Emma refined her language and made sure her points were as clear as possible in the final draft. She also double-checked that she added all the missing citations, and she made sure to format the paper correctly, with a title, a standard 12-point font, and double spacing.

"Words are about experience." Conversation with Robert Pinsky

## Final Draft

Baldwin 1

Proper heading: Name, Prof., Class, Date

Emma Baldwin

Professor Stoller

English 102

3 October 2008

Title that includes author and work

The Power of Paradox in Li-Young Lee's "Eating Alone"

On a first reading, Li-Young Lee's poem "Eating Alone" seems to make little sense. The speaker's conclusion that he is lonely *and* has everything he wants is not logical, as loneliness implies a lack of fulfillment. However, a closer reading shows that the entire poem is created out of contradictory elements. Through contrasts of imagery, tone, and the literal events of the poem, Lee uses paradox to fully express the speaker's grief over the father's death.

Thesis statement

Discussion of first of three elements mentioned in thesis statement

Perhaps the most striking feature of the poem is its imagery. Lee uses precise imagery that appeals to all five senses: we see, along with the speaker, "the shovel, leaning where I had / left it, in the flickering, deep green shade" (lines 18–19); we hear the water from "the icy metal spigot" (7); we feel the cold ground and the cold water (2, 7); we taste and smell "sweet green peas / fried in onions. Shrimp braised in sesame / oil and garlic" (20–22). Yet while the images reaffirm a living being's ability to see, hear, touch, taste, and smell, they also suggest death. The poem begins with the speaker picking "the last" produce so that "The garden is bare now" (1, 2), and Lee further describes the ground as "cold, / brown and old" (2–3). Such images suggest that all has been harvested and that winter is coming—traditional ways of symbolizing death. Even the image in line 5, "I turn, a cardinal vanishes," suggests the fleeting, changeable nature of all that surrounds the speaker, who himself is shown in the act of turning. Thus, the images seem to contradict themselves: on the one hand, they make the reader feel connected to the physical world, but on the other hand, they are cold, fleeting images that connote death.

textual support

textual support

Conclusion about significance of imagery

Baldwin 2

Discussion of second of three elements mentioned in thesis statement

Although the poem never directly states that the father is dead, the imagery, the speaker's act of remembering in the second stanza, and details like the father's difficulty bending years ago suggest the father's age and his subsequent passing. In a poem about death, one might expect the diction to be elevated, perhaps even to the level of Biblical language. One might also expect overt sadness or lamentation over the death of a family member. Lee follows neither of these expectations. Instead, the syntax is straightforward, so that statements like "Once, years back, I walked beside my father / among the windfall pears" sound as though they are said in casual conversation (8–9). This technique of understatement creates a contrast between the level of subject matter and the way that subject matter is expressed. The contrast highlights that even though death is a major and mystical event, it has become a fact of daily life for this speaker. The understated tone of the poem, then, creates the sense that the speaker's grief is so constant and present that he has integrated it into his everyday life.

textual support

Conclusion about significance of tone

Discussion of third of three elements mentioned in thesis statement

Several other contrasts are embedded in the poem. First is the matter of time. Lee presents a young man speaking in the present while remembering a scene from his past. But beyond a simple past/present contrast, Lee adds the element of immediate past versus distant past. The present action is the young man picking the onions, cleaning them, then using them to cook. The distant past is the memory that takes place in the second stanza, "years back" (8), while the immediate past is the occurrence recounted in the third stanza that happened "this morning" (15). The purpose of the immediate past is that it links the past and present. In that stanza, he sees his father waving at him in the current moment; then he recognizes it is only a shovel in the shade, making the speaker painfully aware in the present of all he has lost from the past. In this way, the moment of father and shovel confusion

Conclusion about significance of events in poem

Baldwin 3

encapsulates two realities—the past reality that his father was once alive, and the present reality that the father is dead.

Further discussion of third element mentioned in thesis statement

Similarly, there are other instances where life and death are placed in immediate proximity to highlight the contradicting halves. The title, "Eating Alone," and the fact that the poem ends with the speaker preparing his food, emphasizes the act of eating. Eating sustains life; therefore, the speaker engages in an action that highlights his state as a living being, even as he thinks of his father, who is dead. The hornet in the rotten pear also places life and death in the same space. A rotten pear connotes decay, which equates with death, while the spinning hornet is clearly alive.

Conclusion paragraph

Restatement of thesis, but with further nuance than in intro

Lee, then, builds contradictory elements into every aspect of his poem—within the imagery, between tone/syntax/diction and subject, and in the timing of the literal events of the poem. By using so many contrasts, Lee sets us up to understand the paradoxical last lines: "Shrimp braised in sesame / oil and garlic. And my own loneliness. / What more could I, a young man, want" (21–23). That loneliness is necessary to complete what the young man wants is difficult to reconcile. But in the context of a poem where Lee has shown death alongside life, past and present brushing shoulders in the same instant, and everyday speech coupled with as great an event as death, we instinctively understand that it is in the intersection of contradictory elements that fullness is achieved—whether that be a full life, or a full expression of grief.

Broadening of argument to entire poem

Shows how all three elements mentioned in thesis lead to understanding the poem as a whole

Work Cited

Lee, Li-Young. "Eating Alone." *Literature: Craft & Voice.* Eds. Nicholas Delbanco and Alan Cheuse. New York: McGraw-Hill, 2009. 49. Print.

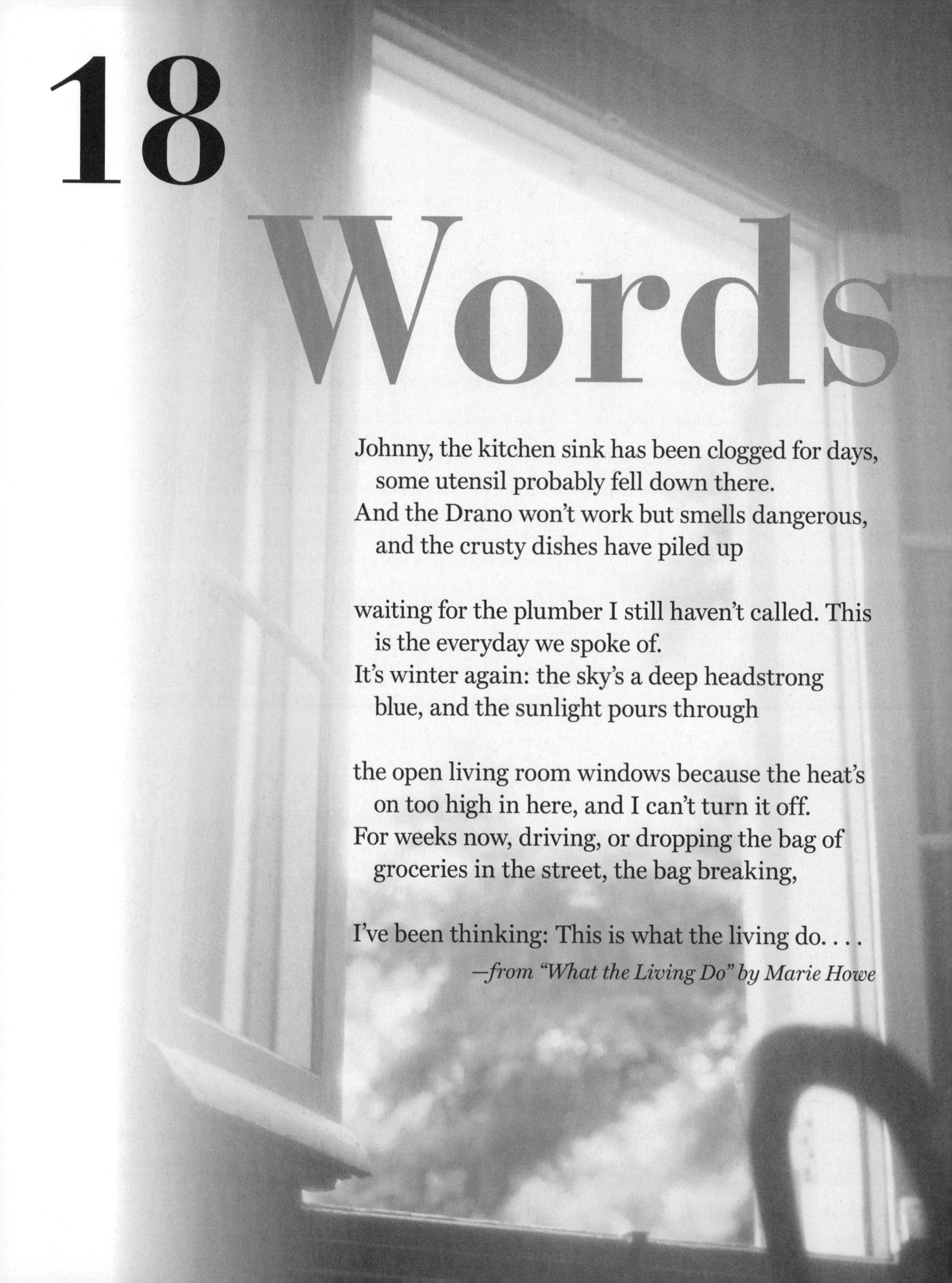

# 18 Words

Johnny, the kitchen sink has been clogged for days,
some utensil probably fell down there.
And the Drano won't work but smells dangerous,
and the crusty dishes have piled up

waiting for the plumber I still haven't called. This
is the everyday we spoke of.
It's winter again: the sky's a deep headstrong
blue, and the sunlight pours through

the open living room windows because the heat's
on too high in here, and I can't turn it off.
For weeks now, driving, or dropping the bag of
groceries in the street, the bag breaking,

I've been thinking: This is what the living do. . . .

*—from "What the Living Do" by Marie Howe*

*"I love Anglo-Saxon. I just like 'rock,' 'stone,' 'dirt,' 'blood.' . . . I would much prefer the four-letter word quite literally like 'rock' to 'boulder' even. I love the simplicity of those words, the thing closest to the thing."*

Conversation with Marie Howe, available on video at www.mhhe.com/delbanco1e

IN the autobiographical poem "What the Living Do," Marie Howe reflects on the aftermath of her brother's death, personally addressing him as if she were writing a letter. She catalogs the details of everyday existence, its mundane irritations as well as its surprising beauty. The poem is a testament both to remembrance and to continuity. The series of observations culminates in the quiet recognition that these commonplace tasks constitute the way that life, in its varying majesty and modesty, continues for the bereaved.

Poets try to find and then select language appropriate to their subject matter. The resulting selection is called **diction,** the choice of words by an author or speaker. A poem about war might sound percussive, even violent. A love poem's language can seem as lush and comforting as an embrace. So, *how* an experience or feeling is expressed in language is just as important to the poet as *what* that experience or feeling consists of.

This poet writes with great clarity. She chooses language immediately understood by the attentive reader. It's almost as though we're eavesdropping on the speaker as she voices these intimate thoughts to her deceased brother. Look at how plainspoken and declarative the language is: "the kitchen sink has been clogged for days," "the heat's on too high," and "I've been thinking: This is what the living do."

In her interview, Marie Howe expresses fondness for the blunt words we've inherited from Anglo-Saxon (or Old English), the language spoken in Britain centuries ago—before the introduction of Latinate words on the heels of the Norman Conquest in 1066. "I just like 'rock,' 'stone,' 'dirt,' 'blood.' . . . I love the simplicity of those words, the thing closest to the thing." This respect for simplicity is reflected in the precision and candor of "What the Living Do." It's a poem committed to honest contemplation and emotion. "I . . . decided to write—to give myself a break—a letter to my brother John, who I missed," Howe says. "So I just wrote 'Johnny, the kitchen sink has been clogged for days,' because it actually was. 'And the Drano won't work,' because it didn't. And I kept going and just kept writing and writing."

The British poet Samuel Taylor Coleridge defined poetry, in 1835, as "the best words in the best order." More than a century later, American poet William Carlos Williams remarked that a poem is "a machine made of words." Both of these quotes wryly reiterate the necessity for language to fit and work properly within a particular poem's context and meaning. (This is also true for writers of prose fiction and drama, of course; every artist hates imprecision and strives to be exact. But it's particularly the case in poetry, where diction takes pride of place.) When you read poetry, you will want to consider how writers choose the kind of language they do, and how they go about fitting words together and putting them in the "best order."

*(CONTINUED ON PAGE 68)*

*. . . when something huge happens, people don't use big language.*

*. . . I fear for the actual.*

# Q&A
# *A Conversation on Writing*

## Marie Howe

### Writing As Discovery

I want to make one thing perfectly clear. I don't know what I'm doing when I'm writing. . . . For me at least, that a [writer] starts off knowing what she's going to say is something I thought for a long time. Now I know that . . . it's quite the opposite—that the writing itself brought me into an experience I didn't know I was going to have. My brother had died. He was my dearest friend. He was twenty-eight years old.

### Poetry in Real Time

I really wanted "What the Living Do" to have . . . the startling reality of the actual. . . . I fear for the actual. It's losing to the virtual. . . . [Think about] what we're able to do with computer technology without having to see or hear anybody. . . . I think that poetry reminds us [of the actual]—it has to do with time as well, right? Why it's difficult to read poetry [i]s not because it's hard to understand, at least for me, it's because it's so painful to slow down. To . . . read a poem is to live in time in a way that is almost unbearable . . . to be all here, this very moment.

### Advice on Reading Poetry

Plunge, don't be embarrassed. . . . When I got out of graduate school, I moved to Cambridge. There were all these other writers and poets living there, and . . . we would say to each other "I don't get Wallace Stevens." . . . And someone would say, "I do. Let's meet Thursday at three." . . . Every week we would meet with our friends and just talk about poems we didn't understand. And it was such a joy not to be embarrassed.

The oldest of nine children, Marie Howe (b. 1950) grew up in Rochester, New York. After teaching high school for a time, Howe earned her master of fine arts degree in poetry from Columbia University, where she studied with poet laureate Stanley Kunitz. Her first major success came in 1987 when Margaret Atwood selected Howe's *The Good Thief* (1988) as the winner of the National Poetry Series. Her next collection of poems, *What the Living Do* (1997), was written after her brother's death from AIDS, and is largely an elegy for him. Her third book of poetry, *The Kingdom of Ordinary Time,* was published in 2008. Howe's work is characterized by an open avowal of emotion—the sense of loss as well as hope; she's a thoroughly *personal* poet with an uninflected voice.

**To watch this entire interview and hear the author read from her poetry, go to www.mhhe.com/delbanco1e.**

**RESEARCH ASSIGNMENT** In her interview, Howe mentions "what happens, happens in between" in language. Listen to her interview. What does Howe mean by this? How does her example relate to "What the Living Do"?

**AS YOU READ** Pay close attention to the kind of language Howe uses. Be aware of how her fondness for simple, direct words (rock, stone, dirt, and blood) affects her diction and attitude to the subject of this poem. Think about the way "the everyday we spoke of" appears here again and again.

# What the Living Do (1997)

Johnny, the kitchen sink has been clogged for days,
some utensil probably fell down there.
And the Drano won't work but smells dangerous,
and the crusty dishes have piled up

waiting for the plumber I still haven't called. This is
the everyday we spoke of.
It's winter again: the sky's a deep headstrong blue,
and the sunlight pours through

the open living room windows because the heat's
on too high in here, and I can't turn it off.
For weeks now, driving, or dropping a bag of
groceries in the street, the bag breaking,

I've been thinking: This is what the living do. And
yesterday, hurrying along those
wobbly bricks in the Cambridge sidewalk, spilling
my coffee down my wrist and sleeve,

I thought it again, and again later, when buying a
hairbrush: This is it.
Parking. Slamming the car door shut in the cold.
What you called *that yearning.*

What you finally gave up. We want the spring to
come and the winter to pass. We want
whoever to call or not call, a letter, a kiss—we want
more and more and then more of it.

But there are moments, walking, when I catch a
glimpse of myself in the window glass,
say, the window of the corner video store, and I'm
gripped by a cherishing so deep

for my own blowing hair, chapped face, and
unbuttoned coat that I'm speechless:

I am living, I remember you.

# Writing from Reading

### Summarize

1 List the activities that "the living do."

### Analyze Craft

2 Contrast the shorter sentences with the longer ones. Do they serve different purposes?

3 Why do you think Howe uses familiar nouns like "Drano" or "video store"?

### Analyze Voice

4 Discuss how tone informs or helps to convey the emotions in this poem. How would you characterize the tone?

5 Notice how many gerunds—present participles such as "driving," "dropping," "hurrying," "walking"—she employs. What does that do to the tense of the action, and what would happen to this "conversation" if it were in the past?

### Synthesize Summary and Analysis

6 In this poem, Howe lists the activities of everyday life. How does her choice of words reinforce the subject of the poem?

### Interpret the Poem

7 What is Howe trying to say about the living as opposed to those who are no longer with us?

8 Howe indicates she is "speechless" when she sees her reflection in a storefront window. What does her speechlessness represent?

9 How would you describe the main theme or themes of "What the Living Do"?

*CONTINUED FROM PAGE 65*

## WORD CHOICE: VARIETIES OF DICTION

**Poetic diction** describes an especially lofty and elevated language characteristic of poetry written before the nineteenth century. A tradition inherited from the classical verse of Greek and Latin, poetic diction was used to separate poetic speech from common speech. Poets believed that verse, in its ambition to demonstrate the full power of language, demanded its own heightened vocabulary. As such, ordinary objects received flowery and exotic description. Britain's most famous poet of the Victorian era, Alfred, Lord Tennyson, uses this diction when he calls grass "the herb" and a horse a "charger." In this same vein, the eighteenth-century British poet and critic Alexander Pope memorably names a pair of scissors "the glitt'ring Forfex." Pope's example of poetic diction (represented here by an apostrophe) employs **elision,** the omission of a vowel or consonant sound within or between words. Words like "o'er" were substituted for "over" and "ne'er" for "never." In addition to dramatizing the language, this also allowed for added flexibility within a poem's meter.

"This is the secret of poets. . . . They actually read the dictionary the way some people would read spy novels."

Conversation with Carolyn Forché

### A BRIEF HISTORY OF POETIC DICTION

Neoclassical poets (c. 1600–1800) chose subjects and words they felt were refined and therefore appropriate for serious poetry, often relying on Greek and Latin (*classical*) verse for inspiration. The Romantic movement in poetry inaugurated a steady change from poetic diction to more everyday modes of speech. William Wordsworth, a leading British Romantic poet, wrote in 1802 in a preface to his celebrated collection of poems *Lyrical Ballads,* "There will also be found in these volumes little of what is usually called poetic diction; I have taken as much pains to avoid it as others ordinarily take to produce it." In the United States in the twentieth century, Robert Frost notably adopted a similar poetic stance, seeking to voice his poems with what he called the "sound of sense," a phrase Frost used to mean the actual sound of spoken language. From the Romantic era of Wordsworth to Frost's modern period to the present moment, poets have chosen their words with increasing freedom.

While there is no strict line clearly separating divisions of diction, poets' selection of language can be divided into three levels, from the most extravagantly phrased lines of poetic diction to the direct and straightforward. These levels of speech are generally referred to as

- Formal (flowery, grand, and elaborate)
- Middle (educated standard English)
- Informal (everyday speech)

**Formal diction** refers to complex, grammatically proper, and often polysyllabic language in writing. It sounds grandiloquent—a "formal" word—and tends not to resemble the sort of talk we hear in our daily lives. Listen to the speaker in John Keats's "Ode on a Grecian Urn." He stands, likely in a museum, before an ancient Greek vase and becomes captivated, stanza after stanza, by the different rural scenes painted on its sides: images of men pursuing women, of lovers, of trees, of religious rituals.

## John Keats (1795–1821)

Although John Keats died of tuberculosis at age twenty-five, he had already composed poetry of such a caliber that he remains one of the best-known and most admired British Romantic poets. Though he believed himself a failure and wanted his epitaph to read "Here lies one whose name is writ in water," nothing could be further from the truth; "Posthumous Keats," as one of his biographers, the poet Stanley Plumly, puts it, lives on. His actual life, however, was never an easy one; his parents died when he was young, he watched his brother Tom die of tuberculosis, his poetry was generally unsuccessful until after his own demise, and he was unable to marry the woman he loved because of his poverty and failing health. Having studied to be a doctor, he could recognize "arterial blood" when he coughed it up in Rome and pronounced his own death sentence there; the house where he died (by the Spanish Steps) as well as the last house where he lived in London are both museums now. John Keats combined a nature deeply sensitive to beauty with a literary talent that allowed him to render his verses with a grace and eloquence paralleled perhaps only by Shakespeare. His celebrated poems "Lamia" and "La Belle Dame sans Merci" and his odes were all written in a great burst of creativity in 1819.

**AS YOU READ** Note the first word of the poem, "Thou." Words like "Thou," "Thee," and "Thy" suggest an archaic form of "You" and "Your" that was seldom heard in Keats's day. Note also how the poem argues that what's lost remains, what's gone endures, and ask yourself how this relates to the poet's illness and premonition of death.

**TIP** **FOR INTERACTIVE READING . . .** As you read "Ode on a Grecian Urn," circle or write down other words that you would characterize as formal.

# Ode on a Grecian Urn (1819)

I.

Thou still unravished bride of quietness,
Thou foster-child of silence and slow Time,
Sylvan historian, who canst thus express
A flowery tale more sweetly than our rhyme:
What leaf-fringed legend haunts about thy shape
Of deities or mortals, or of both,
In Tempe or the dales of Arcady?
What men or gods are these? What maidens loth?
What mad pursuit? What struggle to escape?
What pipes and timbrels? What wild ecstasy?

II.

Heard melodies are sweet, but those unheard
Are sweeter; therefore, ye soft pipes, play on;
Not to the sensual ear, but, more endear'd,
Pipe to the spirit ditties of no tone:
Fair youth, beneath the trees, thou canst not leave
Thy song, nor ever can those trees be bare;
Bold Lover, never, never canst thou kiss,
Though winning near the goal—yet, do not grieve;
She cannot fade, though thou hast not thy bliss,
For ever wilt thou love, and she be fair!

III.

Ah, happy, happy boughs! that cannot shed
Your leaves, nor ever bid the Spring adieu;
And, happy melodist, unwearièd,
For ever piping songs for ever new;
More happy love! more happy, happy love!
For ever warm and still to be enjoy'd,
For ever panting, and for ever young;
All breathing human passion far above,
That leaves a heart high-sorrowful and cloy'd,
A burning forehead, and a parching tongue.

IV.

Who are these coming to the sacrifice?
To what green altar, O mysterious priest,
Lead'st thou that heifer lowing at the skies,
And all her silken flanks with garlands drest?
What little town by river or sea shore,
Or mountain-built with peaceful citadel,
Is emptied of its folk, this pious morn?
And, little town, thy streets for evermore
Will silent be; and not a soul to tell
Why thou art desolate, can e'er return.

V.

O Attic shape! Fair attitude! with brede
Of marble men and maidens overwrought,
With forest branches and the trodden weed;
Thou, silent form, dost tease us out of thought
As doth eternity: Cold Pastoral!
When old age shall this generation waste,
Thou shalt remain, in midst of other woe
Than ours, a friend to man, to whom thou say'st,
"Beauty is truth, truth beauty,"—that is all
Ye know on earth, and all ye need to know.

# Writing from Reading

## Summarize

1 Rewrite each stanza in a couple of sentences using everyday speech.

2 Who or what is the poet addressing in the poem?

## Analyze Craft

3 Why do you think Keats uses the word "still" in the first line of the poem? Does the word supply more than one meaning? And what does he mean by "unravished"?

4 List examples of elision in the poem.

5 In the final stanza the speaker calls the urn a "Cold Pastoral!" Look up the word *pastoral* in a dictionary. Which definition, the adjective or noun, do you think Keats intends to invoke? Why do you think he chooses this word?

## Analyze Voice

6 Describe the mood conveyed in the poem. What words has Keats chosen to evoke this particular mood?

7 How does the use of formal diction help establish a sense of the speaker's attitude?

## Synthesize Summary and Analysis

8 Compare the formal diction in Keats's poem to your rewritten stanzas from question 1. What does Keats accomplish by choosing the kinds of words he does in this poem?

9 How does the formal poetic diction add to the theme of beauty in this poem?

## Interpret the Poem

10 Why do you think Keats decided to use a Grecian urn as opposed to pottery from other time periods?

11 Explain why you agree or disagree with the famous last lines of this poem,

"Beauty is truth, truth beauty,"—
that is all Ye know on earth,
and all ye need to know.

Missing the showy grandiosity of formal diction, **middle diction** is characterized by sophisticated word usage and grammatical accuracy. It is educated language, but not extravagant—a blend of "common" speech and "elevated" diction, sometimes within the same line. Mostly, however, the language is simple and straightforward. At this point in our discussion of diction, it seems appropriate to repeat a pair of points made previously.

1. Every English poem is a blend of formal and informal speech, but
2. No "natural" speaker would be able to rhyme words such as "telephone" with "bone" or "drum" with "come" so effortlessly. So there is craft involved in this particular voice.

In W. H. Auden's "Funeral Blues," the poet goes from realistic (Unplug the clocks, give the dog a bone, quit playing the piano or talking on the phone) to romantic and excessive—from requiring the plausible to asking the impossible.

# W. H. Auden (1907–1973)

Wystan Hugh Auden is one of the most important British poets of the twentieth century (he became an American citizen, but he was born in England and lived there for the majority of his life). With great technical agility and a near-total command of poetic form, Auden could have been a kind of erudite "ivory-tower" artist, remaining aloof from the world. But he allowed his own time to color his poetry, writing about the literal wasteland created by the Great Depression, using the ideas of Sigmund Freud and Karl Marx to examine England's political problems, and gathering the rhythms of colloquial speech alongside his masterful versification. In later life, his poetry moved from the social consciousness of his early work to more personal and even religious poems; both serious and playful, W. H. Auden was continually able to put craft in the service of voice, and to put both craft and voice to use in the hunt for wisdom. After the following poem was featured in the movie "Four Weddings and a Funeral," this lament for a friend's death was widely read again.

**AS YOU READ** Note the role of sound in this poem—the perfect rhymes in couplets (up till the very last line). Though seemingly casual, rhymes such as "overhead/Dead" and "doves/gloves" in the second stanza reveal how well wrought Auden's lines are. Notice, for example, how the only rhyme that's less than true is the final one; the poet surely could have written "wood," not "woods," or found some other way to make the end rhyme absolute. Ask yourself why the speaker doesn't make the last line a true rhyme and if this poem is understated or overstated as an expression of grief.

**TIP**

**FOR INTERACTIVE READING . . .** Auden uses several images in this poem. List these images.

## Funeral Blues (1940)

Stop all the clocks, cut off the telephone,
Prevent the dog from barking with a juicy bone,
Silence the pianos and with muffled drum
Bring out the coffin, let the mourners come.

Let aeroplanes circle moaning overhead
Scribbling on the sky the message He is Dead.
Put crêpe bows round the white necks of the public doves,
Let the traffic policemen wear black cotton gloves.

He was my North, my South, my East and West,
My working week and my Sunday rest,
My noon, my midnight, my talk, my song;
I thought that love would last forever: I was wrong.

The stars are not wanted now; put out every one,
Pack up the moon and dismantle the sun,
Pour away the ocean and sweep up the woods;
For nothing now can ever come to any good.

# Writing from Reading

### Summarize

1 What is the speaker responding to in this poem, and what does the title convey?

2 How does the speaker feel about the subject of the poem?

3 How do such phrases as "muffled drum," "mourners," and "crêpe bows," the traditional trappings of a funeral, contrast with the actual occasion of the poem?

### Analyze Craft

4 Describe the diction in this poem. When does it seem formal or informal?

5 What emotions or meaning come to mind when you read "the white necks of the public doves"? What comes to mind when you read other images?

### Analyze Voice

6 Describe tone in the poem. Is it uniformly mournful? If not, where does the tone shift, and where does it remind you of the blues?

7 There's wild exaggeration in the last stanza's set of instructions: "pack up the moon and dismantle the sun"—as if we could indeed "pour away the ocean" and "put out" the stars. What does this tell us about the emotion of the speaker?

### Synthesize Summary and Analysis

8 How many sentences make up this poem? Discuss the consistency of the arrangement of sentences—how do they affect or reflect the poem's subject?

### Interpret the Poem

9 Compare the last lines of this poem to "What the Living Do." What does this poem say about death? Explain how it is the same as or different from Howe's "What the Living Do."

10 Look at John Donne's "A Valediction: Forbidding Mourning" in the "For Review and Further Study" section of this chapter. Compare Auden's use of the compass with that of Donne's.

A majority of poets today compose in language that sounds like the speech we hear in daily life. **Informal diction** is conversational, plainspoken language and often makes use of slang, contractions, and mainstream expressions. It might sound like a remark across a dinner table, or resemble something you overhear in the course of a regular day.

Gwendolyn Brooks grew up on Chicago's South Side, and many of her poems describe and explore the lives of everyday African Americans in urban twentieth-century America. The following poem, "We Real Cool," speaks in the collective voice of a group of young men shooting pool. Not only does the poem employ informal diction, it simultaneously exemplifies **dialect,** the variety of language spoken by a particular group of people (in this case, young black men during the 1960s). In turn, dialect usually features **colloquial language,** familiar and conversational speech. Lastly, we can see in this poem a bit of **jargon,** words with specific meaning for a particular group of people. Poets assign language like this to speakers in order to convey a vivid sense of who inhabits a poem, what that person is like or what he or she wants.

> "Gwendolyn Brooks is one of my favorite poets and what I particularly love about her besides the musicality of her poems—because she works quite often with formal structures—are the voices. She has so many different voices that she can write in." Conversation with Al Young

# Gwendolyn Brooks (1917–2000)

Born in Topeka, Kansas, and raised in Chicago, Gwendolyn Brooks would grow up to become the first African-American woman to win the Pulitzer Prize for poetry. Her early work, such as *A Street in Bronzeville* (1945), took for its subject the frustrated hopes of urban blacks; her later work became increasingly concerned with black identity, particularly the female perspective. Brooks is known for her bold use of language, often in new applications of old forms like the sonnet.

**AS YOU READ** Notice the diction Brooks uses to form our sense of these individuals and their lives. Notice also how much gets compressed into and expressed by twenty-four words.

## We Real Cool (1960)

*The Pool Players.*
*Seven at the Golden Shovel.*

We real cool. We
Left school. We

Lurk late. We
Strike straight. We

Sing sin. We
Thin gin. We

Jazz June. We
Die soon.

# Writing from Reading

### Summarize

1 Who is the "We" of the poem? What happens to this "We"?

### Analyze Craft

2 How does the informal diction of the poem affect your sense of the speaker? What does the poet mean by such phrases as "thin gin" and "jazz June"?

### Analyze Voice

3 Advising readers on how to recite this poem aloud, Brooks wrote, "Say the 'We' softly." Why do you think she wanted this word quieter than others? What does it reveal about the confidence of the speaker?

### Synthesize Summary and Analysis

4 Describe the author's attitude toward the pool players.

### Interpret the Poem

5 How is the name of the pool hall meaningful?

6 How does the final line affect (and change) the poem's meaning?

## GENERAL VS. SPECIFIC LANGUAGE

Also at work within any poet's choice of diction is the decision to lean toward language that is specific or language that is more general. **Concrete** diction is language referring to a specific, definite thing. Words like "lawn mower," "beer bottle," and "streetlight" are concrete because they represent actual objects you can perceive with your senses. **Abstract** diction is language referring to a more general or conceptual thing or quality. Because words like "progress," "justice," and "calm" do not refer to things you can see or touch, they are abstractions. Your sense of what constitutes "calm" may be slightly or even radically different from the next person's. An abstraction is, thus, an idea that means something a little different to everyone.

Most poets find that concrete language can help make an abstraction come more vividly to life for a reader. Rather than say, abstractly, "Now that the night becomes calm . . ." poet Richard Jackson writes, "Now that the earth, sky and wind settle into night's still pool. . . ." His line gives us concrete language (earth, sky, wind, pool) in order to more tangibly embody his particular idea of "calm."

"I think . . . that there's a mastery over [language] once you name [something]. So yes, once I have got it down, once I have got it right, it's not as frightening anymore." Conversation with Thomas Lynch

Most poets do not use abstract or concrete diction uniformly. They make their selection word by word, moving back and forth between the general and the particular, in order to best serve their purposes. Note how in Auden's "Funeral Blues," the poet blends the metaphoric and specific with the declarative and abstract statement. By saying "He was my North, my South, my East and West," the poet suggests that his dead friend was a kind of compass, encircling the whole world; later, that the dead man "was" every day of the week and every hour of each day ("My noon, my midnight"), both "talk" and "song."

Here are two celebrated poems that incorporate both concrete and abstract language. In the first, a speaker commemorates his devotion by comparing his love to the elements of a season. In the second, a speaker stands next to his love and looks out onto England's ocean cliffs, lamenting his loss of faith in the world's goodness.

# William Shakespeare (1564–1616)

The truth is we actually know more about the historical figure called William Shakespeare than about most other men or women of the period. He was born in Stratford, England, in April 1564. His father was a successful merchant of the town who later fell on hard times; he attended local schools. In November 1582 he married Anne Hathaway, who was eight years his senior; six months later she bore him a daughter and, in 1585, a pair of twins. In 1597, the playwright purchased New Place, a fine house in Stratford-on-Avon—a sign that he had prospered in his own chosen career. Shakespeare spent most of his working life in the city of London, as one of a troupe of "players" called the Lord Chamberlain's Men. He was an actor in the group, as well as its principal playwright. This was the troupe that in 1599 built the great Globe Theater, which stood on the south bank of the Thames outside city regulations and housed the performances of a number of Shakespeare's plays. Under the patronage of King James I (King of England from 1603 to 1625, following the death of Elizabeth I), the company became known as The King's Men. Shakespeare's poetry includes long narrative poems such as "Venus and Adonis" and "The Rape of Lucrece," and the 154 sonnets. By most counts he also composed some 37 plays. A few fragments of disputed authorship survive, but Shakespeare's pre-eminence as playwright is based on the work produced between 1591 and 1611—twenty years of unmatched productivity and enduring art. A collection of 35 plays appeared posthumously in 1623, published by two other members of The King's Men, John Heminge and Henry Condell. Shakespeare retired to New Place, most likely in 1611, and died on April 23, 1616. Contemporaries wrote often about him—competitively, at first, then respectfully, and after his death, in terms of extravagant praise.

**AS YOU READ** Try to identify Shakespeare's use of general and specific language. Consider why he chose the abstract or concrete language that you find. It's worth mentioning here also that "Thou" was a more common form of address in the early seventeenth century—a singular and intimate form of the plural "You"—than would have been the case for Keats two centuries later.

# Shall I compare thee to a summer's day?

**(1609)**

Shall I compare thee to a summer's day?
Thou art more lovely and more temperate:
Rough winds do shake the darling buds of May,
And summer's lease hath all too short a date;
Sometime too hot the eye of heaven shines,
And often is his gold complexion dimmed,
And every fair from fair sometime declines,
By chance, or nature's changing course, untrimmed:
But thy eternal summer shall not fade,
Nor lose possession of that fair thou ow'st,
Nor shall death brag thou wand'rest in his shade,
When in eternal lines to time thou grow'st.
So long as men can breathe, or eyes can see,
So long lives this, and this gives life to thee.

# Writing from Reading

### Summarize

1 List the ways the speaker's beloved is lovelier than a summer day.

### Analyze Craft

2 Compare the language in the final couplet to the language that precedes it. Where does the diction seem concrete? Where does it seem abstract?

### Analyze Voice

3 How does the praise set the tone for the poem? What is the speaker's attitude in the poem? What does he mean by such phrases as "the darling buds of May" or "the eye of heaven"?

### Synthesize Summary and Analysis

4 Explain how the poet uses comparison in the poem.

### Interpret the Poem

5 What is the "this" the speaker mentions in the final line? How does it "give life"?

6 It could be argued that the closing statement here is boastful (as well as, it turns out, correct). Remember that the poem's subject has to do with life's and beauty's brevity. Is there a kind of consolation in the statement that art lasts?

# Matthew Arnold (1822–1888)

The British poet Matthew Arnold was also a literary critic and a commentator on society and education. Interestingly, Arnold stopped writing poetry after 1850, turning more and more to "public" matters under discussion in England. The poetry he did create was principally about the individual in a modern, industrial world, often marked by a melancholy tone. "Dover Beach," widely read during Arnold's lifetime, survives as his best-known poem, and despite its bleak outlook, it was written while he was on his honeymoon. (The next poem here, "The Dover Bitch," makes ironic use of that fact.) Though influential and much honored, Arnold did not make his living as a writer; instead, he worked first as a secretary, then as an inspector of schools, and wrote his poetry and essays on the side.

**AS YOU READ** Consider how the poet's use of concrete and abstract imagery establishes mood within the poem. What, for instance, does Arnold mean by "the sea of faith," and who might he describe as "ignorant armies" that clash? It might help to know that the "white cliffs of Dover" bear roughly the same relation to the idea of England as the Statue of Liberty or the Grand Canyon do to the idea of the United States. For more on Sophocles and the Aegean Sea, look at chapter 32 on Greek drama.

# Dover Beach (1867)

The sea is calm tonight.
The tide is full, the moon lies fair
Upon the straits; on the French coast the light
Gleams and is gone; the cliffs of England stand,
Glimmering and vast, out in the tranquil bay.
Come to the window, sweet is the night-air!
Only, from the long line of spray
Where the sea meets the moon-blanched land,
Listen! you hear the grating roar
Of pebbles which the waves draw back, and fling,
At their return, up the high strand,
Begin and cease, and then again begin,
With tremulous cadence slow, and bring
The eternal note of sadness in.

Sophocles long ago
Heard it on the Aegean, and it brought
Into his mind the turbid ebb and flow
Of human misery; we
Find also in the sound a thought,
Hearing it by this distant northern sea.

The Sea of Faith
Was once, too, at the full, and round earth's shore
Lay like the folds of a bright girdle furled.
But now I only hear
Its melancholy, long, withdrawing roar,
Retreating, to the breath
Of the night-wind, down the vast edges drear
And naked shingles of the world.

Ah, love, let us be true
To one another! for the world which seems
To lie before us like a land of dreams,
So various, so beautiful, so new,
Hath really neither joy, nor love, nor light,
Nor certitude, nor peace, nor help for pain;
And we are here as on a darkling plain
Swept with confused alarms of struggle and flight,
Where ignorant armies clash by night.

# Writing from Reading

### Summarize

**1** What is meant by "the turbid ebb and flow / Of human misery"?

### Analyze Craft

**2** How does the concrete description of the sea ("long line of spray," "pebbles") compare or contribute to the speaker's more abstract thoughts?

### Analyze Voice

**3** Describe how the speaker's mood changes throughout the poem. What does he want, and when?

### Synthesize Summary and Analysis

**4** Describe how word choice in the poem contributes to the overall mood of the poem.

### Interpret the Poem

**5** What might the poet mean by "the eternal note of sadness" in the first stanza?

**6** Look up the word *elegy.* Is this an elegy? If so, to what?

## ALLUSION

Poets often refer or allude to the work of other poets; it is, after all, a way of maintaining tradition and tipping a cap to the past. Matthew Arnold's nineteenth-century poem refers to "Sophocles long ago" and compares the present world situation to what the Greek dramatist once heard and thought; "The Dover Bitch" refers to Dover Beach in a less serious but similar way. Both poets and poems are allusive; there's an added dimension to and pleasure in the reading when you know what went before.

# Anthony Hecht (1923–2004)

As an undergraduate at Bard College in New York, Anthony Hecht fell in love with poetry, but his pursuit of it was interrupted by World War II, in which he served as an army infantryman. After the war, he studied at Kenyon College in Ohio and at Columbia University, where he received his master's degree. He spent the majority of his teaching career at the University of Rochester in upstate New York. His poetry consciously engages in the broader literary traditions, which means his poems are more formal than those of most of his contemporaries and often include references to other works of literature and art. His second collection of poetry, *The Hard Hours* (1967), won the Pulitzer Prize, and Hecht counted among his many honors the position of Poet Laureate from 1982 to 1984.

**AS YOU READ** Refer to Matthew Arnold's poem "Dover Beach." What has changed in "The Dover Bitch," and what stays the same? As you consider the allusion to Dover Beach in the title, ask yourself why Hecht might have responded to Arnold's poem as he did.

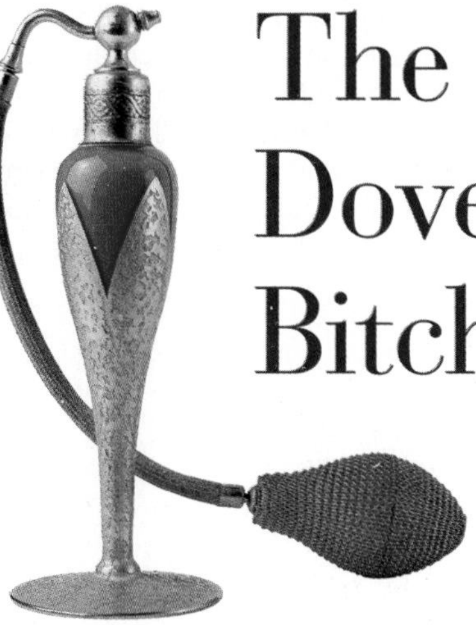

# The Dover Bitch (1967)

*A Criticism of Life: for Andrews Wanning*

So there stood Matthew Arnold and this girl
With the cliffs of England crumbling away behind them,
And he said to her, "Try to be true to me,
And I'll do the same for you, for things are bad
All over, etc., etc."
Well now, I knew this girl. It's true she had read
Sophocles in a fairly good translation
And caught that bitter allusion to the sea,
But all the time he was talking she had in mind
The notion of what his whiskers would feel like
On the back of her neck. She told me later on
That after a while she got to looking out
At the lights across the channel, and really felt sad,
Thinking of all the wine and enormous beds
And blandishments in French and the perfumes.
And then she got really angry. To have been brought
All the way down from London, and then be addressed
As a sort of mournful cosmic last resort
Is really tough on a girl, and she was pretty.
Anyway, she watched him pace the room
And finger his watch-chain and seem to sweat a bit,
And then she said one or two unprintable things.
But you mustn't judge her by that. What I mean to say is,
She's really all right. I still see her once in a while
And she always treats me right. We have a drink
And I give her a good time, and perhaps it's a year
Before I see her again, but there she is,
Running to fat, but dependable as they come.
And sometimes I bring her a bottle of *Nuit d'Amour*.

# Writing from Reading

### Summarize

1 This poem could be looked at as a variation of "Dover Beach" by Matthew Arnold. In your own words, write a few sentences in prose that summarize what happens in each poem.

### Analyze Craft

2 Take your summary of the two poems and look at the differences between your prose language, Hecht's humorous diction, and Arnold's high diction. Point to the differences.

### Analyze Voice

3 Does the tone of this poem change as it proceeds? (*Nuit d'Amour*, which means "Night of Love," is a cheap perfume.)

### Synthesize Summary and Analysis

4 To what extent does this poem echo Arnold's "Dover Beach," and to what extent does it merely parody (comically imitate) it?

### Interpret the Poem

5 How is this poem "a criticism of life," as the dedication states?

Sometimes allusiveness can be confined to a title. Philip Larkin's grim plaint about the approaching (and unavoidable) reality of death uses no metaphorical language and seems in opposition to the fancy titular word *aubade* (traditionally associated with a poem or song about lovers parting at dawn). The poet announces he's up before dawn, "waking at four to soundless dark," and the bulk of what follows describes what he fears. As "slowly light strengthens, and the room takes shape," he speaks without adornment—with none of the romantic associations of a "Dawn Song"—about the dark to come.

# Philip Larkin (1922–1985)

Philip Larkin, perhaps the most influential British poet since World War II, bears a literary kinship to his predecessor Thomas Hardy (see Hardy's "The Convergence of the Twain" in chapter 19 and "The Darkling Thrush" in the Anthology of Poems for Further Reading): both are marked by a pessimistic outlook expressed in unsentimental lines that present the mundane details of daily life. Also like Hardy, Larkin wrote novels in addition to his poetry—*Jill* (1946) and *A Girl in Winter* (1947). Larkin is chiefly remembered for his verse, however, and he was part of a group of poets called "The Movement," who embraced poetry that confronted the current day head-on. Larkin, who made his career as a librarian, was well appreciated in his lifetime; collections like *The Less Deceived* (1955) and *High Windows* (1974) cemented his reputation and led to his being offered the position of Poet Laureate—an honor he refused because of the public attention such a post would bring.

**AS YOU READ** **Ask yourself why this poem is written in the present tense, and if the speaker's feelings change as the lines proceed. Look for both hopelessness and any signs of hope.**

## Aubade (1980)

I work all day, and get half drunk at night.
Waking at four to soundless dark, I stare.
In time the curtain-edges will grow light.
Till then I see what's really always there:
Unresting death, a whole day nearer now,
Making all thought impossible but how
And where and when I shall myself die.
Arid interrogation: yet the dread
Of dying, and being dead,
Flashes afresh to hold and horrify.

The mind blanks at the glare. Not in remorse
—The good not used, the love not given, time
Torn off unused—nor wretchedly because
An only life can take so long to climb
Clear of its wrong beginnings, and may never:
But at the total emptiness forever,
The sure extinction that we travel to
And shall be lost in always. Not to be here,
Not to be anywhere,
And soon; nothing more terrible, nothing more true.

This is a special way of being afraid
No trick dispels. Religion used to try,
That vast moth-eaten musical brocade
Created to pretend we never die,
And specious stuff that says *No rational being*
*Can fear a thing it cannot feel,* not seeing
that this is what we fear—no sight, no sound,
No touch or taste or smell, nothing to think with,
Nothing to love or link with,
The anesthetic from which none come round.

And so it stays just on the edge of vision,
A small unfocused blur, a standing chill
That slows each impulse down to indecision.
Most things may never happen: this one will,
And realization of it rages out
In furnace-fear when we are caught without
People or drink. Courage is no good:
It means not scaring others. Being brave
Lets no one off the grave.
Death is no different whined at than withstood.

Slowly light strengthens, and the room takes shape.
It stands plain as a wardrobe, what we know,
Have always known, know that we can't escape
Yet can't accept. One side will have to go.
Meanwhile telephones crouch, getting ready to ring
In locked-up offices, and all the uncaring
Intricate rented world begins to rouse.
The sky is white as clay, with no sun.
Work has to be done.
Postmen like doctors go from house to house.

# Writing from Reading

## Summarize

1 In a dictionary or literature glossary, look up the word *aubade.* How does this poem resemble and/or differ from the definition?

## Analyze Craft

2 Would you characterize this poem's diction as formal, middle, or informal? What word choices inform your answer?

3 Describe the kind of word choice you observe in the second-to-last line of each stanza.

## Analyze Voice

4 What is the speaker's attitude toward his subject matter? What mood pervades the poem, and where does the poet insist on that mood? What emotions does it represent?

## Synthesize Summary and Analysis

5 How is the title of the poem reflected in the mood of the poem? What words reinforce this mood?

## Interpret the Poem

6 What do you think "that vast moth-eaten musical brocade" and "the uncaring intricate rented world" mean?

7 To what is the poet referring when he writes "It stands plain as a wardrobe, what we know"?

## DENOTATION AND CONNOTATION

Poets choose language based not only on what their diction as a whole will evoke but also on the associations offered by individual words. Selecting language for this additional purpose further distinguishes poetry from non-literary writing. Poets bring to their work a complicated and varied set of perceptions tied to particular word meanings. When you read the instructions in a recipe, for instance, the words hold true to their most apparent, literal meanings. The honey you add to a cookie recipe doesn't *imply* anything or suggest some veiled association. This wouldn't necessarily be the case, however, if you saw the word *honey* in a poem.

"I love it when someone says something, and someone else says another thing and that's all there is. And what happens, happens in between." Conversation with Marie Howe

Most words contain both denotation and connotation. Denotation is the most direct and specific meaning of a word. In its denotative meaning, honey is a sugary, sticky liquid substance produced by bees from flower nectar. The same word also carries connotation, meanings and implications that are suggested beyond a word's literal definition. These associations come from the history of a word's past usage, the circumstances in which it has been spoken and understood. By connotation, honey suggests sweetness and richness, and perhaps something highly prized. Or take the word *snake*. In its simplest dictionary definition, it's a long, legless reptile. However, the connotations expressed by "snake" might include associations of sneakiness, danger, or even evil.

We process denotation and connotation constantly in our lives. From the world of marketing and advertising, products and services are offered to us with careful attention paid to the wider, connotative possibilities of language. We are not just sold products themselves; we are also sold the associations they communicate. A salesperson might suggest a more "affordable" item rather than calling it "cheap" because of the negative connotations of that latter word. An "assisted living community" sounds more welcoming and pleasant than "nursing home" because words like "assist," "living," and "community" connote a much more positive and supportive atmosphere than the worrisome medical implications of "nursing." In the business world, "downsizing" implies, through connotation, associations of efficiency and productivity. For some managers, this word is preferable to terms like "laying off" or "firing," which suggest a bleaker outcome.

Connotation is crucial in poetry because it enriches words' meanings; it widens their perceived associations. In a writing genre where language is compact and economical, connotative meaning further extends a poem's potential scope and meaning.

"Most things are not going to be, as we know, new; but the way they are phrased, the way they are positioned in context might make us and should make us re-engage our lives." Conversation with Stephen Dunn

In the following two poems, notice how the speakers' word choice suggests a kind of transformation. In "The Fish," Elizabeth Bishop gives us a speaker intently observing a fish she has just caught. The poem shows us the intensity and specificity of her observation, and the meditation such observation inspires. Note the kind of image-heavy language Bishop uses throughout the poem to describe her subject. She introduces the animal as a "grunting . . . battered" creature, but by the end of the poem, the speaker has come to see the fish as resilient and strong. For James Wright's "A Blessing," a phrase like "I would like to hold the slenderer one in my arms" connotes a kind of reverence bordering on love. This change in the speaker in both poems is illustrated, in part, by word choice and its connotations.

# Elizabeth Bishop (1911–1979)

An interest in geography and exploration, a tendency toward quiet understatement, and an unflinching sense of honesty make Elizabeth Bishop a unique and much-celebrated poet, a recipient of both the Pulitzer Prize and the National Book Award. She never saw her parents after the age of five—her father had died when she was an infant and her mother was permanently institutionalized—and she moved from Massachusetts to Nova Scotia, then back to Massachusetts while still a child. Later in life, she settled in Brazil for nearly two decades before moving back to the States and taking a professorship at Harvard. Her work includes *North & South—A Cold Spring* (1955), *Questions of Travel* (1965), *The Complete Poems* (published in 1969 although she continued to publish poetry after that), and her more autobiographical work *Geography III* (1976).

**AS YOU READ** Focus on Bishop's diction, particularly her descriptive language. Circle or make note of adjectives in the poem that describe the fish.

## The Fish (1946)

I caught a tremendous fish
and held him beside the boat
half out of water, with my hook
fast in a corner of its mouth.
He didn't fight.
He hadn't fought at all.
He hung a grunting weight,
battered and venerable
and homely. Here and there
his brown skin hung in strips
like ancient wallpaper,
and its pattern of darker brown
was like wallpaper:
shapes like full-blown roses
stained and lost through age.
He was speckled with barnacles,
fine rosettes of lime,
and infested
with tiny white sea-lice,
and underneath two or three
rags of green weed hung down.
While his gills were breathing in

the terrible oxygen
—the frightening gills,
fresh and crisp with blood,
that can cut so badly—
I thought of the coarse white flesh
packed in like feathers,
the big bones and the little bones,
the dramatic reds and blacks
of his shiny entrails,
and the pink swim-bladder
like a big peony.
I looked into his eyes
which were far larger than mine
but shallower, and yellowed,
the irises backed and packed
with tarnished tinfoil
seen through the lenses
of old scratched isinglass.
They shifted a little, but not
to return my stare.
—It was more like the tipping
of an object toward the light.
I admired his sullen face,
the mechanism of his jaw,
and then I saw
that from his lower lip
—if you could call it a lip—
grim, wet, and weaponlike,
hung five old pieces of fish-line,
or four and a wire leader
with the swivel still attached,
with all their five big hooks
grown firmly in his mouth.
A green line, frayed at the end
where he broke it, two heavier lines,
and a fine black thread
still crimped from the strain and snap
when it broke and he got away.
Like medals with their ribbons
frayed and wavering,
a five-haired beard of wisdom
trailing from his aching jaw.
I stared and stared
and victory filled up
the little rented boat,
from the pool of bilge
where oil had spread a rainbow
around the rusted engine
to the bailer rusted orange,
the sun-cracked thwarts,
the oarlocks on their strings,
the gunnels—until everything
was rainbow, rainbow, rainbow!
And I let the fish go.

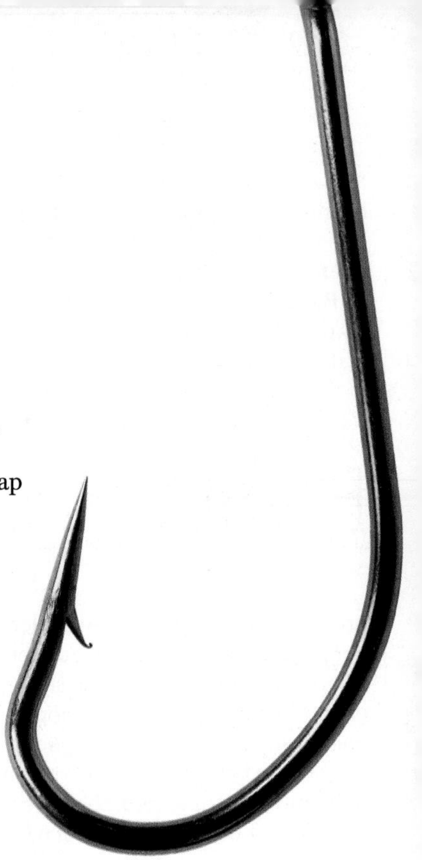

# Writing from Reading

### Summarize

1 In a few sentences, write the facts of what has happened in this poem.

### Analyze Craft

2 How does Bishop describe the fish? What connotations do these adjectives express?

### Analyze Voice

3 In a dictionary, look up the word *terrible,* which Bishop uses in line 23. In what ways does it differ from—or reinforce—the word *tremendous* in line 1? How do its meanings—primary and secondary—reflect the speaker's attitude toward the fish?

### Synthesize Summary and Analysis

4 How does the speaker's attitude change through the poem?

5 Contrast the basic denotative title ("The Fish") with the language Bishop uses to describe the creature. Why do you think she uses such a simple designation?

### Interpret the Poem

6 Explore why the speaker in the poem lets the fish go.

# James Wright (1927–1980)

James Wright was born into a working-class family in the steel-making town of Martin's Ferry, Ohio. He began writing poetry in high school and went on to earn degrees at Kenyon College, the University of Vienna, and the University of Washington. Wright won the Yale Series of Younger Poets award in 1957 with his collection of poems *The Green Wall.* Stylistically, in the 1960s Wright moved from a formal style to a more open form of verse. His subject matter often focused on issues of social concern, particularly the divide between the working and middle classes. In 1971 he won a Pulitzer Prize for his *Collected Poems.* Wright's life was cut short at age fifty-two by cancer; in 2004 his son, Franz Wright, won the Pulitzer Prize for Poetry for his book *Walking to Martha's Vineyard.*

**AS YOU READ** Consider how nature relates to the animal world and how two kinds of animals—pony and poet—relate to each other. It might also be useful to consult the interview with Robert Hass, who talks of another of Wright's works, "Autumn Begins in Martin's Ferry, Ohio," in chapter 25.

## A Blessing (1963)

Just off the highway to Rochester, Minnesota,
Twilight bounds softly forth on the grass.
And the eyes of those two Indian ponies
Darken with kindness.
They have come gladly out of the willows
To welcome my friend and me.
We step over the barbed wire into the pasture
Where they have been grazing all day, alone.
They ripple tensely, they can hardly contain their happiness
That we have come.
They bow shyly as wet swans. They love each other.
There is no loneliness like theirs.
At home once more,
They begin munching the young tufts of spring in the darkness.
I would like to hold the slenderer one in my arms,
For she has walked over to me
And nuzzled my left hand.
She is black and white,
Her mane falls wild on her forehead,
And the light breeze moves me to caress her long ear
That is delicate as the skin over a girl's wrist.
Suddenly I realize
That if I stepped out of my body I would break
Into blossom.

# Writing from Reading

### Summarize

1 The speaker in this poem is describing a natural setting. Describe that setting in your own words.

### Analyze Craft

2 Characterize the language of the poem. How does Wright describe nature? Why do you think Wright chooses this kind of language?

### Analyze Voice

3 How specific is the speaker about the poem's setting? How does the sense of place change as the poem progresses?

### Synthesize Summary and Analysis

4 How does the poem prepare the reader for the final three lines?

### Interpret the Poem

5 What is the "blessing" in the poem? What realization does the speaker arrive at, and when?

## WORD ORDER

In committing their ideas to the page, poets must do more than consider just the formality, denotations, and connotations of their speech. They must also decide how to arrange words within the lines of a poem. **Syntax** is this arrangement, the way that words and phrases combine to form sentences and make meaning. Syntax can refer to individual word placement and order, as well as the overall length and shape of a sentence. At its simplest, English grammar is grounded in word order that follows the sequence of *subject* + *verb* + *object*, as in a basic statement like "The man ate a hamburger." Changing the order of such a sentence ("A hamburger ate the man") will dramatically alter its implications.

"All the time, from when I can remember, from when I was a child, I thought obsessively about the sounds of words—the cad*ences* of *sentences*, cad*ence* of *sentence ess*. Take a word at random, 'carpet.' . . . What if you turn it inside out: 'predicate' or 'particle'? That's what my mind does, compulsively. And I can't remember a time in my life when I didn't do it." Conversation with Robert Pinsky

So, word order is another potentially powerful tool for the fashioning of meaning. Take a famous example from Robert Frost. He begins "Stopping by Woods on a Snowy Evening" with a sentence whose syntax may seem strange: "Whose woods these are I think I know." A reader might expect the speaker to say, "I think I know whose woods these are." Frost, however, sets up an **inversion,** a reversal of expected or traditional word order. Partially this choice aids the poem's sounds, its rhyme and meter.

But the unexpected syntax additionally allows Frost some extra nuance of meaning. *Ending* the line with "I think I know" instead of *opening* with it contributes to the poem's sense of uncertainty—as well as to a gathering certainty, because the speaker moves from the half-convinced "think" to the decisive "know."

> "That's another aspect of poetry. I just love to say [the words]. I love to have the words in my mouth. I love those cadences . . . the . . . music, sound, and . . . rather exotic diction . . . speaking quite directly to my life and my concerns."
>
> Conversation with Stephen Dunn

## Robert Frost (1874–1963)

For a brief biography of Robert Frost, see the Casebook on American Plain Style, chapter 27.

**AS YOU READ** Ask yourself what this poem would sound and look like if it didn't rhyme, and look for the complex simplicities of the structure here.

**TIP**

**FOR INTERACTIVE READING . . .** Underline or list the examples of repetition in the poem.

# Stopping by Woods on a Snowy Evening (1923)

Whose woods these are I think I know.
His house is in the village though;
He will not see me stopping here
To watch his woods fill up with snow.

My little horse must think it queer
To stop without a farmhouse near
Between the woods and frozen lake
The darkest evening of the year.

He gives his harness bells a shake
To ask if there is some mistake.
The only other sound's the sweep
Of easy wind and downy flake.

The woods are lovely, dark and deep,
But I have promises to keep,
And miles to go before I sleep,
And miles to go before I sleep.

# Writing from Reading

### Summarize

**1** Describe the situation and the landscape, the weather and the time of day.

**2** To whom is the speaker in the poem speaking?

### Analyze Craft

**3** Why do you think Frost inverts word order in the first line of the poem? Are there additional examples of this technique, and if not, why not?

**4** The title word is "Stopping"—a gerund—but the speaker and the horse have already stopped. What does this suggest about this particular journey? Has it, for example, happened before and might it happen again?

### Analyze Voice

**5** How would you describe the mood conveyed in the poem? What words has Frost chosen to evoke this mood, and what does the word *queer* suggest?

**6** How does the use of informal diction establish a sense of the speaker's attitude?

### Synthesize Summary and Analysis

**7** There's not a single tri-syllabic (three-syllable) word in the four stanzas. How does this support the casual/conversational feel of the whole?

**8** Discuss the "music" in this poem—in terms of both the imagery of the harness bells and the actual rhyme scheme.

### Interpret the Poem

**9** Why do you think Frost decides to attribute thoughts to the horse, and what does this suggest about the "natural" world?

**10** What "promises" do you think the speaker might be bound to keep? Is there a suggestion that sleep equals death?

In each of the examples that follow, keep an eye (and ear) out for word order, the particular sequence of words—what's predictable and what's surprising in the poets' choices. Punctuation, too, can change the way a poem *sounds* as well as how it *looks;* consider, for example, the way that the formality of diction in Wallace Stevens' peom contrasts with the lowercase (uncapitalized) language of Lucille Clifton. Pay particular attention to the way a change of emphasis suggests a change of tone.

# Wallace Stevens (1879–1955)

Wallace Stevens's conventional life seems at odds with the stunning imagery and unexpected moves of his poetry. He spent years struggling in New York, eventually bowing to his father's disapproval of the literary life and going late to law school. Ultimately, he settled in Hartford, Connecticut, and worked as an executive at the Hartford Accident and Indemnity Company for nearly forty years. He published in literary journals and corresponded with poets such as William Carlos Williams but largely led a life apart from literary circles. Stevens's business life restricted his writing to evenings and summers, but despite this, he cemented his reputation as one of the most important twentieth-century American poets with collections including *Harmonium* (1923, 1931), *Ideas of Order* (1935), *The Man with the Blue Guitar* (1937), and *The Auroras of Autumn* (1950).

**AS YOU READ** Underline or make note of examples of unusual word order, and imagine the poem if it had been written without these constructions.

# The Emperor of Ice-Cream

(1923)

Call the roller of big cigars,
The muscular one, and bid him whip
In kitchen cups concupiscent curds.
Let the wenches dawdle in such dress
As they are used to wear, and let the boys
Bring flowers in last month's newspapers.
Let be be finale of seem.
The only emperor is the emperor of ice-cream.

Take from the dresser of deal,
Lacking the three glass knobs, that sheet
On which she embroidered fantails once
And spread it so as to cover her face.
If her horny feet protrude, they come
To show how cold she is, and dumb.
Let the lamp affix its beam.
The only emperor is the emperor of ice-cream.

# Writing from Reading

## Summarize

1 Who are the various people assembled in this poem? Why are they there together? What is the occasion in this poem?

2 Try to put "Let be be finale of seem" in your own words.

3 What do you think is being described in the lines "And spread it so as to cover her face. / If her horny feet protrude, they come / To show how cold she is, and dumb"?

4 Rewrite the poem in plain English.

## Analyze Craft

5 How would you describe Stevens's syntax (the way the words are arranged) throughout the poem? Does its style serve a point or purpose?

## Analyze Voice

6 What is the mood of the poem? How does the title contribute to this mood? How does word order? Word choice? (Why, for example, might he have chosen words like "concupiscent" and "wenches"?) Be specific.

## Synthesize Summary and Analysis

7 What is the function of humor in this poem? How do subject, word choice, and word order contribute to the humor in the poem?

8 Stevens puts words in unusual order. What is the effect of this order on the poem's tone? How would the poem be different if the words were put in more ordinary sequence? What do you gain? What do you lose?

## Interpret the Poem

9 What does ice cream represent to the speaker in the poem?

10 Who is the emperor of ice cream?

# Lucille Clifton (b. 1936)

Born in Depew, New York, Lucille Clifton is the author of nine collections of poetry as well as a prolific author of children's books. In a plainspoken manner, Clifton writes about her personal history as a woman and African American, at times using her own family's genealogy to give voice to common issues of identity. Her poems reflect a pared-down style, bypassing conventional forms of capitalization, punctuation, and line length. Currently she is Distinguished Professor of the Humanities at St. Mary's College in Maryland, a post she has held since 1991. A former poet laureate of the state of Maryland, in 2007 Clifton became the first black woman to win the Lilly Poetry Prize for lifetime achievement in poetry.

**AS YOU READ** Consider how Clifton's use or lack of use of capitalization and punctuation affects your sense of the poet's voice.

## Homage to my hips (1991)

these hips are big hips
they need space to
move around in.
they don't fit into little
petty places, these hips
are free hips.
they don't like to be held back.
these hips have never been enslaved,
they go where they want to go
they do what they want to do.
these hips are mighty hips.
these hips are magic hips.
i have known them
to put a spell on a man and
spin him like a top!

# Writing from Reading

### Summarize

1 Describe what the poem says hips need.

2 Describe what hips do.

3 What does it mean that hips can "put a spell on a man"?

### Analyze Craft

4 Discuss the use of words like "free," "enslaved," "mighty," and "magic." What connotative meanings do these words evoke? How do they contribute to the poem's central meaning?

### Analyze Voice

5 How does the speaker's tone create a sense of defiance alongside the celebration in this poem? Note how the title word "Homage" affects everything that follows.

### Synthesize Summary and Analysis

6 What aspects of word choice and syntax contribute to the poem's humor?

### Interpret the Poem

7 What do hips represent to the speaker?

# Walt Whitman (1819–1892)

It is almost impossible to overestimate Walt Whitman's influence on American poetry, and indeed on the American spirit. Born on Long Island, New York, Whitman held a variety of jobs including office clerk, journalist, teacher, printer, and carpenter. He created one work of poetry, *Leaves of Grass,* first published in 1855; with each subsequent edition, Whitman added more poems, eventually titling each group of poems, among them the Calamus poems, Children of Adam, and Drum Taps. Known for its freedom of line, optimism, and expansiveness, his poetry celebrates many occupations and classes of people, thus making him a poet inextricably linked to the spirit of democracy and the broad frontier of the West (even though he lived most of his life on the East Coast). His poetry is also marked by an admiration of physicality and the body, which made his work seem scandalous to many nineteenth-century Americans. His darkest poems are those he wrote during the Civil War and after the death of his hero, Abraham Lincoln. Whitman served as a nurse for the Union troops, but his expansive compassion extends to all soldiers, regardless of their allegiance. Perhaps his greatest legacy to future poets was his unconventional abandoning of established poetic form—Whitman wrote in long, confident lines—and his free use of subject matter that made all aspects of life fair game for inclusion.

**AS YOU READ** Notice how the speaker starts by addressing the tide and the clouds; next he addresses "crowds of men and women" as well as the voyagers of the future ("years hence"). If Marie Howe's "What the Living Do" is a "private" poem, and Whitman's is a "public" one, look at the difference here between the "I"s.

# Crossing Brooklyn Ferry (1891–1892)

1

Flood-tide below me! I see you face to face!
Clouds of the west—sun there half an hour high—I see you also face to face.
Crowds of men and women attired in the usual costumes, how curious you are to me!
On the ferry-boats the hundreds and hundreds that cross, returning home, are more curious to me than you suppose,
And you that shall cross from shore to shore years hence are more to me, and more in my meditations, than you might suppose.

2

The impalpable sustenance of me from all things at all hours of the day,
The simple, compact, well-join'd scheme, myself disintegrated, every one disintegrated yet part of the scheme,
The similitudes of the past and those of the future,
The glories strung like beads on my smallest sights and hearings, on the walk in the street and the passage over the river,
The current rushing so swiftly and swimming with me far away,
The others that are to follow me, the ties between me and them,
The certainty of others, the life, love, sight, hearing of others.

Others will enter the gates of the ferry and cross from shore to shore,
Others will watch the run of the flood-tide,
Others will see the shipping of Manhattan north and west, and the heights of Brooklyn to the south and east,

Others will see the islands large and small;
Fifty years hence, others will see them as they cross, the sun half an hour high,
A hundred years hence, or ever so many hundred years hence, others will see them,
Will enjoy the sunset, the pouring-in of the flood-tide, the falling-back to the sea of the ebb-tide.

3

It avails not, time nor place—distance avails not,
I am with you, you men and women of a generation, or ever so many generations hence,
Just as you feel when you look on the river and sky, so I felt,
Just as any of you is one of a living crowd, I was one of a crowd,
Just as you are refresh'd by the gladness of the river and the bright flow, I was refresh'd,
Just as you stand and lean on the rail, yet hurry with the swift current, I stood yet was hurried,
Just as you look on the numberless masts of ships and the thick-stemm'd pipes of steamboats, I look'd.

I too many and many a time cross'd the river of old,
Watched the Twelfth-month sea-gulls, saw them high in the air floating with motionless wings, oscillating their bodies,
Saw how the glistening yellow lit up parts of their bodies and left the rest in strong shadow,
Saw the slow-wheeling circles and the gradual edging toward the south,
Saw the reflection of the summer sky in the water,
Had my eyes dazzled by the shimmering track of beams,
Look'd at the fine centrifugal spokes of light round the shape of my head in the sunlit water,
Look'd on the haze on the hills southward and south-westward,
Look'd on the vapor as it flew in fleeces tinged with violet,
Look'd toward the lower bay to notice the vessels arriving,
Saw their approach, saw aboard those that were near me,
Saw the white sails of schooners and sloops, saw the ships at anchor,
The sailors at work in the rigging or out astride the spars,
The round masts, the swinging motion of the hulls, the slender serpentine pennants,
The large and small steamers in motion, the pilots in their pilot-houses,
The white wake left by the passage, the quick tremulous whirl of the wheels,
The flags of all nations, the falling of them at sunset,
The scallop-edged waves in the twilight, the ladled cups, the frolicsome crests and glistening,
The stretch afar growing dimmer and dimmer, the gray walls of the granite storehouses by the docks,

On the river the shadowy group, the big steam-tug closely flank'd on each side
by the barges, the hay-boat, the belated lighter,
On the neighboring shore the fires from the foundry chimneys burning high
and glaringly into the night,
Casting their flicker of black contrasted with wild red and yellow light over
the tops of houses, and down into the clefts of streets.

4

These and all else were to me the same as they are to you,
I loved well those cities, loved well the stately and rapid river,
The men and women I saw were all near to me,
Others the same—others who look back on me because I look'd forward to them,
(The time will come, though I stop here to-day and to-night.)

5

What is it then between us?
What is the count of the scores or hundreds of years between us?

Whatever it is, it avails not—distance avails not, and place avails not,
I too lived, Brooklyn of ample hills was mine,
I too walk'd the streets of Manhattan island, and bathed in the waters
around it,
I too felt the curious abrupt questionings stir within me,
In the day among crowds of people sometimes they came upon me,
In my walks home late at night or as I lay in my bed they came upon me,
I too had been struck from the float forever held in solution,
I too had receiv'd identity by my body,
That I was I knew was of my body, and what I should be I knew I should be
of my body.

6

It is not upon you alone the dark patches fall,
The dark threw its patches down upon me also,
The best I had done seem'd to me blank and suspicious,
My great thoughts as I supposed them, were they not in reality meagre?
Nor is it you alone who know what it is to be evil,
I am he who knew what it was to be evil,
I too knitted the old knot of contrariety,
Blabb'd, blush'd, resented, lied, stole, grudg'd,
Had guile, anger, lust, hot wishes I dared not speak,
Was wayward, vain, greedy, shallow, sly, cowardly, malignant,
The wolf, the snake, the hog, not wanting in me,
The cheating look, the frivolous word, the adulterous wish, not wanting,
Refusals, hates, postponements, meanness, laziness, none of these wanting,
Was one with the rest, the days and haps of the rest,
Was call'd by my nighest name by clear loud voices of young men as they saw
me approaching or passing,
Felt their arms on my neck as I stood, or the negligent leaning of their flesh
against me as I sat,
Saw many I loved in the street or ferry-boat or public assembly, yet never told
them a word,
Lived the same life with the rest, the same old laughing, gnawing, sleeping,
Play'd the part that still looks back on the actor or actress,
The same old role, the role that is what we make it, as great as we like,
Or as small as we like, or both great and small.

7
Closer yet I approach you,
What thought you have of me now, I had as much of you—I laid in my stores in advance,
I consider'd long and seriously of you before you were born.

Who was to know what should come home to me?
Who knows but I am enjoying this?
Who knows, for all the distance, but I am as good as looking at you now, for all you cannot see me?

8
Ah, what can ever be more stately and admirable to me than mast-hemm'd Manhattan?
River and sunset and scallop-edg'd waves of flood-tide?
The sea-gulls oscillating their bodies, the hay-boat in the twilight, and the belated lighter?
What gods can exceed these that clasp me by the hand, and with voices I love call me promptly and loudly by my nighest name as I approach?
What is more subtle than this which ties me to the woman or man that looks in my face?
Which fuses me into you now, and pours my meaning into you?

We understand then do we not?
What I promis'd without mentioning it, have you not accepted?
What the study could not teach—what the preaching could not accomplish is accomplish'd, is it not?

9
Flow on, river! flow with the flood-tide, and ebb with the ebb-tide!
Frolic on, crested and scallop-edg'd waves!
Gorgeous clouds of the sunset! drench with your splendor me, or the men and women generations after me!
Cross from shore to shore, countless crowds of passengers!
Stand up, tall masts of Mannahatta! stand up, beautiful hills of Brooklyn!
Throb, baffled and curious brain! throw out questions and answers!
Suspend here and everywhere, eternal float of solution!
Gaze, loving and thirsting eyes, in the house or street or public assembly!
Sound out, voices of young men! loudly and musically call me by my nighest name!
Live, old life! play the part that looks back on the actor or actress!
Play the old role, the role that is great or small according as one makes it!
Consider, you who peruse me, whether I may not in unknown ways be looking upon you;

Be firm, rail over the river, to support those who lean idly, yet haste with the hasting current;
Fly on, sea-birds! fly sideways, or wheel in large circles high in the air;
Receive the summer sky, you water, and faithfully hold it till all downcast eyes have time to take it from you!
Diverge, fine spokes of light, from the shape of my head, or any one's head, in the sunlit water!
Come on, ships from the lower bay! pass up or down, white-sail'd schooners, sloops, lighters!
Flaunt away, flags of all nations! be duly lower'd at sunset!
Burn high your fires, foundry chimneys! cast black shadows at nightfall! cast red and yellow light over the tops of the houses!
Appearances, now or henceforth, indicate what you are,
You necessary film, continue to envelop the soul,
About my body for me, and your body for you, be hung our divinest aromas,
Thrive, cities—bring your freight, bring your shows, ample and sufficient rivers,
Expand, being than which none else is perhaps more spiritual,
Keep your places, objects than which none else is more lasting.

You have waited, you always wait, you dumb, beautiful ministers,
We receive you with free sense at last, and are insatiate hence forward,
Not you any more shall be able to foil us, or withhold yourselves from us,
We use you, and do not cast you aside—we plant you permanently within us,
We fathom you not—we love you—there is perfection in you also,
You furnish your parts toward eternity,
Great or small, you furnish your parts toward the soul.

# Writing from Reading

## Summarize

1 What is your first impression of this poem? What is the speaker doing?

2 In one paragraph, recount what happens here.

## Analyze Craft

3 Find descriptions that seem characteristic of the poem's diction. How would you characterize them? How does the language differ from other poets you've read?

## Analyze Voice

4 Describe your sense of the speaker. What is his tone? What is important to him and how can you tell?

5 How does Whitman establish a relationship between his poetic voice and the reader? What is this relationship like?

## Synthesize Summary and Analysis

6 Do the long lines and the diction contribute to the tone of the poem? Explain how they do or do not reinforce the subject of the poem.

## Interpret the Poem

7 What do you think Whitman means by the following lines?

"Flow on, river! flow with the flood-tide,
and ebb with the ebb-tide!
Frolic on, crested and scallop-edg'd
waves!
Gorgeous clouds of the sunset! drench
with your splendor me, or the men
and women generations after me!"

8 Can you say that the poem demonstrates a particularly American way of seeing the world? Why?

# Reading for Words

When reading for words, ask yourself what kind of diction the poet has used and how the poet's diction helps to convey a poem's style.

| | | |
|---|---|---|
| **Formal Diction** | Lofty, ceremonial, and explicitly serious word choice in poetry | EXAMPLE "Thou still unravished bride of quietness" |
| **Middle Diction** | A blend of "common" speech and "elevated" diction | EXAMPLE "Let aeroplanes circle moaning overhead" |
| **Informal Diction** | Conversational, plainspoken language; often makes use of slang, contractions, and mainstream expressions | EXAMPLE "Johnny, the kitchen sink has been clogged for days" |
| **Are there specialized uses of language in a poem?** | *Dialect:* A style of language spoken by and associated with a particular region or group of people<br>*Colloquial Language:* Familiar, conversational language | EXAMPLE "We real cool"<br>EXAMPLE "We / Thin gin. We / Jazz June." |
| **How does the writer mix concrete and abstract words?** | *Concrete:* Specific, physical language describing something perceivable to the senses<br>*Abstract:* Vocabulary referring to something conceptual, not physically material | EXAMPLE "Rough winds do shake the darling buds of May"<br>EXAMPLE "The sea of faith . . ." |
| **What connotations do the words evoke beyond their denotations?** | *Denotation:* The literal, dictionary definition of a word<br>*Connotation:* The non-literal associations and impressions a word conveys to a reader. | EXAMPLE "Snake: A long, legless reptile"<br>EXAMPLE "The wolf, the snake, the hog, not wanting in me.<br>The cheating look, the frivolous word, the adulterous wish, not wanting." |

| | | |
|---|---|---|
| **How does the order of the words, the punctuation, and the syntax (the rhythm and shape of the sentence) enhance the meaning of the poem?** | *Inversion:* A change in the normal, expected order of words | EXAMPLE "Whose woods these are I think I know" versus "I think I know whose woods these are." |

# Writing about Words

1. Write an analysis of the spiritual conflicts imagined in Stevens's "The Emperor of Ice-Cream."
2. Compare attitudes toward religion and/or spirituality between any of the following poems: Arnold's "Dover Beach," Hecht's "The Dover Bitch," Stevens's "The Emperor of Ice-Cream," and Wright's "A Blessing."
3. Both Stevens's "The Emperor of Ice-Cream" and Larkin's "Aubade" deal with the theme of death and mortality. Contrast the tone and meaning by describing the differences between the two poets' language choices. If you wish, you can add Auden's "Funeral Blues" to this mix.
4. Address similarities and differences between tone and language in Brooks's "We Real Cool" and Clifton's "Homage to my hips."
5. Compare the connotations in word choices associated with Robert Frost's horse and speaker in "Stopping by Woods on a Snowy Evening" to those in James Wright's "A Blessing."

# For Review and Further Study

## Wanda Coleman (b. 1946)

### The ISM (1983)

tired i count the ways in which it determines my life
permeates everything. it's in the air
lives next door to me in stares of neighbors
meets me each day in the office. its music comes out the radio
drives beside me in my car. strolls along with me
down supermarket aisles
it's on television
and in the streets even when my walk is casual/undefined
it's overhead flashing lights
i find it in my mouth
*when i would speak of other things*

**Questions for Interactive Reading and Writing**

1. What does this title suggest, and why does the poet declare it "permeates everything"?
1. Why is there a slash between the words "casual" and "undefined"?
2. Why is the last line italicized?
3. Would you call this poem an example of high, mid-level, or informal diction? Why?

## Billy Collins (b. 1941)

### The Names (2002)

Yesterday, I lay awake in the palm of the night.
A fine rain stole in, unhelped by any breeze,
And when I saw the silver glaze on the windows,
I started with A, with Ackerman, as it happened,
Then Baxter and Calabro,
Davis and Eberling, names falling into place
As droplets fell through the dark.

Names printed on the ceiling of the night.
Names slipping around a watery bend.
Twenty-six willows on the banks of a stream.

In the morning, I walked out barefoot
Among thousands of flowers
Heavy with dew like the eyes of tears,
And each had a name—
Fiori inscribed on a yellow petal
Then Gonzalez and Han, Ishikawa and Jenkins.

Names written in the air
And stitched into the cloth of the day.
A name under a photograph taped to a mailbox.
Monogram on a torn shirt,
I see you spelled out on storefront windows
And on the bright unfurled awnings of this city.
I say the syllables as I turn a corner—
Kelly and Lee,
Medina, Nardella, and O'Connor.

When I peer into the woods,
I see a thick tangle where letters are hidden
As in a puzzle concocted for children.
Parker and Quigley in the twigs of an ash,
Rizzo, Schubert, Torres, and Upton,
Secrets in the boughs of an ancient maple.

Names written in the pale sky.
Names rising in the updraft amid buildings.
Names silent in stone
Or cried out behind a door.
Names blown over the earth and out to sea.

In the evening—weakening light, the last swallows.
A boy on a lake lifts his oars.
A woman by a window puts a match to a candle,
And the names are outlined on the rose clouds—
Vanacore and Wallace,
(let X stand, if it can, for the ones unfound)
Then Young and Ziminsky, the final jolt of Z.

Names etched on the head of a pin.
One name spanning a bridge, another undergoing a tunnel.
A blue name needled into the skin.
Names of citizens, workers, mothers and fathers,
The bright-eyed daughter, the quick son.
Alphabet of names in a green field.
Names in the small tracks of birds.
Names lifted from a hat
Or balanced on the tip of the tongue.
Names wheeled into the dim warehouse of memory.
So many names, there is barely room on the walls of the heart.

### Questions for Interactive Reading and Writing

1. Why does Collins first select the names, from "Ackerman" to "Eberling," and what do they convey?
2. In the sequence of names that follow, "Gonzalez and Han," and so on, what is he trying to say—if anything—about the nature of America?
3. Is a phrase like "the walls of the heart" concrete or abstract? Or both?

## e. e. cummings (1894–1962)

*For a biography of e. e. cummings, see chapter 25.*

### in Just- (1920)

in Just-
spring          when the world is mud-
luscious the little
lame balloonman

whistles          far          and wee

and eddieandbill come
running from marbles and
piracies and it's
spring

when the world is puddle-wonderful

the queer
old balloonman whistles
far          and          wee
and bettyandisbel come dancing

from hop-scotch and jump-rope and

it's
spring
and
    the

        goat-footed

balloonMan          whistles
far
and
wee

### Questions for Interactive Reading and Writing

1. Discuss the line arrangements here, and the use of lowercase letters.
2. Why does e. e. cummings conjoin the names of the marble-playing boys, the dancing girls, and the balloonman?
3. What does the repetition of "far and wee" suggest, and did he mean to say, instead, "far and wide"?

## John Donne (1572–1631)

*For a biography of John Donne, see chapter 22.*

### A Valediction: Forbidding Mourning (1633)

As virtuous men pass mildly away,
  And whisper to their souls to go,
Whilst some of their sad friends do say,
  "Now his breath goes," and some say, "No."
So let us melt, and make no noise,
  No tear-floods, nor sigh-tempests move;
'Twere profanation of our joys
  To tell the laity our love.
Moving of th' earth brings harms and fears;
  Men reckon what it did, and meant;
But trepidation of the spheres,
  Though greater far, is innocent.
Dull sublunary lovers' love
  —Whose soul is sense—cannot admit
Of absence, 'cause it doth remove
  The thing which elemented it.
But we by a love so much refined,
  That ourselves know not what it is,
Inter-assurèd of the mind,
  Care less, eyes, lips and hands to miss.
Our two souls therefore, which are one,
  Though I must go, endure not yet
A breach, but an expansion,
  Like gold to aery thinness beat.
If they be two, they are two so
  As stiff twin compasses are two;
Thy soul, the fix'd foot, makes no show
  To move, but doth, if th' other do.
And though it in the centre sit,
  Yet, when the other far doth roam,
It leans, and hearkens after it,
  And grows erect, as that comes home.

Such wilt thou be to me, who must,
Like th' other foot, obliquely run;
Thy firmness makes my circle just,
And makes me end where I begun.

### Questions for Interactive Reading and Writing

1. See the extended image of the compass here. The Metaphysical poets—of whom Donne was a leading member—called such extended comparison a "conceit." Point out its several uses in the text.
2. To whom is the poet speaking when he writes, "Our two souls"? What's concrete, what abstract in Donne's word choice here?
3. The poet begins by discussing death and ends by celebrating life—is all this signaled by the four words of the title? If so, how?

# Alan Dugan (1923–2003)

## Love Song: I and Thou (1961)

Nothing is plumb, level or square:
the studs are bowed, the joists
are shaky by nature, no piece fits
any other piece without a gap
or pinch, and bent nails
dance all over the surfacing
like maggots. By Christ
I am no carpenter. I built
the roof for myself, the walls
for myself, the floors
for myself, and got
hung up in it myself. I
danced with a purple thumb
at this house-warming, drunk
with my prime whiskey: rage.
Oh, I spat rage's nails
into the frame-up of my work:
it held. It settled plumb,
level, solid, square and true
for that great moment. Then
it screamed and went on through,
skewing as wrong the other way.
God damned it. This is hell,
but I planned it, I sawed it,
I nailed it, and I
will live in it until it kills me.
I can nail my left palm
to the left-hand crosspiece but
I can't do everything myself.
I need a hand to nail the right,
a help, a love, a you, a wife.

### Questions for Interactive Reading and Writing

1. What is the speaker's attitude toward himself in this poem? Is this a flattering self-portrait? What is the effect of that?
2. Discuss the extended metaphor in this poem. In what ways does the house reveal the character of the speaker? How would you describe the speaker's looks, character, and personality based on what you know about this house?
3. Discuss the references to Christ in the poem. How does the crucifixion reference at the end affect the tone of the poem?

# Louise Glück (b. 1943)

## Song of Obstacles (1985)

When my lover touches me, what I feel in my body
is like the first movement of a glacier over the earth,
as the ice shifts, dislodging great boulders, hills
of solemn rock: so, in the forests, the uprooted trees
become a sea of disconnected limbs—
And, where there are cities, these dissolve too,
the sighing gardens, all the young girls
eating chocolates in the courtyard, slowly
scattering the colored foil: then, where the city was,
the ore, the unearthed mysteries: so I see
that ice is more powerful than rock, than mere
resistance—

Then for us, in its path, time doesn't pass,
not even an hour.

### Questions for Interactive Reading and Writing

1. This poem is written in the first person. Who is the "I," the "us," and how do these individuals connect to such large entities as "glacier," "sea," and "city"?
2. Discuss the diction here—high, middle, low?—and give examples of each.
3. In this short poem, Louise Glück manages to talk of "young girls / eating chocolates" as well as "unearthed mysteries"—what's abstract, what's concrete, and why?

# Samuel Hazo (b. 1928)

## Just Words (1999)

In Arabic a single word
describes the very act
of taking a position.
Greeks
pronounce three syllables
to signify the sense of doom
that all Greeks fear when things
are going very well.
As for
the shameful ease we feel
when bad news happens
to someone else, including
friends?
In Greek—one word.
To designate a hose that funnels
liquid fire down the turret
of a tank in battle, the Germans
speak one word.
It's three
lines long but still one word.
And as for John, Matthew,
Mark and Luke?
There's not
a surname in the lot.
With just
one name they match in memory
the immortality of martyrs.
The longer
they're dead, the more they live. . . .
I praise whatever mates
perception with precision!
It asks
us only to be spare and make
the most of least.
It simplifies
and lets each word sound final
as a car door being shut
but perfect as a telegram to God.

### Questions for Interactive Reading and Writing

1. Does Hazo intend a pun in his title's first word? Discuss the two possible meanings of "just."
2. This brief poem refers to "Arabic," "Greeks," "Germans," and the long reach of history. How do the lines and particular words support this wide range of referents, and does Hazo succeed?
3. Of the four gospel-writers, the speaker says "There's not a surname in the lot." What is he suggesting here, and what do you make of the arrangement of the poem's last three words?

# Naomi Shihab Nye (b. 1952)

## The World in Translation (1995)

It was a long climb out of the soil.
She counted off whole continents
as she lifted each foot,
imagined her dark years falling away like husks.
Soon she could feel objects come to life
in her hand, the peel of banana,
a lightly waxed pepper,
she accepted these into her home,
placed them in bowls where they could be watched.
There was nothing obscure about melons,
nothing involved about yams.
If she were to have anything to do with the world,
these would be her translators,
through these she would learn secrets of dying,
how to do it gracefully as the peach,
softening in silence,
or the mango, finely tuned to its own skin.

### Questions for Interactive Reading and Writing

1. Consider the specificity of "she lifted each foot" and the improbable generality of "She counted off whole continents." Does the juxtaposition (the placing of one line right after the other) work?
2. List the fruits and vegetables named here. What is it about the changing condition of a piece of fruit that teaches the poet about living and dying?
3. How does the title organize Nye's poem, and what are "the secrets of dying"?

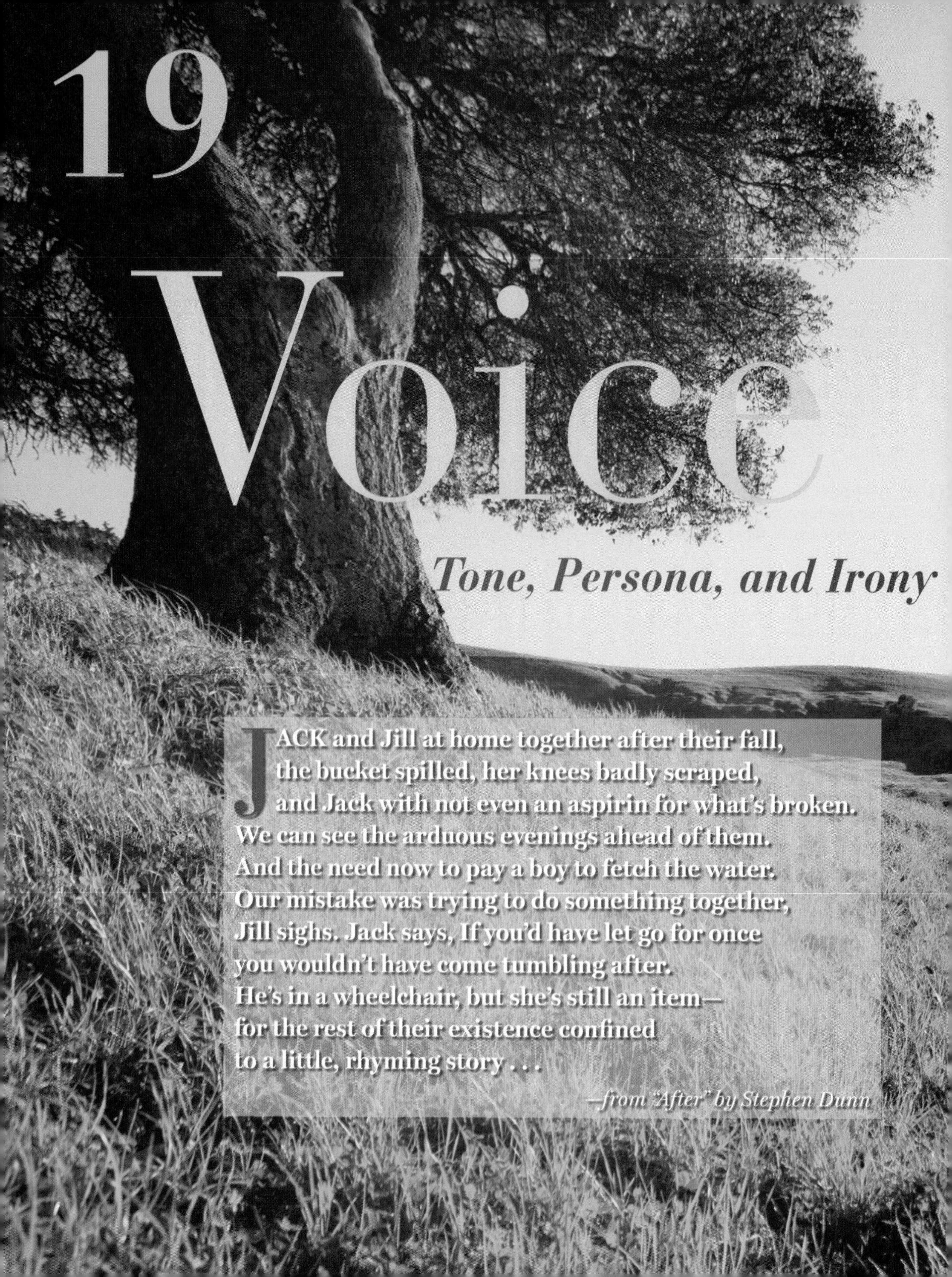

# 19

# Voice

## *Tone, Persona, and Irony*

JACK and Jill at home together after their fall,
the bucket spilled, her knees badly scraped,
and Jack with not even an aspirin for what's broken.
We can see the arduous evenings ahead of them.
And the need now to pay a boy to fetch the water.
Our mistake was trying to do something together,
Jill sighs. Jack says, If you'd have let go for once
you wouldn't have come tumbling after.
He's in a wheelchair, but she's still an item—
for the rest of their existence confined
to a little, rhyming story . . .

*—from "After" by Stephen Dunn*

*"Tone is the author's attitude toward subject, but it's a rather large scaffolding or coloring of subject matter that when you're listening to someone talk—if you're like me, you're making judgments about that person: Would I want to go out to dinner with him, let's say. What kind of guy is he? . . . You do that with inflection, with pauses, irony."*

Conversation with Stephen Dunn, available on video at http://www.mhhe.com/delbanco1e

HERE'S a poem that reports on conversation and relies on **voice.** The poet speaks to us as readers; at the same time he speaks to himself. His diction is as informal as was Marie Howe's in "What the Living Do." Note the contractions ("He's in a wheelchair"), the slang ("she's still an item"), and the general flavor of written language as speech. Stephen Dunn wittily imagines the repercussions for two famous nursery rhyme characters "after" their untimely fall down a hill. The premise here, of course, is comic and even a bit bizarre. Jack and Jill sit at home after their accident like an old married couple, aching and depressed, blaming one another for their predicament. The "little, rhyming story" with which all of us are familiar—"Jack and Jill went up the hill / to fetch a pail of water"—becomes something unfamiliar, *new,* and that unfamiliarity has much to do with **tone.**

Despite his humorous premise, Dunn manages to use the tale of Jack and Jill to reflect on multifaceted themes of intimacy, transgression, and fate. Notice how Jack's "in a wheelchair" because—according to the original poem—he's the one who "fell down / and broke his crown," and her knees are "badly scraped." As you'll see, by the end of "After" the "fallout" of their story has something to say to all of us about coping with misfortune. "The fundamental business of making do," as the poet puts it, transforms what we take for granted—a childhood nursery rhyme—into something with which we must deal.

The lines seem wry, and a little cynical, and matter-of-fact, or all these things at once. Whenever you think about the attitude expressed, you're undoubtedly thinking about the poem's tone. Whenever you consider whose voice you're hearing as you read, you're thinking about the poem's **persona,** the speaker delivering his or her language to the audience.

On the subject of rendering voice in a poem, Stephen Dunn acknowledges the power of **irony,** the use of words to indicate an opposite or unexpected meaning. As he puts it, "irony is a way of managing experience, and thus keeping it at a distance, while at its best being a way of recognizing and opening up experience by delivering simultaneous awareness." A poem like "After" asks us to ponder the emotional lives of a pair of nursery rhyme characters, and asks us to smile at and simultaneously sympathize with the ways we confront our own hardship.

By looking carefully at the artist's choice of tone, persona, and irony, we can improve our sense of the ways poets manage our experience as readers.

*CONTINUED ON PAGE 106*

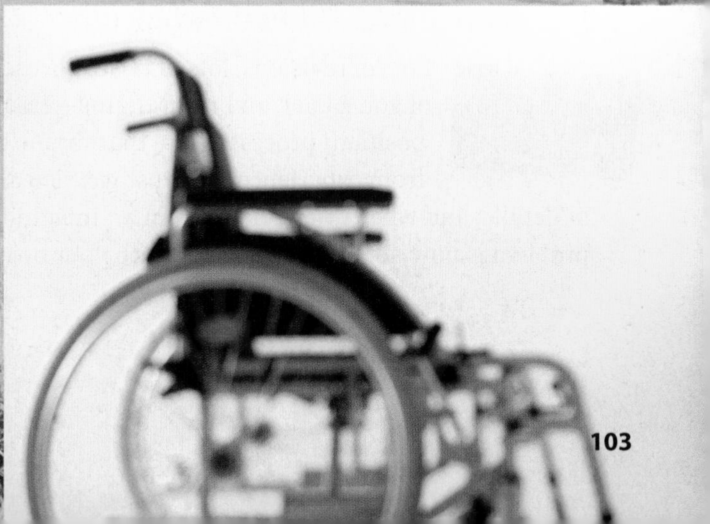

*I was a very silent child and boy and even grown-up for a while . . .*

*Literature brought the world to me.*

# Q&A

# *A Conversation on Writing*

## Stephen Dunn

### Poetry Makes Us Part of the World

I think one of the reasons people don't get into poetry . . . [is] they don't quite believe it has anything to do with their lives. Certainly for me, that was the case, and I didn't come to poetry seriously till after college when I started to find those poems that addressed . . . the things that I had inklings about that I was largely inarticulate about. When we find those stories or poems or novels that make us feel part of the world, [we find] . . . the things that we say are secret . . . the things we've not confessed to anybody. Good literature, whether it's poetry or any of the other genres, has a way of bringing us into the common fold, of making us part of the world.

### Poetry As a Challenge to Personal Experience

I'm sure you all have heard this, when somebody says, "Oh, I can relate to that." They like to relate to that rather than be subverted, rather than to have their ideas challenged. . . . What I want from good poems is to be offered another way into experience. I don't want to have my experience confirmed.

### Revision and Our Own Invention

Lots of revisions, lots of false moves, lots of altering, lots of going back and rearranging—essentially, the [composition] process is like that for me. When I'm working from experience I'm most worried about my selection of details, and when I'm working from an imaginative premise, the problem is how not to be too in love with your own invention.

Born in Forest Hills, New York (1939), Stephen Dunn quit a corporate job to try his hand at writing. Early on, he was an accomplished basketball player, and there's a way in which his skills as athlete translate into the effortless grace of his diction; there's a fluid ease of motion in the lines. He earned a master's in creative writing from Syracuse University, and has taught creative writing at Richard Stockton University in New Jersey since 1974. The author of a collection of essays on craft and a dozen books of poetry, Dunn won the Pulitzer Prize in 2001 for his collection *Different Hours*. Dunn's poetry takes the everyday for its subject; as he puts it in an interview, "I think most of our lives are made up of both things visible and things interior, with a large chunk of them being interior. So whenever I've been able to arrive at clarities about that which is elusive about dailyness, that has pleased me."

To watch this entire interview and hear the author read from his work, go to **www.mhhe.com/delbanco1e**.

**RESEARCH ASSIGNMENT** After you have watched the interview, comment on Dunn's attitude toward irony in poetry. How does he describe the way irony functions in his poem "After"? What part does irony play in Dunn's idea of engagement with poetry? How does he (or how doesn't he) achieve this ironic engagement in his poem "After"?

**AS YOU READ** In "After," Dunn delivers a humorous narrative. At first you may find this poem, a sort of sequel to the old Jack and Jill nursery rhyme, merely funny. As you read more deeply, look for ways the poem reveals an intricate sympathy, a seriousness, and the narrator's darker, ironic attitude.

# After (2002)

Jack and Jill at home together after their fall,
the bucket spilled, her knees badly scraped,
and Jack with not even an aspirin for what's broken.
We can see the arduous evenings ahead of them.
And the need now to pay a boy to fetch the water.
Our mistake was trying to do something together,
Jill sighs. Jack says, If you'd have let go for once
you wouldn't have come tumbling after.
He's in a wheelchair, but she's still an item—
for the rest of their existence confined
to a little rhyming story. We tell it to our children,
who laugh, already accustomed to disaster.
We'd like to teach them the secrets
of knowing how to go too far,
but Jack is banging with his soup spoon,
Jill is pulling out her hair. Out of decency
we turn away, as if it were possible to escape
the drift of our lives, the fundamental business
of making do with what's been left us.

# Writing from Reading

## Summarize

1 What has Dunn added to or altered in the story of the nursery rhyme?

## Analyze Craft

2 How does Dunn introduce irony into the nursery rhyme?

3 What makes this poem feel so playful? Compare its use of a previous text, the nursery rhyme about Jack and Jill, with Anthony Hecht's treatment of Matthew Arnold's "Dover Beach" (chapter 18).

## Analyze Voice

4 Who is "we" in this poem? Why does Dunn use "we"?

5 Describe the speaker's tone in this poem. Why does Dunn choose this kind of voice for the subject matter?

## Synthesize Summary and Analysis

6 How does Dunn marry a playful tone with a melancholy message?

## Interpret the Poem

7 When the poem says "we turn away," what do you think "we" turn away *from*?

*(CONTINUED FROM PAGE 103)*

"The first level of [a poem's] meaning is simply to be moved and to hear a speaker, to hear voice giving voice to what is within the poet." Conversation with Carolyn Forché

## TONE

On a daily basis, sometimes hardly conscious of it, we interpret the language we hear. We know to listen for clues that indicate to us exactly how people intend their language. By putting extra emphasis on one word in a sentence, the ordinary question "Are you going to eat that?" can suddenly become the more surprised "Are you going to *eat* that?" If, instead, the speaker asks "Are you going to eat *that?*" the question focuses on the thing about to be eaten rather than the act of consumption. The word choice is exactly the same, but the meaning is quite different. If the emphasis falls on the word *you,* a fourth meaning may become central: how come *you* get to eat that and I can't? All this has to do with **intonation,** the *way* a thing gets said. We make interpretive distinctions by tuning in to **tone of voice,** the particular communicative quality of a person's speech.

"A poem is . . . like a musical score for human speech. . . . You come and you read the poem and you play the voice."

Conversation with Li-Young Lee

In poetry, language works in similar, equally subtle ways. As you're reading a poem, analyzing the intentions of word choice and word order, you will often find a kind of implicit meaning emerges from these lines. In poetry, **tone** is an attitude conveyed toward a poem's subject as suggested by the poet's language. No one element of poetry establishes tone by itself. It is a kind of cumulative effect, resulting from all of poetry's components, including word choice and arrangement, figures of speech, rhythm, and diction and sound.

Tone in poetry is as variable as the different voices you hear every day on the street, capable of humor, seriousness, contemplation, desperation, anger, or any other emotion. A love poem designed to woo its recipient might do so seriously, with soaring language; or it might work just as effectively with comedy, using wordplay. There's no one right tone for a thought or idea, just the prerogative of the author who wishes to best communicate his or her intended meaning.

"Once you get the poem right . . . you sound like yourself talking to yourself. It's that voice that we hear just before we fall asleep, the voice that we start out the day with when everything seems to fall into place." Conversation with Thomas Lynch

The following poems illustrate a range of tones, from the restrained to the emotional to the ambivalent. The first selection describes the internal and external experiences of a World War II aviator operating the gun on the belly of a large bomber.

# Randall Jarrell (1914–1965)

Born in Tennessee, Randall Jarrell spent part of his childhood in California before returning to his native state for an education at Vanderbilt University. He published his first collection of poetry, *Blood for a Stranger* (1942), in the same year that he enlisted in the Army Air Corps, in which he served during World War II. After the war, he taught at the Women's College of the University of North Carolina until his death at age fifty-one, when he was hit by a car. Jarrell's poetry is sensitive to the pain of his speakers, whether domestic housewives or soldiers fighting in World War II. In addition to winning the National Book Award for *The Woman at the Washington Zoo* (1960), Jarrell held the position of Poet Laureate. He was also an unusually influential literary critic, championing poetry by Walt Whitman and Robert Frost, and helping to establish the success of such poets as Elizabeth Bishop and William Carlos Williams.

**AS YOU READ** Think about how the tone of the language (for example, "wet fur froze," "black flak and the nightmare fighters") helps the poem communicate an attitude or particular atmosphere. Notice, also, the bleak efficiency here; it's a poem of only five lines.

# The Death of the Ball Turret Gunner (1945)

From my mother's sleep I fell into the State,
And I hunched in its belly till my wet fur froze.
Six miles from earth, loosed from the dream of life,
I woke to black flak and the nightmare fighters.
When I died they washed me out of the turret with a hose.

# Writing from Reading

### Summarize

1 Describe the fate the flyer imagines for himself.

### Analyze Craft

2 Why do you think the word *state* is capitalized?

3 What images are used in this poem?

### Analyze Voice

**4** How would you characterize the tone of the poem? Does it seem like an unusual or an apt choice for a poem about war?

### Synthesize Summary and Analysis

**5** How does the description of the flyer's experience show the horror he is imagining?

### Interpret the Poem

**6** How does the tone of the poem's final line contrast with the image it describes?

**7** Is this an anti-war poem or a heroic poem? How do you think the speaker feels about war?

Sometimes a poem's tone is especially subtle or multilayered. Theodore Roethke's "My Papa's Waltz" is one such work. A memory of the poet's father playfully dancing with his son, the poem entertains different attitudes simultaneously. We start with the knowledge that the father is drunk—or at least has been drinking—and that the boy hangs on "like death" because it's hard to follow where the dancing adult leads. The father doesn't fully realize how much he is bending or stretching the bond of love between parent and child. The mother, watching, frowns. By poem's end, however, the dance becomes a kind of elegy, with the speaker "still clinging" to the memories of childhood and the strong if implicit suggestion that the father is dead. These emotions in opposition—fear, delight, disapproval—are bodied forth in a domestic scene, as from kitchen to bedroom "we romped."

## Theodore Roethke (1908–1963)

Growing up, Theodore Roethke loved to spend time in the greenhouse his father and uncle owned in Saginaw, Michigan. This was a lifelong fascination; his poems are full of imagery and metaphor that hinge on the natural world. Unsentimental in his portrayal of nature, Roethke was equally unafraid to put his own feelings and experiences into his poems, making him the forerunner of confessional poets like Anne Sexton and Sylvia Plath. His collections were widely acclaimed: *The Waking* (1953) won the Pulitzer Prize, and *Words for the Wind* (1958) won the National Book Award, as did his posthumous *The Far Field* (1964). His mental health was precarious and his mood swings large, but Roethke was a celebrated and devoted teacher; he spent most of his teaching life at the University of Washington.

**AS YOU READ** Think about how the poet's feelings about memory might have more than one dimension. Consider also how the rhyme of the poem reinforces its meaning and tone using slant rhymes, rather than exact rhymes. In the final two stanzas, however, it's as if the boy gets the hang of his father's waltzing rhythm and can follow along exactly once he gets into the "swing of things" at poem's end.

TIP

**FOR INTERACTIVE READING . . .** Circle the approximate, or slant, rhymes, such as "dizzy" and "easy" or "pans" and "countenance." Note the waltz time and dance step involved.

# My Papa's Waltz (1948)

The whiskey on your breath
Could make a small boy dizzy;
But I hung on like death:
Such waltzing was not easy.

We romped until the pans
Slid from the kitchen shelf;
My mother's countenance
Could not unfrown itself.

The hand that held my wrist
Was battered on one knuckle;
At every step you missed
My right ear scraped a buckle.

You beat time on my head
With a palm caked hard by dirt,
Then waltzed me off to bed
Still clinging to your shirt.

# Writing from Reading

### Summarize

1 What has happened in this poem?

2 How does the mother feel about what has happened? Is it clear how the child feels?

### Analyze Craft

3 Pick out phrases and words that indicate the speaker remembers his father's behavior fondly.

4 Pick out phrases and words that indicate the speaker remembers his father's behavior negatively or critically.

### Analyze Voice

5 Who is the speaker in this poem?

6 Do you think the poem's variation in tone is purposeful? Discuss why or why not.

### Synthesize Summary and Analysis

7 How does the innocence of the child's perspective allow us to draw our own conclusions about what happened here?

### Interpret the Poem

8 Discuss the significance of the poem's final line. What if Roethke did not include this image of the boy "still clinging"? Would that change your sense of the poem's tone?

In contrast to the tone and word choice of poets like Stephen Dunn and Theodore Roethke, Wallace Stevens employs a diction that sounds formal and even stately. This is not "conversational" language—a poet talking to himself and us as audience; rather, it is a carefully arranged and presented series of pronouncements, insisting on attentiveness on the reader's part. In this poem—which first appeared in *Poetry* magazine in 1915, although Stevens later revised and enlarged it—he details an aging woman's religious dilemma, a conflict between traditional religious piety and individual, personal spiritual exploration.

# Wallace Stevens (1879–1955)

For a brief biography of Wallace Stevens, see chapter 18.

**AS YOU READ** Consider "Sunday Morning" in the terms that we've been using: as a series of different poetic elements that establish tone. One way of reading this poem is in terms of its ambitious range of referents—to the Holy Land, to Greek gods and "the blood of paradise," etc.; another is to read about an old woman in the sun, drinking a cup of coffee and wondering what happens when she dies.

**TIP**

**FOR INTERACTIVE READING . . .** Make note of or circle words like "death" or that pertain to death, both obviously (as in "tomb" or "grave") or implicitly where you think Stevens might be making a reference to death. Underline or note words or phrases that are used repeatedly in the poem.

## Sunday Morning (1915)

I

Complacencies of the peignoir, and late
Coffee and oranges in a sunny chair,
And the green freedom of a cockatoo
Upon a rug, mingle to dissipate
The holy hush of ancient sacrifice.
She dreams a little, and she feels the dark
Encroachment of that old catastrophe,
As a calm darkens among water-lights.
The pungent oranges and bright, green wings
Seem things in some procession of the dead,
Winding across wide water, without sound.
The day is like wide water, without sound,
Stilled for the passing of her dreaming feet
Over the seas, to silent Palestine,
Dominion of the blood and sepulchre.

II

She hears, upon that water without sound,
A voice that cries, "The tomb in Palestine
Is not the porch of spirits lingering;
It is the grave of Jesus, where he lay."
We live in an old chaos of the sun,
Or old dependency of day and night,
Or island solitude, unsponsored, free,
Of that wide water, inescapable.
Deer walk upon our mountains, and the quail
Whistle about us their spontaneous cries;
Sweet berries ripen in the wilderness;
And, in the isolation of the sky,
At evening, casual flocks of pigeons make
Ambiguous undulations as they sink,
Downward to darkness, on extended wings.

III

She says, "I am content when wakened birds,
Before they fly, test the reality
Of misty fields, by their sweet questionings;
But when the birds are gone, and their warm fields
Return no more, where, then, is paradise?"
There is not any haunt of prophecy,
Nor any old chimera of the grave,
Neither the golden underground, nor isle
Melodious, where spirits gat them home,
Nor visionary South, nor cloudy palm
Remote on heaven's hill, that has endured
As April's green endures; or will endure
Like her remembrance of awakened birds,
Or her desire for June and evening, tipped
By the consummation of the swallow's wings.

IV

She says, "But in contentment I still feel
The need of some imperishable bliss."
Death is the mother of beauty; hence from her,
Alone, shall come fulfillment to our dreams
And our desires. Although she strews the leaves
Of sure obliteration on our paths—
The path sick sorrow took, the many paths
Where triumph rang its brassy phrase, or love
Whispered a little out of tenderness—
She makes the willow shiver in the sun
For maidens who were wont to sit and gaze
Upon the grass, relinquished to their feet.
She causes boys to bring sweet-smelling pears
And plums in ponderous piles. The maidens taste
And stray impassioned in the littering leaves.

V

Supple and turbulent, a ring of men
Shall chant in orgy on a summer morn
Their boisterous devotion to the sun—
Not as a god, but as a god might be,
Naked among them, like a savage source.
Their chant shall be a chant of paradise,
Out of their blood, returning to the sky;
And in their chant shall enter, voice by voice,
The windy lake wherein their lord delights,
The trees, like serafim, and echoing hills,
That choir among themselves long afterward.
They shall know well the heavenly fellowship
Of men that perish and of summer morn—
And whence they came and whither they shall go,
The dew upon their feel shall manifest.

# Writing from Reading

## Summarize

1 What does the title indicate about the subject of the poem? What activities are typical of a Sunday morning?

2 What information about the situation of the poem—*when* it takes place, *where* it takes place, *what's* at stake or being talked about—do you obtain from the poem's first section?

## Analyze Craft

3 In his interview, Stephen Dunn talks about reciting this poem on Sunday mornings with his wife and about Stevens's "exotic" diction. What about the words chosen for this poem might make Dunn describe Stevens's word choices as exotic? Why do you think Stevens chooses to use language like this?

### Analyze Voice

4 Look at the opening phrase "Complacencies of the peignoir" or the penultimate one of the second stanza, "Ambiguous undulations as they sink," and consider Stevens's voice. What uses does he make of the language of everyday speech, and how does he alter and heighten it? Note the places where he *does* use everyday language or commonplace objects—such as "coffee and oranges" or "sweet berries ripen in the wilderness." How does this kind of juxtaposition create a voice and tone for this poem?

5 Where in the poem does the speaker hint that the woman is old?

### Synthesize Summary and Analysis

6 Each of the stanzas has precisely fifteen lines. How does this formal arrangement serve the poet's purpose, and what does the repetition of such words as "wide water" accomplish?

### Interpret the Poem

7 What is the "old catastrophe" mentioned in the first section? Compare stanza 5 here to John Keats's meditation on a Grecian urn (chapter 18). Do he and Stevens have a similar reaction to the past?

Anne Bradstreet was one of the first poets in the American colonies and inarguably our country's first acclaimed female poet. Unbeknownst to Bradstreet, friends of hers saw to the publication of her poems in London in a collection titled *The Tenth Muse, Lately Sprung Up in America,* in 1650. Written in 1678, the following poem introduced a later edition of that volume and voices Bradstreet's mixed feelings about the book's earlier, unauthorized publication.

# Anne Bradstreet (1612–1672)

Among the earliest Puritans to settle the American colonies, Anne Bradstreet suffered the hardships of an educated Englishwoman brought to the harsh conditions of a struggling colony. Nevertheless, as her poetry attests, she loved her husband, her home, and her children. It was rare for a Puritan woman to write poetry, and equally rare that she was educated in Latin, Hebrew, Greek, medicine, and theology. The mother of eight children and wife to the governor of Massachusetts, Bradstreet shared most of her poems only with family and friends. However, her brother-in-law took a collection of her poems to England, where they were published as *The Tenth Muse, Lately Sprung Up in America* (1650). Echoing Plato's praise of Sappho, this work by the "tenth muse" was the first book by a New Englander ever to be published.

**AS YOU READ** Words like "thou" were common in Anne Bradstreet's day; in this poem, they are not examples of elevated poetic diction but, rather, are everyday speech. "Thou" was the informal or diminutive form of "you," and so the very first word of the poem suggests a kind of intimacy with the "offspring" addressed. Notice the ways in which "the author" compares "her book" to a child and the self-effacing claim that her brain is "feeble." She's both proud and apologetic, both serious and tongue-in-cheek, and the mixture of these elements is part of the poem's great charm.

# The Author to Her Book

**(1678)**

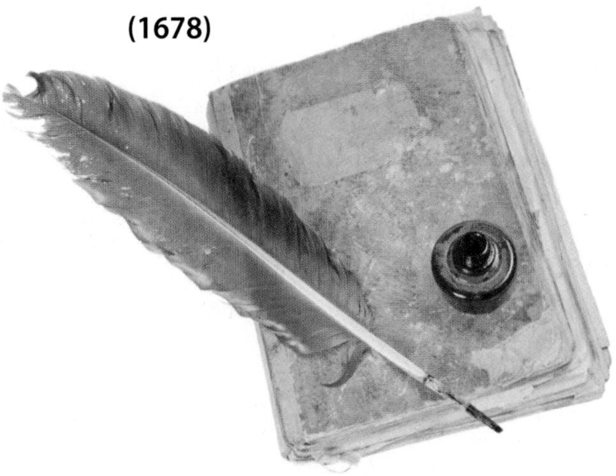

Thou ill-formed offspring of my feeble brain,
Who after birth didst by my side remain,
Till snatched from thence by friends, less wise than true,
Who thee abroad exposed to public view,
Made thee in rags, halting to th' press to trudge,
Where errors were not lessened (all may judge).
At thy return my blushing was not small,
My rambling brat (in print) should mother call.
I cast thee by as one unfit for light,
Thy visage was so irksome in my sight;
Yet being mine own, at length affection would
Thy blemishes amend, if so I could.
I washed thy face, but more defects I saw,
And rubbing off a spot still made a flaw.
I stretched thy joints to make thee even feet,
Yet still thou run'st more hobbling than is meet;
In better dress to trim thee was my mind,
But nought save home-spun cloth, i' th' house I find.
In this array, 'mongst vulgars mayst thou roam.
In critics' hands, beware thou dost not come,
And take thy way where yet thou art not known;
If for thy Father asked, say, thou hadst none;
And for thy Mother, she alas is poor,
Which caused her thus to send thee out of door.

# Writing from Reading

## Summarize

1 Who or what is the speaker addressing? To what does "ill-formed offspring of my feeble brain" refer?

2 List the complaints the speaker has about her book.

3 Why in the last lines are we told "thy Mother . . . is poor"?

## Analyze Craft

4 Discuss how the poet compares a book to a child. How do these lines about the book also reveal her thoughts on motherhood?

## Analyze Voice

5 How does the speaker's attitude toward her book change as the poem progresses?

## Synthesize Summary and Analysis

6 How does the ambivalence the speaker expresses toward her book contrast with the imagery of motherhood and a mother's attitude toward a child? How do these go together in this poem?

## Interpret the Poem

7 What does the line "If for thy Father asked, say, thou hadst none" suggest to you about the author's feelings toward the book?

# For Review and Further Study

## Charlotte Mew (1869–1928)

### I So Liked Spring (1915)

I so liked Spring last year
  Because you were here;—
    The thrushes too—
Because it was these you so liked to hear—
    I so liked you.

  This year's a different thing,—
    I'll not think of you.
But I'll like Spring because it is simply Spring
    As the thrushes do.

#### Questions for Interactive Reading and Writing

1. Summarize the history of the relationship described.
2. There is an element of surprise in the poem. How does Mew create this surprise?
3. Notice there's only one three-syllable word—"different"—in the poem's nine lines. There's an essential simplicity to the diction throughout, but the situation is a complicated one. Discuss.
4. What word choices create the note of melancholy on which this poem ends?

## Gary Soto (b. 1952)

### Mexicans Begin Jogging (1981)

At the factory I worked
In the fleck of rubber, under the press
Of an oven yellow with flame,
Until the border patrol opened
Their vans and my boss waved for us to run.
"Over the fence, Soto," he shouted,
And I shouted that I was American.
"No time for lies," he said, and pressed
A dollar in my palm, hurrying me
Through the back door.
Since I was on his time, I ran
And became the wag to a short tail of Mexicans—
Ran past the amazed crowds that lined
The streets and blurred like photographs, in rain.
I ran from that industrial road to the soft
Houses where people paled at the turn of an autumn sky.
What could I do but yell *vivas*
To baseball, milkshakes, and those sociologists
Who would clock me
As I jog into the next century
On the power of a great, silly grin.

#### Questions for Interactive Reading and Writing

1. What is the action in the poem? What is the misunderstanding?
2. There's good humor here, even in the face of a legal absurdity, and the title word *jogging* suggests a kind of leisure activity of the middle class. What clues does the title reveal about the poem's tone?
3. What does the line "Since I was on his time, I ran" tell us about the speaker?
4. Discuss how Soto frames himself in the group of Mexican workers. Does he feel separate from or unified with them?
5. Note the phrase "great, silly grin" with which the poem closes, and the way the poet likens what he's doing to a kind of *corrida,* or running with the bulls. Why does Soto have a "great, silly grin" for the next century?

## William Stafford (1914–1993)

### Traveling through the Dark (1962)

Traveling through the dark I found a deer
dead on the edge of the Wilson River road.
It is usually best to roll them into the canyon:
that road is narrow; to swerve might make more dead.

By glow of the tail-light I stumbled back of the car
and stood by the heap, a doe, a recent killing;
she had stiffened already, almost cold.
I dragged her off; she was large in the belly.

My fingers touching her side brought me the reason—
her side was warm; her fawn lay there waiting,
alive, still, never to be born.
Beside that mountain road I hesitated.

The car aimed ahead its lowered parking lights;
under the hood purred the steady engine.
I stood in the glare of the warm exhaust turning red;
around our group I could hear the wilderness listen.

I thought hard for us all—my only swerving—
then pushed her over the edge into the river.

### Questions for Interactive Reading and Writing

1. What happens here, and how does the word *usually* establish tone?
2. What does the poet learn when he touches the dead doe? Why does he hesitate? Identify the words that give you clues about the speaker's attitude and why "I hesitated."
3. How does the word *still* do double duty in the phrase "alive, still, never to be born"?
4. Notice the narrative ease of the poem, the uninflected voice. Travel the distance between line 3—"It is usually best to roll them into the canyon"—and what happens at poem's end. Who does the speaker mean by "our group" and how does "the wilderness listen"? What does "my only swerving" suggest, and what do you imagine the speaker thought as he "pushed her over the edge"? How would you describe the tone of the poem, and does it seem appropriate to the scene's subject?
5. Can you detect an implied meaning in the title? Describe the interaction of man and nature here.

# William Carlos Williams (1883–1963)

*For a brief biography of William Carlos Williams, see chapter 20.*

## This Is Just to Say (1934)

I have eaten
the plums
that were in
the icebox

and which
you were probably
saving
for breakfast

Forgive me
they were delicious
so sweet
and so cold

### Questions for Interactive Reading and Writing

1. What does the word *just* imply—"only" or "fairly" or both? Why is the title a part of the poem that follows? Compare the tone of "This Is Just to Say" to the tone of Samuel Hazo's "Just Words" in the previous chapter.
2. What is the past action narrated and why has the poet narrated it?
3. Does this feel like an actual poem to you? Why or why not?
4. Williams avoids punctuation, but he does capitalize "Forgive." Why? What effect does this produce?
5. Discuss the tone here. Is it sincere? Comic? Apologetic?
6. How much does this simple poem tell the reader about the speaker? Who is the "you" addressed?
7. Think of Wordsworth's definition of a poem as "emotion recollected in tranquility." Would you say Williams agrees?
8. Imagine that you found this note on the icebox door or kitchen table as you come down to breakfast after your guest has left. What would be your reaction?

## PERSONA

In some poems, like Anne Bradstreet's, we can be confident that the speaker of a poem is a version of the poet himself or herself. This is equally the case for the poems you've just looked at by Mew, Soto, Stafford, and Williams; most often, when a poet says "I," we can associate that first-person pronoun with the life and mind of the speaker. At other times, a poet "throws" his or her voice—becoming a character other than "I" even when the first-person pronoun is used. Researching a bit of biographical information can help us make an informed decision about this. Knowing, for example, that the poet Ben Jonson lost his eldest son to plague helps us understand that the speaking voice of the following poem is indeed Jonson's.

> "It seems to me that because a poem is a score for the human voice—a voice implies a speaker. So in a way every poem is a portrait of a speaker." Conversation with Li-Young Lee

## Ben Jonson (1573–1637)

Born in Westminster, England, Ben Jonson rose to become a well-known and respected playwright, England's poet laureate, and the author of many masques—that is, spectacles that included drama, poetry, and song performed to entertain the court. Jonson's satirical eye led him to create a brand of comedy that consisted of eccentric characters who represent various types of human temperament, as in *Every Man in His Humour* (1598). Though a scholar and a skilled lyrical poet, Jonson was a man of large appetites and volatile temper (he was nearly executed for killing a man in a duel). Among his most famous works are *Volpone* (1606), *The Alchemist* (1610)—both comedies written for the stage—and *The Forest* (1616), a collection of lyrics and epigrams.

**AS YOU READ** **Note the opposition of the first word "Farewell" and the poem's title. How does this establish tone and serve notice that "joy" has been lost?**

# On My First Son

**(1616)**

Farewell, thou child of my right hand, and joy;
My sin was too much hope of thee, loved boy:
Seven years thou wert lent to me, and I thee pay,
Exacted by the fate, on the just day.
O could I lose all father now! for why
Will man lament the state he should envy,
To have soon 'scaped world's and flesh's rage,
And, if no other misery, yet age?
Rest in soft peace, and asked, say, "Here doth lie
Ben Jonson his best piece of poetry."
For whose sake henceforth all his vows be such
As what he loves may never like too much.

# Writing from Reading

### Summarize

1 What is the situation revealed in the poem and the poet's attitude?

2 What does he mean by "why / Will man lament the state he should envy," and does the poet truly wish for death?

### Analyze Craft

3 Notice the six rhyming couplets of this poem and the two spots where the rhymes are less than exact. What is meant by "Ben Jonson his best piece of poetry"?

4 How old is the child to whom the father says farewell, and what does the poet wish for himself?

### Analyze Voice

5 Technically, this poem is an elegy—a lament for a dear dead child. What words and phrases establish that "lament," and what does the poet promise himself in the final two lines?

### Synthesize Summary and Analysis

6 "Rest in soft peace" adds a word to "Rest in peace." Who does the poet imagine might ask his "soft" son to identify himself, and where, and when?

### Interpret the Poem

7 If age is necessarily linked to misery, can the speaker find comfort in the fact that his son "soon 'scaped world's and flesh's rage"? What is the overall tone of the poem, and does "First Son" in the title suggest that there are or will be more?

While we can say with confidence that Jonson is speaking from his own experience, this is not always necessarily the case. Poets—like novelists and playwrights—often imagine an experience, inventing both speakers and scene. Did Edgar Allan Poe, for instance, really hear a bird crying outside his home, as he asserts in "The Raven"? Did Robert Frost really find himself once, on a walk through the woods, facing two separate roads to choose from, as in "The Road Not Taken" (see chapter 28)? While it's quite possible these poems borrow, perhaps even heavily, from real life, we shouldn't automatically assume they are precise autobiographical accounts. Rather, we think of a poem's speaking voice as a potentially separate entity. This is called a **persona,** a poem's speaker that may or may not use the voice of the poet.

> "One person, of course, can have 20,000 different kinds of voices." Conversation with Marie Howe

One way to read a poem is, in effect, to measure the distance between the voice of the poet and the voice of the persona delivering the lines. In the **dramatic monologue** "My Last Duchess," for example (see chapter 16), it's perfectly clear that the first-person pronoun of the speaker does not belong to the poet himself; Robert Browning was no duke. He is, in fact, unsympathetic to the man who's showing off his collection of art and arranging a new marriage, and asks us as readers to notice things the character would deny. In the poem "Herbert White" by Frank Bidart (see "For Review and Further Study" on page 127), there's an absolute distance established between writer and speaker; as Bidart observes, he wrote this poem to explore "All that I am not."

**A HISTORY OF PERSONA**

The Latin word *persona* derives from the ancient Etruscan word for "mask," and it recalls the ancient Greek practice of actors wearing masks to portray different roles. That the voice of a poem may not be in fact the same as that of the poet is an ancient literary distinction. Aristotle writes in *Poetics,* "The poet may imitate by narration—in which case he can either take another personality . . . or speak in his own person, unchanged—or he may present all his characters as living and moving before us." In more recent times, twentieth-century literary scholars sometimes discouraged readers from assuming that even a first-person poem could be autobiographical. Despite these protests from literary critics, many poets readily concede that the speaker using the first person in their poems is, indeed, an autobiographical "I." A group of writers in the 1950s and 1960s, including Robert Lowell, W. D. Snodgrass, Sylvia Plath, and Anne Sexton, were dubbed "confessional poets." This indicated a deeply personal style by poets unafraid to confront painful private history.

"Until the advent of the romantics, the 'I' was very rare in poetry. . . . Poetry was used to memorize . . . to commemorate, to narrate history, to catechize. . . . [Now] . . . this fictitious 'I' . . . pops up in just about 90 percent of contemporary American poetry. . . . To take on different voices and different characterizations is a challenge and a lot more creative." Conversation with Al Young

Sylvia Plath's poem "Daddy" is sometimes called autobiographical. Indeed, the poem is an angry and raw cry of resistance aimed at the poet's father, Otto Plath, who died when she was still a child. Haunted by three decades of grief and memories of her stern father, Plath fashions a poem that voices a bitter response to his lasting psychological grip.

While Plath borrows heavily from real life in her descriptions in the poem, we shouldn't be too quick to call the "I" of this poem a literal version of the poet. Plath uses, among other references, violent Nazi and Holocaust imagery to describe the father figure of this poem. Otto Plath, however, immigrated to America in 1900 and was never affiliated with the Nazi party or known to be physically abusive. Likewise, to accentuate the poem's conflict, Plath's speaker links herself to a Jewish identity whereas Plath herself was raised primarily in the Unitarian Christian tradition. So, while some descriptions and references in the poem echo authentic aspects of Plath's life, the poem is itself a creative fusion of real-life and fictional elements. Because of this, "Daddy" is a poem that helps us understand why it's important to treat the distinction between poet and persona with care.

"If we can forget ourselves, we can become someone the poem can speak through." Conversation with Marie Howe

# Sylvia Plath (1932–1963)

Born in Massachusetts, Sylvia Plath was a successful student and earned her B.A. *summa cum laude* from Smith College. She was awarded a Fulbright scholarship and went to England, where she met and married poet Ted Hughes. Hughes later left Plath and their two young children; Plath responded with a frenzy of creative outpouring, writing her famous *Ariel* poems in the few months leading up to her suicide at age thirty. She had attempted to take her own life between her junior and senior years of college, and her autobiographical novel *The Bell Jar* (1963) focuses on a heroine who attempts suicide. Plath's poetry is marked by violent imagery contained in clear, precise diction; especially in the *Ariel* poems, she invents a poetic self that has a romantic, larger-than-life quality characteristic of poems in the confessional voice.

**AS YOU READ** This poem uses direct address—from "I" to "you" in the first stanza, and by the second stanza we know that a child addresses a father. As the speaker addresses the father, note if and when her tone changes or shifts.

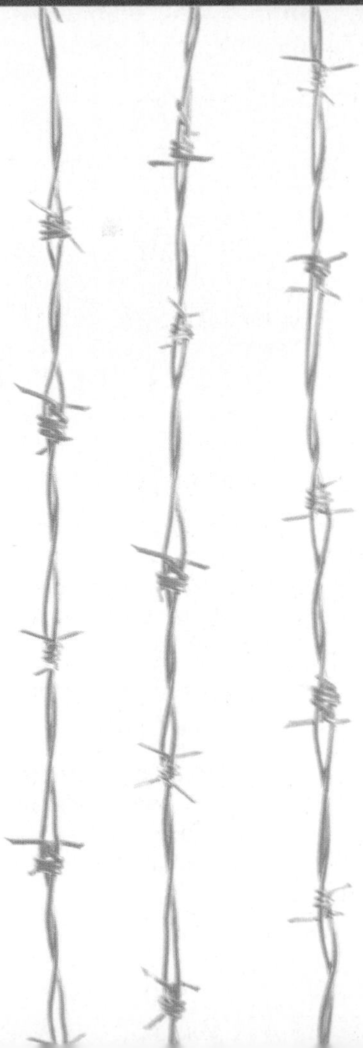

## Daddy (1966)

You do not do, you do not do
Any more, black shoe
In which I have lived like a foot
For thirty years, poor and white,
Barely daring to breathe or Achoo.

Daddy, I have had to kill you.
You died before I had time—
Marble-heavy, a bag full of God,
Ghastly statue with one gray toe
Big as a Frisco seal

And a head in the freakish Atlantic
Where it pours bean green over blue
In the waters off beautiful Nauset.
I used to pray to recover you.
Ach, du

In the German tongue, in the Polish town
Scraped flat by the roller
Of wars, wars, wars.
But the name of the town is common.
My Polack friend

Says there are a dozen or two.
So I never could tell where you
Put your foot, your root,
I never could talk to you.
The tongue stuck in my jaw.

It stuck in a barb wire snare.
Ich, ich, ich, ich,
I could hardly speak.
I thought every German was you.
And the language obscene

An engine, an engine
Chuffing me off like a Jew.
A Jew to Dachau, Auschwitz, Belsen.
I began to talk like a Jew.
I think I may well be a Jew.

The snows of the Tyrol, the clear beer
  of Vienna
Are not very pure or true.
With my gypsy ancestress and my
  weird luck
And my Taroc pack and my Taroc pack
I may be a bit of a Jew.

I have always been scared of *you*,
With your Luftwaffe, your gobbledygoo.
And your neat mustache
And your Aryan eye, bright blue.
Panzer-man, panzer-man, O You—

Not a God but a swastika
So black no sky could squeak through
Every woman adores a Fascist,
The boot in the face, the brute
Brute heart of a brute like you.

You stand at the blackboard daddy,
In the picture I have of you,
A cleft in your chin instead of your foot
But no less a devil for that, no not
Any less the black man who

Bit my pretty red heart in two.
I was ten when they buried you.
At twenty I tried to die
And get back, back, back to you.
I thought even the bones would do.

But they pulled me out of the sack,
And they stuck me together with glue.
And then I knew what to do.
I made a model of you,
A man in black with a Meinkampf look

And a love of the rack and the screw.
And I said I do, I do.
So daddy, I'm finally through.
The black telephone's off at the root,
The voices just can't worm through.

If I've killed one man, I've killed two—
The vampire who said he was you
And drank my blood for a year,
Seven years, if you want to know.
Daddy, you can lie back now.

There's a stake in your fat black heart
And the villagers never liked you.
They are dancing and stamping on you.
They always *knew* it was you.
Daddy, daddy, you bastard, I'm through.

# Writing from Reading

## Summarize

1 Describe the situation of this poem—who's speaking to whom? How does the poet address her dead father? What does she accuse him of, and why?

## Analyze Craft

2 Notice the use of German in this poem and the reference to *Mein Kampf* (Adolf Hitler's autobiographical book). Look at the way the poet compares her father to a vampire ("There's a stake in your fat black heart") and the various references to murder and suicide. What mood does this create?

3 Identify the colloquial language here ("Daddy, daddy, you bastard" or "breathe Achoo"). Why does she choose this language and end the poem with the assertion "I'm through"?

## Analyze Voice

4 Give examples of the poet's anger, even rage. Are there any gentle moments in the poem, any suggestions of love or forgiveness? (Consider Theodore Roethke's poem "My Papa's Waltz" by way of contrast.)

5 Notice how often the speaker says "you"—to someone no longer hears. Look at the rhyme scheme and the insistent repetitive pattern of sound. How would you describe the way repetition contributes to the tone of this poem?

### Synthesize Summary and Analysis

6 The Ben Jonson poem has a father speaking to his dead child, and the Sylvia Plath poem consists of a daughter addressing her dead father. How do the tones and attitudes seem similar, how different; which emotions govern which?

### Interpret the Poem

7 This monologue is one sided; there's no second point of view or position to be heard. In some sense it's both a *diatribe* and a *polemic* (look up these terms in your dictionary). Does Plath come to terms with her memories at poem's end?

# Rita Dove (b. 1952)

Rita Dove was born in Akron, Ohio, and graduated summa cum laude from Miami University in Ohio. She spent a year in Germany on a Fulbright scholarship, then earned an M.F.A. at the University of Iowa before becoming a professor herself. Her ability to render poems that resonate on both a personal and a larger historical level—in addition to her sensitivity toward language and poetic form—has earned her poetry widespread acclaim. Her collection *Thomas and Beulah* (1986) tells the story of her grandparents in short lyrical poems that beautifully render mundane moments; it was awarded the Pulitzer Prize. Less than a decade later, she became the youngest poet to be appointed Poet Laureate, a position she held from 1993 to 1995. She currently teaches at the University of Virginia.

**AS YOU READ** Think of the resonance of the word *master,* and how it suggests both the history of slavery and a competence at mathematics—in the former case it's used as a noun, in the latter as a verb. These fourteen lines suggest the poem belongs, although loosely, to the traditional sonnet form (see chapter 24); in form therefore it refers to the past but, in tone, it is contemporary.

# Flash Cards (1989)

In math I was the whiz kid, keeper
of oranges and apples. *What you don't understand,*
*master,* my father said; the faster
I answered, the faster they came.

I could see one bud on the teacher's geranium,
one clear bee sputtering at the wet pane.
The tulip trees always dragged after heavy rain
so I tucked my head as my boots slapped home.

My father put up his feet after work
and relaxed with a highball and *The Life of Lincoln.*
After supper we drilled and I climbed the dark

before sleep, before a thin voice hissed
numbers as I spun on a wheel. I had to guess.
*Ten,* I kept saying, *I'm only ten.*

# Writing from Reading

### Summarize

**1** Describe the place and, perhaps, the time of this poem. How far removed would you say the speaker is at the time of writing?

**2** Is it important to know that the poet is African American? What are flash cards? What kind of student is the speaker? Does the term "whiz kid" seem deserved?

### Analyze Craft

**3** If this poem appears autobiographical to you—if, in other words, the persona feels like the poet herself—what part of the poem suggests this? If not, why not?

**4** To be "spun on a wheel" is an ancient Greek form of torture. "After supper we drilled" might be another such torture. Does this poem convey a feeling of triumph or grief?

### Analyze Voice

**5** What do you think the speaker means by "keeper / of oranges and apples"?

**6** In the final line, we're twice given a number—"ten"—as the child's age. Does the tone or attitude seem childlike or adult?

### Synthesize Summary and Analysis

**7** Describe the relationship the speaker has with the father figure. How would you characterize the two figures in the poem? What changes; what stays the same?

### Interpret the Poem

**8** What does "the faster / I answered, the faster they came" suggest about life's problems? How does *The Life of Lincoln* connect to the poem's subject, and what is the attitude here?

Sometimes a persona need not even be a *person* in the first place. This may seem strange, but it can produce brilliantly inventive results. In "Golden Retrievals" Mark Doty puts together an engaging combination of persona and Asian spirituality, using his dog for the poem's wise speaker. The practice of Zen Buddhism calls for its adherents to try to live, consciously, in the present moment. Who better to exemplify this attention to the here and now than a golden retriever?

## Mark Doty (b. 1953)

Although born in Tennessee, Mark Doty moved frequently when he was young, so he felt, as he puts it, that "I grew up with a sense that home was something one constructed or carried around inside. I grew up loving books because they were reliable company." Doty's poetry, which has won awards including the National Book Critics Circle Award and the T. S. Eliot Prize, was impacted by the death of his partner, Wally, from AIDS. In addition to two collections of poetry that consciously engage with this event, *My Alexandria* (1993) and *Atlantis* (1995), Doty also wrote a memoir on the subject, *Heaven's Coast* (1996). He currently lives in Texas and teaches at the University of Houston.

**AS YOU READ** Remember Samuel Taylor Coleridge's notion of "the willing suspension of disbelief." Do you believe this poem is spoken by a dog? Look for ways Doty creates the dog as speaker in this poem.

# Golden Retrievals

(1998)

Fetch? Balls and sticks capture my attention
seconds at a time. Catch? I don't think so.
Bunny, tumbling leaf, a squirrel who's—oh
joy—actually scared. Sniff the wind, then

I'm off again: muck, pond, ditch, residue
of any thrillingly dead thing. And you?
Either you're sunk in the past, half our walk,
thinking of what you can never bring back,

or else you're off in some fog concerning
—tomorrow, is that what you call it? My work:
to unsnare time's warp (and woof!), retrieving,
my haze-headed friend, you. This shining bark,

a Zen master's bronzy gong, calls you here,
entirely, now: bow-wow, bow-wow, bow-wow.

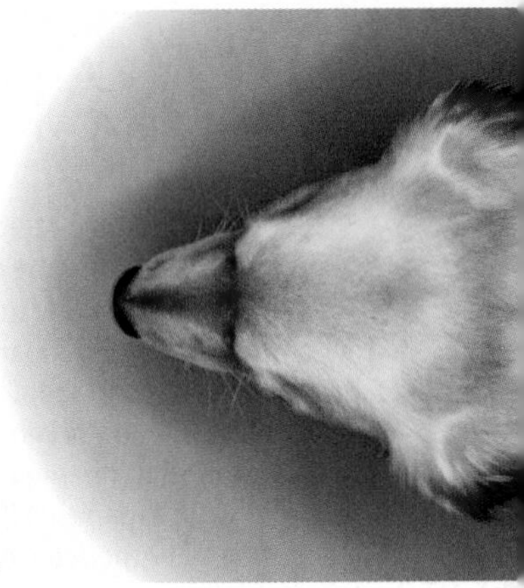

# Writing from Reading

### Summarize

1 Who is the speaker here, and to whom does he speak?

### Analyze Craft

2 "It's a dog's life," as they say. Provide details of that life from the available text. How persuasive is the poet when he writes "bow-wow, bow-wow, bow-wow"?

### Analyze Voice

3 What does the dog perceive that his human master fails to? What are his preoccupations, and what concerns the man?

4 Notice the parenthetical joke ("and woof"). How does this help establish tone?

### Synthesize Summary and Analysis

5 What does the poet-persona mean by "My work: / to unsnare time's warp . . . retrieving, / my haze-headed friend, you"?

6 If a dog is "man's best friend," what does he teach his companion?

### Interpret the Poem

7 Why would the author want to use the dog as a speaker for this poem? Who does the dog represent for the author? For you?

Often a persona entails a shift of gender as opposed to species. The contemporary poet Ai is well known for writing poems using personae separate from herself. While her poems sometimes comment on the African-American experience she herself has witnessed, the speakers of these poems are often characters she wholly creates. In the following poem, she adopts the persona of a man witnessing the 1992 race riots in Los Angeles.

## Ai (b. 1947)

"I am the child of a scandalous affair my mother had with a Japanese man she met at a streetcar stop," Ai comments of her own beginnings. (She legally changed her name to Ai, which means "love" in Japanese.) Born in Texas, of Native American, African, Irish, and Japanese descent, Ai grew up in Arizona, San Francisco, and Las Vegas. Her poetry most often takes the form of dramatic monologues, and she explores personalities as diverse as Marilyn Monroe, Leon Trotsky, and J. Edgar Hoover, and dark topics ranging from domestic to public violence. Her collection *Vice* (1999) won the National Book Award, and she received the Lamont Poetry Award from the Academy of American Poets for *Killing Floor* (1979). Ai holds an M.F.A. from the University of California, Irvine, and currently teaches at Oklahoma State University.

**AS YOU READ** Consider the "I" of this poem and try to establish its relation to the first-person pronoun of the poet herself. Pay attention to the tense of the narrative—the present tense—and how it reports on what happened on the specific date of the title.

# Riot Act, April 29, 1992 (1993)

I'm going out and get something.
I don't know what.
I don't care.
Whatever's out there, I'm going to get it.
Look in those shop windows at boxes
and boxes of Reeboks and Nikes
to make me fly through the air
like Michael Jordan
like Magic.
While I'm up there, I see Spike Lee.
Looks like he's flying too
straight through the glass
that separates me
from the virtual reality
I watch every day on TV.
I know the difference between
what it is and what it isn't.
Just because I can't touch it
doesn't mean it isn't real.
All I have to do is smash the screen,
reach in and take what I want.
Break out of prison.
South Central homey's newly risen
from the night of living dead,
but this time he lives,
he gets to give the zombies
a taste of their own medicine.
Open wide and let me in,
or else I'll set your world on fire,
but you pretend that you don't hear.

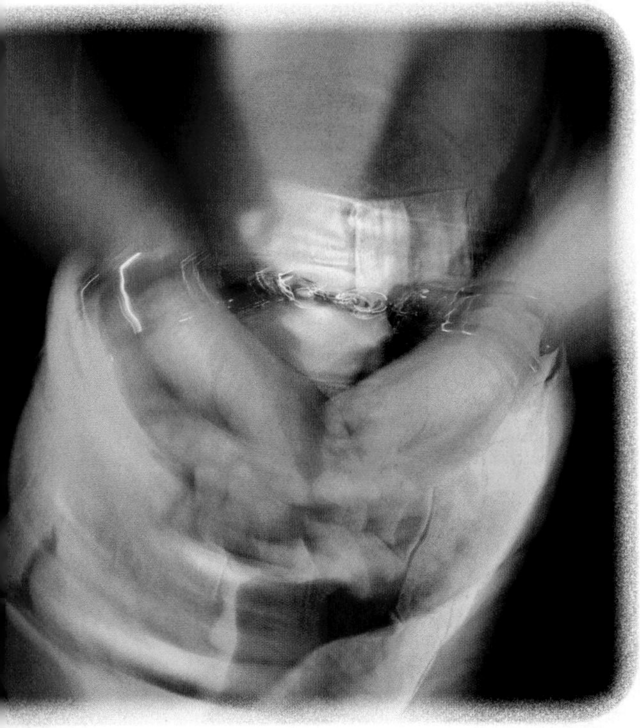

You haven't heard the word is coming down
like the hammer of the gun
of this black son, locked out of the big house,
while massa looks out the window and sees only smoke.
Massa doesn't see anything else,
not because he can't,
but because he won't.
He'd rather hear me talking about mo' money,
mo' honeys and gold chains
and see me carrying my favorite things
from looted stores
than admit that underneath my Raider's cap,
the aftermath is staring back
unblinking through the camera's lens,
courtesy of CNN,
my arms loaded with boxes of shoes
that I will sell at the swap meet
to make a few cents on the declining dollar.
And if I destroy myself
and my neighborhood
"ain't nobody's business, if I do,"
but the police are knocking hard
at my door
and before I can open it,
they break it down
and drag me in the yard.
They take me in to be processed and charged,
to await trial,
while Americans forget
the day wealth finally trickled down
to the rest of us.

# Writing from Reading

### Summarize

1 Describe the action in the poem. Who is the speaker and the poem's "I"?

### Analyze Craft

2 There are many references, here, to contemporary culture—"Raider's cap," "CNN," etc. Michael Jordan, Magic (Johnson), and Spike Lee were three major "players" on the contemporary scene in 1992. How does this help "date" the speaker?

3 Notice the tense shift at poem's end—present to past. Track the activity throughout.

### Analyze Voice

4 The phrase "ain't nobody's business, if I do" comes from a Billie Holliday song. How much of this is celebration and how much of this is "the blues"?

### Synthesize Summary and Analysis

5 Describe ways in which the poet constructs her speaker's character. If he were standing in a police lineup (as at poem's end), could you pick him out?

### Interpret the Poem

6 What is the poet's attitude toward her persona here?

The great Irish poet William Butler Yeats had a notion of "the mask" or "anti-self" and sometimes wrote—as in the "Crazy Jane" sequence—from a woman's point of view. In the poem that follows, he attempts to enter into the consciousness of someone obviously "other" than his own self, and the effect is both dramatic and, somehow, impersonal.

## William Butler Yeats (1865–1939)

For a brief biography of William Butler Yeats, see chapter 16.

**AS YOU READ** Listen for the two separate voices in conversation—the Bishop and Crazy Jane—and decide which of the points of view (either or both) you share.

# Crazy Jane Talks with the Bishop (1932)

I met the Bishop on the road
And much said he and I.
"Those breasts are flat and fallen now
Those veins must soon by dry;
Live in a heavenly mansion,
Not in some foul sty."

"Fair and foul are near of kin,
And fair needs foul," I cried.
"My friends are gone, but that's a truth
Nor grave nor bed denied,
Learned in bodily lowliness
And in the heart's pride.

"A woman can be proud and still
When on love intent;
But Love has pitched his mansion in
The place of excrement;
For nothing can be sole or whole
That has not been rent."

# Writing from Reading

### Summarize

1 Who are the speakers here, and what's the nature of their argument?

2 Assuming that the poet shares the opinion of his title character, what would seem to be Yeats's beliefs as to "fair and foul"?

### Analyze Craft

3 Why does "Crazy Jane" have a name and "the Bishop" merely a title?

4 These eighteen lines follow a fixed pattern, and each stanza rhymes in the second, fourth, and final line. What does that do to emphasis, and who has the last word?

### Analyze Voice

5 What does the speaker mean by "Love has pitched his mansion in / the place of excrement"? Literally? Metaphorically?

6 Comment on the double meanings in the final stanza: "whole" and "sole" and "rent."

### Synthesize Summary and Analysis

7 What ideas about religion—behavior in this life, and the question of the afterlife—are presented here?

8 Discuss the oppositions of body and soul, the church and the fallen woman, faith and physical appearance. Can they be reconciled?

### Interpret the Poem

9 Yeats wrote a series of poems from the point of view of an invented character whom he based upon an old woman who lived in a cottage in Gort, a small village near Galway in western Ireland. What does he admire in her, and why would he use *her* language to make what would appear to be *his* point?

# For Review and Further Study

## Frank Bidart (b. 1939)

### Herbert White (1973)

"When I hit her on the head, it was good,

and then I did it to her a couple of times,—
but it was funny,—afterwards,
it was as if somebody else did it . . .

Everything flat, without sharpness, richness or line.

Still, I liked to drive past the woods where she lay,
tell the old lady and the kids I had to take a piss,
hop out and do it to her . . .

The whole buggy of them waiting for me
made me feel good;
but still, just like I knew all along,
she didn't move.

When the body got too discomposed,
I'd just jack off, letting it fall on her . . .

—It sounds crazy, but I tell you
sometimes it was *beautiful*—; I don't know how
to say it, but for a minute, everything was possible—;
and then,
then,—
well, like I said, she didn't move: and I saw,
under me, a little girl was just lying there in the mud:

and I knew I couldn't have done that,—
somebody *else* had to have done that,—
standing above her there,
in those ordinary, shitty leaves. . . .

—One time, I went to see Dad in a motel where he was
staying with a woman; but she was gone;
you could smell the wine in the air; and he started,
real embarrassing, to cry . . .
He was still a little drunk,
and asked me to forgive him for
all he hadn't done—; but, What the shit?
Who would have wanted to stay with Mom? with
bastards
not even his own kids?

I got in the truck, and started to drive,
and saw a little girl—
who I picked up, hit on the head, and
screwed, and screwed, and screwed, and screwed, then

buried,
in the garden of the motel . . .

—You see, ever since I was a kid I wanted
to *feel* things make sense: I remember

looking out the window of my room back home,—
and being almost suffocated by the asphalt;
and grass; and trees; and glass;
just *there*, just *there*, doing nothing!
not saying anything! filling me up—
but also being a wall; dead, and stopping me;
—how I wanted to see beneath it, cut

beneath it, and make it
somehow, come alive . . .

*The salt of the earth;*
Mom once said, 'Man's spunk is the salt of the earth . . .'

—That night, at that Twenty-nine Palms Motel
I had passed a million times on the road, everything

fit together; was alright;
it seemed like
everything *had* to be there, like I had
spent years
trying, and at last finally finished drawing this
huge circle . . .

—But then, suddenly I knew
somebody *else* did it, some bastard
had hurt a little girl—; the motel
I could see again, it had been
itself all the time, a lousy
pile of bricks, plaster, that didn't seem to
have to be there,—but *was*, just by chance . . .

—Once, on the farm, when I was a kid,
I was screwing a goat; and the rope around his neck
when he tried to get away
pulled tight;—and just when I came,
he *died* . . .
I came back the next day; jacked off over his body;
but it didn't do any good . . .

Mom once said:
'Man's spunk is the salt of the earth, and grows kids.'

I tried so hard to come; more *pain* than anything else;
but didn't do any good . . .

—About six months ago, I heard Dad remarried,
so I drove over to Connecticut to see him and see
if he was happy.
She was twenty-five years younger than him:
she had lots of little kids, and I don't know why,
I felt shaky . . .
I stopped in front of the address; and
snuck up to the window to look in . . .
—There he was, a kid
six months old on his lap, laughing
and bouncing the kid, happy in his old age
to play the papa after years of sleeping around,—
it twisted me up . . .
To think that what he wouldn't give me,
he *wanted* to give them . . .

I could have killed the bastard . . .

—Naturally, I just got right back in the car,
and believe me, was determined, determined,
to head straight for home . . .

but the more I drove,
I kept thinking about getting a girl,
and the more I thought I shouldn't do it,
the more I had to—

I saw her coming out of the movies,
saw she was alone, and
kept circling the blocks as she walked along them,
saying, 'You're going to leave her alone.'
'You're going to leave her alone.'

—The woods were scary!
As the seasons changed, and you saw more and more
of the skull show through, the nights became clearer.
and the buds,—erect like nipples . . .

—But then, one night,
nothing worked . . .
Nothing in the sky
would blur like I wanted it to;
and I couldn't, *couldn't*,
get it to seem to me
that somebody *else* did it . . .

I tried, and tried, but there was just me there,
and her, and the sharp trees
saying, 'That's you standing there.
You're . . .
just you.'

I hope I fry.

—Hell came when I saw
MYSELF . . .
and couldn't stand
What I see . . ."

## Questions for Interactive Reading and Writing

1. Who is the speaker here, and whom does he address?
2. As a dramatic monologue, this poem offers a character at war with all our notions of decency—and, in some sense, at war with himself. Note the places in the poem where he comments on and tries to understand his own behavior.
3. Note the usages of dialogue—remembered and overheard speech.
4. How does Bidart make such a heinous character human? Describe the voice of the character, and what he means by "funny. . . ." Note the slang—"did it," "screwed," etc., and discuss how this helps establish the verisimilitude—the seeming truth—of the voice.
5. Dark parts of the human psyche are the subject here, but the speaker does complete his confession by saying, "I hope I fry." Is he sincere?
6. There's a famous line by the French philosopher-playwright Jean-Paul Sartre: "Hell is other people." At the end of this monologue, however, the speaker Herbert White says, "Hell came when I saw / MYSELF." Discuss.
7. This example of a modern-day dramatic monologue explores a son's reaction to his relationship to his father—and the murderous perversity in which the speaker engages. It was considered a tour de force (great achievement) when it was first published and awarded the National Book Critics Good Reads for 2008. How do you reconcile the loathsome character with the art that brought him into being?

# Juan Felipe Herrera (b.1948)

## Autobiography of a Chicano Teen Poet (1987)

*For Rosita, RIP, Alvnita & Chente & Tito &*
*Julie & Chelita & Yooyee & Beto Jr & Ray G.*

I am a downtown boy, handcuffed
when I was eleven
for being accomplice to armed robbery.

I speak shoeshine parlor brown and serve
as the only usher in *Club Sufrimiento 2001.*

You can call me Johnny B. Nice.

Tender hollow-eyed whores and
busted novelists in spiderweb trenchcoats
are partners in the law firm where I live.

Thelonious Monk,
Janis Joplin, sip with me when you can.
I am out here playing my blues,
my autobiography of penny arcade rendezvous.

From here I can see the Mayor.
He just got three years probation for perjury
and now he's working for the "homeless."
Who was he working for in the first place?

I used to go to church, but the wind-up doll got tired
and couldn't speak proper English anymore.
So, God punished it and drove it into the wilderness
where it found a color film of a Wonderkid
selling Language and Infinity to the lost on Inferno
Street.
But, the translation wasn't bilingual, even though
they showed it at the Casino with triple porno movie.

My brother died in the ring,
stabbed 14 times by the King of Desire.
All the electric guitars moaned in the pawnshops
and my mother grew smaller with memory.

Above me,
the phosphor light coughs and sweats.

I can't wait to see the red-striped cellophane
from cigarette packs—whirl
into a fire at the center of the street.

## Questions for Interactive Reading and Writing

1. Herrera is known for his interest in spoken word poetry and jazz. Can you imagine this piece as a performance? Why or why not?
2. Herrera was raised in California by parents who were immigrants and farmworkers. He himself was educated at the University of California, Los Angeles, and Stanford University, yet his poetry speaks to his roots. How does this poem appeal to those who may have similar experiences?
3. References abound to musicians such as Thelonius Monk and Janis Joplin, and it helps to know what they stood for and what their music sounds like. Look up these musicians on the internet. Why do you think they are referred to in this poem?

# Natasha Trethewey (b. 1966)

## Letter Home (2002)

*—New Orleans, November 1910*

Four weeks have passed since I left, and still
I must write to you of no work. I've worn down
the soles and walked through the tightness
of my new shoes, calling upon the merchants,
their offices bustling. All the while I kept thinking
my plain English and good writing would secure
for me some modest position. Though I dress each day
in my best, hands covered with the lace gloves
you crocheted—no one needs a *girl*. How flat
the word sounds, and heavy. My purse thins.
I spend foolishly to make an appearance of quiet
industry, to mask the desperation that tightens
my throat. I sit watching—

though I pretend not to notice—the dark maids
ambling by with their white charges. Do I deceive
anyone? Were they to see my hands, brown
as your dear face, they'd know I'm not quite
what I pretend to be. I walk these streets
a white woman, or so I think, until I catch the eyes
of some stranger upon me, and I must lower mine,
a *negress* again. There are enough things here
to remind me who I am. Mules lumbering through
the crowded streets send me into reverie, their footfall
the sound of a pointer and chalk hitting the blackboard
at school, only louder. Then there are women, clicking
their tongues in conversation, carrying their loads
on their heads. Their husky voices, the wash pots
and irons of the laundresses call to me. Here,

I thought not to do the work I once did, back-bending
and domestic; my schooling a gift—even those half days
at picking time, listening to Miss J—. How
I'd come to know words, the recitations I practiced
to sound like her, lilting, my sentences curling up
or trailing off at the ends. I read my books until
I nearly broke their spines, and in the cotton field,
I repeated whole sections I'd learned by heart,
spelling each word in my head to make a picture
I could see, as well as a weight I could feel
In my mouth. So now, even as I write this
And think of you at home, Good-bye

is the waving map of your palm, is
a stone on my tongue.

## Questions for Interactive Reading and Writing

1. Trethewey's first work focused on prostitutes in New Orleans in the early 1900s. In this poem, she creates a character looking for work and becoming ever more desperate. How does Trethewey present her? Describe the voice of the character here.
2. Why would Trethewey want to create this persona, this voice?
3. What tone does the poem establish? What words show the speaker's unease?

## IRONY

In life as well as in writing, we detect tone by careful or instinctive observation. Sometimes, whether we're conscious of it or not, we pick up on a difference between what someone says and what they actually mean. As in other literary genres, in poetry this difference is called **irony,** a discrepancy between what a poem says and what it means.

If you've ever encountered the old story of Robin Hood, you may remember that one of Robin's closest friends is a man called Little John. You may also remember that there's actually nothing little about Little John. He's huge, in fact, burly and fat. Calling him "Little" ultimately draws our attention, playfully, to his considerable size. This nickname is a simple example of **verbal irony,** a statement in which the stated meaning is very different from (or the opposite of) the implied meaning.

> "[The] best ironist is profoundly alert to the world—alert, hears the doubleness of things, works that doubleness. It's a . . . keenness of attention, and rather than keep the world away, it interrogates that world—it tries to measure it."
>
> Conversation with Stephen Dunn

One of the most familiar forms of verbal irony is **sarcasm,** a critical use of spoken approval to express implied disapproval. Who hasn't heard, at some point, a phrase like, "Oh, yeah, you look *great* in that hat," or "This is the best vacation ever," when in fact the hat looks ridiculous and it rains the whole week?

## Paul Laurence Dunbar (1872–1906)

Born in Dayton, Ohio, to parents who had been slaves, Paul Laurence Dunbar is remembered chiefly for his poetry, although he also wrote short stories and novels. The only black student in his high school class, Dunbar was class poet and published poems in Dayton newspapers. Although his race at first relegated him to a job as an elevator operator, Dunbar continued to write and soon had a national reputation. While some of his work protests racism, much of it—particularly his poems written in dialect—has been criticized for perpetuating harmful stereotypes of blacks in the Old South. Still, he is recognized as the foremost black poet at the turn of the twentieth century, despite a career cut short by his death from tuberculosis at age thirty-three.

**AS YOU READ** Irony is double-edged. Look for language that suggests the speaker is seemingly above the battle. Look for words that are insulting. Notice how the poet puts these together in the poem.

# To a Captious Critic (1901)

Dear critic, who my lightness so deplores,
Would I might study to be prince of bores,
Right wisely would I rule that dull estate—
But, sir, I may not, till you abdicate.

# Writing from Reading

### Summarize

1 This is a brief letter to a critic written as a poem. Look up the word *captious,* then speculate on what the critic has done to trigger this response.

### Analyze Craft

2 How would you describe the language used in this poem? Formal? Informal? Is poetic diction employed?

3 List the images in the poem. How do these set up the twist in the last line of the poem?

4 Some of the phrasing puts unlikely words together, such as "prince" and "bore." What other phrases like this do you find in this poem?

### Analyze Voice

5 How does the speaker feel about the critic? What in the poem reveals his feelings? How would you describe the poem's tone?

6 Although the tone sounds as though it comes directly out of the eighteenth-century satirical poetry of Alexander Pope, what aspects of this brief poem reveal it is written by a more modern voice?

### Synthesize Summary and Analysis

7 What does the letter form enable the speaker to accomplish in this poem?

8 Contrast the diction in this poem with the point of the poem.

9 How does the speaker use humor in this poem, and how does he mask insult as respect?

### Interpret the Poem

10 Dunbar was praised and criticized for his use of dialect. In writing a poem like this, elevated in language and formal in tone, what point do you think he desires to make?

Because verbal irony can suggest implicit scorn, it's often a good choice for writing that seeks to criticize or attack an idea. **Satire** does this—it's an artistic critique, sometimes quite heated, on some aspect of human immorality or absurdity. In the two poems that follow—one written about World War I, the other about World War II—the poets Wilfred Owen and Kenneth Fearing use both irony and satire to establish attitude—saying, in effect, that far from something to celebrate, war is hell.

# Wilfred Owen (1893–1918)

Wilfred Owen, a British poet, is invariably associated with World War I, and with good reason—his best poetry takes the war for its subject, and he himself served and was killed in the war. A poet from a young age, Owen went to France to teach English in 1913, the year before the war broke out. He enlisted in 1917 and was hospitalized for shell shock later that year. In the hospital, Owen met Siegfried Sassoon, whose war poetry inspired Owen to achieve a new level of maturity in his own poems. Owen's carefully structured poems use physical imagery to create a visual record of war horrors, while using pararhyme—that is, words with the same consonants but different vowels—to give an auditory sense of the discord of war. Owen was killed in action one week before the war's end.

**AS YOU READ** The poem's Latin title means "It Is Sweet and Proper." As you read, look for contrasting vivid flashes of news about the miseries and dangers of the battlefield.

## Dulce et Decorum Est (1920)

Bent double, like old beggars under sacks,
Knock-kneed, coughing like hags, we cursed through sludge,
Till on the haunting flares we turned our backs
And towards our distant rest began to trudge.
Men marched asleep. Many had lost their boots
But limped on, blood-shod. All went lame; all blind;
Drunk with fatigue; deaf even to the hoots
Of tired, outstripped Five-Nines that dropped behind.

Gas! GAS! Quick, boys!—An ecstasy of fumbling,
Fitting the clumsy helmets just in time;
But someone still was yelling out and stumbling
And floundering like a man in fire or lime . . .
Dim, through the misty panes and thick green light,
As under a green sea, I saw him drowning.

In all my dreams, before my helpless sight,
He plunges at me, guttering, choking, drowning.

If in some smothering dreams you too could pace
Behind the wagon that we flung him in,
And watch the white eyes writhing in his face,
His hanging face, like a devil's sick of sin;
If you could hear, at every jolt, the blood
Come gargling from the froth-corrupted lungs,
Obscene as cancer, bitter as the cud
Of vile, incurable sores on innocent tongues,—
My friend, you would not tell with such high zest
To children ardent for some desperate glory,
The old Lie: Dulce et decorum est
Pro patria mori.

# Writing from Reading

## Summarize

1 Who is "bent double" in this poem?

2 What kind of "gas" is being alluded to in the second stanza? Why is everyone "fumbling" in response? How could gas cause someone to drown?

3 What is happening to the person who is "floundering"?

## Analyze Craft

4 The speaker uses numerous images to describe the scene: "like old beggars under sacks," "sludge." List several images from the last stanza. How do these images build suspense in the poem?

5 Wilfred Owen was very young when he composed this poem, but he describes his soldier-comrades in the terms of old age and disease using ordinary, unpoetic words like "coughing." How do these word choices set the scene described in this poem?

## Analyze Voice

6 Discuss such phrases as "An ecstasy of fumbling" or "incurable sores on innocent tongues." Why does the speaker use contrasting words like "ecstasy" (a word meaning exquisite delight) and "fumbling," or "incurable" and "innocent"? Given that irony provides a kind of double take on a situation, what do words like these reveal about the author's feelings about war?

## Synthesize Summary and Analysis

7 The poem's title says one thing, and the poem describes the opposite experience. The Latin at poem's end means, roughly, "It is sweet and proper to die for one's country." The images would suggest nothing sweet about it. What is "The old Lie"? How does the poet's vivid description of war's horror prepare the reader for the last lines of this poem?

## Interpret the Poem

8 World War I erased a generation of young men (including the poet). Is this poem mostly a witness to the poet's own experiences, or is this a social commentary? Would you call the poem propaganda? Could you imagine another poem in which the experiences of the soldiers could be rendered in beautiful language? Is there an argument in this poem, and if so, how convincing is the argument to you?

Published in 1938, when the Nazis began to mobilize throughout Europe, this poem employs satirical verbal irony to criticize not only the brutality of war but also the ways in which potential soldiers are recruited. Fashioned in the form of a newspaper want ad, the poem ironically invites applicants to volunteer to die.

# Kenneth Fearing (1902–1961)

Born in Oak Park, Illinois, Kenneth Fearing was raised mostly by an eccentric aunt. After attending the University of Wisconsin, Fearing went to New York where he supported himself in part by writing pulp fiction, much of which bordered on pornography. His first collection of poems, *Angel Arms* (1929), introduced him as a poet of his age with a bitter sense of irony toward the working classes as well as the wealthier. He published poems regularly in *The New Yorker,* although he also went through periods of writing prose. Active in left-wing politics, Fearing was known for his pessimism, cynicism, and misanthropy. A longtime smoker and heavy drinker, Fearing died of cancer while still in his fifties.

**AS YOU READ** Locate and list the advertising slogans in these lines. Consider who the "we" and the "you" in the poem are.

# AD (1938)

*Wanted:* Men;
Millions of men are *wanted at once* in a big new field;
*New, tremendous, thrilling, great.*
If you've ever been a figure in the chamber of horrors,
If you've ever escaped from a psychiatric ward,
If you thrill at the thought of throwing poison into wells, have
heavenly visions of people, by the thousands, dying in flames—

*You are the very man we want*
We mean business and our business is *you*
*Wanted:* A race of brand-new men.

Apply: Middle Europe;
No skill needed;
No ambition required; no brains wanted and no character allowed;

*Take a permanent job in the coming profession*
Wages: *Death.*

# Writing from Reading

## Summarize

1 What is being advertised in this poem?

## Analyze Craft

2 "Dulce et decorum est" is a kind of advertising slogan in Latin; this "ad" employs a more modern tone. What advertising slogans are used? How do they build momentum toward the ironic last line?

## Analyze Voice

3 How do phrases like "if you've ever escaped from a psychiatric ward" work with the slick, hollow words of marketing to reveal what the speaker feels about World War II? What does his choice of these phrases tell you about his feelings about the war?

## Synthesize Summary and Analysis

4 With what ads are you familiar today? Do they use phrases similar to those used in this poem? Compare the kinds of things that are advertised today to what is being advertised in this poem. Why would the speaker use ads as a description of military recruitment?

## Interpret the Poem

5 "Dulce et decorum est" is written about World War I, in which gas was a factor in trench warfare; World War II, which has been described as "The Good War," relied more on bombs. Technologies may have changed, but is Fearing making the same case as Owen about war? Why or why not?

**Situational irony** occurs when a poem portrays a situation in which what happens is the opposite of what's expected to happen. In the following poem, note how our understanding of the gentleman Richard Cory is shaped. Throughout the poem, we hear of his remarkable fortune, manner, and appearance. His fellow townspeople think his life vastly superior to their own. By the end of the poem, however, we realize Richard Cory's life may have been very different from how it appeared on the surface.

## Edwin Arlington Robinson (1869–1935)

A native of Maine, Edwin Arlington Robinson devoted his life to poetry, struggling with poverty for many years. He studied at Harvard for two years, and his writing eventually won the admiration of Theodore Roosevelt, who arranged for Robinson to work in a New York customs house. Robinson's poetry gradually became more successful, from his first, self-published collection *The Children of the Night* (1897) to his *Collected Poems* (1921), which won the first Pulitzer Prize for Poetry. With his mastery of traditional forms, his portraits of characters like Miniver Cheevy, and his interest in Arthurian legend, Robinson won two more Pulitzers for *The Man Who Died Twice* (1924) and *Tristram* (1927).

**AS YOU READ** **Notice the rhyming pattern in these quatrains, the way everything's perfectly ordered and in place. The final line therefore doubly reverses expectation that all will be "right" in the end.**

### Richard Cory (1897)

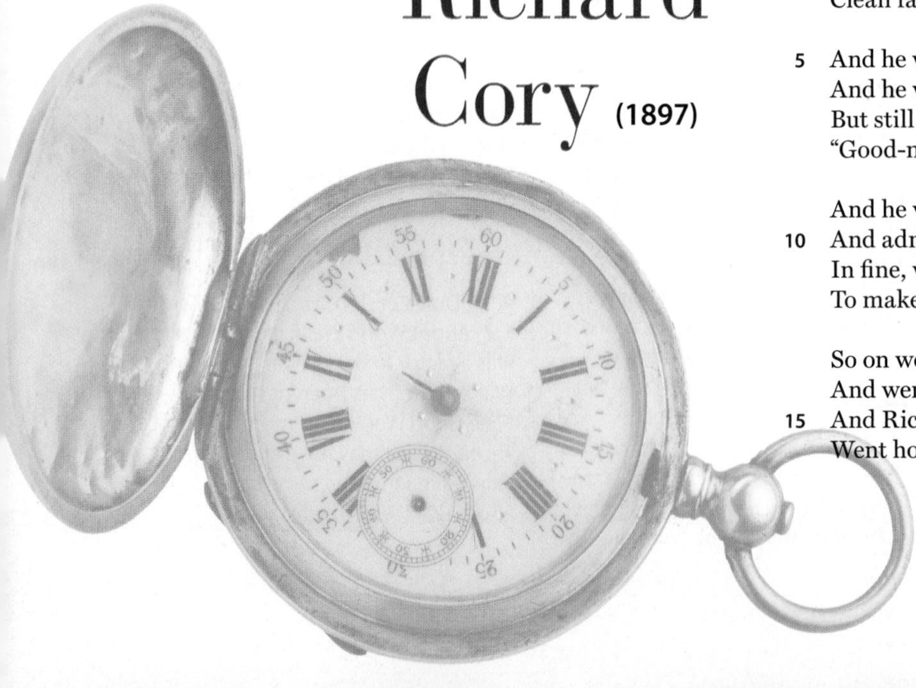

Whenever Richard Cory went down town,
We people on the pavement looked at him:
He was a gentleman from sole to crown,
Clean favored and imperially slim.

And he was always quietly arrayed,
And he was always human when he talked,
But still he fluttered pulses when he said,
"Good-morning," and he glittered when he walked.

And he was rich—yes, richer than a king—
And admirably schooled in every grace:
In fine, we thought that he was everything
To make us wish that we were in his place.

So on we worked, and waited for the light,
And went without the meat, and cursed the bread;
And Richard Cory, one calm summer night,
Went home and put a bullet through his head.

# Writing from Reading

### Summarize

1 What happens here, and who tells the story? Who are "we"?

### Analyze Craft

2 How do the ballad-like feel of these stanzas and the singsong pattern make the disruption of the final line all the more disturbing and harsh-sounding.

3 What would happen if, instead of "one calm summer night," Robinson had written "one dark and stormy night"?

### Analyze Voice

4 This story is told in the past tense, and therefore the speaker knows what has happened. Why does he save the worst for last?

### Synthesize Summary and Analysis

5 This poem is presented without verbal irony, but the situation is ironic in the extreme. How does Robinson make you understand Richard Cory's situation without providing all the facts?

### Interpret the Poem

6 What would you describe as "the moral" here?

A literary convention familiar to readers of classical drama, **dramatic irony** (sometimes called **tragic irony**) refers to a situation in which the reader knows (or is made aware of) more about a character's circumstances than the character himself knows. **Cosmic irony** occurs when forces beyond the characters' control, like God or fate or the supernatural, foil their plans or expectations. Thomas Hardy's famous poem "The Convergence of the Twain" responds to the sinking of the *Titanic,* which struck an iceberg and sank, killing 1,500 people. Hardy suggests that the vain human "Pride of Life" that conceived of such a glorious ship could not overcome "The Immanent Will," the cosmic forces that formed the iceberg that doomed the ship.

# Thomas Hardy (1840–1928)

A British writer proud of his long life span, Thomas Hardy lived at a time when rural England was becoming increasingly industrialized and modern, a fact that figures into his fiction as well as his poetry. Originally trained as an architect, Hardy was drawn to writing and began his career as a novelist, publishing titles that are still well known today, including *Far from the Madding Crowd* (1874), *The Mayor of Casterbridge* (1886), and *Tess of the D'Urbervilles* (1891). But when *Jude the Obscure* (1895) received harsh criticism, Hardy—at the age of fifty-five—gave up novel writing and turned instead to poetry. His poems, like his fiction, are imbued with his bleak, pessimistic outlook, and where his fiction captures characters with strong passions who must nevertheless submit to an unkind and indifferent fate, his poetry equally transmits a passionate sense of loss, as in the poems written following his wife's death, known collectively as *Veteris Vestigiae Flammae* (1914).

**AS YOU READ** Note the regularity in these eleven stanzas and thirty-three lines—and how it all builds to a shock for which the reader is prepared (as opposed to, say, the shock of "Richard Corey").

# The Convergence of the Twain

**(1912)**

## *Lines on the loss of the "Titanic"*

I
In a solitude of the sea
Deep from human vanity,
And the Pride of Life that planned her, stilly couches she.

II
Steel chambers, late the pyres
Of her salamandrine fires,
Cold currents thrid, and turn to rhythmic tidal lyres.

III
Over the mirrors meant
To glass the opulent
The sea-worm crawls—grotesque, slimed, dumb, indifferent.

IV
Jewels in joy designed
To ravish the sensuous mind
Lie lightless, all their sparkles bleared and black and blind.

V
Dim moon-eyed fishes near
Gaze at the gilded gear
And query: "What does this vaingloriousness down here?"

VI
Well: while was fashioning
This creature of cleaving wing,
The Immanent Will that stirs and urges everything

VII
Prepared a sinister mate
For her—so gaily great—
A Shape of Ice, for the time far and dissociate.

VIII
And as the smart ship grew
In stature, grace, and hue,
In shadowy silent distance grew the Iceberg too.

IX
Alien they seemed to be:
No mortal eye could see
The intimate welding of their later history,

X
Or sign that they were bent
by paths coincident
On being anon twin halves of one august event,

XI
Till the Spinner of the Years
Said "Now!" And each one hears,
And consummation comes, and jars two hemispheres.

# Writing from Reading

## Summarize

1 What is the story behind the actual *Titanic*?

2 How does Hardy relate the building of the ship to the forming of the iceberg?

3 Who is the "Spinner of the Years"?

## Analyze Craft

4 Notice the formal arrangements here and the shock with which the poem ends. How does Hardy use language to create this shock?

5 Note the "intimate welding" of iceberg and ship. How does Hardy make them "twin halves"?

## Analyze Voice

6 "Anon" means "soon" in formal poetic diction, and "august" means "important/consequential." How does the word "Now!" make all this more immediate, and what does the poet mean by "consummation comes"?

## Synthesize Summary and Analysis

7 Discuss what you think Hardy means by "no mortal eye" when he describes the *Titanic*'s fate.

## Interpret the Poem

8 The poet censures "vaingloriousness." Does he suggest that this in some way contributes to the sinking? What is his attitude here?

Stephen Dunn confronts an imagined terrorist in this poem, simultaneously expressing dismay, anger, and fundamental human empathy. While full of feeling, "To a Terrorist" still manages to seem quiet and thoughtful; its voice is somber and far less playful than the voice of "After." Notice how the word "Still" in stanza 4 suggests a kind of conversation; Dunn balances the emotion of the poem with solemn commentary. It's as if the speaker's continuing with a line of inner argument, adding another point to points already made. His poem does more than try to just express emotional reactions. It also tries to *understand* someone unknown and upsetting to the speaker.

# Stephen Dunn (b. 1939)

See Dunn's brief biography earlier in this chapter.

**AS YOU READ** Think about why a writer would ever address a poem to a violent fanatic. Also, consider how Dunn's choice of tone in the poem helps communicate the feelings and experience he seeks to explore, and how another choice of tone (a more severe or enraged attitude, for example) would have affected your reading.

# To a Terrorist (1988)

For the historical ache, the ache passed down
which finds its circumstance and becomes
the present ache, I offer this poem

without hope, knowing there's nothing,
not even revenge, which alleviates
a life like yours. I offer it as one

might offer his father's ashes
to the wind, a gesture
when there's nothing else to do.

Still, I must say to you:
I hate your good reasons.
I hate the hatefulness that makes you fall

in love with death, your own included.
Perhaps you're hating me now,
I who own my own house

and live in a country so muscular,
so smug, it thinks its terror is meant
only to mean well, and to protect.

Christ turned his singular cheek,
one man's holiness another's absurdity.
Like you, the rest of us obey the sting,

the surge. I'm just speaking out loud
to cancel my silence. Consider it an old impulse,
doomed to become mere words.

The first poet probably spoke to thunder
and, for a while, believed
thunder had an ear and a choice.

# Writing from Reading

## Summarize

1 Who is the speaker and who the imagined audience here? What is the conversation's subject, and how does Christ enter in?

## Analyze Craft

2 "The first poet probably spoke to thunder" begins the final stanza. How does this comparison relate to the subject of this poem, and does thunder have "an ear and a choice"?

## Analyze Voice

3 Do you think this poem's speaker is the poet or a separate persona?

4 How would you describe the speaker's tone in this poem? Why does Dunn choose this kind of voice for the subject matter?

## Synthesize Summary and Analysis

5 The poet writes, "I offer this poem / without hope." How does that help situate what poems can and can't do?

## Interpret the Poem

6 This poem was written many years before the tragedy of September 11, 2001. Does this affect your reading of the poem? Why or why not?

# For Review and Further Study

## e. e. cummings (1894–1962)

*For a brief biography of e. e. cummings, see chapter 24.*

### next to of course god america i (1926)

"next to of course god america i
love you land of the pilgrims' and so forth oh
say can you see by the dawn's early my
country 'tis of centuries come and go
and are no more what of it we should worry
in every language even deafanddumb
thy sons acclaim your glorious name by gorry
by jingo by gee by gosh by gum
why talk of beauty what could be more beautiful than these heroic happy dead
who rushed like lions to the roaring slaughter
they did not stop to think they died instead
then shall the voice of liberty be mute?"

He spoke. And drank rapidly a glass of water

#### Questions for Interactive Reading and Writing

1. There are slogans here, and snippets of formulaic speech; what is e. e. c ummings's attitude toward the speaker? Does he share that persona's views?
2. How do the lowercase nouns and lack of punctuation and conjoined words (deafanddumb) help establish tone, and how would you describe the speaker's voice?
3. Like the poem by Dorothy Parker included next in this chapter, this borrows—and bends—the form of a sonnet. How do you read the last line?

## Dorothy Parker (1893–1967)

### Sonnet for the End of a Sequence (1944)

So take my vows and scatter them to sea;
Who swears the sweetest is no more than human.
And say no kinder words than these of me:
"Ever she longed for peace, but was a woman!
And thus they are, whose silly female dust
Needs little enough to clutter it and bind it,
Who meet a slanted gaze, and ever must
Go build themselves a soul to dwell behind it."

For now I am my own again, my friend!
This scar but points the whiteness of my breast;
This frenzy, like its betters, spins an end,
And now I am my own. And that is best.
Therefore, I am immeasurably grateful
To you, for proving shallow, false, and hateful.

#### Questions for Interactive Reading and Writing

1. Is this a personal or persona poem, or both? How would you describe the "I"?
2. Would you describe this poem's tone as ironic or sarcastic, and were you surprised by the final couplet?
3. Would you call this a love poem, a "hate" poem, both?

# Reading for Voice

| When Reading for Voice, Ask Yourself . . . | | |
|---|---|---|
| **What is the speaker's predominant tone in the poem—joyful, mournful, bewildered, or confused—and how does it help convey the poem's meaning?** | *Tone:* The vocal quality of a person's speech that helps convey meaning. In a poem, an attitude conveyed toward a poem's subject as suggested by the poet's language. | EXAMPLE: "When I died they washed me out of the turret with a hose." |
| **Who is the speaker in the poem, and why has the poet chosen to use this persona? What does the persona allow the poet to represent more clearly? What is the poet's attitude toward the speaker in the poem?** | *Persona:* A poem's speaker that may or may not be the same voice as the poet. | EXAMPLE: "Fetch? Balls and sticks capture my attention / seconds at a time." |
| **Is irony used to help establish the speaker's attitude toward the subject?** | *Verbal Irony:* The use of words to express something dissimilar to (or the opposite of) their literal meaning. | EXAMPLE: "Millions of men are *wanted at once* in a big new field; / *New, tremendous, thrilling, great.*" |
| | *Sarcasm:* A form of verbal irony using spoken approval to express implied disapproval. | EXAMPLE: "Oh, yeah, you look *great* in that hat." |
| | *Situational Irony:* An outcome that turns out to be very different from what was expected. | EXAMPLE: "And Richard Cory, one calm summer night, / Went home and put a bullet through his head." |
| | *Dramatic Irony / Tragic Irony:* A discrepancy that is detectable to audience but not to a character or characters. | EXAMPLE: "'next to of course god america i / love you land of the pilgrims' and so forth oh" |
| | *Cosmic Irony:* A discrepancy between what characters hope for or expect and what supernatural forces, fate, or God provide. | EXAMPLE: "The Immanent Will that stirs and urges everything" |

# Writing about Voice

1. Compare the relationships of speaker to father figure in Sylvia Plath's "Daddy," Theodore Roethke's "My Papa's Waltz," and Rita Dove's "Flash Cards."
2. Compare the speakers' attitudes toward war and conflict in "To a Terroist" by Stephen Dunn, "AD" by Kenneth Fearing, "Dulce et Decorum Est," by Wilfred Owen, and "next to of course god america i" by e. e. cummings.
3. Consider the tone of William Stafford's "Traveling through the Dark." How does it reflect the conflict and hesitation the speaker faces, and how does Stafford's tone help convey this hesitation?
4. Analyze the interplay of tone and word choice in Wallace Stevens's "Sunday Morning." How does Stevens's language and attitude toward the subject matter help communicate his character's religious deliberations?
5. Write a short, informal imagined biography for the speaker of one of the following poems: "Riot Act" by Ai; "Golden Retrievals" by Mark Doty; "Herbert White" by Frank Bidart. Use specific material in the poems to help support your invented history.
6. Consider the attitude of Ben Jonson's address to his son and Anne Bradstreet's to her book. Move through the poems and explain, in writing, what we learn. Be specific as to what the poem reveals.
7. What is Thomas Hardy saying about the irony of human existence in "Convergence of the Twain"? Compare it with what Edward Arlington Robinson is saying in "Richard Cory." What do these poems tell us about the way their authors look at life, at death, and how what may seem like an accident is fate?

IT is foolish
to let a young redwood
grow next to a house.

Even in this
one lifetime,
you will have to choose.

*—from "Tree" by Jane Hirshfield*

**JANE Hirshfield tells us in her interview, "Now the tree is real and the house is real. Both actually exist, and as the poem says, the house is cluttered with unique things. It's a real dilemma. Eventually the house and the tree won't be able to occupy the same bit of earth. But a house and a tree are also archetypes and images."**

**In the case of a tree, you have the image of an object and you also have the larger symbol of what a tree means as archetype: the particular instance that represents the whole. This specific tree, a redwood growing in a specific place, has also come to represent the idea of natural versus man-made things. It embodies—or stands as a symbol for—the ideas of containment and growth.**

# 20 Imagery

*"The wider the field of senses a poem draws on, the more fully felt and alive its world is going to be in the mind of the reader."*

Conversation with Jane Hirshfield, available on video at http://www.mhhe.com/delbanco1e

"Tree" and its author belong to a tradition of nature writing, of close attention paid to the physical world. In this chapter, we focus on the **image,** the thing seen for and by itself, as well as the **symbol,** what that same thing might stand for or represent. Poetry comes across mainly in terms of an attitude-generating cluster of words, creating vivid sensory (visual, aural, or tactile) impressions through language. Images work in the service of diction and tone; they generate emotion and establish mood. In the case of Hirshfield, the impetus has been provided by the sight of a nearby tree—a "young redwood" that the poet understands will grow much larger over time. Building on that particular sight and specific visual cue, this poem moves out to the general case.

# & Symbol

*Image is a field where the powers of body and mind can meet.*

# Q&A

*Poetry is a kind of thinking and feeling done with the whole body, mind, and heart.*

# A Conversation on Writing

## Jane Hirshfield

### Thinking with the Body

Image is one of the most powerful ways a poem both carries meaning and changes and enlarges it, which is the work that every good poem is trying to do. Image is a field where the powers of body and mind can meet. Everything that we know of the world is constructed on the bedrock of sense experience. . . . Poetry is a kind of thinking and feeling done with the whole body, mind, and heart.

### The Meaning of an Image

Every image is also a portrait of a state of soul. Rain in a poem is almost never only rain. In one poem it might be grief; in another it might be renewal after long thirst or after the drought of loneliness. Image in poetry is an enormously flexible, intimate, and powerful tool just because it hands experience from one person's consciousness into another's directly, with the solidity, multiplicity, and subtlety of actual life, which doesn't arrive with interpretations attached. A poem can add some direction to this, but the image itself is sometimes the only thing that's needed.

### Meditations on the Ordinary

One of the things that has happened to poetry as it's become more contemporary is more and more things have become the subject of poems, and one of the things which has come into poetry in the twentieth and twenty-first centuries is poems about very ordinary objects, meditations on objects which you wouldn't ordinarily think of as

worthy of that important thing we think of as poetry, and yet in fact poetry's work is to see the ordinary world . . . and turn that into something which expounds into larger realms, more resonance, more feeling. It lets you have a bigger life than you would have had if you only saw a button as simply a thing that holds your shirt closed.

Jane Hirshfield lives in a small white cottage in Marin County, California, surrounded by the trees, flowers, and animals that often appear in her poems. Born in New York City in 1953, she was among the first female graduates of Princeton University. Hirshfield has published six books of poetry, including *After* ( 2006), *Given Sugar, Given Salt* (2001), *The Lives of the Heart* (1997), *The October Palace* (1994), *Of Gravity & Angels* (1988), and *Alaya* (1982); essays about poetry, *Nine Gates: Entering the Mind of Poetry* (1997); and several anthologies of women poets. Early in her career, Hirshfield dedicated three years to the study of Zen practice, and her poetry reflects this lifelong involvement in Buddhism. Many poems focus on the natural world and our human condition within it. Hirshfield has received major honors for her poetry, including, in 2004, the seventieth Academy Fellowship for distinguished poetic achievement by the Academy of American Poets.

**To watch this entire interview and hear the author read from her poetry, go to www.mhhe.com/delbanco1e.**

**RESEARCH ASSIGNMENT** In the interview, Hirshfield describes how she uses her own experiences to construct the imagery in her poems. After watching the interview, how would you describe the meaning that Hirshfield herself assigns to her poem "Tree"?

**AS YOU READ** Monitor any visual images that come to you. Can you picture the poet's description of this scene in your mind's eye?

## *Two Poems by Jane Hirshfield*

# Tree (2000)

It is foolish
to let a young redwood
grow next to a house.

Even in this
one lifetime,
you will have to choose.

That great calm being,
this clutter of soup pots and books—

Already the first branch-tips brush at the window.
Softly, calmly, immensity taps at your life.

# Writing from Reading

### Summarize

1 Describe the physical growth of the redwood tree and how it is impinging on the house.

### Analyze Craft

2 What use is the poet making of the literal growth of the tree?

3 Can you picture it? From what literal vantage point does the poet view the tree?

### Analyze Voice

4 Is the poet in a panic about the situation? Or does she speak calmly? Is she trying to accept the growth of the tree as part of the progress, or lack of it, in her own life? How does this affect her choice of words?

### Synthesize Summary and Analysis

5 How does the poet employ the actual tree in order to speak about something greater than just one single redwood?

### Interpret the Poem

6 Do you detect a rhythmic progress in the few stanzas of this poem? If the poet states the problem, wrestles with it, and somehow resolves it, in what particular context does that occur? Would you say the poem speaks to us about a situation in the natural world or in a more abstract philosophical fashion about the situation of our own lives?

*CONTINUED FROM PAGE 145*

Here's another of her close examinations of an object—in this case a man-made as opposed to a natural thing. As the poem continues, the image of a button becomes "its own story, completed." And once again the poet ("I tell you") speaks directly to her readers, inviting us to enter the world of her scrupulous words.

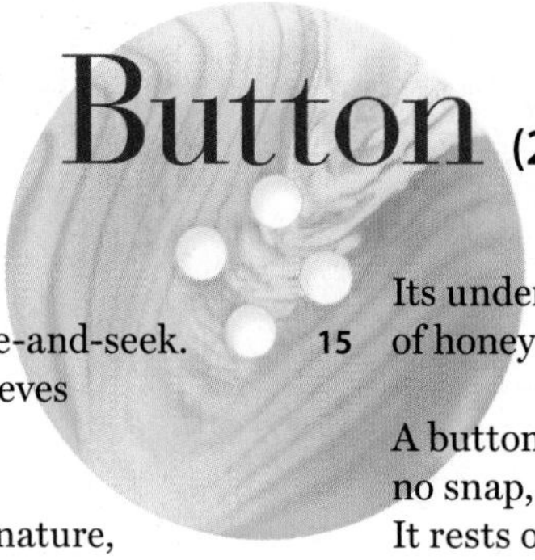

# Button (2000)

It likes both to enter and to leave,
actions it seems to feel as a kind of hide-and-seek.
It knows nothing of what the cloth believes
of its magus-like powers.

If fastening and unfastening are in its nature,
it doesn't care about its nature.

It likes the caress of two fingers
against its slightly thickened edges.
It likes the scent and heat of the proximate body.
The exhilaration of the washing is its wild pleasure.

Amoralist, sensualist, dependent of cotton thread,
its sleep is curled like a cat to a patch of sun,
calico and round.

Its understanding is the understanding
of honey and jasmine, of letting what happens come.

A button envies no neighboring button,
no snap, no knot, no polyester-braided toggle.
It rests on its red-checked shirt in serene disregard.

It is its own story, completed.

Brevity and longevity mean nothing to a button carved
of horn.

Nor do old dreams of passion disturb it,
though once it wandered the ten thousand grasses
with the musk-fragrance caught in its nostrils;
though once it followed—it did, I tell you—that wind
for miles.

# Writing from Reading

### Summarize

1 The poet speaks of a simple, even humble, object from our everyday lives. How does she describe it, in how many ways, and on how many levels of meaning?

### Analyze Craft

2 Is there a specific term we can use to describe the way the poet uses the object in the poem? As what sort of living thing does the poet describe the button?

3 How can a button have a "story"?

4 How does the poet work to make us feel a certain way about the button?

### Analyze Voice

5 What attitude does she express toward the object? What central words or phrases alert you to this?

6 What is the effect of the phrase "it did, I tell you," which the poet sets apart from the rest of the last line?

### Synthesize Summary and Analysis

7 How does the poet raise a simple everyday object into something greater than itself?

### Interpret the Poem

8 Picture the button in all of the states of being or manifestations in which the poet describes it. How important is it that the poet employs the word "horn" to explain the button's origins?

Some of the earliest poetry based almost entirely on image is that of Japanese **haiku.** In haiku (a poetic form containing—in Japanese—seventeen syllables in three lines of five, seven, and five syllables each), two images are juxtaposed in a way that allows a reader to create his or her own understanding of the meaning; the images themselves carry the poem. Haiku also traditionally contain some natural-world reference to a particular season, and so an image from nature is at the heart of each of the following two haiku, one by the eighteenth–nineteenth-century poet Kobayashi Issa (who Hirshfield discusses in her interview) and the other by the seventeenth-century poet Matsuo Bashō, generally considered the first to perfect the haiku form.

> "Every time I heard my parents recite ancient . . . poetry . . . my own experience was that I was hearing language that was manifesting something older and something mysterious and something beautiful that I couldn't account for, and I wanted to be a part of that." Conversation with Li-Young Lee

# Kobayashi Issa (1763–1827)

The Japanese poet used simply the pen name Issa and brought a highly personal voice to the haiku form, using dialect and colloquial language and confessing his personal doubts and loneliness. Issa was born in Kashiwabara, the son of a farmer, and lost his mother at three and his devoted grandmother as a teenager. By age fifteen, Issa had left for Edo (present-day Tokyo), where he entered a school for haiku poets. He spent much of his adult life wandering Japan before settling once again in Kashiwabara, where he married and tried to start a family. All four of his children died in infancy, and his first wife died in childbirth. His poetry, which was influenced by Buddhist themes of sin and compassion, uses simple language to articulate human experiences (as in his collection *The Year of My Life,* 1819, which captures his life events, among them his daughter's death). Despite his hardships, he brings the small pleasures of daily life into the more than 20,000 haiku he wrote in his lifetime.

## On a branch (c. 1800)

On a branch
floating downriver
a cricket, singing.

*—translated by Jane Hirshfield*

# Matsuo Bashō (1644–1694)

A Japanese master of the haiku, Matsuo Bashō spent his youth as a servant to a master with whom he had a close friendship. Bashō's first published poetry appeared in 1664, but when his master died two years later, Bashō became a wanderer. He continued to publish poetry, however, and his reputation grew; he soon had a group of twenty students. The students so respected their teacher that they built him a hut, complete with a *bashō*—or banana tree—outside its door, from which he adopted his nickname. Famous in his lifetime, Bashō took four long journeys in Japan during which he visited friends and wrote poetry and travel journals including *The Records of a Weather-Exposed Skeleton* (1684–1688). Bashō's haiku are marked by a precision of imagery—both visual and auditory—that conveys human emotion.

## A caterpillar (c. 1680)

A caterpillar,
this deep in fall—
still not a butterfly.

*—translated by Robert Hass*

# Writing from Reading

### Summarize

1 Describe the images evoked in both haikus. Note the use of present tense and, in Bashō, the absence of verbs.

### Analyze Craft

2 The Japanese original of this form has a precise number of syllables and usually includes at least two varieties of necessary words, one to denote the season and one to end the poem on a certain emotional note; it is written all in one sentence. How does the English form of the haiku differ from the original? What is the role of the image?

### Analyze Voice

3 Is there a similarity between the two poets? What makes for this kinship aside from the form of the poems?

4 How does the subject matter affect the voice of the speaker?

### Synthesize Summary and Analysis

5 These poems are composed in a specific syllabic form, each focusing on a situation in nature that has meaning for the observer and reader. What limitations does this bring, what freedoms?

### Interpret the Poem

6 Each of these situations, tiny in scope, suggests something much larger about nature and about human life. See if you can make the leap between the cricket and the caterpillar and our own problems of living in crisis or living with time.

Like Jane Hirshfield, but nearly a century earlier, Ezra Pound was much impressed by poetry from Asia—particularly Chinese verse and Japanese haiku, with their brief evocations of things closely seen. Living in Paris and taking the metro (the French term for the subway), he made this striking comparison of urban commuters and the petals on a tree. There's no explicit discussion or association, no essay-like analysis of the way light-colored faces cluster in the station's darkness—but the "unnatural" or man-made crowd of commuters seems suddenly to have become a "natural" thing, a part of nature's blooming. What the poet sees is what compels his (and therefore our) attention. No moral here, or conclusion to draw; there is just an image, defined by Pound as "an intellectual and an emotional complex in an instant of time."

# Ezra Pound (1885–1972)

Regarded as a crucial modern American poet, Ezra Pound helped foster the careers of important Modernists like James Joyce, T. S. Eliot, and Ernest Hemingway. Pound grew up in Pennsylvania and moved to London in 1908. Later, he would move to Italy and become a supporter of Benito Mussolini, for which in 1945 he was arrested and incarcerated for more than a decade in a Washington, D.C., mental hospital. But before he became a politically controversial figure, Pound forged a bridge between American and European avant-gardes, launching the Imagist movement—which advocated poems pared down to an image without any abstraction—early in his career. He later moved away from Imagism, but elements of its stark, precise quality remained in his poetry. His major works, "Hugh Selwyn Mauberley: Life and Contacts" (1920) and "The Cantos"—written over many years—reflect Modernist techniques such as shifts in time and point of view, an eclectic inclusion of material, and a wide-ranging diction.

**AS YOU READ** Notice the influence of haiku here—the compression of language and centrality of image all caught "in an instant of time."

# In a Station of the Metro (1916)

The apparition of these faces in the crowd;
Petals on a wet, black bough.

# Writing from Reading

### Summarize

**1** What action does this poem describe and what, if anything, goes on?

### Analyze Craft

**2** How does the word *apparition* color the poem that follows; what emotion does it convey?

### Analyze Voice

**3** Who is speaking here, and to whom? If the Hirshfield poem yokes the man-made to the natural world, how do these "petals on a wet, black bough" seem similar to or different from her thoughts about a tree?

### Synthesize Summary and Analysis

**4** We've already used more words in the discussion of this poem than are contained in the poem itself. In what ways does Pound's brevity reinforce his notion of an image as an "intellectual and emotional complex in an instant of time"? In what ways does the image convey an idea or feeling about more time than just a single moment?

### Interpret the Poem

**5** The title sets the scene, the poem provides the image. Would the feel of the whole be altered if the title read, instead, "At a Football Game" or "On a Bus"?

Pound and several of his fellow poets founded a movement called **Imagism,** which gave the object *seen* in a poem precedence over any other aspect of the poem. The American expatriate Hilda Doolittle, or H.D., as she signed her work, was one of Pound's partners in this "school" or "movement"—also believing in the elemental power of the image. In her poems, as in Pound's, we look at the thing itself, even as the poet attempts to suggest that details of the natural world evoke a meaning beyond their mere physical presence.

## H.D. (Hilda Doolittle; 1886–1961)

Born in Bethlehem, Pennsylvania, H.D. became friends with William Carlos Williams and Ezra Pound at the University of Pennsylvania. In 1911, she took a summer trip to London, which turned into a lifelong residency abroad and which launched her poetry career when she reconnected with Pound. Under his influence, she became an Imagist, interested in pared-down verses that portrayed only immediate, real objects. Later, she moved away from Imagism, cultivating her interest in mythology and composing book-length poems about World War II: *The Walls Do Not Fall* (1944), *Tribute to the Angels* (1945), and *The Flowering of the Rod* (1946).

**AS YOU READ** In "Sea Poppies" what we look at is the thing itself. The image of sea poppies is in sharp focus in this poem. Ask yourself, how does the poet attempt to suggest that details of the natural world evoke a meaning beyond their mere physical nature?

# Sea Poppies

**(1916)**

Amber husk
fluted with gold,
fruit on the sand
marked with a rich grain,

treasure
spilled near the shrub-pines
to bleach on the boulders:

your stalk has caught root
among wet pebbles
and drift flung by the sea
and grated shells
and split conch-shells.

Beautiful, wide-spread,
fire upon leaf,
what meadow yields
so fragrant a leaf
as your bright leaf?

# Writing from Reading

### Summarize

1 Write your own "snapshot" of this poem.

### Analyze Craft

2 List ways in which the poet tries to make the reader *see* sea poppies. What words are most effective here as description and which ones (such as "beautiful") convey value judgments instead?

3 Compare this with Marianne Moore's "The Fish" in chapter 22. Both poems use an image from the natural world; however, the line structure of the Moore poem emphasizes sound over imagery. How does H.D.'s poem keep the image in focus and Moore's poem shift our attention to sound?

### Analyze Voice

4 How large a role, if any, does voice play in this poem? How might a more prominent presence alter the tone of this poem?

### Synthesize Summary and Analysis

5 Explain how the image takes you to a higher level of understanding of the poem's meaning.

### Interpret the Poem

6 Notice how, in the last stanza, H.D. repeats the word *leaf* three times. What effect does this achieve?

The short poems of William Carlos Williams, the physician from Patterson, New Jersey, illustrate a great deal about that modern tendency in poetry defined by Pound as imagism. Here the "thing itself"—an object seen and not discussed or analyzed—becomes the poet's focus and the poem's primary concern. Gertrude Stein's famous pronouncement that "a rose is a rose is a rose" shares much the same aesthetic—or, as Williams puts it (in his 1944 poem "A Sort of Song"), "No ideas but in things."

On first reading, the following brief poem seems to be about almost nothing. There are echoing sounds such as "glazed" and "rain," or "white" and "beside," and the lines have a similar rhythm, but if you recite these words they may well sound like a casual overheard sentence—not a formal arrangement of language in a structured shape. The formality of Williams's work is less than obvious: a thing you have to look closely at in order to notice at all. In fact, there's a nearly haiku-like compression of

> "So there's the ordinary shape of the thing and the way that you would say it . . . and if you piece them out on the page, you can convey the feeling by getting this shape absolutely."
>
> Conversation with Robert Hass

and shape to the work. The poet presents us with a couple of objects, a red wheelbarrow glazed with rainwater standing in a yard alongside a bunch of white chickens. Together, the poem's formal elements ingrain in our memory the image of the barrow and the chickens and the rain. The life evoked by objects—in a barnyard or a garden patch, and in particular weather—grows as vivid here as though it were *painted,* and as fixed within our memory as though it had been framed. In this way, a poem that seems at first glance quite casual puts forward an image of eternal order and upholds the importance, in a democratic contemporary fashion (very conversational, very American), of each and every thing and every one of us.

## William Carlos Williams (1883–1963)

William Carlos Williams was born in Rutherford, New Jersey, the same town in which he would die eighty years later. This fact is consistent with one of Williams's most fundamental beliefs about poetry: that one ought to write about one's own locale. Williams had many other strong ideas about poetry, among them that the poet should focus only on concrete details and images rather than trying to convey abstract ideas. Although friends with Ezra Pound and T. S. Eliot, Williams in many ways stands in opposition to their complex references and international emphases; unlike his contemporaries, he spent little time abroad. Considered one of the most important of twentieth-century poets, Williams made his living as a doctor with a specialization in pediatrics (he delivered more than 2,000 babies!). His touchstone work, *Paterson,* is an epic in five books—the third of which won the National Book Award in 1950—about Paterson, New Jersey.

**AS YOU READ** Notice how Williams divides "wheel" and "barrow" or "rain" and "water" in a line break; others might have written "wheelbarrow" or "rainwater," but the space between the words and lines allows us to consider how those objects separate or fuse.

# The Red Wheelbarrow (1923)

so much depends
upon

a red wheel
barrow

glazed with rain
water

beside the white
chickens.

# Writing from Reading

### Summarize

1 What images do you see in this poem? How are they connected?

### Analyze Craft

2 What does Williams accomplish by beginning each line with a lowercase letter?

3 Why does Williams say "a" red wheelbarrow instead of "the" red wheelbarrow?

### Analyze Voice

4 What's *not* said is just as important as what's included here. What has been left out, and how would the poem change if it were included in the poem?

### Synthesize Summary and Analysis

5 How does the casual tone combine with the structure to make the poem's point?

### Interpret the Poem

6 The only statement in the entire poem that does not describe a physical thing is the opening line—"so much depends." You can read the first line, in effect, as either "very much depends" or "therefore much depends," and the interpretation of the phrase shifts back and forth accordingly. How much of the meaning of this poem depends on the phrasing of this statement?

Another representation of the importance of the image comes in the following poem—again, very plainly presented—by the twentieth-century American poet Wallace Stevens. This self-described **anecdote**—a personal remembrance or brief story—also takes as its topic the *things* of the world, though a jar upon a hill is somehow more surprising than a wheelbarrow in a backyard. A secondary meaning of the word *jar* is "discord" or "disruption," and the imagined "gray and bare" object cleans up what's "slovenly." Perhaps no clearer testimonial to the power of an image (and what poetry can accomplish by "foregrounding" such an image) exists than "Anecdote of the Jar."

# Wallace Stevens (1879–1955)

For a brief biography of Wallace Stevens, see chapter 18.

**AS YOU READ** Notice how the poem's first word is "I," infusing the poet himself with the pride of positioning the important jar. How does this act of shaping—"like nothing else in Tennessee"—organize and change what is around it?

## Anecdote of the Jar (1923)

I placed a jar in Tennessee,
And round it was, upon a hill.
It made the slovenly wilderness
Surround that hill.

The wilderness rose up to it,
And sprawled around, no longer wild.
The jar was round upon the ground
And tall and of a port in air.

It took dominion everywhere.
The jar was gray and bare.
It did not give of bird or bush,
Like nothing else in Tennessee.

# Writing from Reading

### Summarize

1 Describe the jar. Could you draw it?

2 What words does Stevens use to convey the image? Does it represent a Mason jar, a ceramic jug, a particular bowl you have seen?

### Analyze Craft

3 Notice how the last word of the first line and the last word of the poem are the same (this is true also of the final word in lines 2 and 4). Then there are three perfect rhymes ("air," "everywhere," "bare"). What does this tell you about the "shaping impulse" on the poet's part?

### Analyze Voice

4 Can you read this poem as a companion text to William Carlos Williams's "The Red Wheelbarrow"? In what ways is the voice different, in what ways the same?

### Synthesize Summary and Analysis

5 How does the act of *seeing* itself connect to the name of the state repeated twice—at the end of the poem's first and last lines? How different would this anecdote be if the poet had located his jar in Nevada or Rhode Island?

### Interpret the Poem

6 How much *depends* on the jar in Tennessee, the jar that "took dominion everywhere"? What if the poet had not "placed a jar in Tennessee"? Would the world—or, even more grandly, the universe—be different?

**ALLEGORY AND PARABLE**

**Allegory** and **parable** are related to symbol and are both extended narratives in which people, places, and things function more like conventional symbols directly representing such attributes as good, evil, redemption, hell, or heaven. One of the most famous poetic allegories is Dante's *Divine Comedy.* A parable, like the Fishes and the Loaves from the Gospel of Matthew in the New Testament, is usually an allegory but also a teaching tale with a moral.

Coming up now is another domestic image, another familiar object closely seen: the image of "The Blue Bowl." In this poem, "we" engage in other matters; we work and eat and sleep and attempt to forget what's been buried. The bowl itself—plastic, ceramic, tin, china?—disappears from sight, but the sense of its absent presence remains. In that sense, it stands as a symbol—as well as a literal burial container—of what is cherished and lost.

> "Poetry . . . bring[s] image . . . and symbol to bear on unspeakable love or hurt or loss or hate or whatever happens to be." Conversation with Thomas Lynch

Here is a crucial distinction between image and symbol. If, as William Carlos Williams puts it, there are "no ideas but in things," there are certain "things" within our culture that stand—almost inescapably—for "ideas." A jar in Tennessee or a wheelbarrow glazed with rain are specific images, but say such words as "dove" or "cross" or "crown" and it's impossible not to imagine what else they represent. A dove means *peace* as well as bird, a cross means *suffering and sacrifice* as well as arrangement of wood. The connotations of the word *crown* are those of *power, majesty,* but when Christ wears a crown of thorns we know what that headgear signifies instead. The word for this, in pictorial terms, is **iconography**—put a scepter or skull in a painting, and the viewer is supposed to know what those objects represent. In earlier times, these were almost **conventional** associations: *a* stands for one thing, *b* stands for another, and so on and so forth. More modern poets, however, tend to create their own symbols and go against the grain. So when Jane Kenyon makes "the blue bowl" *stand* for something, she's making that object symbolic in a literary way, a way that is specific to its context in the poem, a way it had not been before.

## Jane Kenyon (1947–1995)

Born in Ann Arbor, Michigan, Jane Kenyon remained there through her undergraduate and graduate education at the University of Michigan. While at the university, Kenyon met poet Donald Hall, whom she married. The couple settled in the New Hampshire home that had been in Hall's family for generations. There, Kenyon began to take her poetry seriously and published four collections, which met with high praise for their portrayals of New England, the cycles of nature, and the depression with which she struggled. She died at age forty-seven of leukemia.

**AS YOU READ** Ask yourself who is the "we" of this poem, and notice that the title tells you something—the bowl's color—that the body of the text does not include.

# The Blue Bowl (1990)

Like primitives we buried the cat
with his bowl. Bare-handed
we scraped sand and gravel
back into the hole.
They fell with a hiss
and thud on his side,
on his long red fur, the white feathers
between his toes, and his
long, not to say aquiline, nose.

We stood and brushed each other off.
There are sorrows keener than these.

Silent the rest of the day, we worked,
ate, stared, and slept. It stormed
all night; now it clears, and a robin
burbles from a dripping bush
like the neighbor who means well
but always says the wrong thing.

# Writing from Reading

### Summarize

1 Why does Kenyon give this poem the title she does?

### Analyze Craft

2 It would seem that in this poem the image of the bowl takes on itself the emotion of the situation—the death and burial of a beloved pet. Is it a visible presence once dropped into the ground?

### Analyze Voice

3 We're told by the poet that "There are sorrows keener than these." What are those sorrows? How does this contribute to the mood of the poem?

### Synthesize Summary and Analysis

4 How much of a role does the bowl play in this poem? Is it all-encompassing, like the jar in Tennessee in the Stevens poem?

### Interpret the Poem

5 If the burbling robin seems to be saying "the wrong thing," what does the poet suggest here about the possibility of consolation, and does she instead imply that it's better to be "silent the rest of the day"?

## POEMS AND PAINTINGS

Put the "blue" from the title of "The Blue Bowl" together with the other two colors mentioned in Kenyon's poem ("long red fur, the white feathers"), and you have the colors of the American flag. This very American poem may not be suggesting anything in particular about the American way of life, but it's hard not to think of red, white, and blue as somehow representative colors—as well as, in and of themselves, vivid particular hues. Our discussion of voice in the previous chapter had largely to do with the sound and the diction of verse, what we *hear* as tone of voice. The "blue bowl" points to what we *see*. Poets have always also had a fascination for the visual, the pictorial representation of things; when William Carlos Williams focuses on a wheelbarrow or chickens, he too insists on telling us that they are red and white. Many poets work with particular paintings in mind, taking verbal cues from the images provided by a work of visual art. Here are three.

# W. H. Auden (1907–1973)

For a brief biography of W. H. Auden, see chapter 18.

**AS YOU READ** Notice that this poem begins, as the title tells us, in a particular place with the poet examining a particular painting. But the opening statement is nonetheless a generality—a blank to be filled in by what he, studying, sees.

# Musée des Beaux Arts (1940)

About suffering they were never wrong,
The Old Masters: how well, they understood
Its human position; how it takes place
While someone else is eating or opening a window or just walking dully along;
How, when the aged are reverently, passionately waiting
For the miraculous birth, there always must be
Children who did not specially want it to happen, skating
On a pond at the edge of the wood:
They never forgot

That even the dreadful martyrdom must run its course
Anyhow in a corner, some untidy spot
Where the dogs go on with their doggy life and the torturer's horse
Scratches its innocent behind on a tree.

In Breughel's *Icarus*, for instance: how everything turns away
Quite leisurely from the disaster; the ploughman may
Have heard the splash, the forsaken cry,
But for him it was not an important failure; the sun shone
As it had to on the white legs disappearing into the green
Water; and the expensive delicate ship that must have seen
Something amazing, a boy falling out of the sky,
Had somewhere to get to and sailed calmly on.

## Brueghel's *Fall of Icarus*

*Pieter Brueghel the Elder.* Landscape with the Fall of Icarus, *c. 1554–1555. Oil on panel (transferred to canvas), 2′ 5″ x 3′ 8 1/8″. Musées Royaux des Beaux-Arts de Belgique, Brussels. © akg-images.*

"Beneath their flight / the fisherman while casting his long rod, / or the tired shepherd leaning on his crook, / or the rough plowman as he raised his eyes, / astonished might observe them on the wing, / and worship them as Gods" (Ovid, lines 338–343). In Brueghel's painting, the characters are all in place, but their reactions, as Auden observes in the following poem, demonstrate a resignation far from the astonishment Ovid describes. The plowman turns his head to the ground, the fisherman keeps his eyes on the water, and the boat, with its sails billowed out toward the horizon, keeps sailing. In the bottom right, away from the focus, fallen Icarus drowns, kicking his feet at the sunny sky.

# Writing from Reading

### Summarize

1 What is happening when suffering "takes place" in this poem? What is the suffering that Auden is referring to? What is the first and final point that Auden makes?

### Analyze Craft

2 This is a work of art about a work of art. How does the tone differ from, say, a poem about a button or a tree?

3 Look at the rhyme pattern of the last eight lines. How does what we hear help establish what we see, and why should the poem's last words be "calmly on"?

### Analyze Voice

4 Discuss a phrase like "the dogs go on with their doggy life" or "for him it was not an important failure."

### Synthesize Summary and Analysis

5 The second stanza of this poem evokes an individual canvas by a particular painter. How much does it help to have a visual image of the image evoked here?

6 How faithful has the poet been to the Brueghel painting described?

### Interpret the Poem

7 Why do you think Icarus dies off at the edge of the composition and not stage center? What is the poet saying, by way of this image, about the importance of "great events" and their place in daily life?

# Anne Carson (b. 1950)

Growing up in Ontario, Canada, Anne Carson developed a love for the classics when one of her high school teachers taught her ancient Greek during school lunch hours. Carson eventually earned her bachelor's, master's, and doctorate from the University of Toronto, and today is a professor of classics and comparative literature at the University of Michigan. Her interest in the classics is reflected in her work: *Autobiography of Red* (1998), a novel-length poem, is a recasting of a Greek myth in the present day, while *Plainwater* (1996), a collection of poetry and prose, includes a conversation with a seventh-century B.C. poet. She has immersed herself in the world of Greek theatre and translated the work of the poet Sappho. Carson has received awards including a MacArthur Foundation award and a Guggenheim Fellowship.

**AS YOU READ** Ask yourself how faithful the verbal "tone" here is to the visual mood of the Hopper painting.

# Automat

**(2000)**

Night work
  neon milk
  powdered
  silk
Girl de luxe

Girl work
  plate glass love
  lone
  glove
Night de luxe

Girl work
  smell of black
  down
  the back
Night de luxe

Night work
  *clamo*
  *ad te*
  *Domine*
Girl de luxe

# Edward Hopper's *Automat* (1927)

A lone woman sits in an automat sipping a cup of coffee. She is well dressed, not a vagrant, but her missing glove and downcast eyes suggest hurry or distraction. Hopper's intention in the painting is ambiguous. An opaque black window dominates the scene, reflecting only rows of lights from the apparently empty automat. The lone woman's skin is the brightest part of the painting, contrasting sharply with the void of the window, and (for the painting's time) perhaps more than slightly suggesting female sexuality. Consider the coin-operated, Prohibition-era setting: Is the woman trapped, lonely, or waiting? Hopper's work frequently appears to capture a scene immediately before or after the action has occurred; as in *Automat,* it is often difficult to know which is the case.

*Edward Hopper (American, 1882–1967).* Automat. *1927. Oil on Canvas; 36" x $28^{1}/_{8}$". Des Moines Art Center Permanent Collections; Purchased with fund from the Edmundson Art Foundation, Inc., 1958.2.*

# Writing from Reading

## Summarize

**1** How would you describe the poet's response to the painting?

## Analyze Craft

**2** Does the poem seem at all "painterly"? How does it employ visual material?

**3** Does the rhyming make clear Carson's response? What effect do the repetitive images have?

## Analyze Voice

**4** Can you identify the needs and interests of the speaker based on her voice? Is the poet singing the praises of the girl or judging her?

## Synthesize Summary and Analysis

**5** How would you characterize the effect of the poem compared with the effect of the painting? How does the painting affect your reaction to the poem?

## Interpret the Poem

**6** Does the quotation in devotional Latin add to the mystery of the poem or make the poem clearer to you? It might help to know that the Latin *clamo ad te Domine* means "I cry out, God, to you."

# Cathy Song (b. 1950)

Cathy Song was born in Hawaii of Korean and Chinese descent. She left Hawaii to complete her education—a B.A. from Wellesley College and an M.A. from Boston University—but returned with her husband and children several years later. Her first collection of poetry, *Picture Bride* (1982), was named for the practice of arranged marriages between Asians in America and women in Asia based on exchanged photographs—the practice by which Song's grandmother came to America at the age of twenty-three. The collection won the Yale Series of Younger Poets Prize. Since then, Song has published two more collections of poetry, which have continued her examination of family ties that *Picture Bride* established.

**AS YOU READ** Go back and forth to the painting and notice the accuracy or freedom of the poet with respect to the original.

# Girl Powdering Her Neck (1983)

## *from an ukiyo-e print by Utamaro*

The light is the inside
sheen of an oyster shell,
sponged with talc and vapor,
moisture from a bath.
A pair of slippers
are placed outside
the rice-paper doors.
She kneels at a low table
in the room,
her legs folded beneath her
as she sits on a buckwheat pillow.

Her hair is black
with hints of red,
the color of seaweed
spread over rocks.

Morning begins the ritual
wheel of the body,
the application of translucent skins.
She practices pleasure:

*Kitigawa Utamaro (1753–1806). c. 1795.* Woman Powdering Her Neck. *Musee des Arts Asiatiques–Guimet, Paris, France.*

# Kitagawa Utamaro's *Girl Powdering Her Neck* (c. 1750)

Painted as a study of the "floating world" (the translation of "ukiyo-e"), this print depicts a geisha preparing herself in a daily ritual. The Japanese term "ukiyo" connotes the frivolity and passing nature of the nouveau riche way of life that Utamaro depicts. Prints such as this were common in Utamaro's time (mid-1700s) because they could be cheaply mass produced. Common subjects were actors, sumo wrestlers, and groups of women. A distinct aspect of many Utamaro prints is their depiction of women alone, often shown only from the waist up. The personal, individual focus of this print engenders its depth and appeal; note how even the artist's signature becomes part of the composition.

the pressure of three fingertips
applying powder.
Fingerprints of pollen
some other hand will trace.

The peach-dyed kimono
patterned with maple leaves
drifting across the silk,
falls from right to left
in a diagonal, revealing
the nape of her neck
and the curve of a shoulder
like the slope of a hill
set deep in snow in a country
of huge white solemn birds.
Her face appears in the mirror,
a reflection in a winter pond,
rising to meet itself.

She dips a corner of her sleeve
like a brush into water
to wipe the mirror;
she is about to paint herself.
The eyes narrow
in a moment of self-scrutiny.
The mouth parts
as if desiring to disturb
the placid plum face;
break the symmetry of silence.
But the berry-stained lips,
stenciled into the mask of beauty,
do not speak.

Two chrysanthemums
touch in the middle of the lake
and drift apart.

# Writing from Reading

### Summarize

**1** The poet views a print by an eighteenth-century Japanese artist. Do you find that her poem is a description only?

### Analyze Craft

**2** How does the poet make her attitudes and emotions known even as she seems to describe rather straightforwardly what she sees in the print? How do the metaphors she employs suggest her attitude toward the subject?

### Analyze Voice

**3** Is there anything in her choice of words that reveals her emotions about the situation or image in the print? Does the vividness of the colors contribute to this effect?

### Synthesize Summary and Analysis

**4** The poet's reproduction in language of the Utamaro print reveals certain ways of seeing that are as much interpretive as descriptive. Can you describe some of these?

### Interpret the Poem

**5** The modern American woman of Asian descent looks at the old Japanese print and finds herself in it in many ways, and yet there are differences. Which might these be?

# Poems for Review and Further Study

## Robert Bly (b. 1926)

### Driving to Town Late to Mail a Letter (1962)

It is a cold and snowy night. The main street is deserted.
The only things moving are swirls of snow.
As I lift the mailbox door, I feel its cold iron.
There is a privacy I love in this snowy night.
Driving around, I will waste more time.

#### Questions for Interactive Reading and Writing

1. This poem is written in the present tense and, in the last line, suggests the future as well. How does that reference enhance the sense of the immediate presence?
2. Why does the speaker emphasize the feel of the iron of the mailbox? How does that contribute to the scene and setting? Is it an image, a symbol—both?
3. A letter is a form of communication, yet the poet seems to value what he calls "privacy." How is this ironic?
4. Contrast the normal sense of urgency in the completion of a task such as this with the poet's apparent desire to "waste" time.

## John Dryden (1631–1700)

### A Song for St. Cecilia's Day, 1687 (1687)

I

From harmony, from heavenly harmony
    This universal frame began:
    When Nature underneath a heap
        Of jarring atoms lay,
    And could not heave her head,
The tuneful voice was heard from high,
    "Arise, ye more than dead."

Then cold, and hot, and moist, and dry,
In order to their stations leap,
And Music's power obey.
From harmony, from heavenly harmony,
This universal frame began:
From harmony to harmony
Through all the compass of the notes it ran,
The diapason closing full in man.

II

What passion cannot music raise and quell?
When Jubal struck the chorded shell,
His listening brethren stood around,
And, wondering, on their faces fell
To worship that celestial sound.
Less than a god they thought there could not dwell
Within the hollow of that shell,
That spoke so sweetly, and so well.
What passion cannot Music raise and quell!

III

The trumpet's loud clangor
Excites us to arms,
With shrill notes of anger,
And mortal alarms.
The double double double beat
Of the thundering drum
Cries: "Hark! the foes come;
Charge, charge! 'tis too late to retreat."

IV

The soft complaining flute,
In dying notes discovers
The woes of hopeless lovers,
Whose dirge is whispered by the warbling lute.

V

Sharp violins proclaim
Their jealous pangs and desperation,
Fury, frantic indignation,
Depth of pains, and height of passion,
For the fair, disdainful dame.

VI

But O! what art can teach,
What human voice can reach,
The sacred organ's praise?
Notes inspiring holy love,
Notes that wing their heavenly ways
To mend the choirs above.

VII

Orpheus could lead the savage race;
And trees uprooted left their place,
Sequacious of the lyre:
But bright Cecilia raised the wonder higher;
When to her organ vocal breath was given,
An angel heard, and straight appeared,
Mistaking earth for heaven.

*Grand Chorus*

As from the power of sacred lays
The spheres began to move,
And sung the great Creator's praise
To all the blest above;
So when the last and dreadful hour
This crumbling pageant shall devour,
The trumpet shall be heard on high,
The dead shall live, the living die,
And Music shall untune the sky.

## Questions for Interactive Reading and Writing

1. One of the ways to consider this "song" is to look at the length of the stanzas, the beat and rhythm of the lines, the way the separate component parts function as a whole. There's a great deal of music here. How do the rhyme schemes of the stanzas, their regularity and variety, help you hear the music? (In the last nine-line stanza, for example, the last three lines have the same single-word rhyme—"high," "die," "sky"—almost as though the poet made sure "The trumpet shall be heard.")
2. Pick out the solo instruments described. There are trumpets and flutes, violins and drums, lyres and organs—all making music together. How do they blend to make an orchestra, "the compass of the notes"?
3. How does Dryden help us picture "heavenly harmony"? What images do you come away with on first reading of the poem?
4. In the composition of the cosmos, as Dryden and his contemporaries saw it, one string untuned meant the possibility of discord or disharmony, and the possibility of the entire enterprise coming apart. What does Dryden think will happen if the links among instruments come apart in "the last and dreadful hour"?

# Paul Laurence Dunbar (1872–1906)

*For a brief biography of Paul Laurence Dunbar, see chapter 19.*

## Farm House by the River (1903)

I know a little country place
  Where still my heart doth linger,
And o'er its fields is every grace
  Lined out by memory's finger.
Back from the lane where poplars grew
  And aspens quake and quiver,
There stands all bath'd in summer's glow
  A farm house by the river.

Its eaves are touched with golden light
  So sweetly, softly shining,
And morning glories full and bright
  About the doors are twining.
And there endowed with every grace
  That nature's hand could give her,
There lived the angel of the place
  In the farm house by the river.

Her eyes were blue, her hair was gold,
  Her face was bright and sunny;
The songs that from her bosom rolled
  Were sweet as summer's honey.
And I loved her well, that maid divine,
  And I prayed the Gracious Giver,
That I some day might call her mine
  In the farm house by the river.

Twas not to be—but God knows best.
  His will for aye be heeded!
Perhaps amid the angels' bliss,
  My little love was needed.
Her spirit from its thralldom torn
  Went singing o'er the river,
And that sweet life my heart shall mourn
  Forever and forever.

She dies one morn at early light
  When all the birds are singing,
And Heaven itself in pure delight
  Its bells of joy seemed ringing.
They laid her dust where soon and late
  The solemn grasses quiver,
And left alone and desolate
  The farm house by the river.

### Questions for Interactive Reading and Writing

1. Describe the rhyme scheme. How does the tone of the poem and the rhyme compare to the ballad in chapter 25?
2. The poet speaks of the loss of an Eden-like setting. Where might he be living that the loss of the farmhouse seems so sharp and deep? What else besides the place by the river has the poet lost?
3. List the images and symbols that Dunbar employs to evoke his lost love.

# John Keats (1795–1821)

*For a brief biography of John Keats, see chapter 18.*

## Ode to a Nightingale (1819)

I

My heart aches, and a drowsy numbness pains
  My sense, as though of hemlock I had drunk,
Or emptied some dull opiate to the drains
  One minute past, and Lethe-wards had sunk:
'Tis not through envy of thy happy lot,
  But being too happy in thine happiness,—
    That thou, light-wingéd Dryad of the trees,
      In some melodious plot
  Of beechen green and shadows numberless,
    Singest of summer in full-throated ease.

II

O, for a draught of vintage! that hath been
  Cooled a long age in the deep-delvéd earth,
Tasting of Flora and the country green,
  Dance, and Provençal song, and sunburnt mirth!
O for a beaker full of the warm South,
  Full of the true, the blushful Hippocrene,
    With beaded bubbles winking at the brim,
      And purple-stainéd mouth;
  That I might drink, and leave the world unseen,
    And with thee fade away into the forest dim:

III

Fade far away, dissolve, and quite forget
  What thou among the leaves hast never known,
The weariness, the fever, and the fret
  Here, where men sit and hear each other groan;

Where palsy shakes a few, sad, last gray hairs,
Where youth grows pale, and spectre-thin, and dies;
Where but to think is to be full of sorrow
And leaden-eyed despairs,
Where Beauty cannot keep her lustrous eyes,
Or new Love pine at them beyond tomorrow.

IV

Away! away! for I will fly to thee,
Not charioted by Bacchus and his pards,
But on the viewless wings of Poesy,
Though the dull brain perplexes and retards:
Already with thee! tender is the night,
And haply the Queen-Moon is on her throne,
Clustered around by all her starry Fays;
But here there is no light,
Save what from heaven is with the breezes blown
Through verdurous glooms and winding mossy ways.

V

I cannot see what flowers are at my feet,
Nor what soft incense hangs upon the boughs,
But, in embalméd darkness, guess each sweet
Wherewith the seasonable month endows
The grass, the thicket, and the fruit-tree wild;
White hawthorn, and the pastoral eglantine;
Fast fading violets covered up in leaves;
And mid-May's eldest child,
The coming musk-rose, full of dewy wine,
The murmurous haunt of flies on summer eves.

VI

Darkling I listen; and, for many a time
I have been half in love with easeful Death,
Called him soft names in many a muséd rhyme,
To take into the air my quiet breath;
Now more than ever seems it rich to die,
To cease upon the midnight with no pain,
While thou art pouring forth thy soul abroad
In such an ecstasy!
Still wouldst thou sing, and I have ears in vain—
To thy high requiem become a sod.

VII

Thou wast not born for death, immortal Bird!
No hungry generations tread thee down;
The voice I hear this passing night was heard
In ancient days by emperor and clown:
Perhaps the selfsame song that found a path
Through the sad heart of Ruth, when, sick for home,
She stood in tears amid the alien corn;
The same that ofttimes hath
Charmed magic casements, opening on the foam
Of perilous seas, in faery lands forlorn.

VIII

Forlorn! the very word is like a bell
To toll me back from thee to my sole self!
Adieu! the fancy cannot cheat so well
As she is famed to do, deceiving elf.
Adieu! adieu! thy plaintive anthem fades
Past the near meadows, over the still stream,
Up the hill side; and now 'tis buried deep
In the next valley-glades:
Was it a vision, or a waking dream?
Fled is that music:—Do I wake or sleep?

## Questions for Interactive Reading and Writing

1. What would "a beaker full of the warm South" look like? Can you drink it? What about "hemlock" or some "dull opiate" instead?
2. The phrase "tender is the night" (stanza 4) was used by F. Scott Fitzgerald as the title of one of his novels. What do the words convey?
3. Track the poet's attitude to the image or symbol of the nightingale through the stanzas. How near is it, how far away?
4. How does the poet, by guessing, describe what "I cannot see"?
5. This poem and Jane Kenyon's "The Blue Bowl" (earlier in this chapter) are both meditations on death. How does Keats's use of the nightingale image compare to Kenyon's use of the cat's blue bowl?

# Shirley Geok-Lin Lim (b. 1944)

## Scavenging on a Double Bluff (2007)

I

My children call these wish-stones, Anne said,
studying the warm brown quartz
I had picked with its perfect elongated
white circle; when that circle is
unbroken, that's what makes them wishes.
I wished she had not told me this.
All week I thought of getting another
down by Double Bluff Beach.
This afternoon I take the time to bike
and walk. Some of us can pick up unbroken
spindles where others see only fragments

and shell bits; can gather a dozen
in a minute, whole and bleached.
Rocks lie everywhere on mud flats.
Serpentine, granite, sandstone, calcite,
agate: igneous and sedimentary,
names enough to fill my pockets.
I find the colors, lines, and shapes
as I find spindles in the shore litter.
Starving at six makes one grow up sharp
at scavenging, and I have seen
strangers turn dubious at my luck.
My eyes stoop to the search.
I do not stop for the blue herons
or the far islands and inlets. The heron
hunts with me, hour after hour,
although I no longer know what it is
I wish for: love, money, position,
picked up like these shells and stones
that weigh down my backpack.

II

What is the difference between
having nothing and too much?
"You have too much," one complimented,
then asked for my things. But that's beside
the point. It's the work of finding
gives them meaning—work of a mind
honed for surviving. The Chinese,
as I found in Shanghai, at the garden
of the Minor Administrator, prefer
edges of unequally worn stone,
spying buttes, peaks, crags, and scarps
lift up against wear and centuries.
I must have never been Chinese.
I like my rocks smooth and worn
through millennia of water, storm, and tide;
round as the round of loaves; circles
of breasts hurting with milk
on round pillows; as a lunar month finds
an open Oh!, a yellow wheel;
round scrotum swollen at touch.
Complete as unbroken bands
of color, stones that are wishes.
I scavenge dandelion leaves, chicory,
wild onions, beach plums, thimbleberries.
I'm scavenging in case of a famine;
in case I'll have to go hungry,
wishes worn smooth, worn daily,
in my round mouth, my anxious hand.

### Questions for Interactive Reading and Writing

1. What is the occasion of the poem? When and where does it take place? What biographical details do we learn about the poet? How do these help us understand what she is doing there on the beach?
2. How does the poet manage to suggest that scavenging for stones on a beach is an action in which we can find some symbolic meaning? What techniques does she use to encourage us to think about the occasion in this fashion?
3. Where does the poet take us in the second part of the poem? To a new location? To a new stage of thinking about the scavenging in part 1?
4. How is the speaker of this poem different in the way she speaks about stones from, say, the friend who collects stones Carolyn Forché speaks of in her poem "The Museum of Stones" (chapter 15)? How does this poet's approach contrast, if it does, with Forché's approach?

# Amy Lowell (1874–1925)

## Patterns (1914)

I walk down the garden paths,
And all the daffodils
Are blowing, and the bright blue squills.
I walk down the patterned garden-paths
In my stiff, brocaded gown.
With my powdered hair and jeweled fan,
I too am a rare
Pattern. As I wander down
The garden paths.

My dress is richly figured,
And the train
Makes a pink and silver stain
On the gravel, and the thrift
Of the borders.
Just a plate of current fashion,
Tripping by in high-heeled, ribboned shoes.
Not a softness anywhere about me,
Only whalebone and brocade.
And I sink on a seat in the shade
Of a lime tree. For my passion
Wars against the stiff brocade.
The daffodils and squills
Flutter in the breeze

As they please.
And I weep;
For the lime-tree is in blossom
And one small flower has dropped upon my bosom.

And the plashing of waterdrops
In the marble fountain
Comes down the garden-paths.
The dripping never stops.
Underneath my stiffened gown
Is the softness of a woman bathing in a marble basin,
A basin in the midst of hedges grown
So thick, she cannot see her lover hiding,
But she guesses he is near,
And the sliding of the water
Seems the stroking of a dear
Hand upon her.
What is Summer in a fine brocaded gown!
I should like to see it lying in a heap upon the ground.
All the pink and silver crumpled up on the ground.

I would be the pink and silver as I ran along the paths,
And he would stumble after,
Bewildered by my laughter.
I should see the sun flashing from his sword-hilt and the
  buckles on his shoes.
I would choose
To lead him in a maze along the patterned paths,
A bright and laughing maze for my heavy-booted lover,
Till he caught me in the shade,
And the buttons of his waistcoat bruised my body as he
  clasped me,
Aching, melting, unafraid.
With the shadows of the leaves and the sundrops,
And the plopping of the waterdrops,
All about us in the open afternoon—
I am very likely to swoon
  With the weight of this brocade,
  For the sun sifts through the shade.

Underneath the fallen blossom
In my bosom,
Is a letter I have hid.
It was brought to me this morning by a rider from the
  Duke.
"Madam, we regret to inform you that Lord Hartwell
Died in action Thursday se'nnight."
As I read it in the white, morning sunlight,
The letters squirmed like snakes.
"Any answer, Madam," said my footman.
"No," I told him.
"See that the messenger takes some refreshment.
No, no answer."
And I walked into the garden,
Up and down the patterned paths,
In my stiff, correct brocade.
The blue and yellow flowers stood up proudly in the sun,
Each one.
I stood upright too,
Held rigid to the pattern
By the stiffness of my gown.
Up and down I walked,
Up and down.

In a month he would have been my husband.
In a month, here, underneath this lime,
We would have broken the pattern;
He for me, and I for him,
He as Colonel, I as Lady,
On this shady seat.
He had a whim
That sunlight carried blessing.
And I answered, "It shall be as you have said."
Now he is dead.

In Summer and in Winter I shall walk
Up and down
The patterned garden-paths
In my stiff, brocaded gown.
The squills and daffodils
Will give place to pillared roses, and to asters, and
  to snow.
I shall go
Up and down,
In my gown.
Gorgeously arrayed,
Boned and stayed.
And the softness of my body will be guarded from
  embrace
By each button, hook, and lace.
For the man who should loose me is dead,
Fighting with the Duke in Flanders,
In a pattern called a war.
Christ! What are patterns for?

## Questions for Interactive Reading and Writing

1. Describe the occasion of the poem. What is the primary emotion felt by the speaker? Does this woman out of history seem remote from the American experience of the poet? Why might Lowell have chosen this particular woman as the speaker?
2. How does "my stiff, brocaded gown . . . each button, hook, and lace" compare with the button in Jane

Hirshfield's poem in this chapter? What image do the words evoke?

3. How does the outer appearance of the woman—her manner, her way of dressing—contrast with her inner state of being? How does the final expressive outburst make that emotion clear?

# Cleopatra Mathis (b. 1914)

## Lilacs (1983)

They open before we have had a chance
to be unkind to each other.
In the dark the tiny whorls
unfold around the stem, candlelit
against the window; the infrequent dark
where our bodies gather and fill.
The lilacs bloom in their time,
the flowers dry in the billowing tree
which I will cut back
and further back.
What is desire
but a stone to bargain with? a longing
that says *be something else,*
until each holds the other
against change. The year turns,
the tree's frame empties,

empties again. If I could need
only what is given—
the way the limbs protect themselves
in spite of weather. Another dark
conceals the latent buds.
It's true, I am closed
between a past and future winter;
any fear is made bearable when it repeats,
when it's mutable and brief.

### Questions for Interactive Reading and Writing

1. Emotion might seem abstract as a subject. How does the poet make it palpable and concrete?
2. The lilacs "bloom in their time." Does the poet's sense of time coincide with or differ from the time of nature?
3. How does the perfection of nature contrast with the poet's sense of needing more than she is given?
4. Compare this poem to Amy Lowell's "Patterns." How might you argue that "Lilacs" is a response to "Patterns"?

# Howard Nemerov (1920–1991)

## The Blue Swallows (1967)

Across the millstream below the bridge
Seven blue swallows divide the air
In shapes invisible and evanescent,
Kaleidoscopic beyond the mind's
Or memory's power to keep them there.

"History is where tensions were,"
"Form is the diagram of forces."
Thus, helplessly, there on the bridge,
While gazing down upon those birds—
How strange, to be above the birds!—
Thus helplessly the mind in its brain
Weaves up relation's spindrift web,
Seeing the swallows' tails as nibs
Dipped in invisible ink, writing . . .

Poor mind, what would you have them write?
Some cabalistic history
Whose authorship you might ascribe
To God? to Nature? Ah, poor ghost,
You've capitalized your Self enough.
That villainous William of Occam
Cut out the feet from under that dream
Some seven centuries ago.
It's taken that long for the mind
To waken, yawn and stretch, to see
With opened eyes emptied of speech
The real world where the spelling mind
Imposes with its grammar book
Unreal relations on the blue
Swallows. Perhaps when you will have
Fully awakened, I shall show you
A new thing: even the water
Flowing away beneath those birds
Will fail to reflect their flying forms,
And the eyes that see become as stones
Whence never tears shall fall again.

O swallows, swallows, poems are not
The point. Finding again the world,
That is the point, where loveliness
Adorns intelligible things
Because the mind's eye lit the sun.

### Questions for Interactive Reading and Writing

1. Where does this poem take place, and who is the "I"?
2. In the final stanza, the poet asserts that "poems are not / The point." Does he mean this, and, if so, what is the point "where loveliness / Adorns intelligible things"?
3. Look up William of Occam and decide why he is "villainous."
4. Would you call these swallows an image or a symbol or both? Why?

# Pablo Neruda (1904–1973)

*For a biography of Pablo Neruda, see chapter 16.*

## The Stolen Branch (1952)

In the night we shall go in
to steal
a flowering branch.

We shall climb over the wall
in the darkness of the alien garden,
two shadows in the shadow.

Winter is not yet gone,
and the apple tree appears
suddenly changed
into a cascade of fragrant stars.

In the night we shall go in
up to its trembling firmament,
and your little hands and mine
will steal the stars.

And silently,
to our house,
in the night and the shadow,
with your steps will enter
perfume's silent step
and with starry feet
the clear body of spring.

*—translated by Donald D. Walsh*

### Questions for Interactive Reading and Writing

1. A crime committed in a garden—are there biblical undertones or overtones to this image?
2. Who are the transgressors? "Thieves"? Why does the speaker celebrate their act?
3. In what part of the daily cycle does the act take place? In what season? What does this setting suggest about the motives of the speaker and his companion?
4. If a critic or an instructor were to suggest that Neruda has written a love poem, how would you respond?

# Octavio Paz (1914–1998)

## Motion (1962)

If you are the amber mare
  I am the road of blood
If you are the first snow
  I am he who lights the hearth of dawn
If you are the tower of night
  I am the spike burning in your mind
If you are the morning tide
  I am the first bird's cry
If you are the basket of oranges
  I am the knife of the sun
If you are the stone altar
  I am the sacrilegious hand
If you are the sleeping land
  I am the green cane
If you are the wind's leap
  I am the buried fire
If you are the water's mouth
  I am the mouth of moss
If you are the forest of the clouds
  I am the axe that parts it
If you are the profaned city
  I am the rain of consecration
If you are the yellow mountain
  I am the red arms of lichen
If you are the rising sun
  I am the road of blood

*—translated by Eliot Weinberger*

### Questions for Interactive Reading and Writing

1. The speaker makes a series of tentative ("if") declarations. Whom is he addressing and why?
2. Do all of the pairings seem to complement each other on first reading? If not, which seem more mysterious or obscure? Which suggest violence? Which suggest peace or pacification? Which, if any, seem to suggest that the poet is Mexican?
3. How is the effect of the chant-like quality of this poem similar to or different from the repetitive list-like structure of Carole Satyamurti's "I Shall Paint My Nails Red," which follows?

# Carole Satyamurti (b. 1939)

## I Shall Paint My Nails Red (1998)

Because a bit of colour is a public service.

Because I am proud of my hands.

Because it will remind me I'm a woman.

Because I will look like a survivor.

Because I can admire them in traffic jams.

Because my daughter will say ugh.

Because my lover will be surprised.

Because it is quicker than dyeing my hair.

Because it is a ten-minute moratorium.

Because it is reversible.

### Questions for Interactive Reading and Writing

1. Contemporary poets are often eclectic in their approach to their work, taking material and form from many different aspects of life and art. Here the poet uses the ordinary form of a list in order to express a less than ordinary emotion. How many areas of life does she mention—besides love and gender—in these ten lines?
2. Make a thumbnail sketch of this woman. Where might she live? What is her current marital status? How old might she be?
3. How would you describe her voice?

# Sarah Teasdale (1884–1933)

## I Am Not Yours (1915)

I am not yours, not lost in you,
Not lost, although I long to be
Lost as a candle lit at noon,
Lost as a snowflake in the sea.

You love me, and I find you still
A spirit beautiful and bright,
Yet I am I, who long to be
Lost as a light is lost in light.

Oh plunge me deep in love—put out
My senses, leave me deaf and blind,
Swept by the tempest of your love,
A taper in a rushing wind.

### Questions for Interactive Reading and Writing

1. The expression of love here seems quite erratic and even close to violence. How does the rhyme scheme contrast with the emotion of the poem?
2. What disturbs the poet about her love? How do the images suggest her state?
3. Compare this poem with those by Amy Lowell and Cleopatra Mathis in this chapter. What are the similarities, what are the differences?

# Reading for Images and Symbols

| | | |
|---|---|---|
| When reading for image, look for language that generates a certain attitude or mental picture using words and language that create vivid visual, aural, and tactile impressions. | | |
| ***Image:*** the literal representation of any "thing" described—the way it looks. | | |
| **When reading for image, ask yourself** | • What senses (sight, sound, touch, smell, taste) has the poet evoked with an image?<br>• What kinds of words are used to make the image vivid?<br>• What associations (meanings) do you connect with those word choices? | EXAMPLE: "Amber husk / fluted with gold, / fruit on the sand / marked with rich grain" |
| ***Symbol:*** an image that stands for or represents something beyond the thing itself | | |
| **When reading for symbol, ask yourself** | • Is the title a tip-off to a centrally important image, one that is likely to be a symbol?<br>• Does the poem focus on a particular image?<br>• Is an image repeated and returned to in a poem? If so, it is likely to be a symbol.<br>• How is that symbolic image used? The description will point to its deeper meaning. | EXAMPLE: "Button" |
| **Pay attention to common associations** | *Conventional association:* An association made so frequently that one thing has come to traditionally represent the other. | EXAMPLE: Dove = peace; shooting star = wish |

| | | |
|---|---|---|
| **When reading poetry from earlier times, consider conventional associations from the period. Remember to read in context.** | *Iconography:* When one symbol always engenders certain meanings. | EXAMPLE: Skull and crossbones = death |
| **Remember that modern poets may try to create fresh symbols through context.** | *Literary symbolism:* Symbolism that is created through the context of a poem. | EXAMPLE: A blue bowl represents death and sorrow *in the context* of Jane Kenyon's poem. |

# Writing about Images and Symbols

1. Consider the various creatures and landscapes in the poems of this chapter and write a brief essay comparing and contrasting their functions; consider also the attitude of each of the poets to each. Contrast, for example, the chickens described by William Carlos Williams with the nightingale in Keats's poem or Hirshfield's tree with the image in the Pound poem.
2. Take any poem in this chapter and focus on its imagery. At what point does a central image (the jar on the hill in Tennessee, the plums in the refrigerator, etc.) attain the status of symbol?
3. As W. H. Auden suggests of the Old Masters, "About suffering they were never wrong." Find images that evoke "suffering" in five of the poems included here. Compare the way poets such as Paul Laurence Dunbar deal with this emotion, what images they use to portray death and loss.

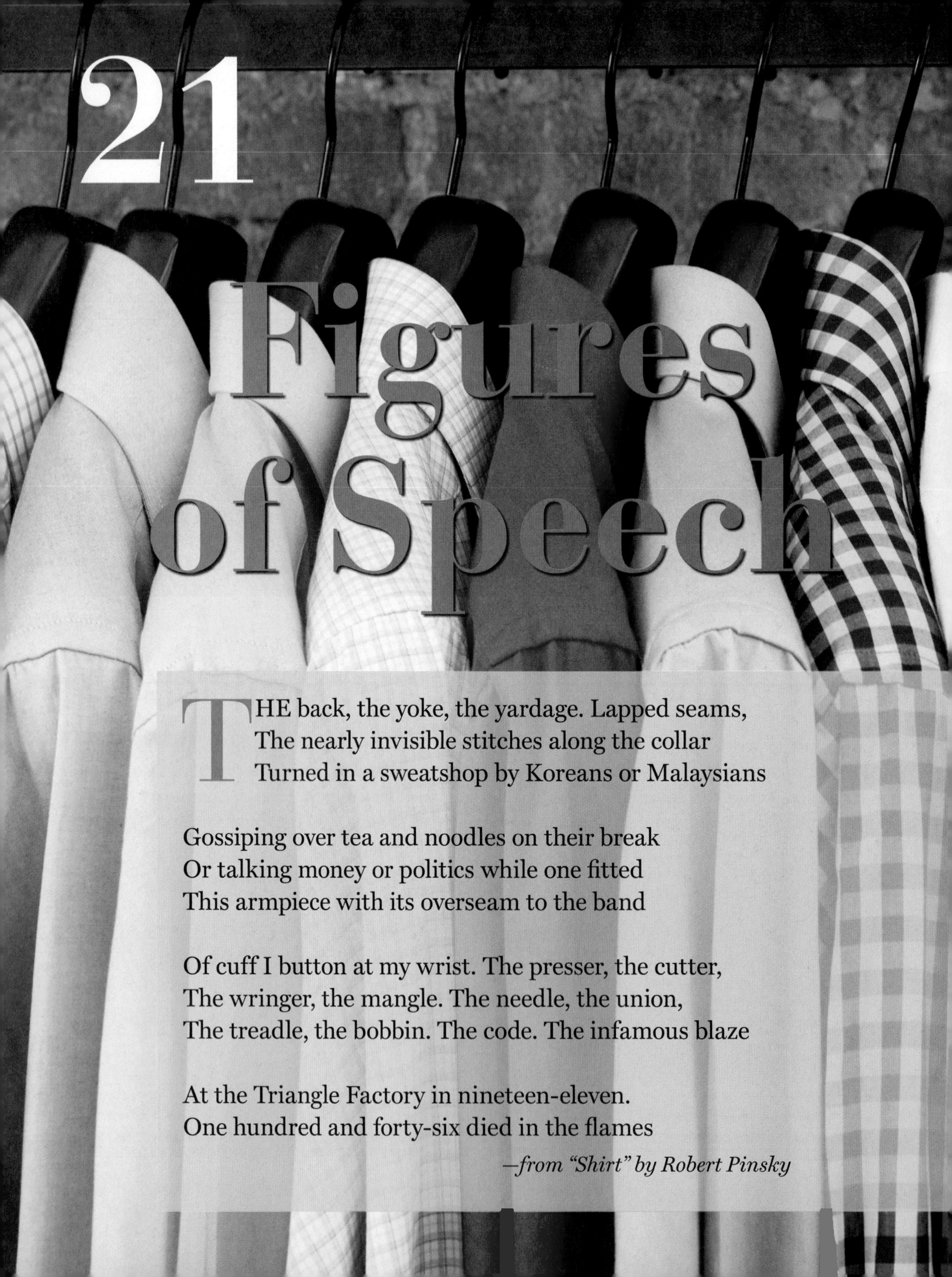

# 21

# Figures of Speech

THE back, the yoke, the yardage. Lapped seams,
The nearly invisible stitches along the collar
Turned in a sweatshop by Koreans or Malaysians

Gossiping over tea and noodles on their break
Or talking money or politics while one fitted
This armpiece with its overseam to the band

Of cuff I button at my wrist. The presser, the cutter,
The wringer, the mangle. The needle, the union,
The treadle, the bobbin. The code. The infamous blaze

At the Triangle Factory in nineteen-eleven.
One hundred and forty-six died in the flames

—*from "Shirt" by Robert Pinsky*

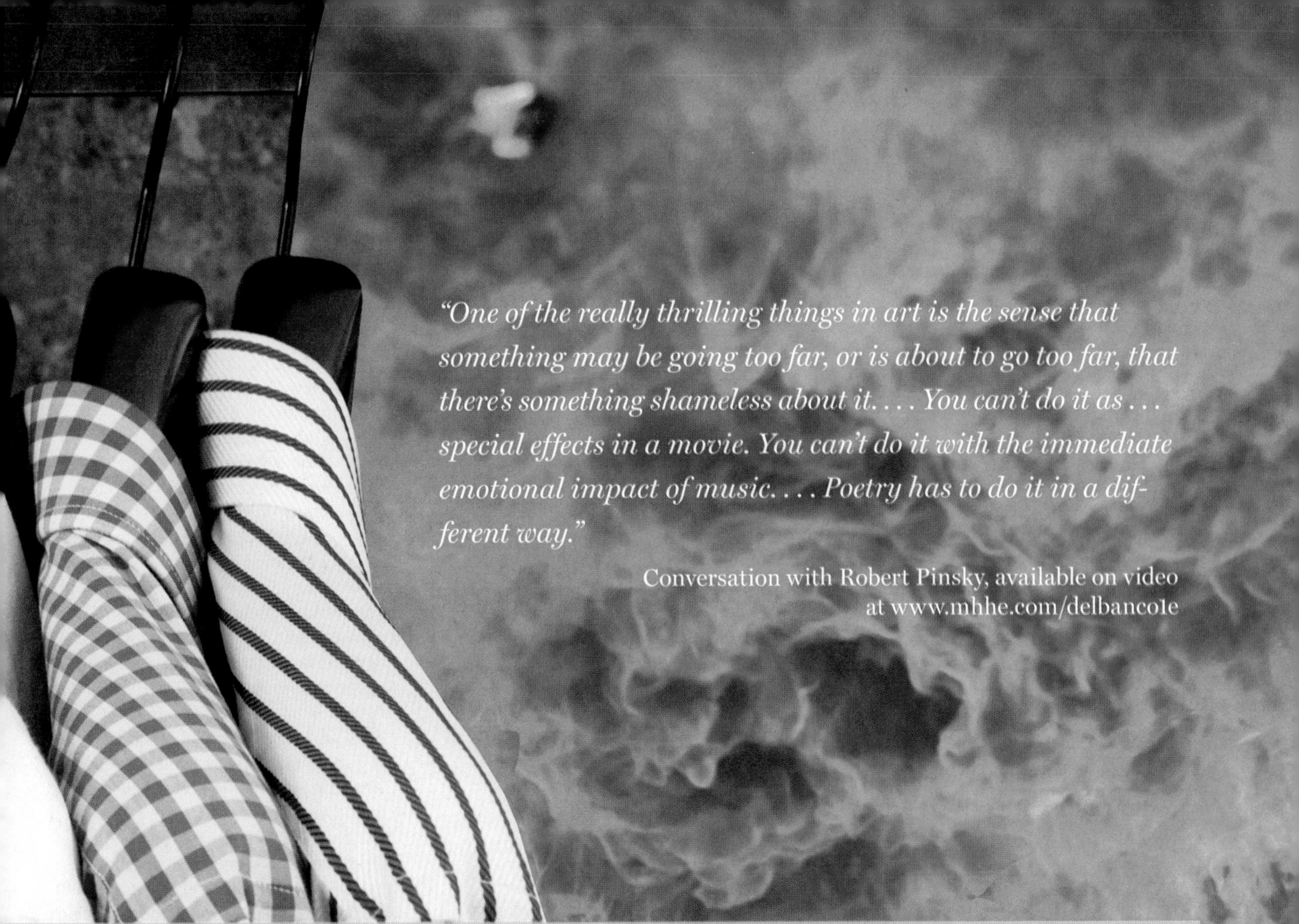

*"One of the really thrilling things in art is the sense that something may be going too far, or is about to go too far, that there's something shameless about it. . . . You can't do it as . . . special effects in a movie. You can't do it with the immediate emotional impact of music. . . . Poetry has to do it in a different way."*

Conversation with Robert Pinsky, available on video at www.mhhe.com/delbanco1e

IN his poem "Shirt," Robert Pinsky gives the reader a great deal of information about the construction of a shirt, the way the fabric gets transformed and shaped for sale and use. This is no technical manual or instruction pamphlet; his intention is to establish a relation between the historical past and the actual shirt-wearing present. When he uses words like "yoke" or "union," he evokes both a literal attribute of fabric and the larger meaning of "yoke" and "union": the language means two things at once. A strategy like this employs **figurative language;** it describes one thing by relating it to something else. People use **figures of speech** every day, and poets use them consciously—nonliteral comparisons that vividly illustrate an idea or theme.

Figures of speech allow writers to make connections and comparisons between seemingly unlike objects and actions. These connections require a particular capacity to perceive relationships between dissimilar things. As Robert Pinsky suggests in his interview, the ability to create metaphor may be a natural gift, an innate talent. "Putting two unlike things together," Pinsky says, "and finding out how they're alike is like being able to jump high or run fast." Very few poets have *no* such gift; indeed, it may be the tell-tale sign of a poet's calling. A person who sees the world only literally is far more likely to be a writer of prose fiction or criticism or drama than a writer who engages in the craft of poetry. One thing suggests another and word leads on to word; image leads to image, sound to sight. The very phrase "figures of speech" makes an implicit linkage, connecting something visual to something spoken and reminding us that language must be both seen and heard.

*I do like that feeling of information accumulating.*

# Q&A

*I'm as likely to refer to the Captain Easy comic strip as I am to the* Aeneid.

# *A Conversation on Writing*

## Robert Pinsky

### The Presence of the Past in Everything

That the past is present in everything is just a deep conviction for me. . . . I grew up in a town where my mother and father went to the same high school as me. My father and I both had Miss Scott for home-room. . . . Long Branch is a very historical town. . . . Grant, Lincoln, and Mrs. Lincoln visited Long Branch. Diamond Jim Brady went to stay there with Lillian Russell. . . . I grew up with a sense . . . that there's always lore and information behind everything. . . . I want the reader [of my poems] to know that the presence of information is there. . . . I do like that feeling of information accumulating.

### Writing As an Amateur Collector of Information

I've never mastered a subject. I've never become a scholarly expert in anything at all. I always make mistakes about dates. Most of the information in my poems is slightly wrong, and frequently made up altogether. . . . I was not a successful student in high school. I was a real failure, a literal failure, in junior high school. In the eighth grade I was in the "dumb class," also called the "bad class." . . . I'm as likely to refer to the Captain Easy comic strip as I am to the *Aeneid*.

### The Mystery of Making a Metaphor

Somebody says that the one thing you can't teach or learn is the making of a metaphor—the ability to see resemblances, or to conceive resemblances. Putting two unlike things together and finding how they're alike is like being able to . . . reproduce a tune perfectly the first time you hear it. . . . like the mysterious way one person can hear a tune and play . . . It comes from nowhere. . . . of all the things you do in writing—it's the thing that's most unlike anything you can figure out.

A New Jersey boy from birth (1940) through his undergraduate years at Rutgers University, Robert Pinsky originally hoped to be a musician. When he changed his focus to poetry in college, however, the change was not wholly unexpected; as a child, he loved the sounds of words, even if he was too young to understand them. This love of language combined with his compelling intellect has made his poetry in collections like *Sadness and Happiness* (1975), *The Figured Wheel: New and Collected Poems 1966–1996* (1996), and *Jersey Rain* (2000) so striking. His translation of the first volume of Dante's *Divine Comedy* (1995) became a best-seller; his work on *The Life of David* (2005) was a close examination of that biblical hero's consequence, and his recent collections of verse include *First Things to Hand* (2006) and *Gulf Music* (2007). In addition to being a Stegner Fellow at Stanford University, Pinsky counts among his honors a Pulitzer Prize nomination, an American Academy of Arts and Letters award, and the position of Poet Laureate of the United States. Pinsky currently teaches in the graduate program at Boston University and edits the poetry for the online journal *Slate*.

**To watch this entire interview and hear the author read from his work, go to www.mhhe.com/delbanco1e.**

**RESEARCH ASSIGNMENT** After you have seen the video, discuss the different ways history informs Robert Pinsky's undertaking in writing "Shirt." List some of the historical references Pinsky mentions in his interview. How does knowing the history of the shirt impact your understanding of the poem? Explain how knowing the history enhanced, detracted from, or was a neutral factor in your enjoyment of "Shirt." Why is history so important to Pinsky?

**AS YOU READ** Consider the variety of historical connections Pinsky makes. The poem seeks to bridge subjects and elements as diverse as the famous fire at the shirt factory, sweatshops, American slavery, the twentieth-century immigrant experience, and seventeenth-century British poet George Herbert. Alongside these references are words from the world of sewing and tailoring, like "yoke," "mangle," and "bobbin." Pinksy uses this *jargon,* technical language specific to a trade, craft, or profession, to further connect the centuries-old history of garment-making to the culture and events of the poem.

# Shirt (1990)

The back, the yoke, the yardage. Lapped seams,
The nearly invisible stitches along the collar
Turned in a sweatshop by Koreans or Malaysians

Gossiping over tea and noodles on their break
Or talking money or politics while one fitted
This armpiece with its overseam to the band

Of cuff I button at my wrist. The presser, the cutter,
The wringer, the mangle. The needle, the union,
The treadle, the bobbin. The code. The infamous blaze

At the Triangle Factory in nineteen-eleven.
One hundred and forty-six died in the flames
On the ninth floor, no hydrants, no fire escapes—

The witness in a building across the street
Who watched how a young man helped a girl to step
Up to the windowsill, then held her out

Away from the masonry wall and let her drop.
And then another. As if he were helping them up
To enter a streetcar, and not eternity.

A third before he dropped her put her arms
Around his neck and kissed him. Then he held
Her into space, and dropped her. Almost at once

He stepped up to the sill himself, his jacket flared
And fluttered up from his shirt as he came down,
Air filling up the legs of his gray trousers—

Like Hart Crane's Bedlamite, "shrill shirt ballooning."
Wonderful how the pattern matches perfectly
Across the placket and over the twin bar-tacked

Corners of both pockets, like a strict rhyme
Or a major chord. Prints, plaids, checks,
Houndstooth, Tattersall, Madras. The clan tartans

Invented by mill-owners inspired by the hoax of Ossian,
To control their savage Scottish workers, tamed
By a fabricated heraldry: MacGregor,

Bailey, MacMartin. The kilt, devised for workers
To wear among the dusty clattering looms.
Weavers, carders, spinners. The loader,

The docker, the navvy. The planter, the picker, the sorter
Sweating at her machine in a litter of cotton
As slaves in calico headrags sweated in fields:

George Herbert, your descendant is a Black
Lady in South Carolina, her name is Irma
And she inspected my shirt. Its color and fit

And feel and its clean smell have satisfied
Both her and me. We have culled its cost and quality
Down to the buttons of simulated bone,

The buttonholes, the sizing, the facing, the characters
Printed in black on neckband and tail. The shape,
The label, the labor, the color, the shade. The shirt.

# Writing from Reading

### Summarize

1 What connections does the poet make between the people, objects, and events in the poem?

### Analyze Craft

2 Why do you think this poem is so full of people and objects?

3 How does the recurring motif of clothing help link historical periods throughout the poem?

### Analyze Voice

4 What attitude does the poet express toward the events described here? Would you call this poem a political statement, a social statement, a moral statement—or all of these? Why?

### Synthesize Summary and Analysis

5 As Pinsky says, "The associations [in the poem] aren't random. They're historical." What figurative leap does the poet take?

### Interpret the Poem

6 Figures of speech enact the same sort of rich connectivity that the poem explores in its diverse historical references. Link the details of shirt making to the larger story here.

## FIGURATIVE LANGUAGE

While all genres of writing (and everyday speech) employ figures of speech, poetry—given its especially condensed and vivid discourse—relies crucially and consistently on figurative language. Poets invent nonliteral descriptions like this because figures of speech allow them, in Pound's phrase, to "make it new." They can help amplify a reader's understanding, or they can intensify a reader's imagination. Most importantly, they can also help a writer create a description whose comparisons illustrate a theme or idea in a more purposeful way.

"Here's what poetry can do. Imagine you're a caterpillar. There's an awful shrug and suddenly you're beautiful for as long as you live."

Conversation with Stephen Dunn

In *Romeo and Juliet,* when the hopelessly infatuated young Romeo looks up to Juliet on her balcony, he whispers, "But, soft! What light through yonder window breaks? It is the east, and Juliet is the sun." Shakespeare has Romeo describe Juliet's radiant, powerful beauty in terms of the radiant, powerful sun. Does Romeo really believe this teenage girl he likes has somehow *become* the sun? Certainly not.

If Shakespeare had instead written, "Who's coming out there by the window? It's that lovely girl I met last night," we would understand his meaning. However, these wholly literal lines would lack the added, richer associations we find in Shakespeare's language—elements like the renewal of the sun rising in the east ending the dark night, and the warmth and sheer beauty of sunlight above us. For Romeo, the sight of Juliet is as beautiful and rejuvenating as a perfect new dawn. It's no accident that Shakespeare adds these figurative associations to his scene—he wants his language to do more for the reader than simply make literal sense.

Understanding how to identify and talk about figures of speech is an important tool for better appreciating poetry. It's one of the ways that the heightened, melodious language of poetry has grown so distinctive. Here are two further examples of figurative speech. In the first instance, the novelist and poet Michael Ondaatje makes a series of rapid comparisons between "your voice" and the series of sounds it evokes; look for the insistent use of "like" in this witty and playful poem. In the second example—again by Robert Pinsky—the poet reimagines television, describing it variously as a container, a showcase for "dreams," and as a means of comfort and escape. Pinsky is more literal and direct, but via the speaker's imagination, a familiar electronic appliance becomes transformed into a series of new images and new ways of thinking about the device itself.

# Michael Ondaatje (b. 1943)

Born in Sri Lanka, Michael Ondaatje emigrated to England and then to Canada, where he has made his home since 1962. Although he is perhaps best known for his novel *The English Patient* (1992), which was made into an Academy Award–winning film, Ondaatje began by writing poetry, and today has published more than a dozen collections of poetry. Among his better-known collections are *There's a Trick with a Knife I'm Learning to Do: Poems, 1963–1978* (1978), and *The Cinnamon Peeler: Selected Poems* (1991); both won the Governor General's Award, one of Canada's most prestigious literary prizes. His fiction suggests Ondaatje's poetic sense: in books like *In the Skin of a Lion* (1987) and *Anil's Ghost* (2000), Ondaatje creates image-driven narrative that often reads more like poetry than prose.

**AS YOU READ** Recite this poem; read it aloud, and listen for its unlikely music—the combination of sounds.

# Sweet Like a Crow (1989)

"The Sinhalese are without a doubt one of the least musical people in the world. It would be quite impossible to have less sense of pitch, line, or rhythm."

*Paul Bowles*

Your voice sounds like a scorpion being pushed
through a glass tube
like someone has just trod on a peacock
like wind howling in a coconut
like a rusty bible, like someone pulling barbed wire
across a stone courtyard, like a pig drowning,
a vattacka being fried
a bone shaking hands
a frog singing at Carnegie Hall.

Like a crow swimming in milk,
like a nose being hit by a mango
like the crowd at the Royal-Thomian match,
a womb full of twins, a pariah dog
with a magpie in its mouth
like the midnight jet from Casablanca
like Air Pakistan curry,
a typewriter on fire, like a spirit in the gas
which cooks your dinner, like a hundred
pappadans being crunched, like someone
uselessly trying to light 3 Roses matches in a dark room,
the clicking sound of a reef when you put your head into the sea,
a dolphin reciting epic poetry to a sleepy audience,
the sound of a fan when someone throws brinjals at it,
like pineapples being sliced in the Pettah market
like betel juice hitting a butterfly in mid-air
like a whole village running naked onto the street
and tearing their sarongs, like an angry family
pushing a jeep out of the mud, like dirt on the needle,
like 8 sharks being carried on the back of a bicycle
like 3 old ladies locked in the lavatory
like the sound I heard when having an afternoon sleep
and someone walked through my room in ankle bracelets.

# Writing from Reading

### Summarize

1 What is the significance of the epigraph by Paul Bowles in this poem? How does the poet respond?

### Analyze Craft

2 How does the sequence of comparisons help establish tone?

### Analyze Voice

3 Which comparisons here seem serious and which seem lighthearted? Is it difficult to make the distinction?

### Synthesize Summary and Analysis

4 The title of this poem suggests something unlikely; we don't tend to think of crows as "sweet." What is the attitude of the speaker to "your voice," and how would you describe the speaker's voice itself?

### Interpret the Poem

5 Is this an act of friendship or enmity? How would you—if the poet were making these connections to the sound of *your* voice—respond?

# Robert Pinsky (b. 1940)

See the brief biography of Robert Pinsky at the beginning of this chapter.

**AS YOU READ** "To Television" is an old-fashioned ode to a relatively modern piece of technology. Pinsky contrasts his own way of seeing television with the popular notion that it's a kind of "window." Notice how Pinsky avoids the familiar critique of television as "garbage" or a narcotic and how he uses figurative language to diversify our sense of a familiar object.

## To Television (2004)

Not a "window on the world"
But as we call you,
A box a tube

Terrarium of dreams and wonders.
Coffer of shades, ordained
Cotillion of phosphors
Or liquid crystal

Homey miracle, tub
Of acquiescence, vein of defiance.
Your patron in the pantheon would be Hermes

Raster dance,
Quick one, little thief, escort
Of the dying and comfort of the sick,

In a blue glow my father and little sister sat
Snuggled in one chair watching you
Their wife and mother was sick in the head
I scorned you and them as I scorned so much

Now I like you best in a hotel room,
Maybe minutes
Before I have to face an audience: behind
The doors of the armoire, box
Within a box—Tom & Jerry, or also brilliant
And reassuring, Oprah Winfrey.

Thank you, for I watched, I watched
Sid Caesar speaking French and Japanese not
Through knowledge but imagination,
His quickness, and Thank You, I watched live
Jackie Robinson stealing

Home, the image—O strung shell—enduring
Fleeter than light like these words we
Remember in: they too winged
At the helmet and ankles.

# Writing from Reading

### Summarize

1 How does Pinsky link TV to the ancient Greek god Hermes, the winged messenger who communicated between the human and celestial realms? How does television function as an "escort" and a companion, easing the hardship of the ill?

### Analyze Craft

2 Terms like "box," "terrarium," "coffer," "cotillion," "miracle," and "tub" suggest that television does not provide a wide, public panorama so much as a smaller, private experience of perception. How does the poet make his point, and make you read this poem—consider its title—as a traditional "ode," an elevated, formal lyric poem usually written in praise?

### Analyze Voice

3 In the terms we've considered before—high, middle, low—describe the poet's tone of voice and the diction here.

### Synthesize Summary and Analysis

4 Later in the poem, Pinsky expresses gratitude for the events and people he's viewed on television. How does he reach this conclusion?

### Interpret the Poem

5 Is it necessary to identify such cultural references as Sid Caesar and Jackie Robinson in order to follow this poet's intention? How does he link the literal and figurative aspects of our culture?

## SIMILE AND METAPHOR

Similes and metaphors, the two most commonly used figures of speech, express resemblances between two unlike things. A **simile** is a direct comparison of two distinct things using the words "like" or "as." If you say that "your friend runs *like* a cheetah" or "your brother's voice is shrill *as* a police siren," your comparisons are similes. By highlighting what two things have in common, poets direct a reader's attention to out-of-the-ordinary, often provocative associations.

You've just read Michael Ondaatje's "Sweet Like a Crow," which uses simile as its foundation. Canadian poet Margaret Atwood shows us, in a brief love lyric, just how radical a departure from ordinary speech a simile can provide.

**A BRIEF HISTORY OF FIGURATIVE LANGUAGE**

Creating new meanings by comparing unlike objects is an ancient practice, observed in even the earliest preserved oral literatures. Aristotle posited that metaphor helped describe, artistically, that which otherwise couldn't be identified and could likewise amplify the persuasive power of a speaker's language. While classical Western tradition—the literatures of ancient Greece and Rome—handed down traditions of figurative language (simile, metaphor, metonymy, and many more) familiar to modern English speakers, non-Western cultures developed their own subtly special figures of speech. Asian, African, and Middle Eastern literatures, for example, each incorporate complex, culturally informed figurative associations. The fact that any language's figures of speech are sometimes very difficult for foreign speakers to construe attests to their individual, social connotations. It's true in American culture, too. Expressions in American English like "I need to make some dough" or "that was a piece of cake" remind us how individual, even obscure, our own culture's figurative language can be.

# Margaret Atwood (b. 1939)

Margaret Atwood, a Canadian writer, is known for both her novels and her poetry, in addition to her short fiction, nonfiction, and children's books. A poet since age sixteen, she has published more than fifteen books of poetry, among them *The Animals in That Country* (1968), *Two-Headed Poems* (1978), and *Morning in the Burned House* (1995), which won the Trillium Award. Her work often engages with ancient mythology and gender relations, and she describes her own poetry as having "a texture of sound which is at least as important to me as the 'argument.'"

**AS YOU READ** Watch this domestic image from the ordinary world turn on itself and grow harsh.

## you fit into me (1971)

you fit into me
like a hook into an eye
a fish hook
an open eye

# Writing from Reading

### Summarize

**1** The poet makes a complex relationship—between two lovers, or partners—into a seemingly simple image. How does the simile of the hook turn dangerous?

### Analyze Craft

**2** The hook and eye suggest some aspect of clothing or, perhaps, a crocheting instrument and clasp. The "fit" seems painless until the third line and second part of the comparison—a fish hook that snags an eye. Suddenly the image grows painful and bloody and wrenching. How does the snug fit become an open wound?

### Analyze Voice

**3** Do you detect a certain harshness on the speaker's part? What is her attitude here?

### Synthesize Summary and Analysis

**4** A simple image transforms itself, using simile, into something much more complex. How does the poet make this happen?

### Interpret the Poem

**5** Does life often offer such brutal domestic truths as this?

# Jane Kenyon (1947–1995)

For a brief biography of Jane Kenyon, see chapter 20.

**AS YOU READ** Notice that the title points to the poem's last word. Is this an instance of "back to back"?

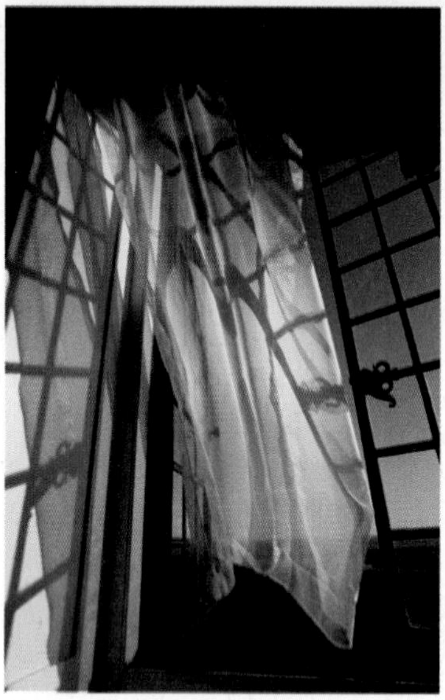

## The Suitor (1978)

We lie back to back. Curtains
lift and fall,
like the chest of someone sleeping.
Wind moves the leaves of the box elder;
they show their light undersides,
turning all at once
like a school of fish.
Suddenly I understand that I am happy.
For months this feeling
has been coming closer, stopping
for short visits, like a timid suitor.

# Writing from Reading

### Summarize

1 Describe, in your own words, the physical images the poem's similes evoke.

### Analyze Craft

2 How do the similes help describe the speaker's sudden understanding? Do the two usages of "like" seem natural or forced?

### Analyze Voice

3 Do you hear anything complex—in terms of its tonality—in this simple declaration? Does Kenyon's choice of words underline the simplicity of the emotion?

### Synthesize Summary and Analysis

4 What role does the natural world play in the poet's turn toward a new understanding of her situation?

### Interpret the Poem

5 Who is being courted? Who is the suitor?

A **metaphor** also closely compares two dissimilar things but *without* using words such as "like" or "as." While a simile suggests that X is *like* Y, a metaphor states that X *is* Y. This can make for even bolder, more emphatic turns of phrase. When converted into a metaphor, the simile "My uncle's funny as a clown" becomes "My uncle's a clown." By referring to the person as a clown directly, the metaphor intensifies the sentiment.

Metaphors create an explicit, or specifically stated, connection, as was apparent when Pinsky's "television" morphed into a "terrarium of dreams," among other images. Occasionally, however, a poet's metaphor is implicit—hinted at, but not directly expressed. If, in an argument, a sister tells her brother, "You're such a chicken," she's using an explicit metaphor to compare the boy to a skittish bird. If the brother retorts, "Quit your yapping," he implies that his sister's teasing sounds to him like an obnoxious barking dog. This is called **implied metaphor**—the comparison is only suggested, never stated plainly. Because the brother does not call his sister a "yapping dog" overtly, the metaphor of his sister as dog remains implicit, if still discourteous.

The American poet Sylvia Plath makes delightfully diverse use of the versatility of metaphorical language in the following poem. She piles on image after image at an almost comic rate.

# Sylvia Plath (1932–1963)

For a brief biography of Sylvia Plath, see chapter 19.

**AS YOU READ** Note how many objects and images the speaker figuratively equates herself to, and how they challenge the reader with a sort of poetic brainteaser.

## Metaphors (1960)

I'm a riddle in nine syllables,
An elephant, a ponderous house,
A melon strolling on two tendrils.
O red fruit, ivory, fine timbers!
This loaf's big with its yeasty rising.
Money's new-minted in this fat purse.
I'm a means, a stage, a cow in calf.
I've eaten a bag of green apples,
Boarded the train there's no getting off.

# Writing from Reading

### Summarize

1 How are different metaphors in the poem related to one another?

### Analyze Craft

2 Why do you think Plath chooses nine syllables per line? And nine lines?

### Analyze Voice

3 Is the speaker here happy or sad, regretting her condition or celebrating it?

### Synthesize Summary and Analysis

4 Are these all metaphors for pregnancy? If so, is the "I" of the poem in the early or late stages of pregnancy?

### Interpret the Poem

5 Since the poem announces in its title that this will be a sequence of metaphors, does it deliver on its promise?

Sometimes poets will use an **extended metaphor,** or a figurative analogy that's woven through a poem. Poetry provides an emphasis on detailed and focused imagery. Because of this, it's an especially effective medium in which to broaden a comparison and enlarge it through several lines. Once again we can take an example from Shakespeare, whose sonnet in chapter 18 alerts the reader in the opening line that he is deploying an extended metaphor. "Shall I compare thee to a summer's day?" offers a kind of hint, a signal from poet to reader to look for the variety of ways he will compare a midsummer day—its best and worst qualities—to the object of his affection. Indeed, virtually every line proceeding from that opening extends the comparison. Here extended metaphor frames the reader's comprehension and offers us a chance, at length, to see Shakespeare's subject the way *he* does.

> "Charlie Simic says that a poem is like an antique pinball machine with metaphors instead of balls. So everything in the poem, if you think of it this way, knocks against everything else."
>
> Conversation with Carolyn Forché

The following is another "love" poem, in which the poet compares herself and her partner to a pair of automobiles conjoined by jumper cables.

# Linda Pastan (b. 1932)

Linda Pastan grew up in a traditional Jewish household in the Bronx. She earned her B.A. from Radcliffe and an M.A. from Brandeis. A married woman with three children, Pastan reflects on domestic life in compressed, lyrical poems. Her later poetry takes up themes of aging and mortality. Collected in books including *A Perfect Circle of Sun* (1971), *The Five Stages of Grief* (1978), and *Queen of a Rainy Country* (2006), Pastan's poetry has won, among other awards, a Pushcart Prize, the Dylan Thomas Award, and the Alice Fay di Castagnola Award from the American Poetry Society. She lives in Maryland with her husband, Ira, a noted molecular biologist.

**AS YOU READ** The French would call this a "jeu d'esprit"—a game of wit—and the metaphysical poets such as John Donne and Andrew Marvell would call it an extended "conceit." Notice how it's also a sustained if implicit comparison: woman=car.

## Jump Cabling (1984)

When our cars touched
When you lifted the hood          of mine
To see the intimate workings          underneath,
When we were bound          together
By a pulse of pure          energy,
When my car like the          princess
In the tale woke with          a start,
I thought why not ride the rest of the way together.

# Writing from Reading

### Summarize

**1** What does the "pulse of pure energy" refer to?

### Analyze Craft

**2** How do metaphors in this poem help illustrate the speaker's thoughts on the person fixing her car?

### Analyze Voice

**3** Imagine the poet were male and the "princess" a prince. What would change, what stay the same?

### Synthesize Summary and Analysis

**4** The figurative language describing a "charge" is sustained. In what ways is the image of the poem's title developed here throughout?

**5** Compare the relationship described in Pastan's poem to the relationships in Atwood's "you fit into me" and Shakespeare's "Shall I compare thee to a summer's day?" (chapter 18). How does the various use of metaphors differ? How are they similar?

### Interpret the Poem

**6** What does the space in the layout of the poem represent?

Because extended metaphor is a tempting and sometimes complex means of explaining an impression, writers can lose track of how these figurative creations work. Occasionally an extended comparison will fail because the analogies within it become inconsistent or don't make sense in relation to one another. A **mixed metaphor** results when a writer uses at least two separate, mismatched comparisons in one statement. The effect is usually confusing, and sometimes comic, too. Look at this example: "When you're a big fish in a small pond, you don't want to end up with your tail between your legs." The speaker here mixes an old metaphor about being a fish with another old metaphor about being a dog. The combination of unrelated metaphors ends up baffling us more than clarifying the parts of the comparison.

In "Symposium," Paul Muldoon purposefully strings together a sequence of mixed metaphors. The poet replaces one formulaic phrase with another, and the substitutions make the familiar seem strange. As you read, consider what effect this conscious jumbling has on your interpretation of the poem itself.

## Paul Muldoon (b. 1951)

Born in Northern Ireland, Paul Muldoon worked in radio and television for the British Broadcasting Corporation before becoming a professor of poetry at Oxford University. He later accepted a professorship at Princeton University, where he still teaches today. Muldoon's poetry is marked by wit and a propensity for surprising twists, and though much of it is lighthearted in tone, he incorporates serious subject matter and makes frequent use of allusions. His collections include *New Weather* (1973), *The Annals of Chile* (1994), and the Pulitzer Prize–winning *Moy Sand and Gravel* (2002), among others. Recently, he was named poetry editor of *The New Yorker* magazine.

**AS YOU READ** **Notice the wit here, the intentional use of cliché and the mixture of snippets of speech.**

# Symposium

**(1995)**

You can bring a horse to water but you can't make it hold
its nose to the grindstone and hunt with the hounds.
Every dog has a stitch in time. Two heads? You've been sold
one good turn. One good turn deserves a bird in the hand.

A bird in the hand is better than no bread.
To have your cake is to pay Paul.
Make hay while you can still hit the nail on the head.
For want of a nail the sky might fall.

People in glass houses can't see the wood
for the new broom. Rome wasn't built between two stools.
Empty vessels wait for no man.

A hair of the dog is a friend indeed.
There's no fool like the fool
who's shot his bolt. There's no smoke after the horse is gone.

# Writing from Reading

### Summarize

1 What is a symposium? Does the title contribute to your reading of the poem?

### Analyze Craft

2 Here the figurative language makes unexpected connections between disparate things. Does the use of discontinuity itself become a metaphor for a way of speaking about ordinarily indescribable situations?

### Analyze Voice

3 Who's speaking here, and who is the "Paul" that gets paid in the second stanza?

### Synthesize Summary and Analysis

4 This poem is full of old metaphorical sayings and advice. What happens to the meaning of these phrases when they're garbled together and mixed?

### Interpret the Poem

5 Do you think this poem has an implicit meaning or message, or is it merely wordplay?

## HYPERBOLE AND UNDERSTATEMENT

While metaphor and simile are the poet's most often utilized figures of speech, other forms of figurative language help writers achieve vivid description. **Hyperbole,** sometimes called overstatement, is another type of figure of speech that uses verbal exaggeration to make a point. For example, after consuming a large meal, you might say, "I couldn't possibly eat another bite." Unless you're in some kind of medical distress, however, you're likely physically able to eat *something.* This exaggeration simply helps drive home the extent of just how full you feel.

Commemorating the first battle of the American Revolution in his poem "Concord Hymn," Ralph Waldo Emerson describes the first fired rifle round as "the shot heard round the world." Emerson uses hyperbole to tell a truth—that the whole world was ultimately affected by the events in 1775 in the battles of Lexington and Concord.

Metaphor can also help create **understatement,** a purposeful tool in description. This is a kind of opposite to hyperbole. Calling Albert Einstein a "pretty smart guy" actually helps communicate, by downplaying the language, just how brilliant the man was. Such American poets as Robert Frost and William Carlos Williams often rely on understatement to emphasize a point.

## SYNECDOCHE AND METONYMY

**Synecdoche** is a figure of speech that uses a piece or part of a thing to represent the thing in its entirety. At a party, for example, you might ask your host, "Can I have another glass?" Because you're using the word *glass* (part of the thing) not to mean an empty cup, but to instead signify a small container filled with water, ice cubes, and maybe a slice of lemon (the whole thing), the word *glass* is a synecdoche for the entire contents—container, ice, water, lemon, and all. "Was this the face that launched a thousand ships?" writes the British poet Christopher Marlowe, referring to Helen of Troy, the beautiful queen whose abduction leads to the Trojan War in Homer's *Iliad.*

Here "the face" is a synecdoche for the woman in total. In the sentence "After my old Chevy broke down for good, I had to buy some new wheels," the speaker uses "wheels" as a synecdoche to indicate that a whole new vehicle was purchased, not just four new individual wheels. The parts represent a greater whole.

> "Poetry gives us an opportunity to do things that prose doesn't."
>
> Conversation with Al Young

Occasionally, synecdoche is also used the other way around—a whole object used to represent a smaller part. "The police had to come and break up the party." We understand in this statement that *individuals* on a police force (part of a whole), and not the entire police force, nor every police force in the world for that matter (a whole), came to subdue the gathering. In this case, "the police" is a synecdoche for those particular, identifiable people wearing the badges.

# Czeslaw Milosz (1911–2004)

Poet and translator Czeslaw Milosz was born in Lithuania and grew up closely tied to ancient folk traditions, living in a society that in subsequent decades was destroyed by the Nazis and political turmoil in Eastern Europe. Although raised in a Polish village, he left Poland in 1951 because he opposed the government. He lived in Paris and the United States (he taught Polish literature at the University of California, Berkeley), an exile "in both an outward and inward sense," as an award committee once described him—"a stranger for whom the physical exile is really a reflection of a metaphysical, or even religious, spiritual exile applying to humanity in general." In addition to his poetry, which he wrote in Polish, Milosz wrote a partially autobiographical novel, *The Seizure of Power* (1953), about the Communist regime in Poland. Among his many prestigious awards is the Nobel Prize in Literature, which he received in 1980.

**AS YOU READ** **Let yourself imagine an anecdote from your own life, some years ago, in which the part can represent the whole.**

## Encounter (1936)

We were riding through frozen fields in a wagon at dawn.
A red wing rose in the darkness.

And suddenly a hare ran across the road.
One of us pointed to it with his hand.

That was long ago. Today neither of them is alive,
Not the hare, nor the man who made the gesture.

O my love, where are they, where are they going
The flash of a hand, streak of movement, rustle of pebbles.
I ask not out of sorrow, but in wonder.

*—translated by Czeslaw Milosz and Lillian Vallee*

# Writing from Reading

### Summarize

1 The poet uses an anecdote from his life for a larger purpose than just to tell the story. Can you think of an anecdote of your own that might serve the same purpose as this one?

### Analyze Craft

2 Where is there an instance of synecdoche in this poem?

### Analyze Voice

3 What does the incremental rise in emphasis at the beginning of line 5 and again at the beginning of line 7 bring to the tone of this poem?

### Synthesize Summary and Analysis

4 The poet employs an anecdote as an illustration of some higher matter. Is the poem more autobiographical than philosophical, or vice versa?

### Interpret the Poem

5 What do you think the speaker means by "wonder"? What is he speculating on?

Synecdoche is considered a form of metonymy, a slightly more general figure of speech. **Metonymy** uses an identifying emblem or closely associated object to represent a thing in its entirety. "Hired gun" is metonymy for an individual paid to shoot people. The gun itself doesn't get hired or paid; it is simply the object associated with the assassin. In the sentence "She really loves reading Harry Potter," the popular books are represented by the name of the main character. People don't, technically, read the *character;* they read the books—the physical objects with pages and words—in which Harry Potter appears.

# Diane Wakoski (b. 1937)

A native of California, Diane Wakoski is known for her intensely personal poetry. Often compared to Beat poets, Wakoski dispenses with traditional rhyme and meter, and her poems seem close to prose at times. Still, they are packed with physical imagery, symbol, and allegory as she seeks to create a personal mythology (take, for example, her poem "The Father of My Country," which features George Washington as her adopted father). She has published over forty collections of poetry, among them *Emerald Ice: Selected Poems 1962–1987* (1988) and the four-volume *Archaeology of Movies and Books* (1990–1995), and has taught at Michigan State University since 1976.

**AS YOU READ** Catalogue the outpouring of seemingly unrelated images.

# Inside Out (1988)

I walk the purple carpet into your eye
carrying the silver butter server
but a truck rumbles by,
        leaving its black tire prints on my foot
and old images        the sound of banging screen doors on hot
    afternoons and a fly buzzing over the Kool-Aid spilled on
    the sink
flicker, as reflections on the metal surface.

Come in, you said,
inside your paintings, inside the blood factory, inside the
old songs that line your hands, inside
eyes that change like a snowflake every second,
inside spinach leaves holding that one piece of gravel,
inside the whiskers of a cat,
inside your old hat, and most of all inside your mouth where you
grind the pigments with your teeth, painting
with a broken bottle on the floor, and painting
with an ostrich feather on the moon that rolls out of my mouth.

You cannot let me walk inside you too long inside
the veins where my small feet touch
bottom.
You must reach inside and pull me
like a silver bullet
from your arm.

# Writing from Reading

### Summarize

1 The poet speaks of intimacy in an outpouring of images. Can you paraphrase the poem?

### Analyze Craft

2 Where in the poem does the speaker use metonymy to represent the intended listener?

3 Do the "veins" the speaker mentions represent synecdoche or metonymy?

### Analyze Voice

4 Does the intensity of tone match the occasion of the poem?

### Synthesize Summary and Analysis

5 How does the outpouring of images express the poet's inner feeling?

### Interpret the Poem

6 Nurturing and violent, lyrical, and urgent—to what end do all of these attributes come together in the poem?

## PERSONIFICATION AND APOSTROPHE

It's a natural habit to perceive human qualities and emotions in nonhuman things. We see ants moving in a line on the sidewalk and think of marching soldiers. A hurricane might blow "angrily," or a tomato plant wilt "with a sigh." A line of trees swaying in a strong wind momentarily reminds us of dancers. Skyscrapers might look like the hunched shoulders of men and women waiting in a gargantuan line. These are examples of **personification,** figures of speech in which writers ascribe human traits or behavior to something inhuman. In "The Gone Years," contemporary American poet Alice Fulton describes darkness coming at the end of the day: "Night pockets the house / in a blue / muffle . . ." The poet personifies night so it can place a building in its pocket.

Taking in a panoramic morning view of London, William Wordsworth describes the city in the following poem.

## William Wordsworth (1770–1850)

For a brief biography of William Wordsworth, see chapter 15.

**AS YOU READ** Situate yourself in the place and time—the poem's "occasion"—and imagine yourself by Wordsworth's side as he speaks.

# Composed upon Westminster Bridge, September 3, 1802 (1807)

Earth has not anything to show more fair:
Dull would he be of soul who could pass by
A sight so touching in its majesty:
This City now doth, like a garment, wear
The beauty of the morning; silent, bare,
Ships, towers, domes, theatres, and temples lie
Open unto the fields, and to the sky;
All bright and glittering in the smokeless air.
Never did sun more beautifully steep
In his first splendor valley, rock, or hill;
Ne'er saw I, never felt, a calm so deep!
The river glideth at his own sweet will:
Dear God! the very houses seem asleep;
And all that mighty heart is lying still!

# Writing from Reading

### Summarize

1 Paraphrase the first line of the poem in your own words.

### Analyze Craft

2 Identify moments of personification in the poem.

### Analyze Voice

3 What do the personified comparisons in the poem suggest to you about the speaker's perception of London?

4 Notice how Wordsworth uses both "never" and " ne'er." Is this for the sake of meter only? Why does he write "glideth" instead of "glides"?

### Synthesize Summary and Analysis

5 You will notice (see chapter 24) that this poem is a sonnet—a fourteen-line arrangement with a turn at the end of line 8. How does the poet link those seemingly opposite things—an urban view and a pastoral one—within a sonnet's shape?

### Interpret the Poem

6 This poem celebrates London and lists its "ships, towers, domes, theatres, and temples." Is there any warning here, or sense of a body at risk?

## William Blake (1757–1827)

For a brief biography of William Blake, see the Case Study on Art and Poetry, chapter 26.

**AS YOU READ** Notice how abstract the "sunflower" is. Could you draw the particular flower, having read the poem?

# Ah! Sun-flower (1793)

Ah! sun-flower! weary of time,
Who countest the steps of the Sun,
Seeking after that sweet golden clime
Where the traveler's journey is done;

Where the youth pined away with desire,
And the pale virgin shrouded in snow,
Arise from their graves and aspire,
Where my sun-flower wishes to go.

# Writing from Reading

### Summarize

1 What metaphorical place does the sunflower "seek"?

### Analyze Craft

2 In addition to personification, what other figures of speech can you find in the poem?

### Analyze Voice

3 Again, there's a consciously archaic diction—"countest" as opposed to "counts." Why?

### Synthesize Summary and Analysis

4 The poet personifies the sunflower both by comparing it to "the youth . . . and the pale virgin" and by suggesting that the flower is "weary of time" and "wishes to go" to the landscape described in the first stanza. What does this suggest about the similarities between the natural and the human world?

### Interpret the Poem

5 Why do you think Blake chooses a sunflower for the speaker to address?

Additional figures of speech invoke imagined human elements within poems. **Apostrophe** describes a figure of speech in which a writer calls out to an unseen person, force, or personified idea. Apostrophe derives from an ancient Greek term meaning a "turning away," and it often marks a moment of digression in which a poem's speaker pauses and turns to an invisible presence, often for counsel, in complaint, or for comfort. In "Ode on a Grecian Urn" (chapter 18), John Keats addresses, using apostrophe, a decorative Greek vase:. "Thou still unravished bride of quietness," he writes, speaking symbolically to the urn, "Thou foster-child of silence and slow time."

# Gabriella Mistral (1889–1957)

The first Latin American woman to win the Nobel Prize for Literature, Lucila Godoy y Alcayaga was born in Chile. A schoolteacher, she had a passionate love affair with a railroad worker when she was twenty years old. When her lover committed suicide, she began to write poetry and later adopted the pseudonym Gabriella (after the biblical angel) Mistral (a Mediterranean wind and the surname of an author she admired). She was involved in education reform in Mexico and Chile; she served as a delegate to the League of Nations, where she helped found UNICEF; and she worked as consul in Spain, France, Italy, Portugal, and Guatemala. Her poetry, as in the collection *Desolación* (1922), is full of sorrow, but also full of compassion toward children, as in *Ternura* (1924).

**AS YOU READ** Ask yourself why the poet finds the tree worthy of her attention.

# Fugitive Woman (1954)

Festival tree, branches wide,
loose cascade, lively freshness
falling steeply at my back:
Who told you to stop me
and sound out my name?

Under a tree, I was only
washing the journeys from my feet
with my shadow for a road
and dust for a skirt.

How lovely that you throw out your limbs
and that you lower your head,
without grasping that I
don't have ten years to learn
your green cross that has no blood
and the disk of your pedestal!

Examine me, cedar-pine,
with your vertical eyes,
and don't move or uproot
your feet from the living soil:
your new feet can't take it
with scrapes from the cactuses
and bites from the cliffs.

There's a kind of restlessness,
like a hissing that runs
from the simmering zodiac
to the bristling grass.
The whole night is alive
with negations and affirmations,
those of the Angel who commands you
and mine who fights against him;

and a wreck of a woman
wails for her cedar of Lebanon
fallen and covered by night,
who's going to leave at dawn
knowing neither road nor dust
and without ever seeing again
his circle of two thousand pines.

Oh, tree of mine, surrendered
senseless to the blizzard
to dog day and to beast
to the hazard of the tempest.
Pine wandering over the earth!

*—translated by Randall Couch*

# Writing from Reading

## Summarize

**1** Here the poet talks to a tree (as did William Blake to a sunflower). Is she also talking to herself and others? In what ways?

**2** What does "his circle of two thousand pines" suggest? What does the reference to "cedar of Lebanon" mean?

## Analyze Craft

**3** Discuss figures of speech such as "shadow for a road" and "dust for a skirt." How does the poet achieve her desired effects?

## Analyze Voice

**4** Does the speaker's voice seem natural? Slightly elevated in tone? Rising to a grand occasion?

## Synthesize Summary and Analysis

**5** An address to a tree that speaks of higher values and actions—is it possible for you to accept this as a way of speaking about life and the world?

## Interpret the Poem

**6** What is the larger subject?

## PARADOX AND OXYMORON

Poets often deal in **paradox,** seemingly contradictory statements that when closely examined, have a deeper, sometimes complicated, meaning. "Youth," say some stodgy adults, paraphrasing George Bernard Shaw, "is wasted on the young." Though this saying seems to contradict itself by definition, the expression means to explain that the older we get, the more we value the vitality and innocence of our younger years. In poetry, paradox attempts to tell a truth of perception or emotion despite an apparent leap in logic. "Love," says the ancient poet Ovid, "is a kind of warfare." A leap like this intends to make the reader think more deeply or subtly about a subject. Consider how Bashō, a seventeenth-century Japanese poet, uses the haiku form to pose a paradox to the listener.

> "Be completely open—innocent, if you will—of the poem. Walk in, just like it's water, and say 'What is this?'"
>
> Conversation with Marie Howe

# Matsuo Bashō (1644–1694)

For a brief biography of Matsuo Bashō, see chapter 20.

**AS YOU READ** Notice how the title word is repeated at the end of the first and the third line.

## Kyoto (c. 1680)

Even in Kyoto—
Hearing the cuckoo's cry
I long for Kyoto.

—*translated by Robert Hass*

# Writing from Reading

### Summarize

1 Why and how do you think the speaker longs for a place and town (Kyoto) he has not left?

2 What do you think is the significance of the birdsong the speaker mentions?

### Analyze Craft

3 If you include the title, there are twelve words in this poem—of which three are the same. What does this repetition suggest?

### Analyze Voice

4 What's being said here and what, paradoxically, is left unsaid?

### Synthesize Summary and Analysis

5 What does this poem suggest about the poet's sense of time and place?

### Interpret the Poem

6 Is there a place about which you feel the way Bashō feels and, if so, why?

**Oxymoron** is a version of paradox that combines contradictory words into a compact, often two-word term. Oxymorons can be amusing, as in "jumbo shrimp" or "definite maybe," but they can also illustrate a writer's particular emotional or spiritual reflection. When Shakespeare calls "parting . . . sweet sorrow," he's making an oxymoronic linkage and saying, in effect, that opposites attract.

The poet William Butler Yeats includes an oxymoronic comparison in the end of his poem "The Fisherman." Yeats was preoccupied throughout his life with the political and spiritual plight of his fellow Irish citizens. Here the speaker imagines an idealized, mythic Irish reader for his poems: "a wise and simple" fisherman who is both "cold and passionate"—terms we commonly believe to be in opposition but that are joined here.

# William Butler Yeats (1865–1939)

For a brief biography of William Butler Yeats, see chapter 15.

**AS YOU READ** Notice how "a man who does not exist" becomes the central figure of the poem.

# The Fisherman (1919)

Although I can see him still.
The freckled man who goes
To a grey place on a hill
In grey Connemara clothes
At dawn to cast his flies,
It's long since I began
To call up to the eyes
This wise and simple man.
All day I'd looked in the face
What I had hoped 'twould be
To write for my own race
And the reality;
The living men that I hate,
The dead man that I loved,
The craven man in his seat,
The insolent unreproved,
And no knave brought to book
Who has won a drunken cheer,
The witty man and his joke
Aimed at the commonest ear,
The clever man who cries
The catch-cries of the clown,
The beating down of the wise
And great Art beaten down.

Maybe a twelvemonth since
Suddenly I began,
In scorn of this audience,
Imagining a man,
And his sun-freckled face,
And grey Connemara cloth,
Climbing up to a place
Where stone is dark under froth,
And the down-turn of his wrist
When the flies drop in the stream;
A man who does not exist,
A man who is but a dream;
And cried, 'Before I am old
I shall have written him one
poem maybe as cold
And passionate as the dawn.'

# Writing from Reading

## Summarize

1 Describe the figure of the fisherman that the speaker imagines. What details do we have?

## Analyze Craft

2 Notice that the second stanza begins with the word "Maybe" and repeats that word in the next-to-last line.

3 Look at the rhyme scheme here—the "true" and "near" or approximate rhymes.

## Analyze Voice

4 How would you describe the speaker's attitude toward himself?

## Synthesize Summary and Analysis

5 What does the poet hope to accomplish, and why? Why does he leave his first imagined audience behind "in scorn," and whose attention does he hope to capture instead?

## Interpret the Poem

6 Describe the "one poem" the speaker wants to write for the fisherman. Does the description seem self-contradictory?

## PUN

Often lighthearted in nature, a **pun** is a play on words that reveals different meanings in words that are similar or even identical. We generally think of puns as silly and perhaps trivial, as in an old joke like "A bigamist loves not too many, but *two* well." Sometimes, however, writers use puns to capitalize on two separate meanings of a word and emphasize a point. "Ask for me tomorrow," says the stabbed Mercutio to Romeo in *Romeo and Juliet,* "and you shall find me a grave man." Here, "grave" suggests both a seriousness of manner and the final resting place where Mercutio, who realizes he's dying, is inevitably headed. By exploiting this double meaning, Shakespeare deepens our understanding of the play's action and the character of Mercutio himself.

> "A poem requires whether consciously or unconsciously some kind of change into a new realization, whether large or small."
>
> Conversation with Jane Hirshfield

Sometimes a punned double meaning underscores humor and critique simultaneously, as in the following poem.

# A. R. Ammons (1926–2001)

Archie Randolph Ammons was born in North Carolina to a tobacco farmer. While on a Navy destroyer escort in the South Pacific during World War II, Ammons began to write poetry. Published at his own expense, his first collection, *Ommateum* (1955), sold hardly any copies, but his poetry career took off eight years later with his second collection. In all, he published almost thirty collections and won many of the most prestigious awards including the National Book Award for *Garbage* (1993) and again for his *Collected Poems: 1951–1971* (1972), and the National Book Critics Circle Award for *A Coast of Trees* (1981). A professor of creative writing at Cornell University, Ammons was known as a nature poet interested in exploring the poet's consciousness; critic Harold Bloom described him as a transcendentalist in the vein of Ralph Waldo Emerson.

**AS YOU READ** Consider this poem as an epigram—a short, pithy saying—as well as a pun.

## Their Sex Life (1991)

One failure on
Top of another

# Writing from Reading

**Summarize**

1 What scene do these two lines describe, and what's personified?

**Analyze Craft**

2 Which words in the poem suggest a double meaning?

**Analyze Voice**

3 Is the poet bitter or sympathetic? Is this poem witty or sad?

**Synthesize Summary and Analysis**

4 How does the visual look of the poem and its line breaks contribute to meaning and humor?

**Interpret the Poem**

5 If these lines had no title, how would their meaning change?

## HUMOR

Poetry sometimes has a reputation for seriousness and even downright gloominess. And while it's true that poems often explore somber and intensely reflective themes, many poets put the elastic tools of language to comedic use. In this chapter, we have already seen such writers as Paul Muldoon and A. R. Ammons indulge in witty wordplay. Poems like these remind us that humorous use of tools like simile, metaphor, and other figures of speech amplifies our perspective on a topic just as interestingly as the use of serious figurative language.

When people invent witty or even vulgar comparisons to describe a situation, they almost always incorporate figures of speech familiar to readers; the comedy may even depend on it. Think of an expression like "It's cold as a well digger's ass," or "The ice on the road's as slippery as snot on a doorknob." Whether you delight in off-color speech like this or find it repulsive, it's inarguably dependent on vivid figurative language.

A good poem can, in fact, be a lot like a good joke—it can jolt our expectation and open up a new and unexpected way of understanding the human condition. To laugh at a joke is to accept a certain degree of shocked surprise; this holds just as true for a peculiar figure of speech. As a result, writers often find that they can use comic analogies to make a reader simultaneously laugh and think seriously. Both results require the same kind of intelligence.

Look at how a rich combination of metaphors, similes, personification, and other figures heightens both absurdity and credible emotion in the following poem.

# Julie Sheehan (b. 1964)

Julie Sheehan, originally from Iowa, won an award for each of her first two poetry collections: the Poetry Out Loud Prize for *Thaw* (2001) and the Barnard Women Poets Prize for *Orient Point* (2006). She earned her degrees from Yale and Columbia, and her poetry has appeared in publications such as *Ploughshares, Kenyon Review,* and *The Best American Poetry 2005.* A new American voice, Sheehan offers a view of the contemporary world in her energetic lines, often with a dose of wry humor. She describes her second collection as "a collage of quilted rhetorics—some more traditional, some experimental, often exploring touchy subjects."

**AS YOU READ** Notice how the title and first line—as well as much that follows—play off against the expectation of a love poem; compare to Elizabeth Barrett Browning's "How do I love thee?" (chapter 23).

# Hate Poem (2005)

I hate you. Truly I do.
Everything about me hates everything about you.
The flick of my wrist hates you.
The way I hold my pencil hates you.
The sound made by my tiniest bones were they trapped in the jaws of a
moray eel hates you.
Each corpuscle singing in its capillary hates you.

Look out! Fore! I hate you.

The blue-green jewel of sock lint I'm trying to dig from under my third
toenail, left foot, hates you.
The history of this keychain hates you.
My sigh in the background as you pick out the cashews hates you.
The goldfish of my genius hates you.
My aorta hates you. Also my ancestors.

A closed window is both a closed window and an obvious symbol of how
I hate you.

My voice curt as a hairshirt: hate.
My hesitation when you invite me for a drive: hate.
My pleasant "good morning": hate.
You know how when I'm sleepy I nuzzle my head under your arm? Hate.
The whites of my target-eyes articulate hate. My wit practices it.
My breasts relaxing in their holster from morning to night hate you.
Layers of hate, a parfait.
Hours after our latest row, brandishing the sharp glee of hate,
I dissect you cell by cell, so that I might hate each one individually and
at leisure.
My lungs, duplicitous twins, expand with the utter validity of my hate,
which can never have enough of you,
Breathlessly, like two idealists in a broken submarine.

# Writing from Reading

### Summarize

**1** We often call a relationship—consider Margaret Atwood's poem "you fit into me"—an example of a "love-hate ambivalence." How does the term apply to these lines?

### Analyze Craft

**2** How do figurative comparisons underscore humor and emotion in this poem? List examples of hyperbole.

### Analyze Voice

**3** Is the "I" here a specific first person, and how does it become a representative "I"?

### Synthesize Summary and Analysis

**4** On the composition of "I Hate You" Julie Sheehan wrote, "It occurred to me, as probably to many, that since hate requires as much passion as love, the two emotions can be described in indistinguishable terms." Note places in the poem where the language used to describe hate seems indistinguishable from or similar to love.

### Interpret the Poem

**5** Is this poem entirely comic, or does Sheehan explore a "legitimate" theme as well?

# For Review and Further Study

## John Keats (1795–1821)

*For a brief biography of John Keats, see chapter 18.*

### To Autumn (1819)

I

Season of mists and mellow fruitfulness,
  Close bosom-friend of the maturing sun;
Conspiring with him how to load and bless
  With fruit the vines that round the thatch-eves run;
To bend with apples the mossed cottage-trees,
  And fill all fruit with ripeness to the core;
    To swell the gourd, and plump the hazel shells
With a sweet kernel; to set budding more,
  And still more, later flowers for the bees,
  Until they think warm days will never cease,
    For summer has o'er-brimmed their clammy cells.

II

Who hath not seen thee oft amid thy store?
  Sometimes whoever seeks abroad may find
Thee sitting careless on a granary floor,
  Thy hair soft-lifted by the winnowing wind;
Or on a half-reaped furrow sound asleep,
  Drowsed with the fume of poppies, while thy hook
    Spares the next swath and all its twinèd flowers:
And sometimes like a gleaner thou dost keep
  Steady thy laden head across a brook;
  Or by a cider-press, with patient look,
    Thou watchest the last oozings hours by hours.

III

Where are the songs of spring? Ay, where are they?
  Think not of them, thou hast thy music too—
While barrèd clouds bloom the soft-dying day,
  And touch the stubble-plains with rosy hue;
Then in a wailful choir the small gnats mourn
  Among the river swallows, borne aloft
    Or sinking as the light wind lives or dies;
And full-grown lambs loud bleat from hilly bourn;
  Hedge-crickets sing; and now with treble soft
  The redbreast whistles from a garden-croft,
    And gathering swallows twitter in the skies.

### Questions for Interactive Reading and Writing

1. The title of the poem tells you it is a direct address to the season of autumn. What kind of "personality" does Keats create for autumn? How does that personality change over the course of the poem?
2. Determine the rhyme scheme of the three stanzas. Does it ever differ? Discuss the ways the rhyme scheme complements the theme and tone of the poem.
3. Identify instances of personification in this poem besides the overarching personification of autumn.
4. Discuss the significance of the three numbered stanzas in the poem. What changes between them, and what stays the same?

## Marge Piercy (b. 1934)

### The Secretary Chant (1973)

My hips are a desk.
From my ears hang
chains of paper clips.
Rubber bands form my hair.
My breasts are wells of mimeograph ink.
My feet bear casters.
Buzz. Click.
My head
is a badly organized file.
My head is a switchboard
where crossed lines crackle.
My head is a wastebasket
of worn ideas.
Press my fingers
and in my eyes appear
credit and debit.
Zing. Tinkle.
My navel is a reject button.
From my mouth issue canceled reams.
Swollen, heavy, rectangular
I am about to be delivered
of a baby
Xerox machine.
File me under W
because I wonce
was a woman.

### Questions for Interactive Reading and Writing

1. A secretary speaks of herself in a particular fashion. How would you describe it?
2. Discuss how figurative language in this poem portrays ideas of work. Does it help or hurt to know that "secretary" is also the name for a piece of furniture?
3. Why do you think Marge Piercy avoids the words *like* and *as* in the images in her poem?
4. Why does Piercy intentionally spell "once" with a "w" at the end of "The Secretary Chant"?
5. The secretary describes her life in a special voice. Would the opposite—a calm recitation of her duties—affect you in the same way?
6. How does work organize this woman's life? How might it affect our own lives?

# Theodore Roethke (1908–1963)

*For a brief biography of Theodore Roethke, see chapter 19.*

## Root Cellar (1948)

Nothing would sleep in that cellar, dank as a ditch,
Bulbs broke out of boxes hunting for chinks in the dark,
Shoots dangled and drooped,
Lolling obscenely from mildewed crates,
Hung down long yellow evil necks, like tropical snakes.
And what a congress of stinks!—
Roots ripe as old bait,
Pulpy stems, rank, silo-rich,
Leaf-mold, manure, lime, piled against slippery planks.
Nothing would give up life:
Even the dirt kept breathing a small breath.

### Questions for Interactive Reading and Writing

1. Describe the trip our eyes—and noses—take through this underground world.
2. In what way does word choice here reflect the atmosphere of the cellar the speaker describes?
3. Identify similes and moments of personification in the poem.
4. How do these figures convey a sense of life and vitality among simple inanimate objects that might otherwise appear lifeless?
5. What does the poem's setting suggest about the speaker's perspective on life and death? How would the poem be different if it were set in a vibrant garden?
6. Does the poet sound urgent or matter-of-fact as he describes what he sees and smells?
7. A trip through the root cellar adds up to more than meets the eye—and nose. What makes the rank journey worthwhile?

# Walt Whitman (1819–1892)

*For a brief biography of Walt Whitman, see chapter 18.*

## A Noiseless Patient Spider (1891)

A noiseless patient spider,
I mark'd where on a little promontory it stood isolated,
Mark'd how to explore the vacant vast surrounding,
It launch'd forth filament, filament, filament, out of itself,
Ever unreeling them, ever tirelessly speeding them.

And you O my soul where you stand,
Surrounded, detached, in measureless oceans of space,
Ceaselessly musing, venturing, throwing, seeking the spheres to connect them,
Till the bridge you will need be form'd, till the ductile anchor hold,
Till the gossamer thread you fling catch somewhere, O my soul.

### Questions for Interactive Reading and Writing

1. Describe the spider's surroundings. How does the speaker align himself with these surroundings?
2. What do you think the speaker wants to "catch" with his soul? How does he connect this desire with the spider's activity?
3. Why do you think Whitman chooses a spider for his comparison? What characteristics of the spider does he explore?
4. Examine the figurative language here, and what the spider stands for.

# Nancy Willard (b. 1936)

## Saint Pumpkin (1982)

Somebody's in there.
Somebody's sealed himself up
in the round room,
this hassock upholstered in rind,
this padded cell.
He believes if nothing unbinds him
he'll live forever.

Like our first room
it is dark and crowded.
Hunger knows no tongue
to tell it.
Water is glad there.
In this room with two navels
somebody wants to be born again.

So I unlock the pumpkin.
I carve out the lid
from which the stem raises
a dry handle on a damp world.
Lifting, I pull away
wet webs, vines on which hang
the flat tears of the pumpkin,

like fingernails or the currency
of bats. How the seeds shine,
as if water had put out
hundreds of lanterns.
Hundreds of eyes in the windless wood
gaze peacefully past me,
hacking the thickets,
and now a white dew beads the blade.
Has the saint surrendered
himself to his beard?
Has his beard taken root in his cell?

Saint Pumpkin, pray for me,
because when I looked for you, I found nothing,
because unsealed and unkempt, your tomb rots,
because I gave you a false face
and a light of my own making.

### Questions for Interactive Reading and Writing

1. The central "figure" of this poem is a person—perhaps someone holy—who has sealed himself inside a pumpkin. Do you find this implausible at poem's start and plausible by poem's end? If so, why, if not, why not?
2. Discuss the various similes—the usages of "like"—and metaphors in this poem.
3. Is there an irony in the tone of the poet's address to this inanimate object?
4. In the final stanza, the poet apostrophizes "Saint Pumpkin" and speaks to it directly. Discuss this poem in terms of the actions described and faith expressed. What sort of worship takes place?
5. Can we find the holy in the ordinary things of this world?

# Reading for Figures of Speech

When reading for ***figures of speech,*** identify places where a writer describes one thing in terms of another in order to make a theme or idea feel fresh and new, richer than a literal description would be.

| | | |
|---|---|---|
| **Look for the words *like* or *as* that show a comparison is being used for illustration.** | *Simile:* Uses the words *like* or *as* to compare two things. *X* is like *Y*. | EXAMPLE: "you fit into me / like a hook into an eye" |
| **Look for comparisons that merge two unlike objects to create a more vivid association.** | *Metaphor:* Compares two things *without using* the words *like* or *as*. *X* is *Y*.<br>*Does the language suggest a comparison without explicitly naming the thing being compared?*<br>*Implied metaphor*<br>*Is something being described using several direct, parallel comparisons?*<br>*Extended metaphor* | EXAMPLE: "What light through yonder window breaks? It is the east, and Juliet is the sun."<br>EXAMPLE: "Quit your yapping."<br>EXAMPLE: "When our cars touched / When you lifted the hood of mine / To see the intimate workings underneath, / When we were bound together / By a pulse of pure energy" |
| **Look for objects or ideas used to represent a larger whole.** | *Synecdoche: The use of a part or piece of a thing that represents the thing in its entirety.*<br>*Metonymy: The use of an identifying emblem or closely associated object to represent a thing in its entirety.* | EXAMPLE: My best friend just got some new wheels. "Wheels"=a new car<br>EXAMPLE: The White House released a statement today. "White House"=the President |
| **Consider who (or what) is being described or addressed by the speaker.** | *Is it an animal or inanimate object?*<br>*Personification:* Endows a nonhuman thing with human qualities.<br>*Is someone or something not "present" otherwise in the poem?*<br>*Apostrophe:* Addresses an unseen person, thing, or idea. | EXAMPLE: "This City now doth, like a garment, wear / The beauty of the morning"<br>EXAMPLE: "Where are we going, Walt Whitman?" |

| | | |
|---|---|---|
| **Ask yourself if comparisons that seem to contradict each other are used to trigger a fresh understanding, or if they are merely confusing.** | *Oxymoron:* Combines two contradictory terms that use contradiction to make a point. | EXAMPLE: "cold / and passionate as the dawn." |
| | *Paradox:* States a self-contradictory position to trigger a fresh concept or comprehension. | EXAMPLE: "Youth is wasted on the young." |
| | *Pun:* Uses words that are spelled or sound alike to suggest, often humorously, more than one idea. | EXAMPLE: "Writing with a broken pencil is pointless." |
| | *Mixed metaphor:* Combines two incompatible metaphors, often resulting in nonsense or confusion. | EXAMPLE: "You can bring a horse to water but you can't make it hold / its nose to the grindstone." |
| **Does the description make a point through exaggeration or restraint?** | *Hyperbole:* Describes a thing or experience using purposeful exaggeration. | EXAMPLE: "The shot heard round the world." |
| | *Understatement:* Downplays a description to make a point or comparison. | EXAMPLE: "I think I know enough of hate / To know that for destruction ice / Is also great / And would suffice." |

# Writing about Figures of Speech

1. Compare the different approaches to metaphor that poets take in "Jump Cabling," "The Suitor," and "Hate Poem."
2. Both William Wordsworth and William Butler Yeats have poems in this chapter in which the speaker watches someone or something in admiration. What's literal, what's figurative in the scene observed?
3. Analyze the use of comic similes to make meaning in "Their Sex Life," "Symposium," and "Sweet Like a Crow."
4. Robert Pinsky's "Shirt" uses figurative language sparingly, but vividly. Discuss the purpose of his literal imagery and how it differs from the purpose of his figurative language. Compare the figurative and nonfigurative language in "Shirt" and "To Television."
5. What is the role of the title in "Metaphors," "Fugitive Woman," and "Saint Pumpkin" regarding the addition of implicit or explicit meaning?

# 22 Sound, Rhyme, & Rhythm

OF all our private parts the heart knows best
that love and grieving share the one body
and keeps a steady iambic tally
of this life's syllables, stressed and unstressed.

—*from "Iambs for the Day of Burial" by Thomas Lynch*

*"The idea that you could play with words is what for me writing poems has always been, sort of a wordplay. It really doesn't matter much to me what the subject is: the subject presents itself after the line presents itself, after the sort of acoustic hook is set in the ear."*

Conversation with Thomas Lynch, available on video at www.mhhe.com/delbanco1e

AS you see in "Iambs for the Day of Burial," the way the **sounds** of language work together with **rhyme** and **rhythm** can dramatically affect the way we experience a poem. Here Lynch makes the claim that the beat of the heart—*da-dum, da-dum, da-dum*—is a "steady iambic tally." Referring to one of poetry's most common rhythms, he relates the pulse to "stressed and unstressed" syllables. Poetry, he seems to say, has our very life force within it. The words are simply words, the sounds are sounds we've heard before, and a pattern exists in each sentence. However, a poet chooses particular words in a conscious attempt to shape the meaning of his poems; *sound* and *sense* are, in effect, two sides of one coin.

Although the language of poetry is sometimes difficult to understand, it's important to remember what you already know: all speech is sound. When we worry over the meaning of a poem, as though it were a foreign language or a code to crack, the answer to a poem's puzzle is often its "acoustic hook," the arrangement of sounds that draws us into the poem. When a sound repeats itself, we call that echo *rhyme*. The pattern of such repetition, and the way the poet places the words, even the syllables, in sequence, creates the poem's rhythm. "Iambs for the Day of Burial" aptly makes the claim that rhythm is as natural as breath. The sound of our pulse beating, the way we walk or dance, what our fingers do while tapping on a keyboard are *naturally* rhythmic, and if that word had been, instead, *unnaturally*, it would still have a rhythm though the rhythm would have changed. To understand a poem, as Lynch observes in his interview, it sometimes help to tap it out.

*I've always said that writers are readers who go karaoke . . .*

Q&A

*Language knows you better than yourself.*

# *A Conversation on Writing*

## Thomas Lynch

### The Heartbeat in Poetry

I have this vexing habit—to some people—of sort of tapping things out that are occurring to me acoustically. . . . I've always been drawn to the notion that Wordsworth could work out his poetry—and Shakespeare his own poetry—by keeping an ear to their own metabolic strain, their own breathing and heartbeat, and the notion that there is some connection between language and a natural order: *da-dum, da-dum, da-dum.* It has this appeal to my ear.

### Becoming Accountable to Your Own Language

I've always said that writers are readers who go karaoke: They first get up in front of the microphone and sing songs, do cover pieces. Then pretty soon they begin to sound like themselves talking to themselves. I don't know what it was for me. I can remember writing poems that were sort of all borrowings from Yeats and Emily Dickinson, and Edward Arlington Robinson, and Michael Heffernan, and anyone else who I came across. Most of the notions were borrowed from maybe other books that I was reading, not poetry. But at some point you become accountable to the language yourself.

### Poetry As Self-Prophecy

I'm aware of this about poetry, and I'm certain musicians must be aware about it with music, and painters with color and image: that it knows you better than yourself. It will make its way into the world, "it" being whatever language wants to do with you. Language knows you better than [you know] yourself. So the poems, when I look back at them now, they were almost prophetic. They knew things about me that came to be true, that I didn't know at the time. But the language did, from whatever part. The words kept pushing themselves onto the page. It knew things. It still does. So I trust it I suppose.

"We need a way to say unspeakable things, and funerals do. So do poems," Thomas Lynch—poet, essayist, and undertaker—once said in an interview. Born in Michigan in 1948, Lynch took over his father's funeral parlor in 1974, and he has been the undertaker for the town of Milford, Michigan, ever since. His poetry—collected in *Skating with Heather Grace* (1986), *Grimalkin* (1994), and *Still Life in Milford* (1998)—explores the intersections of life, death, sex, grief, and other profound aspects of the human experience. Among his books of nonfiction are *The Undertaking—Life Studies from the Dismal Trade,* which won the Heartland Prize for Nonfiction and the American Book Award, and *Bodies in Motion and at Rest,* a collection of essays that won the Great Lakes Book Award. Lynch's written work and commentaries have appeared in prominent venues including *The New York Times,* NPR, *The Washington Post,* and a PBS *Frontline* feature, among many others.

**To watch the entire interview and hear the author read from his work, go to www.mhhe.com/delbanco1e.**

**RESEARCH ASSIGNMENT** In his interview, Lynch quotes Yeats as saying about poetry: "It comes by the ear." Lynch weighs the influence of the Catholic church and its liturgy, even childhood prayers, on his understanding of meter and the importance of language. He says "all language has double edges." What does he mean by this, and how is his understanding of double edges in language related to his work, particularly in his poem "Liberty"?

**AS YOU READ** Consider what the poet means by "life's syllables, stressed and unstressed."

# Iambs for the Day of Burial (1998)

Of all our private parts the heart knows best
that love and grieving share the one body
and keeps a steady iambic tally
of this life's syllables, stressed and unstressed.
Our pulse divided by our breathing equals
pleasure measured in pentameters,
pain endured in oddly rhyming pairs:
sadness, gladness, sex and death, nuptials,
funerals. Love made and love forsaken—
each leaves us breathless and beatified,
more than the sum of parts that lived and died
of love or grief. Both leave the heart broken.

# Writing from Reading

### Summarize

1 Imagine these twelve lines are spoken at a grave, linking love and grief. How does the poet develop that linkage and establish the connection?

### Analyze Craft

2 This is a poem about its own making and structure. Give examples of "pentameters . . . and oddly rhyming pairs." Does the strategy work?

### Analyze Voice

3 Lynch is a professional undertaker as well as a poet; his family has operated Lynch & Sons Funeral Home in Milford, Michigan, for decades. How is Lynch's profession reflected by any of his word choices or the tone of the poem? What about the poem is surprising, considering the poet's frequent interaction with the dead?

### Synthesize Summary and Analysis

4 What connections are there between the rhythm of this poem and its subject matter? Why is this particular rhythm appropriate? Identify places where there is deviation in the rhythm. How do these deviations contribute to the overarching gravity of the poem?

### Interpret the Poem

5 Discuss the idea that love and grief "both leave the heart broken." Do you agree?

## SOUND

From its earliest presence in religious ritual and public entertainment, poetry has been written to accompany music; no form of writing is more closely associated with song and sound. "Musical thought" is how the Scottish writer Thomas Carlyle defined the genre. "[Poetry is] a sonorous molded shape of form," said the Russian poet Osip Mandelstam.

Poets have always paid special attention to the musical elements of their own language. This attention differentiates poetry from language used only to communicate information. Poetry's special sound effects of stresses, rhymes, and repetitions invite a reader to inspect, carefully, the texture and sound of words. A poet chooses language based on sound as well as on meaning. We read, for example, the word *glassy* and can perceive smooth surfaces beneath the double "s" sound. We say the word *trickle* and hear the light, small splashes of water from a kitchen sink faucet. When a writer uses a variety of active verbs, we feel velocity and action evoked in a poem. When a writer fills a line with **monosyllabic** (one-syllable) words, we perceive important emphasis and purpose. Think, for instance, of that memorable catchphrase for insecticide: "Raid kills bugs dead." Or, as in the last two words from the poem by Gerard Manley Hopkins near the end of this chapter, the simple finality of "Praise him."

> "'Meter' comes from the word for 'measure,' so the meters are measures of language in a line. . . . It is very different from music. It has to do with the pace of the language and how everything in the poem is about patterns of vowels, patterns of consonants, patterns of sounds, patterns of stresses . . . even if you can't quite hear the words or make them out . . . you hear a kind of beautiful . . . patterning of meaning." Conversation with Carolyn Forché

When poets arrange the sounds of words together, either purposefully or by sheer instinct, to produce a pleasing effect, they create **euphony,** musically pleasing poetic language. An opening like this from one of Lord Byron's love poems helps illustrate how euphonious language can mirror a poem's emotions:

*She walks in beauty, like the night*
*Of cloudless climes and starry skies;*
*And all that's best of dark and bright*
*Meet in her aspect and her eyes. . . .*

The agreeable flow of the language itself (notice, for instance, how often the "i" gets repeated) helps reinforce Byron's loving description. "Like/night/climes/skies/ bright/ eyes" all sound out a chorus of praise.

In contrast, when poets describe something unpleasant or dissonant, they often employ **cacophony,** harsh-sounding, grating, or even hard-to-pronounce syllables. Listen to these cacophonous lines by Jonathan Swift, who wanted to make fun of the pretty language of nature poetry of his day in this description of a rainstorm flooding London. If you read these lines aloud—and even though their last words rhyme—you'll likely feel your mouth squeezing the sounds out with difficulty:

*Sweeping from butchers stalls, dung, guts, and blood,*
*Drowned puppies, stinking sprats, all drenched in mud,*
*Dead cats and turnip-tops, come tumbling down the flood.*

Not exactly the subject matter we associate with English verse!

You don't have to know all of the following terms to read and enjoy a poem. By learning, however, to recognize the musical effects of sound, you will strengthen your understanding of a poem's meaning and dimensions.

"The poem is made out of the sounds." Conversation with Robert Pinsky

Safe and sound. Drunk and disorderly. Back to basics. Our language is full of catchy phrases like these that repeat their opening sounds. The effect is both memorable and musical. **Alliteration** describes this technique—the repetition of the initial consonant sounds of a sequence of words. Like many forms of repetition, this technique links sound and sense together and intensifies their combined power. As the sounds echo each other, they pull together the meanings of words. Alliterative linkage flourished in our language long before the habit of connecting lines by end-rhyme: It was with us from the start of English verse.

Also demonstrating a kind of kinship between sounds is **consonance,** a repetition of *consonant* sounds or similar patterns in neighboring words. The words

*taken and token*
*whole and whale*

employ consonance in its most familiar definition, within words that are identical except for differing vowels. Consonance also refers, moreover, to a sentence like,

*Calmly, he called to the mule in the old field*

with its repeated rolling "l."

## OLD ENGLISH ALLITERATIVE VERSE

One of the primary sources of our contemporary lexicon, Old English is the language of the oldest surviving poetry born in Britain. Alliteration is closely associated with this early verse and was used—more often than rhyme—to establish the structure of the Old English poetic line. In this tradition, two short half-lines are divided by a break but unified by alliterated, stressed syllables. These repeated consonants give Old English alliterative verse a distinctive and robust sound, ideal for the dramatic public performances in which these poems might have been heard.

**Assonance** is a kind of flip side to consonance. It's the repetition of the same *vowel* sound in neighboring words. Used for musical effect and for poetic emphasis, assonance can tie ideas together in a poem over the course of different phrases and lines.

Robert Herrick's "Delight in Disorder" (for the whole poem, see the Anthology of Poems for Further Reading, chapter 29) employs assonance in the second and third lines of this opening stanza. Note how the shared "o" vowel sound helps join the images of the clothing together:

*A sweet disorder in the dress*
*Kindles in clothes a wantonness.*
*A lawn about the shoulders thrown*
*Into a fine distraction . . .*

Sometimes the various sound elements of poetry combine to evoke the very thing their language describes. **Onomatopoeia** is a use of words that imitate the sounds they refer to. Think of words like *buzz* or *pop* or *sizzle.* We hear what they portray in the very sounds they make. When they appear in poetry or song ("clickety-clack along the track"), they further unify sound and meaning.

Listen to these lines describing the natural landscape by Alfred Lord Tennyson:

*The moan of doves in immemorial elms,*
*And murmuring of innumerable bees.*

Can you associate the doves' cry with the words *moan* and *immemorial*? Can you, in a sense, "hear" the low buzz of the bees in *murmuring* and *innumerable*?

The words *immemorial, murmuring,* and *innumerable* are **polysyllabic,** meaning they have many syllables, as opposed to the monosyllabic, or single syllable—"The moan of doves in . . . elms." In this regard, one of the glories of English is its ability to marry monosyllabic Anglo-Saxon directness with polysyllabic Latin and medieval French, a discourse brought to England when William the Conqueror, in 1066, declared that *his* would be the language of the court. English poets ever since the Norman Conquest have had a grab bag of **sonorities** to choose from, and the word *sonority* itself is just a fancy Latinate way of saying *sound.*

Think of English as a mighty river with several tributaries. By now the waters are thoroughly mixed (a process that continues yearly), and it takes analysis to separate them out. You don't have to be a linguist and fluent in foreign languages to get a sense of which words are simple, which complex—or, by extension, which language they might have derived from and what their root meaning might be.

Here the poet Seamus Heaney stresses Anglo-Saxon, making a kind of onomatopoetic statement about the way his ancestors worked. In the 218 words of "Digging," there are only six that have three syllables and none that have more. The six polysyllabic words (gravelly, flowerbeds, potatoes, grandfather, sloppily, awaken) all refer to matters of the earth or family or physical behavior. For in the end the poet claims that working with a pen is just as hard as working in a garden or bog. Note how the poem's final words are each monosyllabic, stressed, and equally a kind of "digging"; the two skills seem akin.

# Seamus Heaney (b. 1939)

Described as "the best Irish poet since W. B. Yeats," Seamus Heaney is—like Yeats—both Irish and a Nobel Prize laureate. Since he was born to a Roman Catholic family in a Protestant area of Ireland, it is perhaps not surprising that Heaney's poetry portrays Ireland's political problems. However, this is only one aspect of Heaney's poetry; his poems convey a deep sense of history, both personal and collective, in verses marked by quiet compression. In addition to the poetry collected in books like *Death of a Naturalist* (1966) and *Opened Ground* (1999), Heaney is known for his translations, most notably *Beowulf,* and his criticism. He has taught at Harvard for part of each year since 1981 but otherwise lives in Dublin.

**AS YOU READ** Consider how sound works to mimic the meaning of words, or to intensify their overall effect.

# Digging (1966)

Between my finger and my thumb
The squat pen rests; snug as a gun.

Under my window, a clean rasping sound
When the spade sinks into gravelly ground:
My father, digging. I look down

Till his straining rump among the flowerbeds
Bends low, comes up twenty years away
Stooping in rhythm through potato drills
Where he was digging.

The coarse boot nestled on the lug, the shaft
Against the inside knee was levered firmly.
He rooted out tall tops, buried the bright edge deep
To scatter new potatoes that we picked
Loving their cool hardness in our hands.

By God, the old man could handle a spade
Just like his old man.

My grandfather cut more turf in a day
Than any other man on Toner's bog.
Once I carried him milk in a bottle
Corked sloppily with paper. He straightened up
To drink it, then fell to right away
Nicking and slicing neatly, heaving sods
Over his shoulder, digging down and down
For the good turf. Digging.

The cold smell of potato mould, the squelch and slap
Of soggy peat, the curt cuts of an edge
Through living roots awaken in my head.
But I've no spade to follow men like them.

Between my finger and my thumb
The squat pen rests.
I'll dig with it.

# Writing from Reading

### Summarize

1 Why do you think the speaker repeats the title word often in the poem? What other "-ing" (participial) words does he use? Are they related to one another? How does their sound echo their meaning?

### Analyze Craft

2 Find instances of consonance and assonance in the poem. How do they work to connect or unify the language?

3 Read this poem aloud. How would you describe the sound of the language? How does this description seem to fit or contrast with the poem's subject?

### Analyze Voice

4 Can you make an analogy between the work the poet describes and his own way of making lines?

### Synthesize Summary and Analysis

5 Making a poem about work in his family, the poet discovers a link to his own present labors. Do you find that physical labor and creative labor are equivalent?

### Interpret the Poem

6 Is this a poem of justification or celebration?

# For Review and Further Study

## John Keats (1795–1821)

*For a brief biography of John Keats, see chapter 18.*

### Bright star, would I were as steadfast as thou art (1838)

Bright star, would I were steadfast as thou art—
Not in lone splendour hung aloft the night
And watching, with eternal lids apart,
Like nature's patient, sleepless Eremite,
The moving waters at their priestlike task
Of pure ablution round earth's human shores,
Or gazing on the new soft-fallen mask
Of snow upon the mountains and the moors—
No—yet still steadfast, still unchangeable,
Pillow'd upon my fair love's ripening breast,
To feel for ever its soft fall and swell,
Awake for ever in a sweet unrest,
Still, still to hear her tender-taken breath,
And so live ever—or else swoon to death.

#### Questions for Interactive Reading and Writing

1. This is an **apostrophe** (see chapter 21)—a poem in which the speaker speaks, improbably enough, to a personified object, a star—addressing it in the informal second person "thou." How does this establish tone?
2. As with Kelly Cherry's "The Raiment We Put On" (later in this chapter), this is a perfect Shakespearean sonnet with an occasional near rhyme. Why is this particular poem suited to the sonnet form?
3. Look up "Eremite," "ablution," and any other words that may confuse you here. "Splendour" is the British spelling, and natural enough for Keats, but why would he have put an apostrophe in "Pillow'd"? And why does he—remember Keats died of tuberculosis at twenty-five—conclude with "swoon to death"?
4. The word *steadfast* is used twice and the word *still* appears four times, the word *ever* three. How does this affect the poem's music, and how would you describe such a line as "To feel for ever its soft fall and swell"?

## Edna St. Vincent Millay (1892–1950)

### Only until this cigarette is ended (1921)

Only until this cigarette is ended,
A little moment at the end of all,
While on the floor the quiet ashes fall,
And in the firelight to a lance extended,
Bizarrely with the jazzing music blended,
The broken shadow dances on the wall,
I will permit my memory to recall
The vision of you, by all my dreams attended.
And then adieu,—farewell!—the dream is done.
Yours is a face of which I can forget
The color and the features, every one,
The words not ever, and the smiles not yet;
But in your day this moment is the sun
Upon a hill, after the sun has set.

#### Questions for Interactive Reading and Writing

1. Paraphrase this sonnet and compare it to Kelly Cherry's use of "I" and "you" in her sonnet, "The Raiment We Put On" (later in this chapter).
2. How much time elapses in the poem? What does this suggest about the speaker's mood and thoughts? How much actual control do you believe she has over her thoughts?
3. Can you explain the paradox (seemingly contradictory statement) of the final two lines?
4. From Sappho to Shakespeare to Millay and beyond, poets have written about love and its pains and losses. How close to despair do you find Millay in this poem compared to other love poems you have read? How close to joy?

## Christina Rossetti (1830–1894)

### A Birthday (1861)

My heart is like a singing bird
  Whose nest is in a watered shoot;
My heart is like an apple-tree
  Whose boughs are bent with thick-set fruit;
My heart is like a rainbow shell
  That paddles in a halcyon sea;
My heart is gladder than all these,
  Because my love is come to me.

Raise me a dais of silk and down;
  Hang it with vair and purple dyes;
Carve it in doves and pomegranates,
  And peacocks with a hundred eyes;
Work it in gold and silver grapes,
  In leaves and silver fleur-de-lys;
Because the birthday of my life
  Is come, my love is come to me.

### Questions for Interactive Reading and Writing

1. Discuss the repetitions here, as well as variation. Lines 1, 3, 5, and 7 make a kind of chorus, and the last lines of the two stanzas are similar. How does this compare to the ballad form?
2. Although this poem was written roughly 150 years ago, it uses a consciously "archaic" diction—perhaps medieval, perhaps even biblical in tone. How do words like "halcyon" and "vair" and "fleurs-de-lys" contribute to this effect?
3. "A singing bird" appears in the first line, and there are other birds throughout. Does the speaker compare herself to these creatures; if so, why?
4. The second stanza is couched in the imperative mode—as a series of orders to be obeyed. This is a poem of celebration, edging up to excess; list the similes.
5. What does Rosetti mean by "the birthday of my life"?

## RHYME

The sound component most often associated with poetry is called rhyme. **Rhyme (rime)** consists of the echoing repetition of sounds in end syllables of words, often (though not always) at the end of a line of poetry. Rhyme offers one of the primary pleasures of verse; all children are alert to it, and a sound repeated is a sound remembered. "Jack Sprat could eat no fat" and "Old Mother Hubbard went to the cupboard" remain alive as nursery rhymes because of their emphatic repetition.

> "Nursery rhymes [with] those really adorable rhythms that just stay in the head—that was my first sense of the pleasure of language." Conversation with Robert Hass

That said, it's a misconception to think all poetry *has* to rhyme. This mistaken notion has resulted in a lot of bad poetry and greeting cards with awkward or forced rhyming language. Of course you've already seen in this book many successful poems that don't rely on the device, and—as our brief discussion of Anglo-Saxon poetry suggests—the technique of end-rhyme consonance was not always part of the genre. Elegant rhyme, however, can make a poem feel connected and whole, and it often surprises the reader with an unexpected or evocative connection. The linkage between words like "solitaire" and "easy chair" or "greenery" and "scenery" makes for a kind of equation—one word equals another in the mind's ear, and the echo enhances effect.

In the first such pairing, the rhyme comes in the final syllable: *aire* and *air,* in the second there's also **internal rhyme;** *green* and *scene* are rhyming words, and *greenery* and *scenery* sound therefore entirely alike. Had the words been *greenish* and *scenario,* there still would be internal rhyme but the sound of the whole would be changed. Poets have at their disposal many different variations of rhyme, and part of the pleasure of writing a poem derives from this choice of technique. So, too, should we as readers *notice* the use that has been made of rhyme.

"Rhyme . . . is a form of relationship and connection, of encounter and metamorphosis. . . . There is something charged and magnetic about a good rhyme, something unsuspected and inevitable, utterly surprising and unforeseen and yet also binding and necessary. It is as if the poet called up the inner yearning for words to find each other." Conversation with Edward Hirsch

Take these lines in Robert Frost's poem (for the whole poem, see chapter 18):

*The woods are lovely, dark and deep,*
*But I have promises to keep,*
*And miles to go before I sleep,*
*And miles to go before I sleep.*

These are **end rhymes,** rhyming sounds that conclude the four lines of the stanza. Frost chose to repeat the end rhyme for each of his quatrain's four lines and repeat the third line verbatim; this act of willed repetition has much to do with the action described, and how the speaker here will keep on moving through the dark.

If, however, Frost had written "The woods are lovely, dark and deep, / But I have promises I've made, / And miles to go before I'm home, / And miles to go before I rest," our response would be quite different. We might acquire *some* sense of the poem's famous meditation, and its meaning would not change. The substance stays the same. On the whole, however, these modified phrases lose their mournful, musical connectivity; the *sound* is an important—even a crucial—part of *sense.* It's not an accident that one of the synonyms for *language* is *tongue;* we sound out what we see.

While we usually think of rhyme as solely a sound device, **eye rhyme** (also called **sight rhyme**) refers to words that share similar spellings but—when spoken—have different sounds. Words like "lint" and "pint" or "full" and "lull" exemplify eye rhyme, as does the final, sometimes confounding couplet of this old children's song:

*The itsy bitsy spider climbed up the water spout*
*Down came the rain and washed the spider out*
*Out came the sun and dried up all the rain*
*And the itsy bitsy spider climbed up the spout again.*

In contemporary English, *again* does not rhyme with *rain,* and so these lines may introduce kids to their first example of eye rhyme; in its original usage, however, the two words were likely true rhymes. In the seventeenth-century English speech of William Shakespeare's time, it seems probable that the "o" in "love" and "move" was pronounced in the same way, so when Prince Hamlet says "doubt that the sun doth move / but never doubt I love" he's using consonance, not dissonance, to make his point; how words look and how they sound are not always one and the same.

"One of the beauties of formal verse is that it's . . . very memorable. You have a rhyme scheme perhaps to guide your memory. I think the reason that rhyme patterns were established in the first place was as a mnemonic so that we would be able to memorize."

Conversation with Carolyn Forché

In **exact rhyme** (also **pure, perfect,** or **true rhyme**), the final vowel and consonant sounds are identical, regardless of spelling. For most readers, it's the most familiar form. Think of "heard" and "word" or "simple," "pimple," and "dimple." Rhymes like these offer a clear, bright connectivity of sound.

In eighteenth-century England, Alexander Pope composed the following piece in **heroic couplets,** two successive rhyming lines in iambic pentameter (the most commonly used metric pattern in English literature). In addition to the musical pleasure that rhythm can bring to a poem, rhyme schemes can organize a poem in central ways. The heroic couplet scheme of *AA/BB*, for example, is very different from *AB/AB* or *AB/BA*, and one of the most useful ways to look at the craft of poetry is to look for the rhyme scheme involved. Heroic couplets stress the connection between each of the paired lines.

# Alexander Pope (1688–1744)

Born in London, Alexander Pope suffered from a bone disease as a child, and consequently never grew taller than four and a half feet. What he lacked in stature, he more than made up for in literary genius. Largely self-educated and self-sufficient—his translations of the *Iliad* and the *Odyssey* earned him enough money to buy an estate and live solely as a man of letters—Pope became the leading poet of his day, thanks to his mastery of style, the heroic couplet, and satirical writing. His sparkling wit attacked not only his contemporaries, in works like *The Dunciad* (1728), but also great works of literature, like *Paradise Lost* in his famous mock-epic *The Rape of the Lock* (1714). Pope also composed verse that showed his appreciation of beauty, including *Pastorals* (1709) and *Windsor Forest* (1713).

**AS YOU READ** **Note how the rhyme scheme helps notate the repetitions of sound and puts a kind of emphasis on the meaning here.**

# [True ease in writing comes from art, not chance]

## *—from "An Essay on Criticism"* (1711)

True ease in writing comes from art, not chance, a
As those move easiest who have learned to dance. a
'Tis not enough no harshness gives offense, b
The sound must seem an echo to the sense: b
Soft is the strain when Zephyr gently blows, c
And the smooth stream in smoother numbers flows; c
But when loud surges lash the sounding shore, d
The hoarse, rough verse should like the torrent roar; d
When Ajax strives some rock's vast weight to throw, e
The line too labors, and the words move slow; e
Not so, when swift Camilla scours the plain, f
Flies o'er the unbending corn, and skims along
the main. f
Hear how Timotheus' varied lays surprise, g
And bid alternate passions fall and rise! g

# Writing from Reading

## Summarize

1 The poet offers a disquisition (formal explanation, discussion of a subject) on the relation of sound and sense in poetry. Why might he be taking this up as a subject? Have you seen any poets before Pope working on this idea?

## Analyze Craft

2 Describe the paradox in comparing "ease" to "art." What is the effect of this comparison?

3 What is the meaning of the phrase "smoother numbers"?

4 Look up the classical references: Ajax, Camilla, etc. What is the function of these allusions?

## Analyze Voice

5 What, if anything, distinguishes the poet's rhyming couplets from that of songs or poems presented as songs in verse?

## Synthesize Summary and Analysis

6 These rhyming couplets provide some lessons on the relation of craft and voice. Which rhymes do you consider the smoothest, and which rhymes here trouble you?

## Interpret the Poem

7 Does a poem such as this veer too much toward didactism—over-explicit instruction—or philosophy?

There are many variations of patterns available as rhyme—some that the ear can respond to, such as those of nursery rhymes or those of rhyming couplets. Most of us can also *hear* the echo in the first four lines *(AB/AB)* of Lord Byron's "She walks in beauty . . ." (night/skies/bright/eyes) or the *AB/AB* in the first stanza of "Leda and the Swan" by William Butler Yeats (for the whole poem, see chapter 16). In this poem, the god Zeus assumes the form of a swan and rapes the girl Leda, in the process fathering the famously beautiful Helen of Troy. Note the rhyme scheme is less obvious than that of Byron, and think of how the rhyming words differ (*still/bill* versus *caressed/breast*).

*A sudden blow: the great wings beating still* a
*Above the staggering girl, her thighs caressed* b
*By the dark webs, her nape caught in his bill,* a
*He holds her helpless breast upon his breast.* b

Some rhyme schemes are more elaborate, such as the first lines of "Pied Beauty" (by Gerard Manley Hopkins, later in this chapter): *ABC/ABC.* In other cases—if a rhyme is eight or twelve lines distant—the ear will likely fail to retain the sound as echo, though the eye might perhaps notice a repeated word. If, for instance, we write "many" again, you might remember that we used that word in the first sentence of the previous paragraph, but it likely won't function as an echoing *sound* (as would the words *found* or *ground*). The presence or absence of patterned repetition is a crucial factor in how a poem works.

**Slant rhyme** (also called **near, imperfect,** or **off rhyme**) refers to a case in which vowel or consonant sounds are similar but not exactly the same. Examples include word combinations like

*heap, rap, tape*
*aluminum, linoleum*

"Sometimes . . . rhymes clink. The sound is too aggressive. I mean, if I ever have to read *breath* and *death* again, I think it will kill me. . . . Maybe because I'm a modern person, half rhymes often sound more beautiful to me than full rhymes. They . . . de-emphasize the rhyming and emphasize more the sound patterning and make it sound more natural." Conversation with Edward Hirsch

In contrast to the vivid precision of exact rhymes, slant rhyme provides a subtler, sometimes natural-sounding correlation of sound. Yeats uses both exact (*still, bill*) and slant rhyme (*caressed, breast*) in "Leda and the Swan," and unlike Pope, Yeats does not use the end rhyme to create a hard stop at the close of each line but allows the sentence to spill over for a more natural sound. The use of exact, slant, or no rhyme contributes to the poem's voice, as does the way the rhyme fits into the sentence structure of the poem's individual lines.

Thomas Lynch also incorporates both exact and slant rhyme in "Iambs for the Day of Burial." Look at the first four lines of that poem, with the precise rhyming pattern of "best" and "stressed" and the slant rhyme of "body" and "tally." Then see how he repeats yet varies that pattern—ending with "forsaken" and "broken" as slant rhymes and "beatified" and "died" as perfect rhymes.

In chapter 18, for example, we included Elizabeth Bishop's poem "The Fish" as a way of showing the use and value of clear, simple, direct American English. Marianne Moore uses a similar diction in her poem of the same title, "The Fish." Moore introduces rhyme into the poem in a way that plays with echoing: the ear hears *and-stand* or *green-submarine* as exact rhymes.

## Marianne Moore (1887–1972)

Born near Saint Louis, Missouri, Marianne Moore was educated at Bryn Mawr. She lived her adult life with her mother in New York City, where she was an ardent fan of the Dodgers (then located in the New York borough of Brooklyn). Although a modernist and contemporary of Ezra Pound, William Carlos Williams, and H.D., Moore refused to conform to any standard but her own. Her stanzas are unique, composed of lines that count syllables, rather than stresses, and that often hide their rhyme internally. A lover of animals, Moore often uses them or other everyday objects as a springboard for deeper exploration in her poems. In addition to actively publishing her poetry, Moore was an astute literary critic. Poets including Elizabeth Bishop, Richard Wilbur, and Randall Jarrell cite Moore as influential to their poetry.

**AS YOU READ** Watch for the way these lines mirror the motion of a swimming fish.

# The Fish

**(1921)**

wade
through black jade.
Of the crow-blue mussel-shells, one keeps
adjusting the ash-heaps;
opening and shutting itself like

an
injured fan.
The barnacles which encrust the side
of the wave, cannot hide
there for the submerged shafts of the

sun,
split like spun
glass, move themselves with spotlight swiftness
into the crevices—
in and out, illuminating

the
turquoise sea
of bodies. The water drives a wedge
of iron through the iron edge
of the cliff; whereupon the stars,

pink
rice-grains, ink-
bespattered jelly-fish, crabs like green
lilies, and submarine
toadstools, slide each on the other.

All
external
marks of abuse are present on this
defiant edifice—
all the physical features of

ac-
cident—lack
of cornice, dynamite grooves, burns, and
hatchet strokes, these things stand
out on it; the chasm-side is

dead.
Repeated
evidence has proved that it can live
on what can not revive
its youth. The sea grows old in it.

# Writing from Reading

### Summarize

1 Go through each stanza and indicate what is being described.

### Analyze Craft

2 Discuss the use of exact rhyme in the poem with respect to the poem's shape. What contrast do you find between the traditional style of the rhyme scheme and the structure of the poem?

3 Are all the rhymes exact? What other varieties of rhyme do you see in the poem?

4 How does the hyphen in the word *accident* affect our usual expectations for that word? How does it set up the rhyme with *lack*?

### Analyze Voice

5 "All the physical features"—as the poet puts it—announce themselves here; from the very first word and its immediate rhyme ("wade," then three words later, "jade") to the strange shape of the lines and stanzas, we are introduced to a particular way of seeing/saying, an individual use of language.

### Synthesize Summary and Analysis

6 Go through the poem and "read" its rhyme scheme. Which rhymes seem surprising? Which seem to link words together as concepts?

### Interpret the Poem

7 The *arrangement* of the poem—its rhythm, rhyme, and line lengths—takes center stage here. Based on the images and sounds with which Moore composes the poem, what "fishy" point is the poet trying to make?

Perhaps the leading exponent of slant rhyme in our literature is "the belle of Amherst," Emily Dickinson. The words *despair* and *fear* in the brief poem that follows are somehow enlarged and given a kind of kinship—though the poem considers their "difference"—by their associated sounds.

> "When I started to realize that there were words that rhymed in English, it felt like magic to me. . . . I thought, *wren* and *yarn* must share something other than just words. So forever in my mind those tiny little birds and yarn were conflated: they shared not just names." Conversation with Li-Young Lee

# Emily Dickinson (1830–1886)

For a brief biography of Emily Dickinson, see the Case Study on American Plain Style, chapter 28.

**AS YOU READ** Try reading this poem aloud several times, allowing the meaning to emerge not just from the statements but also from the way they follow along in brief lines.

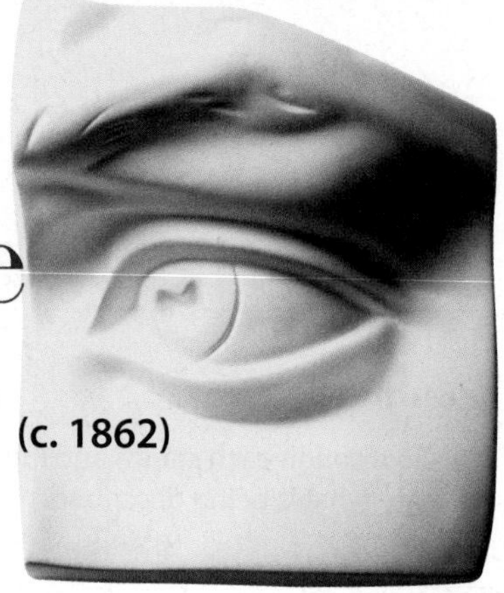

# The difference between Despair (c. 1862)

The difference between Despair
And Fear—is like the One
Between the instant of a Wreck
And when the Wreck has been—

The Mind is smooth—no Motion—
Contented as the Eye
Upon the Forehead of a Bust—
That knows—it cannot see—

# Writing from Reading

## Summarize

1 How would you describe the difference between despair and fear?

## Analyze Craft

2 What constitutes a "statement" in poetry as opposed to a message or statement in a document or newspaper story?

3 Find instances of consonance and assonance in the poem. How do they work to connect or unify the language in the poem?

## Analyze Voice

4 Read this poem aloud. How would you describe the language? How does this description seem to fit or contrast with the poem's subject?

5 Notice the shift between the first stanza, in which the poet presents a thought or idea, and the second, in which she focuses on the organ of thought. Can you explain the shift?

## Synthesize Summary and Analysis

6 What kind of a wreck would the poet in her time be thinking of?

## Interpret the Poem

7 How can "the Eye / Upon the Forehead of a Bust" know it cannot see?

**Masculine rhyme** (also **rising rhyme**) refers to end rhymes of polysyllabic words with a stressed final syllable, as in "remove" and "approve," and rhymes of monosyllabic words, like "good" and "wood." In contrast, **feminine rhyme** refers to rhymes between polysyllabic words in which the final syllable is unstressed. Examples include "bother" and "father" or "monkey" and "funky." A good poet is conscious of the distinction between masculine and feminine rhymes and the effects they produce. A **rhyme scheme** refers to the pattern of rhyme throughout a particular poem. To notate a rhyme scheme, we represent each new end rhyme with a lowercase letter following its line (as you saw with the poems by Pope and Yeats). When a sound recurs, we use the same letter to mark the repeated rhyme.

# For Review and Further Study

## Julia Alvarez (b. 1950)

### Woman's Work (1994)

Who says a woman's work isn't high art?
She'd challenge as she scrubbed the bathroom tiles.
Keep house as if the address were your heart.

We'd clean the whole upstairs before we'd start
downstairs. I'd sigh, hearing my friends outside.
Doing her woman's work was a hard art

to practice when the summer sun would bar
the floor I swept till she was satisfied.
She kept me prisoner in her housebound heart.

She'd shine the tines of forks, the wheels of carts,
cut lacy lattices for all her pies.
Her woman's work was nothing less than art.

And, I, her masterpiece since I was smart,
was primed, praised, polished, scolded and advised
to keep a house much better than my heart.

I did not want to be her counterpart!
I struck out . . . but became my mother's child:
a woman working at home on her art,
housekeeping paper as if it were her heart.

#### Questions for Interactive Reading and Writing

1. Look at the rhyme scheme here—the exact and slant rhymes. Notate the rhyme scheme. What impact does the rhyme scheme have on your understanding of the poem?
2. In the next chapter (Fixed Poetic Forms), we discuss the villanelle. How does this poem follow and then diverge from that form?
3. The speaker remembers her mother and her mother's domestic behavior. What does she herself practice as a "woman's work"? And how does this connect to the work of Seamus Heaney in "Digging"?
4. Is there a linkage here, or opposition, between the tasks of housekeeping and "her art"?
5. What is the significance of the line "And, I, her masterpiece since I was smart"?

## Kelly Cherry (b. 1940)

### The Raiment We Put On (1994)

Do you remember? We were in a room
with walls as warm as anybody's breath,
and music wove us on its patterning loom,
the complicated loom of life and death.
Your hands moved over my face like small clouds.
(Rain fell into a river and sank, somewhere.)
I moved among your fingers, brushed by the small crowds
of them, feeling myself known, everywhere,
and in that desperate country so far from here,
I heard you say my name over and over,
your voice threading its way into my ear.
I will spend my days working to discover
the pattern and its meaning, what you meant,
what has been raveled and what has been rent.

#### Questions for Interactive Reading and Writing

1. What does the title have to do with the text as such?
2. What effect do the vowel sounds in words such as *loom* and *over* have on your understanding of the poem?
3. What does the poet mean by "raveled" and "rent" in the last line?
4. The poem is told in first person and directed at a second-person "you." The first-person plural "We" suggests that it's a shared memory. However, we don't know the name of "you" or "I"—even though "I heard you say my name over and over." Look at the use of pronouns here. What impression is created by the use of pronouns without actual names?

# Marilyn Nelson (b. 1946)

## Chopin (1989)

It's Sunday evening. Pomp holds the receipts
of all the colored families on the Hill
in his wide lap, and shows which white store cheats
these patrons, who can't read a weekly bill.
His parlor's full of men holding their hats
and women who admire his girls' good hair.
Pomp warns them not to vote for Democrats,
controlling half of Hickman from his chair.
The varying degrees of cheating seen,
he nods toward the piano. Slender, tall,
a Fisk girl passing-white, almost nineteen,
his Blanche folds the piano's paisley shawl
and plays Chopin. And blessed are the meek
who have to buy in white men's stores next week.

### Questions for Interactive Reading and Writing

1. Beyond the physical setting, there is the social and political situation. Based on the information in the poem, describe the place, the time, the social and political relations. Why, for example, is the rich man who "holds the receipts" called "Pomp"?
2. The rhyme scheme seems calm and yet appealing. Can we assume a similarity between the rhyme scheme and the piano piece referred to in the poem? Why is this possible?
3. What is the effect on the ironic tone of the poem of the use of the conjunctions—"and. . . . And . . ."—in the next-to-last line?
4. The sonnet form, invented by an Italian poet and perfected by an English genius—Shakespeare—gives us here a portrait of a moment in modern black American life. What seems universal about this poetic form? What seems particular to the time?

## RHYTHM

As much as it depends on patterns and repetition of sound, poetry also relies on patterns and repetition of rhythm. The classic phrase *rhythm and meter* may sound intimidating with its old-fashioned, mathematical connotation, but the rhythm in our language is actually very natural. Human beings are instinctively tuned to rhythm. It's tied to our heartbeat, our breathing, our walking, the passage of our days and weather, the way we learn to shoot a basketball or dance. The word itself comes from an ancient Greek term meaning "flow," which may after all these centuries still be the simplest way of defining the concept.

"The first way to study [a poem] is to say a poem out loud. . . . If you say those words out loud . . . your breath pattern is flowing through your body in exactly the way it flowed through [the poet's body] when he said those words. . . . Poetry is [a] kind of existential breath sculpture." Conversation with Robert Hass

### Stresses and Pauses

The English language depends on rhythmical variation to create meaning even on a basic level. Whether conscious of it or not, we all tend to process the meaning of language through its patterns of sound emphasis. In other words, we don't ask a question like "HEY CAN I BORROW YOUR CAR TONIGHT?" with the same emphasis on each sound in the sentence. If we spoke like that, we'd sound like a robot from an old science fiction movie. Instead, the sentence becomes a collection of subtly contrasting emphases, perhaps, "HEY, can I BORrow your CAR toNIGHT?" These changes are

"There are different kinds of silences. There's a silence of mystery, then there's the silence of secrets—like 'I know something but I'm not telling.' Or there's the silence of 'I know something but I forgot what it is.' So there are all kinds of different silences, and they have different colors, and different ranges, and different depths, and different widths. I think in poetry we're using language a lot of times to inflect those different silences." Conversation with Li-Young Lee

called **stresses** (or **accents**), the emphasis or "push" we put on the pitch (the musical quality), duration, or volume of a syllable.

The same holds just as true for a line or sentence as for a single word. Heroic couplets, for example, tend to be **end-stopped**—meaning they insist upon their rhyming emphasis and don't encourage the reader to continue without pause. **Enjambment** (from a French word meaning "stride" or "encroach") consists of the running-over of a phrase from one line into another, so that closely related words belong to different lines. This makes the rhythm of the sentence seem more closely akin to natural speech, and it's very often used in *open* or *free* verse (see chapter 24.) A **caesura** is a pause, usually in the middle of a line, that marks a kind of rhythmic division—a place to catch your breath. All these are ways of organizing the sound and sense of poetry, *craft* in the service of *voice.*

We stress the *first* syllables of words like

***BA****lance*
***STITCH****ing*
***TEEN****age*

The second syllable of each word receives a stress in words like

*be****CAUSE***
*gui****TAR***
*a****ROUND***

In combination, all these words in our language create diverse rhythmic sounds. Hence, **rhythm** refers to this sequence of stressed and unstressed sounds in a poem. There's an inescapable music in the five brief stanzas in "Sadie and Maud," by Gwendolyn Brooks, with their perfect *B* rhymes in lines 2 and 4:

# Gwendolyn Brooks (1917–2000)

For a brief biography of Gwendolyn Brooks, see chapter 18.

**AS YOU READ** Notice the rhyme scheme, and how it contributes to the singsong effect.

# Sadie and Maud (1945)

Maud went to college.
Sadie stayed at home.
Sadie scraped life
With a fine-tooth comb.

She didn't leave a tangle in.
Her comb found every strand.
Sadie was one of the livingest chits
In all the land.

Sadie bore two babies
Under her maiden name.
Maud and Ma and Papa
Nearly died of shame.

When Sadie said her last so-long
Her girls struck out from home.
(Sadie had left as heritage
Her fine-tooth comb.)

Maud, who went to college,
Is a thin brown mouse.
She is living all alone
In this old house.

# Writing from Reading

## Summarize

1 List the way these two histories are similar or different. What is Sadie's "last so-long," and how does the poet feel about the way Maud lives?

## Analyze Craft

2 Describe the poem's rhythm. Is it in a tightly controlled metrical form, or does it sound more like natural speech? Why do you think this is?

3 Discuss sound in the final line of the poem. Why do you think Brooks chooses monosyllabic words here?

## Analyze Voice

4 "Ma and Papa" are referred to the way that Sadie might say it, and not as "mother and father." How does this contribute to the tone of the whole, and what does "livingest chits" suggest?

## Synthesize Summary and Analysis

5 This poem tells a story of hardship as well as a kind of pleasure. How does the rhyme scheme affect your reading of the poem's subject matter?

## Interpret the Poem

6 Fairy tales and nursery rhymes often deal in opposition—think, for example, of the story of the city mouse and the country mouse or the tortoise and the hare. What moral here—if any—does Brooks suggest we draw?

# METER

**Meter** refers to a sequence of stressed and unstressed syllables that forms an essentially regular pattern in lines of poetry. A poem's meter functions like the bass line or drumbeat to a piece of music, keeping time and arranging a poem's sounds. One unique feature of poetry (as compared, for example, to fiction) is that these rhythmic stresses are often arranged in specific intervals. We measure these patterns of stresses to understand how poets shape, simultaneously, their sound and the reader's understanding. The unit of measurement with which we examine meter is called a **foot,** usually a group of two or three syllables containing a single stress. This study is a component of **prosody,** the analysis of a poem's rhythm and metrical structures.

## Scansion

**Scansion** is the process of determining the metrical pattern of a **line** of poetry by marking its stresses and feet. We most often use a / symbol to mark a stressed syllable and a ~ to indicate an unstressed syllable. Also, we use a vertical line | (sometimes through a word, when needed) to mark divisions between feet. The most common foot in English and American poetry is the **iambic foot,** an unstressed syllable followed by a stressed syllable, as in the word *subLIME.*

> "The only reason we scan is so that we can learn to hear it, learn to hear that music when we read, and learn to hear what poetry's music is." Conversation with Carolyn Forché

The following chart notes the four chief metrical feet in poetry in English:

**COMMON METRIC FEET**

| FOOT/VERSE FORM | STRESSES | EXAMPLE |
|---|---|---|
| **iamb/iambic** | ~ / | because, and then |
| **trochee/trochaic** | / ~ | evil, pizza |
| **anapest/anapestic** | ~ ~ / | understand, in the east |
| **dactyl/dactyllic** | / ~ ~ | merrily, happening |

Other, less common syllable patterns include **spondees** (two stressed syllables), **pyrrhics** (two unstressed syllables), **amphibrachs** (three syllables: unstressed, stressed, unstressed), and **cretic/amphimacer** (three syllables: stressed, unstressed, stressed).

We also measure meter by the number of feet a line of poetry contains. The name of the foot combines with the number of feet; this constitutes the overall metrical form of a poem.

**Number of Feet Per Line**

| | | | |
|---|---|---|---|
| **monometer:** | one foot | **pentameter:** | five feet |
| **dimeter:** | two feet | **hexameter:** | six feet |
| **trimeter:** | three feet | **heptameter:** | seven feet |
| **tetrameter:** | four feet | **octameter:** | eight feet |

When discussing the meter of a poem, we combine the type of metrical foot used in a poem with the number of feet in a line. So, for example, we use the term **iambic pentameter** to refer to a line of poetry with five iambs.

### COMMON METRIC PATTERNS

**Iambic pentameter:** five iambs, as in these lines: "When I have fears that I may cease to be . . ." —John Keats

**Blank verse** refers to lines of unrhymed iambic pentameter. Used in dramatic Renaissance poetry, it has lasted through the centuries and found its way into the work of modernists like Robert Frost, Wallace Stevens, and Elizabeth Bishop.

**Iambic tetrameter** is a line containing four iambs: "Because I could not stop for death . . ." —Emily Dickinson

**Trochaic tetrameter** is a line containing four trochees. Here are two lines from the poem "The Song of Hiawatha": "Heavy with the heat and silence / Grew the afternoon of Summer . . ." —Henry Wadsworth Longfellow

**Anapestic trimeter** is a line that contain three anapests, as in these lines: "From the center all round to the sea / I am lord of the fowl and the brute . . ." —William Cowper

**Dactylic tetrameter** is a line that contains four dactyls, as in these flowing lines: "Just for a handful of silver he left us, / Just for a riband to stick in his coat. . . ." —Robert Browning

"Poetry comes from a time when we didn't have all this electronic gear and screens and so forth. You had the human body and the human voice. . . . You know, the word 'foot' in poetry comes from the days when people would actually dance so that you measured what was said by bodily movements. I think it will always be that way for . . . people who really cut past all the intellectual trappings of poetry and get back to the emotions." Conversation with Al Young

The following light poem by Samuel Taylor Coleridge demonstrates, in sound, the various kinds of metrical feet while it simultaneously explains them. Coleridge may seem pedantic in his definitions, but in his time he could take words like "Amphibrachys" and "Amphimacer" for granted, and he's being playful here.

# Samuel Taylor Coleridge (1772–1834)

One of the leading poets of the Romantic period in England, Samuel Taylor Coleridge first planned with Robert Southey—future Poet Laureate—to begin a utopian society in Pennsylvania. When their plans fell through, Coleridge turned to a writing career. In 1797 he forged a close friendship with William Wordsworth. The two published *Lyrical Ballads,* the seminal work of the Romantic period in which Coleridge's famous "The Rime of the Ancient Mariner" first appeared. Coleridge is also known for pioneering the form of "conversation poems"—poems that begin with a speaker addressing somebody in the present, then follow the mind as it travels in meditation before returning to the present; "The Eolian Harp" and "This Lime-Tree Bower My Prison" are prime examples. Coleridge gave lectures and drew a small following as a talented conversationalist until his death in 1834.

**AS YOU READ** See if you can scan this poem with a pencil to find the stresses and feet.

# Trochee trips from long to short (1806)

Trochee trips from long to short;
From long to long in solemn sort
Slow Spondee stalks; strong foot! yet ill able
Ever to come up with Dactyl's trisyllable.
Iambics march from short to long;—
With a leap and a bound the swift Anapests throng;
One syllable long, with one short at each side,
Amphibrachys hastes with a stately stride;—
First and last being long, middle short, Amphimacer
Strikes his thundering hoofs like a proud high-bred Racer.

If Derwent be innocent, steady, and wise,
And delight in the things of earth, water, and skies;
Tender warmth at his heart, with these metres to show it,
With sound sense in his brains, may make Derwent a poet,—
May crown him with fame, and must win him the love
Of his father on earth and his Father above.
   My dear, dear child!
Could you stand upon Skiddaw, you would not from its whole ridge
See a man who so loves you as your fond S. T. Coleridge.

# Writing from Reading

### Summarize

1 What might have prompted the poet to write this playful but instructive treatment of rhyme schemes?

### Analyze Craft

2 Define each of the rhymes as Coleridge outlines them.

### Analyze Voice

3 Who is the person—the poet—behind these lines?

### Synthesize Summary and Analysis

4 The poet reenacts the basic meters of poetry. Does he follow Pope (see the excerpt from "An Essay on Criticism" earlier in this chapter) in this?

### Interpret the Poem

5 What is the meaning of this poem beyond the instructional purpose?

## METRICAL VARIATION

After all this discussion about the balancing act between rhythm and meter, it may sound strange (or even frustrating) to hear that poets writing in formal structures are often liable to break free occasionally of their own chosen metrical form. As the poet Paul Muldoon once wrote, "Form is a straitjacket the way that a straitjacket was a straitjacket for Houdini." In comparing rhythm, rhyme, and meter to a famous magician's escape act, Muldoon suggests that the traditional formal constraints can be used purposefully and then evaded; *too* regular a use of rhythm and meter can be dull. **Doggerel,** an obviously patterned piece of rhyme, can sometimes seem almost childish and, when extensive, boring; these are rules that can be broken once they have been learned.

Sound can speed a poem's language up ("reeling round and round") or slow it down ("steadfast, he stood up straight"). In the poem by Gerard Manley Hopkins that follows, note the repeated consonants. "Swift" and "slow," "sweet" and "sour" might seem to have opposite meanings, but they are connected by sound; alliteration yokes together the variety of images Hopkins celebrates in the natural world. In the first stanza, "glory" links in sound to "God" and "couple-color" achieves its comparison to "cow" both through sound and sight. So, alliteration not only increases the musicality of the poem but also helps unify the language of a poem that is, itself, *about* unity. The metrical variation of Hopkins's poem—and his work in general—is what he called **sprung verse,** and it's a perfect example of change within consistency.

# Gerard Manley Hopkins (1844–1889)

An English poet of the Victorian era, Gerard Manley Hopkins is often grouped with the Modernist poets because of his innovative poetic form. Hopkins was educated at Oxford and began writing verse there. Three years into his education, he converted to Roman Catholicism and burned his poetry, fearing it interfered with his devotion to God. Seven years later, when a shipwreck killed five nuns, Hopkins asked permission from the church to write a poem commemorating the occurrence. From 1876 onward, Hopkins wrote poems that show God's presence and design in every earthly thing, in verses of sprung meter—lines with a set amount of stresses but with a liberality of unstressed syllables. Hopkins's poetic ear is almost unparalleled, but rather than court literary celebrity, he spent his life as a priest and a teacher. His poetry was not published until thirty years after his premature death from typhoid fever.

**AS YOU READ** Think about the effects of sound on your understanding of a poem's descriptions and overall meaning. Read the poem silently, then aloud. Consider how your perceptions change.

# Pied Beauty (1877)

Glory be to God for dappled things—
For skies of couple-color as a brinded cow;
For rose-moles all in stipple upon trout that swim;
Fresh-firecoal chestnut-falls; finches' wings;
Landscape plotted and pieced—fold, fallow, and plough;
And all trades, their gear and tackle and trim.

All things counter, original, spare, strange;
Whatever is fickle, freckled (who knows how?)
With swift, slow; sweet, sour; adazzle, dim;
He fathers-forth whose beauty is past change:
Praise him.

# Writing from Reading

### Summarize

1 Think of this poem as a kind of sermon delivered by Father Hopkins. What does he urge his readership or congregation to do? What does the word *Pied* mean?

### Analyze Craft

2 Note the repeated consonants. "Swift" and "slow," "sweet" and "sour" might seem to have opposite meanings, but they are connected by sound. How does alliteration yoke together the variety of images Hopkins celebrates in the natural world?

### Analyze Voice

3 In the first stanza "glory" links in sound to "God" and "couple-color" achieves its comparison to "cow" both sonically and visually. Locate other examples of this technique. How does this sonorous connection emphasize the speaker's praise in this poem?

### Synthesize Summary and Analysis

4 The last two words here are simple—monosyllabic—and solemn. If you were to recite this poem, would the last line be quiet or loud?

### Interpret the Poem

5 How does alliteration not only increase the musicality of the poem but also help demonstrate that "Pied Beauty" is, itself, *about* unity?

# For Review and Further Study

## Anonymous Scottish Ballad

### Bonnie Barbara Allan (date unknown)

It was in and about the Martinmas time,
When the green leaves were afalling,
That Sir John Graeme, in the West Country,
Fell in love with Barbara Allan.

He sent his men down through the town,
To the place where she was dwelling:
"Oh haste and come to my master dear,
Gin ye be Barbara Allan."

O hooly, hooly rose she up,
To the place where he was lying,
And when she drew the curtain by:
"Young man, I think you're dying."

"O it's I'm sick, and very, very sick,
And 'tis a' for Bonnie Allan."—
"O the better for me ye's never be,
Tho your heart's blood were aspilling."

"O dinna ye mind, young man," she said,
"When ye was in the tavern adrinking,
That ye made the health gae round and round,
And slighted Barbara Allan?"

He turned his face unto the wall,
And death was with him dealing:
"Adieu, adieu, my dear friends all,
And be kind to Barbara Allan."

And slowly, slowly raise her up,
And slowly, slowly left him,
And sighing said she could not stay,
Since death of life had reft him.

She had not gane a mile but twa,
When she heard the dead-bell ringing,
And every jow that the dead-bell geid,
It cried, "Woe to Barbara Allan!"

"O mother, mother, make my bed!
O make it saft and narrow!
Since my love died for me today,
I'll die for him tomorrow."

**Questions for Interactive Reading and Writing**

1. This poem has often been set to music and performed—what in its *sound* feels like *song?*
2. Do the repetitions here enhance or undermine tone?
3. Paraphrase this story in prose. What, if anything, is gained, and what gets lost?

## Amy Clampitt (1920–1994)

### John Donne in California (1990)

Is the Pacific Sea my home? Or is
Jerusalem? pondered John Donne,
who never stood among these strenuous,
huge, wind-curried hills, their green
gobleted just now with native poppies'
opulent red-gold, where New World lizards run
among strange bells, thistles wear the guise
of lizards, and one shining oak is poison;

or cast an eye on lofted strong-arm
redwoods' fog-fondled silhouette,
their sapling wisps among the ferns in time
more his (perhaps) than our compeer: here at
the round earth's numbly imagined rim,
its ridges drowned in the irradiating vat
of evening, the land ends; the magnesium
glare whose unbridged nakedness is bright
beyond imaging, begins. John Donne,
I think, would have been more at home
than the frail wick of metaphor I've brought
to see by, and cannot, for the conflagration
of this nightfall's utter strangeness.

**Questions for Interactive Reading and Writing**

1. What is it about California—and perhaps life itself—that the poet finds so confounding?
2. Do the rhythms of the poem, with their slant rhymes and somewhat obscure metaphors—"irradiating vat of evening," for example—dramatize a sense of the poet's confusions?

3. Read the following poem by John Donne to which this poem refers. Clampitt's line "Is the Pacific sea my home?" is a direct quotation from Donne's "Hymn to God, My God, In My Sickness." What is it about home in the Donne poem that Clampitt presumes is suitable for this occasion?

# John Donne (1572–1631)

*For a brief biography of John Donne, see chapter 25.*

## Hymn to God, My God, In My Sickness (1633)

Since I am coming to that Holy room,
  Where, with Thy choir of saints for evermore,
I shall be made Thy music; as I come
  I tune the instrument here at the door,
  And what I must do then, think here before;

Whilst my physicians by their love are grown
  Cosmographers, and I their map, who lie
Flat on this bed, that by them may be shown
  That this is my south-west discovery,
  Per fretum febris, by these straits to die;

I joy, that in these straits I see my west;
  For, though those currents yield return to none,
What shall my west hurt me? As west and east
  In all flat maps—and I am one—are one,
  So death doth touch the resurrection.

Is the Pacific sea my home? Or are
  The eastern riches? Is Jerusalem?
Anyan, and Magellan, and Gibraltar?
  All straits, and none but straits, are ways to them
  Whether where Japhet dwelt, or Cham, or Shem.

We think that Paradise and Calvary,
  Christ's cross and Adam's tree, stood in one place;
Look, Lord, and find both Adams met in me;
  As the first Adam's sweat surrounds my face,
  May the last Adam's blood my soul embrace.

So, in His purple wrapp'd, receive me, Lord;
  By these His thorns, give me His other crown;
And as to others' souls I preach'd Thy word,
  Be this my text, my sermon to mine own,
  "Therefore that He may raise, the Lord throws down."

### Questions for Interactive Reading and Writing

1. What is the occasion for the poem?
2. What overarching metaphors does Donne employ? Do they work together or seem contradictory?
3. What pun does he make on the word *straits*? What does he mean by "first Adam" and "last Adam"?
4. Is "death doth touch" in line 15 an example of assonance?
5. Where does the "turn" of the poem occur? What does the poet mean by "my sermon to mine own"?
6. How does the speaker's sickness and impending death become, for him, a triumph?

# Sonia Sanchez (b. 1934)

## Poem at Thirty (1966)

it is midnight
no magical bewitching
hour for me
i know only that
i am here waiting
remembering that
once as a child
i walked two
miles in my sleep.
did i know
then where i
was going?
traveling. i'm
always traveling.
i want to tell
you about me
about nights on a
brown couch when
i wrapped my
bones in lint and
refused to move.
no one touches
me anymore.
father do not
send me out
among strangers.
you you black man
stretching scraping
the mold from your body.
here is my hand.
i am not afraid
of the night.

### Questions for Interactive Reading and Writing

1. Christina Rosetti was thirty-one when she composed "A Birthday." How is it similar to "Poem at Thirty"? How is it dissimilar?
2. How is sleepwalking, the poem's central metaphor, related to what the poet calls "traveling"?
3. Does the situation in the last few lines seem obscure? How might you describe it?
4. How would you describe the way the poem sounds in your ear? In his interview, Thomas Lynch talks about a poet beginning to sound like himself or herself. Can you detect such growth in this poem?
5. Discuss the diction/tone of "Poem at Thirty." Why do you think the poet uses a lowercase "i"?

## Kevin Young (b. 1970)

### Jook (2003)

You have me
to you quite addicted

dear, my hands
in your mouth,

my wet-
nurse, succor,

cure. That old
booze

of you's
what I want,

dry gin, new
world, Old Crow.

### Questions for Interactive Reading and Writing

1. Find a dictionary definition of "jook." How do the meanings help you understand the plight of the speaker? To whom is he speaking? Why does he use this central metaphor?
2. Why does he start with an inversion—not writing "You have me quite addicted to you" instead? Why does he end with the name of a whiskey, "Old Crow"?
3. The poet uses pun—"succor"—and melds rhythms and sounds—"booze of you's"—to create a certain effect. How would you describe that effect?
4. How does the theme of addiction and drinking add to the understanding of the speaker's situation?
5. Some of the earliest poems we know, such as Sappho's work, present love as an illness or an addiction. What changes if you read Young's poem in this context?

# Reading for Sound, Rhyme, and Rhythm

When reading for *sound, rhyme,* and *rhythm,* examine how the sounds of the words work together with rhyme and rhythm to draw the reader into the poem and shape its meaning.

| | | |
|---|---|---|
| **What kinds of words has the poet chosen (monosyllabic, polysyllabic, harsh, or melodious)?** | *Euphony:* Musically pleasing poetic language. | EXAMPLE: "She walks in beauty, like the night / Of cloudless climes and starry skies / And all that's best of dark and bright / Meet in her aspect and her eyes." |
| | *Cacophony:* Harsh-sounding poetic language. | EXAMPLE: "Sweeping from butchers stalls, dung, guts, and blood, / Drowned puppies, stinking sprats, all drenched in mud / Dead cats and turnip-tops, come tumbling down the flood." |

| | | |
|---|---|---|
| **Has the poet used the repetition of consonant or vowel sounds in the poem?** | *Alliteration:* The repetition of the initial consonant sounds of nearby words.<br>*Consonance:* A repetition of consonants or consonant patterns in neighboring words.<br>*Assonance:* The repetition of vowel sounds or vowel patterns in neighboring words. | EXAMPLE: I'm *r*ight as *r*ain, *r*eading in my *r*oom.<br>EXAMPLE: Ca*l*m*l*y he ca*l*led to the mu*l*e in the o*l*d fie*l*d.<br>EXAMPLE: The r*ai*n c*a*me again, s*a*me as yesterd*ay*. |
| **Do words in the poem sound like what they represent?** | *Onomatopoeia:* The use of words that imitate the sounds they refer to. | EXAMPLE: *Snap, crackle, pop* |
| **Is rhyme used in the poem?** | *Is there rhyme within the lines?*<br>*Internal rhyme:* Rhyming between words in the same line, or words in the middle of two different phrases.<br>*Does the rhyme come at the end of the lines?*<br>*End rhyme:* Rhyming sounds that conclude lines of poetry.<br>*Which syllable of the end word is stressed?*<br>*Masculine rhyme:* End rhyme between polysyllabic words with a stressed final syllable, or between monosyllabic words.<br>*Feminine rhyme:* End rhyme between polysyllabic words with unstressed final syllables.<br>*Are the sounds in the rhyme identical?*<br>**Identical:**<br>*Exact rhyme:* Rhyme in which the end sounds of words are identical.<br>**Not identical:**<br>*Slant rhyme:* Rhyme in which the sounds are similar but do not rhyme.<br>*Eye rhyme:* Words that are spelled similarly but do not rhyme. | EXAMPLE: "the *grains* beyond *age,* the dark *veins* of her mother"<br>EXAMPLE: "The itsy bitsy spider climbed up the water *spout* / Down came the rains and washed the spider *out*"<br>EXAMPLE: "I showed admirable re*move* / but mom did not ap*prove.*"<br>EXAMPLE: "Making money's a *bo*ther / so I just ask *fa*ther."<br>EXAMPLE: "bat" and "cat"<br>EXAMPLE: "cat" and "barette"<br>EXAMPLE: "lint" and "pint" |

| | | |
|---|---|---|
| **Where do the lines break, where does the poem speed up, and where does it slow down?** | *End-stopped lines:* Lines that don't encourage the reader to continue without pause.<br>*Enjambment:* The running-over of a phrase from one line into another, so that closely related words belong to different lines. | EXAMPLE: "Trochee trips from long to short; / From long to long in solemn sort"<br>EXAMPLE: "Is the Pacific Sea my home? Or is / Jerusalem? pondered John Donne" |
| **How do sounds work together in a line to create a rhythm of stressed and unstressed syllables?** | *What pattern of stresses has the poet used to shape the sound of the lines in a poem?*<br>~ / ~ / ~ / ~ / ~ /<br>"Of all our private parts the heart knows best" | |
| **How are the stressed and unstressed syllables grouped together in a line?** | **Foot** — **Marks** — **Example**<br>*Iamb* — ~ / — be'*cause*, and' *then*<br>*Trochee* — / ~ — *e'*vil, *pi'*zza<br>*Anapest* — ~ ~ / — un'der'*stand*, in' the' *east*<br>*Dactyl* — / ~ ~ — *mer'*ri'ly, *hap'*pen'ing | |
| **What is the meter of the line?** | *Count the number of feet in a line to determine the meter.*<br>Common meters include:<br>*Monometer:* One foot; *Dimeter:* Two feet<br>*Trimeter:* Three feet; *Tetrameter:* Four feet<br>*Pentameter:* Five feet; *Hexameter:* Six feet<br>*Heptameter:* Seven feet; *Octameter:* Eight feet<br>EXAMPLE: ""Of all our private parts the heart knows best" is five iambic feet; five feet = *pentameter.* | |
| **Is there inconsistent meter (metrical variation) in the poem?** | *Sprung verse:* A rhythm that imitates ordinary speech by putting stresses on words that would not be stressed in consistent metrical patterns. | EXAMPLE: ""Whatever is fickle, freckled (who knows how?)" |

# Writing about Sound, Rhyme, and Rhythm

1. Compare the sounds of the language in Thomas Lynch's "Iambs for the Day of Burial" and Seamus Heaney's "Digging."
2. Consider how sound underscores the subject and themes of Kelly Cherry's "The Raiment We Put On" and Gwendolyn Brooks's "Sadie and Maud"; both use plainspoken language. This is true of the work of Julia Alvarez and Sonia Sanchez as well. Examine how the rhythm of each poem affects (or changes) the reader's understanding of this plainspoken tone.
3. Examine the use of sonic effects like alliteration, assonance, consonance, onomatopoeia, and/or other effects in John Keats's "Bright Star. . . ." and Gerard Manley Hopkins's "Pied Beauty."
4. Look at the poems in this chapter by Marianne Moore, Alexander Pope, and Samuel Taylor Coleridge. Discuss the ways their subject is self-reflexive (a poem about poetry itself).
5. Find a metered poem in this chapter (or another in the book) and identify moments where the poet varies the rhythm. Comment on the purpose and the effect of this variation.

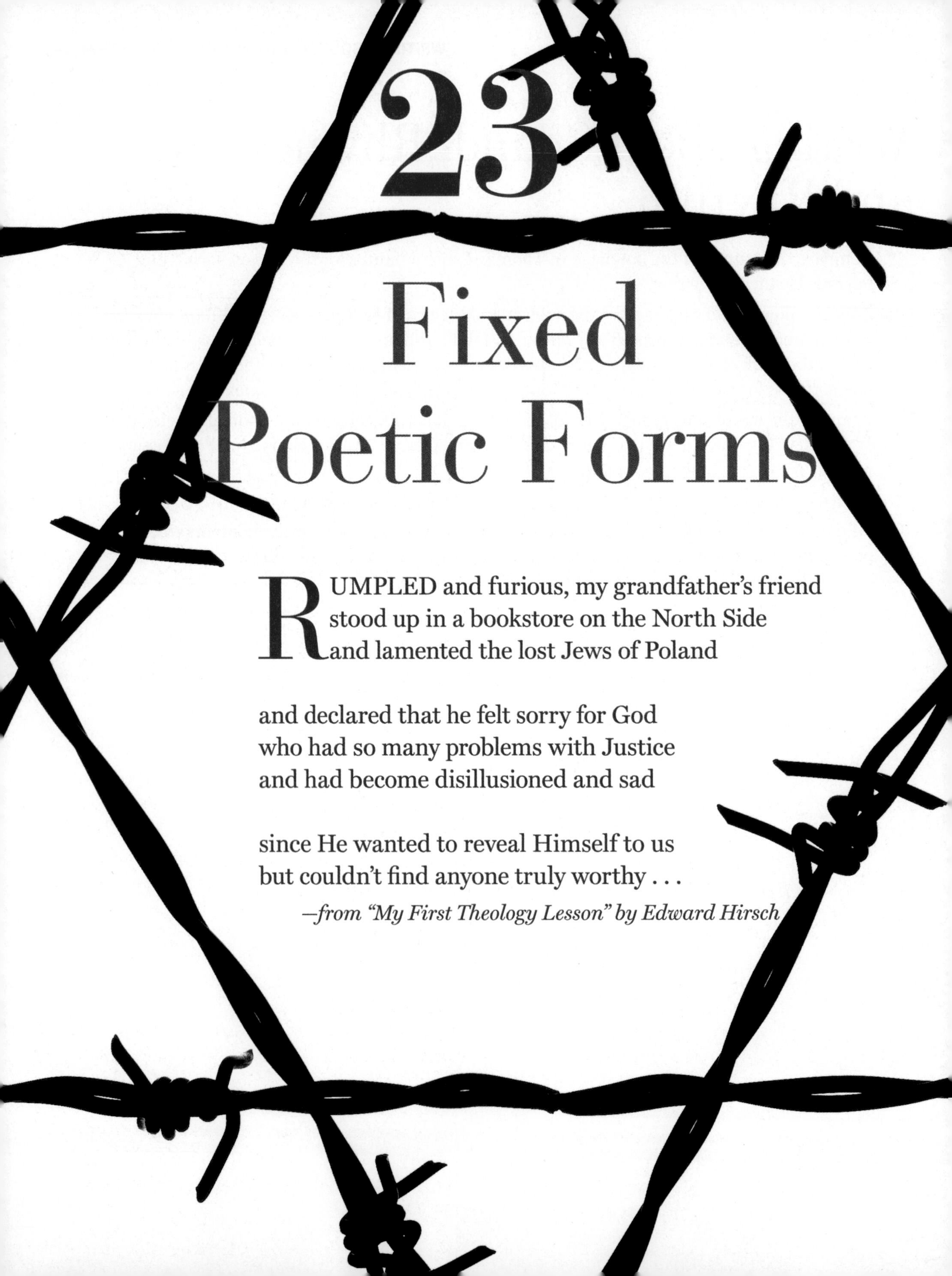

# 23 Fixed Poetic Forms

RUMPLED and furious, my grandfather's friend
stood up in a bookstore on the North Side
and lamented the lost Jews of Poland

and declared that he felt sorry for God
who had so many problems with Justice
and had become disillusioned and sad

since He wanted to reveal Himself to us
but couldn't find anyone truly worthy . . .

*—from "My First Theology Lesson" by Edward Hirsch*

*"The only way you can write a good formal poem is if you can control the form. . . . The form becomes the way in which you can express what you need to say. . . . And if you can use the form as a vehicle in that way, then you can . . . write a good poem. Otherwise, the form will control you."*

Conversation with Edward Hirsch, available on video at www.mhhe.com/delbanco1e

COMPOSING in a poetic form that's been a fixture in literature for more than 700 years, Edward Hirsch shapes this episode from his childhood on the North Side of Chicago.

Gathered for conversation in a bookstore, a group of Jewish men (including the poet's grandfather) listen as a colleague angrily laments the apparent retreat of God from the modern world. In the wake of the twentieth century's violence and the savagery of the Holocaust, God has seemingly withdrawn, unable to find "anyone truly worthy" to receive Him on the earth. This is the position maintained by the grandfather's "furious . . . friend." For the poem's speaker, recollecting the argument many years later, this lament constitutes an early lesson on the nature of religion.

Before committing any idea or memory to verse, poets begin, literally, with an infinite number of possibilities for framing their ideas on the page. In this case, Hirsch weds his poetic intention to the shape and form of the sonnet, a fourteen-line poem traditionally associated with argumentation and persuasion. As he points out in the interview, "The thing that seems to identify [a sonnet] as a sonnet is a structural principle. Some kind of argument is set up and resolved or refuted or avoided."

In trying to re-create a passionate discussion about the nature of God, Hirsch uses a form that matches his purposes ideally. "So here I have," he says, "a . . . kind of furious argument, and here I've got to try and tame it. . . . I've got to find a way to formalize it so that someone else can experience what I experienced. And here the sonnet form helped me."

For much of poetry's millennia-old lifetime, poets have been attracted to set patterns in which to arrange their work. Historically these patterns have served different purposes. To begin with, poets echoed formal designs observable by artists in nature. In turn, the patterns followed the music of religious rituals that celebrate natural cycles; these ritual observances were often expressed as poetry. Also, the means for writing language down and reading it aloud haven't previously been as accessible as is today's familiar word-processing technology. Thus, on a more practical level, formal structures served as early mnemonic devices—mental tools for storing and remembering the hundreds of lines a poet might need to recall in a public performance.

The word *poem* comes from an ancient Greek expression meaning "something made"; the different ways poets *construct* their poems are therefore fundamental to our understanding of the genre. As you'll see, the meaning of a poem and the arrangement of its language combine in a kind of marriage of structure and purpose.

*Poems take place in our lives . . .*

# Q&A

*Sometimes you want to capture something that's more complicated.*

# *A Conversation on Writing*

## Edward Hirsch

### How to Think about Form: The Sonnet

A form like the sonnet . . . exists in poetry not just because some people like me like to write them. . . . It must be serving some kind of function. . . . Otherwise it would die out. They're just too hard, these forms. They're too hard to write. They take too much thinking. There must be a reason for them; otherwise they'd just collapse. . . . And . . . the thing that seems to identify [a sonnet] as a sonnet is a structural principle. Some kind of argument is set up and resolved or refuted or avoided.

### The Poetry in Our Lives

Poems take place in our lives . . . because we're human and we're trying to explain and understand what it means to be alive. They're not there so teachers can get you to memorize what the nature of a poetic form is. They're not there for medicinal purposes, to cure you of something. . . . They're there . . . to help you think about what it means to love someone, and what it means to be dying, and what it means to have someone dying on you, and what it means to dislike someone, and what it means to be enraged . . . complicated and multiple [feelings that] have all kinds of nuances.

### Why Can't You Just Say What You Mean?

Why can't you just say what you mean? . . . Well, there are a lot of reasons. . . . Sometimes you want to capture something that's more complicated. You don't just love your father; you love your father, but you also hate him. You love him and you hate him at the same time. . . . If you just tell them, it doesn't mean anything. . . . But in a poem you can capture that combination of feelings.

As Chicago-born (b. 1950) Edward Hirsch says in his interview for this book, "I began writing poetry in high school the way almost everyone begins writing poetry. It was really emotional desperation." Although he has advanced and refined his poetry—as evidenced by awards that include the National Book Critics Circle Award and the American Academy of Arts & Letters Award for Literature—emotion still lies at its heart. Equally able to portray the emptiness of a world without God at its center and the sense of hope we might gain from art, Hirsch's verse often uses formal structures or the shape of elegies, though his more recent poetry departs into free verse. In addition to award-winning collections like *For the Sleepwalkers* (1981) and *Wild Gratitude* (1986), Hirsch has written essays that have appeared in *The New Yorker* and a best-selling book, *How to Read a Poem: And Fall in Love with Poetry* (1999), as well as a regular poetry column for *The Washington Post.* After teaching at the University of Houston for nearly two decades, Hirsch now serves as the president of the J. S. Guggenheim Memorial Foundation.

**To watch this entire interview and hear the author read from his work, go to www.mhhe.com/delbanco1e.**

**RESEARCH ASSIGNMENT** Discuss how Hirsch describes choosing the sonnet form for the event he wants to describe. Why did he think it an apt choice?

**AS YOU READ** Consider how the subject matter suits the sonnet form Hirsch has chosen. Examine how his use of a fixed form helps organize and deliver the anger and dismay the "grandfather's friend" feels about the world.

# My First Theology Lesson (2003)

Rumpled and furious, my grandfather's friend
stood up in a bookstore on the North Side
and lamented the lost Jews of Poland

and declared that he felt sorry for God
who had so many problems with Justice
and had become disillusioned and sad

since He wanted to reveal Himself to us
but couldn't find anyone truly worthy
(it was always the wrong time or place

in our deranged and barbaric century)
and so withdrew into His own radiance
and left us a limited mind and body

to contemplate the ghostly absence,
ourselves alone in a divine wilderness.

# Writing from Reading

### Summarize

**1** Describe the situation here. Why does the speaker feel "sorry for God," and is that an expression of blasphemy or faith?

### Analyze Craft

**2** Discuss the formal features of this sonnet. What kind of rhymes does Hirsch use? Is the poem composed in strict meter?

### Analyze Voice

**3** What language suggests that the poem is a kind of argument, a laying out of rhetorical positions? What is present, for example, in "the ghostly absence"?

### Synthesize Summary and Analysis

**4** The title "My First Theology Lesson" suggests there have been others. Would you say the poet now agrees with the position voiced here, or does he seem opposed to it?

### Interpret the Poem

**5** Why does the poet refer to this episode as a "theology lesson"? If "a divine wilderness" suggests the Garden of Eden, what has happened to that wilderness today?

## FORM, FIXED FORM, OPEN FORM

All literature has shape. Like architects designing a building, poets must consider how they wish to arrange and enclose their language, how to best give it foundation and structure. Sometimes these designs follow patterns that have existed for centuries, and sometimes they are wholly new creations. In some cases, a poet knows in advance exactly how a poem's language will be arranged; at other times, he or she makes this decision during the process of composition itself. Regardless of these creative choices on the part of the writer, every poem possesses **form,** an overall shape and structure; if that structure has been long established, its shape will have a name.

"Metrical poetry in English mean[s] balancing unstressed and stressed syllables . . . as a kind of . . . building block. . . . You could make a little waltz form of that rhythm [and] . . . do it forever and ever." Conversation with Robert Hass

Though our contemporary language is extensive in vocabulary and intonation, each word edges up against the next and becomes part of the whole. We use the term **fixed form** (or **closed form**) to describe an arrangement of text that requires a poet to obey set written combinations. These will include line length, meter, stanza structure, and rhyme scheme. Over centuries, poets have invented fixed forms and borrowed forms from other languages to suit their needs. These combinations help poets give shape and order to the emotion or experience they wish to convey. By understanding the patterns and overall trajectory of a fixed form, you'll learn what to expect from the genres (how a sonnet, for example, takes on a different subject from a villanelle) and how poets both innovate and imitate previous traditions.

Keep in mind that poets working in a fixed form don't necessarily feel that they must conform to *every* part of a formal design. Think of it this way: As a child, you may have played a game with your friends and changed the rules a little to make the contest more exciting or interesting. Writers share this affection for flexibility. They may vary their work to better fit their intentions, or purposefully stray from formal expectations in hopes of changing a poem's design.

"We've all heard poems [where] the rhymes seemed just there to fill out the forms. . . . The form is dead in that way. It is not alive. The form is controlling you." Conversation with Edward Hirsch

**Open form** (or **free verse**) refers to poetry ungoverned by metrical or rhyme schemes. Although it became fashionable in the twentieth century, the tradition of writing without strict adherence to formal constraints dates to the Psalms of the Bible and probably even further back. Using meaning to guide a poem's overall shape, poets writing in open form do not so much abandon form as use formal elements like rhyme, rhythm, and line length to individually embody their intentions. Because the blank page provides a kind of silent canvas on which to inscribe sound in language, poets can use the combination of white space and interesting syntax to create their own form and structure. Look, for example, at the poems in this book by e. e. cummings and you'll get a sense of open form's ability to devise its own particular meaning and order.

Some people think that open form poetry goes so far as to invite the reader into the creative process itself. By personally considering and then connecting a poem's form and substance, readers can participate in the creation of a poem's meaning. We'll talk about open form poetry in more detail in the next chapter; what follows is a close examination of forms that have long been—by contrast—closed and fixed.

## THE BUILDING BLOCKS OF FORM

To best understand how poets conceive and construct fixed forms, it's important to recognize some of the components that contribute to a poem's particular shape. Becoming familiar with the architecture of verse is useful—even crucial—in this context. Here are a few examples.

The most basic unit of poetry is, of course, the **line,** a row of words containing phrases and/or sentences. Like the paragraphs in a work of prose, poetry is governed by groupings of lines. A **stanza** is a unit of two or more lines, set off by an extra line space, often sharing the same rhythm and meter. (**Blank verse** is a form of such grouping in which the line, as opposed to the stanza, provides the central organizational arrangement.)

In a fixed form poem, a stanza will contain or develop a consistent idea and demonstrate a regular rhyme scheme (as discussed in more depth later in this chapter). The term originates from an old Italian word meaning "stopping place" or "room";

"Poetry is like architecture in that we're using the materiality of language, but we're also using silence, interspaciousness, as part of the medium in poetry. So a lot of times it's like the use of space in architecture; we're using silence—that's the real habitation." Conversation with Li-Young Lee

if you think of a poem as a work of architecture, you can imagine a stanza as a kind of chamber of language that contains a thought. In addition to arranging lines into stanzas, poets also arrange stanzas into defined groupings. Though there are no rules about how a poet should or shouldn't create stanzas, tradition has generated a handful of set stanza patterns.

Here are a pair of stanzas in the *abab* rhyme pattern. Such patterns make up a poem's **rhyme scheme** (for more information, see Rhyme in chapter 22). These stanzas come from a poem itself called "Stanzas," written in 1838 by Mary Shelley—best known as the author of *Frankenstein* (1818). Try to picture this "room" as a rectangle or square in which the walls are perfectly proportioned and the lines are parallel:

*But gentle sleep shall veil my sight,*
*And Psyche's lamp shall darkling be,*
*When, in the visions of the night,*
*Thou dost renew thy vows to me.*

*Then come to me in dreams, my love,*
*I will not ask a dearer bliss;*
*Come with the starry beams, my love,*
*And press mine eyelids with thy kiss.*

"Think of the stanza—'stanza' comes from the word for a room. So in the poem, each stanza is like a room in a house. And something happens in that room. Often the first stanza is like the entryway of the house. It brings you into the poem, it is [the] foyer. Then you . . . are in the more public rooms, and the poem eventually lets you into its private rooms." Conversation with Carolyn Forché

In its strictest sense, a **couplet** (also discussed in chapter 22) is two lines of poetry forming a unit of meaning. Often couplets are rhymed, strung together without a break, and share the same meter. One such form is the **heroic couplet,** two lines of rhymed iambic pentameter. Organized in small double steps, heroic couplets create a sort of chain that helps a long poem flow forward. Along with John Dryden, Alexander Pope is credited with perfecting heroic couplets in English poetry. Here's a brief excerpt from his "Essay on Man" (1733) featuring this particular fixed form:

*Know then thyself, presume not God to scan;* *a*
*The proper study of mankind is Man.* *a*
*Placed on this isthmus of a middle state,* *b*
*A being darkly wise, and rudely great.* *b*

Less common than the couplet, a **tercet** is a group of three lines of poetry. Sometimes the term **triplet** is specifically substituted, meaning a three-line stanza in which all the lines rhyme.

Probably the best-known fixed form using tercets is **terza rima,** a fixed form featuring the interlocking rhyme scheme *aba, bcb, cdc, ded,* etc. Invented and then popularized by the medieval Italian poet Dante Alighieri, terza rima is the exclusive fixed form of his epic *Divine Comedy,* which includes the sections "Inferno," "Purgatorio," and "Paradiso."

Echoing Dante, Percy Bysshe Shelley employs terza rima in his "Ode to the West Wind" (1820), which appears in its entirety later in the chapter. Here are the first three tercets:

*O wild West Wind, thou breath of Autumn's being,* *a*
*Thou, from whose unseen presence the leaves dead* *b*
*Are driven, like ghosts from an enchanter fleeing,* *a*

*Yellow, and black, and pale, and hectic red,* *b*
*Pestilence-stricken multitudes: O thou,* *c*
*Who chariotest to their dark wintry bed* *b*

*The winged seeds, where they lie cold and low,* *c*
*Each like a corpse within its grave, until* *d*
*Thine azure sister of the Spring shall blow . . .* *c*

**Quatrains,** four-line stanzas, are the most popular stanzaic form in English poetry. Easily varied in meter, line length, and rhyme scheme, the quatrain is highly

"I think part of the pleasure of reading poetry is to know the intricacy of its prosody because you see content and form are completely intertwined. They emerge out of each other. Often the content is discovered because of the form." Conversation with Carolyn Forché adaptable. You'll find dozens of poems in this book employing it, in both fixed and open form poetry. Worth noting here in particular is the traditional **ballad stanza,** a quatrain in which the first and third lines possess four stresses, while the second and fourth have three stresses. You can still find this arrangement, popular as a song form since the Middle Ages, in works that span the past several hundred years, including modern poetry and contemporary music lyrics. For example, such contemporary composers as Bob Dylan often use the traditional ballad stanzaic form. Here is an example of an English ballad, "Lament of the Border Widow," from centuries ago.

*My love he built me a bonny bower,*
*And clad it a' wi' lilye flour,*
*A brawer bower ye ne'er did see,*
*Than my true love he built for me.*

A variation on ballad meter, **common measure** uses iambic quatrains with the same alternating four-stress/three-stress meter but sometimes with an *abab* rhyme scheme.

## THE SONNET

Easily the most recognizable fixed form in poetry, the **sonnet** (*sonneto,* "little sound" or "little song," in Italian) is a fourteen-line poem in a recognizable pattern of rhyme, often metered in iambic pentameter.

The fourteenth-century Italian poet Francesco Petrarch (1304–1374) is credited as the first master of this form, in which he wrote about his unrequited love, Laura.

> "I . . . remember . . . writing sonnets. . . . I think it was some point in the mid-1980s . . . you could put fourteen lines on a postcard and mail it for fourteen cents. We thought, well, this was the postal service imitating art. And so we [sent] . . . fourteeners just back and forth and back. . . . As postage rates went up, we started writing more epic poems and putting them in envelopes." Conversation with Thomas Lynch

The form he perfected came to be known as the **Petrarchan** (or **Italian**) **sonnet** and is the most frequently used sonnet form. The Petrarchan sonnet consists of an **octave** (eight lines) and then a **sestet** (six lines).

**PETRARCHAN SONNET**

Fourteen lines
Two stanzas, eight lines/six lines

*abbaabba*

*cdecde* or *cdcdcd*

Since its inception, generations upon generations of poets have tried their hands at the Petrarchan sonnet, often choosing love as a subject matter for the tightly controlled form. A celebrated example by Elizabeth Barrett Browning follows.

# Elizabeth Barrett Browning (1806–1861)

England's most respected female poet in her lifetime, Elizabeth Barrett Browning showed by her own example that women could be educated and important artists. Her education took place at home, and she learned Greek by sitting in on her brother's tutoring sessions. This traditionally male knowledge enabled her to engage with literary and scholarly culture in a serious way. Although she was an invalid confined to her father's house, her elopement with Robert Browning when she was thirty-nine restored her health. In addition to *Sonnets from the Portuguese* (1850), a sequence of love sonnets that contains her much-quoted "How do I love thee?", one of her most famous works is *Aurora Leigh* (1857), a "novel-poem," as she described it. The book follows a young woman's rise to become a great poet and champions the current day as a time worth writing about. Barrett Browning's poetry engages with social issues, and true to Victorian fashion, she used her pen to impart moral instruction.

**AS YOU READ** Look for the shape of the whole—the way a question gets answered in a very different kind of "argument" than is the case with Hirsch.

# How do I love thee? Let me count the ways (1850)

How do I love thee? Let me count the ways.
I love thee to the depth and breadth and height
My soul can reach, when feeling out of sight
For the ends of being and ideal grace.
I love thee to the level of every day's
Most quiet need, by sun and candle-light.
I love thee freely, as men strive for right.
I love thee purely, as they turn from praise.
I love thee with the passion put to use
In my old griefs, and with my childhood's faith.
I love thee with a love I seemed to lose
With my lost saints. I love thee with the breath,
Smiles, tears, of all my life; and, if God choose,
I shall but love thee better after death.

# Writing from Reading

### Summarize

1 Writing to her husband, Robert, how does Elizabeth Barrett Browning record her love?

### Analyze Craft

2 Employing the sonnet form, with its careful rhyme scheme and meter, gives the poem a discipline that subtly increases its seriousness. Identify the rhyme scheme and the repetitions here.

### Analyze Voice

3 The poem is emphatic in its devotion and phrased with intensity. This is not a whimsical little love lyric. It's a serious dedication, an essential catalog of the speaker's affection. How does the last line emphasize that seriousness, and what does the promise tell you about the speaker?

### Synthesize Summary and Analysis

4 What better form to "count" these measures of her love than a sonnet with its carefully measured formal patterns? What aspects of meaning would the poem lose if you translated it into lines of prose?

### Interpret the Poem

5 "I love thee with the breath, / Smiles, tears, of all my life." What does this mean, and how is its meaning affected by the line that follows?

Not all sonnets, however, make romantic love their concern, as we saw with this chapter's opening poem, "My First Theology Lesson." Indeed, the form is often used for a speaker to muse analytically on a thought, idea, or sentiment. Traditionally, after a sonnet's first octave introduces its subject, the remaining sestet begins with a turn that

> "I think part of the pleasure of reading poetry is to know the intricacies of its prosody because, you see, content and form are completely intertwined, they emerge out of each other. Often the content is discovered because of the form."
>
> Conversation with Carolyn Forché

proposes some kind of answer or resolution to the subject at hand. Many poets have maintained this essential notion of an argument and counterargument, eight lines of "call" and six of "response." John Keats demonstrates this structure in the following sonnet. Here the poet analyzes the transformative power of reading the Greek poet Homer in a noted translation by George Chapman.

## John Keats (1795–1821)

For a brief biography of John Keats, see chapter 18.

**AS YOU READ** Note the rhyme scheme and repeating sounds (fourteen lines with four rhymes), the thoroughly formal arrangement that looks at something new.

# On First Looking into Chapman's Homer (1816)

Much have I traveled in the realms of gold,
And many goodly states and kingdoms seen;
Round many western islands have I been
Which bards in fealty to Apollo hold.
Oft of one wide expanse had I been told
That deep-browed Homer rules as his demesne;
Yet did I never breathe its pure serene
Till I heard Chapman speak out loud and bold:
Then felt I like some watcher of the skies
When a new planet swims into his ken;
Or like stout Cortez when with eagle eyes
He stared at the Pacific—and all his men
Looked at each other with a wild surmise—
Silent, upon a peak in Darien.

# Writing from Reading

### Summarize

1 Does this poem present a particular idea or case? What does the speaker want to explain?

### Analyze Craft

2 Do you notice a turn in this poem? What language signals the shift from octave to sestet?

### Analyze Voice

3 What are the "realms of gold" and what is the "wild surmise"? Is the speaker in the poem talking to himself here or making a point to his readership that they should also read Chapman's Homer? What does he mean by "bards in fealty to Apollo"?

### Synthesize Summary and Analysis

4 This sonnet is, as we have seen, a traditional form—but the poem reports on "first" discovery. How does it marry the ancient and new, the "new planet" and old ocean?

### Interpret the Poem

5 Though Keats accidentally confuses the explorer Cortez with Balboa (the first European to see the Pacific Ocean from a peak in Panama), why do you think he compares reading Homer to the life of a famous explorer?

Here Keats follows the traditional shape of the Petrarchan or Italian sonnet—but there are others as well. Readers familiar with Shakespeare's love poetry will likely recognize a different fourteen-line pattern from the octet/sestet form. English poets, faced with a language less conducive to natural rhyming than Italian, found a slightly reduced rhyme scheme a bit easier to work with. Known as the **Shakespearean** (also **English** or **Elizabethan**) **sonnet,** this fixed form is composed of three quatrains and a terminal (final) couplet, all in iambic pentameter and rhymed *abab cdcd efef gg.*

**SHAKESPEAREAN SONNET**

Fourteen lines
Three quatrains and a final couplet

*abab cdcd efef gg*

You'll see sonnets in this form often, and no small number in this very book (see, for example, Shakespeare's "Shall I compare thee to a summer's day?", chapter 18).

"Now . . . Italian is very, very rich in rhymes. The Russian poet Osip Mandelstam said—writing about Dante—that Italian is like baby talk because everything rhymes with everything else. Rhyming is much more difficult in English. . . . The Shakespearean model . . . rhymes but uses different rhymes in each of the four-line stanzas. . . . It gives you more room to move in." Conversation with Edward Hirsch

Though the Elizabethan sonnet took new liberties with rhyme, many of these "newer" sonnets preserved the Petrarchan sonnet's argumentative eight-line "call" and six-line "response." See how Shakespeare uses the sonnet's tight rhetorical structure first to worry through his troubled emotions and then to find some comfort.

# William Shakespeare (1565–1616)

For a brief biography of William Shakespeare, see chapter 33.

**AS YOU READ** Look for evidence of what Hirsch called an "argument" here. What are the opposing positions, and do they become reconciled?

# When, in disgrace with Fortune and men's eyes (1609)

When, in disgrace with Fortune and men's eyes
I all alone beweep my outcast state,
And trouble deaf heaven with my bootless cries,
And look upon myself and curse my fate,
Wishing me like to one more rich in hope,
Featured like him, like him with friends possessed,
Desiring this man's art, and that man's scope,
With what I most enjoy contented least,
Yet in these thoughts myself almost despising,
Haply I think on thee, and then my state,
Like to the lark at break of day arising
From sullen earth, sings hymns at heaven's gate;
  For thy sweet love remembered such wealth brings
  That then I scorn to change my state with kings.

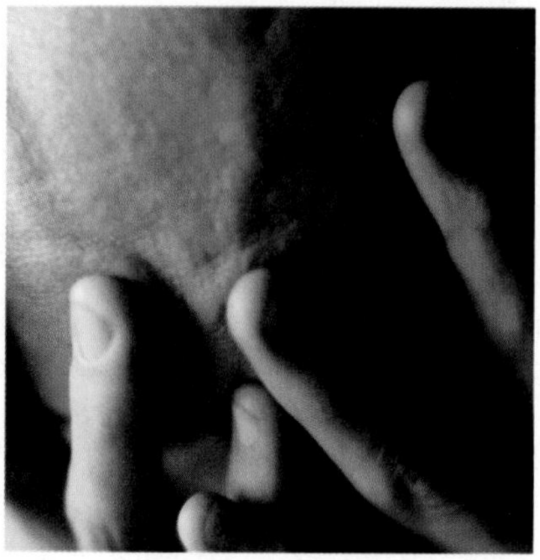

# Writing from Reading

### Summarize

1 This poem deals with the opposition between public and private life, the outer trappings of success and the inner sense of satisfaction or reward. If the speaker feels "outcast" and "in disgrace," why should he "scorn to change my state with kings"?

### Analyze Craft

2 Discuss how this poem is structured. Where do you detect changes in thought or tone?

3 How many sections do you perceive in the poem? How does the rhyme scheme signal section breaks?

### Analyze Voice

4 Notice the implicit pun between "haply"—which means "by accident"—and "happily." Look also at the distinction between "deaf heaven" and "at heaven's gate." How do we get from the one to the other, and how does the voice manage both?

### Synthesize Summary and Analysis

5 If this poem contained no metrical pattern or rhyme scheme, do you think it would illustrate its ideas as effectively? Why or why not?

### Interpret the Poem

6 Less directly a love poem than Elizabeth Barrett Browning's, this sonnet is nonetheless devoted to "thy sweet love remembered." How does the final couplet, with its emphatic *gg* rhyme, help make that point?

Fairly or unfairly, the sonnet is nowadays viewed as an antique form. The poet Robert Bly has been quoted as saying that when he edited a literary magazine in the 1960s, "We sent rejection slips saying things like, 'The sonnet is the place where old professors go to die,' and then [writers would] write us insulting letters. . . ." Nevertheless, sonnet practitioners have continued to work, and brilliantly, within the poem's boundaries. Sometimes contemporary writers follow only very loosely the formal obligations of the sonnet, composing fourteen lines and rhyming them freely and in no regular pattern. Here's one witty contemporary example that takes four versions of the sonnet form (with the third one only approximating it) and strings them together as a story or "saga" in the conversational mode.

> "If you come away from school, and you know what a sonnet is, but you never want to read one again, then your education has failed you." Conversation with Edward Hirsch

# Maxine Kumin (b. 1925)

Maxine Kumin was born in Philadelphia and educated at Radcliffe. Her career as a poet has spanned more than forty-five years, from her first collection *Halfway* (1961) to her recent *Still to Mow* (2007), and she has garnered honors including the Pulitzer Prize and the position of Poet Laureate in the state of New Hampshire. Her poetry leans toward formal verse, but she is often read and written of in conjunction with confessional poets such as Sylvia Plath and Anne Sexton. Kumin and Sexton shared a close friendship and were, at times, collaborators. A fondness for and knowledge of the rural life—Kumin gardens and raises horses in New Hampshire—has characterized her memoirs and essays as well.

**AS YOU READ** Notice the formality of the opening line in "1. Lifestyle"—"begetters" is no doubt a conscious echo of Shakespeare's language (he dedicated his collection of sonnets to their "onlie begetter")—and the slang use of "hereabouts" in line 2.

## Saga (1991)

I. Lifestyle

Invincible begetters, assorted Scutzes
have always lived hereabouts in the woods
trapping beaver or fox, poaching enough
deer to get by on. Winters, they barricade
their groundsills with spoiled hay, which can ignite
from a careless cigarette or chimney spark.
In the fifties, one family barely got out
when the place lit up like the Fair midway at dark.

The singular name of Scutz, it is thought, derives
from *skuft*, Middle Dutch for the nape one is strung up by.
Hangmen or hanged, they led the same snug lives
in an Old World loft adjoining the pigsty
as now, three generations tucked in two
rooms with color tv, in the New.

II. Leisure

The seldom-traveled dirt road by their door
is where, good days, the Scutzes take their ease.
It serves as living room, garage, *pissoir*
as well as barnyard. Hens scratch and rabbits doze
under cars jacked up on stumps of trees.
Someone produces a dozen bottles of beer.
Someone tacks a target to a tire
across the road and hoists it seductively
human-high. The Scutzes love to shoot.
Later, they line the empty bottles up.

The music of glassbreak gladdens them. The brute
sound of a bullet widening a rip
in rubber, the rifle kick, the powder smell
pure bliss. Deadeyes, the Scutzes lightly kill.

III. Shelter

Old doors slanted over packing crates
shelter the Scutzes' several frantic dogs
pinioned on six-foot chains they haven't been
loosed from since January of '91
when someone on skis crept up in snow fog
and undid all of their catches in the night.
Each of the Scutzes' dogs has a dish or plate
to eat from, usually overturned in the dirt.
What do they do for water? Pray for rain.
What do they do for warmth? Remember when
they lay in the litter together, a sweet
jumble of laundry, spotted and stained.

O we are smug in the face of the Scutzes, we
who stroll past their domain, its aromas of ripe decay,
its casual discards mottled with smut and pee.
What do we neighbors do? Look the other way.

IV. Self-fulfilled Prophecy

If Lonnie Scutz comes back, he's guaranteed
free room and board in the State's crowbar hotel.
His girlfriend Grace, a toddler at her heels
and in her arms a grubby ten-month jewel,
looks to be pregnant again, but not his seed.
It's rumored this one was sired by his dad.

Towheads with skyblue eyes, they'll go to school
now and then, struggle to learn to read
and write, forget to carry when they add,
be mocked, kept back or made to play the fool
and soon enough drop out. Their nimble code,
*hit first or get hit*, supplants the Golden Rule.

It all works out the way we knew it would.
They'll come to no good end, the Scutzes' kids.

# Writing from Reading

## Summarize

**1** Who's speaking here, and to whom; why does the speaker say "we"? What is the story told?

## Analyze Craft

**2** Diagram the various versions of the sonnet form in these sections. Why, do you think, is the third such sonnet ("Shelter"), as a form, inexact?

## Analyze Voice

**3** In terms we've used before—high diction, middle diction—discuss the narrative tone and the narrator's "speaking" voice.

## Synthesize Summary and Analysis

**4** Consider William Faulkner's "A Rose for Emily" (chapter 12) and discuss the way the narrator there also employs a collective townsperson's voice. What's different; what's the same?

**5** "What do we neighbors do? Look the other way." How do you reconcile this with the close attention paid by the poet to the story of the Scutzes, and does the poet endorse "non-intervention" or wish that behavior might change?

## Interpret the Poem

**6** This poem about the rural poor refers to Middle Dutch, the Old World, the Golden Rule and uses French words such as *pissoir* while describing a family whose code is *"hit first or get hit."* How does the series of sonnets help fuse the old and the new?

**THE SONNET'S WORLD TOUR**

When Francesco Petrarch published his *Canzoniere* (Song-book) in the fourteenth century in Italy, he could not have imagined the immense impact his collection would have on future readers of world literature. A sequence of 366 poems including 317 sonnets, the volume was widely successful in its own time, and it directly influenced the poetry, within his own lifetime, of his noted poet-contemporaries Boccacio and Geoffrey Chaucer. By the mid-sixteenth century, Petrarch's sonnets had reached scholars throughout western Europe, and the form had already become a fixture of poetic genres in a plentiful number of European languages. In England in particular during this time, Sir Thomas Wyatt (1503–1542) imported the Italian sonnet to English poetry and helped introduce its now trademark closing couplet. Henry Howard, the Earl of Surrey (1517–1547), is credited with first employing the English rhyme scheme of *abab cdcd efef gg*. It's not too much to say that these two men, taking their inspiration from Petrarch, helped inaugurate modern English poetry. From Edmund Spenser and Shakespeare, who each added his own characteristic flourishes to the sonnet form, to Keats and Elizabeth Barrett Browning, to W. B. Yeats and T. S. Eliot, to living poets who are even at this moment trying their hand at the form in any number of countries, the sonnet's hold on the Western poetic imagination is extraordinary and unmatched.

## THE VILLANELLE

The sonnet is just one of the dozens of fixed forms that came "across channel" to England from a foreign language. Another is the **villanelle,** from France, a much more rigorous formal exercise than the sonnet, consisting of nineteen lines and only two rhymes, all in iambic pentameter.

The villanelle, with its Italian root word *villano* meaning "peasant," is a "rural" or "rustic" form with a full refrain or repetition of the first and third lines in song-like fashion. Though its word origin is in Italy, French troubadours are responsible for the form of villanelle we recognize today. In medieval Europe, wandering poets or troubadours plied their trade by demonstrating technical proficiency; their subject matter was limited and their dexterity limitless—as these forms suggest.

The technical arrangement of the villanelle requires five three-line stanzas, or tercets, and a final quatrain. The first and third lines of the first tercet recur alternately in the following stanzas as a refrain and form a final couplet. Why this nineteen-line poem proved popular and an eighteen- or twenty-line version of the same variety has no name is one of the mysteries of tradition, but it has something to do with the power of repetition: the repeated lines add up to more than mere parts of the whole. One of the best-known villanelles in English comes from the twentieth-century Welsh poet Dylan Thomas.

**VILLANELLE**

Nineteen lines
Five tercets/final quatrain

*aba aba aba aba aba abab*

The first and third lines of the tercets recur (the poem's opening line is the final line of the second and fourth stanzas, and the last line of the first stanza is the final line of the third and fifth stanzas) and form a final couplet.

# Dylan Thomas (1914–1953)

Born in Wales, Dylan Thomas decided not to go to college so that he could focus immediately on writing. His *18 Poems* (1934), published when he was twenty, brought him instant critical acclaim for the bold diction and imagery contained in formal structures. In addition to other collections of poetry like *Deaths and Entrances* (1946) and *In Country Sleep* (1951), Thomas also wrote prose—as in his autobiographical sketches *Portrait of the Artist As a Young Dog* (1940)—and plays, as in his successful radio script *Under Milk Wood* (1954). Most of his poetry takes for its theme the unity of the life-and-death cycle, capturing the paradox of living because of death and dying because of life. Although he married in his early twenties and had three children, Thomas lived a bohemian lifestyle, giving boisterous readings in the United States and drinking heavily toward the end of his life. He died suddenly, at thirty-nine, from the effects of alcoholism.

**AS YOU READ** Almost an incantation, this poem gains strength from its lack of variety; listen for the "chorus" and repeated sounds and lines as you read this poem aloud.

## Do not go gentle into that good night (1952)

Do not go gentle into that good night,
Old age should burn and rave at close of day;
Rage, rage against the dying of the light.

Though wise men at their end know dark is right,
Because their words had forked no lightning they
Do not go gentle into that good night.

Good men, the last wave by, crying how bright
Their frail deeds might have danced in a green bay,
Rage, rage against the dying of the light.

Wild men who caught and sang the sun in flight,
And learn, too late, they grieved it on its way,
Do not go gentle into that good night.

Grave men, near death, who see with blinding sight
Blind eyes could blaze like meteors and be gay,
Rage, rage against the dying of the light.

And you, my father, there on the sad height,
Curse, bless me now with your fierce tears, I pray.
Do not go gentle into that good night.
Rage, rage against the dying of the light.

# Writing from Reading

### Summarize

**1** Who's speaking, and to whom? What does "good night" here signify, or "the dying of the light"?

### Analyze Craft

**2** This poem, a desperate plea from the speaker to his declining father to "rage against" death, becomes especially dramatic and poignant in its choral lines. What effect do the repetitions create?

### Analyze Voice

**3** As the American poet Robert Hass has said of the form's repetition, "The effect is mesmerizing; it makes of the music of the poem a kind of haunted waltz." Why is this form appropriate for this speaker and his audience?

### Synthesize Summary and Analysis

**4** Notice that it takes until the final stanza for the poet to address his father directly—making a particular instance out of the general case. How does this heighten the tone and deepen the emotion expressed here?

### Interpret the Poem

**5** The mode of this syntax is imperative, a series of commands. Yet it is also a kind of prayer ("Curse, bless me now with your fierce tears, I pray."). What does that juxtaposition—a blessing, a curse—signify?

Here's another of the best-known villanelles in the language—though a little less formally strict than Thomas's. As Elizabeth Bishop's poem proceeds, the repetition causes the lines to sound as though they're actually trying, deliberately, to convince the speaker (and reader) of a difficult premise. As the poet-critic J. D. McClatchy writes of the final quatrain: "The whole stanza is in danger of breaking apart, and breaking down. In this last line the poet's voice literally cracks. The villanelle—that strictest and most intractable of verse forms—can barely control the grief, yet helps the poet keep her balance."

## Elizabeth Bishop (1911–1979)

For a brief biography of Elizabeth Bishop, see chapter 18.

**AS YOU READ** Note how the repeated refrains of the poem change slightly, both in form and in context. How do the emotions generated by loss and losing enlarge in repetition?

# One Art (1976)

The art of losing isn't hard to master;
so many things seem filled with the intent
to be lost that their loss is no disaster.

Lose something everyday. Accept the fluster
of lost door keys, the hour badly spent.
The art of losing isn't hard to master.

Then practice losing further, losing faster:
places, and names, and where it was you meant
to travel. None of these will bring disaster.

I lost my mother's watch. And look! my last, or
next-to-last, of three loved houses went.
The art of losing isn't hard to master.

I lost two cities, lovely ones. And, vaster,
some realms I owned, two rivers, a continent.
I miss them, but it wasn't a disaster.

—Even losing you (the joking voice, a gesture
I love) I shan't have lied. It's evident
the art of losing's not too hard to master
though it may look like (*Write* it!) like disaster.

# Writing from Reading

## Summarize

**1** Since it's so often repeated, the opening line (or "topic sentence") of a villanelle must be worth hearing more than once. What do you think the poet means by "the art of losing," and which examples does she use?

## Analyze Craft

**2** Determine the poem's rhyme scheme. Where do you notice Bishop using slant rhymes?

## Analyze Voice

**3** What does J. D. McClatchy mean when he says the poet's voice "cracks" in the final stanza? How does the final stanza seem to "break down"?

## Synthesize Summary and Analysis

**4** Does the significance of the repeated lines seem to change as the poem reflects on increasingly serious losses? Why or why not?

**5** How would you compare this to Keats's "On First Looking into Chapman's Homer"?

## Interpret the Poem

**6** What do you think the speaker means by losing "two cities"? And "some realms I owned"? Does this remind you of Keats' "On First Looking into Chapman's Homer"?

## THE SESTINA

Another form that derives from the French is the sestina. An even more elaborately constructed poem than the villanelle, a **sestina** consists of six stanzas composed of six lines each. Featuring word repetition rather than rhyme, the final word of each line in the first stanza is repeated in a different order in the following five stanzas.

**SESTINA**

Six stanzas, six lines each

The final word of each line in the first stanza is repeated in a different order in the following five stanzas.

The concluding stanza, the envoi ("farewell"), summarizes the main idea.

Again it's difficult to know why this *particular* technical form has come down through the centuries, but the challenge of the sestina continues to engage modern poets; Ezra Pound, T. S. Eliot, and other twentieth-century poets have tried it on for size. As another poem by Elizabeth Bishop demonstrates, the sestina concludes with a three-line **envoi,** or "farewell." The final words of the first stanza are repeated in a different order in the second stanza, and the third, and so on, until the envoi (in which the same six words appear) has gathered force and meaning.

**AS YOU READ** Put yourself in the scene, in the house, in the season, as the poet does as she imagines this moment out of childhood.

# Sestina (1956)

September rain falls on the house.
In the failing light, the old grandmother
sits in the kitchen with the child
beside the Little Marvel Stove,
reading the jokes from the almanac,
laughing and talking to hide her tears.

She thinks that her equinoctial tears
and the rain that beats on the roof of the house
were both foretold by the almanac,
but only known to a grandmother.
The iron kettle sings on the stove.
She cuts some bread and says to the child,

*It's time for tea now;* but the child
is watching the teakettle's small hard tears
dance like mad on the hot black stove,
the way the rain must dance on the house.
Tidying up, the old grandmother
hangs up the clever almanac

on its string. Birdlike, the almanac
hovers half open above the child,
hovers above the old grandmother
and her teacup full of dark brown tears.
She shivers and says she thinks the house
feels chilly, and puts more wood in the stove.

*It was to be,* says the Marvel Stove.
*I know what I know,* says the almanac.
With crayons the child draws a rigid house
and a winding pathway. Then the child
puts in a man with buttons like tears
and shows it proudly to the grandmother.

But secretly, while the grandmother
busies herself about the stove,
the little moons fall down like tears
from between the pages of the almanac
into the flower bed the child
has carefully placed in the front of the house.

*Time to plant tears,* says the almanac.
The grandmother sings to the marvelous stove
and the child draws another inscrutable house.

# Writing from Reading

### Summarize

1 Write down the story the poem tells.

### Analyze Craft

2 The poem, as many do, has a turn, this one coming at the beginning of the sixth stanza, announced by the word *but*. What seems different here from the first five stanzas?

### Analyze Voice

3 How would you describe the poet's tone? Be specific about the word *tears*.

### Synthesize Summary and Analysis

4 How does the rhyme scheme help the story unfold? How might the story seem different in a different rhyme scheme?

### Interpret the Poem

5 How does the repetition enforce or not enforce the sense of the timelessness of childhood? Is the sestina form particularly suited for this kind of mood, or is it merely a variation on ways to create the mood?

## THE PANTOUM

Another formal arrangement in verse—which comes to our language also from the French, by way of Malaysia—is the pantoum. A kind of variation on the villanelle, its lines are grouped into quatrains, and there can be as many or as few of them as the poet chooses. Its music, however, is even more demanding than that of the sestina or the villanelle. (The composer Maurice Ravel called the second movement of his Piano Trio in A minor a "Pantoum." It's likely not an accident that the poet Donald Justice, whose pantoum follows, was trained as a composer and first hoped to be a musician.) The "fixed form" pantoum consists of quatrains with a rhyme scheme of *abab*, and it says everything twice; the lines of the poem may vary in length. For all quatrains except the first, the first line of the current quatrain repeats the second line of the preceding quatrain; the third line of the current stanza repeats the fourth of the preceding quatrain—though in the following pantoum the rhyme scheme has been abandoned and the repetition is inexact.

**PANTOUM**

Quatrains

Rhyme scheme for each quatrain: *abab*

The first line repeats the second line of the preceding quatrain, except for the first quatrain.
The third line repeats the final line of the preceding quatrain.
The second line of the final quatrain repeats the third line of the first quatrain.
The last line repeats the first line of the first quatrain.

# Donald Justice (1925–2004)

A native of Miami, Florida, Donald Justice had an illustrious career as both poet and professor. Among his more than ten books of verse—some of which combine poetry and prose—is the Pulitzer Prize–winning *Selected Poems* (1979). Justice's poetry reflects the sadness and isolation of twentieth-century life, first in formal verse early in his career, then in more experimental verse mid-career, and finally in a return to formal verse. He taught at a number of American universities, both public and private, including the University of Missouri, Syracuse, the University of California, Princeton, the University of Virginia, and the University of Iowa. In 2003, he was offered the post of Poet Laureate but declined because of his failing health.

**AS YOU READ** Consider how "the usual sorrows" get changed by repetition, and how the poem's slow progression differs from the repetitions of a villanelle.

# Pantoum of the Great Depression (1994)

Our lives avoided tragedy
Simply by going on and on,
Without end and with little apparent meaning.
Oh, there were storms and small catastrophes.

Simply by going on and on
We managed. No need for the heroic.
Oh, there were storms and small catastrophes.
I don't remember all the particulars.

We managed. No need for the heroic.
There were the usual celebrations, the usual sorrows.
I don't remember all the particulars.
Across the fence, the neighbors were our chorus.

There were the usual celebrations, the usual sorrows
Thank God no one said anything in verse.
The neighbors were our only chorus,
And if we suffered we kept quiet about it.

At no time did anyone say anything in verse.
It was the ordinary pities and fears consumed us,
And if we suffered we kept quiet about it.
No audience would ever know our story.

It was the ordinary pities and fears consumed us.
We gathered on porches; the moon rose; we were poor.
What audience would ever know our story?
Beyond our windows shone the actual world.

We gathered on porches; the moon rose; we were poor.
And time went by, drawn by slow horses.
Somewhere beyond our windows shone the world;
But the Great Depression had entered our souls like fog.

And time went by, drawn by slow horses.
We did not ourselves know what the end was.
The Great Depression had entered our souls like fog.
We had our flaws, perhaps a few private virtues.

But we did not ourselves know what the end was.
People like us simply go on.
We have our flaws, perhaps a few private virtues,
But it is by blind chance only that we escape tragedy.

And there is no plot in that; it is devoid of poetry

# Writing from Reading

### Summarize

**1** How far distant is this memory; is it personal, and how can you tell? Track the usage of "I" and "we."

### Analyze Craft

**2** Make a diagram of the formal elements here, the repeated rhymes and lines.

### Analyze Voice

**3** When the poet writes "At no time did anyone say anything in verse," how far do you think his tongue is in his cheek? When he writes "No audience would ever know our story," how does he prove that untrue?

### Synthesize Summary and Analysis

**4** This is, in part, a poem about the making of poetry. But when Justice writes "there is no plot in that," he seems to be also referring to prose. How close does the poem come to being a story?

### Interpret the Poem

**5** "The Great Depression" refers to a specific moment in our nation's history, but it can signify, as well, a mood of melancholy and inertia. How do the public and private meanings of the phrase connect?

# Erica Funkhouser (b. 1949)

Erica Funkhouser teaches writing at the Massachusetts Institute of Technology. She has published five collections of poetry: *Earthly* (2008), *The Actual World* (1997), *Pursuit* (2002), *Sure Shot and Other Poems* (1992), and *Natural Affinities* (1983). Her poems are inspired by everyday objects and nature and have appeared in prestigious venues including *The Paris Review, Ploughshares, The Atlantic Monthly,* and *The New Yorker.* She also has an interest in the Lewis and Clark Expedition and was a contributor to the PBS *Lewis and Clark* series, directed by Ken Burns. She lives in Essex, Massachusetts.

**AS YOU READ** If Donald Justice's pantoum is about "depression," look for the tone and emotional register in this exact example of the fixed form.

# First Pantoum of Summer (2003)

One sleep depletes, another fills the well.
Our night's companion shapes the coming day.
My bed, half empty, rattled like a cell
when you took off for town. I couldn't stay.

Our night's companion shapes the coming day,
and where we make our bed can make us weep.
When you took off for town, I couldn't stay.
I fell into these words—a second sleep.

Where we make our bed can make us weep
or leave us clean and clear and ravenous.
I fell into these words—a second sleep,
a summer sleep, the windows generous.

You left me clean and clear and ravenous.
I drank new air, a warm and welcome stream
of summer sleep, the windows generous.
Here or away, you lead me out of dream.

I drank new air, a warm and welcome stream.
My bed, half empty, rattled like a cell.
Here or away, you lead me out of dream.
One sleep depletes, another fills the well.

# Writing from Reading

### Summarize

1 If this is a love poem, to whom is it addressed and why? Why does the speaker focus on a particular season?

### Analyze Craft

2 How does the speaker create what she calls a "second sleep"? And if this is the "first pantoum of summer," can you find evidence there will be a second or a third?

### Analyze Voice

3 Describe the speaker's tone. Is it affectionate, disappointed, or angry? Or a mixture of emotions?

### Synthesize Summary and Analysis

4 Does the poet describe—or lament the variations of sleep when with a loved one? Can you make a sketch of the absent lover based on details in the poem?

### Interpret the Poem

5 How do repetition and variation bring the deep expression of the poet's situation to our attention?

## HAIKU

Poets since Homer have worked in several other shorter poetic forms that demand attention. One of these is the distinctive Eastern variety of short poem, the **haiku,** put forward first by Japanese poets in the sixteenth century. The original verse form calls for seventeen syllables and three lines: five/seven/five. In part because of its succinctness and brevity, the form presents a single idea, image, or feeling: Its focus is like that of a photographic snapshot. In chapter 20, Jane Hirshfield discussed the influence of haiku on her work, and there we also saw Ezra Pound's Imagist description of passengers in the Paris metro; his definition of the image as the connection of idea and emotion in an instant of time is wholly captured here. Translators who put these poems into English try to approximate the original verse faithfully, which sometimes means breaking out of the original five/seven/five metrical pattern.

**HAIKU**

Translators try to approximate the Japanese seventeen syllables and three-line (five/seven/five) structure.

You'll see in these poems by three of Japan's most revered haiku masters (translated by Robert Hass, another modern-day poet who has been inspired by haiku) an elegant attention to quiet, meditative, sometimes humorous moments—it's as if they're translating little bits of time itself onto the page.

**AS YOU READ** Try reading the three haikus one after another, for the fleeting pleasure and lingering emotion that each one generates.

# Matsuo Bashō (1644–1694)

For a brief biography of Matsuo Bashō, see chapter 20.

## Deep autumn

**(c. 1600)**

Deep autumn—
my neighbor,
how does he live, I wonder?

*—translated by Robert Hass*

# Yosa Buson (1716–1784)

Yosa Buson was born near modern-day Osaka, Japan. He modeled his poetry as well as his life after those of the great haiku master Matsuo Bashō; like Bashō, he spent a period traveling in northern Japan. Buson himself became a master poet known for his ability to blend older, elegant forms with pieces of contemporary life. Buson eventually settled in Kyoto and perfected his artistry not just in poetry but in painting, calligraphy, and in the practice of the meditative tea ceremony as well.

# Tethered horse (c. 1700)

Tethered horse;
snow
in both stirrups.

*—translated by Robert Hass*

# Kobayashi Issa (1763–1828)

For a brief biography of Issa, see chapter 20.

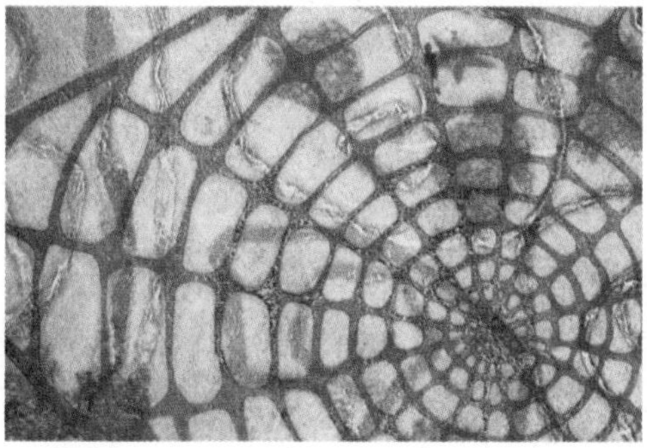

# Don't worry, spiders (c. 1800)

Don't worry, spiders,
I keep house
casually.

*—translated by Robert Hass*

# Writing from Reading

### Summarize

1 How do each of these haiku touch on the cycles of the seasons?

### Analyze Craft

2 These poems have been "Englished" and do not have the precise number of syllables contained in the original. Does that make a difference, and, if not, why not?

### Analyze Voice

3 In two of these three haiku, the first-person pronoun has been used. How personal or impersonal is "I"?

4 The form tends to make the poet speak about the smallest details of everyday life. What kind of tone does that create?

### Synthesize Summary and Analysis

5 How do the separate lines affect your perception of these images? How would your perception differ if all three lines of a haiku were strung together on one line?

### Interpret the Poem

6 Imagine the moments in which each of these haiku were triggered. How do you envision what's going on? Where are the poets in relation to what they're observing? Which of these moments of observation do you relate to?

## EPIGRAM

**Epigrams** are very short, often satirical poems on a single subject. Their primary function, besides deploying wit, is to make a pointed commentary of some kind. Shakespeare said that brevity is the soul of wit, and Samuel Taylor Coleridge puts both soul and wit into play.

**AS YOU READ** Poetry, as we have seen, is a condensed form and an intensive use of language; the epigram is an extreme example of poetic form since it reduces matters to their very briefest expression. Note the way, however, that these condensed meanings expand and enlarge with each rereading in these five epigrams.

# Samuel Taylor Coleridge (1772–1834)

For a brief biography of Samuel Taylor Coleridge, see chapter 22.

# What Is an Epigram? (1802)

What is an epigram? A dwarfish whole;
Its body brevity, and wit its soul.

# Langston Hughes (1902–1967)

For a brief biography of Langston Hughes, see the Case Study on Langston Hughes and His Contemporaries, chapter 26.

# Prayer (1955)

Oh, God of dust and rainbows, help us see
That without dust the rainbow would not be.

# J. V. Cunningham (1911–1985)

James Vincent Cunningham was born in Maryland but considered Montana his home state, as his family moved there when he was three years old. Cunningham is most identified with the epigram, and although his short, witty poems were well appreciated by his colleagues, he never gained much recognition in his lifetime. A successful high school student, Cunningham was unable to attend college following his graduation because his father's death made it necessary for him to get a job. When he lost that job because of the stock market crash in 1929, Cunningham became a poor wanderer, working odd jobs until poet Yvor Winters invited him to come to Stanford University, where Winters taught. Cunningham earned his bachelor's degree and doctorate at Stanford, which enabled him to launch a career in the academy. Although he taught at several universities, he spent the majority of his time at Brandeis University.

## Two Epigrams (1942)

53
On a cold night I came through the cold rain
And false snow to the wind shrill on your pane
With no hope and no anger and no fear.
Who are you? and with whom do you sleep here?

76
Good Fortune, when I hailed her recently,
Passed by me with the intimacy of shame
As one that in the dark had handled me
And could no longer recollect my name.

# A. R. Ammons (1926–2001)

For a brief biography of A. R. Ammons, see chapter 21.

## Small Song (1970)

The reeds give
way to the

wind and give
the wind away.

# Writing from Reading

### Summarize

1 What actually occurs in each of the preceding epigrams?

### Analyze Craft

2 Wit would seem to be a crucial component of these poems, as Coleridge suggests. But there is melancholy here as well. How would you describe the tone of "Small Songs" for example? What about its meaning is suggested by its shape?

### Analyze Voice

3 How does the statement made by an epigram, which makes a single point and not a counterargument, differ from the statement made by a sonnet?

### Synthesize Summary and Analysis

4 Paraphrase these epigrams and compare the points they make. What makes the form appropriate for this type of statement?

### Interpret the Poems

5 If the haiku is an Eastern form and the epigram Western, what similarities do you see in both forms and what seems different? How do these forms effect a different way of seeing everyday life?

## LIMERICK

Unlike the other fixed forms we've examined, the **limerick** originates in the English language. It's a light, often humorous verse form consisting of five anapestic (two short syllables followed by one long one) lines, with a rhyme scheme of *aabba*. The first, second, and fifth lines consist of three feet, while the third and fourth lines consist of two feet.

Though the limerick is considered light and unserious (sometimes downright vulgar), in the hands of a skillful poet it can be quite an impressive display of technique.

**AS YOU READ** Read these three poems aloud, and with emphasis; see how they depend on rhyme.

# Edward Lear (1812–1888)

Edward Lear was born in 1812 outside of London, the twentieth child of stockbroker Jeremiah Lear and his wife Ann. Following poor investments in the market, the Lears fell on hard times, and Edward's upbringing was entrusted to his sister Ann, twenty-one years his senior. At age six, Edward became prone to epileptic seizures, a condition that at the time was often associated with demonic possession. Nevertheless, despite his poor health, Lear began to sell poetry and illustrations at age fifteen; and by age nineteen he earned his living illustrating birds for the scientific book *Illustrations of the Family of Psittacidae, or Parrots* (1830). His first book of poetry, *A Book of Nonsense,* was published in 1846 and contributed greatly to the popularity of the limerick form. He published *The History of the Seven Families of the Lake Pipple-Popple* in 1865, and his most famous work, *The Owl and the Pussycat,* in 1867. Lear spent most of his life traveling abroad in the Mediterranean, and he published several more volumes of illustrated poetry before his death in San Remo, Italy, in 1888.

# There was an Old Man with a gong (1846)

There was an Old Man with a gong,
Who bumped at it all the day long;
But they called out, "Oh, law!
you're a horrid old bore!"
So they smashed that Old Man with a gong.

Most limericks, whether proper or vulgar, include a place-name at poem's start. Their lilting singsong rhyme pattern can also make them appropriate for children's rhymes, as in the following.

## J. D. Landis (b. 1942)

James David Landis was born in Springfield, Massachusetts, attended Yale University, and spent much of his career as a publishing executive in New York. The author of such novels as *Longing* (2000) and *Artist of the Beautiful* (2005), he has written many books for young adults, such as *The Sisters Impossible* (1979), *Daddy's Girl* (1984), and *The Band Never Dances* (1989). His collection of poems for children, *Cars on Mars, and 49 Other Poems for Kids on Earth,* appeared in 2008.

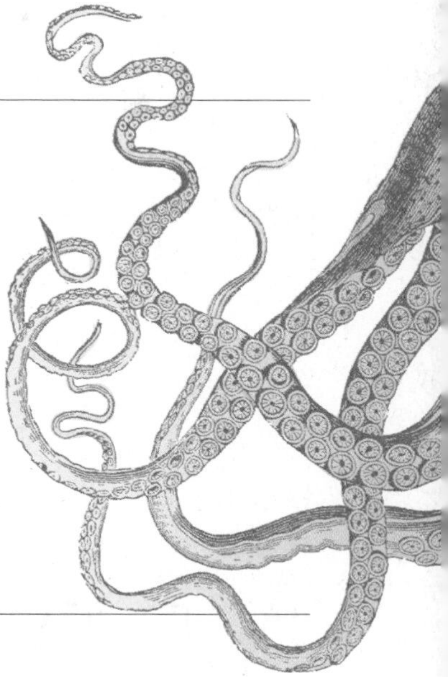

# Starvation Diet (2008)

There was once a fat man from Madrid
Who was told to eat nothing but squid.
He chewed and he chewed.
He chewed and he chewed.
But of squid he could never get rid.

## Laurence Perrine (b. 1915)

Laurence Perrine has published numerous collections of poetry, among them *Sound and Nonsense: Original Limericks* (1994), as well as several influential textbooks, including the poetry anthology *Sound and Sense.* With a B.A. from Oberlin College and a Ph.D. from Yale, Perrine began his teaching career in 1946 at Southern Methodist University, where he taught until his retirement in 1980. Perrine also served as president of the National Council of Teachers of English.

# The limerick's never averse (1982)

The limerick's never averse
To expressing itself in a terse
   Economical style,
   And yet, all the while,
The limerick's *always* a verse.

## Writing from Reading

### Summarize

1 What is constant in this form, and what—if anything—varies?

### Analyze Craft

2 Think of a limerick as a puzzle to be solved—five lines that are "*always* a verse." How does the poet move from "never" to "always," and how does the rhyme scheme here support the poet's point?

### Analyze Voice

3 If epigrams depend on wit, a limerick can't exist without it—or, at least, without good (and sometimes bawdy) humor. Based on the examples in this chapter, what distinction do you draw between humor and wit?

### Synthesize Summary and Analysis

4 The third of these three limericks is both an example of the form and a definition of it; it leaves out the place-name, however. Of these three examples, therefore, only the second is fully "fixed" as a traditional limerick. What are the ways in which such a form can be both rigid and supple?

### Interpret the Poem

5 Poets love wordplay and engage in it often. How serious can this form be?

## ELEGY

On a more somber note, an **elegy** is a poem of lamentation memorializing the dead or contemplating some nuance of life's melancholy. In its original incarnation in ancient Greece, it employed a fixed form of dactylic hexameter and iambic pentameter couplets. Over the centuries, the form has evolved and expanded beyond its early metrical features. A contemporary elegy need not conform to its original classical structure, but it will still reflect a speaker's solemn attention to aspects of grief and mortality.

# A. E. Housman (1859–1936)

A British poet with a bleak outlook, Alfred Edward Housman published only two small volumes of poetry in his lifetime, *A Shropshire Lad* (1896) and *Last Poems* (1922); a third, arguably inferior collection was published posthumously. Despite this limited output, Housman said a lot in a little; his stanzas are compressed yet achieve a sense of poignancy over the fleeting nature of youth and life. Housman also had a reputation as a Latin literature scholar and critic and taught Latin at Cambridge University despite having failed his final exams as an undergraduate at Oxford.

**AS YOU READ** Picture a ceremony, a formal event, at which the poet might read this poem as a tribute.

# To an Athlete Dying Young (1896)

The time you won your town the race
We chaired you through the market-place;
Man and boy stood cheering by,
And home we brought you shoulder-high.

Today, the road all runners come,
Shoulder-high we bring you home,
And set you at your threshold down,
Townsman of a stiller town.

Smart lad, to slip betimes away
From fields where glory does not stay,
And early though the laurel grows
It withers quicker than the rose.

Eyes the shady night has shut
Cannot see the record cut,
And silence sounds no worse than cheers
After earth has stopped the ears:

Now you will not swell the rout
Of lads that wore their honors out,
Runners whom renown outran
And the name died before the man.

So set, before its echoes fade,
The fleet foot on the sill of shade,
And hold to the low lintel up
The still-defended challenge-cup.

And round that early-laureled head
Will flock to gaze the strengthless dead,
And find unwithered on its curls
The garland briefer than a girl's.

# Writing from Reading

### Summarize

1 What does Housman accomplish in his description of the athlete as a "Smart lad, to slip betimes away"?

### Analyze Craft

2 How does the poet use details from the world of sports to move the poem along?

3 Why do you think the poet chooses formal-sounding couplets for his elegy?

### Analyze Voice

4 Does the diction—the word choice elected—sound as formal as the rhyme scheme? What is the speaker's relationship to the athlete?

### Synthesize Summary and Analysis

5 The rhyme and the diction together create a certain effect, and the speaker offers comfort. Does the attitude lend distance to the poem or make it seem more sympathetic, and in what ways?

### Interpret the Poem

6 Compare this to Ben Jonson's "envy" in his elegy "On My First Son" in chapter 19. In what ways are they similar? In what ways different? How would you describe the feelings in each poem about youth?

While the contemporary everyday reader may not know for whom Housman's elegy is composed, W. H. Auden's elegy for the Irish poet William Butler Yeats addresses the death of a literary giant. Living poets often feel a kinship with the great poets of the past. In the case of Auden and Yeats, the sense of kinship was fresh and vital, so that Auden mourned Yeats's death as he might have mourned that of a close relative. Note how Auden remarks on the scope of Yeats's death, how the event is simultaneously momentous and anonymous.

## W. H. Auden (1907–1973)

For a brief biography of W. H. Auden, see chapter 18.

**AS YOU READ** Consider the logic of associating death with the coldest season of the year.

# In Memory of W. B. Yeats (1940)

## *[D. January 1939]*

I

He disappeared in the dead of winter:
The brooks were frozen, the air-ports almost deserted,
And snow disfigured the public statues;
The mercury sank in the mouth of the dying day.
O all the instruments agree
The day of his death was a dark cold day.

Far from his illness
The wolves ran on through the evergreen forests,
The peasant river was untempted by the fashionable quays;
By mourning tongues
The death of the poet was kept from his poems.

But for him it was his last afternoon as himself,
An afternoon of nurses and rumours;
The provinces of his body revolted,
The squares of his mind were empty,
Silence invaded the suburbs,
The current of his feeling failed; he became his admirers.

Now he is scattered among a hundred cities
And wholly given over to unfamiliar affections;
To find his happiness in another kind of wood
And be punished under a foreign code of conscience.
The words of a dead man
Are modified in the guts of the living.

But in the importance and noise of to-morrow
When the brokers are roaring like beasts on the floor of the Bourse,
And the poor have the sufferings to which they are fairly accustomed,
And each in the cell of himself is almost convinced of his freedom;
A few thousand will think of this day
As one thinks of a day when one did something slightly unusual.
O all the instruments agree
The day of his death was a dark cold day.

II

You were silly like us: your gift survived it all;
The parish of rich women, physical decay,
Yourself; mad Ireland hurt you into poetry.
Now Ireland has her madness and her weather still,
For poetry makes nothing happen: it survives
In the valley of its saying where executives
Would never want to tamper; it flows south
From ranches of isolation and the busy griefs,
Raw towns that we believe and die in; it survives,
A way of happening, a mouth.

III

Earth, receive an honoured guest;
William Yeats is laid to rest:
Let the Irish vessel lie
Emptied of its poetry.

Time that is intolerant
Of the brave and innocent,
And indifferent in a week
To a beautiful physique,

Worships language and forgives
Everyone by whom it lives;
Pardons cowardice, conceit,
Lays its honours at their feet.

Time that with this strange excuse
Pardoned Kipling and his views,
And will pardon Paul Claudel,
Pardons him for writing well.

In the nightmare of the dark
All the dogs of Europe bark,
And the living nations wait,
Each sequestered in its hate;

Intellectual disgrace
Stares from every human face,
And the seas of pity lie
Locked and frozen in each eye.

Follow, poet, follow right
To the bottom of the night,
With your unconstraining Voice
Still persuade us to rejoice;

With the farming of a verse
Make a vineyard of the curse,
Sing of human unsuccess
In a rapture of distress;

In the deserts of the heart
Let the healing fountain start,
In the prison of his days,
Teach the free man how to praise.

# Writing from Reading

### Summarize

1 The death of the Irish poet is a day to remember for Auden. Why do you think he honors Yeats in such a formal way?

### Analyze Craft

2 Nature itself seems to be dying, or at least in mourning. With what images and metaphors does Auden achieve this effect? Why does Auden compare the dying poet to a country or city, with "provinces," "squares," "suburbs"?

### Analyze Voice

3 Do you hear a personal or public voice when you listen to this speaker, a private or collective grief? What language from the poem supports your answer?

### Synthesize Summary and Analysis

4 An elegy, elaborate or simple, speaks of life as well as death. Does this statement seem accurate to you? How does Auden's lament refer to what continues as well as to what has stopped?

### Interpret the Poem

5 Discuss the meaning of the lines "The death of the poet was kept from his poems" and ". . . he became his admirers." What does Auden suggest here about the relationship of the poet to his own poetry?

# Theodore Roethke (1907–1973)

For a brief biography of Theodore Roethke, see chapter 19.

**AS YOU READ** Try to put yourself in the mind of the speaker of the poem, the teacher lamenting the death of his student.

# Elegy for Jane (1953)

## *My Student Thrown by a Horse*

I remember the neckcurls, limp and damp as tendrils;
And her quick look, a sidelong pickerel smile;
And how, once startled into talk, the light syllables leaped for her,
And she balanced in the delight of her thought,
A wren, happy, tail into the wind,
Her song trembling the twigs and small branches.
The shade sang with her;
The leaves, their whispers turned to kissing;
And the mold sang in the bleached valleys under the rose.

Oh, when she was sad, she cast herself down into such a pure depth,
Even a father could not find her:
Scraping her cheek against straw;
Stirring the clearest water.

My sparrow, you are not here,
Waiting like a fern, making a spiny shadow.
The sides of wet stones cannot console me,
Nor the moss, wound with the last light.

If only I could nudge you from this sleep,
My maimed darling, my skittery pigeon.
Over this damp grave I speak the words of my love:
I, with no rights in this matter,
Neither father nor lover.

# Writing from Reading

### Summarize

1 The poem presents a sorrowful occasion, in which the poet tries to speak through his pain. Can you paraphrase his speech?

### Analyze Craft

2 What metaphors does the poet employ to achieve his end? Do they all come from nature, and in what ways, if any, do they appear "artificial"?

### Analyze Voice

3 What new and unexpected textures does this poet add to the generic voice of the poet mourning for the beloved dead?

### Synthesize Summary and Analysis

4 Do you think the poet has found the proper metaphors, images, and tone in order to make his grief memorable for a reader? What makes them memorable to you?

### Interpret the Poem

5 How do we express great sorrow at the loss of those we love but who are not our kin? Is there a sorrow we feel beyond that which comes from knowing of an individual death, and how would you describe it?

## ODE

Like the elegy, the **ode** no longer obliges the poet to a specific rhyme scheme or stanza length. It does, however, take a recognizable shape in its celebration of a quality or condition or situation. The main features of this variety of lyric are an elaborate stanzaic structure, a certain ceremonial feel in tone and style, and a sense of address—whether to a private or a public issue. By the nineteenth century, the ode form was more frequently dedicated to abstract subjects than to specific public figures or events.

Despite numerous variations on the ode form over time, the essential nature of the form has remained the same: a poem that declares its topic in the title, and then considers an idea or object or mood at length.

In Shelley's "Ode to the West Wind," the speaker calls to the coming autumn wind and asks it to "make me thy lyre," to project his words beyond the boundaries of both his physical location and his physical body.

# Percy Bysshe Shelley (1792–1822)

The life of Percy Bysshe Shelley, a British Romantic poet, was marked by nonconformity. He was expelled from Oxford University because he had coauthored a pamphlet called *The Necessity of Atheism;* shortly thereafter, he married the daughter of a tavern owner when both he and his wife were still teenagers. He eventually grew estranged from his wife and fell in love with Mary Wollstonecraft Godwin (daughter of Mary Wollstonecraft and future author of *Frankenstein*); he then invited his wife to live with him and Mary as a sister. After his wife's apparent suicide, Shelley married Mary and the couple moved to Italy, where over the course of four years, Shelley wrote his most important works: *Prometheus Unbound, Adonais,* and his famous poems "Hymn to Intellectual Beauty," "Ode to the West Wind," and "Ozymandias." An idealist who believed in intellectual beauty rather than God, Shelley's poetry champions hope and imagination. He drowned, surprised by a storm while sailing, before his thirtieth birthday.

**AS YOU READ** Consider the language and the situation here: the poet speaking to the wind itself.

## Ode to the West Wind (1820)

I

O wild West Wind, thou breath of Autumn's being,
Thou, from whose unseen presence the leaves dead
Are driven, like ghosts from an enchanter fleeing,

Yellow, and black, and pale, and hectic red,
Pestilence-stricken multitudes: O thou,
Who chariotest to their dark wintry bed

The wingèd seeds, where they lie cold and low,
Each like a corpse within its grave, until
Thine azure sister of the Spring shall blow

Her clarion o'er the dreaming earth, and fill
(Driving sweet buds like flocks to feed in air)
With living hues and odors plain and hill:

Wild Spirit, which art moving everywhere;
Destroyer and preserver; hear, oh, hear!

II

Thou on whose stream, mid the steep sky's commotion,
Loose clouds like earth's decaying leaves are shed,
Shook from the tangled boughs of Heaven and Ocean,

Angels of rain and lightning: there are spread
On the blue surface of thine airy surge,
Like the bright hair uplifted from the head

Of some fierce Maenad, even from the dim verge
Of the horizon to the zenith's height,
The locks of the approaching storm. Thou dirge

Of the dying year, to which this closing night
Will be the dome of a vast sepulcher,
Vaulted with all thy congregated might

Of vapors, from whose solid atmosphere
Black rain, and fire, and hail will burst: oh, hear!

III

Thou who didst waken from his summer dreams
The blue Mediterranean, where he lay,
Lulled by the coil of his crystàlline streams,

Beside a pumice isle in Baiae's bay,
And saw in sleep old palaces and towers
Quivering within the wave's intenser day,

All overgrown with azure moss and flowers
So sweet, the sense faints picturing them! Thou
For whose path the Atlantic's level powers

Cleave themselves into chasms, while far below
The sea-blooms and the oozy woods which wear
The sapless foliage of the ocean, know

Thy voice, and suddenly grow gray with fear,
And tremble and despoil themselves: oh, hear!

IV

If I were a dead leaf thou mightest bear;
If I were a swift cloud to fly with thee;
A wave to pant beneath thy power, and share

The impulse of thy strength, only less free
Than thou, O uncontrollable! If even
I were as in my boyhood, and could be

The comrade of thy wanderings over Heaven,
As then, when to outstrip thy skyey speed
Scarce seemed a vision; I would ne'er have striven

As thus with thee in prayer in my sore need.
Oh, lift me as a wave, a leaf, a cloud!
I fall upon the thorns of life! I bleed!

A heavy weight of hours has chained and bowed
One too like thee: tameless, and swift, and proud.

V

Make me thy lyre, even as the forest is:
What if my leaves are falling like its own!
The tumult of thy mighty harmonies

Will take from both a deep, autumnal tone,
Sweet though in sadness. Be thou, Spirit fierce,
My spirit! Be thou me, impetuous one!

Drive my dead thoughts over the universe
Like withered leaves to quicken a new birth!
And, by the incantation of this verse,

Scatter, as from an unextinguished hearth
Ashes and sparks, my words among mankind!
Be through my lips to unawakened earth

The trumpet of a prophecy! O Wind,
If Winter comes, can Spring be far behind?

# Writing from Reading

## Summarize

1 The speaker describes the wind in various ways throughout the poem, for example, as "the trumpet of a prophecy" at the poem's end. Identify these descriptions of the wind. What do they tell you about how the speaker sees the wind?

## Analyze Craft

2 How does this poem reflect the definition of an ode, as a formal, elevated celebration and reflection? What about the "west wind" is the speaker praising?

## Analyze Voice

3 How do the poem's sections govern the speaker's emotions and thinking? How do the poem's attention and focus change over the trajectory of the different sections?

## Synthesize Summary and Analysis

4 What is the importance of nature as it's described over the course of the poem? How would you characterize nature's power, according to Shelley's speaker?

## Interpret the Poem

5 What does the spirit embodied by the wind represent?

# For Review and Further Study

## Louise Bogan (1897–1970)

### The Changed Woman (1923)

The light flower leaves its little core
Begun upon the waiting bough.
Again she bears what she once bore
And what she knew she re-learns now.

The cracked glass fuses at a touch,
The wound heals over, and is set
In the whole flesh, and is not much
Quite to remember or forget.

Rocket and tree, and dome and bubble
Again behind her freshened eyes
Are treacherous. She need not trouble.
Her lids will know them when she dies.

And while she lives, the unwise, heady
Dream, ever denied and driven,
Will one day find her bosom ready—
That never thought to be forgiven.

#### Questions for Interactive Reading

1. Can you imagine one specific occasion for this poem, or does it speak of many similar events? "Flower" and "bough" connect the "she" in the woman of the title to the natural world. "Cracked glass" and "wound" suggest trouble and pain. How might such images contribute to the overall person suggested in the title?
2. What "change," if any, occurs in the poem? What does this suggest about the change in the woman of whom the poem speaks?
3. Does the formal presentation of deep pain and sorrow remind you of other poems about women with lives in turmoil?

## Nikki Giovanni (b. 1943)

### Knoxville, Tennessee (1968)

I always like summer
best
you can eat fresh corn
from daddy's garden
and okra
and greens
and cabbage
and lots of
barbecue
and buttermilk
and homemade ice-cream
at the church picnic
and listen to
gospel music
outside
at the church
homecoming
and go to the mountains with
your grandmother
and go barefooted
and be warm
all the time
not only when you go to bed
and sleep

#### Questions for Interactive Reading

1. The poet depicts this world as a place of distinct seasons. What effect does the list of a Southern summer's pleasures create for you?
2. Implicit in the poem is a waking world and a world of night, and also an inside world and an outside world. Why does the poet focus on the waking part and the outside part in this poem?
3. Does the reference to "daddy's garden" call to mind an image beyond the seemingly ordinary setting of the poem?
4. Does the plain, straightforward natural voice of the poem mask anything more complex and difficult? Or should we take the poem at face value and accept the speaker's simple delight in summer?

## Marilyn Hacker (b. 1942)

### Elektra on Third Avenue (1974)

At six, when April chills our hands and feet
walking downtown, we stop at Clancy's Bar
or Bickford's, where the part-time hustlers are,
scoffing between the mailroom and the street.
Old pensioners appraise them while they eat,

and so do we, debating half in jest
which piece of hasty pudding we'd like best.
I know you know I think your mouth is sweet
as anything exhibited for sale,
fresh coffee cake or boys fresh out of jail,
which tender hint of incest brings me near
to ordering more coffee or more beer.
The homebound crowd provides more youth to cruise.
We nurse our cups, nudge knees, and pick and choose.

### Questions for Interactive Reading

1. A traditional form and an old myth, the story of Electra, have been brought together to create a New York street scene. Why might the poet have chosen this way to present the emotion—and story—of this poem?
2. Do some of the juxtapositions of phrases—"fresh coffee cake or boys fresh out of jail"—seem shocking? Do any others seem as strong?
3. Can you detect a playful quality to the poem overall? In what way does this reflect the possibility that the poet has described a game she plays with her lover?

## Seamus Heaney (b. 1939)

*For a brief biography of Seamus Heaney, see chapter 22.*

### Mid-Term Break (1966)

I sat all morning in the college sick bay
Counting bells knelling classes to a close,
At two o'clock our neighbors drove me home.

In the porch I met my father crying—
He had always taken funerals in his stride—
And Big Jim Evans saying it was a hard blow.

The baby cooed and laughed and rocked the pram
When I came in, and I was embarrassed
By old men standing up to shake my hand

And tell me they were "sorry for my trouble,"
Whispers informed strangers I was the eldest,
Away at school, as my mother held my hand

In hers and coughed out angry tearless sighs.
At ten o'clock the ambulance arrived
With the corpse, stanched and bandaged by the nurses.

Next morning I went up into the room. Snowdrops
And candles soothed the bedside; I saw him
For the first time in six weeks. Paler now,

Wearing a poppy bruise on the left temple,
He lay in the four foot box as in a cot.
No gaudy scars, the bumper knocked him clear.

A four foot box, a foot for every year.

### Questions for Interactive Reading

1. How much do we learn about the speaker's life in this poem?
2. Why do you think Heaney employs such a thorough amount of narrative detail in this elegy?
3. How does the final line of the poem contrast with the detail of the preceding lines?

## Andrew Hudgins (b.1951)

### Elegy for My Father, Who Is Not Dead (1991)

One day I'll lift the telephone
and be told my father's dead. He's ready.
In the sureness of his faith, he talks
about the world beyond this world
as though his reservations have
been made. I think he wants to go,
a little bit—a new desire
to travel building up, an itch
to see fresh worlds. Or older ones.
He thinks that when I follow him
he'll wrap me in his arms and laugh,
the way he did when I arrived
on earth. I do not think he's right.
He's ready. I am not. I can't
just say good-bye as cheerfully
as if he were embarking on a trip
to make my later trip go well.
I see myself on deck, convinced
his ship's gone down, while he's convinced
I'll see him standing on the dock
and waving, shouting, Welcome back.

### Questions for Interactive Reading

1. Usually the poet speaks in an elegy of someone already dead. What makes this poem distinct from other elegies?
2. How does the father-son theme enhance the traditional form? The father has his "faith." Does the son have values he holds to?

3. What effect does the poet create by including an image of his own birth? Do the images of travel and a voyage seem appropriate for an elegy?
4. With what line does the poem seem to turn back against its original statement?

# Dorianne Laux (b. 1952)

## The Shipfitter's Wife (1999)

I loved him most
when he came home from work,
his fingers still curled from fitting pipe,
his denim shirt ringed with sweat,
and smelling of salt, the drying weeds
of the ocean. I'd go to where he sat
on the edge of the bed, his forehead
anointed with grease, his cracked hands
jammed between his thighs, and unlace
the steel-toed boots, stroke his ankles,
and calves, the pads and bones of his feet.
Then I'd open his clothes and take
the whole day inside me—the ship's
gray sides, the miles of copper pipe,
the voice of the first man clanging
off the hull's silver ribs. Spark of lead
kissing metal. The clamp, the winch,
the white fire of the torch, the whistle
and the long drive home.

### Questions for Interactive Reading

1. How does the woman describe her husband? Since this is a past-tense set of memories, and if she loved him "most" when he came home from work, how far removed is the remembered past?
2. Why do you think the speaker floods this poem with specific, concrete images?
3. Would you call this poem an elegy? Why or why not?

# Jacqueline Osherow (b. 1956)

## Song for the Music in the Warsaw Ghetto (1996)

Pity the tune bereft of singers
Pity the tone bereft of chords
Where shall we weep? By which waters?
Pity the song bereft of words
Pity the harps hung on rifles
The unsuspected cunning in each hand
Pity the shrill, bewildered nightingales
How could they sing in that strange land?

Pity the string that has no bow
Pity the flute that has no breath
Pity the rifle's muted solo
Pity its soundless aftermath

### Questions for Interactive Reading

1. List some of the paradoxes in the poem—as in tune without singers, tone without chords, and so on.
2. How many times does the poet repeat the word *pity*? What effect does this create?
3. "Where shall we weep? By which waters?" From where in the Bible is the poet quoting? Does her use of this allusion broaden or narrow the context of the poem?
4. The destruction of the Warsaw Ghetto leaves, as the poet puts it in the image of the rifle's "solo," a "soundless aftermath." Do you find this paradoxical? Why?
5. Does the poem have an "aftermath" in your mind? Reread the poem, then give examples of the language you remember, and explain why.

# Robert Pinsky (b. 1940)

*For a brief biography of Robert Pinsky, see chapter 21.*

## Sonnet (1983)

Afternoon sun on her back,
calm irregular slap
of water against a dock.

Thin pines clamber
over the hill's top—
nothing to remember,

only the same lake
that keeps making the same
sounds under her cheek

and flashing the same color.
No one to say her name,
no need, no one to praise her,

only the lake's voice—over
and over, to keep it before her.

### Questions for Interactive Reading and Writing

1. Contrast the regular rhythms of the form with the apparent calm and relaxed nature of the subject of the poem. Do the half rhymes—"lake . . . cheek," "color . . . her"—suggest anything about the essence of the subject? Why do you think the poet chose the sonnet form and not a less fixed form for this particular poem?
2. How old might the woman be? Can you make an argument that the "her" of the poem might be a young girl? What evidence—one way or the other—does the poet provide?
3. If you were going to make a painting of the same subject as the poem—a portrait of a woman on a dock at lakeside on a summer afternoon—what colors might you use? Would you, in the spirit of the poem, make a realistic portrait? Or would it be more abstract, less distinct? Explain why you would make these choices.

## Mary Jo Salter (b. 1954)

### Video Blues (1999)

My husband has a crush on Myrna Loy,
and likes to rent her movies, for a treat.
It makes some evenings harder to enjoy.

The list of actresses who might employ
him as their slave is too long to repeat.
(My husband has a crush on Myrna Loy,

Carole Lombard, Paulette Goddard, coy
Jean Arthur with that voice as dry as wheat . . .)
It makes some evenings harder to enjoy.

Does he confess all this just to annoy
a loyal spouse? I know I can't compete.
My husband has a crush on Myrna Loy.

And can't a woman have her dreamboats? Boy,
I wouldn't say my life is incomplete,
but some evening I could certainly enjoy

two hours with Cary Grant as *my* own toy.
I guess, though, we were destined not to meet.
My husband has a crush on Myrna Loy
which makes some evenings harder to enjoy.

### Questions for Interactive Reading and Writing

1. How would you describe the mood of this poem. Sad? Wistful? Dejected? Disappointed? Resigned? Confused? Or a comic combination of all these?
2. Why do you think the poet chose this particular form, the villanelle, over, say, the sonnet form or free verse? Is there something special about the subject that suits this form?
3. Does the distracted video-watching husband of the poem have any counterpart in spouses from earlier times? Or is he a particularly contemporary individual?

## Gjertrud Schnackenberg (b. 1953)

### Snow Melting (1982)

Snow melting when I left you, and I took
This fragile bone we'd found in melting snow
Before I left, exposed beside a brook
Where raccoons washed their hands. And this, I know,

Is that raccoon we'd watched for every day.
Though at the time her wild human hand
Had gestured inexplicably, I say
Her meaning now is more than I can stand.

We've reasons, we have reasons, so we say,
For giving love, and for withholding it.
I who would love must marvel at the way
I know aloneness when I'm holding it,

Know near and far as words for live and die,
Know distance, as I'm trying to draw near,
Growing immense, and know, but don't know why,
Things seen up close enlarge, then disappear.

Tonight this small room seems too huge to cross.
And my life is that looming kind of place.
Here, left with this alone, and at a loss
I hold an alien and vacant face

Which shrinks away, and yet is magnified—
More so than I seem able to explain.
Tonight the giant galaxies outside
Are tiny, tiny on my windowpane.

### Questions for Interactive Reading and Writing

1. Write down the pattern of the rhymes. Had you noticed them when you first read the poem, or did the subject catch you up in its intensity? How would you describe the subject of the poem?
2. Does the image of melting snow contrast in fruitful ways with the pain and sorrow felt by the speaker? Does it represent any part of the way she feels, and what does the word "melting" convey?
3. How long ago did the speaker depart? How many seasons of thaw away from that event does she appear to be?
4. What might be the "meaning" of the long-dead raccoon's gesture?
5. In what way are the galaxies outside the window "tiny, tiny"?

## David Wojahn (b. 1953)

### The Assassination of John Lennon As Depicted by the Madame Tussaud Wax Museum, Niagara Falls, Ontario, 1987 (1990)

Smuggled human hair from Mexico
Falls radiant upon the waxy O

Of her scream. Shades on, leather coat and pants, Yoko
On her knees—like the famous Kent State photo

Where the girl can't shriek her boyfriend alive, her arms
Windmilling Ohio sky.
A pump in John's chest heaves

To mimic death throes. The blood is made of latex.
His glasses: broken on the plastic sidewalk.

A scowling David Chapman, his arms outstretched,
His pistol barrel spiraling fake smoke

In a siren's red wash, completes the composition,
And somewhere background music plays "Imagine"

Before the tableau darkens. We push a button
To renew the scream.
The chest starts up again.

### Questions for Interactive Reading and Writing

1. How does this poem echo the conventions of the sonnet, in terms of meter and/or rhyme? How does it diverge from them?
2. Does this sonnet seem to deliberate on an idea or message? Why do you think the "we" speaker wants to start the chest up again?
3. Does it seem strange to write about a rock and roll singer in this centuries-old form? Why or why not?
4. What is the nature of this singular event in the pop culture world that allows the poet to elevate it nearly to the level of modern myth?

# Reading for Fixed Forms

When reading for fixed forms, note patterns in line length, meter, stanza structure, and rhyme scheme, and consider how the poem uses these preestablished schemes.

| | |
|---|---|
| **How is the poem broken up visually?** | *Stanza:* Unit of two or more lines, set off by a space, and often sharing the same rhythm and meter.<br>*Notice lines grouped by rhyme, meter, or purpose.*<br>**Two lines:** *Couplet:* Two lines of poetry that form a unit of meaning.<br>*Heroic couplet:* Two lines of rhymed, iambic pentameter.<br>**Three lines:** *Tercet:* A three-line stanza.<br>*Triplet:* A tercet in which all three lines rhyme.<br>*Terza rima:* Tercets of interlocking rhymes with the middle line rhyming with the first and third lines of the preceding tercet: *aba, bcb, cdc, ded,* etc.<br>**Four lines:** *Quatrain:* A four-line stanza.<br>*Ballad stanza:* Quatrain consisting of alternating four-stress and three-stress lines, usually rhymed *abcb.*<br>*Common measure:* A ballad stanza popular to hymns, consistently iambic, and usually featuring an *abcb* or *abab* rhyme scheme. |
| **Are there fourteen lines in the poem?** | *Sonnet:* Fourteen-line poem, usually in iambic pentameter, with a varied rhyme scheme that employs a call-and-response structure with an answer in the final two lines.<br>*Petrarchan (Italian) sonnet:* A sonnet consisting of an octave rhyming *abbaabba* and of a sestet using any arrangement of two or three additional rhymes, such as *cdcdcd* or *cdecde.*<br>*Shakespearean (English, Elizabethan) sonnet:* A sonnet comprising three quatrains and a final couplet in iambic pentameter with the rhyme scheme *abab cdcd efef gg.* |
| **Is the poem only a few lines?** | *Haiku:* An unrhymed Japanese poem, often featuring observations on nature, generally written in three lines of five, seven, and five syllables.<br>*Epigram:* A short poem highlighting a witty idea, satirical thought, or condensed comment.<br>*Limerick:* A humorous poem of five usually anapestic lines with the rhyme scheme of *aabba.* |

| | |
|---|---|
| **Are lines repeated?** | *Villanelle:* A poem consisting of five tercets and a concluding quatrain. Each tercet rhymes *aba* and the final quatrain rhymes *abaa*. The poem's opening line repeats as the final line of the second and fourth stanzas and in the second-to-last line of the poem. The last line of the first stanza repeats as the final line of the third and fifth stanzas and is also the final line of the poem overall.<br>*Sestina:* A poem of six six-line stanzas and a three-line envoi, usually unrhymed, in which each stanza repeats the end words of the lines of the first stanza, but in different order, the envoi using the six words again, three in the middle of the lines and three at the end.<br>*Envoi:* A short closing stanza in certain verse forms, such as the ballade or sestina, summarizing its main ideas.<br>*Pantoum:* A variation on the villanelle, consisting of an unspecified number of quatrains with the rhyme scheme *abab*. The first line of each quatrain repeats the second line of the preceding quatrain, and the third line repeats the final line of the preceding quatrain. In the final quatrain, the second line repeats the third line of the first quatrain, and the last line of the poem repeats the first line of the poem. |
| **What is the tone of the poem?** | *Elegy:* A mournful poem lamenting the dead or reflecting somberly on life's hardship.<br>*Ode:* An elevated, formal lyric poem often written in commemoration of someone or an abstract subject. |

# Writing about Fixed Forms

1. Analyze the argumentative/rhetorical purposes of Hirsch's "My First Theology Lesson" and Kumin's "Saga."
2. Compare and contrast Shakespeare's attitude toward love in two different sonnets (see chapter 15 and chapter 18, for example). Pay special attention to how he uses the sonnet's architecture to build his meaning.
3. Compare the form of one haiku and one epigram from the chapter. Can a haiku be an epigram?
4. Compare the speaker's relationship to his subject matter in Shelley's "Ode to the West Wind" and Keats's "Ode on a Grecian Urn" (chapter 18).
5. How does the tone and approach to meditating on death and mortality differ in "In Memory of W. B. Yeats," "To an Athlete Dying Young," and "The Shipfitter's Wife"?
6. How does the form support the poets' reflections on time and familial structure in Thomas's "Do not go gentle into that good night" and Bishop's "One Art"?

# 24 Open Form

ALL the new thinking is about loss.
In this it resembles all the old thinking.
The idea, for example, that each particular erases
the luminous clarity of a general idea. That the clown-
faced woodpecker probing the dead sculpted trunk
of that black birch is, by his presence,
some tragic falling off from a first world
of undivided light. Or the other notion that,
because there is in this world no one thing
to which the bramble of *blackberry* corresponds,
a word is elegy to what it signifies.

*—from "Meditation at Lagunitas" by Robert Hass*

*"Starting with Walt Whitman, people began to experiment with not having a set number of lines or preconditions for the writing, of just letting it flow out and see what happens, and that got to be called free verse, open form. There's nothing particularly complicated about understanding it. You just say it out loud. If you say words . . . in a certain pattern, if you start just saying, as I'm saying to you now, [words] in sentences with pauses . . . , if you reflect in the way you put those down on the page, those rhythms, you'll get this thing I was saying, which is the emotion of the rhythm of the truth of the experience that the piece of writing is talking about."*

Conversation with Robert Hass, available on video at www.mhhe.com/delbanco1e

ROBERT Hass's poem "Meditation at Lagunitas" is an intimate reflection on words—their purpose and power, their often profound connections to memory. "All the new thinking is about loss," says the poem's speaker, and, "a word is elegy to what it signifies." By poem's end, the repetition of the word *blackberry* has become a vocal testament to the sensual potential of language; you can see and hear and touch and feel it, *taste* the word. The poet reacts critically to the academic idea that language may be unable to capture the individual essence of a "particular" thing or object, and that language itself may misrepresent the physical specifics we wordlessly see and feel. Hass's poem asserts the reverse. Words, he writes, really do make manifest by naming our memories and sensations. Words can serve us as powerfully and immediately as memories from childhood or of love.

To best embody the ideas and images he sets out to express, Hass has chosen **open form.** The term describes poetry that employs the sounds and rhythms of natural speech, repetition, grammatical variation, and organized patterns of imagery rather than formal rhyming structures. And instead of metrical feet, the line itself is the chief rhythmical unit we use to examine the individual components of an open form poem. So, how a line is arranged, and where it breaks, can be absolutely crucial to understanding a poem of this kind. "Meditation at Lagunitas" delves into complicated issues of language and memory yet is grounded in candid, vivid images and memories. As you listen to Hass read and discuss the poem in his interview, think about why he chose this particular form and about how different the poem would feel in formal fixed meter and rhyme.

*When I first heard poems, I felt like somebody was telling me the truth.*

*. . . Our consciousness is huge and mostly unexplored . . .*

# Q&A
# A Conversation on Writing
## Robert Hass

### Poetry Goes with Equality in America

The country was founded by people who believe that, in order to save your soul, you had to learn to read. . . . So women were taught to read as well as men . . . , and the first book of poetry published in the United States was published by a woman. The first book of poems published by a black person, an African in the United States, was published by a woman. . . . So our country has been, from the start, one in which the attainment of literacy was a very powerful tool. . . . From the beginning, the core of it in some way had been the ability to read and figure out poetry.

### Sound and the Size of Our Inner World

There's a way in which a poem or a story or something opens the size of the inner world to you, one's own inner world. You know, our consciousness is huge and mostly unexplored, and sometimes, something will, like throwing a stone into a well, give you a sense of those depths. For me, if I remember rightly, it was a poem in a school textbook by Tennyson. The lines I remember are "Blow, bugles, blow, set the wild echoes flying, / And answer, echoes, answer, dying, dying, dying." It seems corny to me now, but at the time, something opened in me to that sound that I now think had to do with the sense of the size of our inner life, the vastness of our capacity for loneliness, for happiness, for wonder.

### The Emotional Truthfulness of Poems

I grew up in a house where there were drinking problems. In families that are troubled, there's a lot of denial. Nobody tells the truth much about anything. . . . A lot of it is kindness; it's short of hypocrisy. In some families, in some parts of the world, in dysfunctional institutions of all kinds, nobody ever tells the truth about anything, you know. When I first heard poems, I felt like somebody was telling me the truth.

Native to California—where he continues to live and teach—Robert Hass (b. 1941) has shaped his poetry through the lush landscape that frequently enters into his poems. His first book of poetry, *Field Guide* (1973), the name of which signals Hass's environmental interest, won the Yale Series of Younger Poets Prize. His subsequent collections, along with his work as translator—from Polish and Japanese, among other languages—compose Hass's body of creative work, which is known for its meditative quality and haiku-like clarity. In addition to winning the National Book Award and the Pulitzer Prize for his collection *Time and Materials* (2007), Hass held the position of Poet Laureate from 1995 to 1997. He used his term to bring poetry into areas he deemed devoid of imagination, such as the corporate world.

**To watch this entire interview and hear the author read from his work, go to www.mhhe.com/delbanco1e.**

**RESEARCH ASSIGNMENT** In his interview, Hass talks about trying to translate Czeslaw Milosz, a poet exiled from Poland and teaching with him at the University of California, Berkeley. What was his experience? What did it teach him about translation? Contrast his experience with that of Ezra Pound, whom he discusses as the translator of a Chinese poem, "A River-Merchant's Wife." Why does Hass say that translation makes the world accessible to us but at the same time is impossible?

**AS YOU READ** Listen for what seems conversational here, even prosaic, and for what makes this "meditation" inescapably a poem.

# Meditation at Lagunitas

(1979)

All the new thinking is about loss.
In this it resembles all the old thinking.
The idea, for example, that each particular erases
the luminous clarity of a general idea. That the clown-
faced woodpecker probing the dead sculpted trunk
of that black birch is, by his presence,
some tragic falling off from a first world
of undivided light. Or the other notion that,
because there is in this world no one thing
to which the bramble of *blackberry* corresponds,
a word is elegy to what it signifies.
We talked about it late last night and in the voice
of my friend, there was a thin wire of grief, a tone
almost querulous. After a while I understood that,
talking this way, everything dissolves: *justice,*
*pine, hair, woman, you* and *I.* There was a woman
I made love to and I remembered how, holding
her small shoulders in my hands sometimes,
I felt a violent wonder at her presence
like a thirst for salt, for my childhood river
with its island willows, silly music from the pleasure boat,
muddy places where we caught the little orange-silver fish
called *pumpkinseed.* It hardly had to do with her.
Longing, we say, because desire is full
of endless distances. I must have been the same to her.
But I remember so much, the way her hands dismantled bread,
the thing her father said that hurt her, what
she dreamed. There are moments when the body is as numinous
as words, days that are the good flesh continuing.
Such tenderness, those afternoons and evenings,
saying *blackberry, blackberry, blackberry.*

# Writing from Reading

### Summarize

1 Try to describe the situation here—the setting, the speaker, the intended audience. Where is "Lagunitas," for example, and what does it have to do with the text that follows?

2 In a dictionary, look up the word *numinous* and relate it to the experience described here.

### Analyze Craft

3 Do you think these choices of setting, speaker, and audience were conscious and premeditated or sheer instinct on the part of the poet, or perhaps a combination of all these?

### Analyze Voice

4 Do the speaker's memories of a past love remind you of vivid memories in your own life? What language in the poem reminds you of these memories?

5 Why do you think the details remain in the speaker's mind?

### Synthesize Summary and Analysis

6 What does the poet mean by "a word is elegy to what it signifies"? And what does he mean by "the body is numinous as words"?

### Interpret the Poem

7 Discuss the "tenderness" of the repeated final word. Is this finally a poem about loss—as in the opening assertion—or gain?

## OPEN FORM POETRY

The presence of formal meter in a poem gives us rhythmic intervals we perceive much like a steady musical beat. While this meter may sometimes vary (allowing a poet flexibility of diction, voice, and meaning), it stays generally consistent over the course of a poem. Closed, metrical forms like this dominated poetry in English for hundreds of years. However, such formality was never the whole story; there have always been what we call "open forms" as well. While we may associate open form poetry with contemporary poets, we can see it as early as the King James Bible's Psalms and "Song of Songs," in which English translators attempted to evoke the text's original Hebrew cadences. The "Song of Songs" is often regarded as an allegorical series of love poems between humanity and God, as in these joyful lines depicting the beginning of spring (the "turtle" described in the last line is a translation of "turtle dove"):

*My beloved spake, and said unto me, Rise up, my love,*
*my fair one, and come away.*
*For, lo, the winter is past, the rain is over and gone;*
*The flowers appear on the earth; the time of the singing*
*of birds is come,*
*and the voice of the turtle is heard in our land. . . .*

In open form poetry, meter, stanza arrangement, and set rhyme schemes are never completely abandoned, but the poet feels less obligated to employ those techniques as if they were strict rules. Instead, the practitioner takes sounds and shape not from a preset formal pattern of meter and rhyme, but from the writer's own individual preference—a preference that might well vary from day to day and subject to subject, as well as line by line. Between the late nineteenth and early twentieth centuries, many poets began to reject the formal obligations that had long been a part of the genre. By this design, they allowed the poetic line (its extent, internal sounds, images, pauses, and breaks) to help shape the form.

> "It's no accident that all the great books—the great religious books, the Bible, the Koran, the Sutras—are composed in poetry. So, poetry I think is our original primal language, and I think that when we find ourselves in situations of distress or novelty, we automatically start thinking that way and expressing ourselves that way."
>
> Conversation with Al Young

## *VERS LIBRE,* FREE VERSE, AND OPEN FORM

The term *open form* was coined to avoid the misleading connotations of the other commonly used term for unmetered poetry, "free verse." "Free verse" is derived from the designation *vers libre,* a school of seventeenth-century French poetry (*vers libre* means "free verse" in French). "Open form" avoids the conclusion that poetry of this kind is completely ungoverned or unconcerned with craft. While skilled free verse poets may not always strictly observe rules of rhythm and rhyme, they are careful to fashion their lines with conscious attention to form, sound, and shape.

The New York–born poet Walt Whitman is often credited with inaugurating the widespread use of free verse in modern and contemporary poetry. His volume of poems *Leaves of Grass,* first published in 1855, took imaginative liberties with line length, rhyme, repetition, and word choice. No one had ever heard poems quite like Whitman's before. In this brief opening section from "Song of Myself," one of the poems in *Leaves of Grass,* note the surprising liberties Whitman takes with his language, his line length, his direct address to "you" the reader, and the fresh sound of his voice.

# Walt Whitman (1819–1892)

For a brief biography of Walt Whitman, see chapter 18.

**AS YOU READ** Imagine yourself in a shared space with Whitman—the "you" to whom the "I" speaks. He's embarked on a long monologue. What might be your response?

# Song of Myself (1855)

I Celebrate myself, and sing myself,
And what I assume you shall assume,
For every atom belonging to me as good belongs to you.

I loafe and invite my soul,
I lean and loafe at my ease observing a spear of summer grass.

My tongue, every atom of my blood, form'd from this soil, this air,
Born here of parents born here from parents the same, and their parents the same,
I, now thirty-seven years old in perfect health begin,
Hoping to cease not till death.

Creeds and schools in abeyance,
Retiring back a while sufficed at what they are, but never forgotten,
I harbor for good or bad, I permit to speak at every hazard,
Nature without check with original energy.

# Writing from Reading

### Summarize

**1** It's hard to summarize these lines, because they begin a very long poem indeed. How do they set the stage?

### Analyze Craft

**2** What do you notice about the line length here—its random nature as opposed to patterns? What does that tell you about freedom and "original energy"?

### Analyze Voice

**3** As it happens, Whitman's hope—that we would "cease not till death"—was realized; he worked at this poem for all his long life. What is modest or boastful about a phrase like "Born here of parents born here from parents the same, and their parents the same . . ."?

### Synthesize Summary and Analysis

**4** What sort of claims for art and life does the poet make here, and how do they seem "revolutionary"?

### Interpret the Poem

**5** Why does the poet claim that he will let "Nature without check" do the speaking?

Walt Whitman is, as suggested above, a major presence in the world of American letters. Poets often tip their caps to the work of other poets—as in Anthony Hecht's response to Matthew Arnold's "Dover Beach" (see chapter 18). In the For Review and Further Study section of this chapter, the poet Allen Ginsberg remembers his great predecessor while shopping in California, a state Whitman never visited.

Here a contemporary American Indian author responds to the white-bearded ghost of an artist he, too, can treasure as an ancestor, even though there's something almost comic in the juxtaposition of basketball to Whitman's Civil War. In "Defending Walt Whitman," Sherman Alexie employs a number of formal techniques to tell a brief allegorical story about poetry and sport. Alexie writes with a design dictated by image and the emotions generated by the occasion of the poem: basketball and the life of young American Indian boys. Yet the nation's first major "free" poet takes center stage in his title. There is, with Whitman's "presence" in the poem, an awareness of tradition even while the artist struggles to report on change. When Alexie claims, about Whitman, that "this game belongs to him," he's celebrating poetry as well.

## Sherman Alexie (b. 1966)

Sherman Alexie grew up on the Spokane Indian Reservation in Washington (he is of Spokane/Coeur d'Alene descent). He attended college with the goal of becoming a doctor. His career as a poet took off shortly after graduation; by 1993, he had received two major fellowships and published two books of poetry. Next, he turned to short stories with *The Lone Ranger and Tonto Fistfight in Heaven* (1993) and then produced a novel, *Reservation Blues* (1995). He also wrote the screenplay for the award-winning, independently produced film *Smoke Signals* (1998). His signature blend of irony, humor, cynicism, and critique of modern Native American life has won him many honors including the PEN/Hemingway award, the PEN/Malamud award, and the Pushcart Prize. In 2007, he received the National Book Award for Young People's Literature with *The Absolutely True Diary of a Part-Time Indian*. He calls Seattle home.

**AS YOU READ** Think of this as a kind of conversation between the contemporary and the ancestral, the living and the dead.

# Defending Walt Whitman (1996)

Basketball is like this for young Indian boys, all arms and legs
and serious stomach muscles. Every body is brown!
These are the twentieth-century warriors who will never kill,
although a few sat quietly in the deserts of Kuwait,
waiting for orders to do something, do something.

God, there is nothing as beautiful as a jump shot
on a reservation summer basketball court
where the ball is moist with sweat
and makes a sound when it swishes through the net
that causes Walt Whitman to weep because it is so perfect.

There are veterans of foreign wars here,
whose bodies are still dominated
by collarbones and knees, whose bodies still respond
in the ways that bodies are supposed to respond when we are young.
Every body is brown! Look there, that boy can run
up and down this court forever. He can leap for a rebound
with his back arched like a salmon, all meat and bone
synchronized, magnetic, as if the court were a river,
as if the rim were a dam, as if the air were a ladder
leading the Indian boy toward home.

Some of the Indian boys still wear their military haircuts
while a few have let their hair grow back.
It will never be the same as it was before!
One Indian boy has never cut his hair, not once, and he braids it
into wild patterns that do not measure anything.
He is just a boy with too much time on his hands.
Look at him. He wants to play this game in bare feet.

God, the sun is so bright! There is no place like this.
Walt Whitman stretches his calf muscles
on the sidelines. He has the next game.
His huge beard is ridiculous on the reservation.
Some body throws a crazy pass and Walt Whitman catches it with quick hands.
He brings the ball close to his nose
and breathes in all of its smells: leather, brown skin, sweat, black hair,
burning oil, twisted ankle, long drink of warm water,
gunpowder, pine tree. Walt Whitman squeezes the ball tightly.
He wants to run. He hardly has the patience to wait for his turn.
"What's the score?" he asks. He asks, "What's the score?"

Basketball is like this for Walt Whitman. He watches these Indian boys
as if they were the last bodies on earth. Every body is brown!
Walt Whitman shakes because he believes in God.
Walt Whitman dreams of the Indian boy who will defend him,
trapping him in the corner, all flailing arms and legs
and legendary stomach muscles. Walt Whitman shakes
because he believes in God. Walt Whitman dreams
of the first jump shot he will take, the ball arcing clumsily
from his fingers, striking the rim so hard that it sparks.
Walt Whitman shakes because he believes in God.
Walt Whitman closes his eyes. He is a small man and his beard
is ludicrous on the reservation, absolutely insane.
His beard makes the Indian boys righteously laugh. His beard frightens
the smallest Indian boys. His beard tickles the skin
of the Indian boys who dribble past him. His beard, his beard!

God, there is beauty in every body. Walt Whitman stands
at center court while the Indian boys run from basket to basket.
Walt Whitman cannot tell the difference between
offense and defense. He does not care if he touches the ball.
Half of the Indian boys wear T-shirts damp with sweat
and the other half are bareback, skin slick and shiny.
There is no place like this. Walt Whitman smiles.
Walt Whitman shakes. This game belongs to him.

# Writing from Reading

## Summarize

1 Think of this poem as a discussion of the impact of the past. What has changed; what stays the same?

## Analyze Craft

2 Why do you think Alexie repeats certain phrases and words?

## Analyze Voice

3 How does the language of this poem compare to language in poems in this book by Walt Whitman himself? "Defending" is something a basketball player must do, and it means "standing up for" or "taking the side of" as well. How would you describe the diction and the poet's tone?

## Synthesize Summary and Analysis

4 Whitman wrote at length about the Civil War; Alexie here refers to "the deserts of Kuwait" and the first Gulf War. How does he treat his "warriors," and what does he respect?

## Interpret the Poem

5 Discuss the imaginary presence in this poem of Walt Whitman attending a pickup basketball game on an American Indian reservation. What connections do you think Alexie wants to make here among Whitman, Native Americans, basketball, and war?

Modern writers have disagreed on the place of open form poetry in the wider arena of English and American literature. Many believe open form poetry reflects a democratic spirit, an opportunity to use the musical potential of the poetic line with greater fulfillment and flexibility. Others think that poetry unconcerned with rhythmic structure is simply amateurish. Robert Frost famously compared the writing of free verse poetry to a game of tennis with no net.

It is hard to disagree that the prevalence of open form poetry has helped facilitate a lot of bland, lightweight poems and that it even perpetuates the misconception that "anything can be a poem." As British novelist A. S. Byatt writes, "Free verse has come to represent democracy, equal opportunity, and self-expression. But in bulk and unaware of the forms from which it has been freed . . . it can be extremely depressing."

Practitioners of open form poetry insist that a successful poem "finds" a form using the poet's instinct and intent, and that the absence of iambic pentameter or end

> "You know, free verse to me . . . is nothing less than . . . a discovery, and we haven't even got to the bottom of it yet. We're only scratching the surface because ultimately free verse is a form of writing in which the poem is completely organized by instances of coincidence . . . stanzas are units of coincidence and lines become units of coincidence, and the whole poem becomes organized with that in mind. . . . It sounds simple, but it's a lot harder to do than one would think." Conversation with Li-Young Lee

rhyme (or other traditional devices) does not condemn a poem to pointlessness. In other words, when you write a poem you have definitely created a form of some kind, and that form in turn creates impressions in the reader. Of this aspect of composition, poet C. D. Wright says, "Poetry without form is a fiction. But that there is a freedom in words is the larger fact, and in poetry, where formal restrictions can bear down heavily, it is important to remember the cage is never locked."

Next a pair of open form poems by a pair of American masters—one dead, one still at work—demonstrate how supple the technique can be, and how personal. When e. e. cummings argues for the primacy of feeling and writes "who pays any attention / to the syntax of things," he's arguing, in effect, for the value of open form verse—breaking the rules of syntax in the subsequent phrase by leaving out the first-person pronoun that should "properly" be there before "will never wholly kiss you." And in this poem, certainly, "feeling is first."

# e. e. cummings (1894 –1962)

Born in Cambridge, Massachusetts, Edward Estlin Cummings earned both his undergraduate and graduate degrees from Harvard. Although at first he wrote poetry modeled after the pre-Raphaelites and other classical forms, he soon developed his own innovative style that focused on the poem's appearance on the page, a lack of capitalization, and a free, liberal use of words (he often turned verbs into nouns and vice versa). His poems appear complex and are pleasing orally, yet the ideas behind them are often simple messages against conformity and in favor of love. Consistent with his bohemian spirit, e. e. cummings made a career of being an artist, both in poetry and in drawing/painting. In addition to his poetry collections, such as *Tulips and Chimneys* (1923), e. e. cummings wrote a series of lectures that he delivered at Harvard, though by his request they were called "nonlectures" and later published as *Six Nonlectures* (1953).

**AS YOU READ** **Place the poem somewhere between the loosest of sonnets and the most restricted free verse.**

## since feeling is first (1926)

since feeling is first
who pays any attention
to the syntax of things
will never wholly kiss you;

wholly to be a fool
while Spring is in the world

my blood approves,
and kisses are a far better fate
than wisdom
lady i swear by all flowers.    Don't cry
—the best gesture of my brain is less than
your eyelids' flutter which says

we are for each other:then
laugh,leaning back in my arms
for life's not a paragraph

And death i think is no parenthesis

# Writing from Reading

### Summarize

1 Do you agree or disagree with the assessment that this is a love poem, said in modern language, by an old-fashioned soul? Why?

### Analyze Craft

2 What controls the progress of the poem? Is it the unfolding of the anecdote of the kiss or the deeply ingrained sense of form that the poet never really wholly disregards?

### Analyze Voice

3 The pun-making poet—wholly= holy—is also a fun-making poet. What is the link between free verse in this instance and the freeing of the poet's sense of humor?

### Synthesize Summary and Analysis

4 The poet attempts to create an order (syntax) based on feelings, and the result is either delightful or frivolous. Which do you find it to be?

### Interpret the Poem

5 What is the role in this poem of instinct versus intellect?

# Galway Kinnell (b. 1927)

Born in Providence, Rhode Island, Galway Kinnell was educated at Princeton and the University of Rochester. In addition to serving in the U.S. Navy, Kinnell also worked for the Congress of Racial Equality during the civil rights movement. His poetry, including his book-length poem on the Vietnam War, *The Book of Nightmares* (1971), demonstrates a deep awareness of the nation's life. More often, however, Kinnell's poetry shows a consciousness of the natural world and of death, but in such a way that it is energetic rather than filled with despair. Kinnell has taught at many universities, and his *Selected Poems* (1980) won both the Pulitzer Prize and the National Book Award.

**AS YOU READ** **Think about how individual choices of rhythm, language, sound, pauses, line length, and endings help this piece become more than sentences of prose cut into shorter lines.**

**TIP**

**FOR INTERACTIVE READING . . .** Look for repetitions of words and make note of them.

# After Making Love We Hear Footsteps (1980)

For I can snore like a bullhorn
or play loud music
or sit up talking with any reasonably sober Irishman
and Fergus will only sink deeper
into his dreamless sleep, which goes by all in one flash,
but let there be that heavy breathing
or a stifled come-cry anywhere in the house
and he will wrench himself awake
and make for it on the run—as now, we lie together,
after making love, quiet, touching along the length of our bodies,
familiar touch of the long-married,
and he appears—in his baseball pajamas, it happens,
the neck opening so small he has to screw them on—
and flops down between us and hugs us and snuggles himself to sleep,
his face gleaming with satisfaction at being this very child.

In the half darkness we look at each other
and smile
and touch arms across this little, startlingly muscled body—
this one whom habit of memory propels to the ground of his making,
sleeper only the mortal sounds can sing awake,
this blessing love gives again into our arms.

# Writing from Reading

### Summarize

1 Why is this poem in two stanzas? How does the second respond to the first?

### Analyze Craft

2 Are there rhymes in this poem? Do they help connect the elements contained?

3 How many sentences make up this poem? Why do you think Kinnell chooses to write so few separate sentences in a poem with so many lines?

### Analyze Voice

4 How would you describe the speaker's attitude toward his child?

### Synthesize Summary and Analysis

5 Open form poets often consider the line the principal unit of sense and meaning. How do individual lines in the poem help create a sense of order or form?

### Interpret the Poem

6 What does the poet mean by "this one whom habit of memory propels to the ground of his making," and can you read this poem as a text about the making of poetry itself?

In the spirit of the "free" and "open" possibilities of contemporary poetry, C. K. Williams creates a narrative with lines much longer than those of most unmetered verse. "Tar" conveys deep emotion by means of a story line or set of anecdotes (incidents) composed in very long lines. "Three Mile Island" refers to the location of a nuclear plant in Pennsylvania and a meltdown there in 1979.

# C. K. Williams (b. 1936)

Born in Newark, New Jersey, Charles Kenneth Williams turned to poetry at age nineteen, after he had finished his required English courses at the University of Pennsylvania, where he earned his degree. Williams's ten books of poetry—including the Pulitzer Prize–winning *Repair* (1999) and the National Book Award–winning *The Singing* (2003)—emphasize the pain of human existence in lines that are unconventionally long. The length of his lines is reminiscent of Whitman, though he wholly lacks Whitman's optimism. Williams was a group therapist for troubled adolescents in Philadelphia, edited materials in psychiatry and architecture, and is currently at Princeton University, continuing an academic career that has included Columbia, George Mason, and Drexel Universities.

**AS YOU READ** **Pay attention to the line breaks. They depend on a visual cue. It would have been simple enough to keep words like "atmosphere" or "Susquehanna" or "clinging" as single words, not hyphenated ones, but Williams calls our attention to the way lines fuse or break apart. That hurtling description of risk and wreckage enters the narrative at least in part by way of its line length; there's no chance to pause for breath.**

TIP

**FOR INTERACTIVE READING . . .** Look up the word *tar* in a dictionary and think about how this word connects the national event in the poem with the personal housework that is going on.

# Tar (1983)

The first morning of Three Mile Island: those first disquieting, uncertain, mystifying hours.
All morning a crew of workmen have been tearing the old decrepit roof off our building,
and all morning, trying to distract myself, I've been wandering out to watch them
as they hack away the leaden layers of asbestos paper and disassemble the disintegrating drains.
After half a night of listening to the news, wondering how to know a hundred miles downwind
if and when to make a run for it and where, then a coming bolt awake at seven
when the roofers we've been waiting for since winter sent their ladders shrieking up our wall,
we still know less than nothing: the utility company continues making little of the accident,
the slick federal spokesmen still have their evasions in some semblance of order.
Surely we suspect now we're being lied to, but in the meantime, there are the roofers,
setting winch-frames, sledging rounds of tar apart, and there I am, on the curb across, gawking.

I never realized what brutal work it is, how matter-of-factly and harrowingly dangerous.
The ladders flex and quiver, things skid from the edge, the materials are bulky and recalcitrant.
When the rusty, antique nails are levered out, their heads pull off; the under-roofing crumbles.
Even the battered little furnace, roaring along as patient as a donkey, chokes and clogs,
a dense, malignant smoke shoots up, someone has to fiddle with a cock, then hammer it,
before the gush and stench will deintensify, the dark, Dantean broth wearily subside.
In its crucible, the stuff looks bland, like licorice, spill it, though, on your boots or coveralls,
it sears, and everything is permeated with it, the furnace gunked with burst and half-burst bubbles,
the men themselves so completely slashed and mucked they seem almost from another realm, like trolls.
When they take their break, they leave their brooms standing at attention in the asphalt pails,
work gloves clinging like Brer Rabbit to the bitten shafts, and they slouch along the precipitous lip,
the enormous sky behind them, the heavy noontime air alive with shimmers and mirages.

Sometime in the afternoon I had to go inside: the advent of our vigil was upon us.
However much we didn't want to, however little we would do about it, we'd understood:
we were going to perish of all this, if not now, then soon, if not soon, then someday.
Someday, some final generation, hysterically aswarm beneath an atmosphere as unrelenting as rock,
would rue us all, anathematize our earthly comforts, curse our surfeits and submissions.
I think I know, though I might rather not, why my roofers stay so clear to me and why the rest,
the terror of that time, the reflexive disbelief and distancing, all we should hold on to, dims so.
I remember the president in his absurd protective booties, looking absolutely unafraid, the fool.
I remember a woman on the front page glaring across the misty Susquehanna at those looming stacks.
But, more vividly, the men, silvered with glitter from the shingles, clinging like starlings beneath the eaves.
Even the leftover carats of tar in the gutter, so black they seemed to suck the light out of the air.
By nightfall kids had come across them: every sidewalk on the block was scribbled with obscenities and hearts.

# Writing from Reading

## Summarize

1 An "occasional" poem takes a specific event or date as its subject. What is the occasion for this poem?

## Analyze Craft

2 Compare the line length here with the lines in Walt Whitman's "Song of Myself." This poem is not, of course, a celebration, but what effect does choosing long lines have in this poem?

3 Sometimes the language in "Tar" feels very plainspoken and conversational; at other times it sounds elevated and more traditionally poetic. Where do these changes happen? What kind of events or images do they describe? What is their significance?

## Analyze Voice

4 What do you think the poet means by "I think I know, though I might rather not" or "I remember"? Do these lines set a tone for this poem? What other lines can you point to that create the poem's tone?

## Synthesize Summary and Analysis

5 The poem takes place amid a real-life national crisis. What is the relationship of the event at Three Mile Island and Williams's description of the housework going on in his building?

## Interpret the Poem

6 As this is a poem of political and social commentary, is it surprising that these lines should end as they do, and in what ways does "the terror of that time" transform itself into graffiti—as in "obscenities and hearts"?

The poet Sharon Olds describes internal wreckage, though she, too, deals with "obscenities and hearts." Here, too, the language is that of everyday discourse, the experience described a common one—but shot through with the power of erotic and psychological encounter.

# Sharon Olds (b. 1942)

Born in California, Sharon Olds received a B.A. from Stanford University and a Ph.D. from Columbia University. Her award-winning poetry collections include *The Dead and the Living* (1983), which won the National Book Critics Circle Award, and *The Father* (1992), which was shortlisted for the T. S. Eliot Prize. A poet in the confessional tradition of poets such as Anne Sexton and Sylvia Plath—that is, poetry that takes the poet's personal life as its subject—Olds writes on themes of the body, family life, sex, and violence. She currently teaches at New York University and has been involved as a founder and teacher of the creative writing program for the physically disabled at Goldwater Hospital in New York City.

**AS YOU READ** Ask yourself if this is a poem about morality or whether it has another subject.

# Sex without Love (1984)

How do they do it, the ones who make love
without love? Beautiful as dancers,
gliding over each other like ice-skaters
over the ice, fingers hooked
inside each other's bodies, faces
red as steak, wine, wet as the
children at birth whose mothers are going to
give them away. How do they come to the
come to the    come to the    God    come to the
still waters, and not love
the one who came there with them, light
rising slowly as steam off their joined
skin? These are the true religious,
the purists, the pros, the ones who will not
accept a false Messiah, love the
priest instead of the God. They do not
mistake the lover for their own pleasure,
they are like great runners: they know they are alone
with the road surface, the cold, the wind,
the fit of their shoes, their over-all cardio-
vascular health—just factors, like the partner
in the bed, and not the truth, which is the
single body alone in the universe
against its own best time.

# Writing from Reading

### Summarize

1 The poet meditates on the question of sex and love. What conclusion does the speaker in the poem draw about this realationship?

### Analyze Craft

2 Discuss the poem's lineation and lack of stanza breaks. Why do you think Olds makes these choices?

3 What other poetic techniques suggest this poem's open form style has specific intentions?

### Analyze Voice

4 The poem incorporates many similes. How do they help express the speaker's attitude toward the subject matter?

### Synthesize Summary and Analysis

5 The poet takes up a question important to moralists and romantics alike. With whom does she seem to stand?

### Interpret the Poem

6 What does the poem imply about the relation of love and sex in the context of our lives? Can we ever feel as though we are together with someone and not terribly alone?

# Robert Hass (b. 1941)

For a brief biography of Robert Hass, see the beginning of this chapter.

## Dragonflies Mating (1996)

I

The people who lived here before us
also loved these high mountain meadows on summer mornings.
They made their way up here in easy stages
when heat began to dry the valleys out,
following the berry harvest probably and the pine buds:
climbing and making camp and gathering,
then breaking camp and climbing and making camp and gathering.
A few miles a day. They sent out the children
to dig up bulbs of the mariposa lilies that they liked to roast
at night by the fire where they sat talking about how this year
was different from last year. Told stories,
knew where they were on earth from the names,
owl moon, bear moon, gooseberry moon.

II

Jaime de Angulo (1934) was talking to a Channel Island Indian
in a Santa Barbara bar. You tell me how your people said
the world was made. Well, the guy said, Coyote was on the mountain
and he had to pee. Wait a minute, Jaime said,
I was talking to a Pomo the other day and he said
Red Fox made the world. They say Red Fox, the guy shrugged,
we say Coyote. So, he had to pee
and he didn't want to drown anybody, so he turned toward the place
where the ocean would be. Wait a minute, Jaime said,
if there were no people yet, how could he drown anybody?
The Channelleño got a funny look on his face. You know,
he said, when I was a kid, I wondered about that,
and I asked my father. We were living up toward Santa Ynez.
He was sitting on a bench in the yard shaving down fence posts
with an ax, and I said, how come Coyote was worried about people
when he had to pee and there were no people? The guy laughed.
And my old man looked up at me with this funny smile
and said, You know, when I was a kid, I wondered about that.

III

Thinking about that story just now, early morning heat,
first day in the mountains, I remembered stories about sick Indians
and—in the same thought—standing on the free throw line.

St. Raphael's parish, where the northern-most of the missions
had been, was founded as a hospital, was named for the angel
in the scriptures who healed the blind man with a fish

he laid across his eyes—I wouldn't mind being that age again,
hearing those stories, eyes turned upward toward the young nun
in her white, fresh-smelling, immaculately laundered robes.—

The Franciscan priests who brought their faith in God
across the Atlantic, brought with the baroque statues and metalwork
crosses
and elaborately embroidered cloaks, influenza and syphilis and the
coughing disease.

Which is why we settled an almost empty California.
There were drawings in the mission museum of the long, dark wards
full of small brown people, wasted, coughing into blankets,

the saintly Franciscan fathers moving patiently among them.
It would, Sister Marietta said, have broken your hearts to see it.
They meant so well, she said, and such a terrible thing

came here with their love. And I remembered how I hated it
after school—because I loved basketball practice more than anything
on earth—that I never knew if my mother was going to show up

well into one of those weeks of drinking she disappeared into,
and humiliate me in front of my classmates with her bright, confident
eyes,
and slurred, though carefully pronounced words, and the appalling

impromptu sets of mismatched clothes she was given to
when she had the dim idea of making a good impression in that state.
Sometimes from the gym floor with its sweet, heady smell of varnish

I'd see her in the entryway looking for me, and I'd bounce
the ball two or three times, study the orange rim as if it were,
which it was, the true level of the world, the one sure thing

the power in my hands could summon. I'd bounce the ball
once more, feel the grain of the leather in my fingertips and shoot.
It was a perfect thing; it was almost like killing her.

IV

When we say "mother" in poems,
we usually mean some woman in her late twenties
or early thirties trying to raise a child.

We use this particular noun
to secure the pathos of the child's point of view
and to hold her responsible.

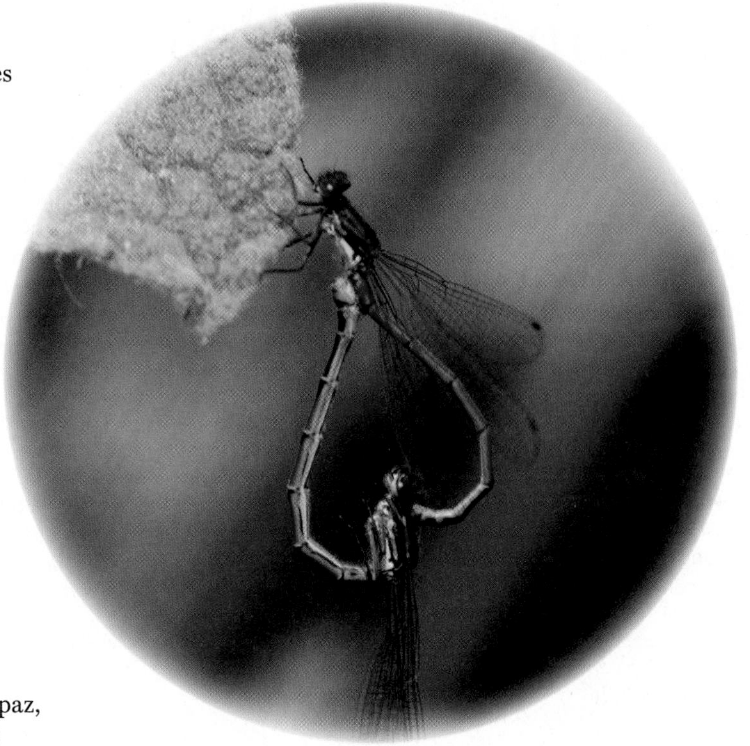

V

If you're afraid now?
Fear is a teacher.
Sometimes you thought that
Nothing could reach her,
Nothing can reach you.
Wouldn't you rather
sit by the river, sit
On the dead bank,
Deader than winter,
Where all the roots gape?

VI

This morning in the early sun,
steam rising from the pond the color of smoky topaz,
a pair of delicate, copper-red, needle-fine insects
are mating in the unopened crown of a Shasta daisy
just outside your door. The green flowerheads look like wombs
or the upright, supplicant bulbs of a vegetal pre-erection.
The insect lovers seem to be transferring the cosmos into each other
by attaching at the tail, holding utterly still, and quivering intently.

I think (on what evidence?) that they are different from us.
That they mate and are done with mating.
They don't carry all this half-mated longing up out of childhood
and then go looking for it everywhere.
And so, I think, they can't wound each other the way we do.
They don't go through life dizzy or groggy with their hunger,
kill with it, smear it on everything, though it is perhaps also true
that nothing happens to them quite like what happens to us
when the blue-backed swallow dips swiftly toward the green pond
and the pond's green-and-blue reflected swallow marries it a moment
in the reflected sky and the heart goes out to the end of the rope
it has been throwing into abyss after abyss, and a singing shimmers
from every color the morning has risen into.

My insect instructors have stilled, they are probably stuck together
in some bliss and minute pulse of after-longing
evolution worked out to suck the last juice of the world
into the receiver body. They can't separate probably
until it is done.

# Writing from Reading

### Summarize

**1** The poet arrives at a certain location and catches sight of the dragonflies. What happens next? Where do his thoughts take him? Break down each subsequent numbered part and paraphrase it.

### Analyze Craft

**2** The poet employs a number of techniques, including several from prose narrative, to move his poem along. What effect does he create using anecdote and dialogue?

**3** As we have seen elsewhere, Robert Hass is very interested in—and a translator of—the brief Japanese form of haiku. Yet this is a long and nontraditional poem, quite different in form and content from a poem of only seventeen syllables. What similarities do you find between the attitudes Hass and the haiku poets express?

### Analyze Voice

**4** "Fear is a teacher." What other emotion, besides fear, does the poet feel along with the calm he conveys?

### Synthesize Summary and Analysis

**5** The poet observes the natural world and looks into himself as well, touching on local and personal history. Have you encountered other poets who do this? Who? Is there a tradition into which Hass's poem seems to fall?

### Interpret the Poem

**6** What wisdom for human behavior and life does the poet find in the mating habits of these insects?

## VISUAL POETRY

Poets writing outside of fixed forms occasionally decide to shape their lines into a recognizable picture. **Visual** (or **concrete**) **poetry** is poetry written in the shape of something it describes. In his poem "Easter Wings," George Herbert works within a noticeable rhyme scheme (*ababacdcdc*) and metric regularity, but he arranges the lines in an unconventional form. His verse is not "free," but neither is it organized by a previous tradition; no series of earlier poems has this particular *shape.*

# George Herbert (1593–1633)

Born into a prominent Welsh family, George Herbert was one of ten children, all of whom his mother raised alone after their father's early death. Educated at Trinity College, Cambridge, Herbert held the post of public orator, or spokesman, for the university. Although his election to Parliament suggested a political career, he became a minister to a rural parish in 1630, where he served until his death from consumption. Herbert's reputation as a poet rests solely on one volume, *The Temple* (1633), published posthumously; the rest of his poetry has been lost. *The Temple,* however, shows a great range, not only in poetic style—from lengthy poems to short lyrics, shape poems, acrostics, and sonnets—but also in feeling, as Herbert concerned himself with his relationship to God.

**AS YOU READ** Go back and forth between the lines and a glance at the shape.

# Easter Wings (1633)

Lord, who createdst man in wealth and store,
Though foolishly he lost the same,
Decaying more and more,
Till he became
Most poor:
With thee
O let me rise
As larks, harmoniously,
And sing this day thy victories:
Then shall the fall further the flight in me.
My tender age in sorrow did begin:
And still with sicknesses and shame
Thou didst so punish sin,
That I became
Most thin.
With thee
Let me combine
And feel this day thy victory
For, if I imp my wing on thine,
Affliction shall advance the flight in me.

# Writing from Reading

### Summarize

**1** This poem celebrates the resurrection of Jesus Christ on Easter, as described in the New Testament. In what ways is this poem a prayer?

### Analyze Craft

**2** How does the shape reflect the subject of the poem?

**3** Which places here in the poem's winged form reflect or combine with specific syntax or diction choices? What is the effect?

### Analyze Voice

**4** Does the form of prayerful speech give the sound of the poem a shape?

### Synthesize Summary and Analysis

**5** The poet seeks to give physical as well as aural shape to his words. Does this seem appropriate—or a playful trick?

### Interpret the Poem

**6** Why might Herbert have viewed poetry and prayer as similar activities? How do you distinguish between this poem and a prayer?

"Easter Wings" is quite a different entity when read aloud than when looked at in silence. And because he knew his work would be physically published, Herbert wrote with the assumption that the poem would be viewed. This is an assumption that the ancient Greek poet Homer or the *Beowulf* poet, for example, could not have made. The later poet's audience would *view* as well as *listen to* the verse, and the visual component matters at least as much as how the poem sounds.

# John Hollander (b. 1929)

Scholar and poet John Hollander was born in New York City, educated at Columbia University and Indiana University, and taught for decades at Yale. His first collection of poetry, *A Crackling of Thorns* (1958), won the Yale Series of Younger Poets Award, launching a career that would yield seventeen books of poetry, eight well-respected books of literary criticism, and more than twenty edited works. Hollander's love of music, which led him to write liner notes for albums to support himself between his master's degree and Ph.D., resulted in his writing opera librettos and lyrics for composers including Milton Babbitt and George Perle.

**AS YOU READ** **Follow the shape, but also ponder the meaning below the surface of the shape.**

## Swan and Shadow

**(1969)**

Dusk
Above the
water hang the
loud
flies
Here
O so
gray
then
What          A pale signal will appear
When          Soon before its shadow fades
Where          Here in this pool of opened eye
In us          No Upon us As at the very edges
of where we take shape in the dark air
this object bares its image awakening
ripples of recognition that will
brush darkness up into light
even after this bird this hour both drift by atop the perfect sad instant now
already passing out of sight
toward yet-untroubled reflection
this image bears its object darkening
into memorial shades Scattered bits of
light          No of water Or something across
water          Breaking up No Being regathered
soon          Yet by then a swan will have
gone          Yes out of mind into what
vast
pale
hush
of a
place
past
sudden dark as
if a swan
sang

# Writing from Reading

### Summarize

1 How is what happens in the image of the top swan reflected in the image of the bottom swan?

### Analyze Craft

2 Discuss how the poem's capitalization, lack of punctuation, and syntax relate to (or contrast with) the clear shape of the poem visually. Do these elements emerge out of the necessity of rendering a clear image, or do they serve other purposes?

3 Why the image of a swan? Where else have you seen it in myth and poetry?

### Analyze Voice

4 Is there anything in the way the poet shapes the poem that might make for confusion if it were read aloud?

### Synthesize Summary and Analysis

5 Discuss Hollander's combination of visual representation and language. What aspects of the poem strike you as particularly interesting or important? Does it hold together on its own as an interesting poem or require the visual form to complete it?

6 Compare the language and tone in the "swan" section of the poem versus the "shadow" section of the poem. Does the poem acknowledge a shift between the image and the image's shadow?

### Interpret the Poem

7 Our lives in time, our own ephemeral images—how does the poem speak to such questions?

# Chen Li (b. 1954)

A Taiwanese poet, Chen Li has contributed to Taiwan's letters both his original work and his translations—in collaboration with his wife Chan Fen-ling—of poets including Pablo Neruda and Seamus Heaney. Li has gone through several stages in his own poetry, first taking up Modernist technique, then demonstrating political and social consciousness, and finally broadening to an eclectic mix of subject matter. Li has presented his poetry at the Rotterdam International Poetry Festival. His work has further reached a wide audience with its English, French, Dutch, and Japanese translations. He teaches at the Hualien Girls Middle School and National Dong Hwa University.

**AS YOU READ** The translator of this poem noted the following about this untranslatable poem: The Chinese character 兵 (pronounced "bing") means "soldier." 乒 and 乓 (pronounced "ping" and "pong"), which look like one-legged soldiers, are two onomatopoeic words imitating sounds of collision or gunshots. The character 丘 (pronounced "chiou") means "hill."

# War Symphony (1995)

兵兵兵兵兵兵兵兵兵兵兵兵兵兵兵兵兵兵兵兵兵兵兵兵
兵兵兵兵兵兵兵兵兵兵兵兵兵兵兵兵兵兵兵兵兵兵兵兵
兵兵兵兵兵兵兵兵兵兵兵兵兵兵兵兵兵兵兵兵兵兵兵兵
兵兵兵兵兵兵兵兵兵兵兵兵兵兵兵兵兵兵兵兵兵兵兵兵
兵兵兵兵兵兵兵兵兵兵兵兵兵兵兵兵兵兵兵兵兵兵兵兵
兵兵兵兵兵兵兵兵兵兵兵兵兵兵兵兵兵兵兵兵兵兵兵兵
兵兵兵兵兵兵兵兵兵兵兵兵兵兵兵兵兵兵兵兵兵兵兵兵
兵兵兵兵兵兵兵兵兵兵兵兵兵兵兵兵兵兵兵兵兵兵兵兵
兵兵兵兵兵兵兵兵兵兵兵兵兵兵兵兵兵兵兵兵兵兵兵兵
兵兵兵兵兵兵兵兵兵兵兵兵兵兵兵兵兵兵兵兵兵兵兵兵
兵兵兵兵兵兵兵兵兵兵兵兵兵兵兵兵兵兵兵兵兵兵兵兵
兵兵兵兵兵兵兵兵兵兵兵兵兵兵兵兵兵兵兵兵兵兵兵兵
兵兵兵兵兵兵兵兵兵兵兵兵兵兵兵兵兵兵兵兵兵兵兵兵
兵兵兵兵兵兵兵兵兵兵兵兵兵兵兵兵兵兵兵兵兵兵兵兵
兵兵兵兵兵兵兵兵兵兵兵兵兵兵兵兵兵兵兵兵兵兵兵兵
兵兵兵兵兵兵兵兵兵兵兵兵兵兵兵兵兵兵兵兵兵兵兵兵

兵兵兵兵兵兵兵乒兵兵兵兵兵兵兵乓兵兵兵兵兵兵兵乒
兵兵兵乓兵兵乒兵兵兵乒乒兵兵乒乓兵兵乒乓兵兵乓乓
乒乒兵兵兵兵乓乓乓乓兵兵乒乒乓乓乒乓兵乓兵兵乓乓
兵乒兵乒乒乒乓乓兵兵乒乒乓乓乓乓乒乒乓乓乒兵乓乓
乒兵乓乓乒兵乓乓乒乒乓乓乒乒乓乓乒乒乓乓乒乒乓乓
乒乒乓乓乒乒乓乓乒乒乓乓乒乒乓乓乒乒乓乓乒乒乓乓
乒乒乓乓乒乒乓乓乒乒乓乓乒乒乓乓乒乒乓乓乒乒乓乓
乒乓乒乓乒乓乒乓乒乓乒乓乒乓乒乓乒乓乒乓乒乓乒乓
乒乓乒乓乒乒乓乓乒乓乒乓乒乒乓乓乒乓乒乓乒乒乓乓
乒乒乒乒乒乒乒乒乓乓乓乓乓乓乓乓乒乒　乒乒乒　乓
乓乓　乒乓乒乒　乒　乓　　乒乒　　　乒乒　　乓乓
乒乒　　乓乒　乒　乓　　乒　乓　乒乒乒　　乓　乒
乒乒　乓　乓乓　乒　　乒　　乓　　乒　乓　　乒
乒　　　　　　　乓乓　　　　　　　乓　　　　乒　乓
　乒　　　乓　　　　　乒　　　　　　乓　　　　乓
　　　　乒　　　　　　　　　　　　　　　　　乓

丘丘丘丘丘丘丘丘丘丘丘丘丘丘丘丘丘丘丘丘丘丘丘丘
丘丘丘丘丘丘丘丘丘丘丘丘丘丘丘丘丘丘丘丘丘丘丘丘
丘丘丘丘丘丘丘丘丘丘丘丘丘丘丘丘丘丘丘丘丘丘丘丘
丘丘丘丘丘丘丘丘丘丘丘丘丘丘丘丘丘丘丘丘丘丘丘丘
丘丘丘丘丘丘丘丘丘丘丘丘丘丘丘丘丘丘丘丘丘丘丘丘
丘丘丘丘丘丘丘丘丘丘丘丘丘丘丘丘丘丘丘丘丘丘丘丘
丘丘丘丘丘丘丘丘丘丘丘丘丘丘丘丘丘丘丘丘丘丘丘丘
丘丘丘丘丘丘丘丘丘丘丘丘丘丘丘丘丘丘丘丘丘丘丘丘
丘丘丘丘丘丘丘丘丘丘丘丘丘丘丘丘丘丘丘丘丘丘丘丘
丘丘丘丘丘丘丘丘丘丘丘丘丘丘丘丘丘丘丘丘丘丘丘丘
丘丘丘丘丘丘丘丘丘丘丘丘丘丘丘丘丘丘丘丘丘丘丘丘
丘丘丘丘丘丘丘丘丘丘丘丘丘丘丘丘丘丘丘丘丘丘丘丘
丘丘丘丘丘丘丘丘丘丘丘丘丘丘丘丘丘丘丘丘丘丘丘丘
丘丘丘丘丘丘丘丘丘丘丘丘丘丘丘丘丘丘丘丘丘丘丘丘
丘丘丘丘丘丘丘丘丘丘丘丘丘丘丘丘丘丘丘丘丘丘丘丘
丘丘丘丘丘丘丘丘丘丘丘丘丘丘丘丘丘丘丘丘丘丘丘丘

# Writing from Reading

## Summarize

1 Given the pictorial nature of the Chinese characters, the poem is telling a story as much through images as it is through sounds. What picture do you see here?

## Analyze Craft

2 Can you get the sense of this "sound" poem about battle without saying it out loud? What does it sound like when you read it aloud?

3 How does the noise of the back and forth—"ping . . . pong"—of saying the Chinese characters create a verbal dramatization of a scene of war?

4 Does the sound of "chiou" resolve the previous back and forth of sounds?

## Analyze Voice

5 Chinese is a highly musical language with the meaning of words often tied to the pitch at which the word is spoken. Given the differences between the tonal nature of the Chinese language and that of European languages, why might you find it difficult to hear the poet's voice without adding the sound of your own voice?

## Synthesize Summary and Analysis

6 The sound of the poem works to become the meaning of the poem. Where have you encountered this concept in your reading of other poems?

## Interpret the Poem

7 Would it be possible to make a poem such as this in English? Explain.

# Dylan Thomas (1914–1953)

For a brief biography of Dylan Thomas, see chapter 23.

**AS YOU READ** Allow your eye to guide you to meanings in the shape. Why does the "I" link the two parts?

# Vision and Prayer (1945)

Who
Are you
Who is born
In the next room
So loud to my own
That I can hear the womb
Opening and the dark run
Over the ghost and the dropped son
Behind the wall thin as a wren's bone?
In the birth bloody room unknown
To the burn and turn of time
And the heart print of man
Bows no baptism
But dark alone
Blessing on
The wild
Child.
I
Must lie
Still as stone
By the wren bone
Wall hearing the moan
Of the mother hidden
And the shadowed head of pain
Casting tomorrow like a thorn
And the midwives of miracle sing
Until the turbulent new born
Burns me his name and his flame
And the winged wall is torn
By his torrid crown
And the dark thrown
From his loin
To bright
Light.

# Writing from Reading

## Summarize

**1** The poet hears the sounds of his son's birth. How does he focus his attentiveness?

## Analyze Craft

**2** Why does the poet choose to give this particular shape to his lines? Does it enhance their meaning? Does it intensify emotion? What metaphors does he employ also to this end?

## Analyze Voice

**3** However odd the shape of the poem, does the voice seem normal for the occasion? Where does it veer toward a prayerful tone?

## Synthesize Summary and Analysis

**4** The particular shape works together with the feeling about the situation to create a particular effect. How is this related to the larger question of how form guides emotion in all poems?

## Interpret the Poem

**5** How does this event fit into the larger questions of life and death? What is the significance of the "I" on its own central line?

## PROSE POEMS

We may be accustomed to think that line breaks are required of poetry. Some writers, however, compose poems in dense, compact units of unbroken lines. **Prose poems** use the devices and imagery characteristic of traditionally lined poetry, but in compact units. French poets of the nineteenth century inaugurated the modern use of the form, and it has seen consistent usage in twentieth-century poetry in English as well. There's no clearly defined line separating the prose poem from the short short story. The mere fact that a poet intends a piece to be read and heard as a prose poem is reason enough to consider it so, as in this example from Carolyn Forché.

# Carolyn Forché (b. 1950)

For a brief biography of Carolyn Forché, see chapter 15.

**AS YOU READ** Picture the scene, as you would for a short story or a movie. Night, a Central American nation, a family dinner. An American poet and her companion are guests of the military man.

# The Colonel (1982)

What you have heard is true. I was in his house. His wife carried a tray of coffee and sugar. His daughter filed her nails, his son went out for the night. There were daily papers, pet dogs, a pistol on the cushion beside him. The moon swung bare on its black cord over the house. On the television was a cop show. It was in English. Broken bottles were embedded in the walls around the house to scoop the kneecaps from a man's legs or cut his hands to lace. On the windows there were gratings like those in liquor stores. We had dinner, rack of lamb, good wine, a gold bell was on the table for calling the maid. The maid brought green mangoes, salt, a type of bread. I was asked how I enjoyed the country. There was a brief commercial in Spanish. His wife took everything away. There was some talk then of how difficult it had become to govern. The parrot said hello on the terrace. The colonel told it to shut up, and pushed himself from the table. My friend said to me with his eyes: say nothing. The colonel returned with a sack used to bring groceries home. He spilled many human ears on the table. They were like dried peach halves. There is no other way to say this. He took one of them in his hands, shook it in our faces, dropped it into a water glass. It came alive there. I am tired of fooling around he said. As for the rights of anyone, tell your people they can go fuck themselves. He swept the ears to the floor with his arm and held the last of the wine in the air. Something for your poetry, no? he said. Some of the ears on the floor caught this scrap of his voice. Some of the ears on the floor were pressed to the ground.

# Writing from Reading

### Summarize

**1** Carolyn Forché has said that this event in fact took place—and announces "I [she herself] was in his house" at poem's start. What kind of truth is she telling, and how does she seem to respond?

### Analyze Craft

**2** What symbolism is evoked by the poem's final disturbing image of ears catching "this scrap of his voice" and ears "pressed to the ground"?

### Analyze Voice

**3** How does the language here feel more like a story than a poem? How does the plain language intensify the speaker's story?

### Synthesize Summary and Analysis

**4** With unbroken lines, this prose poem forms a thick block of text. How does this form reflect the poem's subject and title character?

### Interpret the Poem

**5** Who is the "you" the speaker mentions in the opening line? Does she intend someone specific? And how does the "I am tired of fooling around . . ." get differentiated from the speaker's "I"?

# Louis Jenkins (b. 1942)

Although born in Enid, Oklahoma, and raised for some time in Kansas, Louis Jenkins is a thirty-year resident of Duluth, Minnesota, and has been called by Garrison Keillor the "great wit of the North." A master of prose poetry, Jenkins is the author of eleven books of poetry, including most recently *North of the Cities* (2007), *Four Places on Lake Superior's North Shore* (2005), and *Distance from the Sun* (2004). His book of prose poetry, *Nice Fish* (1995), won the Minnesota Book Award in 1995. Says Jenkins, "I write some poems that are lines, but to me prose poems seem to be comfortable. It has a casual quality to it that other verse does not."

**AS YOU READ** Think about where you would break the lines if this were a traditionally lineated poem. Consider the effect the prose form has on the language and the tone overall.

## Football

**(1995)**

I take the snap from center, fake to the right, fade back . . . I've got protection. I've got a receiver open downfield. . . . What the hell is this? This isn't a football, it's a shoe, a man's brown leather oxford. A cousin to a football maybe, the same skin, but not the same, a thing made for the earth, not the air. I realize that this is a world where anything is possible and I understand, also, that one often has to make do with what one has. I have eaten pancakes, for instance, with that clear corn syrup on them because there was no maple syrup and they weren't very good. Well, anyway, this is different. (My man downfield is waving his arms.) One has certain responsibilities, one has to make choices. This isn't right and I'm not going to throw it.

# Writing from Reading

### Summarize

**1** Why do you think the poet chooses the prose poem to describe this comic, imaginary event?

### Analyze Craft

**2** What elements from traditionally lineated poetry can you find in this poem?

### Analyze Voice

**3** How does the statement "I realize that this is a world where anything is possible" prefigure the last sentence, and what does refusal entail?

### Synthesize Summary and Analysis

**4** At what point in the poem do you come to recognize that this is an imagined event and not an actual game?

### Interpret the Poem

**5** Can there be any connection between the strange substitution of the shoe for a football and corn syrup on pancakes? Why do you think the speaker is reminded of the breakfast?

## Ray Gonzalez (1952)

Ray Gonzalez is the author of sixteen books of poetry, nonfiction, and fiction. Recent titles include *Renaming the Earth: Personal Essays* (2008) and *Consideration of the Guitar* (2005). Gonzalez's 1996 collection, *Heat Arrivals,* won the PEN/Josephine Miles Book Award. He is also an author of short stories and the editor of twelve poetry anthologies. Gonzalez is the poetry editor of *The Bloomsbury Review* and publisher of *Luna,* a journal of poetry. He is a full Professor of English and teaches in the MFA program at the University of Minnesota in Minneapolis.

**AS YOU READ** Keep track of the story of the ritual and the chain of images.

# Corn Face Mesilla[1] (2002)

Someone dissolves into yesterday's climber who made it to the top of the night walk, the massive snow capped mountain in his dream waiting for him to select certain animals to play with. Someone plants a grain of sand in one of those closed eyes and the pain is positioned to show him how the harvest will be. Someone doesn't understand and decides to stand in front of the rock wall and look up forever, condemned and called as a corn follower who made it this far without dropping the bundle of husks

[1]Mesilla, New Mexico, is a small town between Las Cruces, New Mexico, and El Paso, Texas.

on his back. Someone doesn't want to be identified, so the fields are never cleared of rocks, the galleries never illuminated with bloody portraits, the meeting at the lake never held, the ceremony never disrupted by the enemies of the magnolia trees. Someone survives the picking of the corn and becomes an unknown woman standing on a great block of ice, her ability to be worshipped reinforced by the autumn return of a thousand birds flying out of a sun that blinds everything first before rising in the sky to look beyond the fields.

# Writing from Reading

### Summarize

1 The poet observes and describes a participant—"someone"—in an Indian corn harvest ritual. Make a description of the ritual with the clues given in the poem.

### Analyze Craft

2 What effect does the poet create by the repetition of "someone"? If you separated each line with a space, how would the effect change, or would it remain the same?

### Analyze Voice

3 The poet creates a chant-like effect by using repetition. Why is repetition so important to this poem?

### Synthesize Summary and Analysis

4 The poet employs chant-like lines in a prose-like block of language to tell the story of what may possibly be a ritual he sees in a dream. Does it seem possible that a series of simple lines of prose can create such an effect? What does it suggest to you about the line between poetry and prose?

### Interpret the Poem

5 Who is the subject of the dream? Who is the dreamer?

# For Review and Further Study

## Marilyn Chin (b. 1955)

### Turtle Soup (1987)

You go home one evening tired from work,
and your mother boils you turtle soup.
Twelve hours hunched over the hearth
(who knows what else is in that cauldron).

You say, "Ma, you've poached the symbol of long life;
that turtle lived four thousand years, swam
the Wei, up the Yellow, over the Yangtze.
Witnessed the Bronze Age, the High Tang,
grazed on splendid sericulture."
(So, she boils the life out of him.)

"All our ancestors have been fools.
Remember Uncle Wu who rode ten thousand miles
to kill a famous Manchu and ended up
with his head on a pole? Eat, child,
its liver will make you strong."

"Sometimes you're the life, sometimes the sacrifice."
Her sobbing is inconsolable.
So, you spread that gentle napkin
over your lap in decorous Pasadena.

Baby, some high priestess has got it wrong.
The golden decal on the green underbelly
says "Made in Hong Kong."

Is there nothing left but the shell
and humanity's strange inscriptions,
the songs, the rites, the oracles?

*—for Ben Huang*

### Questions for Interactive Reading and Writing

1. This poem reports on a domestic scene. How would you describe it, including location?
2. How "free" do you find the form of this poem? How "free" do you find the lines? Do you notice any near rhymes?
3. What evidence of a clash of cultures or generations do you see in the poem?
4. What is the poem's tone?
5. What does the poet mean by "humanity's strange inscriptions"?

# Sandra Cisneros (b. 1954)

## Pumpkin Eater (1994)

I'm no trouble.
Honest to God I'm not.
I'm not

the kind of woman
who telephones in the middle of the night,
—who told you that?—
splitting the night like machete.
Before and after.  After.  Before.
No, no, not me.
I'm not

the she who slings words bigger than rocks,
sharper than Houdini knives,
verbal Molotovs.
The one who did that—*yo no fuí*—
that wasn't me.

I'm no hysteric,
terrorist,
emotional anarchist.

I keep inside a pumpkin shell.
There I do very well.
Shut a blind eye to where
my pumpkin-eater roams.
I keep like fruitcake.
Subsist on air.
Not a worry nor care.
Please.
I'm as free for the taking
as the eyes of Saint Lucy.
No trouble at all.

I swear, I swear, I swear . . .

### Questions for Interactive Reading and Writing

1. How does the buildup of emotion influence the form of this poem?
2. What does the speaker's emphatic and repeated denials suggest about her situation and possibly even her character?
3. What effect on your understanding of her, and the poem itself, does the invocation of the nursery rhyme have?
4. Look up the reference to "the eyes of Saint Lucy." What impact does that reference have on the meaning of the poem?

# Mari Evans (b. 1923)

## Spectrum (1968)

Petulance is purple
happiness pink
ennui chartreuse
and love
—I think
is blue
like midnight sometimes
or a robin's egg
sometimes

### Questions for Interactive Reading and Writing

1. Describe the moods or emotional states the poet lists. Why does she attach a color to each of them? Do you find an order in the list?
2. Love is two shades of blue. How would you distinguish between them?
3. Is the poet speaking of love in a general sense or about a particular instance? Explain.

4. How does the conjunction "and" shift the poem toward its main subject? How does the last word—the repetition of "sometimes"—change the meaning of the poem?

# Allen Ginsberg (1926–1997)

## A Supermarket in California (1955)

What thoughts I have of you tonight, Walt Whitman, for I walked down the sidestreets under the trees with a headache self-conscious looking at the full moon.
In my hungry fatigue, and shopping for images, I went into the neon fruit supermarket, dreaming of your enumerations!
What peaches and what penumbras! Whole families shopping at night! Aisles full of husbands! Wives in the avocados, babies in the tomatoes!—and you, García Lorca, what were you doing down by the watermelons?

I saw you, Walt Whitman, childless, lonely old grubber, poking among the meats in the refrigerator and eyeing the grocery boys.
I heard you asking questions of each: Who killed the pork chops? What price bananas? Are you my Angel?
I wandered in and out of the brilliant stacks of cans following you, and followed in my imagination by the store detective.
We strode down the open corridors together in our solitary fancy tasting artichokes, possessing every frozen delicacy, and never passing the cashier.

Where are we going, Walt Whitman? The doors close in an hour. Which way does your beard point tonight?
(I touch your book and dream of our odyssey in the supermarket and feel absurd.)
Will we walk all night through solitary streets? The trees add shade to shade, lights out in the houses, we'll both be lonely.
Will we stroll dreaming of the lost America of love past blue automobiles in driveways, home to our silent cottage?
Ah, dear father, graybeard, lonely old courage-teacher, what America did you have when Charon quit poling his ferry and you got out on a smoking bank and stood watching the boat disappear on the black waters of Lethe?

### Questions for Interactive Reading and Writing

1. An American poet on the West Coast speaks to an American East Coast poet of an earlier day. What kinship does the modern poet feel for the older writer?
2. Why does the poet choose a California supermarket for the setting of this poem?
3. Where is the "poetry" in this freely told story?
4. How would you describe the leap the poet makes from the line "Aisles full of husbands . . ." to "wives in the avocados, babies in the tomatoes . . .?"
5. Who is García Lorca? Why is it fitting that he should appear to the poet also?
6. What is the technical device the poet uses when he addresses Whitman by means of carrying his book of poems?

# Lorna Goodison (b. 1947)

## On Becoming a Tiger (2000)

The day that they stole her tiger's-eye ring
was the day that she became a tiger.
She was inspired by advice received from Rilke

who recommended that, if the business of drinking
should become too bitter,
that one should change oneself into wine.

The tiger was actually always asleep
inside her, she had seen it
stretched out, drowsing and inert

when she lay upon her side and stared
for seven consecutive days into a tall mirror
that she had turned on its side.

Her focus had penetrated all exterior
till at last she could see within her
a red glowing landscape of memory and poems,

a heart within her heart
and lying there big, bright, and golden
was the tiger, wildly darkly striped.

At night she dreams that her mother
undresses her and discovers that, under
her outerwear, her bare limbs are marked
of the huge and fierce cat of Asia
with the stunning golden quartz eyes.

She has taken to wearing long dresses
to cover the rounded tail coiling behind her.
She has filled her vases with tiger lilies

and replaced her domestic cat
with a smaller relative of hers, the ocelot.
At four in the morning she practices stalking

up and down the long expanse of the hall.
What are the ingredients in tiger's milk?
Do tigers ever mate for life?

Can she rewrite the story of Little Black Sambo?
Can a non-tiger take a tiger for a wife?
To these and other questions,

she is seeking urgent answers
now that she is living an openly
tigerly life.

## Questions for Interactive Reading and Writing

1. How do the three-line stanzas serve to control the movement of the poem?
2. The poet refers to the German poet Rainer Maria Rilke and a metaphor about transformation. Rilke's sonnet 29 (in *Sonnets to Orpheus*) contains the lines, "What is your most painful experience? / If your drink is bitter, turn into wine." How does the Goodison poem reflect that advice?
3. How does the kinship the speaker feels with the imaginary tiger affect her everyday activities?
4. What part, if any, does race play in the poem?

# D. H. Lawrence (1885–1930)

*For a brief biography of D. H. Lawrence, see chapter 9.*

## Snake (1921)

A snake came to my water-trough
On a hot, hot day, and I in pajamas for the heat,
To drink there.

In the deep, strange-scented shade of the great dark
carob-tree
I came down the steps with my pitcher
And must wait, must stand and wait, for there he was at
the trough before me.

He reached down from a fissure in the earth-wall in the
gloom
And trailed his yellow-brown slackness soft-bellied
down, over the edge of the stone trough
And rested his throat upon the stone bottom,
And where the water had dripped from the tap, in a
small clearness,
He sipped with his straight mouth,
Softly drank through his straight gums, into his slack
long body,
Silently.
Someone was before me at my water-trough,
And I, like a second comer, waiting.
He lifted his head from his drinking, as cattle do,
And looked at me vaguely, as drinking cattle do,
And flickered his two-forked tongue from his lips, and
mused a moment,
And stooped and drank a little more,
Being earth-brown, earth-golden from the burning
bowels of the earth
On the day of Sicilian July, with Etna smoking.

The voice of my education said to me
He must be killed,
For in Sicily the black, black snakes are innocent, the
gold are venomous.

And voices in me said, If you were a man
You would take a stick and break him now, and finish
him off.

But must I confess how I liked him,
How glad I was he had come like a guest in quiet, to
drink at my water-trough

And depart peaceful, pacified, and thankless,
Into the burning bowels of this earth?

Was it cowardice, that I dared not kill him?
Was it perversity, that I longed to talk to him? Was it
humility, to feel so honored?
I felt so honored.

And yet those voices:
*If you were not afraid, you would kill him!*

And truly I was afraid, I was most afraid,
But even so, honored still more
That he should seek my hospitality
From out the dark door of the secret earth.

He drank enough
And lifted his head, dreamily, as one who has drunken,
And flickered his tongue like a forked night on the air, so black,
Seeming to lick his lips,
And looked around like a god, unseeing, into the air,
And slowly turned his head,
And slowly, very slowly, as if thrice adream,
Proceeded to draw his slow length curving round
And climb again the broken bank of my wall-face.

And as he put his head into that dreadful hole,
And as he slowly drew up, snake-easing his shoulders, and entered farther,
A sort of horror, a sort of protest against his withdrawing into that horrid black hole,
Deliberately going into the blackness, and slowly drawing himself after,
Overcame me now his back was turned.

I looked round, I put down my pitcher,
I picked up a clumsy log
And threw it at the water-trough with a clatter.

I think it did not hit him,
But suddenly that part of him that was left behind convulsed in undignified haste.
Writhed like lightning, and was gone
Into the black hole, the earth-lipped fissure in the wall-front,
At which, in the intense still noon, I stared with fascination.

And immediately I regretted it.
I thought how paltry, how vulgar, what a mean act!
I despised myself and the voices of my accursed human education.

And I thought of the albatross
And I wished he would come back, my snake.

For he seemed to me again like a king,
Like a king in exile, uncrowned in the underworld,
Now due to be crowned again.

And so, I missed my chance with one of the lords
Of life.
And I have something to expiate:
A pettiness.

### Questions for Interactive Reading and Writing

1. Why should we consider this description of an encounter between man and snake a poem and not prose? Can you read it as if it were a letter? What separates this text from plain prose?
2. In what ways does the poet-speaker find the meeting with the snake a test of his modern beliefs and values? What biblical symbol stands behind the image of this particular snake? What biblical test of beliefs and values?
3. What in particular surprises the man about his own behavior?
4. Why does the image of the "earth-lipped fissure in the wall-front" frighten him?
5. Why does he call his education "accursed"?
6. What is the overall outcome of the encounter, and how does the poet characterize it?

# Denise Levertov (1923–1997)

## The Ache of Marriage (1964)

The ache of marriage:

thigh and tongue, beloved,
are heavy with it,
it throbs in the teeth

We look for communion
and are turned away, beloved,
each and each

It is leviathan and we
in its belly
looking for joy, some joy
not to be known outside it

two by two in the ark of
the ache of it.

### Questions for Interactive Reading and Writing

1. Is this poem a celebration or a complaint or lament? Whom is the poet addressing?
2. What are the central metaphors the poet uses for marriage?

3. How do the sounds of the poem—the arrangement of the consonants and vowels—reflect the argument of the poem?
4. Does the poet find any relief from the "ache"?

# Alberto Alvaro Rios (b. 1952)

## Nani (1982)

Sitting at her table, she serves
the sopa de arroz to me
instinctively, and I watch her,
the absolute mamá, and eat words
I might have had to say more
out of embarrassment. To speak,
now-foreign words I used to speak,
too, dribble down her mouth as she serves
me albóndigas. No more
than a third are easy to me.
by the stove she does something with words
and looks at me only with her
back. I am full. I tell her
I taste the mint, and watch her speak
smiles at the stove. All my words
make her smile. Nani never serves
herself, she only watches me
with her skin, her hair. I ask for more.

I watch the mamá warming more
tortillas for me. I watch her
fingers in the flame for me.
Near her mouth, I see a wrinkle speak
of a man whose body serves
the ants like she serves me, then more words
from more wrinkles about children, words
about this and that, flowing more
easily from these other mouths. Each serves
as a tremendous string around her,
holding her together. They speak
Nani was this and that to me
and I wonder just how much of me
will die with her, what were the words
I could have been, was. Her insides speak
through a hundred wrinkles, now, more
than she can bear, steel around her,
shouting, then, What is this thing she serves?

She asks me if I want more.
I own no words to stop her.
Even before I speak, she serves.

### Questions for Interactive Reading and Writing

1. What is the relation between the speaker and Nani?
2. Do you need to know the English names of the dishes Nani serves in order to understand the poem?
3. What is the connection between food and words? How does the poet establish this as a metaphor?
4. Why does the poet emphasize Nani's "wrinkles"?
5. How would the effect of the poem change if it were written in rhyming couplets?

# Robert Sward (b. 1933)

## God Is in the Cracks (2006)

"Just a tiny crack separates this world
from the next, and you step over it
every day,
God is in the cracks."
Foot propped up, nurse hovering, phone ringing.
"Relax and breathe from your heels.
Now, that's breathing.
So, tell me, have you enrolled yet?"

"Enrolled?"

"In the Illinois College of Podiatry."

"Dad, I have a job. I teach."

"Ha! Well, I'm a man of the lower extremities."

"Dad, I'm fifty-three."

"So what? I'm eighty. I knew you
before you began wearing shoes.
Too good for feet?" he asks.
"*I. Me. Mind:*
That's all I get from your poetry.
Your words lack feet. Forget the mind.
Mind is all over the place. There's no support.
You want me to be proud of you? Be a foot man.
Here, son," he says, handing me back my shoes,
"try walking in these.
Arch supports. Now there's a subject.
Some day you'll write about arch supports."

### Questions for Interactive Reading and Writing

1. The poem contains informal dialogue reminiscent of a scene in a contemporary short story. Why doesn't the poet give us the setting? Can you imagine a setting to go along with it?
2. What does the father mean by "God is in the cracks," and is he possibly referring to that well-known phrase, "The Devil's in the details"? Does the poet offer a similar opinion in the poem itself?
3. What might the father mean when he says that his son's words, and, presumably, his poetry, lack feet?
4. How many references are there in this short poem to shoes and feet? What effect do these create? How would you describe the overall effect of the poem—is it humorous? bittersweet? pathetic? sorrowful? Or is there another way entirely to describe it?

## James Wright (1927–1980)

*For a brief biography of James Wright, see chapter 18.*

### Autumn Begins in Martins Ferry, Ohio (1959)

In the Shreve High football stadium,
I think of Polacks nursing long beers in Tiltonsville,
And gray faces of Negroes in the blast furnace at
  Benwood,
And the ruptured night watchman of Wheeling Steel,
Dreaming of heroes.

All the proud fathers are ashamed to go home.
Their women cluck like starved pullets,
Dying for love.

Therefore,
Their sons grow suicidally beautiful
At the beginning of October,
And gallop terribly against each other's bodies.

### Questions for Interactive Reading and Writing

1. Try a paraphrase of the poem. The setting should give you the meaning of the line about the sons who "gallop terribly against each other's bodies."
2. Describe the social structure of life in Martin's Ferry, Ohio, based on statements in the poem.
3. How do the lives people lead here stand against the way they dream of "heroes"? Why might the "proud fathers" be "ashamed to go home"?
4. Where does the poem turn?
5. Does the contrast between the women—the wives—who are "dying for love" and the sons who "grow suicidally beautiful" make sense?
6. How essentially American is this poem? Can you imagine a French version? A Mexican version? An Iraqi version?

# Reading for Open Form

When reading for open form, look for poetry that employs a structure determined by its own purpose and uses its own line lengths, line breaks, and rhythm (especially the rhythms of natural speech) instead of traditional patterns of meter, stanza structure, and rhyme.

| | |
|---|---|
| **Is there repetition in the poem?** | EXAMPLE: "because there is in this world no one thing / to which the bramble of *blackberry* corresponds, / . . . saying *blackberry, blackberry, blackberry.*" |

| | |
|---|---|
| **Is there grammatical variation in the poem?** | EXAMPLE: "since feeling is first / who pays any attention / to the syntax of things / will never wholly kiss you // wholly to be a fool / while Spring is in the world" |
| **Are there organized patterns of imagery?** | EXAMPLE: "Even the battered little furnace, roaring along as patient as a donkey, chokes and clogs, / a dense, malignant smoke shoots up, someone has to fiddle with a cock, then hammer it, / before the gush and stench will deintensify, the dark, Dantean broth wearily subside." |
| **How does the line itself create a rhythmical unit?** | EXAMPLE: "I Celebrate myself, and sing myself"<br><br>EXAMPLE: "Someone dissolves into yesterday's climber who made it to the top of the night walk" |
| **How is a line arranged? Where does it break to create its own visual effect?** | EXAMPLE: "And so, I missed my chance with one of the lords<br>Of life.<br>And I have something to expiate:<br>A pettiness."<br><br>EXAMPLE: "Easter Wings"—shaped in triangles like angel wings |

# Writing about Open Form

1. Using Wright's "Autumn Begins in Martins Ferry, Ohio," analyze the poem's use of open form elements (including line length, sound, and stanza structure).
2. Divide one of the three prose poems included in this chapter into a lined poem with separate stanzas. Then, write an informal explanation of your line breaks and stanza breaks. Include observations on how your reading of the poem transforms with your formal changes.
3. Begin with Whitman's "Song of Myself" and then read through the two subsequent poems in this chapter that invoke Whitman (by Alexie and Ginsberg). Discuss how these two more contemporary poets both imitate and break from Whitman's form and subject matter.
4. Using "Easter Wings" or "Swan and Shadow," examine the linkage between a poem's subject and its shape. Consider how different the poem would be if it did not visually depict an object.

# 25 Song & Spoken Word

IN one slow move you slithered and drizzled
snail trails all up and down eroded maps of me.
Doo-wop, stone-slow of step, sticks to you, lasts.

*—from "Doo-Wop: The Moves" by Al Young*

*"A lot of people are mystified by the relationship . . . between poetry and song, and I've always been surprised that people can't hear how obvious that relationship is. . . . Put your hand to your heart and hear that iambic beat. Everything around us is in tempo and works through rhythm and works through a kind of musicality."*

Conversation with Al Young, available on video at www.mhhe.com/delbanco1e

VERSE and song are kissing cousins. In chapter 15, we included a lyric likely set to music by Sappho and a song by Robert Burns; in chapter 16, we talked about the origins of poetry as song, with sacred verses such as the Song of Solomon. In fact, each of our previous chapters on poetry has—to a greater or lesser degree—linked the *craft* of poetry to attributes of *voice*. What could be more musical than rhythm? When a poet chooses words, they are selected for pitch and tone. The word *sonnet* itself means "little song." Words such as *rhythm, pitch,* and *tone* belong to the vocabulary of music and musicians; the word *lyric* attests to this connection. You can almost hear the sliding on the dance floor in "Doo-Wop: The Moves" with "in one slow move you slithered." There are, of course, certain kinds of poetry that focus on the eye, not ear, but by and large poetry is intended to be heard as well as seen.

Poetry began as recitation; it's in the genre's DNA. It goes all the way back to the origins of the Greek epic, when the Greek *rhapsodes,* festival poetry performers, chanted the lines of the long poems of war and peace. Sappho supposedly said her poems out loud for the delectation of a small group of devotees. The bardic tradition *requires* speech and even a kind of rhythmic song in order to reach its audience; there were no books, but there were lyres and harps. The blind bard Homer invokes the Muse, so that she may "sing" in and through him, telling the tale of the wrath of Achilles. Centuries later, the great Latin epic *The Aeneid* does much the same; Virgil begins his account of the escape from Troy and founding of Rome with the invocation of "Arms and the man I *sing*. . . ." In this way, poetry reaches beyond the page, relying on verbal performance and aspiring to song.

The following lines from the former Poet Laureate of the state of California make clear this poet's love of music and musicality in language. Al Young has written album liner notes for Motown records and two volumes of memoirs based on his life with popular music, jazz, and hip-hop. He is also an outspoken proponent of spoken word poetry and poetry as a public forum. As it was for ancient bards, for Young poetry is something resembling pure song.

*The poem is there for the human body to sound or to act out.*

# Q&A

*. . . all of poetry is yet to be created . . .*

# A Conversation on Writing

## Al Young

### Music and Language

Music is just naturally related to language and language to music. . . . When you're looking at a poem on a page, that is not the poem. The poem is there for the human body to sound or to act out. And each of us reciting the same Emily Dickinson poem or Langston Hughes poem will in fact bring a new poem into being. In the same way that you have Yo-Yo Ma playing a Bach cello concerto and you have . . . a cellist with the Kronos Quartet—they'll play it completely differently. The same notes, but they don't mean anything until someone brings feeling to it, brings a personal voice to it.

### Poetry, Hip-Hop, and Spoken Word

With most kids who get into poetry now, they have no problem relating it to music because a lot of them started as hip-hop or rap or spoken word aficionados or performers. And when you go to the poetry clubs, you see how excited they are to be actually saying something using those rhythms and inflections. And I've noticed that a student . . . who will not write a paper on a social situation or a political situation now, will get up at a poetry club or a rap performance and will say all kinds of things, many of them insightful and nuanced.

### Poetry and Live Audiences

Poetry becomes a joy when you're doing it to a live audience. . . . People are moving with your rhythms and your inflections and you're not alone. . . . You're just talking to each other and using poetry to do it. So, I think that—to paraphrase Ralph Waldo Emerson, who said somewhere—all of American literature is yet to be written. Well, all of poetry is yet to be created, and I think the future of poetry is quite healthy.

Al Young was born (1939) in Biloxi, Mississippi, raised in the rural South and Detroit, and eventually made his way to California, where he was named state Poet Laureate in 2005. Young's career has ranged from poet and novelist to screenwriter for Sidney Poitier and Bill Cosby. He has also taught creative writing at a number of universities, including Stanford and several campuses of the University of California. Young has an interest in jazz and blues and performs stories and poems to musical accompaniment. A recipient of Guggenheim, Fulbright, and National Endowment for the Arts Fellowships, Young currently lives in Berkeley, California.

**To watch this entire interview and hear the author read "Doo-Wop: The Moves" and other poems, go to www.mhhe.com/delbanco1e.**

**RESEARCH ASSIGNMENT** After watching the interview with Al Young, describe his view of traditional forms of poetry, such as the sonnet, and the music of poetry. Playing devil's advocate, disagree with Young's view and then turn around and support his view. Explore your own views on what makes music in poetry.

**AS YOU READ** Say the poem out loud and give yourself over to the pleasurable relation of word and rhythm, just as you would to a piece of music or a popular song.

# Doo-Wop: The Moves (2006)

Let's make no bones about it—whatever
this means or ever meant to you. Darling,
you know your way through what I'm about
to say. Doo-wop still steals the moment,
this sizzling thrill of closeness; the slowness
of our touch too much, too messy to process.

Back when dawn rose off the river, we'd feel it.
Feel felt like enough when flowering was new
and not easy to handle. Neither was breathing.
All that light funneling in from Canada, ferried
over the river while you put a move on my heart.

Heart and soul, flesh and bone—doo-wop
was known to sabotage. All across the land
White Citizens Councils shouted and warned:
Negro music is corrupting White youth. Boycott
Negro Music. We were young, too. You pressed
your hand behind my neck, you kissed my mouth.

Wham! So who'd kissed whom? You still wonder?
In one slow move you slithered and drizzled
snail trails all up and down eroded maps of me.
Doo-wop, stone-slow of step, sticks to you, lasts.

The doo-wop mind cries: O baby you know
I love you, always thinking of you, I place no one
above you, and you know I'll never snub you.
Under doo-wop's spell, you make no bones.
You shake your perfumed boodie. You go for keeps.

# Writing from Reading

## Summarize

1 What has the speaker remembered here? What happened between him and his "darling"?

## Analyze Craft

2 This poem announces, in its title, that it's a "Doo-Wop" musical tribute. In the poem, how do the doo-wop lyrics and the sound of doo-wop music get replicated in the lines of the poem?

3 How much of the poem's success depends on saying it, or trying to sing it, out loud?

4 Which phrases or lines distinguish the poem from a popular song?

## Analyze Voice

5 How would you describe the tone of this poem?

6 What is the poet's attitude toward this particular variety of song? Toward music in general?

7 Do you find that the allusions to politics and history enhance the poem or weigh too heavily on it?

**Synthesize Summary and Analysis**

8 How does the speaker's love of music increase the power of his emotion toward the person he loves?

9 Why does he turn to music to express his emotions?

**Interpret the Poem**

10 How do love, music, politics, race all come together in this poem?

"Is poetry an aural or written art? For me, it's both. As time goes on, the way the poem looks is really important to me. But also the way it sounds. And I'm trying to find the perfect coincidence of the way the poem looks, the way it sounds, the way it means, the silence and the speech in the poem" Conversation with Li-Young Lee

## RHYTHM AND SOUND

From Homer onward, poets have used rhythmical patterns and sounds. These rise from the page to emulate something chanted, attesting to the radically musical nature of Western poetry. Rhythm is one of the elemental qualities that separates poetry from ordinary speech and is the central technique in poetic song. (See chapter 22 for a fuller discussion of rhythm.) The most popular hits on the radio engage you with their "beat"; you can dance (or at least tap your foot) to them. Poet and classical scholar Laura Fargas writes about the overwhelming power of the three-syllable clusters (/ ~ ~) of dactylic hexameter, the traditional meter of ancient Greek poetry: "You couldn't vary from its rhythm if you wanted to. Think of griot chanting, or prayer chanting in

"Twenty-five hundred years ago, Homer, some guy stood up and chanted this poem about a war on the Turkish coast that has become a founding epic of western civilization. You can say out those rhythms. . . . Rhythms, they say, that in Greek sound like the surge of the sea that ships sailed across to fight that war."

Conversation with Robert Hass

Hebrew, Arabic, or Hindi, to get a sense of the basic sound, and then allow for variations for emphasis that a really good performer could use to make the story more vivid at appropriate moments—hesitations, hastenings, variations in tone of voice."

*Voice* is also an integral part of any song—the human voice it is written for and the poet's voice that embodies and produces it. We can never fully *define* it, but we can try to *describe* it. What should we pay attention to in voice? We note, for example, the poet's use of sounds (see chapter 22) such as *alliteration* (when the first letter of a word is repeated, as in *Five **m**iles **m**eandering with a **m**azy **m**otion*), *assonance* (when vowels within words are repeated, as in *Where **A**lph, the sacred river r**a**n / through c**a**verns measureless to m**a**n),* consonance (when consonants within words are repeated, as in *for the whole / Of the sea is hilly with whales*), and *rhyme* (ran—man). Rhythmical patterns are important, but voice connects its author to an audience, and often the voice is more important than individual authorship in creating a song's or poem's context.

# Anonymous

**AS YOU READ** Try to imagine what circumstances might have prompted the unknown poet to compose these lines.

## Western Wind (c. 1500)

Western wind, when will thou blow
  The small rain down can rain?
Christ, if my love were in my arms
  And I in my bed again!

# Writing from Reading

### Summarize

1 In what circumstance does the anonymous poet find himself? Herself?

### Analyze Craft

2 For you, what is the most compelling line or image in the poem, and why does it strike you?

3 What effect does the word *Christ* have on the poem? If it were omitted, how would the poem change?

4 How do sounds—rhyme, rhythm, repetition, alliteration, and so on—make this poem song-like?

### Analyze Voice

5 "Western Wind" accomplishes much in a small space; list everything that you know about the speaker's situation and feelings.

6 This poem is a lament and outcry in a difficult time by an anonymous speaker. Does the anonymity of the speaker make the poem more or less effective? Or does it not matter?

### Synthesize Summary and Analysis

7 Most lyric poetry laments loss and absence. What distinguishes this anonymous lyric from others of its kind (such as the fragment by Sappho in chapter 15 or Leonard Cohen's "For Anne" in chapter 16)?

### Interpret the Poem

8 What does the last line suggest in coming after the previous three?

## BALLAD

In twenty-first-century popular music, the word *ballad* is used to describe slow, often confessional songs. Traditionally, a **ballad** is a song or poem that tells a lively or tragic story in simple language, using rhyming four-line stanzas and a set meter (see chapter 22 for more on meter). Whoever first composed the following ballad was, in the artistic sense, detached; the maker does not criticize the king's malevolent decision to send his noble warriors to their deaths at sea. This historical ballad—its hero was a fighter-sailor of the thirteenth century—would have been the work of many hands, and we have no way of knowing who first "wrote" it.

> "The well that I always go back to is actually folk material. I was listening to Leadbelly the other day and just was amazed at what he was singing. Each line takes a remarkable leap into another reality and we accept it because it's sung, and so it sort of disarms our intellectual acumen, and we accept all these fantastic leaps."
>
> Conversation with Al Young

# Anonymous

**AS YOU READ** Focus on the story, but also notice that the rhyming and its effects enhance the story itself.

## Sir Patrick Spence (1765)

The King sits in Dumferling toune,
  Drinking the blude-reid wine:
"O whar will I get guid sailor,
  To sail this schip of mine?"

Up and spak an eldern knicht,
  Sat at the kings richt kne:
"Sir Patrick Spence is the best sailor
  That sails upon the se."

The king has written a braid letter,
  And signed it wi' his hand,
And sent it to Sir Patrick Spence,
  Was walking on the sand.

The first line that Sir Patrick red,
  A loud lauch lauchèd he;
The next line that Sir Patrick red,
  The teir blinded his ee.

"O wha is this has don this deid,
  This ill deid don to me,
To send me out this time o' the yeir,
  To sail upon the se!

"Mak haste, mak haste, my mirry men all,
  Our guid schip sails the morne."
"O say na sae, my master deir,
  For I feir a deadlie storme.

"Late late yestreen I saw the new moone,
Wi' the auld moone in hir arme,
And I feir, I feir, my deir master,
That we will cum to harme."

O our Scots nobles wer richt laith
To weet their cork-heild schoone,
Bot lang owre a' the play wer play'd,
Thair hats they swam aboone.

O lang, lang may their ladies sit,
Wi' thair fans into their hand,
Or ere they se Sir Patrick Spence
Cum sailing to the land.

O lang, lang may the ladies stand,
Wi' their gold kems in their hair,
Waiting for thair ain deir lords,
For they'll se thame na mair.

Haf owre, half owre to Aberdour,
It's fiftie fadom deip,
And thair lies guid Sir Patrick Spence,
Wi' the Scots lords at his feit.

# Writing from Reading

## Summarize

1 Read (or chant) this poem out loud. Did you find that the old-fashioned spellings and words were easier to understand this way? Paraphrase each stanza. What is the plot of the poem?

## Analyze Craft

2 How does the rhythmical pattern, the use of language, or the use of rhyme contribute to the poem's song-like quality?

## Analyze Voice

3 How would you describe the tone of this ballad?

4 We do not know who the original author of "Sir Patrick Spence" is—but the poem does have a voice that distinguishes it from other songs. How would you describe the voice of this particular work *or* the voice of a folk ballad (using specific examples from this poem as evidence)?

5 Look up any unfamiliar words and replace them with modern-day approximations. How does this change the poem's voice?

## Synthesize Summary and Analysis

6 The technical components of the poem, and its musical qualities, create a moving story about loyalty, love, and history. Can you name some contemporary ballads that work in similar fashion?

7 Compare this traditional Scottish ballad with another, "Bonnie Barbara Allen" in chapter 22. How is the rhythm similar? What other similarities do you find?

## Interpret the Poem

8 What lessons does the anonymous poet put forward about life?

## SONGS OF THE COUNTRYSIDE: PASTORAL POETRY

As a poetic form, song itself emerges out of the conventions of peasant life in small towns and in the countryside, in the so-called **pastoral** (as in "countryside") **poetry** of the Roman poets. Anonymous lyrics from the thirteenth through early sixteenth centuries in England continue the tradition. As with "Western Wind" and the early

"Poems come from poems, songs come from songs. They come from experience. You bring your own experience to everything that flows through you." Conversation with Robert Hass

ballads, we cannot name the author or do much more than approximate the date and place of composition; although we do not know their tunes, these early poems have the feel of something sung. By the sixteenth century, we do know the names of the authors, and at least something about them as individuals. Here English poet Christopher Marlowe gives us his version of a country boy's plea to his pastoral love. No shepherd is likely to have engaged in courtship in this way, but Marlowe imagines what it might be like to sing in rhyming couplets about these shared "delights."

# Christopher Marlowe (1564–1593)

Born in Canterbury, Christopher Marlowe was to become the playwright and poet who paved the way for Elizabethan drama, including Shakespeare's work. While on scholarship at Corpus Christi College in Cambridge, Marlowe also served as a spy in the queen's secret service, which kept the Protestant queen safe from Catholic plots. Meanwhile, he cultivated a brilliant literary career with five dramas, among them *Tamburlaine* and *Doctor Faustus,* in which he perfected the blank verse form that Shakespeare would use in his plays. Marlowe also wrote poetry, though much of it is lost. The circumstances of his death at age twenty-nine are unclear; a widespread version holds that he was stabbed in a tavern fight, reportedly in an argument over the bill. Modern research suggests that his death may have been linked to his espionage activity.

**AS YOU READ** Think of a song in a musical in which the singer dressed in a shepherd's costume calls out to the object of his affections.

# The Passionate Shepherd to His Love (c. 1599)

Come live with me and be my love,
And we will all the pleasures prove
That valleys, groves, hills, and fields,
Woods, or steepy mountain yields.

And we will sit upon rocks,
Seeing the shepherds feed their flocks,
By shallow rivers to whose falls
Melodious birds sing madrigals.

And I will make thee beds of roses
And a thousand fragrant posies,
A cap of flowers, and a kirtle
Embroidered all with leaves of myrtle;

A gown made of the finest wool
Which from our pretty lambs we pull;
Fair lined slippers for the cold,
With buckles of the purest gold;

A belt of straw and ivy buds,
With coral clasps and amber studs:
And if these pleasures may thee move,
Come live with me and be my love.

The shepherds' swains shall dance and sing
For thy delight each May morning:
If these delights thy mind may move,
Then live with me and be my love.

# Writing from Reading

## Summarize

**1** What exactly is the shepherd promising?

**2** How might a city dweller serenade his or her love interest? Write "The Passionate Lawyer to Her Love," "The Passionate Waiter to His Love" (or something similar).

## Analyze Craft

**3** What are some of the pastoral, or supposedly natural, images in this poem?

**4** In what ways is this poem like many contemporary love songs, and how is it different? Consider tone, style, and various aspects of language and word choice as well as content in your response.

## Analyze Voice

**5** As suggested, it's unlikely that a shepherd *in reality* would speak to his lover in rhyming couplets. Why can he speak this way in a poem?

## Synthesize Summary and Analysis

**6** The poet constructs a rarefied variety of a song in order to express certain otherwise inexpressible emotions. Why does he choose a song to express his emotions?

## Interpret the Poem

**7** Why does this poem idealize life in this fashion? Look at three very different love poems in this chapter—"Doo-Wop: The Moves," "Western Wind," and "A Song." What is the place of idealization in love poetry?

## SHAKESPEARE IN SONG

William Shakespeare incorporates song in certain plays, mainly the comedies or those late plays that contain both dark and light situations. Many of his dances performed onstage in verbal silence had musical accompaniment—and when (*Henry IV* 1.3.1) the stage directions say *"Here the lady sings a Welsh song,"* it's not necessarily the case that Shakespeare wrote what she performed. Some scholars argue that some of his songs are in fact folk tunes or ditties not of his own composition; others bear the particular stamp of the playwright's particular language. The following **dirge,** or funeral song, from *Cymbeline* is sung for a character the speakers believe to be dead (but who is really in disguise).

# William Shakespeare (1564–1616)

For a brief biography of William Shakespeare, see chapter 18.

**AS YOU READ** Consider how the song helps give the audience some breathing room in the middle of the dramatic action.

# Fear no more the heat o' the sun

## —*from* Cymbeline (c. 1608–1610)

Fear no more the heat o' the sun,
  Nor the furious winter's rages;
Thou thy worldly task hast done,
  Home art gone, and ta'en thy wages:
Golden lads and girls all must,
As chimney-sweepers, come to dust.

Fear no more the frown o' the great;
  Thou art past the tyrant's stroke:
Care no more to clothe and eat;
  To thee the reed is as the oak:
The scepter, learning, physic, must
All follow this, and come to dust.

Fear no more the lightning flash,
  Nor the all-dreaded thunder stone;
Fear not slander, censure rash;
  Thou hast finished joy and moan:
All lovers young, all lovers must
Consign to thee, and come to dust.

No exorciser harm thee!
  Nor no witchcraft charm thee!
Ghost unlaid forbear thee!
  Nothing ill come near thee!
Quiet consummation have;
And renownéd be thy grave!

# Writing from Reading

### Summarize

1 Paraphrase this song into straightforward language. What is being expressed?

### Analyze Craft

2 What is particularly musical about the punctuation of this dirge? In your response, consider the repetition of exclamation points in the final stanza.

3 In the last stanza, the meter and rhythm of the poem change. How does it change—and why? See chapter 22 for more on meter.

### Analyze Voice

4 Why does the voice seem impersonal? Who is speaking here?

### Synthesize Summary and Analysis

5 How does the tone in this funeral song include great wit and irony and remain true to its funereal purpose?

### Interpret the Poem

6 How does the pun that ends the first stanza—"chimney-sweepers, come to dust"—affect the meaning of the poem?

7 If you were directing a production of *Cymbeline,* what kind of music (and/or sound effects) would you use to accompany or help voice this funeral song?

## LANGUAGE AS MELODY

Sometimes the poet drops the pretense of having a character perform, as in Marlowe's shepherd's serenade to his love, and creates his or her own song. Consider the usually more somber John Donne's playful outburst on the subject of love, and constancy or lack of it. Donne's rhyming poem seems to aspire to the condition of music. The lyrical line is **melodious** (tuneful, like a melody), but it is not by itself a **melody** (the linear succession of various musical pitches recognized as a unit).

# John Donne (1572–1631)

John Donne (pronounced *Dunn*) was born into a Catholic family in London, England, at a time when Catholics were persecuted under the Protestant crown. He converted to the Church of England while in his twenties, the decade in which he wrote his famous *Satires* and *Songs and Sonnets.* In 1601, Donne secretly married his employer's niece, Ann More, which so angered his employer that he fired Donne and had him imprisoned for a short period. Donne then struggled with poverty, especially since he and Ann had twelve children. Eventually, under pressure from the king, Donne became a clergyman and was famous for his intelligent and riveting sermons. He imbued his poetry with his wit as well as his passionate disposition—interested in sex and love, yet with a faith in God and an acute awareness of his own mortality. His poems are known for both his use of conceit (or extended metaphor) and his ability to capture and articulate the paradoxes of human existence.

**AS YOU READ** Enjoy the rhymes and the striking images of meteors, of the Devil's foot, and of mermaids, all in the service of a lament.

# Song (1633)

Go and catch a falling star,
Get with child a mandrake root,
Tell me where all past years are,
Or who cleft the Devil's foot;
Teach me to hear mermaids singing,
Or to keep off envy's stinging,
And find
What wind
Serves to advance an honest mind.

If thou be'st born to strange sights,
Things invisible to see,
Ride ten thousand days and nights,
Till Age snow white hairs on thee,
Thou, when thou return'st, wilt tell me
All strange wonders that befell thee,
And swear
Nowhere
Lives a woman true, and fair.

If thou find'st one, let me know,
Such a pilgrimage were sweet—
Yet do not, I would not go,
Though at next door we might meet;
Though she were true, when you met her,
And last, till you write your letter,
Yet she
Will be
False, ere I come, to two or three.

# Writing from Reading

### Summarize

**1** Why do you think this poem is titled "Song"?

### Analyze Craft

**2** How do the rhythmical patterns in this poem suggest music, and/or how would they lend themselves well to accompaniment? Use specific examples in your response.

**3** What is the effect of the pair of two-word lines near the end of each stanza? Consider how these lines affect the poem visually and aurally.

### Analyze Voice

**4** Who is the speaker addressing, and for what purpose?

### Synthesize Summary and Analysis

**5** Does this poem seem to be a lament in the form of a song about one of life's apparent—to the poet at least—inconstancies, or is it just a bit of inspired fun? What language do you see that suggests it might be both?

### Interpret the Poem

**6** If this poem were set to music, how might such music sound? Describe what you think it should sound like—and how it might change in tone or timbre as the song progresses.

**7** What are the particular aspects of life and love that this poet laments? How would you defend or disagree with his lament?

## NATIVE AMERICAN POETRY

On our own continent, the earliest songs were, of course, Indian worship chants. For example, the "Night Chant" was part of a nine-day healing ritual that also included the creation of sand paintings and the performance of sacred dances. The aim was to restore a patient (often someone who had become blind, deaf, or paralyzed) to a state of health and harmony. A medicine man would lead the guests in a call-and-response of chanting and singing. The "Night Chant" was passed down orally through generations. The chant involves an invocation of nature, characterized by repetition, and is ultimately a song of comfort, with repeated lines like "The Rainbow returned with me," and a long sequence of restoration based on a slightly varied line:

> *Beautifully my children to me are restored*
> *Beautifully my wife is to me restored . . .*

Two lines near the conclusion of the chant declare,

> *In beauty may I walk*
> *All day long may I walk.*

Compare these lines to the final lines of Joy Harjo's song below.

# Joy Harjo (b. 1951)

Some poets, such as American Indian poet and composer Joy Harjo, set their own work to music. A member of the Muscogee (Creek) Indian tribe, Harjo was born in Tulsa, Oklahoma. She changed her major from art to poetry before completing her B.A. at the University of New Mexico. From there, she earned an M.F.A. at the Iowa Writers Workshop. In addition to producing eight collections of poems, Harjo is a musician. She performed on saxophone with her band, Poetic Justice before going solo. Her CDs feature both her playing and her poetry. She currently teaches at the University of New Mexico.

**AS YOU READ** See if you think that the text is complete without the voice of the singer and the music.

# Morning Song (2001)

The red dawn is now rearranging the earth
*Thought by thought*
*Beauty by beauty*
Each sunrise a link on the ladder
*Thought by thought*
*Beauty by beauty*
The ladder the backbone
Of shimmering deity
*Thought by thought*
*Beauty by beauty*
Child stirring in the web of your mother
Don't be afraid
Old man turning to walk through the door
Do not be afraid

# Writing from Reading

### Summarize

1 Rewrite this poem in complete sentences.

### Analyze Craft

2 Why does it serve so many poems and songs well to break traditional rules of syntax? How do songs create their own rules? What are the "rules" in Harjo's poem?

3 What is the relationship between the images in the poem? Consider especially: "Child stirring in the web of your mother" and "Old man turning to walk through the door."

4 How does Harjo use long and short lines to achieve musical effects?

### Analyze Voice

5 What is the purpose of this song? How does the voice sound to you?

### Synthesize Summary and Analysis

6 Why does it seem appropriate for this to be a "morning" song rather than a poem associated with another part of the day?

### Interpret the Poem

7 What does the refrain "Thought by thought / Beauty by beauty" mean or suggest? How does it work in the context of the larger song? Why is the line "Don't be afraid" repeated as "Do not be afraid"?

## SPOKEN WORD PIONEERS

Poetry, from earliest times, has not lacked for performance. In the United States, the recitation of poetry was a standard educational experience until recently, but poetry from the 1950s and '60s written by the so-called **Beat** generation was recited, chanted, and sometimes even sung. *Beat*—the very word suggests the rhythmic *beating* out of emphases, repeated sound, and public as opposed to private aspects of delivery. (One of the leading Beat poets was Allen Ginsberg, whose "Supermarket in California" appears in chapter 24.) With the Beats, as with what we're calling **spoken word** poetry today, the written form of a poem seems secondary to the performance of it; the *scene* was not a silent one—much more akin to theater than what Dylan Thomas called "my craft or sullen art."

"The poetry reading was beginning to be a kind of public event that people went to . . . because of the Beat scene. It seemed really cool to go to the Anxious Asp or the Green Street Cafe or the Coexistence Bagel Shop . . . and hear spoken poetry read. It made it seem alive and accessible and not something in books."

Conversation with Robert Hass

Although the evolution of spoken word poetry can be traced as far back as the Beats, it may be best to begin with the precursors to rap, from the late sixties, and then go on to look at how rap songs influenced spoken word. What we know as **rap** is also oral in its presentation, but the performers are as much singers and musicians as poets. Improvisation plays its part, as does choral response or repetition; these artists are most often young, and their diction is colloquial, street-smart. They gather together in back rooms or ballrooms, chanting their work out loud as part of a competition; sometimes the audience appoints itself as arbiter, ranking with applause; more formally there are actual judges to rate the "show." Rap has also led to the syncopated fusion of one of today's most popular music forms, **hip-hop.**

# The Last Poets (1968)

"Born" on May 19, 1968, for a Malcolm X birthday celebration, The Last Poets have been called the grandfathers of rap. Although the combination of members shifted over the years, the group's mission was always clear: to express the feelings behind the Black Arts Movement of the 1960s and the overall experience of being black in America. Their angry, revolutionary poetry set to music appeared on albums including *The Last Poets* (1970) and *This Is Madness* (1971). The group—consisting of Gylan Kain, Abiodun Oyewole, David Nelson, Felipe Luciano, Umar Bin Hassan, Jalal Nurdidin, and Suliaman El-Hadi—took its name from a poem by South African poet Keorapetse Kgositsile, who wrote that he lived in the last generation that knew poetry because guns were replacing it.

**AS YOU READ** Ask yourself how much or how little you can associate yourself with the emotion called up in the poem.

# My people (1984)

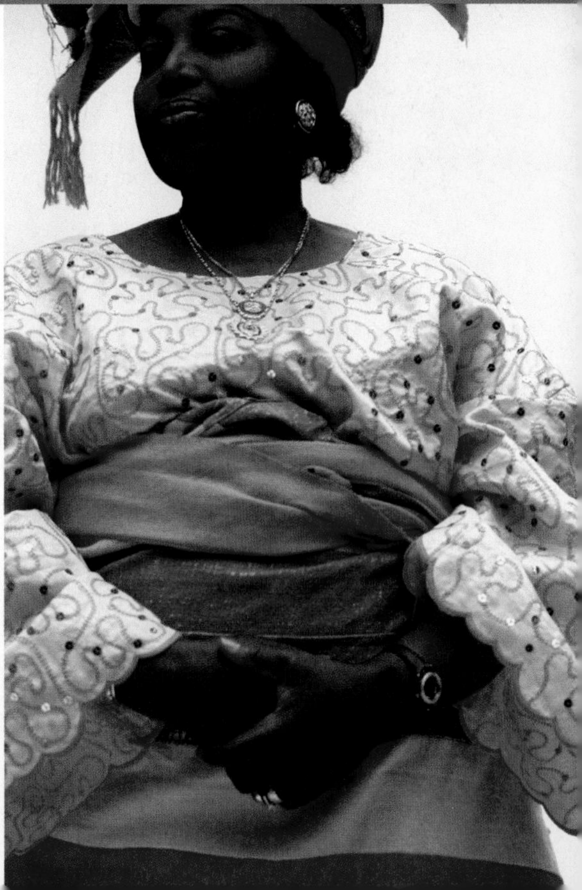

My people are Black, beige, yellow
Brown and beautiful
A garden of life
with a love as sweet as scuppernong wine
growing in muddy waters
making brown babies with
pink feet and quick minds
My people warm sometimes hot
always cool always together
My people let's be together
understand that we've lived together
understand that we've died together
understand My brother that I've
smelled your piss in my hallway
and it smell just like mine
understand that I love your woman
my sister and her rare beauty
is reason enough for a revolution
yes sister my honest sister

I have had ugly moments with you
but you are the only beauty I've ever known
Yes sister my honest sister
you are the joy in my smile
you are the reality of my dreams
you are the only sister I have
and I need you
I need you to feed the children
of our race
I need you to feed the lovers of our race
I need you to be the summer of my winters
I need you because
you are the natural life in the living
at night there is a moon
to make the Blackness be felt
I am that Blackness
filling up the world
with My soul
and the world knows me
You are that moon
my moon Goddess shining down light
on my Black face
that fills the universe
My moon I am your sun
and I shall take this peace
of light and build a world
for you my sister
Sometimes the waters are rough
and the hungry tide swallows the shore
washing away all memories
of children's footsteps
playing in the sand
where is the world I promised my son?
must he push back the tide
and build the world
that I have rapped about
Am I so godly until I forget
what a man is?
Am I so right until
there is no room for patience
My brother Oh in brother
father of a son
father of a warrior
My brother the sun
My brother the warrior
Be the beginning and the end
for my sister
Be the revolution for our world
turn yourself into yourself
and then onto this disordered world
and arrange the laughter for joy
the tears for sorrow
Turn purple pants, alligator shoes
leather jackets, brown boots
polka dot ties, silk suits,
Turn miniskirts, false eyelashes,
red wigs, afro wigs, Easter bonnets,
bellbottoms turn this confusion
into Unity Unity
so that the sun will follow
our foot steps in the day
so that the moon will glow
in our living rooms at night
so that food, clothing, and shelter
will be free
because we are born free
to have the world as our playground
My people.

# Writing from Reading

### Summarize

1 The poets celebrate their identity as a social and racial group. What aspects are celebrated?

### Analyze Craft

2 What techniques do you discern at work in the poem? Does the addressee of the poem change or remain the same?

### Analyze Voice

3 What role does pride play in the establishment of the voice?

4 How would you describe the importance of the voice to the success of the poem?

### Synthesize Summary and Analysis

5 Which basic techniques and emphasis in voice make the poem work?

### Interpret the Poem

6 Is the audience for the poem exclusive to the group lauded in the poem or does "My people" have a broader appeal?

What we describe as **slam** includes all varieties of poetry and poets, from local café poets to Poets Laureate of the United States. Spoken word advocate Nancy Schwalb credits Marc Smith with inventing the poetry slam in Chicago in 1979 or '80, as a way to bring poetry down from the ivory tower and into the streets. It has done so—to an increasing, and increasingly devoted audience—all across America (and with no signs of slowing) ever since. Issues of race and gender appear in much of this work, as do politics and personal relations, love, hate, envy, worry about life, and death. In other words, spoken word poetry is much like all poetry down through the ages. It just swings a little more.

# Marc Smith (b. 1950)

The founder of the poetry slam, Marc Smith was born in southeast Chicago. He organized the first poetry slam at Chicago's Green Mill Tavern in 1987, where the weekly slam has continued for more than twenty years. He brings a sense of rhythm and drama to his performance of spoken word poetry, which has pleased audiences at venues including Lincoln Center, the Kennedy Center, the Art Institute of Chicago, and the Queensland Poetry Fest in Australia. Smith has contributed to the anthologies *The Spoken Word Revolution* (2003) and *The Spoken Word Revolution Redux* (2007); he has also written and produced two plays, *Flea Market, a night of monologues* and *A House Party for Henry.*

**AS YOU READ** **Envision the various settings of each stanza. Consider how the voice of the speaker changes in each different place.**

# Dusty Blues (1996)

The moon, when swinging trumpets blow,
Goes blue as red the rhythm cuts
The rain with saucy cinder-beats;
And blackbirds hop the high hot lines.

(It's a scats madder scene.)

In cellar grays where notes collide
The bulb's half eclipse cleaves a brain;
And "Death," the wailing madman cries,
"Leaves me half breaths, baby."

Oh the wind that crosses elms at night
Flows through the tubes of tacit life
Proclaiming in its haunting moan,
"All is senseless, Pops."

But the brew within the brassy stove
Cooks clean to alabaster bones;
And "Fame" the jiving jazzman's told,
"Hangs with the blackbirds
Up on those high hot lines!"

It's a blue-back crooked dream.

# Writing from Reading

### Summarize

1 Describe in plain speech the various settings the poem travels through.

### Analyze Craft

2 How does Smith transition from one setting to the next, and how does he bring the poem full circle at the end?

### Analyze Voice

3 Consider whether the speaker of dialogue in the poem is one person or many different people. What clues in the language make you think so?

### Synthesize Summary and Analysis

4 Describe the speaker of this poem. Based on your answer, who do you think is speaking back?

### Interpret the Poem

5 Does the poem speak to a particular generation in a particular time and place, or does it have a more universal appeal?

## THE SECOND WAVE

Today, slams are one of the most popular public forums for poetry. Surrounded by new technology, we live in a time of multiple sounds and modes of presentation, creating multimedia performance poems, along with the traditional public theater of the slams. It's been possible to read Wallace Stevens, Percy Bysshe Shelley, or William Butler Yeats and the rest in silence; what follows are a set of texts that need to be *performed*.

# *Three Spoken Word Poems*

**AS YOU READ** Read these poems out loud and compare them to your favorite rap or hip-hop tunes.

## Kenneth Carroll (b. 1959)

Kenneth Carroll has been integral to poetry in Washington, D.C., where he was born and continues to live. He has served as D.C. site coordinator for WritersCorps, as president of the African American Writers Guild, and as a board member of the Poetry Committee of Greater Washington. He also taught high school English in Washington for a number of years and has performed his poetry at the Kennedy Center and the Library of Congress. His work (including his poetry, essays, short stories, and plays) has appeared in numerous journals and magazines. His collection *So What! For the White Dude Who Said This Ain't Poetry* was published in 1997.

# So What! (for the white dude who said dis ain't poetry) (1997)

a faucet dripping arrogance in sycophantic half steps
a literary tarzan trying to save the natives from they own ignorance
short on knowledge, long on knowing he instructs without reference,
ain't poetry?

"no dialectics needed sambo, your thing just is not poetry,"
said the gold coast representative
never been in the mines
never sweated riches but 'bwana knows best'

a minute man wit a culture 30 seconds old
ain't poetry?    mmmm . . .
maybe if i throwed soup cans in it
or something obscure dark & cryptic
alluded to hackneyed over hyped dead writers
& avoided references to the dark continent of
my origin this work could be saved

ain't poetry?
minute rice analysis
cracker instant oats
pour in europe and stir: a cold water recipe
. . . meanwhile my village dances to simmering rhythms
spiced by intellectual development measured in tens
of thousands of years

homer, his lips stuck to the chilly nipple
of his mother's frozen breast,
could only dream civilizations
as dark men & women built pyramids
& shaped words to fit eternity
poets retired & came back as ancestor spirits
while greece contemplated a working alphabet & gods
but this shit ain't poetry cause johnny come lately say so
. . . and he should know

ain't poetry?
our systems were a mystery
alexander burned all that he & aristotle couldn't understand
the ensuing blaze warmed the icecapade continent
as the pillaging plagiarizers worked their un magic in the fire's light

ain't poetry?
the sails on your scholar ship are bloody
you scribble death upon the pages on the world
persecuting your brightest stars, preferring
whoring scribes who search for insignificance
to entertain the inane
. . . so dis ain't poetry . . . so you dis'n me?

ain't poetry, huh?    ain't india either sucka!
what is round, rotating and will never
fit into a box marked trite poetic conventions:
the world and its inhabitants
you are trying to fold the world in half
to place it neatly into your square mind

ain't poetry?
ain't dat a bitch!
a new jack dis
half empty memory banks
culture validated by gun powder
your qualifications are shaky
like a bamboo bridge stretched across
the white supremacist waters of your existence
you are still preaching the missionary position
as the natives re-read the karma sutra

a day late, a dollar short
always missing the bus
you are peeing in the snow
while we design a papyrus for the living
a patronizing peeping tom
seeing in but unable to decipher
without an oxford interpreter

we are a black fire
burning across the pages of your random house guide
to modern american poetry
where you cannot find references to shine or even signifying monkeys
we have left your meter in shambles
as we laugh at you tripping over lemons piled on the steps

the drumming you hear coming from the hills ain't poetry either
(but of course it is!)
it is the maroons planning your demise
it is ritual music and david walker's appeal
it is brown hips dancing verses
it is what it feels like to be kissed by full lips

it is natural
like sun ra returning in a charlie parker space ship
from galaxies wit' no names
while europe sails the wrong way
in search of a short cut to imperialism

damn columbus, you are lost and desperate
and denying the only music you really hear
you riffin' with a trumpet that plays one note
while the planet be's and bops
like coltrane star hopping through
the theloniosphere as a white boy
from downbeat points to the heavens & screams,
"that ain't music, that ain't music!"

we are like miles,
a black whirlwind
wit a red trumpet,
blowing blue stanzas
saying, so what!
yeah goddamn it
SO WHAT!**

# Lawson Fusao Inada (b. 1938)

When Lawson Inada's grandparents immigrated from Japan to California, they might not have imagined their grandson would be a poet important to the beginning of Asian American literature. Inada was born in Fresno, California, and interned in one of the many camps in which Japanese Americans were confined during World War II. As a teenager, Inada fell in love with jazz music, and although he abandoned his aspirations to become a jazz musician, he cites jazz as the biggest influence on his poetry. In addition to his collections—which were published by major publishing houses, a first for Asian American poetry—Inada enjoyed performing his poems to music. He is a professor emeritus of Southern Oregon University and the state of Oregon's Poet Laureate.

# Grandmother

**(1997)**

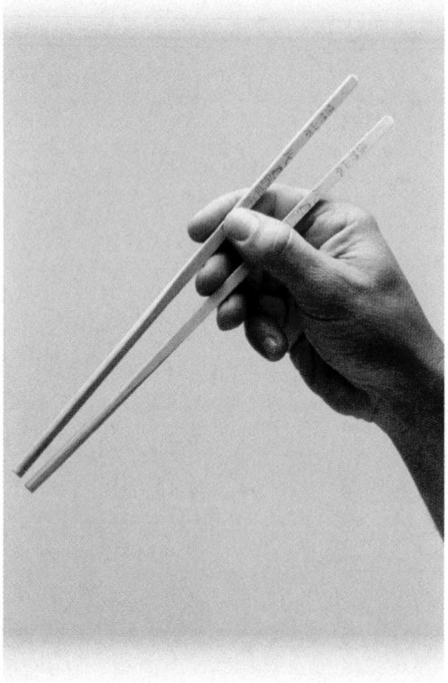

*for Grandmother Miju Inada and Yoshiko Saito*

Except for the fact that Grandmother taught me
chopsticks and Japanese before forks and English,
my relationship with Her wasn't all that much.

As a matter of fact, Grandmother, with Her old-
fashioned ways, was actually somewhat of an extravagant source of confusion and distraction.

For example, just to waste time on a rainy day
in a boring barrack room in our ordinary
concentration camp in Arkansas, She'd say:

"The Great God Thunder is very powerful.
Listen to Him. When He storms, be careful.
Or He will send Lightning to take your navel!"

Or, on just another quiet night in Colorado,
on the way to the shower house, She may pause
in the warm desert sand to simply say:

"Ah, the Full Moon! Look closely, Grandson.
It's the same Moon, and the same Story.
'Two Rabbits with Mallets Pounding Rice.'"

Time passes. Grandmother passes. I've learned
the facts since. Still, in some storms I feel
a twitch, and in the still of certain nights,

with the right chopsticks, I can eat with
the Rabbits who have scattered all the Rice.

## Emily XYZ (c. 1958)

Emily XYZ is a spoken word poet who has been active on the poetry scene in New York City since the early 1980s. She is best known for her two-voice arrangements of her poetry, which she performs with Myers Bartlett. Before hitting her stride with the two-voice arrangement, Emily XYZ staged poetry for up to eight voices. She has released a book, *The Emily XYZ Songbook* (2005), complete with a CD on which she and Bartlett perform to electronic music composed by Virgil Moorefield. Some of her poems have been successful recordings, such as "Who Shot Sadat?" and "Slot Machine," which was featured on the PBS TV series *The United States of Poetry*.

# Ship of State of Fools (2002)

It's October and a big battle is shaping up
not with the Diamondbacks
not with the Democrats
but between our fundamentalists
and their fundamentalists.

Our fundamentalists say
it's time for them to pay the price in blood
for all the trouble they've caused in the world
by being such violent wackos all the time
and having no respect whatsoever
for human life.

Their fundamentalists say
it's time for you to pay the price in blood
for all the trouble you've caused in the world
by being such fucking assholes all the time
and having no respect whatsoever
for human life.

One thing is for sure:

The driver of this car will not be killed
The second in command will not be killed
The loan will remain in effect
and even if it's hit,
the car will not roll over

But the passengers
had better look out
and the pedestrians
had better look out
and the people who live by the road
thinking they're safe
thinking, This is what we voted for
should be ready:

Red lights will be run
All directions will be right
Hatred will come in for the kill
History will do its thing again.

# Writing from Reading

## Summarize

**1** Envision these poems in competition with one another at a poetry slam. Give your vote, from 1 to 10, to each poem and explain your judgment.

## Analyze Craft

**2** Compare the rhythm in each of these poems.

**3** How is rhyme used to create a rhythmic beat?

## Analyze Voice

**4** What's gained by oral presentation of the poems, and what—while reading them in silence—is lost?

## Synthesize Summary and Analysis

**5** Each of these poems seems to depend on a publicly displayed relation among sound, rhythm, and meaning. Is this traditional in poetry or some new shift of emphasis?

## Interpret the Poems

**6** "There appears to be a relation between political awareness of individual lives in the contemporary United States and the rise of spoken word and its variations," writes the probably pseudonymous Prof. I.M. Hipp. Test out this critic's idea about spoken word poetry. Do you agree or disagree with him, and why?

# For Review and Further Study

## Miguel Algarin (b. 1941)

### HIV (1997)

I. *Revelation*
Revel at ion,
Rebel at I on a course
To regret erections,
To whip the cream in my scrotum
Till it hardens into unsweetened,
Unsafe revved elations
Of milk turned sour
By the human body,
Of propagation of destruction.
The epiphany: I am unsafe,
You who want me
Know that I who want you,
Harbor the bitter balm of defeat.

II. *Salvation*
If I were to show you
How to continue holding on,
I would not kiss you,
I would not mix my fluids with yours,
For your salvation
Cannot bear the live weight
Of your sharing liquids with me.

III. *Language*
To tell,
To talk,
To tongue into sounds
How I would cleanse you with urine,
How my tasting tongue would wash your body,
How my saliva and sperm would bloat you,
To touch you in our lovemaking
And not tell you
Would amount to murder.
To talk about how to language this
So that you would still languish
In my unsafe arms and die,
Seems beyond me,
I would almost rather lie
But my tongue muscle moves involuntarily
To tell of the danger in me.

IV. *Of Health*
To use my full and willing
Body to reveal and speak
The strength that I impart
Without fear,
Without killing,
Without taking away what I would give,
To use my man's tongue
To share,
To give,
To lend,
To exact nothing,
To receive all things,
To expand my macho
And let the whole world
Into the safety of my mature masculinity.

V. *Quarantine*
Sometimes I fear touching your plump ear lobes,
I might contaminate you.
Sometimes I refuse odors that would
Drive my hands to spread your thick thighs.
Sometimes closing my ears to your voice
Wrenches my stomach and I vomit to calm wanting.
Can it be that I am the bearer of plagues?
Am I poison to desire?
Do I have to deny yearning for firm full flesh
So that I'll not kill what I love?
No juices can flow 'tween you and me.
Quicksand will suck me in.

### Questions for Interactive Reading and Writing

1. What is the occasion for the poem? To whom is the poet speaking?
2. Describe the emotions felt and expressed by the poet.
3. Why does the poet break the poem into numbered parts?
4. What is the effect of the explicit language and imagery?

# Jimmy Santiago Baca (b. 1952)

## Choices (1986)

An acquaintance at Los Alamos Labs
who engineers weapons
black x'd a mark where I live
on his office map.
Star-wars humor. . . .
He exchanged muddy boots
and patched jeans
for a white intern's coat
and black polished shoes.
A month ago, after butchering a gouged bull,
we stood on a pasture hill,
and he wondered with pained features
where money would come from
to finish his shed, plant alfalfa,
and fix his tractor.
Now his fingers
yank horsetail grass,
he crimps herringbone tail-seed
between teeth, and grits out words,
"Om gonna buy another tractor
next week. More land too."
Silence between us is gray water
let down in a tin pail
in a deep, deep well,
a silence
milled in continental grindings
millions of years ago.
I throw my heart
into the well, and it falls
a shimmering pebble to the bottom.
Words are hard
to come by, "Would have lost everything
I've worked for, not takin' the job."
His words try to
retrieve
my heart
from the deep well.
We walk on in silence,
our friendship
rippling away.

### Questions for Interactive Reading and Writing

1. Describe the setting. What is the relationship between the speaker and the other man?
2. How would you make a short story out of this material?
3. What is the tone, the feel of the poem?
4. What effect does the poet create by employing the image of the "tin pail / in a deep, deep well"?
5. The poet first speaks of his "acquaintance" but then ends the poem by talking about his "friendship" for the man. What, if anything, has changed over the course of the poem that would justify the two different ways of speaking about the other man?

# Lewis Carroll (1832–1898)

## Jabberwocky (1871)

'Twas brillig, and the slithy toves
  Did gyre and gimble in the wabe:
All mimsy were the borogoves,
  And the mome raths outgrabe.

"Beware the Jabberwock, my son!
  The jaws that bite, the claws that catch!
Beware the Jubjub bird, and shun
  The frumious Bandersnatch!"

He took his vorpal sword in hand:
  Long time the manxome foe he sought—
So rested he by the Tumtum tree,
  And stood awhile in thought.

And, as in uffish thought he stood,
  The Jabberwock, with eyes of flame,
Came whiffling through the tulgey wood,
  And burbled as it came!

One, two! One, two! And through and through
  The vorpal blade went snicker-snack!
He left it dead, and with its head
  He went galumphing back.

"And, hast thou slain the Jabberwock?
Come to my arms, my beamish boy!
O frabjous day! Callooh, Callay!"
He chortled in his joy.

'Twas brillig, and the slithy toves
Did gyre and gimble in the wabe;
All mimsy were the borogoves,
And the mome raths outgrabe.

### Questions for Interactive Reading and Writing

1. For all of its nonsense, do you hear a pattern as you recite the poem? What is the "sense" in such "nonsense," and how does Carroll invent his words or reinvigorate his language? Describe the pattern.
2. Compare the language of "Jabberwocky" to the ballad of "Sir Patrick Spence" earlier in this chapter. How does Carroll's use of sounds create a more dreamlike—or nightmarish—story than the jaunty narrative of "Sir Patrick Spence"?
3. Why might you find pleasure in the saying of this poem? Why not? What is your reaction to the nonsense words?

## Gil Scott-Heron (b. 1949)

### The Revolution Will Not Be Televised (1970)

You will not be able to stay home, brother.
You will not be able to plug in, turn on and cop out.
You will not be able to lose yourself on scag and
skip out for beer during commercials because
The revolution will not be televised.

The revolution will not be televised.
The revolution will not be brought to you by Xerox in
four parts without commercial interruption.
The revolution will not show you pictures of Nixon
blowing a bugle and leading a charge by John Mitchell,
General Abramson and Spiro Agnew to eat hog maws
confiscated from a Harlem sanctuary.
The revolution will not be televised.

The revolution will not be brought to you by
The Schaeffer Award Theatre and will not star
Natalie Wood and Steve McQueen or Bullwinkle
and Julia.
The revolution will not give your mouth sex appeal.
The revolution will not get rid of the nubs.
The revolution will not make you look five pounds
thinner.
The revolution will not be televised, brother.

There will be no pictures of you and Willie Mae
pushing that shopping cart down the block on the
dead run
or trying to slide that color tv in a stolen ambulance.
NBC will not be able to predict the winner at 8:32 on
reports from twenty-nine districts.
The revolution will not be televised.

There will be no pictures of pigs shooting down brothers
on the instant replay.
There will be no pictures of pigs shooting down brothers
on the instant replay.
There will be no slow motion or still lifes of Roy
Wilkins strolling through Watts in a red, black
and green liberation jumpsuit that he had been
saving for just the proper occasion.

Green Acres, Beverly Hillbillies and Hooterville Junction
will no longer be so damned relevant
and women will not care if Dick finally got down with
Jane
on *Search for Tomorrow*
because black people will be in the streets looking for
*A Brighter Day.*
The revolution will not be televised.

There will be no highlights on the *Eleven O'Clock News*
and no pictures of hairy armed women liberationists
and Jackie Onassis blowing her nose.
The theme song will not be written by Jim Webb or
Francis Scott Key
nor sung by Glen Campbell, Tom Jones, Johnny Cash,
Englebert Humperdink or Rare Earth.
The revolution will not be televised.

The revolution will not be right back after a
message about a white tornado, white lightning or white
people.
You will not have to worry about a dove in your bedroom,
the tiger in your tank or the giant in your toilet bowl.
The revolution will not go better with Coke.
The revolution will not fight germs that may cause bad
breath.
The revolution *will* put you in the driver's seat.
The revolution will not be televised
will not be televised
not be televised
be televised
The revolution will be no re-run, brothers.
The revolution will be LIVE.

### Questions for Interactive Reading and Writing

1. What role does politics play in the beginning of the poem?
2. How does rhythm play a role in the development of meaning?
3. Is there in the poem a social critique of modern American society that you can appreciate without accepting the idea of political revolution?
4. How does spoken word poetry invite a political perspective?

# Langston Hughes (1902–1967)

*For a brief biography of Langston Hughes, see chapter 26, the Case Study on Langston Hughes and His Contemporaries.*

## The Blues (1958)

When the shoe strings break
On *both* your shoes
And you're in a hurry—
That's the blues.

When you go to buy a candy bar
And you've lost the dime you had—
Slipped through a hole in your pocket somewhere—
That's the blues, too, *and bad!*

### Questions for Interactive Reading and Writing

1. What attracts a poet like Hughes to the blues form? (See the casebook on Langston Hughes, chapter 26.)
2. Can you imagine someone singing this to the accompaniment of a piano and bass?

# Audre Lorde (1934–1992)

## The Electric Slide Boogie (1993)

New Year's Day 1:16 AM
and my body is weary beyond
time to withdraw and rest
ample room allowed me in everyone's head
but community calls
right over the threshold
drums beating through the walls
children playing their truck dramas
under the collapsible coatrack
in the narrow hallway outside my room

The TV lounge next door is wide open
it is midnight in Idaho
and the throb easy subtle spin
of the electric slide boogie
step-stepping
around the corner of the parlor
past the sweet clink
of dining room glasses
and the edged aroma of slightly overdone
dutch-apple pie
all laced together
with the rich dark laughter
of Gloria
and her higher-octave sisters

How hard it is to sleep
in the middle of life.

### Questions for Interactive Reading and Writing

1. How would you describe the holiday spirit of the poem, given the time the poet reveals in it?
2. What elements does the poet use to capture "the throb easy subtle spin" of the dance?
3. What are the greatest contrasting images of the poem?
4. Are the last two lines a complaint or a celebration?

# Willie Perdomo (b. 1967)

## Postcards of El Barrio (1996)

are rarely ever
sent to me

hanging off a broken stick
a dull red, white and blue flag
one star instead of fifty
blows a hot breeze
of bullet beans

congas y timbales bingbangbongboom
down the block and back,
our blood stands on its toes
and we start to dance

winos lean over their canes and begin
a different story with the same ending:
"Geronimo wasn't shit compared to Papo"

chickens, rats, rabbits and cats are
tired of walking on broken glass gardens
they wait for the city to come
and knock all the gates down

once in a full blue moon
rising above crumbling gray rooftops
I see a morenito sitting on a stoop
licking the melting pineapple
ice off his palms

the violent revolutions
of red and white police sirens upset the sky blue peace
of neon crucifixions slow orange and yellow bulbs
race around the rims of stained bodega canopies
hiding from the rain
Old Man Jimmy
sings the blues

postcards of El Barrio
are rarely ever sent to me.

### Questions for Interactive Reading and Writing

1. Read the poem aloud. How do the rhythms make your voice sound?
2. What does the poet mean by "our blood stands on its toes"?
3. Why is the poem itself in a sense a postcard of El Barrio?

## Quincy Troupe (b. 1943)

### Poem Reaching towards Something (1997)

we walk through a calligraphy of hats slicing off
  foreheads
ace-deuce cocked, they slant, razor sharp, clean
through imagination, our spirits knee-deep in what we
  have forgotten
entrancing our bodies now to dance, like enraptured
  water lilies—
my memory & me—the rhythm in liquid stride of a
  certain look—
rippling eyeballs through breezes—
riffling choirs of trees where a trillion slivers of sunlight
  prance

across filigreeing leaves, a zillion voices of bamboo reeds
green with summer's saxophone burst
wrap themselves, like transparent prisms of dew—
drops around images, laced with pearls & rhinestones
perhaps it is through this, or the decoding of syllables
that we learn speech, that sonorous river of broken
  mirrors
carrying our dreams, assaulted by pellets of raindrops, the prisons of words entrapping us between
  parentheses—
two bat wings curving into cynical smiles

still, there is something here that needs explaining
  beyond
the hopelessness of miles, the light at the end of the
  midnight tunnel—
some say it is a train coming right at us—
where do the tumbling words spend themselves after
  they have spent
all meaning residing in the warehouse of language
after they have slipped like smoke
from our lips, where do the symbols they carry stop
  everything
put down roots, cleanse themselves of everything but
  clarity—
though here eye might be asking a little too much of any
  poet's head
full as it is with double-entendres
still, there are these hats slicing foreheads off in the
  middle
of crowds, the calligraphy of this penumbra slanting
ace-deuce cocked, carrying the perforated legacy of
  bebop, these bold
peccadillo, pirouetting pellagras, razor-sharp-clean,
  they cut
into our rip-tiding dreams carrying their whirlpooling
  imaginations
their rivers of schemes assaulted by pellets of raindrops, these broken mirrors reflecting sonorous
words entrapping us between parentheses—
two hat wings curved, imprisoning the world

## Questions for Interactive Reading and Writing

1. Who is the "we" throughout this poem? Using plain language, describe the situation.
2. Is there a physical setting in this poem? Describe it using details from the poem.
3. How does Troupe's use of "eye" in place of the pronoun "I" in line 25 affect the poem?

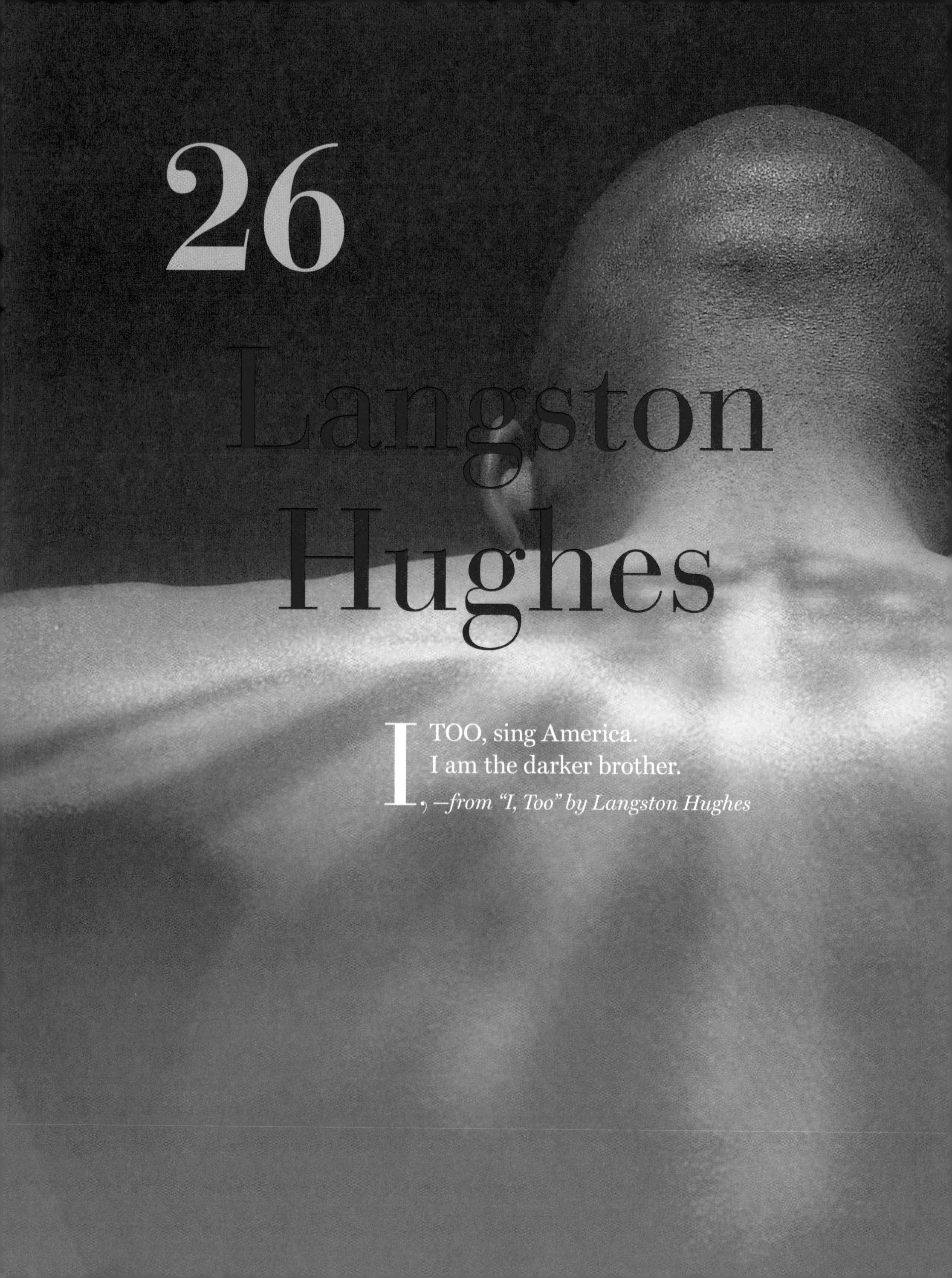

# 26

# Langston Hughes

I, TOO, sing America.
I am the darker brother.

*—from "I, Too" by Langston Hughes*

*"In the last decade something beyond the watch and guard of statistics has happened in the life of the American Negro. . . . The Sociologist, the Philanthropist, the Race-leader are not unaware of the New Negro, but they are at a loss to account for him. He simply cannot be swathed in their formula. For the younger generation is vibrant with a new psychology; the new spirit is awake in the masses, and under the very eyes of the professional observers is transforming what has been a perennial problem into the progressive phases of contemporary Negro life."*

—from "The New Negro" by Alain Locke

# A Case Study on *Langston Hughes and His Contemporaries*

## *Langston Hughes*



## *Hughes's Contemporaries*

# *The Harlem Renaissance*

The historical moment in which Langston Hughes and his contemporaries lived was crucial to launching their careers. All came of age during the Harlem Renaissance, a movement that took place in the 1920s and early 1930s, a time of cultural awakening for African Americans in terms of literature, music, art, theater, and political thinking.

The Cotton Club, a famous night club in Harlem where Duke Ellington, Cab Calloway, and other gifted black musicians played for an exclusively white clientele.

Josephine Baker (1906–1975), although also known for appearing in men's clothing, was more popular for her tendency to perform onstage in the nude.

## The New Culture of Harlem

The Harlem Renaissance is named after the cultural activity—the fiction, poetry, and essays about black life in America—that flourished mainly in a two-mile section of Manhattan in New York City in which many African Americans settled—200,000 blacks lived there by 1928—in the great migration of blacks to find employment and education in the North. Harlem served as the epicenter of the Harlem Renaissance, as it boasted clubs where musicians including Duke Ellington, Louis Armstrong, and Bessie Smith performed; theaters such as the Apollo for black entertainers; and a common neighborhood in which important writers lived, among them Jean Toomer, Claude McKay, and Zora Neale Hurston (see chapter 14, Stories for Further Reading, for Hurston's "Gilded Six-Bits").

Fats Waller (1904–1943) and his hot jazz epitomized the music of the "rent party," a party thrown in an apartment in Harlem to help the tenant pay Harlem's high rents.

In addition to the writers, musicians, and artists, social thinkers such as W. E. B Du Bois were important advocates of black rights and education. Whites, too, were active in the Harlem Renaissance; the photographer Carl Van Vechten, for example, was a close friend of Langston Hughes's who supported the renaissance and admired the work of blacks, though at the time most of the black population was not touched by this cultural awakening.

## "Negro Vogue"

"Madame is of the opinion that little of artistic merit is now being produced in America except that which is being done by Negroes," wrote Countee Cullen after meeting with the (white) Claire Goll. Indeed, whites were drawn to African-American culture, and particularly the night life of Harlem—so much so that one of Harlem's most famous clubs, the Cotton Club, catered to an exclusively white clientele. While this interest in black culture brought national attention to the work of black artists, people like Du Bois feared that it might fuel stereotypes of black society. Still, new venues such as *Crisis* and *Opportunity*—both important magazines for black audiences staffed by leading writers of the Harlem Renaissance—offered an unprecedented outlet for thought and literature.

Duke Ellington (1899–1974), one of America's most influential jazz composers, and the Duke Ellington Orchestra, with its growling trumpet, street rhythms, and the influence of classical music, were broadcast from the Cotton Club. Ellington called it simply "the American Music."

# Langston Hughes (1902–1967)

For Langston Hughes, life was—as he put it—"no crystal stair." Hughes was born in Joplin, Missouri, in 1902; his parents divorced when he was quite young. His father left for Mexico, hoping to find a society less hostile to blacks, and his mother moved away to pursue her personal interests. Hughes was raised by his grandmother in Kansas, who told him her first husband had been killed with John Brown's men raiding Harper's Ferry; sometimes she wrapped his bullet-torn shawl around the child. Although this may have helped nurture Hughes's sense of pride in his race, his childhood was a lonely one, marked by longing for his mother. After his grandmother's death, he moved at age thirteen to Illinois and then to Cleveland to live with his mother, who never provided the maternal love that Hughes so desired.

Cleveland, where he attended high school, set the stage for the rest of his life in two central ways. First, he was active in many clubs at school and immensely popular. Second, he published poems while still in high school. "The Negro Speaks of Rivers" appeared just after his graduation at age nineteen. Still in his early twenties, he won the admiration of poet Vachel Lindsay when, as a busboy at a Washington, D.C., hotel, he put three of his poems next to Lindsay's plate. Even a small sampling of Hughes's poetry—such as we include in this chapter—makes clear the talent and ambition Hughes demonstrated from an early age. He wanted to be a poet, following his favorite forefathers, Walt Whitman and Carl Sandburg, but more, he wanted to celebrate his race, to show whites and blacks alike the beauty and integrity of the common African-American masses.

The year 1926 was an important one for Hughes. After traveling abroad—in France, Spain, and the Soviet Union—and holding a variety of jobs, Hughes entered Lincoln University, from which he would earn his bachelor's degree three years later. He then settled in Harlem, an African-American section of New York City. Hughes lived there during the time of the Harlem Renaissance, when black culture thrived and produced great artists, musicians, and writers, who were for the first time reaching black and white audiences alike. Foremost among these artists was Hughes, who had two early publications of major importance. His first collection of poems, *The Weary Blues,* earned much acclaim, and an essay appeared in *The Nation* called "The Negro Artist and the Racial Mountain," an essay that was both Hughes's personal manifesto and the manifesto of his generation of Harlem Renaissance artists. In it, he speaks against what he calls the "high-class Negro"—blacks who adopt a white way of life and try to fit in with the conventions of white middle-class culture. Instead, he celebrates the "low-down folks, the so-called common element." To Hughes, blacks who are genuine in their way of life are preferable; as he writes, "they still hold their own individuality in the face of American standardizations." The essay concludes with a clear statement of intention: "We younger Negro artists who create now intend to express our individual dark-skinned selves without fear or shame. If white people are pleased we are glad. If they are not, it doesn't matter."

Hughes followed his own dictum as stated in these last lines of "The Negro Artist and the Racial Mountain," for his poetry celebrates black identity, particularly the "low-down folks," in several ways. First, the "I" in these poems is not meant as a specific person but embodies the entire black race by claiming all their experiences—the difficult and admirable alike—in personal terms. "The Negro Speaks of Rivers", "I, Too," and "A New Song" are all written by adopting the voice of a "collective consciousness"—that is, a single speaker who transcends time and place as he recounts the experiences of an entire group. Second, Hughes's poetry is characterized by the directness of his thoughts, a "plain style" (see casebook on Dickinson and Frost) reflecting a long tradition in American literature that extends back to the Puritans, who favored simplicity over adornment. Third, Hughes's poetry consciously salutes and imitates the musical forms of blues and jazz. Hughes describes his 1951 collection *Montage of a Dream Deferred* as growing from popular African-American music. He explains "this poem on contemporary Harlem, like be-bop, is marked by conflicting changes, sudden nuances, sharp and impudent interjections, broken rhythms, and passages sometimes in the manner of a jam session, sometimes the popular song, punctuated by the riffs, runs, breaks, and distortions of the music of a community in transition."

Hughes expressed his black identity in poetry, fiction, nonfiction, children's books, plays, librettos, and a popular newspaper column featuring the character Jesse B. Semple, nicknamed "Simple." In all his work, Hughes celebrated African-American identity, focusing on the urban black population and mimicking what he saw to be at the heart of that population: blues and jazz. Despite Hughes's innovation using dialect, jazz, blues, and black culture in his poetry, he was barely able to make a living with his pen. He once referred to himself as a "literary sharecropper" as he pieced together a career filled with great accomplishments and occasional critical failures. Although in later years Hughes became controversial because of his far left political views, those around him invariably knew him to be a kind man with a celebratory sense of humanity, and he remained popular with readers and audiences throughout his life; even being ordered by Senator Joseph McCarthy to appear before his infamous committee on un-American activities because of socialist political views did not diminish his career. Hughes's credo can be summed up as "to my mind, it is the duty of the younger Negro artist, if he accepts any duties at all from outsiders, to change through the force of his art that old whispering 'I want to be white,' hidden in the aspirations of his people, to 'Why should I want to be white? I am Negro—and beautiful.'"

# The Poetry of Langston Hughes

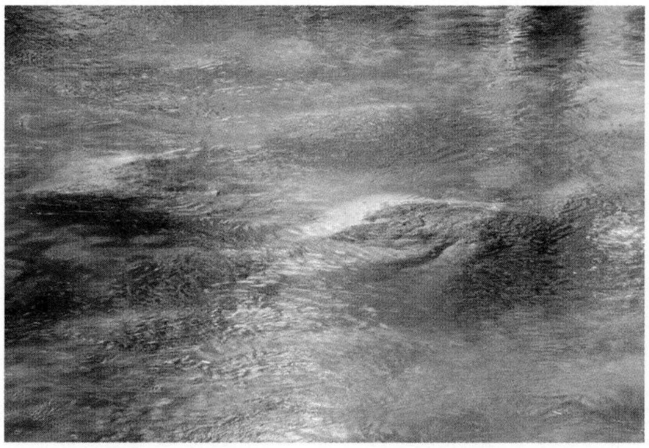

## The Negro Speaks of Rivers (1921)

I've known rivers:
I've known rivers ancient as the world and older than the flow of human blood in human veins.

My soul has grown deep like the rivers.

I bathed in the Euphrates when dawns were young.
I built my hut near the Congo and it lulled me to sleep.
I looked upon the Nile and raised the pyramids above it.
I heard the singing of the Mississippi when Abe Lincoln went down to New Orleans, and I've seen its muddy bosom turn all golden in the sunset.

I've known rivers:
Ancient, dusky rivers.

My soul has grown deep like the rivers.

### Questions for Critical Thinking

1. Highlight the repeated phrases and lines in this poem. What effect does Hughes achieve with these repetitions?
2. Make a list of everything the word *rivers* connotes to you. How do these connotations enhance your reading of the poem?

## Mother to Son (1922)

Well, son, I'll tell you:
Life for me ain't been no crystal stair.
It's had tacks in it,
And splinters,
And boards torn up,
And places with no carpet on the floor—
Bare.
But all the time
I'se been a-climbin' on,
And reachin' landin's,
And turnin' corners,
And sometimes goin' in the dark
Where there ain't been no light.
So boy, don't you turn back.
Don't you set down on the steps
'Cause you finds it's kinder hard.
Don't you fall now—
For I'se still goin', honey,
I'se still climbin',
And life for me ain't been no crystal stair.

### Questions for Critical Thinking

1. Review what you learned about persona in chapter 20. How does this poem compare to one of Robert Browning's dramatic monologues such as "My Last Duchess" (in chapter 16)?
2. What is the controlling metaphor in this poem?

## Negro (1922)

I am a Negro:
  Black as the night is black,
  Black as the depths of my Africa.

I've been a slave:
  Caesar told me to keep his door-steps clean.
  I brushed the boots of Washington.

I've been a worker:
  Under my hand the pyramids arose.
  I made mortar for the Woolworth Building.

I've been a singer:
  All the way from Africa to Georgia
  I carried my sorrow songs.
  I made ragtime.

I've been a victim:
  The Belgians cut off my hands in the Congo.
  They lynch me still in Mississippi.

I am a Negro:
  Black as the night is black,
  Black like the depths of my Africa.

### Questions for Critical Thinking

1. Describe the relation between the repeated statement in the first and last stanzas and the specific descriptions.
2. Could you substitute other racial or ethnic identities and still have the same poem? Why or why not?

## I, Too (1925)

I, too, sing America.

I am the darker brother.
They send me to eat in the kitchen
When company comes,
But I laugh,
And eat well,
And grow strong.

Tomorrow,
I'll be at the table
When company comes.
Nobody'll dare
Say to me,
"Eat in the kitchen,"
Then.

Besides,
They'll see how beautiful I am
And be ashamed—

I, too, am America.

### Questions for Critical Thinking

1. "I sing America" is a phrase from Walt Whitman's "I Hear America Singing." Why is Hughes tipping his cap to his white predecessor, and how is he stressing a kind of separate identity when he writes "I, too, sing America"?
2. Scan this poem's meter. Even though it is free verse, what patterns do you see within the poem? What do you think is the significance of where those patterns fall?

## The Weary Blues (1925)

Droning a drowsy syncopated tune,
Rocking back and forth to a mellow croon,
  I heard a Negro play.
Down on Lenox Avenue the other night
By the pale dull pallor of an old gas light
  He did a lazy sway. . . .
  He did a lazy sway. . . .
To the tune o' those Weary Blues.
With his ebony hands on each ivory key
He made that poor piano moan with melody.
  O Blues!
Swaying to and fro on his rickety stool
He played that sad raggy tune like a musical fool.
  Sweet Blues!
Coming from a black man's soul.
  O Blues!
In a deep song voice with a melancholy tone
I heard that Negro sing, that old piano moan—
  "Ain't got nobody in all this world,
    Ain't got nobody but ma self.
    I's gwine to quit ma frownin'
    And put ma troubles on the shelf."

Thump, thump, thump, went his foot on the floor.
He played a few chords then he sang some more—
  "I got the Weary Blues
    And I can't be satisfied.
    Got the Weary Blues
    And can't be satisfied—
    I ain't happy no mo'
    And I wish that I had died."

And far into the night he crooned that tune.
The stars went out and so did the moon.
The singer stopped playing and went to bed
While the Weary Blues echoed through his head.
He slept like a rock or a man that's dead.

### Questions for Critical Thinking

1. How does the voice shift after the last blues stanza? What effect does this have on your response to the poem?
2. How is the Harlem street scene that Hughes creates here typical or idealized?

## Po' Boy Blues (1926)

When I was home de
Sunshine seemed like gold.
When I was home de
Sunshine seemed like gold.
Since I come up North de
Whole damn world's turned cold.

I was a good boy,
Never done no wrong.
Yes, I was a good boy,
Never done no wrong,
But this world is weary
An' de road is hard an' long.

I fell in love with
A gal I thought was kind.
Fell in love with
A gal I thought was kind.
She made me lose ma money
An' almost lose ma mind.

Weary, weary,
Weary early in de morn.
Weary, weary,
Early, early in de morn.
I's so weary
I wish I'd never been born.

### Questions for Critical Thinking

1. In what ways does this poem interact with the blues?
2. Given the colloquial quality of this poem, which word choices seem important to you and why?

## Song for a Dark Girl (1927)

Way Down South in Dixie
  (Break the heart of me)
They hung my black young lover
  To a cross roads tree.

Way Down South in Dixie
  (Bruised body high in air)
I asked the white Lord Jesus
  What was the use of prayer.

Way Down South in Dixie
  (Break the heart of me)
Love is a naked shadow
  On a gnarled and naked tree.

### Questions for Critical Thinking

1. How would you describe the character the poet has created to sing these lines?
2. How does the historical and social material work with or against the musical aspect of the poem?

## The Dream Keeper (1932)

Bring me all of your dreams,
You dreamers,
Bring me all of your
Heart melodies
That I may wrap them
In a blue cloud-cloth
Away from the too-rough fingers
Of the world.

### Questions for Critical Thinking

1. How does one wrap a heart melody in a cloud-cloth, and why should the world have fingers? Attack or defend the use of figurative language here.
2. Freewrite a page or two comparing this poem to "Harlem (Dream Deferred)." Pay particular attention to differences in tone, imagery, and diction.

## Minstrel Man (1932)

Because my mouth
Is wide with laughter
And my throat
Is deep with song,
You do not think
I suffer after
I have held my pain
So long?

Because my mouth
Is wide with laughter,
You do not hear
My inner cry?
Because my feet
Are gay with dancing,
You do not know
I die?

### Questions for Critical Thinking

1. What patterns do you see in this poem's structure? In its metric foot? In its rhyme?
2. How is this poem a particular discussion of a particular form of entertainment, a general statement about the black man's role in society, or both?

## Quiet Girl (Ardella) (1926)

I would liken you
To a night without stars
Were it not for your eyes.
I would liken you
To a sleep without dreams
Were it not for your songs.

### Questions for Critical Thinking

1. How would you describe the form of this poem? Does it remind you of a traditional form, or is it closer to the blues?
2. Compare this poem to such love songs as Leonard Cohen's "For Anne" (chapter 15) or William Shakespeare's "Shall I compare thee to a summer's day?" (chapter 18). What is different, what similar in tone?

## Let America Be America Again (1936)

Let America be America again.
Let it be the dream it used to be.
Let it be the pioneer on the plain
Seeking a home where he himself is free.

(America never was America to me.)

Let America be the dream the dreamers dreamed—
Let it be that great strong land of love
Where never kings connive nor tyrants scheme
That any man be crushed by one above.

(It never was America to me.)

O, let my land be a land where Liberty
Is crowned with no false patriotic wreath,
But opportunity is real, and life is free,
Equality is in the air we breathe.

(There's never been equality for me,
Nor freedom in this "homeland of the free.")

*Say, who are you that mumbles in the dark?*
*And who are you that draws your veil across the stars?*

I am the poor white, fooled and pushed apart,
I am the Negro bearing slavery's scars.
I am the red man driven from the land,
I am the immigrant clutching the hope I seek—
And finding only the same old stupid plan
Of dog eat dog, of mighty crush the weak.

I am the young man, full of strength and hope,
Tangled in that ancient endless chain
Of profit, power, gain, of grab the land!
Of grab the gold! Of grab the ways of satisfying need!
Of work the men! Of take the pay!
Of owning everything for one's own greed!

I am the farmer, bondsman to the soil.
I am the worker sold to the machine.
I am the Negro, servant to you all.
I am the people, humble, hungry, mean—
Hungry yet today despite the dream.
Beaten yet today—O, Pioneers!
I am the man who never got ahead,
The poorest worker bartered through the years.

Yet I'm the one who dreamt our basic dream
In the Old World while still a serf of kings,
Who dreamt a dream so strong, so brave, so true,
That even yet its mighty daring sings
In every brick and stone, in every furrow turned
That's made America the land it has become.
O, I'm the man who sailed those early seas
In search of what I meant to be my home—
For I'm the one who left dark Ireland's shore,
And Poland's plain, and England's grassy lea,
And torn from Black Africa's strand I came
To build a "homeland of the free."

The free?

Who said the free? Not me?
Surely not me? The millions on relief today?
The millions shot down when we strike?
The millions who have nothing for our pay?
For all the dreams we've dreamed
And all the songs we've sung
And all the hopes we've held
And all the flags we've hung,
The millions who have nothing for our pay—
Except the dream that's almost dead today.

O, let America be America again—
The land that never has been yet—
And yet must be—the land where *every* man is free.
The land that's mine—the poor man's, Indian's, Negro's, ME—
Who made America,
Whose sweat and blood, whose faith and pain,
Whose hand at the foundry, whose plow in the rain,
Must bring back our mighty dream again.

Sure, call me any ugly name you choose—
The steel of freedom does not stain.
From those who live like leeches on the people's lives,
We must take back our land again,
America!

O, yes,
I say it plain,
America never was America to me,
And yet I swear this oath—
America will be!

Out of the rack and ruin of our gangster death,
The rape and rot of graft, and stealth, and lies,
We, the people, must redeem
The land, the mines, the plants, the rivers.
The mountains and the endless plain—
All, all the stretch of these great green states—
And make America again!

### Questions for Critical Thinking

1. Highlight the parts of this poem that use repetition. What is the effect of repetition here? You might want to compare your answer to your response to the first question that accompanies "The Negro Speaks of Rivers" to get a better understanding of how Hughes uses the device.
2. Examine the punctuation in this poem. How does Hughes build the emotion of the poem with punctuation?

## A New Song (1938)

I speak in the name of the black millions
Awakening to action.
Let all others keep silent a moment.
I have this word to bring,
This thing to say,
This song to sing:

Bitter was the day
When I bowed my back
Beneath the slaver's whip.

That day is past.

Bitter was the day
When I saw my children unschooled,
My young men without a voice in the world,
My women taken as the body-toys
Of a thieving people.

That day is past.

Bitter was the day, I say,
When the lyncher's rope
Hung about my neck,
And the fire scorched my feet,
And the oppressors had no pity,
And only in the sorrow songs
Relief was found

That day is past.

I know full well now
Only my own hands,
Dark as the earth,
Can make my earth-dark body free.
O, thieves, exploiters, killers,
No longer shall you say
With arrogant eyes and scornful lips:
"You are my servant,
Black man—
I, the free!"

That day is past—

For now,
In many mouths—
Dark mouths where red tongues burn
And white teeth gleam—
New words are formed,
Bitter
With the past
But sweet
With the dream.
Tense,
Unyielding,
Strong and sure,
They sweep the earth—

Revolt! Arise!

The Black
And White World
Shall be one!
The Worker's World!

The past is done!

A new dream flames
Against the
Sun!

## Questions for Critical Thinking

1. Compare the overall message of this poem with the message in "Let America Be America Again." Which do you find more compelling for Hughes's social context? Which do you find more compelling for today's society?
2. Remembering that Hughes had far left political views—that is, like many of his generation, he sympathized with socialism—where do you see his political views reflected in this poem? Which parts, if any, seem above politics to you?

## Ballad of the Landlord (1940)

Landlord, landlord,
My roof has sprung a leak.
Don't you 'member I told you about it
Way last week?

Landlord, landlord,
These steps is broken down.
When you come up yourself
It's a wonder you don't fall down.

Ten Bucks you say I owe you?
Ten Bucks you say is due?
Well, that's Ten Bucks more'n I'll pay you
Till you fix this house up new.

What? You gonna get eviction orders?
You gonna cut off my heat?
You gonna take my furniture and
Throw it in the street?

Um-huh! You talking high and mighty.
Talk on—till you get through.
You ain't gonna be able to say a word
If I land my fist on you.

*Police! Police!*
*Come and get this man!*
*He's trying to ruin the government*
*And overturn the land!*

Copper's Whistle!
Patrol bell!
Arrest.

Precinct Station.
Iron cell.
Headlines in press:

MAN THREATENS LANDLORD
TENANT HELD NO BAIL
JUDGE GIVES NEGRO 90 DAYS IN COUNTY JAIL

### Questions for Critical Thinking

1. Where do you think the poet might have found the material for the story within his poem?
2. Describe the situation that the poet makes use of, and discuss the process by which he transforms the "news" into his subject here.

## Dream Boogie (1951)

Good morning, daddy!
Ain't you heard
The boogie-woogie rumble
Of a dream deferred?
Listen closely:
You'll hear their feet
Beating out and beating out a—

*You think*
*It's a happy beat?*

Listen to it closely:
Ain't you heard
something underneath
like a—

*What did I say?*

Sure,
I'm happy!
Take it away!

*Hey, pop!*
*Re-bop!*
*Mop!*

*Y-e-a-h!*

### Questions for Critical Thinking

1. Does such playfulness as we find in these lines have its place in good poetry? Why or why not?
2. How does the poet bend a traditional musical form to his own purposes? Why does he do it?

## Harlem (Dream Deferred) (1951)

What happens to a dream deferred?

Does it dry up
like a raisin in the sun?
Or fester like a sore—
And then run?
Does it stink like rotten meat?
Or crust and sugar over—
like a syrupy sweet?

Maybe it just sags
like a heavy load.

*Or does it explode?*

### Questions for Critical Thinking

1. How would you describe the rhyme in this poem? What effect does it create?
2. What impact does the last line have on your understanding of the rest of the poem?

## Motto (1951)

I play it cool
And dig all jive.
That's the reason
I stay alive.

My motto,
As I live and learn,
is:
*Dig And Be Dug*
*In Return.*

### Questions for Critical Thinking

1. Rewrite this poem without using slang. What does this reveal about the voice in the poem?
2. Compare your new version with Hughes's version. What is gained by using slang?

## Night Funeral In Harlem (1951)

Night funeral
In Harlem:

*Where did they get*
*Them two fine cars?*

Insurance man, he did not pay—
His insurance lapsed the other day—
Yet they got a satin box
For his head to lay.

Night funeral
In Harlem:

*Who was it sent*
*That wreath of flowers?*

Them flowers came
from that poor boy's friends—
They'll want flowers, too,
When they meet their ends.

Night funeral
In Harlem:

*Who preached that*
*Black boy to his grave?*

Old preacher-man
Preached that boy away—
Charged Five Dollars
His girl friend had to pay.

Night funeral
In Harlem:

When it was all over
And the lid shut on his head
and the organ had done played
and the last prayers been said
and six pallbearers
Carried him out for dead
And off down Lenox Avenue
That long black hearse done sped,
The street light
At his corner
Shined just like a tear—

That boy that they was mournin'
Was so dear, so dear
To them folks that brought the flowers,
To that girl who paid the preacher-man—
It was all their tears that made
  That poor boy's
  Funeral grand.

  Night funeral
  In Harlem.

### Questions for Critical Thinking

1. How does this poem achieve a musical effect? Keep in mind that it comes from the jazz-inspired collection *Montage of a Dream.*
2. There are several speakers here, and a kind of chorus. Who are the speakers, and what does each contribute to the narrative of the poem?

## Theme for English B (1951)

The instructor said,

*Go home and write*
*a page tonight.*
*And let that page come out of you—*
*Then, it will be true.*

I wonder if it's that simple?
I am twenty-two, colored, born in Winston-Salem.
I went to school there, then Durham, then here
to this college on the hill above Harlem.
I am the only colored student in my class.
The steps from the hill lead down into Harlem,
through a park, then I cross St. Nicholas,
Eighth Avenue, Seventh, and I come to the Y,
the Harlem Branch Y, where I take the elevator
up to my room, sit down, and write this page:

It's not easy to know what is true for you and me
at twenty-two, my age. But I guess I'm what
I feel and see and hear, Harlem, I hear you:
hear you, hear me—we two—you, me, talk on this page.
(I hear New York, too.) Me—who?
Well, I like to eat, sleep, drink, and be in love.
I like to work, read, learn, and understand life.
I like a pipe for a Christmas present,
or records—Bessie, bop, or Bach.
I guess being colored doesn't make me *not* like
the same things other folks like who are other races.
So will my page be colored that I write?
Being me, it will not be white.

But it will be
a part of you, instructor.
You are white—
yet a part of me, as I am a part of you.
That's American.
Sometimes perhaps you don't want to be a part of me.
Nor do I often want to be a part of you.
But we are, that's true!
As I learn from you,
I guess you learn from me—
although you're older—and white—
and somewhat more free.

This is my page for English B.

### Questions for Critical Thinking

1. Given the sentence-like and conversational quality of many of the lines, what elements make this a poem, rather than an essay?
2. Given your knowledge of the facts of Hughes's life, it's obvious that the "I" who speaks in this poem is neither directly autobiographical nor the "I" of the poet himself. Who, then, is the speaker?

*Hughes wrote the following essay in 1926, the same year that his first collection of poetry,* The Weary Blues, *appeared to great acclaim. "The Negro Artist and the Racial Mountain" stands as his personal manifesto even as it speaks to the entire generation of the Harlem Renaissance. It celebrates the "so-called common element," the genuine black artists who stay true to their heritage. At the same it serves as a call to arms for all Negro artists and intellectuals to resist white middle-class standards and express their individuality.*

## The Negro Artist and the Racial Mountain (1926)

1 One of the most promising of the young Negro poets said to me once, "I want to be a poet—not a Negro poet," meaning, I believe, "I want to write like a white poet"; meaning subconsciously, "I would like to be a white poet"; meaning behind that, "I would like to be white." And I was sorry the young man said that, for no great poet has ever been afraid of being himself. And I doubted then that, with his desire to run away spiritually from his race, this boy would ever be a great poet. But this is the mountain standing in the way of any true Negro art in America—this urge within the race toward whiteness, the desire to pour racial individuality into the mold of American standardization, and to be as little Negro and as much American as possible.

2 But let us look at the immediate background of this young poet. His family is of what I suppose one would call the Negro middle class: people who are by no means rich yet never uncomfortable nor hungry—smug, contented, respectable folk, members of the Baptist church. The father goes to work every morning. He is a chief steward at a large white club. The mother sometimes does fancy sewing or supervises parties for the rich families of the town. The children go to a mixed school. In the home they read white papers and magazines. And the mother often says "Don't be like niggers" when the children are bad. A frequent phrase from the father is, "Look how well a white man does things." And so the word white comes to be unconsciously a symbol of all virtues. It holds for the children beauty, morality, and money. The whisper of "I want to be white" runs silently through their minds. This young poet's home is, I believe, a fairly typical home of the colored middle class. One sees immediately how difficult it would be for an artist born in such a home to interest himself in interpreting the beauty of his own people. He is never taught to see that beauty. He is taught rather not to see it, or if he does, to be ashamed of it when it is not according to Caucasian patterns. . . .

3 But then there are the low-down folks, the so-called common element, and they are the majority—may the Lord be praised! The people who have their hip of gin on Saturday nights and are not too important to themselves or the community, or too well fed, or too learned to watch the lazy world go round. They live on Seventh Street in Washington or State Street in Chicago and they do not particularly care whether they are like white folks or anybody else. Their joy runs, bang! into ecstasy. Their religion soars to a shout. Work maybe a little today, rest a little tomorrow. Play awhile. Sing awhile. O, let's dance! These common people are not afraid of spirituals, as for a long time their more intellectual brethren were, and jazz is their child. They furnish a wealth of colorful, distinctive material for any artist because they still hold their own individuality in the face of American standardizations. And perhaps these common people will give to the world its truly great Negro artist, the one who is not afraid to be himself. Whereas the better-class Negro would tell the artist what to do, the people at least let him alone when he does appear. And they are not ashamed of him—if they know he exists at all. And they accept what beauty is their own without question. . . .

Most of my own poems are racial in theme and treatment, derived from the life I know. In many of them I try to grasp and hold some of the meanings and rhythms of jazz. I am as sincere as I know how to be in these poems and yet after every reading I answer questions like these from my own people: Do you think Negroes should always write about Negroes? I wish you wouldn't read some of your poems to white folks. How do you find anything interesting in a place like a cabaret? Why do you write about black people? You aren't black. What makes you do so many jazz poems? 4

But jazz to me is one of the inherent expressions of Negro life in America; the eternal tom-tom beating in the Negro soul—the tom-tom of revolt against weariness in a white world, a world of subway trains, and work, work, work; the tom-tom of joy and laughter, and pain swallowed in a smile. Yet the Philadelphia clubwoman is ashamed to say that her race created it and she does not like me to write about it. The old subconscious "white is best" runs through her mind. Years of study under white teachers, a lifetime of white books, pictures, and papers, and white manners, morals, and Puritan standards made her dislike the spirituals. And now she turns up her nose at jazz and all its manifestations—likewise almost everything else distinctly racial. She doesn't care for the Winold Reiss' portraits of Negroes because they are "too Negro." She does not want a true picture of herself from anybody. She wants the artist to flatter her, to make the white world believe that all Negroes are as smug and 5

as near white in soul as she wants to be. But, to my mind, it is the duty of the younger Negro artist, if he accepts any duties at all from outsiders, to change through the force of his art that old whispering "I want to be white," hidden in the aspirations of his people, to "Why should I want to be white? I am a Negro—and beautiful."

6 So I am ashamed for the black poet who says, "I want to be a poet, not a Negro poet," as though his own racial world were not as interesting as any other world. I am ashamed, too, for the colored artist who runs from the painting of Negro faces to the painting of sunsets after the manner of the academicians because he fears the strange unwhiteness of his own features. An artist must be free to choose what he does, certainly, but he must also never be afraid to do what he must choose.

7 Let the blare of Negro jazz bands and the bellowing voice of Bessie Smith singing the Blues penetrate the closed ears of the colored near intellectuals until they listen and perhaps understand. Let Paul Robeson singing "Water Boy," and Rudolph Fisher writing about the streets of Harlem, and Jean Toomer holding the heart of Georgia in his hands, and Aaron Douglas's drawing strange black fantasies cause the smug Negro middle class to turn from their white, respectable, ordinary books and papers to catch a glimmer of their own beauty. We younger Negro artists who create now intend to express our individual dark-skinned selves without fear or shame. If white people are pleased we are glad. If they are not, it doesn't matter. We know we are beautiful. And ugly too. The tom-tom cries and the tom-tom laughs. If colored people are pleased we are glad. If they are not, their displeasure doesn't matter either. We build our temples for tomorrow, strong as we know how, and we stand on top of the mountain, free within ourselves.

### Questions for Critical Thinking

1. Hughes identifies two groups within the African-American race. What are these groups? List their characteristics, then state which group Hughes admires more. Why?
2. Describe Hughes's feelings toward jazz. According to Hughes, why is jazz important? What does it express?
3. Based on this essay, write a one-paragraph summary of Hughes's mission as a black artist.

# Countee Cullen (1903–1946)

A prominent voice of the Harlem Renaissance, Cullen rivaled and at times surpassed Langston Hughes in his lifetime. Although he was immensely popular in the 1920s and early 1930s, relatively little is known about the childhood of the boy who would grow up to become the "black Keats." He was most likely born in Louisville, Kentucky. Although he went by the name Countee Porter early in life, by early adolescence, he had been adopted by the Cullen family, and he enjoyed a close relationship with his Cullen father, who led a church in Harlem, and spent his young adulthood in Harlem.

Early success with his poetry collections *Color* (1925), *Copper Sun* (1927), *The Ballad of the Brown Girl* (1927), and *The Black Christ* (1929), all published in a four-year period; his receipt of a Guggenheim Fellowship that allowed him to live in France for a year and write; and his high-profile marriage to Yolande Du Bois, the only daughter of the famous African-American activist W. E. B. Du Bois, all promised the making of an exceptional poet and role model and cemented his reputation as the great "crossover" poet—a black man who wrote in the style of classically white poetry. While Hughes made it clear in "The Negro Artist and the Racial Mountain" that he planned to be a poet who celebrated his race, Countee Cullen made the following statement in the *Brooklyn Eagle:*

> If I am going to be a poet at all, I am going to be POET and not NEGRO POET. This is what has hindered the development of artists among us. Their one note has been the concern with their race. That is all very well, none of us can get away from it. I cannot at times. You will see it in my verse. The consciousness of this is too poignant at times. I cannot escape it. But what I mean is this: I shall not write of negro subjects for the purpose of propaganda. That is not what a poet is concerned with. Of course, when the emotion rising out of the fact that I am a negro is strong, I express it. But that is another matter.

Cullen's career peaked early; he began writing less, and his marriage ended in divorce a year after it began. He took a job teaching French and English at a junior high school where he taught until his death at age forty-two.

# Incident (1925)

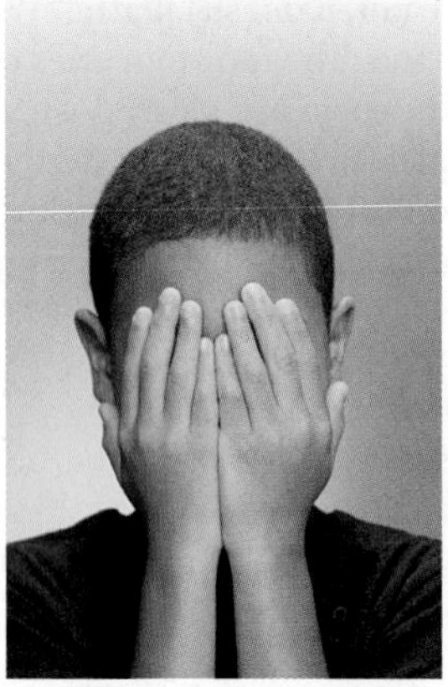

Once riding in old Baltimore,
Heart-filled, head-filled with glee,
I saw a Baltimorean
Keep looking straight at me.

Now I was eight and very small,
And he was no whit bigger,
And so I smiled, but he poked out
His tongue, and called me, "Nigger."

I saw the whole of Baltimore
From May until December;
Of all the things that happened there
That's all that I remember.

### Questions for Critical Thinking

1. This poem is more straightforward than other classical poems that Cullen wrote. Why do you think Cullen chose to make it that way? How would its impact change if it were written in elevated language or a more complex form?
2. Discuss the difference in the rhyme pattern, in these four-line stanzas, between the first and third lines and the second and fourth. Also discuss the enjambment in lines 7 and 8. How does the conversational "tone" here get supported or undermined by the poem's formal structure?

# Helene Johnson (1907–1995)

Helene Johnson came to New York in 1926 to attend the awards ceremony for the winners of *Opportunity* magazine's poetry contest—she had received an honorable mention—and stayed. Langston Hughes's friend and collaborator on "Mule Bone," Zora Neale Hurston (see chapter 14, Stories for Further Reading), lived in the same apartment building, and her cousin, the writer Dorothy West, was nearby in Harlem. Johnson was close to many writers during this time, and Countee Cullen published her work in his anthology *Caroling Dusk*. After her marriage to William Warner Hubbel and the birth of their daughter, she wrote less. When they separated, she moved back home to Boston but later returned to New York, where she died. The subject of race and identity is framed in Johnson's work by lyrical formal verse, as it is in the following poem, "Sonnet to a Negro in Harlem."

# Sonnet to a Negro in Harlem (1927)

You are disdainful and magnificent—
Your perfect body and your pompous gait,
Your dark eyes flashing solemnly with hate;
Small wonder that you are incompetent
To imitate those whom you so despise—
Your shoulders towering high above the throng,
Your head thrown back in rich, barbaric song,
Palm trees and mangoes stretched before your eyes.
Let others toil and sweat for labor's sake
And wring from grasping hands their meed of gold.
Why urge ahead your supercilious feet?
Scorn will efface each footprint that you make.
I love your laughter arrogant and bold.
You are too splendid for this city street!

### Questions for Critical Thinking

1. Do you find this description in the poem similar to that of an actual painting? List the details you learn from the poem. Which details would you also learn from an actual painting, and which are unique to verse? Are any details missing that you would get only from a real picture?
2. How critical is this depiction of the subject? Do you find elements of admiration along with the negative elements?

# Claude McKay (1889–1948)

Jamaican-born Claude McKay brought in a more defiant tone than that of Langston Hughes, but like Hughes his subject was race. He had grown up hearing from his father about his West African Ashanti traditions and how his grandfather had been enslaved by whites. He published two collections while still living in Jamaica, *Songs of Jamaica* (1912), celebrating the life of Jamaican farmers, and *Constab Ballads* (1912), deriding the treatment of dark-skinned blacks by whites and mulattos. These books earned him the medal of the Jamaican Institute of the Arts and Sciences. McKay arrived in the United States, where he studied agriculture first at Booker T. Washington's Tuskegee Institute in Alabama and later at Kansas State College. After two years, he decided instead to make his living as a writer and moved to Harlem. He was close to radicals, often publishing his work in Greenwich Village political magazines, and he lived for a time in England, where he worked at *Workers' Dreadnought.* He returned to America in 1921. Writers like Hughes and McKay were "The New Writers" that Alain Locke described in his essay "The New Negro." McKay shaped the imagination and subject matter of black writers and did so by writing his unflinching condemnations of bigotry in formal verse, as he does in the following sonnet, "The White City."

# The White City (1922)

I will not toy with it nor bend an inch.
Deep in the secret chambers of my heart
I muse my life-long hate, and without flinch
I bear it nobly as I live my part.
My being would be a skeleton, a shell,
If this dark Passion that fills my every mood,
And makes my heaven in the white world's hell,
Did not forever feed me vital blood.
I see the mighty city through a mist—
The strident trains that speed the goaded mass,
The poles and spires and towers vapor-kissed,
The fortressed port through which the great ships pass,
The tides, the wharves, the dens I contemplate,
Are sweet like wanton loves because I hate.

### Questions for Critical Thinking

1. What does the title tell you about the subject of the somewhat difficult poem? What is its subject?
2. How difficult is it to interpret this poem once you identify the subject? What is your interpretation?

# Jessie Redmon Fauset (1884–1961)

Jessie Redmon Fauset was raised by her father, the Reverend Redmon Fauset, and his wife, Annie, outside Philadelphia. She went to public schools in Philadelphia until she graduated with a scholarship to Cornell. She was the first woman to graduate Phi Beta Kappa at Cornell and the first black woman to be admitted to that prestigious academic organization nationally. After teaching Latin and French in Baltimore and Washington, D.C. (where her race did not bar her from getting a teaching job), Fauset went back to school at the University of Pennsylvania to earn her master's degree. She began working for the magazine *Crisis* under W. E. B. Du Bois in 1918 and became its literary editor in 1919. She nurtured the talents of many, including Langston Hughes, whom she recognized early in his career. When she invited him to lunch, he was so nervous he asked if he could bring his gregarious mother (which he did) to make sure the lunch went smoothly. Fauset's home was often the meeting place for literary discussions, sometimes held in French. She had exacting standards as an editor and was of central importance in shaping the talent that was burgeoning in this time in Harlem.

# Touché (1927)

Dear, when we sit in that high, placid room,
"Loving" and "doving" as all lovers do,
Laughing and leaning so close in the gloom,—

What is the change that creeps sharp over you?
Just as you raise your fine hand to my hair,
Bringing that glance of mixed wonder and rue?

"Black hair," you murmur, "so lustrous and rare,
Beautiful too, like a raven's smooth wing;
Surely no gold locks were ever more fair."

Why do you say every night that same thing?
Turning your mind to some old constant theme,
Half meditating and half murmuring?

Tell me, that girl of your young manhood's dream,
Her you loved first in that dim long ago—
Had *she* blue eyes? Did *her* hair goldly gleam?

Does *she* come back to you softly and slow,
Stepping wraith-wise from the depths of the past?
Quickened and fired by the warmth of our glow?

There, I've divined it! My wit holds you fast.
Nay, no excuses; 'tis little I care,
I knew a lad in my own girlhood's past,—
Blue eyes he had and such waving gold hair!

### Questions for Critical Thinking

1. What role does race play in this affair between two dark-haired and, presumably, dark-skinned lovers? How does the matter of race engender doubt in the lover's mind?
2. How does the formal and even archaic diction and tone (words like "rue" and "nay") compare with the writing of Toomer or Hughes? What do these aesthetic choices reveal about Redmon Fauset's work?

# Jean Toomer (1894–1967)

Jean Toomer insisted that he was "of no race," a mix of "Scotch, Welsh, German, English, French, Dutch, Spanish and some dark blood," but his great work *Cane* (1923) is a modernist study by turns of black life in rural Georgia and black life in urban Chicago and Washington, D.C., and an autobiographical synthesis of the two. It includes poems and sketches as well as prose and immediately became a central text for African Americans of his time. Toomer was born in Washington, D.C.; his father abandoned the family a year after he was born. He and his mother moved in with her parents, where Toomer spent his early years. Race was an issue early on but with a twist; Toomer's maternal grandfather had achieved some success as a politician in southern Louisiana, and though he claimed to be black, Toomer himself did not believe it was true. When Toomer 's mother remarried, they relocated to New Rochelle, New York. He never graduated from college, though he attended several, and claimed Alain Locke had "tricked" him into including his work in *The New Negro.* In the 1920s he began a long association with George I. Gurdjieff, a Greek-Armenian spiritualist, and he tried to recruit his friends, African-American writers such as Nella Larsen and Wallace Thurman, to Gurdjieff's Unitism. In later life, Toomer moved away from Gurdjieff, married, and became a Quaker. The following poem, "Reapers," appears in *Cane.*

# Reapers (1923)

Black reapers with the sound of steel on stones
Are sharpening scythes. I see them place the hones
In their hip-pockets as a thing that's done,
And start their silent swinging, one by one.
Black horses drive a mower through the weeds,
And there, a field rat, startled, squealing bleeds,
His belly close to ground. I see the blade,
Blood-stained, continue cutting weeds and shade.

### Questions for Critical Thinking

1. The poet observes workers in the field. How does he use language and rhythm to convey a sense of danger?
2. How does Toomer use the word *reaper* to raise the physical activity in the poem to a higher level of meaning?

# Angelina Weld Grimké (1880–1958)

Angelina Weld Grimké's paternal great-aunts were white Southern abolitionists; she and her sister publicly acknowledged their brother's child from a union with a slave, Nancy Weston. Her father, a lawyer with a Harvard law degree, had married their mother, Sarah Stanly of Boston, though Sarah's father, a clergyman, disapproved of the match, and she eventually abandoned the marriage and her children. She never saw Angelina again. Angelina's father doted on her, and she continued her family tradition in her first work, a play, *Rachel,* which, according to the playbill, was "the first attempt to use the stage for race propaganda in order to enlighten the American people relative to the lamentable condition of ten million of Colored citizens in this free republic." Her output was small, but her poetry is characterized by lyricism and the address of life as a woman. She married Theodore Dwight Weld and remained close friends with a widely published African-American writer of the time, Georgia Douglas Johnson.

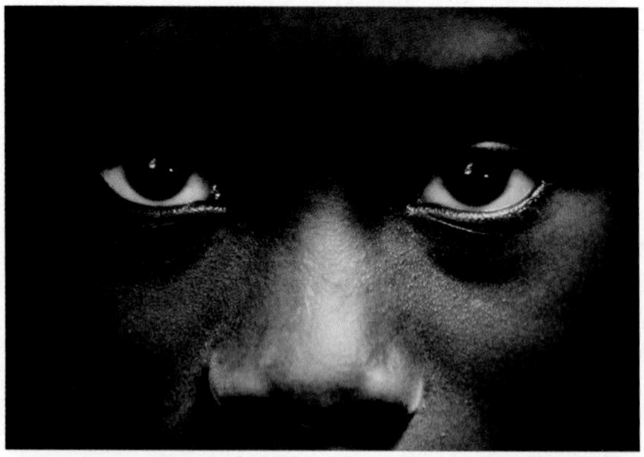

# Fragment (c. 1930)

I am the woman with the black black skin
I am the laughing woman with the black black face
I am living in the cellars and in every crowded place
   I am toiling just to eat
   In the cold and in the heat
      And I laugh
I am the laughing woman who's forgotten how to weep
I am the laughing woman who's afraid to go to sleep

### Questions for Critical Thinking

1. Does the ironic juxtaposition of laughter and destitution seem evident to you?
2. Why does the poet employ irony here? What does she gain? What do you gain as a reader?

# Getting Started: A Research Project

Research is a skill that will carry you through your college career. To help acquaint you with the research process, the materials you need for this project are made available on our website (**www.mhhe.com/delbanco1e**). Other ideas for research projects and sources appear at the end of this chapter.

Although a popular and iconic figure for the Harlem Renaissance, Langston Hughes did share the spotlight with other outspoken literary figures during the period. One such person was Countee Cullen, whose poem "Incident" appears earlier in this chapter. Like Hughes, Cullen was not raised by his biological parents, he was very successful in high school, and he was a published poet in his late teenage years. Although both would become prominent voices of the Harlem Renaissance, their messages were not always the same.

Information on Cullen's background and a timeline of his accomplishments can be found at **www.mhhe.com/delbanco1e**. You will also find a variety of essays related to Cullen, Hughes, and the other writers of their generation. As you conduct your research, ask yourself what ties these diverse writers together as voices of the Harlem Renaissance, and consider how their messages resonate in modern society.

The Harlem Renaissance and the poets associated with it often dealt with race, and it was in many ways a racial movement, but it was more than that. It was a cultural awakening, a celebration of music like blues and jazz, an explosion of new art and theater and political thinking. In the same way, the key players like Langston Hughes or Countee Cullen were not just poets. They wrote essays, plays, and novels. They worked in colloquialisms and formal voices. They wrote about private experiences as well as public issues.

Go to **www.mhhe.com/delbanco1e** for essays and resources on topics centered on Langston Hughes and the poets of his time.

1. Focus on one pair of poets, such as Hughes and Cullen. Read the quote from Cullen's brief biography earlier in this chapter. Contrast Cullen's statement with Hughes's arguments in his essay "The Negro Artist and the Racial Mountain." Note how Hughes refers to a "Negro poet" in the first line of the essay. Compare Hughes's and Cullen's ideas about being a "Negro poet." Write a definition of "Negro poet" from each man's point of view. Now consider how the two definitions compare, and how they are different.
2. Discuss how blues and jazz influenced literature during the Harlem Renaissance.
3. Both Hughes and Cullen experienced highs and lows of popularity. Consider the timelines of their lives and careers, as well as the social atmosphere of their era, and discuss the various factors surrounding each figure's prominence and decline.

# Further Suggestions for Writing and Research

1. If you have an interest in music, particularly in blues and jazz, reread Hughes's poem "Harlem (Dream Deferred)" and some of the blues poems in preparation for reading at least two of the articles listed below—including one from the Hughes scholar Onwuchekwa Jemie. Drawing upon these articles, write an essay in which you present a critical reading of "Harlem," interweaving the significance of its form as a jazz poem.
   - Johnson, Charles S. "Jazz Poetry and Blues." *Critical Essays on Langston Hughes.* Ed. Edward J. Mullen. Boston: G. K. Hall & Co., 1986. See pages 143–147.
   - Jemie, Onwuchekwa. "Jazz, Jive, and Jam." *Langston Hughes: An Introduction to the Poetry.* New York: Columbia UP, 1976. 57–96. Print.

2. Look up Wallace Thurman in the *Encyclopedia of the Harlem Renaissance*. Read selections from Thurman's novel *The Blacker the Berry* (1929) and from his satirical critique of the Harlem Renaissance in *Infants of the Spring* (1932). Argue a case for the complexity of the years of the Harlem Renaissance, in which not all the artists and writers making up this so-called movement take a positive view of the world in which they move.
3. Look up the paintings of Jacob Lawrence, a painter who was another of Langston Hughes's contemporaries during the Harlem Renaissance. The word *renaissance* means, literally, "born again." This is not a religious term but a cultural one; in the European Renaissance of the fifteenth and sixteenth centuries the ideals of antiquity were rediscovered, and artists and writers tried to express the "classical" ideals as derived from Greece and Rome. The name Harlem comes from the Dutch city of Haarlem, the home of many of the first settlers of New Amsterdam (New York City's original name). To what degree do artists like Langston Hughes and Jacob Lawrence pay conscious attention to their own history, and what are they suggesting should be "born again" in this new/old form of art? What's innovative and what's traditional in their work; how much influence do African or Caribbean roots have in the flowering of the Harlem Renaissance? Cite specific examples. What role did music play?
4. There are several other twentieth-century examples of artists in community. To pick a few, there's expatriate Paris (Gertrude Stein, Ernest Hemingway, F. Scott Fitzgerald, Pablo Picasso, etc.), London's Bloomsbury (Virginia Woolf, Vanessa Stephen, E. M. Forster, Lytton Strachey, etc.), and a group of novelists near the southern English town of Rye (Henry James, Joseph Conrad, Ford Madox Ford, and Stephen Crane). How does the idea of collegiality—a shared aesthetic, shared pleasure in each other's company—pertain to the Harlem Renaissance? How does the idea of regionalism (discussed in the Case Studies on Regionalism in chapter 12) play a role in the work—from music to literature—of the Harlem Renaissance? When Josephine Baker sings "Harlem on My Mind" in Paris, or James Baldwin (whose story "Sonny's Blues" can be found in chapter 14) goes to Paris with recordings of Billie Holiday and Bessie Smith, what does that say about the value and power of place?

# Some Sources for Research

**Online Sources:**

1. Alexander, Elizabeth. "The Black Poet as Canon-Maker: Langston Hughes, New Negro Poets, and American poetry's segregated past." *PoetryFoundation.org*. 2004. Web. <http://www.poetryfoundation.org/archive/feature.html?id=177377>.

2. Giaimo, Paul. "Ethnic outsiders: the hyper-ethnicized narrator in Langston Hughes and Fred L. Gardaphe." *MELUS* 28 (2003): 133-147. Web. 18 March 2009. <http://www.articlearchives.com/humanities-social-science/literature-literature/942664-1.html>.
3. Graham, Maryemma. "The beat goes on." *The New Crisis* Jan/Feb (2002). Web. 29 March 2009. <http://findarticles.com/p/articles/mi_qa3812/is_200201/ai_n9041756>.
4. Lamb, Robert Paul. "'A Little Yellow Bastard Boy': Paternal Rejection, Filial Insistence, and the Triumph of African American Cultural Aesthetics in Langston Hughes's 'Mulatto.'" *College Literature* 35.2 (2008): 126-153. Web. 18 March 2009. <http://findarticles.com/p/articles/mi_qa3709/is_200804/ai_n25419543?tag=content;col1>.
5. The Poetry Foundation. "Langston Hughes." *PoetryFoundation.org.* 2009. Web. <http://www.poetryfoundation.org/archive/poet.html?id=3340>.
6. Scott, Jonathan. "Advanced, repressed, and popular: Langston Hughes during the cold war." *College Literature* 33.2 (2006): 30-51. Web. 19 March 2009. <http://www.accessmylibrary.com/coms2/summary_0286-15272890_ITM>.

**Print Sources:**

1. Beckman, Wendy Hart. *Artists and Writers of the Harlem Renaissance.* Berkeley Heights, NJ: Enslow Publishers, 2002. Print.
2. Bloom, Harold, ed. *The Harlem Renaissance.* Philadelphia: Chelsea House Publishers, 2004. Print.
3. Carroll, Anne Elizabeth. *Word, Image, and the New Negro: Representation and Identity in the Harlem Renaissance.* Bloomington: Indiana UP, 2005. Print.
4. Douglas, Ann. *Terrible Honesty: Mongrel Manhattan in the 1920's.* Farrar, Strauss, and Giroux, 1995. Print.
5. Harper, Donna Akiba Sullivan. *Not So Simple: The "Simple" Stories By Langston Hughes.* Columbia, MO: University of Missouri Press, 1995. Print.
6. Jones, Sharon L. *Rereading the Harlem Renaissance: Race, Class, and Gender in the Fiction of Jessie Fauset, Zora Neale Hurston, and Dorothy West.* Westport, CT: Greenwood Press, 2002. Print.
7. Krasner, David. *A Beautiful Pageant: African American Theatre, Drama, and Performance in the Harlem Renaissance, 1910-1927.* New York: Palgrave Macmillan, 2002. Print.
8. Rampersad, Arnold. *The Life of Langston Hughes.* 2 vols. New York: Oxford UP, 2002. Print.
9. Schumacher, Julie A., ed. *The Harlem Renaissance.* Logan, IA: Perfection Learning, 2001. Print.

**For examples of student papers, see chapter 3, "Common Writing Assignments" and chapter 5, "Writing the Research Paper," in the Handbook for Writing from Reading.**

# 27 Art & Poetry A Case Study on *William Blake*

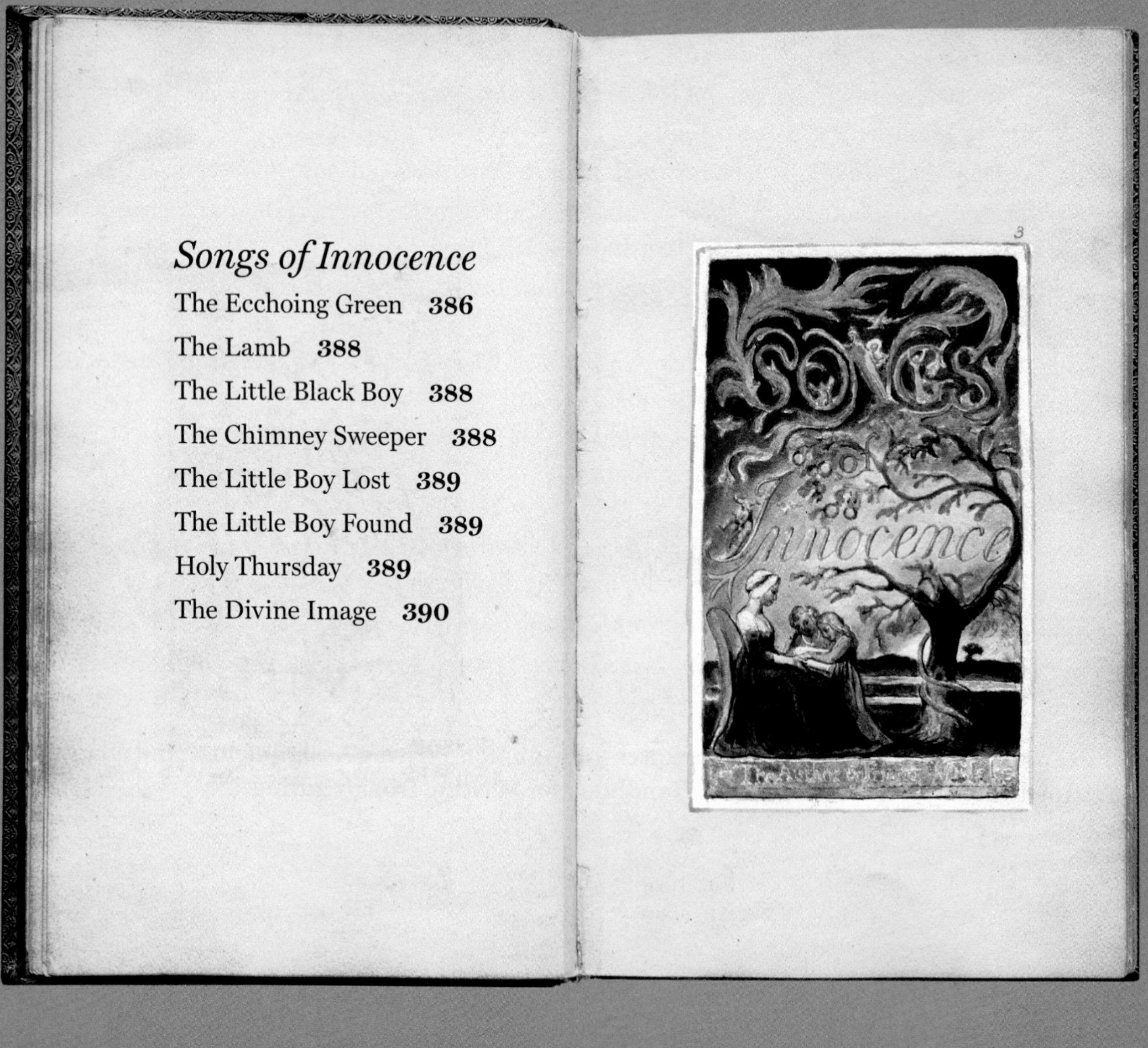


*Songs of Innocence*

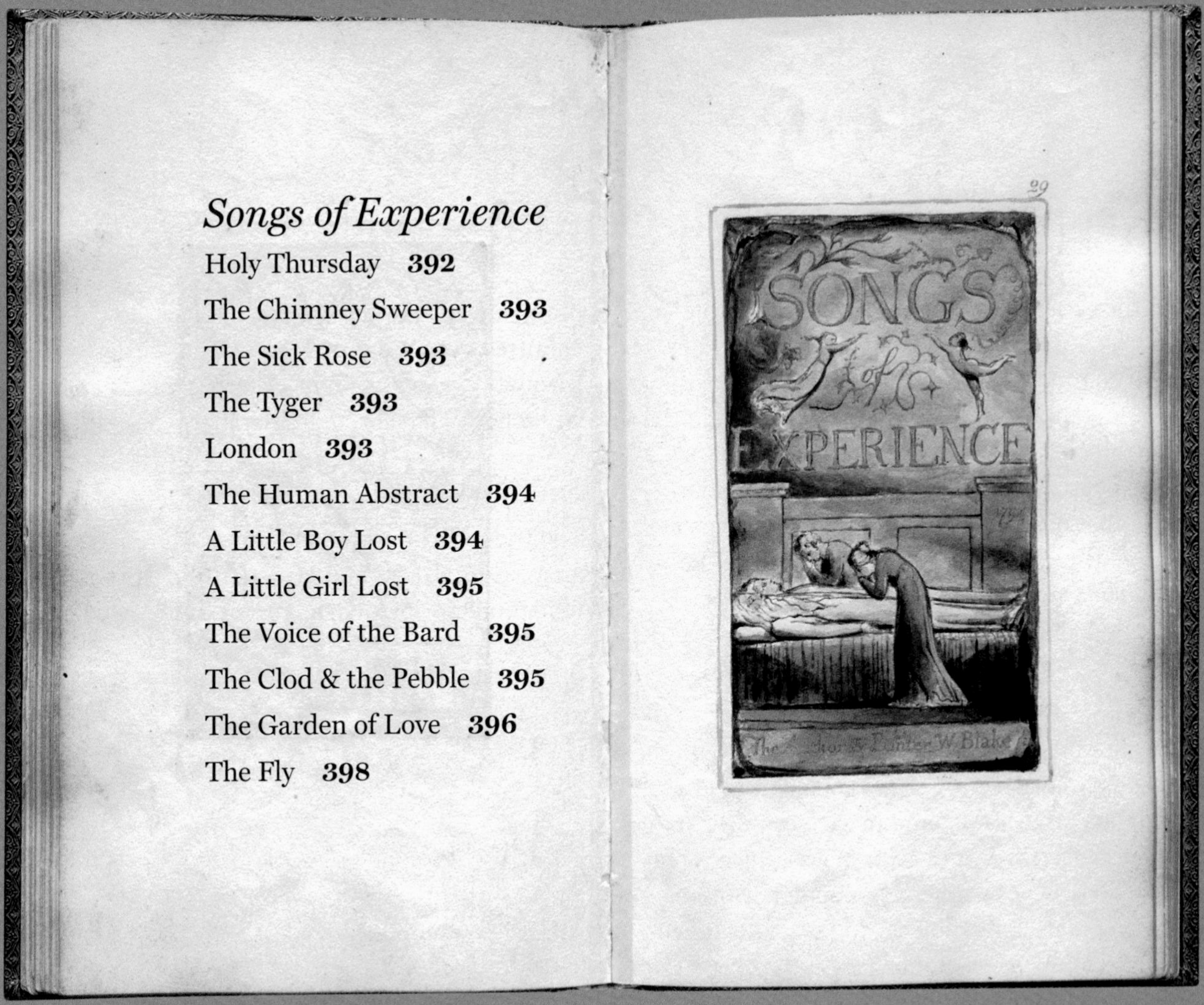


*"I have this morning been reading a strange publication—viz. Poems with very wild and interesting pictures, as the swathing, etched (I suppose) but it is said—printed and painted by the Author, W. Blake. He is a man of Genius . . . certainly a mystic emphatically. You may perhaps smile at my calling another Poet, a Mystic; but verily I am in the very mire of commonplace common-sense compared with Mr. Blake."*

—Samuel Taylor Coleridge upon reading *Songs of Innocence and of Experience*
(from a letter written by Coleridge, February 1818)

# *Blake in Context*

## Eighteenth-Century London

With the exception of three years, William Blake lived his entire life in London. As the center of British commerce and culture, London—like the rest of England—experienced much change in the late eighteenth and early nineteenth centuries. Blake's poetry and art show an acute consciousness of the social changes and problems of his day, a consciousness that appears in poems like "London," "The Chimney Sweeper," "The Little Black Boy," and "The Sick Rose."

### Social Unrest

Both the American Revolution (1775–1783) and the French Revolution (1789–1799) took place in the late eighteenth century, and in each case, the monarchy was overthrown in favor of creating a republic. The British government responded by more tightly regulating its subjects and cracking down on treasonous speech and behavior. Blake himself faced a treason trial in 1803 after a British soldier accused him of cursing the crown. Although Blake's innocence was proven and he was acquitted, the experience continued to haunt him.

### Slavery

In 1788, parliament began an investigation of the slave trade, and a year later, Olaudah Equiano published his best-selling autobiography, which revealed how he had risen from slavery and earned an education. By 1792, the House of Commons was in favor of ending slavery, and in 1807, the law officially ending slavery in Britain was passed. However, many free blacks who lived in London struggled with extreme poverty and racial prejudice from whites. In "The Little Black Boy," Blake captures the voice of a child who has suffered from inequality; it is only in heaven that he and the white boy will be brought together.

### Industry

The Industrial Revolution—that is, the change from an agricultural, rural society to the urban world of manufacturing—began in this time period. The

A photo of chimney sweeps, taken in 1877.

first cotton mill in Britain appeared in 1771, and by the beginning of the nineteenth century, the rise of industry had created a large population of poor urban laborers. Among these laborers who faced long shifts, unsafe conditions, and stifling tasks were children who worked because they were orphans or belonged to an impoverished family.

The chimney sweeping trade was particularly notorious for its maltreatment of child laborers. Children as young as four years old, and more commonly around six to eight years old, were sold as apprentices to master chimney sweepers, many of whom did not provide for the children but made them subsist by begging. Jonas Hanway, an active protester against child labor, gave a picture of the deplorable condition of child chimney sweepers in his 1767 letter published in the *London Chronicle:* "Chimney-sweepers ought to breed their own children to the business, then perhaps they will wash, clothe and feed them. As it is, they do neither, and these poor black urchins have no protectors and are treated worse than a humane person would treat a dog. . . . They often beg in the streets, and seem to be in much more real need than common beggars." Children were popular with the chimney sweeping profession because their small bodies allowed them to climb into fireplace flues; this occupation, however, almost certainly led to an early death—if not from suffocation in the flue, then from cancer and other diseases resulting from constant exposure to soot. Note that "poor black urchins" refers not to skin color but to skin blackened by soot.

A portrait of Mary Wollstonecraft, pregnant with her daughter, painted by John Opie in 1797.

## Women's Rights

Women had almost no rights in the late eighteenth century. When a woman married, she and all her possessions became her husband's property. Further, she was not allowed to initiate a court case, and thus had no form of redress for any abuses she suffered at the hands of her husband or others. Although there were some voices that began to call for more equal treatment—most notably Mary Wollstonecraft, whose 1792 *Vindication of the Rights of Women* argued that men as well as women had been corrupted by the inequality of the genders—women were educated only in domestic accomplishments, like music, drawing, and Romance languages. Furthermore, a girl's virginity before marriage was essential to her worth, and therefore women were expected to be pure and modest. Only a few occupations—such as those of governess or nurse—were considered appropriate for women, making marriage necessary to their economic stability.

# William Blake (1757–1827)

"Genius," "mad," "mystic"—each of these words was applied to William Blake by his contemporaries. Although he lived in relative obscurity and died completely misunderstood, Blake has come to be recognized as one of the most imaginative writers and artists ever to have lived. A lifelong resident of London, Blake was writing poetry by age twelve. At fourteen, he began an apprenticeship with James Brasire, an engraver who taught in a classical style considered out-of-date by most of his colleagues. A few years after completing his seven-year apprenticeship, Blake married Catherine Boucher. Boucher was illiterate, but Blake soon taught her both to read and to be his assistant in producing art that accompanied his own writing.

Unlike that of most other poets, William Blake's craft includes the tangible aspect of visual art—painting, drawing, engraving, and printing. His poems—themselves small masterpieces of symbol and sound—are best studied in conjunction with the illustrations and illuminated designs that Blake made to accompany them in a time-consuming process of etching the words and image backward on a copper plate so that the printed page would turn out the proper way, ready for Blake to paint it by hand. His collection of poems *Songs of Innocence and of Experience* (1794), for example, includes elaborate illustrations that Blake made by etching wax on copper plates, then printing from those plates, and finally painting the printed images by hand. Blake earned a meager living by illustrating children's books and accepting patronage from wealthy benefactors, but for the most part he lived his life in poverty.

Further, his craft is notable because of the singularity of the mind behind the works. In contemporary terms, we might call Blake "antiestablishment"—against the conventional philosophy, politics, and religion of his day. Blake was also a supporter of the French Revolution, which began in 1789 and which many of the English regarded as a threat to their own system of government. At the same time, Blake, a dreamer with a strong interest in mythology and the Bible, valued the imagination over all else and therefore found himself in conflict with the prevailing philosophy of his day, known as The Enlightenment, which valued the authority of rational thought over religious belief. Despite his adherence to Christian views and his love of the Bible, he portrayed the institution of the church of his time as a repressive force. In his poem "The Garden of Love" (which appears later in this chapter), for example, the church is associated with binding people's desires with its forbidding presence.

Blake wrote a series of prophetic works, consciously engaging in the tradition of great English writers like Edmund Spenser (1552–1599) and John Milton (1608–1674), both of whom had written book-length poems of their own. *America: A Prophecy* and *Europe: A Prophecy* show Blake's hatred of social and political tyranny, while *The Book of Urizen* attacks religious tyranny. These themes appear in earlier works as well, particularly *Songs of Innocence and of Experience,* which Blake subtitled "showing the two contrary states of the human soul." Originally, Blake composed just *Songs of Innocence* in 1789, but he added *Songs of Experience* five years later. Just as the two books can stand separately, so does each poem have its individual merit. But, just as Blake combined the two books, so, too, are there parallels connecting the poems: a version of "The Chimney Sweeper" appears in *Innocence* and another appears in *Experience;* "The Tyger" in *Experience* is the counterpart to "The Lamb" in *Innocence;* the "Introduction" in each section achieves a similar purpose but with an opposing view.

"Of all the conditions which arouse the interest of the psychologist, none assuredly is more attractive than the union of genius and madness in single remarkable minds, which, while on the one hand they compel our admiration by their great mental powers, yet on the other move our pity by their claims to supernatural gifts. Of such is the whole race of ecstatics, mystics, seers of visions, and dreamers of dreams, and to their list we have now to add another name, that of William Blake."

—H. C. Robinson, 1811
(from his essay "William Blake, artist, poet, and religious mystic" published 1811)

Title page from *Songs of Innocence.*

# Selected Poems from *Songs of Innocence*

## The Ecchoing Green

The Sun does arise,
And make happy the skies;
The merry bells ring
To welcome the Spring;
The sky-lark and thrush,
The birds of the bush,
Sing louder around
To the bells' chearful sound,
While our sports shall be seen
On the Ecchoing Green.

Old John, with white hair,
Does laugh away care,
Sitting under the oak,
Among the old folk.
They laugh at our play,
And soon they all say:
"Such, such were the joys
When we all, girls & boys,
In our youth time were seen
On the Ecchoing Green."

Till the little ones, weary,
No more can be merry;
The sun does descend,
And our sports have an end.
Round the laps of their mothers
Many sisters and brothers,
Like birds in their nest,
Are ready for rest,
And sport no more seen
On the darkening Green.

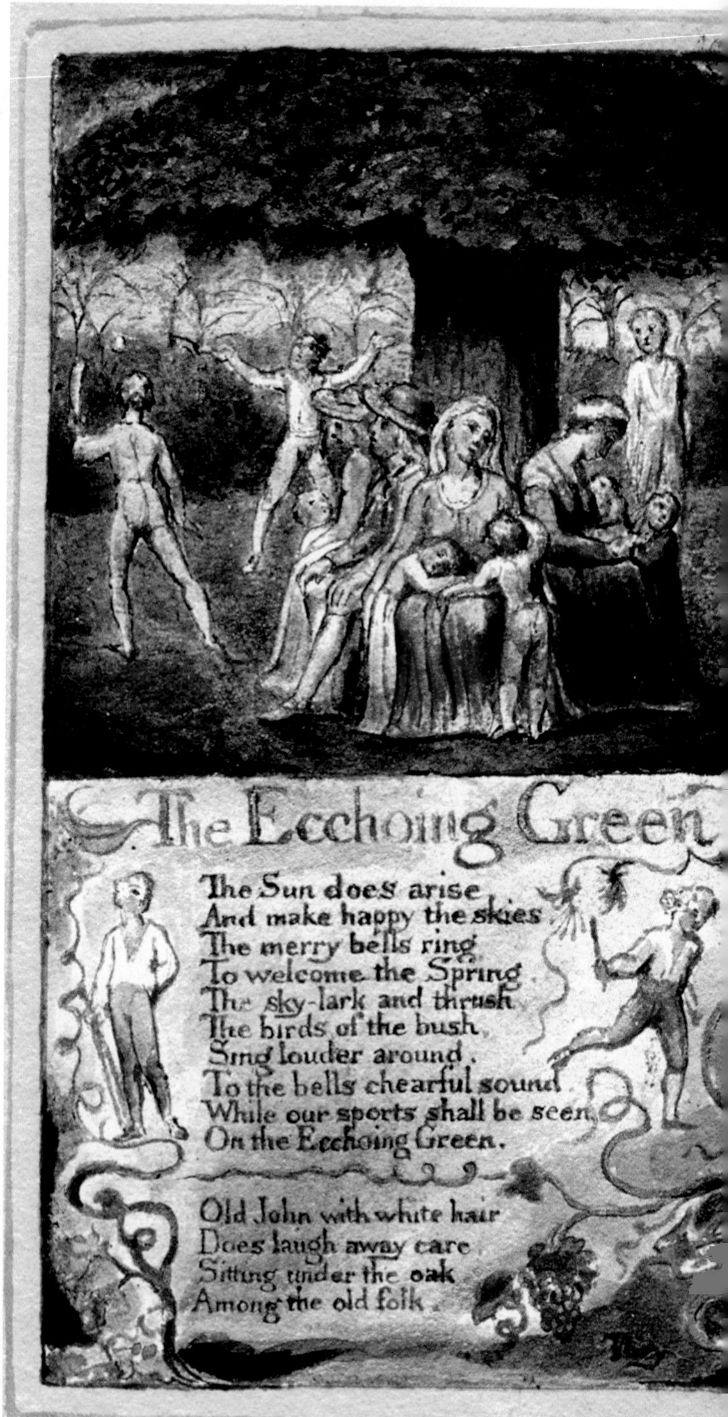


**Question for Critical Thinking**

Underline the imagery in "The Ecchoing Green." How would you describe the imagery? Does it change or remain the same throughout the poem?

(1794)

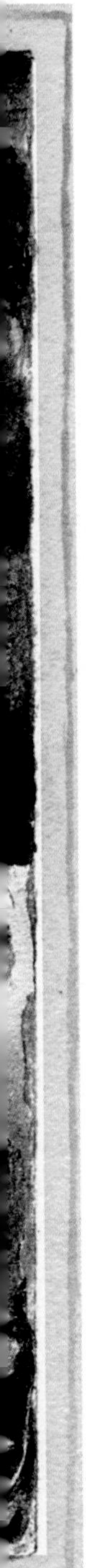

They laugh at our play.
And soon they all say
Such such were the joys.
When we all girls & boys.
In our youth-time were seen,
On the Ecchoing Green.

Till the little ones weary
No more can be merry
The sun does descend,
And our sports have an end:
Round the laps of their mothers
Many sisters and brothers
Like birds in their nest.
Are ready for rest:
And sport no more seen,
On the darkening Green.

## The Lamb

Little lamb, who made thee?
Dost thou know who made thee?
Gave thee life, & bid thee feed
By the stream & o'er the mead;
Gave thee clothing of delight,
Softest clothing, wooly, bright;
Gave thee such a tender voice,
Making all the vales rejoice?
Little Lamb, who made thee?
Dost thou know who made thee?

Little Lamb, I'll tell thee,
Little Lamb, I'll tell thee:
He is called by thy name,
For he calls himself a Lamb.
He is meek & he is mild;
He became a little child.
I a child, & thou a lamb.
We are called by his name.
Little Lamb, God bless thee!
Little Lamb, God bless thee!

### Question for Critical Thinking

Make a list of all the things you associate with a lamb. You might want to think about literal lambs as well as the symbol of the lamb in Christian tradition. In general, are these pleasant connotations? Or are there darker connotations as well? If so, how does the poem deal with these darker undercurrents?

## The Little Black Boy

My mother bore me in the southern wild,
And I am black, but O! my soul is white;
White as an angel is the English child,
But I am black as if bereav'd of light.

My mother taught me underneath a tree,
And, sitting down before the heat of day,
She took me on her lap and kissed me,
And pointing to the east, began to say:

"Look on the rising sun: there God does live,
And gives his light, and gives his heat away;
And flowers and trees and beasts and men receive
Comfort in morning, joy in the noonday.

"And we are put on earth a little space,
That we may learn to bear the beams of love;
And these black bodies and this sunburnt face
Is but a cloud, and like a shady grove.

"For when our souls have learn'd the heat to bear,
The cloud will vanish; we shall hear his voice,
Saying: 'Come out from the grove, my love & care,
And round my golden tent like lambs rejoice.'"

Thus did my mother say, and kissed me;
And thus I say to little English boy:
When I from black and he from white cloud free,
And round the tent of God like lambs we joy,

I'll shade him from the heat, till he can bear
To lean in joy upon our father's knee;
And then I'll stand and stroke his silver hair,
And be like him, and he will then love me.

### Question for Critical Thinking

Refer to the "Blake in Context" section, and after reading it, summarize "The Little Black Boy," being sure to use the historical context to figure out what is being said in this poem.

## The Chimney Sweeper

When my mother died I was very young,
And my father sold me while yet my tongue
Could scarcely cry "'weep! 'weep! 'weep! 'weep!"
So your chimneys I sweep, & in soot I sleep.

There's little Tom Dacre, who cried when his head,
That curl'd like a lamb's back, was shav'd: so I said
"Hush, Tom! never mind it, for when your head's bare
You know that the soot cannot spoil your white hair."

And so he was quiet, & that very night,
As Tom was a-sleeping, he had such a sight!
That thousands of sweepers, Dick, Joe, Ned & Jack,
Were all of them lock'd up in coffins of black.

And by came an Angel who had a bright key,
And he open'd the coffins & set them all free;
Then down a green plain leaping, laughing, they run,
And wash in a river, and shine in the Sun.

Then naked & white, all their bags left behind,
They rise upon clouds and sport in the wind;
And the Angel told Tom, if he'd be a good boy,
He'd have God for his father, & never want joy.

And so Tom awoke; and we rose in the dark,
And got with our bags & our brushes to work.
Tho' the morning was cold, Tom was happy & warm;
So if all do their duty they need not fear harm.

### Question for Critical Thinking

Victor N. Paananen argues that "The finest poems of the *Songs of Innocence* are those in which there is some admission of the hardships actually faced by the innocents . . . but in these poems the innocent view can be seen as easily rising above adversity." In what ways does Tom Dacre's dream raise the chimney sweepers from their harsh reality? Do you see any patterns of imagery present in his dream?

## The Little Boy Lost

"Father! father! where are you going?
O do not walk so fast.
Speak, father, speak to your little boy,
Or else I shall be lost."

The night was dark, no father was there;
The child was wet with dew;
The mire was deep, & the child did weep,
And away the vapour flew.

### Question for Critical Thinking

Brainstorm several different ways you understand "father" in this poem. In other words, what might "father" represent beyond the child's biological parent?

## The Little Boy Found

The little boy lost in the lonely fen,
Led by the wand'ring light,
Began to cry; but God, ever nigh,
Appear'd like his father in white.

He kissed the child & by the hand led
And to his mother brought,
Who in sorrow pale, thro' the lonely dale,
Her little boy weeping sought.

### Question for Critical Thinking

Many critics argue that "The Little Boy Lost" and "The Little Boy Found" are two parts of the same poem; in other words, something is lost if a person reads just one half. In what ways does "The Little Boy Found" answer "The Little Boy Lost"? Does it change your understanding of "father"? Of the enigmatic "vapour" in "The Little Boy Lost"?

## Holy Thursday

'Twas on a Holy Thursday, their innocent faces clean,
The children walking two & two, in red & blue & green,
Grey-headed beadles walk'd before, with wands as white as snow,
Till into the high dome of Paul's they like Thames' waters flow

O what a multitude they seem'd, these flowers of London town!
Seated in companies they sit with radiance all their own.
The hum of multitudes was there, but multitudes of lambs,
Thousands of little boys & girls raising their innocent hands.

Now like a mighty wind they raise to heaven the voice of song,
Or like harmonious thunderings the seats of Heaven among.
Beneath them sit the aged men, wise guardians of the poor;
Then cherish pity, lest you drive an angel from your door.

### Question for Critical Thinking

Scan this poem, being sure to identify the meter and rhyme scheme. Then underline places where Blake deviates from the established pattern. What significance do you see to these changes? In your opinion, what certain ideas does Blake highlight with these deviations?

## The Divine Image

To Mercy, Pity, Peace, and Love
All pray in their distress;
And to these virtues of delight
Return their thankfulness.

For Mercy, Pity, Peace, and Love
God, our father dear,
And Mercy, Pity, Peace, and Love
Man, his child and care.

For Mercy has a human heart,
Pity a human face,
And Love, the human form divine,
And Peace, the human dress.

Then every man, of every clime
That prays in his distress,
Prays to the human form divine,
Love, Mercy, Pity, Peace.

And all must love the human form,
In heathen, turk, or jew;
Where Mercy, Love, & Pity dwell
There God is dwelling too.

### Question for Critical Thinking

Summarize the message you believe Blake conveys in this poem. (Hint: You might pay particular attention to the second and fifth stanzas.) You might also consider how it resonates with or mirrors Christian beliefs.

Title page from *Songs of Experience*.

# Selected Poems from *Songs of Experience* (1794)

## Holy Thursday

Is this a holy thing to see
In a rich and fruitful land,
Babes reduc'd to misery,
Fed with cold and usurous hand?

Is that trembling cry a song?
Can it be a song of joy?
And so many children poor?
It is a land of poverty!

And their sun does never shine,
And their fields are bleak & bare,
And their ways are fill'd with thorns:
It is eternal winter there.

For where-e'er the sun does shine,
And where-e'er the rain does fall,
Babe can never hunger there,
Nor poverty the mind appall.

### Question for Critical Thinking

Underline the imagery that Blake associates with the impoverished children. How would you characterize this imagery? What does it suggest about the children's lives?

## The Chimney Sweeper

A little black thing among the snow,
Crying "'weep! 'weep!" in notes of woe!
"Where are thy father & mother? say?"
"They are both gone up to the church to pray.

"Because I was happy upon the heath,
And smil'd among the winter's snow,
They clothed me in the clothes of death,
And taught me to sing the notes of woe.

"And because I am happy & dance & sing,
They think they have done me no injury,
And are gone to praise God & his Priest & King,
Who make up a heaven of our misery."

**Question for Critical Thinking**

What words contribute to the overall idea that others live well because the chimney sweeps perform miserable labor? In your response, consider the connotations of color and seasons.

## The Sick Rose

O Rose, thou art sick!
The invisible worm
That flies in the night,
In the howling storm,

Has found out thy bed
Of crimson joy,
And his dark secret love
Does thy life destroy.

**Question for Critical Thinking**

The rose and the worm act as symbols in this poem. What might they represent?

## The Tyger

Tyger! Tyger! burning bright
In the forests of the night,
What immortal hand or eye
Could frame thy fearful symmetry?

In what distant deeps or skies
Burnt the fire of thine eyes?
On what wings dare he aspire?
What the hand dare sieze the fire?

And what shoulder, & what art,
Could twist the sinews of thy heart?
And when thy heart began to beat,
What dread hand? & what dread feet?

What the hammer? what the chain?
In what furnace was thy brain?
What the anvil? what dread grasp
Dare its deadly terrors clasp?

When the stars threw down their spears,
And water'd heaven with their tears,
Did he smile his work to see?
Did he who made the Lamb make thee?

Tyger! Tyger! burning bright
In the forests of the night,
What immortal hand or eye,
Dare frame thy fearful symmetry?

**Question for Critical Thinking**

Describe the tone of this poem. What word choices help create this mood?

## London

I wander thro' each charter'd street,
Near where the charter'd Thames does flow,
And mark in every face I meet
Marks of weakness, marks of woe.

In every cry of every Man,
In every Infant's cry of fear,
In every voice, in every ban,
The mind-forg'd manacles I hear.

How the Chimney-sweeper's cry
Every black'ning Church appalls;
And the hapless Soldier's sigh
Runs in blood down Palace walls.

But most thro' midnight streets I hear
How the youthful Harlot's curse
Blasts the new born Infant's tear,
And blights with plagues the Marriage hearse.

### Question for Critical Thinking

Make a list of the people mentioned in this poem. How does each act as a symbol? In other words, what part of society does each represent?

## The Human Abstract

Pity would be no more
If we did not make somebody Poor;
And Mercy no more could be
If all were as happy as we.

And mutual fear brings peace,
Till the selfish loves increase:
Then Cruelty knits a snare,
And spreads his baits with care.

He sits down with holy fears,
And waters the ground with tears;
Then Humility takes its root
Underneath his foot.

Soon spreads the dismal shade
Of Mystery over his head;
And the Catterpiller and Fly
Feed on the Mystery.

And it bears the fruit of Deceit,
Ruddy and sweet to eat;
And the Raven his nest has made
In its thickest shade.

The Gods of the earth and sea
Sought thro' Nature to find this Tree;
But their search was all in vain:
There grows one in the Human Brain.

### Question for Critical Thinking

As this poem progresses, it develops a complex metaphor. In a paragraph, explain the metaphor, exploring how it is appropriate for talking about abstract concepts like Humility, Mystery, and Deceit.

## A Little Boy Lost

"Nought loves another as itself,
Nor venerates another so,
Nor is it possible to Thought
A greater than itself to know:

"And Father, how can I love you
Or any of my brothers more?
I love you like the little bird
That picks up crumbs around the door."

The Priest sat by and heard the child,
In trembling zeal he siez'd his hair:
He led him by his little coat,
And all admir'd the Priestly care.

And standing on the altar high,
"Lo! what a fiend is here!" said he,
"One who sets reason up for judge
Of our most holy Mystery."

The weeping child could not be heard,
The weeping parents wept in vain;
They strip'd him to his little shirt,
And bound him in an iron chain;

And burn'd him in a holy place,
Where many had been burn'd before:
The weeping parents wept in vain.
Are such things done on Albion's shore?

### Question for Critical Thinking

As the introduction to this chapter points out, Blake, who subscribed to Christian beliefs, thought the church was a negative force because it was repressive. How does he develop that idea in this poem? You might pay particular attention to the images he uses.

## A Little Girl Lost

*Children of the future Age*
*Reading this indignant page,*
*Know that in a former time*
*Love! sweet Love! was thought a crime.*

In the Age of Gold,
Free from winter's cold,
Youth and maiden bright
To the holy light,
Naked in the sunny beams delight.

Once a youthful pair,
Fill'd with softest care,
Met in garden bright
Where the holy light
Had just remov'd the curtains of the night.

There, in rising day
On the grass they play;
Parents were afar,
Strangers came not near,
And the maiden soon forgot her fear.

Tired with kisses sweet,
They agree to meet
When the silent sleep
Waves o'er heaven's deep,
And the weary tired wanderers weep.

To her father white
Came the maiden bright;
But his loving look,
Like the holy book,
All her tender limbs with terror shook.

"Ona! pale and weak!
To thy father speak:
O, the trembling fear!
O, the dismal care!
That shakes the blossoms of my hoary hair."

### Question for Critical Thinking

How would you describe the poem's attitude toward sexual activity? What poetic devices suggest this attitude? You might also want to read the paragraph on women's rights in the "Blake in Context" section.

## The Voice of the Bard

Youth of delight, come hither,
And see the opening morn,
Image of truth new-born.
Doubt is fled & clouds of reason,
Dark disputes & artful teazing.
Folly is an endless maze,
Tangled roots perplex her ways.
How many have fallen there!
They stumble all night over bones of the dead,
And feel they know not what but care,
And wish to lead others, when they should be led.

### Question for Critical Thinking

What does "Image of truth new-born" describe? After you have formed your answer, ask yourself whether the lines that follow surprise you. Describe the contrast between the opening three lines and the rest of the poem.

## The Clod & the Pebble

"Love seeketh not Itself to please,
Nor for itself hath any care,
But for another gives its ease,
And builds a Heaven in Hell's despair."

So sang a little Clod of Clay
Trodden with the cattle's feet,
But a Pebble of the brook
Warbled out these metres meet:

"Love seeketh only Self to please,
To bind another to Its delight,
Joys in another's loss of ease,
And builds a Hell in Heaven's despite."

### Question for Critical Thinking

In a single sentence, summarize what the Clod says in the first four lines; then do the same for the Pebble's statement in the last four lines. Which has the more optimistic point of view?

## The Garden of Love

I went to the Garden of Love,
And saw what I never had seen:
A Chapel was built in the midst,
Where I used to play on the green.

And the gates of this Chapel were shut,
And "Thou shalt not" writ over the door;
So I turn'd to the Garden of Love
That so many sweet flowers bore;

And I saw it was filled with graves,
And tomb-stones where flowers should be;
And Priests in black gowns were walking
their rounds,
And binding with briars my joys & desires.

### Questions for Critical Thinking

Reread the last two lines of the poem, noting how they do not follow the meter or rhyme scheme of the rest of the poem. What is the effect of deviating from the pattern in these last lines? How does the new pattern mirror what takes place in these lines?

# Making Connections

### *Songs of Innocence and of Experience*

Review the poems, one from *Innocence* and one from *Experience,* in the following order: "The Ecchoing Green" and "The Garden of Love"; "The Lamb" and "The Tyger"; "The Chimney Sweeper" and "The Chimney Sweeper"; "The Divine Image" and "The Human Abstract"; "Holy Thursday" and "Holy Thursday." Then, pick one pair that you find particularly interesting and make a list of the differences between the two poems, paying particular attention to diction, imagery, rhyme, meter, and the speaker's point of view. How do these differences change the meaning of the poems between *Innocence* and *Experience*?

### Reading Text and Image

1. Consider the illustration for "The Garden of Love." Does the tone of the illustration match the tone of the poem? Explain your answer, being sure to mention specific details from the illustration.
2. Examine the illustration for "Holy Thursday." Then, in a few sentences, summarize what appears to be taking place at the top and sides of the illustration. Is this narrative the same as the poem's? If not, what new ideas does the illustration introduce that are not present in the poem?
3. What symbols in the illustration for "The Ecchoing Green" represent leisure? How do the decorative portions—rather than the main illustrations—support the idea of the poem?
4. Examine the frontispieces to *Songs of Innocence* and *Songs of Experience.* Compare and contrast these pages and ask yourself, "What statement does Blake make about innocence versus experience?"

Frontispiece from *Songs of Innocence.*

Frontispiece from *Songs of Experience.*

# Getting Started: A Research Project

As suggested earlier, research is a skill that will carry you through your college career. To help acquaint you with the research process, the materials you need for this project are available on our website (**www.mhhe.com/delbanco1e**). Other ideas for research projects and sources appear at the end of this chapter.

## *Learning to Read Images*

**Critical Readings on William Blake's "The Fly"**

- The William Blake Archive. Ed. Morris Eaves, Robert Essick, and Joseph Viscomi. 8 Sept. 2003. 17 Sept. 2003 <www.blakearchive.org/main.html>.
- Simpson, Michael. "Who Didn't Kill Blake's Fly: Moral Law and the Rule of Grammar in 'Songs of Experience.'" *Style* 30.2 (1996): 220–40.
- The William Blake Archive at www.blakearchive.org.

After looking at G. S. Morris's reading of "The Fly," examine the artwork from the title page of *Songs of Innocence* and the title page of *Songs of Experience* as printed in this chapter. Use the questions to guide your interpretation of the images.

1. Summarize what each picture portrays. Speculate on what the woman's role is—mother, governess, or something else.
2. After you've created a summary you feel is accurate, explain how the concepts of innocence and experience relate to the story the pictures tell.
3. Compare the foliage surrounding the words. What differences do you notice? What might these differences represent about the states of innocence and experience?
4. Compare the lettering. Is the font appropriate for the words? Why or why not?
5. Thinking of all the elements listed above—lettering, ornamentation, and pictoral narrative—what statements can you make about innocence versus experience? (Begin by listing all the words that come to mind when you look at each picture, for example, innocence = happy, experience = sad.)

### The Fly

Little Fly,
Thy summer's play
My thoughtless hand
Has brush'd away.

Am not I
A fly like thee?
Or art not thou
A man like me?

For I dance,
And drink, & sing,
Till some blind hand
Shall brush my wing.

If thought is life
And strength & breath,
And the want
Of thought is death;

Then am I
A happy fly,
If I live
Or if I die.

# Further Suggestions for Writing and Research

Many critics argue that we cannot achieve a full understanding of Blake's poems without "reading" the illustrations that go along with them. To see the complete set of illustrations, visit the William Blake Archive at www.blakearchive.org, a website maintained by the nation's leading Blake scholars. Which common Blakean themes do these pictures represent, like innocence and experience, the portrayal of religion, the portrayal of British society, the portrayal of nature, and the portrayal of mythological or religious figures?

## Some Sources for Research

### Online Sources:

1. Eaves, Morris, Robert Essick, and Joseph Viscomi. *The William Blake Archive*. Web. <www.blakearchive.org>.

### Print Sources:

1. Bentley, G. E., Jr. *Blake Books: Annotated Catalogues of William Blake's Writings in Illuminated Printing, in Conventional Typography and in Manuscript*. Oxford: Clarendon Press, 1977. Print.
2. Bentley, G. E., Jr. *The Stranger from Paradise: A Biography of William Blake*. New Haven, CT: Yale UP, 2001. Print.
3. Bentley, G. E., Jr., ed. *William Blake: The Critical Heritage*. London: Routledge, 1975. Print.
4. Bindman, David. "Blake as a Painter." *The Cambridge Companion to William Blake*. Ed. Morris Eaves. Cambridge: Cambridge University Press, 2003. 85–109. Print.
5. Bloom, Harold. *The Visionary Company: a Reading of English Romantic Poetry*. Ithaca, NY: Cornell University Press, 1971. Print.
6. Cervo, Nathan A. "Blake's 'The Garden of Love.'" *Explicator*, 59.3 (2001): 121–122. Print.
7. Eaves, Morris, ed. *The Cambridge Companion to William Blake*. Cambridge: Cambridge University Press, 2003. Print.
8. Graves, Roy Neil. "Blake's 'London.'" *Explicator*, 63.3 (2005): 131–136. Print.
9. Lambert, Stephen, Jr. "Blake's 'London.'" *Explicator*, 53.3 (1995): 141–143. Print.
10. Rawlinson, Nick. *William Blake's Comic Vision*. New York: Palgrave Macmillan, 2003. Print.

**For examples of student papers, see chapter 3, Common Writing Assignments, and chapter 5, Writing the Research Paper, in the Handbook for Writing from Reading.**

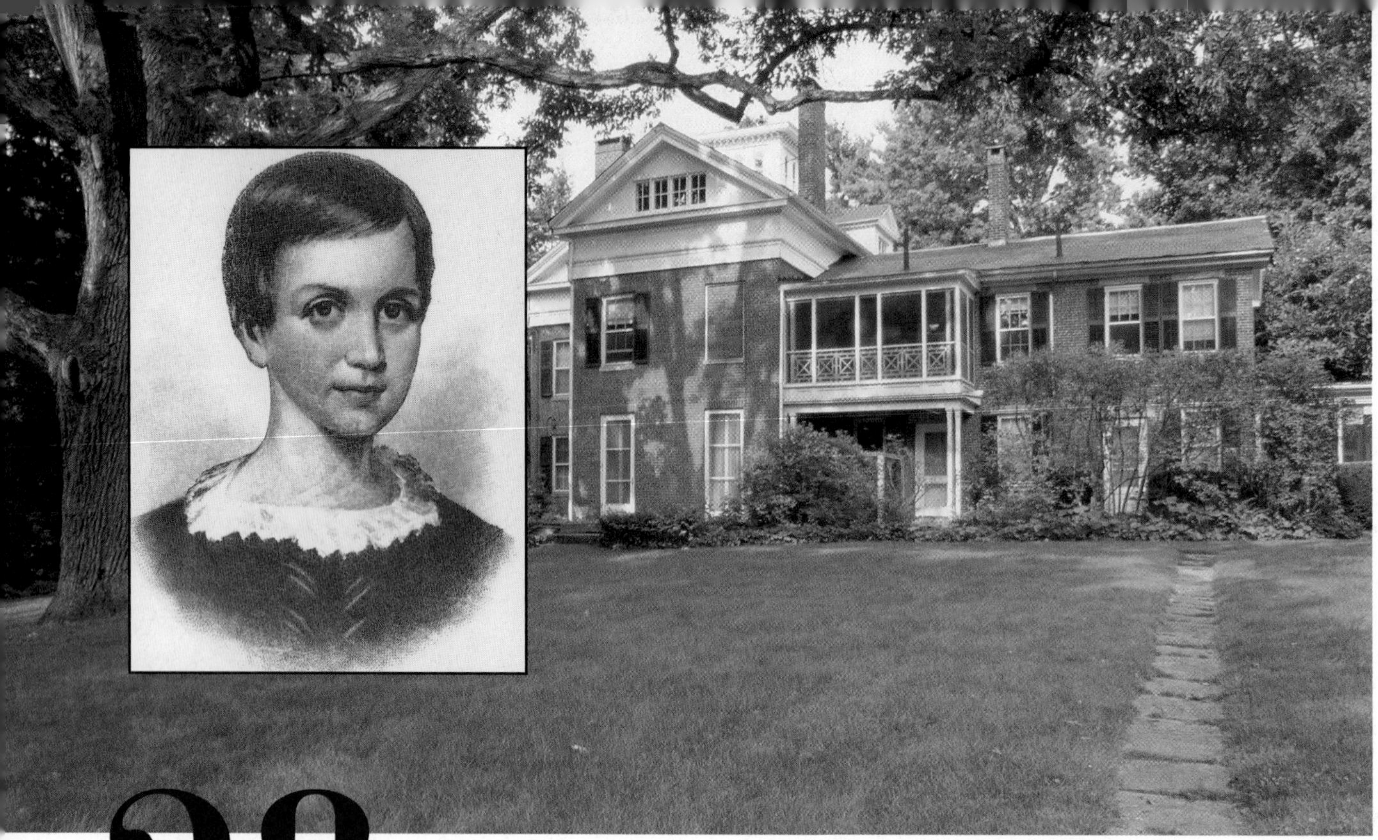

# 28

# American Plain Style

## A Case Study on *Emily Dickinson and Robert Frost*

*"It seems to me that in great poems, in the great poems of Frost, in the great poems of Dickinson . . . they're actually thinking in poetry, they're not taking some idea and poeticizing it; or they're not taking some idea and embellishing it. . . . What's manifested is thinking by imagination."*

Conversation with Li-Young Lee

## *Emily Dickinson*



## *Robert Frost*

# *The Roots of American Plain Style*

No one was more reclusive than Emily Dickinson; no one more widely recognized than Robert Frost. However, they have much in common. Both gave the best parts of their lives to their art; both worked at it unceasingly. Each was eloquent as a letter writer; each was described by others as a "Yankee crank." More importantly, both were original makers and forgers of the American Plain Style. As you have likely observed from the examples so far in this textbook, there are many different approaches to poetry. However, studying plain style allows us to get at the heart of a major split within the genre—"two roads" that, as Robert Frost observes, "diverged."

In American poetry, the divergence in style occurred between poets who write highly symbolic and complex verse in the vein of Wallace Stevens and those who write distilled or pared-down work that focuses on the world around us, such as William Carlos Williams. Think of the difference between Stevens's "jar in Tennessee" (chapter 20) and Williams's "red wheelbarrow" (chapter 20), and you'll get some sense of what we mean. However, this American split has its origin much further back; it came ashore with the Puritan settlers who first inhabited New England. The Puritans, as you may recollect from history, sought religious freedom from what they saw as corruption in the English church. They eschewed the formal pomp and ceremony associated with worship in the Catholic church in favor of a simple and "pure" devotion to God. In other words, "plain"-ness was a way of life, as reflected in their plain clothes, their plain houses of worship, and their simple forms of entertainment—all aspects that allowed them to focus not on a worldly existence but on a godly one.

This belief in plainness as the best way of approaching God permeated Puritan discourse as well. Remember Anne Bradstreet's comparison of her book to her child (chapter 19) or the noticing eye ("I") of Walt Whitman (chapter 24); their use of domestic particulars would not have seemed appropriate before. In early American sermons, you can see a wide embrace of the language of everyday speech. In a sermon titled "Sinners in the Hands of an Angry God," the eighteenth-century New England minister Jonathan Edwards declared, "The God that holds you over the pit of hell, much as one holds a spider, or some loathsome insect, over the fire, abhors you, and is dreadfully provoked; his wrath towards you burns like fire." Here Edwards uses earthy images of spiders and fire to great rhetorical effect.

"Robert Frost . . . is the most cunning and uncanny American poet who ever lived. . . . He refuses to say something is something when it isn't. . . . To rest in that is such a pleasure."

Conversation with Marie Howe

Given the strong Puritan influence in New England, which shaped the society surrounding Emily Dickinson, it's relatively easy to trace that tradition of plain speech in America. Dickinson—along with Whitman and later, Frost—brought an early turn in poetry to plain style. These poets, who confronted the American wilderness and understood that their ancestors had literally done so, brought a view of nature as concrete rather than as an abstract entity. Plain style, then, brought a split from both florid poetic language and elevated treatment of nature: In short, it brought poetry "down to earth."

## The Plain Style

Through plain style, both Dickinson and Frost have left their separate yet shared imprint on the contemporary mode of utterance in verse. By this we mean a way of *saying* that involves a way of *seeing:* straightforward, uncluttered language shaped into poetical form. Enjambment is common, since it makes the poem's line breaks seem less obvious or end-stopped, and rhyme, though widespread, feels unforced. The tone is unpretentious and the vocabulary serviceable; it's the surprising shift of emphasis, not the surprising (or obscure, or arcane) word that counts. Nothing they write is hard to read, but much of it demands close reading before we understand. What's sometimes difficult to follow in this pair of poets is the thought process itself, the sudden leap of intuition or juxtaposition—in Dickinson's case by way of dashes—of what might seem disconnected.

Dickinson rarely glories in the play of "wit" for its own sake. She does love wordplay and the way sounds edge up against each other, but there's an almost confessional impulse in her truth-telling work. Frost, too, is schooled in poetic tradition and studiously familiar with those who wrote before. Although his "homespun" style was always intended to seem offhand and conversational; no matter how intricate the form or thought, the manner of speaking is *plain.*

In the largest sense this style is democratic. Best read aloud, the poems that follow have the rhythms of natural speech (we've included twice as many by Dickinson, because her work is brief). Between them, these two artists provide a portrait of America in its period of growth and maturation, its increasing sense of what's at risk, what's still to be discovered, and what must be preserved.

# Emily Dickinson (1830–1886)

Like other writers whose eccentricities turn into legend over time, Emily Dickinson lives in the popular imagination as a recluse who dressed in all white and never left her room. While it is true that she dressed in white, and that she preferred living in her father's house her entire life, she cultivated relationships with people both near—like her sister-in-law, Susan Gilbert, who lived next door—and far, like her literary critic friend Thomas Wentworth Higginson, with whom she maintained a correspondence for more than twenty years.

Born in Amherst, Massachusetts, she lived her life in almost total obscurity. Raised in a Puritan, New England atmosphere, and in a devoutly religious family, Dickinson herself did not give the public confession of her faith that was expected of her and eventually refused to attend conventional church services. She attended Mount Holyoke Female Seminary—a few miles from Amherst—but returned home after her first year because she was acutely homesick. Though her family was prosperous and prominent, she became a kind of hermit, remaining in the village and writing her "odd" poetry for herself alone. She spent her days reading, writing letters, and composing more than 2,000 poems. Only a handful of these poems were published in her lifetime, and those by the initiative of family and friends, not her own effort. Dickinson preferred self-publication, which for her meant binding by hand forty volumes of her handwritten poetry. She did conceive of the work as a "letter to the world," but it was delivered posthumously; her present fame would not have been imagined and could not have been predicted at the time. When her poems were discovered upon her death, her younger sister, Lavinia, was instrumental in getting them published; however, the editors normalized much of Dickinson's punctuation (they eliminated her characteristic dashes) and syntax so that it read much like any other nineteenth-century verse.

It was not until the 1950s that her original intention was restored by an editor working with her fascicles (handwritten manuscripts). Today, along with Whitman, Dickinson is recognized for creating a uniquely American poetic voice—hers marked by its simplicity of structure and diction, its hymn-like rhythms, and its odd punctuation.

## Success is counted sweetest (c. 1859)

Success is counted sweetest
By those who ne'er succeed.
To comprehend a nectar
Requires sorest need.

Not one of all the purple Host
Who took the Flag today
Can tell the definition
So clear of Victory

As he defeated—dying—
On whose forbidden ear
The distant strains of triumph
Burst agonized and clear!

### Questions for Critical Thinking

1. What does the speaker mean by "To comprehend a nectar / Requires sorest need"? Paraphrase these lines.
2. If Dickinson had ended the poem after the first stanza, the overall meaning of the poem (which you paraphrased in the question above) would still come across. What, then, would be lost by removing the last two stanzas? In other words, how do those stanzas expand upon the meaning set up in the first stanza?

## I taste a liquor never brewed— (c. 1860)

I taste a liquor never brewed—
From Tankards scooped in Pearl—
Not all the Vats upon the Rhine
Yield such an Alcohol!

Inebriate of Air—am I—
And Debauchee of Dew—
Reeling—thro endless summer days—
From inns of Molten Blue—

When "Landlords" turn the drunken Bee
Out of the Foxglove's door—
When Butterflies—renounce their "drams"—
I shall but drink the more!

Till Seraphs swing their snowy Hats—
And Saints—to windows run—
To see the little Tippler
Leaning against the—Sun—

### Questions for Critical Thinking

1. On what is this speaker drunk? Underline where you find the answer, and then paraphrase it in your own words.
2. Scan this poem to discover its meter. Keeping in mind that a typical hymn stanza has alternating lines of eight syllables and six syllables, consider how this poem relates to a hymn. Does this relation enhance the meaning of this poem?

## Some keep the Sabbath going to Church— (c. 1860)

Some keep the Sabbath going to Church—
I keep it, staying at Home—
With a Bobolink for a Chorister—
And an Orchard, for a Dome—

Some keep the Sabbath in Surplice—
I just wear my Wings—
And instead of tolling the Bell, for Church,
Our little Sexton—sings.

God preaches, a noted Clergyman—
And the sermon is never long,
So instead of getting to Heaven, at last—
I'm going, all along.

### Questions for Critical Thinking

1. In line 6, the speaker says "I just wear my Wings." What does she mean?
2. Highlight all the words that have to do with the church. Then underline the words that have to do with nature. How does diction support the message of this poem?

## Safe in their Alabaster Chambers— (1861)

Safe in their Alabaster Chambers—
Untouched by Morning—
And untouched by Noon—
Lie the meek members of the Resurrection—
Rafter of Satin—and Roof of Stone!

Grand go the Years—in the Crescent—above them—
Worlds scoop their arcs—
And Firmaments—row—
Diadems—drop—and Doges—surrender—
Soundless as dots—on a Disc of Snow—

### Questions for Critical Thinking

1. Who are the safe ones?
2. Does nature seem sympathetic to their condition, or indifferent?
3. The second stanza suggests a relation between time and history and the subjects of the poem. How would you describe it?
4. Interpret the line in the second stanza "Soundless as dots—on a disc of snow—" in relation to the first three lines of the stanza. Are the dots the years, worlds, jewels, and rulers referred to there? If so, what does the line mean?

## I like a look of Agony (c. 1861)

I like a look of Agony,
Because I know it's true—
Men do not sham Convulsion,
Nor simulate, a Throe—

The Eyes glaze once—and that is Death—
Impossible to feign
The Beads upon the Forehead
By homely Anguish strung

### Questions for Critical Thinking

1. What does the speaker mean by the beads "Anguish" strings on the forehead? Describe the mental image you get from the last two lines.
2. Describe the speaker's tone in this poem. Is his or her stance toward suffering surprising to you? How does it affect the way you read the poem?

## Wild Nights—Wild Nights! (c. 1861)

Wild Nights—Wild Nights!
Were I with thee
Wild Nights should be
Our luxury!

Futile—the Winds—
To a Heart in port—
Done with the Compass—
Done with the Chart!

Rowing in Eden—
Ah, the Sea!
Might I but moor—Tonight
In Thee!

### Questions for Critical Thinking

1. What is the effect of repeating the phrase "Wild Nights"?
2. Discuss the erotic component of this poem. Does the speaker describe physical love or yearn for spiritual union with something abstract? Or both?

## There's a certain Slant of light (c. 1861)

There's a certain Slant of light,
Winter Afternoons—
That oppresses, like the Heft
Of Cathedral Tunes—

Heavenly Hurt, it gives us—
We can find no scar,
But internal difference,
Where the Meanings, are—

None may teach it—Any—
'Tis the Seal Despair—
An imperial affliction
Sent us of the Air—

When it comes, the Landscape listens—
Shadows—hold their breath—
When it goes, 'tis like the Distance
On the look of Death—

### Questions for Critical Thinking

1. Explain the central metaphor—the oppressive nature of a certain way the light falls on a winter afternoon. Can you link this feeling created in the poet by the light with any modern condition or state of mind?
2. Interpret the meaning of the listening landscape. Is it only in New England that such a condition might occur? Could a poet in Florida or Texas or California make a similar poem?

## I felt a Funeral, in my Brain (c. 1861)

I felt a Funeral, in my Brain,
And Mourners to and fro
Kept treading—treading—till it seemed
That Sense was breaking through—

And when they all were seated,
A Service, like a Drum—
Kept beating—beating—till I thought
My Mind was going numb—

And then I heard them lift a Box
And creak across my Soul
With those same Boots of Lead, again,
Then Space—began to toll,

As all the Heavens were a Bell,
And Being, but an Ear,
And I, and Silence, some strange Race
Wrecked, solitary, here—

And then a Plank in Reason, broke,
And I dropped down, and down—
And hit a World, at every plunge,
And Finished knowing—then—

### Questions for Critical Thinking

1. Read the poem a second time. As you do so, underline any place where a particular sound comes to mind. What techniques allow Dickinson to create a sense of hearing what the speaker hears?
2. Paying particular attention to the last stanza, explain what you think "happens" in this poem. What clues in the poem lead you to your conclusion?
3. The brain surfaces in several of Dickinson's poems. Describe the brain as it is portrayed in this poem (i.e., does it feel claustrophobic or expansive? what type of activity does it harbor? what types of words does Dickinson use in relation to the brain?, etc.). Then do the same for her poem "The Brain—is wider than the Sky" (p. 409). What are the similarities and differences? In your analysis, examine the significance of using "the brain" rather than "the heart" or "the soul."

## I'm Nobody! Who are you? (c. 1861)

I'm Nobody! Who are you?
Are you—Nobody—Too?
Then there's a pair of us!
Don't tell! they'd advertise—you know!

How dreary—to be—Somebody!
How public—like a Frog—
To tell one's name—the livelong June—
To an admiring Bog!

### Questions for Critical Thinking

1. To whom is the poet speaking? Who is "they"? Why would they "advertise" the speaker and the addressee of the poem? What would they advertise about the two?
2. Do you find the pairing of "Somebody" and "Frog" jarring or sensible?
3. How do frogs "tell" their names to the bog?
4. What effect does the adjective "admiring" have on "Bog," or vice versa?

## The Soul selects her own Society— (c. 1862)

The Soul selects her own Society—
Then—shuts the Door—
To her divine Majority—
Present no more—

Unmoved—she notes the Chariots—
  pausing—
At her low Gate—
Unmoved—an Emperor be kneeling
Upon her Mat—

I've known her—from an ample nation—
Choose One—
Then—close the Valves of her attention—
Like Stone—

### Questions for Critical Thinking

1. Paraphrase this poem. What statement is the speaker making about the soul?
2. Without reviewing the poem, make a list of images you remember in it. Now read the poem again, and make a list of images that are in it. Compare the two lists. How does Dickinson's use of imagery enhance the meaning of the poem?

## After great pain, a formal feeling comes— (c. 1862)

After great pain, a formal feeling comes—
The Nerves sit ceremonious, like Tombs—
The stiff Heart questions was it He, that bore,
And Yesterday, or Centuries before?

The Feet, mechanical, go round—
Of Ground, or Air, or Ought—
A Wooden way
Regardless grown,
A Quartz contentment, like a stone—

This is the Hour of Lead—
Remembered, if outlived,
As Freezing persons, recollect the Snow—
First—Chill—then Stupor—then the letting go—

### Questions for Critical Thinking

1. What pain might the poet be trying to describe? How many varieties of metaphor does the poet employ here to describe it?
2. Who is the "He" of line 3?
3. Do you find any possibility for hope in the final stanza?

## Much madness is divinest Sense— (c. 1862)

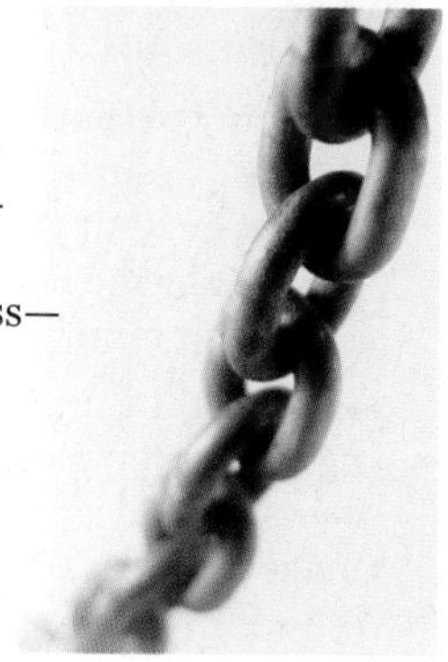

Much Madness is divinest Sense—
To a discerning Eye—
Much Sense—the starkest Madness—
'Tis the Majority
In this, as All, prevail—
Assent—and you are sane—
Demur—you're straightway
  dangerous—
And handled with a Chain—

### Questions for Critical Thinking

1. Circle any of the words that you need to double-check in the dictionary. You may want to choose words that are critical to the poem, such as "madness" and "sense," even if you believe you know their meaning. Then write the dictionary definition on a separate sheet of paper. Are the words' shades of meaning different from what you had expected?
2. The argument of this poem is based on a paradox: "Much Madness is divinest Sense . . . Much Sense—the starkest Madness." In your own words, what does the speaker mean by this contradiction?
3. Can you think of fictional characters who act in a way that appears mad to others, but which is actually sane? Going further, can you think of people you know, either personally or at large, whose "madness" leads them to go against the majority?

## I died for Beauty—but was scarce (c. 1862)

I died for Beauty—but was scarce
Adjusted in the Tomb
When One who died for Truth, was lain
In an adjoining Room—

He questioned softly "Why I failed"?
"For Beauty", I replied—
"And I—for Truth—Themself are One—
We Brethren, are," He said—

And so, as Kinsmen, met a Night—
We talked between the Rooms—
Until the Moss had reached our lips—
And covered up—Our names—

### Questions for Critical Thinking

1. Given that one of Dickinson's major influences was the English poet John Keats, read Keats's "Ode on a Grecian Urn" (chapter 18). How do the two relate? Can you find any evidence that Dickinson may have had Keats's poem in mind when she wrote hers, or is there insufficient support for that conclusion?
2. What is the mood of this poem? Which words and images lead to your reading of the tone?

## I heard a Fly buzz—when I died— (c. 1862)

I heard a Fly buzz—when I died—
The Stillness in the Room
Was like the Stillness in the Air—
Between the Heaves of Storm—

The Eyes around—had wrung them dry—
And Breaths were gathering firm
For that last Onset—when the King
Be witnessed—in the Room—

I willed my Keepsakes—Signed away
What portion of me be
Assignable—and then it was
There interposed a Fly—

With Blue—uncertain stumbling Buzz—
Between the light—and me—
And then the Windows failed—and then
I could not see to see—

### Questions for Critical Thinking

1. What effect does the last line have? Why do you think "I could not see to see" fits better than simply "I could not see"?
2. Why does Dickinson select a fly as opposed to, say, a bird or a bee?

## The Brain—is wider than the Sky— (c. 1862)

The Brain—is wider than the Sky—
For—put them side by side—
The one the other will contain
With ease—and You—beside—

The Brain is deeper than the sea—
For—hold them—Blue to Blue—
The one the other will absorb—
As Sponges—Buckets—do—

The Brain is just the weight of God—
For—Heft them—Pound for Pound—
And they will differ—if they do—
As Syllable from Sound—

### Questions for Critical Thinking

1. How does the "weight of God" relate to the brain? What does the speaker suggest by making this comparison?
2. What techniques does Dickinson use to *illustrate* the vastness of the brain as well as describe it?

## I started Early—Took my Dog— (1862)

I started Early—Took my Dog—
And visited the Sea—
The Mermaids in the Basement
Came out to look at me—

And Frigates—in the Upper Floor
Extended Hempen Hands—
Presuming Me to be a Mouse—
Aground—upon the Sands—

But no Man moved Me—till the Tide
Went past my simple Shoe—
And past my Apron—and my Belt
And past my Bodice—too—

And made as He would eat me up—
As wholly as a Dew
Upon a Dandelion's Sleeve—
And then—I started—too—

And He—He followed—close behind—
I felt His Silver Heel
Upon my Ankle—Then my Shoes
Would overflow with Pearl—

Until We met the Solid Town—
No One He seemed to know—
And bowing—with a Mighty look—
At me—The Sea withdrew—

### Questions for Critical Thinking

1. Some critics read this as a poem about a sexual encounter. Which lines support such a reading? Which images seem to stand for something other than merely a surreal landscape?
2. Besides the sexual encounter theory we suggested in question 1, what else might the poem be about? How does the meaning of the symbols change as your reading changes?

## Because I could not stop for Death— (1863)

Because I could not stop for Death—
He kindly stopped for me—
The Carriage held but just Ourselves—
And Immortality.

We slowly drove—He knew no haste
And I had put away
My labor and my leisure too,
For His Civility—

We passed the School, where Children strove
At Recess—in the Ring—
We passed the Fields of Gazing Grain—
We passed the Setting Sun—

Or rather—He passed Us—
The Dews drew quivering and chill—
For only Gossamer, my Gown—
My Tippet—only Tulle—

We paused before a House that seemed
A Swelling of the Ground—
The Roof was scarcely visible—
The Cornice—in the Ground—

Since then—'tis Centuries—and yet
Feels shorter than the Day
I first surmised the Horses' Heads
Were toward Eternity—

### Questions for Critical Thinking

1. Is there a rhyme scheme in this poem? If not, how do the words work together to create the semblance of such a scheme?
2. Using two different colors, highlight the words you don't know; then highlight the words that you think Dickinson has used to the best possible effect. Do you find that "difficult" diction is the most effective, or simpler phrasing? Explain your answer.

## One need not be a Chamber— to be Haunted— (c. 1863)

One need not be a Chamber—to be Haunted—
One need not be a House—
The Brain has Corridors—surpassing
Material Place—

Far safer, of a Midnight Meeting
External Ghost
Than its interior Confronting—
That Cooler Host.

Far safer, through an Abbey gallop,
The Stones a'chase—
Than Unarmed, one's a'self encounter—
In lonesome Place—

Ourself behind ourself, concealed—
Should startle most—
Assassin hid in our Apartment
Be Horror's least.

The Body—borrows a Revolver—
He bolts the Door—
O'erlooking a superior spectre—
Or More—

### Questions for Critical Thinking

1. What psychological state might have prompted the poet to make this poem?
2. List the metaphors—what does the fact that they are architectural suggest about the poet and the poem? Does she derive the idea only from the traditional myths about haunted houses?
3. Who or what is the ghost in this little ghost story?
4. Do you find her assumptions to be antiquated or modern enough for you to sympathize with?

## A narrow Fellow in the Grass (c. 1865)

A narrow Fellow in the Grass
Occasionally rides—
You may have met him—did you not
His notice instant is—

The Grass divides as with a Comb—
A spotted shaft is seen—
And then it closes at your feet
And opens further on—

He likes a Boggy Acre
A Floor too cool for Corn—
Yet when a Boy, and Barefoot
I more than once at Noon

Have passed, I thought, a Whip lash
Unbraiding in the Sun
When stooping to secure it
It wrinkled, and was gone—

Several of Nature's People
I know, and they know me—
I feel for them a transport
Of Cordiality—

But never met this Fellow
Attended, or alone
Without a tighter breathing
And Zero at the Bone.

### Questions for Critical Thinking

1. Underline the rhyming words in this poem. Then identify what type of rhyme occurs in each instance (i.e., end rhyme, internal rhyme, assonance, consonance, eye rhyme, etc.). What does the rhyme scheme contribute to the poem?
2. Although the speaker never states who or what the "narrow Fellow" is, you can figure it out from context clues. What is the "narrow Fellow"?

## The Bustle in a House (c. 1866)

The Bustle in a House
The Morning after Death
Is solemnest of industries
Enacted upon Earth—

The Sweeping up the Heart
And putting Love away
We shall not want to use again
Until Eternity.

### Questions for Critical Thinking

1. How are the near rhymes of lines 2 and 4, and lines 6 and 8, appropriate to that which is taking place? In other words, why do you think Dickinson did not use exact rhymes in those lines?
2. Many of Dickinson's two-stanza poems put forth something concrete in the first stanza and something abstract in the second stanza. Identify how this poem follows that pattern. How does thinking of the concrete action in the first stanza enhance your understanding of the metaphor in the second stanza?

## Tell all the Truth but tell it slant— (c. 1868)

Tell all the Truth but tell it slant—
Success in Circuit lies
Too bright for our infirm Delight
The Truth's superb surprise

As Lightning to the Children eased
With explanation kind
The Truth must dazzle gradually
Or every man be blind—

### Question for Critical Thinking

1. Paraphrase what the speaker means by telling the truth "slant." This famous phrase has often been used as a working definition of Dickinson's poetry in particular and of the art of poetry in general. What does the phrase suggest about the value of the poet's understanding of the word?

## There is no Frigate like a Book (c. 1873)

There is no Frigate like a Book
To take us Lands away
Nor any Coursers like a Page
Of prancing Poetry—
This Traverse may the poorest take
Without oppress of Toll—
How frugal is the Chariot
That bears the Human soul.

### Questions for Critical Thinking

1. Explain how the idea expressed in the last two lines is appropriate for a plain-style poet (see chapter 25).
2. Notice how all the comparisons suggest movement. How is the idea of movement appropriate to reading? Explore your ideas in a short essay.

# Robert Frost (1874–1963)

Like Emily Dickinson, Robert Frost, too, lived in New England—mostly New Hampshire and Vermont. Unlike her, however, he died when much celebrated at the age of nearly ninety. By then he was the nation's unofficial laureate, had garnered every prize worth having (among them the Bollingen Prize, a Congressional Medal) and had recited "The Gift Outright" for an audience of millions at President John F. Kennedy's inauguration. Robert Frost, known as a New England poet, was born in San Francisco, where he spent his childhood until age eleven. His family then relocated to Massachusetts, where they traced their roots back several generations. Frost determined as a teenager that he would be a poet, and that he would marry his high school sweetheart and co-valedictorian Elinor White. But their courtship was not fairy-tale: They separated for college, and she twice refused his marriage proposals before at last agreeing in 1895. He and Elinor taught school after they were married, and Frost then spent two years studying at Harvard. He did not take a degree and spent the next decade farming and composing many of the poems that would make up his early collections. In 1912, Frost relocated (with Elinor and their four children) to England, with the express purpose of writing poetry. His first two collections, *A Boy's Will* and *North of Boston*, were published in England to great success. By the time Frost returned to New England, his poetry had been published in both England and the United States, and his reputation as a leading poet was secure.

From 1917 onward, Frost spent his career as a "bardic" figure—his way of referring to the public recitations of his poetry he liked to give—and as a professor at Amherst College. Yet while his rural New England imagery and easy manner of public appearance won him a large audience and a reputation as a simple New England farmer, the reality of Frost's life was grimmer. His poetry shows a constant struggle to find order in chaos. On a more literal level, his personal life fell apart in the 1930s: His favorite daughter died after giving birth, he lost his beloved Elinor to a heart attack, one of his sons committed suicide in 1940, and another daughter was committed to a mental institution. Still, by the time of his death in 1963, Frost had won four Pulitzer Prizes, received more than forty honorary degrees, and was perhaps the best-known and most widely respected poet of the time, a status confirmed by John F. Kennedy's request that Frost recite a poem at his inauguration.

"Well, you know, I remember finally reading Frost as other than a folksy poet, [as] somebody who is essentially a philosophical poet, I thought, which was exciting." Conversation with Stephen Dunn

## Mowing (1913)

There was never a sound beside the wood but one,
And that was my long scythe whispering to the ground.
What was it it whispered? I knew not well myself;
Perhaps it was something about the heat of the sun,
Something, perhaps, about the lack of sound—
And that was why it whispered and did not speak.
It was no dream of the gift of idle hours,
Or easy gold at the hand of fay or elf:
Anything more than the truth would have seemed too weak
To the earnest love that laid the swale in rows,
Not without feeble-pointed spikes of flowers
(Pale orchises), and scared a bright green snake.
The fact is the sweetest dream that labor knows.
My long scythe whispered and left the hay to make.

### Questions for Critical Thinking

1. A scythe whispering in the grass brings to mind an auditory image. Read the poem aloud and identify words and phrases that mimic this whispering.
2. The penultimate line contains simple diction but a complex thought: "The fact is the sweetest dream that labor knows." Write a paragraph in which you reflect on this statement.

## After Apple-Picking (1914)

My long two-pointed ladder's sticking through a tree
Toward heaven still,
And there's a barrel that I didn't fill
Beside it, and there may be two or three
Apples I didn't pick upon some bough.
But I am done with apple-picking now.
Essence of winter sleep is on the night,
The scent of apples: I am drowsing off.
I cannot rub the strangeness from my sight
I got from looking through a pane of glass
I skimmed this morning from the drinking trough
And held against the world of hoary grass.
It melted, and I let it fall and break.
But I was well
Upon my way to sleep before it fell,
And I could tell
What form my dreaming was about to take.
Magnified apples appear and disappear,
Stem end and blossom end,

And every fleck of russet showing clear.
My instep arch not only keeps the ache,
It keeps the pressure of a ladder-round.
I feel the ladder sway as the boughs bend.
And I keep hearing from the cellar bin
The rumbling sound
Of load on load of apples coming in.
For I have had too much
Of apple-picking: I am overtired
Of the great harvest I myself desired.
There were ten thousand thousand fruit to touch,
Cherish in hand, lift down, and not let fall.
For all
That struck the earth,
No matter if not bruised or spiked with stubble,
Went surely to the cider-apple heap
As of no worth.
One can see what will trouble
This sleep of mine, whatever sleep it is.
Were he not gone,
The woodchuck could say whether it's like his
Long sleep, as I describe its coming on,
Or just some human sleep.

### Questions for Critical Thinking

1. Looking at the subject, where does the story of the speaker's work end and the story of his dreaming begin?
2. How does the ice on the surface of the drinking trough follow a progression to what he sees in the dream?

## Mending Wall (1914)

Something there is that doesn't love a wall,
That sends the frozen-ground-swell under it
And spills the upper boulders in the sun;
And makes gaps even two can pass abreast.
The work of hunters is another thing:
I have come after them and made repair
Where they have left not one stone on a stone,
But they would have the rabbit out of hiding,
To please the yelping dogs. The gaps I mean,
No one has seen them made or heard them made,
But at spring mending-time we find them there.
I let my neighbor know beyond the hill;
And on a day we meet to walk the line

And set the wall between us once again.
We keep the wall between us as we go.
To each the boulders that have fallen to each.
And some are loaves and some so nearly balls
We have to use a spell to make them balance:
"Stay where you are until our backs are turned!"
We wear our fingers rough with handling them.
Oh, just another kind of outdoor game,
One on a side. It comes to little more:
There where it is we do not need the wall:
He is all pine and I am apple orchard.
My apple trees will never get across
And eat the cones under his pines, I tell him.
He only says, "Good fences make good neighbors."
Spring is the mischief in me, and I wonder
If I could put a notion in his head:
"*Why* do they make good neighbors? Isn't it
Where there are cows? But here there are no cows.
Before I built a wall I'd ask to know
What I was walling in or walling out,
And to whom I was like to give offense.
Something there is that doesn't love a wall,
That wants it down." I could say "Elves" to him,
But it's not elves exactly, and I'd rather
He said it for himself. I see him there
Bringing a stone grasped firmly by the top
In each hand, like an old-stone savage armed.
He moves in darkness as it seems to me,
Not of woods only and the shade of trees.
He will not go behind his father's saying,
And he likes having thought of it so well
He says again, "Good fences make good neighbors."

### Questions for Critical Thinking

1. This poem has some beautiful imagery. Highlight two or three of the images you like best. What in those images draws you to them?
2. Identify where the mood shifts in this poem. Does it change more than once? Do you think the last line is consistent with what leads up to it?

## Birches (1915)

When I see birches bend to left and right
Across the lines of straighter darker trees,
I like to think some boy's been swinging them.
But swinging doesn't bend them down to stay.
Ice-storms do that. Often you must have seen them
Loaded with ice a sunny winter morning
After a rain. They click upon themselves
As the breeze rises, and turn many-coloured

As the stir cracks and crazes their enamel.
Soon the sun's warmth makes them shed crystal shells
Shattering and avalanching on the snow-crust
Such heaps of broken glass to sweep away
You'd think the inner dome of heaven had fallen.
They are dragged to the withered bracken by the load,
And they seem not to break; though once they are bowed
So low for long, they never right themselves:
You may see their trunks arching in the woods
Years afterwards, trailing their leaves on the ground,
Like girls on hands and knees that throw their hair
Before them over their heads to dry in the sun.
But I was going to say when Truth broke in
With all her matter-of-fact about the ice-storm,
I should prefer to have some boy bend them
As he went out and in to fetch the cows—
Some boy too far from town to learn baseball,
Whose only play was what he found himself,
Summer or winter, and could play alone.
One by one he subdued his father's trees
By riding them down over and over again
Until he took the stiffness out of them,
And not one but hung limp, not one was left
For him to conquer. He learned all there was
To learn about not launching out too soon
And so not carrying the tree away
Clear to the ground. He always kept his poise
To the top branches, climbing carefully
With the same pains you use to fill a cup
Up to the brim, and even above the brim.
Then he flung outward, feet first, with a swish,
Kicking his way down through the air to the ground.
So was I once myself a swinger of birches.
And so I dream of going back to be.
It's when I'm weary of considerations,
And life is too much like a pathless wood
Where your face burns and tickles with the cobwebs
Broken across it, and one eye is weeping
From a twig's having lashed across it open.
I'd like to get away from earth awhile
And then come back to it and begin over.
May no fate wilfully misunderstand me
And half grant what I wish and snatch me away
Not to return. Earth's the right place for love:
I don't know where it's likely to go better.

I'd like to go by climbing a birch tree—
And climb black branches up a snow-white trunk
Toward heaven, till the tree could bear no more,
But dipped its top and set me down again.
That would be good both going and coming back.
One could do worse than be a swinger of birches.

### Questions for Critical Thinking

1. The poem starts in the first person ("When I see birches . . .") and ends with a general—even impersonal—assertion ("One could do worse . . ."). How and where does the voice shift?
2. Why does the poet capitalize "Truth" in line 21? And how would you describe the tone of the phrase "I don't know where it's likely to go better" (line 53)?

## "Out, Out—" (1916)

The buzz-saw snarled and rattled in the yard
And made dust and dropped stove-length sticks of wood,
Sweet-scented stuff when the breeze drew across it.
And from there those that lifted eyes could count
Five mountain ranges one behind the other
Under the sunset far into Vermont.
And the saw snarled and rattled, snarled and rattled,
As it ran light, or had to bear a load.
And nothing happened: day was all but done.
Call it a day, I wish they might have said
To please the boy by giving him the half hour
That a boy counts so much when saved from work.
His sister stood beside them in her apron
To tell them "Supper." At the word, the saw,
As if to prove saws knew what supper meant,
Leaped out at the boy's hand, or seemed to leap—
He must have given the hand. However it was,
Neither refused the meeting. But the hand!
The boy's first outcry was a rueful laugh,
As he swung toward them holding up the hand
Half in appeal, but half as if to keep
The life from spilling. Then the boy saw all—
Since he was old enough to know, big boy
Doing a man's work, though a child at heart—
He saw all spoiled. "Don't let him cut my hand off—
The doctor, when he comes. Don't let him, sister!"
So. But the hand was gone already.
The doctor put him in the dark of ether.
He lay and puffed his lips out with his breath.
And then—the watcher at his pulse took fright.
No one believed. They listened at his heart.
Little—less—nothing!—and that ended it.
No more to build on there. And they, since they
Were not the one dead, turned to their affairs.

### Questions for Critical Thinking

1. Rewrite this poem as a short story and then compare your work with Frost's. What is emphasized in your version that is not in Frost's, and vice versa?
2. How is nature portrayed in this poem? Describe the relationship between the nature description and the events of the poem.

## The Road Not Taken (1916)

Two roads diverged in a yellow wood,
And sorry I could not travel both
And be one traveler, long I stood
And looked down one as far as I could
To where it bent in the undergrowth;

Then took the other, as just as fair,
And having perhaps the better claim,
Because it was grassy and wanted wear;
Though as for that the passing there
Had worn them really about the same,

And both that morning equally lay
In leaves no step had trodden black.
Oh, I kept the first for another day!
Yet knowing how way leads on to way,
I doubted if I should ever come back.

I shall be telling this with a sigh
Somewhere ages and ages hence:
Two roads diverged in a wood, and I—
I took the one less traveled by,
And that has made all the difference.

### Questions for Critical Thinking

1. Explain the larger meaning of this poem. What do the paths stand for? What does it mean that one is less traveled than the other?
2. Write a short profile of the speaker, based on clues from the poem. Is he daring? Individualistic? Indecisive? For each trait you mention, cite the line or lines that support your inference.

## Fire and Ice (1923)

Some say the world will end in fire,
Some say in ice.
From what I've tasted of desire
I hold with those who favor fire.
But if it had to perish twice,
I think I know enough of hate
To say that for destruction ice
Is also great
And would suffice.

### Questions for Critical Thinking

1. Scan this poem for both rhyme and meter. Identify places where the irregularities in rhyme or meter emphasize what is being said.
2. If you were given the text of the poem without the poet's name, would you be able to identify it as Frost's? Why or why not? In other words, what in this poem seems characteristic of Frost, and what deviates from his typical poem?

## Nothing Gold Can Stay (1923)

Nature's first green is gold,
Her hardest hue to hold.
Her early leaf's a flower;
But only so an hour.
Then leaf subsides to leaf.
So Eden sank to grief.
So dawn goes down to day.
Nothing gold can stay.

### Questions for Critical Thinking

1. There's a stanza in Thomas Nashe's sixteenth-century poem "Elegy in Times of Pestilence" that reads:

   Brightness falls from the air
   Queens have died young and fair
   Beauty is but a flower
   Which wrinkles must devour
   Dust hath closed Helen's eye
   I am sick, I must die.
   *Lord have mercy upon us*

   To what degree does Frost's "Nothing Gold Can Stay" echo this refrain? Compose your answer in a short essay.
2. Scan this poem for rhyme and meter. What is the relationship between the form and what is being said?

## Acquainted with the Night (1928)

I have been one acquainted with the night.
I have walked out in rain—and back in rain.
I have outwalked the furthest city light.

I have looked down the saddest city lane.
I have passed by the watchman on his beat
And dropped my eyes, unwilling to explain.

I have stood still and stopped the sound of feet
When far away an interrupted cry
Came over houses from another street,

But not to call me back or say good-by;
And further still at an unearthly height,
One luminary clock against the sky

Proclaimed the time was neither wrong nor right
I have been one acquainted with the night.

### Questions for Critical Thinking

1. What is the tone? Which words create this tone?
2. On a literal level, the poem ends with a clock against the night sky. How do you interpret this image on a metaphorical level? Going further, what do you think it means to be "acquainted with the night"?

## Desert Places (1936)

Snow falling and night falling fast, oh, fast
In a field I looked into going past,
And the ground almost covered smooth in snow,
But a few weeds and stubble showing last.

The woods around it have it—it is theirs.
All animals are smothered in their lairs,
I am too absent-spirited to count;
The loneliness includes me unawares.

And lonely as it is, that loneliness
Will be more lonely ere it will be less—
A blanker whiteness of benighted snow
With no expression, nothing to express

They cannot scare me with their empty spaces
Between stars—on stars where no human race is.
I have it in me so much nearer home
To scare myself with my own desert places.

### Questions for Critical Thinking

1. Frost in the fourth stanza refers to a statement by the sixteenth-century French philosopher Blaise Pascal—"The infinite spaces between the stars frightens me." How does the landscape he creates in the poem align with that statement?
2. What can you learn from Frost's style of making complex ideas clear that may help you with your own poetry or prose?

## Design (1936)

I found a dimpled spider, fat and white,
Oh a white heal-all, holding up a moth
Like a white piece of rigid satin cloth—
Assorted characters of death and blight
Mixed ready to begin the morning right,
Like the ingredients of a witches' broth—
A snow-drop spider, a flower like a froth,
And dead wings carried like a paper kite.

What had the flower to do with being white,
The wayside blue and innocent heal-all?
What brought the kindred spider to that height,
Then steered the white moth thither in the night?
What but design of darkness to appall?—
If design govern in a thing so small.

### Questions for Critical Thinking

1. How would you define "design" in the context of this poem? What connotations does it have?
2. What significance does the speaker give to the color white in this poem? What does the all-white imagery bring to mind for you?

## The Gift Outright (1942)

The land was ours before we were the land's.
She was our land more than a hundred years
Before we were her people. She was ours
In Massachusetts, in Virginia,
But we were England's, still colonials,
Possessing what we still were unpossessed by,
Possessed by what we now no more possessed.
Something we were withholding made us weak
Until we found out that it was ourselves
We were withholding from our land of living,
And forthwith found salvation in surrender.

Such as we were we gave ourselves outright
(The deed of gift was many deeds of war)
To the land vaguely realizing westward,
But still unstoried, artless, unenhanced,
Such as she was, such as she would become.

### Questions for Critical Thinking

1. Frost once called "The Gift Outright" "a history of the United States in sixteen lines." What does he mean by this, and do you agree?
2. Do you read the last line as optimistic or pessimistic? Explain your answer.

## The Silken Tent (1942)

She is as in a field a silken tent
At midday when a sunny summer breeze
Has dried the dew and all its ropes relent,
So that in guys it gently sways at ease,
And its supporting central cedar pole,
That is its pinnacle to heavenward
And signifies the sureness of the soul,
Seems to owe naught to any single cord,
But strictly held by none, is loosely bound
By countless silken ties of love and thought
To everything on earth the compass round,
And only by one's going slightly taut
In the capriciousness of summer air
Is of the slightest bondage made aware.

### Questions for Critical Thinking

1. Who is the subject of the poem? How does the speaker make his feelings toward and understanding of her known?
2. Why a tent? Why silk? Why a suggestion of a tie between earth and heaven? What goes "taut"? What does that signify?

# Getting Started: A Research Project

Choose Emily Dickinson or Robert Frost and examine the poet by exploring his or her biography, historical context, and select critical perspectives on his or her work; then make connections among the three.

## *Emily Dickinson*

### Critical Readings on Emily Dickinson

*The Letters of Emily Dickinson.* Thomas H. Johnson. Cambridge, MA: Harvard University Press, 1986.
Dickinson's "The soul selects her own society." Bernhard Frank. *The Explicator,* January 1, 2000.
*Comic Power in Emily Dickinson.* Suzanne Juhasz, Cristanne Miller, and Martha Nell Smith. Austin: University of Texas Press, 1993.

### Exploring Biography

Emily Dickinson's sole literary confidant and critic was an editor at the *Atlantic Monthly,* Thomas Wentworth Higginson. Dickinson initiated contact with him after reading an article in which Higginson called for new writers. Her hunger for responses to her work and literary discourse is clear from her reply to his first letter, but Dickinson and Higginson did not meet face-to-face for more than eight years after their initial correspondence when Higginson at last made a trip to Amherst in 1870. He wrote a letter to his wife describing his meeting with Dickinson. Dickinson and Higginson continued to exchange letters, however, and Dickinson describes herself in several of her early letters to him. These self-descriptions offer a unique glimpse of her home life and self-image. Based on Dickinson's account of her family life and the comments Higginson relays about her father and mother, what type of home life did Dickinson seem to have? How might this have impacted her poetry, in terms of both content and the act of creating it?

### Exploring Historical Context

Although Dickinson excludes herself in her letters when she says her family is religious, what statements does she make that indicate her Puritan background?

### Exploring Critical Perspectives

Based on any prior knowledge of Emily Dickinson you may have and on your current reading of her in these select articles, are you surprised by Juhasz, Miller, and Smith's reading of Dickinson as comic? How does this challenge or agree with your conception of Dickinson? Do you agree with their view?

### Making Connections

Select one of Dickinson's quotations that Higginson recorded. Review her poems and see if the sentiment in her quote is reflected in one of them. When you have found one that resonates, write an essay connecting the personal philosophy with the poetic expression.

## *Robert Frost*

### Critical Readings on Robert Frost

*Selected Letters of Robert Frost.* Lawrence Thompson, ed. New York: Holt, 1964.
*Robert Frost and the Darkness of Nature,* Roberts W. French. Critical Essays on Robert Frost. *The English Record,* 1978: 155–62.
"Frost's 'Mending Wall,'" A. R. Coulthard. *The Explicator* 45, no. 2 (1987): 40–42.

### Exploring Biography

From these two letters to his friends John T. Bartlett and Sidney Cox, in which Frost describes his poetic technique, how would you characterize Frost's personality? Is there anything in the letter that surprises you, or challenges your perception of Frost as a person?

### Exploring Historical Context

In the letter to Sidney Cox, Frost says that poetry should not "tell all to the last scrapings of the brain pan." What contemporary trend in poetry does he seem to be railing against? You might review the work of such poets as Sylvia Plath, Anne Sexton, and Robert Lowell with an eye to secrets told.

### Exploring Critical Perspectives

Coulthard argues that Frost himself was unaware of the negative portrayal of the speaker. Does this seem like a solid claim to you? Why or why not? Write a short essay evaluating the fairness of Coulthard's conjecture on Frost's intent.

Given what you know about Frost as a person, and given what you have read of his letters, evaluate Coulthard's conclusion that the poem "exposes Frost's cold mind posing as a warm heart." Do you see evidence of this in other poems? Or does this seem to be another image of the poet that is not necessarily true? Compose your thoughts in an essay.

### Making Connections

Based on just these two letters, what would you imagine Frost's manifesto on poetry to be? Which of his poems seem to follow his dictates?

# Further Suggestions for Writing and Research

1. Emily Dickinson's publication history is uniquely complex, because of the heavy editing done in the 1890s, which scholars then undid in the 1950s to create a version more faithful to her original poems. Research the progression of editions of Dickinson's work, along with the critical reception—that is, how critics and the public reacted to her poetry as each edition appeared. Write your findings into an essay, being sure to cite your sources. You may want to consult the resources listed below, although you can certainly find a host of information on Dickinson at your college's library:
   - *Guide to Emily Dickinson's Collected Poems.* Online resource: www.poets.org/page.php/prmID/308
   - *Critical Essays on Emily Dickinson.* Paul J. Ferlazzo, ed. Boston: G. K. Hall, 1984.
     - Two anonymous reviews from 1890, pp. 28–29.
     - Anonymous review of British edition, 1904, pp. 50–52.
     - "Emily Dickinson Complete" by Arlin Turner, 1956, pp. 113–16.
   - *A Companion to Emily Dickinson.* Martha Nell Smith and Mary Loeffelholz, eds. Malden, MA: Blackwell, 2008.
     - "Reading Dickinson in Her Context: The Fascicles" by Eleanor Elson Heginbotham, pp. 288–307.
2. Robert Frost appeals to an odd mix of audience—on the one hand, he is known and recited by the general public, including schoolchildren, while on the other, he is recognized in literary circles for his sophisticated versification and hauntingly dark subtext. This research topic asks you to find out how he was received by yet another group: other poets who were his contemporaries. The following three articles give a glimpse of how Ezra Pound, Amy Lowell, and Randall Jarrell reacted to Frost. Read their essays, noting the specific strengths and weaknesses each points to in Frost. Then write your own essay evaluating their reactions. Is Pound's opinion more accurate than Lowell's? Do you agree with Jarrell the most? This is the type of question you will answer in your essay, being sure to use support from Frost's poems in your discussion of his identified strengths and weaknesses. Finally, you may find it useful to review some of Pound's, Lowell's, and Jarrell's own poetry (these poets have work of their own in *Literature: Craft and Voice*) and see how it compares. Each of the following essays appears in *Critical Essays on Robert Frost,* Philip L. Gerber, ed., Boston: G. K. Hall, 1982.
   - "Modern Georgics," Ezra Pound, pp. 19–21.
     - Original Source: *Poetry* (December 1914).
   - "North of Boston," Amy Lowell, pp. 22–25.
     - Original Source: *The New Republic,* February 20, 1915, pp. 81–82.
   - "Tenderness and Passive Sadness," Randall Jarrell, pp. 112–13.
     - Original Source: *The New York Times Book Review,* June 1, 1947.

# Some Sources for Research


## Emily Dickinson

### Online Source:

*The Emily Dickinson Journal. Project MUSE.* The John Hopkins UP, 2009. Web. <http://muse.jhu.edu/journals/emily_dickinson_journal/>.

### Print Sources:

1. Ferlazzo, Paul J., ed. *Critical Essays on Emily Dickinson.* Boston: G. K. Hall, 1984. Print.
2. Higginson, Thomas Wentworth. "An Open Portfolio." *Critical Essays on Emily Dickinson.* Ed. Paul J. Ferlazzo. Boston: G. K. Hall, 1984. 23. Print.
3. Johnson, Thomas H., ed. *The Letters of Emily Dickinson.* Cambridge: Harvard UP, 1986. Print.
4. Loeffelholz, Mary. *Dickinson and the Boundaries of Feminist Theory.* Urbana Chicago: University of Illinois Press, 1991. Print.
5. Whicher, George Frisbie. *This Was a Poet: Emily Dickinson.* Charles Scribner's Sons: New York, 1938. Print.
6. Wolff, Cynthia Griffin. *Emily Dickinson.* Knopf: New York, 1986. Print.
7. Mudge, Jean McClure. *Emily Dickinson and the Image of Home.* Amherst: University of Massachusetts Press, 1975. Print.
8. Patterson, Rebecca. *Emily Dickinson's Imagery.* Amherst: University of Massachusetts Press, 1979. Print.
9. Sewall, Richard. *The Life of Emily Dickinson.* New York: Harvard UP: 1980. Print.

## Robert Frost

### Online Source:

The Poetry Foundation. "Robert Frost." *PoetryFoundation.org.* 2009. Web. <http://www.poetryfoundation.org/archive/poet.html?id=2361>.

### Print Sources:

1. Brower, Reuben A. *The Poetry of Robert Frost: Constellations of Intention.* New York: Oxford UP, 1963. Print.
2. Brodsky, Joseph, Seamus Heaney, and Derek Walcott. *Homage to Robert Frost.* New York: Farrar, Straus, and Giroux, 1996. Print.
3. Gerber, Philip L., ed. *Critical Essays on Robert Frost.* Boston: G. K. Hall, 1982. Print.
4. Meyers, Jeffrey. *Robert Frost: A Biography.* Boston: Houghton Mifflin, 1996. Print.
5. Parini, Jay. *Robert Frost: A Life.* New York: Henry Holt, 1999. Print.
6. Poirier, Richard. *Robert Frost, the Work of Knowing.* New York: Oxford UP, 1977. Print.
7. Sergeant, Elizabeth Shipley. *Robert Frost, The Trial by Existence.* New York: Holt, Rinehart & Winston, 1966. Print.
8. Thompson, Lawrence, ed. *Selected Letters of Robert Frost.* New York: Holt, Rinehart and Winston, 1964. Print.


**For examples of student papers, see chapter 3, Common Writing Assignments, and chapter 5, Writing the Research Paper, in the Handbook for Writing from Reading.**

# 29

# An Anthology of Poetry for Further Reading

# Kim Addonizio (b. 1954)

## First Poem for You (1994)

I like to touch your tattoos in complete
darkness, when I can't see them. I'm sure of
where they are, know by heart the neat
lines of lightning pulsing just above
your nipple, can find, as if by instinct, the blue
swirls of water on your shoulder where a serpent
twists, facing a dragon. When I pull you
to me, taking you until we're spent
and quiet on the sheets, I love to kiss
the pictures in your skin. They'll last until
you're seared to ashes; whatever persists
or turns to pain between us, they will still
be there. Such permanence is terrifying.
So I touch them in the dark; but touch them, trying.

# Gloria Anzaldúa (1942–2004)

## To live in the Borderlands means you (1987)

are neither *hispana india negra española*
*ni gabacha, eres mestiza, mulata,* half-breed
caught in the crossfire between camps
while carrying all five races on your back
not knowing which side to turn to, run from;

To live in the Borderlands means knowing
that the *india* in you, betrayed for 500 years,
is no longer speaking to you,
that *mexicanas* call you *rajetas,*
that denying the Anglo inside you
is as bad as having denied the Indian or the Black;

*Cuando vives en la frontera*
people walk through you, the wind steals your voice,
you're a *burra, buey,* scapegoat,
forerunner of a new race,
half and half—both woman and man, neither—
a new gender;

To live in the Borderlands means to
put *chile* in the borscht,
eat whole wheat *tortillas,*
speak Tex-Mex with a Brooklyn accent;
be stopped by *la migra* at the border checkpoints;

Living in the Borderlands means you fight hard to
resist the gold elixir beckoning from the bottle,
the pull of the gun barrel,
the rope crushing the hollow of your throat;

In the Borderlands
you are the battleground
where enemies are kin to each other;
you are at home, a stranger,
the border disputes have been settled
the volley of shots have shattered the truce
you are wounded, lost in action
dead, fighting back;

To live in the Borderlands means
the mill with the razor white teeth wants to shred off
your olive-red skin, crush out the kernel, your heart
pound you pinch you roll you out
smelling like white bread but dead;

To survive the Borderlands
you must live *sin fronteras*
be a crossroads.

# W. H. Auden (1907–1973)

*For a brief biography of W. H. Auden, see chapter 18.*

## The Unknown Citizen (1940)

*(To JS/07/M/378*
*This Marble Monument*
*Is Erected by the State)*

He was found by the Bureau of Statistics to be
One against whom there was no official complaint,
And all the reports on his conduct agree
That, in the modern sense of an old-fashioned word, he
was a saint,
For in everything he did he served the Greater Community.
Except for the War till the day he retired
He worked in a factory and never got fired,
But satisfied his employers, Fudge Motors Inc.
Yet he wasn't a scab or odd in his views,
For his Union reports that he paid his dues,
(Our report on his Union shows it was sound)
And our Social Psychology workers found
That he was popular with his mates and liked a drink.
The Press are convinced that he bought a paper every day
And that his reactions to advertisements were normal in
every way.
Policies taken out in his name prove that he was fully
insured,

And his Health-card shows he was once in hospital but left it cured.
Both Producers Research and High-Grade Living declare
He was fully sensible to the advantages of the Instalment Plan
And had everything necessary to the Modern Man,
A phonograph, a radio, a car and a frigidaire.
Our researchers into Public Opinion are content
That he held the proper opinions for the time of year;
When there was peace, he was for peace; when there was war, he went.
He was married and added five children to the population,
Which our Eugenist says was the right number for a parent of his generation,
And our teachers report that he never interfered with their education.
Was he free? Was he happy? The question is absurd:
Had anything been wrong, we should certainly have heard.

# Anne Bradstreet (1612–1672)

*For a brief biography of Anne Bradstreet, see chapter 19.*

## To my Dear and Loving Husband (1678)

If ever two were one, then surely we.
If ever man were lov'd by wife, then thee;
If ever wife was happy in a man,
Compare with me ye women if you can.
I prize thy love more than whole Mines of gold,
Or all the riches that the East doth hold.
My love is such that Rivers cannot quench,
Nor ought but love from thee, give recompence.
Thy love is such I can no way repay,
The heavens reward thee manifold I pray.
Then while we live, in love lets so persever,
That when we live no more, we may live ever.

# Emily Brontë (1818–1848)

## Come Walk with Me (1902)

Come, walk with me,
There's only thee,
To bless my spirit now.
We used to love on winter nights,
To wander through the snow;
Can we not woo back old delights?
The clouds rush dark & wild.
They fleck with shade our mountains bright
The same as long ago,
And on the horizon rest at last
In looming masses piled;
While moonbeams flash & fly so fast
We scarce can say they smiled.

Come walk with me, come walk with me,
We were not once so few;
But death has stolen our company,
As sunshine steals the dew.
He took them one by one, and we
Are left, the only two;
So closer would my feelings twine
Because they have no stay but thine.

"Nay call me not; it may not be;
Is human love so true?
Can friendship's flower droop for years
And then revive anew?
No; though the soil be wet with tears,
How fair soe're it grew;
The vital sap once perished
Will never flow again.
And surer than that dwelling dread,
The narrow dungeon of the dead,
Time parts the hearts of men.

# Robert Browning (1812–1889)

*For a brief biography of Robert Browning, see chapter 16.*

## Meeting at Night (1845)

I

The gray sea and the long black land;
And the yellow half-moon large and low;
And the startled little waves that leap
In fiery ringlets from their sleep,
As I gain the cove with pushing prow,
And quench its speed i' the slushy sand.

II

Then a mile of warm sea-scented beach;
Three fields to cross till a farm appears;
A tap at the pane, the quick sharp scratch
And blue spurt of a lighted match,
And a voice less loud, through its joys and fears,
Than the two hearts beating each to each!

## Parting at Morning (1845)

Round the cape of a sudden came the sea,
And the sun looked over the mountain's rim:
And straight was a path of gold for him,
And the need of a world of men for me.

# George Gordon, Lord Byron (1788–1824)

*For a brief biography of Lord Byron, see chapter 16.*

## She Walks in Beauty (1815)

I

She walks in beauty, like the night
  Of cloudless climes and starry skies;
And all that's best of dark and bright
  Meet in her aspect and her eyes:
Thus mellowed to that tender light
  Which heaven to gaudy day denies.

II

One shade the more, one ray the less,
  Had half impaired the nameless grace
Which waves in every raven tress,
  Or softly lightens o'er her face;
Where thoughts serenely sweet express
  How pure, how dear their dwelling place.

III

And on that cheek, and o'er that brow,
  So soft, so calm, yet eloquent,
The smiles that win, the tints that glow,
  But tell of days in goodness spent,
A mind at peace with all below,
  A heart whose love is innocent!

# John Ciardi (1916–1986)

## Most Like an Arch This Marriage (1958)

Most like an arch—an entrance which upholds
and shores the stone-crush up the air like lace.
Mass made idea, and idea held in place.
A lock in time. Inside half-heaven unfolds.

Most like an arch—two weaknesses that lean
into a strength. Two fallings become firm.
Two joined abeyances become a term
naming the fact that teaches fact to mean.

Not quite that? Not much less. World as it is,
what's strong and separate falters. All I do
at piling stone on stone apart from you
is roofless around nothing. Till we kiss
I am no more than upright and unset.
It is by falling in and in we make
the all-bearing point, for one another's sake,
in faultless failing, raised by our own weight.

# Judith Ortiz Cofer (b. 1952)

## Quinceañera (1987)

My dolls have been put away like dead
children in a chest I will carry
with me when I marry.
I reach under my skirt to feel
a satin slip bought for this day. It is soft
as the inside of my thighs. My hair
has been nailed back with my mother's
black hairpins to my skull. Her hands
stretched my eyes open as she twisted
braids into a tight circle at the nape
of my neck. I am to wash my own clothes
and sheets from this day on, as if
the fluids of my body were poison, as if
the little trickle of blood I believe
travels from my heart to the world were
shameful. Is not the blood of saints and
men in battle beautiful? Do Christ's hands
not bleed into your eyes from His cross?
At night I hear myself growing and wake
to find my hands drifting of their own will
to soothe skin stretched tight
over my bones.
I am wound like the guts of a clock,
waiting for each hour to release me.

# Samuel Taylor Coleridge (1772–1834)

*For a brief biography of Samuel Taylor Coleridge, see chapter 22.*

## Kubla Khan (1797–1798)
## *Or A Vision in a Dream. A Fragment*

In Xanadu did Kubla Khan
A stately pleasure dome decree:
Where Alph, the sacred river, ran
Through caverns measureless to man
  Down to a sunless sea.
So twice five miles of fertile ground
With walls and towers were girdled round:

And there were gardens bright with sinuous rills,
Where blossomed many an incense-bearing tree;
And here were forests ancient as the hills,
Enfolding sunny spots of greenery.

But oh! that deep romantic chasm which slanted
Down the green hill athwart a cedarn cover!
A savage place! as holy and enchanted
As e'er beneath a waning moon was haunted
By woman wailing for her demon lover!
And from this chasm, with ceaseless turmoil seething,
As if this earth in fast thick pants were breathing,
A mighty fountain momently was forced:
Amid whose swift half-intermitted burst
Huge fragments vaulted like rebounding hail,
Or chaffy grain beneath the thresher's flail:
And 'mid these dancing rocks at once and ever
It flung up momently the sacred river.
Five miles meandering with a mazy motion
Through wood and dale the sacred river ran,
Then reached the caverns measureless to man,
And sank in tumult to a lifeless ocean:
And 'mid this tumult Kubla heard from far
Ancestral voices prophesying war!

The shadow of the dome of pleasure
Floated midway on the waves;
Where was heard the mingled measure
From the fountain and the caves.
It was a miracle of rare device,
A sunny pleasure dome with caves of ice!

A damsel with a dulcimer
In a vision once I saw:
It was an Abyssinian maid,
And on her dulcimer she played,
Singing of Mount Abora.
Could I revive within me
Her symphony and song,
To such a deep delight 'twould win me,
That with music loud and long,
I would build that dome in air,
That sunny dome! those caves of ice!
And all who heard should see them there,
And all should cry, Beware! Beware!
His flashing eyes, his floating hair!
Weave a circle round him thrice,
And close your eyes with holy dread,
For he on honey-dew hath fed,
And drunk the milk of Paradise.

## e. e. cummings (1894–1962)

*For a brief biography of e. e. cummings, see chapter 24.*

### l(a (1923)

l(a
le
af
fa

ll

s)
one
l

iness

### anyone lived in a pretty how town (1940)

anyone lived in a pretty how town
(with up so floating many bells down)
spring summer autumn winter
he sang his didn't he danced his did.

Women and men(both little and small)
cared for anyone not at all
they sowed their isn't they reaped their same
sun moon stars rain

children guessed(but only a few
and down they forgot as up they grew
autumn winter spring summer)
that noone loved him more by more

when by now and tree by leaf
she laughed his joy she cried his grief
bird by snow and stir by still
anyone's any was all to her

someones married their everyones
laughed their cryings and did their dance
(sleep wake hope and then)they
said their nevers they slept their dream

stars rain sun moon
(and only the snow can begin to explain
how children are apt to forget to remember
with up so floating many bells down)

one day anyone died i guess
(and noone stooped to kiss his face)
busy folk buried them side by side
little by little and was by was

all by all and deep by deep
and more by more they dream their sleep
noone and anyone earth by april
wish by spirit and if by yes.

Women and men(both dong and ding)
summer autumn winter spring
reaped their sowing and went their came
sun moon stars rain

### Buffalo Bills (1923)

Buffalo Bill's
defunct
who used to
ride a watersmooth-silver
stallion
and break onetwothreefourfive pigeonsjustlikethat
Jesus

he was a handsome man
and what i want to know is
how do you like your blueeyed boy
Mister Death

## John Donne (1572–1631)

*For a brief biography of John Donne, see chapter 25.*

### Death Be Not Proud (c. 1610)

Death, be not proud, though some have callèd thee
Mighty and dreadful, for thou art not so;
For those whom thou think'st thou dost overthrow
Die not, poor Death, nor yet canst thou kill me.
From rest and sleep, which but thy pictures be,
Much pleasure; then from thee much more must flow,
And soonest our best men with thee do go,
Rest of their bones, and soul's delivery.
Thou art slave to fate, chance, kings, and desperate men,
And dost with poison, war, and sickness dwell,
And poppy or charms can make us sleep as well
And better than thy stroke; why swell'st thou then?
One short sleep past, we wake eternally
And death shall be no more; Death, thou shalt die.

### The Flea (1633)

Mark but this flea, and mark in this,
How little that which thou deniest me is;
Me it sucked first, and now sucks thee,
And in this flea our two bloods mingled be.
Thou know'st that this cannot be said
A sin, or shame, or loss of maidenhead,
Yet this enjoys before it woo,
And pampered swells with one blood made of two,
And this, alas, is more than we would do.

Oh stay, three lives in one flea spare,
Where we almost, nay more than married are.
This flea is you and I, and this
Our marriage bed and marriage temple is;
Though parents grudge, and you, we are met,
And cloistered in these living walls of jet.
Though use make you apt to kill me,
Let not to that, self-murder added be,
And sacrilege, three sins in killing three.

Cruel and sudden, hast thou since
Purpled thy nail in blood of innocence?
Wherein could this flea guilty be,
Except in that drop which it sucked from thee?
Yet thou triumph'st, and say'st that thou
Find'st not thyself nor me the weaker now;
'Tis true; then learn how false fears be:
Just so much honor, when thou yield'st to me,
Will waste, as this flea's death took life from thee.

### The Sun Rising (1633)

Busy old fool, unruly Sun,
Why dost thou thus
Through windows, and through curtains call on us?
Must to thy motions lovers' seasons run?
Saucy pedantic wretch, go chide
Late schoolboys and sour prentices,
Go tell court huntsmen that the King will ride,
Call country ants to harvest offices;
Love, all alike, no season knows nor clime,
Nor hours, days, months, which are the rags of time.

Thy beams, so reverend and strong
Why shouldst thou think?
I could eclipse and cloud them with a wink,
But that I would not lose her sight so long;
If her eyes have not blinded thine,
Look, and tomorrow late, tell me,
Whether both th' Indias of spice and mine
Be where thou leftst them, or lie here with me.
Ask for those kings whom thou saw'st yesterday,
And thou shalt hear, All here in one bed lay.

She is all states, and all princes I,
Nothing else is.
Princes do but play us; compared to this,
All honor's mimic, all wealth alchemy.

Thou, sun, art half as happy as we,
In that the world's contracted thus;
Thine age asks ease, and since thy duties be
To warm the world, that's done in warming us.
Shine here to us, and thou art everywhere;
This bed thy center is, these walls thy sphere.

# H.D. (Hilda Doolittle) (1886–1961)

*For a brief biography of H.D., see chapter 20.*

## Heat (1916)

O wind, rend open the heat.
cut apart the heat,
rend it to tatters.

Fruit cannot drop
through this thick air—
fruit cannot fall into heat
that presses up and blunts
the points of pears
and rounds the grapes.

Cut the heat—
plough through it,
turning it on either side
of your path

# T. S. Eliot (1888–1965)

## The Love Song of J. Alfred Prufrock (1915)

*S'io credesse che mia risposta fosse*
*A persona che mai tornasse al mondo,*
*Questa fiamma staria senza più scosse.*
*Ma perciocche giammai di questo fondo*
*Non tornò vivo alcun, s'i'odo il vero,*
*Senza tema d'infamia ti rispondo.*°

Let us go then, you and I,
When the evening is spread out against the sky
Like a patient etherized upon a table;
Let us go, through certain half-deserted streets,
The muttering retreats
Of restless nights in one-night cheap hotels
And sawdust restaurants with oyster-shells:
Streets that follow like a tedious argument
Of insidious intent
To lead you to an overwhelming question . . .
Oh, do not ask, "What is it?"
Let us go and make our visit.

In the room the women come and go
Talking of Michelangelo.

The yellow fog that rubs its back upon the window-panes
The yellow smoke that rubs its muzzle on the window-panes
Licked its tongue into the corners of the evening,
Lingered upon the pools that stand in drains,
Let fall upon its back the soot that falls from chimneys,
Slipped by the terrace, made a sudden leap,
And seeing that it was a soft October night,
Curled once about the house, and fell asleep.

And indeed there will be time
For the yellow smoke that slides along the street,
Rubbing its back upon the window-panes;
There will be time, there will be time
To prepare a face to meet the faces that you meet;
There will be time to murder and create,
And time for all the works and days of hands
That lift and drop a question on your plate;
Time for you and time for me,
And time yet for a hundred indecisions,
And for a hundred visions and revisions,
Before the taking of a toast and tea.

In the room the women come and go
Talking of Michelangelo.

And indeed there will be time
To wonder, "Do I dare?" and, "Do I dare?"
Time to turn back and descend the stair,
With a bald spot in the middle of my hair—
[They will say: "How his hair is growing thin!"]
My morning coat, my collar mounting firmly to the chin,
My necktie rich and modest, but asserted by a simple pin—
[They will say: "But how his arms and legs are thin!"]
Do I dare
Disturb the universe?
In a minute there is time
For decisions and revisions which a minute will reverse.

For I have known them all already, known them all:
Have known the evenings, mornings, afternoons,
I have measured out my life with coffee spoons;
I know the voices dying with a dying fall
Beneath the music from a farther room.
So how should I presume?

°If I believed that my reply were made
To one to who the world would e'er return,
The flame without more flickering would stand still;
But inasmuch as never from this depth
Did anyone return, if I hear true,
Without the fear of infamy I answer.

And I have known the eyes already, known them all—
The eyes that fix you in a formulated phrase,
And when I am formulated, sprawling on a pin,
When I am pinned and wriggling on the wall,
Then how should I begin
To spit out all the butt-ends of my days and ways?
And how should I presume?

And I have known the arms already, known them all—
Arms that are braceleted and white and bare
[But in the lamplight, downed with light brown hair!]
Is it perfume from a dress
That makes me so digress?
Arms that lie along a table, or wrap about a shawl.
And should I then presume?
And how should I begin?

. . . . .

Shall I say, I have gone at dusk through narrow streets
And watched the smoke that rises from the pipes
Of lonely men in shirt-sleeves, leaning out of windows? . . .

I should have been a pair of ragged claws
Scuttling across the floors of silent seas.

. . . . .

And the afternoon, the evening, sleeps so peacefully!
Smoothed by long fingers,
Asleep . . . tired . . . or it malingers,
Stretched on the floor, here beside you and me.
Should I, after tea and cakes and ices,
Have the strength to force the moment to its crisis?
But though I have wept and fasted, wept and prayed,
Though I have seen my head [grown slightly bald] brought in upon a platter,
I am no prophet—and here's no great matter;
I have seen the moment of my greatness flicker,
And I have seen the eternal Footman hold my coat, and snicker,
And in short, I was afraid.

And would it have been worth it, after all,
After the cups, the marmalade, the tea,
Among the porcelain, among some talk of you and me,
Would it have been worth while,
To have bitten off the matter with a smile,
To have squeezed the universe into a ball
To roll it toward some overwhelming question,
To say: "I am Lazarus, come from the dead,
Come back to tell you all, I shall tell you all"—
If one, settling a pillow by her head,
Should say: "That is not what I meant at all.
That is not it, at all."

And would it have been worth it, after all,
Would it have been worth while,
After the sunsets and the dooryards and the sprinkled streets,
After the novels, after the teacups, after the skirts that trail along the floor—
And this, and so much more?—
It is impossible to say just what I mean!
But as if a magic lantern threw the nerves in patterns on a screen:
Would it have been worth while
If one, settling a pillow or throwing off a shawl,
And turning toward the window, should say:
"That is not it at all,
That is not what I meant, at all."

. . . . .

No! I am not Prince Hamlet, nor was meant to be;
Am an attendant lord, one that will do
To swell a progress, start a scene or two,
Advise the prince; no doubt, an easy tool,
Deferential, glad to be of use,
Politic, cautious, and meticulous;
Full of high sentence, but a bit obtuse;
At times, indeed, almost ridiculous—
Almost, at times, the Fool.

I grow old . . . I grow old . . .
I shall wear the bottoms of my trousers rolled.

Shall I part my hair behind? Do I dare to eat a peach?
I shall wear white flannel trousers, and walk upon the beach.
I have heard the mermaids singing, each to each.

I do not think that they will sing to me.

I have seen them riding seaward on the waves
Combing the white hair of the waves blown back
When the wind blows the water white and black.

We have lingered in the chambers of the sea
By sea-girls wreathed with seaweed red and brown
Till human voices wake us, and we drown.

# Louise Erdrich (b. 1954)

## Dear John Wayne (1984)

August and the drive-in picture is packed.
We lounge on the hood of the Pontiac
surrounded by the slow-burning spirals they sell

at the window, to vanquish the hordes of mosquitoes.
Nothing works. They break through the smoke screen for
blood.

Always the lookout spots the Indian first,
spread north to south, barring progress.
The Sioux or some other Plains bunch
in spectacular columns, ICBM missiles,
feathers bristling in the meaningful sunset.

The drum breaks. There will be no parlance.
Only the arrows whining, a death-cloud of nerves
swarming down on the settlers
who die beautifully, tumbling like dust weeds
into the history that brought us all here
together: this wide screen beneath the sign of the bear.

The sky fills, acres of blue squint and eye
that the crowd cheers. His face moves over us,
a thick cloud of vengeance, pitted
like the land that was once flesh. Each rut,
each scar makes a promise: *It is*
*not over, this fight, not as long as you resist.*

*Everything we see belongs to us.*

A few laughing Indians fall over the hood
slipping in the hot spilled butter.
*The eye sees a lot, John, but the heart is so blind.*
*Death makes us owners of nothing.*
He smiles, a horizon of teeth
the credits reel over, and then the white fields

again blowing in the true-to-life dark.
The dark films over everything.
We get into the car
scratching our mosquito bites, speechless and small
as people are when the movie is done.
We are back in our skins.

How can we help but keep hearing his voice,
the flip side of the sound track, still playing:
*Come on, boys, we got them*
*where we want them, drunk, running.*
*They'll give us what we want, what we need.*
Even his disease was the idea of taking everything.
Those cells, burning, doubling, splitting out of their skins.

# Rhina Espaillat (b. 1932)

## Bilingual/Bilingüe (1998)

My father liked them separate, one there,
one here (allá y aquí), as if aware

that words might cut in two his daughter's heart
(el corazón) and lock the alien part

to what he was—his memory, his name
(su nombre)—with a key he could not claim.

"English outside this door, Spanish inside,"
he said, "y basta." But who can divide

the world, the word (mundo y palabra) from
any child? I knew how to be dumb

and stubborn (testaruda); late, in bed,
I hoarded secret syllables I read

until my tongue (mi lengua) learned to run
where his stumbled. And still the heart was one.

I like to think he knew that, even when,
proud (orgulloso) of his daughter's pen,

he stood outside mis versos, half in fear
of words he loved but wanted not to hear.

# Linda Gregg (b. 1942)

## Something Scary (1985)

Over the phone Joel tells me
his marriage is suddenly miraculous.
That his wife is glad now about us.
Is even grateful.
"We have crossed a border," he says.
I listen, knowing myself too far gone
to last more than a day.
Remembering him in that dark room
with the shades down saying,
"You don't need the sun. You carry
a brightness in you." And me saying
nothing, burning alone lying there
like the terrible brightness of heaven.

# Kimiko Hahn (b. 1955)

## The Details We Fall For (1994)

Shifting to fifth and swinging behind a Harley
he could be you: black helmet, gloved fists—
on that spin down some LA boulevard,
the heat of February sweating the streets,
my hands around your waist in our first contact
since I married a second time still not to you.

What were those weird trees,
Dr. Seuss illustrations, cocktail mixers?
and what about all that pink—
bungalows, latex buns, tanning billboards—
details instructing the interior landscape
we ride through even, or especially in sleep.
I'm back in New York.
So to the driver behind me:
don't tail the woman behind the guy on the motorcycle.
She's working on a rough draft.

## Donald Hall (b. 1928)

### Letter with No Address (1996)

Your daffodils rose up
and collapsed in their yellow
bodies on the hillside
garden above the bricks
you laid out in sand, squatting
with pants pegged and face
masked like a beekeeper's
against the black flies.
Buttercups circle the planks
of the old wellhead
this May while your silken
gardener's body withers or moulds
in the Proctor graveyard.
I drive and talk to you crying
and come back to this house
to talk to your photographs.

There's news to tell you:
Maggie Fisher's pregnant.
I carried myself like an egg
at Abigail's birthday party
a week after you died,
as three-year-olds bounced
uproarious on a mattress.
Joyce and I met for lunch
at the mall and strolled weepily
through Sears and B. Dalton.

Today it's four weeks
since you lay on our painted bed
and I closed your eyes.
Yesterday I cut irises to set
in a pitcher on your grave;
today I brought a carafe
to fill it with fresh water.
I remember the bone-pain,
vomiting, and delirium. I remember
the pond afternoons.

My routine
is established: coffee;
the *Globe;* breakfast;
writing you this letter
at my desk. When I go to bed
to sleep after baseball,
Gus follows me into the bedroom
as he used to follow us.
Most of the time he flops
down in the parlor
with his head on his paws.

Once a week I drive to Tilton
to see Dick and Nan.
Nan doesn't understand much
but she knows you're dead;
I feel her fretting. The tune
of Dick and me talking
seems to console her.

You know now
whether the soul survives death.
Or you don't. When you were dying
you said you didn't fear
punishment. We never dared
to speak of Paradise.

At five a.m., when I walk outside,
mist lies thick on hayfields.
By eight, the air is clear,
cool, sunny with the pale yellow
light of mid-May. Kearsarge
rises huge and distinct,
each birch and balsam visible.
To the west the waters
of Eagle Pond waver
and flash through popples just
leafing out.

Always the weather,
writing its book of the world,
returns you to me.
Ordinary days were best,
when we worked over poems
in our separate rooms.
I remember watching you gaze
out the January window
into the garden of snow
and ice, your face rapt
as you imagined burgundy lilies.

Your presence in this house
is almost as enormous
and painful as your absence.
Driving home from Tilton,
I remember how you cherished
that vista with its center
the red door of a farmhouse
against green fields.
Are you past pity?
If you have consciousness now,
if something I can call
"you" has something
like "consciousness," I doubt
you remember the last days.
I play them over and over:
I lift your wasted body
onto the commode, your arms
looped around my neck, aiming
your bony bottom so that
it will not bruise on a rail.
Faintly you repeat,
"Momma, Momma."

You lay
astonishing in the long box
while Alice Ling prayed
and sang "Amazing Grace"
a capella. Three times today
I drove to your grave.
Sometimes, coming back home
to our circular driveway,
I imagine you've returned
before me, bags of groceries upright
in the back of the Saab,
its trunklid delicately raised
as if proposing an encounter,
dog-fashion, with the Honda.

# Thomas Hardy (1840–1928)

*For a brief biography of Thomas Hardy, see chapter 19.*

## The Darkling Thrush (1900)

I leant upon a coppice gate
  When Frost was specter-gray,
And Winter's dregs made desolate
  The weakening eye of day.
The tangled bine-stems scored the sky
  Like strings of broken lyres,
And all mankind that haunted nigh
  Had sought their household fires.

The land's sharp features seemed to be
  The Century's corpse outleant,
His crypt the cloudy canopy,
  The wind his death-lament.
The ancient pulse of germ and birth
  Was shrunken hard and dry,
And every spirit upon earth
  Seemed fervorless as I.

At once a voice arose among
  The bleak twigs overhead
In a full-hearted evensong
  Of joy illimited;
An aged thrush, frail, gaunt, and small,
  In blast-beruffled plume,
Had chosen thus to fling his soul
  Upon the growing gloom.

So little cause for carolings
  Of such ecstatic sound
Was written on terrestrial things
  Afar or nigh around,
That I could think there trembled through
  His happy good-night air
Some blessed Hope, whereof he knew
  And I was unaware.

# George Herbert (1593–1633)

*For a brief biography of George Herbert, see chapter 24.*

## Love (1633)

Love bade me welcome: yet my soul drew back,
  Guilty of dust and sin.
But quick-eyed Love, observing me grow slack
  From my first entrance in,
Drew nearer to me, sweetly questioning
  If I lacked anything.

"A guest," I answered, "worthy to be here":
  Love said, "You shall be he."
"I, the unkind, ungrateful? Ah, my dear,
  I cannot look on thee."
Love took my hand, and smiling did reply,
  "Who made the eyes but I?"

"Truth, Lord; but I have marred them; let my shame
  Go where it doth deserve."
"And know you not," says Love, "who bore the blame?"
  "My dear, then I will serve."
"You must sit down," says Love, "and taste my meat."
  So I did sit and eat.

# Robert Herrick (1591–1674)

## Upon Julia's Clothes (1648)

Whenas in silks my Julia goes,
Then, then, methinks, how sweetly flows
The liquefaction of her clothes.

Next, when I cast mine eyes and see
That brave vibration each way free,
Oh, how that glittering taketh me!

## Delight in Disorder (1648)

A sweet disorder in the dress
Kindles in clothes a wantonness.
A lawn about the shoulders thrown
Into a fine distraction;
An erring lace, which here and there
Enthralls the crimson stomacher;
A cuff neglectful, and thereby
Ribbons to flow confusedly;
A winning wave, deserving note,
In the tempestuous petticoat;
A careless shoestring, in whose tie
I see a wild civility:
Do more bewitch me than when art
Is too precise in every part.

## To the Virgins, to Make Much of Time (1646)

Gather ye rosebuds while ye may,
  Old time is still a-flying;
And this same flower that smiles today,
  Tomorrow will be dying.

The glorious lamp of heaven, the sun,
  The higher he's a-getting,
The sooner will his race be run,
  And nearer he's to setting.

That age is best which is the first,
  When youth and blood are warmer;
But being spent, the worse, and worst
  Times still succeed the former.

Then be not coy, but use your time,
  And while ye may, go marry;
For having lost but once your prime,
  You may forever tarry.

# Gerard Manley Hopkins (1844–1889)

*For a brief biography of Gerard Manley Hopkins, see chapter 22.*

## God's Grandeur (1877)

The world is charged with the grandeur of God.
  It will flame out, like shining from shook foil;
  It gathers to a greatness, like the ooze of oil
Crushed. Why do men then now not reck his rod?
Generations have trod, have trod, have trod;
  And all is seared with trade; bleared, smeared with toil;
  And wears man's smudge and shares man's smell:
    the soil
Is bare now, nor can foot feel, being shod.

And for all this, nature is never spent;
  There lives the dearest freshness deep down things;
And though the last lights off the black West went
  Oh, morning, at the brown brink eastward, springs—
Because the Holy Ghost over the bent
  World broods with warm breast and with ah! bright
    wings.

## The Windhover (1877)

*To Christ our Lord*

I caught this morning morning's minion, king-
  dom of daylight's dauphin, dapple-dawn-drawn
    Falcon, in his riding
  Of the rolling level underneath him steady air, and
    striding
High there, how he rung upon the rein of a wimpling
  wing
In his ecstasy! then off, off forth on swing,
  As a skate's heel sweeps smooth on a bow-bend: the
    hurl and gliding
  Rebuffed the big wind. My heart in hiding
Stirred for a bird,—the achieve of, the mastery of the thing!

Brute beauty and valour and act, oh, air, pride, plume, here
  Buckle! AND the fire that breaks from thee then,
    a billion
Times told lovelier, more dangerous, O my chevalier!

  No wonder of it: shéer plód makes plough down sillion
Shine, and blue-bleak embers, ah my dear,
  Fall, gall themselves, and gash gold-vermillion.

# A. E. Housman (1859–1936)

## Loveliest of trees, the cherry now (1896)

Loveliest of trees, the cherry now
Is hung with bloom along the bough,
And stands about the woodland ride
Wearing white for Eastertide.

Now, of my threescore years and ten,
Twenty will not come again,
And take from seventy springs a score,
It only leaves me fifty more.

And since to look at things in bloom
Fifty springs are little room,
About the woodlands I will go
To see the cherry hung with snow.

## When I was one-and-twenty (1896)

When I was one-and-twenty
  I heard a wise man say,
"Give crowns and pounds and guineas
  But not your heart away;
Give pearls away and rubies
  But keep your fancy free."
But I was one-and-twenty,
  No use to talk to me.

When I was one-and-twenty
  I heard him say again,
"The heart out of the bosom
  Was never given in vain;
'Tis paid with sighs a plenty
  And sold for endless rue."
And I am two-and-twenty,
  And oh, 'tis true, 'tis true.

# Ben Jonson (1573?–1637)

*For a brief biography of Ben Jonson, see chapter 19.*

## To Celia (1616)

Drink to me only with thine eyes,
  And I will pledge with mine;
Or leave a kiss but in the cup,
  And I'll not look for wine.
The thirst that from the soul doth rise
  Doth ask a drink divine;
But might I of Jove's nectar sup,
  I would not change for thine.
I sent thee late a rosy wreath,
  Not so much honoring thee,
As giving it a hope that there
  It could not withered be.
But thou thereon didst only breathe,
  And sent'st it back to me;
Since when it grows and smells, I swear,
  Not of itself, but thee.

# John Keats (1795–1821)

*For a brief biography of John Keats, see chapter 18.*

## La Belle Dame sans Merci (1819)

Ah, what can ail thee, wretched wight,
  Alone and palely loitering?
The sedge is wither'd from the lake,
  And no birds sing.

Ah, what can ail thee, wretched wight,
  So haggard and so woe-begone?
The squirrel's granary is full,
  And the harvest's done.

I see a lily on thy brow,
  With anguish moist and fever dew;
And on thy cheek a fading rose
  Fast withereth too.

I met a lady in the meads
  Full beautiful—a faery's child;
Her hair was long, her foot was light,
  And her eyes were wild.

I set her on my pacing steed,
  And nothing else saw all day long,
For sideways would she lean, and sing
  A faery's song.

I made a garland for her head,
  And bracelets too, and fragrant zone;
She look'd at me as she did love,
  And made sweet moan.

She found me roots of relish sweet,
  And honey wild, and manna dew;
And sure in language strange she said—
  "I love thee true."

She took me to her elfin grot,
And there she gazed, and sighed deep,
And there I shut her wild wild eyes
So kiss'd to sleep.

And there we slumber'd on the moss,
And there I dream'd—Ah! woe betide!
The latest dream I ever dream'd
On the cold hill side.

I saw pale kings, and princes too,
Pale warriors, death-pale were they all;
They cried—"La Belle Dame sans Merci
Hath thee in thrall!"

I saw their starved lips in the gloam,
With horrid warning gaped wide,
And I awoke, and found me here
On the cold hill side.

And this is why I sojourn here,
Alone and palely loitering,
Though the sedge is wither'd from the lake,
And no birds sing.

# Yusef Komunyakaa (b. 1947)

## Facing It (1988)

My black face fades,
hiding inside the black granite.
I said I wouldn't
dammit: No tears.
I'm stone. I'm flesh.
My clouded reflection eyes me
like a bird of prey, the profile of night
slanted against morning. I turn
this way—the stone lets me go.
I turn that way—I'm inside
the Vietnam Veterans Memorial
again, depending on the light
to make a difference.
I go down the 58,022 names,
half-expecting to find
my own in letters like smoke.
I touch the name Andrew Johnson;
I see the booby trap's white flash.
Names shimmer on a woman's blouse
but when she walks away
the names stay on the wall.
Brushstrokes flash, a red bird's
wings cutting across my stare.
The sky. A plane in the sky.
A white vet's image floats
closer to me, then his pale eyes
look through mine. I'm a window.
He's lost his right arm
inside the stone. In the black mirror
a woman's trying to erase names:
No, she's brushing a boy's hair.

# Emma Lazarus (1849–1887)

## The New Colossus (1883)

Not like the brazen giant of Greek fame,
With conquering limbs astride from land to land;
Here at our sea-washed, sunset gates shall stand
A mighty woman with a torch, whose flame
Is the imprisoned lightning, and her name
Mother of Exiles. From her beacon-hand
Glows world-wide welcome; her mild eyes command
The air-bridged harbor that twin cities frame.
"Keep, ancient lands, your storied pomp!" cries she
With silent lips. "Give me your tired, your poor,
Your huddled masses yearning to breathe free,
The wretched refuse of your teeming shore.
Send these, the homeless, tempest-tost to me,
I lift my lamp beside the golden door!"

# Thomas Lynch (b. 1948)

*For a brief biography of Thomas Lynch, see chapter 22.*

## Liberty (1998)

Some nights I go out and piss on the front lawn
as a form of freedom—liberty from
porcelain and plumbing and the Great Beyond
beyond the toilet and the sewage works.
Here is the statement I am trying to make:
to say I am from a fierce bloodline of men
who made their water in the old way, under stars
that overarched the North Atlantic where
the River Shannon empties into sea.
The ex-wife used to say, "Why can't you pee
in concert with the most of humankind
who do their business tidily indoors?"
It was gentility or envy, I suppose,
because I could do it anywhere, and do
whenever I begin to feel encumbered.
Still, there is nothing, here in the suburbs,
as dense as the darkness in West Clare
nor any equivalent to the nightlong wind
that rattles in the hedgerow of whitethorn there
on the east side of the cottage yard in Moveen.

It was market day in Kilrush, years ago:
my great-great-grandfather bargained with tinkers
who claimed it was whitethorn that Christ's crown was
made from.
So he gave them two and six and brought them home—
mere saplings then—as a gift for the missus,
who planted them between the house and garden.
For years now, men have slipped out the back door
during wakes or wedding feasts or nights of song
to pay their homage to the holy trees
and, looking up into that vast firmament,
consider liberty in that last townland where
they have no crowns, no crappers and no ex-wives.

# Archibald MacLeish (1892–1982)

## Ars Poetica (1926)

A poem should be palpable and mute
As a globed fruit,

Dumb
As old medallions to the thumb,

Silent as the sleeve-worn stone
Of casement ledges where the moss has grown—

A poem should be wordless
As the flight of birds.

-

A poem should be motionless in time
As the moon climbs,

Leaving, as the moon releases
Twig by twig the night-entangled trees,

Leaving, as the moon behind the winter leaves,
Memory by memory the mind—

A poem should be motionless in time
As the moon climbs.

-

A poem should be equal to:
Not true.

For all the history of grief
An empty doorway and a maple leaf.

For love
The leaning grasses and two lights above the sea—

A poem should not mean
But be.

# Andrew Marvell (1621–1678)

## To His Coy Mistress (1681)

Had we but world enough, and time,
This coyness, lady, were no crime.
We would sit down, and think which way
To walk, and pass our long love's day.
Thou by the Indian Ganges' side
Shouldst rubies find; I by the tide
Of Humber would complain. I would
Love you ten years before the Flood,
And you should, if you please, refuse
Till the conversion of the Jews.
My vegetable love should grow
Vaster than empires, and more slow;
An hundred years should go to praise
Thine eyes, and on thy forehead gaze;
Two hundred to adore each breast,
But thirty thousand to the rest:
An age at least to every part,
And the last age should show your heart.
For, lady, you deserve this state,
Nor would I love at lower rate.

But at my back I always hear
Time's wingèd chariot hurrying near;
And yonder all before us lie
Deserts of vast eternity.
Thy beauty shall no more be found,
Nor, in thy marble vault, shall sound
My echoing song; then worms shall try
That long-preserved virginity,
And your quaint honor turn to dust,
And into ashes all my lust:
The grave's a fine and private place,
But none, I think, do there embrace.
Now therefore, while the youthful hue
Sits on thy skin like morning dew,
And while thy willing soul transpires
At every pore with instant fires,
Now let us sport us while we may,
And now, like amorous birds of prey,
Rather at once our time devour
Than languish in his slow-chapped power.
Let us roll all our strength and all
Our sweetness up into one ball,
And tear our pleasures with rough strife
Thorough the iron gates of life:
Thus, though we cannot make our sun
Stand still, yet we will make him run.

# Gerda Mayer (b. 1927)

## Narcissus (1980)

What he liked in her voice
was his name
called over & over
and the mirrorlike look
in the weeping eyes of his lover;
in the end, left her
on a chill mountain shelf,
in a damp cave
with her wits and her words astray,
to devote himself
to himself.

Then the gods with indolent yawns
took a high hand with him for
such eNOR
mous self-love
was considered by others a bore.

Changed to a flower
he stood by the river
a sad case
of rooted vanity;
he never forgave
the reflecting water
for rippling his face.

# James Merrill (1926–1995)

## The Victor Dog (1972)

*For Elizabeth Bishop*

Bix to Buxtehude to Boulez,
The little white dog on the Victor label
Listens long and hard as he is able.
It's all in a day's work, whatever plays.

From judgment, it would seem, he has refrained.
He even listens earnestly to Bloch,
Then builds a church upon our acid rock.
He's man's—no—he's the Leiermann's best friend,

Or would be if hearing and listening were the same.
*Does* he hear? I fancy he rather smells
Those lemon-gold arpeggios in Ravel's
"Les jets d'eau du palais de ceux qui s'aiment."

He ponders the Schumann Concerto's tall willow hit
By lightning, and stays put. When he surmises
Through one of Bach's external boxwood mazes
The oboe pungent as a bitch in heat,

Or when the calypso decants its raw bay rum
Or the moon in *Wozzeck* reddens ripe for murder,
He doesn't sneeze or howl; just listens harder.
Adamant needles bear down on him from

Whirling of outer space, too black, too near—
But he was taught as a puppy not to flinch,
Much less to imitate his bête noire Blanche
Who barked, fat foolish creature, at King Lear.

Still others fought in the road's filth over Jezebel,
Slavered on hearths of horned and pelted barons.
His forebears lacked, to say the least, forbearance.
Can nature change in him? Nothing's impossible.

The last chord fades. The night is cold and fine.
His master's voice rasps through the grooves' bare groves.
Obediently, in silence like the grave's
He sleeps there on the still-warm gramophone

Only to dream he is at the première of a Handel
Opera long thought lost—*Il Cane Minore.*
Its allegorical subject is his story!
A little dog revolving round a spindle

Gives rise to harmonies beyond belief,
A cast of stars . . . Is there in Victor's heart
No honey for the vanquished? Art is art.
The life it asks of us is a dog's life.

# W. S. Merwin (b. 1927)

## For the Anniversary of My Death (1967)

Every year without knowing it I have passed the day
When the last fires will wave to me
And the silence will set out
Tireless traveller
Like the beam of a lightless star

Then I will no longer
Find myself in life as in a strange garment
Surprised at the earth
And the love of one woman
And the shamelessness of men
As today writing after three days of rain
Hearing the wren sing and the falling cease
And bowing not knowing to what

# John Milton (1608–1674)

## [Of Man's first disobedience]
### —*from "Paradise Lost"* (1667)

Of Man's first disobedience, and the fruit
Of that forbidden Tree, whose mortal taste
Brought death into the world, and all our woe,
With loss of Eden, till one greater Man
Restore us, and regain the blissful seat,
Sing, Heavenly Muse, that on the secret top
Of Oreb, or of Sinai, didst inspire
That shepherd, who first taught the chosen seed
In the beginning how the Heavens and Earth
Rose out of Chaos: or, if Sion hill
Delight thee more, and Siloa's brook that flowed
Fast by the oracle of God, I thence
Invoke thy aid to my adventurous song,
That with no middle flight intends to soar
Above the Aonian mount, while it pursues
Things unattempted yet in prose or rhyme.
And chiefly thou, O Spirit, that dost prefer
Before all temples the upright heart and pure,
Instruct me, for thou know'st; thou from the first
Wast present, and, with mighty wings outspread,
Dove-like sat'st brooding on the vast Abyss,
And mad'st it pregnant: what in me is dark
Illumine, what is low raise and support;
That to the highth of this great argument
I may assert Eternal Providence,
And justify the ways of God to men.

## When I consider how my light is spent (1655?)

When I consider how my light is spent,
  Ere half my days, in this dark world and wide,
  And that one talent which is death to hide
  Lodged with me useless, though my soul more bent
To serve therewith my Maker, and present
  My true account, lest he returning chide;
  "Doth God exact day-labor, light denied?"
  I fondly ask; but Patience to prevent
That murmur, soon replies, "God doth not need
  Either man's work or his own gifts; who best
  Bear his mild yoke, they serve him best. His state
Is kingly. Thousands at his bidding speed
  And post o'er land and ocean without rest:
  They also serve who only stand and wait."

# Wilfred Owen (1893–1918)

*For a brief biography of Wilfred Owen, see chapter 19.*

## Anthem for Doomed Youth (1917)

What passing-bells for these who die as cattle?
  Only the monstrous anger of the guns.
  Only the stuttering rifles' rapid rattle
Can patter out their hasty orisons.
No mockeries now for them; no prayers nor bells,
  Nor any voice of mourning save the choirs,—
The shrill, demented choirs of wailing shells;
  And bugles calling for them from sad shires.
What candles may be held to speed them all?
  Not in the hands of boys, but in their eyes
Shall shine the holy glimmers of good-byes.
  The pallor of girls' brows shall be their pall;
Their flowers the tenderness of patient minds,
And each slow dusk a drawing-down of blinds.

# Grace Paley (1922–2007)

## Here (2001)

Here I am in the garden laughing
an old woman with heavy breasts
and a nicely mapped face

how did this happen
well that's who I wanted to be

at last    a woman
in the old style    sitting
stout thighs apart under
a big skirt    grandchild sliding
on    off my lap    a pleasant
summer perspiration

that's my old man across the yard
he's talking to the meter reader
he's telling him the world's sad story
how electricity is oil or uranium
and so forth    I tell my grandson
run over to your grandpa    ask him
to sit beside me for a minute    I
am suddenly exhausted by my desire
to kiss his sweet explaining lips

# Linda Pastan (b. 1932)

*For a brief biography of Linda Pastan, see chapter 21.*

## Ethics (1980)

In ethics class so many years ago
our teacher asked this question every fall:
if there were a fire in a museum
which would you save, a Rembrandt painting
or an old woman who hadn't many
years left anyhow? Restless on hard chairs
caring little for pictures or old age
we'd opt one year for life, the next for art
and always half-heartedly. Sometimes
the woman borrowed my grandmother's face
leaving her usual kitchen to wander
some drafty, half-imagined museum.
One year, feeling clever, I replied
why not let the woman decide herself?
Linda, the teacher would report, eschews
the burdens of responsibility.
This fall in a real museum I stand
before a real Rembrandt, old woman,
or nearly so, myself. The colors
within this frame are darker than autumn,
darker even than winter—the browns of earth,
though earth's most radiant elements burn
through the canvas. I know now that woman
and painting and season are almost one
and all beyond saving by children.

# Molly Peacock (b. 1947)

## Desire (1984)

It doesn't speak and it isn't schooled,
like a small foetal animal with wettened fur.
It is the blind instinct for life unruled,
visceral frankincense and animal myrrh.
It is what babies bring to kings,
an eyes-shut, ears-shut medicine of the heart
that smells and touches endings and beginnings
without the details of time's experienced *part-*
*fit-into-part-fit-into-part.* Like a paw,
it is blunt; like a pet who knows you
and nudges your knee with its snout—but more raw
and blinder and younger and more divine, too,
than the tamed wild—it's the drive for what is real,
deeper than the brain's detail: the drive to feel.

# Sylvia Plath (1932–1963)

*For a brief biography of Sylvia Plath, see chapter 19.*

## Mirror (1963)

I am silver and exact. I have no preconceptions.
Whatever I see I swallow immediately
Just as it is, unmisted by love or dislike.
I am not cruel, only truthful—
The eye of a little god, four-cornered.
Most of the time I meditate on the opposite wall.
It is pink, with speckles. I have looked at it so long
I think it is a part of my heart. But it flickers.
Faces and darkness separate us over and over.

Now I am a lake. A woman bends over me,
Searching my reaches for what she really is.
Then she turns to those liars, the candles or the moon.
I see her back, and reflect it faithfully.
She rewards me with tears and an agitation of hands.
I am important to her. She comes and goes.
Each morning it is her face that replaces the darkness.
In me she has drowned a young girl, and in me an old
woman
Rises toward her day after day, like a terrible fish.

# Edgar Allan Poe (1809–1849)

## Annabel Lee (1849)

It was many and many a year ago,
In a kingdom by the sea,
That a maiden there lived whom you may know
By the name of Annabel Lee;
And this maiden she lived with no other thought
Than to love and be loved by me.

*She* was a child and *I* was a child,
In this kingdom by the sea,
But we loved with a love that was more than love—
I and my Annabel Lee—
With a love that the wingéd seraphs of Heaven
Coveted her and me.

And this was the reason that, long ago,
In this kingdom by the sea,
A wind blew out of a cloud by night
Chilling my Annabel Lee;
So that her highborn kinsmen came
And bore her away from me,

To shut her up in a sepulchre
  In this kingdom by the sea.

The angels, not half so happy in Heaven,
  Went envying her and me:
Yes! that was the reason (as all men know,
  In this kingdom by the sea)
That the wind came out of the cloud, chilling
  And killing my Annabel Lee.

But our love it was stronger by far than the love
  Of those who were older than we—
  Of many far wiser than we—
And neither the angels in Heaven above
  Nor the demons down under the sea,
Can ever dissever my soul from the soul
  Of the beautiful Annabel Lee:

For the moon never beams without bringing me dreams
  Of the beautiful Annabel Lee;
And the stars never rise but I see the bright eyes
  Of the beautiful Annabel Lee;
And so, all the night-tide, I lie down by the side
Of my darling, my darling, my life and my bride,
  In her sepulchre there by the sea—
  In her tomb by the side of the sea.

# Ezra Pound (1885–1972)

*For a brief biography of Ezra Pound, see chapter 20.*

## The River-Merchant's Wife: A Letter (1915)

While my hair was still cut straight across my forehead
I played about the front gate, pulling flowers.
You came by on bamboo stilts, playing horse,
You walked about my seat, playing with blue plums.
And we went on living in the village of Chokan:
Two small people, without dislike or suspicion.

At fourteen I married My Lord you.
I never laughed, being bashful.
Lowering my head, I looked at the wall.
Called to, a thousand times, I never looked back.

At fifteen I stopped scowling,
I desired my dust to be mingled with yours
Forever and forever and forever.
Why should I climb the lookout?

At sixteen you departed,
You went into far Ku-tō-en, by the river of swirling eddies,
And you have been gone five months.
The monkeys make sorrowful noise overhead.

You dragged your feet when you went out.
By the gate now, the moss is grown, the different mosses,
Too deep to clear them away!
The leaves fall early this autumn, in wind.
The paired butterflies are already yellow with August
Over the grass in the West garden;
They hurt me. I grow older.
If you are coming down through the narrows of the river
  Kiang,
Please let me know beforehand,
And I will come out to meet you
As far as Chō-fū-Sa.

# Sir Walter Raleigh (1552–1618)

## The Nymph's Reply to the Shepherd (1600)

If all the world and love were young,
And truth in every shepherd's tongue,
These pretty pleasures might me move
To live with thee and be thy love.

Time drives the flocks from field to fold
When rivers rage and rocks grow cold,
And Philomel becometh dumb;
The rest complains of cares to come.

The flowers do fade, and wanton fields
To wayward winter reckoning yields;
A honey tongue, a heart of gall,
Is fancy's spring, but sorrow's fall.

The gowns, thy shoes, thy beds of roses,
Thy cap, thy kirtle, and thy posies
Soon break, soon wither, soon forgotten—
In folly ripe, in reason rotten.

Thy belt of straw and ivy buds,
Thy coral clasps and amber studs,
All these in me no means can move
To come to thee and be thy love.

But could youth last and love still breed,
Had joys no date nor age no need,
Then these delights my mind might move
To live with thee and be thy love.

## Dudley Randall (1914–2000)

### The Ballad of Birmingham (1969)

*(On the bombing of a church in Birmingham, Alabama, 1963)*

"Mother dear, may I go downtown
Instead of out to play,
And march the streets of Birmingham
In a Freedom March today?"

"No, baby, no, you may not go,
For the dogs are fierce and wild,
And clubs and hoses, guns and jails
Aren't good for a little child."

"But, mother, I won't be alone.
Other children will go with me,
And march the streets of Birmingham
To make our country free."

"No, baby, no, you may not go,
For I fear those guns will fire.
But you may go to church instead
And sing in the children's choir."

She has combed and brushed her night-dark hair,
And bathed rose petal sweet,
And drawn white gloves on her small brown hands,
And white shoes on her feet.

The mother smiled to know that her child
Was in the sacred place,
But that smile was the last smile
To come upon her face.

For when she heard the explosion,
Her eyes grew wet and wild.
She raced through the streets of Birmingham
Calling for her child.

She clawed through bits of glass and brick,
Then lifted out a shoe.
"O, here's the shoe my baby wore,
But, baby, where are you?"

## Ishmael Reed (b. 1938)

### beware: do not read this poem (1972)

tonite, *thriller* was
abt an ol woman, so vain she
surrounded herself w/
   many mirrors

It got so bad that finally she
locked herself indoors & her
whole life became the
   mirrors

one day the villagers broke
into her house, but she was too
swift for them. she disappeared
   into a mirror
each tenant who bought the house
after that, lost a loved one to
   the ol woman in the mirror:
   first a little girl
   then a young woman
   then the young woman/s husband

the hunger of this poem is legendary
it has taken in many victims
back off from this poem
it has drawn in yr feet
back off from this poem
it has drawn in yr legs
back off from this poem
it is a greedy mirror
you are into this poem. from
   the waist down
nobody can hear you can they?
this poem has had you up to here
      belch
this poem aint got no manners
you cant call out frm this poem
relax now & go w/ this poem
move & roll on to this poem

      do not resist this poem
      this poem has yr eyes
      this poem has his head
      this poem has his arms
      this poem has his fingers
      this poem has his fingertips

this poem is the reader & the
reader this poem

statistic: the US bureau of missing persons reports
that in 1968 over 100,000 people disappeared
leaving no solid clues
nor trace only
a space in the lives of their friends

# Henry Reed (1914–1986)

## Naming of Parts (1946)

Today we have naming of parts. Yesterday,
We had daily cleaning. And tomorrow morning,
We shall have what to do after firing. But today,
Today we have naming of parts. Japonica
Glistens like coral in all of the neighboring gardens,
And today we have naming of parts.

This is the lower sling swivel. And this
Is the upper sling swivel, whose use you will see,
When you are given your slings. And this is the piling swivel,
Which in your case you have not got. The branches
Hold in the gardens their silent, eloquent gestures,
Which in our case we have not got.

This is the safety-catch, which is always released
With an easy flick of the thumb. And please do not let me
See anyone using his finger. You can do it quite easy
If you have any strength in your thumb. The blossoms
Are fragile and motionless, never letting anyone see
Any of them using their finger.

And this you can see is the bolt. The purpose of this
Is to open the breech, as you see. We can slide it
Rapidly backwards and forwards: we call this
Easing the spring. And rapidly backwards and forwards
The early bees are assaulting and fumbling the flowers:
They call it easing the Spring.

They call it easing the Spring: it is perfectly easy
If you have any strength in your thumb: like the bolt,
And the breech, and the cocking-piece, and the point of balance,
Which in our case we have not got; and the almond-blossom
Silent in all of the gardens and the bees going backwards and forwards,
For today we have the naming of parts.

# Adrienne Rich (b. 1929)

## Aunt Jennifer's Tigers (1951)

Aunt Jennifer's tigers prance across a screen,
Bright topaz denizens of a world of green.
They do not fear the men beneath the tree;
They pace in sleek chivalric certainty.

Aunt Jennifer's fingers fluttering through her wool
Find even the ivory needle hard to pull.
The massive weight of Uncle's wedding band
Sits heavily upon Aunt Jennifer's hand.

When Aunt is dead, her terrified hands will lie
Still ringed with ordeals she was mastered by.
The tigers in the panel that she made
Will go on prancing, proud and unafraid.

## Diving into the Wreck (1973)

First having read the book of myths,
and loaded the camera,
and checked the edge of the knife-blade,
I put on
the body-armor of black rubber
the absurd flippers
the grave and awkward mask.
I am having to do this
not like Cousteau with his
assiduous team
aboard the sun-flooded schooner
but here alone.

There is a ladder.
The ladder is always there
hanging innocently
close to the side of the schooner.
We know what it is for,
we who have used it.
Otherwise
it is a piece of maritime floss
some sundry equipment.

I go down.
Rung after rung and still
the oxygen immerses me
the blue light
the clear atoms
of our human air.

I go down.
My flippers cripple me,
I crawl like an insect down the ladder
and there is no one
to tell me when the ocean
will begin.

First the air is blue and then
it is bluer and then green and then
black I am blacking out and yet
my mask is powerful
it pumps my blood with power
the sea is another story
the sea is not a question of power
I have to learn alone
to turn my body without force
in the deep element.

And now: it is easy to forget
what I came for
among so many who have always
lived here
swaying their crenellated fans
between the reefs
and besides
you breathe differently down here.

I came to explore the wreck.
The words are purposes.
The words are maps.
I came to see the damage that was done
and the treasures that prevail.
I stroke the beam of my lamp
slowly along the flank
of something more permanent
than fish or weed

the thing I came for:
the wreck and not the story of the wreck
the thing itself and not the myth
the drowned face always staring
toward the sun
the evidence of damage
worn by salt and away into this threadbare beauty
the ribs of the disaster
curving their assertion
among the tentative haunters.

This is the place.
And I am here, the mermaid whose dark hair
streams black, the merman in his armored body.
We circle silently
about the wreck
we dive into the hold.
I am she: I am he

whose drowned face sleeps with open eyes
whose breasts still bear the stress
whose silver, copper, vermeil cargo lies
obscurely inside barrels
half-wedged and left to rot
we are the half-destroyed instruments
that once held to a course
the water-eaten log
the fouled compass

We are, I am, you are
by cowardice or courage
the one who find our way
back to this scene
carrying a knife, a camera
a book of myths
in which
our names do not appear.

## Wendy Rose (b. 1948)

### Leaving Port Authority for the St. Regis Rezz (1989)

I saw a mesa
between two buildings,
a row of tall
thin houses on top
bare like the desert I know,
the roofs occurring
in clumps like greasewood. O Wendy, he said,
looking at his fingernails,
that's Weehawken.

Well
one way or another
we'll get some
where soon
for I have seen crow
dancing on the snow,
a hawk on Henry Street,
smoke plumes on the lips
of streetkids,
mesas
along the Hudson.
I am getting ready.

# Christina Rossetti (1830–1894)

## Echo (1862)

Come to me in the silence of the night;
Come in the speaking silence of a dream;
Come with soft rounded cheeks and eyes as bright
As sunlight on a stream;
Come back in tears,
O memory, hope, love of finished years.

O dream how sweet, too sweet, too bitter sweet,
Whose wakening should have been in Paradise,
Where souls brimful of love abide and meet;
Where thirsting longing eyes
Watch the slow door
That opening, letting in, lets out no more.

Yet come to me in dreams, that I may live
My very life again though cold in death:
Come back to me in dreams, that I may give
Pulse for pulse, breath for breath:
Speak low, lean low,
As long ago, my love, how long ago.

# Carl Sandburg (1878–1967)

## Fog (1916)

The fog comes
on little cat feet.

It sits looking
over harbor and city
on silent haunches
and then moves on.

# Anne Sexton (1928–1974)

## Letter Written on a Ferry while Crossing Long Island Sound (1961)

I am surprised to see
that the ocean is still going on.
Now I am going back
and I have ripped my hand
from your hand as I said I would
and I have made it this far
as I said I would
and I am on the top deck now
holding my wallet, my cigarettes
and my car keys
at 2 o'clock on a Tuesday
in August of 1960.

Dearest,
although everything has happened,
nothing has happened.
The sea is very old.
The sea is the face of Mary,
without miracles or rage
or unusual hope,
grown rough and wrinkled
with incurable age.

Still,
I have eyes.
These are my eyes:
the orange letters that spell
ORIENT on the life preserver
that hangs by my knees;
the cement lifeboat that wears
its dirty canvas coat;
the faded sign that sits on its shelf
saying KEEP OFF.
Oh, all right, I say,
I'll save myself.

Over my right shoulder
I see four nuns
who sit like a bridge club,
their faces poked out
from under their habits,
as good as good babies who
have sunk into their carriages.
Without discrimination
the wind pulls the skirts
of their arms.
Almost undressed,
I see what remains:
that holy wrist,
that ankle,
that chain.

Oh God,
although I am very sad,
could you please
let these four nuns
loosen from their leather boots
and their wooden chairs
to rise out

over this greasy deck,
out over this iron rail,
nodding their pink heads to one side,
flying four abreast
in the old-fashioned side stroke;
each mouth open and round,
breathing together
as fish do,
singing without sound.

Dearest,
see how my dark girls sally forth,
over the passing lighthouse of Plum Gut,
its shell as rusty
as a camp dish,
as fragile as a pagoda
on a stone;
out over the little lighthouse
that warns me of drowning winds
that rub over its blind bottom
and its blue cover;
winds that will take the toes
and the ears of the rider
or the lover.

There go my dark girls,
their dresses puff
in the leeward air.
Oh, they are lighter than flying dogs
or the breath of dolphins;
each mouth opens gratefully,
wider than a milk cup.
My dark girls sing for this.
They are going up.
See them rise
on black wings, drinking
the sky, without smiles
or hands
or shoes.
They call back to us
from the gauzy edge of paradise,
*good news, good news.*

# William Shakespeare (1564–1616)

*For a brief biography of William Shakespeare, see chapter 18.*

## Let me not to the marriage of true minds (1609)

Let me not to the marriage of true minds
Admit impediments; love is not love
Which alters when it alteration finds,
Or bends with the remover to remove:
O, no, it is an ever-fixèd mark,
That looks on tempests and is never shaken;
It is the star to every wand'ring bark,
Whose worth's unknown, although his highth be taken.
Love's not Time's fool, though rosy lips and cheeks
Within his bending sickle's compass come;
Love alters not with his brief hours and weeks,
But bears it out even to the edge of doom.
  If this be error and upon me proved,
  I never writ, nor no man ever loved.

## Not marble, nor the gilded monuments (1609)

Not marble, nor the gilded monuments
Of princes, shall outlive this powerful rhyme;
But you shall shine more bright in these contents
Than unswept stone, besmeared with sluttish time.
When wasteful war shall statues overturn,
And broils root out the work of masonry,
Nor Mars his sword nor war's quick fire shall burn
The living record of your memory.
'Gainst death and all-oblivious enmity
Shall you pace forth; your praise shall still find room
Even in the eyes of all posterity
That wear this world out to the ending doom.
  So, till the judgment that yourself arise,
  You live in this, and dwell in lovers' eyes.

## That time of the year thou mayest in me behold (1609)

That time of year thou mayest in me behold
When yellow leaves, or none, or few, do hang
Upon those boughs which shake against the cold,
Bare ruined choirs, where late the sweet birds sang.
In me thou seest the twilight of such day
As after sunset fadeth in the west;
Which by and by black night doth take away,
Death's second self that seals up all in rest.
In me thou seest the glowing of such fire
That on the ashes of his youth doth lie,
As the deathbed whereon it must expire,
Consumed with that which it was nourish'd by.
  This thou perceiv'st, which makes thy love more strong,
  To love that well, which thou must leave ere long.

# Percy Bysshe Shelley (1792–1822)

## Ozymandias (1818)

I met a traveller from an antique land
Who said: Two vast and trunkless legs of stone
Stand in the desert. . . Near them, on the sand,
Half sunk, a shattered visage lies, whose frown,
And wrinkled lip, and sneer of cold command,
Tell that its sculptor well those passions read
Which yet survive, stamped on these lifeless things,
The hand that mocked them, and the heart that fed:
And on the pedestal these words appear:
"My name is Ozymandias, king of kings:
Look on my works, ye Mighty, and despair!"
Nothing beside remains. Round the decay
Of that colossal wreck, boundless and bare
The lone and level sands stretch far away.

# Jane Shore (b. 1947)

## My Mother's Chair (2004)

Coming home late, I'd let myself in
with my key, tiptoe up the stairs,
and there she was, in the family room,
one lamp burning, reading her newspaper
in her velvet-and-chrome swivel chair

as though it were perfectly natural
to be wide awake at 2 A.M.,
feet propped on the matching
ottoman, her orthopedic shoes
underneath, two empty turtle shells.

Like a mummy equipped for the afterlife,
she'd have her ashtray and Kents handy,
her magnifying mirror,
and tweezers and eyeglass case,
her crossword puzzle dictionary.

Glancing up and down, she never
appeared to be frisking me, even when,
just seconds before, coming home
from a date, at the front door,
I'd stuck my tongue into a boy's mouth.

I'd sit on the sofa and bum her cigarettes,
and as the room filled up with smoke,
melding our opposite temperaments,
we'd talk into the night, like diplomats
agreeing to a kind of peace.

I'd feign indifference—so did she—
about what I was doing out so late.
When I became a mother myself,
my mother was still the sentry at the gate,
waiting up, guarding the bedrooms.

After her funeral, her chair sat empty.
My father, sister, husband, and I
couldn't bring ourselves to occupy it.
Only my daughter climbed up its base
and spun herself round and round.

In the two years my father lived alone
in the apartment over their store,
I wonder, did he ever once
sit down on that throne, hub
around which our family had revolved.

After my father died, the night
before I left the place for good,
the building sold, the papers signed,
before the moving vans drove away,
dividing the cartons and the furniture

between my sister's house and mine,
a thousand miles apart,
I sat on the sofa—my usual spot—
and stared at the blank TV, the empty chair;
then I rose, and walked across the room,

and sank into her ragged cushions,
put my feet up on her ottoman,
rested my elbows on the scuffed armrests,
stroked the brown velvet like fur.
The headrest still smelled like her!

Swiveling the chair to face the sofa,
I looked at things from her point of view:
*What do you need it for?*
So I left it behind, along with the blinds
the meat grinder, the pressure cooker.

# Gary Soto (b. 1952)

## Saturday at the Canal (1991)

I was hoping to be happy by seventeen.
School was a sharp check mark in the roll book,
An obnoxious tuba playing at noon because our team
Was going to win at night. The teachers were
Too close to dying to understand. The hallways

Stank of poor grades and unwashed hair. Thus,
A friend and I sat watching the water on Saturday,
Neither of us talking much, just warming ourselves
By hurling large rocks at the dusty ground
And feeling awful because San Francisco was a postcard
On a bedroom wall. We wanted to go there,
Hitchhike under the last migrating birds
And be with people who knew more than three chords
On a guitar. We didn't drink or smoke,
But our hair was shoulder length, wild when
The wind picked up and the shadows of
This loneliness gripped loose dirt. By bus or car,
By the sway of train over a long bridge,
We wanted to get out. The years froze
As we sat on the bank. Our eyes followed the water,
White-tipped but dark underneath, racing out of town.

# Wallace Stevens (1879–1955)

*For a brief biography of Wallace Stevens, see chapter 18.*

## Disillusionment of Ten O'Clock (1923)

The houses are haunted
By white night-gowns.
None are green,
Or purple with green rings,
Or green with yellow rings,
Or yellow with blue rings.
None of them are strange,
With socks of lace
And beaded ceintures.
People are not going
To dream of baboons and periwinkles.
Only, here and there, an old sailor,
Drunk and asleep in his boots,
Catches tigers
In red weather.

## Thirteen Ways of Looking at a Blackbird (1917)

I

Among twenty snowy mountains,
The only moving thing
Was the eye of the blackbird.

II

I was of three minds,
Like a tree
In which there are three blackbirds.

III

The blackbirds whirled in the autumn winds.
It was a small part of the pantomime.

IV

A man and a woman
Are one.
A man and a woman and a blackbird
Are one.

V

I do not know which to prefer—
The beauty of inflections
Or the beauty of innuendoes,
The blackbird whistling
Or just after.

VI

Icicles filled the long window
With barbaric glass.
The shadow of the blackbird
Crossed it, to and fro.
The mood
Traced in the shadow
An indecipherable course.

VII

O thin men of Haddam,
Why do you imagine golden birds?
Do you not see how the blackbird
Walks around the feet
Of the women about you?

VIII

I know noble accents
And lucid, inescapable rhythms;
But I know, too,
That the blackbird is involved
In what I know.

IX

When the blackbird flew out of sight,
It marked the edge
Of one of many circles.

X

At the sight of blackbirds
Flying in a green light,
Even the bawds of euphony
Would cry out sharply.

XI

He rode over Connecticut
In a glass coach.
Once, a fear pierced him,
In that he mistook
The shadow of his equipage
For blackbirds.

XII

The river is moving.
The blackbird must be flying.

XIII

It was evening all afternoon.
It was snowing
And it was going to snow.
The blackbird sat
In the cedar-limbs.

# Sir Philip Sydney (1554–1586)

## To the Sad Moon (1591)

With how sad steps, O Moon, thou climb'st the skies!
How silently, and with how wan a face!
What! may it be that even in heavenly place
That busy archer his sharp arrows tries?
Sure, if that long-with-love-acquainted eyes
Can judge of love, thou feel'st a lover's case;
I read it in thy looks; thy languished grace
To me, that feel the like, thy state descries.
Then, even of fellowship, O Moon, tell me,
Is constant love deemed there but want of wit?
Are beauties there as proud as here they be?
Do they above love to be loved, and yet
Those lovers scorn whom that love doth possess?
Do they call virtue there ungratefulness?

# Alfred, Lord Tennyson (1809–1892)

## Ulysses (1842)

It little profits that an idle king,
By this still hearth, among these barren crags,
Matched with an aged wife, I mete and dole
Unequal laws unto a savage race,
That hoard, and sleep, and feed, and know not me.
I cannot rest from travel; I will drink
Life to the lees. All times I have enjoyed
Greatly, have suffered greatly, both with those
That loved me, and alone; on shore, and when
Through scudding drifts the rainy Hyades
Vexed the dim sea. I am become a name;
For always roaming with a hungry heart
Much have I seen and known—cities of men
And manners, climates, councils, governments,
Myself not least, but honored of them all,—
And drunk delight of battle with my peers,
Far on the ringing plains of windy Troy.
I am a part of all that I have met;
Yet all experience is an arch wherethrough
Gleams that untraveled world whose margin fades
Forever and forever when I move.
How dull it is to pause, to make an end,
To rust unburnished, not to shine in use!
As though to breathe were life! Life piled on life
Were all too little, and of one to me
Little remains; but every hour is saved
From that eternal silence, something more,
A bringer of new things; and vile it were
For some three suns to store and hoard myself,
And this gray spirit yearning in desire
To follow knowledge like a sinking star,
Beyond the utmost bound of human thought.
  This is my son, mine own Telemachus,
To whom I leave the scepter and the isle,
Well-loved of me, discerning to fulfill
This labor, by slow prudence to make mild
A rugged people, and through soft degrees
Subdue them to the useful and the good.
Most blameless is he, centered in the sphere
Of common duties, decent not to fail
In offices of tenderness, and pay
Meet adoration to my household gods,
When I am gone. He works his work, I mine.
  There lies the port; the vessel puffs her sail;
There gloom the dark, broad seas. My mariners,
Souls that have toiled, and wrought, and thought with me,
That ever with a frolic welcome took
The thunder and the sunshine, and opposed
Free hearts, free foreheads—you and I are old;
Old age hath yet his honor and his toil.
Death closes all; but something ere the end,
Some work of noble note, may yet be done,
Not unbecoming men that strove with gods.
The lights begin to twinkle from the rocks;
The long day wanes; the slow moon climbs; the deep
Moans round with many voices. Come, my friends,
'Tis not too late to seek a newer world.
Push off, and sitting well in order smite

The sounding furrows; for my purpose holds
To sail beyond the sunset, and the baths
Of all the western stars, until I die.
It may be that the gulfs will wash us down;
It may be we shall touch the Happy Isles,
And see the great Achilles, whom we knew.
Though much is taken, much abides; and though
We are not now that strength which in old days
Moved earth and heaven, that which we are, we are,
One equal temper of heroic hearts,
Made weak by time and fate, but strong in will
To strive, to seek, to find, and not to yield.

# Anne Waldman (b. 1945)

## Bluehawk (1991)

Monk's gone
            blown
those keys
    his
        alone
unlock

            a heart-mind

sway
    swipe those tears away

            Monk's gone
            Monk's gone

*(pause)*
            a minor chord
    asymmetry
            (accent on the "try")
    push limits
            all his own
    &
    music of the spheres
            (song the gong)
    gone
    Monk's gone
            old Buddha fingers gone
                        bluehawk

                                    in the sky
            soars high

# Phyllis Wheatley (1753–1784)

## On Being Brought from Africa to America (1773)

'Twas mercy brought me from my *Pagan* land,
Taught my benighted soul to understand
That there's a God, that there's a *Saviour* too:
Once I redemption neither sought nor knew.
Some view our sable race with scornful eye,
"Their colour is a diabolic die."
Remember, *Christians, Negros,* black as *Cain,*
May be refin'd, and join th' angelic train.

# Richard Wilbur (b. 1921)

## The Writer (1976)

In her room at the prow of the house
Where light breaks, and the windows are tossed with linden,
My daughter is writing a story.

I pause in the stairwell, hearing
From her shut door a commotion of typewriter-keys
Like a chain hauled over a gunwale.

Young as she is, the stuff
Of her life is a great cargo, and some of it heavy:
I wish her a lucky passage.

But now it is she who pauses,
As if to reject my thought and its easy figure.
A stillness greatens, in which

The whole house seems to be thinking,
And then she is at it again with a bunched clamor
Of strokes, and again is silent.

I remember the dazed starling
Which was trapped in that very room, two years ago;
How we stole in, lifted a sash

And retreated, not to affright it;
And how for a helpless hour, through the crack of the door,
We watched the sleek, wild, dark

And iridescent creature
Batter against the brilliance, drop like a glove
To the hard floor, or the desk-top,

And wait then, humped and bloody,
For the wits to try it again; and how our spirits
Rose when, suddenly sure,

It lifted off from a chair-back,
Beating a smooth course for the right window
And clearing the sill of the world.

It is always a matter, my darling,
Of life or death, as I had forgotten. I wish
What I wished you before, but harder.

# William Carlos Williams (1883–1963)

*For a brief biography of William Carlos Williams, see chapter 20.*

## Spring and All (1923)

By the road to the contagious hospital
under the surge of the blue
mottled clouds driven from the
northeast—a cold wind. Beyond, the
waste of broad, muddy fields
brown with dried weeds, standing and fallen

patches of standing water
the scattering of tall trees

All along the road the reddish
purplish, forked, upstanding, twiggy
stuff of bushes and small trees
with dead, brown leaves under them
leafless vines—

Lifeless in appearance, sluggish
dazed spring approaches—

They enter the new world naked,
cold, uncertain of all
save that they enter. All about them
the cold, familiar wind—

Now the grass, tomorrow
the stiff curl of wildcarrot leaf
One by one objects are defined—
It quickens: clarity, outline of leaf

But now the stark dignity of
entrance—Still, the profound change
has come upon them: rooted they
grip down and begin to awaken

# William Wordsworth (1770–1850)

*For a brief biography of William Wordsworth, see chapter 15.*

## London, 1802 (1802)

Milton! thou shouldst be living at this hour:
England hath need of thee: she is a fen
Of stagnant waters: altar, sword, and pen,
Fireside, the heroic wealth of hall and bower,
Have forfeited their ancient English dower
Of inward happiness. We are selfish men;
Oh! raise us up, return to us again;
And give us manners, virtue, freedom, power.
Thy soul was like a Star, and dwelt apart;
Thou hadst a voice whose sound was like the sea:
Pure as the naked heavens, majestic, free,
So didst thou travel on life's common way,
In cheerful godliness; and yet thy heart
The lowliest duties on herself did lay.

## The World Is Too Much with Us (1807)

The world is too much with us; late and soon,
Getting and spending, we lay waste our powers;
Little we see in Nature that is ours;
We have given our hearts away, a sordid boon!
This Sea that bares her bosom to the moon,
The winds that will be howling at all hours,
And are up-gathered now like sleeping flowers,
For this, for everything, we are out of tune;
It moves us not.—Great God! I'd rather be
A Pagan suckled in a creed outworn;
So might I, standing on this pleasant lea,
Have glimpses that would make me less forlorn;
Have sight of Proteus rising from the sea;
Or hear old Triton blow his wreathéd horn.

## The Solitary Reaper (1807)

Behold her, single in the field,
Yon solitary Highland Lass!
Reaping and singing by herself;
Stop here, or gently pass!
Alone she cuts and binds the grain,
And sings a melancholy strain;
O listen! for the Vale profound
Is overflowing with the sound.

No Nightingale did ever chaunt
More welcome notes to weary bands
Of travelers in some shady haunt,
Among Arabian sands;
A voice so thrilling ne'er was heard
In springtime from the Cuckoo bird,
Breaking the silence of the seas
Among the farthest Hebrides.

Will no one tell me what she sings?—
Perhaps the plaintive numbers flow
For old, unhappy, far-off things,
And battles long ago;
Or is it some more humble lay,
Familiar matter of today?
Some natural sorrow, loss, or pain,
That has been, and may be again?

Whate'er the theme, the Maiden sang
As if her song could have no ending;
I saw her singing at her work,
And o'er the sickle bending—
I listened, motionless and still;
And, as I mounted up the hill,
The music in my heart I bore,
Long after it was heard no more.

# James Wright (1927–1980)

*For a brief biography of James Wright, see chapter 18.*

## Lying in a Hammock at William Duffy's Farm in Pine Island, Minnesota (1963)

Over my head, I see the bronze butterfly,
Asleep on the black trunk,
Blowing like a leaf in green shadow.
Down the ravine behind the empty house,
The cowbells follow one another
Into the distances of the afternoon.
To my right,
In a field of sunlight between two pines,
The droppings of last year's horses
Blaze up into golden stones.
I lean back, as the evening darkens and comes on.
A chicken hawk floats over, looking for home.
I have wasted my life.

# William Butler Yeats (1865–1939)

*For a brief biography of William Butler Yeats, see chapter 15.*

## The Second Coming (1921)

Turning and turning in the widening gyre
The falcon cannot hear the falconer;
Things fall apart; the center cannot hold;
Mere anarchy is loosed upon the world,
The blood-dimmed tide is loosed, and everywhere
The ceremony of innocence is drowned;
The best lack all conviction, while the worst
Are full of passionate intensity.

Surely some revelation is at hand;
Surely the Second Coming is at hand:
The Second Coming! Hardly are those words out
When a vast image out of *Spiritus Mundi*
Troubles my sight: somewhere in sands of the desert
A shape with lion body and the head of a man,
A gaze blank and pitiless as the sun,
Is moving its slow thighs, while all about it
Reel shadows of the indignant desert birds.
The darkness drops again; but now I know
That twenty centuries of stony sleep
Were vexed to nightmare by a rocking cradle,
And what rough beast, its hour come round at last,
Slouches towards Bethlehem to be born?

## When You Are Old (1893)

When you are old and grey and full of sleep,
And nodding by the fire, take down this book,
And slowly read, and dream of the soft look
Your eyes had once, and of their shadows deep;

How many loved your moments of glad grace,
And loved your beauty with love false or true,
But one man loved the pilgrim soul in you,
And loved the sorrows of your changing face;

And bending down beside the glowing bars,
Murmur, a little sadly, how Love fled
And paced upon the mountains overhead
And hid his face amid a crowd of stars.

# Glossary of Literary Terms

**Abstract** A short **summary** at the beginning of a scholarly article that states the **thesis,** the major points of **evidence,** and the **conclusion** of the article.
**Abstract Diction** Language referring to a general or conceptual thing or quality, such as *progress,* or *justice.*
**Accent** The vocal emphasis on a syllable in a word. Often used interchangeably with **stress,** which sometimes refers to emphasis within a line of poetry, rather than a single word.
**Accentual Meter** A kind of **meter** or verse measure that uses a fixed number of stressed syllables in each line, although based on a number of unstressed syllables may vary. Accentual meters often can be heard in rap music and children's rhymes.
**Accentual-Syllabic Verse** A verse form that uses a fixed number of **stresses** and syllables per line. This is the most common verse form in English poetry, and includes, for example, **iambic pentameter,** where each line has five **stressed** syllables and five unstressed syllables.
**Act** A subdivision of the action of a play, similar to a chapter in a book. Acts generally occur during a change in **scenery,** cast of **characters,** or mood, and the end of an act usually suggests the advancement of time in the play. Acts are often divided into subunits called **scenes.**
**Allegory** A story in which major elements such as **character**s and settings represent universal truths or moral lessons in a one-to-one correspondence.
**Alliteration** The repetition of the initial consonant sounds of a sequence of words.
**Allusion** A reference to another work of art or literature, or to a person, place, or event outside the text.
**Amphibrach** A syllable pattern characterized by three syllables in the order *unstressed, stressed, unstressed.*
**Amphitheater** A stage surrounded on all sides by the audience, who watch the action from above.
***Anagnorisis*** In **tragedy,** a change from ignorance to knowledge, producing love or hate between the persons destined by the poet for good or bad fortune.
**Anagram** A word or phrase created using the letters that spell a different word or phrase. For example, *dirty room* is an anagram for *dormitory.*
**Analyze** To take a text apart and examine its elements: the different written devices the author uses (such as **point of view, plot,** and imagery) and the **voice** the author brings to the piece (**tone,** word choice).
**Anapestic Meter** A **meter** using feet with two unstressed syllables followed by a **stressed** syllable.
**Anecdote** A personal remembrance or brief story.
**Antagonist** A **character** in **conflict** with the **protagonist.** A story's **plot** often hinges on a protagonist's conflict with an antagonist.
**Anticlimax** The opposite of a **climax;** a point in a narrative that is striking for its *lack* of excitement, intensity, or emphasis. An anticlimax generally occurs at a point of high action where a true climax is expected to occur.
**Antihero** A main **character** who acts outside the usual lines of heroic behavior (brave, honest, true).
**Apostrophe** A **figure of speech** in which a writer directly addresses an unseen person, force, or personified idea. The term *apostrophe* derives from the Greek term meaning *turning away* and often marks a digression.
**Approximate Rhyme** *See* **Slant Rhyme.**
**Archetypal Criticism** *See* **Mythological Criticism.**
**Archetype** An **image** or **symbol** with a universal meaning that evokes a common emotional reaction in readers.
**Arena Theater** Also called *Theater in the Round,* an arena stage is surrounded on all sides by the audience, with all the action taking place on a stage in the center.
**Argument** A position or perspective based on a **claim** that can be supported with **evidence.**
**Aside** In drama, a remark made by an actor to the audience, which the other **characters** do not hear. This convention is sometimes discernable in fiction writing, when a self-conscious **narrator** breaks the flow of the narrative to make a remark directly to the reader.
**Assonance** A repetition of vowel sounds or patterns in neighboring words.
**Auditory Imagery** **Images** that appeal to a reader's sense of hearing.
**Augustan Age** A distinct period in early-eighteenth-century neoclassical English literature characterized by formal structure and diction. This Augustan Age is named after the great period of Roman literature during Emperor Augustus's reign, when Ovid, Horace, and Virgil were writing. Famous writers of the English Augustan Age were Alexander Pope, Thomas Gray, and Jonathan Swift.
**Authorial Intrusion** *See* **Editorial Omniscience.**

**Ballad Stanza** A **quatrain** in which the first and third lines possess four stresses, while the second and fourth have three stresses. The **rhyme scheme** is often *abcb.*
**Ballad** A song or poem that tells a lively or tragic story in simple language using rhyming four-line **stanzas** and a set **meter.**
***Bathos*** An error that occurs when a writer attempts elevated language but is accidentally trite or ridiculous; a sort of **anticlimax.**
**Beat Generation** A group of writers in the 1950s and '60s who represented the counterculture to 1950s American prosperity. The word "beat" comes from the slang for being down and worn out, suggesting their weariness with mainstream culture and their adoption of a freespirited attitude. Jack Kerouac's *On the Road* and Allen Ginsberg's poem "Howl" are major works of the Beat Generation.
**Bibliography** A list of the works consulted in the preparation of a paper, containing adequate information for readers to locate the source materials themselves.
***Bildungsroman*** A **coming of age story** that details the growth or maturity of a youth, usually an adolescent. The term is German, meaning "**novel** of formation."
**Biographical Criticism** **Literary criticism** that emphasizes the belief that literature is created by authors whose

unique experiences shape their writing and therefore can inform our reading of their work. Biographical critics research and use an author's biography to interpret the text as well as the author's stated intentions or comments on the process of composition itself. These critics often consult the author's memoirs to uncover connections between the author's life and the author's work. They may also study the author's rough drafts to trace the evolution of a given text or examine the author's library to discern potential influences on the author's work.

**Biography** The factual account of a person's life.

**Blank Verse** Unrhymed **iambic pentameter,** often used in Shakespeare's plays or for epic subject matter, as in Milton's *Paradise Lost.*

**Blues** A form of music that originated in the Deep South. Descended from African-American spirituals and work songs, the blues reflects the hardships of life and love in its lyrics. Most blues songs follow a form made of three phrases equal in length: a first phrase, a second that repeats the first phrase, and a third phrase different from the first two that concludes the verse.

**Box Set** *See* **Proscenium Stage.**

**Brainstorming** A process of generating and collecting ideas on a topic.

**Burlesque** A work of drama or literature that ridicules its subject matter through exaggerated mockery and broad **comedy.**

**Cacophony** Harsh-sounding, grating, or even hard-to-pronounce language.

**Caesura** A pause, usually in the middle of a line, that marks a kind of rhythmic division.

**Canon** In a literary context, the group of works considered by academics and scholars to be essential to and representative of the body of respected literature.

***Carpe diem*** Latin for *seize the day.* A phrase used commonly in poetry that emphasizes the brevity of life and the importance of living in the moment.

**Catharsis** The purging of emotions which the audience experiences as a result of the powerful **climax** of a classical **tragedy**; the sense of relief and renewal experienced through art.

**Central Intelligence** Henry James's term for the **narrator** of a story—distinct from the author—whose impressions and ideas shape the telling of the story and determine the details revealed.

**Character** The depiction of human beings (and nonhumans) within a story.

**Characters** The actors (human and nonhuman) in a story.

**Characteristics** The physical and mental attributes of a **character,** established through **characterization.**

**Characterization** The way a writer crafts and defines a **character**'s personality to give an insight into that character's thoughts and actions.

**Charting** A technique for generating ideas that involves placing related concepts and themes in a chart to view their relationships.

**Chorus** A group of amateurs and trained actors who participated in traditional Greek plays. The chorus represents a group of citizens with worries and questions, expressed in poetry and music and dance movement.

**Claim** An idea or stance on a particular subject; a defendable claim is necessary for a strong **thesis.**

**Classifications of Drama** These four categories are generally assigned to Shakespeare's theater, but are commonly used in reference to the works of other **playwrights. Histories** focus on the reign of kings from the past, from Julius Caesar to Henry V. Because histories naturally contain very astute and sometimes troubling political commentaries, playwrights had to limit their subjects to rulers of the distant past. **Comedies** are plays for entertainment, and as a convention end in the marriage of two main **characters.** A comedic **plot** generally begins with a complication or misunderstanding between two lovers, which is complicated by further scheming and misunderstandings until finally a **resolution** is attained and the two are wed. **Tragedies** are darker plays, with more complex **characters** and more dire consequences, usually dramatizing the fall from a high state of life of a royal or special **character. Romances** (from the French *roman,* which means an "extended narrative") involve lovers whose potential happiness is complicated by misunderstandings, mistaken identities, and any number of other difficulties. Although similar in plot to a **comedy,** a romance play does not guarantee a happy ending.

**Cliché** A **figure of speech** that has been used so commonly that it has become trite. The use of cliché may suggest an ironic tone.

**Climax** The narrative's turning point in a struggle between opposing forces. The point of highest **conflict** in a story.

**Close Reading** The **explication** of a text in order to **analyze** the ways in which distinct formal elements interact to create a unified artistic experience for the reader.

**Closed Couplet** A pair of rhymed lines that capture one complete idea. If the couplet is **end-stopped** and in **iambic pentameter,** it is called a **heroic couplet.**

**Closed Denouement** A **resolution** to a story that leaves no loose ends.

**Closed Form** *See* **Fixed Form.**

**Closet Drama** A piece of literature written as though for the stage, but intended only to be read.

**Collective Unconscious** A set of **characters, plots, symbols,** and **images** that each evoke a universal response.

**Colloquial Speech** Familiar and conversational speech.

**Comedy** A type of drama that deals with light or humorous subject matter and usually includes a happy ending. The opposite of **tragedy.** *See* **Classifications of Drama.**

**Comedy of Manners** A work of **satire** that pokes fun at human behavior in particular social circles. Since a comedy of manners concerns itself with social interactions, it tends to reveal the **characters'** foibles or follies as they try to appear or act in a certain way.

**Comic Relief** A **character** or situation that provides humor in the midst of a work that is predominantly serious. A classic example is the bumbling Falstaff, a character in Shakespeare's *Henry IV* who makes the audience laugh, even as England's fate hangs in the balance.

**Coming of Age Story** A story that follows a **character's** physical, emotional, or spiritual maturation, often from youth into adulthood. *See* ***Bildungsroman.***

**Common Measure** A variation on **ballad** meter that uses **iambic quatrains** with the first and third lines containing four feet (**tetrameter**) and the second and fourth containing three feet (**trimeter**). The rhyme scheme is often *abab* rhyme. Common measure, also called *common meter,* is the **meter** most associated with hymns.

**Comparison** Looking at two or more texts, **characters,** authors, or other items side by side to draw similarities between them.

**Conceit** A complex comparison or **metaphor** that extends throughout a poem

**Conclusion** The final idea and **resolution** of a text. In a good essay, the conclusion not only reiterates the **thesis** but offers a reason for its significance or a reflection that pushes it toward a broader meaning beyond the essay itself. In a story or play, the conclusion refers to the resolution or **dénouement.**

**Concrete Diction** Language referring to a specific, definite thing or quality, such as *lawn mower* or *street light.*

**Concrete Poetry** Also called *visual poetry.* Poetry written in the shape of something it describes.

**Confessional Poetry** Poetry that includes pieces of a poet's autobiography or personal experience. This mode of poetry was prevalent in the mid-twentieth century with poets like Sylvia Plath, Anne Sexton, and Robert Lowell.

**Conflict** The central problem in a story. The source of tension between the **protagonist** and **antagonist.**

**Connotation** The associations a word carries beyond its literal meaning. Connotations are formed by the context of the word's popular usage; for example, *green,* aside from being a color, connotes money. The opposite of **denotation.**

**Consonance** A repetition of consonant sounds or similar patterns in neighboring words.

**Context** The literary, historical, biographical, or poetical situation that influences the writing of a work of literature.

**Contextual Reading** Reading and interpreting a story while mindful of its author, the time and place it was written, the traditions of its form, and the criticism it explicitly or implicitly responds to.

**Contrast** Looking at two or more texts, **characters,** authors, or other items side by side to highlight the differences between them.

**Convention** In literature, a feature or element of a **genre** that is commonly used and therefore widely accepted—and expected—by readers and writers alike. For example, it is a convention of Shakespearean **comedy** to end with a marriage.

**Conventional Symbols** **Symbols** that have accrued a widely accepted **interpretation** through their repeated use in literature and the broader culture. For example, spring and winter are conventional symbols of birth and death, as they appear with that meaning in Shakespeare's works through Frost's poetry. Colors, too, can be used as conventional symbols; in contemporary society, a pink ribbon is a conventional symbol of breast cancer awareness.

**Cosmic Irony** A literary convention where forces beyond the control of **characters**—such as God or fate or the supernatural—foil plans or expectations.

**Couplet** Two lines of poetry forming one unit of meaning. Couplets are often **rhymed,** strung together without a break, and share the same **meter.**

***Cothurni*** Tall boots, worn by actors in the Ancient Greek theater, which served both to elevate an actor and make him more visible to the massive crowds, and also to make the **character**s seem larger than life.

**Craft** As a noun, craft refers to the elements that comprise a story; as a verb, craft refers to the process of making or fashioning a story out of those elements.

**Cretic** Also called *Amphimacer.* A syllable pattern characterized by three syllables in the order *stressed, unstressed, stressed.*

**Crisis** *See* **Climax.**

**Critical Reading** A process of digesting and understanding a text so you can appreciate not just the ideas it presents or the story it tells, but how it presents those ideas, why it presents them, and how those ideas exist in a certain context. Critical reading involves **summary, analysis, synthesis,** and **interpretation.**

**Critique** A **summary** accompanied by one's own personal opinion and perspectives.

**Cultural Studies** This critical perspective was developed mainly in England in the sixties by New Left writers, social philosophers, and sociologists. Cultural studies incorporates the techniques of literary analysis to **analyze** social life and social movements as though they were written texts.

**Dactylic Meter** A **meter** in which the foot contains a stressed syllable followed by two unstressed syllables.

**Deconstruction** A critical approach to analyzing literature based on the idea that texts do not have a single, stable meaning or **interpretation.** Deconstructionists seek to break down literature to reveal the inevitable inconsistency or lack of unity in even the most successful and revered texts, believing that the author's intentions have no bearing on the meaning of the text to the reader.

**Decorum** A certain level of propriety appropriate to a given text. As well as demanding a certain level of **diction,** decorum can also have bearing on the **characters, setting,** and **plot** events of a piece of literature.

**Denotation** The literal meaning of a word. The opposite of **connotation.**

**Denouement** The period after the story's **climax** when **conflicts** are addressed and/or resolved. Includes the **falling action** and **resolution** of a story.

***Deus ex machina*** Latin for *God from the machine;* a literary device, often seen in drama, where a **conflict** is resolved by unforeseen and often far-fetched means.

**Dialect** **Dialogue** written to phonetically or grammatically replicate a particular **sound,** cadence, **rhythm,** or emphasis in a **character's** speech.

**Dialogue** Spoken interaction between two or more **characters.** A **characterization** technique that can signal class, education, intelligence, ethnicity, and attitude in the characters involved.

**Diction** An author's or **character's** distinctive choice of words and style of expression.

**Didactic Literature** Literature, such as a fable or **allegory,** written to instruct or teach a moral.

**Dimeter** A poetic **meter** comprised of two poetic feet.

**Dirge** A funeral song.

**Doggerel** An obviously patterned piece of **rhyme,** often lunging or twisting word order in order to get a rhyme. Doggerel can sometimes seem almost childish and, when extensive, boring.

**Drama** A term that comes from the Greek word for doing or acting and refers to a literary work that is represented through performance.

**Dramatic Irony** A situation in which an author or **narrator** lets the reader know more about a situation than a **character** does.

**Dramatic Monologue** A poem in which a **character** addresses another character or the reader. Dramatic monologues are offshoots of the epic form.

**Dramatic Poetry** Poetry in which the speaker of the poem is not the poet. Dramatic poetry often tells a story.

**Dramatic Point of View** A **third-person point of view** in which the **narrator** presents only bare details and the **dialogue** of other **characters**.

**Dramatic Question** The overarching challenge or issue in a piece of drama—the complication which the events of a play work to resolve.

**Dynamic Character** A **character** whose personality and behavior alter over the course of the action in response to challenges and changing circumstances.

**Dramatis Personae** "People of the play"; a list of the **characters** in a play, usually one of the first elements of a script.

**Echo Verse** Poetry in which words at the ends of lines or **stanzas** are repeated, mimicking an echo.

**Economic Determinist Criticism** *See* **Marxist Criticism.**

**Editorial Omniscience** A **narrator** inserts his or her own commentary about **character**s or events into the narrative.

**Electra Complex** The female version of the **Oedipus Complex,** the Electra Complex suggests that female children are hostile toward their mothers because of subconscious sexual attraction to their fathers.

**Elegy** A poem of lamentation memorializing the dead or contemplating some nuance of life's melancholy. Early Greek elegies employed a fixed form of **dactylic hexameter** and **iambic pentameter couplets.**

**Elision** The omission of a vowel or consonant sound within or between words, such as "ne'er" for "never" and "o'er" for "over." Elision dramatizes language and allows for flexibility within a poem's **meter.**

**Ellipses** Three periods placed in succession (. . .) to illustrate that something has been omitted.

**End Rhyme** **Rhyme** that occurs at the end of two or more lines of poetry. An example of end rhyme can be found in "The Love Song of J. Alfred Prufrock": "Let us go through certain half-deserted streets, / The muttering retreats."

**End-stopped Line** A line that ends with a full stop or period.

**Endnote** Information placed at the end of a text in an explanatory note. In a research paper, endnotes are used to comment on sources or provide additional analysis that is slightly tangential to the focus of your paper. An endnote is indicated by a superscript number ( $^{1}$ ) in the text itself, which corresponds to a numbered explanatory note at the end.

**English Sonnet** *See* **Shakespearean Sonnet.**

**Enjambment** The running over of a phrase from one line into another so that closely related words belong to different lines.

**Envoi** The final **stanza** of a **sestina,** which summarizes the entire poem. Envoi is French for *farewell.*

**Epic** A long **narrative poem,** traditionally recited publicly, whose subject matter reflects the values of the culture from which it came by portraying important legends or heroes. Classical epics include the *Odyssey* and the *Aeneid,* while English epics include *Beowulf* and *Paradise Lost.*

**Epigram** A short, often satirical observation on a single subject.

**Epigraph** A quotation or brief passage from another source, included at the beginning of a piece of literature. Writers use epigraphs to suggest a major theme or idea in their work.

**Epiphany** A sudden realization or new understanding achieved by a **character** or speaker. In many short stories, the character's epiphany is the **climax** of the story.

**Episode** A unified event or incident within a longer narrative.

***Episodia*** The scenes of a Greek tragedy, divided by ***stasimon*** from the **Chorus.**

**Epistolary Novel** A novel written in the form of letters between two or more **characters,** or in the form of diary entries. Epistolary novels were particularly popular in the eighteenth century.

**Ethnic Studies** A critical approach to literature that seeks to give voice to literature that has previously been overlooked in the traditionally Euro-centric worldview—not simply by including ethnically diverse literature in the **canon,** but by attention to historically underrepresented groups, like African Americans and Native Americans.

**Euphony** Musically pleasing poetic language.

**Evidence** Reliable information, such as statistics, expert opinions, and anecdotes, used to support a **claim** in an **argument.**

**Exact Rhyme** A rhyme in which the final vowel and consonant sounds are identical, regardless of spelling. Also called *pure rhyme, perfect rhyme,* and *true rhyme.*

***Exodos*** The concluding scene of a Greek **tragedy.**

**Explication** a **close reading** of any text where the goal is to logically **analyze** details within the text itself to uncover deeper meanings or contradictions.

**Exposition:** The narrative presentation of necessary information about the **character, setting,** or character's history provided to make the reader care what happens to the characters in the story.

**Expressionism** A mode of theater in which the playwright attempts to portray his or her subjective emotions in a symbolic way on stage.

**Extended Metaphor** A figurative analogy that is woven through a poem.

**Eye Rhyme** Words that share similar spellings but—when spoken—have different sounds. For example, *lint* and *pint.* Also called *Sight Rhyme.*

**Fables** A short narrative in which the **characters** (often animals or inanimate things) illustrate a lesson. The characters in fables are *actors* rather than **symbols.**

**Fairy Tale** A story, usually for children, that involves magical creatures or circumstances and usually has a happy ending.

**Falling Action** The events following the **climax** and leading up to the **resolution.** These events reveal how the **protagonist** has been impacted by and dealt with the preceding **conflicts** of the story.

**Falling Meter** A **meter** comprised of feet that begin with a stressed syllable, followed by an unstressed syllable or syllables. **Trochaic** and **dactylic** feet both create falling meter, which is named for the effect of *falling* from the initial stressed syllable to the unstressed.

**Fantasy** A literary **genre** that uses magical **characters** or circumstances.

**Farce** A work of drama or literature that uses broad, often physical **comedy,** exaggerated **characters,** absurd situations, and improbable **plot** twists to evoke laughter without intending social criticism.

**Feminine Rhyme** Rhymes between multisyllable words in which the final syllable is unstressed, such as *bother* and *father.* Also called *falling rhyme.*

**Feminist Criticism** An approach to literary criticism that highlights literature written by women and the exploration of the experience of female **characters;** also a critical examination of the ways in which female characters are viewed with prejudice, are subjugated to male interests, or are simply overlooked in literature.

**Fiction** A genre of literature that describes events and **characters** invented by the author.

**Figurative Language** Language that describes one thing by relating it to something else.

**Figure of Speech** A technique of using language to describe one thing in terms of another, often comparing two unlike objects, such as *the sun* and *the face of the beloved,* to condense and heighten the effect of language, particularly the effect of **imagery** or **symbolism** in a poem.

**First-Person Narrator** The story is narrated by a **character** in the story, identified by use of the pronoun *I* or the plural first-person, *we.*

**Fixed Form** An arrangement of text that requires a poet to obey set written combinations, including line length, **meter, stanza** structure, and **rhyme scheme.** Also called ***closed form.***

**Flashback** The device of moving back in time to a point before the primary action of the story.

**Flat Character** A **character** with a narrow range of speech or action. Flat characters are predictable and do not develop over the course of the **plot.**

**Foil** A **character** who contrasts with the central character, often with the purpose of emphasizing some trait in the central character. For example, a cruel sister emphasizes the other sister's kindness.

**Folklore** A traditional **canon** of stories, sayings, and **characters.**

**Folktale** A short, often fantastic tale passed down over time.

**Foot** The smallest unit of measure in poetic **meter.** A foot usually contains a stressed syllable and one or two unstressed syllables. **Meter** is formed when the same foot repeats more than once. For example, in **iambic pentameter,** *iambic* refers to the type of foot (an unstressed syllable followed by a stressed syllable), while *pentameter* tells us that there are five (pent) iambic feet in each line.

**Footnote** Like an **endnote,** a way to include commentary on sources or other information tangential to the focus of a text. A footnote occurs at the bottom of the page on which the subject is most closely addressed. To create a footnote, a superscript number ($^1$) is placed in the text itself and corresponds to the number of the explanatory note at the bottom of the page.

**Foreshadowing** A hint about **plot** elements to come, both to advance the plot and build **suspense.**

**Form** The shape, structure, and style of a poem, as distinguishable from, but integral to, the content or substance of the poem.

**Formal Diction** Complex, grammatically proper, and often polysyllabic language in writing. It sounds grandiloquent—a *formal* word—and tends not to resemble the sort of talk heard in daily life.

**Formalist Criticism** An approach to literary criticism that considers a successful text to be a complete, independent, unified artifact whose meaning and value can be understood purely by analyzing the interaction of its formal and technical components, such as **plot, imagery,** structure, style, **symbol,** and **tone.** Rather than drawing their textual interpretations from *extrinsic* factors such as the historical, political, or biographical context of the work, formalist critics focus on the text's *intrinsic* formal elements.

**Found Poem** A poem created from already existing text that the poet reshapes and presents in poetic form. Text may come from advertisements, labels on household items, newspapers, magazines, or any other printed source not intended originally as poetry. A poet may piece together several sources like a collage, or he/she might take a short text exactly as it is and insert line breaks.

**Fourth Wall** The *invisible wall* of the stage, through which the audience views the action.

**Free Verse** Poetry in which the poet does not adhere to a preset metrical or **rhyme scheme.** Free verse has become increasingly prevalent since the nineteenth century, when it was first used. *See* **Open Form.**

**Freewrite** Writing continuously to generate ideas, without worrying about mistakes.

**Gay and Lesbian Criticism** A critical approach that is similar to **feminist criticism** in its quest to uncover previously overlooked undertones and themes in literature. Gay and lesbian criticism seeks to identify underlying homosexual themes in literature.

**Gender Criticism** A critical approach to literature that seeks to understand how gender and sexual identity reflect upon the interpretation of literary works. Feminist criticism and gay and lesbian criticism are derivatives of gender criticism.

**Genre** A literary category or form, such as the short story or novel, or a specific type of fiction, such as science fiction or mystery.

**Groundlings** "Standing room only" spectators in the Elizabethan theater who paid a penny to stand on the ground surrounding the stage.

**Haiku** A poetic form containing seventeen syllables in three lines of five, seven, and five syllables each. Haiku traditionally contain a natural-world reference or central **image.**

***Hamartia*** A tragic flaw or weakness in a tragic **character** that leads to his or her downfall. **Hubris** is a type of *hamartia.*

**Heptameter** A poetic **meter** that consists of seven feet in each line.

**Hero/Heroine** The **protagonist** of a story, often possessing positive traits such as courage or honesty.

**Heroic Couplet** Two successive rhyming lines in **iambic pentameter.**

**Hexameter** A poetic **meter** that consists of six feet in each line. If the six feet are **iambic,** the line is known as an alexandrine, which was the preferred line of French epic poetry.

**High Comedy** **Comedy,** often a satire of upper-class society, that relies on sophisticated wit and **irony.**

**Hip Hop** An intensely rhythmical form of popular music developed by African-Americans and Latinos in the 1970s in which vocalists deploy rhyme—known as rap—over the rhythm.

**Historical Criticism** An approach to **literary criticism** that emphasizes the relationship between a text and its historical context. When interpreting a text, historical critics highlight the cultural, philosophical, and political movements and ideologies prevalent during the text's creation and reception.

**Historical Fiction** A type of fiction writing wherein the author bases his or her **characters, plot,** or **setting** on actual people, events, or places.

**Histories** *See* **Classifications of Drama.**

**Hubris** Excessive arrogance or pride. In classical literature, the hero's tragic flaw was often hubris, which caused his downfall in the tragedy.

**Hyperbole** A type of figurative speech that uses verbal exaggeration to make a point. Hyperbole is sometimes called ***overstatement.***

**Iamb** A poetic **foot** consisting of an unstressed syllable followed by a stressed syllable.

**Iambic Meter** A poetic **meter** created when each line contains more than one **iamb** (a unit with an unstressed syllable followed by a stressed syllable).

**Iambic Pentameter** A poetic **meter** in which each line contains five feet, predominantly iambs. Iambic pentameter is the most commonly used meter in English poetry, comprising **sonnets,** much of Shakespeare's plays, Milton's *Paradise Lost,* Wordsworth's *The Prelude* and Wallace Stevens' "Sunday Morning."

**Iconography** **Symbols** that commonly engender a certain meaning. For example, a skull equals *death,* and a dove equals *peace.*

**Image** A sensory impression created by language. Not all images are visual pictures; an image can appeal to any of the five senses, emotions, or the intellect.

**Imagism** A poetic practice wherein the *thing itself*—the object seen and not discussed or **analyzed**—becomes the poet's focus and the poem's primary concern. Imagism is associated with poets like Ezra Pound and William Carlos Williams.

**Impartial Omniscience** A **narrator** who remains neutral, relating events and **characters'** thoughts without passing judgment or offering an opinion.

**Implied Metaphor** A suggested comparison that is never stated plainly.

**Impressionism** In literature, a style of writing that focuses on a **protagonist**'s reactions to external events rather than the events themselves.

**Indirect Discourse** A **narrator**'s description of an action or event as experienced by a **character** in the story.

**Informal Diction** An author's use of words that are conversational or easily understood, as opposed to elevated or formal language. For example, using *you* instead of *thou.*

**Initial Alliteration** The repetition of consonant or vowel sounds in the middle of a line of poetry.

**Initiation Story** *See* **Coming of Age Story** and ***Bildungsroman.***

***In medias res*** Latin for *in the middle of things.* A term applied when a story begins with relevant story events already having occurred.

**Innocent Narrator** *See* **Naïve Narrator.**

**Intentional Fallacy** The practice by **formalist** critics of discerning or trusting an author's own stated purpose for the meaning of a text.

**Interior Monologue** A **character's** conscious or unconscious thought processes, narrated as they occur, with only minimal-seeming guidance from the **narrator.**

**Internal Alliteration** The repetition of consonant or vowel sounds in the middle of a line of poetry.

**Internal Refrain** The repetition of words or phrases within the lines of a poem.

**Internal Rhyme** **Rhyme** that occurs within a line. The placement of internal rhyme can vary; for example, a word in the middle of the line might rhyme with the word at the end of that same line, or both rhyming words might occur in the middle of two consecutive lines.

**Interpret** The act of **interpretation.**

**Interpretation** The process of contributing to the overall understanding of some aspect of a work in order to illuminate its meaning.

**In-Text Parenthetical Citation** A reference within the body of a paper that links a **quotation, paraphrase,** or **summary** from another source to its full citation in the list of **works cited.**

**In the Round** *See* **Arena Theater.**

**Inverted Syntax** A reversal of expected or traditional word order, often used to aid a poem's sounds, **rhyme,** and/ or **meter.**

**Ironic Point of View** Describes a **narrator** who does not understand the significance of the events of a story.

**Irony** A **tone** characterized by a distance between what occurs and what is expected to occur, or between what is said and what is meant.

**Italian Sonnet** *See* **Petrarchan Sonnet.**

**Jargon** Words used with specific meaning for a particular group of people. For example, *starboard* in nautical jargon refers to the right side of a ship.

**Journal Entry** A writing exercise that expands **freewriting** into a more focused discussion that reflects a growing understanding of a topic.

**Language, Tone, and Style** The elements that conjure a story's particular flavor and **voice,** as achieved by means of the words the author chooses and the **rhythm** with which he or she puts the words together

**Language** The words of a story, including **syntax** (how words or other elements of the sentence are arranged) and **diction** (what words the author chooses).

**Levels of Diction** Refers to the three major categories of diction: high, middle, and low diction. The level of diction a writer uses determines whether the words in the work will be formal or informal, poetic or conversational, etc.

**Limerick** A light, often humorous verse form consisting of five **anapestic** (two short syllables followed by one long one) lines, with a rhyme scheme of *aabba*. The first, second, and fifth lines consist of three feet, while lines three and four consist of two feet.

**Limited Omniscient Narrator** A **third-person narrator** who enters into the mind of only one **character** at a time. This narrator serves more as an interpreter than a source of the main **character's** thoughts.

**Line** A row of words containing phrases and/or sentences. The line is a defining feature of poetry, in which there are often set amounts of syllables or poetic feet in each line.

**Literary Ballad** A story told in **ballad** form.

**Literary Criticism** The acts of analyzing, interpreting, and commenting on literature.

**Literary Epic** *See* **Epic.**

**Literary Theory** The body of criticism and schools of thought (such as **Feminist, Deconstructionist,** or **Biographical** Criticism) that govern how we study literature.

**Low Comedy** An informal brand of **comedy** that uses crude humor and **slapstick.**

**Lyric** A short poem with a central pictorial **image** written in an uninflected (direct and personal) **voice.**

**Madrigal** A variety of contrapuntal song that originated in 16th-century Italy. Madrigal features secular verse sung by two or more voices without instrumental accompaniment.

**Magic Realism** A type of fiction in which something "magical" happens in an otherwise realistic world. The form is particularly associated with Latin American writers like Gabriel García Márquez. Unlike **fantasy** or science fiction, magic realism generally has only one fantastical element and the rest relies on realistic **characters** and settings. Notable examples in this book are Franz Kafka's *The Metamorphosis* and Aimee Bender's "The Rememberer."

**Marxist Criticism** Marxist or Economic Determinist Criticism is based on the writings of Karl Marx, who argued that economic concerns shape lives more than anything else, and that society is essentially a struggle between the working classes and the dominant capitalist classes. Rather than assuming that culture evolves naturally or autonomously out of individual human experience, Marxist critics maintain that culture—including literature—is shaped by the interests of the dominant or most powerful social class.

**Masculine Rhyme** The **end rhymes** of multisyllable words with a stressed final syllable, such as *remove* and *approve*. Also called rising rhyme.

**Melodrama** A literary work, mainly a stage play, movie, or television play or show in which **characters** display exaggerated emotions and the **plot** takes sensational turns, sometimes accompanied by music intended to lead the audience's feelings.

**Melody** The linear succession of various musical pitches recognized as a unit.

**Metafiction** A work of fiction that self-consciously draws attention to itself as a work of fiction. Rather than upholding the standard pretense, prevalent in realist fiction, that a story creates or refers to a "real world" beyond the text, metafiction self-consciously reveals the fact and sometimes the manner of its own construction. Metafiction is often associated with **postmodernism,** but examples of metafiction also occur in many other literary movements.

**Metaphor** A close comparison of two dissimilar things that creates a fusion of identity between the things that are compared. A metaphor joins two dissimilar things *without* using words such as *like* or *as*. While a **simile** suggests that X is *like* Y a metaphor states that X *is* Y.

**Meter** A measure of verse, based on regular patterns of sound.

**Metonymy** A **figure of speech** that uses an identifying emblem or closely associated object to represent another object. For example, the phrase *the power of the purse* makes little sense literally (there is no purse that has power), but in the metonymical sense, *purse* stands for money.

**Middle Diction** Poetic language characterized by sophisticated word usage and grammatical accuracy. Middle diction reads as educated, cultured language but is not extravagant like **poetic diction.**

**Mime** The act of performing a play without words.

**Miracle Plays** During the tenth century, when drama was suppressed by the church, these anonymous plays were acted out as religious instruction for the benefit of spectators who could not read the Bible.

**Mixed Metaphor** A failed comparison that results when a writer uses at least two separate, mismatched comparisons in one statement—to confusing, and sometimes comical effect. For example, *The early bird strikes when the iron's hot!*

**Monologue** A single **character's** discourse, without interaction or interruption by other **characters.**

**Monometer** A poetic **meter** comprised of one poetic foot.

**Monosyllabic** A word with one syllable.

**Moral** The lesson taught by a piece of **didactic literature** such as a fable. A moral is often phrased simply and memorably.

**Morality Play** A form of drama in which the figures on stage taught right and proper behavior—morality—to those who watched.

**Motif** A pattern of **imagery** or a concept that recurs throughout a work of literature.

**Motivation** A **character's** reason for doing something.

**Mystery Play** A play that enacted stories of the Bible, such as the Creation or the Crucifixion. These plays appeared during the tenth century, when drama was suppressed in England.

**Myth** The pre-Classical Greek word for sacred story or religious narrative, which by the Classical period had come to mean **plot,** as used in Aristotle's *Poetics*.

**Mythological Criticism** Also called the *archetypal approach,* mythological criticism stems from the work of Carl Jung, a Swiss psychoanalyst (and contemporary of Freud) who argued that humans share in a **collective unconscious,** or a set of **characters,** plots, symbols, and **images** that each evoke a universal response. Jung calls these recurring elements **archetypes,** and likens them to *instincts*—knowledge or associations with which humans are born. Mythological critics **analyze** the ways in which such archetypes function in literature and attempt to explain the power that literature has over us or the reasons why certain texts continue to hold power over audiences many centuries after their creation.

**Naïve Narrator** An unreliable **narrator** who remains unaware of the full complexity of events in the story being told, often due to youth, innocence, or lack of cultural awareness.

**Narrative Poem** A poem that tells a story. Examples include Tennyson's "The Charge of the Light Brigade," Longfellow's "The Midnight Ride of Paul Revere," and most ballads.

**Narrator** The **character** or consciousness that tells a story. For specific types of narrators, see **First-Person Narrator, Second-Person Narrator, Third-Person narrator, Omniscient Narrator, Limited Omniscient Narrator, Impartial Omniscience, Editorial Omniscience, Naïve Narrator,** and **Unreliable Narrator.**

**Naturalistic Theater** Drama that shines a light on the painful realities and problems of everyday life.

**Near Rhyme** *See* **Slant Rhyme.**

**New Criticism** *See* **Formalist Criticism.**

**New Historicism** A critical approach that emerged as a reaction to **new criticism**'s disregard of historical context, but also in response to the perceived shortcomings of older methods of **historical criticism.** Rather than focusing on texts in the **canon** as representations of the most powerful or dominant historical movements, new historicists give equal or greater attention to less dominant texts and non-literary texts (newspapers, pamphlets, legal documents, medical documents, etc.). New historicists attempt to highlight overlooked or suppressed texts, particularly those that express deviation from the dominant culture of the time. In this way, new historicists study not just the historical context of a major literary text, but the complex relationship between texts and culture, or the ways in which literature can challenge as well as support a given culture.

**Nonfiction Novel** A presentation of real events using the craft and technique of a fiction novel.

**Novel** A long fictional work. Because of their greater length, novels are typically complex and may follow more than one **character** or **plot.**

**Novella** A short novel, which generally means it has more complexity than a short story but without the usual length of a novel.

**Objective Point of View** The story is told by an observer who relates only facts, providing neither commentary nor insight into the **character's** thoughts or actions.

**Observer** A **first-person narrator** who does not participate in the action of the story.

**Octameter** A poetic **meter** that consists of eight feet in each line.

**Octave** Eight lines of poetry grouped together in a **stanza** or a unit of thought, as in the **Petrarchan sonnet** where the octave sets up a thought or feeling that the following **sestet** resolves.

**Ode** An elevated, formal **lyric** poem often written in ceremony to someone or to an abstract subject. In Greek **tragedy,** a song and dance performed by the **Chorus** between ***episodia***.

**Oedipus Complex:** Sigmund Freud's theory of behavior (derived from the **plot** of Sophocles's *Oedipus the King*) which holds that male children are jealous of the father because of their sexual attraction to the mother. In *Oedipus the King,* Oedipus kills his father and sleeps with his mother.

**Off Rhyme** *See* **Slant Rhyme.**

**O. Henry Ending** A short story ending that consists of a sudden surprise, often ironic or coincidental in nature, named for the short story writer O. Henry, who frequently ended his stories in this way. A classic example is O. Henry's "The Gift of the Magi" in which a husband and wife each give something precious of theirs to purchase a gift for the other; the ending reveals that each has sacrificed the very thing that would have allowed him or her to enjoy the gift received from their spouse.

**Omniscient Narrator** A **third-person narrator** who observes the thoughts and describes the actions of multiple **characters** in the story. The omniscient narrator can see beyond the physical actions and **dialogue** of **characters** and is able to reveal the inner thoughts and emotions of anyone in the story.

**One-Act Play** A play that consists of a single act that contains the entire action of the play. One-act plays usually portray a single **scene** with an exchange among a smaller number of **characters**; for example, Edward Albee's *The Zoo Story*.

**Onomatopoeia** The use of words that imitate the sounds they refer to, such as *buzz* or *pop*.

**Open Denouement** A **resolution** to a story that leaves loose ends and does not completely resolve the overarching **conflict.**

**Open Form** Poetry ungoverned by metrical or rhyme schemes. Also called free verse.

**Orchestra** The open area in front of the stage (or ***skene***) in the Greek **amphitheater.**

**Overstatement** *See* **Hyperbole.**

**Oxymoron** A version of **paradox** that combines contradictory words into a compact, often two-word term, such as *jumbo shrimp* or *definitely maybe.*

***Paean*** The final choral **ode** of a Greek **tragedy.**

**Pantoum** A variation on the **villanelle,** consisting of an unspecified number of **quatrains** with the rhyme scheme *abab*. The first line of each quatrain repeats the second line of the preceding quatrain, and the third line repeats the final line of the preceding quatrain. In the final quatrain, the second line repeats the third line of the first quatrain, and the last line of the poem repeats the first line of the poem.

**Parable** A short narrative that illustrates a lesson using comparison to familiar **characters** and events. The characters and events in parables often have obvious significance as **symbols** and **allegories.**

***Parados*** The **Chorus**' first **ode** in a Greek **tragedy.**

**Paradox** Seemingly contradictory statements that, when closely examined, have a deeper, sometimes complicated, meaning.
**Parallelism** The arrangement of words or phrases in a grammatically similar way.
**Paraphrase** Condensing a passage or idea from an existing text into your own words. Paraphrase does not mean simply changing the words from the original; rather, it should re-present the original in a way that demonstrates your understanding of it.
**Parody** Mimicking another author or work of literature in such a way as to make fun of the original, often by exaggerating its characteristic aspects.
**Participant narrator** A **first-person narrator** who takes part in the action of the story.
**Pastoral Poetry** A variety of poem in which life in the countryside, mainly among shepherds, is glorified and idealized.
**Pentameter** A poetic **meter** that consists of five feet in each line.
***Peripeteia*** An element of Greek **tragedy,** *peripeteia* occurs when an action has the opposite result of what was intended. In a **tragedy,** this generally occurs at a turning point for the **hero** and signals his downfall.
**Persona** A poem's speaker, which may or may not use the **voice** of the poet.
***Personae*** Masks, often representative of certain **iconography** and familiar **characters,** worn by actors in the Ancient Greek theater to enable one actor to perform as many **characters.** *Personae* often were designed to project an actor's voice to the far rows of the **amphitheater.**
**Personification** A **figure of speech** in which a writer ascribes human traits or behavior to something inhuman.
**Persuasion** The process of using **analysis** and logical **argument** to prove the validity of a certain **interpretation** or **point of view.**
**Petrarchan (Italian) Sonnet** A sonnet consisting of an **octave** and a **sestet,** all in **iambic pentameter,** with the rhyme scheme *abbaabba cdecde* or *abbaabba cdcdcd.* The **volta,** or turn, typically occurs between the octave and sestet, around line nine of the poem.
**Plagiarism** The act of taking credit for another's work or ideas.
**Play** A work of drama, usually performed before an audience.
**Players** Traveling actors, men and boys, who spoke their lines for pay.
**Play Review** The critique of a play.
**Playwright** The author of a dramatic work.
**Plot** The artful arrangement of incidents in a story, with each incident building on the next in a series of causes and effects.
**Poetic Diction** Lofty and elevated language, used traditionally in poetry written before the nineteenth century to separate poetic speech from common speech.
**Point of View** The perspective from which the story is told to the reader.
**Polysyllabic** A word that has many syllables.
**Portmanteau Word** A word invented by combining two other words to achieve the effect of both. Lewis Carroll's poem "Jabberwocky" is comprised largely of portmanteau words such as *slithy,* which means *slimy* and *lithe.*
**Postcolonialism** A critical approach to **literary criticism** that seeks to offer views of relations between the colonizing West and colonized nations and regions that differed sharply from the conventional Western perspectives.
**Poststructuralist Criticism** Criticism based on the belief that texts do not have a single, stable meaning or **interpretation,** in part because language itself is filled with ambiguity, multiple meanings, and meanings that can change with time or context.
**Precís** *See* **Summary Paper.**
**Preview** The process of gathering information about a piece of literature before you read it.
**Problem Play** A play about a social problem, written with an aim to create awareness of the problem.
**Prologue** The introduction to a literary work.
**Proscenium Stage** A realistic **setting** with three flat walls (two flat sides, and a ceiling) that simulates a room; the audience views the action through the missing **fourth wall.**
**Prose Poem** A poem that uses the devices and **imagery** characteristic of traditionally lined poetry, but in compact units without clearly defined line breaks.
**Prosody** The analysis of a poem's rhythm and metrical structures.
**Protagonist** The main figure (or principal actor) in a work of literature. A story's **plot** hinges equally on the protagonist's efforts to realize his or her desires and to cope with failure if and when plans are thwarted and desires left unfulfilled.
**Psalm** A sacred song, usually written to or in honor of a deity.
**Psychoanalytic Criticism** Also called *psychological criticism,* this approach in a sense studies **characters** and authors as one would patients, looking in the text for evidence of childhood trauma, repressed sexual impulses, preoccupation with death, and so on. Through the lens of psychology critics attempt to explain the motivations and meanings behind characters' actions. Psychological critics also use textual and biographical evidence as a means to better understand the author's psychology, as well as examine the process and nature of literary creation, studying the ways in which texts create an emotional and intellectual effect for their readers and authors.
**Pun** A play on words that reveals different meanings in words that are similar or even identical.
**Pyrrhic** A poetic foot characterized by two unstressed syllables.

**Quantitative Meter** A type of poetry that counts the length of syllables, rather than the emphasis they receive (as in **accentual meter** and syllabic verse). Quantitative meter primarily appears in Greek and Latin poetry and is rarely used in English since English vowel lengths are not clearly quantified.
**Quatrain** A four-line **stanza.** Quatrains are the most popular stanzaic form in English poetry because they are easily varied in **meter,** line length, and **rhyme scheme.**
**Queer Theory** The idea that power is reflected in language and that discourse itself shapes our sense of who we are and how we define ourselves sexually.

**Rap** An oral form of poetry that is akin to spoken word, but distinguished by musical qualities and choral repetitions. *See* **Hip Hop.**
**Reader-Response Criticism** The reader-response approach emphasizes that the reader is central to the writer-text-reader interaction. Reader-response critics believe a literary work is not complete until someone reads and **interprets** it. Such critics acknowledge that because each reader has a different set of experiences and views, each reader's response to a text may be different.
**Realism** A mode of literature in which the author depicts **characters** and scenarios that could occur in real life. Unlike **fantasy** or **surrealism,** realism seeks to represent the world as it is.
**Recognition** The moment in a **tragedy** when the **hero** comes to recognize the actuality of events and is no longer under illusion.
**Refrain** A line or **stanza** that is repeated at regular intervals in a poem or song.
**Resolution** The end of the story, where the **conflict** is ultimately resolved and the effects of the story's events on the **protagonist** become evident.
**Restoration Comedy** A bawdy play about fallen virtue and infidelity that

became popular after the Puritans were displaced in England in the mid-seventeenth century.

**Retrospect** *See* **Flashback.**

**Reversal** *See* ***Peripeteia.***

**Rhyme** The echoing repetition of sounds in the end syllables of words, often (though not always) at the end of a line of poetry.

**Rhyme Scheme** The pattern of **rhyme** throughout a particular poem.

**Rhythm** The sequence of stressed and unstressed sounds in a poem.

**Rising Action** Story events that increase tension and move the plot toward the climax.

**Rising Meter** A **meter** comprised of feet that begin with an unstressed syllable, followed by a stressed syllable or syllables. **Iambic** and **anapestic** feet both create rising meter, which is named for the effect of *rising* from the initial unstressed syllable to the stressed.

**Romance** *See* **Classifications of Drama.**

**Romantic Comedy** A type of **comedy** in which two would-be/should-be lovers find each other after a series of misunderstandings and false starts.

**Round Character** A **character** with complex, multifaceted characteristics. Round characters behave as real people. For example, a round **hero** may suffer temptation, and a round **villain** may show compassion.

**Run-On Line** A line of poetry that, when read, does not come to a natural conclusion where the line breaks. *See* **Enjambment.**

**Sarcasm** Verbal irony that is intended in a mean-spirited, malicious, or critical way.

**Satire** An artistic critique, sometimes heated, on some aspect of human immorality or absurdity.

**Satiric Comedy** A derisive and dark **comedy** in which there is no promise that good will prevail.

**Satyr Play** An often obscene satirical fourth play, provided after a trilogy of tragedies, meant to provide **comic relief.**

**Scansion** The process of determining the metrical pattern of a line of poetry by marking its stresses and feet.

**Scene** A defined moment of action or interaction in a story usually confined to a single **setting.** Scenes are the building blocks of a story's **plot.**

**Scenery** The set pieces and stage decorations onstage during the performance of a play.

**Scratch Outline** A multi-tiered, ordered list of topics that should be covered in a paper. A scratch outline goes into deeper detail than a topic outline.

**Screenplay** A script that is specifically tailored and structured for television or film rather than the stage.

**Script** The written text of a play, which may include set descriptions and actor cues.

**Second-Person Narrator** A **narrator** who addresses the character as *you,* often involving the reader by association.

**Semiotics** The study of how meaning is attached to and communicated by symbols.

**Sentence Outline** An outline that uses complete sentences instead of brief words or phrases.

**Sestet** Six lines of poetry grouped together in a stanza or a unit of thought, as in the **Petrarchan sonnet** where the last six lines of the poem resolve the idea or question set up by the initial **octave.**

**Sestina** A poem of six six-line **stanzas** and a three-line **envoi,** usually unrhymed, in which each stanza repeats the end words of the lines of the first stanza, but in different order, the envoi using the six words again, three in the middle of the lines and three at the end.

**Setting** The time and place where the story occurs. Setting creates expectations for the types of **characters** and situations encountered in the story.

**Shakespearean (English) Sonnet** A **sonnet** form composed of three quatrains and a final couplet, all in **iambic pentameter** and rhymed *abab cdcd efef gg.* The **volta,** or turn, occurs in the final **couplet** of the poem.

**Short Story** A brief fictional narrative that attempts to dramatize or illustrate the effect or meaning of a single incident or small group of incidents in the life of a single **character** or small group of characters.

**Simile** A direct comparison of two dissimilar things using the words *like* or *as.*

**Situational Irony** A situation portrayed in a poem when what occurs is the opposite or very different from what's expected to occur.

***Skene*** The stage in the Greek **amphitheater.**

**Slam** Poetry in a variety of styles, performed competitively in clubs and halls.

**Slant Rhyme** A case in which vowel or consonant sounds are similar but not exactly the same, such as *heap* and *rap* and *tape.* Also called *near rhyme, imperfect rhyme* and *off rhyme.*

**Slapstick** A type of low **comedy** characterized by unexpected, often physical humor. A classic example of slapstick is the man walking along who accidentally slips on a banana peel.

**Social Environment** A study of **setting** that considers era and location as well as a **character's** living and working conditions.

**Sociological Criticism** The study of literary texts as products of the cultural, political, and economic context of the author's time and place.

**Soliloquy** A **monologue** delivered by a **character** in a play who is alone onstage. Soliloquies generally have a **character** revealing his or her thoughts to the audience.

**Sonnet** A poem of fourteen lines of **iambic pentameter** in a recognizable pattern of **rhyme.** Sonnets contain a **volta,** or turn, in which the last lines resolve or change direction from the controlling idea of the preceding lines.

**Sound** The rhythmic structure of the lines of a poem, which draws the reader in, often utilizing **rhyme** and created through word choice and word order.

**Spoken Word Poetry** Poetry that derives from the **Beat** poets, characterized by emphasis of the *performance* of a poem over the written form. Spoken word often employs improvisation.

**Spondee** A poetic foot characterized by two stressed syllables.

**Stage Directions** Cues, included by the playwright in the script of a play, which inform the actions of the actors during the play.

**Stanza** A unit of two or more lines, set off by a space, often sharing the same **rhythm** and **meter.**

***Stasimon*** In Greek **tragedy,** an ode performed by the **Chorus** which interprets and responds to the preceding scene.

**Static Character** A **character,** often flat, who does not change over the course of the story.

**Stock Character** A **character** who represents a concept or type of behavior, such as a "mean teacher" or "mischievous student," and offers readers the comfort of repetition and reliability.

**Stream of Consciousness:** A **character's** thoughts are presented flowing by in free association, and the literary convention that rules is that there is no writer mediating the consciousness of the subject.

**Stress** The vocal emphasis on a syllable in a line of verse, largely a matter of pitch.

**Structuralism** Structuralist literary critics work from the belief that a given work of literature can be fully understood only when a reader considers the system of conventions, or the *genre* to which it belongs or responds.

**Style** The characteristic way in which any writer uses language.

**Subplot** A **plot** that is not the central plot of the work, but nonetheless appears in the same work. Longer works, like **novels** and plays, tend to have subplots that might follow side **characters** or somehow affect the action of the main plot.

**Summary** Restating concisely the main ideas of a text without adding opinion or commentary. The best approach to summary is to divide the text into its major sections and then write a sentence for each section stating its main idea.

**Summary Paper** A short paper that represents the main ideas of the text as the author has presented them, excluding any subjective ideas or interpretations.

**Surrealism** A technique of the modern theater in which the realms of conscious and unconscious experience are fused together to create a total reality. In this way the fiction writer, poet, and **playwright,** tap into the resources of the unconscious mind and the imagination and portray in story on the page or on the modern stage the stuff of human desire, hope, and dreams.

**Suspense** A sense of anticipation or excitement about what will happen and how the **characters** will deal with their newfound predicament.

**Syllabic verse** A verse form that uses a fixed number of syllables per line or stanza, regardless of the number of stressed or unstressed syllables.

**Symbol** Any object, **image, character,** or action that suggests meaning beyond the everyday literal level.

**Symbolic Act** A gesture or action beyond the everyday practical definition.

**Synecdoche** A **figure of speech** that uses a piece or part of a thing to represent the thing in its entirety. For example, in the Biblical saying that man does not live by bread alone, *bread* stands for the larger concept of food or physical sustenance.

**Synopsis** A **summary** or **précis** of a work.

**Syntax** The meaningful arrangement of words and phrases. Syntax can refer to word placement and order, as well as the overall length and shape of a sentence.

**Synthesis** The act of bringing together the ideas and observations generated by reading and analysis in order to make a concrete statement about a work.

**Tactile Imagery** Imagery that appeals to a reader's sense of touch.

**Tercet** A group of three lines of poetry, sometimes called a **triplet** when all three lines rhyme.

**Terminal Refrain** Repeated lines which appear at the end of each **stanza** in a poem.

**Terza Rima** A **tercet** fixed form featuring the interlocking rhyme scheme *aba, bcb, cdc, ded,* etc.

**Tetrameter** A poetic **meter** that contains four feet in each line.

**Theme** The central or underlying meanings of a literary work.

**Thesis Statement** A sentence, usually but not always included in a paper's introductory paragraph, that defines a paper's purpose and argument.

**Thesis** A paper's purpose and **argument,** defined by the **thesis statement** and proved by the paper's **conclusion.**

**Third-Person Narrator** A **narrator** who is outside the story. The narrator refers to all the **characters** in the story with the pronouns *he, she,* or *they.*

**Tiring House** In the Elizabethan theater, a room, adjoined to the stage, in which actors changed their costumes.

**Tone** The author's attitude toward his or her **characters** or subject matter.

**Topic Outline** A multi-tiered organization of a paper's topics and **arguments,** used to structure a paper.

**Tragedy** A dramatic form in which **characters** face serious and important challenges that end in disastrous failure or defeat for the **protagonist.** *See* **Classifications of Drama.**

**Tragic Flaw** In classical literature, the hero's weakness that causes his downfall.

**Tragic Hero** A heroic **protagonist** who from the beginning, due to some innate flaw in his **character** or some unforeseeable mistake (*see* **Tragic Flaw**), is doomed. The inevitability of a tragic hero's demise inspires sympathy in the audience.

**Tragic Irony** The situation in a **tragedy** where the audience is aware of the **tragic hero's** fate although the **character** has not yet become aware.

**Tragicomedy** A play with the elements of **tragedy** that ends happily.

**Transferred Epithet** A description that pairs an adjective with a noun that does not logically follow, such as *silver sounds.*

**Trimeter** A poetic **meter** that contains three feet in each line.

**Triplet** A **tercet** of three rhymed lines.

**Trochaic Meter:** A poetic **meter** created when each line contains more than one **trochee** (a unit with a stressed syllable followed by an unstressed syllable). Trochaic meter is a type of **falling meter.**

**Trochee** A poetic **foot** consisting of a stressed syllable followed by an unstressed syllable. The opposite of an **iamb,** and so sometimes called an "inverted foot," often beginning a line of **iambic pentameter.**

**Understatement** A purposeful underestimation of something, used to emphasize its actual magnitude.

**Unreliable Narrator** A **narrator** who cannot be trusted to present an undistorted account of the action because of inexperience, ignorance, personal bias, intentional deceptiveness, or even insanity.

**Verbal Irony** A statement in which the stated meaning is very different (sometimes opposite) from the implied meaning.

**Verisimilitude** How alike an imitation is to its original. The goal of literature, especially when written in the mode of realism, is to provide a likeness, or a verisimilitude, of real life.

**Verse** A broad term to describe poetic lines.

***Vers libre*** *See* **Free Verse.**

**Villanelle** A poem consisting of five **tercets** and a concluding **quatrain.** Each tercet rhymes *aba* and the final quatrain rhymes *abaa.* The poem's opening line repeats as the final line of the second and fourth stanzas, and in the second-to-last line of the poem. The last line of the first **stanza** repeats as the final line of the third and fifth stanzas and is also the final line of the poem overall.

**Visual imagery** **Imagery** and descriptions that appeal to a reader's sense of sight.

**Voice** The unique sound of an author's writing, created by elements such as **diction, tone,** and sentence construction.

**Volta** In a sonnet, the turn where a shift in thought or emotion occurs. In the **Petrarchan sonnet,** the **volta** occurs between the **octave** and the **sestet;** in the **Shakespearean sonnet,** the ending couplet provides the volta.

**Vulgate** A term to describe the common people, often used in reference to a level of speech or **diction.**

**Well-made Play** A type of theater popularized in France. Well-made plays feature a three-act sequence that *poses* a problem, *complicates* and then *resolves* it; usually that **resolution** comes when a **character's** past is revealed. The first act offers *exposition,* the second a *situation,* the third an unraveling or *completion.* Meticulous plotting and **suspense** are components of this mode of theater.

**Working Bibliography** A list of all the sources consulted in preparing a paper, as well as all the information necessary to cite them in the final list of works cited.

**Works Cited** A list of all the primary and secondary sources consulted in the creation of a paper.

# Credits

Kim Addonizio: "First Poem for You" from *The Philosopher's Club*. Reprinted by permission of Kim Addonizio.

Ai: "Riot Act, April 29, 1992" from *Greed* by Ai. Copyright © 1993 by Ai. Used by permission of W. W. Norton & Company, Inc.

Sherman Alexie: "Defending Walt Whitman" reprinted from *The Summer of Black Widows*, © 1996 by Sherman Alexie, by permission of Hanging Loose Press.

Miguel Algarin: "HIV" from *Love is Hard*. Reprinted by permission of the author.

Julia Alvarez: "Woman's Work" from *Homecoming*. Copyright © 1984, 1996 by Julia Alvarez. Published by Plume, an imprint of Penguin Group (USA); originally published by Grove Press. Reprinted by permission of Susan Bergholz Literary Services, New York, NY and Lamy, NM. All rights reserved.

A. R. Ammons: "Their Sex Life," "Small Song," from *The Really Short Poems of A. R. Ammons* by A. R. Ammons. Copyright © 1990 by A. R. Ammons. Used by permission of W. W. Norton & Company, Inc.

Gloria Anzaldúa: "To live in the borderlands means you" from *Borderlands/LaFrontera: The New Mestiza*. Copyright © 1987, 1999 by Gloria Anzaldúa. Reprinted by permission of Aunt Lute Books www.auntlute.com.

Margaret Atwood: "you fit into me" from *Power Politics* copyright © 1971, 1996 by Margaret Atwood. Reprinted by permission of House of Anansi Press, Toronto.

W.H. Auden: "Funeral Blues," "Musée des Beaux Arts," "The Unknown Citizen," "In Memory of W. B. Yeats" all copyright 1940 and renewed 1968 by W. H. Auden from *Collected Poems by W. H. Auden*. Used by permission of Random House, Inc.

Jimmy Santiago Baca: "Choices" is reprinted by permission of the author.

Frank Bidart: "Herbert White" from *In the Western Night: Collected Poems 1965–1990* by Frank Bidart. Copyright © 1990 by Frank Bidart. Reprinted by permission of Farrar, Straus and Giroux, LLC.

Elizabeth Bishop: "The Fish" and "One Art" from *The Complete Poems 1927–1979* by Elizabeth Bishop. Copyright © 1979, 1983 by Alice Helen Methfessel. Reprinted by permission of Farrar, Straus and Giroux, LLC.

Robert Bly: "Driving to Town Late to Mail a Letter" from *Silence in the Snowy Field*, reprinted by permission of the author.

Louise Bogan: "Changed Woman" from *The Blue Estuaries* by Louise Bogan. Copyright © 1968 by Louise Bogan. Copyright renewed1996 by Ruth Limmer. Reprinted by permission of Farrar, Straus and Giroux, LLC.

Gwendolyn Brooks: "We Real Cool" and "Sadie and Maud" from *Blacks* by Gwendolyn Brooks. Reprinted by consent of Brooks Permissions.

Kenneth Carroll: "So What!" (for the White Dude who said dis ain't poetry) from *So What! (for the White Dude who said this ain't poetry)*, reprinted by permission of Bunny and the Crocodile Press.

Anne Carson: "Automat" from *Men in the Off Hours* by Anne Carson, copyright © 2000 by Anne Carson. Used by permission of Alfred A. Knopf, a division of Random House, Inc.

Kelly Cherry: "The Raiment We Put On" from *Hazard and Prospect*. Reprinted by permission of Louisiana State University Press.

Marilyn Chin: "Turtle Soup" from The *Phoenix Gone, The Terrace Empty* (Minneapolis: Milkweed Editions, 1994). Copyright © 1994 by Marilyn Chin. Reprinted with permission from Milkweed Editions.

John Ciardi: "Most Like an Arch This Marriage" from *Collected Poems* by John Ciardi. Reprinted by permission of The Estate of John Ciardi.

Sandra Cisneros: "Pumpkin Eater" from *Loose Woman*. Copyright © 1994 by Sandra Cisneros. Published by Vintage Books, a division of Random House, Inc. and originally in hardcover by Alfred A. Knopf, Inc. Reprinted by permission of Susan Bergholz Literary Services, New York, NY and Lamy, NM. All rights reserved.

Amy Clampitt: "John Donne in California" from *The Collected Poems of Amy Clampitt* by Amy Clampitt, copyright © 1997 by the Estate of Amy Clampitt. Introduction copyright © 1997 by Mary Jo Salter. Used by permission of Alfred A. Knopf, a division of Random House, Inc.

Lucille Clifton: "homage to my hips" copyright © 1980 by Lucille Clifton. First appeared in *Two-Headed Woman*, published by The University of Massachusetts Press. Reprinted by permission of Curtis Brown, Ltd.

Judith Ortiz Cofer: "Quinceañera" is reprinted with permission from the publisher of *Terms of Survival* by Judith Ortiz Cofer (© 1987 Arte Publico Press—University of Houston).

Leonard Cohen: "For Anne" from *The Spice-Box of Earth* by Leonard Cohen. Copyright © 1961 by Leonard Cohen. Reprinted by permission of R K Management, LLC.

Wanda Coleman: "The ISM" from *Imagoes*. Reprinted by permission of the author.

Billy Collins: "The Names" reprinted by permission of the author.

Countee Cullen: "Incident" from *Color*, Copyright 1925 by Harper & Bros., NY. Copyrights held by the Amistad Research Center, Tulane University, Administered by Thompson and Thompson, Brooklyn, NY.

E.E. Cummings: "next to of course god america i," "l(a", "since feeling is first", "Buffalo Bill's," "in Just-," "anyone lived in a pretty how town" from Complete Poems: 1904–1962 by E.E. Cummings, edited by George J. Firmage. Copyright 1923, 1925, 1926, 1931, 1935, 1938, 1939, 1940, 1944, 1945, 1946, 1947, 1948, 1949, 1950, 1951, 1952, 1953, 1954, © 1955, 1956, 1957, 1958, 1959, 1960, 1961, 1962, 1963, 1966, 1967, 1968, 1972, 1973, 1974, 1975, 1976, 1977, 1978, 1979, 1980, 1981, 1982, 1983, 1984, 1985, 1986, 1987, 1988, 1989, 1990, 1991 by the Trustees for the E. E. Cummings Trust. Copyright © 1973, 1976, 1978, 1979, 1981, 1983, 1985, 1991 by George James Firmage. Used by permission of Liveright Publishing Corporation.

J.V. Cunningham: Epigram #9 and #24 from *The Poems of J.V. Cunningham*, edited with an Introduction and Commentary by Timothy Steele. Reprinted with the permission of Swallow Press/Ohio University Press, Athens, Ohio (www.ohioswallow.com).

William Dickey: "Therefore" from *The Rainbow Grocery*.

Emily Dickinson: "Because I could not stop for death," "I'm nobody! Who are you?" One need not be a chamber to be haunted," "There is no frigate like a book," "There's a certain slant of light," "I heard a fly buzz when I died," "Tell all the truth, but tell it slant," "The brain is wider than the sky," "A narrow fellow in the grass," "The difference between despair," "Safe in their alabaster chambers," "I died for beauty but was scarce," "Much madness is divinest sense," "Some keep the Sabbath going to church," "I started early, took my dog," "Wild nights! Wild nights!" "I felt a funeral in my brain," "The soul selects her own society," "I taste a liquor never brewed," "The bustle in a house," "Success is counted sweetest," "After great pain a formal feeling comes" reprinted by permission of the publishers and the Trustees of Amherst College from *The Poems of Emily Dickinson*, Thomas H. Johnson, ed., Cambridge, Mass: The Belknap Press of Harvard University Press, Copyright © 1951, 1955, 1979, 1983 by the President and Fellows of Harvard College.

Mark Doty: "Golden Retrievals" from *Sweet Machine* by Mark Doty. Copyright © 1998 by Mark Doty. Reprinted by permission of HarperCollins Publishers.

Rita Dove: "Flash Cards" from *Grace Notes* by Rita Dove. Copyright © 1989 by Rita Dove. Used by permission of the author and W. W. Norton & Company, Inc.

Alan Dugan: "Love Song: I and Thou" from *Poems Seven: New and Complete Poetry.* Copyright © 2001 by Alan Dugan. Reprinted with the permission of Seven Stories Press, www.sevenstories.com.

Stephen Dunn: "Poem for People That Are Understandably Too Busy to Read Poetry" from *Work and Love* by Stephen Dunn. Reprinted by permission of the author. "To a Terrorist" from *Between Angels* by Stephen Dunn. Copyright © 1989 by Stephen Dunn. "After" from *Different Hours* by Stephen Dunn. Copyright © 2000 by Stephen Dunn. Used by permission of W. W. Norton & Company, Inc.

T.S. Eliot: "The Love Song of J. Alfred Prufrock" from *Prufrock and Other Observations,* reprinted by permission of Faber and Faber Ltd.

Emily XYZ: "Ship of State of Fools" reprinted by permission of the author.

Louise Erdrich: "Dear John Wayne" from *Jacklight* by Louise Erdrich. Copyright © 1984 by Louise Erdrich, reprinted with permission of The Wylie Agency, Inc.

Rhina P. Espaillat: "Bilingual/Bilingue" from *Where Horizons Go.* Reprinted by permission of the author.

Mari Evans: "Spectrum" from *Where Is All the Music?*(1968). Copyright © Mari Evans.

Jesse Redmond Fauset: "Touché" in *Caroling Dusk,* edited, and with a foreword by Countee Cullen.

Kenneth Fearing: "AD" is reprinted by the permission of Russell & Volkening as agents for the author. Copyright © 1938 by Kenneth Fearing, renewed in 1966 by the Estate of Kenneth Fearing.

Carolyn Forché: "The Colonel" from *The Country Between Us* by Carolyn Forché. Copyright © 1981 by Carolyn Forché. Originally appeared in *Women's International Resource Exchange.* Reprinted by permission of HarperCollins Publishers. "The Museum of Stones" from *The New Yorker* March 26, 2007. Copyright © 2007 by Carolyn Forché. Reprinted by permission of William Morris Agency, LLC on behalf of the author.

Robert Frost: "Design," "Nothing Gold Can Stay," "Acquainted with the Night," "The Gift Outright," "Fire and Ice," "The Silken Tent," "Desert Places," "and "Come In" from *The Poetry of Robert Frost* edited by Edward Connery Lathem. Copyright 1923, 1928, 1969 by Henry Holt and Company, copyright 1936, 1942, 1951, 1956 by Robert Frost, copyright 1964, 1970 by Lesley Frost Ballantine. Reprinted by permission of Henry Holt and Company, LLC.

Erica Funkhouser: "First Pantoum of Summer" from *Earthly: Poems by Erica Funkhouser.* Copyright © 2008 by Erica Funkhouser. Reprinted by permission of Houghton Mifflin Harcourt Publishing Company. All rights reserved.

Allen Ginsberg: "A Supermarket in California" from *Collected Poems 1947–1980* by Allen Ginsberg. Copyright © 1955 by Allen Ginsberg. Reprinted by permission of HarperCollins Publishers.

Nikki Giovanni: "Knoxville, Tennessee" by Nikki Giovanni, reprinted by permission of the author.

Bhagavad Gita: "The Arjuna Speech" translated by Stephen Mitchell from *Bhagavad Gita* translated by Stephen Mitchell, copyright © 2000 by Stephen Mitchell. Used by permission of Harmony Books, a division of Random House, Inc.

Louise Glück: "Song of Obstacles" from *The First Four Books of Poems* by Louise Glück. Copyright 1968, 1971, 1972, 1973, 1974, 1975, 1976, 1977, 1978, 1979, 1980, 1985, 1995 by Louise Glück. Reprinted by permission of HarperCollins Publishers. *Firstborn, Descending Figure, House on Marshland, Triumph of Achilles,* Ecco Press.

Ray Gonzalez: "Corn Face Mesilla" from *Human Crying Daisies* by Ray Gonzalez. Reprinted by permission of Red Hen Press.

Lorna Goodison: "On Becoming a Tiger" from *Women's Worlds* by Lorna Goodison. Reprinted by permission of the author.

Linda Gregg: "Something Scary" Copyright © 2001 Linda Gregg. Reprinted from *Too Bright to See & Alma* by Linda Gregg with the permission of Graywolf Press, Saint Paul, Minnesota.

Angelina Weld Grimke: "Fragment" reprinted by permission of the Moorland-Spingarn Research Center, Howard University.

H.D. (Hilda Doolittle): "Heat" from *Collected Poems, 1912–1944,* copyright © 1982 by The Estate of Hilda Doolittle. Reprinted by permission of New Directions Publishing Corp.

Robert Hass: "Meditation at Lagunitas" from *Praise* by Robert Hass. Copyright © 1979 by Robert Hass. "Dragonflies Mating" from *Sun Under Wood: New Poems* by Robert Hass. Copyright © 1996 by Robert Hass. Reprinted by permission of HarperCollins Publishers." Tethered Horse" by Buson, "Don't worry, spiders" by Issa and "Kyoto," "a caterpillar" and "Deep autumn" by Basho from *The Essential Haiku: Versions of Basho, Buson & Issa,* edited with an Introduction by Robert Hass. Introduction and selection copyright © 1994 by Robert Hass. Unless otherwise noted, all translations copyright © 1994 by Robert Hass. All reprinted by permission of HarperCollins Publishers.

Marilyn Hacker: "Elektra on Third Avenue." Copyright © 1974 by Marilyn Hacker from *Selected Poems: 1965–1990* by Marilyn Hacker. Used by permission of W. W. Norton & Company, Inc.

Kimiko Hahn: "The Details We Fall For" from *Volatile.* Copyright ©1999 by Kimiko Hahn. Reprinted by permission of Hanging Loose Press.

Donald Hall: "Letter with No Address" from *Without: Poems* by Donald Hall. Copyright © 1998 by Donald Hall. Reprinted by permission of Houghton Mifflin Company. All rights reserved.

Joy Harjo: "Morning Song" from *A Map to the Next World: Poems and Tales* by Joy Harjo. Copyright © 2000 by Joy Harjo. Used by permission of W.W. Norton & Company, Inc.

Robert Hayden: "Those Winter Sundays," Copyright © 1966 by Robert Hayden, from *Collected Poems of Robert Hayden* by Robert Hayden, edited by Frederick Glaysher. Used by permission of Liveright Publishing Corporation.

Samuel Hazo: "Just Words" from *As They Sail.* Copyright © 1999 by Samuel Hazo. Reprinted with the permission of the University of Arkansas Press, www.uapress.com.

Seamus Heaney: "Digging" and "Mid-Term Break" from *Opened Ground: Selected Poems 1966–1996* by Seamus Heaney. Copyright © 1998 by Seamus Heaney. Reprinted by permission of Farrar, Straus and Giroux, LLC and Faber and Faber Limited.

Anthony Hecht: "The Dover Bitch" from *Collected Earlier Poems* by Anthony Hecht, copyright © 1990 by Anthony E. Hecht. Used by permission of Alfred A. Knopf, a division of Random House, Inc.

Gil Scott-Heron: "The Revolution Will Not Be Televised." Written by Gil Scott-Heron. Used by permission of Bienstock Publishing Company.

Juan Felipe Herrera: "Autobiography of a Chicano Teen Poet" from *187 Reasons Mexicans Cross the Border* by Juan Felipe Herrera. Reprinted by permission of City Lights Books.

Edward Hirsch: "My First Theology Lesson" from *Lay Back the Darkness: Poems* by Edward Hirsch. Copyright © 2003 by Edward Hirsch. Used by permission of Alfred A. Knopf, a division of Random House, Inc.

Hirshfield, Jane: "Tree" and "Button" from *Given Sugar, Given Salt* by Jane Hirshfield. Copyright © 2001 by Jane Hirshfield. Reprinted by permission of HarperCollins Publishers.

John Hollander: "Swan and the Shadow" from *Types of Shape* by John Hollander. Reprinted by permission of Yale University Press.

Marie Howe: "What the Living Do" from *What the Living Do* by Marie Howe. Copyright © 1997 by Marie Howe. Used by permission of W. W. Norton & Company, Inc.

Andrew Hudgins: "Elegy for My Father, Who Is Not Dead" from *The Never-Ending: New Poems* by Andrew Hudgins. Copyright © 1991 by Andrew Hudgins. Reprinted by permission of Houghton Mifflin Harcourt Publishing Company. All rights reserved.

Langston Hughes: "Po' Boy Blues," "The Dream Keeper," "I, Too," "Theme for English B," "The Negro Speaks of Rivers," "Mother to Son," "Let America Be America Again," "Harlem (2), " "Negro, " "Prayer [1]," "Motto," "Ballad of the Landlord," "A New Song," "Dream Boogie, "The Weary Blues,"

"Song for a Dark Girl," "Minstrel Man," "Night Funeral in Harlem," "The Blue," "Ardella" edited by Arnold Rampersad with David Roessel, Associate Editor, from *The Collected Poems of Langston Hughes* by Langston Hughes, edited by Arnold Rampersad with David Roessel, Associate Editor, copyright © 1994 by The Estate of Langston Hughes. Used by permission of Alfred A. Knopf, a division of Random House, Inc. Excerpt from "The Negro Artist and the Racial Mountain" Copyright 1926 by Langston Hughes. Reprinted by permission of Harold Ober Associates Incorporated. First published in *The Nation*.

Lawson Fusao Inada: "Grandmother" from *Drawing the Line* copyright © 1997 by Lawson Fusao Inada. Reprinted with the permission of Coffee House Press, Minneapolis, MN www.coffeehousepress.org.

Issa: "On a branch" by Kobayashi Issa, translation © 2004 Jane Hirshfield; used by permission of Jane Hirshfield.

Randall Jarrell: "The Death of the Ball Turret Gunner" from *The Complete Poems* by Randall Jarrell. Copyright © 1969, renewed, 1997 by Mary von S. Jarrell. Reprinted by permission of Farrar, Straus and Giroux, LLC.

Louis Jenkins: "Football" from *An Almost Human Gesture*, Eighties Press and Ally Press, 1987. Reprinted by permission of Louis Jenkins.

Donald Justice: "Pantoum of the Great Depression" from *New and Selected Poems* by Donald Justice, coypright © 1995 by Donald Justice. Used by permission of Alfred A. Knopf, a division of Random House, Inc.

Jane Kenyon: "The Suitor" and "The Blue Bowl" copyright © 1997 The Estate of Jane Kenyon. Reprinted from *Otherwise: New & Selected Poems* with the permission of Graywolf Press, Saint Paul, Minnesota.

Galway Kinnell: "After Making Love We Hear Footsteps" from *Mortal Acts, Mortal Words* by Galway Kinnell. Coyright © 1980 by Galway Kinnell. Reprinted by permission of Houghton Mifflin Harcourt Publishing Company. All rights reserved.

Yusef Komunyakaa: "Facing It" from *Dien Kai Dau*. © 1988 by Yusef Komunyakaa and reprinted by permission of Wesleyan University Press.

Maxine Kumin: "Saga" from *Poetry*, Fall 1991, reprinted by permission of Maxine Kumin and the Anderson Literary Agency, Inc.

J.D. Landis: "Starvation Diet" from *Cars on Mars*, reprinted by permission of the author.

Philip Larkin: "Aubade" from *Collected Poems* by Philip Larkin. Copyright © 1988, 2003 by the Estate of Philip Larkin. Reprinted by permission of Farrar, Straus and Giroux, LLC and Faber and Faber Limited.

Dorianne Laux: "The Shopfitter's Wife" from *Smoke*. Copyright © 2000 by Dorianne Laux. Reprinted with the permission of BOA Editions, Ltd., www.boaeditions.org.

Li-Young Lee: "Eating Together" and "Eating Alone" from *Rose*. Copyright © 1986 by Li-Young Lee. Reprinted by permission of BOA Editions, Ltd., www.boaeditions.org.

Denise Levertov: "The Ache of Marriage" by Denise Levertov from *Poems 1960–1967*, copyright © 1966 by Denise Levertov. Reprinted by permission of New Directions Publishing Corp.

Chen Li: "A War Symphony" from *The Edge of the Island* by Chen Li.

Shirley Geok-lin Lim: "Scavenging on a Double Bluff" from *Tilting the Continent* by Shirley Geok-lin Lim is reprinted by permission of the author.

Audre Lorde: "The Electric Slide Boogie" from *The Marvelous Arithmetics of Distance: Poems 1987–1992* by Audre Lorde. Copyright © 1993 by Audre Lorde. Used by permission of W. W. Norton & Company, Inc.

Thomas Lynch: "Liberty" and "Iambs for the day of burial" by Thomas Lynch. Reprinted by permission of the author.

Archibald MacLeish: "Ars Poetica" from *Collected Poems 1917–1982* by Archibald MacLeish. Copyright © 1985 by The Estate of Archibald MacLeish. Reprinted by permission of Houghton Mifflin Harcourt Publishing Company. All rights reserved.

Cleopatra Mathis: "Lilacs" from *Crazyhorse*, Spring 1982 is reprinted by permission of the author.

Gerda Mayer: "Narcissus" from *Monkey on the Analyst's Couch* by Gerda Mayer. Ceolfrith Press, 1980.

James Merrill: "The Victor Dog" from *Collected Poems* by James Merrill, edited by J. D. McClatchy and Stephen Yesner, copyright © 2001 by the Literary Estate of James Merrill at Washington University. Used by permission of Alfred A. Knopf, a division of Random House, Inc.

W.S. Merwin: "For the Anniversary of My Death" from *The Second Four Books of Poems* by W. S. Merwin. Copyright © 1967 by W. S. Merwin. Reprinted with permission of The Wylie Agency, Inc.

Charlotte Mew: "I So Liked Spring" from *Collected Poems & Selected Prose* by Charlotte Mew. Reprinted by permission of Carcanet Press Limited.

Edna St. Vincent Millay: "Not In A Silver Casket Cool With Pearls" copyright © 1921, 1931, 1948, 1958 by Edna St. Vincent Millay and Norma Millay Ellis. All rights reserved. Reprinted by permission of Elizabeth Barnett, Literary Executor, The Millay Society.

Czeslaw Milosz: "Encounter" from *The Collected Poems: 1931–1987* by Czeslaw Milosz. Copyright © 1988 by Czeslaw Milosz Royalties, Inc.

Gabriella Mistral: "Fugitive Woman" from *Madwomen*, reprinted by permission of the University of Chicago Press.

Marianne Moore: "The Fish" reprinted with the permission of Scribner, a Division of Simon & Schuster, Inc., from *The Collected Poems of Marianne Moore* by Marianne Moore. Copyright © 1935 by Marianne Moore. Copyright renewed © 1963 by Marianne Moore & T.S. Eliot. All rights reserved.

Paul Muldoon: "Symposium" from *Poems: 1968–1998* by Paul Muldoon. Copyright © 2001 by Paul Muldoon. Reprinted by permission of Farrar, Straus and Giroux, LLC. This poem originally appeared in *The New Yorker*.

Marilyn Nelson Waniek: "Chopin" from *The Homeplace*, reprinted by permission of Louisiana State University Press from *The Homeplace: Poems by Marilyn Nelson Waniek*. Copyright © 1990 by Marilyn Nelson Waniek.

Howard Nemerov: "The Blue Swallows" from *The Blue Swallows: The Collected Poems of Howard Nemerov*. Reprinted by permission of Margaret Nemerov.

Pablo Neruda: "Sonnet LXVI" from *100 Love Sonnets: Cien Sonetos De Amor* by Pablo Neruda, translated by Stephen Tapscott. Copyright © Pablo Neruda 1959 and Fundacion Pablo Neruda, Copyright © 1986 by the University of Texas Press. By permission of the University of Texas Press. "The Stolen Branch" by Pablo Neruda, translated by Donald D. Walsh, from *The Captain's Verses*, copyright © 1972 by Pablo Neruda and Donald D. Walsh. Reprinted by permission of New Directions Publishing Corp.

Naomi Shihab Nye: "The World in Translation" from *Words Under the Words: Selected Poems*, by Naomi Shihab Nye. Reprinted by permission of the author.

Sharon Olds: "Sex Without Love" from *The Dead and the Living* by Sharon Olds, copyright © 1987 by Sharon Olds. Used by permission of Alfred A. Knopf, a division of Random House, Inc.

Mary Oliver: "At Blackwater Pond" from *New and Selected Poems* by Mary Oliver. Copyright © 1992 by Mary Oliver. Reprinted by permission of Beacon Press, Boston.

Michael Ondaatje: "Sweet Like a Crow" from *Running in the Family*, copyright © 1982 Michael Ondaatje. Reprinted by permission of Michael Ondaatje. Trident Media Group, LLC.

Jacqueline Osherow: "Sonnet for the Music in the Warsaw Ghetto" from *With a Moon in Transit* by Jacqueline Osherow. Copyright © 1996 by Jacqueline Osherow. Used by permission of Grove/Atlantic.

Grace Paley: "Here" from *Begin Again: Collected Poems* by Grace Paley. Copyright © 2000 by Grace Paley. Reprinted by permission of Farrar, Straus and Giroux, LLC.

Dorothy Parker: "Sonnet for the End of a Sequence" from *The Portable Dorothy Parker* by Dorothy Parker, edited by Marion Meade, copyright 1928, renewed © 1956 by Dorothy Parker. Used by permission of Viking Penguin, a division of Penguin Group (USA) Inc.

Linda Pastan: "Jump Cabling" from *Light Year 85* by Linda Pastan. Reprinted by permission of Jean V. Naggar Literary Agency, Inc. "Ethics" from *Waiting for My Life* by Linda Pastan. Copyright © 1981 by Linda Pastan. Used by permission of W. W. Norton & Company, Inc.

Octavio Paz: "Motion" translated by Eliot Weinberger, from *The Collected Poems of Octavio Paz 1957–1987*, copyright © 1986 by Octavio Paz and

Eliot Weinberger. Reprinted by permission of New Directions Publishing Corp.

Molly Peacock: "Desire" from *Cornucopia: New and Selected Poems* by Molly Peacock. Copyright © 2000 by Molly Peacock. Used by permission of W. W. Norton & Company, Inc.

Willie Perdomo: "Postcards of El Barrio" from *Where a Nickel Costs a Dime* by Willie Perdomo. Copyright © 1996 by Willie Perdomo. Used by permission of W. W. Norton & Company, Inc. NA

Laurence Perrine: "The limerick's never averse" reprinted by permission of Doug Perrine.

Marge Piercy: "The secretary chant" from *Circles on the Water* by Marge Piercy, copyright © 1982 by Marge Piercy. Used by permission of Alfred A. Knopf, a division of Random House, Inc.

Robert Pinsky: "Shirt" from *The Want Bone* by Robert Pinsky. Copyright © 1990 by Robert Pinsky. Pinsky. Reprinted by permission of HarperCollins Publishers. "Sonnet" from *The Figured Wheel: New and Collected Poems 1966–1996* by Robert Pinsky. Copyright © 1996 by Robert Pinsky. "To Television" from *Jersey Rain* by Robert Pinsky. Copyright © 2000 by Robert Pinsky. Reprinted by permission of Farrar, Straus and Giroux, LLC.

Sylvia Plath: "Daddy" from *Ariel* by Sylvia Plath. Copyright © 1963 by Ted Hughes. "Metaphors" and "Mirrors" from *Crossing the Water* by Sylvia Plath. Copyright © 1971 by Ted Hughes. Reprinted by permission of HarperCollins Publishers and Faber and Faber Ltd.

Dudley Randall: "Ballad of Birmingham" from *Cities Burning* by Dudley Randall. Reprinted by permission of Broadside Press.

Henry Reed: "Naming of Parts" from *A Map of Verona.* Reprinted by permission of The Royal Literary Fund.

Adrienne Rich: "Aunt Jennifer's Tigers" copyright © 2002, 1951 by Adrienne Rich. "Living in Sin" copyright © 2002, 1955 by Adrienne Rich. "Diving into the Wreck" copyright © 2002 by Adrienne Rich. Copyright © 1973 by W. W. Norton & Company, Inc. from *The Fact of a Doorframe: Selected Poems 1950–2001* by Adrienne Rich. Used by permission of the author and W. W. Norton & Company, Inc.

Ranier Maria Rilke: "Archaic Torso of Apollo" from *The Selected Poetry of Ranier Maria Rilke* by Ranier Maria Rilke, translated by Stephen Mitchell. Used by permission of Random House, Inc.

Alberto Rios: "Nani" from *Whispering to Fool the Wind* by Alberto Ríos. Reprinted by permission of the author.

Theodore Roethke: "My Papa's Waltz", copyright 1942 by Hearst Magazines, Inc. "Root Cellar" copyright 1943 by Modern Poetry Association, Inc. "Elegy for Jane," copyright 1950 by Theodore Roethke, from *Collected Poems of Theodore Roethke* by Theodore Roethke. Used by permission of Doubleday, a division of Random House, Inc.

Wendy Rose: "Leaving Port Authority for the St. Regis Rez" from *What the Mohawk Made the Hopi Say* by Wendy Rose. Reprinted by permission of the author.

Rumi: "Some Kiss We Want" from *The Soul of Rumi: A New Collection of Ecstatic Poems,* translated by Coleman Barks. Copyright © 2001 by Coleman Barks. Reprinted by permission of HarperCollins Publishers.

Mary Jo Salter: "Video Blues" from *A Kiss in Space: Poems* by Mary Jo Salter, copyright © 1999 by Mary Jo Salter. Used by permission of Alfred A. Knopf, a division of Random House, Inc.

Sonia Sanchez: "Poem at Thirty" from *I've Been a Woman,* copyright © 1978, 1985 by Sonia Sanchez. Reprinted by permission of Third World Press, Inc., Chicago, Illinois

Carole Satyamurti: "I Shall Paint My Nails Red" from Carole Satyamurti, *Stitching the Dark: New & Selected Poems* (Bloodaxe Books, 2005). Reprinted by permission of Bloodaxe Books.

Gjertrud Schnackenberg: "Snow Melting" from *Supernatural Love: Poems 1976–1992* by Gjertrud Schnackenberg. Copyright © 2000 by Gjertrud Schnackenberg. Reprinted by permission of Farrar, Straus and Giroux, LLC.

Anne Sexton: "Letter Written on a Ferry While Crossing Long Island Sound" from *All My Pretty Ones* by Anne Sexton. Copyright © 1962 by Anne Sexton, renewed 1990 by Linda G. Sexton. Reprinted by permission of Houghton Mifflin Harcourt Company.

Julie Sheehan: "Hate Poem" from *Orient Point* by Julie Sheehan. Copyright © 2006 by Julie Sheehan. Used by permission of W. W. Norton & Company, Inc.

Jane Shore: "My Mother's Chair" from *A Yes or No Answer: Poems* by Jane Shore. Copyright © 2008 by Jane Shore. Reprinted by permission of Houghton Mifflin Harcourt Company. All rights reserved

Marc Smith: "Dusty Blues" and "The Father Has Faded" from *Crowdpleaser* by Marc Smith. Copyright © 1996. Reprinted by permission of the author.

Cathy Song: "Girl Powdering Her Neck" from *Picture Bride* by Cathy Song. Copyright © 1983. Reprinted by permission of Yale University Press.

Gary Soto: "Mexicans Begin Jogging" from *New and Selected Poems* © 1995 by Gary Soto. Used with permission of Chronicle Books LLC, San Francisco. ChronicleBooks.com. "Saturday at the Canal" from *A Fire in My Hands* by Gary Soto. Copyright © 2006, 1999 by Gary Soto. Reprinted by permission of Houghton Mifflin Harcourt Company. All rights reserved.

William Stafford: "Traveling Through the Dark" copyright 1998 The Estate of William Stafford. Reprinted from *The Way It Is: New & Selected Poems* with the permission of Graywolf Press, Saint Paul, Minnesota.

Robert Sward: "God is in the Cracks" from *God is in the Cracks* by Robert Sward. Reprinted by permission of the author.

The Last Poets: "My People" by The Last Poets.

Dylan Thomas: "Vision and Prayer (part I)" copyright © 1946 by New Directions Publishing Corp. "Do Not Go Gentle Into That Good Night" copyright © 1952 by Dylan Thomas. Both poems from *The Poems of Dylan Thomas.* Reprinted by permission of New Directions Publishing Corp.

Jean Toomer: "Reapers" from *Cane* by Jean Toomer. Copyright 1923 by Boni & Liveright, renewed 1951 by Jean Toomer. Used by permission of Liveright Publishing Corporation.

Natasha Trethewey: "Letter Home" copyright 2002 Natasha Trethewey. Reprinted from *Bellocq's Ophelia* with the permission of Graywolf Press, Saint Paul, Minnesota.

Quincy Troupe: "Poem Reaching Toward Something" from *Transcircularities: New & Selected Poems.* Copyright © 2001 Quincy Troupe. Reprinted with the permission of Coffee House Press, www.coffeehousepress.com.

Diane Wakoski: "Inside Out" from *Emerald Ice: Selected Poems 1962–1987* by Diane Wakoski. Reprinted by permission of Black Sparrow Books, an imprint of David R. Godine, Publishers, Inc. Copyright © 1988 by Diane Wakoski.

Anne Waldman: "Bluehawk" is reprinted by permission of the author.

Richard Wilbur: "The Writer" from *The Mind-Reader,* copyright © 1971 and renewed 1999 by Richard Wilbur, reprinted by permission of Houghton Mifflin Harcourt Publishing Company.

Nancy Willard: "Saint Pumpkin" from *Swimming Lessons: New and Selected Poems* by Nancy Willard, copyright © 1966 by Nancy Willard. Used by permission of Alfred A. Knopf, a division of Random House, Inc.

William Carlos Williams: "Spring and All: Section I" "The Red Wheelbarrow," and "This Is Just to Say" by William Carlos Williams, from *The Collected Poems: Volume I 1909–1939,* copyright © 1938 by New Directions Publishing Corp. Reprinted by permission of New Directions Publishing Corp.

C.K. Williams: "Tar" from *Collected Poems* by C.K. Williams. Copyright © 2006 by C.K. Williams Reprinted by permission of Farrar, Straus and Giroux, LLC.

David Wojahn: "The Assassination of John Lennon as Depicted by the Madame Tussaud Wax Museum, Niagara Falls, Ontario, 1987" from *Mystery Train,* by David Wojhan, © 1990. Reprinted by permission of the University of Pittsburgh Press.

James Wright: "Lying in a Hammock at William Duffy's Farm in Pine Island, Minnesota" from *Above the River: The Complete Poems* © 1963 by James Wright and reprinted by permission of Wesleyan University Press. "Autumn Begins in Martin's Ferry, Ohio" and "A Blessing" from *The Branch Will Not Break.* © 1963 by James Wright and reprinted by permission of Wesleyan University Press.

W. B. Yeats: "Leda and the Swan" and "Sailing to Byzantium" reprinted with the permission of Scribner, a Division of Simon & Schuster Adult Publishing Group, from *The Complete Works of W.B. Yeats, Volume I: The Poems,* edited by Richard J Finneran, copyright © 1928 by The Macmillan Company. Copyright renewed © 1956 by Georgie Yeats. "Crazy Jane Talks with the Bishop" from *The Complete Works of W. B. Yeats, Volume I: The Poems,* edited by Richard J. Finneran. Copyright © 1933 by The Macmillan Company. Copyright renewed © 1961 by Bertha Georgie Yeats. "The Second Coming" from *The Complete Works of W. B. Yeats, Volume I: The Poems,* edited by Richard J. Finneran. Copyright © 1924 by The Macmillan Company. Copyright renewed © 1952 by Bertha Georgie Yeats. All rights reserved.

Kevin Young: "Jook" from *Jelly Roll* by Kevin Young, copyright © 2003 by Kevin Young. Used by permission of Alfred A. Knopf, a division of Random House, Inc.

Al Young: "Doo Wop: The Moves" from *Coastal Nights and Inland Afternoons: Poems 2001–2006* by Al Young. Angel City Press. Reprinted by permission of the author.

# Photo Credits

**Page ii–iii:** (Red Door) Mark Lewis/Getty Images, (Field of Sunflowers) Herbert Kehrer/Zefa/Corbis, (Sunflower) Brand X Pictures/Punchstock, (Woman) Photo of Jasmin Tokatlian courtesy of Miroslav Wiesner; **2:** 2002 Watson & Spierman/Jupiterimages; **3:** Tim McGuire/Corbis; **5:** Brand X Pictures/PunchStock; **5:** The McGraw-Hill Companies, Inc/Ken Karp photographer; **9:** LOC [LC-USZ62-42949]; **10:** Pach Brothers/Corbis; **11:** Kaz Chiba/Getty Images; **12T:** EclectiCollections/Fotosearch; **12B:** Royalty-Free/Corbis; **14T:** University of Texas' Perry Castaneda collection; **14B:** Getty Images; **16T:** Jon Chase photo/Harvard News Office; **16B:** Ingram Publishing/AGE Fotosearch; **17:** Library of Congress (LOC) [LC-USZ62-87604]; **20:** The McGraw-Hill Companies, Inc./Ken Cavanagh Photographer; **21:** Stockbyte; **22:** Robert Levin/Corbis; **23:** DLILLC/Corbis; **27:** AP Photo; **28:** Ingram Publishing/SuperStock; **29:** LOC [LC-USZ62-87604]; **30:** Fototeca Storica Nazionale/Getty Images; **32:** LOC [LC-USZ61-307]; **33:** Kaz Chiba/Getty Images; **35T:** LOC [LC-USZ62-123319]; **35B:** Ingram Publishing/Alamy; **39:** Design Pics/PunchStock; **41:** LOC [LC-USZ62-48982]; **42:** Royalty-Free/Corbis; **46:** Gay Bumgarner/Getty Images; **47:** 2008 Jupiterimages; **49T:** Burke Triolo Productions/Getty Images; **49B:** C Squared Studios/Getty Images ; **64:** Eiji Yanagi/Photonica/Getty Images; **65:** Photodisc/PunchStock; **69:** LOC [LC-USZ62-70369]; **72T:** LOC [LC-USZ62-93465]; **72B:** Digital Vision/ Getty Images; **74:** Royalty-Free/Corbis; **75:** LOC [LC-USZC4-6527]; **76:** C Squared Studios/Getty Images; **77:** LOC [LC-USZ62-36767]; **79:** Image Club ; **83:** PhotoLink/Getty Images; **84:** Stockbyte; **85:** Imagestate Media (John Foxx)/Imagestate; **87T:** LOC [LC-USZ62-120744]; **87B:** Brand X Pictures/PunchStock; **90:** The McGraw-Hill Companies, Inc./Lars A. Niki; **91T:** LOC [LC-DIG-cwpbh-00752]; **91B:** LOC [LC-DIG-ppmsca-08969]; **92:** Royalty-Free/Corbis; **94:** Library of Congress, Prints and Photographs Division [LC-DIG-ppmsca-09854] ; **105:** Jupiterimages/Imagesource; **102:** Drew Kelly Photography/zefa/Corbis; **103:** Bananastock/Jupiterimages; **110:** Imagestate Media (John Foxx)/Imagestate; **111:** Digital Vision/ PunchStock ; **113:** iStockphoto.com/Viktor Pravdi; **116T:** LOC [SWANN - no. 775f]; **116B:** Photodisc; **119:** Brand X Pictures/PunchStock; **120:** Photodisc/Getty Images; **121T:** Photo by Fred Viebahn; **121B:** Chet Phillips/ Getty Images; **122:** Photo by Mark Lacy; **123:** Brand X Pictures/PunchStock; **124:** Photo by Charlie M. P. Sirait; **125:** Brand X Pictures; **126T:** LOC [LC-USZ62-87604]; **126B:** Royalty-Free/Corbis; **131:** LOC [LC-USZ62-108239]; **133:** JupiterImages ; **134:** LOC [LC-USZ62-108026]; **135:** Royalty-Free/Corbis; **136:** iStockphoto.com/Diana Didyk; **138:** Iceberg: Digital Vision/Getty Images; **138:** Jewel: Brand X Pictures/PunchStock; **144:** Huntstock, Inc/Alamy; **144:** Tooga/The Image Bank/Getty Images; **144:** Andy Ryan/Riser/Getty Images; **147:** 1995 Zedcor, Inc.; **148:** iStockphoto.com/Once Upon a Time Creations; **149:** Anthony Ise/Getty Images; **154:** LOC [LC-USZ62-109601]; **155:** iStockphoto.com/Radient Byte; **157:** Courtesy of Donald Hall; **158:** Hemera Technologies/Alamy; **159:** LOC [LC-USZ62-93465]; **160:** Brueghel, Pieter the Elder (c.1525-1569). Landscape with the Fall of Icarus. Musee d'Art Ancien, Musees Royaux des Beaux-Arts, Brussels, Belgium. Photo Credit : Scala/Art Resource, NY; **161:** Courtesy of Peter Smith; **162:** Edward Hopper (American, 1882-1967). Automat. 1927. Oil on canvas; 36 x 28 1/8 in. Des Moines Art Center Permanent Collections; Purchased with fund from the Edmundson Art Foundation, Inc., 1958.2.; **163:** Courtesy of Douglas Davenport; **164:** Kitagawa Utamaro (1753-1806). Woman Powdering Her Neck. Musee des Arts Asiatiques-Guimet, Paris, France. Photo Credit: Réunion des Musées Nationaux/Art Resource, NY; **176:** Rick Lew/Getty Images; **177:** Bill Stormont/Corbis; **179:** LOC [LC-USZ62-93789] ; **180:** The McGraw-Hill Companies, Inc./Lars A. Niki, photographer; **182:** IT Stock/PunchStock; **183B:** Purestock/PunchStock; **185:** Glenn Mitsui/Getty Images; **186T:** Photo by Donald Hall; **186B:** Rim Light/PhotoLink/Getty Images; **187:** Imagestate Media (John Foxx)/Imagestate; **189T:** Courtesy of Oliver Pastan; **189B:** Comstock/JupiterImages; **190T:** Courtesy of Paul Muldoon; **190B:** Royalty-Free/Corbis; **192:** image100/PunchStock; **195T :** University of Texas' Perry Castaneda Collection; **195B:** Andrew Ward/Life File/Getty Images; **196T:** LOC [LC-USZ62-103583]; **196B:** Don Bishop/Getty Images; **198:** Kaz Chiba/Getty Images; **199:** Burke/Triolo Productions/Getty Images; **200T:** LOC [LC-USZ62-87604]; **202T:** Courtesy of the Division of Rare and Manuscript Collections, Cornell University Library; **202B:** Ryan McVay/Getty Images; **203:** Photo by Miles Thorsen.; **204:** Ingram Publishing/AGE Fotostock; **210:** Tom Grill/Corbis; **211R:** simple stock shots/ Getty; **211L:** Guy Thouvenin/Photolibrary; **213:** D. Normark/PhotoLink/ Getty Images; **217:** iStockphoto.com/Robert Pinna; **223:** LOC [LC-USZ62-101955]; **224:** Royalty-Free/Corbis; **225:** LOC [LC-USZ62-90564]; **226:** Photodisc/Getty Images; **230:** Nick Koudis/Getty Images; **235:** Digital Vision/PunchStock; **242:** Chris Stein/Digital Vision/Getty Images; **243:** Gil Cohen Magen/Reuters/Corbis; **245:** PhotoLink/Getty Images; **250T:** LOC [LC-DIG-ggbain-03571]; **250B:** Digital Vision/PunchStock; **251:** LOC [LC-USZ62-70369]; **252:** Brand X Pictures/PunchStock; **253:** LOC [LC-USZC4-6527]; **254:** Mel Curtis/Getty Images; **255B:** Sharon Hudson/Corbis; **258T:** LOC [LC-USZ62-70369]; **258B:** ©iStockphoto.com/René Mansi; **260:** Laurent Hamels/Photoalto/PictureQuest; **261:** Creatas Images/Punchstock; **263B:** LOC, FSA/OWI Collection, [LC-DIG-fsa-8a26538]; **264:** Photo by Nubar Alexanian; **265:** Punchstock/Image Source; **267:** Harnett/Hanzon/Getty Images; **268B:** Royalty-Free/Corbis; **269T:** Kaz Chiba/Getty Images; **269M:** Courtesy of the Division of Rare and Manuscript Collections, Cornell University Library; **269B:** Creatas/ PunchStock; **271:** 1995 Zedcor, Inc.; **273:** Ingram Publishing/SuperStock; **274:** LOC [LC-USZ62-93465]; **275:** Doug Sherman/Geofile; **277:** iStockphoto.com/AJ Studios; **278:** NPS photo by R. Lake; **279:** iStockphoto.com/

Cunfek; **288:** Fresh Food Images/Photolibrary; **289:** Visuals Unlimited/Getty Images; **291:** PhotoAlto/PunchStock; **293T:** LOC [LC-DIG-cwpbh-00752]; **293B:** Royalty-Free/Corbis; **295:** Kim Steele/Getty Images; **296:** LOC [LC-USZC4-5181]; **298T:** LOC [LC-USZ62-111603]; **298B:** PhotoAlto/Glasshouse Images; **299:** Courtesy of Wild Duck Review; **300:** Adam Crowley/Getty Images; **301:** Photo by Catherine Mauger; **302:** Brand X Pictures/PunchStock; **303:** Don Hamerman Photography; **304:** Digital Vision/Getty Images; **305:** MedioImages/PunchStock; **307:** iStockphoto.com/Eric Etman; **313:** LOC [LC-USZ62-78972]; **315B:** iStockphoto.com/Lepas2004; **316:** Comstock/PunchStock; **317T:** Courtesy of Ray Gonzalez; **317B:** PhotoLink/Getty Images; **326:** Blend Images/Hill Street Studios/Veer; **327:** Michael Ochs Archives/Getty Images; **329:** Jupiterimages/Brand X Pictures; **331:** Andy Sotiriou/Getty Images; **333:** Digital Vision; **335:** The Palma Collection/Getty Images; **336T:** LOC [LC-USZC4-6527]; **336B:** Royalty-Free/Corbis; **338:** Angelo Cavalli/Getty Images; **339T:** Photo by Paul Abdoo; **339B:** PhotoLink/Getty Images; **341:** Tim Hall/Getty Images; **342:** Digital Vision; **343:** Courtesy of Marc Smith; **344:** Darren Hopes/Getty Images; **345:** Courtesy of Kenneth Carroll; **346:** Fancy/Veer; **347T:** Darren Hopes/Getty Images; **347B:** © Richard Green; **348T:** Pixtal/SuperStock; **348B:** Courtesy of Emily XYZ; **349:** MIXA/PunchStock; **356:** Ingram Publishing/AGE Fotostock; **358L:** Michael Ochs Archives/Getty Images; **358R:** Michael Ochs Archives/Getty Images; **359L:** LOC [LC-USZ62-123107]; **359R:** LOC [LC-USZ62-129808]; **360:** LOC [LC-USZ62-111447]; **361T:** Bruce Heinemann/Getty Images; **361B:** Philip Coblentz/Brand X Pictures/PictureQuest; **362:** Punchstock/Stockbyte; **363T:** Digital Vision/Getty Images; **363B:** Brand X Pictures/PunchStock; **364T:** LOC [LC-USZC4-2814]; **364B:** Getty Images/Stockbyte; **365:** Steve Hamblin/Alamy; **366:** Lisa Zador/Getty Images; **367T:** PhotoAlto; **367B:** Darren Hopes/Getty Images; **368:** D. Falconer/PhotoLink/Getty Images; **371:** LOC [LC-USZ62-42529]; **372:** Image Source/PunchStock; **373T:** Lifesize/Getty Images; **373B:** LOC [LC-USZ62-105919]; **374:** Jack Hollingsworth/Corbis; **375:** Anthony Saint James/Getty Images; **376:** iStockphoto.com/Peeter Viisimaa; **369:** Royalty-Free/Corbis; **370:** Brian Barneclo; **380 - 381:** LOC, The Lessing J. Rosenwald Collection; **381:** LOC, The Lessing J. Rosenwald Collection; **382:** NMPFT/RPS/SSPL/The Image Works;**383:** LOC [LC-USZ62-64309]; **384:** LOC [LC-USZ62-103583]; **386 - 397:** LOC, The Lessing J. Rosenwald Collection; **400:** James Marshall/Corbis; **401:** Time & Life Pictures/Getty Images; **402:** Royalty-Free/Corbis; **403:** Digital Vision/PunchStock; **404T:** LOC [LC-USZ62-90564]; **404B:** Digital Vision/Getty Images; **405L:** Creatas/Punchstock; **405R:** Royalty-Free/Corbis; **406:** Ingram Publishing/SuperStock; **407T:** Ingram Publishing/AGE Fotostock; **407B:** Digital Vision/PunchStock; **408:** Getty Images; **409L:** IT Stock Free/Alamy; **409R:** Royalty-Free/Corbis; **410:** Royalty-Free/Corbis; **411L:** Corbis; **411R:** Ryan McVay/Getty Images; **412T:** Digital Vision Ltd./SuperStock; **412B:** LOC [LC-USZ62-120744]; **413:** Pixtal/age fotostock; **414:** PhotoLink/Getty Images; **415:** Brand X Pictures/Punchstock; **416T:** Design Pics/PunchStock; **416B:** Royalty-Free/Corbis; **417L:** iStockphoto.com/kirschbam; **417R:** Digital Vision; **421:** Raymond Forbes/AGE Fotostock/Photolibrary; **H-1:** Andre Jenny/Alamy; **H-97:** Michael Ochs Archives /Getty Images; **H-98:** Frank Driggs Collection/Getty Images; **H-107:** "Book Cover" © 2000 from, FROM SLAVERY TO FREEDOM BY John H. Franklin and Evelyn Higginbotham. Used by permission of the McGraw-Hill Companies.

# Index

Note: Page references in **boldface** refer to literary works included in their entirety.

# NOTES

# NOTES

# NOTES

# NOTES

# About the Authors

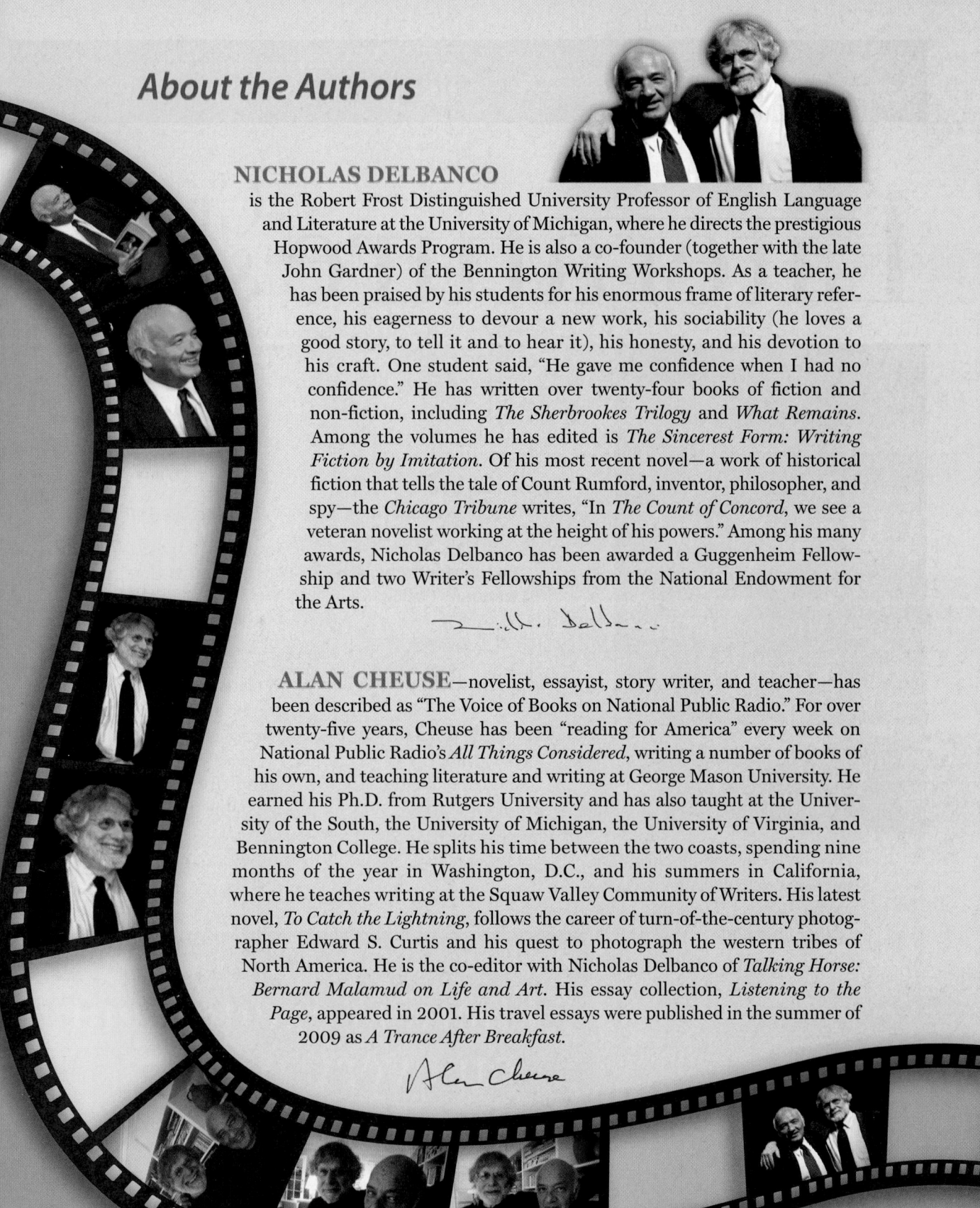

**NICHOLAS DELBANCO** is the Robert Frost Distinguished University Professor of English Language and Literature at the University of Michigan, where he directs the prestigious Hopwood Awards Program. He is also a co-founder (together with the late John Gardner) of the Bennington Writing Workshops. As a teacher, he has been praised by his students for his enormous frame of literary reference, his eagerness to devour a new work, his sociability (he loves a good story, to tell it and to hear it), his honesty, and his devotion to his craft. One student said, "He gave me confidence when I had no confidence." He has written over twenty-four books of fiction and non-fiction, including *The Sherbrookes Trilogy* and *What Remains*. Among the volumes he has edited is *The Sincerest Form: Writing Fiction by Imitation*. Of his most recent novel—a work of historical fiction that tells the tale of Count Rumford, inventor, philosopher, and spy—the *Chicago Tribune* writes, "In *The Count of Concord*, we see a veteran novelist working at the height of his powers." Among his many awards, Nicholas Delbanco has been awarded a Guggenheim Fellowship and two Writer's Fellowships from the National Endowment for the Arts.

**ALAN CHEUSE**—novelist, essayist, story writer, and teacher—has been described as "The Voice of Books on National Public Radio." For over twenty-five years, Cheuse has been "reading for America" every week on National Public Radio's *All Things Considered*, writing a number of books of his own, and teaching literature and writing at George Mason University. He earned his Ph.D. from Rutgers University and has also taught at the University of the South, the University of Michigan, the University of Virginia, and Bennington College. He splits his time between the two coasts, spending nine months of the year in Washington, D.C., and his summers in California, where he teaches writing at the Squaw Valley Community of Writers. His latest novel, *To Catch the Lightning*, follows the career of turn-of-the-century photographer Edward S. Curtis and his quest to photograph the western tribes of North America. He is the co-editor with Nicholas Delbanco of *Talking Horse: Bernard Malamud on Life and Art*. His essay collection, *Listening to the Page*, appeared in 2001. His travel essays were published in the summer of 2009 as *A Trance After Breakfast*.

Student Praise for

# Literature | Craft & Voice

Hundreds of students have compared Literature: Craft & Voice to their current literature text.

## WHAT STUDENTS HAVE TO SAY

'It is very interesting and modern. Readers will actually enjoy reading the stories ... I love this literature book."

–WHITLEY COPE,
Tulsa Community College

---

"Breaking the book into three volumes is genius. One huge book can be much harder to navigate."

–MATT LITTREL,
Midlands Technical College

"*Literature: Craft & Voice* has a distinct quality of invitation... It feels less like a strict textbook and more like a suggested recreational reading book, which I appreciate and enjoy."

–VINCENT NUNCHUCK,
Saint Johns River Community College

---

"*[Literature: Craft & Voice]* gives a more detailed understanding about literature. It's like it actually puts you in the middle of the stories."

–CHRISTA ALLEN,
Tarrant County College

"I would choose to continue reading this text because it's more fun to read; the pictures and images in the text catch your eye and help [you] relate to the text."

–LEONIDES LOPEZ,
LaGuardia Community College

---

"*Craft & Voice* ...makes the reading a little easier to tackle... Being a student with specific learning issues ... I was motivated to jump into the reading in the *Craft & Voice* book."

–JESSICA LONGO,
County College of Morris

"There is excitement on every page."

–TYLER COOK,
Midlands Technical College

A SPECIAL THANK YOU FROM THE AUTHORS ...

Nicholas DELBANCO

Alan CHEUSE

"We wish to express our gratitude to all the professors who shared our texts with their students and provided us with invaluable feedback."

PAUL ANDREWS, Saint Johns River Community College • CHRISTIAN CLARK, College of Southern Nevada • CHAD HAMMETT, Texas State University • MELODY HARGRAVES, Saint Johns River Community College • REBECCA HEINTZ, Polk Community College • HEIDI JOHNSEN, LaGuardia Community College • RUTH McADAMS, Tarrant County College • LOUISE McKINNEY, Georgia Perimeter College • DOROTHY MINOR, Tulsa Community College • DEBORAH PRICKETT, Jacksonville State University • KATHY SANCHEZ, Lone Star College—Tomball • LINDA SMITH, Midlands Technical College • JIM RAWLINS, Sussex County Community College • BILL STEPHENSON, Santa Fe College • JANE WILLIAMS, Arizona Western College • ROD WOEHLER, Santa Fe College • SANDER ZULAUF, County College of Morris

## STUDENT PRAISE FOR CONVERSATIONS ON WRITING

"It was very helpful and interesting to hear the story being told by the author. Hearing the author makes [the story] easier to understand."

–MAYGEN EUBANKS,
Tarrant County College

"We watched the author video before we had to write our first paper and how much I could relate to him just amazed me."

–JOSH POWELL,
Saint Johns River Community College

---

"Hearing the story being read by the author gave me a different perspective and allowed me to understand the text in a different way."

–TOMMY MODERIE,
Santa Fe College

"I was drawn to the author's speech and the way that she read her story. It makes me understand the author better because now I get to see the author explain her own story and her reasons for writing it. She describes and goes into detail about herself personally, and her background, which opens me up to the author."

–LARRY ODELUSI,
Tarrant County College

# Conversations on Writing

**CHAPTER 1** John Updike
**Reading a Story for Its Elements**
*"Your job as a writer of fiction is not to present an ideal world but to try to present the world that you see and hear around you."*

**CHAPTER 2** Richard Ford
**Going Further with Reading**
*"Writing stories is much more mosaical than it is linear."*

Amy Tan
*"I think of fiction as being subversive in a good way. It seduces you."*

**CHAPTER 3** Jamaica Kincaid
**Writing about Fiction**
*"The advice I would give anyone who wants to write is: Read a lot."*

**CHAPTER 4** T. Coraghessan Boyle
**Plot**
*"You don't really know what the story means until you have written it, and until you find out what the ending is."*

**CHAPTER 5** Gish Jen
**Character**
*"I think [character's] where the conflict comes from and I think it's where the plot comes from: that's where the story comes from."*

**CHAPTER 6** Barry Lopez
**Setting**
*"I think setting is often part of what determines the nature of the story, and the nature of the characters."*

**CHAPTER 7** ZZ Packer
**Point of View**
*"I think that in the end voice and craft together can make for an incredibly powerful story, because you end up using all your tools of craft to render a voice believable."*

**CHAPTER 8** Aimee Bender
**Language, Tone, and Style**
*"There isn't a story that doesn't have tone or theme. Those are just things that come from the language itself."*

**CHAPTER 9** Chimamanda Ngozi Adichie
**Theme**
*"If I must think in terms of theme, I would think about multiple themes, that a story can do so many things at the same time."*

**CHAPTER 10** Tim O'Brien
**Symbol**
*"Symbolism has to do with what objects of the world end up meaning to us. The object has meaning, has resonance and has echoes, and that's what symbolism for me really is."*

**CHAPTER 11** Joyce Carol Oates
**Fiction As Social Commentary**
*"I've always been very interested in holding a kind of mirror, sometimes a slightly distorting mirror, up to contemporary American society."*

**CHAPTER 12** William Kittredge
**American Regionalism and Sense of Place**
*"I think one of the ways to not somehow lose track of your dreams is to keep expanding what you see and find in the world."*

Dagoberto Gilb
*"I absolutely think place is everything. I think place is a character."*

**CHAPTER 14** Amy Hempel
**An Anthology of Stories for Further Reading**
*"One of the things that interests me most in story writing is that . . . there's a point where it stops being your story and becomes the story's story."*

**CHAPTER 15** Carolyn Forché
**Reading a Poem in Its Elements**
*"I think the more we know about how a poem makes its rhythms and musics and patternings, the more deeply we can enter into the poem."*

**CHAPTER 16** Stephen Mitchell
**Going Further: An Interactive Reading**
*"There's a whole world of beauty and profundity out there for people who don't know poetry—that's just waiting for you."*

## Videos available online at http://www.mhhe.com/delbanco1e

**CHAPTER 17** Li-Young Lee
**Writing about Poetry**
*"The minute I wake up I feel as if I'm in the presence of a poem: the whole cosmos, the whole world, seems to exist to me like a giant poem."*

**CHAPTER 18** Marie Howe
**Words**
*"It's the greatest feeling in the whole world, to be in the hands of something bigger than oneself."*

**CHAPTER 19** Stephen Dunn
**Voice**
*"So that good literature has a way of bringing us into the common fold, of making us part of the world."*

**CHAPTER 20** Jane Hirshfield
**Imagery and Symbol**
*"Image is one of the most powerful ways a poem both carries meaning and changes and enlarges it, which is the work that every good poem is trying to do."*

**CHAPTER 21** Robert Pinsky
**Figures of Speech**
*"I think one of the thrills of art is the sense that something may be going too far, or is about to go too far."*

**CHAPTER 22** Thomas Lynch
**Sound**
*"It does embolden you once you get a poem right. And there is a pleasure to it, I must say. And the pleasure is acoustic."*

**CHAPTER 23** Edward Hirsch
**Fixed Forms**
*"The only way you can write a good formal poem is if you can control the form, so that the form becomes the way in which you can express what you need to say."*

**CHAPTER 24** Robert Hass
**Open Forms**
*"Poetry is about catching the way we speak and the way things are said, and the rhythms of it, and making a shape from it."*

**CHAPTER 25** Al Young
**Spoken Word and Song**
*"Poetry is a wonderful opportunity to do two things at once. You can say something or not say something and you can sing through language."*

**CHAPTER 30** Marian Seldes
**Reading and Viewing a Play in Its Elements**
*"One of the wonderful things about reading a play is that you can go back and read the page again. You can take your time with it. Lovingly."*

**CHAPTER 31** Edward Albee
**Going Further: An Interactive Reading**
*"If art isn't engaging or troubling in some sense, it is a total waste of time."*

**CHAPTER 32** Edwin Wilson
**Writing about Drama**
*"In writing, whatever it is, you reread it and you'll be amazed at some of the changes you want to make to your own work."*

**CHAPTER 33** Gregory Nagy
**Ancient Greek Drama: Sophocles**
*"Imagine looking down at a sea of faces, twenty thousand pairs of eyes are weeping simultaneously, twenty thousand people have their hair stand on end in terror."*

**CHAPTER 34** Ralph Williams
**A Case Study on William Shakespeare**
*"One of the frightening and thrilling aspects of Shakespeare's plays is the constant reminder of how tentative it is that life turns out to be tragedy or comedy."*

**CHAPTER 35** Arthur Miller
**Modern Drama**
*"All we can hope for is to illuminate something so that people can make up their own minds based upon the reality of the situation."*

Ruben Santiago-Hudson
*"When you can sit down and open up a book and spend time in a whole different world—no matter whether it's five minutes or an hour—that's a privilege."*

**CHAPTER 36** Arthur Kopit
**A Case Study on Contemporary Theater**
*"To fully get a play, you need to imagine the impact on a crowd. The play is not complete until the audience completes it."*

# Literature

## Drama: Craft and Voice

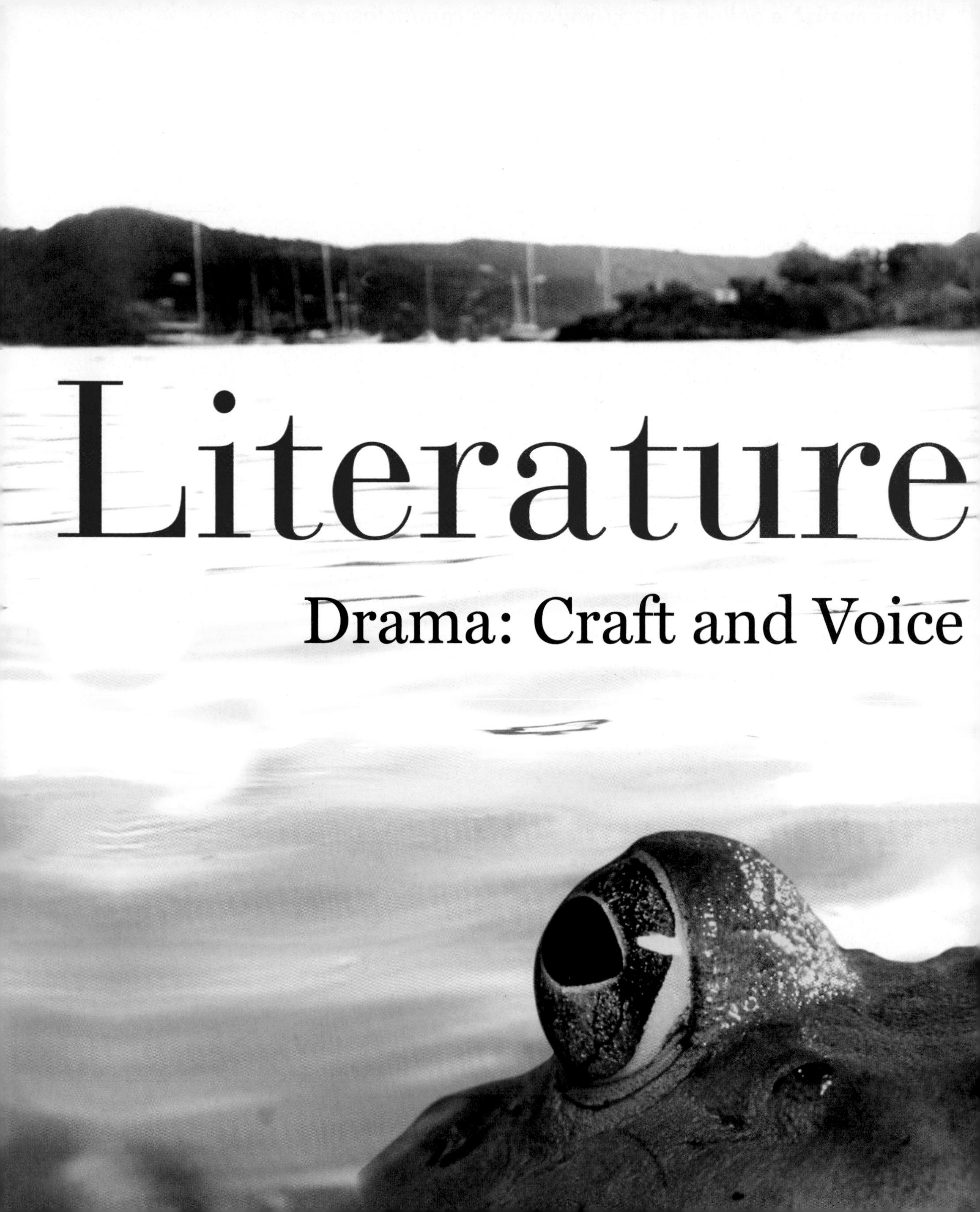

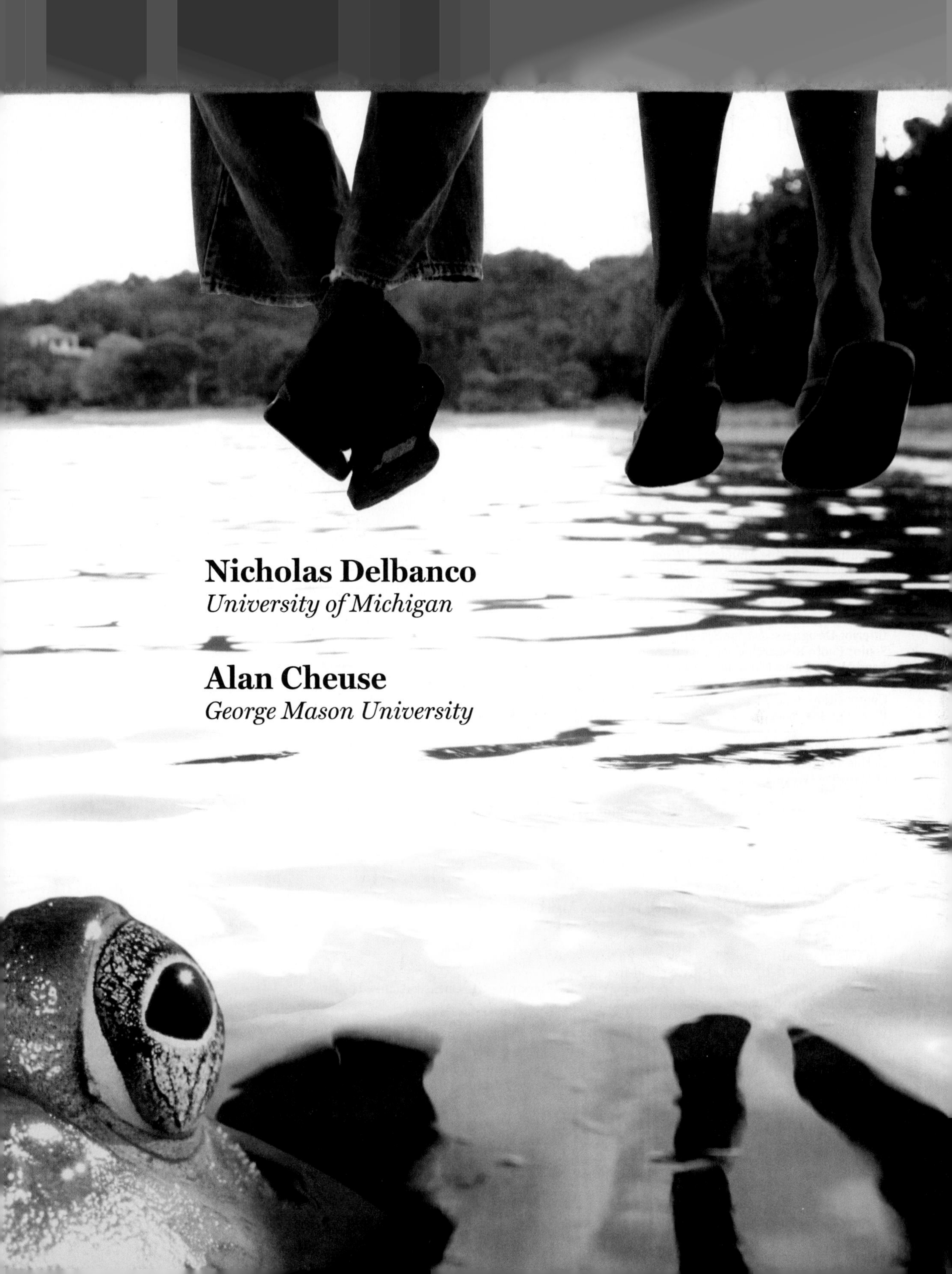


**Nicholas Delbanco**
*University of Michigan*

**Alan Cheuse**
*George Mason University*

# To Our Students

Higher Education

Published by McGraw-Hill, an imprint of The McGraw-Hill Companies, Inc., 1221 Avenue of the Americas, New York, NY 10020. 

This book is printed on acid-free paper.

5 6 7 8 9 0 DOW/DOW 0

ISBN: 978-0-07-721422-7
MHID: 0-07-721422-6

Editor in Chief: *Michael Ryan*
Publisher: *Lisa Moore*
Executive Marketing Manager: *Allison Jones*
Editorial Coordinator: *Stephen Sachs*
Production Editor: *Jasmin Tokatlian*
Manuscript Editor: *Susan Norton*
Cover Designer: *Jeanne Schreiber*
Interior Designers: *Jeanne Schreiber and Linda Robertson*
Senior Photo Research Coordinator: *Nora Agbayani*
Lead Media Project Manager: *Ron Nelms*
Production Supervisor: *Louis Swaim*
Composition: *9.25/11.25 Miller Roman by Thompson Type*
Printing: *45# NewPage Orion Gloss, R. R. Donnelley & Sons/Willard, OH*

Cover: © (Red Door) Mark Lewis/Getty Images, (Field of Sunflowers) Herbert Kehrer/Zefa/Corbis, (Sunflower) Brand X Pictures/Punchstock, (Woman) Photo of Jasmin Tokatlian courtesy of Miroslav Wiesner.

Credits: The credits section for this book begins on page C-1 and is considered an extension of the copyright page.

**Library of Congress Cataloging-in-Publication Data**

Delbanco, Nicholas.
Literature : craft and voice / Nicholas Delbanco, Alan Cheuse.—1st ed.
p. cm.
Includes index.
3 vols. planned.
ISBN-13: 978-0-07-721422-7 (v. 1 : acid-free paper)
ISBN-10: 0-07-721422-6 (v. 1 : acid-free paper) 1. Literature. I. Cheuse, Alan. II. Title.
PN45.D457 2009
800—dc22

2008051003

# Contents

## DRAMA

*Video interview with the authors available online at www.mhhe.com/delbancopreview*



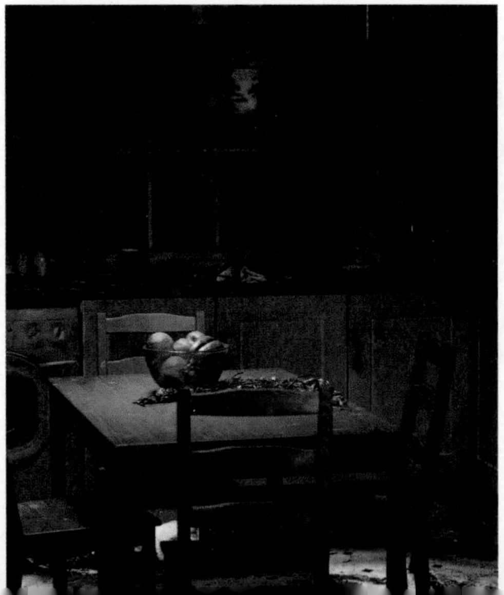

# 32 Writing about Drama 46

# 33 Ancient Greek Drama

# 30 Reading & Viewing a Play in its Elements

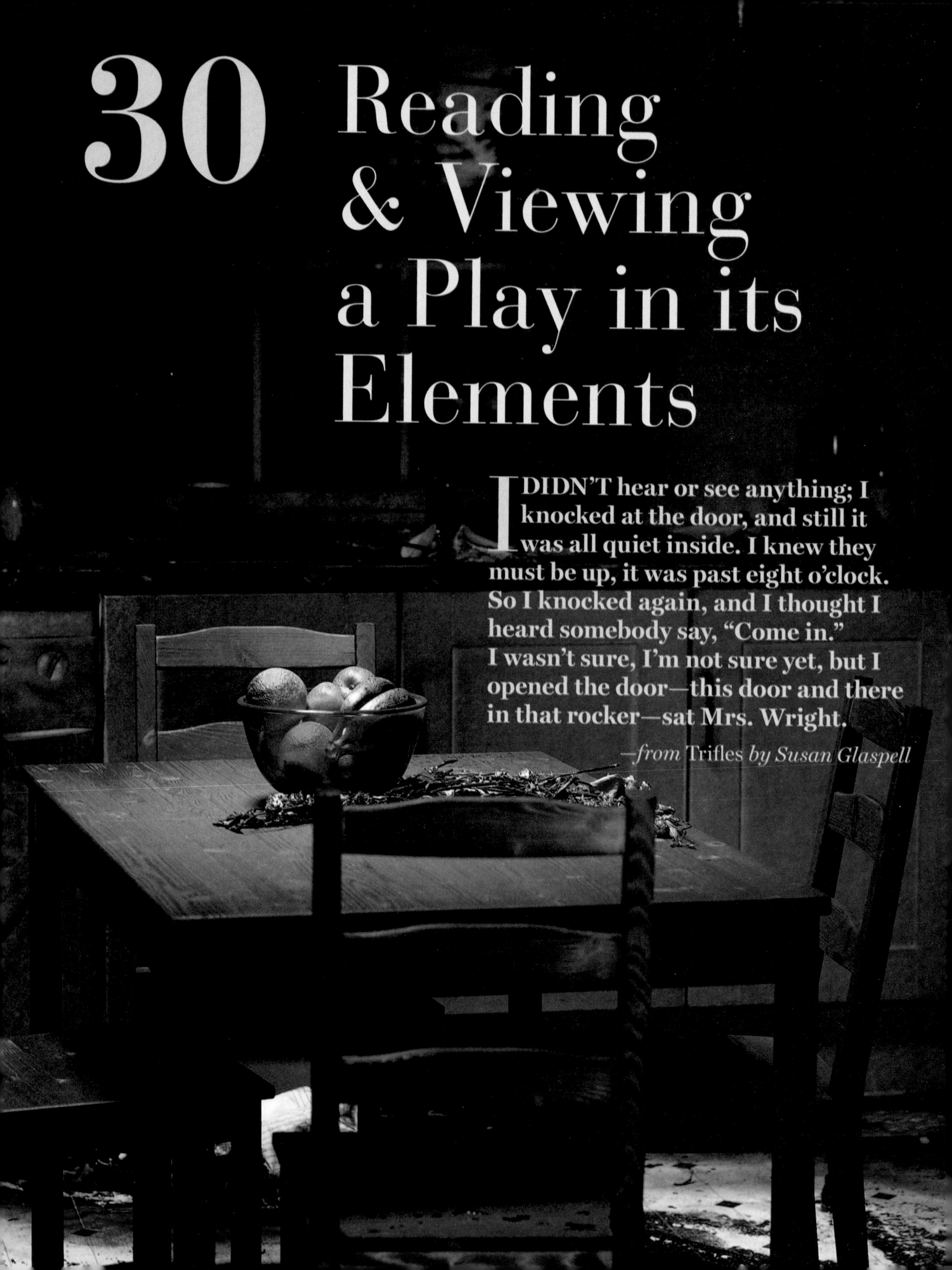

I DIDN'T hear or see anything; I knocked at the door, and still it was all quiet inside. I knew they must be up, it was past eight o'clock. So I knocked again, and I thought I heard somebody say, "Come in." I wasn't sure, I'm not sure yet, but I opened the door—this door and there in that rocker—sat Mrs. Wright.

—*from* Trifles *by Susan Glaspell*

*"I remember once being in a play, and it was the day we were going to open, and the director said to us, 'Try to remember what you felt when you first read this play.' And I thought that was such a wonderful thing to say. It wasn't, 'Use everything I've told you up until this moment,' and blah blah blah about the rehearsal. No. It was your reaction, your personal reaction to the play. So if you have a book full of plays, you are adding yourself to it."*

Conversation with Marian Seldes, available on video at www.mhhe.com/delbanco1e

## A FIRST READING

Of our three principal genres, drama is the one least studied and—in a way—least familiar. You have been exposed to poetry and fiction since you first heard nursery rhymes or fairy tales; you have no doubt read many more books than you've attended plays. But consider how many scripts you've watched enacted in movies and on television screens. The rules of this particular game have been with us since the dawn of Western culture, and there are those who argue—as did William Shakespeare—that "All the world's a stage, and all the men and women merely players." Theater is everywhere around us; we make an "exit" or an "entrance" each time we walk through a door. When you say, "That guy's a character" or "That girl's a prima donna," you're using the language of theater; when you decide what clothes to wear, you're dressing for a role. It's in the way we move and speak, the very air we breathe. When reading drama, you ask yourself many of the same basic questions you ask when watching a movie or TV show: What is all this about? Why is it happening to this person? What does it mean?

The first exposure to a play (as with poetry or fiction) is a crucial one. You will recognize if the play is funny or tragic—comedy and tragedy being two of the fundamental types of drama. Pay attention to your reaction to the story line, the themes that seem to be implied, the way the characters interact, and how you feel about the situation as you read along. A first reading of the script of *Trifles*, for example, reveals a problem—a mystery to be solved—and makes clear the basic elements of the plot. A man is dead; his wife is under suspicion. A neighbor recounts what he found in the Wright house. From his story we hear—secondhand—Mrs. Wright's statement about the circumstances of her husband's death. When reading for the first time, as Edwin Wilson says in another interview in this book, "Let yourself experience your own feelings as you go through . . . a play."

- Read with a pen or pencil in hand.
- Be forthright. Are you enjoying the play? What elements of the play make for enjoyment? Characters? Plot?
- Analyze the action and the motives of the characters. What are they seeking at the beginning of the play?
- Examine the relationship between the characters and the plot. How does what happens grow out of the characters' decisions and actions?
- What is the play's tone? How does the dialogue sound in your ear?

*CONTINUED ON PAGE 13*

*It's like a miracle for me every time.*

# Q&A A Conversation on Reading Drama

*Every playwright awakens something in you you didn't know was there.*

## Marian Seldes

### An Actor's View: Teaching Yourself to Read a Play

You can teach yourself how to read a play. . . . You just read the words the characters say, not worry[ing] too much about who's saying what. . . . When you've read it one way through, you'll have no difficulty in recognizing, Oh, that's the grandmother. Oh, that's . . . the doctor, of course. Oh, that's the beautiful woman . . . because no one else could speak that way.

### Being Alone with a Script

When . . . someone sends you a script, you can pick it up whenever you want to, and part of the thrill is that you're alone with it. You're not sharing this experience with anybody else; it's yours. That frees your imagination. Even if the playwright gives a detailed description of where the play takes place or how the characters look, he can't control your mind, and you invent your play. For me, reading a script for the first time is one of the adventures of being in the theater.

### Writing in the Margins

I think it's a good idea to write your thoughts down. . . . Write down what interests you. When I was young, you weren't allowed to write in the margin of a book. . . . I write things in the script, the acting script, the acting version of a play that I do. . . . Your opinions are as important as everybody else's—especially when you are in communion with a writer you care about: Write it down.

To see the entire interview with Marian Seldes, go to **www.mhhe.com/delbanco1e.**

**RESEARCH ASSIGNMENT** In her interview, Seldes talks about having a playwright at the staging of a play and indicates the answers to the questions she would ask are "all in the play." How does this influence her reading of a script?

Marian Seldes is one of America's foremost actors, having appeared on Broadway and off-Broadway in plays by Tennessee Williams and Edward Albee, among many others, as well as having played in numerous films and television productions. Her many honors include Obie, Drama Desk, and Tony awards in recognition of her achievements in live American theater as well as induction into the Theater Hall of Fame.

# Susan Glaspell (1876–1948)

Born in Davenport, Iowa, the daughter of a pioneer family, Susan Glaspell graduated from Drake University. She worked as a reporter until she decided to devote her time to fiction writing. Although she wrote nine novels (some of which were best sellers) and many short stories, she is best known for her contribution to American drama. She married George Cook, who encouraged Glaspell to write drama, and in 1916 they co-founded the Provincetown Players, a group of playwrights and actors that performed innovative drama. Glaspell's one-act plays were particularly well received. Among her contributions to the group was the way she encouraged the young Eugene O'Neill, who became one of the most important twentieth-century American dramatists. Glaspell's play *Alison's House* (1930), which is based on Emily Dickinson's life, won the Pulitzer Prize, but her early one-act *Trifles* (1916) is generally considered her finest achievement.

**AS YOU READ** Ask yourself how many kinds of investigations are under way in this brief play among the five people—the country attorney, the sheriff and his wife, and a neighboring farmer and his wife—who have come to investigate the scene of the death.

**TIP** **FOR INTERACTIVE READING . . .** Note in the text any references to Mrs. Hale's regrets.

# Trifles (1916)

## CHARACTERS

**GEORGE HENDERSON,** *county attorney*
**HENRY PETERS,** *sheriff*
**LEWIS HALE,** *a neighboring farmer*
**MRS. PETERS**
**MRS. HALE**

**SCENE:** *The kitchen in the now abandoned farmhouse of John Wright, a gloomy kitchen, plainly left without having been put in order—unwashed pans under the sink, a loaf of bread outside the bread-box, a dish-towel on the table—other signs of incompleted work. Door opens rear and enter sheriff followed by* COUNTY ATTORNEY *and* HALE. *The* SHERIFF *and* HALE *are men in middle life, the* COUNTY ATTORNEY *is a young man; all are much bundled up and go at once to the stove. They are followed by the two women—the* SHERIFF*'s wife first; she is a slight wiry woman, a thin nervous face.* MRS. HALE *is larger and would ordinarily be called more comfortable looking, but she is disturbed now and looks fearfully about as she enters. The women have come in slowly, and stand close together near the door.*

**COUNTY ATTORNEY:** *(Rubbing his hands)* This feels good. Come up to the fire, ladies.

**MRS. PETERS:** *(Takes a step forward and looks around)* I'm not—cold.

**SHERIFF:** *(Unbuttoning his overcoat and stepping away from the stove as if to mark the beginning of official business)* Now, Mr. Hale, before we move things about, you explain to Mr. Henderson just what you saw when you came here yesterday morning.

**COUNTY ATTORNEY:** By the way, has anything been moved? Are things just as you left them yesterday?

**SHERIFF:** *(Looking all about)* It's just the same. When it dropped below zero last night I thought I'd better send Frank out this morning to make a fire for us—no use getting pneumonia with a big case on, but I told him not to touch anything except the stove—and you know Frank.

**COUNTY ATTORNEY:** Somebody should have been left here yesterday.

**SHERIFF:** Oh—yesterday. When I had to send Frank to Morris Center for that man who went crazy—I want you to know I had my hands full yesterday. I knew you could get back from Omaha by today and as long as I went over everything here myself—

**COUNTY ATTORNEY:** Well, Mr. Hale, tell just what happened when you came here yesterday morning.

**HALE:** Harry and I had started to town with a load of potatoes. We came along the road from my place and as I got here I said, "I'm going to see if I can't get John Wright to go in with me on a party telephone." I spoke to Wright about it once before and he put me off, saying folks talked too much anyway, and all he asked was peace and quiet—I guess you know about how much he talked himself, but I thought maybe if I went to the house and talked about it before his wife, though I said to Harry that I didn't know as what his wife wanted made much difference to John—

**COUNTY ATTORNEY:** Let's talk about that later, Mr. Hale. I do want to talk about that, but tell now just what happened when you got to the house.

**HALE:** I didn't hear or see anything; I knocked at the door, and still it was all quiet inside. I knew they must be up, it was past eight o'clock. So I knocked again, and I thought I heard somebody say, "Come in." I wasn't sure, I'm not sure yet, but I opened the door—this door *(jerking a hand backward)* and there in that rocker—*(pointing to it)* sat Mrs. Wright. *(All look at the rocker)*

**COUNTY ATTORNEY:** What—was she doing?

**HALE:** She was rockin' back and forth. She had her apron in her hand and was kind of—pleating it.

**COUNTY ATTORNEY:** And how did she—look?

**HALE:** Well, she looked queer.

**COUNTY ATTORNEY:** How do you mean—queer?

**HALE:** Well, as if she didn't know what she was going to do next. And kind of done up.

**COUNTY ATTORNEY:** How did she seem to feel about your coming?

**HALE:** Why, I don't think she minded—one way or other. She didn't pay much attention. I said, "How do, Mrs. Wright, it's cold, ain't it?" And she said, "Is it?"—and went on kind of pleating at her apron. Well, I was surprised; she didn't ask me to come up to the stove, or to set down, but just sat there, not even looking at me, so I said, "I want to see John." And then she—laughed. I guess you would call it a laugh. I thought of Harry and the team outside, so I said a little sharp: "Can't I see John?" "No," she says, kind o' dull like. "Ain't he home?" says I. "Yes," says she, "he's home." "Then why can't I see him?" I asked her, out of patience. "'Cause he's dead," says

she. *"Dead?"* says I. She just nodded her head, not getting a bit excited, but rockin' back and forth. "Why—where is he?" says I, not knowing what to say. She just pointed upstairs—like that *(himself pointing to the room above)*. I got up, with the idea of going up there. I walked from there to here—*(pointing)*—then I says, "Why, what did he die of?" "He died of a rope round his neck," says she, and just went on pleatin' at her apron. Well, I went out and called Harry. I thought I might—need help. We went upstairs and there he was—lyin'—

**COUNTY ATTORNEY:** I think I'd rather have you go into that upstairs, where you can point it all out. Just go on now with the rest of the story.

**HALE:** Well, my first thought was to get that rope off. It looked—*(stops, his face twitches)*—but Harry, he went up to him, and he said, "No, he's dead all right, and we'd better not touch anything." So we went back down stairs. She was still sitting that same way. "Has anybody been notified?" I asked. "No," says she, unconcerned. "Who did this, Mrs. Wright?" said Harry. He said it business-like—and she stopped pleatin' of her apron. "I don't know," she says. "You don't *know?*" says Harry. "No," says she. "Weren't you sleepin' in the bed with him?" says Harry. "Yes," says she, "but I was on the inside." "Somebody slipped a rope round his neck and strangled him and you didn't wake up?" says Harry. "I didn't wake up," she said after him. We may have looked as if we didn't see how that could be, for after a minute she said, "I sleep sound." Harry was going to ask her more questions but I said maybe we ought to let her tell her story first to the coroner, or the sheriff, so Harry went fast as he could to Rivers' place, where there's a telephone.

**COUNTY ATTORNEY:** And what did Mrs. Wright do when she knew that you had gone for the coroner?

**HALE:** She moved from that chair to this one over here, *(pointing to a small chair in the corner)* and just sat there with her hands held together and looking down. I got a feeling that I ought to make some conversation, so I said I had come in to see if John wanted to put in a telephone, and at that she started to laugh, and then she stopped and looked at me—scared. *(*COUNTY ATTORNEY, *who has had his notebook out, makes a note)* I dunno, maybe it wasn't scared. I wouldn't like to say it was. Soon Harry got back, and then Dr. Lloyd came, and you, Mr. Peters, and so I guess that's all I know that you don't.

**COUNTY ATTORNEY:** *(Looking around)* I guess we'll go upstairs first—and then out to the barn and around there. *(To* SHERIFF*)* You're convinced that there was nothing important here—nothing that would point to any motive?

**SHERIFF:** Nothing here but kitchen things.

**COUNTY ATTORNEY:** *(Opens the door of a cupboard closet. Gets up on a chair and looks on a shelf. Pulls his hand away, sticky)* Here's a nice mess. *(The women draw nearer)*

**MRS. PETERS:** Oh, her fruit; it did freeze. *(To* COUNTY ATTORNEY*)* She worried about that when it turned so cold. She said the fire'd go out and her jars would break.

**SHERIFF:** Well, can you beat the women! Held for murder and worrying about her preserves.

**COUNTY ATTORNEY:** *(Setting his lips firmly)* I guess before we are through she may have something more serious than preserves to worry about.

**HALE:** Well, women are used to worrying over trifles. *(The two women move a little closer together)*

**COUNTY ATTORNEY:** *(With the gallantry of a young politician)* And yet, for all their worries, what would we do without the ladies? *(The women do not unbend. He goes to the sink, takes a dipperful of water from pail and pouring it into basin, washes his hands. Starts to wipe them on the roller towel, turns it for a cleaner place)* Dirty towels! *(Kicks his foot against pans under the sink)* Not much of a housekeeper, would you say, ladies?

**MRS. HALE:** *(Stiffly)* There's a great deal of work to be done on a farm.

**COUNTY ATTORNEY:** *(With conciliation)* To be sure. And yet *(with a little bow to her)* I know there are some Dickson county farmhouses which do not have such roller towels. *(Gives it a pull to expose its full length again)*

**MRS. HALE:** Those towels get dirty awful quick. Men's hands aren't always as clean as they might be.

**COUNTY ATTORNEY:** Ah, loyal to your sex, I see. But you and Mrs. Wright were neighbors. I suppose you were friends, too.

**MRS. HALE:** *(Shaking her head)* I've not seen much of her of late years. I've not been in this house—it's more than a year.

**COUNTY ATTORNEY:** And why was that? You didn't like her?

**MRS. HALE:** I liked her all well enough. Farmer's wives have their hands full, Mr. Henderson. And then—

**COUNTY ATTORNEY:** Yes—?

**MRS. HALE:** *(Looking about)* It never seemed a very cheerful place.

**COUNTY ATTORNEY:** No—it's not cheerful. I shouldn't say she had the homemaking instinct.

**MRS. HALE:** Well, I don't know as Wright had, either.

**COUNTY ATTORNEY:** You mean that they didn't get on very well?

**MRS. HALE:** No, I don't mean anything. But I don't think a place'd be any cheerfuller for John Wright's being in it.

**COUNTY ATTORNEY:** I'd like to talk more of that a little later. I want to get the lay of things upstairs now. *(Moves to stair door, followed by the two men)*

**SHERIFF:** I suppose anything Mrs. Peters does'll be all right. She was to take in some clothes for her, you know, and a few little things. We left in such a hurry yesterday.

**COUNTY ATTORNEY:** Yes, but I would like to see what you take, Mrs. Peters, and keep an eye out for anything that might be of use to us.

**MRS. PETERS:** Yes, Mr. Henderson. *(The women listen to the men's steps on the stairs, then look about the kitchen)*

**MRS. HALE:** I'd hate to have men coming into my kitchen, snooping around and criticizing. *(Arranges pans under sink which the county attorney had shoved out of place)*

**MRS. PETERS:** Of course it's no more than their duty.

**MRS. HALE:** Duty's all right, but I guess that deputy sheriff that came out to make the fire might have got a little of this on. *(Gives roller towel a pull)* Wish I'd thought of that sooner. Seems mean to talk about her for not having things slicked up when she had to come away in such a hurry.

**MRS. PETERS:** *(Going to table at side, lifts one end of towel that covers a pan)* She had bread set. *(Stands still)*

**MRS. HALE:** *(Her eyes fixed on a loaf of bread outside bread-box. Moves slowly toward it)* She was going to put this in there. *(Picks up loaf, then abruptly drops it. In a manner of returning to familiar things)* It's a shame about her fruit. I wonder if it's all gone. *(Gets up on a chair and looks)* I think there's some here that is all right, Mrs. Peters. Yes—here; *(holding it toward the window)* this is cherries, too. *(Looking again)* I declare I believe that's the only one. *(Gets down, bottle in her hand. Goes to sink and wipes it off on the outside)* She'll feel awful bad after all her hard work in the hot weather. I remember the afternoon I put up my cherries last summer. *(Puts bottle on table. With a sigh starts to sit down in rocking-chair. Before she is seated realizes what chair it is; with a slow look at it, steps back. The chair which she has touched rocks back and forth)*

**MRS. PETERS:** Well, I must get those things from the front room closet. *(Starts to door left, looks into the other room, steps back)* You coming with me, Mrs. Hale? You could help me carry them. *(Both women go out; reappear,* MRS. PETERS *carrying a dress and skirt,* MRS. HALE *following with a pair of shoes)*

**MRS. PETERS:** My, it's cold in there. *(Puts clothes on table, goes up to stove)*

**MRS. HALE:** *(Holding up skirt and examining it)* Wright was close. I think maybe that's why she kept so much to herself. She didn't even belong to the Ladies Aid. I suppose she felt she couldn't do her part, and then you don't enjoy things when you feel shabby. She used to wear pretty clothes and be lively, when she was Minnie Foster, one of the town girls singing in the choir. But that was—oh, that was thirty years ago. This all you was to take in?

**MRS. PETERS:** She said she wanted an apron. Funny thing to want, for there isn't much to get you dirty in jail, goodness knows. But I suppose just to make her feel more natural. She said they was in the top drawer in this cupboard. Yes, here. And then her little shawl that always hung behind the door. *(Looks on stair door)* Yes, here it is.

**MRS. HALE:** *(Abruptly moving toward her)* Mrs. Peters?

**MRS. PETERS:** Yes, Mrs. Hale?

**MRS. HALE:** Do you think she did it?

**MRS. PETERS:** *(In a frightened voice)* Oh, I don't know.

**MRS. HALE:** Well, I don't think she did. Asking for an apron and her little shawl. Worrying about her fruit.

**MRS. PETERS:** *(Starts to speak, glances up, where footsteps are heard in the room above. In a low voice)* Mr. Peters says it looks bad for her. Mr. Henderson is awful sarcastic in a speech and he'll make fun of her sayin' she didn't wake up.

**MRS. HALE:** Well, I guess John Wright didn't wake when they was slipping that rope under his neck.

**MRS. PETERS:** No, it's strange. It must have been done awful crafty and still. They say it was such a—funny way to kill a man, rigging it all up like that.

**MRS. HALE:** That's just what Mr. Hale said. There was a gun in the house. He says that's what he can't understand.

**MRS. PETERS:** Mr. Henderson said coming out that what was needed for the case was a motive; something to show anger, or—sudden feeling.

**MRS. HALE:** *(Standing by table)* Well, I don't see any signs of anger around here, but *(puts hand on dish-towel in middle of table, stands looking at table, one half of which is clean, the other half messy)* It's wiped to here. *(Makes a move as if to finish work, then turns and looks at loaf of bread beside the bread-box. Drops towel. In that voice of coming back to familiar things)* Wonder how they are finding things upstairs. I hope she had it a little more red-up up there. You know, it seems kind of *sneaking*. Locking her up in town and then coming out here and trying to get her own house to turn against her!

**MRS. PETERS:** But Mrs. Hale, the law is the law.

**MRS. HALE:** I spose't is. *(Unbuttoning her coat)* Better loosen up your things, Mrs. Peters. You won't feel them when you go out.

**MRS. PETERS:** *(Taking off fur tippet, goes to hang it on hook at back of room, stands looking at the under part of the small table)* She was piecing a quilt. *(Brings large sewing basket to table front and they look at the bright pieces)*

**MRS. HALE:** It's log cabin pattern. Pretty, isn't it? I wonder if she was goin' to quilt it or just knot it? *(Footsteps have been heard coming down the stairs. The* SHERIFF *enters followed by* HALE *and* HENDERSON*)*

**SHERIFF:** They wonder if she was going to quilt it or just knot it. *(The men laugh, the women look abashed)*

**COUNTY ATTORNEY:** *(Rubbing his hands over the stove)* Frank's fire didn't do much up there, did it? Well, let's go out to the barn and get that cleared up. *(Exeunt men door rear)*

**MRS. HALE:** *(Resentfully)* I don't know as there's anything so strange, our takin' up our time with little things while we're waiting for them to get the evidence. *(Sits down, smoothing out block with decision)* I don't see as it's anything to laugh about.

**MRS. PETERS:** *(Apologetically)* Of course they've got awful important things on their minds. *(Pulls up a chair and sits by the table)*

**MRS. HALE:** *(Examining another block)* Mrs. Peters, look at this one. Here, this is the one she was working on, and look at the sewing! All the rest of it has been so nice and even. And look at this! It's all over the place! Why, it looks as if she didn't know what she was about! *(After she has said this they look at each other, then start to glance back at the door. After an instant* MRS. HALE *has pulled at a knot and ripped the sewing)*

**MRS. PETERS:** Oh, what are you doing, Mrs. Hale?

**MRS. HALE:** *(Mildly)* Just pulling out a stitch or two that's not sewed very good. *(Threading a needle)* Bad sewing always made me fidgety.

**MRS. PETERS:** *(Nervously)* I don't think we ought to touch things.

**MRS. HALE:** I'll just finish up this end. *(Suddenly stopping and leaning forward)* Mrs. Peters?

**MRS. PETERS:** Yes, Mrs. Hale?

**MRS. HALE:** What do you suppose she was so nervous about?

**MRS. PETERS:** Oh—I don't know. I don't know as she was nervous. I sometimes sew awful queer when I'm just tired. *(*MRS. HALE *starts to say something, looks at her, compresses her lips a little, goes on sewing)* Well, I must get these things wrapped up. They may be through sooner than we think. *(Piling apron and other things up together)* I wonder where I can find a piece of paper, and string.

**MRS. HALE:** In that cupboard, maybe.

**MRS. PETERS:** *(Looking in cupboard)* Why, here's a birdcage. *(Holds it up)* Did she have a bird, Mrs. Hale?

**MRS. HALE:** Why, I don't know whether she did or not—I've not been here for so long. There was a man around last year selling canaries cheap, but I don't know as she took one; maybe she did. She used to sing real pretty herself.

**MRS. PETERS:** *(Glancing around)* Seems funny to think of a bird here. But she must have had one, or why would she have a cage? I wonder what happened to it.

**MRS. HALE:** I s'pose maybe the cat got it.

**MRS. PETERS:** No, she didn't have a cat. She's got that feeling some people have about cats—being afraid of them. My cat got in her room and she was real upset and asked me to take it out.

**MRS. HALE:** My sister Bessie was like that. Queer, ain't it?

**MRS. PETERS:** *(Examining cage)* Why, look at this door. It's broke. One hinge is pulled apart.

**MRS. HALE:** *(Looking too)* Looks as if someone must have been rough with it.

**MRS. PETERS:** Why, yes. *(Puts cage on table)*

**MRS. HALE:** I wish if they're going to find any evidence they'd be about it. I don't like this place.

**MRS. PETERS:** But I'm awful glad you came with me, Mrs. Hale. It would be lonesome for me sitting here alone.

**MRS. HALE:** It would, wouldn't it? *(Dropping sewing, voice falling)* But I tell you what I do wish, Mrs. Peters. I wish I had come over sometimes when *she* was here. I—*(looking around the room)*—wish I had.

**MRS. PETERS:** But of course you were awful busy, Mrs. Hale—your house and your children.

**MRS. HALE:** I could've come. I stayed away because it weren't cheerful—and that's why I ought to have come. I—I've never liked this place. Maybe because it's down in a hollow and you don't see the road. I dunno what it is, but it's a lonesome place and always was. I wish I had come over to see Minnie Foster sometimes. I can see now— *(shakes her head)*

**MRS. PETERS:** Well, you mustn't reproach yourself, Mrs. Hale. Somehow we just don't see how it is with other folks until—something comes up.

**MRS. HALE:** Not having children makes less work—but it makes a quiet house, and Wright out to work all day, and no company when he did come in. Did you know John Wright, Mrs. Peters?

**MRS. PETERS:** Not to know him; I've seen him in town. They say he was a good man.

**MRS. HALE:** Yes—good; he didn't drink, and kept his word as well as most, I guess, and paid his debts. But he was a hard man, Mrs. Peters. Just to pass the time of day with him—*(shivers)* Like a raw wind that gets to the bone. *(Pauses, her eye falling on the cage)* I should think she would 'a wanted a bird. But what do you suppose went with it?

**MRS. PETERS:** I don't know, unless it got sick and died. *(She reaches over and swings the broken door, swings it again, both women watch it)*

**MRS. HALE:** You weren't raised round here, were you? *(MRS. PETERS shakes her head)* You didn't know—her?

**MRS. PETERS:** Not till they brought her yesterday.

**MRS. HALE:** She—come to think of it, she was kind of like a bird herself—real sweet and pretty, but kind of timid and—fluttery. How—she—did—change. *(Silence; then as if struck by a happy thought and relieved to get back to everyday things)* Tell you what, Mrs. Peters, why don't you take the quilt in with you? It might take up her mind.

**MRS. PETERS:** Why, I think that's a real nice idea, Mrs. Hale. There couldn't possibly be any objection to it, could there? Now, just what would I take? I wonder if her patches are in here—and her things. *(Both look in sewing basket)*

**MRS. HALE:** Here's some red. I expect this has got sewing things in it. *(Brings out a fancy box)* What a pretty box. Looks like something somebody would give you. Maybe her scissors are in here. *(Opens box. Suddenly puts her hand to her nose)* Why—*(MRS. PETERS bends nearer, then turns her face away)* There's something wrapped up in this piece of silk.

**MRS. PETERS:** Why, this isn't her scissors.

**MRS. HALE:** *(Lifting the silk)* Oh, Mrs. Peters—it's *(MRS. PETERS bends closer)*

**MRS. PETERS:** It's the bird.

**MRS. HALE:** *(Jumping up)* But, Mrs. Peters—look at it! Its neck! Look at its neck! It's all—other side *to.*

**MRS. PETERS:** Somebody—wrung—its—neck. *(Their eyes meet. A look of growing comprehension, of horror. Steps are heard outside.* MRS. HALE *slips box under quilt pieces, and sinks into her chair. Enter* SHERIFF *and* COUNTY ATTORNEY. MRS. PETERS *rises)*

**COUNTY ATTORNEY:** *(As one turning from serious things to little pleasantries)* Well, ladies, have you decided whether she was going to quilt it or knot it?

**MRS. PETERS:** We think she was going to—knot it.

**COUNTY ATTORNEY:** Well, that's interesting, I am sure. *(Looking at bird-cage)* Has the bird flown?

**MRS. HALE:** *(Piling more quilt pieces over the box)* We think the—cat got it.

**COUNTY ATTORNEY:** *(Preoccupied)* Is there a cat? *(*MRS. HALE *glances in a quick covert way at* MRS. PETERS*)*

**MRS. PETERS:** Well, not *now.* They're superstitious, you know. They leave.

**COUNTY ATTORNEY:** *(To* PETERS, *in the manner of continuing an interrupted conversation)* No sign at all of anyone having come from the outside. Their own rope. Now let's go up again and go over it piece by piece. *(They start upstairs)* It would have to have been someone who knew just the—*(*MRS. PETERS *sinks into her chair. The two women sit there not looking at one another, but as if peering into something and at the same time holding back. When they talk now it is in the manner of feeling their way over strange ground, as if afraid of what they are saying, but as if they can not help saying it)*

**MRS. HALE:** She liked the bird. She was going to bury it in that pretty box.

**MRS. PETERS:** *(In a whisper)* When I was a girl—my kitten—there was a boy took a hatchet, and before my eyes—and before I could get there—*(covers her face an instant)* If they hadn't held me back I would have—*(catches herself, looks upstairs where steps are heard, falters weakly)*—hurt him.

**MRS. HALE:** *(With a slow look around her)* I wonder how it would seem never to have had any children around. *(Pause)* No, Wright wouldn't like the bird—a thing that sang. She used to sing. He killed that, too.

**MRS. PETERS:** *(Moving uneasily)* We don't know who killed the bird.

**MRS. HALE:** I knew John Wright.

**MRS. PETERS:** It was an awful thing was done in this house that night, Mrs. Hale. Killing a man while he slept, slipping a rope around his neck that choked the life out of him.

**MRS. HALE:** His neck. Choked the life out of him. *(Her hand goes out and rests on the bird-cage)*

**MRS. PETERS:** *(With rising voice)* We don't know who killed him. We don't *know.*

**MRS. HALE:** *(Her own feeling not interrupted)* If there'd been years and years of nothing, then a bird to sing to you, it would be awful—still, after the bird was still.

**MRS. PETERS:** *(Something within her speaking)* I know what stillness is. When we homesteaded in Dakota, and my first baby died—after he was two years old, and me with no other then—

**MRS. HALE:** *(Moving)* How soon do you suppose they'll be through, looking for the evidence?

**MRS. PETERS:** I know what stillness is. *(Pulling herself back)* The law has got to punish crime, Mrs. Hale.

**MRS. HALE:** *(Not as if answering that)* I wish you'd seen Minnie Foster when she wore a white dress with blue ribbons and stood up there in the choir and sang. *(Suddenly looking around the room)* Oh, I *wish* I'd come over here once in a while! That was a crime! That was a crime! Who's going to punish that?

**MRS. PETERS:** *(Looking upstairs)* We mustn't—take on.

**MRS. HALE:** I might have known she needed help! I know how things can be—for women. I tell you, it's queer, Mrs. Peters. We live close together and we live far apart. We all go through the same things—it's all just a different kind of the same thing— *(Brushes her eyes, then seeing the bottle of fruit, reaches out for it)* If I was you I wouldn't tell her her fruit was gone. Tell her it *ain't.* Tell her it's all right. Take this in to prove it to her. She—she may never know whether it was broke or not.

**MRS. PETERS:** *(Picks up the bottle, looks about for something to wrap it in; takes petticoat from clothes brought from front room, very nervously begins winding that around it. In a false voice)* My, it's a good thing the men couldn't hear us. Wouldn't they just laugh! Getting all stirred up over a little thing like a—dead canary. As if that could have anything to do with—with—wouldn't they *laugh! (The men are heard coming down stairs)*

**MRS. HALE:** *(Muttering)* Maybe they would—maybe they wouldn't.

**COUNTY ATTORNEY:** No, Peters, it's all perfectly clear except a reason for doing it. But you know juries when it comes to women. If there was some definite thing. Something to show—something to make a story about—a thing that would connect up with this strange way of doing it—*(The women's eyes meet for an instant. Enter* HALE *from outer door)*

**HALE:** Well, I've got the team around. Pretty cold out there.

**COUNTY ATTORNEY:** I'm going to stay here a while by myself. *(To* SHERIFF*)* You can send Frank out for me, can't you? I want to go over everything. I'm not satisfied that we can't do better.

**SHERIFF:** Do you want to see what Mrs. Peters is going to take in?

**COUNTY ATTORNEY:** *(Goes to the table. Picks up apron, laughs)* Oh, I guess they're not very dangerous things the ladies have picked out. *(Moves a few things about, disturbing the quilt pieces which cover the box. Steps back)* No, Mrs. Peters doesn't need supervising. For that matter, a sheriff's wife is married to the law. Ever think of it that way, Mrs. Peters?

**MRS. PETERS:** Not—just that way.

**SHERIFF:** *(Chuckling)* Married to the law. *(Moves toward front room)* I just want you to come in here a minute, George. We ought to take a look at these windows.

**COUNTY ATTORNEY:** Oh, windows!

**SHERIFF:** We'll be right out, Mr. Hale. *(Exit* HALE *door rear.* SHERIFF *follows the* COUNTY ATTORNEY *through door left. The two women's eyes follow them out.* MRS. HALE *rises, hands tightly together, looking intensely at* MRS. PETERS, *whose eyes make a slow turn, finally meeting* MRS. HALE'S. *A moment* MRS. HALE *holds her, then her own eyes point the way to the spot where the box is concealed. Suddenly* MRS. PETERS *throws back quilt pieces and tries to put box in the bag she is wearing. It is too big. She opens box, starts to take bird out, cannot touch it, goes to pieces, stands there helpless. Sound of a knob turning in the other room.* MRS. HALE *snatches box and puts it in the pocket of her big coat. Enter* COUNTY ATTORNEY *and* SHERIFF.

**COUNTY ATTORNEY:** *(Facetiously)* Well, Henry, at least we found out that she was not going to quilt it. She was going to—what is it you call it, ladies?

**MRS. HALE:** *(Hand against her pocket)* We call it—knot it, Mr. Henderson.

# Writing from Reading

## Summarize

1 Scan the script for references to Mrs. Wright's life. What do you know about her before and after her marriage?

2 List the "trifles" in this play. What do they have in common?

3 Who is the central character in the play? Who stands in opposition to this character?

## Analyze Craft

4 What is the significance of setting the play during winter?

5 What is the significance of the kitchen as a setting for this play?

## Analyze Voice

6 Identify an exchange of dialogue that you found particularly powerful and explain why. How does it promote or portray the conflict and theme of the play?

## Synthesize Summary and Analysis

7 Compare the themes of "Trifles" to those of Kate Chopin's "The Story of an Hour" (in Fiction). How do Glaspell and Chopin, writing in the same country and at roughly the same time, approach the issues of the thwarted housewife?

## Interpret the Play

8 What is the attitude of the women toward the men, the men toward the women?

9 What is the relationship between Mrs. Hale's regrets and her instinct to protect Mrs. Wright?

10 Which character goes through the most dramatic change in the course of the play? What is the change, and how does it come about?

11 How are power and powerlessness represented in the play?

*CONTINUED FROM PAGE 3*

## A CLOSER LOOK

The term **drama** comes from the Greek word for *performing an action* or *doing*—and playwrights almost always intend their work to be brought to life on a stage by actors (except in the case of **closet dramas,** which are plays written to be read aloud rather than performed). Even the term we use to refer to the author of a dramatic work—**playwright** (not play-*write*)—reflects the three-dimensionality of a play: a *wright* is a medieval term for one skilled in manufacturing three-dimensional items, such as a shipwright or a wheelwright. The word suggests "maker," or "craftsman"; a carefully built thing has been well *wrought.*

> "A play exists on the page completely as an artwork if it is an artwork, but for anybody to really involve themselves in it . . . it has to be performed." Conversation with Edward Albee

In fact, much of the world's great theater—from Sophocles (chapter 33) to Shakespeare (chapter 34)—had no life on the page *before* or *separate from* enactment on the stage. The playwright did not print out notes for actors or the audience to read. Thus, the original staging had nothing to do with words on a page. Drama had everything to do with how the play worked in performance. Dramas can occur on a **proscenium stage,** a raised platform with a missing fourth wall through which we as audience watch the action (see chapter 34 on Shakespeare). In other cases, the play may be presented **in the round,** where the audience surrounds the actors, or in an **amphitheater,** where the audience looks down on the drama (see chapter 33 on Greek drama). When the philosopher Aristotle asserted that much of the physical action of Greek drama must take place offstage, this was in part a function of necessity. The ancient

Proscenium stage

Theater in the round

Amphitheater

Greeks could not mount battle or death scenes persuasively in their amphitheaters—and so the audience learned of such events after the fact. No contemporary director would miss a chance to stage a combat or a love scene, but Glaspell apparently chose to keep the second-floor rooms of the farm offstage because it simplifies the issues of production. First, the production needs only one set—which allows for economy. Second, when the men go offstage and upstairs, they're gone; the women can pursue their inquiries alone. Even the simplest of dramas is multidimensional in conception.

**THE ORIGINS OF DRAMA**

Drama grew in part out of pre-classical Greek religious ceremonies and the public performances of poetry, Homer's *Iliad* and *Odyssey* in particular. These were not put into written form until after the Homeric epics were copied down in the sixth century B.C.E.; thanks to the collectors and librarians of the early Arab world, scrolls of papyrus with the texts of poems and the play scripts remained safe in libraries across the Mediterranean long after the decline of Greek civilization.

## Elements of Drama

*Trifles* is a one-act play, a small miracle of compression that occurs in a single location and in one continuous action. A full-length play generally has three to five **acts,** and these divisions function in ways similar to fiction, as though they were chapters in a book that shift to a new location, mood, time, or configuration of characters. Acts, in turn, are divided into **scenes,** smaller segments of dramatic action. Here are one student's notes on how scenes work even in this one-act play.

**Student Note on Scenes in *Trifles***

The action comes in waves, one associated with the male characters, the other with the female.

> "There's something in there that's very sensitive to who you are, and things that are important to you. Attach yourself to that person and own that. So when you're reading, that's you. We've all been there. So find yourself in the play. Get inside the play, don't stay outside the play." Conversation with Ruben Santiago-Hudson

As you read through a play the first time, get to know the **characters.** The list of characters is found at the beginning of the play. (In the classical period of Greek theater, discussed in chapter 33, this list would be called **Dramatis Personae,** or "people of the play.") Just as in fiction, you will find a **protagonist,** who is the central character (the lead actor in the play), and an **antagonist,** who is a character or force that opposes the protagonist. A student's notes on characters in *Trifles* follow:

**Student Notes on Characters in *Trifles***

*Men are rational: The men—the county attorney, the sheriff, and their witness, the farmer—are rational investigators, trying to establish a motive for the crime.

*Women are emotional: The women feel their way toward understanding, sorting through memories. The women are, in the words of the neighboring farmer, "worrying over trifles."

Irony: While the men go elsewhere in the house to search for clues, the women find the truth, the essence, of what has happened here.

A playwright must use the characters to move forward the play's **plot**—the important events in the story. The central incident in *Trifles*—the death of Mr. Wright—occurs before the onstage action begins, and is therefore introduced by means of **exposition,** a literary technique by which a character presents necessary background information. In addition to exposition, the plot unfolds in **dialogue,** the conversations

> "Don't just try to figure out the character. If you don't put the character in the plot, you'll never figure out the character. Character and plot are supposed to be organically interwoven."
>
> Conversation with Gregory Nagy

that occur between the characters. When you read a play, notice how the complications the characters face crystallize in a **conflict,** leading to **rising action,** an intensification of the predicament. The moment of greatest tension is the play's **climax** or turning point. Frequently, the climax causes a character to change in some way or at least to gain new understanding as a result of the conflict or crisis. The conclusion of the play, or the resolution of conflicts that follows the climax, is referred to as the **denouement,** a French word that literally means "untying." In the denouement, the knots of the story are untied and conflicts are further resolved. A longer play than *Trifles* might also include a **subplot** or two—secondary stories that involve characters other than the central figure in the play.

The play's **setting**—the location of the action—as depicted onstage is called the **set.** Glaspell describes the set she envisions down to a loaf of bread beside the bread-box and a dish towel on the table. The playwright's instructions on how actors are to move and position themselves onstage, as well as how they are to deliver certain lines—the **stage directions**—usually appear in parentheses and in italics in the **script,** which consists mainly of dialogue and staging instructions. At various points in *Trifles,* Glaspell instructs actors to unbutton a coat, point, look at the rocker, twitch, or speak stiffly.

**Student Notes on the Staging in *Trifles***

The kitchen is cluttered, ill-tended. In the mess of things, of "trifles," the women do find evidence:

- the frenzied stitches in the farm wife's quilting,
- the empty birdcage, and then
- the dead songbird with a twisted neck, an emblem of the crime and a clear if metaphorical motive. The wife—like the bird—has been caged and strangled.

Susan Glaspell's stage directions clarify that the women know what they have found: "Their eyes meet. A look of growing comprehension, of horror. Steps are heard outside."

Finally, consider the theme of the play, the **dramatic** or **central question** that drives the story of the play. For *Trifles* you have to ask yourself what kind of woman, under what sort of pressure, would commit murder? The desperation of the housewife's act is anything but a "trifle"; her situation was profound enough to yield lethal results.

## Sample Student Response to *Trifles*

Ness 1

James Ness

Professor Crane

ENGL 1202

October 22, 2008

*Trifles:* Song and Stillness

At first sight, Susan Glaspell's *Trifles* is a play about a wife suffering at the hands of a coldhearted and arrogant husband. At the end of her rope, she finally goes mad and kills him. But the play also explores what happens in a marriage when one partner fails to communicate with another or care about her happiness. Even more importantly, it reveals the differences between the way men and women view themselves and each other, and it tells a lot about the way these views affect marriage.

Early on, Mr. Hale reveals a lot about the way Wright treated his wife: he "didn't know as what his [Wright's] wife wanted made much difference" (6) to him. Clearly, her needs and desires in life didn't matter much to him. Perhaps he was just selfish. Later on, Mrs. Hale reveals more about the Wrights' marriage when, after finding the broken bird cage, she describes the house in which they lived as a "lonesome place" (10). It "weren't cheerful," she says, and she compares Mr. Wright to "raw wind that gets to the bone" (10). Mrs. Hale also says that Minnie Foster "was kind of like a bird herself" (10) before she married Wright. It is at this point that Mrs. Hale and Mrs. Peters find the bloody, dead canary which Mr. Wright killed and which his wife wrapped up in silk and placed in an expensive box.

The finding of the broken bird cage and the dead canary is also important because they are symbols of the Wrights' marriage. In fact, the canary might very well refer to Mrs. Wright, who, as Mrs. Hale tells us, "used to wear pretty

Ness 2

clothes and be lively, when she was Minnie Foster, one of the town girls singing in the choir" (11). The cage symbolizes the cheerless house in which Mr. Wright kept her. This idea is reinforced later in the play when Mrs. Hale says "Wright wouldn't like the bird—a thing that sang. She used to sing. He killed that, too" (11). There's a good chance that Wright objected to his wife's singing, made her quit the choir, and kept her from socializing with her neighbors.

The fact that Wright killed the bird completes the picture of his character as a coldhearted, arrogant, and violent person. But it also reveals an even more important aspect of the play's theme. Remember that the women come upon the dead bird after searching for some quilt patches to take to Mrs. Wright, who has been arrested. Their motive is to cheer her up while she is in jail. Of course, these are the kinds of female actions and thoughts that Mr. Hale refers to earlier in the play when he claims that "women are used to worrying over trifles" (11). This was said in reaction to hearing that Mrs. Wright was worried that her house had gotten cold and that her preserve jars would freeze and crack. However, the women's natural instinct to comfort someone in pain—what the men in this play might call a trifle—reveals the murder's motive, a motive that the men in the play have no success in finding no matter how hard they search.

Work Cited

Glaspell, Susan. *Trifles. Literature: Craft & Voice.* Eds. Nicholas Delbanco and Alan Cheuse. New York: McGraw-Hill, 2009. Print.

## Types of Drama

To read drama critically, you need in addition to the literary elements of plot and character, a basic vocabulary of theatrical forms and conventions. The two most common dramatic forms are tragedy and comedy, and both date at least as far back as the drama of ancient Greece (chapter 33).

- In **tragedy,** characters face serious and important challenges that end in disastrous failure or defeat for the protagonist.
- In **comedy,** life usually turns out well for the main character, and the primary purpose of the play is to amuse the audience.

> "What we try to do is illuminate something so that people can make up their own minds based upon the reality of the situation rather than the mythology. And if one can do that, it's enough."
>
> Conversation with Arthur Miller

Within these two large groupings there are a number of variations and blendings, such as **tragicomedies** (where the protagonist isn't defeated but there is a downturn in his or her situation), **melodramas** (where the forces of good and evil are in absolute and often violent opposition), and **problem plays** (which explore social issues, such as *Trifles'* exploration of a woman's place and power (or powerlessness) in the home.

## Tragedy

The structure of Greek tragedy shapes tragic drama even today (a fuller discussion of Greek tragedy can be found in chapter 33). Tragedy in real life might be brought on by a natural disaster or wartime or personal heartache, but tragedy in drama begins and ends with the qualities found in the main character: the **hero.** A hero is more than just the protagonist, or lead character, in a play. The hero's nature must be such that in some way the audience feels admiration for his or her qualities (wisdom, generosity, bravery, and love of family) and must feel compassion and fear when the character falls. The audience finds the hero at least in some degree sympathetic.

In a tragedy, the hero stands in conflict with forces larger than himself. These might be an unjust society (as in many modern plays, see chapter 35) or it might be another human being, a villain (as in the conflict between Othello and Iago in Shakespeare's *Othello,* chapter 34). Often the adversary might consist of fate itself, as in

> "The heart of drama . . . has been . . . really since it began . . . character types and the conflict and the encounter with character types. And I don't care whether you go back to . . . the Greek theater . . . you have . . . this conflict of characters."
>
> Conversation with Edwin Wilson

Sophocles' *Oedipus the King,* about whose hero it was prophesied that he would kill his father and marry his mother (chapter 33). However, *external* forces don't turn the hero into a **tragic hero.** Rather, from the beginning there is something about the hero's character that undermines what the audience finds sympathetic, and this **tragic flaw**—be it arrogance or jealousy or stubbornness—speeds along the hero's downfall.

Sophocles' *Oedipus the King* is the very prototype of the tragic mode of drama, from the five-act structure to the noble position of the central figure and the inevitable trajectory of decline. The proximity to power is a significant attribute of the hero. Even today we can see the voyeuristic fascination with the fall from grace of a politician because of a sex scandal or a celebrity because of drug abuse or violence. In classical tragic drama, however, the hero proves his or her heroic stature by accepting the justice of the punishment for mortal flaws. Several tragedies and the many faces of the tragic hero will be more fully studied in chapters and casebooks on ancient Greek drama, Shakespeare, and modern drama that appear later in this volume.

### Comedy

Comedy stands as the countervailing force to tragedy. Laughter illuminates the human condition just as effectively as tears. As in tragedy, the main characters will possess weaknesses, though unlike tragic figures, the main characters fall short of heroism and do not appear to be the larger-than-life people who show what our best selves can be. These characters are much more likely to prick our pride with the revelation that we are no more heroic than is the frog who requires the princess's kiss. To be sure, we can find comic characters written into a tragedy for **comic relief,** but a comedy in general is a play that makes us laugh at our flaws and ultimately forgive ourselves for our foibles.

**Satyr plays**—named for the half horse/half man mythological characters full of mischief and vulgar sexuality—employed excess, unrestrained sexuality, and outlandish characters. They might well be akin to the exaggerated presentation of modern-day **burlesque,** with its sexual innuendo, striptease, and **slapstick** or **farce.** A man who slips on a banana peel, or a character with a three-foot nose, belongs to the broad comic mode of burlesque. Satyr plays were part of Greek festivals, and out of these grew Aristophanes' great comedies of invective, ridicule, and political satire, the most famous of which is *Lysistrata,* in which the wives of soldiers withhold sex from their husbands until the men are willing to end the war. Some **satiric comedies** can be violent, crude, and nasty—biting commentaries on the human condition without any guarantee that good will prevail.

Other forms of comedies evolved from this early Greek theater, such as the **comedy of manners,** which shines an indulgent light on the hypocrisy of the social elite, and, much later, **restoration drama**—bawdy plays of fallen virtue and infidelity, which played to sold-out houses in London after the Puritans were displaced from power. Today we're familiar with **romantic comedy,** where two would-be/should-be lovers find each other after a series of misunderstandings and false starts. A play such as this gently pokes fun at the difficulties of finding love and of keeping one's dignity in the search for it. Whether a play uses **high comedy**—wordplay and wit—or **low comedy**—gags and pratfalls—its storyline contains the unexpected; the French philosopher Henri Bergson argued that this unexpectedness was a crucial part of the comedic mode. Further, the one all-embracing definition of comedy, separating this mode from tragedy, is that it is a kind of play that ends happily—or, in any case, with its main players still alive.

> "When you are reading a . . . comedy, it helps to know something about the history of the time in which it was written. Because what was making the public laugh, not when they were in the theater? Who was the king at that time? Who was the queen? Who were the serfs? Who were the slaves? Who were the masters? What was the situation politically? And so on. If you have that in your head, or if you . . . look it up, I think it makes all plays more interesting."
>
> Conversation with Marian Seldes

In that vein, we offer you *The Wedding Story* by Julianne Homokay, a satiric one-act comedy about romantic relationships. Look at this modern parable about marriage—in both its ideal and its actual state—and compare Homokay's attitude toward gender relations to those in *Trifles,* a play first performed in 1916. When Glaspell wrote her play, women were not allowed to serve on juries, so if Mrs. Wright were to go on trial, she would not have been judged by a "jury of her peers." In fact, as the play makes clear, the men who judge her would have little understanding of her motives or her life. We look at such relationships through a different kind of lens in *The Wedding*. Compare how the storyteller in *The Wedding Story* conjures up his characters, making creatures of his imagination who take on the flesh-and-blood guise of "Bride" and "Groom," and then start to answer back.

# Julianne Homokay (b. 1966)

Julianne Homokay holds an M.F.A. in playwriting from the University of Nevada, Las Vegas and has put it to use writing plays such as *Judy Gray, Living Roanoke,* and *Cottonmouth.* She also collaborated on a musical version of *Around the World in 80 Days* that debuted at the Fulton Opera House in Lancaster, Pennsylvania. She has taught at the Fulton Opera House and currently teaches at Pasadena City College. Her many honors include a grant from the Nevada Arts Council and a term as playwright-in-residence at Franklin and Marshall College. She lives in Los Angeles.

**AS YOU READ** Look for evidence of role reversal, both on the storyteller's and on the characters' part.

# The Wedding Story (2000)

## CHARACTERS

**STORYTELLER**

**BRIDE**

**GROOM**

**SETTING:** *A land where grass is always green, the sun is always shining, and fences are always white picket.*

**TIME:** *A sunny day in sunny June, the height of the perfect wedding season. In Vermont.*

*[Lights up on the* STORYTELLER *reading from a leatherbound volume with gilded pages.]*

**STORYTELLER:** *(closing the volume)* The End. Good night, sleep tight, don't let the bedbugs bite. What? You want to hear another one? But it's a school night. Okay, okay, just this once. I'm such a pushover. What type of story shall we hear?

*[ad lib if the audience yells out suggestions]*

How about a fairy tale for our times? A field of dreams fenced in by white picket, a story of the young man and woman we all hope to be someday? Too bad, that's what you're getting.

*[The* STORYTELLER *opens the volume back up. Lights up on* BRIDE *and* GROOM *in traditional garb standing on top of a wedding cake.]*

Once upon a time there was a young woman, pretty as a day in June.

*[The* BRIDE *does the royal wave.]*

A young man stood by her side, smart as a whip and handsome as a polo horse.

*[The* GROOM *salutes.]*

They met in high school and fell in love on a merry day in May.

*[The* BRIDE *and* GROOM *whisper to each other.]*

Before long, the young man dropped to his knee, pulled a diamond from his pocket, and won the young woman's hand in marriage.

**BRIDE:** Uh, excuse us, Mr. Storyteller?

*[The* STORYTELLER *looks back at them, confused. The* BRIDE *and* GROOM *smile and wave. The* STORYTELLER *waves back.]*

**STORYTELLER:** Moving right along. With the blessings of their compatible—

**BRIDE:** Mr. Storyteller!

**STORYTELLER:** Excuse me a moment. *(to* BRIDE*)* Yes, what is it?

**BRIDE:** We didn't exactly meet in high school.

**STORYTELLER:** Yes you did, it says so right here.

**BRIDE:** We met in a bar.

**GROOM:** And we dated on and off for five years while she experimented with foreigners.

**STORYTELLER:** How nice. Well. For our purposes, let's say you met in high school, shall we?

*[back to the kids]*

So. With the blessings of their compatible families, the young man and woman were to be Bride and Groom.

**BRIDE:** *(to* GROOM*)* Wait a minute. As I recall, you kept breaking it off.

**GROOM:** What?

**BRIDE:** Yeah. Then you'd want me back the minute I had a new boyfriend.

**GROOM:** You certainly didn't waste any time running into the arms of the first guy who had an accent.

**STORYTELLER:** *(to* BRIDE *and* GROOM*)* Sssssh. Let's don't argue in front of the impressionable youngsters. *(to children)* The bride soon set in on the wedding preparations.

**BRIDE:** *(to* GROOM*)* I never realized you were a racist.

**GROOM:** I'm not, I was fine with the fact you'd slept with black men.

**BRIDE:** You're assuming that "racism" automatically refers to African-Americans. Isn't that a form of racism itself?

**STORYTELLER:** Excuse me, ma'am, sir, firmie those bouches so I can return to the story thank you.

**GROOM:** By all means. Don't let anything silly like our issues get in your way.

**STORYTELLER:** Look, will you play along? The children will have ample opportunity to be disillusioned later, let's just have a nice bedtime story, okay? Okay.

*[to the children]*

AS I WAS SAYING, the preparations. They were to be married in a beautiful church—

**GROOM:** *(under his breath)* Drive-thru chapel in Vegas.

**STORYTELLER:** —followed by an elegant reception at an old inn in Vermont.

**BRIDE:** *(under her breath)* Back room at the Star Dust Lounge.

**STORYTELLER:** The bride put Martha Stewart to shame as she had the evening designed to the last detail—

**GROOM:** *(to* BRIDE*)* Ha! That really sounds like you.

**STORYTELLER:** —from the linen napkins to the centerpieces of purple freesia and Italian ruscus.

**BRIDE:** *(to* GROOM*)* I think he was invited to someone else's wedding.

**GROOM:** And why is he assuming the bride always has the taste? Does it never occur to anyone that the groom might want to participate? I worked my way though law school as a floral designer, that's how I know freesia is all wrong for a centerpiece, except maybe as an accent flower.

**BRIDE:** You were a floral designer?

**GROOM:** You need to base your arrangement on a more substantial bloom, like a lily or an orchid.

**BRIDE:** Brad, is there something you want to tell me?

**STORYTELLER:** Actually, there is something I want to tell these youngsters so they can get to bed at a decent hour. THE STORY.

**BRIDE:** Well huffy huff huff.

**STORYTELLER:** SO, they had their flawless reception for 300 guests at a turn-of-the-century inn in Vermont—

**BRIDE:** You know, we're not from Vermont. We've never even been to Vermont.

**STORYTELLER:** —at which all had a delightful time.

**GROOM:** *(to* BRIDE*)* What do you mean is there something I want to tell you?

**STORYTELLER:** Immediately following the splendid reception—

**BRIDE:** I mean, is there something you haven't been honest with me about? With yourself about?

**GROOM:** Like what?

**STORYTELLER:** The bride, at the tender age of 24—
*[The* GROOM *laughs out loud.]*
WHAT? WHAT'S SO FUNNY?

**GROOM:** She's not even close to 24.

**STORYTELLER:** Now just wait a minute here, Buster Brown, whose story is this?

**BRIDE/GROOM:** Ours.

**STORYTELLER:** Wrong. This is a fairy tale, I'm going for prototypes.

**BRIDE:** But I'm 35.

**STORYTELLER:** In this story, you're 24. The average American woman gets married at 24.

**BRIDE:** How old's that make him?

**STORYTELLER:** 27. Why, how old is he really?

**GROOM:** I'm the one that's 24.

**STORYTELLER:** Isn't that a little young to be getting married?

**BRIDE:** How come 24's okay for me but not for him?

**STORYTELLER:** You're the woman. You're supposed to be younger.

**BRIDE:** Jesus.

**STORYTELLER:** Now, before I was interrupted for the umpteenth time, boys and girls, I was saying that after the reception, the 24-year-old bride was whisked away in a horse-drawn carriage by her 27-year-old Prince Charming.

**BRIDE:** Whisked away where?

**STORYTELLER:** I don't know. To . . . the . . . airport.

**BRIDE:** Which one?

**STORYTELLER:** The Airport of . . . Vermont.

**BRIDE:** There's one in Burlington and one in Montpelier.

**GROOM:** How did you know that?

**BRIDE:** I majored in geography.

**GROOM:** You did?

**BRIDE:** *(to* STORYTELLER*)* So Mr. Fancy Pants, which one was it?

**STORYTELLER:** The one where you caught your flight to Hawaii for your honeymoon.

**BRIDE:** This whole fairy tale is completely out of hand. Anyone knows there's no flights from Vermont to Hawaii. You have to fly through Logan or LAX. Or both. And anyway, I highly doubt they'd let the horses in the terminal.

**STORYTELLER:** Oh, for God's sake, what's the big deal in telling the children a nice little story?

**BRIDE:** No one's life turns out like that. How many of those kids will live up to your version of the story? None! They can't, it's too much pressure. It's like why Catholic women are all messed up, you can't be a virgin AND be a mother. And Brad, I probably shouldn't have married you to begin with.

**GROOM:** Shayna, how can you say that?

**BRIDE:** You're probably gay.

**GROOM:** What?

**BRIDE:** Oh c'mon, how many straight male floral designers do you know?

**GROOM:** That's what you thought I needed to be honest about?

**BRIDE:** You didn't even know I majored in Geography! Listen, if we're talking averages here, most people don't get married in Vermont. They get married in their one-horse hometowns that have WalMarts and bad zoning.

**STORYTELLER:** What's wrong with that?

**BRIDE:** NOTHING. THAT'S MY POINT. MOST people do get married in their hometowns. MOST people cheat on their spouses or end up in counseling or sell everything they own to get into a lousy nursing home. Put that in your fairy tale and smoke it.

**STORYTELLER:** No one's smoking anything. There are children present.

**BRIDE:** And God forbid we tell them what life is really like.

**GROOM:** She's got a point there. You're opening yourself up for multiple class-action suits, Mister.

**STORYTELLER:** Fine. I've had it. You want the truth, the whole truth, and nothing but the truth, the whole enchilada, the proverbial hook, line, and sinker? Well far be it from me to give these little souls something to which to aspire.

**BRIDE/GROOM:** Do it! Do it! *(ad lib)*

**STORYTELLER:** I'm warning you, it won't be pretty.

**BRIDE/GROOM:** We stand warned.

**STORYTELLER:** I'm such a pushover.

*[opens the volume back up]*

Once upon a time in a trailer park not so far away, there lived a woman approaching middle age who drank a lot of bourbon, smoked a pack a day, hung out in places where they throw peanut shells on the floor—

**BRIDE:** All right already.

**STORYTELLER:** —and a young, slightly effeminate man who took it up the ass once from a fellow Eagle Scout, but since it only happened once when he was 17 and drunk on Kahlua, he still considered himself straight.

**GROOM:** Hey hey hey.

**STORYTELLER:** The woman and the man met in a bar one night where they got drunk and slept together afterwards at her place. Since the woman felt guilty about the one-night stand, she felt she needed to make a legitimate relationship out of the encounter to justify the sex, even though she really prefers black men. To stay deep in the dark closet, the man proposed to the woman, and since she's 35 and, let's face it, not getting any younger, she accepted his pathetic offer because it was a real ego boost to have snagged a hot stud eleven years younger than she, even if he does have the occasional problem getting a stiffy with her because he's really gay. Although the man offered to plan the entire wedding with his best friend Steve, the woman insisted they hire a horse-drawn carriage to drop them off at the Airport of Vermont, from which they took six connecting flights to Las Vegas to get married by an Elvis impersonator. To celebrate, they showed up at the Star Dust Lounge, at which they bought all the bar patrons cheeseballs and Budweiser. When they arrived back home in Weehawken, New Jersey, the Groom, unable to suppress his inner self for a moment longer, took up with a drag queen from SoHo, and the Bride, realizing she'd never be a mother, consoled herself with vodka and Xanax and died of a somewhat accidental overdose three years later. The Groom, now 27, took up wearing cowboy hats and chaps, and made the unfortunate mistake of traveling to Wyoming on business where he was dragged to his death behind a 4x4 by a bunch of homophobic rednecks. The drag queen wrote a show about the three of them in which he played all the parts, won a Genius Grant, and landed his own talk show on New York City cable access.

*[shuts book, exits]*

I bid you good night and sweet dreams, children. The End.

**BRIDE/GROOM:** *(ad lib, following the* STORYTELLER *off)* Uh, Mr. Storyteller, wait, it's okay, you can tell the other version, etc. . . .

# Writing from Reading

## Summarize

1 What is the story the storyteller wants to tell? What story gets told?

## Analyze Craft

2 What is the effect of the encounters between the bride and groom and the storyteller? How do these interactions create humor?

3 The play speaks to contemporary social arrangements involving love and social life. How would you describe the tone of the play? What is accomplished by this particular tone?

## Analyze Voice

4 The back-and-forth between the couple and the storyteller—and between themselves—makes for three distinct voices. Describe each. Does any one seem dominant at first? Does that condition last for the entire play?

5 Does the first speech the storyteller offers depend on a response to his question—"How about? . . ." When he says "Too bad, that's what you're getting," he's addressing both his invisible onstage audience of children and the audience in the hall. How does this strategy implicate the listener/viewer in the tale as told?

## Synthesize Summary and Analysis

6 Does the presentation about the perfect wedding made by the storyteller to the bride and groom seem closer to fantasy or reality, and why?

7 In this play, a realistic bedtime story about love and the beginning of marriage veers toward the comical. What is inherently comic about the situation? Might the storyteller have told about the meeting, courtship, and marriage in another way?

8 What effect does the storyteller create by insisting on his version of reality? How does the difference between the storyteller's first and second story and the story "play" out?

9 How well suited to the stage are the themes of "illusion" and "reality" here?

## Interpret the Play

10 What does the use of the bedtime fairy tale tell us about the story the playwright wants to tell?

# Suggestions for Writing

1. Both *Trifles* and *The Wedding Story* deal with the institution of marriage, its expectations and disappointments. The older play does so in an essentially tragic mode, the contemporary one in an essentially comic vein. Give examples of each, focusing on tone.
2. Imagine turning a poem (Robert Browning's "My Last Duchess," for example) or a story (like Anton Chekhov's "Rapture") into a play. What are the issues you will face in terms of physical (re)presentation?
3. Speculate on the role of theater in today's society. Is it important to have traditional staged theater? Has theater been sidelined by movies, TV, the Internet, and YouTube? Speculate on the theatrical aspects of all of these, using specific examples.

# 31 Going Further with Reading

## *Reading for the Stage*

A DIRECTOR might push an actor trying to find a connection to his or her character in exactly this fashion: Go deeper! After reading an entire play and beginning to explore the story line and how the characters make sense to you, you are ready to go deeper into the matter of understanding a play in all its elements and writing about it with an audience in mind. Reading a play allows you to be, as actress Marian Seldes says in her interview, "alone with it. . . . That frees your imagination." As you go deeper, imagine yourself as the actors, the director, and the audience.

- As the actor you're onstage delivering lines to the other actors and responding to an audience
- As the director you're trying to draw the audience into the play as a whole through lighting, costumes, setting, and characters
- As the audience you're seeing actors on a stage and responding to how you are drawn into the play

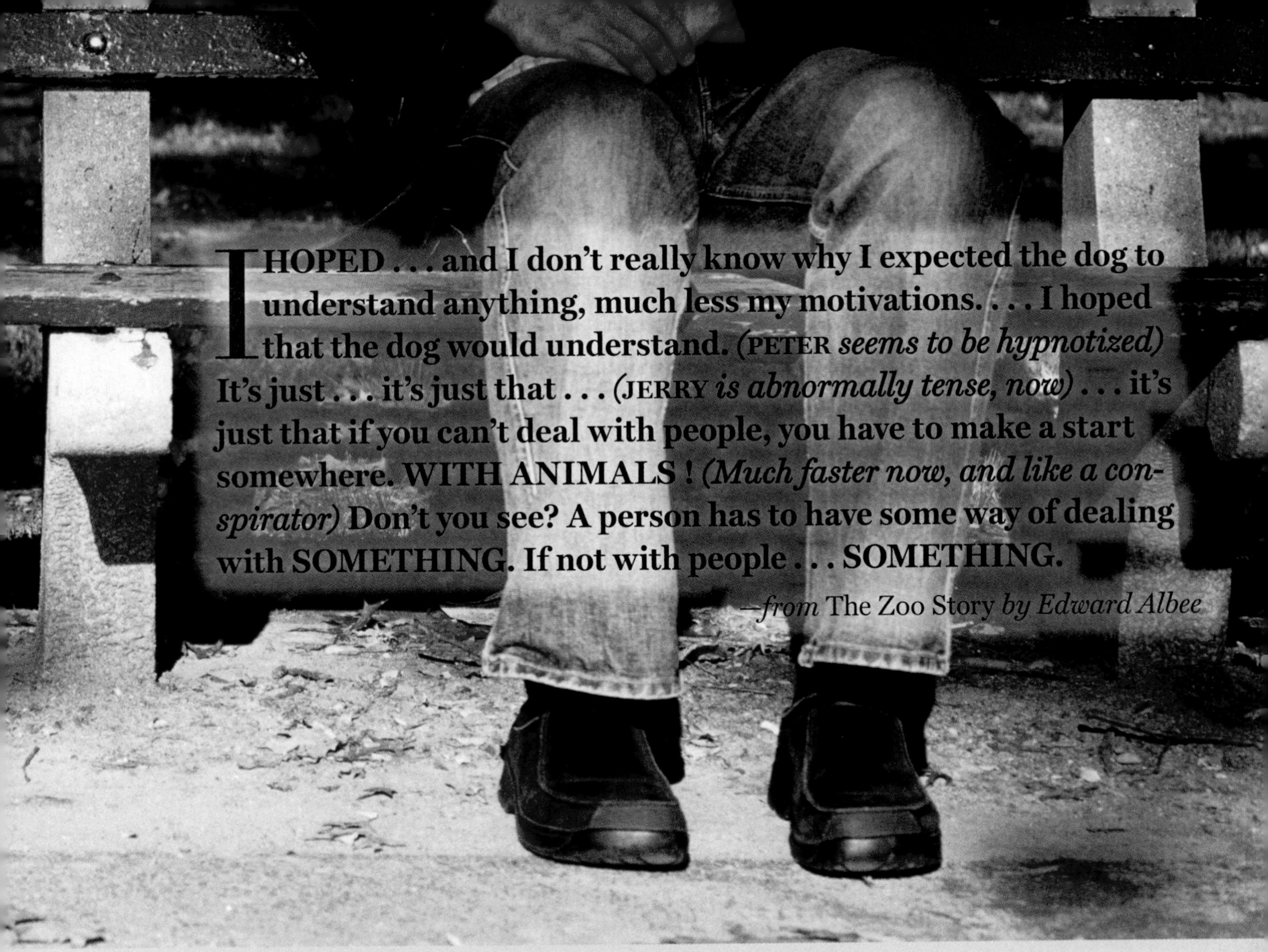

**I HOPED . . . and I don't really know why I expected the dog to understand anything, much less my motivations. . . . I hoped that the dog would understand. *(*PETER *seems to be hypnotized)* It's just . . . it's just that . . . *(*JERRY *is abnormally tense, now)* . . . it's just that if you can't deal with people, you have to make a start somewhere. WITH ANIMALS ! *(Much faster now, and like a conspirator)* Don't you see? A person has to have some way of dealing with SOMETHING. If not with people . . . SOMETHING.**

—*from* The Zoo Story *by Edward Albee*

When you read the play in the context of the stage, try to hear the voices of the actors. Decide if the words I love you, for example, are spoken as if for the first time by a younger romantic or as if for the thousandth time by an old seducer. See the characters' movements across the stage, the clothes they wear, the spotlights on them, and the objects they hold. Considering these extra dimensions, you are staging the play in what the critic Francis Fergusson called "the theater of the mind."

*CONTINUED ON PAGE 44*

*"No two people see the same play. No two performances of the same production are identical. And there's more than one way to skin a cat. Why, I don't know, but there is."*

Conversation with Edward Albee

*Art changes people if they wish to be changed*

Q&A

*Entertainment is misunderstood.*

# *A Conversation on Writing*

## Edward Albee

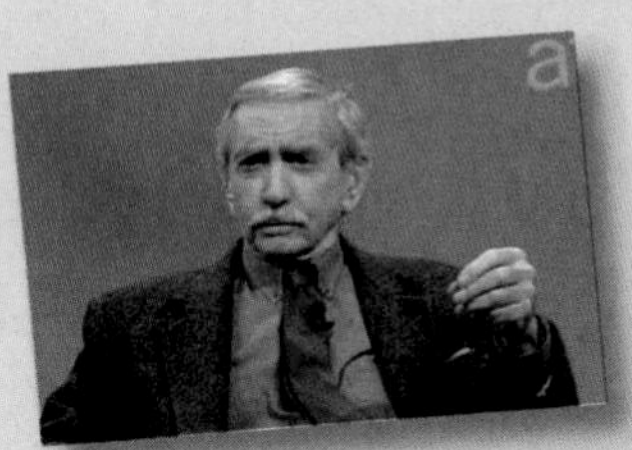

### *The Zoo Story* and the Writing Life

Well, I wrote poetry from the age of eight to twenty-eight when I quit because I was getting better but not better enough, and I wrote two terrible novels in my teens, really very bad novels . . . and since I decided I was a creative writer, which meant I didn't have to be able to think coherently in a straight line . . . essays were beyond me too . . . so I started writing plays. . . . When *The Zoo Story* opened in German in Berlin and got good reviews and it opened in New York in English and got good reviews, I guess it encouraged me to think maybe . . . [I] should go on with this.

### Entertainment

I think a playwright's obligation is to be coherent, to not waste people's time, to do something onstage that makes people think, makes them perhaps reconsider some of their values—accept change, not accept change—to have something in which they are participating, not just some kind of escapist entertainment that will just slide right off the mind. . . . Entertainment is misunderstood. Entertainment seems these days to mean something at which you do not have to think, at which you don't have any troubling experiences. But if art isn't engaging or troubling in some sense, it is a total waste of time.

### The Experience in the Text

The intention is there in the text. The intention is the experience of the play that I had while I was writing it. Because when I write a play . . . I see it, I hear it as a play being performed in front of me, and that's what I want to see on the stage—the same experience that I had while writing it.

**This interview with Edward Albee was conducted by Jesse Green for the *Times Talks* program sponsored by *The New York Times* on the occasion of Albee's eightieth birthday.**

## A STUDENT'S INITIAL REACTION TO *THE ZOO STORY*

When I look at this, I imagine from the title that animals are likely to play a role. Two men are sitting on a park bench. The playwright gives some guidance in stage directions in italics. If I imagine acting out the two parts, how would I draw the audience into the play?

# An Interactive Reading from Edward Albee's *The Zoo Story*

**JERRY:** Do you mind if I ask you questions?

**PETER:** Oh, not really.

**JERRY:** I'll tell you why I do it; I don't talk to many people—except to say like: give me a beer, or where's the john, or what time does the feature go on, or keep your hands to yourself, buddy. You know—things like that.

**PETER:** I must say I don't . . .

**JERRY:** But every once in a while I like to talk to somebody, really *talk;* like to get to know somebody, know all about him.

**PETER:** *(Lightly laughing, still a little uncomfortable)* And am I the guinea pig for today?

**JERRY:** On a sun-drenched Sunday afternoon like this? Who better than a nice married man with two daughters and . . . uh . . . a dog? *(PETER shakes his head)* No? Two dogs. *(PETER shakes his head again)* Hm. No dogs? *(PETER shakes his head, sadly)* Oh, that's a shame. But you look like an animal man. CATS? *(PETER nods his head, ruefully)* Cats! But, that can't be your idea. No, sir. Your wife and daughters? *(PETER nods his head)* Is there anything else I should know?

**PETER:** *(He has to clear his throat)* There are . . . there are two parakeets. One . . . uh . . . one for each of my daughters.

**JERRY:** Birds.

**PETER:** My daughters keep them in a cage in their bedroom.

**JERRY:** Do they carry disease? The birds.

**PETER:** I don't believe so.

**JERRY:** That's too bad. If they did you could set them loose in the house and the cats could eat them and die, maybe. *(PETER looks blank for a moment, then laughs)* And what else? What do you do to support your enormous household?

**PETER:** I . . . uh . . . I have an executive position with a . . . a small publishing house. We . . . uh . . . we publish textbooks.

**JERRY:** That sounds nice; very nice.

The role of questioner gives Jerry more power, almost like a detective. I would cast someone with a bigger presence for his role than for Peter's.

Drinking beer and calling the bathroom "john" gives clues that his character is "low brow," perhaps; Peter isn't—foils to each other?

The first animal mentioned in "Zoo Story" is not a zoo animal at all! I think of guinea pigs as docile household pets, kept in a cage.

I wonder why Jerry is so interested in Peter's pets. Their dialogue seems to say that having cats makes Peter less "manly."

Birds are another caged pet. Parakeets especially are common household birds (it would be different if he owned cardinals or toucans, say).

The interaction of animals becomes disturbing when Jerry puts it this way. Why would he say this? And why would he imagine Peter's pets are diseased in the first place?

If these two are foils, how might I represent that on stage?

We know from clues early on that this is New York's Central Park. There are lots of ways I can imagine staging this—just two benches on a stage, or a more elaborate park backdrop. But I think it would be interesting to do it outside.

Cues for very expressive gestures. Peter shows how he feels without saying it.

Cue for clearing throat and the amount of ellipses make it seem like he says this hesitantly.

Peter reacts hesitantly to Jerry's jab. I think I'd play them as a kind of boxing match with Jerry dancing around Peter throwing punches that Peter politely dodges

# Edward Albee (b. 1928)

Edward Albee was adopted as an infant into a wealthy New York family. His privileged upbringing included limousine rides to see Broadway productions and access to his parents' library, even though the young Albee got in trouble for actually reading the books that his parents maintained for looks only. After expulsion from three prep schools and Trinity College in Connecticut, he had a falling out with his parents that caused a twenty-year estrangement. Living on his own, Albee worked odd jobs until he wrote his first play, *The Zoo Story,* as a thirtieth birthday present to himself. Its debut in America brought the freshest approach to drama on the American stage since Eugene O'Neill and Thornton Wilder. Financially supported to begin with by stipends from his grandparents, Albee made a successful career of writing, and in his long productive life as playwright has garnered three Pulitzer Prizes. He might have received a fourth had not the recommendation of the committee to award the Pulitzer Prize to arguably his best and most important play, *Who's Afraid of Virginia Woolf?* (1962), been overturned because of the play's controversial sexual content. In 1966 the play was made into a movie starring Elizabeth Taylor and Richard Burton. Although Albee's plays have met with varying levels of success, *The Zoo Story* has remained significant to American drama, and some credit it as one of the biggest influence on off-Broadway works. In 2005 Albee was awarded the Special Tony Award for Lifetime Achievement.

**AS YOU READ** Ask yourself what the play's title conveys, and why Albee might have wished to call his play a "story." Make notes about how you would move the actors around on the set if you were directing this play.

# The Zoo Story (1958)

*—for William Flanagan*

## CHARACTERS

**PETER** *A man in his early forties, neither fat nor gaunt, neither handsome nor homely. He wears tweeds, smokes a pipe, carries horn-rimmed glasses. Although he is moving into middle age, his dress and his manner would suggest a man younger.*

**JERRY** *A man in his late thirties, not poorly dressed, but carelessly. What was once a trim and lightly muscled body has begun to go to fat; and while he is no longer handsome, it is evident that he once was. His fall from physical grace should not suggest debauchery; he has, to come closest to it, a great weariness.*

**THE SCENE** *It is Central Park; a Sunday afternoon in summer; the present. There are two park benches, one toward either side of the stage; they both face the audience. Behind them: foliage, trees, sky. At the beginning, Peter is seated on one of the benches.*

*(As the curtain rises,* PETER *is seated on the bench stage-right. He is reading a book. He stops reading, cleans his glasses, goes back to reading.* JERRY *enters.)*

**JERRY:** I've been to the zoo. *(*PETER *doesn't notice)* I said, I've been to the zoo. MISTER, I'VE BEEN TO THE ZOO!

**PETER:** Hm? . . . What? . . . I'm sorry, were you talking to me?

**JERRY:** I went to the zoo, and then I walked until I came here. Have I been walking north?

**PETER:** *(Puzzled)* North? Why . . . I . . . I think so. Let me see.

**JERRY:** *(Pointing past the audience)* Is that Fifth Avenue?

**PETER:** Why yes; yes, it is.

**JERRY:** And what is that cross street there; that one, to the right?

**PETER:** That? Oh, that's Seventy-fourth Street.

**JERRY:** And the zoo is around Sixty-fifth Street; so, I've been walking north.

**PETER:** *(Anxious to get back to his reading)* Yes; it would seem so.

**JERRY:** Good old north.

**PETER:** *(Lightly, by reflex)* Ha, ha.

**JERRY:** *(After a slight pause)* But not due north.

**PETER:** I . . . well, no, not due north; but, we . . . call it north. It's northerly.

**JERRY:** *(Watches as* PETER, *anxious to dismiss him, prepares his pipe)* Well, boy; *you're* not going to get lung cancer, are you?

**PETER:** *(Looks up, a little annoyed, then smiles)* No, sir. Not from this.

**JERRY:** No, sir. What you'll probably get is cancer of the mouth, and then you'll have to wear one of those things Freud wore after they took one whole side of his jaw away. What do they call those things?

**PETER:** *(Uncomfortable)* A prosthesis?

**JERRY:** The very thing! A prosthesis. You're an educated man, aren't you? Are you a doctor?

**PETER:** Oh, no; no. I read about it somewhere; *Time* magazine, I think. *(He turns to his book)*

**JERRY:** Well, *Time* magazine isn't for blockheads.

**PETER:** No, I suppose not.

Peter sits reading before Jerry's arrival, in this 2006 production starring Paul Christophe and Pitt Simon.

**JERRY:** *(After a pause)* Boy, I'm glad that's Fifth Avenue there.

**PETER:** *(Vaguely)* Yes.

**JERRY:** I don't like the west side of the park much.

**PETER:** Oh? *(Then, slightly wary, but interested)* Why?

**JERRY:** *(Offhand)* I don't know.

**PETER:** Oh. *(He returns to his book)*

**JERRY:** *(He stands for a few seconds, looking at* PETER, *who finally looks up again, puzzled)* Do you mind if we talk?

**PETER:** *(Obviously minding)* Why . . . no, no.

**JERRY:** Yes you do; you do.

**PETER:** *(Puts his book down, his pipe out and away, smiling)* No, really; I don't mind.

**JERRY:** Yes you do.

**PETER:** *(Finally decided)* No; I don't mind at all, really.

**JERRY:** It's . . . it's a nice day.

**PETER:** *(Stares unnecessarily at the sky)* Yes. Yes, it is; lovely.

**JERRY:** I've been to the zoo.

**PETER:** Yes, I think you said so . . . didn't you?

**JERRY:** I bet you've got TV, huh?

**PETER:** Why yes, we have two; one for the children.

**JERRY:** You're married!

**PETER:** *(With pleased emphasis)* Why, certainly.

**JERRY:** It isn't a law, for God's sake.

**PETER:** No . . . no, of course not.

**JERRY:** And you have a wife.

**PETER:** *(Bewildered by the seeming lack of communication)* Yes!

**JERRY:** And you have children.

**PETER:** Yes; two.

**JERRY:** Boys?

**PETER:** No, girls . . . both girls.

**JERRY:** But you wanted boys.

**PETER:** Well . . . naturally, every man wants a son, but . . .

**JERRY:** *(Lightly mocking)* But that's the way the cookie crumbles?

**PETER:** *(Annoyed)* I wasn't going to say that.

**JERRY:** And you're not going to have any more kids, are you?

**PETER:** *(A bit distantly)* No. No more. *(Then back, and irksome)* Why did you say that? How would you know about that?

**JERRY:** The way you cross your legs, perhaps; something in the voice. Or maybe I'm just guessing. Is it your wife?

**PETER:** *(Furious)* That's none of your business! *(A silence)* Do you understand? *(JERRY nods. PETER is quiet now)* Well, you're right. We'll have no more children.

**JERRY:** *(Softly)* That *is* the way the cookie crumbles.

**PETER:** *(Forgiving)* Yes . . . I guess so.

**JERRY:** Do you mind if I ask you questions?

**PETER:** Oh, not really.

**JERRY:** I'll tell you why I do it; I don't talk to many people—except to say like: give me a beer, or where's the john, or what time does the feature go on, or keep your hands to yourself, buddy. You know—things like that.

**PETER:** I must say I don't . . .

**JERRY:** But every once in a while I like to talk to somebody, really *talk;* like to get to know somebody, know all about him.

**PETER:** *(Lightly laughing, still a little uncomfortable)* And am I the guinea pig for today?

**JERRY:** On a sun-drenched Sunday afternoon like this? Who better than a nice married man with two daughters and . . . uh . . . a dog? *(PETER shakes his head)* No? Two dogs. *(PETER shakes his head again)* Hm. No dogs? *(PETER shakes his head, sadly)* Oh, that's a shame. But you look like an animal man. CATS? *(PETER nods his head, ruefully)* Cats! But, that can't be your idea. No, sir. Your wife and daughters? *(PETER nods his head)* Is there anything else I should know?

**PETER:** *(He has to clear his throat)* There are . . . there are two parakeets. One . . . uh . . . one for each of my daughters.

**JERRY:** Birds.

**PETER:** My daughters keep them in a cage in their bedroom.

**JERRY:** Do they carry disease? The birds.

**PETER:** I don't believe so.

**JERRY:** That's too bad. If they did you could set them loose in the house and the cats could eat them and die, maybe. *(PETER looks blank for a moment, then laughs)* And what else? What do you do to support your enormous household?

**PETER:** I . . . uh . . . I have an executive position with a . . . a small publishing house. We . . . uh . . . we publish textbooks.

**JERRY:** That sounds nice; very nice. What do you make?

**PETER:** *(Still cheerful)* Now look here!

**JERRY:** Oh, come on.

**PETER:** Well, I make around two hundred thousand a year, but I don't carry more than forty dollars at any one time . . . in case you're a . . . a holdup man . . . ha, ha, ha.

**JERRY:** *(Ignoring the above)* Where do you live? *(PETER is reluctant)* Oh, look; I'm not going to rob you, and I'm not going to kidnap your parakeets, your cats, or your daughters.

**PETER:** *(Too loud)* I live between Lexington and Third Avenue, on Seventy-fourth Street.

**JERRY:** That wasn't so hard, was it?

**PETER:** I didn't mean to seem . . . ah . . . it's that you don't really carry on a conversation; you just ask questions. And I'm . . . I'm normally . . . uh . . . reticent. Why do you just stand there?

**JERRY:** Say, what's the dividing line between upper-middle-middle-class and lower-upper-middle-class?

**PETER:** My dear fellow, I . . .

**JERRY:** Don't my dear fellow me.

Jerry and Peter begin their conversation.

**PETER:** *(Unhappily)* Was I patronizing? I believe I was; I'm sorry. But, you see your question about the classes bewildered me.

**JERRY:** And when you're bewildered you become patronizing?

**PETER:** I . . . I don't express myself too well, sometimes. *(He attempts a joke on himself)* I'm in publishing, not writing.

**JERRY:** *(Amused, but not at the humor)* So be it. The truth *is: I* was being patronizing.

**PETER:** Oh, now; you needn't say that.

*(It is at this point that* JERRY *may begin to move about the stage with slowly increasing determination and authority, but pacing himself, so that the long speech about the dog comes at the high point of the arc)*

**JERRY:** All right. Who are your favorite writers? Baudelaire and Stephen King?

**PETER:** *(Wary)* Well, I like a great many writers; I have a considerable catholicity of taste, if I may say so. Those two men are fine, each in his way. *(Warming up)* Baudelaire, of course . . . uh . . . is by far the finer of the two, but Stephen King has a place . . . in our . . . uh . . . national . . .

**JERRY:** Skip it.

**PETER:** I . . . sorry.

**JERRY:** Do you know what I did before I went to the zoo today? I walked all the way up Fifth Avenue from Washington Square; all the way.

**PETER:** Oh; you live in Greenwich Village! *(This seems to enlighten* PETER*)*

**JERRY:** No, I don't. I took the subway down to the Village so I could walk all the way up Fifth Avenue to the zoo. It's one of those things a person has to do; sometimes a person has to go a very long distance out of his way to come back a short distance correctly.

**PETER:** *(Almost pouting)* Oh, I thought you lived in Greenwich Village.

**JERRY:** What were you trying to do? Make sense out of things? Bring order? The old pigeonhole bit? Well, that's easy; I'll tell you. I live in a four-story brownstone roominghouse on the Upper West Side between Columbus Avenue and Central Park West. I live on the top floor; rear; west. It's a laughably small room, and one of my walls is made of beaverboard; this beaverboard separates my room from another laughably small room, so I assume that the two rooms were once one room, a small room, but not necessarily laughable. The room beyond my beaverboard wall is occupied by a colored queen who always keeps his door open; well, not always but *always* when he's plucking his eyebrows, which he does with Buddhist concentration. This colored queen has rotten teeth, which is rare, and he has a Japanese kimono, which is also pretty rare; and he wears this kimono to and from the john in the hall, which is pretty frequent. I mean, he goes to the john a lot. He never bothers me, and he never brings anyone up to his room. All he does is pluck his eyebrows, wear his kimono and go to the john. Now, the two front rooms on my floor are a little larger, I guess; but they're pretty small, too. There's a Puerto Rican family in one of them, a husband, a wife, and some kids; I don't know how many. These people entertain a lot. And in the other front room, there's somebody living there, but I don't know who it is. I've never seen who it is. Never. Never ever.

**PETER:** *(Embarrassed)* Why . . . why do you live there?

**JERRY:** *(From a distance again)* I don't know.

**PETER:** It doesn't sound like a very nice place . . . where you live.

**JERRY:** Well, no; it isn't an apartment in the East Seventies. But, then again, I don't have one wife, two daughters, two cats and two parakeets. What I do have, I have toilet articles, a few clothes, a hot plate that I'm not supposed to have, a can opener, one that works with a key, you know; a knife, two forks, and two spoons, one small, one large; three plates, a cup, a saucer, a drinking glass, two picture frames, both empty, eight or nine books, a pack of pornographic playing cards, regular deck, an old Western Union typewriter that prints nothing but capital letters, and a small strongbox without a lock which has in it . . . what? Rocks! Some rocks . . . sea-rounded rocks I picked up on the beach when I was a kid. Under which . . . weighed down . . . are some letters . . . please letters . . . please why don't you do this, and please when will you do that letters. And when letters, too. When will you write? When will

Jerry talks about his apartment.

you come? When? These letters are from more recent years.

**PETER:** *(Stares glumly at his shoes, then)* About those two empty picture frames . . . ?

**JERRY:** I don't see why they need any explanation at all. Isn't it clear? I don't have pictures of anyone to put in them.

**PETER:** Your parents . . . perhaps . . . a girl friend . . .

**JERRY:** You're a very sweet man, and you're possessed of a truly enviable innocence. But good old Mom and good old Pop are dead . . . you know? . . . I'm broken up about it, too . . . I mean really. BUT. That particular vaudeville act is playing the cloud circuit now, so I don't see how I can look at them, all neat and framed. Besides, or, rather, to be pointed about it, good old Mom walked out on good old Pop when I was ten and a half years old; she embarked on an adulterous turn of our southern states . . . a journey of a year's duration . . . and her most constant companion . . . among others, among many others . . . was a Mr. Barleycorn. At least, that's what good old Pop told me after he went down . . . came back . . . brought her body north. We'd received the news between Christmas and New Year's, you see, that good old Mom had parted with the ghost in some dump in Alabama. And, without the ghost . . . she was less welcome. I mean, what was she? A stiff . . . a northern stiff. At any rate, good old Pop celebrated the New Year for an even two weeks and then slapped into the front of a somewhat moving city omnibus, which sort of cleaned things out family-wise. Well no; then there was Mom's sister, who was given neither to sin nor the consolations of the bottle. I moved in on her, and my memory of her is slight excepting I remember still that she did all things dourly: sleeping, eating, working, praying. She dropped dead on the stairs to her apartment, my apartment then, too, on the afternoon of my high school graduation. A terribly middle-European joke, if you ask me.

**PETER:** Oh, my; oh, my.

**JERRY:** Oh, your what? But that was a long time ago, and I have no feeling about any of it that I care to admit to myself. Perhaps you can see, though, why good old Mom and good old Pop are frameless. What's your name? Your first name?

**PETER:** I'm Peter.

**JERRY:** I'd forgotten to ask you. I'm Jerry.

**PETER:** *(With a slight, nervous laugh)* Hello, Jerry.

**JERRY:** *(Nods his hello)* And let's see now; what's the point of having a girl's picture, especially in two frames? I have two picture frames, you remember. I never see the pretty little ladies more than once, and most of them wouldn't be caught in the same room with a camera. It's odd, and I wonder if it's sad.

**PETER:** The girls?

**JERRY:** No. I wonder if it's sad that I never see the little ladies more than once. I've never been able to have sex with, or, how is it put? . . . make love to anybody more than once. Once; that's it. . . . Oh, wait; for a week and a half, when I was fifteen and I hang my head in shame that puberty was late . . . I was a h-o-m-o-s-e-x-u-a-l. I mean, I was queer . . . *(Very fast)* . . . queer, queer, queer . . . with bells ringing, banners snapping in the wind. And for those eleven days, I met at least twice a day with the park superintendent's son . . . a Greek boy, whose birthday was the same as mine, except he was a year older. I think I was very much in love . . . maybe just with sex. But that was the jazz of a very special hotel, wasn't it? And now; oh, do I love the little ladies; really, I love them. For about an hour.

**PETER:** Well, it seems perfectly simple to me . . .

**JERRY:** *(Angry)* Look! Are you going to tell me to get married and have parakeets?

**PETER:** *(Angry himself)* Forget the parakeets! And stay single if you want to. It's no business of mine. I didn't start this conversation in the . . .

**JERRY:** All right, all right. I'm sorry. All right? You're not angry?

**PETER:** *(Laughing)* No, I'm not angry.

**JERRY:** *(Relieved)* Good. *(Now back to his previous tone)* Interesting that you asked me about the picture frames. I would have thought that you would have asked me about the pornographic playing cards.

**PETER:** *(With a knowing smile)* Oh, I've seen those cards.

**JERRY:** That's not the point. *(Laughs)* I suppose when you were a kid you and your pals passed them around, or you had a pack of your own.

**PETER:** Well, I guess a lot of us did.

**JERRY:** And you threw them away just before you got married.

**PETER:** Oh, now; look here. I didn't *need* anything like that when I got older.

**JERRY:** No?

**PETER:** *(Embarrassed)* I'd rather not talk about these things.

**JERRY:** So? Don't. Besides, I wasn't trying to plumb your post-adolescent sexual life and hard times; what I wanted to get at is the value difference between pornographic playing cards when you're a kid, and pornographic playing cards when you're older. It's that when you're a kid you use the cards as a substitute for a real experience, and when you're older you use real experience as a substitute for the fantasy. But I imagine you'd rather hear about what happened at the zoo.

**PETER:** *(Enthusiastic)* Oh, yes; the zoo. *(Then, awkward)* That is . . . if you . . .

**JERRY:** Let me tell you about why I went . . . well, let me tell you some things. I've told you about the fourth floor of the roominghouse where I live. I think the rooms are better as you go down, floor by floor. I guess they are; I don't know. I don't know any of the people on the third and second floors. Oh, wait! I do know that there's a lady living on the third floor, in the front. I know because she cries all the time. Whenever I go out or come back in, whenever I pass her door, I always hear her crying, muffled, but . . . very determined. Very determined indeed. But the one I'm getting to, and all about the dog, is the landlady. I don't like to use words that are too harsh in describing people. I don't like to. But the landlady is a fat, ugly, mean, stupid, unwashed, misanthropic, cheap, drunken bag of garbage. And you may have noticed that I very seldom use profanity, so I can't describe her as well as I might.

**PETER:** You describe her . . . vividly.

**JERRY:** Well, thanks. Anyway, she has a dog, and I will tell you about the dog, and she and her dog are the gatekeepers of my dwelling. The woman is bad enough; she leans around in the entrance hall, spying to see that I don't bring in things or people, and when she's had her mid-afternoon pint of lemon-flavored gin she always stops me in the hall, and grabs ahold of my coat or my arm, and she presses her disgusting body up against me to keep me in a corner so she can talk to me. The smell of her body and her breath . . . you can't imagine it . . . and somewhere, somewhere in the back of that pea-sized brain of hers, an organ developed just enough to let her eat, drink, and emit, she has some foul parody of sexual desire. And I, Peter, I am the object of her sweaty lust.

**PETER:** That's disgusting. That's . . . horrible.

**JERRY:** But I have found a way to keep her off. When she talks to me, when she presses herself to my body and mumbles about her room and how I should come there, I merely say: but, Love; wasn't yesterday enough for you, and the day before? Then she puzzles, she makes slits of her tiny eyes, she sways a little, and then, Peter . . . and it is at this moment that I think I might be doing some good in that tormented house . . . a simple-minded smile begins to form on her unthinkable face, and she giggles and groans as she thinks about yesterday and the day before; as she believes and relives what never happened. Then, she motions to that black monster of a dog she has, and she goes back to her room. And I am safe until our next meeting.

**PETER:** It's so . . . unthinkable. I find it hard to believe that people such as that really *are*.

**JERRY:** *(Lightly mocking)* It's for reading about, isn't it?

**PETER:** *(Seriously)* Yes.

**JERRY:** And fact is better left to fiction. You're right, Peter. Well, what I have been meaning to tell you about is the dog; I shall, now.

**PETER:** *(Nervously)* Oh, yes; the dog.

**JERRY:** Don't go. You're not thinking of going, are you?

**PETER:** Well . . . no, I don't think so.

**JERRY:** *(As if to a child)* Because after I tell you about the dog, do you know what then? Then . . . then I'll tell you about what happened at the zoo.

**PETER:** *(Laughing faintly)* You're . . . you're full of stories, aren't you?

**JERRY:** You don't *have* to listen. Nobody is holding you here; remember that. Keep that in your mind.

**PETER:** *(Irritably)* I know that.

**JERRY:** You do? Good.

*(The following long speech, it seems to me, should be done with a great deal of action, to achieve a hypnotic effect on* PETER, *and on the audience, too. Some specific actions have been suggested, but the director and the actor playing* JERRY *might best work it out for themselves)*

ALL RIGHT. *(As if reading from a huge billboard)* THE STORY OF JERRY AND THE DOG! *(Natural again)* What I am going to tell you has something to do with how sometimes it's necessary to go a long distance out of the way in order to come back a short distance correctly; or, maybe I only think that it has something to do with that. But, it's why I went to the zoo today, and why I walked north . . . northerly, rather . . . until I came here. All right. The dog, I think I told you, is a black monster of a beast: an oversized head, tiny, tiny ears, and eyes . . . bloodshot, infected, maybe; and a body you can see the ribs through the skin. The dog is black, all black; all black except for the bloodshot eyes, and . . . yes . . . and an open sore on its . . . *right* forepaw; that is red, too. And, oh yes; the poor monster, and I do believe it's an old dog . . . it's certainly a misused one . . . almost always has an erection . . . of sorts. That's red, too. And . . . what else? . . . oh, yes; there's a gray-yellow-white color, too, when he bares his fangs. Like this: Grrrrrrr! Which is what he did when he saw me for the first time . . . the day I moved in. I worried about that animal the very first minute I met him. Now, animals don't take to me like Saint Francis had birds hanging off him all the time. What I mean is: Animals are indifferent to me . . . like people *(He smiles slightly)* . . . most of the time. But this dog wasn't indifferent. From the very beginning he'd snarl and then go for me, to get one of my legs. Not like he was rabid, you know; he was sort of a stumbly dog, but he wasn't half-assed, either. It was a good, stumbly run; but I always got away. He got a piece of my trouser leg, look, you can see right here, where it's mended; he got that the second day I lived there; but, I kicked free and got upstairs fast, so that was that. *(Puzzles)* I still don't know to this day how the other roomers manage it, but you know what I *think:* I think it had to do only with me. Cozy. So. Anyway, this went on for over a week, whenever I came in; but never when I went out. That's funny. Or, it *was* funny. I could pack up and live in the street for all the dog cared. Well, I thought about it up in my room one day, one of the times after I'd bolted upstairs, and I made up my mind. I decided: First, I'll kill the dog with kindness, and if that doesn't work . . . I'll just kill him. *(*PETER *winces)* Don't react, Peter; just listen. So, the next day I went out and bought a bag of hamburgers, medium rare, no catsup, no onion; and on the way home I threw away all the rolls and kept just the meat.

*(Action for the following, perhaps)*

When I got back to the roominghouse the dog was waiting for me. I half opened the door that led into the entrance hall, and there he was; waiting for me. It figured. I went in, very cautiously, and I had the hamburgers, you remember; I opened the bag, and I set the meat down about twelve feet from where the dog was snarling at me. Like so! He snarled; stopped snarling; sniffed; moved slowly; then faster; then faster toward the meat. Well, when he got to it he stopped, and he looked at me. I smiled; but tentatively, you understand. He turned his face back to the hamburgers, smelled, sniffed some more, and then . . . RRRAAAAGGGGGHHHH, like that . . . he tore into them. It was as if he had never eaten anything in his life before, except like garbage. Which might very well have been the truth. I don't think the landlady ever eats anything but garbage. But. He ate all the hamburgers, almost all at once, making sounds in his throat like a woman. *Then,* when he'd finished the meat, the hamburger, and tried to eat the paper, too, he sat down and smiled. I think he smiled; I know cats do. It was a very gratifying few moments. Then, BAM, he snarled and made for me again. He didn't get me this time, either. So, I got upstairs, and I lay down on my bed and started to think about the dog again. To be truthful, I was offended, and I was damn mad, too. It was six perfectly good hamburgers with not enough pork in them to make it disgusting. I was offended. But, after a while, I decided to try it for a few more days. If you think about it, this dog had what amounted to an antipathy toward me; really. And, I wondered if I mightn't overcome this antipathy. So, I tried it for five more days, but it was always the same: snarl, sniff, move; faster; stare; gobble; RAAGGGHHH; smile; snarl; BAM. Well, now; by this time Columbus Avenue was strewn with hamburger rolls and I was less offended than disgusted. So, I decided to kill the dog.

*(*PETER *raises a hand in protest)*

Oh, don't be so alarmed, Peter; I didn't succeed. The day I tried to kill the dog I bought only one hamburger and what I thought was a murderous portion of rat poison. When I bought the hamburger I asked the man not to bother with the roll, all I wanted was the meat. I expected some reaction from him, like: we don't sell no hamburgers without rolls; or,

Jerry tells Peter about his neighbor's dog.

wha' d'ya wanna do, eat it out'a ya han's? But no; he smiled benignly, wrapped up the hamburger in waxed paper, and said: A bite for ya pussy-cat? I wanted to say: No, not really; it's part of a plan to poison a dog I know. But, you can't say "a dog I know" without sounding funny; so I said, a little too loud, I'm afraid, and too formally: YES, A BITE FOR MY PUSSY-CAT. People looked up. It always happens when I try to simplify things; people look up. But that's neither hither nor thither. So. On my way back to the roominghouse, I kneaded the hamburger and the rat poison together between my hands, at that point feeling as much sadness as disgust. I opened the door to the entrance hall, and there the monster was, waiting to take the offering and then jump me. Poor bastard; he never learned that the moment he took to smile before he went for me gave me time enough to get out of range. BUT, there he was; malevolence with an erection, waiting. I put the poison patty down, moved toward the stairs and watched. The poor animal gobbled the food down as usual, smiled, which made me almost sick, and then, BAM. But, I sprinted up the stairs, as usual, and the dog didn't get me, as usual. AND IT CAME TO PASS THAT THE BEAST WAS DEATHLY ILL. I knew this because he no longer attended me, and because the landlady sobered up. She stopped me in the hall the same evening of the attempted murder and confided the information that God had stuck her puppy-dog a surely fatal blow. She had forgotten her bewildered lust, and her eyes were wide open for the first time. They looked like the dog's eyes. She sniveled and implored me to pray for the animal. I wanted to say to her: Madam, I have myself to pray for, the colored queen, the Puerto Rican family, the person in the front room whom I've never seen, the woman who cries deliberately behind her closed door, and the rest of the people in all roominghouses, everywhere; besides, Madam, I don't understand how to pray. But . . . to simplify things . . . I told her I would pray. She looked up. She said that I was a liar, and that I probably wanted the dog to die. I told her, and there was so much truth here, that I didn't want the dog to die. I didn't, and not just because I'd poisoned him. I'm afraid that I must tell you I wanted the dog to live so that I could see what our new relationship might come to.

(PETER *indicates his increasing displeasure and slowly growing antagonism)*

Please understand, Peter; that sort of thing is important. You must believe me; it *is* important. We have to know the effect of our actions. *(Another deep sigh)* Well, anyway; the dog recovered. I have no idea why, unless he was a descendant of the puppy that guarded the gates of hell or some such resort. I'm not up on my mythology. *(He pronounces the word myth-*o-logy*)* Are you?

(PETER *sets to thinking, but* JERRY *goes on)*

At any rate, and you've missed the eight-thousand-dollar question, Peter; at any rate, the dog recovered his health and the landlady recovered her thirst, in no way altered by the bow-wow's deliverance. When I came home from a movie that was playing on Forty-second Street, a movie I'd seen, or one that was very much like one or several I'd seen, after the landlady told me puppykins was better, I was so hoping for the dog to be waiting for me. I was . . . well, how would you put it . . . enticed? . . . fascinated? . . . no, I don't think so . . . heart-shatteringly anxious, that's it; I was heart-shatteringly anxious to confront my friend again.

(PETER *reacts scoffingly)*

Yes, Peter; friend. That's the only word for it. I was heart-shatteringly et cetera to confront my doggy friend again. I came in the door and advanced, unafraid, to the center of the entrance hall. The beast was there . . . looking at me. And, you know, he looked better for his scrape with the nevermind. I stopped; I looked at him; he looked at me. I think . . . I think we stayed a long time that way . . . still, stone-statue . . . just looking at one another. I looked more into his face than he looked into mine. I mean, I can concentrate longer at looking into a dog's face than a dog can concentrate at looking into mine, or into anybody else's face, for that matter. But during that twenty seconds or two hours that we looked into each other's face, we made contact. Now, here is what I had wanted to happen: I loved the dog now, and I wanted him to love me. I had tried to love, and I had tried to kill, and both had been unsuccessful by themselves. I hoped . . . and I don't really know why I expected the dog to understand anything, much less my motivations . . . I hoped that the dog would understand.

(PETER *seems to be hypnotized)*

It's just . . . it's just that . . . (JERRY *is abnormally tense, now)* . . . it's just that if you can't deal with people, you have to make a start somewhere. WITH ANIMALS! *(Much faster now, and like a conspirator)* Don't you see? A person has to have some way of dealing with SOMETHING. If not with people . . . if not with people . . . SOMETHING. With a bed, with a cockroach, with a mirror . . . no, that's too hard, that's one of the last steps. With a cockroach, with a . . . with a . . . with a carpet, a roll of toilet paper . . . no, not that, either . . . that's a mirror, too; always check bleeding. You see how hard it is to find things? With a street corner, and too many lights, all colors reflecting on the oily-wet streets . . . with a wisp of smoke, a wisp . . . of smoke . . . with . . . with pornographic playing cards, with a strongbox . . . WITHOUT A LOCK . . . with love, with vomiting, with crying, with fury because the pretty little ladies aren't pretty little ladies, with making money with your body which is an act of love and I could prove it, with howling because you're alive; with God. How about that? WITH GOD WHO IS A COLORED QUEEN WHO WEARS A KIMONO AND PLUCKS HIS EYEBROWS, WHO IS A WOMAN WHO CRIES WITH DETERMINATION BEHIND HER CLOSED DOOR . . . with God who, I'm told, turned his back on the whole thing some time ago . . . with . . . someday, with people. *(JERRY sighs the next word heavily)* People. With an idea; a concept. And where better, where ever better in this humiliating excuse for a jail, where better to communicate one single, simple-minded idea than in an entrance hall? Where? It would be A START! Where better to make a beginning . . . to understand and just possibly be understood . . . a beginning of an understanding, than with . . .

*(Here JERRY seems to fall into almost grotesque fatigue)*

than with A DOG. Just that; a dog.

*(Here there is a silence that might be prolonged for a moment or so; then JERRY wearily finishes his story)*

A dog. It seemed like a perfectly sensible idea. Man is a dog's best friend, remember. So: the dog and I looked at each other. I longer than the dog. And what I saw then has been the same ever since. Whenever the dog and I see each other we both stop where we are. We regard each other with a mixture of sadness and suspicion, and then we feign indifference. We walk past each other safely; we have an understanding. It's very sad, but you'll have to admit that it is an understanding. We had made many attempts at contact, and we had failed. The dog has returned to garbage, and I to solitary but free passage. I have not returned. I mean to say, I have *gained* solitary free passage, if that much further loss can be said to be gain. I have learned that neither kindness nor cruelty by themselves, independent of each other, creates any effect beyond themselves; and I have learned that the two combined, together, at the same time, are the teaching emotion. And what is gained is loss. And what has been the result: the dog and I have attained a compromise; more of a bargain, really. We neither love nor hurt because we do not try to reach each other. And, *was* trying to feed the dog an act of love? And, perhaps, was the dog's attempt to bite me *not* an act of love? If we can so misunderstand, well then, why have we invented the word love in the first place?

*(There is silence. JERRY moves to PETER's bench and sits down beside him. This is the first time that JERRY has sat down during the play.)*

The Story of Jerry and the Dog: the end.

*(PETER is silent)*

Well, Peter? *(JERRY is suddenly cheerful)* Well, Peter? Do you think I could sell that story to the *Reader's Digest* and make a couple of hundred bucks for *The Most Unforgettable Character I've Ever Met?* Huh?

*(JERRY is animated, but PETER is disturbed)*

Oh, come on now, Peter; tell me what you think.

**PETER:** *(Numb)* I . . . I don't understand what . . . I don't think I . . . *(Now, almost tearfully)* Why did you tell me all of this?

**JERRY:** Why not?

**PETER:** I DON'T UNDERSTAND!

**JERRY:** *(Furious, but whispering)* That's a lie.

**PETER:** No. No, it's not.

**JERRY:** *(Quietly)* I tried to explain it to you as I went along. I went slowly; it all has to do with . . .

**PETER:** I DON'T WANT TO HEAR ANY MORE. I don't understand you, or your landlady, or her dog . . .

**JERRY:** *Her* dog! I thought it was my . . . No. No, you're right. It *is* her dog. *(Looks at PETER intently, shaking his head)* I don't know what I was thinking about; of course you don't understand. *(In a monotone, wearily)* I don't live in your block I'm not married to two parakeets, or whatever your setup is. I am a *permanent transient,* and my home is the sickening roominghouses on the West Side of New York City, which is the greatest city in the world. Amen.

**PETER:** I'm . . . I'm sorry; I didn't mean to . . .

**JERRY:** Forget it. I suppose you don't quite know what to make of me, eh?

**PETER:** *(A joke)* We get all kinds in publishing. *(Chuckles)*

**JERRY:** You're a funny man. *(He forces a laugh)* You know that? You're a very . . . a richly comic person.

**PETER:** *(Modestly, but amused)* Oh, now, not really. *(Still chuckling)*

**JERRY:** Peter, do I annoy you, or confuse you?

**PETER:** *(Lightly)* Well, I must confess that this wasn't the kind of afternoon I'd anticipated.

**JERRY:** You mean, I'm not the gentleman you were expecting.

**PETER:** I wasn't expecting anybody.

**JERRY:** No, I don't imagine you were. But I'm here, and I'm not leaving.

**PETER:** *(Consulting his watch)* Well, you may not be, but I must be getting home now.

**JERRY:** Oh, come on; stay a while longer.

**PETER:** I really should get home; you see . . .

**JERRY:** *(Tickles* PETER*'s ribs with his fingers)* Oh, come on.

**PETER:** *(He is very ticklish; as* JERRY *continues to tickle him his voice becomes falsetto)* No, I . . . OHHHHH! Don't do that. Stop, stop. Ohhh, no, no.

**JERRY:** Oh, come on.

**PETER:** *(As* JERRY *tickles)* Oh, hee, hee, hee. I must go. I . . . hee, hee, hee. After all, stop, stop, hee, hee, hee, after all, the parakeets will be getting dinner ready soon. Hee, hee. And the cats are setting the table. Stop, stop, and, and . . . *(*PETER *is beside himself now)* and we're having . . . hee, hee . . . uh . . . ho, ho, ho. *(*JERRY *stops tickling* PETER*, but the combination of the tickling and his own mad whimsy has* PETER *laughing almost hysterically. As his laughter continues, then subsides,* JERRY *watches him, with a curious fixed smile.)*

**JERRY:** Peter?

**PETER:** Oh, ha, ha, ha, ha, ha. What? What?

**JERRY:** Listen, now.

**PETER:** Oh, ho, ho. What . . . what is it, Jerry? Oh, my.

**JERRY:** *(Mysteriously)* Peter, do you want to know what happened at the zoo?

**PETER:** Ah, ha, ha. The what? Oh, yes; the zoo. Oh, ho, ho. Well, I had my own zoo there for a moment with . . . hee, hee, the parakeets getting dinner ready, and the . . . ha, ha, whatever it was, the . . .

**JERRY:** *(Calmly)* Yes, that was very funny, Peter. I wouldn't have expected it. But do you want to hear about what happened at the zoo, or not?

**PETER:** Yes. Yes, by all means; tell me what happened at the zoo. Oh, my. I don't know what happened to me.

**JERRY:** Now I'll let you in on what happened at the zoo; but first, I should tell you why I went to the zoo. I went to the zoo to find out more about the way people exist with animals, and the way animals exist with each other, and with people too. It probably wasn't a fair test, what with everyone separated by bars from everyone else, the animals for the most part from each other, and always the people from the animals. But, if it's a zoo, that's the way it is. *(He pokes* PETER *on the arm)* Move over.

**PETER:** *(Friendly)* I'm sorry, haven't you enough room? *(He shifts a little)*

**JERRY:** *(Smiling slightly)* Well, all the animals are there, and all the people are there, and it's Sunday and all the children are there. *(He pokes* PETER *again)* Move over.

**PETER:** *(Patiently, still friendly)* All right. *(He moves some more, and* JERRY *has all the room he might need)*

**JERRY:** And it's a hot day, so all the stench is there, too, and all the balloon sellers, and all the ice cream sellers, and all the seals are barking, and all the birds are screaming. *(Pokes* PETER *harder)* Move over!

**PETER:** *(Beginning to be annoyed)* Look here, you have more than enough room! *(But he moves more, and is now fairly cramped at one end of the bench)*

**JERRY:** And I am there, and it's feeding time at the lions' house, and the lion keeper comes into the lion cage, one of the lion cages, to feed one of the lions. *(Punches* PETER *on the arm, hard)* MOVE OVER!

Peter begins to lose his patience.

**PETER:** *(Very annoyed)* I can't move over any more, and stop hitting me. What's the matter with you?

**JERRY:** Do you want to hear the story? *(Punches* PETER*'s arm again)*

**PETER:** *(Flabbergasted)* I'm not so sure! I certainly don't want to be punched in the arm.

**JERRY:** *(Punches* PETER*'s arm again)* Like that?

**PETER:** Stop it! What's the matter with you?

**JERRY:** I'm crazy, you bastard.

**PETER:** That isn't funny.

**JERRY:** Listen to me, Peter. I want this bench. You go sit on the bench over there, and if you're good I'll tell you the rest of the story.

**PETER:** *(Flustered)* But . . . whatever for? What *is* the matter with you? Besides, I see no reason why I should give up this bench. I sit on this bench almost every Sunday afternoon, in good weather. It's secluded here; there's never anyone sitting here, so I have it all to myself.

**JERRY:** *(Softly)* Get off this bench, Peter; I want it.

**PETER:** *(Almost whining)* No.

**JERRY:** I said I want this bench, and I'm going to have it. Now get over there.

**PETER:** People can't have everything they want. You should know that; it's a rule; people can have some of the things they want, but they can't have everything.

**JERRY:** *(Laughs)* Imbecile! You're slow-witted!

**PETER:** Stop that!

**JERRY:** You're a vegetable! Go lie down on the ground.

**PETER:** Now *you* listen to me. I've put up with you all afternoon.

**JERRY:** Not really.

**PETER:** LONG ENOUGH. I've put up with you long enough. I've listened to you because you seemed . . . well, because I thought you wanted to talk to somebody.

**JERRY:** You put things well; economically, and, yet . . . oh, what is the word I want to put justice to your . . . JESUS, you make me sick . . . get off here and give me my bench.

**PETER:** MY BENCH!

**JERRY:** *(Pushes* PETER *almost, but not quite, off the bench)* Get out of my sight.

**PETER:** *(Regaining his position)* God da . . . mn you. That's enough! I've had enough of you. I will not give up this bench; you can't have it, and that's that. Now, go away.

(JERRY *snorts but does not move)*

Go away, I said.

(JERRY *does not move)*

Get away from here. If you don't move on . . . you're a bum . . . that's what you are. . . . If you don't move on, I'll get a policeman here and make you go.

(JERRY *laughs, stays)*

I warn you, I'll call a policeman.

**JERRY:** *(Softly)* You won't find a policeman around here; they're all over on the west side of the park chasing fairies down from trees or out of the bushes. That's all they do. That's their function. So scream your head off; it won't do you any good.

**PETER:** POLICE! I warn you, I'll have you arrested. POLICE! *(Pause)* I said POLICE! *(Pause)* I feel ridiculous.

**JERRY:** You look ridiculous: a grown man screaming for the police on a bright Sunday afternoon in the park with nobody harming you. If a policeman *did* fill his quota and come sludging over this way he'd probably take you in as a nut.

**PETER:** *(With disgust and impotence)* Great God, I just came here to read, and now you want me to give up the bench. You're mad.

**JERRY:** Hey, I got news for you, as they say. I'm on your precious bench, and you're never going to have it for yourself again.

**PETER:** *(Furious)* Look, you; get off my bench. I don't care if it makes any sense or not. I want this bench to myself; I want you OFF IT!

**JERRY:** *(Mocking)* Aw . . . look who's mad.

**PETER:** GET OUT!

**JERRY:** No.

**PETER:** I WARN YOU!

**JERRY:** Do you know how ridiculous you look *now?*

**PETER:** *(His fury and self-consciousness have possessed him)* It doesn't matter. *(He is almost crying)* GET AWAY FROM MY BENCH!

**JERRY:** Why? You have everything in the world you want; you've told me about your home, and your family, and *your own* little zoo. You have everything, and now you want this bench. Are these the things men fight for? Tell me, Peter, is this bench, this iron and this wood, is this your honor? Is this the thing in the world you'd fight for? Can you think of anything more absurd?

**PETER:** Absurd? Look, I'm not going to talk to you about honor, or even try to explain it to you. Besides, it isn't a question of honor; but even if it were, you wouldn't understand.

**JERRY:** *(Contemptuously)* You don't even know what you're saying, do you? This is probably the first time in your life you've had anything more trying to face than changing your cats' toilet box. Stupid! Don't you have any idea, not even the slightest, what other people *need?*

**PETER:** Oh, boy, listen to you; well, you don't need this bench. That's for sure.

**JERRY:** Yes; yes, I do.

**PETER:** *(Quivering)* I've come here for years; I have hours of great pleasure, great satisfaction, right here. And that's important to a man. I'm a responsible person, and I'm a GROWNUP. This is my bench, and you have no right to take it away from me.

**JERRY:** Fight for it, then. Defend yourself; defend your bench.

**PETER:** You've *pushed* me to it. Get up and fight.

**JERRY:** Like a man?

**PETER:** *(Still angry)* Yes, like a man, if you insist on mocking me even further.

**JERRY:** I'll have to give you credit for one thing; you *are* a vegetable, and a slightly nearsighted one, I think . . .

**PETER:** THAT'S ENOUGH. . . .

**JERRY:** . . . but, you know, as they say on TV all the time—you know—and I mean this, Peter, you have a certain dignity; it surprises me . . .

**PETER:** STOP!

**JERRY:** *(Rises lazily)* Very well, Peter, we'll battle for the bench, but we're not evenly matched.

*(He takes out and clicks open an ugly-looking knife)*

**PETER:** *(Suddenly awakening to the reality of the situation)* You *are* mad! You're stark raving mad! YOU'RE GOING TO KILL ME!

*(But before* PETER *has time to think what to do,* JERRY *tosses the knife at* PETER*'s feet)*

**JERRY:** There you go. Pick it up. You have the knife and we'll be more evenly matched.

Peter brandishes Jerry's knife.

**PETER:** *(Horrified)* No!

**JERRY:** *(Rushes over to* PETER*, grabs him by the collar;* PETER *rises; their faces almost touch)* Now you pick up that knife and you fight with me. You fight for your self-respect; you fight for that goddamned bench.

**PETER:** *(Struggling)* No! Let . . . let go of me! He . . . Help!

**JERRY:** *(Slaps* PETER *on each "fight")* You fight, you miserable bastard; fight for that bench; fight for your manhood, you pathetic little vegetable. *(Spits in* PETER*'s face)* You couldn't even get your wife with a male child.

**PETER:** *(Breaks away, enraged)* It's a matter of genetics, not manhood, you . . . you monster.

*(He darts down, picks up the knife and backs off a little; he is breathing heavily)*

I'll give you one last chance; get out of here and leave me alone!

*(He holds the knife with a firm arm, but far in front of him, not to attack, but to defend)*

**JERRY:** *(Sighs heavily)* So be it!

*(With a rush he charges* PETER *and impales himself on the knife. Tableau: For just a moment, complete silence,* JERRY *impaled on the knife at the end of* PETER*'s still firm arm. Then* PETER *screams, pulls away, leaving the knife in* JERRY. JERRY *is motionless, on point. Then he, too, screams, and it must be the sound of an infuriated and fatally wounded animal. With the knife in him, he stumbles back to the bench that* PETER *had vacated. He crumbles there, sitting, facing* PETER*, his eyes wide in agony, his mouth open)*

**PETER:** *(Whispering)* Oh my God, oh my God, oh my God. . . .

*(He repeats these words many times, very rapidly)*

**JERRY:** *(JERRY is dying; but now his expression seems to change. His features relax, and while his voice varies, sometimes wrenched with pain, for the most part he seems removed from his dying. He smiles)* Peter, thank you, Peter. I mean that now; thank you very much.

*(PETER's mouth drops open. He cannot move; he is transfixed)*

I came unto you *(He laughs, so faintly)* and you have comforted me. Dear Peter.

**PETER:** *(Almost fainting)* Oh my God!

**JERRY:** You'd better go now. Somebody might come by, and you don't want to be here when anyone comes.

**PETER:** *(Does not move, but begins to weep)* Oh my God, oh my God.

**JERRY:** And Peter, I'll tell you something now; you're not really a vegetable; it's all right, you're an animal. You're an animal, too. But you'd better hurry now, Peter. Hurry, you'd better go . . . see?

*(JERRY takes a handkerchief and with great effort and pain wipes the knife handle clean of fingerprints)*

Hurry away, Peter.

*(PETER begins to stagger away)*

Wait . . . wait, Peter. Take your book . . . book. Right here . . . beside me . . . on your bench . . . my bench, rather. Come . . . take your book.

*(PETER starts for the book, but retreats)*

Hurry . . . Peter.

*(PETER rushes to the bench, grabs the book, retreats)*

Jerry lies dead on the park bench.

Very good, Peter . . . very good. Now . . . hurry away.

*(PETER hesitates for a moment, then flees, stage-left)*

Hurry away. . . . *(His eyes are closed now)* Hurry away, your parakeets are making the dinner . . . the cats . . . are setting the table . . .

**PETER:** *(Offstage)* *(A pitiful howl)* OH MY GOD!

**JERRY:** *(His eyes still closed, he shakes his head and speaks; a combination of scornful mimicry and supplication)* Oh . . . my . . . God.

*(He is dead)*

# Writing from Reading

## Summarize

**1** Two men meet in a park in an incident that leads to a disastrous end. Did you have any sense when first reading the play of the conclusion to come?

## Analyze Craft

**2** The setting is spare, there are only two actors, and their dialogue seems low-key, offhand. How does the playwright create suspense and then heighten it by means of their speech?

## Analyze Voice

**3** How would you characterize the diction—the vocabulary and word choice—of the two actors? Use examples from the dialogue to show the difference between the social standing of the establishment figure, Peter, and the outcast, Jerry. Is Jerry's long monologue realistic?

## Synthesize Summary and Analysis

**4** This play focuses partly on isolation and its perils. How does its staging emphasize this condition?

## Interpret the Play

**5** In what ways does the play lead us to see the animal in all of us?

*CONTINUED FROM PAGE 27*

Anyone who's ever sat quietly in a dark room facing forward while another person under a spotlight speaks has had the experience of the theater. In addition to creating characters and dialogue and plot, a playwright must make the play come alive on the stage. In his interview, Edward Albee says everything you need to know about how to stage a play can be found in reading the text itself:

> *The intention is there in the text. The intention is the experience of the play that I had while I was writing it. Because when I write a play . . . I see it, I hear it as a play being performed in front of me, and that's what I want to see on the stage—the same experience that I had while writing it.*

He directs his actors back to the text when they have a question about how to perform a work. The experience of the play can begin with the text, but its success or failure is on the stage, where a lot of its energy and—at its best—its electric feel comes from the vitality of the immediate interaction of live actors with a live audience.

If you are fortunate enough to be able to see a play performed, then you can look at how those elements come alive onstage. It's not perhaps an accident that there are fewer classic works of drama than of poetry or prose; the additional dimension of stagecraft makes the genre all the more demanding and complex. In a short story or poem, a good deal of the action transpires in the reader's mind; in drama, however, it must be played out. You have to get your characters on and off the stage, you have to hear what they're thinking in the form of uttered speech. Dialogue is crucial (though there's a subset of theater called **mime,** in which silence is the rule), and gestures must be clear. Even the simplest of dramas is multidimensional when performed; stage "business" is a major—indeed an inescapable—component of the whole.

"I don't think that the theater is, necessarily, only about entertainment. I think it's entertainment that reaches the soul."

Conversation with Arthur Miller

Your experience of yourself as one person among many in the audience when the curtain goes up is different even from your experience of viewing a movie, where performances don't alter night by night and the actors interact with a camera lens rather than an audience. But even with the movies, your reaction as the audience can depend on whether you watch it at home alone or at a crowded cineplex. Once you've imagined yourself as the director, the actors, and the audience, you can evaluate the director's approach, the actor's efforts and energy, and the attention of the audience as the plot unfolds. Following is part of a *New York Times* review of the first production in America of Edward Albee's first play, *The Zoo Story.* Note how the reviewer comments on the staging, the acting, and the plot.

"Why, when people can play any rock star they want to on a CD, do they flock to a concert in huge numbers? Why, when they can see a political figure on television . . . do they go to a political rally? The reason is for the experience of being with other people, having a communal experience, and being able to share that with other people. The reason theater has withstood the challenges . . . is the experience of going to a live performance." Conversation with Ed Wilson

**Brooks Atkinson's *New York Times* January 15, 1960, review of the opening in America of Edward Albee's *The Zoo Story***

After the banalities of Broadway it tones the muscles and freshens the system to examine the squalor of Off Broadway. . . . [Two actors] sufficed for the short play put on at the Provincetown Playhouse last evening [of] Edward Albee's "The Zoo Story."

The Cast

Jerry . . . . . . . George Maharis
Peter . . . . . . . William Daniels

"The Zoo Story" is a dialogue . . . interesting and well acted by intelligent professionals. Nothing of enduring value is said . . . but [the play] captures some part of the dismal mood that infects many writers today.

Mr. Albee's "The Zoo Story" does not have so much literary distinction. . . . Mr Albee is more the reporter. There are two characters and two benches in his play set in Central Park. A cultivated, complacent publisher is reading a book. An intense, aggressive young man in shabby dress strikes up a conversation with him.

Or, to be exact, a monologue. For the intruder wants to unburden his mind of his private miseries and resentments, and they pour out of him in a flow of wild, scabrous, psychotic details. Since Mr. Albee is an excellent writer and the designer of dialogue and since he apparently knows the city, "The Zoo Story" is consistently interesting and illuminating—odd and pithy. It ends melodramatically as if Mr. Albee had lost control of his material. Although the conclusion is theatrical, it lacks the sense of improvisation that characterizes the main body of the play.

Milton Katselas has staged "The Zoo Story" admirably; and Mr. Maharis' overwrought yet searching intruder, and Mr. Daniels' perplexed publisher are first-rate pieces of acting.

Although the Provincetown bill is hardly glamorous, it has a point of view. Mr. Albee write[s] on the assumption that the human condition is stupid and ludicrous.

# Suggestions for Writing

1. Why does Brooks Atkinson write that the ending is "theatrical," and is that intended as a compliment? Is the rest of the play theatrical? How would you characterize a theater style that is not theatrical?
2. Go to the crime page of your daily or weekly newspaper or your Internet source for news and single out a crime report. Try to reimagine it as a one-act play.
3. Compare your reaction to that of the reviewer. Brooks Atkinson was an important force in American theater of the day and a major factor in the question of whether or not a play would succeed. Find several other articles about this play and compare the current opinion of the importance of *The Zoo Story,* which is still being performed nearly fifty years after its opening night.

*"Writing is a way of thinking. It's a way of thinking about what you have read or what you have seen. It is your mirror to that, your reaction to that, and you have to be sure you're able to say exactly how it was this . . . affected you. . . . So what you are trying to do is not only understand how you felt about something . . . but you want then to communicate that to somebody else. . . . If you are muddy about it, or if you are too repetitious, or whatever the case might be, you have to find that out when you reread it and then you rewrite it."*

Conversation with Edwin Wilson, available online at www.mhhe.com/delbanco1e

# 32 Writing

## FROM READING TO WRITING

WHEN you write about what you read, first think about the title of the work. (What does The Zoo Story say to you?) Find out something about the author. (Edward Albee is a living playwright. He's still writing plays today. In his interview he says that "entertainment is misunderstood," and he wants to write plays that make people think. His plays were influential as "experimental theater.") Then think about the context in which the play was written. (Albee wrote the play in the 1950s and set it in the same time period. In a sense it's a tragedy, since someone dies in the play.) Annotate the work and record your general impressions of the play. (As one student writes, "The surprise ending was really upsetting. I thought the guy was going to try to kill Peter till the end. I was left with a really uneasy feeling about why Jerry would do that.") Your annotations of the play will help you think about how the play works and what it means to you.

Aside from a constant demand that you apply your understanding of what you read to the creation of a good paper about a work of literature, writing about drama requires a slight change in the way you prepare to write your essay. Its form is performance. It comes alive on the stage, not the page. Of the three principal literary modes (fiction, poetry, drama), drama relies most on voice. The actors must enter into the spirit and style of a role; a director should be able to communicate his or her interpretation of a play. To convey that attitude and interpretation, the director and actor establish a focal point of performance—a way of staging (and sometimes improvising on) a text. To write about drama, we do much the same; we imagine the text we are reading as if it were being performed.

# about Drama

*The audience is . . . absolutely necessary.*

# Q&A

*Writing is a way of thinking.*

# *A Conversation on Writing*

## Edwin Wilson

### Writing As a Reporter

One [way to write about a play is] to simply report what happens in the play. This is what this play is about. Here are the characters. Here's what happens in the action. Here's where it takes place in terms of the setting. It takes place in the seventeenth century, the eighteenth century, or in modern times, World War II or the Vietnam War or the war in Iraq. It takes place in a certain time in a certain place with certain characters. And you are in effect being a reporter.

### Experiencing a Play

Maybe you can say to yourself, "I don't really know what's going on in this play." That's a personal reaction. . . . Usually people do decide they like certain kinds of plays and don't like others, which is fine because it's a very individual sort of thing. So another way of writing about a play, and these are not mutually exclusive, but another way of writing about a play is to say how you feel about it. . . . You kind of analyze your feelings too as you go through the play because you shouldn't be locked into just one position. You should let yourself experience your own feelings as you go through reading a play.

### Writing and Revising

There's an old saying . . . that plays are not written, they're rewritten. And what that means is the first time a play is written, it's almost never the finished product. Almost never. . . . Writing is really a process.

**If you would like to view the entire interview with Edwin Wilson, go to www.mhhe.com./delbanco1e.**

**RESEARCH ASSIGNMENT** After viewing the entire video, describe what Edwin Wilson believes to be the special role played by the audience in the theater.

Edwin Wilson was the theater critic for *The Wall Street Journal* for twenty-two years and is the author of *The Theater Experience* as well as coauthor, with Alvin Goldfarb, of *Living Theater: A History* and *Theater: The Lively Art.* He has produced plays on and off-Broadway and the feature film *The Nashville Sound.* Wilson is also the author of two original plays, *The Bettinger Prize* and *Waterfall.*

### Writing about Drama

- Ask yourself which elements (plot, character, setting) will have the biggest impact on the audience.
- Mark where scenes begin and end and show how the action unfolds.
- Note which character in the play changes the most and your own personal reaction to these changes.
- Use act and scene numbers when you quote lines from a play. Also use line numbers if the play is written in verse. For one-act plays, cite by page number.

# A SAMPLE STUDENT ESSAY IN PROGRESS

## Analyze the Assignment

When you write, are you doing an analysis or a review? These are common responses to a play. Make sure you know which you've been asked to write. A review is an argument. If you are asked to write a review (see Brooks Atkinson's review in chapter 31), you will need to include your opinion along with a summary of the work. List the actors, the director (or stage designer and costume designer, if these aspects are included as important points in your review), and the theater where the work is being performed. Then you will need to persuade your reader that your evaluation of the work is worthwhile. Provide your opinion of the work based on how effectively the script engaged you, how effectively the actors drew you in with their performances, and how effectively the director (or stage designer, costume designer, producer) interpreted the play for the stage. If the play is staged often (such as with Shakespeare), you may be able to use a point of comparison in your discussion of the performance you have reviewed.

If you are asked to compare, explain, or analyze, your paper will go beyond a summary of what happened in the play and will require an interpretation. That interpretation in drama will depend on recording how the play works. In the sections that follow you can chart the progress of our student Jim Hanks as he works through his considered response to this assignment:

Assignment: Expand the close reading you completed of Edward Albee's *The Zoo Story* into a 4- to 5-page essay in which you analyze the unfolding of the dramatic action and what it suggests about contemporary life.

Jim thinks he has a kernel of an idea of what "*the unfolding of the dramatic action*" means, beginning with a sense of how to relate the beginning of the play to the unfolding middle and to the shocking conclusion. He also believes he can find his way from what he sees on the stage that the page conjures up in his imagination to "*what it suggests about contemporary life.*" The vague sense he developed as he read the play that drama can serve as a lens through which we better understand our relationship to life and the world has grown for him into a clear idea. He has never been to Central Park in New York City and has never suffered Jerry's problems, or Peter's complacencies, but he can see aspects of his life in new and surprising ways.

## One Student Begins

As Jim Hanks prepares to write about *The Zoo Story* by contemporary playwright Edward Albee, he wonders what he is supposed to focus on and how he will work up the material for his initial draft.

**How do different elements affect the audience?** First, Jim builds his analysis on some practical understanding of the elements and techniques the play employs. He figures out which of the several elements of drama, such as dialogue, character, and setting, seem to have the most impact on the audience.

"To fully get a play, not just this one, but any play, you need to also imagine the impact on a crowd because it means that you are both specific as a person and part of an anonymous group that is responding. And the actors are responding to the audience. The play is not complete until the audience completes it."

Conversation with Arthur Kopit

**Does the play's historical context help provide insight into the play?** After looking at what elements might have the most impact on the audience, Jim assesses the importance of the social and historical context of the play by noting when it was written and whether the piece is written about its own time.

"[I gather] my research, and then I start dealing with relationships. Change comes from what you absorbed from your relationships."

Conversation with Ruben Santiago-Hudson

**What genre of play is it?** Jim feels his way into the tradition and conventions of the play's genre. For example, though a modern play, *The Zoo Story* can in a limited and technical sense also be described as a tragedy (see the discussion of tragedy and comedy in chapter 30), since it entails the death of a protagonist.

But, as your reading will show, there's also much real humor here, and you shouldn't overlook the comic aspects of the text. The term *tragicomedy* might be applied, though Albee would probably resist such a label; tragicomedy is the way another great modern playwright, Samuel Beckett (whom Albee praises in his interview), described his groundbreaking *Waiting for Godot* (a play in which the two characters spend the entire drama awaiting the arrival of a figure called Godot who never arrives and whose mysterious absence is sometimes considered a metaphor for God). Not even a hyphen divides the tragic and the comic mode: *tragicomedy* combines the two in one word.

### A HISTORY OF COMEDY IN TRAGEDY

Greeks appended a satyr play—one of those down-and-dirty comic afterthoughts—to a trilogy of tragedies that were submitted for competition to be performed in their great drama festivals. This ironic mix of high seriousness and low humor—the "comic relief"—is also found in even the darkest plays of William Shakespeare. Although tragicomedies are found as early as Shakespeare as tragic plays with happy endings, modern tragicomedies are a complex blend of serious and light tones that yields dark or satiric results.

"It's a temptation of course to look at [a play] as if it were a short story or a novel, because there are a lot of similarities on the printed page. . . . It's an encounter just between you and what's on the page. . . . You have to begin to visualize . . . in effect, as you begin to read the play, you set the stage . . . then the play begins to unfold." Conversation with Edwin Wilson

## Initial Response

Jim's annotations indicated that he felt surprised and confused by the play's ending. (In this regard he's not so very different from the reviewer for *The New York Times*, Brooks Atkinson, who also questioned the final action.) Jim records his feelings in a short initial response that might later help him see where his interest lies.

Well, that was an unexpected conclusion. Not what I initially expected from a play called *The Zoo Story*. Jerry and Peter were both interesting characters. Strange, even though Jerry does most of the talking, I feel like I know Peter better. The details of his life are clearer in my mind than Jerry's, maybe because they're closer to my own. I can picture the black dog because it was described so much. Why is the anecdote about the dog such a focal point of the play? I mean, Jerry goes on and on about it, but it's not clear what a dog has to do with a "zoo story."

## Explore Your Ideas

As Jim reviews his annotations, he imagines what he might see if he were to watch this play staged. In the "theater" of his mind, he sees two characters and a park setting. He decides to focus first on the characters, trying to figure out his response to them. Then he looks at the setting, comparing the zoo motif to the freedom of the park where the action takes place. He wonders about the mystery of the zoo and what has happened there. How does this relate to the meaning of the action? Jerry's death confuses him. He decides to put down his thoughts in a **freewriting** exercise.

#### Freewriting

What happened at the zoo?! I can't decide if that was frustrating or confusing. Jerry made me uncomfortable. I can't decide how I would react if I was Peter on that bench. I think it would be easier to understand his reaction over the bench if you saw this acted out. You could see the tension building more, the way Jerry forces him off the bench. I wonder what the zoo has to do with this. There were no animals and only two people. The setting is strange too: a wide open park. What animals were there? Cats and birds, and that detailed description of the dog. Were there any cages? Maybe there's a metaphor for a zoo here. I'd like to consider what Jerry and Peter might represent

Next, Jim takes his freewriting responses to a higher level of questioning—and comprehension—by writing a slightly more formal **journal entry.** Here he tries to expand the ideas in his freewriting and organize them into paragraphs.

"It's said to writers, write about what you know. I always like to turn that on its head and say write about what you didn't know you knew." Conversation with Arthur Kopit

**Journaling**

The first thing I noticed when I started *The Zoo Story* was that it was set in a park instead of a zoo. I was surprised because a park is a wide open place, but a zoo is full of cages. When I read more of the play I realized that *The Zoo Story* referred to Jerry's story about his trip to the zoo rather than the events of the play.

But now that I think about it, there are a lot of animal references in this story. Peter says he has cats and birds and Jerry keeps bringing it back up, even at the last line. And Jerry tells the whole long story about trying to bond with his landlady's dog. But cats and birds and dogs aren't really "zoo animals." Maybe there's some meaning in that—a "zoo story" about house pets?

I had trouble understanding the ending of the play because I never really sympathized with Jerry. I felt bad for him mostly, but I couldn't relate to him. It was weird to have a play with only two characters, and then one you can't relate to at all. That might be an interpretation: Peter as the house pet that you get along with, and Jerry as the dog you try to get along with but never can. So what does Jerry's "suicide" mean?

Jim feels like he has hit upon a good idea in the last paragraph of his journal entry. He decides to explore it further. Clarity begins to emerge when he organizes the animal references in the play by listing them under the character most closely associated with the animal. His **brainstorming** session leads him to find a pattern: The domestic animals belong to Peter; the wild animals he associates with Jerry.

> "When my writing is not working for me, then I start listening: listening to music, listening to other writers, listening to other actors, listening to my soul. And then I start writing. And I build, build, build. Then I start learning how to chisel, chisel, chisel down . . . beginning, middle, and end of something that's not only entertaining but [also] educating, and enlightening, and hopefully an experience that will leave you in some way or another changed. And that's how I approach my writing."
>
> Conversation with Ruben Santiago-Hudson

## Brainstorming

| PETER | JERRY |
|---|---|
| • Domestic | • Wild |
| • Cats and parakeets | • Landlady's black dog |
| • Guinea pig | • Zoo as wild place |
| • Caged | • Unable to connect |
| • Holds the knife | • Dies |
| • Conventional | • Nonconformist |

## Develop a Working Thesis

Jim used his brainstorming notes to sharpen his topic and focus his **thesis.** He decided to use the first draft as a "working thesis" and refined it as he revised his paper.

**First-draft thesis**

> Edward Albee reveals a lot about the characters by associating them with different animals.

**Second-draft thesis**

A close reading of *The Zoo Story* reveals an argument about ways to live based on the association of the characters with specific references to animals, wild and caged and free.

**Final thesis**

A close reading of *The Zoo Story* reveals that Albee, using animals as metaphors, has dramatized an argument about two ways to live in the modern world.

## Create a Plan

Jim's brainstorming exercise led him to create the following brief **outline.** His method of working is slightly different from that of the other students we saw in the fiction and poetry sections; he prefers to add to his thesis and support progressively, with each draft, rather than figure out all the details before writing. He will use a comparison/contrast structure to organize his paper.

I. Introduction
II. Peter—Domestic
  A. Cats
  B. Parakeets—caged!
III. Jerry—Wild
  A. Interest in zoo
  B. Landlady's dog
IV. Compare the two men: Domestic vs. Wild
V. Conclusion: A way to understand Jerry's death

## Generate a First Draft

Sitting in front of his blank screen, fingers hovering over the keyboard, Jim takes the leap from reviewing his notes to composing the opening lines of a draft. "Animals are very important to the play . . ." he writes. The point of a first draft is to get ideas onto paper. Then everything can be revisited, reorganized, and refined. The draft allows you to think about your own feelings and experiences in reading or observing a play. You may find it easier to draft the introduction and the conclusion at the end. These sections should answer each other. The introduction introduces the thesis, and the conclusion relates the thesis to a larger issue that explains why the thesis is significant. The paragraphs in the body allow you to use the text to support your thesis.

> "Writing . . . is a very mysterious process. . . . It's so easy to panic, and even in rewriting, look at what the material is. What are you trying to do? You go back to basics. What's this piece about? What do I think it's about? . . . What does this piece want to be?" Conversation with Arthur Kopit

**FIRST DRAFT**

Hanks 1

Jim Hanks

Professor Hernandez

English 1102

February 16, 2009

Animals in *The Zoo Story*

Animals are very important to the play *The Zoo Story*. They factor into a lot of conversations, and it is interesting to see which character talks about which animal. Edward Albee reveals a lot about the characters by associating them with different animals.

Peter talks about his pets because Jerry asks him to. He says he has a cat and two parakeets, which his daughters keep in a cage. The image of caged birds is a strong one—it suggests that a bird who would otherwise fly freely is restrained.

Jerry begins the play by talking about the zoo. The zoo also has cages, but when you think about a zoo, you see that there are wild animals, very unlike cats and parakeets. In a way, then, Jerry aligns himself with wild animals by talking so much about the zoo. But Jerry also talks about his landlady's dog, which he calls "a black monster of a beast" (36). This does not sound like a friendly house dog like the ones we associated with Peter. Yet this is the animal Jerry tries to connect with, and it is significant that Jerry chooses a wild beast with which to establish a relationship (even though his attempt fails).

Hanks 2

Since Peter prefers domestic animals and Jerry prefers wild animals, we can understand something about their characters: Peter is himself domesticated in a 9-to-5 job, while Jerry remains wild and outside of that type of stability. Peter, then, is unable to understand the zoo in the way that Jerry can. Jerry sees the zoo not just as a place for wild animals, but as a place where those animals are separated by bars and cages. Like these animals, Jerry seems unable to connect with those around him.

In the end, then, it is significant that Peter holds the knife that kills Jerry. It seems to mean on a symbolic level that a domesticated life wins out over people who are outside of it. In this way, we can understand Jerry's death as a statement that Albee is making against conventional society.

Work Cited

Albee, Edward. *The Zoo Story. Literature: Craft & Voice.* Eds. Nicholas Delbanco and Alan Cheuse. Vol. 3. New York: McGraw-Hill, 2009. Print.

### Revise Your Draft

Jim was pleased with his first draft in that his ideas about Peter, Jerry, and the animals aligned with them seemed to come together in a logical way. However, after reviewing his notes, he realized that he had not used much from the text to support his claim. He returned to his annotations and reread the sections that had to do with animals. He also highlighted the quotations that would best support his argument.

By rereading and selecting quotations, Jim came to a more nuanced understanding of the play. He realized he could add an additional paragraph analyzing Peter's and Jerry's different understandings of the zoo. Although the kernel of that idea was present in his first draft, he fully expands it in his second draft.

"What you read on the page looks like it's been there forever, but believe me, it hasn't. It's always a struggle to find what you are looking for." Conversation with Arthur Miller

Jim thus makes several major improvements in his second draft. He includes support for his argument from the text itself. He also expands his discussion of quotes from the text, allowing him to more thoroughly analyze the specific language the play uses. Finally, after writing the second draft, Jim rereads his paper and adds annotations. These annotations show him where to refine his language and where to add proper MLA citations when he writes his final draft (see the Handbook for Writing from Reading at the end of this book for information on MLA citation).

## SECOND DRAFT

Hanks 1

Jim Hanks

Professor Hernandez

English 1102

February 20, 2009

Caged or Free?

Animals As Metaphor in Edward Albee's *The Zoo Story*

Better way to start than a preposition?

From the title of Edward Albee's play *The Zoo Story,* the reader is presented with the idea of animals. The meeting between Jerry and Peter is difficult to understand and leaves the reader with many questions. A close reading of *The Zoo Story* reveals an argument about ways to live based on the association of the characters with specific references to animals, wild and caged and free.

Such as?—why the detailed description of the dog, Jerry's suicide . . .

Throughout the play, Peter is closely aligned with domesticated animals. After learning that Peter has a wife and two daughters, Jerry is eager to know what type of pets Peter owns. The animals he guesses are typical pets you would have around the house, like dogs and cats. Peter says that his family owns a cat and two parakeets that his daughters keep in a cage in their bedroom. He also calls himself a guinea pig: When Jerry says he likes to talk to people and learn about them, Peter says, "And am I the guinea pig for today?" (36). In conversation Peter is simply using a popular turn of phrase. But in the context of the larger play, Peter's word choice is extremely significant, because a guinea pig is a passive subject, just like Peter is a passive subject in Jerry's dialogue experiment until Jerry provokes him physically.

"you" too familiar?

Direct quote from play . . . put in quotes and cite!

Discuss significance of birds more?

Break this sentence up to make the point clearer. Mention Peter's conventional life?

The first line of the play has Jerry declaring loudly several times that he has just come from the zoo, associating him with wild animals. The zoo, of course, is filled with wild animals, and even though they are caged they are vastly different from house pets like Peter's cat and birds. The speech where Jerry describes his

Reword sentence to focus on Jerry.

Hanks 2

relationship with the landlady's dog is most significant. Jerry says the dog is "a black monster of a beast" (27). The words "monster" and "beast" tell us that this is not a typical house dog, but one that is practically feral. Jerry also notes the dog's constant erection, which represents an unfulfilled desire. Similarly, Jerry's unfulfilled desire to connect with others is made apparent when he tries to connect with the dog. At best, he and the dog achieve a status of mutual indifference. But it is significant that Jerry chose this wild beast as the object with which to make a start at "dealing" with the world.

Seeing Peter as a domesticated guinea pig and Jerry as a feral dog clarifies their approach to life: Peter is happy to be caged in fulfilling society's expectations through a conventional home, family, and job, but Jerry can't function in such a setting. The closest Peter comes to breaking out of his neat, ordered life is when he mistakenly says he must get home because the parakeets and the cat will be preparing dinner. This slipup makes Peter say, "I had my own zoo there for a moment." Peter has a very shallow understanding of the zoo. He sees it only in the sense of a wild place, with all kinds of animals mixed up together. Jerry's understanding of the zoo is deeper: He describes it as a place where everyone is separated by bars, with all the animals separated from the other animals, and all the people separated from the animals. "But, if it's a zoo, that's the way it is," he says (36). Since Peter and Jerry are domesticated and wild animals, this quote shows that Jerry—the wild animal—views convention not as something that brings comforting order, but as the bars that are divisive and that keep people from connecting to one another.

Everyone knows that the wild animals that populate the zoo are not free to be wild. In the same way, Jerry is not free to be himself in a world of conventions. And just like a wild animal can't flourish in captivity, Jerry can't survive in our oppressive society. Thus, an exploration into the connection between animals and characters

Include more quote to support "erection" discussion.

"us" too familiar

Better paragraph conclusion: So what??

Break into two sentences, emphasize thesis.

Quote from play? Need to cite!

More info: How do we know that?

Confusing sentence . . . just quote Jerry's actual words.

awkward wording.

Assuming too much? Too familiar to the reader?

Need to watch out for these—too familiar for formal paper.

Hanks 3

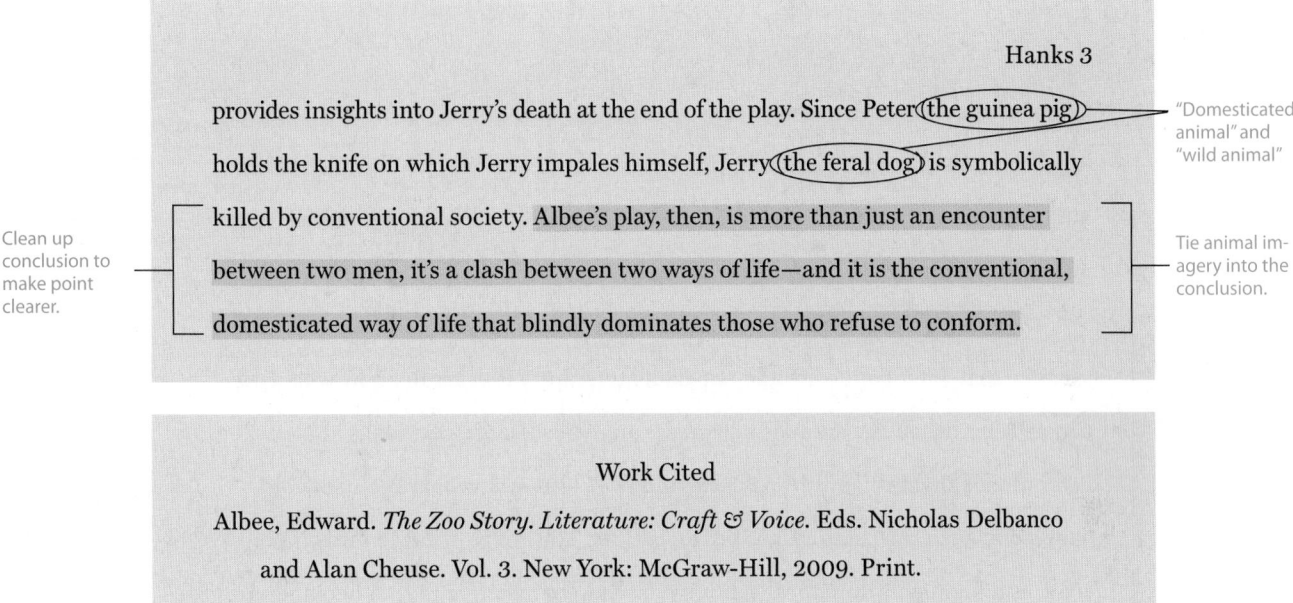

provides insights into Jerry's death at the end of the play. Since Peter (the guinea pig) holds the knife on which Jerry impales himself, Jerry (the feral dog) is symbolically killed by conventional society. Albee's play, then, is more than just an encounter between two men, it's a clash between two ways of life—and it is the conventional, domesticated way of life that blindly dominates those who refuse to conform.

"Domesticated animal" and "wild animal"

Clean up conclusion to make point clearer.

Tie animal imagery into the conclusion.

Work Cited

Albee, Edward. *The Zoo Story*. *Literature: Craft & Voice*. Eds. Nicholas Delbanco and Alan Cheuse. Vol. 3. New York: McGraw-Hill, 2009. Print.

## Edit Your Sentences, Proofread, and Format Your Paper

Jim uses the annotations on his second draft to develop his final draft, in which he fleshes out his character analysis and examines each sentence for clarity. For the final draft, he checks his spelling, word choice, and transitions. He also makes sure he has provided ample evidence from the play itself with quotations and checks to make sure these quotations are correctly formatted in-text references, which correspond to a Work Cited page at the end of his paper (see chapters 3–6 in the Handbook for Writing from Reading). Jim's progress shows his interaction with the story as he continually revises his interpretation.

**FINAL DRAFT**

Hanks 1

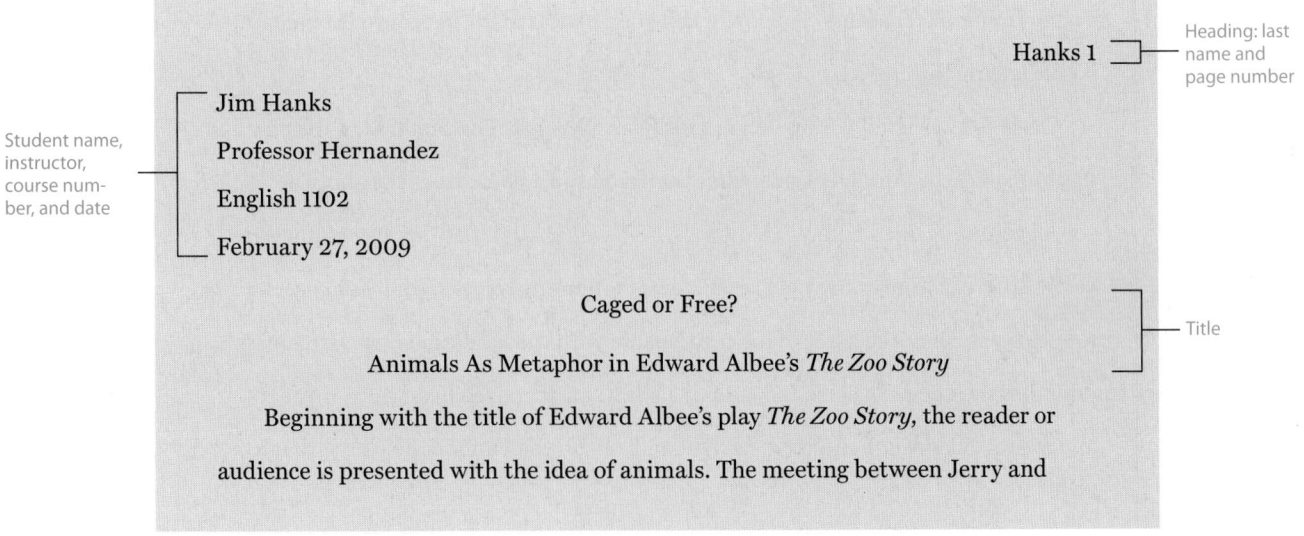

Heading: last name and page number

Jim Hanks

Professor Hernandez

English 1102

February 27, 2009

Student name, instructor, course number, and date

Caged or Free?

Animals As Metaphor in Edward Albee's *The Zoo Story*

Title

Beginning with the title of Edward Albee's play *The Zoo Story*, the reader or audience is presented with the idea of animals. The meeting between Jerry and

Hanks 2

Peter is difficult to understand and leaves the reader with many questions, such as why Jerry tells about his landlady's dog in such detail, and why he ultimately kills himself. A close reading of *The Zoo Story* reveals that Albee, using animals as metaphors, has dramatized an argument about two ways to live in the modern world.

Thesis

Throughout the play, Peter is closely aligned with domesticated animals. After learning that Peter has a wife and two daughters, Jerry is eager to know what type of pets Peter owns. The animals he guesses are typical house pets: dogs and cats. Peter reveals that his family owns a cat and two parakeets, which Peter says his daughters "keep in a cage in their bedroom" (32). The image of caged birds is powerful, as it highlights unnatural captivity; birds were meant to fly, but here they are kept from one of their most basic activities by the cage imposed on them. In fact, all the animals associated with Peter are domesticated. Peter even calls himself a guinea pig: When Jerry says he likes to talk to people and learn about them, Peter says, "And am I the guinea pig for today?" (32). In conversation, Peter is simply using a popular turn of phrase. But in the context of the larger play, Peter's word choice is extremely significant. A guinea pig brings to mind a harmless, large rodent who passes its life in a cage, a passive subject in any experiment. Likewise, Peter is a passive subject in Jerry's dialogue experiment until Jerry provokes him physically. Furthermore, Peter seems caged in, wholly domesticated, by his conventional family life and publishing job.

Textual analysis of Peter's character as domestic

evidence from the play

evidence from the play

Jerry is associated with wild animals from the start. The first line of the play has him declaring loudly several times that he has just come from the zoo. The zoo, of course, is filled with wild animals, and even though they are caged, they are vastly different from house pets like Peter's. Perhaps the most significant speech in the play is Jerry's account of his relationship with the landlady's dog. In it, Jerry describes the dog as "a black monster of a beast: an oversized head, tiny, tiny ears, and eyes . . . bloodshot, infected, maybe; and a body you can see the ribs through

Textual analysis of Jerry's character as wild

evidence from the play

Hanks 3

the skin. [. . .] and an open sore on its . . . *right* forepaw; that is red, too. And, oh yes; the poor monster [. . .] almost always has an erection . . . of sorts. That's red, too" (36). The words "monster" and "beast" tell us that this is not a typical house dog, but one that is practically feral. The attention to the dog's constant erection suggests that he represents unfulfilled desire. As the story unfolds, Jerry, too, has a desire to connect with others, which ultimately goes unfulfilled. His first attempt to connect is with the dog, but he fails. At best, he and the dog achieve a status of mutual indifference. But it is significant that Jerry chooses this wild beast as the object with which to make a start at dealing with the world, for it suggests that he must make peace with what is unconventional before he can deal with the rest of the conventional world.

Synthesis of analysis to develop argument

Seeing Peter as a domesticated guinea pig and Jerry as a feral dog clarifies their approaches to life. While Peter is happy to be caged in fulfilling society's expectations through a conventional home, family, and job, Jerry cannot function in such a setting. The closest Peter comes to breaking out of his neatly ordered life is when he mistakenly says that he must get home because the parakeets and the cat will be preparing dinner. This disruption of conventional order leads Peter to say, "I had my own zoo there for a moment" (39). This quote highlights that Peter, blind to his own captivity in society, has a very shallow understanding of the zoo. He sees it only in the sense of a wild place, with all kinds of animals mixed up together. Jerry, however, shows a deeper understanding when he describes the zoo as a place where "everyone [is] separated by bars from everyone else, the animals for the most part from each other, and always the people from the animals. But, if it's a zoo, that's the way it is" (39). Since metaphorically Peter and Jerry are domesticated and wild animals, this quote shows that Jerry—the untamed one—views convention not as something that brings comforting order, but as divisive bars that keep people from connecting with one another.

Textual support

Textual support

Hanks 4

Conclusion summarizes preceding analysis

The zoo is a place where wild animals that populate it are not free to be wild. Likewise, Jerry is not free to be himself in a world where convention imposes its rules. And just as a wild animal cannot flourish in captivity, neither can Jerry survive in an oppressive society. Thus, an exploration of the connection between animals and the characters provides insight into why Jerry kills himself at the end of the play. Since Peter (the domesticated man) holds the knife on which Jerry impales himself, Jerry (the feral being) is symbolically killed by conventional society. Albee's play, then, is more than just an encounter between two men; it is a clash between two ways of life. By associating the conflicting characters with animal imagery, he illustrates how ultimately it is the conventional, domesticated way of life that blindly dominates those who refuse to conform.

Concluding statement restates and reinforces thesis

Work Cited

Albee, Edward. *The Zoo Story. Literature: Craft & Voice.* Eds. Nicholas Delbanco and Alan Cheuse. Vol. 3. New York: McGraw-Hill, 2009. Print.

# Suggestions for Writing

1. What is the relationship of plot to character in *The Zoo Story*? How do these elements of drama depend on each other in this play?
2. Compare the role of setting in *Trifles* and *The Zoo Story*. Consider how, for example, *Trifles* would change if it were staged at the prison, or how *The Zoo Story* would change if Peter and Jerry ran into one another at a coffee shop.
3. Dialogue drives the action in *The Zoo Story*, but the play was written to be performed. Choose one of the longer monologues (for instance, Jerry's on page 36) and write stage directions for the character not speaking. Cite specific lines that require certain reactions or gestures. How would your directions enhance the audience's experience of the monologue?
4. Focus on an episode of your favorite television drama, if you have one, or a recent movie you enjoyed, and compare it in relation to character and plot to any of these plays. Do television plays and movies stress the same element as these theater pieces? If they differ, how would you describe the differences?

# 33 Ancient Greek Drama

## A Case Study on Sophocles

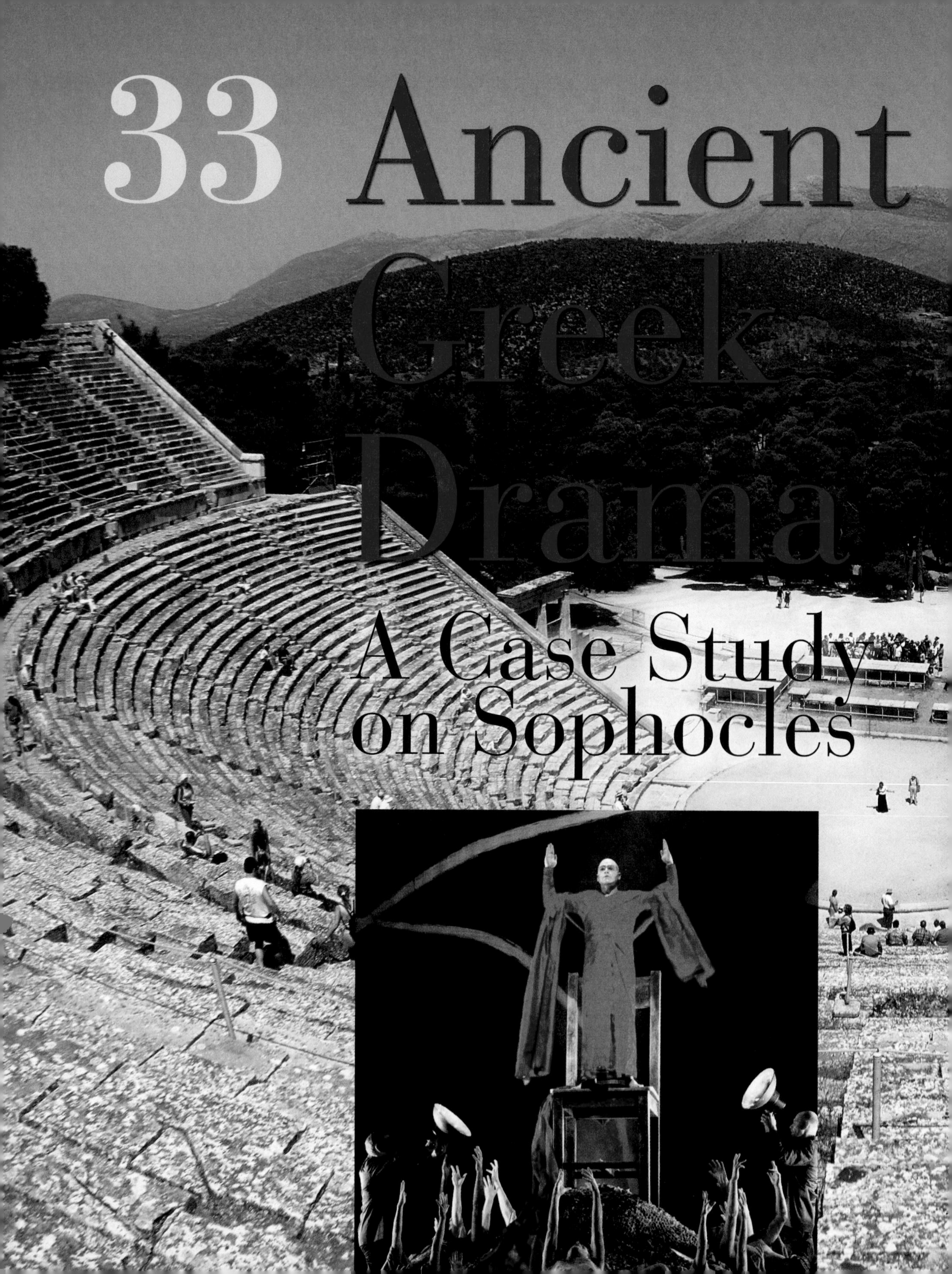

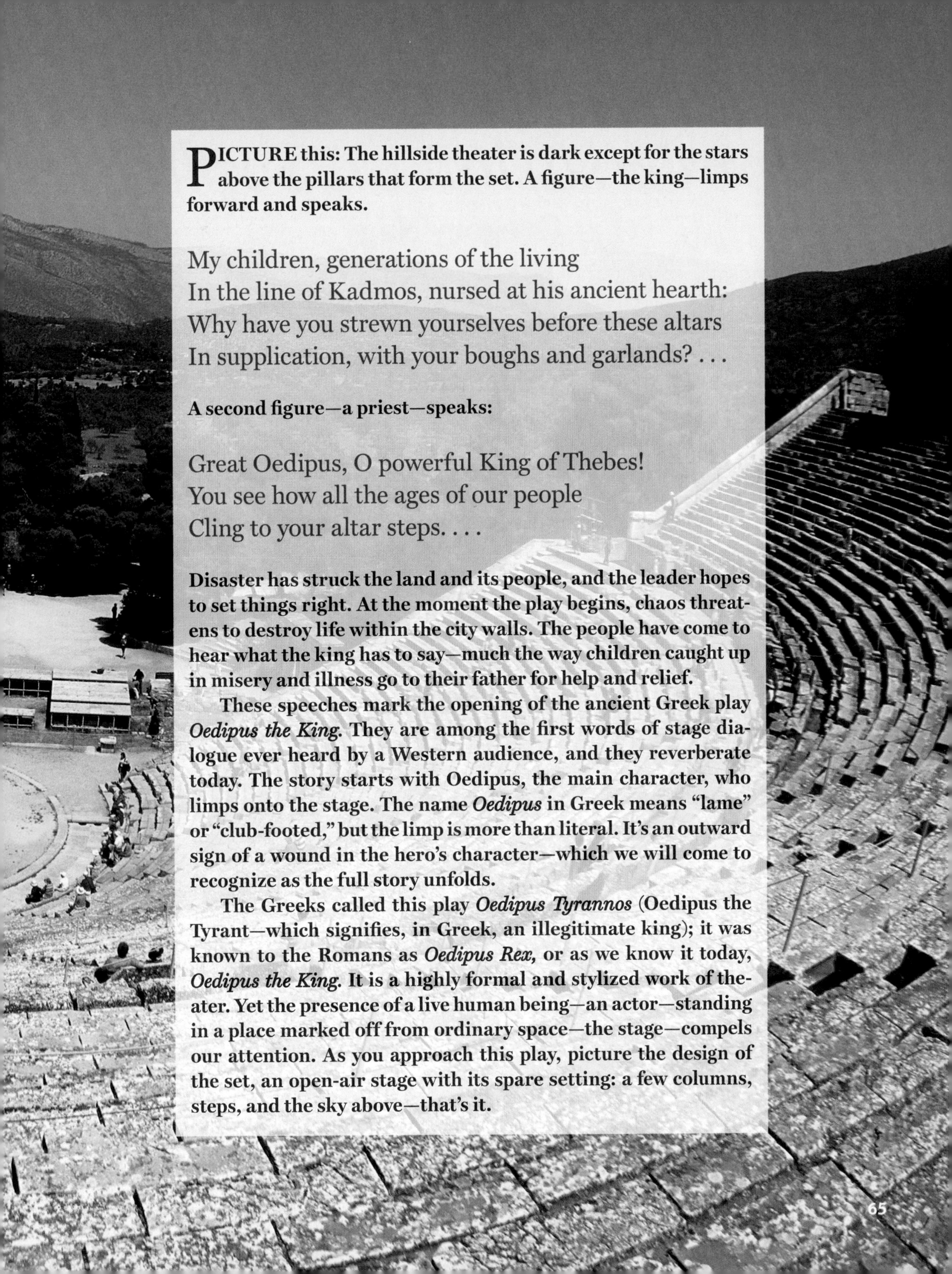

PICTURE this: The hillside theater is dark except for the stars above the pillars that form the set. A figure—the king—limps forward and speaks.

My children, generations of the living
In the line of Kadmos, nursed at his ancient hearth:
Why have you strewn yourselves before these altars
In supplication, with your boughs and garlands? . . .

**A second figure—a priest—speaks:**

Great Oedipus, O powerful King of Thebes!
You see how all the ages of our people
Cling to your altar steps. . . .

Disaster has struck the land and its people, and the leader hopes to set things right. At the moment the play begins, chaos threatens to destroy life within the city walls. The people have come to hear what the king has to say—much the way children caught up in misery and illness go to their father for help and relief.

These speeches mark the opening of the ancient Greek play *Oedipus the King.* They are among the first words of stage dialogue ever heard by a Western audience, and they reverberate today. The story starts with Oedipus, the main character, who limps onto the stage. The name *Oedipus* in Greek means "lame" or "club-footed," but the limp is more than literal. It's an outward sign of a wound in the hero's character—which we will come to recognize as the full story unfolds.

The Greeks called this play *Oedipus Tyrannos* (Oedipus the Tyrant—which signifies, in Greek, an illegitimate king); it was known to the Romans as *Oedipus Rex,* or as we know it today, *Oedipus the King.* It is a highly formal and stylized work of theater. Yet the presence of a live human being—an actor—standing in a place marked off from ordinary space—the stage—compels our attention. As you approach this play, picture the design of the set, an open-air stage with its spare setting: a few columns, steps, and the sky above—that's it.

Pathos *is emotion.*

# Q&A

*We're really the participants of drama.*

# *A Conversation on Sophocles*

## Gregory Nagy

### Drama As Spiritual and Governmental Requirement

In Athens, the classical period, the Golden Age of Greek civilization, all Athenians have to be theatergoers because it's a civic obligation to go to theater. . . . It's not just political . . . it's a religious duty—in fact, festivals and religion go together. . . . It's very important when we look at theater in the fifth century, or even before . . . [that] when the Athenian[s], twenty thousand, thirty thousand of them, go to Athenian state theater, they're going . . . to participate . . . and in this . . . what is achieved is a purification of the body politic, a renewal. . . . We might . . . call it . . . a sacred narrative . . . of . . . heroic values.

### *Pathos* and *Catharsis*

Imagine looking down at a sea of faces, twenty thousand pairs of eyes are weeping simultaneously, twenty thousand people have their hair stand on end in terror. . . . The *pathos*—of the hero, who is . . . larger than life, let's say Oedipus . . . this chemistry brings about *catharsis*. . . . It's a Greek word that means . . . "purification."

### Sophocles As Public Figure

Artists in the ancient world . . . and Sophocles was no exception . . . [were] public figures . . . Sophocles was not only a master dramaturge, he was a master poet, a master composer of music, a master musician. . . . He was everything to the Athenians. When he died in his late eighties . . . there was such an outpouring of emotion that there are many anecdotes about how Sophocles became not only . . . the national poet of the Athenians, but . . . was actually worshipped as a cult hero.

To watch the entire interview online, go to **www.mhhe.com/delbanco1e.**

**RESEARCH ASSIGNMENT** After watching the interview with Nagy, explain how epic poetry and tragic drama were influenced by each other. How would you describe the influence on Sophocles of the tradition of epic poetry in Greece?

Gregory Nagy [Nahzh] is Director of the Center for Hellenic Studies in Washington, D.C., and the Francis Jones Professor of Classical Greek Literature and Professor of Comparative Literature at Harvard University.

"Pathos *is emotion.... That's how we get the borrowing in English.* Pathos. Pathetic. *That shows you the everyday meaning of* pathos. *But, when Oedipus experiences* pathos, *it's not everyday, it's larger than life, it's heroic, it goes back to the heroic world. This is that. That's what happens in theater, that's how the process of* catharsis *happens, that's how the* pathos, *which is the larger-than-life experience of Oedipus, can become part of your life, your emotional life, as you are drawn into this larger-than-life character."*

Conversation with Gregory Nagy, available on video at www.mhhe.com/delbancole

## THE OEDIPUS STORY

Versions of the Oedipus story were part of an oral tradition hundreds of years before Sophocles enacted it as drama. It has its roots in myth, that of the house (or kingdom) of Atreus—a complicated tapestry of guilt and revenge, generational conflict, loss, and gain. The story would have been well known to the Athenian audience; what matters here is not *suspense* (we all know "who done it" already) but *how* the tale is told. Old Thebes, where the action of the play takes place, is ruled by high-minded Oedipus, who appeared one day after the death of the previous king, Laïos. Thebes has been an outpost of civilization in an otherwise wild countryside where bandits reign, terrors lurk, and odd events take place. The city traditionally stands for order, the countryside for chaos, yet Sophocles reverses this—chaos has entered in.

The playwright takes the material of the Oedipus myth, folds and manipulates the time span, and molds it into one of the central texts of our culture, a play whose subject is the essence of human character, the relation of character to destiny or fate, and the links between the middle world of human life and the upper world of the gods. As the play unfolds, the great king discovers that he himself is the cause of the troubles. This truth reveals itself gradually, brought to him in pieces by various characters. At some points, he refuses to believe what he is told; at others, he begs to be told what others prefer not to tell him. Toward the end, Oedipus discovers the truth about himself, and this leads to a desperate act of self-mutilation—which, ironically, turns his vision dark and allows him to "see" for the first time the enormity of his sin.

# Sophocles (496?–406/5 B.C.)

The greatest playwright of the Golden Age of Greek drama, Sophocles, the son of a successful Athenian armorer, attained extraordinary mastery of the dramatic art. He also participated fully in the political life of his city. Early in his life as a creator of plays, he was influenced by the work of his predecessor Aeschylus but went on to stamp his own productions with the particular mark of great character, diction, and dramatic irony that we recognize today. He wrote over a hundred plays, only seven of which have survived in their entirety. Of these *Oedipus The King* remains the pinnacle of Western drama and is the subject of the *Poetics*, the Greek philosopher Aristotle's treatise on the nature of drama. Sophocles' plays were performed at public festivals and employed Athenian citizens as well as trained actors and musicians. Along with those of William Shakespeare, they stand as the most important dramas in the life of Western culture.

## The Oedipus Myth

*Laïos, King of Thebes, is warned in a prophecy that his son will murder him and marry Laïos's wife Iocaste, the Queen of Thebes.*

*To prevent that prophecy from coming true, Laïos orders a herdsman to take his firstborn son into the country and murder him there.*

*The herdsman pities the baby. Instead of killing him, he pierces his feet and gives him to another herdsman to keep. The baby is named Oedipus, which means "swollen foot."*

*The second herdsman takes the baby Oedipus to his master, the King of Corinth, who adopts him and raises him as a prince.*

*Oedipus, now a young man, receives a prophecy that he will kill his father and marry his mother.*

*Assuming the "father" and "mother" of the prophecy are the king and queen of Corinth, Oedipus flees that city for the countryside.*

**AS YOU READ** Picture the design of the amphitheater, with its spare setting of columns and bright air. Read through the play once, and you find that it takes place in this single location, with no change of scene. Only the entrances and exits of the various characters mark the rhythmic development of the action here.

# Oedipus the King (c. 430 B.C.)

*—translated by Dudley Fitts and Robert Fitzgerald*

## CHARACTERS:

**OEDIPUS**

**A PRIEST**

**CREON**

**TEIRESIAS**

**IOCASTE**

**MESSENGER**

**SHEPHERD OF LAÏOS**

**SECOND MESSENGER**

**CHORUS OF THEBAN ELDERS**

*In his travels, Oedipus comes to a crossroads and gets into an argument. His temper gets the better of him, and he murders his opponents, who, unbeknownst to him, include Laïos, Oedipus's true father.*

*Oedipus comes to Thebes, which is threatened by the Sphinx who guards the gate of the city and devours all who cannot answer her riddle.*

*Oedipus solves the Sphinx's riddle. Its riddle solved, the Sphinx throws itself off a cliff and dies.*

*Thankful to Oedipus, and recently having lost its king, the city of Thebes awards him the crown and the Queen, Oedipus's mother Iocaste, as a bride.*

*The prophecies conveyed to Laïos and Oedipus have now come true.*

*Some time later, Thebes suffers plague as a result of "sin" and King Oedipus painfully discovers that he is the sinner.*

**THE SCENE.** *Before the palace of Oedipus, King of Thebes. A central door and two lateral doors open onto a platform which runs the length of the façade. On the platform, right and left, are altars; and three steps lead down into the "orchestra," or chorus-ground. At the beginning of the action these steps are crowded by suppliants who have brought branches and chaplets of olive leaves and who lie in various attitudes of despair.* OEDIPUS *enters.*

## PROLOGUE

**OEDIPUS:** My children, generations of the living
In the line of Kadmos, nursed at his ancient hearth:
Why have you strewn yourselves before these altars
In supplication, with your boughs and garlands?
The breath of incense rises from the city
With a sound of prayer and lamentation
Children,
I would not have you speak through messengers,
And therefore I have come myself to hear you—
I, Oedipus, who bear the famous name.
*[To a* PRIEST:
You, there, since you are eldest in the company,
Speak for them all, tell me what preys upon you,
Whether you come in dread, or crave some blessing:
Tell me, and never doubt that I will help you
In every way I can; I should be heartless
Were I not moved to find you suppliant here.

**PRIEST:** Great Oedipus, O powerful King of Thebes!
You see how all the ages of our people
Cling to your altar steps: here are boys
Who can barely stand alone, and here are priests
By weight of age, as I am a priest of God,
And young men chosen from those yet unmarried;
As for the others, all that multitude,
They wait with olive chaplets in the squares,
At the two shrines of Pallas, and where Apollo
Speaks in the glowing embers.
Your own eyes
Must tell you: Thebes is tossed on a murdering sea
And can not lift her head from the death surge.
A rust consumes the buds and fruits of the earth;
The herds are sick; children die unborn,
And labor is vain. The god of plague and pyre
Raids like detestable lightning through the city,
And all the house of Kadmos is laid waste,
All emptied, and all darkened: Death alone
Battens upon the misery of Thebes.
You are not one of the immortal gods, we know;
Yet we have come to you to make our prayer

The old priest (Eric House) beseeches Oedipus (Douglas Campbell) to find a cure for the plague in *Oedipus Rex* (1957).

As to the man surest in mortal ways
And wisest in the ways of God. You saved us
From the Sphinx, that flinty singer, and the tribute
We paid to her so long; yet you were never
Better informed than we, nor could we teach you:
It was some god breathed in you to set us free.

Therefore, O mighty King, we turn to you:
Find us our safety, find us a remedy,
Whether by counsel of the gods or men.
A king of wisdom tested in the past
Can act in a time of troubles, and act well.
Noblest of men, restore
Life to your city! Think how all men call you
Liberator for your triumph long ago;
Ah, when your years of kingship are remembered,
Let them not say *We rose, but later fell—*
Keep the State from going down in the storm!
Once, years ago, with happy augury,
You brought us fortune; be the same again!
No man questions your power to rule the land:
But rule over men, not over a dead city!
Ships are only hulls, citadels are nothing,
When no life moves in the empty passageways.

**OEDIPUS:** Poor children! You may be sure I know
All that you longed for in your coming here.
I know that you are deathly sick; and yet,
Sick as you are, not one is as sick as I.
Each of you suffers in himself alone
His anguish, not another's; but my spirit
Groans for the city, for myself, for you.
I was not sleeping, you are not waking me.
No, I have been in tears for a long while
And in my restless thought walked many ways.
In all my search, I found one helpful course,
And that I have taken: I have sent Creon,
Son of Menoikeus, brother of the Queen,
To Delphi, Apollo's place of revelation,
To learn there, if he can,
What act or pledge of mine may save the city.
I have counted the days, and now, this very day,
I am troubled, for he has overstayed his time.
What is he doing? He has been gone too long.
Yet whenever he comes back, I should do ill
To scant whatever duty God reveals.

**PRIEST:** It is a timely promise. At this instant
They tell me Creon is here.

**OEDIPUS:** O Lord Apollo!
May his news be fair as his face is radiant!

**PRIEST:** It could not be otherwise: he is crowned with bay,
The chaplet is thick with berries.

**OEDIPUS:** We shall soon know;
He is near enough to hear us now.
*[Enter* CREON

O Prince:
Brother: son of Menoikeus:
What answer do you bring us from the god?

**CREON:** A strong one. I can tell you, great afflictions
Will turn out well, if they are taken well.

**OEDIPUS:** What was the oracle? These vague words
Leave me still hanging between hope and fear.

**CREON:** Is it your pleasure to hear me with all these
Gathered around us? I am prepared to speak,
But should we not go in?

**OEDIPUS:** Let them all hear it.
It is for them I suffer, more than for myself.

**CREON:** Then I will tell you what I heard at Delphi.

In plain words
The god commands us to expel from the land of Thebes
An old defilement we are sheltering.
It is a deathly thing, beyond cure;
We must not let it feed upon us longer.

**OEDIPUS:** What defilement? How shall we rid ourselves of it?

**CREON:** By exile or death, blood for blood. It was
Murder that brought the plague-wind on the city.

**OEDIPUS:** Murder of whom? Surely the god has named him?

**CREON:** My lord: long ago Laïos was our king,
Before you came to govern us.

**OEDIPUS:** I know;
I learned of him from others; I never saw him.

**CREON:** He was murdered; and Apollo commands us now
To take revenge upon whoever killed him.

**OEDIPUS:** Upon whom? Where are they? Where shall we find a clue
To solve that crime, after so many years?

**CREON:** Here in this land, he said.
If we make enquiry,
We may touch things that otherwise escape us.

**OEDIPUS:** Tell me: Was Laïos murdered in his house,
Or in the fields, or in some foreign country?

**CREON:** He said he planned to make a pilgrimage.
He did not come home again.

**OEDIPUS:** And was there no one,
No witness, no companion, to tell what happened?

**CREON:** They were all killed but one, and he got away
So frightened that he could remember one thing only.

**OEDIPUS:** What was that one thing? One may be the key
To everything, if we resolve to use it.

**CREON:** He said that a band of highwaymen attacked them,
Outnumbered them, and overwhelmed the King.

**OEDIPUS:** Strange, that a highwayman should be so daring—
Unless some faction here bribed him to do it.

**CREON:** We thought of that. But after Laïos' death
New troubles arose and we had no avenger.

**OEDIPUS:** What troubles could prevent your hunting down the killers?

**CREON:** The riddling Sphinx's song
Made us deaf to all mysteries but her own.

**OEDIPUS:** Then once more I must bring what is dark to light.
It is most fitting that Apollo shows,
As you do, this compunction for the dead.
You shall see how I stand by you, as I should,
To avenge the city and the city's god,
And not as though it were for some distant friend,
But for my own sake, to be rid of evil.
Whoever killed King Laïos might— who knows?—
Decide at any moment to kill me as well.
By avenging the murdered king I protect myself.

Come, then, my children: leave the altar steps,
Lift up your olive boughs!
One of you go
And summon the people of Kadmos to gather here.
I will do all that I can; you may tell them that.
*[Exit a* PAGE
So, with the help of God,
We shall be saved—or else indeed we are lost.

**PRIEST:** Let us rise, children. It was for this we came,
And now the King has promised it himself.
Phoibos has sent us an oracle; may he descend
Himself to save us and drive out the plague.
*[Exeunt* OEDIPUS *and* CREON *into the palace by the central door. The* PRIEST *and the* SUPPLIANTS *disperse R and L. After a short pause the* CHORUS *enters the orchestra.*

Oedipus (Philip Langridge) addresses the people of Thebes in *Oedipus Rex* (1993).

## PÁRODOS

**CHORUS:** [STROPHE 1
What is God singing in his profound
Delphi of gold and shadow?
What oracle for Thebes, the sunwhipped city?

Fear unjoints me, the roots of my heart tremble.

Now I remember, O Healer, your power, and wonder:
Will you send doom like a sudden cloud, or weave it
Like nightfall of the past?

Speak, speak to us, issue of holy sound:
Dearest to our expectancy: be tender!

The chorus in *Oedipus Rex* (1993).

[ANTISTROPHE 1

Let me pray to Athenê, the immortal daughter of
Zeus,
And to Artemis her sister
Who keeps her famous throne in the market ring,
And to Apollo, bowman at the far butts of heaven—

O gods, descend! Like three streams leap against
The fires of our grief, the fires of darkness;
Be swift to bring us rest!

As in the old time from the brilliant house
Of air you stepped to save us, come again!

Now our afflictions have no end, [STROPHE 2
Now all our stricken host lies down
And no man fights off death with his mind;

The noble plowland bears no grain,
And groaning mothers can not bear—

See, how our lives like birds take wing,
Like sparks that fly when a fire soars,
To the shore of the god of evening.

The plague burns on, it is pitiless, [ANTISTROPHE 2
Though pallid children laden with death
Lie unwept in the stony ways,

And old gray women by every path
Flock to the strand about the altars

There to strike their breasts and cry
Worship of Phoibos in wailing prayers:
Be kind, God's golden child!

[STROPHE 3

There are no swords in this attack by fire,
No shields, but we are ringed with cries.

Send the besieger plunging from our homes
Into the vast sea-room of the Atlantic
Or into the waves that foam eastward to Thrace—

For the day ravages what the night spares—

Destroy our enemy, lord of the thunder!
Let him be riven by lightning from heaven!

[ANTISTROPHE 3

Phoibos Apollo, stretch the sun's bowstring,
That golden cord, until it sing for us,
Flashing arrows in heaven!
Artemis, Huntress,
Race with flaring lights upon our mountains!

O scarlet god, O golden-banded brow,
O Theban Bacchos in a storm of Maenads,
*[Enter* OEDIPUS, *C*
Whirl upon Death, that all the Undying hate!
Come with blinding torches, come in joy!

## SCENE I

**OEDIPUS:** Is this your prayer? It may be answered.
Come,
Listen to me, act as the crisis demands,
And you shall have relief from all these evils.

Until now I was a stranger to this tale,
As I had been a stranger to the crime.
Could I track down the murderer without a clue?
But now, friends,
As one who became a citizen after the murder,
I make this proclamation to all Thebans:
If any man knows by whose hand Laïos, son of
Labdakos,
Met his death, I direct that man to tell me
everything,
No matter what he fears for having so long
withheld it.
Let it stand as promised that no further trouble
Will come to him, but he may leave the land in
safety.

Moreover: If anyone knows the murderer to be
foreign,
Let him not keep silent: he shall have his reward
from me.
However, if he does conceal it; if any man
Fearing for his friend or for himself disobeys this
edict,
Hear what I propose to do:

I solemnly forbid the people of this country,
Where power and throne are mine, ever to receive that man
Or speak to him, no matter who he is, or let him
Join in sacrifice, lustration, or in prayer.
I decree that he be driven from every house,
Being, as he is, corruption itself to us: the Delphic
Voice of Zeus has pronounced this revelation.
Thus I associate myself with the oracle
And take the side of the murdered king.

As for the criminal, I pray to God—
Whether it be a lurking thief, or one of a number—
I pray that that man's life be consumed in evil and wretchedness.
And as for me, this curse applies no less
If it should turn out that the culprit is my guest here,
Sharing my hearth.
You have heard the penalty.
I lay it on you now to attend to this
For my sake, for Apollo's, for the sick
Sterile city that heaven has abandoned.
Suppose the oracle had given you no command:
Should this defilement go uncleansed for ever?
You should have found the murderer: your king,
A noble king, had been destroyed!
Now I,
Having the power that he held before me,
Having his bed, begetting children there
Upon his wife, as he would have, had he lived—
Their son would have been my children's brother,
If Laïos had had luck in fatherhood!
(But surely ill luck rushed upon his reign)—
I say I take the son's part, just as though
I were his son, to press the fight for him
And see it won! I'll find the hand that brought
Death to Labdakos' and Polydoros' child,
Heir of Kadmos' and Agenor's line.

Oedipus vows to find King Laïos's murderer in *Oedipus Rex* (1957).

And as for those who fail me,
May the gods deny them the fruit of the earth,
Fruit of the womb, and may they rot utterly!
Let them be wretched as we are wretched, and worse!

For you, for loyal Thebans, and for all
Who find my actions right, I pray the favor
Of justice, and of all the immortal gods.

**CHORAGOS:** Since I am under oath, my lord, I swear
I did not do the murder, I can not name
The murderer. Might not the oracle
That has ordained the search tell where to find him?

**OEDIPUS:** An honest question. But no man in the world
Can make the gods do more than the gods will.

**CHORAGOS:** There is one last expedient—

**OEDIPUS:** Tell me what it is.
Though it seem slight, you must not hold it back.

**CHORAGOS:** A lord clairvoyant to the lord Apollo,
As we all know, is the skilled Teiresias.
One might learn much about this from him, Oedipus.

**OEDIPUS:** I am not wasting time:
Creon spoke of this, and I have sent for him—
Twice, in fact; it is strange that he is not here.

**CHORAGOS:** The other matter—that old report—seems useless.

**OEDIPUS:** Tell me. I am interested in all reports.

**CHORAGOS:** The King was said to have been killed by highwaymen.

**OEDIPUS:** I know. But we have no witnesses to that.

**CHORAGOS:** If the killer can feel a particle of dread,
Your curse will bring him out of hiding!

**OEDIPUS:** No.
The man who dared that act will fear no curse.
*[Enter the blind seer* TEIRESIAS, *led by a* PAGE

**CHORAGOS:** But there is one man who may detect the criminal.
This is Teiresias, this is the holy prophet
In whom, alone of all men, truth was born.

**OEDIPUS:** Teiresias: seer: student of mysteries,
Of all that's taught and all that no man tells,
Secrets of Heaven and secrets of the earth:

Blind though you are, you know the city lies
Sick with plague; and from this plague, my lord,
We find that you alone can guard or save us.
Possibly you did not hear the messengers?
Apollo, when we sent to him,
Sent us back word that this great pestilence
Would lift, but only if we established clearly
The identity of those who murdered Laïos.
They must be killed or exiled.
Can you use
Birdflight or any art of divination
To purify yourself, and Thebes, and me
From this contagion? We are in your hands.
There is no fairer duty
Than that of helping others in distress.

**TEIRESIAS:** How dreadful knowledge of the truth can be
When there's no help in truth! I knew this well,
But made myself forget. I should not have come.

**OEDIPUS:** What is troubling you? Why are your eyes so cold?

**TEIRESIAS:** Let me go home. Bear your own fate, and I'll
Bear mine. It is better so: trust what I say.

**OEDIPUS:** What you say is ungracious and unhelpful
To your native country. Do not refuse to speak.

**TEIRESIAS:** When it comes to speech, your own is neither temperate
Nor opportune. I wish to be more prudent.

**OEDIPUS:** In God's name, we all beg you—

**TEIRESIAS:** You are all ignorant.
No; I will never tell you what I know.
Now it is my misery; then, it would be yours.

Teiresias (Harry Peeters) tells Oedipus he is the source of the plague in *Oedipus Rex* (1993).

**OEDIPUS:** What! You do know something, and will not tell us?
You would betray us all and wreck the State?

**TEIRESIAS:** I do not intend to torture myself, or you.
Why persist in asking? You will not persuade me.

**OEDIPUS:** What a wicked old man you are! You'd try a stone's
Patience! Out with it! Have you no feeling at all?

**TEIRESIAS:** You call me unfeeling. If you could only see
The nature of your own feelings . . .

**OEDIPUS:** Why,
Who would not feel as I do? Who could endure
Your arrogance toward the city?

**TEIRESIAS:** What does it matter!
Whether I speak or not, it is bound to come.

**OEDIPUS:** Then, if "it" is bound to come, you are bound to tell me.

**TEIRESIAS:** No, I will not go on. Rage as you please.

**OEDIPUS:** Rage? Why not!
And I'll tell you what I think:
You planned it, you had it done, you all but
Killed him with your own hands: if you had eyes,
I'd say the crime was yours, and yours alone.

**TEIRESIAS:** So? I charge you, then,
Abide by the proclamation you have made:
From this day forth
Never speak again to these men or to me;
You yourself are the pollution of this country.

**OEDIPUS:** You dare say that! Can you possibly think you have
Some way of going free, after such insolence?

**TEIRESIAS:** I have gone free. It is the truth sustains me.

**OEDIPUS:** Who taught you shamelessness? It was not your craft.

**TEIRESIAS:** You did. You made me speak. I did not want to.

**OEDIPUS:** Speak what? Let me hear it again more clearly.

**TEIRESIAS:** Was it not clear before? Are you tempting me?

**OEDIPUS:** I did not understand it. Say it again.

**TEIRESIAS:** I say that you are the murderer whom you seek.

**OEDIPUS:** Now twice you have spat out infamy. You'll pay for it!

**TEIRESIAS:** Would you care for more? Do you wish to be really angry?

**OEDIPUS:** Say what you will. Whatever you say is worthless.

**TEIRESIAS:** I say you live in hideous shame with those
Most dear to you. You can not see the evil.

**OEDIPUS:** It seems you can go on mouthing like this for ever.

**TEIRESIAS:** I can, if there is power in truth.

**OEDIPUS:** There is:
But not for you, not for you,
You sightless, witless, senseless, mad old man!

**TEIRESIAS:** You are the madman. There is no one here
Who will not curse you soon, as you curse me.

**OEDIPUS:** You child of endless night! You can not hurt me
Or any other man who sees the sun.

**TEIRESIAS:** True: it is not from me your fate will come.
That lies within Apollo's competence,
As it is his concern.

**OEDIPUS:** Tell me:
Are you speaking for Creon, or for yourself?

**TEIRESIAS:** Creon is no threat. You weave your own doom.

**OEDIPUS:** Wealth, power, craft of statesmanship!
Kingly position, everywhere admired!
What savage envy is stored up against these,
If Creon, whom I trusted, Creon my friend,
For this great office which the city once
Put in my hands unsought—if for this power
Creon desires in secret to destroy me!

He has bought this decrepit fortune-teller, this
Collector of dirty pennies, this prophet fraud—
Why, he is no more clairvoyant than I am!
Tell us:
Has your mystic mummery ever approached the truth?
When that hellcat the Sphinx was performing here,
What help were you to these people?
Her magic was not for the first man who came along:

Teiresias (Donald Davis) prophesies Oedipus's downfall in *Oedipus Rex* (1957).

It demanded a real exorcist. Your birds—
What good were they? or the gods, for the matter of that?
But I came by,
Oedipus, the simple man, who knows nothing—
I thought it out for myself, no birds helped me!
And this is the man you think you can destroy,
That you may be close to Creon when he's king!
Well, you and your friend Creon, it seems to me,
Will suffer most. If you were not an old man,
You would have paid already for your plot.

**CHORAGOS:** We can not see that his words or yours
Have been spoken except in anger, Oedipus,
And of anger we have no need. How can God's will
Be accomplished best? That is what most concerns us.

**TEIRESIAS:** You are a king. But where argument's concerned
I am your man, as much a king as you.
I am not your servant, but Apollo's.
I have no need of Creon to speak for me.

Listen to me. You mock my blindness, do you?
But I say that you, with both your eyes, are blind:
You can not see the wretchedness of your life,
Nor in whose house you live, no, nor with whom.
Who are your father and mother? Can you tell me?
You do not even know the blind wrongs
That you have done them, on earth and in the world below.
But the double lash of your parents' curse will whip you
Out of this land some day, with only night
Upon your precious eyes.
Your cries then—where will they not be heard?
What fastness of Kithairon will not echo them?

And that bridal-descant of yours—you'll know
it then,
The song they sang when you came here to Thebes
And found your misguided berthing.
All this, and more, that you can not guess at now,
Will bring you to yourself among your children.

Be angry, then. Curse Creon. Curse my words.
I tell you, no man that walks upon the earth
Shall be rooted out more horribly than you.

**OEDIPUS:** Am I to bear this from him?—Damnation
Take you! Out of this place! Out of my sight!

**TEIRESIAS:** I would not have come at all if you had not
asked me.

**OEDIPUS:** Could I have told that you'd talk nonsense,
that
You'd come here to make a fool of yourself, and
of me?

**TEIRESIAS:** A fool? Your parents thought me sane
enough.

**OEDIPUS:** My parents again!—Wait: who were my
parents?

**TEIRESIAS:** This day will give you a father, and break
your heart.

**OEDIPUS:** Your infantile riddles! Your damned
abracadabra!

**TEIRESIAS:** You were a great man once at solving
riddles.

**OEDIPUS:** Mock me with that if you like; you will find
it true.

**TEIRESIAS:** It was true enough. It brought about
your ruin.

**OEDIPUS:** But if it saved this town?

**TEIRESIAS:** *[To the* PAGE*:*
Boy, give me your hand.

**OEDIPUS:** Yes, boy; lead him away.
—While you are here
We can do nothing. Go; leave us in peace.

**TEIRESIAS:** I will go when I have said what I have
to say.
How can you hurt me? And I tell you again:
The man you have been looking for all this time,
The damned man, the murderer of Laïos,
The man is in Thebes. To your mind he is foreign-
born,
But it will soon be shown that he is a Theban,
A revelation that will fail to please.
A blind man,
Who has his eyes now; a penniless man, who is
rich now;
And he will go tapping the strange earth with
his staff.
To the children with whom he lives now he will be
Brother and father—the very same; to her
Who bore him, son and husband—the very same
Who came to his father's bed, wet with his father's
blood.

Enough. Go think that over.
If later you find error in what I have said,
You may say that I have no skill in prophecy.
*[Exit* TEIRESIAS, *led by his* PAGE.
OEDIPUS *goes into the palace.*

## ODE I

**CHORUS:** The Delphic stone of prophecies [STROPHE 1
Remembers ancient regicide
And a still bloody hand.
That killer's hour of flight has come.
He must be stronger than riderless
Courses of untiring wind,
For the son of Zeus armed with his father's thunder
Leaps in lightning after him;
And the Furies follow him, the sad Furies.

Holy Parnassos' peak of snow [ANTISTROPHE 1
Flashes and blinds that secret man,
That all shall hunt him down:
Though he may roam the forest shade
Like a bull gone wild from pasture
To rage through glooms of stone.
Doom comes down on him; flight will not avail him;
For the world's heart calls him desolate,
And the immortal Furies follow, for ever follow.

But now a wilder thing is heard [STROPHE 2
From the old man skilled at hearing Fate in the
wingbeat of a bird.
Bewildered as a blown bird, my soul hovers and can
not find
Foothold in this debate, or any reason or rest of
mind.
But no man ever brought—none can bring
Proof of strife between Thebes' royal house,
Labdakos' line, and the son Polybos;
And never until now has any man brought word
Of Laïos' dark death staining Oedipus the King.

Divine Zeus and Apollo hold [ANTISTROPHE 2
Perfect intelligence alone of all tales ever told;
And well though this diviner works, he works in his own night;
No man can judge that rough unknown or trust in second sight,
For wisdom changes hands among the wise.
Shall I believe my great lord criminal
At a raging word that a blind old man let fall?
I saw him, when the carrion woman faced him of old,
Prove his heroic mind! These evil words are lies.

## SCENE II

**CREON:** Men of Thebes:
I am told that heavy accusations
Have been brought against me by King Oedipus.

I am not the kind of man to bear this tamely.

If in these present difficulties
He holds me accountable for any harm to him
Through anything I have said or done—why, then,
I do not value life in this dishonor.
It is not as though this rumor touched upon
Some private indiscretion. The matter is grave.
The fact is that I am being called disloyal
To the State, to my fellow citizens, to my friends.

**CHORAGOS:** He may have spoken in anger, not from his mind.

**CREON:** But did you not hear him say I was the one
Who seduced the old prophet into lying?

**CHORAGOS:** The thing was said; I do not know how seriously.

Creon (Douglas Rain) and Oedipus quarrel in *Oedipus Rex* (1957).

**CREON:** But you were watching him! Were his eyes steady?
Did he look like a man in his right mind?

**CHORAGOS:** I do not know.
I can not judge the behavior of great men.
But here is the King himself.
*[Enter* OEDIPUS

**OEDIPUS:** So you dared come back.
Why? How brazen of you to come to my house,
You murderer!
Do you think I do not know
That you plotted to kill me, plotted to steal my throne?
Tell me, in God's name: am I coward, a fool,
That you should dream you could accomplish this?
A fool who could not see your slippery game?
A coward, not to fight back when I saw it?
You are the fool, Creon, are you not? hoping
Without support or friends to get a throne?
Thrones may be won or bought: you could do neither.

**CREON:** Now listen to me. You have talked; let me talk, too.
You can not judge unless you know the facts.

**OEDIPUS:** You speak well: there is one fact; but I find it hard
To learn from the deadliest enemy I have.

**CREON:** That above all I must dispute with you.

**OEDIPUS:** That above all I will not hear you deny.

**CREON:** If you think there is anything good in being stubborn
Against all reason, then I say you are wrong.

**OEDIPUS:** If you think a man can sin against his own kind
And not be punished for it, I say you are mad.

**CREON:** I agree. But tell me: what have I done to you?

**OEDIPUS:** You advised me to send for that wizard, did you not?

**CREON:** I did. I should do it again.

**OEDIPUS:** Very well. Now tell me:
How long has it been since Laïos—

**CREON:** What of Laïos—

**OEDIPUS:** Since he vanished in that onset by the road?

**CREON:** It was long ago, a long time.

**OEDIPUS:** And this prophet,
Was he practicing here then?

**CREON:** He was; and with honor, as now.

**OEDIPUS:** Did he speak of me that time?

**CREON:** He never did;
At least, not when I was present.

**OEDIPUS:** But . . . the enquiry?
I suppose you held one?

**CREON:** We did, but we learned nothing.

**OEDIPUS:** Why did the prophet not speak against me then?

**CREON:** I do not know; and I am the kind of man
Who holds his tongue when he has no facts to go on.

**OEDIPUS:** There's one fact that you know, and you could tell it.

**CREON:** What fact is that? If I know it, you shall have it.

**OEDIPUS:** If he were not involved with you, he could not say
That it was I who murdered Laïos.

**CREON:** If he says that, you are the one that knows it!—
But now it is my turn to question you.

**OEDIPUS:** Put your questions. I am no murderer.

**CREON:** First, then: You married my sister?

**OEDIPUS:** I married your sister.

**CREON:** And you rule the kingdom equally with her?

**OEDIPUS:** Everything that she wants she has from me.

**CREON:** And I am the third, equal to both of you?

**OEDIPUS:** That is why I call you a bad friend.

**CREON:** No. Reason it out, as I have done.
Think of this first: Would any sane man prefer
Power, with all a king's anxieties,
To that same power and the grace of sleep?
Certainly not I.
I have never longed for the king's power—only his rights.
Would any wise man differ from me in this?
As matters stand, I have my way in everything
With your consent, and no responsibilities.
If I were king, I should be a slave to policy.
How could I desire a scepter more
Than what is now mine—untroubled influence?
No, I have not gone mad; I need no honors,
Except those with the perquisites I have now.
I am welcome everywhere; every man salutes me,
And those who want your favor seek my ear,
Since I know how to manage what they ask.
Should I exchange this ease for that anxiety?
Besides, no sober mind is treasonable.
I hate anarchy
And never would deal with any man who likes it.
Test what I have said. Go to the priestess
At Delphi, ask if I quoted her correctly.
And as for this other thing: if I am found
Guilty of treason with Teiresias,
Then sentence me to death! You have my word
It is a sentence I should cast my vote for—
But not without evidence!
You do wrong
When you take good men for bad, bad men for good.
A true friend thrown aside—why, life itself
Is not more precious!
In time you will know this well:
For time, and time alone, will show the just man,
Though scoundrels are discovered in a day.

**CHORAGOS:** This is well said, and a prudent man would ponder it.
Judgments too quickly formed are dangerous.

**OEDIPUS:** But is he not quick in his duplicity?
And shall I not be quick to parry him?
Would you have me stand still, hold my peace, and let
This man win everything, through my inaction?

**CREON:** And you want—what is it, then? To banish me?

**OEDIPUS:** No, not exile. It is your death I want,
So that all the world may see what treason means.

**CREON:** You will persist, then? You will not believe me?

**OEDIPUS:** How can I believe you?

**CREON:** Then you are a fool.

**OEDIPUS:** To save myself?

**CREON:** In justice, think of me.

**OEDIPUS:** You are evil incarnate.

**CREON:** But suppose that you are wrong?

**OEDIPUS:** Still I must rule.

**CREON:** But not if you rule badly.

**OEDIPUS:** O city, city!

**CREON:** It is my city, too!

**CHORAGOS:** Now, my lords, be still. I see the Queen,
Iocastê, coming from her palace chambers;
And it is time she came, for the sake of you both.
This dreadful quarrel can be resolved through her.
*[Enter* IOCASTE

**IOCASTE:** Poor foolish men, what wicked din is this?
With Thebes sick to death, is it not shameful
That you should rake some private quarrel up?
*[To* OEDIPUS:
Come into the house.
—And you, Creon, go now:
Let us have no more of this tumult over nothing.

**CREON:** Nothing? No, sister: what your husband plans for me
Is one of two great evils: exile or death.

**OEDIPUS:** He is right.
Why, woman I have caught him squarely
Plotting against my life.

**CREON:** No! Let me die
Accurst if ever I have wished you harm!

**IOCASTE:** Ah, believe it, Oedipus!
In the name of the gods, respect this oath of his
For my sake, for the sake of these people here!

**CHORAGOS:** [STROPHE 1
Open your mind to her, my lord. Be ruled by her, I beg you!

**OEDIPUS:** What would you have me do?

**CHORAGOS:** Respect Creon's word. He has never spoken like a fool,
And now he has sworn an oath.

**OEDIPUS:** You know what you ask?

**CHORAGOS:** I do.

**OEDIPUS:** Speak on, then.

**CHORAGOS:** A friend so sworn should not be baited so,
In blind malice, and without final proof.

**OEDIPUS:** You are aware, I hope, that what you say
Means death for me, or exile at the least.

**CHORAGOS:** [STROPHE 2
No, I swear by Helios, first in Heaven!
May I die friendless and accurst,
The worst of deaths, if ever I meant that!
It is the withering fields
That hurt my sick heart:
Must we bear all these ills,
And now your bad blood as well?

**OEDIPUS:** Then let him go. And let me die, if I must,
Or be driven by him in shame from the land of Thebes.
It is your unhappiness, and not his talk,
That touches me.
As for him—
Wherever he goes, hatred will follow him.

**CREON:** Ugly in yielding, as you were ugly in rage!
Natures like yours chiefly torment themselves.

**OEDIPUS:** Can you not go? Can you not leave me?

**CREON:** I can.
You do not know me; but the city knows me,
And in its eyes I am just, if not in yours.
*[Exit* CREON

**CHORAGOS:** [ANTISTROPHE 1
Lady Iocastê, did you not ask the King to go to his chambers?

**IOCASTE:** First tell me what has happened.

**CHORAGOS:** There was suspicion without evidence; yet it rankled
As even false charges will.

**IOCASTE:** On both sides?

**CHORAGOS:** On both.

**IOCASTE:** But what was said?

**CHORAGOS:** Oh let it rest, let it be done with!
Have we not suffered enough?

**OEDIPUS:** You see to what your decency has brought you:
You have made difficulties where my heart saw none.

**CHORAGOS:** [ANTISTROPHE 2
Oedipus, it is not once only I have told you—
You must know I should count myself unwise
To the point of madness, should I now forsake you—
You, under whose hand,
In the storm of another time,
Our dear land sailed out free.
But now stand fast at the helm!

**IOCASTE:** In God's name, Oedipus, inform your wife as well:
Why are you so set in this hard anger?

**OEDIPUS:** I will tell you, for none of these men deserves
My confidence as you do. It is Creon's work,
His treachery, his plotting against me.

**IOCASTE:** Go on, if you can make this clear to me.

**OEDIPUS:** He charges me with the murder of Laïos.

**IOCASTE:** Has he some knowledge? Or does he speak from hearsay?

**OEDIPUS:** He would not commit himself to such a charge,
But he has brought in that damnable soothsayer
To tell his story.

**IOCASTE:** Set your mind at rest.
If it is a question of soothsayers, I tell you
That you will find no man whose craft gives knowledge
Of the unknowable.
Here is my proof:
An oracle was reported to Laïos once
(I will not say from Phoibos himself, but from
His appointed ministers, at any rate)
That his doom would be death at the hands of his own son—
His son, born of his flesh and of mine!

Now, you remember the story: Laïos was killed
By marauding strangers where three highways meet:
But his child had not been three days in this world
Before the King had pierced the baby's ankles
And left him to die on a lonely mountainside.

Thus, Apollo never caused that child
To kill his father, and it was not Laïos' fate
To die at the hands of his son, as he had feared.
This is what prophets and prophecies are worth!
Have no dread of them.
It is God himself
Who can show us what he wills, in his own way.

**OEDIPUS:** How strange a shadowy memory crossed my mind,
Just now while you were speaking; it chilled my heart.

**IOCASTE:** What do you mean? What memory do you speak of?

Iocaste (Eleanor Stuart) comforts her husband Oedipus in *Oedipus Rex* (1957).

**OEDIPUS:** If I understand you, Laïos was killed
At a place where three roads meet.

**IOCASTE:** So it was said;
We have no later story.

**OEDIPUS:** Where did it happen?

**IOCASTE:** Phokis, it is called: at a place where the Theban Way
Divides into the roads toward Delphi and Daulia.

**OEDIPUS:** When?

**IOCASTE:** We had the news not long before you came
And proved the right to your succession here.

**OEDIPUS:** Ah, what net has God been weaving for me?

**IOCASTE:** Oedipus! Why does this trouble you?

**OEDIPUS:** Do not ask me yet.
First, tell me how Laïos looked, and tell me
How old he was.

**IOCASTE:** He was tall, his hair just touched
With white; his form was not unlike your own.

**OEDIPUS:** I think that I myself may be accurst
By my own ignorant edict.

**IOCASTE:** You speak strangely.
It makes me tremble to look at you, my King.

**OEDIPUS:** I am not sure that the blind man can not see.
But I should know better if you were to tell me—

**IOCASTE:** Anything—though I dread to hear you ask it.

**OEDIPUS:** Was the King lightly escorted, or did he ride
With a large company, as a ruler should?

**IOCASTE:** There were five men with him in all: one was a herald,
And a single chariot, which he was driving.

**OEDIPUS:** Alas, that makes it plain enough!
But who—
Who told you how it happened?

**IOCASTE:** A household servant,
The only one to escape.

**OEDIPUS:** And is he still
A servant of ours?

**IOCASTE:** No; for when he came back at last
And found you enthroned in the place of the dead king,
He came to me, touched my hand with his, and begged
That I would send him away to the frontier district
Where only the shepherds go—
As far away from the city as I could send him.
I granted his prayer; for although the man was a slave,
He had earned more than this favor at my hands.

**OEDIPUS:** Can he be called back quickly?

**IOCASTE:** Easily.
But why?

**OEDIPUS:** I have taken too much upon myself
Without enquiry; therefore I wish to consult him.

**IOCASTE:** Then he shall come.
But am I not one also
To whom you might confide these fears of yours?

**OEDIPUS:** That is your right; it will not be denied you,
Now least of all; for I have reached a pitch
Of wild foreboding. Is there anyone
To whom I should sooner speak?

Polybos of Corinth is my father.
My mother is a Dorian: Meropê.
I grew up chief among the men of Corinth
Until a strange thing happened—
Not worth my passion, it may be, but strange.

At a feast, a drunken man maundering in his cups
Cries out that I am not my father's son!

I contained myself that night, though I felt anger
And a sinking heart. The next day I visited
My father and mother, and questioned them. They stormed,
Calling it all the slanderous rant of a fool;
And this relieved me. Yet the suspicion

Iocaste (Jessye Norman) talks with her husband Oedipus in *Oedipus Rex* (1993).

Remained always aching in my mind;
I knew there was talk; I could not rest;
And finally, saying nothing to my parents,
I went to the shrine at Delphi.
The god dismissed my question without reply;
He spoke of other things.
Some were clear,
Full of wretchedness, dreadful, unbearable:
As, that I should lie with my own mother, breed
Children from whom all men would turn their eyes;
And that I should be my father's murderer.

I heard all this, and fled. And from that day
Corinth to me was only in the stars
Descending in that quarter of the sky,
As I wandered farther and farther on my way
To a land where I should never see the evil
Sung by the oracle. And I came to this country
Where, so you say, King Laïos was killed.

I will tell you all that happened there, my lady.

There were three highways
Coming together at a place I passed;
And there a herald came towards me, and a chariot
Drawn by horses, with a man such as you describe
Seated in it. The groom leading the horses
Forced me off the road at his lord's command;
But as this charioteer lurched over towards me
I struck him in my rage. The old man saw me
And brought his double goad down upon my head
As I came abreast.
He was paid back, and more!
Swinging my club in this right hand I knocked him
Out of his car, and he rolled on the ground.
I killed him.

I killed them all.
Now if that stranger and Laïos were—kin,
Where is a man more miserable than I?
More hated by the gods? Citizen and alien alike
Must never shelter me or speak to me—
I must be shunned by all.
And I myself
Pronounced this malediction upon myself!

Think of it: I have touched you with these hands,
These hands that killed your husband. What defilement!

Am I all evil, then? It must be so,
Since I must flee from Thebes, yet never again
See my own countrymen, my own country,
For fear of joining my mother in marriage
And killing Polybos, my father.
Ah,
If I was created so, born to this fate,
Who could deny the savagery of God?

O holy majesty of heavenly powers!
May I never see that day! Never!
Rather let me vanish from the race of men
Than know the abomination destined me!

**CHORAGOS:** We too, my lord, have felt dismay at this.
But there is hope: you have yet to hear the shepherd.

**OEDIPUS:** Indeed, I fear no other hope is left me.

**IOCASTE:** What do you hope from him when he comes?

**OEDIPUS:** This much:
If his account of the murder tallies with yours,
Then I am cleared.

**IOCASTE:** What was it that I said
Of such importance?

Iocaste promises Oedipus she will send for the shepherd in *Oedipus Rex* (1957).

**OEDIPUS:** Why, "marauders," you said,
Killed the King, according to this man's story.
If he maintains that still, if there were several,
Clearly the guilt is not mine: I was alone.
But if he says one man, singlehanded, did it,
Then the evidence all points to me.

**IOCASTE:** You may be sure that he said there were several;
And can he call back that story now? He can not.
The whole city heard it as plainly as I.
But suppose he alters some detail of it:
He can not ever show that Laïos' death
Fulfilled the oracle: for Apollo said
My child was doomed to kill him; and my child—
Poor baby!—it was my child that died first.

No. From now on, where oracles are concerned,
I would not waste a second thought on any.

**OEDIPUS:** You may be right.
But come: let someone go
For the shepherd at once. This matter must be settled.

**IOCASTE:** I will send for him.
I would not wish to cross you in anything,
And surely not in this.—Let us go in.
*[Exeunt into the palace*

## ODE II

**CHORUS:** [STROPHE 1
Let me be reverent in the ways of right,
Lowly the paths I journey on;
Let all my words and actions keep
The laws of the pure universe
From highest Heaven handed down.
For Heaven is their bright nurse,
Those generations of the realms of light;
Ah, never of mortal kind were they begot,
Nor are they slaves of memory, lost in sleep:
Their Father is greater than Time, and ages not.

The tyrant is a child of Pride [ANTISTROPHE 1
Who drinks from his great sickening cup
Recklessness and vanity,
Until from his high crest headlong
He plummets to the dust of hope.
That strong man is not strong.
But let no fair ambition be denied;
May God protect the wrestler for the State
In government, in comely policy,
Who will fear God, and on His ordinance wait.

[STROPHE 2

Haughtiness and the high hand of disdain
Tempt and outrage God's holy law;
And any mortal who dares hold
No immortal Power in awe
Will be caught up in a net of pain:
The price for which his levity is sold.
Let each man take due earnings, then,
And keep his hands from holy things,
And from blasphemy stand apart—
Else the crackling blast of heaven
Blows on his head, and on his desperate heart;
Though fools will honor impious men,
In their cities no tragic poet sings.

[ANTISTROPHE 2

Shall we lose faith in Delphi's obscurities,
We who have heard the world's core
Discredited, and the sacred wood
Of Zeus at Elis praised no more?
The deeds and the strange prophecies
Must make a pattern yet to be understood.
Zeus, if indeed you are lord of all,
Throned in light over night and day,
Mirror this in your endless mind:
Our masters call the oracle
Words on the wind, and the Delphic vision blind!
Their hearts no longer know Apollo,
And reverence for the gods has died away.

## SCENE III

*[Enter* IOCASTE

**IOCASTE:** Princes of Thebes, it has occurred to me
To visit the altars of the gods, bearing
These branches as a suppliant, and this incense.
Our King is not himself: his noble soul
Is overwrought with fantasies of dread,
Else he would consider
The new prophecies in the light of the old.
He will listen to any voice that speaks disaster,
And my advice goes for nothing.
*[She approaches the altar, R.*
To you, then, Apollo,
Lycean lord, since you are nearest, I turn in prayer.
Receive these offerings, and grant us deliverance
From defilement. Our hearts are heavy with fear
When we see our leader distracted, as helpless sailors
Are terrified by the confusion of their helmsman.
*[Enter* MESSENGER

The messenger from Corinth (Tony Van Bridge) delivers his message to Oedipus in *Oedipus Rex* (1957).

**MESSENGER:** Friends, no doubt you can direct me:
Where shall I find the house of Oedipus,
Or, better still, where is the King himself?

**CHORAGOS:** It is this very place, stranger; he is inside.
This is his wife and mother of his children.

**MESSENGER:** I wish her happiness in a happy house,
Blest in all the fulfillment of her marriage.

**IOCASTE:** I wish as much for you: your courtesy
Deserves a like good fortune. But now, tell me:
Why have you come? What have you to say to us?

**MESSENGER:** Good news, my lady, for your house and your husband.

**IOCASTE:** What news? Who sent you here?

**MESSENGER:** I am from Corinth.
The news I bring ought to mean joy for you,
Though it may be you will find some grief in it.

**IOCASTE:** What is it? How can it touch us in both ways?

**MESSENGER:** The word is that the people of the Isthmus
Intend to call Oedipus to be their king.

**IOCASTE:** But old King Polybos—is he not reigning still?

**MESSENGER:** No. Death holds him in his sepulchre.

**IOCASTE:** What are you saying? Polybos is dead?

**MESSENGER:** If I am not telling the truth, may I die myself.

**IOCASTE:** *[To a* MAIDSERVANT:
Go in, go quickly; tell this to your master.

O riddlers of God's will, where are you now!
This was the man whom Oedipus, long ago,
Feared so, fled so, in dread of destroying him—
But it was another fate by which he died.

*[Enter* OEPIDUS, *C*

**OEDIPUS:** Dearest Iocastê, why have you sent for me?

**IOCASTE:** Listen to what this man says, and then tell me
What has become of the solemn prophecies.

**OEDIPUS:** Who is this man? What is his news for me?

**IOCASTE:** He has come from Corinth to announce your father's death!

**OEDIPUS:** Is it true, stranger? Tell me in your own words.

**MESSENGER:** I can not say it more clearly: the King is dead.

**OEDIPUS:** Was it by treason? Or by an attack of illness?

**MESSENGER:** A little thing brings old men to their rest.

**OEDIPUS:** It was sickness, then?

**MESSENGER:** Yes, and his many years.

**OEDIPUS:** Ah!
Why should a man respect the Pythian hearth, or
Give heed to the birds that jangle above his head?
They prophesied that I should kill Polybos,
Kill my own father; but he is dead and buried,
And I am here—I never touched him, never,
Unless he died of grief for my departure,
And thus, in a sense, through me. No. Polybos
Has packed the oracles off with him underground.
They are empty words.

**IOCASTE:** Had I not told you so?

**OEDIPUS:** You had; it was my faint heart that betrayed me.

**IOCASTE:** From now on never think of those things again.

**OEDIPUS:** And yet—must I not fear my mother's bed?

**IOCASTE:** Why should anyone in this world be afraid,
Since Fate rules us and nothing can be foreseen?
A man should live only for the present day.
Have no more fear of sleeping with your mother:
How many men, in dreams, have lain with their mothers!
No reasonable man is troubled by such things.

**OEDIPUS:** That is true; only—
If only my mother were not still alive!
But she is alive. I can not help my dread.

**IOCASTE:** Yet this news of your father's death is wonderful.

**OEDIPUS:** Wonderful. But I fear the living woman.

**MESSENGER:** Tell me, who is this woman that you fear?

**OEDIPUS:** It is Meropê, man; the wife of King Polybos.

**MESSENGER:** Meropê? Why should you be afraid of her?

**OEDIPUS:** An oracle of the gods, a dreadful saying.

**MESSENGER:** Can you tell me about it or are you sworn to silence?

**OEDIPUS:** I can tell you, and I will.
Apollo said through his prophet that I was the man
Who should marry his own mother, shed his father's blood
With his own hands. And so, for all these years
I have kept clear of Corinth, and no harm has come—
Though it would have been sweet to see my parents again

**MESSENGER:** And is this the fear that drove you out of Corinth?

**OEDIPUS:** Would you have me kill my father?

**MESSENGER:** As for that
You must be reassured by the news I gave you.

**OEDIPUS:** If you could reassure me, I would reward you.

**MESSENGER:** I had that in mind, I will confess: I thought
I could count on you when you returned to Corinth.

**OEDIPUS:** No. I will never go near my parents again.

**MESSENGER:** Ah, son, you still do not know what you are doing—

**OEDIPUS:** What do you mean? In the name of God tell me!

The messenger from Corinth (Michio Tatara) delivers his message to Oedipus in *Oedipus Rex* (1993).

**MESSENGER:** —If these are your reasons for not going home.

**OEDIPUS:** I tell you, I fear the oracle may come true.

**MESSENGER:** And guilt may come upon you through your parents?

**OEDIPUS:** That is the dread that is always in my heart.

**MESSENGER:** Can you not see that all your fears are groundless?

**OEDIPUS:** How can you say that? They are my parents, surely?

**MESSENGER:** Polybos was not your father.

**OEDIPUS:** Not my father?

**MESSENGER:** No more your father than the man speaking to you.

**OEDIPUS:** But you are nothing to me!

**MESSENGER:** Neither was he.

**OEDIPUS:** Then why did he call me son?

**MESSENGER:** I will tell you:
Long ago he had you from my hands, as a gift.

**OEDIPUS:** Then how could he love me so, if I was not his?

**MESSENGER:** He had no children, and his heart turned to you.

**OEDIPUS:** What of you? Did you buy me? Did you find me by chance?

**MESSENGER:** I came upon you in the crooked pass of Kithairon.

**OEDIPUS:** And what were you doing there?

**MESSENGER:** Tending my flocks.

**OEDIPUS:** A wandering shepherd?

**MESSENGER:** But your savior, son, that day.

**OEDIPUS:** From what did you save me?

**MESSENGER:** Your ankles should tell you that.

**OEDIPUS:** Ah, stranger, why do you speak of that childhood pain?

**MESSENGER:** I cut the bonds that tied your ankles together.

**OEDIPUS:** I have had the mark as long as I can remember.

**MESSENGER:** That was why you were given the name you bear.

**OEDIPUS:** God! Was it my father or my mother who did it?
Tell me!

**MESSENGER:** I do not know. The man who gave you to me
Can tell you better than I.

**OEDIPUS:** It was not you that found me, but another?

**MESSENGER:** It was another shepherd gave you to me.

**OEDIPUS:** Who was he? Can you tell me who he was?

**MESSENGER:** I think he was said to be one of Laïos' people.

**OEDIPUS:** You mean the Laïos who was king here years ago?

**MESSENGER:** Yes; King Laïos; and the man was one of his herdsmen.

**OEDIPUS:** Is he still alive? Can I see him?

**MESSENGER:** These men here
Know best about such things.

**OEDIPUS:** Does anyone here
Know this shepherd that he is talking about?
Have you seen him in the fields, or in the town?
If you have, tell me. It is time things were made plain.

**CHORAGOS:** I think the man he means is that same shepherd
You have already asked to see. Iocastê perhaps
Could tell you something.

**OEDIPUS:** Do you know anything
About him, Lady? Is he the man we have summoned?
Is that the man this shepherd means?

**IOCASTE:** Why think of him?
Forget this herdsman. Forget it all.
This talk is a waste of time.

**OEDIPUS:** How can you say that,
When the clues to my true birth are in my hands?

**IOCASTE:** For God's love, let us have no more questioning!
Is your life nothing to you?
My own is pain enough for me to bear.

**OEDIPUS:** You need not worry. Suppose my mother a slave,
And born of slaves: no baseness can touch you.

**IOCASTE:** Listen to me, I beg you: do not do this thing!

**OEDIPUS:** I will not listen; the truth must be made known.

**IOCASTE:** Everything that I say is for your own good!

**OEDIPUS:** My own good
Snaps my patience, then; I want none of it.

**IOCASTE:** You are fatally wrong! May you never learn who you are!

**OEDIPUS:** Go, one of you, and bring the shepherd here.
Let us leave this woman to brag of her royal name.

**IOCASTE:** Ah, miserable!
That is the only word I have for you now.
That is the only word I can ever have.
*[Exit into the palace*

**CHORAGOS:** Why has she left us, Oedipus? Why has she gone
In such a passion of sorrow? I fear this silence:
Something dreadful may come of it.

**OEDIPUS:** Let it come!
However base my birth, I must know about it.
The Queen, like a woman, is perhaps ashamed
To think of my low origin. But I
Am a child of Luck; I can not be dishonored.
Luck is my mother; the passing months, my brothers,
Have seen me rich and poor.
If this is so,
How could I wish that I were someone else?
How could I not be glad to know my birth?

## ODE III

**CHORUS:** [STROPHE
If ever the coming time were known
To my heart's pondering,
Kithairon, now by Heaven I see the torches
At the festival of the next full moon,
And see the dance, and hear the choir sing
A grace to your gentle shade:
Mountain where Oedipus was found,
O mountain guard of a noble race!
May the god who heals us lend his aid,
And let that glory come to pass
For our king's cradling-ground.

[ANTISTROPHE
Of the nymphs that flower beyond the years,
Who bore you, royal child,
To Pan of the hills or the timberline Apollo,
Cold in delight where the upland clears,
Or Hermês for whom Kyllenê's heights are piled?
Or flushed as evening cloud,
Great Dionysos, roamer of mountains,
He—was it he who found you there,
And caught you up in his own proud
Arms from the sweet god-ravisher
Who laughed by the Muses' fountains?

## SCENE IV

**OEDIPUS:** Sirs: though I do not know the man,
I think I see him coming, this shepherd we want:
He is old, like our friend here, and the men
Bringing him seem to be servants of my house.
But you can tell, if you have ever seen him.
*[Enter* SHEPHERD *escorted by servants*

**CHORAGOS:** I know him, he was Laïos' man. You can trust him.

**OEDIPUS:** Tell me first, you from Corinth: is this the shepherd
We were discussing?

**MESSENGER:** This is the very man.

**OEDIPUS:** [*To* SHEPHERD
Come here. No, look at me. You must answer
Everything I ask.—You belonged to Laïos?

**SHEPHERD:** Yes: born his slave, brought up in his house.

**OEDIPUS:** Tell me: what kind of work did you do for him?

**SHEPHERD:** I was a shepherd of his, most of my life.

**OEDIPUS:** Where mainly did you go for pasturage?

**SHEPHERD:** Sometimes Kithairon, sometimes the hills near-by.

**OEDIPUS:** Do you remember ever seeing this man out there?

**SHEPHERD:** What would he be doing there? This man?

**OEDIPUS:** This man standing here. Have you ever seen him before?

**SHEPHERD:** No. At least, not to my recollection.

**MESSENGER:** And that is not strange, my lord. But I'll refresh
His memory: he must remember when we two
Spent three whole seasons together, March to September,
On Kithairon or thereabouts. He had two flocks;
I had one. Each autumn I'd drive mine home
And he would go back with his to Laïos' sheepfold.—
Is this not true, just as I have described it?

**SHEPHERD:** True, yes; but it was all so long ago.

**MESSENGER:** Well, then: do you remember, back in those days,
That you gave me a baby boy to bring up as my own?

**SHEPHERD:** What if I did? What are you trying to say?

**MESSENGER:** King Oedipus was once that little child.

**SHEPHERD:** Damn you, hold your tongue!

**OEDIPUS:** No more of that!
It is your tongue needs watching, not this man's.

**SHEPHERD:** My King, my Master, what is it I have done wrong?

**OEDIPUS:** You have not answered his question about the boy.

**SHEPHERD:** He does not know . . . He is only making trouble . . .

**OEDIPUS:** Come, speak plainly, or it will go hard with you.

**SHEPHERD:** In God's name, do not torture an old man!

**OEDIPUS:** Come here, one of you; bind his arms behind him.

**SHEPHERD:** Unhappy king! What more do you wish to learn?

**OEDIPUS:** Did you give this man the child he speaks of?

**SHEPHERD:** I did.
And I would to God I had died that very day.

**OEDIPUS:** You will die now unless you speak the truth.

**SHEPHERD:** Yet if I speak the truth, I am worse than dead.

**OEDIPUS:** Very well; since you insist upon delaying—

**SHEPHERD:** No! I have told you already that I gave him the boy.

**OEDIPUS:** Where did you get him? From your house? From somewhere else?

**SHEPHERD:** Not from mine, no. A man gave him to me.

**OEDIPUS:** Is that man here? Do you know whose slave he was?

**SHEPHERD:** For God's love, my King, do not ask me any more!

Oedipus interrogates the shepherd (Eric House) in *Oedipus Rex* (1957).

**OEDIPUS:** You are a dead man if I have to ask you again.

**SHEPHERD:** Then . . . Then the child was from the palace of Laïos.

**OEDIPUS:** A slave child? or a child of his own line?

**SHEPHERD:** Ah, I am on the brink of dreadful speech!

**OEDIPUS:** And I of dreadful hearing. Yet I must hear.

**SHEPHERD:** If you must be told, then . . .
They said it was Laïos' child;
But it is your wife who can tell you about that.

**OEDIPUS:** My wife!—Did she give it to you?

**SHEPHERD:** My lord, she did.

**OEDIPUS:** Do you know why?

**SHEPHERD:** I was told to get rid of it.

**OEDIPUS:** An unspeakable mother!

**SHEPHERD:** There had been prophecies . . .

**OEDIPUS:** Tell me.

**SHEPHERD:** It was said that the boy would kill his own father.

**OEDIPUS:** Then why did you give him over to this old man?

**SHEPHERD:** I pitied the baby, my King,
And I thought that this man would take him far away
To his own country.
He saved him—but for what a fate!
For if you are what this man says you are,
No man living is more wretched than Oedipus.

**OEDIPUS:** Ah God!
It was true!
All the prophecies!
—Now,
O Light, may I look on you for the last time!
I, Oedipus,
Oedipus, damned in his birth, in his marriage damned,
Damned in the blood he shed with his own hand!
*[He rushes into the palace*

The chorus in *Oedipus Rex* (1957).

## ODE IV

**CHORUS:** Alas for the seed of men. [STROPHE 1

What measure shall I give these generations
That breathe on the void and are void
And exist and do not exist?

Who bears more weight of joy
Than mass of sunlight shifting in images,
Or who shall make his thought stay on
That down time drifts away?

Your splendor is all fallen.

O naked brow of wrath and tears,
O change of Oedipus!
I who saw your days call no man blest—
Your great days like ghósts góne.

That mind was a strong bow. [ANTISTROPHE 1

Deep, how deep you drew it then, hard archer,
At a dim fearful range,
And brought dear glory down!

You overcame the stranger—
The virgin with her hooking lion claws—
And though death sang, stood like a tower
To make pale Thebes take heart.

Fortress against our sorrow!

True king, giver of laws,
Majestic Oedipus!
No prince in Thebes had ever such renown,
No prince won such grace of power.

And now of all men ever known [STROPHE 2
Most pitiful is this man's story:
His fortunes are most changed, his state
Fallen to a low slave's
Ground under bitter fate.

O Oedipus, most royal one!
The great door that expelled you to the light
Gave at night—ah, gave night to your glory:
As to the father, to the fathering son.

All understood too late.

How could that queen whom Laïos won,
The garden that he harrowed at his height,
Be silent when that act was done?

But all eyes fail before time's eye, [ANTISTROPHE 2
All actions come to justice there.
Though never willed, though far down the deep past,
Your bed, your dread sirings,
Are brought to book at last.

Child by Laïos doomed to die,
Then doomed to lose that fortunate little death,
Would God you never took breath in this air
That with my wailing lips I take to cry:

For I weep the world's outcast.

I was blind, and now I can tell why:
Asleep, for you had given ease of breath
To Thebes, while the false years went by.

## ÉXODOS

*[Enter, from the palace,* SECOND MESSENGER

**SECOND MESSENGER:** Elders of Thebes, most honored in this land,
What horrors are yours to see and hear, what weight
Of sorrow to be endured, if, true to your birth,
You venerate the line of Labdakos!
I think neither Istros nor Phasis, those great rivers,
Could purify this place of the corruption
It shelters now, or soon must bring to light—
Evil not done unconsciously, but willed.

The greatest griefs are those we cause ourselves.

**CHORAGOS:** Surely, friend, we have grief enough already;
What new sorrow do you mean?

**SECOND MESSENGER:** The Queen is dead.

**CHORAGOS:** Iocastê? Dead? But at whose hand?

**SECOND MESSENGER:** Her own.
The full horror of what happened you can not know,
For you did not see it; but I, who did, will tell you
As clearly as I can how she met her death.

When she had left us,
In passionate silence, passing through the court,
She ran to her apartment in the house,
Her hair clutched by the fingers of both hands.
She closed the doors behind her; then, by that bed
Where long ago the fatal son was conceived—
That son who should bring about his father's death—
We heard her call upon Laïos, dead so many years,
And heard her wail for the double fruit of her marriage,
A husband by her husband, children by her child.

Exactly how she died I do not know:
For Oedipus burst in moaning and would not let us
Keep vigil to the end: it was by him
As he stormed about the room that our eyes were caught.
From one to another of us he went, begging a sword,
Cursing the wife who was not his wife, the mother
Whose womb had carried his own children and himself.
I do not know: it was none of us aided him,
But surely one of the gods was in control!
For with a dreadful cry
He hurled his weight, as though wrenched out of himself,
At the twin doors: the bolts gave, and he rushed in.
And there we saw her hanging, her body swaying
From the cruel cord she had noosed about her neck.
A great sob broke from him, heartbreaking to hear,
As he loosed the rope and lowered her to the ground.

I would blot out from my mind what happened next!
For the King ripped from her gown the golden brooches
That were her ornament, and raised them, and plunged them down

The second messenger comes to announce his bad news in *Oedipus Rex* (1957).

Straight into his own eyeballs, crying, "No more,
No more shall you look on the misery about me,
The horrors of my own doing! Too long you have known
The faces of those whom I should never have seen,
Too long been blind to those for whom I was searching!
From this hour, go in darkness!" And as he spoke,
He struck at his eyes—not once, but many times;
And the blood spattered his beard,
Bursting from his ruined sockets like red hail.

So from the unhappiness of two this evil has sprung.
A curse on the man and woman alike. The old
Happiness of the house of Labdakos
Was happiness enough: where is it today?
It is all wailing and ruin, disgrace, death—all
The misery of mankind that has a name—
And it is wholly and for ever theirs.

**CHORAGOS:** Is he in agony still? Is there no rest for him?

**SECOND MESSENGER:** He is calling for someone to lead him to the gates
So that all the children of Kadmos may look upon
His father's murderer, his mother's—no,
I can not say it!
And then he will leave Thebes,
Self-exiled, in order that the curse
Which he himself pronounced may depart from the house.
He is weak, and there is none to lead him,
So terrible is his suffering.
But you will see:
Look, the doors are opening; in a moment
You will see a thing that would crush a heart of stone.
*[The central door is opened;* OEDIPUS, *blinded, is led in*

**CHORAGOS:** Dreadful indeed for men to see.
Never have my own eyes
Looked on a sight so full of fear.

Oedipus!
What madness came upon you, what daemon
Leaped on your life with heavier
Punishment than a mortal man can bear?
No: I can not even
Look at you, poor ruined one.
And I would speak, question, ponder,
If I were able. No.
You make me shudder.

The blinded Oedipus addresses his people in *Oedipus Rex* (1957).

**OEDIPUS:** God. God.
Is there a sorrow greater?
Where shall I find harbor in this world?
My voice is hurled far on a dark wind.
What has God done to me?

**CHORAGOS:** Too terrible to think of, or to see.

**OEDIPUS:** O cloud of night, [STROPHE 1
Never to be turned away: night coming on,
I can not tell how: night like a shroud!

My fair winds brought me here.
O God. Again
The pain of the spikes where I had sight,
The flooding pain
Of memory, never to be gouged out.

**CHORAGOS:** This is not strange.
You suffer it all twice over, remorse in pain,
Pain in remorse.

**OEDIPUS:** Ah dear friend [ANTISTROPHE 1
Are you faithful even yet, you alone?
Are you still standing near me, will you stay here,
Patient, to care for the blind?
The blind man!
Yet even blind I know who it is attends me,
By the voice's tone—
Though my new darkness hide the comforter.

**CHORAGOS:** Oh fearful act!
What god was it drove you to rake black
Night across your eyes?

**OEDIPUS:** Apollo. Apollo. Dear [STROPHE 2
Children, the god was Apollo.
He brought my sick, sick fate upon me.
But the blinding hand was my own!
How could I bear to see
When all my sight was horror everywhere?

**CHORAGOS:** Everywhere; that is true.

**OEDIPUS:** And now what is left?
Images? Love? A greeting even,
Sweet to the senses? Is there anything?
Ah, no, friends: lead me away.
Lead me away from Thebes.
Lead the great wreck
And hell of Oedipus, whom the gods hate.

**CHORAGOS:** Your fate is clear, you are not blind to that.
Would God you had never found it out!

**OEDIPUS:** [ANTISTROPHE 2
Death take the man who unbound
My feet on that hillside
And delivered me from death to life! What life?
If only I had died,
This weight of monstrous doom
Could not have dragged me and my darlings down.

**CHORAGOS:** I would have wished the same.

**OEDIPUS:** Oh never to have come here
With my father's blood upon me! Never
To have been the man they call his mother's husband!
Oh accurst! Oh child of evil,
To have entered that wretched bed—
the selfsame one!
More primal than sin itself, this fell to me.

**CHORAGOS:** I do not know how I can answer you.
You were better dead than alive and blind.

**OEDIPUS:** Do not counsel me any more. This punishment
That I have laid upon myself is just.
If I had eyes,
I do not know how I could bear the sight
Of my father, when I came to the house of Death,
Or my mother: for I have sinned against them both
So vilely that I could not make my peace
By strangling my own life.
Or do you think my children,
Born as they were born, would be sweet to my eyes?
Ah never, never! Nor this town with its high walls,
Nor the holy images of the gods.
For I,
Thrice miserable!—Oedipus, noblest of all the line
Of Kadmos, have condemned myself to enjoy
These things no more, by my own malediction
Expelling that man whom the gods declared
To be a defilement in the house of Laïos.
After exposing the rankness of my own guilt,
How could I look men frankly in the eyes?
No, I swear it,
If I could have stifled my hearing at its source,
I would have done it and made all this body
A tight cell of misery, blank to light and sound:
So I should have been safe in a dark agony
Beyond all recollection.
Ah Kithairon!
Why did you shelter me? When I was cast upon you,
Why did I not die? Then I should never
Have shown the world my execrable birth.

Ah Polybos! Corinth, city that I believed
The ancient seat of my ancestors: how fair
I seemed, your child! And all the while this evil
Was cancerous within me!
For I am sick
In my daily life, sick in my origin.

O three roads, dark ravine, woodland and way
Where three roads met: you, drinking my father's blood,
My own blood, spilled by my own hand: can you remember
The unspeakable things I did there, and the things
I went on from there to do?
O marriage, marriage!
The act that engendered me, and again the act
Performed by the son in the same bed—
Ah, the net
Of incest, mingling fathers, brothers, sons,
With brides, wives, mothers: the last evil
That can be known by men: no tongue can say
How evil!
No. For the love of God, conceal me
Somewhere far from Thebes; or kill me; or hurl me
Into the sea, away from men's eyes for ever.

Come, lead me. You need not fear to touch me.
Of all men, I alone can bear this guilt.
*[Enter* CREON

**CHORAGOS:** We are not the ones to decide; but Creon here
May fitly judge of what you ask. He only
Is left to protect the city in your place.

**OEDIPUS:** Alas, how can I speak to him? What right have I
To beg his courtesy whom I have deeply wronged?

**CREON:** I have not come to mock you, Oedipus,
Or to reproach you, either.
*[To* ATTENDANTS:
—You, standing there:
If you have lost all respect for man's dignity,
At least respect the flame of Lord Helios:
Do not allow this pollution to show itself
Openly here, an affront to the earth
And Heaven's rain and the light of day. No, take him
Into the house as quickly as you can.
For it is proper
That only the close kindred see his grief.

**OEDIPUS:** I pray you in God's name, since your courtesy
Ignores my dark expectation, visiting
With mercy this man of all men most execrable:
Give me what I ask—for your good, not for mine.

**CREON:** And what is it that you would have me do?

**OEDIPUS:** Drive me out of this country as quickly as may be
To a place where no human voice can ever greet me.

**CREON:** I should have done that before now—only,
God's will had not been wholly revealed to me.

**OEDIPUS:** But his command is plain: the parricide
Must be destroyed. I am that evil man.

**CREON:** That is the sense of it, yes; but as things are,
We had best discover clearly what is to be done.

**OEDIPUS:** You would learn more about a man like me?

**CREON:** You are ready now to listen to the god.

**OEDIPUS:** I will listen. But it is to you
That I must turn for help. I beg you, hear me.

The woman in there—
Give her whatever funeral you think proper:
She is your sister.
—But let me go, Creon!
Let me purge my father's Thebes of the pollution
Of my living here, and go out to the wild hills,
To Kithairon, that has won such fame with me,
The tomb my mother and father appointed for me,
And let me die there, as they willed I should.
And yet I know
Death will not ever come to me through sickness
Or in any natural way: I have been preserved
For some unthinkable fate. But let that be.

The blinded Oedipus speaks to Creon in *Oedipus Rex* (1957).

As for my sons, you need not care for them.
They are men, they will find some way to live.
But my poor daughters, who have shared my table,
Who never before have been parted from their father—
Take care of them, Creon; do this for me.
And will you let me touch them with my hands
A last time, and let us weep together?
Be kind, my lord,
Great prince, be kind!
Could I but touch them,
They would be mine again, as when I had my eyes.
*[Enter* ANTIGONE *and* ISMENE, *attended*
Ah, God!
It is my dearest children I hear weeping?
Has Creon pitied me and sent my daughters?

**CREON:** Yes, Oedipus: I knew that they were dear to you
In the old days, and know you must love them still.

**OEDIPUS:** May God bless you for this—and be a friendlier
Guardian to you than he has been to me!

Children, where are you?
Come quickly to my hands: they are your brother's—
Hands that have brought your father's once clear eyes
To this way of seeing—
Ah dearest ones,
I had neither sight nor knowledge then, your father
By the woman who was the source of his own life!
And I weep for you—having no strength to see you—,
I weep for you when I think of the bitterness
That men will visit upon you all your lives.
What homes, what festivals can you attend
Without being forced to depart again in tears?

And when you come to marriageable age,
Where is the man, my daughters, who would dare
Risk the bane that lies on all my children?
Is there any evil wanting? Your father killed
His father; sowed the womb of her who bore him;
Engendered you at the fount of his own existence!
That is what they will say of you.
Then, whom
Can you ever marry? There are no bridegrooms for you,
And your lives must wither away in sterile dreaming.

O Creon, son of Menoikeus!
You are the only father my daughters have,
Since we, their parents, are both of us gone for ever.
They are your own blood: you will not let them
Fall into beggary and loneliness;
You will keep them from the miseries that are mine!
Take pity on them; see, they are only children,
Friendless except for you. Promise me this,
Great Prince, and give me your hand in token of it.
[CREON *clasps his right hand*

Children:
I would say much, if you could understand me,
But as it is, I have only this prayer for you:
Live where you can, be as happy as you can—
Happier, please God, than God has made your father!

**CREON:** Enough. You have wept enough. Now go within.

**OEDIPUS:** I must; but it is hard.

**CREON:** Time eases all things.

**OEDIPUS:** But you must promise—

**CREON:** Say what you desire.

**OEDIPUS:** Send me from Thebes!

**CREON:** God grant that I may!

**OEDIPUS:** But since God hates me . . .

**CREON:** No, he will grant your wish.

**OEDIPUS:** You promise?

**CREON:** I can not speak beyond my knowledge.

**OEDIPUS:** Then lead me in.

**CREON:** Come now, and leave your children.

**OEDIPUS:** No! Do not take them from me!

**CREON:** Think no longer
That you are in command here, but rather think
How, when you were, you served your own destruction.
*[Exeunt into the house all but the* CHORUS*;*
CHORAGOS *chants directly to the audience:*

**CHORAGOS:** Men of Thebes: look upon Oedipus.

This is the king who solved the famous riddle
And towered up, most powerful of men.
No mortal eyes but looked on him with envy,
Yet in the end ruin swept over him.

Let every man in mankind's frailty
Consider his last day; and let none
Presume on his good fortune until he find
Life, at his death, a memory without pain.

Oedipus, blinded, faces his fate in *Oedipus Rex* (1993).

# Writing from Reading

## Summarize

1 Write an outline of the story behind the plot. What is the first incident in the dramatized story of the rise and fall of King Oedipus? The second?

## Analyze Craft

2 Given what you know about the story of the myth, you can see that the play opens when the story is quite far along in its unfolding. Why does the playwright, having the entire story to work with, choose to begin where he does? Would the play have the same effect if it began in Oedipus's infancy? Or with the story of the shepherd? Or with an opening at the death of Iocaste and then flashing back to the moment when the messenger returns from the oracle?

3 How many actors does the play have? Imagine the visual effect of King Oedipus wearing the mask. What if the actor wore no mask? How might that affect the way you view the scene in your mind? How does Iocaste's action contribute to the deepening of the drama and its forward motion? What is the role of the shepherd? What is the role of the chorus?

4 A series of ironic revelations—or "reversals"—helps propel the play forward. Identify at least two and discuss.

## Analyze Voice

5 Dialogue in a play such as this reveals character at the same time that it advances the story. How does Oedipus's first exchange of dialogue with Iocaste create a certain false mood of calm? Contrast it with their round of dialogue after the shepherd has made his speech.

6 How does the collective voice of the chorus differ from the speech of the individual actors? How might Sophocles have choreographed the citizen chorus? What moves would they make? How would a contemporary chorus move? What music and moves would you use if you were staging a contemporary version of the play?

## Synthesize Summary and Analysis

7 The playwright has chosen to dramatize a major Greek myth, but in such a way as to maximize its impact on the audience. His presentation of the Oedipus story establishes the template for all future drama in the West and sets forward a series of dramatic techniques that playwrights will find invaluable. How might you imagine a major American playwright dramatizing the story of George Washington or Abraham Lincoln or Martin Luther King.

## Interpret the Play

8 The largest questions—those of fate and human destiny—come to the surface here. In *Oedipus the King,* we have a thoughtful concerned leader—a good man—who fulfills a tragic prophecy. What role do his actions have in his fulfillment of this prophecy? What does his reaction to the knowledge that he has fulfilled this dreadful prophecy tell us about Oedipus's character? What is the play's answer to the human dilemma of how to live a good life?

## Ancient Greek Drama

Western culture today owes a very great deal to the Greeks. Our sense of narrative was born on the lips of Greek poets reciting heroic tales of their ancestors; plays such as *Oedipus* were part of seasonal daylong competitions staged in open-air amphitheaters with seats built into the sides of hills, creating an atmosphere that somewhat resembles that of "March Madness" or the Super Bowl in our contemporary sports arenas. (A better analogy might be to a political rally, where a famous entertainer warms up the waiting crowd.) In the golden period of Greek culture, these plays, which the Athenians considered the highest creations of their best artists, became a central part of civic life. They simultaneously portrayed the honored past and the difficulties of life in the moment and projected a future in which human life coexisted with that of the gods. Everyone in democratic Athens participated, either as part of the play or as part of the audience.

"The Greeks came in the daytime to a huge amphitheater . . . perhaps they brought some food; they probably brought their families with them . . . and spent the whole day there. And when the night came, the night would come in the play too."
Conversation with Marian Seldes

The plays honored the history of Athens, and—as Athens was in a protracted war with Sparta—also honored the power of the gods and goddesses who might be prevailed upon for protection. What we today call patriotism comingled with religious ritual as Athenians fulfilled their obligation as good citizens to attend the festivals. In his interview, Gregory Nagy discusses how Athenian citizens in the tens of thousands were required to attend the annual theatrical festivals of tragedy and comedy. He describes the way all free Athenians would share simultaneously in the emotion of the play's hero; this participation made even more powerful the connection they felt with their heroic past.

### WAR AND *OEDIPUS THE KING*

The first historian, Herodotus, in his history of the Greco-Persian War, now and then offers genealogies that link kings and heroes of the Greeks' immediate past in a long line of kinship to heroes out of mythology. (Thucydides, the second great Greek historian, focused more on politics and tactics in his *History of the Peloponnesian War*, his narrative about the war between Athens and Sparta.) However, the difference between genealogy and chronology and the shaped and remade element of time in a work of art shows itself clearly in the presentation of mythological stories in classic Greek tragic theater. We get the essence of the myth, in all its depth and breadth, without watching the entire history in sequential detail.

What were the forces in Greek life that gave rise to the theatrical spectacles of ancient Greece? We have to look to Greek religion for an answer, because drama, in its original form, was inseparable from ritual observance and collective worship. The system of faith, as best we can tell from scattered references throughout Greek drama and later commentaries, was grounded in the pantheon of gods and goddesses from Homeric times. Dramatic theater evolved out of ceremonies celebrating Dionysus, the god of change and transformation.

"Theater . . . was taken so seriously that we might as well call it . . . a sacred narrative. . . . It's as real as what history might be to us." Conversation with Gregory Nagy

In *The Birth of Tragedy*, nineteenth-century German philosopher Friedrich Nietzsche argues that a priest would lead the Dionysian ceremonies surrounding the planting of the grain; over time, he became the first actor, speaking through a mask. Later, as this art form evolved, a second actor appeared, challenging the statements of the first, and dramatic conflict was born. We can't say exactly how much time passed between the early ceremonies of Dionysus—ceremonies presided over by priests wearing sacred masks—and the first appearance of a play (with actors wearing masks), a work of art that was steeped in the old religion but no longer a part of it. However long the period between early religious ceremonies and the great theatrical festivals of Athens might have been, the Greeks would have considered these myths to be true stories of the origins of their present culture. Sophocles' play is, therefore, a sacred story transformed into a work of art.

"Sophocles . . . occupies a special place . . . as having . . . 'the most comprehensive soul.'" Conversation with Ralph Williams

The United States is a diverse culture. But in order to try and imagine the relation of Greek drama to Greek culture allow yourself to picture an America in which no one held any religious view other than Christianity—no Jews, no Muslims, no Buddhists, and certainly no atheists—and several times a year greatly gifted playwrights tried out in competition full-length (three- to five-act) plays on various aspects of Christian belief, from the Christmas story to the Easter story and everything in between, and everyone in every city came either to work in the productions or to sit as part of the audience.

### Conventions of Greek Drama

Sophocles is not, of course, the only playwright of consequence from the classic period. Others include Aeschylus, the author of a trilogy of plays about another doomed dynasty (*Agamemnon, The Libation Bearers* or *Electra,* and *Eumenides* or *The Furies*), and Euripides, among whose surviving works are *Alcestis, The Phoenician Women,* and *The Bacchae.* Routinely, three such plays would be presented in succession at a festival—followed by a fourth, or **satyr** play, which provided a kind of comic relief (for more information on satyr plays, see chapter 30). The great Greek comic playwright Aristophanes is the author of such texts as *Lysistrata* and *The Frogs,* and the comic mask is just as central to the idea of Greek theater as the tragic one. So some fourth performance would likely have followed Sophocles' trilogy, which includes the story of Oedipus's children's fate (*Antigone*) and the old king's death (*Oedipus at Colonus*).

"Greek plays . . . are thrilling and almost more modern than any other plays I can think of, including plays that are being written now. They're clean. There's no extra word in them. And there are no stage directions—there don't need to be." Conversation with Marian Seldes

In his interview, Gregory Nagy tells us that in addition to being poets, playwrights were musical composers—and in the case of Sophocles, both a musician and a singer. He put this talent to work in the creation of one of the major elements in his drama, the singing-chanting-dancing **chorus.** Here amateurs honored to be included in the play worked side by side with trained actors to portray a group of representative citizens with worries and questions, expressed in poetry and music and dance movement. The presence of the chorus immediately puts us in a special state of awareness; it's almost as if we witness the life of their emotions as well as the music of their fears.

The all-male casts wore **masks,** enabling one actor to appear onstage as many different characters, and elevated shoes (***cothurni***). The mask also served as an amplification device so that members of the audience seated at some distance could hear the actor's words. Imagine what it would be like to see this frozen face and hear a

"Actors do perform with masks. . . . These performances are . . . dialogues, it's a form of verse. . . . Technically, when actors have a dialogue with each other, representing heroes and the heroic world . . . it is, shall we say, modified song . . . there is a melodic contour to it, but it's not full-blown singing. By contrast, when the chorus sings, that is full-blown music, that's singing and dancing." Conversation with Gregory Nagy

solemn voice speaking through the mouth hole, a voice that you, as spectator, identify as coming from a god or goddess. The shoes would have made the actors taller, larger than life. This formality may, on first reading, make these ancient dramas seem overly regulated or ritualistic for modern tastes. However, when you consider the material that the play puts forward—murder, incest, child abuse, and a madness that questions language that comes directly from the gods—you can see how the playwright achieves a certain stability with all of this potentially frenzied subject matter by grounding the intense emotions in such a formal fashion.

The **amphitheater** was outdoors and unroofed, with seats built into the side of a hill. In acoustical terms, the amphitheater is an almost perfect amplifying structure; in this way—thousands of years before the microphone—a single voice could make its way up to the most distant rows. The seats came partway around the **orchestra,** which was the area in front of the ***skene*** (or stage), where the chorus sang and danced. The actors played several roles and changed in a building behind the *skene* that could be designed as part of the setting for the play. Sometimes actors played gods who, when lowered from the roof of the building with a chariot-like machine (***deus ex machina***), could physically rescue a character from danger when the action in the play itself didn't provide an escape. The backdrop for *Oedipus the King* would have been spare, those few columns providing a single setting for the entire play, with all eyes on Oedipus from his first entrance to his final moments onstage.

By convention, each play was composed of five parts and arranged in what is sometimes called the Apollonian mode, after the Greek god Apollo. In the early Greek religion, Dionysus was the god of change and transformation and Apollo the god of form and stability. This tension between the stability of form and the frenzy of the content dramatizes an ancient polarity in Greek culture, and in all Western culture that grows from it: the struggle between the so-called Dionysian mode and the Apollonian mode. After a reading of this play, you can see how the mad chaotic energy and devastating content of the play itself is balanced by the orderliness of a sculpted Apollonian five-part structure.

The first part is the **prologue,** in which the audience learns of the problem of the play—the complication that the characters, and especially the hero or protagonist, must face.

**The *prologue* in Oedipus the King.** *As the Oedipus story begins, in the prologue we learn that the kingdom is suffering from a plague, and the king is seeking a cure. He has consulted the oracle in hope of a message from the gods that might rid the city of its sickness. His duty demands that he rid the city of the murderer whose presence has brought the plague to Thebes.*

Following the prologue is the ***parados,*** the chorus's first **ode**—the song and dance of the chorus. Like an ancient version of the football stadium wave, the members of the chorus weave and bend; they dance and chant their reaction to the problem presented in the prologue.

**The *parados* in Oedipus the King.** *Turning one way ("strophe") and then another ("antistrophe") and using their voices as well as movement, the chorus members declare their worry and confusion about the situation that has overtaken the city they love. What does the oracle say? We're afraid. How will it affect us? Let us pray to Athena for help. The fields are barren, so are the women, the plague continues to ravage us. The chorus calls on the gods to come to the aid of the tortured city.*

Next comes a series of ***episodia,*** or scenes. Each scene is followed by another choral ode, or ***stasimon,*** the chorus's interpretation of and response to the action of the preceding scene, including the final choral poem—dubbed the ***paean***—before the last scene of the play.

**The *episodia* in Oedipus the King.** *In the first of four scenes, Oedipus and Iocaste learn more and more about the problem with the plague, until what they take to be the truth becomes completely reversed. Irony is the great driving engine of the plot. Each action Oedipus takes produces the opposite of the result he seeks. The audience knows exactly how things will turn out and watches the great man writhing in the web of his own destiny. To reiterate, as the play unfolds, the great king discovers that he himself is the cause of the troubles. This truth reveals itself gradually, brought to him in pieces by these various characters. At some points, he refuses to believe what he is told; at others, he begs to be told what others prefer not to tell him. Oedipus struggles against his own nature and against the fate constructed for him by the gods.*

Last, we have the **exodos,** the concluding scene, followed by the final lines from the chorus. The king speaks, and the chorus reflects out loud in its specially choreographed fashion on what he means, questioning, chanting, swaying, bending.

**The *exodos* in *Oedipus the King.*** *Toward the end, the truth Oedipus discovers about his role in the death of the old king and his marriage to Iocaste leads him to a desperate act of violent self-mutilation. Paradoxically, however, once blind he truly "sees." The graceful exodos serves as a sculpted, stabile vehicle for the destructive energy of his mad recognition. The final words of the chorus provide a caution that no matter how powerful and well situated someone may appear at the beginning, those who offend the gods will pay for the offense and be brought low. The chorus assures us that no one is off the hook until he or she is dead.*

*Let every man in mankind's frailty*
*Consider his last day; and let none*
*Presume on his good fortune until he find*
*Life, at his death, a memory without pain.*

## Greek Tragedy

We usually talk about Greek tragedy as a style in itself, a particular art form that treats characters and life in a certain fashion, that is to say, presents its stories as illustrative of the lives of "high" figures. These are kings, mainly, who because of a **tragic flaw** in their character—in the case of Oedipus, his inability to contain his anger mixed with a nearly uncontrollable sense of pride, or arrogance (**hubris**)—fall into death or misery or disrepute. The Greek concept of **hamartia,** defined as a mistake or error in judgment, is the essential element in tragedy. In other words, the offense to the gods may be committed in ignorance, as was the case with Oedipus, but it will not go unpunished. His misfortune is brought about not by villainy but rather by circumstances and errors of understanding and goes beyond the notion of a single tragic flaw.

> "If the exaltation of tragic action were truly a property of the high-bred character alone, it is inconceivable that the mass of mankind should cherish tragedy above all other forms, let alone be capable of understanding it." Conversation with Arthur Miller

**Dramatic** or **tragic irony** sums up the relation between the play and its contemporary audience, the citizens of classical Athens, and gives birth to a particular relation between all art and the audience in modern times. The hero cannot know his fate, may not even be aware of his offense, but the audience does know. Strutting across the stage, our hero is unaware of what his past action propels him toward. **Peripeteia,** or *reversal of circumstances,* is an element of Greek tragedy meaning that an action has the opposite result of what was intended. The classical hero's change of fortune may be surprising and unpredictable to him, the opposite of what he might naturally expect to happen based on his action. Nonetheless, the result of the hero's action appears inevitable to an audience steeped in the myth that gave rise to the play and serves as a continually troubling reminder of the fragility of human life and action. If you take Oedipus as a model, you can see that the Greeks viewed all life as transient, an existence built out of a series of ironic reversals.

Aristotle, one of the most significant philosophers of ancient Greece, made his assessment of the play *Oedipus the King* in his *Poetics,* a collection of lectures his students put together from their notes; it has survived as one of the major documents of classic Greek culture. He describes how tragedy is founded on the playwright's successful yoking of favored myths and an intuitive awareness of what one of Aristotle's later devotees, the twentieth-century literary critic Kenneth Burke, describes as the "tragic rhythm of action." That tragic rhythm consists of a movement from, as Burke puts it, *purpose* to *passion* to *perception.* **Anagnorisis,** or *recognition* (the original Greek way of describing what Burke calls "perception"), is "a change from ignorance to knowledge, producing love or hate between the persons destined by the poet for good or bad fortune"; it is the apparent wisdom that comes out of all the reversals and suffering.

"Oedipus learns . . . to have more humility as he goes through the play. . . . And . . . as the character learns, we learn."

Conversation with Edwin Wilson

In his interview, Gregory Nagy describes the audience as participants in the dramatic experience of tragedy. The audience can see what the outcome will be, but the characters cannot. Those who witness have an advantage over the characters in the play but also a feeling of apprehension or, in some cases, sorrow. This combination of pity—*look what happened to that poor character*—and fear—*there but for the grace of God go I*—is commonly defined as ***catharsis.*** It is a complicated mix of emotions and central to the experience of theater. By invoking and purging the emotions of pity and fear in the audience, the play ideally creates a ***catharsis*** (purgation), or emotional renewal, in the spectators, and with this a vision of wholeness. A well-intentioned man, a hero, goes down, and his goodness, greatness even, allows him to see the justice in his demise; his acceptance of his fate makes the tragedy complete. For us in the modern world, such a play as *Oedipus* produces a recognition of our own roles in life, of how we are all strutting across the stage without being fully aware of what our past actions might mean. The impact of the tragic form of drama is probably greater than that of any other ancient creation.

# Reading Greek Tragedy

When reading or viewing Greek tragedy, it's useful to keep in mind the vocabulary of the theater.

**Basic performance conventions and stage techniques of Greek tragedy:**

- **Dramatic poems:** Poems meant to be performed with a particular meter and design.
- **Chorus:** Amateur and professional actors who represent the citizens in a Greek tragedy.
- ***Personae*** (masks) and ***cothurni*** (elevated shoes): Devices to amplify an actor's voice and appearance, both to make him larger than life and to project the performance to the back rows of the amphitheater.
- ***Deus ex machina:*** A practical reference to a "god" (***deus***) who was lowered by machine (***ex machina***) onto the stage to physically rescue characters from harm. The language is Latin, but the device itself originated with the Greeks.

| | |
|---|---|
| **Five-part structure of most Greek tragedies:** | • **Prologue:** The introduction of the play, in which the audience learns the conflict that the protagonist must face.<br>• ***Parados:*** The Chorus's first *ode* (song), offering an interpretation of the conflict learned in the Prologue.<br>• ***Episodia:*** A series of scenes, usually debates between characters, in which the action and events of the play are presented.<br>• ***Stasimon:*** The Chorus's interpretation and response to the preceding scene.<br>• ***Exodos:*** The concluding scene, including the final lines from the Chorus. |
| **Literary conventions of Greek tragedy that shape the audience's reaction to plot events:** | • **Tragic hero:** A "high" figure—typically a king—who, because of some character flaw or inevitable mistake, falls into death, misery, or disrepute.<br>• **Dramatic irony:** The audience's recognition of the hero's errors or fate before that of the hero.<br>• **Tragic flaw:** The personality trait or fated mistake that leads to a tragic hero's downfall.<br>  • **Hubris:** The sin of pride. A common tragic flaw characterized by arrogance and quick temper.<br>  • ***Hamartia:*** An error or mistake in judgment. Although a mistake may be committed out of good intention or ignorance, it will not go unpunished.<br>• ***Peripeteia:*** An action that has a result opposite to the intention.<br>• ***Anagnorisis:*** The wisdom that results from reversals (*peripeteia*) and suffering.<br>• **Catharsis:** The emotional renewal created by an audience's feelings of pity and terror for a tragic hero, resulting in the recognition that the hero's tragic fate was just and that his acceptance of that fate makes the tragedy complete. |

# Getting Started: A Research Project

Research is a skill that will carry you through your college career. To help acquaint you with the research process, the materials you need for this project are made available on our website (*www.mhhe.com/delbanco1e*). Other ideas for research projects and sources appear at the end of this chapter.

Chances are you have heard of the Oedipus complex, a term that surfaces now and again in popular culture. But you may not know that the Oedipus complex was first identified by the seminal psychoanalyst Sigmund Freud, who based his idea of the complex on Sophocles' play *Oedipus the King.* Since Freud identified the Oedipus complex in his *Interpretation of Dreams,* his theory has shaped psychoanalysis both as it relates to the study of human psychology and as it relates to the theory of psychoanalysis as a form of literary criticism.

Our website will provide you with several articles that will help you understand the Oedipus complex and its potential applications. First, read the excerpt of Freud's *Interpretation of Dreams* in which he defines the Oedipus complex. Then, read the interview with scholar Jean-Pierre Vernant on the enduring value of tragedy and its relationship to Freud's theories. Refer to Haven McClure's introduction to his book *The Modern Reader's Hamlet* to get an idea of how the Oedipus complex is evident in other works of literature—in this case, Shakespeare's *Hamlet.* And finally, read Sarah Boxer's *New York Times* article to see the many challenges to Freud's theory over time.

After consulting these sources, choose one of the prompts below to get you started on writing a research paper.

1. Write a paper in which you define the Oedipus complex based on Freud's description of it. Then, describe challenges to Freud's theory, from the interview with Jean-Pierre Vernant, from Sarah Boxer's article, and from your own ideas. Conclude your paper with your own evaluation of Freud's theory, based on your reading of *Oedipus the King* and your responses to the articles you have researched.
2. Choose one literary work—whether a short story, novel, or play—in which you see the Oedipus complex, or a version of it, at work. Write a paper in which you examine how the Oedipus complex appears in that work, even if it doesn't literally align with the circumstances of *Oedipus the King.* (You might, for example, choose to examine the parent/child conflict in works like Willa Cather's "Paul's Case" or the budding sexuality of a character like the narrator of James Joyce's "Araby" in our *Fiction* volume. Or, you might offer your own reading of the Oedipus complex in the next chapter on *Hamlet.*)

# Further Suggestions for Writing and Research

1. A distinctive feature of Greek theater—and one that has survived—is the chorus. Visit *www.mhhe.com/delbanco1e* to listen to the entire interview with Gregory Nagy, taking notes on what he says about the Greek chorus. Using one of the sources below, you may wish to do some more research into the original function of the chorus. Then, locate a copy of *A Chorus Line,* the hit Broadway musical that was made into a 1985 film directed by Richard Attenborough and starring Michael Douglas and Alyson Reed. Write an essay in which you compare the use of the Greek chorus in *Oedipus* with the use of the choric effect in *A Chorus Line.* Support your ideas with specific examples from your reading of *Oedipus,* your understanding of Nagy's interview, and any other source you consult in learning about the Greek chorus.
   - Ley, Graham. "Chorus." *A Short Introduction to the Ancient Greek Theater.* Chicago: University of Chicago Press, 2006. 30–33. Print.
   - Weiner, Albert. "The Function of the Tragic Greek Chorus." *Theatre Journal* 32.2 (May 1980): 205–212. Print.
   - Zarifi, Yana. "Chorus and Dance in the Ancient World." *The Cambridge Companion to Greek and Roman Theatre.* Ed. Marianne McDonald and J. Michael Walton. New York: Cambridge University Press, 2007. 227–246. Print.
2. If it weren't for translation, *Oedipus the King* would be known only to the few people who could read ancient Greek. Fortunately, many translators have created versions of *Oedipus the King* in English—like the one printed in this chapter. To understand a few of the characteristics of Sophocles' Greek, read Robert Fitzgerald's notes to his translation of *Oedipus the King,* as listed in the sources below. You can use the additional resources to learn more about the problems and challenges of translation.

Find a passage of *Oedipus the King* that you particularly enjoyed or found memorable. Then, find another translation of the same play. Write a paper in which you compare the two translators' choices, drawing upon your research to help you analyze the translators' work.

- Sophocles. *The Oedipus Cycle.* Trans. Dudley Fitts and Robert Fitzgerald. New York: Harvest Books, 2002. Print. See especially pp. 181–185, Robert Fitzgerald's commentary on his translation.
- Venuti, Lawrence, ed. *The Translation Studies Reader.* 2nd ed. New York: Routledge, 2004. Print.
- Walton, J. Michael. "Sophocles' *Oedipus Tyrannus:* Words and Concepts." *Found in Translation: Greek Drama in English.* New York: Cambridge University Press, 2006. 85–105. Print.

# Some Sources for Research

Aristotle. *Poetics.* New York: Penguin, 1997. Print.

Bloom, Harold, ed. *Sophocles.* Philadelphia: Chelsea House, 2003. Print.

Burton, Reginald William Boteler. *The Chorus in Sophocles' Tragedies.* New York: Oxford University Press, 1980. Print.

Dodds, E. R. "On Misunderstanding the *Oedipus Rex.*" *Greece & Rome* 13.1 (April 1966): 37–49. Print.

Frosh, Stephen. "Oedipus Complex." *Key Concepts in Psychoanalysis.* New York: New York University Press, 2003. pp. 62–73. Print.

Haigh, A. E. *The Tragic Drama of the Greeks.* Oxford: Clarendon Press, 1946. Print.

Knox, Bernard. *The Heroic Temper: Studies in Sophoclean Tragedy.* Berkeley: University of California Press, 1983. Print.

——. *Word and Action: Essays on the Ancient Theater.* Baltimore: Johns Hopkins University Press, 1979. Print.

Ley, Graham. *A Short Introduction to the Ancient Greek Theater.* Chicago: University of Chicago Press, 2006. Print.

McDonald, Marianne, and Michael J. Walton, eds. *The Cambridge Companion to Greek and Roman Theatre.* New York: Cambridge University Press, 2007. Print.

Webster, T. B. L. *An Introduction to Sophocles.* London: Methuen, 1969. Print.

**For examples of student papers, see chapter 3, Common Writing Assignments, and chapter 5, Writing the Research Paper, in the Handbook for Writing from Reading.**

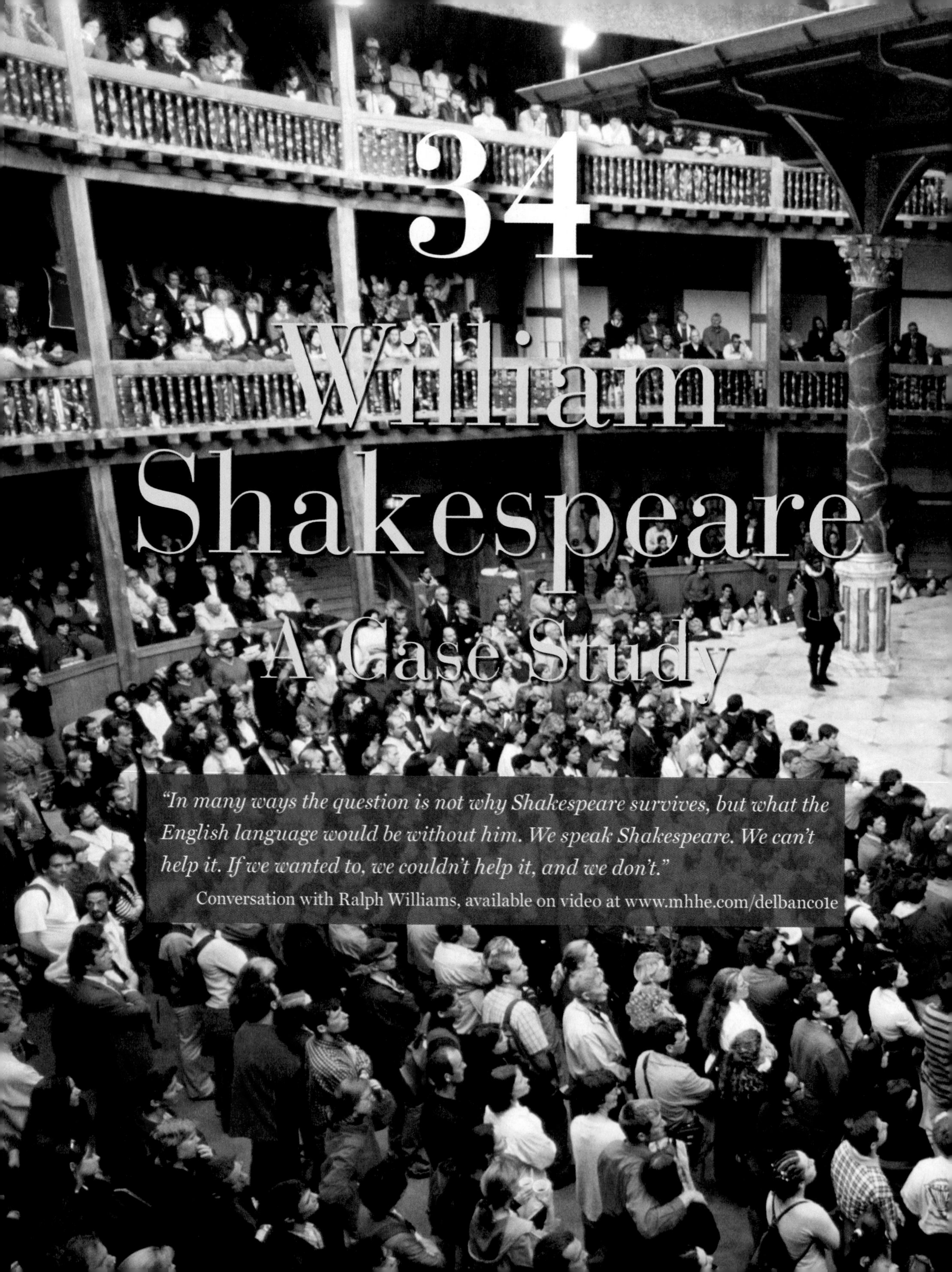

# 34 William Shakespeare: A Case Study

*"In many ways the question is not why Shakespeare survives, but what the English language would be without him. We speak Shakespeare. We can't help it. If we wanted to, we couldn't help it, and we don't."*

Conversation with Ralph Williams, available on video at www.mhhe.com/delbanco1e

**IMAGINE yourself in the open air of an Elizabethan public theater on a sunny afternoon. You're standing elbow to elbow in a throng of commoners—drinkers and brawlers, pickpockets and prostitutes. The curtain opens and Hamlet enters with three players, the traveling actors who will perform the play the mad prince has written to confront his treacherous uncle. The occasion is of utmost importance, and the players have only a few hours to memorize their parts. Dire and passionate, Hamlet instructs them in Act III, Scene II:**

HAMLET: Speak the speech, I pray you, as I pronounced it to you, trippingly on the tongue. But if you mouth it, as many of our players do, I had as lief the town crier spoke my lines. Nor do not saw the air too much with your hand, thus, but use all gently; for in the very torrent, tempest, and, as I may say, whirlwind of your passion, you must acquire and beget a temperance that may give it smoothness.

**Notice what he demands: natural speech, gentle gestures, an even temper. Contrast these pointers with the demands of the Greek theater: booming delivery to reach the thousands of gathered citizens of Athens, large gestures that can be seen from the back row of an amphitheater, tall shoes, padded garb, and a mask that makes natural expression impossible. In the Elizabethan theater, acting was not a stylized civic performance; rather, as Hamlet reminds his actors, "the purpose of playing, whose end, both at the first and now, was and is to hold, as 't were, the mirror up to nature."**

**Whereas the previous chapter presented a tragedy that depicts nobility and civic responsibility, this chapter presents three plays whose subjects are the passions of humanity. *Hamlet* is a play rich in plot and subplot, full of mirrors and doubling tales. The complications of Prince Hamlet himself, as well as his charm and intelligence, demand agility in performance; his quicksilver wit and self-awareness make for a nearly irresistible combination, and a *modern* one. By the time we first encounter him, however, he's steeped in sadness, brooding. He's the dark prince. What Hamlet mourns is understandable: his father's death. Understandably, also, he's upset by the "hot haste" with which his mother has married her husband's (Hamlet's father's) brother.**

*(CONTINUED ON PAGE 177)*

*As you begin to read the play, you set the stage.*

# A Conversation on Shakespeare

*We speak Shakespeare. We can't help it.*

## Ralph Williams

### Why Does Shakespeare Endure?

There are a number of reasons, I think, that Shakespeare endures. . . . He's the rain forest of our language . . . in fact . . . the first user of thousands of words . . . and he is one of the great creators of beauty. . . . You can't solve . . . the pain of life. But you can set beauty against it and maybe endure it. . . . "When we're born, we cry that we are come to this great stage of fools." Of youth . . . "Come kiss me, sweet and twenty, youth's the stuff will not endure." As we reach times of despair . . . "Out out, brief candle, life's but a walking shadow, a poor player that struts and frets his hour upon the stage and then is heard no more." The phrases, the lines, are the vocabulary of our lives really. . . . He lasts for that reason.

### Shakespeare's Moral Imagination

Shakespeare imagined a Richard III . . . who in defense of his claim to the throne orders the two young children of his elder brother, the one who had been king, killed. . . . Then in speaking with the man who oversaw the murder, says to him, "But come to me after dinner and I will hear the process of their deaths." This is evil at a depth which rings absolutely true of a sociopath, a psychopathic murderer. . . . On the other end he can imagine a . . . Desdemona [from *Othello*]. . . . It's that range of moral imagination . . . that makes Shakespeare such an astonishing companion and voice for us all in our human journeys.

To watch this entire interview, go to **www.mhhe.com/delbanco1e.**

**RESEARCH ASSIGNMENT** After you have watched his interview, describe how Ralph Williams sees the categories of comedy and tragedy affecting Shakespeare's plays. Do you agree with Williams's assessment of Shakespeare's bravura?

Ralph Williams is the Arthur F. Thurnau Professor in the Department of English Language and Literature and Adjunct Lecturer in Near Eastern Studies, College of Literature, Science, and the Arts at the University of Michigan. Since 2000 he has collaborated with the Royal Shakespeare Company on its Residency Program.

# William Shakespeare (1564–1616)

Although the speaker here is praising Cleopatra, queen of Egypt, these lines from *Antony and Cleopatra* seem an apt description of Shakespeare the playwright himself:

> Age cannot wither her, nor custom stale
> Her infinite variety. Other women cloy
> The appetites they feed, but she makes hungry
> Where most she satisfies.

The "infinite variety" of William Shakespeare's talent has raised many questions as to his actual identity. Some argue that he must have been a nobleman, citing his knowledge of courtly behavior; others insist he was a commoner because of his detailed knowledge of country matters. Scholars have suggested aristocrats such as the Earl of Oxford or Sir Phillip Sidney used the name "Shakespeare" as a pseudonym. Others propose the translator John Florio or Shakespeare's dead rival Christopher Marlowe. But, time and again, the name seems to fit no one so well as the glove maker's son from the small British town of Stratford-on-Avon.

The truth is, we actually know more about the historical figure called William Shakespeare, born in April 1564, than about most other men or women of the period. His father was a successful merchant of the town who later fell on hard times; he attended local schools, where he learned some Latin and a little Greek. Anne Hathaway was twenty-six, eight years older than William Shakespeare, when they obtained a marriage license in November 1582; she bore him a daughter six months later and, in 1585, a pair of twins. In 1597, the playwright purchased New Place, a fine house in Stratford-on-Avon—a sign that he had prospered in his own chosen career.

William Shakespeare spent most of his working life in the city of London, as one of a troupe of players called the Lord Chamberlain's Men. He was an actor in the group as well as its principal playwright. This was the troupe that in 1599 built the great Globe Theater, which stood on the south bank of the Thames outside city regulations and housed the performances of a number of Shakespeare's plays. Under the patronage of King James I (king of England from 1603 to 1625, following the death of Elizabeth I), the company became known as the King's Men. A bare-bones summary of his life leaves out, of course, the crucial thing: the work itself. It exists in two separate genres: poetry and plays. His poetry, which we have looked at elsewhere, includes long narrative poems such as "Venus and Adonis" and "The Rape of Lucrece" and the 154 sonnets (see chapter 16 on reading further in poetry and chapter 25 on song and spoken word poetry). By most counts he also composed some 37 plays. A few fragments of disputed authorship survive, but Shakespeare's pre-eminence as playwright is based on the work produced between 1591 and 1611—twenty years of unmatched productivity and enduring art. A collection of 35 plays appeared posthumously in 1623, published by two other members of the King's Men, John Heminge and Henry Condell.

Shakespeare retired to New Place, most likely in 1611, and died on April 23, 1616. Contemporaries wrote often about him—competitively, at first, then respectfully, and after his death, in terms of extravagant praise.

## TIPS FOR READING SHAKESPEARE

- *Take it slow.* The characters in Shakespeare's plays speak often in poetry and seldom in language intended to imitate everyday speech. Read lines carefully and take note of annotations where they occur. If language seems especially lofty, or especially straightforward, ask yourself why that is appropriate to the lines being delivered or to the character speaking.
- *Read out loud.* Shakespeare intended his plays not to be read but to be performed. If you are hung up on a line, don't hesitate to give it a voice. Unfamiliar words and phrases can become clearer in meaning when you hear them aloud.
- *Imagine the experience.* The theaters of Elizabethan England did not have elaborate sets, and plays were staged outdoors on sunny afternoons. Thus, playwrights had to work the physical situation into their characters' speech. Notice cues that the moon is in the sky, the ocean is nearby, or snow is falling outside, and use them to construct a mental picture of the action taking place.
- *Become the audience.* The commoners in Shakespeare's audience would have experienced many of the same challenges you do interpreting Shakespeare's poetic, sometimes invented, language. To some extent you must let language, familiar and unfamiliar, carry itself forward. You will want to perform deeper analysis on certain lines when crafting a paper, but for your first reading you should focus less on dissecting the language and more on appreciating the action of the play.
- *Consider watching a staged or filmed production* of the play *after* your first reading. This can lend clarity to difficult portions of the play and also help identify aspects of the play worthy of critical analysis. Ask yourself about the differences and similarities between the way you envisioned the play and the way it is performed. Why have certain aspects been interpreted differently? What qualities of Shakespeare's language contribute to similarities across interpretations?

**AS YOU READ** Note the chances Hamlet has to kill Claudius—most obviously in Act III, Scene III. Why do you think he hesitates?

# Hamlet, Prince of Denmark (c. 1600)

*—edited by David Bevington*

## CHARACTERS

**GHOST** *of Hamlet, the former King of Denmark*

**CLAUDIUS,** *King of Denmark, the former King's brother*

**GERTRUDE,** *Queen of Denmark, widow of the former King and now wife of Claudius*

**HAMLET,** *Prince of Denmark, son of the late King and of Gertrude*

**POLONIUS,** *councillor to the King*

**LAERTES,** *his son*

**OPHELIA,** *his daughter*

**REYNALDO,** *his servant*

**HORATIO,** *Hamlet's friend and fellow student*

**VOLTIMAND, CORNELIUS, ROSENCRANTZ, GUILDENSTERN, OSRIC, A GENTLEMAN, A LORD,** *members of the Danish court*

**BERNARDO, FRANCISCO, MARCELLUS,** *officers and soldiers on watch*

**FORTINBRAS,** *Prince of Norway*

**CAPTAIN** *in his army*

*Three or Four* **PLAYERS,** *taking the roles of* **PROLOGUE, PLAYER KING, PLAYER QUEEN,** *and* **LUCIANUS**

*Two* **MESSENGERS**

**FIRST SAILOR**

*Two* **CLOWNS,** *a gravedigger and his companion*

**PRIEST**

**FIRST AMBASSADOR** *from England*

*Lords, Soldiers, Attendants, Guards, other Players, Followers of Laertes, other Sailors, another Ambassador or Ambassadors from England*

**SCENE:** *Denmark]*

**1.1** *Enter* BERNARDO *and* FRANCISCO, *two sentinels, [meeting].*

**BERNARDO:** Who's there?

**FRANCISCO:** Nay, answer me. Stand and unfold yourself.

**BERNARDO:** Long live the King!

**FRANCISCO:** Bernardo?

**BERNARDO:** He.

**FRANCISCO:** You come most carefully upon your hour.

**BERNARDO:** 'Tis now struck twelve. Get thee to bed, Francisco.

**FRANCISCO:** For this relief much thanks. 'Tis bitter cold,
And I am sick at heart.

**BERNARDO:** Have you had quiet guard?

**FRANCISCO:** Not a mouse stirring.

**BERNARDO:** Well, good night.
If you do meet Horatio and Marcellus,
The rivals of my watch, bid them make haste.

*Enter* HORATIO *and* MARCELLUS.

**FRANCISCO:** I think I hear them.—Stand, ho! Who is there?

**HORATIO:** Friends to this ground.

**MARCELLUS:** And liegemen to the Dane.

**FRANCISCO:** Give you good night.

**MARCELLUS:** O, farewell, honest soldier. Who hath relieved you?

**FRANCISCO:** Bernardo hath my place. Give you good night.

*Exit* FRANCISCO.

**MARCELLUS:** Holla! Bernardo!

**BERNARDO:** Say, what, is Horatio there?

**HORATIO:** A piece of him.

Horatio (Nicholas Farrell), Marcellus (Jack Lemmon), and Bernardo (Ian McElhinney) gape at the ghost of the dead king in the 1996 film directed by Kenneth Branagh.

**BERNARDO:** Welcome, Horatio. Welcome, good Marcellus.

**HORATIO:** What, has this thing appeared again tonight?

**BERNARDO:** I have seen nothing.

**MARCELLUS:** Horatio says 'tis but our fantasy,
And will not let belief take hold of him
Touching this dreaded sight twice seen of us.
Therefore I have entreated him along
With us to watch the minutes of this night,
That if again this apparition come
He may approve our eyes and speak to it.

**HORATIO:** Tush, tush, 'twill not appear.

**BERNARDO:** Sit down awhile,
And let us once again assail your ears,
That are so fortified against our story,
What we have two nights seen.

**HORATIO:** Well, sit we down,
And let us hear Bernardo speak of this.

**BERNARDO:** Last night of all,
When yond same star that's westward from the pole
Had made his course t' illume that part of heaven
Where now it burns, Marcellus and myself,
The bell then beating one—

*Enter* GHOST.

**MARCELLUS:** Peace, break thee off! Look where it comes again!

---

**1.1 Location: Elsinore castle. A guard platform.**
**2 me** (Francisco emphasizes that *he* is the sentry currently on watch.) **unfold yourself** reveal your identity **14 rivals** partners **16 ground** country, land **17 liegemen to the Dane** men sworn to serve the Danish king **18 Give** i.e., may God give

**27 fantasy** imagination **30 along** to come along **31 watch** keep watch during **33 approve** corroborate **37 What** with what **39 Last . . . all** i.e., this *very* last night. (Emphatic.) **40 pole** polestar, north star **41 his** its. **illume** illuminate

The ghost of King Hamlet (Brian Blessed) approaches.

**BERNARDO:** In the same figure like the King that's dead.

**MARCELLUS:** Thou art a scholar. Speak to it, Horatio.

**BERNARDO:** Looks 'a not like the King? Mark it, Horatio.

**HORATIO:** Most like. It harrows me with fear and wonder.

**BERNARDO:** It would be spoke to.

**MARCELLUS:** Speak to it, Horatio.

**HORATIO:** What are thou that usurp'st this time of night,
Together with that fair and warlike form
In which the majesty of buried Denmark
Did sometime march? By heaven, I charge thee, speak!

**MARCELLUS:** It is offended.

**BERNARDO:** See, it stalks away.

**HORATIO:** Stay! Speak, speak! I charge thee, speak!
*Exit* GHOST.

**MARCELLUS:** 'Tis gone and will not answer.

**BERNARDO:** How now, Horatio? You tremble and look pale.
Is not this something more than fantasy?
What think you on 't?

---

**46 scholar** one learned enough to know how to question a ghost properly **47 'a** he **49 It . . . to** (It was commonly believed that a ghost could not speak until spoken to.) **50 usurp'st** wrongfully takes over **52 buried Denmark** the buried King of Denmark **53 sometime** formerly **59 on 't** of it

**HORATIO:** Before my God, I might not this believe
Without the sensible and true avouch
Of mine own eyes.

**MARCELLUS:** Is it not like the King?

**HORATIO:** As thou art to thyself.
Such was the very armor he had on
When he the ambitious Norway combated.
So frowned he once when, in an angry parle,
He smote the sledded Polacks on the ice.
'Tis strange.

**MARCELLUS:** Thus twice before, and jump at this dead hour,
With martial stalk hath he gone by our watch.

**HORATIO:** In what particular thought to work I know not,
But in the gross and scope of mine opinion
This bodes some strange eruption to our state.

**MARCELLUS:** Good now, sit down, and tell me, he that knows,
Why this same strict and most observant watch
So nightly toils the subject of the land,
And why such daily cast of brazen cannon
And foreign mart for implements of war,
Why such impress of shipwrights, whose sore task
Does not divide the Sunday from the week.
What might be toward, that this sweaty haste
Doth make the night joint-laborer with the day?
Who is 't that can inform me?

**HORATIO:** That can I;
At least, the whisper goes so. Our last king,
Whose image even but now appeared to us,
Was, as you know, by Fortinbras of Norway,
Thereto pricked on by a most emulate pride,
Dared to the combat; in which our valiant Hamlet—
For so this side of our known world esteemed him—
Did slay this Fortinbras; who by a sealed compact
Well ratified by and law and heraldry
Did forfeit, with his life, all those his lands
Which he stood seized of, to the conqueror;

---

**61 sensible** confirmed by the senses. **avouch** warrant, evidence **65 Norway** King of Norway **66 parle** parley **67 sledded** traveling on sleds. **Polacks** Poles **69 jump** exactly **70 stalk** stride **71 to work** i.e., to collect my thoughts and try to understand this **72 gross and scope** general drift **74 Good now** (An expression denoting entreaty or expostulation.) **76 toils** causes to toil. **subject** subjects **77 cast** casting **78 mart** buying and selling **79 impress** impressment, conscription **81 toward** in preparation **87 Thereto . . . pride** (Refers to old Fortinbras, not the Danish King.) **pricked on** incited. **emulate** emulous, ambitious **89 this . . . world** i.e., all Europe, the Western world **90 sealed** certified, confirmed **93 seized** possessed

Against the which a moiety competent
Was gagèd by our king, which had returned
To the inheritance of Fortinbras
Had he been vanquisher, as, by the same cov'nant
And carriage of the article designed,
His fell to Hamlet. Now, sir, young Fortinbras,
Of unimprovèd mettle hot and full,
Hath in the skirts of Norway here and there
Sharked up a list of lawless resolutes
For food and diet to some enterprise
That hath a stomach in 't, which is no other—
As it doth well appear unto our state—
But to recover of us, by strong hand
And terms compulsatory, those foresaid lands
So by his father lost. And this, I take it,
Is the main motive of our preparations,
The source of this our watch, and the chief head
Of this posthaste and rummage in the land.

**BERNARDO:** I think it be no other but e'en so.
Well may it sort that this portentous figure
Comes armèd through our watch so like the King
That was and is the question of these wars.

**HORATIO:** A mote it is to trouble the mind's eye.
In the most high and palmy state of Rome,
A little ere the mightiest Julius fell,
The graves stood tenantless, and the sheeted dead
Did squeak and gibber in the Roman streets;
As stars with trains of fire and dews of blood,
Disasters in the sun; and the moist star
Upon whose influence Neptune's empire stands
Was sick almost to doomsday with eclipse.
And even the like precurse of feared events,
As harbingers preceding still the fates
And prologue to the omen coming on,
Have heaven and earth together demonstrated
Unto our climatures and countrymen.

*Enter* GHOST.

But soft, behold! Lo, where it comes again!
I'll cross it, though it blast me. *(It spreads his arms.)*
Stay, illusion!
If thou hast any sound or use of voice,
Speak to me!
If there be any good thing to be done
That may to thee do ease and grace to me,
Speak to me!
If thou art privy to thy country's fate,
Which, happily, foreknowing may avoid,
O, speak!
Or if thou has uphoarded in thy life
Extorted treasure in the womb of earth,
For which, they say, you spirits oft walk in death,
Speak of it! *(The cock crows.)* Stay and speak!—Stop it,
Marcellus.

**MARCELLUS:** Shall I strike at it with my partisan?

**HORATIO:** Do, if it will not stand. *[They strike at it.]*

**BERNARDO:** 'Tis here!

**HORATIO:** 'Tis here! *[Exit* GHOST.*]*

**MARCELLUS:** 'Tis gone.
We do it wrong, being so majestical,
To offer it the show of violence,
For it is as the air invulnerable,
And our vain blows malicious mockery.

**BERNARDO:** It was about to speak when the cock crew.

**HORATIO:** And then it started like a guilty thing
Upon a fearful summons. I have heard
The cock, that is the trumpet to the morn,
Doth with his lofty and shrill-sounding throat
Awake the god of day, and at his warning,
Whether in sea or fire, in earth or air,
Th' extravagant and erring spirit hies
To his confine; and of the truth herein
This present object made probation.

**MARCELLUS:** It faded on the crowing of the cock.
Some say that ever 'gainst that season comes
Wherein our Savior's birth is celebrated,

---

**94 Against the** in return for. **moiety competent** corresponding portion **95 gagèd** engaged, pledged. **had returned** would have passed **96 inheritance** possession **97 cov'nant** i.e., the *sealed compact* of line 90 **98 carriage . . . designed** carrying out of the article or clause drawn up to cover the point **100 unimprovèd mettle** untried, undisciplined spirits **101 skirts** outlying regions, outskirts **102 Sharked up** gathered up, as a shark takes fish. **list** i.e., troop. **resolutes** desperadoes **103 For food and diet** i.e., they are to serve as *food,* or "means," *to some enterprise;* also they serve in return for the rations they get **104 stomach** (1) a spirit of daring (2) an appetite that is fed by the *lawless resolutes* **110 head** source **111 rummage** bustle, commotion **113 sort** suit **115 question** focus of contention **116 mote** speck of dust **117 palmy** flourishing **119 sheeted** shrouded **121 As** (This abrupt transition suggests that matter is possibly omitted between lines 120 and 121.) **trains** trails **122 Disasters** unfavorable signs or aspects. **moist star** i.e., moon, governing tides **123 Neptune** god of the sea. **stands** depends **124 sick . . . doomsday** (See Matthew 24:29 and Revelation 6:12.) **125 precurse** heralding, foreshadowing **126 harbingers** forerunners. **still** continually **127 omen** calamitous event

**129 climatures** regions **130 soft** i.e., enough, break off **131 cross** stand in its path, confront. **blast** wither, strike with a curse. **s.d. his** its **137 privy to** in on the secret of **138 happily** haply, perchance **144 partisan** long-handled spear **156 trumpet** trumpeter **160 extravagant and erring** wandering beyond bounds. (The words have similar meaning.) **hies** hastens **162 probation** proof **164 'gainst** just before

This bird of dawning singeth all night long,
And then, they say, no spirit dare stir abroad;
The nights are wholesome, then no planets strike,
No fairy takes, nor witch hath power to charm,
So hallowed and so gracious is that time.

**HORATIO:** So have I heard and do in part believe it.
But, look, the morn in russet mantle clad
Walks o'er the dew of yon high eastward hill.
Break we our watch up, and by my advice
Let us impart what we have seen tonight
Unto young Hamlet; for upon my life,
This spirit, dumb to us, will speak to him.
Do you consent we shall acquaint him with it,
As needful in our loves, fitting our duty?

**MARCELLUS:** Let's do 't, I pray, and I this morning know
Where we shall find him most conveniently.

*Exeunt.*

## 1.2

*Flourish. Enter* CLAUDIUS, *King of Denmark,* GERTRUDE *the Queen, [the] Council, as* POLONIUS *and his son* LAERTES, HAMLET, *cum aliis [including* VOLTIMAND *and* CORNELIUS*].*

**KING:** Though yet of Hamlet our dear brother's death
The memory be green, and that it us befitted
To bear our hearts in grief and our whole kingdom
To be contracted in one brow of woe,
Yet so far hath discretion fought with nature
That we with wisest sorrow think on him
Together with remembrance of ourselves.
Therefore our sometime sister, now our queen,
Th' imperial jointress to this warlike state,
Have we, as 'twere with a defeated joy—
With an auspicious and a dropping eye,
With mirth in funeral and with dirge in marriage,
In equal scale weighing delight and dole—
Taken to wife. Nor have we herein barred
Your better wisdoms, which have freely gone
With this affair along. For all, our thanks.
Now follows that you know young Fortinbras,
Holding a weak supposal of our worth,

**168 strike** destroy by evil influence **169 takes** bewitches **170 gracious** full of grace

**1.2. Location: The castle.**
**s.d. as** i.e., such as, including. **cum aliis** with others **1 our** my. (The royal "we"; also in the following lines.) **8 sometime** former **9 jointress** woman possessing property with her husband **11 With . . . eye** with one eye smiling and the other weeping **13 dole** grief **17 that you know** what you know already, that; or, that you be informed as follows **18 weak supposal** low estimate

Claudius (Basil Sydney) and Gertrude (Eileen Herlie) greet the court in the 1948 film directed by Laurence Olivier.

Or thinking by our late dear brother's death
Our state to be disjoint and out of frame,
Co-leaguèd with this dream of his advantage,
He hath not failed to pester us with message
Importing the surrender of those lands
Lost by his father, with all bonds of law,
To our most valiant brother. So much for him.
Now for ourself and for this time of meeting.
Thus much the business is: we have here writ
To Norway, uncle of young Fortinbras—
Who, impotent and bed-rid, scarcely hears
Of this his nephew's purpose—to suppress
His further gait herein, in that the levies,
The lists, and full proportions are all made
Out of his subject; and we here dispatch
You, good Cornelius, and you, Voltimand,
For bearers of this greeting to old Norway,
Giving to you no further personal power
To business with the King more than the scope
Of these dilated articles allow. *[He gives a paper.]*
Farewell, and let your haste commend your duty.

**CORNELIUS, VOLTIMAND:** In that, and all things, will we show our duty.

**KING:** We doubt it nothing. Heartily farewell.

*[Exeunt* VOLTIMAND *and* CORNELIUS.*]*

**21 Co-leaguèd with** joined to, allied with. **dream . . . advantage** illusory hope of having the advantage. (His only ally is this hope.) **23 Importing** pertaining to **24 bonds** contracts **29 impotent** helpless **31 His** i.e., Fortinbras'. **gait** proceeding **31–33 in that . . . subject** since the levying of troops and supplies is drawn entirely from the King of Norway's own subjects **38 dilated** set out at length **39 let . . . duty** let your swift obeying of orders, rather than mere words, express your dutifulness **41 nothing** not at all

And now, Laertes, what's the news with you?
You told us of some suit; what is 't, Laertes?
You cannot speak of reason to the Dane
And lose your voice. What wouldst thou beg, Laertes,
That shall not be my offer, not thy asking?
The head is not more native to the heart,
The hand more instrumental to the mouth,
Than is the throne of Denmark to thy father.
What wouldst thou have, Laertes?

**LAERTES:** My dread lord,
Your leave and favor to return to France,
From whence though willingly I came to Denmark
To show my duty in your coronation,
Yet now I must confess, that duty done,
My thoughts and wishes bend again toward France
And bow them to your gracious leave and pardon.

**KING:** Have you your father's leave? What says Polonius?

**POLONIUS:** H'ath, my lord, wrung from me my slow leave
By laborsome petition, and at last
Upon his will I sealed my hard consent.
I do beseech you, give him leave to go.

**KING:** Take thy fair hour, Laertes. Time be thine,
And thy best graces spend it at thy will!
But now, my cousin Hamlet, and my son—

**HAMLET:** A little more than kin, and less than kind.

**KING:** How is it that the clouds still hang on you?

**HAMLET:** Not so, my lord. I am too much in the sun.

**QUEEN:** Good Hamlet, cast thy nighted color off,
And let thine eye look like a friend on Denmark.
Do not forever with thy vailèd lids
Seek for thy noble father in the dust.
Thou know'st 'tis common, all that lives must die,
Passing through nature to eternity.

**HAMLET:** Ay, madam, it is common.

**QUEEN:** If it be,
Why seems it so particular with thee?

**HAMLET:** Seems, madam? Nay, it is. I know not "seems."
'Tis not alone my inky cloak, good Mother,
Nor customary suits of solemn black,
Nor windy suspiration of forced breath,
No, nor the fruitful river in the eye,
Nor the dejected havior of the visage,
Together with all forms, moods, shapes of grief,
That can denote me truly. These indeed seem,
For they are actions that a man might play.
But I have that within which passes show;
These but the trappings and the suits of woe.

**KING:** 'Tis sweet and commendable in your nature, Hamlet,
To give these mourning duties to your father.
But you must know your father lost a father,
That father lost, lost his, and the survivor bound
In filial obligation for some term
To do obsequious sorrow. But to persever
In obstinate condolement is a course
Of impious stubbornness. 'Tis unmanly grief.
It shows a will most incorrect to heaven,
A heart unfortified, a mind impatient,
An understanding simple and unschooled.
For what we know must be and is as common
As any the most vulgar thing to sense,
Why should we in our peevish opposition
Take it to heart? Fie, 'tis a fault to heaven,
A fault against the dead, a fault to nature,
To reason most absurd, whose common theme
Is death of fathers, and who still hath cried,
From the first corpse till he that died today,
"This must be so." We pray you, throw to earth
This unprevailing woe and think of us
As of a father; for let the world take note,

---

**44 the Dane** the Danish king **45 lose your voice** waste your speech **47 native** closely connected, related **48 instrumental** serviceable **51 leave and favor** kind permission **56 bow . . . pardon** entreatingly make a deep bow, asking your permission to depart **58 H'ath** he has **60 sealed** (as if sealing a legal document). **hard** reluctant **62 Take thy fair hour** enjoy your time of youth **63 And . . . will** and may your finest qualities guide the way you choose to spend your time **64 cousin** any kin not of the immediate family **65 A little . . . kind** i.e., closer than an ordinary nephew (since I am stepson), and yet more separated in natural feeling (with pun on *kind* meaning "affectionate" and "natural," "lawful." This line is often read as an aside, but it need not be. The King chooses perhaps not to respond to Hamlet's cryptic and bitter remark.) **67 the sun** i.e., the sunshine of the King's royal favor (with pun on *son*) **68 nighted color** (1) mourning garments of black (2) dark melancholy **69 Denmark** the King of Denmark **70 vailèd lids** lowered eyes

**72 common** of universal occurrence. (But Hamlet plays on the sense of "vulgar" in line 74.) **75 particular** personal **78 customary** (1) socially conventional (2) habitual with me **79 suspiration** sighing **80 fruitful** abundant **81 havior** expression **82 moods** outward expression of feeling **92 obsequious** suited to obsequies or funerals. **persever** persevere **93 condolement** sorrowing **96 unfortified** i.e., against adversity **97 simple** ignorant **99 As . . . sense** as the most ordinary experience **104 still** always **105 the first corpse** (Abel's) **107 unprevailing** unavailing, useless

You are the most immediate to our throne,
And with no less nobility of love
Than that which dearest father bears his son
Do I impart toward you. For your intent
In going back to school in Wittenberg,
It is most retrograde to our desire,
And we beseech you bend you to remain
Here in the cheer and comfort of our eye,
Our chiefest courtier, cousin, and our son.

**QUEEN:** Let not thy mother lose her prayers, Hamlet.
I pray thee, stay with us, go not to Wittenberg.

**HAMLET:** I shall in all my best obey you, madam.

**KING:** Why, 'tis a loving and a fair reply.
Be as ourself in Denmark. Madam, come.
This gentle and unforced accord of Hamlet
Sits smiling to my heart, in grace whereof
No jocund health that Denmark drinks today
But the great cannon to the clouds shall tell,
And the King's rouse the heaven shall bruit again,
Respeaking earthly thunder. Come away.
*Flourish. Exeunt all but* HAMLET.

**HAMLET:** O, that this too sullied flesh would melt,
Thaw, and resolve itself into a dew!
Or that the Everlasting had not fixed
His canon 'gainst self-slaughter! O God, God,
How weary, stale, flat, and unprofitable
Seem to me all the uses of this world!
Fie on 't, ah fie! 'Tis an unweeded garden
That grows to seed. Things rank and gross in nature
Possess it merely. That it should come to this!
But two months dead—nay, not so much, not two.
So excellent a king, that was to this
Hyperion to a satyr, so loving to my mother
That he might not beteem the winds of heaven
Visit her face too roughly. Heaven and earth,
Must I remember? Why, she would hang on him
As if increase of appetite had grown
By what it fed on, and yet within a month—
Let me not think on 't; frailty, thy name is woman!—
A little month, or ere those shoes were old
With which she followed my poor father's body,
Like Niobe, all tears, why she, even she—
O God, a beast, that wants discourse of reason,
Would have mourned longer—married with my uncle,
My father's brother, but no more like my father
Than I to Hercules. Within a month,
Ere yet the salt of most unrighteous tears
Had left the flushing in her gallèd eyes,
She married. O, most wicked speed, to post
With such dexterity to incestuous sheets!
It is not, nor it cannot come to good.
But break, my heart, for I must hold my tongue.

*Enter* HORATIO, MARCELLUS, *and* BERNARDO.

**HORATIO:** Hail to your lordship!

**HAMLET:** I am glad to see you well.
Horatio!—or I do forget myself.

**HORATIO:** The same, my lord, and your poor servant ever.

**HAMLET:** Sir, my good friend; I'll change that name with you.
And what make you from Wittenberg, Horatio?
Marcellus.

**MARCELLUS:** My good lord.

**HAMLET:** I am very glad to see you. *[To* BERNARDO.*]* Good even, sir.—
But what in faith make you from Wittenberg?

**HORATIO:** A truant disposition, good my lord.

**HAMLET:** I would not hear your enemy say so,
Nor shall you do my ear that violence
To make it truster of your own report
Against yourself. I know you are no truant.
But what is your affair in Elsinore?
We'll teach you to drink deep ere you depart.

---

**109 most immediate** next in succession **112 impart toward** i.e., bestow my affection on. **For** as for **113 to school** i.e., to your studies. **Wittenberg** famous German university founded in 1502 **114 retrograde** contrary **115 bend you** incline yourself **120 in all my best** to the best of my ability **124 to** i.e., at. **grace** thanksgiving **125 jocund** merry **127 rouse** drinking of a draft of liquor. **bruit again** loudly echo **128 thunder** i.e., of trumpet and kettledrum, sounded when the King drinks; see 1.4.8–12 **129 sullied** defiled. (The early quartos read *sallied;* the Folio, *solid.*) **132 canon** law **134 all the uses** the whole routine **137 merely** completely **139 to** in comparison to **140 Hyperion** Titan sun-god, father of Helios. **satyr** a lecherous creature of classical mythology, half-human but with a goat's legs, tail, ears, and horns **141 beteem** allow

**147 or ere** even before **149 Niobe** Tantalus' daughter, Queen of Thebes, who boasted that she had more sons and daughters than Leto; for this, Apollo and Artemis, children of Leto, slew her fourteen children. She was turned by Zeus into a stone that continually dropped tears. **150 wants . . . reason** lacks the faculty of reason **155 gallèd** irritated, inflamed **156 post** hasten **157 incestuous** (In Shakespeare's day, the marriage of a man like Claudius to his deceased brother's wife was considered incestuous.) **163 change that name** i.e., give and receive reciprocally the name of "friend" (rather than talk of "servant") **164 make you from** are you doing away from

**HORATIO:** My lord, I came to see your father's funeral.

**HAMLET:** I prithee, do not mock me, fellow student;
I think it was to see my mother's wedding.

**HORATIO:** Indeed, my lord, it followed hard upon.

**HAMLET:** Thrift, thrift, Horatio! The funeral baked meats
Did coldly furnish forth the marriage tables.
Would I had met my dearest foe in heaven
Or ever I had seen that day, Horatio!
My father!—Methinks I see my father.

**HORATIO:** Where, my lord?

**HAMLET:** In my mind's eye, Horatio.

**HORATIO:** I saw him once. 'A was a goodly king.

**HAMLET:** 'A was a man. Take him for all in all,
I shall not look upon his like again.

**HORATIO:** My lord, I think I saw him yesternight.

**HAMLET:** Saw? Who?

**HORATIO:** My lord, the King your father.

**HAMLET:** The King my father?

**HORATIO:** Season your admiration for a while
With an attent ear till I may deliver,
Upon the witness of these gentlemen,
This marvel to you.

**HAMLET:** For God's love, let me hear!

**HORATIO:** Two nights together had these gentlemen,
Marcellus and Bernardo, on their watch,
In the dead waste and middle of the night,
Been thus encountered. A figure like your father,
Armèd at point exactly, cap-à-pie,
Appears before them, and with solemn march
Goes slow and stately by them. Thrice he walked
By their oppressed and fear-surprisèd eyes
Within his truncheon's length, whilst they, distilled
Almost to jelly with the act of fear,
Stand dumb and speak not to him. This to me
In dreadful secrecy impart they did,
And I with them the third night kept the watch,
Where, as they had delivered, both in time,
Form of the thing, each word made true and good,

Hamlet (Kevin Kline) addresses Horatio (Peter Francis James) in the 1990 film directed by Kevin Kline.

The apparition comes. I knew your father;
These hands are not more like.

**HAMLET:** But where was this?

**MARCELLUS:** My lord, upon the platform where we watch.

**HAMLET:** Did you not speak to it?

**HORATIO:** My lord, I did,
But answer made it none. Yet once methought
It lifted up its head and did address
Itself to motion, like as it would speak;
But even then the morning cock crew loud,
And at the sound it shrunk in haste away
And vanished from our sight.

**HAMLET:** 'Tis very strange.

**HORATIO:** As I do live, my honored lord, 'tis true,
And we did think it writ down in our duty
To let you know of it.

**HAMLET:** Indeed, indeed, sirs. But this troubles me.
Hold you the watch tonight?

**ALL:** We do, my lord.

**HAMLET:** Armed, say you?

**ALL:** Armed, my lord.

**HAMLET:** From top to toe?

**ALL:** My lord, from head to foot.

**HAMLET:** Then saw you not his face?

---

**179 hard** close **180 baked meats** meat pies **181 coldly** i.e., as cold leftovers **182 dearest** closest (and therefore deadliest) **183 Or ever** before **186 'A** he **193 Season your admiration** restrain your astonishment **194 attent** attentive **199 dead waste** desolate stillness **201 at point** correctly in every detail. **cap-à-pie** from head to foot **205 truncheon** officer's staff. **distilled** dissolved **206 act** action, operation **208 dreadful** full of dread

**217–218 did . . . speak** began to move as though it were about to speak **219 even then** at that very instant

**HORATIO:** O, yes, my lord, he wore his beaver up.

**HAMLET:** What looked he, frowningly?

**HORATIO:** A countenance more in sorrow than in anger.

**HAMLET:** Pale or red?

**HORATIO:** Nay, very pale.

**HAMLET:** And fixed his eyes upon you?

**HORATIO:** Most constantly.

**HAMLET:** I would I had been there.

**HORATIO:** It would have much amazed you.

**HAMLET:** Very like, very like. Stayed it long?

**HORATIO:** While one with moderate haste might tell a hundred.

**MARCELLUS, BERNARDO:** Longer, longer.

**HORATIO:** Not when I saw 't.

**HAMLET:** His beard was grizzled—no?

**HORATIO:** It was, as I have seen it in his life,
A sable silvered.

**HAMLET:** I will watch tonight.
Perchance 'twill walk again.

**HORATIO:** I warrant it will.

**HAMLET:** If it assume my noble father's person,
I'll speak to it though hell itself should gape
And bid me hold my peace. I pray you all,
If you have hitherto concealed this sight,
Let it be tenable in your silence still,
And whatsoever else shall hap tonight,
Give it an understanding but no tongue.
I will requite your loves. So, fare you well.
Upon the platform twixt eleven and twelve
I'll visit you.

**ALL:** Our duty to your honor.

**HAMLET:** Your loves, as mine to you. Farewell.
*Exeunt [all but* HAMLET*].*
My father's spirit in arms! All is not well.
I doubt some foul play. Would the night were come!
Till then sit still, my soul. Foul deeds will rise,
Though all the earth o'erwhelm them, to men's eyes.
*Exit.*

**232 beaver** visor on the helmet **233 What** how **242 tell** count **245 grizzled** gray **247 sable silvered** black mixed with white **248 warrant** assure you **253 tenable** held **261 doubt** suspect

Laertes (Nathaniel Parker) warns Ophelia (Helena Bonham Carter) to be careful of Hamlet in the 1990 film directed by Franco Zeffirelli.

## 1.3 *Enter* LAERTES *and* OPHELIA, *his sister.*

**LAERTES:** My necessaries are embarked. Farewell.
And, sister, as the winds give benefit
And convoy is assistant, do not sleep
But let me hear from you.

**OPHELIA:** Do you doubt that?

**LAERTES:** For Hamlet, and the trifling of his favor,
Hold it a fashion and a toy in blood,
A violet in the youth of primy nature
Forward, not permanent, sweet, not lasting,
The perfume and suppliance of a minute—
No more.

**OPHELIA:** No more but so?

**LAERTES:** Think it no more.
For nature crescent does not grow alone
In thews and bulk, but as this temple waxes
The inward service of the mind and soul
Grows wide withal. Perhaps he loves you now,
And now no soil nor cautel doth besmirch
The virtue of his will; but you must fear,
His greatness weighed, his will is not his own.
For he himself is subject to his birth.
He may not, as unvalued persons do,
Carve for himself, for on his choice depends
The safety and health of this whole state,

**1.3. Location: Polonius' chambers.**
**3 convoy is assistant** means of conveyance are available **6 toy in blood** passing amorous fancy **7 primy** in its prime, springtime **8 Forward** precocious **9 suppliance** supply, filler **11 crescent** growing, waxing **12 thews** bodily strength. **temple** i.e., body **14 Grows wide withal** grows along with it **15 soil** blemish. **cautel** deceit **16 will** desire **17 His greatness weighed** if you take into account his high position **20 Carve** i.e., choose

And therefore must his choice be circumscribed
Unto the voice and yielding of that body
Whereof he is the head. Then if he says he loves you,
It fits your wisdom so far to believe it
As he in his particular act and place
May give his saying deed, which is no further
Than the main voice of Denmark goes withal.
Then weigh what loss your honor may sustain
If with too credent ear you list his songs,
Or lose your heart, or your chaste treasure open
To his unmastered importunity.
Fear it, Ophelia, fear it, my dear sister,
And keep you in the rear of your affection,
Out of the shot and danger of desire.
The chariest maid is prodigal enough
If she unmask her beauty to the moon.
Virtue itself scapes not calumnious strokes.
The canker galls the infants of the spring
Too oft before their buttons be disclosed,
And in the morn and liquid dew of youth
Contagious blastments are most imminent.
Be wary then; best safety lies in fear.
Youth to itself rebels, though none else near.

**OPHELIA:** I shall the effect of this good lesson keep
As watchman to my heart. But, good my brother,
Do not, as some ungracious pastors do,
Show me the steep and thorny way to heaven,
Whiles like a puffed and reckless libertine
Himself the primrose path of dalliance treads,
And recks not his own rede.

*Enter* POLONIUS.

**LAERTES:** O, fear me not.
I stay too long. But here my father comes.
A double blessing is a double grace;
Occasion smiles upon a second leave.

**POLONIUS:** Yet here, Laertes? Aboard, aboard, for shame!
The wind sits in the shoulder of your sail,
And you are stayed for. There—my blessing with thee!
And these few precepts in thy memory
Look thou character. Give thy thoughts no tongue,
Nor any unproportioned thought his act.
Be thou familiar, but by no means vulgar.
Those friends thou hast, and their adoption tried,
Grapple them unto thy soul with hoops of steel,
But do not dull thy palm with entertainment
Of each new-hatched, unfledged courage. Beware
Of entrance to a quarrel, but being in,
Bear 't that th' opposèd may beware of thee.
Give every man thy ear, but few thy voice;
Take each man's censure, but reserve thy judgment.
Costly thy habit as thy purse can buy,
But not expressed in fancy; rich, not gaudy,
For the apparel oft proclaims the man,
And they in France of the best rank and station
Are of a most select and generous chief in that.
Neither a borrower nor a lender be,
For loan oft loses both itself and friend,
And borrowing dulleth edge of husbandry.
This above all: to thine own self be true,
And it must follow, as the night the day,
Thou canst not then be false to any man.
Farewell. My blessing season this in thee!

**LAERTES:** Most humbly do I take my leave, my lord.

**POLONIUS:** The time invests you. Go, your servants tend.

**LAERTES:** Farewell, Ophelia, and remember well
What I have said to you.

**OPHELIA:** 'Tis in my memory locked,
And you yourself shall keep the key of it.

**LAERTES:** Farewell. *Exit* LAERTES.

**POLONIUS:** What is 't, Ophelia, he hath said to you?

---

**23 voice and yielding** assent, approval **26 in . . . place** in his particular restricted circumstances **28 main voice** general assent. **withal** along with **30 credent** credulous. **list** listen to **34 keep . . . affection** don't advance as far as your affection might lead you. (A military metaphor.) **36 chariest** most scrupulously modest **37 If she unmask** if she does no more than show her beauty. **moon** (Symbol of chastity.) **39 canker galls** cankerworm destroys **40 buttons** buds. **disclosed** opened **41 liquid dew** i.e., time when dew is fresh and bright **42 blastments** blights **44 Youth . . . rebels** youth is inherently rebellious **47 ungracious** ungodly **49 puffed** bloated, or swollen with pride **51 recks** heeds. **rede** counsel. **fear me not** don't worry on my account **53 double** (Laertes has already bid his father good-bye.) **54 Occasion . . . leave** happy is the circumstance that provides a second leave-taking. (The goddess Occasion, or Opportunity, smiles.)

**59 Look** be sure that. **character** inscribe **60 unproportioned** badly calculated, intemperate. **his** its **61 familiar** sociable. **vulgar** common **62 and their adoption tried** and also their suitability for adoption as friends having been tested **64 dull thy palm** i.e., shake hands so often as to make the gesture meaningless **65 courage** young man of spirit **67 Bear 't that** manage it so that **69 censure** opinion, judgment **70 habit** clothing **71 fancy** excessive ornament, decadent fashion **74 Are . . . that** are of a most refined and well-bred preeminence in choosing what to wear **77 husbandry** thrift **81 season** mature **83 invests** besieges, presses upon

**OPHELIA:** So please you, something touching the Lord Hamlet.

**POLONIUS:** Marry, well bethought.
'Tis told me he hath very oft of late
Given private time to you, and you yourself
Have of your audience been most free and bounteous.
If it be so—as so 'tis put on me,
And that in way of caution—I must tell you
You do not understand yourself so clearly
As it behooves my daughter and your honor.
What is between you? Give me up the truth.

**OPHELIA:** He hath, my lord, of late made many tenders
Of his affection to me.

**POLONIUS:** Affection? Pooh! You speak like a green girl,
Unsifted in such perilous circumstance.
Do you believe his tenders, as you call them?

**OPHELIA:** I do not know, my lord, what I should think.

**POLONIUS:** Marry, I will teach you. Think yourself a baby
That you have ta'en these tenders for true pay
Which are not sterling. Tender yourself more dearly,
Or—not to crack the wind of the poor phrase,
Running it thus—you'll tender me a fool.

**OPHELIA:** My lord, he hath importuned me with love
In honorable fashion.

**POLONIUS:** Ay, fashion you may call it. Go to, go to.

**OPHELIA:** And hath given countenance to his speech, my lord,
With almost all the holy vows of heaven.

**POLONIUS:** Ay, springes to catch woodcocks. I do know,
When the blood burns, how prodigal the soul
Lends the tongue vows. These blazes, daughter,
Giving more light than heat, extinct in both
Even in their promise as it is a-making,
You must not take for fire. From this time
Be something scanter of your maiden presence.
Set your entreatments at a higher rate
Than a command to parle. For Lord Hamlet,
Believe so much in him that he is young,
And with a larger tether may he walk
Than may be given you. In few, Ophelia,
Do not believe his vows, for they are brokers,
Not of that dye which their investments show,
But mere implorators of unholy suits,
Breathing like sanctified and pious bawds,
The better to beguile. This is for all:
I would not, in plain terms, from this time forth
Have you so slander any moment leisure
As to give words or talk with the Lord Hamlet.
Look to 't, I charge you. Come your ways.

**OPHELIA:** I shall obey, my lord. *Exeunt.*

## 1.4 *Enter* HAMLET, HORATIO, *and* MARCELLUS

**HAMLET:** The air bites shrewdly; it is very cold.

**HORATIO:** It is a nipping and an eager air.

**HAMLET:** What hour now?

**HORATIO:** I think it lacks of twelve.

**MARCELLUS:** No, it is struck.

**HORATIO:** Indeed? I heard it not.
It then draws near the season
Wherein the spirit held his wont to walk.
*A flourish of trumpets, and two pieces go off [within].*
What does this mean, my lord?

**HAMLET:** The King doth wake tonight and takes his rouse,
Keeps wassail, and the swaggering upspring reels;

---

**91 Marry** i.e., by the Virgin Mary. (A mild oath.) **95 put on** impressed on, told to **98 behooves** befits **100 tenders** offers **103 Unsifted** i.e., untried **108 sterling** legal currency. **Tender** hold, look after, offer **109 crack the wind** i.e., run it until it is broken-winded **110 tender me a fool** (1) show yourself to me as a fool (2) show me up as a fool (3) present me with a grandchild. (*Fool* was a term of endearment for a child.) **113 fashion** mere form, pretense. **Go to** (An expression of impatience.) **114 countenance** credit, confirmation **116 springes** snares. **woodcocks** birds easily caught; here used to connote gullibility **117 prodigal** prodigally

**120 it** i.e., the promise **122 something** somewhat **123 entreatments** negotiations for surrender. (A military term.) **124 parle** discuss terms with the enemy. (Polonius urges his daughter, in the metaphor of military language, not to meet with Hamlet and consider giving in to him merely because he requests an interview.) **125 so . . . him** this much concerning him **127 In few** briefly **128 brokers** go-betweens, procurers **129 dye** color or sort. **investments** clothes. (The vows are not what they seem.) **130 mere implorators** out-and-out solicitors **131 Breathing** speaking **132 for all** once for all, in sum **134 slander** abuse, misuse. **moment** moment's **136 Come your ways** come along

**1.4. Location: The guard platform.**
**1 shrewdly** keenly, sharply **2 eager** biting **3 lacks of** is just short of **5 season** time **6 held his wont** was accustomed **s.d. pieces** i.e., of ordnance, cannon **8 wake** stay awake and hold revel. **takes his rouse** carouses **9 wassail** carousal. **upspring** wild German dance. **reels** dances

And as he drains his drafts of Rhenish down,
The kettledrum and trumpet thus bray out
The triumph of his pledge.

**HORATIO:** Is it a custom?

**HAMLET:** Ay, marry, is 't,
But to my mind, though I am native here
And to the manner born, it is a custom
More honored in the breach than the observance.
This heavy-headed revel east and west
Makes us traduced and taxed of other nations.
They clepe us drunkards, and with swinish phrase
Soil our addition; and indeed it takes
From our achievements, though performed at height,
The pith and marrow of our attribute.
So, oft it chances in particular men,
That for some vicious mole of nature in them,
As in their birth—wherein they are not guilty,
Since nature cannot choose his origin—
By their o'ergrowth of some complexion,
Oft breaking down the pales and forts of reason,
Or by some habit that too much o'erleavens
The form of plausive manners, that these men
Carrying, I say, the stamp of one defect,
Being nature's livery or fortune's star,
His virtues else, be they as pure as grace,
As infinite as man may undergo,
Shall in the general censure take corruption
From that particular fault. The dram of evil
Doth all the noble substance often dout
To his own scandal.

*Enter* GHOST.

**HORATIO:** Look, my lord, it comes!

**10 Rhenish** Rhine wine **12 The triumph . . . pledge** i.e., his feat in draining the wine in a single draft **15 manner** custom (of drinking) **16 More . . . observance** better neglected than followed **17 east and west** i.e., everywhere **18 taxed of** censured by **19 clepe** call. **with swinish phrase** i.e., by calling us swine **20 addition** reputation **21 at height** outstandingly **22 The pith . . . attribute** the essence of the reputation that others attribute to us **24 for** on account of. **mole of nature** natural blemish in one's constitution **26 his** its **27 their o'ergrowth . . . complexion** the excessive growth in individuals of some natural trait **28 pales** palings, fences (as of a fortification) **29 o'erleavens** induces a change throughout (as yeast works in dough) **30 plausive** pleasing **32 nature's livery** sign of one's servitude to nature. **fortune's star** the destiny that chance brings **33 His virtues else** i.e., the other qualities of *these men* (line 30) **34 may undergo** can sustain **35 general censure** general opinion that people have of him **36–38 The dram . . . scandal** i.e., the small drop of evil blots out or works against the noble substance of the whole and brings it into disrepute. To *dout* is to blot out. (A famous crux.)

Hamlet (Kenneth Branagh) goes with Marcellus and Horatio to confront the ghost.

**HAMLET:** Angels and ministers of grace defend us!
Be thou a spirit of health or goblin damned,
Bring with thee airs from heaven or blasts from hell,
Be thy intents wicked or charitable,
Thou com'st in such a questionable shape
That I will speak to thee. I'll call thee Hamlet,
King, father, royal Dane. O, answer me!
Let me not burst in ignorance, but tell
Why thy canonized bones, hearsèd in death,
Have burst their cerements; why the sepulcher
Wherein we saw thee quietly inurned
Hath oped his ponderous and marble jaws
To cast thee up again. What may this mean,
That thou, dead corpse, again in complete steel,
Revisits thus the glimpses of the moon,
Making night hideous, and we fools of nature
So horridly to shake our disposition
With thoughts beyond the reaches of our souls?
Say, why is this? Wherefore? What should we do?

*[The* GHOST*] beckons [*HAMLET*].*

**HORATIO:** It beckons you to go away with it,
As if it some impartment did desire
To you alone.

**MARCELLUS:** Look with what courteous action
It wafts you to a more removèd ground.
But do not go with it.

**39 ministers of grace** messengers of God **40 Be thou** whether you are. **spirit of health** good angel **41 Bring** whether you bring **42 Be thy intents** whether your intentions are **43 questionable** inviting question **47 canonized** buried according to the canons of the church. **hearsèd** coffined **48 cerements** grave clothes **49 inurned** entombed **52 complete steel** full armor **53 glimpses of the moon** pale and uncertain moonlight **54 fools of nature** mere men, limited to natural knowledge and subject to nature **55 So . . . disposition** to distress our mental composure so violently **59 impartment** communication

**HORATIO:** No, by no means.

**HAMLET:** It will not speak. Then I will follow it.

**HORATIO:** Do not, my lord!

**HAMLET:** Why, what should be the fear?
I do not set my life at a pin's fee,
And for my soul, what can it do to that,
Being a thing immortal as itself?
It waves me forth again. I'll follow it.

**HORATIO:** What if it tempt you toward the flood, my lord,
Or to the dreadful summit of the cliff
That beetles o'er his base into the sea,
And there assume some other horrible form
Which might deprive your sovereignty of reason
And draw you into madness? Think of it.
The very place puts toys of desperation,
Without more motive, into every brain
That looks so many fathoms to the sea
And hears it roar beneath.

**HAMLET:** It wafts me still.—Go on, I'll follow thee.

**MARCELLUS:** You shall not go, my lord.

*[They try to stop him.]*

**HAMLET:** Hold off your hands!

**HORATIO:** Be ruled. You shall not go.

**HAMLET:** My fate cries out,
And makes each petty artery in this body
As hardy as the Nemean lion's nerve.
Still am I called. Unhand me, gentlemen.
By heaven, I'll make a ghost of him that lets me!
I say, away!—Go on, I'll follow thee.

*Exeunt* GHOST *and* HAMLET.

**HORATIO:** He waxes desperate with imagination.

**MARCELLUS:** Let's follow. 'Tis not fit thus to obey him.

**HORATIO:** Have after. To what issue will this come?

**MARCELLUS:** Something is rotten in the state of Denmark.

**HORATIO:** Heaven will direct it.

**MARCELLUS:** Nay, let's follow him.

*Exeunt.*

**1.5** *Enter* GHOST *and* HAMLET.

**HAMLET:** Whither wilt thou lead me? Speak. I'll go no further.

**GHOST:** Mark me.

**HAMLET:** I will.

**GHOST:** My hour is almost come,
When I to sulfurous and tormenting flames
Must render up myself.

**HAMLET:** Alas, poor ghost!

**GHOST:** Pity me not, but lend thy serious hearing
To what I shall unfold.

**HAMLET:** Speak, I am bound to hear.

**GHOST:** So art thou to revenge, when thou shalt hear.

**HAMLET:** What?

**GHOST:** I am thy father's spirit,
Doomed for a certain term to walk the night,
And for the day confined to fast in fires,
Till the foul crimes done in my days of nature
Are burnt and purged away. But that I am forbid
To tell the secrets of my prison house,
I could a tale unfold whose lightest word
Would harrow up thy soul, freeze thy young blood,
Make thy two eyes like stars start from their spheres,
Thy knotted and combinèd locks to part,
And each particular hair to stand on end
Like quills upon the fretful porcupine.
But this eternal blazon must not be
To ears of flesh and blood. List, list, O, list!
If thou didst ever thy dear father love—

**HAMLET:** O God!

**GHOST:** Revenge his foul and most unnatural murder.

---

**65 fee** value **69 flood** sea **71 beetles o'er** overhangs threateningly (like bushy eyebrows). **his** its **73 deprive . . . reason** take away the rule of reason over your mind **75 toys of desperation** fancies of desperate acts, i.e., suicide **81 My fate cries out** my destiny summons me **82 petty** weak. **artery** (through which the vital spirits were thought to have been conveyed) **83 Nemean lion** one of the monsters slain by Hercules in his twelve labors. **nerve** sinew **85 lets** hinders **89 Have after** let's go after him. **issue** outcome

**91 it** i.e., the outcome

**1.5. Location: The battlements of the castle.**
**7 bound** (1) ready (2) obligated by duty and fate. (The Ghost, in line 8, answers in the second sense.) **12 fast** do penance by fasting **13 crimes** sins. **of nature** as a mortal **14 But that** were it not that **17 harrow up** lacerate, tear **18 spheres** i.e., eye-sockets, here compared to the orbits or transparent revolving spheres in which, according to Ptolemaic astronomy, the heavenly bodies were fixed **19 knotted . . . locks** hair neatly arranged and confined **22 eternal blazon** revelation of the secrets of eternity

The ghost (Paul Scofield) tells Hamlet of Claudius's betrayal.

**HAMLET:** Murder?

**GHOST:** Murder most foul, as in the best it is,
But this most foul, strange, and unnatural.

**HAMLET:** Haste me to know 't, that I, with wings as swift
As meditation or the thoughts of love,
May sweep to my revenge.

**GHOST:** I find thee apt;
And duller shouldst thou be than the fat weed
That roots itself in ease on Lethe wharf,
Wouldst thou not stir in this. Now, Hamlet, hear.
'Tis given out that, sleeping in my orchard,
A serpent stung me. So the whole ear of Denmark
Is by a forgèd process of my death
Rankly abused. But know, thou noble youth,
The serpent that did sting thy father's life
Now wears his crown.

**HAMLET:** O, my prophetic soul! My uncle!

**GHOST:** Ay, that incestuous, that adulterate beast,
With witchcraft of his wit, with traitorous gifts—
O wicked wit and gifts, that have the power
So to seduce!—won to his shameful lust
The will of my most seeming-virtuous queen.
O Hamlet, what a falling off was there!
From me, whose love was of that dignity
That it went hand in hand even with the vow
I made to her in marriage, and to decline
Upon a wretch whose natural gifts were poor
To those of mine!
But virtue, as it never will be moved,
Though lewdness court it in a shape of heaven,
So lust, though to a radiant angel linked,
Will sate itself in a celestial bed
And prey on garbage.
But soft, methinks I scent the morning air.
Brief let me be. Sleeping within my orchard,
My custom always of the afternoon,
Upon my secure hour thy uncle stole,
With juice of cursèd hebona in a vial,
And in the porches of my ears did pour
The leprous distillment, whose effect
Holds such an enmity with blood of man
That swift as quicksilver it courses through
The natural gates and alleys of the body,
And with a sudden vigor it doth posset
And curd, like eager droppings into milk,
The thin and wholesome blood. So did it mine,
And a most instant tetter barked about,
Most lazar-like, with vile and loathsome crust,
All my smooth body.
Thus was I, sleeping, by a brother's hand
Of life, of crown, of queen at once dispatched,
Cut off even in the blossoms of my sin,
Unhouseled, disappointed, unaneled,
No reckoning made, but sent to my account
With all my imperfections on my head.
O, horrible! O, horrible, most horrible!
If thou hast nature in thee, bear it not.
Let not the royal bed of Denmark be
A couch for luxury and damnèd incest.
But, howsoever thou pursues this act,
Taint not thy mind nor let thy soul contrive
Against thy mother aught. Leave her to heaven
And to those thorns that in her bosom lodge,
To prick and sting her. Fare thee well at once.
The glowworm shows the matin to be near,
And 'gins to pale his uneffectual fire.
Adieu, adieu, adieu! Remember me. *[Exit.]*

---

**28 in the best** even at best **33 shouldst thou be** you would have to be. **fat** torpid, lethargic **34 Lethe** the river of forgetfulness in Hades **36 orchard** garden **38 forgèd process** falsified account **39 abused** deceived **43 adulterate** adulterous **44 gifts** (1) talents (2) presents **50 even with the vow** with the very vow **53 To** compared to

**54 virtue, as it** as virtue **55 shape of heaven** heavenly form **57 sate . . . bed** cease to find sexual pleasure in a virtuously lawful marriage **62 secure** confident, unsuspicious **63 hebona** a poison. (The word seems to be a form of *ebony,* though it is thought perhaps to be related to *henbane,* a poison, or to *ebenus,* "yew.") **64 porches of my ears** ears as a porch or entrance of the body **65 leprous distillment** distillation causing leprosylike disfigurement **69 posset** coagulate, curdle **70 eager** sour, acid **72 tetter** eruption of scabs. **barked** covered with a rough covering, like bark on a tree **73 lazar-like** leperlike **76 dispatched** suddenly deprived **78 Unhouseled** without having received the Sacrament. **disappointed** unready (spiritually) for the last journey. **unaneled** without having received extreme unction **79 reckoning** settling of accounts **82 nature** i.e., the promptings of a son **84 luxury** lechery **90 matin** morning **91 his** its

**HAMLET:** O all you host of heaven! O earth! What else?
And shall I couple hell? O, fie! Hold, hold, my heart,
And you, my sinews, grow not instant old,
But bear me stiffly up. Remember thee?
Ay, thou poor ghost, whiles memory holds a seat
In this distracted globe. Remember thee?
Yea, from the table of my memory
I'll wipe away all trivial fond records,
All saws of books, all forms, all pressures past
That youth and observation copied there,
And thy commandment all alone shall live
Within the book and volume of my brain,
Unmixed with baser matter. Yes, by heaven!
O most pernicious woman!
O villain, villain, smiling, damnèd villain!
My tables—meet it is I set it down
That one may smile, and smile, and be a villain.
At least I am sure it may be so in Denmark.
*[Writing.]*
So, uncle, there you are. Now to my word:
It is "Adieu, adieu! Remember me."
I have sworn 't.

*Enter* HORATIO *and* MARCELLUS.

**HORATIO:** My lord, my lord!

**MARCELLUS:** Lord Hamlet!

**HORATIO:** Heavens secure him!

**HAMLET:** So be it.

**MARCELLUS:** Hilo, ho, ho, my lord!

**HAMLET:** Hillo, ho, ho, boy! Come, bird, come.

**MARCELLUS:** How is 't, my noble lord?

**HORATIO:** What news, my lord?

**HAMLET:** O, wonderful!

**HORATIO:** Good my lord, tell it.

**HAMLET:** No, you will reveal it.

**HORATIO:** Not I, my lord, by heaven.

**MARCELLUS:** Nor I, my lord.

Hamlet (Mel Gibson) swears his companions to secrecy.

**HAMLET:** How say you, then, would heart of man once think it?
But you'll be secret?

**HORATIO, MARCELLUS:** Ay, by heaven, my lord.

**HAMLET:** There's never a villain dwelling in all Denmark
But he's an arrant knave.

**HORATIO:** There needs no ghost, my lord, come from the grave
To tell us this.

**HAMLET:** Why, right, you are in the right.
And so, without more circumstance at all,
I hold it fit that we shake hands and part,
You as your business and desire shall point you—
For every man hath business and desire,
Such as it is—and for my own poor part,
Look you, I'll go pray.

**HORATIO:** These are but wild and whirling words, my lord.

**HAMLET:** I am sorry they offend you, heartily;
Yes, faith, heartily.

**HORATIO:** There's no offense, my lord.

**HAMLET:** Yes, by Saint Patrick, but there is, Horatio,
And much offense too. Touching this vision here,
It is an honest ghost, that let me tell you.

---

**94 couple** add. **Hold** hold together **95 instant** instantly **98 globe** (1) head (2) world **99 table** tablet, slate **100 fond** foolish **101 saws** wise sayings. **forms** shapes or images copied onto the slate; general ideas. **pressures** impressions stamped **108 tables** writing tablets. **meet it is** it is fitting **111 there you are** i.e., there, I've written that down against you **116 secure him** keep him safe **119 Hillo . . . come** (A falconer's call to a hawk in air. Hamlet mocks the hallooing as though it were a part of hawking.)

**127 once** ever **130 arrant** thoroughgoing **133 circumstance** ceremony, elaboration **142 Saint Patrick** (The keeper of Purgatory and patron saint of all blunders and confusion.) **143 offense** (Hamlet deliberately changes Horatio's "no offense taken" to "an offense against all decency.") **144 an honest ghost** i.e., a real ghost and not an evil spirit

For your desire to know what is between us,
O'ermaster 't as you may. And now, good friends,
As you are friends, scholars, and soldiers,
Give me one poor request.

**HORATIO:** What is 't, my lord? We will.

**HAMLET:** Never make known what you have seen tonight.

**HORATIO, MARCELLUS:** My lord, we will not.

**HAMLET:** Nay, but swear 't.

**HORATIO:** In faith, my lord, not I.

**MARCELLUS:** Nor I, my lord, in faith.

**HAMLET:** Upon my sword. *[He holds out his sword.]*

**MARCELLUS:** We have sworn, my lord, already.

**HAMLET:** Indeed, upon my sword, indeed.

**GHOST** *(cries under the stage)*: Swear.

**HAMLET:** Ha, ha, boy, sayst thou so? Art thou there, truepenny?
Come on, you hear this fellow in the cellarage.
Consent to swear.

**HORATIO:** Propose the oath, my lord.

**HAMLET:** Never to speak of this that you have seen,
Swear by my sword.

**GHOST** *[beneath]*: Swear. *[They swear.]*

**HAMLET:** *Hic et ubique?* Then we'll shift our ground.
*[He moves to another spot.]*
Come hither, gentlemen,
And lay your hands again upon my sword.
Swear by my sword
Never to speak of this that you have heard.

**GHOST** *[beneath]*: Swear by his sword. *[They swear.]*

**HAMLET:** Well said, old mole. Canst work i' th' earth so fast?
A worthy pioner!—Once more remove, good friends.
*[He moves again.]*

**HORATIO:** O day and night, but this is wondrous strange!

**HAMLET:** And therefore as a stranger give it welcome.
There are more things in heaven and earth, Horatio,
Than are dreamt of in your philosophy.
But come;
Here, as before, never, so help you mercy,
How strange or odd soe'er I bear myself—
As I perchance hereafter shall think meet
To put an antic disposition on—
That you, at such times seeing me, never shall,
With arms encumbered thus, or this headshake,
Or by pronouncing of some doubtful phrase
As "Well, we know," or "We could, an if we would,"
Or "If we list to speak," or "There be, an if they might,"
Or such ambiguous giving out, to note
That you know aught of me—this do swear,
So grace and mercy at your most need help you.

**GHOST** *[beneath]*: Swear. *[They swear.]*

**HAMLET:** Rest, rest, perturbèd spirit! So, gentlemen,
With all my love I do commend me to you;
And what so poor a man as Hamlet is
May do t' express his love and friending to you,
God willing, shall not lack. Let us go in together,
And still your fingers on your lips, I pray.
The time is out of joint. O cursèd spite
That ever I was born to set it right!
*[They wait for him to leave first.]*
Nay, come, let's go together. *Exeunt.*

## 2.1 *Enter old* POLONIUS *with his man [*REYNALDO*].*

**POLONIUS:** Give him this money and these notes, Reynaldo.
*[He gives money and papers.]*

**REYNALDO:** I will, my lord.

---

**153 In faith . . . I** i.e., I swear not to tell what I have seen. (Horatio is not refusing to swear.) **155 sword** i.e., the hilt in the form of a cross **156 We . . . already** i.e., we swore *in faith* **159 truepenny** honest old fellow **164 s.d. They swear** (Seemingly they swear here, and at lines 170 and 190, as they lay their hands on Hamlet's sword. Tripled oaths would have particular force; these three oaths deal with what they have seen, what they have heard, and what they promise about Hamlet's *antic disposition.*) **165 Hic et ubique** here and everywhere (Latin.) **172 pioner** foot soldier assigned to dig tunnels and excavations

**174 as a stranger** i.e., needing your hospitality **176 your philosophy** this subject called "natural philosophy" or "science" that people talk about **178 so help you mercy** as you hope for God's mercy when you are judged **181 antic** fantastic **183 encumbered** folded **185 an if** if **186 list** wished. **There . . . might** i.e., there are people here (we, in fact) who could tell news if we were at liberty to do so **187 giving out** intimation. **note** draw attention to the fact **188 aught** i.e., something secret **192 do . . . you** entrust myself to you **194 friending** friendliness **195 lack** be lacking **196 still** always **197 The time** the state of affairs. **spite** i.e., the spite of Fortune **199 let's go together** (Probably they wait for him to leave first, but he refuses this ceremoniousness.)

**2.1. Location: Polonius' chambers.**

**POLONIUS:** You shall do marvelous wisely, good Reynaldo,
Before you visit him, to make inquire
Of his behavior.

**REYNALDO:** My lord, I did intend it.

**POLONIUS:** Marry, well said, very well said. Look you, sir,
Inquire me first what Danskers are in Paris,
And how, and who, what means, and where they keep,
What company, at what expense; and finding
By this encompassment and drift of question
That they do know my son, come you more nearer
Than your particular demands will touch it.
Take you, as 'twere, some distant knowledge of him,
As thus, "I know his father and his friends,
And in part him." Do you mark this, Reynaldo?

**REYNALDO:** Ay, very well, my lord.

**POLONIUS:** "And in part him, but," you may say, "not well.
But if 't be he I mean, he's very wild,
Addicted so and so," and there put on him
What forgeries you please—marry, none so rank
As may dishonor him, take heed of that,
But, sir, such wanton, wild, and usual slips
As are companions noted and most known
To youth and liberty.

**REYNALDO:** As gaming, my lord.

**POLONIUS:** Ay, or drinking, fencing, swearing,
Quarreling, drabbing—you may go so far.

**REYNALDO:** My lord, that would dishonor him.

**POLONIUS:** Faith, no, as you may season it in the charge.
You must not put another scandal on him
That he is open to incontinency;
That's not my meaning. But breathe his faults so quaintly
That they may seem the taints of liberty,
The flash and outbreak of a fiery mind,
A savageness in unreclaimèd blood,
Of general assault.

**REYNALDO:** But, my good lord—

**POLONIUS:** Wherefore should you do this?

**REYNALDO:** Ay, my lord, I would know that.

**POLONIUS:** Marry, sir, here's my drift,
And I believe it is a fetch of warrant.
You laying these slight sullies on my son,
As 'twere a thing a little soiled wi' the working,
Mark you,
Your party in converse, him you would sound,
Having ever seen in the prenominate crimes
The youth you breathe of guilty, be assured
He closes with you in this consequence:
"Good sir," or so, or "friend," or "gentleman,"
According to the phrase or the addition
Of man and country.

**REYNALDO:** Very good, my lord.

**POLONIUS:** And then, sir, does 'a this—'a does—what was I about to say? By the Mass, I was about to say something. Where did I leave?

**REYNALDO:** At "closes in the consequence."

**POLONIUS:** At "closes in the consequence," ay, marry.
He closes thus: "I know the gentleman,
I saw him yesterday," or "th' other day,"
Or then, or then, with such or such, "and as you say,
There was 'a gaming," "there o'ertook in 's rouse,"
"There falling out at tennis," or perchance
"I saw him enter such a house of sale,"
Videlicet a brothel, or so forth. See you now,
Your bait of falsehood takes this carp of truth;
And thus do we of wisdom and of reach,
With windlasses and with assays of bias,

---

**3 marvelous** marvelously **4 inquire** inquiry **7 Danskers** Danes **8 what means** what wealth (they have). **keep** dwell **10 encompassment** roundabout talking. **drift** gradual approach or course **11–12 come . . . it** you will find out more this way than by asking pointed questions (*particular demands*) **13 Take you** assume, pretend **19 put on** impute to **20 forgeries** invented tales. **rank** gross **22 wanton** sportive, unrestrained **27 drabbing** whoring **29 season** temper, soften **31 incontinency** habitual sexual excess **32 quaintly** artfully, subtly **33 taints of liberty** faults resulting from free living

**35–36 A savageness . . . assault** a wildness in untamed youth that assails all indiscriminately **41 fetch of warrant** legitimate trick **43 soiled wi' the working** soiled by handling while it is being made, i.e., by involvement in the ways of the world **45 converse** conversation. **sound** i.e., sound out **46 Having ever** if he has ever. **prenominate crimes** before-mentioned offenses **47 breathe** speak **48 closes . . . consequence** takes you into his confidence in some fashion, as follows **50 addition** title **60 o'ertook in 's rouse** overcome by drink **61 falling out** quarreling **63 Videlicet** namely **64 carp** a fish **65 reach** capacity, ability **66 windlasses** i.e., circuitous paths. (Literally, circuits made to head off the game in hunting.) **assays of bias** attempts through indirection (like the curving path of the bowling ball, which is biased or weighted to one side)

By indirections find directions out.
So by my former lecture and advice
Shall you my son. You have me, have you not?

**REYNALDO:** My lord, I have.

**POLONIUS:** God b' wi' ye; fare ye well.

**REYNALDO:** Good my lord.

**POLONIUS:** Observe his inclination in yourself.

**REYNALDO:** I shall, my lord.

**POLONIUS:** And let him ply his music.

**REYNALDO:** Well, my lord.

**POLONIUS:** Farewell. *Exit* REYNALDO.

*Enter* OPHELIA.

How now, Ophelia, what's the matter?

**OPHELIA:** O my lord, my lord, I have been so affrighted!

**POLONIUS:** With what, i' the name of God?

**OPHELIA:** My lord, as I was sewing in my closet,
Lord Hamlet, with his doublet all unbraced,
Not hat upon his head, his stockings fouled,
Ungartered, and down-gyvèd to his ankle,
Pale as his shirt, his knees knocking each other,
And with a look so piteous in purport
As if he had been loosèd out of hell
To speak of horrors—he comes before me.

**POLONIUS:** Mad for thy love?

**OPHELIA:** My lord, I do not know,
But truly I do fear it.

**POLONIUS:** What said he?

**OPHELIA:** He took me by the wrist and held me hard.
Then goes he to the length of all his arm,
And, with his other hand thus o'er his brow
He falls to such perusal of my face
As 'a would draw it. Long stayed he so.
At last, a little shaking of mine arm
And thrice his head thus waving up and down,
He raised a sigh so piteous and profound
As it did seem to shatter all his bulk

Ophelia (Kate Winslet) tells Polonius (Richard Briers) of her encounter with Hamlet.

And end his being. That done, he lets me go,
And with his head over his shoulder turned
He seemed to find his way without his eyes,
For out o' doors he went without their helps,
And to the last bended their light on me.

**POLONIUS:** Come, go with me, I will go seek the King.
This is the very ecstasy of love,
Whose violent property fordoes itself
And leads the will to desperate undertakings
As oft as any passion under heaven
That does afflict our natures. I am sorry.
What, have you given him any hard words of late?

**OPHELIA:** No, my good lord, but as you did command
I did repel his letter and denied
His access to me.

**POLONIUS:** That hath made him mad.
I am sorry that with better heed and judgment
I had not quoted him. I feared he did but trifle
And meant to wrack thee. But beshrew my jealousy!
By heaven, it is as proper to our age
To cast beyond ourselves in our opinions
As it is common for the younger sort
To lack discretion. Come, go we to the King.
This must be known, which, being kept close, might move
More grief to hide than hate to utter love.
Come. *Exeunt.*

---

**67 directions** i.e., the way things really are **69 have** understand **70 b' wi'** be with **72 in yourself** in your own person (as well as by asking questions) **79 closet** private chamber **80 doublet** close-fitting jacket. **unbraced** unfastened **82 down-gyvèd** fallen to the ankles (like gyves or fetters) **84 in purport** in what is expressed **93 As** as if (also in line 97) **97 bulk** body

**104 ecstasy** madness **105 property** nature. **fordoes** destroys **114 quoted** observed **115 wrack** ruin, seduce. **beshrew my jealousy** a plague upon my suspicious nature **116 proper . . . age** characteristic of us (old) men **117 cast beyond** overshoot, miscalculate. (A metaphor from hunting.) **120 known** made known (to the King). **close** secret **120–121 might . . . love** i.e., might cause more grief (because of what Hamlet might do) by hiding the knowledge of Hamlet's strange behavior to Ophelia than unpleasantness by telling it

**2.2** *Flourish. Enter* KING *and* QUEEN, ROSENCRANTZ, *and* GUILDENSTERN *[with others].*

**KING:** Welcome, dear Rosencrantz and Guildenstern.
Moreover that we much did long to see you,
The need we have to use you did provoke
Our hasty sending. Something have you heard
Of Hamlet's tranformation—so call it,
Sith nor th' exterior nor the inward man
Resembles that it was. What it should be,
More than his father's death, that thus hath put him
So much from th' understanding of himself,
I cannot dream of. I entreat you both
That, being of so young days brought up with him,
And sith so neighbored to his youth and havior,
That you vouchsafe your rest here in our court
Some little time, so by your companies
To draw him on to pleasures, and to gather
So much as from occasion you may glean,
Whether aught to us unknown afflicts him thus
That, opened, lies within our remedy.

**QUEEN:** Good gentlemen, he hath much talked of you,
And sure I am two men there is not living
To whom he more adheres. If it will please you
To show us so much gentry and good will
As to expend your time with us awhile
For the supply and profit of our hope,
Your visitation shall receive such thanks
As fits a king's remembrance.

**ROSENCRANTZ:** Both Your Majesties
Might, by the sovereign power you have of us,
Put your dread pleasures more into command
Than to entreaty.

**GUILDENSTERN:** But we both obey,
And here give up ourselves in the full bent
To lay our service freely at your feet,
To be commanded.

**KING:** Thanks, Rosencrantz and gentle Guildenstern.

**QUEEN:** Thanks, Guildenstern and gentle Rosencrantz.
And I beseech you instantly to visit
My too much changèd son. Go, some of you,
And bring these gentlemen where Hamlet is.

**GUILDENSTERN:** Heavens make our presence and our practices
Pleasant and helpful to him!

**QUEEN:** Ay, amen!

*Exeunt* ROSENCRANTZ *and* GUILDENSTERN *[with some attendants].*

*Enter* POLONIUS

**POLONIUS:** Th' ambassadors from Norway, my good lord,
Are joyfully returned.

**KING:** Thou still hast been the father of good news.

**POLONIUS:** Have I, my lord? I assure my good liege
I hold my duty, as I hold my soul,
Both to my God and to my gracious king;
And I do think, or else this brain of mine
Hunts not the trail of policy so sure
As it hath used to do, that I have found
The very cause of Hamlet's lunacy.

**KING:** O, speak of that! That do I long to hear.

**POLONIUS:** Give first admittance to th' ambassadors.
My news shall be the fruit to that great feast.

**KING:** Thyself do grace to them and bring them in.

*[Exit* POLONIUS.*]*

He tells me, my dear Gertrude, he hath found
The head and source of all your son's distemper.

**QUEEN:** I doubt it is no other but the main,
His father's death and our o'erhasty marriage.

*Enter* AMBASSADORS *[*VOLTIMAND *and* CORNELIUS, *with* POLONIUS*].*

**KING:** Well, we shall sift him.—Welcome my good friends!
Say, Voltimand, what from our brother Norway?

**VOLTIMAND:** Most fair return of greetings and desires.
Upon our first, he sent out to suppress
His nephew's levies, which to him appeared

---

**2.2. Location: The castle.**

**2 Moreover that** besides the fact that **6 Sith nor** since neither **7 that** what **11 of . . . days** from such early youth **12 And sith so neighbored to** and since you are (or, and since that time you are) intimately acquainted with. **havior** demeanor **13 vouchsafe your rest** please to stay **16 occasion** opportunity **18 opened** being revealed **22 gentry** courtesy **24 supply . . . hope** aid and furtherance of what we hope for **26 As fits . . . remembrance** as would be a fitting gift of a king who rewards true service **27 of** over **28 dread** inspiring awe **30 in . . . bent** to the utmost degree of our capacity. (An archery metaphor.)

**38 practices** doings **42 still** always **44 hold** maintain. **as** as firmly as **47 policy** sagacity **52 fruit** dessert **53 grace** honor (punning on *grace* said before a *feast,* line 52) **56 doubt** fear, suspect. **main** chief point, principal concern **58 sift him** question Polonius closely **59 brother** fellow king **60 desires** good wishes **61 Upon our first** at our first words on the business

Polonius (Ian Holm) discusses Hamlet with Claudius (Alan Bates) and Gertrude (Glenn Close).

To be a preparation 'gainst the Polack,
But, better looked into, he truly found
It was against Your Highness. Whereat grieved
That so his sickness, age, and impotence
Was falsely borne in hand, sends out arrests
On Fortinbras, which he, in brief, obeys,
Receives rebuke from Norway, and in fine
Makes vow before his uncle never more
To give th' assay of arms against Your Majesty.
Whereon old Norway, overcome with joy,
Gives him three thousand crowns in annual fee
And his commission to employ those soldiers,
So levied as before, against the Polack,
With an entreaty, herein further shown, *[giving a paper]*
That it might please you to give quiet pass
Through your dominions for this enterprise
On such regards of safety and allowance
As therein are set down.

**KING:** It likes us well,
And at our more considered time we'll read,
Answer, and think upon this business.
Meantime we thank you for your well-took labor.
Go to your rest; at night we'll feast together.
Most welcome home! *Exeunt* AMBASSADORS.

**POLONIUS:** This business is well ended.
My liege, and madam, to expostulate
What majesty should be, what duty is,
Why day is day, night night, and time is time,
Were nothing but to waste night, day, and time.
Therefore, since brevity is the soul of wit,
And tediousness the limbs and outward flourishes,
I will be brief. Your noble son is mad.
Mad call I it, for, to define true madness,
What is 't but to be nothing else but mad?
But let that go.

**QUEEN:** More matter, with less art.

**POLONIUS:** Madam, I swear I use no art at all.
That he's mad, 'tis true; 'tis true 'tis pity,
And pity 'tis 'tis true—a foolish figure,
But farewell it, for I will use no art.
Mad let us grant him, then, and now remains
That we find out the cause of this effect,
Or rather say, the cause of this defect,
For this effect defective comes by cause.
Thus it remains, and the remainder thus.
Perpend.
I have a daughter—have while she is mine—
Who, in her duty and obedience, mark,
Hath given me this. Now gather and surmise.
*[He reads the letter.]* "To the celestial and my soul's idol, the most beautified Ophelia"—
That's an ill phrase, a vile phrase; "beautified" is a vile phrase. But you shall hear. Thus: *[He reads.]*
"In her excellent white bosom, these, etc."

**QUEEN:** Came this from Hamlet to her?

**POLONIUS:** Good madam, stay awhile, I will be faithful. *[He reads.]*
"Doubt thou the stars are fire,
Doubt that the sun doth move,
Doubt truth to be a liar,
But never doubt I love.
O dear Ophelia, I am ill at these numbers. I have not art to reckon my groans. But that I love thee best, O most best, believe it. Adieu.
Thine evermore, most dear lady, whilst this machine is to him, Hamlet."
This in obedience hath my daughter shown me,
And, more above, hath his solicitings,

---

**66 impotence** helplessness **67 borne in hand** deluded, taken advantage of. **arrests** orders to desist **69 in fine** in conclusion **71 give th' assay** make trial of strength, challenge **79 On . . . allowance** i.e., with such considerations for the safety of Denmark and permission for Fortinbras **80 likes** pleases **81 considered** suitable for deliberation **86 expostulate** expound, inquire into

**90 wit** sense or judgment **98 figure** figure of speech **103 For . . . cause** i.e., for this defective behavior, this madness, has a cause **105 Perpend** consider **108 gather and surmise** draw your own conclusions **113 In . . . bosom** (The letter is poetically addressed to her heart.) **these** i.e., the letter **115 stay** wait. **faithful** i.e., in reading the letter accurately **118 Doubt** suspect **120 ill . . . numbers** unskilled at writing verses **121 reckon** (1) count (2) number metrically, scan **124 machine** i.e., body **126 more above** moreover

Gertrude (Julie Christie), Claudius (Derek Jacobi), and Polonius discuss Hamlet.

As they fell out by time, by means, and place,
All given to mine ear.

**KING:** But how hath she
Received his love?

**POLONIUS:** What do you think of me?

**KING:** As of a man faithful and honorable.

**POLONIUS:** I would fain prove so. But what might you think,
When I had seen this hot love on the wing—
As I perceived it, I must tell you that,
Before my daughter told me—what might you,
Or my dear Majesty your queen here, think,
If I had played the desk or table book,
Or given my heart a winking, mute and dumb,
Or looked upon this love with idle sight?
What might you think? No, I went round to work,
And my young mistress thus I did bespeak:
"Lord Hamlet is a prince out of thy star;
This must not be." And then I prescripts gave her,
That she should lock herself from his resort,
Admit no messengers, receive no tokens.
Which done, she took the fruits of my advice;
And he, repellèd—a short take to make—
Fell into a sadness, then into a fast,
Thence to a watch, thence into a weakness,
Thence to a lightness, and by this declension
Into the madness wherein now he raves,
And all we mourn for.

**KING** *[to the* QUEEN*]*: Do you think 'tis this?

**QUEEN:** It may be, very like.

**POLONIUS:** Hath there been such a time—I would fain know that—
That I have positively said "'Tis so,"
When it proved otherwise?

**KING:** Not that I know.

**POLONIUS:** Take this from this, if this be otherwise.
If circumstances lead me, I will find
Where truth is hid, though it were hid indeed
Within the center.

**KING:** How may we try it further?

**POLONIUS:** You know sometimes he walks four hours together
Here in the lobby.

**QUEEN:** So he does indeed.

**POLONIUS:** At such a time I'll loose my daughter to him.
Be you and I behind an arras then.
Mark the encounter. If he love her not
And be not from his reason fall'n thereon,
Let me be no assistant for a state,
But keep a farm and carters.

**KING:** We will try it.

*Enter* HAMLET *[reading on a book].*

**QUEEN:** But look where sadly the poor wretch comes reading.

**POLONIUS:** Away, I do beseech you both, away.
I'll board him presently. O, give me leave.

*Exeunt* KING *and* QUEEN *[with attendants].*

How does my good Lord Hamlet?

---

**127 fell out** occurred. **by** according to **128 given . . . ear** i.e., told me about **131 fain** gladly **136 played . . . table book** i.e., remained shut up, concealing the information **137 given . . . winking** closed the eyes of my heart to this **138 with idle sight** complacently or incomprehendingly **139 round** roundly, plainly **140 bespeak** address **141 out of thy star** above your sphere, position **142 prescripts** orders **143 his resort** his visits **148 watch** state of sleeplessness

**149 lightness** lightheadedness. **declension** decline, deterioration (with a pun on the grammatical sense) **151 all we** all of us, or, into everything that we **156 Take this from this** (The actor probably gestures, indicating that he means his head from his shoulders, or his staff or office or chain from his hands or neck, or something similar.) **159 center** middle point of the earth (which is also the center of the Ptolemaic universe). **try** test, judge **162 loose** (as one might release an animal that is being mated) **163 arras** hanging, tapestry **165 thereon** on that account **167 carters** wagon drivers **168 sadly** seriously **170 board** accost. **presently** at once. **give me leave** i.e., excuse me, leave me alone. (Said to those he hurries offstage, including the King and Queen.)

**HAMLET:** Well, God-a-mercy.

**POLONIUS:** Do you know me, my lord?

**HAMLET:** Excellent well. You are a fishmonger.

**POLONIUS:** Not I, my lord.

**HAMLET:** Then I would you were so honest a man.

**POLONIUS:** Honest, my lord?

**HAMLET:** Ay, sir. To be honest, as this world goes, is to be one man picked out of ten thousand.

**POLONIUS:** That's very true, my lord.

**HAMLET:** For if the sun breed maggots in a dead dog, being a good kissing carrion—Have you a daughter?

**POLONIUS:** I have, my lord.

**HAMLET:** Let her not walk i' the sun. Conception is a blessing, but as your daughter may conceive, friend, look to 't.

**POLONIUS** *[aside]*: How say you by that? Still harping on my daughter. Yet he knew me not at first; 'a said I was a fishmonger. 'A is far gone. And truly in my youth I suffered much extremity for love, very near this. I'll speak to him again.—What do you read, my lord?

**HAMLET:** Words, words, words.

**POLONIUS:** What is the matter, my lord?

**HAMLET:** Between who?

**POLONIUS:** I mean, the matter that you read, my lord.

**HAMLET:** Slanders, sir; for the satirical rogue says here that old men have gray beards, that their faces are wrinkled, their eyes purging thick amber and plum-tree gum, and that they have a plentiful lack of wit, together with most weak hams. All which, sir, though I most powerfully and potently believe, yet I hold it not honesty to have it thus set down, for yourself, sir, shall grow old as I am, if like a crab you could go backward.

**POLONIUS** *[aside]*: Though this be madness, yet there is method in 't.—Will you walk out of the air, my lord?

**HAMLET:** Into my grave.

**POLONIUS:** Indeed, that's out of the air. *[Aside.]* How pregnant sometimes his replies are! A happiness that often madness hits on, which reason and sanity could not so prosperously be delivered of. I will leave him and suddenly contrive the means of meeting between him and my daughter.—My honorable lord, I will most humbly take my leave of you.

**HAMLET:** You cannot, sir, take from me anything that I will more willingly part withal—except my life, except my life, except my life.

*Enter* GUILDENSTERN *and* ROSENCRANTZ.

**POLONIUS:** Fare you well, my lord.

**HAMLET:** These tedious old fools!

**POLONIUS:** You go to seek the Lord Hamlet. There he is.

**ROSENCRANTZ** *[to* POLONIUS*]*: God save you, sir!

*[Exit* POLONIUS.*]*

**GUILDENSTERN:** My honored lord!

**ROSENCRANTZ:** My most dear lord!

**HAMLET:** My excellent good friends! How dost thou, Guildenstern? Ah, Rosencrantz! Good lads, how do you both?

**ROSENCRANTZ:** As the indifferent children of the earth.

**GUILDENSTERN:** Happy in that we are not overhappy. On Fortune's cap we are not the very button.

**HAMLET:** Nor the soles of her shoe?

**ROSENCRANTZ:** Neither, my lord.

**HAMLET:** Then you live about her waist, or in the middle of her favors?

**GUILDENSTERN:** Faith, her privates we.

---

**172 God-a-mercy** God have mercy, i.e., thank you **174 fishmonger** fish merchant **182 a good kissing carrion** i.e., a good piece of flesh for kissing, or for the sun to kiss **184 i' the sun** in public (with additional implication of the sunshine of princely favors). **Conception** (1) understanding (2) pregnancy **188 'a** he **194 matter** substance (But Hamlet plays on the sense of "basis for a dispute.") **199 purging** discharging. **amber** i.e., resin, like the resinous *plum-tree gum* **201 wit** understanding **203 honesty** decency, decorum **204 old** as old

**207 out of the air** (The open air was considered dangerous for sick people.) **210 pregnant** quick-witted, full of meaning. **happiness** felicity of expression **212 prosperously** successfully **213 suddenly** immediately **217 withal** with **220 old fools** i.e., old men like Polonius **228 indifferent** ordinary, at neither extreme of fortune or misfortune **234 favors** i.e., sexual favors **235 her privates we** i.e., (1) we are sexually intimate with Fortune, the fickle goddess who bestows her favors indiscriminately (2) we are her private citizens

**HAMLET:** In the secret parts of Fortune? O, most true, she is a strumpet. What news?

**ROSENCRANTZ:** None, my lord, but the world's grown honest.

**HAMLET:** Then is doomsday near. But your news is not true. Let me question more in particular. What have you, my good friends, deserved at the hands of Fortune that she sends you to prison hither?

**GUILDENSTERN:** Prison, my lord?

**HAMLET:** Denmark's a prison.

**ROSENCRANTZ:** Then is the world one.

**HAMLET:** A goodly one, in which there are many confines, wards, and dungeons, Denmark being one o' the worst.

**ROSENCRANTZ:** We think not so, my lord.

**HAMLET:** Why then 'tis none to you, for there is nothing either good or bad but thinking makes it so. To me it is a prison.

**ROSENCRANTZ:** Why then, your ambition makes it one. 'Tis too narrow for your mind.

**HAMLET:** O God, I could be bounded in a nutshell and count myself a king of infinite space, were it not that I have bad dreams.

**GUILDENSTERN:** Which dreams indeed are ambition, for the very substance of the ambitious is merely the shadow of a dream.

**HAMLET:** A dream itself is but a shadow.

**ROSENCRANTZ:** Truly, and I hold ambition of so airy and light a quality that it is but a shadow's shadow.

**HAMLET:** Then are our beggars bodies, and our monarchs and outstretched heroes the beggars' shadows. Shall we to the court? For, by my fay, I cannot reason.

**ROSENCRANTZ, GUILDENSTERN:** We'll wait upon you.

---

**237 strumpet** prostitute (A common epithet for indiscriminate Fortune; see line 493.) **248 confines** places of confinement. **wards** cells **260 the very . . . ambitious** that seemingly very substantial thing that the ambitious pursue **265 bodies** i.e., solid substances rather than shadows (since beggars are not ambitious) **266 outstretched** (1) far-reaching in their ambition (2) elongated as shadows **267 fay** faith **268 wait upon** accompany, attend. (But Hamlet uses the phrase in the sense of providing menial service.)

Hamlet (Kevin Kline) talks with Rosencrantz (Philip Goodwin) and Guildenstern (Reg E. Cathey) in the 1990 film directed by Kevin Kline.

**HAMLET:** No such matter. I will not sort you with the rest of my servants, for, to speak to you like an honest man, I am most dreadfully attended. But, in the beaten way of friendship, what make you at Elsinore?

**ROSENCRANTZ:** To visit you, my lord, no other occasion.

**HAMLET:** Beggar that I am, I am even poor in thanks; but I thank you, and sure, dear friends, my thanks are too dear a halfpenny. Were you not sent for? Is it your own inclining? Is it a free visitation? Come, come, deal justly with me. Come, come. Nay, speak.

**GUILDENSTERN:** What should we say, my lord?

**HAMLET:** Anything but to the purpose. You were sent for, and there is a kind of confession in your looks which your modesties have not craft enough to color. I know the good King and Queen have sent for you.

**ROSENCRANTZ:** To what end, my lord?

**HAMLET:** That you must teach me. But let me conjure you, by the rights of our fellowship, by the consonancy of our youth, by the obligation of our ever-preserved love, and by what more dear a better proposer could charge you withal, be even and direct with me whether you were sent for or no.

---

**269 sort** class, categorize **271 dreadfully attended** waited upon in slovenly fashion **272 beaten way** familiar path, tried-and-true course. **make** do **276 too dear a halfpenny** (1) too expensive at even a halfpenny, i.e., of little worth (2) too expensive *by* a halfpenny in return for worthless kindness **277 free** voluntary **280 Anything but to the purpose** anything except a straightforward answer. (Said ironically.) **282 modesties** sense of shame. **color** disguise **285 conjure** adjure, entreat **286–287 the consonancy of our youth** our closeness in our younger days **288 better** more skillful **289 charge** urge. **even** straight, honest

**ROSENCRANTZ** *[aside to* GUILDENSTERN*]*: What say you?

**HAMLET** *[aside]*: Nay, then, I have an eye of you.—If you love me, hold not off.

**GUILDENSTERN:** My lord, we were sent for.

**HAMLET:** I will tell you why; so shall my anticipation prevent your discovery, and your secrecy to the King and Queen molt no feather. I have of late—but wherefore I know not—lost all my mirth, forgone all custom of exercises; and indeed it goes so heavily with my disposition that this goodly frame, the earth, seems to me a sterile promontory; this most excellent canopy, the air, look you, this brave o'erhanging firmament, this majestical roof fretted with golden fire, why, it appeareth nothing to me but a foul and pestilent congregation of vapors. What a piece of work is a man! How noble in reason, how infinite in faculties, in form and moving how express and admirable, in action how like an angel, in apprehension how like a god! The beauty of the world, the paragon of animals! And yet, to me, what is this quintessence of dust? Man delights not me—no, nor woman neither, though by your smiling you seem to say so.

**ROSENCRANTZ:** My lord, there was no such stuff in my thoughts.

**HAMLET:** Why did you laugh, then, when I said man delights not me?

**ROSENCRANTZ:** To think, my lord, if you delight not in man, what Lenten entertainment the players shall receive from you. We coted them on the way, and hither are they coming to offer you service.

**HAMLET:** He that plays the king shall be welcome; His Majesty shall have tribute of me. The adventurous knight shall use his foil and target, the lover shall not sigh gratis, the humorous man shall end his part in peace, the clown shall make those laugh whose lungs are tickle o' the sear, and the lady shall say her mind freely, or the blank verse shall halt for 't. What players are they?

**ROSENCRANTZ:** Even those you were wont to take such delight in, the tragedians of the city.

**HAMLET:** How chances it they travel? Their residence, both in reputation and profit, was better both ways.

**ROSENCRANTZ:** I think their inhibition comes by the means of the late innovation.

**HAMLET:** Do they hold the same estimation they did when I was in the city? Are they so followed?

**ROSENCRANTZ:** No, indeed are they not.

**HAMLET:** How comes it? Do they grow rusty?

**ROSENCRANTZ:** Nay, their endeavor keeps in the wonted pace. But there is, sir, an aerie of children, little eyases, that cry out on the top of question and are most tyrannically clapped for 't. These are now the fashion, and so berattle the common stages—so they call them—that many wearing rapiers are afraid of goose quills and dare scarce come thither.

**HAMLET:** What, are they children? Who maintains 'em? How are they escoted? Will they pursue the quality no longer than they can sing? Will they not say afterwards, if they should grow themselves to common players—as it is most like, if their means are no better—their writers do them wrong to make them exclaim against their own succession?

---

**292 of** on **293 hold not off** don't hold back **295–296 so . . . discovery** in that way my saying it first will spare you from revealing the truth **297 molt no feather** i.e., not diminish in the least **302 brave** splendid **303 fretted** adorned (with fretwork, as in a vaulted ceiling) **304–305 congregation** mass **305 piece of work** masterpiece **307 express** well-framed, exact, expressive **308 apprehension** power of comprehending **310 quintessence** the fifth essence of ancient philosophy, beyond earth, water, air, and fire, supposed to be the substance of the heavenly bodies and to be latent in all things **318 Lenten entertainment** meager reception (appropriate to Lent) **319 coted** overtook and passed by **322 tribute** (1) applause (2) homage paid in money. **of** from **323 foil and target** sword and shield **324 gratis** for nothing. **humorous man** eccentric character, dominated by one trait or "humor" **325 in peace** i.e., with full license

**326 tickle o' the sear** easy on the trigger, ready to laugh easily. (A *sear* is part of a gunlock.) **327 halt** limp **330 tragedians** actors **331 residence** remaining in their usual place, i.e., in the city **333 inhibition** formal prohibition (from acting plays in the city) **334 late** recent. **innovation** i.e., the new fashion in satirical plays performed by boy actors in the "private" theaters; or possibly a political uprising; or the strict limitations set on the theaters in London in 1600 **338–363 How . . . load too** (The passage, omitted from the early quartos, alludes to the so-called War of the Theaters, 1599–1602, the rivalry between the children's companies and the adult actors.) **339 keeps** continues. **340 wonted** usual **aerie** nest **341 eyases** young hawks. **cry . . . question** speak shrilly, dominating the controversy (in decrying the public theaters) **342 tyrannically** outrageously **343 berattle** berate, clamor against. **common stages** public theaters **344 many wearing rapiers** i.e., many men of fashion, afraid to patronize the common players for fear of being satirized by the poets writing for the boy actors **345 goose quills** i.e., pens of satirists **347 escoted** maintained **348 quality** (acting) profession. **no longer . . . sing** i.e., only until their voices change **350 common** regular, adult. **like** likely **350–351 if . . . better** if they find no better way to support themselves **352 succession** i.e., future careers

**ROSENCRANTZ:** Faith, there has been much to-do on both sides, and the nation holds it no sin to tar them to controversy. There was for a while no money bid for argument unless the poet and the player went to cuffs in the question.

**HAMLET:** Is 't possible?

**GUILDENSTERN:** O, there has been much throwing about of brains.

**HAMLET:** Do the boys carry it away?

**ROSENCRANTZ:** Ay, that they do, my lord—Hercules and his load too.

**HAMLET:** It is not very strange; for my uncle is King of Denmark, and those that would make mouths at him while my father lived give twenty, forty, fifty, a hundred ducats apiece for his picture in little. 'Sblood, there is something in this more than natural, if philosophy could find it out.

*A flourish [of trumpets within].*

**GUILDENSTERN:** There are the players.

**HAMLET:** Gentlemen, you are welcome to Elsinore. Your hands, come then. Th' appurtenance of welcome is fashion and ceremony. Let me comply with you in this garb, lest my extent to the players, which, I tell you, must show fairly outwards, should more appear like entertainment than yours. You are welcome. But my uncle-father and aunt-mother are deceived.

**GUILDENSTERN:** In what, my dear lord?

**HAMLET:** I am but mad north-north-west. When the wind is southerly I know a hawk from a handsaw.

*Enter* POLONIUS.

**POLONIUS:** Well be with you, gentlemen!

**HAMLET:** Hark you, Guildenstern, and you too; at each ear a hearer. That great baby you see there is not yet out of his swaddling clouts.

**ROSENCRANTZ:** Haply he is the second time come to them, for they say an old man is twice a child.

**HAMLET:** I will prophesy he comes to tell me of the players. Mark it.—You say right, sir, o' Monday morning, 'twas then indeed.

**POLONIUS:** My lord, I have news to tell you.

**HAMLET:** My lord, I have news to tell you. When Roscius was an actor in Rome—

**POLONIUS:** The actors are come hither, my lord.

**HAMLET:** Buzz, buzz!

**POLONIUS:** Upon my honor—

**HAMLET:** Then came each actor on his ass.

**POLONIUS:** The best actors in the world, either for tragedy, comedy, history, pastoral, pastoral-comical, historical-pastoral, tragical-historical, tragical-comical-historical-pastoral, scene individable, or poem unlimited. Seneca cannot be too heavy, nor Plautus too light. For the law of writ and the liberty, these are the only men.

**HAMLET:** O Jephthah, judge of Israel, what a treasure hadst thou!

**POLONIUS:** What a treasure had he, my lord?

**HAMLET:** Why,
"One fair daughter, and no more,
The which he lovèd passing well."

**POLONIUS** *[aside]*: Still on my daughter.

**HAMLET:** Am I not i' the right, old Jephthah?

---

**353 to-do** ado **354 tar** set on (as dogs) **355–357 There . . . question** i.e., for a while, no money was offered by the acting companies to playwrights for the plot to a play unless the satirical poets who wrote for the boys and the adult actors came to blows in the play itself **361 carry it away** i.e., win the day **362–363 Hercules . . . load** (Thought to be an allusion to the sign of the Globe Theatre, which was Hercules bearing the world on his shoulders.) **365 mouths** faces **367 ducats** gold coins. **in little** in miniature. **'Sblood** by God's (Christ's) blood **368–369 philosophy** i.e., scientific inquiry **372 appurtenance** proper accompaniment **373 comply** observe the formalities of courtesy **374 garb** i.e., manner. **my extent** that which I extend, i.e., my polite behavior **375 show fairly outwards** show every evidence of cordiality **376 entertainment** a (warm) reception **379 north-north-west** just off true north, only party **380 hawk, handsaw** i.e., two very different things; though also perhaps meaning a mattock (or *hack*) and a carpenter's cutting tool, respectively; also birds, with a play on *hernshaw,* or heron

**384 swaddling clouts** cloths in which to wrap a newborn baby **385 Haply** perhaps **392 Roscius** a famous Roman actor who died in 62 B.C. **394 Buzz** (An interjection used to denote stale news.) **400 scene individable** a play observing the unity of place; or perhaps one that is unclassifiable, or performed without intermission **401 poem unlimited** a play disregarding the unities of time and place; one that is all-inclusive. **Seneca** writer of Latin tragedies. **402 Plautus** writer of Latin comedy. **law . . . liberty** dramatic composition both according to the rules and disregarding the rules **403 these** i.e., the actors **404 Jephthah . . . Israel** (Jephthah had to sacrifice his daughter; see Judges 11. Hamlet goes on to quote from a ballad on the theme.) **409 passing** surpassingly

**POLONIUS:** If you call me Jephthah, my lord, I have a daughter that I love passing well.

**HAMLET:** Nay, that follows not.

**POLONIUS:** What follows then, my lord?

**HAMLET:** Why,
"As by lot, God wot,"
and then, you know,
"It came to pass, as most like it was"—
the first row of the pious chanson will show you more, for look where my abridgement comes.

*Enter the* PLAYERS.

You are welcome, masters; welcome, all. I am glad to see thee well. Welcome, good friends. O, old friend! Why, thy face is valanced since I saw thee last. Com'st thou to beard me in Denmark? What, my young lady and mistress! By 'r Lady, your ladyship is nearer to heaven than when I saw you last, by the altitude of a chopine. Pray God your voice, like a piece of uncurrent gold, be not cracked within the ring. Masters, you are all welcome. We'll e'en to 't like French falconers, fly at anything we see. We'll have a speech straight. Come, give us a taste of your quality. Come, a passionate speech.

**FIRST PLAYER:** What speech, my good lord?

**HAMLET:** I heard thee speak me a speech once, but it was never acted, or if it was, not above once, for the play, I remember, pleased not the million; 'twas caviar to the general. But it was—as I received it, and others, whose judgments in such matters cried in the top of mine—an excellent play, well digested in the scenes, set down with as much modesty as cunning. I remember one said there were no sallets in the lines to make the matter savory, nor no matter in the phrase that might indict the author of affectation, but called it an honest method, as wholesome as sweet, and by very much more handsome than fine. One speech in 't I chiefly loved: 'twas Aeneas' tale to Dido, and thereabout of it especially when he speaks of Priam's slaughter. If it live in your memory, begin at this line: let me see, let me see—
"The rugged Pyrrhus, like th' Hyrcanian beast"—
'Tis not so. It begins with Pyrrhus:
"The rugged Pyrrhus, he whose sable arms,
Black as his purpose, did the night resemble
When he lay couchèd in the ominous horse,
Hath now this dread and black complexion smeared
With heraldry more dismal. Head to foot
Now is he total gules, horridly tricked
With blood of fathers, mothers, daughters, sons,
Baked and impasted with the parching streets,
That lend a tyrannous and a damnèd light
To their lord's murder. Roasted in wrath and fire,

Hamlet (Kenneth Branagh) talks with the players.

**417 lot** chance. **wot** knows **419 like** likely, probable **420 row** stanza. **chanson** ballad, song **421 my abridgement** something that cuts short my conversation; also, a diversion **424 valanced** fringed (with a beard) **425 beard** confront, challenge (with obvious pun) **426 young lady** i.e., boy playing women's parts. **By 'r Lady** by Our Lady **428 chopine** thick-soled shoe of Italian fashion **429 uncurrent** not passable as lawful coinage. **cracked . . . ring** i.e., changed from adolescent to male voice, no longer suitable for women's roles. (Coins featured rings enclosing the sovereign's head; if the coin was cracked within this ring, it was unfit for currency.) **430 e'en to 't** go at it **432 straight** at once. **quality** professional skill **438 caviar to the general** caviar to the multitude, i.e., a choice dish too elegant for coarse tastes **439–440 cried in the top of** i.e., spoke with greater authority than **440 digested** arranged, ordered **441 modesty** moderation, restraint. **cunning** skill **442 sallets** i.e., something savory, spicy improprieties

**444 indict** convict **446 handsome** well-proportioned. **fine** elaborately ornamented, showy **449 Priam's slaughter** the slaying of the ruler of Troy, when the Greeks finally took the city **451 Pyrrhus** a Greek hero in the Trojan War, also known as Neoptolemus, son of Achilles—another avenging son. **Hyrcanian beast** i.e., tiger. (On the death of Priam, see Virgil, *Aeneid*, 2.506 ff.; compare the whole speech with Marlowe's *Dido Queen of Carthage*, 2.1.214 ff. On the *Hyrcanian* tiger, see *Aeneid*, 4.366–367. Hyrcania is on the Caspian Sea.) **453 rugged** shaggy, savage. **sable** black (for reasons of camouflage during the episode of the Trojan horse) **455 couchèd** concealed. **ominous horse** fateful Trojan horse, by which the Greeks gained access to Troy **457 dismal** ill-omened **458 total gules** entirely red. (A heraldic term.) **tricked** spotted and smeared. (Heraldic.) **460 impasted** crusted, like a thick paste. **with . . . streets** by the parching heat of the streets (because of the fires everywhere) **461 tyrannous** cruel **462 their lord's** i.e., Priam's

And thus o'ersizèd with coagulate gore,
With eyes like carbuncles, the hellish Pyrrhus
Old grandsire Priam seeks."
So proceed you.

**POLONIUS:** 'Fore God, my lord, well spoken, with good accent and good discretion.

**FIRST PLAYER:** "Anon he finds him
Striking too short at Greeks. His antique sword,
Rebellious to his arm, lies where it falls,
Repugnant to command. Unequal matched,
Pyrrhus at Priam drives, in rage strikes wide,
But with the whiff and wind of his fell sword
Th' unnervèd father falls. Then senseless Ilium,
Seeming to feel this blow, with flaming top
Stoops to his base, and with a hideous crash
Takes prisoner Pyrrhus' ear. For, lo! His sword,
Which was declining on the milky head
Of reverend Priam, seemed i' th' air to stick.
So as a painted tyrant Pyrrhus stood,
And, like a neutral to his will and matter,
Did nothing.
But as we often see against some storm
A silence in the heavens, the rack stand still,
The bold winds speechless, and the orb below
As hush as death, anon the dreadful thunder
Doth rend the region, so, after Pyrrhus' pause,
A rousèd vengeance sets him new a-work,
And never did the Cyclops' hammers fall
On Mars's armor forged for proof eterne
With less remorse than Pyrrhus' bleeding sword
Now falls on Priam.
Out, out, thou strumpet Fortune! All you gods
In general synod take away her power!
Break all the spokes and fellies from her wheel,
And bowl the round nave down the hill of heaven
As low as to the fiends!"

**POLONIUS:** This is too long.

**463 o'ersizèd** covered as with size or glue **464 carbuncles** large fiery-red precious stones thought to emit their own light **469 antique** ancient, long-used **471 Repugnant** disobedient, resistant **473 fell** cruel **474 unnervèd** strengthless. **senseless Ilium** inanimate citadel of Troy **476 his** its **478 declining** descending. **milky** white-haired **480 painted** i.e., painted in a picture **481 like . . . matter** i.e., as though suspended between his intention and its fulfillment **483 against** just before **484 rack** mass of clouds **485 orb** globe, earth **487 region** sky **489 Cyclops** giant armor makers in the smithy of Vulcan **490 proof eterne** eternal resistance to assault **491 remorse** pity **494 synod** assembly **495 fellies** pieces of wood forming the rim of a wheel **496 nave** hub. **hill of heaven** Mount Olympus

Hamlet and Polonius discuss the play with the players.

**HAMLET:** It shall to the barber's with your beard.— Prithee, say on. He's for a jig or a tale of bawdry, or he sleeps. Say on; come to Hecuba.

**FIRST PLAYER:** "But who, ah woe! had seen the moblèd queen"—

**HAMLET:** "The moblèd queen"?

**POLONIUS:** That's good. "Moblèd queen" is good.

**FIRST PLAYER:** "Run barefoot up and down, threat'ning the flames
With bisson rheum, a clout upon that head
Where late the diadem stood, and, for a robe,
About her lank and all o'erteemèd loins
A blanket, in the alarm of fear caught up—
Who this had seen, with tongue in venom steeped,
'Gainst Fortune's state would treason have pronounced.
But if the gods themselves did see her then
When she saw Pyrrhus make malicious sport
In mincing with his sword her husband's limbs,
The instant burst of clamor that she made,
Unless things mortal move them not at all,
Would have made milch the burning eyes of heaven,
And passion in the gods."

**POLONIUS:** Look whe'er he has not turned his color and has tears in 's eyes. Prithee, no more.

**500 jig** comic song and dance often given at the end of a play **501 Hecuba** wife of Priam **502 who . . . had** anyone who had (also in line 510). **moblèd** muffled **505 threat'ning the flames** i.e., weeping hard enough to dampen the flames **506 bisson rheum** blinding tears. **clout** cloth **507 late** lately **508 all o'erteemèd** utterly worn out with bearing children **511 state** rule, managing. **pronounced** proclaimed **517 milch** milky, moist with tears. **burning eyes of heaven** i.e., heavenly bodies **518 passion** overpowering emotion **519 whe'er** whether

**HAMLET:** 'Tis well; I'll have thee speak out the rest of this soon.—Good my lord, will you see the players well bestowed? Do you hear, let them be well used, for they are the abstract and brief chronicles of the time. After your death you were better have a bad epitaph than their ill report while you live.

**POLONIUS:** My lord, I will use them according to their desert.

**HAMLET:** God's bodikin, man, much better. Use every man after his desert, and who shall scape whipping? Use them after your own honor and dignity. The less they deserve, the more merit is in your bounty. Take them in.

**POLONIUS:** Come, sirs. *[Exit.]*

**HAMLET:** Follow him, friends. We'll hear a play tomorrow. *[As they start to leave,* HAMLET *detains the* FIRST PLAYER.*]* Dost thou hear me, old friend? Can you play *The Murder of Gonzago?*

**FIRST PLAYER:** Ay, my lord.

**HAMLET:** We'll ha 't tomorrow night. You could, for a need, study a speech of some dozen or sixteen lines which I would set down and insert in 't, could you not?

**FIRST PLAYER:** Ay, my lord.

**HAMLET:** Very well. Follow that lord, and look you mock him not. *(Exeunt* PLAYERS.*)* My good friends, I'll leave you till night. You are welcome to Elsinore.

**ROSENCRANTZ:** Good my lord!

*Exeunt [*ROSENCRANTZ *and* GUILDENSTERN*].*

**HAMLET:** Ay, so, goodbye to you.—Now I am alone.
O, what a rogue and peasant slave am I!
Is it not monstrous that this player here,
But in a fiction, in a dream of passion,
Could force his soul so to his own conceit
That from her working all this visage wanned,
Tears in his eyes, distraction in his aspect,
A broken voice, and his whole function suiting
With forms to his conceit? And all for nothing!
For Hecuba!
What's Hecuba to him, or he to Hecuba,
That he should weep for her? What would he do
Had he the motive and the cue for passion
That I have? He would drown the stage with tears
And cleave the general ear with horrid speech,
Made mad the guilty and appall the free,
Confound the ignorant, and amaze indeed
The very faculties of eyes and ears. Yet I,
A dull and muddy-mettled rascal, peak
Like John-a-dreams, unpregnant of my cause,
And can say nothing—no, not for a king
Upon whose property and most dear life
A damned defeat was made. Am I a coward?
Who calls me villain? Breaks my pate across?
Plucks off my beard and blows it in my face?
Tweaks me by the nose? Gives me the lie i' the throat
As deep as to the lungs? Who does me this?
Ha, 'swounds, I should take it; for it cannot be
But I am pigeon-livered and lack gall
To make oppression bitter, or ere this
I should ha' fatted all the region kites
With this slave's offal. Bloody, bawdy villain!
Remorseless, treacherous, lecherous, kindless villain!
O, vengeance!
Why, what an ass am I! This is most brave,
That I, the son of a dear father murdered,
Prompted to my revenge by heaven and hell,
Must like a whore unpack my heart with words
And fall a-cursing, like a very drab,
A scullion! Fie upon 't, foh! About, my brains!
Hum, I have heard
That guilty creatures sitting at a play
Have by the very cunning of the scene
Been struck so to the soul that presently
They have proclaimed their malefactions;
For murder, though it have no tongue, will speak

---

**523 bestowed** lodged **524 abstract** summary account **529 God's bodikin** by God's (Christ's) little body, *bodykin.* (Not to be confused with *bodkin,* "dagger.") **531 after** according to **540 ha 't** have it **541 study** memorize **552 But** merely **553 force . . . conceit** bring his innermost being so entirely into accord with his conception (of the role) **554 from her working** as a result of, or in response to, his soul's activity. **wanned** grew pale **555 aspect** look, glance **556–557 his whole . . . conceit** all his bodily powers responding with actions to suit his thought

**563 the general ear** everyone's ear. **horrid** horrible **564 appall** (Literally, make pale.) **free** innocent **565 Confound the ignorant** i.e., dumbfound those who know nothing of the crime that has been committed. **amaze** stun **567 muddy-mettled** dull-spirited. **peak** mope, pine **568 John-a-dreams** a sleepy, dreaming idler. **unpregnant of** not quickened by **570 property** i.e., the crown; also character, quality **571 damned defeat** damnable act of destruction **572 pate** head **574 Gives . . . throat** calls me an out-and-out liar **576 'swounds** by his (Christ's) wounds **577 pigeon-livered** (The pigeon or dove was popularly supposed to be mild because it secreted no gall.) **578 bitter** i.e., bitter to me **579 region kites** kites (birds of prey) of the air **580 offal** entrails **581 Remorseless** pitiless. **kindless** unnatural **583 brave** fine, admirable. (Said ironically.) **587 drab** whore **588 scullion** menial kitchen servant (apt to be foul-mouthed). **About** about it, to work **591 cunning** art, skill. **scene** dramatic presentation **592 presently** at once

With most miraculous organ. I'll have these players
Play something like the murder of my father
Before mine uncle. I'll observe his looks;
I'll tent him to the quick. If 'a do blench,
I know my course. The spirit that I have seen
May be the devil, and the devil hath power
T' assume a pleasing shape; yea, and perhaps,
Out of my weakness and my melancholy,
As he is very potent with such spirits,
Abuses me to damn me. I'll have grounds
More relative than this. The play's the thing
Wherein I'll catch the conscience of the King. *Exit.*

**3.1** *Enter* KING, QUEEN, POLONIUS, OPHELIA, ROSENCRANTZ, GUILDENSTERN, *lords.*

**KING:** And can you by no drift of conference
Get from him why he puts on this confusion,
Grating so harshly all his days of quiet
With turbulent and dangerous lunacy?

**ROSENCRANTZ:** He does confess he feels himself distracted,
But from what cause 'a will by no means speak.

**GUILDENSTERN:** Nor do we find him forward to be sounded,
But with a crafty madness keeps aloof
When we would bring him on to some confession
Of his true state.

**QUEEN:** Did he receive you well?

**ROSENCRANTZ:** Most like a gentleman.

**GUILDENSTERN:** But with much forcing of his disposition.

**ROSENCRANTZ:** Niggard of question, but of our demands
Most free in his reply.

**QUEEN:** Did you assay him
To any pastime?

**ROSENCRANTZ:** Madam, it so fell out that certain players
We o'erraught on the way. Of these we told him,
And there did seem in him a kind of joy
To hear of it. They are here about the court,
And, as I think, they have already order
This night to play before him.

**POLONIUS:** 'Tis most true,
And he beseeched me to entreat Your Majesties
To hear and see the matter.

**KING:** With all my heart, and it doth much content me
To hear him so inclined.
Good gentlemen, give him a further edge
And drive his purpose into these delights.

**ROSENCRANTZ:** We shall, my lord.
*Exeunt* ROSENCRANTZ *and* GUILDENSTERN.

**KING:** Sweet Gertrude, leave us too,
For we have closely sent for Hamlet hither,
That he, as 'twere by accident, may here
Affront Ophelia.
Her father and myself, lawful espials,
Will so bestow ourselves that seeing, unseen,
We may of their encounter frankly judge,
And gather by him, as he is behaved,
If 't be th' affliction of his love or no
That thus he suffers for.

**QUEEN:** I shall obey you.
And for your part, Ophelia, I do wish
That your good beauties be the happy cause
Of Hamlet's wildness. So shall I hope your virtues
Will bring him to his wonted way again,
To both your honors.

**OPHELIA:** Madam, I wish it may.
*[Exit* QUEEN.*]*

**POLONIUS:** Ophelia, walk you here.—Gracious, so please you,
We will bestow ourselves. *[To* OPHELIA.*]* Read on this book, *[giving her a book]*
That show of such an exercise may color
Your loneliness. We are oft to blame in this—
'Tis too much proved—that with devotion's visage
And pious action we do sugar o'er
The devil himself.

**KING** *[aside]*: O, 'tis too true!
How smart a lash that speech doth give my conscience!
The harlot's cheek, beautied with plastering art,

---

**598 tent** probe. **the quick** the tender part of a wound, the core. **blench** quail, flinch **603 spirits** humors (of melancholy) **604 Abuses** deludes **605 relative** cogent, pertinent

**3.1. Location: The castle.**
**1 drift of conference** directing of conversation **7 forward** willing. **sounded** questioned **12 disposition** inclination **13 Niggard** stingy. **question** conversation **14 assay** try to win **17 o'erraught** overtook

**26 edge** incitement **29 closely** privately **31 Affront** confront, meet **32 espials** spies **41 wonted** accustomed **43 Gracious** Your Grace (i.e., the King) **44 bestow** conceal **45 exercise** religious exercise. (The book she reads is one of devotion.) **color** give a plausible appearance to **46 loneliness** being alone **47 too much proved** too often shown to be true, too often practiced

Is not more ugly to the thing that helps it
Than is my deed to my most painted word.
O heavy burden!

**POLONIUS:** I hear him coming. Let's withdraw, my lord.

*[The* KING *and* POLONIUS *withdraw.]*

*Enter* HAMLET. *[*OPHELIA *pretends to read a book.]*

**HAMLET:** To be, or not to be, that is the question:
Whether 'tis nobler in the mind to suffer
The slings and arrows of outrageous fortune,
Or to take arms against a sea of troubles
And by opposing end them. To die, to sleep—
No more—and by a sleep to say we end
The heartache and the thousand natural shocks
That flesh is heir to. 'Tis a consummation
Devoutly to be wished. To die, to sleep;
To sleep, perchance to dream. Ay, there's the rub,
For in that sleep of death what dreams may come,
When we have shuffled off this mortal coil,
Must give us pause. There's the respect
That makes calamity of so long life.
For who would bear the whips and scorns of time,
Th' oppressor's wrong, the proud man's contumely,
The pangs of disprized love, the law's delay,
The insolence of office, and the spurns
That patient merit of th' unworthy takes,
When he himself might his quietus make
With a bare bodkin? Who would fardels bear,
To grunt and sweat under a weary life,
But that the dread of something after death,
The undiscovered country from whose bourn
No traveler returns, puzzles the will,
And makes us rather bear those ills we have
Than fly to others that we know not of?
Thus conscience does make cowards of us all;
And thus the native hue of resolution
Is sicklied o'er with the pale cast of thought,
And enterprises of great pitch and moment

**53 to** compared to. **the thing** i.e., the cosmetic **56 s.d. withdraw** (The King and Polonius may retire behind an arras. The stage directions specify that they "enter" again near the end of the scene.) **59 slings** missiles **66 rub** (Literally, an obstacle in the game of bowls.) **68 shuffled** sloughed, cast. **coil** turmoil **69 respect** consideration **70 of . . . life** so long-lived, something we willingly endure for so long (also suggesting that long life is itself a calamity) **72 contumely** insolent abuse **73 disprized** unvalued **74 office** officialdom. **spurns** insults **75 of . . . takes** receives from unworthy persons **76 quietus** acquaintance; here, death **77 a bare bodkin** a mere dagger, unsheathed. **fardels** burdens **80 bourn** frontier, boundary **85 native hue** natural color, complexion **86 cast** tinge, shade of color **87 pitch** height (as of a falcon's flight). **moment** importance

Hamlet (Laurence Olivier) talks with Ophelia (Jean Simmons).

With this regard their currents turn awry
And lose the name of action.—Soft you now,
The fair Ophelia. Nymph, in thy orisons
Be all my sins remembered.

**OPHELIA:** Good my lord,
How does your honor for this many a day?

**HAMLET:** I humbly thank you; well, well, well.

**OPHELIA:** My lord, I have remembrances of yours,
That I have longèd long to redeliver.
I pray you, now receive them. *[She offers tokens.]*

**HAMLET:** No, not I, I never gave you aught.

**OPHELIA:** My honored lord, you know right well you did,
And with them words of so sweet breath composed
As made the things more rich. Their perfume lost,
Take these again, for to the noble mind
Rich gifts wax poor when givers prove unkind.
There, my lord. *[She gives tokens.]*

**HAMLET:** Ha, ha! Are you honest?

**OPHELIA:** My lord?

**HAMLET:** Are you fair?

**OPHELIA:** What means your lordship?

**HAMLET:** That if you be honest and fair, your honesty should admit no discourse to your beauty.

**88 regard** respect, consideration. **currents** courses **89 Soft you** i.e., wait a minute, gently **90 orisons** prayers **104 honest** (1) truthful (2) chaste **106 fair** (1) beautiful (2) just, honorable **108 your honesty** your chastity **109 discourse to** familiar dealings with

**OPHELIA:** Could beauty, my lord, have better commerce than with honesty?

**HAMLET:** Ay, truly, for the power of beauty will sooner transform honesty from what it is to a bawd than the force of honesty can translate beauty into his likeness. This was sometime a paradox, but now the time gives it proof. I did love you once.

**OPHELIA:** Indeed, my lord, you made me believe so.

**HAMLET:** You should not have believed me, for virtue cannot so inoculate our old stock but we shall relish of it. I loved you not.

**OPHELIA:** I was the more deceived.

**HAMLET:** Get thee to a nunnery. Why wouldst thou be a breeder of sinners? I am myself indifferent honest, but yet I could accuse me of such things that it were better my mother had not borne me: I am very proud, revengeful, ambitious, with more offenses at my beck than I have thoughts to put them in, imagination to give them shape, or time to act them in. What should such fellows as I do crawling between earth and heaven? We are arrant knaves all; believe none of us. Go thy ways to a nunnery. Where's your father?

**OPHELIA:** At home, my lord.

**HAMLET:** Let the doors be shut upon him, that he may play the fool nowhere but in 's own house. Farewell.

**OPHELIA:** O, help him, you sweet heavens!

**HAMLET:** If thou dost marry, I'll give thee this plague for thy dowry: be thou as chaste as ice, as pure as snow, thou shalt not escape calumny. Get thee to a nunnery, farewell. Or, if thou wilt needs marry, marry a fool, for wise men know well enough what monsters you make of them. To a nunnery, go, and quickly too. Farewell.

**OPHELIA:** Heavenly powers, restore him!

**HAMLET:** I have heard of your paintings too, well enough. God hath given you one face, and you make yourselves another. You jig, you amble, and you lisp, you nickname God's creatures, and make your wantonness your ignorance. Go to, I'll no more on 't; it hath made me mad. I say we will have no more marriage. Those that are married already—all but one—shall live. The rest shall keep as they are. To a nunnery, go. *Exit.*

Hamlet (Mel Gibson) raves at Ophelia.

**OPHELIA:** O, what a noble mind is here o'erthrown!
The courtier's, soldier's, scholar's, eye, tongue, sword,
Th' expectancy and rose of the fair state,
The glass of fashion and the mold of form,
Th' observed of all observers, quite, quite down!
And I, of ladies most deject and wretched,
That sucked the honey of his music vows,
Now see that noble and most sovereign reason
Like sweet bells jangled out of tune and harsh,
That unmatched form and feature of blown youth
Blasted with ecstasy. O, woe is me,
T' have seen what I have seen, see what I see!

*Enter* KING *and* POLONIUS.

**KING:** Love? His affections do not that way tend;
Nor what he spake, though it lacked form a little,
Was not like madness. There's something in his soul
O'er which his melancholy sits on brood,
And I do doubt the hatch and the disclose

---

**110–111 commerce** dealings, intercourse **114 his** its **115 sometime** formerly. **a paradox** a view opposite to commonly held opinion. **the time** the present age **119 inoculate** graft, be engrafted to **119–120 but . . . it** that we do not still have about us a taste of the old stock, i.e., retain our sinfulness **122 nunnery** convent (with possibly an awareness that the word was also used derisively to denote a brothel) **123–124 indifferent honest** reasonably virtuous **127 beck** command **142 monsters** (An allusion to the horns of a cuckold.) **you** i.e., you women

**147 jig** dance. **amble** move coyly **148 you nickname . . . creatures** i.e., you give trendy names to things in place of their God-given names **148–149 make . . . ignorance** i.e., excuse your affectation on the grounds of pretended ignorance **149 on 't** of it **156 expectancy** hope. **rose** ornament **157 The glass . . . form** the mirror of true self-fashioning and the pattern of courtly behavior **158 Th' observed . . . observers** i.e., the center of attention and honor in the court **160 music** musical, sweetly uttered **163 blown** blooming **164 Blasted** withered. **ecstasy** madness **166 affections** emotions, feelings **169 sits on brood** sits like a bird on a nest, about to *hatch* mischief (line 170) **170 doubt** fear. **disclose** disclosure, hatching

Will be some danger; which for to prevent,
I have in quick determination
Thus set it down: he shall with speed to England
For the demand of our neglected tribute.
Haply the seas and countries different
With variable objects shall expel
This something-settled matter in his heart,
Whereon his brains still beating puts him thus
From fashion of himself. What think you on 't?

**POLONIUS:** It shall do well. But yet do I believe
The origin and commencement of his grief
Sprung from neglected love.—How now, Ophelia?
You need not tell us what Lord Hamlet said;
We heard it all.—My lord, do as you please,
But, if you hold it fit, after the play
Let his queen-mother all alone entreat him
To show his grief. Let her be round with him;
And I'll be placed, so please you, in the ear
Of all their conference. If she find him not,
To England send him, or confine him where
Your wisdom best shall think.

**KING:** It shall be so.
Madness in great ones must not unwatched go.
*Exeunt.*

## 3.2 *Enter* HAMLET *and three of the* PLAYERS.

**HAMLET:** Speak the speech, I pray you, as I pronounced it to you, trippingly on the tongue. But if you mouth it, as many of our players do, I had as lief the town crier spoke my lines. Nor do not saw the air too much with your hand, thus, but use all gently; for in the very torrent, tempest, and, as I may say, whirlwind of your passion, you must acquire and beget a temperance that may give it smoothness. O, it offends me to the soul to hear a robustious periwig-pated fellow tear a passion to tatters, to very rags, to split the ears of the groundlings, who for the most part are capable of nothing but inexplicable dumb shows and noise. I would have such a fellow whipped for o'erdoing Termagant. It out-Herods Herod. Pray you, avoid it.

**FIRST PLAYER:** I warrant your honor.

**HAMLET:** Be not too tame neither, but let your own discretion be your tutor. Suit the action to the word, the word to the action, with this special observance, that you o'erstep not the modesty of nature. For anything so o'erdone is from the purpose of playing, whose end, both at the first and now, was and is to hold as 't were the mirror up to nature, to show virtue her feature, scorn her own image, and the very age and body of the time his form and pressure. Now this overdone or come tardy off, though it makes the unskillful laugh, cannot but make the judicious grieve, the censure of the which one must in your allowance o'erweigh a whole theater of others. O, there be players that I have seen play, and heard others praise, and that highly, not to speak it profanely, that, neither having th' accent of Christians nor the gait of Christian, pagan, nor man, have so strutted and bellowed that I have thought some of nature's journeymen had made men and not made them well, they imitated humanity so abominably.

**FIRST PLAYER:** I hope we have reformed that indifferently with us, sir.

**HAMLET:** O, reform it altogether. And let those that play your clowns speak no more than is set down for them; for there be of them that will themselves laugh, to set on some quantity of barren spectators to laugh too, though in the meantime some necessary question of the play be then to be considered. That's villainous,

---

**173 set it down** resolved **174 For . . . of** to demand **176 variable objects** various sights and surroundings to divert him **177 This something . . . heart** the strange matter settled in his heart **178 still** continually **179 From . . . himself** out of his natural manner **186 queen-mother** queen and mother **187 round** blunt **189 find him not** fails to discover what is troubling him

**3.2. Location: The castle.**
**3 our players** players nowadays. **I had as lief** I would just as soon **9 robustious** violent, boisterous. **periwig-pated** wearing a wig **11 groundlings** spectators who paid least and stood in the yard of the theater **12 capable of** able to understand. **dumb shows** mimed performances, often used before Shakespeare's time to precede a play or each act

**14 Termagant** a supposed deity of the Mohammedans, not found in any English medieval play but elsewhere portrayed as violent and blustering **14 Herod** Herod of Jewry. (A character in *The Slaughter of the Innocents* and other cycle plays. The part was played with great noise and fury.) **20 modesty** restraint, moderation **21 from** contrary to **24 scorn** i.e., something foolish and deserving of scorn **24–25 the very . . . time** i.e., the present state of affairs **25 his** its. **pressure** stamp, impressed character **26 come tardy off** inadequately done **27 the unskillful** those lacking in judgment **28 the censure . . . one** the judgment of even one of whom **28–29 your allowance** your scale of values **31 not . . . profanely** (Hamlet anticipates his idea in lines 34–35 that some men were not made by God at all.) **32 Christians** i.e., ordinary decent folk **33 nor man** i.e., nor any human being at all **35 journeymen** laborers who are not yet masters in their trade **36 abominably** (Shakespeare's usual spelling, *abhominably,* suggests a literal though etymologically incorrect meaning, "removed from human nature.") **37–38 indifferently** tolerably **41 of them** some among them **42 barren** i.e., of wit

Hamlet coaches the First Player (Ben Thom).

and shows a most pitiful ambition in the fool that uses it. Go make you ready. *[Exeunt* PLAYERS.*]*

*Enter* POLONIUS, GUILDENSTERN, *and* ROSENCRANTZ.

How now, my lord, will the King hear this piece of work?

**POLONIUS:** And the Queen too, and that presently.

**HAMLET:** Bid the players make haste. *[Exit* POLONIUS.*]*
Will you two help to hasten them?

**ROSENCRANTZ:** Ay, my lord. *[Exeunt they two.]*

**HAMLET:** What ho, Horatio!

*Enter* HORATIO.

**HORATIO:** Here, sweet lord, at your service.

**HAMLET:** Horatio, thou art e'en as just a man
As e'er my conversation coped withal.

**HORATIO:** O, my dear lord—

**HAMLET:** Nay, do not think I flatter,
For what advancement may I hope from thee
That no revenue hast but thy good spirits
To feed and clothe thee? Why should the poor be flattered?
No, let the candied tongue lick absurd pomp,
And crook the pregnant hinges of the knee
Where thrift may follow fawning. Dost thou hear?
Since my dear soul was mistress of her choice
And could of men distinguish her election,
Sh' hath sealed thee for herself, for thou hast been
As one, in suffering all, that suffers nothing,
A man that Fortune's buffets and rewards
Hast ta'en with equal thanks; and blest are those
Whose blood and judgment are so well commeddled
That they are not a pipe for Fortune's finger
To sound what stop she please. Give me that man
That is not passion's slave, and I will wear him
In my heart's core, ay, in my heart of heart,
As I do thee.—Something too much of this.—
There is a play tonight before the King.
One scene of it comes near the circumstance
Which I have told thee of my father's death.
I prithee, when thou seest that act afoot,
Even with the very comment of thy soul
Observe my uncle. If his occulted guilt
Do not itself unkennel in one speech,
It is a damnèd ghost that we have seen,
And my imaginations are as foul
As Vulcan's stithy. Give him heedful note,
For I mine eyes will rivet to his face,
And after we will both our judgments join
In censure of his seeming.

**HORATIO:** Well, my lord.
If 'a steal aught the whilst this play is playing
And scape detecting, I will pay the theft.

*[Flourish.] Enter trumpets and kettledrums,* KING, QUEEN, POLONIUS, OPHELIA, *[*ROSENCRANTZ, GUILDENSTERN, *and other lords, with guards carrying torches].*

**HAMLET:** They are coming to the play. I must be idle.
Get you a place. *[The* KING, QUEEN, *and courtiers sit.]*

**KING:** How fares our cousin Hamlet?

**HAMLET:** Excellent i' faith, of the chameleon's dish: I eat the air, promise-crammed. You cannot feed capons so.

**KING:** I have nothing with this answer, Hamlet. These words are not mine.

---

**48 presently** at once **54 my . . . withal** my dealings encountered **59 candied** sugared, flattering **60 pregnant** compliant **61 thrift** profit **63 could . . . election** could make distinguishing choices among persons **64 sealed thee** (Literally, as one would seal a legal document to mark possession.)

**68 blood** passion. **commeddled** commingled **70 stop** hole in a wind instrument for controlling the sound **78 very . . . soul** your most penetrating observation and consideration **79 occulted** hidden **80 unkennel** (As one would say of a fox driven from its lair.) **81 damnèd** in league with Satan **83 stithy** smithy, place of stiths (anvils) **86 censure of his seeming** judgment of his appearance or behavior **87 If 'a steal aught** if he gets away with anything **89 idle** (1) unoccupied (2) mad **91 cousin** i.e., close relative **92 chameleon's dish** (Chameleons were supposed to feed on air. Hamlet deliberately misinterprets the King's *fares* as "feeds." By his phrase *eat the air* he also plays on the idea of feeding himself with the promise of succession, of being the *heir.*) **93 capons** roosters castrated and *crammed* with feed to make them succulent **94 have . . . with** make nothing of, or gain nothing from **95 are not mine** do not respond to what I asked

**HAMLET:** No, nor mine now. *[To* POLONIUS.*]* My lord, you played once i' th' university, you say?

**POLONIUS:** That did I, my lord, and was accounted a good actor.

**HAMLET:** What did you enact?

**POLONIUS:** I did enact Julius Caesar. I was killed i' the Capitol; Brutus killed me.

**HAMLET:** It was a brute part of him to kill so capital a calf there.—Be the players ready?

**ROSENCRANTZ:** Ay, my lord. They stay upon your patience.

**QUEEN:** Come hither, my dear Hamlet, sit by me.

**HAMLET:** No, good Mother, here's metal more attractive.

**POLONIUS** *[to the* KING*]*: O, ho, do you mark that?

**HAMLET:** Lady, shall I lie in your lap?

*[Lying down at* OPHELIA's *feet.]*

**OPHELIA:** No, my lord.

**HAMLET:** I mean, my head upon your lap?

**OPHELIA:** Ay, my lord.

**HAMLET:** Do you think I meant country matters?

**OPHELIA:** I think nothing, my lord.

**HAMLET:** That's a fair thought to lie between maids' legs.

**OPHELIA:** What is, my lord?

**HAMLET:** Nothing.

**OPHELIA:** You are merry, my lord.

**HAMLET:** Who, I?

**OPHELIA:** Ay, my lord.

**HAMLET:** O God, your only jig maker. What should a man do but be merry? For look you how cheerfully my mother looks, and my father died within 's two hours.

**OPHELIA:** Nay, 'tis twice two months, my lord.

**HAMLET:** So long? Nay then, let the devil wear black, for I'll have a suit of sables. O heavens! Die two months ago, and not forgotten yet? Then there's hope a great man's memory may outlive his life half a year. But, by 'r Lady, 'a must build churches, then, or else shall 'a suffer not thinking on, with the hobbyhorse, whose epitaph is "For O, for O, the hobbyhorse is forgot."

*The trumpets sound. Dumb show follows.*

*Enter a* KING *and a* QUEEN *[very lovingly]; the* QUEEN *embracing him, and he her. [She kneels, and makes show of protestation unto him.] He takes her up, and declines his head upon her neck. He lies him down upon a bank of flowers. She, seeing him asleep, leaves him. Anon comes in another man, takes off his crown, kisses it, pours poison in the sleeper's ears, and leaves him. The* QUEEN *returns, finds the* KING *dead, makes passionate action. The Poisoner with some three or four come in again, seem to condole with her. The dead body is carried away. The Poisoner woos the* QUEEN *with gifts; she seems harsh awhile, but in the end accepts love.*

*[Exeunt* PLAYERS.*]*

**OPHELIA:** What means this, my lord?

**HAMLET:** Marry, this' miching mallico; it means mischief.

**OPHELIA:** Belike this show imports the argument of the play.

*Enter* PROLOGUE.

**HAMLET:** We shall know by this fellow. The players cannot keep counsel; they'll tell all.

**OPHELIA:** Will 'a tell us what this show meant?

---

**96 nor mine now** (Once spoken, words are proverbially no longer the speaker's own—and hence should be uttered warily.) **103 brute** (The Latin meaning of *brutus,* "stupid," was often used punningly with the name Brutus.) **part** (1) deed (2) role **104 calf** fool **105 stay upon** await **108 metal** substance that is *attractive,* i.e., magnetic, but with suggestion also of *mettle,* "disposition" **114 country matters** sexual intercourse (making a bawdy pun on the first syllable of *country)* **119 Nothing** the figure zero or naught, suggesting the female sexual anatomy. (*Thing* not infrequently has a bawdy connotation of male or female anatomy, and the reference here could be male.)

**123 only jig maker** very best composer of jigs, i.e., pointless merriment. (Hamlet replies sardonically to Ophelia's observation that he is merry by saying, "If you're looking for someone who is really merry, you've come to the right person.") **125 within 's** within this (i.e., these) **128 suit of sables** garments trimmed with the fur of the sable and hence suited for a wealthy person, not a mourner (but with a pun on *sable,* "black," ironically suggesting mourning once again) **132 suffer . . . on** undergo oblivion **133 For . . . forgot** (Verse of a song occurring also in *Love's Labor's Lost,* 3.1.27–28. The hobbyhorse was a character made up to resemble a horse and rider, appearing in the morris dance and such May-game sports. This song laments the disappearance of such customs under pressure from the Puritans.) **135 this' miching mallico** this is sneaking mischief **137 Belike** probably. **argument** plot **140 counsel** secret

**HAMLET:** Ay, or any show that you will show him. Be not you ashamed to show, he'll not shame to tell you what it means.

**OPHELIA:** You are naught, you are naught. I'll mark the play.

**PROLOGUE:** For us, and for our tragedy,
Here stooping to your clemency,
We beg your hearing patiently. *[Exit.]*

**HAMLET:** Is this a prologue, or the posy of a ring?

**OPHELIA:** 'Tis brief, my lord.

**HAMLET:** As woman's love.

*Enter [two* PLAYERS *as]* KING *and* QUEEN.

**PLAYER KING:** Full thirty times hath Phoebus' cart gone round
Neptune's salt wash and Tellus' orbèd ground,
And thirty dozen moons with borrowed sheen
About the world have times twelve thirties been,
Since love our hearts and Hymen did our hands
Unite commutual in most sacred bands.

**PLAYER QUEEN:** So many journeys may the sun and moon
Make us again count o'er ere love be done!
But, woe is me, you are so sick of late,
So far from cheer and from your former state,
That I distrust you. Yet, though I distrust,
Discomfort you, my lord, it nothing must.
For women's fear and love hold quantity;
In neither aught, or in extremity.
Now, what my love is, proof hath made you know,
And as my love is sized, my fear is so.
Where love is great, the littlest doubts are fear;
Where little fears grow great, great love grows there.

**PLAYER KING:** Faith, I must leave thee, love, and shortly too;
My operant powers their functions leave to do.
And thou shalt live in this fair world behind,
Honored, beloved; and haply one as kind
For husband shalt thou—

**PLAYER QUEEN:** O, confound the rest!
Such love must needs be treason in my breast.
In second husband let me be accurst!
None wed the second but who killed the first.

**HAMLET:** Wormwood, wormwood.

**PLAYER QUEEN:** The instances that second marriage move
Are base respects of thrift, but none of love.
A second time I kill my husband dead
When second husband kisses me in bed.

**PLAYER KING:** I do believe you think what now you speak,
But what we do determine oft we break.
Purpose is but the slave to memory,
Of violent birth, but poor validity,
Which now, like fruit unripe, sticks on the tree,
But fall unshaken when they mellow be.
Most necessary 'tis that we forget
To pay ourselves what to ourselves is debt.
What to ourselves in passion we propose,
The passion ending, doth the purpose lose.
The violence of either grief or joy
Their own enactures with themselves destroy.
Where joy most revels, grief doth most lament;
Grief joys, joy grieves, on slender accident.
This world is not for aye, nor 'tis not strange
That even our loves should with our fortunes change;
For 'tis a question left us yet to prove,
Whether love lead fortune, or else fortune love.
The great man down, you mark his favorite flies;
The poor advanced makes friends of enemies.
And hitherto doth love on fortune tend;

---

**142–143 Be not you** provided you are not **145 naught** indecent. (Ophelia is reacting to Hamlet's pointed remarks about not being ashamed to show all.) **148 stooping** bowing **150 posy . . . ring** brief motto in verse inscribed in a ring **153 Phoebus' cart** the sun-god's chariot, making its yearly cycle **154 salt wash** the sea. **Tellus** goddess of the earth, of the *orbèd ground* **155 borrowed** i.e., reflected **157 Hymen** god of matrimony **158 commutual** mutually. **bands** bonds **163 distrust** am anxious about **164 Discomfort** distress. **nothing** not at all **165 hold quantity** keep proportion with one another **166 In . . . extremity** i.e., women fear and love either too little or too much, but the two, fear and love, are equal in either case **167 proof** experience **168 sized** in size **172 operant powers** vital functions. **leave to do** cease to perform

**173 behind** after I have gone **178 None** i.e., let no woman. **but who** except the one who **179 Wormwood** i.e., how bitter. (Literally, a bitter-tasting plant.) **180 instances** motives. **move** motivate **181 base . . . thrift** ignoble considerations of material prosperity **186 Purpose . . . memory** our good intentions are subject to forgetfulness **187 validity** strength, durability **188 Which** i.e., purpose **190–191 Most . . . debt** it's inevitable that in time we forget the obligations we have imposed on ourselves **195 enactures** fulfillments **196–197 Where . . . accident** the capacity for extreme joy and grief go together, and often one extreme is instantly changed into its opposite on the slightest provocation **198 aye** ever **202 down** fallen in fortune **203 The poor . . . enemies** when one of humble station is promoted, you see his enemies suddenly becoming his friends **204 hitherto** up to this point in the argument, or, to this extent. **tend** attend

The players perform Hamlet's play.

For who not needs shall never lack a friend,
And who in want a hollow friend doth try
Directly seasons him his enemy.
But, orderly to end where I begun,
Our wills and fates do so contrary run
That our devices still are overthrown;
Our thoughts are ours, their ends none of our own.
So think thou wilt no second husband wed,
But die thy thoughts when thy first lord is dead.

**PLAYER QUEEN:** Nor earth to me give food, nor heaven light,
Sport and repose lock from me day and night,
To desperation turn my trust and hope,
An anchor's cheer in prison be my scope!
Each opposite that blanks the face of joy
Meet what I would have well and it destroy!
Both here and hence pursue me lasting strife
If, once a widow, ever I be wife!

**HAMLET:** If she should break it now!

**PLAYER KING:** 'Tis deeply sworn. Sweet, leave me here awhile;
My spirits grow dull, and fain I would beguile
The tedious day with sleep.

**PLAYER QUEEN:** Sleep rock thy brain,
And never come mischance between us twain!

*[He sleeps.] Exit [*PLAYER QUEEN*].*

**HAMLET:** Madam, how like you this play?

**QUEEN:** The lady doth protest too much, methinks.

**HAMLET:** O, but she'll keep her word.

**KING:** Have you heard the argument? Is there no offense in 't?

**HAMLET:** No, no, they do but jest, poison in jest. No offense i' the world.

**KING:** What do you call the play?

**HAMLET:** *The Mousetrap.* Marry, how? Tropically. This play is the image of a murder done in Vienna. Gonzago is the Duke's name, his wife, Baptista. You shall see anon. 'Tis a knavish piece of work, but what of that? Your Majesty, and we that have free souls, it touches us not. Let the galled jade wince, our withers are unwrung.

*Enter* LUCIANUS.

This is one Lucianus, nephew to the King.

**OPHELIA:** You are as good as a chorus, my lord.

**HAMLET:** I could interpret between you and your love, if I could see the puppets dallying.

**OPHELIA:** You are keen, my lord, you are keen.

**HAMLET:** It would cost you a groaning to take off mine edge.

**OPHELIA:** Still better, and worse.

**HAMLET:** So you mis-take your husbands. Begin, murderer; leave thy damnable faces and begin. Come, the croaking raven doth bellow for revenge.

---

**205 who not needs** he who is not in need (of wealth) **206 who in want** he who, being in need. **try** test (his generosity) **207 seasons him** ripens him into **209 Our . . . run** what we want and what we get go so contrarily **210 devices still** intentions continually **211 ends** results **214 Nor** let neither **215 Sport . . . night** may day deny me its pastimes and night its repose **217 anchor's cheer** anchorite's or hermit's fare. **my scope** the extent of my happiness **218–219 Each . . . destroy** may every adverse thing that causes the face of joy to turn pale meet and destroy everything that I desire to see prosper. **blanks** causes to blanch or grow pale **220 hence** in the life hereafter **224 spirits** vital spirits

**228 doth . . . much** makes too many promises and protestations **230 argument** plot **231–233 offense . . . offense** cause for objection . . . actual injury, crime **232 jest** make believe **235 Tropically** figuratively. (The First Quarto reading, *trapically,* suggests a pun on *trap* in *Mousetrap.*) **237 Duke's** i.e., King's. (A slip that may be due to Shakespeare's possible source, the alleged murder of the Duke of Urbino by Luigi Gonzaga in 1538.) **239 free** guiltless **240 galled jade** horse whose hide is rubbed by saddle or harness **240–241 withers** the part between the horse's shoulder blades **241 unwrung** not rubbed sore **243 chorus** (In many Elizabethan plays, the forthcoming action was explained by an actor known as the "chorus"; at a puppet show, the actor who spoke the dialogue was known as an "interpreter," as indicated by the lines following.) **244 interpret** (1) ventriloquize the dialogue, as in a puppet show (2) act as pander **245 puppets dallying** (With suggestion of sexual play, continued in *keen,* "sexually aroused," *groaning,* "moaning in pregnancy," and *edge,* "sexual desire" or "impetuosity.") **246 keen** sharp, bitter **249 Still . . . worse** more keen, always *bettering* what other people say with witty wordplay, but at the same time more offensive **250 So** even thus (in marriage). **mis-take** take falseheartedly and cheat on. (The marriage vows say "for better, for worse.")

**LUCIANUS:** Thoughts black, hands apt, drugs fit, and time agreeing,
Confederate season, else no creature seeing,
Thou mixture rank, of midnight weeds collected,
With Hecate's ban thrice blasted, thrice infected,
Thy natural magic and dire property
On wholesome life usurp immediately.
*[He pours the poison into the sleeper's ear.]*

**HAMLET:** 'A poisons him i' the garden for his estate. His name's Gonzago. The story is extant, and written in very choice Italian. You shall see anon how the murderer gets the love of Gonzago's wife.
*[*CLAUDIUS *rises.]*

**OPHELIA:** The King rises.

**HAMLET:** What, frighted with false fire?

**QUEEN:** How fares my lord?

**POLONIUS:** Give o'er the play.

**KING:** Give me some light. Away!

**POLONIUS:** Lights, lights, lights!
*Exeunt all but* HAMLET *and* HORATIO.

**HAMLET:**
"Why, let the stricken deer go weep,
The hart ungallèd play.
For some must watch, while some must sleep;
Thus runs the world away."
Would not this, sir, and a forest of feathers—if the rest of my fortunes turn Turk with me—with two Provincial roses on my razed shoes, get me a fellowship in a cry of players?

**HORATIO:** Half a share.

Hamlet and Horatio (Stephen Dillane) discuss the result of their scheme.

**HAMLET:** A whole one, I.
"For thou dost know, O Damon dear,
This realm dismantled was
Of Jove himself, and now reigns here
A very, very—pajock."

**HORATIO:** You might have rhymed.

**HAMLET:** O good Horatio, I'll take the ghost's word for a thousand pound. Didst perceive?

**HORATIO:** Very well, my lord.

**HAMLET:** Upon the talk of the poisoning?

**HORATIO:** I did very well note him.

*Enter* ROSENCRANTZ *and* GUILDENSTERN.

**HAMLET:** Aha! Come, some music! Come, the recorders.
"For if the King like not the comedy,
Why then, belike, he likes it not, perdy."
Come, some music.

**GUILDENSTERN:** Good my lord, vouchsafe me a word with you.

**HAMLET:** Sir, a whole history.

**GUILDENSTERN:** The King, sir—

---

**254 Confederate season** the time and occasion conspiring (to assist the murderer). **else** otherwise. **seeing** seeing me **256 Hecate's ban** the curse of Hecate, the goddess of witchcraft **257 dire property** baleful quality **259 estate** i.e., the kingship **260 His** i.e., the King's **264 false fire** the blank discharge of a gun loaded with powder but no shot **269–272 Why . . . away** (Probably from an old ballad, with allusion to the popular belief that a wounded deer retires to weep and die; compare with *As You Like It,* 2.1.33–66.) **270 ungallèd** unafflicted **271 watch** remain awake **272 Thus . . . away** thus the world goes **273 this** i.e., the play. **feathers** (Allusion to the plumes that Elizabethan actors were fond of wearing.) **274 turn Turk with** turn renegade against, go back on **275 Provincial roses** rosettes of ribbon, named for roses grown in a part of France. **razed** with ornamental slashing **275–276 fellowship . . . players** partnership in a theatrical company **276 cry** pack (of hounds)

---

**279 Damon** the friend of Pythias, as Horatio is friend of Hamlet; or, a traditional pastoral name **280–282 This realm . . . pajock** i.e., Jove, representing divine authority and justice, has abandoned this realm to its own devices, leaving in his stead only a peacock or vain pretender to virtue (though the rhyme-word expected in place of *pajock* or "peacock" suggests that the realm is now ruled over by an "ass"). **280 dismantled** stripped, divested **290 recorders** wind instruments of the flute kind **292 perdy** (A corruption of the French *par dieu,* "by God.")

**HAMLET:** Ay, sir, what of him?

**GUILDENSTERN:** Is in his retirement marvelous distempered.

**HAMLET:** With drink, sir?

**GUILDENSTERN:** No, my lord, with choler.

**HAMLET:** Your wisdom should show itself more richer to signify this to the doctor, for for me to put him to his purgation would perhaps plunge him into more choler.

**GUILDENSTERN:** Good my lord, put your discourse into some frame and start not so wildly from my affair.

**HAMLET:** I am tame, sir. Pronounce.

**GUILDENSTERN:** The Queen, your mother, in most great affliction of spirit, hath sent me to you.

**HAMLET:** You are welcome.

**GUILDENSTERN:** Nay, good my lord, this courtesy is not of the right breed. If it shall please you to make me a wholesome answer, I will do your mother's commandment; if not, your pardon and my return shall be the end of my business.

**HAMLET:** Sir, I cannot.

**ROSENCRANTZ:** What, my lord?

**HAMLET:** Make you a wholesome answer; my wit's diseased. But, sir, such answer as I can make, you shall command, or rather, as you say, my mother. Therefore no more, but to the matter. My mother, you say—

**ROSENCRANTZ:** Then thus she says: your behavior hath struck her into amazement and admiration.

**HAMLET:** O wonderful son, that can so stonish a mother! But is there no sequel at the heels of this mother's admiration? Impart.

**ROSENCRANTZ:** She desires to speak with you in her closet ere you go to bed.

**HAMLET:** We shall obey, were she ten times our mother. Have you any further trade with us?

**ROSENCRANTZ:** My lord, you once did love me.

**HAMLET:** And do still, by these pickers and stealers.

**ROSENCRANTZ:** Good my lord, what is your cause of distemper? You do surely bar the door upon your own liberty if you deny your griefs to your friend.

**HAMLET:** Sir, I lack advancement.

**ROSENCRANTZ:** How can that be, when you have the voice of the King himself for your succession in Denmark?

**HAMLET:** Ay, sir, but "While the grass grows"—the proverb is something musty.

*Enter the* PLAYERS *with recorders.*

O, the recorders. Let me see one. *[He takes a recorder.]* To withdraw with you: why do you go about to recover the wind of me, as if you would drive me into a toil?

**GUILDENSTERN:** O, my lord, if my duty be too bold, my love is too unmannerly.

**HAMLET:** I do not well understand that. Will you play upon this pipe?

**GUILDENSTERN:** My lord, I cannot.

**HAMLET:** I pray you.

**GUILDENSTERN:** Believe me, I cannot.

**HAMLET:** I do beseech you.

**GUILDENSTERN:** I know no touch of it, my lord.

**HAMLET:** It is as easy as lying. Govern these ventages with your fingers and thumb, give it breath with your mouth, and it will discourse most eloquent music. Look you, these are the stops.

---

**299 retirement** withdrawal to his chambers **300 distempered** out of humor. (But Hamlet deliberately plays on the wider application to any illness of mind or body, as in lines 335–336, especially to drunkenness.) **302 choler** anger. (But Hamlet takes the word in its more basic humoral sense of "bilious disorder.") **305 purgation** (Hamlet hints at something going beyond medical treatment to blood-letting and the extraction of confession.) **308 frame** order. **start** shy or jump away (like a horse; the opposite of *tame* in line 309) **314 breed** (1) kind (2) breeding, manners **316 pardon** permission to depart **325 admiration** bewilderment **330 closet** private chamber

**334 pickers and stealers** i.e., hands. (So called from the catechism, "to keep my hands from picking and stealing.") **337 liberty** i.e., being freed from *distemper* (line 336); but perhaps with a veiled threat as well. **deny** refuse to share **342 While . . . grows** (The rest of the proverb is "the silly horse starves"; Hamlet may not live long enough to succeed to the kingdom.) **343 something** somewhat. **s.d. Players** actors **345 withdraw** speak privately **345–346 recover the wind** get to the windward side (thus driving the game into the *toil,* or "net") **346 toil** snare **347–348 if . . . unmannerly** if I am using an unmannerly boldness, it is my love that occasions it **349 I . . . that** i.e., I don't understand how genuine love can be unmannerly **356 ventages** finger-holes or *stops* (line 359) of the recorder

**GUILDENSTERN:** But these cannot I command to any utterance of harmony. I have not the skill.

**HAMLET:** Why, look you now, how unworthy a thing you make of me! You would play upon me, you would seem to know my stops, you would pluck out the heart of my mystery, you would sound me from my lowest note to the top of my compass, and there is much music, excellent voice, in this little organ, yet cannot you make it speak. 'Sblood, do you think I am easier to be played on than a pipe? Call me what instrument you will, though you can fret me, you cannot play upon me.

*Enter* POLONIUS.

God bless you, sir!

**POLONIUS:** My lord, the Queen would speak with you, and presently.

**HAMLET:** Do you see yonder cloud that's almost in shape of a camel?

**POLONIUS:** By the Mass and 'tis, like a camel indeed.

**HAMLET:** Methinks it is like a weasel.

**POLONIUS:** It is backed like a weasel.

**HAMLET:** Or like a whale.

**POLONIUS:** Very like a whale.

**HAMLET:** Then I will come to my mother by and by. *[Aside.]* They fool me to the top of my bent.—I will come by and by.

**POLONIUS:** I will say so. *[Exit.]*

**HAMLET:** "By and by" is easily said. Leave me, friends.
*[Exeunt all but* HAMLET.*]*
'Tis now the very witching time of night,
When churchyards yawn and hell itself breathes out
Contagion to this world. Now could I drink hot blood
And do such bitter business as the day
Would quake to look on. Soft, now to my mother.
O heart, lose not thy nature! Let not ever
The soul of Nero enter this firm bosom.
Let me be cruel, not unnatural;
I will speak daggers to her, but use none.
My tongue and soul in this be hypocrites:
How in my words soever she be shent,
To give them seals never my soul consent! *Exit.*

## 3.3 *Enter* KING, ROSENCRANTZ, *and* GUILDENSTERN.

**KING:** I like him not, nor stands it safe with us
To let his madness range. Therefore prepare you.
I your commission will forthwith dispatch,
And he to England shall along with you.
The terms of our estate may not endure
Hazard so near 's as doth hourly grow
Out of his brows.

**GUILDENSTERN:** We will ourselves provide.
Most holy and religious fear it is
To keep those many many bodies safe
That live and feed upon Your Majesty.

**ROSENCRANTZ:** The single and peculiar life is bound
With all the strength and armor of the mind
To keep itself from noyance, but much more
That spirit upon whose weal depends and rests
The lives of many. The cess of majesty
Dies not alone, but like a gulf doth draw
What's near it with it; or it is a massy wheel
Fixed on the summit of the highest mount,
To whose huge spokes ten thousand lesser things
Are mortised and adjoined, which, when it falls,
Each small annexment, petty consequence,
Attends the boisterous ruin. Never alone
Did the King sigh, but with a general groan.

**KING:** Arm you, I pray you, to this speedy voyage,
For we will fetters put about this fear,
Which now goes too free-footed.

**ROSENCRANTZ:** We will haste us.
*Exeunt gentlemen [*ROSENCRANTZ *and* GUILDENSTERN*].*

*Enter* POLONIUS.

---

**365 sound** (1) fathom (2) produce sound in **366 compass** range (of voice) **367 organ** musical instrument **370 fret** irritate (with a quibble on *fret,* meaning the piece of wood, gut, or metal that regulates the fingering on an instrument) **374 presently** at once **382 by and by** quite soon **383 fool me** trifle with me, humor my fooling. **top of my bent** limit of my ability or endurance. (Literally, the extent to which a bow may be bent.) **387 witching time** time when spells are cast and evil is abroad **392 nature** natural feeling **393 Nero** murderer of his mother, Agrippina

**397 How . . . soever** however much by my words. **shent** rebuked **398 give them seals** i.e., confirm them with deeds

**3.3. Location: The castle.**
**1 him** i.e., his behavior **3 dispatch** prepare, cause to be drawn up **5 terms of our estate** circumstances of my royal position **7 Out of his brows** i.e., from his brain, in the form of plots and threats **8 religious fear** sacred concern **11 single and peculiar** individual and private **13 noyance** harm **15 cess** decease, cessation **16 gulf** whirlpool **17 massy** massive **20 mortised** fastened (as with a fitted joint). **when it falls** i.e., when it descends, like the wheel of Fortune, bringing a king down with it **21 Each . . . consequence** i.e., every hanger-on and unimportant person or thing connected with the King **22 Attends** participates in **24 Arm** prepare

**POLONIUS:** My lord, he's going to his mother's closet.
Behind the arras I'll convey myself
To hear the process. I'll warrant she'll tax him home,
And, as you said—and wisely was it said—
'Tis meet that some more audience than a mother,
Since nature makes them partial, should o'erhear
The speech, of vantage. Fare you well, my liege.
I'll call upon you ere you go to bed
And tell you what I know.

**KING:** Thanks, dear my lord.

*Exit* [POLONIUS].

O, my offense is rank! It smells to heaven.
It hath the primal eldest curse upon 't,
A brother's murder. Pray can I not,
Though inclination be as sharp as will;
My stronger guilt defeats my strong intent,
And like a man to double business bound
I stand in pause where I shall first begin,
And both neglect. What if this cursèd hand
Were thicker than itself with brother's blood,
Is there not rain enough in the sweet heavens
To wash it white as snow? Whereto serves mercy
But to confront the visage of offense?
And what's in prayer but this twofold force,
To be forestallèd ere we come to fall,
Or pardoned being down? Then I'll look up.
My fault is past. But O, what form of prayer
Can serve my turn? "Forgive me my foul murder"?
That cannot be, since I am still possessed
Of those effects for which I did the murder:
My crown, mine own ambition, and my queen.
May one be pardoned and retain th' offense?
In the corrupted currents of this world
Offense's gilded hand may shove by justice,
And oft 'tis seen the wicked prize itself
Buys out the law. But 'tis not so above.
There is no shuffling, there the action lies

Hamlet sits armed in the confessional. Claudius prays, but he hesitates.

In his true nature, and we ourselves compelled,
Even to the teeth and forehead of our faults,
To give in evidence. What then? What rests?
Try what repentance can. What can it not?
Yet what can it, when one cannot repent?
O wretched state, O bosom black as death,
O limèd soul that, struggling to be free,
Art more engaged! Help, angels! Make assay.
Bow, stubborn knees, and heart with strings of steel,
Be soft as sinews of the newborn babe!
All may be well. *[He kneels.]*

*Enter* HAMLET.

**HAMLET:** Now might I do it pat, now 'a is a-praying;
And now I'll do 't. *[He draws his sword.]* And so 'a goes
to heaven,
And so am I revenged. That would be scanned:
A villain kills my father, and for that,
I, his sole son, do this same villain send
To heaven.
Why, this is hire and salary, not revenge.
'A took my father grossly, full of bread,
With all his crimes broad blown, as flush as May;
And how his audit stands who knows save heaven?
But in our circumstance and course of thought
'Tis heavy with him. And am I then revenged,

---

**28 arras** screen of tapestry placed around the walls of household apartments. (On the Elizabethan stage, the arras was presumably over a door or discovery space in the tiring-house facade.) **29 process** proceedings. **tax him home** reprove him severely **31 meet** fitting **33 of vantage** from an advantageous place, or, in addition **37 the primal eldest curse** the curse of Cain, the first murderer; he killed his brother Abel **39 Though . . . will** though my desire is as strong as my determination **41 bound** (1) destined (2) obliged. (The King wants to repent and still enjoy what he has gained.) **46–47 Whereto . . . offense** what function does mercy serve other than to meet sin face to face? **49 forestallèd** prevented (from sinning) **56 th' offense** the thing for which one offended **57 currents** courses **58 gilded hand** hand offering gold as a bribe. **shove by** thrust aside **59 wicked prize** prize won by wickedness **61 There** i.e., in heaven. **shuffling** escape by trickery. **the action lies** the accusation is made manifest. (A legal metaphor.)

**62 his** its **63 to the teeth and forehead** face to face, concealing nothing **64 give in** provide. **rests** remains **68 limèd** caught as with birdlime, a sticky substance used to ensnare birds **69 engaged** entangled. **assay** trial. (Said to himself.) **73 pat** opportunely **75 would be scanned** needs to be looked into, or, would be interpreted as follows **80 grossly, full of bread** i.e., enjoying his worldly pleasures rather than fasting. (See Ezekiel 16:49.) **81 crimes broad blown** sins in full bloom. **flush** vigorous **82 audit** account. **save** except for **83 in . . . thought** as we see it from our mortal perspective

To take him in the purging of his soul,
When he is fit and seasoned for his passage?
No!
Up, sword, and know thou a more horrid hent.
*[He puts up his sword.]*
When he is drunk asleep, or in his rage,
Or in th' incestuous pleasure of his bed,
At game, a-swearing, or about some act
That has no relish of salvation in 't—
Then trip him, that his heels may kick at heaven,
And that his soul may be as damned and black
As hell, whereto it goes. My mother stays.
This physic but prolongs thy sickly days. *Exit.*

**KING:** My words fly up, my thoughts remain below.
Words without thoughts never to heaven go. *Exit.*

## 3.4 *Enter* [QUEEN] GERTRUDE *and* POLONIUS.

**POLONIUS:** 'A will come straight. Look you lay home to him.
Tell him his pranks have been too broad to bear with,
And that Your Grace hath screened and stood between
Much heat and him. I'll shroud me even here.
Pray you be round with him.

**HAMLET** *(within)*: Mother, Mother, Mother!

**QUEEN:** I'll warrant you, fear me not.
Withdraw, I hear him coming.
*[POLONIUS hides behind the arras.]*

*Enter* HAMLET.

**HAMLET:** Now, Mother, what's the matter?

**QUEEN:** Hamlet, thou hast thy father much offended.

**HAMLET:** Mother, you have my father much offended.

**QUEEN:** Come, come, you answer with an idle tongue.

**HAMLET:** Go, go, you question with a wicked tongue.

**QUEEN:** Why, how now, Hamlet?

**HAMLET:** What's the matter now?

**QUEEN:** Have you forgot me?

**HAMLET:** No, by the rood, not so:
You are the Queen, your husband's brother's wife,
And—would it were not so!—you are my mother.

**QUEEN:** Nay, then, I'll set those to you that can speak.

**HAMLET:** Come, come, and sit you down; you shall not budge.
You go not till I set you up a glass
Where you may see the inmost part of you.

**QUEEN:** What wilt thou do? Thou wilt not murder me?
Help, ho!

**POLONIUS** *[behind the arras]*: What ho! Help!

**HAMLET** *[drawing]*: How now? A rat? Dead for a ducat, dead!
*[He thrusts his rapier through the arras.]*

**POLONIUS** *[behind the arras]*: O, I am slain!
*[He falls and dies.]*

**QUEEN:** O me, what hast thou done?

**HAMLET:** Nay, I know not. Is it the King?

**QUEEN:** O, what a rash and bloody deed is this!

**HAMLET:** A bloody deed—almost as bad, good Mother,
As kill a king, and marry with his brother.

**QUEEN:** As kill a king!

**HAMLET:** Ay, lady, it was my word.
*[He parts the arras and discovers* POLONIUS.*]*
Thou wretched, rash, intruding fool, farewell!
I took thee for thy better. Take thy fortune.
Thou find'st to be too busy is some danger.—
Leave wringing of your hands. Peace, sit you down,
And let me wring your heart, for so I shall,
If it be made of penetrable stuff,
If damnèd custom have not brazed it so
That it be proof and bulwark against sense.

**QUEEN:** What have I done, that thou dar'st wag thy tongue
In noise so rude against me?

---

**86 seasoned** matured, readied **88 know . . . hent** await to be grasped by me on a more horrid occasion. **hent** act of seizing **89 drunk . . . rage** dead drunk, or in a fit of sexual passion **91 game** gambling **92 relish** trace, savor **95 stays** awaits (me) **96 physic** purging (by prayer), or, Hamlet's postponement of the killing

**3.4. Location: The Queen's private chamber.**
**1 lay home** thrust to the heart, reprove him soundly **2 broad** unrestrained **4 Much heat** i.e., the King's anger. **shroud** conceal (with ironic fitness to Polonius' imminent death. The word is only in the First Quarto; the Second Quarto and the Folio read "silence.") **5 round** blunt **10 thy father** i.e., your stepfather, Claudius **12 idle** foolish

**15 forgot me** i.e., forgotten that I am your mother. **rood** cross of Christ **18 speak** i.e., to someone so rude **25 Dead for a ducat** i.e., I bet a ducat he's dead; or, a ducat is his life's fee **34 busy** nosey **38 damnèd custom** habitual wickedness. **brazed** brazened, hardened **39 proof** armor. **sense** feeling

Hamlet confides in Gertrude.

**HAMLET:** Such an act
That blurs the grace and blush of modesty,
Calls virtue hypocrite, takes off the rose
From the fair forehead of an innocent love
And sets a blister there, makes marriage vows
As false as dicers' oaths. O, such a deed
As from the body of contraction plucks
The very soul, and sweet religion makes
A rhapsody of words. Heaven's face does glow
O'er this solidity and compound mass
With tristful visage, as against the doom,
Is thought-sick at the act.

**QUEEN:** Ay me, what act,
That roars so loud and thunders in the index?

**HAMLET** *[showing her two likenesses]*: Look here upon this picture, and on this,
The counterfeit presentment of two brothers.
See what a grace was seated on this brow:
Hyperion's curls, the front of Jove himself,
An eye like Mars to threaten and command,
A station like the herald Mercury
New-lighted on a heaven-kissing hill—
A combination and a form indeed
Where every god did seem to set his seal
To give the world assurance of a man.
This was your husband. Look you now what follows:
Here is your husband, like a mildewed ear,

**45 sets a blister** i.e., brands as a harlot **47 contraction** the marriage contract **48 sweet religion makes** i.e., makes marriage vows **49 rhapsody** senseless string **49–52 Heaven's . . . act** heaven's face blushes at this solid world compounded of the various elements, with sorrowful face as though the day of doom were near, and is sick with horror at the deed (i.e., Gertrude's marriage) **53 index** table of contents, prelude or preface **55 counterfeit presentment** portrayed representation **57 Hyperion's** the sun-god's. **front** brow **58 Mars** god of war **59 station** manner of standing. **Mercury** winged messenger of the gods **60 New-lighted** newly alighted **62 set his seal** i.e., affix his approval **65 ear** i.e., of grain

Blasting his wholesome brother. Have you eyes?
Could you on this fair mountain leave to feed
And batten on this moor? Ha, have you eyes?
You cannot call it love, for at your age
The heyday in the blood is tame, it's humble,
And waits upon the judgment, and what judgment
Would step from this to this? Sense, sure, you have,
Else could you not have motion, but sure that sense
Is apoplexed, for madness would not err,
Nor sense to ecstasy was ne'er so thralled,
But it reserved some quantity of choice
To serve in such a difference. What devil was 't
That thus hath cozened you at hoodman-blind?
Eyes without feeling, feeling without sight,
Ears without hands or eyes, smelling sans all,
Or but a sickly part of one true sense
Could not so mope. O shame, where is thy blush?
Rebellious hell,
If thou canst mutine in a matron's bones,
To flaming youth let virtue be as wax
And melt in her own fire. Proclaim no shame
When the compulsive ardor gives the charge,
Since frost itself as actively doth burn,
And reason panders will.

**QUEEN:** O Hamlet, speak no more!
Thou turn'st mine eyes into my very soul,
And there I see such black and grainèd spots
As will not leave their tinct.

**HAMLET:** Nay, but to live
In the rank sweat of an enseamèd bed,
Stewed in corruption, honeying and making love
Over the nasty sty!

**66 Blasting** blighting **67 leave** cease **68 batten** gorge. **moor** barren or marshy ground (suggesting also "dark-skinned") **70 heyday** state of excitement. **blood** passion **72 Sense** perception through the five senses (the functions of the middle or sensible soul) **74 apoplexed** paralyzed. (Hamlet goes on to explain that, without such a paralysis of will, mere madness would not so err, nor would the five senses so enthrall themselves to *ecstasy* or lunacy; even such deranged states of mind would be able to make the obvious choice between Hamlet Senior and Claudius.) **err** so err **76 But** but that **77 To . . . difference** to help in making a choice between two such men **78 cozened** cheated. **hoodman-blind** blindman's bluff. (In this game, says Hamlet, the devil must have pushed Claudius toward Gertrude while she was blindfolded.) **80 sans** without **82 mope** be dazed, act aimlessly **84 mutine** incite mutiny **85–86 be as wax . . . fire** melt like a candle or stick of sealing wax held over the candle flame **86–89 Proclaim . . . will** call it no shameful business when the compelling ardor of youth delivers the attack, i.e, commits lechery, since the *frost* of advanced age burns with as active a fire of lust and reason perverts itself by fomenting lust rather than restraining it **92 grainèd** dyed in grain, indelible **93 leave their tinct** surrender their color **94 enseamèd** saturated in the grease and filth of passionate lovemaking **95 Stewed** soaked, bathed (with a suggestion of "stew," brothel)

Hamlet kneels by Polonius's (Brian Murray) dead body.

**QUEEN:** O, speak to me no more!
These words like daggers enter in my ears.
No more, sweet Hamlet!

**HAMLET:** A murderer and a villain,
A slave that is not twentieth part the tithe
Of your precedent lord, a vice of kings,
A cutpurse of the empire and the rule,
That from a shelf the precious diadem stole
And put it in his pocket!

**QUEEN:** No more!

*Enter* GHOST *[in his nightgown].*

**HAMLET:** A king of shreds and patches—
Save me, and hover o'er me with your wings,
You heavenly guards! What would your gracious figure?

**QUEEN:** Alas, he's mad!

**HAMLET:** Do you not come your tardy son to chide,
That, lapsed in time and passion, lets go by
Th' important acting of your dread command?
O, say!

**GHOST:** Do not forget. This visitation
Is but to whet thy almost blunted purpose.
But look, amazement on thy mother sits.
O, step between her and her fighting soul!
Conceit in weakest bodies strongest works.
Speak to her, Hamlet.

**HAMLET:** How is it with you, lady?

**QUEEN:** Alas, how is 't with you,
That you do bend your eye on vacancy,
And with th' incorporal air do hold discourse?
Forth at your eyes your spirits wildly peep,
And, as the sleeping soldiers in th' alarm,
Your bedded hair, like life in excrements,
Start up and stand on end. O gentle son,
Upon the heat and flame of thy distemper
Sprinkle cool patience. Whereon do you look?

**HAMLET:** On him, on him! Look you how pale he glares!
His form and cause conjoined, preaching to stones,
Would make them capable.—Do not look upon me,
Lest with this piteous action you convert
My stern effects. Then what I have to do
Will want true color—tears perchance for blood.

**QUEEN:** To whom do you speak this?

**HAMLET:** Do you see nothing there?

**QUEEN:** Nothing at all, yet all that is I see.

**HAMLET:** Nor did you nothing hear?

**QUEEN:** No, nothing but ourselves.

**HAMLET:** Why, look you there, look how it steals away!
My father, in his habit as he lived!
Look where he goes even now out at the portal!

*Exit* GHOST.

**QUEEN:** This is the very coinage of your brain.
This bodiless creation ecstasy
Is very cunning in.

**HAMLET:** Ecstasy?
My pulse as yours doth temperately keep time,
And makes as healthful music. It is not madness
That I have uttered. Bring me to the test,

---

**100 tithe** tenth part **101 precedent lord** former husband. **vice** buffoon. (A reference to the Vice of the morality plays.) **106 shreds and patches** i.e., motley, the traditional costume of the clown or fool **111 lapsed** delaying **112 important** importunate, urgent **116 amazement** distraction

**118 Conceit** imagination **122 incorporal** immaterial **124 as . . . alarm** like soldiers called out of sleep by an alarum **125 bedded** laid flat. **like life in excrements** i.e., as though hair, an outgrowth of the body, had a life of its own. (Hair was thought to be lifeless because it lacks sensation, and so its standing on end would be unnatural and ominous.) **127 distemper** disorder **130 His . . . conjoined** his appearance joined to his cause for speaking **131 capable** receptive **132–133 convert . . . effects** divert me from my stern duty **134 want . . . blood** lack plausibility so that (with a play on the normal sense of *color*) I shall shed colorless tears instead of blood **141 habit** clothes. **as** as when **143 very** mere **144–145 This . . . in** madness is skillful in creating this kind of hallucination

And I the matter will reword, which madness
Would gambol from. Mother, for love of grace,
Lay not that flattering unction to your soul
That not your trespass but my madness speaks.
It will but skin and film the ulcerous place,
Whiles rank corruption, mining all within,
Infects unseen. Confess yourself to heaven,
Repent what's past, avoid what is to come,
And do not spread the compost on the weeds
To make them ranker. Forgive me this my virtue;
For in the fatness of these pursy times
Virtue itself of vice must pardon beg,
Yea, curb and woo for leave to do him good.

**QUEEN:** O Hamlet, thou hast cleft my heart in twain.

**HAMLET:** O, throw away the worser part of it,
And live the purer with the other half.
Good night. But go not to my uncle's bed;
Assume a virtue, if you have it not.
That monster, custom, who all sense doth eat,
Of habits devil, is angel yet in this,
That to the use of actions fair and good
He likewise gives a frock or livery
That aptly is put on. Refrain tonight,
And that shall lend a kind of easiness
To the next abstinence; the next more easy;
For use almost can change the stamp of nature,
And either . . . the devil, or throw him out
With wondrous potency. Once more, good night;
And when you are desirous to be blest,
I'll blessing beg of you. For this same lord,
*[pointing to* POLONIUS*]*
I do repent; but heaven hath pleased it so
To punish me with this, and this with me,
That I must be their scourge and minister.
I will bestow him, and will answer well
The death I gave him. So, again, good night.
I must be cruel only to be kind.
This bad begins, and worse remains behind.
One word more, good lady.

**QUEEN:** What shall I do?

**HAMLET:** Not this by no means that I bid you do:
Let the bloat king tempt you again in bed,
Pinch wanton on your cheek, call you his mouse,
And let him, for a pair of reechy kisses,
Or paddling in your neck with his damned fingers,
Make you to ravel all this matter out
That I essentially am not in madness,
But mad in craft. 'Twere good you let him know,
For who that's but a queen, fair, sober, wise,
Would from a paddock, from a bat, a gib,
Such dear concernings hide? Who would do so?
No, in despite of sense and secrecy,
Unpeg the basket on the house's top,
Let the birds fly, and like the famous ape,
To try conclusions, in the basket creep
And break your own neck down.

**QUEEN:** Be thou assured, if words be made of breath,
And breath of life, I have no life to breathe
What thou hast said to me.

**HAMLET:** I must to England. You know that?

**QUEEN:** Alack,
I had forgot. 'Tis so concluded on.

**HAMLET:** There's letters sealed, and my two schoolfellows,
Whom I will trust as I will adders fanged,
They bear the mandate; they must sweep my way
And marshal me to knavery. Let it work.
For 'tis the sport to have the enginer

**150 reword** repeat word for word **151 gambol** skip away **152 unction** ointment **154 skin** grow a skin for **155 mining** working under the surface **158 compost** manure **159 this my virtue** my virtuous talk in reproving you **160 fatness** grossness. **pursy** flabby, out of shape **162 curb** bow, bend the knee. **leave** permission **168 who . . . eat** which consumes all proper or natural feeling, all sensibility **169 Of habits devil** devil-like in prompting evil habits **171 livery** an outer appearance, a customary garb (and hence a predisposition easily assumed in time of stress) **172 aptly** readily **175 use** habit. **the stamp of nature** our inborn traits **176 And either** (A defective line, usually emended by inserting the word *master* after *either,* following the Fourth Quarto and early editors.) **178–179 when . . . you** i.e., when you are ready to be penitent and seek God's blessing, I will ask your blessing as a dutiful son should **182 their scourge and minister** i.e., agent of heavenly retribution. (By *scourge,* Hamlet also suggests that he himself will eventually suffer punishment in the process of fulfilling heaven's will.)

**183 bestow** stow, dispose of. **answer** account or pay for **186 This** i.e., the killing of Polonius. **behind** to come **189 bloat** bloated **190 Pinch wanton** i.e., leave his love pinches on your cheeks, branding you as wanton **191 reechy** dirty, filthy **192 paddling** fingering amorously **193 ravel . . . out** unravel, disclose **195 in craft** by cunning. **good** (Said sarcastically; also the following eight lines.) **197 paddock** toad. **gib** tomcat **198 dear concernings** important affairs **199 sense and secrecy** secrecy that common sense requires **200 Unpeg the basket** open the cage, i.e., let out the secret **201 famous ape** (In a story now lost.) **202 try conclusions** test the outcome (in which the ape apparently enters a cage from which birds have been released and then tries to fly out of the cage as they have done, falling to its death) **203 down** in the fall; utterly **211–212 sweep . . . knavery** sweep a path before me and conduct me to some *knavery* or treachery prepared for me **212 work** proceed **213 enginer** maker of military contrivances

Hoist with his own petard, and 't shall go hard
But I will delve one yard below their mines
And blow them at the moon. O, 'tis most sweet
When in one line two crafts directly meet.
This man shall set me packing.
I'll lug the guts into the neighbor room.
Mother, good night indeed. This counselor
Is now most still, most secret, and most grave,
Who was in life a foolish prating knave.—
Come, sir, to draw toward an end with you.—
Good night, Mother.
*Exeunt [separately,* HAMLET *dragging in* POLONIUS*].*

## 4.1 *Enter* KING *and* QUEEN, *with* ROSENCRANTZ *and* GUILDENSTERN.

**KING:** There's matter in these sighs, these profound heaves.
You must translate; 'tis fit we understand them.
Where is your son?

**QUEEN:** Bestow this place on us a little while.
*[Exeunt* ROSENCRANTZ *and* GUILDENSTERN.*]*
Ah, mine own lord, what have I seen tonight!

**KING:** What, Gertrude? How does Hamlet?

**QUEEN:** Mad as the sea and wind when both contend
Which is the mightier. In his lawless fit,
Behind the arras hearing something stir,
Whips out his rapier, cries, "A rat, a rat!"
And in this brainish apprehension kills
The unseen good old man.

**KING:** O heavy deed!
It had been so with us, had we been there.
His liberty is full of threats to all—
To you yourself, to us, to everyone.
Alas, how shall this bloody deed be answered?
It will be laid to us, whose providence
Should have kept short, restrained, and out of haunt
This mad young man. But so much was our love,
We would not understand what was most fit,
But, like the owner of a foul disease,
To keep it from divulging, let it feed
Even on the pith of life. Where is he gone?

**QUEEN:** To draw apart the body he hath killed,
O'er whom his very madness, like some ore
Among a mineral of metals base,
Shows itself pure: 'a weeps for what is done.

**KING:** O Gertrude, come away!
The sun no sooner shall the mountains touch
But we will ship him hence, and this vile deed
We must with all our majesty and skill
Both countenance and excuse.—Ho, Guildenstern!

*Enter* ROSENCRANTZ *and* GUILDENSTERN.

Friends both, go join you with some further aid.
Hamlet in madness hath Polonius slain,
And from his mother's closet hath he dragged him.
Go seek him out, speak fair, and bring the body
Into the chapel. I pray you, haste in this.
*[Exeunt* ROSENCRANTZ *and* GUILDENSTERN.*]*
Come, Gertrude, we'll call up our wisest friends
And let them know both what we mean to do
And what's untimely done . . . . . . . .
Whose whisper o'er the world's diameter,
As level as the cannon to his blank,
Transports his poisoned shot, may miss our name
And hit the woundless air. O, come away!
My soul is full of discord and dismay. *Exeunt.*

## 4.2 *Enter* HAMLET.

**HAMLET:** Safely stowed.

**ROSENCRANTZ, GUILDENSTERN** *(within)*: Hamlet! Lord Hamlet!

---

**214 Hoist with** blown up by. **petard** an explosive used to blow in a door or make a breach **214–215 't shall . . . will** unless luck is against me, I will **215 mines** tunnels used in warfare to undermine the enemy's emplacements; Hamlet will countermine by going under their mines **217 in one line** i.e., mines and countermines on a collision course, or the countermines directly below the mines. **crafts** acts of guile, plots **218 set me packing** set me to making schemes, and set me to lugging (him), and, also, send me off in a hurry **223 draw . . . end** finish up (with a pun on *draw*, "pull")

**4.1. Location: The castle.**
**s.d. Enter . . . Queen** (Some editors argue that Gertrude never exits in 3.4 and that the scene is continuous here, as suggested in the Folio, but the Second Quarto marks an entrance for her and at line 35 Claudius speaks of Gertrude's *closet* as though it were elsewhere. A short time has elapsed, during which the King has become aware of her highly wrought emotional state.) **1 matter** significance. **heaves** heavy sighs **11 brainish apprehension** headstrong conception **12 heavy** grievous **13 us** i.e., me. (The royal "we"; also in line 15.)

**16 answered** explained **17 providence** foresight **18 short** i.e., on a short tether. **out of haunt** secluded **22 divulging** becoming evident **25 ore** vein of gold **26 mineral** mine **32 countenance** put the best face on **40 And . . . done** (A defective line; conjectures as to the missing words include *So, haply, slander* [Capell and others]; *For, haply, slander* [Theobald and others]; and *So envious slander* [Jenkins].) **41 diameter** extent from side to side **42 As level** with as direct aim. **his blank** its target at point-blank range **44 woundless** invulnerable

**4.2. Location: The castle.**

Rosencrantz and Guildenstern question Hamlet about Polonius's body.

**HAMLET:** But soft, what noise? Who calls on Hamlet? O, here they come.

*Enter* ROSENCRANTZ *and* GUILDENSTERN.

**ROSENCRANTZ:** What have you done, my lord, with the dead body?

**HAMLET:** Compounded it with dust, whereto 'tis kin.

**ROSENCRANTZ:** Tell us where 'tis, that we may take it thence
And bear it to the chapel.

**HAMLET:** Do not believe it.

**ROSENCRANTZ:** Believe what?

**HAMLET:** That I can keep your counsel and not mine own. Besides, to be demanded of a sponge, what replication should be made by the son of a king?

**ROSENCRANTZ:** Take you me for a sponge, my lord?

**HAMLET:** Ay, sir, that soaks up the King's countenance, his rewards, his authorities. But such officers do the King best service in the end. He keeps them, like an ape, an apple, in the corner of his jaw, first mouthed to be last swallowed. When he needs what you have gleaned, it is but squeezing you, and, sponge, you shall be dry again.

**ROSENCRANTZ:** I understand you not, my lord.

**HAMLET:** I am glad of it. A knavish speech sleeps in a foolish ear.

**ROSENCRANTZ:** My lord, you must tell us where the body is and go with us to the King.

---

**12–13 That . . . own** i.e., that I can follow your advice (by telling where the body is) and still keep my own secret **13 demanded of** questioned by **14 replication** reply **16–17 countenance** favor **17 authorities** delegated power, influence **24 sleeps in** has no meaning to

**HAMLET:** The body is with the King, but the King is not with the body. The King is a thing—

**GUILDENSTERN:** A thing, my lord?

**HAMLET:** Of nothing. Bring me to him. Hide fox, and all after! *Exeunt [running].*

## 4.3 *Enter* KING, *and two or three.*

**KING:** I have sent to seek him, and to find the body.
How dangerous is it that this man goes loose!
Yet must not we put the strong law on him.
He's loved of the distracted multitude,
Who like not in their judgment, but their eyes,
And where 'tis so, th' offender's scourge is weighed,
But never the offense. To bear all smooth and even,
This sudden sending him away must seem
Deliberate pause. Diseases desperate grown
By desperate appliance are relieved,
Or not at all.

*Enter* ROSENCRANTZ, *[*GUILDENSTERN,*]* *and all the rest.*

How now, what hath befall'n?

**ROSENCRANTZ:** Where the dead body is bestowed, my lord,
We cannot get from him.

**KING:** But where is he?

**ROSENCRANTZ:** Without, my lord; guarded, to know your pleasure.

**KING:** Bring him before us.

**ROSENCRANTZ:** Ho! Bring in the lord.

*They enter [with* HAMLET*].*

---

**28–29 The . . . body** (Perhaps alludes to the legal commonplace of "the king's two bodies," which drew a distinction between the sacred office of kingship and the particular mortal who possessed it at any given time. Hence, although Claudius' body is necessarily a part of him, true kingship is not contained in it. Similarly, Claudius will have Polonius' body when it is found, but there is no kingship in this business either.) **31 Of nothing** (1) of no account (2) lacking the essence of kingship, as in lines 28–29 and note **31–32 Hide . . . after** (An old signal cry in the game of hide-and-seek, suggesting that Hamlet now runs away from them.)

**4.3. Location: The castle.**
**4 of** by. **distracted** fickle, unstable **5 Who . . . eyes** who choose not by judgment but by appearance **6 scourge** punishment. (Literally, blow with a whip.) **weighed** sympathetically considered **7 To . . . even** to manage the business in an unprovocative way **9 Deliberate pause** carefully considered action **10 appliance** remedies

Claudius asks Hamlet about Polonius.

**KING:** Now, Hamlet, where's Polonius?

**HAMLET:** At supper.

**KING:** At supper? Where?

**HAMLET:** Not where he eats, but where 'a is eaten. A certain convocation of politic worms are e'en at him. Your worm is your only emperor for diet. We fat all creatures else to fat us, and we fat ourselves for maggots. Your fat king and your lean beggar is but variable service—two dishes, but to one table. That's the end.

**KING:** Alas, alas!

**HAMLET:** A man may fish with the worm that hath eat of a king, and eat of the fish that hath fed of that worm.

**KING:** What dost thou mean by this?

**HAMLET:** Nothing but to show you how a king may go a progress through the guts of a beggar.

**KING:** Where is Polonius?

**HAMLET:** In heaven. Send thither to see. If your messenger find him not there, seek him i' th' other place yourself. But if indeed you find him not within this month, you shall nose him as you go up the stairs into the lobby.

**KING** *[to some attendants]*: Go seek him there.

**HAMLET:** 'A will stay till you come. *[Exeunt attendants.]*

**KING:** Hamlet, this deed, for thine especial safety—
Which we do tender, as we dearly grieve
For that which thou hast done—must send thee hence
With fiery quickness. Therefore prepare thyself.
The bark is ready, and the wind at help,
Th' associates tend, and everything is bent
For England.

**HAMLET:** For England!

**KING:** Ay, Hamlet.

**HAMLET:** Good.

**KING:** So is it, if thou knew'st our purposes.

**HAMLET:** I see a cherub that sees them. But come, for England! Farewell, dear mother.

**KING:** Thy loving father, Hamlet.

**HAMLET:** My mother. Father and mother is man and wife, man and wife is one flesh, and so, my mother. Come, for England! *Exit.*

**KING:** Follow him at foot; tempt him with speed aboard.
Delay it not. I'll have him hence tonight.
Away! For everything is sealed and done
That else leans on th' affair. Pray you, make haste.
*[Exeunt all but the* KING.*]*
And, England, if my love thou hold'st at aught—
As my great power thereof may give thee sense,
Since yet thy cicatrice looks raw and red
After the Danish sword, and thy free awe
Pays homage to us—thou mayst not coldly set
Our sovereign process, which imports at full,
By letters congruing to that effect,
The present death of Hamlet. Do it, England,
For like the hectic in my blood he rages,
And thou must cure me. Till I know 'tis done,
Howe'er my haps, my joys were ne'er begun *Exit.*

---

**20 politic worms** crafty worms (suited to a master spy like Polonius). **e'en** even now **21 Your worm** your average worm. (Compare *your fat king and your lean beggar* in line 23.) **diet** food, eating (with a punning reference to the Diet of Worms, a famous *convocation* held in 1521) **24 variable service** different courses of a single meal **28 eat** eaten (Pronounced *et.*) **32 progress** royal journey of state

**42 tender** regard, hold dear. **dearly** intensely **45 bark** sailing vessel **46 tend** wait. **bent** in readiness **52 cherub** (Cherubim are angels of knowledge. Hamlet hints that both he and heaven are onto Claudius' tricks.) **58 at foot** close behind, at heel **61 leans on** bears upon, is related to **62 England** i.e., King of England. **at aught** at any value **63 As . . . sense** for so my great power may give you a just appreciation of the importance of valuing my love **64 cicatrice** scar **65 free awe** voluntary show of respect **66 coldly set** regard with indifference **67 process** command. **imports at full** conveys specific directions for **68 congruing** agreeing **69 present** immediate **70 hectic** persistent fever **72 haps** fortunes

**4.4** *Enter* FORTINBRAS *with his army over the stage.*

**FORTINBRAS:** Go, Captain, from me greet the Danish king.
Tell him that by his license Fortinbras
Craves the conveyance of a promised march
Over his kingdom. You know the rendezvous.
If that His Majesty would aught with us,
We shall express our duty in his eye;
And let him know so.

**CAPTAIN:** I will do 't, my lord

**FORTINBRAS:** Go softly on.
*[Exeunt all but the* CAPTAIN.*]*

*Enter* HAMLET, ROSENCRANTZ, *[*GUILDENSTERN,*] etc.*

**HAMLET:** Good sir, whose powers are these?

**CAPTAIN:** They are of Norway, sir.

**HAMLET:** How purposed, sir, I pray you?

**CAPTAIN:** Against some part of Poland.

**HAMLET:** Who commands them, sir?

**CAPTAIN:** The nephew to old Norway, Fortinbras.

**HAMLET:** Goes it against the main of Poland, sir,
Or for some frontier?

**CAPTAIN:** Truly to speak, and with no addition,
We go to gain a little patch of ground
That hath in it no profit but the name.
To pay five ducats, five, I would not farm it;
Nor will it yield to Norway or the Pole
A ranker rate, should it be sold in fee.

**HAMLET:** Why, then the Polack never will defend it.

**CAPTAIN:** Yes, it is already garrisoned.

**HAMLET:** Two thousand souls and twenty thousand ducats
Will not debate the question of this straw.
This is th' impostume of much wealth and peace,
That inward breaks, and shows no cause without
Why the man dies. I humbly thank you, sir.

**CAPTAIN:** God b' wi' you, sir. *[Exit.]*

**ROSENCRANTZ:** Will 't please you go, my lord?

**HAMLET:** I'll be with you straight. Go a little before.
*[Exeunt all except* HAMLET.*]*
How all occasions do inform against me
And spur my dull revenge! What is a man,
If his chief good and market of his time
Be but to sleep and feed? A beast, no more.
Sure he that made us with such large discourse,
Looking before and after, gave us not
That capability and godlike reason
To fust in us unused. Now, whether it be
Bestial oblivion, or some craven scruple
Of thinking too precisely on th' event—
A thought which, quartered, hath but one part wisdom
And ever three parts coward—I do not know
Why yet I live to say "This thing's to do,"
Sith I have cause, and will, and strength, and means
To do 't. Examples gross as earth exhort me:
Witness this army of such mass and charge,
Led by a delicate and tender prince,
Whose spirit with divine ambition puffed
Makes mouths at the invisible event,
Exposing what is mortal and unsure
To all that fortune, death, and danger dare,
Even for an eggshell. Rightly to be great
Is not to stir without great argument,
But greatly to find quarrel in a straw
When honor's at the stake. How stand I, then,
That have a father killed, a mother stained,
Excitements of my reason and my blood,
And let all sleep, while to my shame I see
The imminent death of twenty thousand men
That for a fantasy and trick of fame
Go to their graves like beds, fight for a plot

---

**4.4. Location: The coast of Denmark.**
**2 license** permission **3 the conveyance of** escort during **6 duty** respect. **eye** presence **9 softly** slowly, circumspectly **10 powers** forces **16 main** main part **18 addition** exaggeration **21 To pay** i.e., for a yearly rental of. **farm it** take a lease of it **23 ranker** higher. **in fee** fee simple, outright **27 debate . . . straw** settle this trifling matter **28 impostume** abscess

**33 inform against** denounce, betray; take shape against **35 market of** profit of, compensation for **37 discourse** power of reasoning **38 Looking before and after** able to review past events and anticipate the future **40 fust** grow moldy **41 oblivion** forgetfulness. **craven** cowardly **42 precisely** scrupulously. **event** outcome **46 Sith** since **47 gross** obvious **48 charge** expense **49 delicate and tender** of fine and youthful qualities **51 Makes mouths** makes scornful faces. **invisible event** unforeseeable outcome **53 dare** could do (to him) **54–57 Rightly . . . stake** true greatness does not normally consist of rushing into action over some trivial provocation; however, when one's honor is involved, even a trifling insult requires that one respond greatly (?) **57 at the stake** (A metaphor from gambling or bear-baiting.) **59 Excitements of** promptings by **62 fantasy** fanciful caprice, illusion. **trick** trifle, deceit **63 plot** plot of ground

Whereon the numbers cannot try the cause,
Which is not tomb enough and continent
To hide the slain? O, from this time forth
My thoughts be bloody or be nothing worth! *Exit.*

**4.5** *Enter* HORATIO, [QUEEN] GERTRUDE, *and a* GENTLEMAN.

**QUEEN:** I will not speak with her.

**GENTLEMAN:** She is importunate,
Indeed distract. Her mood will needs be pitied.

**QUEEN:** What would she have?

**GENTLEMAN:** She speaks much of her father, says she hears
There's tricks i' the world, and hems, and beats her heart,
Spurns enviously at straws, speaks things in doubt
That carry but half sense. Her speech is nothing,
Yet the unshapèd use of it doth move
The hearers to collection; they yawn at it,
And botch the words up fit to their own thoughts,
Which, as her winks and nods and gestures yield them,
Indeed would make one think there might be thought,
Though nothing sure, yet much unhappily.

**HORATIO:** 'Twere good she were spoken with, for she may strew
Dangerous conjectures in ill-breeding minds.

**QUEEN:** Let her come in. *[Exit* GENTLEMAN.*]*
*[Aside.]* To my sick soul, as sin's true nature is,
Each toy seems prologue to some great amiss.
So full of artless jealousy is guilt,
It spills itself in fearing to be spilt.

*Enter* OPHELIA *[distracted].*

**OPHELIA:** Where is the beauteous majesty of Denmark?

**QUEEN:** How now, Ophelia?

**OPHELIA** *(she sings)*:
"How should I your true love know
From another one?
By his cockle hat and staff,
And his sandal shoon."

**QUEEN:** Alas, sweet lady, what imports this song?

**OPHELIA:** Say you? Nay, pray you, mark.
"He is dead and gone, lady, *(Song.)*
He is dead and gone;
At his head a grass-green turf,
At his heels a stone."
O, ho!

**QUEEN:** Nay, but Ophelia—

**OPHELIA:** Pray you, mark.
*[Sings.]* "White his shroud as the mountain snow"—

*Enter* KING.

**QUEEN:** Alas, look here, my lord.

**OPHELIA:** "Larded with sweet flowers; *(Song.)*
Which bewept to the ground did not go
With true-love showers."

**KING:** How do you, pretty lady?

**OPHELIA:** Well, God 'ild you! They say the owl was a baker's daughter. Lord, we know what we are, but know not what we may be. God be at your table!

**KING:** Conceit upon her father.

**OPHELIA:** Pray let's have no words of this; but when they ask you what it means, say you this:
"Tomorrow is Saint Valentine's day, *(Song.)*
All in the morning betime,
And I a maid at your window,
To be your Valentine.
Then up he rose, and donned his clothes,
And dupped the chamber door,
Let in the maid, that out a maid
Never departed more."

---

**64 Whereon . . . cause** on which there is insufficient room for the soldiers needed to engage in a military contest **65 continent** receptacle, container

**4.5. Location: The castle.**
**2 distract** distracted **5 tricks** deceptions. **hems** makes "hmm" sounds. **heart** i.e., breast **6 Spurns . . . straws** kicks spitefully, takes offense at trifles. **in doubt** obscurely **8 unshapèd use** incoherent manner **9 collection** inference, a guess at some sort of meaning. **yawn** gape, wonder; grasp. (The Folio reading, *aim*, is possible.) **10 botch** patch **11 Which** which words. **yield** deliver, represent **12 thought** intended **13 unhappily** unpleasantly near the truth, shrewdly **15 ill-breeding** prone to suspect the worst and to make mischief **18 toy** trifle. **amiss** calamity **19–20 So . . . spilt** guilt is so full of suspicion that it unskillfully betrays itself in fearing betrayal **20 s.d. Enter Ophelia** (In the First Quarto, Ophelia enters, "playing on a lute, and her hair down, singing.")

**25 cockle hat** hat with cockleshell stuck in it as a sign that the wearer had been a pilgrim to the shrine of Saint James of Compostela in Spain **26 shoon** shoes **38 Larded** decorated **40 showers** i.e., tears **42 God 'ild** God yield or reward. **owl** (Refers to a legend about a baker's daughter who was turned into an owl for being ungenerous when Jesus begged a loaf of bread.) **45 Conceit** brooding **49 betime** early **53 dupped** did up, opened

Ophelia (Diane Venora), having gone mad, speaks to the king and queen.

**KING:** Pretty Ophelia—

**OPHELIA:** Indeed, la, without an oath, I'll make an end on 't:
*[Sings.]* "By Gis and by Saint Charity,
Alack, and fie for shame!
You men will do 't, if they come to 't;
By Cock, they are to blame.
Quoth she, 'Before you tumbled me,
You promised me to wed.'"
He answers:
"'So would I ha' done, by yonder sun,
An thou hadst not come to my bed.'"

**KING:** How long hath she been thus?

**OPHELIA:** I hope all will be well. We must be patient, but I cannot choose but weep to think they would lay him i' the cold ground. My brother shall know of it. And so I thank you for your good counsel. Come, my coach! Good night, ladies, good night, sweet ladies, good night, good night. *[Exit.]*

**KING** *[to* HORATIO*]*: Follow her close. Give her good watch, I pray you.

*[Exit* HORATIO.*]*

O, this is the poison of deep grief; it springs
All from her father's death—and now behold!
O Gertrude, Gertrude,
When sorrows come, they come not single spies,
But in battalions. First, her father slain;
Next, your son gone, and he most violent author
Of his own just remove; the people muddied,
Thick and unwholesome in their thoughts and whispers
For good Polonius' death—and we have done but greenly,
In hugger-mugger to inter him; poor Ophelia
Divided from herself and her fair judgment,
Without the which we are pictures or mere beasts;
Last, and as much containing as all these,
Her brother is in secret come from France,
Feeds on this wonder, keeps himself in clouds,
And wants not buzzers to infect his ear
With pestilent speeches of his father's death,
Wherein necessity, of matter beggared,
Will nothing stick our person to arraign
In ear and ear. O my dear Gertrude, this,
Like to a murdering piece, in many places
Gives me superfluous death. *A noise within.*

**QUEEN:** Alack, what noise is this?

**KING:** Attend!
Where is my Switzers? Let them guard the door.

*Enter a* MESSENGER.

What is the matter?

**MESSENGER:** Save yourself, my lord!
The ocean, overpeering of his list,
Eats not the flats with more impetuous haste
Than young Laertes, in a riotous head,
O'erbears your officers. The rabble call him lord,
And, as the world were now but to begin,
Antiquity forgot, custom not known,
The ratifiers and props of every word,
They cry, "Choose we! Laertes shall be king!"
Caps, hands, and tongues applaud it to the clouds,
"Laertes shall be king, Laertes king!"

---

**59 Gis** Jesus **62 Cock** (A perversion of "God" in oaths; here also with a quibble on the slang word for penis.) **67 An** if **79 spies** scouts sent in advance of the main force

**82 remove** removal. **muddied** stirred up, confused **84 greenly** in an inexperienced way, foolishly **85 hugger-mugger** secret haste **88 as much containing** as full of serious matter **90 Feeds . . . clouds** feeds his resentment or shocked grievance, holds himself inscrutable and aloof amid all this rumor **91 wants** lacks. **buzzers** gossipers, informers **93 necessity** i.e., the need to invent some plausible explanation. **of matter beggared** unprovided with facts **94–95 Will . . . ear** will not hesitate to accuse my (royal) person in everybody's ears **96 murdering piece** cannon loaded so as to scatter its shot **97 Gives . . . death** kills me over and over **99 Attend** i.e., guard me **100 Switzers** Swiss guards, mercenaries **102 overpeering of his list** overflowing its shore, boundary **103 flats** i.e., flatlands near shore. **impetuous** violent (perhaps also with the meaning of *impiteous* [*impitious*, Q2], "pitiless") **104 head** insurrection **106 as** as if **108 The ratifiers . . . word** i.e., *antiquity* (or tradition) and *custom* ought to confirm (*ratify*) and underprop our every word or promise **110 Caps** (The caps are thrown in the air.)

**QUEEN:** How cheerfully on the false trail they cry!
*A noise within.*
O, this is counter, you false Danish dogs!

*Enter* LAERTES *with others.*

**KING:** The doors are broke.

**LAERTES:** Where is this King?—Sirs, stand you all without.

**ALL:** No, let's come in.

**LAERTES:** I pray you, give me leave.

**ALL:** We will, we will.

**LAERTES:** I thank you. Keep the door. *[Exeunt followers.]* O thou vile king,
Give me my father!

**QUEEN** *[restraining him]*: Calmly, good Laertes.

**LAERTES:** That drop of blood that's calm proclaims me bastard,
Cries cuckold to my father, brands the harlot
Even here, between the chaste unsmirchèd brow
Of my true mother.

**KING:** What is the cause, Laertes,
That thy rebellion looks so giantlike?
Let him go, Gertrude. Do not fear our person.
There's such divinity doth hedge a king
That treason can but peep to what it would,
Acts little of his will. Tell me, Laertes,
Why thou art thus incensed. Let him go, Gertrude.
Speak, man.

**LAERTES:** Where is my father?

**KING:** Dead.

**QUEEN:** But not by him.

**KING:** Let him demand his fill.

**LAERTES:** How came he dead? I'll not be juggled with.
To hell, allegiance! Vows, to the blackest devil!
Conscience and grace, to the profoundest pit!
I dare damnation. To this point I stand,

Ophelia, driven mad, approaches the king and queen.

That both the worlds I give to negligence,
Let come what comes, only I'll be revenged
Most throughly for my father.

**KING:** Who shall stay you?

**LAERTES:** My will, not all the world's.
And for my means, I'll husband them so well
They shall go far with little.

**KING:** Good Laertes,
If you desire to know the certainty
Of your dear father, is 't writ in your revenge
That, swoopstake, you will draw both friend and foe,
Winner and loser?

**LAERTES:** None but his enemies.

**KING:** Will you know them, then?

**LAERTES:** To his good friends thus wide I'll ope my arms,
And like the kind life-rendering pelican
Repast them with my blood.

**KING:** Why, now you speak
Like a good child and a true gentleman.
That I am guiltless of your father's death,
And am most sensibly in grief for it,
It shall as level to your judgment 'pear
As day does to your eye. *A noise within.*

**LAERTES:** How now, what noise is that?

---

**113 counter** (A hunting term, meaning to follow the trail in a direction opposite to that which the game has taken.) **123 between** in the middle of **126 fear our** fear for my **127 hedge** protect, as with a surrounding barrier **128 can . . . would** can only peep furtively, as through a barrier, at what it would intend **129 Acts . . . will** (but) performs little of what it intends **133 juggled with** cheated, deceived **136 To . . . stand** I am resolved in this

**137 both . . . negligence** i.e., both this world and the next are of no consequence to me **139 throughly** thoroughly **141 My will . . . world's** I'll stop (*stay*) when my will is accomplished, not for anyone else's **142 for** as for **146 swoopstake** i.e., indiscriminately. (Literally, taking all stakes on the gambling table at once. *Draw* is also a gambling term, meaning "take from.") **151 pelican** (Refers to the belief that the female pelican fed its young with its own blood.) **152 Repast** feed **155 sensibly** feelingly **156 level** plain

*Enter* OPHELIA.

**KING:** Let her come in.

**LAERTES:** O heat, dry up my brains! Tears seven times salt
Burn out the sense and virtue of mine eye!
By heaven, thy madness shall be paid with weight
Till our scale turn the beam. O rose of May!
Dear maid, kind sister, sweet Ophelia!
O heavens, is 't possible a young maid's wits
Should be as mortal as an old man's life?
Nature is fine in love, and where 'tis fine
It sends some precious instance of itself
After the thing it loves.

**OPHELIA:**
"They bore him barefaced on the bier, *(Song.)*
Hey non nonny, nonny, hey nonny,
And in his grave rained many a tear—"
Fare you well, my dove!

**LAERTES:** Hadst thou thy wits and didst persuade revenge,
It could not move thus.

**OPHELIA:** You must sing "A-down a-down," and you "call him a-down-a." O, how the wheel becomes it! It is the false steward that stole his master's daughter.

**LAERTES:** This nothing's more than matter.

**OPHELIA:** There's rosemary, that's for remembrance; pray you, love, remember. And there is pansies; that's for thoughts.

**LAERTES:** A document in madness, thoughts and remembrance fitted.

**OPHELIA:** There's fennel for you, and columbines. There's rue for you, and here's some for me; we may call it herb of grace o' Sundays. You must wear your rue with a difference. There's a daisy. I would give you some violets, but they withered all when my father died. They say 'a made a good end— *[Sings.]*
"For bonny sweet Robin is all my joy."

**LAERTES:** Thought and affliction, passion, hell itself,
She turns to favor and to prettiness.

**OPHELIA:**
"And will 'a not come again? *(Song.)*
And will 'a not come again?
No, no, he is head.
Go to thy deathbed,
He never will come again.

"His beard was as white as snow,
All flaxen was his poll.
He is gone, he is gone,
And we cast away moan.
God ha' mercy on his soul!"
And of all Christian souls, I pray God. God b' wi' you.
*[Exit, followed by* GERTRUDE.*]*

**LAERTES:** Do you see this, O God?

**KING:** Laertes, I must commune with your grief,
Or you deny me right. Go but apart,
Make choice of whom your wisest friends you will,
And they shall hear and judge twixt you and me.
If by direct or by collateral hand
They find us touched, we will our kingdom give,
Our crown, our life, and all that we call ours
To you in satisfaction; but if not,
Be you content to lend your patience to us,
And we shall jointly labor with your soul
To give it due content.

**LAERTES:** Let this be so.
His means of death, his obscure funeral—
No trophy, sword, nor hatchment o'er his bones,
No noble rite, nor formal ostentation—
Cry to be heard, as 'twere from heaven to earth,
That I must call 't in question.

---

**160 virtue** faculty, power **161 paid with weight** repaid, avenged equally or more **162 beam** crossbar of a balance **166 fine in** refined by **167 instance** token **168 After . . . loves** i.e., into the grave, along with Polonius **173 persuade** argue cogently for **175–176 You . . . a-down-a** (Ophelia assigns the singing of refrains, like her own "Hey non nonny," to others present.) **176 wheel** spinning wheel as accompaniment to the song, or refrain **177 false steward** (The story is unknown.) **178 This . . . matter** this seeming nonsense is more eloquent than sane utterance **179 rosemary** (Used as a symbol of remembrance both at weddings and at funerals.) **180 pansies** (Emblems of love and courtship; perhaps from French *pensées*, "thoughts.") **182 document** instruction, lesson **184 fennel** (Emblem of flattery.) **columbines** (Emblems of unchastity or ingratitude.) **185 rue** (Emblem of repentance—a signification that is evident in its popular name, *herb of grace.*)

**187 with a difference** (A device used in heraldry to distinguish one family from another on the coat of arms, here suggesting that Ophelia and the others have different causes of sorrow and repentance; perhaps with a play on *rue* in the sense of "ruth," "pity.") **daisy** (Emblem of dissembling, faithlessness.) **188 violets** (Emblems of faithfulness.) **191 Thought** melancholy. **passion** suffering **192 favor** grace, beauty **199 poll** head **207 whom** whichever of **209 collateral hand** indirect agency **210 us touched** me implicated **217 trophy** memorial. **hatchment** tablet displaying the armorial bearings of a deceased person **218 ostentation** ceremony **220 That** so that. **call 't in question** demand an explanation

**KING:** So you shall,
And where th' offense is, let the great ax fall.
I pray you, go with me. *Exeunt.*

## 4.6 *Enter* HORATIO *and others.*

**HORATIO:** What are they that would speak with me?

**GENTLEMAN:** Seafaring men, sir. They say they have letters for you.

**HORATIO:** Let them come in. *[Exit* GENTLEMAN.*]*
I do not know from what part of the world
I should be greeted, if not from Lord Hamlet.

*Enter* SAILORS.

**FIRST SAILOR:** God bless you, sir.

**HORATIO:** Let him bless thee too.

**FIRST SAILOR:** 'A shall, sir, an 't please him. There's a letter for you, sir—it came from th' ambassador that was bound for England—if your name be Horatio, as I am let to know it is. *[He gives a letter.]*

**HORATIO** *[reads]*: "Horatio, when thou shalt have overlooked this, give these fellows some means to the King; they have letters for him. Ere we were two days old at sea, a pirate of very warlike appointment gave us chase. Finding ourselves too slow of sail, we put on a compelled valor, and in the grapple I boarded them. On the instant they got clear of our ship, so I alone became their prisoner. They have dealt with me like thieves of mercy, but they knew what they did: I am to do a good turn for them. Let the King have the letters I have sent, and repair thou to me with as much speed as thou wouldest fly death. I have words to speak in thine ear will make thee dumb, yet are they much too light for the bore of the matter. These good fellows will bring thee where I am. Rosencrantz and Guildenstern hold their course for England. Of them I have much to tell thee. Farewell.
He that thou knowest thine, Hamlet."
Come, I will give you way for these your letters,
And do 't the speedier that you may direct me
To him from whom you brought them. *Exeunt.*

**4.6. Location: The castle.**
**9 an 't** if it **10 th' ambassador** (Evidently Hamlet. The sailor is being circumspect.) **13–14 overlooked** looked over **14 means** means of access **16 appointment** equipage **21 thieves of mercy** merciful thieves **23 repair** come **26 bore** caliber, i.e., importance **31 way** means of access

## 4.7 *Enter* KING *and* LAERTES.

**KING:** Now must your conscience my acquittance seal,
And you must put me in your heart for friend,
Sith you have heard, and with a knowing ear,
That he which hath your noble father slain
Pursued my life.

**LAERTES:** It well appears. But tell me
Why you proceeded not against these feats
So crimeful and so capital in nature,
As by your safety, greatness, wisdom, all things else,
You mainly were stirred up.

**KING:** O, for two special reasons,
Which may to you perhaps seem much unsinewed,
But yet to me they're strong. The Queen his mother
Lives almost by his looks, and for myself—
My virtue or my plague, be it either which—
She is so conjunctive to my life and soul
That, as the star moves not but in his sphere,
I could not but by her. The other motive
Why to a public count I might not go
Is the great love the general gender bear him,
Who, dipping all his faults in their affection,
Work like the spring that turneth wood to stone,
Convert his gyves to graces, so that my arrows,
Too slightly timbered for so loud a wind,
Would have reverted to my bow again
But not where I had aimed them.

**LAERTES:** And so have I a noble father lost,
A sister driven into desperate terms,
Whose worth, if praises may go back again,
Stood challenger on mount of all the age
For her perfections. But my revenge will come.

**KING:** Break not your sleeps for that. You must not think
That we are made of stuff so flat and dull
That we can let our beard be shook with danger
And think it pastime. You shortly shall hear more.

**4.7. Location: The castle.**
**1 my acquittance seal** confirm or acknowledge my innocence **3 Sith** since **6 feats** acts **7 capital** punishable by death **9 mainly** greatly **11 unsinewed** weak **15 conjunctive** closely united. (An astronomical metaphor.) **16 his** its. **sphere** one of the hollow spheres in which, according to Ptolemaic astronomy, the planets were supposed to move **18 count** account, reckoning, indictment **19 general gender** common people **21 Work** operate, act. **spring** i.e., a spring with such a concentration of lime that it coats a piece of wood with limestone, in effect gilding and petrifying it **22 gyves** fetters (which, gilded by the people's praise, would look like badges of honor) **23 slightly timbered** light. **loud** (suggesting public outcry on Hamlet's behalf) **24 reverted** returned **27 terms** state, condition **28 go back** i.e., recall what she was **29 on mount** set up on high

I loved your father, and we love ourself;
And that, I hope, will teach you to imagine—

*Enter a* MESSENGER *with letters.*

How now? What news?

**MESSENGER:** Letters, my lord, from Hamlet:
This to Your Majesty, this to the Queen.
*[He gives letters.]*

**KING:** From Hamlet? Who brought them?

**MESSENGER:** Sailors, my lord, they say. I saw them not.
They were given me by Claudio. He received them
Of him that brought them.

**KING:** Laertes, you shall hear them.—
Leave us. *[Exit* MESSENGER.*]*
*[He reads.]* "High and mighty, you shall know I am set naked on your kingdom. Tomorrow shall I beg leave to see your kingly eyes, when I shall, first asking your pardon, thereunto recount the occasion of my sudden and more strange return. Hamlet."
What should this mean? Are all the rest come back?
Or is it some abuse, and no such thing?

**LAERTES:** Know you the hand?

**KING:** 'Tis Hamlet's character. "Naked"!
And in a postscript here he says "alone."
Can you devise me?

**LAERTES:** I am lost in it, my lord. But let him come.
It warms the very sickness in my heart
That I shall live and tell him to this teeth,
"Thus didst thou."

**KING:** If it be so, Laertes—
As how should it be so? How otherwise?—
Will you be ruled by me?

**LAERTES:** Ay, my lord,
So you will not o'errule me to a peace.

**KING:** To thine own peace. If he be now returned,
As checking at his voyage, and that he means
No more to undertake it, I will work him
To an exploit, now ripe in my device,
Under the which he shall not choose but fall;
And for his death no wind of blame shall breathe,

Claudius and Laertes (Michael Cumpsty) read Hamlet's letters.

But even his mother shall uncharge the practice
And call it accident.

**LAERTES:** My lord, I will be ruled,
The rather if you could devise it so
That I might be the organ.

**KING:** It falls right.
You have been talked of since your travel much,
And that in Hamlet's hearing, for a quality
Wherein they say you shine. Your sum of parts
Did not together pluck such envy from him
As did that one, and that, in my regard,
Of the unworthiest siege.

**LAERTES:** What part is that, my lord?

**KING:** A very ribbon in the cap of youth,
Yet needful too, for youth no less becomes
The light and careless livery that it wears
Than settled age his sables and his weeds
Importing health and graveness. Two months since
Here was a gentleman of Normandy.
I have seen myself, and served against, the French,
And they can well on horseback, but this gallant
Had witchcraft in 't; he grew unto his seat,
And to such wondrous doing brought his horse
As had he been incorpsed and demi-natured

**45 naked** destitute, unarmed, without following **47 pardon** permission **50 abuse** deceit. **no such thing** not what it appears **51 character** handwriting **53 devise** explain to **57 Thus didst thou** i.e., here's for what you did to my father **58 As . . . otherwise** how can this (Hamlet's return) be true? Yet how otherwise than true (since we have the evidence of his letter)? **60 So** provided that **62 checking at** i.e., turning aside from (like a falcon leaving the quarry to fly at a chance bird). **that** if **64 device** devising, invention

**67 uncharge the practice** acquit the stratagem of being a plot **70 organ** agent, instrument **73 Your . . . parts** i.e., all your other virtues **76 unworthiest siege** least important rank **79 no less becomes** is no less suited by **81 his sables** its rich robes furred with sable. **weeds** garments **82 Importing . . . graveness** signifying a concern for health and dignified prosperity; also, giving an impression of comfortable prosperity **85 can well** are skilled **88 As . . . demi-natured** as if he had been of one body and nearly of one nature (like the centaur)

Claudius persuades Laertes to his plans.

With the brass beast. So far he topped my thought
That I in forgery of shapes and tricks
Come short of what he did.

**LAERTES:** A Norman was 't?

**KING:** A Norman.

**LAERTES:** Upon my life, Lamord.

**KING:** The very same.

**LAERTES:** I know him well. He is the brooch indeed
And gem of all the nation.

**KING:** He made confession of you,
And gave you such a masterly report
For art and exercise in your defense,
And for your rapier most especial,
That he cried out 'twould be a sight indeed
If one could match you. Th' escrimers of their nation,
He swore, had neither motion, guard, nor eye
If you opposed them. Sir, this report of his
Did Hamlet so envenom with his envy
That he could nothing do but wish and beg
Your sudden coming o'er, to play with you.
Now, out of this—

**LAERTES:** What out of this, my lord?

**KING:** Laertes, was your father dear to you?
Or are you like the painting of a sorrow,
A face without a heart?

**LAERTES:** Why ask you this?

**89 topped** surpassed **90 forgery** imagining **94 brooch** ornament **96 confession** testimonial, admission of superiority **98 For . . . defense** with respect to your skill and practice with your weapon **101 escrimers** fencers **106 sudden** immediate. **play** fence

**KING:** Not that I think you did not love your father,
But that I know love is begun by time,
And that I see, in passages of proof,
Time qualifies the spark and fire of it.
There lives within the very flame of love
A kind of wick or snuff that will abate it,
And nothing is at a like goodness still,
For goodness, growing to a pleurisy,
Dies in his own too much. That we would do,
We should do when we would; for this "would" changes
And hath abatements and delays as many
As there are tongues, are hands, are accidents,
And then this "should" is like a spendthrift sigh,
That hurts by easing. But, to the quick o' th' ulcer:
Hamlet comes back. What would you undertake
To show yourself in deed your father's son
More than in words?

**LAERTES:** To cut his throat i' the church.

**KING:** No place, indeed, should murder sanctuarize;
Revenge should have no bounds. But good Laertes,
Will you do this, keep close within your chamber.
Hamlet returned shall know you are come home.
We'll put on those shall praise your excellence
And set a double varnish on the fame
The Frenchman gave you, bring you in fine together,
And wager on your heads. He, being remiss,
Most generous, and free from all contriving,
Will not peruse the foils, so that with ease,
Or with a little shuffling, you may choose
A sword unbated, and in a pass of practice
Requite him for your father.

**LAERTES:** I will do 't,
And for that purpose I'll anoint my sword.

**112 begun by time** i.e., created by the right circumstance and hence subject to change **113 passages of proof** actual instances that prove it **114 qualifies** weakens, moderates **116 snuff** the charred part of a candlewick **117 nothing . . . still** nothing remains at a constant level of perfection **118 pleurisy** excess, plethora. (Literally, a chest inflammation.) **119 in . . . much** of its own excess. **That** that which **121 abatements** diminutions **122 As . . . accidents** as there are tongues to dissuade, hands to prevent, and chance events to intervene **123 spendthrift sigh** (An allusion to the belief that sighs draw blood from the heart.) **124 hurts by easing** i.e., costs the heart blood and wastes precious opportunity even while it affords emotional relief. **quick o' th' ulcer** i.e., heart of the matter **128 sanctuarize** protect from punishment. (Alludes to the right of sanctuary with which certain religious places were invested.) **130 Will you do this** if you wish to do this **132 put on those shall** arrange for some to **134 in fine** finally **135 remiss** negligently unsuspicious **136 generous** noble-minded **139 unbated** not blunted, having no button. **pass of practice** treacherous thrust

I bought an unction of a mountebank
So mortal that, but dip a knife in it,
Where it draws blood no cataplasm so rare,
Collected from all simples that have virtue
Under the moon, can save the thing from death
That is but scratched withal. I'll touch my point
With this contagion, that if I gall him slightly,
It may be death.

**KING:** Let's further think of this,
Weigh what convenience both of time and means
May fit us to our shape. If this should fail,
And that our drift look through our bad performance,
'Twere better not assayed. Therefore this project
Should have a back or second, that might hold
If this did blast in proof. Soft, let me see.
We'll make a solemn wager on your cunnings—
I ha 't!
When in your motion you are hot and dry—
As make your bouts more violent to that end—
And that he calls for drink, I'll have prepared him
A chalice for the nonce, whereon but sipping,
If he by chance escape your venomed stuck,
Our purpose may hold there. *[A cry within.]* But stay, what noise?

*Enter* QUEEN.

**QUEEN:** One woe doth tread upon another's heel,
So fast they follow. Your's sister's drowned, Laertes.

**LAERTES:** Drowned! O, where?

**QUEEN:** There is a willow grows askant the brook,
That shows his hoar leaves in the glassy stream;
Therewith fantastic garlands did she make
Of crowflowers, nettles, daisies, and long purples,
That liberal shepherds give a grosser name,
But our cold maids do dead men's fingers call them.
There on the pendent boughs her crownet weeds
Clamb'ring to hang, an envious sliver broke,
When down her weedy trophies and herself
Fell in the weeping brook. Her clothes spread wide,
And mermaidlike awhile they bore her up,
Which time she chanted snatches of old lauds,
As one incapable of her own distress,
Or like a creature native and endued
Unto that element. But long it could not be
Till that her garments, heavy with their drink,
Pulled the poor wretch from her melodious lay
To muddy death.

**LAERTES:** Alas, then she is drowned?

**QUEEN:** Drowned, drowned.

**LAERTES:** Too much of water hast thou, poor Ophelia,
And therefore I forbid my tears. But yet
It is our trick; nature her custom holds,
Let shame say what it will. *[He weeps.]* When these are gone,
The woman will be out. Adieu, my lord.
I have a speech of fire that fain would blaze,
But that this folly douts it. *Exit.*

**KING:** Let's follow, Gertrude.
How much I had to do to calm his rage!
Now fear I this will give it start again;
Therefore let's follow. *Exeunt.*

**5.1** *Enter two* CLOWNS *[with spades and mattocks].*

**FIRST CLOWN:** Is she to be buried in Christian burial, when she willfully seeks her own salvation?

**SECOND CLOWN:** I tell thee she is; therefore make her grave straight. The crowner hath sat on her, and finds it Christian burial.

**FIRST CLOWN:** How can that be, unless she drowned herself in her own defense?

---

**142 unction** ointment. **mountebank** quack doctor **144 cataplasm** plaster or poultice **145 simples** herbs. **virtue** potency **146 Under the moon** i.e., anywhere (with reference perhaps to the belief that herbs gathered at night had a special power) **148 gall** graze, wound **151 shape** part we propose to act **152 drift . . . performance** intention should be made visible by our bungling **155 blast in proof** burst in the test (like a cannon) **156 cunnings** respective skills **159 As** i.e., and you should **161 nonce** occasion **162 stuck** thrust. (From *stoccado,* a fencing term.) **167 askant** aslant **168 hoar leaves** white or gray undersides of the leaves **170 long purples** early purple orchids **171 liberal** free-spoken. **a grosser name** (The testicle-resembling tubers of the orchid, which also in some cases resemble *dead men's fingers,* have earned various slang names like "dogstones" and "cullions.") **172 cold** chaste **173 pendent** overhanging. **crownet** made into a chaplet or coronet

**174 envious sliver** malicious branch **175 weedy** i.e., of plants **178 lauds** hymns **179 incapable of** lacking capacity to apprehend **180 endued** adapted by nature **188 It is our trick** i.e., weeping is our natural way (when sad) **189–190 When . . . out** when my tears are all shed, the woman in me will be expended, satisfied **192 douts** extinguishes. (The Second Quarto reads "drowns.")

**5.1. Location: A churchyard.**
**s.d. Clowns** rustics **2 salvation** (A blunder for "damnation," or perhaps a suggestion that Ophelia was taking her own shortcut to heaven.) **4 straight** straightway, immediately. (But with a pun on *strait,* "narrow.") **crowner** coroner. **sat on her** conducted an inquest on her case **5 finds it** gives his official verdict that her means of death was consistent with

**SECOND CLOWN:** Why, 'tis found so.

**FIRST CLOWN:** It must be *se offendendo,* it cannot be else. For here lies the point: if I drown myself wittingly, it argues an act, and an act hath three branches—it is to act, to do, and to perform. Argal, she drowned herself wittingly.

**SECOND CLOWN:** Nay, but hear you, goodman delver—

**FIRST CLOWN:** Give me leave. Here lies the water; good. Here stands the man; good. If the man go to this water and drown himself, it is, will he, nill he, he goes, mark you that. But if the water come to him and drown him, he drowns not himself. Argal, he that is not guilty of his own death shortens not his own life.

**SECOND CLOWN:** But is this law?

**FIRST CLOWN:** Ay, marry, is 't—crowner's quest law.

**SECOND CLOWN:** Will you ha' the truth on 't? If this had not been a gentlewoman, she should have been buried out o' Christian burial.

**FIRST CLOWN:** Why, there thou sayst. And the more pity that great folk should have countenance in this world to drown or hang themselves, more than their even-Christian. Come, my spade. There is no ancient gentlemen but gardeners, ditchers, and grave makers. They hold up Adam's profession.

**SECOND CLOWN:** Was he a gentleman?

**FIRST CLOWN:** 'A was the first that ever bore arms.

**SECOND CLOWN:** Why, he had none.

**FIRST CLOWN:** What, art a heathen? How dost thou understand the Scripture? The Scripture says Adam digged. Could he dig without arms? I'll put another question to thee. If thou answerest me not to the purpose, confess thyself—

**SECOND CLOWN:** Go to.

**FIRST CLOWN:** What is he that builds stronger than either the mason, the shipwright, or the carpenter?

**SECOND CLOWN:** The gallows maker, for that frame outlives a thousand tenants.

**FIRST CLOWN:** I like thy wit well, in good faith. The gallows does well. But how does it well? It does well to those that do ill. Now thou dost ill to say the gallows is built stronger than the church. Argal, the gallows may do well to thee. To 't again, come.

**SECOND CLOWN:** "Who builds stronger than a mason, a shipwright, or a carpenter?"

**FIRST CLOWN:** Ay, tell me that, and unyoke.

**SECOND CLOWN:** Marry, now I can tell.

**FIRST CLOWN:** To 't.

**SECOND CLOWN:** Mass, I cannot tell.

*Enter* HAMLET *and* HORATIO *[at a distance].*

**FIRST CLOWN:** Cudgel thy brains no more about it, for your dull ass will not mend his pace with beating; and when you are asked this question next, say "a grave maker." The houses he makes lasts till doomsday. Go get thee in and fetch me a stoup of liquor.

*[Exit* SECOND CLOWN. FIRST CLOWN *digs.]*

*Song.*

"In youth, when I did love, did love,
Methought it was very sweet,
To contract—O—the time for—a—my behove,
O, methought there—a—was nothing—a—
meet."

**HAMLET:** Has this fellow no feeling of his business, 'a sings in grave-making?

**HORATIO:** Custom hath made it in him a property of easiness

**HAMLET:** 'Tis e'en so. The hand of little employment hath the daintier sense.

---

**8 found so** determined so in the coroner's verdict **9 se offendendo** (A comic mistake for *se defendendo,* a term used in verdicts of justifiable homicide.) **12 Argal** (Corruption of *ergo,* "therefore.") **14 goodman** (An honorific title often used with the name of a profession or craft.) **17 will he, nill he** whether he will or no, willy-nilly **22 quest** inquest **26 there thou sayst** i.e., that's right **27 countenance** privilege **29 even-Christian** fellow Christians. **ancient** going back to ancient times **31 hold up** maintain **33 bore arms** (To be entitled to bear a coat of arms would make Adam a gentleman, but as one who bore a spade, our common ancestor was an ordinary delver in the earth.) **37 arms** i.e., the arms of the body **39 confess thyself** (The saying continues, "and be hanged.")

**43 frame** (1) gallows (2) structure **46 does well** (1) is an apt answer (2) does a good turn **52 unyoke** i.e., after this great effort, you may unharness the team of your wits **55 Mass** by the Mass **60 stoup** two-quart measure **61 In . . . love** (This and the two following stanzas, with nonsensical variations, are from a poem attributed to Lord Vaux and printed in *Tottel's Miscellany,* 1557. The *O* and *a* [for "ah"] seemingly are the grunts of the digger.) **63 To contract . . . behove** i.e., to shorten the time for my own advantage. (Perhaps he means to *prolong* it.) **64 meet** suitable, i.e., more suitable **65 'a** that he **67–68 property of easiness** something he can do easily and indifferently **70 daintier sense** more delicate sense of feeling

**FIRST CLOWN:** *Song.*

"But age with his stealing steps
Hath clawed me in his clutch,
And hath shipped me into the land,
As if I had never been such."

*[He throws up a skull.]*

**HAMLET:** That skull had a tongue in it and could sing once. How the knave jowls it to the ground, as if 'twere Cain's jawbone, that did the first murder! This might be the pate of a politician, which this ass now o'erreaches, one that would circumvent God, might it not?

**HORATIO:** It might, my lord.

**HAMLET:** Or of a courtier, which could say, "Good morrow, sweet lord! How dost thou, sweet lord?" This might be my Lord Such-a-one, that praised my Lord Such-a-one's horse when 'a meant to beg it, might it not?

**HORATIO:** Ay, my lord.

**HAMLET:** Why, e'en so, and now my Lady Worm's, chapless, and knocked about the mazard with a sexton's spade. Here's fine revolution, an we had the trick to see 't. Did these bones cost no more the breeding but to play at loggets with them? Mine ache to think on 't.

**FIRST CLOWN:** *Song.*

"A pickax and a spade, a spade,
For and a shrouding sheet;
O, a pit of clay for to be made
For such a guest is meet."

*[He throws up another skull.]*

**HAMLET:** There's another. Why may not that be the skull of a lawyer? Where be his quiddities now, his quillities, his cases, his tenures, and his tricks? Why does he suffer this mad knave now to knock him about the sconce with a dirty shovel, and will not tell him of his action of battery? Hum, this fellow might be in 's time a great buyer of land, with his statutes, his recognizances, his fines, his double vouchers, his recoveries. Is this the fine of his fines and the recovery of his recoveries, to have his fine pate full of fine dirt? Will his vouchers vouch him no more of his purchases, and double ones too, than the length and breadth of a pair of indentures? The very conveyances of his lands will scarcely lie in this box, and must th' inheritor himself have no more, ha?

The First Clown (Billy Crystal) shows off a skull.

**HORATIO:** Not a jot more, my lord.

**HAMLET:** Is not parchment made of sheepskins?

**HORATIO:** Ay, my lord, and of calves' skins too.

**HAMLET:** They are sheep and calves which seek out assurance in that. I will speak to this fellow.—Whose grave's this, sirrah?

**FIRST CLOWN:** Mine, sir.

*[Sings.]* "O, pit of clay for to be made
For such a guest is meet."

**HAMLET:** I think it be thine, indeed, for thou liest in 't.

**FIRST CLOWN:** You lie out on 't, sir, and therefore 'tis not yours. For my part, I do not lie in 't, yet it is mine.

---

**73 into the land** i.e., toward my grave (?) (But note the lack of rhyme in *steps, land.*) **76 jowls** dashes (with a pun on *jowl,* "jawbone") **78 politician** schemer, plotter **79 o'erreaches** circumvents, gets the better of (with a quibble on the literal sense) **89 chapless** having no lower jaw. **mazard** i.e., head. (Literally, a drinking vessel.) **90 revolution** turn of Fortune's wheel, change. **an** if **91 trick to see** knack of seeing **91–92 cost . . . but** involve so little expense and care in upbringing that we may **92 loggets** a game in which pieces of hard wood shaped like Indian clubs or bowling pins are thrown to lie as near as possible to a stake **95 For and** and moreover **99 quiddities** subtleties, quibbles. (From Latin *quid,* "a thing.") **100 quillities** verbal niceties, subtle distinctions. (Variation of *quiddities.*) **tenures** the holding of a piece of property or office, or the conditions or period of such holding **102 sconce** head

**103 action of battery** lawsuit about physical assault **104–105 statutes, recognizances** legal documents guaranteeing a debt by attaching land and property **105–106 fines, recoveries** ways of converting entailed estates into "fee simple" or freehold **105 double** signed by two signatories. **vouchers** guarantees of the legality of a title to real estate **106–108 fine of his fines . . . fine pate . . . fine dirt** end of his legal maneuvers . . . elegant head . . . minutely sifted dirt **110 pair of indentures** legal document drawn up in duplicate on a single sheet and then cut apart on a zigzag line so that each pair was uniquely matched. (Hamlet may refer to two rows of teeth or dentures.) **110–111 conveyances** deeds **111 box** (1) deed box (2) coffin. ("Skull" has been suggested.) **112 inheritor** possessor, owner **117 assurance in that** safety in legal parchments **118 sirrah** (A term of address to inferiors.)

**HAMLET:** Thou dost lie in 't, to be in 't and say it is thine. 'Tis for the dead, not for the quick; therefore thou liest.

**FIRST CLOWN:** 'Tis a quick lie, sir; 'twill away again from me to you.

**HAMLET:** What man dost thou dig it for?

**FIRST CLOWN:** For no man, sir.

**HAMLET:** What woman, then?

**FIRST CLOWN:** For none, neither.

**HAMLET:** Who is to be buried in 't?

**FIRST CLOWN:** One that was a woman, sir, but, rest her soul, she's dead.

**HAMLET:** How absolute the knave is! We must speak by the card, or equivocation will undo us. By the Lord, Horatio, this three years I have took note of it: the age is grown so picked that the toe of the peasant comes so near the heel of the courtier, he galls his kibe.—How long hast thou been grave maker?

**FIRST CLOWN:** Of all the days i' the year, I came to 't that day that our last king Hamlet overcame Fortinbras.

**HAMLET:** How long is that since?

**FIRST CLOWN:** Cannot you tell that? Every fool can tell that. It was that very day that young Hamlet was born—he that is mad and sent into England.

**HAMLET:** Ay, marry, why was he sent into England?

**FIRST CLOWN:** Why, because 'a was mad. 'A shall recover his wits there, or if 'a do not, 'tis no great matter there.

**HAMLET:** Why?

**FIRST CLOWN:** 'Twill not be seen in him there. There the men are as mad as he.

**HAMLET:** How came he mad?

**FIRST CLOWN:** Very strangely, they say.

**HAMLET:** How strangely?

**FIRST CLOWN:** Faith, e'en with losing his wits.

**HAMLET:** Upon what ground?

**FIRST CLOWN:** Why, here in Denmark. I have been sexton here, man and boy, thirty years.

**HAMLET:** How long will a man lie i' th' earth ere he rot?

**FIRST CLOWN:** Faith, if 'a be not rotten before 'a die—as we have many pocky corpses nowadays, that will scarce hold the laying in—'a will last you some eight year or nine year. A tanner will last you nine year.

**HAMLET:** Why he more than another?

**FIRST CLOWN:** Why, sir, his hide is so tanned with his trade that 'a will keep out water a great while, and your water is a sore decayer of your whoreson dead body *[He picks up a skull.]* Here's a skull now hath lien you i' th' earth three-and-twenty years.

**HAMLET:** Whose was it?

**FIRST CLOWN:** A whoreson mad fellow's it was. Whose do you think it was?

**HAMLET:** Nay, I know not.

**FIRST CLOWN:** A pestilence on him for a mad rogue! 'A poured a flagon of Rhenish on my head once. This same skull, sir, was, sir, Yorick's skull, the King's jester.

**HAMLET:** This?

**FIRST CLOWN:** E'en that.

**HAMLET:** Let me see. *[He takes the skull.]* Alas, poor Yorick! I knew him, Horatio, a fellow of infinite jest, of most excellent fancy. He hath bore me on his back a thousand times, and now how abhorred in my imagination it is! My gorge rises at it. Here hung those lips that I have kissed I know not how oft. Where be your gibes now? Your gambols, your songs, your flashes of merriment that were wont to set the table on a roar? Not one now, to mock your own grinning? Quite chopfallen? Now get you to my lady's chamber and tell her, let her paint an inch

---

**126 quick** living **137 absolute** strict, precise **138 by the card** i.e., with precision. (Literally, by the mariner's compass-card, on which the points of the compass were marked.) **equivocation** ambiguity in the use of terms **139 took** taken **140 picked** refined, fastidious **141–142 galls his kibe** chafes the courtier's chilblain

**160 ground** cause. (But, in the next line, the gravedigger takes the word in the sense of "land," "country.") **165 pocky** rotten, diseased. (Literally, with the pox, or syphilis.) **166 hold the laying in** hold together long enough to be interred. **last you** last. (*You* is used colloquially here and in the following lines.) **171 sore** i.e., terrible, great. **whoreson** i.e., vile, scurvy **172–173 lien you** lain. (See the note at line 166.) **179 Rhenish** Rhine wine **185 bore** borne **187 My gorge rises** i.e., I feel nauseated **190 were wont** used **191–192 mock your own grinning** mock at the way your skull seems to be grinning (just as you used to mock at yourself and those who grinned at you) **192 chopfallen** (1) lacking the lower jaw (2) dejected

Hamlet speaks to the skull tossed to him by the First Clown.

thick, to this favor she must come. Make her laugh at that. Prithee, Horatio, tell me one thing.

**HORATIO:** What's that, my lord?

**HAMLET:** Dost thou think Alexander looked o' this fashion i' th' earth?

**HORATIO:** E'en so.

**HAMLET:** And smelt so? Pah! *[He throws down the skull.]*

**HORATIO:** E'en so, my lord.

**HAMLET:** To what base uses we may return, Horatio! Why may not imagination trace the noble dust of Alexander till 'a find it stopping a bunghole?

**HORATIO:** 'Twere to consider too curiously to consider so.

**HAMLET:** No, faith, not a jot, but to follow him thither with modesty enough, and likelihood to lead it. As thus: Alexander died, Alexander was buried, Alexander returneth to dust, the dust is earth, of earth we make loam, and why of that loam whereto he was converted might they not stop a beer barrel?
Imperious Caesar, dead and turned to clay,
Might stop a hole to keep the wind away.
O, that that earth which kept the world in awe
Should patch a wall t' expel the winter's flaw!

*Enter* KING, QUEEN, LAERTES, *and the corpse [of* OPHELIA, *in procession, with* PRIEST, lords, *etc.]*

But soft, but soft awhile! Here comes the King,
The Queen, the courtiers. Who is this they follow?
And with such maimèd rites? This doth betoken
The corpse they follow did with desperate hand
Fordo its own life. 'Twas of some estate.
Couch we awhile and mark.

*[He and* HORATIO *conceal themselves.* OPHELIA*'s body is taken to the grave.]*

**LAERTES:** What ceremony else?

**HAMLET** *[to* HORATIO*]*: That is Laertes, a very noble youth. Mark.

**LAERTES:** What ceremony else?

**PRIEST:** Her obsequies have been as far enlarged
As we have warranty. Her death was doubtful,
And but that great command o'ersways the order
She should in ground unsanctified been lodged
Till the last trumpet. For charitable prayers,
Shards, flints, and pebbles should be thrown on her.
Yet here she is allowed her virgin crants,
Her maiden strewments, and the bringing home
Of bell and burial.

**LAERTES:** Must there no more be done?

**PRIEST:** No more be done.
We should profane the service of the dead
To sing a requiem and such rest to her
As to peace-parted souls.

**LAERTES:** Lay her i' th' earth,
And from her fair and unpolluted flesh
May violets spring! I tell thee, churlish priest,
A ministering angel shall my sister be
When thou liest howling.

**HAMLET** *[to* HORATIO*]*: What, the fair Ophelia!

**QUEEN** *[scattering flowers]*: Sweets to the sweet! Farewell.
I hoped thou shouldst have been my Hamlet's wife.
I thought thy bride-bed to have decked, sweet maid,
And not t' have strewed thy grave.

**LAERTES:** O, treble woe
Fall ten times treble on that cursèd head

---

**194 favor** aspect, appearance **204 bunghole** hole for filling or emptying a cask **205 curiously** minutely **208 modesty** plausible moderation **211 loam** mortar consisting chiefly of moistened clay and straw **213 Imperious** imperial **216 flaw** gust of wind **217 soft** i.e., wait, be careful

**219 maimèd** mutilated, incomplete **221 Fordo** destroy. **estate** rank **222 Couch we** let's hide, lie low **227 warranty** i.e., ecclesiastical authority **228 great . . . order** orders from on high overrule the prescribed procedures **229 She should . . . lodged** she should have been buried in unsanctified ground **230 For** in place of **231 Shards** broken bits of pottery **232 crants** garlands betokening maidenhood **233 strewments** flowers strewn on a coffin **233–234 bringing . . . burial** laying the body to rest, to the sound of the bell **237 such rest** i.e., to pray for such rest **238 peace-parted souls** those who have died at peace with God **240 violets** (See 4.5.188 and note.) **242 howling** i.e., in hell

Ophelia is put to rest.

Whose wicked deed thy most ingenious sense
Deprived thee of! Hold off the earth awhile,
Till I have caught her once more in mine arms.
*[He leaps into the grave and embraces* OPHELIA.*]*
Now pile your dust upon the quick and dead,
Till of this flat a mountain you have made
T' o'ertop old Pelion or the skyish head
Of blue Olympus.

**HAMLET** *[coming forward]*: What is he whose grief
Bears such an emphasis, whose phrase of sorrow
Conjures the wandering stars and makes them stand
Like wonder-wounded hearers? This is I,
Hamlet the Dane.

**LAERTES** *[grappling with him]*: The devil take thy soul!

**HAMLET:** Thou pray'st not well.
I prithee, take thy fingers from my throat,
For though I am not splenitive and rash,
Yet have I in me something dangerous,
Which let thy wisdom fear. Hold off thy hand.

**KING:** Pluck them asunder.

**QUEEN:** Hamlet, Hamlet!

**ALL:** Gentlemen!

**HORATIO:** Good my lord, be quiet.
*[*HAMLET *and* LAERTES *are parted.]*

**HAMLET:** Why, I will fight with him upon this theme
Until my eyelids will no longer wag.

**QUEEN:** O my son, what theme?

**HAMLET:** I loved Ophelia. Forty thousand brothers
Could not with all their quantity of love
Make up my sum. What wilt thou do for her?

**KING:** O, he is mad, Laertes.

**QUEEN:** For love of God, forbear him.

**HAMLET:** 'Swounds, show me what thou'lt do.
Woo't weep? Woo't fight? Woo't fast? Woo't tear thyself?
Woo't drink up eisel? Eat a crocodile?
I'll do 't. Dost come here to whine?
To outface me with leaping in her grave?
Be buried quick with her, and so will I.
And if thou prate of mountains, let them throw
Millions of acres on us, till our ground,
Singeing his pate against the burning zone,
Make Ossa like a wart! Nay, an thou'lt mouth,
I'll rant as well as thou.

**QUEEN:** This is mere madness,
And thus awhile the fit will work on him;
Anon, as patient as the female dove
When that her golden couplets are disclosed,
His silence will sit drooping.

**HAMLET:** Hear you, sir.
What is the reason that you use me thus?
I loved you ever. But it is no matter.
Let Hercules himself do what he may,
The cat will mew, and dog will have his day.
*Exit* HAMLET.

---

**248 ingenious sense** a mind that is quick, alert, of fine qualities **253–254 Pelion, Olympus** sacred mountains in the north of Thessaly; see also *Ossa*, below, at line 286 **255 emphasis** i.e., rhetorical and florid emphasis. (*Phrase* has a similar rhetorical connotation.) **256 wandering stars** planets **257 wonder-wounded** struck with amazement **258 the Dane** (This title normally signifies the King; see 1.1.17 and note.) **259 s.d. grappling with him** The testimony of the First Quarto that *"Hamlet leaps in after Laertes"* and the "Elegy on Burbage" ("Oft have I seen him leap into the grave") seem to indicate one way in which this fight was staged; however, the difficulty of fitting two contenders and Ophelia's body into a confined space (probably the trapdoor) suggests to many editors the alternative, that Laertes jumps out of the grave to attack Hamlet.) **262 splenitive** quick-tempered

**270 wag** move (A fluttering eyelid is a conventional sign that life has not yet gone.) **276 forbear him** leave him alone **277 'Swounds** by His (Christ's) wounds **278 Woo't** wilt thou **279 drink up** drink deeply. **eisel** vinegar. **crocodile** (Crocodiles were tough and dangerous, and were supposed to shed hypocritical tears.) **282 quick** alive **285 his pate** his head, i.e., top. **burning zone** zone in the celestial sphere containing the sun's orbit, between the tropics of Cancer and Capricorn **286 Ossa** another mountain in Thessaly. (In their war against the Olympian gods, the giants attempted to heap Ossa on Pelion to scale Olympus.) **an** if. **mouth** i.e., rant **287 mere** utter **290 golden couplets** two baby pigeons, covered with yellow down. **disclosed** hatched **294–295 Let . . . day** i.e., (1) even Hercules couldn't stop Laertes' theatrical rant (2) I, too, will have my turn; i.e., despite any blustering attempts at interference, every person will sooner or later do what he or she must do

**KING:** I pray thee, good Horatio, wait upon him.
*[Exit]* HORATIO.
*[To* LAERTES.*]* Strengthen your patience in our last night's speech;
We'll put the matter to the present push.—
Good Gertrude, set some watch over your son.—
This grave shall have a living monument.
An hour of quiet shortly shall we see;
Till then, in patience our proceeding be. *Exeunt.*

## 5.2 *Enter* HAMLET *and* HORATIO.

**HAMLET:** So much for this, sir; now shall you see the other.
You do remember all the circumstance?

**HORATIO:** Remember it, my lord!

**HAMLET:** Sir, in my heart there was a kind of fighting
That would not let me sleep. Methought I lay
Worse than the mutines in the bilboes. Rashly,
And praised by rashness for it—let us know
Our indiscretion sometimes serves us well
When our deep plots do pall, and that should learn us
There's a divinity that shapes our ends,
Rough-hew them how we will—

**HORATIO:** That is most certain.

**HAMLET:** Up from my cabin,
My sea-gown scarfed about me, in the dark
Groped I to find out them, had my desire,
Fingered their packet, and in fine withdrew
To mine own room again, making so bold,
My fears forgetting manners, to unseal
Their grand commission; where I found, Horatio—
Ah, royal knavery!—an exact command,
Larded with many several sorts of reasons
Importing Denmark's health and England's too,
With, ho! such bugs and goblins in my life,
That on the supervise, no leisure bated,
No, not to stay the grinding of the ax,
My head should be struck off.

**HORATIO:** Is 't possible?

**HAMLET** *[giving a document]*: Here's the commission. Read it at more leisure.
But wilt thou hear now how I did proceed?

**HORATIO:** I beseech you.

**HAMLET:** Being thus benetted round with villainies—
Ere I could make a prologue to my brains,
They had begun the play—I sat me down,
Devised a new commission, wrote it fair.
I once did hold it, as our statists do,
A baseness to write fair, and labored much
How to forget that learning, but, sir, now
It did me yeoman's service. Wilt thou know
Th' effect of what I wrote?

**HORATIO:** Ay, good my lord.

**HAMLET:** An earnest conjuration from the King,
As England was his faithful tributary,
As love between them like the palm might flourish,
As peace should still her wheaten garland wear
And stand a comma 'tween their amities,
And many suchlike "as"es of great charge,
That on the view and knowing of these contents,
Without debatement further more or less,
He should those bearers put to sudden death,
Not shriving time allowed.

**HORATIO:** How was this sealed?

**HAMLET:** Why, even in that was heaven ordinant.
I had my father's signet in my purse,
Which was the model of that Danish seal;
Folded the writ up in the form of th' other,
Subscribed it, gave 't th' impression, placed it safety,
The changeling never known. Now, the next day

---

**297 in** i.e., by recalling **298 present push** immediate test **300 living** lasting. (For Laertes' private understanding, Claudius also hints that Hamlet's death will serve as such a monument.) **301 hour of quiet** time free of conflict

**5.2. Location: The castle.**
**1 see the other** hear the other news **6 mutines** mutineers. **bilboes** shackles. **Rashly** on impulse. (This adverb goes with lines 12 ff.) **7 know** acknowledge **8 indiscretion** lack of foresight and judgment (not an indiscreet act) **9 pall** fail, falter, go stale. **learn** teach **11 Rough-hew** shape roughly **13 sea-gown** seaman's coat. **scarfed** loosely wrapped **14 them** i.e. Rosencrantz and Guildenstern **15 Fingered** pilfered, pinched. **in fine** finally, in conclusion **20 Larded** garnished. **several** different **21 Importing** relating to **22 bugs, goblins** bugbears, hobgoblins. **in my life** i.e., to be feared if I were allowed to live

**23 supervise** reading. **leisure bated** delay allowed **24 stay** await **30–31 Ere . . . play** before I could consciously turn my brain to the matter, it had started working on a plan **32 fair** in a clear hand **33 statists** statesmen **34 baseness** i.e., lower-class trait **36 yeoman's** i.e., substantial, faithful, loyal **37 effect** purport **38 conjuration** entreaty **40 palm** (An image of health; see Psalms 92:12.) **41 still** always. **wheaten garland** (Symbolic of fruitful agriculture, of peace and plenty.) **42 comma** (Indicating continuity, link.) **43 "as"es** (1) the "whereases" of a formal document (2) asses. **charge** (1) import (2) burden (appropriate to asses) **47 shriving time** time for confession and absolution **48 ordinant** directing **49 signet** small seal **50 model** replica **51 writ** writing **52 Subscribed** signed (with forged signature). **impression** i.e., with a wax seal **53 changeling** i.e., substituted letter. (Literally, a fairy child substituted for a human one.)

Was our sea fight, and what to this was sequent
Thou knowest already.

**HORATIO:** So Guildenstern and Rosencrantz go to 't.

**HAMLET:** Why, man, they did make love to this employment.
They are not near my conscience. Their defeat
Does by their own insinuation grow.
'Tis dangerous when the baser nature comes
Between the pass and fell incensèd points
Of mighty opposites.

**HORATIO:** Why, what a king is this!

**HAMLET:** Does it not, think thee, stand me now upon—
He that hath killed my king and whored my mother,
Popped in between th' election and my hopes,
Thrown out his angle for my proper life,
And with such cozenage—is 't not perfect conscience
To quit him with this arm? And is 't not to be damned
To let this canker of our nature come
In further evil?

**HORATIO:** It must be shortly known to him from England
What is the issue of the business there.

**HAMLET:** It will be short. The interim is mine,
And a man's life no more than to say "one."
But I am very sorry, good Horatio,
That to Laertes I forgot myself,
For by the image of my cause I see
The portraiture of his. I'll court his favors.
But, sure, the bravery of his grief did put me
Into a tow'ring passion.

**HORATIO:** Peace, who comes here?

*Enter a Courtier [*OSRIC*].*

**OSRIC:** Your lordship is right welcome back to Denmark.

**HAMLET:** I humbly thank you, sir. *[To* HORATIO.*]* Dost know this water fly?

**HORATIO:** No, my good lord.

**HAMLET:** Thy state is the more gracious, for 'tis a vice to know him. He hath much land, and fertile. Let a beast be lord of beasts, and his crib shall stand at the King's mess. 'Tis a chuff, but, as I say, spacious in the possession of dirt.

**OSRIC:** Sweet lord, if your lordship were at leisure, I should impart a thing to you from His Majesty.

**HAMLET:** I will receive it, sir, with diligence of spirit. Put your bonnet to his right use; 'tis for the head.

**OSRIC:** I thank you lordship, it is very hot.

**HAMLET:** No, believe me, 'tis very cold. The wind is northerly.

**OSRIC:** It is indifferent cold, my lord, indeed.

**HAMLET:** But yet methinks it is very sultry and hot for my complexion.

**OSRIC:** Exceedingly, my lord. It is very sultry, as 'twere—I cannot tell how. My lord, His Majesty bade me signify to you that 'a has laid a great wager on your head. Sir, this is the matter—

**HAMLET:** I beseech you, remember:

*[*HAMLET *moves him to put on his hat.]*

**OSRIC:** Nay, good my lord; for my ease, in good faith. Sir, here is newly come to court Laertes—believe me, an absolute gentleman, full of most excellent differences, of very soft society and great showing. Indeed, to speak feelingly of him, he is the card or calendar of gentry, for you shall find in him the continent of what part a gentleman would see.

**HAMLET:** Sir, his definement suffers no perdition in you, though I know to divide him inventorially

---

**54 was sequent** followed **58 defeat** destruction **59 insinuation** intrusive intervention, sticking their noses in my business **60 baser** of lower social station **61 pass** thrust. **fell** fierce **62 opposites** antagonists **63 stand me now upon** become incumbent on me now **65 election** (The Danish monarch was "elected" by a small number of high-ranking electors.) **66 angle** fishhook. **proper** very **67 cozenage** trickery **68 quit** requite, pay back **69 canker** ulcer **69–70 come In** grow into **74 a man's . . . "one"** one's whole life occupies such a short time, only as long as it takes to count to 1 **79 bravery** bravado

**86–88 Let . . . mess** i.e., if a man, no matter how beastlike, is as rich in livestock and possessions as Osric, he may eat at the King's table **87 crib** manger **88 chuff** boor, churl. (The Second Quarto spelling, *chough,* is a variant spelling that also suggests the meaning here of "chattering jackdaw.") **93 bonnet** any kind of cap or hat. **his** its **97 indifferent** somewhat **99 complexion** temperament **105 for my ease** (A conventional reply declining the invitation to put his hat back on.) **107 absolute** perfect **107–108 differences** special qualities **108 soft society** agreeable manners. **great showing** distinguished appearance **109 feelingly** with just perception. **card** chart, map. **calendar** guide **110 gentry** good breeding **110–111 the continent . . . see** one who contains in him all the qualities a gentleman would like to see. (A *continent* is that which contains.) **112 definement** definition. (Hamlet proceeds to mock Osric by throwing his lofty diction back at him.) **perdition** loss, diminution **113 you** your description. **divide him inventorially** enumerate his graces

Osric (Robin Williams) tells Hamlet of the duel.

would dozy th' arithmetic of memory, and yet but yaw neither in respect of his quick sail. But, in the verity of extolment, I take him to be a soul of great article, and his infusion of such dearth and rareness as, to make true diction of him, his semblable is his mirror and who else would trace him his umbrage, nothing more.

**OSRIC:** Your lordship speaks most infallibly of him.

**HAMLET:** The concernancy, sir? Why do we wrap the gentleman in our more rawer breath?

**OSRIC:** Sir?

**HORATIO:** Is 't not possible to understand in another tongue? You will do 't, sir, really.

**HAMLET:** What imports the nomination of this gentleman?

**OSRIC:** Of Laertes?

**HORATIO** *[to* HAMLET*]*: His purse is empty already; all 's golden words are spent.

**HAMLET:** Of him, sir.

**OSRIC:** I know you are not ignorant—

**HAMLET:** I would you did, sir. Yet in faith if you did, it would not much approve me. Well, sir?

**OSRIC:** You are not ignorant of what excellence Laertes is—

**HAMLET:** I dare not confess that, lest I should compare with him in excellence. But to know a man well were to know himself.

**OSRIC:** I mean, sir, for his weapon; but in the imputation laid on him by them, in his meed he's unfellowed.

**HAMLET:** What's his weapon?

**OSRIC:** Rapier and dagger.

**HAMLET:** That's two of his weapons—but well.

**OSRIC:** The King, sir, hath wagered with him six Barbary horses, against the which he has impawned, as I take it, six French rapiers and poniards, with their assigns, as girdle, hangers, and so. Three of the carriages, in faith, are very dear to fancy, very responsive to the hilts, most delicate carriages, and of very liberal conceit.

**HAMLET:** What call you the carriages?

**HORATIO** *[to* HAMLET*]*: I knew you must be edified by the margent ere you had done.

**OSRIC:** The carriages, sir, are the hangers.

**HAMLET:** The phrase would be more germane to the matter if we could carry a cannon by our sides; I would it might be hangers till then. But, on: six Barbary horses against six French swords, their assigns, and three liberal-conceited carriages; that's the French bet against the Danish. Why is this impawned, as you call it?

---

**114 dozy** dizzy. **115 yaw** swing unsteadily off course. (Said of a ship.) **neither** for all that. **in respect of** in comparison with **115–116 in . . . extolment** in true praise (of him) **116–117 of great article** one with many articles in his inventory **117 infusion** essence, character infused into him by nature. **dearth and rareness** rarity **118 make true diction** speak truly **118–119 semblable** only true likeness **119 who . . . trace** any other person who would wish to follow. **umbrage** shadow **122 concernancy** import, relevance **123 rawer breath** unrefined speech that can only come short in praising him **125–126 to understand . . . tongue** i.e., for you, Osric, to understand when someone else speaks your language. (Horatio twits Osric for not being able to understand the kind of flowery speech he himself uses, when Hamlet speaks in such a vein. Alternatively, all this could be said to Hamlet.) **126 You will do 't** i.e., you can if you try, or, you may well have to try (to speak plainly) **127 nomination** naming

**135 approve** commend **138–140 I dare . . . himself** I dare not boast of knowing Laertes' excellence lest I seem to imply a comparable excellence in myself. Certainly, to know another person well, one must know oneself. **141 for** i.e., with **141–142 imputation . . . them** reputation given him by others **142 meed** merit. **unfellowed** unmatched **145 but well** but never mind **147 he** i.e., Laertes. **impawned** staked, wagered **148 poniards** daggers **149 assigns** appurtenances. **hangers** straps on the sword belt (*girdle*), from which the sword hung. **and so** and so on **149–150 carriages** (An affected way of saying *hangers;* literally, gun carriages.) **150 dear to fancy** delightful to the fancy **150–151 responsive** corresponding closely, matching or well adjusted **151 delicate** (i.e., in workmanship) **152 liberal conceit** elaborate design **155 margent** margin of a book, place for explanatory notes

**OSRIC:** The King, sir, hath laid, sir, that in a dozen passes between yourself and him, he shall not exceed you three hits. He hath laid on twelve for nine, and it would come to immediate trial, if your lordship would vouchsafe the answer.

**HAMLET:** How if I answer no?

**OSRIC:** I mean, my lord, the opposition of your person in trial.

**HAMLET:** Sir, I will walk here in the hall. If it please His Majesty, it is the breathing time of day with me. Let the foils be brought, the gentleman willing, and the King hold his purpose, I will win for him an I can; if not, I will gain nothing but my shame and the odd hits.

**OSRIC:** Shall I deliver you so?

**HAMLET:** To this effect, sir—after what flourish your nature will.

**OSRIC:** I commend my duty to your lordship.

**HAMLET:** Yours, yours. *[Exit* OSRIC.*]* 'A does well to commend it himself; there are no tongues else for 's turn.

**HORATIO:** This lapwing runs away with the shell on his head.

**HAMLET:** 'A did comply with his dug before 'a sucked it. Thus has he—and many more of the same breed that I know the drossy age dotes on—only got the tune of the time and, out of an habit of encounter, a kind of yeasty collection, which carries them through and through the most fanned and winnowed opinions; and do but blow them to their trial, the bubbles are out.

*Enter a* LORD.

**LORD:** My lord, His Majesty commended him to you by young Osric, who brings back to him that you attend him in the hall. He sends to know if your pleasure hold to play with Laertes, or that you will take longer time.

**HAMLET:** I am constant to my purposes; they follow the King's pleasure. If his fitness speaks, mine is ready; now or whensoever, provided I be so able as now.

**LORD:** The King and Queen and all are coming down.

**HAMLET:** In happy time.

**LORD:** The Queen desires you to use some gentle entertainment to Laertes before you fall to play.

**HAMLET:** She well instructs me. *[Exit* LORD.*]*

**HORATIO:** You will lose, my lord.

**HAMLET:** I do not think so. Since he went into France, I have been in continual practice; I shall win at the odds. But thou wouldst not think how ill all's here about my heart; but it is no matter.

**HORATIO:** Nay, good my lord—

**HAMLET:** It is but foolery, but it is such a kind of gaingiving as would perhaps trouble a woman.

**HORATIO:** If your mind dislike anything, obey it. I will forestall their repair hither and say you are not fit.

**HAMLET:** Not a whit, we defy augury. There is special providence in the fall of a sparrow. If it be now, 'tis not to come; if it be not to come, it will be now; if it be not now; yet it will come. The readiness is all. Since no man of aught he leaves knows, what is 't to leave betimes? Let be.

*A table prepared. [Enter] trumpets, drums, and officers with cushions;* KING, QUEEN, *[*OSRIC,*] and all the state; foils, daggers, [and wine borne in;] and* LAERTES.

---

**164 laid** wagered **165 passes** bouts. (The odds of the betting are hard to explain. Possibly the King bets that Hamlet will win at least five out of twelve, at which point Laertes raises the odds against himself by betting he will win nine.) **168 vouchsafe the answer** be so good as to accept the challenge. (Hamlet deliberately takes the phrase in its literal sense of replying.) **173 breathing time** exercise period. **Let** i.e., if **177 deliver you** report what you say **180 commend** commit to your favor. (A conventional salutation, but Hamlet wryly uses a more literal meaning, "recommend," "praise," in line 182.) **182–183 for 's turn** for his purposes, i.e., to do it for him **184 lapwing** (A proverbial type of youthful forwardness. Also, a bird that draws intruders away from its nest and was thought to run about with its head in the shell when newly hatched; a seeming reference to Osric's hat.) **186 comply . . . dug** observe ceremonious formality toward his nurse's or mother's teat **188 drossy** laden with scum and impurities, frivolous **tune** temper, mood, manner of speech. **189 an habit of encounter** a demeanor in conversing (with courtiers of his own kind) **190 yeasty** frothy. **collection** i.e., of current phrases **190–191 carries . . . opinions** sustains them right through the scrutiny of persons whose opinions are select and refined. (Literally, like grain separated from its chaff. Osric is both the chaff and the bubbly froth on the surface of the liquor that is soon blown away.) **192 and do** yet do **192–193 blow . . . out** test them by merely blowing on them, and their bubbles burst **197 that** if **200 If . . . ready** if he declares his readiness, my convenience waits on his **203 In happy time** (A phrase of courtesy indicating that the time is convenient.) **204–205 entertainment** greeting **213–214 gaingiving** misgiving **216 repair** coming **221–222 Since . . . Let be** since no one has knowledge of what he is leaving behind, what does an early death matter after all? Enough; don't struggle against it.

**KING:** Come, Hamlet, come and take this hand from me.
*[The* KING *puts* LAERTES' *hand into* HAMLET*'s.]*

**HAMLET** *[to* LAERTES*]:* Give me your pardon, sir. I have done you wrong,
But pardon 't as you are a gentleman.
This presence knows,
And you must needs have heard, how I am punished
With a sore distraction. What I have done
That might your nature, honor, and exception
Roughly awake, I here proclaim was madness.
Was 't Hamlet wronged Laertes? Never Hamlet.
If Hamlet from himself be ta'en away,
And when he's not himself does wrong Laertes,
Then Hamlet does it not, Hamlet denies it.
Who does it, then? His madness. If 't be so,
Hamlet is of the faction that is wronged;
His madness is poor Hamlet's enemy.
Sir, in this audience
Let my disclaiming from a purposed evil
Free me so far in your most generous thoughts
That I have shot my arrow o'er the house
And hurt my brother.

**LAERTES:** I am satisfied in nature,
Whose motive in this case should stir me most
To my revenge. But in my terms of honor
I stand aloof, and will no reconcilement
Till by some elder masters of known honor
I have a voice and precedent of peace
To keep my name ungored. But till that time
I do receive your offered love like love,
And will not wrong it.

**HAMLET:** I embrace it freely,
And will this brothers' wager frankly play.—
Give us the foils. Come on.

**LAERTES:** Come, one for me.

**HAMLET:** I'll be your foil, Laertes. In mine ignorance
Your skill shall, like a star i' the darkest night,
Stick fiery off indeed.

**LAERTES:** You mock me, sir.

**HAMLET:** No, by this hand.

**226 presence** royal assembly **227 punished** afflicted **229 exception** disapproval **236 faction** party **241 That I have** as if I had **242 in nature** i.e., as to my personal feelings **243 motive** prompting **247 voice** authoritative pronouncement. **of peace** for reconciliation **248 name ungored** reputation unwounded **251 frankly** without ill feeling or the burden of rancor **253 foil** thin metal background that sets a jewel off (with pun on the blunted rapier for fencing) **255 Stick fiery off** stand out brilliantly

Laertes (Michael Maloney) and Hamlet duel.

**KING:** Give them the foils, young Osric. Cousin Hamlet,
You know the wager?

**HAMLET:** Very well, my lord.
Your Grace has laid the odds o' the weaker side.

**KING:** I do not fear it; I have seen you both.
But since he is bettered, we have therefore odds.

**LAERTES:** This is too heavy. Let me see another.
*[He exchanges his foil for another.]*

**HAMLET:** This likes me well. These foils have all a length?
*[They prepare to play.]*

**OSRIC:** Ay, my good lord.

**KING:** Set me the stoups of wine upon that table.
If Hamlet give the first or second hit,
Or quit in answer of the third exchange,
Let all the battlements their ordnance fire.
The King shall drink to Hamlet's better breath,
And in the cup an union shall he throw
Richer than that which four successive kings
In Denmark's crown have worn. Give me the cups,
And let the kettle to the trumpet speak,
The trumpet to the cannoneer without,
The cannons to the heavens, the heaven to earth,
"Now the King drinks to Hamlet." Come, begin.
*Trumpets the while.*
And you, the judges, bear a wary eye.

**HAMLET:** Come on, sir.

**259 laid the odds o'** bet on, backed **261 is bettered** has improved; is the odds-on favorite. (Laertes' handicap is the "three hits" specified in line 166.) **263 likes me** pleases me **267 Or . . . exchange** i.e., or requites Laertes in the third bout for having won the first two **269 better breath** improved vigor **270 union** pearl. (So called, according to Pliny's *Natural History*, 9, because pearls are *unique,* never identical.) **273 kettle** kettledrum

**LAERTES:** Come, my lord. *[They play.* HAMLET *scores a hit.]*

**HAMLET:** One.

**LAERTES:** No.

**HAMLET:** Judgment.

**OSRIC:** A hit, a very palpable hit.

*Drum, trumpets, and shot. Flourish. A piece goes off.*

**LAERTES:** Well, again.

**KING:** Stay, give me drink. Hamlet, this pearl is thine.

*[He drinks, and throws a pearl in* HAMLET*'s cup.]*

Here's to thy health. Give him the cup.

**HAMLET:** I'll play this bout first. Set it by awhile.
Come. *[They play.]* Another hit; what say you?

**LAERTES:** A touch, a touch, I do confess 't.

**KING:** Our son shall win.

**QUEEN:** He's fat and scant of breath.
Here, Hamlet, take my napkin, rub thy brows.
The Queen carouses to thy fortune, Hamlet.

**HAMLET:** Good madam!

**KING:** Gertrude, do not drink.

**QUEEN:** I will, my lord, I pray you pardon me.

*[She drinks.]*

**KING** *[aside]*: It is the poisoned cup. It is too late.

**HAMLET:** I dare not drink yet, madam; by and by.

**QUEEN:** Come, let me wipe thy face.

**LAERTES** *[to* KING*]*: My lord, I'll hit him now.

**KING:** I do not think 't.

**LAERTES** *[aside]*: And yet it is almost against my conscience.

**HAMLET:** Come, for the third, Laertes. You do but dally.
I pray you, pass with your best violence;
I am afeard you make a wanton of me.

**LAERTES:** Say you so? Come on. *[They play.]*

**OSRIC:** Nothing neither way.

**289 fat** not physically fit, out of training **290 napkin** handkerchief **291 carouses** drinks a toast **301 pass** thrust **302 make . . . me** i.e., treat me like a spoiled child, trifle with me

**LAERTES:** Have at you now!

*[*LAERTES *wounds* HAMLET*; then, in scuffling, they change rapiers, and* HAMLET *wounds* LAERTES.*]*

**KING:** Part them! They are incensed.

**HAMLET:** Nay, come, again. *[The* QUEEN *falls.]*

**OSRIC:** Look to the Queen there, ho!

**HORATIO:** They bleed on both sides. How is it, my lord?

**OSRIC:** How is 't, Laertes?

**LAERTES:** Why, as a woodcock to mine own springe, Osric;
I am justly killed with mine own treachery.

**HAMLET:** How does the Queen?

**KING:** She swoons to see them bleed.

**QUEEN:** No, no, the drink, the drink—O my dear Hamlet—
The drink, the drink! I am poisoned. *[She dies.]*

**HAMLET:** O villainy! Ho, let the door be locked!
Treachery! Seek it out. *[*LAERTES *falls. Exit* OSRIC.*]*

**LAERTES:** It is here, Hamlet. Hamlet, thou art slain.
No med'cine in the world can do thee good;
In thee there is not half an hour's life.
The treacherous instrument is in thy hand,
Unbated and envenomed. The foul practice
Hath turned itself on me. Lo, here I lie,
Never to rise again. Thy mother's poisoned.
I can no more. The King, the King's to blame.

**HAMLET:** The point envenomed too? Then, venom, to thy work. *[He stabs the* KING.*]*

**ALL:** Treason! Treason!

**KING:** O, yet defend me, friends! I am but hurt.

**HAMLET** *[forcing the* KING *to drink]*: Here, thou incestuous, murderous, damnèd Dane,
Drink off this potion. Is thy union here?
Follow my mother. *[The* KING *dies.]*

**305 s.d. in scuffling, they change rapiers** (This stage direction occurs in the Folio. According to a widespread stage tradition, Hamlet receives a scratch, realizes that Laertes' sword is unbated, and accordingly forces an exchange.) **309 woodcock** a bird, a type of stupidity or as a decoy. **springe** trap, snare **320 Unbated** not blunted with a button. **practice** plot **328 union** pearl. (See line 270; with grim puns on the word's other meanings: marriage, shared death.)

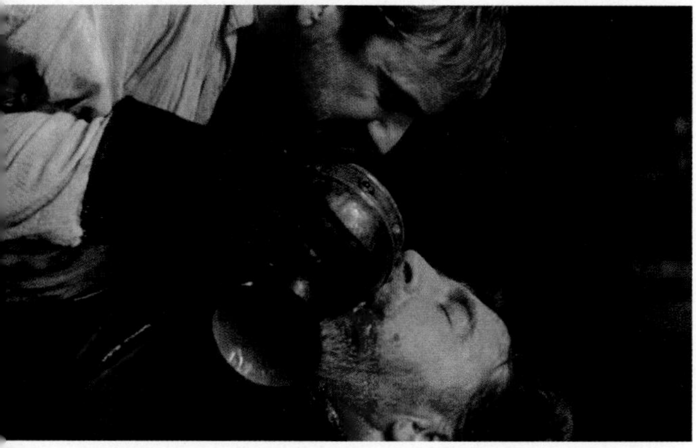

Hamlet forces Claudius to drink the poisoned wine.

**LAERTES:** He is justly served.
It is a poison tempered by himself.
Exchange forgiveness with me, noble Hamlet.
Mine and my father's death come not upon thee,
Nor thine on me! *[He dies]*

**HAMLET:** Heaven make thee free of it! I follow thee.
I am dead, Horatio. Wretched Queen, adieu!
You that look pale and tremble at this chance,
That are but mutes or audience to this act,
Had I but time—as this fell sergeant, Death,
Is strict in his arrest—O, I could tell you—
But let it be. Horatio, I am dead;
Thou livest. Report me and my cause aright
To the unsatisfied.

**HORATIO:** Never believe it.
I am more an antique Roman than a Dane.
Here's yet some liquor left.
*[He attempts to drink from the poisoned cup.* HAMLET *prevents him.]*

**HAMLET:** As thou'rt a man,
Give me the cup! Let go! By heaven, I'll ha 't.
O God, Horatio, what a wounded name,
Things standing thus unknown, shall I leave behind me!
If thou didst ever hold me in thy heart,
Absent thee from felicity awhile,
And in this harsh world draw thy breath in pain
To tell my story. *A march afar off [and a volley within].*
What warlike noise is this?

*Enter* OSRIC.

**OSRIC:** Young Fortinbras, with conquest come from Poland,
To th' ambassadors of England gives
This warlike volley.

**HAMLET:** O, I die, Horatio!
The potent poison quite o'ercrows my spirit.
I cannot live to hear the news from England,
But I do prophesy th' election lights
On Fortinbras. He has my dying voice.
So tell him, with th' occurrents more and less
Which have solicited—the rest is silence. *[He dies.]*

**HORATIO:** Now cracks a noble heart. Good night, sweet prince,
And flights of angels sing thee to thy rest!
*[March within.]*
Why does the drum come hither?

*Enter* FORTINBRAS, *with the [English]* AMBASSADORS *[with drum, colors, and attendants].*

**FORTINBRAS:** Where is this sight?

**HORATIO:** What is it you would see?
If aught of woe or wonder, cease your search.

**FORTINBRAS:** This quarry cries on havoc. O proud Death,
What feast is toward in thine eternal cell,
That thou so many princes at a shot
So bloodily hast struck?

**FIRST AMBASSADOR:** The sight is dismal,
And our affairs from England come too late.
The ears are senseless that should give us hearing,
To tell him his commandment is fulfilled,
That Rosencrantz and Guildenstern are dead.
Where should we have our thanks?

**HORATIO:** Not from his mouth,
Had it th' ability of life to thank you.
He never gave commandment for their death.
But since, so jump upon his bloody question,
You from the Polack wars, and you from England,
Are here arrived, give order that these bodies

---

**330 tempered** mixed **336 chance** mischance **337 mutes** silent observers. (Literally, actors with nonspeaking parts.) **338 fell** cruel. **sergeant** sheriff's officer **339 strict** (1) severely just (2) unavoidable. **arrest** (1) taking into custody (2) stopping my speech **343 Roman** (Suicide was an honorable choice for many Romans as an alternative to a dishonorable life.)

**355 o'ercrows** triumphs over (like the winner in a cockfight) **358 voice** vote **359 occurrents** events, incidents **360 solicited** moved, urged. (Hamlet doesn't finish saying what the events have prompted—presumably, his acts of vengeance, or his reporting of those events to Fortinbras.) **366 quarry** heap of dead. **cries on havoc** proclaims a general slaughter **367 feast** i.e., Death feasting on those who have fallen. **toward** in preparation **374 his** i.e., Claudius' **377 jump** precisely, immediately. **question** dispute, affair

High on a stage be placèd to the view,
And let me speak to th' yet unknowing world
How these things came about. So shall you hear
Of carnal, bloody, and unnatural acts,
Of accidental judgments, casual slaughters,
Of deaths put on by cunning and forced cause,
And, in this upshot, purposes mistook
Fall'n on th' inventors' heads. All this can I
Truly deliver.

**FORTINBRAS:** Let us haste to hear it,
And call the noblest to the audience.
For me, with sorrow I embrace my fortune.
I have some rights of memory in this kingdom,
Which now to claim my vantage doth invite me.

**HORATIO:** Of that I shall have also cause to speak,
And from his mouth whose voice will draw on more.
But let this same be presently performed,
Even while men's minds are wild, lest more mischance
On plots and errors happen.

**380 stage** platform **384 judgments** retributions. **casual** occurring by chance **385 put on** instigated. **forced cause** contrivance **391 of memory** traditional, remembered, unforgotten **392 vantage** favorable opportunity **394 voice . . . more** vote will influence still others **395 presently** immediately **397 On** on the basis of; on top of

Hamlet is laid to rest.

**FORTINBRAS:** Let four captains
Bear Hamlet, like a soldier, to the stage,
For he was likely, had he been put on,
To have proved most royal; and for his passage,
The soldiers' music and the rite of war
Speak loudly for him.
Take up the bodies. Such a sight as this
Becomes the field, but here shows much amiss.
Go bid the soldiers shoot.

*Exeunt [marching, bearing off the dead bodies; a peal of ordnance is shot off].*

**399 put on** i.e., invested in royal office and so put to the test **400 passage** i.e., from life to death **402 Speak** (let them) speak **404 Becomes the field** suits the field of battle

# Writing from Reading

## Summarize

**1** Think of this play as a revenge tragedy, a story of justice played out. Describe how Hamlet chooses to avenge his father's murder and the result of his choice. During the course of the play, what wrongs are righted? In what ways do innocent people suffer or succeed?

**2** This is a complex play with many subplots that mirror the main plot of Hamlet's revenge. Consider, for instance, that Laertes also loves Ophelia, is also of noble birth and travels abroad. He is an excellent fencer, and also has a father who has been killed. How does his story amplify that of the prince?

**3** What is the plot of the play within the play? Does the play have the effect Hamlet hopes for?

## Analyze Craft

**4** How would you describe Hamlet's character? How does indecision help the tragedy unfold?

**5** How would you describe Ophelia's character: her history, her education and upbringing, her feelings for her father and brother and lover? What causes Ophelia to go mad (is it a single event, or a combination of causes that makes her drown herself?), and what effect does her suicide have on the play?

**6** How do you imagine Claudius and Gertrude? How old are they? In what sort of physical health? What attitude do they have? What in the play makes you imagine them this way?

**7** Laertes is a kind of shadow twin to Hamlet. As suggested in question 2, he too is noble and a fine fencer, and his father has also been killed. What differences in character make him, in effect, the king's pawn and the unwitting agent of Prince Hamlet's death?

8 How do the secondary characters—the gravedigger, Fortinbras, Horatio, etc.—advance the action? What perspectives and what commentary do they offer?

### Analyze Voice

9 How do the speeches and high formal tone of the royal characters contrast with the speech of the low characters? Give examples.

10 Do you have any sympathy for the character Claudius when he admits, "Oh, my offence is rank"? What about *rank* in the court? Find other examples of Shakespeare's use of double meaning and puns (as, for example, when Hamlet flirts with and teases Ophelia before the play's performance).

11 Do "these few precepts" that Polonius offers to his son make sense? What of the advice he gives his daughter? Given the solemn nature of this advice, what in his character makes Hamlet thinks him a "rash, intruding fool"? What does the difference between what seems like wise advice and Polonius's character allow us to discover in the play?

12 Focus on the humor in the text. Study the gravediggers' scene and try to play it for laughs.

### Synthesize Summary and Analysis

13 Why would Shakespeare set this play in Denmark and the somewhat distant past? It is, after all, a story about regicide (the killing of a king). What risks would he have taken if he set the tale in England instead?

14 Why did Shakespeare mount a play within the play, and what kind of commentary does it offer on the larger text? How is this similar to or different from the play staged within Hamlet's *A Midsummer Night's Dream* (also in this chapter)?

### Interpret the Play

15 Is Hamlet's story tragic? If so, what makes his story tragic?

16 Does Hamlet choose the most efficient path to avenge his father's murder? At play's end, is everything redeemed?

*CONTINUED FROM PAGE 105*

**THE ORIGINS OF THE HAMLET STORY**

The particular source of this play derives from an old Norse legend in which we first hear of a character called Amlothi, whose name has been translated as "desperate in battle" and is recorded in *Historica Danica* of Saxo Grammaticus (a book printed in 1514). The seed story of Hamlet is used by the French writer Belleforest in his *Histoires Tragiques* (1576), and scholars show Shakespeare did read it. Indeed, the playwright rarely made up his stories out of whole cloth. He was familiar with Plutarch and Holinshed (historians of the classical and medieval world respectively); he adapted histories and voyage accounts and other authors' narratives for most of his career. The father's murder and the sweetheart's madness (sometimes the Ophelia figure is a courtesan, sometimes a princess) and the duel with an exchange of swords all figure in previous sources—but the character of Hamlet is something Shakespeare filled out on his own.

## THE ELIZABETHAN THEATER

From time to time—in periods of plague, for instance, or when the authorities found the crowd's behavior too unruly—the theaters were closed down. To avoid the complications stemming from these unpredictable gaps in business, Shakespeare's troupe,

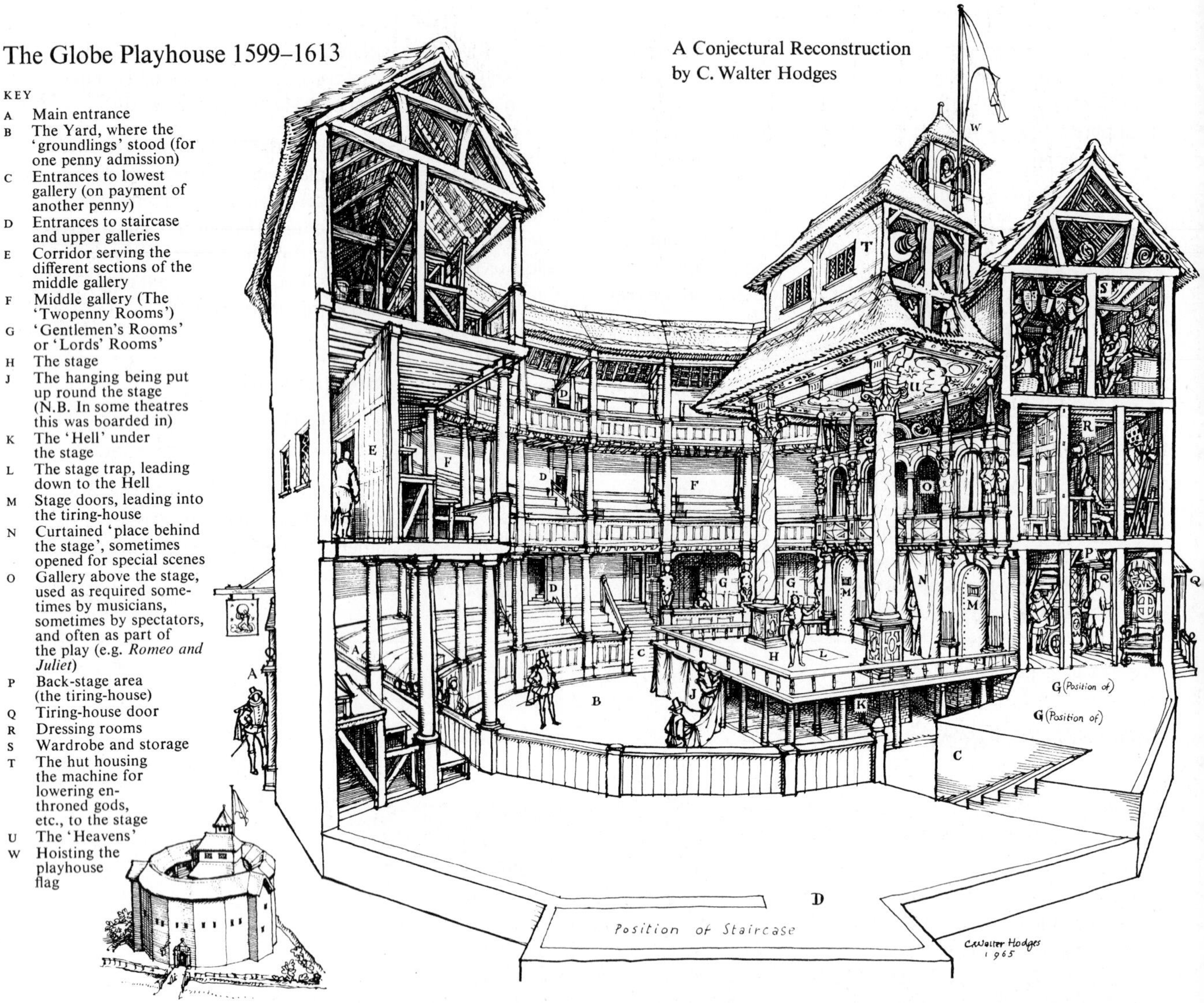
The Globe Playhouse 1599–1613
A Conjectural Reconstruction
by C. Walter Hodges
KEY
A Main entrance
B The Yard, where the 'groundlings' stood (for one penny admission)
C Entrances to lowest gallery (on payment of another penny)
D Entrances to staircase and upper galleries
E Corridor serving the different sections of the middle gallery
F Middle gallery (The 'Twopenny Rooms')
G 'Gentlemen's Rooms' or 'Lords' Rooms'
H The stage
J The hanging being put up round the stage (N.B. In some theatres this was boarded in)
K The 'Hell' under the stage
L The stage trap, leading down to the Hell
M Stage doors, leading into the tiring-house
N Curtained 'place behind the stage', sometimes opened for special scenes
O Gallery above the stage, used as required sometimes by musicians, sometimes by spectators, and often as part of the play (e.g. *Romeo and Juliet*)
P Back-stage area (the tiring-house)
Q Tiring-house door
R Dressing rooms
S Wardrobe and storage
T The hut housing the machine for lowering enthroned gods, etc., to the stage
U The 'Heavens'
W Hoisting the playhouse flag
G (Position of)
G (Position of)
Position of Staircase
C Walter Hodges 1965

the Lord Chamberlain's Men, decided to build its own space in 1599. The **Globe Theater,** constructed on the model of a tavern, stood on the south bank of the Thames River, beyond the city limits and the close watch of the law; it could accommodate—by some estimates—as many as three thousand.

Before the construction of the Globe Theater, the central stage was often a courtyard of taverns or inns. Today, an audience at a boxing match or football game is probably more similar to the Elizabethan clientele than is the well-heeled, well-behaved audience at a Broadway show. Like Greek theater, these stages made for sparse sets. There was only a **tiring house** hidden by a curtain behind the **arena stage**—in essence, a platform—that allowed quick costume changes between scenes. The stage was open to the sky to take advantage of natural light. Similar to the Greek amphithe-

"I have always felt that the . . . works that last . . . address the condition of mankind at any one time. They're not simply private emotional works. . . . They're reflecting the larger reality of the time. And I think that's true with Shakespeare. . . . The original purpose or color of creative art was always the community." Conversation with Arthur Miller

ater, surrounded on three sides, the Elizabethan theater would have been three stories high, each story with a gallery from which patrons could watch; those who paid an additional penny could be seated and look down.

Not since the fall of Rome had theater played such a role in public life, bringing in a boisterous and broad mix of society, from nobles, including Queen Elizabeth herself, to **groundlings,** who paid a penny to stand on the ground surrounding the stage. Puritans decried theaters as brothels, and Queen Elizabeth censored plays closely due to their enormous influence. Shakespeare himself wrote only of royalty that was long gone, since predicting the future or commenting on royalty of the day could have had dire consequences. The theater was a highly competitive place that vied for public support as well as for patrons, sponsoring aristocrats who might order a private performance or commission a celebratory work.

Traveling **players**—hired men and boys who spoke their lines for pay—acted out the plays of the day, and it is just such a group of actors Prince Hamlet is hiring in Act III, Scene II, when he decides to get his message of revenge to the murderous king. Players were always males, with boys usually playing women's roles. The costumes worn by players were generally very elaborate—brightly colored and visually appealing. Acting companies owned a wide variety of costumes for players to wear, some of which held certain conventions and connotations—such as a robe that represented invisibility. And since these costumes were expensive and not readily replaced, the playwright had to "tailor" his lines accordingly. In the beginning of another Shakespeare

"You don't want to lose faith in the plays you love. I can separate the written word from a performance . . . I've seen poor performances of Shakespeare. Particularly the comedies, which are more difficult to do than the tragedies. And I think, Oh don't spoil this play for me! I still love it, I'm still faithful to it, I love this play." Conversation with Marian Seldes

play, *The Tempest,* there's a storm conjured up by Prospero, the great magician, and his servant Ariel. Shakespeare describes how the shipwrecked crew washes up upon the island, writing "On their sustaining garments not a blemish / But fresher than before." In the movies nowadays we'd no doubt show the sailors wet and bedraggled, their "sustaining garments" torn—but in Elizabethan England the costumes would need to stay dry and "fresher than before."

## LANGUAGE ONSTAGE

When the character Jacques in Shakespeare's *As You Like It* famously pronounces that "All the world's a stage, and all the men and women merely players," he may well have been describing the great Globe Theater itself. Though it contained no elaborate scenery, the size of the stage and the structure of the building offered occasions for action; when Orlando, in the same play, hangs his love letters to Rosalind on trees of the Forest of Arden, he almost surely did so from the columns of the Globe. Props and furniture could be employed, and elaborate costumes worn, but "the willing suspension of disbelief"—which Samuel Taylor Coleridge argued "constitutes poetic faith"—was necessary, always, for those theatergoers who came to listen and look. The prologue to *Henry V* admits as much—indeed, is close to apologetic when the speaker asks:

*Can this cockpit hold*
*The vasty fields of France? Or may we cram*
*Within this wooden O the very casques*
*That did affright the air at Agincourt?*

Mostly the answer was yes. Scene after scene in Shakespeare is introduced by vivid description, a speech about a battlefield or palace, a lyric evocation of a forest or the stars. In Act V, Scene 1, of *The Merchant of Venice,* one character observes,

*How sweet the moonlight sits upon this bank!*
*Here will we sit and let the sounds of music*
*Creep in our ears. Soft stillness and the night*
*Become the touches of sweet harmony.*
*Sit, Jessica. Look how the floor of heaven*
*Is thick inlaid with patens of bright gold . . .*

There's no need for stage directions once the scene has been set in such elegant style. Lorenzo, the speaker, is wooing his heart's darling—Jessica, the daughter of Shylock, the Merchant of Venice—looking up while, no doubt, music plays. The opening phrase

"[Shakespeare's] plays are capable of an endless number of good productions. . . . There are no stage directions, so they're endlessly fertile as performance." Conversation with Ralph Williams

of this courtship scene is "The moon shines bright," and though the play was first presented on a London afternoon, we're transported, via the artist's verbal prowess, to the Venetian night.

The configuration of this arena theater gave rise to a convention of drama called the **aside**—a speech directed to the audience only, that the other actors onstage do not appear to hear. The aside can deliver background information to the audience, without the actors having to act it out or act upon it. More importantly, it is used to create a connection between the actor and the audience, to make them partners or co-conspirators. In this way, the audience gains access to secrets and ironies, and to inner thoughts that are withheld from other characters. Another dramatic convention that arose in this era was the **soliloquy,** a monologue delivered by a character standing alone onstage. A soliloquy gives the audience deep access to a character's inner world, as it does in *Hamlet,* when the troubled prince reveals the extent of his dilemmas.

### THE ORIGINS OF DRAMA IN THE CHRISTIAN CHURCH

Around the tenth century, drama, which had been suppressed by the Church as a pagan ritual, became part of the Christian Mass. These dramas were anonymous works intended less as entertainments than as a form of religious instruction. In other words, those who could not read the Bible could watch it being acted out and profit from the "show." **Miracle plays,** one type of drama in this tradition, enacted the lives of the saints. **Mystery plays,** a second type, brought to life stories of the Bible—such as the Creation or the Crucifixion. *The Second Shepherd's Play* (c. 1400), for example, told the story of Christ's birth. Allegory (see chapter 20 in the poetry volume for more on allegory) enters into theatrical productions of the third type—**morality plays.** In this form of drama, the figures onstage taught right and proper behavior—morality—to those who watched. In one well-known morality play, *Everyman,* the titular character is called before God to make his reckoning. Other characters in this play have names such as Kindred, Knowledge, and Beauty. In the end, however, none of those other figures cares enough about Everyman's plight to accompany him and help him plead his case in heaven. Only Good Deeds is up to that task—thus, the moral lesson that good deeds are what matter in life.

## SHAKESPEARE'S CONFOUNDING DIVERSITY

No matter how useful we find it to be, the business of categorization began only after Shakespeare's death. Critics tend to divide the playwright's compositions for theater into four categories.

- **Histories** focus on the reign of kings from the past, from Julius Caesar to Henry V. Because histories naturally contain very astute and sometimes troubling political commentaries, playwrights had to limit their subjects to rulers of the distant past.
- **Comedies** are plays for entertainment and as a convention end in the marriage of two main characters. A comedic plot generally begins with a complication or misunderstanding between two lovers, which is complicated by further scheming and misunderstandings until finally a resolution is attained and the two are wed.
- **Tragedies** are darker plays, with more complex characters and more dire consequences. Tragedies commonly feature murder and as a convention end in a funeral—usually the death of the main character himself.
- **Romances** (from the French *roman,* which means an "extended narrative") involve lovers whose potential happiness is complicated by misunderstandings, mistaken identities, and any number of other difficulties. Although similar in plot to a comedy, a romance play does not guarantee a happy ending.

These categories are loose and overlapping units, and as Ralph Williams discusses in his interview, Shakespeare may have taken a bravura delight in confounding definitions, which in any case are more a matter of critical convenience than of theatrical

"One of the most frightening and thrilling aspects of Shakespeare's plays is the constant reminder of how tentative a thing it is that life turns out to be tragedy or comedy, or some mixture of the two." Conversation with Ralph Williams form. Even the darkest of Shakespeare's plays have some comedic component, called **comic relief**—such as the banter between Hamlet and his bewildered old friends Rosencrantz and Guildenstern—which gives the audience a breather from the tension and can also serve to emphasize the tragic elements of the play.

Many plays belong to more than one category. *Macbeth* and *King Lear*, for example, take place in the distant "historical" past but belong to the group called *tragedies. Romeo and Juliet* is a story of complicated love, but it has a famously tragic ending. Plays such as *Measure for Measure* and *The Merchant of Venice*—which don't fit obviously into these four categories—are often referred to as **problem plays.**

## *A MIDSUMMER NIGHT'S DREAM*

This particular comedy was written and performed roughly five years earlier than *Hamlet,* and its style is very different, its purpose to amuse. The "dream" announced in the title is crucial to the play. Often hallucinatory and sometimes edging up to nightmare, dream is the operative mode here. There are three sets of players:

- Athenians of noble rank
- A group of "rude mechanicals" (by which Shakespeare means tradesmen who work at such crafts as tailoring, carpentry, weaving)
- The King and Queen of the Fairies along with their court

The first group (Theseus and Hippolyta and their attendants) is supremely rational and a little dull; the second and third set of players are susceptible to dreaming and a good deal more fun. The King and Queen of the Fairies are as much alive, as physical and needy, as the humans portrayed here; Oberon and Titania may have supernatural powers, but their marriage, with its jealousies and passions, is portrayed in "natural" terms.

"In comic plays, the playwright so often is referring to what is happening in his world, in the real world, at the moment . . . and . . . making fun." Conversation with Marian Seldes

The events of the play begin with the imminent wedding of Theseus, the Duke of Athens, and his Amazonian queen Hippolyta. Eager for his daughter to marry at the same wedding, a nobleman named Egeus orders Hermia to marry her suitor Demetrius. Hermia refuses because she is in love with another man named Lysander, with whom she makes plans to elope in the forest. Hermia makes the mistake of confiding in her friend Helena, who herself has eyes for Demetrius. Thus, when Hermia and Lysander flee to the forest to marry, they are pursued by Helena and Demetrius, who have been informed of their scheme.

Meanwhile, the fairies in the third group of players listed above are up to their own antics. Oberon, King of the Fairies, and his Queen Titania have arrived in the woods to celebrate the wedding of Theseus and Hippolyta; however, the King and Queen are estranged because Titania will not give over her Indian love child, a "changeling" she keeps by her side. Following a very human argument between husband and wife, Oberon orders his servant Puck to enchant Titania with a flower so she will fall in love with the next person she sees (who ends up being the player Bottom, whose head has recently been transformed by Puck into that of an ass). The events of the play unfold from these confusions, with plenty of enchanting and magically induced love. Ultimately all get what they want, or at least what they deserve, and not without some help from the lingering effects of Puck's mischievous magic.

"Shakespeare's plays are society-driven in a lot of ways, but also class-driven. There are regular people, the common man, and then you have the hierarchy . . . the warriors, the soldiers, the clowns." Conversation with Ruben Santiago-Hudson

Of the three groups of players involved in this web of comedy, the most surprising and original are Bottom and his friends; their performance in the final act of "A tedious brief scene of young Pyramis / and his love Thisbe; very tragical mirth" is a triumph of comic invention. "How shall we find the concord of this discord?" Theseus asks, and when he and members of his court—along with us as audience—view the foolishness within the play, they laugh at happy length. The low humor of Quince, Bottom, Flute, Snout, Snug, and Starveling stands in contrast to the high seriousness of the nobles and their intended nuptials: In musical terms they serve as counterpoint or variation on the theme. That's the point, after all, of "tragical mirth"; they're just as strange bedfellows as are the Queen of the Fairies and a man with the head of an ass. The "rude mechanicals" may not *intend* to be funny, may think themselves serious "players," but Shakespeare stacks the comic deck.

How he does so is in part by *incongruity.* There's pretension and lack of self-knowledge in the way the workers mount their play; the "bumpkin" who believes himself a hero is a comic figure. Shakespeare's making jokes, as well, about his own profession; when Bottom "struts his stuff," he's doing what bad actors do (and what

"Bottom and Snout and the group have the most hilarious imaginings of what it might be to act. . . . And Shakespeare here is hilariously . . . parodying . . . the infelicities of the theater of the time." Conversation with Ralph Williams

Hamlet had cautioned the players against). The idea of Pyramis and Thisbe making love through a make-believe wall is full of **satiric** excess and the gestures of **burlesque;** this scene is often staged in **broad** and **slapstick** terms. (See chapter 31 for more on comedy and its variations.) Lines like these are hard to take seriously, easy to find foolish (and the watching royals cue us that it's all right to laugh):

*But stay, O spite!*
*But mark, poor knight,*
*What dreadful dole is here!*
*Eyes, do you see?*
*How can it be?*
*O dainty duck! O dear!*

The first and final point, and the one that's worth repeating, is that reading William Shakespeare and hearing him and watching him, especially in a play like this, should be *fun.* As Puck, or Robin Goodfellow, says at the close of the performance: "Give me your hands, if we be friends / And Robin shall restore amends." He's asking for applause, approval; the promised result is that the several sets of lovers will live "happily ever after." The first lines of Puck's final speech capture the tone of the whole:

*If we shadows have offended,*
*Think but this, and all is mended,*
*That you have but slumbered here*
*While these visions did appear.*

**AS YOU READ** Pay special attention to Puck's role in the events of the play. To what extent is he a "director" of this play? When he says, "Lord, what fools these mortals be," does he refer to the actors or the audience or both?

# A Midsummer Night's Dream (c. 1595)

## CHARACTERS

**THESEUS,** *Duke of Athens*

**HIPPOLYTA,** *Queen of the Amazons, betrothed to Theseus*

**PHILOSTRATE,** *Master of the Revels*

**EGEUS,** *father of Hermia*

**HERMIA,** *daughter of Egeus, in love with Lysander*

**LYSANDER,** *in love with Hermia*

**DEMETRIUS,** *in love with Hermia and favored by Egeus*

**HELENA,** *in love with Demetrius*

**OBERON,** *King of the Fairies*

**TITANIA,** *Queen of the Fairies*

**PUCK,** *or* **ROBIN GOODFELLOW**

**PEASEBLOSSOM, COBWEB, MOTE, MUSTARDSEED,** *fairies attending Titania*

*Other* **FAIRIES** *attending*

| | | |
|---|---|---|
| **PETER QUINCE,** *a carpenter,* | *representing* | **PROLOGUE** |
| **NICK BOTTOM,** *a weaver,* | | **PYRAMUS** |
| **FRANCIS FLUTE,** *a bellows mender* | | **THISBE** |
| **TOM SNOUT,** *a tinker,* | | **WALL** |
| **SNUG,** *a joiner,* | | **LION** |
| **ROBIN STARVELING,** *a tailor,* | | **MOONSHINE** |

*Lords and Attendants on Theseus and Hippolyta*

**SCENE:** *Athens, and a wood near it]*

**1.1** *Enter* THESEUS, HIPPOLYTA, *[and* PHILOSTRATE,*] with others.*

**THESEUS:** Now, fair Hippolyta, our nuptial hour
Draws on apace. Four happy days bring in
Another moon; but, O, methinks, how slow
This old moon wanes! She lingers my desires,
Like to a stepdame or a dowager
Long withering out a young man's revenue.

**HIPPOLYTA:** Four days will quickly steep themselves in night;
Four nights will quickly dream away the time;
And then the moon, like to a silver bow
New bent in heaven, shall behold the night
Of our solemnities.

**THESEUS:** Go, Philostrate,
Stir up the Athenian youth to merriments.
Awake the pert and nimble spirit of mirth.
Turn melancholy forth to funerals;
The pale companion is not for our pomp.
*[Exit* PHILOSTRATE.*]*
Hippolyta, I wooed thee with my sword
And won thy love doing thee injuries;
But I will wed thee in another key,
With pomp, with triumph, and with reveling.

*Enter* EGEUS *and his daughter* HERMIA, *and* LYSANDER, *and* DEMETRIUS.

**EGEUS:** Happy be Theseus, our renownèd duke!

**THESEUS:** Thanks, good Egeus. What's the news with thee?

**EGEUS:** Full vexation come I, with complaint
Against my child, my daughter Hermia.—
Stand forth, Demetrius.—My noble lord,
This man hath my consent to marry her.—
Stand forth, Lysander.—And, my gracious Duke,
This man hath bewitched the bosom of my child.
Thou, thou Lysander, thou hast given her rhymes

Egeus (Nicholas Selby) brings his daughter Hermia (Helen Mirren) before the duke in the 1968 film directed by Peter Hall.

And interchanged love tokens with my child.
Thou hast by moonlight at her window sung
With feigning voice verses of feigning love,
And stol'n the impression of her fantasy
With bracelets of thy hair, rings, gauds, conceits,
Knacks, trifles, nosegays, sweetmeats—messengers
Of strong prevailment in unhardened youth.
With cunning hast thou filched my daughter's heart,
Turned her obedience, which is due to me,
To stubborn harshness. And, my gracious Duke,
Be it so she will not here before Your Grace
Consent to marry with Demetrius,
I beg the ancient privilege of Athens:
As she is mine, I may dispose of her,
Which shall be either to this gentleman
Or to her death, according to our law
Immediately provided in that case.

**THESEUS:** What say you, Hermia? Be advised, fair maid.
To you your father should be as a god—
One that composed your beauties, yea, and one
To whom you are but as a form in wax
By him imprinted, and within his power
To leave the figure or disfigure it.
Demetrius is a worthy gentleman.

**1.1. Location: Athens. Theseus' court.**
**4 lingers** postpones, delays the fulfillment of **5 stepdame** stepmother. **a dowager** i.e., a widow (whose right of inheritance from her dead husband is eating into her son's estate) **6 withering out** causing to dwindle **7 steep themselves** saturate themselves, be absorbed in **11 solemnities** festive ceremonies of marriage **15 companion** fellow. **pomp** ceremonial magnificence **16 with my sword** i.e., in a military engagement against the Amazons, when Hippolyta was taken captive **19 triumph** public festivity

**31 feigning** (1) counterfeiting (2) faining, desirous **32 And . . . fantasy** and made her fall in love with you (imprinting your image on her imagination) by stealthy and dishonest means **33 gauds** playthings. **conceits** fanciful trifles **34 Knacks** knickknacks **35 prevailment in** influence on **39 Be it so** if **45 Immediately** directly, with nothing intervening **51 leave** i.e., leave unaltered. **disfigure** obliterate

**HERMIA:** So is Lysander.

**THESEUS:** In himself he is;
But in this kind, wanting your father's voice,
The other must be held the worthier.

**HERMIA:** I would my father looked but with my eyes.

**THESEUS:** Rather your eyes must with his judgment look.

**HERMIA:** I do entreat Your Grace to pardon me.
I know not by what power I am made bold,
Nor how it may concern my modesty
In such a presence here to plead my thoughts;
But I beseech Your Grace that I may know
The worst that may befall me in this case
If I refuse to wed Demetrius.

**THESEUS:** Either to die the death or to abjure
Forever the society of men.
Therefore, fair Hermia, question your desires,
Know of your youth, examine well your blood,
Whether, if you yield not to your father's choice,
You can endure the livery of a nun,
For aye to be in shady cloister mewed,
To live a barren sister all your life,
Chanting faint hymns to the cold fruitless moon.
Thrice blessèd they that master so their blood
To undergo such maiden pilgrimage;
But earthlier happy is the rose distilled
Than that which, withering on the virgin thorn,
Grows, lives, and dies in single blessedness.

**HERMIA:** So will I grow, so live, so die, my lord,
Ere I will yield my virgin patent up
Unto his lordship, whose unwishèd yoke
My soul consents not to give sovereignty.

**THESEUS:** Take time to pause, and by the next new moon—
The sealing day betwixt my love and me
For everlasting bond of fellowship—
Upon that day either prepare to die
For disobedience to your father's will,
Or else to wed Demetrius, as he would,
Or on Diana's altar to protest
For aye austerity and single life.

**DEMETRIUS:** Relent, sweet Hermia, and, Lysander, yield
Thy crazèd title to my certain right.

**LYSANDER:** You have her father's love, Demetrius;
Let me have Hermia's. Do you marry him.

**EGEUS:** Scornful Lysander! True, he hath my love,
And what is mine my love shall render him.
And she is mine, and all my right of her
I do estate unto Demetrius.

**LYSANDER:** I am, my lord, as well derived as he,
As well possessed; my love is more than his;
My fortunes every way as fairly ranked,
If not with vantage, as Demetrius';
And, which is more than all these boasts can be,
I am beloved of beauteous Hermia.
Why should not I then prosecute my right?
Demetrius, I'll avouch it to his head,
Made love to Nedar's daughter, Helena,
And won her soul; and she, sweet lady, dotes,
Devoutly dotes, dotes in idolatry
Upon this spotted and inconstant man.

**THESEUS:** I must confess that I have heard so much,
And with Demetrius thought to have spoke thereof;
But, being overfull of self-affairs,
My mind did lose it. But, Demetrius, come,
And come, Egeus, you shall go with me;
I have some private schooling for you both.
For you, fair Hermia, look you arm yourself
To fit your fancies to your father's will,
Or else the law of Athens yields you up—
Which by no means we may extenuate—
To death or to a vow of single life.
Come, my Hippolyta. What cheer, my love?
Demetrius and Egeus, go along.
I must employ you in some business
Against our nuptial, and confer with you
Of something nearly that concerns yourselves.

**EGEUS:** With duty and desire we follow you.

*Exeunt [all but* LYSANDER *and* HERMIA*].*

**LYSANDER:** How now, my love, why is your cheek so pale?
How chance the roses there do fade so fast?

---

**54 kind** respect. **wanting** lacking. **voice** approval **60 concern** befit **65 die the death** be executed by legal process **68 blood** passions **70 livery** habit, costume **71 aye** ever. **mewed** shut in. (Said of a hawk, poultry, etc.) **76 earthlier happy** happier as respects this world. **distilled** i.e., to make perfume **80 patent** privilege **88 Or** either **89 protest** vow

**92 crazèd** cracked, unsound **98 estate unto** settle or bestow upon **99 as well derived** as well born and descended **100 possessed** endowed with wealth **101 fairly** handsomely **102 vantage** superiority **106 head** i.e., face **110 spotted** i.e., morally stained **113 self-affairs** my own concerns **116 schooling** admonition **117 look you arm** take care you prepare **118 fancies** likings, thoughts of love **120 extenuate** mitigate, relax **123 go** i.e., come **125 Against** in preparation for **126 nearly that** that closely

Hermia and Lysander (David Warner) plan their marriage.

**HERMIA:** Belike for want of rain, which I could well
Beteem them from the tempest of my eyes.

**LYSANDER:** Ay me! For aught that I could ever read,
Could ever hear by tale or history,
The course of true love never did run smooth;
But either it was different in blood—

**HERMIA:** O cross! Too high to be enthralled to low.

**LYSANDER:** Or else misgrafted in respect of years—

**HERMIA:** O spite! Too old to be engaged to young.

**LYSANDER:** Or else it stood upon the choice of friends—

**HERMIA:** O hell, to choose love by another's eyes!

**LYSANDER:** Or if there were a sympathy in choice,
War, death, or sickness did lay siege to it,
Making it momentany as a sound,
Swift as a shadow, short as any dream,
Brief as the lightning in the collied night
That in a spleen unfolds both heaven and earth,
And ere a man hath power to say "Behold!"
The jaws of darkness do devour it up.
So quick bright things come to confusion.

**HERMIA:** If then true lovers have been ever crossed,
It stands as an edict in destiny.
Then let us teach our trial patience,
Because it is a customary cross,
As due to love as thoughts, and dreams, and sighs,
Wishes, and tears, poor fancy's followers.

**LYSANDER:** A good persuasion. Therefore, hear me, Hermia:
I have a widow aunt, a dowager
Of great revenue, and she hath no child.
From Athens is her house remote seven leagues;
And she respects me as her only son.
There, gentle Hermia, may I marry thee,
And to that place the sharp Athenian law
Cannot pursue us. If thou lovest me, then,
Steal forth thy father's house tomorrow night;
And in the wood, a league without the town,
Where I did meet thee once with Helena
To do observance to a morn of May,
There will I stay for thee.

**HERMIA:** My good Lysander!
I swear to thee, by Cupid's strongest bow,
By his best arrow with the golden head,
By the simplicity of Venus' doves,
By that which knitteth souls and prospers loves,
And by that fire which burned the Carthage queen
When the false Trojan under sail was seen,
By all the vows that ever men have broke,
In number more than ever women spoke,
In that same place thou hast appointed me
Tomorrow truly will I meet with thee.

**LYSANDER:** Keep promise, love. Look, here comes Helena.

*Enter* HELENA.

**HERMIA:** God speed, fair Helena! Whither away?

**HELENA:** Call you me fair? That "fair" again unsay.
Demetrius loves your fair. O happy fair!
Your eyes are lodestars, and your tongue's sweet air
More tunable than lark to shepherd's ear

---

**130 Belike** very likely **131 Beteem** grant, afford **135 blood** hereditary station **136 cross** vexation **137 misgrafted** ill grafted, badly matched **139 friends** relatives **141 sympathy** agreement **143 momentany** lasting but a moment **145 collied** blackened (as with coal dust), darkened **146 in a spleen** in a swift impulse, in a violent flash. **unfolds** reveals **149 quick** quickly; also, living, alive. **confusion** ruin **150 ever crossed** always thwarted

**152 teach . . . patience** i.e., teach ourselves patience in this trial **155 fancy's** amorous passion's **156 persuasion** doctrine **160 respects** regards **165 without** outside **167 do . . . May** perform the ceremonies of May Day **170 best arrow** (Cupid's best gold-pointed arrows were supposed to induce love; his blunt leaden arrows, aversion.) **171 simplicity** innocence. **doves** i.e., those that drew Venus' chariot **173, 174 Carthage queen, false Trojan** (Dido, Queen of Carthage, immolated herself on a funeral pyre after having been deserted by the Trojan hero Aeneas.) **180 fair** fair-complexioned (generally regarded by the Elizabethans as more beautiful than a dark complexion) **182 your fair** your beauty (even though Hermia is dark complexioned). **happy fair** lucky fair one **183 lodestars** guiding stars. **air** music **184 tunable** tuneful, melodious

When wheat is green, when hawthorn buds appear.
Sickness is catching. O, were favor so,
Yours would I catch, fair Hermia, ere I go;
My ear should catch your voice, my eye your eye,
My tongue should catch your tongue's sweet melody.
Were the world mine, Demetrius being bated,
The rest I'd give to be to you translated.
O, teach me how you look and with what art
You sway the motion of Demetrius' heart.

**HERMIA:** I frown upon him, yet he loves me still.

**HELENA:** O, that your frowns would teach my smiles such skill!

**HERMIA:** I give him curses, yet he gives me love.

**HELENA:** O, that my prayers could such affection move!

**HERMIA:** The more I hate, the more he follows me.

**HELENA:** The more I love, the more he hateth me.

**HERMIA:** His folly, Helena, is no fault of mine.

**HELENA:** None, but your beauty. Would that fault were mine!

**HERMIA:** Take comfort. He no more shall see my face.
Lysander and myself will fly this place.
Before the time I did Lysander see
Seemed Athens as a paradise to me.
O, then, what graces in my love do dwell,
That he hath turned a heaven unto a hell?

**LYSANDER:** Helen, to you our minds we will unfold.
Tomorrow night, when Phoebe doth behold
Her silver visage in the watery glass,
Decking with liquid pearl the bladed grass,
A time that lovers' flights doth still conceal,
Through Athens' gates have we devised to steal.

**HERMIA:** And in the wood, where often you and I
Upon faint primrose beds were wont to lie,
Emptying our bosoms of their counsel sweet,
There my Lysander and myself shall meet,
And thence from Athens turn away our eyes
To seek new friends and stranger companies.
Farewell, sweet playfellow. Pray thou for us,
And good luck grant thee thy Demetrius!
Keep word, Lysander. We must starve our sight
From lovers' food till morrow deep midnight.

**LYSANDER:** I will, my Hermia. *(Exit* HERMIA.*)* Helena, adieu.
As you on him, Demetrius dote on you!
*Exit* LYSANDER.

**HELENA:** How happy some o'er other some can be!
Through Athens I am thought as fair as she.
But what of that? Demetrius thinks not so;
He will not know what all but he do know.
And as he errs, doting on Hermia's eyes,
So I, admiring of his qualities.
Things base and vile, holding no quantity,
Love can transpose to form and dignity.
Love looks not with the eyes, but with the mind,
And therefore is winged Cupid painted blind.
Nor hath Love's mind of any judgment taste;
Wings and no eyes figure unheedy haste.
And therefore is Love said to be a child,
Because in choice he is so oft beguiled.
As waggish boys in game themselves forswear,
So the boy Love is perjured everywhere.
For ere Demetrius looked on Hermia's eyne,
He hailed down oaths that he was only mine;
And when this hail some heat from Hermia felt,
So he dissolved, and showers of oaths did melt.
I will go tell him of fair Hermia's flight.
Then to the wood will he tomorrow night
Pursue her; and for this intelligence
If I have thanks, it is a dear expense.
But herein mean I to enrich my pain,
To have his sight thither and back again. *Exit.*

## 1.2

*Enter* QUINCE *the carpenter, and* SNUG *the joiner, and* BOTTOM *the weaver, and* FLUTE *the bellows mender, and* SNOUT *the tinker, and* STARVELING *the tailor.*

**QUINCE:** Is all our company here?

**BOTTOM:** You were best to call them generally, man by man, according to the scrip.

---

**186 favor** appearance, looks **190 bated** excepted **191 translated** transformed **193 sway** control. **motion** impulse **197 affection** passion. **move** arouse **204–205 Before . . . to me** (Hermia seemingly means that love has led to complications and jealousies, making Athens hell for her.) **209 Phoebe** Diana, the moon **210 glass** mirror **212 still** always **215 faint** pale **216 counsel** secret thought **219 stranger companies** the company of strangers

**226 o'er . . . can be** can be in comparison to some others **231 admiring of** wondering at **232 holding no quantity** i.e., unsubstantial, unshapely **236 Nor . . . taste** i.e., nor has Love, which dwells in the fancy or imagination, any *taste* or least bit of judgment or reason **237 figure** are a symbol of **239 in choice** in choosing. **beguiled** self-deluded, making unaccountable choices **240 waggish** playful, mischievous. **game** sport, jest **242 eyne** eyes. (Old form of plural.) **248 intelligence** information **249 a dear expense** i.e., a trouble worth taking on my part, or a begrudging effort on his part. **dear** costly

**1.2 Location: Athens.**
**2 generally** (Bottom's blunder for "individually.") **3 scrip** scrap. (Bottom's error for "script.")

**QUINCE:** Here is the scroll of every man's name which is thought fit, through all Athens, to play in our interlude before the Duke and the Duchess on his wedding day at night.

**BOTTOM:** First, good Peter Quince, say what the play treats on, then read the names of the actors, and so grow to a point.

**QUINCE:** Marry, our play is "The most lamentable comedy and most cruel death of Pyramus and Thisbe."

**BOTTOM:** A very good piece of work, I assure you, and a merry. Now, good Peter Quince, call forth your actors by the scroll. Masters, spread yourselves.

**QUINCE:** Answer as I call you. Nick Bottom, the weaver.

**BOTTOM:** Ready. Name what part I am for, and proceed.

**QUINCE:** You, Nick Bottom, are set down for Pyramus.

**BOTTOM:** What is Pyramus? A lover or a tyrant?

**QUINCE:** A lover, that kills himself most gallant for love.

**BOTTOM:** That will ask some tears in the true performing of it. If I do it, let the audience look to their eyes. I will move storms; I will condole in some measure. To the rest—yet my chief humor is for a tyrant. I could play Ercles rarely, or a part to tear a cat in, to make all split.

"The raging rocks
And shivering shocks
Shall break the locks
Of prison gates;
And Phibbus' car
Shall shine from far
And make and mar
The foolish Fates."

This was lofty! Now name the rest of the players. This is Ercles' vein, a tyrant's vein. A lover is more condoling.

**QUINCE:** Francis Flute, the bellows mender.

**FLUTE:** Here, Peter Quince.

**QUINCE:** Flute, you must take Thisbe on you.

**FLUTE:** What is Thisbe? A wandering knight?

**QUINCE:** It is the lady that Pyramus must love.

**5–6 interlude** play **10 grow to** come to **11 Marry** (A mild oath; originally the name of the Virgin Mary.) **16 Bottom** (As a weaver's term, a *bottom* was an object around which thread was wound.) **23 condole** lament, arouse pity **24 humor** inclination, whim **25 Ercles** Hercules. (The tradition of ranting came from Seneca's *Hercules Furens*.) **tear a cat** i.e., rant. **make all split** i.e., cause a stir, bring the house down **30 Phibbus' car** Phoebus', the sun god's, chariot

Quince (Sebastian Shaw) persuades Bottom (Paul Rogers) to play Pyramus.

**FLUTE:** Nay, faith, let not me play a woman. I have a beard coming.

**QUINCE:** That's all one. You shall play it in a mask, and you may speak as small as you will.

**BOTTOM:** An I may hide my face, let me play Thisbe too. I'll speak in a monstrous little voice: "Thisne, Thisne!" "Ah, Pyramus, my lover dear! Thy Thisbe dear, and lady dear!"

**QUINCE:** No, no, you must play Pyramus, and Flute, you Thisbe.

**BOTTOM:** Well, proceed.

**QUINCE:** Robin Starveling, the tailor.

**STARVELING:** Here, Peter Quince.

**QUINCE:** Robin Starveling, you must play Thisbe's mother. Tom Snout, the tinker.

**SNOUT:** Here, Peter Quince.

**QUINCE:** You, Pyramus' father; myself, Thisbe's father; Snug, the joiner, you, the lion's part; and I hope here is a play fitted.

**SNUG:** Have you the lion's part written? Pray you, if it be, give it me, for I am slow of study.

**QUINCE:** You may do it extempore, for it is nothing but roaring.

**43 That's all one** it makes no difference **44 small** high-pitched **45 An** if. (Also at line 68.)

**BOTTOM:** Let me play the lion too. I will roar that I will do any man's heart good to hear me. I will roar that I will make the Duke say, "Let him roar again, let him roar again."

**QUINCE:** An you should do it too terribly, you would fright the Duchess and the ladies, that they would shriek; and that were enough to hang us all.

**ALL:** That would hang us, every mother's son.

**BOTTOM:** I grant you, friends, if you should fright the ladies out of their wits, they would have no more discretion but to hang us; but I will aggravate my voice so that I will roar you as gently as any sucking dove; I will roar you an 'twere any nightingale.

**QUINCE:** You can play no part but Pyramus; for Pyramus is a sweet-faced man, a proper man as one shall see in a summer's day, a most lovely gentlemanlike man. Therefore you must needs play Pyramus.

**BOTTOM:** Well, I will undertake it What beard were I best to play it in?

**QUINCE:** Why, what you will.

**BOTTOM:** I will discharge it in either your straw-color beard, your orange-tawny beard, your purple-in-grain beard, or your French-crown-color beard, your perfect yellow.

**QUINCE:** Some of your French crowns have no hair at all, and then you will play barefaced. But, masters, here are your parts. *[He distributes parts.]* And I am to entreat you, request you, and desire you to con them by tomorrow night, and meet me in the palace wood, a mile without the town, by moonlight. There will we rehearse; for if we meet in the city, we shall be dogged with company, and our devices known. In the meantime I will draw a bill of properties, such as our play wants. I pray you, fail me not.

**BOTTOM:** We will meet, and there we may rehearse most obscenely and courageously. Take pains, be perfect. Adieu.

Oberon (Rupert Everett) sits in his fairy court in the 1999 film directed by Michael Hoffman.

**QUINCE:** At the Duke's oak we meet.

**BOTTOM:** Enough. Hold, or cut bowstrings. *Exeunt.*

**2.1** *Enter a* FAIRY *at one door, and* ROBIN GOODFELLOW *[*PUCK*] at another.*

**PUCK:** How now, spirit, whither wander you?

**FAIRY:**
Over hill, over dale,
Thorough bush, thorough brier,
Over park, over pale,
Thorough flood, thorough fire,
I do wander everywhere,
Swifter than the moon's sphere;
And I serve the Fairy Queen,
To dew her orbs upon the green.
The cowslips tall her pensioners be.
In their gold coats spots you see;
Those be rubies, fairy favors;
In those freckles live their savors.
I must go seek some dewdrops here
And hang a pearl in every cowslip's ear.
Farewell, thou lob of spirits; I'll be gone.
Our Queen and all her elves come here anon.

**PUCK:** The King doth keep his revels here tonight.
Take heed the Queen come not within his sight.
For Oberon is passing fell and wrath,

---

**74 aggravate** (Bottom's blunder for "moderate.") **75 roar you** i.e., roar for you. **sucking dove** (Bottom conflates *sitting dove* and *sucking lamb,* two proverbial images of innocence.) **76 an 'twere** as if it were **78 proper** handsome **84 discharge** perform **your** i.e., you know the kind I mean **85–86 purple-in-grain** dyed a very deep red. (From *grain,* the name applied to the dried insect used to make the dye.) **86 French-crown-color** i.e., color of a French crown, a gold coin **88 crowns** heads bald from syphilis, the "French disease" **91 con** learn by heart **95 devices** plans **96 draw a bill** draw up a list **99 obscenely** (An unintentionally funny blunder, whatever Bottom meant to say.) **100 perfect** i.e., letter-perfect in memorizing your parts

**102 Hold . . . bowstrings** (An archers' expression, not definitely explained, but probably meaning here "keep your promises, or give up the play.")

**2.1 Location: A wood near Athens.**
**3 Thorough** through **4 pale** enclosure **7 sphere** orbit **9 dew** sprinkle with dew. **orbs** circles, i.e., fairy rings (circular bands of grass, darker than the surrounding area, caused by fungi enriching the soil) **10 pensioners** retainers, members of the royal bodyguard **12 favors** love tokens **13 savors** sweet smells **16 lob** country bumpkin **17 anon** at once **20 passing fell** exceedingly angry. **wrath** wrathful

Because that she as her attendant hath
A lovely boy, stolen from an Indian king;
She never had so sweet a changeling.
And jealous Oberon would have the child
Knight of his train, to trace the forests wild.
But she perforce withholds the lovèd boy,
Crowns him with flowers, and makes him all her joy.
And now they never meet in grove or green,
By fountain clear, or spangled starlight sheen,
But they do square, that all their elves for fear
Creep into acorn cups and hide them there.

**FAIRY:** Either I mistake your shape and making quite,
Or else you are that shrewd and knavish sprite
Called Robin Goodfellow. Are not you he
That frights the maidens of the villagery,
Skim milk, and sometimes labor in the quern,
And bootless make the breathless huswife churn,
And sometimes make the drink to bear no barm,
Mislead night wanderers, laughing at their harm?
Those that "Hobgoblin" call you, and "Sweet Puck,"
You do their work, and they shall have good luck.
Are you not he?

**PUCK:** Thou speakest aright;
I am that merry wanderer of the night.
I jest to Oberon and make him smile
When I a fat and bean-fed horse beguile,
Neighing in likeness of a filly foal;
And sometimes lurk I in a gossip's bowl
In very likeness of a roasted crab,
And when she drinks, against her lips I bob
And on her withered dewlap pour the ale.
The wisest aunt, telling the saddest tale,
Sometimes for three-foot stool mistaketh me;
Then slip I from her bum, down topples she,
And "Tailor" cries, and falls into a cough;
And then the whole choir hold their hips and laugh,
And waxen in their mirth, and neeze, and swear
A merrier hour was never wasted there.
But, room, fairy! Here comes Oberon.

**FAIRY:** And here my mistress. Would that he were gone!

*Enter [OBERON] the King of Fairies at one door, with his train, and [TITANIA] the Queen at another, with hers.*

**OBERON:** Ill met by moonlight, proud Titania.

**TITANIA:** What, jealous Oberon? Fairies, skip hence.
I have forsworn his bed and company.

**OBERON:** Tarry, rash wanton. Am not I thy lord?

**TITANIA:** Then I must be thy lady; but I know
When thou hast stolen away from Fairyland
And in the shape of Corin sat all day,
Playing on pipes of corn and versing love
To amorous Phillida. Why art thou here
Come from the farthest step of India,
But that, forsooth, the bouncing Amazon,
Your buskined mistress and your warrior love,
To Theseus must be wedded, and you come
To give their bed joy and prosperity.

**OBERON:** How canst thou thus for shame, Titania,
Glance at my credit with Hippolyta,
Knowing I know thy love to Theseus?
Didst not thou lead him through the glimmering night
From Perigenia, whom he ravishèd?
And make him with fair Aegles break his faith,
With Ariadne and Antiopa?

**TITANIA:** These are the forgeries of jealousy;
And never, since the middle summer's spring,
Met we on hill, in dale, forest, or mead,

---

**23 changeling** child exchanged for another by the fairies **25 trace** range through **26 perforce** forcibly **29 fountain** spring. **starlight sheen** shining starlight **30 square** quarrel **33 shrewd** mischievous. **sprite** spirit **35 villagery** village population **36 Skim milk** i.e., steal the cream. **quern** hand mill (where Puck presumably hampers the grinding of grain) **37 bootless** in vain. (Puck prevents the cream from turning to butter.) **huswife** housewife **38 barm** head on the ale. (Puck prevents the barm or yeast from producing fermentation.) **39 Mislead night wanderers** i.e., mislead with false fire those who walk abroad at night (hence earning Puck his other names of Jack o' Lantern and Will o' the Wisp) **40 Those . . . Puck** i.e., those who call you by the names you favor rather than those denoting the mischief you do **45 bean-fed** well fed on field beans **47 gossip's** old woman's **48 crab** crab apple **50 dewlap** loose skin on neck **51 aunt** old woman. **saddest** most serious **54 Tailor** (possibly because she ends up sitting cross-legged on the floor, looking like a tailor, or else referring to the *tail* or buttocks) **55 choir** company

**56 waxen** increase. **neeze** sneeze **57 wasted** spent **58 room** stand aside, make room **63 wanton** headstrong creature **66, 68 Corin, Phillida** (Conventional names of pastoral lovers.) **67 corn** (Here, oat stalks.) **69 step** farthest limit of travel, or, perhaps, *steep*, "mountain range" **71 buskined** wearing half-boots called buskins **75 Glance . . . Hippolyta** make insinuations about my favored relationship with Hippolyta **78 Perigenia** i.e., Perigouna, one of Theseus' conquests. (This and the following women are named in Thomas North's translation of Plutarch's "Life of Theseus.") **79 Aegles** i.e., Aegle, for whom Theseus deserted Ariadne according to some accounts **80 Ariadne** the daughter of Minos, King of Crete, who helped Theseus to escape the labyrinth after killing the Minotaur; later she was abandoned by Theseus. **Antiopa** Queen of the Amazons and wife of Theseus; elsewhere identified with Hippolyta but here thought of as a separate woman **82 middle summer's spring** beginning of midsummer **83 mead** meadow

Titania (Michelle Pfeiffer) argues with Oberon.

By pavèd fountain or by rushy brook,
Or in the beachèd margent of the sea,
To dance our ringlets to the whistling wind,
But with thy brawls thou hast disturbed our sport.
Therefore the winds, piping to us in vain,
As in revenge, have sucked up from the sea
Contagious fogs which, falling in the land,
Hath every pelting river made so proud
That they have overborne their continents.
The ox hath therefore stretched his yoke in vain,
The plowman lost his sweat, and the green corn
Hath rotted ere his youth attained a beard;
The fold stands empty in the drownèd field,
And crows are fatted with the murrain flock;
The nine-men's morris is filled up with mud,
And the quaint mazes in the wanton green
For lack of tread are undistinguishable.
The human mortals want their winter here;
No night is now with hymn or carol blessed.
Therefore the moon, the governess of floods,
Pale in her anger, washes all the air,
That rheumatic diseases do abound.
And thorough this distemperature we see
The seasons alter: hoary-headed frosts
Fall in the fresh lap of the crimson rose,
And on old Hiems' thin and icy crown
An odorous chaplet of sweet summer buds
Is, as in mockery, set. The spring, the summer,
The childing autumn, angry winter, change
Their wonted liveries, and the mazèd world
By their increase now knows not which is which.
And this same progeny of evils comes
From our debate, from our dissension.
We are their parents and original.

**OBERON:** Do you amend it, then. It lies in you.
Why should Titania cross her Oberon?
I do but beg a little changeling boy
To be my henchman.

**TITANIA:** Set your heart at rest.
The fairy land buys not the child of me.
His mother was a vot'ress of my order,
And in the spicèd Indian air by night
Full often hath she gossiped by my side
And sat with me on Neptune's yellow sands,
Marking th' embarkèd traders on the flood,
When we have laughed to see the sails conceive
And grow big-bellied with the wanton wind;
Which she, with pretty and with swimming gait,
Following—her womb then rich with my young
squire—
Would imitate, and sail upon the land
To fetch me trifles, and return again
As from a voyage, rich with merchandise.
But she, being mortal, of that boy did die;
And for her sake do I rear up her boy,
And for her sake I will not part with him.

**OBERON:** How long within this wood intend you stay?

**TITANIA:** Perchance till after Theseus' wedding day.
If you will patiently dance in our round
And see our moonlight revels, go with us;
If not, shun me, and I will spare your haunts.

**OBERON:** Give me that boy, and I will go with thee.

**TITANIA:** Not for thy fairy kingdom. Fairies, away!
We shall chide downright, if I longer stay.
*Exeunt* [TITANIA *with her train*].

---

**84 pavèd** with pebbled bottom. **rushy** bordered with rushes **85 in** on. **margent** edge, border **86 ringlets** dances in a ring. (See *orbs* in line 9.) **to** to the sound of **90 Contagious** noxious **91 pelting** paltry **92 continents** banks that contain them **93 stretched his yoke** i.e., pulled at his yoke in plowing **94 corn** grain of any kind **96 fold** pen for sheep or cattle **97 murrain** having died of the plague **98 nine-men's morris** i.e., portion of the village green marked out in a square for a game played with nine pebbles or pegs **99 quaint mazes** i.e., intricate paths marked out on the village green to be followed rapidly on foot as a kind of contest. **wanton** luxuriant **101 want** lack. **winter** i.e., regular winter season; or, proper observances of winter, such as the *hymn* or *carol* in the next line (?) **103 Therefore** i.e., as a result of our quarrel **104 washes** saturates with moisture **105 rheumatic diseases** colds, flu, and other respiratory infections **106 distemperature** disturbance in nature

---

**109 Hiems'** the winter god's **112 childing** fruitful, pregnant **113 wonted liveries** usual apparel. **mazèd** bewildered **114 their increase** their yield, what they produce **116 debate** quarrel **117 original** origin **121 henchman** attendant, page **123 was . . . order** had taken a vow to serve me **127 traders** trading vessels. **flood** flood tide **129 wanton** (1) playful (2) amorous **130 swimming** smooth, gliding **140 round** circular dance **142 spare** shun

**OBERON:** Well, go thy way. Thou shalt not from this grove
Till I torment thee for this injury.
My gentle Puck, come hither. Thou rememb'rest
Since once I sat upon a promontory,
And heard a mermaid on a dolphin's back
Uttering such dulcet and harmonious breath
That the rude sea grew civil at her song,
And certain stars shot madly from their spheres
To hear the sea-maid's music?

**PUCK:** I remember.

**OBERON:** That very time I saw, but thou couldst not,
Flying between the cold moon and the earth
Cupid, all armed. A certain aim he took
At a fair vestal thronèd by the west,
And loosed his love shaft smartly from his bow
As it should pierce a hundred thousand hearts;
But I might see young Cupid's fiery shaft
Quenched in the chaste beams of the watery moon,
And the imperial vot'ress passèd on,
In maiden meditation, fancy-free.
Yet marked I where the bolt of Cupid fell:
It fell upon a little western flower,
Before milk-white, now purple with love's wound,
And maidens call it love-in-idleness.
Fetch me that flower; the herb I showed thee once.
The juice of it on sleeping eyelids laid
Will make or man or woman madly dote
Upon the next live creature that it sees.
Fetch me this herb, and be thou here again
Ere the leviathan can swim a league.

**PUCK:** I'll put a girdle round about the earth
In forty minutes. *[Exit.]*

**OBERON:** Having once this juice,
I'll watch Titania when she is asleep
And drop the liquor of it in her eyes.
The next thing then she waking looks upon,
Be it on lion, bear, or wolf, or bull,
On meddling monkey, or on busy ape,
She shall pursue it with the soul of love.
And ere I take this charm from off her sight,
As I can take it with another herb,
I'll make her render up her page to me.
But who comes here? I am invisible,
And I will overhear their conference.

*Enter* DEMETRIUS, HELENA *following him.*

**DEMETRIUS:** I love thee not; therefore pursue me not.
Where is Lysander and fair Hermia?
The one I'll slay; the other slayeth me.
Thou toldst me they were stol'n unto this wood;
And here am I, and wood within this wood
Because I cannot meet my Hermia.
Hence, get thee gone, and follow me no more.

**HELENA:** You draw me, you hardhearted adamant!
But yet you draw not iron, for my heart
Is true as steel. Leave you your power to draw,
And I shall have no power to follow you.

**DEMETRIUS:** Do I entice you? Do I speak you fair?
Or rather do I not in plainest truth
Tell you I do not nor I cannot love you?

**HELENA:** And even for that do I love you the more.
I am your spaniel; and, Demetrius,
The more you beat me I will fawn on you.
Use me but as your spaniel, spurn me, strike me,
Neglect me, lose me; only give me leave,
Unworthy as I am, to follow you.
What worser place can I beg in your love—
And yet a place of high respect with me—
Than to be usèd as you use your dog?

**DEMETRIUS:** Tempt not too much the hatred of my spirit,
For I am sick when I do look on thee.

**HELENA:** And I am sick when I look not on you.

**DEMETRIUS:** You do impeach your modesty too much
To leave the city and commit yourself
Into the hands of one that loves you not,
To trust the opportunity of night
And the ill counsel of a desert place
With the rich worth of your virginity.

**HELENA:** Your virtue is my privilege. For that
It is not night when I do see your face,

---

**146 from** go from **149 Since** when **151 dulcet** sweet. **breath** voice, song **152 rude** rough **157 all** fully. **certain** sure **158 vestal** vestal virgin. (Contains a complimentary allusion to Queen Elizabeth as a votaress of Diana and probably refers to an actual entertainment in her honor at Elvetham in 1591.) **by** in the region of **159 loosed** released **160 As** as if **161 might** could **164 fancy-free** free of love's spell **165 bolt** arrow **168 love-in-idleness** pansy, heartsease **171 or . . . or** either . . . or **174 leviathan** sea monster, whale **176 forty** (Used indefinitely.)

**192 and wood** and mad, frantic (with an obvious wordplay on *wood,* meaning "woods") **195 adamant** lodestone, magnet (with pun on *hardhearted,* since adamant was also thought to be the hardest of all stones and was confused with the diamond) **197 Leave you** give up **199 speak you fair** speak courteously to you **214 impeach** call into question **215 To leave** by leaving **218 desert** deserted **220 virtue** goodness or power to attract. **privilege** safeguard, warrant. **For that** because

Therefore I think I am not in the night;
Nor doth this wood lack worlds of company,
For you, in my respect, are all the world.
Then how can it be said I am alone
When all the world is here to look on me?

**DEMETRIUS:** I'll run from thee and hide me in the brakes,
And leave thee to the mercy of wild beasts.

**HELENA:** The wildest hath not such a heart as you.
Run when you will. The story shall be changed:
Apollo flies and Daphne holds the chase,
The dove pursues the griffin, the mild hind
Makes speed to catch the tiger—bootless speed,
When cowardice pursues and valor flies!

**DEMETRIUS:** I will not stay thy questions. Let me go!
Or if thou follow me, do not believe
But I shall do thee mischief in the wood.

**HELENA:** Ay, in the temple, in the town, the field,
You do me mischief. Fie, Demetrius!
Your wrongs do set a scandal on my sex.
We cannot fight for love, as men may do;
We should be wooed and were not made to woo.
*[Exit* DEMETRIUS.*]*
I'll follow thee and make a heaven of hell,
To die upon the hand I love so well. *[Exit.]*

**OBERON:** Fare thee well, nymph. Ere he do leave this grove
Thou shalt fly him, and he shall seek thy love.
*Enter* PUCK.
Hast thou the flower there? Welcome, wanderer.

**PUCK:** Ay, there it is. *[He offers the flower.]*

**OBERON:** I pray thee, give it me.
I know a bank where the wild thyme blows,
Where oxlips and the nodding violet grows,
Quite overcanopied with luscious woodbine,

Puck (Stanley Tucci) shows the magic flower to Oberon.

With sweet muskroses and with eglantine.
There sleeps Titania sometime of the night,
Lulled in these flowers with dances and delight;
And there the snake throws her enameled skin,
Weed wide enough to wrap a fairy in.
And with the juice of this I'll streak her eyes
And make her full of hateful fantasies.
Take thou some of it, and seek through this grove.
*[He gives some love juice.]*
A sweet Athenian lady is in love
With a disdainful youth. Anoint his eyes,
But do it when the next thing he espies
May be the lady. Thou shalt know the man
By the Athenian garments he hath on.
Effect it with some care, that he may prove
More fond on her than she upon her love;
And look thou meet me ere the first cock crow.

**PUCK:** Fear not, my lord, your servant shall do so.
*Exeunt [separately].*

## 2.2 *Enter* TITANIA, *Queen of Fairies, with her train.*

**TITANIA:** Come, now a roundel and a fairy song;
Then, for the third part of a minute, hence—
Some to kill cankers in the muskrose buds,
Some war with reremice for their leathern wings
To make my small elves coats, and some keep back
The clamorous owl, that nightly hoots and wonders
At our quaint spirits. Sing me now asleep.
Then to your offices, and let me rest.

---

**224 in my respect** as far as I am concerned, in my esteem **227 brakes** thickets **231 Apollo . . . chase** (In the ancient myth, Daphne fled from Apollo and was saved from rape by being transformed into a laurel tree; here it is the female who *holds the chase,* or pursues, instead of the male.) **232 griffin** a fabulous monster with the head and wings of an eagle and the body of a lion. **hind** female deer **233 bootless** fruitless **235 stay** wait for, put up with. **questions** talk or argument **240 Your . . . sex** i.e., the wrongs that you do me cause me to act in a manner that disgraces my sex **244 upon** by **249 blows** blooms **250 oxlips** flowers resembling cowslip and primrose **251 woodbine** honeysuckle

**252 muskroses** a kind of large, sweet-scented rose. **eglantine** sweetbrier, another kind of rose **253 sometime of** for part of **255 throws** sloughs off, sheds **256 Weed** garment **257 streak** anoint, touch gently **266 fond on** doting on

**2.2 Location: The wood.**
**1 roundel** dance in a ring **2 the third . . . minute** (Indicative of the fairies' quickness.) **3 cankers** cankerworms (i.e., caterpillars or grubs) **4 reremice** bats **7 quaint** dainty

FAIRIES *sing.*

**FIRST FAIRY:**
You spotted snakes with double tongue,
Thorny hedgehogs, be not seen;
Newts and blindworms, do no wrong;
Come not near our Fairy Queen.

**CHORUS** *[dancing]*:
Philomel, with melody
Sing in our sweet lullaby;
Lulla, lulla, lullaby, lulla, lulla, lullaby.
Never harm
Nor spell nor charm
Come our lovely lady nigh.
So good night, with lullaby.

**FIRST FAIRY:**
Weaving spiders, come not here;
Hence, you long-legged spinners, hence!
Beetles black, approach not near;
Worm nor snail, do no offense.

**CHORUS** *[dancing]*:
Philomel, with melody
Sing in our sweet lullaby;
Lulla, lulla, lullaby, lulla, lulla, lullaby.
Never harm
Nor spell nor charm
Come our lovely lady nigh.
So good night, with lullaby.

*[*TITANIA *sleeps.]*

**SECOND FAIRY:**
Hence, away! Now all is well.
One aloof stand sentinel.

*[Exeunt* FAIRIES, *leaving one sentinel.]*

*Enter* OBERON *[and squeezes the flower on* TITANIA*'s eyelids].*

**OBERON:** What thou seest when thou dost wake,
Do it for thy true love take;
Love and languish for his sake.
Be it ounce, or cat, or bear,
Pard, or boar with bristled hair,
In thy eye that shall appear
When thou wak'st, it is thy dear.
Wake when some vile thing is near. *[Exit.]*

*Enter* LYSANDER *and* HERMIA.

**LYSANDER:** Fair love, you faint with wandering in the wood;
And to speak truth, I have forgot our way.
We'll rest us, Hermia, if you think it good,
And tarry for the comfort of the day.

**HERMIA:** Be it so, Lysander. Find you out a bed,
For I upon this bank will rest my head.

**LYSANDER:** One turf shall serve as pillow for us both;
One heart, one bed, two bosoms, and one troth.

**HERMIA:** Nay, good Lysander, for my sake, my dear,
Lie further off yet. Do not lie so near.

**LYSANDER:** O, take the sense, sweet, of my innocence!
Love takes the meaning in love's conference.
I mean that my heart unto yours is knit,
So that but one heart we can make of it;
Two bosoms interchainèd with an oath—
So then two bosoms and a single troth.
Then by your side no bed-room me deny,
For lying so, Hermia, I do not lie.

**HERMIA:** Lysander riddles very prettily.
Now much beshrew my manners and my pride
If Hermia meant to say Lysander lied.
But, gentle friend, for love and courtesy
Lie further off, in human modesty.
Such separation as may well be said
Becomes a virtuous bachelor and a maid,
So far be distant; and, good night, sweet friend.
Thy love ne'er alter till thy sweet life end!

**LYSANDER:** Amen, amen, to that fair prayer, say I,
And then end life when I end loyalty!
Here is my bed. Sleep give thee all his rest!

**HERMIA:** With half that wish the wisher's eyes be pressed!

*[They sleep, separated by a short distance.]*

*Enter* PUCK.

**PUCK:** Through the forest have I gone,
But Athenian found I none

**9 double** forked **11 Newts** water lizards (considered poisonous, as were *blindworms* —small snakes with tiny eyes—and spiders) **13 Philomel** the nightingale. (Philomela, daughter of King Pandion, was transformed into a nightingale, according to Ovid's *Metamorphoses* 6, after she had been raped by her sister Procne's husband, Tereus.) **23 offense** harm **32 sentinel** (Presumably Oberon is able to outwit or intimidate this guard.) **36 ounce** lynx **37 Pard** leopard

**48 troth** faith, trothplight **51 take . . . innocence** i.e., interpret my intention as innocent **52 Love . . . conference** i.e., when lovers confer, love teaches each lover to interpret the other's meaning lovingly **58 lie** tell a falsehood (with a riddling pun on *lie,* "recline") **60 beshrew** curse. (But mildly meant.) **63 human** courteous (and perhaps suggesting "humane," the Quarto spelling) **71 With . . . pressed** i.e., may we share your wish, so that your eyes too are *pressed,* closed, in sleep

On whose eyes I might approve
This flower's force in stirring love.
Night and silence.—Who is here?
Weeds of Athens he doth wear.
This is he, my master said,
Despisèd the Athenian maid;
And here the maiden, sleeping sound,
On the dank and dirty ground.
Pretty soul, she durst not lie
Near this lack-love, this kill-courtesy.
Churl, upon thy eyes I throw
All the power this charm doth owe.
*[He applies the love juice.]*
When thou wak'st, let love forbid
Sleep his seat on thy eyelid.
So awake when I am gone,
For I must now to Oberon. *Exit.*

*Enter* DEMETRIUS *and* HELENA, *running.*

**HELENA:** Stay, though thou kill me, sweet Demetrius!

**DEMETRIUS:** I charge thee, hence, and do not haunt me thus.

**HELENA:** O, wilt thou darkling leave me? Do not so.

**DEMETRIUS:** Stay, on thy peril! I alone will go. *[Exit.]*

**HELENA:** O, I am out of breath in this fond chase!
The more my prayer, the lesser is my grace.
Happy is Hermia, wheresoe'er she lies,
For she hath blessèd and attractive eyes.
How came her eyes so bright? Not with salt tears;
If so, my eyes are oftener washed than hers.
No, no, I am as ugly as a bear,
For beasts that meet me run away for fear.
Therefore no marvel though Demetrius
Do, as a monster, fly my presence thus.
What wicked and dissembling glass of mine
Made me compare with Hermia's sphery eyne?
But who is here? Lysander, on the ground?
Dead, or asleep? I see no blood, no wound.
Lysander, if you live, good sir, awake.

**LYSANDER** *[awaking]*: And run through fire I will for thy sweet sake.
Transparent Helena! Nature shows art,
That through thy bosom makes me see thy heart.
Where is Demetrius? O, how fit a word
Is that vile name to perish on my sword!

**HELENA:** Do not say so, Lysander; say not so.
What though he love your Hermia? Lord, what though?
Yet Hermia still loves you. Then be content.

**LYSANDER:** Content with Hermia? No! I do repent
The tedious minutes I with her have spent.
Not Hermia but Helena I love.
Who will not change a raven for a dove?
The will of man is by his reason swayed,
And reason says you are the worthier maid.
Things growing are not ripe until their season;
So I, being young, till now ripe not to reason.
And, touching now the point of human skill,
Reason becomes the marshal to my will
And leads me to your eyes, where I o'erlook
Love's stories written in love's richest book.

**HELENA:** Wherefore was I to this keen mockery born?
When at your hands did I deserve this scorn?
Is 't not enough, is 't not enough, young man,
That I did never—no, nor never can—
Deserve a sweet look from Demetrius' eye,
But you must flout my insufficiency?
Good troth, you do me wrong, good sooth, you do,
In such disdainful manner me to woo.
But fare you well. Perforce I must confess
I thought you lord of more true gentleness.
O, that a lady, of one man refused,
Should of another therefore be abused! *Exit.*

**LYSANDER:** She sees not Hermia. Hermia, sleep thou there,
And never mayst thou come Lysander near!
For as a surfeit of the sweetest things
The deepest loathing to the stomach brings,
Or as the heresies that men do leave
Are hated most of those they did deceive,
So thou, my surfeit and my heresy,
Of all be hated, but the most of me!
And, all my powers, address your love and might
To honor Helen and to be her knight! *Exit.*

---

**74 approve** test **85 owe** own **92 darkling** in the dark **93 on thy peril** i.e., on pain of danger to you if you don't obey me and stay **94 fond** doting **95 my grace** the favor I obtain **96 lies** dwells **102–103 no marvel . . . thus** i.e., no wonder that Demetrius flies from me as from a monster **105 compare** vie. **sphery eyne** eyes as bright as stars in their spheres **110 Transparent** (1) radiant (2) able to be seen through, lacking in deceit. **art** skill, magic power

**121 will** desire **124 ripe not** (am) not ripened **125 touching** reaching. **point** summit. **skill** judgment **127 o'erlook** read **129 Wherefore** why **135 Good troth, good sooth** i.e., indeed, truly **138 lord of** i.e., possessor of. **gentleness** courtesy **139 of** by **140 abused** ill treated **145–146 as . . . deceive** as renounced heresies are hated most by those persons who formerly were deceived by them **148 Of . . . of** by . . . by **149 address** direct, apply

Lysander (Dominic West) tells the sleeping Hermia (Anna Friel) to stay away from him.

**HERMIA** *[awaking]*: Help me, Lysander, help me! Do thy best
To pluck this crawling serpent from my breast!
Ay me, for pity! What a dream was here!
Lysander, look how I do quake with fear.
Methought a serpent ate my heart away,
And you sat smiling at his cruel prey.
Lysander! What, removed? Lysander! Lord!
What, out of hearing? Gone? No sound, no word?
Alack, where are you? Speak, an if you hear;
Speak, of all loves! I swoon almost with fear.
No? Then I well perceive you are not nigh.
Either death, or you, I'll find immediately.

*Exit. [The sleeping* TITANIA *remains.]*

**3.1** *Enter the clowns [*QUINCE, SNUG, BOTTOM, FLUTE, SNOUT, *and* STARVELING*].*

**BOTTOM:** Are we all met?

**QUINCE:** Pat, pat; and here's a marvelous convenient place for our rehearsal. This green plot shall be our stage, this hawthorn brake our tiring-house, and we will do it in action as we will do it before the Duke.

**BOTTOM:** Peter Quince?

**QUINCE:** What sayest thou, bully Bottom?

**BOTTOM:** There are things in this comedy of Pyramus and Thisbe that will never please. First, Pyramus must draw a sword to kill himself, which the ladies cannot abide. How answer you that?

---

**156 prey** act of preying **159 an if** if **160 of all loves** for love's sake

**3.1. Location: The action is continuous.**
**s.d. clowns** rustics
**2 Pat** on the dot, punctually **4 brake** thicket. **tiring-house** attiring area, hence backstage **7 bully** i.e., worthy, jolly, fine fellow

**SNOUT:** By 'r lakin, a parlous fear.

**STARVELING:** I believe we must leave the killing out, when all is done.

**BOTTOM:** Not a whit. I have a device to make all well. Write me a prologue, and let the prologue seem to say, we will do no harm with our swords, and that Pyramus is not killed indeed; and for the more better assurance, tell them that I, Pyramus, am not Pyramus but Bottom the weaver. This will put them out of fear.

**QUINCE:** Well, we will have such a prologue, and it shall be written in eight and six.

**BOTTOM:** No, make it two more: let it be written in eight and eight.

**SNOUT:** Will not the ladies be afeard of the lion?

**STARVELING:** I fear it, I promise you.

**BOTTOM:** Masters, you ought to consider with yourself, to bring in—God shield us!—a lion among ladies is a most dreadful thing. For there is not a more fearful wildfowl than your lion living, and we ought to look to 't.

**SNOUT:** Therefore another prologue must tell he is not a lion.

**BOTTOM:** Nay, you must name his name, and half his face must be seen through the lion's neck, and he himself must speak through, saying thus or to the same defect: "Ladies," or "Fair ladies, I would wish you," or "I would request you," or "I would entreat you, not to fear, not to tremble; my life for yours. If you think I come hither as a lion, it were pity of my life. No, I am no such thing; I am a man as other men are." And there indeed let him name his name, and tell them plainly he is Snug the joiner.

**QUINCE:** Well, it shall be so. But there is two hard things: that is, to bring the moonlight into a chamber; for, you know, Pyramus and Thisbe meet by moonlight.

---

**12 By 'r lakin** by our ladykin, i.e., the Virgin Mary. **parlous** perilous, alarming **14 when all is done** i.e., when all is said and done **16 Write me** i.e., write at my suggestion. (*Me* is used colloquially.) **22 eight and six** alternate lines of eight and six syllables, a common ballad measure **28 lion among ladies** (A contemporary pamphlet tells how, at the christening in 1594 of Prince Henry, eldest son of King James VI of Scotland, later James I of England, a "blackamoor" instead of a lion drew the triumphal chariot, since the lion's presence might have "brought some fear to the nearest.") **29–30 fearful** fear-inspiring **37 defect** (Bottom's blunder for "effect.") **39 my life for yours** i.e., I pledge my life to make your lives safe **40–41 it were . . . life** i.e., I should be sorry, by my life; or, my life would be endangered

Bottom (Kevin Kline) and the players meet to discuss their performance.

**SNOUT:** Doth the moon shine that night we play our play?

**BOTTOM:** A calendar, a calendar! Look in the almanac. Find out moonshine, find out moonshine.

*[They consult an almanac.]*

**QUINCE:** Yes, it doth shine that night.

**BOTTOM:** Why then may you leave a casement of the great chamber window where we play open, and the moon may shine in at the casement.

**QUINCE:** Ay; or else one must come in with a bush of thorns and a lantern and say he comes to disfigure, or to present, the person of Moonshine. Then there is another thing: we must have a wall in the great chamber; for Pyramus and Thisbe, says the story, did talk through the chink of a wall.

**SNOUT:** You can never bring in a wall. What say you, Bottom?

**BOTTOM:** Some man or other must present Wall. And let him have some plaster, or some loam, or some roughcast about him, to signify wall; or let him hold his fingers thus, and through that cranny shall Pyramus and Thisbe whisper.

**QUINCE:** If that may be, then all is well. Come, sit down, every mother's son, and rehearse your parts. Pyramus, you begin. When you have spoken your speech, enter into that brake, and so everyone according to his cue.

*Enter* ROBIN *[*PUCK*].*

**PUCK** *[aside]*: What hempen homespuns have we swaggering here
So near the cradle of the Fairy Queen?
What, a play toward? I'll be an auditor;
An actor, too, perhaps, if I see cause.

**QUINCE:** Speak, Pyramus. Thisbe, stand forth.

**BOTTOM** *[as* PYRAMUS*]*: "Thisbe, the flowers of odious savors sweet—"

**QUINCE:** Odors, odors.

**BOTTOM:** "—Odors savors sweet;
So hath thy breath, my dearest Thisbe dear.
But hark, a voice! Stay thou but here awhile,
And by and by I will to thee appear." *Exit.*

**PUCK:** A stranger Pyramus than e'er played here. *[Exit.]*

**FLUTE:** Must I speak now?

**QUINCE:** Ay, marry, must you; for you must understand he goes but to see a noise that he heard, and is to come again.

**FLUTE** *[as* THISBE*]*: "Most radiant Pyramus, most lily-white of hue,
Of color like the red rose on triumphant brier,
Most brisky juvenal and eke most lovely Jew,
As true as truest horse that yet would never tire.
I'll meet thee, Pyramus, at Ninny's tomb."

**QUINCE:** "Ninus' tomb," man. Why, you must not speak that yet. That you answer to Pyramus. You speak all your part at once, cues and all. Pyramus, enter. Your cue is past; it is "never tire."

**FLUTE:** O—"As true as truest horse, that yet would never tire."

*[Enter* PUCK, *and* BOTTOM *as* PYRAMUS *with the ass head.]*

**BOTTOM:** "If I were fair, Thisbe, I were only thine."

---

**55–56 bush of thorns** bundle of thornbush fagots (part of the accoutrements of the man in the moon, according to the popular notions of the time, along with his lantern and his dog) **56 disfigure** (Quince's blunder for "figure.") **57 present** represent **64–65 roughcast** a mixture of lime and gravel used to plaster the outside of buildings

**72 hempen homespuns** i.e., rustics dressed in clothes woven of coarse, homespun fabric made from hemp **73 cradle** i.e., Titania's bower **74 toward** about to take place **83 A stranger . . . here** (Either Puck refers to an earlier dramatic version played in the same theater, or he has conceived of a plan to present a "stranger" Pyramus than ever seen before.) **89 triumphant** magnificent **90 brisky juvenal** lively youth. **eke** also. **Jew** (An absurd repetition of the first syllable of *juvenal* and an indication of how desperately Quince searches for his rhymes.) **93 Ninus** mythical founder of Nineveh (whose wife, Semiramis, was supposed to have built the walls of Babylon where the story of Pyramus and Thisbe takes place) **95 part** (An actor's *part* was a script consisting only of his speeches and their cues.) **97 s.d. with the ass head** (This stage direction, taken from the Folio, presumably refers to a standard stage property.) **98 fair** handsome. **were** would be

**QUINCE:** O, monstrous! O, strange! We are haunted.
Pray, masters! Fly, masters! Help!
*[Exeunt* QUINCE, SNUG, FLUTE, SNOUT, *and* STARVELING.*]*

**PUCK:** I'll follow you, I'll lead you about a round,
Thorough bog, thorough bush, thorough brake, thorough brier.
Sometimes a horse I'll be, sometimes a hound,
A hog, a headless bear, sometimes a fire;
And neigh, and bark, and grunt, and roar, and burn,
Like horse, hound, hog, bear, fire, at every turn. *Exit.*

**BOTTOM:** Why do they run away? This is a knavery of them to make me afeard.

*Enter* SNOUT.

**SNOUT:** O Bottom, thou art changed! What do I see on thee?

**BOTTOM:** What do you see? You see an ass head of your own, do you? *[Exit* SNOUT.*]*

*Enter* QUINCE.

**QUINCE:** Bless thee, Bottom, bless thee! Thou art translated. *Exit.*

**BOTTOM:** I see their knavery. This is to make an ass of me, to fright me, if they could. But I will not stir from this place, do what they can. I will walk up and down here, and will sing, that they shall hear I am not afraid. *[He sings.]*
The ouzel cock so black of hue,
With orange-tawny bill,
The throstle with his note so true,
The wren with little quill—

**TITANIA** *[awaking]*: What angel wakes me from my flowery bed?

**BOTTOM:** *[sings]*
The finch, the sparrow, and the lark,
The plainsong cuckoo gray,
Whose note full many a man doth mark,
And dares not answer nay—
For indeed, who would set his wit to so foolish a bird? Who would give a bird the lie, though he cry "cuckoo" never so?

**TITANIA:** I pray thee, gentle mortal, sing again.
Mine ear is much enamored of thy note;
So is mine eye enthrallèd to thy shape;
And thy fair virtue's force perforce doth move me
On the first view to say, to swear, I love thee.

**BOTTOM:** Methinks, mistress, you should have little reason for that. And yet, to say the truth, reason and love keep little company together nowadays—the more the pity that some honest neighbors will not make them friends. Nay, I can gleek upon occasion.

**TITANIA:** Thou art as wise as thou art beautiful.

**BOTTOM:** Not so, neither. But if I had wit enough to get out of this wood, I have enough to serve mine own turn.

**TITANIA:** Out of this wood do not desire to go.
Thou shalt remain here, whether thou wilt or no.
I am a spirit of no common rate.
The summer still doth tend upon my state,
And I do love thee. Therefore, go with me.
I'll give thee fairies to attend on thee,
And they shall fetch thee jewels from the deep,
And sing while thou on pressèd flowers dost sleep.
And I will purge thy mortal grossness so
That thou shalt like an airy spirit go.
Peaseblossom, Cobweb, Mote, and Mustardseed!

*Enter four* FAIRIES *[*PEASEBLOSSOM, COBWEB, MOTE, *and* MUSTARDSEED*]*.

**PEASEBLOSSOM:** Ready.

**COBWEB:** And I.

**MOTE:** And I.

**MUSTARDSEED:** And I.

**ALL:** Where shall we go?

**TITANIA:** Be kind and courteous to this gentleman.
Hop in his walks and gambol in his eyes;
Feed him with apricots and dewberries,
With purple grapes, green figs, and mulberries;
The honey bags steal from the humble-bees,

---

**101 about a round** roundabout **104 fire** will-o'-the-wisp **114 translated** transformed **120 ouzel cock** male blackbird **122 throstle** song thrush **123 quill** (Literally, a reed pipe; hence, the bird's piping song.) **126 plainsong** singing a melody without variations **128 dares . . . nay** i.e., cannot deny that he is a cuckold **129 set his wit to** to employ his intelligence to answer **130 give . . . lie** call the bird a liar **131 never so** ever so much

**135 thy . . . force** the power of your unblemished excellence **141 gleek** jest **144–145 serve . . . turn** answer my purpose **148 rate** rank, value **149 still . . . state** always waits upon me as a part of my royal retinue **154 mortal grossness** materiality (i.e., the corporal nature of a mortal being) **156 Mote** i.e., speck. (The two words *moth* and *mote* were pronounced alike, and both meanings may be present.) **160 in his eyes** in his sight (i.e., before him) **161 dewberries** blackberries

And for night tapers crop their waxen thighs
And light them at the fiery glowworms' eyes,
To have my love to bed and to arise;
And pluck the wings from painted butterflies
To fan the moonbeams from his sleeping eyes.
Nod to him, elves, and do him courtesies.

**PEASEBLOSSOM:** Hail, mortal!

**COBWEB:** Hail!

**MOTE:** Hail!

**MUSTARDSEED:** Hail!

**BOTTOM:** I cry your worship's mercy, heartily. I beseech your worship's name.

**COBWEB:** Cobweb.

**BOTTOM:** I shall desire you of more acquaintance, good Master Cobweb. If I cut my finger, I shall make bold with you.—Your name, honest gentleman?

**PEASEBLOSSOM:** Peaseblossom.

**BOTTOM:** I pray you, commend me to Mistress Squash, your mother, and to Master Peascod, your father. Good Master Peaseblossom, I shall desire you of more acquaintance too.—Your name, I beseech you, sir?

**MUSTARDSEED:** Mustardseed.

**BOTTOM:** Good Master Mustardseed, I know your patience well. That same cowardly, giantlike ox-beef hath devoured many a gentleman of your house. I promise you, your kindred hath made my eyes water ere now. I desire you of more acquaintance, good Master Mustardseed.

**TITANIA:** Come wait upon him; lead him to my bower.
The moon methinks looks with a watery eye;
And when she weeps, weeps every little flower,
Lamenting some enforcèd chastity.
Tie up my lover's tongue; bring him silently.

*Exeunt.*

**174 I cry . . . mercy** I beg pardon of your worships (for presuming to ask a question) **177 I . . . acquaintance** I crave to be better acquainted with you **178–179 If . . . you** (Cobwebs were used to stanch bleeding.) **181 Squash** unripe pea pod **182 Peascod** ripe pea pod **186–187 your patience** what you have endured. (Mustard is eaten with beef.) **189 water** (1) weep for sympathy (2) smart, sting **194 she weeps** i.e., she causes dew **195 enforcèd** forced, violated; or, possibly, constrained (since Titania at this moment is hardly concerned about chastity) **196 Tie . . . tongue** (Presumably Bottom is braying like an ass.)

Titania (Judi Dench), enchanted, kisses the transformed Bottom.

**3.2** *Enter [*OBERON,*] King of Fairies.*

**OBERON:** I wonder if Titania be awaked;
Then, what it was that next came in her eye,
Which she must dote on in extremity.

*[Enter]* ROBIN GOODFELLOW *[PUCK].*

Here comes my messenger. How now, mad spirit?
What night-rule now about this haunted grove?

**PUCK:** My mistress with a monster is in love.
Near to her close and consecrated bower,
While she was in her dull and sleeping hour,
A crew of patches, rude mechanicals,
That work for bread upon Athenian stalls,
Were met together to rehearse a play
Intended for great Theseus' nuptial day.
The shallowest thickskin of that barren sort,
Who Pyramus presented, in their sport
Forsook his scene and entered in a brake.
When I did him at this advantage take,
An ass's noll I fixèd on his head.
Anon his Thisbe must be answerèd,
And forth my mimic comes. When they him spy,
As wild geese that the creeping fowler eye,
Or russet-pated choughs, many in sort,

**3.2 Location: The wood.**
**5 night-rule** diversion or misrule for the night. **haunted** much frequented **7 close** secret, private **8 dull** drowsy **9 patches** clowns, fools. **rude mechanicals** ignorant artisans **10 stalls** market booths **13 barren sort** stupid company or crew **14 presented** acted **15 scene** playing area **17 noll** noddle, head **19 mimic** burlesque actor **20 fowler** hunter of game birds **21 russet-pated choughs** reddish brown or gray-headed jackdaws. **in sort** in a flock

Rising and cawing at the gun's report,
Sever themselves and madly sweep the sky,
So, at his sight, away his fellow fly;
And, at our stamp, here o'er and o'er one falls;
He "Murder!" cries and help from Athens calls.
Their sense thus weak, lost with their fears thus strong,
Made senseless things begin to do them wrong,
For briers and thorns at their apparel snatch;
Some, sleeves—some, hats; from yielders all things catch.
I led them on in this distracted fear
And left sweet Pyramus translated there,
When in that moment, so it came to pass,
Titania waked and straightway loved an ass.

**OBERON:** This falls out better than I could devise.
But has thou yet latched the Athenian's eyes
With the love juice, as I did bid thee do?

**PUCK:** I took him sleeping—that is finished too—
And the Athenian woman by his side,
That, when he waked, of force she must be eyed.

*Enter* DEMETRIUS *and* HERMIA.

**OBERON:** Stand close. This is the same Athenian.

**PUCK:** This is the woman, but not this the man.
*[They stand aside.]*

**DEMETRIUS:** O, why rebuke you him that loves you so?
Lay breath so bitter on your bitter foe.

**HERMIA:** Now I but chide; but I should use thee worse,
For thou, I fear, hast given me cause to curse.
If thou hast slain Lysander in his sleep,
Being o'er shoes in blood, plunge in the deep,
And kill me too.
The sun was not so true unto the day
As he to me. Would he have stolen away
From sleeping Hermia? I'll believe as soon
This whole earth may be bored, and that the moon
May through the center creep, and so displease
Her brother's noontide with th' Antipodes.
It cannot be but thou hast murdered him;
So should a murder look, so dead, so grim.

**DEMETRIUS:** So should the murdered look, and so should I,
Pierced through the heart with your stern cruelty.
Yet you, the murderer, look as bright, as clear
As yonder Venus in her glimmering sphere.

**HERMIA:** What's this to my Lysander? Where is he?
Ah, good Demetrius, wilt thou give him me?

**DEMETRIUS:** I had rather give his carcass to my hounds.

**HERMIA:** Out, dog! Out, cur! Thou driv'st me past the bounds
Of maiden's patience. Hast thou slain him, then?
Henceforth be never numbered among men.
O, once tell true, tell true, even for my sake:
Durst thou have looked upon him being awake?
And hast thou killed him sleeping? O brave touch!
Could not a worm, an adder, do so much?
An adder did it; for with doubler tongue
Than thine, thou serpent, never adder stung.

**DEMETRIUS:** You spend your passion on a misprised mood.
I am not guilty of Lysander's blood,
Nor is he dead, for aught that I can tell.

**HERMIA:** I pray thee, tell me then that he is well.

**DEMETRIUS:** And if I could, what should I get therefor?

**HERMIA:** A privilege never to see me more.
And from thy hated presence part I so.
See me no more, whether he be dead or no. *Exit.*

**DEMETRIUS:** There is no following her in this fierce vein.
Here therefore for a while I will remain.
So sorrow's heaviness doth heavier grow
For debt that bankrupt sleep doth sorrow owe,
Which now in some slight measure it will pay,
If for his tender here I make some stay.
*[He] lie[s] down [and sleeps].*

**OBERON:** What hast thou done? Thou hast mistaken quite
And laid the love juice on some true love's sight.

---

**23 Sever** i.e., scatter **30 from . . . catch** i.e., everything preys on those who yield to fear **36 latched** fastened, snared **40 of force** perforce **48 Being o'er shoes** having waded in so far **53 whole** solid **55 Her brother's** i.e., the sun's. **th' Antipodes** the people on the opposite side of the earth (where the moon is imagined bringing night to noontime) **57 dead** deadly, or deathly pale

**62 to** to do with **68 once** once and for all **70 brave touch!** fine stroke! (Said ironically.) **71 worm** serpent **72 doubler** (1) more forked (2) more deceitful **74 passion** violent feelings. **misprised mood** anger based on misconception **78 therefor** in return for that **84 heavier** (1) harder to bear (2) more drowsy **85 bankrupt** (Demetrius is saying that his sleepiness adds to the weariness caused by sorrow.) **86–87 Which . . . stay** i.e., to a small extent, I will be able to "pay back" and hence find some relief from sorrow, if I pause here awhile (*make some stay*) while sleep "tenders," or offers, itself by way of paying the debt owed to sorrow

Of thy misprision must perforce ensue
Some true loved turned, and not a false turned true.

**PUCK:** Then fate o'errules, that, one man holding troth,
A million fail, confounding oath on oath.

**OBERON:** About the wood go swifter than the wind,
And Helena of Athens look thou find.
All fancy-sick she is and pale of cheer
With sighs of love, that cost the fresh blood dear.
By some illusion see thou bring her here.
I'll charm his eyes against she do appear.

**PUCK:** I go, I go, look how I go,
Swifter than arrow from the Tartar's bow. *[Exit.]*

**OBERON** *[applying love juice to* DEMETRIUS' *eyes]*:
Flower of this purple dye,
Hit with Cupid archery,
Sink in apple of his eye.
When his love he doth espy,
Let her shine as gloriously
As the Venus of the sky.
When thou wak'st, if she be by,
Beg of her for remedy.

*Enter* PUCK.

**PUCK:** Captain of our fairy band,
Helena is here at hand,
And the youth, mistook by me,
Pleading for a lover's fee.
Shall we their fond pageant see?
Lord, what fools these mortals be!

**OBERON:** Stand aside. The noise they make
Will cause Demetrius to awake.

**PUCK:** Then will two at once woo one;
That must needs be sport alone.
And those things do best please me
That befall preposterously.
*[They stand aside.]*

*Enter* LYSANDER *and* HELENA.

**LYSANDER:** Why should you think that I should woo in scorn?
Scorn and derision never come in tears.
Look when I vow, I weep; and vows so born,
In their nativity all truth appears.
How can these things in me seem scorn to you,
Bearing the badge of faith to prove them true?

**HELENA:** You do advance your cunning more and more.
When truth kills truth, O, devilish-holy fray!
These vows are Hermia's. Will you give her o'er?
Weigh oath with oath, and you will nothing weigh.
Your vows to her and me, put in two scales,
Will even weigh, and both as light as tales.

**LYSANDER:** I had no judgment when to her I swore.

**HELENA:** Nor none, in my mind, now you give her o'er.

**LYSANDER:** Demetrius loves her, and he loves not you.

**DEMETRIUS** *[awaking]*: O Helen, goddess, nymph, perfect, divine!
To what, my love, shall I compare thine eyne?
Crystal is muddy. O, how ripe in show
Thy lips, those kissing cherries, tempting grow!
That pure congealèd white, high Taurus' snow,
Fanned with the eastern wind, turns to a crow
When thou hold'st up thy hand. O, let me kiss
This princess of pure white, this seal of bliss!

**HELENA:** O spite! O hell! I see you all are bent
To set against me for your merriment.
If you were civil and knew courtesy,
You would not do me thus much injury.
Can you not hate me, as I know you do,
But you must join in souls to mock me too?
If you were men, as men you are in show,
You would not use a gentle lady so—
To vow, and swear, and superpraise my parts,
When I am sure you hate me with your hearts.
You both are rivals, and love Hermia,
And now both rivals to mock Helena.
A trim exploit, a many enterprise,
To conjure tears up in a poor maid's eyes

---

**90 misprision** mistake **92 that . . . troth** in that, for each man keeping true faith in love **93 confounding . . . oath** i.e., breaking oath after oath **95 look** i.e., be sure **96 fancy-sick** lovesick. **cheer** face **97 sighs . . . blood** (An allusion to the physiological theory that each sigh costs the heart a drop of blood.) **99 against . . . appear** in anticipation of her coming **101 Tartar's bow** (Tartars were famed for their skill with the bow.) **104 apple** pupil **113 fee** privilege, reward **114 fond pageant** foolish spectacle **119 alone** unequaled **121 preposterously** out of the natural order

**124 Look when** whenever **124–125 vows . . . appears** i.e., vows made by one who is weeping give evidence thereby of their sincerity **127 badge** identifying device such as that worn on servants' livery (here, his tears) **128 advance** carry forward, display **129 truth kills truth** i.e., one of Lysander's vows must invalidate the other **133 tales** lies **139 show** appearance **141 Taurus** a lofty mountain range in Asia Minor **142 turns to a crow** i.e., seems black by contrast **144 seal** pledge **146 set against** attack **150 in souls** i.e., heart and soul **153 superpraise** overpraise. **parts** qualities **157 trim** pretty, fine. (Said ironically.)

With your derision! None of noble sort
Would so offend a virgin and extort
A poor soul's patience, all to make you sport.

**LYSANDER:** You are unkind, Demetrius. Be not so.
For you love Hermia; this you know I know.
And here, with all good will, with all my heart,
In Hermia's love I yield you up my part;
And yours of Helena to me bequeath,
Whom I do love, and will do till my death.

**HELENA:** Never did mockers waste more idle breath.

**DEMETRIUS:** Lysander, keep thy Hermia; I will none.
If e'er I loved her, all that love is gone.
My heart to her but as guestwise sojourned,
And now to Helen is it home returned,
There to remain.

**LYSANDER:** Helen, it is not so.

**DEMETRIUS:** Disparage not the faith thou dost not know,
Lest, to thy peril, thou aby it dear.
Look where thy love comes; yonder is thy dear.

*Enter* HERMIA.

**HERMIA:** Dark night, that from the eye his function takes,
The ear more quick of apprehension makes;
Wherein it doth impair the seeing sense,
It pays the hearing double recompense.
Thou art not by mine eye, Lysander, found;
Mine ear, I thank it, brought me to thy sound.
But why unkindly didst thou leave me so?

**LYSANDER:** Why should he stay, whom love doth press to go?

**HERMIA:** What love could press Lysander from my side?

**LYSANDER:** Lysander's love that would not let him bide—
Fair Helena, who more engilds the night
Than all yon fiery oes and eyes of light.
Why seek'st thou me? Could not this make thee know
The hate I bear thee made me leave thee so?

**HERMIA:** You speak not as you think. It cannot be.

---

**159 sort** character, quality **160 extort** twist, torture **169 will none** i.e., want no part of her **171 to . . . sojourned** only visited with her **175 aby** pay for **177 his** its **187 engilds** gilds, brightens with a golden light **188 oes** spangles (here, stars)

Hermia bemoans Lysander's betrayal to Demetrius (Christian Bale).

**HELENA:** Lo, she is one of this confederacy!
Now I perceive they have conjoined all three
To fashion this false sport, in spite of me.
Injurious Hermia, most ungrateful maid!
Have you conspired, have you with these contrived
To bait me with this foul derision?
Is all the counsel that we two have shared—
The sisters' vows, the hours that we have spent
When we have chid the hasty-footed time
For parting us—O, is all forgot?
All schooldays' friendship, childhood innocence?
We, Hermia, like two artificial gods
Have with our needles created both one flower,
Both on one sampler, sitting on one cushion,
Both warbling of one song, both in one key,
As if our hands, our sides, voices, and minds
Had been incorporate. So we grew together,
Like to a double cherry, seeming parted,
But yet an union in partition,
Two lovely berries molded on one stem;
So, with two seeming bodies but one heart,
Two of the first, like coats in heraldry,
Due but to one and crownèd with one crest.
And will you rend our ancient love asunder,
To join with men in scorning your poor friend?
It is not friendly, 'tis not maidenly.
Our sex, as well as I, may chide you for it,
Though I alone do feel the injury.

**HERMIA:** I am amazèd at your passionate words.
I scorn you not. It seems that you scorn me.

---

**194 in spite of me** to vex me **196 contrived** plotted **197 bait** torment, as one sets on dogs to bait a bear **198 counsel** confidential talk **203 artificial** skilled in art or creation **208 incorporate** of one body **211 lovely** loving **213–214 Two . . . crest** i.e., we have two separate bodies, just as a coat of arms in heraldry can be represented twice on a shield but surmounted by a single crest

**HELENA:** Have you not set Lysander, as in scorn,
To follow me and praise my eyes and face?
And made your other love, Demetrius,
Who even but now did spurn me with his foot,
To call me goddess, nymph, divine, and rare,
Precious, celestial? Wherefore speaks he this
To her he hates? And wherefore doth Lysander
Deny your love, so rich within his soul,
And tender me, forsooth, affection,
But by your setting on, by your consent?
What though I be not so in grace as you,
So hung upon with love, so fortunate,
But miserable most, to love unloved?
This you should pity rather than despise.

**HERMIA:** I understand not what you mean by this.

**HELENA:** Ay, do! Persever, counterfeit sad looks,
Make mouths upon me when I turn my back,
Wink each at other, hold the sweet jest up.
This sport, well carried, shall be chronicled.
If you have any pity, grace, or manners,
You would not make me such an argument.
But fare ye well. 'Tis partly my own fault,
Which death, or absence, soon shall remedy.

**LYSANDER:** Stay, gentle Helena; hear my excuse,
My love, my life, my soul, fair Helena!

**HELENA:** O excellent!

**HERMIA** *[to* LYSANDER*]*: Sweet, do not scorn her so.

**DEMETRIUS** *[to* LYSANDER*]*: If she cannot entreat, I can compel.

**LYSANDER:** Thou canst compel no more than she entreat.
Thy threats have no more strength than her weak prayers.
Helen, I love thee, by my life, I do!
I swear by that which I will lose for thee,
To prove him false that says I love thee not.

**DEMETRIUS** *[to* HELENA*]*: I say I love thee more than he can do.

**LYSANDER:** If thou say so, withdraw, and prove it too.

**DEMETRIUS:** Quick, come!

**HERMIA:** Lysander, whereto tends all this?

**LYSANDER:** Away, you Ethiope!
*[He tries to break away from* HERMIA.*]*

**DEMETRIUS:** No, no; he'll
Seem to break loose; take on as you would follow,
But yet come not. You are a tame man. Go!

**LYSANDER** *[to* HERMIA*]*: Hang off, thou cat, thou burr!
Vile thing, let loose,
Or I will shake thee from me like a serpent!

**HERMIA:** Why are you grown so rude? What change is this,
Sweet love?

**LYSANDER:** Thy love? Out, tawny Tartar, out!
Out, loathèd med'cine! O hated potion, hence!

**HERMIA:** Do you not jest?

**HELENA:** Yes, sooth, and so do you.

**LYSANDER:** Demetrius, I will keep my word with thee.

**DEMETRIUS:** I would I had your bond, for I perceive
A weak bond holds you. I'll not trust your word.

**LYSANDER:** What, should I hurt her, strike her, kill her dead?
Although I hate her, I'll not harm her so.

**HERMIA:** What, can you do me greater harm than hate?
Hate me? Wherefore? O me, what news, my love?
Am not I Hermia? Are you not Lysander?
I am as fair now as I was erewhile.
Since night you loved me; yet since night you left me.
Why, then you left me—O, the gods forbid!—
In earnest, shall I say?

**LYSANDER:** Ay, by my life!
And never did desire to see thee more.
Therefore be out of hope, of question, of doubt;
Be certain, nothing truer. 'Tis no jest
That I do hate thee and love Helena.

**HERMIA** *[to* HELENA*]*: O me! You juggler! You cankerblossom!
You thief of love! What, have you come by night
And stol'n my love's heart from him?

**HELENA:** Fine, i' faith!
Have you no modesty, no maiden shame,

---

**230 tender** offer **232 grace** favor **237 sad** grave, serious **238 mouths** i.e., mows, faces, grimaces. **upon** at **239 hold . . . up** keep up the joke **240 carried** managed **242 argument** subject for a jest **248 entreat** i.e., succeed by entreaty **255 withdraw . . . too** i.e., withdraw with me and prove your claim in a duel. (The two gentlemen are armed.)

**257 Ethiope** (Referring to Hermia's relatively dark hair and complexion; see also *tawny Tartar* six lines later.) **258 take on as** act as if, make a fuss as if **260 Hang off** let go **264 med'cine** i.e., poison **265 sooth** truly **268 weak bond** i.e., Hermia's arm (with a pun on *bond,* "oath," in the previous line) **272 what news** what is the matter **274 erewhile** just now **282 cankerblossom** worm that destroys the flower bud, or wild rose

Helena (Diana Rigg) hides from Hermia between Lysander and Demetrius (Michael Jayston).

No touch of bashfulness? What, will you tear
Impatient answers from my gentle tongue?
Fie, fie! You counterfeit, you puppet, you!

**HERMIA:** "Puppet"? Why, so! Ay, that way goes the game.
Now I perceive that she hath made compare
Between our statures; she hath urged her height,
And with her personage, her tall personage,
Her height, forsooth, she hath prevailed with him.
And are you grown so high in his esteem
Because I am so dwarfish and so low?
How low am I, thou painted maypole? Speak!
How low am I? I am not yet so low
But that my nails can reach unto thine eyes.
*[She flails at* HELENA *but is restrained.]*

**HELENA:** I pray you, though you mock me, gentlemen,
Let her not hurt me. I was never curst;
I have no gift at all in shrewishness;
I am a right maid for my cowardice.
Let her not strike me. You perhaps may think,
Because she is something lower than myself,
That I can match her.

**HERMIA:** Lower? Hark, again!

**HELENA:** Good Hermia, do not be so bitter with me.
I evermore did love you, Hermia,
Did ever keep your counsels, never wronged you,
Save that, in love unto Demetrius,

---

**288 puppet** (1) counterfeit (2) dwarfish woman (in reference to Hermia's smaller stature) **289 Why, so** i.e., Oh, so that's how it is **300 curst** shrewish **302 right** true **304 something** somewhat

I told him of your stealth unto this wood.
He followed you; for love I followed him.
But he hath chid me hence and threatened me
To strike me, spurn me, nay, to kill me too.
And now, so you will let me quiet go,
To Athens will I bear my folly back
And follow you no further. Let me go.
You see how simple and how fond I am.

**HERMIA:** Why, get you gone. Who is 't that hinders you?

**HELENA:** A foolish heart, that I leave here behind.

**HERMIA:** What, with Lysander?

**HELENA:** With Demetrius.

**LYSANDER:** Be not afraid; she shall not harm thee, Helena.

**DEMETRIUS:** No, sir, she shall not, though you take her part.

**HELENA:** O, when she is angry, she is keen and shrewd.
She was a vixen when she went to school;
And though she be but little, she is fierce.

**HERMIA:** "Little" again? Nothing but "low" and "little"?
Why will you suffer her to flout me thus?
Let me come to her.

**LYSANDER:** Get you gone, you dwarf!
You minimus, of hindering knotgrass made!
You bean, you acorn!

**DEMETRIUS:** You are too officious
In her behalf that scorns your services.
Let her alone. Speak not of Helena;
Take not her part. For, if thou dost intend
Never so little show of love to her,
Thou shalt aby it.

**LYSANDER:** Now she holds me not.
Now follow, if thou dar'st, to try whose right,
Of thine or mine, is most in Helena *[Exit.]*

**DEMETRIUS:** Follow? Nay, I'll go with the, cheek by jowl.
*[Exit, following* LYSANDER.*]*

---

**310 stealth** stealing away **312 chid me hence** driven me away with his scolding **314 so** if only **317 fond** foolish **323 keen** fierce, cruel. **shrewd** shrewish **329 minimus** diminutive creature. **knotgrass** a weed, an infusion of which was thought to stunt the growth **333 intend** give sign of **335 aby** pay for **338 cheek by jowl** i.e., side by side

**HERMIA:** You, mistress, all this coil is 'long of you.
Nay, go not back.

**HELENA:** I will not trust you, I,
Nor longer stay in your curst company.
Your hands than mine are quicker for a fray;
My legs are longer, though, to run away. *[Exit.]*

**HERMIA:** I am amazed and know not what to say. *Exit.*

*[*OBERON *and* PUCK *come forward.]*

**OBERON:** This is thy negligence. Still thou mistak'st,
Or else committ'st thy knaveries willfully.

**PUCK:** Believe me, king of shadows, I mistook.
Did not you tell me I should know the man
By the Athenian garments he had on?
And so far blameless proves my enterprise
That I have 'nointed an Athenian's eyes;
And so far am I glad it so did sort,
As this their jangling I esteem a sport.

**OBERON:** Thou seest these lovers seek a place to fight.
Hie therefore, Robin, overcast the night;
The starry welkin cover thou anon
With drooping fog as black as Acheron,
And lead these testy rivals so astray
As one come not within another's way.
Like to Lysander sometimes frame thy tongue,
Then stir Demetrius up with bitter wrong;
And sometimes rail thou like Demetrius.
And from each other look thou lead them thus,
Till o'er their brows death-counterfeiting sleep
With leaden legs and batty wings doth creep.
Then crush this herb into Lysander's eye, *[giving herb]*
Whose liquor hath this virtuous property,
To take from thence all error with his might
And make his eyeballs roll with wonted sight.
When they next wake, all this derision
Shall seem a dream and fruitless vision,
And back to Athens shall the lovers wend
With league whose date till death shall never end.
Whiles I in this affair do thee employ,
I'll to my queen and beg her Indian boy;
And then I will her charmèd eye release
From monster's view, and all things shall be peace.

**PUCK:** My fairy lord, this must be done with haste,
For night's swift dragons cut the clouds full fast,
And yonder shines Aurora's harbinger,
At whose approach ghosts, wand'ring here and there,
Troop home to churchyards. Damnèd spirits all,
That in crossways and floods have burial,
Already to their wormy beds are gone.
For fear lest day should look their shames upon,
They willfully themselves exile from light
And must for aye consort with black-browed night.

**OBERON:** But we are spirits of another sort.
I with the Morning's love have oft made sport,
And, like a forester, the groves may tread
Even till the eastern gate, all fiery red,
Opening on Neptune with fair blessèd beams,
Turns into yellow gold his salt green streams.
But notwithstanding, haste, make no delay.
We may effect this business yet ere day. *[Exit.]*

**PUCK:** Up and down, up and down,
I will lead them up and down.
I am feared in field and town.
Goblin, lead them up and down.
Here comes one.

*Enter* LYSANDER.

**LYSANDER:** Where art thou, proud Demetrius? Speak thou now.

**PUCK** *[mimicking* DEMETRIUS*]***:** Here, villain, drawn and ready. Where art thou?

**LYSANDER:** I will be with thee straight.

**PUCK:** Follow me, then,
To plainer ground.

*[*LYSANDER *wanders about, following the voice.]*

*Enter* DEMETRIUS.

---

**339 coil** turmoil, dissension. **'long of** on account of **340 go not back** i.e., don't retreat. (Hermia is again proposing a fight.) **352 so far** at least to this extent. **sort** turn out **353 As** in that **355 Hie** hasten **356 welkin** sky **357 Acheron** river of Hades (here representing Hades itself) **359 As** that **361 wrong** insults **365 batty** batlike **366 this herb** i.e., the antidote (mentioned in 2.1.184) to love-in-idleness **367 virtuous** efficacious **368 his** its **369 wonted** accustomed **370 derision** laughable business **373 date** term of existence

**379 dragons** (Supposed by Shakespeare to be yoked to the car of the goddess of night or the moon.) **380 Aurora's harbinger** the morning star, precursor of dawn **383 crossways . . . burial** (Those who had committed suicide were buried at crossways, with a stake driven through them; those who intentionally or accidentally drowned (in *floods* or deep water) would be condemned to wander disconsolately for lack of burial rites.) **387 for aye** forever **389 the Morning's love** Cephalus, a beautiful youth beloved by Aurora; or perhaps the goddess of the dawn herself **390 forester** keeper of a royal forest **399 Goblin** Hobgoblin. (Puck refers to himself.) **402 drawn** with drawn sword **403 straight** immediately **404 plainer** more open. **s.d. Lysander wanders about** (Lysander may exit here, but perhaps not; neither exit nor reentrance is indicated in the early texts.)

**DEMETRIUS:** Lysander! Speak again!
Thou runaway, thou coward, art thou fled?
Speak! In some bush? Where dost thou hide thy head?

**PUCK** *[mimicking* LYSANDER*]*: Thou coward, art thou bragging to the stars,
Telling the bushes that thou look'st for wars,
And wilt not come? Come, recreant; come, thou child,
I'll whip thee with a rod. He is defiled
That draws a sword on thee.

**DEMETRIUS:** Yea, art thou there?

**PUCK:** Follow my voice. We'll try no manhood here.
*Exeunt.*

*[*LYSANDER *returns.]*

**LYSANDER:** He goes before me and still dares me on.
When I come where he calls, then he is gone.
The villain is much lighter-heeled than I.
I followed fast, but faster he did fly,
That fallen am I in dark uneven way,
And here will rest me. *[He lies down.]* Come, thou gentle day!
For if but once thou show me thy gray light,
I'll find Demetrius and revenge this spite. *[He sleeps.]*

*[Enter]* ROBIN *[*PUCK*] and* DEMETRIUS.

**PUCK:** Ho, ho, ho! Coward, why com'st thou not?

**DEMETRIUS:** Abide me, if thou dar'st; for well I wot
Thou runn'st before me, shifting every place,
And dar'st not stand nor look me in the face.
Where art thou now?

**PUCK:** Come hither. I am here.

**DEMETRIUS:** Nay, then, thou mock'st me. Thou shalt buy this dear,
If ever I thy face by daylight see.
Now go thy way. Faintness constraineth me
To measure out my length on this cold bed.
By day's approach look to be visited.
*[He lies down and sleeps.]*

*Enter* HELENA.

**HELENA:** O weary night, O long and tedious night,
Abate thy hours! Shine comforts from the east,
That I may back to Athens by daylight
From these that my poor company detest;

Puck, invisible, taunts the bewildered Demetrius (Christian Bale).

And sleep, that sometimes shuts up sorrow's eye,
Steal me awhile from mine own company.
*[She lies down and] sleep[s].*

**PUCK:** Yet but three? Come one more;
Two of both kinds makes up four.
Here she comes, curst and sad.
Cupid is a knavish lad,
Thus to make poor females mad.

*[Enter* HERMIA.*]*

**HERMIA:** Never so weary, never so in woe,
Bedabbled with the dew and torn with briers,
I can no further crawl, no further go;
My legs can keep no pace with my desires.
Here will I rest me till the break of day.
Heavens shield Lysander, if they mean a fray!
*[She lies down and sleeps.]*

**PUCK:** On the ground
Sleep sound.
I'll apply
To your eye,
Gentle lover, remedy.
*[He squeezes the juice on* LYSANDER*'s eyes.]*
When thou wak'st,
Thou tak'st
True delight
In the sight
Of thy former lady's eye;
And the country proverb known,
That every man should take his own,
In your waking shall be shown:
Jack shall have Jill;
Naught shall go ill;
The man shall have his mare again, and all shall be well. *[Exit. The four sleeping lovers remain.]*

---

**409 recreant** cowardly wretch **412 try** test **422 Abide** confront, face. **wot** know **426 buy** aby, pay for. **dear** dearly **432 Abate** lessen, shorten

**439 curst** ill-tempered **461 Jack shall have Jill** (Proverbial for "boy gets girl.")

**4.1** *Enter [*TITANIA,*] Queen of Fairies, and [*BOTTOM *the] clown, and* FAIRIES*; and [*OBERON,*] the King, behind them.*

**TITANIA:** Come, sit thee down upon this flowery bed,
While I thy amiable cheeks do coy,
And stick muskroses in thy sleek smooth head,
And kiss thy fair large ears, my gentle joy.
*[They recline.]*

**BOTTOM:** Where's Peaseblossom?

**PEASEBLOSSOM:** Ready.

**BOTTOM:** Scratch my head, Peaseblossom. Where's Monsieur Cobweb?

**COBWEB:** Ready.

**BOTTOM:** Monsieur Cobweb, good monsieur, get you your weapons in your hand, and kill me a red-hipped humble-bee on the top of a thistle; and, good monsieur, bring me the honey bag. Do not fret yourself too much in the action, monsieur; and, good monsieur, have a care the honey bag break not. I would be loath to have you overflown with a honey bag, signor. *[Exit* COBWEB.*]* Where's Monsieur Mustardseed?

**MUSTARDSEED:** Ready.

**BOTTOM:** Give me your neaf, Monsieur Mustardseed. Pray you, leave your courtesy, good monsieur.

**MUSTARDSEED:** What's your will?

**BOTTOM:** Nothing, good monsieur, but to help Cavalery Cobweb to scratch. I must to the barber's, monsieur, for methinks I am marvelous hairy about the face; and I am such a tender ass, if my hair do but tickle me I must scratch.

**TITANIA:** What, wilt thou hear some music, my sweet love?

**BOTTOM:** I have a reasonable good ear in music. Let's have the tongs and the bones.
*[Music: tongs, rural music.]*

**4.1 Location: The action is continuous. The four lovers are still asleep onstage. (Compare with the Folio stage direction: "They sleep all the act.")**
**2 amiable** lovely. **coy** caress **19 neaf** fist **20 leave your courtesy** i.e., stop bowing, or put on your hat **22–23 Cavalery** cavalier. (Form of address for a gentleman.) **23 Cobweb** (Seemingly an error, since Cobweb has been sent to bring honey, while Peaseblossom has been asked to scratch.) **29 tongs . . . bones** instruments for rustic music. (The tongs were played like a triangle, whereas the bones were held between the fingers and used as clappers.) **s.d. Music . . . music** (This stage direction is added from the Folio.)

Bottom is entertained by Titania.

**TITANIA:** Or say, sweet love, what thou desirest to eat.

**BOTTOM:** Truly, a peck of provender. I could munch your good dry oats. Methinks I have a great desire to a bottle of hay. Good hay, sweet hay, hath no fellow.

**TITANIA:** I have a venturous fairy that shall seek
The squirrel's hoard, and fetch thee new nuts.

**BOTTOM:** I had rather have a handful or two of dried peas. But, I pray you, let none of your people stir me. I have an exposition of sleep come upon me.

**TITANIA:** Sleep thou, and I will wind thee in my arms.
Fairies, begone, and be all ways away.
*[Exeunt* FAIRIES.*]*
So doth the woodbine the sweet honeysuckle
Gently entwist; the female ivy so
Enrings the barky fingers of the elm.
O, how I love thee! How I dote on thee!
*[They sleep.]*

*Enter* ROBIN GOODFELLOW *[*PUCK*].*

**OBERON** *[coming forward]*: Welcome, good Robin. Seest thou this sweet sight?
Her dotage now I do begin to pity.
For, meeting her of late behind the wood
Seeking sweet favors for this hateful fool,
I did upbraid her and fall out with her.
For she his hairy temples then had rounded
With coronet of fresh and fragrant flowers;
And that same dew, which sometime on the buds
Was wont to swell like round and orient pearls,

**31 peck of provender** one-quarter bushel of grain **33 bottle** bundle. **fellow** equal **37 stir** disturb **38 exposition of** (Bottom's phrase for "disposition to.") **40 all ways** in all directions **41 woodbine** bindweed, a climbing plant that twines in the opposite direction from that of honeysuckle **48 favors** i.e., gifts of flowers **52 sometime** formerly **53 orient pearls** i.e., the most beautiful of all pearls, those coming from the Orient

Stood now within the pretty flowerets' eyes
Like tears that did their own disgrace bewail.
When I had at my pleasure taunted her,
And she in mild terms begged my patience,
I then did ask of her her changeling child,
Which straight she gave me, and her fairy sent
To bear him to my bower in Fairyland.
And, now I have the boy, I will undo
This hateful imperfection of her eyes.
And, gentle Puck, take this transformèd scalp
From off the head of this Athenian swain,
That he, awaking when the other do,
May all to Athens back again repair,
And think no more of this night's accidents
But as the fierce vexation of a dream.
But first I will release the Fairy Queen.

*[He squeezes an herb on her eyes.]*

Be as thou wast wont to be;
See as thou wast wont to see.
Dian's bud o'er Cupid's flower
Hath such force and blessèd power.
Now, my Titania, wake you, my sweet queen.

**TITANIA** *[awaking]*: My Oberon! What visions have I seen!
Methought I was enamored of an ass.

**OBERON:** There lies your love.

**TITANIA:** How came these things to pass?
O, how mine eyes do loathe his visage now!

**OBERON:** Silence awhile. Robin, take off his head.
Titania, music call, and strike more dead
Than common sleep of all these five the sense.

**TITANIA:** Music, ho! Music, such as charmeth sleep!

*[Music.]*

**PUCK** *[removing the ass head]*: Now, when thou wak'st, with thine own fool's eyes peep.

**OBERON:** Sound, music! Come, my queen, take hands with me,
And rock the ground whereon these sleepers be.

*[They dance.]*

Now thou and I are new in amity,
And will tomorrow midnight solemnly
Dance in Duke Theseus' house triumphantly,
And bless it to all fair prosperity.
There shall the pairs of faithful lovers be
Wedded, with Theseus, all in jollity.

**PUCK:** Fairy King, attend, and mark:
I do hear the morning lark.

**OBERON:** Then, my queen, in silence sad,
Trip we after night's shade.
We the globe can compass soon,
Swifter than the wandering moon.

**TITANIA:** Come, my lord, and in our flight
Tell me how it came this night
That I sleeping here was found
With these mortals on the ground.

*Exeunt [*OBERON, TITANIA, *and* PUCK*].*
*Wind horn [within].*

*Enter* THESEUS *and all his train;*
*[*HIPPOLYTA, EGEUS*].*

**THESEUS:** Go, one of you, find out the forester,
For now our observation is performed;
And since we have the vaward of the day,
My love shall hear the music of my hounds.
Uncouple in the western valley; let them go.
Dispatch, I say, and find the forester.

*[Exit an* ATTENDANT.*]*

We will, fair queen, up to the mountain's top
And mark the musical confusion
Of hounds and echo in conjunction.

**HIPPOLYTA:** I was with Hercules and Cadmus once
When in a wood of Crete they bayed the bear
With hounds of Sparta. Never did I hear
Such gallant chiding; for, besides the groves,
The skies, the fountains, every region near
Seemed all one mutual cry. I never heard
So musical a discord, such sweet thunder.

**THESEUS:** My hounds are bred out of the Spartan kind,
So flewed, so sanded; and their heads are hung
With ears that sweep away the morning dew;
Crook-kneed, and dewlapped like Thessalian bulls;

---

**65 other** others **66 repair** return **72 Dian's bud** (Perhaps the flower of the *agnus castus,* or chaste-tree, supposed to preserve chastity; or perhaps referring simply to Oberon's herb by which he can undo the effects of "Cupid's flower," the love-in-idleness of 2.1.166–168.) **81 these five** i.e., the four lovers and Bottom **82 charmeth** brings about, as though by a charm **87 solemnly** ceremoniously

**94 sad** sober **103 observation** i.e., observance to a morn of May (1.1.167) **104 vaward** vanguard, i.e., earliest part **106 Uncouple** set free for the hunt **111 Cadmus** mythical founder of Thebes. (This story about him is unknown.) **112 bayed** brought to bay **113 hounds of Sparta** (A breed famous in antiquity for its hunting skill.) **114 chiding** i.e., yelping **118 kind** strain, breed **119 So flewed** similarly having large hanging chaps or fleshy covering of the jaw. **sanded** of sandy color **121 dewlapped** having pendulous folds of skin under the neck

The lovers, Helena (Calista Flockhart), Demetrius, Lysander, and Hermia, are discovered.

Slow in pursuit, but matched in mouth like bells,
Each under each. A cry more tunable
Was never holloed to nor cheered with horn
In Crete, in Sparta, nor in Thessaly.
Judge when you hear. *[He sees the sleepers.]* But soft!
What nymphs are these?

**EGEUS:** My lord, this is my daughter here asleep,
And this Lysander; this Demetrius is;
This Helena, old Nedar's Helena.
I wonder of their being here together.

**THESEUS:** No doubt they rose up early to observe
The rite of May, and hearing our intent,
Came here in grace of our solemnity.
But speak, Egeus. Is not this the day
That Hermia should give answer of her choice?

**EGEUS:** It is, my lord.

**THESEUS:** Go bid the huntsmen wake them with their horns.

*[Exit an* ATTENDANT.*]*

*Shout within. Wind horns. They all start up.*

Good morrow, friends. Saint Valentine is past.
Begin these woodbirds but to couple now?

**LYSANDER:** Pardon, my lord. *[They kneel.]*

**THESEUS:** I pray you all, stand up. *[They stand.]*

I know you two are rival enemies;
How comes this gentle concord in the world,
That hatred is so far from jealousy
To sleep by hate and fear no enmity?

**LYSANDER:** My lord, I shall reply amazedly,
Half sleep, half waking; but as yet, I swear,
I cannot truly say how I came here.
But, as I think—for truly would I speak,
And now I do bethink me, so it is—
I came with Hermia hither. Our intent
Was to be gone from Athens, where we might,
Without the peril of the Athenian law—

**EGEUS:** Enough, enough, my lord; you have enough.
I beg the law, the law, upon his head.
They would have stol'n away; they would, Demetrius,
Thereby to have defeated you and me,
You of your wife and me of my consent,
Of my consent that she should be your wife.

**DEMETRIUS:** My lord, fair Helen told me of their stealth,
Of this their purpose hither to this wood,
And I in fury hither followed them,
Fair Helena in fancy following me.
But, my good lord, I wot not by what power—
But by some power it is—my love to Hermia,
Melted as the snow, seems to me now
As the remembrance of an idle gaud
Which in my childhood I did dote upon;
And all the faith, the virtue of my heart,
The object and the pleasure of mine eye,
Is only Helena. To her, my lord,
Was I betrothed ere I saw Hermia,
But like a sickness did I loathe this food;
But, as in health, come to my natural taste,
Now I do wish it, love it, long for it,
And will forevermore be true to it.

**THESEUS:** Fair lovers, you are fortunately met.
Of this discourse we more will hear anon.
Egeus, I will overbear your will;
For in the temple, by and by, with us
These couples shall eternally be knit.
And, for the morning now is something worn,
Our purposed hunting shall be set aside.
Away with us to Athens. Three and three,
We'll hold a feast in great solemnity.
Come, Hippolyta.

*[Exeunt* THESEUS, HIPPOLYTA, EGEUS, *and train.]*

---

**122–123 matched . . . each** i.e., harmoniously matched in their various cries like a set of bells, from treble down to bass **123 cry** pack of hounds. **tunable** well tuned, melodious **124 cheered** encouraged **126 soft** i.e., gently, wait a minute **130 wonder of** wonder at **133 in . . . solemnity** in honor of our wedding ceremony **138 Saint Valentine** (Birds were supposed to choose their mates on Saint Valentine's Day.)

**143 jealousy** suspicion **151 where** wherever; or, to where **152 Without** outside of, beyond **156 defeated** defrauded **160 hither** in coming hither **162 in fancy** driven by love **166 idle gaud** worthless trinket **181 for** since. **something** somewhat **184 in great solemnity** with great ceremony

**DEMETRIUS:** These things seem small and undistinguishable,
Like far-off mountains turnèd into clouds.

**HERMIA:** Methinks I see these things with parted eye,
When everything seems double.

**HELENA:** So methinks;
And I have found Demetrius like a jewel,
Mine own, and not mine own.

**DEMETRIUS:** Are you sure
That we are awake? It seems to me
That yet we sleep, we dream. Do not you think
The Duke was here, and bid us follow him?

**HERMIA:** Yea, and my father.

**HELENA:** And Hippolyta.

**LYSANDER:** And he did bid us follow to the temple.

**DEMETRIUS:** Why, then, we are awake. Let's follow him,
And by the way let us recount our dreams.

*[Exeunt the lovers.]*

**BOTTOM** *[awaking]*: When my cue comes, call me, and I will answer. My next is "Most fair Pyramus." Heigh-ho! Peter Quince! Flute, the bellows mender! Snout, the tinker! Starveling! God's my life, stolen hence and left me asleep! I have had a most rare vision. I have had a dream, past the wit of man to say what dream it was. Man is but an ass if he go about to expound this dream. Methought I was—there is no man can tell what. Methought I was—and methought I had—but man is but a patched fool if he will offer to say what methought I had. The eye of man hath not heard, the ear of man hath not seen, man's hand is not able to taste, his tongue to conceive, nor his heart to report, what my dream was. I will get Peter Quince to write a ballad of this dream. It shall be called "Bottom's Dream," because it hath no bottom; and I will sing it in the latter end of a play, before the Duke. Peradventure, to make it the more gracious, I shall sing it at her death. *[Exit.]*

---

**188 parted** i.e., improperly focused **190–191 like . . . mine own** i.e., like a jewel that one finds by chance and therefore possesses but cannot certainly consider one's own property **202 God's** may God save **205 go about** attempt **208 patched** wearing motley, i.e., a dress of various colors **209 offer** venture **209–212 The eye . . . report** (Bottom garbles the terms of 1 Corinthians 2:9.) **213 ballad** (The proper medium for relating sensational stories and preposterous events.) **214–215 hath no bottom** is unfathomable **217 her** Thisbe's (?)

**4.2** *Enter* QUINCE, FLUTE, *[*SNOUT, *and* STARVELING*].*

**QUINCE:** Have you sent to Bottom's house? Is he come home yet?

**STARVELING:** He cannot be heard of. Out of doubt he is transported.

**FLUTE:** If he come not, then the play is marred. It goes not forward. Doth it?

**QUINCE:** It is not possible. You have not a man in all Athens able to discharge Pyramus but he.

**FLUTE:** No, he hath simply the best wit of any handicraft man in Athens.

**QUINCE:** Yea, and the best person too, and he is a very paramour for a sweet voice.

**FLUTE:** You must say "paragon." A paramour is, God bless us, a thing of naught.

*Enter* SNUG *the joiner.*

**SNUG:** Masters, the Duke is coming from the temple, and there is two or three lords and ladies more married. If our sport had gone forward, we had all been made men.

**FLUTE:** O sweet bully Bottom! Thus hath he lost sixpence a day during his life; he could not have scaped sixpence a day. An the Duke had not given him sixpence a day for playing Pyramus, I'll be hanged. He would have deserved it. Sixpence a day in Pyramus, or nothing.

*Enter* BOTTOM.

**BOTTOM:** Where are these lads? Where are these hearts?

**QUINCE:** Bottom! O most courageous day! O most happy hour!

**BOTTOM:** Masters, I am to discourse wonders. But ask me not what; for if I tell you, I am no true Athenian. I will tell you everything, right as it fell out.

**QUINCE:** Let us hear, sweet Bottom.

---

**4.2 Location: Athens.**
**4 transported** carried off by fairies; or, possibly, transformed **8 discharge** perform **9 wit** intellect **11 person** appearance **14 a . . . naught** a shameful thing **17–18 we . . . men** i.e., we would have had our fortunes made **19–20 sixpence a day** i.e., as a royal pension **25 hearts** good fellows **28 am . . . wonders** have wonders to relate

**BOTTOM:** Not a word of me. All that I will tell you is that the Duke hath dined. Get your apparel together, good strings to your beards, new ribbons to your pumps; meet presently at the palace; every man look o'er his part; for the short and the long is, our play is preferred. In any case, let Thisbe have clean linen; and let not him that plays the lion pare his nails, for they shall hang out for the lion's claws. And, most dear actors, eat no onions nor garlic, for we are to utter sweet breath; and I do not doubt but to hear them say it is a sweet comedy. No more words. Away! Go, away!
*[Exeunt.]*

**5.1** *Enter* THESEUS, HIPPOLYTA, *and* PHILOSTRATE, *[lords, and attendants].*

**HIPPOLYTA:** 'Tis strange, my Theseus, that these lovers speak of.

**THESEUS:** More strange than true. I never may believe
These antique fables nor these fairy toys.
Lovers and madmen have such seething brains,
Such shaping fantasies, that apprehend
More than cool reason ever comprehends.
The lunatic, the lover, and the poet
Are of imagination all compact.
One sees more devils than vast hell can hold;
That is the madman. The lover, all as frantic,
Sees Helen's beauty in a brow of Egypt.
The poet's eye, in a fine frenzy rolling,
Doth glance from heaven to earth, from earth to heaven;
And as imagination bodies forth
The forms of things unknown, the poet's pen
Turns them to shapes and gives to airy nothing
A local habitation and a name.
Such tricks hath strong imagination
That, if it would but apprehend some joy,
It comprehends some bringer of that joy;
Or in the night, imagining some fear,
How easy is a bush supposed a bear!

**HIPPOLYTA:** But all the story of the night told over,
And all their minds transfigured so together,
More witnesseth than fancy's images
And grows to something of great constancy;
But, howsoever, strange and admirable.

*Enter lovers:* LYSANDER, DEMETRIUS, HERMIA, *and* HELENA.

**THESEUS:** Here come the lovers, full of joy and mirth.
Joy, gentle friends! Joy and fresh days of love
Accompany your hearts!

**LYSANDER:** More than to us
Wait in your royal walks, your board, your bed!

**THESEUS:** Come now, what masques, what dances shall we have,
To wear away this long age of three hours
Between our after-supper and bedtime?
Where is our usual manager of mirth?
What revels are in hand? Is there no play
To ease the anguish of a torturing hour?
Call Philostrate.

**PHILOSTRATE:** Here, mighty Theseus.

**THESEUS:** Say, what abridgment have you for this evening?
What masque? What music? How shall we beguile
The lazy time, if not with some delight?

**PHILOSTRATE** *[giving him a paper]*: There is a brief how many sports are ripe.
Make choice of which Your Highness will see first.

**THESEUS** *[reads]*: "The battle with the Centaurs, to be sung
By an Athenian eunuch to the harp"?
We'll none of that. That have I told my love,
In glory of my kinsman Hercules.
*[He reads.]* "The riot of the tipsy Bacchanals,
Tearing the Thracian singer in their rage"?
That is an old device; and it was played

---

**32 of** out of **34 strings** (to attach the beards) **35 pumps** light shoes or slippers. **presently** immediately **37 preferred** selected for consideration

**5.1 Location: Athens. The palace of Theseus.**
**1 that** that which **2 may** can **3 antique** old-fashioned (punning, too, on *antic*, "strange," "grotesque"). **fairy toys** trifling stories about fairies **5 fantasies** imaginations. **apprehend** conceive, imagine **6 comprehends** understands **8 compact** formed, composed **11 Helen's** i.e., of Helen of Troy, pattern of beauty. **brow of Egypt** i.e., face of a gypsy **20 bringer** i.e., source **21 fear** object of fear

**25 More . . . images** testifies to something more substantial than mere imaginings **26 constancy** certainty **27 howsoever** in any case. **admirable** a source of wonder **32 masques** courtly entertainments **39 abridgment** pastime (to abridge or shorten the evening) **42 brief** short written statement, summary **44 battle . . . Centaurs** (Probably refers to the battle of the Centaurs and the Lapithae, when the Centaurs attempted to carry off Hippodamia, bride of Theseus' friend Pirothous. The story is told in Ovid's *Metamorphoses* 12.) **47 kinsman** (Plutarch's "Life of Theseus" states that Hercules and Theseus were near kinsmen. Theseus is referring to a version of the battle of the Centaurs in which Hercules was said to be present.) **48–49 The riot . . . rage** (This was the story of the death of Orpheus, as told in *Metamorphoses* 11.) **50 device** show, performance

When I from Thebes came last a conqueror.
*[He reads.]* "The thrice three Muses mourning for the death
Of Learning, late deceased in beggary"?
That is some satire, keen and critical,
Not sorting with a nuptial ceremony.
*[He reads.]* "A tedious brief scene of young Pyramus
And his love Thisbe; very tragical mirth"?
Merry and tragical? Tedious and brief?
That is, hot ice and wondrous strange snow.
How shall we find the concord of this discord?

**PHILOSTRATE:** A play there is, my lord, some ten words long,
Which is as brief as I have known a play;
But by ten words, my lord, it is too long,
Which makes it tedious. For in all the play
There is not one word apt, one player fitted.
And tragical, my noble lord, it is,
For Pyramus therein doth kill himself.
Which, when I saw rehearsed, I must confess,
Made mine eyes water; but more merry tears
The passion of loud laughter never shed.

**THESEUS:** What are they that do play it?

**PHILOSTRATE:** Hardhanded men that work in Athens here,
Which never labored in their minds till now,
And now have toiled their unbreathed memories
With this same play, against your nuptial.

**THESEUS:** And we will hear it.

**PHILOSTRATE:** No, my noble lord,
It is not for you. I have heard it over,
And it is nothing, nothing in the world;
Unless you can find sport in their intents,
Extremely stretched and conned with cruel pain
To do you service.

**THESEUS:** I will hear that play;
For never anything can be a miss
When simpleness and duty tender it.
Go, bring them in; and take your places, ladies.
*[*PHILOSTRATE *goes to summon the players.]*

**52–53 The thrice . . . beggary** (Possibly an allusion to Spenser's *Teares of the Muses,* 1591, though "satires" deploring the neglect of learning and the creative arts were commonplace.) **55 sorting with** befitting **59 strange** (Sometimes emended to an adjective that would contrast with *snow,* just as *hot* contrasts with *ice.*) **74 toiled** taxed. **unbreathed** unexercised **75 against** in preparation for **80 stretched** strained. **conned** memorized **83 simpleness** simplicity

Duke Theseus (Derek Godfrey), seated beside his wife Hippolyta (Barbara Jefford), bids the players approach.

**HIPPOLYTA:** I love not to see wretchedness o'ercharged,
And duty in his service perishing.

**THESEUS:** Why, gentle sweet, you shall see no such thing.

**HIPPOLYTA:** He says they can do nothing in this kind.

**THESEUS:** The kinder we, to give them thanks for nothing.
Our sport shall be to take what they mistake;
And what poor duty cannot do, noble respect
Takes it in might, not merit.
Where I have come, great clerks have purposèd
To greet me with premeditated welcomes;
Where I have seen them shiver and look pale,
Make periods in the midst of sentences,
Throttle their practiced accent in their fears,
And in conclusion dumbly have broke off,
Not paying me a welcome. Trust me, sweet,
Out of this silence yet I picked a welcome;
And in the modesty of fearful duty
I read as much as from the rattling tongue
Of saucy and audacious eloquence.
Love, therefore, and tongue-tied simplicity
In least speak most, to my capacity.

*[*PHILOSTRATE *returns.]*

**85 wretchedness o'ercharged** social or intellectual inferiors overburdened **86 his service** its attempt to serve **88 kind** kind of thing **91 respect** evaluation, consideration **92 Takes . . . merit** values it for the effort made rather than for the excellence achieved **93 clerks** learned men **97 practiced accent** i.e., rehearsed speech; or, usual way of speaking **105 least** i.e., saying least. **to my capacity** in my judgment and understanding

**PHILOSTRATE:** So please Your Grace, the Prologue is addressed.

**THESEUS:** Let him approach. *[A flourish of trumpets.]*

*Enter the* PROLOGUE *[*QUINCE*].*

**PROLOGUE:** If we offend, it is with our good will.
That you should think, we come not to offend,
But with good will. To show our simple skill,
That is the true beginning of our end.
Consider, then, we come but in despite.
We do not come, as minding to content you,
Our true intent is. All for your delight
We are not here. That you should here repent you,
The actors are at hand; and, by their show,
You shall know all that you are like to know.

**THESEUS:** This fellow doth not stand upon points.

**LYSANDER:** He hath rid his prologue like a rough colt; he knows not the stop. A good moral, my lord: it is not enough to speak, but to speak true.

**HIPPOLYTA:** Indeed, he hath played on his prologue like a child on a recorder: a sound, but not in government.

**THESEUS:** His speech was like a tangled chain: nothing impaired, but all disordered. Who is next?

*Enter* PYRAMUS *[*BOTTOM*], and* THISBE *[*FLUTE*], and* WALL *[*SNOUT*], and* MOONSHINE *[*STARVELING*], and* LION *[*SNUG*].*

**PROLOGUE:** Gentles, perchance you wonder at this show;
But wonder on, till truth make all things plain.
This man is Pyramus, if you would know;
This beauteous lady Thisbe is, certain.
This man with lime and roughcast doth present
Wall, that vile wall which did these lovers sunder;
And through Wall's chink, poor souls, they are content
To whisper. At the which let no man wonder.
This man, with lantern, dog, and bush of thorn,
Presenteth Moonshine; for, if you will know,
By moonshine did these lovers think no scorn
To meet at Ninus' tomb, there, there to woo.
This grisly beast, which Lion hight by name,
The trusty Thisbe coming first by night
Did scare away, or rather did affright;
And as she fled, her mantle she did fall,
Which Lion vile with bloody mouth did stain.
Anon comes Pyramus, sweet youth and tall,
And finds his trusty Thisbe's mantle slain;
Whereat, with blade, with bloody, blameful blade,
He bravely broached his boiling bloody breast.
And Thisbe, tarrying in mulberry shade,
His dagger drew, and died. For all the rest,
Let Lion, Moonshine, Wall, and lovers twain
At large discourse, while here they do remain.

*Exeunt* LION, THISBE, *and* MOONSHINE.

**THESEUS:** I wonder if the lion be to speak.

**DEMETRIUS:** No wonder, my lord. One lion may, when many asses do.

**WALL:** In this same interlude it doth befall
That I, one Snout by name, present a wall;
And such a wall as I would have you think
That had in it a crannied hole or chink,
Through which the lovers, Pyramus and Thisbe,
Did whisper often, very secretly.
This loam, this roughcast, and this stone doth show
That I am that same wall; the truth is so.
And this the cranny is, right and sinister,
Through which the fearful lovers are to whisper.

**THESEUS:** Would you desire lime and hair to speak better?

**DEMETRIUS:** It is the wittiest partition that ever I heard discourse, my lord.

*[*PYRAMUS *comes forward.]*

**THESEUS:** Pyramus draws near the wall. Silence!

**PYRAMUS:** O grim-looked night! O night with hue so black!
O night, which ever art when day is not!
O night, O night! alack, alack, alack,
I fear my Thisbe's promise is forgot.
And thou, O wall, O sweet, O lovely wall,
That stand'st between her father's ground and mine,

---

**106 Prologue** speaker of the prologue. **addressed** ready **113 minding** intending **118 stand upon points** (1) heed niceties or small points (2) pay attention to punctuation in his reading. (The humor of Quince's speech is in the blunders of its punctuation.) **119 rid** ridden. **rough** unbroken **120 stop** (1) stopping of a colt by reining it in (2) punctuation mark **123 recorder** wind instrument like a flute. **government** control **124–125 nothing** not at all **136 think no scorn** think it no disgraceful matter

**138 hight** is called **141 fall** let fall **143 tall** courageous **146 broached** stabbed **150 At large** in full, at length **154 interlude** play **162 right and sinister** i.e., the right side of it and the left; or, running from right to left, horizontally **166 partition** (1) wall (2) section of a learned treatise or oration **169 grim-looked** grim-looking

Thisbe (Sam Rockwell) and Pyramus speak through the wall.

Thou wall, O wall, O sweet and lovely wall,
Show me thy chink, to blink through with mine eyne. *[*WALL *makes a chink with his fingers.]*
Thanks, courteous wall. Jove shield thee well for this.
But what see I? No Thisbe do I see.
O wicked wall, through whom I see no bliss!
Cursed be thy stones for thus deceiving me!

**THESEUS:** The wall, methinks, being sensible, should curse again.

**PYRAMUS:** No, in truth, sir, he should not. "Deceiving me" is Thisbe's cue: she is to enter now, and I am to spy her through the wall. You shall see, it will fall pat as I told you. Yonder she comes.

*Enter* THISBE.

**THISBE:** O wall, full often hast thou heard my moans
For parting my fair Pyramus and me.
My cherry lips have often kissed thy stones,
Thy stones with lime and hair knit up in thee.

**PYRAMUS:** I see a voice. Now will I to the chink,
To spy an I can hear my Thisbe's face.
Thisbe!

**THISBE:** My love! Thou art my love, I think.

**PYRAMUS:**
Think what thou wilt, I am thy lover's grace,
And like Limander am I trusty still.

**THISBE:** And I like Helen, till the Fates me kill.

**PYRAMUS:** Not Shafalus to Procrus was so true.

**THISBE:** As Shafalus to Procrus, I to you.

**PYRAMUS:** O, kiss me through the hole of this vile wall!

**THISBE:** I kiss the wall's hole, not your lips at all.

**PYRAMUS:** Wilt thou at Ninny's tomb meet me straightaway?

**THISBE:** 'Tide life, 'tide death, I come without delay.
*[Exeunt* PYRAMUS *and* THISBE.*]*

**WALL:** Thus have I, Wall, my part dischargèd so;
And, being done, thus Wall away doth go. *[Exit.]*

**THESEUS:** Now is the mural down between the two neighbors.

**DEMETRIUS:** No remedy, my lord, when walls are so willful to hear without warning.

**HIPPOLYTA:** This is the silliest stuff that ever I heard.

**THESEUS:** The best in this kind are but shadows; and the worst are no worse, if imagination amend them.

**HIPPOLYTA:** It must be your imagination then, and not theirs.

**THESEUS:** If we imagine no worse of them than they of themselves, they may pass for excellent men. Here come two noble beasts in, a man and a lion.

*Enter* LION *and* MOONSHINE.

**LION:** You, ladies, you, whose gentle hearts do fear
The smallest monstrous mouse that creeps on floor,
May now perchance both quake and tremble here,
When lion rough in wildest rage doth roar.
Then know that I, as Snug the joiner, am
A lion fell, nor else no lion's dam;
For, if I should as lion come in strife
Into this place, 'twere pity on my life.

**THESEUS:** A very gentle beast, and of a good conscience.

**DEMETRIUS:** The very best at a beast, my lord, that e'er I saw.

**LYSANDER:** This lion is a very fox for his valor.

**THESEUS:** True; and a goose for his discretion.

**DEMETRIUS:** Not so, my lord, for his valor cannot carry his discretion, and the fox carries the goose.

---

**181 sensible** capable of feeling **182 again** in return **185 pat** exactly **192 an** if **194 lover's grace** i.e., gracious lover **195, 196 Limander, Helen** (Blunders for "Leander" and "Hero.") **197 Shafalus, Procrus** (Blunders for "Cephalus" and "Procris," also famous lovers.)

**202 'Tide** betide, come **208 willful** willing. **without warning** i.e., without warning the parents. (Demetrius makes a joke on the proverb "Walls have ears.") **210 in this kind** of this sort. **shadows** likenesses, representations **222 lion fell** fierce lion (with a play on the idea of "lion skin") **228 is . . . valor** i.e., his valor consists of craftiness and discretion **229 a goose . . . discretion** i.e., as discreet as a goose, that is, more foolish than discreet

**THESEUS:** His discretion, I am sure, cannot carry his valor; for the goose carries not the fox. It is well. Leave it to his discretion, and let us listen to the moon.

**MOON:** This lanthorn doth the hornèd moon present—

**DEMETRIUS:** He should have worn the horns on his head.

**THESEUS:** He is no crescent, and his horns are invisible within the circumference.

**MOON:** This lanthorn doth the hornèd moon present;
Myself the man i' the moon do seem to be.

**THESEUS:** This is the greatest error of all the rest. The man should be put into the lanthorn. How is it else the man i' the moon?

**DEMETRIUS:** He dares not come there for the candle, for you see it is already in snuff.

**HIPPOLYTA:** I am aweary of this moon. Would he would change!

**THESEUS:** It appears, by his small light of discretion, that he is in the wane; but yet, in courtesy, in all reason, we must stay the time.

**LYSANDER:** Proceed, Moon.

**MOON:** All that I have to say is to tell you that the lanthorn is the moon, I, the man i' the moon, this thornbush my thornbush, and this dog my dog.

**DEMETRIUS:** Why, all these should be in the lanthorn, for all these are in the moon. But silence! Here comes Thisbe.

*Enter* THISBE.

**THISBE:** This is old Ninny's tomb. Where is my love?

**LION** *[roaring]*: O!

**DEMETRIUS:** Well roared, Lion.

*[*THISBE *runs off, dropping her mantle.]*

**THESEUS:** Well run, Thisbe.

**HIPPOLYTA:** Well shone, Moon. Truly, the moon shines with a good grace.

*[The* LION *worries* THISBE*'s mantle.]*

**THESEUS:** Well moused, Lion.

*[Enter* PYRAMUS; *exit* LION.*]*

**DEMETRIUS:** And then came Pyramus.

**LYSANDER:** And so the lion vanished.

**PYRAMUS:** Sweet Moon, I thank thee for thy sunny beams;
I thank thee, Moon, for shining now so bright;
For, by thy gracious, golden, glittering gleams,
I trust to take of truest Thisbe sight.
But stay, O spite!
But mark, poor knight,
What dreadful dole is here?
Eyes, do you see?
How can it be?
O dainty duck! O dear!
Thy mantle good,
What, stained with blood?
Approach, ye Furies fell!
O Fates, come, come,
Cut thread and thrum;
Quail, crush, conclude, and quell!

**THESEUS:** This passion, and the death of a dear friend, would go near to make a man look sad.

**HIPPOLYTA:** Beshrew my heart, but I pity the man.

**PYRAMUS:** O, wherefore, Nature, didst thou lions frame?
Since lion vile hath here deflowered my dear,
Which is—no, no, which was—the fairest dame
That lived, that loved, that liked, that looked with cheer.
Come, tears, confound,
Out, sword, and wound
The pap of Pyramus;
Ay, that left pap,
Where heart doth hop. *[He stabs himself.]*
Thus die I, thus, thus, thus.
Now am I dead,
Now am I fled;
My soul is in the sky.
Tongue, lose thy light;
Moon, take thy flight. *[Exit* MOONSHINE.*]*
Now die, die, die, die, die. *[*PYRAMUS *dies.]*

**235 lanthorn** (This original spelling, *lanthorn*, may suggest a play on the *horn* of which lanterns were made and also on a cuckold's horns; however, the spelling *lanthorn* is not used consistently for comic effect in this play or elsewhere. At 5.1.134, for example, the word is *lantern* in the original.) **236–237 on his head** (as a sign of cuckoldry) **238 crescent** a waxing moon **245 for** because of, for fear of **246 in snuff** (1) offended (2) in need of snuffing or trimming

**265 moused** shaken, torn, bitten **274 dole** grievous event **280 Furies** avenging goddesses of Greek myth. **fell** fierce **281 Fates** the three goddesses (Clotho, Lachesis, Atropos) of Greek myth who spun, drew, and cut the thread of human life **282 thread and thrum** i.e., everything—the good and bad alike; literally, the warp in weaving and the loose end of the warp **283 Quail** overpower. **quell** kill, destroy **284–285 This . . . sad** i.e., if one had other reason to grieve, one might be sad, but not from this absurd portrayal of passion **290 cheer** countenance **293 pap** breast

**DEMETRIUS:** No die, but an ace, for him; for he is but one.

**LYSANDER:** Less than an ace, man; for he is dead, he is nothing.

**THESEUS:** With the help of a surgeon he might yet recover, and yet prove an ass.

**HIPPOLYTA:** How chance Moonshine is gone before Thisbe comes back and finds her lover?

**THESEUS:** She will find him by starlight.

*[Enter* THISBE.*]*

Here she comes; and her passion ends the play.

**HIPPOLYTA:** Methinks she should not use a long one for such a Pyramus. I hope she will be brief.

**DEMETRIUS:** A mote will turn the balance, which Pyramus, which Thisbe, is the better: he for a man, God warrant us; she for a woman, God bless us.

**LYSANDER:** She hath spied him already with those sweet eyes.

**DEMETRIUS:** And thus she means, videlicet:

**THISBE:**
Asleep, my love?
What, dead, my dove?
O Pyramus, arise!
Speak, speak. Quite dumb?
Dead, dead? A tomb
Must cover thy sweet eyes.
These lily lips,
This cherry nose,
These yellow cowslip cheeks,
Are gone, are gone!
Lovers, make moan.
His eyes were green as leeks.
O Sisters Three,
Come, come to me,
With hands as pale as milk;
Lay them in gore,
Since you have shore
With shears his thread of silk.
Tongue, not a word.
Come, trusty sword,
Come, blade, my breast imbrue!
*[She stabs herself.]*
And farewell, friends.
Thus Thisbe ends.
Adieu, adieu, adieu. *[She dies.]*

**THESEUS:** Moonshine and Lion are left to bury the dead.

**DEMETRIUS:** Ay, and Wall too.

**BOTTOM** *[starting up, as* FLUTE *does also]*: No, I assure you, the wall is down that parted their fathers. Will it please you to see the epilogue, or to hear a Bergomask dance between two of our company?

*[The other players enter.]*

**THESEUS:** No epilogue, I pray you; for your play needs no excuse. Never excuse; for when the players are all dead, there need none to be blamed. Marry, if he that writ it had played Pyramus and hanged himself in Thisbe's garter, it would have been a fine tragedy; and so it is, truly, and very notably discharged. But, come, your Bergomask. Let your epilogue alone. *[A dance.]*
The iron tongue of midnight hath told twelve.
Lovers, to bed, 'tis almost fairy time.
I fear we shall outsleep the coming morn
As much as we this night have overwatched.
This palpable-gross play hath well beguiled
The heavy gait of night. Sweet friends, to bed.
A fortnight hold we this solemnity,
In nightly revels and new jollity. *Exeunt.*

Thisbe mourns the dead Pyramus.

---

**303 ace** the side of the die featuring the single pip, or spot. (The pun is on *die* as a singular of *dice;* Bottom's performance is not worth a whole *die* but rather one single face of it, one small portion.) **304 one** (1) an individual person (2) unique **308 ass** (with a pun on *ace*) **315 mote** small particle **315–316 which . . . which** whether . . . or **320 means** moans, laments (with a pun on the meaning, "lodge a formal complaint"). **videlicet** to wit **333 Sisters Three** the Fates **337 shore** shorn

**341 imbrue** stain with blood **349–350 Bergomask dance** a rustic dance named for Bergamo, a province in the state of Venice **358 iron tongue** i.e., of a bell. **told** counted, struck ("tolled") **361 overwatched** stayed up too late **362 palpable-gross** palpably gross, obviously crude **363 heavy** drowsy, dull

*Enter* PUCK *[carrying a broom].*

**PUCK:**
Now the hungry lion roars,
And the wolf behowls the moon,
Whilst the heavy plowman snores,
All with weary task fordone.
Now the wasted brands do glow,
Whilst the screech owl, screeching loud,
Puts the wretch that lies in woe
In remembrance of a shroud.
Now it is the time of night
That the graves, all gaping wide,
Every one lets forth his sprite,
In the church-way paths to glide.
And we fairies, that do run
By the triple Hecate's team.
From the presence of the sun,
Following darkness like a dream,
Now are frolic. Not a mouse
Shall disturb this hallowed house.
I am sent with broom before,
To sweep the dust behind the door.

*Enter [*OBERON *and* TITANIA,*] King and Queen of Fairies, with all their train.*

**OBERON:**
Through the house give glimmering light,
By the dead and drowsy fire;
Every elf and fairy sprite
Hop as light as bird from brier;
And this ditty, after me,
Sing, and dance it trippingly.

**TITANIA:**
First, rehearse your song by rote,
To each word a warbling note.
Hand in hand, with fairy grace,
Will we sing, and bless this place.

*[Song and dance.]*

**OBERON:**
Now, until the break of day,
Through this house each fairy stray.
To the best bride-bed will we,
Which by us shall blessèd be;
And the issue there create
Ever shall be fortunate.
So shall all the couples three
Ever true in loving be;
And the blots of Nature's hand
Shall not in their issue stand;
Never mole, harelip, nor scar,
Nor mark prodigious, such as are
Despisèd in nativity,
Shall upon their children be.
With this field dew consecrate,
Every fairy take his gait,
And each several chamber bless,
Though this palace, with sweet peace;
And the owner of it blest
Ever shall in safety rest.
Trip away; make no stay;
Meet me all by break of day.

*Exeunt [*OBERON, TITANIA, *and train].*

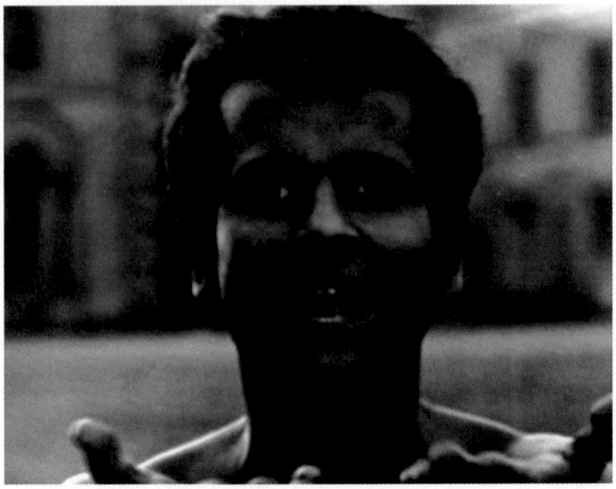

Puck (Ian Holm) delivers his final monologue.

**PUCK** *[to the audience]***:**
If we shadows have offended,
Think but this, and all is mended,
That you have but slumbered here
While these visions did appear.
And this weak and idle theme,
No more yielding but a dream,
Gentles, do not reprehend.
If you pardon, we will mend.
And, as I am an honest Puck,
If we have unearnèd luck
Now to scape the serpent's tongue,
We will make amends ere long;
Else the Puck a liar call.
So, good night unto you all.
Give me your hands, if we be friends,
And Robin shall restore amends. *[Exit.]*

**368 heavy** tired **369 fordone** exhausted **370 wasted brands** burned-out logs **376 Every . . . sprite** every grave lets forth its ghost **379 triple Hecate's** (Hecate ruled in three capacities: as Luna or Cynthia in heaven, as Diana on earth, and as Proserpina in hell.) **382 frolic** merry **385 behind** from behind, or else like sweeping the dirt under the carpet. (Robin Goodfellow was a household spirit who helped good housemaids and punished lazy ones, but he could, of course, be mischievous.) **392 rehearse** recite **400 create** created

**407 prodigious** monstrous, unnatural **410 consecrate** consecrated **411 take his gait** go his way **412 several** separate **420 That . . . here** i.e., that it is a "midsummer night's dream" **423 No . . . but** yielding no more than **425 mend** improve **428 serpent's tongue** i.e., hissing **432 Give . . . hands** applaud **433 restore amends** give satisfaction in return

# Writing from Reading

### Summarize

1 A series of clearly established scenes adds up to a struggle between illusion and reality. Describe the unfolding of the struggle in plain language.

### Analyze Craft

2 Some scholars have suggested that the play itself was commissioned to celebrate a royal wedding or betrothal. As a wedding play, what does this suggest about the condition of marriage? How do Oberon and Titania mirror their mortal counterparts? What does the play's title suggest?

3 What do these "rude mechanicals" tell us about the nature of love?

4 What is the symbolic function of the marriage between Theseus and Hippolyta?

5 Characterize the four young lovers—the two mismatched and then matched pairs. How individual do they seem, or are they interchangeable, and if the latter, is that part of the playwright's point?

### Analyze Voice

6 Why is Bottom so unforgettably comic; what about his behavior reflects on members of the court? When Titania grows passionate about him, is her love truly blind? Look at her protestations of devotion and give examples of what's serious and what's foolish in her speech.

7 This play is a comedy, but in *A Midsummer Night's Dream,* there is danger and the risk of madness or at least delusion. How could this "dream" have been transformed to "nightmare," the comedy to tragedy? The Latin word for "moon"—*luna*—is at the root of "lunatic," and the behavior of the lovers seems more than a little bit crazy when enacted onstage. Analyze the playwright's tone.

### Synthesize Summary and Analysis

8 The play is set in ancient Athens, but the woods are those of Elizabethan England. How easy or uneasy is the fit between the two?

9 How do the fairies help bridge the gap between aristocrat and worker?

10 What do the women have in common here? The men?

11 Compare and contrast the "play within the play," in *A Midsummer Night's Dream* with the one in *Hamlet.*

### Interpret the Play

12 The almost literal lunacy of all this moonlit madness—amorous coupling in the dark, the change of sexual partners, the loss of recognizable identity—evokes a far more pagan set of behaviors than those otherwise permitted to the royal entourage. Are Demetrius, Lysander, Hermia, and Helena very different when "lost" in the woods from when found in court?

13 The themes of marriage and fertility are scarcely new to Shakespeare, but the intersections of society and the primitive world provide his focus now. There are three levels of society here—the kingly, the aristocratic, and the working poor. How do they reflect upon one another, or are they a study in contrasts and the distinctions of class?

## OTHELLO

In his celebration of Shakespeare, the poet Matthew Arnold (see chapter 18) wrote:

> *"Others abide our question. Thou art free. . . ."*

He means by this that, though it's possible to understand or at least imagine the creative processes of authors, Shakespeare outstrips understanding. In his hands, such universal matters as the conflict between good and evil, love and suspicion, nobility and "base" ambition become specific and embodied; figures like those you will encounter in this tragedy—Iago, Desdemona, and Othello—have come to represent evil, trust,

"Shakespeare used the phrase 'holding a mirror up to nature.' It's a mirror in which we can reflect, we can contemplate, we can feel, we can understand. And really the arts do this in a way that nothing else can. They are really the most human of all expressions, the most humane and most human of all enterprises. You can talk about philosophy, you can talk about all kinds of things; but nothing taps in to who we are, who we might be, who we're afraid of, we might become if we don't have the right human qualities—there is something about the arts that touches the wellspring, the really deepest parts of who we are, and makes us more human."
Conversation with Edwin Wilson

and jealousy both in the old allegorical mode (see chapter 20 in Poetry) and in modern terms. *Othello* was most probably composed in 1601, and we know it was performed by 1604; it is, then, the tragedy that follows *Hamlet*—yet with a wholly separate set of characters and problems. The original situation derives from a sixteenth-century tale by Giraldi Cinthio, which portrays the tragedy that ensues when an unnamed Moor in Venice falls in love with the woman Desdemona. But as he had done with the old Norse legend that was the inspiration for *Hamlet,* in *Othello* Shakespeare deepened and changed the sixteenth-century story in important ways.

Two of the most obvious and crucial changes Shakespeare made was to flesh out the main characters of the tragedy and to add new ones. In Othello we see a brand of tortured soul altogether different from that of Hamlet. Indeed, Othello struggles not with vengeance or abandonment but with self-doubt and too much faith in the honesty of those around him. Near the end of the play, Othello says:

*When you shall these unlucky deeds relate,*
*Speak of me as I am; nothing extenuate,*
*Nor set down aught in malice. Then must you speak*
*Of one that loved not wisely but too well;*
*Of one not easily jealous but, being wrought*
*Perplexed in the extreme. . . .*

As you read, decide whether Shakespeare's depiction is the telling or the retelling. Is Othello's story being related with "nothing extenuate," or are we receiving an embellished tale secondhand? Consider the Greek qualities of this tragedy: the nobility of Othello, his fatally short temper, the inevitability of his demise. In what ways is the downfall of Othello larger than life, and in what ways is it poignantly real?

"A mark of the very greatest artists, in my view, is honesty . . . [Shakespeare] allows people to see to the depths of their moral imagination." Conversation with Ralph Williams

**RECONSTRUCTING SHAKESPEARE**

The written texts we have of Shakespeare's plays do not always or exactly match what the actors said. Troupes competed for new stories, and playwrights had no copyright protection, so the managers of the King's Men did not want their pages distributed and used by others. Much of what we have, therefore, was reconstructed afterward, from an actor's or a theatergoer's memory; often the written versions differ. All this by way of saying that versions may contain different spellings—from "sullied" to "solid" to the now generally accepted "sallied"—of a single word.

Pronunciation has also changed in the course of 400 years, and the way the language *sounded* must be deduced; obviously no tape recordings exist. It's a pretty good guess, for example, that the words "love" and "move" were rhyming words—as in Hamlet's poem, "Doubt that the stars are fire / Doubt that the sun doth move / Doubt truth to be a liar / But never doubt I love."

**AS YOU READ** Keep track of the shifts in Othello's attitude and moods—from glad devotion to murderous jealousy and, in the end, a self-destructive self-awareness. Is he deluded or noble, or both?

# Othello, the Moor of Venice (c. 1601)

## CHARACTERS

**OTHELLO,** *the Moor*

**BRABANTIO,** *[a senator,] father to Desdemona*

**CASSIO,** *an honorable lieutenant [to Othello]*

**IAGO,** *[Othello's ancient,] a villain*

**RODERIGO,** *a gulled gentleman*

**DUKE OF VENICE**

**SENATORS** *[of Venice]*

**MONTANO,** *Governor of Cyprus*

**GENTLEMEN** *of Cyprus*

**LODOVICO AND GRATIANO,** *[kinsmen to Brabantio,] two noble Venetians*

**SAILORS**

**CLOWN**

**DESDEMONA,** *[daughter to Brabantio and] wife to Othello*

**EMILIA,** *wife to Iago*

**BIANCA,** *a courtesan [and mistress to Cassio]*

**[A MESSENGER**

**A HERALD**

**A MUSICIAN**

*Servants, Attendants, Officers, Senators, Musicians, Gentlemen*

**SCENE:** *Venice; a seaport in Cyprus]*

**1.1** *Enter* RODERIGO *and* IAGO.

**RODERIGO:** Tush, never tell me! I take it much unkindly
That thou, Iago, who hast had my purse
As if the strings were thine, shouldst know of this.

**IAGO:** 'Sblood, but you'll not hear me.
If ever I did dream of such a matter,
Abhor me.

**RODERIGO:** Thou toldst me thou didst hold him in thy hate.

**IAGO:** Despise me
If I do not. Three great ones of the city,
In personal suit to make me his lieutenant,
Off-capped to him; and by the faith of man,
I know my price, I am worth no worse a place.
But he, as loving his own pride and purposes,
Evades them with a bombast circumstance
Horribly stuffed with epithets of war,
And, in conclusion,
Nonsuits my mediators. For, "Certes," says he,
"I have already chose my officer."
And what was he?
Forsooth, a great arithmetician,
One Michael Cassio, a Florentine,
A fellow almost damned in a fair wife,
That never set a squadron in the field
Nor the division of a battle knows
More than a spinster—unless the bookish theoric,
Wherein the togaed consuls can propose
As masterly as he. Mere prattle without practice
Is all his soldiership. But he, sir, had th' election;
And I, of whom his eyes had seen the proof
At Rhodes, at Cyprus, and on other grounds
Christened and heathen, must be beleed and calmed
By debitor and creditor. This countercaster,
He, in good time, must his lieutenant be,
And I—God bless the mark!—his Moorship's ancient.

**RODERIGO:** By heaven, I rather would have been his hangman.

**IAGO:** Why, there's no remedy. 'Tis the curse of service;
Preferment goes by letter and affection,
And not by old gradation, where each second
Stood heir to th' first. Now, sir, be judge yourself,
Whether I in any just term am affined
To love the Moor.

**RODERIGO:** I would not follow him then.

**IAGO:** O, sir, content you.
I follow him to serve my turn upon him.
We cannot all be masters, nor all masters
Cannot be truly followed. You shall mark
Many a duteous and knee-crooking knave
That, doting on his own obsequious bondage,
Wears out his time, much like his master's ass,
For naught but provender, and when he's old, cashiered.
Whip me such honest knaves. Others there are
Who, trimmed in forms and visages of duty,
Keep yet their hearts attending on themselves,
And, throwing but shows of service on their lords,
Do well thrive by them, and when they have lined their coats,
Do themselves homage. These fellows have some soul,
And such a one do I profess myself. For, sir,
It is as sure as you are Roderigo,
Were I the Moor I would not be Iago.
In following him, I follow but myself—
Heaven is my judge, not I for love and duty,

---

**1.1 Location: Venice. A street.**
**1 never tell me** (An expression of incredulity, like "tell me another one.") **3 this** i.e., Desdemona's elopement **4 'Sblood** by His (Christ's) blood **11 him** i.e., Othello **14 bombast circumstance** wordy evasion. (*Bombast* is cotton padding.) **15 epithets of war** military expressions **17 Nonsuits** rejects the petition of. **Certes** certainly **20 arithmetician** i.e., a man whose military knowledge is merely theoretical, based on books of tactics **22 A . . . wife** (Cassio does not seem to be married, but his counterpart in Shakespeare's source does have a woman in his house. See also 4.1.131.) **24 division of a battle** disposition of a military unit **25 a spinster** i.e., a housewife, one whose regular occupation is spinning. **theoric** theory **26 togaed** wearing the toga. **consuls** counselors, senators. **propose** discuss **29 his** i.e., Othello's **31 Christened** Christian. **beleed and calmed** left to leeward without wind, becalmed. (A sailing metaphor.)

**32 debitor and creditor** (A name for a system of bookkeeping, here used as a contemptuous nickname for Cassio.) **countercaster** i.e., bookkeeper, one who tallies with *counters*, or "metal disks." (Said contemptuously.) **33 in good time** opportunely, i.e., forsooth **34 God bless the mark** (Perhaps originally a formula to ward off evil; here an expression of impatience.) **ancient** standard-bearer, ensign **35 his hangman** the executioner of him **37 Preferment** promotion. **letter and affection** personal influence and favoritism **38 old gradation** step-by-step seniority, the traditional way **40 term** respect. **affined** bound **43 content you** don't you worry about that **46 truly** faithfully **50 cashiered** dismissed from service **51 Whip me** whip, as far as I'm concerned **52 trimmed . . . duty** dressed up in the mere form and show of dutifulness **55 lined their coats** i.e., stuffed their purses **56 Do themselves homage** i.e., attend to self-interest solely **59 Were . . . Iago** i.e., if I were able to assume command, I certainly would not choose to remain a subordinate, or, I would keep a suspicious eye on a flattering subordinate

Iago (Tim McInnerny) tells Roderigo (Sam Crane) his plans in the 2007 production directed by Wilson Milam.

But seeming so for my peculiar end.
For when my outward action doth demonstrate
The native act and figure of my heart
In compliment extern, 'tis not long after
But I will wear my heart upon my sleeve
For daws to peck at. I am not what I am.

**RODERIGO:** What a full fortune does the thick-lips owe
If he can carry 't thus!

**IAGO:** Call up her father.
Rouse him, make after him, poison his delight,
Proclaim him in the streets; incense her kinsmen,
And, though he in a fertile climate dwell,
Plague him with flies. Though that his joy be joy,
Yet throw such changes of vexation on 't
As it may lose some color.

**RODERIGO:** Here is her father's house. I'll call aloud.

**IAGO:** Do, with like timorous accent and dire yell
As when, by night and negligence, the fire
Is spied in populous cities.

---

**62 peculiar** particular, personal **64 native** innate. **figure** shape, intent **65 compliment extern** outward show (conforming in this case to the inner workings and intention of the heart) **67 daws** small crowlike birds, proverbially stupid and avaricious. **I am not what I am** i.e., I am not one who wears his heart on his sleeve **68 full** swelling. **thick-lips** (Elizabethans often applied the term "Moor" to Negroes.) **owe** own **69 carry 't thus** carry this off **72–73 though . . . flies** though he seems prosperous and happy now, vex him with misery **73 Though . . . be joy** although he seems fortunate and happy. (Repeats the idea of line 72.) **74 changes of vexation** vexing changes **75 As it may** that may cause it to. **some color** some of its fresh gloss **77 timorous** frightening **78 and negligence** i.e., by negligence

**RODERIGO:** What ho, Brabantio! Signor Brabantio, ho!

**IAGO:** Awake! What, ho, Brabantio! Thieves, thieves, thieves!
Look to your house, your daughter, and your bags!
Thieves, thieves!

BRABANTIO *[enters] above [at a window].*

**BRABANTIO:** What is the reason of this terrible summons?
What is the matter there?

**RODERIGO:** Signor, is all your family within?

**IAGO:** Are your doors locked?

**BRABANTIO:** Why, wherefore ask you this?

**IAGO:** Zounds, sir, you're robbed! For shame, put on your gown!
Your heart is burst; you have lost half your soul.
Even now, now, very now, an old black ram
Is tupping your white ewe. Arise, arise!
Awake the snorting citizens with the bell,
Or else the devil will make a grandsire of you.
Arise, I say!

**BRABANTIO:** What, have you lost your wits?

**RODERIGO:** Most reverend signor, do you know my voice?

**BRABANTIO:** Not I. What are you?

**RODERIGO:** My name is Roderigo.

**BRABANTIO:** The worser welcome.
I have charged thee not to haunt about my doors.
In honest plainness thou hast heard me say
My daughter is not for thee; and now, in madness,
Being full of supper and distempering drafts,
Upon malicious bravery dost thou come
To start my quiet.

**RODERIGO:** Sir, sir, sir—

**BRABANTIO:** But thou must needs be sure
My spirits and my place have in their power
To make this bitter to thee.

---

**83 s.d. at a window** (This stage direction, from the Quarto, probably calls for an appearance on the gallery above and rearstage.) **85 the matter** your business **88 Zounds** by His (Christ's) wounds **91 tupping** covering, copulating with. (Said of sheep.) **92 snorting** snoring **93 the devil** (The devil was conventionally pictured as black.) **102 distempering** intoxicating **103 Upon malicious bravery** with hostile intent to defy me **104 start** startle, disrupt **106 My spirits and my place** my temperament and my authority of office. **have in** have it in

**RODERIGO:** Patience, good sir.

**BRABANTIO:** What tell'st thou me of robbing? This is Venice;
My house is not a grange.

**RODERIGO:** Most grave Brabantio,
In simple and pure soul I come to you.

**IAGO:** Zounds, sir, you are one of those that will not serve God if the devil bid you. Because we come to do you service and you think we are ruffians, you'll have your daughter covered with a Barbary horse; you'll have your nephews neigh to you; you'll have coursers for cousins and jennets for germans.

**BRABANTIO:** What profane wretch art thou?

**IAGO:** I am one, sir, that comes to tell you your daughter and the Moor are now making the beast with two backs.

**BRABANTIO:** Thou art a villain.

**IAGO:** You are—a senator.

**BRABANTIO:** This thou shalt answer. I know thee, Roderigo.

**RODERIGO:** Sir, I will answer anything. But I beseech you,
If 't be your pleasure and most wise consent—
As partly I find it is—that your fair daughter,
At this odd-even and dull watch o' the night,
Transported with no worse nor better guard
But with a knave of common hire, a gondolier,
To the gross clasps of a lascivious Moor—
If this be known to you and your allowance
We then have done you bold and saucy wrongs.
But if you know not this, my manners tell me
We have your wrong rebuke. Do not believe
That, from the sense of all civility,
I thus would play and trifle with your reverence.
Your daughter, if you have not given her leave,
I say again, hath made a gross revolt,
Tying her duty, beauty, wit, and fortunes
In an extravagant and wheeling stranger
Of here and everywhere. Straight satisfy yourself.
If she be in her chamber or your house,
Let loose on me the justice of the state
For thus deluding you.

Brabantio (Pierre Vaneck) hears the news of his daughter's betrayal in the 1995 film directed by Oliver Parker.

**BRABANTIO:** Strike on the tinder, ho!
Give me a taper! Call up all my people!
This accident is not unlike my dream.
Belief of it oppresses me already.
Light, I say, light! *Exit [above.]*

**IAGO:** Farewell, for I must leave you.
It seems not meet nor wholesome to my place
To be producted—as, if I stay, I shall—
Against the Moor. For I do know the state,
However this may gall him with some check,
Cannot with safety cast him, for he's embarked
With such loud reason to the Cyprus wars,
Which even now stands in act, that, for their souls,
Another of his fathom they have none
To lead their business; in which regard,
Though I do hate him as I do hell pains,

---

**109 grange** isolated country house **110 simple** sincere **114 Barbary** from northern Africa (and hence associated with Othello) **115 nephews** i.e., grandsons. **coursers** powerful horses **116 cousins** kinsmen. **jennets** small Spanish horses. **germans** near relatives **121 a senator** (Said with mock politeness, as though the word itself were an insult.) **122 answer** be held accountable for **124 wise** well-informed **126 odd-even** between one day and the next, i.e., about midnight **127 with** by **128 But with a knave** than by a low fellow, a servant **130 allowance** permission **131 saucy** insolent **134 from** contrary to. **civility** good manners, decency **135 your reverence** the respect due to you

**138 wit** intelligence **139 extravagant** expatriate, wandering far from home. **wheeling** roving about, vagabond. **stranger** foreigner **140 Straight** straightway **144 tinder,** charred linen ignited by a spark from flint and steel, used to light torches or *tapers* (lines 145, 170) **146 accident** occurrence, event **149 meet** fitting. **place** position (as ensign) **150 producted** produced (as a witness) **152 gall** rub; oppress. **check** rebuke **153 cast** dismiss. **embarked** engaged **154 loud reason** unanimous shout of confirmation (in the Senate) **155 stands in act** are going on. **for their souls** to save themselves **156 fathom** i.e., ability, depth of experience **157 in which regard** out of regard for which

Yet for necessity of present life
I must show out a flag and sign of love,
Which is indeed but sign. That you shall surely find him,
Lead to the Sagittary that raisèd search,
And there will I be with him. So farewell. *Exit.*

*Enter [below]* BRABANTIO *[in his nightgown] with servants and torches.*

**BRABANTIO:** It is too true an evil. Gone she is;
And what's to come of my despisèd time
Is naught but bitterness. Now, Roderigo,
Where didst thou see her?—O unhappy girl!—
With the Moor, say'st thou?—Who would be a father?—
How didst thou know 'twas she?—O, she deceives me
Past thought!—What said she to you?—Get more tapers.
Raise all my kindred.—Are they married, think you?

**RODERIGO:** Truly, I think they are.

**BRABANTIO:** O heaven! How got she out? O treason of the blood!
Fathers, from hence trust not your daughters' minds
By what you see them act. Is there not charms
By which the property of youth and maidhood
May be abused? Have you not read, Roderigo,
Of some such thing?

**RODERIGO:** Yes, sir, I have indeed.

**BRABANTIO:** Call up my brother.—O, would you had had her!—
Some one way, some another.—Do you know
Where we may apprehend her and the Moor?

**RODERIGO:** I think I can discover him, if you please
To get good guard and go along with me.

**BRABANTIO:** Pray you, lead on. At every house I'll call;
I may command at most.—Get weapons, ho!
And raise some special officers of night.—
On, good Roderigo. I will deserve your pains.

*Exeunt.*

**159 life** livelihood **162 Sagittary** (An inn or house where Othello and Desdemona are staying, named for its sign of Sagittarius, or Centaur.) **raisèd search** search party roused out of sleep **163 s.d. nightgown** dressing gown. (This costuming is specified in the Quarto text.) **165 time** i.e., remainder of life **175 charms** spells **176 property** special quality, nature **177 abused** deceived **182 discover** reveal, uncover **185 command** demand assistance **187 deserve** show gratitude for

## 1.2 *Enter* OTHELLO, IAGO, *attendants with torches.*

**IAGO:** Though in the trade of war I have slain men,
Yet do I hold it very stuff o' the conscience
To do no contrived murder. I lack iniquity
Sometimes to do me service. Nine or ten times
I had thought t' have yerked him here under the ribs.

**OTHELLO:** 'Tis better as it is.

**IAGO:** Nay, but he prated,
And spoke such scurvy and provoking terms
Against your honor
That, with the little godliness I have,
I did full hard forbear him. But, I pray you, sir,
Are you fast married? Be assured of this,
That the magnifico is much beloved,
And hath in his effect a voice potential
As double as the Duke's. He will divorce you,
Or put upon you what restraint or grievance
The law, with all his might to enforce it on,
Will give him cable.

**OTHELLO:** Let him do his spite.
My services which I have done the seigniory
Shall out-tongue his complaints. 'Tis yet to know—
Which, when I know that boasting is an honor,
I shall promulgate—I fetch my life and being
From men of royal siege, and my demerits
May speak unbonneted to as proud a fortune
As this that I have reached. For know, Iago,
But that I love the gentle Desdemona,
I would not my unhousèd free condition
Put into circumscription and confine
For the sea's worth. But look, what lights come yond?

*Enter* CASSIO *[and certain officers] with torches.*

**1.2 Location: Venice. Another street, before Othello's lodgings.** **2 very stuff** essence, basic material (continuing the metaphor of *trade* from line 1) **3 contrived** premediated **5 yerked** stabbed. **him** i.e., Roderigo **10 . . . him** I restrained myself with great difficulty from assaulting him **12 magnifico** Venetian grandee, i.e., Brabantio **13 in his effect** at his command. **potential** powerful **17 cable** i.e., scope **18 seigniory** Venetian government **19 yet to know** not yet widely known **22 siege** i.e., rank. (Literally, a seat used by a person of distinction.) **demerits** deserts **23 unbonneted** without removing the hat, i.e., on equal terms (? Or "with hat off," "in all due modesty.") **26 unhousèd** unconfined, undomesticated **27 circumscription and confine** restriction and confinement **28 the sea's worth** all the riches at the bottom of the sea. **s.d. officers** (The Quarto text calls for "Cassio with lights, officers with torches.")

**IAGO** Those are the raisèd father and his friends.
You were best go in.

**OTHELLO:** Not I. I must be found.
My parts, my title, and my perfect soul
Shall manifest me rightly. Is it they?

**IAGO:** By Janus, I think no.

**OTHELLO:** The servants of the Duke? And my lieutenant?
The goodness of the night upon you, friends!
What is the news?

**CASSIO:** The Duke does greet you, General,
And he requires your haste-post-haste appearance
Even on the instant.

**OTHELLO:** What is the matter, think you?

**CASSIO:** Something from Cyprus, as I may divine.
It is a business of some heat. The galleys
Have sent a dozen sequent messengers
This very night at one another's heels,
And many of the consuls, raised and met,
Are at the Duke's already. You have been hotly called for;
When, being not at your lodging to be found,
The Senate hath sent about three several quests
To search you out.

**OTHELLO:** 'Tis well I am found by you.
I will but spend a word here in the house
And go with you. *[Exit.]*

**CASSIO:** Ancient, what makes he here?

**IAGO:** Faith, he tonight hath boarded a land carrack.
If it prove lawful prize, he's made forever.

**CASSIO:** I do not understand.

**IAGO:** He's married.

**CASSIO:** To who?

*[Enter* OTHELLO.*]*

**IAGO:** Marry, to—Come, Captain, will you go?

**OTHELLO:** Have with you.

**CASSIO:** Here comes another troop to seek for you.

*Enter* BRABANTIO, RODERIGO, *with officers and torches.*

**IAGO:** It is Brabantio. General, be advised.
He comes to bad intent.

**OTHELLO:** Holla! Stand there!

**RODERIGO:** Signor, it is the Moor.

**BRABANTIO:** Down with him, thief!
*[They draw on both sides.]*

**IAGO:** You, Roderigo! Come, sir, I am for you.

**OTHELLO:** Keep up your bright swords, for the dew will rust them.
Good signor, you shall more command with years
Than with your weapons.

**BRABANTIO:** O thou foul thief, where hast thou stowed my daughter?
Damned as thou art, thou hast enchanted her!
For I'll refer me to all things of sense,
If she in chains of magic were not bound
Whether a maid so tender, fair, and happy,
So opposite to marriage that she shunned
The wealthy curlèd darlings of our nation,
Would ever have, t' incur a general mock,
Run from her guardage to the sooty bosom
Of such a thing as thou—to fear, not to delight.
Judge me the world if 'tis not gross in sense
That thou hast practiced on her with foul charms,
Abused her delicate youth with drugs or minerals
That weakens motion. I'll have 't disputed on;
'Tis probable and palpable to thinking.
I therefore apprehend and do attach thee
For an abuser of the world, a practicer
Of arts inhibited and out of warrant.—
Lay hold upon him! If he do resist,
Subdue him at his peril.

**OTHELLO:** Hold your hands,
Both you of my inclining and the rest.
Were it my cue to fight, I should have known it
Without a prompter.—Whither will you that I go
To answer this your charge?

---

**31 My . . . soul** my natural gifts, my position or reputation, and my unflawed conscience **33 Janus** Roman two-faced god of beginnings **38 matter** business **39 divine** guess **40 heat** urgency **41 sequent** successive **43 consuls** senators **46 about** all over the city. **several** separate **49 makes** does **50 boarded** gone aboard and seized as an act of piracy (with sexual suggestion). **carrack** large merchant ship **51 prize** booty **53 Marry** (An oath, originally "by the Virgin Mary"; here used with wordplay on *married.*) **54 Have with you** i.e., let's go

**55 s.d. officers and torches** (The Quarto text calls for "others with lights and weapons.") **56 be advised** be on your guard **60 Keep up** keep in the sheath **65 refer me** submit my case. **things of sense** commonsense understandings, or, creatures possessing common sense **71 her guardage** my guardianship of her **73 gross in sense** obvious **75 minerals** i.e., poisons **76 weakens motion** impair the vital faculties. **disputed on** argued in court by professional counsel, debated by experts **78 attach** arrest **80 arts inhibited** prohibited arts, black magic. **out of warrant** illegal **83 inclining** following, party

**BRABANTIO:** To prison, till fit time
Of law and course of direct session
Call thee to answer.

**OTHELLO:** What if I do obey?
How may the Duke be therewith satisfied,
Whose messengers are here about my side
Upon some present business of the state
To bring me to him?

**OFFICER:** 'Tis true, most worthy signor.
The Duke's in council, and your noble self,
I am sure, is sent for.

**BRABANTIO:** How? The Duke in council?
In this time of the night? Bring him away.
Mine's not an idle cause. The Duke himself,
Or any of my brothers of the state,
Cannot but feel this wrong as 'twere their own;
For if such actions may have passage free,
Bondslaves and pagans shall our statesmen be.
*Exeunt.*

**1.3** *Enter* DUKE *[and]* SENATORS *[and sit at a table, with lights], and officers. [The* DUKE *and* SENATORS *are reading dispatches.]*

**DUKE:** There is no composition in these news
That gives them credit.

**FIRST SENATOR:** Indeed, they are disproportioned.
My letters say a hundred and seven galleys.

**DUKE:** And mine, a hundred forty.

**SECOND SENATOR:** And mine, two hundred.
But though they jump not on a just account—
As in these cases, where the aim reports
'Tis oft with difference—yet do they all confirm
A Turkish fleet, and bearing up to Cyprus.

**DUKE:** Nay, it is possible enough to judgment.
I do not so secure me in the error
But the main article I do approve
In fearful sense.

The Duke, senators, and officers sit to hear Othello's claims.

**SAILOR** *(within)*: What ho, what ho, what ho!

*Enter* SAILOR.

**OFFICER:** A messenger from the galleys.

**DUKE:** Now, what's the business?

**SAILOR:** The Turkish preparation makes for Rhodes.
So was I bid report here to the state
By Signor Angelo.

**DUKE:** How say you by this change?

**FIRST SENATOR:** This cannot be
By no assay of reason. 'Tis a pageant
To keep us in false gaze. When we consider
Th' importancy of Cyprus to the Turk,
And let ourselves again but understand
That, as it more concerns the Turk than Rhodes,
So may he with more facile question bear it,
For that it stands not in such warlike brace,
But altogether lacks th' abilities
That Rhodes is dressed in—if we make thought of
this,
We must not think the Turk is so unskillful
To leave that latest which concerns him first,
Neglecting an attempt of ease and gain
To wake and wage a danger profitless.

---

**88 course of direct session** regular or specially convened legal proceedings **96 away** right along **97 idle** trifling **100 have passage free** are allowed to go unchecked

**1.3. Location: Venice. A council chamber.**
**s.d. Enter . . . Officers** (The Quarto text calls for the Duke and senators to "sit at a table with lights and attendants.") **1 composition** consistency **3 disproportioned** inconsistent **6 jump** agree. **just** exact **7 the aim** conjecture **11–12 I do not . . . approve** I do not take such (false) comfort in the discrepancies that I fail to perceive the main point, i.e., that the Turkish fleet is threatening

**16 preparation** fleet prepared for battle **19 by** about **20 assay** test. **pageant** mere show **21 in false gaze** looking the wrong way **25 So may . . . it** so also he (the Turk) can more easily capture it (Cyprus) **26 For that** since. **brace** state of defense **27 abilities** means of self-defense **28 dressed in** equipped with **29 unskillful** deficient in judgment **30 latest** last **32 wake** stir up. **wage** risk

**DUKE:** Nay, in all confidence, he's not for Rhodes.

**OFFICER:** Here is more news.

*Enter a* MESSENGER.

**MESSENGER:** The Ottomites, reverend and gracious,
Steering with due course toward the isle of Rhodes,
Have there injointed them with an after fleet.

**FIRST SENATOR:** Ay, so I thought. How many, as you guess?

**MESSENGER:** Of thirty sail; and now they do restem
Their backward course, bearing with frank appearance
Their purposes toward Cyprus. Signor Montano,
Your trusty and most valiant servitor,
With his free duty recommends you thus,
And prays you to believe him.

**DUKE:** 'Tis certain then for Cyprus.
Marcus Luccicos, is not he in town?

**FIRST SENATOR:** He's now in Florence.

**DUKE:** Write from us to him, post-post-haste. Dispatch.

**FIRST SENATOR:** Here comes Brabantio and the valiant Moor.

*Enter* BRABANTIO, OTHELLO, CASSIO, IAGO, RODERIGO, *and officers.*

**DUKE:** Valiant Othello, we must straight employ you
Against the general enemy Ottoman.
*[To* BRABANTIO.*]* I did not see you; welcome, gentle signor.
We lacked your counsel and your help tonight.

**BRABANTIO:** So did I yours. Good Your Grace, pardon me;
Neither my place nor aught I heard of business
Hath raised me from my bed, nor doth the general care
Take hold on me, for my particular grief
Is of so floodgate and o'erbearing nature
That it engluts and swallows other sorrows
And it is still itself.

**DUKE:** Why, what's the matter?

**BRABANTIO:** My daughter! O, my daughter!

**DUKE AND SENATORS:** Dead?

**BRABANTIO:** Ay, to me.
She is abused, stol'n from me, and corrupted
By spells and medicines bought of mountebanks;
For nature so preposterously to err,
Being not deficient, blind, or lame of sense,
Sans witchcraft could not.

**DUKE:** Whoe'er he be that in this foul proceeding
Hath thus beguiled your daughter of herself,
And you of her, the bloody book of law
You shall yourself read in the bitter letter
After your own sense—yea, though our proper son
Stood in your action.

**BRABANTIO:** Humbly I thank Your Grace.
Here is the man, this Moor, whom now it seems
Your special mandate for the state affairs
Hath hither brought.

**ALL:** We are very sorry for 't.

**DUKE** *[To* OTHELLO*]*: What, in your own part, can you say to this?

**BRABANTIO:** Nothing, but this is so.

**OTHELLO:** Most potent, grave, and reverend signors,
My very noble and approved good masters:
That I have ta'en away this old man's daughter,
It is most true; true, I have married her.
The very head and front of my offending
Hath this extent, no more. Rude am I in my speech,
And little blessed with the soft phrase of peace;
For since these arms of mine had seven years' pith,
Till now some nine moons wasted, they have used
Their dearest action in the tented field;
And little of this great world can I speak
More than pertains to feats of broils and battle,
And therefore little shall I grace my cause
In speaking for myself. Yet, by your gracious patience,
I will a round unvarnished tale deliver
Of my whole course of love—what drugs, what charms,

---

**37 injointed them** joined themselves. **after** second, following **39–40 restem . . . course** retrace their original course **40 frank appearance** undisguised intent **42 servitor** officer under your command **43 free duty** freely given and loyal service. **recommends** commends himself and reports to **50 straight** straightway **51 general enemy** universal enemy to all Christendom **52 gentle** noble **55 place** official position **57 particular** personal **58 floodgate** i.e., overwhelming (as when floodgates are opened) **59 engluts** engulfs **60 is still itself** remains undiminished

**62 abused** deceived **65 deficient** defective. **lame of sense** deficient in sensory perception **66 Sans** without **71 After . . . sense** according to your own interpretation. **our proper** my own **72 Stood . . . action** were under your accusation **79 approved** proved, esteemed **82 head and front** height and breadth, entire extent **83 Rude** unpolished **85 since . . . pith** i.e., since I was seven. **pith** strength, vigor **86 Till . . . wasted** until some nine months ago (since when Othello has evidently been not on active duty but in Venice) **87 dearest** most valuable **92 round** plain

Othello (Laurence Fishburne) and Cassio (Nathaniel Parker) stand in defense before the Duke.

What conjuration, and what mighty magic,
For such proceeding I am charged withal,
I won his daughter.

**BRABANTIO:** A maiden never bold;
Of spirit so still and quiet that her motion
Blushed at herself; and she, in spite of nature,
Of years, of country, credit, everything,
To fall in love with what she feared to look on!
It is a judgment maimed and most imperfect
That will confess perfection so could err
Against all rules of nature, and must be driven
To find out practices of cunning hell
Why this should be. I therefore vouch again
That with some mixtures powerful o'er the blood,
Or with some dram conjured to this effect,
He wrought upon her.

**DUKE:** To vouch this is no proof,
Without more wider and more overt test
Than these thin habits and poor likelihoods
Of modern seeming do prefer against him.

**FIRST SENATOR:** But Othello, speak.
Did you by indirect and forcèd courses
Subdue and poison this young maid's affections?
Or came it by request and such fair question
As soul to soul affordeth?

**OTHELLO:** I do beseech you,
Send for the lady to the Sagittary
And let her speak of me before her father.
If you do find me foul in her report,
The trust, the office I do hold of you
Not only take away, but let your sentence
Even fall upon my life.

**DUKE:** Fetch Desdemona hither.

**OTHELLO:** Ancient, conduct them. You best know
the place.
*[Exeunt* IAGO *and attendants.]*
And, till she come, as truly as to heaven
I do confess the vices of my blood,
So justly to your grave ears I'll present
How I did thrive in this fair lady's love,
And she in mine.

**DUKE:** Say it, Othello.

**OTHELLO:** Her father loved me, oft invited me,
Still questioned me the story of my life
From year to year—the battles, sieges, fortunes
That I have passed.
I ran it through, even from my boyish days
To th' very moment that he bade me tell it,
Wherein I spoke of most disastrous chances,
Of moving accidents by flood and field,
Of hairbreadth scapes i' th' imminent deadly breach,
Of being taken by the insolent foe
And sold to slavery, of my redemption thence,
And portance in my travel's history,
Wherein of antres vast and deserts idle,
Rough quarries, rocks, and hills whose heads touch
heaven,
It was my hint to speak—such was my process—
And of the Cannibals that each other eat,
The Anthropophagi, and men whose heads
Do grow beneath their shoulders. These things to
hear
Would Desdemona seriously incline;
But still the house affairs would draw her thence,
Which ever as she could with haste dispatch

**95 withal** with **97–98 her . . . herself** i.e., she blushed easily at herself. (*Motion* can suggest the impulse of the soul or of the emotions, or physical movement.) **99 years** i.e., difference in age. **credit** virtuous reputation **102 confess** concede (that) **104 practices** plots **105 vouch** assert **106 blood** passions **107 dram . . . effect** dose made by magical spells to have this effect **109 more wider** fuller. **test** testimony **110 habits** garments, i.e., appearances. **poor likelihoods** weak inferences **111 modern seeming** commonplace assumption. **prefer** bring forth **113 forcèd courses** means used against her will

**115 question** conversation **125 blood** passions, human nature **126 justly** truthfully, accurately **131 Still** continually **137 moving accidents** stirring happenings **138 imminent . . . breach** death-threatening gaps made in a fortification **141 portance** conduct **142 antres** caverns. **idle** barren, desolate **143 Rough quarries** rugged rock formations **144 hint** occasion, opportunity **146 Anthropophagi** man-eaters. (A term from Pliny's *Natural History*).

She'd come again, and with a greedy ear
Devour up my discourse. Which I, observing,
Took once a pliant hour, and found good means
To draw from her a prayer of earnest heart
That I would all my pilgrimage dilate,
Whereof by parcels she had something heard,
But not intentively. I did consent,
And often did beguile her of her tears,
When I did speak of some distressful stroke
That my youth suffered. My story being done,
She gave me for my pains a world of sighs.
She swore, in faith, 'twas strange, 'twas passing strange,
'Twas pitiful, 'twas wondrous pitiful.
She wished she had not heard it, yet she wished
That heaven had made her such a man. She thanked me,
And bade me, if I had a friend that loved her,
I should but teach him how to tell my story,
And that would woo her. Upon this hint I spake.
She loved me for the dangers I had passed,
And I loved her that she did pity them.
This only is the witchcraft I have used.
Here comes the lady. Let her witness it.

*Enter* DESDEMONA, IAGO, *[and] attendants.*

**DUKE:** I think this tale would win my daughter too.
Good Brabantio,
Take up this mangled matter at the best.
Men do their broken weapons rather use
Than their bare hands.

**BRABANTIO:** I pray you, hear her speak.
If she confess that she was half the wooer,
Destruction on my head if my bad blame
Light on the man!—Come hither, gentle mistress.
Do you perceive in all this noble company
Where most you owe obedience?

**DESDEMONA:** My noble Father,
I do perceive here a divided duty.
To you I am bound for life and education;
My life and education both do learn me
How to respect you. You are the lord of duty;
I am hitherto your daughter. But here's my husband,
And so much duty as my mother showed
To you, preferring you before her father,

Brabantio (Pierre Vaneck) bids Desdemona speak.

So much I challenge that I may profess
Due to the Moor my lord.

**BRABANTIO:** God be with you! I have done.
Please it Your Grace, on to the state affairs.
I had rather to adopt a child than get it.
Come hither, Moor. *[He joins the hands of* OTHELLO *and* DESDEMONA.*]*
I here do give thee that with all my heart
Which, but thou hast already, with all my heart
I would keep from thee.—For your sake, jewel,
I am glad at soul I have no other child,
For thy escape would teach me tyranny,
To hang clogs on them.—I have done, my lord.

**DUKE:** Let me speak like yourself, and lay a sentence
Which, as a grece or step, may help these lovers
Into your favor.
When remedies are past, the griefs are ended
By seeing the worst, which late on hopes depended.
To mourn a mischief that is past and gone
Is the next way to draw new mischief on.
What cannot be preserved when fortune takes,
Patience her injury a mockery makes.
The robbed that smiles steals something from the thief;
He robs himself that spends a bootless grief.

---

**153 pliant** well-suiting **155 dilate** relate in detail **156 by parcels** piecemeal **157 intentively** with full attention, continuously **162 passing** exceedingly **165 made her** created her to be **168 hint** opportunity. (Othello does not mean that she was dropping hints.) **175 Take . . . best** make the best of a bad bargain **184 education** upbringing **185 learn** teach **186 of duty** to whom duty is due

**190 challenge** claim **194 get** beget **196 with all my heart** wherein my whole affection has been engaged **197 with all my heart** willingly, gladly **198 For your sake** on your account **200 escape** elopement **201 clogs** (Literally, blocks of wood fastened to the legs of criminals or convicts to inhibit escape.) **202 like yourself** i.e., as you would, in your proper temper. **lay a sentence** apply a maxim **203 grece** step **205 remedies** hopes of remedy **206 which . . . depended** which griefs were sustained until recently by hopeful anticipation **207 mischief** misfortune, injury **208 next** nearest **209 What** whatever **210 Patience . . . makes** patience laughs at the injury inflicted by fortune (and thus eases the pain) **212 spends a bootless grief** indulges in unavailing grief

**BRABANTIO:** So let the Turk of Cyprus us beguile,
We lose it not, so long as we can smile.
He bears the sentence well that nothing bears
But the free comfort which from thence he hears,
But he bears both the sentence and the sorrow
That, to pay grief, must of poor patience borrow.
These sentences, to sugar or to gall,
Being strong on both sides, are equivocal.
But words are words. I never yet did hear
That the bruised heart was piercèd through the ear.
I humbly beseech you, proceed to th' affairs of state.

**DUKE:** The Turk with a most mighty preparation makes for Cyprus. Othello, the fortitude of the place is best known to you; and though we have there a substitute of most allowed sufficiency, yet opinion, a sovereign mistress of effects, throws a more safer voice on you. You must therefore be content to slubber the gloss of your new fortunes with this more stubborn and boisterous expedition.

**OTHELLO:** The tyrant custom, most grave senators,
Hath made the flinty and steel couch of war
My thrice-driven bed of down. I do agnize
A natural and prompt alacrity
I find in hardness, and do undertake
These present wars against the Ottomites.
Most humbly therefore bending to your state,
I crave fit disposition for my wife,
Due reference of place, and exhibition,
With such accommodation and besort
As levels with her breeding.

**DUKE:** Why, at her father's.

**BRABANTIO:** I will not have it so.

**OTHELLO:** Nor I.

**DESDEMONA:** Nor I. I would not there reside,
To put my father in impatient thoughts
By being in his eye. Most gracious Duke,
To my unfolding lend your prosperous ear,
And let me find a charter in your voice,
T' assist my simpleness.

**DUKE:** What would you, Desdemona?

**DESDEMONA:** That I did love the Moor to live with him,
My downright violence and storm of fortunes
May trumpet to the world. My heart's subdued
Even to the very quality of my lord.
I saw Othello's visage in his mind,
And to his honors and his valiant parts
Did I my soul and fortunes consecrate.
So that, dear lords, if I be left behind,
A moth of peace, and he go to the war,
The rites for why I love him are bereft me,
And I a heavy interim shall support
By his dear absence. Let me go with him.

**OTHELLO:** Let her have your voice.
Vouch with me, heaven, I therefor beg it not
To please the palate of my appetite,
Nor to comply with heat—the young affects
In me defunct—and proper satisfaction,
But to be free and bounteous to her mind.
And heaven defend your good souls that you think
I will your serious and great business scant
When she is with me. No, when light-winged toys
Of feathered Cupid seel with wanton dullness
My speculative and officed instruments,
That my disports corrupt and taint my business,
Let huswives make a skillet of my helm,
And all indign and base adversities
Make head against my estimation!

---

**215–218 He bears . . . borrow** a person well bears out your maxim who can enjoy its platitudinous comfort, free of all genuine sorrow, but anyone whose grief bankrupts his poor patience is left with your saying and his sorrow, too. (*Bears the sentence* also plays on the meaning "receives judicial sentence.") **219–220 These . . . equivocal** these fine maxims are equivocal, either sweet or bitter in their application **222 piercèd . . . ear** i.e., surgically lanced and cured by mere words of advice **225 fortitude** strength **227 substitute** deputy **227 allowed** acknowledged **227–229 opinion . . . on you** general opinion, an important determiner of affairs, chooses you as the best man **230 slubber** soil, sully **231 stubborn** harsh, rough **234 thrice-driven** thrice sifted, winnowed. **agnize** know in myself, acknowledge **236 hardness** hardship **238 bending . . . state** bowing or kneeling to your authority **240 reference . . . exhibition** provision of appropriate place to live and allowance of money **241 accommodation** suitable provision. **besort** attendance **242 levels** equals, suits. **breeding** social position, upbringing

---

**247 unfolding** explanation, proposal. **prosperous** propitious **248 charter** privilege, authorization **252 My . . . fortunes** my plain and total breach of social custom, taking my future by storm and disrupting my whole life. **253–254 My heart's . . . lord** my heart is brought wholly into accord with Othello's virtues; I love him for his virtues **256 parts** qualities **259 moth** i.e., one who consumes merely **260 rites** rites of love (with a suggestion, too, of "rights," sharing) **262 dear** (1) heartfelt (2) costly **263 voice** consent **266 heat** sexual passion. **young affects** passions of youth, desires **267 proper** personal **268 free** generous **269 defend** forbid. **think** should think **272 seel** i.e., make blind (as in falconry, by sewing up the eyes of the hawk during training) **273 speculative . . . instruments** eyes and other faculties used in the performance of duty **274 That** so that. **disports** sexual pastimes. **taint** impair **276 indign** unworthy, shameful **277 Make head** raise an army. **estimation** reputation

**DUKE:** Be it as you shall privately determine,
Either for her stay or going. Th' affair cries haste,
And speed must answer it.

**A SENATOR:** You must away tonight.

**DESDEMONA:** Tonight, my lord?

**DUKE:** This night.

**OTHELLO:** With all my heart.

**DUKE:** At nine i' the morning here we'll meet again.
Othello, leave some officer behind,
And he shall our commission bring to you,
With such things else of quality and respect
As doth import you.

**OTHELLO:** So please Your grace, my ancient;
A man he is of honesty and trust.
To his conveyance I assign my wife,
With what else needful Your Good Grace shall think
To be sent after me.

**DUKE:** Let it be so.
Good night to everyone. *[To* BRABANTIO.*]* And, noble signor,
If virtue no delighted beauty lack,
Your son-in-law is far more fair than black.

**FIRST SENATOR:** Adieu, brave Moor. Use Desdemona well.

**BRABANTIO:** Look to her, Moor, if thou hast eyes to see.
She has deceived her father, and may thee.

*Exeunt [*DUKE, BRABANTIO, CASSIO, SENATORS, *and officers].*

**OTHELLO:** My life upon her faith! Honest Iago,
My Desdemona must I leave to thee.
I prithee, let thy wife attend on her,
And bring them after in the best advantage.
Come, Desdemona. I have but an hour
Of love, of worldly matters and direction,
To spend with thee. We must obey the time.

*Exit [with* DESDEMONA*].*

**RODERIGO:** Iago—

**IAGO:** What sayst thou, noble heart?

**RODERIGO:** What will I do, think'st thou?

**285 of quality and respect** of importance and relevance **286 import** concern **292 delighted** capable of delighting **300 in . . . advantage** at the most favorable opportunity **302 direction** instructions **303 the time** the urgency of the present crisis

**IAGO:** Why, go to bed and sleep.

**RODERIGO:** I will incontinently drown myself.

**IAGO:** If thou dost, I shall never love thee after. Why, thou silly gentleman?

**RODERIGO:** It is silliness to live when to live is torment; and then have we a prescription to die when death is our physician.

**IAGO:** O villainous! I have looked upon the world for four times seven years, and, since I could distinguish betwixt a benefit and an injury, I never found man that knew how to love himself. Ere I would say I would drown myself for the love of a guinea hen, I would change my humanity with a baboon.

**RODERIGO:** What should I do? I confess it is my shame to be so fond, but it is not in my virtue to amend it.

**IAGO:** Virtue? A fig! 'Tis in ourselves that we are thus or thus. Our bodies are our gardens, to the which our wills are gardeners; so that if we will plant nettles or sow lettuce, set hyssop and weed up thyme, supply it with one gender of herbs or distract it with many, either to have it sterile with idleness or manured with industry—why, the power and corrigible authority of this lies in our wills. If the beam of our lives had not one scale of reason to poise another of sensuality, the blood and baseness of our natures would conduct us to most preposterous conclusions. But we have reason to cool our raging motions, our carnal stings, our unbitted lusts, whereof I take this that you call love to be a sect or scion.

**RODERIGO:** It cannot be.

**IAGO:** It is merely a lust of the blood and a permission of the will. Come, be a man. Drown thyself? Drown cats and blind puppies. I have professed me thy friend, and I confess me knit to thy deserving with cables of perdurable toughness. I could never better stead thee than now. Put money in thy purse. Fol-

**308 incontinently** immediately, without self-restraint **312 prescription** (1) right based on long-established custom (2) doctor's prescription **314 villainous** i.e., what perfect nonsense **318 guinea hen** (A slang term for a prostitute.) **321 fond** infatuated. **virtue** strength, nature **322 fig** (To give a fig is to thrust the thumb between the first and second fingers in a vulgar and insulting gesture.) **325 hyssop** a herb of the mint family **326 gender** kind. **distract it with** divide it among **327 idleness** want of cultivation **328 corrigible authority** power to correct **329 beam** balance **330 poise** counterbalance **331 blood** natural passions **333 motions** appetites **334 unbitted** unbridled, uncontrolled **335 sect or scion** cutting or offshoot **341 perdurable** very durable **342 stead** assist low thou the wars; defeat thy favor with an usurped beard. I say, put money in thy purse. It cannot be long that Desdemona should continue her love to the Moor—put money in thy purse—nor he his to her. It was a violent commencement in her, and thou shalt see an answerable sequestration—put but money in thy purse. These Moors are changeable in their wills—fill thy purse with money. The food that to him now is as luscious as locusts shall be to him shortly as bitter as coloquintida. She must change for youth; when she is sated with his body, she will find the error of her choice. She must have change, she must. Therefore put money in thy purse. If thou wilt needs damn thyself, do it a more delicate way than drowning. Make all the money thou canst. If sanctimony and a frail vow betwixt an erring barbarian and a supersubtle Venetian be not too hard for my wits and all the tribe of hell, thou shalt enjoy her. Therefore make money. A pox of drowning thyself! It is clean out of the way. Seek thou rather to be hanged in compassing thy joy than to be drowned and go without her.

**RODERIGO:** Wilt thou be fast to my hopes if I depend on the issue?

**IAGO:** Thou art sure of me. Go, make money. I have told thee often, and I retell thee again and again, I hate the Moor. My cause is hearted; thine hath no less reason. Let us be conjunctive in our revenge against him. If thou canst cuckold him, thou dost thyself a pleasure, me a sport. There are many events in the womb of time which will be delivered. Traverse, go, provide thy money. We will have more of this tomorrow. Adieu.

**RODERIGO:** Where shall we meet i' the morning?

**IAGO:** At my lodging.

**RODERIGO:** I'll be with thee betimes. *[He starts to leave.]*

**IAGO:** Go to, farewell.—Do you hear, Roderigo?

**RODERIGO:** What say you?

**IAGO:** No more of drowning, do you hear?

Iago (Kenneth Branagh) and Roderigo (Michael Maloney) discuss how to deal with Othello.

**RODERIGO:** I am changed

**IAGO:** Go to, farewell. Put money enough in your purse.

**RODERIGO:** I'll sell all my land. *Exit.*

**IAGO:** Thus do I ever make my fool my purse;
For I mine own gained knowledge should profane
If I would time expend with such a snipe
But for my sport and profit. I hate the Moor;
And it is thought abroad that twixt my sheets
He's done my office. I know not if 't be true;
But I, for mere suspicion in that kind,
Will do as if for surety. He holds me well;
The better shall my purpose work on him.
Cassio's a proper man. Let me see now:
To get his place and to plume up my will
In double knavery—How, how?—Let's see:
After some time, to abuse Othello's ear
That he is too familiar with his wife.
He hath a person and a smooth dispose
To be suspected, framed to make women false.
The Moor is of a free and open nature,
That thinks men honest that but seem to be so,
And will as tenderly be led by the nose
As asses are.

---

**343 defeat thy favor** disguise your face. **usurped** (The suggestion is that Roderigo is not man enough to have a beard of his own.) **348 an answerable sequestration** a corresponding separation or estrangement **349 wills** carnal appetites **351 locusts** fruit of the carob tree (see Matthew 3:4), or perhaps honeysuckle **352 coloquintida** colocynth or bitter apple, a purgative **356 Make** raise, collect **357 sanctimony** sacred ceremony **358 erring** wandering, vagabond, unsteady **361 clean . . . way** entirely unsuitable as a course of action **362 compassing** encompassing, embracing **364 fast** true **365 issue** (successful) outcome **368 hearted** fixed in the heart, heartfelt **369 conjuctive** united **372 Traverse** (A military marching term.) **376 betimes** early

---

**386 snipe** woodcock, i.e., fool **388 it is thought abroad** it is rumored **389 my office** i.e., my sexual function as husband **391 do . . . surety** act as if on certain knowledge. **holds me well** regards me favorably **393 proper** handsome **394 plume up** put a feather in the cap of, i.e., glorify, gratify **396 abuse** deceive **397 he** i.e., Cassio **398 dispose** disposition **400 free** frank, generous **open** unsuspicious **402 tenderly** readily

I have 't. It is engendered. Hell and night
Must bring this monstrous birth to the world's light.
*[Exit.]*

**2.1** *Enter* MONTANO *and two* GENTLEMEN.

**MONTANO:** What from the cape can you discern at sea?

**FIRST GENTLEMAN:** Nothing at all. It is a high-wrought flood.
I cannot, twixt the heaven and the main,
Descry a sail.

**MONTANO:** Methinks the wind hath spoke aloud at land;
A fuller blast ne'er shook our battlements.
If it hath ruffianed so upon the sea,
What ribs of oak, when mountains melt on them,
Can hold the mortise? What shall we hear of this?

**SECOND GENTLEMAN:** A segregation of the Turkish fleet.
For do but stand upon the foaming shore,
The chidden billow seems to pelt the clouds;
The wind-shaked surge, with high and monstrous mane,
Seems to cast water on the burning Bear
And quench the guards of th' ever-fixèd pole.
I never did like molestation view
On the enchafèd flood.

**MONTANO:** If that the Turkish fleet
Be not ensheltered and embayed, they are drowned;
It is impossible to bear it out.

*Enter a* [THIRD] GENTLEMAN.

**THIRD GENTLEMAN:** News, lads! Our wars are done.
The desperate tempest hath so banged the Turks
That their designment halts. A noble ship of Venice
Hath seen a grievous wreck and sufferance
On most part of their fleet.

**MONTANO:** How? Is this true?

**THIRD GENTLEMAN:** The ship is here put in,
A Veronesa; Michael Cassio,
Lieutenant to the warlike Moor Othello,
Is come on shore; the Moor himself at sea,
And is in full commission here for Cyprus.

**MONTANO:** I am glad on 't. 'Tis a worthy governor.

**THIRD GENTLEMAN:** But this same Cassio, though he speak of comfort
Touching the Turkish loss, yet he looks sadly
And prays the Moor be safe, for they were parted
With foul and violent tempest.

**MONTANO:** Pray heaven he be,
For I have served him, and the man commands
Like a full soldier. Let's to the seaside, ho!
As well to see the vessel that's come in
As to throw out our eyes for brave Othello,
Even till we make the main and th' aerial blue
An indistinct regard.

**THIRD GENTLEMAN:** Come, let's do so,
For every minute is expectancy
Of more arrivance.

The men return home from overseas.

---

**2.1. Location: A seaport in Cyprus. An open place near the quay.** **2 high-wrought flood** very agitated sea **3 main** ocean (also at line 41) **7 ruffianed** raged **8 mountains** i.e., of water **9 hold the mortise** hold their joints together. (A *mortise* is the socket hollowed out in fitting timbers.) **10 segregation** dispersal **12 chidden** i.e., rebuked, repelled (by the shore), and thus shot into the air **13 monstrous mane** (The surf is like the mane of a wild beast.) **14 the burning Bear** i.e., the constellation Ursa Minor or the Little Bear, which includes the polestar (and hence regarded as the *guards of th' ever-fixèd pole* in the next line; sometimes the term *guards* is applied to the two "pointers" of the Big Bear or Dipper, which may be intended here.) **16 like molestation** comparable disturbance **17 enchafèd** angry **18 If that** if **19 embayed** sheltered by a bay **20 bear it out** survive, weather the storm **23 designment** design, enterprise. **halts** is lame

**24 wreck** shipwreck. **sufferance** damage, disaster **28 Veronesa** i.e., fitted out in Verona for Venetian service, or possibly *Verennessa* (the Folio spelling), i.e., *verrinessa,* a cutter (from *verrinare,* "to cut through") **34 sadly** gravely **38 full** perfect **41 the main . . . blue** the sea and the sky **42 An indistinct regard** indistinguishable in our view **43 is expectancy** gives expectation **44 arrivance** arrival

*Enter* CASSIO.

**CASSIO:** Thanks, you the valiant of the warlike isle,
That so approve the Moor! O, let the heavens
Give him defense against the elements,
For I have lost him on a dangerous sea.

**MONTANO:** Is he well shipped?

**CASSIO:** His bark is stoutly timbered, and his pilot
Of very expert and approved allowance;
Therefore my hopes, not surfeited to death,
Stand in bold cure.

*[A cry] within:* "A sail, a sail, a sail!"

**CASSIO:** What noise?

**A GENTLEMAN:** The town is empty. On the brow o' the sea
Stand ranks of people, and they cry, "A sail!"

**CASSIO:** My hopes do shape him for the governor.

*[A shot within.]*

**SECOND GENTLEMAN:** They do discharge their shot of courtesy;
Our friends at least.

**CASSIO:** I pray you, sir, go forth,
And give us truth who 'tis that is arrived.

**SECOND GENTLEMAN:** I shall. *Exit.*

**MONTANO:** But, good Lieutenant, is your general wived?

**CASSIO:** Most fortunately. He hath achieved a maid
That paragons description and wild fame,
One that excels the quirks of blazoning pens,
And in th' essential vesture of creation
Does tire the enginer.

*Enter [*SECOND*]* GENTLEMAN.

How now? Who has put in?

**SECOND GENTLEMAN:** 'Tis one Iago, ancient to the General.

**CASSIO:** He's had most favorable and happy speed.
Tempests themselves, high seas, and howling winds,
The guttered rocks and congregated sands—
Traitors ensteeped to clog the guiltless keel—
As having sense of beauty, do omit
Their mortal natures, letting go safely by
The divine Desdemona.

**MONTANO:** What is she?

**CASSIO:** She that I spake of, our great captain's captain,
Left in the conduct of the bold Iago,
Whose footing here anticipates our thoughts
A sennight's speed. Great Jove, Othello guard,
And swell his sail with thine own powerful breath,
That he may bless this bay with his tall ship,
Make love's quick pants in Desdemona's arms,
Give renewed fire to our extincted spirits,
And bring all Cyprus comfort!

*Enter* DESDEMONA, IAGO, RODERIGO, *and* EMILIA.

O, behold!
The riches of the ship is come on shore!
You men of Cyprus, let her have your knees.

*[The* GENTLEMEN *make curtsy to* DESDEMONA.*]*

Hail to thee, lady! And the grace of heaven
Before, behind thee, and on every hand
Enwheel thee round!

**DESDEMONA:** I thank you, valiant Cassio.
What tidings can you tell me of my lord?

**CASSIO:** He is not yet arrived, nor know I aught
But that he's well and will be shortly here.

**DESDEMONA:** O, but I fear—How lost you company?

**CASSIO:** The great contention of sea and skies
Parted our fellowship.

*(Within)* "A sail, a sail!" *[A shot.]*

But hark. A sail!

**SECOND GENTLEMAN:** They give their greeting to the citadel.
This likewise is a friend.

**CASSIO:** See for the news.

*[Exit* SECOND GENTLEMAN.*]*

---

**46 approve** admire, honor **51 approved allowance** tested reputation **52 surfeited to death** i.e., overextended, worn thin through repeated application or delayed fulfillment **53 in bold cure** in strong hopes of fulfillment **55 brow o' the sea** cliff-edge **57 My . . . for** I hope it is **58 discharge . . . courtesy** fire a salute in token of respect and courtesy **64 paragons** surpasses. **wild fame** extravagant report **65 quirks** witty conceits. **blazoning** setting forth as though in heraldic language **66–67 in . . . enginer** in her real, God-given, beauty, (she) defeats any attempt to praise her. **enginer** engineer, i.e., poet, one who devises. **s.d. Second Gentleman** (So identified in the Quarto text here and in lines 58, 61, 68, and 96; the Folio calls him a gentleman.) **67 put in** i.e., to harbor

**71 guttered** jagged, trenched **72 ensteeped** lying under water **73 As** as if. **omit** forbear to exercise **74 mortal** deadly **78 footing** landing **79 sennight's** week's **81 tall** splendid, gallant

Good Ancient, you are welcome. *[Kissing* EMILIA.]
Welcome, mistress.
Let it not gall your patience, good Iago,
That I extend my manners; 'tis my breeding
That gives me this bold show of courtesy.

**IAGO:** Sir, would she give you so much of her lips
As of her tongue she oft bestows on me,
You would have enough.

**DESDEMONA:** Alas, she has no speech!

**IAGO:** In faith, too much.
I find it still, when I have list to sleep.
Marry, before your ladyship, I grant,
She puts her tongue a little in her heart
And chides with thinking.

**EMILIA:** You have little cause to say so.

**IAGO:** Come on, come on. You are pictures out of doors,
Bells in your parlors, wildcats in your kitchens,
Saints in your injuries, devils being offended,
Players in your huswifery, and huswives in your beds.

**DESDEMONA:** O, fie upon thee, slanderer!

**IAGO:** Nay, it is true, or else I am a Turk.
You rise to play, and go to bed to work.

**EMILIA:** You shall not write my praise.

**IAGO:** No, let me not.

**DESDEMONA:** What wouldst write of me, if thou shouldst praise me?

**IAGO:** O gentle lady, do not put me to 't,
For I am nothing if not critical.

**DESDEMONA:** Come on, essay.—There's one gone to the harbor?

**IAGO:** Ay, madam.

**DESDEMONA:** I am not merry, but I do beguile
The thing I am by seeming otherwise.
Come, how wouldst thou praise me?

**IAGO:** I am about it, but indeed my invention
Comes from my pate as birdlime does from frieze—
It plucks out brains and all. But my Muse labors,
And thus she is delivered:
If she be fair and wise, fairness and wit,
The one's for use, the other useth it.

**DESDEMONA:** Well praised! How if she be black and witty?

**IAGO:** If she be black, and thereto have a wit,
She'll find a white that shall her blackness fit.

**DESDEMONA:** Worse and worse.

**EMILIA:** How if fair and foolish?

**IAGO:** She never yet was foolish that was fair,
For even her folly helped her to an heir.

**DESDEMONA:** Those are old fond paradoxes to make fools laugh i' th' alehouse. What miserable praise hast thou for her that's foul and foolish?

**IAGO:** There's none so foul and foolish thereunto,
But does foul pranks which fair and wise ones do.

**DESDEMONA:** O heavy ignorance! Thou praisest the worst best. But what praise couldst thou bestow on a deserving woman indeed, one that, in the authority of her merit, did justly put on the vouch of very malice itself?

**IAGO:** She that was ever fair, and never proud,
Had tongue at will, and yet was never loud,
Never lacked gold and yet went never gay,
Fled from her wish, and yet said, "Now I may,"
She that being angered, her revenge being nigh,
Bade her wrong stay and her displeasure fly,
She that in wisdom never was so frail
To change the cod's head for the salmon's tail,
She that could think and ne'er disclose her mind,
See suitors following and not look behind,
She was a wight, if ever such wight were—

---

**100 extend** give scope to. **breeding** training in the niceties of etiquette **105 she has no speech** i.e., she's not a chatterbox, as you allege **107 still** always **list** desire **110 with thinking** i.e., in her thoughts only **111 pictures out of doors** i.e., silent and well-behaved in public **112 Bells** i.e., jangling, noisy, and brazen. **in your kitchens** i.e., in domestic affairs. (Ladies would not do the cooking.) **113 Saints** martyrs **114 Players** idlers, triflers, or deceivers. **huswifery** housekeeping. **huswives** hussies (i.e., women are "busy" in bed, or unduly thrifty in dispensing sexual favors) **116 a Turk** an infidel, not to be believed **121 critical** censorious **122 essay** try **125 The thing I am** i.e., my anxious self

**128 birdlime** sticky substance used to catch small birds. **frieze** coarse woolen cloth **129 labors** (1) exerts herself (2) prepares to deliver a child (with a following pun on *delivered* in line 130) **132 The one's . . . it** i.e., her cleverness will make use of her beauty **133 black** dark-complexioned, brunette **135 a white** a fair person (with wordplay on "wight," a person). **fit** (with sexual suggestion of mating) **138 folly** (with added meaning of "lechery, wantonness"). **to an heir** i.e., to bear a child **139 fond** foolish **141 foul** ugly **142 thereunto** in addition **143 foul** sluttish **147 put . . . vouch** compel the approval **151 gay** extravagantly clothed **152 Fled . . . may** avoided temptation where the choice was hers **154 Bade . . . stay** i.e., resolved to put up with her injury patiently **156 To . . . tail** i.e., to exchange a lackluster husband for a sexy lover (?) (*Cod's head* is slang for "penis," and *tail* for "pudendum.")

**DESDEMONA:** To do what?

**IAGO:** To suckle fools and chronicle small beer.

**DESDEMONA:** O most lame and impotent conclusion! Do not learn of him, Emilia, though he be thy husband. How say you, Cassio? Is he not a most profane and liberal counselor?

**CASSIO:** He speaks home, madam. You may relish him more in the soldier than in the scholar.

*[*CASSIO *and* DESDEMONA *stand together, conversing intimately.]*

**IAGO** *[aside]*: He takes her by the palm. Ay, well said, whisper. With as little a web as this will I ensnare as great a fly as Cassio. Ay, smile upon her, do; I will gyve thee in thine own courtship. You say true; 'tis so, indeed. If such tricks as these strip you out of your lieutenantry, it had been better you had not kissed your three fingers so oft, which now again you are most apt to play the sir in. Very good; well kissed! An excellent courtesy! 'Tis so, indeed. Yet again your fingers to your lips? Would they were clyster pipes for your sake! *[Trumpet within.]* The Moor! I know his trumpet.

**CASSIO:** 'Tis truly so.

**DESDEMONA:** Let's meet him and receive him.

**CASSIO:** Lo, where he comes!

*Enter* OTHELLO *and attendants.*

**OTHELLO:** O my fair warrior!

**DESDEMONA:** My dear Othello!

**OTHELLO:** It gives me wonder great as my content
To see you here before me. O my soul's joy,
If after every tempest come such calms,
May the winds blow till they have wakened death,
And let the laboring bark climb hills of seas
Olympus-high, and duck again as low
As hell's from heaven! If it were now to die,
'Twere now to be most happy, for I fear
My soul hath her content so absolute
That not another comfort like to this
Succeeds in unknown fate.

**161 suckle fools** breastfeed babies. **chronicle small beer** i.e., keep petty household accounts, keep track of trivial matters **164 profane** irreverent, ribald **165 liberal** licentious, free-spoken **166 home** right to the target. (A term from fencing.) **relish** appreciate **167 in** in the character of **168 well said** well done **170 gyve** fetter, shackle **171 courtship** courtesy, show of courtly manners. **You say true** i.e., that's right, go ahead **175 the sir** i.e., the fine gentleman **177 clyster pipes** tubes used for enemas and douches **192 Succeeds . . . fate** i.e., can follow in the unknown future

Othello greets his bride, Desdemona (Irène Jacob).

**DESDEMONA:** The heavens forbid
But that our loves and comforts should increase
Even as our days do grow!

**OTHELLO:** Amen to that, sweet powers!
I cannot speak enough of this content.
It stops me here; it is too much of joy.
And this, and this, the greatest discords be
*[They kiss.]*
That e'er our hearts shall make!

**IAGO** *[aside]*: O, you are well tuned now!
But I'll set down the pegs that make this music,
As honest as I am.

**OTHELLO:** Come, let us to the castle.
News, friends! Our wars are done, the Turks are drowned.
How does my old acquaintance of this isle?—
Honey, you shall be well desired in Cyprus;
I have found great love amongst them. O my sweet,
I prattle out of fashion, and I dote
In mine own comforts.—I prithee, good Iago,
Go to the bay and disembark my coffers.
Bring thou the master to the citadel;
He is a good one, and his worthiness
Does challenge much respect.—Come, Desdemona.—
Once more, well met at Cyprus!

*Exeunt* OTHELLO *and* DESDEMONA *[and all but* IAGO *and* RODERIGO*].*

**198 s.d. They kiss** (The direction is from the Quarto.) **201 set down** loosen (and hence untune the instrument) **202 As . . . I am** for all my supposed honesty **206 desired** welcomed **208 out of fashion** irrelevantly, incoherently (?) **210 coffers** chests, baggage **211 master** ship's captain **213 challenge** lay claim to, deserve

Iago watches from a distance as Othello makes his triumphant entry.

**IAGO** *[to an attendant]*: Do thou meet me presently at the harbor. *[To* RODERIGO.*]* Come hither. If thou be'st valiant—as, they say, base men being in love have then a nobility in their natures more than is native to them—list me. The Lieutenant tonight watches on the court of guard. First, I must tell thee this: Desdemona is directly in love with him.

**RODERIGO:** With him? Why, 'tis not possible.

**IAGO:** Lay thy finger thus, and let thy soul be instructed. Mark me with what violence she first loved the Moor, but for bragging and telling her fantastical lies. To love him still for prating? Let not thy discreet heart think it. Her eye must be fed; and what delight shall she have to look on the devil? When the blood is made dull with the act of sport, there should be, again to inflame it and to give satiety a fresh appetite, loveliness in favor, sympathy in years, manners, and beauties—all which the Moor is defective in. Now, for want of these required conveniences, her delicate tenderness will find itself abused, begin to heave the gorge, disrelish and abhor the Moor. Very nature will instruct her in it and compel her to some second choice. Now, sir, this granted—as it is a most pregnant and unforced position—who stands so eminent in the degree of this fortune as Cassio does? A knave very voluble, no further conscionable than in putting on the mere form of civil and humane seeming for the better compassing of his salt and most hidden loose affection. Why, none, why, none. A slipper and subtle knave, a finder out of occasions, that has an eye can stamp and counterfeit advantages, though true advantage never present itself; a devilish knave. Besides, the knave is handsome, young, and hath all those requisites in him that folly and green minds look after. A pestilent complete knave, and the woman hath found him already.

**RODERIGO:** I cannot believe that in her. She's full of most blessed condition.

**IAGO:** Blessed fig's end! The wine she drinks is made of grapes. If she had been blessed, she would never have loved the Moor. Blessed pudding! Didst thou not see her paddle with the palm of his hand? Didst not mark that?

**RODERIGO:** Yes, that I did; but that was but courtesy.

**IAGO:** Lechery, by this hand. An index and obscure prologue to the history of lust and foul thoughts. They met so near with their lips that their breaths embraced together. Villainous thoughts, Roderigo! When these mutualities so marshal the way, hard at hand comes the master and main exercise, th' incorporate conclusion. Pish! But, sir, be you ruled by me. I have brought you from Venice. Watch you tonight; for the command, I'll lay 't upon you. Cassio knows you not. I'll not be far from you. Do you find some occasion to anger Cassio, either by speaking too loud, or tainting his discipline, or from what other course you please, which the time shall more favorably minister.

**RODERIGO:** Well.

**IAGO:** Sir, he's rash and very sudden in choler, and haply may strike at you. Provoke him that he may, for even out of that will I cause these of Cyprus to

---

**217 base men** even lowly born men **219 list** listen to **220 court of guard** guardhouse. (Cassio is in charge of the watch.) **223 thus** i.e., on your lips **225 but** only **229 the act of sport** sex **231 favor** appearance. **sympathy** correspondence, similarity **233 required conveniences** things conducive to sexual compatibility **234 abused** cheated, revolted. **235 heave the gorge** experience nausea **235–236 Very nature** her very instincts **238 pregnant** evident, cogent **239 in . . . of** as next in line for

**240 voluble** facile, glib. **conscionable** conscientious, conscience-bound **241 humane** polite, courteous **242 salt** licentious **243 affection** passion **243–244 slipper** slippery **245 an eye can stamp** an eye that can coin, create. **advantages** favorable opportunities **248 folly** wantonness. **green** immature **250 found him** sized him up, perceived his intent **252 condition** disposition **253 fig's end** (See 1.3.322 for the vulgar gesture of the fig.) **255 pudding** sausage **259 index** table of contents. **obsure** (i.e., the *lust and foul thoughts,* line 260, are secret, hidden from view) **263 mutualities** exchanges, intimacies **263–264 hard at hand** closely following. **264–265 incorporate** carnal **266 Watch you** stand watch **267 for the command . . . you** I'll arrange for you to be appointed, given orders **270 tainting** disparaging **271 minister** provide **273 choler** wrath **274 haply** perhaps mutiny, whose qualification shall come into no true taste again but by the displanting of Cassio. So shall you have a shorter journey to your desires by the means I shall then have to prefer them, and the impediment most profitably removed, without the which there were no expectation of our prosperity.

**RODERIGO:** I will do this, if you can bring it to any opportunity.

**IAGO:** I warrant thee. Meet me by and by at the citadel. I must fetch his necessaries ashore. Farewell.

**RODERIGO:** Adieu. *Exit.*

**IAGO:** That Cassio loves her, I do well believe 't;
That she loves him, 'tis apt and of great credit.
The Moor, howbeit that I endure him not,
Is of a constant, loving, noble nature,
And I dare think he'll prove to Desdemona
A most dear husband. Now, I do love her too,
Not out of absolute lust—though peradventure
I stand accountant for as great a sin—
But partly led to diet my revenge
For that I do suspect the lusty Moor
Hath leaped into my seat, the thought whereof
Doth, like a poisonous mineral, gnaw my innards;
And nothing can or shall content my soul
Till I am evened with him, wife for wife,
Or failing so, yet that I put the Moor
At least into a jealousy so strong
That judgment cannot cure. Which thing to do,
If this poor trash of Venice, whom I trace
For his quick hunting, stand the putting on,
I'll have our Michael Cassio on the hip,
Abuse him to the Moor in the rank garb—
For I fear Cassio with my nightcap too—
Make the Moor thank me, love me, and reward me
For making him egregiously an ass
And practicing upon his peace and quiet
Even to madness. 'Tis here, but yet confused.
Knavery's plain face is never seen till used. *Exit.*

**276 mutiny** riot. **qualification** appeasement **276–277 true taste** i.e., acceptable state **279 prefer** advance **284 warrant** assure. **by and by** immediately **288 apt** probable. **credit** credibility **294 accountant** accountable **295 diet** feed **304 trace** i.e., train, or follow (?), or perhaps *trash,* a hunting term, meaning to put weights on a hunting dog in order to slow him down **305 For** to make more eager. **stand . . . on** respond properly when I incite him to quarrel **306 on the hip** at my mercy, where I can throw him. (A wrestling term.) **307 Abuse** slander. **rank garb** coarse manner, gross fashion **308 with my nightcap** i.e., as a rival in my bed, as one who gives me cuckold's horns **311 practicing upon** plotting against

## 2.2 *Enter* OTHELLO's HERALD *with a proclamation.*

**HERALD:** It is Othello's pleasure, our noble and valiant general, that, upon certain tidings now arrived, importing the mere perdition of the Turkish fleet, every man put himself into triumph: some to dance, some to make bonfires, each man to what sport and revels his addiction leads him. For, besides these beneficial news, it is the celebration of his nuptial. So much was his pleasure should be proclaimed. All offices are open, and there is full liberty of feasting from this present hour of five till the bell have told eleven. Heaven bless the isle of Cyprus and our noble general Othello!

*Exit.*

## 2.3 *Enter* OTHELLO, DESDEMONA, CASSIO, *and attendants.*

**OTHELLO:** Good Michael, look you to the guard
tonight.
Let's teach ourselves that honorable stop
Not to outsport discretion.

**CASSIO:** Iago hath direction what to do,
But notwithstanding, with my personal eye
Will I look to 't.

**OTHELLO:** Iago is most honest.
Michael, good night. Tomorrow with your earliest
Let me have speech with you. *[To* DESDEMONA.*]*
Come, my dear love,
The purchase made, the fruits are to ensue;
That profit's yet to come 'tween me and you.—
Good night.

*Exit [*OTHELLO, *with* DESDEMONA *and attendants].*

*Enter* IAGO.

**CASSIO:** Welcome, Iago. We must to the watch.

**IAGO:** Not this hour, Lieutenant; 'tis not yet ten o' the clock. Our general cast us thus early for the love of his Desdemona; who let us not therefore blame. He hath not yet made wanton the night with her, and she is sport for Jove.

**2.2. Location: Cyprus. A street.**
**3 mere perdition** complete destruction **4 triumph** public celebration **6 addiction** inclination **8 offices** rooms where food and drink are kept

**2.3. Location: Cyprus. The citadel.**
**2 stop** restraint **3 outsport** celebrate beyond the bounds of **7 with your earliest** at your earliest convenience **9–10 The purchase . . . you** i.e., though married, we haven't yet consummated our love **13 Not this hour** not for an hour yet **14 cast** dismissed **15 who** i.e., Othello

**CASSIO:** She's a most exquisite lady.

**IAGO:** And, I'll warrant her, full of game.

**CASSIO:** Indeed, she's a most fresh and delicate creature.

**IAGO:** What an eye she has! Methinks it sounds a parley to provocation.

**CASSIO:** An inviting eye, and yet methinks right modest.

**IAGO:** And when she speaks, is it not an alarum to love?

**CASSIO:** She is indeed perfection.

**IAGO:** Well, happiness to their sheets! Come, Lieutenant, I have a stoup of wine, and here without are a brace of Cyprus gallants that would fain have a measure to the health of black Othello.

**CASSIO:** Not tonight, good Iago. I have very poor and unhappy brains for drinking. I could well wish courtesy would invent some other custom of entertainment.

**IAGO:** O, they are our friends. But one cup! I'll drink for you.

**CASSIO:** I have drunk but one cup tonight, and that was craftily qualified too, and behold what innovation it makes here. I am unfortunate in the infirmity and dare not task my weakness with any more.

**IAGO:** What, man? 'Tis a night of revels. The gallants desire it.

**CASSIO:** Where are they?

**IAGO:** Here at the door. I pray you, call them in.

**CASSIO:** I'll do 't, but it dislikes me. *Exit.*

**IAGO:** If I can fasten but one cup upon him,
With that which he hath drunk tonight already,
He'll be as full of quarrel and offense
As my young mistress' dog. Now, my sick fool Roderigo,
Whom love hath turned almost the wrong side out,
To Desdemona hath tonight caroused
Potations pottle-deep; and he's to watch.
Three lads of Cyprus—noble swelling spirits,
That hold their honors in a wary distance,
The very elements of this warlike isle—
Have I tonight flustered with flowing cups,
And they watch too. Now, 'mongst this flock of drunkards
Am I to put our Cassio in some action
That may offend the isle.—But here they come.

*Enter* CASSIO, MONTANO, *and* GENTLEMEN; *[servants following with wine].*

If consequence do but approve my dream,
My boat sails freely both with wind and stream.

**CASSIO:** 'Fore God, they have given me a rouse already.

**MONTANO:** Good faith, a little one; not past a pint, as I am a soldier.

**IAGO:** Some wine, ho!

*[He sings.]* "And let me the cannikin clink, clink,
And let me the cannikin clink.
A soldier's a man,
O, man's life's but a span;
Why, then, let a soldier drink."

Some wine, boys!

**CASSIO:** 'Fore God, an excellent song.

**IAGO:** I learned it in England, where indeed they are most potent in potting. Your Dane, your German, and your swag-bellied Hollander—drink, ho!—are nothing to your English.

**CASSIO:** Is your Englishman so exquisite in his drinking?

**IAGO:** Why, he drinks you, with facility, your Dane dead drunk; he sweats not to overthrow your Almain; he gives your Hollander a vomit ere the next pottle can be filled.

---

**21 sounds a parley** calls for a conference, issues an invitation **24 alarum** signal calling men to arms (continuing the military metaphor of *parley,* line 21) **27 stoup** measure of liquor, two quarts. **without** outside. **brace** pair **28–29 fain have a measure** gladly drink a toast **35 for you** in your place. (Iago will do the steady drinking to keep the gallants company while Cassio has only one cup.) **37 qualified** diluted. **37–38 innovation** disturbance, insurrection **38 here** i.e., in my head **44 it dislikes me** i.e., I'm reluctant **47 offense** readiness to take offense

**50 caroused** drunk off **51 pottle-deep** to the bottom of the tankard. **watch** stand watch **52 swelling** proud **53 hold . . . distance** i.e., are extremely sensitive of their honor **54 very elements** typical sort **56 watch** are members of the guard **59 If . . . dream** if subsequent events will only substantiate my scheme **60 stream** current **61 rouse** full draft of liquor **65 cannikin** small drinking vessel **68 span** brief span of time. (Compare Psalms 39:5 as rendered in the Book of Common Prayer: "Thou hast made my days as it were a span long.") **73 potting** drinking **77 drinks you** drinks. **your Dane** your typical Dane **78 sweats not** i.e., need not exert himself. **Almain** German

Iago deludes the drunken Cassio.

**CASSIO:** To the health of our general!

**MONTANO:** I am for it, Lieutenant, and I'll do you justice.

**IAGO:** O sweet England! *[He sings.]*

"King Stephen was and-a worthy peer,
His breeches cost him but a crown;
He held them sixpence all too dear,
With that he called the tailor lown.

He was a wight of high renown,
And thou art but of low degree.
'Tis pride that pulls the country down;
Then take thy auld cloak about thee."

Some wine, ho!

**CASSIO:** 'Fore God, this is a more exquisite song than the other.

**IAGO:** Will you hear 't again?

**CASSIO:** No, for I hold him to be unworthy of his place that does those things. Well, God's above all; and there be souls must be saved, and there be souls must not be saved.

**IAGO:** It's true, good Lieutenant.

**CASSIO:** For mine own part—no offense to the General, nor any man of quality—I hope to be saved.

**IAGO:** And so do I too, Lieutenant.

**CASSIO:** Ay, but, by your leave, not before me; the lieutenant is to be saved before the ancient. Let's have no more of this; let's to our affairs.—God forgive us our sins!—Gentlemen, let's look to our business. Do not think, gentlemen, I am drunk. This is my ancient; this is my right hand, and this is my left. I am not drunk now. I can stand well enough, and speak well enough.

**GENTLEMEN:** Excellent well.

**CASSIO:** Why, very well then; you must not think then that I am drunk. *Exit.*

**MONTANO:** To th' platform, masters. Come, let's set the watch.

*[Exeunt* GENTLEMEN.*]*

**IAGO:** You see this fellow that is gone before.
He's a soldier fit to stand by Caesar
And give direction; and do but see his vice.
'Tis to his virtue a just equinox,
The one as long as th' other. 'Tis pity of him.
I fear the trust Othello puts him in,
On some odd time of his infirmity,
Will shake this island.

**MONTANO:** But is he often thus?

**IAGO:** 'Tis evermore the prologue to his sleep.
He'll watch the horologe a double set,
If drink rock not his cradle.

**MONTANO:** It were well
The General were put in mind of it.
Perhaps he sees it not, or his good nature
Prizes the virtue that appears in Cassio
And looks not on his evils. Is not this true?

*Enter* RODERIGO.

**IAGO** *[aside to him]*: How now, Roderigo?
I pray you, after the Lieutenant; go. *[Exit* RODERIGO.*]*

**MONTANO:** And 'tis great pity that the noble Moor
Should hazard such a place as his own second
With one of an engraffed infirmity.
It were an honest action to say so
To the Moor.

**IAGO:** Not I, for this fair island.
I do love Cassio well and would do much
To cure him of this evil. *[Cry within:* "Help! Help!"*]*
But, hark! What noise?

**82 I'll . . . justice** i.e., I'll drink as much as you **87 lown** lout, rascal **90 pride** i.e., extravagance in dress. **91 auld** old **102 quality** rank

**114 set the watch** mount the guard **118 just equinox** exact counterpart. (*Equinox* is an equal length of days and nights.) **124 watch . . . set** stay awake twice around the clock or *horologe* **133–134 hazard . . . With** risk giving such an important position as his second in command to **134 engraffed** engrafted, inveterate

*Enter* CASSIO, *pursuing* RODERIGO.

**CASSIO:** Zounds, you rogue! You rascal!

**MONTANO:** What's the matter, Lieutenant?

**CASSIO:** A knave teach me my duty? I'll beat the knave into a twiggen bottle.

**RODERIGO:** Beat me?

**CASSIO:** Dost thou prate, rogue? *[He strikes* RODERIGO.*]*

**MONTANO:** Nay, good Lieutenant. *[Restraining him.]*
I pray you, sir, hold your hand.

**CASSIO:** Let me go, sir, or I'll knock you o'er the mazzard.

**MONTANO:** Come, come, you're drunk.

**CASSIO:** Drunk? *[They fight.]*

**IAGO:** *[aside to* RODERIGO*]:* Away, I say. Go out and cry a mutiny.

*[Exit* RODERIGO.*]*

Nay, good Lieutenant.—God's will, gentlemen—
Help, ho!—Lieutenant—sir—Montano—sir—
Help, masters!—Here's a goodly watch indeed!

*[A bell rings.]*

Who's that which rings the bell?—Diablo, ho!
The town will rise. God's will, Lieutenant, hold!
You'll be ashamed forever.

*Enter* OTHELLO *and attendants [with weapons].*

**OTHELLO:** What is the matter here?

**MONTANO:** Zounds, I bleed still.
I am hurt to th' death. He dies! *[He thrusts at* CASSIO.*]*

**OTHELLO:** Hold, for your lives!

**IAGO:** Hold, ho! Lieutenant—sir—Montano—gentlemen—
Have you forgot all sense of place and duty?
Hold! The General speaks to you. Hold, for shame!

**OTHELLO:** Why, how now, ho? From whence ariseth this?
Are we turned Turks, and to ourselves do that
Which heaven hath forbid the Ottomites?
For Christian shame, put by this barbarous brawl!
He that stirs next to carve for his own rage
Holds his soul light; he dies upon his motion.
Silence that dreadful bell. It frights the isle
From her propriety. What is the matter, masters?
Honest Iago, that looks dead with grieving,
Speak. Who began this? On thy love, I charge thee.

**IAGO:** I do not know. Friends all but now, even now,
In quarter and in terms like bride and groom
Devesting them for bed; and then, but now—
As if some planet had unwitted men—
Swords out, and tilting one at others' breasts
In opposition bloody. I cannot speak
Any beginning to this peevish odds;
And would in action glorious I had lost
Those legs that brought me to a part of it!

**OTHELLO:** How comes it, Michael, you are thus forgot?

**CASSIO:** I pray you, pardon me. I cannot speak.

**OTHELLO:** Worthy Montano, you were wont be civil;
Thy gravity and stillness of your youth
The world hath noted, and your name is great
In mouths of wisest censure. What's the matter
That you unlace your reputation thus
And spend your rich opinion for the name
Of a night-brawler? Give me answer to it.

Othello hears from Cassio after the scuffle.

---

**138 s.d. pursuing** (The Quarto text reads "driving in.") **142 twiggen** wicker-covered. (Cassio vows to assail Roderigo until his skin resembles wickerwork or until he has driven Roderigo through the holes in a wickerwork.) **148 mazard** i.e., head. (Literally, a drinking vessel.) **151 mutiny** riot **154 masters** sirs. **s.d. A bell rings** (This direction is from the Quarto, as are *Exit Roderigo* at line 131, *They fight* at line 150, and *with weapons* at line 157.) **155 Diablo** the devil **156 rise** grow riotous **164–165 to ourselves . . . Ottomites** inflict on ourselves the harm that heaven has prevented the Turks from doing (by destroying their fleet)

**167 carve for** i.e., indulge, satisfy with his sword **168 Holds . . . light** i.e., places little value on his life. **upon his motion** if he moves **170 propriety** proper state or condition **174 In quarter** in friendly conduct, within bounds. **in terms** on good terms **175 Devesting them** undressing themselves **178 speak** explain **179 peevish odds** childish quarrel **182 are thus forgot** have forgotten yourself thus **184 wont be** accustomed to be **185 stillness** sobriety **187 censure** judgment **188 unlace** undo, lay open (as one might loose the strings of a purse containing reputation) **189 opinion** reputation

**MONTANO:** Worthy Othello, I am hurt to danger.
Your officer, Iago, can inform you—
While I spare speech, which something now offends me—
Of all that I do know; nor know I aught
By me that's said or done amiss this night,
Unless self-charity be sometimes a vice,
And to defend ourselves it be a sin
When violence assails us.

**OTHELLO:** Now, by heaven,
My blood begins my safer guides to rule,
And passion, having my best judgment collied,
Essays to lead the way. Zounds, if I stir,
Or do but lift this arm, the best of you
Shall sink in my rebuke. Give me to know
How this foul rout began, who set it on;
And he that is approved in this offense,
Though he had twinned with me, both at a birth,
Shall lose me. What? In a town of war
Yet wild, the people's hearts brim full of fear,
To manage private and domestic quarrel?
In night, and on the court and guard of safety?
'Tis monstrous. Iago, who began 't?

**MONTANO** *[to* IAGO*]*: If partially affined, or leagued in office,
Thou dost deliver more or less than truth,
Thou art no soldier.

**IAGO:** Touch me not so near.
I had rather have this tongue cut from my mouth
Than it should do offense to Michael Cassio;
Yet, I persuade myself, to speak the truth
Shall nothing wrong him. This it is, General.
Montano and myself being in speech,
There comes a fellow crying out for help,
And Cassio following him with determined sword
To execute upon him. Sir, this gentleman
*[indicating* MONTANO*]*
Steps in to Cassio and entreats his pause.
Myself the crying fellow did pursue,
Lest by his clamor—as it so fell out—
The town might fall in fright. He, swift of foot,
Outran my purpose, and I returned, the rather
For that I heard the clink and fall of swords
And Cassio high in oath, which till tonight
I ne'er might say before. When I came back—
For this was brief—I found them close together
At blow and thrust, even as again they were
When you yourself did part them.
More of this matter cannot I report.
But men are men; the best sometimes forget.
Though Cassio did some little wrong to him,
As men in rage strike those that wish them best,
Yet surely Cassio, I believe, received
From him that fled some strange indignity,
Which patience could not pass.

**OTHELLO:** I know, Iago,
Thy honesty and love doth mince this matter,
Making it light to Cassio. Cassio, I love thee,
But nevermore be officer of mine.

*Enter* DESDEMONA, *attended.*

Look if my gentle love be not raised up.
I'll make thee an example.

**DESDEMONA:** What is the matter, dear?

**OTHELLO:** All's well now, sweeting;
Come away to bed. *[To* MONTANO.*]* Sir, for your hurts,
Myself will be your surgeon.—Lead him off.
*[*MONTANO *is led off.]*
Iago, look with care about the town
And silence those whom this vile brawl distracted.
Come, Desdemona. 'Tis the soldiers' life
To have their balmy slumbers waked with strife.
*Exit [with all but* IAGO *and* CASSIO*].*

**IAGO:** What, are you hurt, Lieutenant?

**CASSIO:** Ay, past all surgery.

**IAGO:** Marry, God forbid!

**CASSIO:** Reputation, reputation, reputation! O, I have lost my reputation! I have lost the immortal part of myself, and what remains is bestial. My reputation, Iago, my reputation!

**IAGO:** As I am an honest man, I thought you had received some bodily wound; there is more sense in that than in reputation. Reputation is an idle and most false imposition, oft got without merit and lost without deserving. You have lost no reputation at all, unless you repute yourself such a loser. What, man, there are more ways to recover the General again. You are but now cast in his mood—a punishment

---

**193 something** somewhat. **offends** pains **199 blood** passion (of anger). **guides** i.e., reason **200 collied** darkened **201 Essays** undertakes **204 rout** riot **205 approved in** found guilty of **207 town of** town garrisoned for **209 manage** undertake **210 on . . . safety** at the main guardhouse or headquarters and on watch **212 partially affined** made partial by some personal relationship. **leagued in office** in league as fellow officers **222 execute** give effect to (his anger) **223 his pause** him to stop **227 rather** sooner

**235 forget** forget themselves **237 those . . . best** i.e., even those who are well disposed **240 pass** pass over, overlook **248 be your surgeon** i.e., make sure you receive medical attention **263 false imposition** thing artificially imposed and of no real value **266 recover** regain favor with **267 cast in his mood** dismissed in a moment of anger

Iago cleverly advises Cassio (Nick Barber).

more in policy than in malice, even so as one would beat his offenseless dog to affright an imperious lion. Sue to him again and he's yours.

**CASSIO:** I will rather sue to be despised than to deceive so good a commander with so slight, so drunken, and so indiscreet an officer. Drunk? And speak parrot? And squabble? Swagger? Swear? And discourse fustian with one's own shadow? O thou invisible spirit of wine, if thou hast no name to be known by, let us call thee devil!

**IAGO:** What was he that you followed with your sword? What had he done to you?

**CASSIO:** I know not.

**IAGO:** Is 't possible?

**CASSIO:** I remember a mass of things, but nothing distinctly; a quarrel, but nothing wherefore. O God, that men should put an enemy in their mouths to steal away their brains! That we should, with joy, pleasance, revel, and applause transform ourselves into beasts!

**IAGO:** Why, but you are now well enough. How came you thus recovered?

**CASSIO:** It hath pleased the devil drunkenness to give place to the devil wrath. One unperfectness shows me another, to make me frankly despise myself.

**IAGO:** Come, you are too severe a moraler. As the time, the place, and the condition of this country stands, I could heartily wish this had not befallen; but since it is as it is, mend it for your own good.

**CASSIO:** I will ask him for my place again; he shall tell me I am a drunkard. Had I as many mouths as Hydra, such an answer would stop them all. To be now a sensible man, by and by a fool, and presently a beast! O, strange! Every inordinate cup is unblessed, and the ingredient is a devil.

**IAGO:** Come, come, good wine is a good familiar creature, if it be well used. Exclaim no more against it. And, good Lieutenant, I think you think I love you.

**CASSIO:** I have well approved it, sir. I drunk!

**IAGO:** You or any man living may be drunk at a time, man. I'll tell you what you shall do. Our general's wife is now the general—I may say so in this respect, for that he hath devoted and given up himself to the contemplation, mark, and denotement of her parts and graces. Confess yourself freely to her; importune her help to put you in your place again. She is of so free, so kind, so apt, so blessed a disposition, she holds it a vice in her goodness not to do more than she is requested. This broken joint between you and her husband entreat her to splinter; and, my fortunes against any lay worth naming, this crack of your love shall grow stronger than it was before.

**CASSIO:** You advise me well.

**IAGO:** I protest, in the sincerity of love and honest kindness.

**CASSIO:** I think it freely; and betimes in the morning I will beseech the virtuous Desdemona to undertake for me. I am desperate of my fortunes if they check me here.

**IAGO:** You are in the right. Good night, Lieutenant. I must to the watch.

**CASSIO:** Good night, honest Iago. *Exit* CASSIO.

---

**268 in policy** done for expediency's sake and as a public gesture **268–269 would . . . lion** i.e., would make an example of a minor offender in order to deter more important and dangerous offenders **269 Sue** petition **272 slight** worthless **273–274 speak parrot** talk nonsense, rant. (*Discourse fustian*, lines 274–275, has much the same meaning.) **283 wherefore** why **286 applause** desire for applause

**293 moraler** moralizer **299 Hydra** the Lernaean Hydra, a monster with many heads and the ability to grow two heads when one was cut off, slain by Hercules as the second of his twelve labors **306 approved** proved **307 at a time** at one time or another **309–310 in . . . that** in view of this fact, that **311 mark, and denotement** (Both words mean "observation.") **parts** qualities **314 free** generous **317 splinter** bind with splints **318 lay** stake, wager **321 protest** insist, declare **323 freely** unreservedly **325 check** repulse

**IAGO:** And what's he then that says I play the villain,
When this advice is free I give, and honest,
Probal to thinking, and indeed the course
To win the Moor again? For 'tis most easy
Th' inclining Desdemona to subdue
In any honest suit; she's framed as fruitful
As the free elements. And then for her
To win the Moor—were 't to renounce his baptism,
All seals and symbols of redeemèd sin—
His soul is so enfettered to her love
That she may make, unmake, do what she list,
Even as her appetite shall play the god
With his weak function. How am I then a villain,
To counsel Cassio to this parallel course
Directly to his good? Divinity of hell!
When devils will the blackest sins put on,
They do suggest at first with heavenly shows,
As I do now. For whiles this honest fool
Plies Desdemona to repair his fortune,
And she for him pleads strongly to the Moor,
I'll pour this pestilence into his ear,
That she repeals him for her body's lust;
And by how much she strives to do him good,
She shall undo her credit with the Moor.
So will I turn her virtue into pitch,
And out of her own goodness make the net
That shall enmesh them all.

*Enter* RODERIGO.

How now, Roderigo?

**RODERIGO:** I do follow here in the chase, not like a hound that hunts, but one that fills up the cry. My money is almost spent; I have been tonight exceedingly well cudgeled; and I think the issue will be I shall have so much experience for my pains, and so, with no money at all and a little more wit, return again to Venice.

**IAGO:** How poor are they that have not patience!
What wound did ever heal but by degrees?
Thou know'st we work by wit, and not by witchcraft,
And wit depends on dilatory time.
Does 't not go well? Cassio hath beaten thee,
And thou, by that small hurt, hast cashiered Cassio.
Though other things grow fair against the sun,
Yet fruits that blossom first will first be ripe.
Content thyself awhile. By the Mass, 'tis morning!
Pleasure and action make the hours seem short.
Retire thee; go where thou art billeted.
Away, I say! Thou shalt know more hereafter.
Nay, get thee gone. *Exit* RODERIGO.
Two things are to be done.
My wife must move for Cassio to her mistress;
I'll set her on;
Myself the while to draw the Moor apart
And bring him jump when he may Cassio find
Soliciting his wife. Ay, that's the way.
Dull not device by coldness and delay. *Exit.*

## 3.1 *Enter* CASSIO *[and]* MUSICIANS.

**CASSIO:** Masters, play here—I will content your pains—
Something that's brief, and bid "Good morrow,
General." *[They play.]*

*[Enter]* CLOWN.

**CLOWN:** Why, masters, have your instruments been in Naples, that they speak i' the nose thus?

**A MUSICIAN:** How, sir, how?

**CLOWN:** Are these, I pray you, wind instruments?

**A MUSICIAN:** Ay, marry, are they, sir.

**CLOWN:** O, thereby hangs a tail.

**A MUSICIAN:** Whereby hangs a tale, sir?

**CLOWN:** Marry, sir, by many a wind instrument that I know. But, masters, here's money for you. *[He gives money.]* And the General so likes your music that he desires you, for love's sake, to make no more noise with it.

---

**331 free** (1) free from guile (2) freely given **332 Probal** probable, reasonable **334 inclining** favorably disposed. **subdue** persuade **335 framed as fruitful** created as generous **336 free elements** i.e., earth, air, fire, and water, unrestrained and spontaneous **341 her appetite** her desire, or, perhaps, his desire for her **342 function** exercise of faculties (weakened by his fondness for her) **343 parallel** corresponding to these facts and to his best interests **344 Divinity of hell** inverted theology of hell (which seduces the soul to its damnation) **345 put on** further, instigate **346 suggest** tempt **351 repeals him** attempts to get him restored **354 pitch** i.e., (1) foul blackness (2) a snaring substance **358 fills up the cry** merely takes part as one of the pack **361 so much** just so much and no more

**369 cashiered** dismissed from service **370–371 Though . . . ripe** i.e., plans that are well prepared and set expeditiously in motion will soonest ripen into success **377 move** plead **380 jump** precisely **382 device** plot. **coldness** lack of zeal

**3.1. Location: Before the chamber of Othello and Desdemona.** **1 content your pains** reward your efforts **4 speak i' the nose** (1) sound nasal (2) sound like one whose nose has been attacked by syphilis. (Naples was popularly supposed to have a high incidence of venereal disease.) **10 wind instrument** (With a joke on flatulence. The *tail,* line 8, that hangs nearby the *wind instrument* suggests the penis.) **13 for love's sake** (1) out of friendship and affection (2) for the sake of lovemaking in Othello's marriage

**A MUSICIAN:** Well, sir, we will not.

**CLOWN:** If you have any music that may not be heard, to 't again; but, as they say, to hear music the General does not greatly care.

**A MUSICIAN:** We have none such, sir.

**CLOWN:** Then put up your pipes in your bag, for I'll away. Go, vanish into air, away! *Exeunt* MUSICIANS.

**CASSIO:** Dost thou hear, mine honest friend?

**CLOWN:** No, I hear not your honest friend; I hear you.

**CASSIO:** Prithee, keep up thy quillets. There's a poor piece of gold for thee. *[He gives money.]* If the gentlewoman that attends the General's wife be stirring, tell her there's one Cassio entreats her a little favor of speech. Wilt thou do this?

**CLOWN:** She is stirring, sir. If she will stir hither, I shall seem to notify unto her.

**CASSIO:** Do, good my friend. *Exit* CLOWN.

*Enter* IAGO.

In happy time, Iago.

**IAGO:** You have not been abed, then?

**CASSIO:** Why, no. The day had broke
Before we parted. I have made bold, Iago,
To send in to your wife. My suit to her
Is that she will to virtuous Desdemona
Procure me some access.

**IAGO:** I'll send her to you presently;
And I'll devise a means to draw the Moor
Out of the way, that your converse and business
May be more free.

**CASSIO:** I humbly thank you for 't. *Exit [IAGO.]*
I never knew
A Florentine more kind and honest.

*Enter* EMILIA.

**EMILIA:** Good morrow, good Lieutenant. I am sorry
For your displeasure; but all will sure be well.
The General and his wife are talking of it,
And she speaks for you stoutly. The Moor replies
That he you hurt is of great fame in Cyprus
And great affinity, and that in wholesome wisdom
He might not but refuse you; but he protests he loves you
And needs no other suitor but his likings
To take the safest occasion by the front
To bring you in again.

**CASSIO:** Yet I beseech you,
If you think fit, or that it may be done,
Give me advantage of some brief discourse
With Desdemona alone.

**EMILIA:** Pray you, come in.
I will bestow you where you shall have time
To speak your bosom freely.

**CASSIO:** I am much bound to you. *[Exeunt.]*

## 3.2 *Enter* OTHELLO, IAGO, *and* GENTLEMEN.

**OTHELLO** *[giving letters]*: These letters give, Iago, to the pilot,
And by him do my duties to the Senate.
That done, I will be walking on the works;
Repair there to me.

**IAGO:** Well, my good lord, I'll do 't.

**OTHELLO:** This fortification, gentlemen, shall we see 't?

**GENTLEMEN:** We'll wait upon your lordship. *Exeunt.*

## 3.3 *Enter* DESDEMONA, CASSIO, *and* EMILIA.

**DESDEMONA:** Be thou assured, good Cassio, I will do
All my abilities in thy behalf.

**EMILIA:** Good madam, do. I warrant it grieves my husband
As if the cause were his.

**DESDEMONA:** O, that's an honest fellow. Do not doubt, Cassio,
But I will have my lord and you again
As friendly as you were.

**CASSIO:** Bounteous madam,
Whatever shall become of Michael Cassio,
He's never anything but your true servant.

---

**16 may not** cannot **20–21 I'll away** (Possibly a misprint, or a snatch of song?) **24 keep up** do not bring out, do not use. **quillets** quibbles, puns **27–28 a little . . . speech** the favor of a brief talk **29 stir** bestir herself (with a play on *stirring*, "rousing herself from rest") **30 seem** deem it good, think fit **31 In happy time** i.e., well met **43 Florentine** i.e., even a fellow Florentine (Iago is a Venetian; Cassio is a Florentine.) **45 displeasure** fall from favor **47 stoutly** spiritedly

**48 fame** reputation, importance **49 affinity** kindred, family connection **50 protests** insists **52 occasion . . . front** opportunity by the forelock **58 bosom** inmost thoughts

**3.2. Location: The citadel.**
**2 do my duties** convey my respects **3 works** breastworks, fortifications **4 Repair** return, come **6 wait upon** attend

**3.3. Location: The garden of the citadel.**

**DESDEMONA:** I know 't. I thank you. You do love my lord;
You have known him long, and be you well assured
He shall in strangeness stand no farther off
Than in a politic distance.

**CASSIO:** Ay, but, lady,
That policy may either last so long,
Or feed upon such nice and waterish diet,
Or breed itself so out of circumstance,
That, I being absent and my place supplied,
My general will forget my love and service.

**DESDEMONA:** Do not doubt that. Before Emilia here
I give thee warrant of thy place. Assure thee,
If I do vow a friendship I'll perform it
To the last article. My lord shall never rest.
I'll watch him tame and talk him out of patience;
His bed shall seem a school, his board a shrift;
I'll intermingle everything he does
With Cassio's suit. Therefore be merry, Cassio,
For thy solicitor shall rather die
Than give thy cause away.

*Enter* OTHELLO *and* IAGO *[at a distance].*

**EMILIA:** Madam, here comes my lord.

**CASSIO:** Madam, I'll take my leave.

**DESDEMONA:** Why, stay, and hear me speak.

**CASSIO:** Madam, not now. I am very ill at ease,
Unfit for mine own purposes.

**DESDEMONA:** Well, do your discretion. *Exit* CASSIO.

**IAGO:** Ha? I like not that.

**OTHELLO:** What dost thou say?

**IAGO:** Nothing, my lord; or if—I know not what.

**OTHELLO:** Was not that Cassio parted from my wife?

**IAGO:** Cassio, my lord? No, sure, I cannot think it,
That he would steal away so guiltylike,
Seeing you coming.

**OTHELLO:** I do believe 'twas he.

**12 strangeness** aloofness **13 politic** required by wise policy **15 Or . . . diet** or sustain itself at length upon such trivial and meager technicalities **16 breed . . . circumstance** continually renew itself so out of chance events, or yield so few chances for my being pardoned **17 supplied** filled by another person **19 doubt** fear **20 warrant** guarantee **23 watch him tame** tame him by keeping him from sleeping. (A term from falconry.) **out of patience** past his endurance **24 board** dining table. **shrift** confessional **27 solicitor** advocate **28 away** up **34 do your discretion** act according to your own discretion

Desdemona (Zoë Tapper) asks Othello (Eamonn Walker) to pardon Cassio.

**DESDEMONA:** How now, my lord?
I have been talking with a suitor here,
A man that languishes in your displeasure.

**OTHELLO:** Who is 't you mean?

**DESDEMONA:** Why, your lieutenant, Cassio. Good my lord,
If I have any grace or power to move you,
His present reconciliation take;
For if he be not one that truly loves you,
That errs in ignorance and not in cunning,
I have no judgment in an honest face.
I prithee, call him back.

**OTHELLO:** Went he hence now?

**DESDEMONA:** Yes, faith, so humbled
That he hath left part of his grief with me
To suffer with him. Good love, call him back.

**OTHELLO:** Not now, sweet Desdemon. Some other time.

**DESDEMONA:** But shall 't be shortly?

**OTHELLO:** The sooner, sweet, for you.

**DESDEMONA:** Shall 't be tonight at supper?

**OTHELLO:** No, not tonight.

**DESDEMONA:** Tomorrow dinner, then?

**OTHELLO:** I shall not dine at home.
I meet the captains at the citadel.

**49 His . . . take** let him be reconciled to you right away **51 in cunning** wittingly **63 dinner** (The noontime meal.)

**DESDEMONA:** Why, then, tomorrow night, or Tuesday morn,
On Tuesday noon, or night, on Wednesday morn.
I prithee, name the time, but let it not
Exceed three days. In faith, he's penitent;
And yet his trespass, in our common reason—
Save that, they say, the wars must make example
Out of her best—is not almost a fault
T' incur a private check. When shall he come?
Tell me, Othello. I wonder in my soul
What you would ask me that I should deny,
Or stand so mammering on. What? Michael Cassio,
That came a-wooing with you, and so many a time,
When I have spoke of you dispraisingly,
Hath ta'en your part—to have so much to do
To bring him in! By 'r Lady, I could do much—

**OTHELLO:** Prithee, no more. Let him come when he will;
I will deny thee nothing.

**DESDEMONA:** Why, this is not a boon.
'Tis as I should entreat you wear your gloves,
Or feed on nourishing dishes, or keep you warm,
Or sue to you to do a peculiar profit
To your own person. Nay, when I have a suit
Wherein I mean to touch your love indeed,
It shall be full of poise and difficult weight,
And fearful to be granted.

**OTHELLO:** I will deny thee nothing.
Whereon, I do beseech thee, grant me this,
To leave me but a little to myself.

**DESDEMONA:** Shall I deny you? No. Farewell, my lord.

**OTHELLO:** Farewell, my Desdemona. I'll come to thee straight.

**DESDEMONA:** Emilia, come.—Be as your fancies teach you;
Whate'er you be, I am obedient. *Exit [with* EMILIA*].*

**OTHELLO:** Excellent wretch! Perdition catch my soul
But I do love thee! And when I love thee not,
Chaos is come again.

**IAGO:** My noble lord—

**OTHELLO:** What dost thou say, Iago?

**IAGO:** Did Michael Cassio, when you wooed my lady,
Know of your love?

**OTHELLO:** He did, from first to last. Why dost thou ask?

**IAGO:** But for a satisfaction of my thought;
No further harm.

**OTHELLO:** Why of thy thought, Iago?

**IAGO:** I did not think he had been acquainted with her.

**OTHELLO:** O, yes, and went between us very oft.

**IAGO:** Indeed?

**OTHELLO:** Indeed? Ay, indeed. Discern'st thou aught in that?
Is he not honest?

**IAGO:** Honest, my lord?

**OTHELLO:** Honest. Ay, honest.

**IAGO:** My lord, for aught I know.

**OTHELLO:** What dost thou think?

**IAGO:** Think, my lord?

**OTHELLO:** "Think, my lord?" By heaven, thou echo'st me,
As if there were some monster in thy thought
Too hideous to be shown. Thou dost mean something.
I heard thee say even now, thou lik'st not that,
When Cassio left my wife. What didst not like?
And when I told thee he was of my counsel
In my whole course of wooing, thou criedst "Indeed?"
And didst contract and purse thy brow together
As if thou then hadst shut up in thy brain
Some horrible conceit. If thou dost love me,
Show me thy thought.

**IAGO:** My lord, you know I love you.

---

**70 common reason** everyday judgments **71–72 Save . . . best** were it not that, as the saying goes, military discipline requires making an example of the very best men. (*Her* refers to *wars* as a singular concept.) **72 not almost** scarcely **73 a private check** even a private reprimand **76 mammering on** wavering about **80 bring him in** restore him to favor **86 peculiar** particular, personal **88 touch** test **89 poise** weight, heaviness; or equipoise, delicate balance involving hard choice **92 Whereon** in return for which **95 straight** straightway **96 fancies** inclinations

**98 wretch** (A term of affectionate endearment.) **99–100 And . . . again** i.e., my love for you will last forever, until the end of time when chaos will return. (But with an unconscious, ironic suggestion that, if anything should induce Othello to cease loving Desdemona, the result would be chaos.) **123 of my counsel** in my confidence **125 purse** knit **127 conceit** fancy

Othello, jealous of Cassio, is beguiled by Iago.

**OTHELLO:** I think thou dost;
And, for I know thou'rt full of love and honesty,
And weigh'st thy words before thou giv'st them breath,
Therefore these stops of thine fright me the more;
For such things in a false disloyal knave
Are tricks of custom, but in a man that's just
They're close dilations, working from the heart
That passion cannot rule.

**IAGO:** For Michael Cassio,
I dare be sworn I think that he is honest.

**OTHELLO:** I think so too.

**IAGO:** Men should be what they seem;
Or those that be not, would they might seem none!

**OTHELLO:** Certain, men should be what they seem.

**IAGO:** Why, then, I think Cassio's an honest man.

**OTHELLO:** Nay, yet there's more in this.
I prithee, speak to me as to thy thinkings,
As thou dost ruminate, and give thy worst of thoughts
The worst of words.

**IAGO:** Good my lord, pardon me.
Though I am bound to every act of duty,
I am not bound to that all slaves are free to.
Utter my thoughts? Why, say they are vile and false,
As where's that palace whereinto foul things

---

**131 for** because **133 stops** pauses **135 of custom** customary **136 close dilations** secret or involuntary expressions or delays **137 That passion cannot rule** i.e., that are too passionately strong to be restrained (referring to the workings), or, that cannot rule its own passions (referring to the heart). **For** as for **140 none** i.e., not to be men, or not seem to be honest **148 that** that which. **free to** free with respect to

Sometimes intrude not? Who has that breast so pure
But some uncleanly apprehensions
Keep leets and law days, and in sessions sit
With meditations lawful?

**OTHELLO:** Thou dost conspire against thy friend, Iago,
If thou but think'st him wronged and mak'st his ear
A stranger to thy thoughts.

**IAGO:** I do beseech you,
Though I perchance am vicious in my guess—
As I confess it is my nature's plague
To spy into abuses, and oft my jealousy
Shapes faults that are not—that your wisdom then,
From one that so imperfectly conceits,
Would take no notice, nor build yourself a trouble
Out of his scattering and unsure observance.
It were not for your quiet nor your good,
Nor for my manhood, honesty, and wisdom,
To let you know my thoughts.

**OTHELLO:** What dost thou mean?

**IAGO:** Good name in man and woman, dear my lord,
Is the immediate jewel of their souls.
Who steals my purse steals trash; 'tis something, nothing;
'Twas mine, 'tis his, and has been slave to thousands;
But he that filches from me my good name
Robs me of that which not enriches him
And makes me poor indeed.

**OTHELLO:** By heaven, I'll know thy thoughts.

**IAGO:** You cannot, if my heart were in your hand,
Nor shall not, whilst 'tis in my custody.

**OTHELLO:** Ha?

**IAGO:** O, beware, my lord, of jealousy.
It is the green-eyed monster which doth mock
The meat it feeds on. That cuckold lives in bliss
Who, certain of his fate, loves not his wronger;

---

**153 Keep leets and law days** i.e., hold court, set up their authority in one's heart. (*Leets* are a kind of manor court; *law days* are the days courts sit in session, or those sessions.) **154 With** along with. **lawful** innocent **155 thy friend** i.e., Othello **158 vicious** wrong **160 jealousy** suspicious nature **161 then** on that account **162 one** i.e., myself, Iago. **conceits** judges, conjectures **164 scattering** random **169 immediate** essential, most precious **176 if** even if **179–180 doth mock . . . on** mocks and torments the heart of its victim, the man who suffers jealousy **181 his wronger** i.e., his faithless wife. (The unsuspecting cuckold is spared the misery of loving his wife only to discover she is cheating on him.)

Othello is deceived by Iago.

But O, what damnèd minutes tells he o'er
Who dotes, yet doubts, suspects, yet fondly loves!

**OTHELLO:** O misery!

**IAGO:** Poor and content is rich, and rich enough,
But riches fineless is as poor as winter
To him that ever fears he shall be poor.
Good God, the souls of all my tribe defend
From jealousy!

**OTHELLO:** Why, why is this?
Think'st thou I'd make a life of jealousy,
To follow still the changes of the moon
With fresh suspicions? No! To be once in doubt
Is once to be resolved. Exchange me for a goat
When I shall turn the business of my soul
To such exsufflicate and blown surmises
Matching thy inference. 'Tis not to make me jealous
To say my wife is fair, feeds well, loves company,
Is free of speech, sings, plays, and dances well;
Where virtue is, these are more virtuous.
Nor from mine own weak merits will I draw
The smallest fear or doubt of her revolt,
For she had eyes, and chose me. No, Iago,
I'll see before I doubt; when I doubt, prove;
And on the proof, there is no more but this—
Away at once with love or jealousy.

**IAGO:** I am glad of this, for now I shall have reason
To show the love and duty that I bear you
With franker spirit. Therefore, as I am bound,
Receive it from me. I speak not yet of proof.
Look to your wife; observe her well with Cassio.
Wear your eyes thus, not jealous nor secure.
I would not have your free and noble nature,
Out of self-bounty, be abused. Look to 't.
I know our country disposition well;
In Venice they do let God see the pranks
They dare not show their husbands; their best
conscience
Is not to leave 't undone, but keep 't unknown.

**OTHELLO:** Dost thou say so?

**IAGO:** She did deceive her father, marrying you;
And when she seemed to shake and fear your looks,
She loved them most.

**OTHELLO:** And so she did.

**IAGO:** Why, go to, then!
She that, so young, could give out such a seeming,
To seel her father's eyes up close as oak,
He thought 'twas witchcraft! But I am much to blame.
I humbly do beseech you of your pardon
For too much loving you.

**OTHELLO:** I am bound to thee forever.

**IAGO:** I see this hath a little dashed your spirits.

**OTHELLO:** Not a jot, not a jot.

**IAGO:** I' faith, I fear it has.
I hope you will consider what is spoke
Comes from my love. But I do see you're moved.
I am to pray you not to strain my speech
To grosser issues nor to larger reach
Than to suspicion.

**OTHELLO:** I will not.

**IAGO:** Should you do so, my lord,
My speech should fall into such vile success
Which my thoughts aimed not. Cassio's my worthy
friend.
My lord, I see you're moved.

---

**182 tells** counts **185 Poor . . . enough** to be content with what little one has is the greatest wealth of all. (Proverbial.) **186 fineless** boundless **192–193 To follow . . . suspicions** to be constantly imagining new causes for suspicion, changing incessantly like the moon **194 once** once and for all. **resolved** free of doubt, having settled the matter **196 exsufflicate and blown** inflated and blown up, rumored about, or, spat out and flyblown, hence, loathsome, disgusting **197 inference** description or allegation **202 doubt . . . revolt** fear or her unfaithfulness

**212 not** neither. **secure** free from uncertainty **214 self-bounty** inherent or natural goodness and generosity. **abused** deceived **222 go to** (An expression of impatience.) **223 seeming** false appearance **224 seel** blind. (A term from falconry.) **oak** (A close-grained wood.) **228 bound** indebted (but perhaps with ironic sense of "tied") **234 issues** significances. **reach** meaning, scope **238 success** effect, result

**OTHELLO:** No, not much moved.
I do not think but Desdemona's honest.

**IAGO:** Long live she so! And long live you to think so!

**OTHELLO:** And yet, how nature erring from itself—

**IAGO:** Ay, there's the point! As—to be bold with you—
Not to affect many proposèd matches
Of her own clime, complexion, and degree,
Whereto we see in all things nature tends—
Foh! One may smell in such a will most rank,
Foul disproportion, thoughts unnatural.
But, pardon me. I do not in position
Distinctly speak of her, though I may fear
Her will, recoiling to her better judgment,
May fall to match you with her country forms
And happily repent.

**OTHELLO:** Farewell, farewell!
If more thou dost perceive, let me know more.
Set on thy wife to observe. Leave me, Iago.

**IAGO** *[going]*: My lord, I take my leave.

**OTHELLO:** Why did I marry? This honest creature doubtless
Sees and knows more, much more, than he unfolds.

**IAGO** *[returning]*: My lord, I would I might entreat your honor
To scan this thing no farther. Leave it to time.
Although 'tis fit that Cassio have his place—
For, sure, he fills it up with great ability—
Yet, if you please to hold him off awhile,
You shall by that perceive him and his means.
Note if your lady strain his entertainment
With any strong or vehement importunity;
Much will be seen in that. In the meantime,
Let me be thought too busy in my fears—
As worthy cause I have to fear I am—
And hold her free, I do beseech your honor.

**OTHELLO:** Fear not my government.

**IAGO:** I once more take my leave. *Exit.*

**OTHELLO:** This fellow's of exceeding honesty,
And knows all qualities, with a learnèd spirit,
Of human dealings. If I do prove her haggard,
Though that her jesses were my dear heartstrings,
I'd whistle her off and let her down the wind
To prey at fortune. Haply, for I am black
And have not those soft parts of conversation
That chamberers have, or for I am declined
Into the vale of years—yet that's not much—
She's gone. I am abused, and my relief
Must be to loathe her. O curse of marriage,
That we can call these delicate creatures ours
And not their appetites! I had rather be a toad
And live upon the vapor of a dungeon
Than keep a corner in the thing I love
For others' uses. Yet, 'tis the plague to great ones;
Prerogatived are they less than the base.
'Tis destiny unshunnable, like death.
Even then this forkèd plague is fated to us
When we do quicken. Look where she comes.

*Enter* DESDEMONA *and* EMILIA.

If she be false, O, then heaven mocks itself!
I'll not believe 't.

**DESDEMONA:** How now, my dear Othello?
Your dinner, and the generous islanders
By you invited, do attend your presence.

**OTHELLO:** I am to blame.

**DESDEMONA:** Why do you speak so faintly?
Are you not well?

**OTHELLO:** I have a pain upon my forehead here.

**DESDEMONA:** Faith, that's with watching. 'Twill away again.
*[She offers her handkerchief.]*
Let me but bind it hard, within this hour
It will be well.

---

**241 honest** chaste **245 affect** prefer, desire **246 clime . . . degree** country, color, and social position **248 will** sensuality, appetite **249 disproportion** abnormality **250 position** argument, proposition **252 recoiling** reverting. **better** i.e., more natural and reconsidered **253 fall . . . forms** undertake to compare you with Venetian norms of handsomeness **254 happily repent** haply repent her marriage **261 scan** scrutinize **265 his means** the method he uses (to regain his post) **266 strain his entertainment** urge his reinstatement **269 busy** interfering **271 hold her free** regard her as innocent **272 government** self-control, conduct

**275 qualities** natures, types **276 haggard** wild (like a wild female hawk) **277 jesses** straps fastened around the legs of a trained hawk **278 I'd . . . wind** i.e., I'd let her go forever. (To release a hawk downwind was to invite it not to return.) **279 prey at fortune** fend for herself in the wild. **Haply, for** perhaps because **280 soft . . . conversation** pleasing graces of social behavior **281 chamberers** gallants **283 abused** deceived **290 Prerogatived** privileged (to have honest wives). **the base** ordinary citizens. (Socially prominent men are especially prone to the unavoidable destiny of being cuckolded and to the public shame that goes with it.) **292 forkèd** (An allusion to the horns of the cuckold.) **293 quicken** receive life. (*Quicken* may also mean to swarm with maggots as the body festers, as in 4.2.69, in which case lines 292–293 suggest that *even then*, in death, we are cuckolded by *forkèd* worms.) **296 generous** noble **297 attend** await **301 watching** too little sleep

**OTHELLO:** Your napkin is too little.
Let it alone. Come, I'll go in with you.
*[He puts the handkerchief from him, and it drops.]*

**DESDEMONA:** I am very sorry that you are not well.
*Exit [with* OTHELLO*].*

**EMILIA** *[picking up the handkerchief]*: I am glad I have found this napkin.
This was her first remembrance from the Moor.
My wayward husband hath a hundred times
Wooed me to steal it, but she so loves the token—
For he conjured her she should ever keep it—
That she reserves it evermore about her
To kiss and talk to. I'll have the work ta'en out,
And give 't Iago. What he will do with it
Heaven knows, not I;
I nothing but to please his fantasy.

*Enter* IAGO.

**IAGO:** How now? What do you here alone?

**EMILIA:** Do not you chide. I have a thing for you.

**IAGO:** You have a thing for me? It is a common thing—

**EMILIA:** Ha?

**IAGO:** To have a foolish wife.

**EMILIA:** O, is that all? What will you give me now
For that same handkerchief?

**IAGO:** What handkerchief?

**EMILIA:** What handkerchief?
Why, that the Moor first gave to Desdemona;
That which so often you did bid me steal.

**IAGO:** Hast stolen it from her?

**EMILIA:** No, faith. She let it drop by negligence,
And to th' advantage I, being here, took 't up.
Look, here 'tis.

**IAGO:** A good wench! Give it me.

**EMILIA:** What will you do with 't, that you have been so earnest
To have me filch it?

**IAGO** *[snatching it]*: Why, what is that to you?

**303 napkin** handkerchief **304 Let it alone** i.e., never mind **308 wayward** capricious **312 work ta'en out** design of the embroidery copied **315 fantasy** whim **318 common thing** (With bawdy suggestion; *common* suggests coarseness and availability to all comers, and *thing* is a slang term for the pudendum.) **329 to th' advantage** taking the opportunity

Emilia (Anna Patrick) brings Iago Desdemona's handkerchief.

**EMILIA:** If it be not for some purpose of import,
Give 't me again. Poor lady, she'll run mad
When she shall lack it.

**IAGO:** Be not acknown on 't.
I have use for it. Go, leave me. *Exit* EMILIA.
I will in Cassio's lodging lose this napkin
And let him find it. Trifles light as air
Are to the jealous confirmations strong
As proofs of Holy Writ. This may do something.
The Moor already changes with my poison.
Dangerous conceits are in their natures poisons,
Which at the first are scarce found to distaste,
But with a little act upon the blood
Burn like the mines of sulfur.

*Enter* OTHELLO.

I did say so.
Look where he comes! Not poppy nor mandragora
Nor all the drowsy syrups of the world
Shall ever medicine thee to that sweet sleep
Which thou owedst yesterday.

**OTHELLO:** Ha, ha, false to me?

**IAGO:** Why, how now, General? No more of that.

**OTHELLO:** Avaunt! Begone! Thou hast set me on the rack.
I swear 'tis better to be much abused
Than but to know 't a little.

**IAGO:** How now, my lord?

**OTHELLO:** What sense had I of her stolen hours of lust?
I saw 't not, thought it not, it harmed not me.

**335 lack** miss. **Be . . . on 't** do not confess knowledge of it **337 lose** (The Folio spelling, *loose*, is a normal spelling for "lose," but it may also contain the idea of "let go," "release.") **342 conceits** fancies, ideas **343 distaste** be distasteful **344 act** action, working **346 mandragora** an opiate made of the mandrake root **349 thou owedst** you did own

I slept the next night well, fed well, was free and merry;
I found not Cassio's kisses on her lips.
He that is robbed, not wanting what is stolen,
Let him not know 't and he's not robbed at all.

**IAGO:** I am sorry to hear this.

**OTHELLO:** I had been happy if the general camp,
Pioners and all, had tasted her sweet body,
So I had nothing known. O, now, forever
Farewell the tranquil mind! Farewell content!
Farewell the plumèd troops and the big wars
That makes ambition virtue! O, farewell!
Farewell the neighing steed and the shrill trump,
The spirit-stirring drum, th' ear-piercing fife,
The royal banner, and all quality,
Pride, pomp, and circumstance of glorious war!
And O, you mortal engines, whose rude throats
Th' immortal Jove's dread clamors counterfeit,
Farewell! Othello's occupation's gone.

**IAGO:** Is 't possible, my lord?

**OTHELLO:** Villain, be sure thou prove my love a whore!
Be sure of it. Give me the ocular proof,
Or, by the worth of mine eternal soul,
Thou hadst been better have been born a dog
Than answer my waked wrath!

**IAGO:** Is 't come to this?

**OTHELLO:** Make me to see 't, or at the least so prove it
That the probation bear no hinge nor loop
To hang a doubt on, or woe upon thy life!

**IAGO:** My noble lord—

**OTHELLO:** If thou dost slander her and torture me,
Never pray more; abandon all remorse;
On horror's head horrors accumulate;
Do deeds to make heaven weep, all earth amazed;
For nothing canst thou to damnation add
Greater than that.

**IAGO:** O grace! O heaven forgive me!
Are you a man? Have you a soul or sense?
God b' wi' you; take mine office. O wretched fool,
That lov'st to make thine honesty a vice!
O monstrous world! Take note, take note, O world,
To be direct and honest is not safe.
I thank you for this profit, and from hence
I'll love no friend, sith love breeds such offense.

**OTHELLO:** Nay, stay. Thou shouldst be honest.

**IAGO:** I should be wise, for honesty's a fool
And loses that it works for.

**OTHELLO:** By the world,
I think my wife be honest and think she is not;
I think that thou art just and think thou art not.
I'll have some proof. My name, that was as fresh
As Dian's visage, is now begrimed and black
As mine own face. If there be cords, or knives,
Poison, or fire, or suffocating streams,
I'll not endure it. Would I were satisfied!

**IAGO:** I see, sir, you are eaten up with passion.
I do repent me that I put it to you.
You would be satisfied?

**OTHELLO:** Would? Nay, and I will.

**IAGO:** And may; but how? How satisfied, my lord?
Would you, the supervisor, grossly gape on?
Behold her topped?

**OTHELLO:** Death and damnation! O!

**IAGO:** It were a tedious difficulty, I think,
To bring them to that prospect. Damn them then,
If ever mortal eyes do see them bolster
More than their own. What then? How then?
What shall I say? Where's satisfaction?
It is impossible you should see this,
Were they as prime as goats, as hot as monkeys,
As salt as wolves in pride, and fools as gross
As ignorance made drunk. But yet I say,
If imputation and strong circumstances
Which lead directly to the door of truth
Will give you satisfaction, you might have 't.

---

**356 free** carefree **358 wanting** missing **362 Pioners** diggers of mines, the lowest grade of soldiers **363 So** provided **365 big** stately **369 quality** character, essential nature **370 Pride** rich display. **circumstance** pageantry **371 mortal engines** i.e., cannon. (*Mortal* means "deadly.") **372 Jove's dread clamors** i.e., thunder **381 probation** proof **385 remorse** pity, penitent hope for salvation **386 horrors accumulate** add still more horrors **387 amazed** confounded with horror

**391 O wretched fool** (Iago addresses himself as a fool for having carried honesty too far.) **392 vice** failing, something overdone **395 profit** profitable instruction. **hence** henceforth **396 sith** since. **offense** i.e., harm to the one who offers help and friendship **397 Thou shouldst be** it appears that you are. (But Iago replies in the sense of "ought to be.") **399 that** what **403 Dian** Diana, goddess of the moon and of chastity **411 supervisor** onlooker **414 Damn them then** i.e., they would have to be really incorrigible **415 bolster** go to bed together, share a bolster **416 More** other. **own** own eyes **419 prime** lustful **420 salt** wanton, sensual. **pride** heat **422 imputation . . . circumstances** strong circumstantial evidence

Othello, enraged by jealousy, seeks Iago's counsel.

**OTHELLO:** Give me a living reason she's disloyal.

**IAGO:** I do not like the office.
But sith I am entered in this cause so far,
Pricked to 't by foolish honesty and love,
I will go on. I lay with Cassio lately,
And being troubled with a raging tooth
I could not sleep. There are a kind of men
So loose of soul that in their sleeps will mutter
Their affairs. One of this kind is Cassio.
In sleep I heard him say, "Sweet Desdemona,
Let us be wary, let us hide our loves!"
And then, sir, would he grip and wring my hand,
Cry "O sweet creature!", then kiss me hard,
As if he plucked up kisses by the roots
That grew upon my lips; then laid his leg
Over my thigh, and sighed, and kissed, and then
Cried, "Cursèd fate that gave thee to the Moor!"

**OTHELLO:** O monstrous! Monstrous!

**IAGO:** Nay, this was but his dream.

**OTHELLO:** But this denoted a foregone conclusion.
'Tis a shrewd doubt, though it be but a dream.

**IAGO:** And this may help to thicken other proofs
That do demonstrate thinly.

**OTHELLO:** I'll tear her all to pieces.

**IAGO:** Nay, but be wise. Yet we see nothing done;
She may be honest yet. Tell me but this:
Have you not sometimes seen a handkerchief
Spotted with strawberries in your wife's hand?

**427 sith** since **428 Pricked** spurred **443 foregone conclusion** concluded experience or action **444 shrewd doubt** suspicious circumstance **450 Spotted with strawberries** embroidered with a strawberry pattern

**OTHELLO:** I gave her such a one. 'Twas my first gift.

**IAGO:** I know not that; but such a handkerchief—
I am sure it was your wife's—did I today
See Cassio wipe his beard with.

**OTHELLO:** If it be that—

**IAGO:** If it be that, or any that was hers,
It speaks against her with the other proofs.

**OTHELLO:** O, that the slave had forty thousand lives!
One is too poor, too weak for my revenge.
Now do I see 'tis true. Look here, Iago,
All my fond love thus do I blow to heaven.
'Tis gone.
Arise, black vengeance, from the hollow hell!
Yield up, O love, thy crown and hearted throne
To tyrannous hate! Swell, bosom, with thy freight,
For 'tis of aspics' tongues!

**IAGO:** Yet be content.

**OTHELLO:** O, blood, blood, blood!

**IAGO:** Patience, I say. Your mind perhaps may change.

**OTHELLO:** Never, Iago. Like to the Pontic Sea,
Whose icy current and compulsive course
Ne'er feels retiring ebb, but keeps due on
To the Propontic and the Hellespont,
Even so my bloody thoughts with violent pace
Shall ne'er look back, ne'er ebb to humble love,
Till that a capable and wide revenge
Swallow them up. Now, by yond marble heaven,
*[Kneeling]* In the due reverence of a sacred vow
I here engage my words.

**IAGO:** Do not rise yet.
*[He kneels.]* Witness, you ever-burning lights above,
You elements that clip us round about,
Witness that here Iago doth give up
The execution of his wit, hands, heart,
To wronged Othello's service. Let him command,
And to obey shall be in me remorse,
What bloody business ever. *[They rise.]*

**457 the slave** i.e., Cassio **460 fond** foolish (but also suggesting "affectionate") **463 hearted** fixed in the heart **464 freight** burden **465 aspics'** venomous serpents' **466 content** calm **469 Pontic Sea** Black Sea **472 Propontic** Sea of Marmora, between the Black Sea and the Aegean. **Hellespont** Dardanelles, straits where the Sea of Marmora joins with the Aegean **475 capable** ample, comprehensive **476 marble** i.e., gleaming like marble and unrelenting **479 s.d. He kneels** (In the Quarto text, Iago kneels here after Othello has knelt at line 477.) **480 clip** encompass **482 execution** exercise, action. **wit** mind **484 remorse** pity (for Othello's wrongs) **485 ever** soever

**OTHELLO:** I greet thy love,
Not with vain thanks, but with acceptance bounteous,
And will upon the instant put thee to 't.
Within these three days let me hear thee say
That Cassio's not alive.

**IAGO:** My friend is dead;
'Tis done at your request. But let her live.

**OTHELLO:** Damn her, lewd minx! O, damn her, damn her!
Come, go with me apart. I will withdraw
To furnish me with some swift means of death
For the fair devil. Now art thou my lieutenant.

**IAGO:** I am your own forever. *Exeunt.*

**3.4** *Enter* DESDEMONA, EMILIA, *and* CLOWN.

**DESDEMONA:** Do you know, sirrah, where Lieutenant Cassio lies?

**CLOWN:** I dare not say he lies anywhere.

**DESDEMONA:** Why, man?

**CLOWN:** He's a soldier, and for me to say a soldier lies, 'tis stabbing.

**DESDEMONA:** Go to. Where lodges he?

**CLOWN:** To tell you where he lodges is to tell you where I lie.

**DESDEMONA:** Can anything be made of this?

**CLOWN:** I know not where he lodges, and for me to devise a lodging and say he lies here, or he lies there, were to lie in mine own throat.

**DESDEMONA:** Can you inquire him out, and be edified by report?

**CLOWN:** I will catechize the world for him; that is, make questions, and by them answer.

**DESDEMONA:** Seek him, bid him come hither. Tell him I have moved my lord on his behalf and hope all will be well

**CLOWN:** To do this is within the compass of man's wit, and therefore I will attempt the doing it. *Exit* CLOWN.

**487 to 't** to the proof **491 minx** wanton

**3.4 Location: Before the citadel.**
**1 sirrah** (A form of address to an inferior.) **2 lies** lodges. (But the Clown makes the obvious pun.) **13 lie . . . throat** (1) lie egregiously and deliberately (2) use the windpipe to speak a lie **19 moved** petitioned

**DESDEMONA:** Where should I lose that handkerchief, Emilia?

**EMILIA:** I know not, madam.

**DESDEMONA:** Believe me, I had rather have lost my purse
Full of crusadoes; and but my noble Moor
Is true of mind and made of no such baseness
As jealous creatures are, it were enough
To put him to ill thinking.

**EMILIA:** Is he not jealous?

**DESDEMONA:** Who, he? I think the sun where he was born
Drew all such humors from him.

**EMILIA** Look where he comes.

*Enter* OTHELLO.

**DESDEMONA:** I will not leave him now till Cassio
Be called to him.—How is 't with you, my lord?

**OTHELLO:** Well, my good lady. *[Aside.]* O, hardness to dissemble!—
How do you, Desdemona?

**DESDEMONA:** Well, my good lord.

**OTHELLO:** Give me your hand. *[She gives her hand.]* This hand is moist, my lady.

**DESDEMONA:** It yet hath felt no age nor known no sorrow.

**OTHELLO:** This argues fruitfulness and liberal heart.
Hot, hot, and moist. This hand of yours requires
A sequester from liberty, fasting and prayer,
Much castigation, exercise devout;
For here's a young and sweating devil here
That commonly rebels. 'Tis a good hand,
A frank one.

**DESDEMONA:** You may indeed say so,
For 'twas that hand that gave away my heart.

**OTHELLO:** A liberal hand. The hearts of old gave hands,
But our new heraldry is hands, not hearts.

**26 crusadoes** Portuguese gold coins **31 humors** (Refers to the four bodily fluids thought to determine temperament.) **38 argues** gives evidence of. **fruitfulness** generosity, amorousness, and fecundity. **liberal** generous and sexually free **40 sequester** separation, sequestration **41 castigation** corrective discipline. **exercise devout** i.e., prayer, religious meditation, etc. **44 frank** generous, open (with sexual suggestion) **46 The hearts . . . hands** i.e., in former times, people would give their hearts when they gave their hands to something **47 But . . . hearts** i.e., in our decadent times, the joining of hands is no longer a badge to signify the giving of hearts

**DESDEMONA:** I cannot speak of this. Come now, your promise.

**OTHELLO:** What promise, chuck?

**DESDEMONA:** I have sent to bid Cassio come speak with you.

**OTHELLO:** I have a salt and sorry rheum offends me;
Lend me thy handkerchief.

**DESDEMONA:** Here, my lord. *[She offers a handkerchief.]*

**OTHELLO:** That which I gave you.

**DESDEMONA:** I have it not about me.

**OTHELLO:** Not?

**DESDEMONA:** No, faith, my lord.

**OTHELLO:** That's a fault. That handkerchief
Did an Egyptian to my mother give.
She was a charmer, and could almost read
The thoughts of people. She told her, while she kept it
'Twould make her amiable and subdue my father
Entirely to her love, but if she lost it
Or made a gift of it, my father's eye
Should hold her loathèd and his spirits should hunt
After new fancies. She, dying, gave it me,
And bid me, when my fate would have me wived,
To give it her. I did so; and take heed on 't;
Make it a darling like your precious eye.
To lose 't or give 't away were such perdition
As nothing else could match.

**DESDEMONA:** Is 't possible?

**OTHELLO:** 'Tis true. There's magic in the web of it.
A sibyl, that had numbered in the world
The sun to course two hundred compasses,
In her prophetic fury sewed the work;
The worms were hallowed that did breed the silk,
And it was dyed in mummy which the skillful
Conserved of maidens' hearts.

**DESDEMONA:** I' faith! Is 't true?

**OTHELLO:** Most veritable. Therefore look to 't well.

**DESDEMONA:** Then would to God that I had never seen 't!

**OTHELLO:** Ha? Wherefore?

**DESDEMONA:** Why do you speak so startingly and rash?

**OTHELLO:** Is 't lost? Is 't gone? Speak, is 't out o' the way?

**DESDEMONA:** Heaven bless us!

**OTHELLO:** Say you?

**DESDEMONA:** It is not lost; but what an if it were?

**OTHELLO:** How?

**DESDEMONA:** I say it is not lost.

**OTHELLO:** Fetch 't, let me see 't.

**DESDEMONA:** Why, so I can, sir, but I will not now.
This is a trick to put me from my suit.
Pray you, let Cassio be received again.

**OTHELLO:** Fetch me the handkerchief! My mind misgives.

**DESDEMONA:** Come, come,
You'll never meet a more sufficient man.

**OTHELLO:** The handkerchief!

**DESDEMONA:** I pray, talk me of Cassio.

**OTHELLO:** The handkerchief!

**DESDEMONA:** A man that all his time
Hath founded his good fortunes on your love,
Shared dangers with you—

**OTHELLO:** The handkerchief!

**DESDEMONA:** I' faith, you are to blame.

**OTHELLO:** Zounds! *Exit* OTHELLO.

**EMILIA:** Is not this man jealous?

**DESDEMONA:** I ne'er saw this before.
Sure, there's some wonder in this handkerchief.
I am most unhappy in the loss of it.

**EMILIA:** 'Tis not a year or two shows us a man.
They are all but stomachs, and we all but food;

---

**49 chuck** (A term of endearment.) **51 salt . . . rheum** distressful head cold or watering of the eyes **59 charmer** sorceress **61 amiable** desirable **65 fancies** loves **67 her** i.e., to my wife **69 perdition** loss **71 web** fabric, weaving **73 compasses** annual circlings. (The *sibyl,* or prophetess, was two hundred years old.) **74 prophetic fury** frenzy of prophetic inspiration. **work** embroidered pattern **76 mummy** medicinal or magical preparation drained from mummified bodies **77 Conserved of** prepared or preserved out of

**81 startingly and rash** disjointedly and impetuously, excitedly **82 out of the way** lost, misplaced **85 an if** if **93 sufficient** able, complete **94 talk** talk to **95 all his time** throughout his career **105 'Tis . . . man** i.e., you can't really know a man even in a year or two of experience (?), or, real men come along seldom (?) **106 but** nothing but

Othello asks Desdemona for the handkerchief he gave her.

They eat us hungerly, and when they are full
They belch us.

*Enter* IAGO *and* CASSIO.

Look you, Cassio and my husband.

**IAGO** *[to* CASSIO*]*: There is no other way; 'tis she must do 't.
And, lo, the happiness! Go and importune her.

**DESDEMONA:** How now, good Cassio? What's the news with you?

**CASSIO:** Madam, my former suit. I do beseech you
That by your virtuous means I may again
Exist and be a member of his love
Whom I, with all the office of my heart,
Entirely honor. I would not be delayed.
If my offense be of such mortal kind
That nor my service past, nor present sorrows,
Nor purposed merit in futurity
Can ransom me into his love again,
But to know so must be my benefit;
So shall I clothe me in a forced content,
And shut myself up in some other course,
To fortune's alms.

**DESDEMONA:** Alas, thrice-gentle Cassio,
My advocation is not now in tune.
My lord is not my lord; nor should I know him,
Were he in favor as in humor altered.
So help me every spirit sanctified

**107 hungerly** hungrily **110 the happiness** in happy time, fortunately met **113 virtuous** efficacious **115 office** loyal service **117 mortal** fatal **118 nor . . . nor** neither . . . nor **121 But . . . benefit** merely to know that my case is hopeless will have to content me (and will be better than uncertainty) **123 shut . . . in** confine myself to **124 To fortune's alms** throwing myself on the mercy of fortune **125 advocation** advocacy **127 favor** appearance. **humor** mood

As I have spoken for you all my best
And stood within the blank of his displeasure
For my free speech! You must awhile be patient.
What I can do I will, and more I will
Than for myself I dare. Let that suffice you.

**IAGO:** Is my lord angry?

**EMILIA:** He went hence but now,
And certainly in strange unquietness.

**IAGO:** Can he be angry? I have seen the cannon
When it hath blown his ranks into the air,
And like the devil from his very arm
Puffed his own brother—and is he angry?
Something of moment then. I will go meet him.
There's matter in 't indeed, if he be angry.

**DESDEMONA:** I prithee, do so. *Exit [*IAGO*].*
Something, sure, of state,
Either from Venice, or some unhatched practice
Made demonstrable here in Cyprus to him,
Hath puddled his clear spirit; and in such cases
Men's natures wrangle with inferior things,
Though great ones are their object. 'Tis even so;
For let our finger ache, and it indues
Our other, healthful members even to a sense
Of pain. Nay, we must think men are not gods,
Nor of them look for such observancy
As fits the bridal. Beshrew me much, Emilia,
I was, unhandsome warrior as I am,
Arraigning his unkindness with my soul;
But now I find I had suborned the witness,
And he's indicted falsely.

**EMILIA:** Pray heaven it be
State matters, as you think, and no conception
Nor no jealous toy concerning you.

**DESDEMONA:** Alas the day! I never gave him cause.

**EMILIA:** But jealous souls will not be answered so;
They are not ever jealous for the cause,
But jealous for they're jealous. It is a monster
Begot upon itself, born on itself.

**130 within the blank** within point-blank range. (The *blank* is the center of the target.) **140 of moment** of immediate importance, momentous **142 of state** concerning state affairs **143 unhatched practice** as yet unexecuted or undiscovered plot **145 puddled** muddied **148 indues** brings to the same condition **151 observancy** attentiveness **152 bridal** wedding (when a bridegroom is newly attentive to his bride). **Beshrew me** (A mild oath.) **153 unhandsome** insufficient, unskillful **154 with** before the bar of **155 suborned the witness** induced the witness to give false testimony **158 toy** fancy **162 for** because **163 Begot upon itself** generated solely from itself

**DESDEMONA:** Heaven keep that monster from
Othello's mind!

**EMILIA:** Lady, amen.

**DESDEMONA:** I will go seek him. Cassio, walk
hereabout.
If I do find him fit, I'll move your suit
And seek to effect it to my uttermost.

**CASSIO:** I humbly thank your ladyship.

*Exit [*DESDEMONA *with* EMILIA*].*

*Enter* BIANCA.

**BIANCA:** Save you, friend Cassio!

**CASSIO:** What make you from home?
How is 't with you, my most fair Bianca?
I' faith, sweet love, I was coming to your house.

**BIANCA:** And I was going to your lodging, Cassio.
What, keep a week away? Seven days and nights?
Eightscore-eight hours? And lovers' absent hours
More tedious than the dial eightscore times?
O weary reckoning!

**CASSIO:** Pardon me, Bianca.
I have this while with leaden thoughts been pressed;
But I shall, in a more continuate time,
Strike off this score of absence. Sweet Bianca,

*[giving her* DESDEMONA's *handkerchief]*

Take me this work out.

**BIANCA:** O Cassio, whence came this?
This is some token from a newer friend.
To the felt absence now I feel a cause.
Is 't come to this? Well, well.

**CASSIO:** Go to, woman!
Throw your vile guesses in the devil's teeth,
From whence you have them. You are jealous now
That this is from some mistress, some remembrance.
No, by my faith, Bianca.

**BIANCA:** Why, whose is it?

**CASSIO:** I know not, neither. I found it in my chamber.
I like the work well. Ere it be demanded—
As like enough it will—I would have it copied.
Take it and do 't, and leave me for this time.

Cassio gives Bianca (Zawe Ashton) the handkerchief he found in his room.

**BIANCA:** Leave you? Wherefore?

**CASSIO:** I do attend here on the General,
And think it no addition, nor my wish,
To have him see me womaned.

**BIANCA:** Why, I pray you?

**CASSIO:** Not that I love you not.

**BIANCA:** But that you do not love me.
I pray you, bring me on the way a little,
And say if I shall see you soon at night.

**CASSIO:** 'Tis but a little way that I can bring you,
For I attend here; but I'll see you soon.

**BIANCA:** 'Tis very good. I must be circumstanced.

*Exeunt omnes.*

**4.1** *Enter* OTHELLO *and* IAGO.

**IAGO:** Will you think so?

**OTHELLO:** Think so, Iago?

**IAGO:** What,
To kiss in private?

**OTHELLO:** An unauthorized kiss!

**IAGO:** Or to be naked with her friend in bed
An hour or more, not meaning any harm?

---

**170 Save** God save. **make** do **175 Eightscore-eight** one hundred sixty-eight, the number of hours in a week **176 the dial** a complete revolution of the clock **179 continuate** uninterrupted **180 Strike . . . score** settle this account **181 Take . . . out** copy this embroidery for me **182 friend** mistress **190 demanded** inquired for **191 like** likely

**195 addition** i.e., addition to my reputation **200 bring** accompany **204 be circumstanced** be governed by circumstance, yield to your conditions

**4.1 Location: Before the citadel.**

**OTHELLO:** Naked in bed, Iago, and not mean harm?
It is hypocrisy against the devil.
They that mean virtuously and yet do so,
The devil their virtue tempts, and they tempt
heaven.

**IAGO:** If they do nothing, 'tis a venial slip.
But if I give my wife a handkerchief—

**OTHELLO:** What then?

**IAGO:** Why then, 'tis hers, my lord, and being hers,
She may, I think, bestow 't on any man.

**OTHELLO:** She is protectress of her honor too.
May she give that?

**IAGO:** Her honor is an essence that's not seen;
They have it very oft that have it not.
But, for the handkerchief—

**OTHELLO:** By heaven, I would most gladly have
forgot it.
Thou saidst—O, it comes o'er my memory
As doth the raven o'er the infectious house,
Boding to all—he had my handkerchief.

**IAGO:** Ay, what of that?

**OTHELLO:** That's not so good now.

**IAGO:** What
If I had said I had seen him do you wrong?
Or heard him say—as knaves be such abroad,
Who having, by their own importunate suit,
Or voluntary dotage of some mistress,
Convincèd or supplied them, cannot choose
But they must blab—

**OTHELLO:** Hath he said anything?

**IAGO:** He hath, my lord; but, be you well assured,
No more than he'll unswear.

**OTHELLO:** What hath he said?

**IAGO:** Faith, that he did—I know not what he did.

**OTHELLO:** What? What?

**IAGO:** Lie—

**OTHELLO:** With her?

**IAGO:** With her, on her; what you will.

**OTHELLO:** Lie with her? Lie on her? We say "lie on her" when they belie her. Lie with her? Zounds, that's fulsome.—Handkerchief—confessions—handkerchief!—To confess and be hanged for his labor—first to be hanged and then to confess.—I tremble at it. Nature would not invest herself in such shadowing passion without some instruction. It is not words that shakes me thus. Pish! Noses, ears, and lips.—Is 't possible?—Confess—handkerchief!—O devil!

*Falls in a trance.*

**IAGO:** Work on,
My medicine, work! Thus credulous fools are caught,
And many worthy and chaste dames even thus,
All guiltless, meet reproach.—What, ho! My lord!
My lord, I say! Othello!

*Enter* CASSIO.

How now, Cassio?

**CASSIO:** What's the matter?

**IAGO:** My lord is fall'n into an epilepsy.
This is his second fit. He had one yesterday.

**CASSIO:** Rub him about the temples.

**IAGO:** No, forbear.
The lethargy must have his quiet course.
If not, he foams at mouth, and by and by
Breaks out to savage madness. Look, he stirs.
Do you withdraw yourself a little while.
He will recover straight. When he is gone,
I would on great occasion speak with you.

*[Exit* CASSIO.*]*

How is it, General? Have you not hurt your head?

**OTHELLO:** Dost thou mock me?

**IAGO:** I mock you not, by heaven.
Would you would bear your fortune like a man!

**OTHELLO:** A hornèd man's a monster and a beast.

**IAGO:** There's many a beast then in a populous city,
And many a civil monster.

**9 venial** pardonable **17 They have it** i.e., they enjoy a reputation for it **21 raven . . . house** (Allusion to the belief that the raven hovered over a house of sickness or infection, such as one visited by the plague.) **25 abroad** around about **27 voluntary dotage** willing infatuation **28 Convincèd or supplied** seduced or sexually gratified

**36 belie** slander **37 fulsome** foul **38–39 first . . . to confess** (Othello reverses the proverbial *confess and be hanged;* Cassio is to be given no time to confess before he dies.) **40–41 Nature . . . instruction** i.e., without some foundation in fact, nature would not have dressed herself in such an overwhelming passion that comes over me now and fills my mind with images, or in such a lifelike fantasy as Cassio had in his dreams of lying with Desdemona **41 words** mere words **53 lethargy** coma. **his** its **58 on great occasion** on a matter of great importance **60 mock me** (Othello takes Iago's question about hurting his head to be a mocking reference to the cuckold's horns.) **64 civil** i.e., dwelling in a city

**OTHELLO:** Did he confess it?

**IAGO:** Good sir, be a man.
Think every bearded fellow that's but yoked
May draw with you. There's millions now alive
That nightly lie in those unproper beds
Which they dare swear peculiar. Your case is better.
O, 'tis the spite of hell, the fiend's arch-mock,
To lip a wanton in a secure couch
And to suppose her chaste! No, let me know,
And knowing what I am, I know what she shall be.

**OTHELLO:** O, thou art wise. 'Tis certain.

**IAGO:** Stand you awhile apart;
Confine yourself but in a patient list.
Whilst you were here o'erwhelmèd with your grief—
A passion most unsuiting such a man—
Cassio came hither. I shifted him away,
And laid good 'scuse upon your ecstasy,
Bade him anon return and here speak with me,
The which he promised. Do but encave yourself
And mark the fleers, the gibes, and notable scorns
That dwell in every region of his face;
For I will make him tell the tale anew,
Where, how, how oft, how long ago, and when
He hath and is again to cope your wife.
I say, but mark his gesture. Marry, patience!
Or I shall say you're all-in-all in spleen,
And nothing of a man.

**OTHELLO:** Dost thou hear, Iago?
I will be found most cunning in my patience;
But—dost thou hear?—most bloody.

**IAGO:** That's not amiss;
But yet keep time in all. Will you withdraw?
[OTHELLO *stands apart.]*
Now will I question Cassio of Bianca,
A huswife that by selling her desires
Buys herself bread and clothes. It is a creature
That dotes on Cassio—as 'tis the strumpet's plague
To beguile many and be beguiled by one.
He, when he hears of her, cannot restrain
From the excess of laughter. Here he comes.

*Enter* CASSIO.

As he shall smile, Othello shall go mad;
And his unbookish jealousy must conster
Poor Cassio's smiles, gestures, and light behaviors
Quite in the wrong.—How do you now, Lieutenant?

**CASSIO:** The worser that you give me the addition
Whose want even kills me.

**IAGO:** Ply Desdemona well and you are sure on 't.
*[Speaking lower.]* Now, if this suit lay in Bianca's power,
How quickly should you speed!

**CASSIO** *[laughing]*: Alas, poor caitiff!

**OTHELLO** *[aside]*: Look how he laughs already!

**IAGO:** I never knew a woman love man so.

**CASSIO:** Alas, poor rogue! I think, i' faith, she loves me.

**OTHELLO:** Now he denies it faintly, and laughs it out.

**IAGO:** Do you hear, Cassio?

**OTHELLO:** Now he importunes him
To tell it o'er. Go to! Well said, well said.

**IAGO:** She gives it out that you shall marry her.
Do you intend it?

**CASSIO:** Ha, ha, ha!

**OTHELLO:** Do you triumph, Roman? Do you triumph?

**CASSIO:** I marry her? What? A customer? Prithee, bear some charity to my wit; do not think it so unwholesome. Ha, ha, ha!

**OTHELLO:** So, so, so, so! They laugh that win.

**IAGO:** Faith, the cry goes that you shall marry her.

**CASSIO:** Prithee, say true.

**IAGO:** I am a very villain else.

**OTHELLO:** Have you scored me? Well.

---

**67 yoked** (1) married (2) put into the yoke of infamy and cuckoldry **68 draw with you** pull as you do, like oxen who are yoked, i.e., share your fate as cuckold **69 unproper** not exclusively their own **70 peculiar** private, their own. **better** i.e., because you know the truth **72 lip** kiss. **secure** free from suspicion **74 what I am** i.e., a cuckold. **she shall be** will happen to her **77 in . . . list** within the bounds of patience **80 shifted him away** used a dodge to get rid of him **81 ecstasy** trance **83 encave** conceal **84 fleers** sneers. **notable** obvious **88 cope** encounter with, have sex with **90 all-in-all in spleen** utterly governed by passionate impulses **94 keep time** keep yourself steady (as in music) **96 huswife** hussy

**100 restrain** refrain **103 unbookish** uninstructed. **conster** construe **106 addition** title **107 Whose want** the lack of which **111 caitiff** wretch **117 Go to** (An expression of remonstrance.) **Well said** well done **121 Roman** (The Romans were noted for their *triumphs* or triumphal processions.) **122 customer** i.e., prostitute **122–123 bear . . . wit** be more charitable to my judgment **125 They . . . win** i.e., they that laugh last laugh best **126 cry** rumor **128 I . . . else** call me a complete rogue if I'm not telling the truth **129 scored me** scored off me, beaten me, made up my reckoning, branded me

**CASSIO:** This is the monkey's own giving out. She is persuaded I will marry her out of her own love and flattery, not out of my promise.

**OTHELLO:** Iago beckons me. Now he begins the story.

**CASSIO:** She was here even now; she haunts me in every place. I was the other day talking on the seabank with certain Venetians, and thither comes the bauble, and, by this hand, she falls me thus about my neck— *[He embraces* IAGO.*]*

**OTHELLO:** Crying, "O dear Cassio!" as it were; his gesture imports it.

**CASSIO:** So hangs and lolls and weeps upon me, so shakes and pulls me. Ha, ha, ha!

**OTHELLO:** Now he tells how she plucked him to my chamber. O, I see that nose of yours, but not that dog I shall throw it to.

**CASSIO:** Well, I must leave her company.

**IAGO:** Before me, look where she comes.

*Enter* BIANCA *[with* OTHELLO*'s handkerchief].*

**CASSIO:** 'Tis such another fitchew! Marry, a perfumed one.—What do you mean by this haunting of me?

**BIANCA:** Let the devil and his dam haunt you! What did you mean by that same handkerchief you gave me even now? I was a fine fool to take it. I must take out the work? A likely piece of work, that you should find it in your chamber and know not who left it there! This is some minx's token, and I must take out the work? There, give it your hobbyhorse. *[She gives him the handkerchief.]* Wheresoever you had it, I'll take out no work on 't.

**CASSIO:** How now, my sweet Bianca? How now? How now?

**OTHELLO:** By heaven, that should be my handkerchief!

**BIANCA:** If you'll come to supper tonight, you may; if you will not, come when you are next prepared for. *Exit.*

**132 flattery** self-flattery, self-deception **133 beckons** signals **135 seabank** seashore **136 bauble** plaything **137 by this hand** I make my vow **143–144 not . . . to** (Othello imagines himself cutting off Cassio's nose and throwing it to a dog.) **146 Before me** i.e., on my soul **147 'Tis . . . fitchew** what a polecat she is! Just like all the others. **fitchew** (Polecats were often compared with prostitutes because of their rank smell and presumed lechery.) **149 dam** mother **152 A likely . . . work** a fine story **155 hobbyhorse** harlot **159 should be** must be **161 when . . . for** when I'm ready for you (i.e., never)

Bianca enters with the handkerchief.

**IAGO:** After her, after her.

**CASSIO:** Faith, I must. She'll rail in the streets else.

**IAGO:** Will you sup there?

**CASSIO:** Faith, I intend so.

**IAGO:** Well, I may chance to see you, for I would very fain speak with you.

**CASSIO:** Prithee, come. Will you?

**IAGO:** Go to. Say no more. *[Exit* CASSIO.*]*

**OTHELLO** *[advancing]*: How shall I murder him, Iago?

**IAGO:** Did you perceive how he laughed at his vice?

**OTHELLO:** O, Iago!

**IAGO:** And did you see the handkerchief?

**OTHELLO:** Was that mine?

**IAGO:** Yours, by this hand. And to see how he prizes the foolish woman your wife! She gave it him, and he hath given it his whore.

**OTHELLO:** I would have him nine years a-killing. A fine woman! A fair woman! A sweet woman!

**IAGO:** Nay, you must forget that.

**OTHELLO:** Ay, let her rot and perish, and be damned tonight, for she shall not live. No, my heart is turned to stone; I strike it, and it hurts my hand. O, the world hath not a sweeter creature! She might lie by an emperor's side and command him tasks.

**169 Go to** (An expression of remonstrance.)

**IAGO:** Nay, that's not your way.

**OTHELLO:** Hang her! I do but say what she is. So delicate with her needle! An admirable musician! O, she will sing the savageness out of a bear. Of so high and plenteous wit and invention!

**IAGO:** She's the worse for all this.

**OTHELLO:** O, a thousand, a thousand times! And then, of so gentle a condition!

**OTHELLO:** Ay, too gentle.

**OTHELLO:** Nay, that's certain. But yet the pity of it, Iago! O, Iago, the pity of it, Iago!

**IAGO:** If you are so fond over her iniquity, give her patent to offend, for if it touch not you it comes near nobody.

**OTHELLO:** I will chop her into messes. Cuckold me?

**IAGO:** O, 'tis foul in her.

**OTHELLO:** With mine officer?

**IAGO:** That's fouler.

**OTHELLO:** Get me some poison, Iago, this night. I'll not expostulate with her, lest her body and beauty unprovide my mind again. This night, Iago.

**IAGO:** Do it not with poison. Strangle her in her bed, even the bed she hath contaminated.

**OTHELLO:** Good, good! The justice of it pleases. Very good.

**IAGO:** And for Cassio, let me be his undertaker. You shall hear more by midnight.

**OTHELLO:** Excellent good. *[A trumpet within.]* What trumpet is that same?

**IAGO:** I warrant, something from Venice.

*Enter* LODOVICO, DESDEMONA, *and attendants.*

'Tis Lodovico. This comes from the Duke.
See, your wife's with him.

**LODOVICO:** God save you, worthy General!

**OTHELLO:** With all my heart, sir.

**LODOVICO** *[giving him a letter]*: The Duke and the senators of Venice greet you.

**OTHELLO:** I kiss the instrument of their pleasures.

*[He opens the letter, and reads.]*

**DESDEMONA:** And what's the news, good cousin Lodovico?

**IAGO:** I am very glad to see you, signor.
Welcome to Cyprus.

**LODOVICO:** I thank you. How does Lieutenant Cassio?

**IAGO:** Lives, sir.

**DESDEMONA:** Cousin, there's fall'n between him and my lord
An unkind breach; but you shall make all well.

**OTHELLO:** Are you sure of that?

**DESDEMONA:** My lord?

**OTHELLO** *[reads]*: "This fail you not to do, as you will—"

**LODOVICO:** He did not call; he's busy in the paper.
Is there division twixt my lord and Cassio?

**DESDEMONA:** A most unhappy one. I would do much
T' atone them, for the love I bear to Cassio.

**OTHELLO:** Fire and brimstone!

**DESDEMONA:** My lord?

**OTHELLO:** Are you wise?

**DESDEMONA:** What, is he angry?

**LODOVICO:** Maybe the letter moved him;
For, as I think, they do command him home,
Deputing Cassio in his government.

**DESDEMONA:** By my troth, I am glad on 't.

**OTHELLO:** Indeed?

**DESDEMONA:** My lord?

**OTHELLO:** I am glad to see you mad.

**DESDEMONA:** Why, sweet Othello—

**OTHELLO** *[striking her]*: Devil!

**DESDEMONA:** I have not deserved this.

---

**186 your way** i.e., the way you should think of her **190 invention** imagination **193 gentle a condition** wellborn and well-bred **194 gentle** generous, yielding (to other men) **197 fond** foolish. **patent** license **199 messes** portions of meat, i.e., bits **205 unprovide** weaken, render unfit **209 be his undertaker** undertake to dispatch him **215 With all my heart** i.e., I thank you most heartily

**224 unkind** unnatural, contrary to their natures; hurtful **231 atone** reconcile **237 government** office **238 on 't** of it **241 I am . . . mad** i.e., I am glad to see that you are insane enough to rejoice in Cassio's promotion (? Othello bitterly plays on Desdemona's *I am glad.*)

**LODOVICO:** My lord, this would not be believed in Venice,
Though I should swear I saw 't. 'Tis very much.
Make her amends; she weeps.

**OTHELLO:** O devil, devil!
If that the earth could teem with woman's tears,
Each drop she falls would prove a crocodile.
Out of my sight!

**DESDEMONA:** I will not stay to offend you. *[Going.]*

**LODOVICO:** Truly, an obedient lady.
I do beseech your lordship, call her back.

**OTHELLO:** Mistress!

**DESDEMONA** *[returning]*: My lord?

**OTHELLO:** What would you with her, sir?

**LODOVICO:** Who, I, my lord?

**OTHELLO:** Ay, you did wish that I would make her turn.
Sir, she can turn, and turn, and yet go on
And turn again; and she can weep, sir, weep;
And she's obedient, as you say, obedient,
Very obedient.—Proceed you in your tears.—
Concerning this, sir—O well-painted passion!—
I am commanded home.—Get you away;
I'll send for you anon.—Sir, I obey the mandate
And will return to Venice.—Hence, avaunt!
*[Exit* DESDEMONA.*]*
Cassio shall have my place. And, sir, tonight
I do entreat that we may sup together.
You are welcome, sir, to Cyprus.—Goats and monkeys! *Exit.*

**LODOVICO:** Is this the noble Moor whom our full Senate
Call all in all sufficient? Is this the nature
Whom passion could not shake? Whose solid virtue
The shot of accident nor dart of chance
Could neither graze nor pierce?

**IAGO:** He is much changed.

**LODOVICO:** Are his wits safe? Is he not light of brain?

---

**246 very much** too much, outrageous **248 teem** breed, be impregnated **249 falls** lets fall. **crocodile** (Crocodiles were supposed to weep hypocritical tears for their victims.) **255 What . . . sir** (Othello implies that Desdemona is pliant and will do a *turn*, lines 257–259, for any man.) **260 obedient** (With much the same sexual connotation as *turn* in lines 257–259.) **262 passion** i.e., grief **268 Goats and monkeys** (See 3.3.419.)

Othello pumps Emilia (Lorraine Burroughs) for information regarding Desdemona's affair.

**IAGO:** He's that he is. I may not breathe my censure
What he might be. If what he might he is not,
I would to heaven he were!

**LODOVICO:** What, strike his wife?

**IAGO:** Faith, that was not so well; yet would I knew
That stroke would prove the worst!

**LODOVICO:** Is it his use?
Or did the letters work upon his blood
And new-create his fault?

**IAGO:** Alas, alas!
It is not honesty in me to speak
What I have seen and known. You shall observe him,
And his own courses will denote him so
That I may save my speech. Do but go after,
And mark how he continues.

**LODOVICO:** I am sorry that I am deceived in him.
*Exeunt.*

## 4.2 *Enter* OTHELLO *and* EMILIA.

**OTHELLO:** You have seen nothing then?

**EMILIA:** Nor ever heard, nor ever did suspect.

**OTHELLO:** Yes, you have seen Cassio and she together.

**EMILIA:** But then I saw no harm, and then I heard
Each syllable that breath made up between them.

---

**275–277 I may . . . were** i.e., I dare not venture an opinion as to whether he's of unsound mind, as you suggest, but, if he isn't, then it might be better to wish he were in fact insane, since only that could excuse his wild behavior **279 use** custom **280 blood** passions **284 courses will denote** actions will reveal

**4.2. Location: The citadel.**

**OTHELLO:** What, did they never whisper?

**EMILIA:** Never, my lord.

**OTHELLO:** Nor send you out o' the way?

**EMILIA:** Never.

**OTHELLO:** To fetch her fan, her gloves, her mask, nor nothing?

**EMILIA:** Never, my lord.

**OTHELLO:** That's strange.

**EMILIA:** I durst, my lord, to wager she is honest,
Lay down my soul at stake. If you think other,
Remove your thought; it doth abuse your bosom.
If any wretch have put this in your head,
Let heaven requite it with the serpent's curse!
For if she be not honest, chaste, and true,
There's no man happy; the purest of their wives
Is foul as slander.

**OTHELLO:** Bid her come hither. Go.

*Exit* EMILIA.

She says enough; yet she's a simple bawd
That cannot say as much. This is a subtle whore,
A closet lock and key of villainous secrets.
And yet she'll kneel and pray; I have seen her do 't.

*Enter* DESDEMONA *and* EMILIA.

**DESDEMONA:** My lord, what is your will?

**OTHELLO:** Pray you, chuck, come hither.

**DESDEMONA:** What is your pleasure?

**OTHELLO:** Let me see your eyes.
Look in my face.

**DESDEMONA:** What horrible fancy's this?

**OTHELLO** *[to* EMILIA*]*: Some of your function, mistress.
Leave procreants alone and shut the door;
Cough or cry "hem" if anybody come.
Your mystery, your mystery! Nay, dispatch.

*Exit* EMILIA.

**DESDEMONA** *[kneeling]*: Upon my knees, what doth your speech import?
I understand a fury in your words,
But not the words.

**OTHELLO:** Why, what art thou?

**DESDEMONA:** Your wife, my lord, your true
And loyal wife.

**OTHELLO:** Come, swear it, damn thyself,
Lest, being like one of heaven, the devils themselves
Should fear to seize thee. Therefore be double damned:
Swear thou art honest.

**DESDEMONA:** Heaven doth truly know it.

**OTHELLO:** Heaven truly knows that thou art false as hell.

**DESDEMONA:** To whom, my lord? With whom? How am I false?

**OTHELLO** *[weeping]*: Ah, Desdemon! Away, away, away!

**DESDEMONA:** Alas the heavy day! Why do you weep?
Am I the motive of these tears, my lord?
If haply you my father do suspect
An instrument of this your calling back,
Lay not your blame on me. If you have lost him,
I have lost him too.

**OTHELLO:** Had it pleased heaven
To try me with affliction, had they rained
All kinds of sores and shames on my bare head,
Steeped me in poverty to the very lips,
Given to captivity me and my utmost hopes,
I should have found in some place of my soul
A drop of patience. But, alas, to make me
A fixèd figure for the time of scorn
To point his slow and moving finger at!
Yet could I bear that too, well, very well.
But there where I have garnered up my heart,
Where either I must live or bear no life,
The fountain from the which my current runs
Or else dries up—to be discarded thence!
Or keep it as a cistern for foul toads
To knot and gender in! Turn thy complexion there,

---

**14 at stake** as the wager **15 abuse your bosom** deceive you **17 the serpent's curse** the curse pronounced by God on the serpent for deceiving Eve, just as some man has done to Othello and Desdemona. (See Genesis 3:14.) **21–22 she's . . . much** i.e., any procuress or go-between who couldn't make up as plausible a story as Emilia's would have to be pretty stupid **22 This** i.e., Desdemona **23 closet lock and key** i.e., concealer **29 Some . . . function** i.e., practice your chosen profession, that of bawd (by guarding the door) **30 procreants** mating couples **32 mystery** trade, occupation

**38 being . . . heaven** looking like an angel **45 motive** cause **50 they** i.e., heavenly powers **56 time of scorn** i.e., scornful world **57 his** its. **slow and moving finger** i.e., hour hand of the clock, moving so slowly it seems hardly to move at all. (Othello envisages himself as being eternally pointed at by the scornful world as the numbers on a clock are pointed at by the hour hand.) **59 garnered** stored **61 fountain** spring **63 cistern** cesspool **64 knot** couple. **gender** engender. **Turn . . . there** change your color, grow pale, at such a sight

Othello accuses Desdemona of being false.

Patience, thou young and rose-lipped cherubin—
Ay, there look grim as hell!

**DESDEMONA:** I hope my noble lord esteems me honest.

**OTHELLO:** O, ay, as summer flies are in the shambles,
That quicken even with blowing. O thou weed,
Who art so lovely fair and smell'st so sweet
That the sense aches at thee, would thou hadst ne'er been born!

**DESDEMONA:** Alas, what ignorant sin have I committed?

**OTHELLO:** Was this fair paper, this most goodly book,
Made to write "whore" upon? What committed?
Committed? O thou public commoner!
I should make very forges of my cheeks,
That would to cinders burn up modesty,
Did I but speak thy deeds. What committed?
Heaven stops the nose at it and the moon winks;
The bawdy wind, that kisses all it meets,
Is hushed within the hollow mine of earth
And will not hear 't. What committed?
Impudent strumpet!

**DESDEMONA:** By heaven, you do me wrong.

**OTHELLO:** Are not you a strumpet?

**DESDEMONA:** No, as I am a Christian.
If to preserve this vessel for my lord
From any other foul unlawful touch
Be not to be a strumpet, I am none.

**OTHELLO:** What, not a whore?

**DESDEMONA:** No, as I shall be saved.

**OTHELLO:** Is 't possible?

**DESDEMONA:** O, heaven forgive us!

**OTHELLO:** I cry you mercy, then.
I took you for that cunning whore of Venice
That married with Othello. *[Calling out.]* You, mistress,
That have the office opposite to Saint Peter
And keep the gate of hell!

*Enter* EMILIA.

You, you, ay, you!
We have done our course. There's money for your pains. *[He gives money.]*
I pray you, turn the key and keep our counsel. *Exit.*

**EMILIA:** Alas, what does this gentleman conceive?
How do you, madam? How do you, my good lady?

**DESDEMONA:** Faith, half asleep.

**EMILIA:** Good madam, what's the matter with my lord?

**DESDEMONA:** With who?

**EMILIA:** Why, with my lord, madam.

**DESDEMONA:** Who is thy lord?

**EMILIA:** He that is yours, sweet lady.

**DESDEMONA:** I have none. Do not talk to me, Emilia.
I cannot weep, nor answers have I none
But what should go by water. Prithee, tonight
Lay on my bed my wedding sheets, remember;
And call thy husband hither.

**EMILIA:** Here's a change indeed! *Exit.*

**DESDEMONA:** 'Tis meet I should be used so, very meet.
How have I been behaved, that he might stick
The small'st opinion on my least misuse?

*Enter* IAGO *and* EMILIA.

**IAGO:** What is your pleasure, madam? How is 't with you?

---

**65–66 Patience . . . hell** (Even Patience, that rose-lipped cherub, will look grim and pale at this spectacle.) **67 honest** chaste **68 shambles** slaughterhouse **69 quicken** come to life. **with blowing** i.e., with the puffing up of something rotten in which maggots are breeding **72 ignorant sin** sin in ignorance **75 commoner** prostitute **79 winks** closes her eyes. (The moon symbolizes chastity.) **80 bawdy** kissing one and all **81 mine** cave (where the winds were thought to dwell)

**86 vessel** body **92 cry you mercy** beg your pardon **97 course** business (with an indecent suggestion of "trick," turn at sex) **99 conceive** suppose, think **101 half asleep** i.e., dazed **108 go by water** be expressed by tears **112 meet** fitting **113 stick** attach **114 opinion** censure. **least misuse** slightest misconduct

Desdemona seeks the advice of Iago and Emilia regarding Othello's accusations.

**DESDEMONA:** I cannot tell. Those that do teach young babes
Do it with gentle means and easy tasks.
He might have chid me so, for, in good faith,
I am a child to chiding.

**IAGO:** What is the matter, lady?

**EMILIA:** Alas, Iago, my lord hath so bewhored her,
Thrown such despite and heavy terms upon her,
That true hearts cannot bear it.

**DESDEMONA:** Am I that name, Iago?

**IAGO:** What name, fair lady?

**DESDEMONA:** Such as she said my lord did say I was.

**EMILIA:** He called her whore. A beggar in his drink
Could not have laid such terms upon his callet.

**IAGO:** Why did he so?

**DESDEMONA** *[weeping]*: I do not know. I am sure I am none such.

**IAGO:** Do not weep, do not weep. Alas the day!

**EMILIA:** Hath she forsook so many noble matches,
Her father and her country and her friends,
To be called whore? Would it not make one weep?

**DESDEMONA:** It is my wretched fortune.

**IAGO:** Beshrew him for 't!
How comes this trick upon him?

**DESDEMONA:** Nay, heaven doth know.

**EMILIA:** I will be hanged if some eternal villain,
Some busy and insinuating rogue,
Some cogging, cozening slave, to get some office,
Have not devised this slander. I will be hanged else.

**IAGO:** Fie, there is no such man. It is impossible.

**DESDEMONA:** If any such there be, heaven pardon him!

**EMILIA:** A halter pardon him! And hell gnaw his bones!
Why should he call her whore? Who keeps her company?
What place? What time? What form? What likelihood?
The Moor's abused by some most villainous knave,
Some base notorious knave, some scurvy fellow.
O heaven, that such companions thou'dst unfold,
And put in every honest hand a whip
To lash the rascals naked through the world
Even from the east to th' west!

**IAGO:** Speak within door.

**EMILIA:** O, fie upon them! Some such squire he was
That turned your wit the seamy side without
And made you to suspect me with the Moor.

**IAGO:** You are a fool. Go to.

**DESDEMONA:** Alas, Iago,
What shall I do to win my lord again?
Good friend, go to him; for, by this light of heaven,
I know not how I lost him. Here I kneel. *[She kneels.]*
If e'er my will did trespass 'gainst his love,
Either in discourse of thought or actual deed,
Or that mine eyes, mine ears, or any sense
Delighted them in any other form;
Or that I do not yet, and ever did,
And ever will—though he do shake me off
To beggarly divorcement—love him dearly,
Comfort forswear me! Unkindness may do much,
And his unkindness may defeat my life,
But never taint my love. I cannot say "whore."
It does abhor me now I speak the word;

---

**128 callet** whore **135 Beshrew** curse **136 trick** strange behavior, delusion

**137 eternal** inveterate **138 insinuating** ingratiating, fawning, wheedling **139 cogging** cheating. **cozening** defrauding **143 halter** hangman's noose **145 form** appearance, circumstance **148 that** would that. **companions** fellows. **unfold** expose **151 within door** i.e., not so loud **152 squire** fellow **153 seamy side without** wrong side out **155 Go to** i.e., that's enough **160 discourse of thought** process of thinking **161 that** if. (Also in line 163.) **162 Delighted them** took delight **163 yet** still **166 Comfort forswear** may heavenly comfort forsake **167 defeat** destroy **169 abhor** (1) fill me with abhorrence (2) make me whorelike

To do the act that might the addition earn
Not the world's mass of vanity could make me.
*[She rises.]*

**IAGO:** I pray you, be content. 'Tis but his humor.
The business of the state does him offense,
And he does chide with you.

**DESDEMONA:** If 'twere no other—

**IAGO:** It is but so, I warrant. *[Trumpets within.]*
Hark, how these instruments summon you to supper!
The messengers of Venice stays the meat.
Go in, and weep not. All things shall be well.
*Exeunt* DESDEMONA *and* EMILIA.

*Enter* RODERIGO.

How now, Roderigo?

**RODERIGO:** I do not find that thou deal'st justly with me.

**IAGO:** What in the contrary?

**RODERIGO:** Every day thou daff'st me with some device, Iago, and rather, as it seems to me now, keep'st from me all conveniency than suppliest me with the least advantage of hope. I will indeed no longer endure it, nor am I yet persuaded to put up in peace what already I have foolishly suffered.

**IAGO:** Will you hear me, Roderigo?

**RODERIGO:** Faith, I have heard too much, for your words and performances are no kin together.

**IAGO:** You charge me most unjustly.

**RODERIGO:** With naught but truth. I have wasted myself out of my means. The jewels you have had from me to deliver Desdemona would half have corrupted a votarist. You have told me she hath received them and returned me expectations and comforts of sudden respect and acquaintance, but I find none.

**IAGO:** Well, go to, very well.

**RODERIGO:** "Very well"! "Go to"! I cannot go to, man, nor 'tis not very well. By this hand, I think it is scurvy, and begin to find myself fopped in it.

**IAGO:** Very well.

**RODERIGO:** I tell you 'tis not very well. I will make myself known to Desdemona. If she will return me my jewels, I will give over my suit and repent my unlawful solicitation; if not, assure yourself I will seek satisfaction of you.

**IAGO:** You have said now?

**RODERIGO:** Ay, and said nothing but what I protest intendment of doing.

**IAGO:** Why, now I see there's mettle in thee, and even from this instant do build on thee a better opinion than ever before. Give me thy hand, Roderigo. Thou hast taken against me a most just exception; but yet I protest I have dealt most directly in thy affair.

**RODERIGO:** It hath not appeared.

**IAGO:** I grant indeed it hath not appeared, and your suspicion is not without wit and judgment. But, Roderigo, if thou hast that in thee indeed which I have greater reason to believe now than ever—I mean purpose, courage, and valor—this night show it. If thou the next night following enjoy not Desdemona, take me from this world with treachery and devise engines for my life.

**RODERIGO:** Well, what is it? Is it within reason and compass?

**IAGO:** Sir, there is especial commission come from Venice to depute Cassio in Othello's place.

**RODERIGO:** Is that true? Why, then Othello and Desdemona return again to Venice.

**IAGO:** O, no; he goes into Mauritania and takes away with him the fair Desdemona, unless his abode be lingered here by some accident; wherein none can be so determinate as the removing of Cassio.

**RODERIGO:** How do you mean, removing of him?

**IAGO:** Why, by making him uncapable of Othello's place—knocking out his brains.

**RODERIGO:** And that you would have me to do?

**IAGO:** Ay, if you dare do yourself a profit and a right. He sups tonight with a harlotry, and thither will I go to him. He knows not yet of his honorable fortune. If

---

**170 addition** title **171 vanity** showy splendor **172 humor** mood **178 stays the meat** are waiting to dine **183 thou daff'st me** you put me off **183–184 device** excuse, trick **185 conveniency** advantage, opportunity **186 advantage** increase **187 put up** submit to, tolerate **195 deliver** deliver to **196 votarist** nun **197–198 sudden respect** immediate consideration **200 I cannot go to** (Roderigo changes Iago's *go to,* an expression urging patience, to *I cannot go to,* "I have no opportunity for success in wooing.") **202 fopped** fooled, duped

**204 not very well** (Roderigo changes Iago's *very well,* "all right, then," to *not very well,* "not at all good.") **207 satisfaction** repayment. (The term normally means settling of accounts in a duel.) **209 You . . . now** have you finished? **211 intendment** intention **225 engines for** plots against **235 determinate** conclusive **241 harlotry** slut you will watch his going thence, which I will fashion to fall out between twelve and one, you may take him at your pleasure. I will be near to second your attempt, and he shall fall between us. Come, stand not amazed at it, but go along with me. I will show you such a necessity in his death that you shall think yourself bound to put it on him. It is now high suppertime, and the night grows to waste. About it.

**RODERIGO:** I will hear further reason for this.

**IAGO:** And you shall be satisfied. *Exeunt.*

**4.3** *Enter* OTHELLO, LODOVICO, DESDEMONA, EMILIA, *and attendants.*

**LODOVICO:** I do beseech you, sir, trouble yourself no further.

**OTHELLO:** O, pardon me; 'twill do me good to walk.

**LODOVICO:** Madam, good night. I humbly thank your ladyship.

**DESDEMONA:** Your honor is most welcome.

**OTHELLO:** Will you walk, sir?
O, Desdemona!

**DESDEMONA:** My lord?

**OTHELLO:** Get you to bed on th' instant. I will be returned forthwith. Dismiss your attendant there. Look 't be done.

**DESDEMONA:** I will, my lord.
*Exit [*OTHELLO, *with* LODOVICO *and attendants].*

**EMILIA:** How goes it now? He looks gentler than he did.

**DESDEMONA:** He says he will return incontinent,
And hath commanded me to go to bed,
And bid me to dismiss you.

**EMILIA:** Dismiss me?

**DESDEMONA:** It was his bidding. Therefore, good Emilia,
Give me my nightly wearing, and adieu.
We must not now displease him.

**EMILIA:** I would you had never seen him!

**DESDEMONA:** So would not I. My love doth so approve him
That even his stubbornness, his checks, his frowns—
Prithee, unpin me—have grace and favor in them.
*[*EMILIA *prepares* DESDEMONA *for bed.]*

**EMILIA:** I have laid those sheets you bade me on the bed.

**DESDEMONA:** All's one. Good faith, how foolish are our minds!
If I do die before thee, prithee shroud me
In one of these same sheets.

**EMILIA:** Come, come, you talk.

**DESDEMONA:** My mother had a maid called Barbary.
She was in love, and he she loved proved mad
And did forsake her. She had a song of "Willow."
An old thing 'twas, but it expressed her fortune,
And she died singing it. That song tonight
Will not go from my mind; I have much to do
But to go hang my head all at one side
And sing it like poor Barbary. Prithee, dispatch.

**EMILIA:** Shall I go fetch your nightgown?

**DESDEMONA:** No, unpin me here.
This Lodovico is a proper man.

**EMILIA:** A very handsome man.

**DESDEMONA:** He speaks well.

**EMILIA:** I know a lady in Venice would have walked barefoot to Palestine for a touch of his nether lip.

**DESDEMONA** *[singing]*:
"The poor soul sat sighing by a sycamore tree,
Sing all a green willow;
Her hand on her bosom, her head on her knee,
Sing willow, willow, willow.
The fresh streams ran by her and murmured her moans;
Sing willow, willow, willow;
Her salt tears fell from her, and softened the stones—"
Lay by these.
*[Singing.]* "Sing willow, willow, willow—"
Prithee, hie thee. He'll come anon.
*[Singing.]* "Sing all a green willow must be my garland.
Let nobody blame him; his scorn I approve—"
Nay, that's not next.—Hark! Who is 't that knocks?

---

**244 fall out** occur **249 high** fully **250 grows to waste** wastes away

**4.3. Location: The citadel.**
**12 incontinent** immediately

**21 stubbornness** roughness. **checks** rebukes **25 All's one** all right. It doesn't really matter **27 talk** i.e., prattle **29 mad** wild, i.e., faithless **33–34 I . . . hang** I can scarcely keep myself from hanging **36 nightgown** dressing gown **38 proper** handsome **44 willow** (A conventional emblem of disappointed love.) **52 hie thee** hurry. **anon** right away

Emilia helps Desdemona prepare for bed as she sings.

**EMILIA:** It's the wind.

**DESDEMONA** *[singing]*:
"I called my love false love; but what said he then?
Sing willow, willow, willow;
If I court more women, you'll couch with more men."
So, get thee gone. Good night. Mine eyes do itch;
Doth that bode weeping?

**EMILIA:** 'Tis neither here nor there.

**DESDEMONA:** I have heard it said so. O, these men, these men!
Dost thou in conscience think—tell me, Emilia—
That there be women do abuse their husbands
In such gross kind?

**EMILIA:** There be some such, no question.

**DESDEMONA:** Wouldst thou do such a deed for all the world?

**EMILIA:** Why, would not you?

**DESDEMONA:** No, by this heavenly light!

**EMILIA:** Nor I neither by this heavenly light;
I might do 't as well i' the dark.

**DESDEMONA:** Wouldst thou do such a deed for all the world?

**EMILIA:** The world's a huge thing. It is a great price
For a small vice.

**DESDEMONA:** Good troth, I think thou wouldst not.

**EMILIA:** By my troth, I think I should, and undo 't when I had done. Marry, I would not do such a thing for a joint ring, nor for measures of lawn, nor for gowns, petticoats, nor caps, nor any petty exhibition. But for all the whole world! Uds pity, who would not make her husband a cuckold to make him a monarch? I should venture purgatory for 't.

**DESDEMONA:** Beshrew me if I would do such a wrong
For the whole world.

**EMILIA:** Why, the wrong is but a wrong i' the world, and having the world for your labor, 'tis a wrong in your own world, and you might quickly make it right.

**DESDEMONA:** I do not think there is any such woman.

**EMILIA:** Yes, a dozen, and as many
To th' vantage as would store the world they played for.
But I do think it is their husbands' faults
If wives do fall. Say that they slack their duties
And pour our treasures into foreign laps,
Or else break out in peevish jealousies,
Throwing restraint upon us? Or say they strike us,
Or scant our former having in despite?
Why, we have galls, and though we have some grace,
Yet have we some revenge. Let husbands know
Their wives have sense like them. They see, and smell,
And have their palates both for sweet and sour,
As husbands have. What is it that they do
When they change us for others? Is it sport?
I think it is. And doth affection breed it?
I think it doth. Is 't frailty that thus errs?
It is so, too. And have not we affections,
Desires for sport, and frailty, as men have?
Then let them use us well; else let them know,
The ills we do, their ills instruct us so.

**DESDEMONA:** Good night, good night. God me such uses send
Not to pick bad from bad, but by bad mend!

*Exeunt.*

---

**64 abuse** deceive

**76 joint ring** a ring made in separate halves. **lawn** fine linen **77 exhibition** gift **78 Uds** God's **88 To th' vantage** in addition, to boot. **store** populate. **played** (1) gambled (2) sported sexually **90 duties** marital duties **91 pour . . . laps** i.e., are unfaithful, give what is rightfully ours (semen) to other women **93 Throwing . . . us** i.e., jealousy restricting our freedom to see other men **94 scant . . . despite** reduce our allowance to spite us **95 have galls** i.e., are capable of resenting injury and insult **97 sense** physical sense **100 sport** sexual pastime **101 affection** passion **107 uses** habit, practice **108 Not . . . mend** i.e., not to learn bad conduct from others' badness (as Emilia has suggested women learn from men), but to mend my ways by perceiving what badness is, making spiritual benefit out of evil and adversity

Cassio mortally wounds Roderigo.

**5.1** *Enter* IAGO *and* RODERIGO.

**IAGO:** Here stand behind this bulk. Straight will he come.
Wear thy good rapier bare, and put it home.
Quick, quick! Fear nothing. I'll be at thy elbow.
It makes us or it mars us. Think on that,
And fix most firm thy resolution.

**RODERIGO:** Be near at hand. I may miscarry in 't.

**IAGO:** Here, at thy hand. Be bold, and take thy stand.
*[*IAGO *stands aside.* RODERIGO *conceals himself.]*

**RODERIGO:** I have no great devotion to the deed;
And yet he hath given me satisfying reasons.
'Tis but a man gone. Forth, my sword! He dies.
*[He draws.]*

**IAGO:** I have rubbed this young quat almost to the sense,
And he grows angry. Now, whether he kill Cassio
Or Cassio him, or each do kill the other,
Every way makes my gain. Live Roderigo,
He calls me to a restitution large
Of gold and jewels that I bobbled from him
As gifts to Desdemona.
It must not be. If Cassio do remain,
He hath a daily beauty in his life
That makes me ugly; and besides, the Moor
May unfold me to him; there stand I in much peril.
No, he must die. Be 't so. I hear him coming.

*Enter* CASSIO.

**RODERIGO** *[coming forth]*: I know his gait, 'tis he.—
Villain, thou diest!
*[He attacks* CASSIO.*]*

**CASSIO:** That thrust had been mine enemy indeed,
But that my coat is better than thou know'st.
I will make proof of thine.
*[He draws, and wounds* RODERIGO.*]*

**RODERIGO:** O, I am slain! *[He falls.]*

*[*IAGO, *from behind, wounds* CASSIO *in the leg, and exit.]*

**CASSIO:** I am maimed forever. Help, ho! Murder! Murder!

*Enter* OTHELLO.

**OTHELLO:** The voice of Cassio! Iago keeps his word.

**RODERIGO:** O, villain that I am!

**OTHELLO:** It is even so.

**CASSIO:** O, help, ho! Light! A surgeon!

**OTHELLO:** 'Tis he. O brave Iago, honest and just,
That hast such noble sense of thy friend's wrong!
Thou teachest me. Minion, your dear lies dead,
And your unblest fate hies. Strumpet, I come.
Forth of my heart those charms, thine eyes, are blotted;
Thy bed, lust-stained, shall with lust's blood be spotted. *Exit* OTHELLO.

*Enter* LODOVICO *and* GRATIANO.

**CASSIO:** What ho! No watch? No passage? Murder! Murder!

**GRATIANO:** 'Tis some mischance. The voice is very direful.

**CASSIO:** O, help!

**LODOVICO:** Hark!

**RODERIGO:** O wretched villain!

**LODOVICO:** Two or three groan. 'Tis heavy night;
These may be counterfeits. Let's think 't unsafe
To come in to the cry without more help.
*[They remain near the entrance.]*

---

**5.1. Location: A street in Cyprus.**
**1 bulk** framework projecting from the front of a shop **2 bare** unsheathed **11 quat** pimple, pustule. **to the sense** to the quick **14 Live Roderigo** if Roderigo lives **16 bobbled** swindled **21 unfold** expose

**25 coat** (Possibly a garment of mail under the outer clothing, or simply a tougher coat than Roderigo expected.) **26 proof** a test **34 Minion** hussy (i.e., Desdemona) **35 hies** hastens on **36 Forth of** from out **38 passage** people passing by **43 heavy** thick, dark **45 come in to** approach

**RODERIGO:** Nobody come? Then shall I bleed to death.

*Enter* IAGO *[in his shirtsleeves, with a light].*

**LODOVICO:** Hark!

**GRATIANO:** Here's one comes in his shirt, with light and weapons.

**IAGO:** Who's there? Whose noise is this that cries on murder?

**LODOVICO:** We do not know.

**IAGO:** Did not you hear a cry?

**CASSIO:** Here, here! For heaven's sake, help me!

**IAGO:** What's the matter?

*[He moves toward* CASSIO.*]*

**GRATIANO** *[to* LODOVICO*]*: This is Othello's ancient, as I take it.

**LODOVICO** *[to* GRATIANO*]*: The same indeed, a very valiant fellow.

**IAGO** *[to* CASSIO*]*: What are you here that cry so grievously?

**CASSIO:** Iago? O, I am spoiled, undone by villains!
Give me some help.

**IAGO:** O me, Lieutenant! What villains have done this?

**CASSIO:** I think that one of them is hereabout,
And cannot make away.

**IAGO:** O treacherous villains!
*[To* LODOVICO *and* GRATIANO.*]* What are you there?
Come in, and give some help. *[They advance.]*

**RODERIGO:** O, help me there!

**CASSIO:** That's one of them.

**IAGO:** O murderous slave! O villain!

*[He stabs* RODERIGO.*]*

**RODERIGO:** O damned Iago! O inhuman dog!

**IAGO:** Kill men i' the dark?—Where be these bloody thieves?—
How silent is this town!—Ho! Murder, murder!—
*[To* LODOVICO *and* GRATIANO.*]* What may you be?
Are you of good or evil?

**LODOVICO:** As you shall prove us, praise us.

**IAGO:** Signor Lodovico?

**LODOVICO:** He, sir.

**IAGO:** I cry you mercy. Here's Cassio hurt by villains.

**GRATIANO:** Cassio?

**IAGO:** How is 't, brother?

**CASSIO:** My leg is cut in two.

**IAGO:** Marry, heaven forbid!
Light, gentlemen! I'll bind it with my shirt.

*[He hands them the light, and tends to* CASSIO*'s wound.]*

*Enter* BIANCA.

**BIANCA:** What is the matter, ho? Who is 't that cried?

**IAGO:** Who is 't that cried?

**BIANCA:** O my dear Cassio!
My sweet Cassio! O Cassio, Cassio, Cassio!

**IAGO:** O notable strumpet! Cassio, may you suspect
Who they should be that have thus mangled you?

**CASSIO:** No.

**GRATIANO:** I am sorry to find you thus. I have been to seek you.

**IAGO:** Lend me a garter. *[He applies a tourniquet.]* So.—
O, for a chair,
To bear him easily hence!

**BIANCA:** Alas, he faints! O Cassio, Cassio, Cassio!

**IAGO:** Gentlemen all, I do suspect this trash
To be a party in this injury.—
Patience awhile, good Cassio.—Come, come;
Lend me a light. *[He shines the light on* RODERIGO.*]*
Know we this face or no?
Alas, my friend and my dear countryman
Roderigo! No.—Yes, sure.—O heaven! Roderigo!

**GRATIANO:** What, of Venice?

**IAGO:** Even he, sir. Did you know him?

**GRATIANO:** Know him? Ay.

**IAGO:** Signor Gratiano? I cry your gentle pardon.
These bloods accidents must excuse my manners
That so neglected you.

**GRATIANO:** I am glad to see you.

---

**49 cries on** cries out **54 What** who (also at lines 60 and 66) **55 spoiled** ruined, done for **59 make** get **67 praise** appraise

**70 I cry you mercy** I beg your pardon **83 chair** litter **95 gentle** noble **96 accidents** sudden events

**IAGO:** How do you, Cassio? O, a chair, a chair!

**GRATIANO:** Roderigo!

**IAGO:** He, he, 'tis he. *[A litter is brought in.]* O, that's well said; the chair.
Some good man bear him carefully from hence;
I'll fetch the General's surgeon. *[To* BIANCA.*]* For you, mistress,
Save you your labor.—He that lies slain here, Cassio,
Was my dear friend. What malice was between you?

**CASSIO:** None in the world, nor do I know the man.

**IAGO** *[to* BIANCA*]*: What, look you pale?—O, bear him out o' th' air.

*[*CASSIO *and* RODERIGO *are borne off.]*

Stay you, good gentlemen.—Look you pale, mistress?—
Do you perceive the gastness of here eye?—
Nay, if you stare, we shall hear more anon.—
Behold her well; I pray you, look upon her.
Do you see, gentlemen? Nay, guiltiness
Will speak, though tongues were out of use.

*[Enter* EMILIA.*]*

**EMILIA:** 'Las, what's the matter? What's the matter, husband?

**IAGO:** Cassio hath here been set on in the dark
By Roderigo and fellows that are scaped.
He's almost slain, and Roderigo dead.

**EMILIA:** Alas, good gentleman! Alas, good Cassio!

**IAGO:** This is the fruits of whoring. Prithee, Emilia,
Go know of Cassio where he supped tonight.
*[To* BIANCA.*]* What, do you shake at that?

**BIANCA:** He supped at my house, but I therefore shake not.

**IAGO:** O, did he so? I charge you go with me.

**EMILIA:** O, fie upon thee, strumpet!

**BIANCA:** I am no strumpet, but of life as honest
As you that thus abuse me.

**EMILIA:** As I? Faugh! Fie upon thee!

**100 well said** well done **103 Save . . . labor** i.e., never you mind tending Cassio **104 malice** enmity **106 bear . . . air** (Fresh air was thought to be dangerous for a wound.) **107 Stay you** (Lodovico and Gratiano are evidently about to leave.) **108 gastness** terror **109 stare** (Iago pretends to interpret Bianca's wild looks as an involuntary confession of guilt.) **119 know** learn **124 honest** chaste

**IAGO:** Kind gentlemen, let's go see poor Cassio dressed.—
Come, mistress, you must tell 's another tale.
Emilia, run you to the citadel
And tell my lord and lady what hath happed.—
Will you go on afore? *[Aside.]* This is the night
That either makes me or fordoes me quite. *Exeunt.*

**5.2** *Enter* OTHELLO *[with a light], and* DESDEMONA *in her bed.*

**OTHELLO:** It is the cause, it is the cause, my soul.
Let me not name it to you, you chaste stars!
It is the cause. Yet I'll not shed her blood,
Nor scar that whiter skin of hers than snow,
And smooth as monumental alabaster.
Yet she must die, else she'll betray more men.
Put out the light, and then put out the light.
If I quench thee, thou flaming minister,
I can again thy former light restore,
Should I repent me; but once put out thy light,
Thou cunning'st pattern of excelling nature,
I know not where is that Promethean heat
That can thy light relume. When I have plucked thy rose,
I cannot give it vital growth again;
It needs must wither. I'll smell thee on the tree.

*[He kisses her.]*

O balmy breath, that dost almost persuade
Justice to break her sword! One more, one more.
Be thus when thou art dead, and I will kill thee,
And love thee after. One more, and that's the last.

*[He kisses her.]*

So sweet was ne'er so fatal. I must weep,
But they are cruel tears. This sorrow's heavenly;
It strikes where it doth love. She wakes.

**DESDEMONA:** Who's there? Othello?

**OTHELLO:** Ay, Desdemona.

**127 Cassio dressed** Cassio's wounds dressed **132 fordoes** undoes, ruins

**5.2. Location: A bedchamber in the citadel.**
**s.d. in her bed** (Either the curtains are drawn back to reveal the bed in a recessed area backstage, or the bed is "thrust out" onstage as the scene begins.) **1 cause** i.e., cause of justice, the offense itself, which Othello must correct as an agent of justice **5 monumental** i.e., used in making tombs and funeral monuments **7 the light . . . light** the torch or lamp . . . Desdemona's life **8 flaming minister** torch or lamp that serves me **10 repent me** change my mind **11 Thou . . . pattern** you skillfully wrought perfect example **12 Promethean heat** divine fire. (Alluding to the theft of fire from heaven by Prometheus.) **13 relume** rekindle **21 cruel** unrelenting **22 It . . . love** (Compare Hebrews 12:6: "For whom the Lord loveth he chasteneth.")

**DESDEMONA:** Will you come to bed, my lord?

**OTHELLO:** Have you prayed tonight, Desdemon?

**DESDEMONA:** Ay, my lord.

**OTHELLO:** If you bethink yourself of any crime
Unreconciled as yet to heaven and grace,
Solicit for it straight.

**DESDEMONA:** Alack, my lord, what may you mean by that?

**OTHELLO:** Well, do it, and be brief. I will walk by.
I would not kill thy unpreparèd spirit.
No, heaven forfend! I would not kill thy soul.

**DESDEMONA:** Talk you of killing?

**OTHELLO:** Ay, I do.

**DESDEMONA:** Then heaven
Have mercy on me!

**OTHELLO:** Amen, with all my heart!

**DESDEMONA:** If you say so, I hope you will not kill me.

**OTHELLO:** Humh!

**DESDEMONA:** And yet I fear you; for you're fatal then
When your eyes roll so. Why I should fear I know not,
Since guiltiness I know not; but yet I feel I fear.

**OTHELLO:** Think on thy sins.

**DESDEMONA:** They are loves I bear to you.

**OTHELLO:** Ay, and for that thou diest.

**DESDEMONA:** That death's unnatural that kills for loving.
Alas, why gnaw you so your nether lip?
Some bloody passion shakes your very frame.
These are portents; but yet I hope, I hope,
They do not point on me.

**OTHELLO:** Peace, and be still!

**DESDEMONA:** I will so. What's the matter?

**OTHELLO:** That handkerchief which I so loved and gave thee
Thou gav'st to Cassio.

**DESDEMONA:** No, by my life and soul!
Send for the man and ask him.

---

**28 crime** sin **30 Solicit** petition, pray. **straight** immediately **34 forfend** forbid **42 They are . . . you** i.e., if I sinned, it was in loving you more than my father or more than God **48 point on** point at, predict what is to happen to

Othello dispatches Desdemona.

**OTHELLO:** Sweet soul, take heed, take heed of perjury.
Thou art on thy deathbed.

**DESDEMONA:** Ay, but not yet to die.

**OTHELLO:** Yes, presently.
Therefore confess thee freely of thy sin;
For to deny each article with oath
Cannot remove nor choke the strong conception
That I do groan withal. Thou art to die.

**DESDEMONA:** Then Lord have mercy on me!

**OTHELLO:** I say, amen.

**DESDEMONA:** And have you mercy too! I never did
Offend you in my life; never loved Cassio
But with such general warranty of heaven
As I might love. I never gave him token.

**OTHELLO:** By heaven, I saw my handkerchief in 's hand.
O perjured woman! Thou dost stone my heart,
And makes me call what I intend to do
A murder, which I thought a sacrifice.
I saw the handkerchief.

**DESDEMONA:** He found it, then.
I never gave it him. Send for him hither;
Let him confess a truth.

**OTHELLO:** He hath confessed.

**DESDEMONA:** What, my lord?

**OTHELLO:** That he hath used thee.

**DESDEMONA:** How? Unlawfully?

**OTHELLO:** Ay.

---

**56 presently** immediately **59 conception** (1) belief in your guilt (2) plan in my mind **60 groan withal** (1) groan at in sorrow (2) as in giving birth **63 Offend** wrong **64 warranty** sanction **67 stone** turn to stone, harden

**DESDEMONA:** He will not say so.

**OTHELLO:** No, his mouth is stopped;
Honest Iago hath ta'en order for 't.

**DESDEMONA:** O, my fear interprets. What, is he dead?

**OTHELLO:** Had all his hairs been lives, my great revenge
Had stomach for them all.

**DESDEMONA:** Alas, he is betrayed and I undone!
*[She weeps.]*

**OTHELLO:** Out, strumpet! Weep'st thou for him to my face?

**DESDEMONA:** O, banish me, my lord, but kill me not!

**OTHELLO:** Down, strumpet!

**DESDEMONA:** Kill me tomorrow; let me live tonight!

**OTHELLO:** Nay, if you strive—

**DESDEMONA:** But half an hour!

**OTHELLO:** Being done, there is no pause.

**DESDEMONA:** But while I say one prayer!

**OTHELLO:** It is too late.
*Smothers her.*

**EMILIA** *(at the door)*: My lord, my lord! What, ho! My lord, my lord!

**OTHELLO:** What noise is this? Not dead? Not yet quite dead?
I that am cruel am yet merciful;
I would not have thee linger in thy pain.
*[He dispatches her.]*
So, so.

**EMILIA** *(within)*: What, ho! My lord, my lord!

**OTHELLO:** Who's there?

**EMILIA** *[within]*: O, good my lord, I would speak a word with you!

**OTHELLO:** Yes, 'tis Emilia.—By and by.—She's dead.
'Tis like she comes to speak of Cassio's death.—
The noise was here. Ha! No more moving?
Still as the grave. Shall she come in? Were 't good?—
I think she stirs again. No. What's best to do?
If she come in, she'll sure speak to my wife.
My wife! My wife! What wife? I have no wife.
O, insupportable! O heavy hour!
Methinks it should be now a huge eclipse
Of sun and moon, and that th' affrighted globe
Should yawn at alteration.

**EMILIA** *[within]*: I do beseech you
That I may speak with you, O, good my lord!

**OTHELLO:** I had forgot thee. O, come in, Emilia.—
Soft, by and by. Let me the curtains draw.—
*[He closes the bed-curtains and opens the door.]*
Where art thou?

*Enter* EMILIA.

What's the matter with thee now?

**EMILIA:** O, my good lord, yonder's foul murders done!

**OTHELLO:** What, now?

**EMILIA:** But now, my lord.

**OTHELLO:** It is the very error of the moon;
She comes more nearer earth than she was wont,
And makes men mad.

**EMILIA:** Cassio, my lord, hath killed a young Venetian
Called Roderigo.

**OTHELLO:** Roderigo killed?
And Cassio killed?

**EMILIA:** No, Cassio is not killed.

**OTHELLO:** Not Cassio killed? Then murder's out of tune,
And sweet revenge grows harsh.

**DESDEMONA:** O, falsely, falsely murdered!

**EMILIA:** O Lord, what cry is that?

**OTHELLO:** That? What?

**EMILIA:** Out and alas, that was my lady's voice.
*[She opens the bed-curtains.]*
Help, help, ho, help! O lady, speak again!
Sweet Desdemona! O sweet mistress, speak!

**DESDEMONA:** A guiltless death I die.

**EMILIA:** O, who hath done this deed?

**DESDEMONA:** Nobody; I myself. Farewell.
Commend me to my kind lord. O, farewell! *[She dies.]*

---

**76 ta'en order** taken measures **86 Being done** i.e., since justice has begun its relentless course **95 like** likely that **96 here** (The Folio's *high* is possible, suggesting that the commotion of the attack on Cassio was loud.)

**104 yawn** gape in amazement, i.e., move in an earthquake. (According to Pliny, earthquakes often happen during eclipses.) **at alteration** at these cataclysmic events in nature, well suited to express the horror of Desdemona's death **107 Soft** wait a minute **112 error** aberration, irregularity **123 Out** (A cry of dismay, intensifying *alas.*)

**OTHELLO:** Why, how should she be murdered?

**EMILIA:** Alas, who knows?

**OTHELLO:** You heard her say herself it was not I.

**EMILIA:** She said so. I must needs report the truth.

**OTHELLO:** She's like a liar gone to burning hell!
'Twas I that killed her.

**EMILIA:** O, the more angel she,
And you the blacker devil!

**OTHELLO:** She turned to folly, and she was a whore.

**EMILIA:** Thou dost belie her, and thou art a devil.

**OTHELLO:** She was false as water.

**EMILIA:** Thou art rash as fire to say
That she was false. O, she was heavenly true!

**OTHELLO:** Cassio did top her. Ask thy husband else.
O, I were damned beneath all depth in hell
But that I did proceed upon just grounds
To this extremity. Thy husband knew it all.

**EMILIA:** My husband?

**OTHELLO:** Thy husband.

**EMILIA:** That she was false to wedlock?

**OTHELLO:** Ay, with Cassio. Nay, had she been true,
If heaven would make me such another world
Of one entire and perfect chrysolite,
I'd not have sold her for it.

**EMILIA:** My husband?

**OTHELLO:** Ay, 'twas he that told me on her first.
An honest man he is, and hates the slime
That sticks on filthy deeds.

**EMILIA:** My husband?

**OTHELLO:** What needs this iterance, woman? I say thy husband.

**EMILIA:** O mistress, villainy hath made mocks with love!
My husband say she was false?

**OTHELLO:** He, woman;
I say thy husband. Dost understand the word?
My friend, thy husband, honest, honest Iago.

Montano (Nicholas Farrell) and Gratiano (André Oumansky) enter with swords drawn.

**EMILIA:** If he say so, may his pernicious soul
Rot half a grain a day! He lies to th' heart.
She was too fond of her most filthy bargain.

**OTHELLO:** Ha? *[He draws.]*

**EMILIA:** Do thy worst!
This deed of thine is no more worthy heaven
Than thou wast worthy her.

**OTHELLO:** Peace, you were best.

**EMILIA:** Thou hast not half that power to do me harm
As I have to be hurt. O gull! O dolt!
As ignorant as dirt! Thou hast done a deed—
I care not for thy sword; I'll make thee known,
Though I lost twenty lives.—Help! Help, ho, help!
The Moor hath killed my mistress! Murder, murder!

*Enter* MONTANO, GRATIANO, *and* IAGO.

**MONTANO:** What is the matter? How now, General?

**EMILIA:** O, are you come, Iago? You have done well,
That men must lay their murders on your neck.

**GRATIANO:** What is the matter?

**EMILIA** *[to* IAGO*]*: Disprove this villain, if thou be'st a man.
He says thou toldst him that his wife was false.
I know thou didst not; thou'rt not such a villain.
Speak, for my heart is full.

**IAGO:** I told him what I thought, and told no more
Than what he found himself was apt and true.

---

**136 folly** i.e., wantonness, fleshly sin **137 belie** slander **141 else** i.e., if you don't believe me **150 chrysolite** precious topaz **157 iterance** iteration, repetition **158 made mocks with** derided, made sport of

**168 you were best** it would be best for you **170 to be hurt** i.e., to endure hurt. **gull** dupe **184 apt** plausible

Othello confronts Iago.

**EMILIA:** But did you ever tell him she was false?

**IAGO:** I did.

**EMILIA:** You told a lie, an odious, damnèd lie!
Upon my soul, a lie, a wicked lie.
She false with Cassio? Did you say with Cassio?

**IAGO:** With Cassio, mistress. Go to, charm your tongue.

**EMILIA:** I will not charm my tongue; I am bound to speak.
My mistress here lies murdered in her bed—

**ALL** O heavens forfend!

**EMILIA:** And your reports have set the murder on.

**OTHELLO:** Nay, stare not, masters. It is true indeed.

**GRATIANO:** 'Tis a strange truth.

**MONTANO:** O monstrous act!

**EMILIA:** Villainy, villainy, villainy!
I think upon 't—I think I smell 't! O villainy!
I thought so then—I'll kill myself for grief—
O villainy, villainy!

**IAGO:** What, are you mad? I charge you, get you home.

**EMILIA:** Good gentlemen, let me have leave to speak.
'Tis proper I obey him, but not now.
Perchance, Iago, I will ne'er go home.

**OTHELLO:** O! O! O! *[*OTHELLO *falls on the bed.]*

**190 charm** keep silent (as though by a magic spell) **199 then** (Perhaps at 3.3.331–332 and 4.2.137–154.) **205 s.d. Othello . . . bed** (This direction is from the Quarto, as also *He kisses her* at line 19 and *She dies* at line 129.)

**EMILIA:** Nay, lay thee down and roar,
For thou hast killed the sweetest innocent
That e'er did lift up eye.

**OTHELLO** *[rising]*: O, she was foul!
I scarce did know you, uncle. There lies your niece,
Whose breath indeed these hands have newly stopped.
I know this act shows horrible and grim.

**GRATIANO:** Poor Desdemon! I am glad thy father's dead.
Thy match was mortal to him, and pure grief
Shore his old thread in twain. Did he live now,
This sight would make him do a desperate turn,
Yea, curse his better angel from his side,
And fall to reprobance.

**OTHELLO:** 'Tis pitiful. But yet Iago knows
That she with Cassio hath the act of shame
A thousand times committed. Cassio confessed it;
And she did gratify his amorous works
With that recognizance and pledge of love
Which I first gave her. I saw it in his hand;
It was a handkerchief, an antique token
My father gave my mother.

**EMILIA:** O God! O heavenly God!

**IAGO:** Zounds, hold your peace.

**EMILIA:** 'Twill out, 'twill out! I peace?
No, I will speak as liberal as the north.
Let heaven and men and devils, let them all,
All, all, cry shame against me, yet I'll speak.

**IAGO:** Be wise, and get you home.

**EMILIA:** I will not.
*[*IAGO *threatens* EMILIA.*]*

**GRATIANO:** Fie,
Your sword upon a woman?

**EMILIA:** O thou dull Moor! That handkerchief thou speak'st of
I found by fortune and did give my husband;
For often, with a solemn earnestness,
More than indeed belonged to such a trifle,
He begged of me to steal 't.

**IAGO:** Villainous whore!

**207 lift up eye** i.e., lift her eyes to heaven **210 shows** looks **213 Shore . . . thread** sheared the thread of his old age (as Atropos, one of the three Fates, was thought to do) **214 turn** deed **216 reprobance** damnation, i.e., suicide **220 gratify** reward **221 recognizance** token **227 liberal as the north** freely as the north wind (blows) **235 belonged** was appropriate

**EMILIA:** She give it Cassio? No, alas! I found it,
And I did give 't my husband.

**IAGO:** Filth, thou liest!

**EMILIA:** By heaven, I do not, I do not, gentlemen.
O murderous coxcomb! What should such a fool
Do with so good a wife?

**OTHELLO:** Are there no stones in heaven
But what serves for the thunder?—Precious villain!

*[He runs at* IAGO; MONTANO *disarms* OTHELLO. IAGO, *from behind, stabs* EMILIA.*]*

**GRATIANO:** The woman falls! Sure he hath killed his wife.

**EMILIA:** Ay, ay. O, lay me by my mistress' side.

*[Exit* IAGO.*]*

**GRATIANO:** He's gone, but his wife's killed.

**MONTANO:** 'Tis a notorious villain. Take you this weapon,
Which I have here recovered from the Moor.
Come, guard the door without. Let him not pass,
But kill him rather. I'll after that same villain,
For 'tis a damnèd slave.

*Exit [with all but* OTHELLO *and* EMILIA, *who has been laid by* DESDEMONA*'s side].*

**OTHELLO:** I am not valiant neither,
But every puny whipster gets my sword.
But why should honor outlive honesty?
Let it go all.

**EMILIA:** What did thy song bode, lady?
Hark, canst thou hear me? I will play the swan,
And die in music. *[She sings.]* "Willow, willow, willow."
Moor, she was chaste. She loved thee, cruel Moor.
So come my soul to bliss as I speak true.
So speaking as I think, alas, I die. *[She dies.]*

**OTHELLO:** I have another weapon in this chamber;
It was a sword of Spain, the ice-brook's temper—
O, here it is. *[He finds a sword.]* Uncle, I must come forth.

**GRATIANO** *[within]*: If thou attempt it, it will cost thee dear.
Thou hast no weapon, and perforce must suffer.

**OTHELLO:** Look in upon me then and speak with me,
Or, naked as I am, I will assault thee.

*[Enter* GRATIANO.*]*

**GRATIANO:** What is the matter?

**OTHELLO:** Behold, I have a weapon;
A better never did itself sustain
Upon a soldier's thigh. I have seen the day
That, with this little arm and this good sword,
I have made my way through more impediments
Than twenty times your stop. But O, vain boast!
Who can control his fate? 'Tis not so now.
Be not afraid, though you do see me weaponed;
Here is my journey's end, here is my butt
And very seamark of my utmost sail.

*[*GRATIANO *steps back.]*

Do you go back dismayed? 'Tis a lost fear;
Man but a rush against Othello's breast
And he retires. Where should Othello go?

*[He turns to* DESDEMONA.*]*

Now, how dost thou look now? O ill-starred wench!
Pale as thy smock! When we shall meet at compt,
This look of thine will hurl my soul from heaven,
And fiends will snatch at it. Cold, cold, my girl?
Even like thy chastity. O cursèd, cursèd slave!
Whip me, ye devils,
From the possession of this heavenly sight!
Blow me about in winds! Roast me in sulfur!
Wash me in steep-down gulfs of liquid fire!
O Desdemon! Dead, Desdemon! Dead! O! O!

*Enter* LODOVICO, CASSIO *[carried in a litter],* MONTANO, *and* IAGO *[prisoner], with officers.*

**LODOVICO:** Where is this rash and most unfortunate man?

**OTHELLO:** That's he that was Othello. Here I am.

**LODOVICO:** Where is that viper? Bring the villain forth.

*[*IAGO *is led forward.]*

**OTHELLO:** I look down towards his feet; but that's a fable.
If that thou be'st a devil, I cannot kill thee.

*[He wounds* IAGO.*]*

---

**240 coxcomb** fool. (Addressed to Othello.) **242 stones** bolts, such as those used for thunderbolts **243 Precious** i.e., arrant, utter. **s.d. He . . . Emilia** (The Quarto text reads "The Moor runs at Iago. Iago kills his wife." The Quarto also specifies the exit of Iago at line 245 and the death of Emilia at line 260.) **253 whipster** contemptible fellow (one who is always ready to whip out his sword) **254 honor** i.e., the bravery for which one enjoys a soldier's reputation. **honesty** true integrity **262 the icebrook's temper** tempered in ice-cold water

**267 naked** unarmed **273 stop** power (to stop) **276 butt** goal, limit. (An archery term.) **277 seamark** beacon (marking his destination or limit) **278 lost** wasted, unneeded **279 Man . . . rush** wield no more than a reed **282 compt** account, judgment day **285 slave** i.e., Othello himself **290 s.d. in a litter** (The Quarto specifies that Cassio is "in a chair.") **294 towards his feet** i.e., to see if they are cloven, as the devil's are fabled to be

**LODOVICO:** Wrench his sword from him.
*[OTHELLO is disarmed.]*

**IAGO:** I bleed, sir, but not killed.

**OTHELLO:** I am not sorry neither. I'd have thee live,
For in my sense 'tis happiness to die.

**LODOVICO:** O thou Othello, that was once so good,
Fall'n in the practice of a cursèd slave,
What shall be said to thee?

**OTHELLO:** Why, anything,
An honorable murderer, if you will,
For naught I did in hate, but all in honor.

**LODOVICO:** This wretch hath part confessed his villainy.
Did you and he consent in Cassio's death?

**OTHELLO:** Ay.

**CASSIO:** Dear General, I never gave you cause.

**OTHELLO:** I do believe it, and I ask your pardon.
Will you, I pray, demand that demi-devil
Why he hath thus ensnared my soul and body?

**IAGO:** Demand me nothing. What you know, you know.
From this time forth I never will speak word.

**LODOVICO:** What, not to pray?

**GRATIANO:** Torments will ope your lips.

**OTHELLO:** Well, thou dost best.

**LODOVICO:** Sir, you shall understand what hath befall'n,
Which, as I think, you know not. Here is a letter
Found in the pocket of the slain Roderigo;
And here another. *[He produces letters.]* The one of them imports
The death of Cassio, to be undertook
By Roderigo.

**OTHELLO:** O villain!

**CASSIO:** Most heathenish and most gross!

**298 in my sense** to one who feels as I do **300 in the practice** through the plotting, into the snare. **slave** villain **305 consent** agree **314 Torments** torture **322 gross** monstrous

Othello delivers his final words.

**LODOVICO** *[showing another paper]*: Now here's another discontented paper
Found in his pocket too. And this, it seems,
Roderigo meant t' have sent this damnèd villain;
But that belike Iago in the interim
Came in and satisfied him.

**OTHELLO:** O thou pernicious caitiff!—
How came you, Cassio, by that handkerchief
That was my wife's?

**CASSIO:** I found it in my chamber;
And he himself confessed but even now
That there he dropped it for a special purpose
Which wrought to his desire.

**OTHELLO:** O fool, fool, fool!

**CASSIO:** There is besides in Roderigo's letter
How he upbraids Iago, that he made him
Brave me upon the watch, whereon it came
That I was cast; and even but now he spake,
After long seeming dead, Iago hurt him,
Iago set him on.

**LODOVICO** *[to OTHELLO]*: You must forsake this room and go with us.

**323 discontented** full of discontent **326 belike** most likely **327 Came . . . him** interposed and gave him satisfactory explanation **333 wrought . . . desire** worked out as he wished, fitted in with his plan **336 Brave** defy. **whereon it came** whereof it came about **337 cast** dismissed

Your power and your command is taken off,
And Cassio rules in Cyprus. For this slave,
If there be any cunning cruelty
That can torment him much and hold him long,
It shall be his. You shall close prisoner rest
Till that the nature of your fault be known
To the Venetian state.—Come, bring away.

**OTHELLO:** Soft you; a word or two before you go.
I have done the state some service, and they know 't.
No more of that. I pray you, in your letters,
When you shall these unlucky deeds relate,
Speak of me as I am; nothing extenuate,
Nor set down aught in malice. Then must you speak
Of one that loved not wisely but too well;
Of one not easily jealous but, being wrought,
Perplexed in the extreme; of one whose hand,
Like the base Indian, threw a pearl away
Richer than all his tribe; of one whose subdued eyes,
Albeit unusèd to the melting mood,
Drops tears as fast as the Arabian trees
Their medicinable gum. Set you down this;
And say besides that in Aleppo once,
Where a malignant and a turbaned Turk
Beat a Venetian and traduced the state,
I took by th' throat the circumcisèd dog
And smote him, thus *[He stabs himself.]*

**LODOVICO:** O bloody period!

**GRATIANO:** All that is spoke is marred.

**OTHELLO:** I kissed thee ere I killed thee. No way but this,
Killing myself, to die upon a kiss.
*[He kisses* DESDEMONA *and] dies.*

Othello lies dead beside his murdered wife, her maid Emilia, and their betrayer, Iago.

**CASSIO:** This did I fear, but thought he had no weapon;
For he was great of heart.

**LODOVICO** *[to* IAGO*]*: O Spartan dog,
More fell than anguish, hunger, or the sea!
Look on the tragic loading of this bed.
This is thy work. The object poisons sight;
Let it be hid. Gratiano, keep the house,
*[The bed-curtains are drawn]*
And seize upon the fortunes of the Moor,
For they succeed on you. *[To* CASSIO.*]* To you, Lord Governor,
Remains the censure of this hellish villain,
The time, the place, the torture. O, enforce it!
Myself will straight aboard, and to the state
This heavy act with heavy heart relate. *Exeunt.*

---

**341 taken off** taken away **344 hold him long** keep him alive a long time (during his torture) **345 rest** remain **348 Soft you** one moment **351 unlucky** unfortunate **355 wrought** worked upon, worked into a frenzy **356 Perplexed** distraught **357 Indian** (This reading from the Quarto pictures an ignorant savage who cannot recognize the value of a precious jewel. The Folio reading, *Iudean* or *Judean,* i.e., infidel or disbeliever, may refer to Herod, who slew Miriamne in a fit of jealousy, or to Judas Iscariot, the betrayer of Christ.) **358 subdued** i.e., overcome by grief **361 gum** i.e., myrrh **366 s.d. He stabs himself** (This direction is in the Quarto text.) **367 period** termination, conclusion

**372 Spartan dog** (Spartan dogs were noted for their savagery and silence.) **373 fell** cruel **376 Let it be hid** i.e., draw the bed-curtains. (No stage direction specifies that the dead are to be carried offstage at the end of the play.) **keep** remain in **377 seize upon** take legal possession of **378 succeed on** pass as though by inheritance to **379 censure** sentencing

# Writing from Reading

## Summarize

1 The play opens, in effect, with a summary of action previous to the action we witness; it closes with another kind of summary, and one in which Othello demonstrates self-awareness (a quality largely absent in him earlier). At the end of the play (and this is quite similar to Hamlet's request of Horatio), Othello asks that those who survive him will tell his story truly:

"No more of that. I pray you, in your letters,
When you shall these unlucky deeds relate,
Speak of me as I am; nothing extenuate,
Nor set down aught in malice. Then must you speak
Of one that loved not wisely but too well. . . ."

How would you tell his story?

2 If Desdemona were to write letters home to her father and friends, how would she explain herself and her situation?

## Analyze Craft

3 What makes Othello a hero, in the Greek sense of one whose fate is intertwined with those of his people and who discovers that his tragic flaw has led to his demise? What makes his growth through suffering and coming to understand himself sufficient to move us to terror and pity (*catharsis*)? How do you interpret the line in which he says of himself that he "loved not wisely but too well"?

4 Iago has been described as a creature of "motiveless malignity." What motives does he offer for his behavior? What sense do they make? And when he says, at the close of Act 5, "From this time forth I never will speak word," what does his silence suggest?

5 The timeline of the play does not in fact provide an opportunity for Desdemona to betray her husband. Shakespeare must have known this. Why does he compress the action so as to make infidelity improbable if not impossible?

## Analyze Voice

6 Can you distinguish a difference in tone between this play and *Hamlet*? Describe. Pick a soliloquy by Hamlet and Othello and compare them.

7 Othello says about his courtship of Desdemona:

"She loved me for the dangers I had passed,
And I loved her that she did pity them."

What does this suggest about Othello's character? In what ways is this representation accurate or inaccurate?

## Synthesize Summary and Analysis

8 The tale starts out in seeming bliss and ends in total misery. Is that a definition of the tragic mode? And if, as we have seen, Shakespeare mixes low comedy together with high seriousness, what if any comic elements do you find in the play?

9 How closely related is character to plot? How can so great a general be so easily deluded and so completely fooled? Is Othello sane? Give examples to support your answer.

10 To what degree is this a play about empire and armed conflict; how do the domestic wars mirror those between the characters onstage?

## Interpret the Play

11 Is this primarily a play about jealousy—Othello's for Cassio, Iago's for Othello? Is Iago jealous of Othello in ways that mirror or distort the ways the husband grows jealous of his wife?

12 Othello is a well-positioned outcast in society. In what ways is this a play about race relations or class conflict or about power and control?

13 Is this a play about the psychology of insecurity and delusion or, rather, about good and evil in the religious sense?

# Getting Started: A Research Project

Research is a skill that will carry you through your college career. To help acquaint you with the research process, the materials you need for this project are made available on our website (www.mhhe.com/delbanco1e). Other ideas for research projects and sources appear at the end of this chapter.

"Shakespeare has had the status of a secular Bible for the last two centuries," writes critic Harold Bloom in *Shakespeare: The Invention of the Human*. "Textual scholarship on the plays approaches biblical commentary in scope and intensiveness, while the quantity of literary criticism devoted to Shakespeare rivals theological interpretation of the Holy Scripture."

As Bloom points out, the body of critical work on Shakespeare is vast. In part, this is because serious Shakespearean criticism has been growing for more than three centuries!

This research assignment will help you chart some of the major views of Shakespeare throughout the last three centuries by asking you to read two prominent views of Shakespeare: that of Samuel Johnson, the great eighteenth-century critic; and that of Samuel Taylor Coleridge, the nineteenth-century Romantic poet.

Excerpts are available on our website. After reading each of the critics, choose one of the prompts below to get you started on writing a research paper.

1. Read Johnson's and Coleridge's ideas on Shakespeare. Then write a summary of each critic's view. Based on your summaries, evaluate which you find most accurate given your reading of Shakespeare. Then, using one of Shakespeare's plays from this chapter, show how you see the critic's view playing out in the drama.
2. After reading Johnson's and Coleridge's critical perspectives, choose an idea or topic from one of them that you find interesting; for example, you might choose Johnson's idea that Shakespeare holds a mirror to the world, or Coleridge's observation of unity in Shakespeare's plays. Then write a compare/contrast paper in which you examine how each critic develops, complicates, or is silent on that particular idea. As you write, you may want to draw support from not just the critics but also a Shakespeare play you have read.
3. After reading these critics, write your own general statement about Shakespeare based on observations from your reading of Shakespearean drama. In other words, use the three critics as a model for how to write your own critical statement on one or more Shakespearean plays.

# Further Suggestions for Writing and Research

1. Ophelia, in *Hamlet*, is one of Shakespeare's most recognizable female characters. However, critics throughout the centuries—and up through contemporary feminist criticism—have disagreed on how we can best understand her role and herself as a female character. After reviewing Ophelia's lines in *Hamlet*, read the Ophelia research resources that appear on our website at www.mhhe.com/delbanco1e. You will find a nineteenth-century critic, Anna Murphy Jameson, whose *Shakespeare's Heroines*, published in 1832, became one of the earliest works by a female critic to deal directly with Shakespeare's female characters. You can compare her view with that of a contemporary feminist critic, Elaine Showalter, who explains Ophelia's place in feminist criticism. And finally, you can follow our link to a popular painting of Ophelia by nineteenth-century artist John Everett Millais.

Based on your research, write an essay in which you argue for or against a particular interpretation of Ophelia, being sure to support your argument with quotes from the critics and the text itself.

- Jameson, Anna Murphy. *Shakespeare's Heroines.* Ed. Cheri L. Larsen Hoeckley. Ontario: Broadview, 2005. See esp. pp. 177–185.
- Showalter, Elaine. "Representing Ophelia: Women, Madness, and the Responsibilities of Feminist Criticism." *Shakespeare and the Question of Theory.* Ed. Geoffrey Hartman and Patricia Parker. New York: Methuen, 1985. See esp. pp. 77–80.
- John Everett Millais's *Ophelia* at the Tate Gallery. www.tate.org.uk/ophelia/

2. As you have learned from this chapter, Shakespeare's plays are classified as tragedies, comedies, or histories. Using the resources listed below, or others you might find on your own, research Shakespearean comedy and the conventions of the genre, with a particular focus on *A Midsummer Night's Dream.* Write a paper in which you use your research on comedy to show how *A Midsummer Night's Dream* follows, varies from, or complicates the conventions of comedy.
   - Dillon, Janette. "Shakespeare and the Traditions of English Stage Comedy." *A Companion to Shakespeare's Works: Comedies.* Vol. 3. Ed. Richard Dutton and Jean E. Howard. Malden, MA: Blackwell, 2003. pp. 4–22.
   - Snyder, Susan. "The Genres of Shakespeare's Plays." *The Cambridge Companion to Shakespeare.* Ed. Margreta de Grazia and Stanley Wells. New York: Cambridge, 2001. pp. 83–98.
   - Greenblatt, Stephen. "Wooing, Wedding, and Repenting." *Will in the World.* New York: W. W. Norton, 2004. See esp. pp. 133–140.

# Some Sources for Research

### Online Sources

1. Beckman, Katherine, Rebecca Scott, David Covington, Rachel Clark, Aisha Fikes, Anisa Haidary, Caryn Lazzuri, Ginger Simpson, Jane Pisano, Liz Pohland, Teri Cross Davis, Kindra Mizell, Carol Kelly, Niki Jacobsen, Mimi Godfrey, Donnajean Ward, and Sara Weiner, eds. *Folger Shakespeare Library.* Amherst College, 2005. Web. 30 April 2009. <http://www.folger.edu>.
2. Gray, Terry A., ed. *Shakespeare and the Internet.* Terry Gray, 28 April 2009. Web. 30 April 2009. <http://www.Shakespeare.palomar.edu>.
3. "History of the Monarchy." *The Official Website of the British Monarchy.* The Royal Household, 2009. Web. 30 April 2009. <http://www.royal.gov.uk/HistoryoftheMonarchy/HistoryoftheMonarchy.aspx>.

4. Johnson, Samuel. "Preface to Shakespeare." *The Works of Samuel Johnson.* Ed. F. P. Walesby. London: Oxford University Press, 1985. 103–154. Google. Web. 30 April 2009. <http://www.books.google.com/books?id=azsCAAAAQAAJ&pg=PA103&dg="samuel+johnson"+"preface+to+shakespeare"&lr=>.
5. Larque, Thomas, ed. *Shakespeare and his Critics.* N.p., n.d. Web. 30 April 2009. <http://www.shakespearean.org.uk>.
6. *Shakespeare's Globe.* The Shakespeare Globe Trust, 2009. Web. 30 April 2009. <http://www.shakespeares-globe.org>.

**Print Sources**

1. Auden, W. H. "The Joker in the Pack." *Shakespeare's Middle Tragedies: A Collection of Critical Essays.* Ed. David Young. Englewood Cliffs, NJ: Prentice Hall, 1993. 75–90. Print.
2. Bloom, Harold. *Shakespeare: The Invention of the Human.* New York: Riverhead, 1998. Print.
3. Bradley, A. C. *Shakespearean Tragedy: Lectures on Hamlet, Othello, King Lear, Macbeth.* New York: Palgrave Macmillan, 2007. Print.
4. Charney, Maurice. "Shakespeare's Villains." *How to Read Shakespeare.* New York: McGraw-Hill, 1971. Print.
5. De Grazia, Margreta and Stanley Wells, eds. *The Cambridge Companion to Shakespeare.* New York: Cambridge, 2001. Print.
6. Dutton, Richard, and Jean E. Howard, eds. *A Companion to Shakespeare's Works.* 3 vols. Malden, MA; Blackwell, 2003. Print.
7. Empson, William. "Honest in Othello." *The Structure of Complex Words.* Cambridge: Harvard University Press, 1989. 218–249. Print.
8. Knight, George Wilson. "On the Principles of Shakespeare Interpretation." *The Wheel of Fire: Interpretations of Shakespearian Tragedy.* New York: Routledge, 2001. 1–16. Print.
9. Mack, Maynard. "'The Readiness Is All': Hamlet." *Everybody's Shakespeare.* Lincoln: University of Nebraska Press, 1993. 107–128. Print.
10. Poole, Adrian. "Hamlet and Oedipus." *Tragedy: Shakespeare and the Greek Example.* New York: Blackwell, 1987. Print.
11. Zgang, Siyang, and Mason Y. H. Wang. "Hamlet's Melancholy." *Shakespeare and the Triple Play.* Lewisburg, PA: Bucknell University Press, 1988. Print.

**For examples of student papers, see chapter 3, Common Writing Assignments, and chapter 5, Writing the Research Paper, in the Handbook for Writing from Reading.**

# 35 Modern

I DON'T say he's a great man. Willy Loman never made a lot of money. His name was never in the paper. He's not the finest character that ever lived. But he's a human being, and a terrible thing is happening to him. So attention must be paid. . . .

—*from* Death of a Salesman *by Arthur Miller*

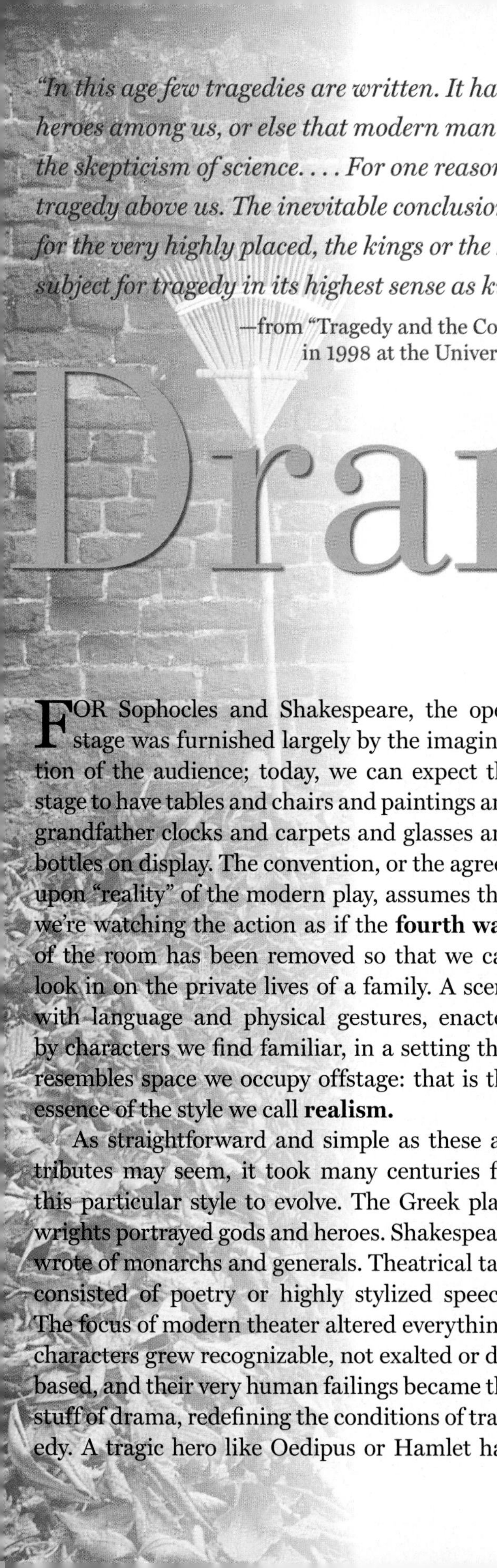

*"In this age few tragedies are written. It has often been held that the lack is due to a paucity of heroes among us, or else that modern man has had the blood drawn out of his organs of belief by the skepticism of science. . . . For one reason or another, we are often held to be below tragedy—or tragedy above us. The inevitable conclusion is, of course, that the tragic mode is archaic, fit only for the very highly placed, the kings or the kingly. . . . I believe that the common man is as apt a subject for tragedy in its highest sense as kings were."*

—from "Tragedy and the Common Man" by Arthur Miller; video of his interview conducted in 1998 at the University of Michigan available online at www.mhhe.com/delbanco1e

# Drama

FOR Sophocles and Shakespeare, the open stage was furnished largely by the imagination of the audience; today, we can expect the stage to have tables and chairs and paintings and grandfather clocks and carpets and glasses and bottles on display. The convention, or the agreed upon "reality" of the modern play, assumes that we're watching the action as if the **fourth wall** of the room has been removed so that we can look in on the private lives of a family. A scene with language and physical gestures, enacted by characters we find familiar, in a setting that resembles space we occupy offstage: that is the essence of the style we call **realism.**

As straightforward and simple as these attributes may seem, it took many centuries for this particular style to evolve. The Greek playwrights portrayed gods and heroes. Shakespeare wrote of monarchs and generals. Theatrical talk consisted of poetry or highly stylized speech. The focus of modern theater altered everything: characters grew recognizable, not exalted or debased, and their very human failings became the stuff of drama, redefining the conditions of tragedy. A tragic hero like Oedipus or Hamlet had to be of elevated rank in society, so that his fate and the fate of the common people can be intertwined. His collapse and fall have consequences for the people of his court and the community at large. His moment of realization provides him with a kind of wisdom that replaces power, and by play's end, the blind Oedipus is truly visionary; when we witness this reversal experience, or so the conventional wisdom about tragic theater would have it, we feel paired emotions of pity and fear, since a hero's death *matters* to us all.

The democratic ideal of the modern world, however, suggests that every man or woman can be a kind of hero. You need not be aristocratic or from an imperial family to have a tale worth telling or a fate that matters to others. *Death of a Salesman* deals with the exigencies of family life, and in unsparing terms. When Willy Loman's wife insists "attention must be finally paid to such a person," she's declaring, in effect, that every single character has his own important history and an aging, ill salesman down on his luck is also in some sense as important as a king.

*(CONTINUED ON PAGE 340)*

*Private theater for profit is a very recent idea.*

*The original purpose . . . of art . . . was always the community.*

Q&A

# A Conversation on Writing

## Arthur Miller

### Radical Drama and Becoming a Playwright

In the '30s the theater in New York was exploding. For the first time probably in its history, it was beginning to reflect real life, which was the Depression. These small radical groups of actors were putting on plays in storefronts and garages, and places like that. . . . Prose seemed to be remote and distant in comparison.

### On His Writing Process

I generally work because I am struck by something somebody has said. Usually playwriting is an aural art. It's not an art of the writer expecting to be read. It's the writer expecting to be heard. So I think that if I hear a character speaking, either one I have invented or one I've confronted, it can start a process of creating.

### Casting *Death of a Salesman*

I remember Lee Cobb, who was the original [Willy Loman]. . . . I imagined the character to be a little guy full of ginger, one of those little salesmen who [look] more or less like a squirrel. Here is Lee looking like a big beef. . . . My son Bobby was a little boy playing to the floor, and at one point Lee looked down—Bobby had done something funny—and he laughed. In that laugh—it was a real hearty laugh—you wanted to just burst out crying because it was so filled with sadness. He was very funny. He could be very funny. But while he was being funny he was dying in front of you. And I knew that was Willy.

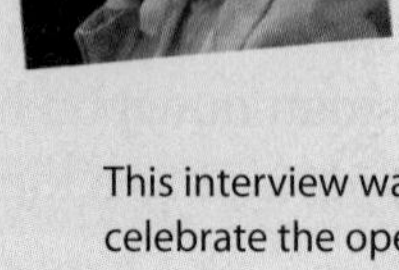

**To watch the entire interview with Arthur Miller, go to www.mhhe.com/delbanco1e**

**RESEARCH ASSIGNMENT** After reading Arthur Miller's interview, how would you describe his ideas on the importance of "making it big" in theater? Do you agree with his position?

This interview was taped at the University of Michigan in April 1998, when the playwright was in Ann Arbor to celebrate the opening of the Arthur Miller Theater at his alma mater.

# Arthur Miller (1915–2005)

Arthur Miller was born in New York City on October 17, 1915; he died at his home in Roxbury, Connecticut, on February 10, 2005. He worked as a playwright for all his long life and was among the most influential artists of his time. The son of Jewish immigrants living on the edge of poverty (his father had a garment manufacturing business that failed in the Depression), he never lost the social awareness or moral alertness that are hallmarks of his work. Though world-famous and much photographed—particularly during his brief marriage to film icon Marilyn Monroe—he remained a spokesman for and champion of the "common man."

In 1934, Miller enrolled at the University of Michigan—and, while a student there, won a Hopwood Award for playwriting. As he records in his autobiography, *Timebends: A Life* (1989), this ratified his sense of a career: "The magical force of making marks on a piece of paper and reaching into another human being, making him see what I had seen and feel my feelings—I had made a new shadow on the earth." His first play, however, *The Man Who Had All the Luck,* opened to negative reviews in 1944, and it was not until *All My Sons* in 1947 that he had a Broadway success. A tragedy about a manufacturer who sells faulty parts to the military in order to save his business, this play deals with many of the themes that characterize Miller's writing: the prospect of commercial failure, the intricacies of family life, the hard moral choices every person must face. Two years thereafter, he produced his most successful play, *Death of a Salesman*—which won both a Pulitzer Prize and a Drama Critics Circle Award. It ran for 700 performances after its first opening, and it's probably safe to say that no week now passes without a production of *Death of a Salesman* somewhere in the world.

Overwhelmed by postwar paranoia and intolerance, Miller wrote the third of his major plays, *The Crucible,* which had its Broadway premiere in 1953. Set in Salem during the witch hunts of the late seventeenth century, this story reports on extraordinary tragedy in ordinary lives. Within three years, Miller was called before the House Un-American Activities Committee and convicted of contempt of Congress for not cooperating in the more modern version of a witch hunt for Communists in the entertainment industry. His steady output continued, however, and his bibliography includes *After the Fall* (1963), *Incident at Vichy* (1964), *The Ride Down Mount Morgan* (1991), and *The Last Yankee* (1993). By his death, he had written essays, stories, a novel, *Focus* (1945), an autobiography, and the dozens of plays for which he remains most celebrated and from which continues to emerge his magisterial voice.

**AS YOU READ** **Compare the main character, Willy Loman, with Oedipus the King. How are they similar and how are they different?**

"What you read on the page looks like it's been there forever, but believe me, it hasn't. It's always a struggle to find what you are looking for. Certainly the play is as much rewritten as it is written." Conversation with Arthur Miller

# Death of a Salesman (1949)

*Certain Private Conversations in Two Acts and a Requiem*

## CHARACTERS

**WILLY LOMAN**
**LINDA**
**BIFF**
**HAPPY**
**BERNARD**
**THE WOMAN**
**CHARLEY**
**UNCLE BEN**
**HOWARD WAGNER**
**JENNY**
**STANLEY**
**MISS FORSYTHE**
**LETTA**

**SCENE:** *The action takes place in* WILLY LOMAN'S *house and yard and in various places he visits in the New York and Boston of today.*

*Throughout the play, in the stage directions, left and right mean stage left and stage right.*

## ACT I

*A melody is heard, played upon a flute. It is small and fine, telling of grass and trees and the horizon. The curtain rises.*

*Before us is the Salesman's house. We are aware of towering, angular shapes behind it, surrounding it on all sides. Only the blue light of the sky falls upon the house and forestage; the surrounding area shows an angry glow of orange. As more light appears, we see a solid vault of apartment houses around the small, fragile-seeming home. An air of the dream clings to the place, a dream rising out of reality. The kitchen at center seems actual enough, for there is a kitchen table with three chairs, and a refrigerator. But no other fixtures are seen. At the back of the kitchen there is a draped entrance, which leads to the living-room. To the right of the kitchen, on a level raised two feet, is a bedroom furnished only with a brass bedstead and a straight chair. On a shelf over the bed a silver athletic trophy stands. A window opens onto the apartment house at the side.*

*Behind the kitchen, on a level raised six and a half feet, is the boys' bedroom, at present barely visible. Two beds are dimly seen, and at the back of the room a dormer window. (This bedroom is above the unseen living-room.) At the left a stairway curves up to it from the kitchen.*

*The entire setting is wholly or, in some places, partially transparent. The roof-line of the house is one-dimensional; under and over it we see the apartment buildings. Before the house lies an apron, curving beyond the forestage into the orchestra. This forward area serves as the back yard as well as the locale of all* WILLY'S *imaginings and of his city scenes. Whenever the action is in the present the actors observe the imaginary wall-lines, entering the house only through its door at the left. But in the scenes of the past these boundaries are broken, and characters enter or leave a room by stepping "through" a wall onto the forestage.*

*From the right,* WILLY LOMAN, *the Salesman, enters, carrying two large sample cases. The flute plays on. He hears but is not aware of it. He is past sixty years of age, dressed quietly. Even as he crosses the stage to the doorway of the house, his exhaustion is apparent. He unlocks the door, comes into the kitchen, and thankfully lets his burden down, feeling the soreness of his palms. A word-sigh escapes his lips—it might be "Oh, boy, oh, boy." He closes the door, then carries his cases out into the living-room, through the draped kitchen doorway.*

LINDA, *his wife, has stirred in her bed at the right. She gets out and puts on a robe, listening. Most often jovial, she has developed an iron repression of her exceptions to* WILLY'S *behavior—she more than loves him, she admires him, as though his mercurial nature, his temper, his massive dreams and little cruelties, served her only as sharp reminders of the turbulent longings within him, longings which she shares but lacks the temperament to utter and follow to their end.*

**LINDA:** *(hearing* WILLY *outside the bedroom, calls with some trepidation)* Willy!

**WILLY:** It's all right. I came back.

**LINDA:** Why? What happened? *(Slight pause.)* Did something happen, Willy?

**WILLY:** No, nothing happened.

**LINDA:** You didn't smash the car, did you?

**WILLY:** *(with casual irritation)* I said nothing happened. Didn't you hear me?

**LINDA:** Don't you feel well?

**WILLY:** I'm tired to the death. *(The flute has faded away. He sits on the bed beside her, a little numb.)* I couldn't make it. I just couldn't make it, Linda.

**LINDA:** *(very carefully, delicately)* Where were you all day? You look terrible.

**WILLY:** I got as far as a little above Yonkers. I stopped for a cup of coffee. Maybe it was the coffee.

**LINDA:** What?

**WILLY:** *(after a pause)* I suddenly couldn't drive any more. The car kept going off onto the shoulder, y'know?

**LINDA:** *(helpfully)* Oh. Maybe it was the steering again. I don't think Angelo knows the Studebaker.

**WILLY:** No, it's me, it's me. Suddenly I realize I'm goin' sixty miles an hour and I don't remember the last five minutes. I'm—I can't seem to—keep my mind to it.

Willy Loman (Dustin Hoffman) talks with his wife, Linda (Kate Reid), in the 1985 film directed by Volker Schlöndorff.

**LINDA:** Maybe it's your glasses. You never went for your new glasses.

**WILLY:** No, I see everything. I came back ten miles an hour. It took me nearly four hours from Yonkers.

**LINDA:** *(resigned)* Well, you'll just have to take a rest, Willy, you can't continue this way.

**WILLY:** I just got back from Florida.

**LINDA:** But you didn't rest your mind. Your mind is overactive, and the mind is what counts, dear.

**WILLY:** I'll start out in the morning. Maybe I'll feel better in the morning. *(She is taking off his shoes.)* These goddam arch supports are killing me.

**LINDA:** Take an aspirin. Should I get you an aspirin? It'll soothe you.

**WILLY:** *(with wonder)* I was driving along, you understand? And I was fine. I was even observing the scenery. You can imagine, me looking at scenery, on the road every week of my life. But it's so beautiful up there, Linda, the trees are so thick, and the sun is warm. I opened the windshield and just let the warm air bathe over me. And then all of a sudden I'm goin' off the road! I'm tellin' ya, I absolutely forgot I was driving. If I'd've gone the other way over the white line I might've killed somebody. So I went on again—and five minutes later I'm dreamin' again, and I nearly—*(He presses two fingers against his eyes.)* I have such thoughts, I have such strange thoughts.

**LINDA:** Willy, dear. Talk to them again. There's no reason why you can't work in New York.

**WILLY:** They don't need me in New York. I'm the New England man. I'm vital in New England.

**LINDA:** But you're sixty years old. They can't expect you to keep traveling every week.

**WILLY:** I'll have to send a wire to Portland. I'm supposed to see Brown and Morrison tomorrow morning at ten o'clock to show the line. Goddammit, I could sell them! *(He starts putting on his jacket.)*

**LINDA:** *(taking the jacket from him)* Why don't you go down to the place tomorrow and tell Howard you've simply got to work in New York? You're too accommodating, dear.

**WILLY:** If old man Wagner was alive I'd a been in charge of New York now! That man was a prince, he was a masterful man. But that boy of his, that Howard, he don't appreciate. When I went north the first time, the Wagner Company didn't know where New England was!

**LINDA:** Why don't you tell those things to Howard, dear?

**WILLY:** *(encouraged)* I will, I definitely will. Is there any cheese?

**LINDA:** I'll make you a sandwich.

**WILLY:** No, go to sleep. I'll take some milk. I'll be up right away. The boys in?

**LINDA:** They're sleeping. Happy took Biff on a date tonight.

**WILLY:** *(interested)* That so?

Willy (Lee J. Cobb) talks with his wife, Linda (Mildred Dunnock), in the 1966 film directed by Alex Segal.

**LINDA:** It was so nice to see them shaving together, one behind the other, in the bathroom. And going out together. You notice? The whole house smells of shaving lotion.

**WILLY:** Figure it out. Work a lifetime to pay off a house. You finally own it, and there's nobody to live in it.

**LINDA:** Well, dear, life is a casting off. It's always that way.

**WILLY:** No, no, some people—some people accomplish something. Did Biff say anything after I went this morning?

**LINDA:** You shouldn't have criticized him, Willy, especially after he just got off the train. You mustn't lose your temper with him.

**WILLY:** When the hell did I lose my temper? I simply asked him if he was making any money. Is that a criticism?

**LINDA:** But, dear, how could he make any money?

**WILLY:** *(worried and angered)* There's such an undercurrent in him. He became a moody man. Did he apologize when I left this morning?

**LINDA:** He was crestfallen, Willy. You know how he admires you. I think if he finds himself, then you'll both be happier and not fight any more.

**WILLY:** How can he find himself on a farm? Is that a life? A farmhand? In the beginning, when he was young, I thought, well, a young man, it's good for him to tramp around, take a lot of different jobs. But it's more than ten years now and he has yet to make thirty-five dollars a week!

**LINDA:** He's finding himself, Willy.

**WILLY:** Not finding yourself at the age of thirty-four is a disgrace!

**LINDA:** Shh!

**WILLY:** The trouble is he's lazy, goddammit!

**LINDA:** Willy, please!

**WILLY:** Biff is a lazy bum!

**LINDA:** They're sleeping. Get something to eat. Go on down.

**WILLY:** Why did he come home? I would like to know what brought him home.

**LINDA:** I don't know. I think he's still lost, Willy. I think he's very lost.

**WILLY:** Biff Loman is lost. In the greatest country in the world a young man with such—personal attractiveness, gets lost. And such a hard worker. There's one thing about Biff—he's not lazy.

**LINDA:** Never.

**WILLY:** *(with pity and resolve)* I'll see him in the morning; I'll have a nice talk with him. I'll get him a job selling. He could be big in no time. My God! Remember how they used to follow him around in high school? When he smiled at one of them their faces lit up. When he walked down the street . . . *(He loses himself in reminiscences.)*

**LINDA:** *(trying to bring him out of it)* Willy, dear, I got a new kind of American-type cheese today. It's whipped.

**WILLY:** Why do you get American when I like Swiss?

**LINDA:** I just thought you'd like a change—

**WILLY:** I don't want a change! I want Swiss cheese. Why am I always being contradicted?

**LINDA:** *(with a covering laugh)* I thought it would be a surprise.

**WILLY:** Why don't you open a window in here, for God's sake?

**LINDA:** *(with infinite patience)* They're all open, dear.

**WILLY:** The way they boxed us in here. Bricks and windows, windows and bricks.

**LINDA:** We should've bought the land next door.

**WILLY:** The street is lined with cars. There's not a breath of fresh air in the neighborhood. The grass don't grow any more, you can't raise a carrot in the back yard. They should've had a law against apartment houses. Remember those two beautiful elm trees out there? When I and Biff hung the swing between them?

**LINDA:** Yeah, like being a million miles from the city.

**WILLY:** They should've arrested the builder for cutting those down. They massacred the neighborhood. *(Lost.)* More and more I think of those days, Linda. This time of year it was lilac and wisteria. And then the peonies would come out, and the daffodils. What fragrance in this room!

**LINDA:** Well, after all, people had to move somewhere.

**WILLY:** No, there's more people now.

**LINDA:** I don't think there's more people. I think—

**WILLY:** There's more people! That's what's ruining this country! Population is getting out of control. The competition is maddening! Smell the stink from that apartment house! And another one on the other side . . . How can they whip cheese?

*On* WILLY*'s last line,* BIFF *and* HAPPY *raise themselves up in their beds, listening.*

**LINDA:** Go down, try it. And be quiet.

**WILLY:** *(turning to* LINDA*, guiltily)* You're not worried about me, are you, sweetheart?

**BIFF:** What's the matter?

**HAPPY:** Listen!

**LINDA:** You've got too much on the ball to worry about.

**WILLY:** You're my foundation and my support, Linda.

**LINDA:** Just try to relax, dear. You make mountains out of molehills.

**WILLY:** I won't fight with him any more. If he wants to go back to Texas, let him go.

**LINDA:** He'll find his way.

**WILLY:** Sure. Certain men just don't get started till later in life. Like Thomas Edison, I think. Or B. F. Goodrich. One of them was deaf. *(He starts for the bedroom doorway.)* I'll put my money on Biff.

**LINDA:** And Willy—if it's warm Sunday we'll drive in the country. And we'll open the windshield, and take lunch.

**WILLY:** No, the windshields don't open on the new cars.

**LINDA:** But you opened it today.

**WILLY:** Me? I didn't. *(He stops.)* Now isn't that peculiar! Isn't that a remarkable—*(He breaks off in amazement and fright as the flute is heard distantly.)*

**LINDA:** What, darling?

**WILLY:** That is the most remarkable thing.

**LINDA:** What, dear?

**WILLY:** I was thinking of the Chevy. *(Slight pause.)* Nineteen twenty-eight . . . when I had that red Chevy—*(Breaks off.)* That funny? I coulda sworn I was driving that Chevy today.

**LINDA:** Well, that's nothing. Something must've reminded you.

**WILLY:** Remarkable. Ts. Remember those days? The way Biff used to simonize that car? The dealer refused to believe there was eighty thousand miles on it. *(He shakes his head.)* Heh! *(To* LINDA.*)* Close your eyes, I'll be right up. *(He walks out of the bedroom.)*

**HAPPY:** *(to* BIFF*)* Jesus, maybe he smashed up the car again!

**LINDA:** *(calling after* WILLY*)* Be careful on the stairs, dear! The cheese is on the middle shelf! *(She turns, goes over to the bed, takes his jacket, and goes out of the bedroom.)*

*Light has risen on the boys' room. Unseen,* WILLY *is heard talking to himself, "Eighty thousand miles," and a little laugh.* BIFF *gets out of bed, comes downstage a bit, and stands attentively.* BIFF *is two years older than his brother* HAPPY, *well built, but in these days bears a worn air and seems less self-assured. He has succeeded less, and his dreams are stronger and less acceptable than* HAPPY*'s.* HAPPY *is tall, powerfully made. Sexuality is like a visible color on him, or a scent that many women have discovered. He, like his brother, is lost, but in a different way, for he has never allowed himself to turn his face toward defeat and is thus more confused and hard-skinned, although seemingly more content.*

**HAPPY:** *(getting out of bed)* He's going to get his license taken away if he keeps that up. I'm getting nervous about him, y'know, Biff?

**BIFF:** His eyes are going.

**HAPPY:** No, I've driven with him. He sees all right. He just doesn't keep his mind on it. I drove into the city with him last week. He stops at a green light and then it turns red and he goes. *(He laughs.)*

**BIFF:** Maybe he's color-blind.

**HAPPY:** Pop? Why he's got the finest eye for color in the business. You know that.

**BIFF:** *(sitting down on his bed)* I'm going to sleep.

**HAPPY:** You're not still sour on Dad, are you, Biff?

**BIFF:** He's all right, I guess.

**WILLY:** *(underneath them, in the living-room)* Yes, sir, eighty thousand miles—eighty-two thousand!

**BIFF:** You smoking?

**HAPPY:** *(holding out a pack of cigarettes)* Want one?

**BIFF:** *(taking a cigarette)* I can never sleep when I smell it.

**WILLY:** What a simonizing job, heh!

**HAPPY:** *(with deep sentiment)* Funny, Biff, y'know? Us sleeping in here again? The old beds. *(He pats his bed affectionately.)* All the talk that went across those two beds, huh? Our whole lives.

**BIFF:** Yeah. Lotta dreams and plans.

**HAPPY:** *(with a deep and masculine laugh)* About five hundred women would like to know what was said in this room.

*They share a soft laugh.*

**BIFF:** Remember that big Betsy something—what the hell was her name—over on Bushwick Avenue?

**HAPPY:** *(combing his hair)* With the collie dog!

**BIFF:** That's the one. I got you in there, remember?

**HAPPY:** Yeah, that was my first time—I think. Boy, there was a pig! *(They laugh, almost crudely.)* You taught me everything I know about women. Don't forget that.

**BIFF:** I bet you forgot how bashful you used to be. Especially with girls.

**HAPPY:** Oh, I still am, Biff.

**BIFF:** Oh, go on.

**HAPPY:** I just control it, that's all. I think I got less bashful and you got more so. What happened, Biff? Where's the old humor, the old confidence? *(He shakes* BIFF*'s knee.* BIFF *gets up and moves restlessly about the room.)* What's the matter?

**BIFF:** Why does Dad mock me all the time?

**HAPPY:** He's not mocking you, he—

**BIFF:** Everything I say there's a twist of mockery on his face. I can't get near him.

**HAPPY:** He just wants you to make good, that's all. I wanted to talk to you about Dad for a long time, Biff. Something's—happening to him. He—talks to himself.

**BIFF:** I noticed that this morning. But he always mumbled.

**HAPPY:** But not so noticeable. It got so embarrassing I sent him to Florida. And you know something? Most of the time he's talking to you.

**BIFF:** What's he say about me?

**HAPPY:** I can't make it out.

**BIFF:** What's he say about me?

Biff (John Malkovich) and Happy (Stephen Lang) talk about their plans.

**HAPPY:** I think the fact that you're not settled, that you're still kind of up in the air . . .

**BIFF:** There's one or two other things depressing him, Happy.

**HAPPY:** What do you mean?

**BIFF:** Never mind. Just don't lay it all to me.

**HAPPY:** But I think if you just got started—I mean—is there any future for you out there?

**BIFF:** I tell ya, Hap, I don't know what the future is. I don't know—what I'm supposed to want.

**HAPPY:** What do you mean?

**BIFF:** Well, I spent six or seven years after high school trying to work myself up. Shipping clerk, salesman, business of one kind or another. And it's a measly manner of existence. To get on that subway on the hot mornings in summer. To devote your whole life to keeping stock, or making phone calls, or selling or buying. To suffer fifty weeks of the year for the sake of a two-week vacation, when all you really desire is to be outdoors, with your shirt off. And always to have to get ahead of the next fella. And still—that's how you build a future.

**HAPPY:** Well, you really enjoy it on a farm? Are you content out there?

**BIFF:** *(with rising agitation)* Hap, I've had twenty or thirty different kinds of jobs since I left home before the war, and it always turns out the same. I just realized it lately. In Nebraska when I herded cattle, and the Dakotas, and Arizona, and now in Texas. It's why I came home now, I guess, because I realized it. This farm I work on, it's spring there now, see? And they've got about fifteen new colts. There's nothing more inspiring or—beautiful than the sight of a mare and a new colt. And it's cool there now, see? Texas is cool now, and it's spring. And whenever spring comes to where I am, I suddenly get the feeling, my God, I'm not gettin' anywhere! What the hell am I doing, playing around with horses, twenty-eight dollars a week! I'm thirty-four years old, I oughta be makin' my future. That's when I come running home. And now, I get here, and I don't know what to do with myself. *(After a pause.)* I've always made a point of not wasting my life, and everytime I come back here I know that all I've done is to waste my life.

**HAPPY:** You're a poet, you know that, Biff? You're a—you're an idealist!

**BIFF:** No, I'm mixed up very bad. Maybe I oughta get married. Maybe I oughta get stuck into something. Maybe that's my trouble. I'm like a boy. I'm not married. I'm not in business, I just—I'm like a boy. Are you content, Hap? You're a success, aren't you? Are you content?

**HAPPY:** Hell, no!

**BIFF:** Why? You're making money, aren't you?

**HAPPY:** *(moving about with energy, expressiveness)* All I can do now is wait for the merchandise manager to die. And suppose I get to be merchandise manager? He's a good friend of mine, and he just built a terrific estate on Long Island. And he lived there about two months and sold it, and now he's building another one. He can't enjoy it once it's finished. And I know that's just what I would do. I don't know what the hell I'm workin' for. Sometimes I sit in my apartment—all alone. And I think of the rent I'm paying. And it's crazy. But then, it's what I always wanted. My own apartment, a car, and plenty of women. And still, goddammit, I'm lonely.

**BIFF:** *(with enthusiasm)* Listen, why don't you come out West with me?

**HAPPY:** You and I, heh?

**BIFF:** Sure, maybe we could buy a ranch. Raise cattle, use our muscles. Men built like we are should be working out in the open.

**HAPPY:** *(avidly)* The Loman Brothers, heh?

**BIFF:** *(with vast affection)* Sure, we'd be known all over the counties!

**HAPPY:** *(enthralled)* That's what I dream about, Biff. Sometimes I want to just rip my clothes off in the middle of the store and outbox that goddam merchandise manager. I mean I can outbox, outrun, and outlift anybody in that store, and I have to take orders from those common, petty sons-of-bitches till I can't stand it any more.

**BIFF:** I'm tellin' you, kid, if you were with me I'd be happy out there.

**HAPPY:** *(enthused)* See, Biff, everybody around me is so false that I'm constantly lowering my ideals . . .

**BIFF:** Baby, together we'd stand up for one another, we'd have someone to trust.

**HAPPY:** If I were around you—

**BIFF:** Hap, the trouble is we weren't brought up to grub for money. I don't know how to do it.

**HAPPY:** Neither can I!

**BIFF:** Then let's go!

**HAPPY:** The only thing is—what can you make out there?

**BIFF:** But look at your friend. Builds an estate and then hasn't the peace of mind to live in it.

**HAPPY:** Yeah, but when he walks into the store the waves part in front of him. That's fifty-two thousand dollars a year coming through the revolving door, and I got more in my pinky finger than he's got in his head.

**BIFF:** Yeah, but you just said—

**HAPPY:** I gotta show some of those pompous, self-important executives over there that Hap Loman can make the grade. I want to walk into the store the way he walks in. Then I'll go with you, Biff. We'll be together yet, I swear. But take those two we had tonight. Now weren't they gorgeous creatures?

**BIFF:** Yeah, yeah, most gorgeous I've had in years.

**HAPPY:** I get that any time I want, Biff. Whenever I feel disgusted. The trouble is, it gets like bowling or something. I just keep knockin' them over and it doesn't mean anything. You still run around a lot?

**BIFF:** Naa. I'd like to find a girl—steady, somebody with substance.

**HAPPY:** That's what I long for.

**BIFF:** Go on! You'd never come home.

**HAPPY:** I would! Somebody with character, with resistance! Like Mom, y'know? You're gonna call me a bastard when I tell you this. That girl Charlotte I was with tonight is engaged to be married in five weeks. *(He tries on his new hat.)*

**BIFF:** No kiddin'!

**HAPPY:** Sure, the guy's in line for the vice-presidency of the store. I don't know what gets into me, maybe I just have an overdeveloped sense of competition or something, but I went and ruined her, and furthermore I can't get rid of her. And he's the third executive I've done that to. Isn't that a crummy characteristic? And to top it all, I go to their weddings! *(Indignantly, but laughing.)* Like I'm not supposed to take bribes. Manufacturers offer me a hundred-dollar bill now and then to throw an order their way. You know how honest I am, but it's like this girl, see. I hate myself for it. Because I don't want the girl, and, still, I take it and—I love it!

**BIFF:** Let's go to sleep.

**HAPPY:** I guess we didn't settle anything, heh?

**BIFF:** I just got one idea that I think I'm going to try.

**HAPPY:** What's that?

**BIFF:** Remember Bill Oliver?

**HAPPY:** Sure, Oliver is very big now. You want to work for him again?

**BIFF:** No, but when I quit he said something to me. He put his arm on my shoulder, and he said, "Biff, if you ever need anything, come to me."

**HAPPY:** I remember that. That sounds good.

**BIFF:** I think I'll go to see him. If I could get ten thousand or even seven or eight thousand dollars I could buy a beautiful ranch.

**HAPPY:** I bet he'd back you. 'Cause he thought highly of you, Biff. I mean, they all do. You're well liked, Biff. That's why I say to come back here, and we both have the apartment. And I'm tellin' you, Biff, any babe you want . . .

**BIFF:** No, with a ranch I could do the work I like and still be something. I just wonder though. I wonder if Oliver still thinks I stole that carton of basketballs.

**HAPPY:** Oh, he probably forgot that long ago. It's almost ten years. You're too sensitive. Anyway, he didn't really fire you.

**BIFF:** Well, I think he was going to. I think that's why I quit. I was never sure whether he knew or not. I know he thought the world of me, though. I was the only one he'd let lock up the place.

**WILLY:** *(below)* You gonna wash the engine, Biff?

**HAPPY:** Shh!

BIFF *looks at* HAPPY, *who is gazing down, listening.* WILLY *is mumbling in the parlor.*

**HAPPY:** You hear that?

*They listen.* WILLY *laughs warmly.*

**BIFF:** *(growing angry)* Doesn't he know Mom can hear that?

**WILLY:** Don't get your sweater dirty, Biff!

*A look of pain crosses* BIFF*'s face.*

**HAPPY:** Isn't that terrible? Don't leave again, will you? You'll find a job here. You gotta stick around. I don't know what to do about him, it's getting embarrassing.

**WILLY:** What a simonizing job!

**BIFF:** Mom's hearing that!

**WILLY:** No kiddin', Biff, you got a date? Wonderful!

**HAPPY:** Go on to sleep. But talk to him in the morning, will you?

**BIFF:** *(reluctantly getting into bed)* With her in the house. Brother!

**HAPPY:** *(getting into bed)* I wish you'd have a good talk with him.

*The light on their room begins to fade.*

**BIFF:** *(to himself in bed)* That selfish, stupid . . .

**HAPPY:** Sh . . . Sleep, Biff.

*Their light is out. Well before they have finished speaking,* WILLY*'s form is dimly seen below in the darkened kitchen. He opens the refrigerator, searches in there, and takes out a bottle of milk. The apartment houses are fading out, and the entire house and surroundings become covered with leaves. Music insinuates itself as the leaves appear.*

**WILLY:** Just wanna be careful with those girls, Biff, that's all. Don't make any promises. No promises of any kind. Because a girl, y'know, they always believe what you tell 'em, and you're very young, Biff, you're too young to be talking seriously to girls.

*Light rises on the kitchen.* WILLY, *talking, shuts the refrigerator door and comes downstage to the kitchen table. He pours milk into a glass. He is totally immersed in himself, smiling faintly.*

**WILLY:** Too young entirely, Biff. You want to watch your schooling first. Then when you're all set, there'll be plenty of girls for a boy like you. *(He smiles broadly at a kitchen chair.)* That so? The girls pay for you? *(He laughs.)* Boy, you must really be makin' a hit.

WILLY *is gradually addressing—physically—a point offstage, speaking through the wall of the kitchen, and his voice has been rising in volume to that of a normal conversation.*

**WILLY:** I been wondering why you polish the car so careful. Ha! Don't leave the hubcaps, boys. Get the chamois to the hubcaps. Happy, use newspaper on the windows, it's the easiest thing. Show him how to do it, Biff! You see, Happy? Pad it up, use it like a pad. That's it, that's it, good work. You're doin' all right, Hap. *(He pauses, then nods in approbation for a few seconds, then looks upward.)* Biff, first thing we gotta do when we get time is clip that big branch over the house. Afraid it's gonna fall in a storm and hit the roof. Tell you what. We get a rope and sling her around, and then we climb up there with a couple of saws and take her down. Soon as you finish the car, boys, I wanna see ya. I got a surprise for you, boys.

**BIFF:** *(offstage)* Whatta ya got, Dad?

**WILLY:** No, you finish first. Never leave a job till you're finished—remember that. *(Looking toward the "big trees.")* Biff, up in Albany I saw a beautiful hammock. I think I'll buy it next trip, and we'll hang it right between those two elms. Wouldn't that be something? Just swingin' there under those branches. Boy, that would be . . .

*Young* BIFF *and Young* HAPPY *appear from the direction* WILLY *was addressing.* HAPPY *carries rags and a pail of water.* BIFF, *wearing a sweater with a block "S," carries a football.*

Willy drinks his milk as he addresses a point offstage.

**BIFF:** *(pointing in the direction of the car offstage)* How's that, Pop, professional?

**WILLY:** Terrific. Terrific job, boys. Good work, Biff.

**HAPPY:** Where's the surprise, Pop?

**WILLY:** In the back seat of the car.

**HAPPY:** Boy! *(He runs off.)*

**BIFF:** What is it, Dad? Tell me, what'd you buy?

**WILLY:** *(laughing, cuffs him)* Never mind, something I want you to have.

**BIFF:** *(turns and starts off)* What is it, Hap?

**HAPPY:** *(offstage)* It's a punching bag!

**BIFF:** Oh, Pop!

**WILLY:** It's got Gene Tunney's signature on it!

HAPPY *runs onstage with a punching bag.*

**BIFF:** Gee, how'd you know we wanted a punching bag?

**WILLY:** Well, it's the finest thing for the timing.

**HAPPY:** *(lies down on his back and pedals with his feet)* I'm losing weight, you notice, Pop?

**WILLY:** *(to* HAPPY*)* Jumping rope is good too.

**BIFF:** Did you see the new football I got?

**WILLY:** *(examining the ball)* Where'd you get a new ball?

**BIFF:** The coach told me to practice my passing.

**WILLY:** That so? And he gave you the ball, heh?

**BIFF:** Well, I borrowed it from the locker room. *(He laughs confidentially.)*

**WILLY:** *(laughing with him at the theft)* I want you to return that.

**HAPPY:** I told you he wouldn't like it!

**BIFF:** *(angrily)* Well, I'm bringing it back!

**WILLY:** *(stopping the incipient argument, to* HAPPY*)* Sure, he's gotta practice with a regulation ball, doesn't he? *(To* BIFF.*)* Coach'll probably congratulate you on your initiative!

**BIFF:** Oh, he keeps congratulating my initiative all the time, Pop.

**WILLY:** That's because he likes you. If somebody else took that ball there'd be an uproar. So what's the report, boys, what's the report?

Willy and his boys, in happier times, discuss the future.

**BIFF:** Where'd you go this time, Dad? Gee we were lonesome for you.

**WILLY:** *(pleased, puts an arm around each boy and they come down to the apron)* Lonesome, heh?

**BIFF:** Missed you every minute.

**WILLY:** Don't say? Tell you a secret, boys. Don't breathe it to a soul. Someday I'll have my own business, and I'll never have to leave home any more.

**HAPPY:** Like Uncle Charley, heh?

**WILLY:** Bigger than Uncle Charley! Because Charley is not—liked. He's liked, but he's not—well liked.

**BIFF:** Where'd you go this time, Dad?

**WILLY:** Well, I got on the road, and I went north to Providence. Met the Mayor.

**BIFF:** The Mayor of Providence!

**WILLY:** He was sitting in the hotel lobby.

**BIFF:** What'd he say?

**WILLY:** He said, "Morning!" And I said, "You got a fine city here, Mayor." And then he had coffee with me. And then I went to Waterbury. Waterbury is a fine city. Big clock city, the famous Waterbury clock. Sold a nice bill there. And then Boston—Boston is the cradle of the Revolution. A fine city. And a couple of other towns in Mass., and on to Portland and Bangor and straight home!

**BIFF:** Gee, I'd love to go with you sometime, Dad.

**WILLY:** Soon as summer comes.

**HAPPY:** Promise?

**WILLY:** You and Hap and I, and I'll show you all the towns. America is full of beautiful towns and fine, upstanding people. And they know me, boys, they know me up and down New England. The finest people. And when I bring you fellas up, there'll be open sesame for all of us, 'cause one thing, boys: I have friends. I can park my car in any street in New England, and the cops protect it like their own. This summer, heh?

**BIFF AND HAPPY:** *(together)* Yeah! You bet!

**WILLY:** We'll take our bathing suits.

**HAPPY:** We'll carry your bags, Pop!

**WILLY:** Oh, won't that be something! Me comin' into the Boston stores with you boys carryin' my bags. What a sensation!

BIFF *is prancing around, practicing passing the ball.*

**WILLY:** You nervous, Biff, about the game?

**BIFF:** Not if you're gonna be there.

**WILLY:** What do they say about you in school, now that they made you captain?

**HAPPY:** There's a crowd of girls behind him everytime the classes change.

**BIFF:** *(taking* WILLY*'s hand)* This Saturday, Pop, this Saturday—just for you, I'm going to break through for a touchdown.

**HAPPY:** You're supposed to pass.

**BIFF:** I'm takin' one play for Pop. You watch me, Pop, and when I take off my helmet, that means I'm breakin' out. Then you watch me crash through that line!

**WILLY:** *(kisses* BIFF*)* Oh, wait'll I tell this in Boston!

BERNARD *enters in knickers. He is younger than* BIFF, *earnest and loyal, a worried boy.*

**BERNARD:** Biff, where are you? You're supposed to study with me today.

**WILLY:** Hey, looka Bernard. What're you lookin' so anemic about, Bernard?

**BERNARD:** He's gotta study, Uncle Willy. He's got Regents next week.

**HAPPY:** *(tauntingly, spinning* BERNARD *around)* Let's box, Bernard!

**BERNARD:** Biff! *(He gets away from* HAPPY.*)* Listen, Biff, I heard Mr. Birnbaum say that if you don't start studyin' math, he's gonna flunk you, and you won't graduate. I heard him!

**WILLY:** You better study with him, Biff. Go ahead now.

**BERNARD:** I heard him!

**BIFF:** Oh, Pop, you didn't see my sneakers! *(He holds up a foot for* WILLY *to look at.)*

**WILLY:** Hey, that's a beautiful job of printing!

**BERNARD:** *(wiping his glasses)* Just because he printed University of Virginia on his sneakers doesn't mean they've got to graduate him, Uncle Willy!

**WILLY:** *(angrily)* What're you talking about? With scholarships to three universities they're gonna flunk him?

**BERNARD:** But I heard Mr. Birnbaum say—

**WILLY:** Don't be a pest, Bernard! *(To his boys.)* What an anemic!

**BERNARD:** Okay, I'm waiting for you in my house, Biff.

BERNARD *goes off. The Lomans laugh.*

**WILLY:** Bernard is not well liked, is he?

**BIFF:** He's liked, but he's not well liked.

**HAPPY:** That's right, Pop.

**WILLY:** That's just what I mean. Bernard can get the best marks in school, y'understand, but when he gets out in the business world, y'understand, you are going to be five times ahead of him. That's why I thank Almighty God you're both built like Adonises. Because the man who makes an appearance in the business world, the man who creates personal interest, is the man who gets ahead. Be liked and you will never want. You take me, for instance. I never have to wait in line to see a buyer. "Willy Loman is here!" That's all they have to know, and I go right through.

**BIFF:** Did you knock them dead, Pop?

**WILLY:** Knocked 'em cold in Providence, slaughtered 'em in Boston.

**HAPPY:** *(on his back, pedaling again)* I'm losing weight, you notice, Pop?

LINDA *enters, as of old, a ribbon in her hair, carrying a basket of washing.*

**LINDA:** *(with youthful energy)* Hello, dear!

**WILLY:** Sweetheart!

**LINDA:** How'd the Chevy run?

**WILLY:** Chevrolet, Linda, is the greatest car ever built. *(To the boys.)* Since when do you let your mother carry wash up the stairs?

Willy, Happy (James Farentino), and Biff (George Segal) scoff at Bernard's (Gene Wilder) attitude toward education.

**BIFF:** Grab hold there, boy!

**HAPPY:** Where to, Mom?

**LINDA:** Hang them up on the line. And you better go down to your friends, Biff. The cellar is full of boys. They don't know what to do with themselves.

**BIFF:** Ah, when Pop comes home they can wait!

**WILLY:** *(laughs appreciatively)* You better go down and tell them what to do, Biff.

**BIFF:** I think I'll have them sweep out the furnace room.

**WILLY:** Good work, Biff.

**BIFF:** *(goes through wall-line of kitchen to doorway at back and calls down)* Fellas! Everybody sweep out the furnace room! I'll be right down!

**VOICES:** All right! Okay, Biff.

**BIFF:** George and Sam and Frank, come out back! We're hangin' up the wash! Come on, Hap, on the double! *(He and* HAPPY *carry out the basket.)*

**LINDA:** The way they obey him!

**WILLY:** Well, that's training, the training. I'm tellin' you, I was sellin' thousands and thousands, but I had to come home.

**LINDA:** Oh, the whole block'll be at that game. Did you sell anything?

**WILLY:** I did five hundred gross in Providence and seven hundred gross in Boston.

**LINDA:** No! Wait a minute, I've got a pencil. *(She pulls pencil and paper out of her apron pocket.)* That makes your commission . . . Two hundred—my God! Two hundred and twelve dollars!

**WILLY:** Well, I didn't figure it yet, but . . .

**LINDA:** How much did you do?

**WILLY:** Well, I—I did—about a hundred and eighty gross in Providence. Well, no—it came to—roughly two hundred gross on the whole trip.

**LINDA:** *(without hesitation)* Two hundred gross. That's . . . *(She figures.)*

**WILLY:** The trouble was that three of the stores were half closed for inventory in Boston. Otherwise I woulda broke records.

**LINDA:** Well, it makes seventy dollars and some pennies. That's very good.

**WILLY:** What do we owe?

**LINDA:** Well, on the first there's sixteen dollars on the refrigerator—

**WILLY:** Why sixteen?

**LINDA:** Well, the fan belt broke, so it was a dollar eighty.

**WILLY:** But it's brand new.

**LINDA:** Well, the man said that's the way it is. Till they work themselves in, y'know.

*They move through the wall-line into the kitchen.*

**WILLY:** I hope we didn't get stuck on that machine.

**LINDA:** They got the biggest ads of any of them!

**WILLY:** I know, it's a fine machine. What else?

**LINDA:** Well, there's nine-sixty for the washing machine. And for the vacuum cleaner there's three and a half due on the fifteenth. Then the roof, you got twenty-one dollars remaining.

**WILLY:** It don't leak, does it?

**LINDA:** No, they did a wonderful job. Then you owe Frank for the carburetor.

**WILLY:** I'm not going to pay that man! That goddam Chevrolet, they ought to prohibit the manufacture of that car!

**LINDA:** Well, you owe him three and a half. And odds and ends, comes to around a hundred and twenty dollars by the fifteenth.

**WILLY:** A hundred and twenty dollars! My God, if business don't pick up I don't know what I'm gonna do!

**LINDA:** Well, next week you'll do better.

**WILLY:** Oh, I'll knock 'em dead next week. I'll go to Hartford. I'm very well liked in Hartford. You know, the trouble is, Linda, people don't seem to take to me.

*They move onto the forestage.*

**LINDA:** Oh, don't be foolish.

**WILLY:** I know it when I walk in. They seem to laugh at me.

**LINDA:** Why? Why would they laugh at you? Don't talk that way, Willy.

WILLY *moves to the edge of the stage.* LINDA *goes into the kitchen and starts to darn stockings.*

**WILLY:** I don't know the reason for it, but they just pass me by. I'm not noticed.

**LINDA:** But you're doing wonderful, dear. You're making seventy to a hundred dollars a week.

**WILLY:** But I gotta be at it ten, twelve hours a day. Other men—I don't know—they do it easier. I don't know why—I can't stop myself—I talk too much. A man oughta come in with a few words. One thing about Charley. He's a man of few words, and they respect him.

**LINDA:** You don't talk too much, you're just lively.

**WILLY:** *(smiling)* Well, I figure, what the hell, life is short, a couple of jokes. *(To himself.)* I joke too much! *(The smile goes.)*

**LINDA:** Why? You're—

**WILLY:** I'm fat. I'm very—foolish to look at, Linda. I didn't tell you, but Christmas time I happened to be calling on F. H. Stewarts, and a salesman I know, as I was going in to see the buyer I heard him say something about—walrus. And I—I cracked him right across the face. I won't take that. I simply will not take that. But they do laugh at me. I know that.

**LINDA:** Darling . . .

**WILLY:** I gotta overcome it. I know I gotta overcome it. I'm not dressing to advantage, maybe.

**LINDA:** Willy, darling, you're the handsomest man in the world—

**WILLY:** Oh, no, Linda.

**LINDA:** To me you are. *(Slight pause.)* The handsomest.

*From the darkness is heard the laughter of a woman.* WILLY *doesn't turn to it, but it continues through* LINDA*'s lines.*

**LINDA:** And the boys, Willy. Few men are idolized by their children the way you are.

*Music is heard as behind a scrim, to the left of the house,* THE WOMAN, *dimly seen, is dressing.*

**WILLY:** *(with great feeling)* You're the best there is, Linda, you're a pal, you know that? On the road—on the road I want to grab you sometimes and just kiss the life outa you.

*The laughter is loud now, and he moves into a brightening area at the left, where* THE WOMAN *has come from behind the scrim and is standing, putting on her hat, looking into a "mirror" and laughing.*

**WILLY:** 'Cause I get so lonely—especially when business is bad and there's nobody to talk to. I get the feeling that I'll never sell anything again, that I won't make a living for you, or a business, a business for the boys. *(He talks through* THE WOMAN*'s subsiding laughter;* THE WOMAN *primps at the "mirror.")* There's so much I want to make for—

**THE WOMAN:** Me? You didn't make me, Willy. I picked you.

**WILLY:** *(pleased)* You picked me?

**THE WOMAN:** *(who is quite proper-looking,* WILLY*'s age)* I did. I've been sitting at that desk watching all the salesmen go by, day in, day out. But you've got such a sense of humor, and we do have such a good time together, don't we?

**WILLY:** Sure, sure. *(He takes her in his arms.)* Why do you have to go now?

**THE WOMAN:** It's two o'clock . . .

**WILLY:** No, come on in! *(He pulls her.)*

**THE WOMAN:** . . . my sisters'll be scandalized. When'll you be back?

**WILLY:** Oh, two weeks about. Will you come up again?

**THE WOMAN:** Sure thing. You do make me laugh. It's good for me. *(She squeezes his arm, kisses him.)* And I think you're a wonderful man.

**WILLY:** You picked me, heh?

**THE WOMAN:** Sure. Because you're so sweet. And such a kidder.

**WILLY:** Well, I'll see you next time I'm in Boston.

**THE WOMAN:** I'll put you right through to the buyers.

**WILLY:** *(slapping her bottom)* Right. Well, bottoms up!

**THE WOMAN:** *(slaps him gently and laughs)* You just kill me, Willy. *(He suddenly grabs her and kisses her roughly.)* You kill me. And thanks for the stockings. I love a lot of stockings. Well, good night.

**WILLY:** Good night. And keep your pores open!

**THE WOMAN:** Oh, Willy!

THE WOMAN *bursts out laughing, and* LINDA*'s laughter blends in.* THE WOMAN *disappears into the dark. Now the area at the kitchen table brightens.* LINDA *is sitting where she was at the kitchen table, but now is mending a pair of her silk stockings.*

**LINDA:** You are, Willy. The handsomest man. You've got no reason to feel that—

**WILLY:** *(coming out of* THE WOMAN*'s dimming area and going over to* LINDA*)* I'll make it all up to you, Linda, I'll—

**LINDA:** There's nothing to make up, dear. You're doing fine, better than—

**WILLY:** *(noticing her mending)* What's that?

**LINDA:** Just mending my stockings. They're so expensive—

**WILLY:** *(angrily, taking them from her)* I won't have you mending stockings in this house! Now throw them out!

LINDA *puts the stockings in her pocket.*

**BERNARD:** *(entering on the run)* Where is he? If he doesn't study!

**WILLY:** *(moving to the forestage, with great agitation)* You'll give him the answers!

**BERNARD:** I do, but I can't on a Regents! That's a state exam! They're liable to arrest me!

**WILLY:** Where is he? I'll whip him, I'll whip him!

**LINDA:** And he'd better give back that football, Willy, it's not nice.

**WILLY:** Biff! Where is he? Why is he taking everything?

**LINDA:** He's too rough with the girls, Willy. All the mothers are afraid of him!

**WILLY:** I'll whip him!

**BERNARD:** He's driving the car without a license!

THE WOMAN*'s laugh is heard.*

**WILLY:** Shut up!

**LINDA:** All the mothers—

Willy and The Woman (Kathy Rossetter) say good-bye in their hotel room.

**WILLY:** Shut up!

**BERNARD:** *(backing quietly away and out)* Mr. Birnbaum says he's stuck up.

**WILLY:** Get outa here!

**BERNARD:** If he doesn't buckle down he'll flunk math! *(He goes off.)*

**LINDA:** He's right, Willy, you've gotta—

**WILLY:** *(exploding at her)* There's nothing the matter with him! You want him to be a worm like Bernard? He's got spirit, personality . . .

*As he speaks,* LINDA, *almost in tears, exits into the living-room.* WILLY *is alone in the kitchen, wilting and staring. The leaves are gone. It is night again, and the apartment houses look down from behind.*

**WILLY:** Loaded with it. Loaded! What is he stealing? He's giving it back, isn't he? Why is he stealing? What did I tell him? I never in my life told him anything but decent things.

HAPPY *in pajamas has come down the stairs;* WILLY *suddenly becomes aware of* HAPPY*'s presence.*

**HAPPY:** Let's go now, come on.

**WILLY:** *(sitting down at the kitchen table)* Huh! Why did she have to wax the floors herself? Everytime she waxes the floors she keels over. She knows that!

**HAPPY:** Shh! Take it easy. What brought you back tonight?

**WILLY:** I got an awful scare. Nearly hit a kid in Yonkers. God! Why didn't I go to Alaska with my brother Ben that time! Ben! That man was a genius, that man was success incarnate! What a mistake! He begged me to go.

**HAPPY:** Well, there's no use in—

**WILLY:** You guys! There was a man started with the clothes on his back and ended up with diamond mines!

**HAPPY:** Boy, someday I'd like to know how he did it.

**WILLY:** What's the mystery? The man knew what he wanted and went out and got it! Walked into a jungle, and comes out, the age of twenty-one, and he's rich! The world is an oyster, but you don't crack it open on a mattress!

**HAPPY:** Pop, I told you I'm gonna retire you for life.

**WILLY:** You'll retire me for life on seventy goddam dollars a week? And your women and your car and your apartment, and you'll retire me for life! Christ's sake, I couldn't get past Yonkers today! Where are you guys, where are you? The woods are burning! I can't drive a car!

CHARLEY *has appeared in the doorway. He is a large man, slow of speech, laconic, immovable. In all he says, despite what he says, there is pity, and, now, trepidation. He has a robe over pajamas, slippers on his feet. He enters the kitchen.*

**CHARLEY:** Everything all right?

**HAPPY:** Yeah, Charley, everything's . . .

**WILLY:** What's the matter?

**CHARLEY:** I heard some noise. I thought something happened. Can't we do something about the walls? You sneeze in here, and in my house hats blow off.

**HAPPY:** Let's go to bed, Dad. Come on.

CHARLEY *signals to* HAPPY *to go.*

**WILLY:** You go ahead, I'm not tired at the moment.

**HAPPY:** *(to* WILLY*)* Take it easy, huh? *(He exits.)*

**WILLY:** What're you doin' up?

**CHARLEY:** *(sitting down at the kitchen table opposite* WILLY*)* Couldn't sleep good. I had a heartburn.

**WILLY:** Well, you don't know how to eat.

**CHARLEY:** I eat with my mouth.

**WILLY:** No, you're ignorant. You gotta know about vitamins and things like that.

**CHARLEY:** Come on, let's shoot. Tire you out a little.

**WILLY:** *(hesitantly)* All right. You got cards?

**CHARLEY:** *(taking a deck from his pocket)* Yeah, I got them. Someplace. What is it with those vitamins?

**WILLY:** *(dealing)* They build up your bones. Chemistry.

**CHARLEY:** Yeah, but there's no bones in a heartburn.

**WILLY:** What are you talkin' about? Do you know the first thing about it?

**CHARLEY:** Don't get insulted.

**WILLY:** Don't talk about something you don't know anything about.

*They are playing. Pause.*

**CHARLEY:** What're you doin' home?

**WILLY:** A little trouble with the car.

**CHARLEY:** Oh. *(Pause.)* I'd like to take a trip to California.

**WILLY:** Don't say.

**CHARLEY:** You want a job?

**WILLY:** I got a job, I told you that. *(After a slight pause.)* What the hell are you offering me a job for?

**CHARLEY:** Don't get insulted.

**WILLY:** Don't insult me.

**CHARLEY:** I don't see no sense in it. You don't have to go on this way.

**WILLY:** I got a good job. *(Slight pause.)* What do you keep comin' in here for?

**CHARLEY:** You want me to go?

**WILLY:** *(after a pause, withering)* I can't understand it. He's going back to Texas again. What the hell is that?

**CHARLEY:** Let him go.

**WILLY:** I got nothin' to give him, Charley, I'm clean, I'm clean.

**CHARLEY:** He won't starve. None a them starve. Forget about him.

**WILLY:** Then what have I got to remember?

**CHARLEY:** You take it too hard. To hell with it. When a deposit bottle is broken you don't get your nickel back.

**WILLY:** That's easy enough for you to say.

**CHARLEY:** That ain't easy for me to say.

**WILLY:** Did you see the ceiling I put up in the living-room?

**CHARLEY:** Yeah, that's a piece of work. To put up a ceiling is a mystery to me. How do you do it?

**WILLY:** What's the difference?

**CHARLEY:** Well, talk about it.

**WILLY:** You gonna put up a ceiling?

**CHARLEY:** How could I put up a ceiling?

**WILLY:** Then what the hell are you bothering me for?

**CHARLEY:** You're insulted again.

**WILLY:** A man who can't handle tools is not a man. You're disgusting.

**CHARLEY:** Don't call me disgusting, Willy.

*Uncle* BEN, *carrying a valise and an umbrella, enters the forestage from around the right corner of the house. He is a stolid man, in his sixties, with a mustache and an authoritative air. He is utterly certain of his destiny, and there is an aura of far places about him. He enters exactly as* WILLY *speaks.*

**WILLY:** I'm getting awfully tired, Ben.

BEN*'s music is heard.* BEN *looks around at everything.*

**CHARLEY:** Good, keep playing; you'll sleep better. Did you call me Ben?

BEN *looks at his watch.*

**WILLY:** That's funny. For a second there you reminded me of my brother Ben.

**BEN:** I only have a few minutes. *(He strolls, inspecting the place.* WILLY *and* CHARLEY *continue playing.)*

**CHARLEY:** You never heard from him again, heh? Since that time?

**WILLY:** Didn't Linda tell you? Couple of weeks ago we got a letter from his wife in Africa. He died.

**CHARLEY:** That so.

**BEN:** *(chuckling)* So this is Brooklyn, eh?

**CHARLEY:** Maybe you're in for some of his money.

**WILLY:** Naa, he had seven sons. There's just one opportunity I had with that man . . .

**BEN:** I must make a train, William. There are several properties I'm looking at in Alaska.

**WILLY:** Sure, sure! If I'd gone with him to Alaska that time, everything would've been totally different.

**CHARLEY:** Go on, you'd froze to death up there.

**WILLY:** What're you talking about?

**BEN:** Opportunity is tremendous in Alaska, William. Surprised you're not up there.

**WILLY:** Sure, tremendous.

**CHARLEY:** Heh?

**WILLY:** There was the only man I ever met who knew the answers.

**CHARLEY:** Who?

**BEN:** How are you all?

**WILLY:** *(taking a pot, smiling)* Fine, fine.

**CHARLEY:** Pretty sharp tonight.

**BEN:** Is Mother living with you?

**WILLY:** No, she died a long time ago.

**CHARLEY:** Who?

**BEN:** That's too bad. Fine specimen of a lady, Mother.

**WILLY:** *(to* CHARLEY*)* Heh?

**BEN:** I'd hoped to see the old girl.

**CHARLEY:** Who died?

**BEN:** Heard anything from Father, have you?

**WILLY:** *(unnerved)* What do you mean, who died?

**CHARLEY:** *(taking a pot)* What're you talkin' about?

**BEN:** *(looking at his watch)* William, it's half-past eight!

**WILLY:** *(as though to dispel his confusion he angrily stops* CHARLEY*'s hand)* That's my build!

**CHARLEY:** I put the ace—

**WILLY:** If you don't know how to play the game I'm not gonna throw my money away on you!

**CHARLEY:** *(rising)* It was my ace, for God's sake!

**WILLY:** I'm through, I'm through!

**BEN:** When did Mother die?

**WILLY:** Long ago. Since the beginning you never knew how to play cards.

**CHARLEY:** *(picks up the cards and goes to the door)* All right! Next time I'll bring a deck with five aces.

**WILLY:** I don't play that kind of game!

**CHARLEY:** *(turning to him)* You ought to be ashamed of yourself!

Willy and Charley (Edward Andrews) play a game of cards as Ben (Albert Dekker) appears.

**WILLY:** Yeah?

**CHARLEY:** Yeah! *(He goes out.)*

**WILLY:** *(slamming the door after him)* Ignoramus!

**BEN:** *(as* WILLY *comes toward him through the wall-line of the kitchen)* So you're William.

**WILLY:** *(shaking Ben's hand)* Ben! I've been waiting for you so long! What's the answer? How did you do it?

**BEN:** Oh, there's a story in that.

LINDA *enters the forestage, as of old, carrying the wash basket.*

**LINDA:** Is this Ben?

**BEN:** *(gallantly)* How do you do, my dear.

**LINDA:** Where've you been all these years? Willy's always wondered why you—

**WILLY:** *(pulling Ben away from her impatiently)* Where is Dad? Didn't you follow him? How did you get started?

**BEN:** Well, I don't know how much you remember.

**WILLY:** Well, I was just a baby, of course, only three or four years old—

**BEN:** Three years and eleven months.

**WILLY:** What a memory, Ben!

**BEN:** I have many enterprises, William, and I have never kept books.

**WILLY:** I remember I was sitting under the wagon in—was it Nebraska?

**BEN:** It was South Dakota, and I gave you a bunch of wild flowers.

**WILLY:** I remember you walking away down some open road.

**BEN:** *(laughing)* I was going to find Father in Alaska.

**WILLY:** Where is he?

**BEN:** At that age I had a very faulty view of geography, William. I discovered after a few days that I was heading due south, so instead of Alaska, I ended up in Africa.

**LINDA:** Africa!

**WILLY:** The Gold Coast!

**BEN:** Principally diamond mines.

**LINDA:** Diamond mines!

**BEN:** Yes, my dear. But I've only a few minutes—

**WILLY:** No! Boys! Boys! *(Young* BIFF *and* HAPPY *appear.)* Listen to this. This is your Uncle Ben, a great man! Tell my boys, Ben!

**BEN:** Why, boys, when I was seventeen I walked into the jungle, and when I was twenty-one I walked out. *(He laughs.)* And by God I was rich.

**WILLY:** *(to the boys)* You see what I been talking about? The greatest things can happen!

**BEN:** *(glancing at his watch)* I have an appointment in Ketchikan Tuesday next week.

**WILLY:** No, Ben! Please tell about Dad. I want my boys to hear. I want them to know the kind of stock they spring from. All I remember is a man with a big beard, and I was in Mamma's lap, sitting around a fire, and some kind of high music.

**BEN:** His flute. He played the flute.

**WILLY:** Sure, the flute, that's right!

*New music is heard, a high, rollicking tune.*

**BEN:** Father was a very great and a very wild-hearted man. We would start in Boston, and he'd toss the whole family into the wagon, and then he'd drive the team right across the country; through Ohio, and Indiana, Michigan, Illinois, and all the Western states. And we'd stop in the towns and sell the flutes that he'd made on the way. Great inventor, Father. With one gadget he made more in a week than a man like you could make in a lifetime.

**WILLY:** That's just the way I'm bringing them up, Ben—rugged, well liked, all-around.

**BEN:** Yeah? *(To* BIFF.*)* Hit that, boy—hard as you can. *(He pounds his stomach.)*

**BIFF:** Oh, no, sir!

**BEN:** *(taking boxing stance)* Come on, get to me. *(He laughs.)*

**WILLY:** Go to it, Biff! Go ahead, show him!

**BIFF:** Okay! *(He cocks his fists and starts in.)*

**LINDA:** *(to* WILLY*)* Why must he fight, dear?

**BEN:** *(sparring with* BIFF*)* Good boy! Good boy!

**WILLY:** How's that, Ben, heh?

**HAPPY:** Give him the left, Biff!

**LINDA:** Why are you fighting?

**BEN:** Good boy! *(Suddenly comes in, trips* BIFF, *and stands over him, the point of his umbrella poised over* BIFF*'s eye.)*

**LINDA:** Look out, Biff!

**BIFF:** Gee!

**BEN:** *(patting* BIFF*'s knee)* Never fight fair with a stranger, boy. You'll never get out of the jungle that way. *(Taking* LINDA*'s hand and bowing):* It was an honor and a pleasure to meet you, Linda.

**LINDA:** *(withdrawing her hand coldly, frightened)* Have a nice—trip.

**BEN:** *(to* WILLY*)* And good luck with your—what do you do?

**WILLY:** Selling.

**BEN:** Yes. Well . . . *(He raises his hand in farewell to all.)*

Willy and Ben have a laugh at Charley.

**WILLY:** No, Ben, I don't want you to think . . . *(He takes Ben's arm to show him.)* It's Brooklyn, I know, but we hunt too.

**BEN:** Really, now.

**WILLY:** Oh, sure, there's snakes and rabbits and—that's why I moved out here. Why, Biff can fell any one of these trees in no time! Boys! Go right over to where they're building the apartment house and get some sand. We're gonna rebuild the entire front stoop now! Watch this, Ben!

**BIFF:** Yes, sir! On the double, Hap!

**HAPPY:** *(as he and* BIFF *run off)* I lost weight, Pop, you notice?

CHARLEY *enters in knickers, even before the boys are gone.*

**CHARLEY:** Listen, if they steal any more from that building the watchman'll put the cops on them!

**LINDA:** *(to* WILLY*)* Don't let Biff . . .

BEN *laughs lustily.*

**WILLY:** You shoulda seen the lumber they brought home last week. At least a dozen six-by-tens worth all kinds a money.

**CHARLEY:** Listen, if that watchman—

**WILLY:** I gave them hell, understand. But I got a couple of fearless characters there.

**CHARLEY:** Willy, the jails are full of fearless characters.

**BEN:** *(clapping* WILLY *on the back, with a laugh at* CHARLEY*)* And the stock exchange, friend!

**WILLY:** *(joining in Ben's laughter)* Where are the rest of your pants?

**CHARLEY:** My wife bought them.

**WILLY:** Now all you need is a golf club and you can go upstairs and go to sleep. *(To Ben).* Great athlete! Between him and his son Bernard they can't hammer a nail!

**BERNARD:** *(rushing in)* The watchman's chasing Biff!

**WILLY:** *(angrily)* Shut up! He's not stealing anything!

**LINDA:** *(alarmed, hurrying off left)* Where is he? Biff, dear! *(She exits.)*

**WILLY:** *(moving toward the left, away from Ben)* There's nothing wrong. What's the matter with you?

**BEN:** Nervy boy. Good!

**WILLY:** *(laughing)* Oh, nerves of iron, that Biff!

**CHARLEY:** Don't know what it is. My New England man comes back and he's bleedin', they murdered him up there.

**WILLY:** It's contacts, Charley, I got important contacts!

**CHARLEY:** *(sarcastically)* Glad to hear it, Willy. Come in later, we'll shoot a little casino. I'll take some of your Portland money. *(He laughs at* WILLY *and exits.)*

**WILLY:** *(turning to Ben)* Business is bad, it's murderous. But not for me, of course.

**BEN:** I'll stop by on my way back to Africa.

**WILLY:** *(longingly)* Can't you stay a few days? You're just what I need, Ben, because I—I have a fine position here, but I—well, Dad left when I was such a baby and I never had a chance to talk to him and I still feel—kind of temporary about myself.

**BEN:** I'll be late for my train.

*They are at opposite ends of the stage.*

**WILLY:** Ben, my boys—can't we talk? They'd go into the jaws of hell for me, see, but I—

**BEN:** William, you're being first-rate with your boys. Outstanding, manly chaps!

**WILLY:** *(hanging on to his words)* Oh, Ben, that's good to hear! Because sometimes I'm afraid that I'm not teaching them the right kind of—Ben, how should I teach them?

**BEN:** *(giving great weight to each word, and with a certain vicious audacity)* William, when I walked into the jungle, I was seventeen. When I walked out I was twenty-one. And, by God, I was rich! *(He goes off into darkness around the right corner of the house.)*

**WILLY:** . . . was rich! That's just the spirit I want to imbue them with! To walk into a jungle! I was right! I was right! I was right!

BEN *is gone, but* WILLY *is still speaking to him as* LINDA, *in nightgown and robe, enters the kitchen, glances around for* WILLY, *then goes to the door of the house, looks out, and sees him. Comes down to his left. He looks at her.*

**LINDA:** Willy, dear? Willy?

**WILLY:** I was right!

**LINDA:** Did you have some cheese? *(He can't answer.)* It's very late, darling. Come to bed, heh?

**WILLY:** *(looking straight up)* Gotta break your neck to see a star in this yard.

**LINDA:** You coming in?

**WILLY:** Whatever happened to that diamond watch fob? Remember? When Ben came from Africa that time? Didn't he give me a watch fob with a diamond in it?

**LINDA:** You pawned it, dear. Twelve, thirteen years ago. For Biff's radio correspondence course.

**WILLY:** Gee, that was a beautiful thing. I'll take a walk.

**LINDA:** But you're in your slippers.

**WILLY:** *(starting to go around the house at the left)* I was right! I was! *(Half to* LINDA, *as he goes, shaking his head.)* What a man! There was a man worth talking to. I was right!

**LINDA:** *(calling after* WILLY*)* But in your slippers, Willy!

WILLY *is almost gone when* BIFF, *in his pajamas, comes down the stairs and enters the kitchen.*

**BIFF:** What is he doing out there?

**LINDA:** Sh!

**BIFF:** God Almighty, Mom, how long has he been doing this?

**LINDA:** Don't, he'll hear you.

**BIFF:** What the hell is the matter with him?

**LINDA:** It'll pass by morning.

**BIFF:** Shouldn't we do anything?

**LINDA:** Oh, my dear, you should do a lot of things, but there's nothing to do, so go to sleep.

HAPPY *comes down the stairs and sits on the steps.*

**HAPPY:** I never heard him so loud, Mom.

**LINDA:** Well, come around more often; you'll hear him. *(She sits down at the table and mends the lining of* WILLY'S *jacket.)*

**BIFF:** Why didn't you ever write me about this, Mom?

**LINDA:** How would I write to you? For over three months you had no address.

**BIFF:** I was on the move. But you know I thought of you all the time. You know that, don't you, pal?

**LINDA:** I know, dear, I know. But he likes to have a letter. Just to know that there's still a possibility for better things.

**BIFF:** He's not like this all the time, is he?

**LINDA:** It's when you come home he's always the worst.

**BIFF:** When I come home?

**LINDA:** When you write you're coming, he's all smiles, and talks about the future, and—he's just wonderful. And then the closer you seem to come, the more shaky he gets, and then, by the time you get here, he's arguing, and he seems angry at you. I think it's just that maybe he can't bring himself to—to open up to you. Why are you so hateful to each other? Why is that?

**BIFF:** *(evasively)* I'm not hateful, Mom.

**LINDA:** But you no sooner come in the door than you're fighting!

**BIFF:** I don't know why. I mean to change. I'm tryin', Mom, you understand?

**LINDA:** Are you home to stay now?

**BIFF:** I don't know. I want to look around, see what's doin'.

**LINDA:** Biff, you can't look around all your life, can you?

**BIFF:** I just can't take hold, Mom. I can't take hold of some kind of a life.

**LINDA:** Biff, a man is not a bird, to come and go with the springtime.

**BIFF:** Your hair . . . *(He touches her hair.)* Your hair got so gray.

**LINDA:** Oh, it's been gray since you were in high school. I just stopped dyeing it, that's all.

**BIFF:** Dye it again, will ya? I don't want my pal looking old. *(He smiles.)*

**LINDA:** You're such a boy! You think you can go away for a year and . . . You've got to get it into your head now that one day you'll knock on this door and there'll be strange people here—

**BIFF:** What are you talking about? You're not even sixty, Mom.

**LINDA:** But what about your father?

**BIFF:** *(lamely)* Well, I meant him too.

**HAPPY:** He admires Pop.

**LINDA:** Biff, dear, if you don't have any feeling for him, then you can't have any feeling for me.

**BIFF:** Sure I can, Mom.

**LINDA:** No. You can't just come to see me, because I love him. *(With a threat, but only a threat, of tears.)* He's

The Lomans argue about Willy.

the dearest man in the world to me, and I won't have anyone making him feel unwanted and low and blue. You've got to make up your mind now, darling, there's no leeway any more. Either he's your father and you pay him that respect, or else you're not to come here. I know he's not easy to get along with—nobody knows that better than me—but . . .

**WILLY:** *(from the left, with a laugh)* Hey, hey, Biffo!

**BIFF:** *(starting to go out after* WILLY*)* What the hell is the matter with him? *(*HAPPY *stops him.)*

**LINDA:** Don't—don't go near him!

**BIFF:** Stop making excuses for him! He always, always wiped the floor with you. Never had an ounce of respect for you.

**HAPPY:** He's always had respect for—

**BIFF:** What the hell do you know about it?

**HAPPY:** *(surlily)* Just don't call him crazy!

**BIFF:** He's got no character—Charley wouldn't do this. Not in his own house—spewing out that vomit from his mind.

**HAPPY:** Charley never had to cope with what he's got to.

**BIFF:** People are worse off than Willy Loman. Believe me, I've seen them!

**LINDA:** Then make Charley your father, Biff. You can't do that, can you? I don't say he's a great man. Willy Loman never made a lot of money. His name was never in the paper. He's not the finest character that ever lived. But he's a human being, and a terrible thing is happening to him. So attention must be paid. He's not to be allowed to fall into his grave like an old dog. Attention, attention must be finally paid to such a person. You called him crazy—

**BIFF:** I didn't mean—

**LINDA:** No, a lot of people think he's lost his—balance. But you don't have to be very smart to know what his trouble is. The man is exhausted.

**HAPPY:** Sure!

**LINDA:** A small man can be just as exhausted as a great man. He works for a company thirty-six years this March, opens up unheard-of territories to their trademark, and now in his old age they take his salary away.

**HAPPY:** *(indignantly)* I didn't know that, Mom.

**LINDA:** You never asked, my dear! Now that you get your spending money someplace else you don't trouble your mind with him.

**HAPPY:** But I gave you money last—

**LINDA:** Christmas time, fifty dollars! To fix the hot water it cost ninety-seven fifty! For five weeks he's been on straight commission, like a beginner, an unknown!

**BIFF:** Those ungrateful bastards!

**LINDA:** Are they any worse than his sons? When he brought them business, when he was young, they were glad to see him. But now his old friends, the old buyers that loved him so and always found some order to hand him in a pinch—they're all dead, retired. He used to be able to make six, seven calls a day in Boston. Now he takes his valises out of the car and puts them back and takes them out again and he's exhausted. Instead of walking he talks now. He drives seven hundred miles, and when he gets there no one knows him any more, no one welcomes him. And what goes through a man's mind, driving seven hundred miles home without having earned a cent? Why shouldn't he talk to himself? Why? When he has to go to Charley and borrow fifty dollars a week and pretend to me that it's his pay? How long can that go on? How long? You see what I'm sitting here and waiting for? And you tell me he has no character? The man who never worked a day but for your benefit? When does he get the medal for that? Is this his reward—to turn around at the age of sixty-three and find his sons, who he loved better than his life, one a philandering bum—

**HAPPY:** Mom!

**LINDA:** That's all you are, my baby! *(To* BIFF.*)* And you! What happened to the love you had for him? You were such pals! How you used to talk to him on the phone every night! How lonely he was till he could come home to you!

**BIFF:** All right, Mom. I'll live here in my room, and I'll get a job. I'll keep away from him, that's all.

**LINDA:** No, Biff. You can't stay here and fight all the time.

**BIFF:** He threw me out of this house, remember that.

**LINDA:** Why did he do that? I never knew why.

**BIFF:** Because I know he's a fake and he doesn't like anybody around who knows!

**LINDA:** Why a fake? In what way? What do you mean?

**BIFF:** Just don't lay it all at my feet. It's between me and him—that's all I have to say. I'll chip in from now on. He'll settle for half my pay check. He'll be all right. I'm going to bed. *(He starts for the stairs.)*

**LINDA:** He won't be all right.

**BIFF:** *(turning on the stairs, furiously)* I hate this city and I'll stay here. Now what do you want?

**LINDA:** He's dying, Biff.

HAPPY *turns quickly to her, shocked.*

**BIFF:** *(after a pause)* Why is he dying?

**LINDA:** He's been trying to kill himself.

**BIFF:** *(with great horror)* How?

**LINDA:** I live from day to day.

**BIFF:** What're you talking about?

**LINDA:** Remember I wrote you that he smashed up the car again? In February?

**BIFF:** Well?

**LINDA:** The insurance inspector came. He said that they have evidence. That all these accidents in the last year—weren't—weren't—accidents.

**HAPPY:** How can they tell that? That's a lie.

**LINDA:** It seems there's a woman . . . *(She takes a breath as):*
BIFF *(sharply but contained):* What woman?
LINDA *(simultaneously):* . . . and this woman . . .

**LINDA:** What?

**BIFF:** Nothing. Go ahead.

**LINDA:** What did you say?

**BIFF:** Nothing. I just said what woman?

**HAPPY:** What about her?

**LINDA:** Well, it seems she was walking down the road and saw his car. She says that he wasn't driving fast at all, and that he didn't skid. She says he came to that little bridge, and then deliberately smashed into the railing, and it was only the shallowness of the water that saved him.

**BIFF:** Oh, no, he probably just fell asleep again.

**LINDA:** I don't think he fell asleep.

**BIFF:** Why not?

**LINDA:** Last month . . . *(With great difficulty.)* Oh, boys, it's so hard to say a thing like this! He's just a big stupid man to you, but I tell you there's more good in him than in many other people. *(She chokes, wipes her eyes.)* I was looking for a fuse. The lights blew out, and I went down the cellar. And behind the fuse box—it happened to fall out—was a length of rubber pipe—just short.

**HAPPY:** No kidding?

**LINDA:** There's a little attachment on the end of it. I knew right away. And sure enough, on the bottom of the water heater there's a new little nipple on the gas pipe.

**HAPPY:** *(angrily)* That—jerk.

**BIFF:** Did you have it taken off?

**LINDA:** I'm—I'm ashamed to. How can I mention it to him? Every day I go down and take away that little rubber pipe. But, when he comes home, I put it back where it was. How can I insult him that way? I don't know what to do. I live from day to day, boys. I tell you, I know every thought in his mind. It sounds so old-fashioned and silly, but I tell you he put his whole life into you and you've turned your backs on him. *(She is bent over in chair, weeping, her face in her hands.)* Biff, I swear to God! Biff, his life is in your hands!

**HAPPY:** *(to* BIFF*)* How do you like that damned fool!

**BIFF:** *(kissing her)* All right, pal, all right. It's all settled now. I've been remiss. I know that, Mom. But now I'll stay, and I swear to you, I'll apply myself. *(Kneeling in front of her, in a fever of self-reproach.)* It's just—you see, Mom, I don't fit in business. Not that I won't try. I'll try, and I'll make good.

**HAPPY:** Sure you will. The trouble with you in business was you never tried to please people.

**BIFF:** I know, I—

**HAPPY:** Like when you worked for Harrison's. Bob Harrison said you were tops, and then you go and do some damn fool thing like whistling whole songs in the elevator like a comedian.

**BIFF:** *(against* HAPPY*)* So what? I like to whistle sometimes.

**HAPPY:** You don't raise a guy to a responsible job who whistles in the elevator!

**LINDA:** Well, don't argue about it now.

**HAPPY:** Like when you'd go off and swim in the middle of the day instead of taking the line around.

**BIFF:** *(his resentment rising)* Well, don't you run off? You take off sometimes, don't you? On a nice summer day?

**HAPPY:** Yeah, but I cover myself!

**LINDA:** Boys!

**HAPPY:** If I'm going to take a fade the boss can call any number where I'm supposed to be and they'll swear to him that I just left. I'll tell you something that I hate to say, Biff, but in the business world some of them think you're crazy.

**BIFF:** *(angered)* Screw the business world!

**HAPPY:** All right, screw it! Great, but cover yourself!

**LINDA:** Hap, Hap!

**BIFF:** I don't care what they think! They've laughed at Dad for years, and you know why? Because we don't belong in this nuthouse of a city! We should be mixing cement on some open plain, or—or carpenters. A carpenter is allowed to whistle!

WILLY *walks in from the entrance of the house, at left.*

**WILLY:** Even your grandfather was better than a carpenter. *(Pause. They watch him.)* You never grew up. Bernard does not whistle in the elevator, I assure you.

**BIFF:** *(as though to laugh* WILLY *out of it)* Yeah, but you do, Pop.

**WILLY:** I never in my life whistled in an elevator! And who in the business world thinks I'm crazy?

**BIFF:** I didn't mean it like that, Pop. Now don't make a whole thing out of it, will ya?

**WILLY:** Go back to the West! Be a carpenter, a cowboy, enjoy yourself!

**LINDA:** Willy, he was just saying—

**WILLY:** I heard what he said!

**HAPPY:** *(trying to quiet* WILLY*)* Hey, Pop, come on now . . .

**WILLY:** *(continuing over* HAPPY*'s line)* They laugh at me, heh? Go to Filene's, go to the Hub, go to Slattery's, Boston. Call out the name Willy Loman and see what happens! Big shot!

**BIFF:** All right, Pop.

**WILLY:** Big!

**BIFF:** All right!

**WILLY:** Why do you always insult me?

**BIFF:** I didn't say a word. *(To* LINDA.*)* Did I say a word?

**LINDA:** He didn't say anything, Willy.

**WILLY:** *(going to the doorway of the living-room)* All right, good night, good night.

**LINDA:** Willy, dear, he just decided . . .

**WILLY:** *(to* BIFF*)* If you get tired hanging around tomorrow, paint the ceiling I put up in the living-room.

**BIFF:** I'm leaving early tomorrow.

**HAPPY:** He's going to see Bill Oliver, Pop.

**WILLY:** *(interestedly)* Oliver? For what?

**BIFF:** *(with reserve, but trying, trying)* He always said he'd stake me. I'd like to go into business, so maybe I can take him up on it.

**LINDA:** Isn't that wonderful?

**WILLY:** Don't interrupt. What's wonderful about it? There's fifty men in the City of New York who'd stake him. *(To* BIFF.*)* Sporting goods?

Willy and the boys discuss their million-dollar ideas.

**BIFF:** I guess so. I know something about it and—

**WILLY:** He knows something about it! You know sporting goods better than Spalding, for God's sake! How much is he giving you?

**BIFF:** I don't know, I didn't even see him yet, but—

**WILLY:** Then what're you talkin' about?

**BIFF:** *(getting angry)* Well, all I said was I'm gonna see him, that's all!

**WILLY:** *(turning away)* Ah, you're counting your chickens again.

**BIFF:** *(starting left for the stairs)* Oh, Jesus, I'm going to sleep!

**WILLY:** *(calling after him)* Don't curse in this house!

**BIFF:** *(turning)* Since when did you get so clean?

**HAPPY:** *(trying to stop them)* Wait a . . .

**WILLY:** Don't use that language to me! I won't have it!

**HAPPY:** *(grabbing* BIFF, *shouts)* Wait a minute! I got an idea. I got a feasible idea. Come here, Biff, let's talk this over now, let's talk some sense here. When I was down in Florida last time, I thought of a great idea to sell sporting goods. It just came back to me. You and I, Biff—we have a line, the Loman Line. We train a couple of weeks, and put on a couple of exhibitions, see?

**WILLY:** That's an idea!

**HAPPY:** Wait! We form two basketball teams, see? Two water-polo teams. We play each other. It's a million dollars' worth of publicity. Two brothers, see? The Loman Brothers. Displays in the Royal Palms—all the hotels. And banners over the ring and the basketball court: "Loman Brothers." Baby, we could sell sporting goods!

**WILLY:** That is a one-million-dollar idea!

**LINDA:** Marvelous!

**BIFF:** I'm in great shape as far as that's concerned.

**HAPPY:** And the beauty of it is, Biff, it wouldn't be like a business. We'd be out playin' ball again . . .

**BIFF:** *(enthused)* Yeah, that's . . .

**WILLY:** Million-dollar . . .

**HAPPY:** And you wouldn't get fed up with it, Biff. It'd be the family again. There'd be the old honor, and comradeship, and if you wanted to go off for a swim or somethin'—well, you'd do it! Without some smart cooky gettin' up ahead of you!

**WILLY:** Lick the world! You guys together could absolutely lick the civilized world.

**BIFF:** I'll see Oliver tomorrow. Hap, if we could work that out . . .

**LINDA:** Maybe things are beginning to—

**WILLY:** *(wildly enthused, to* LINDA*)* Stop interrupting! *(To* BIFF.*)* But don't wear sport jacket and slacks when you see Oliver.

**BIFF:** No, I'll—

**WILLY:** A business suit, and talk as little as possible, and don't crack any jokes.

**BIFF:** He did like me. Always liked me.

**LINDA:** He loved you!

**WILLY:** *(to* LINDA*)* Will you stop! *(To* BIFF.*)* Walk in very serious. You are not applying for a boy's job. Money is to pass. Be quiet, fine, and serious. Everybody likes a kidder, but nobody lends him money.

**HAPPY:** I'll try to get some myself, Biff. I'm sure I can.

**WILLY:** I see great things for you kids, I think your troubles are over. But remember, start big and you'll end big. Ask for fifteen. How much you gonna ask for?

**BIFF:** Gee, I don't know—

**WILLY:** And don't say "Gee." "Gee" is a boy's word. A man walking in for fifteen thousand dollars does not say "Gee!"

**BIFF:** Ten, I think, would be top though.

**WILLY:** Don't be so modest. You always started too low. Walk in with a big laugh. Don't look worried. Start off with a couple of your good stories to lighten things up. It's not what you say, it's how you say it—because personality always wins the day.

**LINDA:** Oliver always thought the highest of him—

**WILLY:** Will you let me talk?

**BIFF:** Don't yell at her, Pop, will ya?

**WILLY:** *(angrily)* I was talking, wasn't I?

**BIFF:** I don't like you yelling at her all the time, and I'm tellin' you, that's all.

**WILLY:** What're you, takin' over this house?

**LINDA:** Willy—

**WILLY:** *(turning on her)* Don't take his side all the time, goddammit!

**BIFF:** *(furiously)* Stop yelling at her!

**WILLY:** *(suddenly pulling on his cheek, beaten down, guilt ridden)* Give my best to Bill Oliver—he may remember me. *(He exits through the living-room doorway.)*

**LINDA:** *(her voice subdued)* What'd you have to start that for? *(*BIFF *turns away.)* You see how sweet he was as soon as you talked hopefully? *(She goes over to* BIFF.*)* Come up and say good night to him. Don't let him go to bed that way.

**HAPPY:** Come on, Biff, let's buck him up.

**LINDA:** Please, dear. Just say good night. It takes so little to make him happy. Come. *(She goes through the living-room doorway, calling upstairs from within the living-room.)* Your pajamas are hanging in the bathroom, Willy!

**HAPPY:** *(looking toward where* LINDA *went out)* What a woman! They broke the mold when they made her. You know that, Biff?

**BIFF:** He's off salary. My God, working on commission!

**HAPPY:** Well, let's face it: he's no hot-shot selling man. Except that sometimes, you have to admit, he's a sweet personality.

**BIFF:** *(deciding)* Lend me ten bucks, will ya? I want to buy some new ties.

**HAPPY:** I'll take you to a place I know. Beautiful stuff. Wear one of my striped shirts tomorrow.

**BIFF:** She got gray. Mom got awful old. Gee, I'm gonna go in to Oliver tomorrow and knock him for a—

**HAPPY:** Come on up. Tell that to Dad. Let's give him a whirl. Come on.

**BIFF:** *(steamed up)* You know, with ten thousand bucks, boy!

**HAPPY:** *(as they go into the living-room)* That's the talk, Biff, that's the first time I've heard the old confidence out of you! *(From within the living-room, fading off.)* You're gonna live with me, kid, and any babe you want just say the word . . . *(The last lines are hardly heard. They are mounting the stairs to their parents' bedroom.)*

**LINDA:** *(entering her bedroom and addressing* WILLY, *who is in the bathroom. She is straightening the bed for him)* Can you do anything about the shower? It drips.

**WILLY:** *(from the bathroom)* All of a sudden everything falls to pieces! Goddam plumbing, oughta be sued, those people. I hardly finished putting it in and the thing . . . *(His words rumble off.)*

**LINDA:** I'm just wondering if Oliver will remember him. You think he might?

**WILLY:** *(coming out of the bathroom in his pajamas)* Remember him? What's the matter with you, you crazy? If he'd've stayed with Oliver he'd be on top by now! Wait'll Oliver gets a look at him. You don't know the average caliber any more. The average young man today—*(he is getting into bed)*—is got a caliber of zero. Greatest thing in the world for him was to bum around.

BIFF *and* HAPPY *enter the bedroom. Slight pause.*

**WILLY:** *(stops short, looking at* BIFF*)* Glad to hear it, boy.

**HAPPY:** He wanted to say good night to you, sport.

**WILLY:** *(to* BIFF*)* Yeah. Knock him dead, boy. What'd you want to tell me?

**BIFF:** Just take it easy, Pop. Good night. *(He turns to go.)*

**WILLY:** *(unable to resist)* And if anything falls off the desk while you're talking to him—like a package or something—don't you pick it up. They have office boys for that.

**LINDA:** I'll make a big breakfast—

**WILLY:** Will you let me finish? *(To* BIFF.*)* Tell him you were in the business in the West. Not farm work.

**BIFF:** All right, Dad.

**LINDA:** I think everything—

**WILLY:** *(going right through her speech)* And don't undersell yourself. No less than fifteen thousand dollars.

**BIFF:** *(unable to bear him)* Okay. Good night, Mom. *(He starts moving.)*

**WILLY:** Because you got a greatness in you, Biff, remember that. You got all kinds a greatness . . . *(He lies back, exhausted.* BIFF *walks out.)*

**LINDA:** *(calling after* BIFF*)* Sleep well, darling!

**HAPPY:** I'm gonna get married, Mom. I wanted to tell you.

**LINDA:** Go to sleep, dear.

**HAPPY:** *(going)* I just wanted to tell you.

**WILLY:** Keep up the good work. *(*HAPPY *exits.)* God . . . remember that Ebbets Field game? The championship of the city?

**LINDA:** Just rest. Should I sing to you?

**WILLY:** Yeah. Sing to me. *(*LINDA *hums a soft lullaby.)* When that team came out—he was the tallest, remember?

**LINDA:** Oh, yes. And in gold.

BIFF *enters the darkened kitchen, takes a cigarette, and leaves the house. He comes downstage into a golden pool of light. He smokes, staring at the night.*

**WILLY:** Like a young god. Hercules—something like that. And the sun, the sun all around him. Remember how he waved to me? Right up from the field, with the representatives of three colleges standing by? And the buyers I brought, and the cheers when he came out—Loman, Loman, Loman! God Almighty, he'll be great yet. A star like that, magnificent, can never really fade away!

*The light on* WILLY *is fading. The gas heater begins to glow through the kitchen wall, near the stairs, a blue flame beneath red coils.*

**LINDA:** *(timidly)* Willy, dear, what has he got against you?

**WILLY:** I'm so tired. Don't talk any more.

BIFF *slowly returns to the kitchen. He stops, stares toward the heater.*

**LINDA:** Will you ask Howard to let you work in New York?

**WILLY:** First thing in the morning. Everything'll be all right.

Linda hums as Willy reminisces.

BIFF *reaches behind the heater and draws out a length of rubber tubing. He is horrified and turns his head toward* WILLY*'s room, still dimly lit, from which the strains of* LINDA*'s desperate but monotonous humming rise.*

**WILLY:** *(staring through the window into the moonlight)* Gee, look at the moon moving between the buildings!

BIFF *wraps the tubing around his hand and quickly goes up the stairs.*

*Curtain.*

## ACT II

*Music is heard, gay and bright. The curtain rises as the music fades away.* WILLY, *in shirt sleeves, is sitting at the kitchen table, sipping coffee, his hat in his lap.* LINDA *is filling his cup when she can.*

**WILLY:** Wonderful coffee. Meal in itself.

**LINDA:** Can I make you some eggs?

**WILLY:** No. Take a breath.

**LINDA:** You look so rested, dear.

**WILLY:** I slept like a dead one. First time in months. Imagine, sleeping till ten on a Tuesday morning. Boys left nice and early, heh?

**LINDA:** They were out of here by eight o'clock.

**WILLY:** Good work!

**LINDA:** It was so thrilling to see them leaving together. I can't get over the shaving lotion in this house!

**WILLY:** *(smiling)* Mmm—

**LINDA:** Biff was very changed this morning. His whole attitude seemed to be hopeful. He couldn't wait to get downtown to see Oliver.

**WILLY:** He's heading for a change. There's no question, there simply are certain men that take longer to get—solidified. How did he dress?

**LINDA:** His blue suit. He's so handsome in that suit. He could be a—anything in that suit!

WILLY *gets up from the table.* LINDA *holds his jacket for him.*

**WILLY:** There's no question, no question at all. Gee, on the way home tonight I'd like to buy some seeds.

**LINDA:** *(laughing)* That'd be wonderful. But not enough sun gets back there. Nothing'll grow any more.

**WILLY:** You wait, kid, before it's all over we're gonna get a little place out in the country, and I'll raise some vegetables, a couple of chickens . . .

**LINDA:** You'll do it yet, dear.

WILLY *walks out of his jacket.* LINDA *follows him.*

**WILLY:** And they'll get married, and come for a weekend. I'd build a little guest house. 'Cause I got so many fine tools, all I'd need would be a little lumber and some peace of mind.

**LINDA:** *(joyfully)* I sewed the lining . . .

**WILLY:** I could build two guest houses, so they'd both come. Did he decide how much he's going to ask Oliver for?

**LINDA:** *(getting him into the jacket)* He didn't mention it, but I imagine ten or fifteen thousand. You going to talk to Howard today?

**WILLY:** Yeah. I'll put it to him straight and simple. He'll just have to take me off the road.

**LINDA:** And Willy, don't forget to ask for a little advance, because we've got the insurance premium. It's the grace period now.

**WILLY:** That's a hundred . . . ?

**LINDA:** A hundred and eight, sixty-eight. Because we're a little short again.

**WILLY:** Why are we short?

**LINDA:** Well, you had the motor job on the car . . .

**WILLY:** That goddam Studebaker!

**LINDA:** And you got one more payment on the refrigerator . . .

Linda helps Willy into his coat.

**WILLY:** But it just broke again!

**LINDA:** Well, it's old, dear.

**WILLY:** I told you we should've bought a well-advertised machine. Charley bought a General Electric and it's twenty years old and it's still good, that son-of-a-bitch.

**LINDA:** But, Willy—

**WILLY:** Whoever heard of a Hastings refrigerator? Once in my life I would like to own something outright before it's broken! I'm always in a race with the junkyard! I just finished paying for the car and it's on its last legs. The refrigerator consumes belts like a goddam maniac. They time those things. They time them so when you finally paid for them, they're used up.

**LINDA:** *(buttoning up his jacket as he unbuttons it)* All told, about two hundred dollars would carry us, dear. But that includes the last payment on the mortgage. After this payment, Willy, the house belongs to us.

**WILLY:** It's twenty-five years!

**LINDA:** Biff was nine years old when we bought it.

**WILLY:** Well, that's a great thing. To weather a twenty-five year mortgage is—

**LINDA:** It's an accomplishment.

**WILLY:** All the cement, the lumber, the reconstruction I put in this house! There ain't a crack to be found in it any more.

**LINDA:** Well, it served its purpose.

**WILLY:** What purpose? Some stranger'll come along, move in, and that's that. If only Biff would take this house, and raise a family . . . *(He starts to go.)* Good-by, I'm late.

**LINDA:** *(suddenly remembering)* Oh, I forgot! You're supposed to meet them for dinner.

**WILLY:** Me?

**LINDA:** At Frank's Chop House on Forty-eighth near Sixth Avenue.

**WILLY:** Is that so! How about you?

**LINDA:** No, just the three of you. They're gonna blow you to a big meal!

**WILLY:** Don't say! Who thought of that?

**LINDA:** Biff came to me this morning, Willy, and he said, "Tell Dad, we want to blow him to a big meal." Be there six o'clock. You and your two boys are going to have dinner.

**WILLY:** Gee whiz! That's really somethin'. I'm gonna knock Howard for a loop, kid. I'll get an advance, and I'll come home with a New York job. Goddammit, now I'm gonna do it!

**LINDA:** Oh, that's the spirit, Willy!

**WILLY:** I will never get behind a wheel the rest of my life!

**LINDA:** It's changing, Willy, I can feel it changing!

**WILLY:** Beyond a question. G'by, I'm late. *(He starts to go again.)*

**LINDA:** *(calling after him as she runs to the kitchen table for a handkerchief)* You got your glasses?

**WILLY:** *(feels for them, then comes back in)* Yeah, yeah, got my glasses.

**LINDA:** *(giving him the handkerchief)* And a handkerchief.

**WILLY:** Yeah, handkerchief.

**LINDA:** And your saccharine?

**WILLY:** Yeah, my saccharine.

**LINDA:** Be careful on the subway stairs.

*She kisses him, and a silk stocking is seen hanging from her hand.* WILLY *notices it.*

**WILLY:** Will you stop mending stockings? At least while I'm in the house. It gets me nervous. I can't tell you. Please.

LINDA *hides the stocking in her hand as she follows* WILLY *across the forestage in front of the house.*

**LINDA:** Remember, Frank's Chop House.

**WILLY:** *(passing the apron)* Maybe beets would grow out there.

**LINDA:** *(laughing)* But you tried so many times.

**WILLY:** Yeah. Well, don't work hard today. *(He disappears around the right corner of the house.)*

**LINDA:** Be careful!

*As* WILLY *vanishes,* LINDA *waves to him. Suddenly the phone rings. She runs across the stage and into the kitchen and lifts it.*

**LINDA:** Hello? Oh, Biff! I'm so glad you called, I just . . . Yes, sure, I just told him. Yes, he'll be there for dinner at six o'clock, I didn't forget. Listen, I was just

Willy notices the stocking that Linda is mending.

dying to tell you. You know that little rubber pipe I told you about? That he connected to the gas heater? I finally decided to go down the cellar this morning and take it away and destroy it. But it's gone! Imagine? He took it away himself, it isn't there! *(She listens.)* When? Oh, then you took it. Oh—nothing, it's just that I'd hoped he'd taken it away himself. Oh, I'm not worried, darling, because this morning he left in such high spirits, it was like the old days! I'm not afraid any more. Did Mr. Oliver see you? . . . Well, you wait there then. And make a nice impression on him, darling. Just don't perspire too much before you see him. And have a nice time with Dad. He may have big news too! . . . That's right, a New York job. And be sweet to him tonight, dear. Be loving to him. Because he's only a little boat looking for a harbor. *(She is trembling with sorrow and joy.)* Oh, that's wonderful, Biff, you'll save his life. Thanks, darling. Just put your arm around him when he comes into the restaurant. Give him a smile. That's the boy . . . Good-by, dear. . . . You got your comb? . . . That's fine. Good-by, Biff dear.

*In the middle of her speech,* HOWARD WAGNER, *thirty-six, wheels in a small typewriter table on which is a wire-recording machine and proceeds to plug it in. This is on the left forestage. Light slowly fades on* LINDA *as it rises on* HOWARD. HOWARD *is intent on threading the machine and only glances over his shoulder as* WILLY *appears.*

**WILLY:** Pst! Pst!

**HOWARD:** Hello, Willy, come in.

**WILLY:** Like to have a little talk with you, Howard.

**HOWARD:** Sorry to keep you waiting. I'll be with you in a minute.

**WILLY:** What's that, Howard?

**HOWARD:** Didn't you ever see one of these? Wire recorder.

**WILLY:** Oh. Can we talk a minute?

**HOWARD:** Records things. Just got delivery yesterday. Been driving me crazy, the most terrific machine I ever saw in my life. I was up all night with it.

**WILLY:** What do you do with it?

**HOWARD:** I bought it for dictation, but you can do anything with it. Listen to this. I had it home last night. Listen to what I picked up. The first one is my daughter. Get this. *(He flicks the switch and "Roll Out the Barrel" is heard being whistled.)* Listen to that kid whistle.

**WILLY:** That is lifelike, isn't it?

**HOWARD:** Seven years old. Get that tone.

**WILLY:** Ts, ts. Like to ask a little favor if you . . .

*The whistling breaks off, and the voice of* HOWARD*'s daughter is heard.*

**HIS DAUGHTER:** "Now you, Daddy."

**HOWARD:** She's crazy for me! *(Again the same song is whistled.)* That's me! Ha! *(He winks.)*

**WILLY:** You're very good!

*The whistling breaks off again. The machine runs silent for a moment.*

**HOWARD:** Sh! Get this now, this is my son.

**HIS SON:** "The capital of Alabama is Montgomery; the capital of Arizona is Phoenix; the capital of Arkansas is Little Rock; the capital of California is Sacramento . . ." *(and on, and on).*

**HOWARD:** *(holding up five fingers)* Five years old, Willy!

**WILLY:** He'll make an announcer some day!

**HIS SON:** *(continuing)* "The capital . . ."

**HOWARD:** Get that—alphabetical order! *(The machine breaks off suddenly.)* Wait a minute. The maid kicked the plug out.

**WILLY:** It certainly is a—

**HOWARD:** Sh, for God's sake!

**HIS SON:** "It's nine o'clock, Bulova watch time. So I have to go to sleep."

**WILLY:** That really is—

**HOWARD:** Wait a minute! The next is my wife.

*They wait.*

**HOWARD'S VOICE:** "Go on, say something." *(Pause.)* "Well, you gonna talk?"

**HIS WIFE:** "I can't think of anything."

**HOWARD'S VOICE:** "Well, talk—it's turning."

**HIS WIFE:** *(shyly, beaten)* "Hello." *(Silence.)* "Oh, Howard, I can't talk into this . . ."

**HOWARD:** *(snapping the machine off)* That was my wife.

**WILLY:** That is a wonderful machine. Can we—

**HOWARD:** I tell you, Willy, I'm gonna take my camera, and my bandsaw, and all my hobbies, and out they go. This is the most fascinating relaxation I ever found.

**WILLY:** I think I'll get one myself.

**HOWARD:** Sure, they're only a hundred and a half. You can't do without it. Supposing you wanna hear Jack Benny, see? But you can't be at home at that hour. So you tell the maid to turn the radio on when Jack Benny comes on, and this automatically goes on with the radio . . .

**WILLY:** And when you come home you . . .

**HOWARD:** You can come home twelve o'clock, one o'clock, any time you like, and you get yourself a Coke and sit yourself down, throw the switch, and there's Jack Benny's program in the middle of the night!

**WILLY:** I'm definitely going to get one. Because lots of time I'm on the road, and I think to myself, what I must be missing on the radio!

**HOWARD:** Don't you have a radio in the car?

**WILLY:** Well, yeah, but who ever thinks of turning it on?

**HOWARD:** Say, aren't you supposed to be in Boston?

**WILLY:** That's what I want to talk to you about, Howard. You got a minute? *(He draws a chair in from the wing.)*

**HOWARD:** What happened? What're you doing here?

**WILLY:** Well . . .

**HOWARD:** You didn't crack up again, did you?

**WILLY:** Oh, no. No . . .

**HOWARD:** Geez, you had me worried there for a minute. What's the trouble?

**WILLY:** Well, tell you the truth, Howard. I've come to the decision that I'd rather not travel any more.

**HOWARD:** Not travel! Well, what'll you do?

**WILLY:** Remember, Christmas time, when you had the party here? You said you'd try to think of some spot for me here in town.

**HOWARD:** With us?

**WILLY:** Well, sure.

**HOWARD:** Oh, yeah, yeah. I remember. Well, I couldn't think of anything for you, Willy.

**WILLY:** I tell ya, Howard. The kids are all grown up, y'know. I don't need much any more. If I could take home—well, sixty-five dollars a week. I could swing it.

**HOWARD:** Yeah, but Willy, see I—

**WILLY:** I tell ya why, Howard. Speaking frankly and between the two of us, y'know—I'm just a little tired.

**HOWARD:** Oh, I could understand that, Willy. But you're a road man, Willy, and we do a road business. We've only got a half-dozen salesmen on the floor here.

**WILLY:** God knows, Howard, I never asked a favor of any man. But I was with the firm when your father used to carry you in here in his arms.

**HOWARD:** I know that, Willy, but—

**WILLY:** Your father came to me the day you were born and asked me what I thought of the name of Howard, may he rest in peace.

**HOWARD:** I appreciate that, Willy, but there just is no spot here for you. If I had a spot I'd slam you right in, but I just don't have a single solitary spot.

*He looks for his lighter.* WILLY *has picked it up and gives it to him. Pause.*

**WILLY:** *(with increasing anger)* Howard, all I need to set my table is fifty dollars a week.

**HOWARD:** But where am I going to put you, kid?

**WILLY:** Look, it isn't a question of whether I can sell merchandise, is it?

**HOWARD:** No, but it's a business, kid, and everybody's gotta pull his own weight.

**WILLY:** *(desperately)* Just let me tell you a story, Howard—

**HOWARD:** 'Cause you gotta admit, business is business.

**WILLY:** *(angrily)* Business is definitely business, but just listen for a minute. You don't understand this. When

I was a boy—eighteen, nineteen—I was already on the road. And there was a question in my mind as to whether selling had a future for me. Because in those days I had a yearning to go to Alaska. See, there were three gold strikes in one month in Alaska, and I felt like going out. Just for the ride, you might say.

**HOWARD:** *(barely interested)* Don't say.

**WILLY:** Oh, yeah, my father lived many years in Alaska. He was an adventurous man. We've got quite a little streak of self-reliance in our family. I thought I'd go out with my older brother and try to locate him, and maybe settle in the North with the old man. And I was almost decided to go, when I met a salesman in the Parker House. His name was Dave Singleman. And he was eighty-four years old, and he'd drummed merchandise in thirty-one states. And old Dave, he'd go up to his room, y'understand, put on his green velvet slippers—I'll never forget—and pick up his phone and call the buyers, and without ever leaving his room, at the age of eighty-four, he made his living. And when I saw that, I realized that selling was the greatest career a man could want. 'Cause what could be more satisfying than to be able to go, at the age of eighty-four, into twenty or thirty different cities, and pick up a phone, and be remembered and loved and helped by so many different people? Do you know? When he died—and by the way he died the death of a salesman, in his green velvet slippers in the smoker of the New York, New Haven, and Hartford, going into Boston—when he died, hundreds of salesmen and buyers were at his funeral. Things were sad on a lotta trains for months after that. *(He stands up.* HOWARD *has not looked at him.)* In those days there was personality in it, Howard. There was respect, and comradeship, and gratitude in it. Today, it's all cut and dried, and there's no chance for bringing friendship to bear—or personality. You see what I mean? They don't know me any more.

**HOWARD:** *(moving away, to the right)* That's just the thing, Willy.

**WILLY:** If I had forty dollars a week—that's all I'd need. Forty dollars, Howard.

**HOWARD:** Kid, I can't take blood from a stone, I—

**WILLY:** *(desperation is on him now)* Howard, the year Al Smith was nominated, your father came to me and—

**HOWARD:** *(starting to go off)* I've got to see some people, kid.

**WILLY:** *(stopping him)* I'm talking about your father! There were promises made across this desk! You mustn't tell me you've got people to see—I put thirty-four years into this firm, Howard, and now I can't pay my insurance! You can't eat the orange and throw the peel away—a man is not a piece of fruit! *(After a pause.)* Now pay attention. Your father—in 1928 I had a big year. I averaged a hundred and seventy dollars a week in commissions.

**HOWARD:** *(impatiently)* Now, Willy, you never averaged—

**WILLY:** *(banging his hand on the desk)* I averaged a hundred and seventy dollars a week in the year of 1928! And your father came to me—or rather, I was in the office here—it was right over this desk—and he put his hand on my shoulder—

**HOWARD:** *(getting up)* You'll have to excuse me, Willy, I gotta see some people. Pull yourself together. *(Going out.)* I'll be back in a little while.

*On* HOWARD*'s exit, the light on his chair grows very bright and strange.*

**WILLY:** Pull myself together! What the hell did I say to him? My God, I was yelling at him! How could I? *(*WILLY *breaks off, staring at the light, which occupies the chair, animating it. He approaches this chair, standing across the desk from it.)* Frank, Frank, don't you remember what you told me that time? How you put your hand on my shoulder, and Frank . . . *(He leans on the desk and as he speaks the dead man's name he accidentally switches on the recorder, and instantly:)*

**HOWARD'S SON:** ". . . of New York is Albany. The capital of Ohio is Cincinnati, the capital of Rhode Island is . . ." *(The recitation continues.)*

**WILLY:** *(leaping away with fright, shouting)* Ha! Howard! Howard! Howard!

**HOWARD:** *(rushing in)* What happened?

**WILLY:** *(pointing at the machine, which continues nasally, childishly, with the capital cities)* Shut it off! Shut it off!

**HOWARD:** *(pulling the plug out)* Look, Willy . . .

**WILLY:** *(pressing his hands to his eyes)* I gotta get myself some coffee. I'll get some coffee . . .

WILLY *starts to walk out.* HOWARD *stops him.*

**HOWARD:** *(rolling up the cord)* Willy, look . . .

**WILLY:** I'll go to Boston.

Howard (Jon Polito) talks to Willy about his job performance.

**HOWARD:** Willy, you can't go to Boston for us.

**WILLY:** Why can't I go?

**HOWARD:** I don't want you to represent us. I've been meaning to tell you for a long time now.

**WILLY:** Howard, are you firing me?

**HOWARD:** I think you need a good long rest, Willy.

**WILLY:** Howard—

**HOWARD:** And when you feel better, come back, and we'll see if we can work something out.

**WILLY:** But I gotta earn money, Howard. I'm in no position to—

**HOWARD:** Where are your sons? Why don't your sons give you a hand?

**WILLY:** They're working on a very big deal.

**HOWARD:** This is no time for false pride, Willy. You go to your sons and you tell them that you're tired. You've got two great boys haven't you?

**WILLY:** Oh, no question, no question, but in the meantime . . .

**HOWARD:** Then that's that, heh?

**WILLY:** All right, I'll go to Boston tomorrow.

**HOWARD:** No, no.

**WILLY:** I can't throw myself on my sons. I'm not a cripple!

**HOWARD:** Look, kid, I'm busy this morning.

**WILLY:** *(grasping* HOWARD's *arm)* Howard, you've got to let me go to Boston!

**HOWARD:** *(hard, keeping himself under control)* I've got a line of people to see this morning. Sit down, take five minutes, and pull yourself together, and then go home, will ya? I need the office, Willy. *(He starts to go, turns, remembering the recorder, starts to push off the table holding the recorder.)* Oh, yeah. Whenever you can this week, stop by and drop off the samples. You'll feel better, Willy, and then come back and we'll talk. Pull yourself together, kid, there's people outside.

HOWARD *exits, pushing the table off left.* WILLY *stares into space, exhausted. Now the music is heard—*BEN's *music—first distantly, then closer, closer. As* WILLY *speaks,* BEN *enters from the right. He carries valise and umbrella.*

**WILLY:** Oh, Ben, how did you do it? What is the answer? Did you wind up the Alaska deal already?

**BEN:** Doesn't take much time if you know what you're doing. Just a short business trip. Boarding ship in an hour. Wanted to say good-by.

**WILLY:** Ben, I've got to talk to you.

**BEN:** *(glancing at his watch)* Haven't the time, William.

**WILLY:** *(crossing the apron to* BEN*)* Ben, nothing's working out. I don't know what to do.

**BEN:** Now, look here, William. I've bought timberland in Alaska and I need a man to look after things for me.

**WILLY:** God, timberland! Me and my boys in those grand outdoors!

**BEN:** You've a new continent at your doorstep, William. Get out of these cities, they're full of talk and time payments and courts of law. Screw on your fists and you can fight for a fortune up there.

**WILLY:** Yes, yes! Linda, Linda!

LINDA *enters as of old, with the wash.*

**LINDA:** Oh, you're back?

**BEN:** I haven't much time.

**WILLY:** No, wait! Linda, he's got a proposition for me in Alaska.

**LINDA:** But you've got—*(To* BEN.*)* He's got a beautiful job here.

**WILLY:** But in Alaska, kid, I could—

**LINDA:** You're doing well enough, Willy!

**BEN:** *(to* LINDA*)* Enough for what, my dear?

**LINDA:** *(frightened of* BEN *and angry at him)* Don't say those things to him! Enough to be Happy right here, right now. *(To* WILLY, *while* BEN *laughs.)* Why must everybody conquer the world? You're well liked, and the boys love you, and someday—*(to* BEN*)*—why, old man Wagner told him just the other day that if he keeps it up he'll be a member of the firm, didn't he, Willy?

**WILLY:** Sure, sure. I am building something with this firm, Ben, and if a man is building something he must be on the right track, mustn't he?

**BEN:** What are you building? Lay your hand on it. Where is it?

**WILLY:** *(hesitantly)* That's true, Linda, there's nothing.

**LINDA:** Why? *(To* BEN.*)* There's a man eighty-four years old—

**WILLY:** That's right, Ben, that's right. When I look at that man I say, what is there to worry about?

**BEN:** Bah!

**WILLY:** It's true, Ben. All he has to do is go into any city, pick up the phone, and he's making his living and you know why?

**BEN:** *(picking up his valise)* I've got to go.

**WILLY:** *(holding* BEN *back)* Look at this boy!

BIFF, *in his high school sweater, enters carrying suitcase.* HAPPY *carries* BIFF*'s shoulder guards, gold helmet, and football pants.*

**WILLY:** Without a penny to his name, three great universities are begging for him, and from there the sky's the limit, because it's not what you do, Ben. It's who you know and the smile on your face! It's contacts, Ben, contacts! The whole wealth of Alaska passes over the lunch table at the Commodore Hotel, and that's the wonder, the wonder of this country, that a man can end with diamonds here on the basis of being liked! *(He turns to* BIFF.*)* And that's why when you get out on that field today it's important. Because thousands of people will be rooting for you and loving you. *(To* BEN, *who has again begun to leave.)* And Ben! when he walks into a business office his name will sound out like a bell and all the doors will open to him! I've seen it, Ben, I've seen it a thousand times! You can't feel it with your hand like timber, but it's there!

Willy and Linda react to Ben's Alaska proposition.

**BEN:** Good-by, William.

**WILLY:** Ben, am I right? Don't you think I'm right? I value your advice.

**BEN:** There's a new continent at your doorstep, William. You could walk out rich. Rich! *(He is gone.)*

**WILLY:** We'll do it here, Ben! You hear me? We're gonna do it here!

*Young* BERNARD *rushes in. The gay music of the Boys is heard.*

**BERNARD:** Oh, gee, I was afraid you left already!

**WILLY:** Why? What time is it?

**BERNARD:** It's half-past one!

**WILLY:** Well, come on, everybody! Ebbets Field next stop! Where's the pennants? *(He rushes through the wall-line of the kitchen and out into the living-room.)*

**LINDA:** *(to* BIFF*)* Did you pack fresh underwear?

**BIFF:** *(who has been limbering up)* I want to go!

**BERNARD:** Biff, I'm carrying your helmet, ain't I?

**HAPPY:** I'm carrying the helmet.

**BERNARD:** How am I going to get in the locker room?

**LINDA:** Let him carry the shoulder guards. *(She puts her coat and hat on in the kitchen.)*

**BERNARD:** Can I, Biff? 'Cause I told everybody I'm going to be in the locker room.

**HAPPY:** In Ebbets Field it's the clubhouse.

**BERNARD:** I meant the clubhouse. Biff!

**HAPPY:** Biff!

**BIFF:** *(grandly, after a slight pause)* Let him carry the shoulder guards.

**HAPPY:** *(as he gives* BERNARD *the shoulder guards)* Stay close to us now.

WILLY *rushes in with the pennants.*

**WILLY:** *(handing them out)* Everybody wave when Biff comes out on the field. *(*HAPPY *and* BERNARD *run off.)* You set now, boy?

*The music has died away.*

**BIFF:** Ready to go, Pop. Every muscle is ready.

**WILLY:** *(at the edge of the apron)* You realize what this means?

**BIFF:** That's right, Pop.

**WILLY:** *(feeling* BIFF*'s muscles)* You're comin' home this afternoon captain of the All-Scholastic Championship Team of the City of New York.

**BIFF:** I got it, Pop. And remember, pal, when I take off my helmet, that touchdown is for you.

**WILLY:** Let's go! *(He is starting out, with his arm around* BIFF, *when* CHARLEY *enters, as of old, in knickers.)* I got no room for you, Charley.

**CHARLEY:** Room? For what?

**WILLY:** In the car.

**CHARLEY:** You goin' for a ride? I wanted to shoot some casino.

**WILLY:** *(furiously)* Casino! *(Incredulously.)* Don't you realize what today is?

**LINDA:** Oh, he knows, Willy. He's just kidding you.

**WILLY:** That's nothing to kid about!

**CHARLEY:** No, Linda, what's goin' on?

**LINDA:** He's playing in Ebbets Field.

**CHARLEY:** Baseball in this weather?

**WILLY:** Don't talk to him. Come on, come on! *(He is pushing them out.)*

**CHARLEY:** Wait a minute, didn't you hear the news?

**WILLY:** What?

**CHARLEY:** Don't you listen to the radio? Ebbets Field just blew up.

**WILLY:** You go to hell! *(*CHARLEY *laughs. Pushing them out.)* Come on, come on! We're late.

**CHARLEY:** *(as they go)* Knock a homer, Biff, knock a homer!

**WILLY:** *(the last to leave, turning to* CHARLEY*)* I don't think that was funny, Charley. This is the greatest day of his life.

**CHARLEY:** Willy, when are you going to grow up?

**WILLY:** Yeah, heh? When this game is over, Charley, you'll be laughing out of the other side of your face. They'll be calling him another Red Grange. Twenty-five thousand a year.

**CHARLEY:** *(kidding)* Is that so?

**WILLY:** Yeah, that's so.

**CHARLEY:** Well, then, I'm sorry, Willy. But tell me something.

**WILLY:** What?

**CHARLEY:** Who is Red Grange?

**WILLY:** Put up your hands. Goddam you, put up your hands!

CHARLEY, *chuckling, shakes his head and walks away, around the left corner of the stage.* WILLY *follows him. The music rises to a mocking frenzy.*

**WILLY:** Who the hell do you think you are, better than everybody else? You don't know everything, you big, ignorant, stupid . . . Put up your hands!

*Light rises, on the right side of the forestage, on a small table in the reception room of* CHARLEY*'s office. Traffic sounds are heard.* BERNARD, *now mature, sits whistling to himself. A pair of tennis rackets and an overnight bag are on the floor beside him.*

**WILLY:** *(offstage)* What are you walking away for? Don't walk away! If you're going to say something say it to my face! I know you laugh at me behind my back. You'll laugh out of the other side of your goddam face after this game. Touchdown! Touchdown! Eighty thousand people! Touchdown! Right between the goal posts.

BERNARD *is a quiet, earnest, but self-assured young man.* WILLY*'s voice is coming from right upstage now.* BERNARD *lowers his feet off the table and listens.* JENNY, *his father's secretary, enters.*

**JENNY:** *(distressed)* Say, Bernard, will you go out in the hall?

**BERNARD:** What is that noise? Who is it?

**JENNY:** Mr. Loman. He just got off the elevator.

**BERNARD:** *(getting up)* Who's he arguing with?

**JENNY:** Nobody. There's nobody with him. I can't deal with him any more, and your father gets all upset everytime he comes. I've got a lot of typing to do, and your father's waiting to sign it. Will you see him?

**WILLY:** *(entering)* Touchdown! Touch—*(He sees Jenny.)* Jenny, Jenny, good to see you. How're ya? Workin'? Or still honest?

**JENNY:** Fine. How've you been feeling?

**WILLY:** Not much any more, Jenny. Ha, ha! *(He is surprised to see the rackets.)*

**BERNARD:** Hello, Uncle Willy.

**WILLY:** *(almost shocked)* Bernard! Well, look who's here! *(He comes quickly, guiltily, to* BERNARD *and warmly shakes his hand.)*

**BERNARD:** How are you? Good to see you.

**WILLY:** What are you doing here?

**BERNARD:** Oh, just stopped by to see Pop. Get off my feet till my train leaves. I'm going to Washington in a few minutes.

**WILLY:** Is he in?

**BERNARD:** Yes, he's in his office with the accountant. Sit down.

**WILLY:** *(sitting down)* What're you going to do in Washington?

**BERNARD:** Oh, just a case I've got there, Willy.

**WILLY:** That so? *(Indicating the rackets.)* You going to play tennis there?

**BERNARD:** I'm staying with a friend who's got a court.

**WILLY:** Don't say. His own tennis court. Must be fine people, I bet.

**BERNARD:** They are, very nice. Dad tells me Biff's in town.

**WILLY:** *(with a big smile)* Yeah, Biff's in. Working on a very big deal, Bernard.

**BERNARD:** What's Biff doing?

**WILLY:** Well, he's been doing very big things in the West. But he decided to establish himself here. Very big. We're having dinner. Did I hear your wife had a boy?

**BERNARD:** That's right. Our second.

**WILLY:** Two boys! What do you know!

**BERNARD:** What kind of a deal has Biff got?

**WILLY:** Well, Bill Oliver—very big sporting-goods man—he wants Biff very badly. Called him in from the West. Long distance, carte blanche, special deliveries. Your friends have their own private tennis court?

**BERNARD:** You still with the old firm, Willy?

**WILLY:** *(after a pause)* I'm—I'm overjoyed to see how you made the grade, Bernard, overjoyed. It's an encouraging thing to see a young man really—really—Looks very good for Biff—very—*(He breaks off, then.)* Bernard—*(He is so full of emotion, he breaks off again.)*

**BERNARD:** What is it, Willy?

**WILLY:** *(small and alone)* What—what's the secret?

**BERNARD:** What secret?

**WILLY:** How—how did you? Why didn't he ever catch on?

**BERNARD:** I wouldn't know that, Willy.

**WILLY:** *(confidentially, desperately)* You were his friend, his boyhood friend. There's something I don't understand about it. His life ended after that Ebbets Field game. From the age of seventeen nothing good ever happened to him.

**BERNARD:** He never trained himself for anything.

**WILLY:** But he did, he did. After high school he took so many correspondence courses. Radio mechanics; television; God knows what, and never made the slightest mark.

**BERNARD:** *(taking off his glasses)* Willy, do you want to talk candidly?

**WILLY:** *(rising, faces* BERNARD*)* I regard you as a very brilliant man, Bernard. I value your advice.

**BERNARD:** Oh, the hell with the advice, Willy. I couldn't advise you. There's just one thing I've always wanted to ask you. When he was supposed to graduate, and the math teacher flunked him—

**WILLY:** Oh, that son-of-a-bitch ruined his life.

**BERNARD:** Yeah, but, Willy, all he had to do was go to summer school and make up that subject.

**WILLY:** That's right, that's right.

**BERNARD:** Did you tell him not to go to summer school?

**WILLY:** Me? I begged him to go. I ordered him to go!

**BERNARD:** Then why wouldn't he go?

**WILLY:** Why? Why! Bernard, that question has been trailing me like a ghost for the last fifteen years. He flunked the subject, and laid down and died like a hammer hit him!

**BERNARD:** Take it easy, kid.

**WILLY:** Let me talk to you—I got nobody to talk to. Bernard, Bernard, was it my fault? Y'see? It keeps going around in my mind, maybe I did something to him. I got nothing to give him.

**BERNARD:** Don't take it so hard.

**WILLY:** Why did he lay down? What is the story there? You were his friend!

**BERNARD:** Willy, I remember, it was June, and our grades came out. And he'd flunked math.

**WILLY:** That son-of-a-bitch!

**BERNARD:** No, it wasn't right then. Biff just got very angry, I remember, and he was ready to enroll in summer school.

**WILLY:** *(surprised)* He was?

**BERNARD:** He wasn't beaten by it at all. But then, Willy, he disappeared from the block for almost a month. And I got the idea that he'd gone up to New England to see you. Did he have a talk with you then?

WILLY *stares in silence.*

**BERNARD:** Willy?

**WILLY:** *(with a strong edge of resentment in his voice)* Yeah, he came to Boston. What about it?

**BERNARD:** Well, just that when he came back—I'll never forget this, it always mystifies me. Because I'd thought so well of Biff, even though he'd always taken advantage of me. I loved him, Willy, y'know? And he came back after that month and took his sneakers—remember those sneakers with "University of Virginia" printed on them? He was so proud of those, wore them every day. And he took them down in the cellar, and burned them up in the furnace. We had a fist fight. It lasted at least half an hour. Just the two of us, punching each other down the cellar, and crying right through it. I've often thought of how strange it was that I knew he'd given up his life. What happened in Boston, Willy?

WILLY *looks at him as at an intruder.*

Willy and Bernard puzzle over Biff's decline.

**BERNARD:** I just bring it up because you asked me.

**WILLY:** *(angrily)* Nothing. What do you mean, "What happened?" What's that got to do with anything?

**BERNARD:** Well, don't get sore.

**WILLY:** What are you trying to do, blame it on me? If a boy lays down is that my fault?

**BERNARD:** Now, Willy, don't get—

**WILLY:** Well, don't—don't talk to me that way! What does that mean, "What happened?"

CHARLEY *enters. He is in his vest, and he carries a bottle of bourbon.*

**CHARLEY:** Hey, you're going to miss that train. *(He waves the bottle.)*

**BERNARD:** Yeah, I'm going. *(He takes the bottle.)* Thanks, Pop. *(He picks up his rackets and bag.)* Good-by, Willy, and don't worry about it. You know. "If at first you don't succeed . . ."

**WILLY:** Yes, I believe in that.

**BERNARD:** But sometimes, Willy, it's better for a man just to walk away.

**WILLY:** Walk away?

**BERNARD:** That's right.

**WILLY:** But if you can't walk away?

**BERNARD:** *(after a slight pause)* I guess that's when it's tough. *(Extending his hand.)* Good-by, Willy.

**WILLY:** *(shaking* BERNARD*'s hand)* Good-by, boy.

**CHARLEY:** *(an arm on* BERNARD*'s shoulder)* How do you like this kid? Gonna argue a case in front of the Supreme Court.

**BERNARD:** *(protesting)* Pop!

**WILLY:** *(genuinely shocked, pained, and happy)* No! The Supreme Court!

**BERNARD:** I gotta run. 'By, Dad!

**CHARLEY:** Knock 'em dead, Bernard!

BERNARD *goes off.*

**WILLY:** *(as* CHARLEY *takes out his wallet)* The Supreme Court! And he didn't even mention it!

**CHARLEY:** *(counting out money on the desk)* He don't have to—he's gonna do it.

**WILLY:** And you never told him what to do, did you? You never took any interest in him.

**CHARLEY:** My salvation is that I never took any interest in anything. There's some money—fifty dollars. I got an accountant inside.

**WILLY:** Charley, look . . . *(With difficulty.)* I got my insurance to pay. If you can manage it—I need a hundred and ten dollars.

CHARLEY *doesn't reply for a moment; merely stops moving.*

**WILLY:** I'd draw it from my bank but Linda would know, and I . . .

**CHARLEY:** Sit down, Willy.

**WILLY:** *(moving toward the chair)* I'm keeping an account of everything, remember. I'll pay every penny back. *(He sits.)*

**CHARLEY:** Now listen to me, Willy.

**WILLY:** I want you to know I appreciate . . .

**CHARLEY:** *(sitting down on the table)* Willy, what're you doin'? What the hell is goin' on in your head?

**WILLY:** Why? I'm simply . . .

**CHARLEY:** I offered you a job. You can make fifty dollars a week. And I won't send you on the road.

**WILLY:** I've got a job.

**CHARLEY:** Without pay? What kind of a job is a job without pay? *(He rises.)* Now, look, kid, enough is enough. I'm no genius but I know when I'm being insulted.

**WILLY:** Insulted!

**CHARLEY:** Why don't you want to work for me?

**WILLY:** What's the matter with you? I've got a job.

**CHARLEY:** Then what're you walkin' in here every week for?

**WILLY:** *(getting up)* Well, if you don't want me to walk in here—

**CHARLEY:** I am offering you a job.

**WILLY:** I don't want your goddam job!

**CHARLEY:** When the hell are you going to grow up?

**WILLY:** *(furiously)* You big ignoramus, if you say that to me again I'll rap you one! I don't care how big you are! *(He's ready to fight.)*

*Pause.*

**CHARLEY:** *(kindly, going to him)* How much do you need, Willy?

**WILLY:** Charley, I'm strapped. I'm strapped. I don't know what to do. I was just fired.

**CHARLEY:** Howard fired you?

**WILLY:** That snotnose. Imagine that? I named him. I named him Howard.

**CHARLEY:** Willy, when're you gonna realize that them things don't mean anything? You named him Howard, but you can't sell that. The only thing you got in this world is what you can sell. And the funny thing is that you're a salesman, and you don't know that.

**WILLY:** I've always tried to think otherwise, I guess. I always felt that if a man was impressive, and well liked, that nothing—

**CHARLEY:** Why must everybody like you? Who liked J. P. Morgan? Was he impressive? In a Turkish bath he'd look like a butcher. But with his pockets on he was very well liked. Now listen, Willy, I know you don't like me, and nobody can say I'm in love with you, but I'll give you a job because—just for the hell of it, put it that way. Now what do you say?

**WILLY:** I—I just can't work for you, Charley.

**CHARLEY:** What're you, jealous of me?

**WILLY:** I can't work for you, that's all, don't ask me why.

**CHARLEY:** *(angered, takes out more bills)* You been jealous of me all your life, you damned fool! Here, pay your insurance. *(He puts the money in* WILLY*'s hand.)*

**WILLY:** I'm keeping strict accounts.

Charley puts money in Willy's hand.

**CHARLEY:** I've got some work to do. Take care of yourself. And pay your insurance.

**WILLY:** *(moving to the right)* Funny, y'know? After all the highways, and the trains, and the appointments, and the years, you end up worth more dead than alive.

**CHARLEY:** Willy, nobody's worth nothin' dead. *(After a slight pause.)* Did you hear what I said?

WILLY *stands still, dreaming.*

**CHARLEY:** Willy!

**WILLY:** Apologize to Bernard for me when you see him. I didn't mean to argue with him. He's a fine boy. They're all fine boys, and they'll end up big—all of them. Someday they'll all play tennis together. Wish me luck, Charley. He saw Bill Oliver today.

**CHARLEY:** Good luck.

**WILLY:** *(on the verge of tears)* Charley, you're the only friend I got. Isn't that a remarkable thing? *(He goes out.)*

**CHARLEY:** Jesus!

CHARLEY *stares after him a moment and follows. All light blacks out. Suddenly raucous music is heard, and a red glow rises behind the screen at right.* STANLEY, *a young waiter, appears, carrying a table, followed by* HAPPY, *who is carrying two chairs.*

**STANLEY:** *(putting the table down)* That's all right, Mr. Loman, I can handle it myself. *(He turns and takes the chairs from* HAPPY *and places them at the table.)*

**HAPPY:** *(glancing around)* Oh, this is better.

**STANLEY:** Sure, in the front there you're in the middle of all kinds a noise. Whenever you got a party, Mr. Loman, you just tell me and I'll put you back here. Y'know, there's a lotta people they don't like it private, because when they go out they like to see a lotta action around them because they're sick and tired to stay in the house by theirself. But I know you, you ain't from Hackensack. You know what I mean?

**HAPPY:** *(sitting down)* So how's it coming, Stanley?

**STANLEY:** Ah, it's a dog's life. I only wish during the war they'd a took me in the Army. I coulda been dead by now.

**HAPPY:** My brother's back, Stanley.

**STANLEY:** Oh, he come back, heh? From the Far West.

**HAPPY:** Yeah, big cattle man, my brother, so treat him right. And my father's coming too.

**STANLEY:** Oh, your father too!

**HAPPY:** You got a couple of nice lobsters?

**STANLEY:** Hundred per cent, big.

**HAPPY:** I want them with the claws.

**STANLEY:** Don't worry, I don't give you no mice. (HAPPY *laughs.)* How about some wine? It'll put a head on the meal.

**HAPPY:** No. You remember, Stanley, that recipe I brought you from overseas? With the champagne in it?

**STANLEY:** Oh, yeah, sure. I still got it tacked up yet in the kitchen. But that'll have to cost a buck apiece anyways.

**HAPPY:** That's all right.

**STANLEY:** What'd you, hit a number or somethin'?

**HAPPY:** No, it's a little celebration. My brother is—I think he pulled off a big deal today. I think we're going into business together.

**STANLEY:** Great! That's the best for you. Because a family business, you know what I mean?—that's the best.

**HAPPY:** That's what I think.

**STANLEY:** 'Cause what's the difference? Somebody steals? It's in the family. Know what I mean? *(Sotto voce.)* Like this bartender here. The boss is goin' crazy what kinda leak he's got in the cash register. You put it in but it don't come out.

**HAPPY:** *(raising his head)* Sh!

**STANLEY:** What?

**HAPPY:** You notice I wasn't lookin' right or left, was I?

**STANLEY:** No.

**HAPPY:** And my eyes are closed.

**STANLEY:** So what's the—?

**HAPPY:** Strudel's comin'.

**STANLEY:** *(catching on, looks around)* Ah, no, there's no—

*He breaks off as a furred, lavishly dressed* GIRL *enters and sits at the next table. Both follow her with their eyes.*

**STANLEY:** Geez, how'd ya know?

**HAPPY:** I got radar or something. *(Staring directly at her profile.)* Oooooooo . . . Stanley.

**STANLEY:** I think that's for you, Mr. Loman.

**HAPPY:** Look at that mouth. Oh, God. And the binoculars.

**STANLEY:** Geez, you got a life, Mr. Loman.

**HAPPY:** Wait on her.

**STANLEY:** *(going to the* GIRL*'s table)* Would you like a menu, ma'am?

**GIRL:** I'm expecting someone, but I'd like a—

**HAPPY:** Why don't you bring her—excuse me, miss, do you mind? I sell champagne, and I'd like you to try my brand. Bring her a champagne, Stanley.

**GIRL:** That's awfully nice of you.

**HAPPY:** Don't mention it. It's all company money. *(He laughs.)*

**GIRL:** That's a charming product to be selling, isn't it?

**HAPPY:** Oh, gets to be like everything else. Selling is selling, y'know.

**GIRL:** I suppose.

**HAPPY:** You don't happen to sell, do you?

**GIRL:** No, I don't sell.

**HAPPY:** Would you object to a compliment from a stranger? You ought to be on a magazine cover.

**GIRL:** *(looking at him a little archly)* I have been.

STANLEY *comes in with a glass of champagne.*

**HAPPY:** What'd I say before, Stanley? You see? She's a cover girl.

**STANLEY:** Oh, I could see, I could see.

**HAPPY:** *(to the* GIRL*)* What magazine?

**GIRL:** Oh, a lot of them. *(She takes the drink.)* Thank you.

**HAPPY:** You know what they say in France, don't you? "Champagne is the drink of the complexion"—Hya, Biff!

BIFF *has entered and sits with* HAPPY.

**BIFF:** Hello, kid. Sorry I'm late.

**HAPPY:** I just got here. Uh, Miss—?

**GIRL:** Forsythe.

**HAPPY:** Miss Forsythe, this is my brother.

**BIFF:** Is Dad here?

**HAPPY:** His name is Biff. You might've heard of him. Great football player.

**GIRL:** Really? What team?

**HAPPY:** Are you familiar with football?

**GIRL:** No, I'm afraid I'm not.

**HAPPY:** Biff is quarterback with the New York Giants.

**GIRL:** Well, that is nice, isn't it? *(She drinks.)*

**HAPPY:** Good health.

**GIRL:** I'm happy to meet you.

**HAPPY:** That's my name. Hap. It's really Harold, but at West Point they called me Happy.

**GIRL:** *(now really impressed)* Oh, I see. How do you do? *(She turns her profile.)*

**BIFF:** Isn't Dad coming?

**HAPPY:** You want her?

**BIFF:** Oh, I could never make that.

**HAPPY:** I remember the time that idea would never come into your head. Where's the old confidence, Biff?

**BIFF:** I just saw Oliver—

**HAPPY:** Wait a minute. I've got to see that old confidence again. Do you want her? She's on call.

**BIFF:** Oh, no. *(He turns to look at the* GIRL.*)*

**HAPPY:** I'm telling you. Watch this. *(Turning to the* GIRL.*)* Honey? *(She turns to him.)* Are you busy?

**GIRL:** Well, I am . . . but I could make a phone call.

**HAPPY:** Do that, will you, honey? And see if you can get a friend. We'll be here for a while. Biff is one of the greatest football players in the country.

**GIRL:** *(standing up)* Well, I'm certainly happy to meet you.

**HAPPY:** Come back soon.

**GIRL:** I'll try.

**HAPPY:** Don't try, honey, try hard.

*The* GIRL *exits.* STANLEY *follows, shaking his head in bewildered admiration.*

**HAPPY:** Isn't that a shame now? A beautiful girl like that? That's why I can't get married. There's not a good woman in a thousand. New York is loaded with them, kid!

**BIFF:** Hap, look—

**HAPPY:** I told you she was on call!

**BIFF:** *(strangely unnerved)* Cut it out, will ya? I want to say something to you.

**HAPPY:** Did you see Oliver?

**BIFF:** I saw him all right. Now look, I want to tell Dad a couple of things and I want you to help me.

**HAPPY:** What? Is he going to back you?

**BIFF:** Are you crazy? You're out of your goddam head, you know that?

**HAPPY:** Why? What happened?

**BIFF:** *(breathlessly)* I did a terrible thing today, Hap. It's been the strangest day I ever went through. I'm all numb, I swear.

**HAPPY:** You mean he wouldn't see you?

**BIFF:** Well, I waited six hours for him, see? All day. Kept sending my name in. Even tried to date his secretary so she'd get me to him, but no soap.

**HAPPY:** Because you're not showin' the old confidence, Biff. He remembered you, didn't he?

**BIFF:** *(stopping* HAPPY *with a gesture)* Finally, about five o'clock, he comes out. Didn't remember who I was or anything. I felt like such an idiot, Hap.

**HAPPY:** Did you tell him my Florida idea?

**BIFF:** He walked away. I saw him for one minute. I got so mad I could've torn the walls down! How the hell did I ever get the idea I was a salesman there? I even believed myself that I'd been a salesman for him! And then he gave me one look and—I realized what a ridiculous lie my whole life has been! We've been talking in a dream for fifteen years. I was a shipping clerk.

**HAPPY:** What'd you do?

**BIFF:** *(with great tension and wonder)* Well, he left, see. And the secretary went out. I was all alone in the waiting-room. I don't know what came over me, Hap. The next thing I know I'm in his office—paneled walls, everything. I can't explain it. I—Hap, I took his fountain pen.

**HAPPY:** Geez, did he catch you?

**BIFF:** I ran out. I ran down all eleven flights. I ran and ran and ran.

**HAPPY:** That was an awful dumb—what'd you do that for?

**BIFF:** *(agonized)* I don't know, I just—wanted to take something, I don't know. You gotta help me, Hap, I'm gonna tell Pop.

**HAPPY:** You crazy? What for?

**BIFF:** Hap, he's got to understand that I'm not the man somebody lends that kind of money to. He thinks I've been spiting him all these years and it's eating him up.

**HAPPY:** That's just it. You tell him something nice.

Willy and Happy celebrate at Stanley's (Tom Signorelli) restaurant.

**BIFF:** I can't.

**HAPPY:** Say you got a lunch date with Oliver tomorrow.

**BIFF:** So what do I do tomorrow?

**HAPPY:** You leave the house tomorrow and come back at night and say Oliver is thinking it over. And he thinks it over for a couple of weeks, and gradually it fades away and nobody's the worse.

**BIFF:** But it'll go on forever!

**HAPPY:** Dad is never so happy as when he's looking forward to something!

WILLY *enters.*

**HAPPY:** Hello, scout!

**WILLY:** Gee, I haven't been here in years!

STANLEY *has followed* WILLY *in and sets a chair for him.* STANLEY *starts off but* HAPPY *stops him.*

**HAPPY:** Stanley!

STANLEY *stands by, waiting for an order.*

**BIFF:** *(going to* WILLY *with guilt, as to an invalid)* Sit down, Pop. You want a drink?

**WILLY:** Sure, I don't mind.

**BIFF:** Let's get a load on.

**WILLY:** You look worried.

**BIFF:** N-no. *(To* STANLEY.*)* Scotch all around. Make it doubles.

**STANLEY:** Doubles, right. *(He goes.)*

**WILLY:** You had a couple already, didn't you?

**BIFF:** Just a couple, yeah.

**WILLY:** Well, what happened, boy? *(Nodding affirmatively, with a smile.)* Everything go all right?

**BIFF:** *(takes a breath, then reaches out and grasps* WILLY'*s hand)* Pal . . . *(He is smiling bravely, and* WILLY *is smiling too.)* I had an experience today.

**HAPPY:** Terrific, Pop.

**WILLY:** That so? What happened?

**BIFF:** *(high, slightly alcoholic, above the earth)* I'm going to tell you everything from first to last. It's been a strange day. *(Silence. He looks around, composes himself as best he can, but his breath keeps breaking the rhythm of his voice.)* I had to wait quite a while for him, and—

**WILLY:** Oliver.

Willy and Biff argue about the meeting with Oliver.

**BIFF:** Yeah, Oliver. All day, as a matter of cold fact. And a lot of—instances—facts, Pop, facts about my life came back to me. Who was it, Pop? Who ever said I was a salesman with Oliver?

**WILLY:** Well, you were.

**BIFF:** No, Dad, I was a shipping clerk.

**WILLY:** But you were practically—

**BIFF:** *(with determination)* Dad, I don't know who said it first, but I was never a salesman for Bill Oliver.

**WILLY:** What're you talking about?

**BIFF:** Let's hold on to the facts tonight, Pop. We're not going to get anywhere bullin' around. I was a shipping clerk.

**WILLY:** *(angrily)* All right, now listen to me—

**BIFF:** Why don't you let me finish?

**WILLY:** I'm not interested in stories about the past or any crap of that kind because the woods are burning, boys, you understand? There's a big blaze going on all around. I was fired today.

**BIFF:** *(shocked)* How could you be?

**WILLY:** I was fired, and I'm looking for a little good news to tell your mother, because the woman has waited and the woman has suffered. The gist of it is that I haven't got a story left in my head, Biff. So don't give me a lecture about facts and aspects. I am not interested. Now what've you got to say to me?

STANLEY *enters with three drinks. They wait until he leaves.*

**WILLY:** Did you see Oliver?

**BIFF:** Jesus, Dad!

**WILLY:** You mean you didn't go up there?

**HAPPY:** Sure he went up there.

**BIFF:** I did. I—saw him. How could they fire you?

**WILLY:** *(on the edge of his chair)* What kind of a welcome did he give you?

**BIFF:** He won't even let you work on commission?

**WILLY:** I'm out! *(Driving.)* So tell me, he gave you a warm welcome?

**HAPPY:** Sure, Pop, sure!

**BIFF:** *(driven)* Well, it was kind of—

**WILLY:** I was wondering if he'd remember you. *(To* HAPPY.*)* Imagine, man doesn't see him for ten, twelve years and gives him that kind of a welcome!

**HAPPY:** Damn right!

**BIFF:** *(trying to return to the offensive)* Pop, look—

**WILLY:** You know why he remembered you, don't you? Because you impressed him in those days.

**BIFF:** Let's talk quietly and get this down to the facts, huh?

**WILLY:** *(as though* BIFF *had been interrupting)* Well, what happened? It's great news, Biff. Did he take you into his office or'd you talk in the waiting-room?

**BIFF:** Well, he came in, see, and—

**WILLY:** *(with a big smile)* What'd he say? Betcha he threw his arm around you.

**BIFF:** Well, he kinda—

**WILLY:** He's a fine man. *(To* HAPPY.*)* Very hard man to see, y'know.

**HAPPY:** *(agreeing)* Oh, I know.

**WILLY:** *(to* BIFF*)* Is that where you had the drinks?

**BIFF:** Yeah, he gave me a couple of—no, no!

**HAPPY:** *(cutting in)* He told him my Florida idea.

**WILLY:** Don't interrupt. *(To* BIFF.*)* How'd he react to the Florida idea?

**BIFF:** Dad, will you give me a minute to explain?

**WILLY:** I've been waiting for you to explain since I sat down here! What happened? He took you into his office and what?

**BIFF:** Well—I talked. And—and he listened, see.

**WILLY:** Famous for the way he listens, y'know. What was his answer?

**BIFF:** His answer was—*(He breaks off, suddenly angry.)* Dad, you're not letting me tell you what I want to tell you!

**WILLY:** *(accusing, angered)* You didn't see him, did you?

**BIFF:** I did see him!

**WILLY:** What'd you insult him or something? You insulted him, didn't you?

**BIFF:** Listen, will you let me out of it, will you just let me out of it!

**HAPPY:** What the hell!

**WILLY:** Tell me what happened!

**BIFF:** *(to* HAPPY*)* I can't talk to him!

*A single trumpet note jars the ear. The light of green leaves stains the house, which holds the air of night and a dream. Young* BERNARD *enters and knocks on the door of the house.*

**YOUNG BERNARD:** *(frantically)* Mrs. Loman, Mrs. Loman!

**HAPPY:** Tell him what happened!

**BIFF:** *(to* HAPPY*)* Shut up and leave me alone!

**WILLY:** No, no! You had to go and flunk math!

**BIFF:** What math? What're you talking about?

**YOUNG BERNARD:** Mrs. Loman, Mrs. Loman!

LINDA *appears in the house, as of old.*

**WILLY:** *(wildly)* Math, math, math!

**BIFF:** Take it easy, Pop!

**YOUNG BERNARD:** Mrs. Loman!

**WILLY:** *(furiously)* If you hadn't flunked you'd've been set by now!

**BIFF:** Now, look, I'm gonna tell you what happened, and you're going to listen to me.

**YOUNG BERNARD:** Mrs. Loman!

**BIFF:** I waited six hours—

**HAPPY:** What the hell are you saying?

**BIFF:** I kept sending in my name but he wouldn't see me. So finally he . . . *(He continues unheard as light fades low on the restaurant.)*

Willy remembers receiving the news of Biff's flunking math.

**YOUNG BERNARD:** Biff flunked math!

**LINDA:** No!

**YOUNG BERNARD:** Birnbaum flunked him! They won't graduate him!

**LINDA:** But they have to. He's gotta go to the university. Where is he? Biff! Biff!

**YOUNG BERNARD:** No, he left. He went to Grand Central.

**LINDA:** Grand—You mean he went to Boston!

**YOUNG BERNARD:** Is Uncle Willy in Boston?

**LINDA:** Oh, maybe Willy can talk to the teacher. Oh, the poor, poor boy!

*Light on house area snaps out.*

**BIFF:** *(at the table, now audible, holding up a gold fountain pen)* . . . so I'm washed up with Oliver, you understand? Are you listening to me?

**WILLY:** *(at a loss)* Yeah, sure. If you hadn't flunked—

**BIFF:** Flunked what? What're you talking about?

**WILLY:** Don't blame everything on me! I didn't flunk math—you did! What pen?

**HAPPY:** That was awful dumb, Biff, a pen like that is worth—

**WILLY:** *(seeing the pen for the first time)* You took Oliver's pen?

**BIFF:** *(weakening)* Dad, I just explained it to you.

**WILLY:** You stole Bill Oliver's fountain pen!

**BIFF:** I didn't exactly steal it! That's just what I've been explaining to you!

**HAPPY:** He had it in his hand and just then Oliver walked in, so he got nervous and stuck it in his pocket!

**WILLY:** My God, Biff!

**BIFF:** I never intended to do it, Dad!

**OPERATOR'S VOICE:** Standish Arms, good evening!

**WILLY:** *(shouting)* I'm not in my room!

**BIFF:** *(frightened)* Dad, what's the matter? *(He and* HAPPY *stand up.)*

**OPERATOR:** Ringing Mr. Loman for you!

**WILLY:** I'm not there, stop it!

**BIFF:** *(horrified, gets down on one knee before* WILLY*)* Dad, I'll make good, I'll make good. *(*WILLY *tries to get to his feet.* BIFF *holds him down.)* Sit down now.

**WILLY:** No, you're no good, you're no good for anything.

**BIFF:** I am, Dad, I'll find something else, you understand? Now don't worry about anything. *(He holds up* WILLY*'s face.)* Talk to me, Dad.

**OPERATOR:** Mr. Loman does not answer. Shall I page him?

**WILLY:** *(attempting to stand, as though to rush and silence the* OPERATOR*)* No, no, no!

**HAPPY:** He'll strike something, Pop.

**WILLY:** No, no . . .

**BIFF:** *(desperately, standing over* WILLY*)* Pop, listen! Listen to me! I'm telling you something good. Oliver talked to his partner about the Florida idea. You listening? He—he talked to his partner, and he came to me . . . I'm going to be all right, you hear? Dad, listen to me, he said it was just a question of the amount!

**WILLY:** Then you . . . got it?

**HAPPY:** He's gonna be terrific, Pop!

**WILLY:** *(trying to stand)* Then you got it, haven't you? You got it! You got it!

**BIFF:** *(agonized, holds* WILLY *down)* No, no. Look, Pop. I'm supposed to have lunch with them tomorrow. I'm just telling you this so you'll know that I can still make an impression, Pop. And I'll make good somewhere, but I can't go tomorrow, see?

**WILLY:** Why not? You simply—

**BIFF:** But the pen, Pop!

**WILLY:** You give it to him and tell him it was an oversight!

**HAPPY:** Sure, have lunch tomorrow!

**BIFF:** I can't say that—

**WILLY:** You were doing a crossword puzzle and accidentally used his pen!

**BIFF:** Listen, kid, I took those balls years ago, now I walk in with his fountain pen? That clinches it, don't you see? I can't face him like that! I'll try elsewhere.

**PAGE'S VOICE:** Paging Mr. Loman!

**WILLY:** Don't you want to be anything?

**BIFF:** Pop, how can I go back?

**WILLY:** You don't want to be anything, is that what's behind it?

**BIFF:** *(now angry at* WILLY *for not crediting his sympathy)* Don't take it that way! You think it was easy walking into that office after what I'd done to him? A team of horses couldn't have dragged me back to Bill Oliver!

**WILLY:** Then why'd you go?

**BIFF:** Why did I go? Why did I go! Look at you! Look at what's become of you!

*Off left,* THE WOMAN *laughs.*

**WILLY:** Biff, you're going to go to that lunch tomorrow, or—

**BIFF:** I can't go. I've got no appointment!

**HAPPY:** Biff, for . . . !

**WILLY:** Are you spiting me?

**BIFF:** Don't take it that way! Goddammit!

**WILLY:** *(strikes* BIFF *and falters away from the table)* You rotten little louse! Are you spiting me?

**THE WOMAN:** Someone's at the door, Willy!

**BIFF:** I'm no good, can't you see what I am?

**HAPPY:** *(separating them)* Hey, you're in a restaurant! Now cut it out, both of you! *(The girls enter.)* Hello, girls, sit down.

THE WOMAN *laughs, off left.*

**MISS FORSYTHE:** I guess we might as well. This is Letta.

**THE WOMAN:** Willy, are you going to wake up?

**BIFF:** *(ignoring* WILLY*)* How're ya, miss, sit down. What do you drink?

**MISS FORSYTHE:** Letta might not be able to stay long.

**LETTA:** I gotta get up very early tomorrow. I got jury duty. I'm so excited! Were you fellows ever on a jury?

**BIFF:** No, but I been in front of them! *(The girls laugh.)* This is my father.

**LETTA:** Isn't he cute? Sit down with us, Pop.

**HAPPY:** Sit him down, Biff!

**BIFF:** *(going to him)* Come on, slugger, drink us under the table. To hell with it! Come on, sit down, pal.

*On* BIFF*'s last insistence,* WILLY *is about to sit.*

**THE WOMAN:** *(now urgently)* Willy, are you going to answer the door!

THE WOMAN*'s call pulls* WILLY *back. He starts right, befuddled.*

**BIFF:** Hey, where are you going?

**WILLY:** Open the door.

**BIFF:** The door?

**WILLY:** The washroom . . . the door . . . where's the door?

**BIFF:** *(leading* WILLY *to the left)* Just go straight down.

WILLY *moves left.*

**THE WOMAN:** Willy, Willy, are you going to get up, get up, get up, get up?

WILLY *exits left.*

**LETTA:** I think it's sweet you bring your daddy along.

**MISS FORSYTHE:** Oh, he isn't really your father!

**BIFF:** *(at left, turning to her resentfully)* Miss Forsythe, you've just seen a prince walk by. A fine, troubled prince. A hard-working, unappreciated prince. A pal, you understand? A good companion. Always for his boys.

**LETTA:** That's so sweet.

**HAPPY:** Well, girls, what's the program? We're wasting time. Come on, Biff. Gather round. Where would you like to go?

**BIFF:** Why don't you do something for him?

**HAPPY:** Me!

**BIFF:** Don't you give a damn for him, Hap?

**HAPPY:** What're you talking about? I'm the one who—

**BIFF:** I sense it, you don't give a good goddam about him. *(He takes the rolled-up hose from his pocket and puts it on the table in front of* HAPPY.*)* Look what I found in the cellar, for Christ's sake. How can you bear to let it go on?

**HAPPY:** Me? Who goes away? Who runs off and—

**BIFF:** Yeah, but he doesn't mean anything to you. You could help him—I can't! Don't you understand what I'm talking about? He's going to kill himself, don't you know that?

**HAPPY:** Don't I know it! Me!

**BIFF:** Hap, help him! Jesus . . . help him . . . Help me, help me, I can't bear to look at his face! *(Ready to weep, he hurries out, up right.)*

**HAPPY:** *(starting after him)* Where are you going?

**MISS FORSYTHE:** What's he so mad about?

**HAPPY:** Come on, girls, we'll catch up with him.

**MISS FORSYTHE:** *(as* HAPPY *pushes her out)* Say, I don't like that temper of his!

**HAPPY:** He's just a little overstrung, he'll be all right!

**WILLY:** *(off left, as* THE WOMAN *laughs)* Don't answer! Don't answer!

**LETTA:** Don't you want to tell your father—

**HAPPY:** No, that's not my father. He's just a guy. Come on, we'll catch Biff, and, honey, we're going to paint this town! Stanley, where's the check! Hey, Stanley!

*They exit.* STANLEY *looks toward left.*

**STANLEY:** *(calling to* HAPPY *indignantly)* Mr. Loman! Mr. Loman!

STANLEY *picks up a chair and follows them off. Knocking is heard off left.* THE WOMAN *enters, laughing.* WILLY *follows her. She is in a black slip; he is buttoning his shirt. Raw, sensuous music accompanies their speech.*

**WILLY:** Will you stop laughing? Will you stop?

**THE WOMAN:** Aren't you going to answer the door? He'll wake the whole hotel.

**WILLY:** I'm not expecting anybody.

**THE WOMAN:** Whyn't you have another drink, honey, and stop being so damn self-centered?

**WILLY:** I'm so lonely.

**THE WOMAN:** You know you ruined me, Willy? From now on, whenever you come to the office, I'll see that you go right through to the buyers. No waiting at my desk any more, Willy. You ruined me.

**WILLY:** That's nice of you to say that.

**THE WOMAN:** Gee, you are self-centered! Why so sad? You are the saddest, self-centeredest soul I ever did see-saw. *(She laughs. He kisses her.)* Come on inside, drummer boy. It's silly to be dressing in the middle of the night. *(As knocking is heard.)* Aren't you going to answer the door?

**WILLY:** They're knocking on the wrong door.

**THE WOMAN:** But I felt the knocking. And he heard us talking in here. Maybe the hotel's on fire!

**WILLY:** *(his terror rising)* It's a mistake.

**THE WOMAN:** Then tell him to go away!

**WILLY:** There's nobody there.

**THE WOMAN:** It's getting on my nerves, Willy. There's somebody standing out there and it's getting on my nerves!

**WILLY:** *(pushing her away from him)* All right, stay in the bathroom here, and don't come out. I think there's a law in Massachusetts about it, so don't come out. It may be that new room clerk. He looked very mean. So don't come out. It's a mistake, there's no fire.

*The knocking is heard again. He takes a few steps away from her, and she vanishes into the wing. The light follows him, and now he is facing Young* BIFF, *who carries a suitcase.* BIFF *steps toward him. The music is gone.*

**BIFF:** Why didn't you answer?

**WILLY:** Biff! What are you doing in Boston?

**BIFF:** Why didn't you answer? I've been knocking for five minutes, I called you on the phone—

**WILLY:** I just heard you. I was in the bathroom and had the door shut. Did anything happen home?

**BIFF:** Dad—I let you down.

**WILLY:** What do you mean?

**BIFF:** Dad . . .

**WILLY:** Biffo, what's this about? *(Putting his arm around* BIFF.*)* Come on, let's go downstairs and get you a malted.

**BIFF:** Dad, I flunked math.

**WILLY:** Not for the term?

**BIFF:** The term. I haven't got enough credits to graduate.

**WILLY:** You mean to say Bernard wouldn't give you the answers?

**BIFF:** He did, he tried, but I only got a sixty-one.

**WILLY:** And they wouldn't give you four points?

**BIFF:** Birnbaum refused absolutely. I begged him, Pop, but he won't give me those points. You gotta talk to him before they close the school. Because if he saw the kind of man you are, and you just talked to him in your way, I'm sure he'd come through for me. The class came right before practice, see, and I didn't go enough. Would you talk to him? He'd like you, Pop. You know the way you could talk.

**WILLY:** You're on. We'll drive right back.

**BIFF:** Oh, Dad, good work! I'm sure he'll change it for you!

**WILLY:** Go downstairs and tell the clerk I'm checkin' out. Go right down.

**BIFF:** Yes, sir! See, the reason he hates me, Pop—one day he was late for class so I got up at the blackboard and imitated him. I crossed my eyes and talked with a lithp.

**WILLY:** *(laughing)* You did? The kids like it?

**BIFF:** They nearly died laughing!

**WILLY:** Yeah? What'd you do?

**BIFF:** The thquare root of thixthy twee is . . . *(*WILLY *bursts out laughing;* BIFF *joins him.)* And in the middle of it he walked in!

WILLY *laughs and* THE WOMAN *joins in offstage.*

**WILLY:** *(without hesitation)* Hurry downstairs and—

**BIFF:** Somebody in there?

**WILLY:** No, that was next door.

THE WOMAN *laughs offstage.*

**BIFF:** Somebody got in your bathroom!

**WILLY:** No, it's the next room, there's a party—

**THE WOMAN:** *(enters, laughing. She lisps this)* Can I come in? There's something in the bathtub, Willy, and it's moving!

WILLY *looks at* BIFF, *who is staring open-mouthed and horrified at* THE WOMAN.

**WILLY:** Ah—you better go back to your room. They must be finished painting by now. They're painting her room so I let her take a shower here. Go back, go back . . . *(He pushes her.)*

**THE WOMAN:** *(resisting)* But I've got to get dressed, Willy, I can't—

**WILLY:** Get out of here! Go back, go back . . . *(Suddenly striving for the ordinary):* This is Miss Francis, Biff, she's a buyer. They're painting her room. Go back, Miss Francis, go back . . .

**THE WOMAN:** But my clothes, I can't go out naked in the hall!

**WILLY:** *(pushing her offstage)* Get outa here! Go back, go back!

BIFF *slowly sits down on his suitcase as the argument continues offstage.*

**THE WOMAN:** Where's my stockings? You promised me stockings, Willy!

**WILLY:** I have no stockings here!

**THE WOMAN:** You had two boxes of size nine sheers for me, and I want them!

**WILLY:** Here, for God's sake, will you get outa here!

**THE WOMAN:** *(enters holding a box of stockings)* I just hope there's nobody in the hall. That's all I hope. *(To* BIFF.*)* Are you football or baseball?

**BIFF:** Football.

**THE WOMAN:** *(angry, humiliated)* That's me too. G'night. *(She snatches her clothes from* WILLY, *and walks out.)*

Humiliated, The Woman encounters Biff inside the hotel room.

**WILLY:** *(after a pause)* Well, better get going. I want to get to the school first thing in the morning. Get my suits out of the closet. I'll get my valise. *(*BIFF *doesn't move.)* What's the matter? *(*BIFF *remains motionless, tears falling.)* She's a buyer. Buys for J. H. Simmons. She lives down the hall—they're painting. You don't imagine—*(He breaks off. After a pause.)* Now listen, pal, she's just a buyer. She sees merchandise in her room and they have to keep it looking just so . . . *(Pause. Assuming command.)* All right, get my suits. *(*BIFF *doesn't move.)* Now stop crying and do as I say. I gave you an order. Biff, I gave you an order! Is that what you do when I give you an order? How dare you cry! *(Putting his arm around* BIFF.*)* Now look, Biff, when you grow up you'll understand about these things. You mustn't—you mustn't overemphasize a thing like this. I'll see Birnbaum first thing in the morning.

**BIFF:** Never mind.

**WILLY:** *(getting down beside* BIFF*)* Never mind! He's going to give you those points. I'll see to it.

**BIFF:** He wouldn't listen to you.

**WILLY:** He certainly will listen to me. You need those points for the U. of Virginia.

**BIFF:** I'm not going there.

**WILLY:** Heh? If I can't get him to change that mark you'll make it up in summer school. You've got all summer to—

**BIFF:** *(his weeping breaking from him)* Dad . . .

**WILLY:** *(infected by it)* Oh, my boy . . .

**BIFF:** Dad . . .

**WILLY:** She's nothing to me, Biff. I was lonely, I was terribly lonely.

**BIFF:** You—you gave her Mama's stockings! *(His tears break through and he rises to go.)*

**WILLY:** *(grabbing for* BIFF*)* I gave you an order!

**BIFF:** Don't touch me, you—liar!

**WILLY:** Apologize for that!

**BIFF:** You fake! You phony little fake! You fake! *(Overcome, he turns quickly and weeping fully goes out with his suitcase.* WILLY *is left on the floor on his knees.)*

**WILLY:** I gave you an order! Biff, come back here or I'll beat you! Come back here! I'll whip you!

STANLEY *comes quickly in from the right and stands in front of* WILLY.

**WILLY:** *(shouts at* STANLEY*)* I gave you an order . . .

**STANLEY:** Hey, let's pick it up, pick it up, Mr. Loman. *(He helps* WILLY *to his feet.)* Your boys left with the chippies. They said they'll see you at home.

*A second waiter watches some distance away.*

**WILLY:** But we were supposed to have dinner together.

*Music is heard,* WILLY*'s theme.*

**STANLEY:** Can you make it?

**WILLY:** I'll—sure, I can make it. *(Suddenly concerned about his clothes.)* Do I—I look all right?

**STANLEY:** Sure, you look all right. *(He flicks a speck off* WILLY*'s lapel.)*

**WILLY:** Here—here's a dollar.

**STANLEY:** Oh, your son paid me. It's all right.

**WILLY:** *(putting it in* STANLEY*'s hand)* No, take it. You're a good boy.

**STANLEY:** Oh, no, you don't have to . . .

**WILLY:** Here—here's some more, I don't need it any more. *(After a slight pause.)* Tell me—is there a seed store in the neighborhood?

**STANLEY:** Seeds? You mean like to plant?

*As* WILLY *turns,* STANLEY *slips the money back into his jacket pocket.*

**WILLY:** Yes. Carrots, peas . . .

**STANLEY:** Well, there's hardware stores on Sixth Avenue, but it may be too late now.

**WILLY:** *(anxiously)* Oh, I'd better hurry. I've got to get some seeds. *(He starts off to the right.)* I've got to get some seeds, right away. Nothing's planted. I don't have a thing in the ground.

WILLY *hurries out as the light goes down.* STANLEY *moves over to the right after him, watches him off. The other waiter has been staring at* WILLY.

**STANLEY:** *(to the waiter)* Well, whatta you looking at?

*The waiter picks up the chairs and moves off right.* STANLEY *takes the table and follows him. The light fades on this area. There is a long pause, the sound of the flute coming over. The light gradually rises on the kitchen, which is empty.* HAPPY *appears at the door of the house, followed by* BIFF. HAPPY *is carrying a large bunch of long-stemmed roses. He enters the kitchen, looks around for* LINDA. *Not seeing her, he turns to* BIFF, *who is just outside the house*

Linda scolds her sons for leaving Willy alone at dinner.

*door, and makes a gesture with his hands, indicating "Not here, I guess." He looks into the living-room and freezes. Inside,* LINDA, *unseen, is seated,* WILLY*'s coat on her lap. She rises ominously and quietly and moves toward* HAPPY, *who backs up into the kitchen, afraid.*

**HAPPY:** Hey, what're you doing up? *(*LINDA *says nothing but moves toward him implacably.)* Where's Pop? *(He keeps backing to the right, and now* LINDA *is in full view in the doorway to the living-room.)* Is he sleeping?

**LINDA:** Where were you?

**HAPPY:** *(trying to laugh it off)* We met two girls, Mom, very fine types. Here, we brought you some flowers. *(Offering them to her.)* Put them in your room, Ma.

*She knocks them to the floor at* BIFF*'s feet. He has now come inside and closed the door behind him. She stares at* BIFF, *silent.*

**HAPPY:** Now what'd you do that for? Mom, I want you to have some flowers—

**LINDA:** *(cutting* HAPPY *off, violently to* BIFF*)* Don't you care whether he lives or dies?

**HAPPY:** *(going to the stairs)* Come upstairs, Biff.

**BIFF:** *(with a flare of disgust, to* HAPPY*)* Go away from me! *(To* LINDA.*)* What do you mean, lives or dies? Nobody's dying around here, pal.

**LINDA:** Get out of my sight! Get out of here!

**BIFF:** I wanna see the boss.

**LINDA:** You're not going near him!

**BIFF:** Where is he? *(He moves into the living-room and* LINDA *follows.)*

**LINDA:** *(shouting after* BIFF*)* You invite him for dinner. He looks forward to it all day—*(*BIFF *appears in his parents' bedroom, looks around, and exits.)*—and then you desert him there. There's no stranger you'd do that to!

**HAPPY:** Why? He had a swell time with us. Listen, when I—*(*LINDA *comes back into the kitchen)*—desert him I hope I don't outlive the day!

**LINDA:** Get out of here!

**HAPPY:** Now look, Mom . . .

**LINDA:** Did you have to go to women tonight? You and your lousy rotten whores!

BIFF *re-enters the kitchen.*

**HAPPY:** Mom, all we did was follow Biff around trying to cheer him up! *(To* BIFF.*)* Boy, what a night you gave me!

**LINDA:** Get out of here, both of you, and don't come back! I don't want you tormenting him any more. Go on now, get your things together! *(To* BIFF.*)* You can sleep in his apartment. *(She starts to pick up the flowers and stops herself.)* Pick up this stuff, I'm not your maid any more. Pick it up, you bum, you!

HAPPY *turns his back to her in refusal.* BIFF *slowly moves over and gets down on his knees, picking up the flowers.*

**LINDA:** You're a pair of animals! Not one, not another living soul would have had the cruelty to walk out on that man in a restaurant!

**BIFF:** *(not looking at her)* Is that what he said?

**LINDA:** He didn't have to say anything. He was so humiliated he nearly limped when he came in.

**HAPPY:** But, Mom, he had a great time with us—

**BIFF:** *(cutting him off violently)* Shut up!

*Without another word,* HAPPY *goes upstairs.*

**LINDA:** You! You didn't even go in to see if he was all right!

**BIFF:** *(still on the floor in front of* LINDA, *the flowers in his hand; with self-loathing)* No. Didn't. Didn't do a damned thing. How do you like that, heh? Left him babbling in a toilet.

**LINDA:** You louse. You . . .

**BIFF:** Now you hit it on the nose! *(He gets up, throws the flowers in the wastebasket.)* The scum of the earth, and you're looking at him!

**LINDA:** Get out of here!

**BIFF:** I gotta talk to the boss, Mom. Where is he?

**LINDA:** You're not going near him. Get out of this house!

**BIFF:** *(with absolute assurance, determination)* No. We're gonna have an abrupt conversation, him and me.

**LINDA:** You're not talking to him!

*Hammering is heard from outside the house, off right.* BIFF *turns toward the noise.*

**LINDA:** *(suddenly pleading)* Will you please leave him alone?

**BIFF:** What's he doing out there?

**LINDA:** He's planting the garden!

**BIFF:** *(quietly)* Now? Oh, my God!

BIFF *moves outside,* LINDA *following. The light dies down on them and comes up on the center of the apron as* WILLY *walks into it. He is carrying a flashlight, a hoe, and handful of seed packets. He raps the top of the hoe sharply to fix it firmly, and then moves to the left, measuring off the distance with his foot. He holds the flashlight to look at the seed packets, reading off the instructions. He is in the blue of night.*

**WILLY:** Carrots . . . quarter-inch apart. Rows . . . one-foot rows. *(He measures it off.)* One foot. *(He puts down a package and measures off.)* Beets. *(He puts down another package and measures again.)* Lettuce. *(He reads the package, puts it down.)* One foot—*(He breaks off as* BEN *appears at the right and moves slowly down to him.)* What a proposition, ts, ts. Terrific, terrific. 'Cause she's suffered, Ben, the woman has suffered. You understand me? A man can't go out the way he came in, Ben, a man has got to add up to something. You can't, you can't—*(*BEN *moves toward him as though to interrupt.)* You gotta consider, now. Don't answer so quick. Remember, it's a guaranteed twenty-thousand-dollar proposition. Now look, Ben, I want you to go through the ins and outs of this thing with me. I've got nobody to talk to, Ben, and the woman has suffered, you hear me?

**BEN:** *(standing still, considering)* What's the proposition?

**WILLY:** It's twenty thousand dollars on the barrelhead. Guaranteed, gilt-edged, you understand?

**BEN:** You don't want to make a fool of yourself. They might not honor the policy.

**WILLY:** How can they dare refuse? Didn't I work like a coolie to meet every premium on the nose? And now they don't pay off? Impossible!

**BEN:** It's called a cowardly thing, William.

**WILLY:** Why? Does it take more guts to stand here the rest of my life ringing up a zero?

**BEN:** *(yielding)* That's a point, William. *(He moves, thinking, turns.)* And twenty thousand—that *is* something one can feel with the hand, it is there.

**WILLY:** *(now assured, with rising power)* Oh, Ben, that's the whole beauty of it! I see it like a diamond, shining in the dark, hard and rough, that I can pick up and touch in my hand. Not like—like an appointment! This would not be another damned-fool appointment, Ben, and it changes all the aspects. Because he thinks I'm nothing, see, and so he spites me. But the funeral—*(Straightening up.)* Ben, that funeral will be massive! They'll come from Maine, Massachusetts, Vermont, New Hampshire! All the old-timers with the strange license plates—that boy will be thunder-struck, Ben, because he never realized—I am known! Rhode Island, New York, New Jersey—I am known, Ben, and he'll see it with his eyes once and for all. He'll see what I am, Ben! He's in for a shock, that boy!

**BEN:** *(coming down to the edge of the garden)* He'll call you a coward.

**WILLY:** *(suddenly fearful)* No, that would be terrible.

**BEN:** Yes. And a damned fool.

**WILLY:** No, no, he mustn't, I won't have that! *(He is broken and desperate.)*

**BEN:** He'll hate you, William.

*The gay music of the Boys is heard.*

**WILLY:** Oh, Ben, how do we get back to all the great times? Used to be so full of light, and comradeship,

Willy discusses his business proposition with Ben.

the sleigh-riding in winter, and the ruddiness on his cheeks. And always some kind of good news coming up, always something nice coming up ahead. And never even let me carry the valises in the house, and simonizing, simonizing that little red car! Why, why can't I give him something and not have him hate me?

**BEN:** Let me think about it. *(He glances at his watch.)* I still have a little time. Remarkable proposition, but you've got to be sure you're not making a fool of yourself.

BEN *drifts off upstage and goes out of sight.* BIFF *comes down from the left.*

**WILLY:** *(suddenly conscious of* BIFF, *turns and looks up at him, then begins picking up the packages of seeds in confusion)* Where the hell is that seed? *(Indignantly.)* You can't see nothing out here! They boxed in the whole goddamn neighborhood!

**BIFF:** There are people all around here. Don't you realize that?

**WILLY:** I'm busy. Don't bother me.

**BIFF:** *(taking the hoe from* WILLY*)* I'm saying good-by to you, Pop. *(*WILLY *looks at him, silent, unable to move.)* I'm not coming back any more.

**WILLY:** You're not going to see Oliver tomorrow?

**BIFF:** I've got no appointment, Dad.

**WILLY:** He put his arm around you, and you've got no appointment?

**BIFF:** Pop, get this now, will you? Everytime I've left it's been a fight that sent me out of here. Today I realized something about myself and I tried to explain it to you and I—I think I'm just not smart enough to make any sense out of it for you. To hell with whose fault it is or anything like that. *(He takes* WILLY*'s arm.)* Let's just wrap it up, heh? Come on in, we'll tell Mom. *(He gently tries to pull* WILLY *to left.)*

**WILLY:** *(frozen, immobile, with guilt in his voice)* No, I don't want to see her.

**BIFF:** Come on! *(He pulls again, and* WILLY *tries to pull away.)*

**WILLY:** *(highly nervous)* No, no, I don't want to see her.

**BIFF:** *(tries to look into* WILLY*'s face, as if to find the answer there)* Why don't you want to see her?

**WILLY:** *(more harshly now)* Don't bother me, will you?

**BIFF:** What do you mean, you don't want to see her? You don't want them calling you yellow, do you? This isn't your fault; it's me, I'm a bum. Now come inside! *(*WILLY *strains to get away.)* Did you hear what I said to you?

WILLY *pulls away and quickly goes by himself into the house.* BIFF *follows.*

**LINDA:** *(to* WILLY*)* Did you plant, dear?

**BIFF:** *(at the door, to* LINDA*)* All right, we had it out. I'm going and I'm not writing any more.

**LINDA:** *(going to* WILLY *in the kitchen)* I think that's the best way, dear. 'Cause there's no use drawing it out, you'll just never get along.

WILLY *doesn't respond.*

**BIFF:** People ask where I am and what I'm doing, you don't know, and you don't care. That way it'll be off your mind and you can start brightening up again. All right? That clears it, doesn't it? *(*WILLY *is silent, and* BIFF *goes to him.)* You gonna wish me luck, scout? *(He extends his hand.)* What do you say?

**LINDA:** Shake his hand, Willy.

**WILLY:** *(turning to her, seething with hurt)* There's no necessity to mention the pen at all, y'know.

**BIFF:** *(gently)* I've got no appointment, Dad.

**WILLY:** *(erupting fiercely)* He put his arm around . . . ?

**BIFF:** Dad, you're never going to see what I am, so what's the use of arguing? If I strike oil I'll send you a check. Meantime forget I'm alive.

**WILLY:** *(to* LINDA*)* Spite, see?

**BIFF:** Shake hands, Dad.

**WILLY:** Not my hand.

**BIFF:** I was hoping not to go this way.

**WILLY:** Well, this is the way you're going. Good-by.

BIFF *looks at him a moment, then turns sharply and goes to the stairs.*

**WILLY:** *(stops him with)* May you rot in hell if you leave this house!

**BIFF:** *(turning)* Exactly what is it that you want from me?

**WILLY:** I want you to know, on the train, in the mountains, in the valleys, wherever you go, that you cut down your life for spite!

**BIFF:** No, no.

**WILLY:** Spite, spite, is the word of your undoing! And when you're down and out, remember what did it. When you're rotting somewhere beside the railroad tracks, remember, and don't you dare blame it on me!

**BIFF:** I'm not blaming it on you!

**WILLY:** I won't take the rap for this, you hear?

HAPPY *comes down the stairs and stands on the bottom step, watching.*

**BIFF:** That's just what I'm telling you!

**WILLY:** *(sinking into a chair at the table, with full accusation)* You're trying to put a knife in me—don't think I don't know what you're doing!

**BIFF:** All right, phony! Then let's lay it on the line. *(He whips the rubber tube out of his pocket and puts it on the table.)*

**HAPPY:** You crazy—

**LINDA:** Biff! *(She moves to grab the hose, but* BIFF *holds it down with his hand.)*

**BIFF:** Leave it there! Don't move it!

**WILLY:** *(not looking at it)* What is that?

**BIFF:** You know goddam well what that is.

**WILLY:** *(caged, wanting to escape)* I never saw that.

**BIFF:** You saw it. The mice didn't bring it into the cellar! What is this supposed to do, make a hero out of you? This supposed to make me sorry for you?

**WILLY:** Never heard of it.

**BIFF:** There'll be no pity for you, you hear it? No pity!

**WILLY:** *(to* LINDA*)* You hear the spite!

**BIFF:** No, you're going to hear the truth—what you are and what I am!

**LINDA:** Stop it!

**WILLY:** Spite!

**HAPPY:** *(coming down toward* BIFF*)* You cut it now!

**BIFF:** *(to* HAPPY*)* The man don't know who we are! The man is gonna know! *(To* WILLY.*)* We never told the truth for ten minutes in this house!

**HAPPY:** We always told the truth!

**BIFF:** *(turning on him)* You big blow, are you the assistant buyer? You're one of the two assistants to the assistant, aren't you?

**HAPPY:** Well, I'm practically—

**BIFF:** You're practically full of it! We all are! And I'm through with it. *(To* WILLY.*)* Now hear this, Willy, this is me.

**WILLY:** I know you!

**BIFF:** You know why I had no address for three months? I stole a suit in Kansas City and I was in jail. *(To* LINDA, *who is sobbing.)* Stop crying. I'm through with it.

LINDA *turns away from them, her hands covering her face.*

**WILLY:** I suppose that's my fault!

**BIFF:** I stole myself out of every good job since high school!

**WILLY:** And whose fault is that?

**BIFF:** And I never got anywhere because you blew me so full of hot air I could never stand taking orders from anybody! That's whose fault it is!

**WILLY:** I hear that!

**LINDA:** Don't, Biff!

**BIFF:** It's goddam time you heard that! I had to be boss big shot in two weeks, and I'm through with it!

**WILLY:** Then hang yourself! For spite, hang yourself!

**BIFF:** No! Nobody's hanging himself, Willy! I ran down eleven flights with a pen in my hand today. And suddenly I stopped, you hear me? And in the middle of that office building, do you hear this? I stopped in the middle of that building and I saw—the sky. I saw the things that I love in this world. The work and the food and time to sit and smoke. And I looked at the pen and said to myself, what the hell am I grabbing this for? Why am I trying to become what I don't want to be? What am I doing in an office, making a contemptuous, begging fool of myself, when all I want is out there, waiting for me the minute I say I know who I am! Why can't I say that, Willy? *(He tries to make* WILLY *face him, but* WILLY *pulls away and moves to the left.)*

**WILLY:** *(with hatred, threateningly)* The door of your life is wide open!

**BIFF:** Pop! I'm a dime a dozen, and so are you!

**WILLY:** *(turning on him now in an uncontrolled outburst)* I am not a dime a dozen! I am Willy Loman, and you are Biff Loman!

BIFF *starts for* WILLY, *but is blocked by* HAPPY. *In his fury,* BIFF *seems on the verge of attacking his father.*

**BIFF:** I am not a leader of men, Willy, and neither are you. You were never anything but a hard-working drummer who landed in the ash can like all the rest of them! I'm one dollar an hour, Willy! I tried seven states and couldn't raise it. A buck an hour! Do you gather my meaning? I'm not bringing home any prizes any more, and you're going to stop waiting for me to bring them home!

**WILLY:** *(directly to* BIFF*)* You vengeful, spiteful mutt!

BIFF *breaks from* HAPPY. WILLY, *in fright, starts up the stairs.* BIFF *grabs him.*

**BIFF:** *(at the peak of his fury)* Pop, I'm nothing! I'm nothing, Pop. Can't you understand that? There's no spite in it any more. I'm just what I am, that's all.

BIFF'*s fury has spent itself, and he breaks down, sobbing, holding on to* WILLY, *who dumbly fumbles for* BIFF'*s face.*

**WILLY:** *(astonished)* What're you doing? What're you doing? *(To* LINDA.*)* Why is he crying?

**BIFF:** *(crying, broken)* Will you let me go, for Christ's sake? Will you take that phony dream and burn it before something happens? *(Struggling to contain himself, he pulls away and moves to the stairs.)* I'll go in the morning. Put him—put him to bed. *(Exhausted,* BIFF *moves up the stairs to his room.)*

**WILLY:** *(after a long pause, astonished, elevated)* Isn't that—isn't that remarkable? Biff—he likes me!

**LINDA:** He loves you, Willy!

**HAPPY:** *(deeply moved)* Always did, Pop.

Biff curses Willy for lying.

**WILLY:** Oh, Biff! *(Staring wildly.)* He cried! Cried to me. *(He is choking with his love, and now cries out his promise.)* That boy—that boy is going to be magnificent!

BEN *appears in the light just outside the kitchen.*

**BEN:** Yes, outstanding, with twenty thousand behind him.

**LINDA:** *(sensing the racing of his mind, fearfully, carefully)* Now come to bed, Willy. It's all settled now.

**WILLY:** *(finding it difficult not to rush out of the house)* Yes, we'll sleep. Come on. Go to sleep, Hap.

**BEN:** And it does take a great kind of a man to crack the jungle.

*In accents of dread,* BEN*'s idyllic music starts up.*

**HAPPY:** *(his arm around* LINDA*)* I'm getting married, Pop, don't forget it. I'm changing everything. I'm gonna run that department before the year is up. You'll see, Mom. *(He kisses her.)*

**BEN:** The jungle is dark but full of diamonds, Willy.

WILLY *turns, moves, listening to* BEN.

**LINDA:** Be good. You're both good boys, just act that way, that's all.

**HAPPY:** 'Night, Pop. *(He goes upstairs.)*

**LINDA:** *(to* WILLY*)* Come, dear.

**BEN:** *(with greater force)* One must go in to fetch a diamond out.

**WILLY:** *(to* LINDA, *as he moves slowly along the edge of the kitchen, toward the door)* I just want to get settled down, Linda. Let me sit alone for a little.

**LINDA:** *(almost uttering her fear)* I want you upstairs.

**WILLY:** *(taking her in his arms)* In a few minutes, Linda. I couldn't sleep right now. Go on, you look awful tired. *(He kisses her.)*

**BEN:** Not like an appointment at all. A diamond is rough and hard to the touch.

**WILLY:** Go on now. I'll be right up.

**LINDA:** I think this is the only way, Willy.

**WILLY:** Sure, it's the best thing.

**BEN:** Best thing!

**WILLY:** The only way. Everything is gonna be—go on, kid, get to bed. You look so tired.

**LINDA:** Come right up.

**WILLY:** Two minutes.

LINDA *goes into the living-room, then reappears in her bedroom.* WILLY *moves just outside the kitchen door.*

**WILLY:** Loves me. *(Wonderingly.)* Always loved me. Isn't that a remarkable thing? Ben, he'll worship me for it!

**BEN:** *(with promise)* It's dark there, but full of diamonds.

**WILLY:** Can you imagine that magnificence with twenty thousand dollars in his pocket?

**LINDA:** *(calling from her room)* Willy! Come up!

**WILLY:** *(calling into the kitchen)* Yes! Yes. Coming! It's very smart, you realize that, don't you, sweetheart? Even Ben sees it. I gotta go, baby. 'By! 'By! *(Going over to* BEN, *almost dancing.)* Imagine? When the mail comes he'll be ahead of Bernard again!

**BEN:** A perfect proposition all around.

**WILLY:** Did you see how he cried to me? Oh, if I could kiss him, Ben!

**BEN:** Time, William, time!

**WILLY:** Oh, Ben, I always knew one way or another we were gonna make it, Biff and I!

**BEN:** *(looking at his watch)* The boat. We'll be late. *(He moves slowly off into the darkness.)*

**WILLY:** *(elegiacally, turning to the house)* Now when you kick off, boy, I want a seventy-yard boot, and get right down the field under the ball, and when you hit, hit low and hit hard, because it's important, boy. *(He swings around and faces the audience.)* There's all kinds of important people in the stands, and the first thing you know . . . *(Suddenly realizing he is alone.)* Ben! Ben, where do I . . . ? *(He makes a sudden movement of search.)* Ben, how do I . . . ?

**LINDA:** *(calling)* Willy, you coming up?

**WILLY:** *(uttering a gasp of fear, whirling about as if to quiet her)* Sh! *(He turns around as if to find his way; sounds, faces, voices, seem to be swarming in upon him and he flicks at them, crying.)* Sh! Sh! *(Suddenly music, faint and high, stops him. It rises in intensity, almost to an unbearable scream. He goes up and down on his toes, and rushes off around the house.)* Shhh!

**LINDA:** Willy?

*There is no answer.* LINDA *waits.* BIFF *gets up off his bed. He is still in his clothes.* HAPPY *sits up.* BIFF *stands listening.*

Willy climbs into the car.

**LINDA:** *(with real fear)* Willy, answer me! Willy!

*There is the sound of a car starting and moving away at full speed.*

**LINDA:** No!

**BIFF:** *(rushing down the stairs)* Pop!

*As the car speeds off, the music crashes down in a frenzy of sound, which becomes the soft pulsation of a single cello string.* BIFF *slowly returns to his bedroom. He and* HAPPY *gravely don their jackets.* LINDA *slowly walks out of her room. The music has developed into a dead march. The leaves of day are appearing over everything.* CHARLEY *and* BERNARD, *somberly dressed, appear and knock on the kitchen door.* BIFF *and* HAPPY *slowly descend the stairs to the kitchen as* CHARLEY *and* BERNARD *enter. All stop a moment when* LINDA, *in clothes of mourning, bearing a little bunch of roses, comes through the draped doorway into the kitchen. She goes to* CHARLEY *and takes his arm. Now all move toward the audience, through the wall-line of the kitchen. At the limit of the apron,* LINDA *lays down the flowers, kneels, and sits back on her heels. All stare down at the grave.*

## REQUIEM

**CHARLEY:** It's getting dark, Linda.

LINDA *doesn't react. She stares at the grave.*

**BIFF:** How about it, Mom? Better get some rest, heh? They'll be closing the gate soon.

LINDA *makes no move. Pause.*

**HAPPY:** *(deeply angered)* He had no right to do that. There was no necessity for it. We would've helped him.

**CHARLEY:** *(grunting)* Hmmm.

**BIFF:** Come along, Mom.

**LINDA:** Why didn't anybody come?

**CHARLEY:** It was a very nice funeral.

**LINDA:** But where are all the people he knew? Maybe they blame him.

**CHARLEY:** Naa. It's a rough world, Linda. They wouldn't blame him.

**LINDA:** I can't understand it. At this time especially. First time in thirty-five years we were just about free and clear. He only needed a little salary. He was even finished with the dentist.

**CHARLEY:** No man only needs a little salary.

**LINDA:** I can't understand it.

**BIFF:** There were a lot of nice days. When he'd come home from a trip; or on Sundays, making the stoop; finishing the cellar; putting on the new porch; when he built the extra bathroom; and put up the garage. You know something, Charley, there's more of him in that front stoop than in all the sales he ever made.

**CHARLEY:** Yeah. He was a happy man with a batch of cement.

**LINDA:** He was so wonderful with his hands.

**BIFF:** He had the wrong dreams. All, all, wrong.

**HAPPY:** *(almost ready to fight* BIFF*)* Don't say that!

**BIFF:** He never knew who he was.

**CHARLEY:** *(stopping* HAPPY*'s movement and reply. To* BIFF*)* Nobody dast blame this man. You don't understand: Willy was a salesman. And for a salesman, there is no rock bottom to the life. He don't put a bolt to a nut, he don't tell you the law or give you medicine. He's a man way out there in the blue, riding on a smile and a shoeshine. And when they start not smiling back—that's an earthquake. And then you get yourself a couple of spots on your hat, and you're finished. Nobody dast blame this man. A salesman is got to dream, boy. It comes with the territory.

The family stands over Willy's grave.

**BIFF:** Charley, the man didn't know who he was.

**HAPPY:** *(infuriated)* Don't say that!

**BIFF:** Why don't you come with me, Happy?

**HAPPY:** I'm not licked that easily. I'm staying right in this city, and I'm gonna beat this racket! *(He looks at* BIFF*, his chin set.)* The Loman Brothers!

**BIFF:** I know who I am, kid.

**HAPPY:** All right, boy. I'm gonna show you and everybody else that Willy Loman did not die in vain. He had a good dream. It's the only dream you can have—to come out number-one man. He fought it out here, and this is where I'm gonna win it for him.

**BIFF:** *(with a hopeless glance at* HAPPY*, bends toward his mother)* Let's go, Mom.

**LINDA:** I'll be with you in a minute. Go on, Charley. *(He hesitates.)* I want to, just for a minute. I never had a chance to say good-by.

CHARLEY *moves away, followed by* HAPPY. BIFF *remains a slight distance up and left of* LINDA. *She sits there, summoning herself. The flute begins, not far away, playing behind her speech.*

**LINDA:** Forgive me, dear. I can't cry. I don't know what it is, but I can't cry. I don't understand it. Why did you ever do that? Help me, Willy, I can't cry. It seems to me that you're just on another trip. I keep expecting you. Willy, dear, I can't cry. Why did you do it? I search and search and I search, and I can't understand it, Willy. I made the last payment on the house today. Today, dear. And there'll be nobody home. *(A sob rises in her throat.)* We're free and clear. *(Sobbing more fully, released.)* We're free. *(*BIFF *comes slowly toward her.)* We're free . . . We're free . . .

BIFF *lifts her to her feet and moves out up right with her in his arms.* LINDA *sobs quietly.* BERNARD *and* CHARLEY *come together and follow them, followed by* HAPPY. *Only the music of the flute is left on the darkening stage as over the house the hard towers of the apartment buildings rise into sharp focus, and*

*The Curtain Falls.*

# Writing from Reading

## Summarize

1 How would you condense the plot into a few lines, to the size of something you might write, say, on the back of a postcard?

2 Explain how the title *Life of a Salesman* compares with the current title? What other titles might describe the play? Which do you prefer and why?

## Analyze Craft

3 Aspects of this play are highly stylized and theatrical—the salesman's hallucinations, for example, and the fade-in and fade-out of characters from his past. How do these imagined conversations alter the concept of realism? Why do they feel appropriate to Willy Loman's collapse?

4 Certain expenses in this play (the price of a drink, the cost of a mortgage) have increased since 1949; others have not. To what extent does this text seem timeless, and what would be the effect of inflating the cost of commodities so as to make them more contemporary?

5 How much of the family dynamic here, in terms of both the siblings and their relation to their parents, grows out of Willy's main desire to sell himself? To what degree does it seem true to your understanding of how families function?

6 Why does Willy feel like a failure? In what ways—as salesman, husband, father—does he succeed? What does his love of gardening suggest?

## Analyze Voice

7 What does Arthur Miller mean when he writes in "Tragedy and the Common Man" (1949) "that the plays we revere, century after century, are the tragedies. In them, and in them alone, lies the belief—optimistic, if you will—in the perfectibility of man. It is time, I think, that we who are without kings, took up this bright thread of our history and followed it to the only place it can possibly lead in our time—the heart and spirit of the average man"?

8 Miller in his lifetime was famous as a voice of conscience, protesting against totalitarianism wherever he found it—and refusing to answer questions from the House Un-American Activities Committee when it subpoenaed him to testify against his "communist" friends. Indeed, one of his crucial plays, *The Crucible,* dealt with the mass hysteria of the Salem witch trials in seventeenth-century America and, by extension, with the hysteria engendered by Joseph McCarthy, junior senator from Wisconsin. In what ways is *Death of a Salesman* a play of social protest, and what are Willy's ideals?

## Synthesize Summary and Analysis

9 To what extent is Willy Loman like the character of Oedipus? Or, more plausibly, to what extent does he remind you of *Hamlet's* Polonius? Loman, however, can be considered as a tragic character; Polonius cannot. Why?

10 The entire action of the play seems to come together in the statement by Linda Loman in which she says of her husband "Attention must be paid." Why does she forgive what her sons resent so much—his infidelities, his drunkenness? What did she know about his life as a traveling salesman and his missed financial chances? What does she want from and for him now?

## Interpret the Play

11 Willy dreams the American dream. In what way does it become a nightmare for him—or does he die content?

*(CONTINUED FROM PAGE 285)*

## FROM THE PALACE TO THE LIVING ROOM, OR, THE ORIGINS OF MODERN THEATER

As you know from your encounters with Greek tragedy and Shakespeare's plays, theater in the West did not begin by depicting ordinary people. In early forms of theater, it was permissible to show ordinary folk as comic and to make fun of the human condition—its pitfalls and pratfalls—in the low or middle class. There was satiric fun to be had at the expense of the common man. The tragic mode was previously reserved, as we have discussed, for elevated members of the society. Middle-class revolutions across Europe brought to power a social class—made up primarily of lawyers, bankers, and landowners—that had served royalty but never before played a dominant role. The fall of monarchies, and the emergence of middle-class democracies driven by industry and finance, gave rise to another sort of audience and another form of theater in western Europe.

> "So whether it's in a play from 1919, or whether it's a play from 1942, or 2010, I approach them all the same: from the truth of that character. . . . Where am I? Who am I? What am I? Why am I here? . . . You always play the truth."
>
> Conversation with Ruben Santiago-Hudson

While kings and queens ruled in Europe, playwrights wrote in a style and took on subjects that catered, at least in part, to the aristocratic audience. With the rise of democratic parliaments, playwrights made a theater for the middle class these legislators represented. In this way marriage and family and various other sorts of everyday social relations replaced the staged deliberations and decisions of kings. Theatergoers wished to see their *own* situations reflected, their *own* society described. In place of the old systems of belief we find a new variety of thought—and therefore a new kind of play. At the start of this chapter we suggested that the movement from palace to living room was a function of the shift in power from monarchy to democracy—and that the possibility of realistic theater was born out of such a shift.

Today it may be difficult to recognize the importance of this distinction in styles, or how much it means even as we witness it. Actors perform the Oedipus play wearing stylized masks that emphasize the difference between the royal family and the audience and the difference between the royals and the gods who rule their lives. Issues of marriage and family in Elizabethan theater are more closely related to matters of kingdom and empire than to domestic relations. Shakespeare's scenes when staged with flair and intelligence remind us of the difference between performers on the stage and our ordinary selves in the audience. Great poetry that it is, the language alone can make us hear—and, by simply hearing, see—the distance between the playwright's characters of high and low station. Here the importance of staging comes, again, to bear. This kind of realistic stage or set design, a **proscenium** stage, forces the playwright to consider the mechanics of staging actors in relation to the audience and to quick, easy, and inexpensive set changes to keep from changing the scenery every time the action shifts.

*Death of a Salesman,* Arthur Miller's most influential work, lies squarely within the tradition of realistic or **naturalistic** theater, theater that shines a light on painful realities. In the course of his lengthy productive career, Miller tried his hand at other modes of representation—writing short experimental plays or ones with an historical context or dabbling in surrealism—but it is his realistic plays that brought his work into the mainstream of American drama. In *Death of a Salesman,* Miller takes his protagonist, a modern-day tragic hero (or **antihero** in that he is not elevated socially or morally), a step further: He is an Everyman in a modern **morality play** (see chapter 34 for more on the medieval morality play).

"America is happiest with a naturalistic play or play that gives the illusion of being naturalistic. . . . We all know that in theater there is no such thing as absolute naturalism. People do not talk the way they do in real life, thank heavens. On stage they talk coherently. . . . We call something naturalistic if it is not highly stylized."

Conversation with Edward Albee

In some ways the American playwright Arthur Miller is the direct inheritor of the playwright who defined the practice of realism onstage: Henrik Ibsen. The nineteenth-century Norwegian Ibsen is the writer who more than any other brought the realistic strategy to the Western stage. Ibsen takes on the difficult and piercing social issues of his period and, to a certain extent, our own. In *A Doll's House* we witness the dramatization of problems that touch on the lives of ordinary middle-class people—the role of women in modern marriage, a struggle about money and employment, the effort to keep up appearances for the outside world. Ibsen highlights the problems of family life, of married life within society—subjects not addressed in any detail in early forms of drama. In his theater we meet people we can legitimately call modern, people mostly like ourselves in recognizable and often unpleasant situations. What made it possible for a playwright to create this sort of play and what makes it possible for an audience to respond to it?

### *METHOD* ACTING—REALISM ONSTAGE

An entirely new style of performance—first propounded by the Russian Konstantin Stanislavski and practiced in America most famously by such graduates of the Actors Studio as Marilyn Monroe and Marlon Brando—made a method out of naturalism onstage. An actor and his or her character should merge so that the role becomes *inhabited* by the person cast in it; the facial tics or accent of a *method* actor were not acquired in the dressing room ten minutes before curtain time but were built into rehearsal and the interpretative process. This notion of identity between the player and the part played is based, of course, on the assumption that behavior must be internalized and is best copied when most natural. Gone were the highly polished performances and perfectly articulated speech of characters in period dress; instead, as some disgruntled reviewers complained, the actors scratched themselves and mumbled and turned their backs on the audience in order to seem *real.*

In nineteenth-century France, the **well-made play** became the norm. Popularized by such playwrights as Eugène Scribe (1791–1861) and Victorien Sardou (1831–1908), this three-act sequence *posed* a problem, *complicated* it, and then *resolved* it; usually that resolution came when a character's past was revealed. The first act offers *exposition,* the second a *situation,* the third an unraveling or *completion.* Meticulous plotting and suspense were components of this mode of theater. Ibsen—who had directed a number of Scribe's well-made plays in Norway—deeply understood how to adapt those cause-and-effect plot arrangements for his own use. Cowardice, hypocrisy, complacency within the expectation of conventional behavior, and a kind of stifled yearning are the problems Ibsen brings to center stage in his drama.

Here's one reason that *A Doll's House* is a **problem play;** it's hard to *read* the central figure and decide if she's a spoiled child or a brave pioneer or some combination of both. Indeed, there have been various interpretations of the role: Nora has been played as everything from victim to victimizer, self-indulgent society matron to selfless ingenue. Nora desires what we desire. The protagonist Nora yearns to become a fully aware human being rather than live as the subservient creature known to society as Torvald's wife. She struggles with confusion as we struggle with confusion. She achieves a breakthrough in her understanding that mirrors our own recognition; her fear of causing embarrassment to and dishonor for her husband feels in many respects contemporary. The way she wrestles with the problem of family duty as opposed to her own individual freedom should seem familiar as well. In any case her progress toward independence feels modern and quite up-to-date. As one of our culture's first great feminist characters, she embodies—in terms of her growth from first to final act—a form of liberation surprising, even shocking, at the time. Here's a portrait of a woman and a family that resonates today.

> "Every playwright awakens something in you you didn't know was there. . . . Ibsen, for example, . . . had such a tremendous influence. . . . His women were as startling and as modern as any woman I've ever worked on. . . . The ideas in Ibsen are so brave and so bold." Conversation with Marian Seldes

## Henrik Ibsen (1828–1906)

Henrik Ibsen, known today as the father of modern drama, was born near Oslo, Norway. Initially wealthy, the Ibsens were left in poverty when their family business failed; Henrik was six years old at the time. As a teenager, he was apprenticed to a pharmacist, but by 1851, he held the position of stage manager and playwright at the Norwegian Theater in Bergen, and after that he worked as a theater director in Norway's capital. Ibsen later lived abroad in Germany and Italy, remaining away from Norway for a twenty-seven-year period because he felt he could better write Norwegian drama from a distance. Supported by stipends from the government, Ibsen devoted himself to writing plays. His work moved theater away from popular nineteenth-century melodramas and into the realm of realism, which allowed him to examine his characters' psychological lives and the individual's conflict with convention and society. Plays such as *A Doll's House* (1879), *Ghosts* (1881), and *Hedda Gabler* (1890) established Ibsen's dramaturgical prowess. In 1891, Ibsen returned to Oslo, where he remained for the rest of his life.

# A Doll's House (1879)

*—translated by B. Farquharson Sharp*

## CHARACTERS

**TORVALD HELMER.**
**NORA, HIS WIFE.**
**DOCTOR RANK.**
**MRS. LINDE.**
**NILS KROGSTAD.**
**HELMERS' THREE YOUNG CHILDREN.**
**ANNE, THEIR NURSE.**
**A HOUSEMAID.**
**A PORTER.**

*(The action takes place in Helmer's house.)*

## ACT I

**SCENE:** *—A room furnished comfortably and tastefully, but not extravagantly. At the back, a door to the right leads to the entrance-hall, another to the left leads to Helmer's study. Between the doors stands a piano. In the middle of the left-hand wall is a door, and beyond it a window. Near the window are a round table, arm-chairs and a small sofa. In the right-hand wall, at the farther end, another door; and on the same side, nearer the footlights, a stove, two easy chairs and a rocking-chair; between the stove and the door, a small table. Engravings on the walls; a cabinet with china and other small objects; a small book-case with well-bound books. The floors are carpeted, and a fire burns in the stove. It is winter.*

*A bell rings in the hall; shortly afterwards the door is heard to open. Enter* NORA, *humming a tune and in high spirits. She is in out-door dress and carries a number of parcels; these she lays on the table to the right. She leaves the outer door open after her, and through it is seen a* PORTER *who is carrying a Christmas Tree and a basket, which he gives to the* MAID *who has opened the door.*

**NORA:** Hide the Christmas Tree carefully, Helen. Be sure the children do not see it till this evening, when it is dressed. *(To the* PORTER, *taking out her purse.)* How much?

**PORTER:** Sixpence.

**NORA:** There is a shilling. No, keep the change. *(The* PORTER *thanks her, and goes out.* NORA *shuts the door. She is laughing to herself, as she takes off her hat and coat. She takes a packet of macaroons from her pocket and eats one or two; then goes cautiously to her husband's door and listens.)* Yes, he is in. *(Still humming, she goes to the table on the right.)*

**HELMER:** *(calls out from his room)* Is that my little lark twittering out there?

**NORA:** *(busy opening some of the parcels)* Yes, it is!

**HELMER:** Is it my little squirrel bustling about?

**NORA:** Yes!

**HELMER:** When did my squirrel come home?

**NORA:** Just now. *(Puts the bag of macaroons into her pocket and wipes her mouth.)* Come in here, Torvald, and see what I have bought.

**HELMER:** Don't disturb me. *(A little later, he opens the door and looks into the room, pen in hand.)* Bought, did you say? All these things? Has my little spendthrift been wasting money again?

**NORA:** Yes but, Torvald, this year we really can let ourselves go a little. This is the first Christmas that we have not needed to economise.

**HELMER:** Still, you know, we can't spend money recklessly.

**NORA:** Yes, Torvald, we may be a wee bit more reckless now, mayn't we? Just a tiny wee bit! You are going to have a big salary and earn lots and lots of money.

**HELMER:** Yes, after the New Year; but then it will be a whole quarter before the salary is due.

**NORA:** Pooh! we can borrow till then.

**HELMER:** Nora! *(Goes up to her and takes her playfully by the ear.)* The same little featherhead! Suppose, now, that I borrowed fifty pounds to-day, and you spent it all in the Christmas week, and then on New Year's Eve a slate fell on my head and killed me, and—

**NORA:** *(putting her hands over his mouth)* Oh! don't say such horrid things!

**HELMER:** Still, suppose that happened,—what then?

**NORA:** If that were to happen, I don't suppose I should care whether I owed money or not.

**HELMER:** Yes, but what about the people who had lent it?

**NORA:** They? Who would bother about them? I should not know who they were.

**HELMER:** That is like a woman! But seriously, Nora, you know what I think about that. No debt, no borrowing. There can be no freedom or beauty about a home life that depends on borrowing and debt. We two have kept bravely on the straight road so far, and we will go on the same way for the short time longer that there need be any struggle.

**NORA:** *(moving towards the stove)* As you please, Torvald.

**HELMER:** *(following her)* Come, come, my little skylark must not droop her wings. What is this! Is my little squirrel out of temper? *(Taking out his purse.)* Nora, what do you think I have got here?

**NORA:** *(turning round quickly)* Money!

**HELMER:** There you are. *(Gives her some money.)* Do you think I don't know what a lot is wanted for housekeeping at Christmas-time?

Nora (Claire Bloom) and Torvald (Anthony Hopkins) Helmer discuss their Christmas plans in the 1973 film directed by Patrick Garland.

**NORA:** *(counting)* Ten shillings—a pound—two pounds! Thank you, thank you, Torvald; that will keep me going for a long time.

**HELMER:** Indeed it must.

**NORA:** Yes, yes, it will. But come here and let me show you what I have bought. And all so cheap! Look, here is a new suit for Ivar, and a sword; and a horse and a trumpet for Bob; and a doll and dolly's bedstead for Emmy,—they are very plain, but anyway she will soon break them in pieces. And here are dress-lengths and handkerchiefs for the maids; old Anne ought really to have something better.

**HELMER:** And what is in this parcel?

**NORA:** *(crying out)* No, no! you mustn't see that till this evening.

**HELMER:** Very well. But now tell me, you extravagant little person, what would you like for yourself?

**NORA:** For myself? Oh, I am sure I don't want anything.

**HELMER:** Yes, but you must. Tell me something reasonable that you would particularly like to have.

**NORA:** No, I really can't think of anything—unless, Torvald—

**HELMER:** Well?

**NORA:** *(playing with his coat buttons, and without raising her eyes to his)* If you really want to give me something, you might—you might—

**HELMER:** Well, out with it!

**NORA:** *(speaking quickly)* You might give me money, Torvald. Only just as much as you can afford; and then one of these days I will buy something with it.

Nora tells Torvald what she would like for Christmas.

**HELMER:** But Nora—

**NORA:** Oh, do! dear Torvald; please, please do! Then I will wrap it up in beautiful gilt paper and hang it on the Christmas Tree. Wouldn't that be fun?

**HELMER:** What are little people called that are always wasting money?

**NORA:** Spendthrifts—I know. Let us do as you suggest, Torvald, and then I shall have time to think what I am most in want of. That is a very sensible plan, isn't it?

**HELMER:** *(smiling)* Indeed it is—that is to say, if you were really to save out of the money I give you, and then really buy something for yourself. But if you spend it all on the housekeeping and any number of unnecessary things, then I merely have to pay up again.

**NORA:** Oh but, Torvald—

**HELMER:** You can't deny it, my dear little Nora. *(Puts his arm around her waist.)* It's a sweet little spendthrift, but she uses up a deal of money. One would hardly believe how expensive such little persons are!

**NORA:** It's a shame to say that. I do really save all I can.

**HELMER:** *(laughing)* That's very true,—all you can. But you can't save anything!

**NORA:** *(smiling quietly and happily)* You haven't any idea how many expenses we skylarks and squirrels have, Torvald.

**HELMER:** You are an odd little soul. Very like your father. You always find some new way of wheedling money out of me, and, as soon as you have got it, it seems to melt in your hands. You never know where it has gone. Still, one must take you as you are. It is in the blood; for indeed it is true that you can inherit these things, Nora.

**NORA:** Ah, I wish I had inherited many of papa's qualities.

**HELMER:** And I would not wish you to be anything but just what you are, my sweet little skylark. But, do you know, it strikes me that you are looking rather—what shall I say—rather uneasy to-day?

**NORA:** Do I?

**HELMER:** You do, really. Look straight at me.

**NORA:** *(looks at him)* Well?

**HELMER:** *(wagging his finger at her)* Hasn't Miss Sweet-Tooth been breaking rules in town to-day?

**NORA:** No; what makes you think that?

**HELMER:** Hasn't she paid a visit to the confectioner's?

**NORA:** No, I assure you, Torvald—

**HELMER:** Not been nibbling sweets?

**NORA:** No, certainly not.

**HELMER:** Not even taken a bite at a macaroon or two?

**NORA:** No, Torvald, I assure you really—

**HELMER:** There, there, of course I was only joking.

**NORA:** *(going to the table on the right)* I should not think of going against your wishes.

**HELMER:** No, I am sure of that; besides, you gave me your word—*(Going up to her.)* Keep your little Christmas secrets to yourself, my darling. They will all be revealed to-night when the Christmas Tree is lit, no doubt.

**NORA:** Did you remember to invite Doctor Rank?

**HELMER:** No. But there is no need; as a matter of course he will come to dinner with us. However, I will ask him when he comes in this morning. I have ordered some good wine. Nora, you can't think how I am looking forward to this evening.

**NORA:** So am I! And how the children will enjoy themselves, Torvald!

**HELMER:** It is splendid to feel that one has a perfectly safe appointment, and a big enough income. It's delightful to think of, isn't it?

**NORA:** It's wonderful!

**HELMER:** Do you remember last Christmas? For a full three weeks beforehand you shut yourself up every evening till long after midnight, making ornaments for the Christmas Tree, and all the other fine things that were to be a surprise to us. It was the dullest three weeks I ever spent!

**NORA:** I didn't find it dull.

**HELMER:** *(smiling)* But there was precious little result, Nora.

**NORA:** Oh, you shouldn't tease me about that again. How could I help the cat's going in and tearing everything to pieces?

**HELMER:** Of course you couldn't, poor little girl. You had the best of intentions to please us all, and that's the main thing. But it is a good thing that our hard times are over.

**NORA:** Yes, it is really wonderful.

**HELMER:** This time I needn't sit here and be dull all alone, and you needn't ruin your dear eyes and your pretty little hands—

**NORA:** *(clapping her hands)* No, Torvald, I needn't any longer, need I! It's wonderfully lovely to hear you say so! *(Taking his arm.)* Now I will tell you how I have been thinking we ought to arrange things, Torvald. As soon as Christmas is over—*(A bell rings in the hall.)* There's the bell. *(She tidies the room a little.)* There's some one at the door. What a nuisance!

**HELMER:** If it is a caller, remember I am not at home.

**MAID:** *(in the doorway)* A lady to see you, ma'am,—a stranger.

**NORA:** Ask her to come in.

**MAID:** *(to* HELMER*)* The doctor came at the same time, sir.

**HELMER:** Did he go straight into my room?

**MAID:** Yes, sir.

(HELMER *goes into his room. The* MAID *ushers in* MRS. LINDE, *who is in travelling dress, and shuts the door.)*

**MRS. LINDE:** *(in a dejected and timid voice)* How do you do, Nora?

**NORA:** *(doubtfully)* How do you do—

**MRS. LINDE:** You don't recognise me, I suppose.

**NORA:** No, I don't know—yes, to be sure, I seem to—*(Suddenly.)* Yes! Christine! Is it really you?

**MRS. LINDE:** Yes, it is I.

**NORA:** Christine! To think of my not recognising you! And yet how could I— *(In a gentle voice.)* How you have altered, Christine!

**MRS. LINDE:** Yes, I have indeed. In nine, ten long years—

**NORA:** Is it so long since we met? I suppose it is. The last eight years have been a happy time for me, I can tell you. And so now you have come into the town, and have taken this long journey in winter—that was plucky of you.

**MRS. LINDE:** I arrived by steamer this morning.

**NORA:** To have some fun at Christmas-time, of course. How delightful! We will have such fun together! But take off your things. You're not cold, I hope. *(Helps her.)* Now we will sit down by the stove, and be cosy. No, take this arm-chair; I will sit here in the rocking-chair. *(Takes her hands.)* Now you look like your old self again; it was only the first moment—You are a little paler, Christine, and perhaps a little thinner.

**MRS. LINDE:** And much, much older, Nora.

**NORA:** Perhaps a little older; very, very little; certainly not much. *(Stops suddenly and speaks seriously.)* What a thoughtless creature I am, chattering away like this. My poor, dear Christine, do forgive me.

**MRS. LINDE:** What do you mean, Nora?

**NORA:** *(gently)* Poor Christine, you are a widow.

**MRS. LINDE:** Yes; it is three years ago now.

**NORA:** Yes, I knew; I saw it in the papers. I assure you, Christine, I meant ever so often to write to you at the time, but I always put it off and something always prevented me.

**MRS. LINDE:** I quite understand, dear.

**NORA:** It was very bad of me, Christine. Poor thing, how you must have suffered. And he left you nothing?

**MRS. LINDE:** No.

**NORA:** And no children?

**MRS. LINDE:** No.

**NORA:** Nothing at all, then.

**MRS. LINDE:** Not even any sorrow or grief to live upon.

**NORA:** *(looking incredulously at her)* But Christine, is that possible?

**MRS. LINDE:** *(smiles sadly and strokes her hair)* It sometimes happens, Nora.

**NORA:** So you are quite alone. How dreadfully sad that must be. I have three lovely children. You can't see them just now, for they are out with their nurse. But now you must tell me all about it.

**MRS. LINDE:** No, no; I want to hear about you.

**NORA:** No, you must begin. I mustn't be selfish to-day; to-day I must only think of your affairs. But there is one thing I must tell you. Do you know we have just had a great piece of good luck?

**MRS. LINDE:** No, what is it?

**NORA:** Just fancy, my husband has been made manager of the Bank!

**MRS. LINDE:** Your husband? What good luck!

**NORA:** Yes, tremendous! A barrister's profession is such an uncertain thing, especially if he won't undertake unsavoury cases; and naturally Torvald has never been willing to do that, and I quite agree with him. You may imagine how pleased we are! He is to take up his work in the Bank at the New Year, and then he will have a big salary and lots of commissions. For the future we can live quite differently—we can do just as we like. I feel so relieved and so happy, Christine! It will be splendid to have heaps of money and not need to have any anxiety, won't it?

**MRS. LINDE:** Yes, anyhow I think it would be delightful to have what one needs.

**NORA:** No, not only what one needs, but heaps and heaps of money.

**MRS. LINDE:** *(smiling)* Nora, Nora, haven't you learnt sense yet? In our schooldays you were a great spendthrift.

**NORA:** *(laughing)* Yes, that is what Torvald says now. *(Wags her finger at her.)* But "Nora, Nora" is not so silly as you think. We have not been in a position for me to waste money. We have both had to work.

**MRS. LINDE:** You too?

**NORA:** Yes; odds and ends, needlework, crotchet-work, embroidery, and that kind of thing. *(Dropping her voice.)* And other things as well. You know Torvald left his office when we were married? There was no prospect of promotion there, and he had to try and earn more than before. But during the first year he over-worked himself dreadfully. You see, he had to make money every way he could, and he worked early and late; but he couldn't stand it, and fell dreadfully ill, and the doctors said it was necessary for him to go south.

**MRS. LINDE:** You spent a whole year in Italy, didn't you?

**NORA:** Yes. It was no easy matter to get away, I can tell you. It was just after Ivar was born; but naturally we had to go. It was a wonderfully beautiful journey, and it saved Torvald's life. But it cost a tremendous lot of money, Christine.

**MRS. LINDE:** So I should think.

**NORA:** It cost about two hundred and fifty pounds. That's a lot, isn't it?

**MRS. LINDE:** Yes, and in emergencies like that it is lucky to have the money.

**NORA:** I ought to tell you that we had it from papa.

**MRS. LINDE:** Oh, I see. It was just about that time that he died, wasn't it?

**NORA:** Yes; and, just think of it, I couldn't go and nurse him. I was expecting little Ivar's birth every day and I had my poor sick Torvald to look after. My dear, kind father—I never saw him again, Christine. That was the saddest time I have known since our marriage.

**MRS. LINDE:** I know how fond you were of him. And then you went off to Italy?

**NORA:** Yes; you see we had money then, and the doctors insisted on our going, so we started a month later.

**MRS. LINDE:** And your husband came back quite well?

**NORA:** As sound as a bell!

**MRS. LINDE:** But—the doctor?

Nora (Juliet Stevenson) catches up with Mrs. Linde (Geraldine James) in the 1992 film directed by David Thacker.

**NORA:** What doctor?

**MRS. LINDE:** I thought your maid said the gentleman who arrived here just as I did, was the doctor?

**NORA:** Yes, that was Doctor Rank, but he doesn't come here professionally. He is our greatest friend, and comes in at least once every day. No, Torvald has not had an hour's illness since then, and our children are strong and healthy and so am I. *(Jumps up and claps her hands.)* Christine! Christine! it's good to be alive and happy!—But how horrid of me; I am talking of nothing but my own affairs. *(Sits on a stool near her, and rests her arms on her knees.)* You mustn't be angry with me. Tell me, is it really true that you did not love your husband? Why did you marry him?

**MRS. LINDE:** My mother was alive then, and was bedridden and helpless, and I had to provide for my two younger brothers; so I did not think I was justified in refusing his offer.

**NORA:** No, perhaps you were quite right. He was rich at that time, then?

**MRS. LINDE:** I believe he was quite well off. But his business was a precarious one; and, when he died, it all went to pieces and there was nothing left.

**NORA:** And then?—

**MRS. LINDE:** Well, I had to turn my hand to anything I could find—first a small shop, then a small school, and so on. The last three years have seemed like one long working-day, with no rest. Now it is at an end, Nora. My poor mother needs me no more, for she is gone; and the boys do not need me either; they have got situations and can shift for themselves.

**NORA:** What a relief you must feel it—

**MRS. LINDE:** No, indeed; I only feel my life unspeakably empty. No one to live for any more. *(Gets up restlessly.)* That was why I could not stand the life in my little backwater any longer. I hope it may be easier here to find something which will busy me and occupy my thoughts. If only I could have the good luck to get some regular work—office work of some kind—

**NORA:** But, Christine, that is so frightfully tiring, and you look tired out now. You had far better go away to some watering-place.

**MRS. LINDE:** *(walking to the window)* I have no father to give me money for a journey, Nora.

**NORA:** *(rising)* Oh, don't be angry with me.

**MRS. LINDE:** *(going up to her)* It is you that must not be angry with me, dear. The worst of a position like mine is that it makes one so bitter. No one to work for, and yet obliged to be always on the look-out for chances. One must live, and so one becomes selfish. When you told me of the happy turn your fortunes have taken—you will hardly believe it—I was delighted not so much on your account as on my own.

**NORA:** How do you mean?—Oh, I understand. You mean that perhaps Torvald could get you something to do.

**MRS. LINDE:** Yes, that was what I was thinking of.

**NORA:** He must, Christine. Just leave it to me; I will broach the subject very cleverly—I will think of something that will please him very much. It will make me so happy to be of some use to you.

**MRS. LINDE:** How kind you are, Nora, to be so anxious to help me! It is doubly kind in you, for you know so little of the burdens and troubles of life.

**NORA:** I—? I know so little of them?

**MRS. LINDE:** *(smiling)* My dear! Small household cares and that sort of thing!—You are a child, Nora.

**NORA:** *(tosses her head and crosses the stage)* You ought not to be so superior.

**MRS. LINDE:** No?

**NORA:** You are just like the others. They all think that I am incapable of anything really serious—

**MRS. LINDE:** Come, come—

**NORA:** —that I have gone through nothing in this world of cares.

**MRS. LINDE:** But, my dear Nora, you have just told me all your troubles.

**NORA:** Pooh!—those were trifles. *(Lowering her voice.)* I have not told you the important thing.

**MRS. LINDE:** The important thing? What do you mean?

**NORA:** You look down upon me altogether, Christine—but you ought not to. You are proud, aren't you, of having worked so hard and so long for your mother?

**MRS. LINDE:** Indeed, I don't look down on any one. But it is true that I am both proud and glad to think that I was privileged to make the end of my mother's life almost free from care.

**NORA:** And you are proud to think of what you have done for your brothers.

**MRS. LINDE:** I think I have the right to be.

**NORA:** I think so, too. But now listen to this; I too have something to be proud and glad of.

**MRS. LINDE:** I have no doubt you have. But what do you refer to?

**NORA:** Speak low. Suppose Torvald were to hear! He mustn't on any account—no one in the world must know, Christine, except you.

**MRS. LINDE:** But what is it?

**NORA:** Come here. *(Pulls her down on the sofa beside her.)* Now I will show you that I too have something to be proud and glad of. It was I who saved Torvald's life.

**MRS. LINDE:** "Saved"? How?

**NORA:** I told you about our trip to Italy. Torvald would never have recovered if he had not gone there—

**MRS. LINDE:** Yes, but your father gave you the necessary funds.

**NORA:** *(smiling)* Yes, that is what Torvald and all the others think, but—

**MRS. LINDE:** But—

**NORA:** Papa didn't give us a shilling. It was I who procured the money.

**MRS. LINDE:** You? All that large sum?

**NORA:** Two hundred and fifty pounds. What do you think of that?

**MRS. LINDE:** But, Nora, how could you possibly do it? Did you win a prize in the Lottery?

**NORA:** *(contemptuously)* In the Lottery? There would have been no credit in that.

**MRS. LINDE:** But where did you get it from, then?

**NORA:** *(humming and smiling with an air of mystery)* Hm, hm! Aha!

**MRS. LINDE:** Because you couldn't have borrowed it.

**NORA:** Couldn't I? Why not?

**MRS. LINDE:** No, a wife cannot borrow without her husband's consent.

**NORA:** *(tossing her head)* Oh, if it is a wife who has any head for business—a wife who has the wit to be a little bit clever—

**MRS. LINDE:** I don't understand it at all, Nora.

**NORA:** There is no need you should. I never said I had borrowed the money. I may have got it some other way. *(Lies back on the sofa.)* Perhaps I got it from some other admirer. When anyone is as attractive as I am—

**MRS. LINDE:** You are a mad creature.

**NORA:** Now, you know you're full of curiosity, Christine.

**MRS. LINDE:** Listen to me, Nora dear. Haven't you been a little bit imprudent?

**NORA:** *(sits up straight)* Is it imprudent to save your husband's life?

**MRS. LINDE:** It seems to me imprudent, without his knowledge, to—

**NORA:** But it was absolutely necessary that he should not know! My goodness, can't you understand that? It was necessary he should have no idea what a dangerous condition he was in. It was to me that the doctors came and said that his life was in danger, and that the only thing to save him was to live in the south. Do you suppose I didn't try, first of all, to get what I wanted as if it were for myself? I told him how much I should love to travel abroad like other young wives; I tried tears and entreaties with him; I told him that he ought to remember the condition I was in, and that he ought to be kind and indulgent to me; I even hinted that he might raise a loan. That nearly made him angry, Christine. He said I was thoughtless, and that it was his duty as my husband not to indulge me in my whims and caprices—as I believe he called them. Very well, I thought, you must be saved—and that was how I came to devise a way out of the difficulty—

**MRS. LINDE:** And did your husband never get to know from your father that the money had not come from him?

**NORA:** No, never. Papa died just at that time. I had meant to let him into the secret and beg him never to reveal it. But he was so ill then—alas, there never was any need to tell him.

**MRS. LINDE:** And since then have you never told your secret to your husband?

**NORA:** Good Heavens, no! How could you think so? A man who has such strong opinions about these things! And besides, how painful and humiliating it would be for Torvald, with his manly independence, to know that he owed me anything! It would upset our mutual relations altogether; our beautiful happy home would no longer be what it is now.

**MRS. LINDE:** Do you mean never to tell him about it?

**NORA:** *(meditatively, and with a half smile)* Yes—some day, perhaps, after many years, when I am no longer as nice-looking as I am now. Don't laugh at me! I mean, of course, when Torvald is no longer as devoted to me as he is now; when my dancing and dressing-up and reciting have palled on him; then it may be a good thing to have something in reserve— *(Breaking off.)* What nonsense! That time will never come. Now, what do you think of my great secret, Christine? Do you still think I am of no use? I can tell you, too, that this affair has caused me a lot of worry. It has been by no means easy for me to meet my engagements punctually. I may tell you that there is something that is called, in business, quarterly interest, and another thing called payment in instalments, and it is always so dreadfully difficult to manage them. I have had to save a little here and there, where I could, you understand. I have not been able to put aside much from my housekeeping money, for Torvald must have a good table. I couldn't let my children be shabbily dressed; I have felt obliged to use up all he gave me for them, the sweet little darlings!

**MRS. LINDE:** So it has all had to come out of your own necessaries of life, poor Nora?

**NORA:** Of course. Besides, I was the one responsible for it. Whenever Torvald has given me money for new dresses and such things, I have never spent more than half of it; I have always bought the simplest and cheapest things. Thank Heaven, any clothes look well on me, and so Torvald has never noticed it. But it was often very hard on me, Christine—because it is delightful to be really well dressed, isn't it?

**MRS. LINDE:** Quite so.

**NORA:** Well, then I have found other ways of earning money. Last winter I was lucky enough to get a lot of copying to do; so I locked myself up and sat writing every evening until quite late at night. Many a time I was desperately tired; but all the same it was a tremendous pleasure to sit there working and earning money. It was like being a man.

**MRS. LINDE:** How much have you been able to pay off in that way?

**NORA:** I can't tell you exactly. You see, it is very difficult to keep an account of a business matter of that kind. I only know that I have paid every penny that I could scrape together. Many a time I was at my wit's end. *(Smiles.)* Then I used to sit here and imagine that a rich old gentleman had fallen in love with me—

**MRS. LINDE:** What! Who was it?

**NORA:** Be quiet!—that he had died; and that when his will was opened it contained, written in big letters, the instruction: "The lovely Mrs. Nora Helmer is to have all I possess paid over to her at once in cash."

**MRS. LINDE:** But, my dear Nora—who could the man be?

**NORA:** Good gracious, can't you understand? There was no old gentleman at all; it was only something that I used to sit here and imagine, when I couldn't think of any way of procuring money. But it's all the same now; the tiresome old person can stay where he is, as far as I am concerned; I don't care about him or his will either, for I am free from care now. *(Jumps up.)* My goodness, it's delightful to think of, Christine! Free from care! To be able to be free from care, quite free from care; to be able to play and romp with the children; to be able to keep the house beautifully and have everything just as Torvald likes it! And, think of it, soon the spring will come and the big blue sky! Perhaps we shall be able to take a little trip—perhaps I shall see the sea again! Oh, it's a wonderful thing to be alive and be happy. *(A bell is heard in the hall.)*

**MRS. LINDE:** *(rising)* There is the bell; perhaps I had better go.

**NORA:** No, don't go; no one will come in here; it is sure to be for Torvald.

**SERVANT:** *(at the hall door)* Excuse me, ma'am—there is a gentleman to see the master, and as the doctor is with him—

**NORA:** Who is it?

Nora tells Mrs. Linde (Anna Massey) about her troubles.

**KROGSTAD:** *(at the door)* It is I, Mrs. Helmer. *(*MRS. LINDE *starts, trembles, and turns to the window.)*

**NORA:** *(takes a step towards him, and speaks in a strained, low voice)* You? What is it? What do you want to see my husband about?

**KROGSTAD:** Bank business—in a way. I have a small post in the Bank, and I hear your husband is to be our chief now—

**NORA:** Then it is—

**KROGSTAD:** Nothing but dry business matters, Mrs. Helmer; absolutely nothing else.

**NORA:** Be so good as to go into the study, then. *(She bows indifferently to him and shuts the door into the hall; then comes back and makes up the fire in the stove.)*

**MRS. LINDE:** Nora—who was that man?

**NORA:** A lawyer, of the name of Krogstad.

**MRS. LINDE:** Then it really was he.

**NORA:** Do you know the man?

**MRS. LINDE:** I used to—many years ago. At one time he was a solicitor's clerk in our town.

**NORA:** Yes, he was.

**MRS. LINDE:** He is greatly altered.

**NORA:** He made a very unhappy marriage.

**MRS. LINDE:** He is a widower now, isn't he?

**NORA:** With several children. There now, it is burning up. *(Shuts the door of the stove and moves the rocking-chair aside.)*

**MRS. LINDE:** They say he carries on various kinds of business.

**NORA:** Really! Perhaps he does; I don't know anything about it. But don't let us think of business; it is so tiresome.

**DOCTOR RANK:** *(comes out of* HELMER*'s study. Before he shuts the door he calls to him)* No, my dear fellow, I won't disturb you; I would rather go in to your wife for a little while. *(Shuts the door and sees* MRS. LINDE.*)* I beg your pardon; I am afraid I am disturbing you too.

**NORA:** No, not at all. *(Introducing him.)* Doctor Rank, Mrs. Linde.

**RANK:** I have often heard Mrs. Linde's name mentioned here. I think I passed you on the stairs when I arrived, Mrs. Linde?

**MRS. LINDE:** Yes, I go up very slowly; I can't manage stairs well.

**RANK:** Ah! some slight internal weakness?

**MRS. LINDE:** No, the fact is I have been overworking myself.

**RANK:** Nothing more than that? Then I suppose you have come to town to amuse yourself with our entertainments?

**MRS. LINDE:** I have come to look for work.

**RANK:** Is that a good cure for overwork?

**MRS. LINDE:** One must live, Doctor Rank.

**RANK:** Yes, the general opinion seems to be that it is necessary.

**NORA:** Look here, Doctor Rank—you know you want to live.

**RANK:** Certainly. However wretched I may feel, I want to prolong the agony as long as possible. All my patients are like that. And so are those who are morally diseased; one of them, and a bad case too, is at this very moment with Helmer—

**MRS. LINDE:** *(sadly)* Ah!

**NORA:** Whom do you mean?

**RANK:** A lawyer of the name of Krogstad, a fellow you don't know at all. He suffers from a diseased moral character, Mrs. Helmer; but even he began talking of its being highly important that he should live.

**NORA:** Did he? What did he want to speak to Torvald about?

**RANK:** I have no idea; I only heard that it was something about the Bank.

**NORA:** I didn't know this—what's his name—Krogstad had anything to do with the Bank.

**RANK:** Yes, he has some sort of appointment there. *(To* MRS. LINDE.*)* I don't know whether you find also in your part of the world that there are certain people who go zealously snuffing about to smell out moral corruption, and, as soon as they have found some, put the person concerned into some lucrative position where they can keep their eye on him. Healthy natures are left out in the cold.

**MRS. LINDE:** Still I think the sick are those who most need taking care of.

**RANK:** *(shrugging his shoulders)* Yes, there you are. That is the sentiment that is turning Society into a sick-house.

Nora, Mrs. Linde, and Dr. Rank (Ralph Richardson) chat about Torvald and Krogstad.

*(NORA, who has been absorbed in her thoughts, breaks out into smothered laughter and claps her hands.)*

**RANK:** Why do you laugh at that? Have you any notion what Society really is?

**NORA:** What do I care about tiresome Society? I am laughing at something quite different, something extremely amusing. Tell me, Doctor Rank, are all the people who are employed in the Bank dependent on Torvald now?

**RANK:** Is that what you find so extremely amusing?

**NORA:** *(smiling and humming)* That's my affair! *(Walking about the room.)* It's perfectly glorious to think that we have—that Torvald has so much power over so many people. *(Takes the packet from her pocket.)* Doctor Rank, what do you say to a macaroon?

**RANK:** What, macaroons? I thought they were forbidden here.

**NORA:** Yes, but these are some Christine gave me.

**MRS. LINDE:** What! I?—

**NORA:** Oh, well, don't be alarmed! You couldn't know that Torvald had forbidden them. I must tell you that he is afraid they will spoil my teeth. But, bah!—once in a way—That's so, isn't it, Doctor Rank? By your leave! *(Puts a macaroon into his mouth.)* You must have one too, Christine. And I shall have one, just a little one—or at most two. *(Walking about.)* I am tremendously happy. There is just one thing in the world now that I should dearly love to do.

**RANK:** Well, what is that?

**NORA:** It's something I should dearly love to say, if Torvald could hear me.

**RANK:** Well, why can't you say it?

**NORA:** No, I daren't; it's so shocking.

**MRS. LINDE:** Shocking?

**RANK:** Well, I should not advise you to say it. Still, with us you might. What is it you would so much like to say if Torvald could hear you?

**NORA:** I should just love to say—Well, I'm damned!

**RANK:** Are you mad?

**MRS. LINDE:** Nora, dear—!

**RANK:** Say it, here he is!

**NORA:** *(hiding the packet)* Hush! Hush! Hush! *(HELMER comes out of his room, with his coat over his arm and his hat in his hand.)*

**NORA:** Well, Torvald dear, have you got rid of him?

**HELMER:** Yes, he has just gone.

**NORA:** Let me introduce you—this is Christine, who has come to town.

**HELMER:** Christine—? Excuse me, but I don't know—

**NORA:** Mrs. Linde, dear; Christine Linde.

**HELMER:** Of course. A school friend of my wife's, I presume?

**MRS. LINDE:** Yes, we have known each other since then.

**NORA:** And just think, she has taken a long journey in order to see you.

**HELMER:** What do you mean?

**MRS. LINDE:** No, really, I—

**NORA:** Christine is tremendously clever at book-keeping, and she is frightfully anxious to work under some clever man, so as to perfect herself—

**HELMER:** Very sensible, Mrs. Linde.

**NORA:** And when she heard you had been appointed manager of the Bank—the news was telegraphed, you know—she travelled here as quick as she could. Torvald, I am sure you will be able to do something for Christine, for my sake, won't you?

**HELMER:** Well, it is not altogether impossible. I presume you are a widow, Mrs. Linde?

**MRS. LINDE:** Yes.

**HELMER:** And have had some experience of book-keeping?

**MRS. LINDE:** Yes, a fair amount.

**HELMER:** Ah! well, it's very likely I may be able to find something for you—

**NORA:** *(clapping her hands)* What did I tell you? What did I tell you?

**HELMER:** You have just come at a fortunate moment, Mrs. Linde.

**MRS. LINDE:** How am I to thank you?

**HELMER:** There is no need. *(Puts on his coat.)* But to-day you must excuse me—

**RANK:** Wait a minute; I will come with you. *(Brings his fur coat from the hall and warms it at the fire.)*

**NORA:** Don't be long away, Torvald dear.

**HELMER:** About an hour, not more.

**NORA:** Are you going too, Christine?

**MRS. LINDE:** *(putting on her cloak)* Yes, I must go and look for a room.

**HELMER:** Oh, well then, we can walk down the street together.

**NORA:** *(helping her)* What a pity it is we are so short of space here; I am afraid it is impossible for us—

**MRS. LINDE:** Please don't think of it! Good-bye, Nora dear, and many thanks.

**NORA:** Good-bye for the present. Of course you will come back this evening. And you too, Dr. Rank. What do you say? If you are well enough? Oh, you must be! Wrap yourself up well. *(They go to the door all talking together. Children's voices are heard on the staircase.)*

**NORA:** There they are! There they are! *(She runs to open the door. The* NURSE *comes in with the children.)* Come in! Come in! *(Stoops and kisses them.)* Oh, you sweet blessings! Look at them, Christine. Aren't they darlings?

**RANK:** Don't let us stand here in the draught.

**HELMER:** Come along, Mrs. Linde; the place will only be bearable for a mother now!

*(*RANK, HELMER, *and* MRS. LINDE *go downstairs. The* NURSE *comes forward with the children;* NORA *shuts the hall door.)*

**NORA:** How fresh and well you look! Such red cheeks!—like apples and roses. *(The children all talk at once while she speaks to them.)* Have you had great fun? That's splendid! What, you pulled both Emmy and Bob along on the sledge?—both at once?—that *was* good. You are a clever boy, Ivar. Let me take her for a little, Anne. My sweet little baby doll! *(Takes the baby from the* MAID *and dances it up and down.)* Yes, yes, mother will dance with Bob too. What? Have you been snowballing? I wish I had been there too! No, no, I will take their things off, Anne; please let me do it, it is such fun. Go in now, you look half frozen. There is some hot coffee for you on the stove.

Torvald greets Mrs. Linde.

*(The* NURSE *goes into the room on the left.* NORA *takes off the children's things and throws them about, while they all talk to her at once.)*

**NORA:** Really? Did a big dog run after you? But it didn't bite you? No, dogs don't bite nice little dolly children. You mustn't look at the parcels, Ivar. What are they? Ah, I daresay you would like to know. No, no—it's something nasty! Come, let us have a game! What shall we play at? Hide and Seek? Yes, we'll play Hide and Seek. Bob shall hide first. Must I hide? Very well, I'll hide first. *(She and the children laugh and shout, and romp in and out of the room; at last* NORA *hides under the table, the children rush in and out for her, but do not see her; they hear her smothered laughter, run to the table, lift up the cloth and find her. Shouts of laughter. She crawls forward and pretends to frighten them. Fresh laughter. Meanwhile there has been a knock at the hall door, but none of them has noticed it. The door is half opened, and* KROGSTAD *appears. He waits a little; the game goes on.)*

**KROGSTAD:** Excuse me, Mrs. Helmer.

**NORA:** *(with a stifled cry, turns round and gets up on to her knees)* Ah! what do you want?

**KROGSTAD:** Excuse me, the outer door was ajar; I suppose someone forgot to shut it.

**NORA:** *(rising)* My husband is out, Mr. Krogstad.

**KROGSTAD:** I know that.

**NORA:** What do you want here, then?

**KROGSTAD:** A word with you.

**NORA:** With me?— *(To the children, gently.)* Go in to nurse. What? No, the strange man won't do mother any harm. When he has gone we will have another game. *(She takes the children into the room on the left, and shuts the door after them.)* You want to speak to me?

**KROGSTAD:** Yes, I do.

**NORA:** To-day? It is not the first of the month yet.

**KROGSTAD:** No, it is Christmas Eve, and it will depend on yourself what sort of a Christmas you will spend.

**NORA:** What do you mean? To-day it is absolutely impossible for me—

**KROGSTAD:** We won't talk about that till later on. This is something different. I presume you can give me a moment?

**NORA:** Yes—yes, I can—although—

**KROGSTAD:** Good. I was in Olsen's Restaurant and saw your husband going down the street—

**NORA:** Yes?

**KROGSTAD:** With a lady.

**NORA:** What then?

**KROGSTAD:** May I make so bold as to ask if it was a Mrs. Linde?

**NORA:** It was.

**KROGSTAD:** Just arrived in town?

**NORA:** Yes, to-day.

**KROGSTAD:** She is a great friend of yours, isn't she?

**NORA:** She is. But I don't see—

**KROGSTAD:** I knew her too, once upon a time.

**NORA:** I am aware of that.

**KROGSTAD:** Are you? So you know all about it; I thought as much. Then I can ask you, without beating about the bush—is Mrs. Linde to have an appointment in the Bank?

**NORA:** What right have you to question me, Mr. Krogstad?—You, one of my husband's subordinates! But since you ask, you shall know. Yes, Mrs. Linde *is* to have an appointment. And it was I who pleaded her cause, Mr. Krogstad, let me tell you that.

**KROGSTAD:** I was right in what I thought, then.

**NORA:** *(walking up and down the stage)* Sometimes one has a tiny little bit of influence, I should hope. Because one is a woman, it does not necessarily follow that—. When anyone is in a subordinate position, Mr. Krogstad, they should really be careful to avoid offending anyone who—who—

**KROGSTAD:** Who has influence?

**NORA:** Exactly.

**KROGSTAD:** *(changing his tone)* Mrs. Helmer, you will be so good as to use your influence on my behalf.

**NORA:** What? What do you mean?

**KROGSTAD:** You will be so kind as to see that I am allowed to keep my subordinate position in the Bank.

**NORA:** What do you mean by that? Who proposes to take your post away from you?

**KROGSTAD:** Oh, there is no necessity to keep up the pretence of ignorance. I can quite understand that your friend is not very anxious to expose herself to the chance of rubbing shoulders with me; and I quite understand, too, whom I have to thank for being turned off.

**NORA:** But I assure you—

**KROGSTAD:** Very likely; but, to come to the point, the time has come when I should advise you to use your influence to prevent that.

**NORA:** But, Mr. Krogstad, I *have* no influence.

**KROGSTAD:** Haven't you? I thought you said yourself just now—

**NORA:** Naturally I did not mean you to put that construction on it. I! What should make you think I have any influence of that kind with my husband?

**KROGSTAD:** Oh, I have known your husband from our student days. I don't suppose he is any more unassailable than other husbands.

**NORA:** If you speak slightingly of my husband, I shall turn you out of the house.

**KROGSTAD:** You are bold, Mrs. Helmer.

**NORA:** I am not afraid of you any longer. As soon as the New Year comes, I shall in a very short time be free of the whole thing.

**KROGSTAD:** *(controlling himself)* Listen to me, Mrs. Helmer. If necessary, I am prepared to fight for my small post in the Bank as if I were fighting for my life.

**NORA:** So it seems.

**KROGSTAD:** It is not only for the sake of the money; indeed, that weighs least with me in the matter. There is another reason—well, I may as well tell you. My position is this. I daresay you know, like everybody else, that once, many years ago, I was guilty of an indiscretion.

**NORA:** I think I have heard something of the kind.

**KROGSTAD:** The matter never came into court; but every way seemed to be closed to me after that. So I took to the business that you know of. I had to do something; and, honestly, I don't think I've been one of the worst. But now I must cut myself free from all that. My sons are growing up; for their sake I must try and win back as much respect as I can in the town. This post in the Bank was like the first step up for me—and now your husband is going to kick me downstairs again into the mud.

**NORA:** But you must believe me, Mr. Krogstad; it is not in my power to help you at all.

**KROGSTAD:** Then it is because you haven't the will; but I have means to compel you.

**NORA:** You don't mean that you will tell my husband that I owe you money?

**KROGSTAD:** Hm!—suppose I were to tell him?

Krogstad (David Calder) confronts Nora with the discrepancy in her father's signature.

**NORA:** It would be perfectly infamous of you. *(Sobbing.)* To think of his learning my secret, which has been my joy and pride, in such an ugly, clumsy way—that he should learn it from you! And it would put me in a horribly disagreeable position—

**KROGSTAD:** Only disagreeable?

**NORA:** *(impetuously)* Well, do it, then!—and it will be the worse for you. My husband will see for himself what a blackguard you are, and you certainly won't keep your post then.

**KROGSTAD:** I asked you if it was only a disagreeable scene at home that you were afraid of?

**NORA:** If my husband does get to know of it, of course he will at once pay you what is still owing, and we shall have nothing more to do with you.

**KROGSTAD:** *(coming a step nearer)* Listen to me, Mrs. Helmer. Either you have a very bad memory or you know very little of business. I shall be obliged to remind you of a few details.

**NORA:** What do you mean?

**KROGSTAD:** When your husband was ill, you came to me to borrow two hundred and fifty pounds.

**NORA:** I didn't know anyone else to go to.

**KROGSTAD:** I promised to get you that amount—

**NORA:** Yes, and you did so.

**KROGSTAD:** I promised to get you that amount, on certain conditions. Your mind was so taken up with your husband's illness, and you were so anxious to get the money for your journey, that you seem to have paid no attention to the conditions of our bargain. Therefore it will not be amiss if I remind you of them. Now, I promised to get the money on the security of a bond which I drew up.

**NORA:** Yes, and which I signed.

**KROGSTAD:** Good. But below your signature there were a few lines constituting your father a surety for the money; those lines your father should have signed.

**NORA:** Should? He did sign them.

**KROGSTAD:** I had left the date blank; that is to say, your father should himself have inserted the date on which he signed the paper. Do you remember that?

**NORA:** Yes, I think I remember—

**KROGSTAD:** Then I gave you the bond to send by post to your father. Is that not so?

**NORA:** Yes.

**KROGSTAD:** And you naturally did so at once, because five or six days afterwards you brought me the bond with your father's signature. And then I gave you the money.

**NORA:** Well, haven't I been paying it off regularly?

**KROGSTAD:** Fairly so, yes. But—to come back to the matter in hand—that must have been a very trying time for you, Mrs. Helmer?

**NORA:** It was, indeed.

**KROGSTAD:** Your father was very ill, wasn't he?

**NORA:** He was very near his end.

**KROGSTAD:** He died soon afterwards?

**NORA:** Yes.

**KROGSTAD:** Tell me, Mrs. Helmer, can you by any chance remember what day your father died?—on what day of the month, I mean.

**NORA:** Papa died on the 29th of September.

**KROGSTAD:** That is correct; I have ascertained it for myself. And, as that is so, there is a discrepancy *(taking a paper from his pocket)* which I cannot account for.

**NORA:** What discrepancy? I don't know—

**KROGSTAD:** The discrepancy consists, Mrs. Helmer, in the fact that your father signed this bond three days after his death.

**NORA:** What do you mean? I don't understand—

**KROGSTAD:** Your father died on the 29th of September. But, look here; your father has dated his signature the 2nd of October. It is a discrepancy, isn't it? *(*NORA *is silent.)* Can you explain it to me? *(*NORA *is still silent.)* It is a remarkable thing, too, that the words "2nd of October" as well as the year, are not written in your father's handwriting but in one that I think I know. Well, of course it can be explained; your father may have forgotten to date his signature, and someone else may have dated it haphazard before they knew of his death. There is no harm in that. It all depends on the signature of the name; and *that* is genuine, I suppose, Mrs. Helmer? It was your father himself who signed his name here?

**NORA:** *(after a short pause, throws her head up and looks defiantly at him)* No, it was not. It was I that wrote papa's name.

**KROGSTAD:** Are you aware that is a dangerous confession?

**NORA:** In what way? You shall have your money soon.

**KROGSTAD:** Let me ask you a question; why did you not send the paper to your father?

**NORA:** It was impossible; papa was so ill. If I had asked him for his signature, I should have had to tell him what the money was to be used for; and when he was so ill himself I couldn't tell him that my husband's life was in danger—it was impossible.

**KROGSTAD:** It would have been better for you if you had given up your trip abroad.

**NORA:** No, that was impossible. That trip was to save my husband's life; I couldn't give that up.

**KROGSTAD:** But did it never occur to you that you were committing a fraud on me?

**NORA:** I couldn't take that into account; I didn't trouble myself about you at all. I couldn't bear you, because you put so many heartless difficulties in my way, although you knew what a dangerous condition my husband was in.

**KROGSTAD:** Mrs. Helmer, you evidently do not realise clearly what it is that you have been guilty of. But I can assure you that my one false step, which lost me all my reputation, was nothing more or nothing worse than what you have done.

**NORA:** You? Do you ask me to believe that you were brave enough to run a risk to save your wife's life?

**KROGSTAD:** The law cares nothing about motives.

**NORA:** Then it must be a very foolish law.

**KROGSTAD:** Foolish or not, it is the law by which you will be judged, if I produce this paper in court.

**NORA:** I don't believe it. Is a daughter not to be allowed to spare her dying father anxiety and care? Is a wife not to be allowed to save her husband's life? I don't know much about law; but I am certain that there must be laws permitting such things as that. Have you no knowledge of such laws—you who are a lawyer? You must be a very poor lawyer, Mr. Krogstad.

**KROGSTAD:** Maybe. But matters of business—such business as you and I have had together—do you think I don't understand that? Very well. Do as you please. But let me tell you this—if I lose my position a second time, you shall lose yours with me. *(He bows, and goes out through the hall.)*

**NORA:** *(appears buried in thought for a short time, then tosses her head)* Nonsense! Trying to frighten me like that!—I am not so silly as he thinks. *(Begins to busy* *herself putting the children's things in order.)* And yet—? No, it's impossible! I did it for love's sake.

**THE CHILDREN:** *(in the doorway on the left)* Mother, the stranger man has gone out through the gate.

**NORA:** Yes, dears, I know. But, don't tell anyone about the stranger man. Do you hear? Not even papa.

**CHILDREN:** No, mother; but will you come and play again?

**NORA:** No, no,—not now.

**CHILDREN:** But, mother, you promised us.

**NORA:** Yes, but I can't now. Run away in; I have such a lot to do. Run away in, my sweet little darlings. *(She gets them into the room by degrees and shuts the door on them; then sits down on the sofa, takes up a piece of needle-work and sews a few stitches, but soon stops.)* No! *(Throws down the work, gets up, goes to the hall door and calls out.)* Helen! bring the Tree in. *(Goes to the table on the left, opens a drawer, and stops again.)* No, no! it is quite impossible!

**MAID:** *(coming in with the Tree)* Where shall I put it, ma'am?

**NORA:** Here, in the middle of the floor.

**MAID:** Shall I get you anything else?

**NORA:** No, thank you. I have all I want.

*(Exit* MAID.*)*

**NORA:** *(begins dressing the tree)* A candle here—and flowers here—. The horrible man! It's all nonsense—there's nothing wrong. The Tree shall be splendid! I will do everything I can think of to please you, Torvald!—I will sing for you, dance for you— *(*HELMER *comes in with some papers under his arm.)* Oh! are you back already?

**HELMER:** Yes. Has any one been here?

**NORA:** Here? No.

**HELMER:** That is strange. I saw Krogstad going out of the gate.

**NORA:** Did you? Oh yes, I forgot, Krogstad was here for a moment.

**HELMER:** Nora, I can see from your manner that he has been here begging you to say a good word for him.

**NORA:** Yes.

**HELMER:** And you were to appear to do it of your own accord; you were to conceal from me the fact of his having been here; didn't he beg that of you too?

**NORA:** Yes, Torvald, but—

**HELMER:** Nora, Nora, and you would be a party to that sort of thing? To have any talk with a man like that, and give him any sort of promise? And to tell me a lie into the bargain?

**NORA:** A lie—?

**HELMER:** Didn't you tell me no one had been here? *(Shakes his finger at her).* My little song-bird must never do that again. A song-bird must have a clean beak to chirp with—no false notes! *(Puts his arm round her waist.)* That is so, isn't it? Yes, I am sure it is. *(Lets her go.)* We will say no more about it. *(Sits down by the stove.)* How warm and snug it is here! *(Turns over his papers.)*

**NORA:** *(after a short pause, during which she busies herself with the Christmas Tree)* Torvald!

**HELMER:** Yes.

**NORA:** I am looking forward tremendously to the fancy-dress ball at the Stenborgs' the day after to-morrow.

**HELMER:** And I am tremendously curious to see what you are going to surprise me with.

**NORA:** It was very silly of me to want to do that.

**HELMER:** What do you mean?

**NORA:** I can't hit upon anything that will do; everything I think of seems so silly and insignificant.

**HELMER:** Does my little Nora acknowledge that at last?

**NORA:** *(standing behind his chair with her arms on the back of it)* Are you very busy, Torvald?

**HELMER:** Well—

**NORA:** What are all those papers?

**HELMER:** Bank business.

**NORA:** Already?

**HELMER:** I have got authority from the retiring manager to undertake the necessary changes in the staff and in the rearrangement of the work; and I must make use of the Christmas week for that, so as to have everything in order for the new year.

**NORA:** Then that was why this poor Krogstad—

**HELMER:** Hm!

**NORA:** *(leans against the back of his chair and strokes his hair)* If you hadn't been so busy I should have asked you a tremendously big favour, Torvald.

**HELMER:** What is that? Tell me.

Nora and Torvald (Trevor Eve) discuss Krogstad's visit.

**NORA:** There is no one has such good taste as you. And I do so want to look nice at the fancy-dress ball. Torvald, couldn't you take me in hand and decide what I shall go as, and what sort of a dress I shall wear?

**HELMER:** Aha! so my obstinate little woman is obliged to get someone to come to her rescue?

**NORA:** Yes, Torvald, I can't get along a bit without your help.

**HELMER:** Very well, I will think it over, we shall manage to hit upon something.

**NORA:** That is nice of you. *(Goes to the Christmas Tree. A short pause.)* How pretty the red flowers look—. But, tell me, was it really something very bad that this Krogstad was guilty of?

**HELMER:** He forged someone's name. Have you any idea what that means?

**NORA:** Isn't it possible that he was driven to do it by necessity?

**HELMER:** Yes; or, as in so many cases, by imprudence. I am not so heartless as to condemn a man altogether because of a single false step of that kind.

**NORA:** No, you wouldn't, would you, Torvald!

**HELMER:** Many a man has been able to retrieve his character, if he has openly confessed his fault and taken his punishment.

**NORA:** Punishment—?

**HELMER:** But Krogstad did nothing of that sort; he got himself out of it by a cunning trick, and that is why he has gone under altogether.

**NORA:** But do you think it would—?

**HELMER:** Just think how a guilty man like that has to lie and play the hypocrite with every one, how he has to wear a mask in the presence of those near and dear to him, even before his own wife and children. And about the children—that is the most terrible part of it all, Nora.

**NORA:** How?

**HELMER:** Because such an atmosphere of lies infects and poisons the whole life of a home. Each breath the children take in such a house is full of the germs of evil.

**NORA:** *(coming nearer him)* Are you sure of that?

**HELMER:** My dear, I have often seen it in the course of my life as a lawyer. Almost everyone who has gone to the bad early in life has had a deceitful mother.

**NORA:** Why do you only say—mother?

**HELMER:** It seems most commonly to be the mother's influence, though naturally a bad father's would have the same result. Every lawyer is familiar with the fact. This Krogstad, now, has been persistently poisoning his own children with lies and dissimulation; that is why I say he has lost all moral character. *(Holds out his hands to her.)* That is why my sweet little Nora must promise me not to plead his cause. Give me your hand on it. Come, come, what is this? Give me your hand. There now, that's settled. I assure you it would be quite impossible for me to work with him; I literally feel physically ill when I am in the company of such people.

**NORA:** *(takes her hand out of his and goes to the opposite side of the Christmas Tree)* How hot it is in here; and I have such a lot to do.

**HELMER:** *(getting up and putting his papers in order)* Yes, and I must try and read through some of these before dinner; and I must think about your costume, too. And it is just possible I may have something ready in gold paper to hang up on the Tree. *(Puts his hand on her head.)* My precious little singing-bird! *(He goes into his room and shuts the door after him.)*

**NORA:** *(after a pause, whispers)* No, no—it isn't true. It's impossible; it must be impossible.

*(The* NURSE *opens the door on the left.)*

**NURSE:** The little ones are begging so hard to be allowed to come in to mamma.

**NORA:** No, no, no! Don't let them come in to me! You stay with them, Anne.

**NURSE:** Very well, ma'am. *(Shuts the door.)*

**NORA:** *(pale with terror)* Deprave my little children? Poison my home? *(A short pause. Then she tosses her head.)* It's not true. It can't possibly be true.

## ACT II

**THE SAME SCENE:** *The Christmas Tree is in the corner by the piano, stripped of its ornaments and with burnt-down candle-ends on its dishevelled branches.* NORA*'s cloak and hat are lying on the sofa. She is alone in the room, walking about uneasily. She stops by the sofa and takes up her cloak.*

**NORA:** *(drops her cloak)* Someone is coming now! *(Goes to the door and listens.)* No—it is no one. Of course, no one will come to-day, Christmas Day—nor to-morrow either. But, perhaps—*(opens the door and looks out)*. No, nothing in the letter-box; it is quite empty. *(Comes forward.)* What rubbish! of course he can't be in earnest about it. Such a thing couldn't happen; it is impossible—I have three little children.

*(Enter the* NURSE *from the room on the left, carrying a big cardboard box.)*

**NURSE:** At last I have found the box with the fancy dress.

**NORA:** Thanks; put it on the table.

**NURSE:** *(doing so)* But it is very much in want of mending.

**NORA:** I should like to tear it into a hundred thousand pieces.

Nora confides in the nurse (Helen Blatch) her fears of being away from the children.

**NURSE:** What an idea! It can easily be put in order—just a little patience.

**NORA:** Yes, I will go and get Mrs. Linde to come and help me with it.

**NURSE:** What, out again? In this horrible weather? You will catch cold, ma'am, and make yourself ill.

**NORA:** Well, worse than that might happen. How are the children?

**NURSE:** The poor little souls are playing with their Christmas presents, but—

**NORA:** Do they ask much for me?

**NURSE:** You see, they are so accustomed to have their mamma with them.

**NORA:** Yes, but, nurse, I shall not be able to be so much with them now as I was before.

**NURSE:** Oh well, young children easily get accustomed to anything.

**NORA:** Do you think so? Do you think they would forget their mother if she went away altogether?

**NURSE:** Good heavens!—went away altogether?

**NORA:** Nurse, I want you to tell me something I have often wondered about—how could you have the heart to put your own child out among strangers?

**NURSE:** I was obliged to, if I wanted to be little Nora's nurse.

**NORA:** Yes, but how could you be willing to do it?

**NURSE:** What, when I was going to get such a good place by it? A poor girl who has got into trouble should be glad to. Besides, that wicked man didn't do a single thing for me.

**NORA:** But I suppose your daughter has quite forgotten you.

**NURSE:** No, indeed she hasn't. She wrote to me when she was confirmed, and when she was married.

**NORA:** *(putting her arms round her neck)* Dear old Anne, you were a good mother to me when I was little.

**NURSE:** Little Nora, poor dear, had no other mother but me.

**NORA:** And if my little ones had no other mother, I am sure you would— What nonsense I am talking! *(Opens the box.)* Go in to them. Now I must—. You will see to-morrow how charming I shall look.

**NURSE:** I am sure there will be no one at the ball so charming as you, ma'am. *(Goes into the room on the left.)*

**NORA:** *(begins to unpack the box, but soon pushes it away from her)* If only I dared go out. If only no one would come. If only I could be sure nothing would happen here in the meantime. Stuff and nonsense! No one will come. Only I mustn't think about it. I will brush my muff. What lovely, lovely gloves! Out of my thoughts, out of my thoughts! One, two, three, four, five, six— *(Screams.)* Ah! there is someone coming—. *(Makes a movement towards the door, but stands irresolute.)*

*(Enter* MRS. LINDE *from the hall, where she has taken off her cloak and hat.)*

**NORA:** Oh, it's you, Christine. There is no one else out there, is there? How good of you to come!

**MRS. LINDE:** I heard you were up asking for me.

**NORA:** Yes, I was passing by. As a matter of fact, it is something you could help me with. Let us sit down here on the sofa. Look here. To-morrow evening there is to be a fancy-dress ball at the Stenborgs', who live above us; and Torvald wants me to go as a Neapolitan fisher-girl, and dance the Tarantella that I learnt at Capri.

**MRS. LINDE:** I see; you are going to keep up the character.

**NORA:** Yes, Torvald wants me to. Look, here is the dress; Torvald had it made for me there, but now it is all so torn, and I haven't any idea—

**MRS. LINDE:** We will easily put that right. It is only some of the trimming come unsewn here and there. Needle and thread? Now then, that's all we want.

**NORA:** It *is* nice of you.

**MRS. LINDE:** *(sewing)* So you are going to be dressed up to-morrow, Nora. I will tell you what—I shall come in for a moment and see you in your fine feathers. But I have completely forgotten to thank you for a delightful evening yesterday.

**NORA:** *(gets up, and crosses the stage)* Well, I don't think yesterday was as pleasant as usual. You ought to have come to town a little earlier, Christine. Certainly Torvald does understand how to make a house dainty and attractive.

**MRS. LINDE:** And so do you, it seems to me; you are not your father's daughter for nothing. But tell me, is Doctor Rank always as depressed as he was yesterday?

**NORA:** No; yesterday it was very noticeable. I must tell you that he suffers from a very dangerous disease. He has consumption of the spine, poor creature. His father was a horrible man who committed all sorts of excesses; and that is why his son was sickly from childhood, do you understand?

**MRS. LINDE:** *(dropping her sewing)* But, my dearest Nora, how do you know anything about such things?

**NORA:** *(walking about)* Pooh! When you have three children, you get visits now and then from—from married women, who know something of medical matters, and they talk about one thing and another.

**MRS. LINDE:** *(goes on sewing. A short silence)* Does Doctor Rank come here every day?

**NORA:** Every day regularly. He is Torvald's most intimate friend, and a great friend of mine too. He is just like one of the family.

**MRS. LINDE:** But tell me this—is he perfectly sincere? I mean, isn't he the kind of man that is very anxious to make himself agreeable?

**NORA:** Not in the least. What makes you think that?

**MRS. LINDE:** When you introduced him to me yesterday, he declared he had often heard my name mentioned in this house; but afterwards I noticed that your husband hadn't the slightest idea who I was. So how could Doctor Rank—?

**NORA:** That is quite right, Christine. Torvald is so absurdly fond of me that he wants me absolutely to himself, as he says. At first he used to seem almost jealous if I mentioned any of the dear folk at home, so naturally I gave up doing so. But I often talk about such things with Doctor Rank, because he likes hearing about them.

**MRS. LINDE:** Listen to me, Nora. You are still very like a child in many things, and I am older than you in many ways and have a little more experience. Let me tell you this—you ought to make an end of it with Doctor Rank.

**NORA:** What ought I to make an end of?

**MRS. LINDE:** Of two things, I think. Yesterday you talked some nonsense about a rich admirer who was to leave you money—

**NORA:** An admirer who doesn't exist, unfortunately! But what then?

**MRS. LINDE:** Is Doctor Rank a man of means?

**NORA:** Yes, he is.

**MRS. LINDE:** And has no one to provide for?

**NORA:** No, no one; but—

**MRS. LINDE:** And comes here every day?

**NORA:** Yes, I told you so.

**MRS. LINDE:** But how can this well-bred man be so tactless?

**NORA:** I don't understand you at all.

**MRS. LINDE:** Don't prevaricate, Nora. Do you suppose I don't guess who lent you the two hundred and fifty pounds?

**NORA:** Are you out of your senses? How can you think of such a thing! A friend of ours, who comes here every day! Do you realise what a horribly painful position that would be?

**MRS. LINDE:** Then it really isn't he?

**NORA:** No, certainly not. It would never have entered into my head for a moment. Besides, he had no money to lend then; he came into his money afterwards.

**MRS. LINDE:** Well, I think that was lucky for you, my dear Nora.

**NORA:** No, it would never have come into my head to ask Doctor Rank. Although I am quite sure that if I had asked him—

**MRS. LINDE:** But of course you won't.

**NORA:** Of course not. I have no reason to think it could possibly be necessary. But I am quite sure that if I told Doctor Rank—

**MRS. LINDE:** Behind your husband's back?

**NORA:** I must make an end of it with the other one, and that will be behind his back too. I *must* make an end of it with him.

**MRS. LINDE:** Yes, that is what I told you yesterday, but—

**NORA:** *(walking up and down)* A man can put a thing like that straight much easier than a woman—

**MRS. LINDE:** One's husband, yes.

**NORA:** Nonsense! *(Standing still.)* When you pay off a debt you get your bond back, don't you?

**MRS. LINDE:** Yes, as a matter of course.

**NORA:** And can tear it into a hundred thousand pieces, and burn it up—the nasty dirty paper!

Nora and Mrs. Linde discuss Dr. Rank and the problem of Krogstad.

**MRS. LINDE:** *(looks hard at her, lays down her sewing and gets up slowly)* Nora, you are concealing something from me.

**NORA:** Do I look as if I were?

**MRS. LINDE:** Something has happened to you since yesterday morning. Nora, what is it?

**NORA:** *(going nearer to her)* Christine! *(Listens.)* Hush! there's Torvald come home. Do you mind going in to the children for the present? Torvald can't bear to see dressmaking going on. Let Anne help you.

**MRS. LINDE:** *(gathering some of the things together)* Certainly—but I am not going away from here till we have had it out with one another. *(She goes into the room on the left, as* HELMER *comes in from the hall.)*

**NORA:** *(going up to* HELMER*)* I have wanted you so much, Torvald dear.

**HELMER:** Was that the dressmaker?

**NORA:** No, it was Christine; she is helping me to put my dress in order. You will see I shall look quite smart.

**HELMER:** Wasn't that a happy thought of mine, now?

**NORA:** Splendid! But don't you think it is nice of me, too, to do as you wish?

**HELMER:** Nice?—because you do as your husband wishes? Well, well, you little rogue, I am sure you did not mean it in that way. But I am not going to disturb you; you will want to be trying on your dress, I expect.

**NORA:** I suppose you are going to work.

**HELMER:** Yes. *(Shows her a bundle of papers.)* Look at that. I have just been into the bank. *(Turns to go into his room.)*

**NORA:** Torvald.

**HELMER:** Yes.

**NORA:** If your little squirrel were to ask you for something very, very prettily—?

**HELMER:** What then?

**NORA:** Would you do it?

**HELMER:** I should like to hear what it is, first.

**NORA:** Your squirrel would run about and do all her tricks if you would be nice, and do what she wants.

**HELMER:** Speak plainly.

**NORA:** Your skylark would chirp about in every room, with her song rising and falling—

**HELMER:** Well, my skylark does that anyhow.

**NORA:** I would play the fairy and dance for you in the moonlight, Torvald.

**HELMER:** Nora—you surely don't mean that request you made to me this morning?

**NORA:** *(going near him)* Yes, Torvald, I beg you so earnestly—

**HELMER:** Have you really the courage to open up that question again?

**NORA:** Yes, dear, you *must* do as I ask; you *must* let Krogstad keep his post in the bank.

**HELMER:** My dear Nora, it is his post that I have arranged Mrs. Linde shall have.

**NORA:** Yes, you have been awfully kind about that; but you could just as well dismiss some other clerk instead of Krogstad.

**HELMER:** This is simply incredible obstinacy! Because you chose to give him a thoughtless promise that you would speak for him, I am expected to—

**NORA:** That isn't the reason, Torvald. It is for your own sake. This fellow writes in the most scurrilous newspapers; you have told me so yourself. He can do you an unspeakable amount of harm. I am frightened to death of him—

**HELMER:** Ah, I understand; it is recollections of the past that scare you.

**NORA:** What do you mean?

**HELMER:** Naturally you are thinking of your father.

**NORA:** Yes—yes, of course. Just recall to your mind what these malicious creatures wrote in the papers about papa, and how horribly they slandered him. I believe they would have procured his dismissal if the Department had not sent you over to inquire into it, and if you had not been so kindly disposed and helpful to him.

**HELMER:** My little Nora, there is an important difference between your father and me. Your father's reputation as a public official was not above suspicion. Mine is, and I hope it will continue to be so, as long as I hold my office.

**NORA:** You never can tell what mischief these men may contrive. We ought to be so well off, so snug and happy here in our peaceful home, and have no cares—you and I and the children, Torvald! That is why I beg you so earnestly—

**HELMER:** And it is just by interceding for him that you make it impossible for me to keep him. It is already known at the Bank that I mean to dismiss Krogstad. Is it to get about now that the new manager has changed his mind at his wife's bidding—

**NORA:** And what if it did?

**HELMER:** Of course!—if only this obstinate little person can get her way! Do you suppose I am going to make myself ridiculous before my whole staff, to let people think that I am a man to be swayed by all sorts of outside influence? I should very soon feel the consequences of it, I can tell you! And besides, there is one thing that makes it quite impossible for me to have Krogstad in the Bank as long as I am manager.

**NORA:** Whatever is that?

**HELMER:** His moral failings I might perhaps have overlooked, if necessary—

**NORA:** Yes, you could—couldn't you?

**HELMER:** And I hear he is a good worker, too. But I knew him when we were boys. It was one of those rash friendships that so often prove an incubus in after life. I may as well tell you plainly, we were once on very intimate terms with one another. But this tactless fellow lays no restraint on himself when other people are present. On the contrary, he thinks it gives him the right to adopt a familiar tone with me, and every minute it is "I say, Helmer, old fellow!" and that sort of thing. I assure you it is extremely painful for me. He would make my position in the Bank intolerable.

**NORA:** Torvald, I don't believe you mean that.

**HELMER:** Don't you? Why not?

**NORA:** Because it is such a narrow-minded way of looking at things.

**HELMER:** What are you saying? Narrow-minded? Do you think I am narrow-minded?

**NORA:** No, just the opposite, dear—and it is exactly for that reason.

**HELMER:** It's the same thing. You say my point of view is narrow-minded, so I must be so too. Narrow-minded! Very well—I must put an end to this. *(Goes to the hall door and calls.)* Helen!

**NORA:** What are you going to do?

**HELMER:** *(looking among his papers)* Settle it. *(Enter* MAID.*)* Look here; take this letter and go downstairs with it at once. Find a messenger and tell him to deliver it, and be quick. The address is on it, and here is the money.

**MAID:** Very well, sir. *(Exit with the letter.)*

**HELMER:** *(putting his papers together)* Now then, little Miss Obstinate.

**NORA:** *(breathlessly)* Torvald—what was that letter?

**HELMER:** Krogstad's dismissal.

**NORA:** Call her back, Torvald! There is still time. Oh, Torvald, call her back! Do it for my sake—for your own sake—for the children's sake! Do you hear me, Torvald? Call her back! You don't know what that letter can bring upon us.

**HELMER:** It's too late.

**NORA:** Yes, it's too late.

**HELMER:** My dear Nora, I can forgive the anxiety you are in, although really it is an insult to me. It is, indeed. Isn't it an insult to think that I should be afraid of a starving quill-driver's vengeance? But I forgive you nevertheless, because it is such eloquent witness to your great love for me. *(Takes her in his arms.)* And that is as it should be, my own darling Nora. Come what will, you may be sure I shall have both courage and strength if they be needed. You will see I am man enough to take everything upon myself.

**NORA:** *(in a horror-stricken voice)* What do you mean by that?

**HELMER:** Everything, I say—

**NORA:** *(recovering herself)* You will never have to do that.

**HELMER:** That's right. Well, we will share it, Nora, as man and wife should. That is how it shall be. *(Caressing her.)* Are you content now? There! there!—not these frightened dove's eyes! The whole thing is only the wildest fancy!—Now, you must go and play through the Tarantella and practise with your tambourine. I shall go into the inner office and shut the door, and I shall hear nothing; you can make as much noise as you please. *(Turns back at the door.)* And when Rank comes, tell him where he will find me. *(Nods to her, takes his papers and goes into his room, and shuts the door after him.)*

**NORA:** *(bewildered with anxiety, stands as if rooted to the spot, and whispers)* He was capable of doing it. He will do it. He will do it in spite of everything.—No, not that! Never, never! Anything rather than that! Oh, for some help, some way out of it! *(The door-bell rings.)* Doctor Rank! Anything rather than that—anything, whatever it is! *(She puts her hands over her face, pulls herself together, goes to the door and opens it.* RANK *is standing without, hanging up his coat. During the following dialogue it begins to grow dark.)*

**NORA:** Good-day, Doctor Rank. I knew your ring. But you mustn't go in to Torvald now; I think he is busy with something.

**RANK:** And you?

**NORA:** *(brings him in and shuts the door after him)* Oh, you know very well I always have time for you.

**RANK:** Thank you. I shall make use of as much of it as I can.

**NORA:** What do you mean by that? As much of it as you can?

**RANK:** Well, does that alarm you?

**NORA:** It was such a strange way of putting it. Is anything likely to happen?

**RANK:** Nothing but what I have long been prepared for. But I certainly didn't expect it to happen so soon.

**NORA:** *(gripping him by the arm)* What have you found out? Doctor Rank, you must tell me.

**RANK:** *(sitting down by the stove)* It is all up with me. And it can't be helped.

**NORA:** *(with a sigh of relief)* Is it about yourself?

**RANK:** Who else? It is no use lying to one's self. I am the most wretched of all my patients, Mrs. Helmer. Lately I have been taking stock of my internal economy. Bankrupt! Probably within a month I shall lie rotting in the churchyard.

**NORA:** What an ugly thing to say!

Dr. Rank (Patrick Malahide) makes his confession to Nora.

**RANK:** The thing itself is cursedly ugly, and the worst of it is that I shall have to face so much more that is ugly before that. I shall only make one more examination of myself; when I have done that, I shall know pretty certainly when it will be that the horrors of dissolution will begin. There is something I want to tell you. Helmer's refined nature gives him an unconquerable disgust at everything that is ugly; I won't have him in my sick-room.

**NORA:** Oh, but, Doctor Rank—

**RANK:** I won't have him there. Not on any account. I bar my door to him. As soon as I am quite certain that the worst has come, I shall send you my card with a black cross on it, and then you will know that the loathsome end has begun.

**NORA:** You are quite absurd to-day. And I wanted you so much to be in a really good humour.

**RANK:** With death stalking beside me?—To have to pay this penalty for another man's sin! Is there any justice in that? And in every single family, in one way or another, some such inexorable retribution is being exacted—

**NORA:** *(putting her hands over her ears)* Rubbish! Do talk of something cheerful.

**RANK:** Oh, it's a mere laughing matter, the whole thing. My poor innocent spine has to suffer for my father's youthful amusements.

**NORA:** *(sitting at the table on the left)* I suppose you mean that he was too partial to asparagus and pâté de foie gras, don't you?

**RANK:** Yes, and to truffles.

**NORA:** Truffles, yes. And oysters too, I suppose?

**RANK:** Oysters, of course, that goes without saying.

**NORA:** And heaps of port and champagne. It is sad that all these nice things should take their revenge on our bones.

**RANK:** Especially that they should revenge themselves on the unlucky bones of those who have not had the satisfaction of enjoying them.

**NORA:** Yes, that's the saddest part of it all.

**RANK:** *(with a searching look at her)* Hm!—

**NORA:** *(after a short pause)* Why did you smile?

**RANK:** No, it was you that laughed.

**NORA:** No, it was you that smiled, Doctor Rank!

**RANK:** *(rising)* You are a greater rascal than I thought.

**NORA:** I am in a silly mood to-day.

**RANK:** So it seems.

**NORA:** *(putting her hands on his shoulders)* Dear, dear Doctor Rank, death mustn't take you away from Torvald and me.

**RANK:** It is a loss you would easily recover from. Those who are gone are soon forgotten.

**NORA:** *(looking at him anxiously)* Do you believe that?

**RANK:** People form new ties, and then—

**NORA:** Who will form new ties?

**RANK:** Both you and Helmer, when I am gone. You yourself are already on the high road to it, I think. What did that Mrs. Linde want here last night?

**NORA:** Oho!—you don't mean to say you are jealous of poor Christine?

**RANK:** Yes, I am. She will be my successor in this house. When I am done for, this woman will—

**NORA:** Hush! don't speak so loud. She is in that room.

**RANK:** To-day again. There, you see.

**NORA:** She has only come to sew my dress for me. Bless my soul, how unreasonable you are! *(Sits down on the sofa.)* Be nice now, Doctor Rank, and to-morrow you will see how beautifully I shall dance, and you can imagine I am doing it all for you—and for Torvald too, of course. *(Takes various things out of the box.)* Doctor Rank, come and sit down here, and I will show you something.

**RANK:** *(sitting down)* What is it?

**NORA:** Just look at those!

**RANK:** Silk stockings.

**NORA:** Flesh-coloured. Aren't they lovely? It is so dark here now, but to-morrow—. No, no, no! you must only look at the feet. Oh well, you may have leave to look at the legs too.

**RANK:** Hm!—

**NORA:** Why are you looking so critical? Don't you think they will fit me?

**RANK:** I have no means of forming an opinion about that.

**NORA:** *(looks at him for a moment)* For shame! *(Hits him lightly on the ear with the stockings.)* That's to punish you. *(Folds them up again.)*

**RANK:** And what other nice things am I to be allowed to see?

**NORA:** Not a single thing more, for being so naughty. *(She looks among the things, humming to herself.)*

**RANK:** *(after a short silence)* When I am sitting here, talking to you as intimately as this, I cannot imagine for a moment what would have become of me if I had never come into this house.

**NORA:** *(smiling)* I believe you do feel thoroughly at home with us.

**RANK:** *(in a lower voice, looking straight in front of him)* And to be obliged to leave it all—

**NORA:** Nonsense, you are not going to leave it.

**RANK:** *(as before)* And not be able to leave behind one the slightest token of one's gratitude, scarcely even a fleeting regret—nothing but an empty place which the first comer can fill as well as any other.

**NORA:** And if I asked you now for a—? No!

**RANK:** For what?

**NORA:** For a big proof of your friendship—

**RANK:** Yes, yes!

**NORA:** I mean a tremendously big favour—

**RANK:** Would you really make me so happy for once?

**NORA:** Ah, but you don't know what it is yet.

**RANK:** No—but tell me.

**NORA:** I really can't, Doctor Rank. It is something out of all reason; it means advice, and help, and a favour—

**RANK:** The bigger a thing it is the better. I can't conceive what it is you mean. Do tell me. Haven't I your confidence?

**NORA:** More than any one else. I know you are my truest and best friend, and so I will tell you what it is. Well, Doctor Rank, it is something you must help me to prevent. You know how devotedly, how inexpressibly deeply Torvald loves me; he would never for a moment hesitate to give his life for me.

**RANK:** *(leaning towards her)* Nora—do you think he is the only one—?

**NORA:** *(with a slight start)* The only one—?

**RANK:** The only one who would gladly give his life for your sake.

**NORA:** *(sadly)* Is that it?

**RANK:** I was determined you should know it before I went away, and there will never be a better opportunity than this. Now you know it, Nora. And now you know, too, that you can trust me as you would trust no one else.

**NORA:** *(rises, deliberately and quietly)* Let me pass.

**RANK:** *(makes room for her to pass him, but sits still)* Nora!

**NORA:** *(at the hall door)* Helen, bring in the lamp. *(Goes over to the stove.)* Dear Doctor Rank, that was really horrid of you.

**RANK:** To have loved you as much as any one else does? Was that horrid?

**NORA:** No, but to go and tell me so. There was really no need—

**RANK:** What do you mean? Did you know—? (MAID *enters with lamp, puts it down on the table, and goes out.)* Nora—Mrs. Helmer—tell me, had you any idea of this?

**NORA:** Oh, how do I know whether I had or whether I hadn't? I really can't tell you— To think you could be so clumsy, Doctor Rank! We were getting on so nicely.

**RANK:** Well, at all events you know now that you can command me, body and soul. So won't you speak out?

**NORA:** *(looking at him)* After what happened?

**RANK:** I beg you to let me know what it is.

**NORA:** I can't tell you anything now.

**RANK:** Yes, yes. You mustn't punish me in that way. Let me have permission to do for you whatever a man may do.

**NORA:** You can do nothing for me now. Besides, I really don't need any help at all. You will find that the whole thing is merely fancy on my part. It really is so—of course it is! *(Sits down in the rocking-chair, and looks at him with a smile.)* You are a nice sort of man, Doctor Rank!—don't you feel ashamed of yourself, now the lamp has come?

**RANK:** Not a bit. But perhaps I had better go—for ever?

**NORA:** No, indeed, you shall not. Of course you must come here just as before. You know very well Torvald can't do without you.

**RANK:** Yes, but you?

**NORA:** Oh, I am always tremendously pleased when you come.

**RANK:** It is just that, that put me on the wrong track. You are a riddle to me. I have often thought that you would almost as soon be in my company as in Helmer's.

**NORA:** Yes—you see there are some people one loves best, and others whom one would almost always rather have as companions.

**RANK:** Yes, there is something in that.

**NORA:** When I was at home, of course I loved papa best. But I always thought it tremendous fun if I could steal down into the maids' room, because they never moralised at all, and talked to each other about such entertaining things.

**RANK:** I see—it is *their* place I have taken.

**NORA:** *(jumping up and going to him)* Oh, dear, nice Doctor Rank, I never meant that at all. But surely you can understand that being with Torvald is a little like being with papa—

*(Enter* MAID *from the hall.)*

**MAID:** If you please, ma'am. *(Whispers and hands her a card.)*

**NORA:** *(glancing at the card)* Oh! *(Puts it in her pocket.)*

**RANK:** Is there anything wrong?

**NORA:** No, no, not in the least. It is only something—it is my new dress—

**RANK:** What? Your dress is lying there.

**NORA:** Oh, yes, that one; but this is another. I ordered it. Torvald mustn't know about it—

**RANK:** Oho! Then that was the great secret.

**NORA:** Of course. Just go in to him; he is sitting in the inner room. Keep him as long as—

**RANK:** Make your mind easy; I won't let him escape. *(Goes into* HELMER'*s room.)*

**NORA:** *(to the* MAID*)* And he is standing waiting in the kitchen?

**MAID:** Yes; he came up the back stairs.

**NORA:** But didn't you tell him no one was in?

**MAID:** Yes, but it was no good.

**NORA:** He won't go away?

**MAID:** No; he says he won't until he has seen you, ma'am.

**NORA:** Well, let him come in—but quietly. Helen, you mustn't say anything about it to any one. It is a surprise for my husband.

**MAID:** Yes, ma'am, I quite understand. *(Exit.)*

**NORA:** This dreadful thing is going to happen! It will happen in spite of me! No, no, no, it can't happen—it shan't happen! *(She bolts the door of* HELMER'*s room. The* MAID *opens the hall door for* KROGSTAD *and shuts it after him. He is wearing a fur coat, high boots and a fur cap.)*

**NORA:** *(advancing towards him)* Speak low—my husband is at home.

**KROGSTAD:** No matter about that.

**NORA:** What do you want of me?

**KROGSTAD:** An explanation of something.

**NORA:** Make haste then. What is it?

**KROGSTAD:** You know, I suppose, that I have got my dismissal.

Krogstad (Denholm Elliott) meets secretly with Nora to reveal his decision.

**NORA:** I couldn't prevent it, Mr. Krogstad. I fought as hard as I could on your side, but it was no good.

**KROGSTAD:** Does your husband love you so little, then? He knows what I can expose you to, and yet he ventures—

**NORA:** How can you suppose that he has any knowledge of the sort?

**KROGSTAD:** I didn't suppose so at all. It would not be the least like our dear Torvald Helmer to show so much courage—

**NORA:** Mr. Krogstad, a little respect for my husband, please.

**KROGSTAD:** Certainly—all the respect he deserves. But since you have kept the matter so carefully to yourself, I make bold to suppose that you have a little clearer idea, than you had yesterday, of what it actually is that you have done?

**NORA:** More than you could ever ever teach me.

**KROGSTAD:** Yes, such a bad lawyer as I am.

**NORA:** What is it you want of me?

**KROGSTAD:** Only to see how you were, Mrs. Helmer. I have been thinking about you all day long. A mere cashier, a quill-driver, a—well, a man like me—even he has a little of what is called feeling, you know.

**NORA:** Show it, then; think of my little children.

**KROGSTAD:** Have you and your husband thought of mine? But never mind about that. I only wanted to tell you that you need not take this matter too seriously. In the first place there will be no accusation made on my part.

**NORA:** No, of course not; I was sure of that.

**KROGSTAD:** The whole thing can be arranged amicably; there is no reason why anyone should know anything about it. It will remain a secret between us three.

**NORA:** My husband must never get to know anything about it.

**KROGSTAD:** How will you be able to prevent it? Am I to understand that you can pay the balance that is owing?

**NORA:** No, not just at present.

**KROGSTAD:** Or perhaps that you have some expedient for raising the money soon?

**NORA:** No expedient that I mean to make use of.

**KROGSTAD:** Well, in any case, it would have been of no use to you now. If you stood there with ever so much money in your hand, I would never part with your bond.

**NORA:** Tell me what purpose you mean to put it to.

**KROGSTAD:** I shall only preserve it—keep it in my possession. No one who is not concerned in the matter shall have the slightest hint of it. So that if the thought of it has driven you to any desperate resolution—

**NORA:** It has.

**KROGSTAD:** If you had it in your mind to run away from your home—

**NORA:** I had.

**KROGSTAD:** Or even something worse—

**NORA:** How could you know that?

**KROGSTAD:** Give up the idea.

**NORA:** How did you know I had thought of *that*?

**KROGSTAD:** Most of us think of that at first. I did, too—but I hadn't the courage.

**NORA:** *(lifelessly)* No more had I.

**KROGSTAD:** *(in a tone of relief)* No, that's it, isn't it—you hadn't the courage either?

**NORA:** No, I haven't—I haven't.

**KROGSTAD:** Besides, it would have been a great piece of folly. Once the first storm at home is over—. I have a letter for your husband in my pocket.

**NORA:** Telling him everything?

**KROGSTAD:** In as lenient a manner as I possibly could.

**NORA:** *(quickly)* He mustn't get the letter. Tear it up. I will find some means of getting money.

**KROGSTAD:** Excuse me, Mrs. Helmer, but I think I told you just now—

**NORA:** I am not speaking of what I owe you. Tell me what sum you are asking my husband for, and I will get the money.

**KROGSTAD:** I am not asking your husband for a penny.

**NORA:** What do you want, then?

**KROGSTAD:** I will tell you. I want to rehabilitate myself, Mrs. Helmer; I want to get on; and in that your husband must help me. For the last year and a half

I have not had a hand in anything dishonourable, and all that time I have been struggling in most restricted circumstances. I was content to work my way up step by step. Now I am turned out, and I am not going to be satisfied with merely being taken into favour again. I want to get on, I tell you. I want to get into the Bank again, in a higher position. Your husband must make a place for me—

**NORA:** That he will never do!

**KROGSTAD:** He will; I know him; he dare not protest. And as soon as I am in there again with him, then you will see! Within a year I shall be the manager's right hand. It will be Nils Krogstad and not Torvald Helmer who manages the Bank.

**NORA:** That's a thing you will never see.

**KROGSTAD:** Do you mean that you will—?

**NORA:** I have courage enough for it now.

**KROGSTAD:** Oh, you can't frighten me. A fine, spoilt lady like you—

**NORA:** You will see, you will see.

**KROGSTAD:** Under the ice, perhaps? Down into the cold, coal-black water? And then, in the spring, to float up to the surface, all horrible and unrecognisable, with your hair fallen out—

**NORA:** You can't frighten me.

**KROGSTAD:** Nor you me. People don't do such things, Mrs. Helmer. Besides, what use would it be? I should have him completely in my power all the same.

**NORA:** Afterwards? When I am no longer—

**KROGSTAD:** Have you forgotten that it is I who have the keeping of your reputation? *(*NORA *stands speechlessly looking at him.)* Well, now, I have warned you. Do not do anything foolish. When Helmer has had my letter, I shall expect a message from him. And be sure you remember that it is your husband himself who has forced me into such ways as this again. I will never forgive him for that. Good-bye, Mrs. Helmer. *(Exit through the hall.)*

Nora tries to pry open the letter box.

**NORA:** *(goes to the hall door, opens it slightly and listens)* He is going. He is not putting the letter in the box. Oh no, no! that's impossible! *(Opens the door by degrees.)* What is that? He is standing outside. He is not going downstairs. Is he hesitating? Can he—? *(A letter drops into the box; then* KROGSTAD*'s footsteps are heard, till they die away as he goes downstairs.* NORA *utters a stifled cry, and runs across the room to the table by the sofa. A short pause.)*

**NORA:** In the letter-box. *(Steals across to the hall door.)* There it lies—Torvald, Torvald, there is no hope for us now!

*(*MRS. LINDE *comes in from the room on the left, carrying the dress.)*

**MRS. LINDE:** There, I can't see anything more to mend now. Would you like to try it on—?

**NORA:** *(in a hoarse whisper)* Christine, come here.

**MRS. LINDE:** *(throwing the dress down on the sofa)* What is the matter with you? You look so agitated!

**NORA:** Come here. Do you see that letter? There, look—you can see it through the glass in the letter-box.

**MRS. LINDE:** Yes, I see it.

**NORA:** That letter is from Krogstad.

**MRS. LINDE:** Nora—it was Krogstad who lent you the money!

**NORA:** Yes, and now Torvald will know all about it.

**MRS. LINDE:** Believe me, Nora, that's the best thing for both of you.

**NORA:** You don't know all. I forged a name.

**MRS. LINDE:** Good heavens—!

**NORA:** I only want to say this to you, Christine—you must be my witness.

**MRS. LINDE:** Your witness? What do you mean? What am I to—?

**NORA:** If I should go out of my mind—it might easily happen—

**MRS. LINDE:** Nora!

**NORA:** Or if anything else should happen to me—anything, for instance, that might prevent my being here—

**MRS. LINDE:** Nora! Nora! you are quite out of your mind.

**NORA:** And if it should happen that there were some one who wanted to take all the responsibility, all the blame, you understand—

**MRS. LINDE:** Yes, yes—but how can you suppose—?

**NORA:** Then you must be my witness, that it is not true, Christine. I am not out of my mind at all; I am in my right senses now, and I tell you no one else has known anything about it; I, and I alone, did the whole thing. Remember that.

**MRS. LINDE:** I will, indeed. But I don't understand all this.

**NORA:** How should you understand it? A wonderful thing is going to happen!

**MRS. LINDE:** A wonderful thing?

**NORA:** Yes, a wonderful thing!—But it is so terrible, Christine; it *mustn't* happen, not for all the world.

**MRS. LINDE:** I will go at once and see Krogstad.

**NORA:** Don't go to him; he will do you some harm.

**MRS. LINDE:** There was a time when he would gladly do anything for my sake.

**NORA:** He?

**MRS. LINDE:** Where does he live?

**NORA:** How should I know—? Yes *(feeling in her pocket)*, here is his card. But the letter, the letter—!

**HELMER:** *(calls from his room, knocking at the door)* Nora!

**NORA:** *(cries out anxiously)* Oh, what's that? What do you want?

**HELMER:** Don't be so frightened. We are not coming in; you have locked the door. Are you trying on your dress?

**NORA:** Yes, that's it. I look so nice, Torvald.

**MRS. LINDE:** *(who has read the card)* I see he lives at the corner here.

**NORA:** Yes, but it's no use. It is hopeless. The letter is lying there in the box.

**MRS. LINDE:** And your husband keeps the key?

**NORA:** Yes, always.

Nora practices her dancing for Torvald.

**MRS. LINDE:** Krogstad must ask for his letter back unread, he must find some pretence—

**NORA:** But it is just at this time that Torvald generally—

**MRS. LINDE:** You must delay him. Go in to him in the meantime. I will come back as soon as I can. *(She goes out hurriedly through the hall door.)*

**NORA:** *(goes to* HELMER*'s door, opens it and peeps in)* Torvald!

**HELMER:** *(from the inner room)* Well? May I venture at last to come into my own room again? Come along, Rank, now you will see— *(Halting in the doorway.)* But what is this?

**NORA:** What is what, dear?

**HELMER:** Rank led me to expect a splendid transformation.

**RANK:** *(in the doorway)* I understood so, but evidently I was mistaken.

**NORA:** Yes, nobody is to have the chance of admiring me in my dress until to-morrow.

**HELMER:** But, my dear Nora, you look so worn out. Have you been practising too much?

**NORA:** No, I have not practised at all.

**HELMER:** But you will need to—

**NORA:** Yes, indeed I shall, Torvald. But I can't get on a bit without you to help me; I have absolutely forgotten the whole thing.

**HELMER:** Oh, we will soon work it up again.

**NORA:** Yes, help me, Torvald. Promise that you will! I am so nervous about it—all the people—. You must give yourself up to me entirely this evening. Not the tiniest bit of business—you mustn't even take a pen in your hand. Will you promise, Torvald dear?

**HELMER:** I promise. This evening I will be wholly and absolutely at your service, you helpless little mortal. Ah, by the way, first of all I will just— *(Goes towards the hall door.)*

**NORA:** What are you going to do there?

**HELMER:** Only see if any letters have come.

**NORA:** No, no! don't do that, Torvald!

**HELMER:** Why not?

**NORA:** Torvald, please don't. There is nothing there.

**HELMER:** Well, let me look. *(Turns to go to the letter-box.* NORA, *at the piano, plays the first bars of the Tarantella.* HELMER *stops in the doorway.)* Aha!

**NORA:** I can't dance to-morrow if I don't practise with you.

**HELMER:** *(going up to her)* Are you really so afraid of it, dear?

**NORA:** Yes, so dreadfully afraid of it. Let me practise at once; there is time now, before we go to dinner. Sit down and play for me, Torvald dear; criticise me, and correct me as you play.

**HELMER:** With great pleasure, if you wish me to. *(Sits down at the piano.)*

**NORA:** *(takes out of the box a tambourine and a long variegated shawl. She hastily drapes the shawl round her. Then she springs to the front of the stage and calls out)* Now play for me! I am going to dance!

*(*HELMER *plays and* NORA *dances.* RANK *stands by the piano behind* HELMER, *and looks on.)*

**HELMER:** *(as he plays)* Slower, slower!

**NORA:** I can't do it any other way.

**HELMER:** Not so violently, Nora!

**NORA:** This is the way.

**HELMER:** *(stops playing)* No, no—that is not a bit right.

**NORA:** *(laughing and swinging the tambourine)* Didn't I tell you so?

**RANK:** Let me play for her.

**HELMER:** *(getting up)* Yes, do. I can correct her better then.

*(*RANK *sits down at the piano and plays.* NORA *dances more and more wildly.* HELMER *has taken up a position beside the stove, and during her dance gives her frequent instructions. She does not seem to hear him; her hair comes down and falls over her shoulders; she pays no attention to it, but goes on dancing. Enter* MRS. LINDE.*)*

**MRS. LINDE:** *(standing as if spell-bound in the doorway)* Oh!—

**NORA:** *(as she dances)* Such fun, Christine!

**HELMER:** My dear darling Nora, you are dancing as if your life depended on it.

**NORA:** So it does.

**HELMER:** Stop, Rank; this is sheer madness. Stop, I tell you! *(*RANK *stops playing, and* NORA *suddenly stands still.* HELMER *goes up to her.)* I could never have believed it. You have forgotten everything I taught you.

**NORA:** *(throwing away the tambourine)* There, you see.

**HELMER:** You will want a lot of coaching.

**NORA:** Yes, you see how much I need it. You must coach me up to the last minute. Promise me that, Torvald!

**HELMER:** You can depend on me.

**NORA:** You must not think of anything but me, either to-day or to-morrow; you mustn't open a single letter—not even open the letter-box—

**HELMER:** Ah, you are still afraid of that fellow—

**NORA:** Yes, indeed I am.

**HELMER:** Nora, I can tell from your looks that there is a letter from him lying there.

**NORA:** I don't know; I think there is; but you must not read anything of that kind now. Nothing horrid must come between us till this is all over.

**RANK:** *(whispers to* HELMER*)* You mustn't contradict her.

**HELMER:** *(taking her in his arms)* The child shall have her way. But to-morrow night, after you have danced—

**NORA:** Then you will be free. *(The* MAID *appears in the doorway to the right.)*

**MAID:** Dinner is served, ma'am.

**NORA:** We will have champagne, Helen.

**MAID:** Very good, ma'am. *(Exit)*

**HELMER:** Hullo!—are we going to have a banquet?

**NORA:** Yes, a champagne banquet till the small hours. *(Calls out.)* And a few macaroons, Helen—lots, just for once!

**HELMER:** Come, come, don't be so wild and nervous. Be my own little skylark, as you used.

**NORA:** Yes, dear, I will. But go in now and you too, Doctor Rank. Christine, you must help me to do up my hair.

**RANK:** *(whispers to* HELMER *as they go out)* I suppose there is nothing—she is not expecting anything?

**HELMER:** Far from it, my dear fellow; it is simply nothing more than this childish nervousness I was telling you of.

*(They go into the right-hand room.)*

**NORA:** Well!

**MRS. LINDE:** Gone out of town.

**NORA:** I could tell from your face.

**MRS. LINDE:** He is coming home to-morrow evening. I wrote a note for him.

**NORA:** You should have let it alone; you must prevent nothing. After all, it is splendid to be waiting for a wonderful thing to happen.

**MRS. LINDE:** What is it that you are waiting for?

**NORA:** Oh, you wouldn't understand. Go in to them, I will come in a moment. *(*MRS. LINDE *goes into the dining-room.* NORA *stands still for a little while, as if to compose herself. Then she looks at her watch.)* Five o'clock. Seven hours till midnight; and then four-and-twenty hours till the next midnight. Then the Tarantella will be over. Twenty-four and seven? Thirty-one hours to live.

**HELMER:** *(from the doorway on the right)* Where's my little skylark?

**NORA:** *(going to him with her arms outstretched)* Here she is!

## ACT III

**THE SAME SCENE:** *The table has been placed in the middle of the stage, with chairs round it. A lamp is burning on the table. The door into the hall stands open. Dance music is heard from the room above.* MRS. LINDE *is sitting at the table idly turning over the leaves of a book; she tries to read, but does not seem able to collect her thoughts. Every now and then she listens intently for a sound at the outer door.*

**MRS. LINDE:** *(looking at her watch)* Not yet—and the time is nearly up. If only he does not—. *(Listens again.)* Ah, there he is. *(Goes into the hall and opens the outer door carefully. Light footsteps are heard on the stairs. She whispers.)* Come in. There is no one here.

**KROGSTAD:** *(in the doorway)* I found a note from you at home. What does this mean?

**MRS. LINDE:** It is absolutely necessary that I should have a talk with you.

**KROGSTAD:** Really? And is it absolutely necessary that it should be here?

**MRS. LINDE:** It is impossible where I live; there is no private entrance to my rooms. Come in; we are quite alone. The maid is asleep, and the Helmers are at the dance upstairs.

**KROGSTAD:** *(coming into the room)* Are the Helmers really at a dance to-night?

**MRS. LINDE:** Yes, why not?

**KROGSTAD:** Certainly—why not?

**MRS. LINDE:** Now, Nils, let us have a talk.

**KROGSTAD:** Can we two have anything to talk about?

**MRS. LINDE:** We have a great deal to talk about.

**KROGSTAD:** I shouldn't have thought so.

**MRS. LINDE:** No, you have never properly understood me.

**KROGSTAD:** Was there anything else to understand except what was obvious to all the world—a heartless woman jilts a man when a more lucrative chance turns up?

**MRS. LINDE:** Do you believe I am as absolutely heartless as all that? And do you believe that I did it with a light heart?

**KROGSTAD:** Didn't you?

**MRS. LINDE:** Nils, did you really think that?

**KROGSTAD:** If it were as you say, why did you write to me as you did at the time?

**MRS. LINDE:** I could do nothing else. As I had to break with you, it was my duty also to put an end to all that you felt for me.

**KROGSTAD:** *(wringing his hands)* So that was it. And all this—only for the sake of money!

Mrs. Linde calls on Krogstad with a plan of her own.

**MRS. LINDE:** You must not forget that I had a helpless mother and two little brothers. We couldn't wait for you, Nils; your prospects seemed hopeless then.

**KROGSTAD:** That may be so, but you had no right to throw me over for anyone else's sake.

**MRS. LINDE:** Indeed I don't know. Many a time did I ask myself if I had the right to do it.

**KROGSTAD:** *(more gently)* When I lost you, it was as if all the solid ground went from under my feet. Look at me now—I am a shipwrecked man clinging to a bit of wreckage.

**MRS. LINDE:** But help may be near.

**KROGSTAD:** It *was* near; but then you came and stood in my way.

**MRS. LINDE:** Unintentionally, Nils. It was only to-day that I learnt it was your place I was going to take in the Bank.

**KROGSTAD:** I believe you, if you say so. But now that you know it, are you not going to give it up to me?

**MRS. LINDE:** No, because that would not benefit you in the least.

**KROGSTAD:** Oh, benefit, benefit—I would have done it whether or no.

**MRS. LINDE:** I have learnt to act prudently. Life, and hard, bitter necessity have taught me that.

**KROGSTAD:** And life has taught me not to believe in fine speeches.

**MRS. LINDE:** Then life has taught you something very reasonable. But deeds you must believe in?

**KROGSTAD:** What do you mean by that?

**MRS. LINDE:** You said you were like a shipwrecked man clinging to some wreckage.

**KROGSTAD:** I had good reason to say so.

**MRS. LINDE:** Well, I am like a shipwrecked woman clinging to some wreckage—no one to mourn for, no one to care for.

**KROGSTAD:** It was your own choice.

**MRS. LINDE:** There was no other choice—then.

**KROGSTAD:** Well, what now?

**MRS. LINDE:** Nils, how would it be if we two shipwrecked people could join forces?

**KROGSTAD:** What are you saying?

**MRS. LINDE:** Two on the same piece of wreckage would stand a better chance than each on their own.

**KROGSTAD:** Christine!

**MRS. LINDE:** What do you suppose brought me to town?

**KROGSTAD:** Do you mean that you gave me a thought?

**MRS. LINDE:** I could not endure life without work. All my life, as long as I can remember, I have worked, and it has been my greatest and only pleasure. But now I am quite alone in the world—my life is so dreadfully empty and I feel so forsaken. There is not the least pleasure in working for one's self. Nils, give me someone and something to work for.

**KROGSTAD:** I don't trust that. It is nothing but a woman's overstrained sense of generosity that prompts you to make such an offer of yourself.

**MRS. LINDE:** Have you ever noticed anything of the sort in me?

**KROGSTAD:** Could you really do it? Tell me—do you know all about my past life?

**MRS. LINDE:** Yes.

**KROGSTAD:** And do you know what they think of me here?

**MRS. LINDE:** You seemed to me to imply that with me you might have been quite another man.

**KROGSTAD:** I am certain of it.

**MRS. LINDE:** Is it too late now?

**KROGSTAD:** Christine, are you saying this deliberately? Yes, I am sure you are. I see it in your face. Have you really the courage, then—?

**MRS. LINDE:** I want to be a mother to someone, and your children need a mother. We two need each other. Nils, I have faith in your real character—I can dare anything together with you.

**KROGSTAD:** *(grasps her hands)* Thanks, thanks, Christine! Now I shall find a way to clear myself in the eyes of the world. Ah, but I forgot—

**MRS. LINDE:** *(listening)* Hush! The Tarantella. Go, go!

**KROGSTAD:** Why? What is it?

**MRS. LINDE:** Do you hear them up there? When that is over, we may expect them back.

**KROGSTAD:** Yes, yes—I will go. But it is all no use. Of course you are not aware what steps I have taken in the matter of the Helmers.

**MRS. LINDE:** Yes, I know all about that.

**KROGSTAD:** And in spite of that have you the courage to—?

**MRS. LINDE:** I understand very well to what lengths a man like you might be driven by despair.

**KROGSTAD:** If I could only undo what I have done!

**MRS. LINDE:** You cannot. Your letter is lying in the letter-box now.

**KROGSTAD:** Are you sure of that?

**MRS. LINDE:** Quite sure, but—

**KROGSTAD:** *(with a searching look at her)* Is that what it all means?—that you want to save your friend at any cost? Tell me frankly. Is that it?

**MRS. LINDE:** Nils, a woman who has once sold herself for another's sake, doesn't do it a second time.

**KROGSTAD:** I will ask for my letter back.

**MRS. LINDE:** No, no.

**KROGSTAD:** Yes, of course I will. I will wait here till Helmer comes; I will tell him he must give me my letter back—that it only concerns my dismissal—that he is not to read it—

**MRS. LINDE:** No, Nils, you must not recall your letter.

**KROGSTAD:** But, tell me, wasn't it for that very purpose that you asked me to meet you here?

**MRS. LINDE:** In my first moment of fright, it was. But twenty-four hours have elapsed since then, and in that time I have witnessed incredible things in this house. Helmer must know all about it. This unhappy secret must be disclosed; they must have a complete understanding between them, which is impossible with all this concealment and falsehood going on.

**KROGSTAD:** Very well, if you will take the responsibility. But there is one thing I can do in any case, and I shall do it at once.

**MRS. LINDE:** *(listening)* You must be quick and go! The dance is over; we are not safe a moment longer.

**KROGSTAD:** I will wait for you below.

**MRS. LINDE:** Yes, do; You must see me back to my door.

**KROGSTAD:** I have never had such an amazing piece of good fortune in my life! *(Goes out through the outer door. The door between the room and the hall remains open.)*

**MRS. LINDE:** *(tidying up the room and laying her hat and cloak ready)* What a difference! what a difference! Some one to work for and live for—a home to bring comfort into. That I will do, indeed. I wish they would be quick and come— *(Listens.)* Ah, there they are now. I must put on my things. *(Takes up her hat and cloak.* HELMER*'s and* NORA*'s voices are heard outside; a key is turned, and* HELMER *brings* NORA *almost by force into the hall. She is in an Italian costume with a large black shawl round her; he is in evening dress, and a black domino which is flying open.)*

**NORA:** *(hanging back in the doorway, and struggling with him)* No, no, no!—don't take me in. I want to go upstairs again; I don't want to leave so early.

**HELMER:** But, my dearest Nora—

**NORA:** Please, Torvald dear—please, *please*—only an hour more.

**HELMER:** Not a single minute, my sweet Nora. You know that was our agreement. Come along into the room; you are catching cold standing there. *(He brings her gently into the room, in spite of her resistance.)*

**MRS. LINDE:** Good-evening.

**NORA:** Christine!

**HELMER:** You here, so late, Mrs. Linde?

**MRS. LINDE:** Yes, you must excuse me; I was so anxious to see Nora in her dress.

**NORA:** Have you been sitting here waiting for me?

**MRS. LINDE:** Yes, unfortunately I came too late, you had already gone upstairs; and I thought I couldn't go away again without having seen you.

**HELMER:** *(taking off* NORA*'s shawl)* Yes, take a good look at her. I think she is worth looking at. Isn't she charming, Mrs. Linde?

**MRS. LINDE:** Yes, indeed she is.

**HELMER:** Doesn't she look remarkably pretty? Everyone thought so at the dance. But she is terribly self-willed, this sweet little person. What are we to do with her? You will hardly believe that I had almost to bring her away by force.

**NORA:** Torvald, you will repent not having let me stay, even if it were only for half an hour.

**HELMER:** Listen to her, Mrs. Linde! She had danced her Tarantella, and it had been a tremendous success, as it deserved—although possibly the performance was a trifle too realistic—a little more so, I mean, than was strictly compatible with the limitations of art. But never mind about that! The chief thing is, she had made a success—she had made a tremendous success. Do you think I was going to let her remain there after that, and spoil the effect? No, indeed! I took my charming little Capri maiden—my capricious little Capri maiden, I should say—on my arm; took one quick turn round the room; a curtsey on either side, and, as they say in novels, the beautiful apparition disappeared. An exit ought always to be effective, Mrs. Linde; but that is what I cannot make Nora understand. Pooh! this room is hot. *(Throws his domino on a chair, and opens the door of his room.)* Hullo! it's all dark in here. Oh, of course—excuse me—. *(He goes in, and lights some candles.)*

**NORA:** *(in a hurried and breathless whisper)* Well?

**MRS. LINDE:** *(in a low voice)* I have had a talk with him.

**NORA:** Yes, and—

**MRS. LINDE:** Nora, you must tell your husband all about it.

**NORA:** *(in an expressionless voice)* I knew it.

**MRS. LINDE:** You have nothing to be afraid of as far as Krogstad is concerned; but you must tell him.

**NORA:** I won't tell him.

**MRS. LINDE:** Then the letter will.

**NORA:** Thank you, Christine. Now I know what I must do. Hush—!

**HELMER:** *(coming in again)* Well, Mrs. Linde, have you admired her?

**MRS. LINDE:** Yes, and now I will say good-night.

**HELMER:** What, already? Is this yours, this knitting?

**MRS. LINDE:** *(taking it)* Yes, thank you, I had very nearly forgotten it.

**HELMER:** So you knit?

**MRS. LINDE:** Of course.

**HELMER:** Do you know, you ought to embroider.

**MRS. LINDE:** Really? Why?

**HELMER:** Yes, it's far more becoming. Let me show you. You hold the embroidery thus in your left hand, and use the needle with the right—like this—with a long, easy sweep. Do you see?

**MRS. LINDE:** Yes, perhaps—

**HELMER:** But in the case of knitting—that can never be anything but ungraceful; look here—the arms close together, the knitting-needles going up and down—it has a sort of Chinese effect—. That was really excellent champagne they gave us.

**MRS. LINDE:** Well,—good-night, Nora, and don't be self-willed anymore.

**HELMER:** That's right, Mrs. Linde.

**MRS. LINDE:** Good-night, Mr. Helmer.

**HELMER:** *(accompanying her to the door)* Good-night, good-night. I hope you will get home all right. I should be very happy to—but you haven't any great distance to go. Good-night, good-night. *(She goes out; he shuts the door after her, and comes in again.)* Ah!—at last we have got rid of her. She's a frightful bore, that woman.

**NORA:** Aren't you very tired, Torvald?

**HELMER:** No, not in the least.

**NORA:** Nor sleepy?

**HELMER:** Not a bit. On the contrary, I feel extraordinarily lively. And you?—you really look both tired and sleepy.

After Mrs. Linde leaves, Torvald has Nora to himself.

**NORA:** Yes, I am very tired. I want to go to sleep at once.

**HELMER:** There, you see it was quite right of me not to let you stay there any longer.

**NORA:** Everything you do is quite right, Torvald.

**HELMER:** *(kissing her on the forehead)* Now my little skylark is speaking reasonably. Did you notice what good spirits Rank was in this evening?

**NORA:** Really? Was he? I didn't speak to him at all.

**HELMER:** And I very little, but I have not for a long time seen him in such good form. *(Looks for a while at her and then goes nearer to her.)* It is delightful to be at home by ourselves again, to be all alone with you—you fascinating, charming little darling!

**NORA:** Don't look at me like that, Torvald.

**HELMER:** Why shouldn't I look at my dearest treasure?—at all the beauty that is mine, all my very own?

**NORA:** *(going to the other side of the table)* You mustn't say things like that to me to-night.

**HELMER:** *(following her)* You have still got the Tarantella in your blood, I see. And it makes you more captivating than ever. Listen—the guests are beginning to go now. *(In a lower voice.)* Nora—soon the whole house will be quiet.

**NORA:** Yes, I hope so.

**HELMER:** Yes, my own darling Nora. Do you know, when I am out at a party with you like this, why I speak so little to you, keep away from you, and only send a stolen glance in your direction now and then?—do you know why I do that? It is because I make believe to myself that we are secretly in love, and you are my secretly promised bride, and that no one suspects there is anything between us.

Dr. Rank stops in to say good-bye to the Helmers.

**NORA:** Yes, yes—I know very well your thoughts are with me all the time.

**HELMER:** And when we are leaving, and I am putting the shawl over your beautiful young shoulders—on your lovely neck—then I imagine that you are my young bride and that we have just come from the wedding, and I am bringing you for the first time into our home—to be alone with you for the first time—quite alone with my shy little darling! All this evening I have longed for nothing but you. When I watched the seductive figures of the Tarantella, my blood was on fire; I could endure it no longer, and that was why I brought you down so early—

**NORA:** Go away, Torvald! You must let me go. I won't—

**HELMER:** What's that? You're joking, my little Nora! You won't—you won't? Am I not your husband—? *(A knock is heard at the outer door.)*

**NORA:** *(starting)* Did you hear—?

**HELMER:** *(going into the hall)* Who is it?

**RANK:** *(outside)* It is I. May I come in for a moment?

**HELMER:** *(in a fretful whisper)* Oh, what does he want now? *(Aloud.)* Wait a minute! *(Unlocks the door.)* Come, that's kind of you not to pass by our door.

**RANK:** I thought I heard your voice, and felt as if I should like to look in. *(With a swift glance round.)* Ah, yes!—these dear familiar rooms. You are very happy and cosy in here, you two.

**HELMER:** It seems to me that you looked after yourself pretty well upstairs too.

**RANK:** Excellently. Why shouldn't I? Why shouldn't one enjoy everything in this world?—at any rate as much as one can, and as long as one can. The wine was capital—

**HELMER:** Especially the champagne.

**RANK:** So you noticed that too? It is almost incredible how much I managed to put away!

**NORA:** Torvald drank a great deal of champagne to-night too.

**RANK:** Did he?

**NORA:** Yes, and he is always in such good spirits afterwards.

**RANK:** Well, why should one not enjoy a merry evening after a well-spent day?

**HELMER:** Well spent? I am afraid I can't take credit for that.

**RANK:** *(clapping him on the back)* But I can, you know!

**NORA:** Doctor Rank, you must have been occupied with some scientific investigation to-day.

**RANK:** Exactly.

**HELMER:** Just listen!—little Nora talking about scientific investigations!

**NORA:** And may I congratulate you on the result?

**RANK:** Indeed you may.

**NORA:** Was it favourable, then?

**RANK:** The best possible, for both doctor and patient—certainty.

**NORA:** *(quickly and searchingly)* Certainty?

**RANK:** Absolute certainty. So wasn't I entitled to make a merry evening of it after that?

**NORA:** Yes, you certainly were, Doctor Rank.

**HELMER:** I think so too, so long as you don't have to pay for it in the morning.

**RANK:** Oh well, one can't have anything in this life without paying for it.

**NORA:** Doctor Rank—are you fond of fancy-dress balls?

**RANK:** Yes, if there is a fine lot of pretty costumes.

**NORA:** Tell me—what shall we two wear at the next?

**HELMER:** Little featherbrain!—are you thinking of the next already?

**RANK:** We two? Yes, I can tell you. You shall go as a good fairy—

**HELMER:** Yes, but what do you suggest as an appropriate costume for that?

**RANK:** Let your wife go dressed just as she is in everyday life.

**HELMER:** That was really very prettily turned. But can't you tell us what you will be?

**RANK:** Yes, my dear friend, I have quite made up my mind about that.

**HELMER:** Well?

**RANK:** At the next fancy-dress ball I shall be invisible.

**HELMER:** That's a good joke!

**RANK:** There is a big black hat—have you never heard of hats that make you invisible? If you put one on, no one can see you.

**HELMER:** *(suppressing a smile)* Yes, you are quite right.

**RANK:** But I am clean forgetting what I came for. Helmer, give me a cigar—one of the dark Havanas.

**HELMER:** With the greatest pleasure. *(Offers him his case.)*

**RANK:** *(takes a cigar and cuts off the end)* Thanks.

**NORA:** *(striking a match)* Let me give you a light.

**RANK:** Thank you. *(She holds the match for him to light his cigar.)* And now good-bye!

**HELMER:** Good-bye, good-bye, dear old man!

**NORA:** Sleep well, Doctor Rank.

**RANK:** Thank you for that wish.

**NORA:** Wish me the same.

**RANK:** You? Well, if you want me to sleep well! And thanks for the light. *(He nods to them both and goes out.)*

**HELMER:** *(in a subdued voice)* He has drunk more than he ought.

**NORA:** *(absently)* Maybe. *(*HELMER *takes a bunch of keys out of his pocket and goes into the hall.)* Torvald! what are you going to do there?

**HELMER:** Empty the letter-box; it is quite full; there will be no be room to put the newspaper in to-morrow morning.

**NORA:** Are you going to work to-night?

**HELMER:** You know quite well I'm not. What is this? Someone has been at the lock.

**NORA:** At the lock—?

**HELMER:** Yes, someone has. What can it mean? I should never have thought the maid—. Here is a broken hairpin. Nora, it is one of yours.

**NORA:** *(quickly)* Then it must have been the children—

**HELMER:** Then you must get them out of those ways. There, at last I have got it open. *(Takes out the contents of the letter-box, and calls to the kitchen.)* Helen!—Helen, put out the light over the front door. *(Goes back into the room and shuts the door into the hall. He holds out his hand full of letters.)* Look at that—look what a heap of them there are. *(Turning them over.)* What on earth is that?

**NORA:** *(at the window)* The letter—No! Torvald, no!

**HELMER:** Two cards—of Rank's.

**NORA:** Of Doctor Rank's?

**HELMER:** *(looking at them)* Doctor Rank. They were on the top. He must have put them in when he went out.

**NORA:** Is there anything written on them?

**HELMER:** There is a black cross over the name. Look there—what an uncomfortable idea! It looks as if he were announcing his own death.

**NORA:** It is just what he is doing.

**HELMER:** What? Do you know anything about it? Has he said anything to you?

**NORA:** Yes. He told me that when the cards came it would be his leave-taking from us. He means to shut himself up and die.

**HELMER:** My poor old friend! Certainly I knew we should not have him very long with us. But so soon! And so he hides himself away like a wounded animal.

**NORA:** If it has to happen, it is best it should be without a word—don't you think so, Torvald?

**HELMER:** *(walking up and down)* He had so grown into our lives. I can't think of him as having gone out of them. He, with his sufferings and his loneliness, was like a cloudy background to our sunlit happiness. Well, perhaps it is best so. For him, anyway. *(Standing still.)* And perhaps for us too, Nora. We two are thrown quite upon each other now. *(Puts his arms round her.)* My darling wife, I don't feel as if I could hold you tight enough. Do you know, Nora, I have often wished that you might be threatened by some great danger, so that I might risk my life's blood, and everything, for your sake.

**NORA:** *(disengages herself, and says firmly and decidedly)* Now you must read your letters, Torvald.

**HELMER:** No, no; not to-night. I want to be with you, my darling wife.

**NORA:** With the thought of your friend's death—

**HELMER:** You are right, it has affected us both. Something ugly has come between us—the thought of the horrors of death. We must try and rid our minds of that. Until then—we will each go to our own room.

**NORA:** *(hanging on his neck)* Good-night, Torvald—Good-night!

**HELMER:** *(kissing her on the forehead)* Good-night, my little singing-bird. Sleep sound, Nora. Now I will read my letters through. *(He takes his letters and goes into his room, shutting the door after him.)*

**NORA:** *(gropes distractedly about, seizes* HELMER*'s domino, throws it round her, while she says in quick, hoarse, spasmodic whispers)* Never to see him again. Never! Never! *(Puts her shawl over her head.)* Never to see my children again either—never again. Never! Never!—Ah! the icy, black water—the unfathomable depths—If only it were over! He has got it now—now he is reading it. Good-bye, Torvald and my children! *(She is about to rush out through the hall, when* HELMER *opens his door hurriedly and stands with an open letter in his hand.)*

**HELMER:** Nora!

**NORA:** Ah!—

**HELMER:** What is this? Do you know what is in this letter?

**NORA:** Yes, I know. Let me go! Let me get out!

**HELMER:** *(holding her back)* Where are you going?

**NORA:** *(trying to get free)* You shan't save me, Torvald!

**HELMER:** *(reeling)* True? Is this true, that I read here? Horrible! No, no—it is impossible that it can be true.

**NORA:** It is true. I have loved you above everything else in the world.

**HELMER:** Oh, don't let us have any silly excuses.

**NORA:** *(taking a step towards him)* Torvald—!

**HELMER:** Miserable creature—what have you done?

**NORA:** Let me go. You shall not suffer for my sake. You shall not take it upon yourself.

**HELMER:** No tragedy airs, please. *(Locks the hall door.)* Here you shall stay and give me an explanation. Do you understand what you have done? Answer me! Do you understand what you have done?

**NORA:** *(looks steadily at him and says with a growing look of coldness in her face)* Yes, now I am beginning to understand thoroughly.

**HELMER:** *(walking about the room)* What a horrible awakening! All these eight years—she who was my joy and pride—a hypocrite, a liar—worse, worse—a criminal! The unutterable ugliness of it all!—For shame! For shame! *(*NORA *is silent and looks steadily at him. He stops in front of her.)* I ought to have suspected that something of the sort would happen. I ought to have foreseen it. All your father's want of principle—be silent!—all your father's want of principle has

Torvald, having read the letter, confronts Nora.

come out in you. No religion, no morality, no sense of duty—. How I am punished for having winked at what he did! I did it for your sake, and this is how you repay me.

**NORA:** Yes, that's just it.

**HELMER:** Now you have destroyed all my happiness. You have ruined all my future. It is horrible to think of! I am in the power of an unscrupulous man; he can do what he likes with me, ask anything he likes of me, give me any orders he pleases—I dare not refuse. And I must sink to such miserable depths because of a thoughtless woman!

**NORA:** When I am out of the way, you will be free.

**HELMER:** No fine speeches, please. Your father had always plenty of those ready, too. What good would it be to me if you were out of the way, as you say? Not the slightest. He can make the affair known everywhere; and if he does, I may be falsely suspected of having been a party to your criminal action. Very likely people will think I was behind it all—that it was I who prompted you! And I have to thank you for all this—you whom I have cherished during the whole of our married life. Do you understand now what it is you have done for me?

**NORA:** *(coldly and quietly)* Yes.

**HELMER:** It is so incredible that I can't take it in. But we must come to some understanding. Take off that shawl. Take it off, I tell you. I must try and appease him some way or another. The matter must be hushed up at any cost. And as for you and me, it must appear as if everything between us were just as before—but naturally only in the eyes of the world. You will still remain in my house, that is a matter of course. But I shall not allow you to bring up the children; I dare not trust them to you. To think that I should be obliged to say so to one whom I have loved so dearly, and whom I still—. No, that is all over. From this moment happiness is not the question; all that concerns us is to save the remains, the fragments, the appearance—

*(A ring is heard at the front-door bell.)*

**HELMER:** *(with a start)* What is that? So late! Can the worst—? Can he—? Hide yourself, Nora. Say you are ill.

*(*NORA *stands motionless.* HELMER *goes and unlocks the hall door.)*

**MAID:** *(half dressed, comes to the door)* A letter for the mistress.

**HELMER:** Give it to me. *(Takes the letter, and shuts the door.)* Yes, it is from him. You shall not have it; I will read it myself.

**NORA:** Yes, read it.

**HELMER:** *(standing by the lamp)* I scarcely have the courage to do it. It may mean ruin for both of us. No, I must know. *(Tears open the letter, runs his eye over a few lines, looks at a paper enclosed, and gives a shout of joy.)* Nora! *(She looks at him questioningly.)* Nora!—No, I must read it once again—. Yes, it is true! I am saved! Nora, I am saved!

**NORA:** And I?

**HELMER:** You too, of course; we are both saved, both you and I. Look, he sends you your bond back. He says he regrets and repents—that a happy change in his life—never mind what he says! We are saved, Nora! No one can do anything to you. Oh, Nora, Nora!—no, first I must destroy these hateful things. Let me see—. *(Takes a look at the bond.)* No, no, I won't look at it. The whole thing shall be nothing but a bad dream to me. *(Tears up the bond and both letters, throws them all into the stove, and watches them burn.)* There—now it doesn't exist any longer. He says that since Christmas Eve you—. These must have been three dreadful days for you, Nora.

**NORA:** I have fought a hard fight these three days.

**HELMER:** And suffered agonies, and seen no way out but—. No, we won't call any of the horrors to mind. We will only shout with joy, and keep saying, "It's all over! It's all over!" Listen to me, Nora. You don't seem to realise that it is all over. What is this?—such a cold, set face! My poor little Nora, I quite understand; you don't feel as if you could believe that I have forgiven you. But it is true, Nora, I swear it; I have forgiven you everything. I know that what you did, you did out of love for me.

**NORA:** That is true.

**HELMER:** You have loved me as a wife ought to love her husband. Only you had not sufficient knowledge to judge of the means you used. But do you suppose you are any the less dear to me, because you don't understand how to act on your own responsibility? No, no; only lean on me; I will advise you and direct you. I should not be a man if this womanly helplessness did not just give you a double attractiveness in my eyes. You must not think any more about the hard things I said in my first moment of consternation, when I thought everything was going to overwhelm me. I have forgiven you, Nora; I swear to you I have forgiven you.

**NORA:** Thank you for your forgiveness. *(She goes out through the door to the right.)*

**HELMER:** No, don't go—. *(Looks in.)* What are you doing in there?

**NORA:** *(from within)* Taking off my fancy dress.

**HELMER:** *(standing at the open door)* Yes, do. Try and calm yourself, and make your mind easy again, my frightened little singing-bird. Be at rest, and feel secure; I have broad wings to shelter you under. *(Walks up and down by the door.)* How warm and cosy our home is, Nora. Here is shelter for you; here I will protect you like a hunted dove that I have saved from a hawk's claws; I will bring peace to your poor beating heart. It will come, little by little, Nora, believe me. To-morrow morning you will look upon it all quite differently; soon everything will be just as it was before. Very soon you won't need me to assure you that I have forgiven you; you will yourself feel the certainty that I have done so. Can you suppose I should ever think of such a thing as repudiating you, or even reproaching you? You have no idea what a true man's heart is like, Nora. There is something so indescribably sweet and satisfying, to a man, in the knowledge that he has forgiven his wife—forgiven her freely, and with all his heart. It seems as if that had made her, as it were, doubly his own; he has given her a new life, so to speak; and she has in a way become both wife and child to him. So you shall be for me after this, my little scared, helpless darling. Have no anxiety about anything, Nora; only be frank and open with me, and I will serve as will and conscience both to you—. What is this? Not gone to bed? Have you changed your things?

**NORA:** *(in everyday dress)* Yes, Torvald, I have changed my things now.

**HELMER:** But what for?—so late as this.

**NORA:** I shall not sleep to-night.

**HELMER:** But, my dear Nora—

**NORA:** *(looking at her watch)* It is not so very late. Sit down here, Torvald. You and I have much to say to one another. *(She sits down at one side of the table.)*

**HELMER:** Nora—what is this?—this cold, set face?

**NORA:** Sit down. It will take some time; I have a lot to talk over with you.

**HELMER:** *(sits down at the opposite side of the table)* You alarm me, Nora!—and I don't understand you.

**NORA:** No, that is just it. You don't understand me, and I have never understood you either—before to-night. No, you mustn't interrupt me. You must simply listen to what I say. Torvald, this is a settling of accounts.

**HELMER:** What do you mean by that?

**NORA:** *(after a short silence)* Isn't there one thing that strikes you as strange in our sitting here like this?

**HELMER:** What is that?

**NORA:** We have been married now eight years. Does it not occur to you that this is the first time we two, you and I, husband and wife, have had a serious conversation?

**HELMER:** What do you mean by serious?

Torvald tries to comfort Nora after his tirade.

**NORA:** In all these eight years—longer than that—from the very beginning of our acquaintance, we have never exchanged a word on any serious subject.

**HELMER:** Was it likely that I would be continually and for ever telling you about worries that you could not help me to bear?

**NORA:** I am not speaking about business matters. I say that we have never sat down in earnest together to try and get at the bottom of anything.

**HELMER:** But, dearest Nora, would it have been any good to you?

**NORA:** That is just it; you have never understood me. I have been greatly wronged, Torvald—first by papa and then by you.

**HELMER:** What! By us two—by us two, who have loved you better than anyone else in the world?

**NORA:** *(shaking her head)* You have never loved me. You have only thought it pleasant to be in love with me.

**HELMER:** Nora, what do I hear you saying?

**NORA:** It is perfectly true, Torvald. When I was at home with papa, he told me his opinion about everything, and so I had the same opinions; and if I differed from him I concealed the fact, because he would not have liked it. He called me his doll-child, and he played with me just as I used to play with my dolls. And when I came to live with you—

**HELMER:** What sort of an expression is that to use about our marriage?

**NORA:** *(undisturbed)* I mean that I was simply transferred from papa's hands into yours. You arranged everything according to your own taste, and so I got the same tastes as you—or else I pretended to, I am really not quite sure which—I think sometimes the one and sometimes the other. When I look back on it, it seems to me as if I had been living here like a poor woman—just from hand to mouth. I have existed merely to perform tricks for you, Torvald. But you would have it so. You and papa have committed a great sin against me. It is your fault that I have made nothing of my life.

**HELMER:** How unreasonable and how ungrateful you are, Nora! Have you not been happy here?

**NORA:** No, I have never been happy. I thought I was, but it has never really been so.

**HELMER:** Not—not happy!

**NORA:** No, only merry. And you have always been so kind to me. But our home has been nothing but a playroom. I have been your doll-wife, just as at home I was papa's doll-child; and here the children have been my dolls. I thought it great fun when you played with me, just as they thought it great fun when I played with them. That is what our marriage has been, Torvald.

**HELMER:** There is some truth in what you say—exaggerated and strained as your view of it is. But for the future it shall be different. Playtime shall be over, and lesson-time shall begin.

**NORA:** Whose lessons? Mine, or the children's?

**HELMER:** Both yours and the children's, my darling Nora.

**NORA:** Alas, Torvald, you are not the man to educate me into being a proper wife for you.

**HELMER:** And you can say that!

**NORA:** And I—how am I fitted to bring up the children?

**HELMER:** Nora!

**NORA:** Didn't you say so yourself a little while ago—that you dare not trust me to bring them up?

**HELMER:** In a moment of anger! Why do you pay any heed to that?

**NORA:** Indeed, you were perfectly right. I am not fit for the task. There is another task I must undertake first. I must try and educate myself—you are not the man to help me in that. I must do that for myself. And that is why I am going to leave you now.

**HELMER:** *(springing up)* What do you say?

**NORA:** I must stand quite alone, if I am to understand myself and everything about me. It is for that reason that I cannot remain with you any longer.

**HELMER:** Nora, Nora!

**NORA:** I am going away from here now, at once. I am sure Christine will take me in for the night—

**HELMER:** You are out of your mind! I won't allow it! I forbid you!

**NORA:** It is no use forbidding me anything any longer. I will take with me what belongs to myself. I will take nothing from you, either now or later.

**HELMER:** What sort of madness is this!

**NORA:** To-morrow I shall go home—I mean, to my old home. It will be easiest for me to find something to do there.

**HELMER:** You blind, foolish woman!

**NORA:** I must try and get some sense, Torvald.

**HELMER:** To desert your home, your husband and your children! And you don't consider what people will say!

**NORA:** I cannot consider that at all. I only know that it is necessary for me.

**HELMER:** It's shocking. This is how you would neglect your most sacred duties.

**NORA:** What do you consider my most sacred duties?

**HELMER:** Do I need to tell you that? Are they not your duties to your husband and your children?

**NORA:** I have other duties just as sacred.

**HELMER:** That you have not. What duties could those be?

**NORA:** Duties to myself.

**HELMER:** Before all else, you are a wife and a mother.

**NORA:** I don't believe in that any longer. I believe that before all else I am a reasonable human being, just as you are—or, at all events, that I must try and become one. I know quite well, Torvald, that most people would think you right; and that views of that kind are to be found in books; but I can no longer content myself with what most people say, or with what is found in books. I must think over things for myself and get to understand them.

**HELMER:** Can you not understand your place in your own home? Have you not a reliable guide in such matters as that?—have you no religion?

**NORA:** I am afraid, Torvald, I do not exactly know what religion is.

**HELMER:** What are you saying?

**NORA:** I know nothing but what the clergyman said, when I went to be confirmed. He told us that religion was this, and that, and the other. When I am away from all this, and am alone, I will look into that matter too. I will see if what the clergyman said is true, or at all events if it is true for me.

**HELMER:** This is unheard of in a girl of your age! But if religion cannot lead you aright, let me try and awaken your conscience. I suppose you have some moral sense? Or—answer me—am I to think you have none?

**NORA:** I assure you, Torvald, that is not an easy question to answer. I really don't know. The thing perplexes me altogether. I only know that you and I look at it in quite a different light. I am learning, too, that the law is quite another thing from what I supposed; but I find it impossible to convince myself that the law is right. According to it a woman has no right to spare her old dying father, or to save her husband's life. I can't believe that.

**HELMER:** You talk like a child. You don't understand the conditions of the world in which you live.

**NORA:** No, I don't. But now I am going to try. I am going to see if I can make out who is right, the world or I.

**HELMER:** You are ill, Nora; you are delirious; I almost think you are out of your mind.

**NORA:** I have never felt my mind so clear and certain as to-night.

**HELMER:** And is it with a clear and certain mind that you forsake your husband and your children?

**NORA:** Yes, it is.

**HELMER:** Then there is only one possible explanation.

**NORA:** What is that?

**HELMER:** You do not love me any more.

**NORA:** No, that is just it.

**HELMER:** Nora!—and you can say that?

**NORA:** It gives me great pain, Torvald, for you have always been so kind to me, but I cannot help it. I do not love you any more.

**HELMER:** *(regaining his composure)* Is that a clear and certain conviction too?

**NORA:** Yes, absolutely clear and certain. That is the reason why I will not stay here any longer.

**HELMER:** And can you tell me what I have done to forfeit your love?

**NORA:** Yes, indeed I can. It was to-night, when the wonderful thing did not happen; then I saw you were not the man I had thought you.

**HELMER:** Explain yourself better. I don't understand you.

**NORA:** I have waited so patiently for eight years; for, goodness knows, I knew very well that wonderful things don't happen every day. Then this horrible misfortune came upon me; and then I felt quite certain that the wonderful thing was going to happen at last. When Krogstad's letter was lying out there, never for a moment did I imagine that you would consent to accept this man's conditions. I was so absolutely certain that you would say to him: Publish the thing to the whole world. And when that was done—

**HELMER:** Yes, what then?—when I had exposed my wife to shame and disgrace?

**NORA:** When that was done, I was so absolutely certain, you would come forward and take everything upon yourself, and say: I am the guilty one.

**HELMER:** Nora—!

**NORA:** You mean that I would never have accepted such a sacrifice on your part? No, of course not. But what would my assurances have been worth against yours? That was the wonderful thing which I hoped for and feared; and it was to prevent that, that I wanted to kill myself.

**HELMER:** I would gladly work night and day for you, Nora—bear sorrow and want for your sake. But no man would sacrifice his honour for the one he loves.

**NORA:** It is a thing hundreds of thousands of women have done.

**HELMER:** Oh, you think and talk like a heedless child.

**NORA:** Maybe. But you neither think nor talk like the man I could bind myself to. As soon as your fear was over—and it was not fear for what threatened me, but for what might happen to you—when the whole thing was past, as far as you were concerned it was exactly as if nothing at all had happened. Exactly as before, I was your little skylark, your doll, which you would in future treat with doubly gentle care, because it was so brittle and fragile. *(Getting up.)* Torvald—it was then it dawned upon me that for eight years I had been living here with a strange man, and had borne him three children—. Oh, I can't bear to think of it! I could tear myself into little bits!

**HELMER:** *(sadly)* I see, I see. An abyss has opened between us—there is no denying it. But, Nora, would it not be possible to fill it up?

**NORA:** As I am now, I am no wife for you.

**HELMER:** I have it in me to become a different man.

**NORA:** Perhaps—if your doll is taken away from you.

Nora, dressed for travel, explains her epiphany to Torvald.

**HELMER:** But to part!—to part from you! No, no, Nora, I can't understand that idea.

**NORA:** *(going out to the right)* That makes it all the more certain that it must be done. *(She comes back with her cloak and hat and a small bag which she puts on a chair by the table.)*

**HELMER:** Nora, Nora, not now! Wait till to-morrow.

**NORA:** *(putting on her cloak)* I cannot spend the night in a strange man's room.

**HELMER:** But can't we live here like brother and sister—?

**NORA:** *(putting on her hat)* You know very well that would not last long. *(Puts the shawl round her.)* Goodbye, Torvald. I won't see the little ones. I know they are in better hands than mine. As I am now, I can be of no use to them.

**HELMER:** But some day, Nora—some day?

**NORA:** How can I tell? I have no idea what is going to become of me.

**HELMER:** But you are my wife, whatever becomes of you.

**NORA:** Listen, Torvald. I have heard that when a wife deserts her husband's house, as I am doing now, he is legally freed from all obligations towards her. In any case I set you free from all your obligations. You are not to feel yourself bound in the slightest way, any more than I shall. There must be perfect freedom on both sides. See, here is your ring back. Give me mine.

**HELMER:** That too?

**NORA:** That too.

**HELMER:** Here it is.

Torvald, alone, gazes around the empty house.

**NORA:** That's right. Now it is all over. I have put the keys here. The maids know all about everything in the house—better than I do. To-morrow, after I have left her, Christine will come here and pack up my own things that I brought with me from home. I will have them sent after me.

**HELMER:** All over! All over!—Nora, shall you never think of me again?

**NORA:** I know I shall often think of you and the children and this house.

**HELMER:** May I write to you, Nora?

**NORA:** No—never. You must not to do that.

**HELMER:** But at least let me send you—

**NORA:** Nothing—nothing—

**HELMER:** Let me help you if you are in want.

**NORA:** No. I can receive nothing from a stranger.

**HELMER:** Nora—can I never be anything more than a stranger to you?

**NORA:** *(taking her bag)* Ah, Torvald, the most wonderful thing of all would have to happen.

**HELMER:** Tell me what would that be!

**NORA:** Both you and I would have to be so changed that—. Oh, Torvald, I don't believe any longer in wonderful things happening.

**HELMER:** But I will believe in it. Tell me! So changed that—?

**NORA:** That our life together would be a real wedlock. Good-bye. *(She goes out through the hall.)*

**HELMER:** *(sinks down on a chair at the door and buries his face in his hands)* Nora! Nora! *(Looks round, and rises.)* Empty. She is gone. *(A hope flashes across his mind.)* The most wonderful thing of all—?

*(The sound of a door shutting is heard from below.)*

# Writing from Reading

### Summarize

1 Some call this much-discussed and widely performed play the first feminist play. This script challenged and in some cases outraged contemporary audiences. In fact, the first German productions of *A Doll's House* in the 1880s had an altered ending at the request of the producers. Ibsen referred to this version as a "barbaric outrage" to be used only in emergencies. What other endings could you imagine that Ibsen might endorse?

### Analyze Craft

2 Dr. Rank assumes the role of the wise, elder statesman—a familiar figure in such theater. In truth, however, he's someone who's ill and even rotting, not elevated. What does his desire for Nora suggest as to his character, and in what if any ways does Ibsen cast him in a sympathetic light?

3 When Nora, in Act III, tells Torvald that they must "sit down and discuss all this that has been happening between us," *A Doll's House* diverges from the final resolution of the well-made play. What do you imagine is the future of the marriage; who has changed, and how?

4 Nora's father is a major figure here, though always offstage. List his characteristics. How does Nora reveal how she feels about her father's characteristics? Does Nora want her husband to have more of her father's qualities, or qualities that are less similar?

### Analyze Voice

5 Descriptive names for Nora include "little skylark," "fascinating, charming little darling," "my darling wife," "my little singing-bird," "little, scared darling," "blind, foolish woman," and "a heedless child." Which of these strikes you as most appropriate—or are they all true? How do they vary in the course of the play?

6 Nora often disguises the truth and—several times—lies in the course of the play. Are these white lies or genuine falsehoods? How do they increase or decrease our trust in her and why?

7 When Nora says that she requires Torvald to help her practice for the dance, what does she imply?

8 The first act takes place on Christmas Eve. Christmas is not, however, presented as a religious holiday and religion as a concept is questioned by Nora in Act III. In fact, it is discussed much more often as a material than a spiritual experience. Does Ibsen here endorse or disapprove of the centrality of material goods over personal connection; what solution does he propose?

9 What overall tone does the play project? In what way does the tone change over the course of the play?

### Synthesize Summary and Analysis

10 The plot contrasts an old way of life with the glimmer of a new way to live. How would you explain this in terms of the struggle between illusion and reality as seen in Greek tragedy?

### Interpret the Play

11 Ibsen believed that "a dramatist's business is not to answer questions, but only to ask them." Would you describe the play's conclusion as closer to comic or tragic in tone? In what ways is it happy or unhappy, and what questions has he asked?

## THE REAL AND THE SURREAL

While Arthur Miller's *Death of a Salesman* represented on the American stage the realist tradition of Ibsen and its overt social criticism, other dramatic techniques came largely into view in the modern theater. **Expressionism,** particularly as practiced by the German playwright Frank Wedekind (1864–1918), whose *Spring Awakening* scandalized audiences with its exploration of sexuality and puberty, draws strongly and mainly on subjective emotions and attempts to find symbolic means to depict them onstage. **Symbolism,** represented by the late works of the Swede August Strindberg (1849–1912) and whose chief practitioner in English is W. B. Yeats (1865–1939), employed poetic techniques by using image, character, or action to suggest meaning beyond the everyday literal level. The deployment of **surrealism,** a technique that bloomed in the early part of the twentieth century in which, as French writer and poet André Breton (1896–1966) suggests in his 1924 "Surrealist Manifesto," the realism of conscious and of unconscious experience are fused together into "an absolute reality, a surreality," added to the ultimate dreamlike quality of the lives onstage. By contrast, Bertolt Brecht's (1898–1956) development of **Epic Theater** brought to the theater a spare and highly stylized set that celebrated ideas over emotions. **Theater of the Absurd** combined comedic elements with a sense of meaninglessness as practiced by Eugene Ionesco (1909–1994), Samuel Beckett (1906–1989), and Edward Albee (chapter 32).

"Someone like Tennessee Williams . . . wrote . . . with a sort of added measure of lyricism and poetry." Conversation with Edwin Wilson

In addition, the American theater's Tennessee Williams's heightened form of realism supplied a poetic overlay to the situation and language, even a kind of *surrealism* in the family dynamic. Williams moves from actual scene to imagined or remembered encounter, and we follow the events almost as though we hallucinate them; the logic of the action is close to the logic of dream.

As Williams—who was born Thomas Lanier Williams, but kept his college nickname "Tennessee"—wrote in *Production Notes to The Glass Menagerie,*

> *Being a memory play,* The Glass Menagerie *can be presented with unusual freedom of convention. Because of its considerably delicate or tenuous material, atmospheric touches and subtleties of direction play a particularly important part. Expressionism and all other unconventional techniques in drama have only one valid aim, and that is a closer approach to truth. When a play employs unconventional techniques, it is not, or certainly shouldn't be, trying to escape its responsibility of dealing with reality, or interpreting experience, but is actually or should be attempting to find a closer approach, a more penetrating and vivid expression of things as they are.*

Much of the rest of that essay—and much of Williams's subsequent work—insists on avoiding "The straight realistic play with its genuine Frigidaire and authentic ice cubes . . . " but his is a kind of lover's quarrel with the idea of realism; he heightens the language of everyday discourse and lowers the lighting so that "the stage is dim." Characters stand in spotlit shafts of light when, turn by turn, they speak, and often what passes for dialogue is a kind of back-and-forth monologue. Nonetheless, the underlying assumption here is that the playwright must scrutinize the real world and portray actual behavior.

"Tennessee was splendid enough a mind to be able to write his women as women, and his men as men. I don't think he was hiding anything. . . . It was only the half-blind straight critics who decided [that if] Tennessee Williams was gay, he must have been lying when he wrote women, which strikes me as being the critical fallacy, as we love to call it." Conversation with Edward Albee

In *The Glass Menagerie,* the family is middle class—southern and shabby genteel. The mother with her insistence on manners and self-deluding remembrance of "gentlemen callers," the crippled daughter Laura and the tortured brother Tom—who attempts to both escape from and come to terms with his heritage—form a traditional family unit (with the father gone). But, as the play's title suggests, things are brittle, breakable, and this particular middle-class "menagerie" is just as much at risk as the Loman clan.

# Tennessee Williams (1911–1983)

Born in Mississippi, Tennessee Williams lived in a small town with his mother and maternal grandparents. His father, a salesman, was frequently away. However, when his father moved the family to St. Louis, Williams grew unhappy—largely because of the taunts his father constantly directed toward him—and turned to writing as an escape. After drifting among three universities, Williams earned a B.A. from the University of Iowa and began a life of wandering and writing plays. He became one of the most important American playwrights of the century, writing masterpiece after masterpiece including *The Glass Menagerie* (1945), *A Streetcar Named Desire* (1947), *Cat on a Hot Tin Roof* (1954), and *Suddenly Last Summer* (1958). Symbolic and poetic, much of his work is set in the South, where his highly developed characters struggle with feelings of isolation. Williams himself struggled with such feelings, as his homosexuality excluded him from mainstream society. Although he won his second Pulitzer Prize in 1955, Williams experienced an artistic and personal decline from that point to the end of his life.

**AS YOU READ** **Trace the intertwining threads of the starkly real and the lyrical element in the language.**

# The Glass Menagerie (1945)

*nobody, not even the rain, has such small hands*

—e. e. cummings

## CHARACTERS

**AMANDA WINGFIELD,** *the mother. A little woman of great but confused vitality clinging frantically to another time and place. Her characterization must be carefully created, not copied from type. She is not paranoiac, but her life is paranoia. There is much to admire in Amanda, and as much to love and pity as there is to laugh at. Certainly she has endurance and a kind of heroism, and though her foolishness makes her unwittingly cruel at times, there is tenderness in her slight person.*

**LAURA WINGFIELD,** *her daughter. Amanda, having failed to establish contact with reality, continues to live vitally in her illusions, but Laura's situation is even graver. A childhood illness has left her crippled, one leg slightly shorter than the other, and held in a brace. This defect need not be more than suggested on the stage. Stemming from this, Laura's separation increases till she is like a piece of her own glass collection, too exquisitely fragile to move from the shelf.*

**TOM WINGFIELD,** *her son. And the narrator of the play. A poet with a job in a warehouse. His nature is not remorseless, but to escape from a trap he has to act without pity.*

**JIM O'CONNOR,** *the gentleman caller. A nice, ordinary, young man.*

**SCENE:** *An alley in St. Louis.*

**PART I:** *Preparation for a Gentleman Caller.*

**PART II:** *The Gentleman Calls.*

**TIME:** *Now and the Past.*

## SCENE I

*The Wingfield apartment is in the rear of the building, one of those vast hivelike conglomerations of cellular living-units that flower as warty growths in overcrowded urban centers of lower middle-class population and are symptomatic of the impulse of this largest and fundamentally enslaved section of American society to avoid fluidity and differentiation and to exist and function as one interfused mass of automatism.*

*The apartment faces an alley and is entered by a fire-escape, a structure whose name is a touch of accidental poetic truth, for all of these huge buildings are always burning with the slow and implacable fires of human desperation. The fire-escape is included in the set—that is, the landing of it and steps descending from it.*

*The scene is memory and is therefore nonrealistic. Memory takes a lot of poetic license. It omits some details; others are exaggerated, according to the emotional value of the articles it touches, for memory is seated predominantly in the heart. The interior is therefore rather dim and poetic.*

*At the rise of the curtain, the audience is faced with the dark, grim rear wall of the Wingfield tenement. This building, which runs parallel to the footlights, is flanked on both sides by dark, narrow alleys which run into murky canyons of tangled clotheslines, garbage cans, and the sinister latticework of neighboring fire-escapes. It is up and down these side alleys that exterior entrances and exits are made, during the play. At the end of* TOM's *opening commentary, the dark tenement wall slowly reveals (by means of transparency) the interior of the ground floor Wingfield apartment.*

*Downstage is the living room, which also serves as a sleeping room for* LAURA, *the sofa unfolding to make her bed. Upstage, center, and divided by a wide arch or second proscenium with transparent faded portieres (or second curtain), is the dining room. In an old-fashioned what-not in the living room are seen scores of transparent glass animals. A blown-up photograph of the father hangs on the wall of the living room, facing the audience, to the left of the archway. It is the face of a very handsome young man in a doughboy's First World War cap. He is gallantly smiling, ineluctably smiling, as if to say, "I will be smiling forever."*

*The audience hears and sees the opening scene in the dining room through both the transparent fourth wall of the building and the transparent gauze portieres of the dining-room arch. It is during this revealing scene that the fourth wall slowly ascends, out of sight. This transparent exterior wall is not brought down again until the very end of the play, during* TOM's *final speech.*

*The narrator is an undisguised convention of the play. He takes whatever license with dramatic convention as is convenient to his purposes.*

TOM *enters dressed as a merchant sailor from alley, stage left, and strolls across the front of the stage to the fire-escape. There he stops and lights a cigarette. He addresses the audience.*

**TOM:** Yes, I have tricks in my pocket, I have things up my sleeve. But I am opposite of a stage magician. He gives you illusion that has the appearance of truth. I give you truth in the pleasant disguise of illusion. To begin with, I turn back time. I reverse it to that quaint period, the thirties, when the huge middle class of America was matriculating in a school for the blind. Their eyes had failed them, or they had failed their eyes, and so they were having their fingers pressed forcibly down on the fiery Braille alphabet of a dissolving economy. In Spain there was revolution. Here there was only shouting and confusion. In Spain there was Guernica. Here there were disturbances of labor, sometimes pretty violent, in otherwise peaceful cities such as Chicago, Cleveland, Saint Louis. . . . This is the social background of the play.

*(Music.)*

The play is memory. Being a memory play, it is dimly lighted, it is sentimental, it is not realistic. In memory everything seems to happen to music. That explains

Tom (Sam Waterston) delivers the opening monologue in the 1973 film directed by Anthony Harvey.

the fiddle in the wings. I am the narrator of the play, and also a character in it. The other characters are my mother, Amanda, my sister, Laura, and a gentleman caller who appears in the final scenes. He is the most realistic character in the play, being an emissary from a world of reality that we were somehow set apart from. But since I have a poet's weakness for symbols, I am using this character also as a symbol; he is the long delayed but always expected something that we live for. There is a fifth character in the play who doesn't appear except in this larger-than-life photograph over the mantel. This is our father who left us a long time ago. He was a telephone man who fell in love with long distances; he gave up his job with the telephone company and skipped the light fantastic out of town. . . . The last we heard of him was a picture post-card from Mazatlán, on the Pacific coast of Mexico, containing a message of two words—"Hello—Goodbye!" and no address. I think the rest of the play will explain itself. . . .

AMANDA*'s voice becomes audible through the portieres.*

*(Legend on screen: "Où sont les neiges.")*

*He divides the portieres and enters the upstage area.*

AMANDA *and* LAURA *are seated at a drop-leaf table. Eating is indicated by gestures without food or utensils.* AMANDA *faces the audience.*

TOM *and* LAURA *are seated in profile.*

*The interior has lit up softly and through the scrim we see* AMANDA *and* LAURA *seated at the table in the upstage area.*

**AMANDA:** *(calling)* Tom?

**TOM:** Yes, Mother.

**AMANDA:** We can't say grace until you come to the table!

**TOM:** Coming, Mother. *(He bows slightly and withdraws, reappearing a few moments later in his place at the table.)*

**AMANDA:** *(to her son)* Honey, don't *push* with your *fingers*. If you have to push with something, the thing to push with is a crust of bread. And chew—chew! Animals have sections in their stomachs which enable them to digest food without mastication, but human beings are supposed to chew their food before they swallow it down. Eat food leisurely, son, and really enjoy it. A well-cooked meal has lots of delicate flavors that have to be held in the mouth for appreciation. So chew your food and give your salivary glands a chance to function!

TOM *deliberately lays his imaginary fork down and pushes his chair back from the table.*

**TOM:** I haven't enjoyed one bite of this dinner because of your constant directions on how to eat it. It's you that makes me rush through meals with your hawk-like attention to every bite I take. Sickening—spoils my appetite—all this discussion of animals' secretion—salivary glands—mastication!

**AMANDA:** *(lightly)* Temperament like a Metropolitan star! *(He rises and crosses downstage.)* You're not excused from the table.

**TOM:** I am getting a cigarette.

**AMANDA:** You smoke too much.

LAURA *rises.*

**LAURA:** I'll bring in the blanc mange.

*He remains standing with his cigarette by the portieres during the following.*

**AMANDA:** *(rising)* No, sister, no, sister—you be the lady this time and I'll be the darky.

**LAURA:** I'm already up.

**AMANDA:** Resume your seat, little sister—I want you to stay fresh and pretty—for gentlemen callers!

**LAURA:** I'm not expecting any gentlemen callers.

**AMANDA:** *(crossing out to kitchenette. Airily)* Sometimes they come when they are least expected! Why, I remember one Sunday afternoon in Blue Mountain—*(Enters kitchenette.)*

**TOM:** I know what's coming!

**LAURA:** Yes. But let her tell it.

**TOM:** Again?

**LAURA:** She loves to tell it.

AMANDA *returns with a bowl of dessert.*

**AMANDA:** One Sunday afternoon in Blue Mountain—your mother received—*seventeen!*—gentlemen callers! Why, sometimes there weren't chairs enough to accommodate them all. We had to send the nigger over to bring in folding chairs from the parish house.

**TOM:** *(remaining at the portieres)* How did you entertain those gentlemen callers?

**AMANDA:** I understood the art of conversation!

**TOM:** I bet you could talk.

**AMANDA:** Girls in those days *knew* how to talk, I can tell you.

Amanda (Katharine Hepburn) clears the table.

**TOM:** Yes?

*(Image:* AMANDA *as a girl on a porch greeting callers.)*

**AMANDA:** They knew how to entertain their gentlemen callers. It wasn't enough for a girl to be possessed of a pretty face and a graceful figure—although I wasn't slighted in either respect. She also needed to have a nimble wit and a tongue to meet all occasions.

**TOM:** What did you talk about?

**AMANDA:** Things of importance going on in the world! Never anything coarse or common or vulgar. *(She addresses* TOM *as though he were seated in the vacant chair at the table though he remains by the portieres. He plays this scene as though he held the book.)* My callers were gentlemen—all! Among my callers were some of the most prominent young planters of the Mississippi Delta—planters and sons of planters!

TOM *motions for music and a spot of light on* AMANDA.

*Her eyes lift, her face glows, her voice becomes rich and elegiac.*

*(Screen legend: "Où sont les neiges.")*

There was young Champ Laughlin who later became vice-president of the Delta Planters Bank. Hadley Stevenson who was drowned in Moon Lake and left his widow one hundred and fifty thousand in Government bonds. There were the Cutrere brothers, Wesley and Bates. Bates was one of my bright particular beaux! He got in a quarrel with that wild Wainwright boy. They shot it out on the floor of Moon Lake Casino. Bates was shot through the stomach. Died in the ambulance on his way to Memphis. His widow was also well-provided for, came into eight or ten thousand acres, that's all. She married him on the rebound—never loved her—carried my picture on him the night he died! And there was that boy that every girl in the Delta had set her cap for! That beautiful, brilliant young Fitzhugh boy from Greene County!

**TOM:** What did he leave his widow?

**AMANDA:** He never married! Gracious, you talk as though all of my old admirers had turned up their toes to the daisies!

**TOM:** Isn't this the first you mentioned that still survives?

**AMANDA:** That Fitzhugh boy went North and made a fortune—came to be known as the Wolf of Wall Street! He had the Midas touch, whatever he touched turned to gold! And I could have been Mrs. Duncan J. Fitzhugh, mind you! But—I picked your *father!*

**LAURA:** *(rising)* Mother, let me clear the table.

**AMANDA:** No dear, you go in front and study your typewriter chart. Or practice your shorthand a little. Stay fresh and pretty!—It's almost time for our gentlemen callers to start arriving. *(She flounces girlishly toward the kitchenette.)* How many do you suppose we're going to entertain this afternoon?

TOM *throws down the paper and jumps up with a groan.*

**LAURA:** *(alone in the dining room)* I don't believe we're going to receive any, Mother.

**AMANDA:** *(reappearing, airily)* What? No one—not one? You must be joking! *(*LAURA *nervously echoes her laugh. She slips in a fugitive manner through the half-open portieres and draws them gently behind her. A shaft of very clear light is thrown on her face against the faded tapestry of the curtains.) (Music: "The Glass Menagerie" under faintly.) (Lightly.)* Not one gentleman caller? It can't be true! There must be a flood, there must have been a tornado!

**LAURA:** It isn't a flood, it's not a tornado, Mother. I'm just not popular like you were in Blue Mountain. . . . *(*TOM *utters another groan.* LAURA *glances at him with a faint, apologetic smile. Her voice catching a little.)* Mother's afraid I'm going to be an old maid.

*(The scene dims out with the "Glass Menagerie" music.)*

## SCENE II

*"Laura, Haven't You Ever Liked Some Boy?"*

*On the dark stage the screen is lighted with the image of blue roses.*

*Gradually* LAURA's *figure becomes apparent and the screen goes out.*

*The music subsides.*

LAURA *is seated in the delicate ivory chair at the small clawfoot table.*

*She wears a dress of soft violet material for a kimono—her hair tied back from her forehead with a ribbon.*

*She is washing and polishing her collection of glass.*

AMANDA *appears on the fire-escape steps. At the sound of her ascent,* LAURA *catches her breath, thrusts the bowl of ornaments away, and seats herself stiffly before the diagram of the typewriter keyboard as though it held her spellbound. Something has happened to* AMANDA. *It is written in her face as she climbs to the landing: a look that is grim and hopeless and a little absurd.*

*She has on one of those cheap or imitation velvety-looking cloth coats with imitation fur collar. Her hat is five or six years old, one of those dreadful cloche hats that were worn in the late twenties, and she is clasping an enormous black patent-leather pocketbook with nickel clasp and initials. This is her full-dress outfit, the one she usually wears to the D.A.R.*

*Before entering she looks through the door.*

*She purses her lips, opens her eyes wide, rolls them upward, and shakes her head.*

*Then she slowly lets herself in the door. Seeing her mother's expression* LAURA *touches her lips with a nervous gesture.*

**LAURA:** Hello, Mother, I was— *(She makes a nervous gesture toward the chart on the wall.* AMANDA *leans against the shut door and stares at* LAURA *with a martyred look.)*

**AMANDA:** Deception? Deception? *(She slowly removes her hat and gloves, continuing the swift suffering stare. She lets the hat and gloves fall on the floor—a bit of acting.)*

Laura (Joanna Miles) gazes at her glass ornaments.

**LAURA:** *(shakily)* How was the D.A.R. meeting? *(*AMANDA *slowly opens her purse and removes a dainty white handkerchief, which she shakes out delicately and delicately touches to her lips and nostrils.)* Didn't you go to the D.A.R. meeting, Mother?

**AMANDA:** *(faintly, almost inaudibly)* —No.—No. *(Then more forcibly.)* I did not have the strength—to go to the D.A.R. In fact, I did not have the courage! I wanted to find a hole in the ground and hide myself in it forever! *(She crosses slowly to the wall and removes the diagram of the typewriter keyboard. She holds it in front of her for a second, staring at it sweetly and sorrowfully—then bites her lips and tears it in two pieces.)*

**LAURA:** *(faintly)* Why did you do that, Mother? *(*AMANDA *repeats the same procedure with the chart of the Gregg Alphabet.)* Why are you—

**AMANDA:** Why? Why? How old are you, Laura?

**LAURA:** Mother, you know my age.

**AMANDA:** I thought that you were an adult; it seems that I was mistaken. *(She crosses slowly to the sofa and sinks down and stares at* LAURA.*)*

**LAURA:** Please don't stare at me, Mother.

AMANDA *closes her eyes and lowers her head. Count ten.*

**AMANDA:** What are we going to do, what is going to become of us, what is the future?

*Count ten.*

**LAURA:** Has something happened, Mother? *(*AMANDA *draws a long breath and takes out the handkerchief again. Dabbing process.)* Mother, has—something happened?

**AMANDA:** I'll be all right in a minute. I'm just bewildered—*(count five)*—by life. . . .

**LAURA:** Mother, I wish that you would tell me what's happened.

**AMANDA:** As you know, I was supposed to be inducted into my office at the D.A.R. this afternoon. *(Image: A swarm of typewriters.)* But I stopped off at Rubicam's Business College to speak to your teachers about your having a cold and ask them what progress they thought you were making down there.

**LAURA:** Oh. . . .

**AMANDA:** I went to the typing instructor and introduced myself as your mother. She didn't know who you were. Wingfield, she said. We don't have any such student enrolled at the school! I assured her she did, that you had been going to classes since early in January. "I wonder," she said, "if you could be talking about that terribly shy little girl who dropped out of school after only a few days' attendance?" "No," I said, "Laura, my daughter, has been going to school every day for the past six weeks!" "Excuse me," she said. She took the attendance book out and there was your name, unmistakably printed, and all the dates you were absent until they decided that you had dropped out of school. I still said, "No, there must have been some mistake! There must have been some mix-up in the records!" And she said, "No—I remember her perfectly now. Her hands shook so that she couldn't hit the right keys! The first time we gave a speed-test, she broke down completely—was sick at the stomach and almost had to be carried into the wash-room! After that morning she never showed up any more. We phoned the house but never got any answer"—while I was working at Famous and Barr, I suppose, demonstrating those—Oh! I felt so weak I could barely keep on my feet. I had to sit down while they got me a glass of water! Fifty dollars' tuition, all of our plans—my hopes and ambitions for you—just gone up the spout, just gone up the spout like that. *(LAURA draws a long breath and gets awkwardly to her feet. She crosses to the Victrola, and winds it up.)* What are you doing?

**LAURA:** Oh! *(She releases the handle and returns to her seat.)*

**AMANDA:** Laura, where have been going when you've gone out pretending that you were going to business college?

**LAURA:** I've just been going out walking.

**AMANDA:** That's not true.

**LAURA:** It is. I just went walking.

**AMANDA:** Walking? Walking? In winter? Deliberately courting pneumonia in that light coat? Where did you walk to, Laura?

**LAURA:** It was the lesser of two evils, Mother. *(Image: Winter scene in park.)* I couldn't go back up. I—threw up—on the floor!

**AMANDA:** From half past seven till after five every day you mean to tell me you walked around in the park, because you wanted to make me think that you were still going to Rubicam's Business College?

**LAURA:** It wasn't as bad as it sounds. I went inside places to get warmed up.

**AMANDA:** Inside where?

**LAURA:** I went in the art museum and the bird-houses at the Zoo. I visited the penguins every day! Sometimes I did without lunch and went to the movies. Lately I've been spending most of my afternoons in the Jewel-box, that big glass house where they raise the tropical flowers.

**AMANDA:** You did all this to deceive me, just for the deception? *(LAURA looks down.)* Why?

**LAURA:** Mother, when you're disappointed, you get that awful suffering look on your face, like the picture of Jesus' mother in the museum!

**AMANDA:** Hush!

**LAURA:** I couldn't face it.

*Pause. A whisper of string.*
*(Legend: "The Crust of Humility.")*

**AMANDA:** *(hopelessly fingering the huge pocketbook)* So what are we going to do the rest of our lives? Stay home and watch the parades go by? Amuse ourselves with the glass menagerie, darling? Eternally play those worn-out phonograph records your father left as a painful reminder of him? We won't have a business career—we've given that up because it gave us nervous indigestion! *(Laughs wearily.)* What is there left but dependency all our lives? I know so well what becomes of unmarried women who aren't prepared to occupy a position. I've seen such pitiful cases in the South—barely tolerated spinsters living upon the grudging patronage of sister's husband or brother's wife!—stuck away in some little mousetrap of a room—encouraged by one in-law to visit another—little birdlike women without any nest—eating the crust of humility all their life! Is that the future that we've mapped out for ourselves? I swear it's the only alternative I can think of! It isn't a very pleasant alternative, is it? Of course—some girls *do marry.* *(LAURA twists her hands nervously.)* Haven't you ever liked some boy?

**LAURA:** Yes. I liked one once. *(Rises.)* I came across his picture a while ago.

**AMANDA:** *(with some interest)* He gave you his picture?

**LAURA:** No, it's in the year-book.

**AMANDA:** *(disappointed)* Oh—a high-school boy.

*(Screen image: JIM as the high school hero bearing a silver cup.)*

**LAURA:** Yes. His name was Jim. *(LAURA lifts the heavy annual from the clawfoot table.)* Here he is in *The Pirates of Penzance.*

Laura and Amanda discuss the future.

**AMANDA:** *(absently)* The what?

**LAURA:** The operetta the senior class put on. He had a wonderful voice and we sat across the aisle from each other Mondays, Wednesdays, and Fridays in the Aud. Here he is with the silver cup for debating! See his grin?

**AMANDA:** *(absently)* He must have had a jolly disposition.

**LAURA:** He used to call me—Blue Roses.

*(Image: Blue roses.)*

**AMANDA:** Why did he call you such a name as that?

**LAURA:** When I had that attack of pleurosis—he asked me what was the matter when I came back. I said pleurosis—he thought that I said Blue Roses! So that's what he always called me after that. Whenever he saw me, he'd holler, "Hello, Blue Roses!" I didn't care for the girl that he went out with. Emily Meisenbach. Emily was the best-dressed girl at Soldan. She never struck me, though, as being sincere. . . . It says in the Personal Section—they're engaged. That's—six years ago! They must be married by now.

**AMANDA:** Girls that aren't cut out for business careers usually wind up married to some nice man. *(Gets up with a spark of revival.)* Sister, that's what you'll do!

LAURA *utters a startled, doubtful laugh. She reaches quickly for a piece of glass.*

**LAURA:** But, Mother—

**AMANDA:** Yes? *(Crossing to photograph.)*

**LAURA:** *(in a tone of frightened apology)* I'm—crippled!

*(Image: Screen.)*

**AMANDA:** Nonsense! Laura, I've told you never, never to use that word. Why, you're not crippled, you just have a little defect—hardly noticeable, even! When people have some slight disadvantage like that, they cultivate other things to make up for it—develop charm—and vivacity—and—*charm!* That's all you have to do! *(She turns again to the photograph.)* One thing your father had *plenty of*—was *charm*!

TOM *motions to the fiddle in the wings.*
*(The scene fades out with music.)*

## SCENE III

*(Legend on the screen: "After the Fiasco—")*
TOM *speaks from the fire-escape landing.*

**TOM:** After the fiasco at Rubicam's Business College, the idea of getting a gentleman caller for Laura began to play a more important part in Mother's calculations. It became an obsession. Like some archetype of the universal unconscious, the image of the gentleman caller haunted our small apartment. . . . *(Image: Young man at door with flowers.)* An evening at home rarely passed without some allusion to this image, this specter, this hope. . . . Even when he wasn't mentioned, his presence hung in Mother's preoccupied look and in my sister's frightened, apologetic manner—hung like a sentence passed upon the Wingfields! Mother was a woman of action as well as words. She began to take logical steps in the planned direction. Late that winter and in the early spring—realizing that extra money would be needed to properly feather the nest and plume the bird—she conducted a vigorous campaign on the telephone, roping in subscribers to one of those magazines for matrons called *The Home-maker's Companion,* the type of journal that features the serialized sublimations of ladies of letters who think in terms of delicate cuplike breasts, slim, tapering waists, rich, creamy thighs, eyes like wood smoke in autumn, fingers that soothe and caress like strains of music, bodies as powerful as Etruscan sculpture.

*(Screen image:* Glamour *magazine cover.)*
AMANDA *enters with phone on long extension cord. She is spotted in the dim stage.*

**AMANDA:** Ida Scott? This is Amanda Wingfield! We *missed* you at the D.A.R. last Monday! I said to myself: She's probably suffering with that sinus condition! How is that sinus condition? Horrors! Heaven have mercy!—You're a Christian martyr, yes, that's what you are, a Christian martyr! Well, I just now happened to notice that your subscription to the *Companion*'s about to expire! Yes, it expires with the next issue, honey!—just when that wonderful new serial by Bessie Mae Hopper is getting off to such an exciting start. Oh, honey, it's something that you can't miss! You remember how *Gone with the Wind* took everybody by storm? You simply couldn't go out if you hadn't read it. All everybody *talked* was Scarlett O'Hara. Well, this is a book that critics already compare to *Gone with the Wind.* It's the *Gone with the Wind* of the post–World War generation!—What?—Burning?—Oh, honey, don't let them burn, go take a look in the oven and I'll hold the wire! Heavens—I think she's hung up!

*(Dim out.)*

*(Legend on screen: "You think I'm in love with Continental Shoemakers?")*

*Before the stage is lighted, the violent voices of* TOM *and* AMANDA *are heard. They are quarreling behind the portieres. In front of them stands* LAURA *with clenched hands and panicky expression.*

*A clear pool of light on her figure throughout this scene.*

**TOM:** What in Christ's name am I—

**AMANDA:** *(shrilly)* Don't you use that—

**TOM:** Supposed to do!

**AMANDA:** Expression! Not in my—

**TOM:** Ohhh!

**AMANDA:** Presence! Have you gone out of your senses?

**TOM:** I have, that's true, *driven* out!

**AMANDA:** What is the matter with you, you—big—big—IDIOT!

**TOM:** Look!—I've got *no thing,* no single thing—

**AMANDA:** Lower your voice!

Amanda scolds her son.

**TOM:** In my life here that I can call my own! Everything is—

**AMANDA:** Stop that shouting!

**TOM:** Yesterday you confiscated my books! You had the nerve to—

**AMANDA:** I took that horrible novel back to the library—yes! That hideous book by that insane Mr. Lawrence. *(*TOM *laughs wildly.)* I cannot control the output of diseased minds or people who cater to them—*(*TOM *laughs still more wildly.)* BUT I WON'T ALLOW SUCH FILTH BROUGHT INTO MY HOUSE! No, no, no, no, no!

**TOM:** House, house! Who pays rent on it, who makes a slave of himself to—

**AMANDA:** *(fairly screeching)* Don't you DARE to—

**TOM:** No, no, *I* mustn't say things! *I've* got to just—

**AMANDA:** Let me tell you—

**TOM:** I don't want to hear any more! *(He tears the portieres open. The upstage area is lit with a turgid smoky red glow.)*

AMANDA'S *hair is in metal curlers and she wears a very old bathrobe, much too large for her slight figure, a relic of the faithless Mr. Wingfield.*

*The upright typewriter and a wild disarray of manuscripts are on the drop-leaf table. The quarrel was probably precipitated by* AMANDA'S *interruption of his creative labor. A chair lying overthrown on the floor.*

*Their gesticulating shadows are cast on the ceiling by the fiery glow.*

**AMANDA:** You *will* hear more, you—

**TOM:** No, I won't hear more, I'm going out!

**AMANDA:** You come right back in—

**TOM:** Out, out, out! Because I'm—

**AMANDA:** Come back here, Tom Wingfield! I'm not through talking to you!

**TOM:** Oh, go—

**LAURA:** *(desperately)* Tom!

**AMANDA:** You're going to listen, and no more insolence from you! I'm at the end of my patience! *(He comes back toward her.)*

**TOM:** What do you think I'm at? Aren't I supposed to have any patience to reach the end of, Mother? I know, I know. It seems unimportant to you, what I'm *doing*—what I *want* to do—having a little *difference* between them! You don't think that—

**AMANDA:** I think you've been doing things that you're ashamed of. That's why you act like this. I don't believe that you go every night to the movies. Nobody goes to the movies night after night. Nobody in their right minds goes to the movies as often as you pretend to. People don't go to the movies at nearly midnight, and movies don't let out at two A.M. Come in stumbling. Muttering to yourself like a maniac! You get three hours' sleep and then go to work. Oh, I can picture the way you're doing down there. Moping, doping, because you're in no condition.

**TOM:** *(wildly)* No, I'm in no condition!

**AMANDA:** What right have you got to jeopardize your job? Jeopardize the security of us all? How do you think we'd manage if you were—

**TOM:** Listen! You think I'm crazy *about* the *warehouse!* *(He bends fiercely toward her slight figure.)* You think I'm in love with the Continental Shoemakers? You think I want to spend fifty-five *years* down there in that—*celotex interior!* with—*fluorescent—tubes!* Look! I'd rather somebody picked up a crowbar and battered out my brains—than go back mornings! I *go*! Every time you come in yelling that God damn "*Rise and Shine!*" "*Rise and Shine!*" I say to myself, "How *lucky dead* people are!" But I get up. I *go!* For sixty-five dollars a month I give up all that I dream of doing and being *ever!* And you say self—*self's* all I ever think of. Why, listen, if self is what I thought of, Mother, I'd be where he is—! *(Pointing to father's picture.)* As far as the system of transportation reaches! *(He starts past her. She grabs his arm.)* Don't grab at me, Mother!

**AMANDA:** Where are you going?

**TOM:** I'm going to the *movies!*

**AMANDA:** I don't believe that lie!

**TOM:** *(crouching toward her, overtowering her tiny figure. She backs away, gasping)* I'm going to opium dens! Yes, opium dens, dens of vice and criminals' hangouts, Mother. I've joined the Hogan gang, I'm a hired assassin, I carry a tommy-gun in a violin case! I run a string of cat-houses in the Valley! They call me Killer, Killer Wingfield, I'm leading a double-life, a simple, honest warehouse worker by day, by night a dynamic *czar* of the *underworld, Mother.* I go to gambling casinos, I spin away fortunes on the roulette table! I wear a patch over one eye and a false mustache, sometimes I put on green whiskers. On those occasions they call me—*El Diablo!* Oh, I could tell you many things to make you sleepless! My enemies plan to dynamite this place. They're going to blow us all sky-high some night! I'll be glad, very happy, and so will you! You'll go up, up on a broomstick, over Blue Mountain with seventeen gentlemen callers! You ugly—babbling old—*witch. . . . (He goes through a series of violent, clumsy movements, seizing his overcoat, lunging to the door, pulling it fiercely open. The women watch him, aghast. His arm catches in the sleeve of the coat as he struggles to pull it on. For a moment he is pinioned by the bulky garment. With an outraged groan he tears the coat off again, splitting the shoulders of it, and hurls it across the room. It strikes against the shelf of* LAURA'*s glass collection, there is a tinkle of shattering glass.* LAURA *cries out as if wounded.)*

*(Music legend: "The Glass Menagerie.")*

**LAURA:** *(shrilly)* *My glass!*—menagerie. . . . *(She covers her face and turns away.)*

*But* AMANDA *is still stunned and stupefied by the "ugly witch" so that she barely notices the occurrence. Now she recovers her speech.*

**AMANDA:** *(in an awful voice)* I won't speak to you—until you apologize! *(She crosses through the portieres and draws them together behind her.* TOM *is left with* LAURA. LAURA *clings weakly to the mantel with her face averted.* TOM *stares at her stupidly for a moment. Then he crosses to shelf. Drops awkwardly to his knees to collect the fallen glass, glancing at* LAURA *as if he would speak but couldn't.)*

*"The Glass Menagerie" music steals in as*

*(The scene dims out.)*

## SCENE IV

*The interior is dark. Faint light in the alley.*

*A deep-voiced bell in a church is tolling the hour of five as the scene commences.*

TOM *appears at the top of the alley. After each solemn boom of the bell in the tower, he shakes a little noise-maker or rattle as if to express the tiny spasm of man in contrast to the sustained power and dignity of the Almighty. This and the unsteadiness of his advance make it evident that he has been drinking.*

*As he climbs the few steps to the fire-escape landing light steals up inside.* LAURA *appears in night-dress, observing* TOM'*s empty bed in the front room.*

TOM *fishes in his pockets for his door-key, removing a motley assortment of articles in the search, including a perfect shower of movie-ticket stubs and an empty bottle. At last he finds the key, but just as he is about to insert it, it slips from his fingers. He strikes a match and crouches below the door.*

**TOM:** *(bitterly)* One crack—and it falls through!

LAURA *opens the door.*

**LAURA:** Tom! Tom, what are you doing?

**TOM:** Looking for a door-key.

**LAURA:** Where have you been all this time?

**TOM:** I have been to the movies.

**LAURA:** All this time at the movies?

**TOM:** There was a very long program. There was a Garbo picture and a Mickey Mouse and a travelogue and a newsreel and a preview of coming attractions. And there was an organ solo and a collection for the milk-fund—simultaneously—which ended up in a terrible fight between a fat lady and an usher!

**LAURA:** *(innocently)* Did you have to stay through everything?

**TOM:** Of course! And, oh, I forgot! There was a big stage show! The headliner on this stage show was Malvolio the Magician. He performed wonderful tricks, many of them, such as pouring water back and forth between pitchers. First it turned to wine and then it turned to beer and then it turned to whisky. I know it was whiskey it finally turned into because he needed somebody to come up out of the audience to help him, and I came up—both shows! It was Kentucky Straight Bourbon. A very generous fellow, he gave souvenirs. *(He pulls from his back pocket a shimmering rainbow-colored scarf.)* He gave me this. This is his magic scarf. You can have it, Laura. You wave it over a canary cage and you get a bowl of gold-fish. You wave it over the gold-fish bowl and they fly away canaries. . . . But the wonderfullest trick of all was the coffin trick. We nailed him into a coffin and he got out of the coffin without removing one nail. *(He has come inside.)* There is a trick that would come in handy for me—get me out of this 2 by 4 situation! *(Flops onto bed and starts removing his shoes.)*

**LAURA:** Tom—Shhh!

**TOM:** What you shushing me for?

**LAURA:** You'll wake up Mother.

**TOM:** Goody, goody! Pay 'er back for all those "Rise an' Shines." *(Lies down, groaning.)* You know it don't take much intelligence to get yourself into a nailed-up coffin, Laura. But who in hell ever got himself out of one without removing one nail?

*As if in answer, the father's grinning photograph lights up. (Scene dims out.)*

*Immediately following: The church bell is heard striking six. At the sixth stroke the alarm clock goes off in* AMANDA*'s room, and after a few moments we hear her calling: "Rise and Shine! Rise and Shine! Laura, go tell your brother to rise and shine!"*

Laura helps her brother into bed.

**TOM:** *(sitting up slowly)* I'll rise—but I won't shine.

*The light increases.*

**AMANDA:** Laura, tell your brother his coffee is ready.

LAURA *slips into front room.*

**LAURA:** Tom! It's nearly seven. Don't make Mother nervous. *(He stares at her stupidly. Beseechingly.)* Tom, speak to Mother this morning. Make up with her, apologize, speak to her!

**TOM:** She won't to me. It's her that started not speaking.

**LAURA:** If you just say you're sorry she'll start speaking.

**TOM:** Her not speaking—is that such a tragedy?

**LAURA:** Please—please!

**AMANDA:** *(calling from the kitchenette)* Laura, are you going to do what I asked you to do, or do I have to get dressed and go out myself?

**LAURA:** Going, going—soon as I get on my coat! *(She pulls on a shapeless felt hat with nervous, jerky movement, pleadingly glancing at* TOM*. Rushes awkwardly for coat. The coat is one of* AMANDA*'s, inaccurately made-over, the sleeves too short for* LAURA*.)* Butter and what else?

**AMANDA:** *(entering upstage)* Just butter. Tell them to charge it.

**LAURA:** Mother, they make such faces when I do that.

**AMANDA:** Sticks and stones may break my bones, but the expression on Mr. Garfinkel's face won't harm us! Tell your brother his coffee is getting cold.

**LAURA:** *(at door)* Do what I asked you, will you, will you, Tom?

*He looks sullenly away.*

**AMANDA:** Laura, go now or just don't go at all!

**LAURA:** *(rushing out)* Going—going! *(A second later she cries out.* TOM *springs up and crosses to the door.* AMANDA *rushes anxiously in.* TOM *opens the door.)*

**TOM:** Laura?

**LAURA:** I'm all right. I slipped, but I'm all right.

**AMANDA:** *(peering anxiously after her)* If anyone breaks a leg on those fire-escape steps, the landlord ought to be sued for every cent he possesses! *(She shuts door. Remembers she isn't speaking and returns to other room.)*

*As* TOM *enters listlessly for his coffee, she turns her back to him and stands rigidly facing the window on the gloomy gray vault of the areaway. Its light on her face with its aged but childish features is cruelly sharp, satirical as a Daumier print.*

*(Music under: "Ave Maria.")*

TOM *glances sheepishly but sullenly at her averted figure and slumps at the table. The coffee is scalding hot; he sips it and gasps and spits it back in the cup. At his gasp,* AMANDA *catches her breath and half turns. Then she catches herself and turns back to window.*

TOM *blows on his coffee, glancing sidewise at his mother. She clears her throat.* TOM *clears his. He starts to rise. Sinks back down again, scratches his head, clears his throat again.* AMANDA *coughs.* TOM *raises his cup in both hands to blow on it, his eyes staring over the rim of it at his mother for several moments. Then he slowly sets the cup down and awkwardly and hesitantly rises from the chair.*

**TOM:** *(hoarsely)* Mother. I—I apologize. Mother. *(*AMANDA *draws a quick, shuddering breath. Her face works grotesquely. She breaks into childlike tears.)* I'm sorry for what I said, for everything that I said, I didn't mean it.

**AMANDA:** *(sobbingly)* My devotion has made me a witch and so I make myself hateful to my children!

**TOM:** No, you *don't.*

**AMANDA:** I worry so much, don't sleep, it makes me nervous!

**TOM:** *(gently)* I understand that.

**AMANDA:** I've had to put up a solitary battle all these years. But you're my right-hand bower! Don't fall down, don't fail!

**TOM:** *(gently)* I try, Mother.

**AMANDA:** *(with great enthusiasm)* Try and you will SUCCEED! *(The notion makes her breathless.)* Why, you—you're just *full* of natural endowments! Both of my children—they're *unusual* children! Don't you think I know it? I'm so—*proud!* Happy and—feel I've—so much to be thankful for but—Promise me one thing, son!

**TOM:** What, Mother?

**AMANDA:** Promise, son, you'll—never be a drunkard!

**TOM:** *(turns to her grinning)* I will never be a drunkard, Mother.

**AMANDA:** That's what frightened me so, that you'd be drinking! Eat a bowl of Purina!

**TOM:** Just coffee, Mother.

**AMANDA:** Shredded wheat biscuit?

**TOM:** No. No, Mother, just coffee.

**AMANDA:** You can't put in a day's work on an empty stomach. You've got ten minutes—don't gulp! Drinking too-hot liquids makes cancer of the stomach. . . . Put cream in.

**TOM:** No, thank you.

**AMANDA:** To cool it.

**TOM:** No! No, thank you, I want it black.

**AMANDA:** I know, but it's not good for you. We have to do all that we can to build ourselves up. In these trying times we live in, all that we have to cling to is—each other. . . . That's why it's so important to—Tom, I—I sent out your sister so I could discuss something with you. If you hadn't spoken I would have spoken to you. *(Sits down.)*

**TOM:** *(gently)* What is it, Mother, that you want to discuss?

**AMANDA:** Laura!

TOM *puts his cup down slowly.*

*(Legend on screen: "Laura.")*

*(Music: "The Glass Menagerie.")*

**TOM:** —Oh.—Laura . . .

**AMANDA:** *(touching his sleeve)* You know how Laura is. So quiet but—still water runs deep! She notices things and I think she—broods about them. *(*TOM *looks up.)* A few days ago I came in and she was crying.

**TOM:** What about?

**AMANDA:** You.

**TOM:** Me?

**AMANDA:** She has an idea that you're not happy here.

**TOM:** What gave her that idea?

**AMANDA:** What gives her any idea? However, you do act strangely. I—I'm not criticizing, understand *that!* I know your ambitions do not lie in the warehouse, that like everybody in the whole wide world—you've had to—make sacrifices, but—Tom—Tom—life's not easy, it calls for—Spartan endurance! There's so many things in my heart that I cannot describe to you! I've never told you but I—*loved* your father. . . .

**TOM:** *(gently)* I know that, Mother.

**AMANDA:** And you—when I see you taking after his ways! Staying out late—and—well, you *had* been drinking the night you were in that—terrifying condition! Laura says that you hate the apartment and that you go out nights to get away from it! Is that true, Tom?

**TOM:** No. You say there's so much in your heart that you can't describe to me. That's true of me, too. There's so much in my heart that I can't describe to *you!* So let's respect each other's—

**AMANDA:** But, why—*why,* Tom—are you always so *restless?* Where do you go to, nights?

**TOM:** I—go to the movies.

**AMANDA:** Why do you go to the movies so much, Tom?

**TOM:** I go to the movies because—I like adventure. Adventure is something I don't have much of at work, so I go to the movies.

**AMANDA:** But, Tom, you go to the movies *entirely too much!*

**TOM:** I like a lot of adventure.

AMANDA *looks baffled, then hurt. As the familiar inquisition resumes he becomes hard and impatient again.* AMANDA *slips back into her querulous attitude toward him.*

*(Image on screen: Sailing vessel with Jolly Roger.)*

**AMANDA:** Most young men find adventure in their careers.

**TOM:** Then most young men are not employed in a warehouse.

**AMANDA:** The world is full of young men employed in warehouses and offices and factories.

**TOM:** Do all of them find adventure in their careers?

**AMANDA:** They do or they do without it! Not everybody has a craze for adventure.

**TOM:** Man is by instinct a lover, a hunter, a fighter, and none of those instincts are given much play at the warehouse!

**AMANDA:** Man is by instinct! Don't quote instinct to me! Instinct is something that people have got away from! It belongs to animals! Christian adults don't want it!

**TOM:** What do Christian adults want, then, Mother?

**AMANDA:** Superior things! Things of the mind and the spirit! Only animals have to satisfy instincts! Surely your aims are somewhat higher than theirs! Than monkeys—pigs—

**TOM:** I reckon they're not.

**AMANDA:** You're joking. However, that isn't what I wanted to discuss.

**TOM:** *(rising)* I haven't much time.

**AMANDA:** *(pushing his shoulders)* Sit down.

**TOM:** You want me to punch in red at the warehouse, Mother?

**AMANDA:** You have five minutes. I want to talk about Laura.

*(Legend: "Plans and Provisions.")*

**TOM:** All right! What about Laura?

**AMANDA:** We have to be making some plans and provisions for her. She's older than you, two years, and nothing has happened. She just drifts along doing nothing. It frightens me terribly how she just drifts along.

**TOM:** I guess she's the type that people call home girls.

**AMANDA:** There's no such type, and if there is, it's a pity! That is unless the home is hers, with a husband!

**TOM:** What?

**AMANDA:** Oh, I can see the handwriting on the wall as plain as I see the nose in front of my face! It's terrifying! More and more you remind me of your father! He was out all hours without explanation—Then *left! Good-bye!* And me with the bag to hold. I saw a letter you got from the Merchant Marine. I know what you're dreaming of. I'm not standing here blindfolded. Very well, then. Then *do* it! But not till there's somebody to take your place.

**TOM:** What do you mean?

**AMANDA:** I mean that as soon as Laura has got somebody to take care of her, married, a home of her own, independent—why, then you'll be free to go wherever you please, on land, on sea, whichever way the wind blows you! But until that time you've got to look out for your sister. I don't say me because I'm old and don't matter! I say for your sister because she's young and dependent. I put her in business college—a dismal failure! Frightened her so it made her sick to her stomach. I took her over to the Young People's League at the church. Another fiasco. She spoke to nobody, nobody spoke to her. Now all she does is fool with those pieces of glass and play those worn-out records. What kind of a life is that for a girl to lead!

**TOM:** What can I do about it?

**AMANDA:** Overcome selfishness! Self, self, self is all that you ever think of! *(*TOM *springs up and crosses to get his coat. It is ugly and bulky. He pulls on a cap with earmuffs.)* Where is your muffler? Put your wool muffler on! *(He snatches it angrily from the closet and tosses it around his neck and pulls both ends tight.)* Tom! I haven't said what I had in mind to ask you.

**TOM:** I'm too late to—

**AMANDA:** *(catching his arms—very importunately. Then shyly.)* Down at the warehouse, aren't there some—nice young men?

**TOM:** No!

**AMANDA:** There *must* be—*some.*

**TOM:** Mother—

*Gesture.*

**AMANDA:** Find out one that's clean-living—doesn't drink and—ask him out for sister!

**TOM:** What?

**AMANDA:** For *sister!* To *meet!* Get *acquainted!*

**TOM:** *(stamping to the door)* Oh, my *go-osh!*

**AMANDA:** Will you? *(He opens the door. Imploringly.)* Will you? *(He starts down.)* Will you? *Will* you, dear?

**TOM:** *(calling back)* YES!

AMANDA *closes the door hesitantly and with a troubled but faintly hopeful expression.*

*(Screen image:* Glamour *magazine cover.)*

*Spot* AMANDA *at phone.*

**AMANDA:** Ella Cartwright? This is Amanda Wingfield! How are you, honey? How is that kidney condition? *(Count five.) Horrors! (Count five.)* You're a Christian martyr, yes, honey, that's what you are, a Christian martyr! Well, I just happened to notice in

Amanda, now hopeful, places a sales call.

my little red book that your subscription to the *Companion* has just run out! I knew that you wouldn't want to miss out on the wonderful serial starting in this new issue. It's by Bessie Mae Hopper, the first thing she's written since *Honeymoon for Three.* Wasn't that a strange and interesting story? Well, this one is even lovelier, I believe. It has a sophisticated society background. It's all about the horsey set on Long Island!

*(Fade out.)*

## SCENE V

*(Legend on screen: "Annunciation.") Fade with music.*

*It is early dusk of a spring evening. Supper has just been finished in the Wingfield apartment.* AMANDA *and* LAURA *in light-colored dresses are removing dishes from the table, in the upstage area, which is shadowy, their movements formalized almost as a dance or ritual, their moving forms as pale and silent as moths.*

TOM, *in white shirt and trousers, rises from the table and crosses toward the fire-escape.*

**AMANDA:** *(as he passes her)* Son, will you do me a favor?

**TOM:** What?

**AMANDA:** Comb your hair! You look so pretty when your hair is combed! *(*TOM *slouches on the sofa with the evening paper. Enormous caption "Franco Triumphs.")* There is only one respect in which I would like you to emulate your father.

**TOM:** What respect is that?

**AMANDA:** The care he always took of his appearance. He never allowed himself to look untidy. *(He throws* *down the paper and crosses to fire-escape.)* Where are you going?

**TOM:** I'm going out to smoke.

**AMANDA:** You smoke too much. A pack a day at fifteen cents a pack. How much would that amount to in a month? Thirty times fifteen is how much, Tom? Figure it out and you will be astounded at what you could save. Enough to give you a night-school course in accounting at Washington U! Just think what a wonderful thing that would be for you, son!

TOM *is unmoved by the thought.*

**TOM:** I'd rather smoke. *(He steps out on landing, letting the screen door slam.)*

**AMANDA:** *(sharply)* I know! That's the tragedy of it. . . . *(Alone, she turns to look at her husband's picture.)*

*(Dance music: "All the World Is Waiting for the Sunrise!")*

**TOM:** *(to the audience)* Across the alley from us was the Paradise Dance Hall. On evenings in spring the windows and doors were open and the music came outdoors. Sometimes the lights were turned out except for a large glass sphere that hung from the ceiling. It would turn slowly about and filter the dusk with delicate rainbow colors. Then the orchestra played a waltz or a tango, something that had a slow and sensuous rhythm. Couples would come outside, to the relative privacy of the alley. You could see them kissing behind ash-pits and telephone poles. This was the compensation for lives that passed like mine, without any change or adventure. Adventure and change were imminent in this year. They were waiting around the corner for all these kids. Suspended in the mist over the Berchtesgaden, caught in the folds of Chamberlain's umbrella—In Spain there was Guernica! But here there was only hot swing music and liquor, dance halls, bars, and movies, and sex that hung in the gloom like a chandelier and flooded the world with brief, deceptive rainbows. . . . All the world was waiting for bombardments!

AMANDA *turns from the picture and comes outside.*

**AMANDA:** *(sighing)* A fire-escape landing's a poor excuse for a porch. *(She spreads a newspaper on a step and sits down, gracefully and demurely as if she were settling into a swing on a Mississippi veranda.)* What are you looking at?

**TOM:** The moon.

**AMANDA:** Is there a moon this evening?

**TOM:** It's rising over Garfinkel's Delicatessen.

**AMANDA:** So it is! A little silver slipper of a moon. Have you made a wish on it yet?

**TOM:** Um-hum.

**AMANDA:** What did you wish for?

**TOM:** That's a secret.

**AMANDA:** A secret, huh? Well, I won't tell mine either. I will be just as mysterious as you.

**TOM:** I bet I can guess what yours is.

**AMANDA:** Is my head so transparent?

**TOM:** You're not a sphinx.

**AMANDA:** No, I don't have secrets. I'll tell you what I wished for on the moon. Success and happiness for my precious children! I wish for that whenever there's a moon, and when there isn't a moon, I wish for it, too.

**TOM:** I thought perhaps you wished for a gentleman caller.

**AMANDA:** Why do you say that?

**TOM:** Don't you remember asking me to fetch one?

**AMANDA:** I remember suggesting that it would be nice for your sister if you brought home some nice young man from the warehouse. I think I've made that suggestion more than once.

**TOM:** Yes, you have made it repeatedly.

**AMANDA:** Well?

**TOM:** We are going to have one.

**AMANDA:** *What?*

**TOM:** A gentleman caller!

*(The Annunciation is celebrated with music.)*
AMANDA *rises.*
*(Image on screen: Caller with bouquet.)*

**AMANDA:** You mean you have asked some nice young man to come over?

**TOM:** Yep. I've asked him to dinner.

**AMANDA:** You really did?

**TOM:** I did!

**AMANDA:** You did, and did he—*accept?*

**TOM:** He did!

**AMANDA:** Well, well—well, well! That's—lovely!

**TOM:** I thought that you would be pleased.

**AMANDA:** It's definite, then?

**TOM:** Very definite.

**AMANDA:** Soon?

**TOM:** Very soon.

**AMANDA:** For heaven's sake, stop putting on and tell me some things, will you?

**TOM:** What things do you want me to tell you?

**AMANDA:** Naturally I would like to know when he's *coming!*

**TOM:** He's coming tomorrow.

**AMANDA:** *Tomorrow?*

**TOM:** Yep. Tomorrow.

**AMANDA:** But, Tom!

**TOM:** Yes, Mother?

**AMANDA:** Tomorrow gives me no time!

**TOM:** Time for what?

**AMANDA:** Preparations! Why didn't you phone me at once, as soon as you asked him, the minute that he accepted? Then, don't you see, I could have been getting ready!

**TOM:** You don't have to make any fuss.

**AMANDA:** Oh, Tom, Tom, Tom, of course I have to make a fuss! I want things nice, not sloppy! Not thrown together. I'll certainly have to do some fast thinking, won't I?

**TOM:** I don't see why you have to think at all.

Tom tells Amanda about the man he's invited over to meet Laura.

**AMANDA:** You just don't know. We can't have a gentleman caller in a pig-sty! All my wedding silver has to be polished, the monogrammed table linen ought to be laundered! The windows have to be washed and fresh curtains put up. And how about clothes? We have to *wear* something, don't we?

**TOM:** Mother, this boy is no one to make a fuss over!

**AMANDA:** Do you realize he's the first young man we've introduced to your sister? It's terrible, dreadful, disgraceful that poor little sister has never received a single gentleman caller! Tom, come inside! *(She opens the screen door.)*

**TOM:** What for?

**AMANDA:** I want to ask you some things.

**TOM:** If you're going to make such a fuss, I'll call it off, I'll tell him not to come.

**AMANDA:** You certainly won't do anything of the kind. Nothing offends people worse than broken engagements. It simply means I'll have to work like a Turk! We won't be brilliant, but we'll pass inspection. Come on inside. *(TOM follows, groaning.)* Sit down.

**TOM:** Any particular place you would like me to sit?

**AMANDA:** Thank heavens I've got that new sofa! I'm also making payments on a floor lamp I'll have sent out! And put the chintz covers on, they'll brighten things up! Of course I'd hoped to have these walls repapered. . . . What is the young man's name?

**TOM:** His name is O'Connor.

**AMANDA:** That, of course, means fish—tomorrow is Friday! I'll have that salmon loaf—with Durkee's dressing! What does he do? He works at the warehouse?

**TOM:** Of course! How else would I—

**AMANDA:** Tom, he—doesn't drink?

**TOM:** Why do you ask me that?

**AMANDA:** Your father *did!*

**TOM:** Don't get started on that!

**AMANDA:** He *does* drink, then?

**TOM:** Not that I know of!

**AMANDA:** Make sure, be certain! The last thing I want for my daughter's a boy who drinks!

**TOM:** Aren't you being a little bit premature? Mr. O'Connor has not yet appeared on the scene!

**AMANDA:** But will tomorrow. To meet your sister, and what do I know about his character? Nothing! Old maids are better off than wives of drunkards!

**TOM:** Oh, my God!

**AMANDA:** Be still!

**TOM:** *(leaning forward to whisper)* Lots of fellows meet girls whom they don't marry!

**AMANDA:** Oh, talk sensibly, Tom—and don't be sarcastic! *(She has gotten a hairbrush.)*

**TOM:** What are you doing?

**AMANDA:** I'm brushing that cow-lick down! What is this young man's position at the warehouse?

**TOM:** *(submitting grimly to the brush and the interrogation)* This young man's position is that of a shipping clerk, Mother.

**AMANDA:** Sounds to me like a fairly responsible job, the sort of job *you* would be in if you just had more *get-up.* What is his salary? Have you any idea?

**TOM:** I would judge it to be approximately eighty-five dollars a month.

**AMANDA:** Well—not princely, but—

**TOM:** Twenty more than I make.

**AMANDA:** Yes, how well I know! But for a family man, eighty-five dollars a month is not much more than you can just get by on. . . .

**TOM:** Yes, but Mr. O'Connor is not a family man.

**AMANDA:** He might be, mightn't he? Some time in the future?

**TOM:** I see. Plans and provisions.

**AMANDA:** You are the only young man that I know of who ignores the fact that the future becomes the present, the present the past, and the past turns into everlasting regret if you don't plan for it!

**TOM:** I will think that over and see what I can make of it.

**AMANDA:** Don't be supercilious with your mother! Tell me some more about this—what do you call him?

**TOM:** James D. O'Connor. The D. is for Delaney.

**AMANDA:** Irish on *both* sides! *Gracious!* And doesn't drink?

**TOM:** Shall I call him up and ask him right this minute?

**AMANDA:** The only way to find out about those things is to make discreet inquiries at the proper moment. When I was a girl in Blue Mountain and it was suspected that a young man drank, the girl whose attentions he had been receiving, if any girl *was,* would sometimes speak to the minister of his church, or rather her father would if her father was living, and sort of feel him out on the young man's character. That is the way such things are discreetly handled to keep a young woman from making a tragic mistake!

**TOM:** Then how did you happen to make a tragic mistake?

**AMANDA:** That innocent look of your father's had everyone fooled! He *smiled*—the world was *enchanted!* No girl can do worse than put herself at the mercy of a handsome appearance! I hope that Mr. O'Connor is not too good-looking.

**TOM:** No, he's not too good-looking. He's covered with freckles and hasn't too much of a nose.

**AMANDA:** He's not right-down homely, though?

**TOM:** Not right-down homely. Just medium homely, I'd say.

**AMANDA:** Character's what to look for in a man.

**TOM:** That's what I've always said, Mother.

**AMANDA:** You've never said anything of the kind and I suspect you would never give it a thought.

**TOM:** Don't be suspicious of me.

**AMANDA:** At least I hope he's the type that's up and coming.

**TOM:** I think he really goes in for self-improvement.

**AMANDA:** What reason have you to think so?

**TOM:** He goes to night school.

**AMANDA:** *(beaming)* Splendid! What does he do, I mean study?

**TOM:** Radio engineering and public speaking!

**AMANDA:** Then he has visions of being advanced in the world! Any young man who studies public speaking is aiming to have an executive job some day! And radio engineering? A thing for the future! Both of these facts are very illuminating. Those are the sort of things that a mother should know concerning any young man who comes to call on her daughter. Seriously or—not.

**TOM:** One little warning. He doesn't know about Laura. I didn't let on that we had dark ulterior motives. I just said, why don't you come have dinner with us? He said okay and that was the whole conversation.

**AMANDA:** I bet it was! You're eloquent as an oyster. However, he'll know about Laura when he gets here. When he sees how lovely and sweet and pretty she is, he'll thank his lucky stars he was asked to dinner.

**TOM:** Mother, you mustn't expect too much of Laura.

**AMANDA:** What do you mean?

**TOM:** Laura seems all those things to you and me because she's ours and we love her. We don't even notice she's crippled any more.

**AMANDA:** Don't say crippled! You know that I never allow that word to be used!

**TOM:** But face facts, Mother. She is and—that's not all—

**AMANDA:** What do you mean "not all"?

**TOM:** Laura is very different from other girls.

**AMANDA:** I think the difference is all to her advantage.

**TOM:** Not quite all—in the eyes of others—strangers—she's terribly shy and lives in a world of her own and those things make her seem a little peculiar to people outside the house.

**AMANDA:** Don't say peculiar.

**TOM:** Face the facts. She is.

*(The dance-hall music changes to a tango that has a minor and somewhat ominous tone.)*

**AMANDA:** In what way is she peculiar—may I ask?

**TOM:** *(gently)* She lives in a world of her own—a world of—little glass ornaments, Mother. . . . *(Gets up.* AMANDA *remains holding brush, looking at him, troubled.)* She plays old phonograph records and—that's about all—*(He glances at himself in the mirror and crosses to door.)*

**AMANDA:** *(sharply)* Where are you going?

**TOM:** I'm going to the movies. *(Out screen door.)*

**AMANDA:** Not to the movies, every night to the movies! *(Follows quickly to screen door.)* I don't believe you always go to the movies! *(He is gone.* AMANDA *looks worriedly after him for a moment. Then vitality and optimism return and she turns from the door. Crossing to portieres.)* Laura! Laura! *(*LAURA *answers from kitchenette.)*

**LAURA:** Yes, Mother.

**AMANDA:** Let those dishes go and come in front! *(*LAURA *appears with dish towel. Gaily.)* Laura, come here and make a wish on the moon!

**LAURA:** *(entering)* Moon—moon?

**AMANDA:** A little silver slipper of a moon. Look over your left shoulder, Laura, and make a wish! *(*LAURA *looks faintly puzzled as if called out of sleep.* AMANDA *seizes her shoulders and turns her at angle by the door.)* Now! Now, darling, *wish!*

**LAURA:** What shall I wish for, Mother?

**AMANDA:** *(her voice trembling and her eyes suddenly filling with tears)* Happiness! Good Fortune!

*The violin rises and the stage dims out.*

## SCENE VI

*(Image: High-school hero.)*

**TOM:** And so the following evening I brought Jim home to dinner. I had known Jim slightly in high school. In high school Jim was a hero. He had tremendous Irish good nature and vitality with the scrubbed and polished look of white chinaware. He seemed to move in a continual spotlight. He was a star in basketball, captain of the debating club, president of the senior class and the glee club and he sang the male lead in the annual light operas. He was always running or bounding, never just walking. He seemed always at the point of defeating the law of gravity. He was shooting with such velocity through his adolescence that you would logically expect him to arrive at nothing short of the White House by the time he was thirty. But Jim apparently ran into more interference after his graduation from Soldan. His speed had definitely slowed. Six years after he left high school he was holding a job that wasn't much better than mine.

*(Image: Clerk.)*

Tom and Amanda discuss what kind of man he is bringing home for Laura.

He was the only one at the warehouse with whom I was on friendly terms. I was valuable to him as someone who could remember his former glory, who had seen him win basketball games and the silver cup in debating. He knew of my secret practice of retiring to a cabinet of the washroom to work on poems when business was slack in the warehouse. He called me Shakespeare. And while the other boys in the warehouse regarded me with suspicious hostility, Jim took a humorous attitude toward me. Gradually his attitude affected the others, their hostility wore off, and they also began to smile at me as people smile at an oddly fashioned dog who trots across their paths at some distance.

I knew that Jim and Laura had known each other at Soldan, and I had heard Laura speak admiringly of his voice. I didn't know if Jim remembered her or not. In high school Laura had been as unobtrusive as Jim had been astonishing. If he did remember Laura, it was not as my sister, for when I asked him to dinner, he grinned and said, "You know, Shakespeare, I never thought of you as having folks!"

He was about to discover that I did. . . .

*(Light upstage.)*

*(Legend on screen: "The Accent of a Coming Foot.")*

*Friday evening. It is about five o'clock of a late spring evening which comes "scattering poems in the sky."*

*A delicate lemony light is in the Wingfield apartment.*

AMANDA *has worked like a Turk in preparation for the gentleman caller. The results are astonishing. The new floor lamp with its rose-silk shade is in place, a colored paper lantern conceals the broken light fixture in the ceiling, new billowing white curtains are at the windows, chintz covers are on chairs and sofa, a pair of new sofa pillows make their initial appearance.*

*Open boxes and tissue paper are scattered on the floor.*

LAURA *stands in the middle with lifted arms while* AMANDA *crouches before her, adjusting the hem of a new dress, devout and ritualistic. The dress is colored and designed by memory. The arrangement of* LAURA*'s hair is changed; it is softer and more becoming. A fragile, unearthly prettiness has come out in* LAURA*: she is like a piece of translucent glass touched by light, given a momentary radiance, not actual, not lasting.*

**AMANDA:** *(impatiently)* Why are you trembling?

**LAURA:** Mother, you've made me so nervous!

**AMANDA:** How have I made you nervous?

**LAURA:** By all this fuss! You make it seem so important!

**AMANDA:** I don't understand you, Laura. You couldn't be satisfied with just sitting home, and yet whenever I try to arrange something for you, you seem to resist it. *(She gets up.)* Now take a look at yourself. No, wait! Wait just a moment—I have an idea!

**LAURA:** What is it now?

AMANDA *produces two powder puffs which she wraps in handkerchiefs and stuffs in* LAURA*'s bosom.*

**LAURA:** Mother, what are you doing?

**AMANDA:** They call them "Gay Deceivers"!

**LAURA:** I won't wear them!

**AMANDA:** You will!

**LAURA:** Why should I?

**AMANDA:** Because, to be painfully honest, your chest is flat.

**LAURA:** You make it seem like we were setting a trap.

**AMANDA:** All pretty girls are a trap, a pretty trap, and men expect them to be. *(Legend: "A Pretty Trap.")* Now look at yourself, young lady. This is the prettiest you will ever be! I've got to fix myself now! You're going to be surprised by your mother's appearance! *(She crosses through portieres, humming gaily.)*

LAURA *moves slowly to the long mirror and stares solemnly at herself.*

*A wind blows the white curtains inward in a slow, graceful motion and with a faint, sorrowful sighing.*

**AMANDA:** *(off stage)* It isn't dark enough yet. *(She turns slowly before the mirror with a troubled look.)*

*(Legend on screen: "This Is My Sister: Celebrate Her with Strings!" Music.)*

The women get ready for dinner.

**AMANDA:** *(laughing, off)* I'm going to show you something. I'm going to make a spectacular appearance!

**LAURA:** What is it, Mother?

**AMANDA:** Possess your soul in patience—you will see! Something I've resurrected from that old trunk! Styles haven't changed so terribly much after all.... *(She parts the portieres.)* Now just look at your mother! *(She wears a girlish frock of yellowed voile with a blue silk sash. She carries a bunch of jonquils—the legend of her youth is nearly revived. Feverishly.)* This is the dress in which I led the cotillion. Won the cakewalk twice at Sunset Hill, wore one spring to the Governor's ball in Jackson! See how I sashayed around the ballroom, Laura? *(She raises her skirt and does a mincing step around the room.)* I wore it on Sundays for my gentlemen callers! I had it on the day I met your father—I had malaria fever all that spring. The change of climate from East Tennessee to the Delta—weakened resistance—I had a little temperature all the time—not enough to be serious—just enough to make me restless and giddy! Invitations poured in—parties all over the Delta! "Stay in bed," said Mother, "you have fever!"—but I just wouldn't.—I took quinine but kept on going, going!—Evenings, dances!—Afternoons, long, long rides! Picnics—lovely!—So lovely, that country in May.—All lacy with dogwood, literally flooded with jonquils!—That was the spring I had the craze for jonquils. Jonquils became an absolute obsession. Mother said, "Honey, there's no more room for jonquils." And still I kept bringing in more jonquils. Whenever, wherever I saw them, I'd say, "Stop! Stop! I see jonquils!" I made the young men help me gather the jonquils! It was a joke, Amanda and her jonquils. Finally there were no more vases to hold them, every available space was filled with jonquils. No vases to hold them? All right, I'll hold them myself! And then I—*(She stops in front of the picture.)* *(Music.)* met your father! Malaria fever and jonquils and then—this—boy.... *(She switches on the rose-colored lamp.)* I hope they get here before it starts to rain. *(She crosses upstage and places the jonquils in bowl on table.)* I gave your brother a little extra change so he and Mr. O'Connor could take the service car home.

**LAURA:** *(with an altered look)* What did you say his name was?

**AMANDA:** O'Connor.

**LAURA:** What is his first name?

**AMANDA:** I don't remember. Oh, yes, I do. It was—Jim!

LAURA *sways slightly and catches hold of a chair.*
*(Legend on screen: "Not Jim!")*

**LAURA:** *(faintly)* Not—Jim!

**AMANDA:** Yes, that was it, it was Jim! I've never known a Jim that wasn't nice!

*(Music: Ominous.)*

**LAURA:** Are you sure his name is Jim O'Connor?

**AMANDA:** Yes. Why?

**LAURA:** Is he the one that Tom used to know in high school?

**AMANDA:** He didn't say so. I think he just got to know him at the warehouse.

**LAURA:** There was a Jim O'Connor we both knew in high school—*(Then, with effort.)* If that is the one that Tom is bringing to dinner—you'll have to excuse me, I won't come to the table.

**AMANDA:** What sort of nonsense is this?

**LAURA:** You asked me once if I'd ever liked a boy. Don't you remember I showed you this boy's picture?

**AMANDA:** You mean the boy you showed me in the year-book?

**LAURA:** Yes, that boy.

**AMANDA:** Laura, Laura, were you in love with that boy?

**LAURA:** I don't know, Mother. All I know is I couldn't sit at the table if it was him!

**AMANDA:** It won't be him! It isn't the least bit likely. But whether it is or not, you will come to the table. You will not be excused.

**LAURA:** I'll have to be, Mother.

**AMANDA:** I don't intend to humor your silliness, Laura. I've had too much from you and your brother, both! So just sit down and compose yourself till they come. Tom has forgotten his key so you'll have to let them in, when they arrive.

**LAURA:** *(panicky)* Oh, Mother—*you* answer the door!

**AMANDA:** *(lightly)* I'll be in the kitchen—busy!

**LAURA:** Oh, Mother, please answer the door, don't make me do it!

**AMANDA:** *(crossing into kitchenette)* I've got to fix the dressing for the salmon. Fuss, fuss—silliness!—over a gentleman caller!

*(Door swings shut.* LAURA *is left alone.*
*(Legend: "Terror!")*

Amanda greets Jim O'Connor (Michael Moriarty).

*She utters a low moan and turns off the lamp—sits stiffly on the edge of the sofa, knotting her fingers together.*

*(Legend on screen: "The Opening of a Door!")*

TOM *and* JIM *appear on the fire-escape steps and climb to landing. Hearing their approach,* LAURA *rises with a panicky gesture. She retreats to the portieres.*

*The doorbell.* LAURA *catches her breath and touches her throat. Low drums.*

**AMANDA:** *(calling)* Laura, sweetheart! The door!

LAURA *stares at it without moving.*

**JIM:** I think we just beat the rain.

**TOM:** Uh-huh. *(He rings again, nervously.* JIM *whistles and fishes for a cigarette.)*

**AMANDA:** *(very, very gaily)* Laura, that is your brother and Mr. O'Connor! Will you let them in, darling?

LAURA *crosses toward kitchenette door.*

**LAURA:** *(breathlessly)* Mother—you go to the door!

AMANDA *steps out of kitchenette and stares furiously at* LAURA. *She points imperiously at the door.*

**LAURA:** Please, please!

**AMANDA:** *(in a fierce whisper)* What is the matter with you, you silly thing?

**LAURA:** *(desperately)* Please, you answer it, *please!*

**AMANDA:** I told you I wasn't going to humor you, Laura. Why have you chosen this moment to lose your mind?

**LAURA:** Please, please, please, you go!

**AMANDA:** You'll have to go to the door because I can't!

**LAURA:** *(despairingly)* I can't either!

**AMANDA:** *Why?*

**LAURA:** I'm *sick!*

**AMANDA:** I'm sick, too—of your nonsense! Why can't you and your brother be normal people? Fantastic whims and behavior! *(*TOM *gives a long ring.)* Preposterous goings on! Can you give me one reason—*(Calls out lyrically.)* COMING! JUST ONE SECOND!—why you should be afraid to open a door? Now you answer it, Laura!

**LAURA:** Oh, oh, oh . . . *(She returns through the portieres. Darts to the Victrola and winds it frantically and turns it on.)*

**AMANDA:** Laura Wingfield, you march right to that door!

**LAURA:** Yes—yes, Mother!

*A faraway, scratchy rendition of "Dardanella" softens the air and gives her strength to move through it. She slips to the door and draws it cautiously open.*

TOM *enters with the caller,* JIM O'CONNOR.

**TOM:** Laura, this is Jim. Jim, this is my sister, Laura.

**JIM:** *(stepping inside)* I didn't know that Shakespeare had a sister!

**LAURA:** *(retreating stiff and trembling from the door)* How—how do you do?

**JIM:** *(heartily, extending his hand)* Okay!

LAURA *touches it hesitantly with hers.*

**JIM:** Your hand's *cold,* Laura!

**LAURA:** Yes, well—I've been playing the Victrola . . .

**JIM:** Must have been playing classical music on it! You ought to play a little hot swing music to warm you up!

**LAURA:** Excuse me—I haven't finished playing the Victrola . . .

*She turns awkwardly and hurries into the front room. She pauses a second by the Victrola. Then catches her breath and darts through the portieres like a frightened deer.*

**JIM:** *(grinning)* What was the matter?

**TOM:** Oh—with Laura? Laura is—terribly shy.

**JIM:** Shy, huh? It's unusual to meet a shy girl nowadays. I don't believe you ever mentioned you had a sister.

**TOM:** Well, now you know. I have one. Here is the *Post Dispatch.* You want a piece of it?

**JIM:** Uh-huh.

**TOM:** What piece? The comics?

**JIM:** Sports! *(Glances at it.)* Ole Dizzy Dean is on his bad behavior.

**TOM:** *(disinterest)* Yeah? *(Lights cigarette and crosses back to fire-escape door.)*

**JIM:** Where are *you* going?

**TOM:** I'm going out on the terrace.

**JIM:** *(goes after him)* You know, Shakespeare—I'm going to sell you a bill of goods!

**TOM:** What goods?

**JIM:** A course I'm taking.

**TOM:** Huh?

**JIM:** In public speaking! You and me, we're not the warehouse type.

**TOM:** Thanks—that's good news. But what has public speaking got to do with it?

**JIM:** It fits you for—executive positions!

**TOM:** Awww.

**JIM:** I tell you it's done a helluva lot for me.

*(Image: Executive at desk.)*

**TOM:** In what respect?

**JIM:** In every! Ask yourself what is the difference between you an' me and men in the office down front? Brains?—No!—Ability?—No! Then what? Just one little thing—

**TOM:** What is that one little thing?

**JIM:** Primarily it amounts to—social poise! Being able to square up to people and hold your own on any social level!

**AMANDA:** *(off stage)* Tom?

**TOM:** Yes, Mother?

**AMANDA:** Is that you and Mr. O'Connor?

**TOM:** Yes, Mother.

**AMANDA:** Well, you just make yourselves comfortable in there.

**TOM:** Yes, Mother.

**AMANDA:** Ask Mr. O'Connor if he would like to wash his hands.

**JIM:** Aw—no—no—thank you—I took care of that at the warehouse. Tom—

**TOM:** Yes?

**JIM:** Mr. Mendoza was speaking to me about you.

**TOM:** Favorably?

**JIM:** What do you think?

**TOM:** Well—

**JIM:** You're going to be out of a job if you don't wake up.

**TOM:** I am waking up—

**JIM:** You show no signs.

**TOM:** The signs are interior.

*(Image on screen: The sailing vessel with Jolly Roger again.)*

**TOM:** I'm planning to change. *(He leans over the rail speaking with quiet exhilaration. The incandescent marquees and signs of the first-run movie houses light his face from across the alley. He looks like a voyager.)* I'm right at the point of committing myself to a future that doesn't include the warehouse and Mr. Mendoza or even a night-school course in public speaking.

**JIM:** What are you gassing about?

**TOM:** I'm tired of the movies.

**JIM:** Movies!

**TOM:** Yes, movies! Look at them—*(A wave toward the marvels of Grand Avenue.)* All of those glamorous people—having adventures—hogging it all, gobbling the whole thing up! You know what happens? People go to the *movies* instead of *moving!* Hollywood characters are supposed to have all the adventures for everybody in America, while everybody in America sits in a dark room and watches them have them! Yes, until there's a war. That's when adventure becomes available to the masses! *Everyone's* dish, not only Gable's! Then the people in the dark room come out of the dark room to have some adventures themselves—Goody, goody—It's our turn now, to go to the South Sea Island—to make a safari—to be exotic, far-off—But I'm not patient. I don't want to wait till then. I'm tired of the *movies* and I am *about* to *move!*

**JIM:** *(incredulously)* Move?

**TOM:** Yes.

**JIM:** When?

**TOM:** Soon!

**JIM:** Where? Where?

*(Theme three: Music seems to answer the question, while* TOM *thinks it over. He searches among his pockets.)*

**TOM:** I'm starting to boil inside. I know I seem dreamy, but inside—well, I'm boiling! Whenever I pick up a shoe, I shudder a little thinking how short life is and what I am doing!—Whatever that means. I know it doesn't mean shoes—except as something to wear on a traveler's feet! *(Finds paper.)* Look—

**JIM:** What?

**TOM:** I'm a member.

**JIM:** *(reading)* The Union of Merchant Seamen.

**TOM:** I paid my dues this month, instead of the light bill.

**JIM:** You will regret it when they turn the lights off.

**TOM:** I won't be here.

**JIM:** How about your mother?

**TOM:** I'm like my father. The bastard son of a bastard! See how he grins? And he's been absent going on sixteen years!

**JIM:** You're just talking, you drip. How does your mother feel about it?

**TOM:** Shhh—Here comes Mother! Mother is not acquainted with my plans!

**AMANDA:** *(enters portieres)* Where are you all?

**TOM:** On the terrace, Mother.

*They start inside. She advances to them.* TOM *is distinctly shocked at her appearance. Even* JIM *blinks a little. He is making his first contact with girlish Southern vivacity and in spite of the night-school course in public speaking is somewhat thrown off the beam by the unexpected outlay of social charm.*

*Certain responses are attempted by* JIM *but are swept aside by* AMANDA*'s gay laughter and chatter.* TOM *is embarrassed but after the first shock* JIM *reacts very warmly. He grins and chuckles, is altogether won over.*

*(Image: Amanda as a girl.)*

**AMANDA:** *(coyly smiling, shaking her girlish ringlets)* Well, well, well, so this is Mr. O'Connor. Introductions entirely unnecessary. I've heard so much about you from my boy. I finally said to him, Tom—good gracious!—why don't you bring this paragon to supper? I'd like to meet this nice young man at the warehouse!—Instead of just hearing him sing your praises so much! I don't know why my son is so stand-offish—that's not Southern behavior! Let's sit down and—I think we could stand a little more air in here! Tom, leave the door open. I felt a nice fresh breeze a moment ago. Where has it gone? Mmm, so warm already! And not quite summer, even. We're going to burn up when summer really gets started. However, we're having—we're having a very light supper. I think light things are better fo' this time of year. The same as light clothes are. Light clothes an' light food are what warm weather calls fo'. You know our blood gets so thick during th' winter—it takes a while fo' us to *adjust* ou'selves!—when the season changes. . . . It's come so quick this year. I wasn't prepared. All of a sudden—heavens! Already summer!—I ran to the trunk an' pulled out this light dress—Terribly old! Historical almost! But feels so good—so good an' co-ol, y'know. . . .

**TOM:** Mother—

**AMANDA:** Yes, honey?

**TOM:** How about—supper?

**AMANDA:** Honey, you go ask Sister if supper is ready! You know that Sister is in full charge of supper! Tell her you hungry boys are waiting for it. *(To* JIM.*)* Have you met Laura?

**JIM:** She—

**AMANDA:** Let you in? Oh, good, you've met already! It's rare for a girl as sweet an' pretty as Laura to be domestic! But Laura is, thank heavens, not only pretty but also very domestic. I'm not at all. I never was a bit. I never could make a thing but angel-food cake. Well, in the South we had so many servants. Gone, gone, gone. All vestiges of gracious living! Gone completely! I wasn't prepared for what the future brought me. All of my gentlemen callers were sons of planters and so of course I assumed that I would be married to one and raise my family on a large piece of land with plenty of servants. But man proposes—and woman accepts the proposal!—To vary that old, old saying a little bit—I married no planter! I married a man who worked for the telephone company!—that gallantly smiling gentleman over there! *(Points to the picture.)* A telephone man who—fell in love with long-distance!—Now he travels and I don't even know where!—But what am I going on for about my—tribulations! Tell me yours—I hope you don't have any! Tom?

**TOM:** *(returning)* Yes, Mother?

**AMANDA:** Is supper nearly ready?

**TOM:** It looks to me like supper is on the table.

**AMANDA:** Let me look—*(She rises prettily and looks through portieres.)* Oh, lovely—But where is Sister?

**TOM:** Laura is not feeling well and she says that she thinks she'd better not come to the table.

**AMANDA:** What?—Nonsense!—Laura? Oh, Laura!

**LAURA:** *(off stage, faintly)* Yes, Mother.

**AMANDA:** You really must come to the table. We won't be seated until you come to the table! Come in, Mr. O'Connor. You sit over there, and I'll—Laura? Laura Wingfield! You're keeping us waiting, honey! We can't say grace until you come to the table!

*The back door is pushed weakly open and* LAURA *comes in. She is obviously quite faint, her lips trembling, her eyes wide and staring. She moves unsteadily toward the table.*

*(Legend: "Terror!")*

*Outside a summer storm is coming abruptly. The white curtains billow inward at the windows and there is a sorrowful murmur and deep blue dusk.*

LAURA *suddenly stumbles—She catches at a chair with a faint moan.*

**TOM:** Laura!

**AMANDA:** Laura! *(There is a clap of thunder.) (Legend: "Ah!") (Despairingly.)* Why, Laura, you *are* sick, darling! Tom, help your sister into the living room, dear! Sit in the living room, Laura—rest on the sofa. Well! *(To the gentleman caller.)* Standing over the hot stove made her ill!—I told her that it was just too warm this evening, but—*(*TOM *comes back in.* LAURA *is on the sofa.)* Is Laura all right now?

**TOM:** Yes.

**AMANDA:** What *is* that? Rain? A nice cool rain has come up! *(She gives the gentleman caller a frightened look.)* I think we may—have grace—now. . . *(*TOM *looks at her stupidly.)* Tom, honey—you say grace!

**TOM:** Oh . . . "For these and all thy mercies—" *(They bow their heads,* AMANDA *stealing a nervous glance at* JIM. *In the living room* LAURA, *stretched on the sofa, clenches her hand to her lips, to hold back a shuddering sob.)* God's Holy Name be praised—

*(The scene dims out.)*

## SCENE VII

*A Souvenir*

*Half an hour later. Dinner is just being finished in the upstage area, which is concealed by the drawn portieres.*

*As the curtain rises* LAURA *is still huddled upon the sofa, her feet drawn under her, her head resting on a pale blue pillow, her eyes wide and mysteriously watchful. The new floor lamp with its shade of rose-colored silk gives a soft, becoming light to her face, bringing out the fragile, unearthly prettiness which usually escapes attention. There is a steady murmur of rain, but it is slackening and stops soon after the scene begins; the air outside becomes pale and luminous as the moon breaks out.*

*A moment after the curtain rises, the lights in both rooms flicker and go out.*

**JIM:** Hey, there, Mr. Light Bulb!

AMANDA *laughs nervously.*

*(Legend: "Suspension of a Public Service.")*

**AMANDA:** Where was Moses when the lights went out? Ha-ha. Do you know the answer to that one, Mr. O'Connor?

**JIM:** No, Ma'am, what's the answer?

**AMANDA:** In the dark! *(*JIM *laughs appreciatively.)* Everybody sit still. I'll light the candles. Isn't it lucky we have them on the table? Where's a match? Which of you gentlemen can provide a match?

**JIM:** Here.

**AMANDA:** Thank you, sir.

**JIM:** Not at all, Ma'am!

**AMANDA:** I guess the fuse has burnt out. Mr. O'Connor, can you tell a burnt-out fuse? I know I can't and Tom is a total loss when it comes to mechanics. *(Sound: Getting up: Voices recede a little to kitchenette.)* Oh, be careful you don't bump into something. We don't want our gentleman caller to break his neck. Now wouldn't that be a fine howdy-do?

**JIM:** Ha-ha! Where is the fuse-box?

Amanda entertains Jim after the lights have gone out.

**AMANDA:** Right here next to the stove. Can you see anything?

**JIM:** Just a minute.

**AMANDA:** Isn't electricity a mysterious thing? Wasn't it Benjamin Franklin who tied a key to a kite? We live in such a mysterious universe, don't we? Some people say that science clears up all the mysteries for us. In my opinion it only creates more! Have you found it yet?

**JIM:** No, Ma'am. All these fuses look okay to me.

**AMANDA:** Tom!

**TOM:** Yes, Mother?

**AMANDA:** That light bill I gave you several days ago. The one I told you we got the notices about?

**TOM:** Oh.—Yeah.

*(Legend: "Ha!")*

**AMANDA:** You didn't neglect to pay it by any chance?

**TOM:** Why, I—

**AMANDA:** Didn't! I might have known it!

**JIM:** Shakespeare probably wrote a poem on that light bill, Mrs. Wingfield.

**AMANDA:** I might have known better than to trust him with it! There's such a high price for negligence in this world!

**JIM:** Maybe the poem will win a ten-dollar prize.

**AMANDA:** We'll just have to spend the remainder of the evening in the nineteenth century, before Mr. Edison made the Mazda lamp!

**JIM:** Candlelight is my favorite kind of light.

**AMANDA:** That shows you're romantic! But that's no excuse for Tom. Well, we got through dinner. Very considerate of them to let us get through dinner before they plunged us into everlasting darkness, wasn't it, Mr. O'Connor?

**JIM:** Ha-ha!

**AMANDA:** Tom, as a penalty for your carelessness you can help me with the dishes.

**JIM:** Let me give you a hand.

**AMANDA:** Indeed you will not!

**JIM:** I ought to be good for something.

**AMANDA:** Good for something? *(Her tone is rhapsodic.)* *You?* Why, Mr. O'Connor, nobody, *nobody's* given me this much entertainment in years—as you have!

**JIM:** Aw, now, Mrs. Wingfield!

**AMANDA:** I'm not exaggerating, not one bit! But Sister is all by her lonesome. You go keep her company in the parlor! I'll give you this lovely old candelabrum that used to be on the altar at the church of the Heavenly Rest. It was melted a little out of shape when the church burnt down. Lightning struck it one spring. Gypsy Jones was holding a revival at the time and he intimated that the church was destroyed because the Episcopalians gave card parties.

**JIM:** Ha-ha.

**AMANDA:** And how about coaxing Sister to drink a little wine? I think it would be good for her! Can you carry both at once?

**JIM:** Sure. I'm Superman!

**AMANDA:** Now, Thomas, get into this apron!

*The door of kitchenette swings closed on* AMANDA'S *gay laughter; the flickering light approaches the portieres.*

LAURA *sits up nervously as he enters. Her speech at first is low and breathless from the almost intolerable strain of being alone with a stranger.*

*(Legend: "I Don't Suppose You Remember Me at All!")*

*In her first speeches in this scene, before* JIM'S *warmth overcomes her paralyzing shyness,* LAURA'S *voice is thin and breathless as though she has run up a steep flight of stairs.*

JIM'S *attitude is gently humorous. In playing this scene it should be stressed that while the incident is apparently unimportant, it is to* LAURA *the climax of her secret life.*

**JIM:** Hello there, Laura.

**LAURA:** *(faintly)* Hello. *(She clears her throat.)*

**JIM:** How are you feeling now? Better?

**LAURA:** Yes. Yes, thank you.

**JIM:** This is for you. A little dandelion wine. *(He extends it toward her with extravagant gallantry.)*

**LAURA:** Thank you.

**JIM:** Drink it—but don't get drunk! *(He laughs heartily.* LAURA *takes the glass uncertainly; laughs shyly.)* Where shall I set the candles?

**LAURA:** Oh—oh, anywhere . . .

**JIM:** How about here on the floor? Any objections?

**LAURA:** No.

Jim brings the candelabrum closer to Laura.

**JIM:** I'll spread a newspaper under to catch the drippings. I like to sit on the floor. Mind if I do?

**LAURA:** Oh, no.

**JIM:** Give me a pillow?

**LAURA:** What?

**JIM:** A pillow!

**LAURA:** *Oh . . . (Hands him one quickly.)*

**JIM:** How about you? Don't you like to sit on the floor?

**LAURA:** Oh—yes.

**JIM:** Why don't you, then?

**LAURA:** I—will.

**JIM:** Take a pillow! *(*LAURA *does. Sits on the other side of the candelabrum.* JIM *crosses his legs and smiles engagingly at her.)* I can't hardly see you sitting way over there.

**LAURA:** I can—see you.

**JIM:** I know, but that's not fair, I'm in the limelight. *(*LAURA *moves her pillow closer.)* Good! Now I can see you! Comfortable?

**LAURA:** Yes.

**JIM:** So am I. Comfortable as a cow. Will you have some gum?

**LAURA:** No, thank you.

**JIM:** I think that I will indulge, with your permission. *(Musingly unwraps it and holds it up.)* Think of the fortune made by the guy that invented the first piece of chewing gum. Amazing, huh? The Wrigley Building is one of the sights of Chicago.—I saw it summer before last when I went up to the Century of Progress. Did you take in the Century of Progress?

**LAURA:** No, I didn't.

**JIM:** Well, it was quite a wonderful exposition. What impressed me most was the Hall of Science. Gives you an idea of what the future will be in America, even more wonderful than the present time is! *(Pause. Smiling at her.)* Your brother tells me you're shy. Is that right, Laura?

**LAURA:** I—don't know.

**JIM:** I judge you to be an old-fashioned type of girl. Well, I think that's a pretty good type to be. Hope you don't think I'm being too personal—do you?

**LAURA:** *(hastily, out of embarrassment)* I believe I *will* take a piece of gum, if you—don't mind. *(Clearing her throat.)* Mr. O'Connor, have you—kept up with your singing?

**JIM:** Singing? Me?

**LAURA:** Yes. I remember what a beautiful voice you had.

**JIM:** When did you hear me sing?

*(Voice offstage in the pause.)*

**VOICE:** *(offstage)* O blow, ye winds, heigh-ho,
A-roving I will go!
I'm off to my love
With a boxing glove—
Ten thousand miles away!

**JIM:** You say you've heard me sing?

**LAURA:** Oh, yes! Yes, very often . . . I—don't suppose you remember me—at all?

**JIM:** *(smiling doubtfully)* You know I have an idea I've seen you before. I had that idea soon as you opened the door. It seemed almost like I was about to remember your name. But the name I started to call you—wasn't a name! And so I stopped myself before I said it.

**LAURA:** Wasn't it—Blue Roses?

**JIM:** *(springing up, grinning)* Blue Roses! My gosh, yes—Blue Roses! That's what I had on my tongue when you opened the door! Isn't it funny what tricks your memory plays? I didn't connect you with the high school somehow or other. But that's where it was; it was high school. I didn't even know you were Shakespeare's sister! Gosh, I'm sorry.

**LAURA:** I didn't expect you to. You—barely knew me!

**JIM:** But we did have a speaking acquaintance, huh?

**LAURA:** Yes, we—spoke to each other.

**JIM:** When did you recognize me?

**LAURA:** Oh, right away!

**JIM:** Soon as I came in the door?

**LAURA:** When I heard your name I thought it was probably you. I knew that Tom used to know you a little in high school. So when you came in the door—Well, then I was—sure.

**JIM:** Why didn't you *say* something, then?

**LAURA:** *(breathlessly)* I didn't know what to say, I was—too surprised!

**JIM:** For goodness' sakes! You know, this sure is funny!

**LAURA:** Yes! Yes, isn't it, though . . .

**JIM:** Didn't we have a class in something together?

**LAURA:** Yes, we did.

**JIM:** What class was that?

**LAURA:** It was—singing—Chorus!

**JIM:** Aw!

**LAURA:** I sat across the aisle from you in the Aud.

**JIM:** Aw.

**LAURA:** Mondays, Wednesdays, and Fridays.

**JIM:** Now I remember—you always came in late.

**LAURA:** Yes, it was so hard for me, getting upstairs. I had that brace on my leg—it clumped so loud!

**JIM:** I never heard any clumping.

**LAURA:** *(wincing at the recollection)* To me it sounded like—thunder!

**JIM:** Well, well, well. I never even noticed.

**LAURA:** And everybody was seated before I came in. I had to walk in front of all those people. My seat was in the back row. I had to go clumping all the way up the aisle with everyone watching!

**JIM:** You shouldn't have been self-conscious.

**LAURA:** I know, but I was. It was always such a relief when the singing started.

**JIM:** Aw, yes, I've placed you now! I used to call you Blue Roses. How was it that I got started calling you that?

**LAURA:** I was out of school a little while with pleurosis. When I came back you asked me what was the matter. I said I had pleurosis—you thought I said Blue Roses. That's what you always called me after that!

**JIM:** I hope you didn't mind.

**LAURA:** Oh, no—I liked it. You see, I wasn't acquainted with many—people. . . .

Laura and Jim look at the old high school annual.

**JIM:** As I remember you sort of stuck by yourself.

**LAURA:** I—I—never have had much luck at—making friends.

**JIM:** I don't see why you wouldn't.

**LAURA:** Well, I—started out badly.

**JIM:** You mean being—

**LAURA:** Yes, it sort of—stood between me—

**JIM:** You shouldn't have let it!

**LAURA:** I know, but it did, and—

**JIM:** You were shy with people!

**LAURA:** I tried not to be but never could—

**JIM:** Overcome it?

**LAURA:** No, I—I never could!

**JIM:** I guess being shy is something you have to work out of kind of gradually.

**LAURA:** *(sorrowfully)* Yes—I guess it—

**JIM:** Takes time!

**LAURA:** Yes—

**JIM:** People are not so dreadful when you know them. That's what you have to remember! And everybody has problems, not just you, but practically everybody has got some problems. You think of yourself as having the only problems, as being the only one who is disappointed. But just look around you and you will see lots of people as disappointed as you are. For instance, I hoped when I was going to high school that I would be further along at this time, six years later, than I am now—You remember that wonderful write-up I had in *The Torch*?

**LAURA:** Yes! *(She rises and crosses to table.)*

**JIM:** It said I was bound to succeed in anything I went into! *(LAURA returns with the annual.)* Holy Jeez! *The Torch! (He accepts it reverently. They smile across it with mutual wonder. LAURA crouches beside him and they begin to turn through it. LAURA's shyness is dissolving in his warmth.)*

**LAURA:** Here you are in *Pirates of Penzance*!

**JIM:** *(wistfully)* I sang the baritone lead in that operetta.

**LAURA:** *(rapidly)* So—*beautifully!*

**JIM:** *(protesting)* Aw—

**LAURA:** Yes, yes—beautifully—beautifully!

**JIM:** You heard me?

**LAURA:** All three times!

**JIM:** No!

**LAURA:** Yes!

**JIM:** All three performances?

**LAURA:** *(looking down)* Yes.

**JIM:** Why?

**LAURA:** I—wanted to ask you to—autograph my program.

**JIM:** Why didn't you ask me to?

**LAURA:** You were always surrounded by your own friends so much that I never had a chance to.

**JIM:** You should have just—

**LAURA:** Well, I—thought you might think I was—

**JIM:** Thought I might think you was—what?

**LAURA:** Oh—

**JIM:** *(with reflective relish)* I was beleaguered by females in those days.

**LAURA:** You were terribly popular!

**JIM:** Yeah—

**LAURA:** You had such a—friendly way—

**JIM:** I was spoiled in high school.

**LAURA:** Everybody—liked you!

**JIM:** Including you?

**LAURA:** I—yes, I—I did, too—*(She gently closes the book in her lap.)*

**JIM:** Well, well, well!—Give me that program, Laura. *(She hands it to him. He signs it with a flourish.)* There you are—better late than never!

**LAURA:** Oh, I—what a—surprise!

**JIM:** My signature isn't worth very much right now. But some day—maybe—it will increase in value! Being disappointed is one thing and being discouraged is something else. I am disappointed but I'm not discouraged. I'm twenty-three years old. How old are you?

**LAURA:** I'll be twenty-four in June.

**JIM:** That's not old age.

**LAURA:** No, but—

**JIM:** You finished high school?

**LAURA:** *(with difficulty)* I didn't go back.

**JIM:** You mean you dropped out?

**LAURA:** I made bad grades in my final examinations. *(She rises and replaces the book and the program. Her voice strained.)* How is—Emily Meisenbach getting along?

**JIM:** Oh, that kraut-head!

**LAURA:** Why do you call her that?

**JIM:** That's what she was.

**LAURA:** You're not still—going with her?

**JIM:** I never see her.

**LAURA:** It said in the Personal Section that you were—engaged!

**JIM:** I know, but I wasn't impressed by that—propaganda!

**LAURA:** It wasn't—the truth?

**JIM:** Only in Emily's optimistic opinion!

**LAURA:** Oh—

*(Legend: "What Have You Done since High School?")*

*JIM lights a cigarette and leans indolently back on his elbows smiling at LAURA with a warmth and charm which light her inwardly with altar candles. She remains by the table and turns in her hands a piece of glass to cover her tumult.*

**JIM:** *(after several reflective puffs on his cigarette)* What have you done since high school? *(She seems not to hear him.)* Huh? *(LAURA looks up.)* I said what have you done since high school, Laura?

**LAURA:** Nothing much.

**JIM:** You must have been doing something these six long years.

**LAURA:** Yes.

**JIM:** Well, then, such as what?

**LAURA:** I took a business course at business college—

**JIM:** How did that work out?

**LAURA:** Well, not very—well—I had to drop out, it gave me—indigestion—

JIM *laughs gently.*

**JIM:** What are you doing now?

**LAURA:** I don't do anything—much. Oh, please don't think I sit around doing nothing! My glass collection takes up a good deal of time. Glass is something you have to take good care of.

**JIM:** What did you say—about glass?

**LAURA:** Collection I said—I have one—*(She clears her throat and turns away again, acutely shy.)*

**JIM:** *(abruptly)* You know what I judge to be the trouble with you? Inferiority complex! Know what that is? That's what they call it when someone low-rates himself! I understand it because I had it, too. Although my case was not so aggravated as yours seems to be. I had it until I took up public speaking, developed my voice, and learned that I had an aptitude for science. Before that time I never thought of myself as being outstanding in any way whatsoever! Now I've never made a regular study of it, but I have a friend who says I can analyze people better than doctors that make a profession of it. I don't claim that to be necessarily true, but I can sure guess a person's psychology, Laura! *(Takes out his gum.)* Excuse me, Laura. I always take it out when the flavor is gone. I'll use this scrap of paper to wrap it in. I know how it is to get it stuck on a shoe. Yep—that's what I judge to be your principal trouble. A lack of confidence in yourself as a person. You don't have the proper amount of faith in yourself. I'm basing that fact on a number of your remarks and also on certain observations I've made. For instance that clumping you thought was so awful in high school. You say that you even dreaded to walk into class. You see what you did? You dropped out of school, you gave up an education because of a clump, which as far as I know was practically nonexistent! A little physical defect is what you have. Hardly noticeable even! Magnified thousands of times by imagination! You know what my strong advice to you is? Think of yourself as *superior* in some way!

**LAURA:** In what way would I think?

**JIM:** Why, man alive, Laura! Just look about you a little. What do you see? A world full of common people! All of 'em born and all of 'em going to die! Which of them has one-tenth of your good points! Or mine! Or anyone else's, as far as that goes—Gosh! Everybody excels in some one thing. Some in many! *(Unconsciously glances at himself in the mirror.)* All you've got to do is discover in *what!* Take me, for instance. *(He adjusts his tie at the mirror.)* My interest happened to lie in electrodynamics. I'm taking a course in radio engineering at night school, Laura, on top of a fairly responsible job at the warehouse. I'm taking that course and studying public speaking.

**LAURA:** Ohhhh.

**JIM:** Because I believe in the future of television! *(Turning back to her.)* I wish to be ready to go up right along with it. Therefore I'm planning to get in on the ground floor. In fact, I've already made the right connections and all that remains is for the industry itself to get under way! Full steam—*(His eyes are starry.) Knowledge*—Zzzzzp! *Money*—Zzzzzzp!—*Power!* That's the cycle democracy is built on! *(His attitude is convincingly dynamic.* LAURA *stares at him, even her shyness eclipsed in her absolute wonder. He suddenly grins.)* I guess you think I think a lot of myself!

**LAURA:** No—o-o-o, I—

**JIM:** Now how about you? Isn't there something you take more interest in than anything else?

**LAURA:** Well, I do—as I said—have my—glass collection—

*A peal of girlish laughter from the kitchen.*

**JIM:** I'm not right sure I know what you're talking about. What kind of glass is it?

**LAURA:** Little articles of it, they're ornaments mostly! Most of them are little animals made out of glass, the tiniest little animals in the world. Mother calls them a glass menagerie! Here's an example of one, if you'd like to see it! This one is one of the oldest. It's nearly thirteen. *(He stretches out his hand.) (Music: "The Glass Menagerie.")* Oh, be careful—if you breathe, it breaks!

**JIM:** I'd better not take it. I'm pretty clumsy with things.

**LAURA:** Go on, I trust you with him! *(Places it in his palm.)* There now—you're holding him gently! Hold him over the light, he loves the light! You see how the light shines through him?

**JIM:** It sure does shine!

**LAURA:** I shouldn't be partial, but he is my favorite one.

**JIM:** What kind of a thing is this one supposed to be?

**LAURA:** Haven't you noticed the single horn on his forehead?

**JIM:** A unicorn, huh?

**LAURA:** Mmm-hmmm!

**JIM:** Unicorns, aren't they extinct in the modern world?

**LAURA:** I know!

**JIM:** Poor little fellow, he must feel sort of lonesome.

**LAURA:** *(smiling)* Well, if he does he doesn't complain about it. He stays on a shelf with some horses that don't have horns and all of them seem to get along nicely together.

**JIM:** How do you know?

**LAURA:** *(lightly)* I haven't heard any arguments among them!

**JIM:** *(grinning)* No arguments, huh? Well, that's a pretty good sign! Where shall I set him?

**LAURA:** Put him on the table. They all like a change of scenery once in a while!

**JIM:** *(stretching)* Well, well, well, well—Look how big my shadow is when I stretch!

**LAURA:** Oh, oh, yes—it stretches across the ceiling!

**JIM:** *(crossing to door)* I think it's stopped raining. *(Opens fire-escape door.)* Where does the music come from?

**LAURA:** From the Paradise Dance Hall across the alley.

**JIM:** How about cutting the rug a little, Miss Wingfield?

**LAURA:** Oh, I—

**JIM:** Or is your program filled up? Let me have a look at it. *(Grasps imaginary card.)* Why, every dance is taken! I'll have to scratch some out. *(Waltz music: "La Golondrina.")* Ahhh, a waltz! *(He executes some sweeping turns by himself then holds his arms toward* LAURA.*)*

**LAURA:** *(breathlessly)* I—can't dance!

**JIM:** There you go, that inferiority stuff!

**LAURA:** I've never danced in my life!

**JIM:** Come on, try!

**LAURA:** Oh, but I'd step on you!

Laura and Jim study the glass unicorn.

**JIM:** I'm not made out of glass.

**LAURA:** How—how—how do we start?

**JIM:** Just leave it to me. You hold your arms out a little.

**LAURA:** Like this?

**JIM:** A little bit higher. Right. Now don't tighten up, that's the main thing about it—relax.

**LAURA:** *(laughing breathlessly)* It's hard not to.

**JIM:** Okay.

**LAURA:** I'm afraid you can't budge me.

**JIM:** What do you bet I can't? *(He swings her into motion.)*

**LAURA:** Goodness, yes, you can!

**JIM:** Let yourself go, now, Laura, just let yourself go.

**LAURA:** I'm—

**JIM:** Come on!

**LAURA:** Trying.

**JIM:** Not so stiff—Easy does it!

**LAURA:** I know but I'm—

**JIM:** Loosen th' backbone! There now, that's a lot better.

**LAURA:** Am I?

**JIM:** Lots, lots better! *(He moves her about the room in a clumsy waltz.)*

**LAURA:** Oh, my!

**JIM:** Ha-ha!

**LAURA:** Goodness, yes you can!

Jim waltzes Laura around the room.

**JIM:** Ha-ha-ha! *(They suddenly bump into the table.* JIM *stops.)* What did we hit on?

**LAURA:** Table.

**JIM:** Did something fall off it? I think—

**LAURA:** Yes.

**JIM:** I hope that it wasn't the little glass horse with the horn!

**LAURA:** Yes.

**JIM:** Aw, aw, aw. Is it broken?

**LAURA:** Now it is just like all the other horses.

**JIM:** It's lost its—

**LAURA:** Horn! It doesn't matter. Maybe it's a blessing in disguise.

**JIM:** You'll never forgive me. I bet that was your favorite piece of glass.

**LAURA:** I don't have favorites much. It's no tragedy, Freckles. Glass breaks so easily. No matter how careful you are. The traffic jars the shelves and things fall off them.

**JIM:** Still I'm awfully sorry that I was the cause.

**LAURA:** *(smiling)* I'll just imagine he had an operation. The horn was removed to make him feel less—freakish! *(They both laugh.)* Now he will feel more at home with the other horses, the ones that don't have horns . . .

**JIM:** Ha-ha, that's very funny! *(Suddenly serious.)* I'm glad to see that you have a sense of humor. You know—you're—well—very different! Surprisingly different from anyone else I know! *(His voice becomes soft and hesitant with a genuine feeling.)* Do you mind me telling you that? *(*LAURA *is abashed beyond speech.)* You make me feel sort of—I don't know how to put it! I'm usually pretty good at expressing things, but—This is something that I don't know how to say! *(*LAURA *touches her throat and clears it—turns the broken unicorn in her hands.) (Even softer.)* Has anyone ever told you that you were pretty?

*Pause: Music.*

*(*LAURA *looks up slowly, with wonder, and shakes her head.)* Well, you are! In a very different way from anyone else. And all the nicer because of the difference, too. *(His voice becomes low and husky.* LAURA *turns away, nearly faint with the novelty of her emotions.)* I wish that you were my sister. I'd teach you to have some confidence in yourself. The different people are not like other people, but being different is nothing to be ashamed of. Because other people are not such wonderful people. They're one hundred times one thousand. You're one times one! They walk all over the earth. You just stay here. They're common as—weeds, but—you—well, you're—*Blue Roses!*

*(Image on screen: Blue Roses.)*
*(Music changes.)*

**LAURA:** But blue is wrong for—roses . . .

**JIM:** It's right for you—You're—pretty!

**LAURA:** In what respect am I pretty?

**JIM:** In all respects—believe me! Your eyes—your hair—are pretty! Your hands are pretty! *(He catches hold of her hand.)* You think I'm making this up because I'm invited to dinner and have to be nice. Oh, I could do that! I could put on an act for you, Laura, and say lots of things without being very sincere. But this time I am. I'm talking to you sincerely. I happened to notice you had this inferiority complex that keeps you from feeling comfortable with people. Somebody needs to build your confidence up and make you proud instead of shy and turning away and—blushing—Somebody ought to—ought to—*kiss* you, Laura! *(His hand slips slowly up her arm to her shoulder.) (Music swells tumultuously.) (He suddenly turns her about and kisses her on the lips. When he releases her* LAURA *sinks on the sofa with a bright, dazed look.* JIM *backs away and fishes in his pocket for a cigarette.) (Legend on screen: "Souvenir.")* Stumble-john! *(He lights the cigarette, avoiding her look. There is a peal of girlish laughter from* AMANDA *in the kitchenette.* LAURA *slowly raises and opens her hand. It still contains the little broken glass* *animal. She looks at it with a tender, bewildered expression.)* Stumble-john! I shouldn't have done that—That was way off the beam. You don't smoke, do you? *(She looks up, smiling, not hearing the question. He sits beside her a little gingerly. She looks at him speechlessly—waiting. He coughs decorously and moves a little farther aside as he considers the situation and senses her feelings, dimly, with perturbation. Gently.)* Would you—care for a—mint? *(She doesn't seem to hear him but her look grows brighter even.)* Peppermint?—Life Saver? My pocket's a regular drug store—wherever I go . . . *(He pops a mint in his mouth. Then gulps and decides to make a clean breast of it. He speaks slowly and gingerly.)* Laura, you know, if I had a sister like you, I'd do the same thing as Tom. I'd bring out fellows—introduce her to them. The right type of boys of a type to—appreciate her. Only—well—he made a mistake about me. Maybe I've got no call to be saying this. That may not have been the idea in having me over. But what if it was? There's nothing wrong about that. The only trouble is that in my case—I'm not in a situation to—do the right thing. I can't take down your number and say I'll phone. I can't call up next week and—ask for a date. I thought I had better explain the situation in case you misunderstood it and—hurt your feelings. . . . *(Pause. Slowly, very slowly,* LAURA*'s look changes, her eyes returning slowly from his to the ornament in her palm.)*

AMANDA *utters another gay laugh in the kitchenette.*

**LAURA:** *(faintly)* You—won't—call again?

**JIM:** No, Laura, I can't. *(He rises from the sofa.)* As I was just explaining, I've—got strings on me, Laura, I've—been going steady! I go out all the time with a girl named Betty. She's a home-girl like you, and Catholic, and Irish, and in a great many ways we—get along fine. I met her last summer on a moonlight boat trip up the river to Alton, on the *Majestic.* Well—right away from the start it was—love! *(Legend: Love!)* *(*LAURA *sways slightly forward and grips the arm of the sofa. He fails to notice, now enrapt in his own comfortable being.)* Being in love has made a new man of me! *(Leaning stiffly forward, clutching the arm of the sofa,* LAURA *struggles visibly with her storm. But* JIM *is oblivious, she is a long way off.)* The power of love is really pretty tremendous! Love is something that—changes the whole world, Laura! *(The storm abates a little and* LAURA *leans back. He notices her again.)* It happened that Betty's aunt took sick, she got a wire and had to go to Centralia. So Tom—when he asked me to dinner—I naturally just accepted the invitation, not knowing that you—that he—that I—*(He stops awkwardly.)* Huh—I'm a stumble-john! *(He flops back on the sofa. The holy candles in the altar of* LAURA*'s face have been snuffed out! There is a look of almost infinite desolation.* JIM *glances at her uneasily.)* I wish that you would—say something. *(She bites her lip which was trembling and then bravely smiles. She opens her hand again on the broken glass ornament. Then she gently takes his hand and raises it level with her own. She carefully places the unicorn in the palm of his hand, then pushes his fingers closed upon it.)* What are you—doing that for? You want me to have him?—Laura? *(She nods.)* What for?

Jim and Laura kiss.

**LAURA:** A—souvenir . . .

*She rises unsteadily and crouches beside the Victrola to wind it up.*

*(Legend on screen: "Things Have a Way of Turning Out So Badly.")*

*(Or image: "Gentleman caller waving good-bye!—Gaily.")*

*At this moment* AMANDA *rushes brightly back in the front room. She bears a pitcher of fruit punch in an old-fashioned cut-glass pitcher and a plate of macaroons. The plate has a gold border and poppies painted on it.*

**AMANDA:** Well, well, well! Isn't the air delightful after the shower? I've made you children a little liquid refreshment. *(Turns gaily to the gentleman caller.)* Jim, do you know that song about lemonade?

"Lemonade, lemonade
Made in the shade and stirred with a spade—
Good enough for any old maid!"

**JIM:** *(uneasily)* Ha-ha! No—I never heard it.

**AMANDA:** Why, Laura! You look so serious!

**JIM:** We were having a serious conversation.

**AMANDA:** Good! Now you're better acquainted!

**JIM:** *(uncertainly)* Ha-ha! Yes.

**AMANDA:** You modern young people are much more serious-minded than my generation. I was so gay as a girl!

**JIM:** You haven't changed, Mrs. Wingfield.

**AMANDA:** Tonight I'm rejuvenated! The gaiety of the occasion, Mr. O'Connor! *(She tosses her head with a peal of laughter. Spills lemonade.)* Oooo! I'm baptizing myself!

**JIM:** Here—let me—

**AMANDA:** *(setting the pitcher down)* There now. I discovered we had some maraschino cherries. I dumped them in, juice and all!

**JIM:** You shouldn't have gone to that trouble, Mrs. Wingfield.

**AMANDA:** Trouble, trouble? Why it was loads of fun! Didn't you hear me cutting up in the kitchen? I bet your ears were burning! I told Tom how outdone with him I was for keeping you to himself so long a time! He should have brought you over much, much sooner! Well, now that you've found your way, I want you to be a very frequent caller! Not just occasional but all the time. Oh, we're going to have a lot of gay times together! I see them coming! Mmm, just breathe that air! So fresh, and the moon's so pretty! I'll skip back out—I know where my place is when young folks are having a—serious conversation!

**JIM:** Oh, don't go out, Mrs. Wingfield. The fact of the matter is I've got to be going.

**AMANDA:** Going, now? You're joking! Why, it's only the shank of the evening, Mr. O'Connor!

**JIM:** Well, you know how it is.

**AMANDA:** You mean you're a young workingman and have to keep workingmen's hours. We'll let you off early tonight. But only on the condition that next time you stay later. What's the best night for you? Isn't Saturday night the best night for you workingmen?

**JIM:** I have a couple of time-clocks to punch, Mrs. Wingfield. One at morning, another one at night!

**AMANDA:** My, but you *are* ambitious! You work at night, too?

**JIM:** No, Ma'am, not work but—Betty! *(He crosses deliberately to pick up his hat. The band at the Paradise Dance Hall goes into a tender waltz.)*

**AMANDA:** Betty? Betty? Who's—Betty! *(There is an ominous cracking sound in the sky.)*

**JIM:** Oh, just a girl. The girl I go steady with! *(He smiles charmingly. The sky falls.)*

*(Legend: "The Sky Falls.")*

**AMANDA:** *(a long-drawn exhalation)* Ohhhh . . . Is it a serious romance, Mr. O'Connor?

**JIM:** We're going to be married the second Sunday in June.

**AMANDA:** Ohhhh—how nice! Tom didn't mention that you were engaged to be married.

**JIM:** The cat's not out of the bag at the warehouse yet. You know how they are. They call you Romeo and stuff like that. *(He stops at the oval mirror to put on his hat. He carefully shapes the brim and the crown to give a discreetly dashing effect.)* It's been a wonderful evening, Mrs. Wingfield. I guess this is what they mean by Southern hospitality.

**AMANDA:** It really wasn't anything at all.

**JIM:** I hope it don't seem like I'm rushing off. But I promised Betty I'd pick her up at the Wabash depot, an' by the time I get my jalopy down there her train'll be in. Some women are pretty upset if you keep 'em waiting.

**AMANDA:** Yes, I know—The tyranny of women! *(Extends her hand.)* Good-bye, Mr. O'Connor. I wish you luck—and happiness—and success! All three of them, and so does Laura—Don't you, Laura?

**LAURA:** Yes!

**JIM:** *(taking her hand)* Good-bye, Laura. I'm certainly going to treasure that souvenir. And don't you forget the good advice I gave you. *(Raises his voice to a cheery shout.)* So long, Shakespeare! Thanks again, ladies—Good night!

*He grins and ducks jauntily out.*

*Still bravely grimacing,* AMANDA *closes the door on the gentleman caller. Then she turns back to the room with a puzzled expression. She and* LAURA *don't dare to face each other.* LAURA *crouches beside the Victrola to wind it.*

**AMANDA:** *(faintly)* Things have a way of turning out so badly. I don't believe that I would play the Victrola. Well, well—well—Our gentleman caller was engaged to be married! Tom!

**TOM:** *(from back)* Yes, Mother?

**AMANDA:** Come in here a minute. I want to tell you something awfully funny.

**TOM:** *(enters with a macaroon and a glass of the lemonade)* Has the gentleman caller gotten away already?

**AMANDA:** The gentleman caller has made an early departure. What a wonderful joke you played on us!

**TOM:** How do you mean?

**AMANDA:** You didn't mention that he was engaged to be married.

**TOM:** Jim? Engaged?

**AMANDA:** That's what he just informed us.

**TOM:** I'll be jiggered! I didn't know about that.

**AMANDA:** That seems very peculiar.

**TOM:** What's peculiar about it?

**AMANDA:** Didn't you call him your best friend down at the warehouse?

**TOM:** He is, but how did I know?

**AMANDA:** It seems extremely peculiar that you wouldn't know your best friend is going to be married!

**TOM:** The warehouse is where I work, not where I know things about people!

**AMANDA:** You don't know things anywhere! You live in a dream; you manufacture illusions! *(He crosses to door.)* Where are you going?

**TOM:** I'm going to the movies.

**AMANDA:** That's right, now that you've had us make such fools of ourselves. The effort, the preparations, all the expense! The new floor lamp, the rug, the clothes for Laura! All for what? To entertain some other girl's fiancé! Go to the movies, go! Don't think about us, a mother deserted, an unmarried sister who's crippled and has no job! Don't let anything interfere with your selfish pleasure! Just go, go, go—to the movies!

Amanda berates Tom for his error.

**TOM:** All right, I will! The more you shout about my selfishness to me the quicker I'll go, and I won't go to the movies!

**AMANDA:** Go, then! Then go to the moon—you selfish dreamer!

TOM *smashes his glass on the floor. He plunges out on the fire-escape, slamming the door.* LAURA *screams—cut by door.*

*Dance-hall music up.* TOM *goes to the rail and grips it desperately, lifting his face in the chill white moonlight penetrating the narrow abyss of the alley.*

*(Legend on screen: "And So Good-Bye . . .")*

TOM's *closing speech is timed with the interior pantomime. The interior scene is played as though viewed through sound-proof glass.* AMANDA *appears to be making a comforting speech to* LAURA *who is huddled upon the sofa. Now that we cannot hear the mother's speech, her silliness is gone and she has dignity and tragic beauty.* LAURA's *dark hair hides her face until at the end of the speech she lifts it to smile at her mother.* AMANDA's *gestures are slow and graceful, almost dancelike, as she comforts the daughter. At the end of her speech she glances a moment at the father's picture—then withdraws through the portieres. At close of* TOM's *speech,* LAURA *blows out the candles, ending the play.*

**TOM:** I didn't go to the moon, I went much further—for time is the longest distance between two places—Not long after that I was fired for writing a poem on the lid of a shoe-box. I left Saint Louis. I descended the steps of this fire-escape for a last time and followed, from then on, in my father's footsteps, attempting to find in motion what was lost in space—I traveled around a great deal. The cities swept about me like dead leaves, leaves that were brightly colored but torn away from the branches. I would have stopped, but I was pursued by something. It always came upon me unawares, taking me altogether by surprise. Perhaps it was a familiar bit of music. Perhaps it was only a piece of transparent glass—Perhaps I am walking along a street at night, in some strange city, before I have found companions. I pass the lighted window of a shop where perfume is sold. The window is filled with pieces of colored glass, tiny transparent bottles in delicate colors, like bits of a shattered rainbow. Then all at once my sister touches my shoulder. I turn around and look into her eyes. . . . Oh, Laura, Laura, I tried to leave you behind me, but I am more faithful than I intended to be! I reach for a cigarette, I cross the street, I run into the movies or a bar, I buy a drink, I speak to the nearest stranger—anything that can blow your candles out! (LAURA *bends over the candles)*—for nowadays the world is lit by lightning! Blow out your candles, Laura—and so good-bye . . .

*She blows the candles out.*

*(The Scene Dissolves.)*

Laura and Amanda sit huddled alone in the dark.

# Writing from Reading

## Summarize

**1** In this day, a small family, living on hopes, dreams, and illusions, seems destined to take a fall. Does the theme seem specific to the time and place, or does it have larger implications?

**2** What are some of the central "problems" in this problem play? What would you describe as its themes?

## Analyze Craft

**3** In Tom Wingfield's first speech, he—and through him the playwright—declares, " I am the opposite of a stage magician. He gives you illusion that has the appearance of truth. I give you truth in the pleasant disguise of illusion." How does this relate to the notion of realistic representation onstage?

**4** In the stage direction, Williams writes of Tom, "His nature is not remorseless, but to escape from a trap he has to act without pity." In what ways does he do so, and how fully does he succeed?

**5** The glass collection—with its fragility, its safe haven on the shelf—is of course Laura's, and it represents her beauty as well as her predicament. In real life, Williams's sister was institutionalized for schizophrenia. How might this experience have contributed to the development of Laura's character, and how does Laura's fantasy life here feel real?

## Analyze Voice

**6** "And so good-bye. . ." is the play's final line as well as the "Legend on screen." Describe the nature of this farewell and the degree of finality. How does Amanda continue, and are things truly over for Laura and Tom? In what ways is this play an act of continuity as well as one of closure?

**7** How would you describe the language of the play? What tone does the language create? Harsh? Lyrical? A mix of tones?

## Synthesize Summary and Analysis

**8** In what ways does the style of the play—the stage directions, the language, and the representation of inner and outer states of the characters—seem to have affinities with *Death of a Salesman*? In what ways does it differ?

## Interpret the Play

**9** Is there something particular to the fate of this family that ties its destiny to eternal illusion, or does the playwright infer that all families are alike in this regard?

## THE BARD OF PITTSBURGH

August Wilson, one of the most widely praised dramatists of the late twentieth century in America, has had a large impact on a subsequent generation of actors and playwrights. We can make an analogy here with Shakespeare and suggest that in his

"August Wilson plays [are] very similar to Tennessee Williams plays [in that] there's somebody fighting for more. . . . The people that he is dealing with, they have been bourgeois . . . a whole way of life that's crumbling, and they're looking for somebody to save them. August Wilson's characters aren't crumbling; they're down, looking for a way to get up." Conversation with Ruben Santiago-Hudson

own way August Wilson is the Shakespeare of the twentieth-century black American experience. He does not, however, deal with kings, and no armies clash just offstage in his theater. Growing out of the realistic tradition, Wilson makes plays that give us a sense of ordinary life in an extraordinary way. His characters dig deeper into themselves than do most people we know, whether we are black or white or red or yellow, and whether in an actual theater or the theater of our minds. *Fences,* arguably his finest creation, is set in Pittsburgh during the 1950s.

# August Wilson (1945–2005)

Raised in a two-room apartment above a garage in Pittsburgh, August Wilson grew up to become an American playwright with two Pulitzer Prizes, several Tony Award nominations, and numerous other awards and fellowships. He was raised by his African-American mother, who had been abandoned by Wilson's German father. When she remarried, the black family moved to a white neighborhood where they were the victims of racist comments and behavior. This, along with his love of the blues as a form of black expression, led Wilson to become a playwright whose central concern was the plight of blacks and the hope of finding healing in black communities. After founding a black theater company in Pittsburgh, Wilson's first major success came with his play *Ma Rainey's Black Bottom* (1984). Two of his plays, *Fences* (1985) and *Joe Turner's Come and Gone* (1986), ran simultaneously on Broadway—a rare achievement. Wilson's body of work functions as a history of black American life in the twentieth century.

**AS YOU READ** Scan the script for the details of the family's life. Find references to Troy Maxon's life at work and at home and with friends.

TIP

**FOR INTERACTIVE READING . . .** Mark the places in the script where you notice that scenes appear to begin and end.

# Fences (1986)

*For Lloyd Richards, who adds to whatever he touches*

*When the sins of our fathers visit us*
*We do not have to play host.*
*We can banish them with forgiveness*
*As God, in His Largeness and Laws.*

—AUGUST WILSON

## CHARACTERS

**TROY MAXSON**

**JIM BONO,** *Troy's friend*

**ROSE,** *Troy's wife*

**LYONS,** *Troy's oldest son by previous marriage*

**GABRIEL,** *Troy's brother*

**CORY,** *Troy and Rose's son*

**RAYNELL,** *Troy's daughter*

**SETTING:** *The setting is the yard which fronts the only entrance to the Maxson household, an ancient two-story brick house set back off a small alley in a big-city neighborhood. The entrance to the house is gained by two or three steps leading to a wooden porch badly in need of paint.*

*A relatively recent addition to the house and running its full width, the porch lacks congruence. It is a sturdy porch with a flat roof. One or two chairs of dubious value sit at one end where the kitchen window opens onto the porch. An old-fashioned icebox stands silent guard at the opposite end.*

*The yard is a small dirt yard, partially fenced, except for the last scene, with a wooden saw horse, a pile of lumber, and other fence-building equipment set off to the side. Opposite is a tree from which hangs a ball made of rags. A baseball bat leans against the tree. Two oil drums serve as garbage receptacles and sit near the house at right to complete the setting.*

**THE PLAY:** *Near the turn of the century, the destitute of Europe sprang on the city with tenacious claws and an honest and solid dream. The city devoured them. They swelled its belly until it burst into a thousand furnaces and sewing machines, a thousand butcher shops and bakers' ovens, a thousand churches and hospitals and funeral parlors and money-lenders. The city grew. It nourished itself and offered each man a partnership limited only by his talent, his guile, and his willingness and capacity for hard work. For the immigrants of Europe, a dream dared and won true.*

*The descendants of African slaves were offered no such welcome or participation. They came from places called the Carolinas and the Virginias, Georgia, Alabama, Mississippi, and Tennessee. They came strong, eager, searching. The city rejected them and they fled and settled along the riverbanks and under bridges in shallow, ramshackle houses made of sticks and tarpaper. They collected rags and wood.*

*They sold the use of their muscles and their bodies. They cleaned houses and washed clothes, they shined shoes, and in quiet desperation and vengeful pride, they stole, and lived in pursuit of their own dream. That they could breathe free, finally, and stand to meet life with the force of dignity and whatever eloquence the heart could call upon.*

*By 1957, the hard-won victories of the European immigrants had solidified the industrial might of America. War had been confronted and won with new energies that used loyalty and patriotism as its fuel. Life was rich, full, and flourishing. The Milwaukee Braves won the World Series, and the hot winds of change that would make the sixties a turbulent, racing, dangerous, and provocative decade had not yet begun to blow full.*

## ACT I

### SCENE I

*It is 1957.* TROY *and* BONO *enter the yard, engaged in conversation.* TROY *is fifty-three years old, a large man with thick, heavy hands; it is this largeness that he strives to fill out and make an accommodation with. Together with his blackness, his largeness informs his sensibilities and the choices he has made in his life.*

*Of the two men,* BONO *is obviously the follower. His commitment to their friendship of thirty-odd years is rooted in his admiration of* TROY*'s honesty, capacity for hard work, and his strength, which* BONO *seeks to emulate.*

*It is Friday night, payday, and the one night of the week the two men engage in a ritual of talk and drink.* TROY *is usually the most talkative and at times he can be crude and almost vulgar, though he is capable of rising to profound heights of expression. The men carry lunch buckets and wear or carry burlap aprons and are dressed in clothes suitable to their jobs as garbage collectors.*

**BONO:** Troy, you ought to stop that lying!

**TROY:** I ain't lying! The nigger had a watermelon this big. *(He indicates with his hands.)* Talking about . . . "What watermelon, Mr. Rand?" I liked to fell out! "What watermelon, Mr. Rand?" . . . And it sitting there big as life.

**BONO:** What did Mr. Rand say?

**TROY:** Ain't said nothing. Figure if the nigger too dumb to know he carrying a watermelon, he wasn't gonna get much sense out of him. Trying to hide that great big old watermelon under his coat. Afraid to let the white man see him carry it home.

**BONO:** I'm like you . . . I ain't got no time for them kind of people.

**TROY:** Now what he look like getting mad cause he see the man from the union talking to Mr. Rand?

**BONO:** He come to me talking about . . . "Maxson gonna get us fired." I told him to get away from me with that. He walked away from me calling you a troublemaker. What Mr. Rand say?

**TROY:** Ain't said nothing. He told me to go down the Commissioner's office next Friday. They called me down there to see them.

**BONO:** Well, as long as you got your complaint filed, they can't fire you. That's what one of them white fellows tell me.

**TROY:** I ain't worried about them firing me. They gonna fire me cause I asked a question? That's all I did. I went to Mr. Rand and asked him, "Why? Why you got the white mens driving and the colored lifting?" Told him, "what's the matter, don't I count? You think only white fellows got sense enough to drive a truck. That ain't no paper job! Hell, anybody can drive a truck. How come you got all whites driving and the colored lifting?" He told me "take it to the union." Well, hell, that's what I done! Now they wanna come up with this pack of lies.

**BONO:** I told Brownie if the man come and ask him any questions . . . just tell the truth! It ain't nothing but something they done trumped up on you cause you filed a complaint on them.

**TROY:** Brownie don't understand nothing. All I want them to do is change the job description. Give everybody a chance to drive the truck. Brownie can't see that. He ain't got that much sense.

**BONO:** How you figure he be making out with that gal be up at Taylors' all the time . . . that Alberta gal?

**TROY:** Same as you and me. Getting just as much as we is. Which is to say nothing.

**BONO:** It is, huh? I figure you doing a little better than me . . . and I ain't saying what I'm doing.

**TROY:** Aw, nigger, look here . . . I know you. If you had got anywhere near that gal, twenty minutes later you be looking to tell somebody. And the first one you gonna tell . . . that you gonna want to brag to . . . is gonna be me.

**BONO:** I ain't saying that. I see where you be eyeing her.

**TROY:** I eye all the women. I don't miss nothing. Don't never let nobody tell you Troy Maxson don't eye the women.

**BONO:** You been doing more than eyeing her. You done bought her a drink or two.

**TROY:** Hell yeah, I bought her a drink! What that mean? I bought you one, too. What that mean cause I buy her a drink? I'm just being polite.

**BONO:** It's alright to buy her one drink. That's what you call being polite. But when you wanna be buying two or three . . . that's what you call eyeing her.

**TROY:** Look here, as long as you known me . . . you ever known me to chase after women?

**BONO:** Hell yeah! Long as I done known you. You forgetting I knew you when.

**TROY:** Naw, I'm talking about since I been married to Rose?

**BONO:** Oh, not since you been married to Rose. Now, that's the truth, there. I can say that.

**TROY:** Alright then! Case closed.

**BONO:** I see you be walking up around Alberta's house. You supposed to be at Taylors' and you be walking up around there.

**TROY:** What you watching where I'm walking for? I ain't watching after you.

**BONO:** I seen you walking around there more than once.

**TROY:** Hell, you liable to see me walking anywhere! That don't mean nothing cause you see me walking around there.

**BONO:** Where she come from anyway? She just kinda showed up one day.

**TROY:** Tallahassee. You can look at her and tell she one of them Florida gals. They got some big healthy women down there. Grow them right up out the ground. Got a little bit of Indian in her. Most of them niggers down in Florida got some Indian in them.

**BONO:** I don't know about that Indian part. But she damn sure big and healthy. Woman wear some big stockings. Got them great big old legs and hips as wide as the Mississippi River.

**TROY:** Legs don't mean nothing. You don't do nothing but push them out of the way. But them hips cushion the ride!

**BONO:** Troy, you ain't got no sense.

**TROY:** It's the truth! Like you riding on Goodyears!

*(*ROSE *enters from the house. She is ten years younger than* TROY. *Her devotion to him stems from her recognition of the possibilities of her life without him: a succession of abusive men and their babies, a life of partying and running the streets, the Church, or aloneness with its attendant pain and frustration. She recognizes* TROY*'s spirit as a fine and illuminating one and she either ignores or forgives his faults, only some of which she recognizes. Though she doesn't drink, her presence is an integral part of the Friday night rituals. She alternates between the porch and the kitchen, where supper preparations are under way.)*

**ROSE:** What you all out here getting into?

**TROY:** What you worried about what we getting into for? This is men talk, woman.

**ROSE:** What I care what you all talking about? Bono, you gonna stay for supper?

**BONO:** No, I thank you, Rose. But Lucille say she cooking up a pot of pigfeet.

**TROY:** Pigfeet! Hell, I'm going home with you! Might even stay the night if you got some pigfeet. You got something in there to top them pigfeet, Rose?

**ROSE:** I'm cooking up some chicken. I got some chicken and collard greens.

**TROY:** Well, go on back in the house and let me and Bono finish what we was talking about. This is men talk. I got some talk for you later. You know what kind of talk I mean. You go on and powder it up.

**ROSE:** Troy Maxson, don't you start that now!

**TROY:** *(Puts his arm around her.)* Aw, woman . . . come here. Look here, Bono . . . when I met this woman . . . I got out that place, say, "Hitch up my pony, saddle up my mare . . . there's a woman out there for me somewhere. I looked here. Looked there. Saw Rose and latched on to her." I latched on to her and told her—I'm gonna tell you the truth—I told her, "Baby, I don't wanna marry, I just wanna be your man." Rose told me . . . tell him what you told me, Rose.

**ROSE:** I told him if he wasn't the marrying kind, then move out the way so the marrying kind could find me.

**TROY:** That's what she told me. "Nigger, you in my way. You blocking the view! Move out the way so I can find me a husband." I thought it over two or three days. Come back—

**ROSE:** Ain't no two or three days nothing. You was back the same night.

**TROY:** Come back, told her . . . "Okay, baby . . . but I'm gonna buy me a banty rooster and put him out there in the backyard . . . and when he see a stranger come, he'll flap his wings and crow . . . " Look here, Bono, I could watch the front door by myself . . . it was that back door I was worried about.

**ROSE:** Troy, you ought not talk like that. Troy ain't doing nothing but telling a lie.

**TROY:** Only thing is . . . when we first got married . . . forget the rooster . . . we ain't had no yard!

**BONO:** I hear you tell it. Me and Lucille was staying down there on Logan Street. Had two rooms with the outhouse in the back. I ain't mind the outhouse none. But when that goddamn wind blow through there in the winter . . . that's what I'm talking about! To this day I wonder why in the hell I ever stayed down there for six long years. But see, I didn't know I could do no better. I thought only white folks had inside toilets and things.

**ROSE:** There's a lot of people don't know they can do no better than they doing now. That's just something you got to learn. A lot of folks still shop at Bella's.

**TROY:** Ain't nothing wrong with shopping at Bella's. She got fresh food.

**ROSE:** I ain't said nothing about if she got fresh food. I'm talking about what she charge. She charge ten cents more than the A&P.

**TROY:** The A&P ain't never done nothing for me. I spends my money where I'm treated right. I go down to Bella, say, "I need a loaf of bread, I'll pay you Friday." She give it to me. What sense that make when I got money to go and spend it somewhere else and ignore the person who done right by me? That ain't in the Bible.

**ROSE:** We ain't talking about what's in the Bible. What sense it make to shop there when she overcharge?

**TROY:** You shop where you want to. I'll do my shopping where the people been good to me.

**ROSE:** Well, I don't think it's right for her to overcharge. That's all I was saying.

**BONO:** Look here . . . I got to get on. Lucille going be raising all kind of hell.

**TROY:** Where you going, nigger? We ain't finished this pint. Come here, finish this pint.

**BONO:** Well, hell, I am . . . if you ever turn the bottle loose.

**TROY:** *(Hands him the bottle.)* The only thing I say about the A&P is I'm glad Cory got that job down there. Help him take care of his school clothes and things. Gabe done moved out and things getting tight around here. He got that job . . . He can start to look out for himself.

**ROSE:** Cory done went and got recruited by a college football team.

**TROY:** I told that boy about that football stuff. The white man ain't gonna let him get nowhere with that football. I told him when he first come to me with it. Now you come telling me he done went and got more tied up in it. He ought to go and get recruited in how to fix cars or something where he can make a living.

**ROSE:** He ain't talking about making no living playing football. It's just something the boys in school do. They gonna send a recruiter by to talk to you. He'll tell you he ain't talking about making no living playing football. It's a honor to be recruited.

**TROY:** It ain't gonna get him nowhere. Bono'll tell you that.

**BONO:** If he be like you in the sports . . . he's gonna be alright. Ain't but two men ever played baseball as good as you. That's Babe Ruth and Josh Gibson. Them's the only two men ever hit more home runs than you.

**TROY:** What it ever get me? Ain't got a pot to piss in or a window to throw it out of.

**ROSE:** Times have changed since you was playing baseball, Troy. That was before the war. Times have changed a lot since then.

**TROY:** How in hell they done changed?

**ROSE:** They got lots of colored boys playing ball now. Baseball and football.

**BONO:** You right about that, Rose. Times have changed, Troy. You just come along too early.

**TROY:** There ought not never have been no time called too early! Now you take that fellow . . . what's that fellow they had playing right field for the Yankees back then? You know who I'm talking about, Bono. Used to play right field for the Yankees.

**ROSE:** Selkirk?

**TROY:** Selkirk! That's it! Man batting .269, understand? .269. What kind of sense that make? I was hitting .432 with thirty-seven home runs! Man batting .269 and playing right field for the Yankees! I saw Josh Gibson's daughter yesterday. She walking around with raggedy shoes on her feet. Now I bet you Selkirk's daughter ain't walking around with raggedy shoes on her feet! I bet you that!

**ROSE:** They got a lot of colored baseball players now. Jackie Robinson was the first. Folks had to wait for Jackie Robinson.

**TROY:** I done seen a hundred niggers play baseball better than Jackie Robinson. Hell, I know some teams Jackie Robinson couldn't even make! What you talking about Jackie Robinson. Jackie Robinson wasn't nobody. I'm talking about if you could play ball then they ought to have let you play. Don't care what color you were. Come telling me I come along too early. If you could play . . . then they ought to have let you play.

*(TROY takes a long drink from the bottle.)*

**ROSE:** You gonna drink yourself to death. You don't need to be drinking like that.

**TROY:** Death ain't nothing. I done seen him. Done wrassled with him. You can't tell me nothing about death. Death ain't nothing but a fastball on the outside corner. And you know what I'll do to that! Lookee here, Bono . . . am I lying? You get one of them fastballs, about waist high, over the outside corner of the plate where you can get the meat of the bat on it . . . and good god! You can kiss it goodbye. Now, am I lying?

**BONO:** Naw, you telling the truth there. I seen you do it.

**TROY:** If I'm lying . . . that 450 feet worth of lying! *(Pause.)* That's all death is to me. A fastball on the outside corner.

**ROSE:** I don't know why you want to get on talking about death.

**TROY:** Ain't nothing wrong with talking about death. That's part of life. Everybody gonna die. You gonna die, I'm gonna die. Bono's gonna die. Hell, we all gonna die.

**ROSE:** But you ain't got to talk about it. I don't like to talk about it.

**TROY:** You the one brought it up. Me and Bono was talking about baseball . . . you tell me I'm gonna drink myself to death. Ain't that right, Bono? You know I don't drink this but one night out of the week. That's Friday night. I'm gonna drink just enough to where I can handle it. Then I cuts it loose. I leave it alone. So don't you worry about me drinking myself to death. 'Cause I ain't worried about Death. I done seen him. I done wrestled with him.

Look here, Bono . . . I looked up one day and Death was marching straight at me. Like Soldiers on Parade! The Army of Death was marching straight at me. The middle of July, 1941. It got real cold just like it be winter. It seem like Death himself reached out and touched me on the shoulder. He touch me just like I touch you. I got cold as ice and Death standing there grinning at me.

**ROSE:** Troy, why don't you hush that talk.

**TROY:** I say . . . what you want, Mr. Death? You be wanting me? You done brought your army to be getting me? I looked him dead in the eye. I wasn't fearing nothing. I was ready to tangle. Just like I'm ready to tangle now. The Bible say be ever vigilant. That's why I don't get but so drunk. I got to keep watch.

**ROSE:** Troy was right down there in Mercy Hospital. You remember he had pneumonia? Laying there with a fever talking plumb out of his head.

**TROY:** Death standing there staring at me . . . carrying that sickle in his hand. Finally he say, "You want bound over for another year?" See, just like that . . . "You want bound over for another year?" I told him, "Bound over hell! Let's settle this now!"

It seem like he kinda fell back when I said that, and all the cold went out of me. I reached down and grabbed that sickle and threw it just as far as I could throw it . . . and me and him commenced to wrestling.

We wrestled for three days and three nights. I can't say where I found the strength from. Everytime it seemed like he was gonna get the best of me, I'd reach way down deep inside myself and find the strength to do him one better.

**ROSE:** Everytime Troy tell that story he find different ways to tell it. Different things to make up about it.

**TROY:** I ain't making up nothing. I'm telling you the facts of what happened. I wrestled with Death for three days and three nights and I'm standing here to tell you about it. *(Pause.)* Alright. At the end of the third night we done weakened each other to where we can't hardly move. Death stood up, throwed on his robe . . . had him a white robe with a hood on it. He throwed on that robe and went off to look for his sickle. Say, "I'll be back." Just like that. "I'll be back." I told him, say, "Yeah, but . . . you gonna have to find me!" I wasn't no fool. I wasn't going looking for him. Death ain't nothing to play with. And I know he's gonna get me. I know I got to join his army . . . his camp followers. But as long as I keep my strength and see him coming . . . as long as I keep up my vigilance . . . he's gonna have to fight to get me. I ain't going easy.

**BONO:** Well, look here, since you got to keep up your vigilance . . . let me have the bottle.

**TROY:** Aw hell, I shouldn't have told you that part. I should have left out that part.

**ROSE:** Troy be talking that stuff and half the time don't even know what he be talking about.

**TROY:** Bono know me better than that.

**BONO:** That's right. I know you. I know you got some Uncle Remus in your blood. You got more stories than the devil got sinners.

**TROY:** Aw hell, I done seen him too! Done talked with the devil.

**ROSE:** Troy, don't nobody wanna be hearing all that stuff.

*(*LYONS *enters the yard from the street. Thirty-four years old,* TROY*'s son by a previous marriage, he sports a neatly trimmed goatee, sport coat, white shirt, tieless and buttoned at the collar. Though he fancies himself a musician, he is more caught up in the rituals and "idea" of being a musician than in the actual practice of the music. He has come to borrow money from* TROY*, and while he knows he will be successful, he is uncertain as to what extent his lifestyle will be held up to scrutiny and ridicule.)*

**LYONS:** Hey, Pop.

**TROY:** What you come "Hey, Popping" me for?

**LYONS:** How you doing, Rose? *(He kisses her.)* Mr. Bono. How you doing?

**BONO:** Hey, Lyons . . . how you been?

**TROY:** He must have been doing alright. I ain't seen him around here last week.

**ROSE:** Troy, leave your boy alone. He come by to see you and you wanna start all that nonsense.

**TROY:** I ain't bothering Lyons. *(Offers him the bottle.)* Here . . . get you a drink. We got an understanding. I know why he come by to see me and he know I know.

**LYONS:** Come on, Pop . . . I just stopped by to say hi . . . see how you was doing.

**TROY:** You ain't stopped by yesterday.

**ROSE:** You gonna stay for supper, Lyons? I got some chicken cooking in the oven.

**LYONS:** No, Rose . . . thanks. I was just in the neighborhood and thought I'd stop by for a minute.

**TROY:** You was in the neighborhood alright, nigger. You telling the truth there. You was in the neighborhood cause it's my payday.

**LYONS:** Well, hell, since you mentioned it . . . let me have ten dollars.

**TROY:** I'll be damned! I'll die and go to hell and play blackjack with the devil before I give you ten dollars.

**BONO:** That's what I wanna know about . . . that devil you done seen.

**LYONS:** What . . . Pop done seen the devil? You too much, Pops.

**TROY:** Yeah, I done seen him. Talked to him too!

**ROSE:** You ain't seen no devil. I done told you that man ain't had nothing to do with the devil. Anything you can't understand, you want to call it the devil.

**TROY:** Look here, Bono . . . I went down to see Hertzberger about some furniture. Got three rooms for two-ninety-eight. That what it say on the radio. "Three rooms . . . two-ninety-eight." Even made up a little song about it. Go down there . . . man tell me I can't get no credit. I'm working every day and can't get no credit. What to do? I got an empty house with some raggedy furniture in it. Cory ain't got no bed. He's sleeping on a pile of rags on the floor. Working every day and can't get no credit. Come back here—Rose'll tell you—madder than hell. Sit down . . . try to figure what I'm gonna do. Come a knock on the door. Ain't been living here but three days. Who know I'm here? Open the door . . . devil standing there bigger than life. White fellow . . . got on good clothes and everything. Standing there with a clipboard in his hand. I ain't had to say nothing. First words come out of his mouth was . . . "I understand you need some furniture and can't get no credit." I liked to fell over. He say "I'll give you all the credit you want, but you got to pay the interest on it." I told him, "Give me three rooms worth and charge whatever you want." Next day a truck pulled up here and two men unloaded them three rooms. Man what drove the truck give me a book. Say send ten dollars, first of every month to the address in the book and every thing will be alright. Say if I miss a payment the devil was coming back and it'll be hell to pay. That was fifteen years ago. To this day . . . the first of the month I send my ten dollars, Rose'll tell you.

**ROSE:** Troy lying.

**TROY:** I ain't never seen that man since. Now you tell me who else that could have been but the devil? I ain't sold my soul or nothing like that, you understand. Naw, I wouldn't have truck with the devil about nothing like that. I got my furniture and pays my ten dollars the first of the month just like clockwork.

**BONO:** How long you say you been paying this ten dollars a month?

**TROY:** Fifteen years!

**BONO:** Hell, ain't you finished paying for it yet? How much the man done charged you?

**TROY:** Aw hell, I done paid for it. I done paid for it ten times over! The fact is I'm scared to stop paying it.

**ROSE:** Troy lying. We got that furniture from Mr. Glickman. He ain't paying no ten dollars a month to nobody.

**TROY:** Aw hell, woman. Bono know I ain't that big a fool.

**LYONS:** I was just getting ready to say . . . I know where there's a bridge for sale.

**TROY:** Look here, I'll tell you this . . . it don't matter to me if he was the devil. It don't matter if the devil give credit. Somebody has got to give it.

**ROSE:** It ought to matter. You going around talking about having truck with the devil . . . God's the one you gonna have to answer to. He's the one gonna be at the Judgment.

**LYONS:** Yeah, well, look here, Pop . . . Let me have that ten dollars. I'll give it back to you. Bonnie got a job working at the hospital.

**TROY:** What I tell you, Bono? The only time I see this nigger is when he wants something. That's the only time I see him.

**LYONS:** Come on, Pop, Mr. Bono don't want to hear all that. Let me have the ten dollars. I told you Bonnie working.

**TROY:** What that mean to me? "Bonnie working." I don't care if she working. Go ask her for the ten dollars if she working. Talking about "Bonnie working." Why ain't you working?

**LYONS:** Aw, Pop, you know I can't find no decent job. Where am I gonna get a job at? You know I can't get no job.

**TROY:** I told you I know some people down there. I can get you on the rubbish if you want to work. I told you that the last time you came by here asking me for something.

**LYONS:** Naw, Pop . . . thanks. That ain't for me. I don't wanna be carrying nobody's rubbish. I don't wanna be punching nobody's time clock.

**TROY:** What's the matter, you too good to carry people's rubbish? Where you think that ten dollars you talking about come from? I'm just supposed to haul people's rubbish and give my money to you cause you too lazy to work. You too lazy to work and wanna know why you ain't got what I got.

**ROSE:** What hospital Bonnie working at? Mercy?

**LYONS:** She's down at Passavant working in the laundry.

**TROY:** I ain't got nothing as it is. I give you that ten dollars and I got to eat beans the rest of the week. Naw . . . you ain't getting no ten dollars here.

**LYONS:** You ain't got to be eating no beans. I don't know why you wanna say that.

**TROY:** I ain't got no extra money. Gabe done moved over to Miss Pearl's paying her the rent and things done got tight around here. I can't afford to be giving you every payday.

**LYONS:** I ain't asked you to give me nothing. I asked you to loan me ten dollars. I know you got ten dollars.

**TROY:** Yeah, I got it. You know why I got it? Cause I don't throw my money away out there in the streets. You living the fast life . . . wanna be a musician . . . running around in them clubs and things . . . then, you learn to take care of yourself. You ain't gonna find me going and asking nobody for nothing. I done spent too many years without.

**LYONS:** You and me is two different people, Pop.

**TROY:** I done learned my mistake and learned to do what's right by it. You still trying to get something for nothing. Life don't owe you nothing. You owe it to yourself. Ask Bono. He'll tell you I'm right.

**LYONS:** You got your way of dealing with the world . . . I got mine. The only thing that matters to me is the music.

**TROY:** Yeah, I can see that! It don't matter how you gonna eat . . . where your next dollar is coming from. You telling the truth there.

**LYONS:** I know I got to eat. But I got to live too. I need something that gonna help me to get out of the bed in the morning. Make me feel like I belong in the world. I don't bother nobody. I just stay with my music cause that's the only way I can find to live in the world. Otherwise there ain't no telling what I might do. Now I don't come criticizing you and how you live. I just come by to ask you for ten dollars. I don't wanna hear all that about how I live.

**TROY:** Boy, your mamma did a hell of a job raising you.

**LYONS:** You can't change me, Pop. I'm thirty-four years old. If you wanted to change me, you should have been there when I was growing up. I come by to see you . . . ask for ten dollars and you want to talk about how I was raised. You don't know nothing about how I was raised.

**ROSE:** Let the boy have ten dollars, Troy.

**TROY:** *(To* LYONS.*)* What the hell you looking at me for? I ain't got no ten dollars. You know what I do with my money. *(To* ROSE.*)* Give him ten dollars if you want him to have it.

**ROSE:** I will. Just as soon as you turn it loose.

**TROY:** *(Handing* ROSE *the money.)* There it is. Seventy-six dollars and forty-two cents. You see this, Bono? Now, I ain't gonna get but six of that back.

**ROSE:** You ought to stop telling that lie. Here, Lyons. *(She hands him the money.)*

**LYONS:** Thanks, Rose. Look . . . I got to run . . . I'll see you later.

**TROY:** Wait a minute. You gonna say, "thanks, Rose" and ain't gonna look to see where she got that ten dollars from? See how they do me, Bono?

**LYONS:** I know she got it from you, Pop. Thanks. I'll give it back to you.

**TROY:** There he go telling another lie. Time I see that ten dollars . . . he'll be owing me thirty more.

**LYONS:** See you, Mr. Bono.

**BONO:** Take care, Lyons!

**LYONS:** Thanks, Pop. I'll see you again.

*(*LYONS *exits the yard.)*

**TROY:** I don't know why he don't go and get him a decent job and take care of that woman he got.

**BONO:** He'll be alright, Troy. The boy is still young.

**TROY:** The *boy* is thirty-four years old.

**ROSE:** Let's not get off into all that.

**BONO:** Look here . . . I got to be going. I got to be getting on. Lucille gonna be waiting.

**TROY:** *(Puts his arm around* ROSE.*)* See this woman, Bono? I love this woman. I love this woman so much it hurts. I love her so much . . . I done run out of ways of loving her. So I got to go back to basics. Don't you come by my house Monday morning talking about time to go to work . . . 'cause I'm still gonna be stroking!

**ROSE:** Troy! Stop it now!

**BONO:** I ain't paying him no mind, Rose. That ain't nothing but gin-talk. Go on, Troy. I'll see you Monday.

**TROY:** Don't you come by my house, nigger! I done told you what I'm gonna be doing.

*(The lights go down to black.)*

## SCENE II

*The lights come up on* ROSE *hanging up clothes. She hums and sings softly to herself. It is the following morning.*

**ROSE:** *(Sings.)*
Jesus, be a fence all around me every day
Jesus, I want you to protect me as I travel on my way.
Jesus, be a fence all around me every day.

*(*TROY *enters from the house.)*

Jesus, I want you to protect me
As I travel on my way.
*(To* TROY.*)* 'Morning. You ready for breakfast? I can fix it soon as I finish hanging up these clothes.

**TROY:** I got the coffee on. That'll be alright. I'll just drink some of that this morning.

**ROSE:** That 651 hit yesterday. That's the second time this month. Miss Pearl hit for a dollar . . . seem like those that need the least always get lucky. Poor folks can't get nothing.

**TROY:** Them numbers don't know anybody. I don't know why you fool with them. You and Lyons both.

**ROSE:** It's something to do.

**TROY:** You ain't doing nothing but throwing your money away.

**ROSE:** Troy, you know I don't play foolishly. I just play a nickel here and a nickel there.

**TROY:** That's two nickels you done thrown away.

**ROSE:** Now I hit sometimes . . . that makes up for it. It always comes in handy when I do hit. I don't hear you complaining then.

**TROY:** I ain't complaining now. I just say it's foolish. Trying to guess out of six hundred ways which way the number gonna come. If I had all the money niggers, these Negroes, throw away on numbers for one week—just one week—I'd be a rich man.

**ROSE:** Well, you wishing and calling it foolish ain't gonna stop folks from playing numbers. That's one thing for sure. Besides . . . some good things come from playing numbers. Look where Pope done bought him that restaurant off of numbers.

**TROY:** I can't stand niggers like that. Man ain't had two dimes to rub together. He walking around with his shoes all run over bumming money for cigarettes. Alright. Got lucky there and hit the numbers . . .

**ROSE:** Troy, I know all about it.

**TROY:** Had good sense, I'll say that for him. He ain't throwed his money away. I seen niggers hit the numbers and go through two thousand dollars in four days. Man bought him that restaurant down there . . . fixed it up real nice. . . . and then didn't want nobody to come in it! A Negro go in there and can't get no kind of service. I seen a white fellow come in there and order a bowl of stew. Pope picked all the meat out of the pot for him. Man ain't had nothing but a bowl of meat! Negro come behind him and ain't got nothing but the potatoes and carrots. Talking about what numbers do for people, you picked a wrong example. Ain't done nothing but make a worser fool out of him than he was before.

**ROSE:** Troy, you ought to stop worrying about what happened at work yesterday.

**TROY:** I ain't worried. Just told me to be down there at the Commissioner's office on Friday. Everybody think they gonna fire me. I ain't worried about them firing me. You ain't got to worry about that. *(Pause.)* Where's Cory? Cory in the house? *(Calls.)* Cory?

**ROSE:** He gone out.

**TROY:** Out, huh? He gone out 'cause he know I want him to help me with this fence. I know how he is. That boy scared of work.

*(GABRIEL enters. He comes halfway down the alley and, hearing TROY's voice, stops.)*

**TROY:** *(Continues.)* He ain't done a lick of work in his life.

**ROSE:** He had to go to football practice. Coach wanted them to get in a little extra practice before the season start.

**TROY:** I got his practice . . . running out of here before he get his chores done.

**ROSE:** Troy, what is wrong with you this morning? Don't nothing set right with you. Go on back in there and go to bed . . . get up on the other side.

**TROY:** Why something got to be wrong with me? I ain't said nothing wrong with me.

**ROSE:** You got something to say about everything. First it's the numbers . . . then it's the way the man runs his restaurant . . . then you done got on Cory. What's it gonna be next? Take a look up there and see if the weather suits you . . . or is it gonna be how you gonna put up the fence with the clothes hanging in the yard?

**TROY:** You hit the nail on the head then.

**ROSE:** I know you like I know the back of my hand. Go on in there and get you some coffee . . . see if that straighten you up. 'Cause you ain't right this morning.

*(TROY starts into the house and sees GABRIEL. GABRIEL starts singing. TROY's brother, he is seven years younger than TROY. Injured in World War II, he has a metal plate in his head. He carries an old trumpet tied around his waist and believes with every fiber of his being that he is the Archangel Gabriel. He carries a chipped basket with an assortment of discarded fruits and vegetables he has picked up in the strip district and which he attempts to sell.)*

**GABRIEL:** *(Singing.)*

Yes, ma'am, I got plums
You ask me how I sell them
Oh ten cents apiece
Three for a quarter
Come and buy now
'Cause I'm here today
And tomorrow I'll be gone

*(GABRIEL enters.)*

Hey, Rose!

**ROSE:** How you doing, Gabe?

**GABRIEL:** There's Troy . . . Hey, Troy!

**TROY:** Hey, Gabe.

*(Exit into kitchen.)*

**ROSE:** *(To GABRIEL.)* What you got there?

**GABRIEL:** You know what I got, Rose. I got fruits and vegetables.

**ROSE:** *(Looking in basket.)* Where's all these plums you talking about?

**GABRIEL:** I ain't got no plums today, Rose. I was just singing that. Have some tomorrow. Put me in a big order for plums. Have enough plums tomorrow for St. Peter and everybody.

(TROY *reenters from kitchen, crosses to steps.)*

*(To* ROSE.*)* Troy's mad at me.

**TROY:** I ain't mad at you. What I got to be mad at you about? You ain't done nothing to me.

**GABRIEL:** I just moved over to Miss Pearl's to keep out from in your way. I ain't mean no harm by it.

**TROY:** Who said anything about that? I ain't said anything about that.

**GABRIEL:** You ain't mad at me, is you?

**TROY:** Naw . . . I ain't mad at you, Gabe. If I was mad at you I'd tell you about it.

**GABRIEL:** Got me two rooms. In the basement. Got my own door too. Wanna see my key? *(He holds up a key.)* That's my own key! Ain't nobody else got a key like that. That's my key! My two rooms!

**TROY:** Well, that's good, Gabe. You got your own key . . . that's good.

**ROSE:** You hungry, Gabe? I was just fixing to cook Troy his breakfast.

**GABRIEL:** I'll take some biscuits. You got some biscuits? Did you know when I was in heaven . . . every morning me and St. Peter would sit down by the gate and eat some big fat biscuits? Oh, yeah! We had us a good time. We'd sit there and eat us them biscuits and then St. Peter would go off to sleep and tell me to wake him up when it's time to open the gates for the judgment.

**ROSE:** Well, come on . . . I'll make up a batch of biscuits.

(ROSE *exits into the house.)*

**GABRIEL:** Troy . . . St. Peter got your name in the book. I seen it. It say . . . Troy Maxson. I say . . . I know him! He got the same name like what I got. That's my brother!

**TROY:** How many times you gonna tell me that, Gabe?

**GABRIEL:** Ain't got my name in the book. Don't have to have my name. I done died and went to heaven. He got your name though. One morning St. Peter was looking at his book . . . marking it up for the judgment . . . and he let me see your name. Got it in there under M. Got Rose's name . . . I ain't seen it like I seen yours . . . but I know it's in there. He got a great big book. Got everybody's name what was ever been born. That's what he told me. But I seen your name. Seen it with my own eyes.

**TROY:** Go on in the house there. Rose going to fix you something to eat.

**GABRIEL:** Oh, I ain't hungry. I done had breakfast with Aunt Jemimah. She come by and cooked me up a whole mess of flapjacks. Remember how we used to eat them flapjacks?

**TROY:** Go on in the house and get you something to eat now.

**GABRIEL:** I got to sell my plums. I done sold some tomatoes. Got me two quarters. Wanna see? *(He shows* TROY *his quarters.)* I'm gonna save them and buy me a new horn so St. Peter can hear me when it's time to open the gates. (GABRIEL *stops suddenly. Listens.)* Hear that? That's the hellhounds. I got to chase them out of here. Go on get out of here! Get out!

(GABRIEL *exits singing.)*

Better get ready for the judgment
Better get ready for the judgment
My Lord is coming down

(ROSE *enters from the house.)*

**TROY:** He gone off somewhere.

**GABRIEL:** *(Offstage.)* Better get ready for the judgment
Better get ready for the judgment morning
Better get ready for the judgment
My God is coming down

**ROSE:** He ain't eating right. Miss Pearl say she can't get him to eat nothing.

**TROY:** What you want me to do about it, Rose? I done did everything I can for the man. I can't make him get well. Man got half his head blown away . . . what you expect?

**ROSE:** Seem like something ought to be done to help him.

**TROY:** Man don't bother nobody. He just mixed up from that metal plate he got in his head. Ain't no sense for him to go back into the hospital.

**ROSE:** Least he be eating right. They can help him take care of himself.

**TROY:** Don't nobody wanna be locked up, Rose. What you wanna lock him up for? Man go over there and fight the war . . . messin' around with them Japs, get half his head blown off . . . and they give him a lousy three thousand dollars. And I had to swoop down on that.

**ROSE:** Is you fixing to go into that again?

**TROY:** That's the only way I got a roof over my head . . . cause of that metal plate.

**ROSE:** Ain't no sense you blaming yourself for nothing. Gabe wasn't in no condition to manage that money. You done what was right by him. Can't nobody say you ain't done what was right by him. Look how long you took care of him . . . till he wanted to have his own place and moved over there with Miss Pearl.

**TROY:** That ain't what I'm saying, woman! I'm just stating the facts. If my brother didn't have that metal plate in his head . . . I wouldn't have a pot to piss in or a window to throw it out of. And I'm fifty-three years old. Now see if you can understand that!

(TROY *gets up from the porch and starts to exit the yard.)*

**ROSE:** Where you going off to? You been running out of here every Saturday for weeks. I thought you was gonna work on this fence?

**TROY:** I'm gonna walk down to Taylors'. Listen to the ball game. I'll be back in a bit. I'll work on it when I get back.

*(He exits the yard. The lights go to black.)*

## SCENE III

*The lights come up on the yard. It is four hours later.* ROSE *is taking down the clothes from the line.* CORY *enters carrying his football equipment.*

**ROSE:** Your daddy like to had a fit with you running out of here this morning without doing your chores.

**CORY:** I told you I had to go to practice.

**ROSE:** He say you were supposed to help him with this fence.

**CORY:** He been saying that the last four or five Saturdays, and then he don't never do nothing, but go down to Taylors'. Did you tell him about the recruiter?

**ROSE:** Yeah, I told him.

**CORY:** What he say?

**ROSE:** He ain't said nothing too much. You get in there and get started on your chores before he gets back. Go on and scrub down them steps before he gets back here hollering and carrying on.

**CORY:** I'm hungry. What you got to eat, Mama?

**ROSE:** Go on and get started on your chores. I got some meat loaf in there. Go on and make you a sandwich . . . and don't leave no mess in there.

(CORY *exits into the house.* ROSE *continues to take down the clothes.* TROY *enters the yard and sneaks up and grabs her from behind.)*

Troy! Go on, now. You liked to scared me to death. What was the score of the game? Lucille had me on the phone and I couldn't keep up with it.

**TROY:** What I care about the game? Come here, woman. *(He tries to kiss her.)*

**ROSE:** I thought you went down Taylors' to listen to the game. Go on, Troy! You supposed to be putting up this fence.

**TROY:** *(Attempting to kiss her again.)* I'll put it up when I finish with what is at hand.

**ROSE:** Go on, Troy. I ain't studying you.

**TROY:** *(Chasing after her.)* I'm studying you . . . fixing to do my homework!

**ROSE:** Troy, you better leave me alone.

**TROY:** Where's Cory? That boy brought his butt home yet?

**ROSE:** He's in the house doing his chores.

**TROY:** *(Calling.)* Cory! Get your butt out here, boy!

(ROSE *exits into the house with the laundry.* TROY *goes over to the pile of wood, picks up a board, and starts sawing.* CORY *enters from the house.)*

**TROY:** You just now coming in here from leaving this morning?

**CORY:** Yeah, I had to go to football practice.

**TROY:** Yeah, what?

**CORY:** Yessir.

**TROY:** I ain't but two seconds off you noway. The garbage sitting in there overflowing . . . you ain't done none of your chores . . . and you come in here talking about "Yeah."

**CORY:** I was just getting ready to do my chores now, Pop . . .

**TROY:** Your first chore is to help me with this fence on Saturday. Everything else come after that. Now get that saw and cut them boards.

(CORY *takes the saw and begins cutting the boards.* TROY *continues working. There is a long pause.)*

**CORY:** Hey, Pop . . . why don't you buy a TV?

**TROY:** What I want with a TV? What I want one of them for?

**CORY:** Everybody got one. Earl, Ba Bra . . . Jesse!

**TROY:** I ain't asked you who had one. I say what I want with one?

**CORY:** So you can watch it. They got lots of things on TV. Baseball games and everything. We could watch the World Series.

**TROY:** Yeah . . . and how much this TV cost?

**CORY:** I don't know. They got them on sale for around two hundred dollars.

**TROY:** Two hundred dollars, huh?

**CORY:** That ain't that much, Pop.

**TROY:** Naw, it's just two hundred dollars. See that roof you got over your head at night? Let me tell you something about that roof. It's been over ten years since that roof was last tarred. See now . . . the snow come this winter and sit up there on that roof like it is . . . and it's gonna seep inside. It's just gonna be a little bit . . . ain't gonna hardly notice it. Then the next thing you know, it's gonna be leaking all over the house. Then the wood rot from all that water and you gonna need a whole new roof. Now, how much you think it cost to get that roof tarred?

**CORY:** I don't know.

**TROY:** Two hundred and sixty-four dollars . . . cash money. While you thinking about a TV, I got to be thinking about the roof . . . and whatever else go wrong here. Now if you had two hundred dollars, what would you do . . . fix the roof or buy a TV?

**CORY:** I'd buy a TV. Then when the roof started to leak . . . when it needed fixing . . . I'd fix it.

**TROY:** Where you gonna get the money from? You done spent it for a TV. You gonna sit up and watch the water run all over your brand new TV.

**CORY:** Aw, Pop. You got money. I know you do.

**TROY:** Where I got it at, huh?

**CORY:** You got it in the bank.

**TROY:** You wanna see my bankbook? You wanna see that seventy-three dollars and twenty-two cents I got sitting up in there?

**CORY:** You ain't got to pay for it all at one time. You can put a down payment on it and carry it on home with you.

**TROY:** Not me. I ain't gonna owe nobody nothing if I can help it. Miss a payment and they come and snatch it right out your house. Then what you got? Now, soon as I get two hundred dollars clear, then I'll buy a TV. Right now, as soon as I get two hundred and sixty-four dollars, I'm gonna have this roof tarred.

**CORY:** Aw . . . Pop!

**TROY:** You go on and get you two hundred dollars and buy one if ya want it. I got better things to do with my money.

**CORY:** I can't get no two hundred dollars. I ain't never seen two hundred dollars.

**TROY:** I'll tell you what . . . you get you a hundred dollars and I'll put the other hundred with it.

**CORY:** Alright, I'm gonna show you.

**TROY:** You gonna show me how you can cut them boards right now.

(CORY *begins to cut the boards. There is a long pause.)*

**CORY:** The Pirates won today. That makes five in a row.

**TROY:** I ain't thinking about the Pirates. Got an all-white team. Got that boy . . . that Puerto Rican boy . . . Clemente. Don't even half-play him. That boy could be something if they give him a chance. Play him one day and sit him on the bench the next.

**CORY:** He gets a lot of chances to play.

**TROY:** I'm talking about playing regular. Playing every day so you can get your timing. That's what I'm talking about.

**CORY:** They got some white guys on the team that don't play every day. You can't play everybody at the same time.

**TROY:** If they got a white fellow sitting on the bench . . . you can bet your last dollar he can't play! The colored guy got to be twice as good before he get on the team. That's why I don't want you to get all tied up in them sports. Man on the team and what it get him? They got colored on the team and don't use them. Same as not having them. All them teams the same.

**CORY:** The Braves got Hank Aaron and Wes Covington. Hank Aaron hit two home runs today. That makes forty-three.

**TROY:** Hank Aaron ain't nobody. That's what you supposed to do. That's how you supposed to play the game. Ain't nothing to it. It's just a matter of timing . . . getting the right follow-through. Hell, I can hit forty-three home runs right now!

**CORY:** Not off no major-league pitching, you couldn't.

**TROY:** We had better pitching in the Negro leagues. I hit seven home runs off of Satchel Paige. You can't get no better than that!

**CORY:** Sandy Koufax. He's leading the league in strikeouts.

**TROY:** I ain't thinking of no Sandy Koufax.

**CORY:** You got Warren Spahn and Lew Burdette. I bet you couldn't hit no home runs off of Warren Spahn.

**TROY:** I'm through with it now. You go on and cut them boards. *(Pause.)* Your mama tell me you done got recruited by a college football team? Is that right?

**CORY:** Yeah. Coach Zellman say the recruiter gonna be coming by to talk to you. Get you to sign the permission papers.

**TROY:** I thought you supposed to be working down there at the A&P. Ain't you suppose to be working down there after school?

**CORY:** Mr. Stawicki say he gonna hold my job for me until after the football season. Say starting next week I can work weekends.

**TROY:** I thought we had an understanding about this football stuff? You suppose to keep up with your chores and hold that job down at the A&P. Ain't been around here all day on a Saturday. Ain't none of your chores done . . . and now you telling me you done quit your job.

**CORY:** I'm going to be working weekends.

**TROY:** You damn right you are! And ain't no need for nobody coming around here to talk to me about signing nothing.

**CORY:** Hey, Pop . . . you can't do that. He's coming all the way from North Carolina.

**TROY:** I don't care where he coming from. The white man ain't gonna let you get nowhere with that football noway. You go on and get your book-learning so you can work yourself up in that A&P or learn how to fix cars or build houses or something, get you a trade. That way you have something can't nobody take away from you. You go on and learn how to put your hands to some good use. Besides hauling people's garbage.

**CORY:** I get good grades, Pop. That's why the recruiter wants to talk with you. You got to keep up your grades to get recruited. This way I'll be going to college. I'll get a chance . . .

**TROY:** First you gonna get your butt down there to the A&P and get your job back.

**CORY:** Mr. Stawicki done already hired somebody else 'cause I told him I was playing football.

**TROY:** You a bigger fool than I thought . . . to let somebody take away your job so you can play some football. Where you gonna get your money to take out your girlfriend and whatnot? What kind of foolishness is that to let somebody take away your job?

**CORY:** I'm still gonna be working weekends.

**TROY:** Naw . . . naw. You getting your butt out of here and finding you another job.

**CORY:** Come on, Pop! I got to practice. I can't work after school and play football too. The team needs me. That's what Coach Zellman say . . .

**TROY:** I don't care what nobody else say. I'm the boss . . . you understand? I'm the boss around here. I do the only saying what counts.

**CORY:** Come on, Pop!

**TROY:** I asked you . . . did you understand?

**CORY:** Yeah . . .

**TROY:** What?!

**CORY:** Yessir.

**TROY:** You go on down there to that A&P and see if you can get your job back. If you can't do both . . . then you quit the football team. You've got to take the crookeds with the straights.

**CORY:** Yessir. *(Pause.)* Can I ask you a question?

**TROY:** What the hell you wanna ask me? Mr. Stawicki the one you got the questions for.

**CORY:** How come you ain't never liked me?

**TROY:** Liked you? Who the hell say I got to like you? What law is there say I got to like you? Wanna stand up in my face and ask a damn fool-ass question like that. Talking about liking somebody. Come here, boy, when I talk to you.

*(*CORY *comes over to where* TROY *is working. He stands slouched over and* TROY *shoves him on his shoulder.)*

Troy (Laurence Fishburne) reminds Cory (Bryan Clark) of the deal they made in this 2006 production directed by Sheldon Epps.

Straighten up, goddammit! I asked you a question . . . what law is there say I got to like you?

**CORY:** None.

**TROY:** Well, alright then! Don't you eat every day? *(Pause.)* Answer me when I talk to you! Don't you eat every day?

**CORY:** Yeah.

**TROY:** Nigger, as long as you in my house, you put that sir on the end of it when you talk to me.

**CORY:** Yes . . . sir.

**TROY:** You eat every day.

**CORY:** Yessir!

**TROY:** Got a roof over your head.

**CORY:** Yessir!

**TROY:** Got clothes on your back.

**CORY:** Yessir.

**TROY:** Why you think that is?

**CORY:** Cause of you.

**TROY:** Aw, hell I know it's 'cause of me . . . but why do you think that is?

**CORY:** *(Hesitant.)* Cause you like me.

**TROY:** Like you? I go out of here every morning . . . bust my butt . . . putting up with them crackers every day . . . cause I like you? You about the biggest fool I ever saw. *(Pause.)* It's my job. It's my responsibility! You understand that? A man got to take care of his family. You live in my house . . . sleep you behind on my bedclothes . . . fill you belly up with my food . . . cause you my son. You my flesh and blood. Not 'cause I like you! Cause it's my duty to take care of you. I owe a responsibility to you!

Let's get this straight right here . . . before it go along any further . . . I ain't got to like you. Mr. Rand don't give me my money come payday cause he likes me. He gives me cause he owe me. I done give you everything I had to give you. I gave you your life! Me and your mama worked that out between us. And liking your black ass wasn't part of the bargain. Don't you try and go through life worrying about if somebody like you or not. You best be making sure they doing right by you. You understand what I'm saying, boy?

**CORY:** Yessir.

**TROY:** Then get the hell out of my face, and get on down to that A&P.

*(ROSE has been standing behind the screen door for much of the scene. She enters as CORY exits.)*

**ROSE:** Why don't you let the boy go ahead and play football, Troy? Ain't no harm in that. He's just trying to be like you with the sports.

**TROY:** I don't want him to be like me! I want him to move as far away from my life as he can get. You the only decent thing that ever happened to me. I wish him that. But I don't wish him a thing else from my life. I decided seventeen years ago that boy wasn't getting involved in no sports. Not after what they did to me in the sports.

**ROSE:** Troy, why don't you admit you was too old to play in the major leagues? For once . . . why don't you admit that?

**TROY:** What do you mean too old? Don't come telling me I was too old. I just wasn't the right color. Hell, I'm fifty-three years old and can do better than Selkirk's .269 right now!

**ROSE:** How's was you gonna play ball when you were over forty? Sometimes I can't get no sense out of you.

**TROY:** I got good sense, woman. I got sense enough not to let my boy get hurt over playing no sports. You been mothering that boy too much. Worried about if people like him.

**ROSE:** Everything that boy do . . . he do for you. He wants you to say "Good job, son." That's all.

**TROY:** Rose, I ain't got time for that. He's alive. He's healthy. He's got to make his own way. I made mine. Ain't nobody gonna hold his hand when he get out there in that world.

**ROSE:** Times have changed from when you was young, Troy. People change. The world's changing around you and you can't even see it.

**TROY:** *(Slow, methodical.)* Woman . . . I do the best I can do. I come in here every Friday. I carry a sack of potatoes and a bucket of lard. You all line up at the door with your hands out. I give you the lint from my pockets. I give you my sweat and my blood. I ain't got no tears. I done spent them. We go upstairs in that room at night . . . and I fall down on you and try to blast a hole into forever. I get up Monday morning . . . find my lunch on the table. I go out. Make my way. Find my strength to carry me through to the next Friday. *(Pause.)* That's all I got, Rose. That's all I got to give. I can't give nothing else.

*(TROY exits into the house. The lights go down to black.)*

## SCENE IV

*It is Friday. Two weeks later. CORY starts out of the house with his football equipment. The phone rings.*

**CORY:** *(Calling.)* I got it! *(He answers the phone and stands in the screen door talking.)* Hello? Hey, Jesse. Naw . . . I was just getting ready to leave now.

**ROSE:** *(Calling.)* Cory!

**CORY:** I told you, man, them spikes is all tore up. You can use them if you want, but they ain't no good. Earl got some spikes.

**ROSE:** *(Calling.)* Cory!

**CORY:** *(Calling to ROSE)* Mam? I'm talking to Jesse. *(Into phone.)* When she say that? *(Pause.)* Aw, you lying, man. I'm gonna tell her you said that.

**ROSE:** *(Calling.)* Cory, don't you go nowhere!

**CORY:** I got to go to the game, Ma! *(Into the phone.)* Yeah, hey, look, I'll talk to you later. Yeah, I'll meet you over Earl's house. Later. Bye, Ma.

*(CORY exits the house and starts out the yard.)*

**ROSE:** Cory, where you going off to? You got that stuff all pulled out and thrown all over your room.

**CORY:** *(In the yard.)* I was looking for my spikes. Jesse wanted to borrow my spikes.

**ROSE:** Get up there and get that cleaned up before your daddy get back in here.

**CORY:** I got to go to the game! I'll clean it up *when I get back.*

*(CORY exits.)*

**ROSE:** That's all he need to do is see that room all messed up.

*(ROSE exits into the house. TROY and BONO enter the yard. TROY is dressed in clothes other than his work clothes.)*

**BONO:** He told him the same thing he told you. Take it to the union.

**TROY:** Brownie ain't got that much sense. Man wasn't thinking about nothing. He wait until I confront them on it . . . then he wanna come crying seniority. *(Calls.)* Hey, Rose!

**BONO:** I wish I could have seen Mr. Rand's face when he told you.

**TROY:** He couldn't get it out of his mouth! Liked to bit his tongue! When they called me down there to the Commissioner's office . . . he thought they was gonna fire me. Like everybody else.

**BONO:** I didn't think they was gonna fire you. I thought they was gonna put you on the warning paper.

**TROY:** Hey, Rose! *(To BONO.)* Yeah, Mr. Rand like to bit his tongue.

*(TROY breaks the seal on the bottle, takes a drink, and hands it to BONO.)*

**BONO:** I see you run right down to Taylors' and told that Alberta gal.

**TROY:** *(Calling.)* Hey Rose! *(To BONO.)* I told everybody. Hey, Rose! I went down there to cash my check.

**ROSE:** *(Entering from the house.)* Hush all that hollering, man! I know you out here. What they say down there at the Commissioner's office?

**TROY:** You supposed to come when I call you, woman. Bono'll tell you that. *(To BONO.)* Don't Lucille come when you call her?

**ROSE:** Man, hush your mouth. I ain't no dog . . . talk about "come when you call me."

**TROY:** *(Puts his arm around ROSE.)* You hear this, Bono? I had me an old dog used to get uppity like that. You say, "C'mere, Blue!" . . . and he just lay there and look at you. End up getting a stick and chasing him away trying to make him come.

**ROSE:** I ain't studying you and your dog. I remember you used to sing that old song.

**TROY:** *(He sings.)*

Hear it ring! Hear it ring!
I had a dog his name was Blue.

**ROSE:** Don't nobody wanna hear you sing that old song.

**TROY:** *(Sings.)*

You know Blue was mighty true.

**ROSE:** Used to have Cory running around here singing that song.

**BONO:** Hell, I remember that song myself.

**TROY:** *(Sings.)*

You know Blue was a good old dog.
Blue treed a possum in a hollow log.

That was my daddy's song. My daddy made up that song.

**ROSE:** I don't care who made it up. Don't nobody wanna hear you sing it.

**TROY:** *(Makes a song like calling a dog.)* Come here, woman.

**ROSE:** You come in here carrying on, I reckon they ain't fired you. What they say down there at the Commissioner's office?

**TROY:** Look here, Rose . . . Mr. Rand called me into his office today when I got back from talking to them people down there . . . it come from up top . . . he called me in and told me they was making me a driver.

**ROSE:** Troy, you kidding!

**TROY:** No I ain't. Ask Bono.

**ROSE:** Well, that's great, Troy. Now you don't have to hassle them people no more.

*(LYONS enters from the street.)*

**TROY:** Aw hell, I wasn't looking to see you today. I thought you was in jail. Got it all over the front page of the *Courier* about them raiding Sefus's place . . . where you be hanging out with all them thugs.

**LYONS:** Hey, Pop . . . that ain't got nothing to do with me. I don't go down there gambling. I go down there to sit in with the band. I ain't got nothing to do with the gambling part. They got some good music down there.

**TROY:** They got some rogues . . . is what they got.

**LYONS:** How you been, Mr. Bono? Hi, Rose.

**BONO:** I see where you playing down at the Crawford Grill tonight.

**ROSE:** How come you ain't brought Bonnie like I told you? You should have brought Bonnie with you, she ain't been over in a month of Sundays.

**LYONS:** I was just in the neighborhood . . . thought I'd stop by.

**TROY:** Here he come . . .

**BONO:** Your daddy got a promotion on the rubbish. He's gonna be the first colored driver. Ain't got to do nothing but sit up there and read the paper like them white fellows.

**LYONS:** Hey, Pop . . . if you knew how to read you'd be alright.

**BONO:** Naw . . . naw . . . you mean if the nigger knew how to *drive* he'd be alright. Been fighting with them people about driving and ain't even got a license. Mr. Rand know you ain't got no driver's license?

**TROY:** Driving ain't nothing. All you do is point the truck where you want it to go. Driving ain't nothing.

**BONO:** Do Mr. Rand know you ain't got no driver's license? That's what I'm talking about. I ain't asked if driving was easy. I asked if Mr. Rand know you ain't got no driver's license.

**TROY:** He ain't got to know. The man ain't got to know my business. Time he find out, I have two or three driver's licenses.

**LYONS:** *(Going into his pocket.)* Say, look here, Pop . . .

**TROY:** I knew it was coming. Didn't I tell you, Bono? I know what kind of "Look here, Pop" that was. The nigger fixing to ask me for some money. It's Friday night. It's my payday. All them rogues down there on the avenue . . . the ones that ain't in jail . . . and Lyons is hopping in his shoes to get down there with them.

**LYONS:** See, Pop . . . if you give somebody else a chance to talk sometime, you'd see that I was fixing to pay you back your ten dollars like I told you. Here . . . I told you I'd pay you when Bonnie got paid.

**TROY:** Naw . . . you go ahead and keep that ten dollars. Put in the bank. The next time you feel like you wanna come by here and ask me for something . . . you go on down there and get that.

**LYONS:** Here's your ten dollars, Pop. I told you I don't want you to give me nothing. I just wanted to borrow ten dollars.

**TROY:** Naw . . . you go on and keep that for the next time you want to ask me.

**LYONS:** Come on, Pop . . . here go your ten dollars.

**ROSE:** Why don't you go on and let the boy pay you back, Troy?

**LYONS:** Here you go, Rose. If you don't take it I'm gonna have to hear about it for the next six months. *(He hands her the money.)*

**ROSE:** You can hand yours over here too, Troy.

**TROY:** You see this, Bono. You see how they do me.

**BONO:** Yeah, Lucille do me the same way.

*(*GABRIEL *is heard singing offstage. He enters.)*

**GABRIEL:** Better get ready for the Judgment! Better get ready for . . . Hey! . . . Hey! . . . There's Troy's boy!

**LYONS:** How are you doing, Uncle Gabe?

**GABRIEL:** Lyons . . . The King of the Jungle! Rose . . . hey, Rose. Got a flower for you. *(He takes a rose from his pocket.)* Picked it myself. That's the same rose like you is!

**ROSE:** That's right nice of you, Gabe.

**LYONS:** What you been doing, Uncle Gabe?

**GABRIEL:** Oh, I been chasing hellhounds and waiting on the time to tell St. Peter to open the gates.

**LYONS:** You been chasing hellhounds, huh? Well . . . you doing the right thing, Uncle Gabe. Somebody got to chase them.

**GABRIEL:** Oh, yeah . . . I know it. The devil's strong. The devil ain't no pushover. Hellhounds snipping at everybody's heels. But I got my trumpet waiting on the judgment time.

**LYONS:** Waiting on the Battle of Armageddon, huh?

**GABRIEL:** Ain't gonna be too much of a battle when God get to waving that Judgment sword. But the people's gonna have a hell of a time trying to get into heaven if them gates ain't open.

**LYONS:** *(Putting his arm around* GABRIEL.*)* You hear this, Pop. Uncle Gabe, you alright!

**GABRIEL:** *(Laughing with* LYONS.*)* Lyons! King of the Jungle.

**ROSE:** You gonna stay for supper, Gabe? Want me to fix you a plate?

**GABRIEL:** I'll take a sandwich, Rose. Don't want no plate. Just wanna eat with my hands. I'll take a sandwich.

**ROSE:** How about you, Lyons? You staying? Got some short ribs cooking.

**LYONS:** Naw, I won't eat nothing till after we finished playing. *(Pause.)* You ought to come down and listen to me play, Pop.

**TROY:** I don't like that Chinese music. All that noise.

**ROSE:** Go on in the house and wash up, Gabe . . . I'll fix you a sandwich.

**GABRIEL:** *(To* LYONS, *as he exits.)* Troy's mad at me.

**LYONS:** What you mad at Uncle Gabe for, Pop?

**ROSE:** He thinks Troy's mad at him cause he moved over to Miss Pearl's.

**TROY:** I ain't mad at the man. He can live where he want to live at.

**LYONS:** What he move over there for? Miss Pearl don't like nobody.

**ROSE:** She don't mind him none. She treats him real nice. She just don't allow all that singing.

**TROY:** She don't mind that rent he be paying . . . that's what she don't mind.

**ROSE:** Troy, I ain't going through that with you no more. He's over there cause he want to have his own place. He can come and go as he please.

**TROY:** Hell, he could come and go as he please here. I wasn't stopping him. I ain't put no rules on him.

**ROSE:** It ain't the same thing, Troy. And you know it.

*(*GABRIEL *comes to the door.)*

Now, that's the last I wanna hear about that. I don't wanna hear nothing else about Gabe and Miss Pearl. And next week . . .

**GABRIEL:** I'm ready for my sandwich, Rose.

**ROSE:** And next week . . . when that recruiter come from that school . . . I want you to sign that paper and go on and let Cory play football. Then that'll be the last I have to hear about that.

**TROY:** *(To* ROSE *as she exits into the house.)* I ain't thinking about Cory nothing.

**LYONS:** What . . . Cory got recruited? What school he going to?

**TROY:** That boy walking around here smelling his piss . . . thinking he's grown. Thinking he's gonna do what he want, irrespective of what I say. Look here, Bono . . . I left the Commissioner's office and went down to the A&P . . . that boy ain't working down there. He lying to me. Telling me he got his job back . . . telling me he working weekends . . . telling me he working after school . . . Mr. Stawicki tell me he ain't working down there at all!

**LYONS:** Cory just growing up. He's just busting at the seams trying to fill out your shoes.

**TROY:** I don't care what he's doing. When he get to the point where he wanna disobey me . . . then it's time for him to move on. Bono'll tell you that. I bet he ain't never disobeyed his daddy without paying the consequences.

**BONO:** I ain't never had a chance. My daddy came on through . . . but I ain't never knew him to see him . . . or what he had on his mind or where he went. Just moving on through. Searching out the New Land. That's what the old folks used to call it. See a fellow moving around from place to place . . . woman to woman . . . called it searching out the New Land. I can't say if he ever found it. I come along, didn't want no kids. Didn't know if I was gonna be in one place long enough to fix on them right as their daddy. I figured I was going searching too. As it turned out I been hooked up with Lucille near about as long as your daddy been with Rose. Going on sixteen years.

**TROY:** Sometimes I wish I hadn't known my daddy. He ain't cared nothing about no kids. A kid to him wasn't nothing. All he wanted was for you to learn how to walk so he could start you to working. When it come time for eating . . . he ate first. If there was anything left over, that's what you got. Man would sit down and eat two chickens and give you the wing.

**LYONS:** You ought to stop that, Pop. Everybody feed their kids. No matter how hard times is . . . everybody care about their kids. Make sure they have something to eat.

**TROY:** The only thing my daddy cared about was getting them bales of cotton in to Mr. Lubin. That's the only thing that mattered to him. Sometimes I used to wonder why he was living. Wonder why the devil hadn't come and got him. "Get them bales of cotton in to Mr. Lubin" and find out he owe him money . . .

**LYONS:** He should have just went on and left when he saw he couldn't get nowhere. That's what I would have done.

**TROY:** How he gonna leave with eleven kids? And where he gonna go? He ain't knew how to do nothing but farm. No, he was trapped and I think he knew it. But I'll say this for him . . . he felt a responsibility toward us. Maybe he ain't treated us the way I felt he should have . . . but without that responsibility he could have walked off and left us . . . made his own way.

**BONO:** A lot of them did. Back in those days what you talking about . . . they walk out their front door and just take on down one road or another and keep on walking.

**LYONS:** There you go! That's what I'm talking about.

**BONO:** Just keep on walking till you come to something else. Ain't you never heard of nobody having the walking blues? Well, that's what you call it when you just take off like that.

**TROY:** My daddy ain't had them walking blues! What you talking about? He stayed right there with his family. But he was just as evil as he could be. My mama couldn't stand him. Couldn't stand that evilness. She run off when I was about eight. She sneaked off one night after he had gone to sleep. Told me she was coming back for me. I ain't never seen her no more. All his women run off and left him. He wasn't good for nobody.

When my turn come to head out, I was fourteen and got to sniffing around Joe Canewell's daughter. Had us an old mule we called Greyboy. My daddy sent me out to do some plowing and I tied up Greyboy and went to fooling around with Joe Canewell's daughter. We done found us a nice little spot, got real cozy with each other. She about thirteen and we done figured we was grown anyway . . . so we down there enjoying ourselves . . . ain't thinking about nothing. We didn't know Greyboy had got loose and wandered back to the house and my daddy was looking for me. We down there by the creek enjoying ourselves when my daddy come up on us. Surprised us. He had them leather straps off the mule and commenced to whupping me like there was no tomorrow. I jumped up, mad and embarrassed. I was scared of my daddy. When he commenced to whupping on me . . . quite naturally I run to get out of the way. *(Pause.)* Now I thought he was mad cause I ain't done my work. But I see where he was chasing me off so he could have the gal for himself. When I see what the matter of it was, I lost all fear of my daddy. Right there is where I become a man . . . at fourteen years of age. *(Pause.)* Now it was my turn to run him off. I picked up them same reins that he had used on me. I picked up them reins and commenced to whupping on him. The gal jumped up and run off . . . and when my daddy turned to face me, I could see why the devil had never come to get him . . . cause he was the devil himself. I don't know what happened. When I woke up, I was laying right there by the creek, and Blue . . . this old dog we had . . . was licking my face. I thought I was blind. I couldn't see nothing. Both my eyes were swollen shut. I layed there and cried. I didn't know what I was gonna do. The only thing I knew was the time had come for me to leave my daddy's house. And right there the world suddenly got big. And it was a long time before I could cut it down to where I could handle it.

Part of that cutting down was when I got to the place where I could feel him kicking in my blood and knew that the only thing that separated us was the matter of a few years.

*(*GABRIEL *enters from the house with a sandwich.)*

**LYONS:** What you got there, Uncle Gabe?

**GABRIEL:** Got me a ham sandwich. Rose gave me a ham sandwich.

**TROY:** I don't know what happened to him. I done lost touch with everybody except Gabriel. But I hope he's dead. I hope he found some peace.

**LYONS:** That's a heavy story, Pop. I didn't know you left home when you was fourteen.

**TROY:** And didn't know nothing. The only part of the world I knew was the forty-two acres of Mr. Lubin's land. That's all I knew about life.

**LYONS:** Fourteen's kinda young to be out on your own. *(Phone rings.)* I don't even think I was ready to be out on my own at fourteen. I don't know what I would have done.

**TROY:** I got up from the creek and walked on down to Mobile. I was through with farming. Figured I could do better in the city. So I walked the two hundred miles to Mobile.

**LYONS:** Wait a minute . . . you ain't walked no two hundred miles, Pop. Ain't nobody gonna walk no two hundred miles. You talking about some walking there.

**BONO:** That's the only way you got anywhere back in them days.

**LYONS:** Shhh. Damn if I wouldn't have hitched a ride with somebody!

**TROY:** Who you gonna hitch it with? They ain't had no cars and things like they got now. We talking about 1918.

**ROSE:** *(Entering.)* What you all out here getting into?

**TROY:** *(To* ROSE.*)* I'm telling Lyons how good he got it. He don't know nothing about this I'm talking.

**ROSE:** Lyons, that was Bonnie on the phone. She say you supposed to pick her up.

**LYONS:** Yeah, okay, Rose.

**TROY:** I walked on down to Mobile and hitched up with some of them fellows that was heading this way. Got up here and found out . . . not only couldn't you get a job . . . you couldn't find no place to live. I thought I was in freedom. Shhh. Colored folks living down there on the riverbanks in whatever kind of shelter they could find for themselves. Right down there under the Brady Street Bridge. Living in shacks made of sticks and tarpaper. Messed around there and went from bad to worse. Started stealing. First it was food. Then I figured, hell, if I steal money I can buy me some food. Buy me some shoes too! One thing led to another. Met your mama. I was young and anxious to be a man. Met your mama and had you. What I do that for? Now I got to worry about feeding you and her. Got to steal three times as much. Went out one day looking for somebody to rob . . . that's what I was, a robber. I'll tell you the truth. I'm ashamed of it today. But it's the truth. Went to rob this fellow . . . pulled out my knife . . . and he pulled out a gun. Shot me in the chest. It felt just like somebody had taken a hot branding iron and laid it on me. When he shot me I jumped at him with my knife. They told me I killed him and they put me in the penitentiary and locked me up for fifteen years. That's where I met Bono. That's where I learned how to play baseball. Got out that place and your mama had taken you and went on to make life without me. Fifteen years was a long time for her to wait. But that fifteen years cured me of that robbing stuff. Rose'll tell you. She asked me when I met her if I had gotten all that foolishness out of my system. And I told her, "Baby, it's you and baseball all what count with me." You hear me, Bono? I meant it too. She say, "Which one comes first?" I told her, "Baby, ain't no doubt it's baseball . . . but you stick and get old with me and we'll both outlive this baseball." Am I right, Rose? And it's true.

**ROSE:** Man, hush your mouth. You ain't said no such thing. Talking about, "Baby you know you'll always be number one with me." That's what you was talking.

**TROY:** You hear that, Bono. That's why I love her.

**BONO:** Rose'll keep you straight. You get off the track, she'll straighten you up.

**ROSE:** Lyons, you better get on up and get Bonnie. She waiting on you.

**LYONS:** *(Gets up to go.)* Hey, Pop, why don't you come on down to the Grill and hear me play?

**TROY:** I ain't going down there. I'm too old to be sitting around in them clubs.

**BONO:** You got to be good to play down at the Grill.

**LYONS:** Come on, Pop . . .

**TROY:** I got to get up in the morning.

**LYONS:** You ain't got to stay long.

**TROY:** Naw, I'm gonna get my supper and go on to bed.

**LYONS:** Well, I got to go. I'll see you again.

**TROY:** Don't you come around my house on my payday.

**ROSE:** Pick up the phone and let somebody know you coming. And bring Bonnie with you. You know I'm always glad to see her.

**LYONS:** Yeah, I'll do that, Rose. You take care now. See you, Pop. See you, Mr. Bono. See you, Uncle Gabe.

**GABRIEL:** Lyons! King of the Jungle!

*(LYONS exits.)*

**TROY:** Is supper ready, woman? Me and you got some business to take care of. I'm gonna tear it up too.

**ROSE:** Troy, I done told you now!

**TROY:** *(Puts his arm around BONO.)* Aw hell, woman . . . this is Bono. Bono like family. I done known this nigger since . . . how long I done know you?

**BONO:** It's been a long time.

**TROY:** I done known this nigger since Skippy was a pup. Me and him done been through some times.

**BONO:** You sure right about that.

**TROY:** Hell, I done know him longer than I known you. And we still standing shoulder to shoulder. Hey, look here, Bono . . . a man can't ask for no more than that. *(Drinks to him.)* I love you, nigger.

**BONO:** Hell, I love you too . . . but I got to get home see my woman. You got yours in hand. I got to go get mine.

*(BONO starts to exit as CORY enters the yard, dressed in his football uniform. He gives TROY a hard, uncompromising look.)*

**CORY:** What you do that for, Pop?

*(He throws his helmet down in the direction of TROY.)*

**ROSE:** What's the matter? Cory . . . what's the matter?

**CORY:** Papa done went up to the school and told Coach Zellman I can't play football no more. Wouldn't even let me play the game. Told him to tell the recruiter not to come.

**ROSE:** Troy . . .

**TROY:** What you Troying me for. Yeah, I did it. And the boy know why I did it.

**CORY:** Why you wanna do that to me? That was the one chance I had.

**ROSE:** Ain't nothing wrong with Cory playing football, Troy.

**TROY:** The boy lied to me. I told the nigger if he wanna play football . . . to keep up his chores and hold down that job at the A&P. That was the conditions. Stopped down there to see Mr. Stawicki . . .

Rose (Angela Bassett) asks Troy why he got Cory kicked off the football team.

Troy tells Cory that he's committed strike one.

**CORY:** I can't work after school during the football season, Pop! I tried to tell you that Mr. Stawicki's holding my job for me. You don't never want to listen to nobody. And then you wanna go and do this to me!

**TROY:** I ain't done nothing to you. You done it to yourself.

**CORY:** Just cause you didn't have a chance! You just scared I'm gonna be better than you, that's all.

**TROY:** Come here.

**ROSE:** Troy . . .

*(*CORY *reluctantly crosses over to* TROY.*)*

**TROY:** Alright! See. You done made a mistake.

**CORY:** I didn't even do nothing!

**TROY:** I'm gonna tell you what your mistake was. See . . . you swung at the ball and didn't hit it. That's strike one. See, you in the batter's box now. You swung and you missed. That's strike one. Don't you strike out!

*(Lights fade to black.)*

# ACT II

## SCENE I

*The following morning.* CORY *is at the tree hitting the ball with the bat. He tries to mimic* TROY, *but his swing is awkward, less sure.* ROSE *enters from the house.*

**ROSE:** Cory, I want you to help me with this cupboard.

**CORY:** I ain't quitting the team. I don't care what Poppa say.

**ROSE:** I'll talk to him when he gets back. He had to go see about your Uncle Gabe. The police done arrested him. Say he was disturbing the peace. He'll be back directly. Come on in here and help me clean out the top of this cupboard.

*(*CORY *exits into the house.* ROSE *sees* TROY *and* BONO *coming down the alley.)*

Troy . . . what they say down there?

**TROY:** Ain't said nothing. I give them fifty dollars and they let him go. I'll talk to you about it. Where's Cory?

**ROSE:** He's in there helping me clean out these cupboards.

**TROY:** Tell him to get his butt out here.

*(*TROY *and* BONO *go over to the pile of wood.* BONO *picks up the saw and begins sawing.)*

**TROY:** *(To* BONO.*)* All they want is the money. That makes six or seven times I done went down there and got him. See me coming they stick out their *hands.*

**BONO:** Yeah. I know what you mean. That's all they care about . . . that money. They don't care about what's right. *(Pause.)* Nigger, why you got to go and get some hard wood? You ain't doing nothing but building a little old fence. Get you some soft pine wood. That's all you need.

**TROY:** I know what I'm doing. This is outside wood. You put pine wood inside the house. Pine wood is inside wood. This here is outside wood. Now you tell me where the fence is gonna be?

**BONO:** You don't need this wood. You can put it up with pine wood and it'll stand as long as you gonna be here looking at it.

**TROY:** How you know how long I'm gonna be here, nigger? Hell, I might just live forever. Live longer than old man Horsely.

**BONO:** That's what Magee used to say.

**TROY:** Magee's a damn fool. Now you tell me who you ever heard of gonna pull their own teeth with a pair of rusty pliers.

**BONO:** The old folks . . . my granddaddy used to pull his teeth with pliers. They ain't had no dentists for the colored folks back then.

**TROY:** Get clean pliers! You understand? Clean pliers! Sterilize them! Besides we ain't living back then. All Magee had to do was walk over to Doc Goldblum's.

**BONO:** I see where you and that Tallahassee gal . . . that Alberta . . . I see where you all done got tight.

**TROY:** What you mean "got tight"?

**BONO:** I see where you be laughing and joking with her all the time.

**TROY:** I laughs and jokes with all of them, Bono. You know me.

**BONO:** That ain't the kind of laughing and joking I'm talking about.

*(CORY enters from the house.)*

**CORY:** How you doing, Mr. Bono?

**TROY:** Cory? Get that saw from Bono and cut some wood. He talking about the wood's too hard to cut. Stand back there, Jim, and let that young boy show you how it's done.

**BONO:** He's sure welcome to it.

*(CORY takes the saw and begins to cut the wood.)*

Whew-e-e! Look at that. Big old strong boy. Look like Joe Louis. Hell, must be getting old the way I'm watching that boy whip through that wood.

**CORY:** I don't see why Mama want a fence around the yard noways.

**TROY:** Damn if I know either. What the hell she keeping out with it? She ain't got nothing nobody want.

**BONO:** Some people build fences to keep people out . . . and other people build fences to keep people in. Rose wants to hold on to you all. She loves you.

**TROY:** Hell, nigger, I don't need nobody to tell me my wife loves me. Cory . . . go on in the house and see if you can find that other saw.

**CORY:** Where's it at?

**TROY:** I said find it! Look for it till you find it!

*(CORY exits into the house.)*

What's that supposed to mean? Wanna keep us in?

**BONO:** Troy . . . I done known you seem like damn near my whole life. You and Rose both. I done know both of you all for a long time. I remember when you met Rose. When you was hitting them baseball out the park. A lot of them old gals was after you then. You had the pick of the litter. When you picked Rose, I was happy for you. That was the first time I knew you had any sense. I said . . . My man Troy knows what he's doing . . . I'm gonna follow this nigger . . . he might take me somewhere. I been following you too. I done learned a whole heap of things about life watching you. I done learned how to tell where the shit lies. How to tell it from the alfalfa. You done learned me a lot of things. You showed me how to not make the same mistakes . . . to take life as it comes along and keep putting one foot in front of the other. *(Pause.)* Rose a good woman, Troy.

**TROY:** Hell, nigger, I know she a good woman. I been married to her for eighteen years. What you got on your mind, Bono?

**BONO:** I just say she a good woman. Just like I say anything. I ain't got to have nothing on my mind.

**TROY:** You just gonna say she a good woman and leave it hanging out there like that? Why you telling me she a good woman?

**BONO:** She loves you, Troy. Rose loves you.

**TROY:** You saying I don't measure up. That's what you trying to say. I don't measure up cause I'm seeing this other gal. I know what you trying to say.

**BONO:** I know what Rose means to you, Troy. I'm just trying to say I don't want to see you mess up.

**TROY:** Yeah, I appreciate that, Bono. If you was messing around on Lucille I'd be telling you the same thing.

**BONO:** Well, that's all I got to say. I just say that because I love you both.

**TROY:** Hell, you know me . . . I wasn't out there looking for nothing. You can't find a better woman than Rose. I know that. But seems like this woman just stuck onto me where I can't shake her loose. I done wrestled with it, tried to throw her off me . . . but she just stuck on tighter. Now she's stuck on for good.

**BONO:** You's in control . . . that's what you tell me all the time. You responsible for what you do.

**TROY:** I ain't ducking the responsibility of it. As long as it sets right in my heart . . . then I'm okay. Cause that's all I listen to. It'll tell me right from wrong every time. And I ain't talking about doing Rose no bad turn. I love Rose. She done carried me a long ways and I love and respect her for that.

**BONO:** I know you do. That's why I don't want to see you hurt her. But what you gonna do when she find out? What you got then? If you try and juggle both of them . . . sooner or later you gonna drop one of them. That's common sense.

**TROY:** Yeah, I hear what you saying, Bono. I been trying to figure a way to work it out.

**BONO:** Work it out right, Troy. I don't want to be getting all up between you and Rose's business . . . but work it so it come out right.

**TROY:** Aw hell, I get all up between you and Lucille's business. When you gonna get that woman that refrigerator she been wanting? Don't tell me you ain't got no money now. I know who your banker is. Mellon don't need that money bad as Lucille want that refrigerator. I'll tell you that.

**BONO:** Tell you what I'll do . . . when you finish building this fence for Rose . . . I'll buy Lucille that refrigerator.

**TROY:** You done stuck your foot in your mouth now!

(TROY *grabs up a board and begins to saw.* BONO *starts to walk out the yard.)*

Hey, nigger . . . where you going?

**BONO:** I'm going home. I know you don't expect me to help you now. I'm protecting my money. I wanna see you put that fence up by yourself. That's what I want to see. You'll be here another six months without me.

**TROY:** Nigger, you ain't right.

**BONO:** When it comes to my money . . . I'm right as fireworks on the Fourth of July.

**TROY:** Alright, we gonna see now. You better get out your bankbook.

(BONO *exits, and* TROY *continues to work.* ROSE *enters from the house.)*

**ROSE:** What they say down there? What's happening with Gabe?

**TROY:** I went down there and got him out. Cost me fifty dollars. Say he was disturbing the peace. Judge set up a hearing for him in three weeks. Say to show cause why he shouldn't be recommitted.

**ROSE:** What was he doing that cause them to arrest him?

**TROY:** Some kids was teasing him and he run them off home. Say he was howling and carrying on. Some folks seen him and called the police. That's all it was.

**ROSE:** Well, what's you say? What'd you tell the judge?

**TROY:** Told him I'd look after him. It didn't make no sense to recommit the man. He stuck out his big greasy palm and told me to give him fifty dollars and take him on home.

**ROSE:** Where's he at now? Where'd he go off to?

**TROY:** He's gone on about his business. He don't need nobody to hold his hand.

**ROSE:** Well, I don't know. Seem like that would be the best place for him if they did put him into the hospital. I know what you're gonna say. But that's what I think would be best.

**TROY:** The man done had his life ruined fighting for what? And they wanna take and lock him up. Let him be free. He don't bother nobody.

**ROSE:** Well, everybody got their own way of looking at it I guess. Come on and get your lunch. I got a bowl of lima beans and some cornbread in the oven. Come on get something to eat. Ain't no sense you fretting over Gabe.

(ROSE *turns to go into the house.)*

**TROY:** Rose . . . got something to tell you.

**ROSE:** Well, come on . . . wait till I get this food on the table.

**TROY:** Rose!

*(She stops and turns around.)*

I don't know how to say this. *(Pause.)* I can't explain it none. It just sort of grows on you till it gets out of hand. It starts out like a little bush . . . and the next thing you know it's a whole forest.

**ROSE:** Troy . . . what is you talking about?

**TROY:** I'm talking, woman, let me talk. I'm trying to find a way to tell you . . . I'm gonna be a daddy. I'm gonna be somebody's daddy.

**ROSE:** Troy . . . you're not telling me this? You're gonna be . . . what?

**TROY:** Rose . . . now . . . see . . .

**ROSE:** You telling me you gonna be somebody's daddy? You telling your *wife* this?

(GABRIEL *enters from the street. He carries a rose in his hand.)*

**GABRIEL:** Hey, Troy! Hey, Rose!

**ROSE:** I have to wait eighteen years to hear something like this.

**GABRIEL:** Hey, Rose . . . I got a flower for you. *(He hands it to her.)* That's a rose. Same rose like you is.

**ROSE:** Thanks, Gabe.

**GABRIEL:** Troy, you ain't mad at me is you? Them bad mens come and put me away. You ain't mad at me is you?

**TROY:** Naw, Gabe, I ain't mad at you.

**ROSE:** Eighteen years and you wanna come with this.

**GABRIEL:** *(Takes a quarter out of his pocket.)* See what I got? Got a brand new quarter.

**TROY:** Rose . . . it's just . . .

**ROSE:** Ain't nothing you can say, Troy. Ain't no way of explaining that.

**GABRIEL:** Fellow that give me this quarter had a whole mess of them. I'm gonna keep this quarter till it stop shining.

**ROSE:** Gabe, go on in the house there. I got some watermelon in the Frigidaire. Go on and get you a piece.

**GABRIEL:** Say, Rose . . . you know I was chasing hellhounds and them bad mens come and get me and take me away. Troy helped me. He come down there and told them they better let me go before he beat them up. Yeah, he did!

**ROSE:** You go on and get you a piece of watermelon, Gabe. Them bad mens is gone now.

**GABRIEL:** Okay, Rose . . . gonna get me some watermelon. The kind with the stripes on it.

*(*GABRIEL *exits into the house.)*

**ROSE:** Why, Troy? Why? After all these years to come dragging this in to me now. It don't make no sense at your age. I could have expected this ten or fifteen years ago, but not now.

**TROY:** Age ain't got nothing to do with it, Rose.

**ROSE:** I done tried to be everything a wife should be. Everything a wife could be. Been married eighteen years and I got to live to see the day you tell me you been seeing another woman and done fathered a child by her. And you know I ain't never wanted no half nothing in my family. My whole family is half. Everybody got different fathers and mothers . . . my two sisters and my brother. Can't hardly tell who's who. Can't never sit down and talk about Papa and Mama. It's your papa and your mama and my papa and my mama . . .

**TROY:** Rose . . . stop it now.

**ROSE:** I ain't never wanted that for none of my children. And now you wanna drag your behind in here and tell me something like this.

**TROY:** You ought to know. It's time for you to know.

**ROSE:** Well, I don't want to know, goddamn it!

**TROY:** I can't just make it go away. It's done now. I can't wish the circumstance of the thing away.

**ROSE:** And you don't want to either. Maybe you want to wish me and my boy away. Maybe that's what you want? Well, you can't wish us away. I've got eighteen years of my life invested in you. You ought to have stayed upstairs in my bed where you belong.

**TROY:** Rose . . . now listen to me . . . we can get a handle on this thing. We can talk this out . . . come to an understanding.

**ROSE:** All of a sudden it's "we." Where was "we" at when you was down there rolling around with some godforsaken woman? "We" should have come to an understanding before you started making a damn fool of yourself. You're a day late and dollar short when it comes to an understanding with me.

**TROY:** It's just . . . She gives me a different idea . . . a different understanding about myself. I can step out of this house and get away from the pressures and problems . . . be a different man. I ain't got to wonder how I'm gonna pay the bills or get the roof fixed. I can just be a part of myself that I ain't never been.

**ROSE:** What I want to know . . . is do you plan to continue seeing her. That's all you can say to me.

**TROY:** I can sit up in her house and laugh. Do you understand what I'm saying. I can laugh out loud . . . and it feels good. It reaches all the way down to the bottom of my shoes. *(Pause.)* Rose, I can't give that up.

**ROSE:** Maybe you ought to go on and stay down there with her . . . if she's a better woman than me.

**TROY:** It ain't about nobody being a better woman or nothing. Rose, you ain't the blame. A man couldn't ask for no woman to be a better wife than you've been. I'm responsible for it. I done locked myself into a pattern trying to take care of you all that I forgot about myself.

**ROSE:** What the hell was I there for? That was my job, not somebody else's.

**TROY:** Rose, I done tried all my life to live decent . . . to live a clean . . . hard . . . useful life. I tried to be a good husband to you. In every way I knew how. Maybe I come into the world backwards, I don't know. But . . . you born with two strikes on you before you come to the plate. You got to guard it closely . . . always looking for the curve-ball on the inside corner. You can't afford to let none get past you. You can't afford a call strike. If you going down . . . you going down swinging. Everything lined up against you. What you gonna do. I fooled them, Rose. I bunted. When I found you and Cory and a halfway decent job . . . I was safe. Couldn't nothing touch me. I wasn't gonna strike out no more. I wasn't going back to the penitentiary. I wasn't gonna lay in the streets with a bottle of wine. I was safe. I had me a family. A job. I wasn't gonna get that last strike. I was on first looking for one of them boys to knock me in. To get me home.

**ROSE:** You should have stayed in my bed, Troy.

**TROY:** Then when I saw that gal . . . she firmed up my backbone. And I got to thinking that if I tried . . . I just might be able to steal second. Do you understand after eighteen years I wanted to steal second.

**ROSE:** You should have held me tight. You should have grabbed me and held on.

**TROY:** I stood on first base for eighteen years and I thought . . . well, goddamn it . . . go on for it!

**ROSE:** We're not talking about baseball! We're talking about you going off to lay in bed with another woman . . . and then bring it home to me. That's what we're talking about. We ain't talking about no baseball.

**TROY:** Rose, you're not listening to me. I'm trying the best I can to explain it to you. It's not easy for me to admit that I been standing in the same place for eighteen years.

**ROSE:** I been standing with you! I been right here with you, Troy. I got a life too. I gave eighteen years of my life to stand in the same spot with you. Don't you think I ever wanted other things? Don't you think I had dreams and hopes? What about my life? What about me. Don't you think it ever crossed my mind to want to know other men? That I wanted to lay up somewhere and forget about my responsibilities? That I wanted someone to make me laugh so I could feel good? You not the only one who's got wants and needs. But I held on to you, Troy. I took all my feelings, my wants and needs, my dreams . . . and I buried them inside you. I planted a seed and watched and prayed over it. I planted myself inside you and waited to bloom. And it didn't take me no eighteen years to find out the soil was hard and rocky and it wasn't never gonna bloom.

But I held on to you, Troy. I held you tighter. You was my husband. I owed you everything I had. Every part of me I could find to give you. And upstairs in that room . . . with the darkness falling in on me . . . I gave everything I had to try and erase the doubt that you wasn't the finest man in the world. And wherever you was going . . . I wanted to be there with you. Cause you was my husband. Cause that's the only way I was gonna survive as your wife. You always talking about what you give . . . and what you don't have to give. But you take too. You take . . . and don't even know nobody's giving!

(ROSE *turns to exit into the house.* TROY *grabs her arm.)*

**TROY:** You say I take and don't give!

**ROSE:** Troy! You're hurting me!

**TROY:** You say I take and don't give.

**ROSE:** Troy . . . you're hurting my arm! Let go!

**TROY:** I done give you everything I got. Don't you tell that lie on me.

**ROSE:** Troy!

**TROY:** Don't you tell that lie on me!

(CORY *enters from the house.)*

**CORY:** Mama!

**ROSE:** Troy. You're hurting me.

**TROY:** Don't you tell me about no taking and giving.

(CORY *comes up behind* TROY *and grabs him.* TROY, *surprised, is thrown off balance just as* CORY *throws a glancing blow that catches him on the chest and knocks him down.* TROY *is stunned, as is* CORY.)

**ROSE:** Troy. Troy. No!

(TROY *gets to his feet and starts at* CORY.)

Troy . . . no. Please! Troy!

(ROSE *pulls on* TROY *to hold him back.* TROY *stops himself.)*

**TROY:** *(To* CORY.) Alright. That's strike two. You stay away from around me, boy. Don't you strike out. You living with a full count. Don't you strike out.

(TROY *exits out the yard as the lights go down.)*

## SCENE II

*It is six months later, early afternoon.* TROY *enters from the house and starts to exit the yard.* ROSE *enters from the house.*

**ROSE:** Troy, I want to talk to you.

**TROY:** All of a sudden, after all this time, you want to talk to me, huh? You ain't wanted to talk to me for months. You ain't wanted to talk to me last night. You ain't wanted no part of me then. What you wanna talk to me about now?

**ROSE:** Tomorrow's Friday.

**TROY:** I know what day tomorrow is. You think I don't know tomorrow's Friday? My whole life I ain't done nothing but look to see Friday coming and you got to tell me it's Friday.

**ROSE:** I want to know if you're coming home.

**TROY:** I always come home, Rose. You know that. There ain't never been a night I ain't come home.

**ROSE:** That ain't what I mean . . . and you know it. I want to know if you're coming straight home after work.

**TROY:** I figure I'd cash my check . . . hang out at Taylors' with the boys . . . maybe play a game of checkers . . .

**ROSE:** Troy, I can't live like this. I won't live like this. You livin' on borrowed time with me. It's been going on six months now you ain't been coming home.

**TROY:** I be here every night. Every night of the year. That's 365 days.

**ROSE:** I want you to come home tomorrow after work.

**TROY:** Rose . . . I don't mess up my pay. You know that now. I take my pay and I give it to you. I don't have no money but what you give me back. I just want to have a little time to myself . . . a little time to enjoy life.

**ROSE:** What about me? When's my time to enjoy life?

**TROY:** I don't know what to tell you, Rose. I'm doing the best I can.

**ROSE:** You ain't been home from work but time enough to change your clothes and run out . . . and you wanna call that the best you can do?

**TROY:** I'm going over to the hospital to see Alberta. She went into the hospital this afternoon. Look like she might have the baby early. I won't be gone long.

**ROSE:** Well, you ought to know. They went over to Miss Pearl's and got Gabe today. She said you told them to go ahead and lock him up.

**TROY:** I ain't said no such thing. Whoever told you that is telling a lie. Pearl ain't doing nothing but telling a big fat lie.

**ROSE:** She ain't had to tell me. I read it on the papers.

**TROY:** I ain't told them nothing of the kind.

**ROSE:** I saw it right there on the papers.

**TROY:** What it say, huh?

**ROSE:** It said you told them to take him.

**TROY:** Then they screwed that up, just the way they screw up everything. I ain't worried about what they got on the paper.

**ROSE:** Say the government send part of his check to the hospital and the other part to you.

**TROY:** I ain't got nothing to do with that if that's the way it works. I ain't made up the rules about how it work.

**ROSE:** You did Gabe just like you did Cory. You wouldn't sign the paper for Cory . . . but you signed for Gabe. You signed that paper.

*(The telephone is heard ringing inside the house.)*

**TROY:** I told you I ain't signed nothing, woman! The only thing I signed was the release form. Hell, I can't read, I don't know what they had on that paper! I ain't signed nothing about sending Gabe away.

**ROSE:** I said send him to the hospital . . . you said let him be free . . . now you done went down there and signed him to the hospital for half his money. You went back on yourself, Troy. You gonna have to answer for that.

**TROY:** See now . . . you been over there talking to Miss Pearl. She done got mad cause she ain't getting Gabe's rent money. That's all it is. She's liable to say anything.

**ROSE:** Troy, I seen where you signed the paper.

**TROY:** You ain't seen nothing I signed. What she doing got papers on my brother anyway? Miss Pearl telling a big fat lie. And I'm gonna tell her about it too! You ain't seen nothing I signed. Say . . . you ain't seen nothing I signed.

*(*ROSE *exits into the house to answer the telephone. Presently she returns.)*

**ROSE:** Troy . . . that was the hospital. Alberta had the baby.

**TROY:** What she have? What is it?

**ROSE:** It's a girl.

**TROY:** I better get on down to the hospital to see her.

**ROSE:** Troy . . .

**TROY:** Rose . . . I got to go see her now. That's only right . . . what's the matter . . . the baby's alright, ain't it?

**ROSE:** Alberta died having the baby.

**TROY:** Died . . . you say she's dead? Alberta's dead?

**ROSE:** They said they done all they could. They couldn't do nothing for her.

**TROY:** The baby? How's the baby?

**ROSE:** They say it's healthy. I wonder who's gonna bury her.

**TROY:** She had family, Rose. She wasn't living in the world by herself.

**ROSE:** I know she wasn't living in the world by herself.

**TROY:** Next thing you gonna want to know if she had any insurance.

**ROSE:** Troy, you ain't got to talk like that.

**TROY:** That's the first thing that jumped out your mouth. "Who's gonna bury her?" Like I'm fixing to take on that task for myself.

**ROSE:** I am your wife. Don't push me away.

**TROY:** I ain't pushing nobody away. Just give me some space. That's all. Just give me some room to breathe.

*(ROSE exits into the house. TROY walks about the yard.)*

**TROY:** *(With a quiet rage that threatens to consume him.)* Alright . . . Mr. Death. See now . . . I'm gonna tell you what I'm gonna do. I'm gonna take and build me a fence around this yard. See? I'm gonna build me a fence around what belongs to me. And then I want you to stay on the other side. See? You stay over there until you're ready for me. Then you come on. Bring your army. Bring your sickle. Bring your wrestling clothes. I ain't gonna fall down on my vigilance this time. You ain't gonna sneak up on me no more. When you ready for me . . . when the top of your list say Troy Maxson . . . that's when you come around here. You come up and knock on the front door. Ain't nobody else got nothing to do with this. This is between you and me. Man to man. You stay on the other side of that fence until you ready for me. Then you come up and knock on the front door. Anytime you want. I'll be ready for you.

*(The lights go down to black.)*

## SCENE III

*The lights come up on the porch. It is late evening three days later.* ROSE *sits listening to the ball game waiting for* TROY. *The final out of the game is made and* ROSE *switches off the radio.* TROY *enters the yard carrying an infant wrapped in blankets. He stands back from the house and calls.*

ROSE *enters and stands on the porch. There is a long, awkward silence, the weight of which grows heavier with each passing second.*

**TROY:** Rose . . . I'm standing here with my daughter in my arms. She ain't but a wee bittie little old thing. She don't know nothing about grownups' business. She innocent . . . and she ain't got no mama.

**ROSE:** What you telling me for, Troy?

*(She turns and exits into the house.)*

**TROY:** Well . . . I guess we'll just sit out here on the porch.

*(He sits down on the porch. There is an awkward indelicateness about the way he handles the baby. His largeness engulfs and seems to swallow it. He speaks loud enough for* ROSE *to hear.)*

A man's got to do what's right for him. I ain't sorry for nothing I done. It felt right in my heart. *(To the baby.)* What you smiling at? Your daddy's a big man. Got these great big old hands. But sometimes he's scared. And right now your daddy's scared cause we sitting out here and ain't got no home. Oh, I been homeless before. I ain't had no little baby with me. But I been homeless. You just be out on the road by your lonesome and you see one of them trains coming and you just kinda go like this . . .

*(He sings as a lullaby.)*

> Please, Mr. Engineer let a man ride the line
> Please, Mr. Engineer let a man ride the line
> I ain't got no ticket please let me ride the blinds

*(ROSE enters from the house. TROY, hearing her steps behind him, stands and faces her.)*

She's my daughter, Rose. My own flesh and blood. I can't deny her no more than I can deny them boys. *(Pause.)* You and them boys is my family. You and them and this child is all I got in the world. So I guess what I'm saying is . . . I'd appreciate it if you'd help me take care of her.

**ROSE:** Okay, Troy . . . you're right. I'll take care of your baby for you . . . cause . . . like you say . . . she's innocent . . . and you can't visit the sins of the father upon the child. A motherless child has got a hard time.

*(She takes the baby from him.)* From right now . . . this child got a mother. But you a womanless man.

*(ROSE turns and exits into the house with the baby. Lights go down to black.)*

## SCENE IV

*It is two months later. LYONS enters from the street. He knocks on the door and calls.*

**LYONS:** Hey, Rose! *(Pause.)* Rose!

**ROSE:** *(From inside the house.)* Stop that yelling. You gonna wake up Raynell. I just got her to sleep.

**LYONS:** I just stopped by to pay Papa this twenty dollars I owe him. Where's Papa at?

**ROSE:** He should be here in a minute. I'm getting ready to go down to the church. Sit down and wait on him.

**LYONS:** I got to go pick up Bonnie over her mother's house.

**ROSE:** Well, sit it down there on the table. He'll get it.

**LYONS:** *(Enters the house and sets the money on the table.)* Tell Papa I said thanks. I'll see you again.

**ROSE:** Alright, Lyons. We'll see you.

*(LYONS starts to exit as CORY enters.)*

**CORY:** Hey, Lyons.

**LYONS:** What's happening, Cory? Say man, I'm sorry I missed your graduation. You know I had a gig and couldn't get away. Otherwise, I would have been there, man. So what you doing?

**CORY:** I'm trying to find a job.

**LYONS:** Yeah I know how that go, man. It's rough out here. Jobs are scarce.

**CORY:** Yeah, I know.

**LYONS:** Look here, I got to run. Talk to Papa . . . he know some people. He'll be able to help get you a job. Talk to him . . . see what he say.

**CORY:** Yeah . . . alright, Lyons.

**LYONS:** You take care. I'll talk to you soon. We'll find some time to talk.

*(LYONS exits the yard. CORY wanders over to the tree, picks up the bat, and assumes a batting stance. He studies an imaginary pitcher and swings. Dissatisfied with the result, he tries again. TROY enters. They eye each other for a beat. CORY puts the bat down and exits the yard. TROY starts into the house as ROSE exits with RAYNELL. She is carrying a cake.)*

**TROY:** I'm coming in and everybody's going out.

**ROSE:** I'm taking the cake down to the church for the bake sale. Lyons was by to see you. He stopped by to pay you your twenty dollars. It's laying in there on the table.

**TROY:** *(Going into his pocket.)* Well . . . here go this money.

**ROSE:** Put it in there on the table, Troy. I'll get it.

**TROY:** What time you coming back?

**ROSE:** Ain't no use in you studying me. It don't matter what time I come back.

**TROY:** I just asked you a question, woman. What's the matter . . . can't I ask you a question?

**ROSE:** Troy, I don't want to go into it. Your dinner's in there on the stove. All you got to do is heat it up. And don't you be eating the rest of them cakes in there. I'm coming back for them. We having a bake sale at the church tomorrow.

*(ROSE exits the yard. TROY sits down on the steps, takes a pint bottle from his pocket, opens it, and drinks. He begins to sing.)*

**TROY:**

Hear it ring! Hear it ring!
Had an old dog his name was Blue
You know Blue was mighty true
You know Blue was a good old dog
Blue trees a possum in a hollow log
You know from that he was a good old dog

*(BONO enters the yard.)*

**BONO:** Hey, Troy.

**TROY:** Hey, what's happening, Bono?

**BONO:** I just thought I'd stop by to see you.

**TROY:** What you stop by and see me for? You ain't stopped by in a month of Sundays. Hell, I must owe you money or something.

**BONO:** Since you got your promotion I can't keep up with you. Used to see you every day. Now I don't even know what route you working.

**TROY:** They keep switching me around. Got me out in Greentree now . . . hauling white folks' garbage.

**BONO:** Greentree, huh? You lucky, at least you ain't got to be lifting them barrels. Damn if they ain't getting heavier. I'm gonna put in my two years and call it quits.

**TROY:** I'm thinking about retiring myself.

**BONO:** You got it easy. You can *drive* for another five years.

**TROY:** It ain't the same, Bono. It ain't like working the back of the truck. Ain't got nobody to talk to . . . feel like you working by yourself. Naw, I'm thinking about retiring. How's Lucille?

**BONO:** She alright. Her arthritis get to acting up on her sometime. Saw Rose on my way in. She going down to the church, huh?

**TROY:** Yeah, she took up going down there. All them preachers looking for somebody to fatten their pockets. *(Pause.)* Got some gin here.

**BONO:** Naw, thanks. I just stopped by to say hello.

**TROY:** Hell, nigger . . . you can take a drink. I ain't never known you to say no to a drink. You ain't got to work tomorrow.

**BONO:** I just stopped by. I'm fixing to go over to Skinner's. We got us a domino game going over his house every Friday.

**TROY:** Nigger, you can't play no dominoes. I used to whup you four games out of five.

**BONO:** Well, that learned me. I'm getting better.

**TROY:** Yeah? Well, that's alright.

**BONO:** Look here . . . I got to be getting on. Stop by sometime, huh?

**TROY:** Yeah, I'll do that, Bono. Lucille told Rose you bought her a new refrigerator.

**BONO:** Yeah, Rose told Lucille you had finally built your fence . . . so I figured we'd call it even.

**TROY:** I knew you would.

**BONO:** Yeah . . . okay. I'll be talking to you.

**TROY:** Yeah, take care, Bono. Good to see you. I'm gonna stop over.

**BONO:** Yeah. Okay, Troy.

*(*BONO *exits.* TROY *drinks from the bottle.)*

**TROY:**

Old Blue died and I dug his grave
Let him down with a golden chain
Every night when I hear old Blue bark
I know Blue treed a possum in Noah's Ark.
Hear it ring! Hear it ring!

*(*CORY *enters the yard. They eye each other for a beat.* TROY *is sitting in the middle of the steps.* CORY *walks over.)*

**CORY:** I got to get by.

**TROY:** Say what? What's you say?

**CORY:** You in my way. I got to get by.

**TROY:** You got to get by where? This is my house. Bought and paid for. In full. Took me fifteen years. And if you wanna go in my house and I'm sitting on the steps . . . you say excuse me. Like your mama taught you.

**CORY:** Come on, Pop . . . I got to get by.

*(*CORY *starts to maneuver his way past* TROY. TROY *grabs his leg and shoves him back.)*

**TROY:** You just gonna walk over top of me?

**CORY:** I live here too!

**TROY:** *(Advancing toward him.)* You just gonna walk over top of me in my own house?

**CORY:** I ain't scared of you.

**TROY:** I ain't asked if you was scared of me. I asked you if you was fixing to walk over top of me in my own house? That's the question. You ain't gonna say excuse me? You just gonna walk over top of me?

**CORY:** If you wanna put it like that.

**TROY:** How else am I gonna put it?

**CORY:** I was walking by you to go into the house cause you sitting on the steps drunk, singing to yourself. You can put it like that.

**TROY:** Without saying excuse me???

*(*CORY *doesn't respond.)*

I asked you a question. Without saying excuse me???

**CORY:** I ain't got to say excuse me to you. You don't count around here no more.

**TROY:** Oh, I see . . . I don't count around here no more. You ain't got to say excuse me to your daddy. All of a sudden you done got so grown that your daddy don't count around here no more . . . Around here in his own house and yard that he done paid for with the sweat of his brow. You done got so grown to where you gonna take over. You gonna take over my house. Is that right? You gonna wear my pants. You gonna go in there and stretch out on my bed. You ain't got to say excuse me cause I don't count around here no more. Is that right?

**CORY:** That's right. You always talking this dumb stuff. Now, why don't you just get out my way?

**TROY:** I guess you got someplace to sleep and something to put in your belly. You got that, huh? You got that? That's what you need. You got that, huh?

**CORY:** You don't know what I got. You ain't got to worry about what I got.

**TROY:** You right! You one hundred percent right! I done spent the last seventeen years worrying about what you got. Now it's your turn, see? I'll tell you what to do. You grown . . . we done established that. You a man. Now, let's see you act like one. Turn your behind around and walk out this yard. And when you get out there in the alley . . . you can forget about this house. See? Cause this is my house. You go on and be a man and get your own house. You can forget about this. Cause this is mine. You go on and get yours cause I'm through with doing for you.

**CORY:** You talking about what you did for me . . . what'd you ever give me?

**TROY:** Them feet and bones! That pumping heart, nigger! I give you more than anybody else is ever gonna give you.

**CORY:** You ain't never gave me nothing! You ain't never done nothing but hold me back. Afraid I was gonna be better than you. All you ever did was try and make me scared of you. I used to tremble every time you called my name. Every time I heard your footsteps in the house. Wondering all the time . . . what's Papa gonna say if I do this? . . . What's he gonna say if I do that? . . . What's Papa gonna say if I turn on the radio? And Mama, too . . . she tries . . . but she's scared of you.

**TROY:** You leave your mama out of this. She ain't got nothing to do with this.

**CORY:** I don't know how she stand you . . . after what you did to her.

**TROY:** I told you to leave your mama out of this!

*(He advances toward* CORY.*)*

**CORY:** What you gonna do . . . give me a whupping? You can't whup me no more. You're too old. You just an old man.

**TROY:** *(Shoves him on his shoulder.)* Nigger! That's what you are. You just another nigger on the street to me!

**CORY:** You crazy! You know that?

**TROY:** Go on now! You got the devil in you. Get on away from me!

**CORY:** You just a crazy old man . . . talking about I got the devil in me.

**TROY:** Yeah, I'm crazy! If you don't get on the other side of that yard . . . I'm gonna show you how crazy I am! Go on . . . get the hell out of my yard.

**CORY:** It ain't your yard! You took Uncle Gabe's money he got from the army to buy this house and then you put him out.

**TROY:** *(Advances on* CORY.*)* Get your black ass out of my yard!

*(*TROY*'s advance backs* CORY *up against the tree.* CORY *grabs up the bat.)*

**CORY:** I ain't going nowhere! Come on . . . put me out! I ain't scared of you.

**TROY:** That's my bat!

**CORY:** Come on!

**TROY:** Put my bat down!

**CORY:** Come on, put me out.

*(*CORY *swings at* TROY*, who backs across the yard.)*

What's the matter? You so bad . . . put me out!

*(*TROY *advances toward* CORY.*)*

**CORY:** *(Backing up.)* Come on! Come on!

**TROY:** You're gonna have to use it! You wanna draw that bat back on me . . . you're gonna have to use it.

**CORY:** Come on! . . . Come on!

*(*CORY *swings the bat at* TROY *a second time. He misses.* TROY *continues to advance toward him.)*

**TROY:** You're gonna have to kill me! You wanna draw that bat back on me. You're gonna have to kill me.

*(*CORY*, backed up against the tree, can go no farther.* TROY *taunts him. He sticks out his head and offers him a target.)*

Come on! Come on!

*(*CORY *is unable to swing the bat.* TROY *grabs it.)*

**TROY:** Then I'll show you.

*(*CORY *and* TROY *struggle over the bat. The struggle is fierce and fully engaged.* TROY *ultimately is the stronger, and takes the bat from* CORY *and stands over him ready to swing. He stops himself.)*

Go on and get away from around my house.

*(*CORY*, stung by his defeat, picks himself up, walks slowly out of the yard and up the alley.)*

**CORY:** Tell Mama I'll be back for my things.

**TROY:** They'll be on the other side of that fence.

*(CORY exits.)*

**TROY:** I can't taste nothing. Helluljah! I can't taste nothing no more. *(TROY assumes a batting posture and begins to taunt Death, the fastball on the outside corner.)* Come on! It's between you and me now! Come on! Anytime you want! Come on! I be ready for you . . . but I ain't gonna be easy.

*(The lights go down on the scene.)*

## SCENE V

*The time is 1965. The lights come up in the yard. It is the morning of TROY's funeral. A funeral plaque with a light hangs beside the door. There is a small garden plot off to the side. There is noise and activity in the house as ROSE, LYONS, and BONO have gathered. The door opens and RAYNELL, seven years old, enters dressed in a flannel nightgown. She crosses to the garden and pokes around with a stick. ROSE calls from the house.*

**ROSE:** Raynell!

**RAYNELL:** Mam?

**ROSE:** What you doing out there?

**RAYNELL:** Nothing.

*(ROSE comes to the door.)*

**ROSE:** Girl, get in here and get dressed. What you doing?

**RAYNELL:** Seeing if my garden growed.

**ROSE:** I told you it ain't gonna grow overnight. You got to wait.

**RAYNELL:** It don't look like it never gonna grow. Dag!

**ROSE:** I told you a watched pot never boils. Get in here and get dressed.

**RAYNELL:** This ain't even no pot, Mama.

**ROSE:** You just have to give it a chance. It'll grow. Now you come on and do what I told you. We got to be getting ready. This ain't no morning to be playing around. You hear me?

**RAYNELL:** Yes, Mam.

*(ROSE exits into the house. RAYNELL continues to poke at her garden with a stick. CORY enters. He is dressed in a Marine corporal's uniform, and carries a duffel-bag. His posture is that of a military man, and his speech has a clipped sternness.)*

**CORY:** *(To RAYNELL.)* Hi. *(Pause.)* I bet your name is Raynell.

**RAYNELL:** Uh huh.

**CORY:** Is your mama home?

*(RAYNELL runs up on the porch and calls through the screen door.)*

**RAYNELL:** Mama . . . there's some man out here. Mama?

*(ROSE comes to the door.)*

**ROSE:** Cory? Lord have mercy! Look here, you all!

*(ROSE and CORY embrace in a tearful reunion as BONO and LYONS enter from the house dressed in funeral clothes.)*

**BONO:** Aw, looka here . . .

**ROSE:** Done got all grown up!

**CORY:** Don't cry, Mama. What you crying about?

**ROSE:** I'm just so glad you made it.

**CORY:** Hey Lyons. How you doing, Mr. Bono.

*(LYONS goes to embrace CORY.)*

**LYONS:** Look at you, man. Look at you. Don't he look good, Rose. Got them Corporal stripes.

**ROSE:** What took you so long?

**CORY:** You know how the Marines are, Mama. They got to get all their paperwork straight before they let you do anything.

**ROSE:** Well, I'm sure glad you made it. They let Lyons come. Your Uncle Gabe's still in the hospital. They don't know if they gonna let him out or not. I just talked to them a little while ago.

**LYONS:** A Corporal in the United States Marines.

**BONO:** Your daddy knew you had it in you. He used to tell me all the time.

**LYONS:** Don't he look good, Mr. Bono?

**BONO:** Yeah, he remind me of Troy when I first met him. *(Pause.)* Say, Rose, Lucille's down at the church with the choir. I'm gonna go down and get the pallbearers lined up. I'll be back to get you all.

**ROSE:** Thanks, Jim.

**CORY:** See you, Mr. Bono.

**LYONS:** *(With his arm around RAYNELL.)* Cory . . . look at Raynell. Ain't she precious? She gonna break a whole lot of hearts.

Cory greets Rose on the day of Troy's funeral.

**ROSE:** Raynell, come and say hello to your brother. This is your brother, Cory. You remember Cory.

**RAYNELL:** No, Mam.

**CORY:** She don't remember me, Mama.

**ROSE:** Well, we talk about you. She heard us talk about you. *(To* RAYNELL.*)* This is your brother, Cory. Come on and say hello.

**RAYNELL:** Hi.

**CORY:** Hi. So you're Raynell. Mama told me a lot about you.

**ROSE:** You all come on into the house and let me fix you some breakfast. Keep up your strength.

**CORY:** I ain't hungry, Mama.

**LYONS:** You can fix me something, Rose. I'll be in there in a minute.

**ROSE:** Cory, you sure you don't want nothing? I know they ain't feeding you right.

**CORY:** No, Mama . . . thanks. I don't feel like eating. I'll get something later.

**ROSE:** Raynell . . . get on upstairs and get that dress on like I told you.

*(*ROSE *and* RAYNELL *exit into the house.)*

**LYONS:** So . . . I hear you thinking about getting married.

**CORY:** Yeah, I done found the right one, Lyons. It's about time.

**LYONS:** Me and Bonnie been split up about four years now. About the time Papa retired. I guess she just got tired of all them changes I was putting her through. *(Pause.)* I always knew you was gonna make something out yourself. Your head was always in the right direction. So . . . you gonna stay in . . . make it a career . . . put in your twenty years?

**CORY:** I don't know. I got six already, I think that's enough.

**LYONS:** Stick with Uncle Sam and retire early. Ain't nothing out here. I guess Rose told you what happened with me. They got me down the workhouse. I thought I was being slick cashing other people's checks.

**CORY:** How much time you doing?

**LYONS:** They give me three years. I got that beat now. I ain't got but nine more months. It ain't so bad. You learn to deal with it like anything else. You got to take the crookeds with the straights. That's what Papa used to say. He used to say that when he struck out. I seen him strike out three times in a row . . . and the next time up he hit the ball over the grandstand. Right out there in Homestead Field. He wasn't satisfied hitting in the seats . . . he want to hit it over everything! After the game he had two hundred people standing around waiting to shake his hand. You got to take the crookeds with the straights. Yeah, Papa was something else.

**CORY:** You still playing?

**LYONS:** Cory . . . you know I'm gonna do that. There's some fellows down there we got us a band . . . we gonna try and stay together when we get out . . . but yeah, I'm still playing. It still helps me to get out of bed in the morning. As long as it do that I'm gonna be right there playing and trying to make some sense out of it.

**ROSE:** *(Calling.)* Lyons, I got these eggs in the pan.

**LYONS:** Let me go on and get these eggs, man. Get ready to go bury Papa. *(Pause.)* How you doing? You doing alright?

(CORY *nods.* LYONS *touches him on the shoulder and they share a moment of silent grief.* LYONS *exits into the house.* CORY *wanders about the yard.* RAYNELL *enters.)*

**RAYNELL:** Hi.

**CORY:** Hi.

**RAYNELL:** Did you used to sleep in my room?

**CORY:** Yeah . . . that used to be my room.

**RAYNELL:** That's what Papa call it. "Cory's room." It got your football in the closet.

*(*ROSE *comes to the door.)*

**ROSE:** Raynell, get in there and get them good shoes on.

**RAYNELL:** Mama, can't I wear these? Them other one hurt my feet.

**ROSE:** Well, they just gonna have to hurt your feet for a while. You ain't said they hurt your feet when you went down to the store and got them.

**RAYNELL:** They didn't hurt then. My feet done got bigger.

**ROSE:** Don't you give me no backtalk now. You get in there and get them shoes on.

*(*RAYNELL *exits into the house.)*

Ain't too much changed. He still got that piece of rag tied to that tree. He was out here swinging that bat. I was just ready to go back in the house. He swung that bat and then he just fell over. Seem like he swung it and stood there with this grin on his face . . . and then he just fell over. They carried him on down to the hospital, but I knew there wasn't no need . . . why don't you come on in the house?

**CORY:** Mama . . . I got something to tell you. I don't know how to tell you this . . . but I've got to tell you . . . I'm not going to Papa's funeral.

**ROSE:** Boy, hush your mouth. That's your daddy you talking about. I don't want hear that kind of talk this morning. I done raised you to come to this? You standing there all healthy and grown talking about you ain't going to your daddy's funeral?

**CORY:** Mama . . . listen . . .

**ROSE:** I don't want to hear it, Cory. You just get that thought out of your head.

**CORY:** I can't drag Papa with me everywhere I go. I've got to say no to him. One time in my life I've got to say no.

**ROSE:** Don't nobody have to listen to nothing like that. I know you and your daddy ain't seen eye to eye, but I ain't got to listen to that kind of talk this morning. Whatever was between you and your daddy . . . the time has come to put it aside. Just take it and set it over there on the shelf and forget about it. Disrespecting your daddy ain't gonna make you a man, Cory. You got to find a way to come to that on your own. Not going to your daddy's funeral ain't gonna make you a man.

**CORY:** The whole time I was growing up . . . living in his house . . . Papa was like a shadow that followed you everywhere. It weighed on you and sunk into your flesh. It would wrap around you and lay there until you couldn't tell which one was you anymore. That shadow digging in your flesh. Trying to crawl in. Trying to live through you. Everywhere I looked, Troy Maxson was staring back at me . . . hiding under the bed . . . in the closet. I'm just saying I've got to find a way to get rid of that shadow, Mama.

**ROSE:** You just like him. You got him in you good.

**CORY:** Don't tell me that, Mama.

**ROSE:** You Troy Maxson all over again.

**CORY:** I don't want to be Troy Maxson. I want to be me.

**ROSE:** You can't be nobody but who you are, Cory. That shadow wasn't nothing but you growing into yourself. You either got to grow into it or cut it down to fit you. But that's all you got to make life with. That's all you got to measure yourself against that world out there. Your daddy wanted you to be everything he wasn't . . . and at the same time he tried to make you into everything he was. I don't know if he was right or wrong . . . but I do know he meant to do more good than he meant to do harm. He wasn't always right. Sometimes when he touched he bruised. And sometimes when he took me in his arms he cut.

When I first met your daddy I thought . . . Here is a man I can lay down with and make a baby. That's the first thing I thought when I seen him. I was thirty years old and had done seen my share of men. But when he walked up to me and said, "I can dance a waltz that'll make you dizzy," I thought, Rose Lee, here is a man that you can open yourself up to and be filled to bursting. Here is a man that can fill all them empty spaces you been tipping around the edges of. One of them empty spaces was being somebody's mother.

I married your daddy and settled down to cooking his supper and keeping clean sheets on the bed. When your daddy walked through the house he was so big he filled it up. That was my first mistake. Not to make him leave some room for me. For my part in the matter. But at that time I wanted that. I wanted a house that I could sing in. And that's what your daddy gave me. I didn't know to keep up his strength I had to give up little pieces of mine. I did that. I took on his life as mine and mixed up the pieces so that you couldn't hardly tell which was which anymore. It was my choice. It was my life and I didn't have to live it like that. But that's what life offered me in the way of being a woman and I took it. I grabbed hold of it with both hands.

By the time Raynell came into the house, me and your daddy had done lost touch with one another. I didn't want to make my blessing off of nobody's misfortune . . . but I took on to Raynell like she was all them babies I had wanted and never had.

*(The phone rings.)*

Like I'd been blessed to relive a part of my life. And if the Lord see fit to keep up my strength . . . I'm gonna do her just like your daddy did you . . . I'm gonna give her the best of what's in me.

**RAYNELL:** *(Entering, still with her old shoes.)* Mama . . . Reverend Tollivier on the phone.

*(ROSE exits into the house.)*

**RAYNELL:** Hi.

**CORY:** Hi.

**RAYNELL:** You in the Army or the Marines?

**CORY:** Marines.

**RAYNELL:** Papa said it was the Army. Did you know Blue?

**CORY:** Blue? Who's Blue?

**RAYNELL:** Papa's dog what he sing about all the time.

**CORY:** *(Singing.)*

Hear it ring! Hear it ring!
I had a dog his name was Blue
You know Blue was mighty true
You know Blue was a good old dog
Blue treed a possum in a hollow log
You know from that he was a good old dog.
Hear it ring! Hear it ring!

*(RAYNELL joins in singing.)*

**CORY AND RAYNELL:**

Blue treed a possum out on a limb
Blue looked at me and I looked at him
Grabbed that possum and put him in a sack
Blue stayed there till I came back
Old Blue's feets was big and round
Never allowed a possum to touch the ground.

Old Blue died and I dug his grave
I dug his grave with a silver spade
Let him down with a golden chain
And every night I call his name
Go on Blue, you good dog you
Go on Blue, you good dog you.

**RAYNELL:**

Blue laid down and died like a man
Blue laid down and died . . .

**BOTH:**

Blue laid down and died like a man
Now he's treeing possums in the Promised Land
I'm gonna tell you this to let you know
Blue's gone where the good dogs go
When I hear old Blue bark
When I hear old Blue bark
Blue treed a possum in Noah's Ark
Blue treed a possum in Noah's Ark.

*(ROSE comes to the screen door.)*

**ROSE:** Cory, we gonna be ready to go in a minute.

**CORY:** *(To RAYNELL.)* You go on in the house and change them shoes like Mama told you so we can go to Papa's funeral.

**RAYNELL:** Okay, I'll be back.

*(RAYNELL exits into the house. CORY gets up and crosses over to the tree. ROSE stands in the screen door watching him. GABRIEL enters from the alley.)*

**GABRIEL:** *(Calling.)* Hey, Rose!

**ROSE:** Gabe?

**GABRIEL:** I'm here, Rose. Hey, Rose, I'm here!

*(ROSE enters from the house.)*

**ROSE:** Lord . . . Look here, Lyons!

**LYONS:** See, I told you, Rose . . . I told you they'd let him come.

**CORY:** How you doing, Uncle Gabe?

**LYONS:** How you doing, Uncle Gabe?

**GABRIEL:** Hey, Rose. It's time. It's time to tell St. Peter to open the gates. Troy, you ready? You ready, Troy. I'm gonna tell St. Peter to open the gates. You get ready now.

The family looks up into the wide-open gates of heaven.

*(GABRIEL, with great fanfare, braces himself to blow. The trumpet is without a mouthpiece. He puts the end of it into his mouth and blows with great force, like a man who has been waiting some twenty-odd years for this single moment. No sound comes out of the trumpet. He braces himself and blows again with the same result. A third time he blows. There is a weight of impossible description that falls away and leaves him bare and exposed to a frightful realization. It is a trauma that a sane and normal mind would be unable to withstand. He begins to dance. A slow, strange dance, eerie and life-giving. A dance of atavistic signature and ritual.* LYONS *attempts to embrace him.* GABRIEL *pushes* LYONS *away. He begins to howl in what is an attempt at song, or perhaps a song turning back into itself in an attempt at speech. He finishes his dance and the gates of heaven stand open as wide as God's closet.)*

That's the way that go!

*BLACKOUT*

# Writing from Reading

## Summarize

1 Which family relationships does the play emphasize; which does it downplay?

## Analyze Craft

2 Explain the importance of the title and how it relates to the play's theme or themes. Of all the elements in the play—dialogue, character, plot, setting, language—which do you think might have the most impact on the audience, and why?

3 Which character goes through the most dramatic change in the course of the play? What evidence do you see of this change?

## Analyze Voice

4 Identify an exchange of dialogue that you found particularly powerful and explain why. How does it promote or portray the conflict and theme of the play?

## Synthesize Summary and Analysis

5 How successful is August Wilson in elevating his working-class characters to the level of the tragic hero portrayed in Greek drama?

6 Throughout the play, stage directions indicate that lines are to be sung. How does the incorporation of song bring the African-American tradition of the blues into the tone of the play? Compare the use of song in *Fences* with the blues poems of Langston Hughes (see chapter 26 in Poetry). How do both use the blues to comment on the African-American experience?

## Interpret the Play

7 Discuss the theme of power and powerlessness as raised in this play.

"August's plays are the blues. Listen to the blues . . . Lightnin' Hopkins . . . Bessie Smith . . . Big Maybell. Listen to these things, listen to the words because they're poetry and they're plays. They're whole dramas told in one song."

Conversation with Ruben Santiago-Hudson

## AN ACTOR'S PERSPECTIVE ON MODERN THEATER AND AUGUST WILSON

As Ruben Santiago-Hudson makes clear in his interview, his mentor and guiding light in the theater was August Wilson. Now that you have read the play, you will begin to see why, among other things, it called out to a young writer and actor like Santiago-Hudson. First performed in 1985, the play has entered the American repertory. Because of its subject matter it has drawn a new audience to theaters and, as the example of Santiago-Hudson suggests, has opened a path for new playwrights and actors to follow.

"I have a sense that—our literature is more and more filled with socially relevant work than it was years back. . . . The escapist notion is always where people want to get out of their troubles. . . . But there's been a lot of literature in the last years that I think is relevant." Conversation with Arthur Miller

### A Glimpse at the Work of Ruben Santiago-Hudson

As Santiago-Hudson suggests, whether in Shakespeare's day or our own, the constant factor is the actor, wrestling with a role, preparing to take the stage. If you happen to watch a DVD of the movie *Lackawanna Blues* (there is currently no publicly available script), you immediately feel a sense of deep emotion, as the movie opens with a telephone call in the middle of the night and a man awakes to pick up the instrument and listen for a moment before announcing that he is on his way. He's going to the upstate New York hospital where the woman who raised him, the owner of a Lackawanna boarding house for black people in the still-segregated mid-1950s, lies dying. The audience is on its way, too, because within seconds we're seeing images from the hospital and then flash back to the '50s to witness, in a dazzling series of cross-cuts, a raucous and joyful Friday night fish fry dance and the birth of the boy the woman will raise to manhood.

"I was raised in a rooming house, pretty much abandoned by my mother. See the film *Lackawanna Blues*. That's my life."

Conversation with Ruben Santiago-Hudson

*Theater can transcend anything.*

Q&A

*You need to feed your soul.*

# *A Conversation on Writing*

## Ruben Santiago-Hudson

### Theater Makes a Person Whole

I choose to do plays first and foremost because I love them. . . . I can't get that love out of me—and I don't want to get it out of me. . . . I have to balance the theater with my film and TV, which is sustenance . . . but theater is the place where I am whole as a human being. . . . The reason I choose theater foremost is not only desire, but need. I need to feel whole because I'm in a business where they don't see you as whole. If you're good at one thing, if you're a good gangster, you're going to be a gangster in twenty films. If you're a good teacher, that's what you're going to be. If you're a good back man, you'll be in the back. . . . In theater, we're all even. Even if somebody's name's above the title, all roles are good roles. . . . So those possibilities are there in theater that I don't find in film.

### August Wilson Speaks Straight into My Heart

My favorite playwright is August Wilson, simply because he speaks to me straight into my heart. But something that's very clear in August Wilson's writing is that he loves the characters. August loves these people. . . . It's the simplicity of his work, the poetry of his work—no matter what their lot in life is. Whether somebody's an elevator operator or somebody is selling refrigerators, we don't know where the refrigerators come from, but he's selling the refrigerators. . . . Some people walk around with the Daily Word; I walk around with August Wilson, because he speaks to me.

**To view the whole interview and hear Ruben Santiago-Hudson read from August Wilson's *Fences*, go to www.mhhe.delbanco1e.**

**RESEARCH ASSIGNMENT:** When Ruben Santiago-Hudson says, "I can't hide" and then is identified as the actor in *Shaft* by a boy at the basketball game, what is the moral of the story and what does the actor tell us about the importance of race?

# Ruben Santiago-Hudson (b. 1956)

Born in Lackawanna, New York, Ruben Santiago-Hudson wrote the autobiographical play *Lackawanna Blues* about his youth in a segregated American steel town. His father, Ruben Santiago, was a Puerto Rican railroad worker. His mother, Alean Hudson, was African American. In *Lackawanna Blues,* Santiago-Hudson portrays his abandonment by his mother, then the community of music and love that embraced him as he was raised by a woman who ran a local boarding house for African Americans. He played over twenty characters in the production of *Lackawanna Blues* and was awarded an Obie. His script was made into an HBO movie directed by George C. Wolfe (2005)—for which Wolfe won the Director's Guild Award for Outstanding Movies for Television—and starring S. Epatha Merkerson, who won an Emmy. Santiago-Hudson graduated from the University of Binghamton and went on to study Shakespeare and classical theater at the Hilberry Classical Repertory Theater. He now lives in New York and has acted in over sixty films and TV movies, including *Devil's Advocate, Blown Away,* and *Shaft,* and the TV miniseries based on Zora Neale Hurston's novel *Their Eyes Were Watching God.* But for writer, director, and actor Santiago-Hudson, who has played opposite Gregory Hines in *Jelly's Last Jam* (also directed by George C. Wolfe) and won a Tony for his performance in August Wilson's *Seven Guitars,* theater remains his first love.

# Lackawanna Blues (2005)

*Adapted from the stage for film by Ruben Santiago-Hudson*

*Director: George C. Wolfe*

*An ensemble cast, starring S. Epatha Merkerson and including Marcus Carl Franklin, Mos Def, Carmen Ejogo, Louis Gossett Jr., Macy Gray, Rosie Perez, Ruben Santiago-Hudson, Liev Schreiber, Jimmy Smits, Lily Santiago, and Trey Santiago.*

Freddie Cobbs (Ruben Santiago-Hudson), a boarder, talks to young Ruben (Marcus Carl Franklin) in the doorway of the boarding house. Why do you think Santiago-Hudson chose to juxtapose his real self with the child acting out his past? How might your interpretation of this scene be affected by your knowledge that the grown man playing Cobbs is the adult version of the boy in the movie?

Rachel "Nanny" Crosby (S. Epatha Merkerson) jokes around with the men gambling at the boarding house fish fry. What do you notice about the men in this image? Do the people in this photo fit your conception of the common man as Santiago-Hudson describes him in his interview?

Young Ruben and Nanny Crosby converse in the restaurant of the boarding house. Consider that *Lackawanna Blues* was written as a one-man performance. How do you imagine such an interaction as staged by only one actor?

An aged and ailing Nanny Crosby is surprised by old friends with donations to fund her medical care. To what extent is this celebration of heroic deeds by a common woman characteristic of modern theater? In what ways? Would you consider Nanny Crosby an "everyman"? Why or why not?

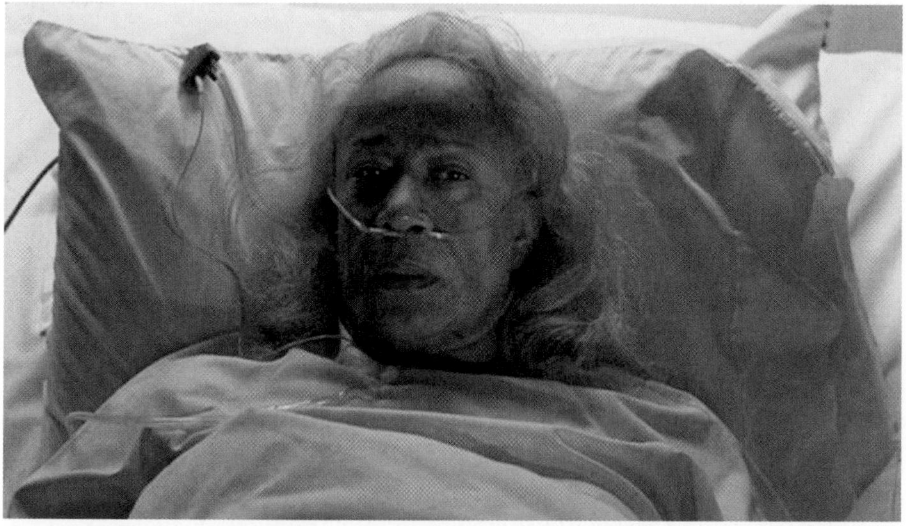

Nanny Crosby, now old and ill, lies in a hospital bed. Would you describe Nanny's death as tragic in the sense of Greek tragedy, or as naturalistic?

# Reading Modern Drama

| When reading or viewing modern drama . . . | |
|---|---|
| **Consider how the play is staged.** | Modern drama commonly is written for the **proscenium stage,** which features an arch through which the main set is visible (and can be separated by a curtain).<br>• Is the set dressing detailed and realistic, as though you are glimpsing the action in a room through the missing **fourth wall**?<br>• Is the set dressing minimal, inviting surrealistic interpretation and imagination? |
| **Identify the structure and aim of the play.** | • **Well-made plays** take place in a three-act sequence: The first act *poses* a problem, the next *complicates* the problem, and the third *resolves* the problem.<br>• **Problem plays** confront a social issue with no clear-cut resolution, often in order to raise awareness of that issue. |
| **Note the conventions of naturalistic theater, which shines a light on the painful realities of life.** | • Is the protagonist an **antihero**—one who is not elevated socially or morally and does not exhibit common heroic characteristics like bravery or morality?<br>• Is the protagonist an **everyman,** a character whose station in life is not unlike that of the audience? The everymen of modern drama are generally ordinary middle-class people struggling with life. |
| **Recognize the difference between realism and surrealism.** | • **Realism** describes acting that features realistic language and physical gestures enacted by characters who are familiar in a setting that resembles the audience's real life.<br>• **Surrealism** describes staging and events that represent an overlap of the conscious and the unconscious experience—often depicting dreams and internal struggles. |
| **Identify instances of symbolism in the play.** | • **Symbolism** occurs when an object, image, character, or action suggests meaning beyond the everyday literal interpretation.<br>• **Expressionist** plays use scenes and onstage cues as **symbols** for characters' subjective emotions. |

# Suggestions for Writing about Modern Drama

1. Taking the long view, choose a modern play that you believe has something approaching the stature and sweep of a classical Greek tragedy and compare and contrast the two theater pieces. Can you make an exact match with respect to questions of tragedy? How do the traditional and modern characters differ in the way they behave? How does the social background of the plays appear to differ? Does it seem possible, given the belief systems of modern life, that a modern play can become truly tragic?
2. What is the role of modern drama in relation to society at large? How does this contrast, if it does contrast, with plays at the origins of Western theater? Does modern drama respond in the fullest possible fashion to the questions of modern psychology and modern life? What to your mind are the greatest problems and questions that arise in our lives today? How do modern plays rise to the level of these problems?
3. Some highly educated and sophisticated critics and instructors might argue that movies are the greatest dramatic creation of the modern age. Do you agree or disagree? Why? What aspects of the film might appear to trump those of the stage play? Which seem to suffer by comparison?

# 36 Contemporary Theater

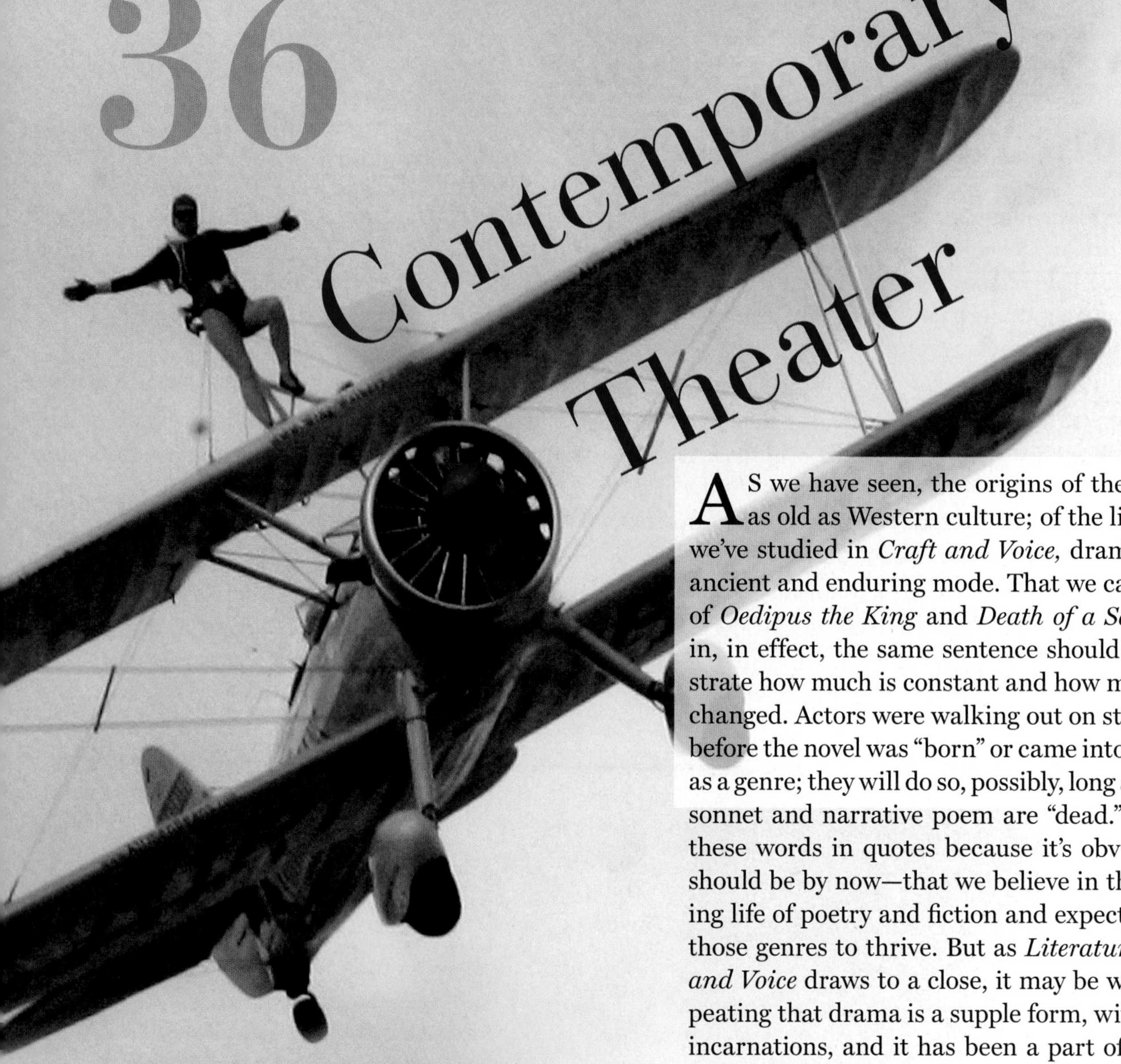

*"How do you begin writing plays? . . . You write some lines, some people get together, they read the lines, they do it in any room. Just somebody reads stage direction, they say it's night, it's cold, it's snowing. Okay. I got it. You know? I don't need, you know, nobody has to say where we gonna get the snowflakes? We'll believe it. And it's fun."*

Conversation on Writing with Arthur Kopit, available online at www.mhhe/delbanco1e

AS we have seen, the origins of theater are as old as Western culture; of the literature we've studied in *Craft and Voice,* drama is the ancient and enduring mode. That we can speak of *Oedipus the King* and *Death of a Salesman* in, in effect, the same sentence should demonstrate how much is constant and how much has changed. Actors were walking out on stage long before the novel was "born" or came into fashion as a genre; they will do so, possibly, long after the sonnet and narrative poem are "dead." We put these words in quotes because it's obvious—or should be by now—that we believe in the ongoing life of poetry and fiction and expect both of those genres to thrive. But as *Literature: Craft and Voice* draws to a close, it may be worth repeating that drama is a supple form, with many incarnations, and it has been a part of human discourse from the start.

Our contemporary world is an eclectic place, a world made up out of individual elements from a variety of sources, systems, and styles. Science, religion, art, business—we draw from all of these realms and more to figure out how to get through working days and dream-filled nights. Technology has altered the speed of communication, and contemporary theater reflects the way we live today. The brevity of television plays and situation comedies (in which scenes are in-

SOUND OF WIND

LIGHTS CHANGE INTO A COOL AND AIRY BLUE. SENSE OF WEIGHTLESSNESS, SERENITY.

IN ANOTHER REALM NOW.

> *Yes, out there walking not holding even danger ever-present*
> *How I loved it love it still no doubt will again hear them*
> *Cheering wisht or waltz away to some place like Rumania . . .*

THE WIND DISAPPEARS.

*Nothing . . .*

THE SERENE BLUE LIGHT BEGINS TO FADE AWAY.
SOME PLACE ELSE NOW THAT SHE IS GOING . . .

—*from* Wings *by Arthur Kopit*

terspersed with commercials), the various possibilities of camera angles in films, the availability of cell-phone cameras, emails, YouTube, Facebook, and the rest, all these have had a transforming effect on the nature of communication and performance. It's not so much a question of information overload as of more rapid transmission; whereas the ancient Greeks might dedicate a day to the production of a trilogy and satyr play, we expect our sound bites to be brief.

Most contemporary playwrights create multi-scene and multi-act plays. But one-act plays have recently emerged as an important part of theatrical discourse. In some sense they bear the same relation to full-length plays as the short story does to the novel; they are necessarily more focused and contained. (In part this has to do with economic reality; one-act plays—with a small cast—are, of course, less expensive to produce.) One playwright who has put his mark on contemporary theater—both in the multi-act and the one-act form—is Arthur Kopit. In his arresting theater piece *Wings,* this New York-born, Harvard-educated playwright evokes the chaos of a stroke patient's perception by breaking with realistic stage setting. *Wings* was first produced as a radio play (available online at *www.mhhe.com/delbanco1e*), and then for television.

Other one-act plays that you will find in this chapter display a remarkable diversity, even as they focus on themes and motifs important to contemporary audiences—family and social relations, and the swift passage of time. Each illuminates the lives we lead together now.

*You've got to be very careful not to censor yourself.*

*The task for the playwright is to find your own play.*

# Q&A

# *A Conversation on Writing*

## Arthur Kopit

### On Doing My Research for *Wings*

The play had been inspired or spurred on by my having observed my father in a stroke, in a massive stroke. He had hardly any speech and I wanted to find some way for myself to see what could it be like. And it was an alien world, clearly. . . . I had done research so that I could be accurate . . . and that included interviewing people that'd had strokes . . . trying to get the speech right, speaking to neurologists, psychiatrists, speech-pathologists, and everything I had observed with my father.

### *Wings* and the Order of Chaos

There really is a sequence. . . . You would have images, which said mostly it's whiteness, dazzling, blinding. . . . Mirrors, of course . . . nothing seen that is not a fragment. At the same time we're hearing sounds . . . Simultaneously with these images . . . the sounds outside of herself, and then Mrs. Stilson's voice.

### How to Read a Play

Some plays don't read very well. . . . You have to see it to realize the impact, because the writing itself is awfully clumsy. . . . A play is written to be performed, but it is also literature. It is also a text. And I think what's crucial for someone reading plays in the course is to also know how would this play on a stage? What is the effect of this? There isn't only one answer.

**To listen to this entire interview and hear the author read from *Wings*, go to www.mhhe/delbanco1e.**

**RESEARCH ASSIGNMENT** In his interview, Kopit talks about writing coming from a "mysterious place" and admonishes writers to write "about what you didn't know you knew." What does he mean by this and how would this compare with your own writing?

# Arthur Kopit (b. 1937)

Born in New York City, Arthur Kopit grew up on Long Island never dreaming of becoming a playwright. However, while a student on scholarship at Harvard, Kopit began to write plays, and his *Oh Dad, Poor Dad, Mama's Hung You in the Closet and I'm Feelin' So Sad* (1960) won a playwriting contest. Soon, Kopit's work was being performed internationally as well as on Broadway, and—though he earned a degree in engineering—he has made his living as a playwright ever since. Kopit's works, though sporadic (at times there has been a nine-year gap between plays, at others, a single year), have been successful because of their special blend of humor, wackiness, innovation, satire, and seriousness. Two of his plays—*Indians* (1969) and *Wings* (1978)—as well as his script for the musical *Nine* (1983) have received Tony Award nominations. He has received prestigious awards and fellowships, including the National Institute of Arts and Letters Award, a Guggenheim, and a Rockefeller grant. Married since 1968, he and his wife, the writer Leslie Garis, have three children

**AS YOU READ** **This play was first produced for the radio. Try to imagine hearing it for the first time, with the images described and the confusion that images, sounds, and Mrs. Stilson's voice would create when going on simultaneously. Imagine yourself coping with the kind of confusion into which Mrs. Stilson awakes.**

# Wings (1978)

## CHARACTERS

**EMILY STILSON**
**AMY**
**DOCTORS**
**NURSES**
**BILLY**
**MR. BROWNSTEIN**
**MRS. TIMMINS**

The play takes place over a period of two years; it should be performed without an intermission.

*I weave in and out of the strange clouds, hidden in my tiny cockpit, submerged, alone, on the magnitude of this weird, unhuman space, venturing where man has never been, perhaps never meant to go. Am I myself a living, breathing, earth-bound body, or is this a dream of death I'm passing through? Am I alive, or am I really dead, a spirit in a spirit world. Am I actually in a plane, or have I crashed on some worldly mountain, and is this the afterlife?*

—Charles Lindbergh, *The Spirit of St. Louis.*

## NOTES ON THE PRODUCTION OF THIS PLAY

*The stage as a void.*

*System of black scrim panels that can move silently and easily, creating the impression of featureless, labyrinthine corridors.*

*Some panels mirrored so they can fracture light, create the impression of endlessness, even airiness, multiply and confuse images, confound one's sense of space.*

*Sound both live and pre-recorded, amplified; speakers all around the theater.*

*No attempt should be made to create a literal representation of* MRS. STILSON*'s world, especially since* MRS. STILSONs' *world is no longer in any way literal.*

*The scenes should blend. No clear boundaries or domains in time or space for* MRS. STILSON *any more.*

*It is posited by this play that the woman we see in the center of the void is the intact inner self of* MRS. STILSON. *This inner self does not need to move physically when her external body (which we cannot see) moves. Thus, we infer movement from the context; from whatever clues we can obtain. It is the same for her, of course. She learns as best she can.*

*And yet, sometimes, the conditions change; then the woman we observe is* MRS. STILSON *as others see her. We thus infer who it is we are seeing from the context, too. Sometimes we see both the inner and outer self at once.*

*Nothing about her world is predictable or consistent. This fact is its essence.*

*The progression of the play is from fragmentation to integration. By the end, boundaries have become somewhat clearer. But she remains always in another realm from us.*

## PRELUDE

AS AUDIENCE ENTERS, A COZY ARMCHAIR VISIBLE DOWNSTAGE IN A POOL OF LIGHT, DARKNESS SURROUNDING IT.

A CLOCK HEARD TICKING IN THE DARK.

LIGHTS TO BLACK.

HOLD.

WHEN THE LIGHTS COME BACK, EMILY STILSON, A WOMAN WELL INTO HER SEVENTIES, IS SITTING IN THE ARMCHAIR READING A BOOK. SOME DISTANCE AWAY, A FLOOR LAMP GLOWS DIMLY. ON THE OTHER SIDE OF HER CHAIR, ALSO SOME DISTANCE AWAY, A SMALL TABLE WITH A CLOCK. THE CHAIR, THE LAMP, AND THE TABLE WITH THE CLOCK ALL SIT ISOLATED IN NARROW POOLS OF LIGHT, DARKNESS BETWEEN AND AROUND THEM.

THE CLOCK SEEMS TO BE TICKING A TRIFLE LOUDER THAN NORMAL.

MRS. STILSON, ENJOYING HER BOOK AND THE PLEASANT EVENING, READS ON SERENELY.

AND THEN SHE LOOKS UP.

THE LAMP DISAPPEARS INTO THE DARKNESS.

BUT SHE TURNS BACK TO HER BOOK AS IF NOTHING ODD HAS HAPPENED; RESUMES READING.

AND THEN, A MOMENT LATER, SHE LOOKS UP AGAIN, AN EXPRESSION OF SLIGHT PERPLEXITY ON HER FACE. FOR NO DISCERNIBLE REASON, SHE TURNS TOWARD THE CLOCK.

THE CLOCK AND THE TABLE IT IS SITTING ON DISAPPEAR INTO THE DARKNESS.

SHE TURNS FRONT. STARES OUT INTO SPACE.

THEN SHE TURNS BACK TO HER BOOK. RESUMES READING. BUT THE READING SEEMS AN EFFORT; HER MIND IS ON OTHER THINGS.

THE CLOCK SKIPS A BEAT.

ONLY AFTER THE CLOCK HAS RESUMED ITS NORMAL RHYTHM DOES SHE LOOK UP. IT IS AS IF THE SKIPPED BEAT HAS ONLY JUST THEN REGISTERED. FOR THE FIRST TIME, SHE DISPLAYS WHAT ONE MIGHT CALL CONCERN.

AND THEN THE CLOCK STOPS AGAIN. THIS TIME THE INTERVAL LASTS LONGER.

THE BOOK SLIPS OUT OF MRS. STILSON'S HANDS; SHE STARES OUT IN TERROR.

BLACKOUT.

NOISE.

*The moment of a stroke, even a relatively minor one, and its immediate aftermath, are an experience in chaos. Nothing at all makes sense. Nothing except perhaps this overwhelming disorientation will be remembered by the victim. The stroke usually happens suddenly. It is a catastrophe.*

*It is my intention that the audience recognize that some real event is occurring; that real information is being received by the victim, but that it is coming in too scrambled and too fast to be properly decoded. Systems overload.*

*And so this section must not seem like utter "noise," though certainly it must be more noisy than intelligible. I do not believe there is any way to be true to this material if it is not finally "composed" in rehearsal, on stage, by "feel." Theoretically, any sound or image herein described can occur anywhere in this section. The victim cannot process. Her familiar world has been rearranged. The puzzle is in pieces. All at once, and with no time to prepare, she has been picked up and dropped into another realm.*

*In order that this section may be put together in rehearsal (there being no one true "final order" to the images and sounds she perceives), I have divided this section into three discrete parts with the understanding that in performance these parts will blend together to form one cohesive whole.*

*The first group consists of the visual images* MRS. STILSON *perceives.*

*The second group consists of those sounds emanating outside herself. Since these sounds are all filtered by her mind, and since her mind has been drastically altered, the question of whether we in the audience are hearing what is actually occurring or only hearing what she believes is occurring is unanswerable.*

*The third group contains* MRS. STILSON*'s words: the words she thinks and the words she speaks. Since we are perceiving the world through* MRS. STILSON*'s senses, there is no sure way for us to know whether she is actually saying any of these words aloud.*

*Since the experience we are exploring is not one of logic but its opposite, there is no logical reason for these groupings to occur in the order in which I have presented them. These are but components, building blocks, and can therefore be repeated, spliced, reversed, filtered, speeded up or slowed down. What should determine their final sequence and juxtaposition, tempi, intensity, is the "musical" sense of this section as a whole; it must pulse and build. An explosion quite literally is occurring in her brain, or rather, a series of explosions: the victim's mind, her sense of time and place, her sense of self, all are being shattered if not annihilated. Fortunately, finally, she will pass out. Were her head a pinball game it would register* TILT*—game over—stop. Silence. And resume again. Only now the victim is in yet another realm. The Catastrophe section is the journey or the fall into this strange and dreadful realm.*

*In the world into which* MRS. STILSON *has been so violently and suddenly transposed, time and place are without definition. The distance from her old familiar world is immense. For all she knows, she could as well be on another planet.*

*In this new world, she moves from one space or thought or concept to another without willing or sometimes even knowing it. Indeed, when she moves in this maze-like place, it is as if the world around her and not she were doing all the moving. To her, there is nothing any more that is commonplace or predictable. Nothing is as it was. Everything comes as a surprise. Something has relieved her of command. Something beyond her comprehension has her in its grip.*

*In the staging of this play, the sense should therefore be conveyed of physical and emotional separation (by the use, for example, of the dark transparent screens through which her surrounding world can be only dimly and partly seen, or by alteration of external sound) and of total immersion in strangeness.*

*Because our focus is on* MRS. STILSON*'s inner self, it is important that she exhibit no particular overt physical disabilities. Furthermore, we should never see her in a wheelchair, even though, were we able to observe her through the doctors' eyes, a wheelchair is probably what she would, more often than not, be in.*

*One further note: because* MRS. STILSON *now processes information at a different rate from us, there is no reason that what we see going on around her has to be the visual equivalent of what we hear.*

## CATASTROPHE

| **IMAGES** | **SOUNDS OUTSIDE HERSELF** | **MRS. STILSON'S VOICE** |
|---|---|---|
| | *(SOUNDS live or on tape, altered or unadorned)* | *(VOICE live or on tape, unaltered or unadorned)* |
| | Of wind. | |
| *Mostly, it is whiteness, dazzling, blinding.* | Of someone breathing with effort, unevenly. | *Oh my God oh my God oh my God—* |
| | Of something ripping, like a sheet. | *—trees clouds houses mostly planes flashing past, images without words, utter disarray disbelief, never seen this kind of thing before!* |
| *Occasionally, there are brief rounds of color, explosions of color, the color red being dominant.* | Of something flapping, the sound suggestive of an old screen door perhaps, or a sheet or sail in the wind. It is a rapid fibrillation. And it is used mostly to mark transitions. It can seem ominous or not. | *Where am I? How'd I get here?* |
| *The mirrors, of course, reflect infinitely. Sense of endless space, endless corridors.* | Of a woman's scream (though this sound should be altered by filters so it resembles other things, such as sirens). | *My leg (What's my leg?) feels wet arms . . . wet too, belly same chin nose everything (Where are they taking me?) something sticky (What has happened to my plane?) feel something sticky.* |
| | Of random noises recorded in a busy city hospital, then altered so as to be only minimally recognizable. | |
| *Nothing seen that is not a fragment. Every aspect of her world has been shattered.* | Of a car's engine at full speed. | *Doors! Too many doors!* |
| | Of a siren (altered to resemble a woman screaming). | *Must have . . . fallen cannot . . . move at all sky . . . (Gliding!) dark cannot . . . talk (Feel as if I'm gliding!).* |
| *Utter isolation.* | Of an airplane coming closer, thundering overhead, then zooming off into silence. | *Yes, feels cool, nice . . . Yes, this is the life all right!* |
| *In this vast whiteness, like apparitions, partial glimpses of doctors and nurses can be seen. They appear and disappear like a pulse. They are never in one place for long. The mirrors multiply their incomprehensibility.* | Of random crowd noises, the crowd greatly agitated. In the crowd, people can be heard calling for help, a doctor, an ambulance. But all the sounds are garbled. | *My plane! What has happened to my plane!* |
| | Of people whispering. | *Help . . .* |

**IMAGES**

*Sometimes the dark panels are opaque, sometimes transparent. Always, they convey a sense of layers, multiplicity, separation. Sense constantly of doors opening, closing, opening, closing.*

*Fragments of hospital equipment appear out of nowhere and disappear just as suddenly. Glimpse always too brief to enable us to identify what this equipment is, or what its purpose.*

MRS. STILSON's *movements seem random. She is a person wandering through space, lost.*

*Finally,* MRS. STILSON *is led by attendants downstage, to a chair. Then left alone.*

**SOUNDS OUTSIDE HERSELF**

Of many people asking questions simultaneously, no question comprehensible.

Of doors opening, closing, opening, closing.

Of someone breathing oxygen through a mask.

**VOICES:** *(garbled)* Just relax. / No one's going to hurt you. / Can you hear us? / Be careful. / You're hurting her! / No, we're not. / Don't lift her, leave her where she is! / Someone call an ambulance! / I don't think she can hear.

**MALE VOICE:** Have you any idea—

**OTHER VOICES:** *(garbled)* Do you know your name? / Do you know where you are? / What year is this? / If I say the tiger has been killed by the lion, which animal is dead?

A hospital paging system heard.

Equipment being moved through stone corridors, vast vaulting space. Endless echoing.

**MRS. STILSON'S VOICE**

*—all around faces of which nothing known no sense ever all wiped out blank like ice I think saw it once flying over something some place all was white sky and sea clouds ice almost crashed couldn't tell where I was heading right side up topsy-turvy under over I was flying actually if I can I do yes do recall was upside down can you believe it almost scraped my head on the ice caps couldn't tell which way was up wasn't even dizzy strange things happen to me that they do!*

*What's my name? I don't know my name!*

*Where's my arm? I don't have an arm!*

*What's an arm?*

*AB-ABC-ABC123DE451212 what? 123—12345678972357 better yes no problem I'm okay soon be out soon be over storm . . . will pass I'm sure. Always has.*

## AWAKENING

*In performance, the end of the Catastrophe section should blend, without interruption, into the beginning of this.*

MRS. STILSON DOWNSTAGE ON A CHAIR IN A POOL OF LIGHT, DARKNESS ALL AROUND HER. IN THE DISTANCE BEHIND HER, MUFFLED SOUNDS OF A HOSPITAL. VAGUE IMAGES OF DOCTORS, NURSES ATTENDING TO SOMEONE WE CANNOT SEE. ONE OF THE DOCTORS CALLS MRS. STILSON'S NAME. DOWNSTAGE, MRS. STILSON SHOWS NO TRACE OF RECOGNITION. THE DOCTOR CALLS HER NAME AGAIN. AGAIN NO RESPONSE. ONE OF THE DOCTORS SAYS, "IT'S POSSIBLE SHE MAY HEAR US BUT BE UNABLE TO RESPOND."

ONE OF THE NURSES TRIES CALLING OUT HER NAME. STILL NO RESPONSE. THE DOCTOR LEAVES. THE REMAINING DOCTORS AND NURSES FADE INTO THE DARKNESS.

ONLY MRS. STILSON CAN BE SEEN.

PAUSE.

**MRS. STILSON:** *Still . . . sun moon too or . . . three times happened maybe globbidged rubbidged uff and firded-forded me to nothing there try again* [WE HEAR A WINDOW BEING RAISED SOMEWHERE BEHIND HER] *window! up and heard* [SOUNDS OF BIRDS] *known them know I know* *them once upon a birds! that's it better getting better soon be out of this.*

PAUSE.

*Out of . . . what?*

PAUSE.

*Dark . . . space vast of . . . in I am or so it seems feels no real clues to speak of.* [BEHIND HER, BRIEF IMAGE OF A DOCTOR PASSING] *Something tells me I am not alone. Once! Lost it. No here back thanks work fast now, yes empty vast reach of space desert think they call it I'll come back to that anyhow down I . . . something what* [BRIEF IMAGE OF A NURSE] *it's SOMETHING ELSE IS ENTERING MY!—no wait got it crashing OH MY GOD! CRASHING! deadstick dead-of-night thought the stars were airport lights upside down was I what a way to land glad no one there to see it, anyhow tubbish blaxed and vinkled I commenshed to uh-oh where's it gone to somewhere flubbished what? with* [BRIEF IMAGES OF HOSPITAL STAFF ON THE MOVE] *images are SOMETHING ODD IS! . . . yes, then there I thank you crawling sands and knees still can feel it hear the wind all alone somehow wasn't scared why a mystery, vast dark track of space, we've all got to die that I know, anyhow then day came light came with it so with this you'd think you'd hope just hold on they will find me I am . . . still intact.*

PAUSE.

*In here.*

LONG SILENCE.

*Seem to be the word removed.*

LONG SILENCE.

*How long have I been here? . . . And wrapped in dark.*

PAUSE.

*Can remember nothing.*

OUTSIDE SOUNDS BEGIN TO IMPINGE; SAME FOR IMAGES. IN THE DISTANCE, AN ATTENDANT DIMLY SEEN PUSHING A FLOOR POLISHER. ITS NOISE RESEMBLES AN ANIMAL'S GROWL.

[TRYING HARD TO BE CHEERY]: *No, definitely I am not alone!*

THE SOUND OF THE POLISHER GROWS LOUDER, SEEMS MORE BESTIAL, VORACIOUS; IT OVERWHELMS EVERYTHING. EXPLOSION! SHE GASPS.

[RAPIDLY AND IN PANIC, SENSE OF GREAT COMMOTION BEHIND HER. A CRISIS HAS OCCURRED] *There I go there I go hallway now it's screaming crowded pokes me then the coolbreeze needle scent of sweetness can see palms flowers flummers couldn't fix the leaking sprouting everywhere to save me help me CUTS UP THROUGH to something movement I am something moving without movement!*

SOUND OF A WOMAN'S MUFFLED SCREAM FROM BEHIND HER. THE SCREAM GROWS LOUDER.

[WITH DELIGHT] *What a strange adventure I am having!*

LIGHTS TO BLACK ON EVERYTHING.

IN THE DARK, A PAUSE.

WHEN HER VOICE IS HEARD AGAIN, IT IS HEARD FIRST FROM ALL THE SPEAKERS. HER VOICE SOUNDS GROGGY, SLURRED. NO LONGER ANY SENSE OF PANIC DISCERNIBLE. A FEW MOMENTS AFTER HER VOICE IS HEARD, THE LIGHTS COME UP SLOWLY ON HER. SOON, ONLY SHE IS SPEAKING; THE VOICE FROM THE SPEAKERS HAS DISAPPEARED.

*Hapst aporkshop fleetish yes of course it's yes the good ol' times when we would mollis I mean collis all around still what my son's name is cannot for the life of me yet face gleams smiles as he tells them what I did but what his name is cannot see it pleasant anyway yes palms now ocean sea breeze wafting floating up and lifting holding weightless and goes swoooping down with me least I . . . think it's me.*

SOUND OF SOMETHING FLAPPING RAPIDLY OPEN AND CLOSED, OPEN AND CLOSED.

SOUND OF WIND.

LIGHTS CHANGE INTO A COOL AND AIRY BLUE. SENSE OF WEIGHTLESSNESS, SERENITY.

IN ANOTHER REALM NOW.

*Yes, out there walking not holding even danger everpresent how I loved it love it still no doubt will again hear them cheering wisht or waltz away to some place like Rumania . . .*

THE WIND DISAPPEARS.

*Nothing . . .*

THE SERENE BLUE LIGHT BEGINS TO FADE AWAY. SOME PLACE ELSE NOW THAT SHE IS GOING.

*Of course beyond that yet 1, 2 came before the yeast rose bubbled and MY CHUTE DIDN'T OPEN PROPERLY! Still for a girl did wonders getting down and it was Charles! no Charlie, who is Charlie? see him smiling as they tell him what I—*

OUTSIDE WORLD BEGINS TO IMPINGE. LIGHTS ARE CHANGING, GROWING BRIGHTER, SOMETHING ODD IS HAPPENING. SENSE OF IMMINENCE. SHE NOTICES.

[BREATHLESS WITH EXCITEMENT]: *Stop hold cut stop wait stop come-out-break-out light can see it ready heart can yes can feel it pounding something underway here light is getting brighter lids I think the word is that's it lifting of their own but slowly knew I should be patient should be what? wait hold on steady now it's spreading no no question something underway here spreading brighter rising lifting light almost yes can almost there a little more now yes can almost see this . . . place I'm . . . in and . . .*

LOOK OF HORROR.

*Oh my God! Now I understand! THEY'VE GOT ME!*

FOR THE FIRST TIME DOCTORS, NURSES, HOSPITAL EQUIPMENT ALL CLEARLY VISIBLE BEHIND HER. ALL ARE GATHERED AROUND SOMEONE WE CANNOT SEE. FROM THE WAY THEY ARE ALL BENDING OVER, WE SURMISE THIS PERSON WE CANNOT SEE IS LYING IN A BED.

LIGHTS DROP ON MRS. STILSON, DOWNSTAGE.

**NURSE:** [TALKING TO THE PERSON UPSTAGE WE CANNOT SEE] Mrs. Stilson, can you open up your eyes?

PAUSE.

**MRS. STILSON:** [SEPARATED FROM HER QUESTIONERS BY GREAT DISTANCE] *Don't know how.*

**DOCTOR:** Mrs. Stilson, you just opened up your eyes. We saw you. Can you open them again?

NO RESPONSE.

Mrs. Stilson . . .?

**MRS. STILSON:** [PROUDLY, TRIUMPHANTLY] *My name then—Mrs. Stilson!*

**VOICE ON A P.A. SYSTEM:** Mrs. Howard, call on three! Mrs. Howard . . . !

**MRS. STILSON:** *My name then—Mrs. Howard?*

LIGHTS FADE TO BLACK ON HOSPITAL STAFF.

SOUND OF WIND, SENSE OF TIME PASSING.

LIGHTS COME UP ON MRS. STILSON. THE WIND DISAPPEARS.

*The room that I am in is large, square. What does large mean?*

PAUSE.

*The way I'm turned I can see a window. When I'm on my back the window isn't there.*

**DOCTOR:** [IN THE DISTANCE, AT BEST ONLY DIMLY SEEN] Mrs. Stilson, can you hear me?

**MRS. STILSON:** *Yes.*

**SECOND DOCTOR:** Mrs. Stilson, can you hear me?

**MRS. STILSON:** *Yes! I said yes! What's wrong with you?*

**FIRST DOCTOR:** Mrs. Stilson, CAN YOU HEAR ME!

**MRS. STILSON:** *Don't believe this—I've been put in with the deaf!*

**SECOND DOCTOR:** Mrs. Stilson, if you can hear us, nod your head.

**MRS. STILSON:** *All right, fine, that's how you want to play it—there!*

SHE NODS.

THE DOCTORS EXCHANGE GLANCES.

**FIRST DOCTOR:** Mrs. Stilson, if you can hear us, NOD YOUR HEAD!

**MRS. STILSON:** *Oh my God, this is grotesque!*

CACOPHONY OF SOUNDS HEARD FROM ALL AROUND, BOTH LIVE AND FROM THE SPEAKERS. IMAGES SUGGESTING SENSATION OF ASSAULT AS WELL.

IMPLICATION OF ALL THESE SOUNDS AND IMAGES IS THAT MRS. STILSON IS BEING MOVED THROUGH THE HOSPITAL FOR PURPOSES OF EXAMINATION, PERHAPS EVEN TORTURE. THE INFORMATION WE RECEIVE COMES IN TOO FAST AND DISTORTED FOR RATIONAL COMPREHENSION. THE REALM SHE IS IN IS TERRIFYING. FORTUNATELY, SHE IS NOT IN IT LONG.

AS LONG AS SHE IS, HOWEVER, THE SENSE SHOULD BE CONVEYED THAT HER WORLD MOVES AROUND HER MORE THAN SHE THROUGH IT.

**WHAT WE HEAR (THE COMPONENTS):** Are we moving you too fast? / Mustlian potid or blastigrate, no not that way this, that's fletchit gottit careful now. / Now put your nose here on this line, would you? That's it, thank you, well done, well done. / How are the wickets today? / [SOUND OF A COUGH] / Now close your— / Is my finger going up or— / Can you feel this? / Can you feel this? / Name something that grows on trees. / Who fixes teeth? What room do you cook in? What year is this? / How long have you been here? / Are we being too rippled shotgun? / Would you like a cup of tea? / What is Jim short for? / Point to your shoulder. / No, your shoulder. / What do you do with a book? / Don't worry, the water's warm. We're holding you, don't worry. In we go, that's a girl!

AND THEN, AS SUDDENLY AS THE ASSAULT BEGAN, IT IS OVER.

ONCE AGAIN, MRS. STILSON ALL ALONE ON STAGE, DARKNESS ALL AROUND HER, NO SENSE OF WALLS OR FURNITURE. UTTER ISOLATION.

**MRS. STILSON:** [TRYING HARD TO KEEP SMILING] *Yes, all in all I'd say while things could be better could be worse, far worse, how? Not quite sure. Just a sense I have. The sort of sense that only great experience can mallees or rake, plake I mean, flake . . . Drake! That's it.*

SHE STARES INTO SPACE.

SILENCE.

IN THE DISTANCE BEHIND HER, TWO DOCTORS APPEAR.

**FIRST DOCTOR:** Mrs. Stilson, who was the first President of the United States?

**MRS. STILSON:** *Washington.*

PAUSE.

**SECOND DOCTOR:** [SPEAKING MORE SLOWLY THAN THE FIRST DOCTOR DID; PERHAPS SHE SIMPLY DIDN'T HEAR THE QUESTION] Mrs. Stilson, who was the first President of the United States?

**MRS. STILSON:** *Washington!*

**SECOND DOCTOR:** [TO FIRST] I don't think she hears herself.

**FIRST DOCTOR:** No, I don't think she hears herself.

THE TWO DOCTORS EMERGE FROM THE SHADOWS, APPROACH MRS. STILSON. SHE LOOKS UP IN TERROR. THIS SHOULD BE THE FIRST TIME THAT THE WOMAN ON STAGE HAS BEEN DIRECTLY FACED OR CONFRONTED BY THE HOSPITAL STAFF. HER INNER AND OUTER WORLDS ARE BEGINNING TO COME TOGETHER.

**FIRST DOCTOR:** Mrs. Stilson, makey your naming powers?

**MRS. STILSON:** What?

**SECOND DOCTOR:** Canju spokeme?

**MRS. STILSON:** Can I what?

**FIRST DOCTOR:** Can do peeperear?

**MRS. STILSON:** *Don't believe what's going on!*

**SECOND DOCTOR:** Ahwill.

**FIRST DOCTOR:** Pollycadjis.

**SECOND DOCTOR:** Sewyladda?

**FIRST DOCTOR:** [WITH A NOD] Hm-hm.

EXIT DOCTORS.

**MRS. STILSON:** [ALONE AGAIN] *How it came to pass that I was captured!* [SHE PONDERS] *Hard to say really. I'll come back to that.*

PAUSE.

*The room that I've been put in this time is quite small, square, what does square mean? . . . Means . . .*

SENSE OF TIME PASSING. THE LIGHTS SHIFT. THE SPACE SHE IS IN BEGINS TO CHANGE ITS SHAPE.

*Of course morning comes I think . . .* [SHE PONDERS] *Yes, and night of course comes . . .* [PONDERS MORE] *Though sometimes . . .*

MRS. STILSON SOME PLACE ELSE NOW. AND SHE IS AWARE OF IT.

*Yes, the way the walls choose to move around me . . . Yes, I've noticed that, I'm no fool!*

A NURSE APPEARS CARRYING A DAZZLING BOUQUET OF FLOWERS. THIS BOUQUET IS THE FIRST REAL COLOR WE HAVE SEEN.

**NURSE:** Good morning! Look what somebody's just sent you! [SHE SETS THEM ON A TABLE] Wish I had as many admirers as you.

EXIT NURSE, SMILING WARMLY.

MRS. STILSON'S EYES ARE DRAWN TO THE FLOWERS. AND SOMETHING ABOUT THEM APPARENTLY RENDERS IT IMPOSSIBLE FOR HER TO SHIFT HER GAZE AWAY. SOMETHING ABOUT THESE FLOWERS HAS HER IN THEIR THRALL.

WHAT IT IS IS THEIR COLOR.

IT IS AS IF SHE HAS NEVER EXPERIENCED COLOR BEFORE. AND THE EXPERIENCE IS SO OVERWHELMING, BOTH PHYSIOLOGICALLY AND PSYCHOLOGICALLY, THAT HER BRAIN CANNOT PROCESS ALL THE INFORMATION. HER CIRCUITRY IS OVERLOADED. IT IS TOO MUCH SENSORY INPUT FOR HER TO HANDLE. AN EXPLOSION IS IMMINENT. IF SOMETHING DOES NOT INTERVENE TO DIVERT HER ATTENTION, MRS. STILSON WILL VERY LIKELY FAINT, PERHAPS EVEN SUFFER A SEIZURE.

A NARROW BEAM OF LIGHT, GROWING STEADILY IN INTENSITY, FALLS UPON THE BOUQUET OF FLOWERS, CAUSING THEIR COLORS TO TAKE ON AN INTENSITY THEMSELVES THAT THEY OTHERWISE WOULD LACK. AT THE SAME TIME, A SINGLE MUSICAL TONE IS HEARD, VOLUME INCREASING.

A NURSE ENTERS THE ROOM.

**NURSE:** May I get you something?

**MRS. STILSON:** [ABSTRACTED, EYES REMAINING ON THE FLOWERS] Yes, a sweater.

**NURSE:** Yes, of course. Think we have one here. [THE NURSE OPENS A DRAWER, TAKES OUT A PILLOW, HANDS THE PILLOW TO MRS. STILSON] Here.

MRS. STILSON ACCEPTS THE PILLOW UNQUESTIONINGLY, EYES NEVER LEAVING THE FLOWERS. SHE LAYS THE PILLOW ON HER LAP, PROMPTLY FORGETS ABOUT IT. THE MUSICAL TONE AND THE BEAM OF LIGHT CONTINUE RELENTLESSLY TOWARD THEIR PEAK.

THE NURSE, OBLIVIOUS OF ANY CRISIS, EXITS.

THE SINGLE TONE AND THE BEAM OF LIGHT CREST TOGETHER.

SILENCE FOLLOWS. THE BEAM DISAPPEARS. THE FLOWERS SEEM NORMAL. THE LIGHTS AROUND MRS. STILSON RETURN TO THE WAY THEY WERE BEFORE THE GIFT OF FLOWERS WAS BROUGHT IN.

**MRS. STILSON:** [SHAKEN] *This is not a hospital of course, and I know it! What it is is a farmhouse made up to look like a hospital. Why? I'll come back to that.*

ENTER ANOTHER NURSE.

**NURSE:** Hi! Haven't seen you in a while. Have you missed me?

**MRS. STILSON:** [NO HINT OF RECOGNITION VISIBLE] What?

**NURSE:** [WARMLY] They say you didn't touch your dinner. Would you like some pudding?

**MRS. STILSON:** No.

**NURSE:** Good, I'll go get you some.

EXIT NURSE, VERY CHEERFULLY.

**MRS. STILSON:** *Yes no question they have got me I've been what that word was captured is it? No it's—Yes, it's captured how? Near as it can figure. I was in my prane and crashed, not unusual, still in all not too common. Neither is it very grub. Plexit rather or I'd say propopic. Well that's that, jungdaball! Anyhow to resume, what I had for lunch? That's not it, good books I have read, good what, done what? Whaaaaat? Do the busy here! Get inside this, rubbidge all around let the vontul do some yes off or it of above semilacrum pwooosh! What with noddygobbit nip-n-crashing inside outside witsit watchit funnel vortex sucking into backlash watchit get-out caught-in spinning ring-grab grobbit help woooosh! cannot stoppit on its own has me where it wants* [AND SUDDENLY SHE IS IN ANOTHER REALM. LIGHTS TRANSFORMED INTO WEIGHTLESS BLUE. SENSE OF EASE AND SERENITY] *Plane! See it thanks, okay, onto back we were and here it is. Slow down easy now. Captured. After crashing, that is what we said or was about to, think it so, cannot tell for sure, slow it slow it, okay here we go . . .* [SPEAKING SLOWER NOW] *captured after crashing by the enemy and brought here to this farm masquerading as a hospital. Why? For I would say offhand information. Of what sort though hard to* *tell. For example, questions such as can I raise my fingers, what's an overcoat, how many nickels in a rhyme, questions such as these. To what use can they be to the enemy? Hard to tell from here. Nonetheless, I would say must be certain information I possess that they want well I won't give it I'll escape! Strange things happen to me that they do! Good thing I'm all right! Must be in Rumania. Just a hunch of course.* [THE SERENE BLUE LIGHT STARTS TO FADE] *Ssssh, someone's coming.*

A NURSE HAS ENTERED. THE NURSE GUIDES MRS. STILSON TO A DOCTOR. THE BLUE LIGHT IS GONE. THE NURSE LEAVES.

THE SPACE MRS. STILSON NOW IS IN APPEARS MUCH MORE "REAL" AND LESS FRAGMENTARY THAN WHAT WE HAVE SO FAR BEEN OBSERVING. WE SEE MRS. STILSON HERE AS OTHERS SEE HER.

**DOCTOR:** Mrs. Stilson, if you don't mind, I'd like to ask you some questions. Some will be easy, some will be hard. Is that all right?

**MRS. STILSON:** Oh yes I'd say oh well yes that's the twither of it.

**DOCTOR:** Good. Okay. Where were you born?

**MRS. STILSON:** Never. Not at all. Here the match wundles up you know and drats flames fires I keep careful always—

**DOCTOR:** Right . . . [SPEAKING VERY SLOWLY, PRECISE ENUNCIATION] Where were you born?

**MRS. STILSON:** Well now well now that's a good thing knowing yushof course wouldn't call it such as I did andinjurations or aplovia could it? No I wouldn't think so. Next?

PAUSE.

**DOCTOR:** Mrs. Stilson, are there seven days in a week?

**MRS. STILSON:** . . . Seven . . . Yes.

**DOCTOR:** Are there five days in a week?

PAUSE.

**MRS. STILSON:** [AFTER MUCH PONDERING] No.

**DOCTOR:** Can a stone float on water?

LONG PAUSE.

**MRS. STILSON:** No.

**DOCTOR:** Mrs. Stilson, can you cough?

**MRS. STILSON:** Somewhat.

**DOCTOR:** Well, would you show me how you cough?

**MRS. STILSON:** Well now well now not so easy what you cromplie is to put these bushes open and—

**DOCTOR:** No no Mrs. Stilson, I'm sorry—I would like to hear you cough.

**MRS. STILSON:** Well I'm not bort you know with plajits or we'd see it wencherday she brings its pillow with the fistils-opening I'd say outward always outward never stopping it.

LONG SILENCE.

**DOCTOR:** Mrs. Stilson, I have some objects here. [HE TAKES A COMB, A TOOTHBRUSH, A PACK OF MATCHES, AND A KEY FROM HIS POCKET, SETS THEM DOWN WHERE SHE CAN SEE] Could you point to the object you would use for cleaning your teeth?

VERY LONG SILENCE.

FINALLY SHE PICKS UP THE COMB AND SHOWS IT TO HIM. THEN SHE PUTS IT DOWN. WAITS.

Mrs. Stilson, here, take this object in your hand. [HE HANDS HER THE TOOTHBRUSH] Do you know what this object is called?

**MRS. STILSON:** [WITH GREAT DIFFICULTY] Tooooooooovvvv . . . bbrum?

**DOCTOR:** Very good. Now put it down.

SHE PUTS IT DOWN.

Now, pretend you have it in your hand. Show me what you'd do with it.

SHE DOES NOTHING.

What does one do with an object such as that, Mrs. Stilson?

NO RESPONSE.

Mrs. Stilson, what is the name of the object you are looking at?

**MRS. STILSON:** Well it's . . . wombly and not at all . . . rigged or tuned like we might twunter or toring to work the clambness out of it or—

**DOCTOR:** Pick it up.

**MRS. STILSON:** [AS SOON AS SHE'S PICKED IT UP] Tooovebram, tooove-britch bratch brush bridge, two-bridge.

**DOCTOR:** Show me what you do with it.

FOR SEVERAL MOMENTS SHE DOES NOTHING.

THEN SHE PUTS IT TO HER LIPS, HOLDS IT THERE MOTIONLESS.

Very good. Thank you.

SHE SIGHS HEAVILY, PUTS IT DOWN.

THE DOCTOR GATHERS UP HIS OBJECTS, LEAVES.

ONCE AGAIN MRS. STILSON ALL ALONE.

SHE STARES INTO SPACE.

THEN HER VOICE IS HEARD COMING FROM ALL AROUND; SHE HERSELF DOES NOT SPEAK.

**HER VOICE:** *Dark now again out the window on my side lying here all alone . . .*

VERY LONG SILENCE.

**MRS. STILSON:** *Yesterday my children came to see me.*

PAUSE.

*Or at least, I was told they were my children. Never saw them before in my life.*

SHE STARES OUT, MOTIONLESS. NO EXPRESSION.

THEN AFTER A WHILE SHE LOOKS AROUND. STUDIES THE DARK FOR CLUES.

*Time has become peculiar.*

AND SHE CONTINUES THIS SCRUTINY OF THE DARK.

BUT IF THIS ACTIVITY STEMS FROM CURIOSITY, IT IS A MILD CURIOSITY AT MOST. NO LONGER DOES SHE CONVEY OR PROBABLY EVEN EXPERIENCE THE EXTREME, DISORIENTED DREAD WE SAW EARLIER WHEN SHE FIRST ARRIVED IN THIS NEW REALM. HER SENSE OF URGENCY IS GONE. INDEED, WERE WE ABLE TO OBSERVE MRS. STILSON CONSTANTLY, WE WOULD INEVITABLY CONCLUDE THAT HER CURIOSITY IS NOW ONLY MINIMALLY PURPOSEFUL; THAT, IN FACT, MORE LIKELY HER INVESTIGATIONS ARE THE ACTIONS, POSSIBLY MERELY THE REFLEX ACTIONS, OF SOMEONE WITH LITTLE OR NOTHING ELSE TO DO.

THIS IS NOT TO DENY THAT SHE IS DESPERATELY TRYING TO PIECE HER SHATTERED WORLD TOGETHER. UNDOUBTEDLY, IT IS THE DOMINANT MOTIF IN HER MIND. BUT IT IS A MOTIF PROBABLY MORE ABSENT FROM HER CONSCIOUSNESS THAN PRESENT, AND THE QUEST IT INSPIRES IS INTERMITTENT AT BEST. HER MENTAL ABILITIES HAVE NOT ONLY BEEN SEVERELY ALTERED, THEY HAVE BEEN DIMINISHED: THAT IS THE TERRIBLE FACT ONE CANNOT DENY.

AND THEN SUDDENLY SHE IS AGITATED.

*Mother! . . . didn't say as she usually . . .*

PAUSE.

*And I thought late enough or early rather first light coming so when didn't move I poked her then with shoving but she didn't even eyes or giggle when I tickled.*

PAUSE.

*What it was was not a trick as I at first had—*

PAUSE.

*Well I couldn't figure, he had never lied, tried to get her hold me couldn't it was useless. Then his face was, I had never known a face could . . . It was like a mask then like sirens it was bursting open it was him then I too joining it was useless. Can still feel what it was like when she held me.*

PAUSE.

*So then well I was on my own. He was all destroyed, had I think they say no strength for this.*

THEN SHE'S SILENT. NO EXPRESSION. STARES INTO SPACE.

ENTER A DOCTOR AND A NURSE.

**DOCTOR:** [WARMLY] Hello Mrs. Stilson.

HE COMES OVER NEXT TO HER. WE CANNOT TELL IF SHE NOTICES HIM OR NOT. THE NURSE, CHART IN HAND, STANDS A SLIGHT DISTANCE AWAY.

You're looking much, much better. [HE SMILES AND SITS DOWN NEXT TO HER. HE WATCHES HER FOR SEVERAL MOMENTS, SEARCHING FOR SIGNS OF RECOGNITION] Mrs. Stilson, do you know why you're here?

**MRS. STILSON:** Well now well now . . .

SHE GIVES IT UP.

SILENCE.

**DOCTOR:** You have had an accident—

| **MRS. STILSON:** [HER WORDS OVERPOWERING HIS] | **DOCTOR:** [TO ALL INTENTS AND PURPOSES, WHAT HE SAYS IS LOST] |
|---|---|
| *I don't trust him, don't trust anyone. Must get word out, send a message where I am. Like a wall between me and others. No one ever gets it right even though I tell them right. They are playing tricks on me, two sides, both not my friends, goes in goes out too fast too fast hurts do the busy I'm all right I talk right why acting all these others like I don't, what's he marking, what's he writing?* | At home. Not in an airplane. It's called a stroke. This means that your brain has been injured and brain tissue destroyed, though we are not certain of the cause. You could get better, and you're certainly making progress. But it's still too soon to give any sort of exact prognosis. [HE STUDIES HER. THEN HE RISES AND MARKS SOMETHING ON HIS CLIPBOARD] |

EXIT DOCTOR AND NURSE.

**MRS. STILSON:** *I am doing well of course!*

PAUSE.

[SECRETIVE TONE] *They still pretend they do not understand me. I believe they may be mad.*

PAUSE.

*No they're not mad, I am mad. Today I heard it. Everything I speak is wronged. SOMETHING HAS BEEN DONE TO ME!*

**DOCTOR:** [BARELY VISIBLE IN THE DISTANCE] Mrs. Stilson, can you repeat this phrase: "We live across the street from the school."

SHE PONDERS.

**MRS. STILSON:** "Malacats on the forturay are the kesterfats of the romancers."

LOOK OF HORROR COMES ACROSS HER FACE; THE DOCTOR VANISHES.

THROUGH THE SCREENS, UPSTAGE, WE SEE A NURSE BRINGING ON A TRAY OF FOOD.

**NURSE:** [BRIGHTLY] Okay ups-a-girl, ups-a-baby, dinnertime! Open wide now, mustn't go dribble-dribble—at's-a-way!

MRS. STILSON SCREAMS, SWINGING HER ARMS IN FURY. IN THE DISTANCE, UPSTAGE, THE TRAY OF FOOD GOES FLYING.

**MRS. STILSON:** [SCREAMING] Out! Get out! Take this shit away! I don't want it! Someone get me out of here!

**NURSE:** [WHILE MRS. STILSON CONTINUES SHOUTING] Help, someone, come quick! She's talking! Good as you or me! It's a miracle! Help! Somebody! Come quick!

WHILE MRS. STILSON CONTINUES TO SCREAM AND FLAIL HER ARMS, NURSES AND DOCTORS RUSH ON UPSTAGE AND SURROUND THE PATIENT WE NEVER SEE.

AND ALTHOUGH MRS. STILSON CONTINUES TO SCREAM COHERENTLY, IN FACT SHE ISN'T ANY BETTER, NO MIRACLE HAS OCCURRED. HER ABILITY TO ARTICULATE WITH APPARENT NORMALCY HAS BEEN BROUGHT ON BY EXTREME AGITATION AND IN NO WAY IMPLIES THAT SHE COULD PRODUCE THESE SOUNDS AGAIN "IF SHE ONLY WANTED"; WILL POWER HAS NOTHING TO DO WITH WHAT WE HEAR.

HER LANGUAGE, AS IT MUST, SOON SLIPS BACK INTO JARGON. SHE CONTINUES TO FLAIL HER ARMS. IN THE BACKGROUND, WE CAN SEE A NURSE PREPARING A HYPODERMIC.

**MRS. STILSON:**—[STRUGGLING] flubdgy please no-mommy-callming holdmeplease to sleeEEEEP SHOOOOP shop shnoper CRROOOOOCK SNANNNNG wuduitcoldly should I gobbin flutter truly HELP ME yessisnofun, snofun, wishes awhin dahd killminsilf if . . . could [IN THE DISTANCE, WE SEE THE NEEDLE GIVEN] OW! . . . would I but . . . [SHE'S BECOMING DROWSY] . . . awful to me him as well moas of all no cantduit . . . jusscantduit . . .

HEAD DROPS.

INTO SLEEP SHE GOES.

EXIT DOCTORS, NURSES.

SOUND OF A GENTLE WIND IS HEARD.

LIGHTS FADE TO BLACK ON MRS. STILSON.

DARKNESS EVERYWHERE; THE SOUND OF THE WIND FADES AWAY.

SILENCE.

LIGHTS UP ON AMY, DOWNSTAGE RIGHT.

THEN LIGHTS UP ON MRS. STILSON STARING INTO SPACE.

**AMY:** Mrs. Stilson?

MRS. STILSON TURNS TOWARD THE SOUND, SEES AMY.

You have had what's called a stroke.

CHANGE OF LIGHTS AND PANELS OPEN. SENSE OF TERRIBLE ENCLOSURE GONE. BIRDS HEARD. WE ARE OUTSIDE NOW. AMY PUTS A SHAWL AROUND MRS. STILSON'S SHOULDERS.

**AMY:** Are you sure that will be enough?

**MRS. STILSON:** Oh yes . . . thhhankyou.

SHE TUCKS THE SHAWL AROUND HERSELF.

THEN AMY GUIDES HER THROUGH THE PANELS AS IF THROUGH CORRIDORS; NO RUSH, SLOW GENTLE STROLL.

THEY EMERGE OTHER SIDE OF STAGE. WARM LIGHT. AMY TAKES IN THE VIEW. MRS. STILSON APPEARS INDIFFERENT.

**AMY:** Nice to be outside, isn't it? . . . Nice view.

**MRS. STILSON:** [STILL WITH INDIFFERENCE] Yes indeed.

THERE ARE TWO CHAIRS NEARBY, AND THEY SIT.

SILENCE FOR A TIME.

**AMY:** Are you feeling any better today?

BUT SHE GETS NO RESPONSE.

THEN A MOMENT LATER, MRS. STILSON TURNS TO AMY; IT IS AS IF AMY'S QUESTION HAS NOT EVEN BEEN HEARD.

**MRS. STILSON:** The thing is . . .

BUT THE STATEMENT TRAILS OFF INTO NOTHINGNESS.

SHE STARES OUT, NO EXPRESSION.

**AMY:** Yes? What?

LONG SILENCE.

**MRS. STILSON:** I can't make it do it like it used to.

**AMY:** Yes, I know. That's because of the accident.

**MRS. STILSON:** [SEEMINGLY OBLIVIOUS OF AMY'S WORDS] The words, they go in sometimes then out they go, I can't stop them here inside or make maybe globbidge to the tubberway or—

**AMY:** Emily. Emily!

**MRS. STILSON:** [SHAKEN OUT OF HERSELF] . . . What?

**AMY:** Did you hear what you just said?

**MRS. STILSON:** . . . Why?

**AMY:** [SPEAKING SLOWLY] You must listen to what you're saying.

**MRS. STILSON:** Did I . . . do . . .

**AMY:** [NODDING, SMILING; CLEARLY NO REPROACH INTENDED] Slow down. Listen to what you're saying.

SILENCE.

**MRS. STILSON:** [SLOWER] The thing is . . . doing all this busy in here gets, you know with the talking it's like . . . sometimes when I hear here [SHE TOUCHES HER HEAD] . . . but when I start to . . . kind more what kind of voice should . . . it's like pfffft! [SHE MAKES A GESTURE WITH HER HAND OF SOMETHING FLYING AWAY]

**AMY:** [SMILING] Yes, I know. It's hard to find the words for what you're thinking of.

**MRS. STILSON:** Well yes.

LONG PAUSE.

And then these people, they keep waiting . . . And I see they're smiling and . . . they keep . . . waiting . . . [FAINT SMILE, HELPLESS GESTURE. SHE STARES OFF]

LONG SILENCE.

**AMY:** Emily.

MRS. STILSON LOOKS UP.

Can you remember anything about your life . . . before the accident?

**MRS. STILSON:** Not sometimes, some days it goes better if I see a thing or smell . . . it . . . remembers me back, you see? And I see things that maybe they were me and maybe they were just some things you know that happens in the night when you . . . [STRUGGLING VISIBLY] have your things closed, eyes.

**AMY:** A dream you mean.

**MRS. STILSON:** [WITH RELIEF] Yes. So I don't know for sure.

PAUSE.

If it was really me.

LONG SILENCE.

**AMY:** Your son is bringing a picture of you when you were younger. We thought you might like that.

NO VISIBLE RESPONSE. LONG SILENCE.

You used to fly, didn't you?

**MRS. STILSON:** [BRIGHTLY] Oh yes indeed! Very much! I walked . . . out . . .

PAUSE.

[SOFTLY, PROUDLY] I walked out on wings.

LIGHTS FADE ON AMY. MRS. STILSON ALONE AGAIN.

*Sitting here on my bed I can close my eyes shut out all that I can't do with, hearing my own talking, others, names that used to well just be there when I wanted now all somewhere else. No control. Close my eyes then, go to—*

SOUND OF SOMETHING FLAPPING RAPIDLY.

A FIBRILLATION.

LIGHTS BECOME BLUE. SENSE OF WEIGHTLESSNESS. SERENITY.

*Here I go. No one talks here. Images coming I seem feel it feels better this way here is how it goes: this time I am still in the middle Stilson in the middle going out walking out wind feels good hold the wires feel the hum down below far there they are now we turn it bank it now we spin! Looks more bad than really is, still needs good balance and those nerves and that thing that courage thing don't fall off! . . . And now I'm out . . . and back and . . .* [WITH SURPRISE] *there's the window.*

LIGHTS HAVE RETURNED TO NORMAL. SHE IS BACK WHERE SHE STARTED.

AMY ENTERS.

**AMY:** Hello, Emily.

**MRS. STILSON:** Oh, Amy! . . . Didn't hear what you was . . . coming here to . . . Oh!

**AMY:** What is it?

**MRS. STILSON:** Something . . . wet.

**AMY:** Do you know what it is?

**MRS. STILSON:** Don't . . . can't say find it word.

**AMY:** Try. You can find it.

**MRS. STILSON:** Wet . . . thing, many, both sides yes.

**AMY:** Can you name them? What they are? You do know what they are.

PAUSE.

**MRS. STILSON:** . . . Tears?

**AMY:** That's right, very good. Those are tears. And do you know what that means?

**MRS. STILSON:** . . . Sad?

**AMY:** Yes, right, well done, it means . . . that you are sad.

## EXPLORATIONS

STAGE DARK.

IN THE DARK, A PIANO HEARD: SOMEONE FOOLING AROUND ON THE KEYBOARD, BRIEF HALTING SNATCHES OF OLD SONGS EMERGING AS THE PRODUCT; WOULD CONSTITUTE A MEDLEY WERE THE SEGMENTS ONLY LONGER, MORE COHESIVE. AS IT IS, SUSPICION AROUSED THAT WHAT WE HEAR IS ALL THE PIANIST CAN REMEMBER.

SOUND OF GENERAL LAUGHTER, HUBBUB.

LIGHTS RISE.

WHAT WE SEE IS A REC ROOM, IN SOME PLACES CLEARLY, IN OTHERS NOT (THE ROOM BEING OBSERVED PARTLY THROUGH THE DARK SCRIM PANELS).

UPSTAGE RIGHT, AN UPRIGHT PIANO, PLAYERS AND FRIENDS GATHERED ROUND. DOCTORS, THERAPISTS, NURSES, ATTENDANTS, PATIENTS, VISITORS CERTAINLY ARE NOT ALL SEEN, BUT THOSE WE DO SEE COME FROM SUCH A GROUP. WE ARE IN THE REC ROOM OF A REHABILITATION CENTER. SOME PATIENTS IN WHEELCHAIRS.

THE ROOM ITSELF HAS BRIGHT COMFORTABLE CHAIRS, PERHAPS A CARD TABLE, MAG-

AZINE RACK, CERTAINLY A TV SET. SOMEONE NOW TURNS ON THE TV.

WHAT EMERGES IS THE SOUND OF ELLA FITZGERALD IN LIVE PERFORMANCE. SHE SINGS SCAT: MELLOW, UPBEAT.

THE PATIENTS AND STAFF PERSUADE THE PIANIST TO CEASE. ELLA'S RIFFS OF SCAT CAST SOMETHING LIKE A SPELL.

MRS. STILSON WANDERS THROUGH THE SPACE.

THE REC ROOM, IT SHOULD BE STRESSED, SHOWS MORE DETAIL AND COLOR THAN ANY SPACE WE'VE SO FAR SEEN. PERHAPS A VASE OF FLOWERS HELPS TO SIGNAL THAT MRS. STILSON'S WORLD IS BECOMING FULLER, MORE INTEGRATED.

MOVEMENTS TOO SEEM NORMAL, SAME FOR CONVERSATIONS THAT GO ON DURING ALL OF THIS, THOUGH TOO SOFTLY FOR US TO COMPREHEND.

THE MUSIC OF COURSE SETS THE TONE. ALL WHO LISTEN ARE IN ITS THRALL.

NEW TIME SENSE HERE, A LANGUOR ALMOST. THE DREAD MRS. STILSON FELT HAS BEEN REPLACED BY AN ACKNOWLEDGMENT OF HER CONDITION, THOUGH NOT AN UNDERSTANDING.

IN THIS TIME BEFORE SHE SPEAKS, AND IN FACT DURING, WE OBSERVE THE LIFE OF THE REC ROOM BEHIND AND AROUND HER. THIS IS NOT A HOSPITAL ANY MORE, AND A KIND OF NORMALCY PREVAILS.

THE SENSE SHOULD BE CONVEYED OF CORRIDORS LEADING TO AND FROM THIS ROOM.

THEN THE MUSIC AND THE REC ROOM SOUNDS GROW DIM; MRS. STILSON COMES FORWARD, LOST IN THE DRIFTS OF A THOUGHT.

**MRS. STILSON:** [RELAXED, MELLOW] *Wonder . . . what's inside of it . . .?*

PAUSE.

*I mean, how does it work? What's inside that . . . makes it work?*

LONG PAUSE. SHE PONDERS.

*I mean when you . . . think about it all . . .*

PAUSE.

*And when you think that it could . . . ever have been . . . possible to . . . be another way . . .*

SHE PONDERS.

BUT IT'S HARD FOR HER TO KEEP IN MIND WHAT SHE'S BEEN THINKING OF, AND SHE HAS TO FIGHT THE NOISE OF THE REC ROOM, ITS INTRUSIVE PRESENCE. LIKE A NOVICE JUGGLER, MRS. STILSON IS UNABLE TO KEEP OUTSIDE IMAGES AND INNER THOUGHTS GOING SIMULTANEOUSLY. WHEN SHE'S WITH HER THOUGHTS, THE OUTSIDE WORLD FADES AWAY. WHEN THE OUTSIDE WORLD IS WITH HER, HER THOUGHTS FADE AWAY.

BUT SHE FIGHTS HER WAY THROUGH IT, AND KEEPS THE THOUGHT IN MIND.

THE REC ROOM, WHOSE NOISE HAS JUST INCREASED, GROWS QUIET.

*Maybe . . . if somehow I could*—[SHE SEARCHES FOR THE WORDS THAT MATCH HER CONCEPT]—*get inside . . .*

PAUSE.

SOUNDS OF THE REC ROOM PULSE LOUDER. SHE FIGHTS AGAINST IT. THE REC ROOM SOUNDS DIMINISH.

*Prob'ly . . . very dark inside . . .* [SHE PONDERS; TRIES TO PICTURE WHAT SHE'S THINKING] *Yes . . . twisting kind of place I bet . . .* [PONDERS MORE] *With lots of . . .* [SHE SEARCHES FOR THE PROPER WORD; FINDS IT] *. . . passageways that . . . lead to . . .* [AGAIN, SHE SEARCHES FOR THE WORD]

THE OUTSIDE WORLD RUSHES IN.

**PATIENT IN A WHEELCHAIR:** [ONLY BARELY AUDIBLE] My foot feels sour.

AN ATTENDANT PUTS A LAP RUG OVER THE PATIENT'S LIMBS. THEN THE REC ROOM, ONCE AGAIN, FADES AWAY.

**MRS. STILSON:** [FIGHTING ON] *. . . lead to . . . something . . . Door! Yes . . . closed off now I . . . guess possib . . . ly for good I mean . . . forever, what does that mean?* [SHE PONDERS]

**ATTENDANT:** Would you like some candy?

**MRS. STILSON:** No.

**ATTENDANT:** Billy made it.

**MRS. STILSON:** No!

THE ATTENDANT MOVES BACK INTO THE SHADOWS.

*Where was I?* [SHE LOOKS AROUND] *Why can't they just . . . let me . . . be when I'm . . .*

LIGHTS START TO CHANGE. HER WORLD SUDDENLY IN FLUX. THE REC ROOM FADES FROM VIEW. SOUNDS OF BIRDS HEARD, DIMLY AT FIRST.

[AWARE OF THE CHANGE AS IT IS OCCURRING] . . . *okay. Slipping out of . . . it and . . .*

MRS. STILSON IN A DIFFERENT PLACE.

*Outside now! How . . . did I do that?*

**AMY:** [EMERGING FROM THE SHADOWS] Do you like this new place better?

**MRS. STILSON:** Oh well oh well yes, much, all . . . nice flowers here, people seem . . . more like me. Thank you.

AMY MOVES BACK TOWARD THE SHADOWS.

*And then I see it happen once again . . .*

AMY GONE FROM SIGHT.

*Amy kisses me. Puts her—what thing is it, arm! yes, arm, puts her arm around my . . .*

PAUSE.

*. . . shoulder, turns her head away so I can't . . .*

PAUSE.

*Well, it knows what she's doing. May not get much better even though I'm here. No, I know that. I know that. No real need for her to . . .*

LONG PAUSE.

*Then she kisses me again.*

PAUSE.

*Walks away . . .*

PAUSE.

LIGHTS CHANGE AGAIN, WORLD AGAIN IN FLUX. NOISES OF THE BUILDING'S INTERIOR CAN BE HEARD LIKE A BABEL, ONLY FLEETINGLY COHERENT. THE REC ROOM SEEN DISSOLVING.

**MRS. STILSON:** *Where am I?*

SHE BEGINS TO WANDER THROUGH A MAZE OF PASSAGEWAYS. THE MIRRORS MULTIPLY HER IMAGE, CREATE A SENSE OF ENDLESSNESS.

*[Note. The following blocks of sound, which accompany her expedition, are meant to blend and overlap in performance and, to that end, can be used in any order and combined in any way desired, except for the last five blocks, numbers 12–16, which must be performed in their given sequence and in a way that is comprehensible. The sounds themselves may be live or pre-recorded; those which are pre-recorded should emanate from all parts of the theater and in no predictable pattern. The effect should be exhilarating and disorienting. An adventure. With terrifying aspects to be sure. But the sense of mystery and adventure must never be so overwhelmed by the terror that it is either lost altogether or submerged to the point of insignificance.*

MRS. STILSON *may be frightened here, but the fear does not prevent her from exploring.*

*She wanders through the labyrinth of dark panels as if they were so many doors, each door leading into yet another realm.]*

**BLOCK 1:** It was but a few years later that Fritsch and Hitzig stimulated the cortex of a dog with an electric current. Here at last was dramatic and indisputable evidence that—

**BLOCK 2:** Would you like me to change the channel?

**BLOCK 3:** . . . presented, I would say, essentially similar conclusions on the behavioral correlates of each cerebral convolution.

**BLOCK 4:** [BEING THE DEEP MALE VOICE, SPEAKING SLOWLY, ENUNCIATING CAREFULLY, THAT ONE HEARS ON THE SPEECH-THERAPY MACHINE KNOWN AS "THE LANGUAGE MASTER"] Mother led Bud to the bed.

**BLOCK 5:** . . . In the laboratory then, through electrical stimulation of neural centers or excisions of areas of the brain, scientists acquired information about the organization of mental activities in the monkey, the dog, the cat, and the rat. The discovery of certain peculiar clinical pictures, reminiscent of bizarre human syndromes, proved of special interest.

**BLOCK 6:** Can you tell me what this object's called?

**BLOCK 7:** ELLA'S RIFFS OF SCAT, AS IF WE WERE STILL IN THE REC ROOM AFTER ALL.

**BLOCK 8:** One has only to glance through the writings of this period to sense the heightened excitement attendant upon these discoveries!

**BLOCK 9:** Possibly some diaschisis, which would of course help account for the apparent mirroring. And then, of course, we must not overlook the fact that she's left-handed.

**BLOCK 10:** Of course, you understand, these theories may all be wrong! [SOUND OF LAUGHTER FROM AN AUDIENCE] Any other questions? Yes, over there, in the corner.

**BLOCK 11:** Mrs. Stilson, this is Dr. Rogans. Dr. Rogans, this is Emily Stilson.

**BLOCK 12:** MALE VOICE: —definite possibility I would say of a tiny subclinical infarct in Penfield's area. Yes? FEMALE VOICE: Are you sure there is a Penfield's area? MALE VOICE: No. [LAUGHTER FROM HIS AUDIENCE] MALE VOICE AGAIN [ITSELF ON THE VERGE OF LAUGHTER]: But *something* is wrong with her! [RAUCOUS LAUGHTER FROM HIS AUDIENCE]

*[Note. Emerging out of the laughter in Block 12, a single musical TONE. This tone increases in intensity. It should carry through Block 16 and into* MRS. STILSON*'s emergence from the maze of panels, helping to propel her into the realm and the memory to which this expedition has been leading.]*

**BLOCK 13:** The controversy, of course, is that some feel it's language without thought, and others, thought without language . . .

**BLOCK 14:** What it is, of course, is the symbol system. Their symbol system's shot. They can't make analogies.

**BLOCK 15:** You see, it's all so unpredictable. There are no fixed posts, no clear boundaries. The victim, you could say, has been cut adrift . . .

**BLOCK 16:** Ah, now you're really flying blind there!

MRS. STILSON EMERGES FROM THE MAZE OF CORRIDORS. SOUND PERHAPS OF WIND, OR BELLS. LIGHTS BLUE, SENSE AGAIN OF WEIGHTLESSNESS, AIRINESS.

**MRS. STILSON:** [IN AWE AND ECSTASY] *As I see it now, the plane was flying BACKWARDS! Really, wind that strong, didn't know it could be! Yet the sky was clear, not a cloud, crystal blue, gorgeous, angels could've lived in sky like that . . . I think the cyclone must've blown in on the Andes from the sea . . .*

BLUE LIGHT FADES. WIND GONE, BELLS GONE, MUSICAL TONE IS GONE.

[COMING OUT OF IT] *Yes . . .* [SHE LOOKS AROUND; GETS HER BEARINGS] *Yes, no question, this . . . place better.* [AND NOW SHE'S LANDED] *All these people just . . . like me, I guess.*

SHE TAKES IN WHERE SHE IS, SEEMS SLIGHTLY STUNNED TO BE BACK WHERE SHE STARTED. SENSE OF WONDERMENT APPARENT.

AN ATTENDANT APPROACHES.

**ATTENDANT:** Mrs. Stilson?

**MRS. STILSON:** [STARTLED] Oh!

**ATTENDANT:** Sorry to—

**MRS. STILSON:** Is it . . . ?

**ATTENDANT:** Yes.

**MRS. STILSON:** Did I . . . ?

**ATTENDANT:** No, no need to worry. Here, I'll take you.

THE ATTENDANT GUIDES MRS. STILSON TO A THERAPY ROOM, THOUGH, IN FACT, MORE LIKELY (ON THE STAGE) THE ROOM ASSEMBLES AROUND HER. IN THE ROOM ARE AMY, BILLY (A MAN IN HIS MIDDLE THIRTIES), MRS. TIMMINS (ELDERLY, IN A WHEELCHAIR), AND MR. BROWNSTEIN (ALSO ELDERLY AND IN A WHEELCHAIR).

THE ATTENDANT LEAVES.

**AMY:** Well! Now that we're all here on this lovely afternoon, I thought that maybe—

**BILLY:** She looks really good.

**AMY:** What?

**BILLY:** This new lady here, can't remember what her name is, no bother, anyhow, she looks really nice all dressed like this, an' I jus' wanna extent a nice welcome here on behalf o' all of us.

THE OTHER PATIENTS MUMBLE THEIR ASSENT.

**AMY:** Well, that is very nice, Billy, very nice. Can any of the rest of you remember this woman's name?

**BILLY:** I seen her I think when it is, yesterday, how's that?

**AMY:** Very good, that's right, you met her for the first time yesterday. Now, can any of you remember her name?

**BILLY:** Dolores.

**AMY:** [LAUGHING SLIGHTLY] No, not Dolores.

**MR. BROWNSTEIN:** She vas, I caught sight ya know, jussaminute, flahtied or vhat, vhere, midda [HE HUMS A NOTE]—

**AMY:** Music.

**MR. BROWNSTEIN:** Yeah right goodgirlie right she vas lissning, I caught slight, saw her vooding bockstond tipping-n-topping de foot vas jussnow like dis. [HE STARTS TO STAMP HIS FOOT]

**AMY:** Mrs. Stilson, were you inside listening to some music just now?

**MRS. STILSON:** Well . . .

PAUSE.

[VERY FAST] Well now I was yes in the what in-the-in-the where the—

**AMY:** [CHEERFULLY] Sssssllow dowwwwn.

THE OTHER PATIENTS LAUGH; MRS. TIMMINS SOFTLY ECHOES THE PHRASE "SLOW DOWN."

[SPEAKING VERY SLOWLY] Listen to yourself talking.

**MRS. STILSON:** [SPEAKING SLOWLY] Well yes, I was . . . listening and it was it was going in . . . good I think, I'd say, very good yes I liked it very nice it made it very nice inside.

**AMY:** Well, good.

**MRS. TIMMINS:** Applawdgia!

**AMY:** Ah, Mrs. Timmins! You heard the music, too?

**MRS. TIMMINS:** [WITH A LAUGH] Ohshorrrrrrn. Yossssso, TV.

**AMY:** Well, good for you! Anyway, I'd like you all to know that this new person in our group is named Mrs. Stilson.

**MR. BROWNSTEIN:** Sssssstaa-illlllsssim.

**AMY:** Right! Well done. Mr. Brownstein!

**MR. BROWNSTEIN:** [LAUGHING PROUDLY] It's vurktiddiDINGobitch!

**AMY:** That's right it's working. I told you it would.

**BILLY:** Hey! Wait, hold on here—jus' remembered!

**AMY:** What's that, Billy?

**BILLY:** You've been holdin' out pay up where is it?

**AMY:** Where . . . is what?

March 2008 production by the Bas Blue Theatre Company in Fort Collins, CO.

**BILLY:** Where is for all what I did all that time labor which you—don't kid me, I see you grinning back there ate up [HE MAKES MUNCHING SOUNDS] so where is it, where's the loot?

**AMY:** For the cheesecake.

**BILLY:** That's right you know it for the cheesecape, own recipe, extra-special, pay up.

**AMY:** [TO MRS. STILSON] Billy is a terrific cook.

**MRS. STILSON:** [DELIGHTED] Oh!

**BILLY:** Well used t' be, not now much what they say, anyhow, hah-hah! See? look, laughing, giggles, tries t' hide it, she knows she knows, scoundrel, thief, can't sleep nights can you, people give their arms whatnots recipe like that one is. Cheapskate. Come on fork over hand it over, don't be chief.

**AMY:** . . . What?

**BILLY:** Don't be chief.

PAUSE.

You know, when someone don' pay, you say he's chief.

**AMY:** [WARMLY, NEARLY LAUGHING] Billy, you're not listening.

**BILLY:** Okay not the word not the right word what's the word? I'll take any help you can give me. [HE LAUGHS]

**AMY:** Cheap.

**BILLY:** That's it that's the word that's what you are, from now on I'm gonna sell my recipes somewheres else.

**AMY:** Billy, say cheap.

HE SIGHS MIGHTILY.

**BILLY:** . . . Chief.

HER EXPRESSION TELLS HIM EVERYTHING.

Not right okay, try again this thing we can, what's its, lessee okay here we go CHARF! Nope. Not right. Ya know really, this could take all day.

**AMY:** Well then, the sooner you do it, the sooner we can go on to what I've planned.

**BILLY:** You've got somethin' planned? You've never got somethin' planned.

**AMY:** I've *always* got something planned.

**BILLY:** Oh come on don' gimme that, you're jus' tryin' to impress this new lady, really nice new lady, Mrs. . . .

**AMY:** Stilson.

**BILLY:** Yeah her, you're jus' tryin'—what's that word again?

**AMY:** Cheap.

**BILLY:** Cheap right okay lessee now—

**AMY:** Billy! You just said it!

**BILLY:** Did I? Good. Then maybe we can go on to somethin' else, such as when you're gonna fork over for the cheesecake, I could be a rich man now.

**AMY:** Billy, I never made the cheesecake.

**BILLY:** I'll bet you've gone sold the recipe to all the stores the whatnot everywhere fancy bigdeal places made a fortune, gonna retire any day t' your farm in New Jersey.

**AMY:** I don't have a farm in New Jersey, *you* have a farm in New Jersey!

**BILLY:** Oh? Then what were you doin' on my farm then?

**AMY:** I wasn't on your farm, Billy, I've been here!

[BILLY STARTS ARGUING ABOUT SOMETHING INCOMPREHENSIBLE AND SEEMINGLY UNRELATED TO FARM LIFE, THE ARGUMENT CONSISTING MOSTLY OF THE RECITATION OF A CONVOLUTED STRING OF NUMBERS; AMY CUTS HIM SHORT BEFORE HE GOES TOO FAR ASTRAY]

Billy, cheap, say cheap!

LONG SILENCE.

**BILLY:** [SIMPLY AND WITHOUT EFFORT] Cheap.

AMY CHEERS.

[OVERJOYED] Cheap!— Cheap-cheap-cheap-cheap-cheap!

**MR. BROWNSTEIN:** I vas hoping you could polsya and git vid mustard all dis out of dis you gottit right good I say hutchit and congratulupsy!

**AMY:** Congratu*lations.*

**MR. BROWNSTEIN:** Yeah right dassit goodgirlie, phhhhew! fin'lly!

LIGHTS FADE TO BLACK ALL AROUND MRS. STILSON. NOTHING SEEN BUT HER.

SILENCE FOR A TIME.

**MRS. STILSON:** *What it was . . . how I heard it how I said it not the same, you would think so but it's not. Sometimes . . . well it just goes in so fast, in-and-out all the sounds. I know they mean—*

PAUSE.

*I mean I know they're . . . well like with me, helping, as their at their in their best way knowing how I guess they practice all the time so I'd say must be good or even better, helps me get the dark out just by going you know sssslowww and thinking smiling . . . it's not easy.*

PAUSE.

*Sometimes . . . how can . . . well it's just I think these death things, end it, stuff like sort of may be better not to listen anything no more at all or trying even talking cause what good's it, I'm so far away! Well it's crazy I don't mean it I don't think, still it's just like clouds that you can't push through. Still you do it, still you try to. I can't hear things same as others say them.*

PAUSE.

*So the death thing, it comes in, I don't ask it, it just comes in, plays around in there, I can't get it out till it's ready, goes out on its own. Same I guess for coming. I don't open up the door.*

SILENCE.

LIGHTS UP ON A CHAIR, SMALL TABLE.

ON THE TABLE, A CASSETTE RECORDER.

MRS. STILSON GOES TO THE CHAIR. SITS. STARES AT THE RECORDER.

A FEW MOMENTS LATER, BILLY AND A DOCTOR ENTER.

**BILLY:** Oh, I'm sorry, I didn't know you was in . . . here or . . .

**MRS. STILSON:** Dr. Freedman said I could . . . use room and his . . . this . . . [SHE GESTURES TOWARD THE RECORDER]

**DOCTOR:** No problem, we'll use another room.

HE SMILES. EXIT BILLY AND DOCTOR.

MRS. STILSON TURNS BACK TO THE MACHINE. STARES AT IT. THEN SHE REACHES OUT, PRESSES A BUTTON.

**DOCTOR'S VOICE:** [FROM CASSETTE RECORDER] All right, essentially, a stroke occurs when there's a stoppage . . . When blood flow ceases in one part of the brain . . . And that brain can no longer get oxygen . . . And subsequently dies. Okay? Now, depending upon which part of the brain is affected by the stroke, you'll see differences in symptoms. Now what you've had is a left cerebral infarction. Oh, by the way, you're doing much, much better. We were very worried when you first arrived . . .

SILENCE.

SHE CLICKS OFF THE RECORDING MACHINE. DOES NOTHING, STARES AT NOTHING. THEN SHE REACHES OUT AND PUSHES THE REWIND BUTTON. THE MACHINE REWINDS TO START OF TAPE. STOPS AUTOMATICALLY. SHE STARES AT THE MACHINE. DEEP BREATH. REACHES OUT AGAIN. PRESSES THE PLAYBACK BUTTON.

**DOCTOR'S VOICE:** All right, essentially, a stroke occurs when there's a stoppage . . . When blood flow ceases in one part of the brain . . . And that brain can no long—

SHE SHUTS IT OFF.

STARES INTO SPACE.

SILENCE.

---

MRS. STILSON WITH AMY SITTING NEXT TO HER ON ANOTHER CHAIR.

**MRS. STILSON:** [STILL STARING INTO SPACE] "Memory" . . .

PAUSE.

**AMY:** Yes, come on, "memory" . . .

NO RESPONSE.

Anything.

STILL NO RESPONSE.

[WARMLY]: Oh, come on, I bet there are lots of things you can talk about . . . You've been going out a lot lately . . . With your son . . . With your niece . . .

PAUSE.

What about Rhinebeck? Tell me about Rhinebeck.

PAUSE.

**MRS. STILSON:** On . . . Saturday . . . [SHE PONDERS] On . . . Sunday my . . . son . . . [PONDERS AGAIN] On Saturday my son . . . took me to see them out at Rhinebeck.

**AMY:** See what?

**MRS. STILSON:** What I used to . . . fly in.

**AMY:** Can you think of the word?

**MRS. STILSON:** . . . What word?

**AMY:** For what you used to fly in.

LONG PAUSE.

**MRS. STILSON:** Planes!

**AMY:** Very good!

**MRS. STILSON:** Old . . . planes.

**AMY:** That is very good. Really!

**MRS. STILSON:** I sat . . . inside one of them. He said it was like the kind I used to . . . fly in and walk . . . out on wings in. I couldn't believe I could have ever done this.

PAUSE.

But he said I did, I had. He was very . . . proud.

PAUSE.

Then . . . I saw my hand was pushing on this . . . stick . . . Then my hand was . . . pulling. Well I hadn't you know asked my hand to do this, it just went and did it on its own. So I said okay Emily, if this is how it wants to do it you just sit back here and watch . . . But . . . my head, it was really . . . hurting bad. And I was up here both . . . sides, you know . . .

**AMY:** Crying.

**MRS. STILSON:** [WITH EFFORT] Yeah.

LONG PAUSE.

And then all at once—it remembered everything!

LONG PAUSE.

But now it doesn't.

SILENCE.

---

FAINT SOUND OF WIND. HINT OF BELLS.

THE SCREENS OPEN.

WE ARE OUTSIDE. SENSE OF DISTANCE OPENNESS. ALL FEELING OF CONSTRAINT IS GONE. AMY HELPS MRS. STILSON INTO AN OVERCOAT; AMY IS IN AN OVERCOAT ALREADY.

**AMY:** Are you sure you'll be warm enough?

**MRS. STILSON:** Oh yes . . .

AND THEY START TO WALK—A LEISURELY STROLL THROUGH A PARK OR MEADOW, SENSE OF WHITENESS EVERYWHERE. THEY HEAD TOWARD A BENCH WITH SNOW ON ITS SLATS. THE SOUND OF WIND GROWS STRONGER.

FAINT SOUND OF AN AIRPLANE OVERHEAD, THE SOUND QUICKLY DISAPPEARING.

**MRS. STILSON:** This is winter, isn't it?

**AMY:** Yes.

**MRS. STILSON:** That was just a guess, you know.

**AMY:** [WITH A WARM, EASY LAUGH] Well, it was a good one, keep it up!

MRS. STILSON LAUGHS.

AMY STOPS BY THE BENCH.

Do you know what this is called?

**MRS. STILSON:** Bench!

**AMY:** Very good! No, I mean what's on top of it.

NO RESPONSE.

What I'm brushing off . . .

STILL NO RESPONSE.

What's falling from the sky . . .

LONG SILENCE.

**MRS. STILSON:** Where do you get names from?

**AMY:** I? From in here, same as you.

**MRS. STILSON:** Do you know how you do it?

**AMY:** No.

**MRS. STILSON:** Then how am I supposed . . . to learn?

**AMY:** [SOFTLY] I don't really know.

MRS. STILSON STARES AT AMY. THEN SHE POINTS AT HER AND LAUGHS.

AT FIRST, AMY DOESN'T UNDERSTAND.

THEN SHE DOES.

AND THEN BOTH OF THEM ARE LAUGHING.

**MRS. STILSON:** Look. You see? [SHE SCOOPS SOME SNOW OFF THE BENCH] If I pick this . . . stuff up in my hand, then . . . I know its name. I didn't have to pick it up to know . . . what it *was*.

**AMY:** No . . .

**MRS. STILSON:** But to find its name . . . [SHE STARES AT WHAT IS IN HER HAND] I had to pick it up.

**AMY:** What's its name?

**MRS. STILSON:** Snow. It's really nuts, isn't it!

**AMY:** It's peculiar!

THEY LAUGH.

THEN, LAUGHTER GONE, THEY SIT; STARE OUT.

SILENCE FOR A TIME.

**MRS. STILSON:** A strange thing happened to me . . .

PAUSE.

I think last night.

**AMY:** Can you remember it?

**MRS. STILSON:** Perfectly.

**AMY:** Ah!

**MRS. STILSON:** I think it may have been . . . you know, when you sleep . . .

**AMY:** A dream.

**MRS. STILSON:** Yes, one of those, but I'm not . . . sure that it was . . . that.

PAUSE. THEN SHE NOTICES THE SNOW IN HER HAND.

Is it all right if I . . . eat this?

**AMY:** Yes! We used to make a ball of it, then pour maple syrup on top. Did you ever do that?

**MRS. STILSON:** I don't know.

PAUSE.

No, I remember—I did!

SHE TASTES THE SNOW. SMILES

AFTER A TIME, THE SMILE VANISHES.

SHE TURNS BACK TO AMY.

Who was that man yesterday?

**AMY:** What man?

**MRS. STILSON:** In our group. He seemed all right.

**AMY:** Oh, that was last week.

**MRS. STILSON:** I thought for sure he was all right! I thought he was maybe, you know, a doctor.

**AMY:** Yes, I know.

**MRS. STILSON:** [SEARCHING HER MEMORY] And you asked him to show you where his . . . hand was.

**AMY:** And he knew.

**MRS. STILSON:** That's right, he raised his hand, he knew. So I thought, why is Amy joking?

SHE PONDERS.

Then you asked him . . . [SHE TRIES TO REMEMBER] . . . where . . . [SHE TURNS TO AMY]

**AMY:** His elbow was.

**MRS. STILSON:** Yes! And he . . . [SHE STRUGGLES TO FIND THE WORD]

**AMY:** [HELPING] Pointed—

**MRS. STILSON:** [AT THE SAME TIME] Pointed! to . . . [BUT THE STRUGGLE'S GETTING HARDER]

**AMY:** The corner of the room.

**MRS. STILSON:** Yes.

PAUSE.

[SOFTLY] That was very . . . scary.

**AMY:** Yes.

MRS. STILSON STARES INTO SPACE.

SILENCE.

What is it that happened to you last night?

**MRS. STILSON:** Oh yes! Well, this . . . *person* . . . came into my room I couldn't tell if it was a man or woman or . . . young or old. I was in my bed and it came. Didn't seem to have to walk just . . . came over to my . . . bed and . . . smiled at where I was.

PAUSE.

And then it said . . . [IN A WHISPER] "Emily . . . we're glad you changed your mind."

PAUSE.

And then . . . it turned and left.

**AMY:** Was it a doctor? [MRS. STILSON SHAKES HER HEAD] One of the staff? [MRS. STILSON SHAKES HER HEAD] How do you know?

**MRS. STILSON:** I just know.

PAUSE.

Then . . . I left my body.

**AMY:** *What?*

**MRS. STILSON:** [WITH GREAT EXCITEMENT] I was on the . . . what's the name over me—

**AMY:** Ceiling?

**MRS. STILSON:** Yes! I was floating like a . . .

**AMY:** Cloud?

MRS. STILSON SHAKES HER HEAD.

Bird?

**MRS. STILSON:** Yes, up there at the—[SHE SEARCHES FOR THE WORD; FINDS IT]—ceiling, and I looked down and I was still there in my bed! Wasn't even scared, which you'd think I would be . . . And I thought, wow! this is the life isn't it?

SOUND OF WIND.

LIGHTS BEGIN TO CHANGE.

AMY RECEDES INTO THE DARKNESS.

*It comes now without my asking . . . Amy is still beside me but I am somewhere else. I'm not scared. It has taken me, and it's clear again. Something is about to happen.*

PAUSE.

AMY NOW COMPLETELY GONE.

MRS. STILSON IN A NARROW SPOT OF LIGHT, DARKNESS ALL AROUND.

*I am in a plane, a Curtiss Jenny, and it's night. Winter. Snow is falling. Feel the tremble of the wings! How I used to walk out on them! Could I have really done— . . . Yes. What I'd do, I'd strap myself with a tether to the stays, couldn't see the tether from below, then out I'd climb! Oh my, but it was wonderful! I could feel the wind! shut my eyes, all alone—FEEL THE SOARING!*

THE WIND GROWS STRONGER.

THEN THE WIND DIES AWAY.

SILENCE.

SHE NOTICES THE CHANGE.

**MRS. STILSON:** *But this is in another time. Where I've been also . . . It is night and no one else is in the plane. Is it . . . remembering?*

PAUSE.

*No . . . No, I'm simply there again!*

PAUSE.

*And I'm lost . . . I am lost, completely lost, have to get to . . . somewhere, Omaha I think. The radio is out, or rather for some reason picks up only Bucharest. Clouds all around, no stars only snow, don't possess a clue to where I am, flying blind, soon be out of gas . . . And then the clouds open up a bit, just a bit, and lights appear below, faint, a hint, like torches. Down I drop! heart pounding with relief, with joy, hoping for a landing place. I'll take anything—a field, a street, and down I drop! No place to land . . . It's a town but the smallest—one tiny street is all, three street lamps, no one on the street, all deserted . . . just a street and some faint light in the middle of darkness. Nothing. Still, down I go! Maybe I can find a name on a railroad station, find out where I am! . . . But I see nothing I can read . . . So I begin to circle, though I know I'm wasting fuel and I'll crash if I keep this up! But somehow, I just can't tear myself away! Though I know I should pull back on the stick, get the nose up, head north into darkness—Omaha must be north! But no, I keep circling this one small silly street in this one small town . . . I'm scared to leave it, that's what, as if I guess once away from it I'll be inside something empty, black, and endless . . .*

PAUSE.

*So I keep circling—madness!—but I love it, what I see below! And I just can't bring myself to give it up, it's that simple—just can't bring myself to give it up!*

PAUSE.

*Then I know I have to. It's a luxury I can't afford. Fuel is running low, almost gone, may be too late anyway, so—*

PAUSE.

*I pull the nose up, kick the rudder, bank, and head out into darkness all in terror! GOD, BUT IT TAKES EFFORT! JUST DON'T WANT TO DO IT! . . . But I do.*

PAUSE.

[SUDDENLY CALM] *Actually, odd thing, once I did, broke free, got into the dark, found I wasn't even scared . . . Or was I?* [SLIGHT LAUGH] *Can't remember . . . Wonder where that town was . . . ?*

PAUSE.

*Got to Omaha all right.*

PAUSE.

*Was it Omaha . . . ?*

PAUSE.

*Yes, I think so . . . Yes, Topeka, that was it!*

PAUSE.

*God, but it was wonderful!* [SLIGHT LAUGH] *Awful scary sometimes, though!*

AMY SEEN IN THE DISTANCE.

**AMY:** Emily! Emily, are you all right!

SUDDEN, SHARP, TERRIFYING FLAPPING SOUND.

MRS. STILSON GASPS.

AMY DISAPPEARS.

**MRS. STILSON:** [RAPIDLY] *Around! There here spins saw it rumple chumps and jumps outgoes inside up and . . . takes it, gives it, okay . . .*

PAUSE.

[EASIER] *Touch her for me, would you?*

PAUSE.

[EVEN EASIER] *Oh my, yes, and here it goes then out . . . there I think on . . . wings? Yes . . .*

PAUSE.

[SOFTLY, FAINT SMILE] *Thank you.*

NO TRACE OF TERROR.

MUSIC. HINT OF BELLS.

LIGHTS TO BLACK.

SILENCE.

# Writing from Reading

### Summarize

1 Mrs. Stilson has a number of problems with perception. List them.

2 In this play a woman suffers a stroke and seeming chaos follows. How does the play's structure mark her progress?

### Analyze Craft

3 The playwright chooses to portray the chaos of what he calls Mrs. Stilson's "catastrophe" by a mix of image, sound, and physical action. If you were directing the play, what would the effect be if you follow his stage directions to the letter? What other choices might you make?

4 What elements of the play do you find familiar? Which do you find innovative?

5 How might Mrs. Stilson's perception problems manifest themselves on stage?

6 How is the author's research into the realm of medicine and neuroscience evident in his presentation of the action? What effect does it have on your reception of the play?

### Analyze Voice

7 Try reading the first few pages and the last few pages aloud. How is speech presented? How does that affect your understanding of the text?

### Synthesize Summary and Analysis

8 Research and insight into character come together on stage for this presentation of one woman's plight. Does the end strike you as a satisfying resolution to the problem?

### Interpret the Play

9 How much does the play speak to your understanding of your own perception of the world?

"People go into the theater now hoping that they'll get out of it and go into movies. . . . The idea of developing actors, writers, who want to be actors and writers for the theater is, I think, diminished. . . . Can we continue to create new plays and new productions and new actors?" Conversation with Arthur Miller

### Experimental Theater

For many theatergoers, contemporary theater has its roots in a slightly earlier period of experimental theater, that variety of post World War II European play that modifies the traditional assumptions and, often, the actual forms of classic theater. The influence of Bertolt Brecht's notions of Epic Theater (in which the playwright favors characters who represent certain ideas as opposed to characters from life) and the Theater of the Absurd (in which the playwright presents life as random seeming and, often, darkly comical) as practiced by Eugene Ionesco, and the so-called Theater of Cruelty of Antonin Artaud (in which the playwright employs shock value in order to jar the audience into a recognition of harsh reality) have all had an impact on contemporary playwrights. Nobel Laureate Samuel Beckett, with such plays as *Waiting for Godot, Endgame,* and *Krapp's Last Tape,* was a transformative presence on the stage and page. The influence of such playwrights can be felt in the work of Edward Albee (chapter 31) and Arthur Kopit, among other American playwrights, and in the work of

> "For a young playwright it doesn't cost anything for anybody to put your play on . . . the way you wrote it. But if it's going to cost a lot of money they get scared and they want to make the play safe." Conversation with Edward Albee

New York City's Living Theater, headed by Julian Beck and Judith Malina. Their productions of Jack Gelber's improvised *The Connection* and Kenneth Brown's *The Brig* had a major impact on the contemporary theater scene, as did Richard Schechner's production of *Dionysus in '69.* Work by such playwrights as Maria Irena Fornes and Liz Swados also enlivened the theater scene.

## Joan Ackermann (b. 1950)

Joan Ackermann is a contemporary playwright whose plays have been produced off-Broadway and in theater venues across the nation. In addition to plays like *Zara Spook and Other Lures* (1993), *The Batting Cage* (1999), *Marcus Is Walking* (1999), *Staying Afloat* (2006), *The Big Picture,* and *The Taster,* Ackermann has written the music and lyrics for a musical—*Isabella: A Young Physician's Primer on the Perils of Love.* She also adapted one of her plays into the screenplay for the film *Off the Map,* which premiered at the Sundance Film Festival in 2003. Beyond her works for the stage, Ackermann is a journalist and has been a special contributor to *Sports Illustrated.* Her articles have also appeared in *The Atlantic Monthly* and *Time,* among other magazines. Ackermann makes her home in the Berkshires of Massachusetts, not far from the Mixed Company Theatre, a company which she cofounded and for which she serves as artistic director. It has been in existence for more than twenty-five years.

**AS YOU READ** **Recall a struggle or competition similar to the one in the audition that you yourself might have experienced.**

# The Second Beam (2004)

## CHARACTERS

**GEORGIA**
**JENNIFER**
**MEG**
**CASTING AGENT**
**PATTI SCHARER**

**PLACE:** An audition waiting room.

*In an audition waiting room, three women—* GEORGIA, JENNIFER, *and* MEG*—sit on folded chairs and study pages from a script. They are all dressed in lab coats as scientists. After a moment, a casting agent opens a door and sticks her head in.*

**CASTING AGENT:** Georgia? *[*GEORGIA *smiles up at her, grabs her stuff and exits. The other two smile at her as she exits into the audition room, closing the door behind her.* MEG *is the older of the two, more mature, grounded.* JENNIFER *is soft-spoken, sweet.]*

**JENNIFER:** *[Approaching* MEG.*]* Pardon me . . . Do you have a tissue? *[*MEG *opens her bag and gives her one. Goes back to studying.* JENNIFER *sits down with the tissue and very discreetly wipes under both her armpits.]* You were at *The Flannerys. [*MEG *looks at her blankly.]* You read for the sister. Of the boxer, with the bad hand. The malpractice suit.

**MEG:** *[Remembering.]* Oh. Right.

**JENNIFER:** I heard that show didn't get picked up. You were at *Mind of a Married Man*, too. The jockey's wife. *[Concerned.]* Are you memorizing that?

**MEG:** *[Friendly.]* No. No, just studying. *[Pause.]*

**JENNIFER:** Do you happen to know who got the part?

**MEG:** Which part. The sister, of the boxer?

**JENNIFER:** No. Yes.

**MEG:** Or the jockey's wife.

**JENNIFER:** Either. Both.

**MEG:** Well, the same actress got them both.

**JENNIFER:** Patti Scharer?

**MEG:** Patti Scharer.

**JENNIFER:** I knew it. Patti Scharer. Patti Scharer. Every part my agent sends me out on, every single part it seems, Patti Scharer gets. Care for a mint? *[*MEG *shakes her head no, takes out a lipstick and puts some on, looking at herself in a small compact mirror.]* Are you doing an accent?

**MEG:** Accent?

**JENNIFER:** For the scientist.

**MEG:** What kind of accent?

**JENNIFER:** Foreign.

**MEG:** I think she's American. *[Pause.]*

**JENNIFER:** *[Concerned.]* So you're not doing an accent? *[*MEG *shakes her head, goes back to studying the pages.]* I was going to do a French accent. Madame Curie. The scientist. You don't think I should?

**MEG:** If you've worked on it that way. It's a choice.

**JENNIFER:** Yes, it is. It's a choice. *[Pause.]* I never know about choices. My agent always says they like it when you make a choice, but I'm not so sure. I've been making choices, strong choices, but . . . they haven't really been panning out for me. *[She discreetly picks something out from between her teeth.]* I really need the work. I really, really, really need the work. I'm sorry, I'll let you concentrate. *[Pause.]* Have you read for him before? *[MEG looks at her.]* Ethan Schroeder. The director. Have you read for him? *[MEG nods. Goes back to her pages, concentrating.]* My friend Annette says he's a monster. She read for him for a movie of the week and he ate his lunch the entire time.

**MEG:** He can be a jerk.

**JENNIFER:** That's all I need. *[She sighs, smooths her skirt.]* Can I just ask you . . . is this lipstick, the color of my lipstick, all right? I've never worn this shade before.

**MEG:** It looks good on you. It's a good color for you.

**JENNIFER:** You think so? Really?

**MEG:** I do. *[Smiling.]* It's a good "choice."

**JENNIFER:** Thanks. I don't know. It felt like a scientist choice. I don't know why. Sometimes you just have to go with your gut. *[MEG nods, goes back to her pages.]*

**JENNIFER:** *[Worrying.]* Patti Scharer. Do you get the light thing? They won't expect us to understand that, do you think? Stopping light? They won't grill us about that.

**MEG:** Probably not.

**JENNIFER:** I don't know. I read for the part of a veterinarian and they acted like they expected me to know everything about a dog's digestive system. I just winged it, talked about heartworm. I've seen them. In a jar. *[MEG doesn't respond.]* It's not just about the money. Truth be known, I'm feeling kind of stuck. *[Pause.]* If he's eating in there, stuffing his mouth with California pizza, Koo-koo-charoo chicken . . . You said you've read for him?

**MEG:** I used to go out with him.

**JENNIFER:** *[Stunned.]* You went out with him? You went out with Ethan Schroeder? *[MEG nods.]*

**JENNIFER:** Ohmygod, I'm so sorry. What I said . . . I didn't mean to call him a monster. Maybe he was just . . . hungry when my friend read for him. Maybe he's perfectly—

**MEG:** It's okay. A lot of people think he's an asshole.

**JENNIFER:** They do. You're not going out with him any more? *[MEG shakes her head.]* You're still friends? I mean, you're okay reading for him?

**MEG:** I really like this part.

**JENNIFER:** *[Not really like it.]* You do?

**MEG:** I do. How often does that happen?

**JENNIFER:** Yeah. Really. You must like this part.

**MEG:** I find the subject fascinating. I've read quite a bit about it.

**JENNIFER:** Oh. So . . . Light travels a hundred and eighty thousand miles an hour . . .

**MEG:** A second.

**JENNIFER:** And . . . *[JENNIFER waits for MEG to explain it.]* Then they stop it in a jar. *[Thinking . . .]* Like heartworm. Preserve it in formaldehyde.

**MEG:** Chilled sodium gas, actually.

**JENNIFER:** It just hangs in there? Frozen?

**MEG:** Well, the light goes out. It gets fainter and fainter as it slows down. The most amazing part to me—it's all amazing—they can revive the light any time by flashing a second beam of light through the gas.

**JENNIFER:** Oh.

**MEG:** They can bring a beam of light to a full stop, hold it, and then send it on its way with a second beam. *[Pause.]*

**JENNIFER:** I like scenes best . . . when I can go deep. Cry. I like emotion. My background is theatre.

**MEG:** Not a lot of emotion in these scenes, not ostensibly.

**JENNIFER:** No. That's why I was thinking the French . . .

**MEG:** Go for the accent.

**JENNIFER:** You think so? *[Another actress enters. She is very appealing, made-up, a knock-out. She takes a seat. Exudes confidence. Both* MEG *and* JENNIFER *look at her, silently, as she takes out many pages and starts going through them.]*

**PATTI:** *[To* JENNIFER, *all business.]* Excuse me, are your pages with the reporter dated May eleventh or May fifteenth? *[*JENNIFER *looks at her pages . . .]*

**JENNIFER:** The reporter? I don't have . . . *[*JENNIFER *flips through, looking . . .]*

**PATTI:** Never mind. *[Noticing . . .]* Meg.

**MEG:** Hi, Patti.

**PATTI:** How *are* you? *[*MEG *nods, friendly, a little guarded.]*

**PATTI:** It's so great to see you, are you here now?

**MEG:** I'm here.

**PATTI:** You know I'd heard that. I ran into Carolyn, she was stage managing *Vanya* at the Taper, she told me you'd moved back.

**MEG:** I did.

**PATTI:** That's great. And you're reading for Ethan?

**MEG:** I am.

**PATTI:** Wow. Wow. *[*PATTI *studies* MEG, *waiting for some kind of response, which is not forthcoming.]*

**MEG:** How's Olivia?

**PATTI:** Olivia is three, God help me. Meg, can I borrow your lipstick, I actually forgot mine.

**MEG:** I'm sorry. I actually left all my makeup in the car.

**PATTI:** Really? What were you thinking? *[*PATTI *maintains her charming smile, miffed underneath.* JENNIFER *stares at* PATTI *in a mixed stupor of defeat and envy.]*

**JENNIFER:** *[Stirring.]* I have some lipstick. You can borrow.

**PATTI:** *[Brightly.]* Great. Thanks. *[*JENNIFER *reaches down into her purse and takes out her lipstick, takes off the cap, and offers it to* PATTI. PATTI, *looking at* JENNIFER*'s lips:]* Oh. Is it the color you're wearing?

**JENNIFER:** Uh-huh.

**PATTI:** That's okay. That color . . . I can't wear that color. But, thanks. *[Mortified,* JENNIFER *looks down at the color, gradually retreats her hand, puts the cover back on and sticks the lipstick back in her purse. Pause as all study the script.]*

**PATTI:** *[To* MEG.*]* I admire you, Meg. I really do. Reading for Ethan. That takes guts.

**MEG:** Not really.

**PATTI:** The way he treated you. You know Carolyn's first A. D. *[*MEG *nods.]* You know they're an item. Ethan and Carolyn. She's pregnant. That's ironic, huh? *[*MEG *did not know this. She flinches slightly. The door opens and* GEORGIA *enters with the casting agent behind her.* GEORGIA *grabs a sweater she left on a chair, waves to the* CASTING AGENT, *exiting.]*

**CASTING AGENT:** Thanks, Georgia. Patti. You made it.

**PATTI:** I'm so sorry I'm late. The 405 was a nightmare.

**CASTING AGENT:** You want to come in? Or do you want to take a minute. Jennifer . . . ? *[*JENNIFER, *discombobulated, jumps up, dropping all her pages as* PATTI *grabs her purse, coat, stands up.]*

**PATTI:** I'm fine. *[*PATTI *heads smoothly into the audition room. The* CASTING AGENT *smiles at* MEG, *looks down at the pages* JENNIFER *has dropped, and exits into the audition room.]*

**JENNIFER:** *[Crying, wiping her nose on her sleeve.]* I'm sorry. Do you have another tissue? *[*MEG *hands her another tissue which* JENNIFER *uses to wipe her nose and wipe away tears.* JENNIFER *grabs her stuff and hurries out.]*

**JENNIFER:** *[Not looking at* MEG.*]* It was very nice meeting you.

**MEG:** Where are you going?

**JENNIFER:** *[Crying, halfway out the door.]* I don't know. Bye.

**MEG:** Wait! *[*JENNIFER *turns and looks at her.]* You can get this part. *[*JENNIFER *is sobbing.]*

**JENNIFER:** I can't get this part.

**MEG:** You can.

**JENNIFER:** I can't. I can't even audition for this part.

**MEG:** Sit down.

**JENNIFER:** What?

**MEG:** Pull yourself together. Sit down.

**JENNIFER:** *[Weepy, discombobulated.]* Where?

**MEG:** On the chair. Go ahead. Sit! *[*JENNIFER *sits back down on her chair, sniffling.]* Here. Put these on. *[*MEG *takes the pair of tortoise-shell glasses she is wearing and gives them to* JENNIFER.*]* Put them on. *[*JENNIFER *does.]*

**JENNIFER:** Why does she want this part? It's not even very big.

**MEG:** Patti Scharer is not going to get this part.

**JENNIFER:** Yes, she is.

**MEG:** No she's not.

**JENNIFER:** *[Crying.]* She's already got it. She's already in there. With the part.

**MEG:** Ethan can't stand Patti Scharer. He's not going to give her this part. He's going to give you this part, because it's your part. *[*JENNIFER, *pauses crying to look at her.]*

**JENNIFER:** He can't stand her?

**MEG:** Jennifer, listen to me. Light . . . is emotion. *[*JENNIFER, *somewhat calmer but still a mess, response to the intensity of* MEG*'s voice. Listens . . .]* Think of light, a beam of light . . . as a story, a story with its own past, its own history. The light has been who knows where, has illuminated who knows what. Maybe it's been traveling for a long, long time—decades, centuries. And somewhere along its journey, it starts to slow down . . . Take a pause, fold into itself . . . *[The lights on them start to dim . . .]* Okay, so . . . Now, I want you to imagine you're at the theatre. You're sitting in the audience, and you're watching a play. You say you love theatre?

**JENNIFER:** *[Blowing her nose.]* I do. Why are you doing this?

**MEG:** So the curtain has just opened, and there are three people on stage, and they're still, not moving. *[Lights keep dimming.]* Who are these people, these characters? What is their past? Their history? We don't know. At the beginning of the play, we don't know anything about them at all. Their pasts are frozen. Suspended. *[The lights stop dimming, and* MEG *and* JENNIFER *are still for a few moments, frozen in close to dark.]* Then the play begins . . . *[Lights start to slowly fade up.]* . . . and we start to learn things about them. Information unfolds. One character leaves. Facts are revealed. We learn that this character really needs something, or this character has a dream, a passion, or maybe this one's been hurt . . . *[A spotlight lights her dimly and gets brighter slowly during the following . . .]* . . . been hurt really, really badly and we don't know how. Within minutes we can learn so much about them. In less than ten minutes, we can see the DNA of their whole lives. Even though there are mysteries, we feel we know them, quite well. Then, there comes that moment, that inevitable pivotal moment in a scene when things turn. The epiphany. The revelation. Something is illuminated. *[The spotlight on her is very bright now. Other lights are up to half full.]*

**JENNIFER:** I think . . . you're probably saying something but I'm not sure what it is. *[*MEG *looks at her. Takes the barrette out of her hair.]*

**MEG:** I think you should put your hair back. Here, take my barrette. *[*MEG *hands her barrette to* JENNIFER, *who puts her hair back.]* That's good. You look . . . like a scientist.

**JENNIFER:** What did Ethan Schroeder do to you that was so bad? *[*MEG *takes a moment to answer.]*

**MEG:** Nothing terribly original. *[*MEG *goes to get her things to leave.]*

**JENNIFER:** You're not going to read for this part?

**MEG:** No.

**JENNIFER:** One thing . . . I do feel emotional, right now. *[A spotlight on* JENNIFER *starts to come up, as all other lights start to fade, including the spotlight on* MEG.*]* For you, mainly.

**MEG:** Use it. Hold it inside. And, I would suggest you drop the accent.

**JENNIFER:** Really?

**MEG:** You don't need it. Another thing . . . when you go in there, tell Ethan he looks like a young Richard Burton.

**JENNIFER:** Okay. I can do that. I can do that.

**MEG:** This is your part. *[All lights are out now except the spotlight on* JENNIFER.*]*

**JENNIFER:** *[Confidently, seriously looking like a scientist.]* I know. This is my part. This is my part. *[The spotlight on* JENNIFER *is up to full. Then it fades out.]*

# Writing from Reading

### Summarize

1 In this play a trio of actresses shows up at an audition, with unexpected results. Describe the temperaments of each of the actresses.

### Analyze Craft

2 How would you characterize the relationships between the two actresses as the scene opens? Does the mood change? If so, what prompts the change? How does the entrance of the third actress affect the situation?

### Analyze Voice

3 How would you describe the overall tone of the play? How is this tone achieved?

### Synthesize Summary and Analysis

4 How does the playwright integrate science—the experiment with the beam of light—into the action of the play?

### Interpret the Play

5 How does the motif of illusion versus reality unfold in this play?

6 Would a male playwright have treated the scene differently, and in what ways?

# David Henry Hwang (b. 1957)

Born in a suburb of Los Angeles, David Henry Hwang has become one of the most prominent Asian-American voices in contemporary drama. His parents, Chinese by birth, met and married in the United States, raising Hwang under his mother's fundamentalist Christian influence. Although Hwang later abandoned fundamentalism, it continues to be an element in his plays. Hwang began writing plays while an undergraduate at Stanford, and his first, *F.O.B,* which stands for "fresh off the boat" in reference to Chinese immigrants, met with great success. His biggest success came with *M. Butterfly,* a play that was performed on Broadway and that brought Hwang a Tony Award and a Pulitzer Prize nomination. Hwang's other projects include collaborations with the composer Phillip Glass on a science-fiction production and on an opera about Christopher Columbus. He also collaborated on the script for the Disney rock musical version of *Aida* and for the screen adaptation of A.S. Byatt's novel *Possession.* Although his work shows great range and variety, it most often concerns itself with the Asian-American identity.

**AS YOU READ** **Think of the work on the railroad performed by all the Chinese laborers who never appear in the play. What is the "dance" the two actors perform against that unseen backdrop of labor.**

# The Dance and the Railroad (1982)

## CHARACTERS

**LONE,** *twenty years old, ChinaMan railroad worker.*

**MA,** *eighteen years old, ChinaMan railroad worker.*

**PLACE** A mountaintop near the transcontinental railroad.

**TIME** June, 1867.

**SYNOPSIS OF SCENES**
*Scene 1. Afternoon*
*Scene 2. Afternoon, a day later.*
*Scene 3. Late afternoon, four days later.*
*Scene 4. Late that night.*
*Scene 5. Just before the following dawn.*

## SCENE 1

*A mountaintop.* LONE *is practicing opera steps. He swings his pigtail around like a fan.* MA *enters, cautiously, watches from a hidden spot.* MA *approaches* LONE.

**LONE:** So, there are insects hiding in the bushes.

**MA:** Hey, listen, we haven't met, but—

**LONE:** I don't spend time with insects.

*[*LONE *whips his hair into* MA*'s face;* MA *backs off;* LONE *pursues him, swiping at* MA *with his hair.]*

**MA:** What the—? Cut it out!

*[*MA *pushes* LONE *away.]*

**LONE:** Don't push me.

**MA:** What was that for?

**LONE:** Don't ever push me again.

**MA:** You mess like that, you're gonna get pushed.

**LONE:** Don't push me.

**MA:** You started it. I just wanted to watch.

**LONE:** You "just wanted to watch." Did you ask my permission?

**MA:** What?

**LONE:** Did you?

**MA:** C'mon.

**LONE:** You can't expect to get in for free.

**MA:** Listen. I got some stuff you'll wanna hear.

**LONE:** You think so?

**MA:** Yeah. Some advice.

**LONE:** Advice? How old are you, anyway?

**MA:** Eighteen.

**LONE:** A child.

**MA:** Yeah. Right. A child. But listen—

**LONE:** A child who tries to advise a grown man—

**MA:** Listen, you got this kind of attitude.

**LONE:** —is a child who will never grow up.

**MA:** You know, the ChinaMen down at camp, they can't stand it.

**LONE:** Oh?

**MA:** Yeah. You gotta watch yourself. You know what they say? They call you "Prince of the Mountain." Like you're too good to spend time with them.

**LONE:** Perceptive of them.

**MA:** After all, you never sing songs, never tell stories. They say you act like your spit is too clean for them, and they got ways to fix that.

**LONE:** Is that so?

**MA:** Like they're gonna bury you in the shit buckets, so you'll have more to clean than your nails.

**LONE:** But I don't shit.

**MA:** Or they're gonna cut out your tongue, since you never speak to them.

**LONE:** There's no one here worth talking to.

**MA:** Cut it out, Lone. Look, I'm trying to help you, all right? I got a solution.

**LONE:** So young yet so clever.

**MA:** That stuff you're doing—it's beautiful. Why don't you do it for the guys at camp? Help us celebrate?

**LONE:** What will "this stuff" help celebrate?

**MA:** C'mon. The strike, of course. Guys on a railroad gang, we gotta stick together, you know.

**LONE:** This is something to celebrate?

**MA:** Yeah. Yesterday, the weak-kneed ChinaMen, they were running around like chickens without a head: "The white devils are sending their soldiers! Shoot us all!" But now, look—day four, see? Still in one piece. Those soldiers—we've never seen a gun or a bullet.

**LONE:** So you're all warrior-spirits, huh?

**MA:** They're scared of us, Lone—that's what it means.

**LONE:** I appreciate your advice. Tell you what—you go down—

**MA:** Yeah?

**LONE:** Down to the camp—

**MA:** Okay.

**LONE:** To where the men are—

**MA:** Yeah?

**LONE:** Sit there—

**MA:** Yeah?

**LONE:** And wait for me.

**MA:** Okay.

*[Pause.]*

That's it? What do you think I am?

**LONE:** I think you're an insect interrupting my practice. So fly away. Go home.

**MA:** Look, I didn't come here to get laughed at.

**LONE:** No, I suppose you didn't.

**MA:** So just stay up here. By yourself. You deserve it.

**LONE:** I do.

**MA:** And don't expect any more help from me.

**LONE:** I haven't gotten any yet.

**MA:** If one day, you wake up and your head is buried in the shit can—

**LONE:** Yes?

**MA:** You can't find your body, your tongue is cut out—

**LONE:** Yes.

**MA:** Don't worry, 'cuz I'll be there.

**LONE:** Oh.

**MA:** To make sure your mother's head is sitting right next to yours.

*[*MA *exits.]*

**LONE:** His head is too big for this mountain. *[Returns to practicing]*

## SCENE 2

*Mountaintop. Next day.* LONE *is practicing.* MA *enters.*

**MA:** Hey.

**LONE:** You? Again?

**MA:** I forgive you.

**LONE:** You . . . what?

**MA:** For making fun of me yesterday. I forgive you.

**LONE:** You can't—

**MA:** No. Don't thank me.

**LONE:** You can't forgive me.

**MA:** No. Don't mention it.

**LONE:** You—! I never asked for your forgiveness.

**MA:** I know. That's just the kinda guy I am.

**LONE:** This is ridiculous. Why don't you leave? Go down to your friends and play soldiers, sing songs, tell stories.

**MA:** Ah! See? That's just it. I got other ways I wanna spend my time. Will you teach me the opera?

**LONE:** What?

**MA:** I wanna learn it. I dreamt about it all last night.

**LONE:** No.

**MA:** The dance, the opera—I can do it.

**LONE:** You think so?

**MA:** Yeah. When I get outa here, I wanna go back to China and perform.

**LONE:** You want to become an actor?

**MA:** Well, I wanna perform.

**LONE:** Don't you remember the story about the three sons whose parents send them away to learn a trade? After three years, they return. The first one says, "I have become a coppersmith." The parents say, "Good. Second son, what have you become?" "I've become a silversmith." "Good—and youngest son, what about you?" "I have become an actor." When the parents hear that their son has become only an actor, they are very sad. The mother beats her head against the ground until the ground, out of pity, opens up and swallows her. The father is so angry he can't even speak, and the anger builds up inside him until it blows his body to pieces—little bits of his skin are found hanging from trees days later. You don't know how you endanger your relatives by becoming an actor.

**MA:** Well, I don't wanna become an "actor." That sounds terrible. I just wanna perform. Look, I'll be rich by the time I get out of here, right?

**LONE:** Oh?

**MA:** Sure. By the time I go back to China, I'll ride in gold sedan chairs, with twenty wives fanning me all around.

**LONE:** Twenty wives? This boy is ambitious.

**MA:** I'll give out pigs on New Year's and keep a stable of small birds to give to any woman who pleases me. And in my spare time, I'll perform.

**LONE:** Between your twenty wives and your birds, where will you find a free moment?

**MA:** I'll play Gwan Gung and tell stories of what life was like on the Gold Mountain.

**LONE:** Ma, just how long have you been in "America"?

**MA:** Huh? About four weeks.

**LONE:** You are a big dreamer.

**MA:** Well, all us ChinaMen here are—right? Men with little dreams—have little brains to match. They walk with their eyes down, trying to find extra grains of rice on the ground.

**LONE:** So, you know all about "America"? Tell me, what kind of stories will you tell?

**MA:** I'll say, "We laid tracks like soldiers. Mountains? We hung from cliffs in baskets and the winds blew us like birds. Snow? We lived underground like moles for days at a time. Deserts? We—"

**LONE:** Wait. Wait. How do you know these things after only four weeks?

**MA:** They told me—the other ChinaMen on the gang. We've been telling stories ever since the strike began.

**LONE:** They make it sound like it's very enjoyable.

**MA:** They said it is.

**LONE:** Oh? And you believe them?

**MA:** They're my friends. Living underground in winter—sounds exciting, huh?

**LONE:** Did they say anything about the cold?

**MA:** Oh, I already know about that. They told me about the mild winters and the warm snow.

**LONE:** Warm snow?

**MA:** When I go home, I'll bring some back to show my brothers.

**LONE:** Bring some—? On the boat?

**MA:** They'll be shocked—they never seen American snow before.

**LONE:** You can't. By the time you get snow to the boat, it'll have melted, evaporated, and returned as rain already.

**MA:** No.

**LONE:** No?

**MA:** Stupid.

**LONE:** Me?

**MA:** You been here awhile, haven't you?

**LONE:** Yes. Two years.

**MA:** Then how come you're so stupid? This is the Gold Mountain. The snow here doesn't melt. It's not wet.

**LONE:** That's what they told you?

**MA:** Yeah. It's true.

**LONE:** Did anyone show you any of this snow?

**MA:** No. It's not winter.

**LONE:** So where does it go?

**MA:** Huh?

**LONE:** Where does it go, if it doesn't melt? What happens to it?

**MA:** The snow? I dunno. I guess it just stays around.

**LONE:** So where is it? Do you see any?

**MA:** Here? Well, no, but . . . *[Pause]* This is probably one of those places where it doesn't snow—even in winter.

**LONE:** Oh.

**MA:** Anyway, what's the use of me telling you what you already know? Hey, c'mon—teach me some of that stuff. Look—I've been practicing the walk—how's this? *[Demonstrates]*

**LONE:** You look like a duck in heat.

**MA:** Hey—it's a start, isn't it?

**LONE:** Tell you what—you want to play some *die siu*?

**MA:** *Die siu?* Sure.

**LONE:** You know, I'm pretty good.

**MA:** Hey, I play with the guys at camp. You can't be any better than Lee—he's really got it down.

*[*LONE *pulls out a case with two dice.]*

**LONE:** I used to play till morning.

**MA:** Hey, us too. We see the sun start to rise, and say, "Hey, if we go to sleep now, we'll never get up for work." So we just keep playing.

**LONE:** *[Holding out dice] Die* or *siu*?

**MA:** *Siu.*

**LONE:** You sure?

**MA:** Yeah!

**LONE:** All right. *[He rolls.] Die!*

**MA:** *Siu!*

*[They see the result.]*

**MA:** Not bad.

*[They continue taking turns rolling through the following section;* MA *always loses.]*

**LONE:** I haven't touched these in two years.

**MA:** I gotta practice more.

**LONE:** Have you lost much money?

**MA:** Huh? So what?

**LONE:** Oh, you have gold hidden in all your shirt linings, huh?

**MA:** Here in "America"—losing is no problem. You know—End of the Year Bonus?

**LONE:** Oh, right.

**MA:** After I get that, I'll laugh at what I lost.

**LONE:** Lee told you there was a bonus, right?

**MA:** How'd you know?

**LONE:** When I arrived here, Lee told me there was a bonus, too.

**MA:** Lee teach you how to play?

**LONE:** Him? He talked to me a lot.

**MA:** Look, why don't you come down and start playing with the guys again?

**LONE:** "The guys."

**MA:** Before we start playing, Lee uses a stick to write "Kill!" in the dirt.

**LONE:** You seem to live for your nights with "the guys."

**MA:** What's life without friends, huh?

**LONE:** Well, why do *you* think I stopped playing?

**MA:** Hey, maybe you were the one getting killed, huh?

**LONE:** What?

**MA:** Hey just kidding.

**LONE:** Who's getting killed here?

**MA:** Just a joke.

**LONE:** That's not a joke, it's blasphemy.

**MA:** Look, obviously you stopped playing 'cause you wanted to practice the opera.

**LONE:** Do you understand that discipline?

**MA:** But, I mean, you don't have to overdo it either. You don't have to treat 'em like dirt. I mean, who are you trying to impress?

*[Pause.* LONE *throws dice into the bushes.]*

**LONE:** Oooops. Better go see who won.

**MA:** Hey! C'mon! Help me look!

**LONE:** If you find them, they are yours.

**MA:** You serious?

**LONE:** Yes.

**MA:** Here. *[Finds the dice]*

**LONE:** Who won?

**MA:** I didn't check.

**LONE:** Well, no matter. Keep the dice. Take them and go play with your friends.

**MA:** Here. *[He offers them to* LONE.] A present.

**LONE:** A present? This isn't a present!

**MA:** They're mine, aren't they? You gave them to me, right?

**LONE:** Well, yes, but—

**MA:** So now I'm giving them to you.

**LONE:** You can't give me a present. I don't want them.

**MA:** You wanted them enough to keep them two years.

**LONE:** I'd forgotten I had them.

**MA:** See, I know, Lone. You wanna get rid of me. But you can't. I'm paying for lessons.

**LONE:** With my dice.

**MA:** Mine now. *[He offers them again.]* Here.

*[Pause.* LONE *runs* MA*'s hand across his forehead.]*

**LONE:** Feel this.

**MA:** Hey!

**LONE:** Pretty wet, huh?

**MA:** Big deal.

**LONE:** Well, it's not from playing *die siu*.

**MA:** I know how to sweat. I wouldn't be here if I didn't.

**LONE:** Yes, but are you willing to sweat after you've finished sweating? Are you willing to come up after you've spent the whole day chipping half an inch off a rock, and punish your body some more?

**MA:** Yeah. Even after work, I still—

**LONE:** No, you don't. You want to gamble, and tell dirty stories, and dress up like women to do shows.

**MA:** Hey, I never did that.

**LONE:** You've only been here a month. *[Pause.]* And what about "the guys"? They're not going to treat you so well once you stop playing with them. Are you willing to work all day listening to them whisper, "That one—let's put spiders in his soup"?

**MA:** They won't do that to me. With you, it's different.

**LONE:** Is it?

**MA:** You don't have to act that way.

**LONE:** What way?

**MA:** Like you're so much better than them.

**LONE:** No. You haven't even begun to understand. To practice every day, you must have a fear to force you up here.

**MA:** A fear? No—it's 'cause what you're doing is beautiful.

**LONE:** No.

**MA:** I've seen it.

**LONE:** It's ugly to practice when the mountain has turned your muscles to ice. When my body hurts too much to come here, I look at the other ChinaMen and think, "They are dead. Their muscles work only because the white man forces them. I live because I can still force my muscles to work for me." Say it. "They are dead."

**MA:** No. They're my friends.

**LONE:** Well, then, take your dice down to your friends.

**MA:** But I want to learn—

**LONE:** This is your first lesson.

**MA:** Look, it shouldn't matter—

**LONE:** It does.

**MA:** It shouldn't matter what I think.

**LONE:** Attitude is everything.

**MA:** But as long as I come up, do the exercises—

**LONE:** I'm not going to waste time on a quitter.

**MA:** I'm not!

**LONE:** Then say it—"They are dead men."

**MA:** I can't.

**LONE:** Then you will never have the dedication.

**MA:** That doesn't prove anything.

**LONE:** I will not teach a dead man.

**MA:** What?

**LONE:** If you can't see it, then you're dead too.

**MA:** Don't start pinning—

**LONE:** Say it!

**MA:** All right.

**LONE:** What?

**MA:** All right. I'm one of them. I'm a dead man too.

*[Pause.]*

**LONE:** I thought as much. So, go. You have your friends.

**MA:** But I don't have a teacher.

**LONE:** I don't think you need both.

**MA:** Are you sure?

**LONE:** I'm being questioned by a child.

*[*LONE *returns to practicing. Silence.]*

**MA:** Look, Lone, I'll come up here every night—after work—I'll spend my time practicing, okay? *[Pause]* But I'm not gonna say that they're dead. Look at them. They're on strike; dead men don't go on strike, Lone. The white devils—they try and stick us with a ten-hour day. We want a return to eight hours and also a fourteen-dollar-a-month raise. I learned the demon English—listen: "Eight hour a day good for white man, alla same good for ChinaMan." These are the demands of live ChinaMen, Lone. Dead men don't complain.

**LONE:** All right, this is something new. But no one can judge the ChinaMen till after the strike.

**MA:** They say we'll hold out for months if we have to. The smart men will live on what we've hoarded.

**LONE:** A ChinaMan's mouth can swallow the earth. *[He takes the dice.]* While the strike is on, I'll teach you.

**MA:** And afterwards?

**LONE:** Afterwards—we'll decide then whether these are dead or live men.

**MA:** When can we start?

**LONE:** We've already begun. Give me your hand.

## SCENE 3

LONE *and* MA *are doing physical exercises.*

**MA:** How long will it be before I can play Gwan Gung?

**LONE:** How long before a dog can play the violin?

**MA:** Old Ah Hong—have you heard him play the violin?

**LONE:** Yes. Now, he should take his violin and give it to a dog.

**MA:** I think he sounds okay.

**LONE:** I think he caused that avalanche last winter.

**MA:** He used to play for weddings back home.

**LONE:** Ah Hong?

**MA:** That's what he said.

**LONE:** You probably heard wrong.

**MA:** No.

**LONE:** He probably said he played for funerals.

**MA:** He's been playing for the guys down at camp.

**LONE:** He should play for the white devils—that will end this stupid strike.

**MA:** Yang told me for sure—it'll be over by tomorrow.

**LONE:** Eight days already. And Yang doesn't know anything.

**MA:** He said they're already down to an eight-hour day and five dollar raise at the bargaining sessions.

**LONE:** Yang eats too much opium.

**MA:** That's doesn't mean he's wrong about this.

**LONE:** You can't trust him. One time—last year—he went around camp looking in everybody's eyes and saying, "Your nails are too long. They're hurting my eyes." This went on for a week. Finally, all the men clipped their nails, made a big pile, which they wrapped in leaves and gave to him. Yang used the nails to season his food—he put it in his soup, sprinkled it on his rice, and never said a word about it again. Now tell me—are you going to trust a man who eats other men's fingernails?

**MA:** Well, all I know is we won't go back to work until they meet all our demands. Listen, teach me some Gwan Gung steps.

**LONE:** I should have expected this. A boy who wants to have twenty wives is the type who demands more than he can handle.

**MA:** Just a few.

**LONE:** It takes years before an actor can play Gwan Gung.

**MA:** I can do it. I spend a lot of time watching the opera when it comes around. Every time I see Gwan Gung, I say, "Yeah. That's me. The god of fighters. The god of adventurers. We have the same kind of spirit."

**LONE:** I tell you, if you work very hard, when you return to China, you can perhaps be the Second Clown.

**MA:** Second Clown?

**LONE:** If you work hard.

**MA:** What's the Second Clown?

**LONE:** You can play the *p'i p'a,* and dance and jump all over.

**MA:** I'll buy them.

**LONE:** Excuse me?

**MA:** I'm going to be rich, remember? I'll buy a troupe and force them to let me play Gwan Gung.

**LONE:** I hope you have enough money, then, to pay audiences to sit through your show.

**MA:** You mean, I'm going to have to practice here every night—and in return, all I can play is the Second Clown?

**LONE:** If you work hard.

**MA:** Am I that bad? Maybe I shouldn't even try to do this. Maybe I should just go down.

**LONE:** It's not you. Everyone must earn the right to play Gwan Gung. I entered opera school when I was ten years old. My parents decided to sell me for ten years to this opera company. I lived with eighty other boys and we slept in bunks four beds high and hid our candy and rice cakes from each other. After eight years, I was studying to play Gwan Gung.

**MA:** Eight years?

**LONE:** I was one of the best in my class. One day, I was summoned by my master, who told me I was to go home for two days, because my mother had fallen very ill and was dying. When I arrived home, Mother was standing at the door waiting, not sick at all. Her first words to me, the son away for eight years, were, "You've been playing while your village has starved. You must go to the Gold Mountain and work."

**MA:** And you never returned to school?

**LONE:** I went from a room with eighty boys to a ship with three hundred men. So, you see, it does not come easily to play Gwan Gung.

**MA:** Did you want to play Gwan Gung?

**LONE:** What a foolish question!

**MA:** Well, you're better off this way.

**LONE:** What?

**MA:** Actors—they don't make much money. Here, you make a bundle, then go back and be an actor again. Best of both worlds.

**LONE:** "Best of both worlds."

**MA:** Yeah!

*[*LONE *drops to the ground, begins imitating a duck, waddling and quacking.]*

**MA:** What are you doing?

*[*LONE *quacks.]*

You're a duck?

*[*LONE *quacks.]*

I can see that.

*[*LONE *quacks.]*

Is this an exercise? Am I supposed to do this?

*[*LONE *quacks.]*

This is dumb. I never seen Gwan Gung waddle.

*[*LONE *quacks.]*

Okay. All right. I'll do it.

*[*MA *and* LONE *quack and waddle.]*

You know, I never realized before how uncomfortable a duck's life is. And you have to listen to yourself quacking all day. Go crazy!

*[*LONE *stands up straight.]*

Now, what was that all about?

**LONE:** No, no. Stay down there, duck.

**MA:** What's the—

**LONE:** *[Prompting]* Quack, quack, quack

**MA:** I don't—

**LONE:** Act your species!

**MA:** I'm not a duck!

**LONE:** Nothing worse than a duck that doesn't know his place.

**MA:** All right. *[Mechanically]* Quack, quack.

**LONE:** More.

**MA:** Quack.

**LONE:** More!

**MA:** Quack, quack, quack!

*[*MA *now continues quacking, as* LONE *gives commands.]*

**LONE:** Louder! It's your mating call! Think of your twenty duck wives! Good! Louder! Project! More! Don't slow down! Put your tail feathers into it! They can't hear you!

*[*MA *is now quacking up a storm.* LONE *exits, unnoticed by* MA.*]*

**MA:** Quack! Quack! Quack! Quack. Quack . . . quack.

*[He looks around.]*

Quack . . . quack . . . Lone? . . . Lone?

*[He waddles around the stage looking.]*

Lone, where are you? Where'd you go?

*[He stops, scratches his left leg with his right foot.]*

C'mon—stop playing around. What is this?

*[*LONE *enters as a tiger, unseen by* MA.*]*

Look, let's call it a day, okay? I'm getting hungry.

*[*MA *turns around, notices* LONE *right before* LONE *is to bite him.]*

Aaaaah! Quack, quack, quack!

*[They face off, in character as animals. Duck—*MA *is terrified.]*

**LONE:** Grrrr!

**MA:** *[As a cry for help]* Quack, quack, quack!

*[*LONE *pounces on* MA. *They struggle, in character.* MA *is quacking madly, eyes tightly closed.* LONE *stands up straight.* MA *continues to quack.]*

**LONE:** Stand up.

**MA:** *[Eyes still closed.]* Quack, quack, quack!

**LONE:** *[Louder]* Stand up!

**MA:** *[Opening his eyes]* Oh.

**LONE:** What are you?

**MA:** Huh?

**LONE:** A ChinaMan or a duck?

**MA:** Huh? Gimme a second to remember.

**LONE:** You like being a duck?

**MA:** My feet fell asleep.

**LONE:** You change forms so easily.

**MA:** You said to.

**LONE:** What else could you turn into?

**MA:** Well, you scared me—sneaking up like that.

**LONE:** Perhaps a rock. That would be useful. When the men need to rest, they can sit on you.

**MA:** I got carried away.

**LONE:** Let's try . . . a locust. Can you become a locust?

**MA:** No. Let's cut this, okay?

**LONE:** Here. It's easy. You just have to know how to hop.

**MA:** You're not gonna get me—

**LONE:** Like this. *[He demonstrates.]*

**MA:** Forget it, Lone.

**LONE:** I'm a locust. *[He begins jumping toward* MA.*]*

**MA:** Hey! Get away!

**LONE:** I devour whole fields.

**MA:** Stop it.

**LONE:** I starve babies before they are born.

**MA:** Hey, look, stop it!

**LONE:** I cause famines and destroy villages.

**MA:** I'm warning you! Get away!

**LONE:** What are you going to do? You can't kill a locust.

**MA:** You're not a locust.

**LONE:** You kill one, and another sits on your hand.

**MA:** Stop following me.

**LONE:** Locusts always trouble people. If not, we'd feel useless. Now, if you became a locust, too . . .

**MA:** I'm not going to become a locust.

**LONE:** Just stick your teeth out!

**MA:** I'm not gonna be a bug! It's stupid!

**LONE:** No man who's just been a duck has the right to call anything stupid.

**MA:** I thought you were trying to teach me something.

**LONE:** I am. Go ahead.

**MA:** All right. There. That look right?

**LONE:** Your legs should be a little lower. Lower! There. That's adequate. So, how does it feel to be a locust? *[*LONE *gets up.]*

**MA:** I dunno. How long do I have to do this?

**LONE:** Could you do it for three years?

**MA:** Three years? Don't be—

**LONE:** You couldn't, could you? Could you be a duck for that long?

**MA:** Look, I wasn't born to be either of those.

**LONE:** Exactly. Well, I wasn't born to work on a railroad, either. "Best of both worlds." How can you be such an insect!

*[Pause.]*

**MA:** Lone . . .

**LONE:** Stay down there! Don't move! I've never told anyone my story—the story of my parents' kidnapping me from school. All the time we were crossing the ocean, the last two years here—I've kept my mouth shut. To you, I finally tell it. And all you can say is, "Best of both worlds." You're a bug to me, a locust. You think you understand the dedication one must have to be in the opera? You think it's the same as working on the railroad.

**MA:** Lone, all I was saying is that you'll go back too, and—

**LONE:** You're no longer a student of mine.

**MA:** What?

**LONE:** You have no dedication.

**MA:** Lone, I'm sorry.

**LONE:** Get up.

**MA:** I'm honored that you told me that.

**LONE:** Get up.

**MA:** No.

**LONE:** No?

**MA:** I don't want to. I want to talk.

**LONE:** Well, I've learned from the past. You're stubborn. You don't go. All right. Stay there. If you want to prove to me that you're dedicated, be a locust till morning. I'll go.

**MA:** Lone, I'm really honored that you told me.

**LONE:** I'll return in the morning. *[Exits.]*

**MA:** Lone? Lone, that's ridiculous. You think I'm gonna stay like this? If you do, you're crazy. Lone? Come back here.

## SCENE 4

*Night.* MA, *alone, as a locust.*

**MA:** Locusts travel in huge swarms, so large that when they cross the sky, they block out the sun, like a storm. Second Uncle—back home—when he was a young man, his whole crop got wiped out by locusts one year. In the famine that followed, Second Uncle lost his eldest son and his second wife—the one he married for love. Even to this day, we look around before saying the word "locust," to make sure Second Uncle is out of hearing range. About eight years ago, my brother and I discovered Second Uncle's cave in back of the stream near our house. We saw him come out of it one day around noon. Later, just before the sun went down, we sneaked in. We only looked once. Inside, there must have been hundreds—maybe five hundred or more—grasshoppers in huge bamboo cages—and around them—stacks of grasshopper legs, grasshopper heads, grasshopper antennae, grasshoppers with one leg, still trying to hop but toppling like trees coughing, grasshoppers wrapped around sharp branches rolling from side to side, grasshopper legs cut off grasshopper bodies, then tied around grasshoppers and tightened till grasshoppers died. Every conceivable kind of grasshopper in every conceivable stage of life and death, subject to every conceivable grasshopper torture. We ran out quickly, my brother and I—we know an evil place by the thickness of the air. Now, I think of Second Uncle. How sad that the locusts forced him to take out his agony on innocent grasshoppers. What if Second Uncle could see me now? Would he cut off my legs? He might as well. I can barely feel them. But then again, Second Uncle never tortured actual locusts, just weak grasshoppers.

## SCENE 5

*Night.* MA *still as a locust.*

**LONE:** *[Off, singing.]*
Hit your hardest
Pound out your tears
The more you try
The more you'll cry
At how little I've moved
And how large I loom
By the time the sun goes down

**MA:** You look rested.

**LONE:** Me?

**MA:** Well, you sound rested.

**LONE:** No, not at all.

**MA:** Maybe I'm just comparing you to me.

**LONE:** I didn't even close my eyes all last night.

**MA:** Aw, Lone, you didn't have to stay up for me. You coulda just come up here and—

**LONE:** For you?

**MA:** —apologized and everything woulda been—

**LONE:** I didn't stay up for you.

**MA:** Huh? You didn't?

**LONE:** No.

**MA:** Oh. You sure?

**LONE:** Positive. I was thinking, that's all.

**MA:** About me?

**LONE:** Well . . .

**MA:** Even a little?

**LONE:** I was thinking about the ChinaMen—and you. Get up, Ma.

**MA:** Aw, do I have to? I've gotten to know these grass-hoppers real well.

**LONE:** Get up. I have a lot to tell you.

**MA:** What'll they think? They take me in, even though I'm a little large, then they find out I'm a human being. I stepped on their kids. No trust. Gimme a hand, will you? *[*LONE *helps* MA *up, but* MA*'s legs can't support him.]* Aw, shit. My legs are coming off. *[He lies down and tries to straighten them out.]*

**LONE:** I have many surprises. First, you will play Gwan Gung.

**MA:** My legs will be sent home without me. What'll my family think? Come to port to meet me and all they get is two legs.

**LONE:** Did you hear me?

**MA:** Hold on. I can't be in agony and listen to Chinese at the same time.

**LONE:** Did you hear my first surprise?

**MA:** No. I'm too busy screaming.

**LONE:** I said, you'll play Gwan Gung.

**MA:** Gwan Gung?

**LONE:** Yes.

**MA:** Me?

**LONE:** Yes.

**MA:** Without legs?

**LONE:** What?

**MA:** That might be good.

**LONE:** Stop that!

**MA:** I'll become a legend. Like the blind man who defended Amoy.

**LONE:** Did you hear?

**MA:** "The legless man who played Gwan Gung."

**LONE:** Isn't this what you want? To play Gwan Gung?

**MA:** No, I just wanna sleep.

**LONE:** No, you don't. Look. Here. I brought you something.

**MA:** Food?

**LONE:** Here. Some rice.

**MA:** Thanks, Lone. And duck?

**LONE:** Just a little.

**MA:** Where'd you get the duck?

**LONE:** Just bones and skin.

**MA:** We don't have duck. And the white devils have been blockading the food.

**LONE:** Sing—he had some left over.

**MA:** Sing? That thief?

**LONE:** And something to go with it.

**MA:** What? Lone, where did you find whiskey?

**LONE:** You know, Sing—he has almost anything.

**MA:** Yeah. For a price.

**LONE:** Once, even some thousand-day-old eggs.

**MA:** He's a thief. That's what they told me.

**LONE:** Not if you're his friend.

**MA:** Sing don't have any real friends. Everyone talks about him bein' tied in to the head of the klan in San Francisco. Lone, you didn't have to do this. Here Have some.

ON THE CENTRAL PACIFIC RAILROAD.

**LONE:** I had plenty.

**MA:** Don't gimme that. This cost you plenty, Lone.

**LONE:** Well, I thought if we were going to celebrate, we should do it as well as we would at home.

**MA:** Celebrate? What for? Wait.

**LONE:** Ma, the strike is over.

**MA:** Shit, I knew it. And we won, right?

**LONE:** Yes, the ChinaMen have won. They can do more than just talk.

**MA:** I told you. Didn't I tell you?

**LONE:** Yes. Yes, you did.

**MA:** Yang told me it was gonna be done. He said—

**LONE:** Yes, I remember.

**MA:** Didn't I tell you? Huh?

**LONE:** Ma, eat your duck.

**MA:** Nine days. In nine days we civilized the white devils. I knew it. I knew we'd hold out till theirs ears started twitching. So that's where you got the duck, right? At the celebration?

**LONE:** No, there wasn't a celebration.

**MA:** Huh? You sure? ChinaMen—they look for any excuse to party.

**LONE:** But I thought *we* should celebrate.

**MA:** Well, that's for sure.

**LONE:** So you will play Gwan Gung.

**MA:** God, nine days. Shit, it's finally done. Well, we'll show them how to party. Make noise. Jump off rocks. Make the mountain shake.

**LONE:** We'll wash your body, to prepare you for the role.

**MA:** What role?

**LONE:** Gwan Gung. I've been telling you.

**MA:** I don't wanna play Gwan Gung.

**LONE:** You've shown the dedication required to become my student, so—

**MA:** Lone, you think I stayed up last night 'cause I wanted to play Gwan Gung?

**LONE:** You said you were like him.

**MA:** I am. Gwan Gung stayed up all night once to prove his loyalty. Well, now I have too. Lone, I'm honored that you told me your story.

**LONE:** Yes . . . That is like Gwan Gung.

**MA:** Good. So let's do an opera about *me*.

**LONE:** What?

**MA:** You wanna party or what?

**LONE:** About you?

**MA:** You said I was like Gwan Gung, didn't you?

**LONE:** Yes, but—

**MA:** Well, look at the operas he's got? I ain't even got one.

**LONE:** Still, you can't—

**MA:** You tell me, is that fair?

**LONE:** You can't do an opera about yourself.

**MA:** I just won a victory, didn't I? I deserve an opera in my honor.

**LONE:** But it's not traditional.

**MA:** Traditional? Lone, you gotta figure any way I could do Gwan Gung wasn't gonna be traditional anyway. I may be as good a guy as him, but he's a better dancer. *[Sings]*

Old Gwan Gung, just sits about
Till the dime-store fighters have had it out
Then he pitches his peach pit
Combs his beard
Draws his sword
And they scatter in fear

**LONE:** What are you talking about?

**MA:** I just won a great victory. I get—whatcha call it?—poetic license. C'mon. Hit the gongs. I'll immortalize my story.

**LONE:** I refuse. This goes against all my training. I try and give you your wish and—

**MA:** Do it. Gimme my wish. Hit the gongs.

**LONE:** I never—I can't.

**MA:** Can't what? Don't think I'm worth an opera? No, I guess not. I forgot—you think I'm just one of those dead men.

*[Silence.* LONE *pulls out a gong.* MA *gets into position.* LONE *hits the gong. They do the following in a mock-Chinese-opera style.]*

**MA:** I am Ma. Yesterday I was kicked out of my house by my three elder brothers, calling me the lazy dreamer of the family. I am sitting here in front of the temple trying to decide how I will avenge this indignity. Here comes the poorest beggar in this village. *[He cues* LONE.*]* He is called Fleaman because his body is the most popular meeting place for fleas from around the province.

**LONE:** *[Singing]*

Fleas in love,
Find your happiness
In the gray scraps of my suit

**MA:** Hello, Flea—

**LONE:** *[Continuing]*

Fleas in need,
Shield your families
In the gray hairs of my beard

**MA:** Hello, Flea—

*[*LONE *cuts* MA *off, continues an extended improvised aria.]*

**MA:** Hello, Fleaman.

**LONE:** Hello, Ma. Are you interested in providing a home for these fleas?

**MA:** No!

**LONE:** This couple here—seeking to start a new home. Housing today is so hard to find. How about your left arm?

**MA:** I may have plenty of my own fleas in time. I have been thrown out by my elder brothers.

**LONE:** Are you seeking revenge? A flea epidemic on your house? *[To a flea]* Get back there. You should be asleep. Your mother will worry.

**MA:** Nothing would make my brothers angrier than seeing me rich.

**LONE:** Rich? After the bad crops of the last three years, even the fleas are thinking of moving north.

**MA:** I heard a white devil talk yesterday.

**LONE:** Oh—with hair the color of a sick chicken and eyes round as eggs? The fleas and I call him Chicken-Laying-an-Egg.

**MA:** He said we can make our fortunes on the Gold Mountain, where work is play and the sun scares off snow.

**LONE:** Don't listen to chicken-brains.

**MA:** Why not? He said gold grows like weeds.

**LONE:** I have heard that it is slavery.

**MA:** Slavery? What do you know, Fleaman? Who told you? The fleas? Yes, I will go to Gold Mountain.

*[Gongs.* MA *strikes a submissive pose to* LONE.*]*

**LONE:** "The one hundred twenty-five dollars passage money is to be paid to the said head of said Hong, who will make arrangements with the coolies, that their wages shall be deducted until the debt is absorbed."

*[*MA *bows to* LONE. *Gongs. They pick up fighting sticks and do a water-crossing dance. Dance ends. They stoop next to each other and rock.]*

**MA:** I have been in the bottom of this boat for thirty-six days now. Tang, how many have died?

**LONE:** Not me. I'll live through this ride.

**MA:** I didn't ask you how you are.

**LONE:** But why's the Gold Mountain so far?

**MA:** We left with three hundred and three.

**LONE:** My family's depending on me.

**MA:** So tell me, how many have died?

**LONE:** I'll be the last one alive.

**MA:** That's not what I wanted to know.

**LONE:** I'll find some fresh air in this hole.

**MA:** I asked, how many have died.

**LONE:** Is that a crack in the side?

**MA:** Are you listening to me?

**LONE:** If I had some air—

**MA:** I asked, don't you see—?

**LONE:** The crack—over there—

**MA:** Will you answer me, please?

**LONE:** I need to get out.

**MA:** The rest here agree—

**LONE:** I can't stand the smell.

**MA:** That a hundred eighty—

**LONE:** I can't see the air—

**MA:** Of us will not see—

**LONE:** And I can't die.

**MA:** Our Gold Mountain dream.

*[*LONE/TANG *dies;* MA *throws his body overboard. The boat docks.* MA *exits, walks through the streets. He picks up one of the fighting sticks, while* LONE *becomes the mountain.]*

**MA:** I have been given my pickax. Now I will attack the mountain.

*[*MA *does a dance of labor.* LONE *sings.]*

**LONE:**

Hit your hardest
Pound out your tears
The more you try
The more you'll cry
At how little I've moved
And how large I loom
By the time the sun goes down

*[Dance stops.]*

**LONE:** This mountain is clever. Buy why shouldn't it be? It's fighting for its life, like we fight for ours.

*[The* MOUNTAIN *picks up a stick.* MA *and the* MOUNTAIN *do a battle dance. Dance ends.]*

**MA:** This mountain not only defends itself—it also attacks. It turns our strength against us.

*[*LONE *does* MA*'s labor dance, while* MA *plants explosives in midair. Dance ends.]*

**MA:** This mountain has survived for millions of years. Its wisdom is immense.

*[*LONE *and* MA *begin a second battle dance. This one ends with them working the battle sticks together.* LONE *breaks away, does a warrior strut.]*

**LONE:** I am a white devil! Listen to my stupid language: "Wha che doo doo blah blah." Look at my wide eyes—like I have drunk seventy-two pots of tea. Look at my funny hair—twisting, turning, like a snake telling lies. *[To* MA*]* Bla bla doo doo tee tee.

**MA:** We don't understand English.

**LONE:** *[Angry]* Bla bla doo doo tee tee!

**MA:** *[With Chinese accent]* Please you-ah speak-ah Chinese?

**LONE:** Oh. Work—uh—one—two—more—work—two—

**MA:** Two hours more? Stupid demons. As confused as your hair. We will strike!

*[Gongs.* MA *is on strike.]*

**MA:** *[In broken English]* Eights hours day good for white man, alla same good for ChinaMan.

**LONE:** The strike is over! We've won!

**MA:** I knew we would.

**LONE:** We forced the white devil to act civilized.

**MA:** Tamed the barbarians!

**LONE:** Did you think—

**MA:** Who woulda thought?

**LONE:** —it could be done?

**MA:** Who?

**LONE:** But who?

**MA:** Who could tame them?

**MA** *and* **LONE:** Only a ChinaMan! *[They laugh.]*

**LONE:** Well, c'mon.

**MA:** Let's celebrate!

**LONE:** We have.

**MA:** Oh.

**LONE:** Back to work.

**MA:** But we've won the strike.

**LONE:** I know. Congratulations! And now—

**MA:** —back to work?

**LONE:** Right.

**MA:** No.

**LONE:** But the strike is over.

*[*LONE *tosses* MA *a stick. They resume their stick battle as before, but* MA *is heard over* LONE*'s singing.]*

| **LONE:** | **MA:** |
|---|---|
| Hit your hardest | Wait. |
| Pound out your tears | I'm tired of this! |
| The more you try | How do we end it? |
| The more you'll cry | Let's stop now, all right? |
| At how little I've moved | Look, I said enough! |
| And how large I loom | |
| By the time the sun goes down | |

*[*MA *tosses his stick away, but* LONE *is already aiming a blow toward it, so that* LONE *hits* MA *instead and knocks him down.]*

**MA:** Oh! Shit . . .

**LONE:** I'm sorry! Are you all right?

**MA:** Yeah. I guess.

**LONE:** Why'd you let go? You can't just do that.

**MA:** I'm bleeding.

**LONE:** That was stupid—where?

**MA:** Here.

**LONE:** No.

**MA:** Ow!

**LONE:** There will probably be a bump.

**MA:** I dunno.

**LONE:** What?

**MA:** I dunno why I let go.

**LONE:** It was stupid.

**MA:** But how were we going to end the opera?

**LONE:** Here. *[He applies whiskey to* MA's bruise.] I don't know.

**MA:** Why didn't we just end it with the celebration? Ow! Careful.

**LONE:** Sorry. But Ma, the celebration's not the end. We're returning to work. Today. At dawn.

**MA:** What?

**LONE:** We've already lost nine days of work. But we got eight hours.

**MA:** Today? That's terrible.

**LONE:** What do you think we're here for? But they listened to our demands. We're getting a raise.

**MA:** Right. Fourteen dollars.

**LONE:** No. Eight.

**MA:** What?

**LONE:** We had to compromise. We got an eight-dollar raise.

**MA:** But we wanted fourteen. Why didn't we get fourteen?

**LONE:** It was the best deal they could get. Congratulations.

**MA:** Congratulations? Look, Lone, I'm sick of you making fun of the ChinaMen.

**LONE:** Ma, I'm not. For the first time. I was wrong. We got eight dollars.

**MA:** We wanted fourteen.

**LONE:** But we got eight hours.

**MA:** We'll go back on strike.

**LONE:** Why?

**MA:** We could hold out for months.

**LONE:** And lose all that work?

**MA:** But we just gave in.

**LONE:** You're being ridiculous. We got eight hours. Besides, it's already been decided.

**MA:** I didn't decide. I wasn't there. You made me stay up here.

**LONE:** The heads of the gangs decide.

**MA:** And that's it?

**LONE:** It's done.

**MA:** Back to work? That's what they decided? Lone, I don't want to go back to work.

**LONE:** Who does?

**MA:** I forgot what it's like.

**LONE:** You'll pick up the technique again soon enough.

**MA:** I mean, what it's like to have them telling you what to do all the time. Using up your strength.

**LONE:** I thought you said even after work, you still feel good.

**MA:** Some days. But others . . . *[Pause]* I get so frustrated sometimes. At the rock. The rock doesn't give in. It's not human. I wanna claw it with my fingers, but that would just rip them up. I want to throw myself head first onto it, but it'd just knock my skull open. The rock would knock my skull open, then just sit there, still, like nothing had happened, like a faceless Buddha. *[Pause]* Lone, when do I get out of here?

**LONE:** Well, the railroad may get finished—

**MA:** It'll never get finished.

**LONE:** —or you may get rich.

**MA:** Rich. Right. This is the Gold Mountain. *[Pause]* Lone, has anyone gone home rich from here?

**LONE:** Yes. Some.

**MA:** But most?

**LONE:** Most . . . do go home.

**MA:** Do you still have the fear?

**LONE:** The fear?

**MA:** That you'll become like them—dead men?

**LONE:** Maybe I was wrong about them.

**MA:** Well, I do. You wanted me to say it before. I can say it now: "They are dead men." Their greatest accomplishment was to win a strike that's gotten us nothing.

**LONE:** They're sending money home.

**MA:** No.

**LONE:** It's not much, I know, but it's something.

**MA:** Lone, I'm not even doing that. If I don't get rich here, I might as well die here. Let my brothers laugh in peace.

**LONE:** Ma, you're too soft to get rich here, naïve—you believed the snow was warm?

**MA:** I've got to change myself. Toughen up. Take no shit. Count my change. Learn to gamble. Learn to win. Learn to stare. Learn to deny. Learn to look at men with opaque eyes.

**LONE:** You want to do that?

**MA:** I will. 'Cause I've got the fear. You've given it to me.

*[Pause.]*

**LONE:** Will I see you here tonight?

**MA:** Tonight?

**LONE:** I just thought I'd ask.

**MA:** I'm sorry, Lone. I haven't got time to be the Second Clown.

**LONE:** I thought you might not.

**MA:** Sorry.

**LONE:** You could have been a . . . fair actor.

**MA:** You coming down? I gotta get ready for work. This is gonna be a terrible day. My legs are sore and my arms are outa practice.

**LONE:** You go first. I'm going to practice some before work. There's still time.

**MA:** Practice? But you said your lost your fear. And you said that's what brings you up here.

**LONE:** I guess I was wrong about that, too. Today, I am dancing for no reason at all.

**MA:** Do whatever you want. See you down at camp.

**LONE:** Could you do me a favor?

**MA:** A favor?

**LONE:** Could you take this down so I don't have to take it all?

*[LONE points to a pile of props.]*

**MA:** Well, okay. *[Pause]* But this is the last time.

**LONE:** Of course, Ma. [MA exits.] See you soon. The last time. I suppose so.

*[LONE resumes practicing. He twirls his hair around as in the beginning of the play. The sun begins to rise. It continues rising until LONE is moving and seen only in shadow.]*

**CURTAIN**

# Writing From Reading

## Summarize

1 Out of historical material, the playwright weaves a fantasylike creation about the relationship between two immigrant laborers. Describe the work situation from which they emerge.

## Analyze Craft

2 How does the playwright make these two characters stand out from the crowd of workers?

3 How do history, myth, and individual desire intersect in the text?

## Analyze Voice

4 Does the dialogue seem real to you? How does its shape and texture differ from what you have heard before?

## Synthesize Summary and Analysis

5 What is the role of Chinese myth and theater in *The Dance and the Railroad*? How do the activities of work and performance come together here?

## Interpret the Play

6 How might this play affect someone's understanding of the making of the American West?

# David Ives (b. 1951)

David Ives was born in Chicago and received his college degree from Northwestern University. While there, he began writing plays. After three years of editing the magazine *Foreign Affairs,* Ives earned an M.F.A. in playwriting from Yale. He is best known for his one-act comedies, such as those collected in *All in the Timing,* the collection that brought him the John Gassner Playwriting Award. In addition to his plays, Ives has contributed articles to magazines including *The New Yorker* and *New York* magazine, and he has also published two children's books. He lives in New York City and has taught at Columbia University.

**AS YOU READ** Consider how slang and stylized language contribute to the comedy.

# Moby Dude, OR: The Three-Minute Whale (2004)

*SFX: sound of waves and gulls. Distant ship's bell.*

*Our Narrator is a stoned-out surfer of seventeen.*

**OUR NARRATOR:** *Call me Ishmael,* dude. Yes, Mrs. Podgorski, I *did* read *Moby-Dick* over the summer like I was supposed to. It was bohdacious. Actually, y'know, it's "Moby-*hyphen*-Dick." The title's got a little hyphen before the "Dick." And what is the meaning of this dash before the "Dick"? *WHOAAA!* Another mystery in this awesome American masterpiece, a peerless allegorical saga of mortal courage, metaphysical ambiguity and maniacal obsession! *What,* Mrs. Podgorski? You don't believe I really *read* Herman Melville's *Moby-Dick Or The Whale*? Five hundred sixty-two pages, fourteen ounces, published 1851, totally tanked its first weekend, re-released in the 1920s as one of the world's gnarliest works of Art? You think I copped all this like off the back of the tome or by watching the crappy 1956 film starring Gregory Peck? Mrs. P., you been chasing my tail since middle school, do *I* get all testy? Do *I* say, what is the plot in under two minutes—besides a whale and a hyphen? *Moby-Dick* in two minutes, huh? Okay, kyool. Let's rip.

*(SFX: ship's bell, close up and sharp, to signal the start and a ticking watch, underneath. Very fast.)*

Fade in the boonies of Massachusetts, eighteen-something. Young dude possibly named Ishmael, like the Bible, meets-cute with, TAA-DAA!, *Queequeg,* a South Sea cannibal with a heart of gold.

*(SFX: cutesy voice going "Awwww.")*

Maybe they're gay.

*(SFX: tongue slurp.)*

Or maybe they represent some east-west, pagan-Christian duality action. Anyway, the two newfound bros go to Mass and hear a sermon about Jonah . . .

*(SFX: one second of church organ.)*

Biblical tie-in, then ship out on Christmas Day (*could be symbolical!*) aboard the USS *Pequod* with its mysterious wacko Captain Ahab . . .

*(SFX: madman laughter.)*

. . . who—*backstory*—is goofyfoot because the equally mysterious momboosaloid white whale Moby-like-the-singer Dick bit his leg off.

*(SFX: chomp.)*

Freudian castration action. I mean he's big and he's got sperm and his last name is "Dick," right? Moby is also a metaphor for God, Nature, Truth, obsessisical love, the world, the past, and white people. Check out Pip the Negro cabin boy who by a *fluke* . . .

*(SFX: rimshot.)*

. . . goes wacko too. Ahab says,

*(SFX: echo effect.)*

*"Bring me the head of the Great White Whale and you win this prize!"*

*(SFX: echo effect out, cash register sound.)*

The crew is stoked, by *NOT* first-mate like-the-coffee-Starbuck. Ahab wants the big one, Starbuck wants the whale juice. Idealism versus capitalism.

*(SFX: an impressed "Whoo.")*

*Radical.* Queequeg tells the carpenter to build him a coffin shaped like a canoe.

*(SFX: theremin.)*

*Foreshadowing!* Then lots of chapters everybody skips about the scientology of whales.

*(SFX: yawn.)*

Cut to . . .

*(SFX: trumpet fanfare.)*

Page 523, the Pacific Ocean. *"Surf's up!"* Ahab sights the Dick. He's totally amped. The boards hit the waves, the crew snakes the Dick for three whole days, bottom of the third Ahab is ten-toes-on-the-nose, he's aggro, Moby goes aerial, Ahab's in the zone, he fires his choicest harpoon, the rope does a 360 round his neck, Ahab crushes out, Moby totals the *Pequod,* everybody eats it 'cept our faithful narrator Ishmael who boogies to safety on Queequeg's coffin . . .

*(SFX: resounding echo effect, deeper voice.)*

*"AND I ONLY AM ESCAPED ALONE TO TELL THEE!"*

*(Resume normal voice.)*

Roll final credits. The End.

*(SFX: ship's bell to signal end of fight. End ticking watch.)*

So what do you say, Mrs. Podgorski? You want to like hang and catch a cup of Starbucks sometime . . . ?—*Tubular!*

*End of play*

# Writing from Reading

### Summarize

**1** A student attempts to summarize Herman Melville's massive masterpiece *Moby-Dick* in under three minutes. Why would that seem appropriate given the life of the average student today?

### Analyze Craft

**2** How does the brevity contribute to the comic effect?

### Analyze Voice

**3** Make a list of surfer terminology. Make a list of mock-serious critical terms. How do these contributes to the voice of the *narrator?*

### Synthesize Summary and Analysis

**4** Take a look at a description of the Herman Melville novel, *Moby-Dick.* In what ways does the play take liberties with the original material? In what ways does it keep the integrity of the material?

### Interpret the Play

**5** The playwright intends to amuse us. What commentary on reading and education does Ives make in the play?

# Denise Chavez (b. 1948)

The American playwright and novelist Denise Chavez has lived in her native New Mexico most of her life. She attended New Mexico State University and received her Masters degree in Dramatic Arts from Trinity University in Texas. After graduation she worked at the Dallas Theater Center and eventually earned an M.F.A. degree from the University of New Mexico . She published her first collection of short stories, called *The Last of the Menu Girls,* in 1986 and since then has gone on to publish novels, more short stories, and plays. She is the founder of the Border Book Festival that is held every year in her hometown of Las Cruces, New Mexico, and devoted to the cause of literature in her native community.

**AS YOU READ** Notice which of the narrator's actions and observations change, and which stay the same, each time she ascends Tortugas Peak.

# Guadalupe × 3 (2009)

## CHARACTERS

**LA MUJER / THE WOMAN (LUPITA, LUPE, MAMA LUPITA)**

## SCENE ONE: EARLY MORNING

*We see the Guadalupe at different ages: seventeen, thirty and seventy-two.*

*At Rise: Early morning around six thirty* A.M. LUPITA, *age seventeen, is climbing Tortugas Peak for the Feast Day of Our Lady of Guadalupe, December 12. Dressed in jeans, or black pants, with a sweat shirt with a pull-over headpiece,* LUPITA *wears a jean jacket and tennis shoes or black hiking shoes. She carries a heavy backpack on her shoulders. She leans on a walking stick and rests from time to time on her climb.*

**LUPITA:** *(Talking to a girlfriend who is climbing with her)*

You've never climbed Tortugas Peak before? Híjole, where have you been? I climb every year with my Granma. She tells me, Lupita Gonzales, this is our tradition and our culture. I've been climbing ever since I was a little girl and I'm sixteen now.

*(looking into a compact and then at the sky)*

So, are you ready? Let's check out our backpacks to see if we have everything we'll need.

*(Opening up the backpack and checking off items inside)*

A candle/veladora de Nuestra Señora de Guadalupe to take up to the altar on the Cerrito. Check. Knife to cut quiotes, the yucca and stool staffs. Check. Colored string to decorate quiote. Check. Bottle of water. Check. Burritos from the Go Burger. Check. Rosary. Check. Cheetoes. Check.

*(looking at the sky)*

It looks like it might snow this year. That's Las Cruces for you.

*(Now at the base of Tortugas Peak)*

Let's go up the middle path. Not the one on the right, that's a goat path and slippery. And not the wild path on the left.

*(Talking to herself)*

Take it slow.

*(Stepping to the side to greet other pilgrims)*

Hello. Good morning.

*(Picking up pace again)*

We're getting higher. Soon you'll be able to see all of Las Cruces and the entire Mesilla Valley. It's real pretty from here.

*(A little tired)*

Rest. Don't go so fast. Pace yourself. That's what my Granma says. Now that she's old, she does the velorio in the church, staying up all night praying the day before the climb because she can't climb anymore. Everyone does what they can, she says, when they can. Whatever you do, do it out of love for La Virgencita.

*(Taking water out of the backpack)*

So you've never come on the climb before? How come? You heard of the climb on December eleventh but you thought it would be too hard? Well, it is and it isn't. You just take it slow and you go down the middle path.

*(Stopping to rest)*

My Granma says that the Guadalupe is the Mother of All the Americas. She's our Mother who is with us always. La Guadalupe es el madre de toda la gente de las Americas. y tenemos que recordar que es nuestra Madre que está con nosotros, siempre. That's what my Granma says in Spanish. The Guadalupe is the Mother of all the Americas and we have to remember that she is with us always.

*(Pausing)*

Chee, my hair is getting all messed up. I don't want nobody to see me flat-headed. Especially Johnny Flores. He's all you know and I'll be all you know. You know. He used to be an esquintle chapito lleno de espinillas with these you know roñas on his arms, anyway, but that was then. Ahora el vato's all you know. I got to have hair, girlfriend!

*(Checking compact and putting on black lipstick)*

So what if he don't like me. I don't care. I'm not climbing for Johnny Flores. I'm climbing for my family and for my manda, my promise to La Virgencita.

*(Stopping to rest)*

What? You don't know the story of La Virgencita? And here you living in Las Cruces and the climb every year in your backyard. Where you been, huh? My abuelita told me the story a long time ago, when I was a little girl . . .

*(Stopping and taking off backpack, sitting on rock, looking out)*

There was this Nativo, this Indio called Juan Diego. He lived in México in 1531, what my Granma calls El Año del Oso, very long ago. One day he was going to early Mass. It was on December 9. Suddenly he heard the most incredible music. Out of a cloud on top of the Cerrito appeared the most beautiful young woman. She wore a blue dress full of stars. Juan Diego knew she was a noblewoman because of her fur-trimmed robe. He knew by her black sash that she was carrying a child. She had a cross around her neck, the symbol of life and death. And the beautiful woman was dark-skinned, like him.

*(Telling the story and becoming the Guadalupe)*

Juanito, Juan Diegüito, the lady called him like a mother would. Where are you going? I am the Mother of the True God, by whom we all live. I want you to go to Bishop Zumárraga, to ask him to build a church for me on this spot so I can care for my children. Juan Diego excused himself from the Beautiful Lady and made his way to the Bishop's house. But he couldn't get in. He returned, very disappointed, to the Beautiful Lady.

*(Getting up)*

Hey, we better start climbing again, it's getting cold. Got to keep moving. I'll tell you the rest of the story as we go along.

*(Pointing out to landscape)*

That's where I live, and over there, that's where my Granma lives, and over there . . .

*(Giggling)*

That's where Johnny Flores lives . . .

*(Making the sign of the cross and then fluffing her hair)*

Que Viva La Virgencita, que Viva!

## SCENE TWO: LATER THAT MORNING

*(LUPE, a thirty-five year old woman, looks out to the landscape for a long time. A sigh of tiredness. She looks unhappy. Looks to the sky. Then out again. She ties her shoelaces. She wears an old pair of jeans, an old black sweatshirt with a scarf of Our Lady of Guadalupe pinned on it. She carries an old resilient Mexican shopping bag full of things.)*

**LUPE:** Long live our Lady of Guadalupe! Que Viva La Virgencita, que Viva!

*(Crossing herself and moving on. She talks to herself as people pass her. She is not in a hurry)*

Got to keep moving! You'd think after all these years of climbing, the walk would get easier.

*(Adjusting her shopping bag)*

Yes, I married Johnny Flores. So now I'm Lupe Gonzales Flores, age thirty-five and counting. Me and Johnny have three kids, el Junior, la Jennifer, y la Vicki.

*(Stopping to rest and look out)*

Poor Johnny! He's a victim of the Gulf War. That stuff they used. He's not right in the head. He drinks a lot. His father died and he don't climb with me anymore like he used to. They think he has a brain tumor. But we don't know. La Jennifer is pregnant from her boyfriend, Manny. La Vicki is driving me

crazy with her texting this texting that, ya me trae con ese teléfono and Junior is in rehab because of the drugs. Yeah, and I'm still working at the K-Mart. In charge of households. Not too many people I know have anything to do with La Martha Stewart. You tell me how many Méxicanos love plaid. And we're not a typical Chicano family. We're going up, up and we're all going to make it. I'm climbing this year for the kids. And Johnny. And for my Granma. It's been sixteen years.

*(Irritated)*

Someone almost fell back there. You have to be very careful or you're going to fall. You know, it makes me happy to see all the kids out here today. So many teenagers and babies, people of all ages! The way they dress! Con esos tattoos y con los arêtes en las cejas o en el ombligo and that cow thing in the nose. Fuchee! What has the world come to? When I was young all we had was black eye liner como la Cleopatra and white lipstick or those textured hose and short skirts. Not that we would have worn them on the climb, my Granma wouldn't have allowed it, no Señorita.

*(To a group of young people)*

Be careful, mi'ja. Giggle. Giggle. The girls, they're so silly. Have you noticed? All they do is talk about boys. Boys!

*(Calling out to the young people)*

Be careful! Cuidado!

*(Tucking her hair under her hat)*

I'm still climbing, Virgencita, after all these years!

*(Stopping to rest on her staff)*

Too many years. Too many stories, too many sorrows, too many too many's! I wish I could take all those kids aside and tell them to wait. Wait! Esperense! Don't be all ready to get married. Just because your honey has a tattoo del Sagrado Corazón aqui en el brazo y otro tattoo aca con el nombre de su Mamá, con la Virgencita all splayed out on his back doesn't mean he's going to be a good provider. I can only talk for myself.

*(An accounting)*

Estoy cansada, Virgencita. I'm tired, Virgencita. Very tired. Bien cansada. Like my Granma used to say, "All of me hurts. Toda la mujer duele."

*(Talking to her Granma)*

I remember how you told me the story of Juan Diego, that story of wonder and majesty. Juan Diego returned to tell the Beautiful Lady that the Bishop had refused to see him. Once again she repeated her request. He left her with the promise that he would return the next day to see the Bishop. The next day, with great difficulty, Juan Diego was admitted to Bishop Zumárraga's chambers. The Bishop did not believe what he had to say and requested proof of the Lady's existence. Juan Diego returned to the Beautiful Lady. She told him to return the following day and that she would give him a sign for the Bishop. But when he returned home, Juan Diego was greeted with the news that his Uncle, Juan Bernardino, was dying. The day came and went and Juan Diego forgot to return to the Beautiful Lady. The next day, Juan Diego was sent to get a priest to give his Uncle the Last Rites. Only then did he remember he had promised the Guadalupe he would go see the Bishop with a sign. And just in case he would run into her, he took another route. Sure enough, La Virgencita met him on the path.

*(In the Guadalupe's Voice)*

The smallest of my children, el más pequeño de mis hijos, where are you going? she asked. Juan Diego told her about his uncle. Do not let your heart be troubled... Am I not here who am your Mother? The Virgencita instructed him to climb the hill and bring her the flowers he would find there. Juan Diego had never seen such exquisite roses. Roses in the wintertime! He took them back to her and the Guadalupe arranged them in his tilma, his poncho made of maguey, and sent him on his way . . .

*(Watching people go by)*

And here I am feeling sorry for myself, Virgencita. There goes a young boy with crutches going up the hill, one crutch forward like an oar and then another . . . One crutch and then another . . . And there's an old woman, descalza, barefooted, without shoes, walking carefully on the rocks, with bloody feet, doing her mand . . . her promise. . . .

*(Getting up and prodding herself)*

I'm over halfway up the mountain, I can see the top of the crest there, and from here it's not so far. I'll get up there and have some water. Then I'll leave our candle up there on the Cerrito, on the altar, out of the wind, near the back, and my prayers will rise high, over Las Cruces, all the way to the Heavens, all the way to God.

*(With reverence)*

Long Live Our Lady of Guadalupe! Que Viva La Virgencita, que Viva!

## SCENE THREE: LATER IN THE MORNING

*(*MAMA LUPITA, *age seventy-three.)*

*(She is waiting by the side of the road at the foot of the mountain, leaning on her walking stick.)*

I'm waiting for the truck to pick me up. Me, Lupita Gonzales Torres. Too old to walk up the mountain anymore. Not since two years ago when I almost fainted. Casi me desmayé. And what good is an old woman that fainted on the side of the road like a costal of chile, a sack of chile? Now I'm going up in style, with the Mayordomo, the Chief of Tortugas Pueblo. They treat me like a queen. La Reina de Las Cruces! That's me. You can call me Mamá Lupita. That's what my kids and grankids all call me.

*(Looking around)*

My grankids started climbing with me last year. That's more than I can say for my kids. La Vicki. La Jennifer. El Junior. Uuuuuque, el Johnny Jr., if he ever gets out of his chair for anything it has to be for a cold beer. And whose fault is it? Mine, Virgencita, for giving in to his father, may he rest in peace. Pobrecito Johnny. I'm climbing for them. And for the soul of my husband, Johnny, may you rest in peace.

*(With her hand on her walking stick)*

I still have my old walking stick. It's served me well all these years. Me ha servido. I've walked this path for more years than you can say mi'ijo. . . .

*(Talking to someone along the path)*

Come on, get in the truck, there's plenty of room. I didn't mean to get in between you and el compadre. Compadre, don't get jealous. No te pongas celosa.

*(Getting comfortable)*

When we get up to the Cerrito, you help me and I'll help you. Me ayudas a caminar, y yo te ayudo a tí. We'll go get the humo, the sacred smoke, we'll cleanse ourselves in the sacred chaparral, and then we'll talk down to our favorite spot, facing the Organ Mountains, and just look at God's wonder. I've brought a little blanket and some food . . .

*(Takes things out of her mochila—a large Guadalupe bag)*

Only the best . . . Kentucky Fried Chicken . . . Extra crispy . . . Que burritos ni que burritos, compadre. No traje burritos este año, porque you know . . . A mi edad me afectan los frijoles . . . when you get older the beans, you know. . . .

*(Resting in the sun)*

We'll sit in the sun like lizards. We'll stay that way un rato, a little while, and then we'll make our quiotes like we do every year. Our wooden yucca staffs will be beautiful like they always are.

*(Looking out)*

Look, there's my house. My neighborhood. The Bank. My Granma grew up there and me and el Johnny and then my kids. And there's Jennifer's house up in Telshor. There's the hospital. And the Bank. You know what they call it. OR rather what the President, Mr. Papen, called it. Papen's Last Erection.

*(Laughing to herself and then crossing herself)*

I can't help myself Madrecita, that's what it's called.

*(Sighing)*

Ay! We'll pray for everybody, eh? Familia—what else is there? Qué más hay, compadre? Remember that you are connected to everyone on this living earth, human, animal, plant, and mineral.

*(Crossing herself again)*

We made it, Bendito sea Dios, otro año de gracia. Y de humilidad. Just like the moment el Obispo, Bishop Zumárraga opened Juan Diego's tilma and out tumbled the beautiful rosas de Casilla. It was in the wintertime. Oh, what a miracle! Juan Diego never gave up and finally the miracle took place that last visit to the Bishop. There, on his robe was imprinted the image of La Virgencita de Guadalupe.

*(With reverence)*

I want to think about where I've been and where I'm going. And I want to give thanks to God and Our Lady of Guadalupe for another year of love and many blessings. Y quiero darle las gracias a Mi Diosito, y especialmente a La Virgencita, por otro año lleno de amor tantas bendiciones.

*(Getting up a little stiff, but still spry)*
*(Looking out)*

Long Live Our Lady of Guadalupe! Que Viva La Virgencita, que Viva!

# Writing from Reading

### Summarize

1 List, and describe, the three stages of Lupita's life.

### Analyze Craft

2 How does the playwright reshape the literal time of Lupita's life?

3 What role does the setting play in the evolution of character?

4 What roles do church rituals play?

### Analyze Voice

5 How much of Lupita's language is high speech; how much is low? Give examples. What is the effect of this voice on the play?

### Synthesize Summary and Analysis

6 What is the function of the story (of the Virgin of Guadalupe) in the story of the play?

### Interpret the Play

7 Three pilgrimages up to the top of a New Mexico peak make up a woman's lifetime. In what way is this celebratory, in what way a description of life's difficulties?

8 How representative of the lives of Chicana women is Lupita's particular life? Can you see similar patterns in the lives of women in your own family, whether Chicana or otherwise?

"Theater is thriving now—it's thriving all over the world . . . You've got these large theaters that produce Broadway-type shows; but you've got hundreds of smaller theaters and theaters like college and university theaters, community theaters, resident theaters. These theaters are producing things and people are going to see them." Conversation with Edwin Wilson

# Getting Started: A Research Project

Research is a skill that will carry you through your college career. To help acquaint you with the research process, the materials you need for this project are made available on our website (www.mhhe.com/delbanco1e). Other ideas for research projects and sources appear at the end of this chapter.

A theater critic is someone who watches a production and then gives a summary of it, including his or her critique of various aspects of the play. Since we can't ask you to go see a live production of Arthur Kopit's *Wings,* we have provided you with excerpts of the original radio version as performed on NPR's *Earplay,* available at our website, www.mhhe.com/delbanco1e. The following assignments will give you the chance to play the critic, using the script printed in this chapter along with the radio clips as sources. You may also consult other resources, including the interview with Arthur Kopit, as directed below.

1. In his interview, Kopit talks about his realization that his research notes on file cards were the start of actually writing the play. "It was the juxtaposition of notes and scenes. I hadn't worked linearly." He also discusses order and sequence, saying that the play's images can appear "in any sequence, although there is a sequence, but just allowing it to be mixed up put the audience in the right way." Compare the reader's sense of time reading the script and the listener's sense of time in the radio play. Are they similar? Different? Give your critical opinion of which techniques related to time are the most or least effective.
2. Some critics explain the end of the play as Mrs. Stilson's tragic death; others, hesitant to say whether she dies, see her possible death as her last, brave act. Form your own critical opinion—or interpretation—of the ending, based on both the radio play and the script. Do you get a different idea from one version than the other? Be sure to support your opinion with quotes from each adaptation. You might also go a step further and, as a critic would do, make an evaluation of which is more successful.
3. "Plays are idiosyncratic," Kopit says in his interview. "They're all idiosyncratic if they're any good." Listen to the excerpt of his interview in which he talks about the playwright's voice. Then, considering both the script and the radio play, write a critical review in which you give an opinion as to how idiosyncratic you believe *Wings* is. Support your opinion with specific examples from either version. Hint: You might first want to explain idiosyncratic in relation to plays, using the dictionary and what Kopit says as tools in forming your definition.

# Suggestions for Writing about Contemporary Theater

1. Read one of the plays as a first-night reviewer might. Write a review of the play based on your immediate reactions to it (see chapter 31 for an example of a play review). Comment on the characters and the plot, describe the setting, the language, and so forth. Make a recommendation for others to read this play or not.
2. Do you find there is a sharp line drawn between what we have called modern theater and experimental theater or do you see experimental theater as a continuation of the modern play? Explain.

# A Handbook for Writing from Reading

# Handbook Contents

# 1 Critical Approaches to Literature

## 1a APPROACH CRITICISM AS AN ONGOING CONVERSATION

Literary theorist Kenneth Burke famously described literary criticism as an ongoing conversation, one that began before we arrived and will continue after we leave. If the thought of engaging in literary criticism intimidates you, think of it instead as adding your voice to those of others who have read the same work of literature and want to talk about it. You need not interpret the work as if you've been the first to read it, and you certainly don't have to feel as though you must deliver the final response. You need only contribute to the conversation.

Whenever we discuss literature, whether we acknowledge our appreciation or disdain for a text, interpret its meanings and mysteries, or cite it as an example of a larger trend in culture, we engage in an act of **literary criticism.** Such responsiveness is all around us and probably has its origins in the genesis of literature itself. The classical philosophers Plato and Aristotle laid the foundations for studying the creation, interpretation, and impact of the written and spoken word—in a sense, they began the conversation we now join.

## 1b USE A CRITICAL APPROACH AS A LENS FOR EXAMINATION

While these classical theories are still relevant, approaches to literature have changed with new developments in human thought. Literary critics and theorists are almost inevitably influenced by major shifts in philosophy, politics, history, science, technology, and economics. For example, the advent of Freud's theories of psychology opened up a way of examining literature by applying psychoanalytic concepts to characters and authors. Later in the century, the feminist movement led critics to apply ideas about gender roles to literary criticism. These borrowings from other fields are particularly influential for twentieth-century theory and criticism, as our discussion of the major approaches to criticism will show.

It may be helpful to think of each of the critical approaches described here as a *lens* through which a piece of literature can be examined. Any work can be looked at from several different points of view, but the lens itself cannot do the interpreting—a reader must do that. Still, the lens provides the reader with a set of guiding principles with which to limit all of the possible questions the reader might ask. For students engaging in literary criticism for the first time, these lenses can be enormously helpful because they narrow down the overwhelming array of possibilities, providing specific approaches to take and questions to ask. Studying and understanding the work of readers who have come before us can make the task of coming up with our own ideas less daunting.

## 1c CONSIDER MULTIPLE APPROACHES

Many of the critical schools described here initially defined themselves in opposition to the dominant theories of their times. It is important to keep in mind, though, that in current practice many critics are comfortable adopting methods from several critical approaches. For example, a reader who considers herself a Marxist critic may draw on historical and deconstructionist theories to help her analyze a work. Each approach described here has its own merits and shortcomings, proponents, and skeptics. These approaches are not necessarily mutually exclusive, and it is possible for critics to choose the most useful strategies from several approaches in their own writing. Though we will refer to "feminist critics" and "formalist critics" in the descriptions below, there are very few scholars who confine themselves solely to one theory without sometimes turning to other approaches.

What follows is an overview of different major critical methods.

### Formalist Criticism

**Formalist criticism** emerged in Russia in the early twentieth century in the work of critics like Boris Eikhenbaum, Viktor Shklovsky, and Mikhail Bakhtin. Their ideas were adopted and further developed in the United States and Great Britain under the heading of **new criticism** by critics such as John Crowe Ransom, Allen Tate, Robert Penn Warren, I. A. Richards, William Wimsatt, T. S. Eliot, and Cleanth Brooks.

Formalists/new critics consider a successful text to be a complete, independent, unified artifact whose meaning and value can be understood purely by analyzing the interaction of its formal and technical components, such as plot, imagery, structure, style, symbol, and tone. Rather than drawing their textual interpretations from *extrinsic* factors such as the historical, political, or biographical context of the work, formalist critics focus on the text's *intrinsic* formal elements. As Cleanth Brooks explains in his article, "The Formalist Critic," published in 1951 in the *Kenyon Review,*

> *. . . the formalist critic is concerned primarily with the work itself. Speculation on the mental processes of the author takes the critic away from the work into biography and psychology. There is no reason, of course, why he should not turn away into biography and psychology. Such explorations are very much worth making. But they should not be confused with an account of the work.*

Formalist criticism relies heavily on **close reading** or explication of the text in order to analyze the ways in which distinct formal elements combine to create a unified artistic experience for the reader. A major tenet of formalism is the notion that form and content are so intertwined that in a successful work of art they cannot be dissevered or separated out.

For formalist or new critics the study and interpretation of literature is an intrinsically valuable intellectual activity rather than a means to advance moral, religious, or political ideologies. There are those who consider this approach to be a limited one—they have argued that formalism can be elitist, willfully dismissive of historical and biographical factors in the work. *All* study of literature has to include at least a component of close reading; the question other critics raise is whether it suffices as a way to approach a text.

## Boris Eikhenbaum (1886–1959)

# The Theory of the Formal Method (1926)

The organization of the Formal method was governed by the principle that the study of literature should be made specific and concrete. All efforts were directed toward terminating the earlier state of affairs, in which literature, as A. Veselovskij observed, was *res nullius.*[1] That was what made the Formalists so intolerant of other "methods" and of eclectics. In rejecting these "other" methods, the Formalists actually were rejecting (and still reject) not methods but the gratuitous mixing of different scientific disciplines and different scientific problems. Their basic point was, and still is, that the object of literary science, as literary science, ought to be the investigation of the specific properties of literary material, of the properties that distinguish such material from material of any other kind, notwithstanding the fact that its secondary and oblique features make that material properly and legitimately exploitable, as auxiliary material, by other disciplines. The point was consummately formulated by Roman Jakobson:

> The object of study in literary science is not literature but "literariness," that is, what makes a given work a *literary* work. Meanwhile, the situation has been that historians of literature act like nothing so much as policemen, who, out to arrest a certain culprit, take into custody (just in case) everything and everyone they find at the scene as well as any passers-by for good measure. The historians of literature have helped themselves to everything—environment, psychology, politics, philosophy. Instead of a science of literature, they have worked up a concoction of home-made disciplines. They seem to have forgotten that those subjects pertain to their own fields of study—to the history of philosophy, the history of culture, psychology, and so on, and that those fields of study certainly may utilize literary monuments as documents of a defective and second-class variety among other materials.

To establish this principle of specificity without resorting to speculative aesthetics required the juxtaposing of the literary order of facts with another such order. For this purpose one order had to be selected from among existent orders, which, while contiguous with the literary order, would contrast with it in terms of functions. It was just such a methodological procedure that produced the opposition between "poetic" language and "practical" language. This opposition [. . .] served as the activating principle for the Formalists' treatment of the fundamental problems of poetics. Thus, instead of an orientation toward a

[1]A legal term describing something that has no ownership.

> history of culture or of social life, towards psychology, or aesthetics, and so on, as had been customary for literary scholars, the Formalists came up with their own characteristic orientation toward linguistics, a discipline contiguous with poetics in regard to the material under investigation, but one approaching that material from a different angle and with different kinds of problems to solve.
>
> from *The Theory of the Formal Method*

## Biographical Criticism

**Biographical criticism** emphasizes the belief that literature is created by authors whose unique experiences shape their writing and therefore can inform our reading of their work. Biographical critics research and use an author's biography to interpret the text as well as the author's stated *intentions* or comments on the process of composition itself. These critics often consult the author's memoirs to uncover connections between the author's life and the author's work. They may also study the author's rough drafts to trace the evolution of a given text or examine the author's library to discern potential influences on the author's work.

Knowledge of an author's biography can surely help readers interpret or understand a text. For example, awareness of Flannery O'Connor's devout Catholicism will make the religious elements of her stories and novels more meaningful to readers. However, as we have just seen, formalist critics reject biographical criticism, arguing that any essential meaning in a text should be discernable to readers purely through close reading. They reject the notion that an author's thought processes and stated *intentions* for a text necessarily define the work's meaning. They call this emphasis on discerning or trusting an author's own stated purpose the **intentional fallacy** and believe a text's meaning must be contained in and communicated only by the text as such.

While biographical criticism was once quite common, in recent decades it is more often used as *part* of a larger critical approach than as the primary critical strategy.

# Gary Lee Stonum (b. 1947)

# Dickinson's Literary Background (1998)

> Books and reading were [Emily] Dickinson's primary access to a world beyond Amherst. We can thus at least be reasonably confident that the cultural contexts of Dickinson's writing are primarily literary, particularly if that term is defined inclusively. Her surviving letters are filled with references to favorite authors, and some of the poems allude in one way or another to recognizable elements of her reading (Pollak, "Allusions"). To be sure, she is by no means a learned poet in the vein of Milton or Pope, writers who can hardly be appreciated without understanding their allusions and allegiances. Yet she is also surely not the unlettered author Richard Chase once unguardedly deemed her, uninfluenced by literary sources in either style or thought.
>
> A few cautions need to be kept in mind as we examine various claims about Dickinson's literary milieu. First, we know very little about how or even whether Dickinson imagined her work as participating in any public enterprise. By con-

trast to Keats, who dreamed of being among the English poets after his death, or a James Joyce, who schemed tirelessly to shape his own reputation, Dickinson hardly trafficked in any cultural arena. We do possess information about the books she read or admired, and we know from the persistent testimony of her letters and poems that she regarded poetry as an exalted calling. Yet, although we can reasonably infer from this a certain broad ambition, we simply do not know if Dickinson regarded her vocation as entailing some sense of a role in literary history or as obliging her to bargain in the cultural marketplace. We do not, for example, know whether or in what respect she regarded herself as a woman poet, in spite of a number of lively arguments supposing that she did.

[. . .] At the writerly end of the spectrum lie the sources Dickinson drew upon or referred to as she wrote, which are of varying importance. Dickinson's regard for Elizabeth Barrett Browning makes it likely that her "Vision of Poets" is a source of "I died for Beauty," as well as or even rather than Keats's now more famous "Ode on a Grecian Urn." On the other hand, the identification is by no means crucial to an understanding of the poem.

The more interesting cases are those in which the source is disputed and identification would make some difference to our reading. Dickinson was notably fond of exotic place-names, most of which she must have come upon in her reading and some of which may carry thematic associations. The reference to "Chimborazo" in "Love—thou are high" may well derive incidentally from Edward Hitchcock's *Elementary Geology,* where it stands among a list of the world's tallest mountains, or it may originate from similarly casual uses in Barrett Browning and Emerson. On the other hand, if we heed Judith Farr's investigations into the influence of contemporary painting, then we might recall that Frederic Church's mammoth painting of Chimborazo was one of the most celebrated luminist canvases of the day. If the poem is read in the latter context, then the "Love" addressed by the poem as like the mountain would function more insistently as a figure of sublime theophany. (The poem also clearly alludes to Exodus 33, the chief biblical commonplace for such an event.)

[. . .] Many of the references in Dickinson's writings are discussed in Jack Capps's indispensable *Emily Dickinson's Reading,* which includes a detailed index of the books and authors she mentions in poems or letters. Capps also surveys the contents of the family library, much of which is now at Harvard. Unfortunately, the usefulness of the library "is limited by the fact that books from the Austin Dickinson and Edward Dickinson household have been mixed and, in most cases, dates of acquisition and individual ownership are uncertain." Likewise, although these volumes include inscriptions, marginalia, and other evidence of use, few of the markings can be confidently traced to the poet herself.

from *Dickinson's Literary Background*

## Historical Criticism

**Historical criticism** emphasizes the relationship between a text and its historical context. When interpreting a text, historical critics highlight the cultural, philosophical, and political movements and ideologies prevalent during the text's creation and reception. Such critics may also use literary texts as a means of studying or promoting a particular movement in history—cultural , political, or otherwise.

Historical critics do extensive research to uncover the social and intellectual trends that influenced the life and work of the author and his or her original audience. This research brings to light allusions, concepts, and vocabulary or word usage that would have been easily understood by the author or the original audience but may elude contemporary readers. Historical critics also study the ways in which the meanings of a given text change over time, looking, for example, at the ways in which Victorians staged or responded to Shakespeare's *A Midsummer Night's Dream.*

One frequent objection to historical criticism is that these methods can reveal more about the context surrounding a text than about the meaning or value of the text itself. Another objection is that historical criticism sometimes views literature simply as an expression of the historical trends of a given era, rather than viewing texts as autonomous, idiosyncratic expressions of a particular author's views. Historical criticism, some argue, oversimplifies the relationship between a text and the prevailing or dominant cultural context, overlooking the possibility that the text may have a subversive, distorted, distanced, or anachronistic relationship to the dominant culture of the author's time.

## Carl Van Doren (1885–1950)

# Mark Twain (1921)

Of the major American novelists Mark Twain derived least from any literary, or at any rate from any bookish, tradition. Hawthorne had the example of Irving, and Cooper had that of Scott, when they began to write; Howells and Henry James instinctively fell into step with the classics. Mark Twain came up into literature from the popular ranks, trained in the school of newspaper fun-making and humorous lecturing, only gradually instructed in the more orthodox arts of the literary profession. He seems to most eyes, however, less indebted to predecessors than he actually was, for the reason that his provenance has faded out with the passage of time and the increase of his particular fame. Yet he had predecessors and a provenance. As a printer he learned the mechanical technique of his trade of letters; as a jocose writer for the newspapers of the Middle West and the Far West at a period when a well established mode of burlesque and caricature and dialect prevailed there, he adapted himself to a definite convention; as a raconteur he not only tried his methods on the most diverse auditors but consciously studied those of Artemus Ward, then the American master of the craft; Bret Harte, according to Mark Twain, "trimmed and trained and schooled me"; and thereafter, when the "Wild Humorist of the Pacific Slope," as it did not at first seem violent to call him, came into contact with professed men of letters, especially Howells, he had already a mastership of his own, though in a second rank.

To be a "humorist" in the United States of the sixties and seventies was to belong to an understood and accepted class. It meant, as Orpheus C. Kerr and John Phœnix and Josh Billings and Petroleum V. Nasby and Artemus Ward had recently and typically been showing, to make fun as fantastically as one liked but never to rise to beauty; to be intensely shrewd but never profound; to touch pathos at intervals but never tragedy. The humorist assumed a name not his own, as Mark Twain did, and also generally a character—that of some rustic sage or adventurous eccentric who discussed the topics of the moment keenly and drolly. Under his assumed character, of which he ordinarily made fun, he claimed a wide license of speech, which did not, however, extend to indecency or to any very serious satire. His fun was the ebullience of a strenuous society, the laughter of escape from difficult conditions. It was rooted fast in that optimism

> which Americans have had the habit of considering a moral obligation. It loved to ridicule those things which to the general public seemed obstacles to the victorious progress of an average democracy; it laughed about equally at idlers and idealists, at fools and poets, at unsuccessful sinners and unsuccessful saints. It could take this attitude toward minorities because it was so confident of having the great American majority at its back, hearty, kindly, fair-intentioned, but self-satisfied and unspeculative. In time Mark Twain partly outgrew this type of fun—or rather, had frequent intervals of a different type and also of a fierce seriousness—but the origins of his art lie there. So do the origins of his ideas lie among the populace, much as he eventually outgrew the evangelical orthodoxy and national complacency and personal hopefulness with which he had first been burdened.
>
> from *The American Novel*

## Psychological or Psychoanalytic Criticism

**Psychoanalytic criticism** originally stemmed, like psychoanalysis itself, from the work of Sigmund Freud. That revolutionary thinker sought to analyze the conscious and subconscious mental workings of his patients by listening to them discuss their dreams, their erotic urges, and their childhoods. Psychoanalytical critics in a sense study characters and authors as they would patients, looking in the text for evidence of childhood trauma, repressed sexual impulses, preoccupation with death, and so on. Through the lens of psychology they attempt to explain the motivations and meanings behind characters' actions. Such critics have, for example, noted Hamlet's Oedipus complex, his desire to kill his (step)father and possess his mother.

At the same time, psychological critics use textual and biographical evidence as a means to better understand the *author's* psychology. They may attribute the somber tone of a group of poems to the poet's contemporaneous loss of a spouse, or may look for patterns in several texts to identify an author's subconscious preoccupations, fears, or motivations. Psychological critics have, for example, attributed sexist tendencies to Hemingway by arguing that women rarely play major roles in his fiction and are often manipulative or emasculating when they do. Others disagree, noting that Hemingway's female characters, while not dominant, frequently offer the story's wisest, most lucid perspectives through what are often the story's most memorable lines of dialogue. To relate these issues to Hemingway's conflicted love for his mother is to consider the work in psychological as well as biographical terms.

Finally, psychoanalytical critics also examine the process and nature of literary creation, studying the ways in which texts create an emotional and intellectual effect for readers and authors. Here too the strategy is most effective when inclusive as opposed to exclusive; this is a useful tool for reading when it's not the *only* approach to a text.

# Kenneth Burke (1897–1993)

# The Poetic Process (1925)

> If we wish to indicate a gradual rise to a crisis, and speak of this as a climax, or a crescendo, we are talking in intellectualistic terms of a mechanism which can often be highly emotive. There is in reality no such general thing as a crescendo. What does exist is a multiplicity of individual artworks each of which

may be arranged as a whole, or in some parts, in a manner which we distinguish as climactic. And there is also in the human brain the potentiality for reacting favorably to such a climactic arrangement. Over and over again in the history of art, different material has been arranged to embody the principle of the crescendo; and this must be so because we "think" in a crescendo, because it parallels certain psychic and physical processes which are at the roots of our experience. The accelerated motion of a falling body, the cycle of a storm, the procedure of the sexual act, the ripening of crops—growth here is not merely a linear progression, but a fruition. Indeed, natural processes are, inevitably, "formally" correct, and by merely recording the symptoms of some physical development we can obtain an artistic development. Thomas Mann's work has many such natural forms converted into art forms, as, in *Death in Venice,* his charting of a sunrise and of the progressive stages in a cholera epidemic. And surely, we may say without much fear of startling anyone, that the work of art utilizes climactic arrangement because the human brain has a pronounced potentiality for being arrested, or entertained, by such an arrangement.

[. . .] Whereupon, returning to the Poetic Process, let us suppose that while a person is sleeping some disorder of the digestion takes place, and he is physically depressed. Such depression in the sleeper immediately calls forth a corresponding psychic depression, while this psychic depression in turn translates itself into the invention of details which will more or less adequately symbolize this depression. If the sleeper has had some set of experiences strongly marked by the feeling of depression, his mind may summon details from this experience to symbolize his depression. If he fears financial ruin, his depression may very reasonably seize upon the cluster of facts associated with this fear in which to individuate itself. On the other hand, if there is no strong set of associations in his mind clustered about the mood of depression, he may invent details which, on waking, seem inadequate to the mood. This fact accounts for the incommunicable wonder of a dream, as when at times we look back on the dream and are mystified at the seemingly unwarranted emotional responses which the details "aroused" in us. Trying to convey to others the emotional overtones of this dream, we laboriously recite the details, and are compelled at every turn to put in such confessions of defeat as "There was something strange about the room," or "For some reason or other I was afraid of this boat, although there doesn't seem to be any good reason now." But the details were not the cause of the emotion; the emotion, rather, dictated the selection of the details. Especially when the emotion was one of marvel or mystery, the invented details seem inadequate—the dream becoming, from the standpoint of communication, a flat failure, since the emotion failed to individuate itself into adequate symbols. And the sleeper himself, approaching his dream from the side of consciousness after the mood is gone, feels how inadequate are the details for conveying the emotion that caused them, and is aware that even for him the wonder of the dream exists only in so far as he still remembers the quality pervading it. Similarly, a dreamer may awaken himself with his own hilarious laughter, and be forthwith humbled as he recalls the witty saying of his dream. For the delight in the witty saying came first (was causally prior) and the witty saying itself was merely the externalization, or individuation, of this delight. Of a similar nature are the reminiscences of old men, who recite the facts of their childhood, not to force upon us the trivialities and minutiae of these experiences, but in the forlorn hope of conveying to us the "overtones" of their childhood, overtones which, unfortunately, are beyond reach of the details which they see in such an incommunicable light, looking back as they do upon a past which is at once themselves and another.

The analogy between these instances and the procedure of the poet is apparent. In this way the poet's moods dictate the selection of details and thus individuate themselves into one specific work of art.

from *The Poetic Process*

### Archetypal, Mythic, or Mythological Criticism

**Archetypal** or **mythological criticism** focuses on the patterns or features that recur through much of literature, regardless of its time period or cultural origins. The archetypal approach to criticism stems from the work of Carl Jung, a Swiss psychoanalyst (and contemporary of Freud) who argued that humans share in a **collective unconscious,** or a set of characters, plots, symbols, and images that each evoke a universal response. Jung calls these recurring elements **archetypes** and likens them to *instincts*—knowledge or associations with which humans are born. Some examples of archetypes are the quest story, the story of rebirth, or the initiation story; others are the good mother, the evil stepmother, the wise old man, the notion that a desert symbolizes emptiness or hopelessness, or that a garden symbolizes fertility or paradise.

Archetypal or mythological critics analyze the ways in which such archetypes function in literature and attempt to explain the power that literature has over us or the reasons why certain texts continue to hold power over audiences many centuries after their creation.

## Northrop Frye (1912–1991)
## The Archetypes of Literature (1951)

We say that every poet has his own peculiar formation of images. But when so many poets use so many of the same images, surely there are much bigger critical problems involved than biographical ones. As Mr. Auden's brilliant essay *The Enchafèd Flood* shows, an important symbol like the sea cannot remain within the poetry of Shelley or Keats or Coleridge: it is bound to expand over many poets into an archetypal symbol of literature. And if the genre has a historical origin, why does the genre of drama emerge from medieval religion in a way so strikingly similar to the way it emerged from Greek religion centuries before? This is a problem of structure rather than origin, and suggests that there may be archetypes of genres as well as of images.

It is clear that criticism cannot be systematic unless there is a quality in literature which enables it to be so, an order of words corresponding to the order of nature in the natural sciences. An archetype should be not only a unifying category of criticism, but itself a part of a total form, and it leads us at once to the question of what sort of total form criticism can see in literature. [. . .] the search for archetypes is a kind of literary anthropology, concerned with the way that literature is informed by pre-literary categories such as ritual, myth and folk tale. We next realize that the relation between these categories and literature is by no means purely one of descent, as we find them reappearing in the greatest classics—in fact there seems to be a general tendency on the part of great classics to revert to them.

[. . .] In the solar cycle of the day, the seasonal cycle of the year, and the organic cycle of human life, there is a single pattern of significance, out of

> which myth constructs a central narrative around a figure who is partly the sun, partly vegetative fertility and partly a god or archetypal human being. [. . .] I supply the following table of its phases:
>
> 1. The dawn, spring and birth phase. Myths of the birth of the hero, of revival and resurrection, of creation and (because the four phases are a cycle) of the defeat of the powers of darkness, winter and death. Subordinate characters: the father and the mother. The archetype of romance and of most dithyrambic and rhapsodic poetry.
> 2. The zenith, summer, and marriage or triumph phase. Myths of apotheosis, of the sacred marriage, and of entering into Paradise. Subordinate characters: the companion and the bride. The archetype of comedy, pastoral and idyll.
> 3. The sunset, autumn and death phase. Myths of fall, of the dying god, of violent death and sacrifice and of the isolation of the hero. Subordinate characters: the traitor and that siren. The archetype of tragedy and elegy.
> 4. The darkness, winter and dissolution phase. Myths of the triumph of these powers; myths of floods and the return of chaos, of the defeat of the hero[. . .] Subordinate characters: the ogre and the witch. The archetype of satire (see, for instance, the conclusion of *The Dunciad*).
>
> from *The Archetypes of Literature*

## Marxist Criticism

**Marxist criticism** is one of the most significant types of **sociological criticism.** Sociological criticism is the study of literary texts as products of the cultural, political, and economic context of the author's time and place. Critics using this approach examine practical factors such as the ways in which economics and politics influence the publishing and distribution of texts, shaping the audience's reception of a text and therefore its potential to influence society. Such factors, of course, may also affect the author's motives or options while writing the text. Sociological critics also identify and analyze the sociological content of literature, or the ways in which authors or audiences may use texts directly or indirectly to promote or critique certain sociological views or values.

Marxist or **economic determinist criticism** is based on the writings of Karl Marx, who argued that economic concerns shape lives more than anything else, and that society is essentially a struggle between the working classes and the dominant capitalist classes. Rather than assuming that culture evolves naturally or autonomously out of individual human experience, Marxist critics maintain that culture—including literature—is shaped by the interests of the dominant or most powerful social class.

Although Marxist critics do not ignore the artistic construction of a literary text, they tend to focus more on the ideological and sociological content of literary texts—such as the ways in which a character's poverty or powerlessness limits his or her choice of actions in a story, making his or her efforts futile or doomed to failure. These critics use literary analysis to raise awareness about the complex and powerful relationship between class and culture. At the same time, some Marxist critics also promote literature or interpretations of literature that can *change* the balance of power between social classes, often by subverting the values of the dominant class, or by inspiring the working classes to heroic or communal rebellion. As Marx wrote, "The philosophers have only *interpreted* the world in various ways; the point is to *change* it."

# Leon Trotsky (1879–1940)
# Literature and Revolution (1924)

The form of art is, to a certain and very large degree, independent, but the artist who creates this form, and the spectator who is enjoying it are not empty machines, one for creating form and the other for appreciating it. They are living people, with a crystallized psychology representing a certain unity, even if not entirely harmonious. This psychology is the result of social conditions. The creation and perception of art forms is one of the functions of this psychology. And no matter how wise the Formalists try to be, their whole conception is simply based upon the fact that they ignore the psychological unity of the social man, who creates and who consumes what has been created.

The proletariat has to have in art the expression of the new spiritual point of view which is just beginning to be formulated within him, and to which art must help him give form. This is not a state order, but an historic demand. Its strength lies in the objectivity of historic necessity. You cannot pass this by, nor escape its force. [. . .] It is unquestionably true that the need for art is not created by economic conditions. But neither is the need for food created by economics. On the contrary, the need for food and warmth creates economics. It is very true that one cannot always go by the principles of Marxism in deciding whether to reject or to accept a work of art. A work of art should, in the first place, be judged by its own law, that is, by the law of art. But Marxism alone can explain why and how a given tendency in art has originated in a given period of history; in other words, who it was who made a demand for such an artistic form and not for another, and why.

It would be childish to think that every class can entirely and fully create its own art from within itself, and, particularly, that the proletariat is capable of creating a new art by means of closed art guilds or circles, or by the Organization for Proletarian Culture, etc. Generally speaking, the artistic work of man is continuous. Each new rising class places itself on the shoulders of its preceding one. But this continuity is dialectic, that is, it finds itself by means of internal repulsions and breaks. New artistic needs or demands for new literary and artistic points of view are stimulated by economics, through the development of a new class, and minor stimuli are supplied by changes in the position of the class, under the influence of the growth of its wealth and cultural power. Artistic creation is always a complicated turning inside out of old forms, under the influence of new stimuli which originate outside of art. In this sense of the word, art is a handmaiden. It is not a disembodied element feeding on itself, but a function of social man indissolubly tied to his life and environment.

from *Literature and Revolution*

## Structuralist Criticism

**Structuralism** emerged in France in the 1950s, largely in the work of scholars like Claude Levi-Strauss and Roland Barthes. They were indebted in part to the earlier work of the Swiss linguist Ferdinand de Saussure, who emphasized that the meanings of words or signs are shaped by the overarching structure of the language or system to which they belong. Similarly, structuralist literary critics work from the belief that a given work of literature can be fully understood only when a reader considers the system of conventions, or the *genre* to which it belongs or responds.

Structuralist critics therefore define and study systematic patterns or structures exhibited by many texts in a given genre. A classic example of this type of study is Vladimir Propp's *Morphology of the Folktale,* in which the critic identifies several key patterns in the plots of folk tales (the hero leaves home, the hero is tested, the hero gains use of a magic agent, etc.). Structuralists thus study the relationship between a given literary text and the larger system of meanings and expectations in the genre or culture from which that text emerges. They also look to literature to study the ways in which meaning is created across culture by means of a system of signs—for example, the pattern of associations that has developed around the images of light (purity, good) and darkness (evil, somber). Here the study of **semiotics** is germane; the way a thing looks to the individual reader or how and what a word *signifies* can change our understanding of a text.

The structuralist approach has been used more frequently and successfully in the study of fiction than poetry. Because of its emphasis on the commonalities within a genre, the structuralist approach has also been helpful to critics attempting to compare works from different time periods or cultures.

## Vladimir Propp (1895–1970)
# Fairy Tale Transformations (1928)

The study of the fairy tale may be compared in many respects to that of organic formation in nature. Both the naturalist and the folklorist deal with species and varieties which are essentially the same. The Darwinian problem of the origin of species arises in folklore as well. The similarity of phenomena both in nature and in our field resists any direct explanation which would be both objective and convincing. It is a problem in its own right. Both fields allow two possible points of view: either the internal similarity of two externally dissimilar phenomena does not derive from a common genetic root—the theory of spontaneous generation—or else this morphological similarity does indeed result from a known genetic tie—the theory of differentiation owing to subsequent metamorphoses or transformations of varying cause and occurrence.

In order to resolve this problem, we need a clear understanding of what is meant by similarity in fairy tales. Similarity has so far been invariably defined in terms of a plot and its variants. We find such an approach acceptable only if based upon the idea of the spontaneous generation of species. Adherents to this method do not compare plots; they feel such comparison to be impossible or, at the very least, erroneous. Without our denying the value of studying individual plots and comparing them solely from the standpoint of their similarity, another method, another basis for comparison may be proposed. Fairy tales can be compared from the standpoint of their composition or structure; their similarity then appears in a new light.

We observe that the actors in the fairy tale perform essentially the same actions as the tale progresses, no matter how different from one another in shape, size, sex, and occupation, in nomenclature and other static attributes.

> This determines the relationship of the constant factors to the variables. The functions of the actors are constant; everything else is a variable. For example:
>
> 1. The king sends Ivan after the princess; Ivan departs.
> 2. The king sends Ivan after some marvel; Ivan departs.
> 3. The sister sends her brother for medicine; he departs.
> 4. The stepmother sends her stepdaughter for fire; she departs.
> 5. The smith sends his apprentice for a cow; he departs.
>
> The dispatch and departure on a quest are constants. The dispatching and departing actors, the motivations behind the dispatch, and so forth, are variables. In later stages of the quest, obstacles impede the hero's progress; they, too, are essentially the same, but differ in the form of imagery.
>
> The functions of the actors may be singled out. Fairy tales exhibit thirty-one functions, not all of which may be found in any one fairy tale; however, the absence of certain functions does not interfere with the order of appearance of the others. Their aggregate constitutes one system, one composition. This system has proved to be extremely stable and widespread. The investigator, for example, can determine very accurately that both the ancient Egyptian fairy tale of the two brothers and the tale of the firebird, the tale of *Morozka,* the tale of the fisherman and the fish, as well as a number of myths follow the same general pattern. An analysis of the details bears this out.
>
> from *Fairy Tale Transformations*

## New Historicism

Both **new historicism** and structuralism owe a debt to the work of the influential French philosopher Michel Foucault. Among other things, Foucault studied the ways in which power dynamics affect human society and, more important, the acquisition and spread of knowledge. Individuals and institutions in positions of power have greater potential to shape the discourse in their field and thus to influence human knowledge and shape the "truth." New historicists look in literary history for "sites of struggle"—developments or texts that illustrate or seek to shift the balance of power.

New historicism emerged as a reaction to new criticism's disregard of historical context, but also in response to the perceived shortcomings of older methods of historical criticism. Rather than focusing on canonical texts as representations of the most powerful or dominant historical movements, new historicists give equal or more attention to marginal texts and non-literary texts (newspapers, pamphlets, legal documents, medical documents, etc.). New historicists attempt to highlight overlooked or suppressed texts, particularly those that express deviation from the dominant culture of the time. In this way, new historicists study not just the historical context of a major literary text, but the complex relationship between texts and culture, or the ways in which literature can challenge as well as support a given culture.

A weakness of this method is implicit in its strength. Those who disagree with Foucault and his followers would stress that the plays of William Shakespeare are more important documents than laundry lists or tax rolls from Elizabethan and Jacobean England—that a work of individual excellence can tell us more about a period than does its census or burial records. Again, it's useful here to remember that critical approaches need not be exclusive, and a sophisticated critic will likely use more than a single strategy when dealing with a text.

## Stephen Greenblatt (b. 1943)
# The Power of Forms in the English Renaissance (1982)

The earlier historicism tends to be monological; that is, it is concerned with discovering a single political vision, usually identical to that said to be held by the entire literate class or indeed the entire population ("In the eyes of the later middle ages," writes Dover Wilson, Richard II "represented the type and exemplar of royal martyrdom" [p. 50]). This vision, most often presumed to be internally coherent and consistent, though occasionally analyzed as the function of two or more elements, has the status of an historical fact. It is not thought to be the product of the historian's interpretation, nor even of the particular interests of a given social group in conflict with other groups. Protected then from interpretation and conflict, this vision can serve as a stable point of reference, beyond contingency, to which literary interpretation can securely refer. Literature is conceived to mirror the period's beliefs, but to mirror them, as it were, from a safe distance.

The new historicism erodes the firm ground of both criticism and literature. It tends to ask questions about its own methodological assumptions and those of others [. . .].

Moreover, recent criticism has been less concerned to establish the organic unity of literary works and more open to such works as fields of force, places of dissension and shifting interests, occasions for the jostling of orthodox and subversive impulses. [. . .] The critical practice represented in this volume challenges the assumptions that guarantee a secure distinction between "literary foreground" and "political background" or, more generally, between artistic production and other kinds of social production. Such distinctions do in fact exist, but they are not intrinsic to the texts; rather they are made up and constantly redrawn by artists, audiences, and readers. These collective social constructions on the one hand define the range of aesthetic possibilities within a given representational mode and, on the other, link that mode to the complex network of institutions, practices, and beliefs that constitute the culture as a whole. In this light, the study of genre is an exploration of the poetics of culture.

from *The Power of Forms in the English Renaissance*

## Gender Criticism

**Feminist criticism** also focuses on sociological determinants in literature, particularly the ways in which much of the world's canonical literature presents a patriarchal or male-dominated perspective. Feminist critics highlight the ways in which female characters are viewed with prejudice, are subjugated to male interests, or are simply overlooked in literature. They highlight these injustices to women and seek to reinterpret texts with special attention to the presentation of women. Feminist critics also study the ways in which women *authors* have been subjected to prejudice, disregard, or unfair interpretation. They attempt to recover and champion little-known or little-valued texts by women authors—who have been marginalized by the male establishment since the formal study of literature began.

Gay and lesbian studies are, if not directly related to feminist criticism, similar in operational strategy. Interpretation of recognized classics may bring a new vantage to bear and cast a new light on old writings; a discussion of "cross-dressing in Shakespeare" or "male bonding in Melville" would belong to this mode of analysis. Here the critic focuses on submerged or hidden aspects of a text, as well as more overt referents; here too a part of the project is to recover lost or little known works of art from earlier generations.

While the focus on overt prejudice is the easiest feature of feminist criticism to recognize, the approach as a whole actually involves much more subtle and nuanced interpretations of texts. As the passage below from Judith Fetterley indicates, feminist critics in some cases find the more subtle traces of male dominance in literature to be the most insidious, because they so easily can go overlooked and pass for the universal or true experience. This puts female readers in the awkward position of doubting the very validity of a female perspective.

**Queer theory** emerged from **gay and lesbian criticism** partly in response to the AIDS epidemic and owes much to Michel Foucault's work on power and discourse and how language itself shapes our sense of who we are. He argues that the idea of being a "homosexual" would have been impossible without psychoanalytic institutions and discourse that created the category of homosexuality. Sexuality is looked upon as straight (or *normative*) or queer (or *non-normative*) and as a social construction rather than an essential component of one's identity. Some believe this undermines a critique of oppression and prejudice toward gays and lesbians.

## Judith Fetterley (b. 1938)

# On the Politics of Literature (1978)

> Literature is political. It is painful to have to insist on this fact, but the necessity of such insistence indicates the dimensions of the problem. John Keats once objected to poetry "that has a palpable design upon us." The major works of American fiction constitute a series of designs on the female reader, all the more potent in their effect because they are "impalpable." One of the main things that keep the design of our literature unavailable to the consciousness of the woman reader, and hence impalpable, is the very posture of the apolitical, the pretense that literature speaks universal truths through forms from which all the merely personal, the purely subjective, has been burned away or at least transformed through the medium of art into the representative. When only one reality is encouraged, legitimized, and transmitted and when that limited vision endlessly insists on its comprehensiveness, then we have the conditions necessary for that confusion of consciousness in which impalpability flourishes. It is the purpose of this book to give voice to a different reality and different vision, to bring a different subjectivity to bear on the old "universality." To examine American fictions in light of how attitudes toward women shape their form and content is to make available to consciousness that which has been largely left unconscious and thus to change our understanding of these fictions, our relation to them, and their effect on us. It is to make palpable their designs.

> American literature is male. To read the canon of what is currently considered classic American literature is perforce to identify as male. Though exceptions to this generalization can be found here and there—a Dickinson poem, a Wharton novel—these exceptions usually function to obscure the argument and confuse the issue: American literature is male. Our literature neither leaves women alone nor allows them to participate. It insists on its universality at the same time that it defines that universality in specifically male terms. "Rip Van Winkle" is paradigmatic of this phenomenon. While the desire to avoid work, escape authority, and sleep through the major decisions of one's life is obviously applicable to both men and women, in Irving's story this "universal" desire is made specifically male. Work, authority, and decision making are symbolized by Dame Van Winkle, and the longing for flight is defined against her. She is what one must escape from, and the "one" is necessarily male. In Mailer's *An American Dream,* the fantasy of eliminating all one's ills through the ritual of scapegoating is equally male: the sacrificial scapegoat is the woman/wife and the cleansed survivor is the husband/male. In such fictions the female reader is co-opted into participation in an experience from which she is explicitly excluded; she is asked to identify with a selfhood that defines itself in opposition to her; she is required to identify against herself.
>
> from *On the Politics of Literature*

## Ethnic Studies and Postcolonialism

**Ethnic studies** emerged after the Civil Rights movement in the United States, but you can find its roots in the pioneering work of W.E.B. DuBois and others of the black arts movement and the Harlem Renaissance. Ethnic studies employs a cross-curricular analysis that is concerned with the social, economic, and cultural aspects of ethnic groups and an approach to literature that includes artistic and cultural traditions that are often pushed to the margins or considered only in relation to a dominant culture. Asian American, Native American, Afro-Caribbean, Italian American, and Latinos are a few of many examples of groups that ethnic studies might explore. Ethnic studies seeks to give voice to literature that has previously been overlooked in the traditionally Eurocentric worldview by reclaiming literary traditions and taking on subjects that explore identity outside the Eurocentric mainstream. But even works that are not written by ethnic writers lend themselves to ethnic studies. For example, a critic wishing to analyze William Faulkner's work from an ethnic studies perspective might focus on his portrayal of African Americans.

Ethnic studies has helped open the American literary **canon**—works deemed essential milestones in a literary tradition—to works by authors outside the white majority. Another far-reaching effect of ethnic studies is that it questions applying traditional modes of literary inquiry (such as feminist and Marxist approaches) to all literature. It suggests that we might be able to learn something more if we approach a text by examining the cultural and social conventions and realities out of which it was created. With the publication in the 1950s of work by Caribbean poet and legislator Aimée Césaire and North African writer Frantz Fanon, the discipline of **postcolonialism** found its beginnings, offering views of relations between the colonizing West and colonized nations and regions that differed sharply from the conventional Western perspectives. The field's modern American academic roots go back to the 1978 publication of *Orientalism* by the late Columbia University scholar Edward Said, a Palestinian by birth, who posits that the concept of the Orient was a projection of the West's ideas of the "other." Many of today's major writers have come out of the old British colonies, from Chinua Achebe to V.S. Naipal to Salman Rushdie, to name a few.

One of the major practitioners of this mode of criticism, Harvard scholar Henry Louis Gates, places such variety of study in a cultural context in which the urgency of the matter becomes plain to hear.

## Henry Louis Gates (b. 1950)

# Loose Canons: Notes on the Culture Wars (1992)

There's no denying that the multicultural initiative arose, in part, because of the fragmentation of American society by ethnicity, class, and gender. To make it the culprit for this fragmentation is to mistake effect for cause. [. . .] Perhaps we should try to think of American culture as a conversation among different voices—even if it's a conversation that some of us weren't able to join until recently. Perhaps we should think about education, as the conservative philosopher Michael Oakeshott proposed, as "an invitation into the art of this conversation in which we learn to recognize the voices," each conditioned, as he says, by a different perception of the world. Common sense says that you don't bracket 90 percent of the world's cultural heritage if you really want to learn about the world.

To insist that we "master our own culture" before learning others only defers the vexed question: What gets to count as "our" culture? What makes knowledge worth knowing? Unfortunately, as history has taught us, an Anglo-American regional culture has too often masked itself as universal, passing itself off as our "common culture," and depicting different cultural traditions as "tribal" or "parochial." So it's only when we're free to explore the complexities of our hyphenated American culture that we can discover what a genuinely common American culture might actually look like. Common sense . . . reminds us that we're all ethnics, and the challenge of transcending ethnic chauvinism is one we all face.

Granted, multiculturalism is no magic panacea for our social ills. We're worried when Johnny can't read. We're worried when Johnny can't add. But shouldn't we be worried, too, when Johnny tramples gravestones in a Jewish cemetery or scrawls racial epithets on a dormitory wall? It's a fact about this country that we've entrusted our schools with the fashioning and refashioning of a democratic policy; that's why the schooling of America has always been a matter of political judgment. But in America, a nation that has theorized itself as plural from its inception, our schools have a very special task.

The society we have made simply won't survive without the values of tolerance. And cultural tolerance comes to nothing without cultural understanding. In short, the challenge facing Americans in the next century will be the shaping, at long last, of a truly common public culture, one responsive to the long-silenced cultures of color. If we relinquish the ideal of America as a plural nation, we've abandoned the very experiment that America represents.

From *Loose Canons: Notes on the Cultural Wars*

### Reader-Response Criticism

The **reader-response** approach emphasizes the role of the reader in the writer-text-reader transaction. Reader-response critics believe a literary work is not complete until someone reads and interprets it. Such critics acknowledge that each reader has a different set of experiences and views; therefore, each reader's response to a text may be different. (Moreover, a single reader may have several and contradictory responses to a work of art depending on the reading-context: a good dinner, a bad breakfast, a single flickering fluorescent bulb—all these affect the way we look at and absorb a page.) This plurality of interpretations is acceptable, even inevitable, since readers are not interpreting a fixed, completed text, but rather *creating* the text as they read it. Reader-response critics do stress that texts limit the possibilities of interpretation; it is not correct for readers to derive an interpretation that textual evidence does not support. So, for instance, it's inappropriate to claim that the character in a story is a vampire because she only ever appears during nighttime scenes in the story—but it's appropriate to compare the housewife in Susan Glaspell's play *Trifles* (chapter 30), to a "caged" bird once we understand the nature of her plight.

Reader-response criticism, moreover, acknowledges the subjectivity of interpretation and aims to discover the ways in which cultural values affect readers' interpretations. Rather than only emphasizing values embodied in an author or literary work, this approach examines the values embodied in the *reader.*

## Wolfgang Iser (1926–2007)
# Interplay between Text and Reader (1978)

Textual models designate only one aspect of the communicatory process. Hence textual repertoires and strategies simply offer a frame within which the reader must construct for himself the aesthetic object. Textual structures and structured acts of comprehension are therefore the two poles in the act of communication, whose success will depend on the degree in which the text establishes itself as a correlative in the reader's consciousness. This "transfer" of text to reader is often regarded as being brought about solely by the text. Any successful transfer however—though initiated by the text—depends on the extent to which this text can activate the individual reader's faculties of perceiving and processing. Although the text may well incorporate the social norms and values of its possible readers, its function is not merely to *present* such data, but, in fact, to use them in order to secure its uptake. In other words, it offers guidance as to what is to be produced, and therefore cannot itself be the product. This fact is worth emphasizing, because there are many current theories which give the impression that texts automatically imprint themselves on the reader's mind of their own accord. This applies not only to linguistic theories but also to Marxist theories, as evinced by the term "Rezeptionsvorgabe"[1] (structured

[1]See Manfred Naumann et al., *Gesellschaft—Literatur—Lesen. Literaturrezeption in theoretischer Sicht* (Aufbau-Verlog, Berlin and Weimar, 1973), p. 35.

prefigurement) recently coined by East German critics. Of course, the text is a "structured prefigurement," but that which is given has to be received, and the *way* in which it is received depends as much on the reader as on the text. Reading is not a direct "internalization," because it is not a one-way process, and our concern will be to find means of describing the reading process as a dynamic *interaction* between text and reader. We may take as a starting-point the fact that the linguistic signs and structures of the text exhaust their function in triggering developing acts of comprehension. This is tantamount to saying that these acts, though set in motion by the text, defy total control by the text itself, and, indeed, it is the very lack of control that forms the basis of the creative side of reading.

This concept of reading is by no means new. In the eighteenth century, Laurence Sterne was already writing in *Tristram Shandy:* ". . . no author, who understands the just boundaries of decorum and good-breeding, would presume to think all: The truest respect which you can pay to the reader's understanding, is to halve this matter amicably, and leave him something to imagine, in his turn, as well as yourself. For my own part, I am eternally paying him compliments of this kind, and do all that lies in my power to keep his imagination as busy as my own."[2] Thus author and reader are to share the game of the imagination, and, indeed, the game will not work if the text sets out to be anything more than a set of governing rules. The reader's enjoyment begins when he himself becomes productive, i.e., when the text allows him to bring his own faculties into play. There are, of course, limits to the reader's willingness to participate, and these will be exceeded if the text makes things too clear or, on the other hand, too obscure: boredom and overstrain represent the two poles of tolerance, and in either case the reader is likely to opt out of the game.

from *Interplay Between Text and Reader (1978)*

## Poststructuralism and Deconstruction

The poststructuralist approach (**poststructuralism**) was primarily developed in France in the late 1960s by Roland Barthes and Jacques Derrida. Poststructuralists believe that texts do not have a single, stable meaning or interpretation, in part because language itself is filled with ambiguity, multiple meanings, and meanings that can change with time or context. Even a simple dictionary definition reveals several multiple uses for each word, and we know that context and tone can expand the number of possible meanings. Moreover, within any work of literature, authors intentionally and unintentionally create even more multiple meanings through sound sense, connotation, or patterns of usage. Poststructuralists revel in the possibility of so many interpretations not just for words but for every element of a text's construction.

Like formalists, poststructuralists use the technique of close reading to focus very precisely on the language and construction of a text. Yet whereas formalists do this in order to develop a sense of the text as a unified artistic whole, poststructuralists "deconstruct" the text, deliberately seeking to reveal the inevitable *inconsistency* or *lack of unity* in even the most successful and revered texts (**deconstruction**). Poststructuralists do not believe that interpretation can reconstruct an author's intentions; they do not even privilege an author's intentions, believing that the text stands apart from the author and may well contain meanings unintended by its maker. These meanings are, in the eyes of poststructuralists, as valid as any other, if textual evidence supports them.

---

[2]Laurence Sterne, *Tristram Shandy II,* 11 (Everyman's Library; London, 1956), p. 79.

Poststructuralists thus reject the notion of "privileged" or standard interpretations and embrace what might sometimes seem like a chaotic approach to literary interpretation. In his book *The Pleasure of the Text,* for example, Roland Barthes presents his random observations on narrative *in alphabetical order,* rather than in the form of a methodically unified argument, since the notion of textual unity is, in his eyes, an illusion.

## Roland Barthes (1915–1980)
# The Death of the Author (1967)

In his story *Sarrasine,* Balzac, describing a castrato disguised as a woman, writes the following sentence: "This was woman herself, with her sudden fears, her irrational whims, her instinctive worries, her impetuous boldness, her fussings, and her delicious sensibility." Who is speaking thus? Is it the hero of the story bent on remaining ignorant of the castrato hidden beneath the woman? Is it Balzac the individual, furnished by his personal experience with a philosophy of Woman? Is it Balzac the author professing "literary" ideas on femininity? Is it universal wisdom? Romantic psychology? We shall never know, for the good reason that writing is the destruction of every voice, of every point of origin. Writing is that neutral, composite, oblique space where our subject slips away, the negative where all identity is lost, starting with the very identity of the body of writing.

No doubt it has always been that way. As soon as a fact is *narrated* no longer with a view to acting directly on reality but intransitively, that is to say, finally outside of any function other than that of the very practice of the symbol itself, this disconnection occurs, the voice loses its origin, the author enters into his own death, writing begins. [. . .] The *author* still reigns in histories of literature, biographies of writers, interviews, magazines, as in the very consciousness of men of letters anxious to unite their person and their work through diaries and memoirs. The image of literature to be found in ordinary culture is tyrannically centered on the author, his person, his life, his tastes, his passions [. . .] The *explanation* of a work is always sought in the man or woman who produced it, as if it were always in the end, through the more or less transparent allegory of the fiction, the voice of a single person, the *author* "confiding" in us.

[. . .] We know now that a text is not a line of words releasing a single "theological" meaning (the "message" of the Author-God) but a multi-dimensional space in which a variety of writings, none of them original, blend and clash. The text is a tissue of quotations drawn from the innumerable centres of culture. [. . .] the writer can only imitate a gesture that is always anterior, never original. His only power is to mix writings, to counter the ones with the others, in such a way as never to rest on any one of them. Did he wish to *express himself,* he ought at least to know that the inner "thing" he thinks to "translate" is itself only a ready-formed dictionary, its words only explainable through other words, and so on indefinitely [. . .]. Succeeding the Author, the scriptor no longer bears within him passions, humours, feelings, impressions, but rather this

> immense dictionary from which he draws a writing that can know no halt: life never does more than imitate the book, and the book itself is only a tissue of signs, an imitation that is lost, infinitely deferred.
>
> Once the Author is removed, the claim to decipher a text becomes quite futile. To give a text an Author is to impose a limit on the text, to furnish it with a final signified, to close the writing. Such a conception suits criticism very well, the latter then allotting itself the important task of discovering the Author (or its hypostases: society, history, psyche, liberty) beneath the work: when the Author has been found, the text is "explained"—victory to the critic. Hence there is no surprise in the fact that, historically, the reign of the Author has also been that of the Critic, nor again in the fact that criticism (be it new) is today undermined along with the author. In the multiplicity of writing, everything is to be *disentangled,* nothing *deciphered;* the structure can be followed, "run" (like the thread of a stocking) at every point and at every level, but there is nothing beneath: the space of writing is to be ranged over, not pierced; writing ceaselessly posits meaning ceaselessly to evaporate it, carrying out a systematic exemption of meaning. In precisely this way literature (it would be better from now on to say *writing*), by refusing to assign a "secret," an ultimate meaning, to the text (and to the world as texts), liberates what may be called an anti-theological activity, an activity that is truly revolutionary since to refuse to fix meaning is, in the end, to refuse God and his hypostases—reason, science, law.
>
> from *The Death of the Author*

## Cultural Studies

The critical perspective usually referred to as **cultural studies** developed mainly in England in the sixties by such New Left writers and sociologists as Raymond Williams, Richard Hoggart, and Stuart Hall. These critics took a sociological approach to literature and their views were colored by the philosophical leftism of such social philosophers as the Italian Antonio Gramsci. The movement grew mainly out of the desire to view social life and social movements from an analytical perspective somewhat akin to the analysis of film and literature.

The American academic branch of this form of criticism also incorporated (mainly in translation) the formal philosophical and critical approaches of a number of French academics including Foucault and other so-called deconstructionists. (Novelist Saul Bellow, affronted by this method, called these writings "Stale chocolates, imported from France. . . ."). Whatever good the English approach might have produced was muted, if not negated, by the French influence, which emphasized viewing society as comprised of various "texts" and imbuing everything from literature to the placement of traffic lights with equal value.

Twentieth-century sociological criticism has been a productive and interesting variety of criticism, as in, for example, studies of the relation of the literacy rate and the rise of the English novel or the effects of the rise of the dime novel in nineteenth-century America or the elevation of film studies to a high place within the university curriculum. Cultural criticism cheerfully blurs the boundaries among the disciplines and acts with a vengeance to blur the lines between high art and popular culture.

# Vincent B. Leitch (b. 1944)
# Poststructuralist Cultural Critique (1992)

Whereas a major goal of New Criticism and much other modern formalistic criticism is aesthetic evaluation of freestanding texts, a primary objective of cultural criticism is cultural critique, which entails investigation and assessment of ruling and oppositional beliefs, categories, practices, and representations, inquiring into the causes, constitutions, and consequences as well as the modes of circulation and consumption of linguistic, social, economic, political, historical, ethical, religious, legal, scientific, philosophical, educational, familial, and aesthetic discourses and institutions. In rendering a judgment on an aesthetic artifact, a New Critic privileges such key things as textual coherence and unity, intricacy and complexity, ambiguity and irony, tension and balance, economy and autonomy, literariness and spatial form. In mounting a critique of a cultural "text," an advocate of postructuralist cultural criticism evaluates such things as degrees of exclusion and inclusion, of complicity and resistance, of domination and letting-be, of abstraction and situatedness, of violence and tolerance, or monologue and polylogue, of quietism and activism, of sameness and otherness, of oppression and emancipation, or centralization and decentralization. Just as the aforementioned system of evaluative criteria underlies the exegetical and judgmental labor of New Criticism, so too does the above named set of commitments undergird the work of poststructuralist cultural critique.

Given its commitments, poststructuralist cultural criticism is, as I have suggested, suspicious of literary formalism. Specifically, the trouble with New Criticism is its inclination to advocate a combination of quietism and asceticism, connoisseurship and exclusiveness, aestheticism and apoliticism. [. . .] The monotonous practical effect of New Critical reading is to illustrate the subservience of each textual element to a higher, overarching, economical poetic structure without remainders. What should be evident here is that the project of poststructuralist cultural criticism possesses a set of commitments and criteria that enable it to engage in the enterprise of cultural critique. It should also be evident that the cultural ethicopolitics of this politics is best characterized, using current terminology, as "liberal" or "leftist," meaning congruent with certain socialist, anarchist, and libertarian ideals, none of which, incidentally, are necessarily Marxian. Such congruence, derived from extrapolating a generalized stance for poststructuralism, constitutes neither a party platform nor an observable course of practical action; avowed tendencies often account for little in the unfolding of practical engagements.

from *Cultural Criticism, Literary Theory, Poststructuralism*

# 2 Writing from Reading

## 2a CONSIDER THE VALUE OF READING IN A DIGITAL AGE

If you want to savor a cup of coffee or a good meal, you will have to linger over it; you can't just gulp it down. In this supercharged world of instant access and the Internet, reading literature helps you slow down long enough to feel, almost firsthand, the experience of characters from nations, cultures, religions, genders, social classes, and temperaments different from your own. Complexity involves consciously sensing multiple aspects of an experience at one time, and reading literature is a training ground for understanding complex situations. In an era when the global economy makes the world smaller every day, this experience can enhance your ability to work with diverse groups of people—both in college and in your career—by helping you see others' points of view clearly. It will also help prepare you for most of the writing you will do in college, where understanding a variety of viewpoints is fundamental to academic thinking.

## 2b MASTER WRITING FROM READING FOR COLLEGE SUCCESS

Not only will you have required reading for almost all courses in college, you will likely be required to write about what you read. Your success will depend on how well you can turn your reading into writing. College writing assignments have a variety of specific purposes, but one of their main benefits is that when you write about what you read you become a better reader as well as a better writer. Your personal reaction causes you to be more attentive to the text, and this focused response contributes to your ability to remember what you've read, clarify your observations, and explore complex relationships. In this chapter you will find a step-by-step approach to any text-based writing assignment, from a short response to a research paper. In the handbook chapter 4, you will find several sample papers for a variety of common writing assignments.

## 2c USE READING STRATEGIES THAT SUPPORT WRITING

Critical reading is a process of digesting and understanding a text so you can appreciate not just the ideas it presents or the story it tells but how it presents those ideas, why it presents them, and the way those ideas exist in a certain context. Below are the three steps for successful critical reading.

**1. Preview the text.** The process of gathering information about a piece of literature before you read it is called *previewing*. When you **preview,** look for information that will help you know how to approach the text. This information can be found in or on the book itself and includes:

- *Date of publication.* Check the copyright page—or, for older classics, you may need to consult the book's introduction or the author's biographical note—to find out when the book or story was published. This will help you determine whether the author was writing about his or her own time, or about a historical period. It might surprise you, for example, to find that Tolstoy wrote *War and Peace* more than fifty years after the time in which the story takes place.
- *Genre.* Sometimes you can tell genre simply from the cover. If it shows a shirtless man gazing at the attractive woman he holds in his arms, you can bet you're in for a romance novel. Knowing whether what you are about to read is fiction or nonfiction, and if it is science fiction, crime, literary, or another form of fiction will help you focus your expectations of your reading experience.
- *The foreword, preface, or other introductory material.* Read the introductory notices to help prepare for your reading. If the selection is part of an anthology or textbook, the surrounding text and questions will be especially helpful in giving your reading direction.
- *The epigraph,* if there is one. An epigraph is a quotation that the author selects and places at the beginning of a work, and it usually alerts you to an important theme.

TIP

### Previewing Non-Literary Works

*If you are reading something that is not a piece of literature, say for another of your college courses or for research on a piece of literature, previewing is still an important step. For non-literary works,*

- Try to identify the purpose of a work and the audience for which it was intended. This information can be found, often in great detail, in the foreword or introduction.
- Also, read the author's biographical note to see if you can identify a bias or school of thought, if the author has one.
- Finally, take note of the context of the work. Scan the copyright page to see where a work was published and by whom. Note how many editions the text has had and if the one you have is current.

**2. Interact with the text: Annotate, keep a journal, take notes.** Reading closely is the first step to writing about literature. A careful reading and simple markup leads to observations that can form the basis of a written response. Annotating a text is a very basic process of noting impressions as they occur throughout a reading. Annotation should be as simple as circling repeated words, underlining interesting phrases, and jotting down brief sets of words. Remember that annotation is a process of *observation;* deeper analysis and interpretation will come later.

Look back at the student's annotation of Jamaica Kincaid's story "Girl" in chapter 3, and notice that this student does not come up with any actual *ideas* in his annotation. Instead, he makes *observations* about what he noticed as he read the story. This is an important distinction. For example, our student, Andrew, noticed that the narrator repeats certain phrases in the story, but he doesn't yet ask why. In fact, by comparing Andrew's original annotation to his final draft, you can see that most of his observations did not make their way into the final paper. He first had to notice many details about the story's tone, patterns, words, and his own reactions before he could start narrowing down the details that would be helpful in firming up his interpretation.

Annotation is a skill that improves with practice like any other. The skill of annotating is best described as learning to *notice what you notice.* Everyone has had the experience of reading a story, poem, or play for the first time and coming across something odd or jarring. Maybe while reading John Updike's "A&P" (chapter 1) you were surprised or even offended by the narrator's comparison of the female mind to a "little buzz like a bee in a glass jar." Students new to reading literature are often tempted to ignore that feeling of surprise, blaming themselves for the disruption. "I must not get what the author is trying to do," they tell themselves, or, "I just don't understand literature." In fact, those feelings are useful, the beginnings of your ideas. Don't ignore them. Even feeling bored by what you read is worth noticing.

## Interactive Readings

*Annotated selections can be found in the following chapters:*

- Anton Chekhov's story "Rapture" (chapter 2)
- Jamaica Kincaid's story "Girl" (chapter 3)
- Carolyn Forché's poem "The Museum of Stones" (chapter 15)
- William Shakespeare's poem "My mistress' eyes are nothing like the sun" (chapter 16)
- Li-Young Lee's poem "Eating Alone" (chapter 17)
- Susan Glaspell's play *Trifles* (chapter 30)
- Edward Albee's play *Zoo Story* (chapter 31)

Keeping a reading journal is a great way to develop all kinds of skills—your observational skills, your writing skills, and even your skill for appreciating literature. Often, instructors will ask you to keep a journal and give you prompts to which you will respond. But whether or not you have that kind of guidance, you can keep your own journal in which you record what you have read, what you thought about it, and what you felt about it. There is no one right way to keep a journal; you may choose to fill it with personal reactions to literature, with ideas for paper topics, or with quotes that you liked and a description of what that quote means to you.

For samples of journal entries as part of the entire writing process, see chapter 3 (Writing about Fiction), chapter 17 (Writing about Poetry), and chapter 32 (Writing about Drama). Our student models from chapters 3 and 17 used their journals as a place to write a slightly more formal and focused response. Their strategy is worth emulating: By focusing their ideas in their journals, each student will be able to look back later in the semester if he or she has an exam—or later in their college career when they want to revisit literature that they enjoyed—and will immediately have a springboard into remembering the Jamaica Kincaid story or the Li-Young Lee poem and what makes it effective.

**3. Read the text again for craft and context.** Reading a good piece of literature is like getting to know somebody new: Your first impression is meaningful, but your second and third impressions can reveal to you entirely different aspects of the work. For a second reading, take into account how the elements of craft work together to create the selection you are reading, and for a third reading, put the selection into context. When was it written? What does its theme say about the perspective of the author on issues or circumstances of the day? It is important to make note of these impressions as well, because they will become the body of information you draw from when you write your responses. The practice of annotation and note taking will not only produce a fuller, more informed response, but will also save you time later.

## 2d MOVE FROM SUMMARY TO INTERPRETATION

When you start to write down your thoughts about a piece of literature, first make sure you understand the basics: What has happened in the selection, who is the main character or speaker, and whose point of view is at stake? This is a summary. Building on summary, you will want to think about the tone and style of the work, to analyze how the story, poem, or play is told. As you analyze, look for the role of the setting (particularly if you're reading a story), or important symbols, repeated words or sounds (which is critical when reading a poem), and the way dialogue pushes the plot forward (a central element in analyzing a play). Your analysis should take special note of who is telling the story; in a poem, identifying the speaker allows you to get underneath the hood of the "machine of words."

When you look at what was said (summary) and how it was said (analysis), you can put these together, bring in the context in which a work was written, and synthesize the work of literature to find themes and subthemes that the substance and style mutually support. You are now prepared to interpret the selection and support your interpretation with points taken from the selection itself. You may take a particular approach (see the preceding chapter on Critical Approaches to Literature) or point of view, and this framework can be useful as you interpret anything you read, whether it is literature or basic prose. Whether or not you take a particular point of view, this approach to reading will set you up to express your thoughts on what is important and meaningful to you in a literary work.

**1. Summarize.** After a first reading, solidify your understanding of the text by *summarizing* what you have read. **Summary** involves condensing a story, poem, or play into your own words, making sure to capture the text's main points. In the case of prose, a summary is much shorter than the original source and is often no more than a paragraph or two in length. For poetry, it may take a line-by-line paraphrase to result in the information you need to condense into the summary of a poem. Before summarizing, you might reread your annotations and notes with an eye toward picking out important points to include.

Remember that summary should be *objective*—focused more on what you saw happen in the work than on how you reacted to it. It should also not get bogged down with details and examples, but should focus on capturing the main events of the story or the main idea if it is a poem or an article.

One easy approach to summarizing is outlined below:

- *Pinpoint the main idea and write it in a sentence.* For a scholarly article, a main idea usually emerges in the thesis or is stated concisely in the conclusion. When you are summarizing a story, the main idea is often contained in the broad trajectory of the main character. For example: "In Alice Munro's *An Ounce of Cure,* the main character embarrasses herself while babysitting by getting drunk to ease her heartache."
- *Break the text into its sections.* Some scholarly sources might already have headings that divide the text for you. In a story or poem, identify the places where shifts occur—scene changes, a change in tone, or other points where the work takes a new direction.
- *Summarize each section's main idea.* As you did in the first step, write a sentence describing the key point the author makes in each section—or for a piece of literature, the key action or idea of the section. Think of this step as writing a topic sentence for each section. For example, the student who wrote the paper on Albee's *Zoo Story,* which appears in chapter 32, summarizes the beginning of Peter and Jerry's conversation and makes a point about the significance of animals in the play. In her discussion, she includes the following summary to support her point that Peter is associated with domesticated animals:

  > *After learning that Peter has a wife and two daughters, Jerry is eager to know what type of pets Peter owns. The animals he guesses are typical house pets: dogs and cats.*

Summaries are sometimes their own goal. See the chapter on Common Writing Assignments for help if your assignment is to write a **summary paper** or a **précis.** For that assignment, your professor is looking for a short paper that represents the main ideas of the text as the writer has presented it—*not* your own ideas or interpretation.

**2. Analyze craft and voice.** Summary helps you understand *what* happened in the text, and you will likely use your summary to support a point. The next step is to **analyze** the text by determining *how* the author created the work. When you analyze, you take the text apart and examine its elements: the different writing devices the author uses (such as point of view, plot, and imagery) and the voice the author brings to the piece (tone, word choice).

**3. Synthesize summary and analysis.** The goal of **synthesis** is to bring together the ideas and observations you've generated in your reading and analysis in order to make a concrete statement about the work you've read. The secret ingredients to synthesis are your own personal opinions and perspectives. (In a research paper, you will want to include the opinions and perspectives from academic sources as well.) Thus, synthesis takes the *what* happened from summary and the *how* it was accomplished from analysis and shapes them into an argument or statement.

**4. Interpret the text.** By *analyzing* a text and *synthesizing* your thoughts into a statement on the text, you will set yourself up to **interpret** a particular element of a work by suggesting what that element means. **Interpretation** means striving to increase understanding of some aspect of a work to illuminate its meaning. Interpretation does not mean identifying one correct answer, one key to unlock a text. Rather, it means taking an argument or statement you've generated through synthesis and using it as an angle from which to enter a work and explore some new, insightful aspect. It is important to remember that an interpretation must have a strong foundation of evidence from the text itself.

## Other Strategies for Exploring Ideas

*A walkthrough of the entire writing process from exploring ideas to writing the final draft can be found in chapter 3 (Writing about Fiction), chapter 17 (Writing about Poetry), and chapter 32 (Writing about Drama). When you're stuck, here are some additional strategies that might get you going again.*

### Freewriting

1 It is all right to start with obvious impressions. Try to answer some of the questions that you asked yourself while annotating the text. Don't worry about finding the "right" answer, and don't limit yourself to just one—there are probably many possible interpretations. *Freewriting* is private writing, just for you. You need not worry about proper spelling or grammar, or even proper sentences and paragraphs.

### Talking

2 Try explaining a story, poem, or play to someone who has never read it before, and encourage that person to ask you questions. If this sounds odd to you, consider what you do after seeing a new movie you had looked forward to seeing.

### Brainstorming

3 If you find it simpler to think in diagrams, your freewrite might take the shape of a web or cluster of related or unrelated impressions. Start with a central idea, literary device, or character that you wish to explore and place that in the center. Then, draw lines to the elements or characteristics associated with your central term.

### Charting

4 Another way to draw connections between your observations is by charting them. This is an especially helpful method if you have identified opposites of some sort in the text, whether it be a hero and a villain, rainy weather and fair weather, or light images and dark images.

## 2e DEVELOP AN ARGUMENT

A literary analysis builds a complex argument around a particular aspect of a work of literature. Summarizing, analyzing, and synthesizing might help you come up with an interpretation that could be your paper's topic, but when you're looking for a topic for a paper, you probably wonder: Where do ideas come from? For all of us, coming up with ideas—and developing those ideas into claims worth writing about—is a challenge.

**Claim:** An argument is based on a claim that requires a defense. It isn't an opinion ("I liked the characters in this story"), and it isn't a fact or a generally recognized truth ("Langston Hughes is one of the most important American poets"). Your essay's claim will be reflected in your thesis (see the following section for guidance on creating a defendable thesis).

**Persuasion:** Aristotle, the same great philosopher who defined tragedy in ancient Greek theater (chapter 33) also defined logic and the art of persuasion. What we call *logic* today Aristotle would have called *analytics*, as in *to analyze*. When we refer to an academic argument, therefore, we are not referring to a fight but rather to a well-reasoned, logical analysis that is based on evidence.

**Evidence:** For literature, the text itself is your most convincing evidence; other kinds of evidence might be statistics, expert opinions, and anecdotes.

## Different Kinds of Source-Based Evidence
## Summary vs. Paraphrase vs. Quotation

*Reference to a source is a form of evidence, and it can take many forms.*

***Summary:*** A boiled down analysis of the line of action or thought in a passage or full text, a summary is used not only to represent your understanding of a text but also as a point of reference that provides context for your argument. See the summary paper in the next chapter on Common Writing Assignments.

***Paraphrase:*** Using your own words, a paraphrase is a restatement ("in other words") of someone else's language that makes a point more clearly than could be made by using the quotation itself. A paraphrase, therefore, may blend your own view with the words of the source. A paraphrase can help you understand a passage, particularly in poetry. Make sure you mention the source when you paraphrase. Use phrases like "According to," "As said in," "We know from."

***Quotation:*** When the meaning of what was said would be distorted or changed in any other words, a quotation needs to be used to make your point. Do not avoid making a point by overusing quotations. A quotation is your evidence out of which you should build a point, using the quotation as a springboard for your own ideas.

You will need to show details, patterns, and ideas from the text when you present your evidence. The tips that follow are possible ways of developing or refining your ideas and then finding the evidence to support them. Together with the critical approaches outlined in the preceding chapter, they offer ways to generate new possibilities to develop an effective argument.

**1. Follow your interests and expertise whenever possible.** If you are a psychology major and the family's interactions in *Death of a Salesman* (chapter 35) remind you of a theory you have just studied in a psychology seminar, don't be afraid to use that knowledge to aid in your interpretation. If you are an avid sailor and that makes you especially interested in analyzing the "open boat" scenes in Stephen Crane's short story (chapter 9), take advantage of your knowledge in creating your argument.

**2. Acknowledge your gut reactions, but then analyze them.** If you found a given text or page extremely frustrating to read, it is absolutely legitimate to admit this to yourself and others. But don't stop there. Ask yourself,

- *What was it that frustrated me so much about this passage?*
- *Was it the slow pace of the action?*
- *Was it my own lack of familiarity with the language used at the time the piece was written?*
- *Was it the fact that the character I most identified with died in the previous scene?*
- *Was it the wordy prose style?*
- *What might have motivated the author to use such convoluted language?*
- *Are there any benefits to it?*

Certainly some works of art will appeal to you more than others; elements of taste and personal preference affect every reading. It is legitimate to say, "I hated that story," and intelligent analysis can come from that reaction if you analyze the ways in which the text creates specific impressions on readers.

Similarly, if you enjoy a text and feel a deep personal connection with it, keep in mind that you will have to ask yourself questions similar to those above to make sure you are being specific in examining the attributes you admire. You need not try to develop negative observations, but make sure that your affection isn't clouding your ability to see all aspects of the work clearly.

**3. Choose a single aspect of the genre to examine.** For instance, look at meter in poetry, voice in fiction, or stage directions in drama. Reread the text closely, looking only at that one aspect. It may be counterintuitive, but it can be especially useful to choose an aspect of the genre that is *not* the most noticeable in the particular text. For instance, most readers notice right away that Elizabeth Bishop's poem "One Art" (chapter 23) is a villanelle, a tricky form that requires a complex rhyme scheme and repetition. It would be easy to comment on her use of the form, but it might be more fruitful, and certainly more original, to think about something less obvious, like the poem's use of images or its rhythm.

**4. Pay attention to detail.** It is a convention of literary criticism to assume that *every* element of a text is potentially significant, no matter how small it seems. Whether or not the author specifically intended everything we notice, once it is written down, everything is fair game for interpretation. When a literary argument does go too far, it is generally *not* because the argument depended on minor details for its support but because it failed to present sufficient evidence or to form a coherent, logical argument. Some of the most insightful interpretations sound as though they are "reading too deeply" into the text until we hear all the supporting evidence and analysis.

Of course, this does not mean that we can arbitrarily assign meaning to any single detail in a text. It is not convincing, for instance, to argue that "Bartleby" (chapter 14) is Melville's rallying cry for Marxism, since there is little evidence for that interpretation in Melville's biography or his other works. The details, however, that might lead to this conclusion—Bartleby's escalating refusal to make copies, his boss's obliviousness to his condition, and the depressing metaphor of Bartleby staring at the brick wall—*could* work together to support a more subtle, complex claim about work and social class in the story. Each of these details on its own does not necessarily carry meaning, but a good paper will *note* them *and put them together* to form a meaningful interpretation.

So, do not be nervous about "reading too deeply" into a text. No claim is too outlandish, no detail too random or seemingly insignificant, no conclusion too far-fetched or implausibly small if your literary argument provides sufficient evidence. "Did Herman Melville *really* mean to use the brick wall as a symbol of class struggle?" you might ask. "Is every tiny detail really so important?" Keep in mind that some interpretations that seemed to be reading too much into the text when they first appeared later became widely accepted. Today's audacious argument might be tomorrow's commonplace one, so don't be afraid to add to the conversation.

**5. Compare the text with other things you have read.** Even if your assignment does not require or allow you to discuss more than one work of art, you may still find it helpful to compare your text to others while in the process of developing your topic. Comparing the spare, straightforward prose of Ernest Hemingway (chapter 7) with the more elaborate prose style of James Joyce (chapter 4), for example, may lead you to useful conclusions about the ways each of these authors uses language. It often helps to look at texts in juxtaposition or opposition; the differences are as important as the similarities.

**6. Pay attention to the things a text does *not* contain.** Thinking about what an author decides to leave out of a text is as revealing as considering what he or she includes. Painters talk about the blank space surrounding an object in a composition, and literary critics often do the same. Looking at the blank space, or what *isn't there,* will cast our subject in relief, enabling us to see it more clearly. Consider which events a play summarizes through dialogue rather than staging; consider whose points of view are left out of a short story; consider why a poet writes without using rhyme. What are the possible motivations for and consequences of those decisions?

**7. Try lumping ideas together.** Sometimes two (or more) minor ideas can combine into one strong one. Let's say your freewrite about Thomas Lynch's poem "Liberty" (chapter 29) turns up an interesting observation: the appearance of the "ex-wife" in line ten tells us that she and the speaker are divorced, which makes the light argument between them suddenly seem more serious. Much later in your freewrite, you notice that it was the great-great-grandfather who bought the plant, but it was "the missus" who planted it.

Neither of these ideas on its own is enough to generate much more, but what if you try putting them together? The ex-wife and the great-great-grandmother are the only two women in a poem about men taking the "liberty" of urinating outside. You find it interesting that the two women seem so different, and they might represent two different responses to male "nature," one American and one Irish. By *lumping* your two separate observations together, you stumble upon a complex and specific idea for an essay.

**8. Or try splitting ideas apart.** You might *split* an unwieldy idea into two or more by narrowing or qualifying it. Narrow a broad observation to just one character, scene, or metaphor. For example, in Flannery O'Connor's "A Good Man Is Hard to Find" (chapter 12) you might notice that every scene in the story contains a moment of foreshadowing that the family will encounter the Misfit. This is a useful observation, but too broad for a short essay. If you instead concentrate on how descriptions of objects foreshadow the end (the car that looks like a hearse, for example), you will find it more manageable to gather evidence and make a clear argument.

**9. Look for patterns.** If an author repeats an image, word, metaphor, gesture, or setting, make note of it. A poem might use words with "sh" sounds in many lines, a story might include images of animals repeatedly, or a play might have two important scenes set in kitchens. Notice these patterns and ask yourself how they are working—is the pattern emphasizing something, providing a sense of comfort, showing the ineffectuality of characters' attempts to change things? Repetition often works together with other aspects of the work and can serve as evidence that the author wanted to emphasize a point.

**10. Look for breaks in the pattern.** Once an author establishes a given pattern, he or she may also disrupt that pattern in a way that compels a reader's attention. If there is a part that seems quite different from the rest of the text, don't ignore it! You can safely assume that such a passage merits special consideration. If a poem is in perfect sonnet form, conforming exactly to the traditional meter and rhyme scheme *except for one line,* it is likely the author wanted this line to disrupt the pattern and create a sense of surprise. If two characters seem alike in almost every regard, look more closely to discover what *distinguishes* them. If a play contains two scenes in the same setting, with nearly the same action, pay attention to the *differences* in these scenes.

## Developing an Argument for Robert Pinsky's "Shirt" (chapter 23)

| | |
|---|---|
| **Follow your interests and expertise whenever possible.** | Maybe your Gender Studies course has been discussing the treatment of women who work in sweatshops; a research paper could combine information about how clothes are made now with Pinsky's description of garment workers in the twentieth century.<br>Or:<br>Let's say your Journalism course has been studying newspaper stories from the turn of the twentieth century. You could use your new knowledge about how stories were written to compare and contrast the *New York Times* coverage of the Triangle Factory fire with the description of the fire in Pinsky's poem. |
| **Acknowledge your gut reactions, but then analyze them.** | This poem at first seems like a mishmash of depressing situations: the sweatshop workers, the girls jumping to their deaths in the Triangle fire, Scottish workers tricked into believing in a fake heritage, slaves growing cotton. All of this is disturbing when combined with the speaker's satisfaction with his new shirt—in the face of the workers' suffering, that satisfaction seems shallow.<br>But these histories are not just tragic, because many of the people in the stories are behaving nobly (like the man who helped girls jump out of the burning building). Maybe Pinsky is saying that every object we own has this kind of tragic history or that our belongings' histories are also positive, because people like Irma are proud of doing good work even if they are exploited. |
| **Choose a single aspect of the genre to examine.** | Some of the more obvious aspects of this poem to write about are Pinsky's use of lists and his inclusion of stories and images from history. Those might lead to good essay topics, but it might be more interesting to look at a less obvious aspect of the poem, such as Pinsky's use of sound. For example, compare the hard, iambic words in the lists of objects with the longer, softer sounds of words in the stories. |
| **Pay attention to detail.** | The speaker's comparison of the matching pattern to "a strict rhyme" makes it seem as though he finds rhyme pleasing—but this poem does not rhyme, which would seem to suggest that its own speaker wouldn't like it.<br>It would be going too far to argue that the speaker of "Shirt" dislikes the poem and is presenting it ironically, based on this one word. However, the observation of the word *rhyme* in an unrhymed poem is intriguing—maybe it could lead to looking for other kinds of rhyme, for instance combinations such as "the back, the yoke" and "sizing and facing." |
| **Compare the text with other things you have read.** | It might be useful to compare this poem to other poems by Robert Pinsky ("To Television," chapter 21) other poems about work ("The Fisherman," chapter 21), or to other poems that closely examine a single object ("The Red Wheelbarrow," chapter 20 and "Anecdote of the Jar," chapter 20). |
| **Pay attention to the things a text does *not* contain.** | You might notice that the poem doesn't contain any information about the speaker except that he has a new shirt. The poem offers no name, no history of the speaker, and no other people in the poem except those he imagines sewing shirts. You might come up with some ideas about what effect this anonymity has on the poem—how would it be different if we knew the speaker's name, his occupation, his tastes and preferences, etc.? |
| **Try lumping and splitting your ideas.** | Let's say you noticed the repeated use of jargon (vocabulary specialized to a specific profession)—terms like *yoke* and *navvy* that most readers will not be familiar with. You are also struck by the detail about Scottish workers being tricked into believing a false story about their heritage. Neither of these observations on its own is very useful, so you try *lumping* them: both the jargon and the lies about heritage are instances of people being left out of some important knowledge because of language.<br>*continued* |

| | |
|---|---|
| | Or you noticed that all the workers in the poem seem to be somehow exploited. Your first idea is to write a research paper exploring the situations of garment workers Pinsky mentions—Koreans and Malaysians, labor unions, the Triangle Factory, Scottish workers, and slaves in the American South. Then you realize this is too much even for a long essay and decide to *split* these possibilities and focus on only one, the Triangle Factory workers' union. |
| **Look for patterns.** | You might notice that most of the poem is made up of sentences that are not grammatically complete but just noun phrases—even some long sentences, like the second one (48 words) are just noun phrases, even though they span multiple stanzas. |
| **Look for breaks in the pattern.** | The pattern breaks in the fourth stanza with "One hundred and forty-six died in the flames . . ." The verb "died" jumps out and seems even more disturbing because it's the first verb in the poem. |

## 2f FORM A DEFENDABLE THESIS

A thesis is not the topic of the paper or the topic sentence to the entire paper. Unlike a topic sentence, a thesis must be more than just a statement of fact. A **thesis** is the writer's argument about the topic of the paper, the controlling idea that he or she will show and develop in the body of the essay. Your interpretation will need to be set forth in a strong arguable thesis. Two strategies may be useful in developing your thesis:

- **Do a focused freewrite.** For example, if you are interested in how Shakespeare uses the seasons symbolically, you might want to highlight all the lines in the sonnets you are addressing that have to do with spring, summer, fall, or winter. It would also be a good idea to write a few sentences about your initial impressions of his handling of the seasons: Does he mention more than one season in a given poem, or does he limit it to one? What details of the season does he incorporate? Is the season mentioned a principal subject of the poem or a subpoint?
- **Write an observation as a sentence.** Then ask yourself which part of the observation you made is arguable. Try to imagine the opposite of your statement. If there is an opposite, you are well on your way to having a thesis. If not, you might try writing another of your observations as a statement, and then see if there is an opposite or argument in your new sentence.

Often, you may find it difficult to know exactly what your argument is until you have made it in the course of writing the paper. That's perfectly fine. Although you want to give yourself the best start possible with a well-planned thesis, don't worry too much about getting your thesis right the first time. Instead, look at the thesis in your first draft as a *working thesis,* one that serves as a diving board to launch you into a draft of your paper. At the end of the paper, chances are you'll have come to a more nuanced understanding of your topic. At that point, you'll want to revise your thesis so that it accurately reflects what you ended up saying in the paper itself. The defendable thesis that follows is arguable, supportable, complex, and purpose-driven.

**1. A thesis must be arguable.** A thesis is not just a statement of fact. Rather, a thesis is your argument, or to put it another way, a meaning you see in the story that not every other reader will necessarily see. Since your idea is not readily apparent to every reader, it is your job over the course of the paper to show why and how you have formed your interpretation. A good way to test whether you have a thesis statement or simply a statement of fact is to ask, "What is the opposite side of this statement? Is that opposite equally arguable?" If it is, you have a good thesis. If not, you either have a statement of fact or a weak argument, one that is widely accepted as true without needing to be explored in a paper.

**INEFFECTIVE THESIS:**

Some of Langston Hughes's poetry was inspired by jazz.

➡ *The statement is a widely accepted fact. Although this particular sentence may function as a good topic sentence or a sentence in the introduction to the paper, it is not an effective thesis statement because there is nothing about it that the writer has to defend.*

**ARGUABLE THESIS:**

Beyond being a jazz poet, Hughes understood the significance of jazz—even as it was being created—and used only those aspects of jazz that express the African-American experience.

➡ *As you will see this arguable thesis is also supportable, complex, and purpose driven. This statement takes a widely accepted fact—that Hughes is a jazz poet—and offers a particular and original interpretation of the significance of jazz in Hughes's poetry. Notice that the sentence is arguable: one could say that Hughes's interest in jazz was for another reason altogether—perhaps that it served the type of free verse he wanted to write or that it gave a popular appeal to his poetry. This thesis promises to show how race is the prominent factor in determining Hughes's use of jazz, and in so doing, it also promises a nuanced discussion of the elements of jazz present in Hughes's poetry.*

**2. A thesis must be supported by the text.** In a good thesis, the writer puts forth a statement that is arguable, or, in other words, a statement of the writer's opinion. It may seem, then, that the writer can say whatever he or she wants in a thesis, but on the contrary, a thesis must be supportable. This support will come primarily from the text itself. You don't want to take your idea and quote the text in a way that misrepresents it, simply to make your idea work. Instead, your thesis should be a reflection of your broad and open reading of the text in question. Although you must ultimately settle on an opinion in your thesis, you must reach that opinion through observation, not through fabrication.

**INEFFECTIVE THESIS:**

Beyond being a jazz poet, Hughes understood the significance of jazz—even as it was being created—and deliberately used very specific elements of jazz to exclude non-musical audiences.

**SUPPORTABLE THESIS:**

> Beyond being a jazz poet, Hughes understood the significance of jazz—even as it was being created—and used only those aspects of jazz that express the African-American experience.

➡ *You may choose to support this with poems that come from Hughes's* Montage of a Dream Deferred *collection, which Hughes identified as being "like be-bop." Also, since the thesis has to do with all of Hughes's jazz poetry, you would want to choose support from poems written at different times in Hughes's career. Whichever poems you choose, you will need to explicate sections of those poems to show how their elements are primarily influenced by race.*

**3. A thesis must be complex, yet focused.** You may not perfect this aspect of your thesis until a later draft, but your goal is to write a thesis that points you toward a topic with enough material to fill a paper. However, it should also be refined enough that the scope of your topic is manageable—that is, in a paper about Shakespeare's sonnets, you need not address the entire evolution of the sonnet form, just one aspect that interests you, such as Shakespeare's symbolic use of the seasons.

**INEFFECTIVE THESIS:**

> Beyond being a jazz poet, Hughes understood the significance of jazz—even as it was being created—and aspects of the jazz form can be found in every one of his poems.

**COMPLEX, YET FOCUSED THESIS:**

> Beyond being a jazz poet, Hughes understood the significance of jazz—even as it was being created—and used only those aspects of jazz that express the African-American experience.

➡ *This thesis has plenty of potential for a long paper. The author can easily limit the scope, however, by choosing a few key poems to use in his or her discussion.*

**4. A thesis must be purpose-driven and significant.** If your thesis is doing its job well, it should lead the reader to answer the question "So what?" As the writer of the paper, you'll want to answer this question yourself over the course of the paper and perhaps more explicitly in your conclusion. But the seed of the answer to "So what?" or "Why is this significant?" lies in the thesis. A good thesis leads the writer (and the reader) to a particular perspective of an aspect of the text, or the writers' oeuvre, or literature in general.

**INEFFECTIVE THESIS:**

Beyond being a jazz poet, Langston Huges was also a big fan of listening to jazz music.

**PURPOSE-DRIVEN THESIS:**

Beyond being a jazz poet, Hughes understood the significance of jazz—even as it was being created—and used only those aspects of jazz that express the African-American experience.

➡ *The purpose of this thesis is to better understand the role of race and jazz in Hughes's poems—an endeavor that may lead to a greater appreciation of Hughes's achievement and a deeper understanding of how to read his poems.*

## 2g CREATE A PLAN

If you have ever printed road directions from websites like MapQuest or Google Maps, you know that they provide step-by-step instructions for how to get from point A to point B. Some students may have such a finely tuned sense of direction that they are able to dive directly into writing a first draft. Or maybe a lucky few simply prefer to see where their writing takes them. Most, however, need some kind of a road map for their paper. An outline provides you with step-by-step instructions on how to get from your introduction (Point A) to your conclusion (Point B). It might help to sketch out an informal plan.

- introduction (includes your thesis and why the thesis is important to you and why you want to explore it in your paper)
- body (indicates the points you will use to support your thesis in a series of paragraphs)
- conclusion (adds a final comment that connects your thesis to a larger issue or places your thesis in a larger context that will make it more meaningful to the person who reads your paper)

Outlines can be very brief and simple or longer and in-depth. You might just write a **scratch outline,** or a list of topics you want to cover. If you're writing a shorter paper that analyzes one work, a **topic outline** might be enough. Topic outlines simply provide the order in which you plan to talk about your broad topics. Look at the student outline in chapter 17, Emma Baldwin's paper on Li-Young Lee's "Eating Alone."

I. Introduction
   A. confusing because last lines contradict
   B. thesis: A close reading shows the entire poem is created out of contradictory elements. Through contrasts of imagery, tone, and the literal events of the poem, Lee uses paradox to give full expression to the grief his speaker feels about his father's death.

II. Imagery
    A. imagery that suggests life
    B. imagery that suggests death
III. Tone
    A. plain language
    B. syntax is not complicated . . .
    C. . . . but subject matter is. This = understatement
IV. Time/Literal Events
    A. present, past "years back," past "this morning"
    B. talk about contrast in time
V. Conclusion
    A. address contrast in last lines
    B. we can understand them in context of poem

Notice how the major headers following the Roman numerals are the topics Emma plans to address: imagery, tone, and events. Supporting ideas can be listed with the alphabet (*A, B, C*). Evidence (quotations, for example) could be numbered in a third level as *1., 2., 3.*

I. Topic
    A. Supporting Idea
        1. Evidence
        2. More Evidence
    B. Second Supporting Idea

Instead of single words or phrases, you might find it more helpful to state every idea in a complete sentence, giving you a **sentence outline** to work from.

Until you have written many papers and learned more about the way your own writing process works best for you, an outline can help you to organize your thoughts and to understand where your paper is headed. Generally, the longer or more complex your paper, the more useful a detailed outline will be. For example, before writing a research paper, you may want to make an outline so detailed that it includes the quotes you plan to integrate. In fact, you may find a full formal outline absolutely necessary.

A more detailed outline example follows for a research paper on Langston Hughes and jazz. The final draft is found in the chapter on Writing the Research Paper. Compare this slice of outline with the third and fourth paragraphs of that paper. Notice how the outline is so detailed that the author had only to flesh out the outline points into complete sentences when writing the actual paper.

II. Blues in the Jazz Age
    A. "The Dream Keeper" and the Jazz Age
        1. Hughes's *The Weary Blues* published in 1925
            a. 1925 was middle of Jazz Age
                1. Marked by energy and optimism
                2. Jazz connoted rebellion
        2. "The Dream Keeper" influenced by blues, not jazz
            b. Part of *The Weary Blues* collection
                1. "The Dream Keeper" reads like abbreviated blues lyrics
                2. Compound words "cloud-cloth" and "too-rough" slow pacing to slow blues pace
    B. The Jazz Age and African-American experience
        1. Jazz Age and the blues have contrasting relationship
            a. Blues related to jazz; jazz grew out of blues roots
            b. Jazz exuberant, blues melancholy

2. Historical context is key
   a. Jazz Age "unprecedented prosperity" ("Roaring Twenties" article) for whites
   b. Great Migration—10% of blacks moved from South to North
      (1) low wages, poor housing conditions
      (2) disease

## 2h DRAFT YOUR PAPER

The word *draft* is used here to help keep the pressure down. Don't worry about spelling and grammar at this stage. Get your thoughts out on paper. *Draft* connotes that what you are writing is not final, that it is a work-in-progress. You will likely revise your first draft, so you will want to save your drafts early and often. Label your drafts so that you can retrace your steps (*draft l, draft 2* . . . or use specific dates to show what the most current draft is). Print the original. Having a hard copy may free you up to tinker and explore.

**Introductions, Conclusions, and Body Paragraphs.** You may find you want to write your introduction last or right before your conclusion but after you've developed the supporting points of the paper. If you do, these two framing paragraphs can speak to each other more obviously, with the introduction stating your thesis and why it matters to you and the conclusion bringing in your thesis and why it might matter to your reader.

TIP

### Drafting Body Paragraphs

- Focus each paragraph on one idea.
- State the main idea of each paragraph in a topic sentence.
- Connect the information clearly in each paragraph to support the topic.
- Make sure the paragraph clearly supports your thesis.

## 2i REVISE YOUR DRAFT

Once you've finished a draft you feel is complete, take a break from your paper—distance can sometimes help you see if your ideas flow as naturally as you thought when you first wrote them. Distance can also help you catch editing mistakes you miss in the heat of developing your ideas. It is also good to get some feedback from a fellow student in your class or a friend. When you come back to your paper, annotate the issues you find. (It is great if you can get your peer to annotate your paper as well.) As you write and revise your paper you have a chance to re-envision how to make your argument clearer and to support it more effectively. In the chapter on Writing the Research Paper you will find the entire final paper for the paragraphs that follow.

## Draft Introductory Paragraph

Jazz poetry, according to the American Academy of Poets website, is "a literary genre defined as poetry necessarily informed by jazz music—that is, poetry in which the poet responds to and writes about jazz." By this definition, Langston Hughes was a jazz poet. Many critics point to specific techniques that Hughes employs to create the effect of jazz. Although the observations are true, such technical readings fail to show the full extent of Hughes's achievement in jazz poetry. More than just a jazz poet, Hughes understood the significance of jazz as it was being created, and he used only the aspects of jazz that expressed the African-American experience.

Which critics? What techniques? May be a good place for an outside source.

In what way? Back up this assertion.

Used how? Maybe back this up. Is there an existing critical argument my claim could respond to in order to create a stronger thesis?

## Revised Introductory Paragraph

Jazz poetry, according to the American Academy of Poets website, is "a literary genre defined as poetry necessarily informed by jazz music—that is, poetry in which the poet responds to and writes about jazz." Langston Hughes was a jazz poet in that his poetry often captured jazz in a literary form. Many critics point to specific techniques that Hughes employs to create the effect of jazz. One such critic is Lionel Davidas, who writes:

> Langston Hughes, in his collection of poems, lavishly uses such characteristics of jazz as repetitions, choruses, riffs, scats, and nonsensical onomatopoeia to achieve musical success as well as audience participation. It is also significant to note that Hughes's poems are often marked by dissonance, discordance, and line irregularity, which all contribute to the representation of the jazz spirit in verse forms. (268)

Although these observations are true, readings like Davidas's fail to show the full extent of Hughes's achievement in jazz poetry. Beyond being a jazz poet, Hughes understood the significance of jazz—even as it was being created—and used only those aspects of jazz that express the African-American experience.

### Draft Supporting Paragraph (Body)

"The Dream Keeper" was published in 1925. At that time, America was in the midst of the "Jazz Age," the period from 1920-1930 marked by energy and optimism. Jazz itself was popular and connoted rebellion. However, Hughes's collection *The Weary Blues* was influenced more by (obviously) the blues than by this new form of jazz. ~~While~~ "The Dream Keeper" doesn't have as obvious a connection to the blues as Hughes's poems that copy blues lyrics directly—such as "Po' Boy Blues"—the repetition early in the poem bears echoes of the repetition characteristic of the blues. Consider the repetition of "Bring me all of your" in the first three lines; typical blues lyrics follow a pattern where the first couplet repeats before a third couplet resolves it, and here half the couplet is repeated and half resolved in both instances. Since Hughes was writing in the "Jazz Age," it may seem surprising that so many of his poems in *The Weary Blues* reflect the blues (lines 1, 3). His decision may in part have been informed by the fact that jazz grew out of the blues, and they were closely related enough that Hughes could use blues and be safe in the jazz realm. But whereas blues are "blue" and melancholy, jazz is "jazzy." The solution to this puzzle is in the historical context. The Roaring Twenties brought "unprecedented prosperity" to the United States ("Roaring Twenties") but it was also the era of the Great Migration, when many African Americans left the south and moved north. Times were difficult for blacks, who faced low wages and poor housing conditions (Marks). So, at the time that Hughes was writing these poems, jazz had two forms: the exuberant, new jazz, and the blues roots it came from. Hughes chose the form—the blues—that best reflected the state of the common black man at the time.

Maybe need some more here—how did jazz, just a music form, connote rebellion?

The discussion here is a little unfounded . . . maybe I need a researched source.

This is too informal! Need to keep an eye out for these.

This explanation is cluttered and a bit confusing; illustrate or clarify.

Reads like a topic sentence. Break the paragraph here?

Cute, but is it meaningful?

Are these common knowledge? Maybe include a brief description.

Maybe I need more research here, since understanding historical context is so important to my argument.

Didn't I see a good image for this when I was researching online? That might help engage the reader here and enrich the discussion of historical context.

Could this point have its own paragraph?

## Revised Supporting Paragraphs (Body)

Hughes first published "The Dream Keeper" in 1925 and included it in his collection *The Weary Blues* the following year (Rampersad 617). At that time, America was in the midst of the "Jazz Age," the period from 1920–1930 marked by energy and optimism. Jazz itself was popular and connoted rebellion as it was associated with nightclubs, sex, and drinking (Tucker, screen 4). But Hughes's collection was clearly influenced more by the blues than by this new form of jazz. The title of the collection suggests the blues takes center stage in these poems, and indeed, "The Dream Keeper" is no exception. While it does not have as overt a connection to the blues as Hughes's poems that replicate blues lyrics directly—such as "Po Boy Blues"—the repetition early in the poem bears echoes of the repetition characteristic of the blues. "Bring me all of your" is repeated twice within the first three lines; the object the addressee is told to bring, however, varies (lines 1, 3). In a way, lines one through three are a compounded version of blues lyrics. Typical blues lyrics follow a pattern where the first couplet repeats before a third couplet resolves it. Here, half the couplet is repeated and half resolved in both instances. Blues also has a hand in the pace of the poem. Compound phrases like "cloud-cloth" and "too-rough" slow the pace of reading, as does the high number of line breaks compared to the small number of words (6, 7).

## Draft Concluding Paragraph

Too familiar, not the right tone for a research paper.

As you can see, "The Dream Keeper" and "Harlem [2]" demonstrate how Hughes effectively incorporated new forms of jazz as they arose. While he does successfully use technical elements of jazz music, to end a reading there would be to miss Hughes's larger achievement. He did not simply adopt jazz technique; he selected only

Embellish conclusion to include new arguments based on content. Remember to restate the argument.

the trends that reflected the African-American experience. He leaves out the "white" sounds of swing and opts instead for the forms of blues and bebop. In so doing, Hughes's poetry captures both the music, as it evolved from blues to bebop, and the African-American experience.

Elaborate or change wording; doesn't sound right.

Tie in history and time period with this, since it's the basis for the argument.

## Revised Concluding Paragraph

As "The Dream Keeper" and "Harlem [2]" demonstrate, Hughes effectively incorporated new forms of jazz as they arose. While he does successfully use formal elements of jazz music, to end a reading there would be to miss Hughes's larger achievement. Hughes did not simply adopt jazz technique; he selected only those trends in jazz that reflected the African-American experience of the time in which he wrote. There is no room in his poetry for the smooth sounds of swing at the hands of whites; instead, he used the true African-American forms of blues and bebop. In so doing, Hughes's poetry captures both the music, as it evolved from blues to bebop, and the African-American experience, as it moved from the blues of the Great Migration to the bitter conflict of continued discrimination.

TIP

## Revising

- *Rethink your introduction:* Have you drawn your readers in by explaining how the topic of your paper is meaningful to you?
- *Rethink your thesis:* Have you changed your mind? Can you make your thesis clearer?
- *Rethink your structure:* Do you have a beginning, a middle, and an end? Do they flow naturally and logically into each other, with each paragraph focusing on an idea that supports your thesis? Are your transitions between ideas and paragraphs effective?
- *Rethink your argument:* Do you have sufficient and convincing evidence to prove your thesis? Does the evidence build logically to your conclusion?
- *Rethink your conclusion:* Have you made your case? Have you connected your thesis to a larger issue that gives it more meaning for your reader?

## 2i EDIT AND FORMAT YOUR PAPER

After you have looked at your paper as a whole, take one more look at its sentence structure, spelling, and formatting. These simple matters, if not done correctly, can interfere with your instructor's good opinion of a well thought-out paper. You may have been making small corrections all along, but consider this last edit your dress rehearsal for making your paper public.

### Questions to Guide Editing

1. Are my sentences wordy?
2. Have I dropped a word out of a sentence?
3. Is my point of view consistent?
4. Does each sentence make sense?
5. Do I have any sentence fragments?
6. Are my commas in the right places?
7. Do my subjects and verbs agree—*single to single/plural to plural?*
8. Are my apostrophe's used correctly—**'s** for singular possession (this *critic's* opinion; Hughes's work); ***s'*** for plural possession when the word ends in **s** (the *singers'* music)?
9. Do my quotation marks represent the exact words of the writer?
10. Have I paraphrased without giving credit to the source?

In addition to formatting your paper with a heading and a title, you will need to follow the formatting guidelines your professor prefers, particularly as you cite sources in your papers:

- *The Modern Language Association* (MLA) provides guidelines for formatting papers and citing sources for courses in the humanities (see handbook chapter 6, MLA Documentation Style Guide).
- *The Chicago Manual of Style* (Chicago or Turabian) is sometimes required for humanities courses where an instructor requires that footnotes be used.
- *The American Psychological Association* (APA) has a different set of formatting guidelines for citing sources in the social sciences.
- *The Council of Science Editors* (CSE) have put together guidelines for papers in mathematics, engineering, computer sciences, and the natural sciences.

Whatever form your instructor wishes you to follow, pay close attention to the conventions for quoting and citing sources that are provided. Mistakes can be misconstrued as plagiarism, and following the correct form will have the added benefit of making your paper consistent and clear. This is the effect you want your paper's design to convey. Variety is the spice of life but not the spice you need for your paper. Be consistent with the features of your design, and make your paper look clean, clear, and serious.

TIP

## Formatting

1. Include a heading on the left with your name, the professor's name, your class, and the date.
2. Center your title (it can be larger than the rest of the type in your paper).
3. Headings within the paper should be the same style and typeface each time.
4. Make your margins wide enough to make the paper easy to read and not so wide as to make your professor suspect you are stretching out thin content.
5. Make your type big enough to be read easily (12-point type is fairly standard) and not so big your professor suspects you are stretching out thin content.
6. Select a common typeface that is easy to read (Times New Roman, for example).
7. Include a caption with any visual in the paper.
8. Double-space your paper.
9. Number the pages.
10. Print on standard 8½ by 11 paper with an ink-jet or laser printer.

# 3 Common Writing Assignments across the Curriculum

## 3a CONNECT WRITING IN COLLEGE TO WRITING BEYOND COLLEGE

In our digital age, we actually write more than ever, and our writing is quite public—on Facebook pages, blogs, or email. Writing after college becomes even more public. Writing for success—especially in the business world—must be succinct, logical, and persuasive. Most professions demand excellent writing skills, even if the job does not seem to depend on writing. According to a recent survey, more than half of major corporations say they take writing skills into consideration when hiring salaried employees—and exceptional writing skills are required for advancement. While it is unlikely you will be asked to write an essay on Coleridge's "Kubla Khan" or Shakespeare's *Hamlet* after graduation, you will very likely be asked to articulate an argument that reveals a better understanding of a complex situation and a complex text or set of texts. Writing about literature is a training ground in dealing with complexity and expressing yourself with clarity

## 3b WRITE TO LEARN ACROSS THE CURRICULUM

The ability to summarize, analyze, synthesize, and critique information is also essential for college writing. In almost all your college courses, you will be asked to respond to something you have read, whether it be a piece of literature, a textbook, a critical article or book, a primary source, a blog, or a website. You may find these sources in a library, in your bookstore, or on the Internet, but whatever the particular assignment, you will have to *show that you understand* the text and *explain* it clearly, and you will have to *develop your own ideas* about how it works and *persuade* your reader that your interpretation is correct.

As you interpret a work of literature, you will use critical thinking skills—from summary to analysis, synthesis, and critique—that require you to look more carefully at how the text has been put together and whether the text effectively accomplishes its purpose. You will use your critical thinking skills in a summary to determine what details to leave out and which ones to keep or in a research paper when you synthesize your research into your presentation. The interpretations that you create in writing about literature employ a number of strategic skills that will prepare you to write throughout your college career:

- Summary
- Analysis
- Synthesis
- Critique

## 3c USE SUMMARY TO DISTILL A TEXT

Summary is used across the curriculum. It is used to condense a whole passage or text and may be a specific part of another paper (where a summary is a necessary reference point for your readers to understand your analysis) or the purpose of your paper as a whole. A summary is useful whenever you need to communicate the content of a text and represent the ideas behind any article or complex essay accurately. Summary is a mainstay of academic writing and is used in a variety of ways in all your courses, including some of the following:

- To summarize a source in order to critique it (as you would in a book review)
- To summarize several sources to reveal the body of knowledge on a particular topic (as in a report)
- To summarize the evidence you have compiled in an argument
- To summarize a critical perspective you are using to analyze a work

The goal of a summary paper (or précis or abstract) is to boil down into a few of your own words a whole text, without using your opinion or commentary. While you do have to decide what to include and what to leave out, your presentation should strive to be fair-minded and neutral. The summary paper is a way for you and your instructor to make sure you understand the main trajectory of action or thought in a reading.

Throughout this text, summary has been invoked to enhance learning, to help you make sure you have understood what has happened in a reading. The summary, therefore, needs to show that you have understood the overarching idea of what you've read. Begin by distilling the text to its single most compelling issue. Unlike a paraphrase, which is something said in another way (see the box on Summary vs. Paraphrase vs. Quotation in the handbook chapter 2 on Writing from Reading), a summary begins with a sentence that is a general condensation of all the *somethings* that were said and done in a text.

Your *interaction* with the text—the notes and annotations you have made while reading—will guide you as you identify how the story, play, or poem unfolds. You may find it useful to break the text into parts and write down each part's main idea. Use your notes or annotations to help you understand the text's twists and turns, its patterns and its allusions, and to explain comprehensively, concisely, and coherently how the main idea is supported by the entire reading.

## Writing a Summary: Just the Facts

- Be neutral; don't include your opinion.
- Begin with a summary sentence of the whole text.
- Be concise; do not paraphrase the whole text.
- Explain how the elements in the reading work with the main idea.
- Look for repetitions and variations that provide insight into the main idea of the text.
- Check the text's context: When was it written? What form does it use?

### Sample Student Summary

Solis 1

Lily Solis

Professor Bennett

Composition 102

30 September 2009

Précis of "Bartleby, the Scrivener"

Begins with a neutral statement that presents the basis for all plot elements in the story.

Herman Melville's short story "Bartleby, the Scrivener" presents a businessman narrator who hires an unusual employee named Bartleby, and who consequently struggles with what to do about Bartleby's behavior. The first-person narrator introduces himself as an elderly gentleman who owns a law office. His three employees, Turkey, Nippers, and Ginger Nut, are so temperamental that the narrator is forced to hire a fourth man to fill in the gaps of their work. He hires Bartleby, who at first works industriously. However, when the narrator asks him to fulfill tasks beyond copying, Bartleby consistently replies "I would prefer not to." This pattern continues, with the narrator becoming more annoyed at Bartleby's refusals and yet feeling unwilling to turn him out. When the narrator discovers that Bartleby is living at the office, he makes an attempt at befriending Bartleby, which Bartleby evades with his usual "prefer not to" responses. Soon, Bartleby stops working entirely, due to damaged eyesight, but even when his eyes improve, Bartleby does nothing but stand all day in the office. The narrator gives Bartleby a friendly ultimatum that he must leave in six days. However, at the end of six days, Bartleby is still there, and the narrator—out of Christian charity—decides to let him remain. Still, Bartleby's presence is a nuisance, and the narrator at last decides to move his offices to another building. He receives complaints from the new tenants, asking him to remove the man he left behind. The narrator

Concise statements introduce major characters and define their roles in the story.

Important element identified specifically.

Concise, neutral statements explain the sequence of action

Solis 2

returns to the old building and offers to Bartleby that he come to the narrator's private home and live there, but Bartleby refuses. A short time later, the narrator learns that Bartleby has been taken to prison as a vagrant. Although the narrator makes provisions for Bartleby to be well-fed in prison, Bartleby refuses to eat, and the narrator visits one day to find him dead. The narrator concludes the story by offering a rumor that Bartleby previously worked in a Dead Letter Office.

Gives story's resolution without offering reader's interpretation.

Work Cited

Melville, Herman. "Bartleby, the Scrivener." *Literature: Craft & Voice.* Eds. Nicholas Delbanco and Alan Cheuse. Vol. 1. New York: McGraw-Hill, 2009. 553–572. Print.

## 3d USE ANALYSIS TO EXAMINE HOW THE PARTS CONTRIBUTE TO THE WHOLE

Like summary, analysis is critical to college writing. In an analysis, you break the selection down into its parts and examine how the parts of a work contribute to the whole. Whether you are writing about irony in Flannery O'Connor or the impact of gunpowder on warfare, your analysis will look at how your source has put together its case, and you will use the source itself as evidence for your analysis. Your thesis will point specifically to the scope of your analysis. Possible analyses include:

- An explication of several aspects of how language is used—most often line by line—to point out the connotations and denotations of words as well as the reinforcing images that are used (see the following paper on William Blake's "The Garden of Love").
- An analysis of one aspect of a specific text, like dialect in Gish Jen's "Who's Irish?" or parallelism in The Museum of Stones by Carolyn Forché (see the Interactive Reading in chapter 15).
- A card report on the various elements of a story, generally only what you can fit on a 5" x 8" index card (see the sample card report at the end of this section).

**1. Explication.** An explication is a kind of analysis that shows how words, images, or other textual elements relate to each other and how these relationships make the meaning of the text clearer. Outside literature, an explication is a close reading of any text where the goal is to logically analyze details within the text itself to uncover deeper meanings or contradictions. According to *Merriam-Webster,* the definition of explicate is "to give a detailed explanation of" or "to develop the implications of; analyze logically." An explication paper does both of these things, as it *gives a detailed* *explanation of* the devices present in order to *analyze logically* the work in question. In other words, the goal of an explication is to unpack the elements of a poem, short passage of fiction or drama, or other text. The thesis statement in an explication is usually a summary of the central idea that all the devices combine to create.

Many explications take a line-by-line or sentence-by-sentence approach. Others organize the paper according to a few elements of craft that seem most meaningful to the work. However you decide to tailor your paper, remember that an explication should touch on more than one element. When explicating fiction or drama, pay attention to character, diction, and tone, and how those connect with larger thematic concerns. In the following paper on a poem, you will see an explanation of the significance of elements like rhyme, meter, diction, simile, metaphor, symbol, imagery, tone, and allusion. Although the author doesn't exactly move line by line through the poem, she does start where the poem starts and walks through it to the end. She organizes her paper in light of the shift she identifies in the poem, which she addresses in the introduction. Notice, too, that her thesis states the sum total of the devices explicated: an overall shift from an innocent state to a repressed state.

## Sample Student Explication

Brown 1

Deborah Brown

Dr. Cranford

English 200

16 September 2007

Title introduces the poem and poet.

Repression and the Church: Understanding Blake's "The Garden of Love"

William Blake's "The Garden of Love" is seemingly appropriate for either *Songs of Innocence* or *Songs of Experience,* for it contains elements of both states. In publishing the poem under the latter, however, Blake suggests that beneath the singsong, child-like quality is a serious message. While the poem begins with colorful imagery and nursery-rhyme rhythm, there is a marked shift as it progresses with an increasingly dark setting and disrupted meter. This shift is triggered by the appearance of a chapel. It is only when considering how this shift occurs that we can fully appreciate how "The Garden of Love" inverts the idea of the church as good, aligning it instead with oppression.

Thesis statement that gives the central idea conveyed by the elements to be explicated.

At the beginning of the poem, several poetic factors work together to create the impression of youthfulness, and therefore a sense of innocence. The meter consists of an iamb followed by two anapestic feet, which makes a beat reminiscent of a nursery rhyme recitation. This nursery rhyme quality is supported by the rhyme scheme which, until the last stanza, follows a regular pattern of abcb. In addition to the structure of the poem, Blake's diction contributes to the child-like voice of the speaker, for he selects

Brown 2

Discuses how each poetic device—meter, rhyme, diction, simile, and imagery—contributes to theme of innocence.

simple words that are, for the most part, monosyllabic. At the most, the words contain two syllables, the longest being "garden" (lines 1, 7), "chapel" (3, 5), and "tombstones" (10). Furthermore, the syntax follows in accord with the simplicity of the diction, as the words are organized in a straightforward, sentence-like manner. The tone comes across as particularly child-like when we consider that seven of the twelve lines in this poem begin with "And," creating the effect of a child who is incapable of forming complex sentences and so advances his story by adding onto the same sentence time and again. The absence of simile and metaphor also lends a lack of complexity to the speaker (although this is certainly not to say that there is a lack of complexity in the poem). In fact, the seeming simplicity of the poem is furthered by the way in which the speaker offers observations rather than reflections. This is set up in the second line when the speaker says, "And saw what I never had seen." The rest of the poem, then, is merely a description of the scene without offering any interpretation. The innocence of the speaker is also established through the imagery at the beginning of the poem. Blake describes the Garden of Love as full of "so many sweet flowers" (8), and he also mentions "the green" (4). These images suggest growth and spring, both of which connote youth. Green especially holds connotations with innocence or a lack of maturity, since both wood that is not yet mature and un-ripened fruit are green.

Specific support from the poem.

Topic sentences identify the shift in the poem.

All of these elements that are associated with childhood and innocence are found at the beginning of the poem. In the second stanza, there is a change in meter with the line, "And the gates of the Chapel were shut" (5). Here, just before the first hint of repression found in the word "shut," Blake has omitted the iamb and included three anapests instead of two. Although still predominantly anapestic, Blake continues to vary the meter, such as in lines 11 and 12 in which he alternates an iamb with an anapest and further deviates from his original form by changing from the abcb end rhyme scheme to internal rhyme—"And binding with *briars* my joys & *desires*" (emphasis added, 12). This altered structure is significant because it indicates that something has changed from the beginning of the poem. To understand this shift, we must first note where the disruptions occur.

Discusses how meter contributes to shift identified in topic sentence.

Specific support from the poem.

The first major disruption of meter comes when Blake writes, "And 'Thou shalt not' writ over the door" (6). Because there are so many monosyllabic words, it is ambiguous where the stresses should lie, yet it is clearly impossible to read this as

Brown 3

strictly anapestic. The result is that "thou shalt not" is emphasized, a message that contrasts the carefree state of "play" (4) in the first stanza. Blake again disrupts the meter when he writes, "And I saw it was filled with graves" (9), which draws attention to the word "graves." Here, too, Blake creates a stark contrast between the image of a garden full of life and the image of a garden filled with graves. Furthermore, the change in the color of Blake's imagery from the first stanza to the last represents a loss of the vibrant nature of youth. What began as a green is now filled with the bleak, monochromatic image of "tombstones where flowers should be" (10) while the priests add to the gloom of the scene by wearing "black gowns" (11). While all these changes are important to note, the key to understanding this poem can be found in the source that sparked this change of setting: a Chapel.

Discusses symbol.

The Chapel in the poem acts as a symbol, a metonymical device that can be taken as a representative of the church as an institution. The shut doors and the phrase "thou shalt not" written over them suggest that the Chapel represents repression. Blake writes that, "A Chapel was built [in the garden's] midst, / Where I used to play on the green" (3, 4), furthering the Chapel—a symbol of religion—as a repressive force by implying that it impedes playing and all the carefree ways that accompany playing. The Priests, who enter the scene with the Chapel, enforce the repression dictated by the church, for they are the ones who end up "binding with briars [the speaker's] joys & desires" (12). Blake's choice of the word "binding" is significant because it implies passivity and restraint; the same qualities are evoked in the idea of routine found in the image of the priests "walking their rounds" (11).

Topic sentence moves discussion towards the thesis.

In addition to the Chapel and the Priests, there are several religious elements that suggest that this poem is making a statement about the church. To begin with, the Garden of Love is in many ways reminiscent of the Garden of Eden. Both house abundant growth and are originally places of innocence. However, they each contain something forbidden which brings a loss of innocence and death. In Eden, it was the forbidden fruit from the Tree of Knowledge that led to sin and ultimately death. The forbidden part in the Garden of Love is the implication of "thou shalt not." The appearance of this forbidding message—a statement of repression—is accompanied by an appearance of graves (representative of death) instead of flowers (representative of growth/life). A second religious element in the poem is the phrase "thou shalt not"

Further explication of symbol.

Identifies allusion.

Brown 4

itself, which alludes to the Bible, and more specifically, the Ten Commandments. These commandments are statements of what man should not do; thus the phrase automatically echoes with connotations of restraint and repression. Another element reminiscent of religion is Blake's use of capitalization. Just as "He" is capitalized as a sign of respect when used in reference to God, so too does Blake capitalize only those words which are related to religion: Garden of Love, Chapel, and Priests. The poem becomes ironic when one considers that it is the Chapel and the Priests, the very objects that the capitalization suggests we should revere, that bring about the change from a place of life and play to a place of restraint and death. It is through these religious allusions that Blake allows the reader to connect the repressive, restrictive setting wrought by the appearance of a Chapel to the church at large as an institution.

Explains significance of Biblical allusions; ties elements previously discussed to thesis.

The diction, imagery, symbols, and allusions used in "The Garden of Love" work together to create a contrast between the energy and youthfulness of innocence found in the first stanza and the repression and death that is increasingly present after the chapel's appearance. In this way, Blake shows that the church turns happy innocence into dark forbidding, creating in a mere twelve lines of poetry a statement against the repressive nature of the church in his time.

Reviews key points of the discussion; restatement and refinement of thesis.

Work Cited

Blake, William. "The Garden of Love." *Literature: Craft & Voice*. Eds. Nicholas Delbanco and Alan Cheuse. Vol. 2. New York: McGraw-Hill, 2009. 396. Print.

**2. Card report.** A card report asks you to represent in a condensed space the various elements of a story. Most instructors require that your report not exceed the amount of information you can fit on a 5" x 8" inch note card, and therefore you must make every word count. As you take apart the pieces of the story, you will naturally forge a deeper understanding of it, and likely a new opinion of the work as a whole. Card reports are a great way to keep track of what you have read and can be an invaluable tool in preparing for exams.

In the following card report, our student, Tessa Harville, was instructed to include the list of information that appears below:

1. Title of the story and date of publication

2. Author's name, dates of birth and death, and the nationality or region (if applicable) with which he/she is associated
3. The name and a brief description of the main character, especially important personality traits
4. Additional characters who play important roles and their major traits
5. The setting, including time and place
6. The type of narration or point of view
7. A summary of the story's major events in the order in which they occur
8. The tone or voice in which the author relates the story
9. The overall style of the work, including (if space allows) short quotes that exemplify the style
10. A brief analysis of irony in the story
11. The theme of the story
12. The major symbols in the story and a brief explanation of what you think each means
13. A critique of the story in which you give your evaluation or opinion of the story in question

As you look at the following model, note the amount of thought and effort to refine language that the student put into the "Critique" portion. Although it is brief, your critique should reflect the amount of thought you might put into a three-page paper.

## Sample Student Card Report

***Front of Card***

Tessa Harville

English 101, Section 2

**Title:** "A Good Man Is Hard to Find" (1955)

**Author:** Flannery O'Connor, 1925-1964, American, Southern writer

**Main Character:** The grandmother, who lives with her son's family and refuses to be ignored. She considers herself a lady, but is stubborn, talkative, and insists on her own way.

**Other Characters:** Bailey, the father of the family, who is grumpy and sullen; Bailey's unnamed wife, who quietly tends the children and is ineffectual; John Wesley and June Star, Bailey's son and daughter who are typical children that bluntly speak their minds and are excited by adventure; and The Misfit, an escaped murderer who philosophizes with the grandmother.

**Setting:** Georgia, presumably around the 1950s, when the story was written. Much of the story recounts a car trip so the scenery changes.

**Narration:** Third-person omniscient; primarily follows grandmother.
**Summary:** 1. The grandmother tries to convince Bailey to take the family to Tennessee for vacation, rather than Florida, and uses the newspaper article she reads about The Misfit as a reason not to travel toward Florida. 2. The family leaves for Florida. The car trip is full of bickering and a restaurant stop where the grandmother talks with the owners about how bad people have become. 3. Back on the road, the grandmother convinces Bailey to take a detour so she can see a plantation she visited years ago. 4. The grandmother's cat, which she snuck into the car, causes an accident while they are on a deserted road looking for the plantation. 5. Three men arrive to help the family. The grandmother recognizes one as The Misfit, and as a result, he has his men shoot the family, one by one. The grandmother is shot last, after a moment of connection with The Misfit in which she sees him as "one of [her] own children" (437).
**Tone/Voice:** The tone is deadpan, with no comments from the narrator. This makes for a reportorial voice with the precision of an acute observer.

***Back of Card***

**Style:** The sentences are straightforward and often declarative: "The grandmother didn't want to go to Florida" (429). The description is vivid but concise: "The car raced roughly along in a swirl of pink dust" (433).
**Irony:** Becomes most apparent after reading the story and looking back, making it dramatic irony. The family does not know to heed the grandmother's preposterous warning about The Misfit before taking the vacation, but the reader knows she is right. The dramatic irony is aided by the large amount of foreshadowing, such as the grandma's remembering the plantation outside of "Toombsboro" (432). The grandmother's behavior is at times ironic—she is concerned with being a lady, but talks too much; she says people should be more respectful, but then uses biased language as she ogles a "pickaninny" (430). The way she causes her own trouble is ironic.

**Theme:** A feeling of connection can transcend the shocking reality of life's brutality.

**Symbols:** The grandmother could symbolize the South: her vanity and pretense to being a lady cause a violent downfall. The family burial ground with "five or six graves" seen from the car is both a foreshadowing tool and symbolic of the family's impending death (431).

**Critique:** Although the story relies on wild coincidence, elements including highly believable characters, perfectly placed description, and economic movement of the plot make this story gripping and a representation of life with all its vanity, surprises, and connections.

## 3e USE A SYNTHESIS TO SHOW RELATIONSHIPS

Synthesis requires two or more sources and shows significant relationships among those sources. The classic synthesis in college writing is the research project, which asks you to look at a topic in depth and from multiple perspectives. The next chapter will follow closely a research paper on the poetry of Langston Hughes, from finding a topic to selecting sources. Here we will look at how that research project is an argument. Another synthesis across the curriculum could be a report on a body of information (on, for example, the effect of AIDS on Africa). The comparison-contrast paper, like the research project, is found in almost every area of college study.

**1. Argument.** The primary goal of an argument paper is to take a position on an issue or form an opinion about a piece of literature and defend that position/opinion using evidence. In a single-source paper (such as the critique of Chekhov's "Rapture" discussed under critique in this chapter), your evidence will be examples and quotations from the text itself. Most of the time, however, an argument paper will be an assignment that involves outside or secondary sources. Secondary sources, such as literary criticism, report, describe, comment on, or analyze a written work other than itself. You can use secondary sources to see what people have learned and written about a topic or an existing work of literature.

Nearly every sample paper cited in this chapter is an argument paper in some sense—a thesis statement in most papers is a type of argument because it posits an opinion that the writer must then support. The best examples of argument papers are the Chekhov student paper, which appears in chapter 2, and the model research project, which appears in the next chapter. In the Chekhov paper, the student argues that the story is incomplete and unsatisfying. Because the student responds to a single source, he supports his argument by citing Chekhov's text directly.

In the research paper on Langston Hughes in the next chapter, the student argues that Langston Hughes uses only those aspects of jazz that reflect the African-American experience. In that paper, the student uses multiple sources to make her argument. To support her points about jazz, she uses secondary sources that provide historical context. To support her reading of jazz devices in Hughes's poems, she relies on quotes taken directly from two of Hughes's poems.

**2. Comparison and contrast.** A compare/contrast paper asks you to consider two works side-by-side and highlight the similarities and differences between them in order to make a point about one or both texts. When you are selecting texts to compare, you must make sure that there is some basis for the comparison—perhaps the works share a common theme; or, they may be vastly different but both products of the same region.

Let's break that definition down a little bit, using the example of comparing *Beowulf* the epic poem with *Beowulf* the 2007 movie version (see chapter 13, Fiction and the Visual Arts, for these two works). The basis for comparison of these sources is self-evident: they are two versions of the same story. After reading the epic and watching the movie, you would ask yourself what the major similarities are and list them. In this case, you might make a list of the characters that the two have in common or the scenes that are common to both text and movie. Then, you should do the same for differences. In the *Beowulf* example, you might note the major plot change that Grendel's mother seduces King Hrothgar and Beowulf, so that they are the fathers of monsters.

As you make your lists, you might further think if some of the items you listed under similarities might in fact hold small differences when examined closely. Continuing with the *Beowulf* example, you might first have noted that Grendel appears in both versions and is a monster in both versions. But as you think about the movie, you might see that, in fact, he seems more distressed than evil.

The following student paper grew out of just such a comparison. Our author, Anthony Melmott, used the similarities and particularly the differences he saw in the two versions of Grendel to make a point about the role of the villain in today's world. Notice how he moves through the paper: after an introduction and an overview of the characters' similarities, Anthony delves into a detailed analysis of how the two differ. He then ties his entire discussion together in the concluding paragraph, and impressively broadens it to make a statement about contemporary society.

## Sample Student Comparison/Contrast Paper

Melmott 1

Anthony Melmott

Professor Wallace

English 150

30 November 2008

Visions of the Villain:

The Role of Grendel in *Beowulf* the Epic and the Movie

Opening sentence establishes the works that will be compared.

In the movie version of *Beowulf,* directed by Robert Zemeckis and released in 2007, there are obvious deviations from the plot of the original epic. Most viewers who are familiar with the epic will readily recognize a major change: Beowulf does not kill Grendel's mother but is instead seduced by her. Clearly, Beowulf in the movie

Melmott 2

version is no longer the hero that he was in the original epic. But what many viewers might miss is that the movie changes more than the hero. Grendel, too, is no longer the evil villain he was in the original epic. Whereas the poem leaves no question that Grendel is a demon with evil intent, the movie portrays him as a tortured, childish soul through differences in his motivation, his power status, and his lineage.

Thesis statement. Also, the mention of three points sets up the organization of the paper.

Discussion of similarities.

The reason that many *Beowulf* movie viewers might miss the change to Grendel's character is that in many respects, he is similar to the original Grendel. In both versions, Grendel is a monster who eats and kills men. His overall trajectory does not change from the epic to the movie: in each, he attacks Hereot's hall and gets away with it until Beowulf comes and tears off his arm, thereby killing him. Even certain details of Grendel's portrayal in the movie echo the original epic. For example, the epic introduces Grendel by calling him an inhabitant of "the abode of monster kind" (14). The movie visually represents him as a monster by making him tall and hideous: his body—which drips with slime—looks as if it is turned inside out. As in the original epic, Grendel appears at night, thus aligning him with darkness in both versions. In these ways, he is meant to be seen as a terrible being in each.

Transition into discussion of differences.

But a little digging suggests otherwise. A major difference between the epic and the movie is that Grendel does not speak in the epic but does speak in the movie. Since Grendel does not speak, and since he is portrayed through narrative rather than visual effect, the epic uses a variety of language to describe Grendel. He is called a "fiend of hell"; "wrathful spirit"; "mighty stalker of the marches" (14); "creature of destruction, fierce and greedy, wild and furious" (15); and a "terrible monster, like a dark shadow of death" (17). All of this language reinforces Grendel's evilness and angry mode of existence. Grendel's fearsome appearance in the movie might lead a viewer to imagine him as the above list describes. However, the movie version allows Grendel to speak, and when he does, we hear a different story. Grendel speaks in Old English, even though the other characters speak in contemporary English, so his lines are difficult to understand. But listening closely reveals that when Beowulf says to Grendel, whose arm is caught in the door, "Your bloodletting days are finished, demon," Grendel replies, "I am not a demon."

Textual support.

Support from the movie.

Melmott 3

On its own, this example could be explained as Grendel lacking the self-awareness that he is a demon. But other details corroborate Grendel's statement. Both of Grendel's attacks are triggered by the loud rollicking of the men in Hereot. As the scene pans from the meadhall to Grendel's underground lair, the noise of the chanting sounds as if it has been submerged. The effect is that we are hearing the men as Grendel hears them—a constant, throbbing, bass line that makes Grendel's membranous ears quiver. When Grendel bursts into full view, his screams are more like cries of anguish than roars meant to frighten. The attention given to Grendel's sensitive ears, his clutching at his head as he screams, and his posture all suggest that he is in physical agony from the parties at Heorot, and thus bursts in to put a stop to it. This is a far less demoniac motivation than that cited in the epic.

In the original, Grendel's first attack reads, "The creature of destruction, fierce and greedy, wild and furious, was ready straight. He seized thirty thanes upon their bed" (15). Nothing in this suggests any sort of pain or anguish that Grendel experiences, as he appears to in the movie. Further, while the movie shows him as provoked, the epic clearly states after that first attack, "It was no longer than a single night ere he wrought more deeds of murder; he recked not of the feud and the crime—he was too fixed in them!" (16). According to the *Oxford English Dictionary,* "reck" means "To take heed or have a care of some thing (or person), so as to be alarmed or troubled thereby, or to modify one's conduct or purpose on that account." In other words, this quote shows that Grendel's killings do not bother him or give him pause because he is so set in his evil ways. Hence, even if Grendel could speak in the original epic, he certainly wouldn't say "I am no demon" and even if he did, we would know by his actions that this was not true. On the contrary, when Grendel utters that line in the movie, we have seen that, indeed, his motivation is not naturally demonic but provocation.

Defines unknown word to add textual support.

Transition sentence that leads into the second point of the thesis.

Consistent with the change in motivation is the change in Grendel's power status from the epic to the movie. In the epic, Grendel holds a reign of terror. Although it is difficult to analyze language in a translation, it is safe to say that the text refers to Grendel in several places as a ruling authority of sorts. One example follows Grendel's

Textual support.

Melmott 4

first series of attacks in which the poem reads, "Thus he tyrannized over them" (16). In another translation, that of Seamus Heaney, the same line reads "So Grendel ruled" (35). Both "rule" and "tyranny" are ways of describing an all-powerful governing body. Later, when he fights Beowulf, Grendel is described as the "master of evils" (43), and in the Heaney translation as "the captain of evil" (47). "Master" and "captain" both refer to someone in charge, someone with power, and both are applied to Grendel in the original epic.

Yet for all the power the epic accords to Grendel, the movie portrays Grendel as child-like. While Grendel has a mother in both versions, only the movie shows Grendel interact with her like a child. After his first attack in the movie, he returns to his lair and speaks with his mother. Throughout their dialogue, he lays on the floor of the cave in a position reminiscent of a fetus. The words he speaks are likewise childish; at one point, he cries out, "The men screamed! The men bellowed and screamed! The men hurt me, hurt my ear." Not only do his simple, repetitive sentences suggest a child's voice, but his fear of and dismay at the men show him to be the opposite of their tyrant, ruler, master, or captain.

Support from the movie.

Transition sentence that leads into the third point of the thesis.

The reduction of Grendel's evilness and power can perhaps be traced to the biggest difference between the epic and the movie's Grendel: that of Grendel's lineage. As mentioned in the introduction, the movie portrays Grendel's mother as a seductress, with the premise that she once seduced King Hrothgar, making Grendel the offspring of Hrothgar and the mother. On the other hand, the original epic is very clear—and frequently emphasizes—that Grendel is a descendent of Cain, who committed the first murder. Referring to Cain, the epic reads, "From him there woke to life all the evil broods, monsters and elves and sea-beasts, and giants too, who long time strove with God" (14–15). There is no room for a human in this description, and certainly not Hrothgar, whom the epic praises as being a "good king." By changing Grendel's parentage, the movie shifts the root of evil from Grendel to Hrothgar. It is because of Hrothgar's past weakness that his kingdom is plagued by the fruit of that very weakness. Grendel, then, is a by-product, a mere pawn in the struggle between Hrothgar's kingdom and the mother's corrupting ways. The mother uses Grendel's

Melmott 5

death as a way to further corrupt the kingdom through her seduction of Beowulf—and Beowulf succumbs.

Brief reiteration of the three points made in the paper.

In the retelling of an existing story—whether that retelling be in the form of a story, a poem, or a movie—there will always be similarities and differences. But the difference in the role of the villain between an epic written in 1000 and a movie filmed in 2007 tells us something about our contemporary society. As we noted briefly in the introduction, Beowulf's seduction makes him less heroic; likewise, we have seen that the movie makes Grendel less villainous in motivation, in power, and in lineage. We might ask ourselves: What does it mean to live in an age where we see heroes as fallible and villains as innocent? The difference between the epic Grendel and the movie Grendel offers an answer: the original villain has been turned into a product of human vice, suggesting that true villainy lies in human behavior. Or, to put it another way, in a world where human deeds are monstrous, there isn't much room for a monster.

Conclusion broadens significance to our own society.

Conclusion explains the implication of the thesis; answers the "so what?" question.

Works Cited

*Beowulf.* Dir. Robert Zemeckis. Perf. Crispin Glover, Anthony Hopkins, Angelina Jolie, and Ray Winstone. Paramount Pictures, 2007. Film.

*Beowulf.* Trans. Seamus Heaney. *The Norton Anthology of English Literature.* 7th ed. Ed. M.H. Abrams and Stephen Greenblatt. New York: W.W. Norton, 2000. 32–99. Print.

*Beowulf.* Trans. Chauncey Brewster Tinker. New York: Newson & Co., 1902. Print.

"Reck." Def. 1b. *The Oxford English Dictionary.* 2nd ed. 1989. Print.

## 3f USE CRITIQUE TO BRING IN YOUR OWN EVALUATION

We define a critique as a summary with your own reasonable opinion. Whether you are asked to critique a reading for an essay exam, the accuracy of a website as a source, or respond to an argument, in most of your courses, you will be required to evaluate the presentation of information.

- What is the work (or performance) trying to accomplish?
- Does it achieve its purpose?
- Do you agree or disagree with the piece, like or dislike it?
- How has the piece created this reaction in you?

**Review.** A critique is a formal evaluation of a text, and one of the most common forms of critique in literature is the review. In a review, you—as the reviewer—get to evaluate the text or, in the case of live theatre, a performance. For an example of a review, see the response to Anton Chekhov's early story "Rapture" in chapter 2. After a few general, opening sentences, the discussion becomes more specific as the student asserts that the main character's lack of change makes the story unsatisfying. The student continues by analyzing the various parts of the story. As your review progresses and you begin to make evaluative statements—such as *The story begins on a strong note but deteriorates; The casting was so well-done that it carries the play from start to finish; The poem's sonnet form is perfect for its content*—you will also need to analyze why you are reacting to the text in that particular way. Particularly strong is his division of the story into three parts:

> *Part one: the clerk runs in, announcing himself, disrupting the household, waking his brothers. Part two: Mitya takes out the newspaper and urges his father to read it aloud. In the closing sequence, a reader may expect something to happen as a result of Mitya's "rapture" that he has become famous because his name is in the paper and on the police record. However, as the ancient philosopher and critic Aristotle might put it, what is the dramatic purpose here? . . . His parents and his siblings humor him instead of contradicting or berating him; thus making change less likely for Mitya. The reader is left to wonder what the point is, and without that concluding action, the dramatic purpose is unclear, and the story is incomplete and ultimately unsatisfying.*

Notice here that the author is not afraid to make bold claims: that the story is incomplete and unsatisfying. You may feel a little intimidated the first time you write a review, especially if the author is well known. Take the Chekhov paper to heart; the validity of an evaluation rests not on how highly you are ranking a noted author but on how your analysis of the story supports your evaluation. In this case, the student has analyzed the structure of the story, and found that in a story set up for a three-part movement, the third part is missing. Therefore, when he claims that the story is incomplete and unsatisfying, we see the author's point.

### Guidelines for Writing Reviews

**Introduce What You Are Evaluating**

- Include the title and author.
- For a live performance, include who performed, when, and under what circumstances (a full house? an outdoor amphitheater?).
- Be clear about what you are evaluating.

**Set Up Your Review with a Summary**

- Your summary is to be used as a reference point for your discussion; you may not want to give the ending away, however.

**Put the Piece into Context**

- What type of work is it? A comedy? A tragedy?
- When was it written?
- If it is a well-known play such as Shakespeare, include any unusual information on the "take" of the director (what's the director's purpose in staging Shakespeare's "Hamlet" in Pakistan, for example).

**Analyze the Text**

- For a play, note the staging, lighting, and costuming as well as the acting.
- Note how the work is structured.
- Look at the individual elements: plot, character, dialogue.
- Determine the purpose of the work.

**Include Your Reasoned Opinion: This Is Your Evaluation**

- Did the work achieve its purpose?
- What is your response to the selection and why?
- Agree or disagree with the presentation of information (whether or not it achieved its purpose).
- Base your agreement or disagreement on evidence.

**End with a Balanced Conclusion**

- Recap the pros and cons of the piece.
- Give your overall reaction.

## 3g FIND AN EFFECTIVE APPROACH TO THE ESSAY EXAM

Timed writing on an exam may seem like an intimidating prospect. Reviewing the tips below will help you learn an effective approach to essay exams, whether you are taking one for a class in English, political science, or psychology.

**1. Prepare.** If you have been diligent in annotating the texts you read and keeping a journal or freewriting exercises, be sure to review these materials before the day of your exam. Jog your memory about each story, poem, novel, or play you have read for the class by reviewing major characters and events of the work, as well as any important information about the authors.

**2. Pace yourself.** When you receive the exam, glance through it to see approximately how much time you should spend on each section. Remember that if an essay is worth, say, 70 percent of the grade, you want to make it a priority to spend sufficient time on it.

**3. Read the assignment carefully.** When you arrive at the essay question, circle key words as you read the assignment. Pay particular attention to the verbs your instructor uses: common choices are *explain, discuss, analyze, compare, contrast, interpret,* and *argue*. Your understanding of the different types of assignments addressed in this chapter can help you here.

## Understanding Essay Exam Assignments

*The words* explain *or* discuss *ask you to engage in a detailed way, much like an explication or a close reading.*

Analyze *should remind you of what you know about an analysis paper—that your job is to explore one element of the text and show how it contributes to the overall work.*

Compare *and* contrast *asks you to find similarities and differences between two items and to suggest what those similarities or differences emphasize or illuminate.*

Argue *is a way of asking you to take a position about an issue, or in the case of a literary text, to defend what you see in the work that may not be readily apparent to others.*

**4. Form a thesis.** In an essay exam, your thesis will likely be a simpler statement than the type of complex argument you would form in a longer research paper or analysis. Look at the phrasing of the question itself to help you shape your thesis.

### EXAMPLE OF AN ESSAY EXAM ASSIGNMENT

➡ *Analyze Frost's use of imagery in "Stopping By Woods on a Snowy Evening."*

### EXAMPLE OF A THESIS THAT RESPONDS TO THE ASSIGNMENT

Frost uses idyllic, New England imagery to disguise a more serious statement about death.

**5. Outline briefly.** Even if you don't typically work from an outline when writing a paper, take a few moments to jot down a brief outline. In an essay exam, even a brief outline will keep you from freezing up entirely. And, if you find you are spending too much time on the first paragraph, you can quickly wrap it up to move on to the next point in your outline. In short, an outline can help you budget time and space in your essay while eliminating the stressful feeling of not knowing where to go next.

**6. Check your work.** Try your best to allow a little extra time in which to read over what you have written. Time constraints often make even the best students leave out words or write sentences that make no sense. Rereading your work will allow you to fix these problems.

Follow our model student, Renee Knox, as she completes the following essay assignment on a timed exam.

## Notes for a Sample Student Essay Exam

Renee identifies key words in the prompt. Already, she knows her paper must focus on the significance of the imagery.

Assignment: Analyze Frost's use of imagery in "Stopping By Woods on a Snowy Evening," reproduced below.

Renee underlines the imagery in the poem and highlights phrases she finds significant.

Renee numbers the lines for easy reference when she quotes in the essay.

**Stopping By Woods On A Snowy Evening**

*Whose woods these are I think I know.*
*His house is in the village though;*
*He will not see me stopping here*
*To watch his woods fill up with snow.*
*My little horse must think it queer*
*To stop without a farmhouse near*
*Between the woods and frozen lake*
*The darkest evening of the year.*
*He gives his harness bells a shake*
*To ask if there is some mistake.*
*The only other sound's the sweep*
*Of easy wind and downy flake.*
*The woods are lovely, dark and deep.*
*But I have promises to keep,*
*And miles to go before I sleep,*
*And miles to go before I sleep.*

Renee notes that many of her underlined phrases bring to mind a farm-like, New England setting. Then she separates out the other images and names their connotations.

Important images: woods, snow, horse, house, village, dark, wind, snowflakes, dark

woods, snow, horse, farmhouse, village=New England; ideal Christmas scene

no farmhouse near, dark, deep, winter=cold, alone, death??

sleep=death?

Renee formulates a thesis based on her observations.

**Thesis:** Frost uses pretty New England imagery to disguise a more serious statement about death.

Renee generates a brief outline to follow. In constructing her essay, she will use a 5 paragraph structure.

I. Introduction and thesis
II. Set up "pretty" imagery
 A. Mention horse
 B. Mention farmhouse
 C. Mention woods
 D. Mention snow
 E. Adds up to ideal Christmas village scene
III. Set up dark imagery and cold effect
 A. Snow
 B. Woods
 C. Wind
 D. Solitary
IV. Discuss symbolic significance of images
 A. Snow=winter=death
 B. Woods=wild, easily lose your way
 C. Sleep=form of death
V. Conclusion—why would Frost do this?

## Sample Student Essay Exam

Knox 1

Renee Knox

Professor Giordano

ENGL 1203

5 November 2008

Renee uses a simple but complete title, in order not to spend too much time on it.

Imagery in Frost's "Stopping By Woods on a Snowy Evening"

Many times in literature, as in life, something appears to be one thing but is actually another. One need only think of tales like "Little Red Riding Hood" in which the woman who appears to be her grandmother turns out to be a wolf. In a similar way, Robert Frost's "Stopping By Woods on a Snowy Evening" appears to be a simple and charming experience. Instead, Frost uses idyllic New England imagery to disguise a more serious statement about death.

Thesis statement. When Renee reread her essay, she changed "pretty" to "idyllic" for more sophisticated diction.

Renee stays on topic by following her outline.

Even in the poem's title, Frost is already using imagery, for the title presents woods, snow, and evening. We can picture an evening scene in which snow is softly falling on woods. And indeed, the speaker is there with his "little horse" (line 5) that wears "harness bells" (9). The mention of a village (2) and a farmhouse (6), even though the speaker is not near them, suggests that villages and farmhouses dot the landscape in which the speaker moves. Put all together—snow, a horse with harness bells, a village, and a farmhouse—Frost's imagery conjures a New England scene that is so quaint, it is exactly the type of scene many people replicate with porcelain villages at Christmas time—it is that perfect.

Renee helps her paper flow by using "however" to signal her transition to her next point.

However, if we look at the nature imagery, we get a much darker picture. While evening might connote a soothing time of leisure after the day's work is done, it is also the time of oncoming dark, as Frost's imagery indicates when he describes it as "the darkest evening of the year" (8). In fact, Frost calls attention to the fact that it is the darkest evening by placing that description in line 8, the exact center of the 16-line poem. Furthermore, he repeats "dark" again when he describes the woods as "dark and deep" (13), adding emphasis to the imagery of dark through repetition. We also know that the evening is cold, and although snow is a part of an idyllic New England Christmas scene, it is equally an unpleasant feeling with bleak connotations. If the world is cold, it means that it is not treating you well. Beyond this kind of cold, there

Knox 2

Renee supports her point with specific examples from the text.

Renee further analyzes the imagery she set up in the previous paragraph to ensure she sufficiently answers the prompt.

is the sensory imagery of the only sound being "the sweep / of easy wind and downy flake" (11-12). In other words, the narrator is not only out in the cold, but he is so alone that he actually hears the snowflakes falling in the wind. When put together with the dark, this is a bleak and lonely scene.

Beyond the sensory unpleasantness of dark and cold, these images have symbolic meaning when placed in the context of other literature. Frost's imagery clearly places this moment in winter, which traditionally symbolizes death, much as spring symbolizes rebirth. Moreover, even though the woods are "lovely," they are also "dark and deep," a place where in much of literature, like Shakespeare's "A Midsummer Night's Dream," characters easily lose themselves or succumb to supernatural forces. Perhaps the woods are "lovely" because their darkness tantalizes the narrator to lose himself, but if you followed such an idea through, the speaker would end up lost and frozen in the dark woods. The last lines reinforce the idea that he is being tempted by death. When recalling himself from gazing into the cold, dark woods, the speaker gives his reason as having "miles to go before I sleep" (15). Sleep, like winter, is another way of suggesting death, for much of literature speaks of death as a type of eternal sleep.

Renee transitions to a brief but insightful conclusion.

Thus, while the scene's first impression is one of a quaint New England night—an impression built through imagery of horse, village, farmhouse, and snow—the cold and dark nature imagery tells another story of death and the temptation to remain in the presence of death. By bringing these two types of imagery together in one poem, Frost perhaps suggests that death is always near, even when we think we are looking at a vivid scene of comfort. Or, to put a more optimistic spin on things, since some of the images overlap (snowy woods are both beautiful and dangerous), Frost might be trying to tell us that death is nothing to fear, that even on the darkest evening, there is still loveliness in the dark of the woods and the sweep of the flake.

In reading Renee's essay, you may have noticed that there were places that sounded a little rough or colloquial and other spots that weren't perfectly explained, such as the end of the fourth paragraph. However, her main ideas are clear and her conclusion compelling. She also used specific support and stayed exactly on topic with what the assignment asked her to do. For these reasons, Renee's essay is well done because the constraints of a timed setting often force the writer to leave a few rough spots. If you have time, do your best to revise, but remember that a timed essay will almost never have the same polished quality as a paper you have had time to think about, draft, and revise.

# 4 Quoting, Paraphrasing, Summarizing, and Avoiding Plagiarism

## 4a KNOW WHAT INFORMATION REQUIRES DOCUMENTATION

When writing from sources—whether a single source, as when you respond to a story, poem, or play you have just read, or multiple sources, as when you include research—you will need to effectively use quotation, paraphrase, and summary in your paper. Quotation, paraphrase, and summary are the evidence you use for your interpretation of a work, and it is common for all three to be employed in the same paper. **Plagiarism** occurs when this material isn't presented accurately. In this chapter, you will find information on how to keep track of the author, title, or URL for any source you have consulted (see also Writing the Research Paper, Avoiding Plagiarism, and Documenting Sources). Keeping track of sources is critical, because how you present your evidence determines more than just how convincing your paper is; it keeps your paper honest by giving your readers

- A framework (who, what, when, where, and how) for your response.
- The specifics in the source that led you to your observations, thoughts, and connections.

Marginal annotations, underlined and highlighted passages, or notes in a reading journal help you trace your response back to specific source material. Your interaction with one text or many provides the basis of your interpretation and the thesis of your paper. Whether you base your paper on a single source or you work with multiple sources, you will likely need to summarize a work to provide your reader with a framework for your analysis. When working with multiple sources, you may also need to summarize a number of critical opinions. It is likely you will paraphrase a short passage to give your reader context for your assessment or the point of view of a scholarly work. Should you be writing about drama, you'll likely quote from the play; should you be discussing a poem, it's almost inevitable that several lines of poetry will be included in your discussion. The guidelines provided here will keep you from plagiarizing when you have summarized, paraphrased, or quoted sources. You will always want to document in your paper where you found the kinds of information listed in the following box.

## Information Requiring Documentation

- Lines from a story, poem, or play
- Opinions, observations, interpretations by writers, critics, and scholars
- Information from expert and/or sponsored sites
- Visual materials, including tables, charts, or graphs
- Footnotes from printed sources
- Statements that are open to debate
- Historical information that is not commonly known
- Statistics, or surveys, census or poll results if you use them

### SAMPLES OF TYPES OF INFORMATION REQUIRING DOCUMENTATION

The whaling industry in nineteenth-century America collapsed when flexible steel hoops replaced whalebone in women's corsets.

A twenty-year Swiss study of organic farming found that organic farms yielded more produce per unit of energy consumed than farms that did not use organic farming methods.

Smoking kills over 418,000 people every year in the United States.

The easiest way to avoid plagiarism is to remember that you must tell your reader the sources of all facts, ideas, and opinions that are taken from others that are not considered common knowledge. If a number of sources contain the same information and that information is widely considered to be true, it is considered common knowledge. For example, in biology, the structure of DNA and the process of cell division or photosynthesis are considered common knowledge. A recent scientific discovery about genetics, however, would not be common knowledge, so you would need to cite the source of this information. When in doubt cite your source; citing is never incorrect.

**COMMON KNOWLEDGE (DOCUMENTATION NOT REQUIRED)**

Millions of soldiers died in the trenches of the Western front in World War I.

Mohandas K. Gandhi was assassinated in 1948.

The cheetah is the fastest-moving land animal.

**Tip for Avoiding Plagiarism and the Web.** What you find on the Web requires extra precaution to make sure you document correctly where you got your information. Do not assume that what you find on the Web is common knowledge. Write in your notes the URL as well as *the date* that you accessed the site. Websites are notoriously prone to change, so this helps you keep your source clear. In your notes, put quotation marks around anything that is a direct quotation (wherever you found the information, print or online) so that you can easily see when you are using another's words. It is easy to cut whole passages from the Internet and paste them into your paper, or to think you have paraphrased when you have quoted if your notes aren't effective. This is plagiarism. Diligence is needed to avoid cobbling together a patchwork of sources without complete and accurate source information.

## 4b USE SOURCES TO SUPPORT YOUR COMMENTARY

Your paper is your own independent thought. A quotation, paraphrase, or summary should be used only if you are going to comment on it in your paper. You can expand upon a quotation, paraphrase, or summary. You can interpret it. You can indicate what you believe the work implies. You can refer to a quotation, paraphrase, or a summary. You can even disagree. Your instructor is looking at your work to make sure you have understood a selection and to see what you have discovered for yourself. So, do not worry that you don't have anything original to say. Few do, even among professionals. *How* you say what you have to say is original to you. Don't apologize by suggesting this is only your opinion ("it seems to me" or "in my opinion"). Make your case. Be confident that, if you have discovered something that is interesting to you, it will also be interesting to your reader.

- A paper with too few references to sources does not provide the evidence you need to support your case.
- A paper with too many references to sources prevents you from making your case because it is overshadowed by the ideas of others.

## TIP: Use Quotation, Summary, Paraphrase

- To support a point
- To present your source's point of view
- To disagree with your source
- To generalize from examples
- To reason through examples
- To make comparisons
- To distinguish fact from opinion
- To provide context

**1. Quotation:** *A word-for-word copy from an original source.* Direct quotation is especially useful when you are writing about literature because the way a writer uses words is central to an understanding of the text You will use quotations as examples of the way a writer uses language. However, you can also use a quotation from another source if a technical term is used that is not easily rephrased or if rephrasing it would change its meaning. You may want to use a quotation when the ideas are so vividly and beautifully expressed that you prefer to avoid paraphrase. Even if you do, a direct quotation is not to be used as a conclusion or summation of your main point in your work. It doesn't stand on its own. You must expand upon any quotation—or paraphrase or summary—that you include in your paper.

**Tip on Avoiding Plagiarism in a Quotation:** Using quotation marks around information from a source while changing or omitting information from that source is a serious error. Use *brackets* **[ ]** around a word or words you insert in a quotation. Use three periods in succession (**ellipses**) **. . .** to show that you have omitted something that was in the original quotation: "He turned green **. . .** but he went on [to steer the ship]."

**ORIGINAL SOURCE** (from page 7 of *The Metaphysical Club* by Louis Menand).

> We think of the Civil War as a war to save the union and to abolish slavery, but before the fighting began most people regarded these as incompatible ideals. Northerners who wanted to preserve the union did not wish to see slavery extended into the territories; some of them hoped it would wither away in the states where it persisted. But many Northern businessmen believed that losing the South would mean economic catastrophe, and many of their employees believed that freeing the slaves would mean lower wages. They feared secession far more than they disliked slavery, and they were unwilling to risk the former by trying to pressure the South into giving up the latter.

➡ ***For more practice with quotation, paraphrase, and summary using this example and many others, visit www.mhhe.com/delbancole.***

**SERIOUS ERROR**

Menand notes that "many Northern businessmen and many of their employees feared secession far more than they disliked slavery, and they were unwilling to risk the former by trying to pressure the South into giving up the latter" (7).

➡ *This sentence is unacceptable because the writer has not used ellipses to indicate where words have been omitted from the quotation.*

**CORRECT QUOTATION**

Menand notes that "many Northern businessmen . . . and many of their employees . . . feared secession far more than they disliked slavery, and they were unwilling to risk the former by trying to pressure the South into giving up the latter" (7).

**2. Paraphrase:** *Someone else's ideas in your own words.* When writing about literature, you may paraphrase some of the story line in order to get to the point you want to make. In research, paraphrase is most often used when you are referring to the work of critics and scholars. If you find that the language you are trying to put into your words is already broken down to its most simple form, or that the language is too perfectly worded to change, you may want to use a quotation instead of a paraphrase. Don't paraphrase if you are not entirely sure you understand the original or you risk misrepresenting its original meaning. One test of a good paraphrase is if you can restate what you are trying to paraphrase without looking at the source.

**Tip on Avoiding Plagiarism in a Paraphrase:** A true paraphrase is not just a few different words, even if you feel the scholar has said something better than you could have said it yourself. *Your words* are the words that matter to your instructor. Just changing a few words—*even when you indicate the source of the paraphrase*—is still plagiarism. In a true paraphrase, the sentence structure is your own. It doesn't sound like the original; it sounds like you.

**PLAGIARISM**

Menand observes that before the Civil War, many Northerners feared secession far more than they disliked slavery, and they were unwilling to risk the former by trying to pressure the South into giving up the latter (7).

➡ *This quotation is plagiarized because it uses the exact words of the source—most of a sentence—without quotation marks.*

**CORRECT PARAPHRASE**

> Menand observes that before the Civil War, many Northerners were afraid that secession would be worse for the country than slavery, and they were not willing to try and force the South to give up slavery for fear that a disastrous Southern secession would follow (7).

**3. Summary:** *A condensation of the main idea or action that includes only the supporting details related directly to that main idea.* Unlike a paraphrase, where a concept or action from a brief passage is explained in your own words, a summary lays out a long passage (such as an act in a play or a whole poem, story, play, or other work). When writing about literature, a plot summary is not enough. A summary sets the stage for an analysis, providing your readers with enough information for them to understand your commentary. In a research paper, summary can also be used to provide examples of a variety of points of view on your topic. Make comparisons between two points of view, then summarize several sources to build upon for your conclusion. (See the chapter on Common Writing Assignments for a discussion of the summary paper.)

**Tip on Avoiding Plagiarism in a Summary:** When you summarize information, you must include information on the source or it will appear as if you are using someone else's ideas as your own. Omitting information in a summary that alters the source's meaning is also unacceptable. Offering an inaccurate interpretation of your source in a summary is not satisfactory either. If the source's words or meaning do not support your argument as fully as you might like, find another source that does.

**PLAGIARISM**

> People believed that the Civil War was a war to save the union and to abolish slavery, but before the fighting began most people regarded these as incompatible ideals.

➡ *The sentence does not acknowledge that the idea comes from a source and is, therefore, an example of plagiarism. Ideas and words from a source cannot be included as if they are your own. You must give credit to the original writer.*

**CORRECT SUMMARY**

> According to Menand, during the Civil War people did not believe both that slavery could be abolished and the union could be saved (7).

## 4c ACKNOWLEDGE YOUR SOURCES

In the case of paraphrases, summaries, and direct quotations, your paper itself must include information about your source (an in-text citation), including an introductory phrase with the author and title, and the page number(s), URL, or line numbers (for a poem or play) placed immediately following the cited material and usually preceding any punctuation marks that divide or end the sentence. (See block quotation later in the next section, p. H-79.)

### IN-TEXT CITATION

> According to Louis Menand in his book on the Civil War, *The Metaphysical Club,* people believed that "the Civil War was a war to save the union and to abolish slavery, but before the fighting began most people regarded these as incompatible ideals" (7).

Professional organizations (such as the Modern Language Association or the American Psychological Association) provide guidelines for how sources should be acknowledged in a paper. MLA guidelines are commonly used in writing for the humanities, and those guidelines are followed here. For more information on how to properly cite electronic and print sources using the MLA documentation styles, see the chapters on Writing the Research Paper and MLA Documentation.

Keep a running list of your sources. The more accurate and complete the information on your sources, the easier it will be to present that source accurately and completely in your paper. In addition to in-text citation, you must also provide a complete and accurate list of all the texts you have consulted in a list at the end of your paper called a **bibliography.** Anything you have cited in your paper must be included in the final bibliography for that paper. Other works, not referenced in your paper, can be included as well. The best way to prevent plagiarism is to make sure you keep precise records of the sources you consult while preparing your paper in a **working bibliography**—a list of all the sources you've used, as well as all the information you'll use to cite them later. For your working bibliography, make sure to include this information:

- The names of all the authors, editors, and/or translators of the piece
- The complete title of the work and relevant chapter title or heading; for Web pages, the name of the site and the page on which the information appears
- The publisher, copyright date, edition, and place of publication should be recorded for sources from books.
- The date, volume, issue, and page number should be included for all sources from periodicals or journals (including those you have pulled up from an online database).
- The URL (complete web address), the date the page was updated, and the date you viewed the page should be recorded for all sources from the Internet.

Plagiarism can be intentional or unintentional. Professors are adept at recognizing papers obtained via the Web—they've likely seen them before! However, unintentional plagiarism carries the same penalties. This chapter should help you avoid plagiarizing unintentionally, and you will soon be found out if your plagiarism is of the other kind.

### Two Kinds of Plagiarism

| | |
|---|---|
| **Intentional plagiarism** | Intentional plagiarism occurs when you buy someone else's work or copy something from a source, usually word for word, and use it without quotation marks or acknowledgment of the source, as if it were your own words. |
| **Unintentional plagiarism** | Unintentional plagiarism can result from careless note taking, such as forgetting to put quotation marks around material you copy, cutting and pasting from the web, and using material you have summarized or paraphrased and forgetting to tell readers the source of that material. |

## 4d FORMAT QUOTATIONS TO AVOID PLAGIARISM

When you integrate your ideas with those of your sources, you will want to format your quotations so that they flow naturally into your sentences and build toward your conclusion. Where possible, keep your quotation brief, four or fewer lines for prose and no more than three for poetry or drama, since you will comment on the entire quotation in your paper. If you include a long quotation (five lines or more for prose or four or more for poetry or drama) make sure you include the entire quotation for your interpretation or analysis. Otherwise, the quotation overshadows your argument instead of supporting it. Introducing a direct quotation into a text can happen in two ways depending on whether it is short or long; each is formatted differently.

- A short quotation within a sentence is identified by quotation marks.
- A long quotation formatted in an indented block of text separated out from a sentence does not use quotation marks.

**1. Refer to your source in an introductory phrase.** Whether your quotation is short or long, however, you will need to introduce it with an introductory (*signal*) phrase. You need to identify the source and the author *before* the quotation. An in-text citation requires that you include the author's full name (without Mr., Miss, Mrs., or Ms.) the first time you quote from the source. Unless there is a long lapse between references to the source, the second time you quote from the same source you should use only the author's last name. Treat women and men equally when you cite them as authors, using the last name only for the second citation and no *Miss, Mrs.,* or *Ms.* Avoid the repetition of *the author says.*

## Verbs to Use in an Introductory Phrase

| | | |
|---|---|---|
| **according to** | **considers** | **notes** |
| **adds** | | |
| **admits** | **declares** | **observes** |
| **aknowledges** | **denies** | |
| **agrees** | **describes** | **points out** |
| **asks** | **disagrees** | **proposes** |
| **asserts** | | **proves** |
| **argues** | **emphasizes** | |
| | **establishes** | **refutes** |
| **believes** | **explains** | **rejects** |
| | **expresses** | **remarks** |
| **charges** | | **reports** |
| **claims** | **finds** | **responds** |
| **comments** | | |
| **compares** | **holds** | **shows** |
| **complains** | | **states** |
| **concedes** | **implies** | **speculates** |
| **concludes** | **insists** | **suggests** |
| **contends** | **interprets** | |
| **continues** | | **warns** |
| | **maintains** | |

**2. Integrate a short quotation in a sentence and always use quotation marks.** Always put a short quotation into quotation marks. Not to do so constitutes plagiarism. Keep your quotations to the point. The source material you quote as a reference should provide backup for the argument you have made. Avoid the temptation to use sources to make your arguments for you, however well the source is worded. References from outside sources, whether they are paraphrased or quoted, are *evidence* or *support* for your own arguments.

You should not use outside sources to make arguments for you.

- Use an introductory phrase to identify the source.
- If the quotation flows into the natural wording of the sentence, begin the quotation with a lowercase letter whether or not the original is capitalized.
- If your introductory phrase ends with a comma, use a capital letter.
- Use quotation marks.
- When quoting poetry in a sentence, use the format of the lines in the poem and break the lines exactly as they appear in the poem with a slash / mark.
- Place periods and commas inside the quotation marks.
- Semicolons, colons, and dashes are placed outside the quotation marks.
- Question marks and exclamation points are sometimes placed inside the quotation marks and sometimes placed outside. If the quotation is itself a question or exclamation, the question mark/exclamation point goes inside the quotation marks.
- Include page numbers for prose, line numbers for poems, act, scene, and line numbers for plays written in verse and page numbers for plays written in prose.

### A SHORT QUOTATION FROM A POEM

> In Robert Frost's "Stopping by Woods on a Snowy Evening," the hypnotic rhythm of the poem is reinforced through the repetition of the speaker's last lines, "And I have miles to go before I sleep / And I have miles to go before I sleep" (lines 15-16).

### INTEGRATING A QUOTATION WITH A LOWERCASE LETTER

> Even certain details of Grendel's portrayal in the movie echo the original epic. For example, the epic introduces him by calling him an inhabitant of "the abode of monster kind" (line 14).

### PERIOD INSIDE QUOTATION MARK

> Blake again disrupts the meter when he writes, "And I saw it was filled with graves" (line 9), which draws attention to the word "graves."
>
> —from the student paper on William Blake's "The Garden of Love" in Common Assignments across the Curriculum.

#### SEMICOLON OUTSIDE QUOTATION MARKS

He is called a "fiend of hell"; "wrathful spirit"; "mighty stalker of the marches" (line 14); "creature of destruction, fierce and greedy, wild and furious" (15); and a "terrible monster, like a dark shadow of death" (17).

—from the student paper on the role of Grendel in *Beowulf,* the epic and the movie, in Common Assignments across the Curriculum.

**3. Set off a long quotation in a block, and don't use quotation marks.** Quotations in block format should be used sparingly because they break up your discussion and can be distracting. If you find that you do not need to refer back to a long quote in several instances, consider using a paraphrase or more precise direct quotation to present the information. If you use a long quotation to support your point, you must set the quote apart:

- Use an introductory phrase to identify the source.
- Punctuate the end of an introductory phrase with a comma or a colon.
- Leave a line of space before and after the long quotation.
- Do not use quotation marks.
- Indent each line of the quotation by ten spaces from the left margin (right margin is not indented).
- Capitalize the first word whether or not it is capitalized in the original unless quoting poetry.
- When quoting poetry, follow the line format exactly as it appears in the poem.
- Double-space.
- Include a page number (or line numbers for a poem) in parentheses after the final punctuation in the quotation.

#### BLOCK QUOTATION

As her spirit wanes, our heroine in Charlotte Perkins Gilman's "Yellow Wallpaper" gives her soliloquy:

> I lie down ever so much now. John says it is good for me, and to sleep all I can. Indeed he started the habit by making me lie down for an hour after each meal. It is a very bad habit, I am convinced, for you see, I don't sleep. And that cultivates deceit, for I don't tell them I'm awake—oh, no! The fact is I'm getting a little afraid of John. (226)

## 4e FORMAT A PARAPHRASE TO AVOID PLAGIARISM

Using paraphrase in your paper is similar to using quotation, but there are some areas that require extra care. Make sure you have understood the text you are paraphrasing; your paraphrase must be true to the original meaning of the text. Don't guess at the meaning of a text by changing a few words and letting it stand for your own idea. This is plagiarism. Even if one part of the text can be construed to support your argument, don't use it if that part doesn't represent the whole source accurately. Make it clear where your ideas end and the ideas of others begin. In addition to giving credit to others for their ideas, a clear transition from your own work to your source materials gives your writing credibility.

- Keep your paraphrase brief.
- Refer to the source in an introductory phrase.
- Include the page number in parentheses after the paraphrase.
- A period, question mark, or exclamation point goes after the page number when the page number is at the end of a sentence.

**ORIGINAL SOURCE MATERIAL**

Although Emily Dickinson was a noted wit in her circle of friends and family, and although her poetry is surely clever, frequently downright funny, and as we shall argue, throughout possessed of a significant comic vision, criticism has paid little attention to her humor. Dickinson's profound scrutiny of life-and-death matters has usually taken precedence in the analysis and evaluation of her work. Yet comedy is a part of that profundity.

—from "Comedy and Audience in Emily Dickinson's Poetry" by Suzanne Juhasz, Cristanne Miller, and Martha Nell Smith (See the McGraw-Hill website for the full text of this article that accompanies the Frost/Dickinson case studies.)

**PARAPHRASE**

Because Emily Dickinson's poetry concerns itself with serious issues like mortality, critics have long overlooked the comedy that aids her poems' success. Those who knew Dickinson personally recognized her smart humor, which shines through her poems but has since gone unnoticed. The authors of the article wish to reverse this trend of neglect, as Dickinson's witty touches are important to understanding her oeuvre.

## 4f FORMAT SUMMARY TO AVOID PLAGIARISM

Summary and paraphrase are certainly related, but they are not the same thing. In general, paraphrase is used for a smaller portion of the original source, and your goal is to capture the spirit of the passage you are paraphrasing, without exactly copying the sentence structure or word choice. Summary is useful for relating a larger idea that you gained from a longer passage of text, as the above example shows.

| Paraphrase | Summary |
|---|---|
| • a relatively short passage<br>• covers every point in the passage<br>• takes up points consecutively<br>• includes no interpretation | • a passage of any length<br>• condenses main idea and support<br>• changes order when necessary<br>• explains point of passage |

When you write a summary, introduce your source and identify the main ideas of the text. Break the discussion of those ideas into sections, and then write a sentence or two in your own words that captures each section.

**ORIGINAL SOURCE**

A figure who played a major role in popularizing swing in the mid-1930s was Benny Goodman. Like Whiteman earlier and Elvis Presley a few decades later, Goodman was a white musician who could successfully mediate between a black American musical tradition and the large base of white listeners making up the majority population in the USA. Wearing glasses and conservative suits—"looking like a high school science teacher,"according to one observer (Stowe 45)—Goodman appeared to be an ordinary, respectable white American. Musically he was anything but ordinary: a virtuoso clarinetist, a skilled improviser who could solo "hot" on up tempo numbers and "sweet" on ballads, and a disciplined bandleader who demanded excellence from his players. [. . .]

In the guise of swing, jazz became domesticated in the 1930s. Earlier, jazz had been associated with gin mills and smoky cabarets, illegal substances (alcohol and drugs) and illicit sex. Swing generally enjoyed a more wholesome reputation, although some preached of the dangers it posed to the morals of young people. This exuberant, extroverted music performed by well-dressed ensembles and their clean-cut leaders entered middle-class households through everyday appliances like the living-room Victrola and the kitchen radio. It reached a wider populace as musicians transported it from large urban centers into small towns and rural areas. Criss-crossing North America by bus, car, and train, big bands played single night engagements in dance halls, ballrooms, theatres, hotels, night clubs, country clubs, military bases, and outdoor pavilions. They attracted hordes of teenagers who came to hear the popular songs of the day and dance the jitterbug, lindy hop and Susie Q. The strenuous touring schedule of big bands was far from glamorous. Nevertheless, musicians who played in these ensembles could symbolize achievement and prove inspirational, as the writer Ralph Ellison recalled from his early years growing up in Oklahoma City. . . .

Mark Tucker and Travis A. Jackson. "Jazz." *Grove Music Online.* Oxford UP. Web. 11 May 2008.

**EXAMPLE OF SUMMARY**

Swing, which became the popular dance music in more reputable venues than just bars and clubs, was usually performed by big bands under the direction of white leaders like Benny Goodman and Glenn Miller. Thus, jazz became mainstream and middle class, unlike the "hot jazz" of the twenties.

# 5 Writing the Research Paper, Avoiding Plagiarism, and Documenting Sources

## 5a UNDERSTAND RESEARCH TODAY

Research today often makes its first stop at the World Wide Web. You might even access the library through your computer. Navigating the research process, therefore, requires critical skills not asked of your predecessors for one of the most common assignments across the curriculum. While the Web makes it more convenient to do your research at three o'clock in the morning if you like, it also brings with it a new set of challenges. Today you don't just find sources, you have to manage the thousands of hits you might get when you google a topic. The Web also makes it more difficult to see what is credible and valid when every site looks largely the same on the computer screen. Plus, the Web makes it easy to create a patchwork cut-and-paste of sources that can lead to unintentional plagiarism. Plagiarism occurs when a source is not properly acknowledged, and whenever you conduct research from outside sources, you run the risk of taking credit for another person's ideas. For more information on acknowledging sources, see our chapter on Quoting, Paraphrasing, Summarizing, and Avoiding Plagiarism.

This chapter will get you started on your research project and also provide guidelines for documentation that keep you from unintentionally plagiarizing someone else's work. How you take notes is more important than ever if you are to distinguish your own work from the work you have found online (or in print). In literature, your instructor is likely to want a variety of sources, not just online references. There are three basic kinds of sources with which you will be working:

- Books
- Print magazines, newspapers, or scholarly journals
- Non-print online sources

The type of source you want to use depends on the type of project you are working on. If you are approaching a piece of literature from a particular critical perspective—like the feminist, Marxist, or psychoanalytical schools of thought discussed in our chapter on Critical Approaches to Literature—your research will likely involve reading literary criticism. If you are embarking on historical criticism or biographical criticism, you will need to gear your research to sources that inform you about a time period or your author's life. This chapter provides a step-by-step walkthrough of the research process. Read the student research paper on Langston Hughes at the end of this chapter to see how these steps look in action.

## 5b CHOOSE A TOPIC

Often, your instructor will assign a topic or provide some guidance. Or, you can find several research topics in this textbook, especially at the end of each case study. We have provided not only the topics, but also a list of good sources to get you started. In addition, there are many relevant secondary sources that you can find for each case study on our website at www.mhhe.com/delbancole. Research projects require a considerable amount of reading and a good deal of thinking. Your job is to make your process and the research project fun. Explore a topic that interests you, and discover new ideas that will help inform your own idea. Break the topic down so that you can manage your research and create a project that teaches you about a subject you enjoy.

**1. Identify what interests you.** Choose your topic, or choose how you want to address your assigned topic, by considering what strikes you as important or interesting in the work of literature you are researching.

**Example:** Our student author, Christine Keenan, was assigned to write a research paper on Langston Hughes. To find a topic, she thought of what she knew about Hughes that interested her. Since Christine loves music, she decided she would like to know more about how jazz influenced Langston Hughes.

**2. Form a question.** Once you have a topic in mind, explore how that aspect of the work is meaningful to you. Do some of the brainstorming exercises that students used to get started in chapter 3, Writing about Fiction, chapter 17, Writing about Poetry, and chapter 32, Writing about Drama. Turn this aspect into a question. Christine made a list of words that she associated with jazz.

*improvisation, be-bop, Duke Ellington, and nightclubs*

She also considered that jazz has several forms including blues, swing, be-bop, and cool jazz. Based on this, she formed the question.

> **Example:** "What elements of jazz influenced Langston Hughes when he wrote his poems?"

**3. Narrow your topic.** She then decided to narrow her question further by picking two poems influenced by jazz, an early poem, "The Dream Keeper," and a later poem, "Harlem [2]."

## 5c FIND AND MANAGE PRINT AND ONLINE SOURCES

The sources you cite in your research should be *reliable* and *relevant*—significant in the context of your current discussion. Refining your keyword search can help prevent information overload and find sources that are pertinent to your topic. Your instructor may have some recommendations for good sources on a topic, and there are also sources listed in this textbook as good starting places. The Web does not offer any guarantees about the accuracy of its content. However, some websites and search engines are better than others for trustworthiness. If your website ends in *.org*, *.edu*, or *.gov*, it's like having a good character reference for the content on the site. If your search engine has preselected source material (such as GoogleScholar) or if you have accessed a library database, you will have saved yourself the painful weeding through of hits that cannot help you. Some tips for finding reliable and relevant sources include:

- *Title.* In a scholarly article or book, the title and subtitle will usually be designed to convey the topic of the piece as specifically as possible. If the title doesn't seem relevant to your topic, that author or piece of work might not be the best source for your discussion.
- *Date of publication.* For print sources, this will often be found on the copyright page of the book. Note not just the copyright of the current edition, but the original copyright. Journals will have dates printed with their issue numbers and often on individual articles themselves to inform the reader when the article's research was originally conducted. A reliable web page will usually print the date last modified at the bottom of the page. Bear in mind that "relevant" doesn't always mean "current." A classic source is one that is a hallmark in the field. If you see a source cited when you're reading sources elsewhere, you've likely come upon a classic work. A current source is just what the word suggests, something written about a topic within the past five years.
- *Abstract.* Most research papers in journals will have **abstracts,** or summaries, that explain the research done, briefly detail the findings, and state the conclusion of the research.
- *Chapter titles or headings.* A perusal of a print source's detailed table of contents can help you determine if the source will contain information useful and relevant to your research. If you are searching for an interpretation of Shakespeare's *Romeo & Juliet* and the index of the book indicates that all mentions of that play occur in a chapter called "Shakespeare: The Fraud," that text might be biased toward a perspective beyond the scope of your paper.

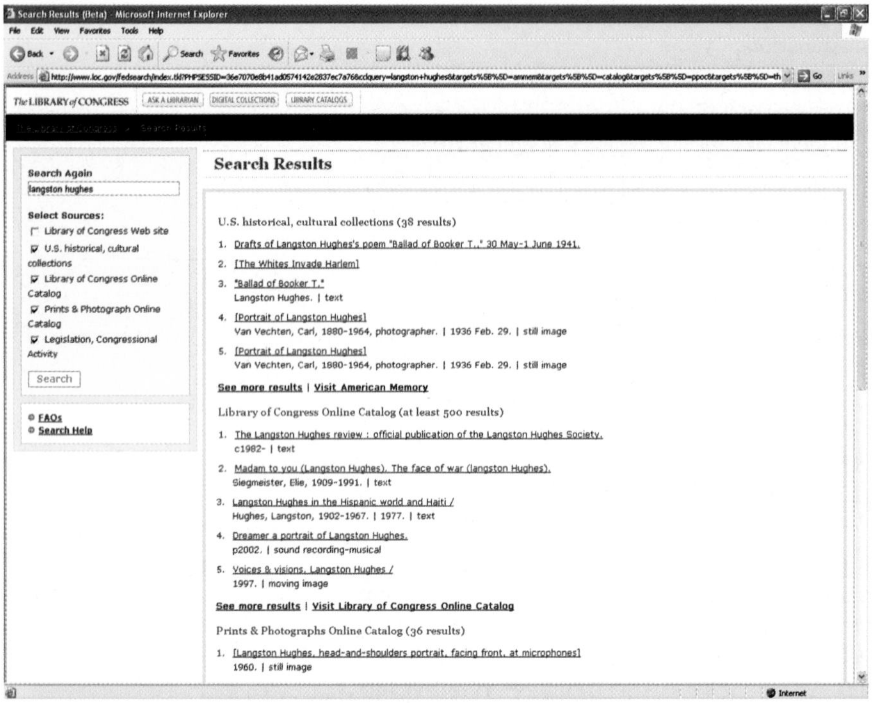


(*Library of Congress search for "Langston Hughes"*)

**1. Refine your keyword search.** Whether you are searching one of your library's databases or the Web, refine your key words by grouping words together, e.g. "Harlem Renaissance." Use *and* or + to bring up sites that have both topics together. Use *or* when you list sites that are for either topic. Two words are better than one to help you narrow the number of sites that come up; use quotation marks around titles or parentheses around key phrases to manage the number of hits as well. To find information on Web pages and avoid the information flood, a good key word search is essential. Experiment with the phrasing of your keyword.

**2. Use more than one search engine.** The Internet brings the world to your door, but don't just google. Use at least three general search engines to locate the sources you need. In addition to Google, you may want to try Yahoo! (http://www.yahoo.com) or WebCrawler (http://www.webcrawler.com). Some sites search several different search engines at once: Library of Congress (http://www.loc.gov) or the Librarian's Index to the Internet (http://www.lii.org). You even have search sites that have already been vetted by experts, such as GoogleScholar (http://scholar.google.com), About.com (http://www.about.com), and Looksmart (http://www.looksmart.com).

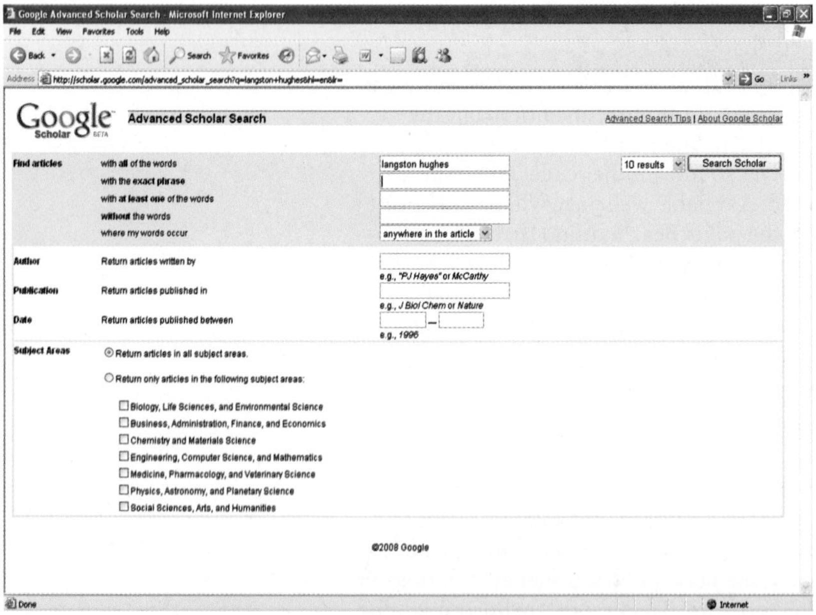


(*Google Scholar Advanced Search Page*)

**3. Use the library, on campus and online.** Check out your library's website. Talk to your librarian. The library is not just a collection of printed texts anymore. Your librarian can help you find the library's computerized catalog of books and discipline-specific encyclopedias, bibliographies, and almanacs, such as the *MLA International Bibliography of Books and Articles on Modern Language and Literature* (also available online) or the *Oxford History of English Literature.* In addition, the librarian can help you locate the library's database of scholarly journals and other electronic resources.

## Databases, Online Periodicals

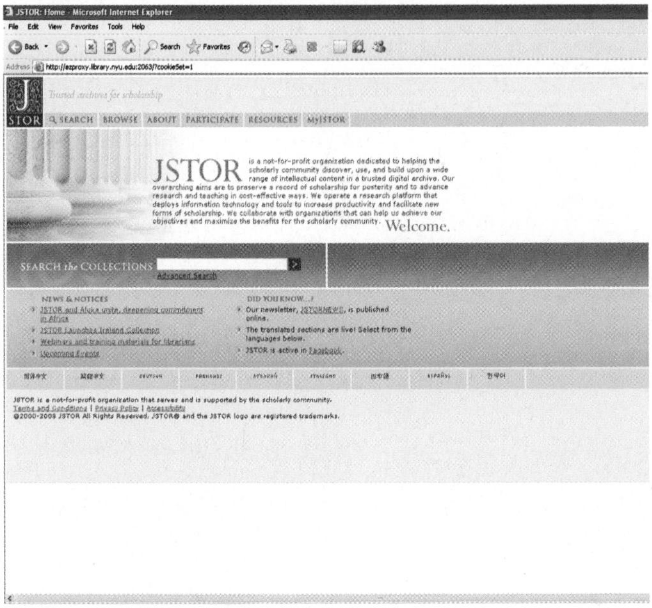


*(JSTOR Online Database)*

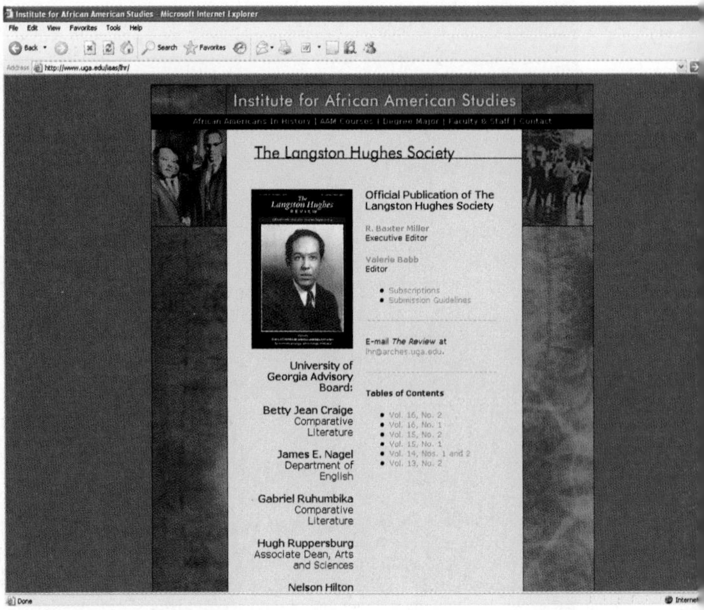


*(Langston Hughes Society online Periodical)*

Library searches can help you find the kinds of sources your professor wants to see on your topic.

> **Example:** Christine used a database through her university's library to do keyword searches using the words "Langston Hughes" and "jazz." She skimmed the results and picked a few that seemed most related to her topic.

### Searching the Internet

*When you go online for help, you may feel all the information is the same. It only looks that way. The Internet serves up information in a couple of ways that it is important for you to differentiate.*

- A *general search* from the entire World Wide Web includes everything that anyone has posted on your topic, from very personal blogs to news groups. You will need to carefully evaluate anything you find in a general search to determine if it is providing information that is reliable.
- An *online database* from your library searches through a collection of reliable published articles and electronic journals. The results of a database search will include only publications and will connect you to abstracts, summaries, or full text (that is, the entire article).

*These film shots illustrate portrayals of the Grendel monster and the Beowulf hero in the movie* Beowulf *(top) and the movie* The 13th Warrior *(bottom).*

## 5d EVALUATE VISUAL SOURCES

A picture is worth a thousand words, or so the old proverb goes. We live in a visual world and visual data is now as easy as a cut-and-paste job off GoogleImage. Like all source information, however, it must be relevant and reliable. Visuals must serve a specific purpose in your paper. A graph or chart can be a useful snapshot of quantitative data. A diagram is a useful flowchart to explain a process. A picture is qualitative evidence that is used to strengthen or amplify your point. If you have taken your visual from the Web or another source, it must be documented in your bibliography and identified in your paper with a caption. The example here is evidence for a paper on adapting the *Beowulf* epic.

## 5e EVALUATE TEXT SOURCES

Sources can be popular or scholarly. A popular source is something you could buy easily at a store, such as *Time* magazine. It will likely have advertisements in it or be advertised to the general public (such as a self-help book like *Rich Dad, Poor Dad*). A scholarly source is generally found through a library rather than a store. The writers focus on discipline-specific rather than broad, general topics and are usually affiliated with a university. These books are likely to have footnotes or include citations to sources and bibliographies. When considering whether a print publication is popular or scholarly, follow these guidelines:

- *Note the publisher of the book, magazine, or journal.* A commercial publisher will probably suggest a popular aim, whereas an academic publisher such as a university press will suggest a scholarly aim.
- *Consider the authors of the articles.* Take note of both the authors' names and their affiliations (generally universities for scholarly articles), and consider how their titles match up with the topic of their article. For instance, Alton Brown might be a name you recognize as an authority from The Food Network, but he would not be a trustworthy expert to cite in a paper on comparative politics.
- *Notice the range of topics in the publication.* A popular publication will usually cover a range of topics to appeal to a wide readership, whereas a scholarly publication will focus on various aspects of one topic.
- *Observe the visual presentation of the publication.* Is it flashy and full of ads and cartoons? Or is it mostly text-based, with fewer but higher quality captioned images?
- *Evaluate the articles themselves.* Academic articles will often be preceded by abstracts that summarize their findings and followed by bibliographies or listings of works cited. Popular articles, on the other hand, may lead in with a catchy line that leaves an unanswered question and will seldom list references.
- *Ask whether the source is refereed or peer reviewed.* A publication may or may not specify this, but most trustworthy scholarly publications accept articles only after they have been reviewed, debated, and accepted by a body of experts in the field. Some research databases will allow you to filter for peer-reviewed publications; or, when in doubt, you can ask your librarian whether a publication has been refereed.

You may find it difficult when using the Web to tell the difference not only between a popular and a scholarly site, but also between a reliable site and one that is biased. The Library of Congress website can be counted on, as can its search engine, so don't just google. Find search engines that will save you the time by leading you to reliable sites. Many of the same guidelines you use for evaluating print sources can apply to evaluating an online publication as well. Some other things you can pay attention to when considering whether an electronic source like a website is reliable include

- *The Web address.* As mentioned earlier, often reliable content will be found on websites with the domains *.org* (non-profit organization), *.edu* (educational institution), *.mil* (military), or *.gov* (United States government). Keep in mind that not all information on a *.org* or *.edu* (or sometimes *.gov* or *.mil*) is reliable. Information on these pages may be biased; or, sometimes, the information might be from a personal page hosted by that specific domain. In this case, you will often notice a tilde (~) followed by a name or personalized "handle" (such as your school ID or AIM screen name) in the Web address.
- *The host of the page.* Is the Web page hosted by a university or academic association? Is it an article of an online encyclopedia? Be careful of sites like Wikipedia, which can claim to be "encyclopedias" or "dictionaries" but may not be accurate. Do not use Wikipedia as a citation in a college paper. You will need to verify the content you find on Wikipedia through another source, and if it is common knowledge (a birth date, for example), it won't need a citation.
- *The visual presentation.* As with print sources, you can tell a lot about a Web page's content and intended audience just by looking at how it is presented. Flashy ads, pop-up windows, intricate backgrounds, complex layouts, and funky colors are all indications that a website might not contain reliable content. A reliable Web page, created by an academic for academic use, will be laid out functionally, without intricate designs or distracting colors.

- *The tone of the information.* Tone is a major indicator of scholarliness and bias. Avoid Web pages that use poor grammar or punctuation or employ colloquial Internet shorthand. Scholarly information will seldom be presented so informally. Also take note of aggravated tone of voice, or hyperbolic claims, or a failure to consider more than one point of view. These are indicators of bias—which might support your point of view, but will detract from the legitimacy of the source as support.

Whenever you are conducting research, if an opinion or piece of information seems fishy or flimsy, you should double-check. If you find that information or point of view in only one place, there's a good chance it is unsupported or not widely agreed upon by the academic community. Many databases now provide information on where an article or book has been cited by other academics in their research; this can be a valuable resource in confirming the reliability of a research source.

## 5f RECOGNIZE UNRELIABLE WEBSITE WARNING SIGNS

The following example shows two websites containing the text of Langston Hughes's poem "Harlem," one unreliable and one reliable. Note the striking differences between the two. Likely your eye will go first to the unreliable site; whereas the reliable site by the Poetry Foundation is designed as a resource, the unreliable site hosted by PoemHunter.com is designed to attract attention and amass visits to the page.

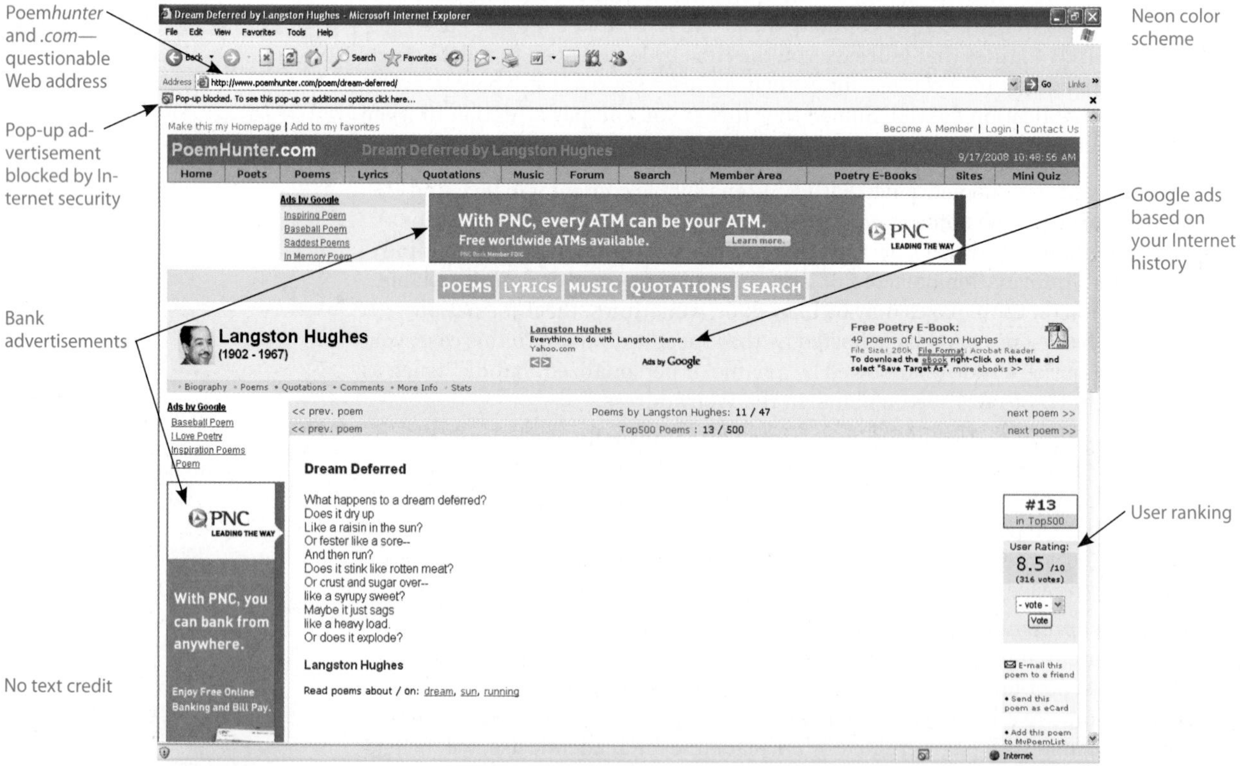

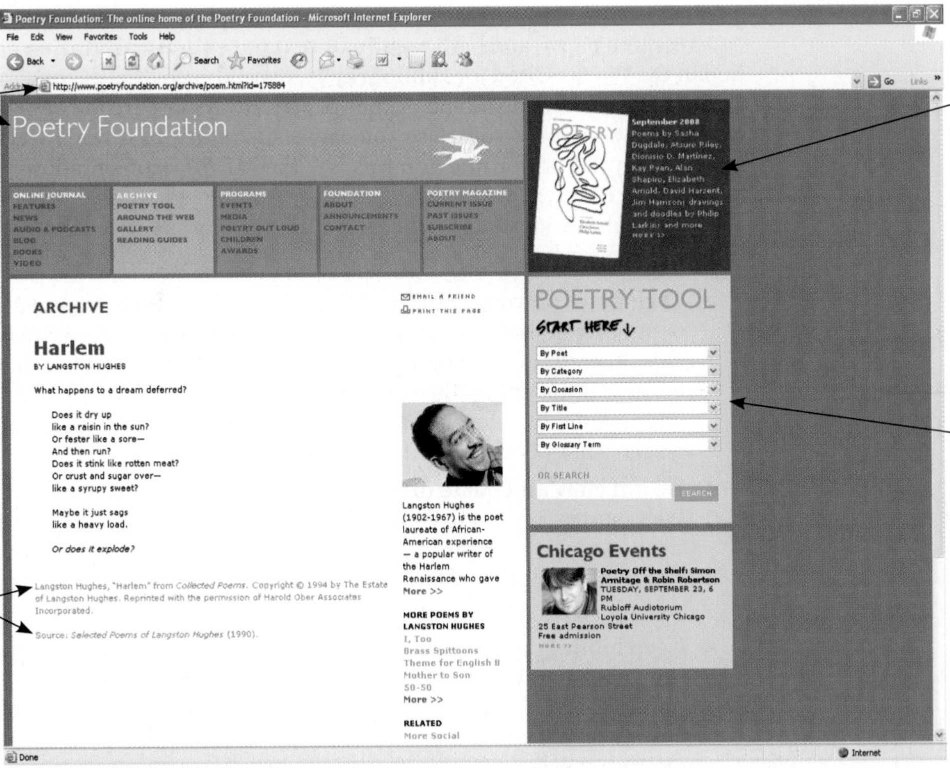


Besides flashy colors and design, there are other major differences between the two. Whereas PoemHunter.com has bank ads (don't ignore that blocked pop-up ad, it's a major clue to unreliability), the Poetry Foundation website advertises only its own publication, *Poetry* magazine, a well-known and respected journal of poetry. Notice also the references that follow the poem text: PoemHunter.com does attribute the author of the poem but does not cite any permission or original publication information.

It will save you time if you can quickly recognize the difference between reliable and unreliable sites. A google search for Langston Hughes's "Harlem" will list PoemHunter.com before the Poetry Foundation, so strong searching skills and judgment are your keys to efficient, effective Web research.

## 5g WORK WITH SOURCES TO AVOID PLAGIARISM

As you collect your sources for your papers, your source notes will protect you from plagiarism. Take careful notes as you read your sources. You may want to use sticky notes to flag specific quotes or passages that you find interesting or of particular relevance to your topic. A necessary part of writing a research paper is the inclusion and citation of outside sources, usually scholarly works from books, journals, and trustworthy Web pages. Because of the risk of plagiarism (taking credit for another's words or ideas), it is important to know the several appropriate ways to include outside information.

There are two different approaches to including outside information into your own research paper, and both require **in-text parenthetical citation** and documentation in the **Works Cited** (or **Bibliography,** depending on the documentation style you are working within) at the end of your paper. Always be sure to copy the bibliographical information of the source so you can easily return to it when writing your paper and properly cite it (for more on this, see the MLA Documentation Style Guide that follows this chapter). All works that have been included in your paper with in-text parenthetical citations must be included in your Works Cited page. Some general tips to avoid plagiarism during research are:

- **Take notes on your sources.** First, when taking notes, make sure to underline or put into quotation marks all direct quotations you copy from books or journals. Record the page numbers and other source information that you'll need for your in-text parenthetical citation. This will help you distinguish your own impressions and conclusions from those that you copied directly and to avoid plagiarism by correctly citing your sources.
- **Do not copy and paste directly into your paper.** Next, when working with Web sources, try not to copy and paste directly into the body of your work; consider instead pasting into a separate document and printing it out to consult alongside your other notes. It's much easier to catch yourself retyping whole passages from another source.
- **Keep bibliographical information.** Finally, choose a documentation style (MLA, APA) early and stick to it as you create the body of your work. Usually your instructor will have assigned you a style for the assignment. If you cannot cite as you write, make sure to note "citation needed" in appropriate places, such as after paraphrases, figures, or direct quotations.

## 5h REFERENCE CITATIONS WITHIN THE PAPER IN THE END-OF-PAPER WORKS CITED PAGE

When you use sources in an MLA -style paper, you must include a parenthetical reference in the body of your paper (for more information, see our chapter on Quoting, Paraphrasing, Summarizing, and Avoiding Plagiarism) and a corresponding entry in a Works Cited page at the end of your paper. The idea is simple: full information about the books, journals, or websites you used in writing your paper appears in a list (the Works Cited page) at the end of your paper. Including all that information in the body of your paper would bog down both you and your reader. Instead, insert a brief reference in parentheses after the word or idea you have borrowed from an outside source. This parenthetical citation does two jobs: (1) It shows your reader exactly which sentences of your paper include ideas that are not your own, and (2) It points the reader to the original source by corresponding with the full citation that occurs in the Works Cited page.

**1. In-text parenthetical reference.** Here, the parenthetical citation tells the reader that the student author has summarized or paraphrased an idea that she found on pages 61 and 62 of a source with an author whose last name is Borshuk.

**SENTENCE FROM STUDENT PAPER:**

Also, the traditionally African-American art form had now been taken over and turned into a commercial success largely by whites, with a few exceptions like Duke Ellington and Count Basie (Borshuk 61-62).

**2. Corresponding entry from works cited page.** Turning to the Works Cited page at the end of the paper, the reader can find the entry beginning with "Borshuk" and know that the information following it is the source from which it came. In this case, the source is a book called *Swinging the Vernacular* by Michael Borshuk. The parenthetical citation and the works cited entry have worked together to inform the reader of the original source of the idea.

Borshuk, Michael. Swinging the Vernacular. New York: Routledge, 2006.

## 5i ORGANIZE YOUR RESEARCH AND DEVELOP A THESIS

**1. Connect your interpretation of a text to various sources.** Consider what each source tells you about your topic. Particularly if you are reading literary criticism, decide whether or not you agree with the critic. If you agree, you may want to use what that critic says to corroborate your reading. If you disagree, use that critic's perspective as a springboard into talking about your own perspective.

**Example:** Christine read the following quote in one of her sources:

> Langston Hughes, in his collection of poems, lavishly uses such characteristics of jazz as repetitions, choruses, riffs, scats, and nonsensical onomatopoeia, to achieve musical success as well as audience participation. It is also significant to note that Hughes's poems are often marked by dissonance, discordance, and line irregularity, which all contribute to the representation of the jazz spirit in verse forms.

Although this quote directly related to her topic, Christine found that she was dissatisfied with the vague way in which most sources—like this one—talked about the jazz elements in Hughes's poems. She began to consider the historical reasons why Hughes might have chosen these specific elements.

**2. Form a working thesis.** Once you have gathered your own ideas and taken notes on your sources, try to state your overall idea in a sentence or two. Most likely, your thesis will have the kernel of the idea that you started with, but it will have become more nuanced by your research. (See more on thesis in our chapter on Writing from Reading.)

**Example:** Christine's original idea was to talk about jazz elements in Hughes's poems. Her research showed her that most critics approach his jazz poetry from a general angle. As a result, she formed the following thesis, which shows a very specific interpretation of why Hughes chose certain jazz elements.

> ***Working thesis:*** Hughes used jazz in a significant way. More than simply feeling jazz's influence generally, Hughes felt the influence of African-American jazz specifically.

**3. Choose your best support.** Review the notes you took on your sources and on the primary text. Select a few quotes that best illustrate a point you want to make. Note ideas that you will want to paraphrase or summarize in your paper, and remember that these are important forms of support as well. For examples of successful summary, paraphrase, and direct quotation refer to our chapter on Quoting, Paraphrasing, Summarizing, and Avoiding Plagiarism and the sample research paper in this chapter.

## 5j DRAFT AND REVISE YOUR DRAFT

Now that you have conducted your research and developed a thesis, you are ready to draft your paper. This is just a first draft, so leave yourself time to revise.

- **Introduction.** Your introduction sets up the rest of your paper.
- **Body.** The body of your paper presents your supporting evidence.
- **Conclusion.** Your conclusion relates your paper to a larger issue.

You may want to share your first draft with a friend or classmate. Then put your draft away and return to it fresh. You may see things you hadn't seen before. When you think through your thesis and look at the supporting evidence for your thesis, you may even find that you've changed your mind. Your thesis can be refined in response to your writing. To see revisions of the introduction, body, and conclusion in the paper on Langston Hughes, go to our Chapter on Writing from Reading. There you will find more on the drafting and revising process.

You can see in-text references and a properly formatted Works Cited page by looking at the student research paper that follows. Other student papers, like the explication of William Blake's "The Garden of Love," which appear in Common Writing Assignments, can also serve as models for in-text references. In that particular paper, note the proper parenthetical citation of lines of poetry rather than page numbers.

Remember, too, that even if you respond to a single source, you should still cite that work. This is especially important when many versions of the same text exist—for example, if you are reading Charlotte Bronte's classic *Jane Eyre* from a Penguin Classics edition, the pagination will be different from the *Jane Eyre* edition published by Oxford World's Classics. Only a full citation in a Works Cited page will tell your reader from which version you are reading. For an example of a single source, see the final draft of the student paper in chapter 3 on Jamaica Kincaid's "Girl."

## Sample Student Research Paper

Christine Keenan

Professor Jackson

English 200

15 May 2008

Title centered; no underline.

From Dream Keeper to Dream Deferred:

Langston Hughes and Jazz Poetry

Quote from website source.

Jazz poetry, according to the American Academy of Poets website, is "a literary genre defined as poetry necessarily informed by jazz music—that is, poetry in which the poet responds to and writes about jazz" ("A Brief Guide to Jazz Poetry"). Langston Hughes was a jazz poet in that his poetry often captured jazz in a literary form. Many critics point to specific techniques that Hughes employs to create the effect of jazz. One such critic is Lionel Davidas, who writes:

Block quote (more than four lines long) from a periodical source.

> Langston Hughes, in his collection of poems, lavishly uses such characteristics of jazz as repetitions, choruses, riffs, scats, and nonsensical onomatopoeia, to achieve musical success as well as audience participation. It is also significant to note that Hughes's poems are often marked by dissonance, discordance, and line irregularity, which all contribute to the representation of the jazz spirit in verse forms. (268)

Establishes a critical reading to which the student responds.

Thesis statement

Although these observations are true, readings like Davidas's fail to show the full extent of Hughes's achievement in jazz poetry. Beyond being a jazz poet, Hughes understood the significance of jazz—even as it was being created—and used only those aspects of jazz that express the African-American experience.

Two of Hughes's collections that have an overt connection to music are *The Weary Blues,* published in 1926, and *Montage of a Dream Deferred,* published in 1951. In the twenty-five years between their publications, jazz music changed dramatically. Two poems, "The Dream Keeper" from *The Weary Blues* and "Harlem [2]" from *Montage of a Dream Deferred,* show how Hughes effectively responded to the current trends in jazz from an African-American perspective.

Author maps out how she will support her thesis.

Topic sentence introduces first poem to be analyzed.

Hughes first published "The Dream Keeper" in 1925 and included it in his collection *The Weary Blues* the following year (Rampersad 617). At that time, America was in the midst of the "Jazz Age," the period from 1920-1930 marked by energy and optimism. Jazz itself was popular and connoted rebellion as it was associated with nightclubs, sex, and drinking (Tucker, screen 4). But Hughes's collection was clearly influenced more by the blues than by this new form of jazz. The title of the collection suggests the blues takes center stage in these poems, and indeed, "The Dream Keeper" is no exception. While it does not have as overt a connection to the blues as Hughes's poems that replicate blues lyrics directly—such as "Po Boy Blues"—the repetition early in the poem bears echoes of the repetition characteristic of the blues. "Bring me all of your" is repeated twice within the first three lines; the object the addressee is told to bring, however, varies (lines 1, 3). In a way, lines one through three are a compounded version of blues lyrics. Typical blues lyrics follow a pattern where the first couplet repeats before a third couplet resolves it. Here, half the couplet is repeated and half resolved in both instances. Blues also has a hand in the pace of the poem. Compound phrases like "cloud-cloth" and "too-rough" slow the pace of reading, as does the high number of line breaks compared to the small number of words (6, 7).

Example of paraphrase.

Student's own analysis.

Since Hughes was writing in the Jazz Age, it may seem surprising that so many of his poems in *The Weary Blues* reflect the blues. In part, his decision may have been informed by the fact that jazz grew out of the blues, and the close relationship of the two forms of music allowed Hughes to use blues and still be in the realm of jazz. But blues is marked by a "blue" or melancholy frame of mind (Oliver, screen 1), not the exuberance of the Jazz Age. Examining the historical context offers an answer for why Hughes chose blues over jazz. While the Roaring Twenties brought "unprecedented prosperity" to the United States ("Roaring Twenties"), it was also the era of the Great Migration, the movement in which ten percent of African Americans left the South and moved North. These were difficult times for blacks, as they faced low wages, poor housing conditions, and disease in the northern cities to which they relocated (Marks). Also, while positive advances did occur in the African-American community, such as the Harlem Renaissance, Emily Bernard has noted that most blacks were not affected

Example of summary.

by the Renaissance—only a so-called talented tenth participated, leaving most blacks to face everyday problems (Bernard xvi-xvii).

Transition paragraph. The first two sentences conclude the blues discussion. The last sentence segues into discussion of the second poem.

To put it simply, jazz at the time that Hughes was writing poems for *The Weary Blues* had two forms: the exuberant new jazz and the blues roots from which it came. Hughes chose the form of music—the blues—that best reflected the state of the common black man. By the time Hughes was writing the poems for *Montage of a Dream Deferred,* however, jazz had changed and once again offered two new forms.

Example of summary.

The 1930s and 40s brought a change to jazz: ensembles of about twelve players began to change the rhythms of jazz into swing. Swing, which became the popular dance music in more reputable venues than just bars and clubs, was usually performed by big bands under the direction of white leaders like Benny Goodman and Glenn Miller.[1] Thus, jazz became mainstream and middle class, unlike the "hot jazz" of the 20s (Tucker, screen 5). Also, the traditionally African-American art form had now been taken over and turned into a commercial success largely by whites, with a few exceptions like Duke Ellington and Count Basie (Borshuk 61-62).

Example of paraphrase.

*Fig. 1* The Glenn Miller Orchestra Source: Photo Gallery. Glenn Miller Orchestra Online. Glenn Miller Productions, Inc. Web. 12 May 2008.

Jazz underwent another major change in the 1940s. Young African-American musicians in Harlem met in informal jam sessions where they began to experiment with nearly every aspect of the music—melody, harmony, and rhythm.[2] Musicians such as Dizzy Gillespie, Thelonious Monk, and Charlie Parker increasingly championed improvisation and creativity over the organized big band aesthetic. Their innovations included "rapid tempo, irregular phrase groups . . . sudden, sharp drum accents, [and] chromatically altered notes" (Tucker, screen 7). This new form of jazz became known as bebop, a form of music that many critics see as "the revolt of young black musicians of the ghetto against the commercialization of 'swing music' of the time" (Lenz 274). In other words, bebop made jazz into a predominantly African-American art once more.

Citation of both paraphrase and direct quote.

*Fig. 2* Tommy Potter, Charlie Parker, Dizzy Gillespie, and John Coltrane—leaders of the bebop movement—pictured at the famous jazz club Birdland, c. 1951. Source: "Charlie Parker, Uptown and Down." *New York Times on the Web. The New York Times.* Web. 12 May 2008.

Topic sentence introduces the second poem to be analyzed.

When Langston Hughes penned "Harlem [2]," two types of jazz existed: the mellow, organized sound of swing and the creative, frantic sound of bebop. For *Montage of a Dream Deferred,* Hughes chose to use the latter jazz form, as his preface to the collection suggests:

Example of paraphrase.

> In terms of current Afro-American popular music and the sources from which it has progressed—jazz, ragtime, swing, blues, boogie-woogie, and be-bop—this poem on contemporary Harlem, like be-bop, is marked by conflicting changes, sudden nuances, sharp and impudent interjections, broken rhythms, and passages sometimes in the manner of the jam session, sometimes the popular song, punctuated by the riffs, runs, breaks, and disc-tortions [sic] of the music of a community in transition. (Rampersad 387)

Citation of line in poem.

Conclusion that shows significance of student's preceding analysis.

Indeed, these bebop-like traits are present in "Harlem [2]": "conflicting changes" and "sudden nuance" can be seen in the series of images Hughes selects; "sharp and impudent interjections" occur in the form of the last line, *"Or does it explode?"* (line 11); and "broken rhythms" are created by the space after the first line and the space before the last line. Hughes, then, successfully reflects bebop technique in his poetry, and in so doing, uses the form of jazz aligned with African Americans, rather than the form of mainstream, middle-class whites.

Topic sentence that introduces a new thread of discussion and analysis.

Reiteration that citation is to poetic line. Avoids confusion with source page numbers found in other citations.

Student's analysis.

Example of summary.

More significant than the blues and bebop form, however, is Hughes's use of blues and bebop content. "The Dream Keeper" and "Harlem [2]" share the theme of dreams, yet each reflects the mindset of the music that influenced it—music that in turn was influenced by the historical events of its day. "The Dream Keeper" is itself dreamy in its imagery of "blue cloud-cloth" and the diction of phrases like "heart melodies" (6, 7). Despite these whimsical elements, the act of tucking away one's dreams so the world will not harm them is a sad one. In fact, the tone of the poem is melancholy, or "blue." Even the one color mentioned in the poem is "blue," which guides the reader toward blue (i.e., sad) feelings (6). This laying aside of dreams is more than the material of blues music; it was also, for many blacks, the reality of the Great Migration. Reading "The Dream Keeper" with the Great Migration in mind makes the poem seem as if it is directly about the blues created by the migration. Blacks were motivated to migrate by the promise of opportunity and freedom from the South's discrimination; once in the North, however, blacks often found limited advancement possibilities in their jobs and continued to suffer from segregation (Marks). In a sense, then, African Americans of the Great Migration often had to lay aside their dreams from the "too-rough fingers" of reality (7).

Student's synthesis of poem and historical context.

Student's analysis.

Similarly, "Harlem [2]" captures the mindset and historical context that gave rise to bebop. Although the dream theme is the same as in "The Dream Keeper," its imagery of "fester[ing] like a sore" and "stink[ing] like rotten meat" suggests an uglier, bitterer side of dreams than anything that appears in "The Dream Keeper" (4, 6). John Lowney's characterization of Harlem is helpful in understanding this shift; he writes, "By the 1940s, Harlem was of course no longer the center of refuge and hope associated with the New Negro Renaissance. Although still a major destination for poor migrant blacks during the Great Depression, Harlem had become better known nationally as an explosive site of urban racial conflict, first in 1935 and then in 1943" (362). Those years saw race riots in Harlem, and racial tension continued to grow as blacks faced discrimination even in the World War II era (362). Lowney notes that "the agitated sound of *Montage* struck many of [Hughes's] contemporaries as a radical departure from the more straightforward 'populist' rhetoric of his best-known work" (369). Indeed, in reflecting bebop's dramatic change from swing, Hughes's poetry also takes a dramatic shift from earlier modes. This shift shows the rising frustration of

Example of direct quotation.

Student's synthesis of poem and historical context.

African Americans whose dreams were no longer the root of melancholy from being tucked away, but were now the product of dreams that continued to be deferred, nearly halfway into the twentieth century.

As "The Dream Keeper" and "Harlem [2]" demonstrate, Hughes effectively incorporated new forms of jazz as they arose. While he does successfully use formal elements of jazz music, to end a reading there would be to miss Hughes's larger achievement. Hughes did not simply adopt jazz technique; he selected only those trends in jazz that reflected the African-American experience of the time in which he wrote. There is no room in his poetry for the smooth sounds of swing at the hands of whites; instead, he used the true African-American forms of blues and bebop. In so doing, Hughes's poetry captures both the music, as it evolved from blues to bebop, and the African-American experience, as it moved from the blues of the Great Migration to the bitter conflict of continued discrimination.

Topic sentence that signals conclusion.

Reiteration of thesis and broadening to encompass Hughes's overall achievement.

Broadens thesis to include historical discussion presented in the body of the paper

Notes

[1]Fig. 1 shows Glenn Miller's orchestra, which exemplifies the white, mainstream big band associated with swing of the 1930s and 1940s.

[2] Fig. 2 represents the smaller, black ensembles associated with bebop in the early 1940s. Comparing the two figures gives a visual representation of the stark difference between the two forms of jazz.

Properly formatted "Notes" section for additional information.

Works Cited

Introduction to a book. — Bernard, Emily. Introduction. *Remember Me to Harlem: The Letters of Langston Hughes and Carl Van Vechten, 1925-1964.* Ed. Bernard. New York: Knopf, 2001. Print.

Book. — Borshuk, Michael. *Swinging the Vernacular.* New York: Routledge, 2006. Print.

"A Brief Guide to Jazz Poetry." *Poets.org*. The American Academy of Poets. Web. 8 May 2008. — Article on a website.

Visual from Web. — "Charlie Parker, Uptown and Down." *New York Times on the Web. The New York Times*. Web. 12 May 2008.

Davidas, Lionel. " 'I, Too, Sing America': Jazz and Blues Techniques and Effects in Some of Langston Hughes's Selected Poems." *Dialectical Anthropology* 26 (2001): 267-272. Print. — Print periodical.

Book. — Hughes, Langston. *Montage of a Dream Deferred.* New York: Henry Holt, 1951. Print.

Hughes, Langston. *The Weary Blues.* New York: Knopf, 1926. Print. — Book.

Article from a database. — Lenz, Gunter. "The Riffs, Runs, Breaks, and Distortions of the Music of a Community in Transition." *The Massachusetts Review* 44.1-2 (Spring 2003): 269-282. *ProQuest.* Web. 11 May 2008.

Lowney, John. "Langston Hughes and the 'Nonsense' of Bebop." *American Literature Online.* Duke University. Web. 11 May 2008. — Online periodical.

Article on a scholarly website. — Marks, Carole. "The Great Migration: African Americans Searching for the Promised Land, 1916-1930." *In Motion: The African-American Migration Experience.* Ed. Howard Dodson and Sylviane A. Diouf. Schomburg Center for Research in Black Culture. Web. 11 May 2008.

Oliver, Paul. "Blues." *Grove Music Online.* Oxford UP. Web. 11 May 2008. — Online music dictionary.

Visual from web. — Photo Gallery. *Glenn Miller Orchestra Online.* Glenn Miller Productions, Inc. Web. 12 May 2008.

Rampersad, Arnold, ed. *The Collected Poems of Langston Hughes.* New York: Knopf, 1995. Print. — Book, emphasis on editor.

Article on a website. — "Roaring Twenties." *JAZZ: A Film by Ken Burns.* PBS. Web. 11 May 2008.

Tucker, Mark and Travis A. Jackson. "Jazz." *Grove Music Online.* Oxford UP. Web. 11 May 2008. — Online music dictionary.

# 6 MLA Documentation Style Guide

## 6a DOCUMENT SOURCES CONSISTENTLY IN APPROPRIATE STYLE

Anytime you use a direct quotation, paraphrase, or summary from a source—in other words, any text or idea that is not your own—you must indicate the author and work from which it came. This is called citing your sources. Different fields of study follow different guidelines for how to format citation. Psychology, for example, requires APA style, while anthropology typically uses the *Chicago Manual of Style*. English and most humanities, however, use MLA style, a format developed and maintained by the Modern Language Association. (For more on documentation styles, see p. H-108.)

This chapter will provide a quick overview and an abbreviated guide to MLA style. For a full description of how to properly cite works, you will want to consult the *MLA Handbook for Writers of Research Papers* (often referred to as simply the *MLA Handbook*), which is the authoritative guide to MLA style. Be sure to consult the 6th edition, which is the most current, as the rules vary slightly from edition to edition.

## 6b DOCUMENT IN-TEXT CITATIONS, MLA STYLE

### 1. Author Named in Parenthesis

A parenthetical reference in MLA consists of the author's last name and the page number from which you are quoting, summarizing, or paraphrasing. The reference comes at the end of the sentence *before* the period. Do *not* insert a comma, hyphen, or other punctuation between the last name and the page number.

**Example:** While documenting sources may take extra time, it is worth it because "your reader might want to see the source for his or her own research" (Smith 42-43).

When you need to cite a page range, simply put a hyphen between the start and end pages, as in the example above. When citing two different pages, separate them with a comma.

**Example:** (Smith 42, 51)

### 2. Author Named in Sentence

If you mention the author's name in the text surrounding the sentence, you need insert only the page number in parentheses.

**Example:** As John Smith points out, "Your reader might want to see the source for his or her own research" (42).

### 3. Two or More Works by the Same Author

If you use two books or articles by John Smith in your paper, you must let your reader know which source you are using by inserting the title of the work into your sentence *or* by abbreviating the title and inserting it in the parenthetical reference as shown below.

**Example:** As John Smith points out in his article "Using Sources," "Your reader might want to see the source for his or her own research" (42).

**Example:** While documenting sources may take extra time, it is worth it because "your reader might want to see the source for his or her own research" (Smith, "Sources" 42).

*For parenthetical references for works with two, three, or more authors, see p. H-108.

### 4. Source of a Long Quotation

When citing a block quotation—one that is four lines or longer in poetry or five lines or longer in prose—indent by one inch and do not include quotation marks. The citation comes *after* the period.

**Example:** Many critics point to specific techniques that Hughes employs to create the effect of jazz. One such critic is Lionel Davidas, who writes:

> Langston Hughes, in his collection of poems, lavishly uses such characteristics of jazz as repetitions, choruses, riffs, scats, and nonsensical onomatopoeia to achieve musical success as well as audience participation. It is also significant to note that Hughes's poems are often marked by dissonance, discordance, and line irregularity, which all contribute to the representation of the jazz spirit in verse forms. (268)

## 6c DOCUMENT LIST OF WORKS CITED, MLA STYLE

To properly format a Works Cited page:

- Begin on a new page, following the end of your paper. If your paper ends on page 5, your Works Cited page will begin on page 6.
- Just like your paper itself, a Works Cited page should be double spaced with one-inch margins.

- At the top of the page, type "Works Cited" and center it. Do not include quotation marks around the words "Works Cited."
- Do not skip spaces. Drop down one double-spaced line, and align your entry to the left.
- If an entry runs longer than one line, indent every line one-half inch (or five spaces) after the first line.
- Put a period at the end of each entry.
- Alphabetize your Works Cited list by the first word of the entry. In most cases, this will be the author's last name.

For an example of a Works Cited page, see the model research paper in the previous chapter on Writing the Research Paper.

## Common Formatting Errors

- Single spacing a Works Cited page
- Adding extra spaces between entries
- Numbering entries

What goes in an entry on a Works Cited page? First determine what type of source it is—a book, a periodical, an online resource. Then follow the instructions in the appropriate section, as follows:

### Citing Book Sources

Authors / Date of Publication / Book Title / Publisher and Place of Publication / Medium

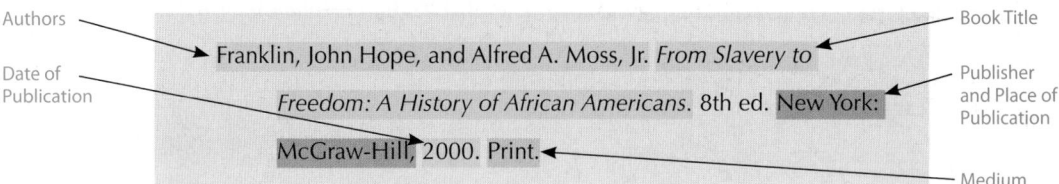

Franklin, John Hope, and Alfred A. Moss, Jr. *From Slavery to Freedom: A History of African Americans.* 8th ed. New York: McGraw-Hill, 2000. Print.

**1. Book with One Author.** Reverse the author's name for alphabetizing, adding a comma after the last name and a period after the first name. The book title follows in italics, followed by a period. Then list the city of publication, followed by a colon. Then the publisher, followed by a comma, then the year, followed by a period. Then list the medium. For how to abbreviate the publisher's name, see Additional Tips, p. H-111.

Borshuk, Michael. *Swinging the Vernacular.* New York: Routledge, 2006. Print.

## Elements in Works Cited Entry: Books

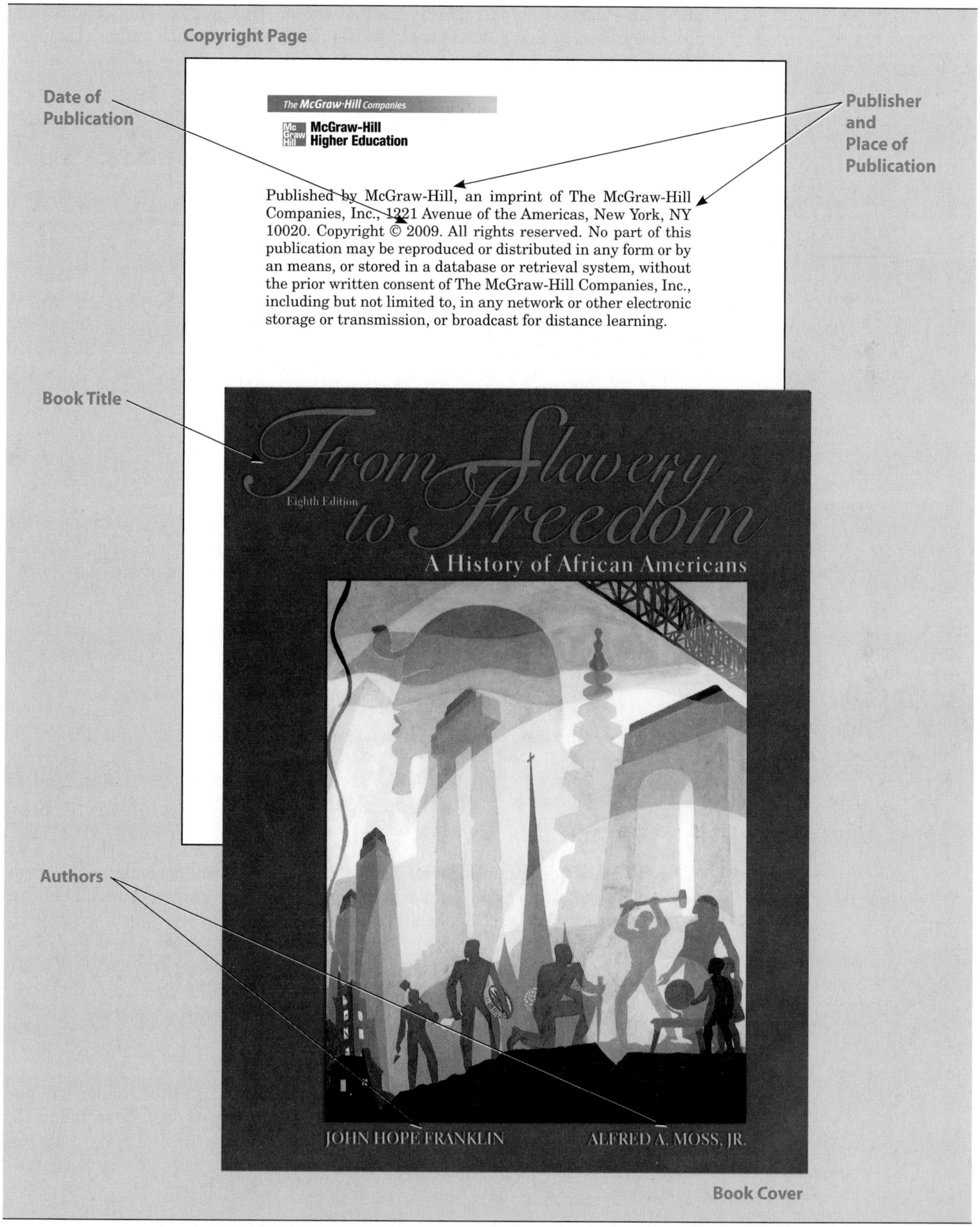
Copyright Page
Date of Publication
Publisher and Place of Publication
The McGraw·Hill Companies
McGraw-Hill Higher Education
Published by McGraw-Hill, an imprint of The McGraw-Hill Companies, Inc., 1221 Avenue of the Americas, New York, NY 10020. Copyright © 2009. All rights reserved. No part of this publication may be reproduced or distributed in any form or by an means, or stored in a database or retrieval system, without the prior written consent of The McGraw-Hill Companies, Inc., including but not limited to, in any network or other electronic storage or transmission, or broadcast for distance learning.
Book Title
From Slavery to Freedom
Eighth Edition
A History of African Americans
Authors
JOHN HOPE FRANKLIN
ALFRED A. MOSS, JR.
Book Cover

**2. Book with Two or Three Authors.** This entry follows the same formula as a book with a single author *except* that you will name the authors in the order listed on the title page. Reverse only the name of the first author. Then add a comma and list additional authors by first name followed by last name. Separate each author's complete name from the next author by a comma.

Gilbert, Sandra M., and Susan Gubar. *The Madwoman in the Attic: The Woman Writer and the Nineteenth-Century Literary Imagination.* New Haven: Yale UP, 2000. Print.

*A parenthetical reference for **two** authors should look like this:

(Gilbert and Gubar 34)

*A parenthetical reference for **three** authors should look like this:

(Gilbert, Gilbert, and Gubar 34)

**3. Book with Four or More Authors.** Indicate the name of the first author appearing on the title page, followed by "et al." (the Latin abbreviation for "and others"). As an alternative, however, you may list the names of all the authors *if convenient.*

Jordan, Frank, et al. *The English Romantic Poets: A Review of Research and Criticism.* New York: MLA, 1985. Print.

*A parenthetical reference for **four or more** authors would look like this:

(Gilbert et al. 34)

**4. Two or More Books by the Same Author.** Follow the same formula as the single book entry, but in this case, you need not repeat the author's name. Instead, indicate the same author with three hyphens and a period.

Bloom, Harold. *The Art of Reading Poetry.* New York: Perennial, 2005. Print.

—. *How to Read and Why.* New York: Scribner, 2000. Print.

**5. Book with an Editor.** In place of an author's name, put the editor's name, followed by a comma and the abbreviation "ed." If there is more than one editor, follow the format for "Book with more than one author" but place a comma and the abbreviation "eds." after the final editor's name listed.

Rampersad, Arnold, ed. *The Collected Poems of Langston Hughes*. New York: Knopf, 1995. Print.

**6. Book with Two Editors.** Use the abbreviation "eds." after the names of the editors.

Opie, Iona, and Peter Opie, eds. *The Oxford Book of Children's Verse*. New York: Oxford, 1973. Print.

**7. Book with an Author and an Editor.** Start with the name of the author, followed by the book title and a period. Then write "Ed." followed by the editor's name in normal order.

Twain, Mark. *Adventures of Huckleberry Finn*. Ed. Henry Nash Smith. Boston: Houghton, 1958. Print.

**8. Book by an Unknown Author.** Begin with the title of the book, followed by the translator or editor (if appropriate). Follow with the publication information. Remember to alphabetize such a book in your Works Cited list by the first major word in the title, *not* by an article (*a*, *an*, or *the*).

*The Bhagavad Gita*. Trans. Eknath Easwaran. Berkeley: Blue Mountain Center for Meditation, 2007. Print.

**9. Work in an Anthology or Chapter in an Edited Book.** Selection author's last name, first name. "Selection or Chapter Title." *Book Title*. Editor's name. City: Publisher, Year. Page numbers of selection. Medium.

Fox, Paula. "The Broad Estates of Death." *The O. Henry Prize Stories*. Ed. Laura Furman. New York: Anchor, 2006. 46-58. Print.

**10. Translation of a Text.** Author's last name, first name. *Title of Book*. Abbreviation "Trans." for "translator." City of publication; publisher, year. Medium.

Alighieri, Dante. *The Divine Comedy*. Trans. John Ciardi. New York: Norton, 1970. Print.

**11. Introduction/Preface/Foreword/Afterword to a Text** If the introduction, preface, foreword, or afterword was written by *someone other than the book's author,* start with the writer and the title of *this* part. Then, indicate the book's title, followed by the word "By" and the name of the book's author in normal order. In the following example, Anita Brookner wrote the introduction to Edith Wharton's novel *The House of Mirth.*

Brookner, Anita. Introduction. *The House of Mirth.* By Edith Wharton. New York: Scribner, 1977. ii- ix. Print.

If the introduction, preface, foreword, or afterword *was written by the author,* use **only** his or her last name preceded by the word "By." In the following example, Thomas Hardy wrote both the book itself and the introduction.

Hardy, Thomas. Introduction. *Tess of the D'Urbervilles.* By Hardy. New York: Barnes and Noble, 1993. Print.

**12. Multivolume Work** If you have taken information from only one of the work's volumes, indicate the number of that volume and abbreviate to "Vol" (no period after "Vol").

Poe, Edgar Allan. *The Collected Works of Edgar Allan Poe.* Ed. Thomas Ollive Mabboth. Vol 2. Cambridge: Harvard UP, 1969. Print.

If you have taken information from more than one volume, indicate the total number of volumes used, abbreviate to "vols" and follow with a period.

Poe, Edgar Allan. *The Collected Works of Edgar Allan Poe.* Ed. Thomas Ollive Mabboth. 2 vols. Cambridge: Harvard UP, 1969. Print.

**13. Book in a Series** Place the name of the series after the medium. Indicate the book's number in the series if available.

Franchere, Hoyt C., ed. *Edwin Arlington Robinson.* New York: Twayne, 1968. Print. Twaynes's United States Authors Series 137.

**14. Encyclopedia Article**

***Signed*** A signed article is one that is attributed to an author.

Invert author's name. "Title of the Article." *Title of the Encyclopedia.* Editor(s). Volume number (if appropriate). City of publication; publisher, year. Page number(s). Medium.

> Merlan, Philip. "Athenian School." *The Encyclopedia of Philosophy.* Ed. Paul Edwards. Vol. 1. New York: Macmillan, 1967. 192-93. Print.

***Unsigned*** An unsigned article is not attributed to an author. Start with the title of the article. Then proceed as above.

> "Pericles." *The Columbia Concise Encyclopedia.* Eds. Judith S. Levey and Agnes Greenhall. New York: Columbia UP, 1983. 655. Print.

**15. Dictionary Definition** "Title of Entry." *Title of Dictionary.* Edition. Year of publication. Medium.

> "Fresco." *Merriam-Webster's Collegiate Dictionary.* 11th ed. 2003. Print.

## Additional Tips

When a book lists multiple cities in which the publisher exists, choose the closest one geographically to put in your citation. For W. W. Norton & Company, which lists New York and London, you would use New York as the city for publication. Also, if the city is relatively unknown, or if there is more than one U.S. city with the same name, indicate the state in addition to the city, as in the following examples:

> Durham, NC: Duke UP
>
> Springfield, IL: Charles C Thomas

You will want to abbreviate or condense the publisher's name. Anytime you see "University Press," you can abbreviate it as "UP." For Southern Methodist University Press, write Southern Methodist UP. Alfred A. Knopf can be condensed to simply "Knopf."

If a book has multiple years on the copyright page, put only the most recent year in your Works Cited entry.

## Citing Periodical Sources

Author — Article Title — Date — Journal Title — Pages — Volume number — Medium

Davidas, Lionel. "'I, Too, Sing America': Jazz and Blues Techniques and Effects in Some of Langston Hughes's Selected Poems." *Dialectical Anthropology* 26 (2001): 267-272. Web.

Journal Title — Page numbers — Date of Publication — Volume — Starting page number — Article Title — Author — Author Affiliation

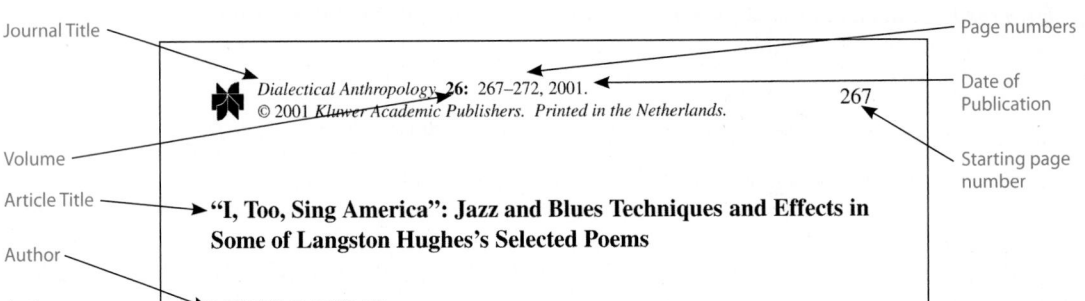

*Dialectical Anthropology* **26:** 267–272, 2001.
© 2001 *Kluwer Academic Publishers. Printed in the Netherlands.* 267

**"I, Too, Sing America": Jazz and Blues Techniques and Effects in Some of Langston Hughes's Selected Poems**

LIONEL DAVIDAS
*Université des Antilles et de la Guyane, Martinique, West Indies*

It is commonly accepted that oral poetry has been greatly influenced by jazz and blues, a phenomenon that developed mainly in the USA. In light of this, we may infer that such poems should logically be considered as mere scores to be deciphered and performed, or records that should be heard rather than read, and that have many of the dynamics of "the music" about them.[1] In point of fact, a significant number of jazz techniques are to be found within the framework of poetry and combine with it to produce a highly personalized mode of free expression, which is the essence and spirit of of jazz creation. As it appears, Langston Hughes's outstanding collection of poems exemplifies the greatest of those qualities of jazz and blues, and his talent truly makes these poems come alive in the same way that jazz and blues music comes alive for the audience as well as for the musicians.

To those who are familiar with such music, it is quite clear that *Selected Poems of Langston Hughes*, a book which reveals the author's personal choice, unquestionably includes blues poetry, as evidenced by the many characteristics of blues music that pervade most of the selected pieces. To start with, it is significant to note that Hughes's poems are not at all static. They are pervaded with lively and active repetitions, and we notice a series of variations within each poem which closely resemble the variations present in a blues song. Many of Hughes's poems exhibit a slow tempo and rhythm which is a common trait to most styles of blues. What is more, there exists some degree of internal variation in breath rhythm that contributes to the blues effect. In addition, those poems definitely seek the interaction of call-and-response, making the reader feel an active participant in the "concert" provided by the poet as musician, as performer.

Periodicals include scholarly journals, magazines, and newspapers. For print periodicals (as opposed to online periodicals), use the following citation formulas.

**1. Article in a Scholarly Journal** Author's last name, first name. "Article Title." *Journal Title* Volume. Issue (Year): Page numbers of article. Medium.

> Davidas, Lionel. "'I, Too, Sing America': Jazz and Blues Techniques and Effects in Some of Langston Hughes's Selected Poems." *Dialectical Anthropology* 26 (2001): 267-272. Print.

Note that not all journals have an issue number, as in the example above. If that is the case, simply include the volume and the year.

**2. Article in a Magazine** Author's last name, first name. "Article Title." *Magazine Title* Day Month Year: Page numbers of article. Medium.

> Lehrer, Jonah. "The Eureka Hunt." *The New Yorker* 28 July 2008: 40-45. Print.

Note that monthly magazines will not have a day with the month; in that case, simply list the month. Also, abbreviate months except for May, June, and July.

**3. Article in a Newspaper** Author's last name, first name. "Article Headline." *Newspaper's Name* Day Month Year: Section letter Page number +. Medium.

> Svrluga, Barry. "Phelps Earns Eighth Gold." *The Washington Post* 17 Aug. 2008: A1+. Print.

Use the plus sign after the page number only if the article is continued on nonconsecutive pages.

**4. Book Review** Start with the reviewer's name, followed by the title of the review (if it has one) in quotation marks. Follow with "Rev. of" (the abbreviation for "review of"), the title of the book, and the name of the book's author preceded by the word "by." The author's name should be in normal order.

In the following example, the reviewer is Robert Kelly; the author of the book is Umberto Eco.

> Kelly, Robert. "Castaway." Rev. of *The Island of the Day Before,* by Umberto Eco. *New York Times* 22 Oct. 1995: BR7. Print.

## Citing Online Resources

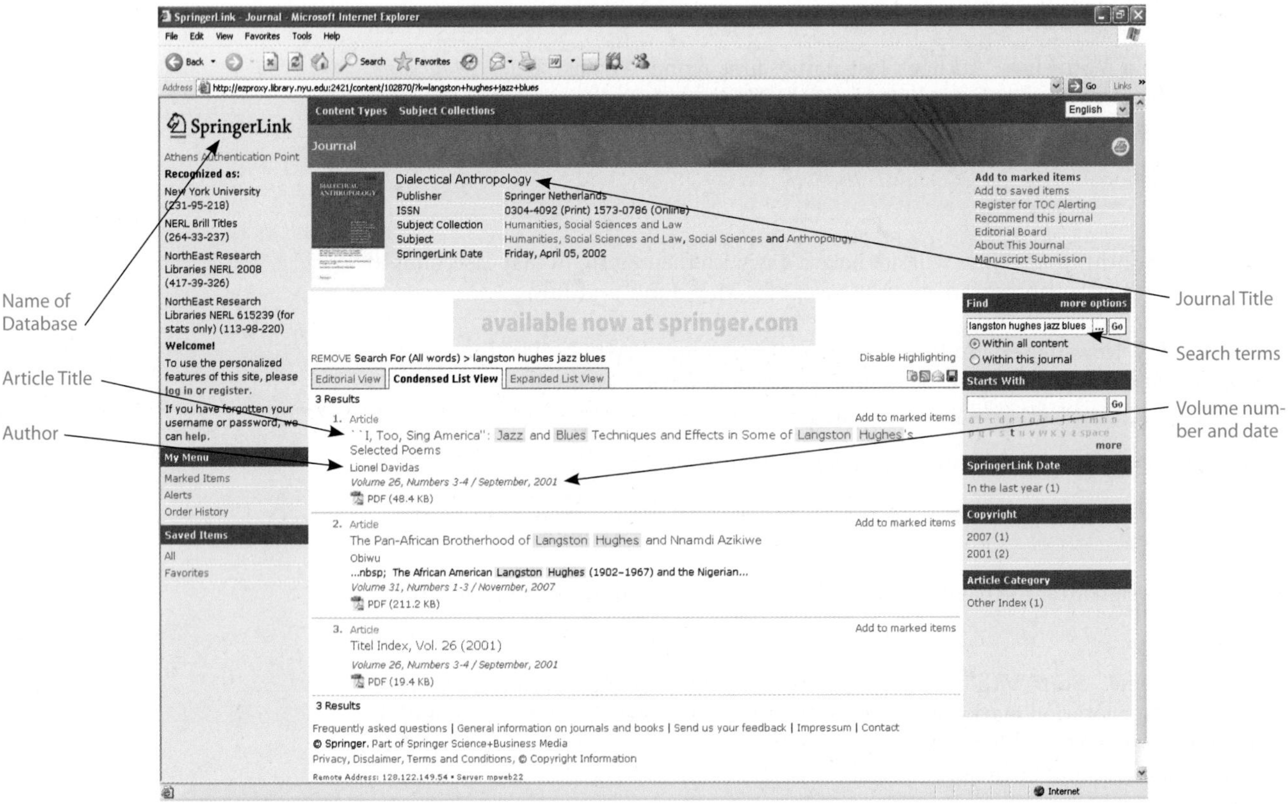


**1. Web Site.** The amount of source information provided varies from Web site to Web site. Include as much of the information below as you can. Remember, too, to choose your online resources wisely. If there is little or no information on the person or institution that created it, you may want to reconsider using it in your paper.

Last name of person responsible for site, first name. *Name of Web site.* Name of publisher, date of publication or last update. Medium. Day you accessed site—Month Year. Note: If no publisher is listed, use the abbreviation "n.p."

> Souther, Randy. *Celestial Timepiece: A Joyce Carol Oates Homepage.* N.p., Web. 8 Oct. 2007.

**2. Article on a Web Site/Part of an Online Scholarly Project.** Segment author's last name, first name. "Title of the Part of the Project." Ed. Name of person responsible for project. Date of publication or update. Name of sponsoring institution. Medium. Date you accessed site.

> "Roaring Twenties." *JAZZ: A Film by Ken Burns.* PBS. Web. 11 May 2008.

*Note that in the above example, the date of the Web site's publication was not available, so the student simply put the date she accessed the site.

**3. Article in an Online Periodical.** Article author's last name, first name. "Article Title." *Periodical's Web site.* Web site sponsor (if available). Day Month Year of publication. Medium. Date you accessed site.

> Lowney, John. "Langston Hughes and the 'Nonsense' of Bebop." *American Literature Online.* June 2000. Web. 11 May 2008.

**4. Article from a Database.** Cite the article as you normally would for a print article, but at the end of your entry add the following information:

*Database Name.* Medium. Date of access.

> Lenz, Gunter. "The Riffs, Runs, Breaks, and Distortions of the Music of a Community in Transition." *The Massachusetts Review* 44.1-2 (Spring 2003): 269-282. *ProQuest.* Web. 11 May 2008.

**5. Online Book.**

***The entire online book.*** Start with the information you would include for any printed book. Follow with the name of the database, project, or other entity in which you found the book. Then, indicate the medium and the date you accessed the book.

> Hardy, Thomas. *Wessex Poems and Other Verses.* New York: Harper, 1898. *Bartleby.com.* Web. 30 Sept. 2008.

***Part of an online book.*** Start with the name of the author, followed by the title of the part of the book you have cited. Then, proceed as above. The following example is an entry for Thomas Hardy's poem "Neutral Tones," which appears in an online book entitled *Wessex Poems and Other Verses.*

Hardy, Thomas. "Neutral Tones." *Wessex Poems and Other Verses.* New York: Harper, 1898. *Bartleby.com.* Web. 30 Sept. 2008.

**6. Online Posting.** Treat an online posting as you would a Web site.

Brantley, Ben. "London Theater Journal: Hitting Bottom." *Artsbeat. New York Times.* 17 July 2008. Web. 29 Sept. 2008.

## Citing Other Media

**1. Audio Recording.** Start with the name of the composer, performer, or conductor—depending on whom you have discussed in your paper. Then, indicate the title of the recording, followed by the name(s) of the composer (s), performer(s), and/or conductor (if they were not mentioned earlier). Follow this with the distributor, the date, and the medium.

Chopin. Frederic. *Chopin: Etudes.* Maurizio Pollini. Deutsche Grammaphon, 1972. CD.

**2. Film.** Begin with the title of the film. Then, write the name of the director preceded by "Dir." (the abbreviation for "director"). Next indicate the name(s) of the principal performer(s) preceded by "Perf." (the abbreviation for "performers"). Follow this with the distributor, the date, and the medium.

*Cinema Paradiso.* Dir. Giuseppe Tornatore. Perf. Phillipe Noiret, Jacques Perrin, Antonella Attilli, Pupella Maggio, and Salvatore Cascio. Miramar, 1988. Film.

**3. Television Program.** Start with the title of the episode in quotation marks. Then, list the title of the program. Follow with the name of the network or channel, the city, the date you viewed the program, and the medium.

"Noah: Myth or Fact." *Into the Unknown with Josh Bernstein.* Discovery Channel, Silver Springs, MD. 15 Aug. 2008. Television.

# Glossary of Literary Terms

**Abstract** A short **summary** at the beginning of a scholarly article that states the **thesis,** the major points of **evidence,** and the **conclusion** of the article.

**Abstract Diction** Language referring to a general or conceptual thing or quality, such as *progress,* or *justice.*

**Accent** The vocal emphasis on a syllable in a word. Often used interchangeably with **stress,** which sometimes refers to emphasis within a line of poetry, rather than a single word.

**Accentual Meter** A kind of **meter** or verse measure that uses a fixed number of stressed syllables in each line, although based on a number of unstressed syllables may vary. Accentual meters often can be heard in rap music and children's rhymes.

**Accentual-Syllabic Verse** A verse form that uses a fixed number of **stresses** and syllables per line. This is the most common verse form in English poetry, and includes, for example, **iambic pentameter,** where each line has five **stressed** syllables and five unstressed syllables.

**Act** A subdivision of the action of a play, similar to a chapter in a book. Acts generally occur during a change in **scenery,** cast of **characters,** or mood, and the end of an act usually suggests the advancement of time in the play. Acts are often divided into subunits called **scenes.**

**Allegory** A story in which major elements such as **characters** and settings represent universal truths or moral lessons in a one-to-one correspondence.

**Alliteration** The repetition of the initial consonant sounds of a sequence of words.

**Allusion** A reference to another work of art or literature, or to a person, place, or event outside the text.

**Amphibrach** A syllable pattern characterized by three syllables in the order *unstressed, stressed, unstressed.*

**Amphitheater** A stage surrounded on all sides by the audience, who watch the action from above.

***Anagnorisis*** In **tragedy,** a change from ignorance to knowledge, producing love or hate between the persons destined by the poet for good or bad fortune.

**Anagram** A word or phrase created using the letters that spell a different word or phrase. For example, *dirty room* is an anagram for *dormitory.*

**Analyze** To take a text apart and examine its elements: the different written devices the author uses (such as **point of view, plot,** and imagery) and the **voice** the author brings to the piece (**tone,** word choice).

**Anapestic Meter** A **meter** using feet with two unstressed syllables followed by a **stressed** syllable.

**Anecdote** A personal remembrance or brief story.

**Antagonist** A **character** in **conflict** with the **protagonist.** A story's **plot** often hinges on a protagonist's conflict with an antagonist.

**Anticlimax** The opposite of a **climax;** a point in a narrative that is striking for its *lack* of excitement, intensity, or emphasis. An anticlimax generally occurs at a point of high action where a true climax is expected to occur.

**Antihero** A main **character** who acts outside the usual lines of heroic behavior (brave, honest, true).

**Apostrophe** A **figure of speech** in which a writer directly addresses an unseen person, force, or personified idea. The term *apostrophe* derives from the Greek term meaning *turning away* and often marks a digression.

**Approximate Rhyme** *See* **Slant Rhyme.**

**Archetypal Criticism** *See* **Mythological Criticism.**

**Archetype** An **image** or **symbol** with a universal meaning that evokes a common emotional reaction in readers.

**Arena Theater** Also called *Theater in the Round,* an arena stage is surrounded on all sides by the audience, with all the action taking place on a stage in the center.

**Argument** A position or perspective based on a **claim** that can be supported with **evidence.**

**Aside** In drama, a remark made by an actor to the audience, which the other **characters** do not hear. This convention is sometimes discernable in fiction writing, when a self-conscious **narrator** breaks the flow of the narrative to make a remark directly to the reader.

**Assonance** A repetition of vowel sounds or patterns in neighboring words.

**Auditory Imagery** **Images** that appeal to a reader's sense of hearing.

**Augustan Age** A distinct period in early-eighteenth-century neoclassical English literature characterized by formal structure and diction. This Augustan Age is named after the great period of Roman literature during Emperor Augustus's reign, when Ovid, Horace, and Virgil were writing. Famous writers of the English Augustan Age were Alexander Pope, Thomas Gray, and Jonathan Swift.

**Authorial Intrusion** *See* **Editorial Omniscience.**

**Ballad Stanza** A **quatrain** in which the first and third lines possess four stresses, while the second and fourth have three stresses. The **rhyme scheme** is often *abcb.*

**Ballad** A song or poem that tells a lively or tragic story in simple language using rhyming four-line **stanzas** and a set **meter.**

***Bathos*** An error that occurs when a writer attempts elevated language but is accidentally trite or ridiculous; a sort of **anticlimax.**

**Beat Generation** A group of writers in the 1950s and '60s who represented the counterculture to 1950s American prosperity. The word "beat" comes from the slang for being down and worn out, suggesting their weariness with mainstream culture and their adoption of a freespirited attitude. Jack Kerouac's *On the Road* and Allen Ginsberg's poem "Howl" are major works of the Beat Generation.

**Bibliography** A list of the works consulted in the preparation of a paper, containing adequate information for readers to locate the source materials themselves.

***Bildungsroman*** A **coming of age story** that details the growth or maturity of a youth, usually an adolescent. The term is German, meaning "**novel** of formation."

**Biographical Criticism** **Literary criticism** that emphasizes the belief that literature is created by authors whose unique experiences shape their writing and therefore can inform our reading of their work. Biographical critics research and use an author's biography to interpret the text as well as the author's stated intentions or comments on the process of composition itself. These critics often consult the author's memoirs to uncover connections between the author's life and the author's work. They may also study the author's rough drafts to trace the evolution of a given text or examine the author's library to discern potential influences on the author's work.

**Biography** The factual account of a person's life.

**Blank Verse** Unrhymed **iambic pentameter,** often used in Shakespeare's plays or for epic subject matter, as in Milton's *Paradise Lost.*

**Blues** A form of music that originated in the Deep South. Descended from African-American spirituals and work songs, the blues reflects the hardships of life and love in its lyrics. Most blues songs follow a form made of three phrases equal in length: a first phrase, a second that repeats the first phrase, and a third phrase different from the first two that concludes the verse.

**Box Set** *See* **Proscenium Stage.**

**Brainstorming** A process of generating and collecting ideas on a topic.

**Burlesque** A work of drama or literature that ridicules its subject matter through exaggerated mockery and broad **comedy.**

**Cacophony** Harsh-sounding, grating, or even hard-to-pronounce language.

**Caesura** A pause, usually in the middle of a line, that marks a kind of rhythmic division.

**Canon** In a literary context, the group of works considered by academics and scholars to be essential to and representative of the body of respected literature.

***Carpe diem*** Latin for *seize the day.* A phrase used commonly in poetry that emphasizes the brevity of life and the importance of living in the moment.

**Catharsis** The purging of emotions which the audience experiences as a result of the powerful **climax** of a classical **tragedy**; the sense of relief and renewal experienced through art.

**Central Intelligence** Henry James's term for the **narrator** of a story—distinct from the author—whose impressions and ideas shape the telling of the story and determine the details revealed.

**Character** The depiction of human beings (and nonhumans) within a story.

**Characters** The actors (human and nonhuman) in a story.

**Characteristics** The physical and mental attributes of a **character,** established through **characterization.**

**Characterization** The way a writer crafts and defines a **character**'s personality to give an insight into that character's thoughts and actions.

**Charting** A technique for generating ideas that involves placing related concepts and themes in a chart to view their relationships.

**Chorus** A group of amateurs and trained actors who participated in traditional Greek plays. The chorus represents a group of citizens with worries and questions, expressed in poetry and music and dance movement.

**Claim** An idea or stance on a particular subject; a defendable claim is necessary for a strong **thesis.**

**Classifications of Drama** These four categories are generally assigned to Shakespeare's theater, but are commonly used in reference to the works of other **playwrights.** **Histories** focus on the reign of kings from the past, from Julius

Caesar to Henry V. Because histories naturally contain very astute and sometimes troubling political commentaries, playwrights had to limit their subjects to rulers of the distant past. **Comedies** are plays for entertainment, and as a convention end in the marriage of two main **characters.** A comedic **plot** generally begins with a complication or misunderstanding between two lovers, which is complicated by further scheming and misunderstandings until finally a **resolution** is attained and the two are wed. **Tragedies** are darker plays, with more complex **characters** and more dire consequences, usually dramatizing the fall from a high state of life of a royal or special **character. Romances** (from the French *roman,* which means an "extended narrative") involve lovers whose potential happiness is complicated by misunderstandings, mistaken identities, and any number of other difficulties. Although similar in plot to a **comedy,** a romance play does not guarantee a happy ending.

**Cliché** A **figure of speech** that has been used so commonly that it has become trite. The use of cliché may suggest an ironic tone.

**Climax** The narrative's turning point in a struggle between opposing forces. The point of highest **conflict** in a story.

**Close Reading** The **explication** of a text in order to **analyze** the ways in which distinct formal elements interact to create a unified artistic experience for the reader.

**Closed Couplet** A pair of rhymed lines that capture one complete idea. If the couplet is **end-stopped** and in **iambic pentameter,** it is called a **heroic couplet.**

**Closed Denouement** A **resolution** to a story that leaves no loose ends.

**Closed Form** *See* **Fixed Form.**

**Closet Drama** A piece of literature written as though for the stage, but intended only to be read.

**Collective Unconscious** A set of **characters, plots, symbols,** and **images** that each evoke a universal response.

**Colloquial Speech** Familiar and conversational speech.

**Comedy** A type of drama that deals with light or humorous subject matter and usually includes a happy ending. The opposite of **tragedy.** *See* **Classifications of Drama.**

**Comedy of Manners** A work of **satire** that pokes fun at human behavior in particular social circles. Since a comedy of manners concerns itself with social interactions, it tends to reveal the **characters'** foibles or follies as they try to appear or act in a certain way.

**Comic Relief** A **character** or situation that provides humor in the midst of a work that is predominantly serious. A classic example is the bumbling Falstaff, a character in Shakesepeare's *Henry IV* who makes the audience laugh, even as England's fate hangs in the balance.

**Coming of Age Story** A story that follows a **character's** physical, emotional, or spiritual maturation, often from youth into adulthood. *See* ***Bildungsroman.***

**Common Measure** A variation on **ballad** meter that uses **iambic quatrains** with the first and third lines containing four feet (**tetrameter**) and the second and fourth containing three feet (**trimeter**). The rhyme scheme is often *abab* rhyme. Common measure, also called *common meter,* is the **meter** most associated with hymns.

**Comparison** Looking at two or more texts, **characters,** authors, or other items side by side to draw similarities between them.

**Conceit** A complex comparison or **metaphor** that extends throughout a poem

**Conclusion** The final idea and **resolution** of a text. In a good essay, the conclusion not only reiterates the **thesis** but offers a reason for its significance or a reflection that pushes it toward a broader meaning beyond the essay itself. In a story or play, the conclusion refers to the resolution or **dénouement.**

**Concrete Diction** Language referring to a specific, definite thing or quality, such as *lawn mower* or *street light.*

**Concrete Poetry** Also called *visual poetry.* Poetry written in the shape of something it describes.

**Confessional Poetry** Poetry that includes pieces of a poet's autobiography or personal experience. This mode of poetry was prevalent in the mid-twentieth century with poets like Sylvia Plath, Anne Sexton, and Robert Lowell.

**Conflict** The central problem in a story. The source of tension between the **protagonist** and **antagonist.**

**Connotation** The associations a word carries beyond its literal meaning. Connotations are formed by the context of the word's popular usage; for example, *green,* aside from being a color, connotes money. The opposite of **denotation.**

**Consonance** A repetition of consonant sounds or similar patterns in neighboring words.

**Context** The literary, historical, biographical, or poetical situation that influences the writing of a work of literature.

**Contextual Reading** Reading and interpreting a story while mindful of its author, the time and place it was written, the traditions of its form, and the criticism it explicitly or implicitly responds to.

**Contrast** Looking at two or more texts, **characters,** authors, or other items side by side to highlight the differences between them.

**Convention** In literature, a feature or element of a **genre** that is commonly used and therefore widely accepted—and expected—

by readers and writers alike. For example, it is a convention of Shakespearean **comedy** to end with a marriage.

**Conventional Symbols** **Symbols** that have accrued a widely accepted **interpretation** through their repeated use in literature and the broader culture. For example, spring and winter are conventional symbols of birth and death, as they appear with that meaning in Shakespeare's works through Frost's poetry. Colors, too, can be used as conventional symbols; in contemporary society, a pink ribbon is a conventional symbol of breast cancer awareness.

**Cosmic Irony** A literary convention where forces beyond the control of **characters**—such as God or fate or the supernatural—foil plans or expectations.

**Couplet** Two lines of poetry forming one unit of meaning. Couplets are often **rhymed,** strung together without a break, and share the same **meter.**

***Cothurni*** Tall boots, worn by actors in the Ancient Greek theater, which served both to elevate an actor and make him more visible to the massive crowds, and also to make the **character**s seem larger than life.

**Craft** As a noun, craft refers to the elements that comprise a story; as a verb, craft refers to the process of making or fashioning a story out of those elements.

**Cretic** Also called *Amphimacer.* A syllable pattern characterized by three syllables in the order *stressed, unstressed, stressed.*

**Crisis** *See* **Climax.**

**Critical Reading** A process of digesting and understanding a text so you can appreciate not just the ideas it presents or the story it tells, but how it presents those ideas, why it presents them, and how those ideas exist in a certain context. Critical reading involves **summary, analysis, synthesis,** and **interpretation.**

**Critique** A **summary** accompanied by one's own personal opinion and perspectives.

**Cultural Studies** This critical perspective was developed mainly in England in the sixties by New Left writers, social philosophers, and sociologists. Cultural studies incorporates the techniques of literary analysis to **analyze** social life and social movements as though they were written texts.

**Dactylic Meter** A **meter** in which the foot contains a stressed syllable followed by two unstressed syllables.

**Deconstruction** A critical approach to analyzing literature based on the idea that texts do not have a single, stable meaning or **interpretation.** Deconstructionists seek to break down literature to reveal the inevitable inconsistency or lack of unity in even the most successful and revered texts, believing that the author's intentions have no bearing on the meaning of the text to the reader.

**Decorum** A certain level of propriety appropriate to a given text. As well as demanding a certain level of **diction,** decorum can also have bearing on the **characters, setting,** and **plot** events of a piece of literature.

**Denotation** The literal meaning of a word. The opposite of **connotation.**

**Denouement** The period after the story's **climax** when **conflicts** are addressed and/or resolved. Includes the **falling action** and **resolution** of a story.

***Deus ex machina*** Latin for *God from the machine;* a literary device, often seen in drama, where a **conflict** is resolved by unforeseen and often far-fetched means.

**Dialect** **Dialogue** written to phonetically or grammatically replicate a particular **sound,** cadence, **rhythm,** or emphasis in a **character's** speech.

**Dialogue** Spoken interaction between two or more **characters.** A **characterization** technique that can signal class, education, intelligence, ethnicity, and attitude in the characters involved.

**Diction** An author's or **character's** distinctive choice of words and style of expression.

**Didactic Literature** Literature, such as a fable or **allegory,** written to instruct or teach a moral.

**Dimeter** A poetic **meter** comprised of two poetic feet.

**Dirge** A funeral song.

**Doggerel** An obviously patterned piece of **rhyme,** often lunging or twisting word order in order to get a rhyme. Doggerel can sometimes seem almost childish and, when extensive, boring.

**Drama** A term that comes from the Greek word for doing or acting and refers to a literary work that is represented through performance.

**Dramatic Irony** A situation in which an author or **narrator** lets the reader know more about a situation than a **character** does.

**Dramatic Monologue** A poem in which a **character** addresses another character or the reader. Dramatic monologues are offshoots of the epic form.

**Dramatic Poetry** Poetry in which the speaker of the poem is not the poet. Dramatic poetry often tells a story.

**Dramatic Point of View** A **third-person point of view** in which the **narrator** presents only bare details and the **dialogue** of other **character**s.

**Dramatic Question** The overarching challenge or issue in a piece of drama—the complication which the events of a play work to resolve.

**Dynamic Character** A **character** whose personality and behavior alter over the course of the action in response to challenges and changing circumstances.

**Dramatis Personae** "People of the play"; a list of the **characters** in a play, usually one of the first elements of a script.

**Echo Verse** Poetry in which words at the ends of lines or **stanzas** are repeated, mimicking an echo.
**Economic Determinist Criticism** *See* **Marxist Criticism.**
**Editorial Omniscience** A **narrator** inserts his or her own commentary about **character**s or events into the narrative.
**Electra Complex** The female version of the **Oedipus Complex,** the Electra Complex suggests that female children are hostile toward their mothers because of subconscious sexual attraction to their fathers.
**Elegy** A poem of lamentation memorializing the dead or contemplating some nuance of life's melancholy. Early Greek elegies employed a fixed form of **dactylic hexameter** and **iambic pentameter couplets.**
**Elision** The omission of a vowel or consonant sound within or between words, such as "ne'er" for "never" and "o'er" for "over." Elision dramatizes language and allows for flexibility within a poem's **meter.**
**Ellipses** Three periods placed in succession (. . .) to illustrate that something has been omitted.
**End Rhyme** **Rhyme** that occurs at the end of two or more lines of poetry. An example of end rhyme can be found in "The Love Song of J. Alfred Prufrock": "Let us go through certain half-deserted streets, / The muttering retreats."
**End-stopped Line** A line that ends with a full stop or period.
**Endnote** Information placed at the end of a text in an explanatory note. In a research paper, endnotes are used to comment on sources or provide additional analysis that is slightly tangential to the focus of your paper. An endnote is indicated by a superscript number ( [1] ) in the text itself, which corresponds to a numbered explanatory note at the end.
**English Sonnet** *See* **Shakespearean Sonnet.**
**Enjambment** The running over of a phrase from one line into another so that closely related words belong to different lines.
**Envoi** The final **stanza** of a **sestina,** which summarizes the entire poem. Envoi is French for *farewell.*
**Epic** A long **narrative poem,** traditionally recited publicly, whose subject matter reflects the values of the culture from which it came by portraying important legends or heroes. Classical epics include the *Odyssey* and the *Aeneid,* while English epics include *Beowulf* and *Paradise Lost.*
**Epigram** A short, often satirical observation on a single subject.
**Epigraph** A quotation or brief passage from another source, included at the beginning of a piece of literature. Writers use epigraphs to suggest a major theme or idea in their work.
**Epiphany** A sudden realization or new understanding achieved by a **character** or speaker. In many short stories, the character's epiphany is the **climax** of the story.
**Episode** A unified event or incident within a longer narrative.
***Episodia*** The scenes of a Greek tragedy, divided by ***stasimon*** from the **Chorus.**
**Epistolary Novel** A novel written in the form of letters between two or more **characters,** or in the form of diary entries. Epistolary novels were particularly popular in the eighteenth century.
**Ethnic Studies** A critical approach to literature that seeks to give voice to literature that has previously been overlooked in the traditionally Euro-centric worldview—not simply by including ethnically diverse literature in the **canon,** but by attention to historically underrepresented groups, like African Americans and Native Americans.
**Euphony** Musically pleasing poetic language.
**Evidence** Reliable information, such as statistics, expert opinions, and anecdotes, used to support a **claim** in an **argument.**
**Exact Rhyme** A rhyme in which the final vowel and consonant sounds are identical, regardless of spelling. Also called *pure rhyme, perfect rhyme,* and *true rhyme.*
***Exodos*** The concluding scene of a Greek **tragedy.**
**Explication** a **close reading** of any text where the goal is to logically **analyze** details within the text itself to uncover deeper meanings or contradictions.
**Exposition:** The narrative presentation of necessary information about the **character, setting,** or character's history provided to make the reader care what happens to the characters in the story.
**Expressionism** A mode of theater in which the playwright attempts to portray his or her subjective emotions in a symbolic way on stage.
**Extended Metaphor** A figurative analogy that is woven through a poem.
**Eye Rhyme** Words that share similar spellings but—when spoken—have different sounds. For example, *lint* and *pint.* Also called *Sight Rhyme.*

**Fables** A short narrative in which the **characters** (often animals or inanimate things) illustrate a lesson. The characters in fables are *actors* rather than **symbols.**
**Fairy Tale** A story, usually for children, that involves magical creatures or circumstances and usually has a happy ending.
**Falling Action** The events following the **climax** and leading up to the **resolution.** These events reveal how the **protagonist** has been

impacted by and dealt with the preceding **conflicts** of the story.

**Falling Meter** A **meter** comprised of feet that begin with a stressed syllable, followed by an unstressed syllable or syllables. **Trochaic** and **dactylic** feet both create falling meter, which is named for the effect of *falling* from the initial stressed syllable to the unstressed.

**Fantasy** A literary **genre** that uses magical **characters** or circumstances.

**Farce** A work of drama or literature that uses broad, often physical **comedy,** exaggerated **characters,** absurd situations, and improbable **plot** twists to evoke laughter without intending social criticism.

**Feminine Rhyme** Rhymes between multisyllable words in which the final syllable is unstressed, such as *bother* and *father.* Also called *falling rhyme.*

**Feminist Criticism** An approach to literary criticism that highlights literature written by women and the exploration of the experience of female **characters**; also a critical examination of the ways in which female characters are viewed with prejudice, are subjugated to male interests, or are simply overlooked in literature.

**Fiction** A genre of literature that describes events and **characters** invented by the author.

**Figurative Language** Language that describes one thing by relating it to something else.

**Figure of Speech** A technique of using language to describe one thing in terms of another, often comparing two unlike objects, such as *the sun* and *the face of the beloved,* to condense and heighten the effect of language, particularly the effect of **imagery** or **symbolism** in a poem.

**First-Person Narrator** The story is narrated by a **character** in the story, identified by use of the pronoun *I* or the plural first-person, *we.*

**Fixed Form** An arrangement of text that requires a poet to obey set written combinations, including line length, **meter, stanza** structure, and **rhyme scheme.** Also called ***closed form.***

**Flashback** The device of moving back in time to a point before the primary action of the story.

**Flat Character** A **character** with a narrow range of speech or action. Flat characters are predictable and do not develop over the course of the **plot.**

**Foil** A **character** who contrasts with the central character, often with the purpose of emphasizing some trait in the central character. For example, a cruel sister emphasizes the other sister's kindness.

**Folklore** A traditional **canon** of stories, sayings, and **characters.**

**Folktale** A short, often fantastic tale passed down over time.

**Foot** The smallest unit of measure in poetic **meter.** A foot usually contains a stressed syllable and one or two unstressed syllables. **Meter** is formed when the same foot repeats more than once. For example, in **iambic pentameter,** *iambic* refers to the type of foot (an unstressed syllable followed by a stressed syllable), while *pentameter* tells us that there are five (pent) iambic feet in each line.

**Footnote** Like an **endnote,** a way to include commentary on sources or other information tangential to the focus of a text. A footnote occurs at the bottom of the page on which the subject is most closely addressed. To create a footnote, a superscript number ($^1$) is placed in the text itself and corresponds to the number of the explanatory note at the bottom of the page.

**Foreshadowing** A hint about **plot** elements to come, both to advance the plot and build **suspense.**

**Form** The shape, structure, and style of a poem, as distinguishable from, but integral to, the content or substance of the poem.

**Formal Diction** Complex, grammatically proper, and often polysyllabic language in writing. It sounds grandiloquent—a *formal* word—and tends not to resemble the sort of talk heard in daily life.

**Formalist Criticism** An approach to literary criticism that considers a successful text to be a complete, independent, unified artifact whose meaning and value can be understood purely by analyzing the interaction of its formal and technical components, such as **plot, imagery,** structure, style, **symbol,** and **tone.** Rather than drawing their textual interpretations from *extrinsic* factors such as the historical, political, or biographical context of the work, formalist critics focus on the text's *intrinsic* formal elements.

**Found Poem** A poem created from already existing text that the poet reshapes and presents in poetic form. Text may come from advertisements, labels on household items, newspapers, magazines, or any other printed source not intended originally as poetry. A poet may piece together several sources like a collage, or he/she might take a short text exactly as it is and insert line breaks.

**Fourth Wall** The *invisible wall* of the stage, through which the audience views the action.

**Free Verse** Poetry in which the poet does not adhere to a preset metrical or **rhyme scheme.** Free verse has become increasingly prevalent since the nineteenth century, when it was first used. *See* **Open Form.**

**Freewrite** Writing continuously to generate ideas, without worrying about mistakes.

**Gay and Lesbian Criticism** A critical approach that is similar to **feminist criticism** in its quest to uncover previously overlooked undertones and themes in literature. Gay and lesbian criticism seeks to identify underlying homosexual themes in literature.

**Gender Criticism** A critical approach to literature that seeks to understand how gender and sexual identity reflect upon the interpretation of literary works. Feminist criticism and gay and lesbian criticism are derivatives of gender criticism.

**Genre** A literary category or form, such as the short story or novel, or a specific type of fiction, such as science fiction or mystery.

**Groundlings** "Standing room only" spectators in the Elizabethan theater who paid a penny to stand on the ground surrounding the stage.

**Haiku** A poetic form containing seventeen syllables in three lines of five, seven, and five syllables each. Haiku traditionally contain a natural-world reference or central **image.**

***Hamartia*** A tragic flaw or weakness in a tragic **character** that leads to his or her downfall. **Hubris** is a type of *hamartia.*

**Heptameter** A poetic **meter** that consists of seven feet in each line.

**Hero/Heroine** The **protagonist** of a story, often possessing positive traits such as courage or honesty.

**Heroic Couplet** Two successive rhyming lines in **iambic pentameter.**

**Hexameter** A poetic **meter** that consists of six feet in each line. If the six feet are **iambic,** the line is known as an alexandrine, which was the preferred line of French epic poetry.

**High Comedy** **Comedy,** often a satire of upper-class society, that relies on sophisticated wit and **irony.**

**Hip Hop** An intensely rhythmical form of popular music developed by African-Americans and Latinos in the 1970s in which vocalists deploy rhyme—known as rap—over the rhythm.

**Historical Criticism** An approach to **literary criticism** that emphasizes the relationship between a text and its historical context. When interpreting a text, historical critics highlight the cultural, philosophical, and political movements and ideologies prevalent during the text's creation and reception.

**Historical Fiction** A type of fiction writing wherein the author bases his or her **characters, plot,** or **setting** on actual people, events, or places.

**Histories** *See* **Classifications of Drama.**

**Hubris** Excessive arrogance or pride. In classical literature, the hero's tragic flaw was often hubris, which caused his downfall in the tragedy.

**Hyperbole** A type of figurative speech that uses verbal exaggeration to make a point. Hyperbole is sometimes called ***overstatement.***

**Iamb** A poetic **foot** consisting of an unstressed syllable followed by a stressed syllable.

**Iambic Meter** A poetic **meter** created when each line contains more than one **iamb** (a unit with an unstressed syllable followed by a stressed syllable).

**Iambic Pentameter** A poetic **meter** in which each line contains five feet, predominantly iambs. Iambic pentameter is the most commonly used meter in English poetry, comprising **sonnets,** much of Shakespeare's plays, Milton's *Paradise Lost,* Wordsworth's *The Prelude* and Wallace Stevens' "Sunday Morning."

**Iconography** **Symbols** that commonly engender a certain meaning. For example, a skull equals *death,* and a dove equals *peace.*

**Image** A sensory impression created by language. Not all images are visual pictures; an image can appeal to any of the five senses, emotions, or the intellect.

**Imagism** A poetic practice wherein the *thing itself*—the object seen and not discussed or **analyzed**—becomes the poet's focus and the poem's primary concern. Imagism is associated with poets like Ezra Pound and William Carlos Williams.

**Impartial Omniscience** A **narrator** who remains neutral, relating events and **characters'** thoughts without passing judgment or offering an opinion.

**Implied Metaphor** A suggested comparison that is never stated plainly.

**Impressionism** In literature, a style of writing that focuses on a **protagonist**'s reactions to external events rather than the events themselves.

**Indirect Discourse** A **narrator**'s description of an action or event as experienced by a **character** in the story.

**Informal Diction** An author's use of words that are conversational or easily understood, as opposed to elevated or formal language. For example, using *you* instead of *thou.*

**Initial Alliteration** The repetition of consonant or vowel sounds in the middle of a line of poetry.

**Initiation Story** *See* **Coming of Age Story** and ***Bildungsroman.***

***In medias res*** Latin for *in the middle of things.* A term applied when a story begins with relevant story events already having occurred.

**Innocent Narrator** *See* **Naïve Narrator.**

**Intentional Fallacy** The practice by **formalist** critics of discerning or trusting an author's own stated purpose for the meaning of a text.

**Interior Monologue** A **character's** conscious or unconscious thought processes, narrated as they occur, with only minimal-seeming guidance from the **narrator.**

**Internal Alliteration** The repetition of consonant or vowel sounds in the middle of a line of poetry.

**Internal Refrain** The repetition of words or phrases within the lines of a poem.

**Internal Rhyme** **Rhyme** that occurs within a line. The placement of internal rhyme can vary; for example, a word in the middle of the line might rhyme with the word at the end of that same line, or both rhyming words might occur in the middle of two consecutive lines.

**Interpret** The act of **interpretation.**

**Interpretation** The process of contributing to the overall understanding of some aspect of a work in order to illuminate its meaning.

**In-Text Parenthetical Citation** A reference within the body of a paper that links a **quotation, paraphrase,** or **summary** from another source to its full citation in the list of **works cited.**

**In the Round** *See* **Arena Theater.**

**Inverted Syntax** A reversal of expected or traditional word order, often used to aid a poem's sounds, **rhyme,** and/or **meter.**

**Ironic Point of View** Describes a **narrator** who does not understand the significance of the events of a story.

**Irony** A **tone** characterized by a distance between what occurs and what is expected to occur, or between what is said and what is meant.

**Italian Sonnet** *See* **Petrarchan Sonnet.**

**Jargon** Words used with specific meaning for a particular group of people. For example, *starboard* in nautical jargon refers to the right side of a ship.

**Journal Entry** A writing exercise that expands **freewriting** into a more focused discussion that reflects a growing understanding of a topic.

**Language, Tone, and Style** The elements that conjure a story's particular flavor and **voice,** as achieved by means of the words the author chooses and the **rhythm** with which he or she puts the words together

**Language** The words of a story, including **syntax** (how words or other elements of the sentence are arranged) and **diction** (what words the author chooses).

**Levels of Diction** Refers to the three major categories of diction: high, middle, and low diction. The level of diction a writer uses determines whether the words in the work will be formal or informal, poetic or conversational, etc.

**Limerick** A light, often humorous verse form consisting of five **anapestic** (two short syllables followed by one long one) lines, with a rhyme scheme of *aabba.* The first, second, and fifth lines consist of three feet, while lines three and four consist of two feet.

**Limited Omniscient Narrator** A **third-person narrator** who enters into the mind of only one **character** at a time. This narrator serves more as an interpreter than a source of the main **character's** thoughts.

**Line** A row of words containing phrases and/or sentences. The line is a defining feature of poetry, in which there are often set amounts of syllables or poetic feet in each line.

**Literary Ballad** A story told in **ballad** form.

**Literary Criticism** The acts of analyzing, interpreting, and commenting on literature.

**Literary Epic** *See* **Epic.**

**Literary Theory** The body of criticism and schools of thought (such as **Feminist, Deconstructionist,** or **Biographical** Criticism) that govern how we study literature.

**Low Comedy** An informal brand of **comedy** that uses crude humor and **slapstick.**

**Lyric** A short poem with a central pictorial **image** written in an uninflected (direct and personal) **voice.**

**Madrigal** A variety of contrapuntal song that originated in 16th-century Italy. Madrigal features secular verse sung by two or more voices without instrumental accompaniment.

**Magic Realism** A type of fiction in which something "magical" happens in an otherwise realistic world. The form is particularly associated with Latin American writers like Gabriel García Márquez. Unlike **fantasy** or science fiction, magic realism generally has only one fantastical element and the rest relies on realistic **characters** and settings. Notable examples in this book are Franz Kafka's *The Metamorphosis* and Aimee Bender's "The Rememberer."

**Marxist Criticism** Marxist or Economic Determinist Criticism is based on the writings of Karl Marx, who argued that economic concerns shape lives more than anything else, and that society is essentially a struggle between the working classes and the dominant capitalist classes. Rather than assuming that culture evolves naturally or autonomously out of individual human experience, Marxist critics maintain that culture—including literature—is shaped by the interests of the dominant or most powerful social class.

**Masculine Rhyme** The **end rhymes** of multisyllable words with a stressed final syllable, such as *remove* and *approve.* Also called rising rhyme.

**Melodrama** A literary work, mainly a stage play, movie, or television play or show in which **characters** display exaggerated emotions and the **plot** takes sensational turns, sometimes accompanied by music intended to lead the audience's feelings.

**Melody** The linear succession of various musical pitches recognized as a unit.

**Metafiction** A work of fiction that self-consciously draws attention to itself as a work of fiction. Rather than upholding the standard pretense, prevalent in realist fiction, that a story creates or refers to a "real world" beyond the text, metafiction self-consciously reveals the fact and sometimes the manner of its own construction. Metafiction is often associated with **postmodernism,** but examples of metafiction also occur in many other literary movements.

**Metaphor** A close comparison of two dissimilar things that creates a fusion of identity between the things that are compared. A metaphor joins two dissimilar things *without* using words such as *like* or *as*. While a **simile** suggests that X is *like* Y a metaphor states that X *is* Y.

**Meter** A measure of verse, based on regular patterns of sound.

**Metonymy** A **figure of speech** that uses an identifying emblem or closely associated object to represent another object. For example, the phrase *the power of the purse* makes little sense literally (there is no purse that has power), but in the metonymical sense, *purse* stands for money.

**Middle Diction** Poetic language characterized by sophisticated word usage and grammatical accuracy. Middle diction reads as educated, cultured language but is not extravagant like **poetic diction.**

**Mime** The act of performing a play without words.

**Miracle Plays** During the tenth century, when drama was suppressed by the church, these anonymous plays were acted out as religious instruction for the benefit of spectators who could not read the Bible.

**Mixed Metaphor** A failed comparison that results when a writer uses at least two separate, mismatched comparisons in one statement—to confusing, and sometimes comical effect. For example, *The early bird strikes when the iron's hot!*

**Monologue** A single **character's** discourse, without interaction or interruption by other **characters.**

**Monometer** A poetic **meter** comprised of one poetic foot.

**Monosyllabic** A word with one syllable.

**Moral** The lesson taught by a piece of **didactic literature** such as a fable. A moral is often phrased simply and memorably.

**Morality Play** A form of drama in which the figures on stage taught right and proper behavior—morality—to those who watched.

**Motif** A pattern of **imagery** or a concept that recurs throughout a work of literature.

**Motivation** A **character's** reason for doing something.

**Mystery Play** A play that enacted stories of the Bible, such as the Creation or the Crucifixion. These plays appeared during the tenth century, when drama was suppressed in England.

**Myth** The pre-Classical Greek word for sacred story or religious narrative, which by the Classical period had come to mean **plot,** as used in Aristotle's *Poetics.*

**Mythological Criticism** Also called the *archetypal approach,* mythological criticism stems from the work of Carl Jung, a Swiss psychoanalyst (and contemporary of Freud) who argued that humans share in a **collective unconscious,** or a set of **characters,** plots, symbols, and **images** that each evoke a universal response. Jung calls these recurring elements **archetypes,** and likens them to *instincts*—knowledge or associations with which humans are born. Mythological critics **analyze** the ways in which such archetypes function in literature and attempt to explain the power that literature has over us or the reasons why certain texts continue to hold power over audiences many centuries after their creation.

**Naïve Narrator** An unreliable **narrator** who remains unaware of the full complexity of events in the story being told, often due to youth, innocence, or lack of cultural awareness.

**Narrative Poem** A poem that tells a story. Examples include Tennyson's "The Charge of the Light Brigade," Longfellow's "The Midnight Ride of Paul Revere," and most ballads.

**Narrator** The **character** or consciousness that tells a story. For specific types of narrators, see **First-Person Narrator, Second-Person Narrator, Third-Person narrator, Omniscient Narrator, Limited Omniscient Narrator, Impartial Omniscience, Editorial Omniscience, Naïve Narrator,** and **Unreliable Narrator.**

**Naturalistic Theater** Drama that shines a light on the painful realities and problems of everyday life.

**Near Rhyme** *See* **Slant Rhyme.**

**New Criticism** *See* **Formalist Criticism.**

**New Historicism** A critical approach that emerged as a reaction to **new criticism**'s disregard of historical context, but also in response to the perceived shortcomings of older methods of **historical criticism.** Rather than focusing on texts in the **canon** as representations of the most powerful or dominant historical movements, new historicists give equal or greater attention to less dominant texts and non-literary texts (newspapers, pamphlets, legal documents, medical documents, etc.). New historicists attempt to highlight overlooked or suppressed texts, particularly those that express deviation from the dominant culture of the time. In this way, new historicists study not just the historical context of a major literary text, but the complex relationship between texts and culture, or the ways in which literature can challenge as well as support a given culture.

**Nonfiction Novel** A presentation of real events using the craft and technique of a fiction novel.

**Novel** A long fictional work. Because of their greater length, novels are typically complex and may follow more than one **character** or **plot.**

**Novella** A short novel, which generally means it has more complexity than a short story but without the usual length of a novel.

**Objective Point of View** The story is told by an observer who relates only facts, providing neither commentary nor insight into the **character's** thoughts or actions.

**Observer** A **first-person narrator** who does not participate in the action of the story.

**Octameter** A poetic **meter** that consists of eight feet in each line.

**Octave** Eight lines of poetry grouped together in a **stanza** or a unit of thought, as in the **Petrarchan sonnet** where the octave sets up a thought or feeling that the following **sestet** resolves.

**Ode** An elevated, formal **lyric** poem often written in ceremony to someone or to an abstract subject. In Greek **tragedy,** a song and dance performed by the **Chorus** between ***episodia***.

**Oedipus Complex:** Sigmund Freud's theory of behavior (derived from the **plot** of Sophocles's *Oedipus the King*) which holds that male children are jealous of the father because of their sexual attraction to the mother. In *Oedipus the King,* Oedipus kills his father and sleeps with his mother.

**Off Rhyme** *See* **Slant Rhyme.**

**O. Henry Ending** A short story ending that consists of a sudden surprise, often ironic or coincidental in nature, named for the short story writer O. Henry, who frequently ended his stories in this way. A classic example is O. Henry's "The Gift of the Magi" in which a husband and wife each give something precious of theirs to purchase a gift for the other; the ending reveals that each has sacrificed the very thing that would have allowed him or her to enjoy the gift received from their spouse.

**Omniscient Narrator** A **third-person narrator** who observes the thoughts and describes the actions of multiple **characters** in the story. The omniscient narrator can see beyond the physical actions and **dialogue** of **characters** and is able to reveal the inner thoughts and emotions of anyone in the story.

**One-Act Play** A play that consists of a single act that contains the entire action of the play. One-act plays usually portray a single **scene** with an exchange among a smaller number of **characters**; for example, Edward Albee's *The Zoo Story.*

**Onomatopoeia** The use of words that imitate the sounds they refer to, such as *buzz* or *pop.*

**Open Denoument** A **resolution** to a story that leaves loose ends and does not completely resolve the overarching **conflict.**

**Open Form** Poetry ungoverned by metrical or rhyme schemes. Also called free verse.

**Orchestra** The open area in front of the stage (or ***skene***) in the Greek **amphitheater.**

**Overstatement** *See* **Hyperbole.**

**Oxymoron** A version of **paradox** that combines contradictory words into a compact, often two-word term, such as *jumbo shrimp* or *definitely maybe.*

***Paean*** The final choral **ode** of a Greek **tragedy.**

**Pantoum** A variation on the **villanelle,** consisting of an unspecified number of **quatrains** with the rhyme scheme *abab.* The first line of each quatrain repeats the second line of the preceding quatrain, and the third line repeats the final line of the preceding quatrain. In the final quatrain, the second line repeats the third line of the first quatrain, and the last line of the poem repeats the first line of the poem.

**Parable** A short narrative that illustrates a lesson using comparison to familiar **characters** and events. The characters and events in parables often have obvious significance as **symbols** and **allegories.**

***Parados*** The **Chorus**' first **ode** in a Greek **tragedy.**

**Paradox** Seemingly contradictory statements that, when closely examined, have a deeper, sometimes complicated, meaning.

**Parallelism** The arrangement of words or phrases in a grammatically similar way.

**Paraphrase** Condensing a passage or idea from an existing text into your own words. Paraphrase does not mean simply changing the words from the original; rather, it should re-present the original in a way that demonstrates your understanding of it.

**Parody** Mimicking another author or work of literature in such a way as to make fun of the original, often by exaggerating its characteristic aspects.

**Participant narrator** A **first-person narrator** who takes part in the action of the story.

**Pastoral Poetry** A variety of poem in which life in the countryside, mainly among shepherds, is glorified and idealized.

**Pentameter** A poetic **meter** that consists of five feet in each line.

***Peripeteia*** An element of Greek **tragedy,** *peripeteia* occurs when an action has the opposite result of what was intended. In a **tragedy,** this generally occurs at a turning point for the **hero** and signals his downfall.

**Persona** A poem's speaker, which may or may not use the **voice** of the poet.

***Personae*** Masks, often representative of certain **iconography** and familiar **characters,** worn by actors in the Ancient Greek theater to enable one actor to perform as many **characters.** *Personae* often were designed to project an actor's voice to the far rows of the **amphitheater.**

**Personification** A **figure of speech** in which a writer ascribes human traits or behavior to something inhuman.

**Persuasion** The process of using **analysis** and logical **argument** to prove the validity of a certain **interpretation** or **point of view.**

**Petrarchan (Italian) Sonnet** A sonnet consisting of an **octave** and a **sestet,** all in **iambic pentameter,** with the rhyme scheme *abbaabba cdecde* or *abbaabba cdcdcd.* The **volta,** or turn, typically occurs between the octave and sestet, around line nine of the poem.

**Plagiarism** The act of taking credit for another's work or ideas.

**Play** A work of drama, usually performed before an audience.

**Players** Traveling actors, men and boys, who spoke their lines for pay.

**Play Review** The critique of a play.

**Playwright** The author of a dramatic work.

**Plot** The artful arrangement of incidents in a story, with each incident building on the next in a series of causes and effects.

**Poetic Diction** Lofty and elevated language, used traditionally in poetry written before the nineteenth century to separate poetic speech from common speech.

**Point of View** The perspective from which the story is told to the reader.

**Polysyllabic** A word that has many syllables.

**Portmanteau Word** A word invented by combining two other words to achieve the effect of both. Lewis Carroll's poem "Jabberwocky" is comprised largely of portmanteau words such as *slithy,* which means *slimy* and *lithe.*

**Postcolonialism** A critical approach to **literary criticism** that seeks to offer views of relations between the colonizing West and colonized nations and regions that differed sharply from the conventional Western perspectives.

**Poststructuralist Criticism** Criticism based on the belief that texts do not have a single, stable meaning or **interpretation,** in part because language itself is filled with ambiguity, multiple meanings, and meanings that can change with time or context.

**Precís** *See* **Summary Paper.**

**Preview** The process of gathering information about a piece of literature before you read it.

**Problem Play** A play about a social problem, written with an aim to create awareness of the problem.

**Prologue** The introduction to a literary work.

**Proscenium Stage** A realistic **setting** with three flat walls (two flat sides, and a ceiling) that simulates a room; the audience views the action through the missing **fourth wall.**

**Prose Poem** A poem that uses the devices and **imagery** characteristic of traditionally lined poetry, but in compact units without clearly defined line breaks.

**Prosody** The analysis of a poem's rhythm and metrical structures.

**Protagonist** The main figure (or principal actor) in a work of literature. A story's **plot** hinges equally on the protagonist's efforts to realize his or her desires and to cope with failure if and when plans are thwarted and desires left unfulfilled.

**Psalm** A sacred song, usually written to or in honor of a deity.

**Psychoanalytic Criticism** Also called *psychological criticism,* this approach in a sense studies **characters** and authors as one would patients, looking in the text for evidence of childhood trauma, repressed sexual impulses, preoccupation with death, and so on. Through the lens of psychology critics attempt to explain the motivations and meanings behind characters' actions. Psychological critics also use textual and biographical evidence as a means to better understand the author's psychology, as well as examine the process and nature of literary creation, studying the ways in which texts create an emotional and intellectual effect for their readers and authors.

**Pun** A play on words that reveals different meanings in words that are similar or even identical.

**Pyrrhic** A poetic foot characterized by two unstressed syllables.

**Quantitative Meter** A type of poetry that counts the length of syllables, rather than the emphasis they receive (as in **accentual meter** and syllabic verse). Quantitative meter primarily appears in Greek and Latin poetry and is rarely used in English since English vowel lengths are not clearly quantified.

**Quatrain** A four-line **stanza.** Quatrains are the most popular stanzaic form in English poetry because they are easily varied in **meter,** line length, and **rhyme scheme.**

**Queer Theory** The idea that power is reflected in language and that discourse itself shapes our sense of who we are and how we define ourselves sexually.

**Rap** An oral form of poetry that is akin to spoken word, but distinguished by musical qualities and choral repetitions. *See* **Hip Hop.**

**Reader-Response Criticism** The reader-response approach emphasizes that the reader is central to the writer-text-reader interaction. Reader-response critics believe a literary work is not complete until someone reads and **interprets** it.

Such critics acknowledge that because each reader has a different set of experiences and views, each reader's response to a text may be different.

**Realism** A mode of literature in which the author depicts **characters** and scenarios that could occur in real life. Unlike **fantasy** or **surrealism,** realism seeks to represent the world as it is.

**Recognition** The moment in a **tragedy** when the **hero** comes to recognize the actuality of events and is no longer under illusion.

**Refrain** A line or **stanza** that is repeated at regular intervals in a poem or song.

**Resolution** The end of the story, where the **conflict** is ultimately resolved and the effects of the story's events on the **protagonist** become evident.

**Restoration Comedy** A bawdy play about fallen virtue and infidelity that became popular after the Puritans were displaced in England in the mid-seventeenth century.

**Retrospect** *See* **Flashback.**

**Reversal** *See* ***Peripeteia.***

**Rhyme** The echoing repetition of sounds in the end syllables of words, often (though not always) at the end of a line of poetry.

**Rhyme Scheme** The pattern of **rhyme** throughout a particular poem.

**Rhythm** The sequence of stressed and unstressed sounds in a poem.

**Rising Action** Story events that increase tension and move the plot toward the climax.

**Rising Meter** A **meter** comprised of feet that begin with an unstressed syllable, followed by a stressed syllable or syllables. **Iambic** and **anapestic** feet both create rising meter, which is named for the effect of *rising* from the initial unstressed syllable to the stressed.

**Romance** *See* **Classifications of Drama.**

**Romantic Comedy** A type of **comedy** in which two would-be/should-be lovers find each other after a series of misunderstandings and false starts.

**Round Character** A **character** with complex, multifaceted characteristics. Round characters behave as real people. For example, a round **hero** may suffer temptation, and a round **villain** may show compassion.

**Run-On Line** A line of poetry that, when read, does not come to a natural conclusion where the line breaks. *See* **Enjambment.**

**Sarcasm** Verbal irony that is intended in a mean-spirited, malicious, or critical way.

**Satire** An artistic critique, sometimes heated, on some aspect of human immorality or absurdity.

**Satiric Comedy** A derisive and dark **comedy** in which there is no promise that good will prevail.

**Satyr Play** An often obscene satirical fourth play, provided after a trilogy of tragedies, meant to provide **comic relief.**

**Scansion** The process of determining the metrical pattern of a line of poetry by marking its stresses and feet.

**Scene** A defined moment of action or interaction in a story usually confined to a single **setting.** Scenes are the building blocks of a story's **plot.**

**Scenery** The set pieces and stage decorations onstage during the performance of a play.

**Scratch Outline** A multi-tiered, ordered list of topics that should be covered in a paper. A scratch outline goes into deeper detail than a topic outline.

**Screenplay** A script that is specifically tailored and structured for television or film rather than the stage.

**Script** The written text of a play, which may include set descriptions and actor cues.

**Second-Person Narrator** A **narrator** who addresses the character as *you,* often involving the reader by association.

**Semiotics** The study of how meaning is attached to and communicated by symbols.

**Sentence Outline** An outline that uses complete sentences instead of brief words or phrases.

**Sestet** Six lines of poetry grouped together in a stanza or a unit of thought, as in the **Petrarchan sonnet** where the last six lines of the poem resolve the idea or question set up by the initial **octave.**

**Sestina** A poem of six six-line **stanzas** and a three-line **envoi,** usually unrhymed, in which each stanza repeats the end words of the lines of the first stanza, but in different order, the envoi using the six words again, three in the middle of the lines and three at the end.

**Setting** The time and place where the story occurs. Setting creates expectations for the types of **characters** and situations encountered in the story.

**Shakespearean (English) Sonnet** A **sonnet** form composed of three quatrains and a final couplet, all in **iambic pentameter** and rhymed *abab cdcd efef gg.* The **volta,** or turn, occurs in the final **couplet** of the poem.

**Short Story** A brief fictional narrative that attempts to dramatize or illustrate the effect or meaning of a single incident or small group of incidents in the life of a single **character** or small group of characters.

**Simile** A direct comparison of two dissimilar things using the words *like* or *as.*

**Situational Irony** A situation portrayed in a poem when what occurs is the opposite or very different from what's expected to occur.

***Skene*** The stage in the Greek **amphitheater.**

**Slam** Poetry in a variety of styles, performed competitively in clubs and halls.

**Slant Rhyme** A case in which vowel or consonant sounds are similar but not exactly the same, such as *heap* and *rap* and *tape*. Also called *near rhyme, imperfect rhyme* and *off rhyme*.

**Slapstick** A type of low **comedy** characterized by unexpected, often physical humor. A classic example of slapstick is the man walking along who accidentally slips on a banana peel.

**Social Environment** A study of **setting** that considers era and location as well as a **character's** living and working conditions.

**Sociological Criticism** The study of literary texts as products of the cultural, political, and economic context of the author's time and place.

**Soliloquy** A **monologue** delivered by a **character** in a play who is alone onstage. Soliloquies generally have a **character** revealing his or her thoughts to the audience.

**Sonnet** A poem of fourteen lines of **iambic pentameter** in a recognizable pattern of **rhyme.** Sonnets contain a **volta,** or turn, in which the last lines resolve or change direction from the controlling idea of the preceding lines.

**Sound** The rhythmic structure of the lines of a poem, which draws the reader in, often utilizing **rhyme** and created through word choice and word order.

**Spoken Word Poetry** Poetry that derives from the **Beat** poets, characterized by emphasis of the *performance* of a poem over the written form. Spoken word often employs improvisation.

**Spondee** A poetic foot characterized by two stressed syllables.

**Stage Directions** Cues, included by the playwright in the script of a play, which inform the actions of the actors during the play.

**Stanza** A unit of two or more lines, set off by a space, often sharing the same **rhythm** and **meter.**

***Stasimon*** In Greek **tragedy,** an ode performed by the **Chorus** which interprets and responds to the preceding scene.

**Static Character** A **character,** often flat, who does not change over the course of the story.

**Stock Character** A **character** who represents a concept or type of behavior, such as a "mean teacher" or "mischievous student," and offers readers the comfort of repetition and reliability.

**Stream of Consciousness:** A **character's** thoughts are presented flowing by in free association, and the literary convention that rules is that there is no writer mediating the consciousness of the subject.

**Stress** The vocal emphasis on a syllable in a line of verse, largely a matter of pitch.

**Structuralism** Structuralist literary critics work from the belief that a given work of literature can be fully understood only when a reader considers the system of conventions, or the *genre* to which it belongs or responds.

**Style** The characteristic way in which any writer uses language.

**Subplot** A **plot** that is not the central plot of the work, but nonetheless appears in the same work. Longer works, like **novels** and plays, tend to have subplots that might follow side **characters** or somehow affect the action of the main plot.

**Summary** Restating concisely the main ideas of a text without adding opinion or commentary. The best approach to summary is to divide the text into its major sections and then write a sentence for each section stating its main idea.

**Summary Paper** A short paper that represents the main ideas of the text as the author has presented them, excluding any subjective ideas or interpretations.

**Surrealism** A technique of the modern theater in which the realms of conscious and unconscious experience are fused together to create a total reality. In this way the fiction writer, poet, and **playwright,** tap into the resources of the unconscious mind and the imagination and portray in story on the page or on the modern stage the stuff of human desire, hope, and dreams.

**Suspense** A sense of anticipation or excitement about what will happen and how the **characters** will deal with their newfound predicament.

**Syllabic verse** A verse form that uses a fixed number of syllables per line or stanza, regardless of the number of stressed or unstressed syllables.

**Symbol** Any object, **image, character,** or action that suggests meaning beyond the everyday literal level.

**Symbolic Act** A gesture or action beyond the everyday practical definition.

**Synecdoche** A **figure of speech** that uses a piece or part of a thing to represent the thing in its entirety. For example, in the Biblical saying that man does not live by bread alone, *bread* stands for the larger concept of food or physical sustenance.

**Synopsis** A **summary** or **précis** of a work.

**Syntax** The meaningful arrangement of words and phrases. Syntax can refer to word placement and order, as well as the overall length and shape of a sentence.

**Synthesis** The act of bringing together the ideas and observations generated by reading and analysis in order to make a concrete statement about a work.

**Tactile Imagery** Imagery that appeals to a reader's sense of touch.

**Tercet** A group of three lines of poetry, sometimes called a **triplet** when all three lines rhyme.

**Terminal Refrain** Repeated lines which appear at the end of each **stanza** in a poem.

**Terza Rima** A **tercet** fixed form featuring the interlocking rhyme scheme *aba, bcb, cdc, ded,* etc.

**Tetrameter** A poetic **meter** that contains four feet in each line.

**Theme** The central or underlying meanings of a literary work.

**Thesis Statement** A sentence, usually but not always included in a paper's introductory paragraph, that defines a paper's purpose and argument.

**Thesis** A paper's purpose and **argument,** defined by the **thesis statement** and proved by the paper's **conclusion.**

**Third-Person Narrator** A **narrator** who is outside the story. The narrator refers to all the **characters** in the story with the pronouns *he, she,* or *they.*

**Tiring House** In the Elizabethan theater, a room, adjoined to the stage, in which actors changed their costumes.

**Tone** The author's attitude toward his or her **characters** or subject matter.

**Topic Outline** A multi-tiered organization of a paper's topics and **arguments,** used to structure a paper.

**Tragedy** A dramatic form in which **characters** face serious and important challenges that end in disastrous failure or defeat for the **protagonist.** *See* **Classifications of Drama.**

**Tragic Flaw** In classical literature, the hero's weakness that causes his downfall.

**Tragic Hero** A heroic **protagonist** who from the beginning, due to some innate flaw in his **character** or some unforeseeable mistake (*see* **Tragic Flaw**), is doomed. The inevitability of a tragic hero's demise inspires sympathy in the audience.

**Tragic Irony** The situation in a **tragedy** where the audience is aware of the **tragic hero's** fate although the **character** has not yet become aware.

**Tragicomedy** A play with the elements of **tragedy** that ends happily.

**Transferred Epithet** A description that pairs an adjective with a noun that does not logically follow, such as *silver sounds.*

**Trimeter** A poetic **meter** that contains three feet in each line.

**Triplet** A **tercet** of three rhymed lines.

**Trochaic Meter:** A poetic **meter** created when each line contains more than one **trochee** (a unit with a stressed syllable followed by an unstressed syllable). Trochaic meter is a type of **falling meter.**

**Trochee** A poetic **foot** consisting of a stressed syllable followed by an unstressed syllable. The opposite of an **iamb,** and so sometimes called an "inverted foot," often beginning a line of **iambic pentameter.**

**Understatement** A purposeful underestimation of something, used to emphasize its actual magnitude.

**Unreliable Narrator** A **narrator** who cannot be trusted to present an undistorted account of the action because of inexperience, ignorance, personal bias, intentional deceptiveness, or even insanity.

**Verbal Irony** A statement in which the stated meaning is very different (sometimes opposite) from the implied meaning.

**Verisimilitude** How alike an imitation is to its original. The goal of literature, especially when written in the mode of realism, is to provide a likeness, or a verisimilitude, of real life.

**Verse** A broad term to describe poetic lines.

***Vers libre*** *See* **Free Verse.**

**Villanelle** A poem consisting of five **tercets** and a concluding **quatrain.** Each tercet rhymes *aba* and the final quatrain rhymes *abaa.* The poem's opening line repeats as the final line of the second and fourth stanzas, and in the second-to-last line of the poem. The last line of the first **stanza** repeats as the final line of the third and fifth stanzas and is also the final line of the poem overall.

**Visual imagery** **Imagery** and descriptions that appeal to a reader's sense of sight.

**Voice** The unique sound of an author's writing, created by elements such as **diction, tone,** and sentence construction.

**Volta** In a sonnet, the turn where a shift in thought or emotion occurs. In the **Petrarchan sonnet,** the **volta** occurs between the **octave** and the **sestet;** in the **Shakespearean sonnet,** the ending couplet provides the volta.

**Vulgate** A term to describe the common people, often used in reference to a level of speech or **diction.**

**Well-made Play** A type of theater popularized in France. Well-made plays feature a three-act sequence that *poses* a problem, *complicates* and then *resolves* it; usually that **resolution** comes when a **character's** past is revealed. The first act offers *exposition,* the second a *situation,* the third an unraveling or *completion.* Meticulous plotting and **suspense** are components of this mode of theater.

**Working Bibliography** A list of all the sources consulted in preparing a paper, as well as all the information necessary to cite them in the final list of works cited.

**Works Cited** A list of all the primary and secondary sources consulted in the creation of a paper.

# Credits

Joan Ackermann: *The Second Beam* copyright © 2004 Joan Ackermann. All rights reserved. Reprinted by permission of Playscripts, Inc. To purchase acting editions of this play, or to obtain stock and amateur performance rights, you must contact: Playscripts, Inc. Website: http://www.playscripts.com.

Edward Albee, *The Zoo Story* copyright © 1959, renewed 1987 by Edward Albee. Reprinted by permission of William Morris Agency, LLC on behalf of the Author.
CAUTION: Professionals and amateurs are hereby warned that *The Zoo Story* is subject to a royalty. It is fully protected under the copyright laws of the United States of America and of all countries covered by the International Copyright Union (including the Dominion of Canada and the rest of the British Commonwealth), the Berne Convention, the Pan-American Copyright Convention and the Universal Copyright Convention as well as all countries with which the United States has reciprocal copyright relations. All rights, including professional/amateur stage rights, motion picture, recitation, lecturing, public reading, radio broadcasting, television, video or sound recording, all other forms of mechanical or electronic reproduction, such as CD-ROM, CD-I, information storage and retrieval systems and photocopying, and the rights of translation into foreign languages, are strictly reserved. Particular emphasis is laid upon the matter of readings, permission for which must be secured from the Author's agent in writing. Inquiries concerning rights should be addressed to: William Morris Agency, LLC. 1325 Avenue of the Americas, New York, NY 10019, Attn: Eric Lupfer. *The Zoo Story* was first produced at the Billy Rose Theatre in NY, USA on October 9, 1968.

Denise Chávez: *Guadalupe × 3* by Denise Chávez is reprinted by permission of the author.

Julianne Homokay: *The Wedding Story* by Julianne Homokay, reprinted by permission of Robert A. Freedman Dramatic Agency, Inc.

David Henry Hwang: *The Dance and the Railroad* from *Trying to Find Chinatown: The Selected Plays of David Henry Hwang* by David Henry Hwang. Copyright © 2000 by David Henry Hwang. Published by Theatre Communications Group. Used by permission of Theatre Communications Group.

David Ives: *Moby-Dude, Or: The Three-Minute Whale* by David Ives. Reprinted by permission of William Craver, agent for David Ives, Paradigm Agency.

Arthur Kopit: *Wings* by Arthur Kopit. Copyright © 1978 by Arthur Kopit. Reprinted by permission of Hill and Wang, a division of Farrar, Straus and Giroux, LLC.

Arthur Miller: *Death of a Salesman* from *Death of a Salesman* by Arthur Miller, copyright 1949, renewed © 1977 by Arthur Miller. Used by permission of Viking Penguin, a division of Penguin Group (USA) Inc.

William Shakespeare: Notes to *Hamlet, Prince of Denmark, A Midsummer Night's Dream,* and *Othello, The Moor of Venice* from *The Complete Works of Shakespeare* 6th edition by David Bevington. Copyright © 2009 by Pearson Education. Reprinted by permission.

Sophocles: *Oedipus Rex* from *Sophocles, the Oedipus Cycle: An English Version* by Dudley Fitts and Robert Fitzgerald, copyright 1949 by Houghton Mifflin Harcourt Publishing Company and renewed 1977 by Cornelia Fitts and Robert Fitzgerald, reprinted by permission of the publisher. CAUTION: All rights, including professional, amateur, motion picture, recitation, lecturing, public reading, radio broadcasting, and television are strictly reserved. Inquiries on all rights should be addressed to Houghton Mifflin Harcourt Publishing Company, Permissions Department, Orlando, FL 32887-6777

Tennessee Williams: *The Glass Menagerie* by Tennessee Williams. Copyright © 1945 The University of The South. Reprinted by permission of Georges Borchardt, Inc. for the Tennessee Williams Estate.

August Wilson: *Fences* from *Fences* by August Wilson, copyright © 1986 by August Wilson. Used by permission of Dutton Signet, a division of Penguin Group (USA) Inc.

# Photo Credits

**Page vi–vii:** Gary John Norman/Getty Images; **vi–vii:** Phototex/Jupiterimages; **2:** SuperStock; **3:** Comstock/PunchStock; **3:** Getty Images/Stockbyte Silver; **5:** Library of Congress (LOC) [LC-USZ62-104649]; **6:** C Squared Studios/Getty Images; **7:** Comstock Images / Alamy; **9:** Mitch Hrdlicka/Getty Images; **10:** Photodisc/Getty Images; **13:** Getty Images / Digital Vision; **14T:** Sheila Burnett/ArenaPAL/Topham/ The Image Works; **14B:** Imagesource/PictureQuest; **18:** Ingram Publishing / Alamy; **21:** Steve Cole/Getty Images; **22:** Comstock/PunchStock; **23:** Stockdisc/PunchStock; **24:** RubberBall Productions; **27:** Panoramic Images /Getty Images; **31:** LOC [LC-USZ62-116769]; **33:** Charles Betz, http://www.betz.lu; **34:** Charles Betz, http://www.betz.lu; **36:** Charles Betz, http://www.betz.lu; **39:** Charles Betz, http://www.betz.lu; **41:** Charles Betz, http://www.betz.lu; **42:** Charles Betz, http://www.betz.lu; **43:** Charles Betz, http://www.betz.lu; **46:** Mike Powell/Getty Images; **64:** Raga Raga/Photolibrary; **64:** ArenaPal/Topham/The Image Works; **67:** The Bridgeman Art Library/Getty Images; **68:** Royalty-Free/Corbis; **97L:** Author's Image/Punchstock; **97R:** 1995 Zedcor, Inc.; **104:** Andrea Pistolesi/Getty Images; **107:** LOC [LC-USZC4-6527]; **178:** Drawing by C. Walter Hodges from his The Globe Restored, published by Oxford University Press © 1968 C. Walter Hodges. Reprinted by permission of Oxford University Press.; **284:** Garden Picture Library/Photolibrary; **284 (play):** ArenaPAL /Topham/The Image Works; **287:** Hulton Archive/Getty Images; **343:** Hulton Archive/Getty Images; **387:** LOC [LC-USZ62-128957]; **421:** Brad Barket/Getty Images; **435:** Craig Schwartz; **441:** Craig Schwartz; **442:** Craig Schwartz; **456:** Craig Schwartz; **464:** Roberto Pfeil/AP Images; **465:** Photo by Brian Miller. Production by the Bas Bleu Theatre Company in Fort Collins, Colorado in March 2008; **484:** Photo by Brian Miller. Production by the Bas Bleu Theatre Company in Fort Collins, Colorado in March 2008; **491:** Courtesy Joan Ackerman; **493:** Tim Rummelhoff; **496:** Paul Hawthorne/Getty Images; **507:** The Granger Collection, New York; **512:** Evan Agostini/Getty Images; **514T:** Art Wolfe/Jason Reed/Getty Images; **514B:** Courtesy Denise Chavez; **517:** Las Cruces Sun-News, Shari Vialpando/AP Images; **H-1:** Andre Jenny/Alamy; **H-97:** Michael Ochs Archives /Getty Images; **H-98:** Frank Driggs Collection/Getty Images; **H-107:** "Book Cover" © 2000 from, FROM SLAVERY TO FREEDOM BY John H. Franklin and Evelyn Higginbotham. Used by permission of the McGraw Hill Companies.

# Index

Note: Page references in **boldface** refer to literary works included in their entirety.